CONTEMPORARY BUSINESS LAW
Principles and Cases

CONTEMPORARY BUSINESS LAW
Principles and Cases

Ralph C. Hoeber, J.D., Ph.D.
Late Emeritus Professor of Business Law
Graduate School of Management
University of California, Los Angeles

J. David Reitzel, M.S., J.D.
Professor of Business Law
California State University, Fresno

Nathan J. Roberts, J.D., LL.M.
Emeritus Professor of Law
Loyola University, Los Angeles

Donald P. Lyden, B.S., J.D.
Professor of Business Law
California State University, Northridge

Gordon B. Severance, J.D., Ph.D.
Professor of Business Law
University of Nevada, Reno

Second Edition

McGraw-Hill Book Company
New York St. Louis San Francisco Auckland Bogotá Hamburg Johannesburg
London Madrid Mexico Montreal New Delhi Panama Paris São Paulo Singapore
Sydney Tokyo Toronto

CONTEMPORARY BUSINESS LAW: Principles and Cases

34567890 DODO 898765432

ISBN 0-07-029165-9

This book was set in Caledonia by The Total Book (BD).
The editor was Kathi A. Benson;
the production supervisor was Charles Hess.
R. R. Donnelley & Sons Company was printer and binder.

Library of Congress Cataloging in Publication Data
Main entry under title:

Contemporary business law.

    Includes index.
    1. Commercial law—United States—Cases.
I. Hoeber, Ralph Carl Louis.
KF888.C62   1982   346.73'07   81-18579
ISBN 0-07-029165-9   347.3067   AACR2

DEDICATION

Contemporary Business Law owes its existence to the late Professor Ralph C. Hoeber, whose sudden death in the summer of 1978 deprived us of an esteemed colleague, leader, and friend.

We cannot adequately describe Ralph's contribution to this book. He organized it and wrote many of the chapters, but after several years of work he realized that the law was too broad and was changing too fast for one person to treat the subject adequately. Hoping to expand the book and preserve the features he prized so highly, he sought out professors of similar view and invited them to join him as coauthors. Then Ralph and his wife Ethel provided the most intensive editorial scrutiny that a business law manuscript has probably ever had. The Hoeber knack for organization, feel for readability, and attention to the policy underlying the law never flagged.

Since Ralph's death, the book has been carried on in his spirit. It reflects the outstanding personal qualities of Ralph Hoeber as a writer and as a teacher of law. We dedicate it with pride to his memory.

J. DAVID REITZEL
DONALD P. LYDEN
NATHAN J. ROBERTS
GORDON B. SEVERANCE

About the Authors

The late RALPH C. HOEBER received a J.D. degree from Stanford University and a Ph.D. from the University of Wisconsin. Professor Hoeber was Emeritus Professor of Business Law at UCLA, having previously taught for the University of Oregon, the University of Hawaii, the University of Wisconsin, and Stanford University. A Past President of the Pacific Southwest Business Law Association, Professor Hoeber was the recipient of numerous academic and professional awards—among them, Phi Beta Kappa and Phi Kappa Phi—and was elected Honorary President of the American Business Law Association.

J. DAVID REITZEL is currently Professor of Business Law, California State University, Fresno, and was formerly Professor and Chairman of the Department of Business Law at The American College, Bryn Mawr. He has also taught at St. Cloud State University, Minnesota. Professor Reitzel holds a J.D. from Indiana University and was admitted to the Indiana Bar in 1969. He is a Senior Staff Editor of the *American Business Law Journal* and has written numerous articles and papers, many dealing with business law education. Professor Reitzel has also served as Chairman of the ABLA Committee on the Teaching and Development of Business Law.

DONALD P. LYDEN holds a J.D. degree from the University of California, Los Angeles. He is currently Professor of Business Law and is a former Chairman of the Department of Business Law, California State University, Northridge. Professor Lyden pioneered a televised college-credit law course offered for nine years throughout California. A member of the California Bar, Professor Lyden is active in several academic and professional organizations. He has also maintained a private law practice in the Los Angeles area since 1959. Professor Lyden is a Past President of the Pacific Southwest Business Law Association.

NATHAN J. ROBERTS, Emeritus Professor of Law at Loyola University, Los Angeles, received a J.D. degree from the University of Florida and a LL. M. from George Washington University. He has previously held positions at the University of California, Santa Barbara, and at the Army Industrial College in Washington, D.C. He is a retired Brigadier General, formerly Assistant Judge Advocate General of the Army for Civil Law. He is a member of Phi Kappa Phi and is a contributing author to *Government Contracts Practice* and to *Basic Techniques of Public Contract Practice* (both published by the Continuing Education of the Bar of California).

GORDON B. SEVERANCE is currently Professor of Business Law at the University of Nevada, Reno. He is Emeritus Professor of Business Law at California State University, Los Angeles, where he previously was Chairman of the Department of Business Law and Finance. He has also taught at Occidental College, California State University, San Diego, and at the University of Southern California. He holds an M.A. degree from Stanford University and J.D. and Ph.D. degrees from the University of Southern California and was elected to Phi Beta Kappa. Professor Severance is Past President of the Pacific Southwest Business Law Association. A specialist in corporation law and real property law, he maintains a private law practice in South Lake Tahoe and in the Los Angeles area. Since 1972 he has also been a Vice President and Director of a Savings and Loan Association.

Contents*

*For more detailed information about content, see the outline of content at the beginning of each chapter.

PART TWO   TORTS AND CRIMES

PART THREE CONTRACTS

PART EIGHT   AGENCY

PART NINE   PARTNERSHIPS; MINOR BUSINESS ORGANIZATIONS

PART TEN   CORPORATIONS

Table of Cases*

*The principal cases are in italic type. Cases discussed or cited in textual material are in roman type.

Preface

PURPOSE

Our purpose in providing a second edition of *Contemporary Business Law* is threefold: to add four new chapters suggested by adopters; to expand the coverage of certain topics; and to incorporate the most recent developments in the field, including many case law developments. In the process, we have concentrated on making the book even more readable than the first edition. Many sections have been rewritten to further clarify difficult concepts. Among the topics that have been considerably revised or expanded are torts, contracts, quasi contracts, commercial paper, and agency.

In the second edition of *Contemporary Business Law*, as in the first, we have attempted above all to provide a sound exposition of business law. The development, the economic and social contexts, and the underlying policies of the law have a place of prominence, for as Lord Coke said, "If by your studie and industrie you make not the reason of the law your owne, it is not possible for you long to retaine it in your memorie." A mastery of the *reason* of the law will, we hope, lead to understanding, evaluation, and appreciation of it—both for students of business and for students who take business law as a general education elective.

Although this book is entitled *Contemporary Business Law*, we have tried to avoid the "business law-legal environment" controversy that has frequently commanded the attention of business educators. We believe that each expression—"business law" and "legal environment of business"—can legitimately encompass both the public and the private law, and that reputable advocates of either label would em-

phasize the nature, functions, policy, and limits of the law and the legal system as these matters relate to business activity.

COVERAGE AND SPECIAL FEATURES

As is pointed out in Chapter 1, most of this book is devoted to those branches of private law that might be considered the foundations of business: the law of torts, property, contracts, sales, secured transactions, commercial paper, agency, partnerships, and corporations. However, we have also dealt with the public law where appropriate to indicate its substantial impact on business. Some chapters and parts of chapters deal with the criminal law, administrative law, and (as the occasion warrants) constitutional law. Others deal with government regulation of business activities, for example, the chapter on securities regulation and various passages elsewhere that discuss federal and state consumer law. And, because financial misfortune is a fact of economic life, we have devoted a chapter to bankruptcy. Now, at the suggestion of many adopters, *Contemporary Business Law* has been expanded by the addition of four chapters—one on insurance; one on wills, estates, and trusts; and two on antitrust law.

This book has ample material for three courses in business law. Some of the material is relatively nontechnical and would be appropriate for an introductory course. Some is more complex and should be presented in intermediate or advanced courses, or even in graduate courses. Most is appropriate for all business students. A few topics, such as bankruptcy, might be of interest mainly to prospective accountants. By a judicious selection of topics, chapters, cases, and problems, instructors can accommodate a broad spectrum of needs.

Contemporary Business Law contains three kinds of chapters. Chapters 1 through 4 are background chapters. These chapters—on the development and nature of law, law in the United States, the court system and civil procedure, and administrative law—are relatively nontechnical and would be suitable as part of an introductory course in law or as supplemental readings for more advanced courses.

Some chapters present an *overview* of a single topic of substantive law. The chapters on business crimes, secured transactions, insurance, and bankruptcy fit into this category. The chapter on business crimes is suitable for a basic course. The other overview chapters are appropriate for intermediate or advanced courses, although the chapter on insurance may be useful in a basic course that first presents the law of contracts.

Most chapters are on *selected aspects* of substantive law topics and examine those aspects in some depth. Most of the chapters on torts, contracts, property, sales, commercial paper, agency, partnerships, and corporations fit into this category. Some of these materials (contracts, torts, business crimes, and possibly sales) are suitable for introductory or intermediate courses. Others, such as commercial paper, are best reserved for intermediate or advanced courses.

Contemporary Business Law is intended for use in departments of business administration, marketing, management, finance, accounting, and business education. The new chapters should enhance the usefulness of the book in two ways. First, the two antitrust chapters serve the needs of institutions that do not offer a separate "legal environment" course but nevertheless wish to focus significant attention on the governmental regulation of business. The antitrust chapters, together with those on administrative law and securities regulation, provide a substantial instructional unit on the regulatory aspects of the law.

Second, the new chapters enhance the usefulness of *Contemporary Business Law* to students of accounting. Because the law affects so many accounting judgments, students of accounting need a deeper and broader exposure to the law than do most business students. The first edition provided the depth of study needed by accounting majors, including a presentation of the Bankruptcy Reform Act of 1978. Now, with the addition of chapters on insurance law, antitrust law, and wills, estate, and trusts, *Contemporary Business Law* provides a breadth of study more in keeping with the demands of the CPA examination.

PEDAGOGICAL AIDS

We are ever mindful of the futility of rote memorization as a technique for studying law. Yet the mastery of basic legal terms, principles, and concepts underlies the ability to explore the law at a more sophisticated level. The end-of-chapter study and discussion questions have been carefully designed to provide students with an opportunity systematically o review and check their comprehension of t ie textual and case materials. Many of these questions encourage students to look more deeply into a principle or topic. The end-of-chapter problems, based on actual cases, encourage the application of legal principles in the discussion, resolution, and evaluation of legal disputes. We hope these activities will lead students to a heightened awareness of the nature, roles, limits, and suitability of the law.

Several other features of this book will also facilitate learning, for example:

1. An outline of content preceding each chapter. The outline provides an overview of the chapter and a framework to aid in study, discussion, review, and retention of important terms, concepts, and principles.

2. An introduction at the beginning of each chapter, to prepare students for the study of the subject matter of the chapter: its importance, its relation to subject matter in other chapters or other areas of law, the major topics or problems to be discussed in the chapter, the general sequence or procedure to be followed in the discussion, etc.

3. Basic terms highlighted by italics and carefully defined in understandable language. For easy reference, an expanded glossary is also included at the end of the book.

4. Principles and rules of law, and policies underlying the law, explained simply but in sufficient depth for accurate understanding.

5. Numerous examples to illustrate the application of principles and rules of law, including several extended examples in particularly difficult areas.

6. Cases interspersed with text material at the spots in the text where they best illustrate the application of the law to business situations.

7. Chapter summaries to put the content of the chapter in perspective and to aid in review and retention of the most important legal terms, concepts, and principles.

8. Questions and problems arranged in a sequence that corresponds to the flow of textual material, and so worded as to provide clues to locating the textual material that provides help in answering the questions or in solving the problems.

9. An expanded table of cases and an index to aid in quick location of textual material.

SUPPLEMENTARY MATERIALS

Additional detailed aids to learning and teaching are available in three separate supplements: A **Student's Study Guide**, and **Instructor's Manual**, and a **Test Bank**. Each of these supplements has been reviewed and revised to correspond with changes in the second edition of the textbook and to incorporate helpful suggestions from teachers and students.

The **Student's Study Guide** has been prepared by Professors James and Deborah Highsmith and Professor Dan Davidson (all at California State University, Fresno). The Study Guide offers general study helps, including aid for reading and briefing cases; chapter review objectives; and independent study questions, including case problems.

The **Instructor's Manual** includes a table of cases, general suggestions concerning course objectives and course formats, tips about preparing for the CPA examination, and specially prepared transparency masters with suggestions about their use. Among the several aids included in the manual for each text chapter is an outline chart keying the cases, study and discussion questions, and case problems to the pertinent topics in the chapter. Also included are expanded case briefs and comments, "back-to-the-chapter" cross references, and solutions to case problems.

The **Test Bank** provides over 1100 test items in a greatly simplified chapter-by-chapter format that can be used easily with or without the aid of a computer. For adopters who have access to a computer, the publisher will provide on request a unique computerized test generation system, the EXAMINER system. Please contact your local McGraw-Hill representative or office for additional information about this easy method to produce and score examinations using a computer.

ACKNOWLEDGMENTS

In the final preparation of the second edition of *Contemporary Business Law*, we were aided by perceptive reviews of revised as well as new chapters—reviews which prompted numerous revisions and additions. We acknowledge with gratitude the work of the following reviewers: Dr. Deborah Bolliteri, State University College at Oswego; Professor Clark Wheeler, Santa Fe Community College; Professor Larry Curtis, Iowa State University; Mr. Thomas Goldman, Bucks County Community College; Professor Jeremy Wiesen, New York University; Professor Walt Ryba, Southern Connecticut State College; Professor Virginia Maurer, University of Florida; Professor Robert Rodgers, Springfield Technical Community College; Professor Elliott Klayman, The Ohio State University; Professor Michael Cane, University of Hawaii; Professor William Purrington, American River College; Professor Ed Graves, American College; Professor Wynona Hall, Central State University; Professor Carol Docan, California State University—Northridge; Professor Gerald Halpern, University of Arkansas; and Professor Robert Schachman, Bloomfield College. In addition, we benefited greatly from the helpful suggestions of users of the book—instructors and students in various parts of the country.

We also acknowledge with gratitude the endless hours of typing, proofreading, and other assistance provided by our wives.

Finally, we would like to extend our special thanks to Dr. Ethel S. Hoeber. A former university professor specializing in the language arts and education, she continued to coordinate the project after her husband's death and to provide extensive editorial assistance. Her years of dedication to this project, her patience, and her careful attention to detail have added immeasurably to the quality of this book in the second edition as in the first.

J. DAVID REITZEL
DONALD P. LYDEN
NATHAN J. ROBERTS
GORDON B. SEVERANCE

PART ONE

LEGAL FOUNDATIONS

Chapter 1

Development and
Nature of Law

Chapter 2

Law in the
United States

Chapter 3

The Court System;
Civil Procedure

Chapter 4

Administrative Law in
the United States

Chapter

1

Development and Nature of Law

Law has been likened to a system of traffic control, sometimes annoying in its restrictions and confusing in its commands, but essential to the orderly conduct of human affairs. Some people see only the "Thou shalt nots" of the law and tend to view the law as oppressive; others see law as a liberating framework within which to pursue creative activities. Because law serves many diverse functions and often bears upon people in unexpected ways, its scope and nature can easily be misunderstood.

Law is a vastly complex system of social control, firmly rooted in a larger social order. This book focuses on one aspect of that social order, business activities, and on the law affecting these activities. The study of business law requires that one give considerable attention to the nature of business activities, to the needs

and desires of persons participating in or affected by those activities, to the functions and rationale of business law, and, frequently, to the historical context within which the law of business developed. As a background to the study of specific business law topics, this chapter discusses the development of law, the nature of law in general, and the nature of business law in particular.

DEVELOPMENT OF LAW

Like most other aspects of society, law has evolved. Some kinds of law have developed more rapidly than others, and at different periods in history. Yet, the evolution of our Anglo-American legal system has parallelled the gen-

3

eral development of Anglo-American society. An examination of how law has developed and how legal philosophy has contributed to that development will be helpful in understanding contemporary law.

Stages in the Development of Law

In primitive societies law as we know it did not exist. People settled their grievances as custom dictated, frequently by means of vengeance and self-help. Often a person who was wronged took far more drastic revenge than the wrong warranted, and life became intolerably violent. By stages, people began to devise legal systems for resolving disputes.

Legal scholars have recognized five overlapping "periods" in the development of Anglo-American law: the Archaic Period, the Strict Period, the Period of Equity, the Period of Maturation, and the Period of Socialization.[1] The first of these periods began shortly after the Romans quit their occupancy of England (and after the Anglo-Saxons reverted to a primitive state of no law).

Archaic Period   The law of the Archaic Period (approximately A.D. 410 to A.D. 1272) was aimed at limiting violence by regulating vengeance and self-help. At first, the avenger was required merely to direct vengeance only toward the wrongdoer. Eventually, the law established a sum of money to be paid for deeds of violence in lieu of vengeance and permitted accused persons to prove their innocence. If an accused person could not demonstrate innocence and either refused to pay or could not pay the fine, the accuser could then take vengeance. The principal rights and duties recognized by the law of the Archaic Period were those of personal safety, family, and property. The only public right (a right which the state asserts for itself) was that of the "king's peace."

Strict Period   During the Strict Period (approximately 1272–1613), the objective of the law was the protection of the social interest in peace and personal security. This objective was promoted by substituting law for force and private warfare. The common law of this time (judge-made decisional law developed through court cases) focused largely upon remedies, which a person sought by acquiring the appropriate writ (writing) from the appropriate official. If there was no writ, there was no remedy. Although the modern consensual contract originated in this period and although the courts began to enforce some oral promises, the chief characteristics of the law were artificial formality, technicality, and rigidity.

Period of Equity   The Period of Equity (circa 1613–1793) was a time of considerable reform of the law. The protection of morals became a major objective of the law, an objective accomplished by developing the law of crimes, torts, property, contracts, and public callings (duties of innkeepers, common carriers, and others). The rigidity and inadequacy of the common law writ system had contributed to the development, during the Strict Period, of a supplemental court of equity—the origins of which date back to about 1270. In the Period of Equity, the court of equity became a substantial force in the law, as did legislation, and the law emphasized duties and justice without undue formality.[2] In the law of evidence and procedure, cross-examination of witnesses took the place of torture, and jurors became deciders of the facts rather than mere witnesses.

During the Period of Equity, the "law merchant" was incorporated into the common law of England, largely through the efforts of Lord Mansfield, Chief Justice of the King's Bench from 1756 to 1788. The law merchant consisted of practical rules of trade and commerce developed over the centuries by European merchants

---

[1]The following paragraphs are based primarily on Hugh E. Willis, *Introduction to Anglo-American Law*, Indiana University Studies, Bloomington, 1951, Chaps. 9–14.

[2]The development of the courts of equity is discussed in Chap. 2 of this volume.

and traders, and enforced in local mercantile courts. These rules were based on the customs of merchants, were international in character, and were devised because no law suitable for trade then existed. The law merchant, as developed in the English common law (judge-made decisional, case law), contributed substantially to our contemporary law of negotiable instruments, insurance, and sales of goods. It also contributed to our law of partnership and agency.

Period of Maturation   Although the history of the United States began in the Period of Equity, the legal history of the United States began in the Period of Maturation (circa 1793–1875). The objective of the law in this period was the protection of property and freedom of contract, in furtherance of the social interests in security (personal and economic safety) and equality of opportunity. The social philosophy and economic theories of the late 1700s were persuasive to the courts. Theories of competition, laissez faire, and individualism became a part of the law; and individuals were permitted to make their own law by means of contracts. This period saw the major development of the law of sales, and since there was more emphasis on rights than on duties, those business firms in the public callings were allowed to limit their liability by contract.

Period of Socialization   The Period of Socialization began about 1875 and continues into the present. A major objective of this period is to encourage the satisfaction of as many human wants as possible and to assure fair play between groups as well as between individuals. Many new social interests have found protection, and the focus of the present period is on resolving conflicts between interests so that the more substantial interest will prevail. For example, in the Period of Maturation, the law recognized relatively few limitations on the rights of individuals to use property or to contract as they pleased, whereas in the present period the law limits the ability of individuals to use property

or contracts in oppressive ways. Similarly, in the Period of Maturation, the tort principle of "no liability without fault" was predominant, whereas in many situations today that principle must give way to a principle of liability without fault. New public callings like insurance have been identified, and freedom of contract in such matters is now curtailed in favor of control and regulation by public commissions.

These five stages of development reveal a progression from the simple and primitive to the complex and civilized, but they also reveal many human needs to which the legal system has responded throughout the ages in essentially the same way. Many principles of equity are formulated and applied today much as they were during the Strict Period; and the need for stability of contract law is as urgent now as it was in the Period of Maturation.

Role of Legal Philosophy in the Development of Law

The law affects virtually all human affairs. How can a legal system so complex, far-flung, and pervasive be given adequate direction in its development? Legal philosophy is a part of the answer. Legal philosophy contributes to the coherence and refinement of law by expressing for lawyers, judges, legislators, legal scholars, and the public some general principles upon which the law has been or should be based. Four major legal philosophies or schools of legal thought have been especially influential in the development of Anglo-American law.[3]

Natural Law   Many centuries before the beginning of the Archaic Period, thinkers such as Socrates, Plato, and Aristotle believed that all aspects of the world, including humankind, have inherent in them perfect and eternal laws

---

[3]The following paragraphs are based primarily on George C. Christie, *Jurisprudence*, West Publishing Company, St. Paul, 1973; and R. W. Dias, "Jurisprudence," *Encyclopaedia Britannica*, Wm. Benton, Chicago, 1966, vol. 13, pp. 149–159.

which they obey; that these ideal *natural laws* can be discovered by reason; and that human (positive) law should conform to natural law. Near the end of the Archaic Period, medieval churchmen adapted this theory to the needs of medieval times, asserting that positive law should emulate the natural law and that the natural law could be known from reason and divine revelation.

Natural law theories had considerable influence until the late 1700s. By that time, legal thinkers had begun to doubt whether natural law theories could meet the needs of complex societies in a scientific age. The need for a legal philosophy of a more practical and scientific orientation gave rise to the analytical and historical schools of legal thought. Legal thinkers of both schools (called "legal positivists") believed that a person cannot understand the law without examining the law itself.

Analytical Jurisprudence The analytical school stressed the need to examine the law as it is, without being misled by conceptions of what the law *ought* to be. The examination ("analysis") of existing law would involve a thorough study of existing social and economic institutions in an effort to determine the elements and nature of law. Jeremy Bentham (1748–1832) and John Austin (1790–1859), both Englishmen, are the best-known analytical positivists.

Historical Jurisprudence The major development of the historical school began with the work of the German Friedrich Karl von Savigny (1779–1861). He thought that the law would be unpersuasive and ineffective unless it were in accord with the spirit of the people, the *Volksgeist*. He viewed custom as the chief manifestation of law and believed that the function of legal specialists was to reflect the *Volksgeist* in technical matters. Savigny developed his theory in an unsuccessful attempt to prevent the adoption in Germany of a comprehensive legal code derived by "reason" in the manner of the natural law lawyers. In England, Sir Henry Maine (1822–1888) developed a theory of legal evolu-

tion by comparative study of Roman, early English, and Hindu institutions. Evolving societies, he thought, develop their law first through fictions, then by equity, and finally by legislation.

Sociological Jurisprudence and American Realism By the end of the Period of Maturation, analytical and historical schools of legal thought were in decline. Both had made important contributions to the general understanding of law, but neither proved adequate for resolving new problems created by changing conditions. The sociological school, with its emphasis on the functions served by law, provides a philosphical basis for today's Period of Socialization. In the view of the German Rudolf von Jhering (1818–1892), the immediate purpose of law is to protect individual interests, but the paramount social purpose of law is to coordinate competing interests for the ultimate good of society. According to the American Roscoe Pound (1870–1964), the task of lawyers is "social engineering." Social engineering requires the accommodation of three kinds of interests: public (state), social (group), and individual.

American realism, pioneered by John Chipman Gray (1839–1915) and Oliver Wendell Holmes (1841–1935), adopts important principles of other schools of legal thought and adds some of its own. Like the positivists, the realists study the law itself and use analytical methods in that study (e.g., distinguish between law and morals; break the law into smaller units for further analysis). Like the sociological school, the realists view the law as functional and emphasize the need to discern the policy underlying the law. The realists, however, focus more explicitly on the jobs that a legal system is called upon to perform. Moreover, believing that general statements of law often obscure the real bases for decision, the realists prefer to look at what officials actually do, rather than at what they say, in resolving legal problems.

None of these legal philosophies has been

totally abandoned. Just as contemporary law contains elements of ancient law, adjusted to meet contemporary needs, so contemporary legal philosophy contains echoes of the past. For example, natural law philosophers sought to express the value-premises underlying the law. Today, the search for values continues, but it concentrates on social interests rather than on divine revelation.

NATURE OF CONTEMPORARY LAW

An understanding of the nature of our contemporary Anglo-American law requires examination of the functions, meaning, characteristics, classifications, and sources of that law.

Functions of Law

Some statements of legal function or purpose apply to the legal system as a whole and suggest a philosophy of government. The Preamble to the Constitution of the United States is an example. According to the Preamble, the Constitution was ordained and established "to form a more perfect Union, establish Justice, insure domestic Tranquility, provide for the common defence, promote the general Welfare, and secure the Blessings of Liberty" for the people of the United States. Other statements of legal function supplement the Preamble in giving direction to governmental activity. Many legal philosophers believe that a major function of law is to encourage the satisfaction of as many human wants as possible with a maximum of fairness and a minimum of friction. Implicit in these broad statements of legal purpose are notions of individual freedoms, limits on those freedoms, and due process of law.

But what constitutes "justice" and "the general welfare"? What human wants should our law sanction in a pluralistic society where people disagree about what is moral and where legitimate needs and aspirations often conflict? Although few clear answers can be found in the literature of the law, there are some guidelines. Most people would agree, for example, that the law should preserve the integrity of the state, maintain freedom of personal action, reinforce the family, and protect privacy. Certain functions of the law are commonly associated with business activities: enforcing intent (contracts and wills), furthering trade, allowing people to acquire and use property, and protecting people from exploitation and fraud. And, of course, the law in general should be stable, predictable, and capable of appropriate change.

Some matters lie outside the purview of the law. The law is not intended, for example, to dictate religious beliefs or to regulate purely family or social relations, although the law does place limits on dangerous practices associated with these matters. Nor is it usually a function of the law to make purely economic decisions for contracting parties.

In determining the limits of the law, the courts encounter many questions:

- What new social interests merit protection?
- Where can the law control effectively?
- Where should the law yield to other kinds of social control?

Meaning of Law

Some definitions of law are too vague to be useful. Some encompass only certain aspects of the law. Some are based on political or social philosophies not germane to the Anglo-American legal system. However, two definitions of law are very useful. Together, they suggest the general nature of Anglo-American law, its purpose in our society, and some of the legal content which will appear in later chapters. The first, a definition formulated by Professor Hugh E. Willis, is particularly helpful:

Law is a scheme of social control which, by means of legal capacities backed and sanctioned by legal redress, delimits personal liberty for the protection of social interests.[4]

In this definition, *social interest* is a need or want of an individual or a group. Preservation of the peace, the protection of individuals and institutions from unwarranted encroachment by others, and the pursuit of economic, political, and cultural progress are social interests recognized and given protection by the law. There are many others.[5]

A *legal capacity* is an ability conferred upon a person or a group, because of some social interest, to control the conduct of others through the power of the state (any sovereign governmental entity).[6] The legal capacities commonly recognized are: rights, privileges, powers, and immunities. The existence of a legal capacity in one person creates a corresponding legal liability in another. For example, where a party to a contract has a right to be paid a sum of money, the other party has a duty or an obligation to pay it.

Legal redress is a mechanism of social control for enforcing a society's standards. Specifically, legal redress is any means (sanction) provided by the law for protecting social interests. Among the sanctions employed by the law are monetary judgments, deprivation of property, fines, and imprisonment.

As used in defining legal redress, the word *sanction* suggests punishment or coercive intervention. But sanction has another meaning important in the law. *Sanction* also means to give authoritative approval or consent to a thing or action. *Sanctioned by the government* means backed, permitted, or protected by the government.

The *social control* referred to in this definition of law is a control exercised by the group over individuals (through the state).[7] In other words, the rights and duties of individuals are determined by deliberate legal process rather than by the whims of an individual.

The second definition of law, one formulated by the American Law Institute, has received wide acceptance:

> Law is the body of principles, standards and rules which the courts of a particular state apply in the decision of controversies brought before them.[8]

In this definition, *state* means any governmental entity. *Rules* are specific directions for conduct, for example, a traffic rule requiring drivers to stop at red traffic signals. A *standard* is a criterion by means of which conduct in a particular situation is assessed. A person must drive a car the way a reasonably prudent person would drive in similar circumstances. Standards such as that of the reasonably prudent person are used in situations too complicated to be governed by specific rules. *Principles* are the fundamental doctrines of the law upon which rules and standards are based. It is a principle of the law that no person shall be unjustly enriched at the expense of another person. Out of this principle have grown various rules for the recovery of money unjustly withheld.

Desirable Characteristics of Law

Professor Lon L. Fuller has identified eight characteristics which a legal system should have.[9] They are:

1   General rules (standards) of conduct

---

[4]Willis, op. cit., p. 13.
[5]Ibid., pp. 15–16.
[6]Ibid., pp. 17–21.

[7]Ibid., p. 15.
[8]Restatement of the Law, Conflicts, The American Law Institute, Philadelphia, 1934, sec. 3. Copyright © 1934, by The American Law Institute. Reprinted with the permission of The American Law Institute.
[9]Lon L. Fuller, *The Morality of Law*, Yale University Press, New Haven, 1969, pp. 46–91.

2 Publication of the laws sufficient to subject them to public criticism

3 A minimum reliance on retroactive laws

4 Clear laws and clear standards of decision, that is, a minimum of obscurity, incoherence, and vagueness

5 As few contradictory laws as possible

6 Law (especially criminal law) within the citizen's capacity for obedience

7 Law which is relatively constant through time

8 Conformity of official action with declared rule

These characteristics are not absolutely attainable, nor are they universally desirable. The retroactive nature of some law provides an example. To limit despotism, the Constitution of the United States prohibits the enactment of ex post facto laws (e.g., laws imposing criminal sanctions upon persons for acts which, when committed, were not criminal). On the other hand, much nonpenal legislation confers remedial benefits on the population, and therefore retroactive application is not legally objectionable. Some judicial decisions create new law, and when they do, the retroactive effect can hardly be avoided.

Classifications of Law

A person frequently encounters descriptive labels in the study of law, some of which are used to classify the law. Some well-known classifications of law are described in the following paragraphs.

Public and Private Law   Law can be classified as either public or private. *Public law* deals with the organization of government and with the relation of the government to the people. It includes constitutional law, administrative law, and criminal law. *Constitutional law* prescribes generally the plan and method according to which the public affairs of a sovereign govern-

mental entity are to be conducted. In our legal system, the important aspects of constitutional law include: the allocation of powers between the federal government and the state governments; the distribution of powers among the executive, judicial, and legislative branches of government (state or federal); and the rights guaranteed to the people. Administrative law and criminal law are discussed later in this chapter and elsewhere in this book.

Private law deals with the relationships among private persons and organizations. Of the many branches of private law, five main branches are fundamental in the study of business law:

1 The *law of contracts* is concerned with the rights and duties arising out of such promises as the law will enforce or otherwise recognize.

2 The *law of property* treats of the ownership, possession, use, and disposition of things. The law of sales, of secured transactions, and of commercial paper (negotiable instruments) is a blend of contract law and property law.

3 The *law of torts* obligates a person who has committed a private wrong other than a breach of contract to make compensation for the wrong.

4 The *law of persons* determines the extent to which various classes of persons (e.g., minors, mental incompetents) are subject to the rights and duties normally recognized in the law.

5 The *law of business relations* includes the law of agency, of partnerships, and of corporations.

International law has public- and private-law aspects of great concern to firms that do business in foreign countries. "Public international law" includes those rules of customary law that control the conduct of independent nations (states) in their relations with one another, for example, the law of war and peace and the law governing the use of the seas. "Private international law" is the branch of a nation's law that is applied to disputes between citizens of different nations to determine which nation's courts and laws shall be used to resolve the dispute. Private international law is similar to the conflict-of-laws principles that are applied in the United States to resolve disputes between citizens of different states. Conflict of state laws is discussed in Chapter 2. The expression "private international law" has also been applied to the "law merchant," a body of commercial law developed long ago by traders who needed a single body of law for resolving disputes between merchants from different countries. The law merchant and its modern counterparts are discussed in Chapter 24 and in other chapters of this book.

Substantive and Procedural Law   *Substantive law* is concerned with the recognition of rights, duties, privileges, and immunities. The law of contracts, property, torts, and business relations are examples. *Procedural law*, on the other hand, specifies any formal steps to be followed in enforcing or asserting rights, duties, privileges, and immunities. Procedural law is also known as *adjective* law, because it is subsidiary in nature to substantive law.

Criminal and Civil Law   The *criminal law* defines offenses against the state (the public) and provides punishments for their commission. Most crimes are defined by legislation, although some statutes merely refer to a crime by its common law name and thereby leave to the courts the task of applying the common law (case law) definition of the offense. The meaning of "common law" is discussed in Chapter 2.

Crimes are prosecuted by governmental officials on behalf of the public. A victim of crime is not permitted to prosecute the accused offender or to take vengeance, but is merely a complaining witness. Only the state may punish crime. However, because the power to punish sometimes led, in England, to governmental tyranny, the Constitution of the United States and the law interpreting it carefully regulate the prosecutory function by providing persons accused of crime with certain basic rights. These include the right to a fair trial. One aspect of a fair trial is the judicially imposed presumption of innocence.

In the United States, the *civil law* is that law under which a person (the plaintiff) may sue another (the defendant) to obtain redress for a wrong committed by the defendant.[10] The usual remedy in a civil suit is compensatory damages, often for a breach of a contract or the commission of a tort; but in some tort litigation, punitive damages have been awarded for particularly offensive misconduct. Sometimes damages are inadequate as a remedy. In such instances, the plaintiff might seek specific performance of a contract, an injunction against threatened harm, or some other equitable remedy. Where an alleged act is both a crime and a tort, the state may prosecute the person who committed the act, and the victim may bring a civil suit against that person to recover damages for any harm suffered.

Sources of Law

The predecessors of law include the customs, the religious and ethical beliefs, and any notions of social policy by which primitive peoples regulated their practical affairs. As society grew more complex, the state emerged, and law replaced custom as the regulator of most practical affairs. Many customs, religious and ethical beliefs, and notions of social policy have influenced the law or have been incorporated into it, but many have not; and the law contains many rules of conduct *not* found in its antecedents.

What, then, may we regard as the sources of contemporary law? In the United States, the law-making power is lodged in the state and federal governments. Our law has legislative, judicial, and administrative sources.

---

[10]The expression "civil law" is also used to describe those legal systems (e.g., the French) whose law is centered around a comprehensive legislative code.

Legislative Sources In its broadest sense, legislation (enacted law) includes federal and state constitutions; federal and state statutes (often called acts); federal treaties; executive orders and proclamations of the President and of the state governors, as authorized by statutes; and ordinances of subdivisions of the states, such as cities and villages.

Judicial Sources Judicial decisions include judicial treatment of statutes and judicial rulings in situations not governed by statutes. Courts treat statutes in two principal ways: (1) A court might declare a statute invalid. A statute will be held invalid if the court decides that the statute is unconstitutional. Occasionally, a court declares a statute invalid ("void") on the ground that it violates public policy. (2) Where a statute is valid but ambiguous or otherwise unclear, judicial interpretation might be required.

In many branches of law, judicial decisions are the main source of law and contribute to an accumulation of judicially developed legal principles called the "common law." The common law of early England represented an attempt to provide uniformity of law. Then, as now, judges often expanded the law by the method of *analogy*; that is, a principle or a rule of law would be applied to situations essentially similar to, but not exactly the same as, the case originally decided. At the same time, however, expansion of the law was (and is) kept in check by the doctrine of *stare decisis*. Under that doctrine, precedents set by decisions in previous cases are to be followed unless there is a compelling reason to depart from them.

Administrative Sources The legislative and the executive branches of government oversee many administrative agencies. The function of these agencies is to attend to matters which the overseers have neither the time nor the expertise to handle. Many of these agencies publish regulations and render decisions which have the force of law.

NATURE OF BUSINESS LAW

Meaning of Business Law

The phrase *business law* does not refer to a single branch of law; rather, it describes those parts of the law most closely connected with typical business activities. Much of the public law affects business directly and substantially. This book discusses some of the public law: criminal law, administrative law, and (as the occasion warrants) constitutional law. Some chapters and parts of chapters deal with governmental regulation of business activities (e.g., the chapters on securities regulation and trade regulation). And there is a chapter on bankruptcy. However, most of the book is devoted to those branches of private law which might be considered the foundations of business: the law of torts, property, contracts, sales, secured transactions, commercial paper, agency, partnerships, and corporations.

Objectives of a Course in Business Law

The main general objective of a course in business law is to help students—majors in business and nonmajors alike—to understand the legal aspects of common business activities. This objective can be broken down into specific objectives, five of which are discussed in the following pages. Some may seem more important than others; the weight to be given to a particular objective will be affected by the student's reasons for studying business law.

Understanding and Applying Legal Principles The first objective of most business law students is to learn the leading principles of business law and to develop some degree of competence in applying them to business problems. In attaining this objective, a student is likely to acquire considerable knowledge of law as it pertains to specific business activities. That knowledge should enable the student to recognize situations in which it is not safe to proceed without competent legal help, and to communicate effectively with a lawyer if the need arises. At the same time, the student will come to recognize that many business decisions having legal implications may safely be made without advice from a lawyer, if those decisions are made in conformance with basic, well-known legal principles. The knowledge acquired in attaining this objective is the foundation for attaining the next three objectives.

Understanding the Relationship between Law and Business Business law students should go beyond the study of relatively narrow legal problems and should develop an understanding of the relationship between law and business. That relationship has at least three major aspects:

• How and why law facilitates business activities
• How and why law constrains business activities
• How law and business adjust to each other

Attention to these aspects (and to the general nature and purposes of law and business) will provide a background and perspective which can be invaluable to business planners and to others.

Recognizing Business Law as Representative of Law in General Every educated person should have some knowledge and appreciation of the law under which she or he lives. For many college students, a business law course is the best source of knowledge about the law as a whole. Although business law is only a sample of law, that sample is a fairly representative one. The history, philosophy, functions, sources, structure, and even the shortcomings of business law are typical of law in general. And business law is representative of other law with regard to how legal disputes are resolved; how values held by legislators, judges, and society affect the development of law; and how law grows to accommodate new needs.

Evaluating the Law In a democratic society, a citizen has a right to comment on the quality of the law and to try to affect its content. To exercise this right responsibly, a citizen should learn how to evaluate the law. A course in business law provides an unusual opportunity to do so. Evaluating the law involves, among other things, identifying the functions and policy of the law, considering the social or economic background of the law, perceiving trends in the law, and understanding the reasons for the trends. In learning to evaluate the law, students will find three kinds of study materials provided in this book helpful:

1 Text material which presents background information and leading principles of law applicable to business transactions
2 Court cases which illustrate the application of legal principles to business transactions
3 Problems which require analysis of facts and the application of legal principles to business transactions

Learning to judge the quality of the law can begin with the evaluation of cases and statutes in light of certain criteria. When evaluating a court case, a student might apply such criteria as: Is the decision a just one? Does it facilitate or hinder ethical and effective business practices? Does it conform to sound social policy? How could the parties have avoided the costs, inconvenience, and uncertainty of litigation? Comparable criteria could be used to evaluate the legislation involved in the course.

Understanding the Roles of Participants in the Legal Process A course in business law contributes directly and indirectly to an understanding of the roles of participants in the legal process. The major figures in that process include litigants, lawyers, judges, jurors, legislators, the heads and staffs of administrative agencies, personnel in the executive branch of government, and legal scholars. Three of these—lawyers, judges, and legal scholars—have significant developmental roles in the legal process as it pertains to the law presented in this book. The roles of the most important participants in the legal process are discussed as appropriate in subsequent chapters.

SUMMARY

Anglo-American law has developed in five overlapping stages or periods. These stages of development reveal a progression from the simple law of ancient times to the complex law of today. A major objective of contemporary law is to encourage the satisfaction of as many human wants as possible and to assure fair play between groups as well as between individuals.

A number of legal philosophies have been influential in the development of Anglo-American law. These schools of legal thought have given direction to the development of law by expressing general principles upon which the law has been or should be based.

Two definitions of law are very useful in the study of law. Professor Willis has defined law as a scheme of social control. The American Law Institute has defined law as a body of principles, standards, and rules used to decide controversies. These definitions, together with the characteristics of law identified as desirable by Professor Fuller suggest the general nature of Anglo-American law, its purpose in our society, and some of the legal content which will appear in later chapters.

For purposes of analysis and study, the law has been classified in a variety of ways, and a number of functions and sources of law have been identified. The antecedents of law include customs and religious beliefs by which primitive peoples regulated their practical affairs. These antecedents and similar contemporary customs and beliefs affect the content of contemporary law. Contemporary law has legislative, judicial, and administrative sources.

The phrase *business law* describes those parts of the law most closely connected with typical business activities. The main general objective of a course in business law is to help students understand the legal aspects of common business activities. The precise nature of that understanding will depend on which of several specific course objectives the student weights most heavily.

STUDY AND DISCUSSION QUESTIONS

1 "Law is a vastly complex system of social control, firmly rooted in a larger social order." How does this statement apply to business law?

2 Five stages or "periods" of legal development are described in the text. What is the major accomplishment, characteristic, or objective of each period?

3 *(a)* What was the "law merchant"? *(b)* How is the law merchant related to contemporary business law?

4 Legal philosophy guides the development of law by expressing some general principles upon which the law has been or should be based. What main guiding belief or principle characterizes each of the following schools of legal thought? *(a)* Natural law philosophy. *(b)* Analytical jurisprudence. *(c)* Historical jurisprudence. *(d)* Sociological jurisprudence.

5 *(a)* What are some of the functions of the law? *(b)* Give examples of some matters which lie outside the purview of the law.

6 Professor Willis and the American Law Institute have defined law in different ways, with different emphases. What does each definition contribute to your understanding of the nature of law?

7 *(a)* Of the eight characteristics which Professor Fuller believes a legal system should have, which characteristic or characteristics do you consider the most important? Why? *(b)* Are there instances in which absolute attainment of one or more of the eight characteristics might be undesirable? Explain.

8 Explain the essential differences between *(a)* public and private law, *(b)* substantive and procedural law, and *(c)* criminal and civil law.

9 *(a)* How are customs, religious and ethical beliefs, and concepts of social policy related to law? *(b)* What are the sources of law in this country? *(c)* What is the principal "output" of each source?

10 *(a)* In litigation, how might a court treat a statute which is relevant to a dispute? *(b)* What is the "common law"? *(c)* Explain the meaning and significance of the "method of analogy." *(d)* Explain the meaning and significance of *"stare decisis."*

11 *(a)* What is meant by "business law"? *(b)* Which branches of private law might be considered the "foundations of business"?

12 Five specific objectives of a business law course are discussed in the text. Which objective or objectives do you consider the most important? Why?

Chapter

2

Law in the United States

In the United States, individuals and organizations have considerable freedom to establish their social and business priorities and to accomplish their goals as they see fit. Opinions, goals, and methods of operation differ and, indeed, are often in direct conflict. To minimize conflict and to provide a framework for orderly social development, the law must accommodate the diverse and often-opposing desires and needs of a huge population. The legal structure required for such a task has become very complicated. Yet, the general nature and content of our law is not beyond understanding. That understanding will be aided by recalling certain basic facts about our system of government.

First, the Constitution of the United States recognizes two levels of government—federal and state. Consequently, we have 51 major governmental entities capable of making law. Through a process of delegation, thousands of smaller governmental entities and subdivisions (United States possessions and territories, cities, counties, towns, etc.) have the power to make law. Second, within each major governmental entity, law comes from judicial, legislative, and administrative sources. Because there are so many lawmakers, there are many conflicting laws. The conflicts may be resolved by resort to "conflict-of-laws" principles and by other means.

This chapter presents an overview of law in the United States. Successive parts of the chapter discuss the constitutional allocation of power in the United States, the common law, enacted law, conflict of laws, some trends toward greater uniformity in state law, and other trends in the law affecting business.

CONSTITUTIONAL ALLOCATION OF POWER IN THE UNITED STATES

The Constitution of the United States allocates governmental power in two principal ways: (1) between the federal and the state governments, and (2) among the three branches of the federal government.

Federal-State Allocation of Powers

As between the federal and the state governments, the federal government has the powers enumerated (expressed) in the Constitution. In addition, under the Constitution the federal government has powers (called implied powers) which are not specifically named in the Constitution but which are necessary and proper for carrying out the enumerated powers. The federal government has, for example, the implied power to incorporate a national bank as a means of carrying out its express powers to impose and collect taxes, to borrow money, to regulate commerce, and to raise and support armies.[1] On the other hand, "The powers not delegated to the United States by the Constitution, nor prohibited by it to the States, are reserved to the States respectively, or to the people."[2] The powers of a state include its "police power," that

is, the power of the state, through its legislature, to limit the personal freedom and property rights of persons for the protection of the public safety, health, and morals and for the promotion of the public convenience and general prosperity. Although the police power of a state is quite broad, it is subject to constitutional limitations such as the due process requirement that there be a rational connection between a police regulation and the general welfare. State laws against crime, residential zoning ordinances, and the regulation of the manufacture and sale of intoxicating liquors are examples of the exercise by a state of its police power.

There is no police power expressly conferred on the federal government. However, the federal government is empowered to regulate interstate commerce, and in the exercise of its commerce and other powers, Congress indirectly exercises control over many of the social and economic problems that the states may attack directly under their police power. The federal antitrust laws, the Civil Rights Act of 1964 prohibiting racial discrimination in interstate commerce, and a variety of federal statutes pertaining to industrial safety are examples of congressional use of the commerce power to control problems which the states can and sometimes do attack directly under their police power.

The powers of the federal government frequently overlap the powers of the state governments. Consequently, both federal and state law may purport to govern a dispute, and conflicts between state and federal law arise. How such conflicts are resolved is discussed later in this chapter.

Although the federal and the state governments have broad regulatory powers, the federal Constitution prohibits the federal government, the state governments, or both, from engaging in certain activities. The first ten Amendments to the Constitution (called the Bill of Rights) protect individuals from governmental oppression. For example, neither the federal

---

[1]*McCulloch v. Maryland*, 4 Wheat. 316, 4 L. Ed. 579 (U.S. Sup. Ct. 1819).
[2]U.S. Constitution, amend. X.

nor the state governments may enact an ex post facto law (a law which imposes a criminal sanction on a person for an act which was not criminal when the law was made). Other constitutional prohibitions help mark the boundaries between federal and state authority. For example, states may not coin money or enter into treaties with foreign countries. Such activities are exclusively federal responsibilities. The federal government also has a broad power to regulate interstate commerce; but the federal government may not tax articles exported from any state or give preference to the ports of one state over the ports of another.

Distribution of Powers within the Federal Government

The federal Constitution distributes federal powers among three branches of government—the legislative, the judicial, and the executive. Each branch of the federal government thus has an area of primary responsibility. Congress has the power to make laws authorized by the Constitution. The federal judiciary has the power to decide cases and controversies. The President of the United States has executive powers and duties. The President is the Commander in Chief of the armed forces, has the power to make treaties (subject to the concurrence of the Senate), and is required to "take Care that the Laws be faithfully executed."

The distribution of powers among the three branches of government is known as the "separation of powers," and it serves two main purposes:

1 It enables each branch of government to exercise its constitutional prerogatives without undue interference by the other branches.

2 It prevents the excessive accumulation and unchecked use of power by a would-be dictator.

However, the separation of powers is not absolute. For efficiency of governmental operation, considerable overlapping of functions is necessary. The judicial power is vested in one Supreme Court and in such inferior courts as the Congress may from time to time establish. Yet, officers who hold hearings for administrative agencies decide controversies, and in so doing they carry out a "quasi-judicial" function. The power to make law is vested in Congress, but the courts frequently decide cases and controversies on topics for which there is no statutory law. To the extent that such decisions have authority as precedent, the courts which make them can be said to make law. In reality the federal government is one of separation and overlap of powers. Most state constitutions follow the model of the federal Constitution with regard to separation and overlap of powers.

As a further protection against the excessive accumulation of power, the powers of a branch of government are limited by powers possessed by one or both of the other branches. For instance, the judicial branch of the federal government has the power to declare legislation and executive exercises of power unconstitutional. Subject to the approval of the Senate, the President fills vacancies in the Supreme Court, and the President may veto legislation. Congress may enact laws affecting the structure of the federal court system and the activities of the President; and by a process of impeachment (accusation), trial, and conviction, Congress may remove the President, the Vice President, and other civil officers of the United States (including members of the judiciary) from office for committing high crimes and misdemeanors. Similar checks and balances are found in the state governments, most of which pattern their constitutions after the federal Constitution.

COMMON LAW IN THE UNITED STATES

When the English colonists came to what is now the United States, they brought with them not only their language and customs but also a system of law consisting of two parts—"common law" and "equity."

The law of England had its beginnings in separate geographical areas of England, and the rules of law differed from one area to another. As the country developed, a need arose for a body of law *common* to the whole population. Judges began to conform their decisions with those of judges from other regions, and the development of the common (national) law of England was under way.

In its early stages the English common law was "an aristocratic law . . . which handled the problems of a tiny group of people . . . lords and ladies, landed gentry, high-ranking clergymen, wealthy merchants."[3] Gradually the common law expanded to aid others. The history of English commercial law provides an example. Because the scope of the early common law was so narrow, merchants developed their own commercial law (called the "law merchant"). After centuries of development, this law merchant was incorporated into the English common law.

Despite some expansion, the English common law did not develop adequately to meet the needs of a growing population. At common law, a person had no cause of action (legal basis for a lawsuit) unless it was already defined in a writ (document) which had to be purchased from the king and presented to the court. Only then would the court hear the controversy. If there was no writ for the kind of injury suffered or if the writ presented did not precisely fit the situation, a person could not obtain legal redress.

The English were faced with a problem. The early English common law limited itself primarily to the recognition of a narrow range of property rights, and the writ system was not well suited to defining new causes of action. To recognize new property rights and to provide additional remedial relief where existing remedies were inadequate, the English developed the law of equity together with a new set of courts to administer that law.[4]

The new courts were known as *courts of chancery* and came to be known in this country as *courts of equity*. The procedure in equity differed in many ways from that required for an action at common law. For example, common law judges were concerned with exact compliance with the technical requirements of writs. In contrast, equity judges encouraged a method of "facts pleading" which enabled the litigants to get quickly to the substance of the controversy.

Thus, the legal system that the English brought to the American colonies consisted essentially of a rigid system of common law supplemented by a separate, more flexible system of equity.

Adoption by States of the Common Law of England

The English system of law (common law as supplemented by equity) was adopted first in the Colonies and then in each of the states except Louisiana.[5] Some of the states adopted it by constitutional provision; others by statute; still others by judicial decision. Although the adopting phraseology was usually the "common law of England," the phrase was always interpreted to mean the common law (decisional or case law) as modified by some (but not all) basic English statutes and as supplemented by equity law. Some states adopted the common law of England as that law existed in 1607, the year in which the first permanent English colony was founded on this continent. Most states adopted the common law as it existed in England in

---

[3]Lawrence M. Friedman, *A History of American Law*, Simon and Schuster, New York, 1973, pp. 21–22.

[4]For a long time equity purported to protect only property rights. In the United States modern equity recognizes and protects a number of personal and civil rights. Dan B. Dobbs, *Law of Remedies*, West Publishing Company, St. Paul, 1973, pp. 534–536 and sec. 2.11.

[5]Louisiana, being of French background, adopted Roman civil law in its French form as the basis of its legal system. However, the criminal law of Louisiana is based on the common law system.

1776, the date of the Declaration of Independence. Much, perhaps most, of the adopted law has since been modified or replaced by law developed in this country.

The common law of England was not adopted in its entirety. It was adopted with modifications to fit the general American scene and with variations to meet differing local needs. That portion of the English law which was "repugnant to or inconsistent with" the federal Constitution or the constitution of the state was not adopted; neither were those parts of English law which are foreign to the American way of life. For example, the law providing for titles of nobility was rejected, as was the law of primogeniture (a system whereby the eldest son has the exclusive right to inherit the estate of his ancestor). Because of the separation of church and state, ecclesiastical law as a separate system of jurisprudence has never been in effect in any state; but such principles of English ecclesiastical law as are consistent with American law and institutions are a part of the common law of each state. As of 1776, the law merchant had not been fully incorporated into the English common law. Therefore the law merchant was adopted by the states with alterations to fit local business customs. English maritime or admiralty law became a part of our federal law.

Merger of Equity Law and the Common Law in the United States

There were historical and political reasons for the existence of separate common law and equity courts in England. But separate courts and different procedures were expensive and inefficient, and in England the common law and the equity courts were merged into a single system by the Judicature Acts of 1873 and 1875. In the United States the merger of law and equity began even earlier.

Procedural Merger of Law and Equity   New York led the way in the merger of law and equity in the United States by adopting in 1848 a code of reformed pleading which had the following provision:

> The distinctions between actions at law and suits in equity . . . are abolished; and there shall be in this state hereafter but one form of action for the enforcement or protection of private rights and the redress of private wrongs, which shall be denominated a civil action.

Most of the states have established a single set of courts and have abolished the procedural distinctions between actions at law and suits in equity.[6] In a few states there is a single set of courts, but many of the procedural distinctions between actions at law and suits in equity have been preserved. Four states have completely separate courts of law and equity, but the degree of procedural difference varies. Virtually all states have adopted the equity technique of relatively informal facts pleading and have abolished the rigid, technical kind of pleading associated with the writ system.

In some states the party who initiates a suit in equity is called the "complainant," and the other party is called the "respondent." In other states these parties are called "plaintiff" and "defendant," as they would be if they were involved in an action at law.

The procedural distinctions between actions at law and suits in equity were abolished for most kinds of federal proceedings by federal rules of civil procedure which went into effect in 1938. One of the rules provides that in federal proceedings other than those in admiralty there "shall be one form of action to be known as a 'civil action.'"

Continued Separate Identity of Equity   The procedural merger of law and equity has been accompanied by a less extensive substantive merger. A number of substantive concepts de-

---

[6]The extent of merger as of 1972 is discussed in Dobbs, op. cit., pp. 81–82 and sec. 2.6.

veloped in equity are now applied in actions at law as well as in suits in equity.[7] However, in terms of general approaches to the resolution of legal problems, law and equity retain distinctly separate identities.

Law and equity differ in the remedies that they provide for plaintiffs. Law courts awarded judgments in the form of money damages. This approach is suitable where harm to the plaintiff can be easily calculated in terms of money. But some types of harm, such as that resulting from a defendant-seller's refusal to convey real estate to the purchaser, cannot be adequately compensated for by a mere payment of money. Therefore, the court of equity devised so-called "extraordinary" (equitable) remedies to supplement the remedy at law (damages). Today, as in pre-colonial times, equitable remedies are applied when the remedy at law is inadequate. Major equitable remedies, such as specific performance and the injunction, are discussed later in this chapter.

Law and equity differ also in the method of enforcing a judgment. To enforce a judgment at law, the person to whom a judgment was awarded must undertake a second legal process, called "execution." Execution of a judgment at law is the process of procuring a writ of execution from the clerk of the court and having the sheriff seize the defendant's property and sell it to satisfy the judgment. In contrast, decrees in equity are enforceable directly against the respondent (defendant) by means of a contempt proceeding. A respondent who refuses to obey a decree in equity can be sent to jail or fined until he or she obeys the decree or shows a willingness to obey.

Law and equity differ in other respects. For example, the Constitution guarantees a jury trial in most actions at law, whereas in equity there is no jury trial; the equity judge decides the facts. And today, as in pre-colonial times,

equitable principles and remedies are available only where the remedy at law is inadequate.

Equity principles and maxims   A main historic function of a common law judge is to resolve disputes by applying existing law (e.g., statutes and prior decisions). Where the law is clear and not obviously outmoded or destructive, common law judges tend to apply it as written. Indeed, applying statutory law as written is required in this country by the separation-of-powers doctrine if the statute in question is constitutional and unambiguous.[8] Common law judges take a similar approach to the interpretation and enforcement of contracts. Because common law judges look to contracts and to existing law for statements of substantive rights, they avoid deciding controversies merely on the basis of their own moral convictions, which might be too lax or too strict.

The court of chancery, on the other hand, was a "court of conscience" whose responsibility was to use wise discretion in supplementing the common law. In exercising this discretion today, courts of equity are guided by equitable principles and by maxims such as "He who comes into equity must come with clean hands." In accordance with this maxim, a complainant in equity will be denied an equitable remedy (such as the specific performance of a contract) if his or her own conduct is illegal or unethical. The overreaching complainant will have to settle for any remedy available at law—damages, if any can be proved.[9]

The equitable doctrine of laches (delay in asserting a legal right) further illustrates the discretionary and flexible nature of equity in balancing the interests of opposing litigants. At

---

[7]Dobbs, op. cit., pp. 41–42.

[8]However, courts have occasionally held such statutes "void as against public policy."

[9]Illegal conduct, such as fraud by a party to a contract, could also bar that person's recovery of damages at law, but merely unethical conduct would not. Under the Uniform Commercial Code (UCC) "unconscionable" conduct constitutes illegality.

law and in equity, there is a need to encourage the bringing of lawsuits while evidence and memories are fresh, and to establish a time at which potential defendants and their business associates may conduct their affairs free from disruptive litigation. At common law a person has a fixed time within which to bring suit. The time is fixed by a "statute of limitations," and the time limit applies uniformly to all cases within the relevant class of lawsuit. For tort actions the statute of limitations period is usually two years; for contract actions, four to six years; for actions for the recovery of real estate, ten, fifteen, or even twenty-one years. In contrast, the equitable doctrine of laches imposes no fixed time limit. A person must bring a suit in equity within a reasonable time, which may vary according to the circumstances of the case. An equity judge may consider many factors in determining what is reasonable. One factor is whether the complainant has delayed bringing suit for such a length of time that the delay itself would cause the respondent substantial or unreasonable harm.

Equitable remedies   The most familiar equitable remedies are the injunction, specific performance of a contract, rescission of a contract, an accounting for profits, and the imposition of a constructive trust. Specific performance, rescission, and other remedies applicable to contracts are discussed in subsequent chapters of this book. Three equitable remedies—injunction, specific performance, and constructive trust—need special mention here.

An *injunction* is a judicial order to do an act or, more commonly, an order to refrain from doing an act which threatens irreparable harm. Temporary and permanent injunctions may be issued in many situations: for example, in labor disputes; in situations involving a nuisance (a use of property in such a way as to harass, annoy, or harm neighbors); and in situations involving violations of civil rights.

Specific performance will be ordered where

(money) damages are inadequate to compensate the nondefaulting party to a contract for the failure of the defaulting party to perform or to deliver the specific thing promised. Damages are inadequate, for example, where the thing to be delivered is unique. A work of art is considered unique, and its purchaser will usually be granted specific performance where the seller can deliver it but refuses to do so. However, a court will not order the specific performance of a contract for personal services even though those services are unique, as this would in effect impose involuntary servitude. Courts of equity also will not make orders whose enforcement is impractical; for example, many large-scale construction contracts would be impractical to enforce specifically.

A *trust* is a legal arrangement in which a person (the "trustee") holds title to and manages property for another person (the "beneficiary"). A trust in the sense just described is an arrangement planned and consented to by some or all of the parties involved. In contrast, a "constructive" trust is a trust imposed by law. A person who has procured property by fraud may be considered by the law to be a constructive trustee of the property wrongfully acquired. A constructive trustee is required to return property to the person who, in fairness, should have it.

Is There a Federal Common Law?

Each state has its own system of decisional law (hereafter called common law) whose rules may vary from those of other states. When litigants are from different states, and when a federal court must decide the case on the basis of common law, which common law does it apply—the common law of one of the states, or some sort of federal common law?

For almost a century the United States Supreme Court held that there was a federal common law separate and distinct from the law of any state. Then, in 1938, that holding was overruled by the case of *Erie Railroad v. Tompkins*.[10] In that case the Court held:

> Except in matters governed by the Federal Constitution or by Acts of Congress, the [substantive] law to be applied in any case is the law of the State. And whether the law of the State shall be declared by its Legislature in a statute or by its highest court in a decision is not a matter of federal concern. There is no federal general common law.

Therefore, when federal courts apply common law in cases involving citizens of different states (called "diversity of citizenship" cases), they apply the substantive common law of the state in which the federal court is sitting, unless the law of a different state is dictated by conflict-of-laws principles discussed later in this chapter.

There is an important qualification of the rule that there is no federal general common law. As pointed out in Chapter 19, the federal courts have developed what is loosely called the "federal common law of contracts" which is applied to contracts between private persons and the United States government. This law is applied because of the need to subject all government contracts to a single (federal) standard of interpretation rather than to varying standards arising from the laws of fifty different states. The same reasoning has also led to the development of a federal common law of commercial paper.

ENACTED LAW IN THE UNITED STATES

Meaning and Classification of Enacted Law

The word "legislation" is ordinarily used to refer to statutes passed by Congress and by state legislatures. But the legislative power of the United States and the various states may be exercised in more than one way. The phrase "enacted law" is usually used to designate the exercise of the legislative power in its broadest aspect.

Enacted law includes the following classes of law:

1 Federal and state constitutions
2 Federal and state statutes (acts)
3 Federal treaties
4 Executive orders and proclamations issued by the President of the United States or by state governors when authorized by statute
5 Administrative rules and regulations when authorized by statute, which have the force and effect of law
6 Ordinances of the subdivisions of the states, such as cities and towns

Rank of Laws in the United States

Rank of Enacted Laws in Order of Authority
Our legal system would be unworkable if law were not ranked in some order of authority. Article 6 of the federal Constitution provides a framework for ranking enacted law. According to Article 6:

> This Constitution, and the Laws of the United States which shall be made in Pursuance thereof; and all Treaties made, or which shall be made, under the Authority of the United States, shall be the supreme Law of the Land; and the Judges in every State shall be bound thereby, any Thing in the Constitution or Laws of any State to the contrary notwithstanding.

By virtue of this Article, the federal Constitution heads all enacted laws in authority. Next below it are the statutes and treaties of the United States. United States statutes and treaties are of equal rank. A later treaty supersedes a prior, inconsistent statute; a later statute supersedes a prior, inconsistent treaty. When federal and state enacted law covers the same subject matter, the federal law prevails, *if valid*.

[10]304 U.S. 64.

When only state law is involved, the state constitution ranks highest, followed by state statutes. Below the statutes come the ordinances of the state's subdivisions.

The relationship between federal and state statutes requires special mention. Federal law can validly regulate only those matters committed to federal authority by the Constitution, that is, those matters within the express and implied powers of the federal government. The regulation of all other matters is reserved to the states (or to the people). Thus, only those constitutional federal statutes which carry out some federal power will take precedence over conflicting state statutes.

Even where a federal statute regulates a federal matter, much nonconflicting state law can coexist. For example, the federal Bankruptcy Code expressly looks to state law for the regulation of certain aspects of bankruptcy. Where federal statutes are silent as to the role of state law, nonconflicting state regulation is valid *except* in three situations summarized briefly as follows:

1 *Where national uniformity of regulation is required.* Courts will strike down any state law on such a topic (as, for example, where a state law purports to regulate the length of railroad trains) even though no federal law exists.

2 *Where the federal government has "preempted the field."* The federal government can preempt (take exclusive control) by expressly denying the states the right to regulate, or by enacting a comprehensive scheme of regulation which by implication precludes state regulation. For example, because the federal government extensively regulates air traffic, a city was precluded from enforcing a noise-control ordinance affecting jet aircraft.[11]

3 *Where the state statute does not usurp federal authority but otherwise violates the Constitution.* For example, a state statute is invalid if it discriminates against interstate commerce or imposes an "undue burden" on interstate commerce. A state statute which imposes a sales tax on milk produced outside the state but not on milk produced within the state discriminates against interstate commerce. A state statute might require an out-of-state firm doing a strictly mail-order business to collect the state's "use" tax. Such a statute imposes an undue burden on interstate commerce and therefore is invalid.[12]

Rank of Common Law in Relation to Enacted Law In terms of substantive coverage, the common law ranks below all classes of enacted law. A rule of common law will be applied only where there is no valid enacted law. However, the fact that the common law ranks below enacted law should not lead us to minimize the role of the courts. They have the exclusive responsibility for determining the common law, and they have the ultimate responsibility for determining the constitutionality and the meaning of enacted law. Moreover, when courts interpret constitutions and statutes, their interpretations affect the content of the enacted law.

Rank of Administrative Rules In addition to the great number of federal and state statutes there are the rules and regulations of federal, state, and local administrative agencies. These rules and regulations have the force and effect of law, and they rank ahead of common law decisions in approximately the way that federal and state statutes do.

Interpretation and Construction of Statutes
Meaning of Interpretation and Construction Interpretation of a statute is the process of discovering and explaining the meaning of any unclear language. *Construction* of a statute is the process of discovering and explaining the

---

[11]*City of Burbank v. Lockheed Air Terminal, Inc.*, 411 U.S. 624 (1973).

[12]*National Bellas Hess v. Dept. of Revenue*, 386 U.S. 753 (1967). A use tax is a tax levied on goods purchased outside a state for use in the state. Its purpose is to prevent residents of a state from escaping the state sales tax merely by buying goods from an out-of-state dealer.

legal effect which the statute is to have. Construing a statute may involve interpreting unclear language, but it mainly involves such tasks as determining the purpose or policy of the statute, deciding how the provisions of a complex statute are related, and deciding to what specific people or things the statute applies. "Interpretation" and "construction" are often used interchangeably.

Need for Authoritative Interpretation The causes of statutory vagueness or ambiguity are many. The legislature might have used general language and left to the courts or administrative agencies the task of applying the statute as specific situations develop. A statute might govern so complex a matter that the statute itself is complex and confusing. A statute might simply have been poorly drafted. Even where a statute is clear, litigants often take opposite positions as to its meaning. Authoritative interpretation is therefore indispensable. Although an administrative agency such as the Internal Revenue Service may have the immediate responsibility for interpreting a statute, ultimately the courts are responsible. When faced with an unclear statute, a court or an agency seeks an interpretation which conforms to the intent of Congress or the legislature and which preserves the usefulness of the statute.

Determination of Constitutionality as a Preliminary to Interpretation Sometimes a statute is alleged to be not only unclear but also unconstitutional. Because of the need to maintain separation of powers, a court normally will not determine the constitutionality of a statute if there is an alternative basis for disposing of the case. Frequently, however, there is no alternative basis for decision, and the court must address the question of constitutionality. In such a situation the court might determine the constitutionality of the statute before interpreting it (although some preliminary interpretation might be required in order to isolate the constitutional issue). The courts have developed two main "tests" for determining the constitutionality of a statute: the "any-rational-purpose" test and the "compelling-interest" test.

Under the *any-rational-purpose test,* a statute is constitutional if it has some rational purpose, even though the purpose found by the court is not the purpose which may have been expressed by the legislature. The use of this test of constitutionality minimizes judicial interference with legislative activities by imposing a light burden of justification on the legislature, and this is the test usually applied.

The *compelling-interest test* is applied where legislation threatens individual rights, such as the right to vote or to exercise freedom of speech. Under the compelling-interest test, legislation will be held unconstitutional unless there is a governmental interest sufficiently compelling to warrant curbing the right in question. Compared to the any-rational-purpose test, the compelling-interest test imposes a heavier burden of justification on the legislature and is therefore less compatible with the separation-of-powers doctrine. For this reason, the courts tend to limit application of the compelling-interest test to infringement of fundamental rights guaranteed by the Constitution.

Common Law Rules of Statutory Construction To aid them in construing statutes, the courts have developed numerous rules of statutory construction. Illustrations of well-known rules of construction follow:

1 The words of a statute are to be construed with reference to its *subject matter*. If they are susceptible of several meanings, that one is to be adopted which best accords with the subject matter to which the statute relates.

2 Words are to be construed in connection with the *context*, and the entire statute is to be read as one complete instrument.

3 The words of a statute are to be taken in their ordinary and *popular meaning*, unless they are technical terms or words of art (words

used in a special sense), in which case they are to be understood in their technical or special sense.

4 Statutes on the same subject are to be *construed* together.

Legislative Rules of Statutory Construction

In each state the rules of statutory construction adopted by the courts have been supplemented by rules enacted by the legislature. These supplemental rules may be in the form of definitions incorporated within a statute and applicable only to it. Good examples of this procedure may be found in Article 1 of the Uniform Commercial Code appearing in Appendix 1 of this book. The supplemental legislative rules may also be expressed as general rules of construction, applicable to all the state's statutes, or perhaps to all the statutes within a particular state code. The following illustrative rules appear in the Civil Code of California:

1 No part of [the Civil Code] is retroactive, unless expressly so declared [Sec. 3].

2 The rule of the common law, that statutes in derogation thereof [i.e., statutes limiting or impairing the common law] are to be strictly construed, has no application to this code. The code establishes the law of the state respecting the subjects to which it relates, and its provisions are to be liberally construed with a view to effect its objects and to promote justice [Sec. 4].

CONFLICT OF STATE LAWS

Within the limits imposed by the federal Constitution, each state has the power to make law as it sees fit. Despite general similarities of coverage, techniques of lawmaking, and methods of dispute resolution, the laws of the states differ in many respects. Some kinds of contracts or contractual provisions are enforceable in some states but not in others. An act may be a tort or a crime in some states, but not in others. Remedies and measures of damage vary from state to state. Tax burdens vary, and so do the requirements for establishing or conducting a business.

If a person's business or personal affairs were confined to a single state, differing state laws would cause little difficulty. But few people can avoid interstate transactions. A person might reside in one state, work in another, own property in a third, and travel in many. So simple an act as buying merchandise from an out-of-state mail-order house involves the possibility of a conflict between state laws. To resolve such conflicts, each state has developed a body of conflict-of-laws principles. These principles are usually treated as a part of the substantive law of the state.

Many suits involving interstate transactions or involving litigants who are citizens of different states are brought in federal courts and require the application of state law. The case of *Erie Railroad v. Tompkins* (mentioned earlier in this chapter) requires the federal court to apply the substantive law of the state in which the federal court sits. However, because the substantive law of that state includes its conflicts principles, the federal court may be required by those principles to apply the law of some other state.

General Principles for Resolving Conflicts of Laws

In a typical conflict-of-laws situation, two or more states have the power to hear the case and to render a binding decision. Usually the plaintiff is a resident of the state in which suit is brought (the "forum" state) or is for some other reason entitled to bring suit there. The defendant may be a resident of another state, or the events which led to the bringing of suit may have occurred there.

The forum state's jurisdiction over the person

of the defendant may be based on *any* of the following:

1   The defendant's residency, citizenship, or presence in the forum state

2   The defendant's consent to the jurisdiction of the forum state (e.g., appearing in its court to defend the suit)

3   The forum state's "long-arm" statute (a statute conferring jurisdiction over out-of-state defendants)

Long-arm statutes are valid if there are sufficient "minimum contacts" between the defendant and the forum state to make its assertion of jurisdiction reasonable. Sufficient minimum contacts might exist, for example, where an out-of-state defendant conducts business within the forum state.

The forum state exercises its jurisdiction over the person of the defendant by delivering to the defendant a summons to appear in court and defend the suit. The service of process (delivery of the summons) meets the constitutional requirement of due process if it gives the defendant reasonable notice of the suit and a reasonable opportunity to be heard. While service personally on the defendant is preferred, delivery of a summons by mail or by some other means may provide due process, depending on the circumstances.[13]

The object of conflict-of-laws principles is to provide the forum court with a means for determining which state law to apply. The following paragraphs state some traditional conflicts rules and illustrate a newer judicial approach to the resolution of conflicts of laws.

Some Traditional Rules That Govern Conflicts of Laws   Suppose that X, a resident of Ohio, while in Pennsylvania, is negligently struck and injured by Y, a driver from New York. X is able in Ohio to secure service of process on Y and sues Y in an Ohio court. Under the traditional conflict-of-laws rule for tort actions, the law of Pennsylvania (the place of injury) is applied by the Ohio court.

Actions concerning contracts are subject to a variety of conflict-of-laws rules. Suppose that X, a resident of Ohio, meets Y, a New York architect, in Pennsylvania and there makes a contract with Y for the design and construction in Ohio of a building. If suit is brought for breach of contract, what law applies? Some early American cases held that the law of the place where the contract was made (Pennsylvania) would apply. Others held that the law of the place where the contract was to be performed (Ohio) would apply. In many conflicts situations today, the courts apply the law of the state which has the most substantial "contacts" with the matter being litigated.

The Grouping-of-Contacts Approach   In the contract illustration just given, Pennsylvania was merely a meeting place, and its law would not be applied under the grouping-of-contacts theory. The law of either Ohio or New York could apply, because both states have contacts with the contract. Which state has the more substantial contacts depends, however, on who breached the contract, what kind of performance has occurred, the nature of the breach, the ability of the forum court to provide an effective remedy, and so on. The grouping-of-contacts method of selecting the law to be applied has also been used in tort cases.

Right of Contracting Parties to Choose Controlling Law

Within limits, the parties to a contract may choose the state law by which they will be bound. As one writer[14] explains:

---

[13]Summons and service of process are discussed in more detail in Chap. 3.

[14]Herbert F. Goodrich, *Handbook of the Conflict of Laws*, West Publishing Company, St. Paul, 1964, p. 203 (4th ed. by Eugene F. Scoles). Quoted with permission of the publisher.

If the parties are all from the same state and there they negotiate and execute a contract to be performed therein, they cannot stipulate that the law of . . . another state having no contact with the transaction shall apply, since this is normally a matter subject to mandatory regulation in the public interest. However, if one party lives in [one state] and the other [in another state] and they are negotiating by mail for a loan, there seems no reason why the regulations of either state are not adequate to protect the public interest. . . . There is often stated a requirement that the state whose law is chosen must have some substantial relationship to the transaction. . . . [But] if the element of free intent of one party is absent, as where the choice-of-law clause is inserted by mistake or fraud, then the clause is ineffective.

TREND TOWARD GREATER UNIFORMITY IN STATE LAW

Two approaches toward greater uniformity in state law are in progress in the United States, and each is achieving a considerable measure of success. One approach is that of encouraging state legislatures to pass uniform legislation. The other approach is that of encouraging courts to apply uniformly stated principles of the common (decisional) law.

Trend toward Uniform State Legislation

The movement to encourage uniform legislation began in 1892 with the founding of the National Conference of Commissioners on Uniform State Laws. The national conference is a body of commissioners appointed by the governors of their respective states. Committees prepare tentative drafts of acts, sometimes employing legal experts for the purpose. Each draft is discussed section by section at the annual meeting of the national conference and may or may

not be sent back to the committee for revision. Through this process of criticism and revision, each uniform act reflects the experience and judgment of lawyers from every part of the United States. When it is finally approved by the national conference, a proposed act is submitted to the American Bar Association for approval, and eventually the act is recommended for adoption by the state legislatures. Over the years, many uniform acts were developed and adopted (e.g., the Uniform Partnership Act and the Uniform Consumer Credit Code). Those dealing with commercial subjects such as commercial paper and sale of goods were eventually incorporated into the Uniform Commercial Code.

Ideally, from the standpoint of facilitating interstate business, the acts proposed by the national conference would be adopted without change and would be interpreted by all courts in a uniform way. The ideal has not been fully realized. A few states have failed to adopt some fundamental uniform acts such as the Uniform Partnership Act. Every state except Louisiana has adopted the Uniform Commercial Code. In 1975 Louisiana adopted in substance four of the Code's eleven Articles and later adopted others. In adopting the Code or parts of it, all the states made numerous changes in order to conform the Code to their laws or to local needs. To the extent of the changes, the Code—as adopted—ceased to be truly uniform. Furthermore, state courts have not always interpreted the same section of the Code in the same way. Yet, despite these shortcomings and variations in legislation and interpretation, substantial uniformity has been achieved.

On certain subjects where uniformity does not seem practical, the national conference prepares "model acts" to guide state legislatures in the drafting of their own acts. Illustrative of model acts are the Model Business Corporation Act and the Model State Administrative Procedure Act.

**Trend toward Uniform
Statements of the Common Law**

The movement to encourage courts to apply uniformly stated principles of common (decisional) law was initiated and is fostered by the American Law Institute, organized in 1923 and composed of eminent members of the bar.

The object of the institute, as expressed in its certificate of incorporation, is "to promote the clarification and simplification of the law and its better adaptation to social needs, to secure the better administration of justice, and to carry on scholarly and scientific legal work." One method by which the institute seeks to attain its object is by preparing and printing a "restatement" of the common law covering each major branch of the law. For example, there is a Restatement of the Law of Contracts, a Restatement of the Law of Agency, and a Restatement of the Law of Torts. The American Law Institute is continually working on the updating of published restatements of the common law.

There is a growing tendency on the part of lawyers, judges, and authors of legal works to quote from the restatements and to view them as persuasive statements of legal principles. However, it should be noted that a restatement, unlike a uniform act which has been adopted by a legislature, is *not* an official statement of law. Its rules and principles are merely persuasive to a court until incorporated into official judicial opinions.

OTHER TRENDS IN THE LAW AFFECTING BUSINESS

This book describes or alludes to a great number of trends in the law affecting business. The law constantly grows and adjusts to meet new needs. Many trends in the law affecting business are of this accommodating nature; but the law also has defects and gaps in coverage, and many of the trends in the law are therefore corrective in nature.

Three major trends or developments in the recent legal history of the United States affect business directly and deserve brief mention here: the development of the administrative regulation of business, the development of consumer protection, and some recent trends in corporate responsibility.

Administrative Regulation of Business

Since the 1930s, the regulation of business by administrative agencies has become a fact of business life. In many instances the regulation is detailed, as in the regulation of the insurance business. Few businesses are entirely unaffected by governmental regulation.

In presenting administrative law, Chapter 4 of this book deals primarily with the development, legal nature, functions, and internal operations of administrative agencies. The substantive law output of administrative agencies is too large and varied to discuss except by way of illustration. Yet, by a careful reading of Chapter 4 and other chapters on substantive law, the reader can detect a number of general trends in the substantive output of administrative agencies. These trends concern the amount, nature, and propriety of governmental regulation and will remain of interest throughout one's business and personal life.

Consumer Protection

Consumer protection has long been an important aspect of American law, but consumer protection law has acquired special significance within the past two or three decades. Consumer protection law can be defined as any law which provides a person with a remedy for injury suffered as a result of the purchase of, use of, or contact with, property or services.

Some chapters of this book are devoted exclusively to topics usually characterized as consumer protection law. The chapters on product liability and securities regulation are examples. Other chapters present consumer protection law as a part of a broader topic of substantive law. Warranties in the sale of real estate, fraud in the law of torts, consumer fraud as an aspect of white-collar crime, and the role of the Federal Trade Commission in the regulation of advertising are examples. Some consumer legislation such as the federal Truth in Lending Act is mentioned briefly, but a detailed study of recent federal and state consumer legislation is beyond the scope of this book. In the discussions of consumer protection, many trends in the substantive law itself will be apparent.

Corporate Responsibility

Problems in business ethics have concerned society for ages. In the 1200s the question was whether trading in goods produced by others should be permitted at all. It took a long time for society to recognize the need for traders and to develop a rationale under which the taking of profits and the charging of interest would be considered legitimate.[15] The business excesses of nineteenth century America brought into focus the question of whether private initiative could be left unchecked. Monopolies and the suppression of labor led to the enactment of the Sherman Antitrust Act, the Clayton Act, and other remedial legislation which placed limitations on business activities. The rise in and possible misuse of power by labor unions has encouraged corrective legislation in this area. In the law of sales, unconscionability as a defense to the enforcement of a contract was incorporated into Article 2 of the Uniform Commercial Code. Much of the conduct covered by that concept was once considered merely unethical. Now it is illegal.

The recognition of corporate responsibility is of increasing interest. The expression *corporate responsibility* describes the obligations of a corporation to act (through its directors, officers, and employees) in a socially acceptable way. At one time corporate conduct was considered

responsible if corporate managers honestly sought maximum profits for the shareholders regardless of the social effect of corporate activities. Natural resources were plentiful, and pollution and environmental destruction were not considered serious problems. Conditions today are much different, and many thoughtful people are seriously questioning whether traditional corporate organization and practices should be allowed to continue. Some of the changes that have been suggested are discussed later in this book, especially in Chapters 42, 44, and 45.

SUMMARY

The Constitution of the United States allocates governmental power between the federal and the state governments and among the three branches of the federal government. The federal government has the powers expressly conferred on it by the Constitution together with implied powers necessary and proper for carrying out the express powers. All other powers are reserved to the states or to the people. In accordance with the doctrine of separation of powers, the Constitution distributes federal powers among the legislative, the judicial, and the executive branches of the federal government. Most state constitutions and governments follow the federal model.

Within the framework established by the Constitution, each state is free to develop its own law. All states except Louisiana adopted some version of the English legal system— common law as supplemented by a separate system of equity. Louisiana made Roman civil law in its French form the basis of its legal system.

In most states common law and equity were merged into a single system as to procedure. The substantive merger was less extensive, and the common law and equity retain separate identities. The remedy at law is damages; equity provides supplemental remedies where the

---

[15]Peter Riesenberg, "Profit and the Church, a Gradual Accommodation," *MBA Magazine*, November 1977.

remedy at law is inadequate. Among the equitable remedies are the injunction, specific performance of a contract, and the imposition of a constructive trust. In cases involving diversity of citizenship the federal courts are required to apply the common law of the state in which the federal court is sitting. That common law includes the state's conflict-of-laws principles.

Enacted law includes federal and state constitutions and statutes, city ordinances, and the like. In general, enacted law outranks common law in authority. However, the courts have the ultimate responsibility for determining the constitutionality and the meaning of enacted law.

Courts and agencies often engage in a process of interpretation and construction of statutes. A court or an agency seeks an interpretation which conforms to the intent of the legislature and which preserves the usefulness of the statute. If called upon to determine the constitutionality of a statute, a court might apply either the any-rational-purpose or the compelling-interest test of constitutionality.

Conflicts between federal and state law are resolved by application of the Supremacy Clause (Article 6) of the Constitution. Conflict of state laws is resolved by application of state conflict-of-laws principles. In many conflicts situations today, the courts apply the law of the state which has the most substantial "contacts" with the matter being litigated. Within limits, the parties to an interstate contract may choose the state law by which they will be bound.

Two major trends toward greater uniformity in state law are now well established. One is the trend toward the adoption of uniform state legislation; the other is the increasing use by judges, lawyers, and others of the restatements of the common law.

Many developments or trends in the recent legal history of the United States affect business directly. They include the development of administrative regulation of business, the development of consumer protection, and some recent trends in corporate responsibility.

STUDY AND DISCUSSION QUESTIONS

1 What factors contribute to the complexity of our law and legal system?

2 (a) How does the Constitution of the United States allocate power between the federal and the state governments? (b) Define and illustrate the police power of the states. (c) Does the federal government have a police power? Explain. (d) The text of this chapter describes two kinds of constitutional prohibition. What is the nature and purpose of each kind of prohibition?

3 (a) How does the Constitution distribute power among branches of the federal government? (b) Explain the meaning and purpose of "separation of powers." (c) Is the separation of powers complete? Why? (d) Illustrate the "checks and balances" of the federal government.

4 (a) What was the original reason for the development of the common law? (b) Why did the English develop a system of equity?

5 (a) How and to what extent did the English common law become a part of our law? (b) To what extent have law and equity been merged in this country? (c) What are the chief differences between law and equity? (d) Describe or define the following equitable remedies: injunction, specific performance, and the imposition of a constructive trust.

6 Explain the significance of *Erie Railroad v. Tompkins.*

7 (a) What constitutes "enacted law"? (b) In order of authority, what is the rank of the different kinds of enacted law? (c) Can state statutes which conflict with federal statutes ever prevail over the federal statutes? Explain. (d) Some nonconflicting state law can coexist with federal statutes which regulate federal matters, but some cannot. Under what circumstances will nonconflicting state law *not* be upheld?

8 (a) Does the low rank of the common law

mean that the courts have an insignificant role in our legal system? Explain. *(b)* What is the rank of administrative rules and regulations?

9 *(a)* Distinguish between interpretation and construction of a statute. *(b)* Why is authoritative interpretation of enacted law necessary?

10 Sometimes a court is called upon to determine the constitutionality of a statute. *(a)* Describe the any-rational-purpose test of constitutionality. *(b)* Describe the compelling-interest test of constitutionality. *(c)* Which of the two tests of constitutionality is more compatible with the separation-of-powers doctrine? Why? *(d)* To what kind of situations is the compelling-interest test applied?

11 Give an illustration of *(a)* a common law rule of statutory construction and *(b)* a legislative rule of statutory construction.

12 *(a)* Describe a situation which would give rise to a conflict of state laws. *(b)* How might the forum court gain jurisdiction over the person of the defendant? *(c)* What is meant by "service of process," and how is it accomplished?

13 *(a)* Give an illustration of a traditional rule for resolving a conflict of laws. *(b)* Explain or illustrate the grouping-of-contacts approach to resolving a conflict of laws. *(c)* Under what circumstances may contracting parties choose the state law by which they will be bound?

14 *(a)* How is a uniform state statute developed? *(b)* Is the adoption of uniform legislation by all the states likely to result in complete uniformity of state law? Why?

15 In legal effect, how does a uniform state law differ from a restatement of the common law?

3

The Court System;
Civil Procedure

Justice and order require some system for the determination of rights and their enforcement. In the United States, the courts constitute a most important part of that system. Beginning with Chapter 4 of this book, actual court cases are presented in the chapters. In order to understand the background of each case, the student must be familiar with the court system and the procedure involved in the trial and appeal of a civil lawsuit.

The first part of this chapter deals with the function and jurisdiction of courts in the United States, the organization of the federal and state courts, and the work of the courts. The remainder of the chapter deals with procedures related to civil lawsuits and with an alternative means of resolving disputes, called "arbitration."

THE COURT SYSTEM

In most states the same court system handles both criminal and civil cases. However, criminal procedure differs greatly from civil procedure. As this book deals with commercial law, the following discussion of the court system and court procedure is centered upon civil law matters. Some aspects of criminal procedure are discussed in Chapter 8.

Function and Jurisdiction of Courts
Function of Courts The word "court" has various meanings. At times it is used as a synonym for judge, as when a judge admonishes an attorney to address his or her remarks "to the court and not to the opposing counsel." At other

times it may be used to indicate the place where a judicial tribunal functions, as in the statement that trials must take place "in court," whereas orders may be signed "in chambers" (judge's office or anteroom). Usually, however, the word "court" is used to mean a tribunal established by the state or federal government for the administration of justice.

The main function of a court is to decide controversies between litigants (parties in a lawsuit). The decision is called a *judgment*. Courts ordinarily do not answer hypothetical questions. For example, a court may enforce a contract which has been breached, but it will not advise a person what his or her rights would be under a contemplated contract. In many states, courts are empowered to declare the rights of the parties to a controversy even though no actual wrong has occurred or is threatened, as long as there is a real dispute of fact or a question of law. Judgments in which rights are declared without ordering the parties to do anything are called *declaratory* judgments. Declaratory judgments are useful because they permit rights to be determined (as under existing leases, contracts, wills of deceased persons, statutes, etc.) before prejudicial action has been taken. Some of the cases presented in later chapters involve requests for declaratory judgments.

Jurisdiction of Courts   The word "jurisdiction" is used in different senses. As used here, *jurisdiction* means the authority or power of a court to hear and decide controversies. In order to process a case, a court must have two kinds of jurisdiction: jurisdiction over the subject matter (type of case) and jurisdiction over the property or the litigants in the case.

Jurisdiction over the subject matter is the authority of a court over the particular kind of case presented to it for decision. For example, a civil court may be without authority to process cases involving an amount in controversy above a certain monetary sum. The proper tribunals to handle various types of civil suits are discussed below. Jurisdiction of a court may be limited by

a defined geographic area. For example, the state courts of New York have authority to handle cases involving lands lying within the state but not involving lands lying elsewhere. Jurisdiction over the parties may be based on residency, citizenship, presence in the state, or a long-arm statute.[1] The methods of bringing the parties before a court will be discussed in the latter part of this chapter under the heading, "Civil Procedure."

Where only one court has the requisite authority to hear and decide a case, the court is said to have *exclusive* jurisdiction. For example, a suit involving admiralty law can be processed only in a federal court. Where two or more courts have authority, they are said to have *concurrent* jurisdiction. In the next section on the federal and state court systems, we will see that in some classes of cases the jurisdiction of the federal courts is exclusive; in other cases, the jurisdiction of the state courts is exclusive; in still others, the federal courts and the state courts have concurrent jurisdiction.

Federal and State Courts

The dual system of federal and state governments has resulted in two sets of courts—federal and state. Most of the cases presented in this textbook are state court decisions, but some are federal. A brief discussion of the federal and state court systems is necessary to understand why a case was heard in a particular tribunal. Before we examine the federal court system, we need to know what judicial power is extended to the federal government by the Constitution of the United States.

Judicial Power of the United States   The Constitution provides that the judicial power of the United States shall extend to certain categories of disputes. A few of the major categories are:

1   Cases arising under the Constitution, acts of Congress, and treaties. Such cases are commonly said to involve a *federal question*.

[1]See Chap. 2, p. 25, second column, and p. 26.

2 Admiralty and maritime cases.

3 Cases affecting ambassadors, other public ministers, and consuls.

4 Controversies to which the United States is a party.

5 Controversies between citizens of different states. Such cases are commonly called *diversity of citizenship* cases.

Federal courts have exclusive jurisdiction over cases in categories (1) through (4). Federal and state courts may have concurrent jurisdiction over diversity of citizenship cases.

Congress has never granted federal courts all the jurisdiction permitted under the Constitution. For example, under present provisions, the federal courts have jurisdiction in suits between private litigants only when the matter in controversy exceeds the sum or value of $10,000, exclusive of interest and costs. In such controversies the jurisdiction of the federal courts is not exclusive, but is concurrent with that of the state courts. When the sum involved is $10,000 or less, the state courts have exclusive jurisdiction.

The Federal Court System The United States Constitution provides that the "judicial power of the United States shall be vested in one Supreme Court, and in such inferior [lower] courts as the Congress may from time to time ordain and establish."[2] At present the federal court system consists of district courts, courts of appeals, the Supreme Court, and various special courts. Figure 3.1 illustrates the federal court system. All judges who serve on a federal court are appointed for the period of their good behavior by the President of the United States, with the advice and consent of the Senate.

District courts The district courts are the trial courts of the federal judicial system. A litigant begins a lawsuit in a United States district court. There is one such court for each federal judicial district. In the less populous states a district covers the whole state; in the more populous states, such as California and New York, there are several federal districts.

Depending upon the volume of litigation, the court may consist of one, two, or more judges. Most cases are tried before a single judge; a few types of cases are tried before a panel of three judges.

Courts of appeals If a litigant is dissatisfied with the judgment rendered by the district court, the litigant may file an appeal with a higher court. The courts of appeals hear all appeals from district courts except for a few classes of cases where appeals may be taken directly to the Supreme Court. They also review orders of federal administrative agencies. In recent years the reviewing of such orders has become one of their important functions.

Originally the judges of these courts traveled a circuit and the courts were called *circuit courts of appeals*. There are at present twelve circuits serving the 50 states. Although judges of the courts of appeals no longer travel regularly, they are still referred to as "circuit judges."

Appeals are usually heard by a panel of three judges. The judges review the trial proceedings in the district court and the evidence presented in the district court to determine if an error of law was made in the trial. For example, a litigant may file an appeal alleging that the district court judge improperly denied a motion or gave the jury an erroneous instruction.

The Supreme Court The chief function of the Supreme Court is its appellate function. Most of the cases it reviews come from the courts of appeals, although a few come from other federal courts and even from the highest state courts. State decisions may be appealed when the issue in the case involves a federal question. A litigant is not entitled as a matter of right to appeal to the United States Supreme Court. This is true even if a case involves a federal question. The Supreme Court has discretion to choose only the cases it deems important enough to hear.

---

[2]U.S. Constitution, Art. III, sec. 1, par. 1.

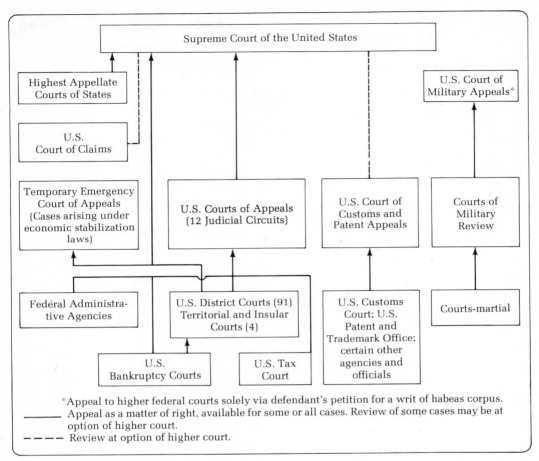

Figure 3.1 Federal court system.

The members of the Supreme Court are called "justices." The Constitution is silent about the size of the Supreme Court, and the number of justices has varied from six to ten. It is now, and for many years has been, nine. There is no requirement that a person be a judge, or even a lawyer, to be appointed to the Supreme Court.

Special courts Congress has from time to time created special courts for limited purposes or for certain geographic areas. The more important special courts, with their jurisdictions briefly indicated, are as follows: (1) Court of Claims: to hear nontort claims against the United States; (2) Customs Court: to decide controversies involving the collection of customs; (3) Court of Customs and Patent Appeals: to review decisions of the Customs Court, the Patent and Trademark Office, and certain other agencies and officials; and (4) miscellaneous courts, including territorial courts (e.g., Guam), United States Military Courts, and the United States Tax Court.

State Court Systems The court systems of the states vary in details but are alike in fundamentals. Every state has a series of local trial

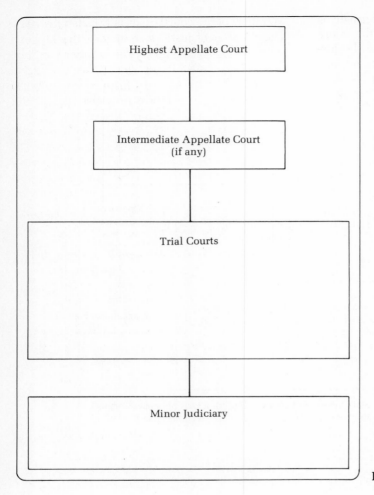

Figure 3.2 A typical state court system.

courts of original jurisdiction and a court of appeals. The dissimilarities consist primarily in the variety of local courts and the distribution of authority among them, in the number of levels of appellate courts, and in the titles given to some of the courts. Figure 3.2 illustrates a typical state court system.

Judges of state courts are selected in various ways. In many states judges of lower courts are elected by the citizens. In some states the governor appoints all lower court judges. In a few states, there is a combination of appointment and election, where judges are appointed

for their first term. If a judge desires to continue in office after the expiration of his or her appointive term, the judge must stand for election. Normally no other candidate's name appears on the ballot; the only decision the voters make is whether the incumbent shall be returned to office.

Trial courts In most states trial courts are divided into two groups—the minor judiciary and other trial courts.

1 *The minor judiciary.* Traditionally, legal cases of minor nature have been handled by officers called "justices of the peace." A justice

of the peace is not required to be, and usually is not, a legally trained person. In the more populous communities of some states, the justice court has been supplemented by a small claims court for the recovery of minor sums of money. In California, justice courts have jurisdiction over civil cases where the amount in controversy is $15,000 or less. The presiding officer is a judge who is or has been a lawyer. Justices of the peace have been abolished.

In larger communities of California (over 40,000 population) the lowest trial court is called a municipal court. It, too, has jurisdiction over civil cases where the amount in controversy is $15,000 or less. In addition, a municipal court judge presides over the small claims court. In small claims court the litigants may not be represented by lawyers, there is no jury, and the amount in controversy may not exceed $750.

2 *Other trial courts.* In every state there is a court of general and original jurisdiction for each county. It may be called the county court, the district court, the superior court, or the circuit court.[3] In California, the jurisdiction of superior courts over civil cases is limited to cases involving an amount in controversy exceeding $15,000. It also has limited jurisdiction to hear appeals from small claims, justice, and municipal courts. In some states, and especially in the more populous counties of some states, the courts of general jurisdiction are supplemented by one or more courts of special jurisdiction. The most commonly found courts of special jurisdiction are criminal courts, equity courts, and probate courts.[4] For example, in Los Angeles County, California, the superior court has almost 200 judges and numerous special courts.

Appellate courts In most states the highest appellate court is called the supreme court.[5]

Members of the court are usually called *justices*. The number of justices serving in the highest state courts varies. Usually the number is either five or seven. In most states the Governor appoints all supreme court justices, although in some states they are elected by the citizens.

Some states have an appellate court intermediate between the trial courts and the state supreme court. In California, for example, a dissatisfied litigant may appeal to the court of appeals, alleging an error of law. As in the federal court system, appeals are heard by a panel of three justices. No new evidence is allowed; the court simply reviews the trial procedure and evidence.

A litigant who is dissatisfied with the decision of the court of appeals may appeal to the state supreme court. In some states appeal to the state supreme court is allowed as a matter of right. In California, an appeal to the supreme court is largely a matter of privilege, and the practice is for the court to grant the privilege only in the most important cases.

CIVIL PROCEDURE

When disputes between individuals or business firms cannot be resolved amicably, litigation often results. This part of the chapter is devoted to a discussion of the steps in the trial of cases, from beginning to end. Knowledge of these steps will be of assistance in understanding the cases presented in later chapters. Often, an appeal is based on a defect alleged to exist in one or more steps in the trial of a case. Terminology varies greatly among the states. The following discussion will provide some familiarity with the most common terms used in civil litigation.

Procedures Prior to Trial
Pleadings Pleadings are the initial written statements presented to the trial court by each party to a civil suit. The function of pleadings is to reduce the controversy to its essential issues.

---

[3]In New York, strangely enough, it is called the "supreme court." In Ohio, it is called the "court of common pleas."

[4]Probate courts in Georgia are called "courts of the ordinary," and in Florida and some other states, "the county judge's court."

[5]In New York the highest appellate court is called the "court of appeals."

Summons and complaint The party who initiates a suit is called the *plaintiff*. The party being sued is called the *defendant*. The plaintiff initiates a lawsuit by filing with the court a statement variously called a declaration, petition, or complaint. The requirements for a complaint in California are typical of those states which have modernized their pleadings. The *complaint* must contain a statement of the facts constituting the cause of action, in ordinary and concise language, and a demand of the relief which the plaintiff claims. For example, the plaintiff may state, "On January 1, the defendant drove his automobile in a negligent manner and collided with the plaintiff, causing great bodily injury." The plaintiff would then request damages in a certain amount, such as $100,000. This request, called the *prayer*, varies according to the nature of the action. For example, in an equity action the plaintiff may seek specific performance or an injunction. The subject of equity and equitable remedies is discussed in Chapter 2.

The plaintiff brings the defendant under the jurisdiction of the court by serving the defendant with a copy of the complaint and a document called a "summons." A *summons* is, in effect, an order of court directing the defendant to appear in court within a certain time period, usually 30 days. In the summons the defendant is advised that, if no action is taken within the 30 days, the plaintiff may take a judgment against the defendant by default. Ordinarily, "serving" a copy of the summons and complaint (called "service of process") is accomplished by handing the papers to the defendant in person. However, there are provisions in most states allowing for "substituted" service when the defendant cannot be found. Such service may be accomplished by mailing or by advertising in a newspaper.

Demurrer After the defendant is "served" the copy of the summons and complaint, defendant must file with the court a responsive pleading within the required time in order to avoid a default judgment. The defendant may challenge the court's jurisdiction or the legal sufficiency of the plaintiff's complaint by means of a demurrer, in some states called a "motion to dismiss." A *demurrer* to a complaint challenging its legal sufficiency, says in effect: "Even if the facts alleged in the complaint be assumed to be true, still the complaint does not state a cause of action against the defendant." For example, suppose Peter alleges in his complaint that Donna promised to meet him at a certain movie theater at 7 P.M. on Saturday night and to attend the movie with him. Peter alleges that Donna failed to appear, breaching her promise, and this caused Peter great mental distress. He asks for $1,000 damages. Donna would likely file a demurrer to the complaint, alleging that the complaint does not state a cause of action recognized at law.

A demurrer raises an issue of law which the court must decide. If the court *sustains* the demurrer, the judge is ruling that plaintiff has failed to state a recognized cause of action. The plaintiff ordinarily is then given time to file an amended complaint. If the plaintiff fails to file an amended complaint, a judgment will be filed against him or her on the basis of the pleadings. If the court *overrules* the demurrer, the judge is ruling that plaintiff has stated a recognized cause of action. The defendant is then given time to file a further pleading. If the defendant fails to do so, judgment will be entered for the plaintiff. Whether the demurrer is sustained or overruled, the losing party has the right of appeal. Many cases in this textbook involve an appeal from a demurrer or motion to dismiss. On appeal the question is: Did the trial court correctly decide the issue of whether the plaintiff stated a recognized cause of action?

Answer and cross-complaint The defendant may file an answer to a complaint or an amended complaint. An *answer* may contain a general denial, that is, the defendant denies everything contained in the complaint, or a specific denial, that is, the defendant denies the truth of one or more of the essential allegations of the complaint and admits the truth of the other allegations. For example, in the illustration above of the complaint filed by Peter, Donna may file an answer containing a general denial of all facts, or she may deny that she promised to meet Peter on the particular Saturday night stated in the complaint.

An answer may contain one or more "affirmative defenses." An *affirmative defense* is an allegation of some new matter as a bar to plaintiff's recovery. For example, suppose that the plaintiff alleges in the complaint that on a specified date the plaintiff lent the defendant the sum of $1,000 and that the defendant has failed to pay it or any portion thereof. If the money was indeed a loan but the defendant has received a discharge in bankruptcy from all debts, the defendant may file an answer admitting the debt, but alleging bankruptcy as an affirmative defense. Other examples of affirmative defenses are statute of limitations and statute of frauds. These and many other defenses are presented in various chapters later in this book. In most states the defendant as part of the answer may assert a counterclaim. A *counterclaim* is an assertion that the defendant has a claim against the plaintiff. Such claim need not be related to the plaintiff's cause of action stated in the complaint. The plaintiff must file an answer to a counterclaim.

In some states, such as California, the defendant may file with an answer a cross-complaint. A *cross-complaint* alleges that the defendant has an independent cause of action against the plaintiff or against a third person. For example, the plaintiff may allege that the defendant breached a contract to deliver goods. The defendant files an answer containing a general denial and cross-complains that the plaintiff defrauded defendant. If a cross-complaint is filed against a third party the cause of action must be related to the plaintiff's complaint, that is, must arise out of the same transaction or involve the same property or controversy. The defendant may ask for relief in the form of damages or an equity remedy. The plaintiff, or third person, who is served with a cross-complaint must file a demurrer or answer to the cross-complaint.

Summary Judgment At various points during the pleading stage of litigation, either party to the lawsuit may make a motion for a "summary judgment." The summary judgment procedure is designed to dispose of suits in which there is no genuine issue of fact for a judge or jury to decide. A hearing is held before the judge to review the pleadings. The parties may file affidavits (sworn statements) of witnesses who would be called by the parties to testify if a trial were held. If the pleadings and affidavits reveal no material issue of fact, the judge makes a ruling that no trial is necessary and enters a judgment for the plaintiff or defendant. Like the demurrer, the summary judgment procedure helps to avoid the expense of unnecessary trials. A judge's granting of a motion for summary judgment may be appealed to a higher court.

Discovery At one time there was a feeling in the legal profession that a lawsuit should be a battle of wits, with each side guarding its case jealously and making the adversary's trial preparations as difficult and onerous as possible. Often the parties did not know until the day of trial what witnesses the other party would call to testify. In order to minimize the element of surprise, to improve and speed up the trial of cases, and to encourage settlements before trial, all states today provide for and encourage the parties to learn as much as possible about the adversary's case prior to trial. There are five major devices for discovery of facts before trial: depositions, interrogatories, inspection of documents and property, physical and mental examinations, and request for admissions.

Depositions A *deposition* is a statement under oath made at a hearing held out of court and after due notice to the other side. Ordinarily, each party will request permission to take the deposition of the other party and the party's key witnesses. A hearing is arranged at the office of one party's attorney. A court reporter records the questions and answers and prepares a written transcript for the witness to sign. In recent years, many courts have encouraged the use of videotape depositions. The need for a written transcript is eliminated; and if the videotape is presented at trial, the judge or jury can view the witness and better evaluate the person's credibility.

Depositions may serve various purposes: to discover what testimony to expect at the trial; to obtain testimony while it is fresh in the mind of a witness; to impeach (discredit) a person's testimony at the trial by showing that the testimony varies from the deposition; to memorialize testimony where there is danger that it may be unavailable at the trial. For example, a deposition may be desirable if a witness is elderly, has a serious illness, or is likely not to be available for the trial. Often, the deposition of an expert witness, such as a doctor or engineer, is taken and used at the trial in place of actual testimony. Expert witnesses receive large fees for testifying at trials and their schedules are often such that it may be difficult to secure their attendance at the trial.

Interrogatories Interrogatories are written questions addressed by one party in a case to the other party. Such questions might elicit information that can be used as a basis for further questions at a deposition hearing or at the trial of the case. An interrogatory may be used to demand a list of the other party's witnesses. Interrogatories are an inexpensive way to obtain information; they can be served informally (usually by mail) and answered at leisure, without the necessity of the presence of a court reporter or opposing attorney. Ordinarily, the answers must be given in writing, under penalty of perjury. As with depositions, the answers can be used for impeachment purposes at a trial.

Inspection of documents and property Either party to a case may secure a court order permitting the party or an agent to inspect, copy, or photograph documents or tangible things in the possession or control of another. For example, in a case where the plaintiff alleges personal injury the defendant may wish to inspect medical or hospital records pertaining to the injury.

Physical and mental examinations When the physical or mental condition of a party is in controversy, the court is empowered to issue an order requiring him or her to submit to an examination by a physician. In many lawsuits both parties will request an examination by physicians. Often, the doctors' opinions as to a party's condition are at odds with one another and the judge or jury must then weigh the credibility of each physician.

Request for admissions Either party may serve upon the other party (usually by mail) a request that he or she admit the genuineness of some document or the truth of some assertion described or set forth in the request. Failure to deny in writing and under oath the genuineness of the document or the truth of the assertion is deemed an admission of its genuineness or truth. The admission relieves the requesting party of the burden of producing proof on that point at the trial.

In general, the information sought by discovery must be relevant to the subject matter of the lawsuit. For example, in most cases it would be improper to ask in a deposition hearing or in an interrogatory for a party or witness to disclose his or her social security number. It is not required that the information sought be used in evidence at a later trial nor that the information be admissible evidence. Thus, a plaintiff is entitled to discover the existence and scope of the defendant's insurance coverage, although such information is not admissible as evidence in a trial.

Pretrial Conference In most states the courts require a pretrial conference in civil suits. A pretrial conference is a meeting of the judge and attorneys, and sometimes the parties, held usually two or three weeks before trial.

The conference serves two purposes. One purpose is to shorten the time of trial by refining or narrowing the issues, clarifying the pleadings through amendments, and placing a limitation on the number of witnesses and exhibits. The second purpose of the pretrial conference is to encourage an out-of-court settlement. At the end of the conference, if no settlement is reached, the judge sets a date for the trial.

Trial of Cases

Sometime before the trial date, the plaintiff and defendant must decide whether the trial will be by judge or by jury. In some suits no jury may be requested, as in suits for equity relief. In other suits either party may request a jury but is not required to do so (i.e., they may "waive" a jury). If either side requests a jury, a deposit of jury fees ordinarily must be made in advance of the trial date. On the day of trial, if the parties still desire a jury, the first step is for the parties to select a jury. (The judge selects the jury in cases tried in federal district courts.) The remaining steps in a trial are substantially the same whether or not a jury is used.

Opening Statements of Counsel Ordinarily, the next step in a civil trial after a jury is selected (if there is one) consists of opening statements by the attorneys for the plaintiff and the defendant. In some states the attorney for the defendant may elect to make an opening statement after plaintiff's evidence has been presented and before defendant presents any evidence. The purpose of the opening statements is to outline the general nature of the case and to indicate the kinds of evidence to be offered, so that the judge or jurors may understand the significance of each item of evidence as it is introduced.

Occasionally, the defendant makes a motion to dismiss at the close of plaintiff's opening statement. Such a motion parallels a demurrer to a complaint. In effect, the defendant states that even if the plaintiff can prove all facts alleged, it does not amount to a cause of action recognized at law. For example, in the previous illustration of Peter's suing Donna for failing to meet him at the movie theater, Donna could make a motion to dismiss at the close of Peter's opening statement and the judge likely would grant her motion. Thus, a judgment would be given to Donna and the trial terminated. A ruling on a motion to dismiss is appealable.

Presentation of Evidence The plaintiff proceeds next to introduce evidence to prove the allegations of the complaint. The word "evidence" is used in different senses. As used here, *evidence* means anything presented at the trial for the purpose of inducing belief in the truth or falsity of some contention. The two chief methods of inducing belief are testimony of witnesses and physical evidence. Testimony is secured by calling a witness, swearing the person in, and asking the person questions. A court reporter records all testimony in trial courts above the justice court level.

When a witness is put on the stand, the person is first examined by the attorney who called the person as a witness. This is called "direct examination" and is followed by a "cross-examination" conducted by the attorney for the other side. Ordinarily, the purpose of cross-examination is to show the witness's lack of credibility, such as by questioning his or her powers of observation. The attorney may try to impeach the witness by showing that the witness's answers to questions differ from those given in a deposition or interrogatories. The cross-examination may be followed by a redirect examination, in order to give the witness an opportunity to explain or modify answers given on cross-examination. The trial judge has discretion to allow the examination to proceed to a re-cross-examination, or even beyond. Physical evidence may consist of objects or documents which have been verified as authentic. Items of physical evidence are called *exhibits* and are tagged with a number for future reference (e.g., "Plaintiff's 1").

The rules of evidence governing the introduction of exhibits and the testimony of witnesses are numerous and technical. These rules may be the basis for a party to "object" to a question of a witness or to the introduction of physical evidence. Many of the rules have as their primary purpose the protection of a jury of lay persons from irrelevant and prejudicial material.

After the plaintiff has called all witnesses for the plaintiff's side and has introduced all physical evidence desired, the plaintiff "rests." At this point the defendant may make a motion for nonsuit (in some states called "a motion to dismiss"). By such a motion the defendant contends that the plaintiff has failed to prove his or her case, as outlined in the complaint and opening statements. If the judge agrees, a judgment of nonsuit is entered in favor of the defendant. If the judge does not agree, the motion will be denied and the defendant proceeds to introduce evidence to contradict the plaintiff's evidence. The defendant calls witnesses and introduces physical evidence in the same manner as did the plaintiff.

When there is a trial by jury, either party, or both, may make a motion for directed verdict at the close of defendant's evidence. By such a motion a party contends that the facts proven are so clear that reasonable people could not differ as to the outcome of the case. If the judge directs a verdict for a party, the judge thereby takes the case away from the jury and then enters a judgment for the party who made the motion. If neither party moves for a directed verdict, the judge may on his or her own motion order a directed verdict.

Arguments of Counsel After all evidence is presented, the attorneys for each party are allowed to make final or closing arguments. These usually take place before the judge's charge to the jury (if there is a jury). In some states, the final arguments of counsel come after the charge to the jury. In the final argument, an attorney will usually review the evidence produced by his or her side and emphasize its adequacy and credibility; discuss the evidence produced by the other side to show its inadequacy and lack of credibility; and indicate the conclusions of fact that may reasonably be drawn from the evidence.

Charge to the Jury When there is a trial by jury, the judge instructs the jurors after closing arguments by both attorneys as to the law to be applied in their deliberations. Normally the judge instructs the jury that its duty is to determine the facts of the case; to accept the law as stated by the judge; and, by applying the law so stated to the facts so determined, to reach a decision for the plaintiff or the defendant. These instructions are a guide to assist the jury in reaching a verdict. For example, the judge may say, "Negligence means the failure to exercise reasonable care to prevent harm to others. If you find that the defendant drove his car 80 miles per hour in a residential area, you must find the defendant has committed the tort of negligence."

Attorneys may, and often do, submit written instructions to the judge which they request the judge to include in the charge to the jury. The refusal to include a requested instruction or to give the instruction in the wording requested is often the basis of an appeal to a higher court.

Verdict of the Jury In a trial by jury, after receiving the judge's instructions, the jury retires to the jury room to consider the evidence and reach a verdict. In federal courts and in many state courts the jury verdict must be unanimous. Some states, such as California, authorize a verdict in a civil action to be reached by vote of three-fourths of the jurors. When the jury has reached its verdict, it returns to the courtroom and in the presence of the judge (and usually in the presence of the parties and their attorneys) announces its verdict. Either side may demand to have the jury *polled*, that is, to have each juror state whether the verdict of the jury is his or her verdict.

The type of verdict just considered—that is, a verdict for plaintiff or defendant reached by applying the law as stated by the judge to the facts as found by the jury—is called a *general verdict.* Another type of verdict is a *special verdict.* Such a verdict generally consists of answers to specific questions asked by the judge without any attempt to reach a decision for either party. The judge then decides the case by applying the law to the facts as given in the special verdict. If a general verdict is given for the defendant, the jurors' functions terminate. However, if the verdict is for the plaintiff in a civil action for damages, the jury must fix the amount of damages to which the plaintiff is entitled.

Judgment; Motions after Trial The last step in the trial of a case is the judgment. A *judgment* is the decision of the court. Normally the judgment in jury trials is based on the verdict of the jury. For example, the judge might simply state that the defendant is liable to plaintiff for $100,000. Often, after the judgment in a jury trial is entered in the court records, the losing party will make a motion for judgment notwithstanding the verdict ("judgment n.o.v."). The judge will grant the motion and enter judgment for the losing party only if there is no substantial evidence to support the decision of the jury. In some states the judge on his or her own motion may reject the jury verdict and enter a judgment for the other party. The party whose verdict is overturned usually will appeal to a higher court.

After the judgment is entered, a motion for a new trial may be made by either party. If the plaintiff wins the case, the defendant may move for a new trial on the ground that the judge committed prejudicial error in the conduct of the trial, or that the damages assessed are excessive. A party may be granted a new trial if the other party, or the party's attorney, was guilty of prejudicial misconduct during the trial. However, a party is not entitled to a new trial if the party's own attorney was negligent or incompetent. A new trial may be granted where the losing party shows new evidence was discovered after the trial. The party must prove that

the evidence is significant and could not have been obtained before trial by due diligence. The plaintiff, although the winner, may move for a new trial on the ground that the damages awarded are insufficient under the evidence. If a motion for a new trial is granted by the judge, the case is again put on the trial calendar. Eventually it will be set for trial before another judge or jury. If the motion is denied, the moving party may appeal. In certain instances, the judge may order a denial of a new trial if the plaintiff consents to a reduction in the amount of the judgment (called a "remittitur"). In some states, the judge may order a new trial unless the defendant consents to an increase in the amount of the judgment (called an "additur"). Figure 3.3 provides a summary of civil litigation procedure.

Appeals

After the entry of judgment, the party who feels dissatisfied by the outcome may file an appeal. Normally the loser appeals; sometimes the winner appeals (e.g., the plaintiff may allege that the damages awarded were inadequate under the evidence); occasionally both parties appeal. The party who files an appeal is called the *appellant.* The other party is called the *appellee,* or the *respondent.*

Review of the Case The appellate court does not retry the case. No new evidence is allowed. Its job is to review the case as conducted in the trial court to see if any error of law was committed. Usually the appellate court limits its review to such questions as: Did the trial judge properly exclude or admit evidence, follow proper procedure, or state or apply the law accurately? If the trial judge committed error, was the error serious enough to warrant reversal of the judge's decision?

Sometimes an appellate court conducts a limited review of the facts found by the trial court. Such a review is necessary in deciding whether a summary judgment or a judgment n.o.v. was warranted. It should be noted, however, that an

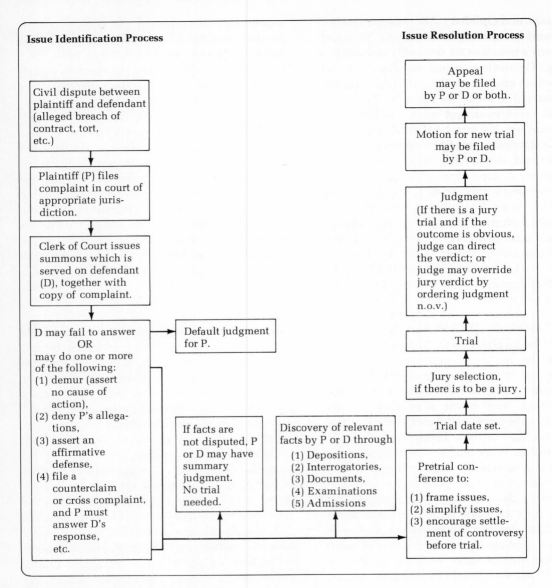

Figure 3.3 Flow of civil litigation.

appellate court will not overturn a trial court's ruling unless the ruling is in serious disharmony with the evidence. The trial judge and jury, having the witnesses physically present, are in a better position than an appellate court to evaluate the credibility of witnesses. The appellate court therefore does not reweigh the evidence. The appellate court reviews the complete record of the trial of the case and listens to oral arguments by the attorneys for both parties. The attorneys submit written "briefs" to support their arguments.

Decision and Opinion After consideration of the record and the arguments made, the appellate court announces its decision (judgment) in writing. The decision is ordinarily accompanied by a written opinion in which the court explains the basis or reasons for its decision. If the appellate justices do not agree unanimously, a dissenting opinion may be written.

If the appellate court finds that no error of law has occurred, it will affirm the judgment of the trial court. If prejudicial error is found, the appellate court may reverse or modify that judgment. When the evidence does not clearly justify a decision for one party or the other, the appellate court may reverse the judgment of the trial court and "remand" the case with directions to hold a new trial or to take other action regarding the case.

ARBITRATION AS AN ALTERNATIVE TO CIVIL LITIGATION

As can be seen from the discussion on the preceding pages, a lawsuit involves complex procedures. The courts in many states are crowded with cases, and there is a long wait for litigants to get to trial. The costs of civil litigation sometimes are staggering. Attorneys' fees, depositions, and fees of expert witnesses are but a few of the items each party to a suit must pay for. Often, the parties to a dispute will avoid litigation by a process called "arbitration."

Arbitration is a nonjudicial method of resolving civil disputes. Rather than file a lawsuit, the disputing parties agree to let a neutral third party decide who is right and who is wrong. The parties select an arbitrator or sometimes a panel of three arbitrators. An arbitrator's decision, called an "award," is binding on the parties and is subject to only a limited judicial review. Usually, a party must show an illegal award, fraud, or gross mistake in order to obtain a judicial review.

As an alternative to litigation, arbitration of disputes has a number of advantages. It is less formal (e.g., the rules of evidence are greatly relaxed), is more efficient (e.g., the parties do not have to wait years for a courtroom), and is less expensive than litigation (e.g., there are no jury fees to pay, and attorney fees are much lower).

However, there are several disadvantages to arbitration. The presiding officer usually is not a judge trained in the law and rules of evidence. Evidence allowed at an arbitration hearing is not subject to the same strict rules of scrutiny as prevail in a court trial. This is a two-edged sword. For example, hearsay evidence which may be prejudicial to a party ordinarily is not allowed in a court of law but is permitted to be introduced at an arbitration hearing. There is no right to a jury in an arbitration; there is only a limited right to appeal an award.

In rare instances, arbitration may be imposed by law (state or federal legislation) and is called *compulsory arbitration*. It is usually limited to public-interest emergency disputes between public employees—such as police officers, fire fighters, and teachers—and their employers. A statute which imposes compulsory arbitration is invalid unless it provides for judicial review of disputed issues or of the award.

SUMMARY

Courts are established to decide actual controversies between parties, not to answer hypothetical questions. In order to process a case, a court must have jurisdiction over the subject matter and jurisdiction over the property or the parties.

In our dual system of federal and state governments, there is a federal court system and a system of state courts. The federal court system consists of district courts, courts of appeals, the Supreme Court, and various special courts. The state court systems typically include several types of trial courts, intermediate appellate courts, and a supreme court. In some classes of cases the federal courts have exclusive jurisdiction, in others the state courts have exclusive jurisdiction, and in still others the federal and state courts have concurrent jurisdiction.

When a dispute is not settled by an agreement out of court and litigation results, the parties must follow a lengthy series of civil procedures before, during, and after a court trial. However, where there is no recognized cause of action or no material question of fact for a judge or jury to decide, judgment can be awarded in the pleadings stage of litigation. During a trial there are various times a party may make motions to terminate the proceedings without further action. A motion for judgment n.o.v. may be made by the losing party. After judgment, a motion for new trial may be made. Judgments at the various stages of litigation are appealable to higher courts.

The function of an appellate court, state or federal, intermediate or supreme, is to review the case as conducted by the trial court to see if any error of law was committed. The appellate court may affirm the decision of the trial court, reverse the decision, or reverse and remand the case for a new trial.

Arbitration, an alternative to litigation, is a nonjudicial method of resolving disputes by private, disinterested persons called *arbitrators*. There are both advantages and disadvantages to arbitration. Compulsory arbitration is usually limited to public-interest emergency disputes.

STUDY AND DISCUSSION QUESTIONS

1 (*a*) What is the function of a court? (*b*) What is the purpose of a declaratory judgment? (*c*) Explain how an action for declaratory judgment is consistent with a court's main function.

2 (*a*) What is the general meaning of jurisdiction? (*b*) Describe and give an illustration of jurisdiction over the subject matter. (*c*) Describe and give an illustration of jurisdiction over the parties. (*d*) Distinguish between exclusive and concurrent jurisdiction.

3 (*a*) Give two examples of classes of cases over which the federal courts have exclusive jurisdiction. (*b*) To what extent do the *state* courts have jurisdiction over cases involving citizens of different states?

4 (*a*) Describe the work of the following federal courts: district courts, courts of appeals, and the Supreme Court. (*b*) Explain who appoints federal judges and the length of their terms of office.

5 (*a*) Describe the courts commonly found in a state court system. (*b*) How are vacancies filled?

6 (*a*) What is the purpose of the pleading stage of litigation? (*b*) What is the "prayer"? (*c*) Describe how process may be served on a defendant.

7 Explain what happens after a judge: (*a*) sustains a demurrer; (*b*) overrules a demurrer.

8 (*a*) List the items a defendant may include in an answer. (*b*) What is a cross-complaint? (*c*) What may a party do who is served with a cross-complaint? (*d*) Contrast a counterclaim and a cross-complaint. (*e*) Why do you think states allow, or even encourage, counterclaims and cross-complaints?

9 (*a*) What is the purpose of a summary judgment? (*b*) How does a motion for summary judgment differ from a demurrer?

10 (*a*) What is the purpose of discovery devices? (*b*) Explain the purpose and use of "deposition," "interrogatory," and "request for admission of facts."

11 What are the purposes of a pretrial conference?

12 (*a*) Briefly describe the difference between opening and closing arguments in a trial. (*b*) What is a motion to dismiss?

13 (*a*) What is an exhibit? (*b*) What is a motion

for nonsuit? *(c)* What is a motion for directed verdict?

14   *(a)* Explain the difference between a general verdict and a special verdict. *(b)* What is a judgment? *(c)* What is a "judgment n.o.v." *(d)* What are the typical grounds for a motion for a new trial?

15   *(a)* Explain how a plaintiff could also be an appellant; an appellee. *(b)* What is the function of an appellate court? *(c)* How does it perform this function? *(d)* To what extent does the appellate court review the facts of the case? Why?

Chapter
4
Administrative Law in
the United States

When we think of law we tend to think only of
courts and legislatures; but much of the law
controlling modern business is the creation of
administrative agencies. They, too, have power
to decide controversies and to formulate rules
and regulations. Many agencies have a more
immediate impact on business than have courts
and legislatures. Some understanding of administrative law is therefore essential in the conduct
of modern business affairs.

This chapter traces the development and
scope of administrative regulation in the United
States and considers the principal legal and
business problems growing out of such regulation.

DEVELOPMENT AND SCOPE OF
ADMINISTRATIVE LAW

Meaning of "Administrative Agency,"
"Administrative Law,"
and "Administrative Process"
The term *administrative agency* is used to mean
any public officer, board, bureau, or
commission—other than legislatures and courts
—having power to determine private rights and
obligations by making rules and rendering decisions. The term has no reference to organizational pattern. It refers equally to agencies
organized within a department of government
(e.g., the Patent and Trademark Office in the

Department of Commerce) and those organized independently of any such department (e.g., the Federal Trade Commission). Administrative agencies have been characterized as "independent" if organized outside the executive departments of government. However, a more meaningful test of "independence" is the "presence or absence of power of the President to discharge the agency head or heads without cause."[1]

Administrative law is any law concerning the powers and procedures of administrative agencies, including the law governing judicial review of administrative action.[2] Administrative law is found in constitutions, statutes, court decisions, and in agency decisions, rules, and regulations. Administrative law does not include the substantive law produced by agencies. The substantive output of an agency is better classified as tax law, labor law, antitrust law, or the like, because that output becomes part of an existing body of substantive law.

Administrative process has various meanings depending on the context. In this chapter the expression means the procedure through which administrative agencies carry on their work.

Rise of Administrative Regulation

Resorting to the use of administrative agencies as a means of social control in the United States goes back almost to the founding of the nation. The first Congress created agencies to implement statutes on the regulation of coastal trade, the collecting of customs, and the payment of veterans' bonuses. During the eighteenth and nineteenth centuries, agencies played a minor role in the regulation of business. Since 1900, however, and particularly from 1930 on, there has been a marked increase in the number of administrative agencies and in their impact on business. Because administrative agencies have achieved great importance only in recent decades, administrative law "as a distinctive part of our legal system" is a recent development. It is now recognized by legal scholars as "an outstanding characteristic of twentieth-century jurisprudence."[3]

A variety of factors account for the marked trend in recent decades toward administrative regulation. Among them are the following:

1 Legislators desire to free themselves, as far as possible, from the need for enacting detailed legislation in order that more time might be available for determining legislative policy. Similarly, legislators seek to free courts from a myriad of small cases in order that judges might have more time for cases requiring the formulation of fundamental legal principles.

2 The increasing complexity of life requires expertness in every field in which government regulates. Legislators and judges generally are not experts in such technical and diverse fields as utility rates, security issues, public health, labor relations, and social insurance.

3 Effective regulation often requires greater uniformity of approach, continuity of supervision, and flexibility of action than could be achieved through traditional legislative and judicial patterns.

4 Behind much agency legislation are (*a*) the belief of legislators that the judicial process "is unduly awkward, slow, and expensive" and (*b*) the demand of the public for a "speedy, cheap, and simple procedure, a procedure which keeps the role of the lawyers to a minimum."[4]

5 There is a need for more effective preventive action than can be achieved through normal legislative and judicial processes. In creating the Securities and Exchange Commission, for

---

[1]Kenneth C. Davis, *Administrative Law and Government*, West Publishing Company, St. Paul, 1975, p. 16.
[2]Ibid., p. 6.

[3]Frank E. Cooper, *Administrative Agencies and the Courts*, Michigan Legal Studies, University of Michigan Law School, Ann Arbor, 1951, p. 3.
[4]Kenneth C. Davis, *Administrative Law*, West Publishing Company, St. Paul, 1951, p. 16.

example, Congress acted in the belief that it is better to prevent fraudulent sales of stock than it is to have the courts give legal redress to plaintiffs injured by fraudulent sales.

6   Most of the great regulatory statutes departed fundamentally from the substantive law evolved by the courts, and proponents of such statutes often feared that conservative courts would construe (interpret) away some of the legislative changes. The desire to secure sympathetic administration of reform legislation is said to be "one of the prime reasons for the growth of the administrative process."[5]

7   When legislators decide to regulate a new industry or to embark upon some program of social control for which there is no adequate basis of experience, they may resort to the administrative process as a means of coping with the problem on an experimental basis. Much of the legislation of the 1930s was experimental in character, and for that reason more administrative agencies were created in that decade than in any peacetime decade in our history.

Current Importance of Administrative Regulation

The present-day importance of administrative regulation is indicated by the number of administrative agencies in existence and by the wide scope of their duties and powers.

Number of Administrative Agencies   The total number of federal, state, and local agencies in the United States is unknown, but it is estimated to run into the thousands. In the federal government alone, there are well over 100 agencies, including 59 specifically characterized as agencies in the *United States Government Manual.*

As the great number of agencies implies, virtually no one escapes agency regulation.

The barber, the plumber, the nurse, the teacher—all practitioners of the many

trades or professions subject to licensing—anyone who uses electricity and telephone or drives an automobile, the farmer selling milk, the laborer injured on a job or [the one who is] out of work—all these and many more are affected in one way or another by rules, regulations, rate schedules, and decisions of state [and federal] administrative agencies and commissions.[6]

The same can be said of small business firms. Large firms doing interstate business may be subject to a staggering amount of administrative regulation—federal, state, and local.

Scope of Agency Powers and Duties   The impact of agency regulation results not only from the number of agencies, but also from the wide scope of powers and duties possessed by some of them. Among the more important duties of the Federal Trade Commission, to give but one illustration, are the following:

- To prevent unfair methods of competition (such as price-fixing agreements and boycotts)
- To prevent false and deceptive advertising of certain products (such as foods, drugs, and cosmetics)
- To prevent practices tending toward monopoly or a substantial lessening of competition (such as price discrimination, exclusive-dealing arrangements, and interlocking directorates)
- To police the use of trademarks.

In carrying out their duties, agencies engage in one or more (usually more) of the following activities: rule making, adjudicating, prosecuting, advising, supervising, and investigating. The Federal Trade Commission engages in all these activities.

---

[5]Ibid., p. 15.

[6]Miles O. Price, Harry Bitner, Shirley Raissi Bysiewicz, *Effective Legal Research,* 4th ed., Little, Brown and Co. (Inc.), Boston, 1979, p. 136. Quoted with permission of the publisher.

LEGAL PROBLEMS RELATING TO ADMINISTRATIVE LAW

The use of the administrative process has raised several problems involving constitutional issues: How can the concentration of legislative, executive, and judicial powers in the hands of a single official or body be justified under the American doctrine of separation of powers? By what right, or at least to what extent, may a legislature delegate powers which the Constitution places in the legislature's own hands? Does the administrative process provide "due process of law"? To what extent may courts review, set aside, or modify rules and decisions of administrative agencies?

Separation of Powers

The doctrine of separation of powers grows out of the provisions of federal and state constitutions creating three branches of government: the legislative, the executive, and the judicial. The courts have often said that "it is a breach of the National fundamental law" for one branch of the government to attempt to divest itself of power through transfer to another branch or to invest itself with power belonging to either of the other branches.[7] Separation of governmental powers serves to prevent the acquisition of tyrannical power by one ruler or one branch of government.

The possession by an administrative agency of legislative, executive, and judicial powers could be viewed as a violation of the separation-of-powers doctrine. Indeed, in the early days of commission regulation of railroads and utilities, the question was often before the courts. However, for some time now the courts have been in agreement that the possession and exercise by agencies of their various powers is not incompatible with the separation-of-powers doctrine.

The courts have concluded that agencies do not have legislative and judicial power, but only "quasi-legislative" and "quasi-judicial" power, that is, the power to make rules and to decide disputes regarding topics properly delegated to them. Agencies are not, like the legislature, independent of the other branches of government, but have only such power as is given by the legislature (which may abolish an agency at any time). Neither do they, like courts, try cases and render judgments but merely hold hearings and issue orders, both of which are subject to review by the courts. These and other controls on the abuse of power of agencies make unnecessary a strict application of the separation-of-powers doctrine to administrative agencies.

Delegation of Powers

Closely related to the doctrine of separation of powers is that of delegation of powers. The early view was that legislative power could not be delegated. The modern view is that delegation of some power is "necessary in order that the exertion of legislative power does not become a futility."[8]

The Supreme Court accomplished the transition from the early to the modern view by resort to two theories: (1) that Congress may enact legislation to become operative upon the happening of some event or state of facts and may leave to others the responsibility of determining when the event or state of facts occurs; (2) that Congress may declare a policy or determine a standard and may empower some officer or agency to fill in the details needed for implementation. The courts have taken a liberal view of what constitutes a declaration of policy or determination of standard. Such phrases as "public convenience, interest, or necessity," "just and reasonable," "fair and equitable," and "excessive profits" have been held to meet constitutional requirements. Similarly, the expression "unfair methods of competition" was

---

[7]The quoted words are from *J. W. Hampton, Jr. & Co. v. United States,* 276 U.S. 394, 406 (1928).

[8]*Sunshine Anthracite Coal Co. v. Adkins,* 310 U.S. 381, 398 (1940).

held to be an adequate standard for the guidance of the Federal Trade Commission in carrying out duties delegated to it.[9] Nevertheless, an agency may not engage in regulatory activities not authorized by statute.

Due Process of Law

The Fifth and Fourteenth Amendments to the federal Constitution prohibit federal and state governments from depriving a person of life, liberty, or property without due process of law. At first the courts interpreted "due process of law" merely as a procedural requirement. No person was to be deprived of life, liberty, or property except in accordance with traditional Anglo-American standards of fair trial. Minimum standards include an impartial tribunal, separation of the prosecuting and judging functions, adequate notice, opportunity to be heard and to confront witnesses, and fair rules of evidence. During the latter part of the nineteenth century, American courts began broadening the concept of due process by applying the due process clauses to the substantive content of laws. A statute would be held to violate the requirement of due process if the statute were arbitrary, unreasonably discriminatory, or demonstrably irrelevant to reasonable legislative policy.[10] Both the substantive and procedural aspects of due process raise important questions in the field of administrative law.

Substantive Due Process in Administrative Agencies Substantive due process requires that the orders, rules, and regulations of an administrative agency not be arbitrary, unreasonably discriminatory, or demonstrably irrelevant to matters properly delegated to the agency. Statutes commonly grant federal and state utility commissions the power to determine utility rates. A rate set so low as to amount to confiscation of a utility's property will be held, on appeal to the courts, to be a deprivation of property without due process. Administrative standards for testing a teacher's competence must be fair and rationally related to the teacher's performance in the classroom.[11]

Procedural Due Process in Administrative Agencies Most agencies are created to develop and implement solutions to complex, emerging problems or to regulate current activities. Their work requires them to perform simultaneously a number of tasks (such as investigation, prosecution, adjudication, and rule making), with a limited number of personnel, within a governmental subunit of relatively small size. The nature of their work often requires an overlapping of functions (such as judging or legislating) to a degree not usually encountered in the three main branches of government. Yet, despite the administrative need for overlapping of function and for efficiency and flexibility of procedure, agencies must provide procedural due process. Administrative agencies are subject to the same *general* requirements for due process that apply to the three main branches of government, but with some modifications befitting the work of the agencies. Three aspects of procedural due process in administrative agencies serve to illustrate.

Procedural due process may require that a person affected by agency action be given notice of the action and an opportunity to be heard. But who is entitled to a hearing, what form must it take, and when must it occur? Does due process require notice and hearing, for example, before an agency may adopt a new rule or regulation? Before a tax official may assess property? Before an agency may grant, refuse to grant, or revoke a license? Must a hearing, if required, always precede all other administrative action?

There is no easy answer to questions such as these. Much agency rule making and other action (but not all) is subject to statutory re-

---

[9]*Atlantic Ref. Co. v. F.T.C.*, 381 U.S. 357 (1965).
[10]*Nebbia v. New York*, 291 U.S. 502 (1934).

[11]Ernest Gellhorn, *Administrative Law in a Nutshell*, West Publishing Company, St. Paul, 1972, p. 165.

quirements of notice and hearings. Whether or not a statute so provides, where agency action is clearly an adjudication of an issue of fact affecting the rights of the parties to the adjudication, due process requires a trial procedure (one involving witnesses, oral and written evidence, cross-examination, etc.). Where agency action clearly is for the purpose of resolving questions of law or policy (e.g., determining "legislative facts" in a rule-making procedure), a less elaborate hearing will suffice. But many actions taken by agencies could be considered as either adjudicatory or legislative. The courts are often called upon to decide what kind of hearing is appropriate.

When administrative action is challenged in court for inadequate notice or hearing, the courts consider a number of factors bearing on the issue. Among these are:

1 The seriousness of the impact of the agency on fundamental individual rights or interests. Where the action of the agency curtails freedom of speech or association, or jeopardizes a person's livelihood, courts tend to require more elaborate hearings.

2 The kind of action being taken by the agency. If misconduct or other circumstances threaten irreparable damage, an agency may be allowed to take temporary or emergency action without a hearing, subject to a requirement of an appropriate hearing as circumstances permit.

3 The existence of a reasonable alternative to a hearing. A hearing may be inferior to an inspection, examination, or testing. "The way to ascertain airworthiness of an airplane . . . is for a skilled inspector to look at the object and make his decision. And the same may often be true of inspecting perishable commodities, quarantining plants, determining the skill of applicants for various kinds of licenses, [and] censoring motion pictures."[12]

4 The need to protect the national security. In rare instances, the right to confront witnesses may be abridged if revealing the source of adverse testimony would seriously threaten the national security.[13]

5 The stage of the proceedings in which notice or a hearing is sought. If a court's review of an allegedly inadequate hearing requires the court to look into the facts, the court's review might provide the requisite hearing in lieu of the hearing sought.

The second illustrative aspect of administrative procedure is the degree to which agencies must maintain separation of functions. It would be unthinkable under our traditional standards for a fair trial for a judge to assume the role of prosecutor or for the lawyer for one of the litigants to be the judge. Strict separation of the investigatory, prosecutorial, and judicial functions is required in the judicial system. Administrative law, on the other hand, generally requires only the degree of functional separation which is needed to produce fair decisions.

Combination of investigation with judging may be bad in such prosecuting agencies as the National Labor Relations Board and the Federal Trade Commission, but it may be harmless and even affirmatively desirable in claims agencies which are as much interested in making payments to the deserving as in withholding payments from the undeserving.[14]

Administrative treatment of the rules of evidence further illustrates the agency approach to procedural due process. Courts refuse to admit certain kinds of "hearsay" evidence (statements made by a witness on the authority of another, and not from personal knowledge or observation). The reason for excluding hearsay evidence is that (despite the often high credibility of the

---

[12]Kenneth C. Davis, *Administrative Law*, 3d ed., West Publishing Company, St. Paul, 1972, p. 173. Quoted with permission of the publisher.

[13]Ibid., pp. 189–192.
[14]Ibid., p. 255.

reporting witness) the maker of the statement is not available in court for cross-examination. The hearsay exclusionary rule has been criticized as arbitrary, as have other exclusionary rules supposedly needed for the protection or guidance of juries. Administrative tribunals, which do not use juries, have often found strict exclusionary rules inappropriate for the administrative process and have taken the lead in relaxing them.

Scope of Judicial Review

The proper scope of judicial review is one of the most important and perplexing problems in the field of administrative law. Considerable progress toward solving the problem at the national level was made in 1946 by the passage of the Federal Administrative Procedure Act, which contains provisions regarding the proper scope of judicial review. The Model State Administrative Procedure Act[15] contains similar provisions for review at the state level.

Under the provisions of the model state act, any person aggrieved by a final decision of an agency is entitled to judicial review. The court may remand, modify, or reverse the decision to the extent that it is:

a In violation of constitutional provisions; or

b In excess of statutory authority or jurisdiction of the agency; or

c Made upon unlawful procedure; or

d Affected by other error of law; or

e Unsupported by competent, material, and substantial evidence in view of the entire record as submitted; or

f Arbitrary or capricious.[16]

Both the model state act and the federal act adopt the "substantial evidence rule." The rule prevents trials de novo (new trials conducted in an appellate court) by requiring courts to accept agency findings when they are based upon substantial evidence. In determining whether there is substantial evidence, the federal courts, at least, must consider the whole record and not just the case presented by one party.[17] The substantial evidence rule also prevents agency decisions from being reversed merely because the court itself would have reached a different conclusion on the basis of the facts found by the agency. The function of courts in reviewing cases is not to determine the facts or the weight thereof but to enunciate and apply the law.

Ordinarily the courts have no difficulty distinguishing between a question of law and a question of fact. However, some agency decisions, when appealed, present a mixed question of law and fact, and the court must decide which aspect (law or fact) predominates so that the court can decide whether to review the agency determination. If the agency determination presents a mixed question of law and fact and the court believes that sound policy requires judicial review of the determination, the court will treat it as one of law; otherwise, it will treat the determination as one of fact. Although policy considerations usually remain inarticulate in judicial opinions, the cases seem to warrant the additional following generalizations:

1 Where the purpose of the agency is to discharge a function essential to the operation of government (as, collection of taxes), judicial review is usually less extensive than where the purpose is control of private business.

2 Where agency action is primarily legislative in character, review is less searching than where the action is primarily judicial in nature.

3 Where agency determination involves a highly technical subject (as, engineering),

---

[15]Promulgated in 1944 by the National Conference of Commissioners of Uniform State Laws. Found in *Uniform Laws Annotated*, Edward Thompson Company, 1957, vol. 90, pp. 179–185.

[16]Subsections (a) to (f) from sec. 12(7) of the act.

[17]*Universal Camera Corp. v. N.L.R.B.*, 340 U.S. 474 (1951).

courts are less likely to upset action taken by an agency than where the subject is one about which the judges may easily educate themselves.

4 Normally, the greater the experience of the agency (Interstate Commerce Commission, for example), the greater is the confidence displayed by the courts in that agency's determinations.

5 The more summary (short, abbreviated) the administrative procedure, the more searching is the judicial review.

6 Up to a certain point, the more the legislature restricts the power of review, the less extensive is the review. For example, if the expressed intent of the legislature is to make final such agency findings as are supported by substantial evidence, courts will give effect to that intention. But courts will not allow themselves to be divested of all power of review. Legislation attempting to do so would be held to be an invasion of one department of the government by another and would be declared unconstitutional.

7 A court will not review action taken by an agency until the petitioner has exhausted his administrative remedies—unless exhaustion of remedies would result in irreparable harm to the petitioner or unless the agency is obviously without jurisdiction.

The case which follows illustrates several principles of administrative law that affect the scope of judicial review.

Case 4.1   **Appeal of Nationwide Insurance Co.**
411 A.2d 1107 (N.H. 1980)

Nationwide Mutual Insurance Company and Nationwide Mutual Fire Insurance Company (Nationwide) petitioned the New Hampshire Insurance Commissioner for a 14% insurance premium rate increase on August 24, 1978, following an increase of 15% granted just three weeks earlier. The commissioner denied the request. Nationwide then requested a hearing which was held on November 28, 1978. The commissioner issued a decision on December 29, 1978, again denying the requested increase on grounds that it was excessive and discriminatory. A rehearing was held on March 26, 1979, at Nationwide's request, and the commissioner reaffirmed his decision. Nationwide then appealed to the New Hampshire Supreme Court for a review of the commissioner's decision.

BOIS, J. Nationwide first argues that the Insurance Commissioner's denial of its requested rate increase was unlawful because [the Commissioner] did not comply with the Administrative Procedure Act (hereinafter APA). . . . We acknowledge that the commissioner's adoption of rules and regulations . . . must be in accordance with procedures established . . . in the APA. Compliance with the APA, however, was not required in this case.

The Insurance Commissioner is directed by statute to disapprove rate schedules which are excessive, inadequate, unreasonable, or unfairly discriminatory. The commissioner disapproved Nationwide's requested rate increase on grounds that it was both excessive and discriminatory. The denial was not

Case 4.1
Continued

founded upon the violation of a rule requiring a flat rate surcharge, but rather upon the commissioner's conclusion in the form of a declaratory ruling that the failure to adopt a flat rate surcharge *in this case* was discriminatory and violative of [the statute]. [Emphasis added.]

. . . The commissioner's decision did not trigger the procedural requirements of the APA, because he did not adopt a "rule" within the meaning of [the APA]. He simply issued a declaratory ruling denying Nationwide's requested rate increase. *See* N.H. Laws 1979, 307:3 ("declaratory rulings" expressly excluded from APA definition of "rule"). However, we caution against the adoption of rules under the guise of issuing declaratory rulings. We would consider a uniform policy that conditions automobile policy rate increases upon adoption by insurers of a flat rate surcharge plan to be a "rule" under [the APA, and compliance with the APA would be required].

Nationwide next argues that the commissioner erred in implementing the requirements of [New Hampshire's ratemaking statute] by considering Nationwide's profits outside the State in its decision, and by not giving "due consideration" to several factors such as Nationwide's past and prospective loss experience and its calculations to establish a reasonable margin for underwriting profit and contingencies.

The broad powers conferred upon the commissioner by [the ratemaking statute] clearly encompass the authority to consider Nationwide's profits outside the State. Furthermore, the record supports a finding that the commissioner reached his decision after giving "due consideration" to the factors enumerated in [the statute], including Nationwide's past and prospective loss experience, and a reasonable margin for underwriting profit and contingencies.

Ratemaking is a technical and highly complex process, and has been delegated to the Insurance Commissioner because he is a specialist in the field. [The statute] does not prescribe the weight to be accorded to the various factors considered by the commissioner in ratemaking, and it is within his discretion to determine both the method to be used in deriving rates and the weight to be given to each factor. Nationwide has not overcome the presumption that the commissioner's decision is prima facie lawful and reasonable. . . .

In his order of May 18, 1979, following the rehearing on March 26, 1979, the commissioner appended certain statistical information which he obtained after the rehearing, indicating a decline in the frequency of claims filed in the State in 1978 from the previous year. The subject of claim frequency was an issue raised by Nationwide at both the original hearing and the rehearing. Because Nationwide was not afforded the opportunity to inspect the data and dispute [their] accuracy, the commissioner's use of such information as a basis for his decision was error. However, we do not find that such error here was prejudicial. There is substantial evidence in the record to support the commissioner's decision without the benefit of such information, and we do not believe that a remand on this issue would alter the result. The doctrine that error must be prejudicial to be reversible applies to decisions of an administrative agency.

Nationwide contends that the commissioner's orders denying the requested rate increase contained insufficient findings of fact to support its rulings, and in the same vein argued that the record did not support the commissioner's decision. The record clearly contained sufficient findings of fact and conclusions based on those facts to enable Nationwide to pursue an adequate appeal. Furthermore, the evidence in the record supports the commissioners decision, and Nationwide has not shown by a clear preponderance of the evidence that his order was unjust or unreasonable. . . .

[The decision of the commissioner is] affirmed.

WORK OF THE AGENCIES— FTC AS AN EXAMPLE

Agencies vary widely in the nature and scope of the work they do. The American Battle Monuments Commission, for example, is charged with a narrow range of responsibilities. Its responsibility is the construction and permanent maintenance of military cemetaries and memorials. Most of its work is routine and custodial. In contrast, the Federal Trade Commission (FTC) is a large and complex agency charged with so many responsibilities that its activities directly affect millions of people. Yet, in terms of the kinds of work it does, the FTC is representative of administrative agencies in general. To illustrate, we turn now to the scope of FTC activities and to the principal techniques of regulation.

Scope of FTC Activities

The basic objective of the FTC is "the maintenance of strongly competitive enterprise as the keystone of the American economic system."[18] In furtherance of that objective, the FTC carries out a wide range of duties. The FTC Act of 1914 prohibits the use in commerce of unfair methods of competition and unfair or deceptive acts or practices. The FTC also has enforcement duties under numerous other acts of Congress, including the federal antitrust laws, the Export Trade Act, the Fair Packaging and Labeling Act, the Lanham Trade-Mark Act, the Trans-Alaska

Pipeline Authorization Act, the Truth in Lending Act, the Fair Credit Reporting Act, and the Magnuson-Moss Warranty Act.

In addition, the FTC has the duty of gathering and making available to the Congress, the President, and the public, factual data concerning economic and business conditions. Reports from the commission include studies of conditions and problems affecting competition, quarterly reports on the financial position and operating results of the nation's manufacturing industries, and annual reports on merger activity and on rates of return for selected manufacturing industries. "Not only have the reports provided the basis for significant legislation, but by spotlighting uneconomic or otherwise objectionable trade practices, they have also led in many instances to voluntary changes in the conduct of business, with resulting benefits to both industry and the public."[19]

Techniques of Regulation

In carrying out its responsibilities, the FTC acts quasi-judicially and quasi-legislatively on a continuing and corrective basis. The FTC "has no authority to punish; its function is to 'prevent,' through cease-and-desist orders and other means, those practices condemned by the law of federal trade regulation."[20] The FTC utilizes two principal enforcement techniques: (1) actions to foster voluntary observance of the law and (2) litigation leading to mandatory orders against the offender.

---

[18]*United States Government Manual*, 1977–1978, Office of the Federal Register, Washington, p. 540.

[19]Ibid., p. 546.
[20]Ibid., p. 540.

Voluntary and Cooperative Action Most law observance is accomplished by voluntary and cooperative procedures which provide business and industry with authoritative guidance and a measure of certainty as to what they may do under the laws administered by the FTC. These procedures include the following:

1 *Advisory opinions.* A business firm may seek an advisory opinion as to whether a proposed course of conduct will be permitted by the FTC. An advisory opinion is binding on the FTC but may be rescinded. If the opinion is rescinded, the requesting party must discontinue the course of conduct but is not subject to penalty for good faith reliance on the opinion.

2 *Trade regulation rules.* Trade regulation rules express the FTC's judgment concerning the substantive requirements of the statutes it administers. A trade regulation rule may be nationwide in effect, or it may be directed only to particular areas, industries, products, or geographical markets. A trade regulation rule is binding on all to whom it is directed, subject to an alleged violator's right to a hearing on the application of the rule to her or him.

3 *Industry guides.* An industry guide is an administrative interpretation of laws administered by the FTC expressed in language easily understood by the nonspecialist. An industry guide enables the members of a particular industry, or industries in general, to abandon unlawful practices voluntarily and simultaneously. If all members follow an industry guide, none will be put at a competitive disadvantage by ceasing the unlawful practice while others continue it. Failure to comply with an industry guide may result in corrective action by the FTC.

FTC Litigation Cases before the FTC originate through complaints filed by consumers, competitors, Congress, or by federal, state, or local agencies. Complaints are screened to determine which ones warrant investigation. Also, the FTC itself may initiate an investigation to determine possible violation of the laws admin-

istered by it. On completion of an investigation, there may be a staff recommendation for an informal settlement of the case, for an issuance of a formal complaint, or for a closing of the matter.

If the FTC decides to issue a formal complaint, the alleged violator (respondent) is served with a copy of the complaint and a copy of an order proposed by the FTC. Before a hearing on the matter takes place, the respondent may "consent" to the order. Under a consent order the respondent does not admit any violation of the law but agrees to discontinue the challenged practice.

If no agreement can be reached, litigation before an administrative law judge usually ensues. After a hearing, the judge issues an initial decision which is appealable to the Commission or is reviewable by the Commission on its own initiative. If an initial decision adverse to the respondent is not appealed within the 30 days allowed, or if an adverse decision is sustained by the Commission upon appeal or review, a cease-and-desist order is issued. The respondent has 60 days after the order is served to appeal it to the appropriate United States court of appeals. The order becomes final if not appealed within the 60 days or if, upon appeal, it is affirmed by the proper courts.

Violation of a final order to cease and desist subjects the offender to a suit by the federal government in a federal district court for the recovery of a civil penalty of not more than $10,000. Where the violation continues, each day of its continuance is a separate violation. Other FTC orders (e.g., consent orders and orders to take corrective action such as affirmative disclosure, divestiture, or restitution) are subject to the same penalties.

The *Trans World Accounts* case which follows presents a typical instance of FTC litigation. The case was decided shortly before the Fair Debt Collection Practices Act became effective. The FTC would now apply that Act to the kind of dispute litigated in *Trans World Accounts*.

Case 4.2   **In the Matter of
Trans World Accounts, Inc.
90 F.T.C. 350 (1977)**

OPINION OF THE COMMISSION

BY DIXON, *Commissioner:* The extraction of money owed from the pockets of those who owe it is a necessary, if not universally revered occupation in a society, like ours, whose growth and prosperity depends so heavily upon the extension of credit. Worthy ends, nonetheless, cannot excuse means which slide beyond education, persuasion, and exhortation into the realm of deception and unfairness. This case involves allegations of such overreaching by a large West Coast collection agency.

Respondents are Trans World Accounts, Inc., (hereinafter Trans World), a full-line collection agency, which contacts over 100,000 consumers per year, and Floyd T. Watkins, its principal shareholder and guiding light. The complaint in this matter . . . charged that respondents had used two sorts of misrepresentations in a series of form notices and letters sent to debtors in an effort to induce payment. Respondents were first alleged to have sent communications in a "yellow window envelope" with the word "TELEGRAM" printed in large black type over the window and on the reverse side. The notice inside was alleged to be a "yellow printed form, styled TELEGRAM." The complaint further alleged that these simulated telegrams misled recipients as to the nature, import, purpose, and urgency of the message they contained. The complaint also charged that statements in the messages to debtors represented that legal action was about to be, or might be taken against the recipients by their creditors when in fact legal action with respect to the debt would not be taken at all during the course of sending the series of form notices and letters, if ever.

A trial was held before Administrative Law Judge (ALJ) Daniel Hanscom who entered an intial decision sustaining the allegations of the complaint and recommended an order to cease and desist. This matter is before the Commission upon the appeal of respondents from the ALJ's decision.

Like many collection agencies, Trans World will take assignment of delinquent accounts, make contact with the debtor, and attempt to collect the debt, retaining as its fee a fixed percentage (often 50 percent) of any amounts recovered. A more commonly employed offering is a series of form letters which may be purchased by creditors for a "flat rate" and are mailed to debtors by Trans World over a period of time, typically 85–90 days for a six-letter series and 60–70 days for a five-letter series. Trans World offers "diplomatic" and "intensive" dunning notices to suit the varied corporate philosophies of its customers. Both series hint, in diplomatic or "intensive" prose, at dire consequences that may befall a debtor who neglects to pay up, but typically the only consequence to afflict a person who ignores one letter is the receipt of another . . . until the flat-rate series is exhausted. Should the debtor pay at any point, he or she may be sent, at the creditor's option, a message of thanks.

I. TELEGRAM

A review of the record leaves no doubt that certain of respondents' collection notices were misleading because they simulated telegraphic communications. The overwhelming similarities between respondents' "telegrams" and Western Union's are set forth in the initial decision. . . .

The materiality of the deception is . . . manifest. We take judicial notice that on some occasions money speaks louder than words. A creditor would not spend $7.95 to convey a message when 13 cents might suffice, unless the message being sent were of the utmost importance and urgency. The obvious conclusion to be drawn from the receipt of a demand to pay, telegraphically communicated at substantial cost, is that precipitous action may follow if immediate response to the message is not made.

The law judge entered two order provisions (paragraphs 1 and 2) addressed to the deceptive telegram count. Paragraph 1 prohibits respondents from using or placing in the hands of others materials which misrepresent that they are telegrams or a telegram. Respondents do not question the applicability of this provision if an order is to be entered. Respondents do, however, object to Paragraph 2 which prohibits the use or placement in the hands of others of materials which "by simulating telegrams or other methods or forms or types of communication misrepresent the nature, import, or urgency of any communication."

We believe [that Paragraph 2 is an] entirely appropriate "fencing in," designed to prevent recurrence in slightly altered form of the violation proven. Indeed, there is evidence of record that the misrepresentation proven has already occurred in slightly different form. Following their discontinuance of the "telegram" format in 1975, respondents switched to the "Trans-O-Gram," a blue and white missive which looks suspiciously like a Western Union Mailgram. . . .

Respondents are entirely free to attract the debtor's attention with all manner of non-deceptive, eye-catching pictures, colors, or words. The order contains no prohibition upon use of such exhortations as "Important Message" to call the reader's attention to what respondents believe to be a communication deserving serious consideration. What is deceptive, however, is for respondents to attempt to convince their readers that a message is of such urgency or importance that they have taken particular pains or spent extra money to deliver it, *when in fact they have not.* We think the order as framed by the ALJ is sufficiently explicit in this regard, but should respondents remain honestly in doubt as to whether any particular format would run afoul of the order, Section 3.61(d) of the Commission's Rules of Practice permits them to obtain an advisory opinion to allay their uncertainty.

II. IMMINENCE OF LEGAL ACTION

We think there can be no question that some of respondents' communications were intended to and had the capacity to convince their readers that legal action to collect a debt was imminent, when in fact it was not. While it appears that respondents sought to avoid certain of the flagrant express misrepresentations that have characterized cases of this sort in the past, the message they did get across differed very little. What, for example, is a reader likely to understand by these words: . . .

> You are hereby directed to appear at our client's office at 9:00 A.M. next Tuesday to protest liability of the above claim. Failure to comply may result in immediate commencement of litigation by our client. If judgment is granted, property, including monies, automobile, credits and bank deposits now in your possession could be attached. If our client receives payment in full prior to the time of protest as scheduled, your appearance will not be required.

. . . Other examples are cited and analyzed by the administrative law judge.
. . . We believe that the record in this case makes perfectly clear that the intention of Trans World . . . was to exhaust the series . . . before deciding whether to take . . . further action in particular cases. Nevertheless, having made no evaluation of individual files to determine whether legal action in any particular case would be warranted; knowing nothing about an account except that it was "delinquent;" not having determined whether the debtor refused to pay because he or she had a legitimate complaint, because he or she had lost a job and was not able to pay, or because he or she was a "deadbeat"; and despite the absence of any present intention on its own part or that of its creditors to take any action, Trans World threatened people with the possibility of being immediately taken to court. . . . We fail to perceive how this can constitute acceptable conduct under a law that prohibits misrepresentations affecting commerce. . . . As noted above, a worthy end does not justify deceptive means. And a false threat of immediate legal action is highly deceptive. . . .

Paragraph 3 of the order speaks to the misrepresentation of legal action. As modified by the Commission it would prohibit respondents from misrepresenting the imminence of legal action, and from misrepresenting that legal action has been, is about to be, or may be initiated or [from] otherwise misrepresenting the likelihood of such action. . . . [However], we do not agree with complaint counsel that the order entered herein should be read to prohibit necessarily any reference to legal action in respondents' flat rate letter series. But such references must be carefully and selectively employed to avoid deception. Respondents should not state or imply that legal action *will* be taken unless they indeed take such action in *all* cases wherein the threat of legal action is not met by payment. And respondents should not state or imply that legal action *may* be taken unless they can demonstrate from their experience that suit is the *ordinary* response to nonpayment. For purposes of the guidance respondents have solicited, suit in more than half the instances on nonpayment will suffice under this order to substantiate a claim that legal action may be taken.

In complying with the foregoing standard, respondents would do well to treat discernible classes of alleged debtors differently, depending upon the likelihood that members of each class will be sued. . . . [For example], if it is true . . . that it is the corporate policy of some clients to pursue nearly all unsatisfied claims, even small ones, through the courts, references to the possibility of eventual legal action would be appropriate in a series of letters drafted for such clients. Distinguishing among discernible classes of debtors can also provide a way for respondents to make mention of possible legal action in a non-deceptive fashion where it might otherwise be improper. For example, when serving a creditor whose policy is to sue infrequently, respondents might nonetheless be able to make non-deceptive mention of possible legal action in some cases by separating out a class of claims that their non-litigious client would ordinarily pursue (for example, bad checks written for large amounts). . . .

[As modified by the Commission], the initial decision is affirmed and adopted as the decision of the Commission.

FINAL ORDER

. . . *It is ordered*, That respondents, Trans World Accounts, Inc., . . . its successors and assigns, and Floyd T. Watkins, individually and as an officer of said corporation . . . do forthwith cease and desist from:

1 Using or placing in the hands of others for use, envelopes, letters, forms or any other materials which by their appearance, content, or otherwise, misrepresent that they are telegrams or a telegram.

2 Using or placing in the hands of others for use, envelopes, letters, forms or any other materials which by simulating telegrams or other methods or forms or types of communication misrepresent the nature, import, or urgency of any communication.

3 Misrepresenting directly or by implication, that legal action with respect to an alleged delinquent debt has been, is about to be, or may be initiated, or otherwise misrepresenting in any manner the likelihood or imminency of legal action.

4 Placing in the hands of others the means and instrumentalities to accomplish any of the matters prohibited in this order, or which fail to comply with the requirements of this order.

It is further ordered, That the respondent shall distribute a copy of this order to each of its operating divisions or departments and to each of its present and future officers, agents, representatives, or employees . . . and that said respondent secure a signed statement acknowledging receipt of said order from each such person.

It is further ordered, That the respondent corporation notify the Commission at least thirty (30) days prior to any proposed change in the corporate respondent such as dissolution, assignment or sale resulting in the emergence of a successor corporation, the creation or dissolution of subsidiaries or any other change in the corporation which may affect compliance obligations arising out of the order.

It is further ordered, That [Floyd T. Watkins] promptly notify the Commission of the discontinuance of his employment with Trans World Accounts, Inc., and of his affiliation with a new business or employment [if such a discontinuance or new affiliation should occur]. In addition, for a period of ten years from the effective date of this order, [Floyd T. Watkins] shall promptly notify the Commission of his affiliation with a new business or employment whose principal activities [include a debt-collection service], or of his affiliation with a new business or employment in which his own duties and responsibilities involve [debt-collection activities].

It is further ordered, That the respondents herein shall, within sixty (60) days from the date this order becomes final, and periodically thereafter as required by the Federal Trade Commission, file with the Commission a written report setting forth in detail the manner and form of their compliance with this order. . . .

IMPACT OF ADMINISTRATIVE REGULATION ON BUSINESS

The impact of administrative regulation on business is difficult to describe and may be impossible to measure. For some businesses, such as the railroads, regulation is pervasive; for other businesses, regulation is partial and perhaps minimal. Whether pervasive or partial, regulation is both quantitative and qualitative. It is easy to count the number of forms to be filled out and fairly easy to list the agencies which directly affect a business firm. It is less easy to identify agencies which indirectly affect business operations or to measure the qualitative aspects of regulation.

A policy of tight credit imposed by the Federal Reserve Board will affect some businesses adversely but help others, and the policy will have different effects on the various operational divisions within a large firm. What is the true impact of this monetary policy? With regard to a single firm, must not the short-term and the long-term effects be considered?

Safety measures required by the Occupational Safety and Health Administration may increase production costs but decrease injury and death among employees. If the increase in production costs were exactly balanced by the decrease in costs caused by injury, what would be the impact of regulation? Would the impact on a firm necessarily be adverse even if the increase in production costs substantially outweighed the decrease in costs due to injury? Should factors other than the purely economic be considered in evaluating the impact of the regulation on the firm?

The remainder of this chapter illustrates the magnitude of business regulation and identifies certain problems confronting business as a result of that regulation. However, no thorough-going qualitative evaluation is attempted.

Example of Regulation of a Business Firm

Suppose the hypothetical firm of Gardner Company, Inc., is engaged in food processing and does business in two states. In the establishment and conduct of its business, the Gardner Company has been subject to the following direct regulation:

1 Before the corporation could come into existence, articles of incorporation had to be approved by the secretary of state of the "domicile" (home) state. Then the firm had to qualify

in the "foreign" state (any state other than the domicile state) before doing business there.

2   Acquiring a permit to sell a public issue of stock in a state necessitated registration of the issue under the provisions of the state "blue-sky" law, and the filing of a complex registration statement with the federal Securities and Exchange Commission.

3   The firm had to acquire licenses for its food-processing activities from federal, state, and local authorities. To receive and retain the licenses, the Gardner Company was required to submit detailed plans for the processing plant to various state and federal agencies, make the plant facilities conform to health, safety, and fire codes, and submit to frequent inspections of the facilities and processes.

4   The Gardner Company is required to file returns for the following taxes: state sales and use taxes, state and federal income taxes, state and federal unemployment taxes, and social security taxes. Gardner is also required to withhold income, unemployment, and social security taxes from employees' wages, and to make its pension plan conform to state and federal laws.

5   Shortly after the Gardner Company opened for business, a labor union sought to organize Gardner's employees. Gardner is required by regulations of the National Labor Relations Board not to commit unfair labor practices.

6   In developing a testing program for prospective employees, Gardner has faced charges of violating the antidiscrimination provisions of the Equal Employment Opportunity Act.

7   The Federal Trade Commission has proposed a consent order under which Gardner would agree to halt certain advertising practices. Beyond that, Gardner must conform all its labeling and packaging to state and federal standards.

8   Gardner proposes to discharge food-processing wastes into a nearby river. Gardner's proposal has met formal objection from local, state, and federal agencies, including the Environmental Protection Agency.

9   The Gardner Company contemplates purchasing a rival food-processing company. The antitrust division of the Justice Department is looking into the matter.

10   The Gardner Company wishes to purchase raw materials from a Russian supplier. The U.S. Customs Service informs the firm that those materials are subject to certain tariffs and quotas, and that no importation from Russia will be permitted unless the firm first acquires a special import license from the State Department.

Practical Problems of Compliance

The illustration has been carried far enough to point out some of the problems which business people face in connection with regulation: keeping informed about administrative requirements, minimizing the cost of complying with the requirements, and preventing the "invasion of private management by public administrators."

Keeping Informed about Administrative Requirements   In the past, business people have found it difficult to keep themselves informed about changes in administrative requirements. New agencies were created from time to time, and the powers of existing agencies were enlarged or redistributed. Agency rules and decisions were for the most part unpublished. Adequate digests and indexes were lacking for such materials as were available in printed form.

Fortunately the situation is changing. Legal principles are becoming crystallized in this field as they have become crystallized elsewhere in the law. A pattern of organizational structure and proceedings begins to emerge, so that knowledge of how one agency operates may give insight into how others operate.

Information is more readily available, particularly at the federal level. The first publication of rules and regulations occurs in the *Federal Register*, issued five days a week. Rules and regulations appearing in the *Register* are reprinted in systematic and organized form in the *Code of Federal Regulations*. The *Register* and the *Code* are useful primarily to the specialist.

The nonspecialist will find much useful information in the annual *United States Government Manual,* available in nearly every library. It contains material on the structure, functions, and personnel of each agency and gives the addresses of district offices. Some states, following the lead of the federal government, have compiled codes of regulations. In all states, rules of some agencies are available gratis or at nominal cost.

Often it is unnecessary for a business person to search official publications for desired information. A letter addressed to an agency, or a telephone call, may be all that is needed. A person may even be able to elicit the help of the agency in filling out a puzzling form.

Minimizing Compliance Costs Coupled with the problem of obtaining information on administrative requirements is that of keeping compliance costs to a reasonable level. "Compliance costs" means the cost of regulation borne by the regulated, as distinct from those borne by the regulator (government). Included are such costs as those of keeping required records, preparing reports, issuing prospectuses, and employing legal counsel.

Not all such costs are compliance costs. When the accumulation of required data results in greater business efficiency, only a portion of the expenditures for such purposes should be allocated to compliance costs. For example, after railroads adopted the uniform system of accounts set up by the Interstate Commerce Commission, many railroads found that their improved financial records resulted in greater efficiency of operation.

In attempting to minimize compliance costs, business firms rightly object to unnecessary or duplicative record keeping. Often, ways and means of reducing such costs can be worked out in conferences between representatives of the agency and of business associations. The consuming public, too, has an interest in keeping such costs within reasonable limits because to the extent that elasticity of demand and conditions of competition allow, business firms pass along compliance costs, as they pass along other costs, by including them in sales prices.

Preventing "Invasion of Private Management" Business people also rightly object to unnecessary regulation of business. The question of what constitutes unnecessary regulation, however, grows less and less clear. It was long thought that a corporate manager was answerable only to the shareholders and that the measure of the manager's success was the degree of profitability attained by the company—at least if profit was attained honestly. Now, in an era of gigantic industrial-nuclear enterprise, vanishing natural resources, and shocking problems of pollution and environmental destruction, serious thinkers believe that corporate managers should consider in their business decisions a broader range of interests than they have heretofore.[21] Many governmental regulators agree, and therein lies the problem. What constitutes an unwarranted invasion of private management by government? As in so many other areas of policy and judgment, there are no easy answers.

In order to limit what they regard as encroachment on managerial rights, business people try to get legislation that is as favorable as possible. They may appear before legislative committees, carry on publicity campaigns, and perhaps even resort to pressure tactics. After a regulatory statute has been passed, they seek to get favorable interpretations through such methods as (1) holding conferences with commissioners and staff members, (2) recommending personnel from industry for appointment to the commission or for employment by the commission, and (3) pressing for the establishment of an industry committee to serve as an advisory council to the commission.[22] When other means fail, relief may be sought by challenging the constitutionality of the legislation or by petitioning for court review of the action of the agency.

---

[21]Christopher D. Stone, *Where the Law Ends,* Harper & Row, New York, 1975.

[22]Vernon A. Mund, *Government and Business,* 2d ed., Harper & Brothers, New York, 1955, pp. 41–42.

SUMMARY

Like the legislatures and the courts, administrative agencies have the power to determine private rights and obligations by making rules and deciding cases. The large number of agencies, the wide scope of their powers, and the great volume of their rules and decisions give some indication of the impact of the action of an agency on modern business.

Administrative law is any law concerning the powers and procedures of administrative agencies, including the law governing judicial review of administrative action. Administrative law does not include the substantive law produced by agencies, which is better classified as tax law, labor law, or the like.

A variety of reasons account for the trend toward administrative regulation. Among them are: (1) the need for expertness in certain fields of regulation; (2) the desire to achieve greater uniformity, continuity, and flexibility in regulation than can be achieved through strictly legislative and judicial means; and (3) the demand of the public for speedy, simple, and inexpensive legal procedures.

Resort to the administrative process as a means of regulation has raised important constitutional issues. Two of these are now well settled. The concentration of "quasi-legislative" and "quasi-judicial" power in the hands of an executive agency is no longer held to be incompatible with the doctrine of separation of powers. It is equally well recognized that under proper safeguards legislatures may delegate some of their power to administrative agencies. Two other issues still occupy the attention of courts: What demands do the due-process clauses of federal and state constitutions make upon agency rules and procedures? What is the permissible scope of judicial review of agency action?

Administrative regulation of business is both quantitative and qualitative, and for that reason the impact of administrative regulation on business may be impossible to measure. From the point of view of business people, the most important problems growing out of regulation are keeping informed about administrative requirements, minimizing the costs of compliance, and preventing the "invasion of private management by public administrators." What constitutes an unwarranted invasion of management by government grows less and less clear.

Agency rules are important supplements to legislative enactments, and agency decisions are important supplements to judicial decisions. Although agency rules may be formulated only within statutory limits and agency decisions are subject to reversal by the courts, it is probably safe to conclude that administrative agencies have a more immediate impact on business than have legislatures and courts.

STUDY AND DISCUSSION QUESTIONS

1   Define *(a)* administrative agency, *(b)* administrative law, and *(c)* administrative process.

2   In the text seven reasons are given for the marked trend toward, and the development of, administrative regulation. Which three reasons seem most important today? Why?

3   What evidence is there of the current importance of administrative regulation?

4   *(a)* What is the purpose of the American doctrine of separation of powers? *(b)* How has concentration of legislative, judicial, and executive powers in the hands of a single agency been justified?

5   *(a)* What were the early and later views of the courts regarding the delegation of power to administrative agencies? *(b)* Under what conditions may a legislative body now delegate power to such agencies?

6   *(a)* What is the due-process-of-law requirement of the federal Constitution? In particular, distinguish between procedural and substantive due process. *(b)* Illustrate how the requirement of substantive due process applies to administrative agencies. *(c)* Illustrate how the requirement of procedural due process applies to administrative agencies.

7 *(a)* Under what circumstances may courts remand, modify, or reverse a decision of an administrative agency? *(b)* What is the purpose of the "substantial evidence rule"? In complying with this rule, what evidence must the federal courts and perhaps the state courts consider? *(c)* What is the function of the courts in reviewing administrative decisions? *(d)* What policy considerations determine the extent of such review?

8 The work of the FTC is representative of the work of administrative agencies in general. Explain how this statement is true with regard to *(a)* the scope of FTC activities and *(b)* the techniques of regulation used by the FTC.

9 The impact of administrative regulation on business is difficult to describe and may be impossible to measure. Why?

10 Even a small business firm is subject to considerable administration regulation. Illustrate.

11 What are some of the best sources to which business people and other citizens can turn for information or help concerning administrative rules and regulations?

12 *(a)* Define compliance costs. What expenditures are included in compliance costs? *(b)* Why is it important to keep compliance costs to a minimum, and how can such costs be minimized?

13 *(a)* What do business people mean by the "invasion of private management" by government officials? *(b)* Are the prerogatives of management clear? Explain. *(c)* How do business people seek to protect managerial prerogatives?

PART TWO

TORTS AND CRIMES

Chapter 5
Nature of Torts; Intentional Torts

Chapter 6
Negligence and Liability without Fault

Chapter 7
**Business Torts:
Interference with Business Rights**

Chapter 8
**Business Crimes:
White-Collar Crimes**

Chapter

5

Nature of Torts;
Intentional Torts

The law of torts is designed to protect individuals and business firms from civil wrongs other than breach of contract. That law is of great importance to everyone. It is especially important to the business person, who may become the victim of a tort at one time or another or may intentionally or unintentionally commit a tort. As will be seen in Chapter 39, a business person may also be responsible to others for torts committed by employees and agents. The proprietor of a small business, as well as the multinational corporation, continually risks being sued in tort by a customer, a fellow business person, or a member of the public.

Most torts are committed unintentionally, either because a person is not paying attention to what he or she is doing or because the person does not know that the particular act is a tort. The moral is clear: we need to acquire a basic knowledge of the nature of torts and of the law relating to the most important types of torts.

NATURE OF TORTS

Meaning of Torts

A *tort* has been defined as "a civil wrong other than breach of contract for which the court will provide a remedy in the form of an action for damages."[1] The courts and legislatures of the various states determine which civil wrongs are actionable, and the law of torts changes as the values and opinions of judges and elected representatives change. New torts are recognized from time to time, and existing torts are applied

---

[1]William L. Prosser, *Handbook of the Law of Torts*, 4th ed., West Publishing Company, St. Paul, 1971, p. 2.

to new fact situations. For example, invasion of the right of privacy was not generally accepted as a tort until the 1930s. Some common law torts have been abolished. For example, a number of torts based on interference with family relations, such as breach of promise to marry and alienation of affections, are no longer recognized in many states.

Tort liability is based on conduct which is socially unreasonable.[2] What is unreasonable depends upon one's point of view. An important consideration in the minds of judges and legislators is the balance between an injured person's claim to protection of person or property and the accused person's claim to freedom of action. There are situations where one person interferes with the personal or property rights of another and no cause of action results. In such situations the accused person's freedom of action is given greater weight than the harm to the aggrieved person. For example, in most states one may be held liable for intentionally inflicting mental distress on another but not for negligently causing mental distress unaccompanied by physical injury. However, when physical injury is caused by negligent conduct the balance shifts to the injured person, and a cause of action is then recognized.

Torts Distinguished from Crimes

A crime and a tort often are similar, and the student must exercise care not to confuse them. A crime may involve harm to the person or property of another or be only a violation of a statutory prohibition. A *crime* is an offense against the sovereign authority, usually punished by fine or imprisonment. Criminal prosecution is brought by the local, state, or federal government.

Because a *tort* is a civil wrong—an interference with private rights—the injured person may obtain, through a civil action against the wrongdoer (tortfeasor), money damages as com-

pensation for an injury. The same act may constitute both a tort and a crime. For example, unjustifiably confining another person within fixed boundaries is the tort of false imprisonment and the crime of kidnapping. Some criminal activities involving business organizations are dealt with in Chapter 8. In these chapters on torts, we are concerned solely with the civil aspects of a person's conduct.

Classes of Torts

Various kinds of civil wrongs are recognized as torts in contemporary law, and they are classified generally according to the nature of the wrongdoer's conduct. The two main classes are: intentional torts and unintentional torts. This chapter deals with the major intentional torts. They are discussed under the following headings: intentional harm to the person, intentional harm to property, and fraud as a tort. The next chapter discusses negligence and liability without fault. Business torts, which involve interference with business rights, are discussed in Chapter 7.

INTENTIONAL HARM TO THE PERSON

Following is a discussion of the major intentional torts involving harm to the person. Battery is the only one involving physical contact with the injured person's body. The other intentional torts involve interference with the person's peace of mind or injury to reputation.

Battery

The tort of *battery* can be defined as the intentional touching of another person without consent or legal justification. The harm may range from permanent disfigurement to merely removing a person's hat without permission or grabbing a plate out of someone's hand. A plaintiff need not be aware of having been touched, as in sleep or in an unconscious state.

In an action for battery there are two major

---

[2]Ibid., p. 6.

defenses available to the defendant: consent and privilege. The plaintiff's consent may be expressed by words or implied from conduct. Parties who participate in athletic contests such as boxing, football, and baseball are assumed to consent to the physical contact normally associated with the sport. However, the tort of battery may occur if a party exceeds the consent given. A common situation presented to the courts involves medical surgery. Let us suppose that Mrs. Abel consents to have Dr. Barr perform an operation on her nose. While Mrs. Abel is unconscious and under an anaesthetic, Dr. Barr decides that she would look much better if her eyelids were also altered, and he performs this procedure. Dr. Barr may be held liable for the tort of battery. The scope of consent may not be exceeded by a physician unless an unforeseen emergency which threatens the patient's life arises during surgery. In such event it is assumed that the patient would consent if he or she were conscious and able to understand the situation.

A person's intentional touching of another without consent may be excused if such conduct is "privileged." The most common privilege asserted is self-defense, which allows one to use reasonable force to prevent personal harm. The privilege applies where the defendant is in actual danger of harm and also where there is no danger but the defendant reasonably believes there is. The privilege is limited to the use of force which reasonably appears to be necessary to protect against the threatened injury. Deadly force may be used only when the defendant has reason to believe he or she is threatened with death or serious physical harm. In some states a person must retreat if he or she can do so safely, rather than use deadly force in self-defense. However, even in those states there is no obligation to retreat if an attack takes place in the defendant's own home.

In many states the privilege of using reasonable force extends to defense of a third person who is in immediate danger of attack. The privilege may also extend to the protection of property where there is danger of immediate damage or wrongful appropriation. Ordinarily, there is no privilege to use deadly force in protection of property. For example, a landowner is privileged to install a spiked wall or fence to prevent trespassers but may be held liable in tort if a thief is injured or killed as a result of the landowner's setting a spring gun or keeping a vicious watchdog at large.

Assault

The tort of *assault* may be defined as intentionally causing another to be in apprehension of an immediate battery. However, a battery need not follow an assault in order for the assault to constitute a tort. The two torts are separate and distinct. In most states a plaintiff in a tort action for assault may not recover damages unless he or she was aware of the defendant's conduct and felt threatened. Thus, a defendant ordinarily will not be liable for pointing a loaded pistol at a person who was unaware of the defendant's conduct. Generally, in order for a plaintiff to establish that he or she was apprehensive, it must be established that the defendant made a threat to use force and had the apparent present ability to carry out this threat. For example, suppose Ann makes an oral threat to shoot Bill while pointing a pistol at him which he believes is loaded. Ann is liable for the tort of assault even though she knows the pistol is unloaded. Apprehension is measured from the point of view of a reasonable person. No legal redress is given to the unusually timid, nor is recovery denied to the unusually brave.

In an action for assault the defendant may assert the defenses of consent and privilege. These defenses were discussed in connection with the tort of battery. Such discussion is equally applicable here. In an action for assault the defendant may not be held liable if the defendant proves he or she acted under the reasonable belief that an attack was imminent, even if the belief was mistaken. Bill, above, is privileged to threaten the use of reasonable force to protect himself. He need not wait until Ann pulls the trigger on the pistol.

False Imprisonment

The tort of *false imprisonment* may be defined generally as intentionally causing the confinement of another without consent or legal justification. There is some disagreement among courts and legal writers whether the plaintiff in a false imprisonment action must prove awareness of imprisonment. A sound argument can be advanced that where the plaintiff has suffered substantial injury he or she should recover damages even if unaware of the confinement.[3] Ordinarily the plaintiff is aware of being imprisoned, and in such a situation no injury need be shown.

Situations involving false imprisonment include confinement caused by: (1) physical restraint on a person's movement, (2) threat of force to one's person or to a member of one's immediate family, (3) force or threat of force directed against a person's property, and (4) refusal to release a person from confinement when there is a duty to do so. Confinement ordinarily means a person is restricted to a

limited area without knowledge of a reasonable means of exit. A situation involving false imprisonment often presented to the courts is one in which a retail merchant detains a customer suspected of shoplifting. In such event, the customer may recover damages for false imprisonment if it can be proved that the customer submitted involuntarily to the merchant's restraint. Where an action is filed against a merchant for false imprisonment, ordinarily the merchant asserts the defense of "shopkeeper's privilege," alleging he or she was justified in detaining the customer. In order to avoid liability, the defendant must prove that he or she had reasonable grounds to believe the plaintiff committed a crime. Limitations on the privilege are discussed in the case below.

The defendant in a false imprisonment action may avoid liability by proving the plaintiff consented to restriction of his or her movement. For example, if a store customer is accused of committing a crime and voluntarily accompanies the merchant to his or her office in an attempt to clear up the matter, the merchant has not committed false imprisonment. Of course, the merchant may be liable if he or she exceeds the consent given, as where the customer is detained for an unreasonable length of time.

---

[3]Ibid., p. 43.

Case 5.1   SuperX Drugs of Kentucky, Inc. v. Rice
554 S.W.2d 903 (Ky. App. 1977)

PARK, Judge. This appeal arises out of an action for false imprisonment brought by plaintiff-appellee, Wanda Rice, against the defendants-appellants, SuperX Drugs of Kentucky, Inc., and a clerk in its Middlesboro store, Leslie Rowland. On the first two trials of the case, the juries were unable to agree on a verdict. On the third trial of the case, the jury returned a verdict in favor of Mrs. Rice, awarding her $75,000 as compensatory damages and $75,000 as punitive damages. SuperX and Rowland appeal from the judgment on this verdict.

. . . According to their evidence, Rowland and an independent salesman, Robertson, observed Mrs. Rice place makeup, lipstick and cologne in a Rose's Department Store sack. At the checkout counter, Mrs. Rice paid for certain other items by means of a social security check. However, according to Rowland and Robertson, Mrs. Rice did not remove the makeup, lipstick and cologne from the Rose's sack or offer to pay for those items. As she was preparing to leave the store, Mrs. Rice was stopped by Rowland who escorted her back to a small room at the rear of the drugstore used as an employee's lounge. When requested, Mrs. Rice emptied the contents of the Rose's sack onto a table, including the three items from the drugstore. According to Rowland, Robertson and the store manager, Hurley, Mrs. Rice admitted taking the three items, and she offered to pay for them. This offer was refused, and the store employees took possession of the three items. At the request of the store manager, Rowland called the police and informed them that they had a shoplifter in "custody." Rowland then went to the Middlesboro city police judge from whom he obtained a warrant for Mrs. Rice's arrest. While the warrant was being obtained, a Middlesboro city policeman arrived at the store. The police officer took Mrs. Rice in the cruiser from the drugstore to the police station where she was subsequently served with the warrant of arrest.

A substantially different story was offered by Mrs. Rice and her daughter Debbie, who was twelve years old at the time of the incident. . . . According to Mrs. Rice, she thought she had paid for the makeup, lipstick and cologne and, in any event had no intent to steal. She denied admitting that she had taken the items, and she asserted that she asked Hurley and Rowland to verify the purchase with the cashier or the sales receipt. . . .

In an effort to give merchants some assistance in dealing with shoplifters, the legislature in 1958 enacted a statute providing merchants a limited defense to charges of false imprisonment. As amended, KRS 433.236(1) provides:

> "A peace officer, security agent of a mercantile establishment, merchant or merchant's employee who has probable cause for believing that goods held for sale by the merchant have been unlawfully taken by a person, and that he can recover same by taking the person into custody, may, *for the purpose of attempting to effect recovery, take the person into custody and detain him in a reasonable manner for a reasonable length of time.*" [Emphasis added.] . . .

Mrs. Rice asserts that KRS 433.236 can provide no defense to SuperX and Rowland. She points out that a merchant is permitted to take a suspected shoplifter into custody and to detain him pursuant to KRS 433.236(1) only for the purpose of recovering the goods from the suspected shoplifter. According to this interpretation of the shoplifting statute, the suspected shoplifter must be released as soon as the goods are recovered. The merchant has no right to detain the person until the arrival of a police officer who can make an arrest. . . .

If a merchant has the right to detain a person in order to recover his property, common sense dictates that the merchant should make some investigation of the facts during the period of detention. Certainly, the merchant will want to verify the person's name and address. With this information, the merchant may find that the person has an extensive shoplifting record with the police. In other cases, the merchant may be able to ascertain that the person's failure to pay for the goods was due to inadvertence rather than criminal intent. . . . On the other hand, the person's refusal to state his or her name can justify the merchant's continued detention of that person. We conclude that a merchant's limited privilege to recover goods believed to have been stolen also includes the privilege to detain the person for the time necessary to make a reasonable investigation of the facts.

. . . Assuming that there was no valid arrest without a warrant pursuant to KRS 433.236(2) when Mrs. Rice was taken into custody at the drugstore by the city policeman, it is clear that there was a valid arrest of Mrs. Rice pursuant to a warrant at the police station. . . . From the point in time when Mrs. Rice was lawfully arrested pursuant to the warrant, her detention could no longer be considered unlawful. . . .

Furthermore, we conclude that the evidence establishes that Mrs. Rice did not suffer any substantial damages from any false imprisonment. By her own estimate, she was detained at the drugstore prior to the arrival of the city police for no more than twenty-five to thirty minutes. According to Mrs. Rice, the trip to the police station took "some five to eight minutes." She estimated that Mr. Rowland arrived at the station with the warrant some five to fifteen minutes afterwards. By her own estimate, the maximum period of her detention prior to being arrested pursuant to the warrant was less than one hour. According to all of the other witnesses, the period of detention was substantially less. . . .

Mrs. Rice's claim for damages is based upon her mental suffering and embarrassment resulting from her detention. However, in an action for false imprisonment, she can recover damages only for that mental suffering and embarrassment endured during the period of less than one hour prior to her arrest. . . . Considering all of the evidence, we are of the opinion that Mrs. Rice was entitled to no more than nominal damages for the period of her detention after the goods were recovered until she was arrested, together with her costs in the trial court.

If the jury believed from the evidence that Mrs. Rice placed the three items on the checkout counter and made an effort to pay for them, then the jury could also find that Rowland did not have probable cause to believe that Mrs. Rice had taken the items unlawfully. If a reasonably prudent person would not have believed Mrs. Rice was shoplifting, then the original detention was unlawful. In such case, Mrs. Rice might be entitled to more than nominal damages. However, it is evident that her damages were not substantial, and the jury's award of $75,000 compensatory damages was clearly excessive.

. . . We find nothing in the record to indicate that Rowland or any other SuperX employee acted in bad faith or that the treatment of Mrs. Rice was grossly in excess of what the circumstances reasonably required, as perceived by Rowland and the other store employees. Under the circumstances, Mrs. Rice was not entitled to an award of punitive damages. It was error for the trial court to submit that issue to the jury.

The judgment of the circuit court is reversed with directions to grant a new trial. . . .

Infliction of Mental Distress

The tort of *infliction of mental distress* can be defined as intentionally or recklessly causing severe mental suffering in another by means of extreme or outrageous conduct or language. Generally, extreme and outrageous misconduct means exceeding all bounds of decent behavior. For example, collection agencies have been held liable to debtors for outrageous high-pressure tactics, and landlords have been held liable to tenants for similar conduct.[4] A person has been held liable for falsely telling a woman that her husband was seriously injured and in a hospital, thus causing the woman to suffer emotional trauma and physical injury.

The courts have been reluctant to impose liability on a defendant who utters obscene or abusive language. There are two reasons for this reluctance: a high regard for freedom of speech and the danger of encouraging groundless or trivial lawsuits. Thus, the citizen in contemporary society must be able to face insults, annoyances, profanity, and discourtesy without legal redress. Although obscene or abusive language ordinarily is not sufficient grounds for a tort action, special circumstances may result in a defendant's being held liable. Innkeepers (operators of motels or hotels), common carriers (railroads, buslines, airlines, etc.), and public utilities (telephone, telegraph, etc.) have been held liable to patrons for language of employees which is profane, indecent, or grossly insulting to people of ordinary sensibilities.

In most states the plaintiff need not suffer physical illness in order to recover damages for the tort of infliction of mental distress. In recent years large awards have been made to plaintiffs who suffered no physical injury. A defendant may be held liable for mental distress inflicted recklessly. For example, a defendant who without excuse inflicts a serious beating on another person may be liable to a member of the person's family who is present and suffers emotional distress.

Defamation

The tort of *defamation* can be defined generally as the intentional or negligent unjustified publication of a false statement that tends to hold a person up to hatred, contempt, or ridicule, or to cause him or her to be shunned or avoided. To hold a defendant liable in an action for defamation, the plaintiff must prove that the false statement was "published," that is, communicated to someone other than the plaintiff. The publication need not be to a large group. Communication to a single person may be enough. For example, delivery of a message to a telegraph company for transmission is a publication to the employee receiving it. The defendant must have intentionally communicated to some third person or must have carelessly permitted the defamatory matter to be communicated. For example, a defendant is negligent if he or she leaves written or visual defamatory matter in a place where other persons will surely see the material.

Defamation involves harm to a person's good name or reputation in the community. In order to constitute a tort, the statement published must be of a nature to reflect upon the defamed person's character or to disgrace him or her. For example, it is defamatory to say falsely that a person is a drunk, a liar, or a crook. The courts have awarded damages to one accused of being a member of the Communist party, to one accused of being the daughter of a murderer, and to a kosher meat dealer accused of selling bacon. When a derogatory statement is published about a large group of people, it is difficult for a member of the group to prove his or her reputation has been harmed. The courts have allowed a member of a small group, such as a jury or a family, to hold a defendant liable in a defamation action, since the defamatory statement could reasonably be interpreted as apply-

---

[4]A debtor who is harassed may have a cause of action under the Fair Debt Collection Practices Act enacted by U.S. Congress, effective March 20, 1978. There are various restrictions on suit but in some respects the remedy provided is more beneficial to the debtor than filing a common law tort action.

ing to each member. No tort is committed if a defamatory statement is published about a person who is dead.

Types of Defamation (Libel and Slander) Defamation includes two torts—libel and slander. *Libel* is defamation committed generally by means of written communication. Libelous matter may be published in a variety of forms. Some examples are newspaper articles, verses, pictures, signs, motion pictures, cartoons, and caricatures. Libel may also involve conduct conveying a defamatory message, such as one person hanging another in effigy or a bank dishonoring a customer's valid check. *Slander* is defamation committed generally by means of oral communication. The defamatory matter is expressed in spoken words and may be communicated person to person or by radio or television.

Occasionally the method of publication of defamatory matter causes difficulty in determining whether the tort is libel or slander. The courts have held that transcribing defamatory language dictated to a stenographer is libel rather than slander. A defamatory statement made in a sound motion picture is also libel.

Defenses There are two major defenses to the tort of defamation: truth and privilege. In most states *truth* is a complete defense to a defamation action. For example, suppose Andrea maliciously and in bad faith publishes the statement "Charles is a criminal," and Charles is a convicted embezzler. Charles could not recover damages from Andrea for defamation. In certain circumstances, he may have a cause of action against Andrea for the tort of invasion of privacy. That tort is discussed in the next section.

The defense of *privilege* is based upon the idea that the defendant should be allowed to publish a defamatory statement in order to further some interest of social importance. In some instances the interest is deemed to be of such great importance that the defendant is given complete or absolute immunity regardless of motive or the reasonableness of conduct.

Absolute privilege protects the following: (1) statements made in a civil or criminal action or quasi-judicial proceeding by the parties, witnesses, lawyers, judges, and jurors, as long as the statements are relevant or pertinent to an issue in the proceeding; (2) statements made by federal and state legislators performing their duties and by witnesses in legislative and quasi-legislative hearings; (3) statements made by superior officers of the executive departments and branches of the federal and state governments in the exercise of their duties (in some states the privilege extends to lower level state officers and local government officials); (4) statements made with consent of the defamed person; (5) statements made between husband and wife; and (6) certain political broadcasts required by federal law.

The defense of qualified or conditional privilege is available to a defendant under circumstances deemed to be of lesser importance than those above. To avoid liability, the defendant must prove the defamatory statement was published to protect some recognized interest in good faith and without malice. Recognized interests include one's own pecuniary interest, membership in an organization, credit standing, and employment record. The following have been held to be proper purposes justifying defamatory communications: to defend one's own reputation against the defamation of another, to warn someone of the misconduct or bad character of a third person where there is a legal or moral duty to speak, and to give information to public officials in the interest of crime prevention or detection. The defense of qualified privilege protects communications by one who is interested in the subject only to other persons who reasonably appear to have legitimate interests in receiving the information. For example, communications between partners, corporate officers, and members of unincorporated associations may be privileged. The privilege may be lost, however, if defamatory matter is published outside the interested group.

If a defendant abuses his or her qualified

privilege, the plaintiff may hold the defendant liable in an action for defamation. The qualified privilege is lost if defendant acts with malice or other improper purpose, does not honestly believe in the truth of the statement, or has no reasonable grounds for believing the statement to be true. *Malice,* as used here, means hatred, spite, or ill will.

A qualified privilege exists to publish defamatory statements about a public figure. The privilege is based on the constitutional protection given to freedom of speech and freedom of press. A defendant who publishes a false defamatory statement about a public official or a public figure may not be held liable unless the defendant acts with "actual malice." *Actual malice* means that the defendant knows the statement is false or shows a reckless disregard of the truth. The courts have held that public officials are those high-ranking government officers, whether executive, legislative, or judicial, who control the conduct of government. No complete definition has yet been given but it is clear that low-level and middle-level public employees are not public officials. Public figures include two groups of people: (1) persons who have achieved fame and notoriety, such as sports figures and well-known entertainers; and (2) persons who voluntarily thrust or inject themselves into the forefront of public controversy in order to influence the outcome of issues, such as consumer advocates and environmentalists. Persons who are involuntarily put in the public eye, such as criminals or attorneys defending persons accused of heinous crimes, are not public figures. The rationale behind the qualified privilege concerning public persons is that they have greater access to the mass media than do private persons and thus can counteract the effect of defamations. Also, those who inject themselves into public controversies must expect to be the object of public discussion.

A defendant who publishes defamatory matter about a private person may not enjoy the constitutional qualified privilege because the private person does not have access to mass media and has not voluntarily thrust himself or herself into the public eye. There are two rules of law that apply where the plaintiff is a private person. (1) If the defendant is a mass medium (newspaper, radio or television broadcaster, etc.), the plaintiff may not recover for defamation in most states unless the defendant either knew the matter was defamatory or was negligent in determining its nature. The rationale for this rule is to protect freedom of the press by requiring the plaintiff to prove the defendant was at least careless. A mass medium may not be held liable without fault. (2) If the defendant as well as the plaintiff is a private person (nonmass medium), the defendant may be held liable whether or not the matter was intended to be defamatory and whether or not the defendant was negligent in determining its defamatory nature. Thus, a private defendant may be liable without fault to a private plaintiff.

Case 5.2   **Brown v. Skaggs-Albertson's Properties, Inc.**
563 F.2d 983 (10th Cir. 1977)

WILLIAM E. DOYLE, Circuit Judge. . . . The problem arose as a result of the plaintiff, Ladonna Brown, giving a check to the [defendant's] store in Oklahoma City, Oklahoma, for the purpose of paying for groceries which she had purchased at one of the stores. There is no irregularity on the face of the check. It was nevertheless returned to the store unpaid due to the fact that Skaggs had failed to endorse the check. . . . It was sent through again without having been endorsed. . . . Thereafter, the store communicated with Craig

Brown, husband of Ladonna . . . and informed Mr. Brown that the check had been returned and would have to be replaced. He agreed to replace it and proceeded on the next day to the defendant's store, where he spoke with an employee concerning a letter saying that as a result of the return of the check the Browns' name was to be placed on a list of problem checks, which list was circulated by an organization called Check Verification Association of Central Oklahoma (CVA). . . .

The CVA would appear from the record to be engaged in acquiring information concerning problem checks. The member stores report to CVA all checks which have been returned to them dishonored and which remain in their possession for seven days. The list is then printed by CVA and circulated to its members. The members have agreed beforehand not to accept checks from people on the list.

Unfortunately, an additional mistake was made. This took place on April 22, 1975, on which day a report was sent in to CVA mistakenly showing that the Browns' check had been returned because of insufficient funds. The report which indicated that the problem had been taken care of was not received by CVA until Friday, April 25. Testimony showed that CVA could have rectified the problem if they had been notified by telephone on Tuesday, April 22. If this had been carried out, the Brown name would have been deleted. As a consequence, however, of the failure to communicate with the CVA immediately after the substitute check was written, an additional check given by Mrs. Brown was rejected at the Skaggs-Albertson's store. The very next day the Browns visited another grocery store where they asked if their check would be accepted. They were told that it could not be because their name was on the list. During the subsequent month the Browns made purchases for cash, and after a month they were told at another store that they were not on the list.

An action was brought . . . in libel. The transaction relied on was alleged injuries resulting to the plaintiffs as a result of a false statement communicated by Skaggs-Albertson to CVA. . . . The cause was submitted to the jury, which returned a verdict against defendant awarding the sum of $20,000 actual damages and $10,000 punitive damages. . . . [Defendant appealed.]

It is not seriously contended by defendant-appellant that the communication from it to CVA was not defamatory. The Oklahoma statute defines libel (12 Okla. Stat. Ann. 1441) as being "a false or malicious unprivileged publication . . . which exposes any person to public hatred, contempt, ridicule or obloquy, or which tends to deprive him of public confidence."

. . . Since the Browns' check was perfectly valid, reporting that they had issued an insufficient funds check clearly indicates guilt of a criminal act of the grade of felony. On its face then, it is defamatory.

[Here] the conditions and relationships are such as to create a qualified privilege occasion. Such exists where the defendant is seeking to vindicate an interest in a reasonable manner and for a proper purpose. It is said that such a privilege exists when the communication is fairly made by a person in the discharge of some public or private duty whether legal or moral or in the conduct of his own affairs in matters where his interest is concerned. See Prosser, *Law of Torts*, 4th ed., pp. 785, 786. Communications, then, in furtherance of legitimate business interests are privileged; but the privilege is qualified, being subject to the communication being within the bounds of the privilege. If it is made for purposes outside the privilege or with malice, the privilege is lost. [Citations.]

[In one of the cases cited] it was recognized that conditional privilege exists in connection with the report on the financial condition of a business to an interested party. Later cases have extended this to recognition of a qualified privilege in connection with reports of credit agencies. Prosser at 790.

It would appear, then, that since CVA is serving a social interest and since also the defendant was carrying out the purposes of CVA by reporting problem checks to it, the occasion here involved was a qualifiedly privileged one— provided the communication was made in good faith and was thus free of malice. Malice in the sense of ill will and an express design to inflict an injury was not present, but it can consist of an unreasonable and wrongful act done intentionally, without just cause. Malice may be inferred in the situation where the defendant has no reasonable basis for believing that the statement is true. This would be the case where there had been a failure to make an adequate investigation.

In the case at bar the conduct involved in the communication to CVA was at the very least negligence. Simple negligence would not, however, be enough to establish implied malice. It must rise to the level of recklessness. In Oklahoma also this is the accepted standard in assessing and awarding punitive damages.

The fact that the check was stamped "endorsement missing" and twice returned for that reason makes the case one of aggravated conduct sufficient for the jury to infer that malice was present. . . .

The only issue for the jury to determine was whether the defendant had exceeded the privilege; whether malice was to be implied, in which case the privilege was lost. . . .

The unjustifiable imputation of the commission of a crime together with the resultant humiliation and embarrassment to the plaintiffs justified the submission to the jury of the issue of damages and justified as well the award which the jury made. . . .

The judgment of the district court is affirmed.

Invasion of Privacy

The tort of invasion of privacy was unknown until 1890 when a legal article was published in which the authors contended that the press was overstepping the bounds of propriety and decency. They urged the recognition of a new tort to provide compensation for the individual who suffered mental pain and distress from a newspaper's invading the bounds of privacy. In the following decades the courts and legislatures of the various states began to recognize this new tort. Today, the overwhelming majority of states provide a remedy for invasion of the individual's right of privacy.

The tort of invasion of privacy usually occurs in one of four forms: (1) The wrongdoer uses a person's name or likeness without consent for business purposes. A typical example is using a public figure's name or picture without consent to advertise a commercial product. (2) The wrongdoer unreasonably intrudes upon a person's physical solitude. Examples include illegal entry of one's home, illegal wiretapping, and unauthorized investigation of one's bank account. (3) The wrongdoer makes public disclosure of private information about a person which is offensive and objectionable. An example is publishing the history and the present identity of a reformed criminal. (4) The wrongdoer publishes information which places a person in a false light. An example is attributing to a successful poet an inferior poem which he or she did not write. When the information published is false and defamatory, the injured person may have an additional cause of action for defamation.

Several defenses are available to a defendant in an action for invasion of privacy. The defendant may assert that the plaintiff has no cause of action because the one whose interest is invaded is dead. For example, a defendant who uses the name or photograph of a deceased public figure for commercial purposes is not liable to the decedent's heirs or close relatives. Consent, express or implied, is a defense to a suit for invasion of privacy. The courts have held that an individual has no right of privacy while in a public place, that one impliedly consents to intrusion upon personal solitude after leaving one's abode. Thus, in the absence of special circumstances no tort is committed if a person's picture is taken while walking along a sidewalk or while sitting as a spectator at a public event.

A defendant in an action for invasion of privacy may assert a constitutional privilege to give publicity to public figures or to publish news or matters of public interest. A public figure's right of privacy is not given the same protection as that of an ordinary person. A similar loss of privacy is suffered by a person who becomes involved in a matter of public interest. For example, one who is the victim of a crime or the witness to a crime has no cause of action if he or she is identified in the news media and the person's personal and family background is exposed to public view. In recent years the courts have held that a defendant who publishes statements concerning a public figure or a person in the news which place him or her in a false light will be liable only if the statements are made with actual malice, that is, knowledge of falsity or reckless disregard of the truth.

Case 5.3   Kinsey v. Macur
165 Cal. Rptr. 608 (Cal. App. 1980)

While Bill Kinsey was in the Peace Corps in Tanzania in 1966, his wife died when they were on a picnic. Kinsey was charged with her murder and spent six months awaiting trial. He was subsequently acquitted. The case attracted some notoriety, including articles published in *Time* magazine. In December 1971, Kinsey met Mary Macur at a cocktail party in San Francisco. At that time he was a graduate student at Stanford University and she worked at a medical institute. For the next five months Kinsey and Macur had a love affair. On April 5, 1972, Kinsey told Macur that he would no longer be seeing her since a woman was coming from England to live with him.

In the fall of 1972, Kinsey accepted a job in Central Africa. He and Sally Allen went to Africa and were subsequently married. Shortly before they left the United States, each received a letter from Macur stating in graphic terms how Kinsey had mistreated Macur. During the time the Kinseys were in Africa they received more letters. Other letters were received by acquaintances of Bill Kinsey and forwarded to him. Some letters accused Bill of murdering his first wife, spending six months in jail for the crime, being a rapist, and other questionable behavior.

On July 9, 1973, Sally and Bill Kinsey filed a complaint for invasion of privacy. On June 28, 1977, after a trial without jury, judgment was entered for Bill Kinsey for $5,000. Macur appealed.

MILLER, Associate Justice. . . . Courts now recognize four separate torts within the broad designation of "invasion of privacy": (1) the commercial appropriation of the plaintiff's name or likeness, . . . (2) intrusion upon the plaintiff's physical solitude or seclusion; (3) public disclosure of true, embarrassing private facts concerning the plaintiff; and (4) publicity which places the plaintiff in a false light in the public eye. . . . In the present case, only the latter two forms of invasion of privacy are alleged.

. . . Except in cases involving physical intrusion, the tort must be accompanied by publicity in the sense of communication to the public in general or to a large number of persons as distinguished from one individual or a few. . . . The interest to be protected is individual freedom from the wrongful publicizing of private affairs and activities which are outside the realm of legitimate public concern. . . .

Appellant [Macur] first contends that her mailing of letters to "perhaps twenty [people] at most" was insufficient publicity to justify a finding that respondent's [Kinsey's] privacy had been invaded. Since these mailings were ostensibly to only a small select group of people, appellant argues that the requirement of mass exposure to the public as opposed to a few people has not been satisfied. Appellant's contention misstates the applicable law. . . .

In the instant case, appellant, in her professed attempts to "tell the whole world what a bastard he is," sought to reach a large group of people whom she knew had nothing in common except the possible acquaintance of Bill Kinsey. . . . Recipients of her letters included the Kinseys, their former spouses, their parents, their neighbors, their parents' neighbors, members of Bill Kinsey's dissertation committee, other faculty and the President of Stanford University. Since this court believes these recipients adequately reflect "mass exposure" we decline to yield to appellant's claim of insufficient publicity. . . .

Appellant next contends that, even if respondent's privacy had been invaded, the invasion was privileged since Kinsey was a public figure. This status, she contends, was achieved "by virtue of his entry into the Peace Corps and through his trial for the murder of his first wife." Given this "public figure" status, she asserts that she may exercise her constitutional privilege to disseminate critical material if done without malice. . . . It is difficult to see

Case 5.3
Continued

how respondent could become a public figure simply because of his participation in the Peace Corps or his employment with the United Nations.

With respect to Kinsey's notoriety by virtue of his trial, respondent was involuntarily thrust into the public limelight through the unfortunate death of his first wife. Offered the opportunity to be released on bail, he declined in favor of waiting some six months in jail for his trial at which time he was acquitted.

In the leading case of *Melvin v. Reid* (1931) 112 Cal. App. 285, 297 P. 91, plaintiff, a prostitute, was charged with murder and acquitted after a very long and very public trial. She abandoned her life of shame, married and assumed a place in respectable society, making many friends who were not aware of the incidents of her earlier life. The court held that she had stated a cause of action for privacy against defendants who had made a movie based entirely on Mrs. Melvin's life some seven years after the trial. . . . Since Kinsey, like Mrs. Melvin, had been acquitted of the murder charge, there is a strong societal interest in allowing him "to melt into the shadows of obscurity" once again.

Appellant argues that her First Amendment right of freedom of speech has been cut off by respondent's right to privacy. She points out that the "only social sanction available to a person wronged is exposure" noting that "people do not always relate damaging information about others in a detached, rational manner, particularly when they feel they have been victimized."

" 'The right "to be let alone" and to be protected from undesired publicity is not absolute but must be balanced against the public interest in the dissemination of news and information consistent with the democratic processes under the constitutional guarantees of freedom of speech and of the press. [Citations.]' " A review of the contents of Macur's letters yields very little that may be considered to be of public interest. . . .

Little of what Macur wrote in her letters to the Kinseys and their acquaintances could be considered "newsworthy." . . . She falsely accused him of murdering his wife and of having spent six months in jail for the crime. . . . The fact that appellant "believed her own allegations" is not relevant to the issue of newsworthiness. Her admission in her opening brief that she had described her experiences with respondent in "graphic, if hysterical detail" is a gross understatement of the truth.

The judgment is affirmed.

Misuse of Legal Procedure

There are three intentional torts involving misuse of legal procedure: malicious prosecution of criminal action, malicious prosecution of civil action, and abuse of process. Often there is overlap between one or more of these torts and torts discussed previously. For example, the wrongful filing of criminal charges or the wrong-

ful instituting of a civil lawsuit may be defamatory and harmful to the defendant's reputation. Also, litigation generally involves publicity and may result in the parties' privacy being invaded. In addition, if wrongful criminal proceedings are instituted, the accused may be falsely imprisoned. The requirements for each of the torts discussed below are difficult for a plaintiff to meet. The requirements have been imposed because of the social policy in favor of encouraging the use of the courts for resolution of legitimate disputes and for bringing criminals to justice.

Malicious Prosecution of Criminal Action The tort of *malicious prosecution of criminal action* can be defined generally as instigating or encouraging criminal proceedings against another when three elements are present: (1) the proceedings terminate in favor of the accused, (2) there is no probable cause for the proceeding, and (3) the instigator has acted maliciously. The student should note that two proceedings are involved. The first is a criminal proceeding in which the person accused of a crime is the defendant; a civil proceeding follows in which the person accused of a crime is the plaintiff and the instigator of the criminal charges is the defendant. If the accused is convicted of the crime charged, he or she may not recover damages in a tort action for malicious prosecution.

As a general rule, the plaintiff in a malicious prosecution action must prove that the prior criminal proceeding terminated in such a way that it cannot be revived, such as by acquittal after trial. The second element, lack of probable cause, may be proven by establishing that the defendant instigator of the criminal proceedings did not honestly believe the accused was guilty or that the defendant's belief was not supported by an appearance such that a reasonable person would have been led to begin criminal proceedings. "Malice" as used in malicious prosecution actions does not mean hatred, spite, or ill will. The plaintiff need prove only that the instigator's primary purpose in bringing the criminal proceedings was something other than bringing an offender to justice.

The defendant may defeat an action of malicious prosecution by proving that although the criminal proceeding terminated in favor of the accused, the plaintiff was in fact guilty of the offense charged.

Malicious Prosecution of Civil Action The majority of states today recognize as a tort the wrongful initiation of a civil suit, usually called malicious prosecution of civil action. The courts generally require the same three elements to be present as in malicious prosecution of criminal action. However, in an action for *malicious prosecution of civil action* there is a fourth element the plaintiff must prove: that he or she suffered actual harm, such as the expenses incurred in defending the civil action or a loss of business.

Abuse of Process The tort of *abuse of process* can be defined as the use of legal process for an improper purpose, as where a person initiates a civil action and uses legal process for an end other than that which it was designed to accomplish. For example, suppose that Cedric files suit for breach of contract against Donna, asking $10,000 in damages, and secures from the court a writ of attachment instructing the sheriff to take possession of her business worth $50,000. If Cedric takes these legal steps in order to force a settlement out of court, he may be liable to Donna for the tort of abuse of process. Such misuse of process is a form of extortion. There is no requirement that the civil action terminate in favor of the injured party or that there be an absence of probable cause. The typical misuse of legal process occurs while litigation is pending and the outcome uncertain. The initiator may, in fact, have probable cause to begin the civil action.

INTENTIONAL HARM TO PROPERTY

Property as used in this discussion refers to things people own, such as land, furniture, and accounts receivable. (The law of property is discussed in Chapters 20, 21, and 22.) The phrase "harm to property" can be used in two senses: in the sense of physical harm (i.e., injury) to the property and in the sense of wrongful interference with the possession of property. The context will make clear in which of the senses the phrase is being used.

Trespass to Real Property

The tort of *trespass to real property* may be defined generally as intentionally and without consent or legal justification entering upon real property in possession of another or causing an object or a third person to enter the property. Real property includes the land and all things imbedded in it or firmly attached to it, such as minerals, trees, fences, and buildings. Thus, one may be held liable in tort for walking across another's lawn, cutting down a neighbor's tree, or painting someone's barn without permission. Real property customarily includes the airspace above the surface of the land and materials below the surface. Thus, a person may be liable for trespass by causing an object to enter the airspace of another without permission. For example, if Arnold has a large tree planted on his land the branches of which extend over the boundary line of his property into the airspace above the land of his neighbor, Betty, Arnold may be liable to Betty in damages for trespass.

A trespasser may be held liable for the harm resulting from trespassing although such harm may not have been anticipated. For example, a trespasser would be liable to property owners if he or she started a small fire for warmth and a spark from the fire caused a major forest fire.

Various defenses are available to the defendant in an action for trespass. The major defenses are: *consent*, express or implied, as where a landowner allows the defendant to walk across his or her land at will; *unavoidable accident*, as where the defendant's car goes out of control and runs onto someone's land; *entry to remove chattels*, as where the defendant enters the land of another to remove equipment that had been taken and placed there; and *necessity*, private or public, as where the defendant dynamites the house of another to stop the spread of a fire that threatens a whole town.

Trespass to Personal Property

The tort of *trespass to personal property* can be defined as intentionally, and without consent or legal justification, taking or damaging personal property in the possession of another. Personal property includes movable or portable things, such as jewelry or furniture. Thus, a person may be held liable in tort for taking another's car temporarily without permission or for unjustifiably injuring an animal that belongs to another. The major defenses available to the defendant in an action for trespass to personal property include consent, unavoidable accident, and necessity.

Conversion

The tort of *conversion* can be defined generally as intentionally and without legal justification seriously interfering with possession of the personal property of another. The following illustrate acts that give rise to a cause of action for conversion: (1) wrongfully taking possession of another's property for an indefinite period, as by stealing; (2) improperly selling or transferring possession of one person's property to another person, as by delivering goods to the wrong person; (3) lawfully acquiring possession of someone's property and later upon demand wrongfully refusing to return the property to the one entitled, as by an artisan keeping goods until an exorbitant repair bill is paid; or (4) destroying another's property or substantially altering it so as to make it unusable, as by killing or maiming someone's animal.

A converter will be liable in damages even though he or she acts in good faith or under a mistake of law or fact. In an action for conversion the plaintiff need not prove the defendant had an evil state of mind or an improper purpose in interfering with possession of the plaintiff's property. Thus, an innocent purchaser of stolen property may be liable for the tort of conversion. However, if one innocently receives lost or stolen property merely for purposes of storage or transportation, the courts would not hold the warehouse or the carrier liable.

Conversion is similar in some respects to the tort of trespass to personal property, but significant differences exist between the two torts. The major difference is the *theory of recovery*. In an action for trespass the plaintiff is compensated for the harm to property or for loss of possession. In an action for conversion the owner recovers the full value of the property at the time and place of conversion. Upon payment of the judgment, the converter becomes the owner of the property. Thus, an action for the tort of conversion is appropriate only when the defendant has so seriously interfered with the plaintiff's possession as to justify a forced sale of the article. An action for trespass is the appropriate remedy for minor interferences resulting in little damage to the plaintiff's goods.

The major defenses available to a defendant in an action for conversion are consent and necessity.

The owner of converted property may not wish to sue for the value of the property but may want the property returned. Possession may be recovered by filing a lawsuit and, without waiting for trial of the case, having the court issue an order called a "writ of replevin." In some states the procedure is called "claim and delivery." The plaintiff must post a bond to protect any legitimate interests the defendant may have.

Case 5.4   **Staub v. Staub**
                          376 A.2d 1129 (Md. App. 1977)

DAVIDSON, Judge. On 5 January 1954, John C. Staub (grandfather) purchased Series H United States Savings Bonds in the amount of $5,000 payable on death to his grandson, John T. Staub, Jr. The grandfather died on 9 March 1954 when his grandson was 17 months old. Thereafter, John T. Staub (father) cashed the interest checks which accrued from the bonds. On 19 May 1955, the father signed the name of John T. Staub, Jr. (son) on a form which requested that the bonds be reissued in the names of John T. Staub, Jr. or John T. Staub. The father continued to cash the interest checks as they accrued. In November, 1959, the father cashed the bonds.

On 5 June 1975, in the Circuit Court for Frederick County, the son, the plaintiff, filed suit against the father, defendant, for trespass and conversion. Compensatory and punitive damages were sought. Judge Samuel T. Barrick found that the father had trespassed on the interest checks between 1954 and 1959, and had converted the bonds in 1959. In essence, he awarded the son $200 plus six percent interest for each of the years between 1954 and 1959 as compensation for the interest which had accrued on the bonds. In addition, he awarded him $5,000 plus six percent interest from November, 1959 as compensation for the bonds. [Plaintiff appealed.]

The son [appellant] first contends that the bonds were converted on 19 May 1955 when the father had them reissued in his or his son's name rather than in November, 1959 when the father cashed them. We do not agree.

. . . Conversion has been defined as a distinct act of ownership or dominion exerted by a person over the personal property of another which either denies the other's right or is inconsistent with it. "The gist of a conversion is not the acquisition of the property by the wrongdoer, but the wrongful deprivation of a person of property to the possession of which he is entitled." Accordingly, a conversion occurs at such time as a person is deprived of property which he is entitled to possess.

Applying this principle to the instant case produces a clear result. Here the record shows that although the father wrongfully added his name to the bonds in 1955, the son was not then deprived of his property. Even after the bonds were reissued, the son as a co-owner could have cashed them at any time. It was not until 1959, when the father cashed the bonds, that the son was deprived of his property. The bonds were converted in 1959 when the father cashed them. The trial court did not err.

The son further contends that as compensatory damages he was entitled not only to an award of $200 plus six percent interest for each of the years between 1954 and 1959, but also to $200 plus six percent interest for each of the years from 1959 to the date of judgment. He maintains that "under a trespass theory of recovery" he is entitled to this additional amount as incidental damages. We do not agree.

There is a distinction between trespass to chattels and conversion and the measure of damages applicable to each. Restatement (Second) of Torts, Topic 2 Conversion (1965) states:

> . . . In trespass the plaintiff may recover for the diminished value of his chattel because of any damage to it, or for the damage to his interest in its possession or use. Usually, although not necessarily, such damages are less than the full value of the chattel itself. In conversion the measure of damages is the full value of the chattel, at the time and place of the tort. When the defendant satisfies the judgment in the action for conversion, title to the chattel passes to him, so that he is in effect required to buy it at a forced judicial sale. Conversion is therefore properly limited, and has been limited by the courts, to those serious, major, and important interferences with the right to control the chattel which justify requiring the defendant to pay its full value." . . .

Here the record shows that the father cashed the bonds in 1959. The trial court properly found that this was so substantial an exercise of dominion and control over the bonds as to constitute a conversion and properly awarded the market value of the bonds at the time of the conversion plus interest to the date of judgment as damages. There is nothing in the record to indicate that the son suffered any other injurious consequence which resulted in a loss greater than the damages awarded. . . .

Finally, the son contends that the trial court erred in refusing to award punitive damages. . . .

Under proper circumstances, punitive damages may be awarded in conversion and trespass actions. In order to recover punitive damages in such actions, an element of aggravation evidenced by conduct of an extraordinary nature characterized by a wanton or reckless disregard for the rights of others, sometimes called implied malice or the legal equivalent of actual malice or legal malice, must accompany the tortious act. . . .

Here there was evidence to show that the father cashed the interest checks and bonds knowing that they belonged to his son. There was also, however, evidence to show that the father cashed the interest checks and bonds in order to preserve financial investments which provided support for his family, including his son. Indeed, he stated that his failure to use the bonds would have caused him to "lose everything" and thus be unable to care for his family. Under these circumstances, the trial court's finding that the father did not act out of evil motives intended to injure his son or with wanton or reckless disregard for his son's rights was not clearly erroneous. Accordingly, punitive damages were properly denied.

Judgment affirmed. Costs to be paid by appellant.

FRAUD AS A TORT

When fraud occurs in connection with a business transaction, the harm suffered is generally of a monetary nature. Fraud sometimes plays an important part in the commission of torts involving harm to the person, as where a battery is committed by inducing the injured person's consent to physical contact by means of a misrepresentation. Because the tort of fraud may involve harm to property and harm to the person, fraud is discussed in a separate part of this chapter. Fraud in connection with the law of contracts is discussed in Chapter 13. A person who is fraudulently induced to enter a contract has a variety of legal remedies available, one of which is to commence a tort action for damages.

Elements of Fraud

To recover in an action for the tort of fraud, sometimes called "deceit," the plaintiff must prove five elements: (1) a false representation of fact; (2) knowledge that the representation was false; (3) intent to induce another to act; (4) justifiable reliance on the representation; and (5) injury resulting from such reliance. Some of the elements are modified in some states, and only the most common provisions of the contemporary law are presented here.

False Representation of Fact   A person may misrepresent by means of actions or by concealment. The word "actions" as used in the tort of fraud includes making an oral or written statement of fact and making a statement by conduct, such as turning back the odometer of a car. Ordinarily silence, or failure to disclose facts of which one has knowledge, is not treated as a false representation. However, there are a growing number of exceptions to this rule reflecting the increasing concern for the consumer's right to full and accurate information. Thus, in a business transaction one party is not permitted to tell a half-truth. For example, if the seller of a lot improved with a residence knows there are two engineers' reports regarding the condition of the soil, one favorable and the other unfavorable, and the seller informs the buyer only of the favorable report, the seller has made a false representation of fact. Another example of false representation by concealment is the following: John Turner makes a statement while he is negotiating with Carol Bates which he believes to be true. Later John obtains information which indicates that the statement he made was untrue or misleading. If John enters into an agreement with Carol without disclosing the new information received, many courts would hold that he has made a false statement of fact.

In recent years there has been a trend in most states to impose a duty of disclosure in any transaction where one party has knowledge of material facts not available to the other party and he or she is aware that the other party is under a misapprehension as to those facts.[5] Material facts are important facts that would affect the person's decision in a transaction. For example, in negotiating for the purchase of a residence, the buyer's decision would be affected by the fact that the house is infested with termites. If the seller knows of the defect and the sale is completed without disclosure of this fact, the seller may be held liable for damages in tort. However, a party is not required to disclose facts that are obvious or that could be discovered by reasonable inspection.

As a general rule a person is not liable in tort for misrepresentations of opinion, value, or law. Each party to a business transaction is presumed to be able to form personal opinions and may not rely upon those of an adversary in the bargaining process.[6] Statements of value and predictions of profits to be made ordinarily are not treated as representations of fact, nor are statements of law treated as representations of fact. However, a person may be held liable for misstatements of opinion, value, or law where the circumstances make it probable that the other party would rely on the statements rather than his or her own judgment. One such situation is where the parties have a relationship of trust and confidence, as between principal and agent or between family members. Another such situation is where one party claims to have superior knowledge which is not available to the other party. Thus, the ordinary person may be expected to rely on the opinion of a real estate broker as to the value of land or the opinion of an attorney upon a point of law, even though the parties are adversaries in a bargaining transaction. Statements of intention usually are treated

as statements of fact. Thus, in most states it is fraud to make a promise without the intent to fulfill it.

Knowledge of Falsity The element of knowledge of falsity exists not only when a person makes a false representation of fact with knowledge of the falsity but also when one makes a statement without any belief as to its truth or with reckless disregard as to whether it is true or false. Thus, a person who represents something as being true of his or her own knowledge but who is in fact completely ignorant of the subject is treated in the law as knowingly making a false statement. Negligent misrepresentation is discussed in Chapter 6, p. 101.

Intent to Induce Action For a plaintiff to establish a cause of action for fraud it must be proven that the defendant intended the plaintiff, or a class of persons to which plaintiff belongs, to believe and act upon the false representation. There is a trend in contemporary law to expand liability and allow recovery to persons who did not directly deal with the defrauding person but whose reliance on his or her representation should have been anticipated. For example, a seller may be held liable not only to an immediate purchaser but also to a remote purchaser for a deliberate misrepresentation contained in a negotiable instrument or a stock certificate. Such documents are intended to be freely transferable, and the seller should reasonably have foreseen that subsequent purchasers would rely on the representation contained in the document.

Justifiable Reliance Justifiable reliance occurs when a person's false representation causes another person justifiably to act or to refrain from acting to his or her detriment. In a fraud action it is not necessary for the plaintiff to prove that the defendant's misrepresentation was the sole cause of the plaintiff's loss. It is sufficient for the plaintiff to prove that the misrepresentation was a substantial factor in influencing a decision. Thus, there may be justifiable reliance where a plaintiff's decision to

---

[5]Prosser, op. cit., p. 697.

[6]Ibid., p. 721.

buy or sell an article was based on information obtained from several sources, including the defendant's false representation.

In some situations one may have difficulty in determining whether reliance was justified. As a general rule the ordinary person may justifiably rely on representations as to the quantity of land or the quality or authenticity of merchandise without making an independent investigation. However, a plaintiff of normal intelligence, ordinary experience, and average education may not justifiably rely on representations that the average person by reasonable investigation should discover are false. A defendant may be held liable for fraud if he or she takes advantage of a plaintiff knowing that the plaintiff is illiterate or unusually gullible. On the other hand, a plaintiff who has special knowledge, experience, and competency may not justifiably rely on the defendant's statements but must exercise his or her own judgment. As stated earlier, the ordinary person is not justified in relying on a defendant's statement of opinion or representation of law unless special circumstances are involved.

Case 5.5   **Butts v. Dragstrem**
349 So. 2d 1205 (Fla. App. 1977)

ERVIN, Judge . . . In early 1973, John Dragstrem [plaintiff] visited his brother, Wayne, who at the time managed a seventeen unit mobile home subdivision in Jacksonville, Florida, which was owned by Butts [defendant]. . . . He advised his brother he was interested in purchasing rental property which would net him at least $1,000.00 per month. His brother consulted Mr. Butts concerning the possibility of Dragstrem's purchasing the property. Butts evinced interest, advising Wayne that his brother could easily make $1,000.00 per month net income, saying he had made at least that much per month for several years in the past.

Between February and October, 1973, Dragstrem spent a considerable portion of his time in the Jacksonville area. He socialized with Butts and his wife and saw them frequently in church. . . . Although Dragstrem was never shown Butts' books of account, he was given a pink slip listing average monthly expenses of $249.00. . . . Butts represented these figures as accurate. Dragstrem, relying on Butts' representations as a Christian brother and on Butts' reputation for honesty agreed to purchase the property for $145,000.00.

After purchasing the property, Dragstrem soon realized that he was unable to make anywhere near the $1,000.00 per month net income Butts had claimed to have made. . . . [Dragstrem filed suit against Butts for the tort of fraud.]

At a deposition of Butts' accountant, taken three weeks prior to trial, Dragstrem learned for the first time that Butts' net monthly income, after subtracting expenses and mortgage payments, was $540.00 per month. At trial Dragstrem testified that following the purchase, his average net monthly income was $490.00. The accountant for Butts, one Rudolph Black, testifying on behalf of Butts . . . testified the net monthly expenses during the 15 months were $480.00, which contrasted sharply with the average monthly figure of

$249.00 supplied by Butts to Dragstrem on the pink slip. [The trial court denied Butts' motion for directed verdict. A judgment was entered in favor of Dragstrem for $42,000. Butts appealed.]

At the outset we conclude there was ample evidence in support of the conclusion that Butts fraudulently misrepresented the average monthly net income he derived from his business. In general, misrepresentations as to past income—as opposed to probable future profits—are proper predicates for alleging fraud. Dragstrem was required, however, to prove also that he relied upon the representation resulting in his injury, which representation was a material fact in inducing the purchase and that he was justified in relying upon the truth of the statement. The right of reliance is also closely bound up with a duty on the part of the representee to use some measure of protection and precaution to safeguard his interests. His justifiable reliance goes to the heart of the problem. In the absence of a showing of a fiduciary or confidential relationship, if there is no accompanying actual deception, artifice, or misconduct, where the means of knowledge are at hand and are equally available to both parties and the subject matter is equally open to their inspection, one disregarding them will not be heard to say that he was deceived by the other's misrepresentations.

Thus, it was necessary for Dragstrem to avail himself of an opportunity to inspect Butts' books. True, Dragstrem testified he asked to see the books, and, according to Dragstrem's testimony, Butts replied he would bring them over in the morning, but the morning never came. Later after the purchase was consummated, the books of account containing only items of income were found upon the premises. Before the sale, however, Dragstrem was advised the name of Butts' bookkeeper yet he made no attempt, until three weeks prior to trial, to ascertain from the accountant what Butts' expenses had been. If there was evidence of active concealment by Butts of his books then a different result might well obtain. There is no such evidence here. We have previously held that where a vendor by his actual deception or misconduct conceals the evidence of a defective condition in such a way as to render it incapable of detection from a reasonable and ordinary inspection, the vendor can no longer rely upon the purchaser's duty to inspect because such conduct by the vendor serves to impair the purchaser's opportunity to make a meaningful inspection.

While Dragstrem had never operated a mobile home park before the purchase, he was not an inexperienced man of business. He had for seven years maintained a small apartment building in Illinois and was thereby not unaware of the attendant problems associated with the maintenance and upkeep of rental properties. There were certain avenues of inquiry which this record does not show Dragstrem pursued. In addition to his failure to consult Butts' accountant, Dragstrem could also have directed appropriate inquiries to his brother concerning what knowledge, if any, he had concerning the income and operational expenses of the subdivision.

It appears Dragstrem's primary justification for his reliance upon Butts' representations was owing to their close personal friendship and mutual religious interests. Unfortunately for Dragstrem's position such a relationship does not create a fiduciary or confidential relationship. True, the relation and correlative duties necessary to give rise to such status need not be legal but may be moral, social, domestic or merely personal. But close friendship is not enough to sustain Dragstrem's action. . . .

Having considered the record before us we determine that Dragstrem had a duty to make a reasonable inquiry of the seller's operational expenses. . . . While it may have required a bit more persistence by Dragstrem to ascertain the truth, there is nothing before us indicating he could not have acquired the requisite knowledge by the exercise of ordinary care. On the facts before us we conclude his failure to discover the truth is attributable to his own negligence.

The lower court erred in denying Butts' motion for directed verdict. The judgment is reversed.

SMITH, Judge, dissenting: In my view the trial court properly concluded that the evidence presented a jury question on the pertinent issues. Butts misrepresented his average monthly expenses at a precise $249.00. Even assuming that inspection of Butts' books of account was reasonably required of Dragstrem as a matter of law, Dragstrem's persistence in his request for inspection would have been unavailing because, as the majority of opinion recognizes, the books contained no information inconsistent with Butts' misrepresentation of expenses. I do not conceive that we are justified in imposing on Dragstrem a duty to interview Butts' accountant in order to verify information so explicitly misrepresented. To so hold as a matter of law imposes an incalculable burden on a prospective purchaser and reduces the seller's precise misrepresentation of facts to the legal insignificance of puffery. The question was one for the jury under proper instructions, concerning which Butts has demonstrated no error. I would affirm.

Resulting Injury The damage suffered as a result of a person's false representation in a business transaction may be slight (loss of a few dollars) or serious (loss of valuable property). In a tort action for fraud the plaintiff must prove that the misrepresentation was the cause of the loss. Thus, if a plaintiff is fraudulently induced to purchase stock as an investment and there is a general decline in the stock market, the loss in value of the stock may not be recovered. The loss was not caused by the false representation which induced the plaintiff to purchase the stock.

Measure of Damages for Fraud

In order to recover damages in a tort action for fraud, the plaintiff must prove that all five elements of fraud were present in the situation involved. If fraud is proved, the judge or jury must determine what damages the plaintiff may recover. In the United States two methods are used to measure damages for fraud. The majority rule is called the "loss-of-bargain" rule. Under this rule the successful plaintiff recovers the difference between the value of the property or service received and the value it would have had if it had been as represented. For example, if the defendant, a professional antique dealer, falsely represents that the desk he or she is selling to the plaintiff is a genuine antique worth $1,000 when in fact it is not genuine and is worth only $150, the plaintiff may recover $850 damages.

The minority rule is called the "out-of-pocket" rule. Under this rule the plaintiff recovers the difference between the value of what was transferred to the defendant and the value of what was received. In the above example, if the plaintiff has paid the defendant $850 for the desk, he or she would recover $700 damages under the minority rule. Under this rule the defendant may be guilty of flagrant misrepresentation, but if what the plaintiff receives is worth the amount paid for it, the plaintiff is not entitled to damages in a fraud action.

SUMMARY

Tort liability is based on conduct which is socially unreasonable. An important part of the determination of what is unreasonable is the balance between an injured person's claim to protection and the accused's claim to freedom of action. Various kinds of civil wrongs are recognized as torts in contemporary law, and they are classified according to the nature of the wrongdoer's conduct. The two main classes are intentional torts and unintentional torts.

The major intentional torts involving harm to the person are battery, assault, false imprisonment, infliction of mental distress, defamation (libel and slander), invasion of privacy, malicious prosecution of criminal action, malicious prosecution of civil action, and abuse of process. Battery is the only one of these torts in which bodily contact is essential. The remaining torts generally involve interference with the other person's peace of mind, or injury to reputation. In an action for tort the defendant may avoid liability by proving one or more defenses, such as consent or privilege.

To constitute the tort of defamation, a false defamatory statement must be communicated to someone other than the one defamed. Infliction of mental distress and invasion of privacy may occur without communication to a third person. Truth is an absolute defense to an action for defamation but is no defense to an action for infliction of mental distress or invasion of privacy.

The torts of malicious prosecution of criminal action, malicious prosecution of civil action, and abuse of process are related to one another and to the torts of defamation and invasion of privacy. These five torts ordinarily involve harm to a person's reputation. A major difference between malicious prosecution of civil action and abuse of process is that an action for abuse of process may be brought prior to the conclusion of the civil action filed by the instigator. There is no requirement that the original action terminate in favor of the injured party.

The major intentional torts involving harm to property are: trespass to real property, trespass to personal property, and conversion. In an action for trespass the plaintiff is compensated for the harm to property or for loss of possession. In an action for conversion, the owner recovers the full value of his or her personal property. Replevin and claim and delivery are remedies to secure the return of the property.

Fraud sometimes plays an important part in the commission of torts involving harm to the person, but it usually arises in connection with business transactions where money or property is involved. The tort of fraud involves intentional misrepresentation committed either by means of one's actions or by concealment of facts, justifiably relied on by another to his or her injury.

STUDY AND DISCUSSION QUESTIONS

1 (*a*) Define the tort of battery. (*b*) List and explain briefly the defenses available to a defendant in an action for battery. (*c*) How does the privilege of self-defense differ from the privilege of protection of one's property?

2 (*a*) What is an assault? (*b*) Explain the statement, "an attempted battery is not necessarily an assault." (*c*) Give an example of a battery that is not preceded by an assault.

3 (*a*) Define false imprisonment. (*b*) Why is it

important for a business person to have some knowledge of this tort?

4 *(a)* Define the tort of infliction of mental distress. *(b)* How does this tort differ from other torts that involve mental distress, such as assault and false imprisonment?

5 *(a)* Define defamation. *(b)* Why do you think publication is required in order to recover for the tort of defamation? *(c)* Explain the difference between libel and slander. *(d)* List and give examples of three types of absolute privilege. *(e)* Explain qualified privilege and how it may be lost. *(f)* Explain the difference between malice and actual malice.

6 *(a)* List and give examples of the four main forms of invasion of privacy. *(b)* How does invasion of privacy differ from defamation? *(c)* List and explain briefly the defenses to an action for invasion of privacy. *(d)* Explain the legal protection given to a public figure's right of privacy.

7 *(a)* List the three torts involving misuse of legal procedure. *(b)* Explain each of the three elements required in an action for malicious prosecution of criminal action. *(c)* What additional element is required in an action for malicious prosecution of civil action? *(d)* Define abuse of process, and explain how it differs from malicious prosecution.

8 *(a)* Define trespass to real property. *(b)* List and explain briefly each of the defenses to this tort. *(c)* Define the torts of trespass to personal property and conversion. *(d)* Explain the major difference between these torts.

9 *(a)* List the five elements of the tort of fraud. *(b)* Explain how fraud may be committed by concealment. *(c)* Give an example of an opinion that may be grounds for an action in fraud. *(d)* Explain how a defendant who misrepresents may be held liable to someone he or she has never dealt with. *(e)* Explain both the majority rule and minority rule of measuring damages in a fraud action.

CASE PROBLEMS

1 Mrs. Turman had been treated for glaucoma for a number of years at the Eye Clinic. She owed the Eye Clinic $46 for services. She had not paid her account, and in May it was assigned to Central Billing Bureau for collection. During the month of June, Mrs. Turman received numerous phone calls from Central informing her that someone from the sheriff's office would come to her house to serve papers on her, that unless she paid in full her husband could lose his job, and that she could lose her home and everything she owned. At one time Central's agent used profane and abusive language and said she could not "care less about Mrs. Turman's being blind" and called her "scum" and a "dead beat." Mrs. Turman suffered severe headaches and was hospitalized because of her state of anxiety. Does Mrs. Turman have a cause of action for infliction of mental distress?

2 Dr. Corey was a vice president at the state university and acted as president while the president was away. At a meeting with a five-member faculty committee chosen to pass on the qualifications for tenure of Dr. Stukuls, Dr. Corey read a letter accusing Dr. Stukuls, a married man, of having attempted to seduce a young woman who was a student in one of his classes. Dr. Corey had taken the letter from the president's private file in the president's absence. Dr. Stukuls filed suit against the university for defamation and wished to show that Dr. Corey acted with malice. The university asserted that it was protected by an absolute privilege. Is the university entitled to an absolute privilege or a qualified privilege?

3 From 1953 until 1973 the Central Intelligence Agency conducted an extensive program of opening first-class mail passing in and out of the country through certain cities. Various criteria were employed in selecting letters for inspection, including the country of origin or destination. Birnbaum, MacMillen, and Avery sent letters to persons in Russia and received letters from persons in Russia, the contents of which were copied by the CIA. No judicial warrants had been obtained, and there is no evidence to suggest probable cause for a warrantless search. None of the three persons was aware until several years later that his mail had been interfered with. Do Birnbaum, MacMillen, and Avery have a cause of action against the CIA for invasion of privacy?

4 Ware Corporation owned real property on Torch Lake and took steps to develop a residential condominium project on the property. Three Lakes Association, composed of individuals owning other property on the lake, filed suit to stop the proposed project, alleging undue pollution would result. That action was called Action 849. Ware Corporation filed an action against the association and various individual members alleging conspiracy, defamation, and interference with contractual relations in obstructing the condominium project. That action, called Action 926, claimed $2.5 million in damages. In Action 926 Ware burdened the association and its members with requests for discovery of evidence and at the same time caused delays in complying with legitimate discovery procedures of the association. Ware Corporation stated it would dismiss Action 926 without receiving any damages if the association would agree not to oppose the proposed condominium project. Is Ware liable for abuse of process?

5 Willie Henderson financed the purchase of a Cadillac automobile through Security Bank. Willie defaulted on his agreement with the bank by letting the insurance on the vehicle lapse and being delinquent in his monthly payments. The bank repossessed the car and sold it. Willie filed suit against the bank for conversion, charging that the repossessor unlawfully broke the lock on Willie's garage door in order to take possession of the car. The bank defended that it was entitled to take possession of the Cadillac and that it neither expressly nor impliedly authorized or ratified the unlawful breaking and entering by the repossessor. Is this a valid defense?

6 Clark, an experienced contractor, built a residence for Aenchbacher containing numerous defects. When Aenchbacher started a fire in the fireplace, the chimney did not function properly, and the room filled with smoke. When rain came, the basement floor became flooded. Aenchbacher contended that Clark was guilty of fraud since he knew of the defects in construction and did not inform Aenchbacher. Also, the defects could not be discovered by the exercise of ordinary prudence and caution. Clark contended that such facts did not constitute the tort of fraud. He also defended that Aenchbacher signed a statement when he moved into the residence that he had carefully inspected the house and was completely satisfied with the workmanship and materials in the house. Does Aenchbacher have a cause of action against Clark for fraud?

Chapter

6

Negligence and Liability without Fault

The contemporary world is crowded and complex. Often it seems impossible for a person to move about or engage in a business transaction without committing a civil wrong to another person. Most people do not intentionally inflict harm on others. However, an individual or business firm may unintentionally harm the person or property of another and become liable in tort for damages. There are two major areas of liability for un ntentional acts: liability for the tort of negligence and liability without fault. The first part of this chapter is devoted to a discussion of the major legal aspects of the tort of negligence and the major defenses available. The last part of the chapter is devoted to several areas of liability without fault and the major defenses available.

NEGLIGENCE

Nature of Negligence

There is no universal definition of the tort of negligence. Many definitions have been given by legal writers, judges, and legislatures. A general definition of *negligence* for our purposes is failure to exercise due care when there is a foreseeable risk of harm to others. The tort of negligence may be illustrated simply by the following comparison. A person who intentionally drives a car into another's car is guilty of the tort of trespass to personal property. One who carelessly drives a car at an excessive rate of speed and cannot stop it in time to avoid a collision is guilty of the tort of negligence.

As stated in the previous chapter, an important consideration in the law of torts is the balance between an injured person's claim to protection of person or property and the accused person's claim to freedom of action. A person's freedom to act is limited by the risk the person creates. A person is held responsible for conduct which creates a risk of harm to others under circumstances where such risk should be apparent. Ordinarily a person is not liable for harm caused by an unavoidable accident.

Elements of Negligence

In order to establish a cause of action for negligence, the plaintiff traditionally is required to prove four elements: (1) the defendant owed a duty to protect the plaintiff against harm; (2) the defendant failed to exercise due care; (3) the plaintiff suffered actual loss or damage; (4) the defendant's negligence was the cause of the plaintiff's injury. The law of negligence continually changes, and many states have modified these elements. The most common provisions of the contemporary law are examined here within the context of procedures and rules of evidence applicable to a civil lawsuit for damages.

Duty of Care The first element, a duty to protect the plaintiff against harm, is commonly called a duty of care. There are many views among legal writers and judges as to who owes a duty of care and when the duty arises. For our purposes it can be stated that a duty of care arises whenever a person should foresee that his or her conduct will create an unreasonable risk of harm to others. For example, driving a car on a deserted highway at an excessive speed does not create a duty of care. Such conduct in a populated area creates an unreasonable risk of harm to others, and the driver owes a duty of care to all persons who foreseeably may be injured.

There are two views concerning the question of to whom the defendant owes a duty of care. The narrow view is that in order to establish the first element of negligence, the plaintiff must prove he or she was within the "zone of danger" created by the defendant's conduct. If the defendant should reasonably have foreseen a risk of harm to this particular plaintiff or to a class of persons to which the plaintiff belongs, then the defendant is held to a duty to exercise due care to avoid harm to the plaintiff. On the other hand, if the plaintiff was outside the zone of danger, the defendant is not held to a duty of care. Thus, the "unforeseen plaintiff" who is injured by the defendant's careless conduct has no cause of action. For example, a person who carelessly starts a fire is liable for damages to the owner on whose land the fire is begun but may not be liable to an owner whose land is burned an unforeseeable distance away.

The broader view, which is probably the majority view in the United States today, is that once the plaintiff establishes that a reasonable person should have foreseen an unreasonable risk of harm to others, the defendant owes a duty of care to anyone injured as a proximate result of his or her failure to exercise care. Under this view the unforeseen plaintiff may recover from the defendant.

Case 6.1   Department of Commerce v. Glick
372 N.E.2d 479 (Ind. App. 1978)

In December 1971, Robert L. Johnson presented himself to the industrial promotions and development division, Department of Commerce, State of Indiana (defendant) as a consultant for a large Eastern concern interested in locating a laser research facility somewhere in Indiana. Hollis, the assistant director of the division, assisted Johnson by preparing and mailing throughout the state a "site-location fact sheet" and referring responses to Johnson. In February 1972, Hollis also arranged several meetings between Johnson and the Hope Improvement Corp. (H.I.C.), an organization of citizens of the Town of Hope, Indiana, interested in attracting business to their town.

At a meeting in March 1972, Johnson stated that he would need $100,000 of local money in order to secure a federal grant of $50 million. In April 1972, upon urging by Hollis to demonstrate their good faith, $25,000 was raised and paid to Johnson. Glick (plaintiff), a member of H.I.C., gave a check for $1,000 and H.I.C. gave the remaining $24,000. Glick signed a note in his own name to H.I.C. to cover the $24,000 advanced. Shortly thereafter Glick learned that Johnson was a "con man." Johnson was later apprehended and convicted of theft by deception. None of the money was recovered, and Glick was forced to pay off the $24,000 note.

Prior to April 1972, Hollis had become suspicious of Johnson because he refused to divulge the name of the company he represented. Hollis made numerous inquiries concerning Johnson and on April 11 requested a report from the Indiana State Police. The report was compiled and showed that Johnson had a lengthy criminal record, including convictions for theft and forgery. The report was not delivered to Hollis until after the $25,000 was delivered to Johnson. Hollis never communicated his suspicions to Glick or other members of H.I.C. and never informed Glick that an arrest report had been requested. Hollis claimed that the state did not investigate persons who came into the office to request information about site location. He added that they did not usually ask a consultant for any background information but just took him or her at face value and sent the information out to local communities interested in new industry. Glick sued the state of Indiana for negligence and received a judgment for $24,000. The state appealed.

LYBROOK, J. The requisite elements of an action in negligence are (1) the existence of a duty on the part of the defendant in relation to the plaintiff; (2) the failure of the defendant to conform his conduct to the standard of care demanded by such duty; and (3) an injury to the plaintiff proximately resulting from such failure. . . .

The first question raised by the State is whether there was sufficient evidence for the jury to find that the State owed Glick a legal duty to ascertain the legitimacy of Johnson as a consultant for an industrial firm. The State argues that the Division of Industrial Promotions and Development of the Department of Commerce did not undertake a special obligation towards Glick as an individual, but merely had a general duty under the statute which created the Division of Industrial Promotion and Development, to assist communities and promote industrial development.

This court has consistently held that the State is liable for the negligence of its employees where employees are performing ministerial tasks. . . .

The record shows that there was evidence sufficient for the jury to hold that the agents of the State were negligent in their actions where they were so suspicious of Johnson that they questioned outside sources concerning Johnson's status as a "consultant." Repeatedly, but unsuccessfully, they sought to discover the name of Johnson's corporate client, and even asked State Police assistance, yet continued to urge Glick, as a director of H.I.C., to secure the "project." Without consulting the available State Police report, they took part in the actual transfer of $24,000 to Johnson. . . .

The State now claims that it was under no duty to anticipate that a crime would be committed resulting in subsequent injury or loss to Glick.

The trial court gave the following instruction to the jury without an objection by the State at the conclusion of all the evidence:

> "Every person is under a duty to exercise his senses and intelligence in his actions in order to avoid injury to others, and where a situation suggests investigation and inspection in order that its dangers may fully appear, duty to make such investigation and inspection is imposed by law."

In light of the evidence above, which shows that the State was not only suspicious of Johnson, but actively investigated his background and prior arrest record through the Indiana State Police, we think that the State had reason to be suspicious of Johnson. It was also reasonably foreseeable that H.I.C. and the investors, including Glick, were in danger of losing their money, particularly where the State's suspicions were not communicated to Glick and the other members of H.I.C. . . .

Finding no error, we affirm the judgment of the trial court.

Failure to Exercise Care   The judge or jury in a lawsuit for negligence must determine if the defendant failed to exercise due care. To assist in this determination, the courts have established a standard of behavior. The standard is that of a hypothetical "reasonable person of ordinary prudence." The judge or jury compares the conduct of the defendant with the presumed conduct of the ordinary prudent person under the same or similar circumstances. If the defendant's conduct does not measure up to the model standard of conduct, the defendant may be held liable for damages for the tort of negligence.

The ordinary prudent person standard Negligence is often described as the failure to do what the ordinary prudent person would do under the same or similar circumstances. The

ordinary prudent person has been described as "a personification of a community ideal of reasonable behavior, determined by the jury's social judgment."[1] However, when evaluating the defendant's behavior, allowances are made if the defendant is handicapped with blindness, deafness, or other physical disability. The defendant's conduct will be judged with a view toward the handicap and the defendant's knowledge of his or her own limitations. Thus, it may be negligence for a person who knows that he or she is subject to epileptic seizures to drive a car. In evaluating the conduct of a defendant who is a minor, the judge or jury does not hold the child to the same standard of conduct as an

---

[1]William L. Prosser, *Handbook of the Law of Torts*, 4th ed., West Publishing Company, St. Paul, 1971, p. 151.

adult. The judge or jury determines what is reasonable to expect from children of like age, intelligence, and experience to the defendant.

Presumed experience and knowledge When the judge or jury applies the ordinary prudent person standard to the defendant's behavior, the defendant is presumed to have knowledge of certain facts. Every adult with a minimum of intelligence is presumed to know such things as: the fact that fire burns and that flammable objects will catch fire; the principles of balance and leverage as applied to the person's own body; the limits of the person's own strength; the normal habits, capacities, and reactions of other human beings; and the dangers involved in explosives, electricity, moving machinery, and firearms. Ordinarily, a defendant will not be excused if he or she denies knowledge of these facts. The courts generally impose this minimum standard of knowledge based on what is common to the community. In addition, a defendant is presumed to know the limits of his or her own knowledge and in certain circumstances may be held liable for negligence for proceeding in the face of ignorance. For example, a lay person may be negligent in attempting to give medical treatment.

A person who possesses or claims to possess superior knowledge or skill is held to a higher standard of conduct than the ordinary prudent person. Physicians, dentists, attorneys, accountants, and other professional persons hold themselves out to the public as having specialized skill and knowledge. In a lawsuit for professional malpractice, the defendant is presumed to have the skill and learning commonly possessed by members of the profession in good standing in the same or a similar community. Failure to possess the presumed knowledge and skill is strong evidence of negligence.

Application of experience and knowledge To exercise due care means to use one's presumed experience and knowledge in such a manner as to prevent an unreasonable risk of harm to others. To determine whether the defendant's conduct was unreasonable, that is, whether he or she breached the duty of care, requires a balancing of factors. The defendant's conduct is judged by (1) the severity of damage that might occur and (2) the probability that such damage will occur, compared with (3) the expense or inconvenience in taking precautions. The defendant is considered negligent if his or her conduct is such that factors (1) and (2) are greater than factor (3). For example, supplying gasoline to another in an open bucket is unreasonable conduct and thus negligent. The risk of probable injury if the gasoline is ignited outweighs the cost or inconvenience of supplying a closed container with a warning label.

The more probable and the more serious the harm, the greater the expense and effort that must be taken to prevent that harm. Thus, the courts have held that a great amount of care must be exercised in dealing with items that are known to be dangerous such as gas, electricity, or elevators. Great care is required when dealing with persons who are known to be irresponsible, such as insane persons or intoxicated persons. In many states the courts have held sellers of alcoholic beverages negligent for furnishing alcohol to customers who are obviously intoxicated. In some states the host of a social gathering has been held liable to a third person who was injured by an intoxicated guest driving a car.

Negligent misrepresentation A person may commit the tort of negligence by means of the misuse of language. For example, one may be liable for making a false statement of fact to another where the person has failed to exercise due care to determine the truth. Most cases of negligent misrepresentation involve defendants in the business of supplying information for the guidance of others, such as accountants, attorneys, title abstractors, etc. The defendant owes a duty of care not only to persons to whom the representation is made but to persons the defendant knows will rely on the representation. For example, an accountant who negligently certifies a financial statement for a client, knowing the client will show the statement to a creditor in order to borrow money, may be held liable for damages caused to the creditor. The liability of accountants is presented in more detail in Chapter 45.

To recover damages for negligent misrepresentation, the plaintiff must prove that he or she was justified in relying on the defendant's statement and suffered harm as a result. Thus, a plaintiff who relies on a casual bystander for information and suffers injury ordinarily may not recover from the bystander for negligent misrepresentation.

Injury to the Plaintiff   The harm suffered as a consequence of another's negligence may be physical (harm to the person or property) or mental (fright, pain). In most lawsuits for negligence, the plaintiff's injury is easily shown and the plaintiff recovers damages for any physical injury. In addition, an award may be made for mental suffering accompanying the physical injury, that is, for pain, suffering, fright, and humiliation. The courts have been reluctant to award damages where the plaintiff's injury is limited solely to fright, shock, or other mental distress. The major objection to recovery for mental distress unaccompanied by physical injury is the danger of fictitious claims.[2] Mental distress is easily simulated and difficult to deny. In most states today, the plaintiff may recover damages for negligent infliction of mental distress only if the defendant causes immediate physical injury to the plaintiff or causes mental distress which is followed by physical harm. For example, a pregnant woman who suffers mental distress from a defendant's negligence may recover damages for mental distress if the distress results in a later miscarriage.

One situation which the courts have great difficulty in resolving is that of a bystander witnessing harm negligently inflicted upon another person. Ordinarily, the courts do not hold the defendant liable to the bystander for the tort of negligence since the defendant could not reasonably foresee mental distress to that person. The bystander is outside the zone of danger created by the defendant's negligence. However, in a few states recovery has been permitted when four elements are present: (1) the injury inflicted on the third person is serious and of a nature to cause mental distress to the bystander; (2) the shock results in physical harm to the bystander; (3) the bystander is a close relative to the person injured; and (4) the bystander is present at the time of the injury to the third person or suffers the shock almost immediately after the accident. Suppose, for example, a mother appeared on the scene of an accident moments after her child had been seriously injured by the defendant's negligence. In some states the mother would be allowed to recover damages if she suffered mental distress and physical harm.

Negligence the Cause of Injury   In order to hold the defendant liable, the plaintiff must prove that the defendant's negligence was the cause of the injury. Sometimes the cause is obvious, as where the defendant carelessly drives a car and collides with the plaintiff. At other times an outside event occurs that contributes to the plaintiff's injuries.

There are two tests commonly used by courts to establish whether the defendant should be held liable for the plaintiff's injury: (1) Was defendant's conduct the actual cause of the plaintiff's injury? (2) Was there proximate cause?

Actual cause   The term *actual cause* (sometimes called *cause in fact*) in general means something without which plaintiff's injury would not have occurred. The test sometimes is referred to as the "but for" test. A court will find that the defendant's conduct is the actual cause of plaintiff's injury if it can be stated that "but for" the defendant's conduct the plaintiff would not have been injured. Actual cause may be a positive act or a failure to act. For example, a

---

[2]Ibid., p. 328.

court would hold that failure of the defendant to fence his or her yard is a cause in fact of a child's drowning in the defendant's pool. If the plaintiff's injury would have occurred without the defendant's conduct, a court ordinarily will hold that the defendant's negligence is not the actual cause of the plaintiff's injury. For example, suppose that Daniel is driving his car knowing that it has defective brakes. A child suddenly darts into his path, and Daniel is unable to stop in time and injures the child. If Daniel could not have avoided hitting the child even if the car had good brakes, his negligence is not the actual cause of the child's injury.

To be the actual cause does not mean that the defendant's conduct must be the *only* cause of the plaintiff's injury. The defendant's conduct must be a material or substantial factor in causing the injury. If there are two or more causes of the plaintiff's injury, they are called "concurring causes."

Proximate cause The second major test of causation is proximate cause. There is no satisfactory definition of "proximate cause." The purpose of proximate cause is to place a limitation on the defendant's liability—a limitation based on considerations of logic, common sense, justice, and precedent.[3] An important consideration in deciding the limit on the defendant's liability is the concept of foreseeability. This concept is utilized in cases where there is direct causation. The defendant's negligence may start a chain of events which results in injury to persons or property not within the defendant's contemplation. For example, suppose the defendant negligently drives his or her car into a truck containing explosives, and the explosives detonate and blow out store windows many feet away, causing injury to persons and property inside. Many courts would not hold the defendant liable to the persons in the store on the rationale that the particular results of the defendant's negligence were unforeseeable. How-

ever, the defendant is liable where it is only the extent of the plaintiff's injury that is not reasonably foreseeable. For example, the defendant is liable where the defendant's negligence causes the aggravation of a plaintiff's unforeseeable previous condition, such as heart disease.

Proximate cause also limits the extent of the defendant's liability when there is an intervening cause. An *intervening cause* is one that occurs after the defendant's negligence and alters the consequences of the defendant's conduct. Such a concurring cause of the plaintiff's injury may be of human or natural origin. An infinite variety of possible intervening causes exists, and it is obvious that a defendant should not always be held liable for the plaintiff's injury. As a general rule the defendant is liable only if the intervening cause of plaintiff's injury is reasonably foreseeable.

To determine if an intervening cause is foreseeable, the judge or jury utilizes the model of the ordinary prudent person. The defendant is presumed to have the experience and knowledge of human and natural behavior discussed previously. Thus, for example, one who negligently leaves explosives in a public place should reasonably foresee that another person may find the explosives, detonate them, and thereby cause injury to a third person. The courts have held that a negligent defendant should reasonably foresee the negligence of others. For example, suppose a defendant who is driving a car injures a pedestrian and negligently leaves the person unconscious in the roadway. If a second driver negligently runs over the pedestrian and the injuries are indivisible, both drivers may be held liable for the plaintiff's injuries. The two negligent drivers are called *joint tortfeasors*. In some instances a negligent defendant should reasonably foresee the commission of a crime or intentional tort by another as an intervening cause of injury to the plaintiff. For example, a landlord has been held liable for failing to protect against, or warn a tenant of, possible harm from criminal assault when the landlord

---

[3]Ibid., p. 249.

knew of past similar incidents and could reasonably foresee a future occurrence.

An intervening cause which is not reasonably foreseeable by the defendant is called a *superseding cause*. If a superseding cause occurs, the defendant will not be held liable since the defendant's negligence is a cause in fact (actual cause) but not the proximate cause of plaintiff's injury. There are some cases in which a defendant has been held liable where there was an unforeseeable intervening cause but the injuries to the defendant were of a type that was foreseeable. For example, in one case a defendant negligently allowed gas vapors to accumulate in the hold of a ship. An explosion was caused by a bolt of lightning that was not foreseeable. The defendant was held liable since explosion and damage to nearby persons and property were foreseeable.

Case 6.2   **Ford v. Jeffries**
379 A.2d 111 (Pa. 1977)

James Jeffries owned a dwelling that was located five or six feet from Mamie Ford's home on the adjoining lot. The property was vacant and in disrepair. Windows were broken, there were holes in the walls, the property harbored large rats, and dogs wandered in and out of the basement. Mamie Ford complained to Jeffries about the condition of the property, but nothing was done. On July 30, 1969, at 2:27 A.M. a fire started in Jeffries' house and damaged parts of the house. Jeffries made no repairs except to place crossboards over broken windows. On September 26, 1969, at approximately 2 A.M., a second fire broke out in Jeffries' house. This fire started on the second floor. Flames ignited the eaves of Ford's home, resulting in almost total destruction of her home.

Ford brought suit against Jeffries for negligence. At trial, after Ford rested her case, Jeffries' motion for nonsuit was granted by the trial judge. Plaintiff Ford appealed.

MANDERINO, J. An order granting a non-suit is proper only if the jury, viewing the evidence and all reasonable inferences arising from it, in the light most favorable to the plaintiff, could not reasonably conclude that the elements of the cause of action have been established. We must therefore review the evidence to determine whether the appellant [Ford] was entitled to have the jury consider whether the appellee [Jeffries] engaged in negligent conduct toward the appellant and, if so, whether appellee's conduct was the proximate cause of the harm suffered by the appellant. . . .

Our review of the evidence leaves no doubt that the jury could reasonably have concluded that the appellee engaged in negligent conduct toward the appellant. . . .

A property owner can reasonably be expected to know that the visible conditions of vacant property in a state of disrepair may attract, for various purposes, children or adults, who, having entered the property, might act, either negligently or intentionally, in a manner that would cause a fire. Such properties "invite" strangers for various purposes and are more likely to be targets for arsonists than are properties maintained in good repair. Appellee's conduct in allowing the property to deteriorate, particularly after the first fire, increased the risk that a fire would occur on the premises. We are unwilling to say, as a matter of law, that the maintenance of a vacant dwelling house in a state of disrepair visible to passersby does not create an unreasonable fire hazard. That hazard in this case was located only five or six feet from appellant's house. A jury question was thus presented as to whether the appellee negligently maintained his property prior to the second fire. The jury should have been permitted to consider the condition of the property, and whether its state of disrepair created an unreasonable risk of harm by fire to appellant's property. . . .

Appellee contends that, as a matter of law, the evidence is insufficient to establish that he was the proximate cause of the harm sustained by the appellant. . . . The issue is whether the defendant's conduct was, on the one hand, a "substantial factor" or a "substantial cause" or, on the other hand, whether the defendant's conduct was an "insignificant cause" or a "negligible cause." The determination of the issue simply involves the making of a judgment as to whether the defendant's conduct, although a cause in the "but for" sense, is so insignificant that no ordinary mind would think of it as a cause for which a defendant should be held responsible. . . .

The determination of whether the conduct of the defendant was a substantial cause or an insignificant cause of plaintiff's harm should not be taken from the jury if the jury may reasonably differ as to whether the conduct of the defendant was a substantial cause or an insignificant cause. Such is the case before us. When one negligently maintains property so as to create a fire hazard to an adjoining property and fire harm results, we refuse to conclude, as a matter of law, that the negligent conduct in maintaining the fire hazard was an insignificant cause. This issue is therefore one for the jury to consider.

The question is also raised as to whether the appellee should escape liability as a matter of law simply because the actual physical force that started the fire is unknown in this case. Although some force may have intervened between appellee's conduct and the resulting harm to the appellant, it cannot be said, as a matter of law, that any such intervening force superseded appellee's conduct. Not every intervening force is a superseding force . . .

Although there are some circumstances under which one is not liable for the intervening act of third persons committing intentional torts or crimes, that principle does not apply in this case because any such acts were within the scope of the risk created by the appellee. Section 448 of the Restatement of Torts, Second, is applicable to the situation before us:

> "The act of a third person in committing an intentional tort or crime is a superseding cause of harm to another resulting therefrom, although the

actor's negligent conduct created a situation which afforded an opportunity to the third person to commit such a tort or crime, *unless the actor at the time of his negligent conduct realized or should have realized the likelihood that such a situation might be created, and that a third person might avail himself of the opportunity to commit such a tort or crime.*" (Emphasis added.)

The condition of appellee's property was such that third persons might avail themselves of the opportunity to commit a tort or a crime. Whether or not appellee should have realized that such a situation had been created is a question for the jury to decide. . . .

The order of the Superior Court is reversed, and the record is remanded to the Court of Common Pleas for further proceedings consistent with this opinion.

Proof of Negligence

In order to recover damages in a lawsuit, the plaintiff has the burden of proving the four elements of negligence. The task is difficult, but occasionally procedural aids are available that help the plaintiff in meeting this burden of proof. Two major aids are: the doctrine of negligence *per se* and the doctrine of *res ipsa loquitur*.

Negligence Per Se The doctrine of "negligence *per se*" permits the plaintiff to use the defendant's violation of a criminal statute as proof that the defendant committed the tort of negligence. A criminal statute establishes a standard of behavior for a community. Thus, a defendant's unexcused violation of a criminal statute constitutes failure to live up to the standard of the ordinary prudent person and therefore is negligence.

Negligence *per se* applies only if the plaintiff is within the class of individuals intended to be protected by the criminal statute and if the harm suffered is of the kind which the statute is intended to prevent. Negligence *per se* is often utilized in a lawsuit resulting from an automobile accident. Suppose, for example, the plaintiff is injured by the defendant's driving a car in excess of the state speed law. State motor vehicle codes carry criminal penalties for viola-

tion and are enacted generally to protect users of highways and public streets. Thus, if the plaintiff is injured by the defendant's automobile on a public street, the plaintiff is within the class of persons to be protected and suffers the kind of harm intended to be prevented. By contrast, let us suppose that the plaintiff is injured by the defendant who is a competent driver but does not possess a valid driver's license. The purpose of the state statute requiring a driver's license is to protect the public against injury by incompetent drivers. Under the circumstances the plaintiff, in meeting the burden of proof in a suit for damages, is not permitted to use defendant's violation as negligence *per se*.

The majority of states treat the defendant's unexcused violation of an applicable criminal statute as conclusive proof of negligence. Thus, in a lawsuit the plaintiff need not submit further evidence to prove the first two elements of a cause of action for negligence; the court ordinarily instructs the jury to find a verdict of negligence. A minority of states hold that violation of a criminal statute is only evidence of negligence which the jury may accept or reject. In all states, to recover damages, the plaintiff must prove the last two elements of a cause of action for negligence: injury and cause.

Case 6.3   **Wolf v. Moughon**
562 S.W.2d 936 (Tex. Civ. App. 1978)

The defendant, Carol Moughon, was driving her car east on Windswept Street in Houston, Texas, at approximately 7 A.M. The plaintiff, Mary Wolf, with her daughter Shannon (also a plaintiff) was driving west on Windswept Street. The streets were wet. As the defendant's car came around a curve, it went up over the right curb and out of control, then came back over the curb into the street and into the left lane of traffic where it collided with plaintiff's vehicle. The defendant testified she was driving between 25 and 30 m.p.h. before the accident. She also testified that she had her brakes repaired two days before and that when she drove the car home from the repair shop she noticed the vehicle would pull to the right each time she applied the brakes. She was returning the car to the repair shop when the accident occurred. The defendant could not definitely say whether or not she had applied the brakes as she came around the curve on Windswept Street.

Plaintiffs filed suit against Carol Moughon for damages for negligence, alleging negligence *per se* in failing to keep her vehicle on the right side of the road in violation of a Texas statute. The defendant alleged unavoidable accident and sudden emergency. The jury failed to find negligence and judgment was entered for the defendant. Plaintiffs moved for judgment n.o.v. and for a new trial. The trial judge overruled both motions and plaintiffs appealed.

EVANS, J. On this appeal plaintiffs are faced with a situation where the jury has returned negative answers to issues upon which they had the burden of proof. Thus, in order to prevail in their appeal, the plaintiffs must demonstrate that the evidence established the defendant's negligence as a matter of law.

Where the legislature has declared that a particular act shall not be done, it fixes a standard of reasonable care, and an unexcused violation of the statute constitutes negligence as a matter of law. The plaintiffs, therefore, have met this burden if the evidence establishes as a matter of law: (1) a violation of a penal standard, (2) which was unexcused. . . .

Since the undisputed facts show that the defendant's vehicle was on the wrong side of the road at the time of the collision, the defendant was required to offer some evidence of a permissible excuse in order to justify her failure to comply with the statute. The excuse must be one which falls within a permissible class such as impossibility, emergency, or incapacity. . . . If the evidence raises more than a mere speculation or suspicion of excuse, it will be considered sufficient.

One type of permissible excuse is where the defendant is confronted by an emergency not due to his own misconduct, such as an unexpected failure in the vehicle's steering or braking system. . . .

Case 6.3
Continued

There are two reasons why the evidence in the case at bar does not raise the issue of a permissible excuse. First, the defendant failed to offer any evidence indicating that the faulty braking system caused her to lose control of the vehicle immediately prior to the accident. There is no affirmative evidence that she applied her brakes before her car first went up over the curb and if there is an inference to be gained from her testimony, it is that she probably did not do so. The evidence, at best, creates only a suspicion that her loss of control might have been due to a faulty braking system. The fact alone that the defendant's brakes were defective does not give rise to the inference that the defective braking system caused the vehicle to jump the curb and go out of control. Under the record before the court, it was just as likely that some other factor such as the defendant's own inadvertence was the cause of her loss of control. The second reason that the evidence falls short of creating an issue of permissible excuse is that there is no showing that the defendant was confronted with an emergency not due to her own misconduct. It is undisputed that for some time prior to the morning of the accident the defendant had been fully aware of the defective condition of her brakes and that she knew of the tendency of the car to pull to the right when the brakes were applied. The fact that a defect is shown does not under all circumstances establish a permissible excuse.

Since the defendant failed to offer evidence showing that the violation of the statute in question was due to a permissible excuse, the trial court erred in refusing to enter the judgment for the plaintiffs. . . .

The judgment of the trial court is reversed. . . .

Res Ispa Loquitur   Occasionally, there is no clear or direct evidence of the defendant's failure to exercise due care but there is circumstantial evidence of negligence. *Res ipsa loquitur* is a Latin phrase meaning "the thing speaks for itself." The doctrine of *res ipsa loquitur* permits the judge or jury to draw from circumstantial evidence the inference that the defendant was negligent. For example, it is reasonable to infer from skid marks on a street that an automobile was driven at an excessive speed. More than one inference may be drawn from circumstantial evidence and *res ipsa loquitur* is merely a rule of evidence in a lawsuit; it does not ensure a verdict in favor of the plaintiff. As in any lawsuit, the defendant may introduce evidence to contradict the inference of negligence or to prove a defense. It is only in the absence of evidence to the contrary that *res ipsa loquitur* would likely result in a verdict for the plaintiff.

In order for the plaintiff to utilize *res ipsa loquitur*, the plaintiff must prove the existence of two elements: (1) the event which caused the plaintiff's injury must be of a kind which ordinarily does not occur in the absence of someone's negligence, and (2) the accident must be caused by an instrumentality within the exclusive control of the defendant. The doctrine has been applied to a wide variety of situations. Some examples are: a falling elevator, the explosion of a boiler, an unexplained plane crash, and a sponge left in a patient following surgery.

When there is more than one explanation of the cause of the event resulting in plaintiff's injury, the plaintiff is not required to eliminate all possible causes or inferences other than negligence. In order to use the *res ipsa loquitur* doctrine in a negligence suit, the plaintiff need only present evidence from which reasonable people can say that on the whole it is more likely that there was negligence associated with the cause of the event than that there was not.[4] However, the plaintiff must eliminate any doubt that the defendant was in exclusive control of the instrumentality causing the injury. Ordinarily, the defendant may not be held liable where the negligence can be attributable to another. Thus, *res ipsa loquitur* does not apply where a spectator is injured by a bottle thrown by an unidentified person from a baseball grandstand, because it is impossible to attribute the negligent conduct to a particular person.

Defenses to Negligence

There are three major defenses to the tort of negligence: contributory negligence, assumption of the risk, and comparative negligence.

Contributory Negligence The defense of *contributory negligence* can be defined as failure by the plaintiff to exercise due care for his or her own safety, which failure is a contributing cause of the plaintiff's injury. To determine whether the plaintiff exercised due care, the model of the ordinary prudent person is utilized. However, there is a difference in approach between determining whether the defendant is negligent and whether the plaintiff is contributorily negligent. In determining whether the plaintiff is guilty of contributory negligence, the judge or jury is concerned about a risk of harm to the plaintiff created by the plaintiff. The plaintiff is required to exercise due care to protect his or her own interest from harm by others. Some legal writers and judges have stated that the defense might better be called "contributory fault."

Much criticism has been leveled at the defense of contributory negligence because it is a complete bar to the plaintiff's recovery. Thus, a plaintiff who is slightly negligent may not recover from a defendant who is greatly negligent. Most states have developed exceptions and

modifications to the defense of contributory negligence, but the defense still is recognized in a substantial number of states.

Assumption of the Risk The defense of *assumption of the risk* may be defined generally as voluntary exposure to a known risk. A common activity involving assumption of the risk is attending a sporting event. Suppose that a spectator at a baseball game is injured by a flying baseball. The spectator files a suit for negligence against the owner of the stadium alleging that the owner failed to provide a protective screen for spectators. The stadium owner may assert the defense that upon entering the stadium the plaintiff assumed the known risk of being hit by a bat or ball. A plaintiff's assumption of the risk may be express or implied. The spectator at a baseball game impliedly consents to the known risks of harm associated with the game. Occasionally the defense of assumption of the risk overlaps the defense of contributory negligence, since exposure to a known risk may also amount to failure to exercise due care for one's own safety.

To determine whether the plaintiff assumed the risk of the defendant's negligence, the judge or jury applies a subjective test. The ordinary prudent person model is not used. The judge or jury considers the particular plaintiff's age, experience, and knowledge, since these are important factors affecting the person's ability to understand and consent to the danger involved in the particular situation.

The defense of assumption of the risk has been criticized because it too is a complete bar to the plaintiff's recovery. As with contributory negligence, the courts have developed exceptions and modifications to the defense in an attempt to reduce the hardship resulting to the plaintiff.

Comparative Negligence The dissatisfaction of the courts with the absolute defenses of contributory negligence and assumption of the risk has led to the adoption of the defense of comparative negligence. For example, in 1975 the California Supreme Court overruled 120

---

[4]Ibid., p. 218.

years of precedent and replaced contributory negligence with comparative negligence. In 1981, the Illinois Supreme Court made the same ruling. The defense of comparative negligence in various forms is now provided either by court decision or by statute in the great majority of states.

In a lawsuit where both the defendant and the plaintiff are negligent, the defense of *comparative negligence* requires the judge or jury to apportion damages between the plaintiff and the defendant according to the fault of each. Thus, for example, if the defendant is found to be 75 percent at fault and the plaintiff is found to be 25 percent at fault, the plaintiff's damages will be reduced by 25 percent. With an unusual fact situation, the plaintiff who is only slightly at fault may actually owe money to the defendant. Thus, if the plaintiff's damages are $5,000 and the plaintiff is 25 percent at fault while the defendant who is 75 percent at fault has damages of $20,000, the plaintiff would owe the defendant $1,250.

The effect of the adoption of the comparative negligence rule on the defense of assumption of the risk varies greatly among the states. In some states the defense has been completely abolished. In other states express assumption of the risk remains as a complete defense, but implied assumption of the risk is treated as a form of comparative negligence, and the plaintiff's damages are reduced. In a few states assumption of the risk, whether express or implied, is retained as an absolute defense.

Case 6.4   Gonzalez v. Garcia
142 Cal. Reptr. 503 (Cal. App. 1977)

Plaintiff Juan Gonzalez, defendant Francisco Garcia, Jack Longest, and Weldon Roberts were coworkers at a power plant on the 10 P.M. to 6 A.M. shift. They were members of a car pool. One day the four men finished work and went to nearby Avila Landing where they drank beer, tequila, and other alcoholic beverages for 3 hours. The plaintiff drank about three beers, the others drank considerably more. About 9 A.M. Roberts went home, and the defendant drove the plaintiff and Longest to a liquor store where Longest and the defendant purchased a bottle of tequila. Plaintiff asked several times to be taken home. He phoned his wife to ask her to pick him up, but there was no answer. Garcia and Longest drank the tequila and drove to a bar for another drink, despite plaintiff's protests. Plaintiff had a glass of beer while defendant and Longest continued to drink tequila. A disturbance arose at the bar, and the police came to investigate. One officer suggested that since plaintiff appeared to be the least intoxicated of the three, he should drive the other two home.

Plaintiff then drove defendant's car to Longest's house. When plaintiff returned to the car after helping Longest inside, defendant was in the driver's seat and insisted on driving. The two argued, and plaintiff tried unsuccessfully to reach his wife again. Finally, plaintiff got into the passenger's seat and the defendant drove off. The plaintiff fell asleep. The defendant apparently lost control of the car and caused it to roll over, landing on its side on the median strip of the freeway. A test indicated the defendant's blood had an alcohol content of .20 and that therefore he was unquestionably intoxicated. Plaintiff sued for damages for negligence, and defendant asserted comparative negligence and assumption of the risk as defenses. The trial judge refused to instruct the jury on assumption of the risk. The jury returned a verdict for plaintiff but found him to be 20 percent responsible for his injuries. Defendant appealed and contended the trial court should have instructed the jury on the defense of assumption of the risk.

STEPHENS, J. The defense of assumption of risk was a late development in the law of negligence. The elements most frequently cited as essential to find assumption of risk are that the plaintiff have actual knowledge of the specific risk, appreciate the magnitude of the danger, and freely and voluntarily encounter it.

Most commentators recognize at least three kinds of assumption of risk: (1) express—where plaintiff, in advance, gives consent to relieve defendant of a legal duty and to take his chances of injury from a known risk; (2) implied—where plaintiff acts reasonably in voluntarily encountering a risk with the knowledge that defendant will not protect him; and (3) implied—where the plaintiff acts unreasonably in voluntarily exposing himself to a risk created by defendant's negligence. . . .

So long as contributory negligence and assumption of risk were both complete bars to recovery, the distinction between the two was never completely clarified, especially with implied assumption of risk. Usually, if a distinction was made, it was based upon the fact that assumption of risk requires knowledge of the danger and intelligent and deliberate acquiescence, whereas contributory negligence is concerned with fault or departure from the reasonable man standard of conduct, frequently inadvertently. Also the standard for determining whether the defense is available is different—assumption of risk using a subjective standard of the particular individual and circumstances, and contributory negligence using an objective, reasonably prudent man standard with which to compare plaintiff's conduct.

Assumption of risk has been rather unpopular due to the harshness of the "all or nothing" recovery, and there has been considerable effort to abolish it completely, particularly in view of the emergence of the comparative negligence doctrine. Nevertheless, where the doctrine of comparative negligence has been accepted, there have been three different approaches to assumption of risk—completely abolishing it as a defense, . . . maintaining it as a complete and separate defense, . . . or merging it to some extent with contributory negligence. . . . In those states which have merged the defenses, there has frequently been a complete merger of implied assumption of risk and contributory negligence, with express assumption of risk remaining as a separate defense. . . . We find this last approach to be the better view and to be the approach most in keeping with the Supreme Court's opinion in *Li*. [*Li v. Yellow Cab Co.*, 13 Cal. 3d 804 (1975).] . . .

In the instant case defendant's negligent driving was the direct cause of plaintiff's injuries, and plaintiff's only contributing negligence was in riding in the same car. Thus, in this case plaintiff's conduct is of the type which is a variant of contributory negligence which "exists when a plaintiff unreasonably undertakes to encounter a specific known risk created by defendant's negligence."

Regardless of the extent of assumption of risk which still exists as a separate defense and complete bar to recovery, in this case plaintiff's conduct clearly falls into the overlapping area, the area of choosing an unreasonable alternative when reasonable ones were available, thereby evidencing a lack of due care for his own safety. Plaintiff had actual knowledge that defendant was intoxicated, he had been advised by a police officer that he should drive, he demonstrated that he probably had knowledge of the risk by his attempts to contact his wife, he had alternatives of remaining at Longest's house or calling a cab and yet he chose to ride with defendant. Where there is a reasonably safe alternative open, the plaintiff's free choice of the more dangerous way is unreasonable and amounts to both contributory negligence and assumption of the risk. To that extent the doctrines are merged under *Li, supra*, into the doctrine of comparative negligence.

The facts do not justify even an inference that the acts of plaintiff included an element in addition to negligence such as waiver of duty, agreement, or other element not a variant of contributory negligence.

There was no error in the court's refusal to give the instruction on assumption of risk as requested.

The judgment is affirmed.

LIABILITY WITHOUT FAULT

The remainder of this chapter is devoted to a discussion of *liability without fault*, sometimes called *strict liability*. As the term implies, there are situations where a person may be held liable for injuring another even though the person has no intent to injure anyone and, in fact, acts with the utmost care to prevent harm to others. In such a situation the conduct of the one causing injury is blameless, yet for reasons of social policy the law requires him or her to compensate the injured person for the loss. The social policy is based largely on the notion that one person has caused injury to another and, although no one is at fault, a system of allocating losses must be developed. The courts reason that liability for the injury should be imposed on the party who can best bear the loss; that party usually is the one who caused the injury.

Liability without fault exists in a variety of areas of contemporary law. All individuals and firms should be aware that whenever their conduct results in injury to another, there is the possibility of being required to compensate the injured person. The law regarding certain situations of strict liability, such as workers' compensation and nuisance, are too extensive to present fully in this text. (Workers' compensation is discussed briefly at p. 801, nuisance at p. 405.) Three areas of strict liability have been selected for discussion here: liability for injuries by animals, liability for injuries from abnormally dangerous activities, and product liability.

Liability for Injuries by Animals
Several rules of law impose liability without fault on the owners of animals. In most states, the owner of an animal that is likely to roam and

injure the person or property of another is liable without fault for damages inflicted when the animal enters upon another's land. Such animals include: cattle, horses, sheep, hogs, turkeys, chickens, and most wild animals, since their natural tendency is to escape.

Either of two rules may apply when the injury occurs on the land of the animal's owner. First, the owner may be liable without fault for injuries inflicted by an animal that is dangerous by its nature and incapable of being domesticated. Such animals include lions, tigers, bears, elephants, and wolves. As a general rule, liability is absolute though the owner has raised the animal as a pet and it has shown no outward signs of being dangerous. The second rule of law that may apply pertains to domestic animals and domesticated wild animals that normally are not likely to injure people. The owner is liable for injuries inflicted only if the owner knows, or has reason to know, of a dangerous propensity in the particular animal. Domestic animals include dogs, cats, sheep, horses, and cows. The courts have held that deer and monkeys are wild animals capable of being domesticated. In many states the legislatures have enacted special statutes which hold an owner liable for injuries from a dog bite, regardless of the owner's knowledge or prior warning.

In a lawsuit to recover damages for injuries inflicted by an animal, the defendant may assert one or more defenses. The defendant may assert assumption of the risk and prove that the plaintiff voluntarily exposed himself or herself to a known risk. The defendant may assert that there is a state statute or local ordinance which protects the defendant from liability for maintaining a dangerous animal. For example, many states have enacted statutes which protect owners of zoos and transporters of dangerous animals from liability, provided they are not guilty of negligence. In most states the defendant is not allowed to assert contributory negligence as a defense. Thus, the plaintiff may have failed to exercise due care for his or her own safety and

yet recover damages for injuries inflicted by the defendant's animal. A plaintiff's recovery may be reduced in many states that have adopted the defense of comparative negligence.

Liability for Injuries from Abnormally Dangerous Activities

As a general rule, one is liable without fault for injuring the person or property of another by an unduly dangerous activity that is inappropriate to the particular locality. Typical examples of such an activity are: crop dusting near livestock, storing quantities of explosives in the heart of a city, and drilling an oil well in a populated area. The courts have held that the following are not considered "inappropriate to the locality": storing gasoline in a service station, maintaining an ordinary fire in a factory, and stocking a small quantity of dynamite for sale in a hardware store. A person who engages in these activities is not liable without fault for injuring another but may be liable for the tort of negligence if the person fails to exercise due care. In the early decades of the twentieth century, flying an airplane was considered an abnormally dangerous activity, and aircraft operators were held strictly liable for harm to others. Today, in most states, the owner or operator of an airplane is held liable only when negligence is proven.

In a lawsuit for abnormally dangerous activities the liability of a defendant is limited by concepts discussed previously, such as proximate cause. The defendant is not liable where the plaintiff's injury is the result of an unforeseeable intervening cause. For example, a defendant has been relieved of liability where his reservoir (abnormally dangerous for the area) was damaged and then carried away by an unprecedented rainstorm. The defendant may assert the defense of assumption of the risk and prove that the plaintiff voluntarily exposed the plaintiff's person or property to a known risk. The defendant may not assert the defense of contributory negligence. Most states have enacted statutes which protect a person or firm from liability for certain hazardous activities. For example, statutes ordinarily protect persons and firms laying gas or electric lines in public streets or doing blasting for the state, provided they are not guilty of negligence.

Product Liability

The law of product liability is complex and has a long history of development. Chapter 26 discusses this history and presents various contemporary theories of liability. This section is devoted to one theory: tort liability for defective products.

The overwhelming majority of states today recognize tort liability without fault for defective products sold to the public. The general rule has been stated as follows: one who sells a defective product that is unreasonably dangerous is liable to the ultimate user or consumer if the seller is engaged in the business of selling such a product and the product reaches the user or consumer without substantial changes in the condition in which it is sold.[5] Under the general rule the seller is liable though the seller exercises all possible care to prevent harm to others. A major reason for adopting this rule of liability without fault is social policy. The courts have repeatedly stated that the risk of injury from defective products should be borne by the manufacturer or seller who can insure against losses and distribute the cost to the public as an expense of doing business.

The courts have had difficulty in defining *a defective product that is unreasonably dangerous*. The usual definition is a product that does not meet the reasonable expectations of the ordinary consumer as to its safety. The product may be a sophisticated aircraft or automobile or a simple glass door or paper cup. The cause of

the defect may vary. The manufacturer may make an unintentional and unavoidable error in production; the design of the product may be defective; or there may be inadequate instructions or warnings.

Liability for a defective product extends to the manufacturer of the product, the wholesaler, the retailer, and the maker of a defective component part. However, liability is not imposed upon a person who is not engaged in the business of supplying goods of the particular kind, as when a private owner sells a defective car to another. (In certain circumstances, a seller may be liable for the torts of fraud or negligence.) Courts recently have held that a business firm, such as a car or truck rental agency, that leases personal property to others may be held liable without fault for injuries caused by a defect in the goods leased.

The courts have allowed persons other than users and purchasers to recover damages for injuries resulting from defective products. However, an injured person must be within the zone of danger. The zone of danger includes all persons who may foreseeably be injured by the defective product, such as family members, guests, or mere bystanders. One may recover for physical injuries, damages to the product itself, and damages to one's property in the vicinity.

Several defenses are available to a defendant in a product liability lawsuit. The defendant may assert that the plaintiff made an abnormal use of the product which the defendant could not reasonably foresee, such as using a glass bottle to hammer a nail. The defendant may assert assumption of the risk as a defense, but not contributory negligence. A number of states permit the defense of comparative negligence in a product liability case. In those states the judge or jury reduces the plaintiff's damages by the proportion of fault attributed to the plaintiff's conduct.

---

[5]Based on sec. 402A, *Restatement (Second) of the Law of Torts*, vol. 2, American Law Institute, St. Paul, 1965.

Case 6.5   **Smith v. United States Gypsum Co.**
612 P.2d 251 (Okla. 1980)

James H. Smith (plaintiff) and his wife, intending to panel their bathroom, bought two gallon cans of Wal-lite, a solvent-based adhesive. The directions on the can were as follows:

"DANGER
EXTREMELY FLAMMABLE
VAPORS MAY CAUSE FLASH FIRE
VAPORS HARMFUL
See cautions on back panel"

The back label carried the following admonitions:

"CONTAINS HEXANE. Vapors may ignite explosively. Prevent buildup of vapors—open windows and doors—use only with cross ventilation. Do not smoke, extinguish all flames and pilot lights; turn off stoves, heaters, electric motors, and other sources of ignition during use and until all vapors are gone. Do not take internally. Avoid prolonged contact with skin and breathing of vapor. Keep away from heat, sparks, and open flame. Close container after each use."

Plaintiff turned off his hot water heater and the pilot light on his kitchen stove and opened the front and back doors. He opened a can of Wal-lite and started to apply the adhesive over the bathroom window which was closed and sealed. Mrs. Smith turned on a fan across the hall from the bathroom. As she reentered the bathroom a blue flame erupted under plaintiff's trowel and an explosion occurred, seriously injuring plaintiff. Plaintiff filed suit against the manufacturer, U.S. Gypsum Co., and the distributor, Chicago Mastic Co., for product liability. A jury trial was held and plaintiff received a judgment for $600,000 damages. Defendants appealed.

DOOLIN, Justice. . . . In *Kirkland v. General Motors Corporation*, 521 P.2d 1353, 1363 (Okla. 1974) this court set out the elements of a cause of action in manufacturers' products liability.

"*First* of all Plaintiff must prove that the product was the cause of the injury; the mere possibility that it might have caused the injury is not enough.
Secondly, Plaintiff must prove that the defect existed in the product, if the action is against the manufacturer, at the time the product left the manufacturer's possession and control. [Citation omitted.] If the action is against the retailer or supplier of the article, then the Plaintiff must prove that the article was defective at the time of sale for public use or consumption or at the time it left the retailer's possession and control.
Thirdly, Plaintiff must prove that the defect made the article

unreasonably dangerous to him or to his property as the term 'unreasonably dangerous' is above defined.''

Unreasonably dangerous is defined as ''dangerous to an extent beyond that which would be contemplated by the ordinary consumer who purchases it, with the ordinary knowledge common to the community as to its characteristics.'' Defendants claim proof of the third element of the cause of action was missing.

There is no question the Wal-lite exploded, probably due to ignition of the vapors by the electric fan. But was the proximate cause an unreasonably dangerous product due to defective design and inadequate warnings, or was it plaintiff's ignoring the warnings on the can?

. . . A manufacturer must anticipate all foreseeable uses of his product. In order to escape being *unreasonably* dangerous, a *potentially* dangerous product must contain or reflect warnings covering all foreseeable uses. These warnings must be readily understandable and make the product safe. . . . Defendants in the present case should have known that some users would install paneling in a room without a window. If the jury found Wal-lite was designed in such a way that the vapors ignited easily, and that warnings and directions did not adequately warn of the dangerous conditions created, it was justified in finding a defect in the product.

If jury found this defect made the product unreasonably dangerous to the consumer, *Kirkland's* third element is satisfied.

Expert testimony at trial indicated the hexane vapors contained in the adhesive were released at a rapid rate if applied as directed on the can. The label instructed the consumer to apply the adhesive with a saw-tooth trowel. The expert opined such use compounded the dangers as this type of application doubled the evaporative rate by making grooves in the mixture. He concluded the release of the vapors into an enclosed space was too rapid to be overcome or guarded against. Plaintiff and his wife both testified the instructions and warnings were read and followed to the best of their ability. They attempted to satisty the ''cross ventilation'' instruction by opening the doors and using the fan.

Defendants claim the evidence shows plaintiff deliberately disregarded the instructions and warnings on the can, resting their case on the fact the bathroom contained no open window. This, they submit, caused the accident, not any defect in the Wal-lite. There is no evidence of such deliberate disregard of the instructions. To the contrary, testimony indicates every attempt was made to heed the warning.

We hold there was sufficient evidence the warnings on the Wal-lite did not prevent the product from being unreasonably dangerous. Proof of the third element was sufficient to send the case to the jury.

Defendants ask us to hold as a matter of law that plaintiff misused the product and voluntarily assumed the risk of a known defect, defenses to a manufacturers' products liability action under *Kirkland v. General Motors, supra.* Use of Wal-lite as an adhesive, its sole purpose, cannot be misuse of the product even if plaintiff used it carelessly as alleged. Evidence does not support defense that plaintiff knew the warnings were inadequate or that its application with a trowel would make the product more dangerous. The existence of the defenses is a jury question. Trial court properly overruled defendants' demurrers to the evidence and motions for directed verdict.

. . . Defendants objected to the testimony of one of plaintiff's expert witnesses, a chemical engineer, that warnings [on the label] appeared to him "to be inadequate," arguing this is testimony as to the ultimate fact. Also they objected to testimony of a psychiatrist [that the] warnings would be vague to a person such as plaintiff.

We feel this is well within permissible testimony of expert witnesses and is not reversible error. Defendants had ample opportunity for cross-examination.

. . .

Judgment affirmed.

SUMMARY

There are two major areas of tort liability for unintentional harm to others: liability for the tort of negligence and liability without fault. Negligence may be defined as the failure to exercise due care when there is a foreseeable risk of harm to others. In order to recover damages in a lawsuit for negligence, the plaintiff must prove four elements: (1) the defendant owed a duty of care to the plaintiff; (2) the defendant failed to exercise due care; (3) the plaintiff suffered actual loss or damage; and (4) the defendant's negligence was the cause of the plaintiff's injury. A duty of care arises when one should foresee that his or her conduct will create an unreasonable risk of harm to others. Whether the defendant has exercised due care is determined by comparing the defendant's behavior to that of the hypothetical ordinary prudent person. The defendant will be held liable if his or her conduct is unreasonable. The harm suffered by the plaintiff may be physical or mental. As a general rule the plaintiff may recover damages for negligent infliction of mental distress only if the plaintiff suffers physical injury from defendant's conduct.

Cause is used to refer to the connection between the defendant's negligence and the plaintiff's injury. Proximate cause is a limitation on the defendant's liability. The plaintiff may recover damages if the defendant's negligence was an actual cause of the plaintiff's injury and there is no superseding cause. Proximate cause includes an intervening cause that is reasonably foreseeable.

Two major procedural doctrines assist the plaintiff in proving that the defendant was negligent. Negligence *per se* permits use of the defendant's unexcused violation of a criminal statute to establish negligence. *Res ipsa loquitur* is used when there is no direct evidence of the defendant's negligence but there is circumstantial evidence from which an inference of negligence can be drawn.

Three major defenses are available to a defendant in a lawsuit for negligence: contributory negligence, assumption of the risk, and comparative negligence. Comparative negligence is provided in the great majority of states and has largely replaced the two other defenses.

There are three major areas of liability without fault (strict liability): liability for injuries by animals, liability for injuries from abnormally dangerous activities, and product liability. In a strict-liability lawsuit the defendant may be held liable though he or she exercises all possible care to prevent harm to others. The defendant may assert the defense of assumption of the risk but ordinarily may not assert contributory negligence of the plaintiff. Some states permit the defendant to assert comparative negligence as a defense in a lawsuit involving product liability.

STUDY AND DISCUSSION QUESTIONS

1 *(a)* Define the tort of negligence. *(b)* List the four elements required to establish a cause of action for negligence.

2 *(a)* What is a "duty of care"? *(b)* Who owes this duty and when does it arise? *(c)* To whom is the duty owed?

3 *(a)* Explain how a judge or jury determines if a defendant has failed to exercise due care. *(b)* How does the age or condition of the defendant affect the determination?

4 *(a)* Give examples of the types of injuries for which a plaintiff may recover damages in a negligence suit. *(b)* List the four elements required for a bystander to recover damages for the tort of negligence.

5 *(a)* Explain the purpose of proximate cause. *(b)* Define and give an example of each of the following terms: "concurring cause," "intervening cause," "superseding cause."

6 *(a)* Explain the doctrine of "negligence *per se.*" *(b)* Under what circumstances does the doctrine apply?

7 *(a)* Explain the doctrine of *res ipsa loquitur.* *(b)* What are the two elements required in order to utilize the doctrine in a lawsuit?

8 *(a)* Define contributory negligence. *(b)* How does this definition differ from the definition of the tort of negligence? *(c)* Define "assumption of the risk." *(d)* Explain how the judge or jury determines if a plaintiff has assumed the risk. *(e)* Explain why, to a plaintiff, the defense

of comparative negligence is more beneficial than either contributory negligence or assumption of the risk.

9 *(a)* Explain the social policy behind strict liability. *(b)* State and give examples of the three rules of law that may apply to injuries by animals. *(c)* In what circumstances may a person be held liable for injuring another by an abnormally dangerous activity?

10 *(a)* State the general rule of liability for injuries from defective products. *(b)* Who may be held liable for injuries from a defective product? *(c)* Who may recover damages for injuries from a defective product? *(d)* What defenses are available to a defendant in a product liability suit?

CASE PROBLEMS

1 Galen Irby was a cab driver for Cab Company. On the night of December 17, Cab Company dispatched Galen to respond to a request for a taxi at 5616 Vernon Avenue in a part of St. Louis known as a high-crime area. While at that address, Galen was murdered. Galen's wife, Anita, filed suit for negligence (wrongful death) against Cab Company, alleging that they owed a duty to exercise due care in dispatching Galen into high-crime areas and to provide means to protect him from intentional criminal acts of third persons. Cab Company filed a motion to dismiss for failure to state a claim upon which relief can be granted. How should the court rule?

2 On February 25, Mrs. Follins was traveling west on Washington Street. Her vehicle was struck on its left side by an automobile driven by Lazzard Barrow, who was driving north on Acadian Way, a two-lane one-way street. Washington Street was under extensive repair by the city. A stop sign that normally controlled westbound traffic on Washington Street had been removed by city employees on February 5.

Mrs. Follins had lived about four blocks from the intersection for over 3 years. She had driven on Washington Street previously. As she approached the intersection she reduced her speed and looked in both directions but did not see traffic approaching from the left or right. There was no impediment to her view. Mrs. Follins filed suit for negligence against Barrow and the city. At trial, Barrow was found free from negligence. The city was held liable on the ground that its removal of the stop sign was permitted for too long a period and the absence of a sign was the cause in fact of the accident. Should the city be held liable?

3 Avis left a rental car unattended in the parking lot at the Miami International Airport with the key in the ignition, the door open, and the car lights flashing. The car was subsequently stolen. The thief operated the car negligently and collided with a car driven by Charlie Vining, severely injuring him. The area around the airport had the highest incidence of auto theft in Dade County. Avis had had vehicles stolen in the past. Vining sued Avis for negligence. The trial court dismissed the complaint, stating that even if Avis were negligent it was not liable because the criminal act of stealing the car broke the chain of causation. Is Avis' negligence the proximate cause of Vining's injuries?

4 On November 14 at 10 A.M. a fire was discovered in a room at the Skyway Motel. The occupant of the room, Charles Hall, a traveling salesperson, died in the fire. Hall had checked into the motel the night before and looked as though he was overly tired or had been drinking. He went to a tavern and had three "mixed shots." Hall bought a new pack of cigarettes before he left the tavern at 12:30 A.M. The Deputy State Fire Marshall concluded the fire probably was started by Hall's smoking cigarettes in bed. His conclusion was based on the physical evidence of the fire: that Hall's right arm had been badly burned, that the fire had burned from the front of his bed's headboard to the back, and that the fire had burned from the top of the mattress to the bottom. May the motel prove a cause of action for negligence against Hall's estate by using the doctrine of *res ipsa loquitur*?

5 Marcos Garcia's automobile was parked in a parallel parking space on the south side of Howard Street. Keith Howard's car was parked in the space directly in front of Garcia's car, both vehicles facing east. Garcia had obtained new license plates for his car, had returned to his car, and had begun to affix the plates to his car. He had difficulty with the front license plate and spent 25 minutes trying to affix it. Howard returned to his automobile and got in, unaware that Garcia was between the rear of his car and the front of Garcia's car. Howard started his car, looked at his rearview mirror, saw only Garcia's car behind his, and slowly backed his car in the parking space. Garcia was crouching, facing his car, and was struck on the left shoulder by the rear bumper of Howard's car. Garcia sued Howard for the tort of negligence. Howard alleged Garcia was guilty of contributory negligence and assumption of the risk. Are the defenses valid?

6 Tasha, a four-and-one-half-year-old girl, visited her friend, Theresa, age ten, at the home of Theresa's grandparents, Mr. and Mrs. Yeager. The Yeagers kept a monkey, named "Mr. Jim," in a cage in the backyard. Theresa told Tasha where she could place her hand so the monkey could reach out and shake hands with her. The monkey bit Tasha's finger, causing serious injury. Mr. Jim had been a family pet for 26 years; he was regularly petted; he played with children and had never before bitten a child. Tasha filed suit for strict liability alleging the monkey was a wild animal. Is Tasha's allegation sufficient for her to recover damages for her injuries?

Chapter

7

Business Torts:
Interference with Business
Rights

The right to engage freely in business and to compete for customers and sales is woven into the economic and social fabric of our national life. Competition stimulates efficiency and inspires innovation and progress; it is a basic ingredient of our expanding economy and ever-rising standard of living. At the same time, competition may inspire some business magnates to embark upon unbridled practices which, if unchecked, could stifle lawful competition or improperly cause financial loss to others. Therefore, to assure equal opportunity to those who desire to engage in commerce and trade, restraints on unfair business practices are imposed by common law and by statute.

NATURE OF BUSINESS TORTS

In Chapters 5 and 6 we dealt with the invasion of, or interference with, the private rights of others, which in law is called a *tort*. In this chapter we will consider those torts which particularly interfere with commercial or business rights. For ease of discussion, we will call such business interference *business torts*. The injured party may be entitled to redress in damages or may be entitled to an injunction prohibiting or restraining the wrongful act if the act would result in irreparable injury without an adequate or complete relief. Some of these improper business practices may also violate criminal statutes and thus constitute crimes as well as torts.

Concepts and methods of doing business change to reflect shifting emphasis caused by such factors as national advertising, the growth of labor unions, and "fair trade" laws; similarly, the criteria as to what practices constitute business torts are not constant. It follows that whether or not a business practice is tortious is not always clear-cut. A court, in reaching its

120

decision, weighs the conflicting interests involved and may find that interests are present in a particular case which excuse or *privilege* an interference with another's business rights.

Most interferences with the business rights of others may be included within the broad generic term "unfair competition." It would be impossible in a chapter of limited length to discuss all the devices considered by the courts to be unfair competition.[1] Excluded from consideration here are such obviously improper acts as harassing a competitor's customers, blocking the ingress or egress of delivery trucks, displaying a sign saying 'Main Entrance' over one's own door adjacent to a competitor's entryway, threatening groundless lawsuits, and paying employees to commit sabotage.

For simplicity, the wide spectrum of business torts is discussed in this chapter under four broad general categories:

- Entering wrongfully into business
- Interfering with business relations
- Disparaging reputation or property
- Engaging in unfair trade practices

In each instance the facts must be examined and the interests of the respective parties viewed in the light of the ethical standards expected of business people. These standards are expressed in statutes (such as those which prohibit combinations in restraint of trade[2]) and in the decisions of the courts.

ENTERING WRONGFULLY INTO BUSINESS

It is a cardinal principle of American free society that a person may engage in any business of his or her choice and compete with other businesses for customers. This broad principle is subject, however, to restrictions. In certain circumstances, merely to engage in a business may violate the legal rights of others. For example, the right of an established business is violated where a competing business is carried on solely for predatory reasons or in violation of some regulatory rule or statute. The right to engage in a particular business is not a license to carry on that business in a manner that ignores restraints imposed by law. Such restraints are discussed in the next chapter.

Entering Business for Predatory Purposes

If a person opens a shop or office with the intention of continuing it only long enough to drive some other firm out of business or out of the neighborhood, there is present only a "simulated" competition. Such a predatory tactic is a violation of another's right to engage in the competitive world.

On the other hand, if a firm opens a business for the primary purpose of accomplishing a legitimate end, such as to make a profit or, in the case of a cooperative, to benefit its members, it would not be held to account for the losses its competitors may suffer unless it stoops to competitive practices the law deems improper. By way of illustration, there would be no violation of the rights of an old "corner store" forced out of business by a big new store which uses such competitive practices as selling at low discount prices, attempting to cut off the old store's source of supply of a fast-selling name-brand article by telling wholesalers they must cease selling such merchandise to the old store if the wholesalers want the new store's business, or threatening to discharge any of its own employees who trade in the old corner store.[3] These practices, in the absence of statutory prohibitions such as antitrust laws, would be

---

[1]Rudolph Callman and Seymour Kleinman, *The Law of Unfair Competition, Trademarks and Monopolies*, 3d ed., Callaghan & Company, Chicago, 1975, secs. 2–4.

[2]For example, the Sherman Antitrust Act, July 2, 1890, 15 U.S.C.A. 1, et seq.

[3]William L. Prosser, *Handbook of the Law of Torts*, 4th ed., West Publishing Company, St. Paul, 1971, sec. 130.

among the legitimate weapons in the war for customers, and the possibility of their use is a normal risk of business life. After termination of his or her employment, a former employee may compete with the ex-employer, provided the employee had not entered into an enforceable noncompetition agreement. However, the employee may not take advantage of trade secrets or of other confidential information learned during the prior employment.

Entering Business in Violation of Law

The privilege of engaging in business is curtailed whenever a governmental unit grants an exclusive franchise to a particular individual or firm. Thus, a state Public Service Commission may grant a franchise to Railway X to construct and operate a railway line between two designated points within the state, and the Federal Communications Commission may grant to a certain broadcasting station the exclusive right to use a designated frequency upon which it may broadcast. Any attempt by an individual or firm to invade an exclusively granted right is subject to a restraining order and possibly to a judgment for damages to the injured firm, or to a fine.

Similarly, the privilege of engaging in a business or profession may be curtailed by a statute requiring approval of an applicant by an examining board. In general, it is the responsibility of the state to take corrective action against a person who does business without the requisite permission. However, many courts permit a licensed member of a profession to bring an action on behalf of the entire protected group to restrain an interloper who attempts to enter the field.

INTERFERING WITH BUSINESS RELATIONS

The second category of business torts, *interfering with business relations*, may consist of inter-fering with contract relations or interfering with employer-employee relations.

Interfering with Business-Contract Relations

Business relationships are generally translated into contracts, either express or implied. The right to engage in a contract and to reap the profits of its performance is a property right closely guarded by law. An improper interference with that right, either by preventing the making of a contract or by interfering with contract performance, is a tort generally called *interference with prospective economic advantages*.[4]

Interfering with the Making of a Contract   A person who *maliciously* induces another not to engage in a contract with a third party commits a business tort if a contract would otherwise have been consummated and if the party aggrieved was damaged because of such interference. "Malice" is a legal term that is not subject to simple definition. In the context of this tort, *malice* means that the interference with the making of a contract was without legal justification or was accomplished through means themselves illegal, as, for instance, through injurious falsehoods or fraud. An example of interference without legal justification would be where an individual, with spiteful motive solely to prevent a particular real estate agent from earning a commission, induces an acquaintance not to purchase a house he was about to buy. An example of interference through illegal means would be where a father, in an effort to prevent the impending sale of a car to his son, threatens to "beat up" a used-car dealer.

If an inducement not to engage in a contract serves a legitimate end and no improper means is used, the action is said to be justifiable or privileged, and there would be no tort. *Bona*

---

[4]*Restatement of the Law (Second) Torts,* American Law Institute, Philadelphia, 1979, vol. 4, sec. 766, (hereafter cited as "*Restatement*").

fide competition—that is, competition using accepted business practices—is the most common instance of a privileged interference with the making of a contract. Thus, wholesaler X may with impunity, by offering a better discount, induce storekeeper Z to buy X's merchandise rather than that of wholesaler Y who had been regularly supplying A in the past; and Y cannot successfully complain that this is an improper interference with a contract of sale which had seemed assured.

Refusing to Deal   Thus far the discussion has considered only the interference by a third party with a prospective contract between other individuals. What of the case where a person seeks to purchase from someone who refuses to sell to him or her? Such an occurrence, although technically not an interference with the making of a contract, is so closely akin to it that its brief consideration is appropriate here.

As a general rule an individual is free to choose whether to sell or not to sell his or her products. However, at certain times, even though no third party is involved, this freedom is curtailed. This curtailment may result directly from statutory mandate, as in the Civil Rights Act of 1964,[5] or somewhat less directly from the requirement in a public utility franchise that the company serve the public without discrimination. Even when no statute or franchise is involved, if a refusal to sell is for the purpose of creating an illegal monopoly, the refusal is improper. Moreover, although an individual acting alone may be privileged to refuse to deal with another, under certain circumstances the refusal is tortious because it is part of a concerted effort with others. Thus, firms A, B, and C, acting independently of one another, may, without violating legal standards, refuse to deal with firm X; but if the three firms enter into an agreement, for example, not to deal with firm X in order to force it out of business or to force it

into a price combine, the refusal to deal with X constitutes a business tort.

Interfering with Contract Performance   As we have seen, the right of an individual to enter into contractual relations is protected by law. The right to expect performance under a contract already entered into is even more fully protected. Any unprivileged interference by a third person which retards, makes more difficult, or prevents performance of a contract or makes its performance of less value to one of the contracting parties is therefore tortious. Inducing a breach of contract is the most common form of this type of business tort.

An individual who induces a breach of contract is liable if three conditions are present: (1) He or she knew of the existence of the contract and intended to bring about its breach. (2) The action was not legally justifiable. (3) The breach was the proximate result of the action.

There can be no breach of contract where there is no valid contract. It is therefore not a tort to induce a party to an illegal agreement to refrain from performing his or her promise. Thus, if C induces A not to pay a bet to B, C has not committed the tort of inducing a breach of contract if the gambling agreement is illegal. Where an oral contract is unenforceable because it is of the type required to be in writing, some courts hold that a person who induces its breach has committed a tort, but most courts do not so hold.

A contract may provide that it is terminable at the will, that is, at the election, of the parties to it. Notwithstanding this freedom, a third person is not privileged, without justification, intentionally to induce a termination of the contract.

The discussion of malice and legal justification with respect to interfering with the *making* of a contract is generally also applicable to the tort of *inducing* a breach of contract. Malice in the sense of intentionally doing a harmful act without legal justification or excuse is necessary to establish the tort of interference with contract performance. Whether malice is present de-

---

[5] Civil Rights Act of 1964, Pub. Law 88–352, July 2, 1964.

pends on the circumstances. The facts may be "so outrageous" that malice may be presumed. On the other hand, the defendant may have acted under such a color of right that a claim of tortious interference fails. For example, assume that A has promised a certain performance to X and that A later promised a similar performance to Y; but A cannot physically fulfill both promises. If X then induces Y to terminate the contract with A, X commits no wrong.[6]

Bona fide competition may furnish legal justification for interfering with the *creation* of a contract. It does not, however, furnish legal justification for inducing a *breach* of contract. Similarly, inducing a breach of contract is not normally excused by the fact that the inducement was free of duress and took the form of mere persuasion. However, inducing a breach of contract by peaceful persuasion is legally excusable where the object sought to be accomplished by the inducement redounds to the public good. Assume, for example, that a labor union goes on strike for better working conditions and pickets an employer's plant. Not wanting to cross the picket line, a third person breaches a contract with the company struck. Clearly the union has induced the breach of contract; yet the union will not be held liable for it is now generally recognized that the public

interest in improved working conditions transcends the right of a contracting party not to have a contract interfered with by a stranger to the contract. But a labor union can be restrained and even held in damages if its actions constitute an unfair labor practice under applicable statutes, such as by engaging in a secondary boycott.[7] A secondary boycott is a combination not merely to refrain from dealing with the person aimed at, or to persuade customers to refrain from dealing with that person (practices which would be legal), but to put coercive pressure upon customers of another firm to cause them to withhold or withdraw their patronage from it.

The same act which gives rise to the business torts of interfering with the making of a contract and of inducing a breach of contract may also give rise to other tort actions. For example, suppose that A writes disparaging statements to B about the quality of C's products and thereby induces B to breach a contract with C. C would have two causes of action against A: one for inducing the breach of contract and one for trade libel, a business tort to be discussed later.

The following case explains the tort of inducing a breach of contract.

---

[6]*Barlow v. Brunswick Corp.*, 311 F. Supp. 209 (E.D. Pa. 1970).

[7]Norris-La Guardia Anti-Injunction Act, 29 U.S.C. 101; National Labor Relations Act, 29 U.S.C. 151; Taft-Hartley Act, 29 U.S.C. 141; *Gilbertson v. McLean*, 341 P.2d 139 (Ore. 1959).

Case 7.1   Imperial Ice Co. v. Rossier
112 P.2d 631 (Cal. 1941)

One Coker was the owner of an ice distribution business in Santa Monica, California. He sold the business to X, agreeing not to engage in a like business in the same territory as long as the purchasers or anyone deriving title from them were in such business. The plaintiff, the Imperial Ice Company, purchased the business from X, including the right to enforce Coker's covenant not to compete. Coker subsequently, in violation of the contract, began selling ice supplied by one Rossier. Plaintiff brought suit against Coker, Rossier, and certain others to restrain Coker from engaging in the ice business and to restrain Rossier from inducing Coker to violate the contract not to compete. The excerpt below involves defendant Rossier whose demurrer (a pleading asserting that the plaintiff had no legal basis to sue) was sustained by the trial court. Plaintiff appealed.

TRAYNOR, J. . . . . The question thus presented to this court is under what circumstances may an action be maintained against a defendant who has induced a third party to violate a contract with the plaintiff.

It is universally recognized that an action will lie for inducing breach of contract by a resort to means in themselves unlawful such as libel, slander, fraud, physical violence, or threats of such action. Most jurisdictions also hold that an action will lie for inducing a breach of contract by the use of moral, social or economic pressures, in themselves lawful, unless there is sufficient justification for such inducement.

Such justification exists when a person induces a breach of contract to protect an interest which has greater social value than insuring the stability of the contract. Thus, a person is justified in inducing the breach of a contract the enforcement of which would be injurious to health, safety, or good morals. The interest of labor in improving working conditions is of sufficient social importance to justify peaceful labor tactics otherwise lawful, though they have the effect of inducing breaches of contracts between employer and employee or employer and customer. In numerous other situations, justification exists depending upon the importance of the interests protected. The presence or absence of ill will, sometimes referred to as "malice," is immaterial, except as it indicates whether or not an interest is actually being protected.

It is well established, however, that a person is not justified in inducing a breach of contract simply because he is in competition with one of the parties to the contract and seeks to further his own economic advantage at the expense of the other. Whatever interest society has in encouraging free and open competition by means not in themselves unlawful, contractual stability is generally accepted as of greater importance than competitive freedom. Competitive freedom, however, is of sufficient importance to justify one competitor in inducing a third party to forsake another competitor if no contractual relationship exists between the latter two. A person is likewise free to carry on his business, including reduction of prices, advertising, and solicitation in the usual lawful manner although some third party may be induced thereby to breach his contract with a competitor in favor of dealing with the advertiser. Again, if two parties have separate contracts with a third, each may resort to any legitimate means at his disposal to secure performance of his contract even though the necessary result will be to cause a breach of the other contract. A party may not, however, under the guise of competition actively and affirmatively induce the breach of a competitor's contract in order to secure an economic advantage over the competitor. The act of inducing the breach must be an intentional one. If the actor had no knowledge of the existence of the

Case 7.1
Continued

contract or his actions were not intended to induce a breach, he cannot be held liable though an actual breach results from his lawful and proper acts.

Had [Rossier] merely sold ice to Coker without actively inducing him to violate his contract, his [Coker's] distribution of the ice in the forbidden territory in violation of his contract would not then have rendered defendants liable. They may carry on their business of selling ice as usual without incurring liability for breaches of contract by their customers. It is necessary to prove that they [Rossier et al.] intentionally and actively induced the breach. Since the complaint alleges that they did so and asks for an injunction on the grounds that damages would be inadequate, it states a cause of action.

The judgment is reversed and cause remanded.

Interfering with Employer-Employee Relations

A trained labor force is a most important element of any successful business organization, requiring time and money to develop. If a trained employee is induced to leave a company in order to work for a competitor, the new employer may gain a considerable economic advantage. Not only will the new employer be saved a costly training cycle, but he or she may also "inherit" some of the other company's customers and perhaps learn something of its trade secrets. A contract of employment, therefore, represents a valuable property right that is given special protection by the law of torts. Interference with the employment relationship is a form of inducing a breach of contract, and thus the legal concepts pertaining to inducing breach of contract generally also apply to the tort of interfering with employer-employee relations.

Newspapers and trade journals regularly carry advertisements of job opportunities, holding out attractive working and living conditions and favorable salary scales to induce qualified persons to apply. Suppose that as a result of such an advertisement an individual leaves the place where he or she is employed. Does this mean that the firm which advertised has committed a tort? No, unless acting with malice it induced the employee to terminate the prior employment.

Malice, in the context of this tort, as in any other inference with business advantage,

means that the wrongdoer intentionally, and without just cause or excuse, interfered with an employer-employee relationship. Just cause or excuse depends upon the facts in the particular situation.

Malice is present when an employee is under a contract of employment and this fact is known to a competitor who nonetheless intentionally entices him or her away. In that event, the fact that the only motive was to satisfy a real need for the individual's services furnishes no defense to the tort.

The contract of employment need not be in writing to be thus protected. An oral understanding that the individual will render service for a specified period will be protected whether or not the employee has begun to work.

If the employee is not under contract for any specific period of time but is free to terminate employment at any time, no tort results if he or she "switches jobs" in response to an offer of higher wages or better working conditions. As one court has said: "In our free economy, social mobility is a chief characteristic. An employee who is dischargeable at will is under no obligation to treat his employer otherwise or with more consideration than he can be treated by [the employer]."[8] This privilege is not, however, a license to an employer to entice employees away from competitors without lawful excuse. If the purpose of inducing the employee to leave a

---

[8]*Sarkes Tarzian, Inc. v. Audio Devices, Inc.*, 166 F. Supp. 250 (S.D. Cal. 1958).

position is not only to gain an employee but also to *injure* the former employer, then the lawful excuse is lost and a tort has been committed. Enticing away a key member of a competitor's sales organization or research department would be wrongful.

In this discussion of inducing breach of contract it was noted that a labor union, under certain circumstances, may induce a breach of contract between an employer and his or her customers. Similarly, a labor union is privileged to invade the employer-employee relationship and, if only legitimate suasion is used, may induce employees to leave their employment at least for the period of a dispute.

Some states have special statutes designed to prevent interference with employment contracts. Since these statutes may so tie an employee to the employer as to approach a condition of peonage, they are strictly construed by the courts.

The protection the law gives to employment contracts is illustrated by the next case.

Case 7.2   **Wear-Ever Aluminum, Inc. v. Townecraft Industries, Inc.**
182 A.2d 387 (N.J. 1962)

Plaintiff, Wear-Ever Aluminum, Inc., manufactures and sells aluminum cooking utensils through house-to-house salesmen called "distributors." The distributors work under a "dealer" who instructs them in the techniques of selling the merchandise. The distributors and dealers are independent contractors. District managers, employees of the plaintiff company, supervise the dealers. The defendant company, Townecraft Industries, carried on a campaign in various cities throughout the United States to recruit Wear-Ever personnel to work for Townecraft. As a result of one social meeting alone, a group of the plaintiff's dealers and about 10 or 15 of its distributors agreed to work for the defendant. The plaintiff brought suit to enjoin the defendant from inducing the plaintiff's employees and distributors from terminating their employment with the plaintiff.

PASHMAN, J.S.C. . . . The general principle to be applied in the area of interference with contractual . . . relations was cogently expressed [as follows]:

"Merely to persuade a person to break his contract, may not be wrongful in law or fact. . . . But if the persuasion be used for the *indirect purpose of injuring the plaintiff, or of benefiting the defendant, at the expense of the plaintiff, it is a malicious act.* . . .
. . . "While a trader may lawfully engage in the sharpest competition with those in like business, by offering extraordinary inducements or by representing his own goods to be better and cheaper than those of his competitors, yet when he oversteps that line and commits an act with the *malicious intent of inflicting injury upon his rival's business,* his conduct is illegal, and if damage ensues from it the injured party is entitled to redress. And it does not matter whether the wrongdoer effects his object by persuasion or by false representation. The courts look through the instrumentality or means employed to the wrong

perpetrated with the malicious intent, and provide the remedy to redress that wrong. . . .

". . . No man can justify an interference with another man's business through fraud or misrepresentation nor by intimidation, obstruction, or molestation. This right to pursue one's business without such interference, and the correlative duty, are fundamentals of a well-ordered society. They inhere basically in the relations of those bound by the social compact. They have their roots in natural justice. . . ." [Citation.]

. . . The fact that the distributors' and dealers' contracts with the plaintiff were terminable at will cannot and does not provide the basis for justification where a third party tortiously interferes with an employment relationship. . . . Justification must be found in facts independent of the nature of the relationship [to] which the law affords protection. The right to terminate a contract at will is one which is peculiarly personal to the contracting parties, and a stranger to the contract may not exercise his will in substitution for the will of either of the parties to the contract.

. . . The conduct of the defendant . . . was designed and intended to promote the interests of the defendant at the expense of the plaintiff. The injury suffered by the plaintiff, i.e., loss of man power and loss of revenue . . . was the ultimate consequence envisioned and planned for by the defendant. The defendant's desire was to build its sales force, and Wear-Ever was as good a source as any to pick from. . . .

. . . [E]ven if the defendant had established that the custom in the trade was to pirate salesmen from competitors, this court would not permit such a custom to justify and legitimize what otherwise would be tortious conduct. The role of the court is to raise the standard of business morality and care, not judicially to sanction tortious activities. Higher standards benefit and protect both the innocent members of an industry and the general public.

. . . I feel that the only effective way to prevent future irreparable injury and to protect the plaintiff . . . is a permanent injunction restraining the defendant from recruiting or attempting to recruit employees, dealers and distributors of the plaintiff. . . .

[Judgment accordingly.]

DISPARAGING REPUTATION OR PROPERTY

In addition to protection in its contract and employee relationships, a firm is also entitled to compete in an orderly business world free from disparagement both of its reputation and of the product which it sells. This part of the chapter deals with: (1) torts involving disparagement of reputation, generally referred to as "defama-tion"; and (2) torts involving disparagement of property, generally referred to as "disparage-ment"[9] or "injurious falsehoods."[10]

Disparagement of Reputation (Defamation)

The tort of defamation involves the unprivileged dissemination, called in law *publication*, of false

---

[9]*Restatement*, op. cit., secs. 623 A, 629.
[10]Prosser, op. cit., sec. 128, p. 915.

and defamatory matter. (Refer to Chapter 5, page 77, where the law of defamation is treated in a broader aspect.) When the publication occurs in written or printed form, the tort is called *libel*. When the publication is oral, the tort is called *slander*. Because of the wide dissemination of material through radio and television broadcasts, some courts consider publication of defamatory matter by radio or television to be libel rather than slander.

To constitute defamation it is not necessary that the defamatory statement mention by name the party affected as long as the statement is reasonably understood to refer to that party. And although the words are ambiguous, if they are used in a particular meaning which makes them defamatory and they are understood in this light, the tort has been committed.

Defamation as a Business Tort Defamation is not confined to business relationships and therefore is not generally considered a business tort. It is included here, however, because defamatory matter may tend to harm another in a business, trade, or profession; or may adversely affect a corporation, partnership, or other business entity in its credit standing; or may otherwise deter people from dealing with it.

Defenses against Defamation Unless changed by state law, truth of the statement made is a complete defense to an action for defamation regardless of the bad faith behind the publication. But to establish this defense the person making the defamatory statement must prove that it was true; the person may not assert the defense that the statement was merely repetition of rumor or gossip. Similarly, X cannot find refuge from liability for a falsehood he or she publishes by attributing the authorship to another, as: "Y said that Company B never pays its bills until it is sued." Although disbelief by the hearer of a false statement about a firm or individual does not prevent the tort from arising, it may mitigate the damages assessed.

Privilege, a justifiable excuse for publishing the actionable matter, is another defense to defamation. There are two kinds of privilege: (1) absolute privilege and (2) qualified, or conditional, privilege.

If a publication is absolutely privileged there is no liability even though the false statement may have been made through malice. By virtue of absolute privilege a member of Congress is immune from suit for a slander he or she may utter in a speech on the floor of Congress, and a witness is immune (although possibily liable for perjury) for a slander uttered when testifying in the course of, and related to, a judicial proceeding.

The more common type of privilege as a defense to defamation is *qualified*, or *conditional*, *privilege*. The defense is given this name because it may be asserted only on condition that the maker of the defamatory falsehood reasonably believes the statement to be true and, without malice, publishes it in furtherance of some recognized interest. For example, a credit bureau, in response to a request from one of its members, furnishes a derogatory credit report on another firm or on an individual, based upon erroneous information; when sued for defamation the bureau successfully may claim its action as qualifiedly privileged. If, however, it circulates a derogatory report indiscriminately, the defense of privilege is absent.

Disparagement of Property

Disparagement of property is a term used to refer collectively to the common law torts of slander of title and slander of quality (commonly referred to as "trade libel").[11]

Slander of Title This tort involves the unprivileged publication of untrue matter which casts doubt upon, or denies, the validity of another's title or interest in any kind of property and which results in financial loss. The disparagement may be accomplished by any conduct reasonably understood to impair the vendibility of property, such as wrongfully filing for record

---

[11]*Restatement*, op. cit., secs. 624, 626.

a mortgage or claim of lien; wrongfully asserting that a third person has some interest in the property; wrongfully stating that the owner cannot deliver possession; or, in bad faith, claiming that use of a competitor's product will result in a patent infringement suit.

Slander of Quality (Trade Libel)   Trade libel is the unprivileged publication of false matter which indicates that another's property lacks the characteristics its vendor claims for it or which indicates that the property is unfit for the purposes for which it is being sold or leased. This tort is akin to slander of title, but here the financial loss is caused by belittling the *quality* of another's property rather than the title to it. Slander of title always involves a statement of fact, but trade libel may be either a false statement of fact or a dishonest expression of opinion made in such circumstances that the vendibility of the property will probably be diminished.

It is not unusual for the same improper publication to constitute both a trade libel and a defamation. Such a situation would exist, for example, when the statement not only disparages the quality of an article but also reflects upon the honesty of the owner or storekeeper who offers it for sale.

Defenses against Disparagement of Property
Just as truth of the statement and privilege of utterance are defenses in actions for defamation, so they are defenses in actions for disparagement of property. As in defamation, the privilege may be either absolute or qualified. Whether the defendant should be held to have a qualified privilege often presents a difficult problem to the courts. A qualified privilege exists when the publication is made in a reasonable manner or, as many courts say, without malice, and to satisfy a purpose which the law recognizes as justifiable.

In a title dispute a rival claimant is qualifiedly privileged to disparage another's title by honestly asserting his or her interest in the property. And a storekeeper is qualifiedly privileged to disparage the quality of a competitor's article by consciously exaggerating or "puffing" the superiority of his or her own merchandise in comparison with the competitor's, provided, however, no direct attack is made on the other's wares by expressing false facts about them. X is privileged to say, for example, "My soap powder washes clothes brighter than A's or B's or anyone else's," even though there is present in this statement the implication that A's or B's product is not of the quality their makers represent in their advertising. This can be considered mere "puffing." But X is not privileged to say, "My soap powder washes clothes brighter than A's or B's because their powder does not completely dissolve in hard water," if that statement is not true.

A statement made to protect the interest of the person to whom the statement was made is privileged only when the person making the disparaging statement believes it to be true and when he or she is under duty to inform the other person. The duty may be a legal duty, as that owing by a real estate agent to his client; or it may arise from a close family relationship; or it may exist because the person to whom the information is given is entitled to it and requests it.

ENGAGING IN UNFAIR TRADE PRACTICES

Individuals engaged in business are entitled to enjoy the trade advantages they create for themselves and to profit from the customer relationships that can be expected to follow the reputation and goodwill they earn. These broad rights, not being susceptible of simple definition, have been characterized as an "interest in prospective economic advantage."[12] This interest may be impaired through a wrongful trade practice by a competitor, or by someone not in direct

---

[12]Prosser, op. cit., sec. 130.

competition but within the merchandising chain from manufacturer to dealer, or even by an individual in an entirely unrelated business. Among such practices are *palming off* one maker's product as that of another, discussed below under the heading of Fraudulent Marketing; the intentional or unintentional infringement by one firm of the trademark or trade name of another firm; and the violation by one firm of the trade secrets of another firm. Where the tort is accomplished by intentionally deceiving the purchasers, there is also a tort against the purchasers—that of *fraudulent representation*. However, it is the tort against the firm with which we are primarily concerned in this discussion of business torts.

Fraudulent Marketing

Falsifying Source or Maker   Any intentional sales representation falsifying the source or maker of a product constitutes fraudulent marketing. Examples of confusion of the source are:

• A store displays a sign, "X Brand," above a stack of shirts on a counter in such a way as to indicate that all of the shirts in the pile are "X Brand," but only one or two actually are that brand

• A dress store has a sign in its window falsely claiming "Dress styles by Madam X"

• A manufacturer falsely tells wholesalers that the motor in an electric tool was approved by Laboratory Z

The damaged party in the tort of fraudulent marketing is the purported manufacturer or source to which the goods have been falsely attributed.

Imitating Physical Appearance or Packaging   Imitating the form or style of another's product or its distinctive wrapping may violate the rights of the business concern whose product is imitated. The imitation may also deceive a prospective purchaser if the imitation amounts to a palming off of one product for another. Such a situation would exist where a company adopts a wrapper or package for its products or uses employees' uniforms or delivery vehicles so similar to those already used by another company that a customer would be confused between the two. However, the law permits considerable latitude in copying the design or style of another concern. In the words of the Restatement of the Law of Torts, the "privilege to engage in business and to compete with others implies a privilege to copy or imitate the physical appearance of another's goods that are not protected by patent or trademark."[13]

Although the copying of a product may be economically harmful to the originator, the courts generally will neither restrain the imitator nor cause the imitator to respond in damages as long as the imitator does not resort to unfair methods in securing the copy or to fraudulent marketing in introducing it to the public. Assume that Company A sends its buyers to Paris where they purchase expensive original couturier dresses to be sold in its dress salon. The dress styles are not patented. Company B, which sells popular-priced dresses, reads in the newspaper that Company A has "original dresses fresh from Paris" for sale. Company B sends a designer to A's store where she carefully examines the Paris dresses displayed there. She then returns to her own store and makes an excellent copy of one of them. Company B puts the imitation on sale for one-fourth the price of A's original but does not advertise the dress as an original Paris model. Company A has no basis for tort action against B. But if we would change this hypothetical case to say that B secured the dress design by bribing one of Company A's employees to show the dress privately so that B's designer could copy it, or if B had promised not to make a copy of the dress but nonetheless did so, then Company B would have secured its copy through improper means and its privilege to imitate would be lost. And where customers

---

[13]*Restatement of the Law (Second) Torts*, vol. 4, sec. 735. Copyright 1979 by The American Law Institute. Reprinted with permission.

are deceived, the tort of unfair marketing would be present.

Although the law permits considerable latitude in copying another's design, the unauthorized appropriation of news distributed by a press association to its members is not permitted. Similarly, the selling of an unauthorized transcription of a presentation or broadcast of the performing arts is tortious.[14]

---

[14]*Fame Publishing Co., Inc. v. Alabama Custom Tape, Inc.*, 507 F. 2d 667 (5th Cir. 1975).

Case 7.3   Zippo Manufacturing Co. v. Manners Jewelers, Inc.
180 F. Supp. 845 (E.D. La. 1960)

Zippo, which manufactures cigarette lighters, seeks to enjoin defendant, a New Orleans jewelry store, from selling foreign imitations of its lighters at cut-rate prices. Defendant displays genuine Zippos in its windows and sells them as well as the foreign brand. Zippo is not protected by patent, all relevant patents having expired. Zippo claims unfair competition and seeks a restraining order.

WRIGHT, D.J. The problem of unfair competition through imitation of product design has given rise to an increasing amount of jurisprudence [litigation], much of which is difficult to reconcile. The difficulty derives largely from a difference in economic philosophy between those who would protect the rights of the public as distinguished from those who would find a property right in the form or design of a manufactured article, which property right would withdraw that form or design from the public domain. Most of the cases recognize that the public interest in competition ordinarily precludes the protection of a property right in form or design; unless protected by copyright or patent, once the form or design in an article is offered to the public, it becomes the property of the public and, absent deceptive identification as to source, may be copied at will by competitors.

The only circumstances under which a manufacturer may protect the form and design of its product is where that form or design identifies the product with the manufacturer, and purchasers are influenced to buy the product because of this identification. . . .

Without question, the Japanese lighters have copied the form of Zippo. Also without question, however, is the fact that these lighters nowhere bear any indication, other than the form and design, of being manufactured by Zippo. As a matter of fact, these lighters are boldly marked on the bottom with their own trade names. Even the fact that they are made in Japan is inscribed there. Under the circumstances, it can hardly be said that the public, acting reasonably, could be, or are likely to be, confused or misled by these lighters. . . .

Zippo's patent rights have long expired. To protect the form in which it merchandised its monopoly would be to prolong the monopoly and to deny the public the consideration for which the patent was granted. When a patent expires, the form as well as the substance of the product patented becomes the property of the public. So it is with Zippo. Purchasers who desire a Zippo-looking lighter at a low price may have one. Competitors who desire to satisfy this demand may do so. The public, having tolerated the patent monopoly, now has its inning.

A temporary injunction will issue restraining the defendant from using the name Zippo and any Zippo advertising displays in merchandising the accused products in suit. The motion for temporary restraining order is otherwise denied.

Infringing a Trademark or Trade Name

A *trademark* is any word, symbol, device, or design adopted and used to identify an article offered for sale and placed on or affixed to it or its container. Place or personal names or words normally descriptive of an article or its use generally may not be trademarked, as such words should be available to anyone. However, if such words are used as a part of a design or device or are so fanciful or uncommon as not normally to be identified with an article, they may then be subject to trademark. The difference may best be explained by two illustrations. "Swiss watch" may not be trademarked to describe a watch made in Switzerland, for any watchmakers there located should be free to so describe their product; but if "Swiss Watch" is the name given to a candy bar, it would be such a fanciful use of the words that it may be adopted as a trademark. As the other illustration, manufacturer John Smith may not use his name as a trademark, for any person by that name is free to use it to identify his product; however, if one of these John Smiths accompanies his name with his picture or other unique design, the entire device may be trademarked to identify the product. Familiar to many generations of consumers is the trademark "Smith Brothers Cough Drops" with the picture of the two bearded brothers on the box.

A firm is entitled to the exclusive use of a trademark it adopts for marketing a product. The *intentional or unintentional* use by another firm of a trademark which is so similar to a previous one that it is likely to confuse prospective purchasers as to the source of the product is the business tort of trademark infringement. The trademark need not necessarily be registered with a state or with the federal government in order to earn protection from infringement. Registration does, however, extend the geographical effectiveness of a trademark and furnishes proof of the date of inception of its use. Registration may also prolong the life of a trademark and entitle its owner to additional legal remedies in the event of infringement.

The term *trade name* is used to indicate a part or all of a firm or corporate name. For example, "Philco" is a trade name for the Philco Corporation. Whether the name of a corporation is to be regarded as a trademark or a trade name, or both, is not entirely clear under the decisions of the courts. However, it is generally recognized that a trademark is applicable to the vendible commodity to which it is affixed, and a trade name applies to a business and its goodwill. The precise difference is usually immaterial, since the law affords protection against the wrongful appropriation of either where confusion or uncertainty results or may result.[15]

Words or devices which have not been made the subject of a trademark or which identify a product after the trademark has expired may be protected from infringement if they have acquired a secondary meaning. A *secondary meaning* is acquired when the name or device connotes in the public mind a specific product

---

[15]*Trade Marks and Unfair Competition*, J. Thomas McCarthy, The Lawyers Co-operative Publishing Co., Rochester, N.Y., 1973.

or source. In that event, use of the name by another company in such a way as to deceive a purchaser constitutes unfair competition. The Supreme Court has said with respect to Coca-Cola:

> The name means a single thing coming from a single source, and well known to the community. . . . In other words "Coca-Cola" probably means to most persons the plaintiff's familiar product to be had everywhere rather than a compound of particular substances. . . . [It] has acquired a secondary significance and has indicated the plaintiff's product alone.[16]

Therefore, if another concern uses a name or mark so similar to Coca-Cola that it deceives or will probably deceive purchasers and cause them to buy a product believing it to be the product of the Coca-Cola Company, unfair competition results. How much time must elapse

---

[16]*Coca-Coca Co. v. Koke Co. of America*, 254 U.S. 143, 146 (1920).

and what extent of usage is necessary before a secondary meaning is acquired by a mark or name is dependent upon the circumstances in each case.

Sometimes a trademark or trade name is so commonly used that it is "understood as a generic or descriptive designation for that *type* of goods."[17] If that situation arises, the trademark or trade name no longer solely identifies a particular source or brand but describes the article in general. What was formerly a trademark or trade name may then be used by anyone to describe the article, provided, of course, there is no attempt to palm off the new product as the original. For example, the word "Vichy" was originally a brand name for a French mineral water. "Vichy" has now become a generic term and can be used by anyone to denote mineral water as long as the source of the product is made clear to the public. The use of the trademark "lite" to describe a beer is the subject of the next case.

---

[17]*Restatement*, op. cit., sec. 735.

Case 7.4 **Miller Brewing Company v. G. Heileman Brewing Company**
561 F. 2d 75 (7th Cir. 1977)

Meister Brau, Inc., secured United States Patent Office trademark approval of labels containing the name "LITE" for beer with no available carbohydrates. Meister Brau later sold its interest in "LITE" trademarks to the plaintiff, Miller Brewing Company. Miller used the term "LITE" upon labels for a beer lower in calories than Miller's regular beer but not entirely without available carbohydrates. Miller spent considerable money advertising the beer. Soon other brewers, including defendant, G. Heileman Brewing Company, marketed reduced-calorie beers labeled or described as "light." Miller filed a trademark infringement action. The district court enjoined Heileman from continuing to sell, advertise, and distribute beer anywhere in the United States under a brand name incorporating the word "Light" and from imitating Miller's labels which had been registered with the Patent Office. Heileman appealed from that order.

TONE, Cir. J. . . . The registrations are prima facie evidence of Miller's exclusive right to use the word "LITE" for beer with no available carbohydrates, not for any beer. . . . Inasmuch as the beer marketed [by Miller] . . . contains available carbohydrates, the registrations are not prima facie evidence of Miller's exclusive right to use the mark on that beer. Thus . . . Miller's brand name "LITE" must be evaluated under the common law of trademarks without the benefit of registration.

The basic principles of trademark law which are applicable here have often been stated . . . and may be briefly summarized. A term for which trademark protection is claimed will fit somewhere in the spectrum which ranges through (1) generic or common descriptive and (2) merely descriptive to (3) suggestive and (4) arbitrary or fanciful. . . .

A generic or common descriptive term is one which is commonly used as the name or description of a kind of goods [e.g., "Consumer Electronics"]. It cannot become a trademark under any circumstances. Using the phonetic equivalent of a common descriptive word, i.e., misspelling it, is of no avail. . . .

A merely descriptive term specifically describes a characteristic or ingredient of an article [e.g., "After Tan Lotion"]. It can, by acquiring a secondary meaning, i.e., becoming 'distinctive of the applicant's goods,' . . . become a valid trademark.

A suggestive term suggests rather than describes an ingredient or characteristic of the goods and requires the observer or listener to use imagination and perception to determine the nature of the goods [e.g., "gobble-gobble" for turkey parts]. Such a term can be protected without proof of a secondary meaning.

An arbitrary or fanciful term [e.g., "Q-Tips"] enjoys the same full protection as a suggestive term but is far enough removed from the merely descriptive not to be vulnerable to possible attack as being merely descriptive rather than suggestive.

'Light' has been widely used in the beer industry for many years to describe a beer's color, flavor, body, or alcoholic content, or a combination of these or similar characteristics. . . . Indeed, state statutes even use 'light beer' as a generic or common descriptive term. 'Light' is clearly a common descriptive word when used with beer. . . . [E]ven if Miller had given its light beer a characteristic not found in other light beers, it could not acquire the exclusive right to use the common descriptive word 'light' as a trademark for that beer. Other brewers whose beers have qualities that make them 'light' as that word has commonly been used remain free to call their beer 'light.' Otherwise a manufacturer could remove a common descriptive word from the public domain by investing his goods with an additional quality, thus gaining the exclusive right to call his wine 'rosé,' his whiskey 'blended' or his bread 'white.'

The word 'light,' including its phonetic equivalent, 'lite,' being a generic or common descriptive term as applied to beer, could not be exclusively appropriated by Miller as a trademark. . . . [T]he preliminary injunction must be reversed.

Infringing a Patent or Copyright

The Constitution authorizes[18] and Congress has enacted patent and copyright laws which give to inventors and authors for an extended period of years the exclusive right to market their "brain children." Patents may be issued for a process (e.g., a way to bond cloth); a machine (e.g., an innovative sewing machine); a manufacture (e.g., a new toy); a composition of matter (e.g., a new plastic); or a plant (e.g., a novel hybrid rose). The duration of such patents is seventeen years.[19] A design patent is granted for a lesser period. To acquire a patent, the applicant must demonstrate to the Patent Office that the invention or discovery satisfies the legal standards. The process or article must be useful, novel, and nonobvious in light of the prior state of the art.

The patent holder gives notice to the public that the article is patented by placing on it the word "Patent" (or "Pat.") and the patent number. Making or selling a patented article without the permission of the patent holder is called a *patent infringement*. This may constitute a business tort of great economic consequence. The patent holder may bring suit to enjoin the infringement and also to ask for damages. Such suits are notoriously involved and costly. As the patent holder may be required to prove the validity of the patent as well as the fact of infringement, the litigation may place in jeopardy the very valuable property right that a patent represents. Therefore, a patent holder, instead of resorting to a lawsuit, may sell to the infringer a license to use the patented product or design.

Copyright protection covers writings and recordings.[20] Although a copyrighted work must be original, it may be substantially similar to a work previously produced by another. A copyright is acquired by placing upon all publicly distributed copies of the work a symbol or abbreviation meaning copyright, the year of first publication, and the name or abbreviation of the name of the owner. Effective January 1, 1978, the duration of a copyright for work created subsequent to that date is for the life of the author plus fifty years after the author's death. Action for infringement of a copyright may not be instituted until the copyright claim is registered with the Copyright Office in the Library of Congress. As in the case of a patent, a copyright may represent a valuable property right, and its infringement—a business tort—may be enjoined and made the basis of a suit for damages. In addition, the court may order the impounding and subsequent destruction of all copies of phonorecords and tapes made or used in violation of the copyright owner's exclusive rights.[21] A person who infringes a copyright willfully and for purposes of commercial advantage may also be subject to fine and imprisonment.

Violating Trade Secrets

A trade secret is any information guarded by a firm because it furnishes the business with a peculiar economic advantage. It might be an engineering process, a formula, use of tools, quality control procedure, customer attitude study, or customer list of a delivery route. In certain instances, a trade secret furnishes the owner with benefits not found in the patent or copyright laws. Companies may find it easier and less expensive to gain the court's protection of a trade secret than to perfect and protect a patent.

Just as a firm is privileged as a normal incident of competition to copy the physical characteristics of a product, it is allowed to copy business methods and processes, provided the information making such imitation possible comes into its possession legitimately. However, if a firm gains the use of another's trade secret dishonestly or through the abuse of a confidence, an unlawful interference with the business rights of another has taken place.

---

[18]U.S. Constitution, Art. 1, sec. 8, cl. 8.
[19]35 U.S.C. 154.
[20]17 U.S.C. 1 et seq.

[21]17 U.S.C. 503.

Case 7.5 **The Anaconda Company v. Metric Tool & Die Company**
485 F. Supp. 410 (E.D. Pa. 1980)

The plaintiff, Anaconda, spent more than two years developing a machine to make flexible metal hose used, among other things, for the protection of telephone cords, a product familiar to all users of coin telephones. Plaintiff became the principal supplier to the Western Electric Company of this flexible hose. Plaintiff kept the machine out of public sight and isolated in its plant, available only to those whose work required access to it. The machine was not patented. Defendant, Metric, desiring to sell that same product to Western Electric, decided to make a similar machine. It was unable to do so and therefore hired two of plaintiff's former employees who had worked with the machine. An attempt to hire others away from Anaconda failed. With information from their two ex-Anaconda employees, plus some of plaintiff's drawings and discarded parts of the machine, the defendant, after about four years, in 1969–70, displaced the plaintiff as the primary supplier of armored telephone cord to Western Electric.

In 1976 a disgruntled former employee of defendant gave the plaintiff photographs of the defendant's machines and a statement concerning its construction. Defendant's machines are practically the same as plaintiff's. Plaintiff, alleging a misappropriation of its trade secrets by industrial piracy, brought suit to enjoin the defendant's further use of its machine and for damages.

The Court's conclusions of law, filed pursuant to the federal Rules of Civil Procedure, in part state:

EDWARD R. BECKER, District Judge. . . . The most comprehensive definition [of a trade secret] is set out in Comment b to the Restatement of Torts, sec. 757 (1939). . . .

> "A trade secret may consist of any formula, pattern, device or compilation of information which is used in one's business and which gives him an advantage over competitors who do not know or use it. . . . Generally it relates to the production of goods, as, for example, a machine or formula for the production of an article. . . .
>
> " . . . The subject of a trade secret must be secret. Matters of public knowledge or of general knowledge in an industry cannot be appropriated by one as his secret. Matters which are completely disclosed by the goods which one markets cannot be his secret. Substantially, a trade secret is known only in the particular business in which it is used. He [the proprietor of the business] may, without losing his protection, communicate it to employees involved in its use. . . .
>
> "The secrecy in which a purported trade secret is shrouded need not be absolute but reasonable precautions under the circumstances must be taken to prevent disclosure to unauthorized parties. The degree

of secrecy must be such that it would be difficult for others to obtain the information without using improper means."

"[A] trade secret can exist in a combination of characteristics and components, each of which, by itself, is in the public domain, but which in unique combination, affords a competitive advantage and is a protectable secret." Here it was the precise configuration, juxtaposition, and assemblage of components and features . . . rather than the breaking of heretofore unknown ground, which made plaintiff's machine unique . . . [and] legally sufficient to constitute a trade secret. . . .

Although Ames and Van Meter [plaintiff's two employees hired by defendant] . . . made no express agreement with Anaconda not to disclose its secrets in the . . . machine, nevertheless their disclosure was wrongful if the nature of their relationship with Anaconda gave rise to an implied duty of nondisclosure. An employee, upon terminating his employment relationship with his employer, is entitled to take with him "the experience, knowledge, memory and skill which he . . . gained while there employed." . . . However, an employee is not entitled to take with him and to disclose his knowledge of the trade secrets or secret processes of his employer. . . . [A] pledge of secrecy is impliedly extracted from the employee, a pledge which he carries with him even beyond the ties of his employment relationship. . . .

We also reject Metric's contention that its . . . machines were independently designed by reverse engineering or other processes. Reverse engineering is a process by which one analyzes a finished product and, working backwards, designs the machine capable of producing such a product. . . .

We find that the Metric machine was created not by reverse engineering, but by application of the knowledge of the Anaconda machine which Ames and Van Meter acquired while working on the Anaconda machine, by use of drawings which Ames had taken from Anaconda, and by direct incorporation of Anaconda winding rolls procured by Ames. . . .

There are two competing views on the theoretical basis for legal protection of trade secrets: the "property" view and the "confidential relationship" view. . . . Justice Holmes stated that the basis of trade secret protection is the "confidential relations" between the parties and not the status of the trade secret as intellectual property. The Holmes view has been rejected by the Pennsylvania Supreme Court [where suit was brought]. . . . Pennsylvania adheres to the "property"view of trade secret law. . . . On that view, the theoretical basis for recovery on a trade secret claim is not merely the breach of a confidential relationship, but also the adverse use of the plaintiff's intellectual property . . . [which view] follows Section 757 of the Restatement of Torts. That section creates a cause of action against a person "who discloses *or uses* another's trade secret."

[The statute of limitations and the principle of laches (plaintiff's delay in seeking equitable relief) were also discussed.]

For the reasons previously stated, . . . we will enter an injunction for 16 months duration [the time which would have been required for the defendant to learn how the machine was made had he attempted to reverse engineer it]. . . . An appropriate order follows.

SUMMARY

While the spirit of competition with its play of interest against interest is inherent in the business world, our free-enterprise economy does not justify conduct which is contrary to the ethical standards expected of business people or to public policy as determined by courts or legislatures. Business practices which violate such standards or policy are business torts and may be crimes as well. A person harmed by a business tort may secure redress in damages, or such a person may secure an injunction against continuance of the tortious act if damages cannot be determined or cannot give adequate relief.

There is a wide variety of business torts. The most frequently recurring ones may be grouped into four broad categories:

- Wrongfully entering into business
- Interfering with business relations
- Disparaging reputation or property
- Engaging in unfair trade practices

Entering into competition with an established firm is not normally a tort, even though it causes the established firm to lose customers and profits. However, under certain circumstances merely engaging in business may violate the rights of others, as where the entry into business is for predatory purposes or in violation of some privilege granted by statute to others.

The right to contract is protected by law. It is therefore a tort for a person unjustifiably to induce another person to refrain from entering into a contract which he or she otherwise would have consummated. The right to receive the performance of a contract already entered into is even more zealously guarded by the law. Although it is not a tort for a person to breach his or her own contract, inducing a person to breach a contract he or she has with another person is a tort. In recent decades numerous cases have involved the tort of inducing a trained and skilled employee or a person of great managerial competence to breach his or her contract of employment in order to work for a competitor firm.

Every business person (and firm) is entitled to compete in an orderly business world free from unprivileged disparagement of reputation, property, and product. Where the unprivileged dissemination of false and defamatory matter tends to injure a person's reputation, it constitutes the tort of slander or of libel, depending on the mode of publication; where it casts doubt on or denies the validity of title to property, it constitutes the tort of slander of title; where it indicates that property or product lacks the characteristics claimed by the owner or producer, it constitutes the tort of trade libel.

Engaging in unfair trade practices has been described as a wrongful interference with a person's "interest in prospective business advantage." The wrongful interference may result from some act or practice of a competitor, or of a person not in direct competition or in the chain of manufacturer to dealer, or even of a person in an entirely unrelated business. The practice may consist of "palming off" a product for that of another firm by false advertising or by imitating the physical appearance or packaging of its product. Or the practice may consist of the infringement of a trademark, patent, or copyright; the intentional or unintentional imitation of a trade name; or the unlawful use of another firm's trade secret. Some of these wrongful practices deceive purchasers and also constitute a tort against them. All these practices cause a diversion of trade and thus constitute a tort against the firm whose trade has been diverted.

STUDY AND DISCUSSION QUESTIONS

1 *(a)*What is the meaning of "business tort"? *(b)*In an economic society that is based on the principle of free enterprise, may there be situations in which a court may appropriately prevent an individual from entering into a business of his or her own choice? Explain and illustrate.

2 *(a)*What is meant by "interfering with business relations"? *(b)*When does interference with the making of a contract become a business tort? *(c)*Give an example of interference with the making of a contract which is legally *justifiable* and one which is legally *unjustifiable.*

3 *(a)*What conditions must be present before an individual is liable for inducing a breach of contract? *(b)*Give an example of a situation where inducing a breach of a legal contract does not result in a business tort. *(c)*What policy considerations justify this freedom of action?

4 *(a)*Why is the performance of an employment contract protected by the courts from unreasonable interference by competitors? *(b)*Do you think that the protection of a contract of employment deserves greater, equal, or less protection from interference than does a contract involving the sale of a house? Why?

5 *(a)* Name and illustrate the two kinds of torts involving disparagement of property. *(b)* What are the legal defenses against such disparagement?

6 *(a)* Give examples of unlawful marketing practices which may be termed "palming off." *(b)* Should the courts restrain a business person from imitating the products of a competitor? Support your answer with the reasons you believe would dictate the court's decision.

7 *(a)* What is a "trademark"? *(b)* Distinguish between a trademark and a trade name. *(c)* What is the significance of "secondary meaning" with regard to a trademark? *(d)* What are the advantages of registering a trademark with a state or with the federal government?

8 *(a)* What is a "trade secret"? *(b)* Give examples of trade secrets. *(c)* Why might a company choose to rely on the protection afforded by a trade secret rather than on that provided by a patent?

CASE PROBLEMS

1 The plaintiff and defendant corporations were both engaged in the manufacture of women's wearing apparel. S, a noted dress designer, entered into a written contract to work for the plaintiff for a period of five years. The agreement required her to devote her full energies to the plaintiff's business and not to compete with it. The defendant company, knowing that S was under contract to the plaintiff, offered her a job and agreed to pay her a larger salary if she would leave the plaintiff and work for the defendant. S did so. The plaintiff sued the defendant for the damages it claimed it sustained because the defendant induced the breach of S's contract. The court held that plaintiff was entitled to recover. Do you agree with this holding? Why or why not?

2 The plaintiff, a retail butcher located in San Francisco, occasionally sold Chinese pork. He refused to join the butchers' union. The defendant, the union, printed and circulated handbills reading in part: "Don't sow the seeds of disease and spread pestilence and death by buying Chinese pork and lard. . . . [Plaintiff] sells Chinese pork and lard." The evidence established was that the Chinese meat sold by the plaintiff was wholesome. He sued the defendant for damages because of the trade libel but offered no proof that the defendant's publication

was malicious. The defendant admitted the publication but denied that it was malicious. Should the plaintiff succeed in his suit?

3 The plaintiff manufactured and sold a "pole lamp," that is, one which stands upright between the floor and ceiling of a room. The defendant, learning of the successful sale of the lamp, marketed a substantially identical one which it sold at retail at a price lower than plaintiff sold them at wholesale. The plaintiff sought to enjoin the defendant's sale of the lamps, claiming unfair competition. The lower court granted an injunction and the defendant appealed. Should the order directing an injunction be sustained?

4 Plaintiff had for many years manufactured and sold various types of nails and other fasteners. The plaintiff corporation designed and produced a nail with a series of annular ribs about the shank which it designated its "Stronghold nail," and which it advertised widely. The plaintiff also registered a design trademark containing the word "Stronghold" which it used on its packages. The defendant company was a direct competitor of the plaintiff and sold the same general type of articles to the same customers. Later the defendant company changed its name to the Stronghold Screw Products Company. Thereafter both companies used the name "Stronghold" in their respective businesses, but there was no proof that the defendant was "palming off" its products as those of the plaintiff company. The plaintiff charged the defendant with appropriating its trademark and with unfair competition and sought to enjoin defendant's use of the word "Stronghold." Should the plaintiff be granted an injunction?

5 Plaintiff, Horlick's Malted Corporation, sells malted milk in packages and bottles for human consumption. Its packages are identified with a drawing of three cows and with writing that states, in part, that the product is manufactured in Racine, Wisconsin. The defendant, Charles Horlick, produces "Horlick Dog Food." His packages bear a drawing of a dog and the statement that the product is manufactured by Horlick, of Horlicksville, Racine, Wisconsin, a short distance from the city of Racine. The name "Horlick" is the family name of both the defendant and the plaintiff. Plaintiff sought to enjoin defendant from using the name Horlick, alleging trademark violation and unfair competition. The trial court issued the requested injunction, and defendant appealed. Should the appellate court sustain the injunction, modify it, or dissolve it?

6 The plaintiff was engaged in cleaning private homes by mass production methods, employing crews of workers whom it had trained. The plaintiff, at considerable effort and expense, developed and screened its customers with most of whom it had contracts. The defendant worked for the plaintiff as a house cleaner and learned the plaintiff's method of doing business. After being in plaintiff's employ for three years, the defendant quit his job and started the same type of business for himself. He solicited the plaintiff's customers whose names and addresses defendant had learned from his employment with the plaintiff. House cleaning is not a unique business and no trade secrets are involved. The plaintiff sought to enjoin the defendant from soliciting its customers. Should the plaintiff be successful in its suit?

Chapter

8

Business Crimes:
White-Collar Crimes

Civil law furnishes the framework upon which commercial enterprises are established and business is conducted. A business law textbook, therefore, properly focuses attention upon the civil law. However, certain criminal activities are so closely linked with the conduct of business that they have become known as "business crimes" or "white-collar crimes."[1] This subject is important to a business person because there is a possibility of suffering loss as a victim of business crime or of being charged with committing such a crime.

It is impossible to compute accurately the cost to the public of white-collar crimes. It has been estimated that losses are "not less than $40-billion annually, which *excludes* the cost to the public and business of price-fixing illegalities and industrial espionage."[2] "The direct cost of business crime surpasses the cost of such conventional crimes as larceny, robbery, burglary, and auto theft."[3]

This chapter will (1) discuss the meaning and impact of business, or white-collar, crimes; (2) briefly explain criminal law principles with rela-

---

[1]The term "economic crime" is also sometimes used. In this chapter the terms business crimes and white-collar crimes will be used interchangeably.

[2]Chamber of Commerce of the United States, *A Handbook on White-Collar Crime*, 1974, p. 5.
[3]John E. Conklin, *Illegal But Not Criminal*, Prentice-Hall, Inc., Englewood Cliffs, N.J., 1977, p. 4.

142

tion to such crimes; and (3) consider a sampling of typical white-collar crimes.

MEANING AND IMPACT OF BUSINESS, OR WHITE-COLLAR, CRIMES

Business, or White-Collar, Crimes Defined

Neither the federal penal code nor state penal statutes characterize any criminal act as a "business," or "white-collar," crime. These crimes have been called a "social concept, not a legal [one]. . . . Any person whose behavior is put into this social category must violate some specific criminal law, not some general law prohibiting white-collar crime."[4]

The term "white-collar crime" was first used to refer to the social class of the offender. It was thought of as a crime committed by a person of respectability and high social status in the course of his occupation. That concept has since been broadened. Although no single definition of these crimes is universally accepted, in this chapter a *business*, or *white-collar*, crime is defined as an illegal act or series of illegal acts

1 Committed by nonviolent means
2 By an individual or corporation
3 Related to a legitimate occupation
4 To obtain business or personal advantage

Business crimes cover a wide spectrum of offenses. They usually involve some sort of fraud, guile, misrepresentation, or the evasion of statutory directions designed for the protection of the public. Such a crime is normally thought of as a wrongful act committed *by* a business entity against another business, or a "rip-off" by a business against the government,

the public, or an individual. For example, a white-collar crime might be a misrepresentation in a financial statement; an unlawful manipulation of a publicly traded stock; or a tax or mail fraud. Among many others, it may be the bribery of a public official; the improper donation of a political contribution; the adulteration of foodstuffs; or false advertising.

Certain crimes in which a business is the *victim* may also be viewed as white-collar crimes. For example, embezzlement or pilferage by an employee, theft of securities by a broker, and insurance fraud fall into this category. Of particular interest are computer-related crimes. Business crimes of this type may be, among others, the programming of a computer to cause money to be credited to an account not entitled to it, the theft of computer time, or the theft of information stored in a computer.

Impact of Business, or White-Collar, Crimes

The financial impact of business crime upon the victimized public is enormous. Unlawful trusts and cartels may cause consumers to pay artificially inflated prices for goods or services. Losses suffered by business enterprises and the increased insurance premiums they must therefore pay are all ultimately passed on to the public. White-collar crimes "may contribute to general social problems. Citizens come to distrust government and business; business distrusts its employees and government; and government loses faith . . . in the probity of business."[5]

Despite the personal interest consumers should have in preventing or punishing business crimes, these wrongs seem to enjoy considerable public tolerance. This may be because white-collar crimes are impersonal, and no one

---

[4]Testimony of Professor Donald R. Cressey before Subcommittee on Crime of the Committee on the Judiciary, House of Representatives, 95th Cong. 1st Sess., Comm. Print no. 2, *New Directions for Federal Involvement in Crime Control*, April 1977, p. 67.

[5]Peter Finn and Alan R. Hoffman, *Prosecution of Economic Crime*, National Institute of Law Enforcement and Criminal Justice, U.S. Department of Justice, March 1976, p. 3.

is physically hurt. Violence is not an element. Moreover, the public has an inherent dislike of big business and big government. Some disgruntled employees believe that thefts from their employers are justifiable. Some corporate managers may be more interested in their company's balance sheets than in the methods they adopt to best their competitors or to secure new business. In this, they may not even perceive themselves as committing criminal acts.

Usually business concerns which have been the victims of white-collar crimes do not seek prosecution of the offender because the financial loss is covered by insurance, because prosecution may be difficult, or because they fear their own image may be tarnished should the loss come into public view.

CRIMINAL LAW PRINCIPLES

A consideration of white-collar, or business, crimes requires a general understanding of criminal law principles.

Nature of Criminal Law

Criminal law is concerned with acts committed or omitted in violation of public law. Because criminal prosecution is an action to protect a public right, it is initiated on behalf and in the name of the state and not in the name of the victim of the crime. This is markedly different from a civil suit between private parties, as for instance, a suit by A against B to collect a past-due debt. In such a dispute the state is not a party. A person found guilty of a crime may also be made the defendant in a separate civil suit wherein the victim claims money damages. (Chapters 5 and 6 discuss in detail intentional and unintentional injuries, called *torts*, inflicted upon another.) Criminal laws reflect the demands of current mores and public policy; accordingly, criminal law is never static. As new and innovative schemes are devised to gain profit or reward, social and legal concepts of

white-collar crimes change, and new criminal laws are enacted to curb them.

Categories of Crimes

There are two categories of criminal acts:[6]

- Felonies
- Misdemeanors

A *felony*, under federal law, is a serious crime punishable by imprisonment for more than 1 year. Under the law of most states, felony is punishable by imprisonment in a state prison.[7] Under either federal or state law a fine may also be imposed upon conviction for a felony. A *misdemeanor* is a lesser crime. It is punishable generally by imprisonment for no more than 1 year in other than a state prison, with or without the imposition of a fine. *Infractions* may also be mentioned. These are minor wrongs which do not have the stature of criminal acts. Among them are such derelictions as traffic offenses, punishable by small fines. Some white-collar crimes are felonies; others are misdemeanors.

Arrest

An individual first feels the force of punitive state action when he or she is arrested. Usually an arrest is accomplished by a police officer. Authority to arrest may be based upon (1) a crime being committed in the presence of the arresting officer, (2) the officer having reason to believe that a *felony* has been committed, or (3) a warrant issued by a court. The Supreme Court, in the landmark case of *Miranda v. State of Arizona* [384 U.S. 436 (1966)], held that an arrested person cannot be interrogated by the police unless first warned of his or her rights, among them, the right to remain silent and the

---

[6]Treason, a betraying or breach of allegiance, is a constitutional crime (U.S. Constitution, Art. 3, sec. 3, cl. 1) and generally is not included within the common categories of criminal acts such as felonies and misdemeanors.

[7]Certain felonies may also be punishable by death in jurisdictions which authorize this punishment.

right to have an attorney present. If this rule is not complied with, a confession, even though voluntary, full, and complete, may not be received in evidence in a subsequent criminal prosecution. Except in unusual circumstances, an arrested person is entitled to be released on bail or upon his or her own recognizance (assurance) to be present in court if so required.

Criminal Prosecution

Criminal prosecution of a felony is initiated by a grand jury indictment or by an information filed by the district (prosecuting) attorney charging an accused with the commission of a crime.[8] At a preliminary hearing the accused enters a plea of either guilty, not guilty, or nolo contendere. By the latter plea the accused, in effect, says, "I do not wish to contest the charge." Such a plea, though not technically a guilty plea, is an implied admission of guilt. By nolo contendere an accused submits himself to the mercy of the court. It is frequently used by defendants charged with business crimes since the plea of nolo contendere cannot be used as evidence of legal guilt in a civil suit. In addition, it precludes the exposure of damaging information which might be publicized in a public trial.

A criminal case ordinarily is tried before a jury.[9] Accused persons cannot be forced to testify against themselves and are presumed innocent until a verdict of guilty is rendered.

Criminal Intent

Most crimes are *malum in se* (evil in themselves). In the commission of such a crime, the actor has an evil purpose or blameworthy intent. To convict, the jury must determine be-

yond a reasonable doubt that a criminal act was committed by the accused while harboring criminal intent (mens rea) or with criminal negligence.[10] Depending upon the wording of the law violated, the accused must be found to have committed the prohibited act "wrongfully," "corruptly," "willfully," "fraudulently," "intentionally," or "feloniously." Such intent is almost invariably proved by inference drawn from the circumstances under which the act was committed. People are presumed to intend the natural consequences of their voluntary acts. Thus, if X, an employee, without permission takes a hand tool owned by his or her employer and pawns it, the jury may presume that X had the intention to deprive the employer of its property permanently, a necessary ingredient of the crime of larceny.

Although a corporation is a legal entity created by statute, without a mind with which to form an intent or a body with which to act, it may be criminally responsible for a business crime. The intent of the corporation's officers and agents who acted for it is imputed to the corporation. That is, the intent of the individuals who acted for the corporation is assumed to be the intent of the corporation. (For a discussion in depth of corporations see Chapters 42 to 46.)

Violations of certain regulatory laws enacted for the safety and health of the community are punishable without proof of criminal intent in the ordinary sense. For instance, to manufacture for sale foodstuffs in unclean premises violates the Federal Food, Drug and Cosmetic Act. Such a wrong is called *malum prohibitum* (evil because prohibited by statute); it does not constitute a common law crime. Conviction for an offense of this type usually results in only a light punishment. A business crime may, depending on the law violated, be either *malum in se* or *malum prohibitum*.

---

[8]The Fifth Amendment to the Constitution provides that "No person shall be held to answer for a capital, or otherwise infamous crime, unless on presentment or indictment of a Grand Jury. . . ."

[9]Article 3, sec. 2, cl. 3 of the U.S. Constitution states, "The Trial of all Crimes . . . shall be by Jury. . . ." Jury trial of either a felony or misdemeanor is not jurisdictional but is a privilege which an accused may waive. *Patton v. United States* 281 U.S. 276 (1930).

[10]In a civil suit a fact is established by a preponderance of the evidence, a lesser degree of proof than that required in a criminal case.

Criminal Penalties

An accused may appeal to a higher court if convicted, but a verdict of not guilty ends the case. Because of the constitutional protection against double jeopardy, an acquittal may not be appealed by the prosecution.[11] An individual found guilty of a white-collar crime may be imprisoned or fined, or both. In white-collar criminal cases the penalties are often small and merely symbolic. The only penalties which may be imposed on a guilty corporation are fines and, in certain circumstances, forfeiture of the company's charter. The fine is sometimes a sum that is but a fraction of the illegal gain.

A number of regulatory-type laws provide that in the event of their breach, an administrative agency such as the Food and Drug Administration, or the Federal Trade Commission, may impose a penalty as a deterrent to future violations. A criminal trial is not involved, and the wrongdoer is not considered to have committed a crime. Such laws may also provide that if the wrong is repeated or is willful and deliberate, the wrongdoer is subject to criminal trial and punishment. However, relatively few corporations are prosecuted for white-collar crimes in which the public is the victim. Instead, by civil action, repetition of the wrongful act is enjoined or a noncriminal penalty is imposed. (For an in-depth discussion of administrative law in the United States see Chapter 4.)

ILLUSTRATIVE BUSINESS CRIMES

Quoting from a Report of the House of Representatives on a case involving the Federal Trade Commission Act, Justice Phillips said, "It is impossible to frame definitions which embrace all unfair [business] practices. There is no limit to human inventiveness in this field. Even if all known unfair practices were specifically defined and prohibited, it would be at once necessary to begin over again."[12] One study lists more than sixty different categories of white-collar crimes.[13] The remainder of this chapter will briefly discuss a sampling of such crimes.

Bankruptcy Frauds

The Bankruptcy Reform Act of 1978 furnishes a means whereby an individual or a business entity may be relieved from oppressive debt. (For a discussion of the Bankruptcy Reform Act in depth see Chapter 49.) Such relief requires that a debtor disclose all of his or her assets after filing a voluntary petition in bankruptcy or after an involuntary petition is filed by the debtor's creditors. A trustee takes possession of the assets (less certain statutory exemptions, if applicable) and distributes them among the creditors according to rules set out in the act. Despite the remedial character of the Bankruptcy Reform Act, it furnishes a fruitful opportunity for the commission of white-collar crime.

Concealment or Transfer of Property The two most common bankruptcy crimes are concealment of the debtor's assets and their fraudulent transfer before or after the petition is filed. Assets may be concealed by methods limited only by the ingenuity of the debtor. A common device is the transfer of property to a trusted friend to be held until the proceedings are completed.

False Statements in Proceedings The intentional omission from required property schedules of information that must be disclosed, and the knowing and willful making of a false oath while testifying in the proceedings are criminal offenses.

---

[11]Fifth Amendment to the Constitution. In civil actions either litigant may appeal.

[12]*American Cyanamid Co. v. Federal Trade Comm.*, 363 F.2d 757, (6th Cir. 1966).

[13]Herbert Edelhertz, *The Nature, Impact and Prosecution of White-Collar Crime*, National Institute of Law Enforcement and Criminal Justice, U.S. Department of Justice, 1970, App. A.

False Claims of Creditors   A creditor who files a false claim against a debtor's estate also commits a criminal act.

Planned Bankruptcies   A planned bankruptcy is a swindle (a "scam") using business credit and the Bankruptcy Reform Act as vehicles. This offense has come to be known in some circles as a "bust out." The basic scheme involves setting up (or buying) a business which deals in merchandise that is readily salable, such as television sets, electrical appliances, or jewelry. Merchandise is purchased on credit and paid for immediately. When a good credit rating is established, the scam operators order a large quantity of merchandise on credit, dispose of it at bargain prices for cash as quickly as possible, and close the business. The creditors file an involuntary petition in bankruptcy against the business. Most likely they recover nothing; frequently the wrongdoers have vanished.

Bribery

Bribery of Public Officials   This offense is the effort to influence a public servant to handle an official matter in a way that serves a private interest.[14] Such a private interest may be, for example:

- to thwart official interference with an illicit activity
- to secure a building permit
- to defeat or effect the passage of an ordinance or statute
- to bring about a decision not to prosecute a criminal act

An offer of a gift or favor is a bribe if it is accompanied by a corrupt intent. If such intent is present, the guise under which the offer or payment is made is immaterial. It may be, for

instance, a donation to a police ball or a political contribution. The bribe offered may be anything the receiver considers to be of value. As an example, it may be money; a physical object such as clothing; a price advantage; inside information which might lead to financial gain; or sexual favors. The crime of bribery is committed when the bribe is tendered; acceptance is not necessary, nor need the intended recipient agree to perform the action sought. However, a corrupt intent is not present when a donor makes a gift merely to create a generally congenial business climate not conditioned upon the recipient's performance of any particular official act.

Bribery of Foreign Officials   Bribes, kickbacks, and other forms of gratuitous payments to foreign officials are sometimes made to obtain new business. They have also been made to avert expropriation or nationalization of property, to avoid expulsion of individuals by foreign governments, and to expedite the performance of routine services. Although such payments may be an accepted way of life in some foreign lands, bribery of government officials is contrary to law in virtually all countries.[15] In the course of the 1972 Watergate investigations the magnitude of this practice by American businesses was revealed. Over three hundred United States firms have since disclosed questionable payments. One aircraft company acknowledged payments of more than $30 million to agents of foreign countries. An oil company made payments to officials of six foreign countries; and a fruit importing company saved itself from onerous foreign taxes by under-the-table payment to appropriate officials.

In 1977 the Foreign Corrupt Practices Act was enacted. It provides that the offer to give anything of value to foreign officials to influence an official act for business purposes is illegal. Any company which violates this law is subject

---

[14]18 U.S.C. 201. Most state bribery statutes are to the same effect as this section of the federal Penal Code.

to a fine of up to $1 million. An officer or director of the company, upon conviction, is liable to a fine of no more than $10,000 and imprisonment of not more than 5 years. The fine cannot be paid by the company.

Commercial Bribery Commercial bribery, including kickbacks and payoffs, recognized as a crime in some states, is bribery in which a public official is not involved. In those states where commercial bribery is not a crime, the aggrieved party has recourse only to civil remedies—most commonly injunctions and actions for damages. There is no general federal law proscribing commercial bribery. However, a number of statutes which impose criminal penalties may be applicable.[16]

Among the objectives for which commercial bribes are given are:

- The securing of new business
- Covering up inferior products and services
- Obtaining inside information concerning competing bids

---

[16]The Clayton Act (15 U.S.C. 16); The Robinson-Patman Act (15 U.S.C. 13); The Sherman Antitrust Act (15 U.S.C. 1); The Federal Alcohol Administration Act (27 U.S.C. 21).

- Acquiring proprietary information
- Preventing work stoppages

For example, to gain competitive advantage a business concern may offer to pay an employee of another firm to betray his or her employer. The employee might be induced to commit acts of industrial espionage such as turning over the employer's pricing schedules, customer lists, or other trade secrets. A manager of a liquor store may be bribed by the salesperson for a certain brand of liquor not to carry a competitor's merchandise, or might accept hidden payments for preferred shelf space.

Kickbacks are a form of commercial bribery. For example, X might offer to pay a prime contractor to secure a subcontract, or an employer performing work on a government construction contract might attempt to circumvent the minimum wage laws by inducing employees to kick back a part of their wages. In 1976 two variants of antikickback laws were passed. They make illegal: (1) an attempt to force an employee to make a political contribution under threat of loss of employment and (2) a threat of discharge from employment on account of political affiliation.

Case 8.1   North Carolina v. Brewer
129 S.E.2d 262 (N.C. 1963)

Brewer, the appellant, was an employee or agent of two companies which manufacture signs. He promised to pay a low-level employee (not an official) of the North Carolina State Highway Commission to write specifications for highway signs in such a manner as to favor the products of Brewer's companies. Brewer was indicted, tried, and convicted (with others) of violating North Carolina's commercial bribery statute (G.S. 14-353) and of conspiracy. Brewer appealed.

PARKER, J. . . . Twelve states have statutes prohibiting the general practice of bribery in commercial relationships or influencing agents, employees and servants in commercial relationships, analogous to our statute codified as G.S.

sec. 14-353. . . . In addition to statutes of this general type, there are seventeen states which have made it a crime to bribe a particular type of employee, notably agents or employees in charge of purchasing or hiring. . . .

G.S. sec. 14-353 . . . provides that "any person who gives, offers, or promises to an . . . employee . . . any gift or gratuity whatever *with intent to influence his action in relation to his* . . . *employer's business*" shall be guilty of a misdemeanor. . . . "If a person does the prohibited act or acts specified in this part of the statute with the intent explicitly stated therein, he is guilty of what is commonly called 'commercial bribery.' . . . The vice of conduct labeled 'commercial bribery,' as related to unfair trade practices, is the advantage which one competitor secures over his fellow competitors by his secret and corrupt dealing with employees or agents of prospective purchasers." Surely a violation of this part of G.S. sec. 14-353 is related to unfair trade practices, and is an unfair method of competition. . . .

The second part of the statute provides that "any . . . employee . . . who requests or accepts a gift or gratuity or a promise to make a gift or to do an act beneficial to himself, *under an agreement or with an understanding that he shall act in any particular manner in relation to his* . . . *employer's* . . . *business*" shall be guilty of a misdemeanor. . . . The plain intent and purpose of this part of G.S. sec. 14-353 is to prohibit any . . . employee . . . from being disloyal and unfaithful to his . . . employer. . . . The Holy Bible in the New Testament, St. Matthew, chapter 6, verse 24 (King James Version), says: "No man can serve two masters: for either he will hate the one, and love the other; or else he will hold to the one, and despise the other." A statement of an eternal truth. . . .

The indictment charges the defendants with a violation of the first two parts of G.S. sec. 14-353. . . .

The activities necessary to accomplish the offenses prohibited by G.S. sec. 14-353, and similar statutes, require no violence, . . . and frequently, if not almost entirely, have no witnesses other than persons implicated or potentially implicated. Once completed, they leave few persons, if any, aware of being damaged. The enforcement problems, which arise from the very nature of the offenses, are extremely difficult, because of lack of evidence. This is probably the prime reason why so few persons have been prosecuted for violating these statutes.

In view of the structure of modern business organizations and the demands made upon the individual by present-day business, both the opportunities and the practice of bribing or unlawfully influencing the agents and employees of others seem to be increasing. There is general agreement that where an . . . employee receives money or other considerations from a person in return for the . . . employee's efforts to further that person's interests in business dealings between him and the . . . employer, such an act or acts on the part of the . . . employee and on the part of the person who gives the money or other consideration to the . . . employee should be prohibited. . . .

All the judgments entered against defendant Brewer . . . are affirmed.

Computer Crimes

Computers handle the financial transactions of government and of practically all large business enterprises. Money circulates not physically but in the form of binary digital information. Some computers print out negotiable instruments; many write checks. Confidential information can be extracted from a computer, an account altered, data rearranged, and all evidence of the transaction erased in seconds by anyone with access to the computer and the special knowledge needed to give it the proper commands. The temptation to manipulate a computer for personal gain is heightened by the impersonality of the machine and the difficulty of detection even through careful auditing. These conditions present a challenge to some individuals to employ their wits and technical know-how to "beat the machine," with the possibility of immense reward. Thefts running into millions of dollars have been committed through computer manipulation.

The February 16, 1981, issue of *Time* magazine, in reporting on a multimillion dollar theft from the Wells Fargo Bank in southern California through computer manipulation, said in part, "No one knows exactly how much computer con men are raking in, but the numbers are big. Federal officials say that the average loss in a bank robbery is $3,200. A typical nonelectric embezzlement comes to $23,500. But the average computer fraud is $430,000." The following examples illustrate the array of schemes that have utilized computers for criminal purposes.[17]

• On the counter of his bank a man put a large number of deposit slips bearing the magnetized-ink number of an account he opened in a fictitious name. Customers who had forgotten to bring their own deposit slips innocently used these "counter slips" to make their deposits. Tellers accepted them with money for deposit. The computer, later sorting the slips, disregarded the handwritten names and, on the basis of the magnetized-ink numbers, credited the deposits to the account of the imaginative criminal. In four days his account accumulated sufficient money for him to withdraw $100,000, whereupon he disappeared without a trace.

• An Internal Revenue Service clerk, by computer manipulation, transferred unclaimed tax credits from various accounts through a chain of other accounts and finally to his own.

• An employee in the accounting department of a large company was authorized to round net salaries down to two decimal places. When he did so through the computer, he transferred the tiny remainder amounts to his own salary account. Thus, the total salary payout balanced correctly, and the felon ultimately made off with thousands of dollars.

• A computer operator ingeniously caused a machine to print 200 extra copies of his own paycheck.

• A computer programmer and part of his staff used their firm's computer and expensive computer time to analyze race-horse handicaps, making several thousand dollars each week.

• By reading discarded manuals, a man discovered a utility company's method of sending supplies to its field workers. Then, by telephone, he instructed the corporation's computer to deliver huge supplies of wire, cable, and other equipment to locations he selected. The deliveries were made, and the criminal sold the material.

• Information representing fictitious purchases was fed into a computer which then issued checks to the fictitious vendor, an accomplice of the computer operator.

• The management of a large finance company which controlled both a mutual fund and an insurance company inflated its assets by programming its computer to show ownership of about 56,000 fictitious insurance policies. Their programmed value was some $2 billion. Other

---

[17]Some of the examples are from Stephen W. Leibholz and Louis D. Wilson, *Users' Guide to Computer Crime* (Chilton Book Company, Radnor, Pa., 1974). Copyright © 1974 by Stephen W. Leibholz and Louis D. Wilson. Reprinted by permission of Chilton Book Company.

insurance companies, in legitimate transactions called "reinsurance," purchased many of the fictitious policies. The purchasers relied on computer readouts furnished them to establish the authenticity and current status of the nonexistent policies. Millions of dollars were lost through the far-reaching swindle.

Banks and business executives hesitate to reveal that their computers have been exploited for criminal purposes. Publicizing such information might raise questions concerning the accuracy of *all* their computer readouts. If a wrongdoer is apprehended, the case is usually disposed of by *plea bargain*[18] without trial. Therefore, despite the large monetary losses involved, few cases dealing with computer crimes are reported. Computer crime is a new phenomenon, and the application of the criminal law to it is still in the formative stage.

---

[18]A plea negotiated between the accused and the prosecutor in exchange for an agreed sentence, to be submitted to the court for approval and imposition. Such procedure saves the state the time and expense of trial in return for a light sentence.

Case 8.2   **Ward v. Superior Court, Alameda County, California**
3 Computer Law Service Reptr. 206 (Super. Ct., Cal. 1972)

ISD, a computer company located in Oakland, California, developed a program it called Plot/Trans. The program makes possible a remote plotting service (presenting data by graphs) from the ISD computer and memory bank in Oakland, through an automatic switching arrangement and telephone wires, to customers far from the ISD office. The Plot/Trans Program saves time and eliminates the need to purchase expensive equipment. Using Plot/Trans, ISD provides remote plotting services at a lower cost than its competitors.

The details of the Plot/Trans Program are stored in ISD's computer memory bank. Access to the program is secured only through a special data telephone using three sets of numbers: (1) the unlisted telephone number of the ISD computer; (2) the site code number of an ISD customer; and (3) the customer's billing number.

In January 1971, defendant Ward was an employee of UCC, a competing computer service company, located in Palo Alto, California. Without authority, using a data telephone, he dialed the appropriate numbers and caused the UCC computer to gain access to the ICS computer in Oakland and to make two printouts of the Plot/Trans Program.

An information, in lieu of an indictment, was filed charging Ward with the theft of a trade secret belonging to ISD in violation of California Penal Code sections 487 and 499c. After a preliminary hearing, defendant filed a demurrer, contending the information stated no offense, and moved to dismiss the information.

SPARROW, J. . . . Section 499c(b) of the Penal Code provides "Every person is guilty of theft who, with intent to deprive or withhold from the owner thereof the control of a trade secret . . . does any of the following: (1) Steals . . .

Case 8.2
Continued

any article representing a trade secret. . . . (2) Having unlawfully obtained access to the article, without authority makes . . . a copy of any article representing a trade secret. . . ." Implicit in the definition of "article" . . . is that it must be something *tangible*, even though the trade secret which the article represents may itself be *intangible*. . . . Defendant Ward did not carry any tangible thing representing ISD's Plot/Trans Program from the ISD computer to the UCC computer unless the impulses which defendant allegedly caused to be transmitted over the telephone wire could be said to be tangible. *It is the opinion of the Court that such impulses are not tangible and hence do not constitute an "Article"* within the definition . . . [of] Section 499c. . . .

However, the preliminary transcript does establish probable cause to believe that the defendant Ward . . . did, without authority of ISD, make a copy [of the Program] through use of the UCC computer, . . . a violation of Section 499c(b). . . .

The record establishes that ISD took "measures to prevent [the Program] from becoming available to other than those selected by the owner, ISD, to have access thereto for limited purposes" within the meaning of Section 499c(a)(3). . . . Anyone using the [secret] numbers for the purpose of securing access to the Plot/Trans Program without the authority of the owner would be acting unlawfully within the meaning of Section 499c(b)(3).

The evidence adduced at the preliminary hearing thus established that: (1) The Plot-Trans Program is secret. . . . (2) The Plot/Trans Program was not generally available to the public; (3) Use by ISD of the Plot/Trans Program gave the latter an advantage over competitors including UCC, the employer of the defendant, who did not know of or use the program. . . .

[A] wrongful appropriation of any trade secret, or article representing it, can properly be charged either as (1) a theft of property under Section 487 of the Penal Code . . . or (2) as a violation of Section 499c of the Penal Code. . . .

There is probable cause to believe that offenses under Sections 499c and 487 of the Penal Code were committed and the defendant committed them. Accordingly, the motion to dismiss the Information . . . is denied and the demurrer is overruled.

Consumer Frauds

Consumers are so often the victims of business crimes that a whole series of offenses have come to be known as *consumer frauds*. Increasingly, federal and state laws are enacted to protect consumers from suppliers of goods and services who may take unfair advantage of their customers.[19] Consumer protection divisions have been established in the offices of the Attorneys General and in many District Attorneys' offices. These divisions are helping the public to recognize when consumer frauds are attempted and to guard against them. The following categories of consumer frauds illustrate the problem.

Appliance Service "Rip-offs" An appliance repair service advertises that its prices are "the

---

[19]Among the federal laws are: The Flammable Fabrics Act, 15 U.S.C. 1191 et seq.; The Fair Packaging and Labeling Act of 1966, 15 U.S.C. 1451 et seq.; The Toxic Substances Control Act, 15 U.S.C. 2601 et seq.; and The Debt Collection Practices Act, 15 U.S.C. 1692 et seq. The Uniform Consumer Credit Code (1974) has been proposed for approval by the several states, and has been adopted by some states.

lowest in town." But when the price of repair of an appliance is not agreed upon in advance, the customer may be exorbitantly charged when he or she seeks return of the article. The same "rip-off" may occur with respect to home service calls.

Automobile Sales and Repair Frauds The mileage indicator (odometer) may be rolled back to conceal the extent of the vehicle's prior use.

A dealer may engage in *low-balling,* that is, inducing a customer to sign a contract and make a "good faith" payment to purchase a new vehicle by quoting a lower than Blue Book price. When the car is delivered, the price is raised to cover equipment and extras not ordered by the purchaser. As the buyer has already signed the contract and made a part payment, believing there is no recourse, he or she resignedly accepts the car at the elevated price.

What appear to be good tires on a second-hand car may, in fact, be old, worn tires which have been regrooved.

In commercial garages unnecessary repairs and services may be suggested by mechanics or the customer may be billed for work that was not performed.

Home Improvement Frauds Salespersons for an unscrupulous company may persuade a homeowner to sign a contract for the application of oil to the house roof "to protect it from the elements." In fact, oiling has no useful effect.

A victim may be induced to have the surface of an asphalt driveway oiled. A valueless light coating of old crankcase oil is applied. It is of no benefit to the driveway and soon disappears.

A contractor is paid for performing work on a house and for all the materials that were used in the work. He intentionally fails to pay his materials suppliers, and the latter file liens against the property. The owner must then pay the suppliers to discharge their liens, thereby, in effect, paying twice for the materials.

Merchandising Frauds In addition to such obvious frauds as false or deceptive advertising, merchants sometimes take advantage of the customer in other ways. Seconds may be sold as perfect merchandise; the price tags on "marked down" articles may show an original price much higher than normal. Salespeople may be instructed to "switch" customers from their interest in advertised "bait" items to other articles which return a greater profit to the store.

Particular advantage may be taken of a customer who signs a retail installment contract. The signed contract may have blank spaces which can be filled in later by the seller to his or her personal advantage.

Warranties may be only orally expressed and not included within the written contract; interest charges may be unreasonable; harsh penalties may be imposed in the event of nonpayment of installments by the unwary customer; and undisclosed finance charges may be exorbitant. To protect the public against unconscionable retail installment contracts "Truth in Lending" statutes have been enacted by Congress and by several states.[20] Violation of such a statute would be a business crime.

[20]For example, the Unruh Act, Calif. Civ. Code, sec. 1801; New York Consolidated Laws, chap. 24A, sec. 6-101; Conn. Gen. Laws, 1958, sec. 36-393.

Case 8.3 People v. Block & Kleaver, Inc.
427 N.Y.S.2d 133 (N.Y. 1980)

Block and Kleaver, Inc., the defendant, was in the business of selling bulk beef at retail. It advertised the meat at prices less than the defendant itself had paid for it and less than those charged by two other retail bulk meat businesses. Each customer who responded to the advertisement was shown the sale beef. It was fatty, discolored, and unappetizing. The customer was told that there would be a weight loss averaging about 54 percent to trim the meat for use. The customer was also shown more appetizing and more expensive beef that had been pretrimmed. Employees represented that its weight loss in preparation for use would be only about 10 percent and that a side of beef would last for about 11 months. As a result customers purchased the more expensive beef. However, the average percentage of its waste in 17 purchases was 31 percent and the beef did not last as long as had been represented.

The defendant was charged with violating sections 190.20 and 190.65 of the Penal Law, proscribing misleading advertising and consumer fraud. After a non-jury trial, the defendant was convicted of both offenses. Pertinent parts of the trial court's opinion follows.

MARK, Judge. . . . Section 190.20 of the Penal Law may be construed in conjunction with Section 396 of the General Business Law. . . . Both statutes proscribe the sale promotional practice known as "bait and switch advertising," "bait advertising," or "fictitious bargain claims." . . . This practice consists of advertising a product at a very low price; a pattern of conduct discouraging the purchase of the advertised article by disparaging the same and exhibiting a poor-appearing specimen of the advertised article; and the resulting switch to the purchase of a product costing more than the one advertised. . . .

This is the exact factual predicate in the instant case, as it was in *People v. Glubo* [158 N.E.2d 699 (N.Y. 1959)].

In that case, the defendant advertised via television a sewing machine which cost $45, for the price of $29.50. A customer who responded was visited by a salesman who would undertake to prove the advertised machine inoperable and point out that it was basically defective and inferior. The salesman would then attempt to persuade the customer to order a better machine at a much higher price. . . . The sole claim of falsity was that the defendant had no intention whatever of selling the advertised machine. . . . The People's case rested on the fact that the defendant advertised for sale a sewing machine it did not intend to sell in order to obtain leads so that it might sell the higher-priced machine. The defendant made no false representation concerning the machines they did sell and the sewing machines sold by the defendants were worth the money paid therefor.

The Court of Appeals held that the conduct of the defendant constituted false advertising and that it was properly convicted. . . .

Accordingly, the defendant corporation [Block & Kleaver, Inc.] is found guilty of the crime of False Advertising in violation of Section 190.20. . . .

Defrauding of different people over [an] extended period, using different means and representations may constitute a scheme and it makes no difference that various deceptions are practiced. . . .

The fact that the employees of the defendant corporation over a period of nine months induced 29 customers to purchase pre-trimmed meat by representing the waste percentage of the sale beef at various high percentages, by misrepresenting the estimated loss of the pre-trimmed beef at various low percentages, by erroneously informing customers that they could save money by purchasing pretrimmed beef and by overestimating the length of time the pretrimmed beef would last, indicates that the defendant was engaged in a scheme to defraud. [Section 190.65 of the Penal Law.]

. . . Even the defendant's subjective intent is unimportant if his criminal culpability is based upon reckless indifference to the truth. . . . Included in this category are half truths . . . and statements implying knowledge where there is no knowlege, expressions of opinion when the speaker has no opinion in fact, and promises made without a reasonable basis that they can be fulfilled. . . .

The defendant corporation cannot defend upon the ground that the misrepresentations of its employees were mere seller's talk. . . . The federal courts have constructed two tests for distinguishing fraudulent representations from puffing.

Under the first test, a seller engages in a fraudulent misrepresentation when he actually invents non-existent attributes. . . . False declarations of value constitute fraud because values are facts. . . . Under the second test, the purchaser is entitled to receive a product conforming to his expectation, and he is defrauded if his expectation is not met. . . . When a buyer receives a product not meeting the specifications represented . . . or the value of the product is less than represented . . . he has been defrauded. . . .

Accordingly, the defendant corporation is found guilty of the crime of Scheme to Defraud . . . in violation of Section 190.65(1) of the Penal Law.

False Claims against the Government

The following hypothetical cases illustrate violations of the False Claims Act[21] and indicate the wide range of the statute.

• Company A had a contract with the government to supply engines. The contract specified that all parts should be new and unused. The engines that Company A delivered had bearings of lesser price because they had been reworked to be "as good as new." Company A submitted its invoice to the government according to the original contract terms.

• Company B worked upon two government contracts—one that was for a price agreed upon in advance (called a fixed price contract) and the other for which Company B was to be reimbursed for its costs plus a predetermined profit (called a cost-type contract). Company B altered some of its workers' time cards to show that they

had spent time on the cost contract while, in fact, they had worked on the fixed-price contract. The government was thus billed for labor costs that should have been paid by Company B.

• Company C made a false statement of material matter in an application to the Federal Commodity Credit Corporation for a loan.

• Company D, in collusion with a government purchasing agent, submitted a bill for 200 desks but shipped only 100 desks to the government warehouse.

• Company E falsely claimed that one of its vehicles which had been hit by a post office truck was completely demolished when, in fact, it was only slightly damaged. Company E submitted a claim to the post office service for the full value of the truck.

• Company F endorsed and deposited to its account two government checks, knowing that they were issued by mistake.

---

[21]31 U.S.C. 231; 18 U.S.C. 287.

Both civil and criminal penalties may be imposed for filing a claim against the United States knowing it to be false or fraudulent. By civil action, a wrongdoer may be made to forfeit and pay to the government the sum of $2,000 and, in addition, double the amount of damages the government may have sustained. If found guilty after a criminal trial, the offender may be fined up to $10,000 and imprisoned for up to 5 years, or both.

Akin to the False Claims Act is the False Statements Act. This statute declares that anyone who knowingly and willfully makes a false, fictitious, or fraudulent statement in any matter within the jurisdiction of any department or agency of the government is guilty of a felony. It differs from the False Claims Act primarily in that there is no requirement that the false statement involve a claim for money.

A claim made contrary to the Medicare-Medicaid Antifraud and Abuse Amendments enacted in 1977 may also constitute a business crime.[22] For instance, a person who makes a false statement or representation of material fact concerning the operations of a health care facility in order that it may qualify as a skilled nursing home commits a felony.

Federal Food, Drug, and Cosmetic Act Offenses

The average consumer has no control over the quality of the food or the effectiveness of the drugs or cosmetics he or she buys. To protect the lives and health of people unable to protect

themselves, Congress enacted the Federal Food, Drug and Cosmetic Act.[23] In its published form the act is 149 pages long. Eighteen prohibited classes of activities are described. Among them are misbranding or adulterating a food, drug, medical device or cosmetic; refusing to permit inspection; giving a false guarantee; and the failure of a drug producer to register with the Food and Drug Administration. The statute also lists many circumstances which constitute the unlawful manufacture or sale of foods, drug products, or cosmetics.

The Federal Food, Drug and Cosmetic Act is implemented by a host of regulations of the Food and Drug Administration. Violations of their many provisions are business crimes. A first violation is punishable as a misdemeanor. Should the offender be again convicted of a violation of the law, or if the wrongdoer had the intent to defraud or mislead, the crime is a felony and is punishable as such.

As the Federal Food, Drug and Cosmetic Act is a public health statute, conviction for its violation requires neither proof of conscious fraud nor awareness of wrongdoing. Thus, the president of a grocery chain, made aware by an FDA inspector that one of the company's warehouses was rodent-infested, was properly convicted of a violation of the act as he had knowledge of the condition of the warehouse and the responsibility and authority either to prevent or correct the violation, yet failed to do so.[24]

---

[22]42 U.S.C. 1395g.

[23]21 U.S.C. 321 et seq.
[24]*United States v. Park*, 421 U.S. 658 (1975).

Case 8.4   United States v. Hohensee
243 F.2d 367 (3rd Cir. 1957)

Adolphus Hohensee was the President of Scientific Living, Inc., and the moving spirit in El Rancho Adolphus Products, Inc. Both of these companies, located in Pennsylvania, manufactured and sold health foods. In January, 1952, Hohensee told the proprietor of a health food store in Phoenix, Arizona, that he intended to lecture on health subjects there. He gave the storekeeper leaflets and advertising copy to be distributed to arouse interest in the lectures. He also provided for stocking the store with El Rancho Adolphus brand products. During February and March, 1952, Hohensee gave his lectures and distributed literature dealing with many chronic diseases and physical complaints. As remedies, the literature suggested diets which included large quantities of El Rancho Adolphus products. At the lectures peppermint tea "was recommended for gall stones, colic, flatulence, headache, rheumatism, high blood pressure, arthritis, prostate trouble, lumbago, fits, convulsions, colitis, tuberculosis, asthma, pin worms and tape worms." Similar fantastic representations were made for the curative properties of wheat germ oil and herb laxatives.

From July through September of 1952, Hohensee lectured in Denver, Colorado. There, representations were made concerning the curative powers of El Rancho Adolphus brands of concentrated broth, whole wheat, peppermint tea leaves, and wheat germ.

The directions on the label of the El Rancho Adolphus peppermint tea leaves packet stated only, "Used as a delicious refreshing table beverage. Take one level teaspoon of Adolphus peppermint for each cup of water, steep for four minutes. Do not boil. Sweeten to taste."

Hohensee, who had been previously convicted of a violation of the Federal Food, Drug and Cosmetic Act, and the two corporations, were indicted and convicted of violating section 321 of the Federal Food, Drug and Cosmetic Act. The three appealed.

McLAUGHLIN, J. . . . The Supreme Court [in *Kordel v. United States*, 1948, 335 U.S. 345, 69 S.Ct. 106, 93 L.Ed 52] reaffirmed its position . . . that this legislation [the Federal Food, Drug and Cosmetic Act] be given a liberal interpretation to effectuate its high purpose of protecting unwary consumers in vital matters of health. The intended uses of the products in the present issue as in Kordel were to cure, ameliorate or prevent diseases. The evidence to prove their uses included both graphic materials distributed and testimony of oral representations to users and prospective users. . . . The crime is that the labels on the containers were insufficient for the purposes for which the products were to be used. The statute prohibits the shipment of any products that are to be used as drugs, and are inadequately labeled for that purpose. . . .

. . . It is argued that since the lectures occurred some weeks after the products were introduced into interstate commerce, there was no proof of a medicinal or curative purpose or use of the products at the time of the shipments from Scranton to Phoenix and Denver. . . . The Supreme Court specifically held [in Kodel] that:

"The false and misleading literature in the present case was designed for use in the distribution and sale of the drug, and it was so used. The fact that it went in a different mail was wholly irrelevant whether we judge the transaction by purpose or result. And to say that the prior or subsequent shipment of the literature disproves that it 'is' misbranded when introduced into commerce . . . is to overlook the integrated nature of the transactions established in this case. . . ."

Hohensee insists that the principle that intent is not an element of the offense charged should not have been applied to him since as a second offender, if convicted, he would be subject to felony penalties. His guilt falls into the felony category not because of evil intent but because of the maximum sentence of three years for second offenders provided by Section 333(a) of 21 U.S.C.A. The Act imposes criminal sanctions as a means of regulating activities so dangerous to the public welfare as not to permit of exception for good faith or ignorance. A person acts at his peril in this field. . . .

The judgments of the district court will be affirmed.

Violations of Securities Laws

The laws and regulations governing the issuance, sale, and purchase of stocks, bonds, and other securities are discussed at length in Chapter 45. However, at this point it is important to mention that securities transactions furnish a fertile field for white-collar crime. Such wrongs involve the purchase or sale of securities through the mails or in interstate commerce by means of fraudulent schemes or contrivances, or they may involve the intentional failure to disclose vital information which an average investor would want to know before entering into a securities transaction.

The following are examples of breaches of the securities laws:

• A broker advises a client to purchase a stock in which the brokerage firm has an interest without first advising the purchaser of that fact.

• A highly advertised patent medicine from which its manufacturer makes large profits is discovered to have dangerous side effects. As a result, it is about to be withdrawn from the market. When the withdrawal of the medicine is publicly announced, the company's stock is certain to go down in value. A company director, with that inside information, sells a large block of the company's stock before the public announcement is made.

• Company AB offers to buy a block of the shares of Company CD in order to gain control of CD and merge it into AB. AB makes statements in its tender offer which are only half-truths as to its financial condition.

• An interest in a limited partnership is sold to an investor without disclosing all the risks that the enterprise will face. The investor buys the partnership interest. Later the partnership fails because of the undisclosed risk.

• A corporation management solicits its shareholders to sign proxy statements so that management can vote the stock at a forthcoming shareholders' meeting. The shareholders are not told in the solicitation that a resolution, of which the company has knowledge, will be presented to the meeting by a dissident stockholder to discontinue bonus payments to the firm's officers.

In each of the above situations a white-collar crime may have been committed. Victims of securities offenses, however, usually seek compensation for their losses through recourse to the civil courts.

Monopolies and Antitrust Offenses

Monopolies and agreements in restraint of trade are classic examples of white-collar crimes. The federal statutes designed to discourage such activities are primarily the Sherman Antitrust Act and the Clayton Act, as amended by the Robinson-Patman Act. The Federal Trade Commission also acts in this area of the law. These acts are discussed in Chapters 47 and 48, dealing with antitrust laws. At this point, only their general purposes, as they bear on white-collar crimes, are noted.

The Sherman Antitrust Act This law, enacted in 1890, makes it illegal to engage in any contract or combination in restraint of interstate or foreign commerce or to monopolize or attempt to monopolize any part of interstate trade. The courts apply a rule of reason to these general prohibitions and hold that whether or not a restraint of trade is unreasonable (and therefore illegal) must be measured by its effect upon the particular business or market affected. However, certain restraints of trade are illegal per se and are not subject to a test of reasonableness. For example, representatives of companies A, B, and C, competitors and the leading forces in their industry, meet each year and agree on the prices they will charge their customers. That is *price fixing* and illegal per se. Or it may be that companies A, B, and C agree that A will sell only east of the Mississippi River, B will sell only to the west of the river, and C will not sell in the United States but will have the Mexican and Canadian markets to itself. That is a per se illegal *division of the markets.*

Breach of the prohibitions imposed by the Sherman Antitrust Act is subject to injunction, and persons injured may secure triple damages in a civil action against the wrongdoers. In addition, the act imposes severe criminal penalties for its violation. By a 1974 amendment, a corporation may be fined up to $1 million and an individual $100,000 or imprisoned up to three years, or both.

The Clayton Act As the Sherman Act is cast in only general terms, its scope rests largely on judicial interpretation. To cure its defects, the Clayton Act was enacted in 1914. It prohibits specific classes of trade practices, the effect of which may be to lessen competition or tend to create a monopoly. For example, one may not engage in a lease or sale with the understanding that the lessee or purchaser will refrain from using the goods of a competitor. The act also attacks restraints of trade by prohibiting a corporation engaged in commerce from acquiring (except for investment purposes) the assets or stock of another company where the effect may be substantially to lessen competition or tend to create a monopoly. Certain corporate directors may not serve as directors of competitor concerns, and if corporations desire to merge, a notification is required with a waiting period before the merger can become effective.

The Robinson-Patman Act This act in effect amends the Clayton Act and aims to correct restraints brought about by price discrimination. It provides that a larger discount, rebate, or allowance may not be made to one customer than to another for the same grade or quantity of goods. Articles may not be sold at unreasonably low prices for the purpose of destroying competition. The act also provides that it is unlawful to give any compensation or discount to a customer except for services or facilities in connection with the purchase or sale of merchandise, and if such payment is made to a customer, a payment of like character must be available to all other customers.

It should be noted that the restrictions against price discrimination do not prevent a seller from selecting customers provided the transaction is bona fide and not in restraint of trade. As an example, Company A may, without violating the law, limit the sale of its high-fashion dresses to only the most prestigious shops in a community.

The Federal Trade Commission is charged with preventing unfair methods of competition and unfair or deceptive practices affecting commerce. After a hearing, the Commission may issue a cease-and-desist order directing the termination of the unfair method of competition. Should that order be ignored, a civil penalty may be imposed.

Case 8.5   **United States v. Continental Group, Inc.**
456 F.Supp. 704 (D.C. Pa. 1978)

Continental Group, Inc., and ten other companies and individuals (the defendants) were competitors engaged in manufacturing consumer paper bags. Such bags, usually made according to customers' specifications, are used for packaging a variety of products—among them pet foods, cookies, coffee, chemicals, and agricultural products. From about 1951 until 1976 the defendants periodically met, discussed, and agreed upon the prices to be charged for consumer paper bags and for the various components involved in their manufacture. Approximately twice a year there were agreed increases in prices. From time to time there were increases in the prices of individual components. Other manufacturers who entered the consumer bag industry were invited to use the price lists agreed upon at the meetings. The parties frequently verified over the telephone the prices they were quoting to their customers to be certain that identical prices were quoted for similar specifications. None of the defendants increased prices on consumer bags without first consulting its competitors. The several competitors monitored the actions of the others by exchanging copies of their price-list changes.

In 1976 the parties were charged in a one-count indictment with having engaged in a continuing combination and conspiracy in unreasonable restraint of trade in violation of the Sherman Antitrust Act. Of the eleven defendants, two pleaded nolo contendere; four were convicted; and five were acquitted. The four convicted filed motions for judgment of acquittal, new trial, and in arrest of judgment.

BECHTLE, C.J. [Portions of the opinion dealing with pleading, charges, and procedural matters are omitted]. . . . [T]o sustain a conviction for a violation of Sec. 1 of the Sherman Act, as amended December 21, 1974, the Government was required to prove: (1) that there existed a conspiracy as charged in the indictment, that the conspiracy was knowingly formed and that the defendants knowingly participated in [it] . . . ; (2) that the conspiracy unreasonably restrained trade; (3) that the restraint was on interstate trade and commerce. . . .

The third element . . . that the restraint was on interstate commerce was stipulated by the parties. . . . To establish that a conspiracy existed, the Government was not required to prove any overt act other than the act of conspiracy. . . . Nor was the Government required to prove any express, informal agreement, by words spoken or written, or simultaneous action. . . . Nor was the Government required to prove that the means to accomplish the unlawful objective were in themselves unlawful.

. . . [T]he Government [was required] to demonstrate that the overall objects, aims or goals of the conspiracy were consciously agreed to and that the defendants knowingly participated in the agreement or conspiracy to achieve the agreed goals. . . . The element of intent that the Government was required to prove was that the defendants acted knowingly in forming and participating in the conspiracy. Proof of specific intent to violate the Sherman Act is not required, for if a defendant charged with a violation of the Sherman Act is found by the jury to have acted knowingly, then that defendant is held to have intended the necessary and direct consequence of his acts, i.e., the resulting unreasonable restraint on trade. . . .

Neither the December 21, 1974, amendment of Sec. 1 of the Sherman Act which increased the penalty for its violation to imprisonment for three years, or the recent decision of the United States Supreme Court in *United States v. United States Gypsum Co.*, 550 F.2d 115 (3d Cir. 1977) Aff'd, [438U.S.422], 57 L.Ed 2d 854 (1978), altered or amended this requirement that the Government prove that the defendants acted knowingly rather than with specific intent. . . .

. . . Congress' December 21, 1974 amendment of Sec. 1 of the Sherman Act altered only the penalty but did not, either explicitly or implicitly . . . alter the substantive elements of the offense.

The second element which the Government was required to prove to support the defendants' convictions . . . was that the conspiracy in which the defendant knowingly participated unreasonably restrained trade and commerce. It is hornbook law, however, that a conspiracy to fix, maintain and stabilize the prices and the terms and conditions of sale is a *per se* violation of the Sherman Act and, thus, the unreasonableness of the restraint is conclusively presumed. . . .

. . . [The] defense theory was . . . that the prices charged by the defendants for consumer bags, although fixed by the conspiracy and not by free market forces, were reasonable prices and, therefore . . . conspiring to fix those prices did not violate Sec. 1 of the Sherman Act . . . based upon [the] . . . belief that specific intent and conduct in unreasonable restraint of trade were essential elements of a Sec. 1 felony charge. [T]hat theory was clearly erroneous. . . .

The [several] motions . . . will be denied.

Theft and Embezzlement

Any consideration of business crimes must recognize that they are not solely entrepreneurial activities. Theft and embezzlement by employees from their employers are also white-collar crimes. A salesperson charges a friend only $2 for a shirt marked $10. Another salesperson overcharges a customer and pockets the overage. Expense accounts are inflated. Shipping clerks steal racks of clothes and sides of beef. It is said that in many businesses internal theft of cash, stock certificates, tools, spare parts, office supplies, and other materials is their most pressing problem. Most of these activities are carried on by people with no criminal records. Detection is difficult, and criminal prosecution —when it is undertaken—furnishes but slight deterrence to others. Yet the losses from this type of white-collar crime are greater than the nationwide robbery and burglary losses combined.[25] Such business crimes have a great financial impact on the economy of the country, as commercial enterprises include such losses in the overhead charges which they pass on to their customers.

---

[25]Mark Lipman, *Stealing—How America's Employees Are Stealing Their Companies Blind*, Harper's Magazine Press, New York, 1973, p. xvi.

SUMMARY

Although there is no generally accepted definition of business, or white-collar, crime, certain nonviolent offenses are so closely related to the conduct of business that they have come to be called by those names. They usually involve fraud or misrepresentation, committed either by or against a business entity for financial gain. In the United States business crimes cause losses of the order of $40 billion each year, and they tend to breed distrust between all segments of society.

Criminal law is concerned with the punishment of violators of public law; civil law deals with disputes between private parties. A criminal prosecution is brought in the name of the state or of the federal government, not in the name of the victim, as in a civil suit. An individual may be liable to criminal prosecution and to a civil suit for damages, both arising from a single wrongful act.

Following a grand jury indictment (or an information by a prosecuting attorney) in a criminal case, an accused is required to plead either guilty, not guilty, or nolo contendere. The latter is tantamount to a plea of guilty but is not an admission of guilt. Defendants, particularly corporations, charged with business crimes, often take advantage of the plea of nolo contendere since a guilty plea or conviction following a plea of not guilty may be used as evidence against the defendant in a subsequent civil suit. If a criminal trial results in a verdict of not guilty, the case ends and the state may not appeal. In a civil suit either litigant may appeal to a higher court.

A crime may be either a felony or a misdemeanor, depending upon the degree of punishment which may be imposed.

A business crime, depending upon the facts, may be either a felony or misdemeanor and may involve a blameworthy intent or be merely a transgression of a regulatory law without such an intent. A corporation may be found guilty of a criminal act requiring proof of intent by imputing to the corporation the intent of the actual wrongdoers who acted in its behalf.

Fine or imprisonment, or both, may be imposed upon a person found guilty of a business, or white-collar, crime. A corporation is subject only to a fine or, in certain instances, forfeiture of charter.

Business crimes are acts which evade the standards established by law pursuant to which business should be conducted. Among the many categories of business crimes are: (1) Bankruptcy frauds; (2) bribery of public officials or officials of foreign lands, and commercial bribery; (3) computer-related crimes; (4) frauds against consumers; (5) false claims against the government; (6) Federal Food, Drug and Cosmetic Act violations; (7) securities laws violations; (8) monopoly and antitrust offenses; and (9) theft and embezzlement by employees against business enterprises.

STUDY AND DISCUSSION QUESTIONS

1 (*a*) What is a business crime? A white-collar crime? (*b*) Why have these names been given to this facet of the law?

2 How do business crimes differ from other crimes, such as robbery?

3 What relation do such offenses have to business law? Explain.

4 (*a*) Can a business be the victim of a white-collar crime? (*b*) Give examples.

5 (*a*) Do business crimes have any effect on the public at large? How? (*b*) On business activities? In what way? (*c*) Why should the public be concerned about such offenses?

6 If an individual is subject to a penalty in a civil court, can that person also be found guilty of a crime arising out of the same facts? Explain.

7 (*a*) What names are given to categories of

crime according to their severity? *(b)* What determines into which category each falls? *(c)* Into what category would you place business crimes?

8 *(a)* What is the difference between a plea of guilty and a plea of nolo contendere? *(b)* Why is a plea of nolo contendere often used when an accused is charged with the commission of a white-collar crime?

9 Give at least three illustrations of how criminal prosecutions differ from civil suits.

10 Distinguish between *malum in se* and *malum prohibitum* offenses.

11 *(a)* What circumstances must be present before an act can be characterized as criminal? *(b)* How are these elements proven?

12 *(a)* Is the degree of proof necessary to establish the existence of a fact in a civil suit the same as that required to establish the existence of criminal intent in a criminal action? *(b)* What degree of proof is necessary in each?

13 *(a)* Under what legal theory can a corporation be guilty of a criminal offense which requires proof of a specific intent? *(b)* How is a corporation punished if found guilty of a white-collar crime?

14 Is there any distinction between the right to appeal a judgment in a civil suit and to appeal a verdict in a criminal prosecution? Explain.

15 Describe three white-collar crimes which may be committed in conjunction with a bankruptcy proceeding.

16 *(a)* Distinguish between bribery and commercial bribery. *(b)* Who is the victim when the offense of bribery is committed? When the offense is *commercial* bribery?

17 *(a)* Explain how a computer can be the instrument of a criminal act. *(b)* Why would you consider this type of business crime important?

18 *(a)* What is a consumer fraud? *(b)* Explain four different types of consumer frauds.

19 Distinguish between a false claim against the government and a false statement on a government form.

20 Why should a violation of the Federal Food, Drug and Cosmetic Act be considered a white-collar crime? Give examples of this type of violation.

21 Assume that an employee of a cookie manufacturing company adulterates the cookie dough. Can an officer of the company who did not participate in, or order an adulteration, be guilty of violating the Federal Food, Drug and Cosmetic Act? Explain.

22 Companies A and B are potential competitors. Both have the technology and capacity to manufacture large and small duplicating machines. They agree that Company A will manufacture and sell only large machines and that B will make and sell only small ones. They do not agree on the prices that each will charge for its products. Does such an agreement violate any laws? Discuss.

23 Why should a theft by an employee from an employer be considered a white-collar crime?

24 Describe three white-collar crimes other than those mentioned in these questions.

25 Why do many white-collar crimes go unprosecuted? Discuss.

PART THREE

CONTRACTS

Chapter 15

Illegal Agreements

Chapter 16

A Writing as a Requirement;
The Parol Evidence Rule

Chapter 17

Rights and Duties of Third Persons

Chapter 18

Performance
and Other Discharge of Contracts;
Remedies for Breach of Contract

Chapter 19

Contracting with the Government

Chapter

9

Introduction to
the Law of Contracts

The contract is one of the most important legal devices ever developed in the quest for economic security and a stable society. Individuals enter into contracts when, for example, they buy a home, visit the dentist, or buy an automobile on the installment plan. Business firms enter into contracts with suppliers of raw materials and parts; with banks, utility companies, and other service institutions; and with employees, investors, and customers. Although governments have considerable power to command obedience, much of their work is accomplished by means of contracts entered into voluntarily. Contracts constitute "binding arrangements for the future," and it is largely by means of such arrangements that the processes of production, exchange, and distribution are carried on in a free enterprise economy.

Freedom of individuals and organizations to contract as they think best is one of the basic elements of a free enterprise system. However, freedom of contract is not absolute. Courts and legislatures alike curtail freedom of contract when in their view the public good so requires.

They are especially likely to control contract provisions where there is considerable inequality of bargaining power between the parties involved, as, for example, there often is between adults and minors, creditors and borrowers, sellers and consumers. As our study of contract law proceeds, we shall encounter numerous examples of limitations on freedom of contract.

NATURE AND IMPORTANCE
OF CONTRACT LAW

Contract law is a body of rules regarding the formation, avoidance, discharge, and enforcement of contracts. A major purpose of contract law is to assure that contracts properly formed are binding on and enforceable by the parties. To carry out this purpose, the law provides procedures by which an aggrieved party can force compliance with the terms of a binding contract or can obtain damages when there is lack of compliance.

167

Contract law is worth attention not only because it governs contractual arrangements but also because it is basic to other areas of law. Much of the law governing sales of goods, commercial paper ("negotiable instruments"), agency, partnerships, corporations, landlord and tenant, and so on is but the application to specialized situations of general contract principles. An understanding of the concepts, principles, and technical vocabulary presented in the chapters on contracts will be helpful in understanding other areas of business law.

NATURE OF CONTRACTS

Meaning of Contract

The commonly accepted definitions of contract are broad. The *Restatement of the Law of Contracts* gives the following definition: "A contract is a promise or a set of promises for the breach of which the law gives a remedy, or the performance of which the law in some way recognizes as a duty."[1] More simply stated, a *contract* is a set of promises that the courts will enforce.

Contracting involves the making of promises, but not all promises are contractual. In response to social situations, people often promise to attend social events but then fail to do so. The failure to attend will not result in legal liability even though the host might have incurred expenses in preparing for the occasion. Any remedy for the broken social promise is to be found in social or moral sanctions against such conduct, and not in the law. The law tends to avoid regulating purely social, private, interpersonal relations.

The widespread breach of business or commercial promises, on the other hand, can create serious economic instability. To reduce economic uncertainty and to protect a party's reasonable expectations, the law makes certain kinds of commercial promises legally enforceable.

Meaning of Promise

Promises are a vital part of contracting, and therefore it is necessary to consider the legal meaning of promise. The *Restatement* defines *promise* as "a manifestation of intention to act or to refrain from acting in a specified way, so made as to justify a promisee in understanding that a commitment has been made."[2] The party who makes a promise is called the "promisor." The one to whom the promise is made is called the "promisee." The *Restatement* definition stresses the expectations of the promisee and the need for stability. A fundamental part of a free enterprise system is the ability to make long-range plans and enforceable commitments.

In communicating a promise, the manifestation of intention may be expressed either in language or in conduct. For example, at an auction, a promise to pay may be inferred from the bidder's act of raising a hand or a card. This is so regardless of any secret intention of the bidder not to pay. In dealing with others, people are usually entitled to rely on external manifestations of intention and are not bound by contrary internal intentions.

When expressed in language, the manifestation need not include the word "promise." Expressions such as "I will pay," "I hereby offer to pay," and "It is understood that I am to pay" are promises to pay. Conversely, the use of the word "promise" does not always express the commitment required for a contract. A person makes no commitment by saying, "I promise to buy from you all the lumber I may care to order during the coming year." Such seeming promis-

---

[1] *Restatement of the Law (Second) Contracts,* The American Law Institute, Philadelphia, 1973, sec. 1. Copyright©1973 by The American Law Institute. Quotations from and comments to the *Restatement* are reprinted with the permission of The American Law Institute. See Chap. 2, p. 28, for explanation and history of the *Restatement.*

[2] *Restatement (Second) Contracts,* sec. 2(1).

es are called "illusory promises." They do not justify a promisee in believing a firm commitment has been made.

Requirements for a Bargained Contract

The usual objective of contracting parties is a bargained-for exchange: money for goods, services for money, goods for services, and so on. Thus, ordinarily a contract involves a transaction in which one person renders a performance or makes a promise in exchange for a return performance or promise.

When a contract takes the usual form of a bargained-for exchange, it must meet the following requirements:

• There must be an agreement, that is, a manifestation of mutual assent reached through offer and acceptance.

• The promise or promises must be supported by consideration.

• There must be two or more competent parties; that is, parties having legal capacity to contract in relation to the subject matter of the agreement.

• The agreement must have a "legal objective"; that is, the agreement must be one that is not void by statute or by rule of common law.

The requirements listed above may be referred to briefly as (1) offer; (2) acceptance; (3) consideration; (4) contractual capacity; and (5) a legal objective. For certain types of contracts there is another requirement: a writing or a legally acceptable substitute. Each of these requirements is discussed in detail in the following chapters.

Some contracts which may appear to meet these requirements are not enforceable. A party may enter into an agreement because of fear, unfair persuasion, or deception by the other party. One party, or both parties, may be laboring under a mistake as to an important fact which affects the bargaining process. Chapter 13 is devoted to a discussion of avoidance of contract when there is no true mutual assent.

Contracts of Adhesion

A traditional assumption underlying contract law is that each of the opposing parties to a contract has sufficient bargaining power that one party cannot take undue advantage of the other. In many situations involving contracts, the negotiating parties are so well matched in terms of bargaining power that each party can look out for his or her own interests. Often, however, one party, usually the borrower or buyer, has no meaningful choice with regard to some or all the terms of the contract. These terms are usually embodied in a "standard-form" contract, called a "contract of adhesion," or "adhesion contract." Rather than permit the form to be varied, the firm (or industry) imposing it will simply not deal with anyone who will not accept its terms. Most contracts for consumer goods, insurance, mortgages, automobiles, and a host of other goods and services are contracts of adhesion. Such contracts usually are enforced despite the weaker party's lack of consent to some (or most) terms.

The efficiencies attending standard-form contracts justify their usage. Many businesses and industries could not function if the terms of each transaction had to be negotiated individually. Transaction costs for inexpensive goods and services could become prohibitive; the insurance industry, which must be able to limit and calculate risk, would be unable to do so if insurance contracts were freely bargainable. Yet, people upon whom contracts of adhesion are imposed are vulnerable to exploitation. Most consumers sign standard-form contracts without reading all the provisions. Often important terms are in small print or on the back of the form. Because of the lack of the bargain element and true mutual assent in adhesion contracts, some provisions of such contracts may be unenforceable. Chapter 15 contains a discussion of adhesion contracts and points out that if a provision of the contract is oppressive, the court will strike down that provision as being unconscionable or contrary to public policy.

CLASSIFICATION OF CONTRACTS

The study and discussion of contract law often involves reference to different kinds of contracts. The following paragraphs describe some common types of contracts and some of their characteristics. A given contract may fit into more than one category, because contracts may be classified on various bases.

Formal and Informal Contracts

A *formal* contract is one to which the law gives special effect because of the form used in creating it. At common law, a written promise or contract to which the promisor's seal was attached was enforceable because the sealed document complied with the formalities prescribed by law, and not because there was any exchange or bargain. In many states the legal effect of a seal has been modified or abolished.

A negotiable instrument such as a check is a formal contract because to create a negotiable instrument, a person must use a particular form or style of language. A negotiable instrument has legal characteristics which differ from those of ordinary contracts. For example, a negotiable instrument is freely transferable and is used as a substitute for money. (Negotiable instruments are discussed in Chapters 30 to 35.)

Informal contracts are those for which the law does not require a particular set of formalities. The requirements listed above for a contract must be met, but the parties to an informal (ordinary) contract may use any style of language they please and the contract may be oral, in the absence of a special statute. Informal contracts are sometimes called "simple" contracts, although they may in fact be very complicated. Most contracts we enter into are informal.

Unilateral and Bilateral Contracts

A *unilateral* contract is one in which only one party makes a promise. "I'll pay you $5 if you mow my lawn" is an offer for a unilateral contract. It can be accepted by the promisee's mowing the lawn. In contrast, a *bilateral* contract is one in which both parties make promises. The statement "I'll pay you $5 to mow my lawn. Will you mow it tomorrow for that price?" is an offer for a bilateral contract because the promisor wants a return promise.

Executory and Executed Contracts

Suppose that Omar says to Mary, "I'll pay you $5 to mow my lawn. Will you mow it tomorrow?" and Mary says "Yes." Omar and Mary have entered into a bilateral contract. However, the contract is *executory* because neither party to it has rendered the promised performance. There are two types of *executed* contracts: partially executed and fully executed. If Mary mows the lawn and Omar pays the $5, the contract is *fully executed* (performed). If Mary mows the lawn but Omar fails to pay, the contract is *partially executed*. The contract could also be said to be *partially executory*, since one party has performed but the other has not.

Express and Implied Contracts

An *express* contract is one in which the terms of the contract are stated in words, either written or spoken. An *implied* contract (sometimes called "implied-in-fact") is one in which the terms of the contract are wholly or partly inferred from conduct or from surrounding circumstances. When Jane, on passing a market where she has an account, picks up a bag of oranges marked "98 cents," holds up the bag, and waits until the clerk nods, a promise to pay 98 cents is implied by the conduct of the parties. In legal effect there is no difference between an express and an implied contract. They differ merely in the manner in which assent is manifested.

QUASI CONTRACTS

Nature of Quasi Contracts

Quasi contracts (sometimes called "implied-in-law" contracts) are not contracts at all; they are obligations imposed by law to prevent unjust enrichment of one person at another's expense. The obligation is created by law, not by mutual assent, and in fact is often imposed contrary to one's wishes. In order to recover in a lawsuit for quasi contract the plaintiff must prove four elements: (1) the plaintiff conferred a benefit on the defendant; (2) the plaintiff expected to be paid for the benefit; (3) the plaintiff was not an intermeddler; and (4) to allow the defendant to retain the benefit conferred without compensating the plaintiff would result in unjust enrichment.

Recovery under Quasi Contract

Quasi-contract recovery is available in a wide variety of situations. Two parties may negotiate a contract which turns out to be unenforceable for one or more reasons. If one party has begun performance and conferred a benefit on the other party, it would be unjust to allow retention of the benefits without compensation. There are occasions when one person will confer benefits on another by mistake. For example, suppose Ben pays Alice, whom he mistakes for his creditor, Carla. Retention of the money by Alice would constitute unjust enrichment. To prevent this result, the law allows debtor Ben to recover payment under quasi-contractual principles. Another situation where quasi contract would apply is one involving emergency care. For example, suppose a physician comes upon an unconscious person lying on a roadside and renders emergency medical services. The physician would be entitled to recover in quasi contract.

The amount of recovery in quasi contract is the reasonable value of services rendered or property expended (money or goods). Thus, the physician above is entitled to the customary rate in the community for the emergency procedures performed.

There are situations where quasi-contract recovery is denied by the courts although the defendant receives a benefit. If the plaintiff did not reasonably expect to be paid for the services or property, the court will deny recovery. For example, a physician who treats a member of his immediate family ordinarily would not be allowed quasi-contract recovery for services rendered. An intermeddler, one who tried to force benefits upon another, would not be allowed quasi-contract recovery. For example, suppose an owner leaves his or her car at a service station for an oil change. When the owner returns, the service station operator states that the car has been given a tune up. The operator would not be allowed to recover in quasi contract for the benefits conferred.

Case 9.1   **Nursing Care Services, Inc. v. Dobos**
                380 So. 2d 516 (Fla. App. 1980)

Mary Dobos (defendant) was admitted to Boca Raton Community Hospital. Her condition was serious and her doctor ordered around-the-clock nursing care. The hospital called upon the plaintiff to provide individualized nursing services. Mrs. Dobos received nursing care in the hospital and, following her release, received two weeks of at-home care. She refused to pay plaintiff for the services, arguing that she never signed a written contract nor orally agreed to be liable.

Testifying about the in-hospital care, she said, "Dr. Rosen did all the work. I don't know what he done, and he says, I needed a nurse." After her release Mrs. Dobos was alert and aware of the nurses. She never tried to fire them and said, "I thought that Medicare would take care of it, or whatever." After a non-jury trial the court denied quasi-contract recovery to plaintiff saying, ". . . There certainly was a service rendered, but . . . I don't think there is sufficient communications and dealings with Mrs. Dobos to make sure that she knew that she would be responsible for those services rendered. . . ." Plaintiff appealed.

HURLEY, J. . . . Contracts implied in law, or as they are more commonly called "quasi contracts," are obligations imposed by law on grounds of justice and equity. Their purpose is to prevent unjust enrichment. Unlike express contracts or contracts implied in fact, quasi contracts do not rest upon the assent of the contracting parties. . . . One of the most common areas in which recovery on a contract implied in law is allowed is that of work performed or services rendered. The rationale is that the defendant would be unjustly enriched at the expense of the plaintiff if she were allowed to escape payment for services rendered or work performed. There is, however, an important limitation. Ordinarily liability is imposed to pay for services rendered by another only when the person for whose benefit they were rendered requested the services or knowingly and voluntarily accepted their benefits. [Citations.]

The law's concern that needless services not be foisted upon the unsuspecting has led to the formulation of the "officious intermeddler doctrine." It holds that where a person performs labor for another without the latter's request or implied consent, however beneficial such labor may be, he cannot recover therefor. A notable exception to this rule, however, is that of emergency aid:

> A person who has supplied things or services to another, although acting without the other's knowledge or consent, is entitled to restitution therefor from the other if he acted unofficiously and with intent to charge therefor, and the things or services were necessary to prevent the other from suffering serious bodily harm or pain, and the person supplying them had no reason to know that the other would not consent to receiving them, if mentally competent, and it was impossible for the other to give consent or, because of extreme youth or mental impairment, the other's consent would have been immaterial. 66 Am. Jur. 2d, Restitution and Implied Contract, § 23.

In the case at bar it is unclear whether Mrs. Dobos, during the period of in-hospital care, understood or intended that compensation be paid. Her condition was grave. She had been placed in the hospital's intensive care unit and thereafter had tubes and other medical equipment attached to her body which necessitated special attention. She was alone, unable to cope and without family assistance. It is worthy of note that at no point during the litigation was there any question as to the propriety of the professional judgment that the patient required special nursing care. To the contrary, the record demonstrates that the in-hospital nursing care was essential to Mrs. Dobos' health and safety. Given these circumstances it would be unconscionable to deny the plaintiff recovery for services which fall squarely within the emergency aid exception.

. . . It is unquestioned that during the at-home recuperation, Mrs. Dobos was fully aware of her circumstances and readily accepted the benefits conferred. Given such facts, we believe the rule set down in *Symon v. J. Rolfe Davis, Inc.,* 245 So.2d 278, 279 (Fla. 4th DCA 1971) must govern:

> It is well settled that where services are rendered by one person for another which are knowingly and voluntarily accepted, the law presumes that such services are given and received in expectation of being paid for, and will imply a promise to pay what they are reasonably worth.

A patient's unannounced misconception that the cost of accepted services will be paid by an insurer or Medicare does not absolve her of responsibility to bear the cost of the services. . . . Accordingly, we remand the cause to the trial court with instructions to enter an amended final judgment for the plaintiff in the sum of $3,723.90 plus interest and court costs.

It is so ordered.

SUMMARY

By means of contracts, individuals and organizations make binding arrangements for the future. Freedom of people to contract as they think best is one of the basic elements of a free enterprise system, but courts and legislatures curtail freedom of contract when they think the public good so requires.

Contract law is a body of rules and procedures regarding the formation, avoidance, discharge, and enforcement of contracts. A major purpose of contract law is to assure that contracts properly formed are binding on and enforceable by the parties.

Most people think of a contract as a bargained-for exchange. The requirements for a contract are: an agreement or mutual assent, reached through offer and acceptance; consideration to support the promise or promises; two or more parties having legal capacity to contract; and a legal objective. For certain kinds of

contracts, a writing or a legally acceptable substitute is also required.

Much of the discussion of contracts in this book presupposes parties of roughly equivalent bargaining power who, because they possess it, can fend for themselves when negotiating a contract. However, there is a vast number of contracts, called "contracts of adhesion," in which one of the parties has no meaningful choice with regard to some or all terms of the contract. Contracts of adhesion serve legitimate economic functions and are usually enforced despite the weaker party's inability to bargain some of the terms. Yet, people upon whom contracts of adhesion are imposed are vulnerable to exploitation and are therefore given protection by the law.

There are various types of contracts, the significance of which will become more apparent in later chapters of this book. Quasi contracts are not contracts at all. They are obligations imposed by law to prevent unjust enrichment of one person at another person's expense.

STUDY AND DISCUSSION QUESTIONS

1   (*a*) Why is the contract of great importance to individuals and to business firms? To a free enterprise economy? (*b*) Give examples of situations in which restrictions of freedom of contract might be necessary.

2   What is a major purpose of contract law?

3   John Doe's Aunt Martha invited John to a family reunion, promising to serve an expensive tropical fruit which was John's favorite. John promised to attend but did not arrive. Aunt Martha sued John for breach of contract. Was there a contract? Explain.

4   (*a*) Explain the meaning of "promise" as used in the law of contracts. (*b*) Define promisor. (*c*) Define promisee. (*d*) Give an example of a promise expressed by conduct.

5   What requirements must a bargained-for exchange ordinarily meet in order to constitute a contract?

6   What is a contract of adhesion?

7   On September 1, Seller and Buyer signed a written agreement which provides that Seller is to deliver certain specified merchandise on September 20 and that Buyer is to pay the specified price on or before October 10. Seller delivers the merchandise as promised. It is October 5 and Buyer has not yet paid for it. Is the contract: (*a*) Formal or informal? (*b*) Bilateral or unilateral? (*c*) Executory or executed? (*d*) Express or implied? Justify each answer.

8   (*a*) Quasi contracts are not contracts at all. Explain. (*b*) What is the underlying purpose of the law of quasi contracts? (*c*) Give examples of situations where quasi-contract principles would apply. (*d*) List the four elements required for quasi-contractual recovery.

Chapter

10
Offer

As stated in Chapter 9, the first requirement for a bargained contract is that there must be an agreement, that is, a manifestation of mutual assent, reached through offer and acceptance. *Manifestation of mutual assent* involves an outward expression of agreement by words or acts. The test is not what a person intends to convey but what his or her words and acts, reasonably interpreted, do convey.

Agreement is normally reached by a process in which one person, the "offeror," makes an offer to another person, the "offeree." The offeree may accept the offer as presented, or may make a counterproposal. Often the parties dicker back and forth over the terms of the proposed contract before reaching final agreement. Thus, there may be a series of "counteroffers" or "conditional acceptances" submitted by both parties. The present chapter deals with offer and counteroffer; the following chapter deals with acceptance.

NATURE OF OFFER

Meaning of Offer
An *offer* is a statement or other conduct by which the offeror confers upon the offeree a legal power to accept the offer and thereby to create a contract. What kind of statement or other conduct is sufficient to constitute an offer? Usually an offer does two things:

1 It expresses or implies a promise by the offeror to render some proposed performance—to do or refrain from doing some stated thing.

2 It requests from the offeree a return promise of performance, or an act.

Offers Distinguished from Other Kinds of Statements
When a person makes a promise, he or she makes a proposal of conduct. Two frequently

175

recurring types of statements which are not proposals of conduct—and which must therefore be distinguished from offers—are statements of ·present intention and negotiatory statements.

Statements of Present Intention   An offer requires a promise (express or implied) from the offeror. Suppose that A says to B, "I am going to sell my camera for $100," and B replies, "I'll take it; here's the $100." Is there a contract? No, because a reasonable person would conclude that A's statement was not a promise. It was nothing more than a statement of fact. Reasonably interpreted, the statement means: "It is my present intention to make an offer at some time in the future."

Negotiatory Statements   Statements which are not in themselves proposals of conduct (promises) but are preliminary thereto are called *negotiatory statements* to distinguish them from offers. Negotiatory statements are used for a variety of purposes—for example, to sound out the other party before making an offer, to maneuver him or her into making the first commitment, or to invite bids—in order to secure the best possible selling or purchasing price. Sometimes negotiations are used for purely exploratory purposes rather than for laying the foundation for an immediately forthcoming offer. Specifications, quantities, prices, discounts, credit terms, delivery dates, and return privileges may have to be explored mutually to determine whether there is even the possibility of a transaction.

Circulars, catalogs, newspaper advertisements, posters, price display cards, and price tags, are usually mere invitations to submit offers. There are at least three reasons why such items usually are not offers: (1) Ordinarily, the items do not contain words of promise. (2) These items are addressed to the public and, if considered to be offers, the number of people who accept could exceed the quantity of goods for sale. (3) It is believed that the sellers ought to be able to choose those with whom they wish to

contract. However, suppose that a newspaper advertisement reads, "To the first ten customers taking advantage of this offer we will sell a Model X Sure-View Television for $199.50 cash." A court would probably have no difficulty in concluding that the advertisement was an offer, since it has three features ordinarily lacking in advertisements for the sale of goods: (1) It professes to be an offer ("this offer"). This feature by itself is of little significance, but when considered in connection with other features of the advertisement, the word "offer" assumes added significance. (2) The advertisement contains promissory language ("we will sell"). (3) The advertisement specifies a quantity ("ten").

Business people sometimes fail to indicate clearly whether they are making an offer or merely laying the groundwork for one. Failure to make the intention clear invites costly litigation and gives the courts the difficult task of ascertaining the intention as a reasonable person would construe it.

In deciding such controversies, the courts will of course consider the language used. But words of themselves are not determinative. Thus, "We quote you a price of $4.50" usually means no more than a willingness to consider an offer to buy at $4.50; but under certain circumstances "quote" may constitute an offer to sell at the quoted price, as in the well-known Fairmount Glass Works case (see Case 10.1 below).

When a court must decide whether a particular proposal was an offer or merely a preliminary negotiation, the court will consider not only the language used but also the surrounding circumstances. Examples of questions which the court might consider:

• *Was the proposal addressed to an individual (or business firm) or to an indefinite group of individuals?* A communication addressed to a group is less likely to be an offer than is one addressed to an individual. It is for this reason that circular letters, advertisements, and other fliers are usually interpreted as being invitations for an offer. Included in this category are advertisements soliciting bids from contractors or subcontractors. No offer is made by the one who advertises because no promise is made to award a contract to any particular person, such as the low bidder. However, notices of reward, although addressed to the public, usually contain an express or implied promise to pay money and are held to be offers.

• *Did the addressee, if an individual, and the sender of the communication have prior business dealings?* A proposal made by a person who has had prior business dealings with the addressee is more likely to be interpreted as an offer than is a proposal made by a stranger.

• *Was there any local or trade custom regard-*

ing the meaning or effect of the proposal? If so, the parties probably intended the proposal to be interpreted in the light of the custom, unless there was substantial evidence of a contrary intention. For example, an advertisement of a public auction usually is not an offer but an invitation for offers. A bidder makes an implied promise to pay a certain sum (offer) by raising his hand. An acceptance occurs when the auctioneer strikes the gavel. Prior to acceptance the bid may be withdrawn or the auctioneer may withdraw the article. However, if an auction is advertised to be "without reserve," the auctioneer cannot withdraw an article and must accept the highest bid.

Case 10.1   **Fairmount Glass Works v. Grunden-Martin Woodenware Co.**
51 S.W. 196 (Ky. 1899)

HOBSON, J. On April 20, 1895, plaintiff [Grunden-Martin Woodenware Co.] wrote defendant [Fairmount Glass Works] the following letter:

"St. Louis, Mo., April 20, 1895. Gentlemen: Please advise us the lowest price you can make us on our order for ten carloads of Mason green jars, complete, with caps, packed one dozen in a case, either delivered here, or f.o.b. care your place, as you prefer. State terms and cash discount. Very truly, Grunden-Martin W.W. Co."

To this letter defendant answered as follows:

"Fairmount, Ind., April 23, 1895. Gentlemen: Replying to your favor of April 20, we quote you Mason fruit jars, complete, in one-dozen boxes, delivered East St. Louis, Ill.: Pints $4.50, quarts $5.00, half gallons $6.50, per gross, for immediate acceptance, and shipment not later than May 15, 1895; sixty days acceptance, or 2 off, cash in ten days. Yours truly, Fairmount Glass Works."

For reply thereto, plaintiff sent the following telegram on April 24, 1895:

"Your letter twenty-third received. Enter order ten carloads as per your quotation. Specifications mailed. [The letter of specifications gave the quantity desired for each size of jar and the date of shipment for the first case.]"

In response to this telegram, defendant sent the following:

Case 10.1
Continued

"April 24, 1895. Impossible to book your order. Output all sold. See letter. Fairmount Glass Works."

Plaintiff insists that, by its telegram sent in answer to the letter of April 23rd, the contract was closed for the purchase of ten carloads of Mason fruit jars. Defendant insists that the contract was not closed by this telegram, and that it had the right to decline to fill the order at the time it sent its telegram of April 24. This is the chief question in the case. The court below gave judgment in favor of plaintiff, and defendant has appealed, earnestly insisting that the judgment is erroneous.

We are referred to a number of authorities holding that a quotation of prices is not an offer to sell, in the sense that a completed contract will arise out of the giving of an order for merchandise in accordance with the proposed terms. There are a number of cases holding that the transaction is not completed until the order so made is accepted. [Citations.]

But each case must turn largely upon the language there used. In this case we think there was more than a quotation of prices, although defendant's letter uses the word "quote" in stating the prices given. The true meaning of the correspondence must be determined by reading it as a whole. Plaintiff's letter of April 20th, which began the transaction, did not ask for a quotation of prices. It reads: "Please advise us the lowest price you can make us on our order for ten carloads of Mason green jars. . . . State terms and cash discount." From this defendant could not fail to understand that plaintiff wanted to know at what price it would sell it ten carloads of these jars; so when, in answer, it wrote: "We quote you Mason fruit jars . . . pints \$4.50, quarts \$5.00, half gallons \$6.50, per gross, for immediate acceptance; . . . 2 off, cash in ten days,"—it must be deemed as intending to give plaintiff the information it had asked for. We can hardly understand what was meant by the words "for immediate acceptance," unless the letter was intended as a proposition to sell at these prices if accepted immediately. In construing every contract, the aim of the court is to arrive at the intention of the parties. In none of the cases to which we have been referred on behalf of defendant was there on the face of the correspondence any such expression of intention to make an offer to sell on the terms indicated. . . .

Defendant also insists that the contract was indefinite because the quantity of each size of the jars was not fixed, that ten carloads is too indefinite a specification of the quantity sold, and that plaintiff had no right to accept the goods to be delivered on different days. The proof shows that "ten carloads" is an expression used in the trade as equivalent to 1,000 gross, 100 gross being regarded a carload. The offer to sell the different sizes at different prices gave the purchaser the right to name the quantity of each size, and, the offer being to ship not later than May 15th, the buyer had the right to fix the time of delivery at any time before that.

Judgment affirmed.

Requirements for an Offer

To constitute a legally sufficient offer, a proposal of conduct (promise) must meet three requirements: (1) it must be made with serious intent, or appear to be so made; (2) it must be reasonably definite and complete; and (3) it must be communicated to the offeree.

Serious Proposal Statements obviously or apparently made in jest or under the stress of great excitement or as bravado or bluff are not offers. If Adams makes a proposal to Brown, Adams' intention will be held by courts to be what a reasonable person in Brown's position would judge Adams' intention to be. Thus, if Brown should realize that a proposal by Adams was made in jest or under the stress of great excitement or as bravado or bluff, the proposal would not constitute a legally effective offer.

The classic case involving a proposal made under the stress of great excitement is *Higgins v. Lessig.*[1] An old harness worth about $15 had presumably been stolen. When the defendant, Lessig, discovered the loss he became "much excited" and using "rough language and epithets" said he would give $100 to any person who found out who the thief was. Plaintiff, who had been present when Lessig made the statement, furnished the information and sought to recover the reward. The trial court found for the plaintiff. However, the appellate court reversed the judgment on the ground that the defendant's language was not to be regarded as a serious proposal but "as the extravagant exclamation of an excited man."

In the following case, the court was called upon to determine whether the plaintiff was warranted in interpreting as a serious proposal of conduct a statement which the defendant contended had been meant as a joke.

---

[1] 49 Ill. App. 459 (1893).

Case 10.2   Barnes v. Treece
549 P.2d 1152 (Wash. App. 1976)

Warren Treece (a defendant) was vice president and a major stockholder of Vend-A-Win, Inc., a corporation engaged primarily in the business of distributing punchboards. On July 24, 1973 Treece spoke before the Washington State Gambling Commission in support of punchboard legitimacy and of Vend-A-Win's application for a temporary license to distribute punchboards. During his speech, Treece stated in effect: "I'll pay a hundred thousand dollars to anyone to find a crooked board. If they find it, I'll pay it." The statement brought laughter from the audience.

The next morning Vernon Barnes (plaintiff), while watching a television news report of the proceedings before the gambling commission, heard Treece's previous statement that $100,000 would be paid to anyone who could produce a crooked punchboard. Barnes also read Treece's statement in a newspaper report of the proceedings. On July 26, Barnes telephoned Treece, announced that he had two crooked punchboards and asked Treece if his earlier statement had been made seriously. Treece assured Barnes that the statement had been made seriously, advised him that the statement was firm, and further informed him that $100,000 was being held safely in escrow.

In accordance with instructions from Treece, Barnes brought one of the punchboards to the Seattle office of Vend-A-Win for inspection. The other punchboard was produced in a hearing before the Washington State Gambling Commission.

Treece and Vend-A-Win each refused to pay Barnes the $100,000, and Barnes instituted legal action against both of them. The trial court held that defendant Treece was personally liable for the $100,000 but dismissed the action against defendant Vend-A-Win. There was an appeal. "The first issue," said the appellate court, "is whether the statement of Treece was the manifestation of an offer which could be accepted." Only so much of the court's opinion as pertains to that issue is included in the following excerpts from the court's opinion.

CALLOW, J. . . . Treece maintains that his statement was made in jest. . . . When expressions are intended as a joke and are understood or would be understood by a reasonable person as being so intended, they cannot be construed as an offer and accepted to form a contract. However, if the jest is not apparent and a reasonable hearer would believe that an offer was being made, then the speaker risks the formation of a contract which was not intended. It is the objective manifestations of the offeror that count and not secret, unexpressed intentions. . . .

The trial court found that there was an objective manifestation of mutual assent to form a contract. . . . The record includes substantial evidence of the required mutual assent to support the finding of the trial court. Although the original statement of Treece drew laughter from the audience, the subsequent statements, conduct, and the circumstances show an intent to lead any hearer to believe the statements were made seriously. There was testimony, though contradicted, that Treece specifically restated the offer over the telephone in response to an inquiry concerning whether the offer was serious. Treece, when given an opportunity to state that an offer was not intended, not only reaffirmed the offer but also asserted that $100,000 had been placed in escrow and directed Barnes to bring the punchboard to Seattle for inspection. The parties met, Barnes was given a receipt for the board, and he was told that the board would be taken to Chicago for inspection. In present day society it is known that gambling generates a great deal of income and that large sums are spent on its advertising and promotion. In that prevailing atmosphere, it was a credible statement that $100,000 would be paid to promote punchboards. The statements of the defendant and the surrounding circumstances reflect an objective manifestation of a contractual intent by Treece and support of the finding of the trial court.

The trial court properly categorized Treece's promise of $100,000 as a valid offer for a unilateral contract. . . .

The judgment is affirmed.

Definite and Complete Terms To be enforceable, a contract must contain reasonably definite and complete terms. The essential terms usually include the names of the parties, the subject matter involved, the price, and the time and place for performance. Sometimes the offer contains all of the essential terms. If the offer by itself does not meet the requirement of reasonable definiteness but requires definite terms in the acceptance, the offer and acceptance together may meet the requirement that the terms of a contract must be reasonably certain.

An example of an offer requiring "such definite terms in the acceptance" was contained in the case of *Minneapolis & St. Louis Railway* (plaintiff) *v. Columbus Rolling Mill* (defendant).[2] The defendant, by letter of December 8, offered to sell plaintiff 2,000 to 5,000 tons of iron rails at a specified price. The plaintiff replied, "Please enter our order for 1,200 tons rails." Since the order was below the minimum quantity specified in the offer, there was no contract. In so deciding, the court said: "This offer [of December 8] would authorize the plaintiff to take at his election any number of tons not less than two thousand nor more than five thousand, on the terms specified." If the plaintiff had elected to take, say, three thousand tons, there would have been a contract, although considered alone the offer was not even reasonably definite as to quantity.

It should be noted that the requirement is not one of absolute definiteness but only of reasonable definiteness. Promises of performance to be rendered "immediately" or "at once" or "promptly" or "as soon as possible" have been held to meet this requirement. Similarly, quantities and prices have been held to be reasonably definite even though qualified by such expressions as "about" or "more or less" or "approximately." But proposals to pay "a fair share of my profits" and to erect "a permanent first-class hotel" have been held not to meet the requirements of reasonable definiteness.

Often the dynamics of business are such that a potential seller or buyer does not wish to specify or is unable to specify an approximate quantity of goods to be sold or purchased. Thus, A may offer to sell to B all the oranges to be grown on A's citrus ranch during the next season; or C may offer to buy from D all the paint required for the next two years in the operation of C's automobile body shop. Most courts hold that such offers are reasonably definite. The Uniform Commercial Code specifically recognizes output and requirements contracts for the sale of goods and sets a standard for their interpretation and performance. (See UCC, Sec. 2–306(1), discussed in Chapter 25.)[3]

A proposal may fail to meet the requirement of reasonably definite and complete terms if some term vital to the proposed agreement has been omitted. Courts have many times held that if the parties fail to make an enforceable agreement, the courts will not make one for them. Thus, if A and B agree that A is to make a suit for B at the price of $150, but there is no agreement concerning the material from which the suit is to be made, a court would refuse to supply the missing term.

It does not follow, however, that all the terms of an offer must necessarily be expressed. Some of them may be *implied*. For example, if a contract fails to mention the time of performance, courts will usually hold that performance within a reasonable time is implied in the offer. Similarly, if a contract fails to mention the price to be paid for the goods or service, courts will hold that a reasonable price was implicit in the offer, at least where it is clear the parties intended to conclude a contract and there is some objective basis for determining what is a

---

[2]119 U.S. 149 (1866); see also Case 10.1, p. 177.

[3]See Chap. 2, p. 27, for explanation and history of the Uniform Commercial Code.

reasonable price. If there is a market price for the specified goods or services, that price will be taken as the reasonable price. However, failure to state a price is sometimes used by courts as evidence that the parties were still negotiating.

Case 10.3   Abrams v. Illinois College of Podiatric Medicine
395 N.E.2d 1061 (Ill. App. 1979)

In early 1973 Jonathan M. Abrams (plaintiff) was admitted to the Illinois College of Podiatric Medicine (College), a private educational institution. In his first semester plaintiff failed Physiology 101. Plaintiff has a minor neurological disturbance which results in a slow rate of reading speed. He was given a re-examination in the course and failed the test. Mr. Abrams was then placed on probation and told that he must successfully complete a two semester sequence, Physiology 101–203, in order to register as a second year student for the 1974–75 academic year. Plaintiff failed the two courses and was dismissed from school.

Plaintiff filed an action against the College alleging breach of contract and seeking: (1) expunction of his dismissal, (2) reinstatement, and (3) an order compelling the College to give due consideration and accommodation to his learning disability. Plaintiff alleges in his complaint that the College was apprised of the difficulty he was having in pursuing the standard curriculum and that the College informed him that he "should not worry . . . that everything would be done to assist him, including figuring out some way to help him." Plaintiff contends this statement by the College gave rise to a binding and enforceable oral contract which was subsequently breached. The College answered the complaint and then filed a motion for judgment on the pleadings. Defendant maintained that plaintiff's complaint failed to state a cause of action as a matter of law. The trial court granted the motion and dismissed plaintiff's complaint with prejudice. Plaintiff appeals.

LINN, J. . . . A binding and enforceable oral contract cannot arise unless the terms of the alleged agreement are sufficiently definite and certain. [Citations.] An "offer must be so definite as to its material terms or require such definite terms in the acceptance that the promises and performances to be rendered by each party are reasonably certain." (Restatement (Second) of Contracts § 32(1) (Tent. Draft No. 1, 1964).) The reason for this rule is obvious.

"A court cannot enforce a contract unless it can determine what it is. It is not enough that the parties think that they have made a contract; they must have expressed their intentions in a manner that is capable of understanding. It is not enough that they have actually agreed, if their expressions, when interpreted in the light of accompanying factors and circumstances, are not such that the court can determine what the terms of that agreement are. Vagueness of expression, indefiniteness and uncertainty as to any of the essential terms of an agreement, have often been held to prevent the creation of an enforceable contract." 1 Corbin on Contracts § 95, at 294 (1963).

We find that the vagueness and indefiniteness of the statement attributable to the College prevents the creation of a binding and enforceable oral contract.

Plaintiff next invokes the general rule that the basic legal relationship between a student and a private university or college is contractual in nature, and the catalogues, bulletins, circulars and regulations of the institution, made available to the student, become a part of that contract. [Citations.]

Plaintiff alleges in his complaint that during the 1973–1974 school year he "did not receive periodic information with respect to his [academic] progress ... nor recommendations for improvement" in violation of the following Student Handbook provision:

> *"Evaluation of the Student*
> It is *desirable* that the instructor should periodically inform the student of his progress. . . . The student should be informed soon after mid-term examinations of his standing *with recommendations, if necessary,* for improvement."

Plaintiff contends that the violations of this provision amounted to a breach of contract. We disagree.

This particular provision in the Student Handbook was *not* an offer or a promise by the College which created a power of acceptance in the plaintiff. The provision was more in the nature of an unenforceable expression of intention, hope, or desire. It did not justify an understanding that a commitment had been made by the College and it was not communicated to the plaintiff in such a way as to invite the payment of tuition in reliance thereon. We find that this provision in the Student Handbook was an expression by the College of an unenforceable expectation which plaintiff did not have the power to transform into a binding contractual obligation. . . .

Affirmed.

Communication to Offeree An offer does not become legally effective until communicated to the person or persons for whom it was intended. "Communicated" literally means "brought to the attention of." The courts hold that an offeree can assent to a proposal which he or she does not know about if, under the circumstances, the offeree should have realized that a proposal was made.

In some situations there is no difficulty in concluding that a person should have been aware that a proposal was being made. For example, a shipper who receives a bill of lading from a carrier should realize that the lengthy document is more than a receipt of goods for shipment and that it contains the terms of a proposed contract. If the shipper accepts the bill of lading, he or she expresses assent to the proposed contract and all the terms legally contained in it, including any term legally limiting the extent of the carrier's liability.

In other situations a question may arise as to

whether a person should have realized that an offer was being made to him or her. The problem most often involves proposals printed on tags attached to goods shipped, on invoices, on folders enclosed with bills or distributed as handbills, on tickets, on claim checks (such as those issued in parking lots, checkrooms, or repair shops), and on letterheads. In any such situation the test of whether communication has occurred is that of reasonableness. Could the customer reasonably be expected to know that an offer was being made to him or her? If so, the offer has been communicated to him or her; if not, there has been *no* communication.

Provisions printed in letterheads have given rise to some litigation. Most courts hold that any provision plainly printed in a letterhead (for example, "All contracts subject to strikes") has been communicated to the offeree regardless of whether he or she reads it. A wise offeror takes no chance but ensures communication by including a specified reference to the printed material. A simple way to do so is to begin the letter with the words "Subject to the provision printed above, we offer you as follows. . . . "

The requirement of communication demands not only that the offer be communicated to the offeree but that it be communicated by the offeror personally or by an agency chosen by him or her. If A in the presence of B dictates an offer addressed to C, and B informs C of the offer without being authorized by A to do so, the requirement of communication has not been met. Neither would it be met if C called upon A while A was out of the office, saw the dictated letter on A's desk, and read it.

DURATION AND TERMINATION OF OFFERS

A legally effective offer gives to the offeree the power to create a contract by acceptance of the offer. This "power of acceptance" continues until the offer is terminated by some legally recognized method. Offers may be terminated by: (1) lapse of time, (2) revocation by the offeror, (3) rejection or counteroffer by the offeree, (4) death or incapacity of the offeror or offeree, (5) loss or destruction of the subject matter of the offer, or (6) illegality arising subsequently to the offer ("supervening illegality").

Termination by Lapse of Time

Specified Time Limitation An offer may be so worded as to terminate on a specified date. Examples are: "This offer to terminate at 5 P.M., October 10"; "This offer to remain open until 5 P.M., October 10." Or the offer may be so worded as to terminate after a specified period of time: "This offer to remain open eight days from date of this letter."

Difficulty arises when the limitation is worded ambiguously. Suppose that an offeror mails a letter which gives the offeree "ten days to accept or reject this offer." Is the offeror's intention to have the ten-day period measured from the date the letter is sent or from the date it is received? Although there is some conflict in court decisions, the usual ruling is that the time runs from the day of receipt by the offeree.

Implied Time Limitation Where an offeror does not specify a time limitation, the offer remains open for a reasonable period of time. What constitutes a reasonable period of time is a question of fact to be determined on the basis of all relevant circumstances, including the subject matter of the offer, the market price situation, any special objective the offeror had in making the offer where that fact is known to the offeree, and the method of communication chosen by the offeror. Thus, an offer to buy or sell corporate stock terminates sooner than an offer to buy or sell land; an offer to sell corporate stock during a period of rapidly fluctuating stock prices terminates sooner than an offer to sell the same stock during periods of relative price stability; an offer which the offeree knows has been made to meet an emergency situation terminates sooner than one not so made; and an offer sent by telegram normally terminates sooner than one sent by letter.

An attempt by the offeree to accept an offer after a specified time or a reasonable time has expired may be considered a counteroffer.

Case 10.4   **Modern Pool Products, Inc. v. Rudel Machinery Co.**
294 N.Y.S.2d 426 (Civ. Ct. City of N.Y. 1968)

This case involved a controversy between Modern Pool Products, Inc. (plaintiff) and Rudel Machinery Company (defendant). Modern Pool Products, Inc., (Pool Products) was located in Greenwich, Connecticut; Rudel Machinery Company (Rudel) was located in New York City. Sometime prior to September 1964, Pool Products made an inquiry of Rudel as to the probable cost of repairing a pipe-bending machine which Pool Products used in the construction of swimming pools. The machine was examined by a representative of Rudel, and on September 16, 1964, Rudel submitted its proposal by letter. The price for parts and labor necessary to restore the machine to working condition was quoted as "$1,600 plus freightage." Pool Products was informed that although Rudel would do the repairing, the work would have to be done in the plant of the Pines Engineering Company in Aurora, Illinois.

Written response from Pool Products did not come until January 14, 1965, when it advised Rudel that the machine would be shipped to the Illinois plant by January 20.

On February 10, 1965, Rudel, by letter, acknowledged that the machine had arrived at the Illinois plant but stated that detailed examination of the interior of the machine had disclosed that more extensive repairs were required than originally contemplated. In this letter Rudel approximated the cost of the repairs and labor to be $3,300 and stated that it would await Pool Products' instructions whether or not to proceed with the work to be done.

In December 1965, Pool Products advised Rudel, by letter, that a decision would be made during the next month. On February 8, 1966, Pool Products notified Rudel that the machine in question had been sold. Thereafter Pool Products sued Rudel for breach of contract for failure to repair the machine at the original price. Plaintiff, Pool Products, contended that it was entitled to recover as damages the reduced market value of the machine resulting from the breach of contract by defendant.

BIRNS, J. . . . The critical question appears to be whether the letters of September 16, 1964 and January 14, 1965 constituted a contract as maintained by plaintiff. If they did, then plaintiff is entitled to damages; if they did not, then obviously the later correspondence created no binding relationship between the parties to this suit (because plaintiff never asked defendant to go ahead with the necessary work), and thus defendant is entitled to judgment.

The application of basic principles of contract law is dispositive of the issues of this case.

It is fundamental that an offer, if not accepted promptly, may be terminated by lapse of time (*Restatement, Law of Contracts,* Section 35). Where no time is fixed in the offer within which acceptance must be made, it is a rule of law that acceptance must be made within a reasonable time (*Restatement,* supra, Section 40(1)). What is a reasonable time may vary with the circumstances (*Restatement,* supra, Section 40(2); 1 Williston on Contracts, Section 54) and is an issue to be resolved upon trial.

There are instances, no doubt, where a court would be warranted in holding that the failure of an offeree to respond within a reasonable time terminated the offer as a matter of law. Such was the holding in *Staples v. Pan American Wallpaper and Paint Co.,* 3 Cir., 63 F.2d 701, where a period of 101 days intervened between the receipt of an offer and its purported acceptance. In most cases where this problem has arisen, the question is considered to be one of fact. . . .

In the case at bar, plaintiff failed to respond to defendant's offer for 114 days. That such an extended period of time was not within the contemplation of the offer can be deduced from the correspondence and surrounding circumstances. For example, the price as quoted was subject to change without notice; the parties involved were not separated by vast distances or prevented from rapid communication.[Citations.]

In addition, the terms of the offer reflect the need for a prompt reply by plaintiff. Defendant's offer stated that if there were an acceptance by plaintiff "it (the rebuilding of the machine) would have to be done at a time which is convenient to both you and Pines Engineering Company, Inc." and "They are currently very busy in their shop and would have to schedule a job like this just as though it were a new machine order. It could very well be that Pines would not want the·machine to arrive for at least 6–8 weeks from now." Thus the current ability of the factory to handle the machine in question required a prompt reply. . . .

Judgment for defendant.

Effect of Delay in Transmission An offer sent by mail or telegram may be delayed in transmission. The question then arises: What effect does the delay have on the duration of the offer?

Where the offer contains a specified termination date, the delay does not extend the life of the offer. If the letter or telegram is received before the specified date, the offeree has only as much time for considering the offer as remains before that date. If the letter or telegram is delivered after the specified date, there is no legally effective offer.

Where the offer does not contain a specified termination date, the effect of the delay depends on whether the offeree knows or has reason to know of the delay. If the offeree knows or has reason to know of the delay, the delay does not extend the life of the offer, even though the delay may have been due to the fault of the offeror. On the other hand, if the offeree does not know or has no reason to know of the delay, the offer remains open for a reasonable time as determined by the circumstances discussed above.

Termination by Revocation

Revocation of offer means the withdrawal of the offer by the offeror. Important legal problems may arise in connection with revocation: (1) Under what circumstances does the offeror have the power to revoke an offer? (2) What is necessary to constitute a revocation? (3) When does revocation take effect?

Power of Revocation   As a general rule, an offeror has the power to revoke an offer at any time before acceptance even though he or she has promised not to do so. Thus, for example, if the offeror specifies "This offer will remain open until October 10," the offeror may revoke the offer on October 5.

Irrevocable offers: options; promissory estop- *pel*   There are several exceptions to the general rule that offers are revocable. If the offeree gives consideration (money, property, etc.) to the offeror to keep the offer open, the offer is irrevocable for the agreed period of time. Such an arrangement is called an "option" or "option contract." Thus, in the example above, if the offeree gives $10 to the offeror to keep the offer open, the offeror can no longer revoke the offer before October 10.

Many courts hold that an offer becomes irrevocable if the offeror should reasonably expect the offer to induce the offeree to change his or her position in reliance on the offer and in fact the offeree does change position in reliance on the offer. This holding of the courts has been called the theory or doctrine of "detrimental reliance" or "promissory estoppel." The offer becomes irrevocable for the stated time period if one is stated, otherwise for a reasonable time.

Case 10.5   Lyon Metal Products v. Hagerman Construction Corp.
391 N.E.2d 1152 (Ind. App. 1979)

Hagerman Construction Corporation (plaintiff) was preparing a bid for the construction of a school. One of the items it was required to bid upon was athletic lockers. On Feb. 12, 1974 Lyon Metal Products, Inc. (defendant) submitted a bid to Hagerman for the lockers in the amount of $16,824. The bid was on a Lyon's quotation form. On the bottom of the form, in small print, was the following: "This quotation is subject to . . . the further condition contained on the reverse side hereof." On the reverse side, in yet smaller print, eight conditions were printed. One said: "This quotation may be withdrawn and is subject to change without notice after 15 days from date of quotation." The specifications for the project, which Lyon read, required that bids remain open for 120 days.

Lyon's bid for the lockers was the lowest of four received by Hagerman and was used by Hagerman in computing its bid. On Feb. 12 Hagerman was informed it was the lowest bidder on the school project. Lyon learned of this three or four days later. On March 1 Hagerman sent Lyon a letter of intent stating that a formal contract would be sent about June 10. Lyon did not respond to this letter. On June 5 a formal contract was sent but was never received by Lyon because of a wrong address. On September 6, 1974 Lyon withdrew its bid and submitted a new price of $28,750. Hagerman obtained the

Case 10.5
Continued

lockers from another supplier for $24,787. Hagerman filed suit against Lyon for damages. The trial court entered judgment for Hagerman in the sum of $7,963 based upon the doctrine of promissory estoppel. Defendant appealed.

GARRARD, Presiding Judge. . . . The doctrine of promissory estoppel, embodied in Section 90 of the Restatement of Contracts, provides that:

"A promise which the promisor should reasonably expect to induce action or forbearance of a definite and substantial character on the part of the promisee and which does induce such action or forbearance is binding if injustice can be avoided only by the enforcement of the promise."

Although the doctrine was traditionally recognized in cases involving donative or gratuitous promises (ex. charitable subscriptions), it is now well accepted that promissory estoppel applies with equal force in commercial transactions, including construction bid cases.

The leading case in this area is *Drennan v. Star Paving Co.* (1958), 51 Cal.2d 409, 333 P.2d 757. The case involved an oral bid by a subcontractor for paving work on a school project on which Drennan, the general contractor, was about to bid. The subcontractor's bid was the lowest and Drennan computed his own bid, using the subcontractor's bid. Drennan was the successful bidder but the subcontractor informed him the next day that it would not do the work at the quoted price. The court applied the doctrine of promissory estoppel to prevent the subcontractor's revocation of the bid, stating:

"Defendant's offer constituted a promise to perform on such conditions as were stated expressly or by implication therein or annexed thereto by operation of law. Defendant had reason to expect that if its bid proved the lowest it would be used by plaintiff. It introduced 'action . . . of a definite and substantial character on the part of the promisee.' . . . It was to its own interest that the contractor be awarded the general contract; the lower the subcontract bid, the lower the general contractor's bid was likely to be and the greater its chance of acceptance and hence the greater defendant's chance of getting the paving subcontract. Defendant had reason not only to expect plaintiff to rely on its bid but to want him to. Clearly defendant had a stake in plaintiff's reliance on its bid. Given this interest and the fact that plaintiff is bound by his own bid, it is only fair that plaintiff should have at least an opportunity to accept defendant's bid after the general contract has been awarded to him." 333 P.2d 759–60.

. . . Our task is to determine whether there was sufficient evidence of probative value in the case at bar to support each of the elements of promissory estoppel, viz: (1) whether Lyon made a definite promise to Hagerman with the reasonable expectation that the promise would induce action of a definite and substantial character on the part of Hagerman; (2) whether the promise induced such action; (3) whether Hagerman acted in justifiable reliance upon the promise to its detriment; and (4) whether injustice can be avoided only by enforcement of the promise. . . .

Lyon offered to supply a given quantity of specified kinds of lockers at a stated price. It realized that if its quote or bid was the lowest received by Hagerman that Hagerman would use the Lyon bid in computing its own bid. In fact, Lyon not only realized that its promise would induce action of a definite and substantial character, it was Lyon's express intention that this would occur. Hagerman did use the Lyon bid in computing its bid, which subsequently bound Hagerman to provide the lockers to the school corporation at the price quoted. Lyon was notified by the letter of intent that Hagerman intended to have Lyon supply the lockers at the quoted price. When Lyon refused to supply the lockers at the price quoted, Hagerman was forced to incur the loss of $7,963.00.

Lyon asserts that Hagerman could not have reasonably relied on its offer since the offer expressly stated that it was subject to withdrawal or modification 15 days after the date it was given. We acknowledge that several cases have stated in dicta that if the bid states that it was revocable or reserves a right of withdrawal or otherwise disclaims any intention to be bound, there could be no reasonable reliance by the general contractor. [Citations.] However, we have determined that there was sufficient evidence of probative value from which the trial court could have found justifiable reliance notwithstanding the 15 day clause. The evidence established that the project specifications required that the bids be held open for 120 days. Lyon's attempted variation of this specification was printed in small letters on the back of its quote along with seven other conditions and the reference to the conditions on the reverse side was itself in small print. Hagerman's agent testified that he barely glanced at the conditions. Lyon made no special effort at any time to apprise Hagerman of the 15 day clause. After it had received the letter of intent which referred to "uncertainty of prices" and the reason for delay in sending the formal contract, Lyon did not inform Hagerman that its bid would be adjusted by increases in prices. Furthermore Langevin, Lyon's agent, testified that more than 120 days had elapsed when the bid was withdrawn in September. From this evidence, the trial court could have inferred that Lyon did not intend the 15 day clause to be the controlling time period but rather the 120 day period found in the specifications. . . . Lyon was aware that Hagerman was low bidder and that Hagerman was relying on it to supply the lockers at the quoted price. The project specifications, of which Lyon was aware, adequately informed it of the extent of its obligations.

For these reasons, we conclude that the trial court did not err in finding that Lyon was liable to Hagerman under the theory of promissory estoppel.

Affirmed.

Other irrevocable offers   Some types of offers are commonly made irrevocable by statute. Among such offers are bids made to governmental agencies (see Chapter 19), and, under Section 2–205 of the Uniform Commercial Code, "firm offers" of merchants. A *firm offer* is a written and signed offer of a merchant to buy or sell goods, where the writing gives assurance that the offer will be held open. Such an offer is not revocable within the time-period provisions of Section 2–205, even though the offeror was not paid to keep the offer open. (Firm offers and the provisions of UCC, Section 2–205 are discussed in Chapter 25.)

A difficult problem arises where the offeror asks for an act which requires time to perform and then, after the requested performance has been begun, serves notice of revocation. Where an offer is made for a unilateral contract, acceptance does not take place until the act has been substantially performed. But to allow repudiation after part performance may work a serious hardship on an offeree who has started performance. Many courts utilize a variant of the detrimental reliance theory so that such hardship to the offeree may be prevented. Most courts take the view that the offer becomes irrevocable as soon as the offeree "begins the invited performance or tenders the beginning of it."[4] The theory behind this view is that the beginning of the invited performance or the tendering of the beginning, creates an option contract. As would be true under any option contract, the offeree who begins performance is not bound to complete performance. The offeree who does not finish but who confers benefits on the offeror may recover in quasi contract the reasonable value of services rendered or property expended. The offeror is not bound to perform the other side of the bargain unless the offeree completes performance within the time stated in the offer, or if no time is stated, within a reasonable time.

What Constitutes Revocation The usual method of revocation is for the offeror to notify the offeree that he or she is withdrawing the offer. No special form of notice is required. Anything suffices which lets the offeree know

that the offeror has reconsidered and no longer intends to enter into the proposed contract. The notice may be given face to face, over the telephone, or by letter or telegram.

Notice of revocation need not come directly from the offeror. If an offeree gets "reliable information" that the offeror has taken "definite action" inconsistent with an intention to enter into the proposed contract, the offeree's power of acceptance is terminated. For example, suppose that John offers to sell his golf clubs to Tom at a certain price and tells him he may have a week to consider the offer. If before the week is up John sells the clubs to Wally, and Tom acquires reliable information to that effect, Tom may no longer accept the offer.

There is one situation in which the common law recognizes revocation as having occurred even though the offeror's change of mind is not known by the offeree. Where an offer has been made to the public generally, as in a published offer to pay a reward, the offer may be withdrawn by giving public notice of revocation. If the same amount of publicity is given to the revocation as was given to the offer, revocation is effective even against a member of the public who knew of the offer but does not know of the publication of notice of revocation.

Effective Date of Revocation The general rule is that a written revocation becomes effective when received.[5] It is received, according to the *Restatement,*

> . . . when the writing comes into possession of the person addressed or of some person authorized by him to receive it for him, or when it is deposited in some place which he has authorized as the place for this or similar communications to be deposited for him.[6]

---

[4]*Restatement of the Law (Second) Contracts,* American Law Institute, Philadelphia, sec. 45(2).

[5]By statute in California, a written revocation becomes effective when posted or put into the course of transmission by any reasonable mode. A few other states have a similar statute.

[6]*Restatement (Second) Contracts,* sec. 69.

Under this provision a written revocation is effective though it is not read or though it does not even reach the hands of the person to whom it is addressed.

Termination by Rejection or Counteroffer

A *rejection* is a manifestation by the offeree of his or her intention not to accept the offer. Rejection terminates the offeree's power of acceptance, unless the offeror has manifested a contrary intention or unless he or she has been paid to keep the offer open.[7] Such rejection may be express or implied by words or conduct.

A *counteroffer* is an offer made by the offeree to an offeror relating to the same matter as the original offer but differing from the original offer in one or more particulars. A counteroffer terminates the original offer unless:

1 The offeror or offeree has manifested a contrary intention, or

2 The offer was, or has become, irrevocable.

---

[7]Ibid., secs. 37 and 35A.

A form of counteroffer is a *conditional acceptance.* For example, if Arnold offers to sell his car to Barbara for $1,500 and Barbara says, "I accept your offer of $1,500 and I will pay you in three equal monthly installments," Barbara has impliedly rejected the offer. However, when an offeree makes a counteroffer or a conditional acceptance, negotiations are not always terminated. The original offeror becomes an offeree and is free to accept the counteroffer or conditional acceptance.

Rejections and counteroffers should be distinguished from requests for information. Suppose an offer is made to sell a house for $40,000. The offeree says, "I am considering your offer, although I think the price is high. Would you be willing to scale it down to $37,500?" Such a response to the offer is not a rejection; on the contrary, it tells the offeror the offer is being kept under advisement. Neither is the response a counteroffer because it contains no promise. It is merely an inquiry.

Case 10.6   Ryder v. Wescoat
535 S.W.2d 269 (Mo. App. 1976)

Wescoat (defendant), in exchange for a valuable consideration, gave Ryder (plaintiff) an option to purchase a 120-acre farm. The option period extended to, and included, September 1. On August 20 Ryder informed Wescoat that he was not going to exercise the option. Shortly thereafter Wescoat obtained a price for doing some bulldozing on the farm, discussed arrangements for doing some liming, and talked with a bank official about obtaining some necessary funds. However, Wescoat had not legally committed himself under any of the arrangements.

On August 30 Ryder caused a contract to be prepared by which he agreed to purchase the 120-acre farm. On the same day, the contract along with a down payment was tendered to Wescoat. Wescoat refused to sign the contract, contending that Ryder's previous rejection terminated his rights under the option contract. Ryder brought an action against Westcoat for specific performance of the agreement to purchase and sell the farm. There was a judgment for defendant Wescoat, and Ryder appealed.

Case 10.6
Continued

TURNAGE, J. This case poses the problem of a rejection on the part of an option holder and a subsequent acceptance within the time limited. . . .

No case has been cited, and diligent research on the part of this court has failed to locate any case involving this precise issue. However, text writers have dealt with the problem. In Simpson on Contracts, 2d ed., Section 23, the author states:

> "Where an offer is supported by a binding contract that the offeree's power of acceptance shall continue for a stated time, will a communicated rejection terminate the offeree's power to accept within the time? On principle, there is no reason why it should. The offeree has a contract right to accept within the time. . . . So an option holder may complete a contract by communicating his acceptance despite the fact that he has previously rejected the offer. Where, however, before the acceptance the offeror has materially changed his position in reliance on the communicated rejection, as by selling or contracting to sell the subject matter of the offer elsewhere, the subsequent acceptance will be inoperative."

To the same effect is Corbin on Contracts, Vol. 1, Section 94, p. 392, 1963. . . . This court adopts the rule stated in *Simpson* and *Corbin* and holds that a rejection of an option which has been purchased for a valuable consideration does not terminate the rights of the option holder unless the optionor has materially changed his position prior to a timely acceptance.

This rule fully protects the rights of both parties. It extends to the optionor the protection he requires in the event a rejection of the option is communicated to him and he thereafter changes his position in reliance thereon to his detriment. At the same time it protects the right of the option holder to have the opportunity to exercise his option for the full period for which he paid, absent the material change in position.

To apply this rule in this case, it must be held [that] Ryder retained his right to exercise the option for the reason Wescoat had not shown any material change in his position between the time of the rejection and the later acceptance.

The judgment in favor of Wescoat is reversed and the cause is remanded with directions to enter a judgment in favor of Ryder. The court shall direct specific performance of the agreement between Ryder and Wescoat for the purchase and sale of the 120-acre farm.

Termination by Death or Incapacity of Offeror or Offeree

Death or incapacity of the offeror or the offeree terminates the ordinary offer whether or not the other party is aware of the occurrence. Probably the most usual kind of legal incapacity terminating an offer is insanity. In some states conviction of a felony results in a person's being deprived of the capacity to enter into contracts.

Death or incapacity does not terminate an

offer which is irrevocable because of consideration, detrimental reliance, etc.

Termination by Loss of Subject Matter; Termination by Supervening Illegality

The loss or destruction of the subject matter of a proposed contract terminates the offer. Thus, if the offer concerns the purchase or sale of a horse and the horse dies before the offer is accepted, the offer is terminated.

If a proposed contract or performance becomes illegal after an offer has been made but *before* it is accepted, the offer is terminated. This method of termination is usually referred to as *supervening illegality*. Suppose that A offers to lend B or B offers to borrow from A the sum of $1,000 for one year at 10 percent interest, and suppose that after the offer is made a statute is passed prohibiting loans at more than 8 percent' interest. If the statute takes effect before the offer is accepted, the statute terminates the offer.

SUMMARY

One of the requirements for a contract is a manifestation of mutual assent. "Manifestation of assent" means an outward expression of assent by words or acts. Mutual assent is reached by means of offer and acceptance. This chapter dealt with offer.

An offer is a statement or other conduct by which the offeror confers upon the offeree a legal power to accept the offer and thereby to create a contract. Offers contain promises and are to be distinguished from statements of present intention and from negotiatory statements. Negotiatory statements are statements which lay the groundwork for or invite the submission of offers. Advertisements, circulars, catalogs, and price tags are usually negotiatory statements, or invitations for offers, rather than offers.

To constitute a legally effective offer, a proposal must meet three requirements:

1 The proposal must appear to be made with serious intent.

2 The proposal must be so definite and complete in its terms, or require such definite terms in the acceptance, that the parties will know their rights and duties and that in the event of litigation a court will be able to determine the extent of the obligations assumed.

3 The proposal must be communicated to the offeree by the offeror or by an agency selected by him or her. An offeree may be bound by terms contained in an invoice, a claim check, or other printed document if the offeree should reasonably be expected under the circumstances to know an offer was being made.

A power of acceptance may be exercised at any time before termination of the offer. An offer may be terminated by: (1) lapse of time, (2) revocation, (3) rejection or counteroffer, (4) death or incapacity of offeror or offeree, (5) loss or destruction of the subject matter of the offer, or (6) illegality arising subsequent to the making of the offer.

The offeror may state a time when the offer will terminate. In the absence of a specified time an offer remains open for a reasonable time. As a general rule, offers are revocable at any time before acceptance. There are several exceptions to this rule. An offer will be irrevocable for a stated time, or for a reasonable time when no date for termination is specified, if: (a) the offeree gives consideration to the offeror ("option contract"); (b) the promissory estoppel doctrine applies; (c) a special statute declares the offer to be irrevocable; or (d) the offer is for a unilateral contract and the offeree begins performance. With certain exceptions, an offer is terminated when the offeree rejects the offer, expressly or impliedly, or submits a counteroffer or conditional acceptance.

STUDY AND DISCUSSION QUESTIONS

1 What is meant by "manifestation of mutual assent" as a requirement for a contract?

2 *(a)* Define "offer"; "negotiatory statement." *(b)* How do the two differ in legal effect? *(c)* What do courts take into account in deciding whether a statement is an offer or a negotiatory statement?

3 What three requirements must a promise meet to constitute an offer?

4 *(a)* What test do courts apply in determining whether a proposal of conduct is seriously intended? *(b)* How should the following statement be qualified in order to make it accurate? "An offer must be so definite in its terms that the promises and the performances to be tendered by each party are reasonably certain." *(c)* What terms are essential to meet this requirement?

5 *(a)* Explain how terms of a written offer may be communicated without the offeree reading those terms. *(b)* How should an offeror protect himself or herself when he or she intends to include in a written offer a condition or term printed on the stationery?

6 *(a)* What is the rule as to termination of offer by lapse of time when a time limitation is specified? When no time limitation is specified? *(b)* How does delay in transmission affect the duration of an offer?

7 *(a)* What is the general rule as to the power of an offeror to revoke his or her offer? *(b)* What is an option contract? *(c)* Explain the doctrine of promissory estoppel. *(d)* When does a written notice of revocation become effective?

8 *(a)* Define "rejection." What effect does rejection have on the offeree's power of acceptance? *(b)* Define "counteroffer." What effect does a counteroffer have on the offeree's power of acceptance? *(c)* What is a conditional acceptance?

9 *(a)* Give an original illustration of termination of offer by loss or destruction of subject matter. *(b)* What is meant by "supervening illegality" as a method of terminating offers?

CASE PROBLEMS

1 Adams invited various brokers to submit proposals for fire and theft insurance. Brown submitted a proposal. In response to Adams' requests, Brown revised his proposal several times at the cost of considerable effort and some expense. *(a)* Is Adams free to reject all of Brown's proposals and to place the insurance with Campbell, another broker? *(b)* Would the answer differ if, on expert analysis, Campbell's proposal were found to be less favorable to Adams than Brown's proposal?

2 Joseph Sidran offered to sell piece goods for the Tanenbaum Textile Company for a commission "of 1 percent of the sale price of said merchandise." The offer made no mention of the duration of the proposed contract nor of the time and place of payment. Were the terms of the offer reasonably definite?

3 Roy Key and Michael Haitchi signed a "Contract" which stated that Key agreed to buy "a house to be built on Lot 9 Lambert Drive Dunmovin S/D Plan No. 603 W.D. Farmer." The contract further provided that it constituted "the sole and entire agreement between the parties." Was the agreement sufficiently definite to constitute a contract?

4 Plaintiff checked a package in a parcel room of a railway station, paid the 10-cent checking charge, and received a claim check which he put into his pocket without reading. In error the package was given out on another claim check. The package contained valuable furs, and plaintiff sued for $1,000. The evidence showed that at the bottom of the claim check, printed in large red letters, was an identifying number, and at the top, in smaller red letters, was the word "Contract." In between the two lines were

eighty-eight words, in fine black type, purporting to contain the terms of contract, one of which limited the liability for loss to $25. No sign containing notice of limitation was posted in the parcel room. Should plaintiff's recovery be limited to $25?

5   Cline sent Caldwell a letter offering to sell a tract of land for $6,000. The letter was dated January 29 and gave Caldwell "eight days in which" to accept or reject the offer. Caldwell received the letter February 2. He sent notification of acceptance on February 8. Had the offer terminated before February 8?

6   Beach offered to contribute $2,000 to a church building fund of $10,000 on condition that the church raise the remaining $8,000. The church raised the $8,000, but before it did so, Beach was adjudged insane, and conservators of his estate were appointed. Can the church recover the promised amount from the estate?

Chapter

11

Acceptance

As we have seen, a contract requires a manifestation of mutual assent, and mutual assent is normally reached by means of offer and acceptance. The previous chapter dealt with offer; the present chapter deals with acceptance. The first part of this chapter is devoted to legal principles which apply to acceptance of offers in general. The next two parts are devoted to principles applicable primarily to acceptance in situations involving unilateral contracts (often referred to as "acceptance of unilateral offers") and to principles applicable primarily to acceptance in situations involving bilateral contracts ("acceptance of bilateral offers"). The last part of the chapter deals with the problem of determining when a contract comes into being where the parties mutually understood that the agreement would be put into writing.

ACCEPTANCE IN GENERAL

In very general terms, *acceptance* is the offeree's manifestation of assent to the terms of the offer in the manner requested by the offeror—that is, either by performing the requested act or by promising to perform it.

An offer may be addressed to a specified person, or to one or more of a specified group of persons, or to the general public. Where an offer is addressed to a specified person, only that person can accept the offer. A party has a right to select and determine with whom he or she will contract. Thus, if A sends B an order for goods made by B, only B can accept that offer. If B hands the order to another manufacturer (C) who fills it without disclosing that C (and not B) made the goods, there is no contract. However, if A, before using the goods, learns that they were made by C, retention or use of them is an acceptance of an offer from C.

When an offer is addressed to one or more of a specified group of persons, the acceptance is not complete until assent has been manifested by the specified person or persons. When an offer is directed to the general public, there may be any number of acceptances or only one acceptance, depending on the intent of the offeror. An offer to pay $100 to anyone who fails to get relief after using a certain remedy is an offer to pay every user who fails to get relief. An offer to sell "to the first person who answers this advertisement" is limited to a single acceptance. When the wording of an offer does not clearly indicate the intent of the offeror, the offer is to be construed (interpreted) as a reasonable person would construe it under all the surrounding circumstances. For example, an offer to pay a reward for certain information should be construed as an offer to pay the first person who furnishes that information. The reasonable supposition is that the offeror does not intend to pay several times for the same information.

Case 11.1   Bachli v. Holt
200 A.2d 263 (Vt. 1964)

Marcella McDuffy engaged an architect to draw up plans and specifications for a restaurant building. The architect drew up plans and specifications and submitted them to several prospective bidders, including Earl Holt (defendant). Due to pressure of other work, Holt returned the plans without submitting a bid. Bids of other contractors were higher than McDuffy had anticipated, and Holt was requested to confer with her and the architect. During one of the conferences, Holt was asked to "figure the job" with the understanding that if his estimate was equal to or higher than the lowest bid, he would be compensated for his effort in making the computation. The figure concluded by Holt was about $10,000 less than that submitted by the previous lowest bidder. The owner then requested Holt to construct the building on a cost-plus basis with a warranty that the total cost would not exceed the lowest bid previously received. To this Holt agreed.

While these negotiations were in process, Holt telephoned William Bachli (plaintiff), a plumbing and heating contractor, telling him that plans and specifications for a plumbing and heating job would be sent to him and asking him "for a price." In a letter dated August 23, 1960, addressed to Earl Holt, Bachli quoted a price of $9,731. The price included labor and materials. Payments were to be made twice monthly upon presentation of requisitions for labor and materials, and final payment was to be made upon completion of the job.

Bachli commenced work on the project, and as the work progressed, he submitted requisitions for payment. Upon receiving the architect's approval of the various requisitions, Holt paid them in the total amount of $7,287. Payments were made by means of his personal checks, but from funds supplied by the owner. When Bachli had completed work on the plumbing and heating systems, Holt refused to make the final payment, for the reason that he had received no funds from the owner with which to make the payment. Bachli sued Holt for the amount of the final payment.

At the trial, plaintiff Bachli contended that his undertaking was solely with defendant Holt. The defendant presented evidence in opposition to plaintiff's contention. This evidence included a letter written by defendant to the owner stating that the architect had engaged the plumbing, heating, and electrical contractors. It stated that Holt waived his usual 5-percent surcharge on the payments to the subcontractors because the architect was to supervise their work. There was no showing that the contents of this letter were communicated to the plaintiff. There was evidence that the plaintiff had endeavored to collect final payment from the owner before proceeding against Holt. And Holt never specifically agreed to pay the plaintiff in the event of the owner's default. There was also evidence that Holt had nothing to do with the problems that developed in connection with the plaintiff's performance, and that these problems were settled by the architect.

Upon this state of the evidence, the trial court submitted but one issue to the jury: "Was there an understanding or agreement mutually entered into between these parties whereby it was intended by both that the plaintiff would perform the [heating and plumbing work and that the defendant would make payment]?" The jury returned a verdict for the plaintiff. The defendant moved for judgment notwithstanding the verdict. The court denied the motion, and defendant appealed.

HOLDEN, C. J. . . . It was the defendant who called upon the plaintiff to submit a bid for the plumbing and heating contract. When the plaintiff complied in his letter of August 23, 1960, he made an offer to the defendant to perform the work specified at the price given. Until this bid was accepted, no rights or liabilities were created. . . .

It is significant that the letter was directed to the defendant alone. The offer could be accepted only by the person to whom it was addressed. Neither the owner nor the architect could accept the bid, since it was extended only to the defendant. A prospective party has the right to select with whom he will contract, and an outsider has no standing to intrude.

It is clear from the defendant's own testimony that there was a binding acceptance [by the defendant] of the plaintiff's offer. Both parties responded accordingly. The plaintiff went on the job and did the work. All prior payments were made by the defendant according to the terms stated in the plaintiff's letter.

An acceptance of a proposal may be accomplished by conduct as effectively as though done verbally where it appears the acts of the parties conform to the terms proposed. If the defendant had some mental reservations that he was acting for the owner, without any personal obligation to compensate the plaintiff, it was for him to openly announce his position. The language and acts of a party to a contract will receive such operation as the opposite party is fairly entitled to afford them under the circumstances. He will not be entitled to claim a different consequence as the result of some undisclosed mental reservation which he had when the contract was made.

. . . [The] jury had adequate reason to find that the plaintiff was entitled to understand that his undertaking was with the defendant as principal contractor. Its conclusion that the plaintiff was justified in looking to the defendant for the full payment of the price . . . was sound in law. The defendant's motion for judgment was properly overruled. . . .

Judgment affirmed.

ACCEPTANCE OF UNILATERAL OFFER

A unilateral offer asks for an *act* of performance in exchange for the offeror's promise, whereas a bilateral offer asks for a *promise* of performance in exchange for the offeror's promise. Three questions merit special attention in connection with acceptance of unilateral offers: (1) Is complete performance a requirement for acceptance of a unilateral offer? (2) Is knowledge of the offer a requirement for acceptance? (3) Is notification of performance a requirement?

Extent of Performance
Required for Acceptance

The offeree accepts an offer for a unilateral contract by performing the act requested with intent to accept. For example, if David says to Mary, "I will pay you $1,000 to paint my house," Mary must paint the entire house in order to recover the $1,000.

Some courts take the view that an offer for a unilateral contract may be accepted by the substantial performance of the requested act, unless the offer provides otherwise. Under this view David's promise would be enforceable when Mary "substantially" finished painting the house. If Mary refused to finish, David could deduct from the $1,000 the cost to have another painter finish the job.

Knowledge of Offer as a
Requirement for Acceptance

Since, as a general rule, the offeree must perform the act requested with intent to accept, knowledge of the existence of an offer is essential. Thus, where an offer to pay a reward has

been published the offer creates a power of acceptance in a person only if that person knew of the offer at the time he or she performed the requested service. Suppose, for example, that Arthur advertises in a newspaper that he will pay a certain reward to any person who finds his lost wallet and returns it and its contents to Arthur. Barbara finds the wallet, discovers that Arthur is the owner, and delivers the wallet and contents to him. If Barbara had no knowledge of the offer at the time she returned the wallet, nearly every court would hold that she has no contractual claim against Arthur.

A difficult legal problem arises when knowledge of an offer comes to the offeree after a partial performance, as where the offeree has secured some of the information requested in an offer of reward before learning of the offer to pay for the information. If the offeree thereafter completes the performance, is there an acceptance? An offeree who learns of an offer after rendering part of the performance requested by the offer becomes entitled to the reward by completing the requested performance, unless the offeror manifested a contrary intention.

Notification of Performance as
a Requirement for Acceptance

As a general rule, when the offer is for a unilateral contract the offeree is not required to notify the offeror that performance of the requested act is complete. The offeree is required to give notice only if the offeror has included notification as part of the offer. However, a number of courts state that if the offeree has reason to believe that the performance will not come to the offeror's attention within a reasonable time, the offeree must exercise reasonable diligence to notify the offeror. Thus, notice might be required if the offeree performs the act requested in a remote area far from the offeror.

ACCEPTANCE OF BILATERAL OFFER

Usually bilateral offers are so worded or are made under such circumstances that the requested promise must be expressed in words. Sometimes, however, the requested promise is to be manifested by the performance of some act. In certain limited situations acceptance of a bilateral offer takes place even though the offeree remains silent and inactive. Each of these three methods of manifesting assent to an offer for a bilateral contract is discussed in the following pages.

Acceptance by Words Expressing Assent

Language by Which Assent May Be Expressed No particular words are required to express assent to a bilateral offer. A desirable way to express assent is to identify the offer and then add "I hereby accept your offer" (or other words indicating unequivocal acceptance). Ambiguous expressions, such as "Your order will receive our prompt and careful attention," lead to controversy over whether there has been an acceptance.

Not infrequently an offeree will purport to accept the offer but will include a term or terms additional to or different from those in the offer. As stated in Chapter 10, such a variation may be a counteroffer or a conditional acceptance and thus a rejection of the offer.

Case 11.2 **Burkhead v. Farlow**
146 S.E.2d 802 (N.C. 1966)

John A. Burkhead, the plaintiff, became interested in purchasing a tract of land from Mr. and Mrs. Farlow, the defendants. During negotiations for the land, the defendants signed the following document, which had been prepared by the plaintiff:

"Option of Purchase
We do hereby option to John A. Burkhead, a certain parcel or tract of land, lying & being in Back Creek Township, Randolph County and described as follows: App. 52 acres of land with 500 ft. more or less fronting the Spero Rd. The purchase $15,000.00, payable upon delivery of deed and acceptance of Title.
"Option expires Oct. 15, 1961.
HIS—Lester M. Farlow.
HER—Dorothy Farlow."

After the above memorandum was signed, the plaintiff asked the defendants for the deed to the property so that he could "put it in the hands of an attorney for a title check." When they gave him the deed, he told them it would be two or three weeks before the title examination could be completed, and that when it was, "the money would be available for them." Approximately two weeks after defendants signed the "Option of Purchase," they notified the plaintiff that they had decided not to sell the property. Upon completion of the title examination, the plaintiff found the title acceptable and brought action for specific performance of an alleged contract for the sale of the real estate. At the close of the plaintiff's evidence, the court allowed the defendants' motion for judgment of nonsuit (that is, the court decided the plaintiff's case was too weak to warrant continuation of the trial). The plaintiff appealed.

SHARP, J. The informal "Option of Purchase" signed by the defendants . . . embodies the terms of the offer of sale and the names of the vendor and vendee. The adequacy of the description of the land to be conveyed is not in question here. . . . The option . . . was a mere offer to sell which defendants might have withdrawn at any time before acceptance. . . .

Plaintiff's evidence, which must be taken as true in considering the motion for nonsuit, tends to show that at the time defendants delivered the option to plaintiff, he orally agreed to buy the property and told defendants the money would be available as soon as the title examination had been completed. "A written option offering to sell, at the election of the optionee, can become binding on the owner by verbal notice to the owner. . . . " [Citation.]

Plaintiff's notice of acceptance was given to defendant-optionors approximately two months before the option expired, and defendants' purported repudiation occurred about two weeks after receipt of this notice. The question which this appeal presents is whether plaintiff unconditionally accepted the offer contained in the option. Defendants contend that plaintiff's acceptance was conditional, in that it was made to depend upon the title examination which had not been completed at the time defendants withdrew their offer.

It is uniformly held that to consummate a valid contract, an acceptance must be unconditional and must not change, add to, or qualify the terms of the offer. It is also the general rule that the optionee's insertion in his acceptance of a condition which merely expresses that which "would be implied in fact or in law by the offer does not preclude the consummation of the contract, since such a condition involves no qualification of the acceptor's assent to the terms of the offer." [Citation.] In any contract to convey land, unless the parties agree differently, the law implies an undertaking on the part of the vendor to convey a good or marketable title to the purchaser. . . .

The narrow question confronting us is whether the terms of plaintiff's acceptance—that when the title examination was completed the money would be available—specified any requirement other than a good or marketable title.

It goes without saying that plaintiff had a right to secure a lawyer's opinion as to the quality of the title. No prudent person would buy land without first having the title examined by a qualified title attorney. . . . All that plaintiff required in this case was "a title check." From these words we can imply only that plaintiff would accept the title if it were ascertained to be [a good title.] . . . We hold that, upon this record, plaintiff's acceptance of the offer contained in the "Option of Purchase" was unconditional. . . .

The judgment of nonsuit is reversed.

Communication of Acceptance The general rule is that the offeree's acceptance of an offer for a bilateral contract must be communicated to the offeror.

It is often said that the offeror is master of the offer. The offeror may specify that acceptance is to be communicated face to face or by telephone, by mail, by telegraph, or by some other medium and that acceptance is to be effective only upon timely receipt of the acceptance. For example, if Steel Corporation in its offer to sell steel to a customer, says, "You must accept this offer by letter received at our home office by October 1," the offeree may not accept by any other medium. Thus, an attempt by the customer to accept by telephone is ineffective as an acceptance but amounts to a counteroffer.

The offeror may dispense with the requirement of notification of acceptance. Suppose that a salesperson for the XYZ Merchandising firm takes an offer from a customer on the firm's (offeree's) order form, that the form contains the statement, "This offer will become a contract when signed by the customer and approved (i.e., accepted) by an executive officer of the XYZ Company," and that the customer—fully aware of the statement—signs the order. By signing the order without requiring notice of XYZ's acceptance, the customer (offeror) may be held to have dispensed with the requirement of notice of acceptance.

Medium of Acceptance; When and Where Acceptance Becomes Effective Usually an offeror makes no specification as to how acceptance is to be made or is to take effect. Often courts are faced with controversies involving such a situation and have the problem of deciding when and where an acceptance becomes effective.

In early times the courts were often faced with that problem when the offer was made by mail. The prevailing rule was that the offeree had power to accept the offer by mailing a letter of acceptance, properly stamped and addressed, within a reasonable time. The contract was regarded as made at the time and place that the letter of acceptance was put into the possession of the post office. The rule is often referred to as the "deposited acceptance," or "mailbox" rule.

There was considerable confusion in the law as to when acceptance became effective where the offer was by mail and the acceptance was by telegraph or where the offer was by telegraph and the acceptance was by mail.

Acceptance by reasonable medium The general rule today is that unless otherwise specified, an offer to make a contract is construed as inviting acceptance by any medium reasonable under the circumstances. The *Restatement* provides that a medium of acceptance is reasonable if: (1) it is the one used by the offeror; (2) it is customary in similar transactions at the time and place the offer is received; or (3) it is appropriate in view of the speed and reliability of the medium used, the prior dealings between offeror and offeree, and usage of trade.[1]

If the offeree uses a "reasonable medium" to accept, the acceptance becomes effective when and at the place where the acceptance is properly dispatched, provided the offer is still open. An acceptance sent from a distance by mail is properly dispatched if it is properly addressed and stamped and if deposited in a mailbox where regular pickups are made.

The "proper dispatch" or "deposited acceptance," rule places the risk of a lost acceptance on the offeror. The rationale is that the offeree needs to know right away that there is a contract, and the offeror, having initiated the contractual relationship, is in a better position than the offeree to detect a loss or lateness of communication.

---

[1]*Restatement of the Law (Second) Contracts*, American Law Institute, Philadelphia, sec. 29(2) and 66.

Case 11.3   **Froling v. Braun**
                235 N.W.2d 168 (Mich. App. 1975)

Joseph Braun (defendant) owned a piece of real property in Bloomfield Hills. Disner, a real estate agent, asked Braun whether he would be willing to sell his property if Disner could get an offer at an acceptable price. Braun was unwilling to give an exclusive listing, but he gave permission to Disner to show the property and receive offers.

Disner received a written offer of $165,000 cash from William Froling (plaintiff) and brought the offer to Braun. Braun rejected the offer, and, through Disner, made a counteroffer of $185,000. Within a few days of receiving the counteroffer, Froling notified Disner that he accepted the counteroffer. Disner neglected to give Braun prompt notice of Froling's acceptance. Before receiving the notice, Braun told Froling's assistant, Walker, that the deal was off. Froling brought suit for specific performance. There was a judgment for the plaintiff, and defendant appealed.

MAHER, J. . . . We agree with the trial judge that a contract for sale of the property was formed by Froling's communication of acceptance of the counter-offer to Disner. . . . [Disner's delay] in notifying Braun of Froling's acceptance [did not prevent] a contract between Braun and Froling. Braun used Disner to transmit the offer to Froling. Absent any contrary indications from Braun, Froling was able [i.e., had the power] to accept in the same manner. . . . "We are of the opinion that the authorities are clear that—'The offeror takes the risk as to the effectiveness of communication if the acceptance is made in the manner either expressly or impliedly indicated by him.'" [Citation.] . . .

The judgment of specific performance in favor of plaintiff Froling . . . [is] affirmed.

Acceptance by other medium   As a general rule, an acceptance by an unreasonable medium is not effective on dispatch, but only upon *receipt* by the offeror (if the offer is still open). If the offeror sends a revocation, it is effective when received by the offeree. In such event, a difficult factual determination must be made when the offeree attempts to accept by an unreasonable medium. If a lawsuit occurs, the judge or jury must decide whether the offeree received the revocation before the offeror received the acceptance.

No acceptance occurs if the offeror has stipulated that a particular medium must be used by the offeree to communicate an acceptance, and the offeree uses a different medium. As stated previously, in such circumstances an attempt by the offeree to accept by a different medium amounts to a counteroffer. Therefore, in analyzing a factual situation, it is critical to determine whether the offeror has required (stipulated) a particular medium for acceptance.

Effect of Acceptance Plus Rejection   There is an important exception to the general rule that a timely acceptance by any reasonable medium becomes effective on proper dispatch. The rule does not apply where the notice of acceptance was preceded by a notice of rejection. The reason for the exception is that the notice of rejection might be the first to reach the offeror, and the offeror should be entitled to rely on a notice of rejection as soon as it is received. To protect the offeror, the law provides that an acceptance dispatched after a rejection has been sent is not effective until received and will not take effect even then unless the offer is still open. In short, when a notice of rejection is followed by a notice of acceptance promptly dispatched, that notice is effective which first reaches the offeror.

Suppose that instead of sending a notice of rejection followed by a notice of acceptance, the offeree sends a notice of acceptance followed by a notice of rejection. In such a situation, courts apply the general rule that a notice of acceptance becomes effective at the time the notice is properly dispatched. However, if the notice of rejection is the first notice to reach the offeror,

and the offeror changes his or her position in reliance on the notice of rejection, the offeree is estopped (barred) from enforcing the contract.

Acceptance by Act Indicating Assent

The acceptance of an offer to enter into a bilateral contract may at times properly be expressed by an act which implies a promise. A nod of the head, the raising of a hand, and the fall of an auctioneer's hammer are common examples. Similarly, taking possession of, or exercising dominion over, something may constitute acceptance. To illustrate: A, a contractor, has a pile of lumber stored on a vacant lot. A tells B to "Take a look at the lumber. If it's worth $80 to you, haul it away." B hauls it away. The act of taking possession of the lumber is an acceptance of the offer and a promise to pay the $80. The offeree who objectively manifests an intent to accept is not permitted to testify that his or her secret intent was otherwise. In the above example, hauling away the lumber is held to be an acceptance, regardless of B's subjective intention.

Case 11.4   Crouch v. Marrs
430 P.2d 204 (Kans. 1967)

In February 1964, Phillip Crouch (plaintiff) wrote the Purex Corporation a letter of inquiry about a silica processing plant which Purex owned but which had not been in use for many years. In the letter Crouch asked whether Purex might be interested in selling the building and its contents, and if so what the lowest price would be. On March 4, Crouch received a letter of reply from Purex Corporation signed by Frank Knox which stated: "We will sell this building and the equipment in and about the building for a total of $500."

On March 19, Crouch wrote to Frank Knox, Purex Corporation, stating that the building was in "pretty bad condition" and asking, "Would you consider taking $300 for what is left?" This letter was not answered.

On April 16, Crouch addressed another letter to Frank Knox, Purex Corporation, which read: "I guess we will buy the building for the amount you quoted, $500. I am sending you a personal check for this amount. It will be 2 or 3 weeks before we can get started, and I presume that we will be allowed all the time that we need to remove the material."

The check was made out to Frank Knox and stated on its face that it was "For Silica building and equipment in and about that building." Knox endorsed the check to the Purex Corporation.

On April 27, Knox sent Crouch the following telegram: "Your counter offer received April 23 is unacceptable. Your check mistakenly deposited by Purex will be recovered and returned to you or Purex check will be issued to you if your check cannot be located."

There followed a letter dated May 16, which read:

"This is a follow-up to our telegram to you of April 27, advising you that your check which we received on April 23 was not acceptable, but that it had been deposited by mistake. Since we were unable to recover your check, we herewith enclose our check for $500 to reimburse you.

We wish to explain that the reason we could not accept your counter-offer of $500 for the mine building and machinery at Meade, Kansas was because we had received and accepted an offer from another party [Martin Asche] prior to receipt of yours on April 23."

Asche sold the building and contents to Roy Marrs, who sold them to others.

Crouch filed an action against Marrs, Purex Corporation, and other defendants.

HATCHER, Commissioner. This was an action to enjoin interference with plaintiff's right of ingress and egress to land on which was located a building he was attempting to salvage. The result of the action was to have the title to the building determined. Judgment was rendered against plaintiff and he appealed. . . .

The appellees [defendants] contend that the appellant's check was cashed through inadvertence or an error in office procedure and under such circumstances the cashing of the check did not constitute an acceptance of appellant's offer. The difficulty with this contention is that there was no evidence of any character as to why the check was cashed. . . .

The question is whether the endorsing and depositing of appellant's check constituted an acceptance of his offer to buy? We think it did. . . .

The endorsing and depositing a check constitutes an acceptance of the offer to buy which accompanies it because the act itself indicates acceptance. An offer may be accepted by performing a specified act as well as by an affirmative answer. Also, where the offeree exercised dominion over the thing offered him—in this instance the check—such exercise constitutes an acceptance of the offer. The rule is well stated in *Autographic Register Co. v. Philip Hano Co.*, 1 Cir., 198 F.2d 208, where it is said:

". . . It is elementary that an offer may be accepted by performing or refraining from performing a specified act as well as by an affirmative answer, and it is stated in Am. Law Inst., *Restatement, Contracts*, Sec. 72(2) as the general rule that 'Where the offeree exercises dominion over things which are offered to him, such exercise of dominion in the

Case 11.4
Continued

absence of other circumstances showing a contrary intention is an acceptance.'" . . .

We are forced to conclude that the acceptance and endorsement of the check accompanying the offer to purchase the property in controversy constituted an acceptance of the offer.

The judgment is reversed with instructions to the district court to quiet plaintiff's title to the building and equipment in controversy against the defendants and enjoin them from interfering with plaintiff's ingress and egress for the purpose of salvaging the property.

[The Commissioner's opinion is] approved by the Court.

Acceptance by Silence and Inaction

As a general rule, silence of the offeree does not constitute acceptance. For example, if Able Company sends an offer to Barbara and states, "If we do not hear from you by June 1, we shall assume you accept our offer," Barbara need not reply. Several states and the federal government have enacted legislation which provides that unordered merchandise received by mail may be treated as a gift. Thus, the recipient may use or dispose of the merchandise without liability.

There can be an acceptance of a bilateral offer, even though the offeree remains silent, if that silence is accompanied by some act from which assent may reasonably be inferred. Following are two examples of situations in which silence and inaction operate as an acceptance.

1 Silence and inaction operate as an acceptance where the offeree in remaining silent and inactive intends to accept the offer. Suppose that A's horse is temporarily in B's possession, and that A sends B an offer to sell the horse for $250. In the letter A says, "I am so sure that you will accept that you need not trouble to write me. Your silence alone will operate as acceptance." *With the intention* of accepting, B makes no reply and remains inactive. There is a contract.

2 Silence and inaction operate as an acceptance where because of previous dealings or otherwise, it is reasonable that the offeree should notify the offeror if he does not intend to accept. For example, a firm which sends out a salesperson to solicit offers "subject to acceptance by the home office" must reject an order it does not care to accept if, in the past, it had invariably filled the customer's orders or informed the customer promptly that it was unable to fill a particular order. Some courts hold that the firm has the duty of rejection even in the absence of a past course of conduct. These courts believe that the initiative taken by the firm in soliciting an order warrants any customer in believing that the order is accepted unless the customer is promptly notified to the contrary so that he or she may place an order elsewhere.

Case 11.5   Corbin-Dykes Electric Co. v. Burr
500 P.2d 632 (Ariz. App. 1972)

General Motors Corporation requested bids from general contractors to construct the central air-conditioning plant at its Mesa proving grounds. The defendant, Walter Burr, a general contractor, was interested in obtaining the contract. He invited bids for the electrical subcontract. Corbin-Dykes Electric Company, the plaintiff, submitted a bid. Burr incorporated Corbin-Dykes' subcontract bid into Burr's general contract bid. All bids were rejected by General Motors because they exceeded the cost estimate, and the project was rebid. The second bid submitted by Burr also included the Corbin-Dykes' subcontract bid. Burr was awarded the general contract, but Burr accepted another bid for the electric subcontract.

Corbin-Dykes objected to the selection of another as the subcontractor and sued Burr for breach of their alleged subcontract. Burr moved for summary judgment, and the motion was granted. Corbin-Dykes appealed from the summary judgment.

EUBANKS, J. . . . [Corbin-Dykes contends] that a custom and usage exists in the trade to the effect that a subcontractor who is listed in the general contractor's bid will receive the subcontract, if the general contractor is successful and is awarded the general contract. This custom and usage would be introduced at the trial, according to Corbin-Dykes, in order to prove the contract existed between it and Burr, or in other words to prove the acceptance by Burr of Corbin-Dykes' bid offer. The record shows that there was no other evidence of acceptance by Burr of the subcontract offer.

In Arizona the law is clear that Corbin-Dykes' bid to Burr was nothing more than an offer to perform the subcontract under specified terms, and that it did not ripen into a contract until it was voluntarily accepted by Burr. . . .

If the law requires an actual voluntary acceptance of Corbin-Dykes' bid by Burr, can this acceptance be established solely by [evidence of] custom and usage in the trade . . . as offered by Corbin-Dykes? We think not.

In order for there to be any contract between Corbin-Dykes and Burr, there must be a manifestation of mutual assent thereto by both, and the acts by which their mutual assent is manifested must show that they intended to do those acts. . . . However, evidence of custom and usage is admissible only where an existing agreement between the parties is ambiguous, to show what the parties intended by their agreement. . . .

Corbin-Dykes relies on no evidence of the acceptance of their offer by Burr except the above referred to custom and usage. . . . In our opinion the record shows no evidence of a voluntary acceptance of the offer. . . . The inclusion of Corbin-Dykes' subcontract bid as a part of the general contract bid did not constitute such an acceptance, and the offer never was accepted by Burr in any other manner.

The summary judgment is affirmed.

AGREEMENT LOOKING FORWARD TO A WRITING

Often parties who are negotiating for a bilateral contract decide at some point in the negotiating process that when agreement is reached it will be put into writing and signed. If agreement is reached, does a contract come into being as soon as the agreement is reached or not until the agreement is put into writing and signed?

The question is easily answered if the parties made clear what their intention was.

Where litigation arises out of the contract and the parties have not made clear what their intention was, the court will try to determine the intention from all the surrounding circumstances. For example, where the contract has many details and is of a type usually put into writing, the court might conclude the intention was that there was to be no binding obligation until the writing was completed. If the parties orally agree on all the details and the transaction involves a small amount of money, the courts might conclude that the parties intended to be bound when the oral agreement was reached and that the writing was to serve merely as a "memorial" (record) of the agreement.

Case 11.6   **Mohler v. Park County School District**
515 P.2d 112 (Colo. App. 1973)

Robert Mohler, the plaintiff, was employed by Park County School District Re-2 as superintendent of schools for the 1970-1971 school year. Mohler's reemployment for the school year 1971-1972 was to be considered at the regular meeting of the board of education of the school district on June 14, 1971; and a special meeting of the board was held on June 3 to discuss his reemployment. At the June 14 meeting, a motion was made, and carried by a vote of 4 to 3, that Mohler be offered a contract as superintendent of schools for the 1971-1972 school year. Mohler was present when the motion was made and responded to the motion, as he had in July of the previous year, by saying, "Thank you." He returned to summer school and made no attempt to seek employment or arrange for job interviews elsewhere.

At a board meeting on July 12, 1971, the board passed the following resolution, by a 6 to 1 majority vote: "Resolved, that the motion made on June 14, 1971, to reemploy Mr. Mohler for the 1971-1972 school year is hereby rescinded." After July 12, Mohler unsuccessfully sought other employment.

Plaintiff Mohler brought an action for breach of an employment contract against the school district and the board of education. A jury returned a verdict in favor of plaintiff in the amount of $14,600. Defendants appealed, contending that the resolution passed by the school board on June 14 did not constitute an offer of employment which plaintiff could accept and that therefore no contract of employment arose. Defendants also contended that the court erred in refusing to give certain tendered instructions.

COYTE, J. . . . We disagree with these contentions. . . .

The evidence disclosed that in the prior year plaintiff had accepted a verbal offer of employment, and that a written contract of employment prepared by defendants' attorney had not been executed until August 10, 1970, some ten days after plaintiff's term of employment began. The board member who made the motion at the June 14, 1971 board meeting testified that he intended the motion to be an offer on the same terms as the previous year. . . . [Plaintiff testified that he intended his reply, "Thank you," to be an acceptance of the offer.]

It is urged by defendants that plaintiff could not have been offered a specific contract because he had not obtained a type "D" school administrator's certificate as required in the 1970 contract. Whether plaintiff's failure to obtain this certificate precluded the offer and acceptance of a binding contract was a question for determination by the jury.

Whether the parties to an oral agreement become bound prior to the drafting and execution of a contemplated formal writing is a question largely of intent on their part. That intent can be inferred from their actions and may be determined by their conduct prior to the time the controversy arose. [If a jury finds] that the parties intended to be bound regardless of a complete writing, a contract must be held to exist. [In the present case] there was evidence introduced from which the jury could determine that the board did offer plaintiff a contract of employment for the 1971-72 school year, and that plaintiff had accepted the offer of employment. . . .

Further, the board between June 14th and July 12th took no action to hire anyone for the position of superintendent of schools, nor was plaintiff advised after the June 14th motion that the board did not consider him reemployed for the next year. . . .

Defendants particularly object to the refusal of the trial court to give two of their tendered instructions. The first of these is not applicable to the facts in this case. It instructed that the mere passing of a resolution by a public board or agency such as the defendant school board does not create a power of acceptance in one who learns of the passing of the resolution in a fortuitous manner. In the instant case, plaintiff was present at the board meeting when the motion was made and passed. . . .

Judgment affirmed.

SUMMARY

Acceptance is the offeree's expression of assent to the terms of an offer proposed by the offeror. Where an offer is addressed to a specified offeree, only that person may accept the offer. Where the offer is addressed to the public, there may be one acceptance or a number of acceptances, depending on the manifested intent of the offeror.

Most courts hold that substantial performance by the offeree with intent to accept is required for the acceptance of a unilateral offer. The offeree is not required to notify the offeror that performance is complete unless the offeror has

so specified in the offer, or the performance will not come to the offeror's attention within a reasonable time.

Usually bilateral offers are so worded that the acceptance (promise) must be expressed in words. Where acceptance is to be by words, any language suffices so long as it identifies the offer and clearly expresses acceptance of the offer. If the offeror stipulates that the acceptance must be communicated by a particular medium, an attempt by the offeree to accept by a different medium is treated as a counteroffer.

Normally an offer for a bilateral contract invites acceptance by any medium reasonable in the circumstances. Acceptance by a reasonable medium becomes effective when and where notification is properly dispatched, provided the offer is still open. If the offeree uses an unreasonable medium, acceptance is effective on receipt.

An acceptance of a bilateral offer may be implied by the offeree's conduct. In such event the offeree's secret intent is immaterial. As a general rule, silence or inaction of the offeree does not constitute acceptance. The offeree's silence may constitute acceptance if the offeree intends to accept or if a previous course of dealing between the parties imposes an obligation to deny acceptance.

Often, parties who are negotiating a bilateral contract decide at some point in the negotiating process that when the agreement is reached it will be put into writing and signed. Later the question may arise as to whether the oral agreement was legally binding as soon as it was reached or not until it was put into writing. The answer depends on what the intent of the parties was.

STUDY AND DISCUSSION QUESTIONS

1 (a)What is meant by "acceptance?" (b)What determines the number of acceptances there may be of an offer addressed to the general public? Illustrate how there could be multiple acceptances.

2 (a)What degree of performance is required for acceptance of a unilateral offer? (b)How does the law prevent hardship to the offeror where an offeree does not complete performance?

3 (a)Why is notification of performance not usually required in unilateral contracts? (b)Under what circumstances is notification of performance required?

4 (a)When must an acceptance be actually communicated to the offeror? Explain and give an example. (b)Define "reasonable medium" of acceptance. (c)Explain how the "proper dis-

patch" rule works. (d)Under the proper dispatch rule, who bears the risk of a lost communication? Why that person?

5 If an offeree uses an unreasonable medium, when and where is the acceptance effective?

6 What is the effect of a rejection preceding a properly and timely dispatched acceptance?

7 (a)In what kind of situation may an act operate as an acceptance of a bilateral offer? (b)Illustrate a situation where silence and inaction might operate as acceptance of a bilateral offer.

8 (a)When does an agreement looking forward to a writing become legally effective? (b)Where an agreement becomes legally effective before it is put into writing, of what value is the writing?

CASE PROBLEMS

1 After negotiations, defendant wrote plaintiff on December 20: "I am planning on going away the first of the year some place. About the ditching you were to do on my farm, go ahead and do the work that you think is needed and I will pay you later on when you send me the bill. I may not see you before I go away." On December 23, plaintiff wrote: "We will be at your ranch ready to extend the ditches for you about January 20th." The court decided that the letter of December 23 was an acceptance. Can this decision be justified?

2 Mullaly sent Grieve an offer to lease him certain land. Grieve, without Mullaly's consent, turned the offer over to Adams. Adams sent Mullaly a lease based on the terms of the offer, but naming himself as lessee. Was there an acceptance of the offer?

3 Certain private individuals offered a reward for information leading to the arrest of an accused person. There were two claimants for the reward: A, who gave correct information to the proper officers but whose information did not

lead to the arrest and B, who gave information leading to the arrest but who did not know about the offer of reward. Is either of the claimants entitled to the reward?

4 H. M. Johnson stated in writing that in return for a designated compensation he would assist Star Iron and Steel Co. (Star Iron) to secure short-term financing from a bank of Johnson's choice. By letter dated October 3, 1969, Star Iron indicated its willingness to accept the terms of Johnson's offer, subject to the condition that Johnson's statement, "bank of my choice," be changed to read "Bank of Tacoma." On October 8, Star Iron withdrew its conditional acceptance. Johnson brought suit for compensation under the theory that Star Iron's letter of October 3 constituted an acceptance of Johnson's offer. Did Star Iron's letter of October 3 constitute an acceptance?

5 On November 2, T submitted to a federal farm mortgage bank a written offer to buy a certain piece of land. The offer specified that acceptance "must be in writing" and must be approved by the executive committee of the bank. While the offer was in the possession of the bank, a notation was placed on it reading: "Approved by the Executive Committee—Nov. 9—A. R. Murray." Later the notation was crossed out and another added: "Reconsidered and rejected—A. R. Murray, Minute Clerk— Date Nov. 17." No notification of acceptance had been sent to T. Was there a contract?

6 Plaintiff and defendant exchanged a series of letters concerning the possible sale of certain land by plaintiff to defendant. After "the terms were pretty well agreed upon," the plaintiff, at defendant's suggestion, made a draft of the agreement and mailed it to defendant. Defendant returned the draft unsigned and with certain amendments written on it. He accompanied the draft with a letter in which he said: "I believe you will find this as near as possible to the conditions which I wrote you in the possible purchase of the land by contract." The letter suggested that if the revised draft was satisfactory to plaintiff, he should have two copies made, sign them, and send them to defendant for his signature. The letter concluded: "I see no reason why we can't close it right up." Plaintiff did as defendant had suggested but defendant refused to sign. Action for breach of contract. Was there a contract?

7 After preliminary negotiations, plaintiff and defendant reached an agreement by the terms of which plaintiff was to buy a half interest in defendant's business and to become a partner in the operation of the business. The two parties agreed that the terms of the agreement were to be reduced to writing, even though the law does not require a partnership agreement to be in writing; that the parties were to meet on July 1 to sign the writing; and that plaintiff was to pay the purchase price at that time. Plaintiff prepared the writing and appeared at the appointed time and place with the purchase money, but defendant did not appear. Learning that defendant had sold his business to others, plaintiff brought action for breach of contract. Was there a contract?

Chapter

12
Consideration

Not all promises are legally enforceable. Purely social promises, such as a promise to love someone, are not enforceable, and some promises made in a commercial context are not. How do the courts distinguish those commercial promises which are enforceable from those which are not?

To be enforceable under the early common law, a promise had to be in writing, and the writing had to bear the seal or insignia of the promisor. The writing and the seal were tangible evidence of an undertaking by the promisor, and the courts were willing to enforce a promise that had been so elaborately and formally prepared.

As society and commerce developed, a need arose for a broader range of promise enforcement. A poor and largely illiterate population conducted much of its business informally and had little time for or understanding of elaborate contractual formalities. By the early fourteenth century, courts were enforcing some kinds of unsealed promises and were seeking some basis —some underlying idea or theory—for determining which unsealed promises should be enforceable. The courts now recognize three bases for the enforcement of unsealed (i.e., "informal") commercial promises:

- Consideration
- Promissory estoppel
- Statutes and decisional law which impose liability in the absence of consideration or in the absence of the justifiable reliance characteristic of promissory estoppel.

THE REQUIREMENT OF CONSIDERATION

The doctrine of consideration arose out of the need to enforce promises made as a part of a bargained-for exchange. A person usually rendered a performance or promised to do so because some other person promised a return performance such as a payment of money. Each person's promise was made "in consideration of" (i.e., in exchange for) the other person's promise, and each promise created an expectation of performance. To protect those expectations, the courts long ago began to enforce informal promises which had been induced by consideration.

Most commercial promises are made in the hope of receiving the benefit of a bargain, and consideration is therefore the most frequent and the most important basis for promise enforcement.

Nature of Consideration

There are various definitions of consideration given by judges and legal writers. For our purposes, *consideration* may be defined as legal detriment to the promisee bargained for by the promisor.

Elements of Consideration Consideration consists of two elements. One of the elements is the "bargained-for" aspect of consideration. The second element is referred to as "legal detriment."

Bargained-for exchange Section 75 of the Restatement (Second) of the Law of Contracts provides in part:

(**1**) To constitute consideration, a performance or a return promise must be bargained for.

(**2**) A performance or return promise is bargained for if it is sought by the promisor in exchange for his promise and is given by the promisee in exchange for that promise.

These statements indicate that there must be a reciprocal relationship between the offeror's promise and the offeree's performance or return promise: the offeror's promise must *induce* the offeree's performance or return promise.

Legal detriment The second element of consideration is that the promisee must incur legal detriment. Legal detriment means the promisee gives up or promises to give up a legal right, or assumes or promises to assume a legal burden. Where the offer is for a unilateral contract there is one promisor and one promisee. Where the offer is for a bilateral contract the parties are at the same time promisors and promisees. As a general rule, in bilateral contracts both parties must incur legal detriment.

Usually the legal detriment incurred by the promisee will be a legal benefit to the promisor but this is not required. Legal detriment does not necessarily mean *actual* detriment. The well-known case of *Hamer v. Sidway*[1] involved a promise by an uncle to pay his nephew $5,000 if he would "refrain from . . . using tobacco" until he was twenty-one. The nephew refrained from doing so. The uncle did not pay, and the nephew sued. The court held that the nephew had a legal right to use tobacco and that when he gave up that right he suffered a legal detriment, even though abstaining might have constituted an actual physical benefit.

By defining consideration in terms of legal rather than actual detriment, courts accomplish two things: (1) leave the problem of economic valuation to the parties to the contract and (2) avoid the difficulty of finding actual detriment in those cases where the promisee is benefited, as in *Hamer v. Sidway*.

---

[1]121 N.Y. App. 538 (1891).

Case 12.1   **Graphic Arts Finishers, Inc. v. Boston Redevelopment Authority**
255 N.E.2d 793 (Mass. 1970)

In an exercise of the power of eminent domain, the Boston Redevelopment Authority (BRA) took buildings which housed the business of Graphic Arts

Finishers (plaintiff). To induce plaintiff to leave the premises without legal action, BRA (defendant) promised to pay plaintiff's relocation expenses which amounted to approximately $130,000. BRA also induced the plaintiff to agree not to liquidate its business.

BRA did not pay all the relocation expenses, and plaintiff brought an action for breach of contract. The trial court sustained defendant's demurrer, and plaintiff appealed.

SPALDING, J. . . . The sufficiency in law of count 1 depends on whether the plaintiff's alleged promises constitute valid consideration for the defendant's promise to pay moving expenses. Since we think that the plaintiff's [promise not to liquidate its business] constitutes consideration, we need not consider the validity of the other two.

The essentials of consideration are summarized in Williston, Contracts (3d ed.) sec. 102A: "[Legal detriment] means giving up something which immediately prior thereto the promisee was privileged to retain, or doing . . . something which he was then privileged not to do. . . . Benefit correspondingly must mean the receiving as the exchange for his promise of some performance or forbearance which the promisor was not previously entitled to receive." The plaintiff's promise to relocate its business and not liquidate clearly is the "doing something which . . . [it] was then privileged not to do." . . .

The defendant's second argument is that the plaintiff's promise was illusory in that it specified no definite time period during which the plaintiff would remain in business and hence was not valid consideration. It is true that a promise that binds one to do nothing at all is illusory and cannot be consideration. *Gill v. Richmond Co-op Assn. Inc.,* 309 Mass. 73, 79-80, 34 N.E.2d 509 (plaintiffs' promise to buy such milk as they might order). But here the plaintiff has bound itself to do something, namely, to relocate and open its business elsewhere. If, after having done so, the plaintiff decided to liquidate, it cannot be said that the original promise was entirely lacking in consideration. The law does not concern itself with the adequacy of consideration; it is enough if it is valuable. The plaintiff's promise is to be distinguished from a promise to relocate if it so desired, which clearly would be illusory. . . .

Order sustaining demurrer reversed.

Movement of Consideration   The consideration (i.e., performance or return promise) demanded by a promisor usually moves from the promisee to the promisor. But it need not necessarily do so. The performance or the return promise may be given to some person other than the promisor if the promisor so requires. Suppose that Brenda Buyer promises to pay $200 for a guitar to be delivered to her son. Susan Seller's promise (made to Brenda) to deliver the guitar to Brenda's son is consideration to Brenda even though her son actually receives the guitar.

"Past Consideration"—No Consideration
The term "past consideration," which is sometimes used, is self-contradictory. Consideration, by its definition, is something given in exchange for a promise and to induce it. Accordingly,

anything which has occurred *before* a promise was made cannot be consideration. Suppose a father writes his son and daughter-in-law: "I am so happy you named your son after me. In consideration of that fact, I promise to pay you $1,000 on the tenth of next month." The promise is unenforceable because the naming of the child was not something bargained for. The fact that a past event cannot be something bargained for has given rise to the statement, "Past consideration is no consideration."

Consideration Distinguished from Motives

Consideration should not be confused with *motives*. "Love and affection" may be compelling motives for making a promise, but they are not words of bargaining. Thus, an uncle may write his nephew: "In consideration of my love and affection, I promise to send you a check for $1,000 on your twenty-first birthday." The uncle bargained for nothing in exchange for his promise. His promise is therefore unsupported by consideration.

Illusory Promise—Not Consideration

Whether a bargained-for promise from an offeree constitutes consideration for the offeror's promise depends on the *content* of the promise. As explained earlier in this chapter, a promise to give up a legal right or a promise to assume a legal burden constitutes consideration. However, certain words of promise do not obligate the "promisor" to any performance. Such words of promise are called *illusory* promises. Suppose, for example, that S offers to deliver to B at a stated price per bushel as many bushels of wheat, not exceeding 5,000, as B may order within the next 30 days. B "accepts," agreeing to buy at that price as many bushels as she shall order from S within the 30-day period. Although B seems to have made a promise, in fact she has not committed herself to purchase any wheat. Her promise is illusory and is not consideration.

If, on the other hand, B had promised to buy as many bushels (not to exceed 5,000) as she would need in her business, the promise would not be illusory. The arrangement is called a "requirements" contract, and B's business needs provide an objective standard for determining some minimum amount of purchase. Because requirements contracts are useful and because the amount to be purchased does not depend solely on the whim of a party to the contract, courts routinely enforce them.

A promise may be rendered illusory if the promisor has an unrestricted right to cancel the contract, such as a right to cancel without notice. If the right to terminate the agreement is restricted in any way, the promise is not illusory. A right to cancel might be conditioned on the happening of some event such as a strike or a war or might require the promisor to give notice, such as 30 days. In such events the promisor incurs detriment. The promisor must perform for some period of time and thus the promise is not illusory.

Adequacy of Consideration

As a general rule, any detriment, no matter how small, may constitute consideration. If courts were to substitute their ideas of relative values for those of the parties as expressed in their agreement, endless litigation, delay, and uncertainty would result. Besides, courts believe that it would be unwarranted interference with freedom of contract if they were to relieve a party from a bad bargain.

Although the requirement of consideration may be met despite great differences in the values exchanged, gross inadequacy of consideration may be relevant in the application of other rules. Such inadequacy (for example, $10,000 in exchange for $3 worth of foreign currency) may help to justify rescission of the contract on the ground of duress, undue influence, or fraud (discussed in Chapter 13) or on the ground of contractual incapacity (discussed in Chapter 14). It may also indicate that a purported consideration was not in fact bargained for but was a mere formality or pretense. Such a sham or "nominal" consideration does not satisfy the requirement of consideration.

Case 12.2   Osborne v. Locke Steel Chain Co.
                 218 A.2d 526 (Conn. 1966)

Plaintiff Osborne began working for Locke Steel Chain Co. in 1912, progressively holding the positions of order clerk, traffic manager, sales representative, sales manager, president, and chairman of the board of Locke Steel Chain Co. (defendant). In 1960, when plaintiff was chairman of the board, the company's six other directors prepared a proposed agreement for Osborne's retirement. Osborne knew nothing of the proposal until it was presented to him at a special meeting of the board. Osborne signed it. The agreement provided that the defendant company would pay Osborne $20,000 during the year ending September 30, 1961, and $15,000 a year thereafter for the remainder of his life. Osborne agreed to hold himself available for consultation and advice with the company and its officers and not to compete with the company in its domestic or foreign markets.

The company made regular payments under the agreement until April 1963. The company requested Osborne to agree to smaller annual payments. He refused, and the company repudiated the agreement and discontinued payments. Osborne brought suit for breach of contract. The trial court rendered judgment in favor of defendant, and Osborne appealed.

COTTER, J. . . . We first pass to the question of consideration . . . the general rule being that in the absence of consideration an executory promise is unenforceable. In defining the elements of the rule, we have stated that consideration consists of "a benefit to the party promising, or a loss or detriment to the party to whom the promise is made." An exchange of promises is sufficient consideration to support a contract. . . .

Under the facts of this case, the recited consideration constituted a benefit to the defendant, as well as a detriment to the plaintiff, and was therefore sufficient consideration. . . . An exclusive right to the counseling of the plaintiff, who had almost fifty years of experience in the defendant's business, including some twenty years in positions of ultimate responsibility, and whose capacities are unchallenged, cannot reasonably be held to be valueless. Exactly what value might be placed on such a right is of course irrelevant to this issue. The doctrine of consideration does not require or imply an equal exchange between the contracting parties.

> "That which is bargained-for by the promisor and given in exchange for the promise by the promisee is not made insufficient as a consideration by the fact that its value in the market is not equal to that which is promised. Consideration in fact bargained for is not required to be adequate in the sense of equality in value." 1 Corbin, Contracts sec. 127. . . .

In the absence of fraud or other unconscionable circumstances, a contract will not be rendered unenforceable at the behest of one of the contracting parties merely because of an inadequacy of consideration. The courts do not unmake bargains unwisely made. The contractual obligation of the defendant in the present case, whether wise or unwise, was supported by consideration, in the form of the plaintiff's promises to give advice and not to compete with the defendant. . . .

One additional aspect of the issue of consideration needs discussion. The defendant has claimed that the agreement was motivated by a desire to compensate the plaintiff during his retirement years for his past services to the company. Judging from certain language in the preamble to the agreement . . . this was undoubtedly true. The general rule is that past services will not constitute a sufficient consideration for an executory promise of compensation for those services. It is well established, however, that if two considerations are given for a promise, only one of which is legally sufficient, the promise is nonetheless enforceable. Since the agreement contained promises by the plaintiff which we have held to constitute sufficient consideration, [the defendant cannot be excused from performance]. . . .

. . . The judgment is set aside.

PROBLEMS RELATING TO CONSIDERATION

The courts must deal with a variety of problems relating to consideration. For example, in some cases the issue is whether there is any consideration to support a promise to accept a lesser performance than that already owed as a result of an existing duty or obligation. In other cases the question is whether a composition agreement requires consideration to be enforceable or what constitutes consideration. These and other problems are discussed in the following paragraphs.

Performance of Existing Legal Duty or Obligation

In general, performing or promising to perform an act which a person is already under a legal obligation to perform is not consideration for a new promise. There are two situations involving existing obligation which call for some discussion: (1) where the promisee is already under contractual duty to the promisor and (2) where the existing obligation is the result of statutory or common law rule.

Existing Contractual Duty Performing or promising to perform a contractual duty which is still in effect is *not* consideration. Suppose that B was under contract with A to build an asphalt road along one side of A's farm for a stated sum, that after partial performance B discovered he would lose money on the job, and that B threatened to quit. In order to persuade B to complete the job, A promised to pay him an additional $10,000. B completed the job. Nearly all courts would hold that there was no consideration given by B and he cannot enforce A's promise. B suffered no legal detriment in completing a job he was already under contractual duty to perform. He did not give up "a legal right"; he had no right to threaten to quit the job even though he would lose money. Such threats are a form of blackmail.

There are exceptions to the general rule of unenforceability, and occasionally courts find legal detriment by the promisee. If the parties to a contract mutually and voluntarily rescind the contract and one party promises to pay a bonus to the other for performing the same duties called for in the original contract, the courts will enforce the promise. Rescission of a contract excuses both parties from further performance. Thus, performing or promising to perform the same acts called for in the original contract is "assuming a legal burden" and constitutes consideration. Another exception to the rule of unenforceability is where the promisee encounters unforeseen difficulties. The courts are reluctant to enforce promises to pay bonuses in such situations and the difficulty must be truly unanticipated. For example, if B in the illustration above would lose money on the job because of a labor strike, increase in cost of materials, or bad weather, A's promise would still not be enforceable. A court might find consideration by B if the cause of his losing money was an unforeseeable flash flood that destroyed all work done to that time.

Case 12.3 **Owens v. City of Bartlett**
528 P.2d 1235 (Kan. 1974)

Owens (plaintiff), a plumbing contractor, was hired by the City of Bartlett (defendant) to install a water distribution system. The written contract stated that no claims for extra work or materials would be allowed unless ordered in writing by the city or its authorized representative. The mayor orally requested extra work and materials which Owens provided and for which the city made payment. Owens encountered unexpected rock. The city ran short of money and fell behind in payments required by the contract. Owens stopped work for three weeks to discuss the payment and rock removal situation, and the city agreed to rent special rock removal equipment. After the project was completed, the city refused to pay for some of the extra work. Owens brought suit to recover the balance due. The trial court rendered judgment for Owens, and the city appealed.

FROMME, J. . . . . Generally a stipulation in a public construction contract that claims for extra work or materials shall be allowed only if ordered in writing by the public entity, is valid and binding upon the parties; and therefore, so long as such a provision remains in effect, no recovery can be had for extra work or materials furnished without a written order in compliance therewith. The stipulation in a public construction contract that extra work or materials must be ordered in writing can be avoided by the parties to the contract where their words, acts, or conduct would amount to a waiver or modification of such provision, or where the public entity by the acts or conduct of its proper officer or representative is estopped to rely on it. . . .

The appellant [City] correctly points out, however, that the ditching and removal of the rock was an obligation of the contractor under the original contract. . . . [This court has stated]:

"The prevailing view in this country [is] that the performance or promise of performance of an act which the promisor is already bound to do does not constitute consideration so long as the original promise is still in effect."

However, if the original provisions of the contract are mutually rescinded by agreement of the parties, the contractor is then free of any obligation to obtain an order in writing for extra work or materials and is no longer obligated to perform the work for the amount specified in the original contract. Rescission depends upon the intention of the parties as shown by their words, acts, or agreement. Parties to a contractual transaction may mutually rescind the transaction although neither party had a right to compel a rescission. . . .

In the present case the parties, throughout the performance of the contract, entirely disregarded the stipulation [requiring a written order]. An extra water hydrant, 600 feet of pipe, footings and lines to a water tower were orally ordered and these resulted in extra work and materials furnished by the contractor over which there is no dispute. When rock was encountered in the ditching, the city through its mayor agreed to and did arrange for special equipment which it rented at the city's expense. The removal of rock was treated the same as other extras. Itemized statements covering at least a portion of the completed extras were submitted by the contractor to the city and at least a portion of these were paid. . . . Such action by the council . . . did not constitute compliance with the provision in the contract that no claim for extra work or materials shall be allowed "unless it is ordered in writing. . . ."

In addition, waiver and modification of the stipulation as to rock removal appears to have occurred at a time when the city was in default. . . . The contractor when confronted by the city's default . . . was justified in shutting down until payments were made. . . . The contractor testified and the trial court impliedly found that the contractor was to be paid for removal of the rock as an extra. A promise to pay additional compensation to a contractor for the performance of an obligation to which he is bound by a contract may be enforceable where it is made in consideration of a waiver of a default by the promisee. . . .

The judgment is affirmed.

Existing Statutory or Common Law Obligation Performance or promise of performance (or forbearance) of an act which a person is under legal obligation to perform (or forbear) because of some statutory or common law rule is *not* consideration. Everyone is obligated not to commit torts and crimes. A witness at a trial is required to tell the truth. The holder of a public office has an obligation to perform the duties of the office. There is therefore no consideration for a promise to pay for immunity from assault, to reward a witness for telling the truth, or to pay a sheriff for making an arrest that comes within the scope of the sheriff's duties. In each instance the promisee is not giving up a legal right or assuming a legal burden.

Part Payment of a Liquidated Claim

A debt (or claim) is said to be liquidated when there is no dispute about the existence of the debt or its amount. The general rule is that part payment of a liquidated debt, made when the debt is due or past due, is not consideration for the creditor's promise to accept the part payment as payment in full. There is no consideration because the debtor has suffered no legal detriment in doing what he or she was already bound to do. This is merely an application of the existing-contractual-duty rule discussed previously. Since the debtor gives no consideration, a creditor can recover the unpaid part of the debt *even after promising to accept the part payment as payment in full.*

The general rule has been criticized as tending to defeat fair dealing and the rightful expectations of the debtor. Consequently, the courts have been "astute to find consideration" if the debtor had done anything at all in connection with the payment that he or she was not under obligation to do. Thus, courts will find that there is consideration if the debtor: (1) gives some inconsequential thing in addition to making the part payment; (2) pays at a place other than that required by the contract; (3) pays in a medium other than required by the contract; or (4) pays a lesser sum before the due date in the contract. The widespread feeling regarding the undesirable results of the general rule has caused some state legislatures to modify or abolish it, such as by allowing a written release by the creditor to extinguish the debt.

Settlement of an Unliquidated Claim

The rule that a part payment does not discharge the debt applies only where the debt is liquidated. A claim is unliquidated when there is an honest dispute about the existence of an indebtedness or, more commonly, about the amount of the indebtedness. Suppose that the owner of a house orders a certain plumbing job without any agreement as to price. After the plumber completes the job he sends a bill for $300. The owner protests that the size of the bill is unreasonable. She suggests a price of $200. The plumber states that $300 is the "going price" for

such a job but that to get the dispute settled, he will accept $250 as payment in full. The owner pays that amount. The agreement to accept $250 is called an "accord." Payment of the amount is called "satisfaction." The plumber may not recover the remaining $50 of his bill. By accepting the settlement he impliedly promises to cancel the balance claimed. The same result occurs if there is no agreement as to price and the homeowner sends a check for $250 marked "payment in full." There is an accord and satisfaction if the plumber cashes the check. The result is the same if, before cashing the check, the plumber crosses out the notation.

The creditor's promise to cancel the balance is supported by consideration, since the debtor suffered a legal detriment in paying more than a court might have required the debtor to pay. However, this reasoning applies only where the debtor asserts his or her objection in good faith. If a court believes that the debtor is trying to take advantage of the creditor, the court will not enforce the creditor's promise.

Occasionally a court is faced with the problem of a debtor owing two separate obligations to a creditor, one liquidated and one not. If the debtor pays the liquidated debt with a check marked "payment in full of all amounts owing" and the creditor cashes the check, the creditor thereby promises to cancel the balance claimed. However, most courts would hold that the promise is unenforceable since the debtor incurred no legal detriment. Paying an undisputed debt is not consideration. The debtor does not give up any legal right. (See Existing Contractual Duty, p. 217 in this chapter.)

Case 12.4 Field Lumber Co. v. Petty
512 P.2d 764 (Wash. App. 1973)

Petty (defendant), a general contractor, made numerous purchases from Field Lumber Co. (plaintiff). Field's ledger statement showed a balance of $1,752.21 in October 1970. Petty acknowledged a balance of $1,091.96 but disputed the difference of $660.25 which represented an allegedly unauthorized $292.60 purchase by an employee and a 1 percent per month finance charge. In early October 1970, Petty mailed a check for $500 to Field Lumber Co. with a letter—clear and definite in its terms—indicating that the check must be accepted in full settlement of the claim or returned. The letter also recited that the funds had been borrowed. In response, Field Lumber Co. notified Petty by telephone that it would require full payment but cashed the $500 check.

Field initiated action to recover the sum alleged to be due and owing. The trial court held that cashing the check under the circumstances discharged Petty from any further liability on the account. Field appealed.

FARRIS, J. . . . We reverse. We recognize the general rule that where a sum due is unliquidated or disputed and a remittance of an amount less than that claimed is sent to the creditor with a statement explaining that it is in full satisfaction of the claim, the acceptance of such a remittance by the creditor constitutes an accord and satisfaction.

However, this rule is not applicable where a portion of the alleged debt in excess of the amount paid is acknowledged and not in dispute. In such a case a debtor cannot unilaterally tender a lesser sum than that which it is agreed is due and owing and rely upon the retention of that sum as full settlement of the debt unless there is some additional consideration given therefor. An accord and satisfaction is founded on contract, and a consideration therefor is as necessary as for any other contract.

The recognition of a debt in a fixed amount and in excess of the $500 which was tendered under the circumstances here precludes the finding of an accord and satisfaction unless there is proof of new consideration. It has long been the rule in this state that payment of an amount admitted to be due can furnish no consideration for an accord and satisfaction of the entire claim.

Here we cannot find a scintilla of evidence indicating that any new consideration was given. Petty did not borrow the sum after agreeing with Field . . . that he would do so if it would be accepted as full settlement. He borrowed the money of his own volition and then simply mailed the check with a letter after efforts had been made and were continuing to be made to recover the full amount. To find an accord and satisfaction here where a definite portion of the alleged debt was acknowledged to be due and owing and therefore liquidated and undisputed would place a creditor at a disadvantage in accepting partial payments from a reluctant debtor, since by doing so he would be jeopardizing his right to receive the balance, even though in law that balance was in fact due him. It is true that courts look with favor on compromise, but this means genuine compromise, arrived at through mutual agreement.

The payment of $500 here was a payment on account; whether the disputed sum of $660.25 is due and owing is a proper subject for litigation. The cause is remanded for determination of the question of the balance due on account.

Reversed and remanded.

Composition Agreement

A composition agreement is an arrangement between a debtor and two or more creditors whereby the debtor, who is unable to pay the full amount owed, agrees to turn his or her assets over to the creditors, and the creditors agree to accept their pro rata portions in *full* satisfaction of their claims. Suppose that D owes $10,000 to A, $6,000 to B, and $4,000 to C. D offers to enter into a composition agreement whereby each creditor will be paid 50 percent of his or her claim. If the creditors agree to cancel the balances owed, a composition results, and upon making the payments, D will be discharged from his obligation to each of the participating creditors.

The question of consideration is sometimes raised by a creditor who wishes to ignore the promise to cancel and to recover the balance owing from the debtor. The debts are liquidated. The debtor does not dispute the existence or amount of any debt. It has been said that consideration may be found:

• In the promise of each creditor to forgo a portion of his or her claim

• In forbearance by the debtor to pay the creditors in unequal portions

• In the action of the debtor in seeking the assent of the creditors[2]

Some courts do not attempt to justify enforcement of composition agreements on the basis of consideration. Instead, those courts base their

---

[2]*Restatement of the Law (Second) Contracts*, American Law Institute, Philadelphia, sec. 83, comment *c*, Compositions with creditors.

decision on the ground of public policy in that they settle a group of claims expeditiously at a minimum of expense to the parties, and such out-of-court settlements lessen the ever-increasing volume of litigation.

A composition agreement applies only to the creditors who enter into the agreement. If in the example above, B had refused to enter into the agreement, B would not have shared in the distribution of D's assets; but B would also not be precluded from attempting later on to collect the full $6,000 owed to him or her.

Forbearance to Sue on a Claim

Every person has a legal right to litigate a valid claim. Giving up the right to sue on a valid claim is a legal detriment, and if bargained for, constitutes consideration. Suppose that Peter and Donna are driving their cars and collide in an intersection. There is some doubt as to who is at fault. Donna promises not to sue Peter if Peter agrees to pay her $2,500. Peter agrees but later changes his mind and refuses to pay the money. Donna sues Peter. Peter's defense is that Donna gave no consideration for his promise. A court would hold that Donna's promise to forbear from suing is giving up a legal right and constitutes legal detriment.

One who agrees not to assert a clearly unfounded claim incurs no legal detriment and cannot enforce a return promise to pay money. In most cases there is doubt as to who is at fault, whether the situation involves an alleged tort or breach of contract. The general rule is that forbearance to sue is consideration if the promisee's claim is doubtful because of uncertainty as to the facts or the law, or if the promisee honestly believes that his or her claim is valid.

Case 12.5   Frasier v. Carter
437 P.2d 32 (Ida. 1968)

D. L. Carter, the plaintiff's attorney and brother, advised the plaintiff, Lena Frasier, regarding her late husband's estate. Under the will, the specific devises and bequests to her were more valuable than her interest in the community property. The will provided that if she failed to waive her community property rights, she would receive her interest in the community property and nothing more. Although attorneys for the executors frequently inquired of Carter and Frasier whether Frasier would waive her interest in the community property, no waiver was filed. Under a decree of distribution rendered by the probate court, Frasier received only her share of the community property.

During an appeal of the decree, Carter wrote to Frasier as follows:

"Dear Lena:

This is to advise and confirm our agreement—that in the event the J. W. Frasier estate case now on appeal is not terminated so that you will receive settlement equal to your share of the estate as you would have done if your waiver had been filed in the estate in proper time, that I will make up any balance to you in payments as suits my convenience and will pay interest on your loss at 6%."

The decree of the probate court was upheld by the state supreme court, and Frasier brought suit to enforce Carter's promise. Carter died. A jury returned a verdict for Frasier, and Carter's executrix appealed.

TAYLOR, J. . . . The principal ground urged for reversal is that the promise of Mr. Carter . . . was without consideration. We think consideration was sufficiently established. . . .

Plaintiff (Frasier) contends that Carter's promise to pay was supported by her forbearance from prosecuting an action against him for his negligence in failing to advise her properly respecting her interest in the Frasier estate. Waiver of, or forbearance to exercise, a right which is not utterly groundless is sufficient consideration to support a contract made in reliance thereon. "Mere forbearance without any request to forbear, or circumstances from which an agreement to forbear may be implied, is not a consideration which will support a promise." [Citation.] However, an agreement to forbear may be implied, and actual forbearance is some evidence of an agreement to forbear. In passing we note that in a letter to counsel for the coexecutors, written after decree of distribution was entered, Carter, in referring to the failure to file a waiver, said: ". . . if anyone is to blame, it is I. . . ." This indicates that he was acting in plaintiff's behalf. . . .

Judgment affirmed.

PROMISES ENFORCEABLE WITHOUT REGARD TO CONSIDERATION

As we have seen, promises generally are enforceable only if the promises are supported by consideration. The rule produces unfortunate results in certain kinds of situations, and so the courts recognize some exceptions to the rule. Those exceptions are discussed in the following pages.

Promises under Seal

In a few states the seal continues to have the effect it had at early common law, that is, the addition of a seal on a writing containing a promise made the promise enforceable, even though the promisor asked for and received nothing in exchange for the promise. In most states the law regarding contracts under seal has been changed by statute. A common statutory provision is that a seal upon an "executory instrument" is presumptive evidence of consideration. In about half the states, statutes purport to abolish the seal so far as contracts are concerned or to abolish the distinction between sealed and unsealed contracts.

States in which the seal is still given its common law effect almost invariably have statutes liberalizing the form which a seal may take. Examples of authorized versions of a seal are: the word "seal," the letters "L.S.," and a scroll or other device made with pen or printed upon the paper and intended to represent a seal. Obviously, the great volume and the fast pace of modern business transactions have caused the seal to lose most of the solemnity and importance it had at common law.

Promises Enforceable Because of Prior Legal Duty

As previously indicated, a past transaction cannot constitute consideration. However, where a person had a contractual duty of performance and the duty was barred by operation of law, a subsequent promise to perform is enforceable, even if the promisor receives nothing in exchange for the new promise. Such a situation may occur where the promise was made (1) following bar of the original duty by operation of the statute of limitations or (2) during bankruptcy.

Promise Following Bar by Statute of Limitations All states have statutes of limitations. Such statutes prescribe time limits within which legal action must be started. A prescribed time limit starts running from the time a cause of action arises. The prescribed periods vary from state to state. They vary mainly according to the kind of cause of action (e.g., torts, contracts, property). In some states the time limitation for bringing an action to recover a debt may be 5 years from the maturity date of the debt if the debt involves an oral promise, and 10 years if the debt is evidenced by a writing or by a document under seal.

A well-recognized rule of law is that a new promise by a debtor to pay a debt which has been barred by the statute of limitations is enforceable. A voluntary part payment or an unqualified acknowledgment of indebtedness is usually interpreted as an implied promise to pay and so comes under the rule just stated. However, statutes in most states provide that a promise to pay a debt or an acknowledgment of indebtedness is not binding unless it is in writing and signed by or on behalf of the promisor.

Because there is no legal duty to pay a debt which has been barred by the statute of limitations, the debtor may attach to the new promise such qualifications or conditions as the debtor wishes. Thus, a promise to pay "one-half of what I owe you and no more" imposes only the obligation stated, as does a promise to pay by the end of the year "if I am able to do so."

Promise during Bankruptcy Prior to the federal Bankruptcy Reform Act of 1978, a promise to pay a debt which had been discharged in bankruptcy required no consideration to make it binding. The new Bankruptcy Code discourages debtors from reaffirming debts since a major purpose of bankruptcy is a "fresh start," free from the burden of debts. The Code imposes a number of conditions to have an enforceable promise, including court approval of a debtor's reaffirmation. It is clear that in the future promises to pay debts in bankruptcy will virtually disappear. The federal requirements are discussed in Chapter 49 under "Discharge hearing; reaffirmation; protection of discharge," p. 1127.

Promises Enforceable Because of Justifiable Reliance (Promissory Estoppel)

Promissory estoppel is an alternative to the contract doctrine of consideration as a basis for promise enforcement. Under the doctrine of promissory estoppel, the promisor is "estopped" (prevented by the law) from avoiding liability for the consequences of the promise. Section 90(1) of the *Restatement (Second)* sets forth the following elements or requirements of the doctrine of promissory estoppel:

1 There must be "a promise which the promisor should reasonably expect to induce action or forbearance on the part of the promisee."

2 The promise must "induce such action or forbearance."

3 The situation must be such that "injustice can be avoided only by enforcement of the promise."

The doctrine of promissory estoppel is of growing importance in the enforcement of commercial promises. It is not usual, for example, for a general contractor to make contracts with subcontractors before obtaining the prime contract. Yet, as indicated in Chapter 10, Case 10.5, general contractors often rely on contractual bids (promises) from subcontractors as the general contractors prepare their own bids and enter into contractual arrangements. If nothing more than traditional contract law were available for the protection of general contractors, they would be unable to enforce the promises (bids) from subcontractors. Promissory estoppel fills a gap in contract law.

Other persons than building contractors may have the benefit of the doctrine of promissory estoppel. In the case of *Hoffman v. Red Owl Stores, Inc.,*[3] the plaintiff sold his business, moved his family to another town, and purchased business property there in reliance on the defendant's assurance that the plaintiff would become the operator of one of defendant's retail grocery stores. When the deal did not materialize, the plaintiff successfully invoked the doctrine of promissory estoppel, even though the defendant's representations did not meet the requirements for a contractual offer

because many of the terms were missing. The elements of promissory estoppel were present: the promisor should have reasonably expected action by the promisee, the promisee did act, and injustice could only be avoided by enforcement of the defendant's promise. The court awarded plaintiff the amounts he had lost and expended in reliance on the promise.

Promises to make gifts of land have been enforced under the promissory estoppel doctrine. In the decided cases the promisee usually proved that he or she, with the knowledge of the promisor, took possession of the land in reliance on the promise of a gift and made improvements.

Charitable Subscriptions

The phrase "charitable subscription" is of wide scope. "Charitable" refers not merely to institutions founded for the purpose of aiding people in unfortunate circumstances; it refers also to such institutions as churches, schools, colleges, libraries, museums, and hospitals. "Subscription" in this context usually means a signed promise by each of several or many persons to contribute a sum of money specified on a subscription form. The word may also be used to refer to a similar promise of payment (usually a large payment) made solely by one person.

Charitable subscriptions have been widely enforced in the United States. Some courts have purportedly found consideration for charitable subscriptions in the exchange of promises among subscribers; other courts have found it in the implied promise of the charity to use the funds in accordance with the terms of the subscription agreement. The difficulty with these and other explanations based on the bargain theory of consideration is that in the typical charitable subscription the promisor does not have a bargaining intent. The promisor intends to make a gift. Consequently, modern courts tend to abandon any attempt to explain enforcement of such subscriptions on the basis of traditional consideration theory and to resort instead to the doctrine of promissory estoppel.

---

[3] 133 N.W.2d 267 (Wis. 1965).

SUMMARY

Not all promises are enforceable. Depending on the state law, a promise may be enforceable because:

1 It is under seal; or

2 It was given in exchange for consideration; or

3 The promise arose out of a prior legal duty which had been discharged by operation of law; or

4 The promisee justifiably relied on the promise to his or her detriment.

Consideration is the most common basis of promise enforcement. Generally, to constitute consideration, a performance or return promise must be bargained for. Moreover, that which is bargained for must be a legal detriment to the promisee. Legal detriment means the promisee gives up or promises to give up a legal right, or assumes or promises to assume a legal burden. The detriment may have little if any monetary value. Usually the legal detriment incurred by the promisee will be a legal benefit to the promisor but this is not required. A promise is illusory if the party is not obligated to any performance or has an unrestricted right to cancel the contract.

The courts must deal with a variety of problems relating to consideration. Performing or promising to perform a contractual duty which is still in effect is not consideration. If the parties to a contract mutually rescind the contract and one party promises to pay a bonus to the other for performing the same duties called for in the original contract, the courts will enforce the promise. A promise to pay a bonus is enforceable if the promisee has encountered unforeseen difficulties in performing the contractual duties. A debtor who makes a part payment of a liquidated debt incurs no legal detriment and may not enforce the creditor's promise to cancel the balance of the debt. The creditor's promise is enforceable if the debtor gives some new consideration or if the debt is unliquidated. Settlement of an unliquidated debt is called "accord and satisfaction." A composition agreement is enforceable by the courts even though the agreement involves liquidated debts. A promise to forbear from suing another person is legal detriment if the one forbearing has a valid claim, has a doubtful claim, or has an honest belief that his or her claim is valid.

Some classes of promises are enforceable despite a lack of consideration. A few states continue the common law practice of enforcing promises under seal even though the promisor asked for and received nothing in exchange for the promise. Where a person makes a new promise to pay a debt which has been barred by operation of law, the new promise may be enforceable even though the debtor received no consideration for the new promise. Finally, under the doctrine of promissory estoppel, a promise not supported by consideration may nevertheless be enforceable where the promisee justifiably relied on the promise to his or her detriment.

STUDY AND DISCUSSION QUESTIONS

1 What is the purpose of consideration and the other bases of promise enforcement?

2 *(a)*With regard to consideration, explain the meaning and purpose of "bargained-for exchange." *(b)* Why do the courts define consideration in terms of "legal" rather than "actual" detriment?

3 *(a)* Illustrate how the consideration demanded by a promisor can move to someone other than the promisor. *(b)* Why does "past consideration" not constitute consideration?

4 Distinguish between "consideration" and "motive."

5 *(a)* Why does an "illusory" promise not constitute consideration? *(b)* Is a promise in a "requirements" contract to purchase "all the wheat I'll need in my business" illusory? Explain. *(c)* Does a promisor's right to cancel a contract always make the promise illusory? Explain.

6 *(a)* Why will courts usually not look into the adequacy of consideration? *(b)* Under what circumstances will courts look into the adequacy of consideration?

7 *(a)* Is the performance of an act which a person is already under a legal obligation to perform consideration for a promise to pay more for the performance? Explain in terms of legal detriment. *(b)* For what reasons might a court enforce a promise to pay extra compensation for the performance of an existing contractual obligation?

8 *(a)* Is part payment of a liquidated debt consideration for the creditor's promise to accept the part payment as payment in full? Explain in terms of legal detriment. *(b)* Under what circumstances will a promise to accept part payment of a liquidated debt be binding on the creditor?

9 Explain how consideration theory is applied to the settlement of an unliquidated claim?

10 Some courts hold that a "composition" agreement lacks consideration; yet such agreements are enforceable. On what ground?

11 *(a)* Does forbearance to sue on a claim constitute consideration? Explain in terms of legal detriment. *(b)* Under what circumstances will forbearance to sue not constitute consideration?

12 In a few states, the addition of a seal to a writing containing a promise makes the promise enforceable. What is the reason for giving a seal this effect?

13 A promise to pay a debt barred by the running of the statute of limitations may be enforceable without consideration. Under what circumstances will such a promise be enforced?

14 What is required for a promise to be enforced under the doctrine of promissory estoppel?

CASE PROBLEMS

1 In 1958, the mother of plaintiff Robert Adair and defendant Ralph Adair deeded a farm to Ralph and his wife Elsie. The deed recited a consideration of $12,000, half the appraised value of the property. The mother received $5,890 and gave approximately $3,500 of that amount to Robert. Ralph gave Robert a note for $3,000 and a mortgage on the property to secure the note. In 1972 the mortgage was recorded, and Robert brought an action to foreclose the mortgage. Ralph died prior to the trial. Defendant Elsie contended that there was no consideration given by Robert for the note and mortgage. Agreeing that there was no consideration, the trial court rendered judgment for Elsie. Robert appealed. Was there consideration for the note and mortgage?

2 Hill, as representative of the Oertel family, agreed to pay Thomas a "finder's fee" of $25,000 for procuring the sale of the controlling stock of the Oertel Brewing Co. Thomas, a director and executive vice president of the company, did arrange the sale of the stock to Brown-Forman Distillers, Inc. However, Hill refused to pay the finder's fee. Hill contended that there was no consideration for the agreement because Thomas's employment as executive vice president, for which he was being paid a salary of $25,000 per year, included the duty to find a buyer for the brewery. Was Thomas entitled to the finder's fee in addition to his salary?

3 Rhoades was divorced in 1971 and ordered to pay $80 per week for child support. He later resigned his employment and accepted another position at a sharply reduced salary. In litigation relating to child support, Rhoades testified that his former wife agreed to accept payments of $50 per week instead of the $80 per week originally ordered. Assume that the former wife agreed to accept the smaller payments. Is her agreement binding on her?

4 Rhea sold land to Smith, who executed a note for $12,500 in part payment. Smith had a right to pay the amount before the due date of the note, and after making payments for four years, he decided to pay off the note. He asked for a discount on the amount owed, which Rhea refused. When Smith asked the bank handling the matter to state the payoff amount, the note teller made an error. Smith paid $2,363.88 less than was owed, and Rhea signed a release before anyone discovered the mistake. Smith refused to make further payment, and Rhea brought suit for the balance of the account. The trial court held that the note was discharged by an accord and satisfaction, and rendered judgment for Smith. Rhea appealed. Was there an accord and satisfaction?

5 British Overseas Airways Corp. (BOAC) decided to construct a new cargo building at New York International Airport. The architect served as BOAC's agent in awarding the general contract to Thatcher Construction Co. Thatcher awarded the structural steel subcontract to Bethlehem Fabricators, Inc., which, because of unhappy prior dealings with Thatcher, insisted on a payment bond. Bonnington, a representative of the architect, told Moser, a representative of Bethlehem, that BOAC had required Thatcher to obtain a payment bond. After the discussion between Bonnington and Moser, BOAC—in order to save itself the $4,250 bond premium—decided not to require a payment bond of Thatcher. Bethlehem performed its contract not knowing of this decision. Thatcher failed to make payments and eventually filed a petition in bankruptcy, leaving a total of $78,115.98 due Bethlehem. Bethlehem sued BOAC for that amount. Under what theories of law might Bethlehem prevail?

Chapter

13

Avoidance of Agreement

If people could escape their contractual obligations for trivial reasons, our economic system could be seriously undermined. In the interest of economic stability, therefore, a court will usually enforce a contract in accordance with its terms without regard to whether a party made a good or a bad bargain. Even a contract of adhesion (standard-form contract) will normally be enforced, as long as the party with the superior bargaining power does not exercise that power in an oppressive way.

Yet, where the circumstances warrant, the courts permit people to avoid their contracts. This chapter and the two which follow discuss a number of situations in which a party to a contract has a right to have a court set the contract aside or modify its terms. This chapter deals with two major bases for avoiding an agreement: (1) a lack of or a defect in the assent required for a bargained contract and (2) certain rights granted by consumer protection statutes to avoid contracts.

AVOIDANCE ON GROUND OF DEFECTIVE ASSENT

The bargain theory of contracts is fundamental to a free enterprise system. It has been assumed in discussing offer, acceptance, and consideration (Chapters 10, 11, and 12) that the parties acted freely in the marketplace so that genuine assent could be achieved. Occasionally that assumption of an environment of free exchange is put in question. One party may coerce the other by various means to assent to an agreement. A party may use a position of trust or confidence to persuade unfairly the other party to enter a contract. There are instances where a party may deliberately lie to another in order to induce the other to assent to a contract. At other times a party may innocently misrepresent an important fact, or both parties may enter a contract holding mistaken beliefs about important facts. A party should not be held to a bargain made under any of the circumstances stated. Following is a discussion of five recognized grounds to avoid a contract: duress, undue influence, fraud, misrepresentation, and mistake, each of which results in defective assent.

Duress

Meaning of Duress Most courts define *duress* as a wrongful threat, by words or conduct, that induces such fear on the part of the person threatened as to overcome his or her free will. Stated in simpler terms, duress is any wrongful coercion by which a person is induced to do something he or she otherwise would not do. In the context of contract law, the act done under coercion is the expression of assent to an offer or counteroffer. The person expressing assent under coercion is said to "act under duress" or "give assent under duress." Typically, the threatening party gains money or property to which he or she is not entitled and the resulting contract is voidable. Two remedies are available to the party coerced: (1) raise duress as a defense in a lawsuit filed by the promisee to enforce the contract or (2) rescind the contract. The remedy of rescission is discussed in the last part of this chapter.

Elements of Duress As indicated in the definition above, the elements which must be present to constitute duress are (1) a wrongful threat, and (2) the overcoming of a party's free will.

Wrongful threat Various kinds of threats constitute duress. The most common kinds are threats to the person, threats to property, and threats to business or to means of earning a living.

Threats to the *person* may take the form of

1 A threat of physical injury to the person threatened or to the person's spouse, child, or other near relative

2 A threat of wrongful imprisonment or prosecution of the person threatened or of the person's spouse, child, or other near relative.

An example of a threat of wrongful prosecution would be the following. Suppose an employer discovers that an employee has stolen merchandise belonging to the employer. The employer threatens to institute criminal proceedings against the employee unless the employee agrees to pay back a sum in excess of the fair value of the merchandise. The employee's assent is given under duress and may be rescinded. The employer has a right to report the commission of a crime but not to use the threat of prosecution for improper gain.

Threats to *property* may take the form of a threat to injure, destroy, seize, or wrongfully withhold real or personal property. There are times when a party may properly assert a lien on goods or threaten to foreclose a mortgage on land. It is when a party threatens to use such measures to force an excessive payment that duress exists. Many courts find duress under such circumstances only if the party coerced has no reasonable alternative but to assent to the excessive payment.

Threats to *a person's business* or to means of earning a livelihood may, under certain circumstances, result in duress. This kind of duress by threat is commonly referred to as *economic duress* or *business compulsion*. The importance of economic duress has greatly increased because of the ever-increasing extent of economic interdependence. Ordinarily a court will not hold that there has been economic duress unless the plaintiff seeking to rescind can prove that irreparable injury to his or her business or to chances of gaining an adequate livelihood would result if the defendant were to carry out the wrongful threat. The threat made by the defendant may consist of threatening to breach a contract under circumstances where the defendant knows the plaintiff would suffer severe economic hardship. Many courts stress the plaintiff's lack of a reasonable alternative as a necessary part of finding duress.

Ordinarily, threatening to file a civil action against someone is not duress. Thus, a party who agrees to pay a sum of money to avoid being sued may not rescind the agreement. However, if the circumstances are appropriate, a court may find economic duress. Suppose, for example, a large corporation threatens to sue a small business person unless the person transfers to the corporation a novel invention discovered by the person. The large corporation knows that by claiming patent infringement and filing an expensive lawsuit, it could cause irreparable injury to the business person. A court would find economic duress if the corporation is attempting to gain something to which it is not entitled. Of course, it would not be duress for

the corporation to file a suit in good faith to protect its lawful rights.

Overcoming of free will In order to constitute duress, the threat must produce fear sufficient to overcome a party's free will. The test in most states is the reaction of the particular individual threatened. The particular individual need not be as brave as the "ordinary reasonable person." The law protects the unusually timid. In the words of the *Restatement:*

> Age, sex, capacity, relation of the parties, attendant circumstances, must all be considered. Persons of a weak or cowardly nature are the very ones that need protection. The courageous can usually protect themselves; timid persons are generally the ones influenced by threats, and the unscrupulous are not allowed to impose upon them because they are so unfortunately constituted.[1]

[1]*Restatement, Contracts*, sec. 492, comment *a*.

Case 13.1   Litten v. Jonathan Logan, Inc.
286 A.2d 913 (Pa. Super. 1971)

CERCONE, J. This is an appeal by Jonathan Logan, Inc., defendant in the court below, from a judgment upon verdicts for plaintiffs. . . .

Plaintiffs are Bernard Litten, his father Irving Litten, and his brother-in-law Harold Romm . . . owners of Princess Fair, Inc., . . . and . . . Roliman, Inc., which companies are engaged in the manufacture, sale and distribution of women's apparel. . . .

Defendant is . . . also engaged in the manufacture, sale and distribution of women's apparel. . . .

Plaintiffs assert the right to recover money damages and [to have] an accounting on the basis of an oral contract of November 1960. . . . Defendant, in June 1960, because it did not have, but desired to have, the particular line of women's wearing apparel manufactured by plaintiffs, offered to purchase plaintiffs' two corporations, Princess Fair and Roliman; to employ plaintiffs for a term of three years, and to give a stock option to Bernard Litten. Plaintiffs refused to sell. In the latter part of September 1960, the plaintiffs' two corporations were in an inventory bind, but were financially solvent and had a net worth in excess of $140,000. At that time plaintiffs were not in drastic financial difficulties. . . . At the urging of the accountant who worked for both parties, the plaintiffs and defendant resumed negotiations for the sale and purchase of plaintiffs' corporations.

In November 1960, plaintiffs and defendant orally agreed that in exchange for all the stock of plaintiffs' two corporations, defendant would pay the corporations' creditors; pay off the corporations' bank loans which were guaranteed by plaintiffs and their wives; pay to plaintiffs any monies remaining in excess of such payments from assets of the corporation; employ plaintiffs for a term of one year, beginning January 1, 1961, at stipulated salaries and give Bernard Litten . . . an option to purchase 5,000 shares of defendant stock at $15 per share, said option to be exercised during the year's employment.

In reliance upon these mutual oral promises plaintiffs made no further effort to resolve their financial situation through other channels or means.

In further reliance upon the oral agreement and upon the good faith and integrity of defendant, plaintiffs, at the insistence of defendant's President and Chairman of the Board [David Schwartz], and on the advice of their attorney, transferred and assigned to defendant, on November 22, 1960, the entire stock of the two corporations. At the same time, plaintiffs waived or relinquished their rights to repayment of loans they had made to the two corporations. Thus, defendant became sole owner of the two corporations and plaintiffs were left depending on defendant to carry out his oral promises. Defendant made an initial payment of $15,000 to the creditors on November 28, 1960. Defendant refused to pay the creditors in full on December 22, 1960, the date fixed, and still refused to pay on January 5, 1961, to which date the time for payment had been extended. The creditors threatened plaintiffs with bankruptcy.

On January 9, 1961, four days after the last date fixed for payment, defendant delivered to plaintiffs a written agreement which defendant said had to be signed that day. The agreement was basically different from the one orally agreed upon and plaintiffs refused to sign. It did not include provision for return of excess monies from liquidation, contained no stock option to Bernard Litten, and no one-year employment clause. Defendant insisted that neither the creditors nor the banks would be paid unless plaintiffs signed the written agreement as prepared by defendant's attorney. Plaintiffs' attorney, who happened to be a brother of defendant's attorney, advised them they had no alternative but to sign. Bernard Litten then telephoned David Schwartz, telling him that he had stolen their business, that he was "putting a gun to his [Litten's] head," and was requiring them to sign a different agreement, to which Schwartz replied that if the agreements were not signed that would be the end of the transaction; he would not pay the creditors. Faced with immediate financial disaster and without immediate legal relief, plaintiffs were compelled to sign the agreement on January 9, 1961.

Continuous requests by plaintiffs of defendant's President and Chairman of the Board that the oral agreement of November 1960 be honored brought no relief for plaintiffs. In fact, because of plaintiff Bernard Litten's insistence that the oral promises of defendant be lived up to, all the plaintiffs who had begun work for defendant were fired within a month and a half to two months after they began work. Before and after the termination of his employment, Bernard attempted to prevail upon their then counsel who was, as already stated, brother of defendant's counsel, to have defendant agree to the original terms or to institute legal action against defendant, but was told to "just take it easy, . . . and let me work on it." Later, when further pressed, plaintiffs' counsel required a $5,000 retainer fee prior to instituting suit, which fee plaintiffs were not in a position to pay. Plaintiffs later acquired the services of their present counsel who instituted suit in their behalf in 1962.

Under the plaintiffs' evidence, as above summarized, the jury was justified in finding that on January 9, 1961, all avenues which plaintiffs could have pursued to find solutions to their financial problems had been closed because of the inescapable economic peril in which defendant had slowly but inexorably placed them after the date of the oral agreement. Plaintiffs, once they had turned over all the stock of their two corporations to defendant had lost independence of decision, arm's-length advantages, and, most important, time and circumstances to control the future of their corporations which they did have prior to the events which tied their economic destiny to the decisions of defendant. . . .

The important elements in the applicability of the doctrine of economic duress or business compulsion are that (1) there exists such pressure of circumstances which compels the injured party to involuntarily or against his will execute an agreement which results in economic loss, and (2) the injured party does not have an *immediate* legal remedy.

Contrary to defendant's contention, the trial court did adequately charge the jury that coercion or duress must be a force exerted by the defendant, for it clearly stated that:

> "Duress exists whenever one person, by the *unlawful act of another* is induced to enter into contractual relations under such circumstances as to indicate that he had been deprived of the exercise of free will. . . . Now, *regardless of the means employed*, duress is shown whenever the force or threat thereof is sufficient to overcome the will of the particular person. (Emphasis supplied.)
>
> A threatened breach of contract ordinarily is not in itself coercive but if failure to receive the promised performance will result in irreparable injury to business, the threat may involve duress. Business compulsion is a species of duress, not the common law duress, but duress clothed in modern dress, and for this reason the early common law doctrine of duress has been expanded to include business compulsion.
>
> Business compulsion is not established merely by proof that consent was secured by the pressure of financial circumstances, but a threat of serious financial loss may be sufficient to constitute duress and

to be ground for relief *where an ordinary suit at law or equity might not be an adequate remedy.* (Emphasis supplied.)" . . .

Defendant's contention that the written contract was fair ignores the issue that the written contract did not contain all the provisions of the oral agreement upon which the plaintiffs agreed to turn over all of the stock of their two corporations to defendant.

There being no reason for our disturbance of the jury's verdict in favor of the plaintiffs, the judgment of the court below is accordingly affirmed.

Undue Influence

Undue influence occurs when one party overcomes the free will of the other party by *unfair persuasion.* In the context of contract law, the act done under the influence of unfair persuasion is the expression of assent to an offer or counteroffer. Many cases involve persons making gifts of money or property or making wills which include large bequests to persons outside one's immediate family. Thus, in the usual case of undue influence there is an unnatural enrichment of one party at the expense of the other party or the other's family.

Unfair persuasion is most likely to occur in situations in which

1 A person is under the domination of another person, or

2 There is such a relationship of trust and confidence (often called a "fiduciary relationship") between two persons that one of them is justified in assuming that his or her best interests will be protected by the other.

In the first category, a person may be under the *domination of another person* because of mental weakness, ignorance, lack of experience, old age, poor health, physical handicap, emotional strain, or financial distress. The situation is well illustrated by the New Jersey case of *Holland v. John*[2] Plaintiff Holland was the heir of a Mrs. Burns who had conveyed her properties to the defendant, a young man who made

his home with Mrs. Burns. At the time she made the conveyance, Mrs. Burns was 80 years of age, afflicted with palsy, and, said the court, under the complete control of John.

> She was like a child, cared for and secluded like a child and was obedient to every word of John, who treated her exactly like a child. John was a good-natured improvident man, fond of drink—indeed boozy at the hearing—who obviously was in need of money. He undoubtedly got what money the old woman had in the bank; he wanted the property, and it is . . . certain that he urged and cajoled the old woman into making these transfers in a way which, under the circumstances, amounted to undue influence.

The second category embraces relationships of trust and confidence, called *fiduciary relationships* such as—parent and child, guardian and ward, husband and wife, physician and patient, attorney and client, pastor and parishioner. Most courts take the position that if it is established that a confidential relationship existed when a transaction was entered into that benefited the trusted person, the burden of proof is on that person to prove the transaction was not procured by undue influence. Thus, for example, if an attorney prepares a will for a client in which the attorney is to receive a large sum of money in preference to the client's legal heirs, a court would require the attorney to prove he or she did not exercise undue influence over the client.

---

[2]60 N.J. Eq. 435 (1899).

Case 13.2   **First National Bank & Trust Co. v. Albert**
238 N.W.2d 827 (Mich. App. 1975)

The First National Bank & Trust Company of Marquette (plaintiff) was the executor of the estate of George Albert, deceased. George Albert died November 24, 1970, leaving as survivors Dr. Sam Albert and Fred Albert (defendants) and four other children. During the summer of 1969, the aged and terminally ill father returned from a Duluth hospital to his home in Ironwood, Michigan. At first, son John lived with his father in the family home and took care of the father's business under a power of attorney. On October 21, 1970 Fred took charge of the father's business under a power of attorney.

By mid-December 1969, the father's illness had deteriorated to the point where the family members agreed that Dr. Sam should take care of the father. Sam agreed to do so, but on condition that he would be paid for his services. In March 1970, Dr. Sam moved the father to Sam's home. Thereafter, he added $45 a day to his monthly bills for the father's care.

On November 12, 1970 the father executed a new power of attorney granting Fred broader powers than he had had under his former power of attorney. Two days thereafter, Sam and Fred signed a note payable to their father, ostensibly in payment of a loan which the father had made to Sam. The note was payable in 10 years and bore no interest.

After the First National Bank & Trust Company was confirmed as executor, it brought an action against Sam and Fred Albert for conversion of estate funds. At the trial, the following questions were asked of, and answered by, Dr. Sam Albert.

"Q. Well Doctor, so you decided you would approach your father for a $30,000 loan and take it as a loan rather than receiving payment on your medical fees on which you would have to report income?"
"A. That's right. . . ."
"Q. Did you suggest the terms, or did your father suggest the terms?"
"A. I suggested the terms of it. I made the request a number of times and I said, 'We will draw up the note,' but he said 'I don't want any note. I want to give it to you.' [But] as a gift I would have to pay a gift tax."

There was a judgment for the plaintiff [executor-bank], and defendants appealed.

ALLEN, J. . . . In a detailed opinion, the trial court ruled in plaintiff's favor, giving as its reasons: (1) the so-called loan to Sam Albert constituted a gift, and, since the power of attorney dated November 12, 1970 did not authorize the attorney in fact to give away the principal's property—either permanently or for any extended period—the attorney in fact exceeded his power; (2) defendants failed to overcome the legal presumption, arising in cases involving a doctor-patient or attorney-client relationship, that the loan was the result of undue influence; . . .

We [think] that the lower court reached the correct results based upon the grounds stated in number 2, above. It is undisputed that there was a doctor-patient relationship between George and Sam Albert. Equally clear is the power of attorney-business relationship between George and Fred Albert. The law deems such to be fiduciary and confidential relationships. A fiduciary relationship also exists where, as in the instant case, one who is enfeebled by poor health and incapable of attending to his business affairs, relies on another to manage his business affairs. In the landmark decision *In re Wood Estate*, 374 Mich. 278, 285, 132 N.W.2d 35, 40 (1965) our Supreme Court recognized that: "Once such a relationship is established and the fiduciary or an interest which he represents benefits therefrom, the law recognizes a presumption that he in whom trust was reposed exercised his influence unduly."

We do not imply that defendants committed intentional fraud in the sense that the term is used in the criminal statutes or as commonly understood by the general public. Neither do we imply that Dr. Sam did not properly care for his father. The record is quite the contrary. But we do state that after a meticulous review of the record, we are [not] convinced that [defendants overcame the presumption of undue influence] arising in cases involving gifts made where there is a doctor-patient or other confidential relationship . . . ; nor [are we convinced] that the trial court erred in its findings of fact.

Affirmed, costs to plaintiff.

Fraud

Fraud as a tort was discussed in detail in Chapter 5 (see pp. 89–94). The five elements of fraud were each analyzed extensively in that chapter. The following discussion assumes knowledge and familiarity with the elements of fraud, and is devoted mainly to fraud in contract situations.

Elements of Fraud in Contract Situations   In the context of contract law, four elements must be proved: (1) a false representation of fact (not of opinion or of law, unless made by an expert); (2) knowledge that the representation was false; (3) intent to induce another to act; and (4) justifiable reliance on the representation. A fifth element, resulting injury, is required in a tort action but need not be proved in a contract case. Thus, a party who is fraudulently induced to enter a contract may get what he or she bargained for and suffer no economic loss, yet that person may rescind the transaction.

Often, contracts contain exculpatory or disclaimer clauses. For example, a clause might provide: "It is agreed that there are no representations of any kind between the parties other than contained in this written contract." Most courts ignore such provisions and allow a party to introduce evidence that he or she was defrauded. In some contracts of sale, the seller will state that the sale is made "as is." Such language gives the seller little protection. Most courts require the seller to disclose to the buyer any material facts known by the seller and not readily apparent to a buyer. Failure to disclose such facts constitutes fraud.

Types of Fraud in Contract Situations
There are two types of fraud relating to contracts: (1) fraud in the *inducement*, and (2) fraud in the *execution*. If all of the elements of the tort of fraud are involved in the inducement of a contract, remedies are available which are not available in other contract situations.

Fraud in the inducement; remedies if tort
Fraud in the inducement of a contract is a common type of fraud. In the typical situation the fraud relates to the nature or quality of goods or services exchanged, rather than the content of an agreement or the nature of the document signed.

When a party has been fraudulently induced to enter a contract, he or she may have a choice of remedies. If the five elements of fraud are established, the defrauded party may: (1) raise fraud as a defense in a lawsuit filed by the promisee to enforce the contract; (2) rescind the contract entered into; or (3) file an action against the promisee for the tort of fraud. If only the first four elements of fraud are proved, the defrauded party may not file an action in tort. The remedy of rescission is discussed in the last part of this chapter. Where a party elects to sue in tort, the party chooses to affirm the contract, keep what he or she has received, and seek damages to compensate for the injury suffered. The two rules for measuring fraud damages are discussed on p. 93.

Case 13.3   **Slater v. KFC Corp.**
621 F.2d 932 (8th Cir. 1980)

Thomas J. Slater filed a tort action alleging that KFC Corporation fraudulently induced him to purchase two franchises for the operation of seafood restaurants. KFC counterclaimed for the cost of certain equipment which it had supplied to Slater and for royalty and advertising fees owing under the franchise agreement. In August 1975 Slater received a letter addressed to all prospective franchisees from KFC concerning a new market concept called "H. Salt Seafood Galley." The letter stated:

Actual market experience has shown that the H. Salt Seafood Galley is an efficient, high volume profit producer.

Slater obtained franchise agreements for two stores, constructed buildings and began operating the restaurants in the summer of 1976. The two galley-restaurants proved unsuccessful and were closed in May 1978. In Slater's suit for fraud he alleged that KFC intentionally concealed its knowledge that from July 1975 through May 1976 KFC's eight test seafood restaurants had a marked decline in profits and thus could no longer be characterized as high volume profit producers.

The franchise agreements set out the following disclaimer in large type:

NO STATEMENT, REPRESENTATION OR OTHER ACT, EVENT OR COMMUNICATION, EXCEPT AS SET FORTH HEREIN, IS BINDING ON THE FRANCHISOR IN CONNECTION WITH THE SUBJECT MATTER OF THIS AGREEMENT.

Following a trial the jury awarded Slater $265,000 in actual and $100,000 in punitive damages and awarded KFC $141,000 on its equipment counterclaim but denied recovery on the counterclaim for royalty and advertising fees. Both parties appealed.

BRIGHT, Circuit Judge. . . . KFC maintains that when Slater sued on these agreements, he became bound by the disclaimer clause. Under this theory, the disclaimer provision effectively insulated KFC from making any actionable misrepresentation. . . .

KFC correctly observes that Missouri law affords an alleged fraud victim an option: he may retain whatever he has received and sue on the contract, or he may return what he has received and sue for rescission and restitution. [Citation.] KFC incorrectly asserts however, that by electing to sue on these agreements Slater affirmed all the contractual terms, including the disclaimer.

A party simply may not, by disclaimer or otherwise, contractually exclude liability for fraud in inducing that contract. *Beshears v. S-H-S Motor Sales Corp.*, 433 S.W.2d 66, 71 (Mo.App. 1968) sets forth the Missouri rule as follows:

> "The rule that all prior and contemporaneous oral agreements and representations are merged in the written contract entered into by the parties does not apply to fraudulent representations made for the purpose of inducing a party to enter into such contract."

Unlike *Beshears*, the fraud in this case arose from KFC's concealment of the decline in volume and profits of the test stores, not from the original representation. Regardless of its source, however, the fraud allegedly induced Slater to enter the franchise agreements. Under the Missouri rule, KFC's contractual disclaimers will not bar a suit based upon fraud which induced the defrauded party to enter into the contract.

. . . Missouri recognizes that fraud may . . . arise by concealment where one contracting party breaches a duty to disclose certain information to the other. We commented on that aspect of Missouri law in *McMahon v. Meredith Corp.*, supra, 595 F.2d at 438–39:

> "A failure to disclose a material fact can be considered to be an implicit representation of the nonexistence of such fact on which a party may rely, but only if the alleged fraud-feasor has a duty to speak. . . ."

Missouri courts have consistently held that a duty to speak may arise under any of three conditions: (1) where there is a fiduciary relationship between the parties or a relationship of confidence; (2) where there is an inequality of condition between the parties; and (3) where one party has superior knowledge not within the fair and reasonable reach of the other party. . . .

Here the jury instructions premised liability upon an affirmative statement which, although true when made, became false in light of subsequent developments. . . .

Our review of the record indicates that Slater produced sufficient evidence to go to the jury on KFC's failure to disclose the downturn in the test stores' performance. Further, the jury could have determined that, as to the undisclosed information, KFC possessed superior knowledge of a material fact not within the fair and reasonable reach of Slater. Accordingly, we hold that KFC was not entitled to a judgment n.o.v. . . .

[The court remanded the case for a new trial on the issues of fraud damages and KFC's counterclaim for royalty and advertising fees. The court affirmed KFC's judgment on its equipment counterclaim. In a footnote the court referred to the counterclaim for royalty and advertising fees under the agreement and stated:]

KFC also maintains that the instruction was erroneous because Slater could not both sue on the contract for fraud and use that fraud to avoid part of his obligations under the contract. We do not reach this issue. We note, however, that damages for fraud might include a portion of amounts paid for advertising and royalty fees based upon KFC's overestimation of the franchises' value. That issue should be submitted to the jury on an instruction which correctly enunciates the rules of damages for fraud.

Fraud in the execution Occasionally, a party is defrauded as to the nature of a document he or she is asked to sign. Such fraud is called "fraud in the execution" or "fraud in the factum." For example, suppose a salesperson demonstrates a vacuum cleaner to a homeowner and at the conclusion of the demonstration has the owner sign a document the salesperson describes as "an acknowledgement of the demonstration." If in fact the document is a contract purporting to obligate the homeowner to purchase a vacuum cleaner the contract is void (of no effect whatsoever). Many courts will find fraud in the execution only if the document signed is entirely different from that which the party is led to believe he or she is signing and if the party was not negligent in signing the document under the circumstances. Void contracts are discussed in the last part of this chapter.

Innocent Misrepresentation

There are similarities between the elements of fraud and the guidelines developed for cases involving innocent misrepresentation (often referred to merely as "misrepresentation"). There are, however, two important differences between the elements of fraud and what might be called the elements of innocent misrepresentation.

1 As the word "innocent" indicates, knowledge of falsity is not an element of innocent misrepresentation.

2 To be of legal consequence, an innocent misrepresentation must be of a material fact, whereas materiality of a representation is not generally regarded as an essential aspect of an action based on fraud. The reason for this difference is that a person "who makes an innocent misrepresentation of an unimportant fact has no reason to suppose that his statement will cause action, but fraud is directed to that very end, or is expected to achieve it."[3]

Innocent misrepresentation is not a tort. Therefore, a party who is induced to enter a contract in reliance on an innocent misrepresentation may either (1) raise misrepresentation as a defense in a lawsuit filed by the promisee to enforce the contract or (2) rescind the contract entered into. The remedy of rescission is discussed later in this chapter.

Mistake

Mistake as used in this discussion means a self-induced error, that is, one not induced by the fraud or misrepresentation of the other contracting party. Some frequently recurring kinds of mistakes are:

---

[3]*Restatement, Contracts*, sec. 476, comment *b*.

- Mistake in connection with words used
- Mutual mistake of fact
- Unilateral mistake of fact
- Mistake of law

Mistake in Connection with Words Used

We have seen that modern law usually takes an objective approach toward expressions of assent. If John, who owns a Ford and a Dodge, means to offer his Ford for sale but inadvertently says, "I'll sell you my Dodge for $495," and Bill replies in good faith, "I accept your offer," there is a contract for the sale of the Dodge. "In good faith" means that Bill must not know or have reason to think that John misspoke. If John's Dodge was reasonably worth $1,500, Bill's attempted acceptance of the offer may be ineffective. An offeree is not allowed to "snap up" an offer that is too good to be true.

Sometimes an offer contains a latent (not yet obvious) ambiguity. In the above illustration there was only one possible meaning of "my Dodge." Suppose, however that John owned two Dodge automobiles, one a 1970 model and one a 1973 model. If John thought he was selling the 1970 Dodge and Bill thought he was buying the 1973 Dodge, there is no contract. Only if both parties actually intended the same subject matter (either car) of the sale would there be a contract.

Another type of mistake may occur in connection with words used and be of such nature that the court will correct the mistake. An error in transcription occurs where the parties have made an oral agreement and in the process of reducing the agreement to writing, a mistake is made with the result that the writing does not correctly state the terms of the oral agreement. Suppose, for example, that Paula orally agrees to sell a parcel of land to Don. The legal description of Paula's land is "Lot 6 of the Blackacre Tract." When a written document is prepared to incorporate all the terms of sale the parcel is described as "Lot 9 of the Blackacre Tract." In this situation either party may seek through court action the remedy of reformation.

Reformation means the court will order that the written document be corrected to conform to the terms of the oral agreement.

Mutual Mistake of Fact   At times both parties to a contract assume the existence of a vital fact and on the basis of that assumption enter into the contract. If they later discover the assumption is false, either party may (1) raise the mistake as a defense in a lawsuit filed by the other to enforce the contract, or (2) rescind the contract. The remedy of rescission is discussed in the last part of this chapter.

A mutual mistake of fact usually means the parties have a false assumption about some *aspect of the subject matter* of the contract (identity or quality, quantity or extent). The existence or nonexistence of the aspect must be vital and basic to the parties' bargain and must not be a matter of opinion. For example, suppose a person buys a violin and both the seller and buyer believe it to be a genuine Stradivarius. The buyer later discovers the violin is an imitation and worth a fraction of the sale price. The buyer may rescind the contract on the grounds of mutual mistake of fact. No rescission would be allowed if both parties expressed their ignorance about violins and simply guessed this one to be a genuine Stradivarius. Where there is "conscious uncertainty" both parties assume risks. A mistake of opinion or judgment is not grounds to avoid a contract. For example, if a person sells a horse because he or she believes the horse is not fast enough to race competitively, the seller may not rescind if the horse later does race successfully and the value of the horse rises.

Occasionally the parties have a false assumption about the *existence of the subject matter* of the contract. For example, they may make an agreement for the sale of specific goods and later discover the goods never existed or are no longer in existence. In such instances there is no contract. However, if the goods exist at the time of agreement, there is a contract even though the goods are destroyed later by an unforeseen occurrence.

Case13.4   **Beachcomber Coins, Inc. v. Boskett**
              400 A.2d 78 (N.J. Super. 1979)

Beachcomber Coins, Inc. (plaintiff), a retail dealer in coins, purchased for $500 a dime purportedly minted in 1916 at Denver. It was later discovered that the "D" on the coin signifying Denver mintage was counterfeited. Boskett had acquired this coin and two others of minor value for a total of $450 and believed the dime to be a genuine rarity. A representative of plaintiff spent from 15 to 45 minutes in close examination of the coin before purchasing it. Upon discovery that the coin was a counterfeit, plaintiff brought an action for rescission, asserting mutual mistake of fact. The trial judge held for defendant (Boskett) on the ground that customary coin dealing procedures were for a dealer to make his own investigation of the genuineness of the coin and to "assume the risk" of his purchase if his investigation is faulty. Plaintiff appealed to the Superior Court, Appellate Division.

CONFORD, P.J. . . . The evidence and trial judge's findings establish this as a classic case of rescission for mutual mistake of fact. As a general rule,

> . . . where parties on entering into a transaction that affects their contractual relations are both under a mistake regarding a fact assumed by them as the basis on which they entered into the transaction, it is voidable by either party if enforcement of it would be materially more onerous to him than it would have been had the fact been as the parties believed it to be. [Citations.]

By way of example, the *Restatement* posits the following:

> A contracts to sell to B a specific bar of silver before them. . . . The parties supposed that the bar is sterling. It has, however, a much larger admixture of base metal. The contract is voidable by B.

Moreover, "negligent failure of a party to know or to discover the facts as to which both parties are under a mistake does not preclude rescission or reformation on account thereof." . . . In the *Riviere* case [*Riviere v. Berla*, 89 N.J.Eq. 596] relief was denied only because the parties could not be restored to the *status quo ante*. In the present case they can be. It is undisputed that both parties believed that the coin was a genuine Denver-minted one. The mistake was mutual in that both parties were laboring under the same misapprehension as to this particular, essential fact. The price asked and paid was directly based on that assumption. That plaintiff may have been negligent in his inspection of the coin (a point not expressly found but implied by the trial judge) does not, as noted above, bar its claim for rescission. [Citation.]

Defendant's contention that plaintiff assumed the risk that the coin might be of greater or lesser value than that paid is not supported by the evidence. It is well established that a party to a contract can assume the risk of being mistaken as to the value of the thing sold. . . . The *Restatement* states the rule this way:

Where the parties know that there is doubt in regard to a certain matter and contract on that assumption, the contract is not rendered voidable because one is disappointed in the hope that the facts accord with his wishes. The risk of the existence of the doubtful fact is then assumed as one of the elements of the bargain. [Citations.]

However, for the stated rule to apply, the parties must be conscious that the pertinent fact may not be true and make their agreement at the risk of that possibility. In this case both parties were certain that the coin was genuine. They so testified. Plaintiff's principal thought so after his inspection, and defendant would not have paid nearly $450 for it otherwise. A different case would be presented if the seller were uncertain either of the genuineness of the coin or of its value if genuine, and had accepted the expert buyer's judgment on these matters. . . .

Reversed.

Unilateral Mistake of Fact   Generally, when one party to an agreement assents on the basis of that party's own mistake, the mistake is not ground for relief. Suppose for example, that Bob Brown, a bidder on a construction project, forgets to include a very expensive item, so that his bid (offer) is materially less than it otherwise would have been. A contract is formed by the acceptance of an offer even though the offer is made under a mistake. However, if a bid is so low that the offeree should realize that a mistake has been made, the offeree would not be entitled to "snap up" the offer. Thus, if several bids around $750,000 and one bid of $570,000 were submitted, the offeree should realize that the low bid, being approximately 25 percent below the average of the other bids, probably was based on an error. When the offeree knows or should know of the offeror's mistake, the mistake is said to be "palpable," and no contract is formed by an attempted acceptance. The rule regarding palpable mistake does not apply to errors in judgment or opinion. Thus, for example, if Roger offers to sell his car for $500 and Sally accepts, knowing the car is a classic and worth $5,000 and that Roger is unaware of this fact, a contract is formed and no relief is available to Roger.

Under certain conditions, a person may be granted relief on the basis of that person's own mistake, even though the other party had no reason to suppose that a mistake had been made. The conditions essential to such relief are:

1   The mistake must be of so grave a consequence that to enforce the contract would be unconscionable.

2   The matter as to which the mistake was made must relate to a material feature of the contract.

3   Generally the mistake must have occurred notwithstanding the exercise of ordinary diligence by the party making the mistake.

4   It must be possible to give relief by way of rescission without serious prejudice to the other party except the loss of the bargain. In other words, it must be possible to put the unmistaken party in *statu quo*.

Relief from a contract entered into with unilateral mistake of fact usually takes the form of rescission. However, the mistaken party may raise mistake as a defense in a lawsuit filed by the promisee to enforce the contract.

Case 13.5   **Clover Park School District v. Consolidated Dairy Products Co.**
550 P.2d 47 (Wash. App. 1976)

Clover Park School District No. 400 (plaintiff) sent invitations to several dairies to submit bids for dairy products for the 1973–74 school year. Among those dairies was the Consolidated Dairy Products Company, doing business as (d/b/a) Darigold Farms (defendant). Bids were to be opened May 25, 1973, at 10 A.M., and the invitation stated that "no bidder may withdraw his bid after the time set for opening unless the award of contract is delayed." Among the products for which bids were sought was milk in an established quantity of 1.5 million half pints. When the bids were opened, Darigold's bid of $0.07013 per half pint proved to be the lowest bid. The next lowest bid was $0.072.

Darigold's Tacoma area manager was on hand for the bid opening and immediately realized that an error had been made in Darigold's bid. He at once notified Clover Park School District of the error. On the same day (May 25) Mr. Izzard, Darigold's farm division general manager, wrote Clover Park requesting permission to withdraw the erroneous bid before the school board meeting scheduled for June 11, 1973. He was informed by letter that his request would be placed before the board of directors at their meeting on June 11 and that the directors "will then make the final decision as to whether or not your bid may be withdrawn." On June 12 Darigold was notified that its bid had been accepted at the meeting of June 11.

On June 14 Darigold's lawyer wrote Clover Park that Darigold "cannot supply" the milk at the erroneous price, but that Foremost Dairies had expressed to Darigold its willingness to supply milk at the erroneous price. However, Foremost changed its mind about supplying milk at the lower price. Then, apparently at Darigold's request, Sanitary Cloverleaf Dairy agreed to supply milk at the lower price and did so until the middle of October when it ceased operations because of insolvency. Clover Park brought an action against Darigold for breach of contract. The trial court gave judgment to Clover Park in the amount of $11,466.70, and Darigold appealed.

On appeal there were three issues: (1) whether a contract was formed; (2) if so, whether Darigold had a right to rescind the contract because of an error in submitting its bid; and (3) if Darigold had such a right, whether it waived that right by its subsequent actions. The following excerpts from the court's opinion deal primarily with the first and second issues.

REED, J. . . . The litigation is traceable to an inadvertent human error in the office of Richard Izzard, Darigold's Farm Division general manager. His usually reliable secretary saw penciled figures on a bid form in the Clover Park bid file and, assuming they were Darigold's bid, typed the price of $0.07013 per half pint on the form subsequently submitted. In reality, the figure she typed represented the previous year's price rather than the intended 1973–74 bid of

$0.079 per half pint. Mr. Izzard would have reviewed the bid figures but was away from the office; the erroneous bid was submitted and proved to be lowest among five bids opened by Clover Park. . . .

We begin with the premise that a bid is no more than an offer to contract. Clover Park's advertisement for bids provided that no bid could be withdrawn after the time for opening. Once the bid was submitted, its acceptance by the school district formed a contract. A. Corbin *Contracts* Section 609, pp. 678–79 (1960). However, the general rule is that communication of the error in computation by Darigold before Clover Park could change its position in reliance on the bid, rendered the contract [formed by Clover Park's acceptance of Darigold's bid] voidable by rescission. 3A Corbin *Contracts*, supra, pp. 680–82.

The propriety of relief from a contract when a mistaken bid calculation is promptly made known to the offeree is discussed in *Donaldson v. Abraham*, 68 Wash. 208, 122 P. 1003 (1912) and *Puget Sound Painters, Inc. v. State*, 45 Wash. 2d 819, 278 P.2d 302 (1954). In those cases, erroneously computed bids were submitted to governmental entities along with mandatory bid bonds, and the error in each case was immediately made known to the offeree. The bidder in each case was successful in preventing forfeiture of its bid bond.

In *Puget Sound Painters, Inc. v. State*, supra, the court set forth guidelines as to when forfeiture of a bid bond should be enjoined—and by clear inference, when a bid contract can be rescinded—where a unilateral and material mistake is made in the offeror's bid and the error is called to the attention of the offeree before he has changed his position in reliance thereon. Under these guidelines relief will be decreed:

> (a) if the bidder acted in good faith, and (b) without gross negligence, (c) if he was reasonably prompt in giving notice of the error in the bid to the other party, (d) if the bidder will suffer substantial detriment by forfeiture, and (e) if the other party's status has not greatly changed, and relief from forfeiture will work no substantial hardship on him.

However, rescission of an agreement . . . must be prompt upon discovery of the facts warranting such an action. When a party fails to take steps to rescind within a reasonable time and instead follows a course of conduct inconsistent therewith, the conclusion follows that he has waived his right of rescission and chosen to continue the contract. . . .

Rather than firmly and unequivocally [keeping] to its initial resolve to refuse to perform . . . Darigold . . . [found another supplier]. Having elected that course, Darigold cannot now claim it always and invariably was in a posture of rescission. . . .

Darigold by its conduct . . . allowed Clover Park to change its position by leading the school district to rely on the belief it did not need to select one of the other bids while time remained to do so. In the end, Clover Park incurred the detriment of extra costs upon rebidding that would have been largely avoided had Darigold forced Clover Park to select another of the original bids. We are persuaded the trial court was correct in finding no genuine issue of material fact as to Darigold's conduct being inconsistent with rescission and demonstrating an intent to permit the contract to stand.

Judgment affirmed.

Mistake of Law Mistake of law means ignorance of law, or a wrong conclusion as to the effect of law upon a known set of facts. In the past the general rule has been stated that no relief will be given to a contracting party for a mistake of law unaccompanied by a mistake of fact. The rule served to expedite the administration of justice by minimizing the ability of a person to escape, on a pretext of ignorance, the obligations imposed by law.

As reasonable as the rule usually is, some law is so complex, contradictory, or poorly drafted that even skilled lawyers have difficulty interpreting it. Some individuals have spent great amounts of time and money in an effort to learn the requirements of the law and to comply with them, only to find themselves inadvertently in violation of the law despite the best efforts of competent attorneys. The injustice of some of the results produced by the rule has led to an increasing number of exceptions and to much criticism. Today, in many states relief for mistake of law is placed on the same basis as relief for mistake of fact. Relief is granted if the mistake of law is either: (1) mutual, or (2) unilateral but palpable.

AVOIDANCE UNDER CONSUMER PROTECTION LAWS

We have in this country a wide variety of federal and state "consumer protection" laws. The legislation is intended to protect people from deceptive advertising, hidden charges for loans, inaccurate credit reports, unfair billing practices, undue loss as the result of lost or stolen credit cards and a host of other evils that befall consumers in their day-to-day transactions. Some of the legislation requires disclosure of interest rates, finance charges, and other contractual terms. A few consumer protection statutes are designed to combat high-pressure tactics and unfair business practices, and these statutes grant consumers a right to avoid (rescind) certain of their contracts. The substance of this great mass of legislation is beyond the scope of this book, but the right of rescission deserves attention.

The statutory right of rescission is associated mainly with consumer credit sales. Under the federal Consumer Credit Protection Act (also known as the Truth-in-Lending Act) a consumer, after entering into a consumer credit transaction involving a lien on the consumer's residence, has 3 days to rescind the transaction. The right to rescind does *not* apply to a first mortgage given to acquire the residence. It *does* apply to any lien given as security for a home improvement or other consumer credit transaction.

A regulation of the Federal Trade Commission grants a consumer 3 days to avoid a home solicitation sale in excess of $25. The purpose of the regulation is to give the consumer a "cooling-off period" to reflect on purchases made in the home. No reason need be given for rescinding the sale within the 3-day period. In addition, various state laws give consumers 3 days to avoid consumer credit sales or credit home improvement transactions, or both.

REMEDIES ASSOCIATED WITH AVOIDANCE

Remedies When Contract Is Voidable

A contract entered into where the assent of one or both parties is defective is said to be "voidable." The defect may be duress, undue influence, fraud, misrepresentation, or mistake. A *voidable* contract means that a party has the option to rescind the contract. The contract is not automatically avoided. Historically, rescission was an equity remedy and the courts imposed certain prerequisites to granting relief. Today in most states in order to rescind, the party seeking rescission must: (1) act promptly upon discovery of the defect; (2) return or offer to return the goods or property received; and (3) demand the return of money or goods transferred to the other party.

Failure to act promptly amounts to ratification of the contract. Where a party has assented to a contract under duress or undue influence, the party (or sometimes a guardian or executor) must act with reasonable promptness after the coercion or domination ceases. Where a party is induced to assent to a contract through fraud or misrepresentation, the truth may not be discovered until some time later. In such event if the party chooses to rescind, he or she must act within a reasonable time after the discovery is made. The same rule applies in situations where a unilateral mistake of fact or a mutual mistake of fact is discovered after a contract is entered into.

Occasionally one party or the other is not able to return goods received. At times the contract calls for performance of a service and the party has partially performed part of the bargain. In such instances the court will grant relief in quasi contract to prevent unjust enrichment. The amount of recovery is the reasonable value of services performed or property consumed.

Remedies When Contract Is Void

In rare cases a contract is said to be "void." Although the term seems logically contradictory, in law a *void contract* is one that is of no effect and never will be. Void contracts take many forms. One form resulting from fraud in the execution is illustrated on page 239. Generally the prerequisites to rescission do not apply where a contract is void. Thus, a party need not act promptly. Failure to act promptly does not amount to ratification. To prevent unjust en-richment, a party may recover in quasi contract the money paid under a void contract, or the reasonable value of services performed or property consumed.

Remedies When Third Persons Are Involved

The difference between voidable and void agreements may be of great importance when the rights of third persons are involved. Suppose that B buys goods from S and resells them to T, a bona fide (good faith) purchaser. If the original transfer of goods from S to B was merely voidable by S (as where S transferred the goods to B on the basis of B's innocent misrepresentation), T obtains good title and may retain the goods without any further obligation to S. After B transfers the goods to a bona fide purchaser, S's only remedy is to sue B to rescind the contract and to obtain from B damages in quasi contract. On the other hand, if a transfer by S was void (as where S had previously been declared insane by a court), S (or a guardian) would be entitled to recover the goods from T even though T is a good faith purchaser. The legal theory is that where a transaction was void, T received no title to the goods.

SUMMARY

Where circumstances warrant, the courts permit people to avoid their contracts. Assent to an offer may be lacking or defective in situations involving duress, undue influence, fraud, innocent misrepresentation, or mistake.

Duress is a wrongful threat, by words or conduct, that induces such fear on the part of the person threatened as overcomes his or her free will. The wrongful threat may be to harm a person or a person's property, to wrongfully prosecute someone; or the threat may consist of economic duress. Often duress involves threatening to use a lawful procedure to gain something to which a person is not entitled.

Undue influence involves overcoming freedom of will through unfair persuasion. The usual case of undue influence involves a transaction resulting in the unnatural enrichment of someone outside a party's immediate family. Contracts induced by duress or undue influence are voidable. A party who assents to a contract under duress or undue influence may raise the defect as a defense in a lawsuit filed by the promisee to enforce the contract, or may rescind the contract.

Fraud requires: (1) a false representation of fact; (2) knowledge that the representation was false; (3) intent to induce another to act; and (4) justifiable reliance on the representation. Agreements resulting from fraud in the inducement of a contract are voidable. A person who has been victimized by fraud in the inducement of a contract may assert fraud as a defense when sued, or may rescind the contract. If a fifth element, resulting injury, is present, the party may have the alternative remedy of affirming the contract and suing in tort to recover damages. Exculpatory or disclaimer clauses in contracts generally are not enforced by the courts. Agreements resulting from fraud in the execution of a contract are void.

Innocent misrepresentation involves neither knowledge of falsity nor intent to deceive. To be of legal consequence, the misrepresentation must be of a material fact. There must also be justifiable reliance and resulting injury. A person injured by innocent misrepresentation may raise the misrepresentation as a defense when sued or may rescind the contract.

Courts may give relief on the ground of *mistake*. A mutual mistake sometimes prevents the formation of a contract, as where each party attaches a different meaning to an ambiguous word in the agreement. Where there is a mistake in transcribing an oral agreement, the court will grant reformation and enforce the contract as corrected. More often a mutual mistake results in a voidable contract, as where the parties are mutually mistaken about the quality of the subject matter or some other fact basic to the agreement. A mutual mistake of opinion or judgment is not grounds for rescission. Ordinarily, unilateral mistake is not grounds for relief. If the mistake is palpable, no contract is formed by an attempted acceptance. Even when the mistake is not palpable, relief may be granted where enforcement of the contract would be unconscionable, the party making the mistake was not negligent, and the other party would not suffer serious prejudice. Today, mistake of law is treated in a manner similar to mistake of fact. Mistake may be asserted as a defense or the mistaken party may rescind the agreement.

A few federal and state consumer protection statutes grant consumers a right to avoid certain of their contracts. Under such statutes a consumer has 3 days from the time of entering a consumer credit sale or loan to avoid the sale or loan, if the loan is secured by a lien on the borrower's residence or if the transaction took place in the consumer's home.

A *voidable* contract is one that a party has the option to rescind. Rescission requires that a party, or a party's representative, (1) act promptly, (2) return or offer to return goods or property received, and (3) demand the return of money or goods transferred. A *void* contract is one that is of no effect and never will be. In cases of either void or voidable contracts, quasi contract may be available to prevent unjust enrichment.

STUDY AND DISCUSSION QUESTIONS

1 *(a)* How do courts define "duress"? *(b)* Give an original example of a wrongful threat: to the person; to property. *(c)* What is meant by "economic duress"?

2 *(a)* Is threatening to institute criminal proceedings against someone always duress? Explain. *(b)* Is threatening civil action against someone duress? Explain.

3 "Undue influence is closely related to duress." *(a)* What is the similarity? *(b)* What is the difference? *(c)* State the two kinds of situations in which undue influence is most likely to occur, and give an example of each.

4 *(a)* List the five elements of the tort of fraud. *(b)* Why is the fifth element necessary in a tort action?

5 *(a)* What is the purpose of including an exculpatory or disclaimer clause in a contract? *(b)* What is the legal effect of such clauses?

6 Differentiate between "fraud in the inducement" and "fraud in the execution."

7 *(a)* What is meant by "innocent misrepresentation" (or simply "misrepresentation")? *(b)* "There are two differences between the elements of fraud and what might be called the elements of misrepresentation." Explain. *(c)* Explain the difference in remedies available to a party induced to enter a contract by fraud and to a party induced by innocent misrepresentation.

8 *(a)* In the context of this chapter, what is the meaning of "mistake"? *(b)* Explain and give an example of a latent ambiguity in the wording of a contract. *(c)* Explain the consequences of a latent ambiguity.

9 *(a)* What is reformation? *(b)* Under what circumstances is reformation available?

10 *(a)* Under what circumstances is mutual mistake grounds for relief from a contract? *(b)* When is mutual mistake not grounds for relief? *(c)* Explain the difference in result if an agreement calls for sale of specific goods where (i) the goods are destroyed before agreement is reached and where (ii) the goods are destroyed after agreement is reached.

11 Under what circumstances will courts grant relief from a contract entered into under a unilateral mistake?

12 *(a)* What rule is to be applied where both parties to an agreement were operating under a mistake of law assumed by them as a basis on which they entered into the transaction? *(b)* Is relief granted where only one party is operating under a mistake of law? Explain.

13 Under some state and federal consumer protection statutes, a consumer has a 3-day "cooling-off period." For what kinds of transactions is this cooling-off period available?

14 *(a)* List the prerequisites to rescind a voidable contract. *(b)* What effect would a failure to act promptly have on a void contract?

15 Whether an agreement is void or voidable may make a great difference where the rights of third persons are concerned. Explain or illustrate.

CASE PROBLEMS

1 Mr. and Mrs. Peterson entered into an agreement with Florence Johnson for the purchase and sale of a certain piece of land for $21,000. Later the real estate agents representing Johnson told the Petersons that their client "was unwilling to sell the property at the price agreed upon," that the Petersons "would not be able to enforce the agreement in a court, and that they would spend 3 years trying unsuccessfully if they insisted on enforcing the agreement." Relying upon the agents' representations, the Petersons released Johnson "from any responsibilities" under the agreement. Subsequently the Petersons sued the agents for fraud, alleging misrepresentations of fact. The agents contended that the alleged misrepresentations were not representations of fact but of opinion or law, and that therefore there was no fraud. Was the contention of the agents sound?

2 Mrs. Korth was obtaining unsatisfactory service from her coal-and-wood furnace. She explained her heating problems to the Holland Furnace Company, and the company sent out a salesman to inspect the furnace and premises. The salesman represented himself to be an expert in the design and installation of furnaces. After making an inspection, he recommended that the furnace be converted to an oil burner and that four of the warm-air pipes be replaced with larger pipes. He told Mrs. Korth that if these changes were made, the furnace would heat the house comfortably and would cut her fuel bills in half.

Mrs. Korth signed a contract for the suggested changes, and the changes were made, but the furnace did not heat adequately and did not reduce fuel bills. Mrs. Korth refused to pay the contract price, and the furnace company sued. The company contended that the salesman was merely expressing an opinion and that there was no false representation of fact. Was there a false representation of fact?

3 Mr. and Mrs. Barylski looked at a house owned by a Mr. and Mrs. Andrews with a view to buying it. On their first visit to the house, the Andrews' real estate agent showed them through the house; on their second visit, Mrs. Andrews showed them the house. The Barylskis purchased the house. Four years later a leak developed in the roof, and water ran down behind the wallboards. In making necessary repairs, the Barylskis discovered that the house had been seriously burned and that the damaged areas had been covered over by new wallboards, wallpaper, and paint. Subsequent inquiry disclosed that concealment of the burned areas was the work of Mr. and Mrs. Andrews. The Barylskis sued the Andrewses for actionable fraud. The defendants contended that two essential elements of fraud were lacking: (**a**) false representation of facts and (**b**) justifiable reliance. Were the defendants' contentions sound?

4 J. J. Ansley and his son, E. C. Ansley, were partners who owned and operated a construction firm. They wanted to rent a heavy John Deere scraper from a certain equipment company. Thomas Clay, an authorized agent of the equipment company, drew up a lease, using for that purpose a printed lease form. The son inquired whether the lease included credit life insurance and was told that it included such insurance in the amount of $25,000. Thereupon the son signed the lease without reading it. Actually the lease did not include credit life insurance. Instead, the lease contained a provision reading, "Notice: Liability insurance coverage for bodily injury and property damage caused to others and life insurance on Lessee are not included." The father died before the lease was terminated. The son brought an action against the equipment company for damages growing out of the "false and fraudulent representations of [the company's] authorized agent." Is the son entitled to recover on the basis of fraud in the execution?

5 Plaintiff was injured by a car driven by the defendant. Plaintiff's doctor told both the plaintiff and the defendant's insurance company that the bruises and cuts which plaintiff had suffered were of a superficial nature. Both parties accepted the doctor's diagnosis. A settlement of $150 was then agreed upon. Later it developed that the doctor had been mistaken in his diagnosis and that plaintiff's injuries were of a serious nature. Plaintiff brought suit for rescission of the settlement. Should he succeed?

6 The School District of Scottsbluff advertised for bids for the construction of a school building. Just before closing time for filing of bids, the Olson Construction Company filed a bid of $68,400. The only other bid was for $89,905. The Olson Company's bid was accepted, and the company was notified of the acceptance. When Olson's vice president learned of the variation in the two bids, he examined the company's estimate sheets. He discovered that an experienced clerk had made a serious error while using an adding machine. The company had been forced to prepare its bid in a great hurry because of slowness of subcontractors in submitting *their* bids. The vice president informed the school district of the error as soon as he discovered and accounted for the error. The school district refused to allow Olson Company to withdraw its bid and eventually sued the company. Which party should win?

Chapter

14

Contractual Capacity
of the Parties

Previous chapters dealt with three requirements for a contract: offer, acceptance, and consideration. A fourth requirement is that there must be two or more parties having legal capacity to contract. Some persons have no legal capacity to contract; some have full contractual capacity. In between these extremes are persons having limited contractual power. Most of their contracts are voidable, but some of their contracts are fully enforceable against them.

Of the persons having limited capacity to contract, minors constitute the largest class. Another class of such persons is referred to in the broad category "mentally incompetent." Still another class of persons having limited contractual capacity ,is made up of persons under the influence of alcohol or other drugs.

The first part of this chapter examines the contractual capacity of minors. The last part discusses the contractual capacity of mentally incompetent persons and persons under the influence of alcohol or other drugs.

CONTRACTUAL CAPACITY OF MINORS

At common law, persons under the age of twenty-one years were called "infants." The term is still widely used in the United States to refer to "underage" persons. However, the modern trend is to refer to such persons as "minors."

From early common law days to the present, the law has sought to protect minors from being bound by their imprudent contracts. Several reasons have been advanced for providing this protection:

• Minors need to be protected from their immaturity, their inexperience, and their tendency to do impulsive buying.

• They are especially likely to be the victims of unscrupulous adults.

• Young minors may not understand the nature and consequences of contracts which they enter into.

The policy of protecting minors is very strong.

The protection takes the form of allowing the minor to avoid or "disaffirm" contracts made with adults. The result often is that adults refuse to enter contracts with persons known to be "under age." Where such a result might actually harm the minor the courts or legislatures have provided the adult with a remedy, thus encouraging the adult to deal with the minor. For example, because a minor must be able to buy food, clothing, and other necessaries, he or she may be liable for them under appropriate circumstances. The subject of necessaries will be examined later in this part of the chapter.

Period of Minority

The age at which the period of minority ends and the minor achieves full contractual capacity does not necessarily correspond with the age or ages that a state sets for other purposes. Thus, a statute in a particular state may set one age when a person has the capacity to make a will, another age for voting in state and local elections, and still another age for legally purchasing liquor.

In many states the age of majority for contract purposes has been lowered from twenty-one to eighteen. Most states follow the common law rule that a person achieves majority the first moment of the day preceding his or her eighteenth (or twenty-first) birthday. Other states have changed the rule in various ways. For example, in some states a person becomes of age on the twenty-first anniversary of birth rather than on the preceding day; in some, women become of age at eighteen; in others, marriage gives women full contractual capacity; in still others, both men and women have full contractual capacity upon marriage. However, states may not establish one age of majority for males and a different age for females unless the classification by gender serves some important governmental objective and is substantially related to the achievement of that objective.[1]

A number of states have a statutory procedure for "judicial emancipation" of minors. The statutes vary in their details, but they all require a petition by or on behalf of the minor and also a court hearing. If the judge finds that removal of disabilities is in the best interests of the minor and that the minor is capable of tending to his or her own affairs or business, the judge will sign an order or decree of emancipation. The effect of the order or decree is to enable the minor to enter into contracts as if the minor were an adult, that is, with an adult's rights and duties.

There is also a form of emancipation by parental consent. This form of emancipation "involves an entire surrender of the right to the care, custody, and earnings of such [minor] child as well as a renunciation of parental duties.[2] This form of emancipation has no effect, however, upon the contractual capacity of the minor.

Disaffirmance of Minors' Voidable Contracts

Meaning of Disaffirmance The general rule is that a minor's contract is voidable by the minor. Exercise of the power of avoidance is commonly referred to as the "disaffirmance" of the contract.

Disaffirmance may be express or implied. It is *express* where the decision to avoid is stated in words, oral or written. No particular form of expression need be used. Any words suffice if they show an unequivocal intention to repudiate the contract. Disaffirmance is *implied* where the repudiation is inferred from conduct. Any act suffices if it is clearly inconsistent with the existence of a contract.

Because the purpose of giving the minor the power of disaffirmance is to protect him or her, the power of disaffirmance is personal to the minor. During his or her lifetime, only the minor or a legally appointed guardian may exercise that power; and upon the minor's death

---

[1]*Craig v. Boren*, 429 U.S. 190, 197 (1976).

[2]*Black's Law Dictionary*, 5th ed., West Publishing Company, St. Paul, 1979. Reprinted with permission from Black's Law Dictionary © Copyright 1979 by West Publishing Co.

the minor's heirs or a personal representative may exercise it. An adult party to a contract with a minor has no similar power of disaffirmance; the adult is bound to the contract unless the minor disaffirms it. Where both parties to the contract are minors, each has the power of disaffirmance.

Case 14.1   **Lamb v. Midwest Mutual Insurance Co.**
296 F. Supp. 131 (W.D. Ark. 1969)

The plaintiff Richard Lamb, a minor, applied for insurance for his motorcycle. As required by statute, the defendant, Midwest Mutual Insurance Co., offered the plaintiff a policy which provided uninsured motorist coverage. The plaintiff rejected the uninsured motorist provision, as he had a right to do under the statute, but he accepted the rest of the policy.

While riding his motorcycle during the policy period, the plaintiff was involved in a collision with an automobile. He sustained injuries and sued the insurance company. In his suit he alleged that the injuries were proximately caused by the automobile driver's negligence, that the driver was an uninsured motorist, and that the plaintiff should not be bound by his written rejection of the uninsured motorist endorsement contained in the insurance policy. The defendant insurance company made a motion for summary judgment.

HENLEY, District Judge. . . . The defendant's motion for summary judgment presents the sole question of whether the plaintiff is bound by the written rejection of uninsured motorist coverage which he executed when he applied for the policy. . . . The plaintiff contends that he is not so bound, and bases his contention solely on his [minority]. In resisting the motion, counsel for plaintiff undertakes to characterize the rejection as a separate contract which plaintiff is free to disaffirm. . . . The Court agrees with counsel on both sides in their view that the question presented is a novel one, and this case seems to be one of first impression.

The Court . . . agrees with the defendant that plaintiff has no claim against the defendant. There is no question that in Arkansas, as elsewhere, a minor has a right to disaffirm a contract for nonnecessaries at any time during his minority and for a reasonable time thereafter. [Citations.] It is safe to assume that in Arkansas the general rule is applicable to an insurance contract entered into by a minor, including a policy of automobile or motorcycle insurance. . . .

It is clear, however, that in the case of such a contract, as in the case of contracts generally, the minor must either affirm or disaffirm the contract as a whole; he cannot accept the benefits and disaffirm the burdens. And a minor is not entitled by reason of his minority to change a contract unilaterally so as to impose upon the other party obligations which he did not assume. It has been well stated that infancy acts "as a shield and not as a sword."

The Court sees nothing in the statute which requires a minor to purchase uninsured motorist insurance if he does not want it, and certainly the Court sees nothing in the statute which requires an insurance company to provide uninsured motorist coverage gratis to a minor who has rejected the coverage and has paid nothing for such protection.

When plaintiff applied to the defendant for liability insurance, the defendant was required under the statute to offer uninsured motorist coverage as well, and it did so. The plaintiff had an option either to reject the coverage or to accept and pay for it. It was necessary, of course, for him to manifest his choice, and he did so by executing the rejection appearing in the application.

In terms of contract law, what plaintiff did when he executed the rejection was to decline an offer which the defendant was required to make but which plaintiff was not required to accept. Thus, as far as uninsured motorist insurance was concerned, there was simply never any contract to be either affirmed or disaffirmed by the minor. He cannot be permitted to change his mind ex post facto and thereby obtain the benefit of coverage which he did not purchase in the first place.

The motion for summary judgment will be sustained, and the complaint will be dismissed.

Requisites for Disaffirmance   Most contracts entered into by minors are not void, but voidable. If the minor chooses to avoid a particular contract, he or she may assert minority as a defense in a lawsuit filed by the adult to enforce the contract, or may file a suit to disaffirm. Most states impose prerequisites to granting relief. These requirements are similar to the requirements for rescission discussed in Chapter 13 (see pages 245–246). In most states in order to disaffirm, the person must: (1) act during minority or within a reasonable time after attaining majority; (2) demand the return of money or goods, if any, transferred to the other party; and (3) return or offer to return any goods or property received.

As stated above, a person may disaffirm the contract during minority or within a reasonable time after reaching majority. What constitutes a reasonable time for disaffirmance is a question of fact and depends on the circumstances. In most states a minor may not disaffirm his or her conveyance of land until after reaching majority. In a few states, such as California, a minor's conveyance of land is void, rather than voidable. Thus, in those states no time limit is imposed on disaffirmance. A void contract is never binding on either party.

Upon disaffirmance the minor is entitled to the return of any property still in the hands of the other contracting party. However, the minor may not recover the property from an innocent third-person ("bona fide") purchaser, that is, from a person who purchased the property without knowing that the seller had purchased it from a minor. The Uniform Commercial Code, Article 2, which pertains to contracts for the sale of *goods*, provides that a person with voidable title has power to transfer a good title to a good faith purchaser for value [UCC, sec. 2–403 (1)]. *Goods* are defined to include all things which are movable, such as automobiles, books, furniture, etc. [UCC, sec. 2–105(1)].

Upon disaffirmance, the minor must return whatever was received if it is still in his or her possession. The courts are not in agreement on whether the minor can disaffirm when unable to return the property received or when able to return it only in damaged condition. The majority view is that the minor may disaffirm even though the property received has been lost, destroyed, or damaged. The justification for this rule is said to be that the same immaturity of judgment which causes minors to enter into improvident contracts causes them to be careless in using and guarding the property received. The minority view is that a minor is not permitted to disaffirm a contract unless he or she is able to restore the other contracting party to the same position the party occupied at the time of contracting. If the minor has sold or exchanged property purchased from the adult and still has the property or money received in the resale or exchange, the minor must transfer the money or replacement property to the adult.

Case 14.2　　**Terrace Co. v. Calhoun**
　　　　　　　　347 N.E.2d 315 (Ill. App. 1976)

When she was thirteen years old, Marilyn Calhoun (defendant) was told of her father's death. At the request of the funeral director she signed two documents. As she signed, the funeral director covered the written portions with his hand. No one told Marilyn the nature of the documents. One was a confession-of-judgment promissory note in the amount of $1,944.72, payable to L. C. Wesley Funeral Home. The other was an assignment of $1,944.72 of Marilyn's beneficial interest in an insurance policy on her father's life. The day after Marilyn signed the documents, Wesley Funeral Home assigned them to the Terrace Company (plaintiff).

Almost 8 months later, when Marilyn was fourteen years old, Terrace filed a complaint to confess judgment on the note against Marilyn. Judgment against her was entered the same day. An attempt to execute the judgment failed.

Marilyn attained majority [eighteen years] on July 7, 1972. A year later, a prospective employer informed her that her credit record was impaired. Marilyn made inquiry and learned for the first time of the judgment by confession. She filed a motion to open the judgment. The motion was granted, and, following a trial, the judgment by confession was restored. Marilyn appealed.

The appellate court considered a number of issues, three of which were: (1) is a promissory note subject to disaffirmance? (2) If so, did defendant disaffirm within a reasonable time? (3) If a promissory note is subject to disaffirmance, what duty of restitution does the defendant have? The following excerpts from the court's opinion relate to these three issues.

MEDJA, J. . . . . The promissory note of a minor is voidable, as are [a minor's] contracts in general. . . . This rule has been applied to both negotiable and nonnegotiable promissory notes, whether issued or accepted by minors.

What constitutes a reasonable time in which to disaffirm has been held to be a period not in excess of that prescribed by the statute of limitations for bringing action after the removal of a disability. [Citations.] However, more recent case law indicates that what constitutes a reasonable time is a question of fact to be determined by the circumstances of a particular case.

In the instant case, the . . . defendant was not advised of the nature and effect of the confession note and assignment of insurance benefits when she signed the documents at the age of 13. It is not disputed that she first learned of the judgment by confession . . . when she was 19 years old, and that 2 months thereafter she filed a motion to open the judgment. We find that under these circumstances defendant disaffirmed the note and assignment within a reasonable time after attaining her majority. . . .

Plaintiff argues that as a condition precedent to disaffirmance, defendant must first return to plaintiff [what defendant received]. A minor cannot retain what he still has of what he received and at the same time recover what he has parted with under the contract. While a minor is under an obligation to make restitution upon disaffirmance, if he no longer has the consideration, he need not return it. The promissory note in the instant case states that it was for the funeral of defendant's father. . . . What plaintiff is asking defendant to return is a funeral service, an intangible which is incapable of being returned. Therefore, restitution is clearly not required under the circumstances.

[The appellate court also found all other issues in favor of the defendant, and reversed the judgment of the trial court.]

Effect of Misrepresentation of Age Most courts hold that a minor who has intentionally misrepresented his or her age is not thereby prevented from avoiding the contract. However, there is conflict of authority on whether the minor is liable in tort for that misrepresentation. It is well established that minors are liable for their torts generally, and the view of most courts is that the minor is liable for the tort of fraud. The minority view is that to hold the minor liable in tort would enable the adult to enforce indirectly a contract admitted to be voidable by the minor.

A minor's intentional misrepresentation of age, or of any other material fact, if justifiably relied on by the adult is grounds for rescission by the adult. The requisites for rescission were discussed in Chapter 13.

Case 14.3 **Kiefer v. Fred Howe Motors, Inc.**
158 N.W.2d 288 (Wis. 1968)

On August 9, 1965, the plaintiff, Steven Kiefer, entered into a contract with the defendant, Fred Howe Motors, Inc. ("dealer"), for the purchase of a 1960 Willys station wagon. Kiefer paid the contract price of $412 and took possession of the car. At the time of the sale, Kiefer was twenty years old, married, and the father of one child. The age of majority was twenty-one.

Kiefer had difficulty with the car. Several attempts to secure some adjustment with the dealer failed, and Kiefer contacted an attorney. The attorney wrote a letter to the dealer advising it that Kiefer was under twenty-one at the time of the sale. The letter tendered return of the automobile and demanded repayment of the purchase price. There was no response, and the plaintiff commenced this action to recover the purchase price. The trial court entered a judgment for the plaintiff, and the defendant appealed.

WILKIE, J. Three issues are presented on this appeal. They are:

1 Should an emancipated minor over the age of eighteen be legally responsible for his contracts?

2 Was the contract effectively disaffirmed?

3 Is the plaintiff liable in tort for misrepresentation [of his age]?

The law governing agreements made during infancy reaches back over many centuries. The general rule is that the contract of a minor . . . is . . . voidable at his option. . . . The general rule is not affected by the minor's status as emancipated or unemancipated.

Appellant (defendant) . . . urges that this court, as a matter of public policy, adopt a rule that an emancipated minor over eighteen years of age be made legally responsible for his contracts.

The underpinnings of the general rule allowing the minor to disaffirm his contracts were undoubtedly the protection of the minor. It was thought that the minor was immature in both mind and experience and that, therefore, he should be protected from his own bad judgments as well as from adults who would take advantage of him. . . .

No one really questions that a line as to age must be drawn somewhere, below which a legally defined minor must be able to disaffirm his contracts for nonnecessities. The law over the centuries has considered this age to be twenty-one. Legislatures in other states have lowered the age. We suggest that the appellant might better seek the change it proposes in the legislative halls rather than this court. . . .

For this court to adopt a rule that the appellant suggests and remove the contractual disabilities from a minor simply because he becomes emancipated, which in most cases would be the result of marriage, would be to suggest that the married minor is somehow vested with more wisdom and maturity than his single counterpart. However, logic would not seem to dictate this result, especially when today a youthful marriage is oftentimes indicative of a lack of wisdom and maturity.

The appellant questions whether there has been an effective disaffirmance of the contract in this case. Williston, while discussing how a minor may disaffirm a contract, states:

> Any act which clearly shows an intent to disaffirm a contract or sale is sufficient for the purpose. Thus a notice by the infant of his purpose to disaffirm, . . . a tender or even an offer to return the consideration or its proceeds to the vendor, . . . is sufficient.

The testimony of Steven Kiefer and the letter from his attorney to the dealer clearly establish that there was an effective disaffirmance of the contract.

Appellant's last argument is that the respondent should be held liable in tort for damages because he misrepresented his age. Appellant would use these damages as a set-off against the contract price sought to be reclaimed by respondent.

. . . There appear to be two possible methods that . . . can be employed to bind a defrauding minor: He may be estopped from denying his alleged majority, in which case the contract will be enforced or contract damages will be allowed; or he may be allowed to disaffirm his contract but be liable in tort for damages. Wisconsin follows the latter approach. . . .

Having established that there is a remedy against a defrauding minor, [we now consider whether] the requisites for a tort action in [fraudulent] misrepresentation are present in this case.

The trial produced conflicting testimony regarding whether Steven Kiefer had been asked his age or had replied that he was "twenty-one." . . . The question of credibility was for the trial court to decide, which it did by holding that Steven did not orally represent that he was "twenty-one." This finding is not contrary to the great weight and clear preponderance of the evidence. . . . The trial court observed that the plaintiff was sufficiently immature looking to arouse suspicion. The appellant never took any affirmative steps to determine whether the plaintiff was in fact over twenty-one. It never asked to see a draft card, identification card, or the most logical indicium of age under the circumstances, a driver's license. Therefore, because there was no intent to deceive, and no justifiable reliance, the appellant's action for misrepresentation must fail.

Judgment affirmed.

Ratification of Minors' Voidable Contracts

Meaning of Ratification   In a broad sense, ratification means the confirmation of a previous act or promise. When used in connection with minors' contracts, ratification means a manifestation of an intention to be bound by a contract entered into during the period of minority. The minor cannot ratify a contract until he or she becomes of age. Any purported ratification during minority is ineffective.

How Contracts May Be Ratified   A contract may be ratified in one of three ways: by express ratification, by implied ratification, or by failure to make a timely disaffirmance. An *express ratification* is one in which the intention to be bound by a contract previously made is express-ed in words. Unless a statute provides otherwise, ratification may be made orally. No particular form of expression is required. Any wording suffices as long as it indicates an intention to be bound. Making a definite promise to perform a contract previously entered into is one way of expressing such an intention. However, a mere acknowledgment by a person that he or she had entered into the contract as a minor, without any indication of an intent to be bound by the contract, is not a ratification.

An *implied ratification* is one in which an intention to be bound is inferred from the person's conduct. For example, suppose that Brenda enters into a contract 3 months before reaching her majority. Under the terms of the contract she receives some diving gear for which she is to pay later. Two months after reaching her majority, she sells the gear. Disposal of the gear is an act inconsistent with an intent to disaffirm and thus may be held to constitute ratification. Other conduct from which ratification may be inferred includes using property purchased for more than a reasonable time after majority and part payment or other performance of contract terms after reaching majority.

It was stated earlier that one of the requisites for disaffirming a minor's contract is to act during minority or within a reasonable time after attaining majority. Failure to disaffirm within a reasonable time after attaining majority results in a ratification. In determining a reasonable time some courts consider whether the contract is executory or executed. These courts permit a person to wait much longer to disaffirm an executory contract than an executed one, provided such delay does not prejudice the other party to the contract.

Contracts Which Minors Cannot Disaffirm

The general rule that minors may avoid their contracts is subject to certain exceptions. Some of these exceptions have been created by statutes. Examples are a statute which provides that minors who are emancipated by court order cannot avoid contracts, a statute providing that minors who open bank accounts in their own names will be fully liable for all of their acts in respect to such accounts, and a statute limiting the rights of minors to avoid the payment of insurance premiums.

Other exceptions to the general rule have been created by court action. For example, minors generally cannot disaffirm their bailbond contracts, on the ground that permitting avoidance "would be contrary to sound public policy." Neither can a minor disaffirm the contract by which he or she obtained money to pay taxes on real property. Some of the court-created exceptions can be explained only on the ground

that on entering into the contract, the minor had promised to do something which the law would require the minor to do even in the absence of a contract. For example, a minor father who contracted to support his illegitimate child is not permitted to avoid the contract, because in entering into the contract he promised to do only what he would be required to do under a rule of the common law.

In most states there are statutes permitting a court to approve certain minors' contracts, such as contracts of employment as an entertainer or professional athlete and contracts compromising tort claims. The minor may not later disaffirm a court-approved contract. Where a minor owns property a court may, upon petition, appoint a guardian to manage the estate of the minor. The guardian may sell the minor's property when appropriate and the sale is not subject to disaffirmance.

Liability of Minors for Necessaries

Ordinarily, a minor's parents or guardian will provide the minor with food, clothing, and housing. If the parent or guardian is unable or unwilling to supply such items, the law makes it possible for the minor to purchase them.

Nature of Liability for Necessaries. A minor who enters into a contract for necessaries may disaffirm the contract in accordance with the general rule regarding minors' contracts. However, the minor may be liable in quasi contract to the provider of the necessaries for the reasonable value of the necessaries provided (See Chapter 9, pages 171–173 for discussion of quasi contract). The law places this liability upon minors mainly for their protection. If minors could avoid all obligation to pay, they might find difficulty in securing necessaries.

The difference in contractual liability and quasi-contractual liability for necessaries may be illustrated by the following. Suppose a minor enters into a contract to lease an apartment for one year at a rental of $200 per month. If, after 3 months, the minor decides to disaffirm the contract and vacate the apartment the minor is liable for $600, the reasonable value of housing provided. If the minor were not permitted to disaffirm such a contract he or she would be liable under contract law for the remaining 9 months' rental.

Goods and Services Recognized as Necessaries Courts have held that food, clothing, shelter, medical services, tools of a trade, and some degree of education come within the classification of necessaries. Other goods and services have also been included by some courts. Examples are a reasonable fee for legal services for the enforcement of a tort claim and a reasonable fee paid to an employment agency for assistance in finding a job for a married minor. A minor who borrows money for the purchase of necessaries and who uses the money for that purpose has the same liability to the lender as if the lender supplied the necessaries. Because of this protection, bankers are more inclined to make such a loan, just as sellers of necessaries are more inclined to make the sale.

"Necessaries" is a relative term. The same goods and services may be recognized as necessaries in one situation and not in another. One of the determinants of whether a good or service is a necessary is the minor's *station in life*. Clothing of high quality and fashion may be a necessary for a minor whose father is a diplomat, but not for one whose father works in a fish cannery. *Marital status* may be an important determinant. Goods and services which are necessaries for a married minor may not be necessaries for an unmarried minor. Perhaps the most impor ant test is the *need* of the minor for the particular article or service at the time it is supplied. For example, food is not a necessary for a minor who has an adequate supply. A minor is not liable for necessaries so long as the minor's parent or guardian is able and willing to supply those necessaries. Broad discretion is granted the parent or guardian in determining how to meet the needs of the minor.

CONTRACTUAL CAPACITY OF CERTAIN OTHER CLASSES OF PERSONS

Mentally Incompetent Persons

Ordinarily, a contract made by a person who is mentally incompetent is voidable, just as a contract made by a minor is voidable and for the same reason—to protect persons unable to protect themselves against imposition. In protecting the mentally incompetent, the law seeks to protect also the justifiable expectations of the other contracting party and society's interest in maintaining the security of transactions.

Test of Mental Incompetency Great progress has been made in understanding that mental incompetency is not the same as insanity. According to a comment in the *Restatement of the Law of Contracts*,

It is now recognized that there is a wide variety of types and degrees of mental incompetency. Among them are congenital deficiencies in intelligence, the mental deterioration of old age, the effects of brain damage caused by accident or organic disease, and mental illnesses evidenced by such symptoms as delusions, hallucinations, delirium, confusion, and depression. . . . A person may be able to understand almost nothing, or only simple routine transactions, or he may be incompetent only with respect to a particular type of transaction.[3]

The general test for determining whether a person is so mentally incompetent as to justify a court in holding his or her contract to be voidable may be stated thus:

• Did the party have, at the time of entering into the contract, sufficient mental capacity to understand the nature and consequences of the transaction?

---

[3]*Restatement of the Law (Second) Contracts*, American Law Institute, Philadelphia, sec. 18c, comment *b*.

• If the person had no such capacity, did the lack of capacity affect the particular transaction?

A person suffering from mental illness may have lucid intervals. A contract made during such an interval is binding on both parties.

Effect of Mental Incompetency If a party at the time of entering into a contract lacks sufficient mental capacity, the contract is voidable and may be rescinded. The usual requisites for rescission must be met. The person, or a guardian or conservator, must: (1) act promptly; (2) demand the return of money or goods; and (3) return or offer to return goods or property received. Mental incompetency may be raised as a defense in a lawsuit filed by the other party to enforce the contract.

In some instances a person may be adjudicated incompetent by a court and the court will appoint a guardian or conservator to care for the person's estate. In rare circumstances an insane person may be committed to a state institution. After an adjudication of mental incompetency or insanity any contracts entered into by the person are void, not voidable. Thus, no time limitation is imposed for rescission and either party to the contract may avoid it.

One who is mentally incompetent is liable in quasi contract for the reasonable value of necessaries.

Case 14.4   **Williams v. Wilson**
335 So. 2d 110 (Miss. 1976)

On July 12, 1968, Willie Ester Williams was committed to the Mississippi State Hospital where, for several months, she was treated for a mental or nervous disorder described as schizophrenia. After this period of treatment, she returned home. On February 10, 1970, she sold 60 acres of land to defendant Woodson Wilson for $3,000. The fair market value of the land on that date was later appraised at $6,500.

Ms. Williams moved to Detroit to live with her son. While there, she underwent a program of treatment for psychotic depression. The doctor treated her from March 5, 1970, (27 days after she executed the deed of sale) to November 1971. In the litigation involved in this case, the doctor testified that "in my opinion the patient was not of sufficient mental capacity on February 10th, 1970, to have understood the purport of a deed and the consideration therefor for sixty acres of land and to have looked after her interest at that time."

A relative of Ms. Williams brought suit on her behalf to have the contract of sale rescinded. The Chancery Court of Itawamba County held that Ms. Williams was competent on February 10, 1970, to execute a deed to Wilson. The plaintiff appealed.

WALKER, J. . . . Except for necessaries suited to his condition in life, a lunatic cannot make a contract. Courts of law, as well as equity, protect persons of unsound mind from the consequences of contracts attempted to be made by them. Against the consequences of mere imprudence, folly, or that deficiency of intellect which makes mistake easy but does not amount to unsound or disordered intellect, even equity affords no relief, unless the other party has made use of this want of intelligence to do a wrongful act. Weakness of understanding is not of itself any objection to the validity of a contract if the capacity remains to see things in their true relations and to form correct conclusions.

The doubtful and uncertain point at which the disposing mind disappears and where incapacity begins can be ascertained only by an examination of all the circumstances of each particular case, to be duly weighed and considered by the court or jury, and in determining the question the common sense and good judgment of the tribunal must be mainly relied on. Generally, when it appears that a person had not strength of mind and reason sufficient to understand the nature and consequences of his act in making a deed or other contract, it may be avoided on the ground of insanity.

. . . The purchaser . . . was put on notice that [Ms. Williams] was probably suffering from a mental disorder. The attorney who examined the title to the property for Wilson testified that he found Willie Ester Williams had been committed some few years prior to [the sale] and that he had brought this to Mr. Wilson's attention. . . . Under the circumstances, it was the duty of the purchaser to make an investigation into the competency of Willie Ester Williams, and, failing to do so, he bought the property at his peril.

This case fits squarely within the holding of [an 1884 Mississippi case] where it was said:

> "Sanity is presumed until the contrary appears, and the burden of proof is on the party alleging insanity to prove it; but when a person is shown to have been generally or habitually insane at any particular period, that condition is presumed to continue, and whoever relies on a lucid interval to support a contract subsequently made with such a lunatic must prove it and show sanity and competence at the time the contract was made."

. . . The evidence in support of a lucid interval . . . should be as strong and demonstrative of such fact as when the object of the proof is to show insanity, and it ought to go to the state and habit of the person, and not to the accidental interview of any individual or to the degree of self-possession in any particular act. . . .

The only evidence tending to show that Willie Ester Williams was in a "lucid interval" at the time she executed the deed to the sixty acres of land to Mr. Wilson came from three witnesses who observed her briefly. . . .

The testimony of the three witnesses falls far short of [that required by Mississippi law]. . . . The testimony of Mr. Reeder covered a momentary period, the testimony of the attorney who handled the transaction covered a period of only fifteen minutes, and the testimony of Mr. Homer Wilson, the agent and cousin of Woodson Wilson, covered [three brief periods]. It could hardly be argued that such testimony based on the observations of lay witnesses over such a short period of time would be sufficient evidence upon which a person could be found insane. Conversely . . . it is not sufficient to show that Willie Ester Williams, who was habitually insane, had a lucid interval on February 10, 1970, and was competent to execute a deed to her property. . . . The chancellor was manifestly wrong in his finding.

Reversed. . . .

Persons under the Influence of Alcohol or Other Drugs

In most respects the law treats the contracts of persons who are acting under the influence of alcohol or other drugs the same way it treats the contracts of mentally incompetent persons. For example, where a guardian has been appointed for the property of a chronic alcoholic, any transaction entered into thereafter by the person is void. Where no guardian has been appointed, an intoxicated person's transactions are usually held to be voidable. Relief will be granted only if the person is so intoxicated or so under the influence of drugs that he or she does not understand the nature and consequences of the contract entered into.

Where the intoxicated person has some understanding of the transaction despite intoxication, avoidance may depend on such circumstances as whether the other party induced the intoxication and whether the consideration for the intoxicated person's promise was inadequate. The requisites for rescission apply to contracts made by an intoxicated or drugged person. Incapacity may be raised as a defense in a lawsuit filed by the other party to enforce the contract.

A person who lacks understanding as a result of using alcohol or other drugs is liable in quasi contract for the reasonable value of necessaries.

Case 14.5   Curry v. Stewart
368 P.2d 297 (Kan. 1962)

In 1913, defendant Edgar Stewart started in the paving contracting business. Two years later his brother, defendant Oscar Stewart, joined him as a partner. In 1941, the plaintiff, Edwin M. Curry, married Edgar's daughter and began working for the Stewarts. In 1946, the Stewarts took Curry and defendant Kenton Stewart (Edgar's son) into the partnership.

Marital troubles developed between Curry and his wife, and Curry began to drink heavily. On at least one occasion Curry was hospitalized for alcoholism. During this time Curry contributed little or nothing to the operation of the business.

Looking for a solution to the problem, Edgar Stewart and Curry had a number of discussions. Early in May 1957 a partnership dissolution agreement was prepared. Curry signed it on May 13. On several occasions thereafter, Curry executed other instruments in furtherance of the dissolution.

On September 17, 1957, Curry filed an action to rescind the dissolution agreement. He alleged that in May 1957 he was ill, intoxicated, and under the influence of sedatives to such an extent that he was in no mental or physical condition to transact business, that the three defendant partners were aware of his condition, and that in the execution of the dissolution agreement he had been overreached and defrauded.

The trial court held the dissolution agreement void on the ground that "during the entire month of May 1957, the plaintiff was mentally incompetent to exercise independent, normal judgment about the transaction of business affairs, or to understand their consequences." The defendants appealed.

PRICE, J. . . . It is noted that in the finding above quoted . . . the trial did *not* find that Curry was *intoxicated* or under the *influence of liquor* when he signed the dissolution agreement on May 13, 1957, which is the *crucial* date in this case. . . .

The rule is that a contract by an alcoholic may not be avoided on [the ground of alcoholism] if at the time of its execution he was sober and in possession of his faculties. One's dissipated condition, standing alone, is not itself a ground for avoiding a contract or deed. An habitual drunkard is not necessarily incompetent as a matter of law; and, in the absence of an adjudication finding an habitual drunkard to be incompetent, in order to avoid his contract or deed on the ground of his incompetency, it must be shown that his mental condition was such *at the time* the contract or deed was made that he lacked the power of reason and was unable to comprehend the nature and consequences of his act in entering into the contract or executing the deed. . . .

It is quite true that on direct examination Curry testified to the effect that on May 13th he was "pushed" into signing the dissolution agreement, and that he was not afforded the opportunity to have a full understanding of "what was going on." On cross-examination, however, he specifically contradicted those statements. When asked if he wanted the court to understand that he was *drunk* at the time the agreement was executed, he replied "No. . . ."

When asked if he was "fully aware" of what was going on *at the time* the agreement was executed he replied in the *affirmative*. He also testified that on a number of occasions prior to May 13th the matter of dissolving the partnership had been discussed, particularly between him and Edgar. Nowhere in his testimony did he state or contend that he was drunk at the time the agreement was signed.

We find no substantial evidence in the record to support the proposition that at the time and place in question Curry was *intoxicated*, or to support the finding by the court of *incompetency* at the time and place in question so as to avoid the agreement. . . .

The judgment is reversed. . . .

SUMMARY

Minors, mentally incompetent persons, and persons under the influence of alcohol or other drugs have limited capacity to contract. Depending on the degree of incapacity and on other factors, the contracts of such persons may be void, voidable, or enforceable.

The law seeks to protect minors from imprudent contracts. As a general rule, therefore, a minor's contract is voidable. A minor may disaffirm a contract while still a minor or within a reasonable time thereafter. Ordinarily a minor may not disaffirm his or her conveyance of land until after reaching majority. In some states a minor's conveyance of land is void.

Upon disaffirmance a minor is entitled to the return of money or property from the other party. Under the Uniform Commercial Code, a minor may not recover property from an innocent third-person purchaser.

Generally, upon disaffirmance of a contract, the minor must return whatever he or she received if still in possession of it. In most states, a minor is not required to make any type of payment if he or she no longer possesses what was received or if it is damaged or depreciated. A minor who intentionally misrepresents his or her age may still disaffirm a contract. However, the minor may be liable for the tort of fraud. In addition, the adult may use such fraud as grounds to rescind the contract with the minor.

Upon reaching the age of majority, a person may ratify contracts made as a minor. Ratification is a manifestation of an intention to be bound by a contract entered into during the period of minority. Ratification may be express or implied, or may result from not disaffirming within a reasonable time after attaining majority.

Minors cannot avoid certain kinds of contracts. For example, minors cannot avoid court-approved contracts, such as contracts of employment as an entertainer or professional athlete, and contracts compromising tort claims. In most states a minor may disaffirm a contract for necessaries but is liable in quasi contract for their reasonable value. Whether a good or service is a necessary depends in great part on the need of the minor for it at the time it is supplied. Necessaries include food, clothing, medical care, shelter, tools of a trade, and education. The item supplied must be appropriate to the minor's station in life and not be supplied by the minor's parent or guardian in order for the minor to be held.

Where a person has been adjudged mentally incompetent and has been placed in the care of a guardian, a contract made by the incompetent person is void. Where there is no adjudication, the contract of such a person is voidable if, when it was made, the person lacked the capacity to understand the nature and consequences of the transaction. The rules regarding the contracts of persons under the influence of alcohol or other drugs are similar. Contracts made by persons lacking in understanding may be rescinded. The usual requisites of rescission must be met. Mental incapacity may be raised as a defense to a lawsuit filed by the other party to enforce the contract. A person lacking in understanding is liable in quasi contract for the reasonable value of necessaries furnished.

STUDY AND DISCUSSION QUESTIONS

1 For what reasons does the law permit minors to avoid their contracts?

2 (*a*) Does minority cease for all purposes when a person becomes "of age"? Explain. (*b*) What is meant by "judicial emancipation" of minors? What is its legal effect?

3 (*a*) What is meant by "disaffirmance" of a contract? (*b*) In general, how may disaffirmance occur? (*c*) Who may exercise a minor's power of disaffirmance?

4 (*a*) What are the requisites for disaffirmance of a contract by a minor? (*b*) When may a minor disaffirm a contract? (*c*) When may a minor disaffirm his or her conveyance of land?

5 (*a*)Upon disaffirmance of a contract, what right does a minor have to recover property he or she gave in performing the contract? (*b*) Must a disaffirming minor always return property received under the contract? Explain.

6 Suppose an adult enters a contract with a minor because the minor misrepresented his or her age. Will the minor be permitted to avoid the contract and to escape liability for any harm caused to the adult by the misrepresentation? Explain.

7 *(a)* With regard to minors' contracts, explain the meaning and legal effect of ratification. *(b)* When may a minor's contract be ratified? *(c)* Illustrate the three ways in which a minor's contract may be ratified.

8 *(a)* Give examples of contracts which a minor may not disaffirm. *(b)* For what reasons may such contracts not be disaffirmed?

9 *(a)* What is the theoretical basis of a minor's liability for "necessaries"? *(b)* For what practical reason is a minor liable for necessaries? *(c)* Give illustrations of necessaries. *(d)* State a general guide for deciding what constitutes a necessary.

10 Explain and illustrate the difference between contractual liability for necessaries and quasi-contractual liability for necessaries.

11 *(a)* The contract of a mentally incompetent person may be voidable. Why? *(b)* What is the general test for determining whether a person is sufficiently competent mentally for his or her contract to be enforced? *(c)* Explain and illustrate a "lucid interval." *(d)* What is the effect of an adjudication of incompetency on contracts made thereafter?

12 *(a)* Under what circumstances may a person avoid his or her contract on the ground of intoxication? *(b)* Why should an intoxicated or drugged person be liable for necessaries?

CASE PROBLEMS

1 Bristol County Stadium, Inc. (defendant) owned and operated an automobile racetrack. To enter a "novice race," Del Santo (plaintiff) was required to sign several documents, one of which was a release for any injury he might sustain on the track. A release is a type of contract in which a person promises not to sue for future injury or loss. In his entry application, Del Santo misrepresented his age to conceal the fact that he was a minor.

During the race, Del Santo's car overturned. Del Santo was not injured then, but he sustained serious injuries when his car was run into by another car a short time later. A few months after attaining his majority, Del Santo sued the defendant for alleged negligence in conducting the race. In bringing suit, Del Santo disaffirmed the release contract on the ground that he was a minor when he signed the release. Should Del Santo be allowed to proceed against the defendant?

2 Frank Dalton, a minor, and his wife bought a house from Conduff and agreed to assume the mortgage to which the property was subject. The age of majority was twenty-one. Dalton became twenty-one years of age on June 13, 1965. Dalton remained in possession of the property until September 1965. During that time five partial payments were made on the mortgage as authorized by a payroll deduction plan established before he became twenty-one. Despite these payments, the mortgage was in default, and the bank which held the mortgage brought suit against Conduff to foreclose it. Conduff, in turn, brought suit against Dalton for breach of his promise to assume the mortgage. Dalton denied liability on the ground of his infancy at the time of the agreement. Conduff contended that Dalton had ratified the agreement. Had Dalton ratified his agreement to assume the mortgage?

3 Gerald Givens, a minor, inherited a piece of real property. A guardian was appointed for him. The guardian borrowed $2,000 from the Wiggins Company on behalf of the minor "for the purpose of paying taxes" due on the land inherited by Givens. The money was used for the intended purpose, but the loan was not repaid. When Givens attained his majority, the Wiggins Company sued for the amount of the loan. Givens' defense was that at the time the loan was made he was a minor and that he now disaffirmed the loan contract. Should Givens be allowed to disaffirm the loan contract?

4 In February 1966, Joseph Fuld contracted to sell to Virgil McPheters a commercial lot which Fuld owned. When Fuld signed the contract, he was in his late eighties and had recently been widowed. Fuld was unable to care for himself and at times appeared unaware that his wife had died prior to the signing of the contract. Once an alert businessman, Fuld had become confused as to business matters, and the contract for the sale of the real estate contained unusual terms. The purchase price was $14,000, although the same property had been appraised in his wife's estate at more than $26,000. Fuld died, and the executor of his estate refused performance of the contract on the ground that on the date of the signing Fuld was incompetent to contract. McPheters brought suit seeking performance of the contract to convey the property. *(a)* What test and guidelines should the court apply in determining whether Fuld was competent to contract? *(b)* Was McPheters entitled to performance of the contract?

5 Margaret Gahr and her husband Charles were contemplating a divorce. They met in a tavern and agreed to meet later at the office of a local lawyer to work out details of a property settlement. They had agreed to divide their property equally. At the meeting, they reviewed their holdings. To accomplish an equal division of their property, they executed a deed to certain real estate. Before the divorce could take place, Charles Gahr died and Margaret remarried. Margaret Gahr Reiner then filed an action in equity to set aside the deed, alleging that she had the meeting with the lawyer and was intoxicated during the meeting. The trial court refused to set aside the deed, and Margaret appealed. Should the deed be set aside?

6 Poole sold real estate to Hudson and took a note and mortgage to secure the purchase price. Hudson failed to pay the debt, and Poole brought an action to foreclose the mortgage. Hudson's defense was that at the time she signed the note and mortgage, she was in a hospital under a doctor's care and under the influence of opiates. She also claimed that she was unaware of the nature and character of the papers she signed. Did Hudson have an adequate defense to the foreclosure action?

Chapter

15

Illegal Agreements

Previous chapters in this series have dealt with four requirements for a contract—offer, acceptance, consideration, and legal capacity of parties. Another requirement is that the agreement must not be illegal.

The first part of this chapter examines illegal agreements in general; the second part, the various types of illegal agreements. The final portion of the chapter discusses the effect of illegality and the extent to which the courts will aid the parties to an illegal agreement.

ILLEGAL AGREEMENTS IN GENERAL

An agreement is illegal if it comes within a class of agreements made illegal by statute or if it is otherwise opposed to public policy. The illegality may be in the nature of the performance promised, in the consideration given for the promise, or in the formation of the agreement (that is, in the act of entering into the agreement).

Agreements Illegal by Statute

Whether a certain class of agreements is made illegal by statute depends upon the intention of the legislature which enacted it. The intention may be expressed in words, as where the statute states that a certain type of agreement is "illegal," "unlawful," "void," or "against public policy." Where the intention is not expressed, the courts may have the difficult task of determining the implied intention. That task is explained by one court as follows:

> The courts take the statute by its four corners and carefully consider the terms of

the statute, its object, the evils it was enacted to remedy, and the effect of holding agreements in violation of it void—for the purpose of ascertaining whether it was the legislative intent to make such agreements void; and if from these considerations it is manifest that the lawmakers had no such intention, the agreement should be held to be legal.[1]

---

[1]*Uhlmann v. Kin Dow*, 193 P. 435 (Or. 1920).

Case 15.1   National Labor Relations Board v. Bratten Pontiac Corp.
406 F.2d 349 (4th Cir. 1969)

In March 1966, nine of twelve automobile salesmen employed by Bratten Pontiac Corp. (defendant) signed authorization cards granting the Teamsters Union the right to represent them as their collective bargaining agent. On March 6, the union advised the company that the union represented a majority of Bratten's employees. The union requested recognition and bargaining. The company acknowledged the letter but made no further immediate reply.

The sales personnel then requested a meeting with George W. Bratten, president of the company. The meeting took place at dinner at a local restaurant. The salesmen expressed dissatisfaction with employment conditions, and Bratten polled them as to their complaints. During the meeting Bratten said, "Why pay someone to negotiate for you when you are grown men? You can negotiate yourself with me." Bratten paid for the dinner for the entire group.

A day or two later, Bratten submitted a "Pay Plan" to the sales staff. It increased a number of fringe benefits and bonuses, and it decreased the commission on the sale of used cars. It also contained an agreement that for the next two years the sales staff "will not enter into any combination or association with the intent or purpose of injuring the company or its property, and that they will not be a party to any hostile act against the company." The entire sales staff signed the pay plan and decided to withdraw their authorization cards.

Upon being informed of their decision, the union took the position that no one on the sales staff could revoke the authorizations. At a representation election consented to by the company and the union, the union lost nine to three. The union filed objections to the company's conduct in affecting the results of the election, and the regional director of the National Labor Relations Board issued an unfair labor practices complaint, charging—among other things—a violation of Section 8(a)(1) of the National Labor Relations Act. The Board concluded that the company had violated Section 8 (a)(1) and ordered the company to recognize and bargain with the union. The company appealed. (Under Section 8(a)(1), it is an "unfair labor practice" for an employer to interfere with the pursuit by employees of rights guaranteed by Section 7 of the Act. Section 7 guarantees "the right to self-organization, to form, join or assist labor organizations, to bargain collectively . . . and to engage in other concerted activities. . . .")

WINTER, Circuit Judge. . . . There was substantial evidence to support the conclusion of a Section 8(a)(1) violation. The actions of the salesmen smack of a perfidious attempt to make the union a tool to assist them in their direct bargaining efforts. Although they had recently authorized the union to act in their behalf, they initiated direct bargaining with the company and invited the major part of the company's response. If this were all that the case consisted of, we might have difficulty in sustaining the Board's conclusion that the company interfered with the Section 7 rights of the employees to unionize. . . . But the record is clear that the company, when presented with the opportunity to deal directly with its salesmen, went well beyond any permissible limit. Leaving aside Bratten's statement at dinner, the permissible inference which may be drawn when benefits are unilaterally conferred while a request to bargain is pending, and the assiduousness of the company's vice president in seeing that the union learned that its constituency had defected, we think that Section 8(a)(1) was violated when the company extracted from its salesmen a two-year agreement not to enter into "any combination or association with the intent or purpose of injuring the company or its property," etc., as the price they must pay for increased employment benefits. . . . We view [this language] as a thinly disguised attempt at preventing salesmen from joining a union or engaging in any union activity for a period of two years. This Section 8(a)(1) proscribes. [Section 103 of the Act] renders such an agreement unenforceable. . . .

Enforcement granted in part and denied in part.

Agreements Which May be Contrary to Public Policy

In the absence of legislation revealing that an agreement is against public policy, the courts may determine which kinds of agreements are so contrary to public policy that they should not be enforced. Some kinds of agreements are so threatening to the public welfare that virtually all agreements of the class, if challenged in court, would be held unenforceable as against public policy. Agreements to commit a crime are an example. Other kinds of agreements and clauses, such as contracts of adhesion and exculpatory clauses, are not necessarily harmful and will be denied enforcement only if misused.

Contracts of Adhesion A *contract of adhesion* ("standard-form" contract) is one in which there is so great a disparity of bargaining power that the weaker party has no choice but to accept the terms imposed by the stronger party or forego the transaction. As was pointed out in Chapter 9, contracts of adhesion serve legitimate functions in our economy and usually are enforced despite the weaker party's possible lack of consent to some or most terms. Yet, because of the great disparity of bargaining power which characterizes contracts of adhesion, people upon whom they are imposed are vulnerable to exploitation. In the absence of an effective bargaining power, what is their protection?

The first protection may well be the innate sense of fairness and responsibility which most business people bring to their business dealings. That failing, the next protection might be a vigorous competition among sellers. Whether motivated by ethical considerations or merely by the pressures of competition, many businesses choose not to exercise their superior bargaining power in oppressive ways. If ethical and competitive protections fail, the courts and the legislatures must intervene. The courts have invalidated contracts or clauses of adhesion in a variety of ways, for example, by (1) holding that because of a lack of consideration, no contract arose or (2) finding that a contract or a clause was contrary to public policy. The concept of unconscionability, discussed later in this chapter and in Chapter 24, has frequently been applied to invalidate clauses of adhesion. More systematic ways of combatting the misuse of adhesive contracts have been suggested and will probably be given increasingly serious attention.[2]

Exculpatory Clauses *Exculpatory* clauses are contractual provisions whose aim is to exempt a contracting party from the payment of damages for his or her own misconduct. Such clauses frequently are challenged in court as

---

[2]See, for example, W. David Slawson, "Standard Form Contracts and Democratic Control of Lawmaking Power," 84 *Harvard Law Review* 529 (1971).

being contrary to public policy. But not all of the challenged clauses are illegal.

Ordinarily, the courts will not enforce exculpatory clauses which relieve a contracting party of responsibility for his or her own criminal conduct, intentional torts, or "gross" negligence. In such instances, the desirability of freedom of contract and the need of the public for stability of contracting give way to other interests. Among these are the need of injured persons for compensation and the more general need of the public for protection against contractual arrangements which, by protecting wrongdoers, might tend to induce a lack of regard for the safety or rights of others. As the following case indicates, however, a clause which exempts a person from liability for his or her own "simple" negligence might or might not be upheld. If the clause is freely consented to by parties of substantially equal bargaining power, it ordinarily will be upheld as an appropriate measure for shifting risk of loss. In contrast, if the clause is a part of a *contract of adhesion* so that the weaker party has no choice but to bear the consequences of the other party's simple negligence, the clause might be invalidated.

Case 15.2   Winterstein v. Wilcom
293 A.2d 821 (Md. Ct. Spec. App., 1972)

Wilcom operated a "drag strip" where, for a fee, persons could engage in automobile timing and acceleration runs. After Winterstein and his wife each signed a document purporting to release Wilcom from liability for any injuries Winterstein might suffer while participating in drag-strip activities, Winterstein paid the fee and entered a speed contest. Near the end of his run, his car hit a 100-pound cylinder head lying on the track, and Winterstein sustained permanent injuries. The cylinder head was not visible to him when he commenced the race, but it was visible to Wilcom's employees who were stationed in a tower to watch for any hazards on the track. Alleging negligence on the part of Wilcom's employees, Winterstein sued Wilcom for damages. The trial court entered a summary judgment in favor of Wilcom, and Winterstein appealed.

ORTH, J. . . . The first question is whether the releases were void as against public policy. . . .

THE GENERAL RULE OF LAW REGARDING EXCULPATORY CLAUSES

In the absence of legislation to the contrary, the law, by the great weight of authority, is that there is ordinarily no public policy which prevents the parties from contracting as they see fit, as to whether the plaintiff will undertake the responsibility of looking out for himself. . . . In other words, the parties may agree that there shall be no obligation [on the part of the defendant] to take precautions and hence no liability for negligence.

EXCEPTIONS TO THE GENERAL RULE

There is a proviso to the general rule. The relationship of the parties must be such that their bargaining be free and open. When one party is at such an obvious disadvantage in bargaining power that the effect of the contract is to put him at the mercy of the other's negligence, the agreement is void as against public policy. . . .

It is also against public policy to permit exculpatory agreements as to transactions involving the public interest, as for example with regard to public utilities, common carriers, innkeepers, and public warehousemen. . . . There has been a definite tendency to expand the exception raised by the proviso to other professional bailees who are under no public duty but [who] deal with the public, such as garagemen, owners of parking lots, and [owners of] parcel checkrooms, because the indispensable need for their services deprives the customer of all real equal bargaining power. . . .

Generally, exculpatory agreements otherwise valid are not construed to cover the more extreme forms of negligence—wilful, wanton, reckless, or gross. Nor do they encompass any conduct which constitutes an intentional tort. And, of course, it is fundamental that if an agreement exempting a defendant from liability for his negligence is to be sustained, it must appear that its terms were known to the plaintiff, and "if he did not know of the provision in his contract and a reasonable person in his position would not have known of it, it is not binding upon him, and the agreement fails for want of mutual consent." [Citation to Prosser omitted.]

TRANSACTIONS AFFECTED WITH A PUBLIC INTEREST

Because an exculpatory provision may not stand if it involves the public interest, our inquiry turns to what transactions are affected with a public interest. In *Tunkl v. Regents of the University of California*, 60 Cal.2d 92, 383 P.2d 441, 32 Cal.Reptr. 33 (1963), the Supreme Court of California [noted that] the courts have revealed a rough outline of that type of transaction in which exculpatory provisions will be held invalid. "Thus the attempted but invalid exemption involves a transaction which exhibits some or all of the following characteristics. It concerns a business of a type generally thought suitable for public regulation. The party seeking exculpation is engaged in performing a service of great importance to the public, which is often a matter of practical necessity for some members of the public. The party holds himself out as willing to perform this service for any member of the public who seeks it, or at least for any member coming within certain established standards. As a result of the essential nature of the service, in the economic setting of the transaction, the party invoking exculpation possesses a decisive advantage of bargaining strength against any member of the public who seeks his services. In exercising a superior bargaining power the party confronts the public with a standardized adhesion contract of exculpation, and makes no provision whereby a purchaser may pay additional reasonable fees and obtain protection against negligence. Finally, as a result of the transaction, the person or property of the purchaser is placed under the control of the seller, subject to the risk of carelessness by the seller or his agents." [The court in *Tunkl* held that an agreement between the U.C.L.A. Medical Center and an entering patient affects the public interest and that, in consequence, an exculpatory provision releasing the hospital from liability for negligence of its employees must be held invalid.]

We note a further refinement. Although the traditional view has been that where the defendant's negligence consists of the violation of a statute the plaintiff may still assume the risk, there is a growing tendency to the contrary where a safety statute enacted for the protection of the public is violated. The rationale is that the obligation and the right so created are public ones which it is not within the power of any private individual to waive.

It is clear that the exculpatory provisions involved in the case before us . . . were under the general rule recognizing the validity of such provisions. There was not the slightest disadvantage in bargaining power between the parties. Winterstein was under no compulsion, economic or otherwise, to race his car. He obviously participated in the speed runs simply because he wanted to do so. . . .

The business operated by Wilcom had none of the characteristics of one affected with the public interest. The legislature . . . has not sought to regulate it. Wilcom is not engaged in performing a service of great importance to the public which is a matter of practical necessity for any member of the public. . . . Since the service is not of an essential nature, Wilcom had no decisive advantage of bargaining strength against any member of the public seeking to participate. Nor was Winterstein so placed under the control of Wilcom that he was subject to the risk of carelessness by Wilcom or his agents. . . .

We do not believe that any safety statute of this state, enacted for the protection of the public, was involved. . . .

We observe that Winterstein did not allege that the negligence he attributed to Wilcom was other than simple negligence; . . . [nor does he say] that he was wronged by an intentional tort. . . . We hold that [the releases] were not void as against public policy.

Judgment affirmed. . . .

COMMON TYPES OF ILLEGAL AGREEMENTS

Because of the great variety of agreements which can be made in violation of statutes and rules of the common law, only a few types of illegal agreements can be discussed here. The types discussed are representative of the more common types of such agreements.

Unconscionable Agreements

For many years, the courts have been developing legal concepts and techniques for combatting undesirable business practices that fall short of established wrongs such as fraud and duress. Out of those efforts has emerged the concept of "unconscionability" which appears in Section 2-302 of the Uniform Commercial Code and Section 234 of the Restatement (Second) of the Law of Contracts. A court may refuse to enforce an unconscionable contract, may delete any unconscionable term and enforce the remainder of the contract, or may so limit the application of any unconscionable term as to avoid any unconscionable result.

Because unconscionability can take so many forms, there is no rigid definition of unconscionability. Instead, the courts apply guidelines such as "oppression" and "unfair surprise" on a case-by-case basis. Any contract or contractual term that oppresses or unfairly surprises a contracting party may be held illegal even though the practice involved does not constitute fraud or some other traditional variety of illegal conduct.

Throughout the years the courts have identified a number of practices which may be held unconscionable if the circumstances warrant. These practices have been classified as either "procedural" or "substantive" unconscionability.[3] The resulting build-up of case law provides specific guidance for the courts as they decide what new practices and variations of old ones should be declared unconscionable.

Procedural unconscionability has to do with an unfair or deceptive process of contract formation. Procedural unconscionability may occur, for example, where a seller, by means of a clause in fine print placed near the end of a complex contract, seeks secretly to deprive a semi-literate buyer of rights which buyers normally would not wish to give up if the topic were discussed. Procedural unconscionability "may also take the form of fraud, sharp practice, high pressure salesmanship, and so on."[4]

Substantive unconscionability has more to do with unreasonably harsh terms of a contract than with a deceptive process of contract formation. An excessively high price might be held unconscionable, as in *Jones v. Star Credit Corporation,* Case 24.3, which appears in Chapter 24 of this volume. Substantive unconscionability also occurs where a seller-creditor in an installment sale of goods or services unduly restricts the buyer-debtor's remedies for breach of contract or unduly expands the creditor's own

[3]James J. White and Robert S. Summers, *Handbook of the Law Under the Uniform Commercial Code,* West Publishing Company, St. Paul, Minn., 1972, sec. 4-2.
[4]Ibid., sec. 4-3

remedial rights. Suppose that a furniture seller, by means of a fine-print clause in an installment-sale contract, retains a security interest in all items sold over a period of years to the buyer, and then seeks to repossess all the furniture because the buyer missed a payment on the last item. If the value of the furniture to be repossessed greatly exceeds the amount of the unpaid debt, or the buyer did not understand the rather unusual consequences of missing a payment, the clause which provides for repossession is likely to be held substantively unconscionable, especially where the agreement is one of adhesion.

In *Williams v. Walker-Thomas Furniture Co.*,[5] the appellate court stated the general test of unconscionability for the trial court to apply to the facts of the case. In *Williams*, the buyer was a welfare mother with seven children and a monthly income of $218. She missed payments on the last item, a stereo set costing $514.95 and had previously made payments of more than $1,400 on a total debt of $1,800. If the seller kept the existence of the repossession clause unknown to Mrs. Williams, or upon her request for an explanation refused to explain the clause or gave misleading information, the transaction would have involved procedural unconscionability. Even if Mrs. Williams understood the provision, however, it would be invalid if so unreasonably harsh as to be substantively unconscionable.

Agreements Not to Compete

Types of Agreements Not to Compete This discussion of agreements not to compete does not include agreements made illegal by the Sherman Act, the Clayton Act, or any other federal or state antitrust act. Such acts deal with monopolies and other large-scale restraints on trade and are discussed in Chapters 47 and 48. The discussion here is limited to three kinds of

------

[5]350 F.2d 445 (D.C. Cir. 1965).

restraints on trade entered into even by small business firms and by the employees of such firms:

• An agreement by the seller of a business not to compete with the buyer

• A partnership agreement in which each partner promises not to compete with the partnership in the event the partner withdraws from the firm

• An agreement by an employee not to compete with the employer after the termination of the employment

Because these agreements purport to prohibit a person from engaging in his or her livelihood, the courts are reluctant to enforce them except for compelling reasons. For what reasons and to what extent may such agreements be enforced?

Agreement by seller of a business Where the owner of a business sells it as a "going concern," the buyer rightfully expects the seller not to withhold or divert any of the assets comprising the business. "Goodwill" is one such asset. It consists of the willingness of customers to deal with the firm. The buyer rightfully expects to receive the continued patronage of the seller's customers (that is, the goodwill) free from the seller's interference, at least until the buyer has had a reasonable opportunity to establish his or her own business reputation.

To protect goodwill, the buyer might require the seller to sign an agreement not to compete with the buyer. The courts hold that such an agreement is enforceable if it imposes no more than a reasonable restraint on the seller. Usually a restraint is reasonable if it is so limited in duration and in territory covered as to protect only the goodwill purchased. The reasonableness of a restraint is a question of fact to be determined from all the circumstances. A covenant by the seller of a small delicatessen store not to compete for 6 months anywhere within the city might be unduly restrictive and unenforceable, whereas a covenant by the seller of a firm doing a statewide business not to compete for 3 years throughout the state might be a reasonable restriction.

Agreement by partners As pointed out later in this volume, under certain conditions the business of a partnership may survive the withdrawal of a partner. Partners may be inadequately protected if a withdrawing partner is allowed to start a business in competition with the surviving business. Many partnership agreements therefore contain a provision restraining a withdrawing partner from competing with the partnership. Such a provision is enforceable if the area and the time limitations contained in the restrictive provision are reasonable.

Agreement by employee By far the most usual type of agreement not to compete occurs in employment contracts which employees are often required to sign. In such a contract, the employee usually promises that upon the termination of the employment, the employee will not compete with the former employer either by setting up a business or by entering the employment of a competitor. Sometimes the employee is required to sign an agreement not to reveal the former employer's trade secrets.

To be enforceable, restrictive provisions in employment contracts must be reasonable, just as restrictive provisions in sale-of-business contracts and in partnership contracts must be reasonable. However, courts are less likely to uphold restrictive covenants in employment agreements than they are to uphold restrictive covenants in either of the other two types of agreements. The chief reason for the reluctance of courts to enforce an employee's promise not to compete is that enforcement may deprive the employee of the opportunity to support his or her dependents in reasonable comfort. Enforcement may also deprive the public of the benefit which could result from the competition be-

tween an employer and the former employee. Even in the absence of a contractual prohibition, however, an employee has no right to reveal the employer's trade secrets. A contract provision prohibiting such conduct usually will be enforced.

Divisibility of Agreements Not to Compete Suppose that Bob Brown, the buyer of a small delicatessen store whose business extends for a twelve-block radius, requires the seller to agree not to compete within a radius of 20 miles. Shortly after the sale, the seller announces that within the next few days she will open a delicatessen store three blocks from her former location. Immediately thereafter the buyer seeks an injunction restraining the seller from carrying out her announced plan.

The situation just described presents a dilemma. Most courts would agree that the buyer has demanded an unreasonably broad restriction on the seller's right to conduct a business. They would also agree that the seller threatens to engage in an unreasonable interference with the goodwill of the buyer's new business. Whom should the courts protect?

Some courts refuse to enforce overly broad restrictions, and thus would deny the buyer injunctive relief. They refuse enforcement in an effort to encourage buyers to be cautious and to draft clauses which will be reasonable. In these jurisdictions, buyers who draft overly broad clauses do so at the risk of losing all protection. Other courts would hold that because a twelve-block limitation would have been reasonable, the restrictive agreement is enforceable at least to that extent. In granting the buyer injunctive relief, these courts treat overly broad agreements as "divisible" or "severable" (partially enforceable), especially where the overbreadth seems inadvertent or where reasonableness of the restriction was difficult to estimate.

A similar problem arises—and a similar split of authority occurs—where an agreement not to compete specifies a time limit greater than necessary to protect the purchaser. Sometimes agreements not to compete mention no time limit. In such instances many courts enforce the agreement if the seller attempts to compete before the expiration of a reasonable time and if the agreement is otherwise reasonable. The case which follows involves both a time and a geographic limitation.

Case 15.3   **Boldt Machinery & Tools, Inc. v. Wallace**
366 A.2d 902 (Pa. 1976)

The plaintiff, Boldt Machinery & Tools, Inc., is a seller and distributor of industrial machinery and tools in parts of Pennsylvania, New York, and Ohio. Glen Wallace, defendant, was employed by Boldt in 1959 as a salesman and was assigned a sales territory which covered parts of Pennsylvania and New York. In 1973, Wallace voluntarily terminated his employment. Upon leaving Boldt, Wallace was employed as a salesman of industrial machinery by Tri-State Machinery Company, a competitor of Boldt, in roughly the same territory he had covered for Boldt, that is, parts of Pennsylvania and New York, but not parts of Ohio.

Boldt contended that Wallace's activities on behalf of Tri-State constituted a breach of the restrictive covenant contained in paragraph 24 of the contract between Boldt and Wallace. Paragraph 24 provides:

> "Upon termination of employment . . . Employee . . . shall not engage directly or indirectly in the sale or distribution of any items regularly sold by Employer in the territory covered by Employer for a period of five years."

Boldt brought suit to enforce the covenant. The chancellor enjoined Wallace from selling or distributing for a period of 5 years items of a type sold by Boldt. The injunction applied to the parts of Pennsylvania, New York, and Ohio serviced by Boldt. Wallace's exceptions to the chancellor's rulings were dismissed by an intermediate appellate court, and Wallace appealed to the Supreme Court of Pennsylvania.

POMEROY, J. . . . Wallace [argues] that paragraph 24 is unenforceable as an impermissible restraint on trade. A post-employment restraint on competition is enforceable if it is ancillary to an employment relationship between the parties, is designed to protect a legitimate business interest of the employer, and is reasonably limited in duration and area. . . .

With respect to protectible interest, appellant contends that Boldt is not entitled to any protection from competition by him because the company did not provide him with any specialized training or skills or with access to any trade secrets. But this argument is based upon too restrictive a view of the interests an employer may legitimately seek to protect by means of such restraints. . . . An employer has a protectible interest in the customer goodwill developed by its employees. . . .

The reasonableness of the temporal and geographic aspects of a restrictive covenant must be determined in light of the nature of the employer's interest sought to be protected. The time should be no longer and the area should be no greater than are reasonably necessary for the protection of that interest. [According to Professor Blake:] "When the restraint is for the purpose of protecting customer relationships, its duration is reasonable only if it is no longer than necessary for the employer to put a new man on the job and for the new employee to have a reasonable opportunity to demonstrate his effectiveness to the customers." . . . The evidence supports the chancellor's determination that effectiveness as a salesman of the industrial machinery here involved is sufficiently difficult to achieve, and customer contact is here sufficiently infrequent, as to justify a five year restraint for the employer's protection. . . .

Turning to appellant's challenge to the geographic extent of the restraint, it will be noted that paragraph 24 pertains to the employer's total trade territory, which the evidence established as western Pennsylvania, southwestern New York, and eastern Ohio. The chancellor enforced this provision to its full extent. . . . [He] erred. An employer's interest in the customer relationships developed by an employee . . . extends no farther than the sales territory to which the employee was assigned. Thus, a restrictive covenant designed to protect this interest is valid only insofar as it is limited to that area. If a covenant which is limited in area is still too widespread, the court should enforce the restraint, but only to the extent of the employee's sales territory. . . .

At trial it was established that, while employed by Boldt, Wallace covered an area comprised of [parts of New York and Pennsylvania]. It is only in this geographical area that Boldt is now entitled to protection from Wallace's competition. . . . The chancellor's decree must be vacated insofar as it enforces the geographic term of the covenant as written, and the case [is] remanded for a determination of the boundaries of Wallace's sales territory for Boldt and for the entry of a decree in light of that determination. . . .

MANDERİNO, J. (in support of reversal). I must express my disagreement with the approach to restrictive covenants taken by the opinion in support of affirmance, and also with the approach taken by Mr. Justice Roberts in his opinion. . . .

Both [of the opinions] agree that as to the territory it covers, the covenant is an illegal restraint of trade as written. . . . Both opinions sanction a judicial rewriting of the illegal covenant to make it legal. I cannot subscribe to such a procedure. It is not a difficult task for an employer to write a legal restrictive covenant into the employment contract. Employers have no incentive to do so, of course, so long as this Court says to such employers: "Write any covenant you wish—if it's illegal, we'll act as your counsel and rewrite it." The rewriting, of course, takes place after a period of time during which the illegal restraint of trade has already intimidated the employee. As I stated in my dissenting opinion in *Sidco Paper Company v. Aaron*, 465 Pa. 586, 351 A.2d 250 (1976):

Case 15.3
Continued

"Such a covenant perpetually hovers over the employee, who must act at his peril when considering termination of employment because he does not know whether he will be faced with a lawsuit challenging his right to obtain new employment, and if challenged by a lawsuit, whether he will suffer economic harm because a court determines *ex post facto* that he violated a covenant, the limitations of which were not clearly spelled out until after a burdensome and costly lawsuit. Thus, an employee faced with a covenant barring him from competing anywhere with a former employer lives under a constant threat that if he finds new employment even in an area not covered by his present employer, he will be faced with litigation."

Gambling Agreements

All states have statutes pertaining to wagering, or (alternately expresssed) gambling. A "wager" is an agreement between two or more persons in which one or some of them shall make a gain and the other or others shall suffer a loss upon the happening of an event in which the only risk of loss is such as the parties created by their agreement. Formerly, most states prohibited wagering and made it a criminal offense. In recent years many states have "modernized" their antigambling statutes and now permit some kinds of regulated gambling. In some states, the state itself conducts a lottery as a means of obtaining revenue. To find out which kinds of wagers are illegal in a particular state, the reader will have to look to the statutes of that state.

Some people think of insurance contracts as a gamble. There is a very real difference, however, between an insurance contract and a gambling agreement. In an insurance contract, the risk of loss is not one created by the agreement itself, but is one that existed prior to the agreement. The risk of loss is simply transferred to the insurer by the agreement. To have a legal insurance contract, the beneficiary (i.e., the person to whom the insurer is to pay any monies due under the contract) must have an "insurable interest" in the thing or person insured. In a fire insurance policy on a dwelling, for example, the insured person must be the owner of the dwell-

ing or at least have some financial interest in it. If there is no insurable interest in the dwelling, there is no risk to be shifted from the would-be insured person to the insurer. If the dwelling burns, any payment received from an insurance company is not a "gain" but an *indemnity* for the loss suffered.

Agreements Involving Usury

Meaning and Effect of Usury To discourage the charging of exorbitant interest, almost every state has a statute or a series of statutes specifying the highest rate of interest which may be charged for a loan of money. *Usury* is the charging of any rate of interest in excess of that permitted by law.

Statutes usually specify a maximum rate of interest of general application for "normal" loans and a series of higher maximum rates for other kinds of loans, for example, loans by pawn brokers and small loan companies. Typically these latter kinds of loans involve small amounts of money, small payments, and relatively high costs of collection. The bookkeeping expenses attending such loans, together with the doubtful creditworthiness of many of the borrowers, warrant higher maximum interest rates.

Nevertheless, maximum interest rates imposed by the legislatures frequently lag behind the market price of credit. When this happens, lenders often divert their funds to more lucrative markets. To encourage lenders to provide businesses with an adequate supply of credit, the laws of many states exempt loans to corporations from the limits imposed by the usury statutes.

The states differ in their treatment of usurious agreements. In some states usurious agreements are void, and the overreaching lender forfeits interest *and* principal. In other states a usurious agreement is voidable, but only as to the amount of interest in excess of the amount permitted by law. In still other states the agreement is voidable as to the usurious amount, and the injured party may recover a penalty of double or triple the usurious amount.

Effect of Usury Limits on Consumer Credit
Statutes imposed usury limits long before the need for massive consumer credit developed or was recognized. When that need developed, the market price of consumer credit was forced up, well beyond the limits imposed by the usury statutes. Lenders who could have served the consumer credit market found more lucrative markets. To encourage more lenders to provide consumer credit, many states enacted installment-loan acts, credit union legislation, and other laws which exempted certain types of loans and lenders from the coverage of the usury statutes.

The courts also recognized the need for more consumer credit and in a number of ways contributed to its availability. Chief among these contributions was the development of the "time-price" doctrine. When a person makes immediate payment for goods at a store, he or she is charged a so-called "cash" price which supposedly represents the lowest price at which the seller is willing to do business. If the buyer is permitted to purchase the goods on a credit (e.g., installment-payment) basis, the seller runs a higher risk of nonpayment. To compensate for the added risk, the seller may charge a higher price (called the time price) for the goods. Under the time-price doctrine, the credit sale of goods is not a loan, and the difference

between the cash price and the time price is not considered interest. This is so even though the difference is commonly expressed in terms of a percentage of the cash price. Thus, credit sales of goods are usually held not to be subject to the usury statutes.

Reform of Credit Extension and Usury Law
Legislatures typically have imposed flat limits on the rates of interest which can legally be charged, and they have left to the courts the task of deciding which methods of interest calculation violate the statutes. Some methods of calculating or expressing interest disguise the actual rate of interest being charged and were originally devised to circumvent the statutory limits on interest. Some of these methods are still in use. They tend to confuse borrowers and to make comparison shopping for credit difficult.

Within recent years there have been significant attempts to reform the law relating to credit extension and usury. The federal Truth-in-Lending Act[6] and the Uniform Consumer Credit Code (UCCC)[7] impose disclosure requirements on the lenders to whom the laws apply. Under both laws, lenders must disclose to borrowers the true cost of credit. Moreover, the cost of credit must be calculated and reported to borrowers in terms they can understand: specifically, in terms of an annual percentage rate as that rate is defined in the applicable law. The UCCC is more than a disclosure statute. It also provides maximum rates of interest which can legally be charged, prohibits false and misleading credit advertising, and imposes other restrictions on lenders. Both the Truth-in-Lending Act and the UCCC apply to all extensions of consumer credit: bank loans, credit sales of goods, and other forms of consumer credit.

---

[6]Officially known as Title I, Consumer Credit Protection Act.

[7]As of November 1980, adopted by Colorado, Idaho, Indiana, Iowa, Kansas, Maine, Oklahoma, South Carolina, Utah, and Wyoming.

Case 15.4   **Overbeck v. Sears, Roebuck and Co.**
349 N.E.2d 286 (Ind. App. 1976)

Karl Overbeck brought a class action seeking recovery of $6 million in allegedly usurious "interest" collected from Indiana credit card customers of defendant Sears, Roebuck & Co. The "Sears Revolving Charge Account" imposed a "finance charge" at an annual percentage rate of 18 percent on unpaid account balances.

The Indiana usury statutes applicable to this case provide in part:

". . . The interest on loans or forbearance of money, goods, or things in action, shall be as follows: . . .

(b) By agreement in writing signed by the party to be charged thereby, and not otherwise, any obligor other than a corporation may lawfully agree to pay any rate of interest not in excess of eight dollars . . . per year per one hundred dollars. . . .

When a greater rate of interest than is hereby allowed shall be contracted for, the contract shall be void as to the usurious interest contracted for; and, if it appears that interest at a higher rate than eight percent has been, directly or indirectly, contracted for by an obligor other than a corporation, the excess of interest over six percent shall be deemed usurious and illegal, and, in an action on a contract affected by such usury, the excess over the legal interest may be recouped by the debtor, whenever it has been reserved or paid before the bringing of the suit."

The trial court granted Sears' motion for summary judgment, and Overbeck appealed.

SULLIVAN, J. . . . Both statutes have been repealed and replaced by the Indiana version of the Uniform Consumer Credit Code (UCCC), which was enacted and became effective after Overbeck's suit was filed but before Sears' successful motion for summary judgment. . . . [The court held that the UCCC does not apply to this case.]

The court below, following the First District's reasoning in *Standard Oil (Indiana) v. Williams*, 153 Ind. App. 489, 288 N.E.2d 170 (1972), concluded that . . . the law is with Sears because: "The statute relating to usury applies only to a loan of money or to the forbearance of a debt, and upon execution of the agreement between the parties, a time price differential sale was entered into and the transaction as between the parties did not represent a loan of money, nor a forbearance on a then existing debt." . . . We hold that the trial court did not err. . . .

We deem it appropriate to respond to a fundamental attack by Overbeck upon the authorities upon which our decision rests. Plaintiff points out that there is a certain unreality inherent in the "time-price differential" theory; that it is at worst pure "fiction" or at best "mathematical and intellectual impurity" to say that Sears' 1.5% monthly finance charge on the unpaid balance is the differential between a cash price for the goods and a "time-price," rather than a "charge . . . for the forbearance to collect the full cash price, or for the use of money. . . ." Plaintiff implies that we should not ignore what we know as men—that a finance charge, which goes up as the length of time which we put off paying for goods bought on credit increases, is nothing more than "interest" for the free use of the seller's goods and our own cash which we would have otherwise parted with when the goods were first obtained. Overbeck agrees with one scholar's view. . . .:

> "prior to the adoption of the UCCC . . . it was generally believed that a charge in excess of eight percent per annum was usurious because the general statute so provided. Cunning lawyers, however, had long ago hoodwinked the courts of other states and Indiana into neutralizing the language of the statute by various devices. One of these was the 'time price differential' theory. . . ."

While the "time-price differential" theory may seem to some a slender reed upon which to rest a judicial determination, it has been termed the "corner-stone of the sales finance industry." The reality of which we must be aware is not the legal nature of the transactions taking place under the terms of the Sears Revolving Charge Account, but the unreality of conducting consumer credit transactions with strict adherence to an 8% per annum ceiling on interest in 1976. As one writer notes:

> "It is generally conceded in the finance industry that extension of consumer credit is significantly more expensive than extension of normal business credit. . . . If, then, retailers presently availing themselves of the immunizing effect of the time-price doctrine are forced to reduce their rates to 'non-usurious' levels, restrictions of credit would presumably result. In an attempt to reduce costs by minimizing losses, retailers might well extend their charge account agreements to only the more secure risks. Consequently, many middle and lower income families may be excluded from what is presently an important avenue of consumer credit." . . .

If the "time-price differential" theory is indeed a fiction, it is one not only recommended by case law but compelled by the realities of our society. . . . Our legislature has laudably acknowledged today's realities and enacted the Uniform Consumer Credit Code to regulate consumer credit transactions.

Having decided that the first basis of decision in the *Standard Oil* case and the court below [is sound], that Sears' revolving charge is not within the purview of the 1879 usury statute because of the "time-price differential" theory, we need not consider whether the enactment of the UCCC after Overbeck filed his complaint justifies summary judgment for Sears.

Affirmed.

Agreements in Violation
of Sunday-Closing Statutes

Many states have statutes prohibiting or regulating certain kinds of Sunday transactions. Such statutes are commonly referred to as Sunday-closing laws or "blue laws" and in colonial times were intended to encourage the practice of religion. Today, the First and the Fourteenth Amendments forbid laws "respecting an establishment of religion, or prohibiting the free exercise thereof."

Nevertheless, Sunday-closing legislation will be upheld if the purpose for it is rational and nonreligious and if the legislation does not violate the due process or equal-protection guarantees of the state or federal constitutions. Sunday-closing laws will be upheld, for example, where they have an economic justification or where they are merely an exercise of a state's police power to provide a day of rest, amusement, and family togetherness.

In some states, Sunday contracts are generally enforced; in others, they are generally ignored. It has been suggested that "in the present climate in which we live," we may expect that Sunday laws will be repealed or that their effects on contracts "will be drastically limited."[8]

Agreements in Violation
of Licensing Statutes

A type of statute that has been the subject of considerable litigation is one requiring a person to obtain a license or certificate or diploma before carrying on an occupation. Thus, licenses may be required of doctors, dentists, lawyers, public accountants, and those engaged in various other professions; of electricians, plumbers, contractors, beauty operators, barbers, and those engaged in various other skilled occupations; of pawnbrokers, wholesalers and retailers

of liquor, operators of restaurants and hotels, and those engaged in various other kinds of businesses.

Usually licensing statutes provide that any person who carries on one of the designated occupations or businesses without having obtained the required license is subject to a fine. Some of the licensing statutes also provide that an unlicensed person cannot recover compensation for services performed. However, many licensing statutes are silent as to whether compensation is or is not recoverable. Where the legislature has not expressed its intention regarding compensation, courts try to determine the presumed intention of the legislature.

As an aid in determining the presumed intention of the legislature, courts look to the character of the statute. Some licensing statutes are regulatory in character. They are designed to protect the public against unprincipled and unqualified persons. Other licensing statutes are revenue-raising measures. The general rule is: If a statute is regulatory, unlicensed persons cannot recover for services rendered or goods delivered; if the statute is a revenue-raising measure, recovery is normally allowed. The rationale behind denying recovery where the statute is regulatory is that the denial of compensation will encourage an unlicensed practitioner to withhold services until he or she has demonstrated (by compliance with the statute) possession of the minimum qualifications thought necessary for the safety of the public.

Whether a statute is of a regulatory or revenue-producing character may well be the most important test in helping courts to determine the presumed intention of the legislature regarding recovery of compensation, but this is not the only available test. Other available tests include: Did the unlicensed person perform his or her contract fully and well? Did the performance endanger public safety, health, or morals? Would denial of recovery cause a substantial loss to the unlicensed person and an undeserved windfall to the other party?

---

[8]John D. Calamari and Joseph M. Perillo, *The Law of Contracts*, West Publishing Company, St. Paul, 1970, p. 558.

Agreements Involving Interference with Governmental Processes

Any agreement which involves interference with the orderly processes of government is against public policy. This statement is true whether the level of government is federal, state, or local; whether the interference consists of corrupting a public official or misleading the official's judgment; or whether the official is in the legislative, executive, administrative, or judicial branch of government. Two representative examples of the kinds of agreements which tend to interfere with the orderly processes of government are: (1) agreements involving interference with the legislative process and (2) agreements involving interference with the administration of justice.

Interference with the Legislative Process Interference with the legislative process occurs most frequently through lobbying. However, not all lobbying is illegal. Anyone has the right to employ a person whose duty is to keep the employer informed about pending legislation which might affect the employer's interests and to try in good faith to persuade legislators to vote for or against proposed legislation. On the other hand, a person does not have the right to employ an agent whose duties include persuasion by bribery, threats, or other improper means. A lobbying agreement of this kind is illegal and thus void. When the legality of a lobbying agreement is challenged in court, the court has the difficult task of scrutinizing the agreement and all relevant evidence to make sure that nothing was contemplated by the parties other than the presentation of facts and arguments in an open and aboveboard manner.

Case 15.5   Troutman v. Southern Railway Co.
441 F.2d 586 (5th Cir. 1971)

In 1963 the Interstate Commerce Commission (ICC) issued an order directing Southern Railway Co. to increase certain rates on grain shipments from the Midwest to the Southeast by approximately 16 percent. The order created a difficult situation for Southern. If allowed to stand, the order, according to Southern, would result in its losing a $13 million investment in "Big John" railroad cars plus a "tremendous" loss of revenue in the future. Wilbanks, a vice president of Southern, turned for help to Robert B. Troutman, an Atlanta attorney (plaintiff).

Troutman had no experience in ICC matters, but he was known to Wilbanks as a personal friend and political ally of President John F. Kennedy. Wilbanks told Troutman that Southern was filing suit in a federal district court in Ohio to enjoin the order of the ICC. He asked Troutman to persuade the President and the Department of Justice to "ditch" the ICC and to enter the case on the side of Southern. Troutman did so, and in the Ohio lawsuit, the ICC order was struck down. Southern failed to compensate Troutman in the agreed manner, and he filed suit for the reasonable value of his services. A jury awarded Troutman the sum of $175,000, and Southern appealed.

WISDOM, Circuit Judge. . . . Southern's first contention is that the district court erred in refusing to grant Southern's motion for judgment notwithstanding the verdict because the evidence conclusively establishes that the contract upon which Troutman sued was "to exert his personal and political influence upon the President of the United States." Southern argues that such a contract is in violation of public policy and unenforceable; therefore, the court erred as a matter of law in failing to render judgment for Southern. We cannot agree.

It is of course true that a contract to influence a public official in the exercise of his duties is illegal and unenforceable when that contract contemplates the use of personal or political influence rather than an appeal to the judgment of the official on the merits of the case. Nevertheless, all citizens possess the right to petition the government for redress of their grievances. To that end, one may employ an agent or attorney to use his influence to gain access to a public official. Moreover, once having obtained an audience, the attorney may fairly present to the official the merits of his client's case and urge the official's support for that position. As the district court well stated, . . . it is "only the elements of 'personal influence' and 'sinister means' [that] will void the contract and deny it enforcement." . . .

Whether the parties in fact entered into a contract calling for the improper exercise of personal influence upon a public official is . . . a question for the jury. . . . In this case the jury concluded that Troutman had agreed with Southern to use his influence merely to gain access to the President and present him the merits of Southern's case; therefore the contract was valid and enforceable. . . .

Affirmed.

Interference with the Administration of Justice   Any agreement which interferes with the administration of justice is illegal. The most direct form of such interference is the bribery of a witness or juror or judge. The bribery need not take the form of a payment of money. Thus, where a judge who is trying a case is up for reelection to office, a promise to swing certain votes in the judge's favor for deciding the case a certain way would constitute bribery.

An agreement which does not directly interfere with the administration of justice will nevertheless be illegal if it tends to interfere with justice. Thus, an agreement to pay a witness who is in the jurisdiction and is subject to subpoena an amount greater than permitted by statute is illegal. The rationale for the rule is that the payment may predispose the witness to favor the party whose witness he or she is rather than to speak the truth. Statutes limiting payment of fees to witnesses commonly exempt expert witnesses from the fee limitation. An agreement to pay an expert any reasonable compensation is legal, provided the agreement does not make payment contingent on the outcome of the case.

The general principle that an agreement which interferes or tends to interfere with the administration of justice is illegal applies not only to civil proceedings but also to criminal proceedings. For example, where a male employee has stolen funds from his employer, a promise by the employee's father to restore the funds if the employer will refrain from pressing charges against the son is contrary to public policy as an interference with the enforcement of the criminal law. The father's promise is therefore unenforceable by the employer. For the same reason, a promise by the employer not to press charges if the father will restore the stolen funds is unenforceable by the father.

Agreements Involving Commission of Crimes and Torts[9]

As previously indicated, a crime is a wrong to the public, whereas a tort is a wrong or injury to an individual or individuals. It would seem to be obvious, therefore, that an agreement to commit a crime or a tort is against public policy and thus illegal.

An agreement which does not call for the commission of a crime is nevertheless illegal if it tends to induce a criminal act. For example, a fire insurance policy issued to Jane Smith on a building in which she has no financial interest (no "insurable interest") may tempt her to set fire to the building in order to collect the insurance money. Similarly, an insurance policy issued to John Doe on the life of Richard Rowe, in whom Doe has no insurable interest, may tempt him to commit murder. Therefore both policies would be invalid.

Just as an agreement tending to induce a criminal act is illegal, so an agreement tending to induce a tortious act is illegal and unenforceable. For example, agreements to exempt a railroad company or public service company from the consequences of its negligence are usually held to be against public policy in that they tend to cause carelessness and thus to result in injury to persons or property. On the other hand, agreements which merely limit the amount of damages for negligent conduct to a reasonable amount do not tend to cause carelessness and are therefore not illegal.

EFFECT OF ILLEGALITY

The preceding discussion of common types of illegal agreements included some comment on specific remedial measures that courts may order when granting relief from an illegal agreement. The rest of this chapter discusses factors which the courts take into consideration when deciding whether a request for remedial relief should be granted.

The General Rule

The general rule is that the courts will aid neither party to an illegal agreement. If the agreement is completely executory, neither party can tender performance and demand performance by the other party or demand damages in lieu of performance. If the agreement is completely executed, neither party can rescind the agreement, tender the performance received, and demand the return of his or her own performance. The general rule is applied even where one party has performed and the other party has not. The party who has performed cannot sue on the basis of the agreement and recover damages or disaffirm the bargain and recover the performance or its value.

The net result of the general rule often is that one wrongdoer is unjustly enriched at the expense of the other wrongdoer. The justification for the general rule is said to be its deterrent effect. Although the rule may have a deterrent effect on the particular plaintiff who has suffered a forfeiture of performance, "its effect on the defendant who has been enriched may be to [make him astute] to find some other person whom he can dupe."[10] And when a wrongdoer's success is observed by other dishonest persons, will they not become similarly astute? The real justification for the general rule is not the deterrent effect but the impropriety of placing the machinery of justice at the disposal of a plaintiff who has broken the law by entering into an illegal bargain.

Exceptions to the General Rule

The law recognizes certain exceptions to the general rule, where the illegal agreement does not involve serious moral turpitude. "Exception," as used in this context, implies that the

---

[9]Agreements involving breach of trust (fiduciary duty), often considered with agreements involving crimes and torts, are discussed in the chapters on agency, partnership, and corporations.

[10]John E. Murray, *Murray on Contracts*, Bobbs-Merrill Company, Indianapolis, 1974, sec. 344.

law permits some kind of remedy, even though the agreement is illegal. What that remedy is depends on the nature of the exception and the law of the state. The most important exceptions to the general rule are discussed in the following pages.

Parties Not Equally at Fault Where the parties to an illegal agreement are both blameworthy, but not equally at fault (not *"in pari delicto"*), and the party who was less at fault has rendered some performance, that party will be allowed to recover the performance or its value.

This principle finds frequent application in cases where the plaintiff has been induced to enter into the illegal agreement by the fraud, duress, or undue influence of the other party to the agreement. For example, suppose that A is indebted to numerous creditors and fears that she may lose substantially all her property. Her lawyer, B, works on these fears and finally induces A to turn over her property to B on the promise that he will return it when A's financial troubles are over. B subsequently refuses to perform his promise, and A sues. Although A's transfer of property was for the purpose of defeating her creditors and was thus illegal, the courts will allow A to recover her property. To refuse to do so would be to reward the more blameworthy of the two parties to the illegal agreement.

Withdrawal from Illegal Agreement Where an illegal bargain has been partly performed but the illegal part of the bargain has not yet been performed, the party who has rendered performance can withdraw from the bargain and recover the performance or its value. The performing party is said to have a *locus poenitentiae*—literally, place or opportunity for repentance. The opportunity to repent is not restricted to situations where one party is less at fault than the other. It applies also where the parties are equally at fault.

A common application of the doctrine of repentance is the withdrawal from a wager in a state where wagers are illegal. Suppose that each party to the wager deposited money with a stakeholder who has agreed to pay the winner of the bet. By depositing money, each party has partially performed the agreement. However, performance of the illegal part of the agreement does not occur until the money is paid to the winner. At any time before such payment occurs, either party is entitled to withdraw from the agreement by giving notice of repudiation to the stakeholder. If the stakeholder ignores a notice of repudiation and pays the wager, the stakeholder is liable to the party who has given notice of repudiation, for the amount of that party's deposit.

Party Protected by Statute Some statutes which make a particular kind of agreement illegal have been designed to protect the members of a certain class of persons. When a member of the protected class enters into such an agreement, that person is usually entitled to some kind of relief, despite the illegality of the transaction. The statute may specify the kind of relief available to a member of the protected class. Where the statute does not specify the remedy, and litigation involving that kind of statute occurs, the court will determine the appropriate remedy. The appropriate remedy under the circumstances may be to grant the right of rescission, as where a member of the protected class has purchased unregistered corporate stocks or bonds. If the general rule of nonenforceability were applied, the shareholders—for whose benefit the statute was enacted—would be unable to get their money back and would therefore suffer an undeserved loss.

Justifiable Ignorance of Facts An agreement may appear to be legal on its face but may nevertheless be illegal because of facts about which one party is justifiably ignorant. For example, suppose that the A Insurance Company has not obtained the license necessary to enable it lawfully to do business. In justifiable ignorance of that fact, B enters into a one-year employment contract with the company. Later

B discovers that the company did not have a license and that B therefore will not be able to perform the work she was hired to do. She at once leaves the company. Is she entitled to recover damages? The courts have held that in a situation such as this, the illegality of the employment agreement does not prevent the employee from recovering damages. Some courts will limit the recovery to the amount of unpaid salary; other courts will permit the employee to recover the same damages that would be recoverable for breach of contract.

Effect of Partial Illegality

Some agreements are illegal only in part, as where part of what is promised is illegal or part of the consideration demanded by the promisor is illegal. In either event, the general rule is that the illegal part taints the whole agreement and makes it void. However, most courts recognize some exceptions to the rule. Courts are loath to apply the rule where the plaintiff would suffer a severe penalty and the illegality is not serious enough, from the public policy standpoint, to justify a severe penalty.

One of the most important exceptions to the rule that a court will not enforce a partly illegal agreement occurs where the agreement is "divisible." The word refers to those situations where the legal part of the agreement can be separated from the illegal part, and the legal part can be enforced without violating the intention of the parties. Some kinds of agreements are clearly divisible, for example, an agreement to sell several articles at a designated price for each article. Even if one of the articles cannot legally be sold, the agreement could be enforced as to the other articles. However, if the agreement had called for the sale of those same articles for one lump sum, the agreement would have been indivisible and void. Where the parties do not by agreement apportion the price among the various promised performances of a divisible contract, the courts will not make the apportionment for them.

Effect Of Knowledge Of Intended Illegal Use

It is well settled that if one party (A) to an agreement has no knowledge that what she is to supply will be used by the other party (B) for an unlawful purpose, A can enforce the agreement. Suppose, for example, that A agrees to rent a dock to B without any knowledge that B intends to use the dock for smuggling goods into the country. If B finds another dock better suited for his purposes and refuses to pay the rent, A can recover damages for breach of contract. On the other hand, if A changes her mind about renting the dock to B, B cannot enforce the agreement. The legal principle involved in this situation is that a person who intends to accomplish an unlawful purpose may not enforce a "facilitating contract," that is, a contract made for the purpose of enabling him or her to accomplish the unlawful purpose.

The courts differ on what the law should be where A knew at the time she entered into the agreement of the unlawful purpose of B. Some courts take the view that A cannot enforce the agreement. Other courts take the view that she can enforce the agreement unless she has the intention of furthering B's unlawful purpose. Still other courts take the view that A can enforce the agreement unless the contemplated wrongful act involved great moral turpitude or the commission of a serious crime.

SUMMARY

An agreement is illegal if it comes within a class of agreements made illegal by statute or if it is held by a court to be against public policy.

Contracts of adhesion and exculpatory clauses may or may not be against public policy, depending on the circumstances. An unconscionable agreement is illegal even though the practice involved does not constitute a traditional variety of illegal conduct.

Agreements not to compete are restraints on

trade, and the courts are reluctant to enforce them except for compelling reasons. Many such restraints are enforceable if properly limited. For example, an agreement by the seller of a business not to compete with the buyer is usually enforceable if so limited in duration and in territory covered by the agreement as to protect only the interest purchased. On the other hand, a restriction which unreasonably deprives a person of the opportunity to engage in gainful employment will not be enforced.

Many other kinds of agreements are illegal. Among them are gambling agreements, agreements to pay a usurious rate of interest, agreements in violation of Sunday-closing laws, agreements involving interference with governmental processes, and agreements requiring or inducing the commission of crimes and torts.

Some classes of illegal agreements present special problems. The law of usury must protect borrowers from overreaching lenders without unduly limiting the supply of consumer credit. Sunday-closing legislation raises constitutional problems. A Sunday-closing law is unconstitutional if its purpose is to establish or prevent the free exercise of religion. However, the law may be constitutional if it has an economic or other nonreligious motivation.

An illegal agreement is unenforceable. As a general rule, the courts will aid neither party to an illegal agreement. The rule is subject to many exceptions. For example, where the parties to an illegal agreement are both blameworthy, but the party who was less at fault has rendered some performance, that party may be allowed to recover the performance or its value. Similarly, a party protected by a statute (for example, a usury statute) may have a statutory remedy or some other remedy despite the illegality of the transaction.

STUDY AND DISCUSSION QUESTIONS

1 Where a statute does not express any intention to make an agreement illegal, how do the courts determine whether the legislature had such an intention?

2 *(a)* If challenged in court, will a contract of adhesion be held void as against public policy? Explain. *(b)* Is a clause which exempts a contracting party from the payment of damages for his or her own negligence enforceable? Explain.

3 *(a)* How may a court treat an unconscionable contract or an unconscionable term of a contract when confronted with a request for remedial relief? *(b)* How is unconscionability related to fraud and duress? *(c)* What is the difference between procedural and substantive unconscionability? Give an illustration of each.

4 Agreements not to compete may be enforceable. *(a)* For what reasons might a court enforce such an agreement? *(b)* Even though there might be a justification for enforcing an agreement not to compete, the agreement will not be enforced unless the restraint it imposes is reasonable. In general, under what circumstances will the restraint be held reasonable? *(c)* Explain or illustrate the dilemma involved in situations where an illegal restraint is alleged to be "divisible."

5 Many gambling agreements are illegal and therefore unenforceable. Is an insurance contract a gambling agreement? Explain.

6 *(a)* What is usury? *(b)* Why might a state provide for different maximum rates for different categories of loans? *(c)* What is the legal effect of a usurious agreement?

7 *(a)* What was the effect of the older usury limits on the availability of consumer credit? *(b)* What measures did the legislatures take to nullify that effect? *(c)* How might the judicial "time-price" doctrine contribute to the availability of consumer credit?

8 How do the Truth-in-Lending Act and the Uniform Consumer Credit Code affect agreements for the extension of credit?

9 Are Sunday-closing laws constitutional? Explain.

10 Suppose a person is required to obtain a license before rendering services. Under what circumstances will a person who fails to obtain the required license be denied the right to enforce an agreement to compensate him or her for services rendered? Why?

11 *(a)* An agreement involving interference with governmental processes is unenforceable. Give an example. *(b)* An agreement tending to induce a tortious act is illegal. Give an example.

12 The courts will aid neither party to an illegal agreement. This general rule is subject to many exceptions. Explain or illustrate each of the following exceptions: *(a)* Agreements involving parties not equally at fault. *(b)* Agreement of a party protected by a statute.

13 *(a)* How do the courts treat agreements which are illegal only in part? *(b)* Explain the rule governing a "facilitating contract."

CASE PROBLEMS

1 Graham leased the land on which his business was situated from the Chicago, R.I. & P. Railway Co. One of its trains derailed because of the negligent operation of the railroad. Graham's place of business was damaged, and the means of public access was impaired for a substantial time. Graham sued the railroad for damages. The railroad filed a motion for summary judgment on the basis of the following clause in the lease: "The Lessee releases the Lessor, its agents, and employees from all liability for loss or damage caused by fire or other casualty by reason of any injury to or destruction of any real or personal property, of any kind, owned by the Lessee, or in which the Lessee is interested, which now is or may hereafter be placed on any part of the leased premises." Should the railroad's motion for summary judgment be granted?

2 Scott, a long-term employee of General Iron and Welding Co. (General), signed a contract of employment as chief engineer. In this capacity he had access to General's design and engineering knowledge, freedom to handle the affairs of the company, and access to the company's customer list. Scott solicited business from customers located throughout Connecticut. General did business in not less than 25 nor more than 75 Connecticut towns in any one year. In 1972, after a salary dispute, Scott left General and took employment with a competitor as a welder. Later he wished to participate in the management of the competitor despite a restrictive clause in his contract with General. The clause forbade him for a period of 5 years from managing a competitor in the state of Connecticut. Scott brought an action for a declaratory judgment to determine the validity of the restrictive covenant. Should the covenant be upheld?

3 Kot had a franchise from Rita Personnel Services International, Inc. (Rita). The franchise agreement provided that upon termination of the agreement, Kot would not compete with Rita in three designated counties in Georgia nor in "any territorial areas in which a franchise has been granted." The franchise agreement was terminated, and Kot began operating a personnel employment service under his own name. Rita sought an injunction to enforce the restrictive clause. Should the injunction be granted?

4 Cagle signed a mortgage note to finance the construction of a residence. The note bore a 10 percent annual interest rate as permitted by law. However, the lender mailed Cagle computerized monthly statements which, as a result of compounding interest and the use of a daily interest factor based on a 360-day year, produced a simple interest rate of 10.6235296 percent per annum. Cagle objected to the interest charges and made no payments. The lender brought a foreclosure action to recover the principal and interest. Cagle sought to cancel the note and mortgage on the basis of usury. Was the transaction usurious?

5 Miller-Davis Co., a general contractor, bid on an atomic energy project. Premier Electrical Construction Co., an electrical subcontractor, wanted to work on the project with Miller-Davis. Miller-Davis and Premier agreed that if Premier submitted higher bids to the general contractor's competitors as "protection" and if Miller-Davis secured the prime contract for the project, Premier would receive the electrical subcontract. Premier carried out the agreement but did not get the subcontract despite being low bidder. Premier sued Miller-Davis for breach of contract. Was Premier entitled to damages?

Chapter

16

A Writing
as a Requirement;
The Parol Evidence Rule

At early common law only written promises were enforceable, and then only if a seal had been attached to the writing. In the 1300s the English courts began to enforce oral promises, and they did so on the basis of testimony of witnesses who were not parties to the contract. If these witnesses could be persuaded to testify falsely, a person could be held to a "contract" into which he or she had not entered. In 1677, to prevent such "frauds and perjuries," the English Parliament enacted the famous Statute of Frauds. Two sections of the statute—Sections 4 and 17—dealt with contracts; other sections dealt with other kinds of writings, such as wills.

Section 17 dealt with contracts for the sale of goods. The section was generally copied in the United States. Eventually it evolved into part of Article 2 of the Uniform Commercial Code. The Article 2 statute of frauds provisions are dis-

cussed in the Sales portion of this volume (Chapter 25). Section 4 of the English Statute dealt with five other important classes of contracts. The American counterparts of Section 4 of the Statute are discussed in the first part of this chapter.[1]

Note that the requirements of the statutes of frauds apply only to *certain* kinds or classes of contracts—those thought to affect such a vital interest of a contracting party that a writing should be required as evidence of contractual intent. Except where a statute of frauds or some other special statute requires a writing for the formation or enforcement of a contract, an oral contract is as enforceable as a written one.

---

[1]In Maryland and New Mexico, the English Statute of Frauds is in force by judicial decision. All other states but Louisiana have statutes similar in content to the English statute.

A party to a written contract may contend that the writing (whether or not required by the statute of frauds) does not express the agreement of the parties. The dissatisfied party may wish to challenge the contents of the writing on the basis of prior inconsistent oral or written statements. That problem is considered in the second part of this chapter, in the discussion of the parol evidence rule, although the question has nothing to do with the statute of frauds.

WRITING REQUIREMENTS UNDER THE STATUTE OF FRAUDS

Classes of Contracts Covered by the Statute

Nearly every state statute of frauds covers the same five classes of contracts that were included in the English Statute of Frauds. The state statutes usually forbid enforcement of a contract which is included in any of the five classes unless the contract is in writing or some memorandum thereof is in writing. The five classes may be summarized as:

1 A contract of an executor or administrator to answer for a duty of the decedent (the executor-administrator provision of the Statute)

2 A contract to answer for the debt or default of another (the suretyship provision)

3 A contract made upon consideration of marriage (the marriage provision)

4 A contract for the sale of an interest in land (the land-contract provision)

5 A contract not performable within a year (the one-year provision)[2]

Although most state statutes of frauds include at least those five classes of contracts, some of the statutes include one or more additional classes of contracts. Examples are a contract to

pay a commission for the sale of land and a contract to leave property by will. The discussion in this chapter is limited to the five basic classes of contracts.

Contract of Executor or Administrator A promise of an executor (or an administrator) to pay the debt of the decedent out of the executor's own funds must be evidenced by a writing. Bereaved family members who happen to be executors are particularly vulnerable to pressures by the decedent's creditors for payment. The writing requirement gives executors a bit more time to consider whether to pay someone else's debt. Under the law of some states the "executor-administrator" situation is treated as one form of suretyship and is covered by the statute-of-frauds provision on suretyship.

Contract to Answer for Debt or Default of Another All the statutes of frauds contain a suretyship provision. The usual wording of the provision is: "A contract to answer for the debt, default, or miscarriage of another must be evidenced by a writing." "Default" means the failure to perform a promise or to discharge an obligation. Suppose that B is under contract to build a house for A and that G has guaranteed the faithful performance of B's obligation. G's promise is a promise to answer for the default of B. "Miscarriage" means any kind o unlawful conduct or wrongful act for which the wrongdoer would be held liable in a civil action. A promise by a fidelity (bonding) company given to an employer to make good any embezzlement of company funds by an employee is a promise to answer for the miscarriage of another. To be within the suretyship provision of the statute, the surety's promise to pay must be made not to the debtor but to the debtor's creditor.

There can be no suretyship agreement unless there are a primary obligation and a secondary (collateral) obligation. In the example involving the building contractor, above, B has the primary obligation (to build a house) and G has the secondary obligation (to pay A if B defaults). G's obligation is called "secondary" because G is not

---

[2]*Restatement of the Law (Second) Contracts*, American Law Institute, Philadelphia, 1973, sec. 178(1).

liable unless B fails to perform his or her obligation. In the example involving the fidelity company, any embezzling employee has the primary obligation to pay; the fidelity company has the secondary obligation.

A contract situation may involve three persons and yet not be a suretyship contract. For example, suppose that B writes to A: "Sell C whatever groceries he needs up to a value of $100, and I will pay for them." If A lets C have $75 worth of groceries, there is only one obligation to pay, and that obligation is B's. C is a third-person beneficiary of the contract between A and B. Now imagine a slightly different situation. Suppose B writes A: "Let C have whatever groceries he needs up to a value of $100, and if he does not pay, I will." If A lets C have $75 worth of groceries, there are two obligations. C has the primary obligation; B has a secondary or collateral obligation. The contract is one of suretyship, and it comes within the suretyship provision of the state's statute of frauds.

The courts have created an exception to the suretyship provision of the statute, which has become known as the "main-purpose" or "leading-object" rule: When the surety's main purpose is to obtain some personal pecuniary or business advantage, the promise is "not within" (or is "taken out of") the statute, and the surety's promise is therefore enforceable even though oral. Suppose D contracts to build a house for S. D then contracts to buy the building materials from C, a supplier of building materials. D gets into financial difficulties and fails to pay for some of the materials furnished. C justifiably refuses to furnish further materials until she receives payment for material already furnished. S fears that a delay may cause him to default on a contract, previously made, for the sale of the house. Faced with this possibility, S orally promises to pay C for materials already furnished and also for those yet to be furnished, if D does not pay for them. S's promise is enforceable, even though it is not in writing and even though it results in a benefit to a third party. The courts view such a benefit as merely an incidental result of S's promise. The main purpose of that promise was to get the house built on schedule.[3] Case 16.1 further illustrates the main-purpose rule.

---

[3]This example is based on *Restatement (Second), Contracts*, sec. 184, illustration 3.

Case 16.1   **Howard M. Schoor Associates v. Holmdel Heights Construction Co.**
343 A.2d 401 (N.J. 1975)

Holmdel Heights Construction Co. was engaged in developing a tract of land for home building. Schoor Associates, Inc., and Schoor Engineering, Inc. (plaintiffs) were engaged to do surveying, engineering, and professional planning work in connection with the development. Some of the bills submitted by the plaintiffs were not paid, and the plaintiffs became concerned.

On April 14, 1970, a conference on financing took place in the office of defendant Alan Sugarman, who owned 18 percent of the capital stock of Holmdel and acted as its attorney. To secure additional financing, further engineering work had to be done at once. According to the plaintiffs and the trial court, Sugarman agreed to pay all of Holmdel's outstanding and future bills in exchange for the plaintiffs' agreement to continue engineering work for Holmdel. The plaintiffs did all the engineering work requested but received no further payment. Holmdel went into receivership, and plaintiffs brought suit against Sugarman for the amounts due them.

The trial court rendered judgment for the plaintiffs. The appellate court reversed the judgment, and the plaintiffs appealed.

MOUNTAIN, J. . . . Defendant contends that his promise . . . is unenforceable under the Statute of Frauds. The relevant section of that act reads as follows: "No action shall be brought upon any of the following agreements or promises, unless the agreement or promise . . . shall be in writing, and signed by the party to be charged . . . (b) A special promise to answer for the debt . . . of another person."

. . . Defendant contends that the promise . . . obligated him only secondarily to pay the debt owed by Holmdel in the event it should default, and that as such it comes squarely within the purview of the statute. Plaintiffs argue that the promise was made largely . . . for the defendant's personal benefit, that it did not create a suretyship relationship but rather was an "original" promise resting upon consideration sought by defendant for his personal ends, and that this being so the promise is not controlled by the statute. This latter argument rests upon what is sometimes referred to as the "leading object or main purpose rule." It has been stated as follows:

"When the leading object of the promise or agreement is to become guarantor or surety to the promisee for a debt for which a third party is and continues to be primarily liable, the agreement, whether made before or after or at the time with the promise of the principal, is within the statute, and not binding unless evidenced by writing. On the other hand, when the leading object of the promisor is to subserve some interest or purpose of his own, notwithstanding [that] the effect is to pay or discharge the debt of another, his promise is not within the statute." 2 Corbin on Contracts . . . 273-74 (1950).

. . . In applying this rule, which we think expresses sound doctrine, it becomes important . . . to determine what interest, purpose or object was sought to be advanced by defendant's promise to pay plaintiff's fees. As noted above, defendant owned 18% of the capital stock of Holmdel Heights Construction Company, for which he paid $10,000. He was also attorney for the corporation and at the time of trial . . . was still owed $14,000 for legal services. . . . Defendant . . . agreed that had the corporation eventually been successful, the amount he would have received upon his investment, together with reasonably anticipated legal fees, would have been a substantial sum. . . .

. . . In many if not most cases the consideration for which the new promise is given will be beneficial *both* to the promisor and to the original debtor. Whether or not the Statute of Frauds will apply is then to depend upon whether this consideration was *mainly* desired for the promisor's benefit or for the benefit of the original debtor. . . .

The present action falls factually within that category of suits where the original debtor is a corporation in which the promisor has a financial interest. Such cases are fairly numerous. Depending upon their particular facts . . . they have been decided both ways.

> "There are many cases in which a shareholder or officer of a corporation or other party interested in its prosperity has promised a contractor that, if he would continue to supply goods or labor under his contract with the corporation in spite of its defaults, the promisor would pay the bill. If the only expected gain to the promisor is in the protection of the value of his shares, the promise is held to be within the statute; but there are cases in which the promisor was found to have received a special benefit that constituted his 'leading object' and made him an original debtor." 2 Corbin, *supra* . . . 298–99.

The interest of defendant Sugarman in inducing plaintiffs to undertake the work that they did after the April 14 conference seems obvious. . . . There is little to support the view that he meant to commit his personal assets to so considerable an extent only to further his client's interest. . . . The consideration was *mainly* desired for his personal benefit.

Accordingly the judgment of the Appellate Division is reversed and the judgment of the [trial court] is hereby reinstated.

Contract upon Consideration of Marriage

The marriage provision in state statutes of frauds may require "a contract upon consideration of marriage" or "a promise in consideration of marriage" to be evidenced by a writing. These phrases, or similarly worded phrases, refer most commonly to a promise to give money or property in exchange for a marriage or promise of marriage. Such bargains are known as property settlements.

In a property settlement, the promise to give money or property ordinarily is specifically enforceable (if in writing), whereas the unperformed promise to marry is not. The courts will not use their equitable powers to force marriage upon the unwilling. However, a refusal to perform the promise to marry is a breach of contract and would confer remedial rights on the other party. For example, the other party (the recipient of the promise to marry) would be entitled to retrieve any property given under the terms of the property settlement.

Often the promise to give money or property is made by a third person, as where Betty's father promises to pay Arnold $5,000 if he will marry Betty. However, the promise need not necessarily be made by a third person. Suppose that Alfred, in proposing to Bertha, says: "If you will marry me, I'll buy you the Cadillac of your choice for your personal use." The promise of Betty's father and the promise of Alfred are both within the statute of frauds, i.e., must be in writing to be enforceable.

The marriage provision does not apply to mutual promises to marry. "It would be imputing to the legislature too great an absurdity to suppose that they had enacted that all our courtships, to be valid, must be in writing."[4] Thus, in many states an exchange of oral promises to marry can create an enforceable contract. But sometimes people have falsely alleged the existence of such a contract in an attempt to

---

[4]*Withers v. Richardson*, 5 T.B. Mon. 94 (Ky. 1844) and other cases cited in Laurence P. Simpson, *Law of Contracts*, West Publishing Company, St. Paul, 1965, p. 152, note 19.

extort payments of money or to embarrass a former lover, and there have been sensational "breach-of-promise" trials. To curb these and other abuses, the legislatures of some states have enacted statutes which provide that the breach of a promise to marry (in a situation involving merely mutual promises to marry) does not give rise to a cause of action.

The statute of frauds marriage provision does not apply to a promise in contemplation of marriage. For example, suppose that two fathers (A and B) orally agree that each will give $5,000 to A's daughter when she marries B's son. She is a third-party beneficiary of the contract between A and B. The promises made by A and B are enforceable even though oral, since the marriage is a condition to the liability of the fathers rather than a consideration bargained for by the daughter.[5] The meaning of "condition" is discussed on p. 335.

Contract for Sale of Interest in Land Under the statute of frauds, a contract for the sale of an interest in land must be evidenced by a writing to be enforceable. The definition of *interest in land* is deferred to a later chapter, where the definition will be much more meaningful. However, a few examples of interests in land may be helpful at this point. Such interests include contracts to sell or buy land; leases of land (unless the lease is within a statutory exception for short-term leases); real estate mortgages; and easements (e.g., a right of way that the owner of one piece of property may have over the land of another person). Case 16.2 discusses a mortgage as an interest in land.

Statutes in most states exempt short-term leases and contracts for short-term leases from the land-contract provisions of the statute of frauds.[6] A lease is usually characterized as "short-term" if it is for a term of a year or less. In most states an oral lease for a one-year term is

valid without regard to when the term is to begin.

Until recently there was considerable confusion in the law regarding whether contracts for the sale of *oil, gas, or other minerals* still in the ground at the time of contracting were contracts for the sale of goods or contracts for the sale of an interest in land. It seems to be well settled now that if the seller is to "sever" the mineral from the land, the contract is for the sale of goods. The UCC as amended in 1972 so provides. If the buyer is to enter on the land and do the severing, the contract is one "affecting land" and "must conform to the Statute of Frauds [provision] affecting the transfer of interests in land" (UCC, Section 2-107, comment 1).

A contract for the sale, apart from the land, of *growing crops* or other things attached to realty and capable of severance without material harm to the land is not a contract for the sale of an interest in land, whether the subject matter is to be severed by the buyer or by the seller. (See UCC, Section 2-107(2); this section is discussed further in Chapter 24, p. 469.) Therefore, a contract for the sale of such property (characterized as goods by the Code) is not required to be in writing by the *land* provision of the statute of frauds. However, if the value of the goods is more than $500, the UCC statute of frauds applies. (Section 2-201, the Code statute of frauds, is discussed in Chapter 25.)

The writing required by the statute of frauds for the sale or purchase of an interest in land should not be confused with the writing (called a "deed") commonly used for actually transferring the interest and having the transfer recorded in the public land records. A deed is a document signed by the "grantor" conveying (transferring) an interest in realty and may be used in connection with either a sale or a gift of the interest to the "grantee." The writing required by the statute of frauds merely provides evidence of an intention to enter a contract. Usually it is not adequate as evidence of a transfer of an interest in land.

---

[5]*Restatement (Second), Contracts*, sec. 192, illustration 5.

[6]Ibid., sec. 193(4).

Case 16.2   **Eastgate Enterprises, Inc. v. Bank and Trust Company**
345 A.2d 279 (Pa. Super. 1975)

The Bank and Trust Company of Old York Road (defendant) held a mortgage on real estate owned by Eastgate Enterprises, Inc. (plaintiff). The Bank foreclosed the mortgage and, as permitted by statute, charged Enterprise for costs and attorney's fees. In order to obtain a release of the mortgage, Enterprise paid costs and fees totaling $9,455.36. Enterprise then brought suit to recover that amount, alleging that the Bank had violated an oral agreement not to foreclose the mortgage. The trial court dismissed Enterprise's complaint on the ground that the oral agreement was unenforceable under the Pennsylvania Statute of Frauds. Enterprise appealed.

SPAETH, J. . . . The Statute of Frauds . . . provides that

"no leases, estates or interests . . . in . . . any . . . lands shall, at any time after the said April 10, 1772, be assigned, granted or surrendered, unless it be by deed or note, in writing, signed by the party so assigning, granting, or surrendering the same. . . ."

Thus, "an *oral* contract to convey *real estate* or to change the title to real estate is a violation of the Statute of Frauds." [Citation.]

"The statute of frauds . . . does not absolutely invalidate an oral contract relating to land but is intended merely to guard against perjury on the part of one claiming under the alleged agreement." [Citation.]

Specific evidence that would make rescission of an oral contract inequitable and unjust will take the contract out of the Statute of Frauds, as, for example, sufficient "part performance" or an admission by the defendant, either in his pleadings or at the trial, of the existence of the contract. The reason for this rule is that such evidence reduces the chances of fraud and perjury and therefore the purpose of the statute is served.

Here there is no suggestion of such evidence. There is only the bare allegation of the oral agreement; the allegation about "negotiating a cancellation" of the agreement to sell to Gino's adds nothing, for the terms of the negotiations are not alleged.

Appellant [Enterprise] contends, however, that an oral agreement not to foreclose a mortgage is not such an agreement as falls within the Statute of Frauds.

To be valid, a mortgage must be in writing. . . . Early cases held that certain parol agreements relating to mortgages were permissible. [One case held that an oral assignment of a mortgage is not invalidated by the statute of frauds. Another held that an oral release may extinguish a mortgage.] The reasoning was that a "mortgage, in Pennsylvania, is literally and legally now understood to be but a bare security for the payment of the money, or performance of other

Case 16.2
Continued

acts therein mentioned; and at most only a chose in action." Subsequent decisions, however, have not accepted this reasoning. . . . Mortgages

"are in form defeasible sales, and in substance [are] grants of specific security or interests in land for the purpose of security. . . . While ordinarily, as to third parties, a mortgage may be only a security for the debt specified in the accompanying bond, it is, as to the mortgagor and the mortgagee, and those claiming under and through them, a conveyance of the land and may be enforced as such whenever the mortgagee deems it necessary so to do in order to enable him to speedily and effectively recover the amount then due on the bond. . . ."

In the present case, the alleged oral agreement not to foreclose was between the mortgagor and mortgagee. As between these parties, the mortgage represented an interest in land [and] was within the Statute of Frauds. . . .[Under the Pennsylvania Statute of Frauds, therefore, a mortgage may not be surrendered unless by a deed or note in writing.]

The order of the lower court is affirmed.

Contract Not Performable within a Year

Like other classes of contracts covered by statutes of frauds, long-term contracts are considered of sufficient importance to warrant a requirement that contractual intent be evidenced by a writing. The dividing line between a long-term contract and a short-term contract has been set at 1 year. However, the distinction between a long-term and a short-term contract is not so simple as it might sound. The courts have tended to interpret the class of long-term contracts narrowly and, consequently, to enforce a variety of oral contracts which might seem long-term but which the courts hold to be short-term.

To most courts, "not to be performed within a year" means "cannot be performed within a year." If performance of the contract could conceivably occur within 1 year, the contract is not within (covered by) the statute and need not be evidenced by a writing. A contract by which A agrees to support B for the rest of B's life could conceivably be performed within a year because there is the possibility that B might die within the year. The contract is enforceable even though oral. On the other hand, full performance of a promise to support B for the

next 4 years could not possibly occur in less than a year. The contract is not enforceable unless evidenced by a writing.

Many oral contracts specify a performance to be rendered for a term of more than one year but nevertheless are terminable at any time for a variety of reasons such as the death or the bankruptcy of one of the parties. Such apparently long-term contracts might or might not be subject to the writing requirement of the statute of frauds. As Case 16.3 illustrates, many courts take the view that the words "not to be performed within a year" refer to actual performance, and that terminability of an oral multi-year contract for reasons other than a completed performance is an insufficient basis for interpreting the contract as short term. Other courts take the opposite view and hold that the possibility of a rightful termination within a year *is* sufficient to take even a multi-year contract outside the statute so that no writing is required for enforceability.

The 1-year period is figured from the time the contract is made. Suppose that A and B enter into a contract on January 1. When does the 1-year period end for that contract? Since the law does not usually count fractions of a day, the 1-year period does not begin to run until January 2. Consequently, the 1-year period ends January 1 of the following year.

"Performed within a year" means fully performed within the year. Consequently, if either party to a contract promises a performance which cannot be fully completed within a year, all the promises in the contract are within the statute and must be evidenced by a writing. "But unlike other provisions of the Statute, the one-year provision does not apply to a contract which is performed on one side at the time [the contract] is made."[7] Thus, if B borrows $15,000 from A, and B promises to repay the loan in three semi-annual payments of $5,000 each, A can enforce the contract against B, even though the contract was oral, because A had completely performed his or her part of the contract at the time the contract was made.

Where one of the parties to an oral long-term contract completes his or her performance, the statute does not prevent enforcement of the promise of the other party.[8] Most courts (but not all) say that full performance by the one party "takes the contract out of the Statute."

---

[7]Ibid., sec. 198, comment *d.*

[8]Ibid., sec. 198(2).

Case 16.3   Gilliland v. Allstate Insurance Co.
388 N.E.2d 68 (Ill. App. 1979)

In an action against defendants Allstate Insurance Company and Sears, Roebuck & Company (Allstate), plaintiff Gilliland alleged the following: On March 15, 1954, he entered an oral contract of employment with Allstate under which defendants agreed to employ him until the time of his retirement at age 62, as long as plaintiff substantially complied with all lawful directions of defendants. At the time of contracting, defendants agreed to give plaintiff notice or warning if he was not fulfilling his duties so that plaintiff would have an opportunity to correct any deficiencies. After one year of employment, plaintiff commenced participation in profit sharing, pension, and savings plans and continued his participation until Allstate terminated his employment in 1972 without good cause and without prior notice or warning. As a result of defendants' breach of the oral contract of employment, plaintiff suffered a loss of profits and earnings and the amount which would have accumulated in the pension fund had he remained employed until retirement.

The circuit court of Cook County dismissed the action, and plaintiff appealed.

PERLIN, J. . . . Plaintiff initially contends that enforcement of the alleged oral contract of employment is not barred by the Statute of Frauds because the contract was capable of being performed within one year.

The [Illinois] Statute of Frauds provides in pertinent part:

["No] action shall be brought, . . . upon any agreement that is not to be performed within the space of one year from the making thereof,

Case 16.3
Continued

unless the promise or agreement upon which such action shall be brought, or some memorandum or note thereof, shall be in writing, and signed by the party to be charged therewith. . . . "

The Statute of Frauds has been interpreted as rendering an oral contract unenforceable only if it is impossible of performance within one year from the time the contract is made. To be outside the statute [so that no writing is required], the contract must be capable of being fully performed within one year and not simply terminated by some contingency such as death or bankruptcy. *Sinclair v. Sullivan Chevrolet Co.*, 45 Ill. App. 2d 10, 195 N.E.2d 250, *aff'd*, 31 Ill. 2d 507, 202 N.E.2d 516.

Plaintiff contends that the oral contract to employ him until age 62 could have been performed within one year because plaintiff could have quit or died or defendants could have terminated plaintiff's employment for good cause within one year. Plaintiff cites *Balstad v. Solem Machine Co.*, 26 Ill. App. 2d 419, 168 N.E.2d 732, in which an oral contract for employment that was of indefinite duration was found to be terminable at will and outside the Statute of Frauds. . . . We conclude that the oral contract [between Gilliland and Allstate] was not of indefinite duration but was allegedly for a term of 36 years—plaintiff would be employed until he reached age 62, at which time he would receive certain benefits. The contract would not have been "performed" had some contingency such as death or bankruptcy occurred; rather, the contract simply would have been terminated. In *Sinclair*, the court held that an employment contract made on May 31, 1960, for a term ending June 6, 1961, could not be performed within one year and was unenforceable under the Statute of Frauds. As in *Sinclair*, the contract in the case at bar extended over a period more than one year and is unenforceable under the Statute of Frauds. . . .

[The court then held that, contrary to the ruling of the lower court, the Illinois statute of *limitations* did not bar plaintiff's action against Allstate for fraudulent misrepresentation.]

Affirmed in part and reversed in part. . . .

Requirements Regarding the Writing

As already indicated, statutes of frauds apply only to certain kinds or classes of contracts. The primary purpose of such statutes is evidentiary—that is, to require reliable evidence that an alleged contract was indeed entered into. To accomplish this purpose, the English Statute of Frauds required that "the agreement . . . or some memorandum or note thereof, shall be in writing." Most states have adopted the same or very similar wording. In a few states the statute requires that "the contract" shall be in writing. In those states the writing must state the basic terms of the contract; a sketchy memo-randum is not sufficient. All states require that the writing be signed.

Certain important questions arise regarding the statutory requirements:

1 What content must the memorandum have?

2 What form may it take?

3 What is a "signature," who must do the signing, and where may the signature be placed?

4 At what time may the memorandum be made and signed?

Content Requirements regarding the content of the memorandum cannot be reduced to an exact formula. However, the courts have developed some "general requisites." To be sufficient evidence of a contract, the memorandum must:

• Identify with reasonable certainty the subject matter of the contract and the parties to it

• Sufficiently indicate that a contract with respect to that subject matter has been made between the parties

• State with reasonable certainty the essential terms of the unperformed promises in the contract.[9]

It should be noted that the law does not require that the subject matter and the parties be identified with precision; they need be indicated only with "reasonable certainty." For example, a memorandum which describes the subject matter of a contract as "my lot on the corner of Grant Street and Fourth Avenue in the County of X, State of Y" is sufficiently definite if the seller owns only one of the four lots on the intersection of Grant Street and Fourth Avenue. Similarly, a party may be identified by name or initials, even though there may be other persons with the same name or initials. "Where there is no dispute as to the parties, a person may be sufficiently identified by possession of a memorandum signed by the other party."[10]

Form The memorandum need take no particular form. It may be in the form of a letter, a receipt, an order blank, an invoice, a check, an entry in an account book, or an entry in a diary. It may consist of several writings "if one of the writings is signed and the writings in the circumstances clearly indicate that they relate to the same transaction."[11]

Signature The signature to a memorandum may consist of the signer's initials or thumbprint or of "any symbol made or adopted with an intention, actual or apparent, to authenticate the writing as that of the signer."[12] Most statutes of frauds have adopted the wording of the English Statute that the memorandum be "signed by the party to be charged." That wording is generally interpreted to mean the party to be charged with breach of contract in any subsequent legal proceeding. When parties enter into a bilateral contract, they cannot tell at the time of contracting which one of them will be "the party to be charged" with breach of contract in the event of subsequent litigation. For his or her own protection, each party should make sure that the other party signs the agreement or memorandum of agreement. Signatures need not appear at any particular place on the memorandum unless the statute provides otherwise.

Time There is no requirement that the memorandum be made at the time the contract is made. Courts differ in their views as to the time. One view is that a memorandum may be made and signed at any time before suit is instituted. The view of the *Restatement* is that the memorandum "may be made or signed at any time before or after the formation of the contract."[13]

---

[9]Ibid., sec. 207 and comment c.
[10]Ibid., sec. 207, comment f.

[11]Ibid., sec. 208.
[12]Ibid., sec. 210 and comment a.
[13]Ibid., sec. 214.

Case 16.4 **McMahan Construction Co. v. Wegehoft Brothers, Inc.**
354 N.E.2d 278 (Ind. App. 1976)

McMahan Construction Co. (defendant) was engaged in building Interstate Highway 465 in Marion County, Indiana. McMahan owned a 10-acre lot (the

Bluff Road property) which it used as a source of fill dirt and gravel. McMahan
needed additional fill dirt, and William Koch, McMahan's construction project
manager, attempted to purchase it from land owned by Wegehoft Bros., Inc.
(plaintiff). The Wegehoft land was adjacent to the Bluff Road property.

Wegehoft agreed to sell fill dirt to McMahan, but on the condition that
McMahan would sell Wegehoft the Bluff Road property. A handwritten
"Memorandum of Agreement" was drafted by Koch and signed by him and
Wegehoft. The document contained the following provisions:

"**A.** Wegehoft Bros. Inc. agree to sell to McMahan dirt and gravel from the
land adjacent to the 4404 Bluff Road property owned by McMahan.

B. McMahan will pay $0.25/cubic yard for the material removed and will
have the material measured by a registered engineer. . . .

E. McMahan will apply payments for the purchase of materials toward the
purchase of the 4404 Bluff Road land if the Wegehoft Bros. so desire.

F. McMahan Const. Co. will give Wegehoft the option to buy approximately 8-½ acres located at 4404 Bluff Road for the price of $5,000. The option [is] to
be exercised between January 1, 1966 and March 30, 1966, or sooner if
McMahan so elects. McMahan [reserves] the mineral rights on the land to
themselves."

Following the signing of the agreement, Wegehoft questioned the legality
of the document, and Koch said he would have an official contract prepared.
Wegehoft never received such a contract. During the next three years,
McMahan removed fill dirt from Wegehoft's property, and Wegehoft made
many inquiries of Koch about the deed to the Bluff Road property.

In November 1968, Wegehoft traveled to McMahan's home office to "settle
up" for the property. McMahan denied that there was an agreement for the sale
of property, and Wegehoft brought this action for specific performance. The
trial court entered judgment for plaintiff, and defendant appealed.

LYBROOK, J. . . . A search of the record reveals that the trial court had
sufficient evidence to support its finding that an oral option contract for the sale
of the 4404 Bluff Road property was created. The record, from appellee's view,
shows that Koch offered to buy and Wegehoft conditionally agreed to sell dirt
from the Wegehoft property, this condition being that the 4404 Bluff Road
property be sold to them at some future date. . . .

The final contention dealing with the first issue and the formation of a
contract relates to the specificity of the contract and the exactness necessary to
allow an order of specific performance to stand. In essence, this is a challenge
to the sufficiency of the writing to [satisfy] the Statute of Frauds. The
Restatement of Contracts sec. 207 (1932) . . . specifies the following as necessary for a sufficient memorandum:

"A memorandum, in order to make enforceable a contract within the
Statute, may be any document or writing, formal or informal, signed by
the party to be charged or by his agent actually or apparently authorized

thereunto, which states with reasonable certainty, (a) each party to the contract either by his own name, or by such a description as will serve to identify him, or by the name or description of his agent, and (b) the land, goods or other subject-matter to which the contract relates, and (c) the terms and conditions of all the promises constituting the contract and by whom and to whom the promises are made."

A reading of the document in question makes it quite apparent that all the prerequisites and requirements for a sufficient memorandum have been met by the document. The parties have obviously been identified and both parties have signed the memorandum. The property to be sold was known to both parties and identified by the best available means, the common mailing address. The document specifies the duties and obligations of each party and is specific as to the price of both the dirt and the land. . . . We thus hold that the trial court was justified in ruling that a contract was created and that the writing was sufficient to [satisfy] the Statute of Frauds. . . .

No error having been demonstrated, we affirm the decision of the trial court. . . .

Consequences of Noncompliance with Requirements

General Rule The general rule is that contracts within the statute of frauds are unenforceable unless evidenced by a writing. However, sometimes a person who knows about the requirement enters into an oral agreement intending later to use lack of compliance with the statute as a means of avoiding contractual liability, if such a course of action suits that person's purposes. Thus, the statute of frauds can itself be used as an instrument of fraud or oppression against persons ignorant of the writing requirement or too lacking in bargaining power to compel a writing.

The courts and the legislatures have developed ways of preventing the injustice which can arise from misuse of the statute-of-frauds writing requirement. One important technique is used in the statute of frauds relating to sales of goods. Under that statute of frauds (Section 2-201 of the Uniform Commercial Code), a writing is only one of several ways to evidence a contract for the sale of goods. Other ways include part performance of an oral contract, admitting to a contract in court, and failure by a merchant to respond to certain kinds of written communications. (The sales statute of frauds is discussed in Chapter 25.)

Long before the development of the Uniform Commercial Code, the courts were taking steps to prevent injustice from the misuse of the writing requirement. The judicial approach was basically to create "exceptions" to the general rule that contracts within the statute of frauds had to be evidenced by a writing.

"Exceptions" to the General Rule In two especially important situations a refusal to enforce an oral contract within the statute of frauds might work an injustice: (1) where one of the parties justifiably relied upon a misrepresentation of the other party and (2) where one of the parties performed his or her part of the oral contract in the justifiable expectation that the other party would perform.

Exception based on justifiable reliance (doctrine of equitable estoppel) It has long been recognized that if one party to a contract has misrepresented (or has concealed) a material fact and the other party has relied on the misrepresentation to his or her detriment, the party who made the misrepresentation is "estopped" (prohibited) from setting up the statute of frauds as a defense.[14]

Suppose, for example, that B says to A, "I have prepared and signed a memorandum of our oral agreement and have just mailed it to you," whereas B had not prepared and signed such a memorandum. If A substantially changes his position in reliance on B's statement and later sues B, B will be estopped from setting up the defense of the statute of frauds, unless (as seems improbable here) A has some other adequate remedy available.

Exception based on justifiable expectation (doctrine of part performance) Outside the law of sales, the doctrine of part performance has a somewhat limited application. If the courts are to give reasonable effect to the writing requirement, they cannot logically enforce an oral contract to which the requirement applies merely because some degree of performance took place.

Yet, in certain situations where there has been a sufficient performance, the courts will not blindly enforce the writing requirement. As stated earlier in this chapter, in most jurisdictions *full* performance by one party to an oral long-term contract "takes the contract out of the Statute." Otherwise, the party who has received the performance could use the statute of frauds to escape any obligation to perform in return. Part performance of an oral long-term contract would *not* render the contract enforceable, although the person who partly performs might be entitled to recover in quasi-contract the value of the part performance.

The judicial doctrine of part performance is applied mainly to oral land contracts. Courts of equity have long held that an oral contract for the sale of land will be specifically enforced when the contract has been partly performed *if*

the purchaser takes action which is "unequivocally referable to the oral agreement" and has reasonably relied on the agreement to his or her substantial detriment.[15] Usually, but not always, "it is necessary for possession of the land to be transferred to the purchaser plus either of the following elements: (1) payment of all or a substantial portion of the purchase price, *or* (2) the making of valuable improvements upon the land by the purchaser."[16]

Modification or Rescission of Contracts Covered by the Statute

Modification of Contract If a contract is modified by a subsequent agreement and the contract as modified is within the statute of frauds, the requirements of the statute must be satisfied. Suppose that A and B enter into an oral contract by the terms of which A is to employ B for a term of 6 months at a stated salary, beginning the first of next month. On the first of that month, on the recommendation of B's former employer, A decides to employ B for a longer time, and A and B orally agree that the period of employment is to be extended to 18 months. The oral agreement as modified exceeds 1 year and therefore must be in writing to be enforceable.

Rescission of Contract The *Restatement* provides that "Notwithstanding the Statute of Frauds, all unperformed duties under an enforceable contract may be discharged by an oral rescission."[17] Suppose that A and B enter into a written contract of employment for a term exceeding 1 year. Later they orally agree to rescind the contract. "The oral agreement is effective and the written contract is rescinded."[18]

All courts do not agree that a land contract may be orally rescinded. The prevailing rule is

---

[14]John E. Murray, *Murray on Contracts*, Bobbs-Merrill Company, Indianapolis, 1974, sec. 333.

[15]Ibid., sec. 328.
[16]*Restatement (Second), Contracts*, sec. 223(1).
[17]Ibid., sec. 222.
[18]Ibid., sec. 222, illustration 1.

that it may be rescinded orally just as other contracts within the statute may be. However, "where land has been transferred by an effective deed, an agreement to rescind the transaction is a contract for the transfer of an interest in land within the Statute of Frauds."[19]

EFFECT OF ADOPTION OF A WRITING: PAROL EVIDENCE RULE

Suppose that the parties to an agreement decide to put their agreement into a writing—whether or not a writing is required—and that later one of the parties sues for breach of contract. The other party contends that part of the writing had been omitted or that the writing incorrectly states part of the agreement. Will she be permitted to introduce evidence in court in support of her contention? Or will the court look solely to the writing in determining the contents of the contract? The answer involves a principle of the law known as the "parol evidence rule."

The Parol Evidence Rule

The purpose of the parol evidence rule is to promote certainty and security of transactions by giving binding effect, insofar as is reasonable, to a writing signed as the final expression of an agreement. Two kinds of writings are of key significance in the application by the courts of the parol evidence rule. The first kind of writing contains only a part of the agreement between the parties, but the writing is regarded by the parties as the final expression of the terms contained in the writing. Such a writing is said to be a "partially integrated agreement." The second kind of writing is regarded by the parties as being a complete and exclusive statement of all the terms of the agreement and is referred to as a "completely integrated agreement."

Under the parol evidence rule, a partially integrated agreement may *not* be contradicted but *may be supplemented* by evidence of prior negotiations or agreements, *oral or written*. A completely integrated agreement *may not be contradicted or supplemented* by evidence of prior negotiations or agreements, oral or written.[20] However, parol evidence *will* be admitted to resolve an ambiguity in an integration (whether partial or complete) and to resolve other questions such as the presence of fraud. A version of the parol evidence rule applicable to the sale of goods is found in Section 2-202 of the Uniform Commercial Code and is discussed in Chapter 25.

Even though the parol evidence rule does not permit an integrated agreement to be contradicted by prior agreements, the rule has no application to agreements entered into subsequent to the writing. Thus, where an integrated contract is modified or rescinded by a subsequent agreement, there is no violation of the parol evidence rule.

Determination of Intention of Parties

Inasmuch as the parol evidence rule applies only to writings which the parties intend as the final expression or integration of their agreement, the question naturally arises: How is the intention of the parties to be determined?

According to the *Restatement of the Law of Contracts*, whether a writing has been adopted as the final or "integrated" agreement is a question of fact to be determined in accordance with all relevant evidence. A written agreement which is apparently "complete on its face is taken to be an integrated agreement in the absence of contrary evidence."[21]

Sometimes the parties declare in writing that they intend it to be a complete expression of their agreement. Courts will usually give effect to such a declaration of intention. Even if the wording of the contract omits a term such as price or time of performance, courts will usually

---

[19]Ibid., sec. 222, comment *c*.

[20]Ibid., secs. 236 and 241.
[21]Ibid., sec. 235, comment *c*.

hold that a reasonable price or a reasonable time was implicit in the writing and that therefore the writing was not necessarily incomplete. However, courts do not always give effect to a declaration of intent. If, for example, the declaration of intent is a term of adhesion, the courts may, if the circumstances warrant, set aside the declaration and admit parol evidence.

Ordinarily, the issue of whether an alleged agreement was integrated is determined by the trial judge in the first instance. After the preliminary determination, such questions as whether the alleged agreement was in fact made and whether the writing is genuine may remain to be decided by the trier of fact.

It should be noted that the parol evidence rule serves to exclude evidence of prior negotiations only where there is a direct conflict between an unambiguous integration and the information sought to be presented to the court. For many purposes, parol evidence of prior negotiations is freely admissible even where there is an integration—for example, as we have seen, to clear up an ambiguity in the integration or to resolve an allegation of fraud. Parol evidence is admissible for other purposes: for example, to determine whether an agreement was illegal or lacked consideration or whether a writing constitutes a full or partial integration.

Case 16.5   **J. C. Penney Co. v. Koff**
              345 So. 2d 732 (Fla. App. 1977)

After 25 months of negotiations, Richard Koff (defendant) entered into a written agreement to purchase from J. C. Penney, Inc. (plaintiff) a tract of land for residential development. At the time of the agreement, the applicable zoning law permitted 28 condominium units per acre. A few months later, but before the closing date established in the agreement, the city changed the zoning law. The revised law permitted only 12 condominium units per acre. Before the date scheduled for closing, defendant gave plaintiff notice of intention to rescind the contract. plaintiff brought an action for specific performance of the contract. Plaintiff appealed from judgment for defendant.

CARLTON, Associate Judge. . . . [Defendant's] primary case in the trial court consisted of attempting to show an ambiguity in the sale and purchase agreement and utilizing various parol testimony and prior correspondence in an attempt to support his position for denial for specific performance. . . . The substance of the parol evidence was to establish that appellee [defendant] because of the change in density requirements between the execution of the contract and the scheduled closing would have a less profitable business venture and that appellee did not intend to be bound by the sale and purchase agreement if there was a change in the density.

Paragraphs 1A, 1C, and 6 of the . . . agreement must be examined for ambiguities. They are as follows:

> "1. . . . Seller shall sell and Purchaser shall purchase good and marketable fee simple title . . . subject to the following: A. Applicable building laws, *zoning ordinances*, laws and other regulations of any

governmental body, subdivision, or agency having jurisdiction existing *at the date of closing of title*, provided the same do not prohibit the construction of residential type units *as permitted* under zoning ordinance category R—4A of the zoning ordinance of the City. . . . C. All covenants, agreements, restrictions and easements of record; provided the same do not prohibit the construction of residential type units *as provided* under zoning ordinance category R—4a of the zoning ordinance. . . . (Emphasis added.)

"6. . . . Seller makes and has made no representation, statement, warranty or guarantee as to the condition, fitness or value of the Premises. The execution of this Agreement has not been procured by any representation, statement, warranty or guarantee not herein contained and Purchaser agrees to accept the Premises *'as is' as of the date hereof."*

Appellee contends that the phrases "as permitted" under Paragraph 1A, "as provided" under Paragraph 1C, and "as is as of the date hereof" under Paragraph 6 were ambiguous and therefore parol evidence should be received by the court to determine what was meant by these phrases.

In reviewing the contract in an attempt to determine its true meaning, the court must review the entire contract without fragmenting any segment or portion.

[Our Supreme Court has held]:

". . . When parties deliberately put their engagement into writing, in such terms as import a legal obligation without any uncertainty as to the object or extent of engagement, it is, as between them, conclusively presumed that the whole engagement and the extent and manner of their undertaking is contained in the writing. . . . No other language is admissible to show what they meant or intended, and for the simple reason that each of them has made [the language] found in the instrument the agreed text of his meaning and intention."

. . . This principle was stated over seventy years ago and continues to be the law of Florida and does bar the consideration of any [extrinsic] evidence to explain or vary the express terms of a contract unless an ambiguity . . . is first found to fairly appear. . . . The courts are allowed to consider extrinsic evidence only when confronting an ambiguous contract provision, and they are barred from using evidence to create an ambiguity to rewrite a contractual provision, or to vary a party's obligation under a contract.

It is necessary to look to the balance of the entire agreement to see what the intent of the parties was. The last clause of Paragraph 6 where "purchaser agrees to accept the premises 'as is' as of the date hereof" can logically be read in conjunction with Paragraph 1A without ambiguity. There is under Paragraph 1A language specifically relating to the zoning question in that appellant agreed to convey good and marketable title subject to zoning "existing at date of closing of title." The court cannot interpret a general clause, the last phrases of Paragraph 6, in a manner directly contrary to a specific clause, Paragraph 1A.

However, there must be an attempt made to give the last phrase in Paragraph 6 a reasonable meaning. Paragraph 6 is obviously a clause inserted to protect the seller by the limitation of representations for which he will be held responsible. There is no ambiguity in that portion of paragraph 1A or of Paragraph 6 sufficient to justify the admission of parol evidence.

Appellee further contends that the phrases "as permitted" under Paragraph 1A and "as provided" under Paragraph 1C are ambiguous. We disagree. The most compelling language in the contract is in Paragraph 1A itself. It is stated that title must be good and marketable subject to zoning regulations "existing at the date of closing of title." The phrase immediately following states "provided the same" (the regulations existing at the date of closing) do not prohibit the construction of residential type units as permitted under zoning ordinance category R—4A. It is obvious that the phrases "as permitted" under 1A and "as provided" under 1C refer to the type of use the land could be put to for the actual construction of various buildings and complexes under the prior zoning provisions and does not refer to a change of density. This phrase relates to when a future zoning ordinance may prohibit the actual construction of an apartment complex. . . .

Therefore, we are of the opinion the agreement . . . is not ambiguous, and extrinsic evidence should not have been admitted to change or alter the express provision in Paragraph 1A. . . .

This cause is hereby reversed and remanded to the court below with direction to enter an order for specific performance in behalf of appellant Penney. . . .

SUMMARY

The statute of frauds applies to classes of contracts thought to affect such a vital interest of a contracting party that a writing should be required as evidence of contractual intent. Except where a statute of frauds or some other special statute requires a writing for the formation or enforcement of a contract, an oral contract is as enforceable as a written one.

The classes of contracts commonly covered by a state statute of frauds are:

1 A contract of an executor or administrator to answer for a duty of the decedent

2 A contract to answer for the debt or default of another

3 A contract made upon consideration of marriage

4 A contract for the sale of an interest in land

5 A contract not performable within 1 year

The Uniform Commercial Code contains a statute of frauds which covers sales of goods.

The primary purpose of a statute of frauds is to require reliable evidence that an alleged contract was indeed entered into. To accomplish this purpose, the statute requires that an agreement covered by the statute, or some memorandum or note thereof, shall be in writing and signed by the person to be charged with breach of contract in any subsequent legal proceeding.

The statute of frauds can itself be used as an instrument of fraud or oppression against persons ignorant of the writing requirement or too lacking in bargaining power to compel a writing.

To prevent injustice which can arise from misuse of the writing requirement, the courts apply the doctrines of equitable estoppel and part performance in the enforcement of some oral contracts. Under some statutes of frauds, such as the one applicable to sales of goods, a writing is only one of several ways to evidence a contract. Other ways include part performance and admitting to a contract in court. If a contract is modified and the contract, as modified, is within the statute of frauds, the modified contract must conform to the requirements of the statute.

A statute of frauds indicates what evidence is required for enforceability of a contract. The parol evidence rule indicates what evidence a court will consider in determining the content of a contract. The parol evidence rule does not, in litigation, permit admission of evidence of an oral or written agreement made prior to an integrated agreement if the prior agreement conflicts with the terms of the integration.

STUDY AND DISCUSSION QUESTIONS

1 The statute of frauds does not apply to all contracts. State the criterion which is generally applied in determining which contracts should be covered by the statute of frauds.

2 *(a)* Why is a promise of an executor to pay the debt of the decedent out of the executor's own funds covered by the statute of frauds? *(b)* Under what circumstance would such a promise be enforceable?

3 A surety's promise to pay the debt, default, or miscarriage of another must be evidenced by a writing to be enforceable. *(a)* Using the terms "primary obligation" and "secondary obligation," illustrate a contract of suretyship. *(b)* Explain the operation and significance of the "main-purpose" rule.

4 *(a)* To what kinds of contracts involving marriage as consideration does the statute of frauds apply? *(b)* To what kinds of such contracts does the statute not apply? Why?

5 *(a)* Explain to which of the following contracts the land-contract provision of the statute of frauds applies: Purchase of land. Lease of land. Mortgage. Contract for sale of oil. Contract for sale of growing crops. *(b)* Distinguish between a deed and the writing required by the statute of frauds for a land contract.

6 *(a)* How do the courts distinguish between contracts which are performable within a year and those which are not? *(b)* What is the significance of the distinction? *(c)* A makes an oral contract to support B for the rest of B's life. Under the statute of frauds, is the oral contract enforceable? Explain.

7 What kind of writing will satisfy the statute of frauds?

8 *(a)* How can the statute of frauds be used as an "instrument of fraud or oppression"? *(b)* Illustrate how *legislatures* have attempted to prevent the injustice which can arise from the misuse of the statute of frauds writing requirement. *(c)* Describe two general ways in which the *courts* have attempted to prevent the injustice arising from the misuse of the statute of frauds writing requirement. *(d)* Under what circumstances might a court enforce an oral land contract?

9 Are oral modifications and rescissions of contracts covered by the statute of frauds? Explain.

10 *(a)* What is the purpose of the parol evidence rule? *(b)* Illustrate the operation of the parol evidence rule.

CASE PROBLEMS

1 Jim & Slim's Tool Supply, Inc., furnished building materials to a subcontractor who was using them in the construction of apartment buildings. The subcontractor defaulted in pay-

ment. The owner of the apartments orally agreed to guarantee payment for materials, and Tool Supply agreed to continue furnishing materials and to forbear from filing a claim of lien against the owner's real property. Later the owner refused to make payment, and Tool Supply brought suit for breach of the agreement. The trial court dismissed the complaint on the ground that enforcement of the agreement was barred by the statute of frauds. Tool Supply appealed. Should the trial court's ruling be upheld?

2 In February 1966, Michael O'Shea, age 35, married a wealthy widow, age 65. In May 1966, the O'Sheas were divorced at the wife's behest. In June 1966, they remarried. The wife sued for divorce again in April 1967. The husband appealed from that portion of the final decree of divorce which awarded all jointly held property to the wife. Before the second marriage, the wife had orally agreed to put her property in their joint names. In return, the husband agreed to remarry her and to give up his job in Michigan, working henceforth only out of Fort Lauderdale, Florida. The husband fully performed his part of the agreement, and after the remarriage the wife put her property in their joint names. Was the husband entitled to half the jointly held property?

3 Hilda A. Anderson worked for Erik H. Skoglund as his housekeeper for about 7 years until Skoglund's death in 1960. She received no wages. In a suit against Skoglund's estate for the reasonable value of her services, Anderson claimed that she worked for Skoglund in reliance on his oral promise that if anything happened to him, she would receive his house. Skoglund died intestate, and Anderson, who was unrelated to him, received nothing. Was Anderson entitled to the house?

4 Kiyose was a university lecturer in a department of East Asian Languages. During this period, the university orally assured him that upon obtaining his Ph.D. he would receive perpetual lifetime appointments at the university, commencing with a 3-year appointment as assistant professor. After obtaining the degree and being appointed to the rank of assistant professor, Kiyose was notified that he would not be reappointed. Kiyose brought suit for breach of the oral agreement. The university contended that the agreement was not enforceable. Was Kiyose's action barred by the statute of frauds?

5 Bernstein was the principal owner of United Packers, Inc., a producer of vienna sausage. Koin owned Ellis Canning Co., a large purchaser of vienna sausage from United. United was on the verge of bankruptcy, and after many attempts to sell the company, Bernstein persuaded Koin to purchase it. Although oral, the purchase agreement was complex, and with the permission of Bernstein and Koin, Koin's attorney tape-recorded Bernstein's explanation of the oral agreement. A dispute developed about other matters, and eventually Koin brought suit for breach of the contract for the sale of the corporation. Was Koin's action barred by the statute of frauds?

6 Sylvia owned some mortgaged real estate. He was in default on mortgage payments, and to avoid foreclosure of the mortgage, he agreed orally to sell the property to Weale. Weale secured a bank commitment to finance the purchase, paid an attorney $150 for examining the title and doing other legal work relating to the property, and spent $2,860 for a survey of the land. In the meantime, Cole learned of the proposed sale, visited the property, and saw the survey work. He then offered to purchase the land, and he and Sylvia signed a contract of sale. Weale and Cole brought separate actions against Sylvia for specific performance. In a single hearing, the trial court granted specific performance to Weale and ordered Cole to file a release of his recorded written purchase agreement. Cole appealed. Was Weale entitled to specific performance?

7 Emery, a farm owner, agreed in writing to sell landfill from his farm to the Caledonia Sand & Gravel Co., a road contractor. Under the written agreement, Caledonia was obliged to restore the excavation area "with the original topsoil . . . or with some other material capable of supporting vegetation, to fertilize and seed the pit area, and to clean up all areas disturbed by the operation to the owner's specifications." Emery was paid for the landfill, but he was dissatisfied with the restoration. He brought suit to recover damages for breach of the restoration agreement. In awarding damages to Emery, the trial court considered parol evidence relating to Emery's understanding that the land would be restored for use as a hayfield. The written agreement made no mention of the use of the land as a hayfield. Was the court in error in considering the parol evidence?

Chapter

17

Rights and Duties
of Third Persons

So far in the discussion of contracts, the emphasis has been on the relationship between contracting parties. A promises to work for B, and B promises to pay A an agreed wage. X promises to sell a new car to Y, and Y promises to pay X an agreed amount of money for it. In everyday life, however, business relationships can be much more complex, and contracts can be used in many different ways to accomplish a variety of business purposes. A might promise to work for B if B will pay an agreed amount of money to C, a "third-person beneficiary." X might promise to sell a car to Y on credit, intending to sell (to Z) Y's promise to pay the agreed amount. The sale to Z of Y's promise to pay is a type of "assignment" of contract rights.

In this chapter, we turn to contracts involving third persons. The first part of the chapter deals with *third-person beneficiary contracts* (sometimes inaccurately referred to as "third-party contracts"). The second and third parts of the chapter deal with the *assignment of contract rights* and the *delegation of contract duties*.

THIRD-PERSON
BENEFICIARY CONTRACTS

Under English law, a person could not sue on a contract unless he or she was one of the contracting parties, that is, either the promisor or the promisee. A mere contract beneficiary had no enforceable rights.[1]

At first, the American courts adopted the English view without much question as to its soundness. But they soon began to break away from the English view. The break finally came in 1859 with the famous case of *Lawrence v.*

---

[1]John Edward Murray, Jr., *Murray on Contracts*, The Bobbs-Merrill Company, Indianapolis, 1974, secs. 276 and 277.

Fox.[2] Defendant Fox had borrowed $300 from a Mr. Holly on the promise to repay the money to Holly's creditor, Lawrence. Fox did not pay, and Lawrence sued. The trial court gave judgment to the plaintiff, and the New York Court of Appeals affirmed the judgment. Courts in other states followed the lead of the New York court in holding that where a promise is "made for the benefit of another, he for whose benefit it is made may bring an action for its breach." Eventually a judicial and statutory trend developed in this country toward recognizing the rights of third-person beneficiaries.[3] Today, most jurisdictions, but not all, recognize such rights.

Who Is a Third-Person Beneficiary?

The performance of a contract may benefit people who have no connection with it and whom the contracting parties had no intention of benefiting. Suppose, for example, that A contracts with B to tear down a disreputable

[2]20 N.Y. 268.
[3]Murray, op. cit., sec. 278.

tenement house owned by B and to build in its place a beautiful apartment building. The contract, if carried out, may well enhance the value of all properties in the neighborhood. In a sense, the owners of these properties are beneficiaries of the contract between A and B, but at best they are merely "incidental beneficiaries," and as such have no rights in the contract. They are not included in the term "third-person beneficiary" as that term is used in this chapter.

To be a third-person beneficiary, the third person must be the intended beneficiary or one of the intended beneficiaries of the promised performance. It is not essential that third-person beneficiaries be identified by name, or even that their identity be known at the date of the agreement. It suffices if the beneficiary or beneficiaries can be identified at the time the performance is due. Thus, a promise by A to pay the claims of all such persons who may be creditors of B at some specified future date sufficiently describes the intended beneficiaries.

In Figure 17.1, A is the promisor, B is the promisee, and T is the third-person beneficiary.

Figure 17.1 Third-Person Beneficiary Contract

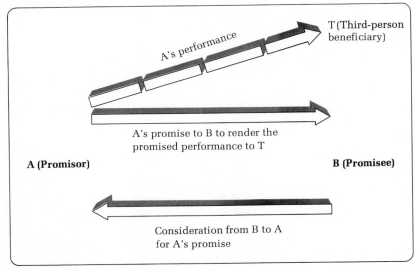

A's performance

T (Third-person beneficiary)

A's promise to B to render the promised performance to T

A (Promisor)

B (Promisee)

Consideration from B to A for A's promise

Case 17.1   **Schell v. Knickelbein**
252 N.W.2d 921 (Wis. 1977)

Mark and Barbara Knickelbein made mortgage payments on their home to Security Savings & Loan Association (Security). The mortgage payments included monthly amounts to cover a homeowners insurance policy, allegedly to be procured by Security on behalf of the Knickelbeins. In 1971, insurance coverage was terminated, allegedly as a result of Security's failure to make the premium payment in accordance with its agreements.

In 1974, Mr. Schell was attacked by a dog owned by the Knickelbeins. Mr. Schell died, and Mrs. Schell (plaintiff) sued the Knickelbeins for negligence, alleging that her husband's death resulted from injuries he received in the attack. In the same action, Mrs. Schell sued Security, alleging that she was a third-party beneficiary of the mortgage contract between the Knickelbeins and Security. The trial court overruled Security's demurrer, and Security appealed.

HANSEN, J. . . . A third party cannot maintain an action as a third party beneficiary if under the contract his was only an "indirect benefit, merely incidental to the contract between the parties." [Citation.] The third party's complaint must allege facts to show that the agreement was entered primarily and directly for his benefit. . . .

In the instant case, the only contract provisions alleged in the second amended complaint are the Knickelbeins' agreement to pay Security money adequate to provide insurance and Security's responsibility to pay the insurance company the premium. The . . . complaint does not allege enough of the contract to show what kind of insurance the parties contemplated. The mortgage contract may have only called for fire and extended coverage insurance that would protect Security's interest in the real estate and the mortgage. The complaint does not allege enough of the contract to show whether Security and the Knickelbeins contemplated securing liability insurance that would protect third parties against the Knickelbeins' negligence. Thus, the complaint does not allege enough of the contract to show that Security and the Knickelbeins entered the agreement for the benefit of Schell or others of her class. Having failed to show that, Schell has failed to allege facts sufficient to maintain an action as a third party beneficiary.

Arguing that as a third party beneficiary she can maintain a direct action against a party who breached a contract to secure insurance, Schell cites three cases from other jurisdictions. . . . However, these cases are distinguishable. In each case the defendant agreed to procure automobile liability insurance which would have paid damages to the plaintiffs, the injured third parties. The Illinois and New Jersey courts reasoned that in entering the agreements to procure the liability insurance, the car owners contemplated, among other things, possible injury to third parties, and the insurance coverage was for the direct benefit of the injured third parties. The rationale of these cases cannot be applied to the instant case because, as noted above, the complaint does not allege enough of the contract to show that Security and the Knickelbeins contemplated securing liability insurance. . . .

Order reversed and cause remanded for further proceedings consistent with this opinion. [Mrs. Schell was given leave to file another amended complaint.]

Types of Third-Person Beneficiary Contracts

There are two types of intended third-person beneficiaries—donee and creditor—and consequently two types of third-person beneficiary contracts. In both types of contracts, the promisee intends a third person to get the benefit of the promised performance. The difference in the two types is the purpose which the promisee has in obtaining the promise to render performance to the third person.

Third-Person Donee Beneficiary Contract

Where the purpose of the promisee in obtaining the promise is to make a gift of the promised performance to the third person, the contract is a third-person donee beneficiary contract. Life insurance provides an example. Suppose that B insures his life with A, a Life Insurance Company, and designates his wife as the beneficiary of the policy. The wife is a third-person beneficiary because performance is to be rendered to her rather than to the husband-promisee. She is a donee beneficiary because the purpose of the husband-promisee was to confer a gift upon her.

Third-Person Creditor Beneficiary Contract

Where the purpose of the promisee in requiring performance to be rendered to a third person is to fulfill a legal obligation which the promisee owes to the third person, the contract is a third-person creditor beneficiary contract. The case of *Lawrence v. Fox*, summarized on p. 313, involved a creditor beneficiary. Holly's purpose in securing Fox's promise to pay Lawrence was to fulfill a legal obligation owed by Holly to Lawrence. Other common examples of creditor beneficiary contracts are the so-called "assump-

tion contracts." Suppose that B purchases A's home, that there is a mortgage on the home, and that as part of the purchase price B agrees to assume the mortgage (that is, to pay off the mortgage debt owed by A). Or suppose that B purchases A's business and that as part of the purchase price B agrees to pay off the firm's creditors. The mortgagee (A's creditor) in the one situation and the firm's creditors in the other are third-person creditor beneficiaries of the assumption contract between A and B.

Justification for Recognizing Rights of Beneficiaries

There is a sound reason for allowing a donee beneficiary to enforce the contract. Only the beneficiary can do so effectively. The promisee has intended to confer a substantial benefit (a gift) upon the beneficiary and not to obtain personal benefit. Therefore, where the promisor breaches the contract, the promisee (who has personally suffered no substantial injury) would be entitled only to nominal damages and to restitution of any consideration given. Unless the beneficiary has a right of enforcement, the purpose of the promisee would be defeated. Whole industries could be adversely affected. Life insurance contracts, for example, would be of doubtful value if surviving beneficiaries could not enforce them.

Unlike a donee beneficiary, a creditor beneficiary has a contract with the debtor-promisee and certain rights of enforcement. The process of enforcement, however, may be cumbersome and may result in unnecessary litigation. Why require a creditor beneficiary to sue the promisee and the promisee to sue the promisor if the same result could be achieved by allowing the beneficiary to sue the promisor directly? Most states group donee and creditor beneficiaries under the heading of "intended beneficiaries" and allow an intended beneficiary to sue a promisor directly for breach of the promise to render a performance to the beneficiary. Of course, the beneficiary has no right of recovery for breach of contract if the promisor has a good defense to the suit. The question then becomes: What defenses against the beneficiary are available to the promisor?

Promisor's Defenses against the Beneficiary

Upon the vesting (establishment) of a beneficiary's rights, the beneficiary acquires a cause of action against the promisor for breach of the beneficial promise, and the promisor may assert any available defense. The general rule is that the promisor may assert any defense against the beneficiary that the promisor could assert against the promisee if the promisee were doing the suing (e.g., fraud, mistake, absence of mutual assent or consideration, lack of capacity, and the like).

When do the rights of a beneficiary vest? One view is that of the *Restatement:* The rights of the beneficiary vest when he or she "brings suit on the contract" or "materially changes his position in justifiable reliance on the promise."[4] A second view is that the beneficiary's rights vest when the contract is made. This view would be applied in those infrequent situations involving a life insurance policy under which the insured person has no right to change the beneficiary. An insured person has no such right unless he or she has specifically reserved it in the policy. However, the vast majority of life insurance policies contain a standard form clause that *does* specifically reserve to the insured person the right to change the beneficiary. Where the

insured person may change the beneficiary, the beneficiary's rights do not vest until the death of the insured person. Until that time the beneficiary has a "mere expectancy" and no rights under the policy to vest.

ASSIGNMENT OF CONTRACT RIGHTS

Business firms and others often sell goods or services on credit and need to convert into immediate cash or credit their customers' promises to pay. Or a creditor might wish to make a gift of his or her debtor's obligation. Whether the creditor's objective is to obtain financing or to make a gift, the creditor may decide to do so by transferring the debtor's promise to pay. Such a transfer is called an "assignment" of the creditor's contract right against the debtor.

Nature of Assignment

In early English history few kinds of contracts were enforced, and those which were enforced involved formal documents and the transfer of physical objects. The transfer of intangibles such as a contract right was difficult to imagine. As trade and commerce developed, so did the need to raise capital by transferring (assigning) contract rights. The English Chancellor met the need by developing a set of principles which made the transfer of contract rights enforceable in courts of equity. Later, the courts of common law adopted nearly all these principles. The English principles or rules were adopted with some variations in the United States and formed the basis for our contemporary law of assignments.

Meaning of Assignment An *assignment* is a manifestation of intention by the owner of an existing right (often a contract right) to make a *present transfer* of the right. The person who transfers or "assigns" the right is the "assignor." Since the right in a contract situation consists of a promise made to the assignor, the assignor may also be called the "promisee" or "obligee"

---

[4]*Restatement of the Law (Second) Contracts,* American Law Institute, Philadelphia, 1973, sec. 142(3).

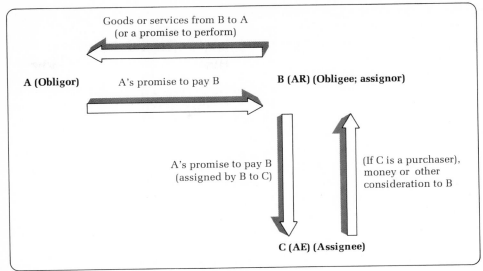

Figure 17.2 Assignment of Contract Rights

or "creditor." The person to whom the right is assigned is the "assignee." As used in this chapter, "transfer" means the extinguishment of the assignor's right to the obligor's performance and the acquisition of a right to such performance by the assignee. Some attempts to make an assignment are legally ineffective. Consequently, courts sometimes distinguish between "attempted" or "purported" assignments and "effective" assignments.

Figure 17.2 illustrates an assignment of a contract right. In that figure, B sells goods or services to A on credit; and A (the obligor)

promises to pay B in the future, perhaps by making installment payments. At this point, B has a contract right against A, but no cash. In order to raise immediate cash, B assigns to C the obligor's promise to pay; and in exchange for the assignor's promise, C (the assignee) gives money (or other consideration) to B. Thus in Figure 17.2, the assignee is a purchaser of the assigned right. If B had made a gift to C of the assigned right, there would of course be no arrow representing movement of consideration from C to B.

Case 17.2   **Factors Etc., Inc. v. Creative Card Co.**
444 F. Supp. 279 (S.D. N.Y. 1977)

Soon after the death of Elvis Presley in 1977, Factors Etc., Inc., and Boxcar Enterprises, Inc., plaintiffs, sought a preliminary injunction to restrain defendant Creative Card Co. from the manufacture, distribution, and sale of any poster or other commercially exploitive souvenir merchandise bearing the likeness of the late entertainer. The plaintiffs alleged that during his life Presley assigned to Boxcar a "right of publicity" which gave Boxcar the exclusive right to promote the Presley likeness.

Two days after Presley's death, Boxcar entered into an agreement which purported to grant to Factors an exclusive license to use the Presley likeness. The defendant contended that Boxcar never acquired the exclusive right to merchandise the Presley name and image and that if Boxcar did have such a right in Presley's lifetime, the right died with the entertainer. In granting the injunction, the court discussed the nature of the "right of publicity."

TENNEY, J. . . . By far the most interesting issue in this case is whether Boxcar had anything to transfer to Factors when it entered into the . . . "exclusive licensing" contract. After consulting the case law and certain commentaries in this field, I have concluded that it did. It appears that a recognized property right, the "right of publicity," inhered in and was exercised by Elvis Presley in his lifetime, that it was assignable by him and was so assigned, that it survived his death and was capable of further assignment.

The "right of publicity" is not a new concept, but, to the detriment of legal clarity, it has often been discussed only under the rubric, "right of privacy." It is said that the right of privacy embraces "four distinct kinds of invasion of four different interests of the plaintiff. . . . Dean Prosser recognized that the fourth species of right of privacy tort, i.e., the appropriation of plaintiff's name or likeness for defendant's benefit, is distinct from "intrusion upon the plaintiff's physical solitude or seclusion," "public disclosure of private facts," or "false light in the public eye," in that "appropriation" is the only one which "involves a use for the defendant's advantage." However, Prosser has failed to discuss the fact that appropriation of plaintiff's name and likeness for defendant's financial advantage has different consequences in a case where the celebrity himself has attempted to commercialize his own name and face. It is evident that courts address intrusions on feelings, reputation and privacy only when an individual has elected not to engage in personal commercialization. By contrast, when a "persona" is in effect a product, and when that product has already been marketed to good advantage, the appropriation by another of that valuable property has more to do with unfair competition than it does with the right to be left alone. . . .

This circuit was in the vanguard in recognizing the right of publicity and its assignability. . . . *Price v. Hal Roach Studios, Inc.*, 400 F. Supp. 836 (S.D. N.Y. 1975) . . . is particularly interesting because it is the only reported decision known to this Court where the right of publicity was deemed descendible [inheritable]. In that case the widows of Stan Laurel and Oliver Hardy and another party claiming the right to exploit the Laurel and Hardy image through merchandise sued to restrain defendants from infringing on that right. Plaintiffs set up the exclusivity of a prior contract covering commercial merchandise which had been entered into by Stan Laurel, Hardy's widow, and the plaintiff licensee. Although there was no evidence to show that the comedians had ever exploited their own personalities through merchandising efforts, the *Price* court, relying on the distinction between a personal right of privacy which is extinguished at death and a valuable, alienable property right in name and image, i.e., the "right of publicity," asked "what policy should operate to cut off this [latter] right at death?" The *Price* court could find none, and on the much stronger facts here presented, this Court adopts that view. There is no reason why the valuable right of publicity—*clearly exercised by and financially benefiting Elvis Presley in life*—should not descend at death like any other intangible property right.

. . . Defendant . . . will be enjoined. . . .

Requirements for Assignment The general rule is that, in the absence of a statute to the contrary, an assignment may be made in any form. Any act or statement, written or oral, indicating an intention to make a present transfer is sufficient. However, statutes in nearly every state require a writing, and sometimes even witnesses or a notary's seal, for the assignment of certain kinds of rights. Common illustrations are statutes regulating the form of assignments of wage claims or corporate shares.

Consideration is not a requirement for an assignment. But courts do not regard a *gift assignment* as having been made until the intended donee of the contract right secures a substantial measure of control over it. If the claim is embodied in or represented by a document, such as a life insurance policy or a bank savings account book, the gift may be accomplished by the surrender of the document.

Until the obligor (A in Figure 17.2) receives *notice* of assignment, the obligor owes no duty to the assignee. Until then, the obligor's only duty is to the assignor-obligee. Upon receipt of notice, the obligor must render performance to the assignee and not to the assignor, unless the assignor has been authorized by the assignee to receive payment for the assignee. Commercial assignees often do find it expedient to authorize assignors to collect assigned customer accounts on behalf of the assignees. But an obligor without notice of assignment cannot be required to pay twice.

Legal Position of the Assignee It is often said that an assignee stands in the shoes of the assignor. The statement means two things:

1 The assignee succeeds to any rights that the assignor may have had at the time of the assignment. These rights include any right of performance (usually, any right to payment) that the assignor had and any other right that the assignor might have had, such as priority of payment in the event of the obligor's insolvency.

2 As illustrated by Case 17.3, the assignee takes the assigned rights subject to defenses of the obligor. The obligor (A) may assert against the assignee any defense which the obligor could have asserted against the assignor (B) (illegality of the contract, failure of consideration which B was supposed to give for A's promise, fraud by B, A's infancy, etc.). The obligor may also assert any defense arising out of a fact which occurred after the assignment was made but before the obligor received notice of the assignment. Examples of such defenses are payment by the obligor, release by the obligee, and mutual modification or rescission of the contract.

Sometimes an obligor receives notice of assignment, and then the obligor and the obligee modify the contract. Under common law principles the assignee's rights are not affected by the modification. However, Article 9 of the Uniform Commercial Code changes the rule for certain security assignments of contract rights not yet fully earned by performance:

"Notwithstanding notification [of assignment], modification of or substitution for the contract made in good faith and in accordance with reasonable commercial standards is effective against an assignee . . . but the assignee acquires corresponding rights under the modified or substituted contract."[5]

Suppose, for example, that A, a corporation, hires B, a construction company, to build a large factory for A. B then hires dozens of subcontractors to complete various parts of the construction project, and the subcontractors, in turn, hire sub-subcontractors. To raise money so that they can procure labor and materials necessary for completing their parts of the project, B and the subcontractors assign their rights to future payments to lenders as collateral for construction loans. The assignees notify A of the assignments and make construction loans to the assignors. Then, because certain kinds of building materials become unavailable, A and B redesign the factory building. The new design results in a 10 percent lower cost for the factory, and all contracts are modified to reflect a 10 percent reduction in payments. Under UCC Section 9-318(2), the reduction of payments is effective against the assignees without their consent. This UCC departure from the common law rule "is a sound and indeed a necessary rule in view of the realities of large scale procurement"[6] where there may be a need to modify hundreds or even thousands of financing arrangements at one time. By use of "termination for convenience" clauses in government contracts, the federal government accomplishes the same result. The subject of contracting with the government is discussed in Chapter 19.

---

[5]UCC sec. 9-318(2).

[6]UCC sec. 9-318, comment 2.

Case 17.3   Chimney Hill Owners' Association, Inc. v. Eastern Woodworking Co.
392 A.2d 423 (Vt. 1978)

Chimney Hill is a recreational second-home development consisting of more than 900 lots and a large area of "common land" containing a clubhouse, indoor and outdoor swimming pools, three tennis courts, 18 miles of roads, and a private underground water system which serves the community. Most owners in the development purchased only one lot. However, approximately 30 owners, including Eastern Woodworking Company (defendant), hold multiple lots in Chimney Hill.

A Declaration of Protective Covenants, Restrictions, and Reservations pertaining to Chimney Hill was executed by Chimney Hill Corporation and recorded in the local Town Clerk's office. Paragraph 10 of the Declaration states that an annual charge shall be assessed against each lot in Chimney Hill and paid "to the grantor, its successors and assigns" for the right to use the common lands and related facilities. Paragraph 10 also states that:

> "This charge shall run with and bind the land . . . and shall be binding upon the grantee or grantees [and] his, her, their, or its heirs, . . . successors and assigns, until May 31, 1988, unless earlier terminated by written release of the grantor, its successors or assigns."

Defendant Eastern purchased eleven lots in 1968. The purchase agreement signed by Eastern and by the president of Chimney Hill Corporation states,

"There will be one annual charge . . . until one or more of the lots have been improved." In 1975, Chimney Hill Corporation conveyed the common land to the Chimney Hill Owners' Association, Inc. (plaintiff). The Association then billed defendant for the annual charge for each of defendant's eleven lots. Defendant paid only one assessment, and the Association brought suit to collect the rest allegedly owed. The trial court awarded judgment to defendant, and plaintiff appealed.

HILL, J. . . . The trial court . . . concluded that Chimney Hill Corporation released Eastern from any obligation to pay on ten of its lots, as long as the lots remained unimproved, by virtue of the language in its sales agreement specifying one annual charge. . . . Finally, the court concluded that these defenses of release and waiver were available and binding on Chimney Hill Corporation's assignee, the plaintiff. . . .

The plaintiff . . . seeks to recover the assessments . . . under the assignment from Chimney Hill Corporation. In the assignment, the Corporation assigned to the plaintiff the right to collect from each owner in Chimney Hill the annual charge provided for in Paragraph 10 of the Declarations. As assignee, however, the plaintiff takes the right to collect subject to all defenses of the obligor against the assignor. . . .

A waiver is the intentional relinquishment or abandonment of a known right and may be evidenced by express words as well as by conduct. A waiver of a covenant may be made . . . by the party for whose benefit it was inserted. . . . The assessment covenant was for the benefit of Chimney Hill Corporation, its successors and assigns, as owner of the common lands, and therefore it was waivable by the corporation during the period it owned the common lands. . . .

As to defendant Eastern, the trial court concluded that defendant possessed a valid release from Chimney Hill Corporation concerning the ten unimproved lots, which was a valid defense to the plaintiff's claim. Paragraph 10(E) of the Declarations reserves to the grantor, Chimney Hill Corporation, its successors and assigns, the right to terminate the annual charge on any of the lots. Eastern's sales agreement, executed by both Eastern and Chimney Hill Corporation, provides that one annual charge only will be assessed on Eastern's eleven lots until one or more have been improved. The sales agreement contains . . . the release contemplated by Paragraph 10(E). . . .

The judgment in favor of Eastern must be affirmed.

Effect of Waiver-of-Defenses Clause Contract forms often contain a clause under which the obligor-buyer "agrees" not to assert against an assignee of the obligee-seller any claim or defense which the obligor may have against the seller. If enforceable, such a provision (called a *waiver-of-defenses clause*) would require the obligor to make payment to the assignee despite a defective performance or other misconduct by the assignor. For any redress, the obligor would have to seek out the seller-assignor, who might be insolvent, recalcitrant, or unavailable for suit.

Case law is in a state of disagreement on the enforceability of waiver-of-defenses clauses. Some jurisdictions have enforced such clauses because they enhance the value of assigned rights. The value of such rights increases as the risk of noncollection decreases. Other jurisdictions have refused to enforce waiver-of-defenses clauses because such clauses often surprise buyers and leave them without effective remedies for defective performances. A recent rule of the Federal Trade Commission renders invalid waiver-of-defenses clauses in *consumer credit* transactions.[7] As to transactions not involving consumer credit, waiver-of-defenses clauses remain enforceable in some states.

Subject to "any statute or decision which establishes a different rule for buyers or lessors of consumer goods," Article 9, Section 9-206(1) of the UCC, makes a waiver-of-defenses clause enforceable as to some defenses, but not as to others. Thus, with regard to assertability of defenses, Article 9 treats a contract with a waiver-of-defenses clause much like a negotiable instrument. The law of negotiable instruments is discussed in Chapters 30 to 35.

Assignments Which Are Not Legally Effective

The law allows most types of contract rights to be assigned. However, to protect the obligor, the law does not recognize an assignment of contract rights where the transfer of the right "would materially change the duty of the obligor, or materially increase the burden or risk imposed upon him by his contract, or materially impair his chance of obtaining a return performance."[8] (The UCC Section

---

[7]*FTC Trade Regulation Rule*, Title 16, *Code of Federal Regulations*, Part 433 (amended and effective April 14, 1977).

[8]*Restatement (Second), Contracts*, sec. 149(2) (a).

2-210(2), relating to the assignment of rights in the sale and purchase of goods, contains language almost identical to that in the quoted passage.) Furthermore, there can be no effective assignment of contract rights where "the assignment is forbidden by statute or is otherwise against public policy," or where "assignment is validly precluded by contract."[9] Some of these situations are illustrated in the paragraphs which follow.

Assignments Materially Varying the Obligor's Duty or Risk The most obvious material change in an obligor's duty is a substantial variation in the nature or quantity of performance to be rendered. Suppose that A is under contract with B to paint B's portrait and that B attempts to assign her rights under the contract to C. Painting B's portrait is not the same as painting C's portrait. If assignment were permitted, the nature of A's performance would be changed. Or suppose that A, a small power company, is under contract to furnish B all the electric power it needs for its business, that B sells the business and attempts to assign to the purchaser the right against the electric company. If the purchaser's needs for power differed materially from B's, the assignment would not be effective unless A consented, because of the unexpected burden A would otherwise face.

Where the change in the duty of the obligor is only in slight and unimportant details, there can be an assignment without the obligor's consent. For example, if a sales contract requires the seller to deliver merchandise COD to the home of the purchaser, the purchaser can effectively assign his or her rights under the contract to a next-door neighbor. The assignment would require a change in the obligor's performance, but only in a slight and unimportant detail. On the other hand, if the assignee lived a considerable distance from the home of the assignor, the change in the seller's performance would be

---

[9]Ibid., sec. 149(2)(*b*) and (*c*).

substantial and the assignment would be ineffective.

Some rights are of such a nature that their transfer causes no substantial change in the obligor's performance. A common example is the right of a creditor to receive payment of money for a completed performance. All that remains is for the obligor to pay, and under the law it can make no difference to the obligor which party receives payment—the creditor, or the creditor's assignee.

An assignor may not unilaterally increase the risk of the obligor. Suppose that B's house is insured by A, a fire insurance company, and that B sells the house to C and assigns the fire insurance policy to her. The assignment is ineffective unless A consents. Presumably one of the risk factors upon which insurance companies base their policies is the safety record of the insured. Allowing insured persons to assign a policy without the consent of the insurer could result in increasing the insurer's risks and in impairing the insurer's ability to insure effectively.

Assignments Forbidden by Statute or Public Policy Federal and state statutes prohibit the assignment of certain types of claims, and regulate the assignment of certain other types. For example, a federal statute makes assignment of claims against the federal government void except where a claim has already been allowed and a federal Treasury warrant for the payment has been issued. This statute serves to minimize litigation against the government. Most states have statutes prohibiting the assignment of future wages and regulating in amount and method the assignment of earned wages, veterans compensation, old age and disability payments, and the like. These statutes tend to protect lower-income families from pressures to commit their incomes far in advance of receipt. An assignment which violates public policy as determined by a court is illegal, even in the absence of a statute prohibiting such an assignment.

Assignment Prohibited by Contract A contract might contain a "nonassignability" clause purporting to prohibit the assignment of rights under the contract. In deciding whether to enforce such a clause, the courts consider the principle of freedom of contract (which would support enforcing the clause) and the policy of free alienation (transfer) of property (which might justify invalidating the clause).

Modern courts recognize that assignments facilitate business transactions. Therefore, wherever possible, the courts will interpret a contract stipulation not to assign as merely a promise not to assign, rather than as an absolute prohibition of assignment. Suppose that A and B stipulate that "neither party shall assign his or her rights under this contract." Most courts interpret such language as a promise not to assign. Under that interpretation, the assignor may be liable for breach of the stipulation, but effective assignment is possible and business activities which depend on effective assignments are not unduly hampered.

In contrast, a stipulation that "no assignment of rights arising under this agreement shall be valid" is too clearly a prohibition of assignment to be interpreted as a promise not to assign. Such a clear prohibition of assignment will be enforced unless the prohibition is against public policy or is otherwise illegal. Many courts consider some prohibitions of assignment to be illegal restraints on alienation and, as such, against public policy. These courts will invalidate, for example, clauses prohibiting the assignment of money claims (including established claims under life insurance policies) and clauses prohibiting the assignment of rights under contracts for the purchase of real estate.

Successive (Dual) Assignments

Sometimes, through mistake, negligence, or dishonesty, a person sells the same claim to two (or more) assignees. Which of the assignees has priority? The majority rule in the United States (the "American rule") is that as between successive assignees of the same right, the first in time has priority. The logic behind the rule is that when an effective assignment is made, the assignor has no further rights which could be subject to a second assignment.

The majority rule is subject to some exceptions. For example, a subsequent assignee prevails where the prior assignee negligently failed to take possession of the documentary evidence of the assignment and thus enabled the assignor to transfer the document to a second assignee. Also, it should be noted that where the first assignment is revocable or voidable, as where a gift has been promised but not delivered, the second assignment is a manifestation of an intent to revoke or avoid, and the second assignee therefore has priority.[10]

The minority American rule (the "English rule") is that the assignee who first notifies the debtor of the assignment has priority. This rule encourages potential assignees to inquire of debtors as to the existence of rival claimants and to take prompt action in notifying debtors of assignments. Assignments of accounts covered by Article 9, Section 9-312(5), of the UCC are subject to a similar "first-to-file" rule of priority. Thus, the so-called minority rule is of considerable importance in the law of assignments.

Partial Assignments

Sometimes a creditor sells only a part of a claim to one assignee and later sells the rest of the claim to another assignee. For example, A owes B $1,000, and B assigns $600 of the claim to AE1 (partial assignee No. 1) and $400 to AE2 (partial assignee No. 2).

Partial assignments are effective subject to the limitation that if the obligor has not contracted to perform separately or has not subsequently consented to do so, no legal proceeding can be maintained against the obligor unless *all* persons entitled to the promised performances

are joined in (made plaintiffs in) the proceeding.[11] AE1 could not sue without joining AE2 in the action, and vice versa. If either of them refused to join in the action, that person could be brought into the proceeding (by the other partial assignee) by being named a party defendant along with the obligor (A). If B had assigned only a part of the claim and kept the rest for himself, he and the assignee would have to join in any legal action to collect the $1,000 from the obligor.

Warranties of the Assignor

Suppose that an assignee tries to collect payment from the obligor but is met with a valid defense. What recourse has the assignee against the assignor? Where an assignment is made for value, the assignor impliedly warrants that:

1 The right assigned actually exists.

2 It is subject to no limitations or defenses other than those stated or apparent at the time of the assignment.

3 The assignor will do nothing to defeat or impair the value of the assignment.

An assignment of a supposed but nonexisting claim is a breach of the first warranty listed above. Assignment of a claim that is subject to the defense of fraud is a breach of the second warranty. The unauthorized collection of the debt by the assignor is a breach of the third warranty.

It will be noted that the list of implied warranties does not include a warranty of the solvency of the debtor. If the assignee is unwilling to assume the risk of the debtor-obligor's nonperformance, he or she should require the assignor to make an express warranty of performance. Where the assignor receives consideration for such a warranty, the assignor will be

---

[10]Ibid., sec. 174, comment *d*.

[11]Ibid., sec. 158(2).

liable to the assignee for failure of the obligor to perform.

DELEGATION OF CONTRACT DUTIES

As we have seen, business people use assignments as a means of converting contract rights that are not yet due into immediate cash or credit. In addition, sometimes business people need to procure a substitute to perform a contractual duty. One way to provide for a substitute performance is to find a person willing to accept a "delegation" of the contractual duty. A delegation of a duty often occurs in conjunction with an assignment of a right.

Meaning of Delegation

There is a fundamental difference between assignment and delegation. An *assignment* is a transfer that, if effective, terminates the assignor's interest in the right that was transferred.

Because the assignor's interest terminates, the assignee acquires the right free from any claim of ownership by the assignor.

Duties are another matter. It is a policy of the law that a person who undertakes a duty should not be able to put it aside casually. A party to a contract is expected to perform the duty or to be responsible for its performance. Because assignment implies a cessation of responsibility, duties may not be assigned without the consent of the other party to the contract. Duties may only be delegated. *Delegation* means no more than that a person under a duty of performance authorizes another person to render the required performance. The person who delegates the duty is often called the *delegator*, and the person to whom the duty is delegated is called the *delegatee*. The delegator (B in Figure 17.3), remains liable to the contract obligee (A, the person entitled to the delegator's performance) for any failure of the delegatee (C) to perform. The delegator will be released from liability to A

Figure 17.3 Assignment of Rights and Delegation of Duties

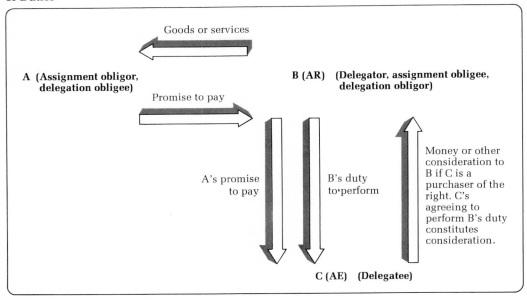

only if A consents to the release. (An arrangement totally releasing the delegator from liability is called a *novation*.)

Figure 17.3 illustrates an assignment of a contract right and a delegation of the assignor's duty of performance. Note that Figure 17.3 is a modification of Figure 17.2 and that for the purposes of delegation, *B* is the obligor and A is the obligee.

Case 17.4   Contemporary Mission, Inc. v. Famous Music Corp.
557 F.2d 918 (2d Cir. 1977)

Contemporary Mission, Inc. (Contemporary), a group of Roman Catholic priests who write, produce, and publish musical compositions and recordings, owned all the rights to a rock opera entitled *Virgin*. In 1972, Contemporary entered a contract with Famous Music Corporation (Famous) in which Famous agreed to manufacture, promote, and sell records made from the master-tape recording of *Virgin*. Tony Martell, the president of Famous, had successfully distributed the rock operas *Tommy* and *Jesus Christ Superstar*.

The following year, Contemporary entered another contract with Famous for the distribution of recordings of musical compositions other than *Virgin*. This contract was called the Crunch Agreement. In 1974, Famous's record division was sold to ABC-Dunhill Record Corporation (ABC Records). Contemporary was told that it would have to look to ABC Records for performance of the contracts. ABC Records refused to perform the contracts, and Contemporary sought to hold Famous liable for breach of contract. The trial court rendered judgment for Contemporary, and Famous appealed. The following excerpts from the appellate opinion pertain only to the Crunch Agreement.

MESKILL, Cir. J. . . . . There is no dispute that the sale of Famous's record division to ABC constituted an assignment of the Crunch agreement to ABC. The assignment of a bilateral contract includes both an assignment of rights and a delegation of duties. The distinction between the two is important.

> "Perhaps more frequently than is the case with other terms of art, lawyers seem prone to use the word "assignment" inartfully, frequently intending to encompass within the term the distinct [concept] of delegation. . . . An assignment involves the transfer of rights. A delegation involves the appointment of another to perform one's duties." J. Calamari & J. Perillo, Contracts sec. 254 (1970).

Famous's arguments with respect to the Crunch agreement ignore this basic distinction, and the result is a distortion of several fundamental principles of contract law.

It is true, of course, as a general rule, that when rights are assigned, the assignor's interest in the rights assigned comes to an end. When duties are delegated, however, the [delegator's] obligation does not end.

> "One who owes money or is bound to any performance whatever cannot

by any act of his own, or by any act in agreement with any other person, except his creditor, divest himself of the duty and substitute the duty of another. . . . This is sufficiently obvious when attention is called to it, for otherwise obligors would find an easy practical way of escaping their obligations." 3 Williston on Contracts sec. 411 (3d ed. 1960).

This is not to say that one may not delegate his obligations. In fact, most obligations can be delegated—as long as performance by the [delegatee] will not vary materially from performance by the [delegator]. The act of delegation, however, does not relieve the [delegator] of the ultimate responsibility to see that the obligation is performed. If the [delegatee] fails to perform, the [delegator] remains liable. . . .

The judgment of the district court is affirmed in all respects except as to its ruling with regard to lost royalties, and the case is remanded to the district court for further proceedings in accordance with this opinion.

Delegable and Nondelegable Duties

Suppose that Bill Brown (B) contracts to render a performance to Alice Allen (A) and that A and B say nothing about delegation. Whether B may delegate his duty to perform may depend on whether a court will characterize the duty as delegable or nondelegable.

The general rule is that a duty may be delegated where performance by the delegatee would be substantially the same to the obligee as would performance by the delegator. Common illustrations of duties which may normally be delegated are the duty to:

• Pay money
• Deliver standard merchandise
• Manufacture ordinary goods
• Build according to a set of plans and specifications (as where a contractor delegates to a subcontractor the installation of electric fixtures)

In contrast, a duty is nondelegable if its performance requires a unique ability or the personal attention of the would-be delegator. Common illustrations of duties which may *not* be delegated (without the consent of the obligee) are the duty to:

• Support a relative
• Provide professional services
• Farm "on shares" (tenant shares output of farm with landlord)
• Represent another as an exclusive sales agent
• Manufacture a special class of high-quality goods
• Render personal services to an employer

For the protection of obligees, the courts enforce contract clauses which forbid the delegation of duties, and this is so even where a duty would otherwise be delegable. Some delegations are forbidden by law, usually because the performance, if delegated, would vary materially from that contracted for.

Case 17.5   Macke Co. v. Pizza of Gaithersburg, Inc.
270 A.2d 645 (Md. 1970)

The defendant Pizza Shops, retail outlets under common ownership, contracted with Virginia Coffee Services, Inc. (Virginia), to have cold-drink vending machines installed in each of their six locations. The machines were owned and serviced by Virginia.

In 1967, The Macke Company (Macke) purchased the assets of Virginia, and Virginia assigned the six vending machine contracts to Macke. The Pizza Shops attempted to terminate the contracts, and Macke brought suit against each of the shops for breach of contract. The court rendered judgment for the defendants, and Macke appealed.

SINGLEY, J. . . . In the absence of a contrary provision—and there was none here—rights and duties under an executory bilateral contract may be assigned and delegated, subject to the exception that duties under a contract to provide personal services may never be delegated, nor [may] rights be assigned, under a contract where *delectus personae* ["choice of the person"] was an ingredient of the bargain. *Crane Ice Cream Co. v. Terminal Freezing & Heating Co.*, 147 Md. 588, 128 A. 280 (1925) held that the right of an individual to purchase ice under a contract which by its terms reflected a knowledge of the individual's needs and reliance on his credit and responsibility could not be assigned to the corporation which purchased his business. [In another case] our predecessors held that an advertising agency could not delegate its duties under a contract which had been entered into by an advertiser who had relied on the agency's skill, judgment and taste.

The six machines were placed on the appellees' premises under a printed "Agreement-Contract." . . . We cannot regard the agreements as contracts for personal services. They were either a license or concession granted Virginia by the appellees, or a lease of a portion of the appellees' premises, with Virginia agreeing to pay a percentage of gross sales as a license or concession fee or as rent, and were assignable by Virginia unless they imposed on Virginia duties of a personal or unique character which could not be delegated.

The appellees earnestly argue that they had dealt with Macke before and had chosen Virginia because they preferred the way it conducted its business. Specifically, they say that service was more personalized, since the president of Virginia kept the machines in working order, that commissions were paid in cash, and that Virginia permitted them to keep keys to the machines so that minor adjustments could be made when needed. Even if we assume all this to be true, the agreements with Virginia were silent as to the details of the working arrangements and contained only a provision requiring Virginia to "install . . . the above listed equipment and . . . maintain the equipment in good operating order and stocked with merchandise."

We think the Supreme Court of California put the problem of personal service in proper focus a century ago when it upheld the assignment of a contract to grade a San Francisco street:

"All painters do not paint portraits like Sir Joshua Reynolds, nor landscapes like Claude Lorraine, nor do all writers write dramas like Shakespeare or fiction like Dickens. Rare genius and extraordinary skill are not transferable, and contracts for their employment are therefore personal, and cannot be assigned. But rare genius and extraordinary skill are not indispensable to the workmanlike digging down of a sand hill or the filling up of a depression to a given level, or the construction of brick sewers with manholes and covers, and contracts for such work are not personal, and may be assigned." *Taylor v. Palmer*, 31 Cal. 240 at 247 (1866).

. . . [T]he difference between the service the Pizza Shops happened to be getting from Virginia and what they expected to get from Macke did not mount up to such a material change in the performance of obligations under the agreements as would justify the appellees' refusal to recognize the assignment. . . . Modern authorities . . . hold that, absent provision to the contrary, a duty may be delegated, . . . and that the promisee cannot rescind, if the quality of the performance remains materially the same. [Citations.]

Judgment reversed. . . .

"Assignment of the Contract"

Contracts sometimes contain a clause prohibiting the assignment of "this contract." The phrase is ambiguous. Did the parties intend to prohibit the assignment of rights or to prohibit the delegation of duties or to prohibit both? The common law rule is that unless circumstances indicate the contrary, a prohibition of assignment of "the contract" or "this contract" is to be construed as barring only the delegation of the assignor's duty of performance. This rule has been adopted by Section 2-210(3) of the UCC and is consistent with the policy that rights should be freely transferrable, but duties should not be.

The phrase, "the contract" or "this contract," is similarly ambiguous when used *in* an assignment. Suppose that on the back of a written contract one of the parties writes "For value received, I assign this contract to Richard Roe. (Signed) John Doe" and that he thereupon hands the written contract to Roe. The courts are not agreed as to whether such language effects both an assignment of rights and a delegation of duties. The Code has resolved the difficulty as far as contracts for the sale of goods are concerned:

"An assignment of 'the contract' or of 'all my rights under the contract' or an assignment in similar general terms is an assignment of rights and, unless the language or the circumstances [as in an assignment for the purpose of securing payment of a debt] indicate the contrary, it is a delegation of performance of the duties of the assignor, and its acceptance by the assignee constitutes a promise by him to perform those duties." (UCC Section 2-210(4). Comment 7 states that the section "is not intended as a complete statement of the law of delegation and assignment but is limited to clarifying a few points doubtful under the case law.")

Liability of the Delegatee

The delegatee (C) is not liable to either the delegator (B) or the delegator's obligee (A) on the delegatee's promise to perform unless the delegatee has received consideration for the promise. Where the delegation of duty occurs in connection with an assignment of rights, the assignment itself furnishes the necessary consideration.

Suppose that B has agreed to supply A with coal and that B delegates to C the duty to supply coal and assigns to C the right to be paid by A for the coal. Because C has received the requisite consideration, C will of course be liable to the delegator (B) for any default in C's performance. Will C also be liable to A (B's obligee)? With regard to the sale of goods, Section 2-210(4) of the UCC provides that C will be liable to A. If the Code does not apply, the answer depends upon whether A is a third-person beneficiary. In the contract between B and C, C promised to perform the obligation B owes A. The contract between B and C is therefore a third-person creditor beneficiary contract. In all but a few states such a contract is enforceable by the third person.

SUMMARY

A person who is not a promisee may acquire rights in a contract in two ways—by the device of a third-person beneficiary contract and by the process of assignment.

A third-person beneficiary contract designates some person other than the promisee as the one who is to receive the promised performance. That person is a donee beneficiary if the purpose of the promisee was to confer a gift upon him or her. The person is a creditor beneficiary if the purpose of the promisee was to secure the discharge of an obligation owing or supposedly owing to the beneficiary. In most states third-person beneficiaries have the right to enforce the promise from which they derive their interest.

An assignment is a manifestation by the owner of an existing right (often, a contract right) of an intent to make a present transfer of the right. An assignee succeeds to any right of performance, priority, or other preference which the assignor had, and the assignee takes the assigned right subject to any defense inherent in the original contract or arising out of a fact which occurred after the assignment was made but before the obligor received notice of assignment.

A contract right can be effectively assigned unless transfer of the right would materially vary the duty of the obligor, increase the obligor's risk under the contract, or impair the obligor's chances of obtaining return performance, or unless assignment of the right is forbidden by law or is validly prohibited by the contract creating the right.

Where a person sells the same claim to two or more persons, the question arises as to which assignee has priority. The majority rule is that the first assignee in time has priority. The minority (and Code) rule is that the assignee who first notifies the debtor of the assignment has priority.

Where a person makes partial assignments of a claim and where the obligor objects to making a number of fractional payments when the contract required only one payment, no legal proceeding can be maintained against the obligor unless the owners of the partial claims join in the proceedings.

An assignor for value impliedly warrants (1) that the right assigned actually exists, (2) that it is subject to no limitations or defenses other than those stated or apparent at the time of the assignment, and (3) that the assignor will do nothing to defeat or impair the value of the assignment.

Duties cannot be assigned, but certain kinds of duties can be delegated. A duty can be delegated unless performance by the delegatee would differ materially from performance by the delegator or unless delegation is forbidden by law or by contract. Unless the delegation obligee consents, delegation of a duty does not relieve the delegator from his or her duty of performance.

A valid prohibition of the assignment of "the contract" bars only the delegation of duties. Under the Code and some case law, the assignment of "this contract" accomplishes both an assignment of rights and a delegation of duties.

STUDY AND DISCUSSION QUESTIONS

1 *(a)* What kind of beneficiary may have rights in a contract to which the beneficiary was not a party? *(b)* Must a person be specifically named as a beneficiary in order to be one? Explain.

2 *(a)* Distinguish between a third-person donee beneficiary contract and a third-person creditor beneficiary contract. *(b)* For what reasons are third-person beneficiaries allowed to enforce the beneficial promises?

3 *(a)* When does a beneficiary acquire a cause of action for breach of a beneficial promise? *(b)* What defenses may the promisor assert against the suing beneficiary?

4 *(a)* For what reasons are assignments of contract rights made? *(b)* Define "assignment" and distinguish it from the creation of rights in a third-person beneficiary.

5 *(a)* Is consideration required for an assignment to be effective? Explain. *(b)* Is notice to the obligor required for an assignment to be effective? Explain.

6 In general, what is the legal position of the person to whom contract rights have been assigned?

7 Under common law principles, an assignee's rights are not affected if the assignor and the obligor modify their contract after the obligor receives notice of the assignment. Article 9 of the Code changes this rule for certain security assignments. Why?

8 *(a)* What is a "waiver-of-defenses clause"? *(b)* If such a clause is enforceable, what is its legal effect? *(c)* Why do some jurisdictions enforce such clauses? Why do some jurisdictions not enforce them? *(d)* What effect does Article 9 of the Code give to waiver-of-defenses clauses covered by that article?

9 *(a)* Under what general circumstances will an assignment of contract rights not be legally effective? *(b)* Give three examples of assignments which would not be legally effective.

10 *(a)* What two policies might the courts consider when deciding whether to enforce a "nonassignability" clause? *(b)* How might a

court interpret a contract stipulation which purports to forbid an assignment? Why?

11 *(a)* With regard to successive assignments of the same contract right, distinguish the "American rule" from the "English rule." *(b)* Which rule do you think is the more sound?

12 Under what circumstances will partial assignments by an assignor be enforced against the obligor?

13 *(a)* Illustrate how the three warranties of the assignor can be breached. *(b)* How might an assignee protect himself or herself against the risk of the debtor-obligor's insolvency?

14 *(a)* For what reason might a business person delegate a contractual duty? *(b)* In terms of legal effect, what is the difference between an assignment of rights and a delegation of duties? *(c)* Why may duties not be assigned? *(d)* Under what circumstances may a delegator be released from liability to the person entitled to the delegator's performance?

15 *(a)* Where the parties to a contract say nothing about the delegation of duties, under what circumstances may the duties be delegated? *(b)* How will a court treat a contract clause which forbids delegation?

16 *(a)* How is a contract clause prohibiting the assignment of "this contract" treated under the common law? The Code? *(b)* How is an assignment of "this contract" treated under the common law? Article 2 of the Code (Sales)?

17 Under what circumstances will a delegatee be liable on his or her promise to perform the delegated duty?

CASE PROBLEMS

1 Niagara Mohawk Power Corp. contracted to supply electric power to a Chevrolet plant. An explosion at the nearby plant of a persulphate manufacturer disrupted Niagara Mohawk's service to the Chevrolet plant, and 600 of

Chevrolet's hourly employees were put out of work for a day. Alleging breach of a contract warranty, these employees and their unions sued Niagara Mohawk for $340,000 in lost wages. Should the Chevrolet employees and their unions prevail?

2 Chevron Oil Co. had an exclusive service station franchise with the New York State Thruway Authority. The franchise contract required Chevron to provide roadside automotive service on a 24-hour basis and to provide sufficient equipment and personnel to service disabled vehicles within thirty minutes from the time a call was assigned to a service vehicle. Kornblut's automobile had a flat tire on the Thruway. New York State Troopers made calls requesting a service truck. After a wait of two and one-half hours, Kornblut—a heavy man unaccustomed to physical exertion—changed the tire with great difficulty, suffered a heart attack, and died 20 days later. His widow sued Chevron for damages resulting from her husband's death. Should she prevail?

3 Bess and Vincent Costanza operated two gift shops. To obtain a business loan, Mr. Costanza executed to the lending bank a mortgage on the Costanza residence and forged his wife's signature on the mortgage agreement. Later, pursuant to a divorce proceeding, the Costanzas signed a separation agreement. It provided that the homestead was to be sold and that the proceeds of the sale were to be applied to payment of the mortgage debt. Mrs. Costanza filed a bill to cancel the forged mortgage. The trial court declared the mortgage void as to her. The bank contended that it was a beneficiary of the separation agreement and that it was therefore entitled to payment of the mortgage debt from the proceeds of the sale. May the bank enforce the separation agreement?

4 Shapiro, the president of a lumber and supply corporation, obtained a loan on behalf of the corporation. As security for the loan, the corporation assigned to the bank the corpora-

tion's rights under construction contracts it was to perform. The corporation experienced financial difficulty, and Shapiro applied the proceeds of the contracts to other corporate debts. Upon failure of the corporation to repay the loan, the bank sued the corporation for the conversion of funds to which the bank was entitled. (Conversion is defined as an unauthorized exercise of the right of ownership over personal property belonging to another, to the exclusion of the owner's rights.) Did the corporation convert the bank's funds?

5 American Biomedical Corp. (ABC) purchased the assets of Health Management Systems, the president of which was John H. Anderson. ABC made the acquisition through American Medical Computer Centers, Inc. (AMCC), a wholly owned subsidiary of ABC formed for the purpose of making the acquisition. Anderson was made president of AMCC under a written personal services agreement with ABC. The agreement was for a term of five years beginning on January 1, 1968. Anderson was to perform "such duties as may be assigned to him." A few months later ABC sold AMCC to Medical Computer Systems, Inc. (MCSI), and assigned to MCSI Anderson's employment agreement. Anderson did not know that the agreement had been assigned, and his duties did not change in any material way. Later Anderson became a vice president of MCSI. In early 1972 he was asked to resign from AMCC and MCSI, and he signed a document releasing MCSI from "any and all claims he may have against them." When Anderson informed ABC that he was ready to accept a new assignment under his employment agreement (which had another year to run), ABC denied any obligation to him. Anderson sued ABC for breach of contract. Was Anderson entitled to damages?

6 Manubenco Enterprises Corp. was a subcontractor for the construction of a housing development. Manubenco engaged a surety to guarantee the completion of the subcontracted work. As a part of the indemnity agreement with the surety, Manubenco assigned to the surety Manubenco's rights to future payments for work completed. Later, to secure financing of the construction work, Manubenco assigned its rights under the construction subcontract to the lending bank. The bank notified the general contractor (obligor) of the assignment, and the general contractor made several "progress payments" to the bank for work completed by Manubenco. Then Manubenco declared itself in default and discontinued work. A dispute arose as to who was entitled to the progress payments. Who should prevail—the surety or the bank?

7 Smith sold a taxicab company to Wrehe. Wrehe made a partial payment, but still owed Smith $15,000 under the contract. With Smith's consent, Wrehe then assigned "the contract" to a corporation. The assignee-corporation made some payments but soon defaulted. Smith sued Wrehe for the balance due under the contract. Wrehe contended that only the assignee was liable to Smith. Was Wrehe liable to Smith?

Chapter

18

Performance
and Other Discharge
of Contracts;
Remedies for
Breach of Contract

The parties to a contract undertake legal duties or obligations, and they usually expect to render the agreed performance. But the circumstances surrounding the making of a contract and its performance often vary from what was originally contemplated. The performance agreed to may have become impossible, it may have been superseded by a subsequent agreement, or the parties may have disagreed as to what kind or degree of performance is required of them by the contract. In such situations the courts may be called on to decide whether a contract has been performed or otherwise "discharged." If the contractual obligations of one party to a contract have not been discharged (that is, extinguished), the other party may be entitled to a remedy for breach of the contract—damages, rescission, or specific performance, for example.

In this chapter we turn to two main questions:

1   Under what circumstances will a party to a contract be released (discharged) from a duty imposed by the contract?

2   Where a contractual duty has not been discharged but has been breached, what remedies are available for its breach?

334

PERFORMANCE AND OTHER DISCHARGE OF CONTRACTS

Meaning of "Discharge" and "Performance"

As applied to contracts, *discharge* means the termination of a contractual obligation. Performance is one method of discharging a contractual obligation. *Performance* of a contract means that the parties have carried out the obligations imposed on them by the contract. Other kinds of discharge involve an agreement to cancel the contract, an agreed performance that has become illegal, or a failure to perform. Whatever the method of or reason for discharge, the discharged party no longer has a duty of performance, and the party to whom the duty was owed is no longer entitled to a remedy for breach of that duty. Of course, a person who performs his or her own duty is entitled to the other party's performance or to some remedy in lieu of that performance, unless the other party is already discharged.

Role of Conditions in Defining and Discharging Duty of Performance

A party to a contract might "condition" his or her performance on the occurrence or nonoccurrence of some fact or event. For example, suppose that X, a Minnesota resident, agrees to work for Y, a Nebraska employer, on condition that X can rent an apartment near the place of employment at least one week before the term of employment is to begin. X's duty to work for Y is conditioned on X's ability to rent an apartment, and X's duty to perform will not be activated unless the condition is satisfied (or is waived by X). Inability of X to rent an apartment ("failure of the condition") discharges X from her duty to work for Y. Or suppose that X, a scientist, agrees to work for Y for 5 years unless a labor dispute prevents X from using the laboratory facilities in Y's factory. The occurrence of such a labor dispute during the term of employment discharges X from her duty to work for Y for the remainder of the 5-year term.

As these examples indicate, contractual conditions contribute to flexibility of contracting. They also help to establish the circumstances under which a contractual duty may be discharged.[1]

Discharge by Performance

In approaching the general topic of discharge, we are concerned with the rights and duties of both parties to a contract. With regard to discharge by performance, we are especially interested in the answers to three questions:

1 How are the precise duties of the parties determined?

2 How does a party to a contract discharge his or her own duty of performance?

3 What is the effect of a defective performance by one party on the duty of the other party?

Determination and Performance of Contractual Duties The duties of contracting parties are determined by reference to the contract. Under the definition of contract ordinarily applied to consensual transactions, "the contract" means the agreement of the parties as that agreement is affected by applicable rules of law. The parties to an agreement may fail to state *all* the terms of the contract. The law then frequently supplies missing terms. Sometimes a party to an agreement wishes to impose burdensome provisions on the other party. Such provisions may be illegal. If a provision is illegal, the courts will not enforce it even though it might have been agreed to by the other party, but will

---

[1] Traditionally, conditions have been classified as conditions "precedent," "subsequent," or "concurrent." These classifications have been challenged as unsound, and the *Restatement of the Law (Second) Contracts* has abandoned some of that terminology. John E. Murray, *Murray on Contracts*, Bobbs-Merrill Co., Indianapolis, 1974, sec. 141.

enforce what remains if the remaining provisions are sufficient to constitute a contract. The contract which identifies the duties of the parties consists, then, of their agreement as supplemented or as restricted by the law.

A party to a contract discharges his or her duty of performance by doing what the contract requires, or in some situations by offering to do what the contract requires (i.e., by "tendering" the required performance). For example, A, who has contracted to repair a roof, discharges his duty by making repairs which conform to standards established by the contract. Where the other party unjustifiably prevents the performance of the work contracted for, A discharges his duty by being "ready, willing, and able" for a reasonable time to make the repairs. The effect of a discharge is to release A from any further duty of performance. Discharge in these circumstances also entitles him (1) to payment of the contract price if the work was performed or (2) to damages for lost profits if he was unjustifiably prevented from performing.

Sometimes a contractor such as A will agree to a no-profit or even to a losing contract—for example to keep a construction crew intact during an economic recession when little work is available. Where A is unjustly prevented from performing such a contract, a measure of damages frequently applied is the reasonable value of services actually rendered by A, often subject, however, to a maximum established by the price called for by the contract. Because of their variety and complexity, no-profit contract situations and the various other measures of damages that might be applied to them are largely beyond the scope of this book. The discharge of performance obligations in sales of goods is discussed in Chapter 27.

Effect of Breach on Performance Obligation of Other Party What kind of breach of contract by one party will result in discharging the other party from his or her duty to perform? There is no simple answer to this question, but there are some guiding principles. These principles have traditionally been discussed under the label of "doctrine of substantial performance." However, the principles are more easily understood in terms of whether the breach of a contract is material or nonmaterial.

A breach of contract is a failure to perform a duty imposed by the contract. A breach may be either "material" or "nonmaterial." A material breach is so serious that the nonbreaching party may be deprived of the benefit that he or she expected to receive from the breaching party's performance. Suppose that A, a seller of coal, contracts with B to deliver five tons of coal to B on the first day of each month for a period of two years. A makes three of the monthly deliveries and receives prompt payment from B, but thereafter makes no more deliveries of coal. A's breach is material because it deprives B of the fuel she needs in her business. In contrast, a nonmaterial breach does not deprive the nonbreaching party of the benefit of the bargain, although a nonmaterial breach may cause inconvenience, annoyance, or extra expense. Short delays in making deliveries of coal or making a delivery of coal which falls a bit short of the quality prescribed by the contract normally would constitute nonmaterial breaches.

A party to whom a contractual duty is owed has a remedy for any breach of that duty, whether the breach is material or not. The availability of remedies for any breach tends to discourage people from treating their contractual commitments lightly. Whether a breach of contract results in *discharge* of the other party is another matter entirely. A nonmaterial breach by A will not discharge B from his or her duty to perform. If the rule were otherwise, the legitimate expectations of parties performing in good faith could easily be defeated, and commerce could be disrupted. On the other hand, a material breach by A can result in great harm to B. Any material breach is therefore cause for the discharge of B, although there is a difference of legal opinion as to when that discharge should occur. The following paragraphs describe typical situations involving material breach.

Situations in which the contract states which breaches are material What is material in some situations might not be in others. Within limits, the courts permit the parties to a contract to determine by their agreement which duties imposed by the contract are material (and whose breach therefore can result in discharge).

Consider, for example, a contract for the sale of land. Usually such a contract specifies the day for "closing," that is, the day upon which the transaction is to be formally completed. Will failure of the seller to convey the land on that day discharge the buyer from the duty to pay? Will the failure of the buyer to make the agreed payment on that day discharge the seller from his or her duty to convey the land? Delay of performance does not necessarily constitute a material breach of the contract.[2] Unless the contract makes timely performance "of the essence" of the contract, one party's minor delay serves only to *postpone* and not to discharge the other party's duty of performance. The other party does, of course, have a remedy for any loss caused by the delay.

The parties to a contract may make time of the essence, that is, provide in effect that a failure of one party to perform by the time stated is material and shall discharge the other party. In the words of Professor Murray:

> If . . . there is a provision in the contract which indicates that the time stated for tender or performance is clearly important and [if] the parties understand that time was genuinely of the essence, failure to perform by that stated time will result in the discharge of the remaining duties of the injured party immediately. . . . The difficulty . . . is to determine whether the parties genuinely intended time to be "of

the essence." If the writing is a printed form containing the stock "time is of the essence" clause, it should not necessarily be given that effect. Even if the writing is not a printed form, the stock phraseology . . . may not indicate that the parties were genuinely concerned that performance take place absolutely no later than the specified date or hour.[3]

With regard to aspects of the contract other than time of performance, the parties may likewise determine what breaches are to be considered material.

Situations in which courts find a breach material Unreasonable delay of performance, delivery of seriously defective goods, and a substantial failure to render the services bargained for have been held to constitute material breaches of contract. Traditionally the courts have held that a material breach immediately discharges the injured party, even where the defective performance was made before the time specified by the contract.[4] Under the *Restatement (Second) of the Law of Contracts* the injured party may be discharged, but not always immediately. Under this newer rule, an uncured (uncorrected) material failure to perform allows the injured party to suspend his or her performance while the breaching party uses any time remaining under the contract to cure the defective performance. If the breaching party cannot cure the defect within the remaining time, the injured party's performance is then discharged.[5] The newer rule prevents the injured party from using a curable material breach as an excuse to escape a contract which, for some reason other than the breach, is no longer attractive to the injured party. A

---

[2]Ibid., sec. 175. (*And see* Arthur L. Corbin, *Corbin on Contracts*, West Publishing Company, St. Paul, 1952, sec. 713.)

[3]Murray, op. cit., pp. 341–342 (citing *Restatement (Second)*, *Contracts*, sec. 267); Corbin, *Contracts*, sec. 715, Accord. Reprinted with permission of the Bobbs-Merrill Company, Inc. All rights reserved.

[4]Murray, op. cit., sec. 167.

[5]Ibid., p. 325.

similar rule applies to sales of goods and is discussed in Chapter 27.

Other Kinds of Discharge

So far we have considered three kinds of discharge: discharge by failure of a condition, discharge of one's own duties by performing them, and discharge of the other party's duty of performance by a material failure to perform one's own duty. We turn now to other kinds of discharge commonly associated with business transactions.

Discharge by Subsequent Agreement   The parties to a contract may wish to put an end to the contract without performing it, or, with a view to performance, they may wish to alter the performance obligations in some way. Subsequent agreements of the parties are useful for such purposes. The following paragraphs briefly describe some common types of subsequent agreements and the extent to which they discharge the obligations imposed by the original contracts.

Mutual rescission   "Rescission" means cancellation of a transaction. In one specific sense, rescission is the voluntary act of putting an end to an executory bilateral contract by means of an agreement to do so.[6] The agreement of rescission is in fact a new contract, agreed to without going to court, in which each party discharges the other by surrendering the rights which were established by the old contract. The mutual surrender of rights constitutes the consideration necessary for, and the performance of, the contract of rescission.

Where one or both parties have partially performed the executory bilateral contract, the question arises whether there is a right to compensation for or return of the partial performances. The courts are not in agreement on this question. Some courts treat mutual rescission as if it were the court-ordered equitable remedy of

rescission (discussed later in this chapter) that must be accompanied by restitution (compensation for or the return of partial performances). Under this view the parties would always be returned to the situation in which they found themselves before the formation of the original contract, regardless of any agreement to the contrary. Most courts hold that the mutual rescission of an executory bilateral contract is itself nothing more than a contract, and that any compensation for or return of partial performances is a matter for the parties to decide.

Accord and satisfaction; substitute contract   Instead of simply putting an end to the original contract, the parties to it may wish to substitute a new set of performance obligations for those imposed by the original contract. To accomplish this result, they may resort to an "accord and satisfaction" or to the very similar "substitute contract."[7] Where the new agreement is not made until after the maturity or breach of the original contract, the new agreement is called an *accord*; and the performance of it (or the acceptance of it by both parties as a substitute for the original contract) is called a *satisfaction*. Where the new agreement is made before the maturity or breach of the original agreement, the new agreement is usually called a *substitute contract*. To be binding on the parties, an accord or a substitute contract must be supported by consideration as explained in Chapter 12, pages 220-221. An accord or a substitute contract discharges the original contract if the parties to the new agreement so intended.

Novation   The purpose of a novation is to accomplish the substitution of parties to a contract, with or without a change in the performance obligations. Suppose that A has a contract with B and that A agrees with B and C that C will perform the obligations imposed on A by the original contract. The resulting contract is a novation. Discharge of the original contract by

---

[6]Ibid., sec. 252.

[7]Ibid., sec. 253.

the novation (new contract) requires the agreement of all the parties affected by the novation.[8] For example, A will not be discharged from the obligations imposed by the original contract unless B, at least, agrees to A's discharge.

Release; contract not to sue In its broad sense, a *release* is any discharge from liability. The release of a contractual obligation is usually accomplished by means of a writing. In some states a written statement of discharge is effective without consideration, if sealed and delivered. In other states a release is invalid unless supported by consideration.

Where one party to a contract promises never to sue the other, the promise, if supported by consideration, constitutes a "contract not to sue" and discharges the other party. However, "a contract never to sue any number less than all of a group of joint, or joint and several, debtors does not operate as a discharge [of the whole group], but is enforceable only according to its literal terms."[9]

Discharge by Impossibility, Frustration, or Impracticability Sometimes the circumstances surrounding a contract change so drastically that the contract originally contemplated (1) cannot be performed, (2) is no longer of value to the obligee (party to whom the performance is owed), or (3) can be performed only with great hardship or loss to the obligor. Accordingly, the party adversely affected might seek a discharge on the ground of impossibility of performance, frustration of purpose, or impracticability of performance.

The expression "impossibility of performance" usually designates situations in which the promised performance literally is no longer possible. Performance is impossible, for example, where the services of a particular person were contracted for, but the person died or became incapacitated before the performance

was due or completed. Other instances of impossibility involve the destruction of an object or a source of supply expressly required for performance of the contract. Sometimes a performance is declared illegal after the contract was made. Although the act contracted for may still be physically possible, the performance may be declared "impossible" because performance would be against the law.

In situations involving frustration of purpose, performance is possible and legal despite the changed circumstances. However, the performance once sought by the frustrated obligee is no longer of value to the obligee. For example, suppose that X has an apartment which commands an excellent view of the Rose Bowl parade and that X agrees to rent the apartment to Y for the day of the parade so that Y can view it in comfort. If a disaster results in the cancellation of the parade, Y's purpose in contracting for the use of the apartment is frustrated. Unless the contract imposed on Y the risk of cancellation, Y may be discharged from the rental contract.

Where a situation involves impracticability of performance, the performance is possible and legal, but it has become so burdensome that the obligor wishes to be relieved of it, as where X agrees to construct a house for a specified price, but the cost of raw materials then rises so high that the builder can no longer make a profit. The circumstances under which an obligor may be discharged on the ground of impracticability from a contract for the sale of goods are discussed in Chapter 27.

The principles governing discharge for impossibility, frustration, or impracticability reflect a concern for the needs of both parties to the contract. Whether a discharge will be granted depends only in part on the degree of difficulty faced by the party seeking discharge. A court will also consider the value of the contract to the other party and any intention of the parties to shift the risk of loss from one to the other.

---

[8]Ibid., sec. 258.
[9]Ibid., sec. 260.

Discharge by Operation of Law In many situations contractual obligations are discharged by law, regardless of the will of the parties. Illustrations include discharges by merger, by unauthorized alteration of a written contract, and by bankruptcy or the "running" of the statute of limitations.

Merger is the fusion or absorption of a lesser thing or right into one of a higher order. The parol evidence rule in the law of contracts provides an example. Under that rule, where the parties to a contract reduce an agreement to writing, under circumstances indicating that it is to be the complete and final expression of their bargain, all prior negotiations (including prior agreements) are merged into the final writing. By operation of law the final writing supersedes and discharges the prior agreements.

For a variety of reasons, some legitimate and some not, people make alterations of written, signed contracts—alterations that are unknown to or unauthorized by one or both parties to the contracts. A bank customer might have forgotten to indorse a check when depositing it; to expedite the check-cashing process, Article 4 of the Uniform Commercial Code permits the bank teller to supply the missing endorsement even without the knowledge of the customer. Although perhaps unknown to the customer, such an alteration is authorized by law and is therefore legitimate; but unauthorized alterations in other contract situations are not. For example, upon reviewing a signed contract, a building contractor might revise the price substantially upward without consulting the other party, or a forger might steal, alter, and cash a signed payroll check. To what extent will unauthorized, illegitimate alterations discharge the original parties to the contracts?

Not all unauthorized alterations of signed contracts result in discharge. Usually a contract is not discharged on the ground of unauthorized alteration unless the alteration is material and is made with fraudulent intent by the obligee or with the obligee's knowledge or consent. Indeed, where an unauthorized material alteration is not fraudulent, or where it is made by a stranger without the knowledge or consent of the obligee, the obligation is enforceable (by a person entitled to enforcement) according to its original tenor (that is, as originally drafted). A nonmaterial unauthorized alteration does not discharge a contract. Thus, the law affords protection against forgery and other dishonesty while protecting persons who have legitimate interests in altered contracts.

A discharge in bankruptcy is granted by a court and releases the debtor from the contractual obligations covered by the discharge. However, many debts are not dischargeable in bankruptcy (alimony, back taxes, and so on), and to be effective, the discharge must be pleaded as a defense to an action on a contract covered by it. The "running" of the statute of limitations (expiration of the time permitted by statute for bringing suit on a contract) bars enforcement of contractual obligations.

REMEDIES FOR BREACH OF CONTRACT; OTHER REMEDIES

Remedies for Breach of Contract

Major Contract Remedies The remedies most commonly sought in a lawsuit for breach of contract are damages (the "legal" remedy discussed in Chapter 2), and specific performance and rescission ("equitable" remedies). A court awards *damages* by ordering a payment of money that represents or compensates for the harm sustained by the plaintiff as a result of the defendant's breach of the contract. A judgment for damages is the sole remedy where a payment of money is an adequate substitute for the performance promised by the breaching party. Suppose that Baxter contracts to sell 5,000 tons of #1 wheat to Carlson, that the price of wheat rises 5 percent above the contract price, and that Baxter breaches the contract by selling all her wheat to Samson. If #1 wheat is readily available from other sources, Carlson's only remedy is a judgment for damages, in an amount sufficient to cover, for example, the higher cost of substitute wheat and any extra expenses required to procure it.

An equitable remedy, *specific performance*, is available where the remedy at law (damages) is inadequate. Damages would be inadequate where the seller of a work of art breaches the contract of sale by refusing to deliver the artwork. The purchaser must have the artwork itself to enjoy its special qualities or to enable others to enjoy them. Therefore, the seller may be compelled by a court of equity specifically to perform the contract by delivering the artwork to the purchaser. Similarly, a contract for the purchase of land, or for the acquisition of some interest in land, is specifically enforceable, since each parcel of real estate is considered under Anglo-American law to have unique physical features or some special commercial value such as a good location that cannot be adequately compensated for by a payment of money. And, as is pointed out in Chapter 27, specific performance may be available to a buyer of goods even though the goods might not be unique. Suppose that Wintergreen, a farmer, contracts to sell his farm's output of corn to Soya, Inc., that a drought ruins much of the country's crop of corn, and that Wintergreen's crop is unharmed. If Wintergreen refuses to deliver the corn to Soya and Soya cannot acquire corn from other sources, Soya is entitled to specific performance of the contract.

Sometimes, however, a court will withhold specific performance even though the remedy at law is inadequate and will instead limit the plaintiff to his or her remedy at law. The courts prefer not to impose offensive personal relationships on contracting parties. A court will not compel the specific performance of a contract for personal services, for example, because to do so would in effect impose involuntary servitude. Nor will the court specifically enforce a contract

to marry or, usually, a contract to enter into a partnership. Courts also refuse to grant specific performance where judicial supervision of the performance is impractical or beyond the ability of the court. Some partnership agreements that do not impose an offensive personal relationship would nevertheless be impractical for the court to enforce specifically, as would some (but not all) contracts to arbitrate and some construction or repair contracts. Large-scale construction contracts would be especially difficult to enforce specifically, and injured parties to such contracts are often left to their remedy at law.

Sometimes a person has a valid reason for rescinding (canceling) a contract—fraud, mistake, duress, and the like—but is uncertain about his or her legal right to do so (or is unable to do so) without the aid of a court. The court-ordered equitable remedy of *rescission* is available. When seeking rescission, the plaintiff petitions the court to order cancellation of the contract and to restore what the plaintiff has parted with. Since the plaintiff must "do equity to receive equity," the plaintiff who seeks court-ordered rescission ordinarily must make or offer restitution of anything the plaintiff received from the defendant under the contract.

As is true with other equitable remedies, a plaintiff might be denied a court-ordered rescission even though the remedy at law is inadequate. Suppose that Watson, in negotiating the sale of his drugstore to Danner, fraudulently overstates the assets of the business by 20 percent. Danner learns of the fraud two weeks after taking possession of the store but continues to operate it for a year while the volume of business declines to almost zero due to Danner's mismanagement. Danner then brings suit in equity to rescind the contract, expecting to return the now worthless drugstore to Watson and to receive from Watson the amount that Danner paid for the business. Danner will be denied the remedy of rescission. Under the principle of laches discussed in Chapter 2, and under the principle that Danner must "do equity to receive equity," Danner must seek rescission (and make a good-faith attempt to return the business) within a reasonable time after learning of Watson's fraud. Here, the business was in sound condition when Danner learned of the fraud. It would be unreasonable to permit Danner to ruin the business over the course of a year and then to return to Watson the worthless remains. Despite being denied the equitable remedy of rescission, however, Danner will be allowed to pursue his legal remedy of damages if the time specified in the applicable statute of limitations has not expired.

Interests Protected by Contract Remedies Remedies for breach of a contract protect three interests of the nonbreaching party: the expectation interest, the reliance interest, and the restitution interest. For illustrative purposes the paragraphs which follow refer mainly to contracts for the sale of goods. However, the remedial principles involved apply as well to contracts for the sale of real estate, to contracts for services, and to other kinds of contracts.

The expectation interest The expectation interest is the interest that a party to a contract has in receiving the benefit of the bargain for which he or she contracted. Where performance has been withheld in breach of the contract, the expectation interest of the nonbreaching party is protected by legal and equitable remedies. Usually the expectation interest is protected by an award of damages sufficient to put the nonbreaching party in as good a position as that party would have been in had the contract been performed. Where damages are inadequate to accomplish that result, the equitable remedy of specific performance may be available as a substitute for voluntary performance of the contract.

The measure of damages necessary to give effect to the expectation interest varies according to the circumstances surrounding the breach of contract. Consider three possible situations in which S, a dealer in construction equipment, contracts on January 1 to sell a tractor to B, a building contractor. The price of the tractor is $10,000, and S is to deliver the tractor on March 1.

1   In breach of the contract, S fails to deliver the tractor, and B must buy that kind of tractor from another dealer for $11,000, the market price on March 1. In this situation the amount of damages necessary to give B the benefit of the bargain is $1,000. This amount is called "general damages." General damages are those which the law presumes to have accrued directly as a result of the wrong complained of, without reference to any special character or circumstances of the plaintiff. General contract damages typically consist of the difference between the contract price and the market price at the time performance is due. If the market price is lower at that time, B suffers no general damages.

2   At the time of contracting, B informs S that the tractor is needed by March 1 so that B can avoid incurring a penalty for breach of a construction contract with C. S promises to deliver the tractor by that date, but never does deliver it. B buys a replacement tractor at a higher market price, but is not able to buy it in time to avoid incurring the penalty. S is liable to B for the difference in the price of the tractors and might be liable for the amount of the penalty B had to pay to C. That amount constitutes "special" or "consequential" damages resulting from S's failure to deliver the tractor by the date promised. S is liable for such damages if they were within the contemplation of S and B when they made their contract.

3   Besides being a building contractor, B is also a retail dealer in construction equipment. At the time of the contract with S, B had a contract for the resale of the tractor. In breach of the contract with B, S fails to deliver the tractor. S is liable in damages to B for the amount of profit S would have made from the resale of the tractor.

If B were the breaching party in these situations, S, the seller, would have remedies which protect the seller's expectation interest. Remedies of a seller of goods are discussed in Chapter 27.

The reliance interest The reliance interest is the interest of the nonbreaching party in recovering costs incurred in preparing for the hoped-for performance. The seller might have altered machinery or contracted for supplies to fill a special order for the buyer. The buyer might have made arrangements to accommodate, sell, or use goods which the seller promised to deliver. In either situation the nonbreaching party suffers a monetary loss which may be recoverable from the breaching party as reliance damages (called "incidental damages" in the Uniform Commercial Code). However, the amount of reliance damages is limited to the reasonable cost of reasonable preparations, and the relying party must deduct any amounts saved as a result of the other party's breach. Furthermore, many reliance costs are compensated for by expectancy remedies. Where the injured party has received an expectancy remedy, duplicative reliance damages will not be allowed.[10]

The restitution interest The restitution interest is the interest of the nonbreaching party in recovering a benefit (amounting to less than full performance) which he or she conferred on the other party. The buyer might have made a partial payment for goods promised but not delivered. The seller might have made a partial delivery of goods for which payment was promised but not made.

The party seeking restitution may wish to recover the property delivered or, instead, to recover its value. A return of the property itself is called "specific restitution"; a payment of the value of the benefit conferred is called "substitutionary restitution"; a return of the property together with compensation for a decrease in the value of the property is called "mixed restitution."[11] Substitutionary restitution is necessary where the benefit cannot be returned—where, for example, services have been ren-

dered or goods have been consumed. Mixed restitution is useful where the property to be restored has been damaged or has depreciated.

Usually some form of restitution accompanies the rescission (cancellation) of a contract. However, as noted earlier in this chapter, restitution need not necessarily accompany rescission. Where rescission of a contract is by subsequent agreement of the parties, many courts, instead of invariably requiring restitution, hold that the parties may decide whether partial performances are to be restored.

Limits on Damage Remedies Within limits, the plaintiff in a suit for contract damages may recover damages for any loss resulting from the defendant's breach. The principal limits on the recovery of damages are reflected

1 In rules concerning causation, certainty, and foreseeability of damages

2 In the requirement that a plaintiff minimize (mitigate) his or her damages where reasonably possible

Causation, certainty, and foreseeability of damages A plaintiff must prove the amount of loss with reasonable certainty. In a suit for general damages, the amount of loss may be determined by reference to market values. Where there is no established market, the amount of loss may be determined by use of an appraiser or by some other means.

The recovery of "special" ("consequential") damages is subject to more complex limits, primarily because special damages represent losses due to special or unusual circumstances surrounding the breach of contract. The principal limits on the recovery of special damages are reflected in rules concerning causation, certainty, and foreseeability of special damages.[12]

• *Causation of special damages* Special damages ordinarily are not recoverable unless

---

[10]Dan B. Dobbs, *Handbook on the Law of Remedies*, West Publishing Company, St. Paul, 1973, p. 791.
[11]Ibid., sec. 4.4.

[12]The discussion which follows is based mainly on Dobbs, op. cit., sec. 12.3.

the defendant's breach was in itself sufficient to cause the loss and was the primary, real, and chief cause of the loss. Nevertheless, some courts find causation present if the breach was a substantial factor in causing the loss.

Suppose that S had promised delivery of parts to B on March 1 so that B could complete the assembly of machines to be shipped to B's customers. S's failure to deliver the parts by the time promised could upset B's production schedule, put B in breach of contracts with her customers, and thereby cause her lost profits or other damages. However, if just before the date set for B's performance, B's employees go on an extended strike, her inability to meet her obligations to her customers would be attributable to the strike, at least temporarily. If S failed to make timely delivery but performed before the end of the strike, S's breach would not be the cause of B's loss.

• *Certainty of special damages*   Suppose that in the situation just described, S's breach caused B's inability to supply her customers with machines. What loss has B sustained as a result of the breach? She might have suffered a loss of profits due to customers' cancellation of their contracts with B, and B's reputation as a supplier of machines might have been harmed. Most courts would consider proof of cancelled contracts sufficiently certain to support an award of damages, especially where the contracts were in writing. Loss of commercial reputation (goodwill) is much more difficult to prove. Some courts refuse to allow damages for loss of goodwill on the ground that goodwill is too speculative and uncertain for adequate proof of loss ever to be made. However, most courts recognize loss of goodwill as a legitimate element of recovery, and they award damages for its loss where proof of loss is adequate.

• *Foreseeability of special damages*   Suppose that a buyer plans to assemble machines and to sell them to thousands of customers. Failure of a supplier to deliver apparently commonplace parts could defeat the buyer's expectations. Should the seller be liable not only for general damages, if any, but also for special damages such as the buyer's lost profits?

With regard to damages, the principal policy of the law is to make the plaintiff "whole," that is, to protect his or her expectancy and reliance interests. Limiting this policy is the somewhat conflicting policy of protecting the defendant from unexpected and potentially ruinous awards of special damages, even though all the damages claimed flowed from the defendant's breach. In an attempt to place a reasonable limit on "remote" damages, American courts have followed *Hadley v. Baxendale*, a famous English case decided in 1854.[13] Under principles stated in or derived from that case, the courts have refused to award special damages unless they were "foreseen by" or were "within the contemplation of" the parties to the contract at the time of contracting.

In developing and applying principles relating to foreseeability damages, some courts were unduly restrictive in awarding special damages. Those courts required an actual agreement by the defendant to pay special damages in the event of his or her breach. The Uniform Commercial Code has rejected the so-called "tacit agreement rule," which required an actual agreement but permitted it to be inferred from conduct. Under the Code, special damages can be within the contemplation of the parties even though there is no actual agreement to pay special damages. It is sufficient that the breaching defendant had at the time of contracting "reason to know" of potential special damages (UCC Section 2-715(2), comment 2).

Mitigation of damages   A plaintiff may not recover damages for losses he or she could reasonably have avoided. This general rule of damages applies to breaches of contract.[14] An employee wrongfully discharged in breach of an employment contract for a term of years has a damage remedy for that breach, but her recovery of damages may be reduced by amounts she could reasonably have earned by taking other suitable employment. A manufacturer who continues to manufacture goods after the buyer repudiates the contract may not be allowed the

---

[13]156 English Reports 145.
[14]Dobbs, op. cit., sec. 12.6.

expenses of the continued manufacture as damages unless the continuation is a commercially reasonable attempt to avoid loss.

The rule illustrated by these examples is called the "rule of avoidable consequences." It is not meant to defeat legitimate claims for damages. Rather, in applying it, the courts intend to disallow damage claims only where (and only to the extent that) a very modest effort by the plaintiff would have reduced the loss sustained.

Other Remedies

In addition to remedies provided by law for breach of contract, there are other remedies relating to contracts. For example, a court may be called upon to rewrite, correct, or otherwise "reform" a contract so that it reveals the bargain of the parties.

We turn now to two other remedies. The first is a remedy for breach of contract provided for by the contract itself—the "agreed upon" remedy of liquidated damages. The second, called a "quasi-contractual" remedy, is available in situations where no contract exists. It is provided by the law to prevent "unjust enrichment."

Liquidated Damages Clauses   A contract may contain a clause which stipulates an amount of damages to be paid for breach of the contract. Or the clause might provide a formula for calculating damages in the event of breach. Such clauses are not enforceable if they are "penal" in nature, that is, if their purpose or effect is to coerce performance of the contract by means of harsh penalties unrelated to actual damages. A court will find a clause penal and unenforceable if it provides for damages unreasonably disproportionate to anticipated losses.

On the other hand, most courts will enforce an agreed ("liquidated") damage clause where two conditions exist at the time of contracting:

1   It appears to the parties that the harm flowing from the breach will be difficult to estimate accurately

2   There is a reasonable relation between the damages agreed on and those expected to occur in the event of breach.[15]

Enforceable liquidated damages clauses take the place of a judicial determination of damages. A liquidated damages clause may be enforceable even though it provides for an amount greater or less than the actual damages sustained.

Quasi-Contractual Remedy   Suppose the following situations:

• X, a doctor, notices an unconscious stranger lying on a roadside and renders emergency medical services. The stranger dies without regaining consciousness.

• X makes improvements on a house under an oral purchase agreement which is not enforceable as a contract because of failure of the parties to comply with the statute of frauds.

• X and Y transport their children to school because the school board refuses to perform its statutory duty to provide transportation.

None of these situations involves a contract. Yet, in each situation X has conferred a benefit on someone. To prevent the "unjust enrichment" of the person benefited (or in the first situation perhaps to encourage the rendering of emergency services), the law provides a restitutionary remedy called "quasi contract." Under the law of quasi contract, the plaintiff may recover the thing conferred if it is specifically restorable. If the thing is not specifically restorable, the plaintiff may recover the reasonable value of the property or services conferred. Quasi contract is discussed in more detail in Chapter 9.

A quasi-contractual remedy is *in lieu of* any contractual remedy that might have been available. Thus, where A has partly performed services called for by her contract with B and has rightfully rescinded it on the ground that full

---

[15]Ibid., sec. 12.5.

performance has become impossible, the contract is discharged. However, A may be entitled to recover in quasi contract the value of her services. In quasi contract, the measure of A's damages is the reasonable value (ordinarily, the market value) of her services and not the price established by the now-ineffective contract.

SUMMARY

Discharge means the termination of a contractual obligation. *Performance* is one method of discharge. Whatever the method, the discharged party no longer has a duty of performance, and the party to whom the duty was owed is no longer entitled to a remedy for breach of that duty.

The performance duties of contracting parties are determined by their contract. The contract is the agreement of the parties (including any conditions) as supplemented or as restricted by the law. A party to a contract discharges his or her duty of performance by doing what the contract requires or, in some situations, by tendering the required performance.

A material breach of contract by one party may discharge the other party. Traditionally, the courts have held that such a breach immediately discharges the injured party. Under a newer rule, an uncured material breach will discharge the injured party only when the material failure to perform cannot be cured. In addition to discharge by performance, by failure of a condition, and by material breach, there are other kinds of discharge. They include discharge by subsequent agreement; by impossibility, frustration, or impracticability; and by operation of law.

Remedies for breach of contract protect three interests of the nonbreaching party: the expectation interest, the reliance interest, and the restitution interest. The *expectation interest* is the interest that a party has in receiving the benefit of the bargain. The *reliance interest* is the interest of a party in recovering costs in-

curred in preparing for the hoped-for performance. The *restitution interest* is the interest of a party in recovering a benefit (amounting to less than full performance) which he or she conferred on the other party.

Within limits, the plaintiff in a suit for contract damages may recover damages for any loss resulting from the defendant's breach. The plaintiff must prove damages with reasonable certainty. The principal limits on the recovery of special damages are reflected in rules concerning causation, certainty, and foreseeability of special damages. A plaintiff may not recover damages for losses which the plaintiff could reasonably have avoided. Where the remedy at law is inadequate, the equitable remedies of specific performance or rescission may be available.

In addition to damages, specific performance, and rescission, there are other remedies relating to contracts. These include reformation and the "agreed" remedy of liquidated damages. For situations where there is no contract, there is a "quasi-contractual" remedy. It is provided by the law to prevent unjust enrichment.

This chapter brings to a close the discussion of general contract law. Special applications of contract law are discussed in the following chapter (Contracting with the Government), in the chapters on sales, and in other parts of this book wherever pertinent.

Cases have been omitted from this chapter because cases on remedies for breach of contract are provided in other parts of the book (see, for example, cases 27.3, 27.5, and 27.6). However, in this chapter the study and discussion questions and the problems on discharge and remedies provide opportunity to apply principles developed here.

STUDY AND DISCUSSION QUESTIONS

1 *(a)* What is the meaning of "discharge"? Of "performance"? *(b)* What is the legal effect of the discharge of a contractual obligation?

2 Illustrate how the use of a condition may help establish the circumstances under which a contractual duty will be discharged.

3 *(a)* How are the precise duties of the parties to a contract determined? *(b)* How may a party to a contract discharge his or her duty of performance? *(c)* Performance entitles the performing party to what?

4 *(a)* Why are remedies available for nonmaterial breaches of contract? *(b)* Why will a nonmaterial breach by one party not discharge the other party to the contract? *(c)* Under what circumstances will a "time-is-of-the-essence" clause be considered material so that a failure of one party to comply with it will discharge the other party? *(d)* When does a discharge take effect? Explain.

5 A contract may be discharged by a subsequent agreement of the parties. *(a)* Define (and where possible explain a common use of) mutual rescission, accord and satisfaction, novation, and release. *(b)* Does mutual rescission necessarily involve a return of partial performances? Explain.

6 How does discharge by impossibility differ from discharge by frustration? From discharge by impracticability? In your answer illustrate each kind of discharge.

7 *(a)* Illustrate discharge by operation of law as a result of merger. *(b)* Under what circumstances will an unauthorized alteration of a written contract discharge the person whose obligation was altered? *(c)* Is a discharge in bankruptcy effective when granted? Explain.

8 *(a)* How does the remedy of damages differ from the remedy of specific performance? *(b)* For what reasons might a court refuse to award specific performance even though the remedy at law (damages) is inadequate? *(c)* Why might a person seek the aid of a court in rescinding a contract? *(d)* Explain why a person might be denied the remedy of rescission even though the remedy at law is inadequate. *(e)* Explain whether being denied an equitable remedy affects the availability of the legal remedy of damages.

9 *(a)* With what remedies may the expectation interest be protected? *(b)* Distinguish between general and special (consequential) damages. *(c)* Illustrate how the measure of damages necessary to give effect to the expectation interest varies.

10 *(a)* Illustrate the reliance interest. *(b)* What are the limits on reliance damages? *(c)* Under what circumstances will a claim for otherwise recoverable reliance damages be disallowed?

11 List three kinds of restitution and describe a typical use for each.

12 There are limits on the recovery of damages, especially on the recovery of special damages. *(a)* Illustrate the requirement of causation of special damages. *(b)* Explain or illustrate the requirement of certainty of special damages. *(c)* What is the purpose of the "foreseeability" requirement? How does the "foreseeability" requirement of the Uniform Commercial Code differ from that imposed by the now-abandoned "tacit agreement rule"?

13 Explain the meaning and operation of the "rule of avoidable consequences."

14 Define "reformation" and illustrate its use.

15 Suppose that X signs a contract which provides that X will pay $3,000 if she fails to render the services required of her by the contract. Under what circumstances might this provision be enforceable?

16 *(a)* Define "quasi-contractual remedy" and describe its typical use. *(b)* What is the relationship between quasi-contractual remedies and contractual remedies?

CASE PROBLEMS

1 The Warrens hired Denison, a builder, to construct a house on the Warrens' property. The contract price was $73,400. After the Warrens took possession of the house, a dispute arose regarding the quality of workmanship. Because of the dispute the Warrens withheld the balance of $48,000 due under the contract and brought suit for a declaratory judgment. In their suit they sought a discharge from their remaining obligations under the contract on the ground that Denison had failed to perform his obligations. The jury found that when the Warrens took possession of the house, it was fit for the ordinary purposes for which houses are used. The jury also found that $2,000 in repairs would be required to correct defective workmanship. Did Denison's defective performance discharge the Warrens from their remaining obligations under the contract?

2 The government required the defendant, Chicago and North Western Transportation Co., to provide intercity rail passenger service. Such service was unprofitable and was becoming more so. In 1965, to provide the required service in the most efficient manner and to minimize losses, defendant leased some depot and track facilities from plaintiff railroad company for a term of 10 years. In 1971 defendant voluntarily joined Amtrak, which was established by federal law to provide a national rail passenger service. By joining Amtrak, defendant was released from its obligation to provide rail passenger service, and defendant immediately terminated its lease with plaintiff.

Plaintiff sued for rentals due under the lease. Defendant contended that its performance should be excused on the ground of frustration of purpose, because a federal takeover of rail passenger service was not anticipated in 1965 when the lease was made. Section 285 of the *Restatement (Second) of the Law of Contracts* applies to this case. It provides: "Where, after a contract is made, a party's principal purpose is substantially frustrated without his fault by the occurrence of an event the nonoccurrence of which was a basic assumption on which the contract was made, his remaining duties to render performance are discharged." Should

the defendant be discharged from liability for the rental payment?

3 Goings leased farm land from Gerken. In December 1974, Gerken and Goings signed a purchase agreement for the property. They agreed to a closing date of March 2, 1975. Goings applied to the Farmers Home Administration (FHA) for a loan. The FHA sent Goings a form agreement entitled "Option to Purchase Real Property." Goings and Gerken signed it. Under this agreement, Goings' option to purchase the property would expire not later than December 8, 1975. His FHA loan was approved in March 1975. No funds were available then, but the FHA thought funds would be available by July 1, 1975. In April 1975, Goings and Gerken signed a third agreement, entitled "Lease With Option to Purchase Agreement." Under it, the lease would expire February 28, 1976; the option to purchase would expire July 1, 1975; and Goings would pay a higher price for the land.

In August 1975, Gerken listed the property with a different realtor. FHA funds finally became available in October 1975, and Goings attempted to complete the purchase of the land. In the meantime Gerken had received three higher offers. He refused to honor the FHA option agreement. Goings brought suit for specific performance, contending that the FHA agreement was the only effective agreement between the parties and that under it he had until December 8, 1975, to complete the transaction. Was the FHA agreement still effective?

4 Dupre, a rice farmer familiar with internal combustion engines, hired Tri-Parish Flying Service to repair an irrigation pump engine that was using oil excessively. Tri-Parish installed new piston rings and said the excessive oil consumption would cease after the rings sealed. The condition persisted, and Dupre made numerous complaints. Tri-Parish assured Dupre that he could continue to use the engine until

Tri-Parish could take it back to the shop for a check after the irrigation season. Before the end of the season the engine threw a rod and was a total loss. Dupre sued for damages for loss of the engine and for partial loss of his rice crop. The trial court held that Dupre was not entitled to damages because, by continuing to use the malfunctioning engine, he had failed to mitigate his damages. Dupre appealed. In a companion suit Tri-Parish sought payment for the repairs. *(a)* Did Dupre violate his duty to mitigate damages? *(b)* If not, to what damages was Dupre entitled? *(c)* Was Tri-Parish entitled to payment for the repairs?

5 D.H.M. Industries, Inc. (plaintiff) leased a 500,000 square foot warehouse to Central Port Warehouses, Inc. (defendant) for a 20-year term at a total rental of $10.5 million. Defendant paid plaintiff a security deposit of $126,525 (about 2 months' rent). The lease provided that if the lease was terminated, plaintiff had the right to retain the security deposit and to collect damages from the defendant. Defendant wrongfully refused to take possession of the premises, thus breaching and terminating the lease. In plaintiff's suit for damages the defendant sought the return of the security deposit, alleging that the lease provision relating to the security deposit imposed a penalty. The trial court held that the amount of the security deposit had been agreed upon as liquidated damages. Was the trial court in error?

6 Fonda Corporation contracted with the Georgia Retardation Center to install a "dry" fire sprinkler system. Fonda took bids from subcontractors. Southern won the bid and began the work. Eventually it became apparent that Southern and Fonda had a mutual misunderstanding at the time of contracting and were thinking of entirely different types of systems. Southern refused to make changes which would have greatly increased its cost of performance. Fonda terminated the agreement with Southern and hired another subcontractor. Southern sued Fonda to recover the $25,911 it had spent in installing parts of the system. To what remedy, if any, was Southern entitled?

Chapter

19

Contracting
with
the Government

To be of practical assistance, a book on business law cannot ignore transactions by the federal government—the largest single purchaser in the United States of supplies, services, and construction. Directly or indirectly, the impact of its purchases is felt by nearly every community and segment of industry, science, and agriculture. Our concern here is not with the effect of this government spending upon the economy but, rather, with the *legal aspects* of its thousands of contracts by means of which such spending is accomplished.

The purpose of this chapter is to provide only a broad overview and brief explanation of this important facet of business law not usually included in a business law text.

NATURE OF GOVERNMENT CONTRACTING

Government Contracting as an Aspect of Business Law

Government contracting is not a separate and distinct division of law such as, for example, security transactions, but rather it is a system of rules by which the totality of business law is applied to this important aspect of business. These rules are not static. From time to time new procedures are developed for the formulation of government contracts or for their administration. While many of the principles to be considered may also apply to contracting with state governments and their political subdivisions, this chapter is limited to a discussion of contracting with the federal government.

In general, the same broad principles of law are applied to government contracts as to other contracts. As in private contracts, there must be a manifestation of mutual assent, adequacy of consideration, competency of parties, and the other familiar requisites of a contract. Similarly, when the issue involves contract performance, the rules are the same whether or not the government is a party. There are, however, significant differences in the more detailed rules. Some of these detailed rules are departures from or exceptions to private contract law. Others are new rules developed to meet situations peculiar to governmental action. The new rules are designed to further the social objectives of the government, or to give small and socially and economically disadvantaged businesses the opportunity to work upon government contracts.

The Meaning of Government Contracting

The phrase "government contracting" may be used in a narrow or in a broad sense. In its narrower context it involves only transactions between an individual or firm, which we will call firm A, and a government agency. In its broader context, which is used in this chapter, it also includes the transactions between firm A and its suppliers for parts or services necessary to the performance by A of its government contract.

The contract between the government and firm A is called a prime contract, and firm A is the *prime contractor*. The subordinate contracts between A and its suppliers are subcontracts, and the firms furnishing these supplies are *subcontractors*. Subcontractors are identified by "tiers" descriptive of the level that each is removed from the government. Thus, a first-tier subcontractor might supply the jet engine to the prime contractor who is building the aircraft, the second-tier subcontractor supplies the turbine fins to the engine maker, and the third-tier subcontractor furnishes the metal to the turbine-fin manufacturer.

Generally, subcontractors have no contractual relationship with or obligation to the government. Hence, there is said to be "no privity of contract" between the subcontractor and the government. However, even though there is no contractual relationship between the government and a subcontractor, many of the provisions of the prime contract are "passed down" to the subcontractor. For example, because of the terms of the prime contract, there may be a clause in the subcontract requiring the subcontractor to open its books for the inspection of government auditors. The terms of the contract between the prime contractor and its subcontractors may, in turn, affect the contracts between the first and second-tier subcontractors and so on through an indefinite number of transactions. Thus, the terms of a government contract affect many more companies than those directly engaged in business with the government.

BASIC LAWS AFFECTING GOVERNMENT CONTRACTING

Government contracting is distinguished from contracting between private parties largely by the laws and regulations which:

1 Define contracting procedures
2 Limit the sources of supply
3 Impose special obligations or restrictions upon the contractor[1]

Laws and Regulations Defining Contracting Procedures

The laws governing procurement by the Army, Navy, and Air Force are assembled and pub-

---

[1]Also peculiar to government contracting are the laws, not here pertinent, which restrict the expenditure of federal funds.

lished in Chapter 137 of Title 10 of the United States Code and are commonly called the Armed Services Procurement Act of 1947. The Office of Federal Procurement Policy in the Office of Management and Budget oversees the Federal Procurement Regulation System (FPRS). The Secretary of Defense publishes the Defense Acquisition Regulation (DAR), formerly known as the Armed Services Procurement Regulation (ASPR). Both titles may be used to identify those publications. DAR is a part of the Defense Procurement Regulation System. "It is a system of policies and regulations to guide managers in the conduct of DoD [Department of Defense] acquisition activities and detailed functional regulations required to govern DoD contractual actions in accordance with applicable law and the need for efficiency."[2]

The nonmilitary departments and agencies of the government make contracts according to the procedures and rules set out in the Federal Procurement Regulations (FPR), promulgated by the General Services Administration.[3]

DAR for military and FPR for nonmilitary procurement are periodically modified and republished to reflect pertinent laws newly enacted by Congress and to incorporate changes in procurement policies. Contractual methods and procedures established by the two sets of regulations are closely coordinated.

Having been promulgated by statutory authority and published in the Code of Federal Regulations, DAR and FPR have the force and effect of law. Government contracting officers may not deviate from the regulations without appropriate approval, and contractors are charged with knowledge of their provisions.[4] Obviously, this places an unusual responsibility upon a firm which does business with the government.

Laws and Regulations
Limiting the Sources of Supply

Manufacturer or Regular Dealer The Walsh-Healey Public Contracts Act requires anyone who would contract with the United States to be a manufacturer or regular dealer.[5] In general, a *regular dealer* is a person or concern owning, operating, or maintaining an establishment where supplies of the general character as those required under the contract are kept in stock for sale to the public in the usual course of business. A *manufacturer* need not make the particular item it bids on as long as it is engaged in a manufacturing business in general.

Preference to American Sources The Buy American Act, as its popular title indicates, gives preference to domestically mined or produced articles unless the domestic price is unreasonably high or the purchase would be inconsistent with the public interest.[6] A contractor who furnishes foreign-source supplies in violation of the Act breaches its contract and may be barred from receiving other government contracts for up to 3 years.

From time to time Congress further limits the sources from which supplies and services may be procured. For example, American cargo carriers must be used if available, and purchases from certain foreign countries may be proscribed.

Preference to Small and Disadvantaged Business Firms The Small Business Act is designed to secure for small and socially and economically disadvantaged business firms a fair proportion of government contracts and subcontracts.[7] Where economically practicable, a purchase may be wholly or partially limited to small business

---

[2]DoD Directive 5000.35, March 23, 1978.
[3]Authorized by the Federal Property and Administrative Services Act of 1949, 40 U.S.C. 486(c) et seq.
[4]*G. L. Christian and Assocs. v. United States*, 312 F.2d 418 (Ct. Cl. 1963).

[5]Act of June 30, 1936, as amended, 41 U.S.C. 35.
[6]Act of March 3, 1933, 41 U.S.C. 10 a-d, and Executive Order No. 10582, December 17, 1954, 19 Fed. Reg. 8723.
[7]Act of July 30, 1953, as amended, 15 U.S.C. 631 et seq. Other significant statutes involving small business may be found in 10 U.S.C. 2301, 41 U.S.C. 253, and 50 U.S.C. App. 2151.

enterprises under a procedure called a "small business set-aside." If an entire procurement is so limited, it is called a "total set-aside"; if only a part of the procurement is limited to small business it is a "partial set-aside."

A *small business* is one that is independently owned and operated, is not dominant in the field in which it is bidding, and is—with its affiliates—within the size limitation fixed by the Small Business Administration. A "certificate of competency" issued by that Administration attests that the firm has the capacity and credit to perform the contract for which it submitted a bid or proposal. Such a determination is conclusive upon a government contracting officer.

Preference to Labor Surplus Areas   Government contracting officers are directed to place, where practicable, contracts in areas designated by the Department of Labor as having "substantial" or "persistent" labor surplus. However, no price differential above that offered by a supplier in an area where no labor surplus exists may be paid to a bidder because it is located in a labor surplus area.

Laws and Regulations Imposing Special Obligations or Restrictions

Government contractors and subcontractors may assume obligations and subject themselves to restrictions not ordinarily present in commercial contracts. In addition to laws concerning the hiring of employees and their hours of work, the laws concerning the following topics should be noted.

Limitation on Assignment of Contract   A government contractor may not delegate its duty of performance by assigning the contract to another to perform. However, a government contract may be assigned to a bank or financial institution as security for a loan.[8] Violation of the Anti-Assignment Act may be considered a

breach of contract, but the prohibition against assignment, which exists for the benefit of the government, may be waived by the government.

Limitation on Profits   In a cost reimbursement type contract, that is, one in which the contractor is repaid all allowable costs plus a fee, the maximum permissible fee is fixed by law. An architect-engineer may receive a fee of 6 percent of the original estimated construction cost. In an ordinary cost type contract the contractor's fee may not exceed 10 percent, and in a research and development contract the fee is limited to 15 percent.

It should be noted that a contractor may be reimbursed only for "allowable" costs. That is, the cost must be reasonable, allocable to the contract, recognized by generally accepted accounting practices, and not specifically excluded by regulations. Profits may also be affected by a law frequently called the "Truth or Consequences Act."[9] This provides that prior to the award of any cost-reimbursement type contract expected to exceed $100,000, the contractor must reveal and certify as being complete, current, and accurate all cost and pricing data. If the agreed price is later found to include substantial amounts which can be attributed to erroneous or incomplete cost or pricing data, the contract price may be reduced accordingly. Even though a profit or fee may be within the limits established by law, it may be subject to reduction pursuant to other applicable legislation.

Submission to Examination of Records   An "examination-of-records" clause appears in all negotiated government contracts. This requires the prime contractor and all subcontractors to retain the books and records pertaining to a contract for a period of at least 3 years after final payment and to permit their examination and audit by government representatives.

---

[8]The Anti-Assignment Act, RS 3737, as amended, 41 U.S.C. 15.

[9]Act of September 10, 1962, Pub. Law 87-653, 10 U.S.C. 2306(f).

Adoption of Cost Accounting Standards   As national defense procurements of large value generally involve the use of cost type contracts, proper contract administration requires the auditing of the costs for which the contractor claims reimbursement. To achieve uniformity, Congress created the Cost Accounting Standards Board.[10] That board periodically publishes bookkeeping standards to be followed by any contractor who has a negotiated contract exceeding $100,000 unless exempt by regulations of the board. The contract price or the costs claimed by the contractor may be adjusted if the contractor or a subcontractor fails to comply with applicable cost accounting standards or fails to file a disclosure of its accounting practices.

Submission to Change or Termination of Contract   Written into all government contracts are clauses which permit the government, without becoming liable for breach, to direct changes in the work to be done provided the changes are within the general scope of the task originally contracted for. As recompense, an equitable adjustment is made in the price or the contractor is granted further time to perform the contract. Under appropriate circumstances, the contractor may be allowed both remedies. A change within the scope of the contract may call for work beyond the contractor's financial or plant capabilities or may interfere with the orderly performance of its commercial work. Nonetheless, having undertaken the basic contract, the contractor must accept this added burden.

Frequently considered a directed change in the contract work, but actually distinct therefrom, is a directed acceleration of the work. *Acceleration* means the required completion of a contract task before its due date. It may be directed by an actual order or constructively

directed by failure of the contracting officer to grant a time extension to which the contractor is entitled. In either event the contractor will be due an equitable adjustment in the contract price to compensate for additional costs.

Under commercial contract practice, a direction by the buyer to the seller to discontinue performance already begun is a breach of contract, and the seller becomes entitled to all anticipated, though unearned, profits. Not so under government contract practice. Every government contract contains a clause that permits the government at any time to terminate the contract for its own convenience. If the contract is so terminated, no action for breach will lie. The contractor's compensation is based upon the degree of completion of the contract and the monies expended in its performance.

Compliance with Nondiscrimination Legislation   It is government policy that there should be no discrimination in employment. Therefore, all government contracts exceeding $10,000 (and in certain circumstances contracts in lesser amounts) are required by Executive order to contain an *equal opportunity* clause. That clause requires a contractor to take affirmative action to ensure that all applicants are considered for employment and that all employees are treated, during employment, without regard to their race, color, religion, sex, or national origin. In the event of noncompliance, among other sanctions, the contract may be terminated or suspended in whole or in part, and the contractor may be declared ineligible to receive further government contracts. Each contractor is required to include a nondiscrimination clause in its subcontracts.

Government contractors are also subject to the Civil Rights Act of 1964 as amended by the Equal Employment Opportunity Act of 1972. In addition, they may not discriminate on the basis of the age of the applicant or employee, and they must take affirmative action in most contracts to employ or advance in employment

---

[10]Act of August 15, 1970, Pub. Law 91-379, 50 U.S.C. App. 2168.

qualified handicapped individuals and qualified disabled veterans, including those of the Vietnam era.

MECHANICS OF GOVERNMENT CONTRACTING

Authority of Government Contracting Officer

The head of each buying or contracting agency of the government does not personally enter into contracts but appoints "contracting officers." They, in turn, make contracts in the name of the United States. The order appointing a contracting officer states the limits of authority of the officer. Often the broad authority of a contracting officer is divided among three individuals: a purchasing contracting officer (PCO) who is authorized to enter into contracts within the dollar limits of his or her authorization; an administrative contracting officer (ACO) who does not enter into contracts personally but oversees and administers contract performance; and a termination contracting officer (TCO) who administers contract terminations.

Of course commercial concerns also contract through agents. But there is a startling difference between the authority of an agent of a commercial concern and an agent of the government. As we shall see later in this book, a commercial agent may act within the limits of *actual or apparent* authority. A government agent, however, may act only within the limits of *actual* authority. This difference marks one of the major peculiarities of government contracting and offers one of the most common pitfalls to an unwary individual who contracts with the government. The difficulty lies in the fact that anyone doing business with the government is presumed to know the limitations upon the authority of the government's agent with whom he or she deals. The government may disassociate itself from its agent when the latter acts

beyond his or her authority, and, as a result, a good faith contractor may be "left holding the bag." But the contractor's position is not entirely hopeless, for the agent's unauthorized act may be subsequently adopted or ratified by someone in the government who initially had authority to authorize the contractual action.

Methods of Selecting the Contractor

A contracting officer about to make a purchase either invites bids by "formal advertising" or, preparatory to negotiation, requests proposals from selected sources he or she believes to be competent. Occasionally the elements of the two methods are combined into a two-step or four-step procedure, discussed later under "Special Methods of Procurement."

Formal Advertising for Bids The contracting officer prepares an "invitation for bids" (IFB) which, with its specifications, describes the articles or services to be procured. The specification reflects the actual needs of the government rather than an item of the highest quality attainable. A specification may be either a design or a performance type. A *design specification* completely describes the manufacturing details required to produce the article. A *performance specification* leaves the choice of design to the contractor, setting out only the performance standards which the article must satisfy. The invitation also defines the bidding instructions, including the date, hour, and place of the bid opening and the contract terms and conditions. The invitation is "advertised" by posting copies in appropriate public places. A synopsis of the desired procurement appears in the *Commerce Business Daily.*[11] In rare instances a procurement may be advertised in the public press. In addition, the contracting officer sends copies of the invitation to prospective bidders whose names appear on bidders' mail-

---

[11] A report of government contracting activities, published daily by the Department of Commerce.

ing lists developed from applications submitted by firms desiring government business. The names of prospective bidders are also secured from trade journals.

After public bid opening at the time specified in the invitation, the contracting officer reviews and evaluates the bids. When this process is completed, the contract is awarded to the responsible bidder whose bid conforms to the invitation and is the most advantageous to the United States—price and other factors considered. These factors include, among others, the bidder's financial ability to perform, its plant capacity, the technical know-how of its staff, and its history of prior performance on other government contracts. An award, therefore, reflects the exercise of judgment by the contracting officer and is not automatically made to the lowest bidder.

An invitation for bids is a call for offers and is not itself an offer. In ordinary commercial practice, the rule is that the offeror may revoke an offer at any time before it is accepted. (Section 2-205, of the Uniform Commercial Code, provides that a merchant's offer in writing to buy or sell goods is irrevocable for a reasonable period, not to exceed 3 months. If a consideration is given to keep a bid open, it is then an option and cannot be withdrawn during the option period.) Under government contract law, however, a bid may be withdrawn or modified *only* before the time set for the bid opening. After the opening, the bid is irrevocable or "firm" and cannot be withdrawn for the period stated in the bid.

A bid must be received by the office issuing the invitation on or before the exact time set for the bid opening. If it is received only a minute or two late, it is a "late bid" and will not be considered for award unless the delay was caused by the fault of the mails, proved by the date and time stamped on registered or certified mail.

Certain special problems sometimes arise in connection with selecting a contract through the process of formal advertising. Chief among them are:

1 Irregularities in bids
2 Mistakes in bids
3 Rights of an unsuccessful bidder

Irregularities in bids In order to be considered for award, a bid must comply in all material respects with the conditions of the invitation. In other words, it must be "responsive." For example, if a bidder omits to furnish required drawings or changes the date or place of delivery from that specified in the invitation, the bid is not responsive. After the bid opening a nonresponsive bid may not be corrected. However, an obvious clerical error in a bid (such as a misplaced decimal point) or a minor irregularity or informality having no effect on the price, quality, or delivery schedule may be corrected by the bidder or the informality may be waived by the contracting officer.

Mistakes in bids Notwithstanding the firm-bid rule, a bidder may, under certain circumstances based on the legal theory of mistake, withdraw or correct a bid. To be permitted to do so, the bidder must supply information from which the contracting officer can with reasonable certainty conclude that the claim of error had basis in fact and was made in good faith.

The correction of a bid is more difficult to accomplish than its withdrawal because correction involves not only proof of mistake but also proof of the bid which had actually been intended.

Should a bid be so much lower than the contracting officer's estimate of costs or so out of line with competing bids as to suggest that there may have been a mistake in the bid, it becomes the responsibility of the contracting officer to advise the bidder of the possibility of mistake and to ask for verification. If the contracting officer awards the bidder the contract without first seeking verification and the contractor later discovers that there has been a mistake, a "mutual mistake" is said to have been made. Under such circumstances the contractor may be relieved of the obligation to perform the contract at the stated bid price, or the contract may be corrected. The modification may not, however, result in a corrected price which exceeds the next higher bid.

A contractor who, after receipt of award of a government contract, discovers that a mistake was made in the bid and that the mistake cannot be characterized as "mutual," may desire to rescind the contract or to seek its reformation. Under appropriate circumstances, such remedy may be effected (1) by the contracting officer under the authority of the Contract Disputes Act of 1978, (2) by the Comptroller General through the exercise of that officer's powers, or (3) by the secretary of the department concerned through the application of Public Law 85-804, when the national defense would thereby be facilitated.

Rights of unsuccessful bidder   An unsuccessful bidder who believes that he or she has been wrongfully denied award of a contract was, until the *Scanwell* case, without legal remedy.[12] Since that case, however, an unsuccessful bidder may seek an injunction against the award's being made to another, and a court may direct that the aggrieved bidder be given the award.

Negotiation   It is the expressed intent of Congress that whenever possible a government procurement will be accomplished through formal advertising. Under certain circumstances, however, it permits the selection of a contractor through negotiation. Some of these circumstances are:

1   To make small purchases
2   To satisfy a public exigency
3   To secure personal or professional services

4   To secure experimental, developmental, or research work
5   To further the interest of national defense or industrial mobilization

When formal advertising is not feasible or practicable and one of the statutory exceptions exists, a contracting officer may secure a contractor through negotiation. The contracting officer does this by requesting proposals or quotations from individuals or firms that he or she deems qualified to perform the work. The contracting officer then discusses all aspects of the intended contract with the prospective contractors. These discussions may be conducted in writing or orally and include the cost, fee, contract terms, and the type of contract to be consummated. The contracting officer selects the offeror who is apparently the best—price and other factors considered—and that offeror becomes the contractor. Although public advertising and the formal bid procedure are not used, competition is still present among the selected offerors in the negotiation process, each being aware that any proposal will be critically weighed against the others. During the several discussions, however, the contracting officer may not disclose to the offerors the names or even the number of their competitors nor, of course, the details of competing proposals.

Special Methods of Procurement   Department of Defense contracting officers sometimes use a hybrid contracting system called "two-step formal advertising." The first step, through a negotiation process, determines the bidders who are qualified to perform the desired task. Then, as a second step, these concerns are asked to bid upon the procurement. A bid from a firm which had not qualified by the first step is not considered.

"Four-step" source selection procedures are applicable to all competitively negotiated research and development acquisitions. These steps are: (1) the submission by business firms of technical proposals and their evaluation by the

---

[12]*Scanwell Labs., Inc. v. Schaffer*, 424 F.2d 859 (D.C. Cir. 1970).

government; (2) the submission and evaluation of the firms' cost proposals; (3) the establishment of the maximum possible contract cost and the tentative selection of a firm to perform the contract; and (4) the negotiation of a definitive contract with that firm.

TYPES OF GOVERNMENT CONTRACTS

Because of the vast array of different articles and services that the government procures, it is only natural that a number of different contract types have been developed. These may be classified by the nature of the goods or services to be procured, by their form, or by the methods used to establish the contractor's compensation.

Types of Contracts by
Nature of the Procurement

Government contracts may be (1) "supply contracts" to produce or furnish personal property, (2) "personal service contracts" to furnish personal services, (3) "research and development contracts" to investigate technical problems or develop new products, (4) "construction contracts" to construct buildings or make other improvements to land, or (5) "facilities contracts" to manage or use government-furnished production facilities (plants or equipment).

Types of Contracts by Form

Contracts are normally written on government standard forms identified by their numbers, such as Standard Forms 23 and 23A for construction contracts and Standard Forms 26, 30, and 32 for supply contracts. While contracting officers have great latitude to tailor the wording of each contract to satisfy the particular situation present, the use of certain clauses is mandatory. Before deviating from a standard form the contracting officer must secure approval from higher authority.

On occasion, because of lack of time, a con-tract is expressed in letter form. Such a letter contains as many of the definitive contract provisions as possible and, as a minimum, expresses the scope of the work, the price and method of payment, and incorporates by reference the clauses required by statute and regulation. Although a letter contract is a binding commitment, it is superseded by a definitive contract at the earliest practicable date, generally within 90 days. Purchase orders and blanket orders are short-form contracts for purchases of small dollar value.

Types of Contracts by
Method of Compensation

Particularly characteristic of government contracting is the variety of ways by which the contract price may be determined. In the commercial world a fixed-price contract is generally used—that is, the contractor's total compensation is agreed upon when the contract is entered into. In addition to fixed-price contracts, the government frequently utilizes, particularly for its larger acquisitions, one of several cost type contract forms. However, the cost type contract may be used only when the contractor has been selected through negotiation and may not be used in conjunction with formal advertising.

Fixed-Price Contracts   These contracts may be (1) firm fixed-price, (2) fixed-price with escalation, (3) fixed-price with price redetermination, or (4) fixed-price incentive. The firm fixed-price contract is the ordinary contract of commercial practice. One with escalation provides for a price increase according to changes in costs of such a basic item as labor, steel, or coal. A fixed-price contract with price redetermination is one in which the price is negotiated after partial performance and the contractor has developed some cost experience. A fixed-price incentive contract is one in which the final contract price is established by application of a formula agreed to at the time the contract is negotiated. The formula involves incentive targets which may include total ultimate costs, performance characteristics, or delivery schedules—or a combination of any of these targets. If the incentive target is reached, the contractor receives an increased profit according to the agreed formula; if the contractor fails to reach the target, profit is diminished in accordance with the formula. A contractor's performance may be such that it receives no profit but suffers a loss on the contract.

Cost Reimbursement Contracts   A cost reimbursement contract is one providing for the payment to the contractor of allowable costs together with an agreed-upon fixed, incentive, or award fee. Rules for determining allowable costs are spelled out in the contracting agency's regulations, as, for example, DAR, Part XV, for the Department of Defense. As a protection to the government, each such cost type contract sets forth an expenditure ceiling above which the contractor will not be paid without prior approval of the contracting officer.

Sometimes a cost type contract provides for payment of costs, but no fee to the contractor. This form is used primarily for research and development work by nonprofit institutions. In certain instances not only does the contractor receive no fee but even agrees to bear some of the costs. A contractor might engage in such an undertaking when it believes that substantial present or future commercial benefit will ensue from performing the contract for the government.

Increasingly, particularly in large and complex contracts, the contractor is paid for costs and an incentive or award fee as arranged instead of a fixed fee. When this type of cost contract is agreed to, a maximum and a minimum fee is established. Within these limits the ultimate fee is adjusted according to the degree of success or failure of the contractor to reach established performance goals. In this respect this contract is similar to a fixed-price incentive contract.

When it is not possible at the time of entering into a contract to estimate the extent or duration of the work or to estimate the costs with any degree of confidence, a time-and-materials or a labor-hour contract may be used. Contracting officers are admonished, however, to engage in such contracts only when no other type of contract will suitably serve.

During World War I a cost-plus-percentage-of-cost type of contract was frequently used. Because such an arrangement encouraged extravagance in the work and unduly increased the government's ultimate costs, the Congress has expressly forbidden its use.

SETTLEMENT OF CONTRACTUAL DISPUTES

Administrative Settlement

The Contract Disputes Act of 1978, 41 U.S.C. 601-613, establishes procedures for the administrative settlement of claims by or against contractors of government contracts. Claims, as defined by that act, include the payment of money, the adjustment or interpretation of contract terms, or other relief arising under or relating to a government contract. For the Department of Defense, the procedures for administrative settlements are contained in section 1-314 of Defense Acquisition Circular 76-24, 28 August 1980. A contractor is required to submit its claim in writing to the contracting officer who, within the dollar limits of his authority, is authorized to settle it. However, a claim in excess of $50,000 must be certified by the contractor that it is submitted in good faith; that the supporting data are accurate and complete; and that the amount requested accurately reflects the contract adjustment for which the contractor believes the government is liable.

A contractor may appeal the contracting officer's decision to the board of contract appeals of the department concerned. Such a board has the same powers of relief as the court of claims possesses. In the Department of Defense, the appeals procedures, established by its board of contract appeals, are published in the Defense Acquisition Regulation. Each board has established its own rules for the presentation of cases, the admissibility of evidence, and the conduct of its hearings. These rules generally are less restrictive than those governing proceedings in a court of law. Under the provisions of the Wünderlich Act, a decision of a board of contract appeals is final and conclusive upon the contractor unless the contractor can convince a court of competent jurisdiction that the decision was "fraudulent, capricious or arbitrary or was so grossly erroneous as necessarily to imply bad faith or was not supported by the evidence."[13]

Resort to a board of contract appeals, composed of employees of the government who, in effect, act as arbitrators or judges of a controversy in which their employer, the government, is a party certainly differs from procedures for the settlement of commercial contract disputes. However, in practice the boards of contract appeals have been found to be impartial; relatively few of their decisions are appealed to the courts.

Judicial Settlement

Through the Tucker Act the government has given blanket consent to be sued in matters arising under contract.[14] The remedies against the United States, however, may differ, and rules of law may be applied which would not apply if both the parties had been private litigants. The court applies what is loosely called the "federal common law of contracts." This body of law is not defined but is fashioned by the courts from the federal statutes, Executive orders, regulations and selected court decisions, the opinions of the Attorney General, and the decisions of the Comptroller General and of the boards of contract appeals. As a result, government contracts are subject to a single judicial standard and interpretation and are not subject to the possible vagaries of the laws of fifty different states.

---

[13]Act of May 11, 1954, 41 U.S.C. 321.

[14]Act of March 3, 1887, as amended, 28 U.S.C. 1346; 1491.

PART FOUR

PROPERTY AND ESTATES

Chapter 20

**Nature and Importance of Property;
Personal Property (Including Bailments)**

Chapter 21

**Real Property: Nature, Acquisition,
and Ownership**

Chapter 22

Interests in Real Property

Chapter 23

Wills, Estates, and Trusts

Chapter

20

Nature and Importance of Property; Personal Property (Including Bailments)

Property forms the foundation of any economic system. Private property constitutes the major portion of the foundation of a free-enterprise economy. The law of property grew out of a need to protect the individual's creations and acquisitions and is an integral part of the philosophy and customs of a free, competitive society. In recent years the institution of private property has come under scrutiny, and many people have explicitly or implicitly questioned the validity of private property. In order to understand the milieu in which we live and to act intelligently in it, we need to know the nature and importance of property, the most important legal principles relating to different types of property, and the reasons underlying contemporary property law.

This chapter deals with the general nature and importance of property, particularly private property, and with the most important aspects of the law of personal property, including the subject of bailments. The next two chapters are devoted to real property.

NATURE AND IMPORTANCE OF PROPERTY

Meaning of Property

The word "property" is used in two different senses. In one sense, property refers to things owned, such as land, automobiles, and shares of stock in a corporation. Lay persons customarily think of property in this sense. Sometimes the law also refers to things as constituting property. For example, a California statute defines property as "the thing of which there may be ownership."[1]

In its other sense, property means the exclusive right to use, possess, enjoy, and dispose of a thing. Used in this sense, "property" refers not to a *thing* but to a collection or bundle of *rights* in that thing. These rights are protected by law. This second concept is the more fundamental one; land and other physical objects can exist where there is no law (e.g., rocks on the moon), but *property rights* can exist only where there is law. As the English philosopher and jurist Jeremy Bentham pointed out, "Property and law are born together and die together. Before laws were made there was no property; take away law, and property ceases."[2]

It should be noted that the bundle of rights referred to is not always held in its entirety by the same person at the same time. For example, an owner of a house may lease it to a tenant for a term of years. In that event, the tenant has the exclusive right to use, possess, and enjoy the house for the lease period. The landlord retains the right to dispose of the house. At the termination of the lease period the owner regains the rights he or she temporarily gave up.

Classes of Property

Many laws are applicable only to certain specified classes or subclasses of property. The main classes of property are tangible and intangible, real and personal, and public and private.

Tangible and Intangible Property   Tangible property consists of things that have a physical existence, such as books, clothing, buildings, and land. Intangible property consists of things that do not exist in physical form but that have economic value, such as patents, copyrights, accounts receivable, and shares of stock.

To understand the concept of intangible property we need to observe an important distinction. We know, for instance, that a stock certificate has a physical existence. It can be seen, touched, endorsed by the owner, and transferred to a purchaser. But the reason it has value and will be accepted by others in the commercial world is that the certificate represents an intangible property right—the right of ownership in a corporate entity. In addition, if the stock certificate is lost or destroyed, it can be replaced without loss of any rights. A person is still a stockholder in a corporation even though the certificate may have been totally destroyed in a fire. A stock certificate is simply *evidence of ownership*, and is not the property itself. The property consists of a bundle of rights that cannot be destroyed by fire.

Real and Personal Property   Real property consists of land, airspace above the land, and all things imbedded in the land or firmly attached to it, such as minerals, trees, fences, and buildings. Personal property is all property that is not real property, and thus includes tangible things that are movable and intangible things that have economic value. However, the term "personal property" is often used in a more limited sense to mean only movable, tangible things, sometimes called "chattels."

It is possible for items to be changed in their classification from real to personal and from personal to real. For example, a tree is real property until it is severed from the land— either by a person cutting it down or by an act of nature, as by wind or flood. When the tree is severed it becomes movable and is reclassified as personal property. The reverse of this situation occurs when personal property becomes attached to land. For example, a building contractor takes movable items, such as lumber and bricks, and firmly affixes them to the land in constructing a house. The items are thereby converted to real property.

Public and Private Property   All property, whether tangible or intangible, real or personal,

---

[1]Calif. Civ. Code, sec. 654.

[2]Quoted in Morris R. Cohen and Felix S. Cohen, *Readings in Jurisprudence and Legal Philosophy*, Little, Brown and Company, Boston, 1951, p. 9.

can be characterized as public or private. The essential difference is in designating who has the right to use, possess, enjoy, and dispose of the particular thing. Private property is that held by an individual or business entity primarily for personal or corporate benefit. Public property is that held by a governmental unit or agency, whether federal, state, or local. To illustrate: a national park and a city recreation center are classified as public property because a governmental unit holds the bundle of rights over the park or recreational center. By contrast, many football and baseball stadiums are held as private property; that is, a private individual or corporation holds the right to use, possess, enjoy, and dispose of the particular thing.

Occasionally, the status of property changes from one class to the other. For example, a person who owns a lot at the beach and allows the public to use the beach frontage, without restriction, may find that after a period of time the beach frontage has become public property. When a governmental unit or agency finds it no longer needs certain items, it may dispose of them to private individuals or business firms. Thus the property becomes private property.

Case 20.1   **Lloyd Corp. v. Tanner**
                407 U.S. 551 (1972)

Lloyd Corporation (Lloyd), owns a large modern retail shopping center in Portland, Oregon called Lloyd Center. Some 60 stores are located within a single large, multi-level building complex sometimes referred to as the "Mall." Within this complex, in addition to the stores, there are parking facilities, malls, private sidewalks, stairways, escalators, gardens, an auditorium and a skating rink. The interior malls are a distinctive feature of the Center, serving both utilitarian and esthetic functions. Essentially, they are private, interior promenades with 10-foot sidewalks serving the stores, and with a center strip 30 feet wide in which flowers and shrubs are planted, and statuary, fountains, benches and other amenities are located. The Center is open generally to the public, with a considerable effort being made to attract shoppers. The Center allows limited use of the malls by the American Legion to sell "Buddy Poppies" for disabled veterans, and by the Salvation Army and Volunteers of America to solicit Christmas contributions. It has denied similar use to other civic and charitable organizations. Political use is also forbidden, except that presidential candidates of both parties have been allowed to speak in the auditorium.

The Center for some eight years had a policy, strictly enforced, against the distribution of handbills within the building complex and its malls. No exceptions were made with respect to handbilling, which was considered likely to annoy customers, to create litter, potentially to create disorders, and generally to be incompatible with the purpose of the Center and the atmosphere sought to be preserved.

On November 14, 1968, the respondents in this case, (plaintiffs in the lower court), Donald M. Tanner and others, distributed within the Center handbill invitations to a meeting of the "Resistance Community" to protest the draft and the Vietnam War. The distribution, made in several different places on the mall walkways by five young people, was quiet and orderly, and there was no littering. There was a complaint from one customer. Security guards informed the respondents that they were trespassing and would be arrested unless they stopped distributing the handbills within the Center. The guards suggested that respondents distribute their literature on the public streets and sidewalks adjacent to but outside of the Center complex. Respondents left the premises as requested "to avoid arrest" and continued the handbilling outside. Subsequently, respondents initiated this suit in the District Court seeking an injunction to restrain Lloyd from interfering with respondents' asserted right to distribute handbills in the shopping center. Lloyd appealed from the District Court's granting of an injunction.

POWELL, J. . . . The basic issue in this case is whether respondents, in the exercise of asserted First Amendment rights, may distribute handbills on Lloyd's private property contrary to its wishes and contrary to a policy enforced against *all* handbilling. In addressing this issue, it must be remembered that the First and Fourteenth Amendments safeguard the rights of free speech and assembly by limitations on *state* action, not on action by the owner of private property used nondiscriminatorily for private purposes only. . . . This court has never held that a trespasser or an uninvited guest may exercise general rights of free speech on property privately owned and used nondiscriminatorily for private purposes only.

Respondents contend, however, that the property of a large shopping center is "open to the public," serves the same purposes as a "business district" of a municipality, and therefore has been dedicated to certain types of public use. The argument is that such a center has sidewalks, streets, and parking areas which are functionally similar to facilities customarily provided by municipalities. It is then asserted that all members of the public, whether invited as customers or not, have the same right of free speech as they would have on the similar public facilities in the streets of a city or town.

The argument reaches too far. The Constitution by no means requires such an attenuated doctrine of dedication of private property to public use. . . .

Nor does property lose its private character merely because the public is generally invited to use it for designated purposes. Few would argue that a free standing store, with abutting parking space for customers, assumes significant public attributes merely because the public is invited to shop. Nor is size alone the controlling factor. The essentially private character of a store and its privately owned abutting property does not change by virtue of being large or clustered with other stores in a modern shopping center. . . .

We hold that there has been no such dedication of Lloyd's privately owned and operated shopping center to public use as to entitle respondents to exercise therein the asserted First Amendment rights. Accordingly, we reverse the judgment and remand the case to the Court of Appeals with directions to vacate the injunction.

It is so ordered.

Legal Protection of Private Property

Private property is vital to the maintenance of a free, competitive society. For this reason, and other reasons discussed below, governments have recognized the need for laws to protect private property.

Methods of Protection of Private Property As we have seen, the concept of property embodies the idea of a bundle of rights; that is, property is the exclusive right to use, possess, enjoy, and dispose of a thing. In regard to private property, an essential part of the definition is the word "exclusive": an individual holds the bundle of rights to the exclusion of the public at large and the government.[3] This concept of *exclusive* rights is deeply ingrained in our society. The law provides protection from interference by others through the law of torts. Much of the law covered in Chapters 5 and 6 is devoted to protection of private property.

Private property is also protected against interference by the government. The United States Constitution provides in the Fifth and Fourteenth Amendments that neither the federal nor any state government shall deprive a person of his life, liberty, or *property* without due process of law. These provisions were added to the Constitution in the belief that the individual was entitled to protection from possible overreaching by the government.

Many state constitutions contain provisions similar to the above, giving further protection to private property. In addition, state legislatures and local city councils have enacted statutes and ordinances imposing criminal penalties for violating the rights of an owner to the exclusive use, possession, and enjoyment of private property.

Reasons for Protection of Private Property The foundation of private property rests on protection of possession, a fact recognized in the familiar colloquialism "possession is nine-tenths of the law." There are good reasons to support legal protection of possession.

For many years it has been recognized that possession of property should be protected in order to avoid breaches of the peace. From earliest recorded history it became apparent that one who possessed an object or plot of land would instinctively fight to keep it from being taken by an aggressor. To avoid such fights, the notion of an intermediary to protect the owner became institutionalized in the form of laws to deter aggression. Today, the citizen's property rights are protected through these laws, enforced by means of a police force and a court system. We all benefit from avoiding the physical violence of "self-help" or vigilante groups associated with a more primitive society.

Another reason advanced for legal protection of possession is that society benefits when resources are developed, not left to lie fallow. Of course, there are limitations to development that have been imposed for the protection of others. But, to the extent we desire application of human knowledge and energy to natural resources, a choice of incentives to promote effective development is involved. There are indications that a person works best on something, whether it be real or personal property, when the benefits of his or her labor can be retained. When a natural resource is developed and society gives protection to the possessor, the incentive to expend individual effort is

---

[3]*Exclusive* does not mean unlimited. There are many restrictions on the use of private property discussed in later pages.

greatly increased. This rationale applies not only to utilization of physical objects, but also to the area of intangibles. The law of patents and copyrights developed from the notion that intellectual effort that results in a valuable invention or creation should be protected from appropriation. This view is the proper response from a society that benefits from such creativity.

In sum, a free enterprise economy requires a framework of legal rules to avoid violence and to encourage individual effort by giving legal protection to possession of private property.

Legal Restrictions on Private Property

Although the scope of this book does not permit a detailed discussion of the legal restrictions on the use, possession, enjoyment, and disposition of private property, some mention should at least be made of the scope and importance of such restrictions. All states have health and safety laws regulating the use of property, motor vehicle laws, zoning ordinances, building codes, and the like. Part of the law of torts restrains an owner of property from using it in such a way that it harms others. An owner can be held liable in damages to a person who is injured on or near the property due to an intentional or negligent act, and in some instances, even if the owner is without fault (see Chapter 21 under the heading, "Duties of Owners").

If a person attempts to transfer property for the purpose of defrauding creditors or evading taxes, the effort may be thwarted by a restraining order. In addition, there are antitrust laws prohibiting the improper use of private property in restraint of free competition.

There are many other legal restrictions on private property, and new restrictions are being created at all levels of government. In today's world, the owner of private property must constantly keep abreast of new rules and regulations in order to plan his or her business transactions intelligently.

PERSONAL PROPERTY (INCLUDING BAILMENTS)

The most important aspects of the law of personal property involve the ownership and possession of such property. The rest of this chapter deals with the acquisition of ownership of personal property and with the temporary possession of such property by someone who is not an owner.

Acquisition of Ownership of Personal Property

Ownership of personal property can be acquired in various ways. We shall discuss in some detail the legal principles governing various methods and the background out of which the principles emerged.

Acquisition by Purchase Probably the most common method of acquiring ownership of personal property is by purchase from an owner. We are all consumers. We purchase goods daily in the marketplace from a variety of sellers. The legal principles relating to these transactions are so extensive that they cannot be treated here. Many principles are covered in the next part of this book that deals with sales (Chapters 24–27). In addition, many rules presented in the law of contracts apply to sales transactions.

Acquisition by Gift Another common method of acquiring ownership of personal property is by gift. A simple definition of a gift is a voluntary transfer of property without consideration. The one who makes the gift is called the "donor", and the one who receives the gift is called the "donee".

Controversies sometimes arise as to whether a gift has been made. In such cases, the courts require three elements to be present in order to establish a valid gift: (1) intent to make a present transfer; (2) delivery, or a satisfactory substitute, and (3) acceptance.

Intent to make present transfer In order to have a valid gift, it is required that the donor intend to make an unconditional present transfer of his or her rights. Statements such as, "Take it, it is yours," or "I want you to have this," are clear indications of the requisite donative intent. Where there is no clear indication of intent and a lawsuit results, the court must determine the intent. It is seldom that someone's subjective intent is entirely clear; and, of necessity, the court will examine the circumstantial evidence of what a donor said and did, and will draw inferences from it. The court must decide if the donor exhibited the intent to make an unconditional present transfer.

Sometimes the law's requirements result in the frustration of a donor's intention. Suppose that an elderly person puts money in an envelope and writes on the outside, "To my nephew, John, upon my death." The person's intent obviously was to retain control over the money until death and to have the transfer occur at that time. That intent is frustrated by the legal rule that a gift requires an unconditional *present* transfer. The desire to retain control over the money and to have the transfer occur at the time of death could be effectuated only by a will. (*Note*: the words "To my nephew, John, upon my death" do not constitute a will. Under the statutes of most states, a will, to be valid, must meet certain formal requirements. One of these requirements is that the instrument must be signed.[4])

Delivery or satisfactory substitute   The requirement of delivery is usually met by physically handing the object to the donee and thereby giving up control and possession of it. No gift occurs if the donor does not give up complete control and possession of the object. For example, if one person says to another, "I want you to have my watch," but continues to wear the watch, no gift is made.

In some situations it is impractical to make

physical delivery of an item, and the law allows a *constructive* (sometimes called *symbolic*) delivery. For example, giving the donee a key to a locker may under some circumstances be recognized as a gift of the contents. With intangible property, where physical delivery is impossible, a symbol may be given to the donee that will be sufficient to constitute a gift of the underlying interest. For instance, delivery of a savings account passbook is usually sufficient to pass ownership of the account to a donee. Even though the particular financial institution usually requires the donor to sign a withdrawal slip before the donee will be recognized as owner, courts would generally hold that title passed to the donee when the passbook was delivered. If the donor were to die or have a change of mind before signing anything, the donee could secure a court order forcing the institution to recognize the donee as owner. The donee's case is based not on mere verbal words of intent, which could be subject to dispute, but on physical possession of a symbol, that is, the passbook.

In order to constitute a gift, delivery of an item need not necessarily be to the donee. Occasionally, a donor will turn over an item to a third person with instructions to deliver it to the donee or to hold it for the benefit of the donee. The question may then arise: Has the donor made an *unconditional* present transfer of his or her rights? The answer will depend upon the relationship of the third person to the donor.

Where the third person is an agent for the donor, there is no present transfer of rights. An agent owes a duty to follow the instructions of his or her principal. Thus, a donor who delivers an object to his or her own agent could have a change of mind at any time and get the object back. Where the donor delivers an item to an agent of the *donee*, the donor does not retain control and there is an unconditional present transfer of rights.

Frequently, the donor will execute a written conveyance of an object. The delivery of such a

---

[4]See Chapter 23 for discussion of the requirements of a will.

document is as effective to transfer ownership as is physical delivery of the object. For example, the gift of an automobile or a boat is usually accomplished by the donor's signing and delivering the certificate of ownership to the donee. Ownership of securities, accounts receivable, and other intangibles is often transferred by means of a written form of assignment.

Acceptance   There are few situations where an intended donee would not wish to receive a gift. However, it is fundamental that a person cannot be forced to accept something the person does not want. Some examples of items a person might not wish to accept as a gift are an automobile with an unpaid purchase price in excess of its current value, stock in a corporation on the verge of bankruptcy, and defective goods that require extensive repairs to be usable.

In a lawsuit in which the issue is whether the alleged donee intended to *accept* the gift offered, the alleged donee ordinarily will testify as to his or her subjective intent. Often, the court will draw inferences from the circumstantial evidence presented. If, for example, acceptance of the gift would impose undue burdens on the intended donee, the court may conclude that there was no acceptance. On the other hand, if the donee's conduct manifests ownership of the article, the court may infer an intent to accept. For example, riding a bicycle received as a birthday present is an act of ownership. It is not necessary for the donee to say, "I accept." In most instances, a gift will result in a benefit to the donee. Therefore, in the absence of contrary evidence, the courts ordinarily will *presume* acceptance by the donee.

Case 20.2   **In re Estate of Stahl**
301 N.E.2d 82 (Ill. App. 1973)

Petitioner, Ursula Stahl, filed a petition in the Estate of Leonard Stahl, deceased, requesting the court to declare that the contents of a certain safety deposit box belonged to her and not to the estate. Petitioner claimed Leonard Stahl made a gift to her of the contents of the box before he died. The contents of the box consisted of government bonds. After a hearing without a jury the court found that the estate was entitled to the contents of the safety deposit box. Petitioner appealed.

SULLIVAN, J. . . . The . . . question presented is whether an inter vivos gift was made by the decedent to petitioner of the contents of a certain safe deposit box. On November 25, 1969, the decedent and petitioner executed a leasing agreement with the Uptown Safe Deposit Company. The terms of the agreement gave co-renter status to the parties and thereby entitled access to either. Previously, the box was solely in the name of the decedent. Decedent also gave petitioner one of two keys, retaining the other for himself. Petitioner testified, without objection, that decedent had expressed a desire that she have the contents therein. It is urged that this court find these acts as having constituted a valid inter vivos gift.

The necessary prerequisites for a valid inter vivos gift are present donative intent of the donor, delivery of the gift to the donee and acceptance of the gift by the donee. [Citation.] It is clear that constructive delivery is permissible, as by a key, [Citation], and a gift will be sustained if the delivery divests the donor of possession and dominion over it and invests the donee with the only means by which possession may be obtained. . . .

The undisputed facts here demonstrate that the delivery was not completed until Leonard Stahl's death. At any time prior to his death he had the ability to withdraw the contents of the safe deposit box by virtue of the duplicate key and therefore a sufficient delivery was negated. [Citation.] We note also from the record certain facts which cast doubt on decedent's donative intent. He did not have the government bonds in the box reissued in the name of petitioner and she did not enter the box until after his death, 15 months after she became a co-renter, nor did she otherwise attempt to exercise any control over the contents of the box prior to his death. [Citation.]

Petitioner having failed to establish by clear and convincing evidence the alleged gift, . . . the decedent did not effectuate a valid inter vivos gift.

For the reasons stated, we affirm the order of the circuit court.

Acquisition by Will or by Descent   When a person dies, with or without leaving a will, the decedent's property passes to others, called beneficiaries or heirs. The subject of wills and inheritances is discussed in Chapter 23. Here, the student simply should note that a common method of acquiring ownership of property is by inheritance from someone who dies.

Acquisition by Taking Possession   A person may acquire ownership of a movable object that is unowned by taking possession of it. *Possession* in its literal sense means control or power over an object. Taking possession of a movable object in today's world is not always sufficient to establish ownership of the object. In an urban, industrial society, few objects are unowned. As stated above, ownership of personal property is usually established in other ways, but one of the primary methods recognized historically was taking possession of something in its natural state.

Wildlife   There are many early court cases involving the acquisition of ownership of wild animals, fish, and bees. Such acquisition often was necessary for survival in a frontier society. At times, more than one person claimed ownership of an animal. Obviously, some rule governing ownership rights in wild animals was re-

quired. The rule that emerged was that ownership of a wild animal was obtained by taking the animal into possession. This rule is still part of our contemporary common law.

Possession, as used here, means depriving an animal of its natural liberty by (1) trapping or capturing it, (2) killing it, (3) mortally wounding it and continuing the chase, or (4) confining it in an enclosed place under private control. For example, if a person catches a wolf or mink in a trap, catches a fish in a net, or kills a wild deer with rifle or arrow, he or she thereby takes possession of the animal and acquires ownership.

Today, a person's survival is seldom at stake, and there are many conservation laws protecting endangered species of animals and birds from capture. All states have established seasons for hunting and fishing, and there is a prerequisite license. Failure to comply with state or local laws usually is a criminal offense. Only within the permissible legal limits outlined by the appropriate governmental unit can a person acquire ownership of wild animals today.

Abandoned property   A contemporary application of the acquisition-by-possession principle may occur today in regard to abandoned chattels. Ownership of an abandoned item may be acquired by taking possession of it with intent to exclude others. For example, if someone finds a broken watch lying in a trash barrel, the person may acquire ownership of it by picking it up and exercising control over it to the exclusion of others. The finder must proceed cautiously, however, and first establish that the article has truly been abandoned. "Abandonment" is the intentional relinquishment of all rights in an object without transferring ownership to another person.

Case 20.3   Menzel v. List
267 N.Y.S.2d 804 (Sup. Ct. 1966)

Plaintiff, Erna Menzel, and her husband bought a painting by Marc Chagall in 1932. The painting was kept in their apartment in Brussels. In March 1941 the Nazis invaded Brussels and plaintiff and her husband fled the country, leaving the painting in their apartment. About March 31, 1941, the Nazis seized the painting as "decadent Jewish art," and left a certification of receipt indicating that the painting had been taken into safekeeping.

After the war Mr. and Mrs. Menzel searched for the painting but were unable to locate it, until in 1962 it was discovered in the possession of the defendant, Albert A. List. Demand was made for return of the painting but List refused. Defendant had purchased the painting from Perls Galleries, a well-known art gallery. Perls had bought the painting in July 1955 from Galerie Art Moderne in Paris. The whereabouts of the painting between 1941 and 1955 are unknown.

A trial was held, and the jury brought in a verdict for the plaintiff and fixed the value of the painting at $22,500. The defendant had moved to set aside the verdict as contrary to the weight of evidence. The court denied the motion, saying that the jury's assessment of the facts was "amply supported by the record."

KLEIN, J. . . . . There remain for disposition, on the motion to set aside, numerous questions of law which have been earnestly and forcefully pressed by able counsel for the defense and vigorously opposed by learned counsel for plaintiff. . . .

Abandonment is defined as a voluntary relinquishment of a known right, with no intent to reclaim . . . ; personal property temporarily abandoned at the approach of the enemy, without the relinquishment of the owner's right of ownership, is neither foreclosed nor forfeited.

The relinquishment here by the Menzels in order to flee for their lives was no more voluntary than the relinquishment of property during a holdup and from the history of their search for the painting, there was obviously a continuing intent to reclaim.

The court finds, accordingly, as a matter of law, that there was here no abandonment.

Nor may this seizure be treated as lawful booty of war by conquering armies.

If the seizure is to be classified at all, it is to be classified as plunder and pillage, as those terms are understood in international and military law.

Booty is defined as property necessary and indispensable for the conduct of war, such as food, means of transportation, and means of communication; and is lawfully taken. . . .

Pillage, or *plunder*, on the other hand, is the taking of private property not necessary for the immediate prosecution of war effort, and is unlawful. Where pillage has taken place, the title of the original owner is not extinguished. . . .

It is of no moment that Perls Galleries may have been a *bona fide* purchaser of the painting, in good faith and for value and without knowledge of the saga of the Menzels. No less is expected of an art gallery of distinction.

Throughout the course of human history, the perpetration of evil has inevitably resulted in the suffering of the innocent, and those who act in good faith. And the principle has been basic in the law that a thief conveys no title as against the true owner. . . .

The jury has found plaintiff to be the sole and rightful owner of the painting. The court has found that she never abandoned it but that it was pillaged and plundered by the Nazis. No title could have been conveyed by them as against the rightful owners. The law stands as a bulwark against the handiwork of evil, to guard to rightful owners the fruits of their labors.

The motion to set aside the verdict is in all respects denied. Judgment may be entered accordingly.

Lost and mislaid property   A different rule of law applies to *lost*, as distinguished from abandoned, property. For instance, suppose Alice's dog wanders away from home and Ben finds and takes care of it. As a finder of lost property Ben acquires a legally protected right of possession against everyone except Alice, the owner. However, since the dog was *not unowned*, Ben does not acquire the rights of an owner.

The distinction between lost and abandoned property is not always easy to make. The test or guideline to apply is the intent of the owner. If the owner unconsciously or unintentionally gave up possession of the chattel, the item is said to be merely lost. If the owner has consciously given up possession, with the intent to relinquish ownership permanently, the item is thereby abandoned. A person's intent is not always obvious. Courts usually consider three factors in determining the intent of the owner in relinquishing possession: (1) location of the item, (2) value of the item, and (3) utility of the item. Trash barrels, public dumps, and roadside areas are all repositories for abandoned items. However, if an item of great value is found in any such place, the item has probably been lost by the owner without any intent to abandon it. If the item is unusable without the expenditure of a large sum of money for repair, it is probable that the owner chose to relinquish possession and ownership permanently.

Another distinction that sometimes is important in determining property rights is whether an item is lost or *mislaid*. An item is said to be lost when the disappearance is a result of something other than the owner's conscious conduct. For example, coins that fall through a hole in a person's pocket are not abandoned or mislaid, but lost. By contrast, an item is said to be mislaid if the owner intentionally placed it somewhere and later cannot remember, for the time being at least, where it was left.

In one respect, the law governing lost and mislaid objects is the same: in neither situation does a finder acquire ownership. The difference in legal effect concerns the right of possession. If the item was mislaid, the owner of the premises where the item was found is entitled to take possession. For example, suppose a customer places his or her sun glasses on a table while having a haircut and then leaves without them. The proprietor of the shop has a right of possession superior to that of a second customer who discovers the glasses. The rationale is that the owner logically can be expected to return to the premises as soon as he or she remembers where the item was left. On the other hand, if the item was lost, the finder is entitled to take possession and retain it against all persons except the rightful owner. For example, if sun glasses are found lying under a seat in a motion picture theater, the courts would most likely conclude that the item was lost, not mislaid, and the finder would be entitled to possession as against the theater owner.

In many states today the finder of a lost article can acquire full ownership of the item under proper circumstances. Usually, the statutes require the finder to take some steps to locate the owner, such as posting a public notice or advertising in a local newspaper. When a specified time has elapsed after the required steps have been taken, the statutes usually allow ownership to pass to the finder.

Acquisition by Accession A person who owns property can acquire ownership of additional property by means of accession. Accession occurs when property is improved or augmented by the labor and materials of another person. For example, if Carol asks David to repair her television set and David replaces several parts, Carol acquires ownership of the parts by accession, provided that the new parts are more or less permanently joined to the

television set. Similarly, if a thief adds parts to the transmission of a stolen car, the owner upon recovery of the car acquires ownership of the parts by accession. But there is this difference in the two situations: the owner of the television set who requested the repair is obligated to pay for the parts and labor, whereas the owner of the stolen car can receive the benefit of the improved car without obligation to pay for the improvement.

Acquisition by Confusion In some unusual cases, ownership of personal property may be acquired by a process called confusion. Confusion of goods occurs when identical goods belonging to different persons are so commingled or intermixed that the owners cannot identify their particular goods. Most of the litigated cases involve grain crops such as wheat or corn, liquids such as wine or oil, or animals such as unbranded cattle. Goods that are identical, or nearly so, are called "fungible." [See UCC Sec. 1-201 (17).]

When several owners voluntarily commingle interchangeable goods, each person becomes the owner of a proportionate part of the entire mass. Thus, if 1,000 bushels of Smith's wheat, 2,000 bushels of Jones's wheat, and 3,000 bushels of Rogers's wheat are inseparably commingled, Smith becomes the owner of an undivided sixth of the 6,000 bushels, Jones becomes the owner of an undivided third part, and Rogers becomes the owner of an undivided half part. This result occurs even if a wrongdoer intentionally and without consent intermixes someone's goods with goods the wrongdoer owns. But, where it is impossible to determine the original value or quantity of the innocent party's goods, most courts hold that ownership of the wrongdoer's goods will pass to the innocent victim by confusion. Thus, the innocent party would acquire ownership of the entire mass without obligation to pay the wrongful party.

Bailments

The subject of bailments does not involve the acquisition of ownership of property. It concerns the temporary possession of personal property by one who is not the owner.

Meaning of Bailment   A bailment may be defined as the legal relation resulting from the transfer of possession of personal property from one person (called the bailor) to another person (called the bailee) under such circumstances that the bailee is under a duty to return the item to the bailor or to dispose of it as directed by the bailor. Two points should be emphasized concerning this definition: (1) a bailment involves the transfer of possession without the transfer of ownership: where possession and ownership are both transferred, the transfer constitutes either a sale or a gift; and (2) the bailor need not be the owner of the property. If B, who has borrowed A's book, lends it to C, B is a bailor as to C. Even a thief may be a bailor.

The transfer of possession of property referred to in the definition above implies voluntary acceptance of the property. Thus, where goods come into a person's possession without the person's knowledge, he or she is not a bailee of the goods. For example, if a person agrees to store an "empty trunk" for a neighbor, the person is not a bailee of an overcoat that the neighbor neglected to remove from the trunk.

Classes of Bailments   Bailments may be classified as gratuitous bailments and nongratuitous bailments. Nongratuitous bailments are usually called "mutual benefit bailments" and are sometimes called "bailments for hire." Table 20.1 (p. 376) illustrates the classification of bailments.

A gratuitous bailment is a bailment in which one of the parties receives a benefit in regard to the bailed article without being obligated to pay for the benefit. The examples in the right-hand column of the table show that the party receiving the benefit is usually the bailor. However, in one situation (gratuitous loan of a thing) the bailee is the party who receives the benefit.

A mutual-benefit bailment is one in which each party is entitled to receive a benefit. Usually, the bailor receives a service with regard to the bailed article and the bailee receives compensation, as can be seen from the examples

contained in the table. However, in one situation (hired use of a thing) the bailee receives the service and the bailor receives the compensation. And in one situation (a pledge or pawn) the bailment relation is not entered into for the purpose of giving or receiving a service with respect to the bailed item, but for the purpose of securing the payment of a debt or the performance of some other obligation.

A special bailment, as can be seen from the table, is one in which the bailee is an innkeeper (hotel, motel, etc.) or common carrier of goods (railroad, airline, etc.). The common law governing special bailments has been so affected both by federal and state statutes and by regulations of federal and state administrative agencies that it is not feasible to discuss in a volume of this size the contemporary law governing this type of bailment.

Creation of Bailments   A bailment is a simple relation, and its formation requires no ceremony. The relation may exist even though there is no contract between the bailor and the bailee. The mere act of one person's transferring possession of personal property to another may result in a bailment relationship between them. The law then imposes certain duties on the parties and gives them certain rights. These rights and duties may be supplemented or modified by a written or oral agreement between the bailor and bailee.

One occurrence that deserves special attention is that of placing a car in a parking lot. Sometimes a bailment is created, while at other times a "lease" or "license" is created. The distinction between the two relations is important should the owner's car be stolen or damaged. A bailee of goods assumes certain duties toward the goods. These duties are discussed in the next section. One who merely leases a parking space to the car owner does not assume the duties of a bailee. Since a bailment results from the transfer of possession, the test to be applied is whether the driver has given up control over the vehicle. For example, if a student drives a car to school, parks the car in

TABLE 20.1

Classification of Bailments

Type of Bailment	Example (E stands for Bailee; R stands for bailor)
Gratuitous bailments For bailor's sole benefit:	
Gratuitous storage of a thing	E allows a neighbor, R, to store his or her car in E's garage without charge
Gratuitous carriage of a thing	E transports R's sofa without charging R for the service
Receiving possession of a thing for the purpose of gratuitously performing work on it	E offers to sharpen R's lawn-mower if he or she will bring it to E's basement; R brings it and leaves it in E's basement
For the bailee's sole benefit: Gratuitous loan of a thing	R lends his or her power saw to E
Mutual-benefit bailments Ordinary bailments for hire	
Compensated storage of a thing	R stores his or her furniture in a commercial warehouse
Receiving possession of a thing for the purpose of performing compensated work on it	R leaves his or her garment with Valet Shop to be cleaned and pressed
Hired use of a thing	E rents a car from the Car Rental Service Co.
Pledge or pawn	R deposits stocks with his or her bank to secure a loan
Special bailments: bailments involving	
Innkeepers as bailees	R (hotel guest) leaves valuables in hotel safe
Common carriers of goods as bailees	R hires E (railroad) to transport merchandise

the student lot, locks the car, and takes the keys, a *lease* of space, not a bailment is created. The driver has not relinquished control over the car. On the other hand, if a person drives to a restaurant where an attendant parks the car, takes the key, and gives the owner a claim check, a *bailment* is created. The driver has given up control; possession has been transferred to the restaurant. Transfer of possession is all that is required: no formal documents need be signed and no particular words need be said.

Case 20.4   Broadview Apartments Co. v. Baughman
350 A.2d 707 (Md. App. 1976)

Glenn H. Baughman, plaintiff (appellee), was a tenant in the Broadview Apartments located in Northwest Baltimore. He paid Broadview $15 a month to park his car in the Broadview Garage. The garage was beneath the apartment building and was an enclosed two-level garage, one in the basement and one on the ground (lobby) level. Each level had a separate entrance and exit. There was no attendant at the lobby level but there was one on the basement level. There was a security guard on duty twenty-four hours a day and each tenant had a key to the garage door.

On the night of November 23, 1966, appellee parked his car in his assigned spot on the lobby level, locked the car, and took the keys with him. When he returned the next day, his car was gone. It was never recovered. Mr. Baughman filed suit for the loss of his automobile. The trial court held that Broadview was a bailee of the car and, as such, was liable for the value of the missing car. Broadview appealed.

MELVIN, J. . . . A bailment is "the relation created through the transfer of the possession of goods or chattels, by a person called the bailor to a person called the bailee, without a transfer of ownership, for the accomplishment of a certain purpose, whereupon the goods or chattels are to be dealt with according to the instructions of the bailor". [Citations.]. . . .

"To constitute a bailment there must be an existing subject-matter, a contract with reference to it which involves possession of it by the bailee, delivery, actual or constructive, and acceptance, actual or constructive." [Citation.]

Once the bailment relationship is proven certain responsibilities flow from the relationship. The bailee in accepting possession of the bailed property assumes the duty of exercising reasonable care in protecting it. . . . If no bailment is shown, and the owner of the property is a mere licensee or lessee of the storage space, then in order to recover against the defendant garage owner the plaintiff would have to prove specific acts of negligence on the part of the defendant proximately causing loss or injury of plaintiff's property. . . .

The courts have uniformly found a delivery of possession to the parking lot operators, and therefore a contract for bailment, where the keys are surrendered with the car or where the car is parked by an attendant. . . . Some other factors which have been considered to be important are: (1) whether there are attendants at the entrances and exits of the lots, (2) whether the car owner receives a claim check that must be surrendered before he can take his car, (3) whether the parking lot is enclosed, and (4) whether the parking lot operator expressly assumes responsibility for the car. No single factor has been viewed as determinative of the issue. The law has probably been best stated in *Osborne v. Cline*, 263 N.Y. 434 at 437, 189 N.E. 483 at 484, where the New York Court of Appeals stated that

> "Whether a person simply hires a place to put his car (licensor-licensee relationship) or whether he has turned its possession over to the care and custody of another (bailee-bailor relationship) depends on the place, the conditions and the nature of the transaction."

In the instant case we think the evidence is legally insufficient to establish that a bailor-bailee relationship existed. Appellee merely rented a parking space monthly; he parked his own car, locked the car and took the keys with him. There was no testimony that Broadview had a set of keys for the car or had any right or authority to move or exercise any control over the car. The parking garage was laid out in such a manner that it was possible for appellee to park his car without any attendant even being aware of his presence in the garage. Appellee entered into the monthly lease arrangement with full knowledge of how the garage operated. He was not required to check his car in or out, and there was no evidence whatsoever that control of the car was ever turned over to the operators of the garage, or that they ever accepted delivery or control. Nor was there any evidence that Broadview expressly contracted or asserted that the car would be safe from theft while in the garage. . . . The mere fact that he paid a monthly rent for an enclosed parking space, . . . does not, standing alone, raise an inference of a bailment contract. . . .

On the record before us, as we have indicated, there is insufficient evidence to warrant a finding of a bailor-bailee relationship between the parties. The trial court was wrong in finding there was such a relationship. . . .

Judgment reversed.

Bailee's Rights and Duties   In a bailment relation, possession of the bailed item passes to the bailee. Along with possession, the bailee acquires certain rights. In return, the bailee assumes certain duties for the protection of the bailor's interests.

Right to possess the bailed property   During the time that a bailment relation exists, the bailee has a right to the exclusive possession of the bailed property. The right of possession is protected by the law of torts, which gives the bailee a cause of action against any person who wrongfully interferes.[5] For instance, if Andrews leaves his pedigreed dog with Happy Valley Kennel while on his vacation and Brown steals the dog, Happy Valley has a cause of action in tort against Brown to secure return of the animal or to recover damages. The bailee's right

_____
[5] See the discussion of the tort of conversion in Chapter 5.

of possession is protected even against the bailor. Suppose that Andrews rents his dog to Smith, to be used by Smith for hunting, and Andrews returns unexpectedly and wrongfully interferes by retaking possession. Smith has a cause of action against Andrews.

Right to use borrowed or rented property Where the purpose of a bailment is the use of the bailed article, the bailee has the right to use the article in a fair and reasonable manner. For example, if George borrows his neighbor's drill and wood bit, he may use them to drill holes in wood. If George attempts to drill through metal or concrete, he is liable for any damage caused to the drill and bit. On the other hand, when the purpose of a bailment is for storage, the bailor does not contemplate any use of the goods and the bailee would be liable for *any* use made of the goods. For example, if Charles boards his horse at a stable and Donna, who works there, rides the horse in a parade, Charles has a cause of action against Donna.

Duty to exercise care   Every bailee owes to the bailor some degree of care in the custody of the bailed article. The traditional view is that the degree of care depends on the type or class of bailment. In a mutual-benefit bailment, the bailee owes a duty of ordinary care; in a bailment for the sole benefit of the bailor, the bailee owes a duty of slight care; in a bailment for the sole benefit of the bailee, the bailee owes a duty of great care. The traditional view has been criticized because the amount of care required is made to depend solely on the circumstances of who benefited from the bailment relation. In addition, juries find it difficult to draw any reasonably clear line of distinction between slight care and ordinary care, or between ordinary care and great care.

These criticisms of the traditional view are causing an increasing number of courts to abandon the three-fold standard of care and to substitute for it a single standard of care. That standard is the degree of care that a reasonable person would exercise under all the circumstances of the case.[6] Among the more important circumstances are the value of the bailed article (jewelry, work of art); the nature of the article (whether easily portable or not, whether easily damaged or not); the facilities available to the bailee for taking care of the bailed article; the experience of the bailee (whether a professional bailee or not); the kind of community (metropolitan city or isolated rural town); and the presence or absence of any benefit to the bailee.

If the bailee is negligent and if the negligence is a proximate cause of damage to the bailor's goods, the bailee may be held liable to the bailor. In the absence of fault, the bailee is not liable. Unless the bailment agreement so provides, the bailee is not an insurer. Thus, if an earthquake or flood occurs and destroys property in the possession of the bailee, the bailee cannot be held liable. Let us suppose, however, that a hurricane warning is announced. The bailee must now take reasonable precautions to protect the bailed property against this foreseeable, known risk, such as boarding up doors and plate glass windows. If the bailee does not do so and the goods are damaged, the bailee may be held liable for negligence.

In the event the bailor sues the bailee because goods were lost or damaged while in the bailee's possession, most courts would say that the bailee is *presumed* to be negligent and that the burden rests on the bailee to prove the precise cause of the loss or damage *and* to prove he or she acted in a reasonable and prudent manner. For example, suppose someone leaves furniture in storage at a warehouse and thereafter a piece is stolen. The presumption is that the storage company was negligent in failing to prevent the theft and is liable. However, if the company can prove that the goods were packed safely and that a night watchman patroled regularly, monitoring with closed-circuit television,

---

[6]Many of the principles discussed in this section are discussed more fully in Chapter 6. See also UCC Sections 7-204 and 7-309 regarding duties of care by warehousemen and carriers.

a court might properly conclude the company had exercised the degree of care expected from a reasonable person and therefore was not liable to the bailor. It is not sufficient merely to show exercise of care. To avoid liability, the bailee also must explain the precise cause of the bailor's loss. The bailee may be held liable for an unexplained loss. There are several views by legal authorities to justify placing this burden on the bailee. One such view is that it is difficult for a bailor to obtain from the bailee or the bailee's employees the information needed to establish negligence. Usually, there are no independent witnesses to testify how a bailed article was lost or damaged. Therefore, the law assists the bailor by establishing a presumption that the bailee was negligent.

Case 20.5   **Clark v. Fields**
          219 N.E.2d 162 (Ill. App. 1966)

EBERSPACHER, J. This is an action brought against [W. B. Fields, defendant] the bailee of an airplane, by the bailors [B. R. Clark and W. H. Jordan, plaintiffs] for the fair cash market value of the airplane which was destroyed in a fire which took place in the backyard of the bailee's home. The jury found for the defendant-bailee, from which judgment this appeal has been taken. . . .

At defendant's direction, the plane was placed in his backyard at a spot designated by him near a small ravine or gulley where he customarily burned his trash. His backyard was 70 to 80 feet wide and 40 to 60 feet deep. It was covered with ordinary grass and the plane was placed some 40 to 50 feet from the defendant's house and some 15 to 20 feet from the gulley where the trash was customarily burned. . . .

A ditch ran from the spot where the plane was placed to the area where the trash was burned. This ditch was filled with dry grass, and the yard surrounding the plane was filled with dry grass.

A week or ten days later, on March 8, 1963, the defendant took some trash out into his backyard to burn. . . .

He dumped the trash in the gulley on the back of his lot, set it on fire, and before it had burned out, was called into his house by his wife to move a refrigerator. When he left, the trash fire was still smouldering. . . .

A short time later the defendant's wife looked out the back window, saw that the airplane was on fire and called to her husband. When the defendant got out there, the grass running from the place where the trash was burned to the place where the airplane was located was on fire and still burning. The entire perimeter of the burned area, and [the area] surrounding the airplane was aflame. The trash that the defendant had dumped and burned was all over the hill. The plane was totally destroyed except for the wings and stabilizer which were not attached to the plane. . . .

The rule relating to the burden of proof in gratuitous bailment cases is stated in *Miles v. International Hotel Co.*, 289 Ill. 320, 327, 124 N.E. 599, 602 as follows:

"The weight of modern authority holds the rule to be that, where the bailor has shown that the goods were received in good condition by the bailee and were not returned to the bailor on demand, the bailor has made out a case of prima facie negligence against the bailee, and the bailee must show that the loss or damage was caused without his fault. [Citing cases.] The effect of this rule is, not to shift the burden of proof from plaintiff to the defendant, but simply the burden of proceeding. The bailor must in all instances prove that the bailee was negligent, but when she shows that the goods which she intrusted to the bailee's care were not delivered upon demand she has made out a prima facie case, or created a presumption of negligence which the bailee may overcome by offering evidence to show that it was not negligent, and if it produces such evidence, the bailor, in order to make out her case, must show that the bailee was, in fact, negligent and that its negligence caused the loss or contributed thereto." . . .

A gratuitous bailee is bound to take such care in the preservation of the property intrusted to him as every prudent man takes of his own goods of like character.

In the instant case, there is no dispute of facts as to who started the fire that eventually caused the loss of the aircraft. The cause of the loss is not a mystery. The defendant started a trash fire and then went back into the house while it was still burning or smouldering. The burden of proceeding as to issue of negligence shifts to bailee after bailor has shown that goods were received in good condition by bailee and not returned to bailor on demand. The defendant has not introduced any evidence showing himself free from negligence. . . .

The judgment of the Circuit Court of St. Clair County is reversed and the cause is remanded with directions to enter judgment in favor of plaintiffs and against the defendant for $4,500.00 and costs. Reversed and remanded with directions.

Limitations of liability In some situations the liability of the bailee may be limited or even eliminated by agreement of the parties. The most common examples involve auto parking lots and check rooms where claim checks or tickets are given to customers. The ticket usually contains language specifying a maximum amount of liability for damage to the bailor's property or disclaiming all liability. This situation is essentially one involving contract law, specifically the rules regarding communication of offers (see Chapter 10). Most courts hold that the bailee can limit liability only if the disclaimer is effectively communicated to the bailor. For instance, if a sign is posted with letters large enough for the average person to see upon entering the establishment, the bailor will be chargeable with *notice* of the terms posted. Ordinarily, the bailor will not be chargeable with notice of terms contained in small print on the back of a ticket stub. In many states, even if the disclaimer is properly communicated, the bailee will be liable for *willful* injury to the bailor's property. (See discussion of exculpatory clauses in Chapter 15, p. 270.)

When a bailor transfers possession of an item

of great value, such as jewelry or a work of art, the bailee should be notified of that fact. In some states, such as California, the statutes limit the bailee's liability in case of loss to the *apparent* reasonable value of the chattel, unless the bailor had specifically notified the bailee of its unusual worth. And, of course, a bailee is not liable for loss of an item within a bailed chattel if the bailee was not aware and had no reason to be aware of the presence of the item.

Duty to return the property In a bailment relation the bailee is obligated to return the bailed property at the termination of the bailment or to dispose of it as directed by the bailor. If the parties have agreed to a specified time period for the bailment, the right to possession of the item automatically reverts to the bailor at the expiration of the period. If the relation is a bailment at will (i.e., no term is specified), the bailor can request return of the goods at any time. In either situation, the bailee must promptly return the goods; if the bailee improperly withholds return of the bailor's property, the bailee may be liable to the bailor in tort.

A bailee may also be liable for wrongfully delivering goods to someone other than the bailor or a person designated by the bailor. A bailee who delivers the property to the wrong person is liable to the bailor for the tort of conversion. The bailee may have been induced to deliver the bailor's property to someone through trickery, fraud, or simple mistake. The bailee's liability for misdelivery, however, is *absolute*, and is not based on negligence or bad faith.

Duty to compensate bailor in rental situations In a mutual-benefit bailment of the type where the bailee hires the use of a thing, the bailee is obligated to compensate the bailor for that use. For example, a person who rents a trailer to haul goods must pay the bailor for the use of the trailer.

Bailor's Duties When a bailment relation is created the bailor has certain rights, namely rights to performance of the duties listed in the preceding section, and the bailor owes certain duties with respect to the bailed property and to the bailee.

Duty to protect bailee from defects in the property Where the bailor knows that the bailee will be using the bailed item and will be exposed to a risk of harm from such use, the bailor must exercise due care to prevent harm to the bailee, the bailee's employees, and the bailee's property from a defect in the bailed property. This is merely an application of the basic tort law of negligence. If the bailor knows of a defect, it must be disclosed to the bailee. For instance, if a person knows there is a loose belt on a power mower that is being loaned to a neighbor, the owner must inform the neighbor of the defect. Where great harm could occur from the use of a bailed item, the bailor is obligated to make an inspection of the article prior to relinquishing possession to the bailee. For example, a car rental agency should inspect a vehicle before it is delivered to the customer-bailee. If the rental agency fails to make an inspection when an inspection would have disclosed a defect in the car, the agency may be held liable for an injury that later occurs as a result of the defect. Rental agencies have been held liable without fault under the law of product liability for injuries caused by a defect in the goods leased. (See Chapter 6, p. 114.)

Case 20.6   Ikeda v. Okada Trucking Co.
393 P.2d 171 (Haw. 1964)

MIZUHA, J. Plaintiff, Kazuto Ikeda, while employed as a carpenter's apprentice by the United Construction Company, was injured by a concrete bucket which fell off a crane which was rented for a concrete pouring job during the construction of a men's dormitory building on the campus of the University of Hawaii.

[Plaintiff brought suit against the owner of the crane and the trial court directed a verdict for the defendant. Plaintiff filed this appeal.]

In the early morning of the day of the accident, United Construction Company's foreman, Hiroji Maeda, rented a crane from defendant, Okada Trucking Company, to complete the pouring of concrete for the building. . . .

The plaintiff's theory was that defendant, as a bailor for hire, breached its duty to furnish a safe chattel by furnishing a crane for pouring concrete which had a hook without the usual safety clasp or locking device, which it knew, or in the exercise of ordinary care should have known, was unsafe for the particular job intended. . . .

The assembled crane which was delivered to the jobsite had a hook which was an open hook, as differentiated from a safety hook. Charles J. Utterback, the sole expert witness on safety engineering, testified:

> "A safety hook is a hook that has a locking device across the throat so that the object being hoisted or pulled by the hook cannot escape while it's being under load, . . . It (the safety clasp or locking device) is a flat piece, spring steel, which is about a quarter of an inch thick and a half an inch wide. It goes across the mouth, what we call the 'throat' here."

The hook in this case had no such safety clasp or locking device. . . . It was his professional opinion that the cause of the accident was the use of an open hook. . . .

Viewing the case as we must from the standpoint most favorable to plaintiff, the defendant knew that the crane was to be used for the purpose of hoisting and pouring concrete. In view of that knowledge, the jury could find that defendant was negligent in supplying an assembled crane including a hook which was unsafe, and that this was a violation of defendant's duty of care. . . .

> "It is now generally agreed that a seller, or other supplier of chattels for a consideration, may be liable for harm to the person or property of a third person who may be expected to be in the vicinity of the chattel's probable use, if he has failed to exercise reasonable care to make the chattel safe for the use for which it is supplied." Prosser, *Torts*, Sec. 84 (2d ed.).
>
> ". . . The law is the 'source' of a duty of the supplier of a chattel to use reasonable care to see that it is reasonably safe for use, even where there is not actual knowledge of the presence of a defect, or knowledge of facts which would indicate that a defect exists, where the nature of the chattel and its use are such 'that it is reasonably certain to place life and limb in peril' when defectively made or repaired, and it is probable that it will be used without inspection by others than a party who could claim the benefit of an implied warranty. . . ." *La Rocca v. Farrington*, 93 N.Y.S.2d 363 at 366, *aff'd*, 301 N.Y. 247. . . .
>
> "The fact that the plaintiff's employer, as lessee of the crane, had an

equal opportunity to discover the defect . . . does not serve to relieve the owner of liability. . . ." *La Rocca v. Farrington*, 301 N.Y. 247 at 250.

While these cases relate to hidden defects the same principle is applicable if

". . . the condition, although readily observable, (is) one which only persons of special experience would realize to be dangerous. In such case if the supplier, having such special experience, knows that the condition involves danger and has no reason to believe that those who use it will have such special experience as will enable them to perceive the danger, he is required to inform them of the risk of which he himself knows and which he has no reason to suppose that they will realize." Restatement, *Torts*, Sec. 388, comment i. . . .

Hence, after a careful review of the evidence, we are of the opinion that there are questions of fact to be presented to the jury as to whether defendant was negligent in supplying an assembled crane including a hook which was not reasonably safe and suitable for the purpose intended and whether such negligence, if any, proximately caused plaintiff's injury. . . .

Reversed and remanded for a new trial.

Duty to compensate bailee in service situations When the purpose of a nongratuitous bailment is performance by the bailee of some service in connection with the bailed item, the bailor has a duty to compensate the bailee for the service. For instance, if a person leaves a car to be repaired at a commercial garage and the mechanic properly performs the service requested, the bailor has a duty to pay for that service. If the bailee is unable to collect for the services, the bailee has a cause of action against the bailor for breach of contract.

Often, the bailee has the privilege of retaining possession of the bailed chattel until his or her just charges are paid. This privilege of retaining possession until compensation is received is called a "possessory lien." In most states there are statutory procedures that enable an unpaid bailee who has a lien on bailed goods to advertise and sell them at public auction, after waiting a specified period of time for payment. See, for examples, UCC Sections 7-210 and 7-308.

SUMMARY

Property law is fundamental to rational government. Private property is an essential part of a free enterprise economy. The word "property" is used in two different senses. In one sense, property refers to things owned. In its other sense, property means the exclusive right to use, possess, enjoy, and dispose of things. The main classes of property are: tangible and intangible, real and personal, public and private. Tangible property consists of things that have a physical existence; intangibles do not exist in physical form but have economic value. Real property is land, airspace above the land, and all things imbedded in the land or firmly attached to it. Personal property is all property that is not real property. Public property is that held by a governmental unit or agency. Private property is that held by an individual or business entity. There are historical as well as practical reasons why rights in private property are protected by law.

The laws relating to personal property are an important part of the milieu in which we live. A person or firm may acquire ownership of personal property by purchase or by gift. The elements of a valid gift are an intent by the donor to make a present transfer; a delivery, or acceptable substitute; and an acceptance by the donee. To acquire ownership in an unowned chattel a person must take possession of it, that is, must exercise control over it. However, the individual must distinguish abandoned articles from lost and mislaid property. The finder of lost or mislaid property does not automatically acquire ownership rights. If the owner does not appear, title to lost property may pass in accordance with local statutes. Other methods of acquiring ownership of personal property are inheritance, accession, and confusion.

A bailment results from the transfer of possession, but not ownership, of personal property by one person (the bailor) to another person (the bailee). There are two major classes of bailments: (1) gratuitous bailments, where only one party receives a benefit from the bailment relationship, and (2) mutual-benefit bailments, sometimes called "bailments for hire."

Both parties to a bailment relationship have certain rights and duties. The bailee has the right to possession of the bailed article and, when appropriate, the right to the use of the bailed article. The bailee has the duty to exercise reasonable care in the custody of the article, to return it to the bailor or to someone designated by the bailor, and, in one situation (hired use of a thing), to compensate the bailor. The bailor must exercise due care to protect the bailee from defects in the bailed item, and in commercial situations involving a service to the item, the bailor must compensate the bailee.

STUDY AND DISCUSSION QUESTIONS

1 *(a)* Discuss the two ways the word "property" is used in the law. *(b)* Define the following: tangible property; intangible property; real property; personal property; public property; private property.

2 *(a)* How is private property protected under the law? *(b)* What are the reasons for the protection of private property? *(c)* Are these reasons valid in today's world? Why or why not?

3 *(a)* Give examples of legal restrictions that the law places on the use, possession, enjoyment, and disposition of private property. *(b)* Why do you think the law imposes these restrictions?

4 *(a)* Define "gift." *(b)* What are the requirements for a gift of personal property? *(c)* What does the term "donative intent" mean? *(d)* Indicate a method that a donor might utilize to make "delivery" of a patent. *(e)* Is acceptance of a gift by the donee usually a problem? Explain.

5 *(a)* How would a person take possession of a wild animal? *(b)* Do you think a person who traps a wild animal that has escaped from a circus acquires ownership of the animal? Why or why not?

6 *(a)* Distinguish between the following: abandoned and lost property; lost and mislaid property. *(b)* Why is it important to determine whether an article is abandoned, lost, or mislaid?

7 *(a)* What is a bailment? *(b)* How does it differ from a gift?

8 State whether you agree, partially agree, or disagree with the following statements, and why. *(a)* A gratuitous bailment is one in which the bailor receives a benefit in regard to the bailed article without being obligated to pay for the benefit. *(b)* A mutual-benefit bailment is one in which the bailor receives a service for which he or she is obligated to pay. *(c)* The bailee's right to the exclusive possession of the bailed property is good against everyone except the bailor. *(d)* A bailee has the right to use the bailed article in a fair and reasonable way.

9 *(a)* State and explain the duties a bailee owes to a bailor. *(b)* State and explain the duties a bailor owes to a bailee.

CASE PROBLEMS

1 On March 10, Juanita had a new certificate of registration to her car issued in the name of her friend, Gussie. The registration on the automobile was transferred because Juanita contemplated receiving welfare assistance, and she believed that such assistance would not be forthcoming as long as she was the owner of an automobile. At the time of the transfer, there was owing to the finance company a balance of $1,726.20. Gussie testified that she and Juanita had agreed that Gussie would assume the balance of payments due, but that if Juanita should return to work she would take the car back and make up to Gussie whatever payments she had made on the loan in the meantime. Gussie made six payments toward the loan, by making payments of $68 each directly to Juanita. At all times the actual custody and possession of the car remained with Juanita, who continued to use and operate the car. Had Juanita made a gift of her car?

2 Harvey purchased an automobile, paying $400 down and signing promissory notes for the balance due. He then gave his friend, Alene, a set of keys to the car and told her he was giving it to her. The next day he repeated the same thing in front of a neighbor and both parties stated before this witness that he had given Alene the automobile. Later that day Harvey was killed. The balance of the purchase price of the automobile was paid by insurance after his death. Does the administrator of Harvey's estate have the right to ownership of the car?

3 On May 16, Geraldine wrote a letter to Elmira College containing the following: "I wish to present and hereby do present and convey title to all of these items as a gift to Elmira College. It is to be understood, however, that I may retain possession of such items as long as I am able to enjoy them." The items referred to consisted of Geraldine's entire collection of paintings, pictures, jade, bronze, and various art objects. There had been many conversations and exchanges of correspondence between the college and Geraldine concerning the possibility of such a gift over a period of approximately 7 months prior to the letter. However, it was not until January of the year following the May 16 letter that any of the articles referred to were actually shipped. Was the letter sufficient to effect a valid gift?

4 Thelma, an employee of Northwestern National Bank, found an unmarked envelope containing $1,500 in currency on the floor of a passageway in the bank. The passageway extended from the vault where the safety boxes were to the section where booths were located for the convenience of safety vault patrons. The area was in the basement of the bank and was restricted to patrons who registered and presented a ticket to a guard. Thelma was employed as an attendant to assist vault customers, and at the time she found the money she was checking to see if anything had been left in the rooms where customers had gone for privacy. She immediately turned the envelope over to the bank. The owner of the money failed to appear and demand his or her property, and Thelma sued the bank for the $1,500, claiming to be the finder of lost property. Was the property lost?

5 Sampson was discussing the purchase of a car with Flack, a used car salesman employed by Birkeland. Sampson took one of Birkeland's cars for a trial drive and left his own car on the dealer's lot for appraisal and determination of trade-in allowance. Flack took Sampson's car from the lot and drove it several blocks to determine its condition. Upon returning to the lot he found the entrance to the lot blocked, and he parked Sampson's car on the opposite side of the public street adjacent to the lot. Sometime later an automobile being pursued by the police collided with Sampson's car and damaged it beyond repair. Are Birkeland and Flack liable for damages to Sampson's car?

6 Dumlao checked into the Franklin Park Hotel. He removed a great deal of clothing from the back seat of his car and then left the car to be parked by a hotel doorman. The hotel bell captain saw Dumlao remove a cosmetic case from the trunk of the car, but he could not view the trunk's other contents, nor was he told that any other items of personal property were in the car. An employee of Atlantic Garage picked up the car, pursuant to an arrangement between it and the hotel. When Dumlao checked out of the hotel 4 or 5 days later, the hotel was unable to deliver the car and could not account for its disappearance. It was later found, missing a cigarette lighter that had been left in the glove compartment, various articles of clothing left in the back seat of the car, and a $1,000 set of drums left in the trunk. Is the Franklin Park Hotel liable for the loss of all of these items?

Chapter

21

Real Property: Nature, Acquisition, and Ownership

This chapter deals with several important aspects of the law of real property. In order to determine the rights and duties of parties in a transaction involving property, it is often necessary to classify the subject matter involved in the transaction as personal or real property. Some examples of areas of the law that are affected by the classification are formal requirements for transfer, taxation, and succession at death. There are a number of statutes and court decisions that attempt to define and classify the physical elements of real property.

Real property may be owned by individuals, by business firms, and by governmental units or agencies. Anyone who contemplates the acquisition of real property should understand the various methods of acquiring ownership, the types of ownership available, and the rights and duties involved in owning real property.

The first part of this chapter is devoted to a discussion of the physical elements customarily included in the term "real property." Special attention is given to the subject of fixtures. The last two parts of the chapter are devoted to acquisition and ownership of real property.

388

PHYSICAL ELEMENTS OF REAL PROPERTY

Land, Airspace, Subsurface

The term "real property" customarily includes the surface of the land, things attached to the land, the airspace above, and materials below the surface. The surface includes things found in nature, such as water and soil, and things added by human effort, such as buildings and crops. Below the surface are found such things as minerals, oil, and gas. The law pertaining to each of these elements is complex and too extensive to be covered in a business law text. However, certain fundamental rules and principles are presented to give some understanding of this area of law.

Airspace   The owner of real property has the right to the airspace above the surface of his or her land. An ancient rule of common law was that ownership extended to the "periphery of the universe." There was little need to question this rule prior to the invention of the airplane. Today, airspace is recognized as an economic resource that should be available for public use, and the landowner's rights have been restricted. The general rule is that the landowner owns that portion of the airspace above the land that the owner can use in connection with the beneficial and convenient enjoyment of the land surface. The owner's control extends to no fixed height, and each case must be decided on its particular facts. The federal government has established a public domain for air transit through the navigable airspace of the United States. Thus, the owner or operator of an aircraft that passes over land owned by another is not necessarily a trespasser. However, it is a trespass to fly below the minimum altitude set by federal regulation or to operate an aircraft in a manner dangerous or annoying to persons below.

Ownership of airspace can be transferred with or without the transfer of the land surface. The transfer usually occurs automatically in connec-tion with transfer of the land surface. However, the separate transfer of airspace is a growing phenomenon in the United States. Such transfer occurs, for example, when a person buys into a high-rise condominium. In effect, the purchaser buys a cube of airspace in the building. Some of the legal aspects of condominiums are discussed later in this chapter.

Water   Water on or below the surface of the land is real property. However, if the water is "severed" from the land and put in a container, its classification is changed to personal property. In arid parts of the western United States local water agencies purchase water as they would purchase any commodity. The water may be transported by pipe or truck and sold to consumers who may live hundreds of miles from the source of the water.

Water is a precious resource, and the public policy of the federal and state governments is to preserve and protect that resource. This policy is reflected in statutes and court decisions that restrict the rights of owners of real property. In most states an owner of real property does not have the right to dig a well and take water from under the land in unlimited quantity. The owner may draw only the amount of water that he or she can reasonably and beneficially use. Likewise, a person who owns a parcel of land bordering on a stream or river has the right (called "riparian right") to take reasonable quantities of water from the stream or river. An owner cannot dam up the stream or dig a channel and divert the entire water flow onto his or her land. The downstream owners of the land bordering the stream also have riparian rights to take water for their reasonable use, and these rights cannot be unreasonably interfered with by an owner upstream.

Crops and Timber   Items that grow on the land, such as trees, shrubs, corn, and potatoes, are considered to be part of the real property. Thus, when real property is transferred by a landowner, any trees and growing crops automatically pass to the transferee, unless the owner specifically reserves rights in them. Ownership of growing trees and crops may be transferred separately from a transfer of the land. Harvested crops and felled trees are classed as personal property. The methods of transferring ownership of personal property were discussed in the previous chapter.

Minerals   All materials below the surface of an owner's land are part of the real property. Minerals, such as gold, silver, and copper, can be of great commercial value. The landowner can transfer ownership of the subsurface separately or as part of a transfer of the real property. Separate ownership of the subsurface normally includes the right to enter upon the surface of the land to remove minerals. The prudent landowner will not transfer ownership of the subsurface without having given due consideration to how much the transfer would restrict use of the surface of the land. A landowner may simply grant a right to others to enter upon the land and remove minerals from the ground, usually on a royalty basis.

Case 21.1   **Buffalo Mining Co. v. Martin**
                   267 S.E.2d 721 (W. Va. 1980)

In 1890 a mineral severance deed was executed which granted all coal and other minerals underlying certain real estate now owned by James and Toni Martin. Buffalo Mining Company acquired mining rights in a coal lease in 1969 from the owner of the mineral rights. Buffalo was involved in mining a large tract of coal, part of which was located under the Martins' property. In order to ventilate its coal mine, Buffalo erected an electric transmission line on the Martins' land. James Martin obstructed the project and Buffalo filed suit to secure an injunction prohibiting the Martins from interfering with the erection of the line. The Martins contended that the power line constituted an unreasonable use of the surface and that the 1890 deed is silent as to the right to erect an electric power line. The trial court granted the injunction and the Martins appealed.

MILLER, J. . . . It is generally recognized that where there has been a severance of the mineral estate and the deed gives the grantee the right to utilize the surface, such surface use must be for purposes reasonably necessary to the extraction of the minerals. [Citations.]

Appellants [Martins] rely heavily on three decisions in which this Court refused to interpret language granting surface rights in connection with deep mining as including the right to strip or auger the surface for coal. [Citations.] These decisions were each based on two grounds. First, at the time of the original severance deed, neither strip nor auger mining was known and therefore could not have been within the contemplation of the parties. Second, and of even more importance, was the fact that these mining methods virtually destroyed the surface for its normal use, . . .

We do not believe that these three decisions are controlling in the present case. The issue here presented involves no claim of any widespread destruction of the surface, but whether the utilization of the surface for an electric power line can be inferred as a reasonable use within the context of the severance deed language. . . .

It would appear from the foregoing cases that where the severance deed contains broad rights for utilization of the surface in connection with underground mining activities and these broad rights are coupled with a number of specific surface uses, courts will be inclined to imply compatible surface uses that are necessary to the underground mining activity. . . .

Despite statements in *West Virginia-Pittsburgh Coal Co. v. Strong*, 129 W. Va. 832, 42 S.E.2d 46 (1947), that the grant of express mining easements restricts or negates implied rights, we do not believe this principle to be controlling in the present case. First, in addition to a number of express surface rights, including the compatible use of telephone and telegraph lines, the severance deed sets forth the general grant of "all proper and reasonable rights and privileges for ventilating and draining the mines and wells." Moreover, we believe that *Strong* was correctly decided on the more fundamental principle that a right to surface use will not be implied where it is totally incompatible with the rights of the surface owner.

Our past cases have demonstrated that any use of the surface by virtue of rights granted by a mining deed must be exercised reasonably so as not to unduly burden the surface owner's use. [Citations.]

We conclude that where implied as opposed to express rights are sought, the test of what is reasonable and necessary becomes more exacting, since the mineral owner is seeking a right that he claims not by virtue of any express language in the mineral severance deed, but by necessary implication as a correlative to those rights expressed in the deed. In order for such a claim to be successful, it must be demonstrated not only that the right is reasonably necessary for the extraction of the mineral, but also that the right can be exercised without any substantial burden to the surface owner. . . .

Affirmed.

Oil and Gas   Oil and gas occupy a unique position in the law because they are substances that flow from one place to another. The law regarding ownership of these physical elements differs in the various states. In most of the major oil-producing states, the landowner does not own any particular oil and gas below the land surface. The owner simply has the exclusive *right to drill* for oil and gas on his or her land and, if some is discovered, to extract it. The landowner may extract oil and gas from an underground pool, even if the boundaries of the pool extend under neighboring land. There are comprehensive state and federal laws restricting the amount of oil and gas that may be extracted. When the likelihood of an oil or gas field exists, the usual practice in most states is for a group of landowners to grant the right to drill to one individual or firm, by means of leases. The typical lease provides that in the event oil or gas is found and is extracted by the driller, the rent that the landlord (or landlords) receives is a royalty based on the amount of oil or gas removed. For example, a common arrangement in oil leases is that the landowner (or landowners) receives the market value at the well of one-eighth of all oil extracted.

Fixtures

General Nature of Fixtures A fixture is an article that was personal property but which has been attached to real property with the intent that it become permanently a part of the realty. Thus, an owner of real property who takes building materials, such as cement, lumber, and pipe, and constructs a residence clearly intends to convert the items of personal property into real property. However, in some situations the affixing party's intent is not clear. If litigation results, the court has the difficult task of determining the probable intent.

Tests of a Fixture In order to determine whether a particular item was intended to be a fixture, the courts have established several objective criteria. These criteria are not always given equal weight by the courts; the relative importance of each test depends on the circumstances of each case. The usual tests are (1) method of attachment, (2) adaptability to use, and (3) relationship of the parties.

Method of attachment When an item is attached to land or to a building or other structure in such a manner that removing the item would cause injury to it or to the real property to which it is attached, the courts consider such attachment strong evidence that the item was intended to be a fixture. One can reasonably infer that items that are attached to a structure by cement or plaster are intended to remain permanently. Heating and air conditioning systems are generally installed in buildings in such a manner that to remove them would cause great injury, and therefore usually are held to be fixtures.

The fact that an item is easily removable without injury to it or to the real property suggests that the intent of the affixing party is to have the item remain personal property. However, ease of removal is not conclusive in determining whether an item was intended to be a fixture.

Adaptability to use An item of personal property that is beneficial or necessary to the ordinary use of the real property to which the item is attached, is likely to be held a fixture, even though the item may be easily removable. For example, doors, windows, and hot-water heaters are usually removable without injury, but courts normally hold such items to be fixtures. These items are necessary to the ordinary use of real property, and the courts infer that the affixing party must have intended the items to be permanently part of the real property. Items that are custom-made for the particular premises, such as wall-to-wall carpeting and built-in kitchen appliances, are also normally held to be fixtures.

The courts seldom hold an item to be a fixture if it is not beneficial or necessary to the ordinary use of the real property. For example, a large pipe organ installed in a home was held to be personal property because it was a musical instrument and not a necessary part of a residence.

Relationship of the parties In order to determine the intent of the party who has attached an item to the realty, the courts also consider as evidence the relationship of the parties to each other. Thus, in litigation involving the right of a tenant to remove an item the tenant has attached to the landlord's real property, the courts will presume that the tenant intended to remove the item at the end of the lease period. Such items are usually held not to be fixtures because a tenant seldom intends to make a gift of personal property to the landlord.

Disputes often arise between the buyer and seller of real property as to whether certain items attached to the premises were intended to be removable by the seller or were intended to pass to the buyer as fixtures. Typical examples of items causing disputes are curtains, bookshelves, and television aerials. If the parties cannot agree and litigation results, the court will first apply the usual tests of method of attachment and adaptability to use. If doubt still exists, the court will generally favor the buyer and hold the disputed item to be a fixture. For example, a television aerial could be classed either as personal or real property, considering the method of attachment (easy to remove) and the adaptability of its use (very beneficial). Most courts would probably declare it to be a fixture and would not allow the seller to remove it.

Case 21.2   Wilmington Suburban Water Corp. v. Board of Assessment
291 A.2d 293 (Del. Super. 1972)

O'HARA, J. This action is an appeal to the Superior Court from a decision of the New Castle County Board of Assessment ("Board") holding certain trade equipment taxable as real property. Appellants [Wilmington Water Corp. et al.] are a group of companies that furnish water for commercial and residential uses within New Castle County. In the conduct of their operations appellants maintain various pipes, mains and storage tanks used in connection with a water distribution system extending throughout the County. The appellant water companies contend in this proceeding that the aforementioned equipment, presently assessed and taxed against the companies by the County, is personal property and, therefore, not properly subject to taxation under the terms of 9 Del. C. Sec. 8101. That statute in express language provides:

> "All real property situated in this State shall be liable to taxation and assessment for public purposes by the county in which the property is located, except as otherwise provided in this chapter." . . .

A complete description of the subject property may be fairly summarized as follows. The water companies own distributional equipment of basically two types, water storage facilities existing above ground and pipelines buried beneath the soil at varying depths throughout the County. Some of the land occupied by the pipelines is owned by the water companies themselves. [Most of the pipelines are laid on land owned by others.] . . .

The water companies also own large storage facilities on property owned by themselves or held under lease. These storage facilities consist of both ground and elevated tanks. The elevated tanks are steel and stand or rest upon metal legs which are bolted to foundations of concrete. The ground storage tanks apparently are not fastened or bolted in any way to the real property, but rest upon the ground by the force of gravity supported in position by a concrete ring or a stone bern type of foundation. These structures, though large, are capable of being removed and, in fact, at least one was so removed from the water company's property in 1968 after a useful life of approximately 30 years. The one tank remaining and situated on leased property is guaranteed long term occupancy if desired by the terms of a 99 year leasehold interest.

The term "real property" is not defined in 9 Del. C. Sec. 8101. When a revenue statute, like any other statute, does not define its terms, it is proper to refer to the common law. At common law the concept of real property included fixtures, articles which by reason of their annexation to land were regarded as part of the freehold. . . . *Wilmington Housing Authority v. Parcel of Land*, 219 A.2d 148 (Del. Sup. Ct. 1966). . . . The Court therein stated:

> "In determining whether or not a chattel has been sufficiently annexed to the realty to become a fixture, the controlling test is the intention of the party making the annexation as disclosed by the surrounding circumstances. To determine this intention, various factors should be considered. Thus, the nature of the chattel, the mode of its annexation, the purpose or use for which the annexation has been made, and the relationship of the annexor to the property, are all to be considered and weighed in determining the question of intention."

The parties have stipulated to the pertinency of the above principles of law, but differ as to its application to the record facts.

The water companies assert that the nature of their chattels and the mode of annexation suggest that they were installed for a temporary purpose and are properly characterized as nontaxable personalty. . . . Furthermore, the manner in which the equipment is affixed to the land allows for its removal. In this connection, it is emphasized that both the inherent right to remove the chattels (from company owned land) and the reserved right to remove pursuant to agreement have, in fact, been exercised with respect to particular links in the water system in a continuing process of repair and replacement. Finally, the water companies argue that the law necessarily implies that a licensee who attaches chattels used in a trade or business upon the land of another with the reservation of a right to remove upon the termination of the privilege intended that the attachment was for a temporary purpose. This follows from the natural presumption that a gift to the owner of property was not intended.

The County, on the other hand, contends that while the subject chattels are removable it is only with great difficulty. Moreover, it is argued that the physical removability of the chattels has no discernible significance in the present case where from the purpose or use for which the annexation was made it may be inferred that the chattels were intended to remain upon the land indefinitely or for a substantial period of time. In this connection, the County suggests that it would be unrealistic to conclude that the water companies ever contemplated the removal of the subject chattels prior to the termination of their useful life where such removal would affect the water supply of New Castle County.

It is the opinion of the Court that the various pipelines, conduits, and storage tanks used in the distribution of water constitute real estate for the purpose of taxation under the common law. . . . In concluding that the subject chattels constitute fixtures at the common law, the Court is persuaded in this instance that controlling significance must be afforded to the purpose or use for which the annexation was made as indicative of an intention on the part of the water companies to accede the chattels to the land permanently. Thus, the Court agrees that given the nature of the service performed and the capital outlay expended it is inconceivable that the water companies contemplated removal of the chattels prior to the expiration of their useful life. Moreover, it is the opinion of this Court that the result reached in this decision is supported by the weight of authority. 57 A.L.R. 869. . . . Having satisfied the criteria set forth in Delaware with respect to fixtures, appellants' equipment is taxable under 9 Del. C. Sec. 8101. . . . It is so ordered.

ACQUISITION OF OWNERSHIP OF REAL PROPERTY

Acquisition by Private Individuals and Firms

Methods of Acquisition There are various methods of acquiring ownership of real property. In some situations an individual (or business firm) participates actively in a transaction to acquire ownership, as where a person contracts to purchase the property. In other situations one acquires ownership without active participation, as where a person inherits the property.

Acquisition by purchase The most common method of acquiring ownership of real property is by purchase from an owner. The legal principles relating to a purchase are presented in the contracts part of this text (Part Three). An oral agreement of purchase of real property is generally not enforceable under the statute of frauds. Almost invariably, a written contract is a part of the real property purchase transaction. The contract may be a standard printed form with blanks filled in, or it may be a lengthy, specially drawn instrument containing many terms and conditions. In either event, the actual transfer of ownership of the real property is accomplished by means of a written document, called a "deed," given by the owner to the purchaser. The various types of deeds and the requirements for a deed are discussed later in this chapter.

Acquisition by gift Another common method of acquiring ownership of real property is by gift. The three elements required to establish a valid gift of personal property were discussed in the previous chapter. The same elements (intent to make a gift, delivery to the donee, and acceptance by the donee) are required to establish a gift of real property. Since physical delivery of real property is impractical, the requirement of delivery is usually met by the owner's signing a deed and handing the deed to the donee or to an agent of the donee.

Acquisition by will or by descent An individual or firm may acquire ownership of real property when someone dies. The owner of real property may have made a will, leaving the property to a named person or firm. If the owner dies without having made a will, the owner's real property passes to his or her heirs in accordance with the law of the state where the real property is located.

Acquisition by adverse possession Occasionally, an individual or firm acquires ownership of real property by adverse possession. The transfer of ownership occurs without the consent of the owner. It is an unusual method of acquisition, largely because compliance with the essential requirements is difficult. In order to acquire ownership of real property by adverse possession, the claimant must take possession of the property and must prove that the occupation of the property was (1) open and notorious, (2) exclusive and hostile to the owner, (3) under claim of right or color of title, and (4) continuous for the statutory period. In some states the claimant must also pay all property taxes levied against the property during the statutory period.

Open and notorious occupation means that the adverse possessor must actually use the real property in such manner as to make his or her presence known. For example, constructing a building, or enclosing land with a fence, or growing a crop would be visible signs of occupancy. Whether the owner observes the activities of the adverse possessor is immaterial. The law simply requires occupancy of such nature that any reasonable person who cared to look would know that the occupant claimed some interest in the property.

In order to establish exclusive and hostile occupancy, the adverse possessor must be a trespasser. The possession must be without the permission of the owner and without recognition of the owner's rights. Obviously, such possession is dangerous because it clearly gives the owner a cause of action against the adverse possessor. If the owner or others use the property at the same time as does the adverse possessor, the claim of adverse possession will fail because the occupancy has not been exclusive.

In most states, the adverse possessor must take possession of the real property either under claim of right or under color of title. Claim of right means the claimant knows he or she is a trespasser, committing a wrongful act, but intends to establish ownership of the real property against all others. Color of title means the adverse possessor has some written document (usually a deed) or judicial decree that appears to transfer ownership but that is legally defective.

In order for an adverse possessor to acquire ownership of real property, the claimant must be in continuous possession for a minimum period specified by state law. The length of this period usually varies from 5 to 20 years.

There are certain situations in which an adverse possessor cannot acquire ownership of real property. For example, an adverse possessor usually cannot acquire ownership of real property held by a governmental agency for public use. Thus, ownership of vacant desert land held by the government cannot be acquired by an adverse possessor who meets all the requirements listed above.

Case 21.3   **Hunt v. Matthews et al.**
505 P.2d 819 (Wash. App. 1973)

CALLOW, J. . . . Plaintiff [Anna M. Hunt] acquired title by deed to that parcel marked "A" on the map. Title was acquired in 1957 after the plaintiff had leased this residential property for a year. She has lived since in a house on the property. In November 1968, she filed a complaint alleging adverse possession of the adjacent parcel "B" under the 10-year statute, RCW 4.16.020.

Defendants Biele and Brody are the contract purchasers of the property to the west of plaintiff's property, their property being bounded on the north by Northeast 95th Street, on the west by Sand Point Way and on the south by the Northern Pacific Railway right-of-way. The . . . property of the defendants includes parcel "B". When plaintiff acquired parcel "A", parcel "B" included an irregular and undefined extension of the lawn then existing on parcel "A". She has maintained the lawn which extended onto defendant's property since she purchased parcel "A", and the lawn presently appears much as it did when she acquired parcel "A". . . . She maintained a garden of approximately 15 feet by 15 feet in an area to the south of the extended lawn, usually spaded the garden in the spring and used a compost pile near the garden area. The plaintiff described her use of parcel "B" as "a lawn and also a garden spot."

Plaintiff did not erect a fence or any structure on parcel "B", but an old fence was standing on part of the western fringe of the disputed area when plaintiff took possession of parcel "A". . . . The western periphery of parcel "B" extending from the south edge of the old fence to the railroad right-of-way is a tangled area of blackberries and bushes. The plaintiff never cut a boundary through this area or maintained it but left it in its wild state as a barrier. . . . Were the actions of the one claiming title by adverse possession sufficiently apparent and blatant to give notice to the original title holder that he was being challenged?

The acts constituting the warning which establishes notice must be made with sufficient obtrusiveness to be unmistakable to an adversary, not carried out with such silent civility that no one will pay attention. The intention to claim title to an area must be objectively exhibited by the claimant. Uninterrupted, open, notorious, hostile, and exclusive possession for 10 years is required. Real property will be taken away from an original owner by adverse possession only when he was or should have been aware and informed that his interest was challenged.

Whether actions are open, notorious, and hostile is a question of fact to be

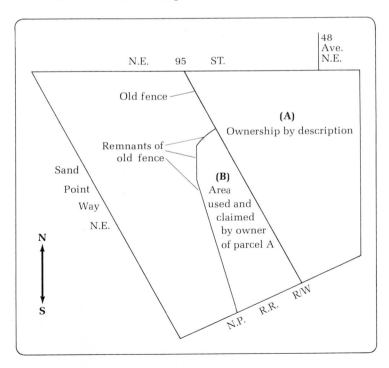

decided by the trier of the fact. The decision is made within the context of the locality, the nature and character of the property, and the use made of it. When a claimant does everything a person could do with particular property, it is evidence of the open hostility of his claim. If he does less, the trier of the fact is justified in concluding that an owner would not be expected to take alarm from such random activity.

The trial court noted that the claimant lived in a residence on her property, but the adjacent property of the defendants was a vacant lot. Greater use of a vacant lot would be required to be notorious to an absentee owner than to one occupying the land who would observe an offensive encroachment daily. . . .

The property must be used beyond the use it would receive because it was handy and convenient and, instead, must be utilized and exploited as by an owner answerable to no one.

The erection of a fence is also a circumstance to be considered by the trial court in ascertaining if the claim was open, notorious, and hostile. The fence in question was not erected or improved by the plaintiff but was allowed to deteriorate. Its existence, under the circumstances, would not convey notice of a claim by the plaintiff. A fence existing as a convenience rather than as an assertion of ownership does not establish notice of a claim. In this light, the evidence was justifiably weighed and found wanting. The fence did not define the boundary of the area claimed by the plaintiff; it did not exclude the defendants from the property; and it did not indicate an affirmative exertion of dominion by the claimant over the property.

The burden of proving the existence of each element of adverse possession is on the claimant. The presumption is in the holder of the legal title. He need not maintain a constant patrol to protect his ownership.

The findings of the trial court are supported by substantial evidence and will not be overturned. The conclusion follows that adverse possession was not proven.

The judgment is affirmed.

Acquisition by accretion Accretion is the gradual increase in soil on the bank of a river or stream from natural depositing of silt or other material. Such increases belong to the owners of the property upon which the soil is deposited. If the waterline in a river, stream, ocean, or lake gradually recedes so that more soil is exposed, this additional land belongs to the owners of the bank or shore line.

Transfer by Deed As stated earlier, the actual transfer of ownership of real property in a purchase or gift transaction is accomplished by deed. A deed is merely a written document used to transfer ownership from one person, called the grantor, to another person, called the grantee.

Types of deeds There are various types of deeds used in the United States to transfer ownership of real property. The more important types are the quitclaim deed, the grant deed, and the warranty deed.

The language in *quitclaim deeds* varies, but a typical wording is "Grantor hereby remises, releases and quitclaims his interest to Grantee."

The legal effect of a quitclaim deed is to transfer to the grantee whatever interest, if any, the grantor may have in the property. If a defect is discovered that results in loss or reduction of ownership of all or part of the real property, the grantee will have no recourse against the grantor.[1]

A *grant deed*, or special warranty deed, as it is called in some states, contains wording such as, "Grantor hereby grants and conveys" certain real property to the grantee. The legal effect of such a deed is to transfer the grantor's ownership to the grantee and to give the grantee some protection if, later on, a defect is discovered in the grantor's title. In many states a statute imposes upon the grantor implied covenants (promises) that (1) the grantor has not transferred the same real property or any interest in it to another grantee and (2) the grantor has not encumbered the property. For example, if Carla grants to James the ownership of timber growing on her land and later grants to Sally ownership of the entire real property, using a grant deed, Sally would have a cause of action against Carla for breach of implied covenant. A grant deed does not protect the grantee against all possible defects, however. Let us suppose that Carla does not have valid ownership of the property because she previously dealt with someone who gave her a forged deed. Neither James nor Sally could recover from Carla because she has not breached either of the implied covenants. In such a situation, the grant deed gives no more protection than does the quitclaim deed.

In most Midwestern and Eastern states the *warranty deed* is the most common type of deed for the transfer of ownership of real property. In such a deed, the grantor expressly warrants (guarantees) to the grantee that ownership is transferred free from all defects or claims. Thus,

in the previous example of a forged deed, both James and Sally would have a cause of action against Carla if she had given each of them a warranty deed.

Requirements for a deed As previously stated, a deed is a written document used to transfer ownership of real property. The requirements for a valid transfer of ownership by deed are (1) a competent grantor, (2) a capable grantee, (3) words of conveyance, (4) adequate description of the real property, (5) proper execution (6) delivery and (7) acceptance. The law relating to each of these requirements is extensive and varies somewhat among the states. A discussion of these requirements is beyond the scope of this text and is reserved for a course in real estate law.

Recording of deeds Ordinarily, if all the above requirements are met, the grantor's ownership of the real property passes to the grantee. However, there is always a danger that a grantor may mistakenly or knowingly give a second deed to the same real property, or a portion of it, to someone else. In order to minimize disputes and hardships that could result from such occurrences, the states have enacted recording statutes.

The recording statutes differ among the states, but essentially the statutes allow a public record to be made of all deeds and other documents affecting real property. An individual or business firm can "record" a deed by filing it at the office of a designated local government official, usually called a county "recorder" or "registrar." The purpose of recording a deed is to put on notice potential subsequent grantees, and other persons interested in the real property, that ownership has passed to the grantee. In many states, an unrecorded deed is void against a subsequent purchaser for value who had no notice or knowledge of the prior deed. In other states (e.g., California), the rule is somewhat different. An unrecorded deed is void against a subsequent purchaser for value who had no

---

[1]The grantee may have a cause of action on other grounds, such as fraud.

notice or knowledge of the prior deed *only* if the later deed is recorded first. This system has been called "a race to the registry." For example, if Alma, the owner of certain real property, gives a deed to Bob and subsequently sells the same real property to Charles and gives him a deed, Charles will acquire the ownership of the real property if he had no knowledge of the deed to Bob and if he records his deed before Bob records his. Bob would thus lose the ownership acquired from Alma, but would have a cause of action against her for damages.

Acquisition by Governmental Units and Agencies

Acquisitions by governmental units and agencies are of increasing significance in contemporary society. The size of government increases continually at all levels—federal, state, and local. As governmental units and agencies expand and new ones are created, a need to acquire real property for personnel, equipment, and supplies is created. In most instances, governmental units and agencies acquire property in the same way as do individuals and business firms. Typically, a governmental unit or agency bargains in the market place for the real property it desires, enters into a written contract of purchase, and receives a deed for the property. Less frequently, a governmental unit or agency acquires ownership through adverse possession or accretion.

There are three other ways in which governmental units and agencies may acquire ownership of real property: through eminent domain, dedication, or escheat.

Acquisition through Eminent Domain Eminent domain, or "condemnation," as it is commonly called, is the right to take private property for public use without the owner's consent.[2] This right is limited by the Fifth and Fourteenth Amendments to the United States Constitution, which require that the owner of property taken through eminent domain be paid just compensation. There is a substantial body of statutes and court cases involving eminent domain. Only a very brief summary of the law on this subject can be presented here.

Before private property can be taken without the owner's consent, the acquiring agency must establish that the taking is for a public use. Early court cases recognized certain obvious public uses, such as streets, highways, military installations, public buildings, and reservoirs. The concept of public use has been steadily broadened over the years, and today courts rarely hold any contemplated use by a governmental unit or agency to be improper. Public use now includes urban renewal projects, automobile parking facilities, rapid-transit lines, and public recreation and entertainment facilities.

The right of eminent domain may be exercised not only by a governmental unit but also by a private corporation entrusted with performance of a public service. For example, a private college can take property necessary for classroom expansion or student housing, and public utility corporations supplying gas, electricity, and telephone service can condemn property for utility lines and poles. In such instances, the corporation acts under delegation of power from the state or federal legislature.

Acquisition through Dedication Dedication of real property is a gift by the owner to a governmental unit or agency on the condition that the property be used for a designated public purpose. The designated purpose might be for a park, street, beach, or historical landmark. The gift can occur during the donor's life or upon his or her death. There is typically a statutory procedure to be followed. The owner makes a formal offer to give certain real property to a city, state, or federal governmental unit or agency, indicating the use or uses to which the property may be put and any other conditions the unit or agency must meet. If the

---

[2]Technically, "eminent domain" and "condemnation" are not synonymous terms. *Eminent domain* is the right to take private property for a public use. *Condemnation* is the legal procedure by which this right is exercised.

appropriate governmental officials decide to accept the gift on the conditions stated, a statute or ordinance is formally passed, and the owner transfers the property to the governmental unit or agency. Thereafter, the government is responsible for the maintenance and operation of the facility.

In certain situations, a "common law" dedication can occur. If an owner of real property makes an offer, express or implied, to give ownership to the public and there is evidence of acceptance by the public, a dedication may take place without formal action. For example, if an owner freely allows the public to do such things as drive across the land, park cars on it, or have picnics on the land, a court may find that a common law dedication has occurred.

Acquisition through Escheat The state government may occasionally acquire ownership of real property by escheat. Earlier, it was pointed out that when the owner of property dies without making a will the decedent's property passes to his or her heirs. Let us suppose a decedent has made no will and has no heirs, that is, no spouse or blood relatives who can inherit the property under state law. When such a situation occurs, the ownership of the property passes to the state. Ownership is said to "escheat" to the state.

TYPES AND INCIDENTS OF OWNERSHIP OF REAL PROPERTY

Types of Ownership of Real Property

Various types of ownership of real property are possible, but no state recognizes all of them. When given a choice, an individual (or firm) must decide which of the available types of ownership will best serve the person's needs or legal position.

Sole Ownership The simplest form of ownership is ownership by a sole individual, business firm, or governmental unit or agency. Where ownership is acquired by purchase or by gift, a deed is executed naming the grantee. Appropriate descriptive words are normally added to the name of the grantee, such as "a single man," "a married woman," "a minor," or "a Delaware corporation."

Joint Tenancy If two or more individuals together acquire a parcel of real property, several types of ownership are available to them. Joint tenancy is not available in all states, but where available, it is one of the types of ownership most often selected by two or more purchasers who are closely related. In a joint tenancy, each cotenant owns an equal, undivided interest in the entire parcel of real property. To illustrate, if Arnold and Betty each buy contiguous 5-acre parcels of land, they are sole owners of their respective parcels and neither of them has an interest in the parcel of the other. But, if Arnold and Betty combine their resources and purchase one parcel of 10 acres as joint tenants, each of them owns an undivided one-half interest in the entire parcel.

The major characteristic of joint tenancy ownership is the "right of survivorship." If one of the joint tenants dies, the interest that he or she had in the property automatically passes to the surviving joint tenant or tenants. Thus, a deceased joint tenant's interest is not subject to disposition by will; nor does it pass to the person's heirs in the absence of a will.

In order for individuals to acquire ownership in joint tenancy by purchase or gift, the deed from the grantor would typically say, "to A and B as joint tenants." If the individuals named in the deed are husband and wife, in some states their ownership is called *tenancy by the entirety*. The characteristics of equal, undivided interests and right of survivorship are the same as those in joint tenancy. There are some differences, however. A major difference is that a joint tenancy may be terminated by one tenant's conveyance of his or her interest in the property to another person. Neither spouse may convey an interest in a tenancy by the entirety without consent of the other spouse.

Tenancy in Common Tenancy in common is similar to joint tenancy in that two or more individuals acquire ownership and each cotenant has an undivided interest in the entire parcel of real property. Tenancy in common differs from joint tenancy in two respects. First, the interests of tenants in common need not be equal. Thus, one cotenant could own an undivided two-thirds interest in a parcel and the other cotenant own the remaining one-third interest. A second difference is that there is no right of survivorship. For example, if Arnold and Betty acquire ownership as tenants in common and Arnold dies, his undivided interest in the real property passes to his heirs or to beneficiaries named in his will.

In order to create a tenancy in common by deed, the deed would typically say, "to A and B as tenants in common." In most states, it would be sufficient to say, "to A and B," since the prevailing rule of law is that a conveyance to two or more persons will be *presumed* to create a tenancy in common in the absence of an express indication otherwise. This rule also applies when individuals acquire co-ownership by will or by descent. For example, if Charles dies leaving a parcel of real property to his children, Dexter and Ephraim, in the absence of some express indication otherwise, the children would acquire ownership of the parcel as tenants in common.

Case 21.4   Zamiska v. Zamiska
296 A.2d 722 (Pa. 1972)

EAGEN, J. Mike Zamiska and George Zamiska were father and son. On December 26, 1957, Mike Zamiska executed a deed conveying the title in certain land to Mike Zamiska and George Zamiska "as joint tenants and as in common with the right of survivorship." Upon his father's death (intestate) on July 18, 1970, George claimed complete title in the land. Other children and grandchildren of Mike Zamiska, claiming the 1957 deed created only a tenancy in common in the grantees, instituted an action in equity asking the court to declare that George's ownership was limited to an undivided one-half interest. The court below ruled the deed created a joint tenancy in the grantees with the right of survivorship and entered a decree granting the defendant's [George Zamiska's] motion for judgment on the pleadings. This appeal followed.

At common law joint tenancies were favored, and the doctrine of survivorship was a recognized incident to a joint estate. But the courts of the United States have generally been opposed to the creation of such estates, the presumption being that all tenants . . . who are not husband and wife . . . hold jointly as tenants in common, unless a clear intention to the contrary is shown.

In Pennsylvania, by the Act of March 31, 1812, the incident of survivorship in joint tenancies (except where the grantees or devisees are husband and wife) was eliminated unless the instrument creating the estate expressly provided that such incident should exist. . . . Whereas before the act, a conveyance or devise to two or more persons (not husband and wife or trustees) was presumed to create a joint tenancy with the right of survivorship unless otherwise clearly stated, the presumption is reversed by the act, with the result that now such a conveyance or devise carries with it no right of survivorship unless clearly expressed, and in the absence of a clearly expressed intent to the contrary, the conveyance or devise creates not a joint tenancy, but a tenancy in common. . . .

Since the issue was decided on the pleadings below, our inquiry is limited to whether the deed involved expressed the intent to create a joint tenancy with the right of survivorship with sufficient clarity to overcome the statutory presumption to the contrary. We conclude it did, as did the court below. Hence, we will affirm.

The pertinent phrase in the deed is "Mike Zamiska and George Zamiska as joint tenants and as in common with the right of survivorship." Appellants contend that the words "with the right of survivorship" conflict with the words "and as in common" and argue since they are part of the same phrase said words are without sense or meaning. The phrase "with the right of survivorship" it is urged is not a clear expression of anything under the circumstances. Consequently, the deed fails to contain a clear expression of intention to create a joint tenancy with the right of survivorship, and instead creates by operation of law an equal tenancy in common between the two grantees.

. . . We cannot disregard the words "with the right of survivorship" in the instant deed as meaningless. It is true that if we were to look merely to the words in the deed "as joint tenants and as in common," we would have an ambiguity since joint tenancy implies the term "survivorship" and "in common" implies the opposite. However, the use of the words "joint tenants" in connection with the operative words "with the right of survivorship" removes the ambiguity and makes it clear that the intention of the parties was to create a joint tenancy, with the passage of the title to the survivor upon the death of the other. . . .

Decree affirmed. Each side to pay own costs.

Community Property Community property is a type of ownership found only in eight states in the United States.[3] Historically, the area within these states was owned by France and Spain, both of which had adopted the civil law system of community property. The system was continued in the states later created out of this area. Each of the eight states has developed its own laws regarding community property, and the subject is too extensive to be covered in a business law text. However, a few general observations can be made.

Community property is usually defined in such a way as to include property acquired by a husband or wife during their marriage, except property acquired by gift, by will, or by descent. This type of ownership is similar to both joint tenancy and tenancy in common in that each person (spouse) owns an undivided interest in a parcel of property. As with joint tenancy, the interests in community property are always equal. As with tenancy in common, either spouse may make a will disposing of his or her one-half interest in community property. If a spouse dies without a will, his or her community interest generally will pass under state statutes to the surviving spouse. Any property owned by a spouse on the date of marriage and any property received by him or her thereafter by

---

[3]Arizona, California, Idaho, Louisiana, Nevada, New Mexico, Texas, and Washington.

gift or inheritance is the *separate property* of that spouse.

Partnership Property Most states have adopted the Uniform Partnership Act. Under the act, real property may be acquired and disposed of in the partnership name. Partnership property may also be held in the name of one or more of the partners. Under the act, each partner is a co-owner of an undivided interest in partnership property as a "tenant in partnership." Upon the death of a partner, his or her interest in partnership property automatically passes to the surviving partner or partners. The subject of partnership property is discussed in more detail in Chapter 40.

Corporate Property A corporation is a legal person or entity. It exists separate from its shareholders and has many legal rights of its own. Among such rights is the right to own real property. Shareholders do not have an ownership interest in property owned by the corporation, but simply own shares of stock in the corporation. Ordinarily, the corporation has the exclusive right to control or dispose of its property. The subject of corporations is treated at some length in Chapters 42 through 46.

Condominiums and Cooperatives In recent years, there has been a tremendous increase in the number of condominiums in the United States. A *condominium* type of ownership is utilized most often for residential purposes, but its use is rapidly expanding to office buildings and commercial property. Briefly stated, condominium ownership involves separate ownership of a unit in a multiunit building, combined with an interest in the common areas and the land. For example, if a grantee acquires ownership of a unit in a high-rise building, the grantee becomes the sole owner of that unit. In effect, the person owns a cube of airspace. Along with the ownership of that unit, the grantee acquires an undivided interest as tenant in common in the ground on which the building stands and in the "common areas" within the building, such as elevators, stairways, hallways, and recreation areas. In some planned communities, a condominium development may consist of a "campus" of buildings. In such developments, the common areas may include a club house, swimming pool, golf course, and other recreational facilities.

The word "cooperative" is used in different senses. As used here, *cooperative* refers to a corporation that is organized for the sole purpose of owning and managing a multiunit building(s), such as an apartment house or an office building, and sells shares of stock in the corporation. A purchase of shares of stock carries with it the right to occupy a unit (apartment or office) in the building. Thus, the shareholder, unlike the purchaser of a condominium unit, does not own the particular unit of the building he or she occupies; all the units are owned by the cooperative. In legal effect, a unit in a condominium is real property, whereas a shareholder in a cooperative owns personal property.

Incidents of Ownership of Real Property

When an individual, firm, or governmental unit or agency acquires ownership of real property there are legal rights and duties that accompany the ownership. These rights and duties exist regardless of the method of acquisition of ownership or the type of ownership acquired.

Rights of Owners Ordinarily, an owner of real property has the exclusive right to use, possess, enjoy, and dispose of the land. The owner's rights extend into the subsurface and the airspace above the surface. The owner can cultivate the land, grow crops, build a house, or install a swimming pool. An owner may give permission to others to use the property or to take minerals from the subsurface, either for temporary periods or for long durations. An owner may use real property as security for a loan or may dispose of the property by gift, by sale, or by will.

Duties of Owners The rights of an owner of real property are not unlimited. There is a growing awareness of the rights of others, and the law imposes certain duties on every property owner. Occasionally some duties are assumed by property owners through agreements with others.

Duties imposed by law   One of the most pervasive of the duties imposed by law is the duty not to create a *nuisance*. For many years the laws of nuisance have prohibited landowners from maintaining anything on their premises that is injurious to the health of others, that is offensive to the senses, or that unreasonably interferes with the comfortable enjoyment of life or property. For example, the following things have been held to be nuisances under the circumstances involved: rock quarry, drop-forging shop, dilapidated wooden building, slaughter-house, airport, emission of smoke or odors, obstruction of a street or river. In recent years, nuisance laws have been enforced more vigorously as a result of public demand to protect the environment from pollution. Liability generally is not based on intent or negligence of the owner, but is imposed by the courts even though the owner is without fault.

Another duty of the property owner is not to *encroach* on a neighbor's property. For example, an owner must not allow the roof of his or her house or the limbs of a tree to over-hang into a neighbor's airspace, nor may an owner allow the roots of a tree to extend into the neighbor's land and interfere with the comfortable enjoyment of the neighbor's property. Still another duty of the property owner is always to exercise *due care* in the use and maintenance of the person's property in order to prevent injury to others. For example, an owner who invites guests to his or her house should remove a child's skates from the entry walk before the guests arrive. This is an application of the tort law of negligence discussed in Chapter 6.

There are many local government regulations imposing duties on owners of real property. The power of local governments to impose these regulations is part of what is known as the "police power." *Police power* is the power to restrict the activity of persons in the interest of public health, safety, morals, and welfare. Such restrictions must not be unreasonable, arbitrary, or discriminatory. Zoning ordinances are enacted by city and county governments to regulate land use. These ordinances generally designate segregated zones or areas where land can be used for residential, agricultural, commercial, or industrial purposes. Zoning ordinances may also regulate the height, size, and appearance of buildings; the size of yards and open spaces; and the amount of off-street parking. Building and safety codes are enacted by city and county governments to regulate the construction, repair, or alteration of buildings. Most local governments have also enacted ordinances enabling the city or county to compel the owner of property to move rubbish or weeds from his or her property, or to remedy unsafe or unsightly conditions on the property.

Case 21.5   Bohannan v. City of San Diego
106 Cal. Rptr. 333 (Cal. App. 1973)

COUGHLIN, J. Plaintiff [W. J. Bohannan] appeals from a judgment in a declaratory relief action rejecting his claim [that] a zoning ordinance is invalid.

On June 30, 1971, the City Council of San Diego adopted Ordinance No. 10608 entitled "Old San Diego Planning District," referred to hereinafter as "the Ordinance," . . . regulating the architectural design of buildings and signs within public view in an area surrounding a state park known as "Old Town."

Case 21.5
Continued

The zoned area, as well as the state park, is the site of the original settlement in San Diego; is of historical significance as the birth place of California; and is the locale of many structures built before 1871.

The purpose of the ordinance is to preserve and enhance the cultural and historical aspects of Old Town for the benefit of the general public. . . .

Plaintiff owns and operates a retail business in the zoned area; brings this class action on behalf of himself and others similarly affected; and contends the ordinance is unconstitutional in that it violates equal protection, due process, and free speech concepts and is not a valid exercise of the police power. . . .

The police power extends to measures designed to promote the public convenience and the general prosperity.

The trial court found the "purpose of the ordinance as shown by the evidence falls within the meaning of 'general welfare' of the public." This finding is supported by the record. Preservation of the image of Old Town as it existed prior to 1871, as reflected in the historical buildings in the area, as a visual story of the beginning of San Diego, and as an educational exhibit of the birth place of California, contributes to the general welfare; gives the general public attendant educational and cultural advantages; and by its encouragement of tourism is of general economic value. . . .

Plaintiff's contention [that] the ordinance provides for the taking of property without compensation in violation of the Constitution is directed to the effect of the provision allegedly requiring the use of materials and architectural styles in remodeling or repairing existing structures "as were used and existed prior to 1871"; and those prescribing the size, location and content of signs.

As to buildings in the area plaintiff contends the practical effect of the ordinance is to render them valueless or substantially reduce their value without compensation. The ordinance does not require the use of such materials and styles "as were used and existed prior to 1871." Instead, it prescribes the use of materials and styles "in general accord with the appearance of the structures built in old San Diego prior to 1871." There is no showing [that] compliance with the provision imposing style requirements upon remodeling or repairing existing buildings in practical effect would render them valueless or substantially less valuable.

As to signs in the area plaintiff makes a similar contention, claiming regulation of their size, location, content and composition deprives their owners of the right to advertise. It is obvious the provision in question does not deprive property owners in the area of the right to use signs; instead, it regulates and restricts that use for the purpose of preserving the historical atmosphere of the area which, for the reasons heretofore stated, is a proper exercise of the police power.

Regulations regarding, and restrictions upon, the use of property in an exercise of the police power for an authorized purpose . . . do not constitute the taking of property without compensation or give rise to constitutional cause for complaint. . . .

The ordinance decrees elimination of non-conforming signs in the area and prescribes a three-year amortization period which plaintiff contends is unreasonable. In support of this contention he directs attention only to two signs in the area, i.e., Shell Oil Company service station signs, which he claims represent an investment of $9,533 and have a life span of 16½ years. There was evidence the cost of the signs, poles and installation in 1967 was $9,533. The only evidence of "life span" was testimony [that] the accounting department of the owner "allows" a life span of 16½ years for signs of this type. The court found as to these signs the evidence "is not sufficient to show the three-year period of amortization is unreasonable." Among other things, the signs were removable to other locations; one of them had been used before; and it may be inferred the poles also could be used elsewhere. There was no evidence upon which to base a finding of the loss, if any, the owner would sustain in removing the signs to another location. Furthermore, plaintiff had the burden of proving the amortization period was unreasonable; and the lack of credible evidence on the issue supports a finding it was reasonable. Whether an amortization period is reasonable depends upon the particular property . . . and each case must be determined on its own facts. In any event the fact the amortization period may be unreasonable as to a particular property does not invalidate its application to other property or invalidate the ordinance of which it is a part.

Plaintiff's contention the ordinance violates free speech concepts is not supported by any argument or citations; it apparently refers to the limitations placed on the design, size, content, and location of signs permitted in the area. The limitations in question do not constitute a denial of the right to advertise as a concomitant of the constitutional guarantee of freedom of speech, but is a permissible regulation in the exercise of the police power. Signs are subject to zoning regulations.

The judgment is affirmed.

Duties created by agreements   In some situations, duties are imposed on the owner of real property by deed or contract. For example, when an individual acquires ownership of a parcel in a subdivision tract (including condominiums and cooperatives) the purchaser usually agrees as a condition of the purchase to assume certain obligations. These obligations are set forth in the deed executed by the subdivider and are imposed for the protection of all present and future owners in the subdivision tract. Thus, each owner might be required to maintain his or her premises in a neat and safe condition at all times. Types of construction and architectural design within the tract are often controlled.

When the purchaser of real property finances all or part of the purchase price by borrowing from a private or institutional lender, certain duties are imposed for the protection of the lender. The borrower generally signs an agreement that includes, among other provisions, the obligation to pay all property taxes and assessments, maintain adequate insurance, keep the premises neat and sanitary, and not to resell the property without consent of the lender.

SUMMARY

The term real property customarily includes the surface of the land, things attached to the land, airspace above, and materials below the surface. Ownership of any of these physical elements of real property can be transferred separately.

A fixture is an article that was personal property but which has been attached to real property with the intent that it become permanently a part of the realty. Controversies arise because the intent of the attacher is not always clear. In such cases, the courts apply three tests: (1) method of attachment; (2) adaptability of the item to the use of the real property; and (3) relationship of the parties.

Individuals and business firms can acquire ownership of real property in several ways. The most common ways are by purchase and by gift. In each such instance, the transfer of ownership is accomplished by means of a deed from the grantor to the grantee. The recording of a deed is not essential to the transfer of ownership from a grantor to a grantee; nevertheless, the deed should be recorded in order to protect the grantee from claims by third persons who may later acquire an interest in the property. Other methods by which individuals and firms may acquire ownership of real property are by adverse possession; by will; and, in the case of individuals, by descent.

Governmental units and agencies—local, state, and federal—frequently acquire ownership of real property. In addition to acquiring ownership by the methods available to individuals and business firms, governmental units and agencies may acquire property by exercising the power of eminent domain. Under this power, private property may be taken for public use without the owner's consent. A governmental unit or agency may receive ownership of property by statutory or common law dedication. A state may acquire ownership of real property by escheat.

Various types of ownership of real property are possible. The list includes: sole ownership, joint tenancy, tenancy by the entirety, tenancy in common, community property, partnership property, corporate property, condominiums, and cooperatives. The right of survivorship exists in a joint tenancy and tenancy by the entirety, but not in the other types of ownership.

Ordinarily, an owner of real property has the exclusive right to use, possess, enjoy, and dispose of the land, airspace, and subsurface. These rights are not unlimited, however; they are limited by duties to others imposed by law and by governmental regulation under the police power. In addition, many duties are assumed by purchasers of real property as part of a contract of purchase in a subdivision tract, or as part of a finance agreement with a lender.

STUDY AND DISCUSSION QUESTIONS

1 *(a)* List the physical elements of real property. *(b)* What is the rule today regarding a landowner's use of airspace? What is the reason for such a rule? *(c)* Explain how each of the following elements might be classified as personal property: water, coal, oil.

2 *(a)* Define a fixture. *(b)* What are the usual tests of a fixture? *(c)* Apply the tests to the following items: window screens, front door key, lawn statuary.

3 *(a)* What must a claimant prove in order to acquire ownership of real property by adverse possession? *(b)* What suggestions could you make to a landowner to help prevent loss of ownership to an adverse possessor?

4 *(a)* What are the essential differences between the following: quitclaim deed; grant deed; warranty deed. *(b)* What are the requirements for a valid deed? *(c)* Should a deed be recorded? Why or why not?

5 *(a)* List and explain the methods by which a governmental unit or agency can acquire ownership of real property. *(b)* What are the distinctions between eminent domain and dedication? *(c)* What is the similarity between them? *(d)* Give an example of each of the two types of dedication.

6 *(a)* In which of the following types of ownership must the owners' interests be equal: joint tenancy, tenancy in common, community property. *(b)* If an owner died without making a will, who would acquire his or her interest in each of the three types of ownership listed?

7 *(a)* List and give examples of several important duties of landowners imposed by law. *(b)* Discuss the justification, pro and con, of impositions of deed restrictions by subdividers.

CASE PROBLEMS

1 Ethyl Corporation has oil-gas-and-mineral leases on a block of about 16,000 acres of land. The corporation has a number of input wells in what is roughly a circle near the outer edge of the block, and a number of output wells within that circle. Ethyl withdraws salt water from the inner wells, extracts from the salt water valuable minerals (one of which is bromine), and then forcibly injects the salt water into the input wells. Such injection facilitates the further withdrawal of salt water from the output wells. Budd owns the minerals in 240 acres lying next to, but outside of, Ethyl's 16,000-acre block. Budd asserts that the recycling operation is draining salt water from the 240 acres and that Ethyl should be made to account to him for his share of the minerals that are being extracted from the salt water. Is Budd entitled to an accounting for a share of the minerals being extracted from the 240 acres?

2 A cable television company provides master television antennas at high, unobstructed points and transmits signals through a system of cables carried on utility company poles to the homes of subscribers to their service. At the terminal points, a cable is suspended from the utility pole to the subscriber's home. The cable then enters the home and with related wiring and equipment is fastened by clamps, screws, and bolts. The portion extending from the utility pole and into the house is called a "housedrop." The portion within the home is called the "interior housedrop." The cable company charges for installation and for monthly service. If service is discontinued, the system is simply disconnected at the utility pole; nothing is removed. The company has no agreement whatever with the subscriber over what can be done with the equipment. The material and labor costs for installation of the housedrops are carried on the company's books as capital assets, and depreciation is taken as a deduction on its federal income tax returns. Should the interior housedrop portion be treated as a fixture owned by the subscriber or as property owned by the cable company?

3 In 1938 George and Amelia Popp executed and delivered a deed to Wachter conveying ownership of some 90 acres of land. Both parties agreed and understood that only land north of Rock Creek Road was intended to be transferred, but by mistake 11 acres of land south of the road were included in the deed. In 1941 Wachter conveyed the 90 acres to Lauf, and in 1955 Lauf conveyed the property to Fitzpatrick. Meanwhile, in 1940 George Popp had died and his widow, Amelia, undertook to convey lands south of Rock Creek Road to Phelps in 1942, including the 11 acres mistakenly deeded in 1938. Phelps deeded to Siebeneck in 1944. Siebeneck fenced the entire area he considered he owned. Rock Creek Road was fenced as the north boundary line, in accordance with the deed description. He used the land for pasturing and feeding cattle continuously until 1962, when he deeded the farm to Boeckmann. All the deeds were promptly recorded following their execution and delivery. Through the years both sets of "owners" paid taxes on the 11 acres south of the road. Boeckmann filed suit against

Fitzpatrick, the record owner, claiming that ownership of the 11 acres was acquired by Siebeneck by adverse possession and transferred to him. Who should win?

4 In 1950 Mrs. Ethel Nevins offered to buy a house for her younger sister, Carrie Johnson. A contract was entered into for the purchase of a home, and Mrs. Nevins paid the down payment of $1,500. The seller executed a deed to Carrie Johnson, who then signed a deed conveying the property to Mrs. Nevins. The deed to Carrie Johnson was recorded. The deed to Mrs. Nevins was held by her but not recorded because she did not want her husband to know of the transaction. Carrie Johnson and her daughter lived in the home. The daughter was informed by her mother and by her aunt, Mrs. Nevins, that if her mother should die, the house would be hers. Carrie Johnson died in 1971, without leaving a will. After the death, Mrs. Nevins recorded the 1950 deed signed by Carrie Johnson, and claimed ownership of the house. The daughter claims ownership by inheritance from her mother. Who owns the property?

5 State National owns the Reymond Building located on the southwest corner of Third and Florida Streets in Baton Rouge. Attached to the north wall of the building is a canopy that projects over the sidewalk and extends several inches over Florida Street. The city claims ownership by dedication of the street and the airspace above it. A subdivision map dated 1837 shows Florida Street to be 64 feet wide. There is no evidence of a formal acceptance of the map by the city. Since 1837, this 64-foot strip has been considered as a main thoroughfare and has been used and maintained by the city. The street was originally 42 feet wide and there was an 11-foot sidewalk on each side of the street. The city initiated a downtown improvement program and after the construction of improvements by the city, the street measured 44 feet wide and each sidewalk measured 10 feet wide. The Reymond Building canopy did not project into Florida Street until the street was widened. Does the city own the street and can it compel State National to remove that portion of the canopy that now projects over the street?

6 Beulah Sharpe enrolled as a member of the Adam Dante health spa and paid for a 1-year membership. The premises contained an exercise area, a locker room, a shower room, and the "spa" area. The shower room and the spa area had tiled floors, and there were no mats on the floors. A small, inconspicuous sign read "Slippery When Wet." On her fifth visit to the spa, Mrs. Sharpe walked barefoot from the shower room past the steam room, sauna room, and sunken whirlpool to the swimming pool. After swimming, she spent a few minutes in the whirlpool and in the sauna room. Then she walked back toward the swimming pool to pick up a towel. Near the whirlpool her feet slipped from under her, and she was seriously injured. At the time of the accident there was no employee of Adam Dante in the spa area. Does Mrs. Sharpe have a cause of action against Adam Dante?

Chapter
22
Interests in Real Property

The subject of interests in real property is important to almost everyone in contemporary society, including persons who are not owners of real property. The three major types of interests in real property are: estates, easements, and liens. Estates in real property range from those involving full ownership to those involving considerably less than full ownership, such as tenancies. Easements and liens are both interests in the real property of *another*. Thus, two persons are always involved—one who owns the real property and one who owns the easement or the lien.

The first part of this chapter is devoted to a discussion of the nature of estates and the different types of estates. Special attention is given to landlord-tenant relations. The last two parts of the chapter are devoted to easements and liens.

ESTATES IN REAL PROPERTY

Meaning and Classification of Estates
One of the most helpful explanations of the meaning of estates in real property is that contained in the following quotation.

The ownership interest that a person has in land is called an "estate." This [interest]

411

may vary in size from absolute ownership, which is called a fee simple estate, to a mere tolerated possession called an estate at sufferance. An estate in land gives the owner of such interest the right to enjoy and possess the land—presently or in the future—for a period of time that may be long or short, definite or indefinite, depending upon the interest owned.[1]

Estates may be classified on various bases. The usual classification is based on duration of enjoyment. On that basis, estates are either "freehold" or "leasehold." *Freehold estates* include those in which the duration of enjoyment is potentially infinite and those in which duration is measured by the life of a person. *Leasehold estates* include those in which the enjoyment is for a specified period of time and those in which the enjoyment is for an unspecified period not intended to be infinite.

Freehold Estates

There are two major types of freehold estates: fee simple estates and life estates. In either type the owner of the interest normally has the present right to use, possess, and enjoy the property. If the owner is not to exercise these rights until some future time, he or she has what is called a "future interest." Although future interests are sometimes discussed independently of freehold estates, they are discussed in this chapter under freehold estates because they generally involve either a fee simple estate or a life estate.

Fee Simple Estate   The estate that owners usually acquire in real property is the fee simple, sometimes referred to as a fee simple absolute, or merely as a "fee." A person owning property in fee simple has the fullest type of ownership—the largest "bundle of rights" possible under the law. The owner has the exclusive

right to possess and enjoy the property, sell it, give it away, lease it to another, or borrow against it. Upon the death of the owner, a fee simple estate passes to the beneficiary or beneficiaries designated in the owner's will, or to the decedent's heirs if there is no will. This process of passing on a fee simple estate from generation to generation may continue indefinitely. There are no technical words required to transfer a fee simple estate from a grantor to a grantee. In most states any properly executed deed is presumed to pass a fee simple estate, in the absence of specific words indicating that a lesser estate is intended. There are other types of fee estates, but complete coverage of this area is reserved for a course in real estate law.

Life Estates   A life estate is an estate the duration of which is measured by the life of a person. For example, a deed to "Alice for life" creates an estate that will automatically end when Alice dies. A deed to "Alice for the life of Ben" creates an estate that will end when Ben dies. In this latter example, if Alice dies before Ben, the unexpired portion of the life estate passes to Alice's heirs or to the beneficiaries under her will. During the existence of a life estate, the holder of the estate (called a "life tenant") has a great many rights. The life tenant can use, possess, and enjoy the property; sell his or her interest; give it to a donee; borrow against it; or lease it to someone and collect the rents. However, any lease given by a life tenand could not continue beyond the duration of the life estate. For example, if Alice, a life tenant, leases the property to Don for 10 years, there is no certainty that Don will be able to remain in possession for the full 10 years. If Alice dies and the life estate ends before the 10-year lease expires, Don must vacate the property.

Although a life tenant has many rights, he or she also has certain duties and obligations. The life tenant must keep all improvements on the property in good repair and must not use or treat the property in such a way as substantially

---

[1] Gerald O. Dykstra and Lillian G. Dykstra, *The Business Law of Real Estate*, Macmillan Company, New York, 1956, p. 82.

to diminish its value. Any such abuse of the property is called "waste." Specific examples of waste are permitting the house or fences to fall into disrepair and removing timber, earth, or minerals unnecessarily. Normally, the life tenant must pay the annual taxes assessed against the property and pay interest on any mortgage or other encumbrance on the property. The reason the law imposes these duties on the life tenant is to protect the value of the property for the person who will take possession at the termination of the life estate.

Future Interests As mentioned earlier, when a person's right to use, possess, and enjoy a parcel of property is to begin at some future time, he or she has a future interest. Of necessity, when a grantor creates a life estate a future interest is also created. Someone will succeed to the use and possession of the property upon termination of the life estate. There are several types of future interests recognized in the law as estates. A discussion of all types is beyond the scope of this text; however, we will discuss two major future interests: reversions and remainders.

Reversions When the owner of real property transfers a life estate to someone or leases the property to someone for a certain period, the owner gives up the present right of possession and enjoyment. When the life estate or lease terminates, someone will succeed to those rights. If the grantor will reacquire the right of possession and enjoyment, he or she is said to own a reversion. For example, if Paul makes a deed conveying certain property to Betty "for her life" and makes no mention of who shall have possession and enjoyment when Betty dies, the general rule of law is that full possession and enjoyment will revert to the grantor. Thus, Paul has a reversion and is referred to as a "reversioner." Paul can transfer his future interest to another. If he dies before Betty, the reversion will pass to Paul's heirs or beneficiaries. When a life estate or lease terminates, the owner of the reversion will have all the rights of an owner of a fee simple estate.

Remainders A remainder is also an estate where possession and enjoyment of realty are to occur in the future, but the person who is to receive possession and enjoyment is someone other than the grantor or the grantor's heirs. For example, if Paul transfers certain real property to Betty "for her life, then to Carol," Carol acquires a remainder. She can transfer her interest in the property to another. If she dies before Betty without having transferred the remainder, it will pass to her heirs or beneficiaries. There are different types of remainders, but a complete discussion of the subject is beyond the scope of this text.

Case 22.1   Root v. Mackey
486 S.W.2d 449 (Mo. 1972)

H. P. Snow was the owner of 280 acres of land. In 1927 he executed and delivered a deed to this land to two of his sons, Sam H. Snow and J. Edgar Snow. The grantor stated in the deed that he retained the right of possession of the land during his life and that, "in case of the death of either or both [of the grantees], the share of such deceased shall revert to the living brothers and sisters."

H. P. Snow died in 1933, leaving Sam and Edgar and five other children surviving him. Sam died in 1934. Edgar died in 1948, leaving several children surviving him. In order to get a court determination of where the title to the land was, the brothers and sisters of Sam and Edgar brought suit in the circuit court, naming the children of Edgar as defendants. The defendants claimed an interest in the land by inheritance from their father. The plaintiffs claimed that Sam and Edgar had had only a life estate and that upon the deaths of the life tenants, the remainder (referred to in the deed as the reversion) passed to them, as "the living brothers and sisters." The trial court, adopting plaintiffs' view, found that title in fee simple vested in the plaintiffs as remaindermen. The defendants appealed. The Supreme Court referred the case to a Special Commissioner.

LAURANCE M. HYDE, Special Commissioner. . . . Obviously this deed was not prepared by a lawyer. Such "do it yourself drafting" frequently makes judicial interpretation necessary and difficult. . . .

Plaintiffs claim that Sam H. Snow and J. Edgar Snow had only life estates. . . . "No particular words are required or are necessary to create a life estate. The use of the term 'life estate' is not necessary, but the intention to create a life estate may be expressed in any equivalent and appropriate language." 31 C.J.S., Estates, sec. 32, p. 56. In *Cross v. Hoch*, 149 Mo. 325, 50 S.W. 786, a will gave certain described land to the testator's daughter Sarah Cross and her heirs but provided: "the property here devised to Sarah Cross be subject to the trust, care, and control of my son Turner Maddox, for her use, and, should the said Sarah Cross die without children, then said property shall be divided among my other daughters." The court held this "a life estate for his daughter Sarah Cross, by necessary implication from the terms of the grant." It was considered that the testator was not a lawyer; that he "evidently used the term 'her heirs' as meaning her 'children.'" The court said it was not the law "that a life estate could only be created by the use of the express term 'life estate,'" but instead "the same intention may be expressed in any appropriate equivalent words."

. . . What is determinative is the restriction on the grantees' right to determine to whom the title goes on the deaths of the grantees, by specifically providing that upon the death of either grantee his living brothers and sisters take his share. This is similar to the provision construed in *Cross v. Hoch*, supra.

Defendants . . . point out the use of the term "revert." . . . However, in *Petty v. Griffith*, Mo. Sup., 165 S.W.2d 412, 416, we held the grantor "did not use 'revert' in its technical sense"; instead we said: "To her it was a word of conveyance or her way of saying she intended the title to the property to go to Beal if he survived Belle Ford Griffith and then to his heirs." We held a life estate was conveyed to Belle Ford Griffith. Our view here, from the entire provisions of the deed, likewise, is that the grantor intended to create life estates in his two sons, the fee to go at the death of either to the living brothers and sisters. . . .

We, therefore, hold that the trial court correctly determined that defendants had no interest in the land involved.

The judgment is affirmed.

PER CURIAM: The foregoing opinion by LAURANCE M. HYDE, Special Commissioner, is adopted as the opinion of the court.

Leasehold Estates

As previously noted, a leasehold estate is an estate in real property having a duration of a specified period of time or an unspecified period not intended to be infinite. The holder of a leasehold estate (called a "tenant" or "lessee") is given the exclusive right to possess and use certain premises during the leasehold period, or term. The owner of the property (called a "landlord" or "lessor") retains a reversion. He or she has all the other rights of a full owner and will normally regain the right to possess and use the premises at the end of the term. *Premises* is a word used frequently in creating leaseholds and may mean land, or a building or part of a building with or without the land.

There are four types of leasehold estates: tenancies for a fixed term, periodic tenancies, tenancies at will, and tenancies at sufferance. Each of these types is discussed below. The first three types normally come into existence by means of an agreement called a lease. The nature and requirements of a lease and the rights and duties of landlord and tenant are such important topics that they warrant special consideration. These topics are discussed in connection with tenancies for a fixed term because the reciprocal rights and duties of the parties ordinarily are fully spelled out in leases for that type of tenancy.

Tenancies for a Fixed Term The most common type of leasehold estate is the tenancy for a fixed term, often referred to as an "estate for years," even though the duration of the tenancy may be for a single year or for a term shorter than a year. The lessor and lessee can agree upon a term of any length, unless a statute provides otherwise. Most states have a statute specifying maximum terms for certain kinds of leases. For example, in California the maximum term for leases on agricultural or horticultural land is 15 years; for oil and gas lands, 99 years; for town and city lots, 99 years.[2] A lease for a term in excess of a statutory maximum is usually held to be invalid.

Nature and requirements of a lease A lease has two aspects. In one of its aspects, a lease is a contract setting forth the reciprocal rights and duties of the lessor and lessee concerning the use and possession of certain property. In its other aspect, a lease is a conveyance of an estate in real property from one person to another.

Although most people think of a lease as a written document, a lease need be in writing only if a statute so requires. Most states have a statute requiring leases for more than 1 year to be in writing. Even when the law does not require a lease to be in writing, sound business policy may require a written lease.

No particular words are necessary to create a valid lease. However, certain items should be mentioned in any kind of a lease: (1) the identification of each of the parties; (2) a designation of the premises leased; (3) the rent to be paid, and the time and manner of its payment; and (4) the term of the lease, including a beginning and ending date.

Rights and duties of landlord and tenant As previously noted, a lease sets forth the reciprocal rights and duties of the parties. The most fundamental right of the *landlord* is the right to receive the rental payments provided for in the lease. If the tenant defaults in the payment, the landlord has a cause of action for the unpaid rent. If the tenant unlawfully remains in possession of the premises, the law provides one or more remedies by which the landlord may regain possession. The most fundamental right

---

[2]Calif. Civ. Code, secs. 717 and 718.

of the *tenant* is to have the exclusive possession of the premises for the agreed term, if the tenant fulfills his or her part of the bargain. Suitable remedies are available to the tenant who is unlawfully deprived of the right of possession.

Leases usually include some provisions concerning rights and duties other than those relating to rent and occupancy. For example, some of the additional provisions customarily included in leases of apartments are that the tenant is to pay all electric and gas bills accruing against the apartment during the term of the lease; that the tenant is not to sublet the apartment or assign the lease without the written consent of the landlord; that the tenant will deliver the premises at the expiration of the term in as good order and repair as when received, natural wear and tear excepted; and that the landlord or an agent shall have the right to enter the premises at any reasonable hour to examine the same and to make repairs. Leases of commercial and industrial properties, involving long terms and properties of great value, usually contain more provisions concerning rights and duties than do leases of residential properties.

Landlords and tenants are subject not only to the rights and duties set forth in a lease but also to those declared by the courts and those specified in statutes. For example, at common law the landlord had no duty to repair or maintain the premises occupied by the tenant during the term of the lease. Recently, there has been an important shift in the attitude of the judiciary toward the rights of tenants of residential property, especially in large metropolitan communities. Stressing the contract aspect of leases, some courts have held that the lessor impliedly warrants (guarantees) the habitability of a dwelling.[3] Thus, the landlord must maintain the

premises in a habitable condition throughout the term of the lease. If the landlord fails to meet this obligation, the tenant can stay in possession *without paying rent*. A number of state legislatures have responded to demands of tenant groups and have enacted statutes requiring the landlord of a building intended for residency to keep it in habitable condition, except for waste or dilapidations caused by the tenant. Generally, such statutes define "habitable" to include at least adequate plumbing, water supply, heating, and sanitation.

Transfer of interests under a lease   The landlord can transfer his or her reversion to another. If the landlord dies without having transferred the reversion, it passes to the person's heirs or beneficiaries. Where the reversion is transferred, the transferee becomes the landlord and is bound by the terms of the lease. The tenant may transfer all or part of the leasehold estate to another, unless the lease prohibits or limits the right to do so.

Periodic Tenancies   A periodic tenancy is an estate in real property that is created for a specified period of time and that will continue for successive periods of the same length, until the tenancy is terminated. The period may be week-to-week, month-to-month, or any term the parties agree upon. Frequently, a periodic tenancy arises by inference from the conduct of the parties. Suppose, for example, that a landlord agreed to rent certain premises to a tenant, that no specified term was agreed upon, but that the tenant agreed to pay rent monthly. In the event of litigation, a court would normally hold that a month-to-month tenancy had been created.

A periodic tenancy continues indefinitely until the parties agree to terminate the tenancy, or one of the parties gives notice of termination. Requirements regarding the method and time of notice vary among the states. A common requirement is that the notice must be given in writing in the same amount of time as the period of tenancy, but not to exceed 30 days. Under such a statute, 1 week's notice would be suffi-

---

[3]Some court cases have extended the obligation of apartment house landlords to include reasonable protection against the commission of crimes, especially in common lobbies, hallways, and stairwells. *Kline v. 1500 Mass. Ave.*, 439 F.2d 477 (D.C. Cir. 1970).

cient to terminate a week-to-week tenancy; and 30 days' notice would be sufficient to terminate a year-to-year tenancy. Generally, no reason for termination need be given by either party. However, in many states a landlord may not terminate a tenancy because the tenant report- ed dilapidations and building or health code violations to the authorities. Such a termination is called "retaliatory eviction." Neither may a landlord terminate a tenancy because the tenant withheld rent or deducted the cost of needed repairs from the rent due.

Case 22.2   **Toms Point Apartments v. Goudzward**
339 N.Y.S.2d 281 (N.Y. Dist. Ct. 1972)

DIAMOND, J. . . . The basic facts are not in dispute. The parties entered into a lease on August 17, 1966, for a two-year period commencing September 1, 1966. The lease was renewed twice, each time for a two-year period. The last renewal expired August 31, 1972.

In October, 1971, the tenant invited a group of fellow tenants to meet in her apartment to consider the possibility of forming a tenant's organization to deal with the landlord with respect to several grievances.

In April, 1972, and again in June, 1972, the tenant was advised that her lease would not be further renewed. Despite notice tenant failed to vacate the premises. On the 5th day of October, 1972, this proceeding was begun [to evict the tenant].

At the trial, the tenant raised the affirmative defense of "retaliatory eviction." She claimed that the landlord's refusal to renew her lease was solely in retaliation for her actions with her fellow tenants in opposing the landlord. The landlord contends that the tenant has failed to sustain the burden of proof required and, further, that the defense of retaliatory eviction does not apply in this case.

Tenant seeks to dismiss the action and have the Court order the landlord to renew the lease on terms equal to those offered other tenants.

The Court has before it the question whether a landlord has the right to pick his tenants and refuse to renew the tenancy of a person he finds undesirable for any reason, or whether that right is affected by the defense of retaliatory eviction. . . .

The defense of retaliatory eviction in a holdover proceeding was not available at common law, nor do we in New York have any statutes specifically prohibiting retaliatory eviction. A few states have recently enacted such statutes. Illinois has declared it to be against public policy for a landlord to "terminate or refuse to renew a lease or tenancy of property used as a residence on the ground that the tenant has complained to any government authority of a bona fide violation of any applicable building code, health ordinance, or similar regulation." [The court then similarly summarized the retaliatory-evictions statutes of Rhode Island, Michigan, Maryland, California, and New Jersey.]

There is no dispute between the parties that absent the defense of retaliatory eviction the Court must grant the landlord's petition of eviction. Testimony at the trial indicates that the tenant did hold a meeting of the tenants in her apartment and that she had testified at a hearing concerning the dismissal of the landlord's custodian. There was some testimony that the tenant had concerned herself with such matters as lack of services, rent increases and inequities in rent. The tenant testified that she complained to the Attorney General's Office regarding the failure of the landlord to pay interest on rent security deposits and that she appeared at a "hearing" of the superintendent who was fired by the landlord. . . .

The first question the Court addresses itself to is the prayer of the tenant that the Court order the landlord to grant her a new lease on the same terms and conditions as other tenants in the same building. In the case of a tenant continuing in possession of leased premises after the expiration of the term of the lease, the rights of the landlord are fixed by statute in New York. The Real Property Law provides that upon a holding over by a tenant whose term is for more than one month, the landlord may proceed in any manner permitted by law to remove the tenant, or, if the landlord accepts rent for any period subsequent to the expiration of the term, there is created a tenancy from month to month. The holdover tenancy created at the election of a landlord is not an extension or prolongation of the original term. It is a new term for a new period, separate and distinct from that which preceded it.

The Court rejects tenant's argument that if the Court finds a retaliatory eviction it should grant the remedy of ordering a *new* lease [emphasis added.] There seems to be no authority, public policy or any other justification for disturbing the well settled law in New York that there is no way, legal or equitable, to compel a renewal of a lease.

In reviewing the New York, Federal, and out of state cases discussed above, the Court finds that the basis for accepting the defense of retaliatory eviction is as follows:

A tenant has the constitutional right such as to discuss the conditions of the building he is living in with his cotenants; to encourage them to use legal means to remedy improper conditions; hold meetings; form tenant's associations; and inform public officials of their complaints. These rights would for all practical purposes be meaningless if the threat of eviction would coerce the most justifiable complaints into a submissive silence.

Failure to recognize the defense of retaliatory eviction might result in the continuation of undesirable housing conditions contrary to the strong public policy of creating and/or maintaining proper housing in New York State. Our Court should not by the granting of an eviction of a complaining tenant encourage the landlord to evade his responsibility to abide by the law.

The Court is in accord with the reasoning behind the acceptance of the defense of retaliatory eviction in an action by a landlord to recover possession. Once having accepted that concept, the Court is faced with the problem as to what elements are necessary to create a valid retaliatory eviction defense. In reviewing the cases we find no definite guidelines to follow.

It seems to this Court that *all* of the following should be present for the tenant to prevail:

1 The tenant must have exercised a constitutional right in the action he undertook.

2 The grievance complained of by the tenant must be bona fide, reasonable, serious in nature, and have a foundation in fact. However, the grievance need not have been adjudicated by the agency reviewing the complaint.

3 The tenant did not create the condition upon which the complaint is based.

4 The grievance complained of must be present at the time the landlord commences his proceeding.

5 The overriding reason the landlord is seeking the eviction is to retaliate against the tenant for exercising his constitutional rights.

Applying the facts in the present case to the above criteria, the Court finds that at the time the landlord commenced this action and, at the present time, none of the original grievances existed. The tenant testified that the tenants' association never came into being; that the tenants had collected the interest due them; that the problem with the superintendent had been resolved. Moreover, the tenant failed to show any current complaint against the landlord. . . .

Final judgment in favor of the landlord against the tenant.

Tenancies at Will A tenancy at will is an estate in real property created by agreement of the parties that the tenant will have the exclusive right to possession for an indefinite period of time not intended to be infinite. Such tenancies arise only in limited circumstances. Two examples of the way in which tenancies at will arise are when the tenant is given possession under a void lease and when the tenant is given possession while negotiations take place for a sale of the property or for a comprehensive written lease.

A tenancy at will can be terminated by either party, but many states require a landlord to give 30 days' written notice. Such a tenancy is automatically terminated upon the death of either party. The tenant cannot assign a tenancy at will to another. Any attempt to do so would automatically terminate the tenancy.

Tenancies at Sufferance A tenancy at sufferance typically arises when a tenant remains in possession after the expiration of a tenancy for a fixed term, without the landlord's consent. In most states the landlord can institute legal action to evict the tenant at sufferance without first giving notice of termination of the tenancy. The tenant woud be liable for the reasonable rental value of the premises for the period the tenant remains in possession after expiration of the tenancy for a fixed term. If the landlord accepts rent from a holdover tenant, a court very likely would hold that a periodic tenancy was created by the conduct of the parties. A landlord should therefore consider carefully the legal consequences before accepting rent from a tenant at sufferance.

EASEMENTS

Meaning of Easement

An easement may be defined as the right to use, or prevent the use of, the real property of another in a specific manner. An example would be the following: Edith grants to Fred, an adjoining landowner, the permanent right to drive his car over a designated portion of her land in order to get to and from the nearest public street. Fred has a right-of-way easement. His land is called the "dominant" tenement or parcel. Edith's land, the land that is subject to the easement, is called the "servient" tenement or parcel.

An easement is an interest in real property, but it is not an estate in real property. We have seen that an estate is an interest that is, or may become, possessory. The owner of an easement does not have the right to possess the servient tenement but merely the right to use it, or to prevent the use of it, in a certain way. The easement for roadway purposes, mentioned above, entitles Fred to drive his car across Edith's land, but does not entitle him to fence it, cultivate it, or exercise the usual rights of an owner of an estate in real property.

Methods of Creating Easements

Creation by Express Grant or Reservation   The most common method of creating an easement is by deed.[4] The owner of real property executes a deed that transfers to the grantee a limited right to use the property of the grantor. For example, Edith executes a deed transferring to her neighbor, Fred, a right of way over her land. In some instances, a grantor transfers ownership of the property to another, but expressly reserves an easement in the property for

the grantor's own purposes. For example, Agnes, the owner of a 10-acre parcel of land, executes a deed transferring to Robert the fee simple ownership in 5 acres, but expressly reserves the right to use a 12-foot strip as a roadway for access to the land retained by her.

Creation by Implied Grant or Reservation   In some situations, an easement may be created by implied grant or reservation. For example, suppose that Archer owns 100 acres of land on which he constructs an irrigation system with an open ditch running from the north portion to the south portion. After several years he transfers ownership of the south portion to Donna without making any mention of an easement. Under these circumstances a court very likely would infer that the parties must have intended Donna to have an easement in Archer's land for irrigation purposes. Such an easement is known as an easement by implied grant. In a similar manner, if Archer had sold the *north* portion of the land to Donna without mention of any easement, a court would be warranted in holding that Archer has an irrigation easement by implied reservation. Several conditions must exist before an easement by implied grant or reservation will be recognized by the courts: (1) the owner of real property must have transferred a portion of it to another person; (2) at the time of the transfer, there must have been a long, obvious use of one portion of the property; and (3) the easement must be reasonably necessary to the beneficial use of the other portion of the property (the dominant tenement).

Creation by Necessity   In rare situations an easement may be created by necessity. Where an owner of real property transfers to a grantee a portion of the owner's property without providing the grantee a means of access, the parcel is said to be *landlocked*. Upon application to a court, the grantee may be given an easement for access to his or her parcel over the retained portion of the grantor's property. Such an easement must be absolutely necessary for the grantee, and not just convenient or desirable. Thus,

---

[4]The types of deeds and the requirements for a valid deed were discussed in the previous chapter under the heading "Transfer by Deed," p. 398.

a grantee who has access to a parcel of land but complains that the only way to get to the parcel is by way of a steep, narrow, winding road cannot expect a court to give an easement by necessity over a flatter portion of the grantor's retained property. If a grantor transfers ownership of real property and retains a portion that is inadvertently landlocked, the grantor is entitled to an easement by necessity over the transferred property.

Case 22.3   **Close v. Rensink**
501 P.2d 1383 (Idaho 1972)

McFADDEN, J. The plaintiffs-appellants in this action are John E. Close, the trustee of the estate of J. W. McTarnahan, deceased, and Daryl Dorsey, the beneficiary of such trust. . . . The defendants-respondents are George C. Rensink, Jr., and his wife, Dorothy L. Rensink, who own certain real property adjoining property previously owned by J. W. McTarnahan during his lifetime. . . .

To assist in understanding the location of the lands and roads involved, a plat reflecting the tracts of land and their ownership and the roadways which are in controversy is set out below. . . .

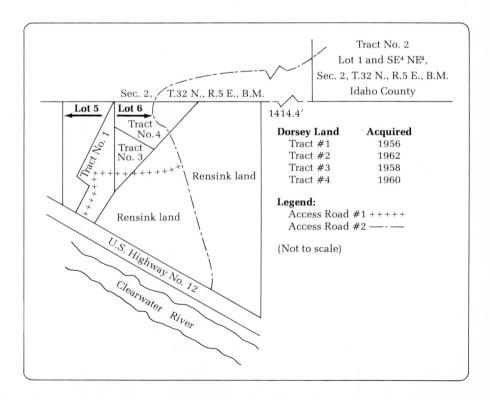

Tract No. 2
Lot 1 and SE⁴ NE⁴,
Sec. 2, T.32 N., R.5 E., B.M.
Idaho County

Sec. 2, T.32 N., R.5 E., B.M.

Lot 5   Lot 6

Tract No. 4

Tract No. 3

Tract No. 1

1414.4'

Rensink land

Rensink land

U.S. Highway No. 12

Clearwater River

Dorsey Land	Acquired
Tract #1	1956
Tract #2	1962
Tract #3	1958
Tract #4	1960

Legend:
Access Road #1 +++++
Access Road #2 —·—

(Not to scale)

The appellants own what is designated on the foregoing map as Tracts nos. 1, 2, 3, and 4. Tract no. 1 was purchased by McTarnahan in 1956 . . . and abutted on what is designated as U.S. Highway No. 12. Tract no. 1 has its own access to the highway and does not utilize any access road in common with the Rensinks. McTarnahan purchased Tract no. 3 from the Rensinks in 1958. This tract abutted Tract no. 1 and was utilized by McTarnahan as the site for a residence he later constructed. In 1960 McTarnahan purchased Tract no. 4 from the Rensinks, which adjoined original Tract no. 1 and Tract no. 3, so that there was one continuous ownership by McTarnahan of Tracts nos. 1, 3, and 4. Tract no. 2 was purchased by McTarnahan in 1962 from Mr. Agee. . . .

The appellants' main contention on this appeal is that they are entitled to an implied easement over the Rensink land for access to Tract no. 4, and in the event that there was no implied easement then they are entitled to an easement by way of necessity to give access to Tract no. 4. While it is unclear from the record, apparently they also contend that they are entitled to an implied easement or way of necessity over the Rensinks' land to give access to Tract no. 2. . . .

In *Davis v. Gowen*, 83 Idaho 204, 360 P.2d 403 (1961), this Court in discussing the elements essential to create an implied easement for right of way stated them as follows:

"To establish an easement by implication in favor of the dominant estate, three essential elements must be made to appear:

1 Unity of title and subsequent separation by grant of dominant estate;

2 Apparent continuous user;

3 The easement must be reasonably necessary to the proper enjoyment of the dominant estate." . . .

In applying these principles of the elements essential to establish an implied easement to the controversy here, it is clear that there can be no implied easement for Tract no. 2. This tract is separate and apart from any lands owned by the Rensinks. Secondly, because Mr. McTarnahan acquired title to Tract no. 2 from a Mr. Agee, who is a stranger to the title now held by the Rensinks, unity of title never existed. . . .

Concerning Tract no. 4 which McTarnahan purchased in 1960, certainly the evidence fails to establish any apparent continuous user of Access Road no. 2 to this tract. . . . While Rensinks still owned Tracts nos. 3 and 4, they logged the timber from this area, at which time Access Road no. 1 was used as a skidroad, and logs were decked near the place where McTarnahan later built his home on Tract no. 3. After the sale of Tract no. 4 to McTarnahan, the use of the respective access roads was greatly limited and then only with the Rensinks' permission. The record discloses that McTarnahan never used Access Road no. 2 except with permission first obtained from the Rensinks. It is undisputed that McTarnahan obtained Tract no. 4, which is a steep hillside, for the purpose of preventing encroachment by others upon his residence; and there is no evidence that Tract no. 4 was ever used for farming or residence purposes. Thus, the requirement for an easement by implication that there be "apparent continuous user" is absent. *Davis v. Gowen*, supra.

It is our conclusion that the appellants failed to establish the basic elements essential to establish an easement or right of way by implication.

As a second ground the appellants contend they are entitled to a right of way by necessity. . . . Concerning Tract no. 2, the district court found that the appellants had other access to this tract by way of Suttler Creek Road, a publicly maintained road. This finding is fully sustained by the evidence. . . .

Tracts nos. 1, 3, and 4 are all adjoining and constitute one integral piece of land under ownership of the appellants. They have access to this land from Highway No. 12, via the road leading from the highway to their residence. Consequently there is access to the outside from the tract as a whole. However, appellants point to the fact that northerly from their residence, Tract no. 3 is steep, hillside land, and Tract no. 4's gradient is even steeper. Further the appellants argue that it is almost impossible to go from Tract no. 3 northerly onto Tract no. 4 by means other than on foot or horseback. Accepting this as true, still the appellants have failed to establish in this record what use they desire to make of Tract no. 4 other than as a means of access to Tract no. 2. . . . Since the appellants failed to establish the use intended to be made of Tract no. 4 when it was acquired, it is difficult to see where a way of necessity to Tract no. 4 over respondents' land arose. In other words the appellants in failing to establish the use to be made of Tract no. 4 at the time of the original conveyance (the basis for a way of necessity), failed to establish any necessity for a right of way to that tract across respondents' land.

The judgment of the trial court is affirmed. Costs to respondents.

Creation by Prescription An easement by prescription arises from use of property contrary to the wishes of the owner. In most states, one who claims such an easement must show use of a portion of another's property that is open and notorious, hostile to the owner, and continuous for the period specified in the state statute. The requirements are very similar to those of adverse possession, discussed in Chapter 21. The difference is that adverse *possession* results in the acquisition of ownership, while adverse *use* results in the acquisition of an easement. A typical example would be the following. Suppose that Mary and Tom are neighbors and almost daily for many years Mary has walked across a corner of Tom's property, eventually making a visible pathway. Tom objected many times during those years, but to no avail. Mary has acquired a prescriptive easement if the statutory period of time has elapsed. Tom is now powerless to prevent Mary from continuing to walk across that corner. In most states Tom could have prevented such an occurrence by posting in plain sight a notice that permission to pass over his property was revocable at any time.

Creation by Dedication In Chapter 21 we discussed dedication as a method of a governmental unit or agency's acquiring ownership of real property (see p. 400). The process of dedication may also be used to create an easement. For example, an owner of land may offer a roadway easement to the local city government. If the city council passes an ordinance accepting the offer, the city acquires an easement by statutory dedication. The owner of the servient tenement retains the right to use the airspace above the roadway and the subsurface below the roadway as part of the fee simple estate.

In recent years, the creation of easements by common law dedication has been asserted in lawsuits between environmental groups and owners of recreation land. Some courts have found that common law dedications have occurred when the evidence showed that the landowners freely allowed the public to camp, picnic, or walk across their property. In some states the property owner can avoid such claims of dedication by posting in plain sight an appropriate sign.

Use and Maintenance of Easements

The owner of an easement may exercise the right to use, or prevent the use of, the servient tenement according to the purpose of the easement and the circumstances surrounding its creation. Where an easement is created by *express grant*, a properly drawn deed will indicate the specific purpose of the easement, such as use of the land for a roadway, or for installa-

tion of power poles. Where an easement is created by *implied grant* or by *prescription*, there has been an obvious, open use that determines the extent of the easement owner's right to use the servient tenement. He or she will be able to use the property in the same manner as it was used previously. Under an easement by *necessity*, the right to use the servient tenement is limited to the purpose that necessitated the creation of the easement, such as use for vehicular access to the nearest public street. An easement by *dedication* allows the servient tenement to be used by the government or the public for the purpose specified in the landowner's express or implied offer.

The owner of an easement has the right and the duty to maintain and repair installations connected with the easement. For example, an easement owner may grade and pave the surface designated in a roadway easement or, if the easement is for utility purposes, the easement owner may enter the servient property to repair and replace water lines or sewer pipes as needed. The owner of the servient tenement may do as he or she wishes with the property so long as he or she does not unreasonably interfere with the use, enjoyment, and maintenance of the easement created.

Case 22.4   Jordan v. Guinn
485 S.W.2d 715 (Ark. 1972)

Mr. and Mrs. Jordan owned a tract of land adjacent to property owned by Esther Guinn, plaintiff [appellee]. For many years there had been a roadway easement 20 feet wide running across the north side of the Jordans' property. The purpose of the easement was to give access to the Guinn property. Mr. Jordan erected a gate across the west end of the roadway and installed a fence across the east end of the roadway. Guinn brought suit against Mr. and Mrs. Jordan to require them to remove both the gate and the fence. The trial court directed their removal. Mr. and Mrs. Jordan appealed.

FOGLEMAN, J. . . . The general rule regarding the obstruction by fences or gates of such private easements by the owner of the servient estate is that a fence may not be erected so as to entirely obstruct the way; but that unless it is expressly stipulated or it appears from the terms of the grant or the surrounding circumstances that the way shall be an open one, without gates, the owner of the servient estate may erect gates across the way if they are so located, constructed or maintained as not unreasonably to interfere with the right of passage, when they are necessary for the preservation and proper and efficient use of the lands constituting the servient estate. . . .

Pertinent factors to be considered include the terms of the grant, the intention of the parties as reflected by the circumstances, the nature and situation of the property and the manner in which it has been used and occupied before and after the grant and the location of gates. . . .

Whatever right the Jordans may have to place obstructions across the easement of appellee Guinn, such obstructions must not be of such a character as to interfere with the reasonable enjoyment of the easement by Esther Guinn, and must be for purposes appropriate to the Jordans' use of their own property, not for the purpose of annoying the easement owner or obstructing her in the use of the way. We find nothing in the evidence to indicate any express agreement that the way would be open or that [Jordan] retained the right to maintain any gates or gaps.

Orville Guinn, father of Esther Guinn, . . . testified that Roy Jordan had closed, blocked or "stopped up" the road by a gate at one end of the Jordan property and a fence at the other and that one could not go into or from his daughter's property over the way after Jordan had placed gates across it. . . . Inez Etheridge stated that Jordan first blocked the way by parking his car in it. Mrs. Jordan testified that in order to give notice that people should not cross the Jordan property a fence was built across the strip about which this dispute arose and that the parking of the Jordan vehicle across it was to protect the interest of the Jordans in keeping that land to themselves. Mr. Jordan also said that he blocked passage over the "road" first by parking a car across it and later by a fence.

We find no evidence that the gate and fence were placed across the way for any purpose relating to appellants' [Jordans'] use of the servient estate or any purpose other than to prevent its use as a means of ingress to and egress from the Guinn property. . . .

It is clear that appellants had no right to completely obstruct the way. From our review of the circumstances and of the evidence pertaining to the use of the easement, we are unable to say that the chancellor's [trial court's] finding that the fence and gate constituted unreasonable obstructions was clearly against the preponderance of the evidence.

The decree is affirmed.

Termination of Easements

There are various ways in which an easement may be terminated or extinguished. The most common method is by a deed from the owner of the easement to the owner of the servient tenement. Some of the other ways in which an easement may be terminated are by (1) abandonment; (2) merger, as where the same person becomes the owner of the easement and the servient tenement, for obviously a person cannot have an easement on his or her own land; (3) destruction of the servient property, as where the tenant in an apartment building has an easement in the common halls and stairways, and the building is destroyed by fire or earthquake; and (4) adverse possession, as where the owner of the servient tenement refuses to recognize the rights of the easement owner and, for the statutory period, occupies the property adversely to the easement owner's rights.

LIENS ON REAL PROPERTY

Meaning and Classification of Liens

In general, a lien is a claim or charge on property as security for the payment of a debt or for the performance of some other obligation. In one sense, a lien is a contingent claim held by a creditor. If the obligation is satisfied, there will be no interference with the debtor's right to use, possess, and enjoy his or her property. On the other hand, if the obligation is not satisfied, the lien holder may take steps (called "foreclosure") to sell the property and to apply proceeds from the sale to the debt.

There are two main classes of liens on real property: *voluntary* liens, which are created with the property owner's consent (mortgages, for example); and *involuntary* liens, which are created without the property owner's consent (mechanics' liens, for example). Only the most important voluntary and involuntary liens are discussed on the following pages.

Voluntary Liens on Real Property

Mortgages A mortgage is the most common type of voluntary lien on real property. The mortgage device is used in connection with many different kinds of credit transactions. Usually, the device is used for either of two purposes. (1) It is used by a property owner as a means of borrowing a substantial sum of money needed for some personal or business reason. The property owner goes to a bank, borrows the money on a promissory note, and executes a mortgage on the owner's home or business property to secure the repayment of the money borrowed. (2) The mortgage device is often the indispensable means of financing the purchase of real property. The person who desires to purchase the property has sufficient cash for a down payment but not enough to pay the balance of the purchase price. If the seller agrees "to carry the mortgage," he or she gives the buyer a deed to the property, and the buyer executes a mortgage on the property in favor of the seller. If the seller does not agree to carry the mortgage, the buyer borrows the money from a lender and executes a mortgage to the lender.

Nature and requirements of a mortgage As implied above, a real estate mortgage is an interest in real property given to secure the performance of some obligation. The two parties to a mortgage are called the "mortgagor" (the borrower or debtor) and the "mortgagee" (the lender or creditor).

The requirements for a valid mortgage parallel the requirements for a valid deed. Under the statute of frauds, a mortgage must be evidenced by a writing. There must be a competent mortgagor named in the document; a named mortgagee; appropriate language to create a lien; an adequate description of the real property; and proper execution, delivery, and acceptance of the mortgage. There is no requirement that a mortgage instrument be recorded in order to create a lien on the property mortgaged. However, the mortgagee should have the instrument recorded at the local county recorder's office as a protection against any subsequent purchaser or any subsequent mortgagee or other lien holder. (Recording was discussed in Chapter 21.)

Rights and duties of the parties The *mortgagor* of real property retains the right to use, possess, enjoy, and dispose of the property. The mortgagor can lease the premises to another and collect rent. He or she can borrow further sums of money from other creditors and give subsequent mortgages to them. If the mortgagor transfers ownership of the property during life or if the property passes at death to his or her heirs or beneficiaries, the transferee takes the property subject to the mortgage. The typical mortgage instrument contains a list of duties to be performed by the mortgagor. Some of the duties customarily included are to repay money borrowed; to repay any future sums that may be advanced by the mortgagee; to keep the premises in good repair; to refrain from committing waste; to pay annual real property taxes; to pay any prior mortgage that may be on the property; and to maintain adequate fire insurance on improvements.

The *mortgagee* has the right to performance of all of the mortgagor's duties. Under the typical mortgage instrument the mortgagee has several duties. The mortgagee has a duty to lend money in accordance with the agreement of the parties. When the mortgagor pays back the loan, the mortgagee owes a duty to execute appropriate documents to remove the lien from the mortgagor's property. In the event foreclosure becomes necessary, the mortgagee owes a duty to act fairly and to follow the statutory procedure of the state. A mortgagee can transfer the mortgage to a third person and assign to such person the right to collect the debt that is secured by the mortgage. Upon the mortgagee's death, the mortgage passes to his or her heirs or beneficiaries. The transferee would be obligated to perform the mortgagee's duties mentioned above.

Case 22.5 **Investors Savings & Loan Association v. Ganz**
416 A. 2d 918 (N.J. Super. Ch. 1980)

Mr. & Mrs. Ganz (defendants) borrowed $50,000 from Investors Savings & Loan Association (plaintiff) to finance the purchase of a home. The loan was secured by a mortgage in favor of the plaintiff. In the mortgage loan application the defendants stated they would occupy the property. The mortgage contained the following condition:

> And it is further agreed that, if the mortgaged premises are not used as the primary place of residence and are not occupied by the Mortgagor during the term of the mortgage loan, then and in such event, the aforesaid principal sum with accrued interest shall, at the option of the Mortgagee, become due and payable immediately, . . .

In October 1979 plaintiff learned that the premises were not occupied by the defendants but were occupied by tenants. Plaintiff demanded that the balance due on the mortgage be paid in full. Defendants have not made this payment and the premises continue to be tenant-occupied. Plaintiff brought suit to foreclose the mortgage. Defendants have filed an answer alleging that the acceleration clause and mortgage requirement that defendants reside in the mortgaged premises are unconscionable, inequitable, create a forfeiture, and thus are of no force and effect. Plaintiff moves for an order granting summary judgment.

KENTZ, J. . . . Where an acceleration clause is express and certain in its terms, such a clause requiring the payment of the entire balance due on the mortgage upon default in the performance of any covenant or condition of the mortgage is held to be a legitimate contractual obligation for credit on condition and not a penalty or forfeiture clause. . . .

The only remaining issue is whether the enforcement of the acceleration clause because of the violation of the owner occupancy requirement would be unconscionable or inequitable. This question appears to be one of first impression in this State.

Defendants contend that before such a clause can be enforced there must be shown some jeopardy or threat to the plaintiff's security and that plaintiff has demonstrated none. Defendants argue that unlike cases in which the mortgagor has defaulted on payments due or in which the identity of the mortgagor changes, defendants here remain responsible for the payments and are ready, willing and able to pay. Thus, they maintain that there is no jeopardy to plaintiff's security in the mortgage by virtue of the fact that they are not living in the premises.

Plaintiff states by affidavit that historically the purpose of a savings and loan association has been to assist persons in acquiring a home in which to reside and that this has always been plaintiff's policy. . . . Plaintiff contends that from its experience nonoccupying owners tend to restrict and minimize property maintenance and upkeep in order to enhance their financial return. Plaintiff argues that such conduct leads to an unreasonable depreciation of the property and jeopardizes the security on which the loan was made. In order to prevent this result, the owner occupancy provision is made a condition of the loan. . . .

When a contract is clear and unambiguous a court is bound to enforce its terms as they are written and the court may not make a better contract for either of the parties. A court has no right to rewrite the contract by substituting new or different provisions from those clearly expressed in the contract. . . .

In applying the foregoing to the facts of this case, I do not find that the owner occupancy requirement is unconscionable or inequitable. Given plaintiff's purpose to promote home ownership, its policy of not making loans except for that reason, . . . it cannot be said that its requirement of owner occupancy as a condition for the granting of a mortgage loan is unjust. Defendants were fully aware of this condition when they freely and voluntarily entered into the mortgage transaction. Furthermore, plaintiff's fear that the lack of owner occupancy might jeopardize its security is not unreasonable.

Since defendants have defaulted, plaintiff has the right to accelerate the due date of the unpaid balance of the debt and to require payment thereof. Such payment having not been made as demanded, summary judgment of foreclosure is appropriate.

Foreclosure of a mortgage; right of redemption   If the mortgagor fails to perform any of the listed duties, the mortgagee has the right to foreclose; that is, steps can be taken to have the real property sold and to apply proceeds from the sale to the debt. The mortgagee may initiate a court proceeding to secure an order of sale. The sheriff or other officer of the court then conducts a sale by auction. At any time prior to the court's entering a decree of foreclosure, the mortgagor can reinstate the mortgage by curing the default; ordinarily, that means making up installment payments that have been missed. Normally, the mortgagor also has a statutory *right of redemption* after a foreclosure sale takes place; that is, a right for a limited time to repurchase the property by payment of the auction sale price to the high bidder.

Trust Deeds   About half the states recognize the trust deed as an acceptable security instrument in real estate transactions. To the creditor, a trust deed has several significant advantages over the mortgage, and in some states the trust deed has virtually replaced the real property mortgage. States that refuse to recognize the trust deed on real property base the refusal on the ground that in the event of foreclosure debtors should have the procedural advantages connected with mortgages.

Nature of a trust deed   A trust deed is a document by which a debtor transfers the title to real property to a disinterested person (called a "trustee") to be held in trust as security for the performance of an obligation, usually the payment of a debt. The trustee is typically given the power to sell the property if the debtor defaults, and to apply proceeds from the sale to the debt.

Since mortgages and trust deeds perform a similar function, they necessarily have many features in common. Most of the preceding discussion concerning mortgages is applicable to trust deeds. However, while there are only two parties to a mortgage, there are three parties to a trust deed: the *trustor* (the debtor), the *beneficiary* (the creditor), and the *trustee*. Although the trustee holds title to the real property, it is a bare legal title, not a true ownership interest. In legal effect, the trust deed is considered to be merely a lien on the real property. If the trustor meets his or her obligations, there will be no interference with the use and possession of the property. When the obligation is satisfied the trustee will execute the necessary documents to reconvey title to the trustor. However, if the trustor-debtor defaults on an obligation, the holding of the title to the real property by the trustee becomes important. The major difference between a mortgage and a trust deed relates to foreclosure, as indicated in the following discussion.

Foreclosure of a trust deed   Under the terms of the typical trust deed the trustee is given the power to sell the property upon default by the debtor-trustor and to apply proceeds from the sale to the debt. In most states that permit the trust deed device, the creditor-beneficiary may elect to have the trustee use the same judicial procedure as for foreclosing a mortgage. However, the creditor ordinarily will elect to foreclose by having the trustee use the power of sale granted in the trust deed. The nonjudicial "power of sale" foreclosure by the trustee has certain advantages for the creditor: (1) it avoids the delay involved in getting a court order for a sale and avoids the expenses of litigation; (2) it can be used even when the statute of limitations period has run on the underlying debt, whereas foreclosure by court action is barred when the statutory period has run; and (3) it allows the trustor no right of redemption after the sale.

To foreclose by power of sale, the trustee simply notifies all interested persons (the debtor, other lienholders) that the trustor has defaulted. After a short period of time allowed for reinstatement of the trust deed, the trustee advertises and conducts an auction sale. Since the trustor has no right of redemption, the purchaser can immediately take possession, make improvements, lease, or even sell the property.

Involuntary Liens on Real Property

There are a number of liens on real property that can be created without the consent or approval of the owner. The statutes relating to such liens are complex and vary widely among the states. Some general aspects of the more important involuntary liens are discussed below.

Mechanics' Liens　At common law, a person who was not paid for performing a service or supplying materials in the improvement of someone's real property had a cause of action solely against the person who requested the service or materials. Today, nearly every state has a statute giving such a person a mechanic's lien on the property he or she helped to improve, provided the person takes the steps required to perfect a claim.

The term "mechanic" is misleading. It does not apply to a person who works on machinery or automobiles; rather, it applies to all types of contractors, subcontractors, laborers, and material suppliers who perform services or supply materials for the improvement of real property. Suppose, for example, that O owns a house and that he or she enters into a contract with C, a general building contractor, to add a room to the house. C, in turn, enters into subcontracts with D, E, and F to do the carpentry work, the electrical wiring, and the painting. Each subcontractor has employees who do the actual work under his or her supervision. C also contracts with M for the lumber and other materials to be used in the construction of the room. Each person mentioned in this example who is not paid for services or materials by the one he or she contracted with is entitled to a lien on O's property, provided the steps are taken as required by statute to perfect the lien.

The mechanics' liens statutes of the various states ordinarily require that a claim-of-lien form be filed or recorded in a specified government office within a limited time period. Some states require that notice of a possible claim be mailed to the property owner. In addition, the claimant ordinarily must initiate a civil action within a certain time period to foreclose the lien. The failure of a claimant to fulfill the statutory requirements will bar the claimant, in most instances, from obtaining the benefits of the mechanic's lien statute; however, such failure will not bar the claimant from pursuing contract law remedies against the party who requested the service or materials.

Attachment Liens　In certain situations an unsecured creditor who has filed an action against a debtor may have the defendant's property seized by the sheriff under a "writ of attachment." The purpose of the seizure is to hold the property pending the outcome of the suit. Where the property is real property, "seizure" consists of having the sheriff record the writ of attachment in the county recorder's office. Upon recording, a lien is created against the property. If the plaintiff-creditor obtains a judgment in the civil action, the plaintiff can have the property sold by foreclosure. If the defendant-debtor prevails in the action, the attachment lien terminates. The United States Supreme Court has severely restricted the creditor's right to attachment, because attachment interferes with the debtor's constitutional right to use and dispose of his or her property *prior* to a court trial.[5]

Judgment Liens　When one party to a lawsuit receives a judgment requiring the other party to pay a sum of money, the party receiving the judgment is thereafter called a judgment creditor; the party against whom the judgment is rendered is called the judgment debtor. If the judgment debtor does not voluntarily pay the judgment, the judgment creditor may, under modern statutes, record the judgment in the county or counties in which the judgment debtor owns real property. When the judgment is

---

[5]*Sniadach v. Family Fin. Corp.*, 395 U.S. 337 (1969).

recorded, it becomes a lien on any real property owned by the judgment debtor in the county. A judgment lien remains a lien on the property until the judgment is satisfied or is rendered inoperative by the expiration of the statutory period. In several states a judgment is valid for a period of 10 years. In some states a judgment may be renewed for one or more statutory periods. Any real property acquired by the judgment debtor during the statutory period or any extension of it would be subjected to the judgment lien.

Execution Liens A judgment creditor often faces the need to take coercive measures to enforce collection of a judgment. One method that may be available is to have the court issue a "writ of execution." Such a writ is directed to the sheriff, ordering the seizure and sale of certain specified property of the judgment debtor. Details of the procedure vary among the states, but usually the sheriff records a notice of execution in the county where the judgment debtor's real property is located. Recording the notice creates a lien on the described parcel of property. Unlike the judgment lien, recording a writ of execution does not create a lien on *all* the judgment debtor's real property in the county, just on the described parcel. The sheriff sets a time and place for foreclosure sale of the specific parcel, advertises, and conducts the sale in the same manner as that of a mortgage foreclosure sale. Some state statutes provide for a redemption period following the sale.

Tax Liens A tax lien is a special type of involuntary lien against real property. It is a lien created by a governmental unit or agency to enforce collection of a tax. There exists a wide variety of taxes in our contemporary society, imposed by various agencies ranging from local townships to the federal government.

The most common tax lien in the United States is the real property tax lien. Generally, the taxing agency is given an *automatic* lien against the taxpayer's real property to secure the payment of real property taxes. The state or local government is not required to file suit or have a trial prior to foreclosure. If the taxes are not paid within the statutory time period, the government can simply publish a notice in the paper and conduct an auction sale. There is typically no redemption period after sale, and the high bidder receives a tax deed immediately.

When the federal government or a state or local governmental taxing agency is attempting to collect an unpaid income tax, employment tax, sales tax, or other nonproperty tax, a lien on the taxpayer's real property is not automatically created. The governmental agency is usually required to record some type of delinquency notice in the county recorder's office. A lien is created by the recording. In order to sell the taxpayer's real property, the taxing agency generally must follow a procedure similar to that for foreclosing a mortgage. Often the taxpayer is given a redemption period after sale to recover his or her property.

SUMMARY

The subject of interests in real property is important to almost everyone in contemporary society, including persons who do not own real property. There are three main types of interests in real property: estates, easements, and liens. An estate in real property is an interest that is, or may become, possessory. Estates are either freeholds or leaseholds. The major freehold estates are the fee simple estate and life estates. The owner of a freehold estate can sell it, give it away, lease it to someone, or borrow against it. The death of an owner of a fee simple estate does not terminate the estate. Upon the owner's death the estate passes to the owner's heirs or to the beneficiaries named in his or her will. A life estate automatically terminates at the death of the person whose life measures the estate.

If the owner of an estate in real property is

not to exercise the right to use, possess, and enjoy the property until some future time, he or she has a future interest. There are two main types of future interests: reversions (where the right of future possession is retained by the grantor) and remainders (where the right of future possession is owned by someone other than the grantor). Leasehold estates are those in which a person acquires the right to exclusive possession of certain premises for a limited period of time. The most common types of leasehold estates are tenancies for a fixed term and periodic tenancies. The laws regarding landlord and tenant relations currently are undergoing analysis by state legislatures and the judiciary. Tenants in contemporary society have acquired more rights than exist in a lease, and landlords are required to assume a corresponding increase in duties.

An easement is an interest in real property, but it is not an estate in real property. An easement is the right to use, or to prevent the use of, the real property of another in a specific manner. Although an easement may give the easement holder a right to limited use of another's property, it does not give the holder the right to possess that property. Easements may be created by express or implied grant or reservation, by necessity, by prescription, and by dedication. Easements may be terminated by deed, by abandonment, by merger, by destruction of the property, and by adverse possession.

A lien is a claim or charge on property as security for an obligation. A creditor who holds a lien on real property has no right to possess or use the property. If the owner of the property does not satisfy his or her obligation to the creditor, the creditor can take steps to foreclose the lien. Foreclosure usually involves a sale of the property at auction and the use of as much of the proceeds as are needed to satisfy the creditor's claim. Two major voluntary liens are the mortgage and the trust deed. A mortgage is a two-party document; a trust deed involves three parties. The steps in foreclosure differ

greatly between them. Because of the differences, creditors prefer to acquire trust deeds in states that permit them, whereas debtors prefer to give a mortgage as security for an obligation. The major involuntary liens on real property are mechanics' liens, attachment liens, judgment liens, execution liens, and tax liens. The procedure for foreclosure of involuntary liens is similar to that for foreclosure of mortgages.

STUDY AND DISCUSSION QUESTIONS

1   (*a*) What is an estate in real property? (*b*) What is the essential difference between the following: freehold estate and leasehold estate; fee simple estate and reversion?

2   (*a*) Explain the two aspects of a lease. (*b*) What are the most important rights of landlord and tenant under a typical lease? (*c*) What duties does a landlord incur under the typical lease? (*d*) What duties does the tenant incur? (*e*) Why would an individual or firm be willing to assume these duties? (*f*) What can a landlord or tenant do if either wishes to be freed from these duties?

3   (*a*) How are the following tenancies created: periodic tenancy; tenancy at will; tenancy at sufferance? (*b*) How can each be terminated?

4   (*a*) What is an easement? (*b*) How does it differ from an estate in real property? (*c*) Define or explain: dominant tenement and servient tenement. (*d*) Why might it be important for you to know whether an easement exists before acquiring ownership of real property?

5   (*a*) List and explain briefly the five methods of creating an easement. (*b*) If you were about to purchase a parcel of real property, what steps could you take to determine whether an easement had been created by any of the five methods? (*c*) Describe the ways in which you could terminate an easement that is no longer desired.

6   (*a*) What is the nature and function of a

lien? *(b)* Explain and give examples of the two main classes of liens.

7 *(a)* What functions do the mortgagor and mortgagee perform in a real estate transaction? *(b)* List the rights of each party under the typical mortgage. *(c)* List the duties of each party. *(d)* How can foreclosure of a mortgage be avoided if threatened?

8 *(a)* Who are the parties to a trust deed? *(b)* What functions does each perform in a business transaction? *(c)* Why would a lender rather have a trust deed than a mortgage?

9 *(a)* What is a mechanic's lien? *(b)* Why do you think the states enacted mechanics' liens statutes? *(c)* What remedy other than a mechanic's lien is available to an unpaid contractor, subcontractor, laborer, or material supplier who benefits someone's real property?

10 *(a)* Explain the differences between an attachment lien and an execution lien. *(b)* Give examples of common types of tax liens that the typical individual or business firm would encounter in today's world.

CASE PROBLEMS

1 W. O. Young had several children. In 1915 he executed a deed conveying to his two daughters, Bertha and Pearl, certain real property and providing as follows: "If either should marry or die, then the property shall belong to the other, and in case both Bertha and Pearl should get married or should die, the property shall revert to the estate of W. O. Young." W. O. Young died in 1918 without having made any other conveyance of the property and without making a will. Bertha Young died unmarried in 1921. Pearl Young died unmarried in 1969. Who now owns the fee simple estate in the real property?

2 In 1940 Mrs. Nitschke and her two children inherited a parcel of real property with a dry cleaning shop on it. The shop was occupied by Doggett under a series of written leases. In 1959, the children acquired the interest of Mrs. Nitschke in the property, but she continued to deal with Doggett concerning the leasing and payment of rents. In 1962 or 1963, after Doggett delivered a written lease form to her so that she could obtain the children's signatures, Mrs. Nitschke told him he did not need a written lease, and that he could have the property for the rest of his life for a rental of $85 per month. Doggett agreed to pay $85 a month so long as he remained a tenant. It is his intent to remain a tenant for the rest of his life. He has a life expectancy of 23 years. Does Doggett have a tenancy for a term or a tenancy at will?

3 Hulse owned vacant land described as Lots 8, 9, and 10 in Block 38. These lots are contiguous and are bordered on the east side by an abandoned railroad right-of-way owned by Adams. The lots are bounded on the north by land owned by others and on the west by the waters of Barnegat Bay. Hulse conveyed Lot 8 to Cale, leaving Lots 9 and 10 as the southerly boundary. Later, Hulse conveyed Lots 9 and 10 to Wanamaker. Wanamaker built a house and garage on his lots. Lot 10 is bounded on its southerly side by a public highway, Albertson Street. Cale claims an easement by necessity over Lots 9 and 10 to get to the street. Wanamaker claims Cale has a ready access from Barnegat Bay. Is Cale entitled to an easement by necessity?

4 In 1958 Gartley conveyed a parcel of land, a strip 50 feet wide and 428 feet long, to the town of Lisbon, reciting in the deed that the parcel was conveyed with the agreement "that it shall be dedicated, improved, and accepted by the Town of Lisbon as a public street." In 1959, after a vote of the inhabitants of Lisbon, the town conveyed this strip to the Maine School Building Authority "subject to rights of the public to use the same as a public street." In 1970 the town voted "to indefinitely postpone" acceptance of the land as a public street. Vachon purchased land abutting the strip conveyed to the town and claims the right to use the strip as a public street for access to his property. The town of Lisbon refuses to improve or formally accept the strip as a public street. Was there a valid dedication by Gartley?

5 The Missouri State Highway Commission instituted a condemnation proceeding in connection with the widening of Lindbergh Boulevard. Damages in the amount of $14,500 were awarded by the commissioners for the land taken. The owners of the land did not accept this amount, and the Highway Commission filed suit in court. A Missouri statute requires the inclusion as parties defendant all persons who have a title appearing of record on the proper records of the county wherein the affected real estate lies. Southern Bank held a note secured by a deed of trust on the land. Is the Highway Commission required to include the trustee named in the deed of trust as a defendant and serve the trustee with a summons?

6 John and Mildred Hawthorne owned real estate on Summit Drive. They gave Assured Corporation a promissory note for $6,600 and secured the note with a trust deed against the real estate. They defaulted, and Assured fore-closed on the real property. At the foreclosure sale Assured was the high bidder at $6,224, which was the total of the balance due under the note plus interest, costs, and attorneys' fees. The Hawthornes had a statutory right of redemption by bidding the amount of the obligation but failed to exercise it. They sued Assured for $12,000, contending that the real estate was worth $38,000 and was subject to trust deeds totaling $26,000 and that Assured should have bid an amount equal to this equity in the property. Is the Hawthornes's contention valid?

7 The statutes in the State of Maine provide, among other things, that a mechanic's lien may be enforced by action against the owner of the property affected if filed within 90 days after the last of the labor, materials, or services are furnished, "and not afterwards." Bellegarde Custom Kitchens supplied materials used in the construction of a home for Jacques. Bellegarde filed an action in court 91 days after the last of the materials were furnished. The 90th day following the furnishing of the materials fell on Sunday. Did the fact that the deadline fell on Sunday excuse noncompliance with the mechanic's lien statute?

Chapter

23

Wills, Estates, and Trusts

When a person dies, his or her property is transferred to others (the heirs) in accordance with the provisions of a valid will or, in the absence of a valid will, in accordance with state inheritance laws. If there are no heirs, the property is transferred (escheats) to the state. As the creation of a significant estate is the aim of most business people, a brief survey of the laws of inheritance is appropriate in a comprehensive business law text.

This chapter traces briefly the development of inheritance laws and then outlines the usual order of entitlement to receive the property that was owned by an individual who had not made a valid will. The chapter next describes the elements of a will and points out the judicial process for the settlement (probate) of estates of persons who die leaving valid wills, and of those who die without leaving wills. The function of trusts as legal devices to control the ownership and uses of property after death are then examined. The chapter closes with a brief overview of death taxes.

INHERITANCE OF INTESTATE ESTATES

Historical Background

The inheritance laws of the 50 states are generally based on the English common law. Under that law, a person who died without leaving a valid will was said to die *intestate*. The real and personal property owned by such a person at the time of death constituted the *intestate estate*. At common law the rules governing the inheritance of intestate real property were different from those dealing with personal property. Real property *descended* to the decedent's eldest son (the rule of primogeniture), and only if there was no male heir would realty descend to a female child. It was not until the Inheritance Act of 1833 that England abandoned that rule. Unlike real property, personal property was *distributed* by ecclesiastical courts according to canon law. Until the Statute of Distribution of 1670 there was controversy in England as to who was entitled to the personal property of one who died intestate. That statute affirmed the policy that the surviving widow and children and their lineal descendants (that is, their children, grandchildren, etc.) were entitled to inherit an intestate's personal property. If there were no surviving widow or children, then the decedent's personal property was distributed between, and inherited by, the next closest kin (blood relatives, also called collateral heirs.)

Current State Practices in Intestate Inheritance

All states have supplanted the English rules of descent and distribution with their own inheritance statutes. However, state inheritance laws (except in Louisiana which applies the civil law) reflect in varying degrees the common law. Although no state distinguishes between the inheritance of real and personal property, state inheritance statutes in other respects are not necessarily uniform. Therefore, if a question of inheritance of intestate property arises, an interested party must refer to state statutes for definitive answer. To encourage the enactment of uniform inheritance laws throughout the United States, the National Conference on Uniform State Laws has developed the Uniform Probate Code (UPC). That Code has been approved by the American Bar Association and has been adopted, often with changes, by a number of states. This chapter, from time to time, refers to the UPC. Since there are no federal inheritance laws, other than taxing statutes, of general application, we will direct our attention to state practices.

Usual Order of Inheritance of Intestate Estates   When a person dies intestate, that is, without leaving a valid will, the following inheritance scheme is generally followed after all estate debts have been paid:

1   If there is a surviving spouse (wife or husband) and one child, the estate is *equally divided* between them; if there is a surviving spouse and more than one surviving child, the spouse receives *one-third* and the children equally divide the remaining *two-thirds;* and if a child or children but no spouse survive the intestate, the child takes, or the children divide equally, the entire estate.[1] If a child who predeceased the intestate leaves issue (e.g., a grand-

---

[1] In those states which apply community property rules, discussed at p. 446, the surviving spouse inherits the community property of a deceased spouse who dies intestate, notwithstanding the fact that there may also be surviving children.

child or great grandchild of the deceased), such grandchild or great grandchild takes the share its deceased parent would have taken had such parent been alive to inherit from the intestate. This is called *taking by representation.*

2 If the spouse and a member of the intestate's immediate family survive, and there are no surviving children or issue of children, the spouse is entitled to *one-half* of the estate and the members of the immediate family receive the *other half.* "Immediate family" consists of the intestate's parents, if living, and, if not, then the intestate's brothers and sisters and, if not living, their issue, by representation.

3 If no spouse or children or issue of children of the intestate survive the intestate, then the entire estate goes to the immediate family and, if no member of the immediate family survives the intestate, then the estate is divided between the intestate's closest next of kin.

4 If there are none of the above categories of people to inherit the intestate's estate, it escheats to the state.

Applying these rules of intestate distribution to a specific example, let us assume that Davis dies intestate, leaving an estate of $300,000 after all debts have been paid. He is survived by his widow (W), one sister (S), one child (C-1), and

two grandchildren (GC-1 and GC-2) who are children of a daughter (C-2) who predeceased Davis. C-2's husband is still living when Davis dies. A distribution of Davis' estate in most states can be diagrammatically shown as in Figure 23.1. In the diagram, the sister (S) gets nothing because heirs in more preferred classes were entitled to divide the entire estate. C-2's husband gets nothing as he is not related by blood to the deceased. GC-1 and GC-2 take their mother's (C-2's) share by representation.

Inheritance of Intestate Estates in Special Situations Inheritance of intestate estates in special situations departs somewhat from the order discussed above.

Adopted Children State intestacy laws offer no uniformity in the treatment of adopted children. Under the common law, followed by some states, an adopted child has a limited right of inheritance from his or her adoptive parents and the adopted child still retains certain rights to inherit from his or her natural parents. Other states theoretically "transplant" the adopted child into the family of the adoptive parents. The adopted child thus acquires all the rights of a natural child of the adoptive parents and is entirely cut off from any right to inherit from a natural parent who may die intestate.

Illegitimate children In all states a child

Figure 23.1 Distribution of a Hypothetical Intestate Estate

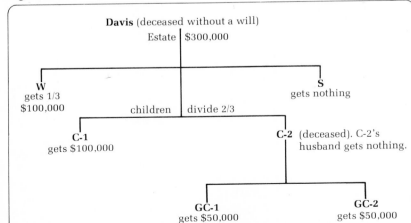

born out of wedlock is an heir of its mother and may also become an heir of its father if *legitimized*, that is, publicly acknowledged by the father to be his child or if the father follows statutory procedures for legitimization. Some states provide that if a "parent and child relationship" existed as defined in the statutes, there is a complete right of inheritance by an illegitimate child from an intestate father.

Advancements to children Practically all states apply the principle of advancements in intestate distribution. This involves a presumption that a parent who dies intestate, survived by more than one child, would desire all of the children to share equally in the parent's bounty. The courts have developed a formula to carry this presumption into effect. The formula takes into account any substantial *advancements* (gifts) previously given by the parent to any of the children. In this way the total benefits the children receive are equalized. Some states do not apply the presumption but require that, for a gift to be considered an advancement, there must be written evidence that it was so intended.

Beneficiary dying simultaneously with intestate A person must survive the intestate in order to become the latter's heir. Because of the increasing frequency of accidents resulting in multiple deaths in which the order of death is impossible to determine, it is necessary that some rule be adopted for such a situation. One solution is that furnished by the Uniform Probate Code (sec. 2-601) which provides that, unless a person outlives the intestate by 120 hours, he or she will be considered to have predeceased the intestate. The Uniform Simultaneous Death Act, adopted by a number of states, offers another approach which is best explained by a hypothetical case. Assume that Arthur and Betty, husband and wife, are killed in an airplane crash and there is no satisfactory proof as to which one died first. Pursuant to that statute, in the settlement of Arthur's estate it will be presumed that he outlived Betty, and in

the settlement of Betty's estate it will be presumed that she outlived Arthur.

Unworthy heirs No person should be permitted to benefit from his own wrong. Therefore, statutes have been enacted which disqualify an heir who causes the death of the decedent. Most states require the homicide to be *intentional* and not accidental and also require a conviction of homicide in a criminal prosecution as a prerequisite for disqualification.

WILLS

Why Make a Will?

If there is no will, a decedent's heirs inherit his or her property according to state law as above outlined. Why, then, should a person go to the trouble and expense of making a will? The answer is that the state distributes an estate in a fixed way while a will expresses personal desires as to who will inherit the property and how it will be divided among the beneficiaries. The state gives no consideration to the needs of those who inherit or if they were even on friendly terms with the decedent. As a result, sometimes remote family members who are total strangers (sometimes called "laughing heirs") inherit when no immediate family exists. Moreover, no provision is made by the state for gifts to a church, to charity, or to close friends. A will is the means by which such personal desires are made known. It is the ultimate expression and the last possible demonstration of affection, compassion, and gratitude to others by an owner of property. A will also makes possible the settlement of an estate, particularly one of appreciable size, with a minimum of delay and expense. Accordingly, it is normal practice for a person to make a will.

It should be borne in mind, however, that a person has no natural or constitutional right to make a will and dispose of his or her property through that means. As the Supreme Court of the United States said in 1896 in the case of

United States v. Perkins, (163 U.S. 625), ". . . most enlightened nations [have] from the earliest historical period, recognized a natural right in children to inherit the property of their parents, [but] . . . we know of no legal principle to prevent the legislature from taking away or limiting the right of testamentary disposition."

Requisites For a Valid Will

A *will* is a declaration of the desires of the maker as to what should be done with his or her property after death. One who makes a will is called a *testator* or, if female, a *testatrix*. As used in this chapter, "testator" refers to either a testator or a testatrix. A person who dies having made a valid will is said to have died *testate*. A will usually names an executor and may also appoint a guardian for minor children. An *executor*, (*executrix* if female) is the *personal representative* of the testator who, after the testator's death, submits the will to a probate court so that it may be proved valid and who then *administers* the estate of the decedent.

To be valid, a will must be in the form and executed in the manner prescribed by law. A provision of a will is ineffective if against public policy. For example, a provision for the payment of a sum of money to someone if he commits a crime would obviously be void as against public policy. Until a maker of a will dies, it is not effective for any purpose and may be modified or revoked at any time. To make a valid will, the testator must have both a testamentary capacity and a testamentary intent.

Testamentary Capacity Testamentary capacity has two elements: (1) the testator must have attained the statutory age (usually 18 years) before the will is executed, and (2) at the time of such execution must have had the mental capacity required by law. As to the first element, if a will is executed while the maker is under age, it does *not* become valid when the maker attains the statutory age. For that maker to have a valid will, he or she must then execute a new one.

Different courts express different tests as to the second element, mental capacity, that is, whether a testator was of sound mind at the time the will was made. It can be said generally that a testator should know that he or she is making a will and has the mental capacity (a) to know who are the natural objects of his or her bounty; (b) to know the nature and extent of his or her property; and (c) be able to make an orderly disposition of it.

A perfect memory is not an element of mental capacity. It is not necessary to know who all of one's relatives are, nor does the testator need to remember all of his or her property, its location or value. It follows that soundness of mind sufficient for mental capacity to make a will is not the same as soundness of mind and mental capacity required to enter into a contract. Ordinarily, less mental capacity is required to make a valid will than to conduct regular business affairs. A testator need not be of average intelligence and, in fact, may have a very low IQ. Even a person under a guardianship may possess sufficient mental capacity to make a valid will. The following case distinguishes between testamentary capacity in the legal sense and mental soundness in the medical sense.

Case 23.1 **Estate of Podgursky**
271 N.W.2d 52 (S.D. 1978)

Eugene Podgursky was admitted to a Veterans Administration Hospital in 1943. He was diagnosed schizophrenic and required supervision. In 1967, through the use of new drugs, he was sufficiently improved to be placed in a foster home. A bank was appointed as his guardian and he was transferred to a foster home run by Mr. and Mrs. Sorenson. In February, 1974, Mrs. Sorenson drove Podgursky to a lawyer's office. There Podgursky told the lawyer that he wanted to make a will. He said that he had no relatives and that his estate consisted solely of personal property (money) which he wanted to leave to the Sorensons. On March 8, 1974, Podgursky returned to the law office where he read the will that had been prepared. The lawyer also explained it to him. Podgursky signed the will before two witnesses. A secretary who talked with him about the will said she "thought he understood it" and "believed Podgursky knew what he was doing."

Podgursky died in January 1976 and the Sorensons offered the will for probate. The United States objected, claiming that Podgursky was not competent to make a will and that, as a veteran without heirs and hospitalized under the care of the Veterans Administration, his property should escheat to the United States under Federal law. After a trial the court found the will to be a valid one. The United States appealed, claiming that Podgursky did not have the testamentary capacity to make a will. Portions of the opinion contrasting the legal and medical views of mental capacity follow.

BIEGELMEIR, Ret. J. . . . The court has held consistently that for the purpose of making a will, one has a sound mind if able, without prompting, to comprehend the nature and extent of his property, the persons who are the natural objects of his bounty and the disposition that he desires to make of such property. . . .

. . . There is a difference in the legal and medical use of the word "sanity." Sanity is not necessarily synonymous with the capacity to make a testamentary disposition. . . . One may lack mental capacity to such an extent that according to medical science he is not of sound mind and memory, and nevertheless retain the mental capacity to execute a will. . . . This distinction was also voiced by the Wyoming Supreme Court when it wrote:

> The requirements of mental soundness in the legal sense, so as to constitute testamentary capacity, are not as rigid as those in the medical sense. A mind legally sound may be medically unsound. . . .

As was said by the Supreme Court of California in *In re Arnold's Estate*, . . .

> It is well settled that mere proof of mental derangement or even of insanity in a medical sense is not sufficient to invalidate a will, but the contestant [the party objecting to the will] is required to go further and prove . . . such a complete mental degeneration as denotes utter incapacity to know and understand those things which the law prescribes as essential to the making of a will. . . .

Briefly summarizing the evidence, it appears all three witnesses for the contestant [United States] were in its employ; that [one doctor] had never examined Podgursky and had never seen him. . . . A VA social worker . . . , who last saw Podgursky in 1970, . . . [said] that Podgursky was 'getting along pretty well then' and that he [Podgursky] 'appreciated the fact that she had gotten him out of the VA hospital.' On the part of the proponents [Sorensons] the attesting witnesses were disinterested and their testimony . . . supports the trial court's findings that Podgursky had the requisite testamentary capacity at the time the will was executed; that he knew he was making a will and the consequences thereof. . . .

The judgment is affirmed.

Proof of testamentary capacity   Some states, before admitting a will to probate, require proof that the testator was of sound mind when the will was executed. The more modern view is that mental competency is presumed by the court until rebutted (disproved).[2] A litigant who seeks to overcome this presumption must prove that the testator was so mentally deficient or deranged, either by accident, sickness, age, or otherwise, or was so under the influence of drugs or of alcohol when executing a will, that testamentary capacity was lacking.

Insane delusion   Testamentary capacity problems may arise when a testator, otherwise entirely sane, disinherits a spouse or other close family member because of some totally irrational fear or belief, entertaining it against all evidence, argument, and reason. Such a person is said to suffer from an insane delusion and to have a mental illness called *monomania*. If the belief affects the disposition of property under a will, the will (or in some states only that particular disposition) is void.

However, an attack against a will on the ground of insane delusion is difficult to establish since a belief which can be attributed to an error of judgment or mistake of fact is held not to be evidence of a delusion. For example, Mary, an elderly woman, lived alone, occasionally visited by her sister, Fran. Fran, by mistake, gave Mary an overly large dose of medicine. This did no harm but Mary, for the rest of her life, was convinced that Fran had tried to poison her. As a consequence, Mary made no provision for Fran in her will. It could be anticipated that a court, if the validity of the will were attacked, would *not* determine that Mary lacked testamentary capacity based upon an insane delusion because the incident of the medicine did, in fact, occur and Mary's belief sprang from a mistaken conclusion from that fact and did not spring spontaneously into her mind.

Testamentary Intent   Testamentary intent is a necessary element of every will. It is present if the testator's words in the will make clear that the instrument is intended to dispose of the signer's property effective only upon his or her death. Although a will makes a gratuitous transfer of property, a transfer by will is not the same as an ordinary gift. To illustrate the difference, let us say that Alice hands her ring to Mabel saying, "Here is my pearl ring. Take it; I give it to you." Alice has made a gift to Mabel who now owns the ring. But if Alice includes in her will a provision stating, "I give my pearl ring to Mabel," this is not a gift at the present time but only the expression of a testamentary intention of what shall be done with the ring after Alice dies. Until that time (because a will does not become effective until the testator's death), Alice remains owner of the ring. At any time before her death Alice may change her mind and sell the ring; give it to someone else, or change her will.

If a bequest in a will is made as a result of fraud, duress, or undue influence on the testator by another, or if the testator is mistaken as to

---

[2]This view is also expressed in sec. 3–407 of the Uniform Probate Code.

the nature of the instrument he or she is signing, the will does not reflect the true intentions of the testator. Thus, testamentary intent is absent.

Effect of fraud Fraud in the execution of a will is similar to deceit in the formation of a contract, discussed at page 239. However, while fraud causes a contract to be *voidable at the election of the aggrieved party, fraud invalidates* a will. However, to invalidate the entire will, the fraud must involve a sufficiently important part of it that the overall testamentary scheme is tainted. If the fraud does not meet this test, then only that portion of the will affected by the fraud becomes invalid.

Effect of duress; undue influence Duress and undue influence mean more than mere advice, persuasion, or the demonstration of extraordinary kindness or attention. (See also the discussion at pages 230–234.) The terms, in this context, refer to actions that cause a will to become the expression of *another's* intent, rather than that of the testator. A will executed under such conditions is void. Duress and undue influence may take many forms. For example, the act might involve some kind of threat (duress) or might involve the subjugation of the testator's mind by someone in a confidential relationship (undue influence). The circumstances which must be present to constitute undue influence and the required burden of proof are illustrated in the following case.

Case 23.2   Estate of Paul Zech
285 N.W.2d 236 (S. D. 1979)

In May of 1967, Paul Zech bought a house, putting the title in the names of Mary Tesch, a niece, and her husband Charles Tesch. In exchange, the Tesches agreed to take care of Paul and his sister Alma, during their remaining years, a service for which they were additionally paid by Paul. In July, 1967, Alma died and Paul continued to live with the Tesch family. In June, 1970, at Mary's request, an attorney came to the house and met with Paul. Paul told the attorney that he wanted to make a new will; he discussed the extent and nature of his property, who his relatives were, and how he wished to dispose of his property. The document was written and then executed in the presence of the attorney and his law partner. Paul left the bulk of his estate to Charles and Mary Tesch. During the next several years, Paul transferred much of his property to them. In 1975 Paul was moved to a nursing home and later a bank was named as his financial conservator. Charles and Mary frequently visited Paul in the nursing home. It does not appear that any other relatives visited him. Paul died in 1977 at 83 years of age.

The 1970 will was offered for probate by the Tesches (proponents). Paul's four other nieces and nephews (the contestants) contested the probate, claiming that the Tesches had exerted undue influence on Paul. Their contention was not sustained and the will was admitted to probate. The contestants appealed.

TICE, Cir. J. . . . The sole issue we must consider is whether the proponents exercised undue influence upon decedent in the making of his will. . . .

It is beyond argument that the proponents were in a confidential relationship with decedent. Mary Tesch assisted decedent with his business affairs, . . . prepared checks for his signature, . . . wrote letters for him under her signature, made deposits and withdrawals from his savings accounts, [and] had access to his safety deposit box. . . . "When a confidential relationship is established the burden of 'going forward with the evidence' shifts to the beneficiary to show that he took no unfair advantage of his dominant position." . . . In the present case the proponents went forward with evidence showing there was a rational explanation for the disposition of decedent's property . . .

Influence, to be undue, must be of such character as to destroy the free agency of the testator and substitute the will of another person for his own. . . . Its essential elements are (1) a person susceptible to such influence, (2) opportunity to exert such influence and effect the wrongful purpose, (3) a disposition to do so for an improper purpose, and (4) a result clearly showing the effect of such influence.

. . . Contestants failed to establish that decedent was a person susceptible to [undue] influence.

It is clear that the proponents had a very close relationship with decedent, and spent much time with him; however, they were never present during, nor in any way a party to, the discussions with the decedent and his counsel in the preparation of his will. . . . 'opportunity alone is not sufficient to warrant an inference of undue influence.' . . . The fact that proponents were the only relatives of decedent who showed an interest in him in his later years and provided for him on a daily basis obviously established the opportunity to exert influence, but it does not establish the exertion of undue influence. . . .

Contestants did not establish that proponents were of a disposition to exert undue influence for an improper purpose. . . . There is no evidence of any cold and calculating plot on the part of the proponents to cajole, coerce, or subtly acquire decedent's estate.

The final element to be considered is whether the will clearly shows the effect of undue influence. It can not be disputed that the proponents stand to benefit handsomely under the terms of decedent's will. . . . In the present case [however], the contestants have failed to establish the necessary prerequisites that would cast the disposition of decedent's property in an unfavorable light. . . . We must conclude that the decedent was appreciative of the many acts of kindness shown to him by the proponents and that he wished to reward them for this behavior. . . .

A testator has the privilege and right to dispose of his property as he chooses within limits and in the manner fixed by statute. The law does not require that he recognize his relatives equally or at all. . . .

Accordingly, the judgment of the trial court must be affirmed. [Two justices dissent.]

Effect of mistake   If a person signs an instrument not knowing that it is a will (called a *mistake in the factum*), there is no testamentary intent and the purported will is void. For instance, if Alice believes that she is signing a deed but actually it is a will, the will is not effective. A different rule is applied, however, where a testator makes a will and for some reason, based upon a mistaken belief, makes or omits to make a bequest to someone. This circumstance is called a *mistake in the inducement* and it does *not* invalidate a will. Suppose Alice hears, erroneously, that her friend Mabel, who lives in a distant city and to whom Alice intended to make a bequest, has recently died. As a result, Alice makes no provision in her will for Mabel. If Mabel should contest Alice's will, the court will not change it to create a provision for Mabel if no fraud was involved. The reason is obvious: to do so would invite no end of litigation over the validity of bequests and the distribution of estates would be needlessly delayed.

Execution of Wills

Some states authorize only one type of will, a *formal* will. Others authorize both formal and *holographic* (also called olographic), that is handwritten, wills. Some also recognize oral or *nuncupative* wills which involve personal property of limited value, usually made by soldiers or sailors in actual military service or while at sea. Because only formal and holographic wills are normally encountered, this chapter focuses upon them.

All courts agree that, to minimize the possibility of fraud, there must be strict compliance with the statutes which define how a will must be executed. If the rules are not followed, even if the intention of the testator is abundantly clear, a court will not admit the will to probate and the maker will have died intestate.

Which laws govern the requirements for a valid will? If a will disposes of real property, the laws of the state or states in which the property is located control the validity of the will insofar as that property is concerned. If a will disposes only of personal property (such as stocks, bonds, bank accounts, furniture, jewelry, etc.), normally the instrument must comply with the laws of the state of the testator's domicile. No federal laws are applicable.

Formal Wills   The usual requirements for a formal will are that it be written, signed, and witnessed. Some states impose additional requirements.

Writing   While a formal will must be in writing, neither the kind of material upon which the writing appears nor the method of the writing is important. For instance, in one case a will was written on wallpaper. Any language may be used.

Dating   Generally, there is no requirement that a formal will must be dated. However, if a testator writes several wills which contain contradictory provisions and none bears a date, the court would have great difficulty determining which was the most recent and therefore the effective will. To avoid what could be long drawn-out and expensive litigation, any will should be dated when it is executed.

Signing   A formal will must be signed by the testator in a manner that complies with state requirements. In most states, the law does not specify the particular place on a will where the testator's signature should be affixed. In some states, however, a will must be signed at the end to assure that no pages purporting to be part of the will are later attached. It is not necessary that a will be signed with the testator's full name. As a general rule, any name intended by the testator to be his or her signature satisfies the statute. "Bubba Smith," "Mommie," or just initials may be held sufficient. Under conditions established by state law, a testator may sign with a mark or the testator's name may be written as his or her signature by another person at the testator's request and in the testator's presence. Thus, a paralyzed person, for example, may execute a valid will.

Witnessing   The testator's signature to a formal will must be witnessed. Most states require two witnesses; others require three. If it is not properly witnessed, the will is void and the maker has died intestate. It is generally held that this requirement of witnessing is satisfied when a testator who has already signed a will outside the presence of witnesses shows the paper to them and acknowledges that the signature on it is his or her signature. Any person capable of understanding that he or she is witnessing the signature may be a witness. The witnesses must sign in the presence of the testator and, in some states, in the presence of each other. The courts do not hold identical views as to what constitutes "in the presence of the testator." Some require that the witnesses be within the testator's sight and others require only a "conscious presence." A court which follows the latter and more liberal view sustained the validity of a will executed by an individual who was lying in a hospital bed unable to move or turn his head, while the witnesses were in another room, looking into his room through an open doorway. In some states, and it is the better practice, the witnesses write their addresses in addition to their names. There is no requirement that a will be notarized and, if a will is not properly witnessed, a notarization does not make it legally effective.

Publishing Some states require that the witnesses be told that the paper being signed is a will. This declaration is called a *publication*. In no state must the witnesses be informed of the contents of the will nor must it be given to them to read.

Filing A completed will is retained by the maker among his or her valuable papers or, at the testator's election, it may be held by an attorney or other person for safekeeping. In some states and under the Uniform Probate Code, a will may be deposited in the local probate office subject to being withdrawn by the testator at any time. Upon the testator's death, the custodian of a will is required to file it with the Probate Court.

Holographic Wills Generally, a *holographic will* is one that is entirely in the testator's own handwriting. In some states only the material parts of such a will must be in the testator's own handwriting. A holographic will must be signed by the testator and, in some states, also dated. The signature to a holographic will may be

placed anywhere on the face of the instrument, not necessarily at the end. A holographic will need not be witnessed. North Carolina requires that, to be effective, a holographic will must be found after the decedent's death among his or her valuable papers or it must have been placed in the hands of some person for safekeeping.

Codicils

A *codicil* is a modification or amendment of, or an addition to, a previously executed will. It must be executed in the same manner as is required in that state for any valid will. In states which recognize holographic wills, a formal will may have holographic codicils and a holographic will may have formal codicils. A will and its codicils are read together. The date on the last codicil executed becomes the new date of the entire will to which it applies. A valid codicil also validates an invalid will and may revive a revoked will. Thus, if the provisions of a will were written as a result of some fraud, and the testator later makes a valid codicil to it, the original will is no longer considered to have been fraudulently inspired.

Incorporation by Reference

To obviate the necessity of copying into a will matters contained in documents such as public records or other papers to which the will refers, the law permits the information contained in documents which are in existence when the will is executed to be incorporated into it *by reference*. For example, instead of laboriously copying into a will or codicil the legal description of a farm which a testator wants to make the subject of a gift by will, it is easier to refer to the book and page number of the public record where the legal description of the property can be found. Almost all states allow such an incorporation by reference provided the will or codicil properly identifies the document or documents to be incorporated and also makes clear that it is (or they are) *in existence when the will is executed*.

Compare a will stating in part, "I give $1,000

to each of the people named in a paper which will be found in my safe deposit box," with, "I give $1,000 to each of the people named in a paper dated June 30, 1980 [a date prior to the execution of the will] which will be found in my safe deposit box." In the first instance the paper may or may not have been written before the will was executed and it cannot be incorporated by reference. In the second example the paper may be incorporated.

Limitations on Devises and Bequests

As a general rule, a competent testator may make any disposition by will he or she desires. A gift of real property is called a *devise;* of personal property a *bequest;* and a bequest of money is usually called a *legacy.* If the testator was of sound mind when the will was executed, the validity of the will is not diminished by the fact that its provisions are unnatural, leaving nothing to members of the testator's immediate family or to close personal friends. However, this general rule is subject to certain exceptions.

Protection of Surviving Spouse   At common law, a widow could not, regardless of the will's provisions, be entirely omitted from sharing in the estate of her deceased husband. She was entitled to a *life estate,* free from his debts, in one-third of the *real property* owned by her deceased husband. This is called the right of *dower.* A widower had a somewhat similar right called *curtesy.* Under the common law and in the few states which still apply these rights, a widow or widower can elect to take that interest instead of the share provided in the deceased spouse's will. This is called "taking against the will."

The right of a surviving spouse, whether widow or widower, has now been expanded by statute. As the assets of most estates today are made up of personal property such as stocks and bonds, money and jewelry, as well as real property, the modern concept aims at assuring to a surviving spouse a fixed portion of *all* the property owned by the deceased. The surviving spouse may elect to receive this designated

share, called a "forced" or "elective" share instead of what a will provides.[3] Eight states protect the surviving spouse through community property laws.[4] Under such laws, all the real and personal property acquired by either spouse as a result of his or her work during the marriage, and all income from such property, is community property. Each spouse owns an undivided one-half interest in all of the community property as the law presumes that the marital estate was created through the joint efforts of both parties. Any real or personal property acquired by either spouse before the marriage, or which after the marriage comes to a spouse from sources other than work, such as by gift or inheritance, is *separate property,* not community property. A decedent may without restriction, by will dispose of his or her separate property and of his or her own half of the community property. But since each spouse owns one-half of all community property, the spouse's half is not inherited by the survivor when one partner to the marriage dies; it was always the survivor's own property and remains so after the death of the other.

Protection of Surviving Children   A parent may, if he or she chooses, disinherit a child and instead make gifts to more distant relatives, friends, or even strangers. Contrary to popular belief, it is not necessary that the child be left one dollar or any other small gift in order to be disinherited. A testator may disinherit a child by specifically so stating or by simply recognizing the existence of the child but leaving him or her nothing.

However, if a child's name is not even mentioned in a parent's will (and in many states if he or she was not otherwise provided for by that parent), the unmentioned child is said to be *pretermitted,* meaning, in a sense, that child was forgotten. A pretermitted child inherits from the deceased parent as though the parent had died without making any will at all, that is,

---

[3]Uniform Probate Code, sec. 2–201 (a), et seq.
[4]See Chapter 21, p. 403.

had died intestate with respect to that child. Any mention of a child by name in a will is sufficient recognition to preclude its pretermission.

Limitations in Unusual Situations Just as an heir, to inherit, must survive an intestate and must not have been convicted of intentionally causing his or her death (discussed at p. 438), so a beneficiary named in a will must survive the testator and must not have been guilty of his or her murder.

Witness as Beneficiary To lessen the possibility of fraud or undue influence, almost all states limit inheritance that may come to anyone who acts as one of the required witnesses to a will. This limitation applies, therefore, to a person who is one of two required witnesses to a will; it does not apply to a person who is one of *three* witnesses in a state which requires only *two* witnesses to a will. The statutes usually provide that a *required* witness may receive no more than he or she would have inherited had the testator died intestate. Thus, if a witness would have received nothing had the testator died intestate, the witness gets nothing from the estate even if the will left a bequest or devise to him or her. The following hypothetical case illustrates this principle. In a state requiring two witnesses, Tess makes a formal will which contains a legacy of $1,000 for her good friend and long-time companion Wendy. Wendy is one of the two witnesses to Tess' will. The will is valid but the legacy to Wendy is void and of no effect. She takes nothing under the will for, not being related to Tess, Wendy could not have inherited from Tess had Tess died intestate.

Revocation of Wills

A will is without legal effect until the testator dies. Therefore, a testator may revoke, that is annul, a will at any time during his or her lifetime. After a will is revoked it cannot again be made effective except by adding a codicil to it. If the revocation was effected by the writing of a later will, some courts allow the revocation of the later will to revive the former one. A will may be revoked either by intentional act of the testator or by operation of law.

Revocation by Act of Testator There are two methods by which a testator may revoke a will: (1) by a physical act upon the document, or (2) by later executing another will which specifically revokes, or is inconsistent with, the previous one.

To revoke by physical act the testator must, with intent to revoke, do something physical to the will which the state says constitutes a revocation. Such acts as burning, tearing, canceling (as by writing "cancelled" across its face or drawing lines through its words), or obliterating the document, revoke a will. Most states permit a revocation of a part of a will by physical act. A revocation of either a formal or holographic will needs no witness to be legally effective. State statutes establish conditions under which a physical act of revocation may be done by another person under the testator's direction.

Revocation by subsequent instrument comes about by the testator making a later will or codicil which expressly revokes the earlier one. If specific words of revocation are not used in the later will, but it is *entirely* inconsistent with the earlier one, courts generally presume that the earlier will has been revoked. An example of entirely inconsistent wills might be: the first makes Arlene, Bess, and Clarise the beneficiaries; the second makes Dorothy, Eve, and Frances the beneficiaries. However, if the second had made Arlene, Eve, and Frances the beneficiaries, the two wills would not have been *entirely* inconsistent and both wills would be read together, possibly resulting in Arlene receiving multiple gifts. To obviate the question of whether a later will revokes a former one, a testator usually begins a will with words such as, "This will revokes all prior wills and codicils made by me at any time."

In an effort to carry out a testator's presumed intentions, the courts apply a principle called *dependent relative revocation*. It is this: if the testator revokes a will (or provision) believing that a new one has been validly executed, but it has not, then the revocation is ignored by the court and the original will (or provision) remains in effect. For example, let us assume that, in a state allowing partial revocation, a clause in Art's properly executed *formal typewritten* will says, "I give Ben my fishing reels." Some time later Art changes his mind about the gift. He draws lines through "Ben" and writes above it, in his own handwriting, "Charles," and dates and initials the change. Has Art revoked the gift to Ben? Yes; drawing lines through words with intent to revoke, is a method of cancellation. Has Art made a valid gift to Charles? No. A formal will must be signed by the testator and properly witnessed. Even assuming that Art's initials constituted a signing, the act was not witnessed so there was no new formal will. Then did Art's actions constitute a valid holograph? The answer must again be "no" because the gift, which now reads, "I give Charles my fishing reels" is partially typed and partially handwritten and thus is not entirely in Art's handwriting. Therefore, if the court were to recognize the revocation, there would be no provision at all covering the reels. Instead, the court, presuming that if Art had known his gift to Charles would fail he would have desired that Ben receive the reels, applies dependent relative revocation and disregards the revocation. By applying this legal legerdemain, Ben is still entitled to the bequest even though the presumption applied by the court may be groundless. The proper way for Art to have made the change would have been, in a state which permits holographs, to write in his own handwriting the complete sentence, "I give my fishing reels to Charles" and to sign and date the insertion. If the state does not recognize holographic wills, the writing, either in his own handwriting or otherwise, must be witnessed as required by law. The better practice would be for Art to write the sentence on a separate paper as a codicil to the will and to sign it and have his signature properly witnessed.

Revocation by Operation of Law At common law, marriage plus the birth of a child automatically revoked a will executed before the marriage. However, now there is little uniformity among the states as to the circumstances which *automatically* cause the revocation of a will. Under the Uniform Probate Code a divorce or annulment automatically revokes a provision in a will in favor of the other spouse. In many states only a divorce accompanied by a property settlement automatically revokes a will. In other states a divorce, even one accompanied by a property settlement, does not cause automatic revocation.

PROBATE

The probate of an estate involves two processes: the first, dealing only with testate estates, is the determination of the validity of a will by a court of competent jurisdiction.[5] The second process deals with both testate and intestate estates. It involves the court appointment of the *executor* or *administrator* who becomes the personal representative of the decedent. The executor or administrator, under the supervision of the court, takes charge of the estate and administers it.

Increasingly, particularly when the estate is small, statutes eliminate the necessity for formal probate and administration and substitute summary, limited, or informal proceedings. In this way, heirs are saved the expense of formal proceedings and they more quickly come into possession of their inheritances.

Probate of Wills
Until probate, a will has no legal effect. After the testator's death, the custodian of the will delivers it to the probate court in the county of decedent's domicile. In many states the failure to produce the will subjects the holder to penalty.

---

[5]Commonly, the court having jurisdiction of estate matters is called the Probate Court. In various states it may be the County Court, the County Judge's Court, the Surrogate Court, the Prerogative Court, the Court of the Ordinary, Orphans' Court, etc.

Procedure   A petition is filed with the court for probate of the will. Probate of a will is not a lawsuit in the ordinary sense because, strictly speaking, there are no parties to the proceedings and all interested persons are bound by the determination of the court as to the will's validity. Probate is a proceeding *in rem,* literally, concerning "the thing."   Proof that the will was executed by the decedent is furnished by a witness to the testator's signature upon it, if that testimony is available. If not, other evidence satisfactory to the court is required. Many states do away with the necessity for such proof by establishing certain circumstances under which a will becomes "self-proved."

If real property in a state other than the state of the decedent's domicile is among the estate assets, the will is also probated in an ancillary (subordinate) proceeding in the state where the property is located because the law of the location of real property controls its inheritance.

Will Contests   During the proceedings for the probate of a will, or within such extended period as may be allowed by statute, a person who has a direct interest in the estate and who would be economically benefited if the will were set aside, may contest its admission to probate. Contest may be based on any claim against the will's validity, such as that it was not properly executed or that the decedent did not have the requisite testamentary capacity or testamentary intent. Statutes usually provide for a jury trial of the issues raised and the ordinary rules of evidence are applied.

Probate Administration—Testate and Intestate Estates

Appointment of Executor; of Administrator   When a will is admitted to probate, the court issues letters testamentary appointing the petitioner, generally the person named in the will, as executor. In unusual circumstances, such as the death, unwillingness, or inability of the named executor to serve, or if the will fails to name an executor, the court appoints an *administrator c.t.a.* (cum testamento annexo, meaning "administrator with the will annexed").

If the decedent died intestate, it may be found advantageous to proceed with a formal probate and not to adopt an abbreviated or summary form of administration. In that event, the surviving spouse or other qualified person applies for letters of administration. After notice to the heirs and a hearing, an administrator is appointed.

The order of priority of those who may be appointed executor or administrator and the requisite qualifications of such an appointee are prescribed by statute. Among the qualifications are attainment of statutory age and capacity to contract. Some states disqualify from appointment persons who are not residents of the state or who are shown to be of poor moral character. Usually an executor or administrator is required to file a bond with the court to protect the estate against improper administration. In most jurisdictions, this requirement may be waived if the will contains a provision stating that the executor need not file a bond.

Functions of Executors and Administrators   The functions of executors of testate estates and administrators of intestate estates, and their obligations to their respective estates, are essentially the same. Each is the *personal representative* of the decedent. As personal representative, the executor or administrator gathers and inventories the assets of the estate; pays taxes and allowable claims; with court approval sells estate property if necessary; and distributes the remainder, if any, to the beneficiaries. In addition, the personal representative may, if the will authorizes or the court approves, carry out the contracts of the decedent and make new contracts for the estate. However, if the representative carries on the decedent's business or makes contracts without authorization, he or she becomes personally responsible for any loss the estate suffers.

Ordinarily, because the administration of an estate should be concluded as speedily as possible, a personal representative is not authorized to invest estate funds. Instead, money must be deposited in a bank in the estate name.

A personal representative is a fiduciary, that is, a person upon whose integrity a special trust and confidence has been imposed. The ethics of ordinary business relations, where parties deal with each other at arm's length, do not apply to this relationship. Instead, a fiduciary is expected to show more than ordinary candor, consideration, and honesty in his or her dealings on behalf of the decedent's estate, acting in its best interests without taking personal advantage of the business he or she conducts. A personal representative is required to exercise the same care in managing the affairs of the estate as a prudent person would do in managing his or her own affairs. Among the representative's duties are: to safeguard and preserve the estate assets; to keep its property in substantial repair and productive; and to pay all taxes that become due so that tax liens are not imposed. The representative may hire experts, such as accountants and lawyers, as the conditions demand and may file and defend lawsuits on behalf of the estate. The representative is not permitted to purchase assets from the estate nor to make any personal gain from the conduct of its affairs. If the representative does make such profit, the money must be returned to the estate. The representative may also be liable to the beneficiaries of the estate for any losses it suffers because of his or her mismanagement, breach of duty, or bad faith actions.

A personal representative is entitled to be compensated for his or her services. In some states the compensation is upon a scale fixed by statute, graduated according to the value of the estate. In other states, the compensation is fixed by the court or by the parties. It is not unusual for the personal representative, particularly when a member of the decedent's family, to waive compensation.

The care that a personal representative owes an estate is the subject of the following case.

Case 23.3   In re Estate of Kurkowski
409 A.2d 357 (Pa. 1979)

Carl Kurkowski died intestate in November, 1973, survived by his wife, Emma, and two minor children by a prior marriage. Emma posted bond and was appointed administratrix of Carl's estate. At the time of his death, Carl was the sole owner of a company which sold and serviced motorcycles. The corporation's capital stock was then worth about $43,800. Emma became the president, secretary and treasurer of the corporation. She continued to run the business without first securing court approval. An insurance company paid $75,000 to the business as beneficiary of a policy on Carl's life.

Emma paid herself a monthly salary, used the company auto for her private purposes, and later traded it for another, taking the title in her own name. She operated the business until August, 1975, then closed it. However, she took no action to liquidate the corporation's assets or to pay its debts. Nine months later the company was placed in receivership and all its assets were sold. All the funds received from the sale were used in paying the administration expenses and priority claims.

In October, 1976, decedent's sons petitioned for an accounting of Carl's estate. The administratrix (Emma) furnished an accounting. Objections to it by the sons were sustained by the court and Emma was surcharged (ordered to pay) $119,000 for having operated the business without court approval. The amount of the surcharge was essentially the value of the company's capital stock at the time of Carl's death, plus the proceeds from the insurance policy. The administratrix appealed the order which held her personally liable to the heirs.

EAGEN, C.J. . . . Even assuming the statutory procedures [requiring court approval before running the business] were not applicable to decedent's business, administratrix nevertheless breached her common law fiduciary duty in failing to liquidate the estate for purposes of distribution to decedent's heirs and, therefore, is chargeable with the losses incurred.

A decedent's personal representative is under a duty to take custody of the estate and administer it in such a way as to preserve and protect the property for distribution to the proper persons within a reasonable time. . . . In the discharge of this duty, he is regarded as a fiduciary and is held to the highest good faith. Moreover, he will be required to exercise the care and diligence which prudent persons ordinarily exercise in their own affairs. A personal representative who fails to use common skill and ordinary business caution may be held liable for losses to the estate which result therefrom. . . .

A personal representative's duty to settle the estate must be viewed with reference to the situation of the assets at the time of decedent's death. Thus, he has no duty to carry on a business conducted by the decedent. On the contrary, a personal representative breaches his trust if he continues to operate a trade or business on behalf of an estate in the absence of testamentary direction, . . . or the consent of all interested persons. . . . If he does so, he will be liable for any loss thereby resulting to the estate. . . .

This . . . rule is subject to the limitation that the personal representative may continue operating a business of the decedent for a limited time without liability for the purpose of selling the business as a going concern or winding up the business by converting the assets into cash or performing existing contracts of the decedent. . . .

In this case, administratrix clearly breached her fiduciary duty as personal representative of the decedent by continuing to operate the business at a loss for a period of twenty months after decedent's death while realizing personal gain in the form of salary and fringe benefits and by eventually abandoning the business without making provision for disposition or liquidation of its assets or payment of the corporate debts. . . .

. . . We find no error in the court's surcharge of administratrix for the full loss of the value of the corporation at the time of the decedent's death plus the additional capital resulting from insurance proceeds paid to the corporation.

Decree affirmed. . . .

Claims against Estates A major purpose of probate administration is to pay the decedent's valid debts and then to distribute the net assets of the estate to the heirs. Therefore, a personal representative receives and considers all claims filed against the estate and, with court approval, pays those found to be valid. Statutes prescribe the time and the manner in which claims must be filed. The time allowed under the so-called "non-claim" statutes varies, but usually it is four months from the date of the publication by the representative of notice to creditors to file claims, usually by advertising in a newspaper of general circulation. If a claim, not otherwise barred by a statute of limitations, is not filed within the prescribed time, then payment is forever barred. State statutes establish the order in which claims against an estate are paid. The costs of administration, funeral expenses and those of the decedent's last illness, statutory family allowances, and taxes take priority in the sequence of payment. Family allowances (payments to a surviving widow and minor children), being entirely statutory, vary from state to state. They are separate and apart from any inheritance and are for their financial support during the administration of the estate.

Distribution of Estates After the costs of administration, taxes, and valid claims have been paid, the personal representative (executor or administrator) accounts to the court and, with its approval, distributes the remaining money and property to the beneficiaries. An intestate estate is distributed in accordance with state inheritance laws. A testate estate is distributed in accordance with the terms of the decedent's will and, if the will does not dispose of all of the assets of an estate, inheritance laws then govern the distribution of the remainder. After the distribution is completed, the personal representative is discharged by the court.

In the following situations an executor may have difficulty in carrying out the provisions of a will (1) when there is ambiguity or mistake in the words of a will; (2) when there are insufficient assets in the estate to satisfy all of the gifts; (3) when a named beneficiary has died; and (4) when described property is not in the estate.

Ambiguity or mistake in will If more than one meaning can be given to a provision of a will, that provision is *ambiguous*. For instance, suppose a will states, "I give my niece, Sarah, $100," and the testator has two nieces named Sarah, one Sarah Smith and one Sarah Jones. Which Sarah inherits the $100? In another will there may be a *mistake* in the description of the beneficiary or of the property covered by the bequest. For example, a will makes a gift "of my house at 684 Oxford Lane." The testator owns no house on Oxford Lane but does own one at 186 Oxford Avenue. Should the named beneficiary inherit the house at 186 Oxford Avenue? In both these situations, a court will endeavor to ascertain the true intent of the testator. The following two hypothetical cases indicate to what degree a court may read meaning into the words of a will to give effect to the wishes of a person who can no longer speak for himself or herself.

1 Alice asks her lawyer to draft her will, leaving, among other gifts, a diamond ring to Mary. The secretary's notes were garbled; therefore the secretary wrote in the will, "I give my———to Mary," intending to fill in the blank space later. Unfortunately, the secretary forgot and the sentence was never completed. Alice, not noticing the omission, signed the will as it was written. Even though, after Alice's death, the lawyer clearly recalls her instructions, a court will not construe the will to make a bequest of the ring to Mary. Such a construction would entail the court's "writing" Alice's will, an undertaking beyond its power.

2 Alice's will states in part, "I give my diamond ring to Mary Lowen." Mary's name is Mary Lincoln. Alice knew no Mary Lowen and intended that Mary Lincoln have her ring. A court could, given adequate evidence, hold that Mary Lincoln was entitled to the ring.

The case that follows illustrates the evidence that a court will consider when called upon to construe an ambiguous will.

Case 23.4   **Matter of Estate of Smith**
580 P.2d 754 (Ariz. 1978)

Hazel Smith died, leaving a will which stated in part:

"III SPECIFIC DEVISE

I devise my money and coin collection to Todd Fehlhaber and Sue Fehlhaber in equal shares, or to the survivor thereof."

"IV DISPOSITION OF RESIDUE OF MY ESTATE

I devise the residue of my estate, consisting of all my property of every nature owned by me at my death . . . and not effectively disposed of by the preceding articles of this will to Juliet D. Rolle and Eleanor J. McQuaid in equal shares."

Rolle and McQuaid (the appellees) were appointed the personal representatives of the decedent. They inventoried the estate. It consisted of various bank accounts having a total value of $75,336.71; 36 coins and six two-dollar bills found in Smith's safe deposit box, appraised at $49; and other property. The appellees filed a petition for court approval of a distribution of the collection of coins and bills (worth $49) to the Fehlhabers as their sole share of the estate. Rolle and McQuaid filed affidavits with the petition, one of which was executed by the attorney who drew the will. In it he said that the testatrix told him she wanted to leave a collection of coins and bills in her safe deposit box to the Fehlhabers and all her other property to Rolle and McQuaid. The Fehlhabers (appellants) objected to the inventory, asserting that all of the bank accounts were "money" and thus part of the "money and coin collection" given to them. Appellants further argued that the lawyer's affidavit was not admissible because it varied the terms of the will.

The court considered the affidavits, found that the word "money" in the will was ambiguous, and determined that the testatrix intended to devise to appellants only the collection of coins and bills in the safe deposit box. The Fehlhabers appealed this interpretation of the will.

HATHAWAY, J. . . . The cardinal rule for construction of wills is to ascertain the intention of the testator. . . . This determination is to be made upon a consideration of the instrument as a whole, and, when necessary or appropriate, the circumstances under which the will was executed. . . . When the language of a will is ambiguous resort may be had to extrinsic evidence in order to ascertain the intention of the testator. . . .

The issue is whether the trial court erred in deciding that there was ambiguity here. An ambiguity is said to exist in an instrument when the written language is fairly susceptible of two or more constructions. . . . We agree that there was an ambiguity in the instant will and it was a patent one.

The term "money" when used in wills is essentially ambiguous. . . . The rule concerning the meaning of "money" is stated *In re Estate of Whitney*, 162 Cal. App.2d 860 . . . (1958):

> 'When used in a will it has no fixed or technical meaning, but is a term of flexible scope having either a restricted or a wide meaning according to the signification which the testator intended to give the word. . . . Where the context of a will discloses the intent of the testator to attribute to the word 'money' a specific meaning which is more comprehensive than the meaning ordinarily given it, that meaning will be adopted. . . .'

We cannot say as a general rule that "money" when used in a will always includes bank deposits. The word may have any meaning which the testamentary intent, as manifested by the will read in the light of proper evidence, imparts to it. . . .

Once having established an ambiguity, parol evidence is admissible for the purpose of explaining it. . . . Parol evidence is not admissible to show what the testator intended to say, but rather to show what he intended by what he did say. . . .

The language used here admits of two constructions. One would limit "money" to the collection of coins and bills and the other would enlarge the term to include much more. From the language alone the intent of the testatrix Smith was not clear. It was therefore proper to resort to extrinsic proof, including the statement of the attorney who drew up the will. . . . [The Fehlhabers are therefore entitled only to the coins and bills found in the safe deposit box.]

Affirmed.

Insufficient assets in estate It sometimes happens that the assets in an estate are insufficient, after all the estate taxes and debts are paid, to complete all of the gifts described in the will. The question then arises, which gifts must be cut down or go unsatisfied? Courts settle the question by classifying bequests into categories and fixing the order in which each category *abates. Abatement* is the reduction or nonpayment of a gift stated in a will. Bequests are classified as follows:

• *Residual gifts:* those payable out of the remainder (residual) of the estate after general, specific, and demonstrative gifts have been paid. "I give all the rest of my property to my friend Mary K. Jones," is an example of a residual gift. This type abates first.

• *General gifts:* those payable out of the general property of the estate but (1) not from any specified source or money, and (2) not part of money or property given as specific or demonstrative gifts, viz: "I give the sum of $250 to Wilfred." These abate next.

• *Specific gifts:* gifts of a particular thing, viz: "I give my General Motors stock to John Baxter." These abate last. [Use of the modifier "my," normally indicates a specific gift.]

• *Demonstrative gifts:* These have characteristics of both general and specific gifts and, as such, abate with them. Demonstrative gifts provide for payment first from a designated source and, if that is not sufficient, then out of the general estate, viz: "I give Mary P. Smith all my Standard Oil Company stock and if that is not worth $10,000, the balance to be paid from my estate."

As a general rule, all gifts of both real and personal property within a class abate at the same rate and the entire class abates before there is any abatement in the next succeeding class.

Named beneficiary deceased If a beneficiary predeceases the testator or renounces a gift, the gift *lapses* and that property may be applied to satisfy other gifts except under two conditions. (a) If the will makes an alternative disposition of the property, such as a gift "to my cousin Arthur, if he is living and, if not, then to my cousin Joseph," and the alternative beneficiary survives the testator, there is no lapse. (b) If an *anti-lapse statute* applies there is no lapse. An anti-lapse statute applies when a gift has been made to a blood relative of the testator who has died before the testator but whose child or children survive the testator. Those children then inherit the gift their deceased parent would have received.

Specific property not in estate If property which is the subject of a *specific* gift (not other types of gifts) is not in the estate, the gift fails and that beneficiary gets nothing. This is called *ademption by extinction.* Thus, if a will makes a gift to Louis of "my Chrysler car," and the testator had exchanged the Chrysler for a Buick, in most states Louis will not inherit the Buick. The majority of courts mechanically apply ademption by extinction without regard to what

may have been the testator's intentions. However, a growing number of courts apply the testator's intentions to the facts and do not impose ademption by extinction if the property described in the will can be followed into some other form of property.

There may also be *ademption by satisfaction.* This occurs when a testator makes a will containing a bequest, for example, to Arthur. Later the testator, in his lifetime, makes a gift to Arthur intending that the gift will satisfy (take the place of) the bequest in the will, but the testator neglects to modify the will accordingly. In such a situation, upon proof of the testator's intention, there is an ademption by satisfaction and Arthur is not entitled to the bequest. Of course, the problem is to establish the testator's intention. Some states and the Uniform Probate Code require a writing by the testator at the time of the gift expressing the intention that it replace the bequest, or a written acknowledgment by the beneficiary to that effect. Other courts rely upon various other types of evidence.

TRUSTS

A trust is a fiduciary relationship in which one person (the *trustee*) holds the legal title to property for the benefit of another (the *beneficiary,* also called *cestui* (usually pronounced "seddy"), or *cestui que trust,* or *trustant.* The following is an example of a simple trust:

Andy, (the *trustor* or *settlor,* that is, the one who makes the trust) conveys to Tidy Bank (the trustee) $300,000 with directions for the bank to pay the interest annually to Andy's children, Beatrice and Barry (the beneficiaries), until the younger of them reaches 30 years of age, at which time the trust fund is to be divided between them if both are still living. If only one child lives to attain that age, the entire trust fund is to be paid to that child. If neither Beatrice nor Barry live to reach 30 years of age, then upon the death of the last child, the entire fund is to be paid to the American Cancer Society.

Express Trusts

An *express trust* is established when a person who has the power to transfer property expresses the intent to create the trust relationship. A trust involving personal property may be created orally, although usually it is created by written instrument. A trust involving real property, to satisfy the Statute of Frauds, must be in writing. The Uniform Probate Code requires the trustee of either an oral or a written trust to register it with the probate court. No particular words are required to establish a trust, but there must be the expression of a trust intent. For instance, if Charles gives $10,000 to his brother Thomas, *instructing* him to use the money to pay Kate's college expenses, a trust comes into being and Thomas has title to the money for the benefit of Kate. However, if Charles gives the money to Thomas while merely expressing the *hope* or *wish* that Thomas will use it for Kate's benefit, no trust is created because a moral obligation but not a legal one is imposed on Thomas. In that event Thomas has complete title to the money and can do with it as he pleases.

Living (Inter Vivos) Trusts; Testamentary Trusts An express trust created in the trustor's lifetime is called a *living* or *inter vivos* trust. A trust created by will is a *testamentary trust*. A living trust may serve as a substitute for a will. It may also drastically lessen the costs of probate and administration of an estate by reducing the amount of property that is subject to the orders of the probate court. To create a living trust, the trustor must transfer assets to the trustee when the trust is created. For example, the Tidy Bank Trust, above, is an express living trust. When it was established, the bank took title to the $300,000 and undertook its management.

A living trust can also be created by the owner (the trustor) segregating money or property of his or her choice, designating himself or herself trustee, and declaring that the money or property is being held for the beneficiary for stated trust purposes. Normally, such a trust is evidenced by a written instrument.

A trustor, when establishing a living trust, may retain the power to change the designated trustee and to modify or revoke the trust. The majority rule is that a trust is irrevocable unless the trustor, when creating the trust, reserves the power to revoke it. The minority rule is that a trust is revocable unless it is made irrevocable when the trust is established.

A testamentary trust, like the will of which it is a part, does not become effective until the death of the testator and, until that time, may be revoked or modified by the testator-trustor. As the trust is not in being until the trustor dies, the assets which makes up the body of the trust are not transferred to the trustee by the trustor in his or her lifetime. They are transferred to the trustee by the executor of the testator-trustor's estate from the estate assets.

Trustee Anyone having the capacity to acquire title to property and to bind the trust by contract may act as a trustee. Usually, a nonresident of the state is required to file a bond to assure the proper administration of the trust. It is common practice to designate a bank or trust company as trustee for a testamentary trust. There is a general rule of equity law that a trust will not be allowed to fail for lack of a trustee. Therefore, if no trustee is named in the trust instrument or if the named trustee declines appointment, or for any reason ceases to act as trustee, a court of equity appoints a trustee so that the trustor's intentions can be carried out.

A trustee, whether serving with or without compensation, is a fiduciary and owes extensive obligations to the beneficiaries. Among them is the duty of absolute loyalty. The trustee must administer the trust in accordance with its terms, exercising at least the degree of care and expertise which a reasonably prudent business person would exercise in dealing with his or her own property and affairs. The trustee must take care of and preserve the trust property, enforcing all rights and claims to which the trust is entitled and defending any action that is brought against it. The trustee must use reasonable care and skill to keep the trust estate productive and may make only such investments as a prudent person would make in the disposition of his own funds, taking into consideration the probable income and the probable safety of the principal. This is called the "prudent investor rule." The trustee is personally liable to the beneficiaries should the estate suffer loss because of the trustee's breach of duties. If the trustee makes a private gain through breach of trust, he or she must turn over those profits to the estate. For instance, let us assume that Thomas, a trustee, exceeding his authority as trustee, borrows $10,000 from the trust. He invests this money in the stock market and, through good fortune, makes a considerable profit. The money Thomas borrowed and the profit belong to the trust estate.

Beneficiary Any person, including minors and incompetent individuals, artificial persons (e.g., corporations and cities), and groups or classes of people may be designated beneficiaries. The particular person need not be specifically named in the trust instrument; it is sufficient if the instrument establishes a formula whereby the beneficiary can be identified. Therefore, unborn children may be the beneficiaries of trusts.

Trust purposes A trust may be established for charitable or for private purposes; it may give the trustee wide discretionary authority and it may prevent a beneficiary from borrowing against funds expected from a trust but not yet received.

1 *Charitable trusts* A charitable trust is not limited to the relief of the poor. A trust solely devoted to any purpose which serves or benefits the general public, such as for the promotion of religion, education, health, the arts, etc., is a *charitable trust*. All other trusts are *private trusts*.

The legal rules for the establishment and administration of charitable trusts are more liberal than those pertaining to private trusts. For instance, a charitable trust can continue indefinitely. In addition, a court of equity, applying what is called the *cy pres doctrine*, may devote the trust property and its funds to another, generally similar, charitable purpose when it is impossible or impracticable to carry out the original purpose for which the trust was established.

2 *Private trusts* It is common practice for a private trust to be established for the care, health, maintenance, support, and education of some particular person or group of people. It need not be so limited, however, and may be for any purpose not contrary to public policy. Unlike a charitable trust, a private trust comes to an end when the purposes for which it was established have been accomplished or can no longer be attained. For example, a trust established to send John through college ends when John is accidentally killed in his freshman year. Also, various provisions of property law prevent a private trust from lasting unduly long.

3 *Discretionary trusts; spendthrift trusts.* A trust can add very useful conditions to an estate. For example, the trustee of either a living or a testamentary trust may be given wide discretionary authority (the trust is then called a *discretionary trust*) to determine how or to whom the trust assets will be paid. In this way the needs of beneficiaries can be reviewed and judged long after the trust is created and the trustor may have died. Most states also allow the establishment of *spendthrift trusts*. In such a trust, the trustor directs that the beneficiary has no rights whatever in the corpus (capital) of the trust nor to its income until it is actually received by such beneficiary. The rights of a beneficiary to the property of a discretionary-spendthrift trust are explained in the following case.

Case 23.5   **In re the Marriage of Rosenblum**
602 P.2d 892 (Colo. 1979)

Gordon and Sandra Rosenblum were married in 1954. They had two children. In 1963 Gordon's mother established a trust consisting of $200,000 worth of stock for him and his children. Gordon and his sister were designated the trustees. The trust, in pertinent part, authorized the trustees, in their absolute discretion, "to distribute all, none, or any part of the net income and principal to any of the beneficiaries." It further provided, "no beneficiary shall have any right or power to enforce the payment of the principal or income to himself or any other person." On Gordon's death none of the money in the trust was to go to his estate but it was to be divided into separate trusts for the children.

Gordon and Sandra's marriage was dissolved in 1977. At that time it was established that Gordon had a yearly income in excess of $80,000 not including any funds received from the trust which was then worth approximately $3,500,000. In the divorce proceedings the joint property was divided between Sandra and Gordon, and Gordon was ordered to make monthly payments for child support and for Sandra's maintenance. The court also determined that Gordon's interest in the increased value of the trust was marital property and ordered that Sandra be paid $500,000 as her share of that increase.

Gordon contended that the trial court erred in treating his rights in the trust as property belonging to him or in ruling that the increase in its value was marital property to which Sandra had any entitlement. On that basis, Gordon appealed.

VAN CISE, J. . . . Where the trust permits the trustees to distribute to a beneficiary . . . so much, if any, of the income and principal as they in their discretion see fit to distribute, a beneficiary has no property interest or rights in the undistributed funds. . . . Although a beneficiary of such a discretionary trust does have rights therein, those rights are merely an expectancy and do not rise to the level of property. . . . [Gordon's] rights in the trust have no cash surrender, loan, redemption, or lump sum value, and no value realizable after death. . . . Neither could the corpus [principal] or income of the trust be reached by his creditors until a distribution occurred. . . .

Thus, we conclude that the husband's rights in the trust are not "property" subject to division as such. . . . The trial court therefore erred in treating the increase in the value of the trust assets as marital property. . . . In this case, the husband's beneficial interest in the discretionary trust has no present value and thus is not "property." Therefore . . . the orders pertaining to . . . payments . . . are reversed and the cause is remanded for a new trial on disposition of assets and liabilities and on maintenance. . . .

[So ordered]

Savings Bank Trusts   A unique form of express trust, called a *savings bank trust* or Totten trust, after the name of the case holding it valid,[6] deserves mention. Such a trust arises when an individual deposits funds in a bank or savings association in his or her name as trustee for another, retaining the deposit book and the right to withdraw the funds. Most states hold that such a deposit presumptively establishes a revocable trust. The minority view is that the deposit creates no trust at all but is merely an attempt to make a testamentary transfer in the depositor's lifetime. The advantages of a savings bank trust are that (1) it can be easily established; (2) the maker (trustor) continues to have control over its funds; (3) it can be established without cost; and (4) upon the maker's death, the beneficiary is immediately entitled to the funds without the necessity of probate.

Resulting Trusts; Constructive Trusts

In addition to express trusts (which include spendthrift, discretionary, private, and charitable trusts), the law also recognizes *resulting trusts* and *constructive trusts*. These two types of trusts arise by operation of law and are actually merely equitable remedies. A *resulting trust* is inferred by a court to effect the return of property to a trustor when, for example, an intended trust could not be carried out. For instance, when the beneficiary of a trust has died and no successor beneficiary is named, there is a resulting trust in favor of the trustor. A *constructive trust* arises where a court finds that a person, having wrongful possession of property, holds it in trust for the owner and the court, to prevent unjust enrichment, orders its return to the rightful owner.

ESTATE TAXATION

Two kinds of taxes are imposed in connection with a decedent's estate: (1) income taxes, and (2) estate or inheritance taxes.

---

[6]*In re Totten*, 71 N.E.748 (N.Y. 1904).

Income Taxes

A person's income tax liability does not die when he or she dies. The personal representative who administers the estate is required to pay from estate assets the income taxes that had accrued against the decedent. In addition, the representative must file income tax returns, called "fiduciary returns," and pay taxes upon the income received by the estate during its administration.

Estate and Inheritance Taxes

The federal government imposes an *estate tax* on the right of the decedent to transmit property after death. The estate tax is graduated according to the taxable value of the estate, reaching a substantial part of that value when the taxable value of an estate reaches $5 million. Among the items included in its taxable value are: the entire value of all property over which the decedent, alone or jointly with others, had the right of control; community property; and policies of insurance owned by or over which the decedent had the right to change the beneficiary. The Internal Revenue Code allows deductions from an estate's gross value of (1) a marital deduction (the exclusion of the value of the property transferred by a decedent to his or her surviving spouse); (2) allowable expenses (such as the costs of administration of the estate, funeral expenses, and certain other indebtednesses); and (3) gifts to charities (in general, those organized and operated exclusively for charitable purposes.)

Practically all states impose either *estate* or *inheritance taxes*. An *inheritance tax*, instead of being imposed on the estate of the decedent, is levied against the beneficiaries for the privilege of receiving an inheritance. Such a tax is graduated according to the value of the inheritance and the relationship of the decedent to the beneficiary. A small tax or no tax at all may be due from the surviving spouse or child, while taxes at higher rates may be due from the more distant relatives or nonrelatives who inherit.

Before a beneficiary receives an inheritance,

all taxes are paid by the decedent's personal representative.

SUMMARY

Property may be inherited under the rules of intestate succession (applicable when a person dies without a will) or pursuant to the provisions of a properly executed will.

A will is not effective until the maker (the testator) dies. To make a valid will, a testator must have both testamentary capacity and testamentary intent. While a person must have a sound mind to make a valid will, it is not necessary that he or she have sufficient mental capacity to carry on business affairs. If a person, in making a will, is subject to the fraud, duress, or undue influence of another, the maker is not expressing testamentary intent and the will is void.

A formal will must be in writing, signed, and witnessed before at least two witnesses. A holographic will (not authorized in all states) must be entirely in the testator's handwriting, signed and, in most states, dated. A holographic will is not witnessed.

While a testator may, in general, make any disposition of property he or she wishes, there are certain exceptions to this rule providing, primarily, protection to a surviving spouse and children.

A testator may revoke a will by later executing a new will or codicil which revokes the earlier one, or by physically acting upon the will in a manner directed by state statute. Depending on the various state statutes, wills may also be revoked by operation of law as a result of a subsequent marriage or divorce or the birth of a child.

The validity of a will is proven in a court proceeding called *probate*. A decedent whose will is admitted to probate is said to die *testate*. A decedent who dies without leaving a valid will is said to die *intestate*. When a will is admitted to probate, an executor is appointed to carry out its provisions. An administrator is appointed by the court to administer the estate of an intestate. Executors and administrators are the personal representatives of the decedents for whom they act. The personal representative takes charge of the assets of the estate, gives notice to creditors to file claims, pays valid claims filed within the period established by law, and then distributes the remaining assets among the beneficiaries.

In the absence of a will the state fixes the portion of the estate each beneficiary will receive. Primarily, a surviving spouse and children inherit an intestate's property. If there are no surviving spouse, children, or immediate family, the closest collateral heirs (blood relatives) of the decedent divide the estate.

A court can interpret a will and decide who inherits in the event a will is ambiguous or a mistake has been made in it.

A trust is a fiduciary relationship with respect to property whereby one person (the trustee) holds the legal title for the benefit of another (the beneficiary). A trust created in the maker's lifetime is a living or *inter vivos* trust. A trust incorporated in a will is a testamentary trust. A trust can add great flexibility to a will; it is one of the major tools of estate planning. A trust that is solely for the benefit of the public is a charitable trust. It is subject to more liberal rules for its formation and administration than is a private trust.

Resulting or constructive trusts are not true trusts but are imposed by legal action as a means of effecting the conveyance of property to the persons entitled to it.

Income taxes upon the income earned by an estate are paid by the personal representative (executor or administrator) of the decedent. In addition, estate taxes, depending on the size of the estate, must be paid to the federal government. Some states impose estate taxes; others, instead, levy inheritance taxes on the beneficiaries, graduated according to the size of the inheritance and the relationship of the beneficiary to the decedent. In either situation, the decedent's personal representative pays all taxes before making distribution of the estate to those who inherit.

STUDY AND DISCUSSION QUESTIONS

1   In a noncommunity property state, if one spouse dies without having made a will, leaving a mother, a surviving spouse and two children, who inherits the decedent's estate and in what shares?

2   If an individual dies without having made a will, leaving both parents and two surviving children but no surviving spouse, who inherits the decedent's estate and in what shares?

3   Arthur and Betty, husband and wife, are killed in an airplane crash. Neither had made a will. They had no children but each left surviving parents. What portion of Betty's estate did Arthur's parents inherit? What portion of Arthur's estate did Betty's parents inherit?

4   The Fifth Amendment to the Constitution provides that no person shall be deprived of property without due process of law. Therefore, would the following statement be a correct statement of the law: It is a principle of United States law, not found in all countries, that the right of a child to inherit the property owned by his or her parent may not be abridged? Explain.

5   Susan graduates from college at 17 years of age. At that time she makes a will dividing her estate in equal shares between the school, her parents, and her sister. Susan becomes a well-known novelist. She dies at 35 years of age, never having married. Susan's two parents and her sister and the school all survive her. Susan made no will other than the one she executed when she graduated. How is Susan's estate divided?

6   Comment upon this statement: If a person has the capacity to enter into a contract, he or she has the capacity to make a will.

7   Contrast a gift by will and one by deed.

8   Contrast fraud and duress in contract law with fraud and duress in the law of wills.

9   *(a)* Distinguish between a holographic will and a formal will. *(b)* Is it correct to say that in most states a person who has a large estate, consisting of both real and personal property, must make a formal will rather than a holographic one? Explain.

10   What is dependent relative revocation?

11   Parties to a marriage are divorced. Each spouse had, during the marriage, made a will in favor of the other. How does the divorce affect their wills? Explain.

12   *(a)* What is meant by the statement that a will is admitted to probate? *(b)* Under what circumstances may it be necessary to probate a will in a state other than that of the decedent's domicile? *(c)* Assume that a will has been admitted to probate; what events next take place with respect to the estate?

13   In general, what are the duties of an executor? Of an administrator?

14   *(a)* What is meant by abatement in the law of wills? *(b)* How does it arise? *(c)* Who brings about an abatement?

15   *(a)* Distinguish between, and give examples of, residual, general, and specific legacies. *(b)* If a decedent dies intestate, is there the same classification of gifts? Explain.

16   Give examples of lapse; ademption by extinction; and ademption by satisfaction in the law of wills.

17   What is meant by a trust?

18   Explain how a trust can add flexibility to a

decedent's estate and extend after death a decedent's control over estate property.

19 Give an example of a savings bank trust.

20 Distinguish between a resulting and a constructive trust.

CASE PROBLEMS

1 There was found among George's effects after his death, a dated paper, written 17 years earlier (the spelling as shown), reading:

> I here buy sent my hand and seal to any one enterseted to my estate, that I give all my monies & estates to my sister Lillian as benefecesitay to all an any.
> Yours truly,
> George

The document was entirely handwritten, on a sheet of paper torn from a notebook. It was offered for probate as George's will. Objection was made because the paper was "unintelligible" and did not express a testamentary intent as it did not say that the gift was to take effect after George's death. Could the writing be considered a valid will? What is the basis for your answer?

2 Paul Weir was a lifelong bachelor. His only relatives were a niece and nephew. Shortly after World War II, Weir met Mrs. Holmead, a widow of about his own age. Until Weir's death in 1971 when he was about 80 years old, he and Mrs. Holmead were constant companions. Weir made a will in 1966, leaving small sums of money to his nephew and to his niece. Mrs. Holmead was the beneficiary of the bulk of his estate. The niece challenged the validity of the will, claiming that it was executed under Mrs. Holmead's undue influence because they were such close friends. Should the will be denied probate?

3 Lloyd Nielson in 1979 executed a valid holographic will. He died soon after. In one paragraph of that 1979 will he stated, "I hereby revoke all wills and codicils heretofore made by me but I still make the gifts set out in paragraph 7g of the will I made on February 3, 1966." Nielson's 1966 will was typewritten and formally executed. The law of the state of Nielson's domicile provides that a holographic will must be entirely written, dated and signed by the hand of the testator. Have the gifts made by paragraph 7g of the 1966 will been revoked or are they still effective?

4 Mrs. C by will left all of her estate to her daughter Viola, with whom she lived. At the time of her death, Mrs. C had two grandchildren, Kyle and Lynn, whose parents had predeceased Mrs. C. Neither Kyle nor Lynn nor their parents were mentioned in Mrs. C's will. The grandchildren believe that they are entitled to a share of their grandmother's estate. Are they correct?

5 A testator made a will which gave to his spouse approximately one-half of his estate. The spouse was one of the attesting witnesses to testator's signature to the will. If the decedent had died without making a will, the spouse would have been entitled to receive only one-third of his estate. To how much of the estate is the widow entitled?

6 Emily, before her marriage to the plaintiff, was the owner of certain property. She conveyed the property by an *inter vivos* trust to a bank as trustee with a grandchild as the beneficiary, reserving to herself all of the income from the property during her lifetime and the right to amend or revoke the trust. Emily later married the plaintiff. She amended the trust several times. After Emily's death, the plaintiff contended that since Emily had retained all of the incidence of ownership of the property she purported to convey to the trust, the conveyance was of no legal effect and therefore the property was still in her estate. Was the plaintiff's contention correct?

7   Bank was the trustee of a testamentary trust which directed Bank to invest the trust monies and to pay the income to Agnes during her lifetime and, after her death, to pay the principal to Charity. Agnes sought to have Bank removed as trustee because it did not consult with her before investing the trust funds and because "Bank should have invested the funds in securities which paid a higher rate of interest although with possibly a greater risk to the principal." Based upon the general discussion of a trustee's duties at page 456–457, do you believe that Agnes is correct?

PART FIVE

SALES AND SECURED TRANSACTIONS

Chapter 24
Introduction to the Law of Sales

Chapter 25
The Sales Contract; Transfer of Title and Risk of Loss

Chapter 26
Product Liability

Chapter 27
Performance of the Sales Contract; Remedies for Breach of Contract

Chapter 28
Secured Transactions

Chapter

24

Introduction to the Law of Sales

People need or want goods of immense variety. To meet this demand, our complex marketing system must handle billions of transactions daily. The principal means for channeling this vast bulk of goods from producers to consumers is the sales contract, and the potential for dispute is great. The law that governs sales of goods must resolve conflicts fairly, but in such a way that the market system remains stable and efficient.

The common law of contract was never well suited to sales of goods. Early in English history, agriculture was the main enterprise, and the land-oriented contract law was too cumbersome for the needs of traders. The traders therefore developed their own commercial law, which was based on the customs of merchants, and enforced it in their own trade organizations.[1] International and unifying in character, the law merchant was fairly well adapted to fast-moving transactions among traders, whose business

originally lay almost entirely outside the established legal-agricultural system.

Eventually, commerce became a principal business activity of the English, and this development affected the history of the law merchant in two ways. First, the law of sales emerged from the law merchant as one of many distinct bodies of commercial law. As early as 500 years ago, the English mercantile courts were applying legal principles characteristic of the law of sales.[2] Second, as commerce assumed more importance in England, the judges began to incorporate the law merchant (and the law of sales) into the common law.

In England the law of sales was put into statutory form by the enactment in 1893 of the Sales of Goods Act. That act formed the basis in the United States of the Uniform Sales Act. The Sales Act was widely enacted by state legislatures, though usually with some modifications. The act was superseded by Article 2 of the Uniform Commercial Code (UCC). The Code,

---

[1]Theodore F. T. Plucknett, *A Concise History of the Common Law*, Little, Brown and Company, Boston, 1956, p. 67.

[2]Ibid., p. 665.

467

and thus the Article on Sales, has been adopted by all the states except Louisiana.[3]

This chapter deals with the nature, policy, and scope of Article 2, with key concepts of the article, and with its relation to certain other articles of the Code. Subsequent chapters in this series present the most important legal principles governing the sale of goods. Principles from Article 2 are supplemented with applicable principles from other parts of the Code and from the common law.

NATURE, POLICY, AND SCOPE OF ARTICLE 2

Nature and Policy of Article 2

The law of sales under Article 2 is based mainly on contract law.[4] Article 2 continues in a revised form most of the content of the Uniform Sales Act and puts into statutory form a number of case-law principles developed both outside and under the Sales Act. Some of the statutory provisions incorporate well-recognized principles of the common law of contracts and property; some choose between conflicting common-law rules; still others represent departures specially adapted to sales of goods in an increasingly complex economy.

The modern-day need for contract rules specially adapted to sales becomes apparent when we consider the complexity of the production process. Consider, for example, the lowly candle—a wick, wax, perfume, coloring, cellophane, cartons, sealing tape, shipping labels, order forms. All these and more must arrive at the manufacturing plant on a schedule that permits the candlemaker to operate efficiently and to meet commitments to buyers who, in turn, may have made commitments to other buyers. For the marketing process to operate efficiently, each person in it must be able to rely on the performance of others, often on the basis of a telephone call across state lines. There is little time to engage in an elaborate contracting process.

The general policy of the UCC is "to simplify, clarify and modernize the law governing commercial transactions; to permit the continued expansion of commercial practices through custom, usage and agreement of the parties; [and] to make uniform the law among the various jurisdictions" [1-102(2)].[5] This policy is implicit in most of the rules of Article 2.

Scope of Article 2

Transactions Included   The drafters of Article 2 state broadly that unless the context otherwise requires, the article applies to *transactions* in goods [2-102]. Yet, many sections of Article 2 make clear that the article applies mainly to sales of goods or to contracts to sell goods, but not to other kinds of transacttions, such as gifts or leases of goods. Why, then, is the term "transaction" used? One writer believes that the drafters intended to encourage courts to apply Code principles "by analogy" to a wider range of commercial transactions than just sales.[6] Buyers injured by defective goods often have the benefit of an Article 2 warranty. A court might be encouraged to imply a similar non-Code warranty in a lease of goods, for example, if similar policy justifies the warranty. Many courts have, in fact, applied Article 2 principles to nonsales transactions.

"Transactions" may have been used for a different reason—to make clear that Article 2 applies to a variety of sales contracts, regardless of the time of performance or title passage. A *sale* consists in the passing of title to goods from the seller to the buyer, in return for a considera-

---

[3]Louisiana has not adopted the UCC as such. Some of the articles have been adopted "in substance," but not Article 2. For more information about the development of the UCC, see Chapter 2, p. 27.

[4]Robert J. Nordstrom, *Handbook of the Law of Sales*, West Publishing, St. Paul, Minn., 1970, p. 1.

[5]Unless otherwise noted, a hyphenated section number refers to a section of the UCC. The numeral before the hyphen is the number of the article in which the section appears; thus here, Art. 1, sec. 102, subsec. (2).

[6]Nordstrom, op. cit., p. 44.

tion called the price (which can be made payable in "money, goods, realty, or otherwise") [2-106(1) and 2-304]. If title passes at the time the sale transaction is entered into, the transaction is called a "present sale." The time of title passage, not the time of payment for or delivery of goods, determines whether the transaction is a present sale. A goods-for-cash supermarket sale is a present sale that is executed by an exchange of goods and money across a counter. However, a present sale can be executory, as in the time purchase of a used automobile.

The present sale is to be distinguished from a "contract to sell." In a contract to sell, the seller agrees to transfer title to the buyer at some future time. This kind of contract is used, for example, where the seller does not yet own existing goods or where the goods have not yet been produced. Under a contract to sell, certain rights do not accrue to the buyer until title to the goods is transferred. But if the title transfer occurs at the designated time, the contract to sell becomes a "sale," and the buyer then acquires the rights in question. Article 2 covers both present sales of goods and contracts to sell goods at a future time. For convenience, the drafters of Article 2 use the term "contract for sale" in reference to both types of transactions [2-106(1)].

Generally, the parties can determine by agreement whether title shall pass at the time of the transaction or at some future time. However, there are some restrictions on when title to goods can pass. Title cannot pass unless the goods are both existing and "identified" (marked or otherwise designated) as the subject of a particular contract. If the buyer and the seller have agreed to a present sale, but the goods are not both existing and identified to the contract, the buyer has a contract for "future goods," which "operates as a contract to sell" [2-105(2)].[7]

The meaning of "goods" is central in determining the scope of Article 2. Section 2-105(1) defines *goods* as "all things (including specially manufactured goods) which are movable at the time of identification to the contract for sale other than the money in which the price is to be paid, investment securities . . . and things in action."[8] Although the primary focus of Article 2 is upon movable things, goods includes the unborn young of animals, growing crops, and certain things attached to realty. Goods also includes money, if the money is a commodity. Thus, coin collections would be considered goods.

Some things are considered to be goods in certain situations and to be real estate in others. If things normally move in commerce as commodities, they may be goods. Thus, goods includes "minerals or the like (including oil and gas) or a structure or its materials to be removed from realty . . . if they are to be severed by the seller . . ." [2-107(1)]. If the buyer is to do the severing, the transaction is considered a contract affecting land and is subject to the real estate statute of frauds and any land-recording requirements. However, growing crops, standing timber, or other things attached to realty are goods, regardless of whether the buyer or the seller is to do the severing, if these things are to be sold apart from the land and if they can be removed without material harm to the land [2-107(2)].[9] Crops and timber are so clearly commercial commodities that their biological connection with the land should be ignored.

Goods are *fungible* if by their nature or by usage of trade one unit is the equivalent of any other unit; unlike units may be treated as fungible by agreement [1-201(17)]. Oil and flour of a particular grade are fungible goods. Fungible goods that are to be sold from an identified mass do not have to be separated from the mass to be identified to the contract. Identification of

---

[7]The meaning and significance of "identification to the contract" are discussed at p. 472.

[8]A *thing in action* (also called "chose in action") is a legal right to recover damages or possession of property by way of court proceedings.

[9]The 1972 amendments to sec. 2-107 treat timber as a growing crop. Under earlier versions of sec. 2-107, timber is treated as goods only if the seller is to do the severing.

fungible goods to the contract occurs as soon as the contract is made [2-502, comment 5]. Another significance of fungibility is that a warehouseman may commingle fungible goods without liability to the owners of different lots. The warehouseman must keep nonfungible goods separate from the goods of others, unless the warehouse receipt provides otherwise [7-207(1)].

Transactions Excluded Transactions involving sales of real estate, personal services, investment securities, and other types of nongoods obviously lie outside the coverage of Article 2. Also excluded are a number of transactions involving goods, but not involving a sale. For instance, Article 2 "does not apply to any transaction which . . . is intended to operate *only* as a security transaction . . ." [2-102; emphasis added].[10] *Pledges* and *chattel mortgages* are intended to operate only as security transactions. However, a conditional sale contract is meant to effect a sale of goods while creating a security interest for the seller, who retains the security interest until the goods are paid for. Article 2 governs the sale aspects of a conditional sale contract, and Article 9 governs the security aspects.

Gifts, leases, and *bailments* may also involve goods, but these transactions usually are not subject to the rules of Article 2. In a gift, title to goods is transferred to the donee, but there is no sale because the title is not transferred for a price. A lease of goods is not a sale because only possession is sold, not title. A bailment is not a sale because the owner retains title and puts someone else in possession of the goods for a limited purpose, such as repair or storage. Yet, many courts are strongly inclined to extend Code principles to non-Code transactions, and especially to leases of goods.

It is not clear to what extent Article 2 applies to transactions involving a mixture of goods and services. Plaintiffs often want the benefit of Article 2 provisions, especially when defective goods cause personal injury, but the case law is in serious conflict. A transfusion of contaminated blood traditionally has been treated as an aspect of medical services and thus as not subject to sales warranties. Courts adopting this position believe that persons who provide essential medical services should be held liable only for negligence or intentional misconduct. More recently, some courts have held that blood and other medical supplies are the subject of sales, and that Article 2 warranties apply. These courts believe that a person injured by a defective product should not have to bear the loss.

Similar conflict is found in decisions involving other types of services and materials contracts. Have beauticians or electricians made a sale of goods to which Article 2 warranty or other rules should apply? Some courts recognize a sale as to the goods. Other courts will consider the mixed contract to be a contract for services, but perhaps will recognize non-Code warranties. A few courts recognize non-Code warranties even in purely services contracts.[11]

---

[10]Article 9, discussed in Chapter 28, covers secured transactions in goods and other personal property.

[11]Richard W. Duesenberg, "Uniform Commercial Code Annual Survey of Legal Developments" (Sales), *The Business Lawyer,* 28:805–808, 1973.

Case 24.1   Ellibee v. Dye
15 UCC Rep. 361 (Pa. Ct. of Com. Pleas, 1973)

ACKER, J. This matter arises from a demurrer to a complaint in assumpsit and trespass. There it is alleged that on May 2, 1972, defendant [Dye] . . . gave a permanent for a fee to the hair of [Ellibee, plaintiff] by applying "French Perm."

Shortly after the treatment, [Ellibee's] hair began to fall out when washing was done by one of defendant's employees. It is alleged that "French Perm" was defective and unreasonably dangerous to plaintiff, and, as a result . . . she suffered certain injuries for which suit is now filed. . . . The fourth cause of action . . . is based on an alleged breach of implied warranty of fitness for the particular purpose for which the material was intended; and an implied warranty of merchantability in that the product was unmerchantable and defective. . . . [D]efendant raises the sole issue of whether there was a sale of the product. . . .

[In] *Hoffman v. Misericordia Hospital of Philadelphia*, 439 Pa. 501, 267 A.2d 867, . . . a demurrer was filed to a complaint . . . claiming breach of implied warranty of merchantability and/or fitness for a particular purpose. The action was for death caused by a transfusion of blood containing hepatitis virus. The claim was that there was no sale. The lower court sustained the demurrer. This was reversed on appeal and remanded with appropriate language applicable to the case at bar . . .:

> "We therefore do not feel obligated to hinge any resolution of the very important issue here raised on the technical existence of a sale. In this respect, we agree with the following statement made by a court of a sister state: 'It seems to us a distortion to take what is, at least arguably, a sale, twist it into shape of a service, and then employ this transformed material in erecting the framework of a major policy decision.' In view of our case law implying warranties in non-sales transactions, it cannot be said with certainty that no recovery is permissible with the claim here made, even if it should ultimately be determined that the transfer of blood from hospital for transfusion into a patient is a service."

. . . [T]he court quotes Comment 2 to Section 2-313 of the Uniform Commercial Code to the effect that the warranty section was not designed in any way to disturb that line of case law growth which has recognized that warranties need not be confined either to sale or contract or to the direct parties to such contract.

Consideration of hospital, doctor, dentist and other medical service cases brings confusing results because of the desire of the courts to protect those who are rendering health and life saving services to the public. Various approaches have been used. . . . *Perlmutter v. Beth David Hospital*, 308, N.Y. 100, 123 N.E.2d 792, . . . in a four-to-three decision denied recovery against a hospital for defective blood. Illinois . . . held . . . that despite the reasoning of Perlmutter, the furnishing of blood by a hospital is a sale for which absolute liability can be held whether the virus is detectable in the blood or not. Other states have resolved the matter by giving immunity to hospitals against strict liability for the furnishing of defective blood. . . . [A Wisconsin federal district] court holds: . . .

> "My decision should not be based on a technical or artificial distinction between sales and services. Rather, I must determine if the policies which support the imposition of strict tort liability would be furthered

by its imposition in this case. In the present context, the question is whether it is in the public interest for the consumer/patient or the supplier/hospital to bear the loss incurred by defective, though nonnegligent, services." . . .

California has recognized that an implied warranty may be found even though the contract is for labor and materials rather than a sale. . . . Although there is a conflict in jurisdictions as to whether the furnishing of materials by a beautician constitutes a sale, a well-reasoned opinion holding a sale is *Newmark v. Gimbel's, Inc.,* 102 N.J. Super. 279, 246 A.2d 11. There, plaintiff, at defendant's establishment, secured a permanent wave, the type being at the suggestion of defendant's representative. Certain injuries were alleged to have resulted. The lower court had concluded that it was merely a transaction between parties amounting to a rendition of services rather than a sale of a product. The appellate court reversed, concluding that there was no good reason for restricting warranties to sales. [The judgment of the appellate court was affirmed by the N.J. Supreme Court, 258 A.2d 697 (1969).] Where one person supplies a product to another, whether or not the transaction be technically considered a sale, warranties should be applicable. . . . The fact that there was no separate charge for the product did not preclude [its] being considered as having been supplied to the customer in a sense justifying the imposition of the implied warranty against injurious defects. . . .

The trend in Pennsylvania law has been to extend warranties in new directions and for situations previously denied. . . .

This court is of the opinion that accepting the facts of plaintiff as true . . . the supplying of the product was a vital part of the performance of the service. Without the product, the service could not have been successfully accomplished. . . . The cost of the service must necessarily have included the cost of the product. If a supplier of a product over the counter would be liable to plaintiff under . . . [a] warranty theory, certainly in logic and reason a beauty shop operator . . . should be held responsible if the product is defective. Plaintiffs in the case at bar must be given the opportunity to prove their case. . . .

. . . [T]he demurrer of defendant is denied.

KEY CONCEPTS OF ARTICLE 2

A number of Code concepts are of general significance in the law of sale as interpretive guides for courts. Some of these concepts are discussed below; others are of equal importance, but they are more conveniently discussed in subsequent chapters.

Identification to the Contract

The parties to a sale may need to know when the sale has occurred, who has a right to insure the goods, or what rights a buyer has to demand the delivery of specific goods. The answers to such questions may depend to some extent upon whether goods have been "identified" (i.e., designated) as the subject of a particular contract of sale.

The parties may make an "explicit agreement" as to when goods will be identified to the contract. In the absence of an explicit agreement, Section 2-501(1) provides the rules. Where the contract is for crops or for the unborn young of animals, identification to the contract usually occurs when the crops are planted or when the animals are conceived. If the contract is for the sale of goods "already existing and identified" (e.g., particular goods owned or possessed by the seller), identification *to the contract* occurs as soon as the contract is made. If the contract is for the sale of "future goods"other than crops or animals (e.g., goods yet to be manufactured or acquired by a supplier for a retailer), identification occurs "when the goods are shipped, marked, or otherwise designated as the goods to which the contract refers."

One important consequence of identifying goods to a contract is that the buyer "obtains a special property and an insurable interest" in the goods. Suppose that B orders 1,000 radios from S. S then manufactures 2,000 radios and marks 1,000 of them as the radios to be shipped to B. According to the title passage rules discussed in the next chapter, B does not yet have title to the radios. However, because the 1,000 radios have been "identified to the contract," B does have a "special property" in the radios and may insure them against loss, as she may wish to do if she pays for them in advance or makes contracts for their resale before receiving them. Furthermore, if S becomes insolvent before delivering the radios, B is entitled to the radios in which she has a special property, and for which she has made arrangements for payment [2-502(1)]. B is thus protected from claims of S's creditors.

Course of Performance; Course of Dealing; Usage of Trade

The courts are frequently called upon to interpret unclear sales contracts. The Code permits the application to sales agreements of many general contract rules concerning interpretation, but the Code "rejects the idea found in many pre-Code cases that certain words have a plain meaning, and that the meaning is to be imposed on the parties."[12] Instead, the meaning intended by the parties to a sales contract is to be determined by their actual language and conduct, "read and interpreted in light of commercial practices and other surrounding circumstances" [1-205, comment 1].

To aid interpretation, the Code gives special prominence to "course of performance," "course of dealing," and "usage of trade." The term *course of performance* refers to how a particular transaction is carried out. There can be no course of performance unless there are repeated occasions for performance, such as several deliveries of coal to be made pursuant to a single contract of sale. Suppose that a contract for the delivery of coal says nothing about how large each delivery shall be. The buyer's acceptance of a series of small deliveries could establish a course of performance that would bind the buyer [2-208(1)].

The term *course of dealing*, on the other hand, refers to a series of transactions, not just the performance of one transaction. A course of dealing (i.e., a pattern of prior business transactions) can establish a background for the interpretation of the immediate transaction [1-205(1)]. Suppose that for each of five previous winters a buyer of home heating oil has always paid the delivery person in cash. The seller's acceptance of this practice establishes a course of dealing upon which the buyer may rely until notified differently.

A *usage of trade* is "any practice or method of dealing having such regularity of observance in a place, vocation or trade as to justify an expectation that it will be observed with respect to the transaction in question" [1-205(2)]. In the seed corn business, for example, it has been held to be a usage of trade that sellers of seed

---

[12]Nordstrom, op. cit., p. 144, n. 47.

corn give no warranties of yield or against disease.[13]

What happens when there is conflict as to the meaning of a contract? The Code provides that (1) express terms of a contract control (have priority over) course of performance, course of dealing, and usage of trade; (2) course of performance controls course of dealing and usage of trade [2-208(2)]; and (3) course of dealing controls usage of trade [1-205(4)].

Good Faith

The concept of good faith is mentioned throughout the Code. Section 1-201(19) defines *good faith* as "honesty in fact in the conduct or transaction concerned." Section 1-203 states the general obligation of good faith: "Every contract or duty within this Act imposes an obligation of good faith in its performance or enforcement." Section 2-103 defines good faith with regard to a

merchant as "honesty in fact and the observance of reasonable commercial standards of fair dealing in the trade." Thus, the requirement of good faith applies to all persons who are subject to the Code, and merchants must be especially careful not to overreach or to cause unwarranted loss to others. For example, in certain instances, a seller has the right to fix a price without consulting the buyer. In fixing such a price, the seller must exercise good faith, perhaps by fixing an objectively determined market price [2-305(2) and comment 3]. Sometimes a merchant buyer has the right to reject delivered goods. Where the seller has no agent or place of business at the market of rejection, the merchant-buyer meets the obligation of good faith by disposing of the rejected goods in accordance with reasonable instructions of the seller, or, in the absence of instructions, by selling perishable goods for the seller's account [2-603(1)]. Failure to act in good faith takes many forms. The following case illustrates one of them.

---

[13]*Bickett v. W. R. Grace & Co., 12 UCC Rep. 629 (D.C., W. Dist. Ky., 1972).*

Case 24.2   Toppert v. Bunge Corp.
377 N.E.2d 324 (Ill. App. 1978)

Plaintiff Charles Toppert, a farmer, signed three contracts for the sale of corn to the defendant Bunge Corporation. Each contract was for 10,000 bushels of corn. Toppert and Bunge discussed a fourth contract, but Toppert never signed and returned the form which Bunge sent him. Plaintiff's father and brother, also farmers, discussed selling their corn to Bunge, but Bunge could not persuade them to sign the contract forms Bunge sent to them.

On November 9, 1973, plaintiff completed the delivery of corn called for by contract number 0355, and commenced delivery under contract number 0364. It was defendant's normal policy to make payment as soon as a contract was performed by a farmer. However, plaintiff was not paid for deliveries made under contract 0355 until his attorney demanded payment. On December 3, 1973, plaintiff completed deliveries under contract 0364 and commenced delivery under contract 0366. Defendant refused to make payment for deliveries made under contract 0364, and plaintiff ceased making deliveries under contract 0366. Discussions involving plaintiff, his father, and his brother ensued, and defendant continued to refuse to pay for the delivered corn. On

June 1, 1974, plaintiff brought suit for the contract price of the corn delivered under contract 0364. The trial court awarded judgment to plaintiff. Defendant appealed.

ALLOY, J. . . . In the testimony before the trial court, defendant's district manager indicated that defendant withheld the amount due plaintiff under contract number 0364 as a wedge to force plaintiff to sign contract number 6079, and also to force plaintiff's brother and father to sign certain contracts with the defendant, so as to assure that all corn under those contracts was delivered. On the basis of the record in this case, we conclude that the trial court could properly determine that defendant's action in withholding payment to plaintiff as leverage against plaintiff's brother and father, in their dealings with the defendant, established a lack of good faith on the part of defendant Bunge in dealing with plaintiff Toppert. . . .

When plaintiff completed deliveries under contract 0364, plaintiff was not in default on the subsequent contracts. Defendant's refusal to pay plaintiff and defendant's imposition of conditions beyond the scope of the contract 0364 were without legal justification and evidenced a lack of good faith on the part of defendant Bunge with respect to payment on that contract. Plaintiff was then justified in requesting adequate assurance of defendant's performance under contract 0366. . . . Defendant's failure to comply with that request constituted, as the court has concluded, a repudiation of contract 0366. . . .

Affirmed.

Unconscionability

Sometimes one party to a contract becomes a victim of contractual wrongdoing by the other. The courts have little difficulty granting appropriate remedies if the impropriety consists of fraud, misrepresentation, or duress. These wrongs are well known, and their elements have been rather clearly worked out in long lines of cases. Article 2 specifically recognizes another category of contractual misconduct called "unconscionability." The essence of unconscionable conduct is oppression or unfair surprise, and the courts have long combatted such conduct indirectly with a variety of techniques.

Section 2-302 gives the court the authority to attack unconscionable conduct directly. If the court finds a contract or any clause of the contract to have been unconscionable at the time it was made, the court may "refuse to enforce the contract as a whole if it is permeated by the unconscionability; or [the court] may strike any single clause or group of clauses which are so tainted or which are contrary to the essential purpose of the agreement; or it may simply limit unconscionable clauses so as to avoid unconscionable results" [2-302, comment 2].[14] As to what specific conduct will be declared unconscionable, Section 2-302 leaves that question for the court to decide as a matter of law on a case-by-case basis. However, the court may take evidence as to what practices are unconscionable. Decided cases and comments to Section 2-302 provide further general guidance.

---

[14]Copyright © 1978 by The American Law Institute and the National Conference of Commissioners on Uniform State Laws. Comments to the Code reprinted with permission of The American Law Institute and the National Conference of Commissioners on Uniform State Laws.

Case 24.3   **Jones v. Star Credit Corp.**
298 N.Y.S.2d 264 (N.Y. Sup. Ct. 1969)

WACHTLER, J. On August 31, 1965, the plaintiffs [Mr. and Mrs. Jones], who are welfare recipients, agreed to purchase a home freezer unit for $900 as the result of a visit from a salesman representing Your Shop At Home Service, Inc. With the addition of the time credit charges, credit life insurance, credit property insurance, and sales tax, the purchase price totaled $1,234.80. Thus far the plaintiffs have paid $619.88 toward their purchase. The defendant [Star Credit Corp.] claims that with various added credit charges paid for an extension of time, there is a balance of $819.81 still due from the plaintiffs. The uncontroverted proof at the trial established that the freezer unit, when purchased, had a maximum retail value of approximately $300. The question is whether this transaction and the resulting contract could be considered unconscionable within the meaning of Section 2-302 of the Uniform Commercial Code. . . .

There was a time when the shield of "caveat emptor" would protect the most unscrupulous in the marketplace—a time when the law, in granting parties unbridled latitude to make their own contracts, allowed exploitive and callous practices which shocked the conscience of both legislative bodies and the courts.

The effort to eliminate these practices has continued to pose a difficult problem. On the one hand it is necessary to recognize the importance of preserving the integrity of agreements and the fundamental right of parties to deal, trade, bargain, and contract. On the other hand there is the concern for the uneducated and often illiterate individual who is the victim of gross inequality of bargaining power, usually the poorest member of the community. . . .

The law is beginning to fight back against those who once took advantage of the poor and illiterate without risk of either exposure or interference. From the common law doctrine of intrinsic fraud we have, over the years, developed common and statutory law which tells not only the buyer but also the seller to beware. This body of laws recognizes the importance of a free enterprise system but at the same time will provide the legal armor to protect and safeguard the prospective victim from the harshness of an unconscionable contract.

Section 2-302 . . . authorizes the court to find, as a matter of law, that a contract or a clause of a contract was "unconscionable at the time it was made," and upon so finding the court may refuse to enforce the contract, excise the objectionable clause or limit the application of the clause to avoid an unconscionable result. "The principle," states the Official Comment to this section, "is one of the prevention of oppression and unfair surprise." It permits a court to accomplish directly what heretofore was so often accomplished by construction of language, manipulations of fluid rules of contract law, and determinations based upon a presumed public policy.

. . . [T]his section is intended to encompass the price term of the agreement. . . . [T]he statutory language itself makes it clear that not only a clause of the contract, but the contract in toto, may be found unconscionable. . . . Indeed, no other provision of an agreement more intimately touches upon the question of unconscionability than does the term regarding prices.

Fraud, in the instant case, is not present; nor is it necessary under the statute. The question which presents itself is whether or not, under the circumstances of this case, the sale of a freezer unit having a retail value of $300 for $900 ($1,439.69 including credit charges and $18 sales tax) is unconscionable as a matter of law. The court believes it is.

Concededly, deciding the issue is substantially easier than explaining it. No doubt, the mathematical disparity between $300, which presumably includes a reasonable profit margin, and $900, which is exorbitant on its face, carries the greatest weight. Credit charges alone exceed by more than $100 the retail value of the freezer. These alone may be sufficient to sustain the decision. Yet, a caveat is warranted lest we reduce the import of Section 2-302 solely to a mathematical ratio formula. . . . The very limited financial resources of the purchaser, known to the sellers at the time of the sale, is entitled to weight in the balance. Indeed, the value disparity itself leads inevitably to the felt conclusion that knowing advantage was taken of the plaintiffs. In addition, the meaningfulness of choice essential to the making of a contract can be negated by a gross inequality of bargaining power. *Williams v. Walker-Thomas Furniture Co.*, 121 U.S. App. D.C. 315, 350 F.2d 445.

There is no question about the necessity and even the desirability of installment sales and the extension of credit. Indeed, there are many, including welfare recipients, who would be deprived of even the most basic conveniences without the use of these devices. Similarly, the retail merchant selling on installment or extending credit is expected to establish a pricing factor which will afford a degree of protection commensurate with the risk of selling to those who might be default prone. However, neither of these accepted premises can clothe the sale of this freezer with respectability. . . .

Having already [been] paid more than $600 toward the purchase of this $300 freezer unit, . . . the defendant has already been amply compensated. In accordance with the statute, the application of the payment provision should be limited to amounts already paid by the plaintiffs and the contract [should] be . . . amended by changing the payments called for therein to equal the amount of payment actually so paid by the plaintiffs.

Merchant

Many sections of Article 2 state rules that have special application to merchants. Some of these rules are intended primarily to expedite sales by replacing those common law rules that might impede the formation or the performance of sales contracts. Others are intended to make explicit the rights or duties of a merchant in transactions with other merchants or with non-merchants. The sections of Article 2 that apply especially to merchants are listed in Table 24.1, together with the purpose of each section.

TABLE 24.1

Sections Having Special Application to Merchants

Section	Topic	Purpose of Section
2-103(1)(b)	Good faith	To provide a higher and more objective test of good faith for the merchant than for the nonmerchant
2-201(2)	Statute of Frauds	To reduce compliance requirements between merchants; thus, to expedite contract formation
2-205	Firm offer	To protect offeree's expectation that certain offers by merchants will remain open without consideration
2-207(2)	Counteroffer	To expedite contract formation between merchants by reducing right to invoke common law counteroffer rules
2-209(2)	Modification of contract	To force evidence (nonmerchant's signature) that nonmerchant agreed to modification of the contract
2-312(3)	Warranty against infringement	To protect buyer against rightful claims of any third person by way of patent or other infringement, where seller is a merchant regularly dealing in goods of the kind
2-314(1)	Warranty of merchantability	To protect buyer in the event that goods are below the standards of quality specified in sec. 2-314(2)
2-326(3)	Rights of merchants' creditors	To make clear when goods may be considered property of the merchant-buyer, and therefore subject to his or her creditors' claims
2-327(1)(c)	Sale on approval	To require merchant-buyer to follow reasonable instructions of seller as to return of goods
2-402(2)	Rights of merchants as to creditors	To permit merchant-seller to retain goods for a reasonable time without being considered fraudulent as to his or her creditors
2-403(2)	Rights of buyers	To protect buyers in ordinary course of business from claims of those who entrust possession of goods to a merchant who deals in goods of that kind
2-509(3)	Risk of loss	To impose risk of loss upon merchant, in certain circumstances, until buyer receives the goods
2-603	Rejection of goods	To require rejecting merchant to take reasonable care of rejected goods; to grant rejecting merchant the right to reasonable payment of caretaking services; to limit his or her obligation to the exercise of good faith
2-605(1)(b)	Rejection of goods	Between merchants, to preclude rejecting buyer from relying on unstated defects where seller has made proper request for a final statement of defects
2-609(2)	Right to adequate assurance of performance	Between merchants, to make commercial standards the basis for judging whether grounds for insecurity as to performance are reasonable

These sections have a variety of purposes. Because of this variety, the term "merchant" is defined in two ways. In its narrower sense, *merchant* means a person "who deals in goods of the kind . . . involved in the transaction" [2-104(1)]. Some of the sections listed in Table 24.1 apply only to merchants in the narrow sense of the term. For example, certain warranty obligations arise only "if the seller is a merchant with respect to goods of that kind" [2-314(1)]. In contrast, a number of sections listed in Table 24.1 deal with nonspecialized business matters that ought to be familiar to any person in business. These sections are to be applied broadly, and *merchant* therefore is fur-

ther defined in the broad sense as (1) a person who "by his occupation holds himself out as having knowledge or skill peculiar to the practices or goods involved in the transaction," and (2) a person "to whom such knowledge or skill may be attributed by his employment of an . . . intermediary who by his occupation holds himself out as having such knowledge or skill" [2-104(1)]. Thus, "even persons such as universities . . . can come within the definition of merchant if they have regular purchasing departments or business personnel who are familiar with business practices . . ." [2-104, comment 3].

Case 24.4   Campbell v. Yokel
313 N.E.2d 628 (Ill. App. 1974)

CREBS, J. . . . Plaintiffs, owners and operators of the Campbell Grain and Seed Company, alleged in the complaint that they had reached an oral agreement on February 7, 1973 with [Yokel and the other] defendant farmers. It was alleged that the defendants agreed to sell and the plaintiffs agreed to purchase 6,800 to 7,200 bushels of yellow soybeans at a price of $5.30 per bushel. Defendants admit that such an agreement was reached but maintain that the agreement was tentative and was not intended to be binding unless a written contract was signed. After the conversation between plaintiffs and defendants on February 7, 1973, the plaintiffs signed and mailed to the defendants a written confirmation of the oral agreement. Defendants received the written confirmation but did not sign it or give any notice of objection to its contents to the plaintiffs. . . .

Defendants refused to deliver any soybeans to the plaintiffs and [on] April 30, 1973, informed the plaintiffs that, since the defendants did not sign the written confirmation, they did not feel bound by an agreement.

Plaintiffs' complaint requested damages or, in the alternative, specific performance of the alleged contract. [Defendants moved for summary judgment and] asserted the statute of frauds as a defense. The circuit court granted the summary judgment motion, holding that . . . the statute of frauds was a defense to the complaint, . . . and that the defendants were not "merchants" within the meaning of Section 2-201(2). Plaintiffs contend that the court erred in finding that the defendant farmers were not "merchants" and that Section 2-201(2) was not applicable. We agree.

[Under Section 2-201, a contract for the sale of goods for the price of $500 or more is not enforceable unless the party to be charged has signed a writing sufficient to indicate a contract of sale. However, this rule is subject to a number of exceptions. One is that *between merchants,* a *non-signing* party who receives a writing sufficient to be enforceable against the sender can usually be held to a contract if he fails to give written notice of objection within 10 days after the writing is received. If the defendant farmers are "merchants," they will be subject to the contract without signing because they did not object in writing within 10 days.]

Very few reviewing courts have attempted to resolve the question of whether a farmer is a "merchant" within the meaning of the . . . Uniform Commercial Code. In *Cook Grains, Inc. v. Fallis,* 239 Ark. 962, 395 S.W.2d 555, a case factually similar to the instant case, the Arkansas Supreme Court held that a farmer is not a "merchant" when he is acting in the capacity of a farmer and that he is acting in such a capacity when he is attempting to sell the commodities that he has raised. In *Oloffson v. Coomer,* 11 Ill. App.3d 918, 296 N.E.2d 871, the appellate court stated, by dictum, that a farmer in the business of growing grain is not a "merchant" with respect to the merchandising of that grain.

We disagree with the decisions in Cook Grains and Oloffson and feel that the reviewing courts in those cases failed to properly interpret the Uniform Commercial Code definition of "merchant." Section 2-104(1) states:

"(1) 'Merchant' means a person who deals in goods of the kind or otherwise by his occupation holds himself out as having knowledge or skill peculiar to the practices or goods involved in the transaction or to whom such knowledge or skill may be attributed by his employment of an agent or broker or other intermediary who by his occupation holds himself out as having such knowledge or skill."

Growing crops are "goods" within the meaning of [Section 2-105(1)]. The above definition of "merchant" leads us to the conclusion that a farmer may be considered a merchant in some instances and that one of the instances exists when the farmer is a person "who deals in goods of the kind . . . involved in the transaction."

The defendants . . . have admitted . . . that they have grown and sold soybeans and other grains for several years. They have sold to the plaintiffs and to other grain companies in the past. We believe that a farmer who regularly sells his crops is a person "who deals in goods of that kind."

[The comments to Section 2-104] state that the term "merchant" applies to a "professional in business" rather than to a "casual or inexperienced seller or buyer." The defendants admittedly were not "casual or inexperienced" sellers. We believe that farmers who regularly market their crops are "professionals" in that business and are "merchants" when they are selling those crops.

Our decision does not place a great burden on farmers. . . . [T]he provisions in Article 2 . . . dealing with "merchants" involve "normal business practices which are or ought to be typical of and familiar to any person in business." The practices involved are "non-specialized business practices such as answering mail." Placing this small burden upon farmers in certain instances lessens the possibility that the statute of frauds would be used as an instrument of fraud. For example, assuming that an oral agreement had been reached in the instant case, that the farmers had received the written confirmation signed by the plaintiffs and that the farmers were not "merchants," the farmers would be in a position to speculate on a contract to which the grain company was bound. If the market price fell after the agreement had been reached, the farmers could produce the written confirmation and enforce the contract. If the market price rose, the farmers could claim the protection of the statute of frauds and sell [their] crop on the open market. Our holding reduces the possibility of this type of practice in cases in which the farmer is a person who regularly sells crops of the kind involved in the transaction at hand. . . .

Reversed and remanded. . . .

RELATION OF ARTICLE 2 TO ARTICLES 6 AND 7

A business deal may involve a number of Code transactions. The price for an Article 2 sale of goods may be paid by use of an Article 3 note or check or an Article 5 letter of credit. The seller may reserve an Article 9 security interest in the goods and pass title by use of an Article 7 warehouse receipt. Article 2 is only one aspect of the law affecting transaction in goods. Articles 6 and 7 may also have to be considered.[15]

Relation of Article 2 to Article 6 on Bulk Transfers

Article 2 encourages sales of goods, and Article 6 discourages fraudulent bulk sales. The function of Article 6 is aptly stated by its drafters:

Many states have bulk sales laws, of varying type and coverage. Their central purpose is to deal with two common forms of commercial fraud, namely: (a) The merchant, owing debts, who sells out his stock in trade to a friend for less than it is worth, pays his creditors less than he owes them, and hopes to come back into the business through the back door some time in the future. (b) The merchant, owing debts, who sells out his stock in trade to anyone for any price, pockets the proceeds, and disappears leaving his creditors unpaid. The first is one form of fraudulent conveyance. The substantive law concerning it has been codified by the Commissioners in the Uniform Fraudulent Conveyance Act. No change in that Act is proposed [by the drafters of Article 6]. . . . The second form of fraud suggested above represents the major bulk sales risk, and its prevention is the central purpose of . . . this Article. Advance notice to the seller's creditors of the impending sale is an important protection against it, since with notice the creditors can take steps to impound the proceeds if they think it necessary. . . .[16]

A bulk sale can be made effective against creditors of the seller in either of two ways: (1) the seller can use the auction procedure prescribed in Section 6-108; or (2) the buyer (transferee) can notify the seller's creditors of the bulk sale. The transferee must deliver the notice personally or send it by registered or certified

---

[15]The titles to Code articles referred to above are as follows: Art. 2, Sales; Art. 3, Commercial Paper; Art. 5, Letters of Credit; Art. 6, Bulk Transfers; Art. 7, Warehouse Receipts, Bills of Lading and Other Documents of Title; and Art. 9, Secured Transactions, Sales of Accounts and Chattel Paper.

[16]Sec. 6-101, excerpts from comments 2–4.

mail "at least ten days before he takes possession of the goods or pays for them, whichever
happens first" [6-105]. A similar notice is required for an auction.

Relation of Article 2 to Article 7 on Documents of Title

Article 2 governs the contract aspects of sales of
goods. Article 7 governs the documents used to
distribute goods; it consolidates and revises
rules of the now superseded Uniform Warehouse Receipts Act, Uniform Bills of Lading
Act, and the provisions of the Uniform Sales Act
relating to negotiation of documents of title.
However, Article 7 does not apply to interstate
or foreign commerce because under the United
States Constitution the federal government has
been charged with responsibility in these areas.
Article 7 must yield to federal law, such as the
federal Bills of Lading Act and the Carriage of
Goods at Sea Act.

> The term document of title . . . includes bill
> of lading, dock warrant, dock receipt,
> warehouse receipt or order for the delivery
> of goods, and . . . any other document
> which in the regular course of business or
> financing is treated as adequately evidencing
> that the person in possession of it is entitled
> to receive, hold and dispose of the
> document and the goods it covers. To be a
> document of title, a document must purport
> to be issued by or addressed to a bailee and
> purport to cover goods in the bailee's
> possession which are either identified or are
> fungible portions of an identified mass.[17]

The two principal documents of title are the
warehouse receipt and the bill of lading. A
warehouse receipt is "a receipt issued by a
person engaged in the business of storing goods
for hire" [1-201(45)]. A *bill of lading* is "a
document evidencing the receipt of goods for
shipment, issued by a person engaged in the

business of transporting or forwarding goods"
[1-201(6)]. A *through bill* of lading is one issued
by a carrier for transport of goods over its own
lines for a certain distance, and then over
connecting lines to the destination [7-302(1)]. A
destination bill of lading is one to be issued at
the destination point instead of the sending
point so that documents will be available when
the goods arrive [comment to 7-305]. This procedure would require some preliminary arrangements between the seller and a bank at the
destination, but it facilitates fast shipments.

Documents of title may be either negotiable
or nonnegotiable. A warehouse receipt, a bill of
lading, or other document of title is negotiable if
by its terms the goods are to be delivered to
bearer or to the order of a named person. Any
other document is nonnegotiable [7-104]. Suppose that S, intending to sell certain goods when
a buyer can be found delivers the goods to W for
storage. W, at S's instruction, makes the warehouse receipt to "S or order." The receipt is
negotiable. When S finds a buyer, she need
merely indorse and deliver the warehouse receipt to the buyer. If S had had the receipt
made to her personally ("to S"), the receipt
would have been nonnegotiable. Such a receipt
would have obligated W to deliver the goods to
S and to no one else, unless S had assigned her
rights to someone else.

The essential difference in legal effect between a negotiable and a nonnegotiable document of title is that the holder of a negotiable
document takes the goods free of many defenses
or claims of others to the goods.[18] Suppose that
W had issued a negotiable warehouse receipt
before receiving delivery of the goods from S. A
holder to whom the document has been duly
negotiated is entitled to the amount of goods
specified in the document, and the holder may
hold W liable for failure to deliver the goods,
despite W's defense that S has not delivered the

---

[17]Sec. 1-201(15).

[18]Negotiability as it pertains to commercial paper is
discussed in Chapters 30–35, especially Chapter 31.

goods to W [7-203]. In general, the holder of a negotiable document may acquire more rights than his transferor had, whereas the assignee of a nonnegotiable document receives only such rights in the goods as the assignor had.

SUMMARY

Sales of goods are subject to an adaptation of contract law called the law of sales. Originating in the law merchant, the law of sales is now found in the Uniform Commercial Code. The general purpose of the Code is to simplify, unify, and modernize the law of commercial transactions, and this policy is implicit in most of the rules of Code Article 2, Sales. Some provisions of Article 2 incorporate well-recognized common law principles; some choose between conflicting common law rules; still others represent departures specially adapted to sales of goods in an increasingly complex economy.

Article 2 applies to present sales of goods and to contracts to sell goods at a future time. For convenience, the drafters of the Code refer to both kinds of contracts as "contracts for sale."

The meaning of goods is central in determining the scope of Article 2. *Goods* means all things that are movable at the time of identification to the contract, other than the money in which the price is to be paid, investment securities, and things in action. Article 2 does not apply to transactions involving nongoods, such as sales of real estate or personal services, nor to exclusively security transactions, gifts, leases, or bailments. However, many courts apply Code principles by analogy to nonsales transactions involving goods. Courts differ in their application of the Code to contracts for a mixture of goods and services.

A number of Code concepts are of general significance in the law of sales as interpretive guides to courts. These concepts include "identification to the contract"; "course of performance, course of dealing, and usage of trade"; "good faith"; "unconscionability"; and "merchant." These concepts emphasize the need in the law of sales to remove certain common law barriers to the formation and the performance of sales contracts, and to make explicit the rights or duties of a merchant in transactions with other merchants or with nonmerchants.

Article 2 is closely related to Article 6. Article 2 deals primarily with sales in the regular course of business while Article 6 deals with bulk sales of stocks-in-trade and is aimed at preventing such bulk sales in fraud of the seller's creditors. Article 2 is indirectly related to Article 7, Documents of Title, in that the person who is in possession of such a document is entitled to receive, hold, and dispose of the document and the goods it covers. Articles 2, 6, and 7, taken together, are a significant part of the legal framework within which the marketing of goods takes place in the United States.

STUDY AND DISCUSSION QUESTIONS

1 *(a)* What needs have led to the establishment of the law of sales? *(b)* To what extent does the law of sales incorporate common law principles?

2 What is the difference between a "present sale" and a "contract to sell" *(a)* in terms of title passage, and *(b)* in terms of function?

3 *(a)* What is the difference between goods and nongoods? *(b)* Why is it necessary to distinguish between goods and nongoods?

4 *(a)* Define "fungible goods." *(b)* How is the term significant?

5 *(a)* List some transactions in goods that are not directly subject to the rules of Article 2. *(b)* In what way may the law governing these transactions be affected by Article 2?

6 Many contracts involve a mixture of goods and services. When asked to apply Article 2 to such transactions, courts respond in various ways. Briefly describe each of the ways.

7 *(a)* Briefly explain how goods may be identified to a contract. What is the significance of "identification to the contract"? *(b)* What is the meaning of "usage of trade"? How is a usage of trade relevant to the law of sales?

8 *(a)* The Code defines "good faith" in two ways. Why are two definitions necessary? *(b)* What are the essential features of unconscionable conduct? *(c)* Who decides what constitutes unconscionable conduct? How is the decision reached?

9 The term "merchant" is defined in two principal ways. Why are two definitions needed?

10 *(a)* What is the purpose of Article 6 on Bulk Transfers? *(b)* By what method is this purpose accomplished?

11 How does Article 7 on Documents of Title pertain to goods?

12 *(a)* Distinguish between negotiable and nonnegotiable documents of title. *(b)* Distinguish between "warehouse receipt" and "bill of lading." *(c)* Distinguish between "through bill" and "destination bill."

CASE PROBLEMS

1 Quality Fruit Buyers, Inc., agreed in writing to sell 50,000 boxes of oranges, which it did not yet own, to Killarney Fruit Co. for future delivery at 40 cents per pound. Quality delivered 20,297 boxes, but refused to deliver the other 29,703 boxes. The market price had risen, and as to the undelivered oranges, Killarney sustained a loss fixed by the Florida Commissioner of Agriculture at $17,331.70. Quality paid this amount to Killarney rather than suffer the loss of its license to do business. Quality then filed suit to recover the amount from Killarney, contending that there was no contract for the

undelivered oranges. (a) Was there a contract for the sale of the undelivered oranges? (b) Explain the significance of the first sentence of Section 2-105(2): "Goods must be both existing and identified before any interest in them can pass."

2 Carrie Mays leased a new Cadillac from S & S Sales of Florida, Inc. S & S assigned rentals to Citizens and Southern National Bank (Bank). Mays was notified of the assignment and began making payments to Bank. Mays eventually ceased making payments, leaving five installments unpaid. Bank brought suit against Mays for the amount due under the lease. Mays defended on the ground that the Cadillac was defective, that the defects constituted a breach of implied warranty under Article 2, and that she could assert the breach of warranty as a defense against Bank's demand for payment. In the lease agreement S & S had made clear its intention to exclude warranties. However, S & S had not excluded warranties in the manner required by Article 2. Was S & S required to use the Article 2 methods of excluding warranties?

3 Blank came into possession of some furniture from a funeral business. In an effort to sell the furniture Blank made an oral agreement with Dubin. Dubin was to pick up and advertise and sell certain parts of the furniture, equipment, and stock-in-trade. Dubin was to receive 20 percent commission on what he sold. Dubin sold the furniture for about $4,700, an amount Blank considered much too low. Blank contends the agreement is within the Statute of Frauds of Article 2 and is therefore unenforceable unless in writing. Does the Article 2 statute of frauds (Section 2-201) apply to the transaction between Blank and Dubin?

4 During an oil shortage, OKC Refining, Inc. (Refinery) canceled its contract to supply Oskey Gasoline & Oil Co., Inc. (Distributor) with gasoline, alleging that Distributor had breached the contract by failing to pay in terms of net gallons. Distributor filed suit, requesting that Refinery be compelled to perform its duties under the contract. In the course of litigation, the following facts concerning the alleged breach were developed. (1) Gasoline expands as its temperature increases. Meters on pipelines measure fuel in both "gross" and "net" quantities, and the difference in measuring technique will result in different gallonages for the same volume of gasoline if the temperature of the gasoline varies from 60°F. (2) From May 1972 to October 1, 1972, Refinery had sold gasoline to Distributor on a gross gallonage basis. (3) On October 1, 1972, Refinery contracted to supply Distributor with gasoline until December 1, 1973. The contract drafted by Refinery's lawyers contained this clause: "The quantity of motor fuel gasoline loaded into trucks shall be determined by truck loading rack meters." Distributor's president added these words: "as computed in gross gallons." (4) Beginning on October 1, 1972, Refinery billed in terms of net gallons, and Distributor paid in terms of gross gallons. Refinery did not object to Distributor's payment in terms of gross gallons until 5 months later, after Refinery had sold 2 million gallons of gasoline to Distributor under the October 1 contract. Applying the concepts of "course of dealing" and "course of performance," decide whether the parties to the October 1 contract objectively intended to deal on the basis of gross gallons.

5 McEntire agreed to sell his 1973 cotton crop to Hart, a cotton merchant. The price agreed upon was somewhat higher than the market price of prior years. After the contract was made, but before the cotton was to be delivered, the cotton market began an unprecedented rise, reaching more than double the price at which McEntire had agreed to sell. McEntire contends that the contract should be voided as unconscionable. Is the contract unconscionable?

6 Fear Ranches, Inc., was looking for breeding cattle to stock its ranch. Perschbacker owned some cattle he had recently purchased from Berry. Perschbacker had made a down payment and was keeping the cattle on Berry's ranch. Fear purchased the cattle from Perschbacker. Berry also had to sign the contract as owner because he had retained a security interest in the cattle, and because the cattle had not been rebranded. Unknown to all parties, the cattle were infected with brucellosis, a disease that causes cows to have a high rate of abortion and makes them unfit for breeding purposes. Fear was forced to sell 1,600 expensive breeding stock as cheaper slaughter animals. Fear sued both Berry and Perschbacker for breach of the implied warranty of merchantability. The court held that the implied warranty of merchantability had been breached because the cattle were not "fit for the ordinary purposes for which such goods are used" (i.e., as breeding animals). However, under Section 2-314(1), a warranty of merchantability is implied in a contract for sale only "if the seller is a merchant with respect to goods of that kind." Berry was a rancher who had sold cattle only to packers as slaughter animals. Perschbacker was a rancher and a bonded trader in livestock. (a) With regard to breeding animals, was Berry a "merchant" as the term is used in Section 2-314(1)? (b) Was Perschbacker?

Chapter

25

The Sales Contract;
Transfer of Title and Risk
of Loss

As we have seen, sellers and buyers of goods have long needed a body of contract law suited to the fast pace of commercial transactions. The drafters of Article 2 of the Uniform Commercial Code have attempted to provide such a body of law, principally by applying to the sale of goods rules of law that make sense in a modern commercial context. For some sales situations, Article 2 provides no rules; instead, the drafters rely upon the general law of contracts to supply the rules. For other sales situations, the drafters have chosen between conflicting general contract rules and have adopted without substantial change the rule that is best suited to sales of goods. For yet other situations, the drafters have found general contract rules to be unsuited to sales. For these situations the drafters have developed new rules or substantially modified old ones.

In this chapter, as well as in other chapters on the sale of goods, attention is given where needed to changes in the law so that the reader will not attempt to apply to a sales transaction a legal principle or rule that is no longer applicable to such a transaction. The first part of the chapter deals with the formation and other aspects of the sales contract, including the rights of good-faith purchasers. The last part of the chapter deals with the transfer of title to goods and with the transfer of risk of loss.

THE SALES CONTRACT

Under the Code, *contract* means the total legal obligation that results from the parties' agreement, as that agreement is affected by the Code and by any other applicable rules of law [1-

486

201(11)]. *Agreement* means the bargain of the parties in fact, as found in their language or by implication from other circumstances, such as course of performance, course of dealing, and usage of trade [1-201(3)]. Since a sales contract includes obligations imposed by the Code and by other law, the parties are obliged at least to act in good faith and to avoid unconscionable conduct. As is discussed later in this chapter, the Code and other law also fill in certain terms left open by the parties. Thus, the agreement of the parties, as supplemented or as limited by law, constitutes the "sales contract."

A contract for the sale of goods must meet traditional requirements for the formation of a contract. As commonly stated, these requirements are mutual assent; consideration; parties having legal capacity to contract; and a legal "object," that is, a purpose not prohibited by law. Contracts for the sale of goods are also subject to traditional legal principles relating to the form and interpretation of contracts. However, most of these aspects of general contract law have been modified somewhat by Article 2 in order to adjust them to sales transactions and to contemporary business needs.

Formation of the Sales Contract

The mutual assent referred to above is normally reached by means of an offer and acceptance. Our first concern, therefore, is with offer and acceptance as they relate specifically to agreements involving the sale of goods.

Offer One of the practical adjustments relating to an offer for the sale of goods is that open terms are permitted in the offer. Usually, the offer will name at least the parties to the sale, the quantity of goods, and the price, but even the price and quantity terms can be left open if the parties intend to conclude a contract for sale and there is a reasonably certain basis for enforcing it. By permitting open terms, Article 2 enables the parties to contract quickly, and to contract in situations where price or quantity information is not immediately available. Open terms are discussed more fully later

under Certainty of Contract Terms. Other adjustments relating to offers are discussed below.

Offer for a unilateral contract One of those other adjustments relates to offers for unilateral contracts. An example of an offer for such a contract is: "Ship 50 cases of X grade sardines at once." At common law this kind of order constituted an offer to enter into a unilateral contract. Consequently, the offer could be accepted only by a shipment made at once. An attempt by the offeree to accept by making an immediate *promise* to ship promptly would be ineffective, and the offeror would be free to revoke the offer. The ability to revoke gives the offeror the opportunity to play the market, often to the surprise and injury of the shipper who is in fact making a prompt shipment. To prevent this kind of injurious surprise, Section 2-206(1)(b) provides, "Unless otherwise unambiguously indicated by the language or circumstances, an . . . offer to buy goods for prompt or current shipment shall be construed as inviting acceptance either by a prompt promise to ship or by the prompt . . . shipment of . . . goods."

Firm offer Another adjustment relates to the revocability of offers. Suppose that S offers to sell a certain piece of real property to B for $50,000, giving B 10 days to decide whether to buy. S may revoke the promise to hold the main offer open for 10 days, unless he or she asked for and received consideration for that promise. In transactions in goods, however, offerees often make commitments in reliance on assurances that "firm offers" will remain open for the promised time. This reliance is especially justified when the assurances are made by merchants. Accordingly, if a merchant states in a signed writing that the offer will be held open, under the Code this statement cannot be revoked merely because consideration was not received [2-205]. The promise to hold the offer open is binding for the time stated or, if no time is stated, for a reasonable time. However, in no event may the period of irrevocability exceed 3 months. For the protection of the offeror, "any such term of assurance on a form supplied by the offeree must be separately signed by the offeror."

Offers in auctions   Some basic law concerning sales by auctions has been codified by Section 2-328. Auctions may be either "with reserve" or "without reserve." These terms indicate whether the auctioneer has reserved the privilege of withdrawing the goods during the bidding process. In an auction *with reserve* the auctioneer is the offeree and has the power of acceptance. As offeree, he or she may reject all bids.[1] In an auction *without reserve* the auctioneer is much like an offeror, with the bidders competing to determine who will win the power of acceptance.[2] After the auctioneer calls for bids in an auction without reserve, the goods cannot be withdrawn unless no bid is made within a reasonable time. In either type of auction (with or without reserve), a bidder may withdraw his or her bid until the auctioneer's announcement of completion of the sale [2-328(3)]. A sale by auction is completed when the auctioneer so announces by the fall of the hammer or in some other customary manner [2-328(2)].

Unless goods "are in explicit terms put up without reserve," an auction is "with reserve" [2-328(3)]. An auction with reserve tends to produce a fair market value. In contrast, an auction "without reserve" tends to produce low prices because the seller has no power to reject low bids. However, the auction without reserve may be useful for moving goods quickly. Where the seller has not stated clearly the kind of auction intended, the law imposes the auction with reserve so that the seller may reject all bids and await a more favorable market.

Acceptance   Suppose that S offers by letter

to sell goods to B, and that B accepts by letter or by telegram. One question that arises concerning the acceptance is whether B's acceptance is effective at the point of dispatch by B or at the point of receipt by S. If B has used an authorized medium of acceptance, the contract usually forms at the point of dispatch.[3] Other questions that arise in connection with acceptance in a sale of goods are: What constitutes an authorized medium of acceptance? What is the effect of a nonconforming "acceptance"? What is the effect of a nonconforming shipment of goods?

Authorized medium of acceptance   Under both the common law and Section 2-206(1), an offeror is entitled to require an offeree to use a particular medium of acceptance. If the offeror requires a medium, it becomes the only authorized medium. If the offeree uses a medium other than the required one, there is no acceptance. The use of a different medium does not necessarily destroy the offeree's power of acceptance, however, because unless otherwise indicated by the offeror, an offer is open for a reasonable time. The offeree therefore may have time remaining to use the required medium of acceptance. Yet, an offeree who is slow to use the required medium faces an increased risk of revocation or other termination of the offer.

Where an offeror says nothing regarding the medium of acceptance, what medium has been authorized? Section 2-206(1) provides, "Unless otherwise unambiguously indicated by the language or circumstances, an offer to make a contract shall be construed as inviting acceptance in any manner and by any medium reasonable in the circumstances." Suppose that S offers by letter to sell goods to B, and that B responds with a telegram of acceptance. Under the Code, the faster telegram is likely to be regarded as a reasonable medium of acceptance effective upon dispatch by B. Suppose, howev-

---

[1]Arthur L. Corbin, *Corbin on Contracts*, West Publishing Company, St. Paul, Minn., 1952, sec. 108.

[2]L. C. B. Gower, "Auction Sales of Goods Without Reserve," *Law Quarterly Review*, **68**:457–460, 1952; also *Restatement of the Law of Contracts, Second*, American Law Institute Publishers, St. Paul, Minn., 1973, sec. 27(1)(b).

---

[3]The "deposited acceptance" or "mailbox" rule is discussed in Chapter 11, under "Medium of Acceptance."

er, that S had made the offer by telegraph and that B had responded with a letter. Some courts have ruled that offerors impliedly authorize only those acceptance media that are at least as fast as the medium used to make the offer. Other courts have looked at the circumstances of each situation before deciding whether the slower letter is a reasonable response to the telegraphed offer.[4] The Code position is that a slower medium may be reasonable, depending upon the circumstances [2-206, comment 1].[5] If the slower medium turns out to be reasonable, the acceptance is effective upon dispatch.

Often the beginning of performance by the offeree is an appropriate method of acceptance. In such a situation, if the offeree begins performance but does not inform the offeror of that fact, the offeror is faced with uncertainty. To reduce this uncertainty, Section 2-206(2) requires the offeree to give notice within a reasonable time that the performance has begun. If the notice is not given, the offeror "may treat the offer as having lapsed before acceptance" and may supply his or her needs elsewhere without liability to the offeree.

Effect of a nonconforming acceptance The common law requirement that the offeree respond exactly to the terms of the offer is incompatible with business needs to routinize transactions. A buyer of goods who wants a warranty may word the order forms so that he or she will obtain the warranty. A seller who wishes to avoid warranty liability will draft his or her acceptance forms accordingly. Since it is unlikely that the forms of buyers and sellers will match exactly, Article 2 provides rules that treat some counteroffers as acceptances. The thrust of these rules is that an agreement for the sale of goods can be enforced even though the acceptance does not mirror the offer; and, where the agreement is *between merchants*, it is possible

for insignificant additional or different terms to become part of the contract without the knowledge of both parties [2-207]. These rules deal with two typical situations. One is that in which an agreement or a contract has been reached "and is followed by one or both parties sending formal memoranda" embodying the terms agreed on, and adding some terms. The other situation is that in which an offer is sent, and a wire or a letter intended as an acceptance adds terms [2-207, comment 1]. Because the rules governing these situations are a substantial departure from the general law of contracts, the rules are discussed in some detail in the following paragraphs. For illustrative purposes, however, the discussion is limited to the offer and acceptance situation.

Under Section 2-207(1), "A definite and seasonable expression of acceptance . . . which is sent within a reasonable time operates as an acceptance even though it states terms additional to or different from those offered. . . ." However, the offeree may condition his or her acceptance on the offeror's assent to the additional or different terms. If the offeree conditions the acceptance on the offeror's assent, no contract arises unless the offeror appropriately consents to the offeree's additional or different terms.

If the offeree does not condition the acceptance on the offeror's assent to the additional terms, they are "to be construed as proposals for addition to the contract. Between merchants such terms become part of the contract unless: (a) the offer expressly limits acceptance to the terms of the offer; (b) they materially alter it; or (c) notification of objection to them . . . is given within a reasonable time" after the additional terms have been communicated [2-207(2)]. Thus, in the law of sales, the offeror must take the initiative to prevent a proposed minor term from becoming a part of the sales contract. Under rule (a), he or she may exclude a proposed minor term by expressly limiting acceptance to the terms of the offer. Under rule (c), he

---

[4]Corbin, op. cit., secs. 78 and 81.

[5]Robert J. Nordstrom, *Handbook of the Law of Sales*, West Publishing Company, St. Paul, Minn., 1970, p. 90, n. 47, interprets this comment.

or she may exclude a proposed minor term by giving timely notification of any objections to the term.

Under rule (b) in the previous paragraph, an additional term that materially alters the offer does not become a part of the contract. Minor terms are reasonably incorporated into the con-tract unless the offeror takes steps to exclude them, but additional terms that could substantially impair the value of the contract to the offeror will not be binding without his or her actual consent. Whether a particular term materially alters the offer is a question for a court to decide.

Case 25.1   **Just Born, Inc. v. Stein, Hall & Co.**
13 U.C.C. Rep. 431 (Pa. Ct. Com. Pleas 1971)

Just Born, Inc. (plaintiff), a candy manufacturer, purchased gelatin from Stein, Hall & Co. (defendant). On six occasions in 1967, plaintiff telephoned orders to defendant and followed these oral communications with written purchase orders specifying the terms of the agreement such as price, quantity, and description of the goods. Thereafter, defendant sent plaintiff a "Sales Acknowledgment Agreement" and shipped the gelatin to plaintiff's plant. The agreement form contained an "Arbitration Clause" which stated:

"Any controversy or claim arising out of or relating to this agreement, or the breach thereof, shall be settled by arbitration in New York, N.Y., pursuant to the rules, then obtaining, of the American Arbitration Association and the laws of New York. Judgment may be entered upon the award in any court having jurisdiction."

The plaintiff found the gelatin unfit for its intended use and filed an action against the defendant. Defendant denied that the gelatin was unfit and petitioned the court for a rule to show cause why the dispute should not be taken to arbitration pursuant to the "Sales Acknowledgment Agreement."

WILLIAMS, J. The issue of whether the present dispute is subject to arbitration may be characterized as the "battle of conflicting forms" used by buyer and seller. . . .

Defendant contends that under the terms of the Uniform Commercial Code, Section 2-207, the "Sales Acknowledgment Agreements" were definite and seasonable acceptances of plaintiff's purchase orders and that the arbitration clause contained therein was an additional term which should be construed as having become part of the contracts. Plaintiff cites Section 2-207 for the opposite proposition, namely that the arbitration clause was an additional term which materially altered the offer to purchase the gelatin and thus did not become part of the contracts between plaintiff and defendant. . . .

Applying Section 2-207 to the facts of the case at bar, it is clear that a contract was formed by the exchange of forms between plaintiff and defendant, and that the arbitration clause contained in defendant's "Sales Acknowledgment Agreement" forms was an additional term. . . .

The pleadings indicate that both plaintiff and defendant are merchants; therefore, the arbitration clause would become a part of the contracts unless it runs afoul of the three caveats of Section 2-207(2). Subsection 2-207(2)(a) and 2-207(2)(c) do not hinder the inclusion of the arbitration clause. Nowhere on plaintiff's purchase order forms did the offers to purchase the gelatin expressly limit acceptance to the terms of the offer. In addition, plaintiff admits that it made no objection to the additional clause as prescribed by subsection 2-207(2)(c).

The parties differ, however, as to whether the arbitration clause is a "material alteration" of the contract within the terms of subsection 2-207(2)(b). Defendant argues that the arbitration clause does not materially alter the contracts but merely sets forth the forum in which any disputes are to be decided without changing the substantive rights of either party with respect to the contracts. Defendant urges the court to follow *Roto-Lith v. Bartlett*, 297 F.2d 497 (1st Cir. 1962), which was the first case to interpret section 2-207. Plaintiff cites *Application of Doughboy Industries*, 233 N.Y.S.2d 488 (1962), and its New York progeny for the opposite proposition that an arbitration clause is a material term and requires the assent of both parties. There appear to be no reported Pennsylvania cases, either trial or appellate, which have construed Section 2-207(2)(b).

In our opinion, *Roto-Lith v. Bartlett* is inapplicable to the case at bar. . . . We do not agree with the court's reasoning in that case and are unwilling to extend it to the present issue.

In *Application of Doughboy Industries*, the New York court ruled that an arbitration clause contained in the seller's form but not in the buyer's form was a "material alteration" and under Section 2-207 did not become a part of the contract between the parties. In determining that the arbitration clause was a "material alteration," the New York court based its conclusion on the well-settled principle that in New York an agreement to arbitrate had to be clear and direct and could not depend upon implication, inveiglement or subtlety. Elaborating on this principle, the court held: "It follows then that the existence of an agreement to arbitrate should not depend solely upon the conflicting fine print of commercial forms which cross one another but never meet. . . ."

The Pennsylvania policy with regard to arbitration agreements is similar to the New York law relied upon by *Doughboy*. In *Scholler Bros., Inc. v. Hagen Corp.* . . . it was held that: ". . . [T]he assent to relinquish a trial by jury is not to be found by mere implication." *Scholler* further noted that: "No technical or formal words are necessary to constitute a reference of a controversy to arbitration, but it must clearly appear that the intention of the parties was to submit their differences to [an arbitration] tribunal and to be bound by the decision reached by that body on deliberation."

Defendant wisely does not contend that there was actual assent or a meeting of the minds to include the arbitration clause in the present case, but urges that it be included by implication under Section 2-207 of the Code.

In our opinion, *Doughboy* is a proper interpretation of Section 2-207 and is consistent with the principle of *Scholler* that an agreement to arbitrate is not to be found by implication. It should be noted that *Doughboy* has been uniformly followed in New York [Citations].

We conclude, therefore, that the arbitration clause contained in defendant's "Sales Acknowledgment Agreement" forms was an additional term which materially altered the offer and, as such, did not become a part of the contract between defendant and plaintiff. . . .

. . . [D]efendant's rule to show cause is denied and dismissed.

Shipment of nonconforming goods as an acceptance In certain situations Article 2 treats a shipment of nonconforming goods as an acceptance. Suppose B orders for prompt shipment 100 bolts of white silk cloth from S for manufacture into ladies' handkerchiefs. S ships 100 bolts of white nylon cloth instead. S has not performed the requested act. At common law, a judge would have held that S has not accepted B's offer and therefore cannot be liable for breach of contract. Under Section 2-206(1)(b), if S ships the nylon without giving B notice that the goods are nonconforming, the shipment is an acceptance and at the same time a breach of contract [2-206, comment 4].[6] This rule should have the effect of discouraging S (and other sellers) from being negligent in filling orders and from substituting slow-moving goods in the hope that the buyer will not notice the substitution. However, if S gives B timely notice that the goods are nonconforming, the shipment is not an acceptance, and S will not be liable for breach of contract. This rule encourages S and other sellers to send substitute goods as an accommodation to B, who may need them to keep his operation going. If B decides to use the goods, there is a contract. If B decides not to use the goods, they may be shipped back at S's expense.

Certainty of Contract Terms The promises in an agreement must be expressed with reasonable certainty if they are to constitute a contract. Yet the most carefully planned contract might contain a vaguely worded promise or might even omit an essential term. Promises may be vague or indefinite as to time or place of payment and still constitute a contract.[7] In dealing with cases involving indefinite promises the common law "endeavors to give a sufficiently clear meaning to offers and promises where the parties intended to enter into a bargain. . . ."[8] Thus, if the parties to a contract have said nothing about price, most courts would hold that a reasonable price was intended, provided there was evidence that the parties intended to enter into a bargain. The common law practice of implying missing terms where such an implication is reasonable was adopted by the Code. Section 2-204(3) states, "Even though one or more terms are left open, a contract for sale does not fail for indefiniteness if the parties have intended to make a contract and there is a reasonably certain basis for giving an appropriate remedy."

However, Article 2 departs from the older common law treatment of some situations involving open terms. Chief among these departures is the treatment of the "agreement to agree." At common law, if the parties agreed to leave an essential term open for future agreement, there was no contract. Article 2 takes a contrary position on open price terms and on some other open terms. The Code provisions on these various kinds of open terms are discussed in the following paragraphs.

Open price term For one or more reasons,

---

[6]Nordstrom, op. cit., p. 88.

[7]*Restatement of the Law of Contracts*, American Law Institute, Philadelphia, 1932, sec. 32, comment b.
[8]Ibid.

the parties to a sales agreement might not state a price for goods to be delivered later. For example, costs of production might not be known at the time of the sale, the market price might be subject to considerable variation, or the parties might have forgotten to state a price. To make the contracting process safer in such situations, Section 2-305 provides:

> The parties if they so intend can conclude a contract for sale even though the price is not settled. In such a case the price is a reasonable price at the time for delivery if (a) nothing is said as to price; or (b) the price is left to be agreed by the parties and they fail to agree; or (c) the price is to be fixed in terms of some agreed market or other standard [and the price is not so fixed].

Where the parties agree that the seller or the buyer is to fix the price, the party who is to fix the price must do so in good faith. Where the price is to be fixed in a manner other than by agreement of the parties, and one party improperly prevents the fixing of the price, the party who is not at fault may treat the contract as cancelled or may himself or herself fix a reasonable price.

Other open terms   Article 2 supplies various other terms for the parties. If the parties do not agree otherwise, they are presumed to have intended a delivery of goods in a single lot [2-307]. Section 2-308 states the place for delivery. Under Section 2-309(1), "The time for shipment or delivery . . . if not provided in this Article or agreed upon shall be a reasonable time." Section 2-310 states the time for pay-

ment, the rights of the buyer to inspect goods, and the starting time for an agreed credit period. The comments to these and other sections make clear that if the parties do not decide the designated matters for themselves, Article 2 will fill the gaps in such a way as to reflect "modern business methods" or "common commercial standards."

Output and requirements terms   Many businesses must plan deliveries of goods months or years in advance, and in amounts that cannot be stated with precision until some future date. Consequently, businesses have long employed "output" and "requirements" contracts. A farmer's contract to sell to B "all the carrots I grow on Greenacre during the 1980 growing season" is an *output contract*. A power company's contract to "buy from you all the X-grade oil that we need to meet our power requirements for the next year" is a *requirements contract*. Once considered illusory or vague by some courts, such statements have come to be routinely enforced.

Article 2 continues the common law policy of permitting output and requirement contracts, and Section 2-306 sets up a standard for their interpretation and performance. An output or a requirements term "means such actual output or requirements as may occur in good faith. . . ." However, "no quantity unreasonably disproportionate to any stated estimate or, in the absence of a stated estimate, to any normal or other comparable prior output or requirements may be tendered or demanded." Thus, Article 2 provides needed contract flexibility and protects the parties from unreasonable variations in output and requirements.

Case 25.2   City of Louisville v. Rockwell Manufacturing Co.
482 F.2d 159 (6th Cir. 1973)

The City of Louisville (defendant) solicited bids in September 1969 for the purchase of approximately 7650 parking meters. Two bids were submitted, one by Rockwell Manufacturing Co., and the other by Duncan Industries, Inc. The City decided to award a contract to Rockwell (plaintiff). On November 29, 1969 an agreement was entered into for the purchase of parking meters. Among the terms of the agreement were the following:

> "Annual Contract thru June 30, 1970 to furnish part of the City's requirements of parking meters, coin boxes and repair parts, in accordance with the following and [with] specifications which were attached to Proposal P-41-58 and which are made a part thereof.
> "APPROXIMATELY:
> "7650 Parking Meters and Coin Boxes to be installed in accordance with the aforementioned specifications. . . .
> "Delivery to be in accordance with schedule 'E' which was made a part of bid P-41-58, and which is made a part hereof." . . .

On December 8, 1969, the City placed an order for 1,000 meters. On December 15, 1969, Rockwell acknowledged receipt of the order. On January 5, 1970, Rockwell notified the City that it had completed the manufacture of the initial order of 1,000 meters and was holding them pending receipt of shipping orders. In the meantime, a change of administration occurred in Louisville. The new City Law Director advised Rockwell's attorney that he considered the agreement with Rockwell null and void and that he had so advised the appropriate city officials. Acting upon the Law Director's advice, the City repudiated its agreement with Rockwell and proceeded to solicit new bids for "approximately 6,000" parking meters. Duncan Industries, Inc. was the successful bidder and a contract was awarded to it.

On May 5, 1970, Rockwell filed an action against the City of Louisville for breach of contract. The trial court concluded that the agreement of November 29, 1969 constituted a contract, that the City had breached the contract, and that Rockwell was entitled to damages. The City appealed. Only so much of the appellate court's opinion as deals with the issue of whether there was a contract is quoted in the following excerpts.

WILSON, J. . . . The initial contention of the City upon this appeal is that the trial court was in error in concluding that an enforceable agreement ever arose between the parties. . . .

The principal thrust of the appellant's [City's] argument appears to be directed to the wording of the agreement itself, and to the contention that the agreement, properly construed, commits the City to no purchase obligation, but is rather in the nature of an option, committing Rockwell to an "open end offer" to sell at a stated price for a stated time. In support of this contention it is emphasized that the agreement dated November 29, 1969, provides that it is an "annual contract through June 30, 1970," that Rockwell is to furnish only "part of the City's requirement for parking meters," the number to be furnished being "approximately 7650 parking meters" and that delivery is to be made only "after receipt of a purchase order" from the City. While it does appear that these matters create a degree of indefiniteness and ambiguity in the agreement, in the light of the full record in this case it does not appear that they render the agreement only an option or an "open end offer," leaving the City wholly uncommitted until such time as it may elect to place an order. While such an argument could better have been advanced prior to the adoption of the Uniform Commercial Code in Kentucky, it would appear to have no merit subsequent to the adoption of that Code. The Code . . . is more liberal than prior law in permitting open terms in a sales contract and in not requiring complete certainty or definiteness. Under the Code, even though one or more terms are left open, a contract for sale does not fail for indefiniteness or lack of mutuality if the parties have intended to make a contract and there is a reasonably certain basis for granting appropriate relief. Section 2-204(3).

Moreover, Section 2-306(1) provides in pertinent part: "A term which measures the quantity by the output of the seller or the requirements of the buyer means such actual output or requirements as may occur in good faith. . . ." Under this provision municipal "requirements" is not too indefinite a term, since it is held to mean the actual good faith requirements of the City when dealing according to commercial standards of fairness. The further provision for furnishing "part" of the City's requirements likewise does not render the agreement illusory or lacking in mutuality, both in light of the full record upon the trial and in light of the further provision in the agreement for furnishing "approximately 7650" parking meters. The word "approximately" when used in this context merely indicates that precision in quantity is not intended, but rather a margin is intended either for excess or deficiency in the quantity stated. The degree of variation thus made permissible depends upon the facts of the particular case. . . .

Although this court cannot concur in the conclusion of the trial court that the subject agreement is without ambiguity, it is the opinion of this court that such ambiguity as exists in the agreement . . . must be resolved in favor of the conclusion that the City contracted to purchase of Rockwell such parking meters as would be required by it during the contract term if the City acted in good faith to carry out its contemplated parking meter installation project. The good faith and commercial fairness standards of the Code require this result. . . .

[The court affirmed the District Court's decision that the City had entered a contract with Rockwell and had breached it.]

Form of the Sales Contract

The parties to a sales contract are not required to use any particular form of contract. Yet, certain rules of law do affect the form of some sales contracts. The Article 2 statute of frauds requires that specified kinds of sales contracts be evidenced by a writing or by some legally acceptable alternative, such as partial performance. The Article 2 parol evidence rule is applied to determine whether a particular kind of writing, when it exists, will be the exclusive evidence of the content of a sales contract.

The Article 2 Statute of Frauds In the 1300s the English courts began to enforce oral contract promises, and they did so on the basis of the testimony of witnesses who were not parties to the contract. If these witnesses could be persuaded to testify falsely, a person could be held to a "contract" into which that person had not entered. In 1677, to prevent such "frauds and perjuries," the English Parliament enacted the famous Statute of Frauds. That statute was the forerunner of a host of statutes of frauds enacted in the United States, including Section 2-201 of the Code.[9]

Section 2-201(1) states, "Except as otherwise provided in this section, a contract for the sale of goods for the price of $500 or more is not enforceable by way of action or defense unless" the party against whom enforcement is sought has signed some writing "sufficient to indicate" that a contract for sale has been made between the parties. What must the writing contain to be "sufficient"? Many courts interpreting non-Code statutes of frauds have required that the writing state with some certainty all the material terms of the contract. Article 2 rejects this approach. The Article requires only that "the writing afford a basis for believing that the offered oral evidence rests on a real transaction," that the writing be signed, and that the writing specify a quantity of goods. The quantity need not be accurately stated, but recovery is limited to the quantity stated. The writing could be sufficient to meet the statute of frauds requirement even though the quality of the goods, the time of delivery, and other terms are omitted [2-201, comment 1].

With regard to two classes of sales transactions, the drafters of Article 2 recognized that certain contracts should be enforceable even though the party against whom enforcement is sought has signed nothing. Both classes of transactions involve situations in which one party would be subjected to unfair surprise if the other party were permitted to cancel an agreement merely because the canceling party has not signed a writing.

The first class consists of transactions "between merchants" in which a writing exists but has not been signed by the person against whom enforcement is sought. Suppose that merchant Brown telephones an offer to dealer Smith to buy a certain cash register for $1,000; that Smith replies over the telephone, "I accept your offer"; and that Smith immediately sends Brown a writing in confirmation of the contract. Under Section 2-201(2), the statute of frauds is satisfied without Brown's signing a memorandum (1) if within a reasonable time Brown receives a writing in confirmation of the contract and the writing is sufficient against the sender (Smith); (2) if the party receiving the writing (Brown) has reason to know its contents; and (3) if he (Brown) does not give written notice of objection to the contents of the writing within 10 days after receiving it.

In the second class of sales transactions there is usually no writing, but there may be convincing alternative evidence that the parties have entered a contract. If a party against whom enforcement of an oral contract is sought admits in court that a contract for sale was made, the oral contract can be enforced to the extent of the quantity of goods admitted [2-201(3)(b)]. If an oral contract has been partially performed, it is enforceable "with respect to goods for which payment has been made and accepted" or with respect to goods "which have been received and accepted" [2-201(3)(c)]. Oral contracts for goods to be specially manufactured for the buyer may also be enforceable. No writing is required for enforcement where (1) the circumstances reasonably indicate that the goods are for the buyer, (2) the goods are not suitable for sale in the ordinary course of the seller's business, and (3) the seller had made either a substantial beginning of their manufacture or commitments for their procurement before receiving notice of repudiation by the buyer [2-201(3)(a)].

The Article 2 Parol Evidence Rule The parol evidence rule as it applies to contracts in general was discussed in the contracts portion of this volume.[10] The adaptation of the rule to agreements for the sale of goods is contained in

---

[9]Corbin, *Contracts*, sec. 275. Non-Code statutes of frauds are discussed in Chapter 16.

[10]See Chapter 16.

Section 2-202 of the Code. Under that section, terms in a "writing intended by the parties as the final expression of their agreement with respect to such terms" are not to be contradicted by evidence of any prior agreement or by evidence of a contemporaneous oral agreement. The same is true of terms agreed to by the parties in confirmatory memoranda (i.e., a memorandum from each party, with the memoranda agreeing on the term in dispute). However, agreed-to terms may be explained or supplemented by course of dealing, by usage of trade, or by course of performance. Agreed-to terms may also be explained or supplemented by evidence of consistent additional terms, unless the judge finds that the parties intended the writing to be not only a "final" but also a "complete and exclusive" statement of terms.

Section 2-202 provides no test for judging whether the writing is actually intended to be the final expression. However, writers on the law of sales believe that the section encourages the judge to consider all reasonable evidence of intention, and to reject an older common law position that an inquiry into finality and completeness should be limited to an inspection of the writing itself.[11]

[11]James J. White and Robert S. Summers, *Handbook of the Law Under the Uniform Commercial Code*, West Publishing Company, St. Paul, Minn., 1972, sec. 2-10.

Case 25.3   **Warren's Kiddie Shoppe, Inc. v. Casual Slacks, Inc.**
Kiddie Shoppe, Inc. v. Casual Slacks, Inc.
171 S.E.2d 643 (Ga. App. 1969)

(In each of these cases Casual Slacks, a manufacturer, was the plaintiff. Both defendants were retail merchants. There was a summary judgment for the plaintiff in each case. Both defendants appealed. The court dealt with both cases in a single opinion because the basic issue was the same in both cases.)

Plaintiff's affidavit showed that on March 5, 1968, defendants placed orders with plaintiff for assorted teenage clothing, and these orders called for delivery during "June–Aug." Plaintiff shipped these goods and thereafter received checks from both defendants. However, these checks reflected substantial deductions from the invoiced prices, and therefore plaintiff refused to accept them and instead brought suit for the full amount of each account.

Defendants' affidavits showed substantially the following facts: The phrase "June–Aug." has a definite meaning in the teenage clothing trade—i.e., the largest shipment of the ordered merchandise is to be received in June with a substantially similar shipment in July, and the balance, which should represent approximately twenty percent of the total order, should arrive in August. In the trade, it is well known that the phrase "June–Aug." means the delivery just specified because this is the period during which parents purchase new clothes for their children's school year commencing in September. Plaintiff was well aware of the significance of this delivery term when he entered into these contracts with defendants. Furthermore, defendants reminded plaintiff on a number of occasions prior to delivery that time was of the essence in these contracts for the reasons above stated.

In spite of this, no shipment whatever was received by defendants until August 15, 1968, and possibly some days later than this, and they were incomplete. Upon receipt of these first shipments, defendants immediately telephoned plaintiff's president and told him that because the goods had been received so late in the pre-school selling season, it would be necessary to mark them down from one-third to one-half off their usual retail price and possibly more in order to sell them at all. Defendants further informed plaintiff's president . . . that by reason of plaintiff's breach in the delivery term of the contracts and the resulting need to sell the goods below their usual retail price, defendants would each have to make an appropriate deduction from the invoiced price of the goods. Defendants later forwarded to plaintiff their checks reflecting these deductions along with letters of explanation.

HALL, J. The plaintiff contends that parol evidence is inadmissible to explain the shipment term "June–Aug." because the term unambiguously meant that the goods could be shipped at any time during June and July and through August 31, while defendants contend that whether or not the term "June–Aug." is ambiguous, evidence of course of dealing and usage of trade is admissible to explain or supplement the written terms of a contract. The Uniform Commercial Code which governs contracts of the kind here involved supports defendants' contention. "Terms with respect to which the confirmatory memoranda of the parties agree or which are otherwise set forth in a writing intended by the parties as a final expression of their agreement with respect to such terms as are included therein may not be contradicted by evidence of any prior agreement or of a contemporaneous oral agreement but may be explained or supplemented (a) by course of dealing or usage of trade or by course of performance;. . . ." Section 2-202.

. . . Comment 1 to Section 2-202 states: "This section definitely rejects [the] premise that the language used has the meaning attributable to such language by rules of construction existing in the law rather than the meaning which arises out of the commercial context in which it was used; . . . ;" Comment 2 states: ". . . [W]ritings are to be read on the assumption that the course of prior dealings between the parties and the usages of trade were taken for granted when the document was phrased. Unless carefully negated they have become an element of the meaning of the words used."

In our opinion, evidence of trade usage was admissible and the question of whether or not the delivery terms of the contract in the instant cases had been breached presented an issue of fact for a jury. . . .

The trial court erred in its judgments granting the plaintiff's motions for summary judgment.

Judgments reversed.

Alteration of the Sales Contract

After a contract has been formed, one or both parties may wish to modify it. There may be a need to change the time or place of delivery, specifications in the goods ordered, warranty obligations, or even the price. At common law, such modifications would not be enforceable unless both parties to the contract had received new consideration. Yet it is common practice for honest people to agree to, and to rely upon, modifications that are not supported by consideration. To expedite legitimate modifications, Section 2-209(1) provides, "An agreement modifying a contract within this Article needs no consideration to be binding."

But not all modifications are legitimately inspired. Sometimes a party to a sale extorts a modification of the contract by threatening to withhold delivery of essential goods unless the purchaser "agrees" to pay more. Pre-Code courts could use the common-law consideration requirement to combat extortion and similar misconduct. The drafters of the Code have provided substitute protections against such misconduct. One protection is the good faith doctrine imposed by UCC Section 1-203. According to a Code comment: "The test of 'good faith' . . . may in some situations require an objectively demonstrable reason for seeking modification" [2-209, comment 2]. Another protection is the requirement that "the statute of frauds section of this Article . . . must be satisfied if the contract as modified is within its provisions [2-209(3)]. Still another protection is that the parties to a signed agreement may require any modification or rescission to be evidenced by a signed writing [2-209(2)]. However, where a "no oral modifications" clause is included in a form supplied by a merchant and the other party is not a merchant, the clause will not be binding on the other party unless he or she signs the clause separately.

Rights of Good Faith Purchasers

Suppose that Cromwell, a dealer in new and used lawn equipment, stole a small tractor from Davis, acquired a similar tractor from Keller at a very low price by means of fraud, and immediately sold both tractors to Aker who knew nothing of how Cromwell acquired them. Then Davis and Keller sue Aker to recover possession of the tractors. What are the rights of Aker, a good faith purchaser for value?

Davis will be allowed to recover the stolen tractor or its value from Aker. A thief has no title (right of ownership) to the property and there-

fore cannot convey title to anyone. Since Davis still owns the tractor, Aker is acting in a manner inconsistent with Davis's ownership and has committed the tort of conversion. Conversion is discussed in Chapter 5. The rule that a thief has no title protects the ownership rights of individuals by tending to limit the market for stolen goods.

Keller, however, may *not* recover either the tractor or its value from Aker. Although defrauded, Keller intentionally transferred the tractor to Cromwell and thus conferred "voidable title" on her. Because Cromwell's title was voidable, Keller could have rescinded the transaction and recovered the tractor if Cromwell still had it; but under Section 2-403, a person who has voidable title has the power to transfer good title to a good faith purchaser for value. Because Cromwell sold the tractor to Aker before Keller could recover it, Aker owns the tractor and Keller is left to seek fraud damages from Cromwell. Section 2-403, by protecting good faith investors from loss of property at the hands of aggrieved prior owners, serves to enhance property values.

To be entitled to take goods free from claims of aggrieved prior owners, a person must (1) be a "purchaser," (2) receive the goods in good faith, and (3) give value for the goods. *Good faith* means "honesty in fact" in the transaction. If the purchaser is a merchant, good faith requires, in addition, conformance to reasonable commercial standards of fair dealing in the trade. For the purposes of Section 2-403, a person gives *value* by giving any consideration sufficient to support a simple contract. Value therefore could consist of an executory (unperformed) promise. (In contrast, under the law of negotiable instruments discussed later in this volume, "value" means *performed* consideration.)

The requirement that the protected person be a "purchaser" can be a source of confusion. In its ordinary sense, the word "purchaser" means a person who buys something, and buying implies the giving of value. But the UCC adopts a broader, technical meaning of "purchaser." Under the UCC, a *purchaser* is a person who takes property by sale, negotiation, mortgage, *gift*, or any other voluntary transaction creating an interest in property. Thus, a donee of a gift can be a purchaser.

Suppose that Cromwell's father owned a tractor, delivered it to Cromwell as a gift, learned that she gave it to Boyd, and brought action to recover the tractor from Boyd on the ground that Cromwell had given no consideration for it. A completed gift of the kind just described is irrevocable, and lack of consideration is not a sufficient legal basis for recovery of the property. Although they are donees, Cromwell and Boyd are "purchasers" in the Code sense. Such a purchaser acquires whatever title the transferor had or whatever limited interest the transferor agreed to transfer, and the purchaser can transfer that title or interest to someone else.

Suppose a different situation in which, by means of duress, Cromwell forced her father to sell his tractor to her at a ridiculously low price. If Cromwell then gave the tractor to Boyd, Cromwell's father could recover it from him even though Boyd acted honestly. The reason is that Cromwell had only a voidable title (because of the duress) *and* that Boyd, although a good faith purchaser in the Code sense, gave no value. If Boyd had been a good faith purchaser *for value*, he would, of course, take the tractor free from the claim of Cromwell's father.

Suppose that Appleseed owns an orchard and gives possession of 500 bushels of her apples to Sander, a wholesale fruit dealer, for storage. Then, contrary to Appleseed's instructions, Sander sells the apples to Wagner for resale in Wagner's grocery stores. Wagner knew nothing of Sander's wrongful act. As between Appleseed and Wagner, who is entitled to the apples?

Appleseed has "entrusted" the apples to Sander. Under Section 2-403, any entrusting of possession of goods to a merchant who deals in goods of that kind gives the merchant power to transfer all rights of the entruster to a buyer in the ordinary course of business. A "buyer in the ordinary course of business" is similar to a good faith purchaser for value and receives the same kind of protection. Wagner, a retail grocer, is such a buyer and may keep the apples free from any claim of Appleseed. However, if Appleseed had stolen the entrusted apples, Appleseed would have had no rights in them, and Wagner would be subject to losing them to the true owner. Case 25.4 presents an entrustment situation.

The concept of protecting the good faith purchaser is found in many branches of the law besides the law of sales. For example, in the law of negotiable instruments (Article 3 of the UCC), holders in due course (similar to good faith purchasers) take negotiable notes and checks free from many defenses of issuers. Similar treatment is accorded good faith purchasers of negotiable securities (Article 8); many retail purchasers of goods subject to security interests (Article 9); and holders of "duly negotiated" documents of title (Article 7). Market values are enhanced, and commerce is benefited, if the good faith purchaser's perception of risk is minimized. Reducing that perception of risk places upon prior owners the burden of taking more care in their transactions, tracking down wrongdoers, and sometimes absorbing loss.

Case 25.4   Carlsen v. Rivera
382 So. 2d 825 (Fla. App. 1980)

Rivera, doing business in Quebec, Canada, as Empire Auto Leasing, Reg'd., leased a 1976 Mercedes Benz to James McEnroe who, Rivera knew, was the owner of an automobile dealership. Later, McEnroe fraudulently obtained title to the car in the name of his agency, Jimmy McEnroe Auto. McEnroe sold the car to Expo Rent-a-Car, Inc., in Fort Lauderdale, Florida. Expo sold the car to Marlin Imports, Inc., which sold it to Carlsen.

Rivera brought an action against Carlsen to recover possession of the car. The trial court held that Rivera leased the car to McEnroe as an individual, that McEnroe stole the car by fraudulently obtaining title, that McEnroe in fact had no title, and that Rivera was therefore entitled to the car or its value together with damages for its wrongful detention. Carlsen appealed.

HERSEY, J. . . . Initially, it is necessary to determine whether there was an entrustment of the automobile. Both under the Code and under prior case law McEnroe could not convey good title or even voidable title if he had stolen the automobile. While it is true that McEnroe is said to have stolen the automobile, he acquired possession lawfully by virtue of the lease agreement. He then committed larceny by forging the title documents, and converted the automobile by selling it. . . . He obtained possession lawfully and could therefore convey a voidable title which could be perfected upon a sale to a buyer in the ordinary course of business. The statutes make it very clear that any delivery of possession and any acquiescence in retention of possession constitutes entrustment. . . . This would obviously include a lease agreement.

Having concluded that there was an entrustment, the second question . . . is whether McEnroe was a merchant who deals in goods of that kind.

The record discloses that McEnroe was actively engaged in the business of selling automobiles. The trial court apparently considered the fact that the lease recited McEnroe's home address rather than his business address as conclusively establishing the intention of the lessor to lease the automobile to McEnroe the individual rather than to McEnroe the automobile dealer. Even assuming this was the intention of the parties to that transaction, the statute clearly does not look to intent but to effect. It is undisputed that McEnroe was in the business of selling cars. In our view that is determinative of this issue. The purpose of [Section 2-403(2)] is to protect the buyer in the ordinary course of business and thus to eliminate impediments to the free flow of commerce. . . .

Quite clearly, then, there was an entrustment of the automobile to a merchant who dealt in goods of that kind.

If McEnroe had sold directly to Carlsen for valid consideration and without notice of the defect in title, then Carlsen would prevail as against the interests of the owner/entruster. Should the result be any different because of the existence of intervening sales? We think not. Carlsen purchased the automobile from Marlin Imports, Inc., which was engaged in the business of selling automobiles. Carlsen had no notice of any defect in the title and in fact obtained a title certificate. Under these circumstances, Carlsen was clearly a buyer in the ordinary course of business. In pre-Code language, McEnroe conveyed voidable title to Expo, who conveyed voidable title to Marlin, who conveyed voidable title to Carlsen, a bona fide [good faith] purchaser for value without notice. The Uniform Commercial Code does not change the result. The buyer in the ordinary course of business obtains good title by virtue of [Section 2-403(2)]. . . .

Reversed and remanded.

TRANSFER OF TITLE
AND RISK OF LOSS

Transfer of Title

In pre-Code law the location of title (ownership) was important in deciding legal issues relating to contracts and to property rights. With regard to sales, Article 2 of the Code has greatly reduced the importance of title as a basis for decision. Yet, even under Article, 2, title remains relevant to a limited number of matters, such as the definition of a sale of goods, the rights of good faith purchasers, and the warranty of title. The Code therefore provides some general rules of title passage, which apply to situations not covered by the other provisions of Article 2. These general rules are discussed in the following paragraphs.

When Title Passes from Seller to Buyer
Subject to two limitations, the parties to a sales contract may decide by explicit agreement when and how title to goods is to pass from the seller to the buyer. The limitations are: (1) Title to the goods cannot pass from the seller to the buyer before the goods have been identified to the contract. (2) Any reservation of "title" by the seller under a contract of sale is limited in effect to the reservation of a security interest and thus does not prevent the passage of basic rights of ownership commonly associated with title. In the absence of an explicit agreement, the passage of title is governed by the rules in Section 2-401.

Under that section, if delivery is to be made by moving the goods, title passes "at the time and place at which the seller completes his performance with reference to the physical delivery of the goods . . . even though a document of title is to be delivered at a different time or place" [2-401(2)]. When does the seller "complete his performance"? The answer depends upon whether the seller has entered into a "shipment" contract or a "destination" contract. The seller has entered into a *shipment contract* if he or she is required *or authorized* to send the goods to the buyer, and the contract does not require him to deliver them at a particular destination. If the seller has entered into a shipment contract, the seller completes performance by putting the goods in the custody of a carrier, and title passes to the buyer at that point. The seller has entered into a *destination contract* if he or she is explicitly required to make delivery at the point of destination. If the contract requires delivery at destination, title passes on tender of delivery there.

Other rules apply where delivery is to be made without moving the goods. If the seller is to deliver a document of title, title passes at the time when and the place where the seller delivers the document. If no documents are to be delivered, title to identified goods passes at the time and place of contracting.

When Title Revests in Seller   As we shall see later, where goods are tendered or delivered, the buyer normally has the right to inspect the goods and to decide whether to accept or to reject them. If title has passed to the buyer and he or she rejects the goods, title revests in the seller, regardless of whether the rejection is rightful or wrongful. Once the buyer accepts the goods, however, title will revest in the seller only if the buyer justifiably revokes acceptance [2-401(4)]. These rules are intended to make clear who has title when there is a dispute about delivery.

Transfer of Risk of Loss

Sometimes goods are lost, damaged, or destroyed without the fault of either the buyer or the seller. Yet, one or the other will have to absorb the loss or try to collect from the business firm responsible for the loss (usually a carrier, a warehouse, or an insurer). Section 2-509(4) permits the parties to determine which one is to bear the risk of loss or how the risk is to be shared. If the parties remain silent as to risk, Article 2 assigns it.

The drafters of Article 2 rejected the common law view that title location should be the basis for assigning the risk of loss. Feelings of responsibility for goods are not necessarily related to who has title, and to impose risk of loss upon title holders often results in unfair surprise. Article 2 provides practical rules that tend to place the risk of loss upon the party (seller or buyer) who is likely to have actual control of the goods, who is likely to insure the goods as they move through the delivery process, or who is likely to be better able to prevent loss. Some of the rules relate to risk of loss in situations involving a breach of contract; others relate to situations involving no breach.

Risk of Loss Where There Is No Breach of Contract The following paragraphs deal with transfer of risk of loss in the most common situations where the parties to a contract are silent as to risk and where there has been no breach of contract: situations involving shipment of goods by carrier, goods held by a bailee, "pick-up" and noncarrier delivery of goods, and goods subject to a right of return. It should be emphasized that the rules relating to these situations apply *only* if the contracting parties have made no agreement to the contrary. This qualification holds for each rule discussed, whether or not the qualification is mentioned in the discussion.

Situations involving shipment of goods by carrier When goods are to be delivered by carrier, the assignment of risk of loss depends upon whether the parties have entered a shipment contract or a destination contract. In a shipment contract, the risk of loss passes from the seller to the buyer "when the goods are duly delivered to the carrier . . . ." [2-509(1)(a)]. In a

destination contract, the risk of loss passes to the buyer "when the goods are there duly so tendered as to enable the buyer to take delivery" from the carrier [2-509(1)(b)]. Section 2-503 states the requirements for a "tender" of delivery.

To determine whether the parties intended a shipment or a destination contract, a court may have to interpret the language of the contract. The court's task is made easier if the parties have used certain standard shipping instructions or terms. Suppose a St. Paul textbook manufacturer promises to ship to a New York buyer 300 textbooks "FOB [free on board] St. Paul." Use of this expression creates a shipment contract, and the risk of loss shifts to the New York buyer when the seller puts the books into the possession of the carrier at St. Paul [2-319(1)(a)]. In contrast, a promise by the St. Paul seller to deliver books "FOB New York" would create a destination contract under which "the seller must at his own expense and risk transport the goods to that place and there tender delivery of them . . ." [2-319(1)(b)]. Similarly, "FAS [free alongside a vessel at] the port of shipment" creates a shipment contract; and "FAS the port of destination" creates a destination contract.

The term *CIF* means that "the price includes in a lump sum the cost of goods and the insurance and freight to the named destination." The term *C&F* or *CF* means that "the price . . . includes cost and freight to the named destination" [2-320(1)]. Despite the word "destination," these terms create a *shipment* contract. If a New York buyer says to a St. Paul seller, "Ship 300 books CIF New York," the buyer in effect appoints the seller as an agent for the purchase of insurance and the payment of freight. By performing the CIF delivery obligations set forth in Section 2-320, the seller shifts the risk of loss to the buyer upon delivery of the goods to a carrier.

Situations involving goods held by bailee Goods stored in a warehouse may be sold and "delivered" without being moved. The risk of loss may be passed from the seller to the buyer in any of three ways: (1) by the buyer's receipt of a negotiable document of title covering the goods; (2) by the bailee's acknowledgment of the buyer's right to possession of the goods; or (3) under certain circumstances, by the buyer's receipt of a nonnegotiable document of title [2-509(2)]. Ordinarily, the recipient of a nonnegotiable document of title takes goods subject to the rights of others. However, with regard to delivery of goods by means of a nonnegotiable document, the buyer is protected from the claims of third parties if, within a reasonable time after the buyer receives the nonnegotiable document, the bailee is notified of the buyer's right to the goods. In the meantime, the risk of the loss of the goods (and of any failure of the bailee to honor the nonnegotiable document of title) remains with the seller [2-503(4)(b)].

Situations involving "pick-up" or noncarrier delivery of goods Suppose that B, by telephone, bought a sofa from S. The parties were silent about risk of loss, but S said, "You may pick up the sofa any morning during the next three days." On the morning of the second day, B arrived to pick up the sofa. However, during the preceding night, the sofa had been destroyed by fire. Who bears the risk of loss?

If S is a merchant, the risk is upon S. Under Section 2-509(3), the risk of loss does not pass from a merchant seller to the buyer until the buyer's *actual receipt* of the goods. This rule applies even though full payment has been made, and the buyer has been notified that the goods are at his or her disposal. The rule also applies where the merchant is to make physical delivery at a place designated by the buyer (e.g., the buyer's place of business or residence). The reason for the rule is that a merchant is likely to have insurance coverage on goods as long as they remain in his or her possession, whereas a buyer is unlikely to have insurance coverage on goods not yet in his or her possession.

If S is a nonmerchant seller, the risk is on B. Under Section 2-509(3), risk of loss passes from a nonmerchant seller to a buyer upon the seller's *tender* of delivery. The seller makes a tender of delivery by making the goods available to the buyer and by giving the buyer any notification reasonably necessary to enable him or her to take delivery [2-503(1)]. Thus, where the seller is a nonmerchant, the risk of loss may pass to the buyer before the buyer actually receives the goods.

Case 25.5   Hayward v. Postma
188 N.W.2d 31 (Mich. App. 1971)

V. J. BRENNAN, J. . . . On February 7, 1967, the plaintiff [Hayward] agreed to purchase a 30-foot Revel Craft Playmate Yacht for $10,000. The total purchase price included a number of options which the dealer was to install after he received the boat from the manufacturer. The parties agreed that defendant [Postma] would deliver the boat to a slip on Lake Macatawa in or about April, 1967.

On March 1, 1967, shortly after the boat arrived at the dealer's showroom, plaintiff executed a security agreement in favor of the defendant seller along with a promissory note in the amount of $13,095.60. The note was subsequently assigned to Michigan National Bank. Clauses 7 and 8 of the security agreement provided:

"(7) Buyer will at all times keep the goods in first class order and repair, excepting any loss, damage or destruction which is fully covered by proceeds of insurance;

"(8) Buyer will at all times keep the goods fully insured against loss, damage, theft and other risks, in such amounts and [with] companies and under such policies . . . satisfactory to the secured party. . . ."

In April of 1967, prior to delivery of the boat, a fire on defendant's premises destroyed part of his inventory of boats including the Revel Craft Playmate. Neither party had obtained insurance. . . . Plaintiff requested the defendant to pay off the promissory note or reimburse him for payments made, and when he [defendant] refused, the plaintiff started suit. . . . The lower court held that the seller bore the risk of loss and entered judgment for plaintiff.

. . . Under the UCC, risk of loss is no longer determined by which party has title to the goods at the time of the loss. It is determined, instead, by rules in the Code covering specific fact situations independent of title. . . . Section 2-509 provides in subsection (3): ". . . risk of loss passes to the buyer on his receipt of the goods if the seller is a merchant; otherwise the risk passes to the buyer on tender of delivery." But for the next subsection of the Code, the solution to this case would be clear, since it is undisputed that the seller was a merchant and that the buyer had not received the goods.

The Code further provides at Section 2-509(4) that: "The provisions of this section are subject to contrary agreement of the parties. . . ." It is the seller's claim that clause 8 in the security agreement declaring that the buyer must "at all times keep the goods fully insured" is equivalent to a contrary agreement of the parties. We do not agree.

The general approach of Article 2 . . . is that freedom of contract prevails; the greater part of it is concerned with detailing what happens where the contract is silent on a particular point. [Section 2-509(3)] was meant to cover the common situation where parties have not agreed on who shall bear the risk of loss. In deciding that the seller should bear the risk of loss while the goods are still in his hands, . . . the Code drafters correctly observed [in a Comment] that it would be highly unusual for the average consumer to carry insurance on an item of personal property weeks or even months before it is delivered to him. The question in our case, then, is whether boilerplate language in a security agreement to the effect that the buyer agrees to keep the goods insured at all times is sufficient to apprise the buyer that he bears the risk of loss on goods he has contracted for, but has not yet received. We think not.

. . . [W]e feel that a contract which shifts the risk of loss to the buyer before he receives the goods is so unusual that a seller who wants to achieve this result must make his intent very clear to the buyer. Fine print in a security agreement concerning insurance does not achieve this result. Clause 8 is entirely vague when it states that insurance is to be carried "at all times." Common experience would dictate that the words "at all times" mean "at all times after one gets possession." . . . We . . . hold that the parties to this contract had not agreed

Case 25.5
Continued

that the buyer would bear the risk of loss prior to his receipt of the goods and that the seller bears the loss under Section 2-509(3). . . .

We do not mean to say that parties may not validly agree on who bears the risk of loss; rather, we hold that if they intend to shift that burden to the buyer before his receipt of the goods, they must do so in clear and unequivocal language. . . .

Affirmed.

Situations involving right to return goods A seller may find a "sale on approval" useful in breaking down the sales resistance of reluctant consumers. A seller who wants to induce a merchant to stock a new product might resort to a "sale or return." These two types of sales transactions are useful for such purposes because the buyers may return the goods even though they conform to the contract.

Yet, a contract that grants a right to return conforming goods does not always indicate whether the parties intended a sale on approval or a sale or return. The distinction is necessary for assigning risk of loss, and Section 2-326(1) provides a guide for making the distinction. If goods are delivered primarily for the buyer's use, the transaction is a *sale on approval*. In a sale on approval, the risk of loss rests on the seller until the buyer accepts (i.e., approves) the goods, unless otherwise agreed by the parties [2-327(1)(a)].

If the goods are delivered primarily for resale, the transaction is a *sale or return*. In a sale or return, the risk of loss passes from the seller to the buyer in accordance with the rules that apply to the particular delivery situation involved. Thus, where goods are shipped by carrier, the risk of loss passes from the seller to the buyer either at the point of shipment or at the point of destination, depending upon the kind of shipping terms used by the parties. If the buyer returns goods in accordance with the sale or return provision of the sales contract, "the return is at the buyer's risk and expense"

[2-327(2)(b)][12] unless otherwise agreed by the parties.

Risk of Loss Where There Is Breach of Contract Where there is a breach of a sales contract, the risk of loss usually falls totally or partially upon the party who breached the contract. Section 2-510 states rules that govern most risk-of-loss situations involving a breach of contract.

Situations involving breach by seller Where the seller's tender or delivery of goods "so fails to conform to the contract as to give [the buyer] a right of rejection, the risk of their loss remains on the seller until cure or acceptance." A seller effects *cure* by correcting the defects in the delivery process or in the goods themselves. A buyer *accepts* goods by taking them as his or her own in a manner indicating that he or she finds the goods satisfactory.[13]

Where a buyer receives goods, accepts them, and later rightfully revokes his acceptance, the buyer "may to the extent of any deficiency in his effective insurance coverage treat the risk of loss as having rested on the seller from the beginning."

Situations involving breach by buyer Where conforming goods have been identified to the contract, and where the buyer repu-

---

[12]The two types of sales also differ with regard to title passage and rights of the buyer's creditors to the goods. Creditors' rights are stated in sec. 2-326(2).

[13]Cure is discussed at p. 542; acceptance is discussed at p. 544.

diates the contract or is otherwise in breach before the risk of loss has passed to him or her, "the seller may to the extent of any deficiency in his effective insurance coverage treat the risk of loss as resting on the buyer for a commercially reasonable time."

Case 25.6   Southland Mobile Home Corp. v. Chyrchel
500 S.W.2d 778 (Ark. 1973)

Gloria Chyrchel, plaintiff, purchased three mobile homes from Southland Mobile Home Corporation, defendant. A service crew employed by Southland and supervised by Barham was to install a new gas range in one of the trailers, hook up electrical and gas lines, and complete similar work. During the installation, Mrs. Chyrchel smelled gas and asked the crew to check for leaks. A few days later, before the installations were completed, an explosion and fire damaged the trailer and made it uninhabitable. Southland refused to refund the purchase price or to replace the trailer. Chyrchel sued Southland for damages, alleging negligence, breach of contract, and breach of warranty. Southland defended on the basis that the sale was complete before the fire, and that the risk of loss therefore had passed to the buyer. The trial court rendered judgment for Chyrchel, and Southland appealed.

HARRIS, J. [We do not] agree that . . . the risk of the loss had passed to the buyer. Mrs. Chyrchel testified that the price included installation of facilities and that everything was to be ready for use of the trailer . . . before acceptance. In fact, she said that her son had signed the acceptance agreement for the other two trailers but that this particular trailer was never accepted nor was any checklist ever presented to her for acceptance. Barham testified that, "We would try our best to get the trailer ready, yes," and he explained that by "ready," he meant water, light, and gas connected so that the trailer could be lived in. Admittedly, this was not done, and the trailer was not ready for occupancy at the time it burned. Appellant [Southland] relies on UCC Section 2-509(3), which it contends placed the risk of loss on appellee [Chyrchel] once the trailer was delivered. . . . [T]here is a quick answer to this contention. Subsection (4) provides that the provisions of this section are subject to a contrary agreement of the parties and to the provisions of the article on effect of breach on risk of loss as stated in Section 2-510. We have already pointed out that in addition to moving the trailer to the Chyrchel lot, there was an agreement to hook up the facilities and thus prepare the trailer for occupancy. . . . This required more from appellant than mere placement of the trailer and can be construed as a contrary agreement which left the risk of loss on the seller/appellant until the installation was completed.

Also, Section 2-510 provides that where delivery of goods so fails to conform to the contract as to give the right of rejection, the risk of loss remains on the seller until cure or acceptance. This section was construed in the case of *William F. Wilke, Inc. v. Cummins Diesel Engines, Inc.*, 252 Md. 611, 250 A.2d 886, where a seller delivered a generator to the job site in a field, but did not perform required field tests called for under the agreement between the buyer and seller. Subsequently, the generator froze, and the question at issue was which party suffered the loss. The court held that "In the absence of a delivery of conforming goods, the risk of damage remained with Cummins, notwithstanding the delivery of the generator to the job site, the receipt of payment from Wilke, and some eight months' delay in start-up." It also stated:

"UCC Section 2-106(2) provides that 'Goods or conduct including any part of a performance are "conforming" or conform to the contract when they are in accordance with the obligations under the contract.' Non-conformity cannot be viewed as a question of the quantity and quality of goods alone, but of the performance of the totality of the seller's contractual undertaking."

The court then said:

"Under the facts of this case, we have no difficulty in holding that the delivery of the generator to the job site, while identifying the goods to the contract, did not amount to a delivery of goods or the performance of obligations conforming to the contract. It could not constitute such a delivery and performance until the generator had been installed, started up, and field tests completed to the satisfaction of the government. Until then, risk of loss remained with Cummins regardless of where title may have stood."

[Judgment of the trial court is] affirmed.

SUMMARY

Sellers and buyers of goods need a body of sales law suited to the fast pace of commercial transactions. To meet contemporary business needs, the drafters of Article 2 have adjusted the general law of contracts in an effort to facilitate sales transactions. Many of these adjustments relate to the formation, form, and alteration of sales contracts. The drafters have also adopted a practical basis for assigning risk of loss in sales contracts.

Article 2 facilitates the formation of sales contracts in a number of ways. The parties to a contract may leave most terms open. Unilateral offers to buy goods for prompt shipment may be accepted either by a prompt shipment or by a prompt promise to ship. Certain firm offers made by a merchant will be irrevocable even though the merchant receives no consideration for the promise to hold an offer open. Offers may be accepted by any means reasonable under the circumstances; and Article 2 provides rules that treat some counteroffers as acceptances. Between merchants, minor additional terms can become part of the contract upon the failure of the offeror to make timely objection, but an additional term that materially alters the offer will not bind the offeror without his or her actual consent.

Under the Code, a shipment of nonconforming goods constitutes an acceptance and a breach of contract. However, if the shipper gives timely notice that the goods are nonconforming, the shipment will be considered an accommodation, and not an acceptance and breach of contract.

The parties to a sales contract are not required to use any particular form of contract. Yet, certain rules of law affect the form of some sales contracts. The Article 2 statute of frauds requires that specified kinds of sales contracts be evidenced by a writing or by some legally acceptable alternative, such as partial performance. The Article 2 parol evidence rule is applied to determine whether a particular kind of writing, when it exists, will be the exclusive evidence of the content of a sales contract.

An agreement modifying a sales contract needs no consideration to be binding. However, modifications must meet the Code test of good faith.

A good faith purchaser for value takes goods free of most claims of aggrieved prior owners.

Article 2 rejects title as a basis for assigning the risk of loss. More pertinent are factors such as who is likely to insure the goods and who has actual control of the goods. The risk-of-loss rules of Article 2 assign loss on the basis of such practical considerations.

STUDY AND DISCUSSION QUESTIONS

1 Explain how and why Article 2 departs from common law rules with regard to *(a)* an offer for a unilateral contract and *(b)* a firm offer.

2 What difference does it make whether an auction is with reserve or without reserve *(a)* Legally? *(b)* Economically?

3 *(a)* Under Article 2, what is the legal significance of characterizing an acceptance as "reasonable"? *(b)* Is a letter of acceptance a reasonable response to a telegraphed offer for the sale of goods?

4 How and why does Article 2 depart from common law rules with regard to *(a)* counterof-

fers? *(b)* shipment of nonconforming goods as an acceptance?

5 *(a)* Why does Article 2 permit open terms in offers for the sale of goods? *(b)* By what legal test will a court determine whether an agreement for the sale of goods is sufficiently certain to be enforced as a contract? *(c)* In accordance with what general standard are open terms in contracts to be filled under Article 2?

6 *(a)* In what ways may the Article 2 statute of frauds be satisfied? *(b)* If a writing is used to satisfy the statute of frauds, what must the writing contain?

7 Explain how the Article 2 parol evidence rule would be applied by a court.

8 Upon what basis are agreements to alter sales contracts enforceable under Article 2? Discuss the roles, if any, of consideration and good faith.

9 *(a)* What is the significance of being a good faith purchaser for value? *(b)* How does the Code meaning of "purchaser" differ from the ordinary meaning? *(c)* What is the significance of being a "buyer in the ordinary course of business"?

10 *(a)* For what matters does location of title remain of importance under Article 2? *(b)* Where there is no agreement between the parties, when does title pass from the seller of goods to the buyer if the goods are shipped by carrier? If the goods are delivered without moving them?

11 What reasoning underlies the Code rules for assigning risk of loss in a sales contract, where the parties are silent as to risk of loss and where neither party is in breach of the contract?

12 Where the parties to a contract are silent as to risk of loss, and where there has been no breach of contract, who bears the risk of loss in the following situations? *(a)* A shipment of goods CIF. *(b)* A return of goods under a sale on approval, where the buyer has not approved the goods. *(c)* A shipment of goods under a sale-or-return, FOB-destination contract, where the goods are lost before they reach the buyer.

13 *(a)* How will a breach of contract affect who bears the risk of loss? *(b)* Where there is a breach of contract, how does insurance coverage affect who bears the risk of loss?

CASE PROBLEMS

1 John Deere Co. repossessed a tractor and advertised it for sale at public auction. The advertisement stated that the tractor would be sold to the highest bidder. Drew bid $1,500, but the auctioneer did not accept the bid; instead, he announced that John Deere had itself bid $1,600, and accordingly the property was "struck down" to John Deere. Drew contends that the auction was without reserve and that John Deere was required to sell the tractor to Drew, the highest lawful bidder. *(a)* Under Section 2-328(3), was the auction without reserve? *(b)* If there is doubt, how might the court hold?

2 Jack and Virginia Brewer were negotiating with McAfee for the purchase of furniture in a house they had bought from McAfee. On April 30, 1971, McAfee sent the Brewers a letter containing a list of furniture he had offered to sell to them, a payment schedule for a total of $8,635 with $3,000 as the first payment, a blank space for the Brewers' signatures, and a clause reading, "If the above is satisfactory please sign and return one copy with the first payment." On June 3, 1971, the Brewers sent the following letter to McAfee: "Enclosing a $3,000 ck.—I've misplaced the two copies of the contract. We're moving into the house on June 12. Please include the red secretary on the contract." McAfee responded with a letter dated June 8, 1971, in which he listed again the furniture itemized in his letter of April 30. The list did not include the red secretary. Had the Brewers accepted the April 30th offer?

3 Dangerfield was a potato buyer, and Markel was a potato farmer. Dangerfield alleged that Markel had breached an oral contract for the sale of 25,000 hundredweight (cwt) of potatoes from the 1972 crop by failing to deliver 15,000 cwt. In court proceedings, Markel filed an answer in which he alleged that Dangerfield had failed to provide for delivery of the 15,000 cwt of potatoes and had failed to make timely payment for the 10,000 cwt of potatoes delivered, thus breaching any agreement. The specified price for the 25,000 cwt of potatoes was in excess of $500. Has the Article 2 statute of frauds (Section 2-201) been satisfied?

4 Dana Debs, Inc., a dress and suit manufacturer in New York City, received a written order from Lady Rose Stores, Inc., Westbury, Long Island, for the purchase of 288 garments. The order was on Lady Rose's printed form, and it advised Dana Debs to "ship via Stuart, 453 W. 57th St., New York City." Stuart Express Co., Inc., picked up the shipment. Later Stuart wrote Dana Debs that the entire shipment had been lost and that Stuart's limit of liability was $1.00 per garment, as indicated in the bill of lading. Dana Debs, the seller, then informed Lady Rose Stores of the loss and presented a bill for $1,756.80, the amount of the loss. Lady Rose contended that a destination contract had been created, and that risk of loss therefore could not pass to Lady Rose until Stuart tendered delivery at the destination. Was this a destination contract?

5 In September 1968, Crump purchased from Lair Distributing Co. a television antenna and tower for the price of $900.00, payable in consecutive monthly installments of $7.50 for 10 years. To secure the payments Crump executed a conditional sales contract. The contract provided that until the full purchase price was paid title would remain in Lair and that Crump would not move the tower and antenna from his premises except with the written consent of Lair. The antenna system was installed by Lair on the premises of Crump, and Crump had uninterrupted use of the system until June 1969, when it was struck by lightning and was severely damaged. Crump contended that Lair should bear the loss. Crump's argument was that he had never been in possession of the antenna system because he was prohibited from moving it from his premises; that not being in possession, he did not "receive" the system according to Section 2-509(3); and that therefore the risk of loss had not passed to him. Did Crump "receive" the antenna system?

6   Klein, a wholesale jeweler, and Lopardo, a retail jeweler, had a long-standing business relationship whereby Klein would deliver jewels to Lopardo, who would sell the jewels to retail customers and pay Klein the agreed price. If unable to sell the jewels, Lopardo would return them to Klein. Approximately 10 days after Lopardo received two diamonds, they were stolen from his jewelry store. Who should bear the loss?

Prior to the industrial revolution, goods produced for sale were relatively simple products, and buyers of such goods usually purchased them directly from the makers. The buyer was expected to examine the goods and to judge for himself whether they were free from defects and fit for his purpose. The idea that the buyer must protect himself from injury became the policy of the common law of contract: caveat emptor ("Let the buyer beware"). Under the law of that era, a person injured by a defective product could not maintain an action for damages unless he or she was "in privity of contract" with the seller. If purchases were made directly from the manufacturer, the privity-of-contract requirement would be met.

During and after the industrial revolution, the doctrine of caveat emptor began to make

less and less sense. Mass production led to the use of middlemen and mass advertising. Increasingly, goods were distributed in packaged form by people who knew little about their quality. Products became vastly more complicated and dangerous. No longer could purchasers easily inspect and judge for themselves the merits of what they bought. A seller's exaggerations became dangerous because purchasers of unfamiliar products were no longer able to question the manufacturer personally, or to recognize false statements if made.

Despite increased danger to the public from defective products, the courts were slow to discard the privity-of-contract requirement. As the use of middlemen increased, the privity requirement became a substantial barrier to the recovery of damages by injured consumers.

Their contracts would normally be with retailers, not with manufacturers, and without privity of contract there could be no recovery of damages from the manufacturers who had produced the defective goods.

During the early 1900s the courts began to deny the validity of the doctrine of privity of contract. In the leading case of *MacPherson v. Buick Motor Co.*, 111 N.E. 1050 (N.Y. 1916),[1] Justice Cardozo stated the principle that the manufacturer of a product had a duty to make the product carefully and that this duty would be owed even to users other than the purchaser; that is, an injured person could have a cause of action against the manufacturer for negligence, even though there was no contract between that person and the manufacturer.

During recent decades, court decisions and legislation (especially the Uniform Commercial Code) have made dramatic changes in the law with respect to who should bear the cost of injury resulting from the use of defective products. The law has developed a number of theories of "product liability" that shift the burden of loss from the injured buyer, user, or bystander to the manufacturer, the wholesaler, or the retailer, and the privity requirement has been virtually abandoned. The most common causes of action available to the injured person are based on negligence, warranty, or "strict liability in tort." Frequently, these causes of action are alleged in the same complaint. If one cause of action does not fit the situation, the plaintiff might succeed with another.

The first part of this chapter is devoted to a brief discussion of negligence as a basis of product liability. The last two parts are devoted to warranties and strict liability as bases of product liability.

NEGLIGENCE AS A BASIS OF PRODUCT LIABILITY

Elements of Negligence

A defendant is liable in negligence if the plaintiff proves four traditional elements of negligence:

1 A duty of care on the part of the defendant—i.e., a duty to conduct oneself reasonably in light of a foreseeable risk of harm to others.

2 A failure of the defendant to exercise due care.

3 A reasonably close causal connection between the misconduct and the resulting injury.

4 Actual loss to the plaintiff.[2]

In negligence and in other product liability cases, the defendant is usually a manufacturer, a distributor, or some other supplier of goods.

The courts have developed a number of tests for determining when a duty of care arises. A manufacturer producing "inherently dangerous" goods, such as explosives or poisons, has a duty to foresee possible dangers of various kinds and to take reasonable measures to prevent harm. Under the *MacPherson* decision a duty of care arises where a thing, if negligently made, may reasonably be expected to cause injury. Under other decisions, a duty of care arises if the goods are to be directly consumed, if the manufacturer can anticipate danger from the normal use of a product, or if the manufacturer can anticipate danger from the use that actually occurred. Under the latter two tests, a manufacturer of caustic drain cleaner could be liable for failure to explain how to use the cleaning material safely, or for failure to provide a safety cap for the protection of children playing with the can. Retailers and other suppliers of goods have duties of care commensurate with the degree of

---

[1]MacPherson had purchased a Buick from a retail dealer and was injured when a defective wheel collapsed. MacPherson sued Buick Motor Co., alleging negligent failure to inspect the wheel. A judgment for MacPherson was affirmed by the New York Court of Appeals.

[2]William L. Prosser, *Handbook of the Law of Torts*, West Publishing Company, St. Paul, Minn., 1964, p. 146. Negligence is discussed in more detail in Chapter 6.

danger they should foresee as retailers or other suppliers.

Negligent conduct takes a variety of forms. Liability has been found for negligent design of a product; for negligent inspection or assembly of parts; for negligent inspection of a finished product; for negligent testing of a product before, during, or after production; and for negligent packaging. Other typical forms of negligence are failure to give adequate instructions for the use of a product, failure to warn of known dangers, and representations made negligently as to the effectiveness of a product.

Limited Usefulness of Negligence as a Basis of Product Liability

From the injured plaintiff's point of view, negligence as a theory of product liability may be useless in some situations. The plaintiff must prove that the defendant's conduct violated a duty of care. Acquiring such proof may require examination of the defendant's manufacturing process or similar matters. Defendants may be reluctant to provide necessary information, and

compelling the provision of such information, if possible at all, can become costly.

Sometimes the requisite causal connection between a particular defendant and the plaintiff's injury cannot be proved. Establishing that a soft drink bottle exploded and injured a shopper does not constitute proof that the bottle manufacturer caused the injury. The injury-causing condition might have occurred while the bottle was in the custody of the wholesaler or the retailer. In a proper case, the doctrine of *res ipsa loquitur* ("the thing speaks for itself") may place upon a defendant the burden of proving that he or she was not negligent. However, the doctrine is not universally available, and its availability usually is premised upon the defendant's exclusive control of the instrumentality that caused the injury. To avoid the difficulties of proof inherent in a negligence suit, or to avoid the defenses of contributory negligence, assumption of risk, or comparative negligence, the plaintiff may decide to pursue a theory of product liability other than negligence.

Case 26.1   Larsen v. General Motors Corp.
391 F.2d 495 (8th Cir. 1968)

FLOYD R. GIBSON, C. J. The plaintiff . . . Larsen received severe bodily injuries while driving, with the consent of the owner, a 1963 Chevrolet Corvair on February 18, 1964. . . . A head-on collision, with the impact occurring on the left front corner of the Corvair, caused a severe rearward thrust of the steering mechanism into the plaintiff's head. . . .

The plaintiff does not contend that the design caused the accident but that because of the design he received injuries he would not have otherwise received or, in the alternative, his injuries would not have been as severe. The rearward displacement of the steering shaft on the left frontal impact was much greater on the Corvair than it would be in other cars that were designed to protect against such a rearward displacement. . . .

The District Court for the District of Minnesota [applying Michigan law] rendered summary judgment in favor of General Motors on the basis that there was no common law duty on the manufacturer "to make a vehicle which would protect a plaintiff from injury in the event of a head-on collision" and dismissed the complaint. A timely appeal was filed. . . .

General Motors . . . views its duty as extending only to producing a vehicle that is reasonably fit for its intended use . . . and that is free from hidden defects; and that the intended use of a vehicle . . . [does] not include its participation in head-on collisions or any other type of impact, regardless of the manufacturer's ability to foresee that such collisions may occur.

The plaintiff maintains that General Motors' view of its duty is too narrow and restrictive and that an automobile manufacturer is under a duty to use reasonable care in the design of the automobile to make it safe to the user for its foreseeable use and that its intended use or purpose is for travel on the streets and highways, including the possibility of impact or collision with other vehicles or stationary objects. . . .

There is a line of cases directly supporting General Motors' contention that negligent design of an automobile is not actionable, where the alleged defective design is not a causative factor in the accident. . . .

. . . Since *MacPherson v. Buick Motor Co.*, the courts have consistently held a manufacturer liable for negligent construction of an automobile. The Courts, however, have been somewhat reluctant to impose liability upon a manufacturer for negligent product design in the automotive field. [The court discussed a number of cases which deny liability in the manufacturer for a variety of reasons, but which nevertheless recognize a duty of care in the design of motor vehicles.]

[In] *Ford Motor Company v. Zahn*, 265 F.2d 729 (8th Cir. 1959), . . . the plaintiff lost [the] sight of one eye on being thrown against a defectively designed ash tray having a jagged edge. The ash tray had nothing to do in a causative way [with] setting up an emergency braking situation, which in turn projected the plaintiff into the ash tray, but the Court recognized a duty to use reasonable care in design, recognized the foreseeability of injury resulting from a defective ash tray so placed, and also recognized the duty resting on the manufacturer to make reasonable inspections or tests to discover defects. . . .

Generally . . . the manufacturer has a duty to use reasonable care under the circumstances in the design of a product but is not an insurer that his product is incapable of producing injury, and this duty of design is met when the article is safe for its intended use and when it will fairly meet any "emergency of use" which is foreseeable. This doctrine has even been extended to cover an unintended use where the injury resulting from that unintended use was foreseeable or should have been anticipated. . . .

We think the "intended use" construction urged [in the present case] by General Motors is much too narrow and unrealistic. Where the manufacturer's negligence in design causes an unreasonable risk to be imposed upon the user of its products, the manufacturer should be liable for the injury caused by its failure to exercise reasonable care in the design. These injuries are readily foreseeable as an incident to the normal and expected use of an automobile.

While automobiles are not made for the purpose of colliding with each other, a frequent and inevitable contingency of normal automobile use will result in collisions and injury-producing impacts. [Statistics omitted.] . . .

This duty of reasonable care in design rests on common law negligence. . . . The Michigan case of *Piercefield v. Remington Arms Company, Inc.*, 375 Mich. 85, 133 N.W.2d 129 (1965), applied the doctrine of strict liability in tort, and gave effect in a case involving a defective shotgun shell, to an implied warranty that a product is reasonably fit for the use intended. We, however, think the duty in this evolving field of law should and can rest, at this time, on general negligence principles, with each state free to supplement common law liability for negligence with a doctrine of strict liability for tort as a matter of social policy expressed by legislative action or judicial decision. The National Traffic and Motor Vehicle Safety Act of 1966 will result in the establishment of minimum safety standards the violation of which may constitute negligence per se. . . .

General Motors, in arguing against what it views as an expanded duty of . . . care in design, makes the statement that this duty "must be considered in its application to all products. Automobile manufacturers cannot be made a special class." With this we quite agree. . . . The courts have imposed this duty perhaps more readily against other manufacturers than against the automotive industry. We, therefore, do not think the automotive industry is being singled out for any special adverse treatment by applying to it general negligence principles in (1) imposing a duty on the manufacturer to use reasonable care in the design of its products . . . and (2) holding that the intended use of automotive product contemplates its travel on crowded and high speed roads and highways that inevitably subject it to the foreseeable hazards of collisions and impacts. . . .

On the second count of plaintiff's petition alleging negligence in failure to warn of an alleged dangerous condition in vehicle design the same principles would apply. We think a cause of action is alleged and that under the law the manufacturer has a duty to inspect and to test for designs that would cause an unreasonable risk of foreseeable injury. . . . [K]nowledge of a defective design gives rise to the reasonable duty on the manufacturer to warn of this condition.

. . . Where the danger is obvious and known to the user, no warning is necessary and no liability attaches for an injury occurring from the reasonable hazards attached to the use of chattels or commodities; but where the dangerous condition is latent it should be disclosed to the user, and non-disclosure should subject the maker or supplier to liability for creating an unreasonable risk. . . . Admittedly, [General Motors] would not sell many cars of this particular model if its sales "pitch" included the cautionary statement that the user is subjected to an extra hazard or unreasonable risk in the event of a head-on collision. But the duty of reasonable care should command a warning of this latent defect that could under certain circumstances accentuate the possibility of severe injury.

General Motors contends that any safety standards in design and equipment should be imposed [only] as envisioned by the National Traffic and Motor Vehicle Safety Act of 1966. . . . Section 108(c) of the Act . . . reads: "Compliance with any Federal motor vehicle safety standard issued under this subchapter does not exempt any person from any liability under common law."

It is apparent that the National Traffic Safety Act is intended to be supplementary of and in addition to the common law of negligence and product liability. The common law is not sterile or rigid and serves the best interests of society by adapting standards of conduct and responsibility that fairly meet the emerging and developing needs of our time. The common law standard of a duty to use reasonable care in light of all the circumstances can at least serve the needs of our society until the legislature imposes higher standards or the courts expand the doctrine of strict liability for tort. The Act is a salutary step in this direction and not an exemption from common law liability.

. . . [W]e reverse and remand for proceedings not inconsistent with this opinion.

WARRANTIES AS A BASIS OF PRODUCT LIABILITY

Much of the law of warranty is found in Article 2 of the Uniform Commercial Code (as modified by recent federal legislation). The warranty provisions of Article 2 are limited by their terms to sales of goods, but as indicated in Chapter 24, those provisions have been applied "by analogy" to some transactions other than sales, such as leases of goods.

Originally, the term "warranty" meant a promise or agreement by the seller that the thing sold had a certain level of quality, or that the seller had title to the thing and could confer ownership upon the buyer. Today, warranties created by the seller's promises or other affirmations of fact are called "express" warranties. Article 2 recognizes express warranties of title and express warranties of quality.

After the industrial revolution, courts began to impose warranty obligations upon the seller without regard to whether the seller intended to make a warranty. Warranties that are imposed by law are called "implied" warranties. Under Article 2, sellers can be subject to implied warranties of quality. Most sellers are also subject to a nonverbal warranty of title under Article 2, but for the reason stated later in this chapter, the nonverbal title warranty is not classified as an implied warranty.

The principal function of a warranty is to establish the characteristics of a thing (kind of ownership or level of quality) to which the purchaser or some other person is entitled as a result of the existence of the warranty. In a sale of goods, a warranty may be the only practical source of remedy for loss due to a defect in the title to or the quality of the goods. A plaintiff is entitled to damages upon proof that a warranty was made (or imposed by law), that the product does not conform to the standard of title or quality established by the warranty, and that the plaintiff suffered harm as a result of the breach of the warranty.

In the following discussion of title and quality warranties, special attention is given to how warranties are made; what kind of ownership or level of quality is established by a warranty; how a seller may exclude warranties; and who, besides the buyer, is protected if a warranty is made.

Warranties of Title

Nature and Scope of Title Warranties If a seller says to a buyer, "I own these goods free and clear," the seller probably has made an express warranty of title under Section 2-313 of the Code. But usually the parties to a sale are silent as to title. If the parties are silent, Section 2-312(1) imposes upon the seller a warranty that "(a) the title conveyed shall be good, and its transfer rightful; and (b) the goods shall be delivered free from any security interest or other lien or encumbrance of which the buyer at the time of contracting has no [actual] knowledge."

Sometimes goods are manufactured and sold in violation of trademark or patent rights. To protect the buyer, Section 2-312(3) imposes upon a merchant seller "regularly dealing in goods of the kind" a warranty that the goods do not infringe upon the trademark or patent of any third party. On the other hand, if a buyer furnishes specifications for goods to be assembled, prepared, or manufactured by the seller, the buyer is responsible for avoiding infringement. The buyer "must hold the seller harmless against any such claim which arises out of compliance with the specifications." The obligations imposed by a warranty against infringement may be varied by agreement of the parties to the sale.

Exclusion or Modification of Title Warranties A seller usually may exclude warranties, but the seller must give notice of the exclusion to the buyer, and the notice must be sufficient to avoid unfair surprise. Sometimes goods are sold "as is" or "with all faults." Section 2-316(3) permits sellers to disclaim "all implied warranties" by the use of such expressions. Are these expressions sufficient to exclude the nonverbal warranty of good title, rightful transfer, and freedom from encumbrances? The answer is no. A person who buys something "as is" may be willing to take his or her chances as to the quality of the thing, but the buyer still expects to become the owner. To protect the buyer from an unexpect-ed exclusion of the nonverbal warranty of title, Article 2 limits the meaning of implied warranty to "implied warranty of quality."

A seller who wishes to exclude the nonverbal warranty of good title must do so under Section 2-312(2). Under that section, the nonverbal warranty of good title may be excluded or modified "only by specific language or by circumstances which give the buyer reason to know that the person selling does not claim title in himself, or that he is purporting to sell only such right or title as he or a third person may have." The "specific language" requirement could be met by the seller's statement that the seller does not warrant title, or that the seller warrants title only to a limited extent. However, the buyer is expected to recognize the fact that in certain circumstances sellers do not warrant title. For example, sales by sheriffs, executors, and foreclosing lienors "are so out of the ordinary commercial course that their peculiar character is immediately apparent to the buyer . . . ; no personal obligation is imposed upon the seller who is purporting to sell only an unknown or limited right" [2-312, comment 5].

Warranties of Quality

Whether express or implied, a warranty of quality establishes a level of quality to which goods must conform if the seller is to avoid liability for breach of warranty. The level of quality established by an express warranty is determined by the seller's statements or other representations. The level of quality established by an implied warranty is measured by the concept of "merchantability" or of "fitness for a particular purpose."

The Code permits a seller to disclaim all implied warranties or, if the seller wishes, to substitute for an implied warranty a less burdensome express warranty. Yet the nature of the marketing process, certain features of the Code, the Magnuson-Moss Warranty Act, and the growing tendency of courts to resolve warranty doubts in favor of consumers limit the opportunities for a seller to escape warranty liability altogether.

Express Warranties of Quality A seller may refrain from making express warranties, but express warranties can arise in ways that the seller might not anticipate. Under Section 2-313(1)(a), "Any affirmation of fact or promise made by the seller to the buyer which relates to the goods and becomes part of the basis of the bargain creates an express warranty. . . ." Any seller who advertises goods is subject to having the advertising claims construed as factual, and some courts have held that a retail seller has adopted the statements made by the manufacturer, even though the retailer personally has said nothing concerning the goods.

Under the Code an express warranty can arise without any verbalization whatever. Any description of the goods (including drawings and sketches) or any sample or model "which is made part of the basis of the bargain" creates an express warranty that the goods will conform to the description, sample, or model [2-313(1)(b) and (c)]. Even a seller who silently adopts specifications furnished by the buyer makes an express warranty that the goods will conform to the specifications. As long as business people make normal use of advertising, models, samples, and descriptions, express warranties are likely to be made.

An express warranty must rest on some statement or other affirmation of fact, not upon mere "sales puffing" of the seller. Despite the strong movement away from caveat emptor, the buyer is expected to detect and discount such nonfactual seller's talk as "a good coat, will wear very good," and "his father was the greatest living dairy bull."[3] Statements made by sellers may range from those that are clearly opinion to those that are clearly fact. In the middle are statements that a court may have to interpret as either fact or opinion. The background against which a statement was made becomes important in interpreting it. Thus, a former garage mechanic who sold a used car to a nurse was held to have made an express warranty when he stated, "This is a car I can recommend . . . it is in A-1 shape."[4]

Under the Code's "basis of the bargain" test, postsale talk may, and often does, create an express warranty. Even though an affirmation is made after a contract has been entered into, the affirmation may create expectations that the product will do what the seller promised. A buyer who opens a carton and reads descriptive information may be led to make a use of the product that he or she would not have made if the seller had remained silent. The statement should be regarded as an indicator of quality level and as an aspect of the bargain.[5] "The precise time when words of description or affirmation are made or samples are shown is not material" [2-313, comment 7]. What is material is whether the description or affirmation of fact in some way defined the quality level of the product. Under the "basis of the bargain" test, assurances that were given at the time of the delivery of the goods, and advertisements that were read after the sale, could create express warranties.

Implied Warranties of Quality Unless warranties are properly excluded, the Code imposes an implied warranty of merchantability, or an implied warranty of fitness for a particular purpose, or both. The warranties differ with regard to who makes the warranties, how the warranties are made, what quality level is established by the warranties, and how the warranties may be disclaimed.

Implied warranty of merchantability Under section 2-314(1), "a warranty that the goods shall be merchantable is implied in a contract for their sale if the seller is a merchant with respect

---

[3]From cases cited in Lawrence Vold, *Handbook of the Law of Sales*, West Publishing Company, St. Paul, Minn., 1959, p. 431.

[4]*Wat Henry Pontiac Co. v. Bradley*, 210 P.2d 348 (Okla. 1949).

[5]Robert J. Nordstrom, *Handbook of the Law of Sales*, West Publishing Company, St. Paul, Minn., 1970, p. 209.

to goods of that kind." The serving of meals by hotels or restaurants had been considered a service by some pre-Code courts. Because contracts for services carried no warranties, a customer injured by unfit food had to seek redress in an action for negligence. Under Article 2 of the Code, "the serving for value of food and drink to be consumed either on the premises or elsewhere is a sale" subject to the warranty of merchantability if the seller is a merchant [2-314(1)]. A seller is a merchant if he deals in goods of the kind sold or if he holds himself out as having knowledge of the goods. Normally, a "person making an isolated sale of goods is not a 'merchant,'" and therefore is not subject to the implied warranty of merchantability. However, the nonmerchant seller of goods is required by the good faith provision of the Code to disclose any material hidden defects of which he or she has knowledge.

Section 2-314(2) establishes minimum standards of merchantability. Fungible goods must be "of fair average quality within the description." All goods must "pass without objection in the trade under the contract description"; be "fit for the ordinary purposes for which such goods are used"; "run . . . of even kind, quality, and quantity within each unit and among all units"; be "adequately contained, packaged, and labeled as the agreement may require"; and "conform to the promises or affirmations of fact made on the container or label if any."

Other attributes of merchantability may arise by usage of trade or through the development of case law. Goods are not usually "fit" for their ordinary purposes unless they can be used safely. The degree of safety required for a product to be considered merchantable is developed in the case law. Some courts hold that goods may be fit for their ordinary purposes even though a few persons suffer allergic reactions or other isolated injuries not common to ordinary people.[6] Whatever the precise meaning of merchantable quality may be, the warranty of merchantability is not breached unless the goods fall below the required level of quality.

---

[6]*Robbins v. Alberto-Culver Co.*, 499 P.2d 1080 (Kan. 1972).

Case 26.2   **Williams v. Braum Ice Cream Stores, Inc.**
15 UCC Rep. 1019 (Okla. App. 1974)

REYNOLDS, J. Plaintiff [Williams] brought this action . . . for breach of implied warranty of merchantability. Defendant's motion for summary judgment was granted. Plaintiff appeals from that ruling.

The uncontroverted facts in the case show that plaintiff purchased a "cherry pecan" ice cream cone from defendant's retail store. . . . Plaintiff ate a portion of the ice cream, and broke a tooth on a cherry pit contained in the ice cream. Plaintiff notified defendant of her injury and subsequently filed this action.

The trial court held that a cherry seed or pit found in ice cream made of natural red cherry halves was a substance natural to such ice cream, and [that] as a matter of law defendant was not liable for injuries resulting from such a natural substance.

There is a division of authority as to the test to be applied where injury is suffered from an object in food or drink sold to be consumed on or off the premises. Some courts hold there is no breach of implied warranty on the part of a restaurant if . . . the substance found in the food is natural to the ingredients of the type of food served. This rule, labeled the "Foreign-natural test" by many jurists, is predicated on the view that the practical difficulties of separation of ingredients in the course of food preparation (bones from meat or fish, seeds from fruit, and nutshell from the nut meat) is a matter of common knowledge. Under this . . . theory, there may be a recovery only if the object is "foreign" to the food served. . . .

The other line of authorities hold that the test to be applied is what should "reasonably be expected" by a customer in the food sold to him.

Section 2-314 provides in pertinent part as follows:

> "(1). . . a warranty that the goods shall be merchantable is implied in a contract for their sale if the seller is a merchant with respect to goods of that kind. Under this section the serving for value of food or drink to be consumed either on the premises or elsewhere is a sale. (2) Goods to be merchantable must be at least such as . . . (c) are fit for the ordinary purposes for which such goods are used. . . ."

The defendant is an admitted "merchant."

In *Zabner v. Howard Johnson's Inc.*, 201 So.2d 824 (Fla. 1967), the court held:

> "The 'Foreign-natural' test as applied as a matter of law by the trial court does not recommend itself to us as being logical or desirable. The reasoning applied in this test is fallacious because it assumes that all substances which are natural to the food in one stage or another of preparation are, in fact, anticipated by the average consumer in the final product served. . . . Categorizing a substance as foreign or natural may have some importance in determining the degree of negligence of the processor of food, but it is not determinative of what is unfit or harmful in fact for human consumption. A nutshell natural to nut meat can cause as much harm as a foreign substance, such as a pebble, piece of wire or glass. All are indigestible and likely to cause injury. Naturalness of the substance to any ingredients in the food served is important only in determining whether the consumer may reasonably expect to find such substance in the particular type of dish or style of food served."

The "reasonable expectation" test as applied to an action for breach of implied warranty is keyed to what is "reasonably" fit. If it is found that the pit of a cherry should be anticipated in cherry pecan ice cream and guarded against by the consumer, then the ice cream was reasonably fit under the implied warranty.

In some instances, objects which are "natural" to the type of food but which are generally not found in the style of the food as prepared, are held to be the equivalent of a foreign substance.

We are not aware of any appellate decision in Oklahoma dealing with this precise issue.

We hold that the better legal theory to be applied in such cases is the "reasonable expectation" theory, rather than the "naturalness" theory as applied by the trial court. What should be reasonably expected by the consumer is a jury question, and the question of whether plaintiff acted in a reasonable manner in eating the ice cream is also a fact question to be decided by the jury. . . .

Reversed and remanded.

[Certiorari to review the decision of the Court of Appeals was denied by the Supreme Court of Oklahoma. 534 P.2d 700 (Okla. 1975).]

Implied warranty of fitness for a particular purpose A warranty of fitness for a particular purpose is implied where, at the time of contracting, two circumstances exist: (1) the seller has reason to know any particular purpose for which the goods are required, and (2) the seller has reason to know that the buyer is relying on the seller's skill or judgment to select or furnish suitable goods [2-315]. A particular purpose "envisages a specific use by the buyer. . . . For example, [ordinary] shoes are generally used for the purpose of walking upon ordinary ground, but a seller may know that a particular pair [of ordinary shoes] was selected to be used for climbing mountains" [2-315, comment 2]. If the seller also has reason to know that the buyer is relying on the seller to furnish suitable shoes, and if the buyer actually does rely on the seller's judgment, a warranty that the shoes are fit for mountain climbing is implied. Merchants and nonmerchants alike can be subject to an implied warranty of fitness.

An increasing number of judges hold that advertising can contribute to the existence of an implied warranty of fitness. A seller who advertises his product expects to persuade buyers that the product is suitable for a certain purpose or purposes. Many sellers also expect to create "brand loyalty" by convincing the buyer that the seller's product is superior to the products of competitors. Sellers who engage in brand-loyalty advertising may well have reason to know of the buyer's particular purpose and of the buyer's reliance on the seller to provide suitable goods. In a context of intense competition and flamboyant advertising, a warranty of fitness might be implied even though the seller never meets the buyer.

Under an implied warranty of fitness, the goods are defective if not fit for the particular purpose for which the goods were furnished. But how is the minimum level of fitness for a particular purpose to be defined? Is a lotion unfit if one user out of millions is allergic to ordinarily safe ingredients? The difficult question, as yet unresolved, is how much harm is tolerable, given the general utility of a product. Most courts hold that a product is fit if it is safe for use by "normal" people. This approach works well enough when the number of unusually sensitive users is very small and their injuries are slight. If injury is widespread or severe, the court could find a breach of the warranty of fitness, find the seller negligent (e.g., for failure to provide conspicuous warnings), or impose strict liability. The problem of defining the minimum level of quality exists also with regard to the warranty of merchantability.

Case 26.3   Swan Island Sheet Metal Works, Inc. v. Troy's Custom Smoking Co., Inc.
619 P.2d 1326 (Ore. App. 1980)

Peter Troy, president and owner of Troy's Custom Smoking Co. (Troy's) asked Swan Island Sheet Metal Works, Inc. (Swan Island) to manufacture two stainless steel crab cookers. The cookers were to be modeled after a crab cooker that Troy's already owned, and were to use gas burners. Troy explained to Bader, president of Swan Island, the use of the cooker and some of the special needs a crab cooker must satisfy. The fabrication of the cooker presented no problems for Swan Island. Bader informed Troy, however, of his lack of knowledge of gas or gas burners. Both men agreed that Swan Island should seek outside expert advice on the design of the burner. Subsequently, Bader told Troy that he could not duplicate the burner on the old cooker and sent Troy a brochure illustrating the type of burner that had been selected by the experts Bader had consulted. The first cooker was delivered to Troy's Beaverton store.

Crab is cooked by dropping it into boiling water, allowing the water to recover to a rolling boil, and then boiling the crab for ten minutes. If the recovery time exceeds ten minutes, or if the cooker cannot sustain a rolling boil, the crab is immersed too long in hot water and the finished product is unmarketable.

Soon after delivery, Swan Island received complaints from Troy's concerning the cooker's performance. The cooker cooked crab too slowly, and the pilot light and burner were difficult to light and keep lit. In attempting to use the cooker, Troy's ruined 1,200 lb. of crab. The cooker never worked properly. Eventually, Troy's returned it to Swan Island without paying for it. Swan Island (plaintiff) brought an action for the price of the cooker, and Troy's (defendant) counterclaimed for damages arising from an alleged breach of an implied warranty of fitness for a particular purpose. The trial court awarded defendant $2,950 in damages. Swan Island appealed.

WARREN, J. . . . The following three conditions are necessary to create a warranty of fitness for a particular purpose: (1) The seller must have reason to know the buyer's particular purpose. (2) The seller must have reason to know that the buyer is relying on the seller's skill or judgment to furnish appropriate goods. (3) The buyer must, in fact, rely upon the seller's skill or judgment. [Citation.]

Plaintiff's major contention is that defendant did not rely on the plaintiff's expertise to furnish a suitable product.

The existence of a warranty of fitness for a particular purpose depends in part on the comparative knowledge and skills of the parties. There can be no justifiable reliance by a buyer possessing equal or superior knowledge or skill with respect to the product purchased by him. Since both Bader and Troy admitted ignorance of the design of gas burners, plaintiff argues, there could be no justifiable reliance by defendant on plaintiff's expertise.

It is uncontested, however, that defendant relied on plaintiff to assemble the expertise necessary to select a suitable burner and design its placement relative to the crab pot. We conclude that where, as here, the parties expressly agree that the seller will seek outside expert advice with respect to the selection and design of a product to be purchased by the buyer, and the buyer relies on the seller to do so, the requirement of reliance . . . is satisfied. Such reliance by

Case 26.3
Continued
the buyer is reasonable. Commercial necessity also justifies such reliance, since a manufacturer must often consult outside specialists on the design and incorporation of component parts into a larger product built and sold by the manufacturer.

Swan Island also argues that Troy's merely relied on it to duplicate an existing crab cooker supplied by Troy's as a model and, therefore, did not rely on Swan Island's skill and judgment. When goods are manufactured in accordance with specifications supplied by the buyer, there is no warranty of fitness for a particular purpose, because the buyer does not rely on the seller's skill or judgment. Here, however, Swan Island did not simply follow Troy's specifications, since a different burner had to be substituted due to the unavailability of a burner to match the one on the old crab cooker.

Swan Island contends that there was no evidence that it was aware of the particular problems unique to cooking crab, and thus that it had no reason to know the particular purpose for which the cooker was required. Bader's testimony indicates, however, that at the time of contracting he was aware that the cooker required certain controls and that a rapid recovery time was essential in order for the cooker to fulfill its intended purpose. . . .

Affirmed.

Exclusion   or   Modification   of   Quality Warranties Once made, an *express* warranty is difficult to disclaim. Section 2-316(1) states a general principle that words or conduct creating an express warranty, and words or conduct negating warranty, shall be construed wherever reasonable as consistent with each other, but that "negation or limitation is inoperative to the extent that such construction is unreasonable." Suppose that S, a used car dealer, makes an express oral warranty in the sale of a used car to B. If the contract that B signs contains a disclaimer of "all warranties, express or implied," the disclaimer will be inoperative. S has taken the trouble to make an express warranty that is calculated to capture B's attention. To give effect to S's disclaimer of his own express warranty would be an unreasonable action.

What if S makes an express oral warranty, but the contract disclaims all warranties and further states that the writing is the final and exclusive expression of the agreement? Will the parol evidence rule of Section 2-202 prevent proof of the oral warranty? It might, but B might be able

to demonstrate that she did not agree that the writing should be considered final and exclusive. Under Section 2-202, the parties must agree. Litigation of this issue is difficult, because at its heart is the credibility of B and S on questions of fact, including the question of whether S actually made the express warranty.[7]

The *implied* warranties of quality may be excluded in either of two principal ways: (1) by the buyer's examining the goods or refusing to examine the goods, or (2) by the use of appropriate exclusionary language. If the buyer examines the goods (or a sample or model) before entering the contract, there is no implied warranty with regard to defects which an examination ought in the circumstances to have revealed to the buyer. Nor is there an implied warranty as to obvious defects if the seller demands that the buyer examine the goods, but the buyer refuses. Making goods available for inspection does not constitute a demand. The seller must

---

[7]Nordstrom, op. cit., p. 215.

make clear that the buyer is assuming the risk of defects which the examination ought to reveal. Exclusion by examination applies only to obvious defects, not to hidden defects; and it applies only to implied warranties, not to express warranties on which the buyer clearly indicates he or she is relying.

Except in certain situations governed by the Magnuson-Moss Warranty Act, a seller who wishes to disclaim implied warranties by using exclusionary language may do so in either of two ways. One, all implied warranties may be excluded by using "expressions like 'as is,' 'with all faults' or other language which in common understanding calls the buyer's attention to the exclusion of warranties and makes plain that there is no implied warranty . . ." [2-316(3)(a)]. Two, implied warranties may also be excluded by complying with the provisions of Section 2-316(2). Under that subsection, an *implied warranty of merchantability* may be excluded orally or by a writing, but the exclusionary language must mention merchantability. If the disclaimer is written, the language of disclaimer must be "conspicuous."[8] Under the same subsection, an *implied warranty of fitness* can be excluded only by a conspicuous writing, but the exclusionary language may be general. A con-

spicuous general statement, such as "There are no warranties which extend beyond the description on the face hereof," is sufficient to exclude an implied warranty of fitness.

Strict compliance with the warranty exclusion provisions of the Code is not always sufficient to exclude an implied warranty. Some courts have held that certain attempts at exclusion are against public policy. In the pre-Code case of *Henningsen v. Bloomfield Motors*, 161 A.2d 69 (N.J. 1960), all automobile manufacturers doing business in New Jersey had adopted the same printed disclaimer of implied warranties and had substituted a "parts only" express warranty. Automobile buyers could not negotiate with the manufacturers for a more extensive warranty. The Supreme Court of New Jersey held that under these circumstances, an attempt by Bloomfield Motors to disclaim an implied warranty of merchantability was against public policy and was therefore invalid. A few courts interpreting the Code have reached similar conclusions, usually on the ground that an attempted disclaimer is unconscionable. With regard to "consumer products," the Magnuson-Moss Warranty Act prohibits or limits the exclusion of implied warranties where a warranty has been made in writing.[9]

---

[8]Conspicuous is defined in sec. 1-201(10).

[9]The statute is discussed on pp. 531–532.

Case 26.4   Century Dodge, Inc. v. Mobley
272 S.E.2d 502 (Ga. App. 1980)

Mobley purchased a new car from Century Dodge, Inc., and later discovered that the car had been involved in an accident. Unable to resolve his differences with Century, Mobley filed a four-count complaint. Count 1 alleged that Century had breached an implied warranty of merchantability and fitness. Count 2 alleged a breach of an express warranty by Century that the automobile purchased by Mobley was new. Counts 3 and 4 alleged fraud and deceit. The contract of sale described the car as "new" and contained a disclaimer of all warranties, express or implied.

The trial court directed a verdict in favor of Century on Counts 1, 2, and 4.

Case 26.4
Continued

Mobley obtained a jury verdict on Count 3, which alleged fraud in the sale of the car, and was awarded $1,750 general damages, $3,575 punitive damages, and $3,575 attorney fees. Century appealed, and Mobley filed a cross-appeal, contending that it was error for the trial court to dismiss Counts 1, 2, and 4. Holding that the trial court had erred on a point of evidence law, the appellate court reversed the judgment for Mobley on Count 3. The court then discussed Mobley's cross-appeal.

SOGNIER, J. . . . Count 2 is a claim for breach of an express warranty that the car Mobley purchased was new, when in fact it had been involved in an accident. We are aware that the contract contained a disclaimer of all warranties, express or implied. We are also aware of the cases upholding such a provision and barring recovery for breach of contract (based on express or implied warranties) when the purchaser has acknowledged such a disclaimer by signing the contract. [Citations.] Under these holdings a purchaser must rely on an action in tort, based on fraud and deceit. Nevertheless, this case differs from those cited because the car purchased was described as new in the contract. Section 2-313(1)(b) provides: "Any description of the goods which is made part of the basis of the bargain creates an express warranty that the goods shall conform to the description." Since the description of the vehicle as new becomes an express warranty under this section, we must turn to Section 2-316(1) as a guide in resolving the conflict between the express warranty and a disclaimer of such warranty in the contract. Section 2-316(1) provides: "Words or conduct relevant to the creation of an express warranty and words or conduct tending to negate or limit warranty shall be construed wherever reasonable as consistent with each other; but subject to the provisions of this Article on parol or extrinsic evidence . . . negation or limitation is inoperative to the extent that such construction is unreasonable."

Applying this rule to the facts of the instant case, we hold it is unreasonable to allow an express warranty contained in a contract (the description as "new") to be negated by a disclaimer of warranty in the same contract, for the two provisions are not consistent with each other. Hence, Mobley's cause of action in Count 2 is not defeated by the disclaimer of warranty. Since the question of whether the car was new is one of fact, it should have been submitted to the jury. Thus, it was error for the court to direct a verdict for Century as to Count 2 of the complaint.

Count 1 of Mobley's complaint was based on an *implied* warranty, and here, the disclaimer thereof would prevail. . . . Count 4 was merely repititious of Count 3 wherein he sued in tort for fraud and deceit. Hence, the trial court was correct in granting a directed verdict as to Counts 1 and 4 of the complaint.

. . . Judgment [on the cross-appeal] affirmed in part and reversed in part. . . .

Cumulation and Conflict of Warranties

Cumulation of Warranties In a sale of goods, a number of warranties may exist concurrently. For example, a merchant seller can be subject to a warranty of title, a warranty against infringement of a patent or a trademark, an implied warranty of merchantability, and an implied warranty of fitness for a particular purpose. In addition, any number of express warranties can be created, including express warranties of merchantability and fitness. To the extent that these express and implied warranties are consistent with one another, the buyer receives an accumulation of express and implied assurances [2-317]. If a warranty of any kind is excluded, the seller remains subject to all warranties that were made or imposed but that were not excluded.

Conflict of Warranties Suppose that a building contractor is interested in a new type of high-strength concrete building block. The contractor inspects a sample, reads the results of a laboratory test conducted by the manufacturer, and purchases from the manufacturer a large quantity of the blocks. The blocks that are delivered conform in strength to the sample but not to the laboratory test results supplied to the buyer as a part of the sales promotion. Which warranty prevails—the one arising from the sample, or the one arising from the test results?

Where there is a conflict of warranties, the intention of the parties determines which warranty is dominant. As an aid in determining that intention, Section 2-317 states three tentative "rules" of construction for the guidance of the court: (1) exact or technical specifications displace an inconsistent sample or model or general language of description; (2) a sample from an existing bulk displaces inconsistent general language of description; and (3) express warranties displace inconsistent implied warranties other than an implied warranty of fitness for a particular purpose. In the situation described in the preceding paragraph, the contractor is entitled to blocks that conform in strength to the specifications stated in the laboratory report.

Third-Party Beneficiaries of Quality Warranties

Suppose that manufacturer M sells a golf cart to wholesaler W, who sells it to retailer R, who sells it to B, who presents it as a gift to her husband H. The cart has a hidden defect that causes it to overturn on a slight grade, injuring H and a bystander X (a stranger) and damaging the golf clubs of both H and X. M, W, and R are merchants, and none has excluded the warranty of merchantability. To whom do the warranties of M, W, and R run? Section 2-318, as amended in 1966, provides three alternative provisions, labeled Alternative A, Alternative B, and Alternative C. Most states have adopted Alternative A or some version of it, and some states have adopted Alternative B or C, or some variation. California has not enacted the section, but relies instead on other consumer law.

The purpose of Section 2-318 is "to give certain beneficiaries the benefit of the same warranty which the buyer received in the contract of sale, thereby freeing such beneficiaries from any technical rules as to 'privity'" [2-318, comment 2]. Although the three alternatives have a common purpose, they differ with regard to who may be a beneficiary, and with regard to the kinds of injury for which a beneficiary may receive a remedy.

Alternative A provides:

A seller's warranty whether express or implied extends to any natural person who is in the family or household of his buyer or who is a guest in his home if it is reasonable to expect that such person may use, consume or be affected by the goods and who is injured in person by breach of the warranty.

This alternative permits recovery of damages only for personal injury, not for injury to property. Bystanders, nonfamily members, and guests in automobiles are unprotected, unless the court is willing to include them in the protected class by some process of interpretation.

Alternative B broadens the class of beneficiaries to whom a seller's warranty extends. The warranty "extends to any natural person who may reasonably be expected to use, consume, or be affected by the goods and who is injured in person by breach of the warranty." To make clear that a seller's warranty does extend to the beneficiaries, Alternatives A and B both provide that "a seller may not exclude or limit the operation of this section."

Alternative C is a variation of Alternative B. It differs from Alternative B in two ways. One, Alternative C extends a seller's warranty to "any person" (not merely to a "natural person") who may reasonably be expected to use, consume, or be affected by the goods. Two, Alternative C permits a beneficiary to recover damages for injury to property (as well as for injury to the

person), unless the seller excludes or limits liability for injury to property. With regard to personal injury, a seller may not exclude or limit the operation of Alternative C.

The drafters of the Code did not intend, by providing Alternatives A, B, and C, to restrict the development of case law regarding third-party beneficiaries of quality warranties. In the case that follows, the Supreme Court of Pennsylvania, in an exercise of its judicial power to impose warranty liability, extends warranty protection beyond that provided by the Pennsylvania legislature.

| Case 26.5 | **Salvador v. I.H. English of Philadelphia, Inc.**
319 A.2d 903 (Pa. 1974) |

ROBERTS, J. In *Kassab v. Central Soya*, 432 Pa. 217, 246 A.2d 848 (1968), this court abolished the requirement of vertical privity in actions for breach of warranty. Today the question is whether the doctrine of horizontal privity should likewise be abandoned.[*] We conclude that the theoretical foundation which once supported horizontal privity has been undermined; we hold that lack of horizontal privity itself may no longer bar an injured party's suit for breach of warranty.

Allegedly as a result of the explosion of a steam boiler on May 22, 1967, at his place of work, Ahmed Salvador [plaintiff] suffered the loss of approximately 77 percent of his ability to hear. On March 29, 1971, Salvador filed a summons in assumpsit naming as defendants his employer, the retail seller of the boiler, and . . . the manufacturers of the exploding steam boiler. A complaint was filed on February 3, 1972, and the manufacturers filed preliminary objections. . . . The trial court sustained the preliminary objections and dismissed the complaint in assumpsit because plaintiff . . . did not allege a contractual relationship with [the manufacturers] and thus horizontal privity was lacking.[†] . . . [T]he Superior Court reversed. That court reasoned that the thrust of *Kassab* was the desire to reach the same result in a lawsuit arising from particular facts whether the action is brought in trespass [tort] or

---

[*Privity is "vertical" if the reference is to the distribution chain: Manufacturer-wholesaler-retailer-buyer (M-W-R-B). Privity is "horizontal" if the reference is to nonpurchaser users or to bystanders.]

[†The Pennsylvania legislature had adopted Alternative A of sec. 2-318. Under Alternative A, a seller's warranty of quality extends to "any natural person who is in the family or household of his buyer or who is a guest in his home."]

assumpsit [contract]. [In this case Salvador's suit in trespass may have been barred by the two-year personal injury statute of limitations.] Concluding that the adoption of section 402A of the *Restatement (Second) of Torts* eliminates the logical basis for both vertical and horizontal privity, the Superior Court held that the *Kassab* rationale dictated abolition of the horizontal privity requirement in breach of warranty actions. [The Superior Court reinstated Salvador's complaint, and the manufacturer appealed.] We affirm [reinstatement of the complaint].

In *Hochgertel v. Canada Dry Corp.*, 409 Pa. 610, 187 A.2d 575 (1963), plaintiff, engaged in his duties as a bartender, was injured by flying glass when a bottle of carbonated soda exploded. He sued Canada Dry, the manufacturer, alleging breach of implied warranties. Because Hochgertel was neither the purchaser, a member of the purchaser's family, nor a guest in purchaser's home, this court held that he could not establish any horizontal privity relationship with the manufacturer. Hence he could not recover.

That decision was based on the Uniform Commercial Code, Section 2-318, "A seller's warranty whether express or implied extends to any natural person who is in the family or household of his buyer or who is a guest in his home if it is reasonable to expect that such person may use, consume or be affected by the goods and who is injured in person by breach of the warranty. . . ."

Although this court determined that Hochgertel as an employee was "definitely in none of these [Section 2-318] categories," it nevertheless recognized that the Code was not dispositive. "Since the Code was not intended to restrict the case law in this field . . . a study of pertinent Pennsylvania authorities is also necessary for the purposes of this decision." [Section 2-318, comment 3 states, "This section expressly includes as beneficiaries within its provisions the family, household, and guests of the purchaser. Beyond this, the section is neutral and is not intended to enlarge or restrict the developing case law on whether the seller's warranties . . . extend to other persons. . . ."] After examining the relevant case law, this court concluded that no Pennsylvania case had extended warranty protection beyond the class of persons enumerated in Section 2-318. The *Hochgertel* court in 1963 declined to do so.

The limitations imposed by *Hochgertel* were quickly challenged. *Yentzer v. Taylor Wine Co.*, 414 Pa. 272, 199 A.2d 463 (1964), decided only one year later on almost identical facts, permitted recovery. There, plaintiff, a hotel employee, purchased a bottle of champagne manufactured by defendant. It was undisputed that Yentzer was acting as an agent of his employer. While preparing to serve the wine to hotel guests, the cork ejected and struck plaintiff in the eye. The trial court concluded that *Hochgertel* controlled, but this court commented: "We do not think that the rigid construction we placed on a seller's warranty in *Hochgertel* should be extended to a situation such as this." We held that even though he acted as the agent of his employer, because the employee had actually purchased the champagne himself, he was a "buyer." . . .

Between *Yentzer* and the present case several significant developments occurred in Pennsylvania products liability law. In 1966, *Webb v. Zern*, 422 Pa. 424, 220 A.2d 853, adopted section 402A as the law of Pennsylvania. This section imposes liability on the seller or manufacturer of a defective product regardless of the lack of proven negligence or the lack of contractual relation [vertical privity] between the seller and the injured party. On the same day, this court issued its opinion in *Miller v. Preitz*, 422 Pa. 383, 221 A.2d 320 (1966), reaffirming the requirement of vertical privity in an action for injuries suffered through a breach of warranty.

Only two years later *Miller* was overruled in *Kassab v. Central Soya*. The Kassabs were purchasers of allegedly defective cattle feed and therefore no question of horizontal privity was presented. The manufacturer . . . , however, argued that it could not be liable because no vertical privity was present, that is, only the retailer and not itself, the manufacturer, had a contractual relation with the plaintiffs.

We noted that our adoption of section 402A in *Webb v. Zern* obliterated any logical basis for retaining the demand for vertical privity. . . .

Kassab dealt only with the issue of vertical privity. The Superior Court nevertheless concluded that *Kassab's* rationale likewise required the abolition of the requirement of horizontal privity in breach of warranty cases. We believe the Superior Court is correct. . . .

Today . . . a manufacturer, by virtue of section 402A, is effectively the guarantor of his products' safety. Our courts have determined that a manufacturer by marketing and advertising his product impliedly represents that it is safe for its intended use. We have decided that no current societal interest is served by permitting the manufacturer to place a defective article in the stream of commerce and then to avoid responsibility for damages caused by the defect. He may not preclude an injured plaintiff's recovery by forcing him to prove negligence in the manufacturing process. Neither may the manufacturer defeat the claim by arguing that the purchaser has no contractual relation to him. Why then should the mere fact that the injured party is not himself the purchaser deny recovery? . . .

Though we must overrule *Hochgertel*, this is not an occasion when a court reexamines its precedents and finding them in error returns to a "correct" view. On the contrary, as we have said, when *Hochgertel* was decided, it was clearly the appropriate accommodation between the law of torts and the law of contracts. Since then Pennsylvania products liability law has progressed, and demands of public policy . . . compel today's decision.

The order of the Superior Court is affirmed.[‡]

[‡It should be noted that the courts of many states give effect to legislative limits on the class of nonpurchasers who may have the benefit of a seller's warranty. The legislative limits on that class are usually found in Alternative A, B, or C of sec. 2-318.]

"Consumer Product" Warranties under Federal Legislation

In 1975 the federal Magnuson-Moss Warranty Act became law.[10] The act differs somewhat from Article 2 of the Code in purpose, scope, and warranty provisions. Some of the warranty provisions of the act supersede some of the warranty provisions of Article 2.

Purpose and Scope of the Magnuson-Moss Warranty Act The Warranty Act has two broad purposes: (1) to improve the adequacy of information available to consumers, prevent deception, and improve competition in the marketing of consumer products, and (2) to encourage warrantors to establish procedures for the informal settlement of disputes with consumers. The act is to be implemented by the Federal Trade Commission through exercise of its rule-making and enforcement powers.

The Warranty Act applies only to consumer products, and only to those consumer products manufactured after January 3, 1975. *Consumer product* means "any tangible personal property which is distributed in commerce and which is normally used for personal, family, or household purposes (including any such property intended to be attached to or installed in any real property . . . .)"[11]

Chief Warranty Provisions of the Act The Warranty Act does not require that a consumer product or any of its components be warranted.[12] However, if a consumer product is warranted in writing, the warranty must, to the extent required by the Federal Trade Commission, fully and conspicuously disclose in simple language the terms and conditions of the warranty. Furthermore, any written warranty must be clearly and conspicuously designated as either a "full warranty" or a "limited warranty,"

unless the warrantor is exempted from the designation requirement by a rule of the Commission.

A warranty is a "full warranty" (and can be so labeled) only if it meets four minimum standards or requirements:

1 Where the product is defective or fails to conform to the written warranty, the warrantor must, without charge, remedy the product within a reasonable time.

2 The warranty may not impose any limitation on the duration of any implied warranty on the product.

3 To be effective, any clause purporting to exclude or limit consequential damages for breach of warranty must conspicuously appear on the face of the warranty.

4 If the product (or a component part) contains a defect or continues to malfunction after a reasonable number of attempts by the warrantor to remedy defects or malfunctions in the product, the warrantor must permit the consumer to elect either a refund of the purchase price or a replacement of the product or part.

If the warrantor replaces a component part, the replacement must include installing the part without charge. A written consumer-product warranty that does not conform to these standards is a "limited warranty."

A full warranty extends from the warrantor to any person who is a consumer with respect to the consumer product. The term "consumer" includes the buyer of a consumer product, any person to whom the product is transferred while its warranty coverage is in effect, and any other person, such as an injured bystander, who is entitled by the terms of the warranty or by state law to the benefit of the warranty.

Extent to Which the Act Supersedes the Code The Warranty Act nullifies conflicting provisions of other warranty legislation. For example, the Code permits the exclusion of implied warranties even where the seller has made a written

---

[10]Magnuson-Moss Warranty–Federal Trade Commission Improvement Act, 15 USCA, secs. 2301–2312.

[11]Ibid., sec. 2301(1).

[12]Ibid., sec. 2302(b)(2).

warranty. Under the Warranty Act, a supplier who makes a written warranty may not disclaim or modify implied warranties. In two situations, the act prohibits entirely the disclaimer or modification of implied warranties: (1) where the supplier makes a full warranty, and (2) where at the time of sale, or within 90 days thereafter, the supplier enters into a service contract with the consumer for the repair or maintenance of the consumer product.[13] Where a supplier makes a *limited* warranty, implied warranties may not be disclaimed or modified as to content. But the supplier may limit the duration of implied warranties to "the duration of a written warranty of reasonable duration, if such limitation is conscionable and is set forth in clear and unmistakable language and [is] prominently displayed on the face of the [limited] warranty."[14] In the sale of a consumer product, these Warranty Act provisions prevail over the conflicting provisions of the Code.

STRICT LIABILITY AS A BASIS OF PRODUCT LIABILITY

Nature and Scope of Strict Liability

Courts use the expression "strict liability" in two senses. In the older sense, *strict liability* means a liability that flows from a breach of a warranty of quality. In its newer sense, and the sense in which the expression is used in this chapter, *strict liability* means a liability based on tort law. Such a liability is often referred to as "strict liability in tort." It is a liability imposed by the law when a defective product has caused injury or when injury results from a justifiable reliance upon a material misrepresentation of the quality of a product. The liability is called "strict" because the plaintiff need not prove "fault" (negligence or fraud) on the part of the defendant. The liability is "in tort" because the existence of the liability does not depend upon the existence of a warranty. Strict liability in tort usually cannot be disclaimed. The ability of sellers to disclaim or otherwise to avoid warranty liability for serious loss explains in large measure the rapid development of strict liability in tort.

Strict liability in tort has had its greatest growth since the early 1960s, when the leading case of *Greenman v. Yuba Power Products, Inc.*, 377 P.2d 897 (Cal. 1963) was decided. In that case, the plaintiff was injured while using a defective power tool that had been purchased by his wife. The court held, "A manufacturer is strictly liable in tort when an article he places on the market, knowing that it is to be used without inspection for defects, proves to have a defect that causes injury to a human being." Section 402A of the *Restatement of the Law of Torts*[15] contains similar language:

> One who sells any product in a defective condition unreasonably dangerous to the user or consumer or to his property is subject to liability for physical harm thereby caused to the ultimate user or consumer, or to his property, if (a) the seller is engaged in the business of selling such a product, and (b) it is expected to and does reach the user or consumer without substantial change in the condition in which it is sold.

This rule applies "although (a) the seller has exercised all possible care in the preparation and sale of his product, and (b) the user or consumer has not bought the product from or entered into any contractual relation with the seller."

Section 402B of the *Restatement* refers to

---

[13]A service contract is "a contract in writing to perform, over a fixed period of time or for a specified duration, services relating to the maintenance or repair (or both) of a consumer product." Ibid., sec. 2301(8).

[14]Ibid., sec. 2308(b).

[15]*Restatement of the Law (Second) Torts*, vol. 2. Copyright © 1965 by The American Law Institute, Philadelphia. Reprinted with the permission of The ALI.

certain situations not necessarily involving a defective product. By advertising, labels, or otherwise, a seller might make to the public "a misrepresentation of material fact concerning the character or quality of a chattel sold by him." A consumer of the chattel who justifiably relies on the misrepresentation and is thereby physically harmed may have a cause of action against the seller. Liability for physical harm flowing from a material misrepresentation is imposed even though the misrepresentation is not made fraudulently or negligently, and even though the consumer has not bought the chattel from or entered into any contractual relation with the seller.

Reasons for Imposing Strict Liability

Judges have stated a number of reasons for imposing strict liability. The reasons most commonly offered include the following. One, users of complex or packaged goods are usually in no position to examine the goods intelligently at the time of purchase, and much advertising is calculated to convince the public that goods may be used safely. Under such circumstances, users of defective goods are especially vulnerable to injury. When a defective product causes injury, the loss should be shifted from the individual to the manufacturer as a cost of doing business. Two, manufacturers are in the best position to distribute loss due to defective products, either by raising the price of their products or by procuring insurance. Three, the imposition of strict liability will exert pressure on manufacturers to police their operations more carefully and to make fewer defective products. Related to these reasons is the tendency of some courts to impose strict liability on everyone in the distribution chain, so that the injured plaintiff will have a better chance of recovering damages. The manufacturer who produced the defective goods may be beyond the reach of the plaintiff, but the manufacturer may be liable to a middleman who has been required to bear the cost of the plaintiff's injury.

Availability of Strict Liability

Strict liability, like the other bases of product liability, is not universally available to injured plaintiffs. The courts of a few states have refused to adopt the doctrine of strict liability in tort. Some of these courts have stated that the decision to adopt strict liability is for the legislature. The courts of certain other states will not impose that doctrine if the plaintiff has suffered only property damage. These courts reserve strict liability for situations involving serious personal injury, preferring to let most product liability matters be governed by the warranty provisions of Article 2, or by other law.[16] Even in situations involving serious personal injury, manufacturers may escape the imposition of strict liability. That doctrine may not apply, for example, where a product has been designated "FOR PROFESSIONAL USE ONLY—NOT FOR PUBLIC SALE," where the manufacturer has sold the product to a professional user, and where the professional user has supplied the product to the injured plaintiff.[17]

However, if strict tort liability is available (as it is in most states) it provides injured plaintiffs with procedural advantages similar to those associated with an action in warranty. The plaintiff may prevail essentially by proving (1) that the doctrine applies to the plaintiff's situation, (2) that the product had a defect when it left the defendant-seller's hands and was unreasonably dangerous to the plaintiff (or that the plaintiff justifiably relied on the defendant's material misrepresentation), and (3) that harm to the plaintiff resulted. Ordinarily, contributory negligence of the plaintiff is not a defense to a suit based on strict liability in tort. But the defendant usually *may* prevail by proving that the plaintiff knew of the defect, understood the danger, and voluntarily assumed the risk.

---

[16]See, for example, *Hawkins Construction Co. v. Matthews Co.*, 209 N.W.2d 643 (Neb. 1973).
[17]*Helene Curtis Industries, Inc. v. Pruitt*, 385 F.2d 841 (5th Cir. 1967), *cert. denied*, 391 U.S. 913 (1968).

Case 26.6   **Martin v. Ryder Truck Rental, Inc.**
353 A.2d 581 (Del. 1976)

The defendant, Ryder Truck Rental, Inc. (Ryder), leased a truck to Gagliardi Brothers, Inc. As a Gagliardi employee was operating the truck, its brakes failed, and the truck struck an automobile which had stopped for a traffic signal. The impact caused the automobile to collide with the vehicle driven by the plaintiff, Dorothy Martin. She was injured, and her car was damaged. She and her husband sued Ryder for damages.

The plaintiffs based their cause of action solely upon the doctrine of strict liability in tort. The Superior Court granted summary judgment in favor of Ryder, holding that the doctrine is not applicable to the factual situation here presented. Plaintiffs appealed.

HERRMANN, C.J. . . . We disagree [with the Superior Court]. We hold today that a bailment-lease of a motor vehicle, entered into in the regular course of a truck rental business, is subject to application of the doctrine of strict tort liability in favor of an injured bystander. . . .

The defendant contends that if the Legislature intended to create a strict liability for bailments for hire, it would have done so in the Uniform Commercial Code. Thus, the threshold question in the instant case is whether, by the enactment of the UCC and the limitation of its . . . warranty provisions to sales, the Legislature has preempted this field of the law of products liability; or whether, the UCC notwithstanding, the courts are free to provide for bailments and leases the alternate, but somewhat conflicting, remedy of strict tort liability.

The warranty provisions of Article 2 . . . are clearly limited to the sales of goods; the statute is "neutral" as to other types of [transactions]. The Official Comment to Section 2-313 reads:

"Although this section is limited in its scope and direct purpose to warranties made by the seller to the buyer as part of a contract for sale, the warranty sections of this Article are not designed in any way to disturb those lines of case law growth which have recognized that warranties need not be confined either to sales contracts or to the direct parties to such a contract. They may arise in other appropriate circumstances such as in the case of bailments for hire. . . . [T]he matter is left to the case law with the intention that the policies of this Act may offer useful guidance in dealing with further cases as they arise."

Manifestly, the Legislature has not preempted, either explicitly or implicitly, the field as to bailments and leases by enactment of the UCC. Hence, we are free, in the common law tradition, to apply the doctrine of strict tort liability to a bailment-lease. The question is whether that course should be adopted; and for that decision, consideration of the nature and evolution of the doctrine is important. Reserved for another day is the question of whether the Legislature has preempted the field as to direct sales cases and whether the warranty provisions of the UCC are, therefore, the exclusive source of strict liability in such cases.

The development of the doctrine of strict tort liability in the law of products liability has evolved rapidly during the past decade, until it has become the prevailing remedy throughout the country. It is now the rule in approximately two-thirds of the states. . . . The doctrine was developed at the outset for application against remote manufacturers for the protection of users and consumers. It has been in a constant state of refinement and extension, however. One of the extensions of the doctrine has been to bailors and lessors; another has been to injured bystanders. . . .

The extension of the doctrine to bailors-lessors has been limited . . . to leases made in the regular course of a rental business. . . . Strict tort liability has been found "peculiarly applicable" to the lessor of motor vehicles in "today's society with 'the growth of the business of renting motor vehicles, trucks and pleasure cars' . . . and the persistent advertising efforts to put one 'in the driver's seat.' " [Citation.]

. . . All of the societal policy reasons leading to the expansion of strict tort liability in sales cases are . . . applicable in this motor vehicle rental case: (1) the concept that the cost of compensating for injuries and damages arising from the use of a defective motor vehicle should be borne by the party who placed it in circulation, who is best able to prevent distribution of a defective product, and who can spread the cost as a risk and expense of the business enterprise; (2) the concept that the defective motor vehicle was placed on the highways in violation of a representation of fitness by the lessor . . . ; and (3) the concept that the imposition upon the lessor of liability without fault will result in general risk-reduction by arousing in the lessor an additional impetus to furnish safer vehicles.

Accordingly, we hold that the doctrine of strict tort liability is applicable to Ryder in the instant case. The remaining question is whether the doctrine is applicable to . . . an injured bystander.

. . . We endorse the rationale of *Elmore v. American Motors Corporation*, 75 Cal. Rptr. 652, 451 P.2d 84 (1969):

> "If anything, bystanders should be entitled to greater protection than the consumer or user where injury to bystanders from the defect is reasonably foreseeable. Consumers and users, at least, have the opportunity to inspect for defects . . . whereas the bystander ordinarily has no such opportunities. . . ."

Bystander recovery is the prevailing rule in the application of the doctrine of strict tort liability by the overwhelming weight of authority. Fairness and

Case 26.6
Continued

logic, as well as the philosophy underlying the doctrine, require that an injured bystander be covered in its application. We so hold.

It is noteworthy that under UCC Section 2-318, an injured bystander may be protected as one "affected by" a defective product in a direct sale situation covered by an implied warranty. Thus, the conclusion reached here is in accord with the public policy underlying Section 2-318. . . .

The judgment below is reversed. . . .

SUMMARY

Prior to the industrial revolution, a person injured by a defective product could not maintain an action for damages unless he or she was in privity of contract with the seller. Since the industrial revolution, a number of theories of product liability have been developed to shift the burden of loss from the injured person to various suppliers of goods, and the privity requirement has been virtually abandoned. Today, the most common causes of action available to the injured person are based on negligence, warranty, or strict liability in tort.

A defendant is liable in negligence if he or she is subject to a duty of care, violates it, and causes harm to the plaintiff. The courts have developed a number of tests for determining when a duty of care arises. The duty can be violated in a variety of ways. However, negligence may be difficult to prove, and it may therefore be less useful than warranty or strict liability as a basis for a lawsuit.

Article 2 of the Uniform Commercial Code provides for warranties of title and warranties of quality. The Article imposes two warranties of title. Unless otherwise agreed, certain merchants are subject to a warranty against infringement of a patent or a trademark. Most sellers are subject to a warranty of good title, rightful transfer, and freedom from encumbrances, unless the warranty is properly excluded.

Quality warranties are classified as express or implied. Any affirmation of fact or promise that relates to the goods and becomes a part of the basis of the bargain creates an express warranty.

An express warranty can be made by showing or adopting a sample, model, or description of the goods.

Article 2 imposes two implied warranties. A warranty of merchantability is implied if the seller is a merchant with respect to goods of the kind sold. This warranty entitles the buyer to goods that are fit for their ordinary purposes. A warranty of fitness for a particular purpose is implied where the seller at the time of contracting (1) has reason to know any particular purpose for which the goods are required and (2) has reason to know that the buyer is relying on the seller's skill or judgment to furnish suitable goods.

A seller may refrain from making express warranties and may exclude implied warranties. Once made, an express warranty is difficult to disclaim. The implied warranties of quality may be excluded in either of two principal ways: by the buyer's examining the goods or refusing to examine them or by the use of appropriate exclusionary language.

A number of warranties may exist at the same time. Under the Code, consistent warranties are cumulative. If warranties are inconsistent, the intention of the parties shall determine which warranty is dominant. A warranty of quality made to a buyer extends also to certain third-party beneficiaries.

The Magnuson-Moss Warranty Act establishes special rules for consumer-product warranties. With regard to consumer products, these rules supersede conflicting provisions of the Uniform Commercial Code and other warranty legislation.

Where a product physically harms a user, the seller may be subject to strict liability in tort. Strict liability may be available where the product is unreasonably dangerous to the user, or where the user has justifiably relied upon the seller's misrepresentation of material fact concerning the nature of the product. One reason commonly offered for the imposition of strict liability is that sellers can best absorb loss and spread it as a cost of doing business.

STUDY AND DISCUSSION QUESTIONS

1 *(a)* With respect to privity of contract, what general change has taken place during the evolution of product liability law? *(b)* Briefly state the reasons for this change.

2 *(a)* What are the elements of negligence? *(b)* As a basis of product liability, negligence might be of limited usefulness to injured plaintiffs. Why?

3 *(a)* What is the principal function of a warranty of title or quality? *(b)* What must a plaintiff prove to obtain damages for loss due to breach of a warranty?

4 *(a)* How may warranties of title be made? *(b)* What ownership attributes may a buyer be assured of under a warranty of title? *(c)* Explain why a nonverbal warranty of title is not classified as an implied warranty under the Code. *(d)* How may nonverbal warranties of title be excluded?

5 *(a)* How may an express warranty of quality be made? *(b)* What would be the best way to avoid the liability that can result from an express warranty? *(c)* Is this method of avoiding liability compatible with normal business practices? *(d)* Describe the problem that exists with regard to express oral warranties and the parol evidence rule.

6 Compare the implied warranty of merchantability with the implied warranty of fitness for a particular purpose with regard to *(a)*

method of creation; *(b)* quality level assured; and *(c)* method of exclusion.

7 *(a)* Suppose a seller orally states, "I do not warrant these goods." What warranties, if any, have been made? *(b)* Give an example of cumulated warranties. *(c)* Illustrate inconsistent warranties and explain how the inconsistency would be resolved under Section 2-317.

8 *(a)* Explain the purpose of Section 2-318. *(b)* Compare Alternatives A, B, and C of Section 2-318 with regard to the class of people protected; the kind of injury protected against.

9 *(a)* What are the purposes of the Magnuson-Moss Warranty Act? *(b)* Explain the meaning of "full warranty" and "limited warranty." *(c)* To what extent does the Warranty Act supersede provisions of the UCC? *(d)* Under what circumstances (and to what extent) does the Warranty Act limit the right granted by Article 2 to exclude implied warranties?

10 *(a)* What is the meaning of "strict liability in tort"? *(b)* The *Restatement of the Law of Torts* describes two principal situations in which strict liability may be imposed. What are these two situations? *(c)* What reasons are commonly offered for the imposition of strict liability in tort?

CASE PROBLEMS

1 Associated Grocers delivered a pallet of produce to the back room of Thriftway Market. On top of the stack of produce was a cardboard box of Chiquita brand bananas. The bananas were unwrapped and the box contained breather holes. On the day of the delivery, Anderson, the produce manager, removed the box of bananas from the top of the stack. When he reached for a lug of radishes that had been under the bananas, a 6-inch "banana" spider leaped from some wet burlap onto his left hand and bit him. Not long thereafter, Anderson died. Assume that Anderson's death was caused by the bite of the spider.

Is Associated Grocers liable to Anderson's estate for Anderson's death? Discuss *(a)* negligence; *(b)* breach of the implied warranty of merchantability; and *(c)* strict liability.

2 Kemin Industries, Inc., manufactured a chemical preparation called "Improved Hay Savor." Its advertised purpose was to retard mold growth in baled hay and to reduce heating so that the hay could be baled at higher moisture levels than would otherwise be possible. The advertising literature specified a moisture level of 25 percent or less before baling. Bigelow purchased Hay Savor from Agway, Inc., the distributor, and sprayed his hay with the chemical. Later, Nelson, a sales representative of Kemin Industries, accompanied Bigelow into the fields where unbaled hay lay drying. The hay contained 32 to 34 percent moisture, ordinarily too much for safe baling. Nelson represented that the hay was safe for baling inasmuch as the hay had been sprayed with Hay Savor. Bigelow then baled the hay despite his better judgment that it was still too green. The hay was placed in the center section of the barn, where a fire later broke out as a result of spontaneous combustion of the wet hay. The hay and the barn were destroyed. Bigelow sued Kemin Industries and Agway, alleging breach of an express warranty that Hay Savor would make the treated hay safe to bale. Kemin contends that it made no warranty because Nelson's statements were made after the sale and therefore could not have been a part of the basis of the bargain. Did Kemin make an express warranty?

3 Holden Chemical Corp. ordered a set of rocker panels, an automobile part, from J. C. Whitney & Co. A rocker panel is a pressed steel panel approximately 6 inches wide, 60 inches long, and one sixteenth of an inch thick. The ends are uneven and form sharp, angular projections. The panels were inserted in a long rectangular cardboard carton without any covering or sheathing, and the ends of the carton were sealed with adhesive tape. The package contained no warning that the ends of the rocker panels were unprotected. Earl Pugh, an employee of Holden Corp., seriously injured his thumb when he reached inside the package to remove the panels. Pugh had never before opened a package of this kind, and he had never seen a rocker panel as a part separate from an automobile. Pugh sued Whitney for breach of the implied warranty of merchantability. Had the warranty been breached?

4 In 1959 a foreman in the Indianapolis plant of Standard Brands, Inc., was killed by the explosion of a large commercial cream separator. The bowl, a 338-pound rotating mass, turned at 6,175 r/min during normal operation. The top and bottom parts of the bowl were held together by a carbon-steel coupling ring. In 5 years of use, the coupling ring had corroded so badly that its original weight of 21½ pounds had diminished to 6¼ pounds. The ring had been soaked nightly in a hot acid solution for one-half hour, scrubbed every Friday with a hot lye solution, and exposed to a 2- or 3-percent salt water solution in the separating operation. De-Laval Separator Co., the manufacturer, had given instructions on cleaning the bowl, but not on cleaning the ring. DeLaval did not advise Standard Brands that the coupling ring might be eaten away by cleaning acids. Between 1960 and 1966 DeLaval had replaced about 80 coupling rings for various customers, including several plants of Standard Brands. Of 10,000 such rings manufactured by DeLaval, this was the first to fail. The executor of the foreman's estate sued DeLaval for negligence and for breach of an implied warranty of fitness. At the close of the case, the trial court directed a verdict for DeLaval under both the negligence and the implied warranty counts. Should the trial court's decision be reversed *(a)* as to the negligence count? *(b)* as to the implied warranty count?

5 In 1961 Hunt purchased a new diesel engine for his fishing boat. The engine, when running, gave off excessive quantities of heavy black smoke that caused the boat to become dirty. Perkins Machinery Co., the seller, was unable to correct the smoking condition. Hunt had the engine removed and sued Perkins for damages, alleging breach of the implied warranty of merchantability. In bold type on the face of the purchase order for the engine were the words, "BOTH THIS ORDER AND ITS ACCEPTANCE ARE SUBJECT TO 'TERMS AND CONDITIONS' STATED IN THIS ORDER." On the back of the order appeared the words "TERMS AND CONDITIONS." Under those words were eleven numbered paragraphs. The third paragraph stated in part, "SELLER MAKES NO WARRANTIES (INCLUDING . . . ANY WARRANTIES AS TO MERCHANTABILITY . . .) EITHER EXPRESS OR IMPLIED." The purchase order had been prepared by Perkins's sales manager from a pad of forms separated by carbon paper. Hunt did not read anything on the back of the order when he signed it. Perkins contended that the disclaimer of warranties was conspicuous, and that the warranty of merchantability was therefore excluded. Was the disclaimer conspicuous?

6 In 1970 Salvatore Realmuto purchased a used 1965 automobile from Straub Motors, Inc. During a road test the motor sputtered. The sales representative said the trouble was caused by the carburetor. A rebuilt carburetor was installed. Six days later the accelerator stuck, and in a matter of seconds the car attained tremendous speed and went out of control. The car was demolished and Realmuto was injured. In Realmuto's suit against Straub Motors, the court had to decide whether Straub Motors had made any warranties. On the face of the sales agreement, the sales representative had written, "30-day warranty" (which he said "would cover parts and labor for 30 days. One hundred percent.") The salesperson also had written on the face of the agreement, "Full State Inspection Guarantee" and "Two years' discount 20 percent parts and labor." The back of the agreement contained the following printed language: "It is expressly agreed that there are no warranties, express or implied, made by either the selling dealer or the manufacturer on the motor vehicle, chassis, or parts furnished hereunder. . . ." On these facts what warranties, if any, did Straub Motors make?

7 Harvey was injured, and his antique railroad pocket watch was broken, when an aluminum stepladder upon which he had been standing collapsed. The ladder had been manufactured by Whitelight Industries, Inc., and had been sold by Sears, Roebuck and Company to William White. The ladder had been loaned to Harvey through a series of other persons. Assume that the warranty of merchantability had been breached. *(a)* To what recovery, if any, would Harvey be entitled under Section 2-318, Alternative A? *(b)* Alternative B? *(c)* Alternative C?

Chapter

27

Performance of the Sales Contract; Remedies for Breach of Contract

In a sales transaction, the seller expects to receive the price and the buyer expects to receive the goods. If one party to a sale cannot or will not perform his or her contractual obligations, the other party may suffer inconvenience, monetary loss, or even a serious disruption of business. To minimize the difficulties that can attend the breach of a sales contract, Article 2 of the Uniform Commercial Code provides a number of remedies for the seller and the buyer. These remedies are available upon a breach or a threatened breach of a performance obligation.

The first part of this chapter discusses the performance obligations of the seller and the buyer and the grounds upon which the seller and the buyer may be excused from performance. The second part of the chapter discusses the seller's remedies and the buyer's remedies for a breach or a threatened breach of a sales contract.

PERFORMANCE OF THE SALES CONTRACT

Performance: General Concepts

Obligations of the Parties　Sellers and buyers "perform" by meeting the obligations that they undertake by entering into a contract. In a sale of goods, "The [general] obligation of the seller is to transfer and deliver and that of the buyer is to accept and pay in accordance with the contract" [2-301]. The agreement of the parties, as supplemented or as limited by law, constitutes "the contract" by which the performance obligations of the parties are to be measured.

Meaning of "Tender"　Sellers and buyers meet their performance obligations by making a "tender" of performance. A "tender" is an offer of performance by one party that, if unjustifiably refused, places the other party in default and

540

permits the party making the tender to exercise remedies for breach of contract.[1] The meaning of tender is discussed in more detail later in this chapter.

The Perfect Tender Rule For the protection of buyers, Article 2 adopts the "perfect tender" rule. Under that rule, the buyer may elect to reject the goods if the goods or the tender of delivery fail *in any respect* to conform to the contract [2-601]. The perfect tender rule is intended to protect the buyer from having to debate the sufficiency of an incomplete performance or from having to track down missing documents. The protection afforded by this rule is especially important to buyers who are geographically distant from sellers. However, the perfect tender rule is frequently relaxed by Article 2, for reasons to be discussed later in this chapter.

Seller's Obligation to Deliver

How Seller Meets the Delivery Obligation The seller meets his or her obligation to deliver the goods by making a tender of delivery. Tender of delivery requires that the seller put and hold conforming goods at the buyer's disposition and give the buyer any notification reasonably necessary to enable the buyer to take delivery [2-503(1)]. Goods are "conforming" when they are in accordance with the obligations under the contract, including any warranty obligations. The tender must be at a reasonable hour, and if the tender is of goods, they must be kept available for the period reasonably necessary to enable the buyer to take possession. Unless otherwise agreed, the buyer must furnish facilities reasonably suited to the receipt of the goods.

Tender Requirements for Common Types of Delivery The specific acts required for an effective tender of delivery vary according to the kind of delivery contemplated by the parties to the sales contract. The parties may have specified a particular kind of delivery. Where the parties were silent as to delivery, the kind of delivery may be a matter for a court to decide by applying the Code sections on open delivery terms.[2] Once the kind of delivery has been established, the specific acts required for an effective tender of delivery can be determined by applying the Code sections on tender. The tender requirements for some common types of delivery are discussed in the following paragraphs.

Delivery involving no shipment of goods Often delivery occurs at the seller's place of business. Suppose that B signs a contract to buy from Dealer S a particular motorboat from S's stock of boats, that the motorboat is to be specially equipped from S's stock of accessories, and that the contract says nothing about the time and place of delivery. Under Article 2, S is obligated to make delivery within a reasonable time [2-309(1)]. Since S is a dealer who has a place of business, and since the boat and accessories are located there, the place for delivery is S's place of business [2-308(a) and (b)]. Under Section 2-503(1), S may tender delivery by notifying B within a reasonable time that the boat is ready for pick-up at S's place of business.

Delivery might involve a bailee. Where goods are in the possession of a bailee and are to be delivered without being moved, the seller can fulfill his or her tender obligation by tendering a negotiable document of title covering the goods or by procuring acknowledgment by the bailee of the buyer's right to possession of the goods [2-503(4)(a)]. There are alternative methods of tendering goods that are in the possession of a bailee [2-503(4)(b)]. All documents required for making the tender must be in correct form.

Delivery involving shipment of goods Unless displaced by a contrary agreement, rules

---

[1] UCC sec. 2-503, comment 1.

[2] Secs. 2-307, 2-308, and 2-309 refer to the manner, place, and time of delivery.

of Article 2 govern tender in common types of deliveries involving a carrier. Under a *shipment* contract,[3] the seller fulfills his or her tender obligation by completing four steps. The seller must (1) put conforming goods in the possession of a carrier, (2) make a reasonable contract for their transportation, (3) obtain and promptly deliver or tender in due form any document necessary to enable the buyer to obtain possession of the goods, and (4) promptly notify the buyer of the shipment [2-504]. If the seller fails to notify the buyer of the shipment, or fails to make a proper contract for the transportation of the goods, the buyer may reject the goods—but only if material delay or loss has occurred. These rules place upon the seller the responsibility for arranging suitable transportation. But they also relax the perfect tender rule to protect the seller from harmless error in making the arrangements.

Under a *destination* contract,[4] the seller fulfills the tender obligation by completing three steps. The seller must (1) put and hold conforming goods at destination for the buyer's disposition, (2) give the buyer any notification reasonably necessary to enable the buyer to take delivery, and (3) tender any required documents in correct form [2-503(3)].

---

[3]*Shipment contract* is defined in Chapter 25.
[4]*Destination contract* is defined in Chapter 25.

Seller's Cure of Improper Delivery   A seller may have the right to "cure" an improper tender or an improper delivery. Suppose S sells a power saw to B and promises delivery on or before June 1. S delivers the saw on May 25, but B rejects it because some parts contracted for are missing. S may give notice of his intention to "cure" the nonconforming delivery and then within the contract time may make a conforming delivery [2-508(1)]. Even where S has taken back the nonconforming goods and refunded the purchase price, he may effect cure before the time for performance expires.

Sometimes the right to cure a defective tender may be exercised after the time set for performance. To mitigate the effects of a surprise rejection of goods, Section 2-508(2) provides: "Where the buyer rejects a nonconforming tender which the seller had reasonable grounds to believe would be acceptable with or without money allowance, the seller may, if he seasonably notifies the buyer, have a further reasonable time to substitute a conforming tender." Suppose that B orders Brand X galvanized pipe for delivery at noon on November 1. At the appointed hour S delivers Brand Y pipe of the same kind and quality for the same price. If B rejects the Brand Y pipe, and if S reasonably believed that the delivery of Brand Y pipe would be acceptable, S is entitled to a further reasonable time to effect a cure.

Case 27.1   Hayes v. Hettinga
228 N.W.2d 181 (Iowa 1975)

In 1968, the plaintiff (Hayes) and the defendant (Hettinga) entered into a contract by which Hayes was to custom make two molds—a lid and a cup—to be used in manufacturing plastic containers for a household air freshener. The plaintiff agreed to make the mold for $12,000. The amount of $6,250 was paid down. The balance was to be paid upon completion of the contract. In the meantime, the defendant had entered into an agreement to sell the finished containers to Earl Harmon Products.

From the start, the plaintiff encountered difficulty in fabricating the molds. The runner system which channeled the hot plastic to the mold cavities failed to operate properly, and part of one mold cracked as the result of an imperfect fit between cores and cavities. Some corrective procedures were undertaken. The modified molds then proved to be unsuitable because they were larger than called for by the plans and drawings. Other troubles developed, and corrections were attempted. After each corrective procedure, the molds were tested. Each time the molds proved unsuitable for the defendant's purpose.

Eventually, the plaintiff-seller brought an action for the price of the molds. The trial court held that the plaintiff had failed to manufacture and deliver satisfactory molds. The trial court also held that the defendant-buyer chose after inspection to reject the tender of delivery; that the buyer had properly communicated his rejection and cancellation to the seller; and that, although the plaintiff had been given many opportunitites to cure defects, there was no cure of the defects.

The plaintiff appealed these holdings.

LEGRAND, J. . . . Plaintiff argues that the defendant accepted the molds by failing to reject them within a reasonable time and by using them to produce the containers. He insists the evidence shows without dispute that, first, 5,000 and, later 50,000 of the plastic lids and cups were run off from his molds and accepted by, or at least used for, defendant. . . . We find the evidence is conflicting on these matters in at least two important respects. Concerning the first, when 5,000 of the plastic parts were run off, there is doubt as to whether these were completed for defendant or at the independent request of Earl Harmon Products after the defendant had rejected the tendered molds. Plaintiff simply failed to show defendant authorized production of any parts. As for the later run of 50,000 containers, there is substantial evidence these were not made from plaintiff's molds at all, but were fabricated from entirely different molds made by May Plastics of Kansas City. Plaintiff failed to establish that defendant's acts constituted acceptance under Section 2-606(1)(c).

There is abundant testimony about the numerous imperfections which plaintiff tried to remedy. After each successive effort to correct the molds, additional tests demonstrated they still did not conform. When all efforts to cure had failed, [the plaintiff breached] the contract by failing to manufacture the molds according to the contract specifications or to make delivery of suitable molds to the defendant. . . . The record supports a finding that after several attempts [by the plaintiff] to remedy a defective product, defendant rejected a tender of non-conforming goods. Since time for the performance of the contract had expired, plaintiff no longer had the unfettered right to "cure" pursuant to Section 2-508(1).

Plaintiff, however, might have extended the time for performance and "cure" under Section 2-508(2), thus depriving defendant of his right to reject, if [the plaintiff] had established: (1) he had reasonable grounds to believe the non-conforming tender would be acceptable; he notified defendant of his intent to cure; and (3) he did cure within a "further reasonable time." . . . The evidence fails to disclose any compliance with Section 2-508(2). . . .

Affirmed. . . .

Buyer's Obligation to Accept and to Pay

Where the seller has properly tendered conforming goods, the buyer is obliged to accept them and to pay the price. However, the buyer's obligations are conditioned on a right to inspect the goods. Where a tender of delivery does not substantially conform to the contract, the buyer may have a right to reject the goods or to revoke any acceptance he or she might have made.

Meaning and Effect of Buyer's Acceptance
Acceptance of goods means "that the buyer, pursuant to the contract, takes [as his own] particular goods which have been appropriated to the contract . . . whether he does so by words, action, or silence when it is time to speak" [2-606, comment 1]. Acceptance may occur in a variety of ways: for example, by the buyer's telling the seller that the goods are conforming, or that the buyer will take or retain them in spite of their nonconformity; by the buyer's failure to make an effective rejection; or by the buyer's doing some act inconsistent with the seller's ownership, such as reselling the goods or incorporating building materials into a building [2-606(1)]. If the buyer's act is wrongful, acceptance does not occur (and the buyer commits the tort of conversion) unless the wrongful act is ratified by the seller.

The legal effect of acceptance is that the buyer becomes obligated to pay the contract price [2-607(3)(a)]. Moreover, a buyer who has accepted a *defective* tender is "barred from any remedy," including a remedy for breach of warranty, unless the seller is notified of the defect within a reasonable time after it has been or should have been discovered. Notice is required so that the seller may take steps to cure a defective performance or, where defective goods are alleged to have caused harm, so that the seller may adequately prepare for negotiation or defense of a lawsuit. What constitutes "reasonable" notice depends on the facts of the case. An injured consumer who is unaware of the notice requirement may be allowed more time to give notice than a merchant would be.

Buyer's Right to Inspect the Goods The buyer may make a reasonable inspection of the goods to see whether they conform to the contract. Usually, the right to inspect may be exercised before payment or acceptance. Accordingly, when the seller is required or authorized to send the goods to the buyer, the buyer may take custody of the goods for the purpose of inspection without being considered to have accepted the goods. With rare exceptions, no agreement by the parties can displace the right of inspection.

Even though the right to inspect usually may be exercised before payment, the buyer can be required by contract to pay first and inspect later. Unless otherwise agreed, CIF, COD, cash against documents, and similar clauses require payment before inspection [2-513(3), 2-320(4), and comment 12].[5] Upon inspection after payment, the buyer may, of course, reject nonconforming goods and have appropriate remedies. And even where the contract requires the buyer to make payment before inspection, the buyer may withhold payment "if the non-conformity appears without inspection" [2-512(1)(a)]. The buyer is not required, for example, to pay for goods that obviously are not the goods ordered.

Buyer's Options on Improper Delivery Within limits imposed by the Code, a buyer may reject an improper tender or an improper delivery of goods. In some situations the buyer may revoke acceptance of defective goods.

Rejection of goods In general, a buyer may reject goods that do not conform to the contract. Specifically, the buyer may "(a) reject the whole; or (b) accept the whole; or (c) accept any commercial unit or units and reject the rest"

---

[5]Sometimes a CIF contract contains a clause providing for payment *on or after arrival* of the goods. The presence of such a clause gives the buyer the right to "such preliminary inspection as is feasible" *before* making payment. Sec. 2-321(3). The clause merely postpones the time for payment. It does not, by itself, change the risk of loss consequences of a CIF contract. If the goods do not arrive, payment is due to the seller when the goods should have arrived.

[2-601]. The meaning of commercial unit is discussed in the *Axion* case, which appears later in this chapter.

The rejection must be made within a reasonable time after delivery or tender of the goods, and the buyer *must "seasonably" notify* the seller of the rejection [2-602(1)]. In addition, the buyer must specify the defects upon which the buyer bases the rejection, if those defects are ascertainable by inspection. The requirement that defects be specified is for the protection of the seller's right to cure any curable defects. "A buyer who merely rejects the delivery without stating his objections to it is probably acting in commercial bad faith and seeking to get out of a deal which has become unprofitable" [2-605, comment 2]. Failure to reject in accordance with Code rules results in acceptance and liability for payment.

The buyer's right of rejection is limited by important Code rules regarding installment contracts. An installment contract is one that requires or authorizes the delivery of goods in separate lots to be separately accepted [2-612(1)]. The buyer may reject a nonconforming installment only if the nonconformity "substantially impairs the value of that installment and cannot be cured . . ." [2-612(2)]. Professor Nordstrom[6] explains the reasons for relaxing the perfect tender rule with regard to installment contracts:

---

[6] Robert J. Nordstrom, *Handbook of the Law of Sales,* West Publishing Company, St. Paul, Minn., 1970, p. 314. Quoted with the permission of the publisher.

The privilege of rejection can be a powerful weapon. In a shipment contract the goods will most often be at the buyer's place of business when they are rejected. The seller—who may be hundreds of miles away—will be called upon to determine whether [the] goods . . . are in fact non-conforming. . . . Further, if the perfect tender rule applies, the seller knows that in any lawsuit he will be called upon to prove that the goods and their tender were in complete conformity with the contract. . . . The time and expense involved for the seller may cause a buyer to reject in the hopes of forcing a compromise price. The Code recognizes the interests of the seller by obligating the buyer to take goods even though they do not conform in every respect to the contract; the Code also recognizes the interests of the buyer by requiring the seller to pay damages for his default, no matter how trivial.

An installment contract may require accurate conformity in quality as a condition to the seller's right to the buyer's acceptance, but only if there is a real need for such conformity. To be enforceable, a provision requiring accurate conformity in quality must "have some basis in reason, must avoid imposing hardship by surprise, and is subject to waiver . . ." [2-612, comment 4, par. 1]. A requirement of strictly accurate conformity might be enforceable in a purchase of surgeon's tools or delicate parts for a space shuttle, but not in a purchase of waste logs to be processed into chipboard.

Case 27.2   **Holiday Manufacturing Co. v. B.A.S.F. Systems, Inc.**
 380 F. Supp. 1096 (D. Neb. 1974)

Holiday Manufacturing Co. (plaintiff) contracted to sell six million plastic cassettes loaded with blank magnetic tape to B.A.S.F. Systems, Inc. (defendant). On April 5, 1971 the defendant buyer cancelled the contract because of "continuous quality problems and delivery delays." The plaintiff brought an action for damages for wrongful cancellation. The defendant denied that the cancellation was wrongful, alleging that the plaintiff's failure to produce goods which conformed to the contract caused the defendant substantial monetary loss.

This case involved several issues. The following excerpts from the court's opinion focus mainly on whether the UCC provision regarding the breach of an installment contract applies to the facts of this case.

SCHATZ, Dist. J. The court finds that [Holiday was to supply] six million cassettes at $.14144 per cassette with delivery to begin in April of 1970 at five hundred thousand cassettes per month until [delivery was] completed. This was an installment contract under Section 2-612(1). The court further finds that this was not a contract in which all of the terms were agreed upon at the time of the contract's formation, but one in which the basic terms were reached and [in which] later refinements concerning what would constitute acceptable cassettes were expected.

. . . Section 2-612 of the UCC states as follows:

". . . (a) An 'installment contract' is one which requires or authorizes the delivery of goods in separate lots to be separately accepted, even though the contract contains a clause 'each delivery is a separate contract' or its equivalent.

"(2) The buyer may reject any installment which is nonconforming if the nonconformity substantially impairs the value of that installment and cannot be cured or if the nonconformity is a defect in the required documents; but if the nonconformity does not fall within subsection (3) and the seller gives adequate assurance of its cure, the buyer must accept that installment.

"(3) Whenever nonconformity or default with respect to one or more installments substantially impairs the value of the whole contract, there is a breach of the whole. But the aggrieved party reinstates the contract if he accepts a nonconforming installment without seasonably notifying of cancellation or if he brings an action with respect only to past installments or demands performance as to future installments."

In determining whether B.A.S.F. acted lawfully or unlawfully in cancelling the purchase orders, Section 2-612(3) governs, and gives B.A.S.F. a right to cancel if the "nonconformity or defect with respect to one or more installments substantially impairs the value of the whole contract" for B.A.S.F. . . . As to what constitutes substantial impairment of the value of the contract, authority is scarce. . . . The question is essentially one of fact and must turn upon the particular circumstances in this case. . . .

There is no question that Holiday's cassette manufacturing project was behind schedule from the start, and that at no point during the existence of the contract was Holiday delivering five hundred thousand cassettes per month. However, nowhere in either the correspondence between Holiday and B.A.S.F. or the interoffice correspondence of B.A.S.F. introduced at trial is there any indication . . . that B.A.S.F. was seriously concerned with Holiday's delivery delays. To the contrary, the evidence shows that B.A.S.F.'s chief concern was production of an acceptable cassette and that B.A.S.F. was quite willing to give Holiday ample time to do this. . . . The court concludes that B.A.S.F.'s use of the Holiday sonic-welded cassette was a potentially very profitable business venture and that the delays which occurred in development of this relatively new product by a manufacturer unfamiliar with cassette production were liberally tolerated by B.A.S.F. [Under these circumstances] B.A.S.F. cannot be permitted to urge this nonperformance as a justification for cancelling the contract.

[The court then discussed the "continuous quality problems." The court listed a number of defects in the cassettes, the dates on which the defects were reported, and the dates upon which the defects were corrected.]

Considering only the information listed in these five paragraphs, the issue of whether these five occasions substantially impaired the value of the cassette contract to B.A.S.F. is a close one. For example, on three occasions the defects were not corrected for approximately two months. Moreover, one of the defects discovered in the tests conducted by B.A.S.F. in mid-March of 1971 had occurred previously—i.e., overwidth of the cassettes. But the court cannot look at these factors alone; it must consider all of the evidence introduced at trial. And when all of this evidence is considered, the court is of the opinion that B.A.S.F. was not justified in cancelling the contract.

First, concerning the instances in which over two months were required for Holiday to correct defects, . . . the court finds that B.A.S.F. evidenced no protest or even serious displeasure concerning these delays.

Second, although the overwidth problem had been noted once earlier, this is the only repetition of any significant defect. The situation here is far different from that in *Sunray D-X Oil Co. v. Great Lakes Carbon Corp.*, 476 P.2d 329 (Okla. 1970), cited by B.A.S.F. where the plaintiff-seller delivered goods which were consistently defective *for the same reason* for almost nine months prior to cancellation of the contract by the defendant-buyer, who had repeatedly notified the seller of the defect.

Third, and . . . most persuasive to the court, on February 16, 1971, and March 9, 1971, B.A.S.F. placed with Holiday purchase orders (Nos. 24469 and 24790) for cassettes *identical* to the cassettes under the original purchase order (No. 20080) in all respects except for the fact that they had no knock-out tabs, a feature having no connection whatsoever with any of the defects later discovered. Certainly these actions by B.A.S.F. must be construed to mean that at the time the purchase orders were given, B.A.S.F. had confidence that Holiday could produce acceptable cassettes. The only significant defects reported after this time were the guidehole spacing and the overwidth. . . . [T]he apparent lack of concern by B.A.S.F. over delivery delays, and the ability of Holiday to cure defects generally in the past, are evidence that the nonconformities discovered in the mid-March tests did not substantially impair the value of the contract to B.A.S.F. . . .

The amount of damages to be awarded Holiday because of the wrongful breach of the contract by B.A.S.F. is also governed by the UCC. [The court then went into detail in estimating damages due under UCC provisions.]

. . . [T]he final amount due Holiday from B.A.S.F. is $137,647.88, less $108,494.32, which is $29,153.56. A separate order will be entered this day rendering judgment in accordance with this opinion.

Revocation of acceptance Suppose that Bartley Buyer (B) accepts goods and later discovers that they are defective. In two principal kinds of situations, B may have a right to revoke his acceptance of goods whose nonconformity *substantially impairs* their value to him [2-608(1) and (2)]. He may revoke his acceptance (1) where he accepted the goods on the reasonable assumption that the substantial nonconformity would be cured and it has not been seasonably cured or (2) where his acceptance was reasonably induced either by the difficulty of discovering the substantial nonconformity before acceptance or by the seller's assurances. B may revoke as to the entire lot of goods accepted or as to any subdivision of the lot that constitutes a "commercial unit." Revocation of acceptance must occur within a reasonable time after B discovers or should have discovered the substantial nonconformity. B may not revoke if the goods have undergone substantial change for reasons other than their own defects.

Case 27.3 Axion Corp. v. G.D.C. Leasing Corp.
269 N.E.2d 664 (Mass. 1971)

Axion Corp. (plaintiff-seller) designed and built a valve-setting machine for G.D.C. Leasing Corp. (defendant-buyer). The buyer later placed an order for two more of the machines. In August 1965 the buyer told the seller that the third machine was useless and that the buyer would not pay for it unless it would meet a "plus or minus five percent" specification. The seller then agreed to take back the third machine at the buyer's expense and to work on it. In January 1966, representatives of the buyer went to the seller's plant to conduct a series of tests. The parties do not agree on the meaning of the specification or on what the tests showed. In February 1966, the buyer notified the seller that it was reserving its rights for recovery of its losses and expenses and that the third machine was unacceptable and would not be paid for. The seller brought an action for the price of the machine. At the close of the evidence in the jury trial, the judge allowed the seller's motion for a directed verdict. The buyer excepted (appealed).

BRAUCHER, J. . . . "The buyer must pay at the contract rate for any goods accepted." Section 2-607(1). The parties appear to agree that the buyer accepted the first two machines, but disagree as to whether the third machine was accepted or rejected. The seller argues that the second and third machines, which were ordered together, delivered together, tested together, and complained of essentially as a unit, together constituted one "commercial unit." Hence, it argues, Section 2-606(2) applies: "Acceptance of a part of any commercial unit is acceptance of that entire unit." . . .

Section 2-105(6) defines "commercial unit" as a unit which "by commercial usage is a single whole for purposes of sale, and division of which materially impairs its character or value on the market or in use." . . .

The buyer here first ordered one machine separately. Later, after the second and third machines were ordered and delivered together, the seller took the third back separately to work on it. There is no evidence that there was a commercial usage to treat two machines as a single whole or that division of a pair of machines materially impaired their character or value, or that acceptance of one produced a materially adverse effect on the other. In these circumstances, it could not be ruled as a matter of law that the two machines constituted a single commercial unit, or that one machine was not a commercial unit.

Alternatively, the seller argues that the buyer accepted the third machine by virtue of Section 2-606(1)(b) by failing to make an effective rejection under Section 2-602(1), which provides: "Rejection of goods must be within a reasonable time after their delivery or tender. It is ineffective unless the buyer seasonably notifies the seller." We think this contention is correct. The buyer received the machine on December 22, 1964, and claims to have determined that it was non-conforming shortly thereafter. Notice of rejection was first given on February 2, 1966. As a matter of law, after delay of more than a year, the notification was not "seasonable," and the rejection was not "within a reasonable time."

. . . Since the goods were accepted, the buyer had the burden of establishing breach. Section 2-607(4). If it met that burden, however, it could in proper circumstances revoke its acceptance under Section 2-608. [Under that section],

> "(1) The buyer may revoke his acceptance of a lot or commercial unit whose non-conformity substantially impairs its value to him if he has accepted it (a) on the reasonable assumption that its non-conformity would be cured and it has not been seasonably cured; or (b) without discovery of such non-conformity if his acceptance was reasonably induced either by the difficulty of discovery before acceptance or by the seller's assurances. . . ."

The buyer contends . . . that the machine was non-conforming [and] that the nonconformity substantially impaired its value to the buyer. . . . We agree with the seller's contention that there is insufficient evidence that the alleged nonconformity substantially impaired the value of the machine to the buyer. . . .

The nonconformity on which the buyer relies for substantial impairment of value is failure of the machine to meet the plus or minus five percent specification. The seller's president testified that when tested, the machine met this requirement. The buyer's general manager, who left the buyer's organization in August 1965, testified that the machines performed well and were used in production, that competitive valves would be far less accurate, in general, than those set by these machines, and that the five percent specification was "unreal" and "meaningless." That testimony does not bind the buyer, but we are not directed to any testimony showing how and to what extent failure to meet the specification impaired the value of the machine. There was vague testimony that a valve set too low might become a nuisance and indirectly might bear on safety, and that if set too high a valve might fail to function as a safety device to protect water heaters; but there was no showing of the bearing of the particular specification on these possibilities or on the manufacture or marketing of valves. On this issue the buyer had the burden of proof, and it failed to sustain that burden.

. . . Since the buyer has accepted the goods and has not revoked the acceptance, the seller may recover the unpaid portion of the price. Section 2-709(1)(a). But if the goods were nonconforming, the buyer may have an offsetting claim for damages. Section 2-714. The buyer claims that there were breaches of express warranties, of an implied warranty of merchantability, and of an implied warranty of fitness for a particular purpose. The burden is on the buyer to establish such breaches. Section 2-607(4). [The court held that the seller had made no express warranties. The court also held that the buyer had proved neither the existence of an implied warranty of fitness nor a breach of the implied warranty of merchantability.]

Exceptions overruled.

Buyer's Obligation to Pay for Goods Accepted B meets her obligation to pay the price by making payment in accordance with the contract. If the parties have not stated how payment is to be made, B may pay in any customary manner, unless the seller demands payment in legal tender and gives any extension of time reasonably necessary to procure it [2-511(2)]. Thus, Article 2 protects B from a surprise demand for cash. For the protection of sellers who accept checks, a buyer's payment by check is conditional and is defeated by dishonor of the check on due presentment to the bank upon which the check was drawn [2-511(3)].

If the parties have not stated the time and the place for payment, Section 2-310 provides the rules: (1) payment is due at the time and place at which the buyer is to receive the goods; (2) where delivery is authorized and made by means of documents of title, payment is due at the time and place at which the buyer is to receive the documents, regardless of where the goods are to be received. Both of these rules are subject to any right of the buyer to inspect the goods before payment. If the goods are lost in transit, and if the risk of loss has shifted to the buyer, the buyer is obligated to make payment at the time and place at which he or she was to receive the goods.

Suppose that a foreign seller ships goods to a New York buyer under a CIF contract and the goods are lost at sea. A CIF contract places the risk of loss on the buyer when the seller properly puts the goods in the custody of the carrier. Because the buyer acquires the risk of loss when the carrier receives the goods, the buyer must pay for them despite their nonarrival and must rely on the insurance provided for in the CIF contract.

Where the parties have agreed to an extension of credit, the credit term governs the time, place, and manner of payment, to the extent that the credit term discusses these matters.

Excuse for Nonperformance or Substitute Performance

If the performance of a contractual obligation becomes more burdensome than the obligated party anticipated, that party might ask to be excused from performance. In general, the parties to a contract are excused from their performance obligations when performance has been rendered impossible or unreasonably burdensome by circumstances beyond the contemplation of the parties at the time of contracting.

Excuse for Nonperformance Article 2 adopts "commercial impracticability" as the principal basis for excusing nonperformance of obligations under a sales contract. The Article also provides rules that apply where an agreed method of payment or delivery fails and a substitute method is sought by the aggrieved party.

Commercial impracticability Unless the seller has assumed a greater obligation, the seller is excused for delay in delivery or for nondelivery of goods if performance has been made impracticable by an unexpected occurrence of the type for which the Code and supplementary law give relief [2-615(a)]. The seller is also excused if the agreed performance has been made impracticable by the seller's compliance in good faith with any applicable foreign or domestic governmental regulation or order. Suppose that a manufacturer agrees to make and sell sophisticated electronics equipment to a buyer in a foreign country. If the foreign buyer's government later unexpectedly forbids the importation of such equipment, the manufacturer may be excused from performance.

The drafters of Article 2 explain the meaning of *commercial impracticability* as follows:

Increased cost alone does not excuse

performance unless the rise in cost is due to some unforeseen contingency which alters the essential nature of the performance. Neither is a rise or a collapse in the market in itself a justification, for that is exactly the type of business risk which business contracts made at fixed prices are intended to cover. But a severe shortage of raw materials or of supplies due to a contingency such as war, embargo, local crop failure, unforeseen shutdown of major sources of supply, or the like, which either causes a marked increase in cost or altogether prevents the seller from securing supplies necessary to his performance, is within the contemplation of this section.[7]

The seller's performance may be totally impracticable, or only partially so. Where commercial impracticability partially impairs the seller's capacity to perform, the seller must allocate production and deliveries among his or her customers in a fair and reasonable manner. Regardless of the degree of impairment, the seller will not be excused from performance unless he or she seasonably notifies the buyer that there will be a delay or nondelivery. If there is a partial impairment, the seller must also inform the buyer of any production or delivery quota to which the buyer is entitled.

In response to the seller's notice of a material delay or an allocation of goods, the buyer may, by written notification to the seller, elect to do one of the following: (1) terminate (and thereby discharge) any unperformed portion of the contract or (2) modify the contract by agreeing to take the available quota [2-616(1)]. The buyer may terminate the whole of an installment contract if the seller's deficiency substantially impairs the value of the whole contract. Where a seller is excused from performance because of unforeseen circumstances, the buyer is also excused, despite any agreement to the contrary [2-616(3)].

---

[7]Sec. 2-615, comment 4.

Case 27.4   **Maple Farms, Inc. v. City School District**
352 N.Y.S.2d 784 (N.Y. Sup. Ct. 1974)

In June 1973, the plaintiff (Maple Farms, Inc.) entered a contract with the defendant school district to supply it with milk for the school year 1973–1974. By December 1973, the price of raw milk was 23% higher than the price of raw milk in June. The plaintiff would lose $7,350.55 if required to supply milk at the December price. The defendant refused to relieve the plaintiff of its contract and to put the contract out for rebidding. Faced with losses on similar contracts with other school districts, the plaintiff brought this action for a declaratory judgment. The plaintiff alleged that the performance of the contract with the defendant school district has been made impracticable by the occurrence of events not contemplated by the parties. The plaintiff requested (by means of a motion for summary judgment) that the contract be terminated.

SWARTWOOD, J. The plaintiff [argues that the substantial increase in the price of raw milk] could not have been foreseen by the parties because it came about in large measure from the agreement of the United States to sell huge amounts of grain to Russia and to a lesser extent [from] unanticipated crop failure.

The legal basis of the plaintiff's request for being relieved of the obligation under the contract award is the doctrine known variously as "impossibility of performance" and "frustration of performance" at common law and as "Excuse by Failure of Presupposed Conditions" under the UCC, Section 2-615. . . .

Performance has been excused at common law where performance has become illegal; where disaster wipes out the means of production; [and] where governmental action prevents performance.

In *Mineral Park Land Co. v. Howard*, 172 Cal. 289, 156 Pac. 458 (1916), the defendants agreed to take all the gravel from the plaintiff's land up to a certain quantity. The defendants took only half the agreed amount because the balance of the gravel was under the water level. The court relieved the defendants from the obligation to pay for the balance under water because it was not within the contemplation of the parties that the gravel under the water level would be taken and secondly because the cost of doing so would be ten to twelve times as expensive. The court stated the common law rule at page 460:

> " 'A thing is impossible in legal contemplation when it is not practicable; and a thing is impracticable when it can only be done at an excessive and unreasonable cost.' . . . We do not mean to intimate that the defendants could excuse themselves by showing the existence of conditions which would make the performance of their obligation more expensive than they had anticipated, or which would entail a loss upon them. But, where the difference in cost is so great as here, and has the effect, as found, of making performance impracticable, the situation is not different from that of a total absence of earth and gravel."

. . . [W]here economic hardship alone is involved, performance will not be excused. This is so even where governmental acts make performance more expensive. Existing circumstances and foreseeability also play a part in determining whether a party should be relieved of his contracts.

The Uniform Commercial Code, Section 2-615, states in part:

"Except so far as a seller may have assumed a greater obligation . . . : (a) Delay in delivery or non-delivery in whole or in part by a seller . . . is not a breach of his duty under a contract for sale if performance as agreed has been made impracticable by the occurrence of a contingency the non-occurrence of which was a basic assumption on which the contract was made. . . ."

[The case of *Transatlantic Financing Corp. v. United States** also involved the doctrine enunciated in Section 2-615, "Excuse by Failure of Presupposed Conditions." The court explained the doctrine in these words:]

"The doctrine ultimately represents the ever shifting line, drawn by courts hopefully responsive to commercial practices and mores, at which the community's interest in having contracts enforced according to their terms is outweighed by the commercial senselessness of requiring performance. When the issue is raised, the court is asked to construct a condition of performance based on the changed circumstances, a process which involves at least three reasonably definable steps. First, a contingency—something unexpected—must have occurred. Second, the risk of the unexpected occurrence must not have been allocated either by agreement or by custom. Finally, occurrence of the contingency must have rendered performance commercially impracticable."

Applying these rules to the facts here we find that the contingency causing the increase of the price of raw milk was not totally unexpected. The president of the plaintiff milk dealer has for at least ten years bid on contracts to supply milk for the defendant school district and is thoroughly conversant with prices and costs. The price from the low point in the year 1972 to the price on the date of the award of the contract in June 1973 had risen nearly 10%, and any businessman should have been aware of the general inflation in this country during the previous years and of the chance of crop failure.

However, should we grant that the first test had been met, and thus that the substantial increase in price was due to the sale of wheat to Russia, poor crops and general market conditions which were unexpected contingencies, then the question of allocation of risk must be met. Here the very purpose of the contract was to guard against fluctuation of the price of half pints of milk as a basis for the school budget. Surely had the price of raw milk fallen substantially, the defendant could not be excused from performance. We can reasonably assume that the plaintiff had to be aware of escalating inflation. It is chargeable with knowledge of the substantial increase of the price of raw milk from the previous

*362 F.2d 312 (D.C. Cir. 1966).

year's low. It had knowledge that for many years the Department of Agriculture had established the price of raw milk and that that price varied. It nevertheless entered into this agreement with that knowledge. It did not provide in the contract any exculpatory clause to excuse it from performance in the event of a substantial rise in the price of raw milk. On these facts the risk of a substantial or abnormal increase in the price of raw milk can be allocated to the plaintiff.

. . . [W]here the circumstances reveal a willingness on the part of the seller to accept abnormal rises in costs, the question of impracticability of performance should be judged by stricter terms than where the contingency is totally unforeseen. . . .

There is no precise point . . . at which an increase in price of raw goods above the norm would be so disproportionate to the risk assumed as to amount to "impracticality" in a commercial sense. However, we cannot say on these facts that the increase here has reached the point of "impracticality" in performance of this contract in light of the risks that we find were assumed by the plaintiff.

The plaintiff's motion is denied and the defendant is granted summary judgment dismissing the complaint.

Casualty to identified (specific) goods Sometimes a contract is for a sale of a specific item or lot of goods that is destroyed or damaged before the buyer actually receives the goods. Suppose that S has on display a dozen Brand X refrigerators of a discontinued model. Eleven are green and one is yellow, and no others of that model are available to S. B makes clear that he needs the yellow refrigerator because it fits the color scheme of his kitchen. B buys the yellow refrigerator, but before S can deliver it, it is destroyed by fire. Is S liable to B for failure to deliver the yellow refrigerator?

Under Section 2-613, the answer is "No." Where the contract "requires for its performance [specific] goods identified when the contract is made, and the goods suffer casualty without fault of either party before the risk of loss passes to the buyer . . . , then if the loss is total, the contract is avoided. . . ." If the loss is partial, "the buyer may nevertheless demand inspection and at his option either treat the contract as avoided or accept the goods with due allowance from the contract price . . . but without further right against the seller." Since S is a merchant, the risk of loss does not pass

to B until he actually receives the goods. Because the loss of the yellow refrigerator is total, S has no obligation to tender the refrigerator, and B has no obligation to pay for it. In contrast, if B had purchased *a* refrigerator of the discontinued model (instead of specifying the yellow one), S would be obliged to tender a Brand X refrigerator and B would be obliged to accept it and to make payment. However, if S's entire stock of the discontinued model had been destroyed, S would be excused from performance on the ground of impracticability.

Excuse for Substitute Performance Sometimes the parties to a sales contract agree to a particular method of delivery or payment. What happens if the agreed method fails—for example, if an agreed type of carrier becomes unavailable without the fault of either party? The parties are required to use a commercially reasonable substitute carrier if one is available [2-614(1)]. If there is no commercially reasonable substitute for the agreed method of delivery, both parties may be excused from their performance obligations on the ground of impracticability.

Where the agreed means or manner of payment fails because of domestic or foreign governmental regulation, the seller is required to make delivery only if the buyer provides a payment that is commercially a substantial equivalent [2-614(2)]. Suppose that Sarah Seller contracts to sell refrigerators to a foreign buyer, and that the buyer's government devalues its currency to one-tenth the value it had at the time of contracting. The seller is entitled to a payment substantially equivalent to the payment agreed upon and may refuse delivery if the substantial equivalent is not forthcoming. Where the buyer has already taken delivery of the goods, payment in accordance with the regulation discharges the buyer's obligation unless the regulation is discriminatory, oppressive, or predatory.

REMEDIES FOR BREACH OF CONTRACT

What Constitutes Breach of Contract

Failure to perform a contractual obligation constitutes a breach of contract. However:

> Unless the parties have otherwise agreed, tender of payment by the buyer and tender of delivery by the seller are concurrent conditions. . . . The practical implication of this rule is that the seller is not in default, even though the date set for delivery has gone by, unless the buyer has tendered the price; and the buyer is not in default, even though the date set for the payment of the price has gone by, unless the seller has tendered the goods.[8]

How can the buyer make a tender (and thus put the seller in default) if the seller is not present at the time and place for tender? The Code provides no rules for this kind of situation, but pre-Code law indicates that the buyer needs only to

> . . . prove that at the time and place that the goods were supposed to have been received, the buyer had sufficient funds . . . and that someone was present with authority to tender the payment had the goods arrived. [Under these circumstances] the failure of the seller to deliver is a default for which he may be held liable in damages.[9]

The doctrine of concurrent conditions notwithstanding, either party to the contract can be put in default, or can put himself or herself in default, before the time set for performance. For example, whenever the circumstances surrounding a sale give either party "reasonable grounds for insecurity," the aggrieved party has a right to adequate assurance of due performance [2-609(1)]. Section 2-609, comment 1, explains the reasons for granting this right to the insecure party:

> If either the willingness or the ability of a party to perform declines materially between the time of contracting and the time for performance, the other party is threatened with the loss of a substantial part of what he has bargained for. A seller needs protection not merely against having to deliver on credit to a shaky buyer, but also against having to procure and manufacture the goods, perhaps turning down other customers. Once he has been given reason to believe that the buyer's performance has become uncertain, it is an undue hardship to force him to continue his own performance. Similarly, a buyer who believes that the seller's deliveries have become uncertain cannot safely wait for the due date of performance when he has been buying to assure himself of materials for his

---

[8]Nordstrom, op. cit., p. 292.

[9]Ibid., p. 340.

current manufacturing or to replenish his stock of merchandise.

Suppose that a buyer's lateness in making payments gives the seller reasonable grounds for insecurity. In such a situation, the buyer's ability to produce reasonable evidence of creditworthiness might constitute an adequate assurance of due performance.

Where an adequate assurance is not forthcoming within a reasonable time not to exceed 30 days, the aggrieved party may treat the contract as breached [2-609(4)]. Failure to provide adequate assurance where such assurance is warranted constitutes a "repudiation" of the contract. A repudiation is a statement or other conduct indicating that the repudiating party will not perform when the time set for performance arrives. Upon a repudiation that will substantially impair the value of the contract to the aggrieved party, that party may suspend his or her own performance. In addition, the aggrieved party may await performance for a commercially reasonable time, or take the remedial steps discussed later in this chapter [2-610]. However, the repudiating party may retract the repudiation "unless the aggrieved party has since the repudiation cancelled [the contract] or materially changed his position or otherwise indicated that he considers the repudiation final" [2-611(1)].

Remedies of Seller and Buyer

As a group, the remedies discussed in this chapter are intended to protect the buyer and the seller from three principal kinds of loss. As Professor Nordstrom explains, "On breach of a contract for the sale of goods, three interests of the parties contend for judicial protection. These are the expectation, reliance, and restitution interests. . . ."[10] The *expectation interest* is the gain that the nondefaulting party expected to make had the defaulting party performed.

The *reliance interest* is the interest of the nondefaulting party in recovering costs incurred in preparing for the hoped-for performance. For instance, the seller might have altered machinery solely to fill a special order for the buyer. The buyer might have made special arrangements to accommodate or sell goods that the seller promised to deliver. The *restitution interest* is the interest of the nondefaulting party in recovering a benefit that that party conferred upon the other party. The buyer might have made a prepayment on the price of the goods; the seller might have made a partial delivery.

Under the general law of contracts, a court intends, by granting a remedy for breach of contract, to put the aggrieved party in as good a position as that party would have been in had the contract been performed. The aim is similar under the law of sales, except that there is perhaps a greater concern in the law of sales for providing remedies attuned to business needs. The sales remedy of *cover*, discussed later in this chapter, permits a buyer to continue his or her business by arranging a purchase in substitution for goods the seller failed to deliver. The right of *cure* enables a seller to correct imperfect deliveries with a minimum of effort and expense, and it prevents a buyer from rejecting essentially sound deliveries on a pretext. Other sales remedies are suited to fast-paced commercial transactions, and buyers and sellers have considerable leeway in choosing remedies appropriate for the situation.

Some remedies for breach of a sales contract have been alluded to in cases presented earlier in this chapter. We now turn to a brief survey of the remedies available to a buyer or a seller for breach of a sales contract.

Remedies of the Seller Remedies are available to a seller where the buyer wrongfully rejects the goods, or wrongfully revokes acceptance of the goods, or fails to make a payment due on or before delivery, or repudiates with respect to a part or the whole of the contract [2-703]. With respect to the goods affected by

---

[10]Ibid., pp. 420–423.

the breach, the seller may do one or more of the following.

1 The seller may withhold delivery of the goods.

2 The seller may stop delivery of goods in the possession of a carrier or other bailee. If the reason for stoppage is the buyer's insolvency, the seller may stop the delivery regardless of its size. But

. . . the right to stop [delivery] for reasons other than insolvency is limited to carload, truckload, planeload or larger shipments. The seller shipping to a [solvent] buyer of doubtful credit can protect himself by shipping C.O.D. Where stoppage occurs for insecurity it is merely a suspension of performance, and if assurances are duly forthcoming from the buyer, the seller is not entitled to resell or divert the goods [2-705, comment 1, pars. 2 and 3].

3 As a preliminary to the remedy of resale or to an action for the price of the goods, the seller may identify conforming goods to the contract. If the goods are unfinished, the seller may either "complete the manufacture and wholly identify the goods to the contract, or cease manufacture and resell for scrap or salvage value, or proceed in any other reasonable manner" [2-704].

4 The seller may resell the goods and recover damages. The resale must be made in good faith and in a commercially reasonable manner. Where the resale price is lower than the contract price, "the seller may recover the difference between the resale price and the contract price, together with any incidental damages . . . but less expenses saved in consequence of the buyer's breach" [2-706(1)]. Incidental damages include (but are not limited to) any commercially reasonable expenses incurred in stopping delivery, transporting and caring for the goods after the buyer's breach, and returning or reselling the goods [2-710].

5 The seller may recover damages for nonacceptance. One measure of damages for nonac-

ceptance or repudiation by the buyer is "the difference between the market price at the time and place for tender and the unpaid contract price, together with any incidental damages . . . but less expenses saved in consequence of the buyer's breach" [2-708(1)]. Where the supply of goods is large and the demand for them is weak, this measure of damages will usually put the seller in as good a position as the buyer's performance would have done. Where a seller has an unlimited supply of eagerly sought goods, however, the seller's loss will not necessarily be revealed by subtracting the market price from the contract price. The seller is in a position to sell an unlimited number of units, but the buyer's default has reduced the number of sales by one. In such a situation, "the measure of damages is the profit (including reasonable overhead) which the seller would have made from full performance by the buyer . . ." [2-708(2)].

6 When the buyer fails to pay the price as it becomes due, the seller may recover the price of the goods. This remedy is limited to *(a)* situations where the buyer has accepted the goods; *(b)* most situations where conforming goods have been lost or damaged after the risk of their loss has passed to the buyer; and *(c)* situations where goods identified to the contract cannot be resold at a reasonable price, for example, where furniture designed in compliance with a customer's order is so garish that it can be sold only as scrap [2-709(1)].

7 To the extent justified by the buyer's breach, the seller may cancel the contract.

8 In a *few* situations, the seller has a right of reclamation, i.e., a right to reclaim the goods. For example, where the contract requires payment on delivery, the goods were delivered, payment was demanded, and the buyer paid by a check that "bounced," the seller may reclaim the goods from the buyer under Section 2-507(2). However, the seller may *not* reclaim the goods from a good-faith purchaser for value to whom the buyer has transferred the goods.

Remedies of the Buyer Remedies are available to a buyer where the seller fails to make delivery, or the seller repudiates with respect to a part or the whole of the contract, or the buyer rightfully rejects the seller's tender, or the buyer justifiably revokes acceptance [2-711]. With respect to the goods affected by the seller's breach (including breach of a warranty), and with respect to goods affected by the buyer's rightful rejection or justifiable revocation, the buyer may do one or more of the following.

1   To the extent warranted by the seller's breach, the buyer may cancel the contract.

2   The buyer may recover so much of the price as has been paid.

3   The buyer may "cover" and have damages as to all the goods affected, whether or not they have been identified to the contract. The buyer *covers* by making or arranging in good faith a substitution of goods for those due from the seller [2-712(1)]. The buyer may also recover from the seller the difference between the cost of cover and the contract price, "together with any incidental or consequential damages . . . but less expenses saved in consequence of the seller's breach" [2-712(2)]. *Incidental damages* resulting from the seller's breach include (but are not limited to) expenses reasonably incurred in inspecting, receiving, transporting, or caring for goods rightfully rejected, and expenses reasonably incurred in effecting cover [2-715(1)]. *Consequential damages* resulting from the seller's breach "include (a) any loss resulting from general or particular requirements and needs of which the seller at the time of contracting had reason to know and which could not reasonably be prevented by cover or otherwise; and (b) injury to person or property proximately resulting from any breach of warranty" [2-715(2)].

4   The buyer may recover damages for nondelivery. The measure of damages for nondelivery or repudiation by the seller is the "difference between the market price, at the time when the buyer learned of the breach, and the contract price, together with any incidental and consequential damages . . . but less expenses saved in consequence of the seller's breach." This

remedy "applies only when and to the extent that the buyer has not covered" [2-713, comment 5].

5   Where an insolvent seller fails to deliver the goods or repudiates the contract, the buyer may obtain identified goods from the insolvent seller [2-502].

6   The buyer may obtain specific performance. "Specific performance may be decreed where the goods are unique or in other proper circumstances" [2-716(1)]. The drafters explain specific performance as it relates to Article 2: "Specific performance is no longer limited to goods which are already specific or ascertained at the time of contracting. The test of uniqueness under this section must be made in terms of the total situation which characterizes the contract." Output and requirements contracts involving a particular source or market present "the typical commercial specific performance situation." However, "uniqueness is not the sole basis of the remedy under this section, for the relief may also be granted 'in other proper circumstances,' and inability to cover is strong evidence of 'other proper circumstances'" [2-716, comment 2].

7   The buyer may exercise a right of replevin [2-716(2)]. *Replevin* is an action taken to acquire possession of goods. Replevin is available to the buyer if the goods are identified to the contract and if (*a*) the buyer is unable to effect cover after reasonable effort; (*b*) the circumstances reasonably indicate such an effort will be unavailing; or (*c*) the seller has shipped the goods under reservation of a security interest, and the buyer has made or tendered satisfaction of the security interest.

In addition to the remedies listed in the preceding paragraphs, a buyer may have a security interest in goods in the buyer's control. On rightful rejection or justifiable revocation of acceptance, the buyer has a security interest in such goods for any payments made on their price, and for expenses of handling and resale [2-711(3)]. A buyer who has accepted goods and given notice of defects may recover damages for loss due to any nonconformity of tender [2-714]. Finally, upon giving proper notice to the seller, the buyer may "deduct all or any part of the damages resulting from any breach of the contract from any part of the price still due under the same contract" [2-717].

Case 27.5   **Thorstenson v. Mobridge Iron Works Co.**
208 N.W.2d 715 (S.D. 1973)

DOYLE, J. Plaintiff Adolph Thorstenson brought an action for damages for breach of contract against defendant Mobridge Iron Works Company. The trial court directed a verdict in favor of defendant and plaintiff appeals.

On December 1, 1967 . . . the defendant agreed to sell to the plaintiff a Case 730 farm tractor and a mounted F-11 Farmhand loader with certain attachments. [The tractor was to be delivered to the buyer's farm, but no delivery date was specified in the contract. In the fall of 1968, defendant notified the plaintiff that there would be no delivery of the equipment as specified in the contract. The defendant contended that the F-11 loader could not be mounted on the 730 Case tractor. In December 1968, plaintiff made a "cover" purchase from a Case dealer of a 730 Case tractor equipped with an F-11 loader, at a price increase of $1,000.] Plaintiff testified the cover purchase was similar equipment while defendant claims it was an "entirely different tractor" from the one specified in their contract. In our view, these disputed questions of fact should have been submitted to a jury. . . .

The trial court limited its directed verdict in favor of the defendant to the issue of damages and found that the plaintiff failed to introduce evidence of any damages sustained.

When a seller fails to make delivery or repudiates, or the buyer rightfully rejects or justifiably revokes a contract, the buyer has certain remedies available by statute. In Section 2-711(1)(a), it is provided that the buyer may: "(1) 'Cover' and have damages under [Section 2-712]." Section 2-712(1) provides that: ". . . the buyer may 'cover' by making in good faith and without unreasonable delay any reasonable purchase of or contract to purchase goods in substitution for those due from the seller." Section 2-712(2) provides: "The buyer may recover from the seller as damages the difference between the cost of cover and the contract price together with any incidental or consequential damages as hereafter defined . . . but less expenses saved in consequence of the seller's breach." It is stated in [the comments to Section 2-712]:

"This section provides the buyer with a remedy aimed at enabling him to obtain the goods he needs thus meeting his essential need. This remedy is the buyer's equivalent to the seller's right to resell.

"The definition of 'cover' . . . envisages . . . a single contract or sale;

[and the definition envisages] goods not identical with those involved but commercially usable as reasonable substitutes under the circumstances of the particular case. . . . The test of proper cover is whether at the time and place the buyer acted in good faith and in a reasonable manner, and it is immaterial that hindsight may later prove that the method of cover used was not the cheapest or most effective. . . .

"This section does not limit cover to merchants. . . . It is the vital and important remedy for the consumer buyer as well. Both are free to use cover; the . . . non-merchant consumer is required only to act in normal good faith. . . ."

From a review of the record it appears there was sufficient evidence of damages to the plaintiff under the statutes quoted above to require the question of damages to be submitted to a jury.

Reversed and remanded for trial. . . .

Limitation of Remedies

The remedies provided by Article 2 may be limited or supplemented by agreement of the parties to the contract [2-719(1)(a)]. However, the right to limit remedies is itself subject to certain restrictions. Any clause purporting to modify or limit the remedial provisions of Article 2 in an unconscionable manner

. . . is subject to deletion, and in that event the remedies made available by this Article are applicable as if the stricken clause had never existed. Similarly . . . where an apparently fair and reasonable clause . . . fails in its purpose or operates to deprive either party of the substantial value of the bargain, it must give way to the general remedy provisions of this Article.[11]

---

[11]Sec. 2-719, comment 1, par. 2.

In transactions involving consumer goods, the limitation of consequential damages for personal injury is prima facie unconscionable, but limitation of damages where the loss is commercial is not [2-719(3)].

Where a supplier of a "consumer product" has made a full warranty under the Magnuson-Moss Warranty Act, consequential damages for breach of a written or implied warranty may not be excluded or limited unless the exclusion or limitation conspicuously appears on the face of the warranty. In other respects, the rules of Article 2 regarding limitation of remedies remain unaffected by the Warranty Act. The limitation of remedies or consequential damages should not be confused with the exclusion of implied warranties. To the extent described in Chapter 26, the Warranty Act prohibits the exclusion of implied warranties.

Case 27.6   Wilson Trading Corp. v. David Ferguson, Ltd.
244 N.E.2d 685 (N.Y. 1968)

JASEN, J. The plaintiff, the Wilson Trading Corporation, entered into a contract of sale with the defendant, David Ferguson, Ltd., for the sale of a specified quantity of yarn. After the yarn was delivered, cut and knitted into sweaters, the finished product was washed. It was during this washing that it was discovered that the color of the yarn had "shaded"—that is, "there was a variation in color from piece to piece and within the pieces." This defect, the defendant claims, rendered the sweaters "unmarketable."

This action for the contract price of the yarn was commenced after the defendant refused payment. As a defense to the action . . . the defendant alleges that "[p]laintiff has failed to perform all of the conditions of the contract on its part required to be performed, and has delivered . . . defective and unworkmanlike goods."

The sales contract provides in pertinent part:

"2. No claims relating to excessive moisture content, short weight, count variations, twist quality or shade shall be allowed *if made after weaving, knitting, or processing*, or more than 10 days of the receipt of shipment. . . . The buyer shall within 10 days of the receipt of the merchandise by himself or agent examine the merchandise for any and all defects." (Emphasis supplied.)

Special Term [the trial court] granted plaintiff summary judgment for the contract price of the yarn sold on the ground that "notice of the alleged breach of warranty for defect in shading was not given within the time expressly limited. . . ." The Appellate Division affirmed, without opinion.

The defendant on this appeal urges that the time limitation provision on claims in the contract was unreasonable since the defect in the color of the yarn was latent and could not be discovered until after the yarn was processed and the finished product washed.

. . . [T]he plaintiff does not seriously dispute the fact that its yarn was unmerchantable, but instead, like Special Term, relies upon the failure of defendant to give notice of the breach of warranty within the time limits prescribed by paragraph two of the contract.

Section 2-607(3)(a) expressly provides that a buyer who accepts goods has a reasonable time after he discovers or should have discovered a breach to notify the seller of such breach. Defendant's affidavits allege that a claim was made immediately upon discovery of the breach of warranty after the yarn was knitted and washed, and that this was the earliest possible moment that the defects could reasonably be discovered in the normal manufacturing process. Defendant's affidavits are, therefore, sufficient to create a question of fact concerning whether notice of the latent defects alleged was given within a reasonable time.

However, the Uniform Commercial Code allows the parties, within limits established by the Code, to modify or exclude warranties and to limit remedies for breach of warranty. The courts below have found that the sales contract bars all claims not made before knitting and processing. Concededly, defendant discovered and gave notice of the alleged breach of warranty after knitting and washing. . . .

Parties to a contract are given broad latitude within which to fashion their own remedies for breach of contract (Section 2-316(4); Sections 2-718, 2-719). Nevertheless, it is clear from the official comments to section 2-719 of the Uniform Commercial Code that it is the very essence of a sales contract that at least minimum adequate remedies be available for its breach.

"If the parties intend to conclude a contract for sale within this Article, they must accept the legal consequence that there be at least a fair quantum of remedy for breach of the obligations or duties outlined in the contract. Thus any clause purporting to modify or limit the remedial provisions of this Article in an *unconscionable manner* is subject to deletion and in that event the remedies made available by this Article are applicable as if the stricken clause had never existed" (Section 2-719, official comment 1; emphasis supplied.)

It follows that contractual limitations upon remedies are generally to be enforced unless unconscionable. . . .

Whether a contract or any clause of the contract is unconscionable is a matter for the court to decide against the background of the contract's commercial setting, purpose, and effect. . . .

However, it is unnecessary to decide the issue of whether the time limitation is unconscionable on this appeal, for Section 2-719(2) provides that the general remedy provisions of the Code apply when "circumstances cause an exclusive or limited remedy to fail of its essential purpose." As explained by the official comments to this section: "where an apparently fair and reasonable clause because of circumstances fails in its purpose or operates to deprive either party of the substantial value of the bargain, it must give way to the general remedy provisions of this Article." . . .

Defendant's affidavits allege that sweaters manufactured from the yarn were rendered unmarketable because of latent shading defects not reasonably discoverable before knitting and processing of the yarn into sweaters. If these factual allegations are established at trial, the limited remedy established by paragraph two [of the contract] has failed its "essential purpose" and the buyer is, in effect, without remedy. The time limitation clause of the contract, therefore, insofar as it applies to defects not reasonably discoverable within the time limits established by the contract, must give way to the general Code rule that a buyer has a reasonable time to notify the seller of breach of contract after he discovers or should have discovered the defect (Section 2-607(3)(a).) . . . [D]efendant's affidavits are sufficient to create a question of fact concerning whether notice was given within a reasonable time after the shading defect should have been discovered.

[Reversed and case remitted.]

SUMMARY

The Uniform Commercial Code provides remedies for a breach or a threatened breach of the performance obligations in a sales contract. The obligation of the seller is to transfer and deliver the goods, and that of the buyer is to accept and pay for them.

The seller meets his or her delivery obligation by making a tender of delivery. Tender requires that the seller put and hold conforming goods at the buyer's disposition and give the buyer any notification reasonably necessary to enable the buyer to take delivery. Within limits imposed by the Code, the buyer may reject a tender that fails in any respect to conform to the contract. The seller has a right to cure an improper tender before, and sometimes after, the time for performance has expired. In an installment contract, the buyer may reject a nonconforming installment only if the nonconformity substantially impairs the value of that installment and cannot be cured.

The buyer's obligation to accept and pay is conditioned on the buyer's right to inspect the goods. Acceptance occurs in a number of ways. The buyer accepts, for example, by signifying that the goods are conforming. Upon acceptance, the buyer becomes obligated to pay the contract price. In two principal situations, the buyer may revoke acceptance of nonconforming goods. Unless otherwise agreed, the buyer may pay by any customary means or in any customary manner. The seller may require payment in legal tender but must give any extension of time reasonably necessary for the buyer to procure such a payment.

The parties to a sales contract may be excused from their performance obligations if the agreed performance has been made commercially impracticable by an unforeseen occurrence that alters the essential nature of the performance. Where an agreed method of payment or delivery fails, the aggrieved party may be entitled to a substitute performance.

A party to the contract is not entitled to a remedy unless the other party is in breach of the contract. Normally, there is no default before the date set for performance. Nor is there usually a default after that time until one party puts the other party in default by tendering the required performance. However, a party can put himself or herself in default before the time set for performance by repudiating the contract. A party can be put in default by circumstances surrounding the sale that give the other party reasonable grounds for insecurity.

An aggrieved seller has available a number of remedies for breach of contract. The seller may, for example, withhold delivery of the goods, stop delivery of goods in the possession of a carrier, or have an action for the price. An aggrieved buyer may cancel the contract, "cover" and have damages as to the goods affected by the seller's breach, or have other remedies.

The remedies of Article 2 may be limited or supplemented by the agreement of the parties to the contract. An unconscionable limitation of remedies is subject to deletion from the contract. Where a supplier of a consumer product makes a full warranty, the Warranty Act requires that an exclusion or limitation of consequential damages appear conspicuously on the face of the warranty.

STUDY AND DISCUSSION QUESTIONS

1 In a contract for the sale of goods, what are the general performance obligations of the buyer and the seller?

2 *(a)* What is the meaning of tender? *(b)* What is the reason for the perfect tender rule?

3 *(a)* In general, how does a seller fulfill the seller's tender obligations? *(b)* What specific acts are required for a seller to fulfill the tender obligation in a shipment contract? *(c)* In what kinds of situations may a seller "cure" an improper tender?

4 *(a)* What constitutes acceptance of goods? *(b)* What is the legal effect of acceptance? *(c)* How is the buyer's right to inspect the goods related to the buyer's obligation to accept the goods? *(d)* How does a COD clause in a sales contract affect the buyer's right to inspect the goods?

5 *(a)* In general, under what circumstances may a buyer reject the seller's tender of delivery? *(b)* With regard to an installment contract, under what circumstances may a buyer reject an installment?

6 In what two principal situations may a buyer revoke acceptance of goods?

7 How does the buyer meet the obligation to pay *(a)* where the parties have not stated how payment is to be made? and *(b)* where the parties have not stated the time and place for payment?

8 *(a)* Explain the meaning and significance of commercial impracticability as an excuse for nonperformance. *(b)* Explain how the concept of commercial impracticability could be applied to a situation involving casualty to identified goods, where the casualty occurs without the fault of either party to the sale of those goods.

9 Illustrate how a substitute performance could excuse the obligation of a party to a sales contract.

10 *(a)* How does the doctrine of concurrent conditions affect the availability of a remedy to a buyer or a seller? *(b)* With regard to default, explain the significance of reasonable grounds for insecurity. *(c)* What is repudiation? *(d)* Under what circumstances may an aggrieved party have a remedy for a repudiation?

11 Remedies for breach of a contract for the sale of goods are meant to protect the expectation, the reliance, and the restitution interests of nondefaulting parties. Define these three terms.

12 *(a)* Under what circumstances may a seller recover the price of goods when the buyer fails to make payment? *(b)* Describe at least three other remedies of the seller.

13 *(a)* Explain the meaning and significance of cover as a buyer's remedy. *(b)* Describe at least three other remedies of the buyer.

14 *(a)* To what extent may a contract for the sale of goods limit the remedies provided by Article 2? *(b)* How does the Magnuson-Moss Warranty Act affect the limitation of remedies in a contract for the sale of goods?

CASE PROBLEMS

1 Allen purchased a mobile home from Performance Motors, Inc. In litigation concerning her obligation to pay for the mobile home, Allen listed a number of defects in manufacture. She testified that the mobile home had never been leveled; that "you could see the ground through the floor"; that "when they were putting it up, I told those men, 'Now this is not right and I do not want it'"; that after the mobile home was installed, she complained to the plaintiff's president continually "from September to the last of December when he hung up on me and said Happy New Year"; that she ceased making monthly payments because of the plaintiff's failure to make the repairs necessary to place the trailer in a usable condition; and that she lived in the mobile home from September to May when plaintiff repossessed it. *(a)* Did Allen accept the mobile home? *(b)* If Allen did accept the mobile home, did she revoke her acceptance?

2 In 1967 Traynor (buyer) ordered 1,736 Christmas trees for resale—1,300 Scotch Pine and 436 of other varieties. The sellers warranted that the trees would be of "top quality." On December 7, the sellers delivered 625 trees. One hundred eighty-five of these trees conformed to the contract and were accepted by the buyer. Three hundred fifteen Scotch Pine were of very poor quality, did not conform to the contract, and were rejected. On December 13, the sellers tendered 71 Douglas Fir and 200 Scotch Pine. The Scotch Pine did not conform to the contract and were rejected. On December 14, 2 days before the final date set for performance, the sellers tendered 600 Scotch

Pine by telephone, stating that those trees were of a different origin from the Scotch Pine sent in the first two deliveries. The buyer refused to accept any further shipment of Scotch Pine, but demanded the other trees due under the contract. Under Section 2-612, relating to breach of installment contracts, was the buyer within his rights in refusing to accept any further shipment of Scotch Pine trees?

3   In 1969 Gramling bought a new International truck from Baltz, a seller of International Harvester equipment. During the next 2 years, the truck failed to function properly. The truck was out of service for long periods, and it often broke down while in use. Repeated efforts of Baltz and two International garages to repair the truck were unavailing. In 1971, just after the expiration of the 2-year warranty period, the truck had to be towed to Memphis for repairs. Gramling was notified that the "block was busted" and repairs would cost $2,700. Gramling refused to pay for the repairs, and he sued Baltz and International Harvester for breach of warranty. The defendants contended that Gramling had operated the truck in excess of 115,000 miles during more than the 2-year warranty period without rejection or revocation of acceptance, and that Gramling therefore should not be awarded damages for breach of warranty. Gramling contended that under Section 2-608, he was entitled to revoke his acceptance even after the warranty period expired. Might Gramling be entitled to revoke his acceptance after the expiration of the warranty period?

4   Mishara Construction Company, Inc. (Mishara) was the general contractor for the construction of a housing project for the elderly. Transit-Mixed Concrete Corp. (Transit) agreed with Mishara to supply the ready-mixed concrete for the project. For several months Transit supplied concrete. Then a labor dispute disrupted work on the job site, and Transit stopped delivering concrete. Although work resumed on June 15, 1967, a picket line was maintained on the site until the completion of the project in 1969. Notwithstanding frequent requests by Mishara, Transit made no further deliveries of concrete. After notifying Transit of its intention, Mishara purchased the rest of its concrete requirements elsewhere. Mishara then sought as damages the additional cost of the replacement concrete. Mishara also sought as damages the expenses of locating an alternate source of concrete. During the litigation, Mishara contended that a labor dispute that makes performance more difficult never constitutes an excuse for nonperformance. (a) Might such a labor dispute excuse Transit from performance? (b) If Transit was not excused from performance, is Mishara entitled to recover from Transit the costs of locating an alternate source of concrete?

5   Brant Development Company (Brant) was to build a large apartment complex. Ellis Manufacturing Company (Ellis) agreed with Brant to supply and install assorted cabinets in the apartment units. Under the contract, Brant was to make payments on or before the tenth of each month for cabinets installed by the twenty-fifth of the preceding month. On November 13, 1967, Ellis delivered material for ten apartment units. Most of these materials were not installed until after November 15; therefore, payment was not due until January 10, 1968. Nevertheless, on December 14, Ellis threatened to discontinue deliveries until payment was made. Brant refused to pay before January 10 and gave Ellis until January 5 to make the next (final) delivery. On January 13, Ellis tendered delivery. In the meantime, Brant had contracted with another subcontractor to complete the work, and Brant refused to accept delivery from Ellis. Ellis sued Brant for breach of contract. During ensuing litigation, Ellis stated that it felt insecure because of Brant's failure to pay as requested and that Ellis was entitled under Section 2-609(1) to withhold delivery until se-

cure. Was Ellis entitled to withhold delivery of the cabinets?

6 In the case upon which the preceding problem was based, Brant alleged that Ellis's withholding delivery of the cabinets resulted in damages to Brant. First, Brant alleged that Ellis's failure to deliver the cabinets delayed completion of the apartments for 30 days and caused Brant a loss of rentals. Second, Brant alleged that he had to make a cover purchase of cabinets for a substantially higher amount than called for in the Ellis contract. *(a)* Does the loss of rentals constitute consequential damages, or only incidental damages? *(b)* If Brant receives damages for the lost rentals, will he be entitled to damages for cover?

7 Posttape Associates purchased Ektachrome Commercial film from Eastman Kodak Co. Posttape used this film to produce a documentary film. During the processing of the film, marks were discovered on the film. These marks made the film commercially useless. Alleging breach of an implied warranty of merchantability, Posttape sued Kodak for damages. Relying on a notice printed on individual film containers, Kodak denied any liability beyond replacement of the film. The notice stated, "This film will be replaced if defective in manufacture, labeling, or packaging, or if damaged or lost by us or any subsidiary company even though by negligence or other fault. Except for such replacement, the sale, processing, or other handling of this film for any purpose is without other warranty or liability. . . ." Assume that this notice was inadequate to exclude the implied warranty of merchantability. *(a)* Could the notice nevertheless constitute a valid limitation of remedies under Sections 2-719 and 1-205(3)? *(b)* Is there any legal requirement that a limitation of remedies be conspicuous?

Chapter

28

Secured Transactions

In the cash society of former times, individuals had to accumulate wealth before they could expand their businesses or undertake new ventures. Opportunities were lost, and economic development was painfully slow. Then business people began to use the money lender's credit to expand their business activities. As commerce and industry developed, credit extension came to be recognized as a valuable economic tool.

Credit extension involves a risk that the debtor will "default", that is, fail to repay a loan or fail to make payment for property bought "on credit." To reduce the risk of loss due to non-payment, creditors may demand some sort of "collateral" ("security") from the debtor. *Collateral* is something of value that can be converted into cash if the debtor defaults.

Security arrangements take many forms. One form, the secured transaction in personal property, is of major commercial significance. However, law that would permit the use of personal property as collateral for loans has developed unevenly. From a patchwork of unsatisfactory security law, the more streamlined Article 9 of the Uniform Commercial Code has evolved.

This chapter discusses the general nature and development of secured transactions law, provides an introduction to contemporary secured transactions law under Article 9, and illustrates the operation of that law in a "case study" involving typical secured transactions.

NATURE OF SECURED TRANSACTIONS AND SECURED TRANSACTIONS LAW

Nature of Secured Transactions

Meaning of Secured Transaction   In its general sense, the term "secured transaction" refers to any arrangement made by agreement of the parties for the purpose of providing the creditor with a backup source of payment if the debtor defaults. In one form of secured transaction, a person or firm called a "surety" makes a backup promise to pay the debt in the event that the debtor defaults. More often the backup source of payment is real or personal property. This chapter focuses on the *secured transaction in personal property*, that is, on transactions in which personal property serves as the collateral.

Distinction between Unsecured and Secured Transactions   Suppliers often sell and deliver goods solely on the basis of the buyer's promise to pay later. If the buyer-debtor refuses to pay, the unsecured seller must rely on a legal claim against the general assets of the debtor. To enforce this right to payment, the seller might have to sue the debtor, obtain judgment, seek execution against the debtor's available property, and garnishee the debtor's wages. Obtaining judgment will be a hollow victory if the debtor has no assets, or leaves the jurisdiction of the court, or actively resists collection attempts. In contrast, a seller who insists on a secured transaction substantially reduces his or her risk of loss. If the debtor defaults, the secured seller will have not only a claim against the general assets of the debtor, but also first rights, as against other creditors, to the specific property that is the subject of the secured transaction.

Nature of Secured Transactions Law

A major principle of contemporary security law is that upon the debtor's default, the secured creditor has the right to the collateral and the debtor has the right to any surplus proceeds realized upon disposition of the collateral but remains personally liable for any deficiency. This "security notion" stands in marked contrast to older ideas that any breach by the debtor, however small, justified imposing upon him or her forfeiture of collateral and loss of all payments made. Contemporary security law attempts an accommodation of competing interests designed to promote the economic welfare of all concerned: debtors, creditors, and the public.

The law of secured transactions is a blend of contract and property law, added to or modified somewhat to serve credit needs. Property law defines and establishes interests of various kinds in the thing owned. Contract law permits and governs the agreements the parties usually use to set up a secured transaction. These familiar principles form the foundation upon which other features of the law of secured transactions have been built.

DEVELOPMENT OF SECURED TRANSACTIONS LAW

Pre-Code Policy and Devices

Before the industrial revolution, the courts refused to enforce against subsequent creditors any secured transaction in personal property that left the debtor in possession of the collateral. The reasoning was that a creditor who put a debtor into possession of unpaid-for property while retaining a "secret lien" on the property created an unwarranted danger for other lenders. Since time purchases were unusual, these other lenders would naturally believe that the debtor owned free and clear all the property over which he or she had the usual owner's control. The security device preferred by the courts of that era was the *pledge*, in which the debtor gave possession of the collateral to the creditor in order to obtain a loan. Since the pledgee-creditor would possess the collateral until the loan was repaid, subsequent creditors would not be likely to overestimate the debtor's wealth.

The industrial revolution dramatically increased credit needs and forced the invention of new financing patterns. As industry developed, producers often lacked sufficient operating capital, even though they might own considerable equipment. The equipment could not be pledged because the owner needed to use it in the business. Lawyers therefore created some security devices intended to allow the borrower to use the collateral while the loan was being repaid. The courts, adhering to their position that the secret lien must be avoided, at first refused to enforce these new arrangements against subsequent creditors, but then slowly relented.

With lawyers and legislatures initiating changes and the courts applying brakes, eventually there emerged a variety of additional security devices. The most important of these were the chattel mortgage and the conditional-sale contract. Under the *chattel mortgage*, the debtor retained possession of the goods ("chattels") used as collateral but transferred to the creditor a defeasible title to the chattel, or, in some states, granted a lien on the chattel. Upon payment of the debt, the title was defeated or the lien was discharged. Under the *conditional-sale contract*, the buyer-debtor received possession of the goods and the seller-creditor retained title until the buyer had performed his or her part of the agreement. These two devices are still in general use.

A third security device, *field warehousing*, developed in response to a need for the financing of inventory. The inventory used as collateral was segregated in a fenced-off area of the borrower's (e.g., a manufacturer's) premises and placed under the control of an independent warehouseman. Field warehousing is no longer a requirement for inventory financing, but it is often used as an optional policing technique by lenders who wish to keep close track of inventory being used as collateral. Two other pre-Code security devices—the "trust receipt" and the "factor's lien"—have become of little more than historical interest to most business people.

By the middle of the 1940s an individual or business firm could acquire an enforceable security interest in most kinds of personal property. Yet, the pre-Code law of secured transactions had many shortcomings. Contributing generally to inadequate protection of the secured creditor were: (1) a variety of security devices, each with its separate filing system; (2) courts willing to invalidate the security transaction that did not fall clearly into the category the lender thought it did; (3) the expense of multiple filing as a hedge against a wrong guess; (4) undeveloped inventory and accounts receivable financing; (5) the necessity of using two or more devices to secure a large loan where different forms of property constituted the collateral; and (6) different treatment by courts and legislatures of similar security devices, and even of devices of the same name. Credit extension could be very tricky and expensive.

Development and Revision of Code Article 9

The growth in credit transactions in the decades just prior to the promulgation of the Uniform Commercial Code[1] created an urgent need for legislation that would correct inadequacies of pre-Code secured transactions law. Article 9, which deals with secured transactions involving personal property, was developed to meet this need.

Despite the great desirability of uniformity in

---

[1]The development of the Code is discussed in Chapter 2.

all areas of commercial law, each state has a sovereign right to depart from the Official Text of the Code. The variations made by adopting legislatures were especially numerous in connection with Article 9. Because of the unusual number of these variations, a "Revised Article 9 of the Uniform Commercial Code" was published in 1972, to replace the 1962 Article 9. Although basic secured transactions principles and techniques remain essentially unaltered, some significant changes were made. References to Article 9 in this chapter are to the 1972 version of the Article, unless otherwise noted. Because some states have not yet adopted the 1972 revision of Article 9, differences between the 1962 and the 1972 versions are pointed out where necessary for the purposes of this chapter.[2]

Policy and Scope of Code Article 9

Policy of Article 9   The general policy or aim of Article 9 is to facilitate business activity by providing the legal framework for safe and efficient credit extension. As stated by the drafters of the Code, "the aim of the Article is to provide a simple and unified structure within which the immense variety of present-day secured financing transactions can go forward with less cost and with greater certainty" [9-101, comment, par. 7].

Nearly all of the provisions of Article 9 contribute directly or indirectly to the accomplishment of this aim. The provision that probably contributes the most is the substitution of the single term *security interest* "for the variety of descriptive terms which had grown up at com-

mon law and under a hundred-year accretion of statutes" [9-101, comment, par. 8]. Security devices are no longer viewed as inherently different from each other but as variations of the same thing—an Article 9 secured transaction whose consequences are spelled out in the Article. Article 9 also substitutes a simplified public-notice *filing system* for the pre-Code system of different files, records, and indexes for each type of security device. "Thus not only is the information contained in the files made more accessible, but the cost of procuring credit information and . . . of maintaining the files is greatly reduced" [9-101, comment, par. 13].

Two other provisions of Article 9 contribute greatly to the aim of the article. One provision establishes a *system of priorities* for resolving disputes where there are two or more conflicting interests in the same collateral. The other provision sets up a *uniform method of liquidating collateral* after default, "regardless of the form of the security device. Instead of the forced sale provisions of many pre-Code statutes which caused economic loss to both secured party and debtor, Article 9 adopts an approach of commercially reasonable liquidation. . . ."[3] The Article 9 provisions referred to in this and the previous paragraph are discussed more fully later in the chapter.

Scope of Article 9   Article 9 places very few limits on the kinds of personal property that can be used as collateral. The article is intended to validate a security interest in any personal property that is or "may become customarily used as commercial security" [9-106, comment, par. 1]. The coverage of Article 9, its exclusions, and its relationships to supplemental legislation are outlined in the article.

Coverage of Article 9   Section 9-102(1) outlines the coverage of Article 9 as follows. "Ex-

---

[2]As of June 1981, the 1972 Revised Article 9 has been adopted by the following states: Arizona, Arkansas, California, Colorado, Connecticut, Florida, Georgia, Hawaii, Idaho, Illinois, Iowa, Kansas, Maine, Maryland, Massachusetts, Michigan, Minnesota, Mississippi, Nebraska, Nevada, New York, North Carolina, North Dakota, Ohio, Oregon, Rhode Island, Texas, Utah, Virginia, West Virginia, Wisconsin.

The 1962 and 1972 amendments to Article 9 are now incorporated in the 1978 Official Text of the UCC.

[3]Oscar Spivak, *Secured Transactions*, pp. 19–20. Copyright © 1963, by The American Law Institute, Philadelphia. Reprinted with the permission of The American Law Institute–American Bar Association Committee on Continuing Professional Education.

cept as otherwise provided in Section 9-104 on excluded transactions, this Article applies (a) to any transaction (regardless of its form) which is intended to create a security interest in personal property or fixtures . . . ; and also (b) to any sale of accounts or chattel paper." Table 28.1, p. 574, lists and illustrates most of the types of personal property covered by Article 9 and indicates the section where each type is defined. Three terms in the section just quoted require brief explanation: fixtures, accounts, and chattel paper.

Fixtures are normally considered part of the real property to which they are annexed. For most purposes, therefore, they are subject to the real estate law of the jurisdiction where they are annexed.[4] Why, then, does Article 9 apply to the security aspects of fixtures? Fixtures begin life as goods and often move in interstate commerce until annexed to realty. If the security aspects of fixture transactions were governed by real estate law, which varies from state to state, fixture creditors would be faced with great uncertainty. Article 9 minimizes such uncertainty by providing a single set of rules that govern the security aspects of fixtures, both before and after annexation.

Chattel paper is a writing, or writings, that evidence both a monetary obligation and a security interest in specific goods. For an example of chattel paper, see Table 28.1. A dealer who has sold goods on credit and has accepted the customer's chattel paper can himself use the chattel paper as collateral for a loan.

Account (usually referred to as account receivable) means "any right to payment for goods sold or leased or for services rendered which is not evidenced by an instrument or chattel paper" (see Table 28.1). Article 9 applies to security interests in, and also to *sales* of, chattel paper and accounts receivable. The article includes sales of these property rights because sales of chattel paper and accounts are often

difficult to distinguish from their use as collateral for a loan. Therefore, the same filing requirements and other rules should apply, and under Article 9 do apply, to both types of transactions.

Exclusions from Article 9 Section 9-104 excludes from Article 9 twelve kinds of security transactions. Assignments of wages as security for debts are excluded because such assignments present important social problems whose solution should be a matter of local regulation. Although most sales of accounts receivable are covered by Article 9, some transfers of accounts are excluded because they have nothing to do with commercial financing—for example, sales of accounts or chattel paper as a part of a sale of the business out of which they arose. In other instances, such as in the use of life insurance as collateral, the transaction is excluded because it is adequately covered by existing law.

SECURED TRANSACTIONS UNDER ARTICLE 9

Nature of a Security Interest
To permit the use of old security devices and the development of new ones, Section 1-201(37) of the Code defines *security interest* broadly as "an interest in personal property or fixtures which secures payment or performance of an obligation." Thus, in the common law pledge, possession by the creditor is the security interest; in a conditional-sale or chattel mortgage transaction, possession is in the debtor and the creditor retains or receives "title" as the security interest.

It is not always clear whether a sale, lease, consignment, or the like, is a secured transaction. Under Section 9-102, the intention of the parties to a transaction determines whether the arrangement is a secured transaction. For example, sellers of goods, in attempts to avoid the claims of buyers' creditors, began to characterize sales of goods as "leases." In a true lease (e.g., lease of a computer), the lessor retains

[4]Fixtures are discussed in Chapter 21.

title and grants possession and usage rights to the lessee. The lessor intends to remain owner. In the security "lease," however, the intention of the "lessor" is not to remain owner, but to sell the goods and reserve a right to retrieve them if payment is not made. Since the "lease" is intended to secure payment of an obligation, the rules of Article 9 must be followed if the seller is to prevail over creditors of the "lessee." Section 1-201(37) emphasizes that a lease is one intended for security if the parties agree that "upon compliance with the terms of the lease the lessee shall become . . . the owner of the property for no additional consideration or for a nominal consideration."

Acquisition of a Security Interest

The business person's interest in the topic of secured transactions may center around what must be done in order to acquire a security interest or to grant one. Article 9 speaks in terms of "attachment" and "perfection." *Attachment* is the name given to the process of creating a security interest and of making it enforceable against the debtor. *Perfection* is the name of the process by which the security interest is made enforceable against subsequent lien creditors and certain other persons having a right in the collateral.

Attachment of a Security Interest   Section 9-203 provides that a security interest is not enforceable against the debtor, and does not attach, unless three attachment "events" have occurred. These events are, in effect, requirements to be met, and are here regarded as requirements.

1   The debtor and the creditor must agree that a security interest is to be created *and* (unless the creditor possesses the collateral) the debtor must sign a security agreement that reasonably identifies the collateral [9-203 and 9-110].

2   Value must be given by the creditor (the "secured party"). If no value is given, there will be no debtor's obligation to be secured. The requirement of value is usually met by making a

loan, by selling goods on credit, or by making a binding commitment to extend credit.

3   The debtor must have rights in the collateral. Under the terms of the security agreement, some or all of the debtor's rights are held by the secured party as the security interest.

Attachment occurs when all three required attachment events have been completed. Diversity of business needs and practices would make inappropriate the imposition of a particular sequence for completing these events, and so, under the Code, the events may occur in any order. Attachment cannot occur earlier than the completion of the last event, but the parties to the security agreement can postpone the time of attachment [9-203(2)].

In recognition of contemporary business practices, Section 9-204 permits the use of an "after-acquired property clause" in commercial secured transactions, except when the collateral is consumer goods.[5] By use of an after-acquired property clause, the creditor obtains a security interest in both present and future assets of the debtor instead of a security interest only in specific assets on hand at the creation of the secured transaction. If the other attachment events have occurred, the after-acquired property is subject to the security interest as soon as the debtor acquires rights in the property. Such a security interest is called a "floating lien." The floating lien is especially useful in inventory financing and in accounts-receivable financing because only one security agreement is needed to grant the creditor a security interest in a shifting mass of collateral. In a similar vein, the *future-advances* provision of Section 9-204 permits the collateral to secure future loans if the security agreement so provides. Thus, without having to enter into a new security agreement for each new loan, the creditor safely and automatically gives value each time he or she extends new credit.

---

[5]The 1962 version of Article 9 also prohibits the use of the after-acquired property clause when the collateral is a farmer's crops. Sec. 9-204(4)(a).

Perfection of a Security Interest Completion of the attachment events results in a security agreement that is enforceable between the secured party and the debtor. However, for maximum protection from others who might claim the collateral or some interest in it, the secured party must *perfect* his or her security interest. Ordinarily, these competing claimants will be other creditors of the debtor, the buyer of the collateral from the debtor, an artisan who has improved the collateral, or the debtor's trustee in bankruptcy. Timely perfection of a security interest gives the secured party priority over most, but not all, of these competing claimants.

Methods of perfection: In general Perfection may be accomplished in three ways: (1) automatically at the completion of the attachment events; (2) by the secured party's taking possession of the collateral; and (3) by the filing of a financing statement in the public records. Table 28.1 indicates which types of perfection may or must be used for particular types of collateral.

1 *Perfection by attachment only:* Article 9 grants the status of perfection to some security interests even though nothing more than attachment has occurred. For example, Section 9-302(1)(d) exempts a "purchase money security interest" (PMSI) in most consumer goods from the general filing requirement.[6] Credit sales of consumer goods are so numerous that to require sellers to file a financing statement for each sale would impose an unreasonable burden on the market system. Since no overt notice-giving step, such as possession by the secured party, is required, the debtor can possess the collateral without invalidating the seller's security interest. Any difficulty caused by the resulting secret lien is thought to be offset by the benefits of more and cheaper credit extension.

Similar reasoning underlies the 21-day and the 10-day temporary perfections available to a variety of secured parties. For example, where collateral must be released to the debtor for storage, further processing, shipping, or similar purposes, Article 9 grants perfection for up to 21 days without filing [9-304(5)]. The 10-day grace period applies to proceeds of the debtor's disposition of collateral and also to PMSIs in fixtures or collateral other than inventory [9-306(3), 9-301(2), 9-313(4)(a), and 9-312(4)]. Within the 21, or 10, days the secured party must either file a financing statement or take possession of the collateral if a longer period of perfection is needed.

2 *Perfection by possession:* For most types of collateral, a security interest is perfected if the secured party possesses the collateral or if a bailee possesses it on behalf of the secured party. The pledge and field warehousing are common examples of perfection by possession. Usually, possession is an alternative to filing, but for some collateral, possession is the required perfection method. For instance, because the public expects the possessor of money to own it, a security interest in money can be perfected only by the secured party's taking possession [9-304(1)].[7]

3 *Perfection by filing:* In order to allow debtors to use the collateral while paying for it, the Code provides that security interests in most kinds of personal property may be perfected by filing a "financing statement." To be legally effective, the statement must be signed by the debtor and must include at least the following information: names of the debtor and the secured party, addresses of both parties, and a statement of types of collateral or a description of the items of collateral. Where the collateral is closely identified with a particular parcel of land, the financing statement must also contain a description of the land concerned [9-402(1)]. The amount of information required in the financing statement has been kept to a minimum because the purpose of filing the statement is merely to give notice "that the secured party who has filed may have a security interest

---

[6]The purchase money security interest is defined in Section 9-107. The 1962 sec. 9-302(1)(c) exempts from the filing requirement "a purchase money security interest in farm equipment having a purchase price not in excess of $2,500." The 1972 revision of Article 9 removed this exemption.

[7]Instruments are treated similarly. See Table 28.1.

TABLE 28.1

Methods of Perfecting Security Interests

Type of Collateral	Where Defined	Perfection Method	Where Indicated
Account (receivable). Example: A buys goods or services, promising to pay later. The promise is an account if not evidenced by an instrument or chattel paper.	9-106	Filing required, but casual or isolated assignments need not be filed. See Section 9-104(f) for assignments not subject to rules of Article 9.	9-302(1)(e) and (g)
Chattel paper. Example: A buys goods from B and signs a promissory note and security agreement. The note and agreement constitute chattel paper.	9-105(1)(b)	Filing or possession by secured party.	9-304(1); 9-305
Document (of title). Example: warehouse receipts, bills of lading, dock warrants, etc. May be negotiable or nonnegotiable.	1-201(15), (45) 7-201(2) 9-105(1)(f)	Filing or possession for negotiable documents. 21-day perfection status is available. For nonnegotiable documents, other rules apply.	9-304(1) 9-304(5) 9-304(3) and (5)
Instrument. Example: Checks, drafts, notes, whether or not negotiable; investment securities.	9-105(1)(i)	Possession only, except where temporary perfection status is granted.	9-304(1` (4), (5)
General intangibles. Example: Patents, copyrights, liquor licenses in some states.	9-106	Filing only.	9-302(1)

in the collateral described. Further inquiry from the parties concerned will be necessary to disclose the complete state of affairs" [9-402, comment 2].

The financing statement described above is not to be confused with a security agreement. However, if a security agreement is in writing, contains the minimum information required for a financing statement, and is signed by the debtor, the security agreement may serve as a financing statement, as may a *signed copy* of the security agreement [9-402(1)].[8]

The proper place to file a financing statement

---

[8] Under the 1962 Article 9, only the debtor is required to sign the security agreement, but both "the debtor and the secured party" must sign the financing statement. This inconsistency in formalities has created unnecessary filing problems. Under the 1972 Article 9, only the debtor need sign a financing statement.

TABLE 28.1 Continued

Type of Collateral	Where Defined	Perfection Method	Where Indicated
Goods	9-105(1)(h)	In general, filing or possession; 21-day perfection status is available.	9-302(1)(a); 9-305 9-304(5)
Consumer goods	9-109(1)	Attachment is sufficient for purchase money security interests in consumer goods. Filing or compliance with a certificate of title statute is required for motor vehicles, boats, trailers, etc. For other security interests in consumer goods, general rules apply.	9-302(1)(d) 9-302(3) 9-302(4); 9-305
Equipment	9-109(2)	Filing, usually.	9-302(1)(a);9-305
Farm products	9-109(3)	Filing.	By implication from 9-109(3)
Inventory	9-109(4)	Filing, usually.	9-302(1)(a)

can be determined only by reference to the relevant state's version of Section 9-401. Because neither central nor local filing is clearly best for all jurisdictions, Section 9-401 "is drafted in a series of alternatives; local considerations of policy will determine the choice to be made" [9-401, comment 1]. Users of the filing system who wish to acquire credit information about thousands of people at once might prefer a centralized filing system. On the other hand, if most credit inquiries about businesses, farmers, and consumers come from local sources, local files may be preferable. There is one point of general agreement, however. If goods are or are to become fixtures, a *fixture filing* is required, and "the proper filing place . . . is in the office where a mortgage on the real estate concerned would be filed or recorded . . ." [9-401, comment 2].[9]

---

[9]Sec. 9-313(1)(b) defines "fixture filing." Other important sections dealing with financing statements and their filing are sec. 9-402(3), which gives an example of a sufficient filing form, and sec. 9-403, on what constitutes filing and the duration for which filing is effective.

Case 28.1   **James Talcott, Inc. v. Franklin National Bank**[*]
                 194 N.W.2d 775 (Minn. 1972)

On February 20, 1968, Noyes Paving Company, debtor, entered into an installment conditional sales contract with Northern Contracting Company,

---

[*]*Note:* All the cases in this chapter were decided on the basis of provisions in the 1962 Official Text of Article 9. However, each case involves only such provisions as remain essentially the same in the 1972 revision of the article.

seller, for two dump trucks and other construction equipment. On the same day, seller assigned the contract to James Talcott, Inc., plaintiff. On February 21, 1968, a financing statement covering "Construction Equipment, Motor Vehicles" was filed with the secretary of state.

On May 1 and May 31, debtor entered into equipment leases with Franklin National Bank of Minneapolis, defendant, covering additional dump trucks and equipment. Each lease provided that debtor, if not in default, could purchase the leased goods at the end of the lease term for $1. Defendant bank did not at that time file a financing statement regarding these leases.

Later in 1968 debtor experienced difficulty in making payments on the conditional sales contract, and on January 30, 1969, debtor and Talcott entered into an agreement extending the time for payment. In consideration for the extension, debtor gave Talcott a security interest "in all goods . . . whether now owned or hereafter acquired." No additional financing statement was filed in connection with the extension agreement. Talcott did not know of the existence of the motor vehicles and equipment listed in the bank's equipment lease.

Debtor defaulted on both the conditional sales contract and the equipment leases. On May 21, Franklin Bank filed copies of the leases as financing statements. Sometime during May 1970, the bank repossessed the leased equipment. Plaintiff Talcott commenced this action for recovery of possession of several motor vehicles, or their value, in which plaintiff claimed a superior security interest. The trial court granted summary judgment in favor of defendant bank. Plaintiff appealed.

RONALD E. HACHEY, J. . . . The issues on appeal are: . . .

1. *Were the leases security agreements?*

. . . It is the clear policy of Art 9 of the code to look to the substance, rather than to the form, of an agreement to determine whether or not it is a security agreement. . . . The words of Section 1-201(37)[†] are unequivocal. An option given to the lessee to purchase the leased property for a nominal consideration does make the lease one intended for security. Hence, the options to buy the equipment in the instant case for the combined sum of $2, nominal in amount when compared to the total rental of $73,303.32, created security interests. . . . We hold, as did the trial court, that the leases in question were security agreements even though they purported to reserve title in the bank.

2. *Did the debtor "own" the leased property so that it is included as secured property under plaintiff's security agreement?*

This question is a part of the critical issue in the case inasmuch as the

---

†In Minnesota (and in some other states) each section of the UCC is preceded by another number. Thus, the Minnesota citation to UCC, sec. 1-201(37) is 336.1-201(37). For the sake of simplicity, the state number preceding the UCC section number is omitted in the excerpts from cases in this chapter.

second security agreement between plaintiff and debtor (the extension agreement of January 30, 1969) gave plaintiff a security interest in "all goods . . . whether now owned or hereafter acquired" by debtor. The issue turns on whether or not debtor can be deemed to have owned the leased property at the time it entered into the extension agreement. . . . The draftsmen of the code intended that its provisions should not be circumvented by manipulation of the locus of title. For this reason, consignment sales, conditional sales, and other arrangements or devices whereby title is retained in the seller for a period following possession by the debtor are all treated under Art 9 as though title had been transferred to the debtor and the creditor-seller had retained only a security interest in the goods. For the purpose of analyzing rights of ownership under Art 9, we hold, based upon the stipulated facts of this case, that defendant had only a security interest in the equipment despite a purported reservation of title and that debtor "owned" the equipment at the time that the extension agreement was executed.

3. *Was the description of the secured property, as it appeared in the extension agreement, sufficient to meet the requirements of Art 9; that is, did the description reasonably identify what was being described?*

. . . A number of courts have sustained security agreements containing descriptions almost as general as the one in question in the instant case. Section 9-203(1)(b) . . . states that [the security agreement] must contain "a description of the collateral." Section 9-110 . . . provides:

> "For the purposes of this article any description of personal property or real estate is sufficient whether or not it is specific if it reasonably identifies what is described."

The principal function of a description of the collateral in a security agreement is to enable the parties themselves or their successors in interest to identify it, particularly if the secured party has to repossess the collateral. . . .

The description of the collateral in the extension agreement . . . included all of the goods then owned, or to be owned in the future, by the debtor. . . . The policy of Art 9 is to uphold security agreements according to their terms. . . . We hold that [the description] suffices within the terms of the statute. We further hold specifically that the description used in the extension agreement between debtor and plaintiff includes the equipment financed by defendant bank.

4. *Was the financing statement, filed at the time the first security agreement was assigned to plaintiff, sufficient to reflect a security interest in the property covered by the extension agreement?*

Defendant argues that plaintiff [Talcott] did not perfect its security interest in the equipment covered by the . . . extension agreement . . . because of the failure to file an amendment to the financing statement. The trial court also followed this line of reasoning in arriving at its decision that plaintiff had not perfected its security interest.

Section 9-402(1) provides that "a financing statement may be filed before a security agreement is made or a security interest otherwise attaches." This is what happened in the instant case. The financing statement filed February 21, 1968, met all requirements of the code since it described by type ("Construction Equipment, Motor Vehicles") not only the property covered by the original sales agreement which was assigned to plaintiff but also the property, which likewise consisted of motor vehicles and construction equipment, financed by defendant. The code does not require a reference in the financing statement to after-acquired property. . . .

The whole purpose of notice filing would be nullified if a financing statement had to be filed whenever a new transaction took place between a secured party and a debtor. Once a financing statement is on file describing property by type, the entire world is warned, not only that the secured party may already have a security interest in the property of that type . . . but that it may later acquire a perfected security interest in property of the same type acquired by the debtor in the future. When the debtor does acquire more property of the type referred to in the financing statement already on file, and when a security interest attaches to that property, the perfection is instantaneous and automatic. Section 9-303(1). . . .

The error of the trial court in the instant matter was apparently prompted by its reliance on Section 9-402(4), which provides that any amendment adding collateral to a financing statement is effective as to the added collateral only from the filing date of the amendment. . . . However, the financing statement originally filed was broad enough to cover the after-acquired collateral. If, for instance, the equipment leases between the debtor and defendant had included items which did not fall within the description "Construction Equipment, Motor Vehicles" (for example, machine tools), then it would have been necessary, in order for plaintiff to perfect its security interest in such different goods, to file either a new financing statement or an amendment to the original one. In either event, the effective date would have been the date of filing. . . .

5. Priority

From an examination of the record, it is clear that Section 9-312(4) [does not give defendant bank priority] inasmuch as defendant's security was not perfected within the allotted time thereunder—that is, no financing statement had been filed at the time that the debtor received the equipment or within 10 days thereafter. Had a financing statement covering the equipment leases been filed at the time the transaction between debtor and defendant took place or within 10 days thereafter, defendant would have had priority under this section of the code. Unfortunate as it may be for defendant, this did not take place; hence Section 9-312(4) does not govern despite the bank's later filing. . . .

The summary judgment for defendant is reversed, and the matter is remanded with directions to enter judgment for plaintiff. . . .

Methods of perfection: Special rules A method of perfection may be appropriate in some business situations but inappropriate in others. Article 9 therefore provides special perfection rules aimed at making the credit extension process practical and fair. Some of these rules are stated in terms of type of collateral and may be located by use of Table 28.1. Special rules of major importance are discussed in the paragraphs that follow.

To encourage sellers of goods to extend credit, Article 9 gives favored treatment to the purchase money security interest (PMSI) defined in Section 9-107. Special rules for perfecting PMSIs are found throughout Article 9. These rules vary according to whether the PMSI is in consumer goods, inventory, collateral other than inventory, or fixtures.

The rule for perfecting a PMSI in fixtures is too complex to be summarized here. It can be found in Section 9-313(4)(a). As noted in Table 28.1, the PMSI in *consumer goods* is perfected as soon as the security interest attaches. A PMSI in collateral other than inventory (such as equipment for a retail store or a machine for a factory) will receive maximum protection only if the security interest is perfected (by filing) no later than 10 days after the debtor receives possession of the collateral [9-312(4)]. (Filing is necessary because the debtor receives possession.)

Frequently, a credit seller of inventory (purchase-money secured party) needs protection from previously filed security interests of conflicting secured parties. To gain this protection, the purchase money secured party must do two things *before* the debtor receives possession of the inventory. The purchase money secured party must (1) perfect his or her interest and (2) give written notice to record holders of conflicting security interests in the inventory that he or she "expects to acquire a purchase

money security interest in inventory of the debtor . . ." [9-312(3)]. Suppose Bank B, under the future-advances provisions of a filed loan agreement, grants Dan Debtor (D) loans for the purchase of inventory. If D is fraudulent or careless, he might keep the money and purchase the inventory on credit, granting to his inventory seller a PMSI in the inventory. The requirement that the inventory seller give advance notice to the bank enables the bank to police D's inventory purchasing activities and thus to avoid possible loss.

A security interest in the *proceeds* of a debtor's disposition of collateral is the subject of other special perfection rules. Suppose that S sells D a lathe and perfects a security interest in the lathe. If D sells the lathe to X, what are S's rights to the proceeds of the sale? Under Section 9-306(2), a security interest in collateral continues in any identifiable cash or noncash proceeds. Section 9-306(3) provides essentially that if the security interest in the original collateral was perfected, the security interest in proceeds remains perfected for 10 days, but then becomes "unperfected" unless the secured party makes a special filing with respect to the proceeds or takes possession of them.[10]

Default

Meaning of Default as Used in Article 9 Part 5 of Article 9 is labeled "Default." Inasmuch as the word "default" is not defined in the Code, the word as used in the article is to be interpreted in its common law meaning of a failure to perform a legal duty. The range of default

---

[10]The 1962 version of Article 9 requires the secured party to make in the financing statement an express claim to proceeds, if he or she wishes to reserve a right in them. The 1972 Revised Article 9 removes the requirement by treating the original filing as an automatic filing with respect to proceeds.

possibilities will depend in part upon what the parties have specified in the security agreement as duties [9-201]. In the absence of adequate contract provisions, the court may have to decide what duties have been undertaken. Misunderstandings and litigation are minimized if the agreement clearly states the rights and duties of the parties.

Rights of Secured Party and Debtor upon Default If the debtor defaults, the provisions of Article 9, Part 5, come into play. These provisions embody three key principles: (1) The secured party should be free to possess and dispose of the collateral efficiently, and he or she usually should be allowed to hold the debtor personally liable for a deficiency if the amount realized upon disposition is insufficient to discharge the debt. (2) The debtor should usually receive surplus proceeds of the collateral and must be protected from unreasonable or wasteful dispositions of the collateral. (3) Secured parties and debtors must be free to structure the security agreement to meet widely varying business needs. In furtherance of these principles, the Code provides a few basic, nonwaivable rules, but leaves much for the parties to decide in the security agreement.

Upon default of the debtor, the secured party usually faces two problems: (1) how to acquire control of the collateral and (2) how to dispose of the collateral in a manner that minimizes loss. Article 9 permits the secured party considerable latitude in repossessing and disposing of the collateral.

Acquisition of Control of Collateral upon Default Unless the secured party possesses the collateral at the time of default, he or she must take steps to acquire control. Under Section 9-501(1), the secured party "may reduce his claim to judgment, foreclose, or otherwise enforce the security interest by any available judicial procedure." Section 9-502 permits the secured party to (1) notify the debtor's account debtor (usually a purchaser "on time" from the debtor) to make payment directly to the secured party, and to (2) "take control of any proceeds to which he is entitled. . . ." Section 9-503 provides that unless otherwise agreed, the secured party may take possession of the collateral after default without judicial process, if he or she can do so without breach of the peace. In lieu of removal of bulky equipment, the secured party may render it unusable and dispose of (e.g., sell) it on the debtor's premises.

Some courts have invalidated repossessions that were accomplished without granting the debtor a prior hearing. The reasoning of these courts is that by failing to provide for a prior hearing, Section 9-503 violates the Fourteenth Amendment to the Constitution, which forbids the states to "deprive any person of life, liberty, or property, without due process of law." However, most courts reason that Section 9-503 repossession activity is private action, not state action, and thus does not violate the due process clause. Underlying many of these decisions is the belief that a requirement of a prior hearing may dry up some types of credit or increase its cost, without significantly increasing the debtor's protection from unwarranted governmental interference.

Disposition of Collateral upon Default Largely to protect the debtor, Article 9 imposes disposition rules that are not subject to change by the security agreement. Section 9-207(1), for instance, imposes upon the secured party a nonwaivable duty of reasonable care "in the custody and preservation of collateral in his possession." This duty applies both before and after the debtor's default [9-501(2)]. Under Section 9-501(3), the debtor is granted rights to (1) a commercially reasonable disposition of collateral, (2) an accounting for surplus proceeds of collateral, (3) a prescribed disposition of consumer goods subject to a security interest if the debtor has paid 60 percent of the cash price, (4) a redemption of collateral that has been taken in settlement of debt, and (5) appropriate remedies if the secured party fails to comply with Part 5.[11] However, the secured party must be allowed to dispose of the collateral efficiently. Therefore, after the debtor defaults, a few of these rights may be waived by the debtor, and the secured party may "sell, lease, or otherwise dispose of any or all of the collateral . . ." [9-504(1)].

The security agreement may spell out in considerable detail the rights and duties of the parties with regard to disposition of collateral. The following points illustrate matters that might be considered for inclusion in the security agreement.

1 If the secured party must exercise his or her rights to the collateral, how is the property to be valued? Collateral is often work in process with no clear market value. The parties should anticipate valuation difficulties when making the security agreement.

---

[11]Sec. 9-507(2) and accompanying comments discuss the meaning of a commercially reasonable disposition; secs. 9-505 and 9-504 and comments, the disposition of consumer goods. Sec. 9-501(3) lists sections pertaining to the other rights listed above.

2 What rights should the parties have if the collateral is inventory or equipment? Accounts, chattel paper, and instruments can be collected without interrupting the business, but removal of inventory or equipment could halt the business. Although the security agreement can provide the secured party with valid before-default rights in collateral, a too-early exercise of rights against inventory or equipment might violate the good faith provision of the Code.

Contract provisions and the rules of Article 9 are but two factors that may affect a secured party's right to repossess and dispose of collateral. Another factor is the prior dealings between the debtor and the secured party. Suppose, for example, that the debtor had been late with some of the payments and that the creditor had accepted the late payments without protest. This pattern of conduct could reasonably cause the debtor to believe that delay in making a future payment would not result in seizure of the collateral. Under such circumstances the secured party may lose the right to repossess the collateral unless he or she notifies the debtor that late payments will no longer be tolerated.

Case 28.2   In re Bishop
482 F.2d 381 (4th Cir. 1973)

Per curiam. Roanoke Industrial Loan & Thrift Corporation appeals from an order of the district court which denied its petition to stay the discharge in bankruptcy of Mrs. Christine J. Bishop while it brought suit in state court to subject property owned by Mr. and Mrs. Bishop . . . to its claim of indebtedness. We affirm the order denying the stay.

[The Bishops] had purchased an outboard motorboat and trailer costing $3,313. They paid $413 down and jointly executed a note for $4,041 representing the balance due, creditor life insurance premiums, and finance charges. The seller assigned the note without recourse to Roanoke along with a purchase money security interest. After paying eight installments aggregating $674, the Bishops defaulted on the note. Roanoke repossessed the boat and its equipment, credited the proceeds from its resale in the amount of $2,000 on the debt, and claimed a deficiency of $1,088 including costs. Several months after the sale, but before Roanoke obtained a judgment for the deficiency, Mrs. Bishop filed a voluntary petition in bankruptcy. . . .

The referee conducted an evidentiary hearing on Roanoke's petition for a stay. He found that Roanoke had failed to comply with the provisions of the Uniform Commercial Code . . . governing the sale of repossessed collateral. Concluding, therefore, that Roanoke was not entitled to collect the deficiency, the referee denied the stay, and the district court affirmed. . . .

Roanoke . . . contends that the bankruptcy court erred in holding that the sale of the Bishop collateral did not comply with the law. We find no merit in this assignment of error.

The Uniform Commercial Code provides that a secured creditor may purchase repossessed collateral only at a public sale unless the collateral is of the type customarily sold in a recognized market, or is subject to standard price quotations.[*]

The evidence disclosed that Roanoke's notice of sale to the Bishops was returned unclaimed. Roanoke then moved the boat to a used car lot. It did not advertise the sale in any newspaper. It posted no signs announcing the event. Roanoke's collection manager testified [that] he mentioned the sale to anyone he thought would be interested. The credit manager, who held the sale, testified that he neither advertised it nor invited anyone to attend. No one passing the lot could have known an auction was taking place. Other than Roanoke's representatives, only two people were present at the sale. The manager admitted that they were probably employees of the used car lot. One of them, possibly both, bid at the sale, but how high they bid is not shown. Roanoke purchased the collateral for $1,500 and subsequently resold it for $2,000, which it credited to Mrs. Bishop's account.

Gilmore, in his commentary on Section 9-504(3) . . . says:

> "Presumably the essence of a 'public sale' is that the relevant public is not only invited to attend but is also informed, by whatever means of publicity may be appropriate, when and where the sale is to be held. If the sale has not been appropriately publicized, it would not be a public sale no matter where it was held or how it was conducted." 2 G. Gilmore, *Security Interests in Personal Property*, 1242 (1965).

. . . We conclude, therefore, that the bankruptcy court's ruling that Roanoke did not conduct a public sale is supported by the evidence and the law.

The commercial code imposes liability on a secured creditor who disposes of collateral without complying with the law.[†] It is silent, however, about the creditor's right to recover a deficiency, and courts have not ruled uniformly on

---

[*The court quoted sec. 9-504(3).]
[†The court quoted sec. 9-507(1), (2).]

this issue. Several courts have held that compliance is a condition precedent to recovery. [Citations.] Other courts hold to the contrary.

In the absence of a definitive ruling by the Supreme Court of Virginia, we cannot say that the bankruptcy court erred in concluding that Roanoke was barred from recovering a deficiency judgment because it disposed of the collateral in a manner not permitted by the code. [Gilmore] advocates this rule . . . and the result is consistent with the pre-code Virginia law.[‡]

But the outcome of this appeal need not rest on speculation about the rule Virginia ultimately will apply to recovery of deficiencies. Even under the alternative theory adopted by some courts, Roanoke cannot prevail. Courts that allow a secured creditor to recover a deficiency although he has not fully complied with the law hold that the debt is not to be credited merely with the proceeds of sale; instead, the debtor must be credited with the amount that reasonably should have been obtained through a lawful sale—that is, the credit must be equivalent to the market value. Logically, the amount of the proceeds is not evidence of the market value, and a creditor who has not complied with the law has the burden of proving by other evidence that the market value is less than the balance due. [Citations.]

Roanoke's credit manager admitted that the collateral did not bring its market value at the sale, but he ventured the opinion that it brought 75 percent of its value. His professional qualifications for making this estimate are not shown. Indeed, he conceded that he could not testify what the collateral actually was worth. Roanoke introduced no other evidence of the market value. Nor did resale of the collateral for an additional $500, and the crediting of this sum on Mrs. Bishop's account, prove that the disposition of the collateral was commercially reasonable or that the aggregate credit of both sales represented the market value of the collateral. Roanoke did not introduce an appraisal of the property or even evidence of sales of comparable property. The resale does not appear to have been made through a broker or dealer, or in the usual manner in any recognized market. Circumstances of the resale, including advertising, were not disclosed. In short, the only proof of market value was the amount the collateral brought at sales that were neither lawful nor commercially reasonable. This proof is insufficient, as a matter of law, to secure a deficiency judgment.

Roanoke has not established its claim under either theory pertaining to recovery of deficiency judgments when a secured creditor does not follow the law in disposing of collateral. We conclude, therefore, that the bankruptcy court properly exercised its equitable jurisdiction by declining to stay the bankrupt's discharge.

The judgment is affirmed.

[‡The Court pointed out in a footnote that "unless displaced by the Uniform Commercial Code, a state's prior commercial law supplements the Code" (so provided in UCC, sec. 1-103) and that "this provision supports the bankruptcy court's application of pre-code Virginia Law."]

Case 28.3   **Michigan National Bank v. Marston**
185 N.W.2d 47 (Mich. App. 1970)

Defendant Marston purchased damaged automobiles and repaired and resold them. In April 1966, defendant purchased for $1,350 a 1965 Imperial convertible which had been gutted by fire. He arranged with the Michigan National Bank (plaintiff) for a 90-day loan but did not reveal to the bank the condition of the car. After receiving the loan, signing the note, and giving the bank a security interest in the car, defendant was injured in an automobile accident and hospitalized for an extended period of time. Ultimately he went into bankruptcy. In September 1966, when the note had not been paid, the bank learned that the car was in storage and that the garage owner was demanding $600 in storage fees.

Upon receiving title from the trustee in bankruptcy in January 1967, the bank tried to sell the car to three dealers in repossessed and damaged cars. Only one dealer, the garage owner, made an offer—$500. The offer was rejected because the offeror was a poor credit risk. The bank brought suit on defendant's note in October 1967.

The trial court, sitting without a jury, determined that defendant's loan had been obtained under false pretenses and was therefore not discharged in the bankruptcy proceedings. The trial court further determined that the bank's obtaining title and attempting to sell the car were commercially reasonable under provisions of the Uniform Commercial Code. There was a judgment for plaintiff bank and defendant appealed.

BORRADAILE, J. . . . As the debt was not discharged in the bankruptcy proceedings, we next consider the question of the propriety of the bank's actions under Article 9 of the Uniform Commercial Code. The basic issue raised is whether the bank, having a security interest in the car and holding title to the car after bankruptcy, was required to dispose of the collateral before bringing suit for the balance owing on the note.

. . . It is defendant's position that under Section 9-505(1), plaintiff was required to dispose of the car under Section 9-504 which in turn provides inter alia for the sale of collateral by secured parties.

Section 9-505(1) states in pertinent part:

> "If the debtor has paid *60% of the cash price in the case of a purchase money security interest in consumer goods or 60% of the loan in the case of another security interest in consumer goods*, and has not signed after default a statement renouncing or modifying his rights under this part *a secured party who has taken possession of collateral must dispose of it under section 9-504*, and if he fails to do so within 90 days after he takes possession the debtor at his option may recover in conversion or under section 9-507(1) on secured party's liability." (Emphasis supplied.)

The proofs below [from the lower court] establish that defendant made no payments at any time on the note. Moreover, defendant has never alleged that he paid "60% of the cash price . . . or 60% of the loan." As the code clearly intends such payment to be a condition precedent to the operation of Section 9-505(1), *supra*, we consider the section to be irrelevant to the instant case.

It is of course basic law that the purpose of collateral is to secure the creditor and increase his chance of recovery in the case of default. The existence of a security interest in no way affects the existence of the debt. It merely provides the secured party with an immediate source of recovery in addition to the standard remedies of an unsecured creditor. Thus, for example, should a sale take place under Section 9-504(2), the debtor remains fully liable for any deficiency after the proceeds are applied to the debt.

. . . Section 9-501(1) provides "the rights and remedies referred to in this subsection are cumulative." In discussing this point Professor Steinheimer has written:

> "The code contemplates considerable flexibility in the default procedures which can be used by the secured party. He can (1) proceed under part 5 of article 9, (2) proceed under appropriate provisions of the security agreement and (3) proceed as a judgment creditor. These procedures are cumulative and may be employed without danger of election of remedies. . . ."[*]

We, therefore, conclude that the intent of the code was to broaden the options open to a creditor after default rather than to limit them under the old theory of election of remedies.

As the facts of the instant case illustrate, defendant's argument, if accepted, could reduce a secured creditor to a position less favorable than an unsecured creditor. Here the collateral was placed by defendant in the physical control of a garageman, resulting in a lien superior to plaintiff's . . . and for an amount quite possibly in excess of the value of the car. If plaintiff were required to sell the collateral, he would have to first pay the garageman or file suit to challenge the propriety of the claim. In either event plaintiff would effectively be increasing the amount owed it by a debtor who has already defaulted and whose assets have been greatly reduced by bankruptcy. We do not believe that the code intended such a strained result. . . .

In the instant case there was no evidence adduced below tending to substantiate either that plaintiff acted in any way other than a commercially reasonable manner or that defendant suffered a loss by plaintiff's failure to sell or return title. This court will not assume unreasonableness or the existence of a loss where neither has been alleged or proven.

Affirmed.

[*Michigan Compiled Laws Annotated, sec. 440.9501 (i.e., UCC, sec. 9-501), Practice Commentary by Roy L. Steinheimer, Jr.]

Priorities among Conflicting Interests

The priorities provisions of Article 9 determine which claimants will prevail when there is a dispute over collateral. Most conflicts fall into one of the four categories discussed below.[12]

Priorities among Conflicting Security Interests in the Same Collateral Conflicting security interests in the same collateral can arise in a number of ways. Often the conflict is between a PMSI of a trade creditor and the security interest of a lender, such as a bank. Suppose that Bank B makes a start-up loan to newly formed Corporation C, and that B includes an after-acquired property clause in the security agreement. If Dealer D thereafter sells C a piece of equipment and retains a PMSI in the equip-

---

[12]Priorities in a fifth category, accessions and commingled goods, are stated in secs. 9-314 and 9-315.

ment, a conflict exists between the security interests of B and D. Under Section 9-312(4), D's PMSI prevails if it was perfected at the time D received possession of the equipment, or within 10 days thereafter. If Supplier S (another trade creditor) sells C some inventory, retains a PMSI in the inventory, and complies with Section 9-312(3), S's PMSI would also prevail over B's security interest. Similar priority rules are found in Section 9-312(1) and (2).

For other situations involving priorities among conflicting interests in the same collateral, Section 9-312(5) provides that "(a) Conflicting security interests rank according to priority in time of filing or perfection. . . . (b) So long as conflicting security interests are unperfected, the first to attach has priority." These rules would apply if, for example, two banks were claiming the same collateral.

Case 28.4   In re Automated Bookbinding Services, Inc.
471 F.2d 546 (4th Cir. 1972)

On November 20, 1968, Automated Bookbinding Services, Inc. (Automated), a Maryland corporation, executed an installment note for $151,267.75 payable to the order of Finance Company of America (FCA). Automated signed a chattel mortgage security agreement to secure the obligation. On November 21, 1968, FCA perfected its security interest by filing in Anne Arundel County, Maryland, a financing statement covering Automated's after-acquired property as well as its present equipment.

On January 30, 1970, Automated contracted with Hans Mueller Corporation (HMC) for the purchase and installation of a new bookbinder. HMC retained a valid purchase money security interest in the machine for an unpaid balance of $51,540. Fifteen cases of component parts for the binder were sent from Europe under a negotiable bill of lading to the order of HMC's shipping agents. On May 22, 1970, HMC mailed an invoice to Automated identifying the binder's parts by particular description and serial numbers, and providing for payment of the balance in cash upon completion of the installation.

Upon HMC's instructions, the shipper directed a common carrier to pick up the 15 crates from dockside in New York and to deliver them to Automated in Maryland. The crates arrived at Automated's plant in Maryland on several dates between May 26, 1970, and June 2, 1970. HMC's employees completed the installation not earlier than June 13 nor later than June 19, 1970. On June

15, HMC filed a financing statement in Anne Arundel County, Maryland, to perfect its purchase money security interest in the binder. Automated filed a petition in bankruptcy on February 24, 1971.

The referee in bankruptcy held that bankrupt Automated received possession of the binder on June 2 when the last crates were delivered, and that since HMC's June 15 filing came more than 10 days after the debtor received possession, HMC lost its Section 9-312(4) priority.[*] On HMC's petition for review of the referee's order, the District Court awarded the right to possession of the binder to HMC. FCA appealed.

The appellate court's opinion discusses a number of Article 9 passages. Only so much of the opinion as concerns the meaning of "possession" under Article 9 is included in the following excerpts from the court's opinion.

SOBELOFF, Sr. Cir. J. . . . This case presents the single issue of which of the two secured creditors, FCA or the purchase money security interest holder HMC, is entitled to the binder. . . .

HMC's claim of priority under Section 9-312(4), as a purchase money security interest holder, depends on how the word "possession," used in that section, is to be defined. . . . [The District Court held that] possession did not occur . . . until the tender of delivery terms the bankrupt bargained for with HMC were completed [and that] installation was a tender of delivery term. . . .

We reject the District Court's holding that possession was received by the bankrupt when [installation was] completed, between June 13 and 19. Such an approach confuses the Article 2 tender of delivery concept with the Article 9 notion of possession.

"Possession" is one of the few terms employed by the Code for which it provides no definition. The Code's general purpose is to create a precise guide for commercial transactions under which businessmen may predict with confidence the results of their dealings. In defining "possession" we must be guided by these considerations as well as by the underlying theories unique to Article 9. . . .

"Possession" is used throughout Article 9 in establishing the filing scheme, in permitting debtors to retain use of collateral, and in providing perfection through means other than filing, such as through the secured party's taking possession. . . . Gilmore, a draftsman of Article 9, explains:

> " 'Receives possession' is evidently meant to refer to the moment when the goods are physically delivered at the debtor's place of business—not to the possibility of the debtor's acquiring rights in the goods at an earlier point by identification or appropriation to the contract or by shipment under a term under which the debtor bears the risk." 2 Gilmore, *Security Interests in Personal Property*, 787 (1965).

[*Sec. 9-312(4) states, "A purchase money security interest in collateral other than inventory has priority over a conflicting security interest in the same collateral if the purchase money security interest is perfected at the time the debtor receives possession of the collateral or within ten days thereafter."]

Case 28.4
Continued

Tender of delivery is a sales concept, employed by Article 2, which binds a buyer and seller to contractual conditions. It affects their rights against each other. It would be a serious error to allow those private conditions to affect the carefully defined rights of creditors under Article 9.

Secured parties are required, in most cases, to file a financing statement in order to perfect their security interest. To define "possession" as requiring completion of [installation] would permit a secured creditor to delay [installation or performance of some other] tender of delivery term and thereby avoid the filing requirement indefinitely. Even if a debtor would have use of the collateral he would not be deemed to have "possession," under the District Court's analysis, and purchase money security interest holders filing after complying with a tender of delivery term, at any future date, would still be entitled to the Section 9-312(4) priority. Such a result would frustrate the purpose of Article 9 and could not have been intended by the drafters.

To summarize, possession under Section 9-312(4) is not dependent upon completion of tender of delivery terms which affect only the buyer and seller of the goods. Since the last of the binder parts were delivered to the bankrupt, in their crates, on June 2, possession of the collateral was received on that date. HMC's failure to file its financing statement until June 15, more than 10 days later, causes it to lose its favored position under Section 9-312(4) and entitles FCA to the binder.

[The court then considered other errors of law in the district court's holdings and concluded by saying that "For all the reasons stated above" the judgment of the district court is reversed and the referee's original order is reinstated.]

Priorities between Security Interests and the Interest of a Third-Person Purchaser Sometimes the conflict is between the secured party and a purchaser from the debtor. Under Section 9-307(1), "a buyer [of goods] in ordinary course of business . . . takes free of a security interest created by his seller even though the security interest is perfected and even though the buyer knows of its existence."[13] This rule applies primarily when a debtor has granted to his or her lender a security interest in inventory and then makes sales from the inventory. The rule is intended to encourage buyers to pay full market values by minimizing the buyers' fear of loss at the hands of unseen creditors of the seller. Similar, but less extensive, protection is given to most purchasers of chattel paper, negotiable instruments, and documents [9-308 and 9-309].

Under Section 9-307(1), the buyer of goods is not necessarily, but could be, a consumer. Section 9-307(2), on the other hand, is interpreted to apply *only when* a purchaser of consumer goods has resold encumbered goods to another consumer.[14] If the original seller (the retailer) has retained a PMSI and perfected it by *attachment only*, his or her PMSI offers no

---

[13]Sec. 1-201(9) defines "buyer in ordinary course of business." If the buyer knows that terms of the security agreement are being violated, the buyer does not come within the definition of buyer in ordinary course of business, and he or she takes *subject to* the security interest.

[14]*Everett National Bank v. Deschuiteneen*, 244 A.2d 196 (N.H. 1968); also *Balon v. Cadillac Automobile Co.*, 303 A.2d 194 (N.H. 1973).

protection against a second consumer who "buys without knowledge of the security interest, for value and for his own personal family or household purposes. . . ." However, if the original seller had perfected *by filing* before the resale to the second consumer, the original seller would be protected from the claim of ownership of all subsequent purchasers.

Priorities of Liens Arising by Operation of Law   Sometimes collateral that is subject to a security interest must be sent out for repairs or improvements. The common law and statutes have long granted a bailee's lien to workers for the value of such services to goods. If a worker is not paid, will his or her bailee's lien have priority over the security interest? Section 9-310 gives priority to common law possessory liens and to most statutory possessory liens for materials or services furnished "with respect to goods subject to a security interest," even though the security interest is perfected. Workers who repair or improve goods in the ordinary course of their business thus have the traditional bailee's lien upon goods in their possession until reasonable payment has been made, unless the statute granting the lien expressly subordinates it to a prior security interest.

Priorities of Security Interests in Fixtures   For reasons of uniformity noted earlier in the chapter, Article 9 governs the creation and priority of security interests in fixtures. The article leaves the definition of the term "fixture" largely up to non-Code real estate law. However, Section 9-313(2) specifically states that "no security interest exists under this Article in ordinary building materials incorporated into an improvement on land." Such security interests are usually covered by local real estate mechanics' lien laws.

The fixture priority rules are best understood by examining the conflicts that the rules are intended to resolve. The usual conflict is between purchase money fixture financers and real estate financers. The real estate financer argues that fixtures should "feed" the real estate mortgage in order to offset building depreciation or otherwise to encourage real estate financing. Fixture financers argue that unless they are allowed to repossess unpaid-for fixtures, fixture credit will diminish and the improvement of real estate will be slowed.

The priority rules of Section 9-313 grant the fixture financer a limited priority. Suppose F sells a furnace to O and reserves a PMSI. Then O annexes the furnace to her house, which is subject to a real estate mortgage in favor of R. To prevail over R, F must perfect his PMSI by a "fixture filing" within 10 days after the furnace is annexed [9-313(4)(a)].[15]

Now suppose that the furnace is to be installed in a new house D is building, and that R is the construction financer. R's *construction mortgage* will prevail over F's PMSI, provided the construction mortgage is recorded "before the goods become fixtures if the goods become fixtures before the completion of the construction [9-313(6)]. The construction mortgage prevails because the drafters of the 1972 Amendments believed that financers of new construction were being unfairly surprised by unfiled security interests in fixtures installed after the construction mortgage was recorded.

In many other fixture priority situations, the first to file prevails [9-313(4)(b)].[16] This rule applies especially to situations in which a fixture has been annexed and a real estate interest has been subsequently granted (usually by mortgage or sale). Other priority situations are covered by Section 9-313, but they are too

---

[15]*Fixture filing* is defined in sec. 9-313(1)(b).

[16]It should be noted that the 1962 fixture priority rules differ substantially from the 1972 rules discussed in the text. One difference is that under the 1962 rules the construction mortgage does not prevail. Another difference is that under the 1962 rules the fixture financer acquires a "permanent" priority over preannexation real estate interests merely by completing the attachment process. However, even under the 1962 rules, the fixture financer must file first to prevail over subsequent real estate interests.

numerous or too complex for discussion in this chapter.

Conflict between Secured Parties and Debtor's Trustee in Bankruptcy

A debtor's bankruptcy raises the question of where the rights of secured parties end and the rights of general creditors begin. If the trustee in bankruptcy successfully challenges a security interest, the collateral becomes a part of the debtor's "estate" to be distributed to general creditors. If the security interest withstands the trustee's challenge, the secured party retains his or her rights in the collateral. To prevail over the trustee, the secured party must have complied not only with Article 9, but also with the federal Bankruptcy Code.

An attempt to create a security interest may run afoul of the Bankruptcy Code in a number of ways. For example, the security agreement may create a "voidable preference." The harm of a voidable preference is that the bankrupt debtor favors a particular creditor with a larger percentage of the debtor's property than other creditors of the same class would receive. Thus, the debtor subverts the distribution scheme of the Bankruptcy Code. A security interest granted "on or within 90 days" of bankruptcy (within 4 months, under the old bankruptcy law) for a debt that was originally unsecured is open to attack as a voidable preference.

The trustee's characteristic vigor in challenging Article 9 security interests should not be mistaken for a desire by the legal system to invalidate security interests generally. A bankruptcy court will not set aside a security interest unless it violates bankruptcy law. Even during the dangerous 90 days preceding bankruptcy, a secured party is permitted to acquire and enforce a security interest, although the secured party must be careful to give value at or very nearly at the time he or she acquires and perfects the interest. The old policy of general invalidation of security interests is gone.

SUMMARY

After the industrial revolution the demand for secured credit intensified, but satisfactory security techniques were slow to develop. The pre-Code law of secured transactions in personal property was marked by many independently developed security devices, gaps in coverage, and a judicial tendency to invalidate non-possessory security interests.

Article 9 of the Uniform Commercial Code brought order, and a clear policy of credit encouragement, to the law of secured transactions in personal property and fixtures. The general aim of Article 9 is to provide the legal framework for safe and efficient credit extension. To accomplish this aim, Article 9 (1) substitutes the term "security interest" for the variety of pre-Code descriptive terms; (2) substitutes a simplified public-notice filing system for the pre-Code system of different files, records, and indexes for each type of security device; (3) establishes a system of priorities for resolving disputes where there are conflicting interests in the same collateral; and (4) sets up a uniform method of liquidating collateral after default.

The secured party receives maximum protection if his or her security interest is attached and perfected. Attachment is the process of creating a security interest and of making it enforceable against the debtor. A security interest attaches upon the completion, in any order, of three attachment "events": (1) agreement between debtor and creditor, in writing unless the creditor possesses the collateral, that a security interest is to be created; (2) the giving of value by the creditor; and (3) acquisition by the debtor of rights in the collateral. Perfection is the process of making the security interest enforceable against others than the debtor. Perfection may be accomplished (1) by attachment only—that is, under certain circumstances perfection occurs automatically at the completion of the attachment events; (2) by the secured party's taking possession of the collateral; or (3) by the secured party's filing a financing statement in the public records. For certain types of collateral, a particular method of perfection is required; for other types, there is a choice of methods. Table 28.1 lists types of collateral and indicates the applicable methods of perfection.

Upon the debtor's default, the secured party has liberal repossession and disposition rights. However, the debtor is entitled to a commercially reasonable disposition of the collateral and cannot be subjected to harsh forfeiture clauses. The debtor is usually entitled to any surplus proceeds realized from disposition of the collateral, but remains personally liable for any deficiency.

Where claimants are in conflict concerning particular collateral, parties having a perfected PMSI usually prevail, even though other claimants completed the attachment and perfection processes earlier. In most other conflict situations, the first to perfect or, if there is no perfection, the first to attach prevails. Priorities in fixtures are more complex because more claimants are involved, but similar priority and disposition rules govern. A trustee in bankruptcy may prevail over secured parties who complied with Article 9 but not with bankruptcy law.

CASE STUDY: ANATOMY OF A SECURED TRANSACTION UNDER ARTICLE 9

Even in a simple business situation, a secured transaction can affect the interests of a number of people. Indeed, the need to balance the conflicting interests of several people at once is the main reason why secured transactions law is so complex. The following case study illustrates the application of common secured transactions principles. Although the business situation is fictitious, it presents a typical set of financing transactions.

The Business Situation

Donald (D), owner of a small general clothing store, decides to expand his business by enlarging the clothing sales operation and adding a small dry-cleaning facility. He must therefore acquire a delivery truck, dry-cleaning equipment, and a new line of men's clothing. D applies to a bank for a loan, listing the following assets that he would be willing to use as collateral:

- A life insurance policy—cash surrender value, $4,000.
- Trade fixtures and equipment worth $7,000.
- 50 shares of stock worth $5,000.
- Accounts receivable for clothing not paid for—face value, $3,000.

Bank officials evaluating D's application must decide which items of proposed collateral are substantial enough to support a loan. They must then classify the acceptable items in order to determine what action is necessary for the bank to become a secured creditor. They reach the following conclusions.

1 The life insurance policy is acceptable collateral. However, according to comment 7 on UCC Section 9-104, direct use of insurance as collateral is not efficiently governed by the Code and is sufficiently regulated by other state law. The bank grants a $4,000 loan on the insurance policy, in accordance with non-Code state law that regulates such loans.

2 The other assets fall within the broad categories of personal property covered by Article 9 and are not excluded by Section 9-104. The bank decides to lend $12,000 on the basis of this collateral.

Later, D makes the following arrangements with other financers.

1 A credit purchase from Gladrags, Inc., of clothing inventory to be paid for in installments out of the proceeds from sales.

2 An installment purchase from Steam Co. of a steam-heating unit for use in the dry-cleaning operation.

3 An installment purchase of a delivery truck from Truck Sales, Inc.

Acquisition of the Security Interest

Attachment and Perfection by the Bank D and the bank meet the attachment requirements of Section 9-203 in the following manner. D already has *rights in the collateral*; the parties *agree* to the creation of a security interest in the collateral; and the bank will give *value* by means of a $12,000 credit to D's account, but not until the security agreement that *describes* the collateral is committed to writing and signed by D. Since the shares of stock will be pledged, they need not be included in the security agreement, but the parties decide to include them as a matter of prudence. Anticipating that D may need to replace trade fixtures or equipment, the parties include an after-acquired property clause in their security agreement. The bank's security interest will not attach to new or replacement property until D acquires it. To expedite future loans, the parties also include a future-advances provision.

The bank officials now draw up and file a financing statement that conforms with the requirements of Section 9-402. The financing statement covers the trade fixtures (which by the real estate law of D's state are specifically exempted from fixture filing), and it covers the other equipment, the accounts receivable, and "any business property which may hereafter be acquired." The financing statement does not mention the shares of stock because a security interest in investment securities must be perfected by the bank's taking possession. The bank takes possession of the shares.

Attachment and Perfection by the Suppliers D and each of the installment sellers complete an attachment process similar to that completed by D and the bank, omitting, however, the after-acquired property and the future-advances provisions from their security agreements. The Code does not state when a debtor acquires rights in the collateral, but rights arise under the general law of contract when the parties enter into a binding agreement. An executory promise, here, to deliver goods, constitutes value under Section 1-201(44).

The sellers of the clothing, steam unit, and delivery truck draw up financing statements. Truck Sales files 5 days after D receives the truck. Gladrags takes the steps required to perfect a PMSI in inventory. Steam Co. makes an ordinary filing before delivery, but it also takes the precautionary step of entering a fixture filing in the local real estate records office before delivering the steam unit to D.

Default and Foreclosure

Soon after the installation of the steam unit and delivery of the clothing and the truck, D's business fails. For 6 months D makes no payments on any of his obligations other than the payments due on the real estate mortgage held by Farmer's Mortgage Co. on D's business premises. All the security agreements define default as the failure of D to make payments when due. The bank, contending that the after-acquired property clause entitles it to all items of business-related personal property and fixtures, institutes foreclosure proceedings. Upon hearing of the bank's suit, the other creditors react as follows.

1 Truck Sales sends an employee to repossess the truck, but when D's employee threatens her with physical harm, she leaves without it.

2 Steam Co., without opposition, renders the

steam unit unusable by removing an electronic monitoring system.

3 Farmer's Mortgage claims the steam unit as part of the real estate.

4 Gladrags, Inc., makes two claims: first, that it is entitled to the suits still in the possession of D, and second, that it is entitled to the proceeds of fifteen suits sold in the course of business or, in the alternative, to repossession of the suits from D's customers.

The bank directs its lawyers to advise it as to the rights of all parties. The lawyers agree that D is in default to all creditors except Farmer's Mortgage, which has been paid each month. The lawyers agree that all creditors have valid security interests and that the problem is to determine priorities.

As to the delivery truck, Truck Sales prevails over the bank because the PMSI was filed within the 10-day grace period permitted by Section 9-312(4). Truck Sales has a Section 9-503 right to repossess the truck, but to avoid a breach of the peace, Truck Sales must obtain a court order and, if necessary, have a law enforcement official carry out the repossession. Under Section 9-504, Truck Sales may then dispose of the truck in a commercially reasonable manner but must account to D for any surplus, calculated by subtracting various expenses of disposition and D's indebtedness from the proceeds. Unless the security agreement provides otherwise, D will be liable for any deficiency.

Steam Co.'s rights are complicated somewhat by the possibility that the steam unit—large, bolted in place, and attached to plumbing and electrical wiring—may be ruled an ordinary fixture and therefore a part of the real estate. If the unit is an ordinary fixture, Steam Co. and Farmer's Mortgage (the real estate creditor) are the rival claimants, and Steam Co. prevails under Section 9-313(4)(a) because it made a timely fixture filing. If the unit is a trade fixture,

the contestants are Steam Co. and the bank (by virtue of the after-acquired property clause), and the purchase money priority rules that aided Truck Sales give Steam Co. priority over the bank. Either way, Steam Co. wins and has the disposal rights and duties of Part 5 of Article 9.

Finally, Gladrags may prevail over the bank in two ways. First, it may repossess the unsold suits, since it complied with Section 9-312(3) in perfecting its PMSI in inventory. Second, Gladrags is entitled to the proceeds of the fifteen suits sold in the course of D's business if it has complied with Section 9-306(2) and (3) as to the perfection of a security interest in proceeds, and with Section 9-312(3) and (5)(a) as to priority of a security interest in proceeds of the sale of inventory. Regardless of whether Gladrags is entitled to the proceeds from the sale of the suits, the purchasers are entitled under Section 9-307(1) to keep them for the reasons indicated in the part of this chapter dealing with the rights of a third-person purchaser.

STUDY AND DISCUSSION QUESTIONS

1 *(a)* Distinguish between secured transactions and unsecured transactions. Give an example of each type. *(b)* What is the purpose of a secured transaction?

2 *(a)* What is a secret lien? Why did the courts usually invalidate such liens in pre-Code days? *(b)* What were the chief weaknesses in pre-Code law that prompted development of Article 9?

3 *(a)* What is the principal aim of Article 9? *(b)* State four provisions of the article that contribute greatly to the accomplishment of this aim.

4 *(a)* Briefly explain the coverage of Article 9. *(b)* Why are security interests in fixtures covered by Article 9 rather than by real estate law?

5 *(a)* What is the Code definition of *security interest*? *(b)* Why is the term defined so broadly? *(c)* Distinguish between a true lease and a "lease" that creates a security interest.

6 *(a)* With reference to a security interest, what is the function of attachment? *(b)* What must be done to accomplish attachment?

7 *(a)* What is meant by floating lien? *(b)* What is the purpose of an after-acquired property clause? Of a future-advances provision?

8 *(a)* What is the legal consequence of perfection of a security interest? *(b)* Name the three methods of perfection. Why are three methods necessary? *(c)* What information must a financing statement contain?

9 *(a)* Why is the purchase money security interest (PMSI) given priority? *(b)* How may a PMSI in inventory be perfected? Why is the procedure relatively complex?

10 *(a)* If the debtor disposes of collateral, how does the secured party acquire a security interest in the proceeds? *(b)* How would the security interest in proceeds be perfected?

11 *(a)* What is the meaning of default? *(b)* Briefly state the general principles that govern the repossession and disposition of collateral upon the debtor's default.

12 *(a)* How may the secured party repossess collateral upon the debtor's default? *(b)* What constitutes a commercially reasonable disposition of collateral?

13 Naming the usual participants, describe a typical conflict situation under each of the following headings: *(a)* Conflicting security interests in the same collateral. *(b)* Conflicting security interests in a fixture.

14 *(a)* What must a secured party do to prevail over the debtor's trustee in bankruptcy? *(b)* Under what circumstances may a secured party

enforce a security interest acquired within 90 days of bankruptcy?

CASE PROBLEMS

(*NOTE:* Each problem in this chapter involves provisions of Article 9 that have not been changed significantly in the 1972 revision. Therefore, each problem is to be solved by applying the relevant provisions of the 1972 revision of Article 9. The relevant provisions of the 1972 revision can be found in the text of the chapter or in Appendix 1.)

1 Blumenstein sold a boat, *Mermaid I*, to Martin Dredging, Inc. (Martin) for use in an Alaskan gold-dredging project. A "Conditional Sale Agreement," intended to give Blumenstein a security interest, was never filed. Martin defaulted in payments. Martin beached *Mermaid I* and purchased and outfitted a surplus minesweeper, the *Mermaid II*. Phillips Insurance Center, Inc., (Phillips) insured *Mermaid II*. Thereafter, the *Mermaid II* was sold to satisfy a judgment for unpaid sailors' wages. Phillips then filed suit against Martin for nonpayment of premiums for the insurance on *Mermaid II* and "attached" *Mermaid I*, thus becoming a lien creditor. A few days earlier Blumenstein had boarded *Mermaid I*, removed some equipment, and prepared the boat for the onset of winter. Section 9-301 of the UCC reads in pertinent part, ". . . an unperfected security interest is subordinate to the rights of a person who becomes a lien creditor before the security interest is perfected." Blumenstein claims *Mermaid I* on the ground that he had perfected his security interest in the boat before Phillips became a lien creditor. Did Blumenstein perfect his security interest?

2 Upon selling a cash register to Borgwald, National Cash Register (NCR) filed a financing statement in the proper places. Because NCR's clerk had misspelled Borgwald's name, the financing statement was indexed and filed under the name of "Boywald." The financing statement was also filed under Borgwald's correctly spelled trade name. A year later Borgwald granted to Valley National Bank (Bank) a security interest in personal property used in his business, including the cash register. The security agreement stated Borgwald's individual name but not the trade name. Bank properly filed a financing statement. Bank contends that NCR's filing was insufficient and that Bank therefore has a superior interest in the cash register. NCR contends that under Section 9-402(8) the filing was sufficient. Was NCR's filing sufficient to give NCR the protection of the filing statute?

3 Rosenblum owed $160,000 to American National Bank of Cheyenne (Bank). On January 11, 1965, to secure the debt and future advances, Rosenblum signed a security agreement covering his bar supplies and equipment and the liquor license that had been issued to him by the City of Cheyenne. A day later a proper financing statement was filed. On May 4, 1966, Rosenblum executed and delivered to Bank an instrument containing his acknowledgment that he was unable to redeem the security interest and his consent that Bank enforce its security interest by arranging for him to sell the collateral "so that the proceeds might be applied to the payment of his debts to the Bank." Bank made the necessary arrangements, and Rosenblum sold the bar supplies for $2,900 and the liquor license for $53,825. The total proceeds were turned over to Bank. Later Rosenblum was adjudicated a bankrupt, and the trustee in bankruptcy claimed the proceeds of the sale of the license. *(a)* Is the license "property" in which Bank can acquire a security interest? See Sections 9-102 and 9-106. *(b)* If the license is property in which Bank can acquire a security interest, does the security interest cover the proceeds from the sale of the license? See Section 9-306. *(c)* If Bank has a security interest

in the proceeds, would Bank necessarily prevail over the trustee? Explain.

4 Waters purchased a new 1970 Ford from Jones Ford, Inc., on April 25, 1969, and signed a security agreement containing default and repossession provisions that could be exercised by the financer, Ford Motor Credit Company (FMCC). One provision of the security agreement stated, "Time is of the essence of this contract." Waters made timely payments from May 1969 through January 1970. Thereafter, his payments were irregular and sometimes untimely. In June 1970, and again in September 1970, Waters received notice of late payment. On January 25, 1971, FMCC, acting through its agent Seagren, repossessed the car by making a duplicate set of keys and driving the car from the parking lot of Waters' place of business. At the time of the repossession, Waters was two months behind in his payments. Waters sued FMCC for wrongful repossession of his car. FMCC's defense was that the repossession was in accordance with the provisions of Section 9-503 of the UCC. Waters contended that FMCC had lost its right to repossess the car. *(a)* Was the repossession in accordance with the provisions of Section 9-503? *(b)* Had FMCC lost its right to repossess the car?

5 Penrose Industries Corporation owned radio WPEN. William and Harry Sylk, the chief officers in control of Penrose, pledged to Old Colony Trust Co. the stock of WPEN. After prolonged default by Penrose, Old Colony gave notice of intent to sell, and did sell, the collateral at a private sale. The Sylks contended that Old Colony's use of a private sale rather than a public sale was commercially unreasonable. In regard to this contention, what do Sections 9-504(3) and 9-507(2) suggest as to the commercial reasonableness of a private sale?

6 The Mar-K-Z Motors and Leasing Co. (Mar-K-Z) was primarily engaged in leasing automobiles, but it also sold automobiles no longer used in the leasing operation. In 1969 Mar-K-Z acquired a new Buick. The certificate of title issued by the Secretary of State showed that Mar-K-Z was the owner, that the automobile was a "lease unit," and that American National Bank (Bank) had a lien on the car in the amount of $6,250. Mar-K-Z leased the Buick for a period of time, and after reacquiring possession of it sold it to Buttel in March 1970. Mar-K-Z made payments to Bank up to March 1970 and thereafter was in default. Bank instituted a replevin action, seeking to recover possession of the car from Buttel. Is Bank entitled to possession of the car under Sections 9-307(1) and 1-201(9)?

7   On May 1, 1968, Mousel agreed in writing to sell his cattle to Daringer. Daringer paid one-half of the purchase price on the date of the agreement and received possession of half of the cattle. The agreement provided that Mousel was to retain possession of the other half of the cattle until he received payment ($58,000) for them and that he was to receive a fair and reasonable charge as "agister" for the care and feeding of the cattle left in his possession. On March 31, 1969, Daringer borrowed $58,000 from State Securities to pay for the cattle and granted that company a security interest in the cattle. The next day State Securities perfected its security interest. A statute of the state reads in part:

When any person shall hire . . . any other person to feed and take care of . . . livestock, the person . . . so . . . hired shall have a first . . . lien upon such property for the feed and care bestowed by him . . . , provided the holders of any prior liens shall have agreed in writing to the contract for the feed and care of the livestock. . . .

Mousel's reasonable charge as an agister was $18,523. State Securities contends that the cattle are not subject to Mousel's lien because State Securities did not agree in writing to the contract for their care. Whose lien should prevail? (See Section 9-310.)

PART SIX

INSURANCE

Chapter 29
Insurance

Chapter

29
Insurance

Everyone faces a risk of economic or financial loss in the conduct of business and personal activities. The sources of loss include negligence, intentional misconduct such as theft and vandalism, disease, labor disputes, war, and natural forces such as flood and earthquakes. Whatever its source, economic loss takes many forms. Among them are loss of or damage to physical assets such as household furnishings, real estate, and business equipment; a decrease in the value of corporate stock and other intangible personal property; loss of income, future productive capacity, and business reputation (goodwill); the loss of any accumulated assets that must be used to pay court-ordered judg-

ments or expenses attending illness, injury, and death; and the loss to a family or business of valuable personal services. Risk management and the prevention of loss are of obvious concern to business people.

To minimize the impact on themselves of economic losses that might occur, individuals and business firms use several techniques of risk management. Among them are hedging (the use of counterbalancing transactions in which losses will be offset by gains), risk control (by, for example, installing safety devices or taking precautions against burglary), risk transfer and distribution (commonly accomplished by means of an insurance contract), and self-insuring (a planned absorption of loss, usually engaged in by companies large enough to take protective measures such as the funding of a special loss account). This chapter deals with insurance, the principal means of transferring and distributing the risk of financial loss. The first part of the chapter discusses the nature of the insurance mechanism. Subsequent parts discuss insurance against personal risk (life and health insurance), insurance against property risks (property and liability insurance), the regulation of the insurance business, and the roles of insurance agents.

THE INSURANCE MECHANISM

Nature and Functions of Insurance

Transfer of Risk; Meaning of "The Insured"
A main function of insurance, the transfer of risk, is accomplished by means of a two-party contract called an "insurance policy." In a typical insurance policy, for a payment called a "premium" an insurance company (the insurer) agrees with another party (usually, the insured) to assume a specified risk that otherwise would have to be borne by the insured or by others such as the insured's family or business associates. The transfer of the risk from the insured to the insurer ordinarily occurs when the insurance contract arises. If the insured suffers a loss covered by the policy, the insurer makes payment in accordance with the terms of the policy, usually to the insured or to a third-party beneficiary. This payment, a compensation or reimbursement for actual loss, is called "indemnity." Suppose Alice pays an insurer $100 to insure her expensive sports car against fire or theft. If the car is destroyed by fire, the insurer will indemnify Alice by paying her the value of the car as of the time of the loss. Thus, by means of insurance, Alice has traded off the possibility of heavy loss for a certain but more moderate cost.

In insurance terminology, "the insured" has two basic meanings—one for property and liability insurance and another for life insurance. In property and liability insurance, "the in-

sured" is any person who is protected by a policy from risk of loss. Suppose that Imelda Smith purchases automobile insurance covering liability for personal injuries resulting from negligent operation of her car. The insurance policy, if typical, will protect Imelda and other licensed drivers to whom she might occasionally lend the car. All such persons are "insureds" under the policy and have a right to reimbursement from the insurer for amounts they are obliged to pay in settlement in claims covered by the policy. Suppose that Imelda's employee drives Imelda's car with her consent and negligently injures Joel Watson. The employee is "an insured" under Imelda's policy, and Watson has a claim against the employee for hospital bills, loss of income, and so on. As an insured, the employee may look to the insurance company for reimbursement for any amount he is required to pay Watson. However, even though the insurer might make payments directly to Watson without litigation, Watson is not himself an insured under Imelda's policy, but is only a claimant against one.

In *life* insurance, "the insured" is the person whose life is the subject of the insurance contract. The death benefit specified by the policy will be paid to someone *other than* the insured —directly to a named third person called the "beneficiary" or to the insured's estate for distribution to others. In life insurance, as in other kinds of insurance, "the insured" will often not be a party to the insurance contract. Suppose that A and B are business partners and that A insures the life of B and names herself (A) as beneficiary of the policy. A and the insurance company are the contracting parties; B is "the insured" (meaning here "the person whose life is the subject of the insurance policy"); and A is the beneficiary as well as the "policyholder" and the "policyowner."

Distribution of Risk: Pooling and Reinsurance Insurers distribute risk of loss mainly by use of two risk-spreading techniques—pooling and reinsurance. *Pooling* is a process of treating as a single group a large number of individual risks of a certain kind so that the *total* loss likely to be sustained by the group of insureds can be accurately estimated. Then individual losses are distributed among all in the pool by requiring all insureds in the pool to pay the same premium per unit of coverage regardless of the amount of loss sustained by any one individual. The premium paid by an individual insured covers the insured's share of predicted *pool* loss, an amount for administrative costs, and insurance company profit (if the insurer is one for profit).

Reinsurance is a contractual arrangement in which an insurance company transfers (cedes) a part of the group risk it has assumed to another insurance organization called a reinsurer. The ceding company is somewhat like an individual who buys insurance; that is, the ceding company pays the reinsurer to assume part of a risk that the ceding company believes might be too great for it to bear alone. By a process of pooling or of further reinsurance, the reinsurer distributes the ceding risk. Distribution occurs also where a ceding company transfers a fraction of its cedable risk to each of several reinsurers. In reinsurance, the ceded company does not assign individual insurance contracts or risks to the reinsurer, but, rather, transfers a portion of the aggregate risk. Therefore, an individual who buys insurance from a ceding company never becomes a party to a reinsurance contract. Reinsurance agreements are strictly between insurance organizations.

Indemnity Principle; Requirement of an Insurable Interest

Indemnity Principle   The principle of indemnity is based on the idea that insurance is a system for distributing losses and not for generating a profit. Therefore, in the event of casualty an insured should be limited to reimbursement (indemnity) for loss actually suffered. Suppose that Jamison has identical medical insurance policies with two different insurers, that each policy will reimburse her for up to $5,000 in hospital expenses in the event of her illness,

that she becomes ill and incurs $5,000 in hospital expenses, and that each policy has a "coordination-of-benefits" clause. Jamison files a claim with each insurer for $5,000 (for a total of $10,000). Under the coordination-of-benefits clauses, Jamison may collect only the amount of her loss and, moreover, *only a proportion* of her loss from each of the companies with which she has a policy. Since she has policies with two companies, she will collect $2,500 from each company and, since neither company is liable for the full amount of her loss, she will receive back from each company an appropriate proportion of the premiums she paid.

Coordination of benefits is consistent with the principle of indemnity. If Jamison were allowed to collect the $10,000 she sought, she would receive $5,000 profit, and premiums charged to all insureds would have to be large enough to provide the profit. Not all insurance policies have coordination-of-benefit clauses, however. Some insurers believe that such clauses impede sales of insurance and create disputes between insurers that delay the settlement of claims.

The principle of indemnity underlies many legal rules governing the interpretation and enforcement of insurance contracts. Examples are rules of law prohibiting the use of insurance contracts as gambling devices and rules (and contract clauses) requiring an insurer to distribute insurance proceeds to persons actually sustaining loss (e.g., the insured's mortgagee) rather than just to the person named in the insurance contract to receive benefits. The application of such rules helps minimize the cost of insurance by reducing the opportunities for a person to make a net gain from the insurance system. The indemnity principle of "reimbursement for actual loss only" is less often applied to life insurance than to other kinds such as property, liability, and health insurance.

Requirement of an Insurable Interest   The principle of indemnity is the source of the general requirement that a person who procures insurance must have an insurable interest in the property or life insured. An *insurable interest* is the financial stake that a person has in property or in someone's life or health. For example, you have an insurable interest in your car but not in mine. In property insurance, five common classes of circumstances give rise to an insurable interest. They are: ownership of and other rights in property; contract rights, as in a contract for the sale of goods; potential legal liability to others; one's acting as a representative in procuring insurance for another; and, in rare instances, a factual expectancy of economic disadvantage from damage to someone else's property (as where a payee of patent royalties sought insurance on the payor-oil processor's filtering plant to offset any decrease of royalties due to fire damage to payor's plant). In a contract for the sale of goods, a buyer obtains an insurable interest in the goods when they are *identified* to the contract (marked or otherwise designated as the subject of a particular contract of sale) even though the buyer might not yet have title to or possession of the goods.[1] In property and liability insurance, the insurable interest need exist only at the time of loss. This rule and the rules relating to identification of goods to a contract permit a person to make arrangements for insurance before acquiring property or being otherwise exposed to risk.

Ordinarily, a person may obtain insurance on his or her own life without regard to insurable interest, but to obtain valid insurance on the life of another, the person procuring the insurance must have an insurable interest, i.e., a financial stake, in the other's life. This requirement will usually be met where there is a close family relationship, as where a person seeks insurance on the life of his or her spouse or minor child to cover the expenses resulting from that person's untimely death. Where an adult seeks insurance on a parent's life, however, or where a person seeks insurance on the life of a brother, sister, uncle, niece, or other such family member, the

courts tend to require a showing of something more than the family relationship itself before holding that there is an insurable interest. The courts differ as to whether an existing financial interest must be shown in such instances. Often much less will do, as where an aunt who had supported her niece from infancy was held to have an insurable interest in the niece's life on the basis of an expectation that the aunt might eventually receive a return benefit from the niece. Where there is no family relationship, an actual financial interest is required. A creditor has an insurable interest in the life of his or her debtor; a business entity has an insurable interest in the life of a key employee; and a partner may have an insurable interest in the life of his or her partner.

In life insurance, the insurable interest need exist only when the policy is taken out. By preserving the validity of the policy beyond the extinguishment of the insurable interest, this rule helps preserve any cash values that might have accumulated, reduces the barriers to free assignability of cash-value policies, and enhances the marketability of life insurance by making clear to the public that policies will be honored. Cash values accumulate in policies where the premium charged exceeds the amount needed for immediate claims, administrative expenses of the insurer, and any profits that might be payable. Assignability of life insurance is discussed later in this chapter.

The requirement of an insurable interest is useful in at least three ways: (1) The existence of an insurable interest is evidence that personal or business economic loss is reasonably anticipated and that the insurance contract is not just a gambling device for making a speculative gain. Insuring the life of a total stranger in the hope of making a large gain from a small investment in premiums involves no insurable interest and results in an unenforceable wagering contract. In contrast, insuring the life of one's business partner may involve an expectation of economic loss to, and consequently an insurable interest

---

[1]The meaning and significance of identification to the contract are discussed in Chapter 24 of this volume.

in, the partner procuring the insurance. (2) The existence of an insurable interest helps pinpoint a specific property right or economic relationship and thus contributes to the proper reimbursement of the person or firm suffering loss. (3) The existence of an insurable interest tends to limit the operation of "moral hazard." *Moral hazard* is any characteristic of a potential recipient of insurance proceeds that will increase the frequency or severity of loss—poor health habits and tendencies toward fraud, arson, murder, accident-proneness, and exaggeration of claims, for example. Thus, if A insures B's car but has no insurable interest in it, A might be tempted to destroy the car to collect the insurance.

Case 29.1   Butler v. Farmers' Insurance Company of Arizona
616 P.2d 46 (Ariz. 1980)

In 1976, James Butler (plaintiff) purchased a 1967 Austin-Healy for $3,500. Butler was unaware that the car had been stolen. Approximately two years after the purchase, the Tucson police seized the car and returned it to its lawful owner. The car was insured against loss, and Butler filed a claim with the insurer for the value of the car. Alleging a lack of insurable interest, the insurer (defendant) refused to reimburse Butler for the loss, offering instead "$55 to $56" as a return of premiums paid. Butler brought suit against the insurer. The trial court granted the insurer's motion for summary judgment, the Court of Appeals reversed the decision of the trial court, and the insurer (the appellee at the Court-of-Appeals level) appealed the decision of the Court of Appeals.

HAYS, J. . . . Appellee [the insurer] based its refusal to reimburse upon a lack of insurable interest. Although the question of whether a bona fide purchaser of stolen commodities may claim this relationship is one of first impression in Arizona, we note that the appellate courts of several jurisdictions have considered this issue and are in disagreement. Some courts, relying upon, *inter alia,* the inability of a seller of stolen property to transfer valid title, deny the innocent purchaser an interest of insurable quality. [Citations.] Other jurisdictions, however, cite principles of real property or public policy in finding the existence of the requisite relationship. [Citations.] . . . It is the considered opinion of this court that a bona fide purchaser of a stolen automobile has an interest sufficient to qualify as insurable.

Any analysis of the insurable interest principle in Arizona must focus initially upon the language of our statutes. The governing standard is set forth in A.R.S. § 20-1105(B):

"Insurable interest" . . . means any actual, lawful and substantial economic interest in the safety or preservation of the subject of the insurance free from loss, destruction or pecuniary [monetary] damage or impairment.

We believe that the innocent purchaser of stolen property falls within this protection and reject any construction to the contrary.

. . . Appellant's interest in conservation of the vehicle was both "lawful" and "substantial." The law is clear that a bona fide purchaser of stolen commodities inherits title defeasible [capable of being made void] by none other than the rightful owner. [As to persons other than the rightful owner, the purchaser] possesses a valid legal claim to the property which will be given full force and effect in a court of law. . . . As against the true owner, moreover, the innocent purchaser may, upon loss or destruction of the stolen merchandise, be held liable in tort for conversion, and therefore has an interest in maintaining the property in an undamaged condition.

In addition, the rule above-stated is not only sustained by the authorities, but is in accord with justice and common sense. Among the vices sought to be discouraged by the insurable interest requirement is the intentional destruction of the covered property in order to profit from the insurance proceeds. We believe this purpose will be furthered where the insured has a financial investment in the property and believes him or herself to be in lawful possession. We see no greater risk of illicit activity under these circumstances than where the insured is, in actuality, the rightful owner. . . .

The opinion of the Court of Appeals is vacated, and this cause is remanded to the trial court for proceedings consistent with this opinion.

Contractual Basis of Insurance

An insurance policy is a contract subject to the general principles of contract law discussed in Chapters 9 to 18. Because the contract of insurance is so common in daily life, we now review some aspects of contract law as they apply to the insurance contract.

Insurance as a Contract of Adhesion Insurance is a contract of adhesion because the typical purchaser has little or no power to negotiate the price or other terms of the insurance contract. The purchaser has discretion regarding the kind and amount of coverage, beneficiary designation, and so on, but otherwise the purchase of insurance is basically a "take it or leave it" proposition in which the terms of a very complex standard form contract are imposed on the purchaser.

As is pointed out in Chapter 9, contracts of adhesion have legitimate uses, and the insurance contract is an example. If all terms of an insurance coverage had to be bargained individually, transaction costs would be prohibitive. If insurers could not use standard-form contracts, the limits of an insurer's liability would be uncertain, insurance companies would face tremendous difficulties in predicting loss, and the price of insurance would be difficult to determine. Yet, as the early history of the insurance business clearly reveals, the adhesive nature of an insurance contract exposes purchasers to exploitation by unscrupulous insurance companies. To preserve the advantages of standard-form insurance contracts while curbing their abuse, administrative agencies control the content of insurance contracts, and the courts construe ambiguous policy terms against the preparer of the contract. Insurance regulation is discussed later in this chapter.

Offer and Acceptance in Insurance Contracts An insurance policy is complex and detailed in part because the insurer must carefully control the nature and extent of liability. Attempts to control liability extend to all aspects of the insurance contract, including the contract formation process. Since the insurer's liability under an insurance policy *usually* arises immediately upon contract formation and can greatly exceed amounts paid in premiums, both the insurer and the insured have a strong interest in how the rules of offer and acceptance will be applied to the question of when an insurance contract arises.[2]

Ordinarily, insurance policies are sold by a representative of the insurer, called an "agent." The extent of the agent's authority to make insurance contracts on behalf of the insurer depends greatly on the kind of insurance involved. In property and liability insurance, the insurer may cancel a policy by giving a legally prescribed amount of notice to the insured and refunding any unearned premiums. Because the property and liability insurer may thus free itself from risks that have become unacceptable, the insurer gives its agents the authority to enter into binding contracts without consulting the company in advance about the merits of each individual contract. Often the agent may orally accept an applicant's offer and bill the applicant later, and the property or liability applicant thereby acquires immediate coverage.

In contrast, the right of a life insurance company to cancel life insurance policies is sharply limited by law. Life insurance companies therefore prefer to check an applicant's health, determine whether there is an insurable interest, and inquire about moral hazard before issuing a policy. To give themselves time to make a proper investigation and to reserve to themselves the decision of whether to grant insurance coverage, life insurers often restrict their agents' authority to accept offers.

---

[2]In most health and disability insurance, and in some life insurance sold to older people, there is a "probationary" period specified, during which benefits are limited or excluded.

In life insurance, the rules of offer and acceptance can be applied to four common situations that might lead to the formation of a life insurance contract.

1 A person fills out an application for insurance but does not pay the first premium. At this time the applicant is considered merely to be inviting the insurer to make an offer. The company then proffers a policy (presents it for acceptance). The company is the offeror. The applicant pays the first premium. The applicant has accepted the offer.

2 A person pays the first premium upon completing the application. The applicant is the offeror. The insurer delivers the policy to the applicant or to the insurer's agent for unconditional delivery to the applicant. The insurer, by making delivery, has accepted the applicant's offer.

3 A person applies for insurance and pays the first premium. The applicant is the offeror. The agent immediately gives the applicant a "conditional receipt" which specifies that the insurance is effective immediately (or as of a certain date) if the applicant is found to be insurable. The insurer has accepted the applicant's offer. If the applicant is not insurable, there is no insurance coverage and the premium will be refunded. If the applicant turns out to have been insurable, coverage occurs at the time specified by the conditional receipt, even though the applicant might, for example, be struck by lightning and die before insurability is determined.

4 The insurance company gives its agent authority to make temporary binding contracts. The agent accepts the applicant's offer by issuing a "binding receipt" or by issuing a temporary insurance policy. The applicant has insurance coverage while the company decides whether or not to grant the requested coverage. The temporary coverage ceases when the company issues a policy (whether or not for the amount originally requested), when the applicant is notified of denial of insurance coverage, or at some other time specified by the company or determinable by law.

Assignability of Insurance Contracts For many reasons, people attempt to assign their insurance policies. A purchaser of real or personal property might seek an assignment of the seller's fire insurance. A person might wish to sell or give away a policy of insurance on his or her life, or might wish to use the policy as collateral security for a loan. Some assignments of insurance are permitted and some are not.

As a general rule, contracts of property and liability insurance are not assignable without the consent of the insurer. If, for example, a homeowner with a good safety record had an absolute right to assign his or her fire insurance policy to a homeowner with a record of serious fires, the assignor could, by assigning the policy, impose a heavier risk on the insurer than warranted by the premium paid by the assignor. To allow the insurer better to screen out unacceptable risks, the law therefore treats most property and liability insurance as a "personal" contract that is not assignable without the consent of the insurer. However, *marine* insurance (essentially, insurance on a ship and its cargo while at sea) usually *may* be assigned without the consent of the insurer. Marine insurance is not so clearly subject to "moral hazard" as other forms of property insurance are, and there is a need in the transshipment of goods to have a type of insurance that is readily transferable. The language of marine insurance policies often implies free assignability, and the law will give effect to an assignment over the objections of the insurer unless the policy contains a clause restricting or prohibiting assignment.

Life insurance tends to be more freely assignable than property and liability insurance is, but assignability of life insurance depends very much on the kind of situation involved. *After the death of the insured*, a life insurance policy is basically a promise by the insurer to pay money and as such is freely assignable (e.g., by

a policyowner such as a creditor) despite any clause that purports to prohibit assignment. The law favors free alienability (transferability) of property, and an obligation merely to pay money usually involves no personal considerations that would warrant enforcing a nonassignability clause.

An assignment of a life insurance policy by the policyowner *during the lifetime of the insured* may or may not be enforceable. Some life insurance policies contain clauses prohibiting assignment by the owner. Although the courts favor free transferability of property, they tend to give effect to nonassignability clauses during the lifetime of the insured, in part because such clauses protect the rights of creditors where insurance is used as security. But many policies contain no prohibition of assignment. Ordinarily a person who has such a policy on his or her own life may assign it and thus make use of the property rights represented by the policy. These rights consist mainly of (1) any cash values that might accumulate before the death of the insured and (2) the face amount of the policy that will be available upon the death of the insured (i.e., the "death benefit"). The courts of *some* states, it should be noted, will not enforce an otherwise valid assignment unless the assignee has an insurable interest in the insured life, but this is a distinctly minority view.[3]

Where an insurance policy names a beneficiary to receive the death benefit, the rights of an assignee to the cash value may conflict with the rights of the beneficiary, since a main function of the cash value is to provide funding for a continuation of the death benefit that the beneficiary expects to receive. If the designation of beneficiary is *irrevocable* (as where no right to change the beneficiary has been reserved by the policy), the rights of the beneficiary prevail over

---

[3]Janice E. Greider and William T. Beadles, *Law and the Life Insurance Contract*, Richard D. Irwin, Inc., Homewood, Ill., 1974, pp. 371–373.

those of the assignee. Where the beneficiary designation is *revocable*, the law varies.[4] In some states the (revocable) beneficiary's rights are considered to be vested (absolute) subject to being divested (taken away). In those states the beneficiary's rights will prevail unless the beneficiary agrees to the contrary or unless the rights of the beneficiary are divested. Divestment can occur only where the change-of-beneficiary procedures outlined in the policy have been followed. In most states, however, the assignee's rights are superior to those of a revocable beneficiary. This majority rule, by protecting the assignee, enables the policyowner to make effective use of the policy as collateral for a loan.

Duties, Defenses, and Rights of Insurers and Others

Duties of Insurer and Insured An insurer has a duty to make prompt payment of valid claims. The statutes of several states provide special remedies to aggrieved persons for unjustified nonpayment or late payment of valid claims. These statutes typically impose on insurers liability for claimants' attorney's fees together with a monetary penalty. As Case 29.2 suggests, the statutes are especially useful in encouraging prompt payment of small claims. In states without such statutes, however, claimants may be at a decided disadvantage. Under common law principles of the United States, litigants generally must pay their own attorney's fees regardless of the outcome of the litigation, and the use of an attorney for a small claim may be impractical.

Liability insurers also have a duty to defend suits against insureds and, where circumstances warrant, a duty to settle claims out of court. The insurer's duty to defend arises, for example, where an injured person files a lawsuit alleging a claim within policy coverage. The insurer's duty to settle claims out of court arises especially

where the facts reveal a claim greatly in excess of policy limits, the validity of the claim is not in serious doubt, and the claimant is willing to accept the policy maximum and to release the insured from liability for the excess. Where the validity of the claim is doubtful, the insurer is not required to settle out of court.

The duties of insureds and other claimants relate primarily to the prompt presentment of claims and to the assistance and cooperation of the insured in lawsuits against the insured. Prompt presentment of claims is a requirement that must be met before the insurer can be held liable for payment of claims. Many policies require that claims be presented within a specified number of days after a loss. *Reasonable* policy provisions requiring notice and proof of loss are enforced by the courts because of the general benefit to the insured public that flows from prompt investigation and settlement of claims. A claimant who fails to make a timely claim or proof of loss will lose the right to a benefit unless there is a valid excuse for delay, as where a person is incapacitated or reasonably believes he or she was not at fault in an automobile accident and chose to rely on the other driver's insurance instead of his or her own.

The duty of assistance and cooperation arises frequently under policies of liability insurance that impose on the insurer a duty to defend the insured against tort claims. The insured is expected to notify the insurer promptly if suit is filed against the insured, and to attend hearings and trials, give evidence, help arrange a settlement, help obtain the attendance of witnesses, refrain from interfering with legitimate defense and settlement efforts, and give any other reasonable assistance and cooperation connected with the trial of the case. However, the insured may not be imposed on unreasonably. The insured does not breach the duty of assistance and cooperation by, for example, refusing to make an expensive trip unless reimbursed for travel expenses.

---

[4]Ibid., pp. 376–377.

Case 29.2   **Fresh Meadows Medical Associates v. Liberty Mutual Insurance Co.**
400 N.E.2d 303 (N.Y. 1979)

Janina Tokarz was injured in an automobile accident. At the time she was a passenger in an automobile operated by a driver insured under a liability policy issued by Liberty Mutual Insurance Company (defendant). Tokarz thereafter incurred a $70 bill for X-ray services rendered by Fresh Meadows Medical Associates (plaintiff). She assigned her claim for payment of this bill to Fresh Meadows, which presented the bill to the insurance carrier. When the carrier declined to make payment, Fresh Meadows submitted its claim to arbitration under section 675 of the Insurance Law, demanding payment by the carrier of the $70 (called "first-party benefits") and associated attorney's fees. Initially the attorney for Fresh Meadows sought a fee of $1,650. Liberty Mutual challenged the amount. The attorney conducted further legal research to substantiate the fee and sought an additional $1,200 for a total fee of $2,850. The arbitrator awarded Fresh Meadows $70 for the X-ray bill and $2,850 for attorney's fees. Liberty Mutual appealed. The Supreme Court (a first-level appellate court in New York) upheld the award. Liberty Mutual appealed, and the Appellate Division reduced the award of attorney's fees to $1,650. Fresh Meadows appealed.

JONES, J. . . . [Only one] issue is presented for our resolution—in awarding an attorney's fee incident to determination of a claim for first-party benefits, did the arbitrator have authority to include services rendered by the attorney in substantiating the claim for counsel fees? We hold that he did.

The relevant provision of section 675 as applicable to this case was found in subdivision 1: "the claimant shall also be entitled to recover his attorney's reasonable fee if a valid claim or portion thereof was overdue and such claim was not paid before the attorney was retained." The insurance carrier contends that the arbitrator had no authority under this section to direct payment of counsel fees for services rendered in justifying the claim for the attorney's fee, that to the extent this arbitrator directed payment for such services he exceeded his authority and that the disposition at the Appellate Division should be upheld.

In enacting section 675 the Legislature reversed the traditional principle in our jurisprudence that each litigant is expected to bear the cost of his attorney's services. In granting the arbitrator authority under the new so-called No-Fault Insurance Law to make an award to the claimant for "his attorney's reasonable fee" if the underlying claim for first-party benefits was valid in whole or in part and had not been paid before the attorney was retained, the precise extent of such authority was not otherwise delineated. It is not disputed that the arbitrator was given authority to award counsel fees for services rendered in proving entitlement to first-party benefits. There is no explicit address in the statute, however, by way either of inclusion or of exclusion to whether the authority extends to the category of services necessarily rendered by the attorney in substantiating his entitlement to an attorney's fee—an issue sometimes referred to by use of the phrase, "a fee on a fee." The statutory provision does not preclude allowance for such services. Nor did the regulations originally issued by the Superintendent of Insurance speak to this issue. . . .

The carrier asserts that the authority exercised by the arbitrator in this instance in granting the supplemental layer of allowances is so contrary to normal jurisprudential principle[s] that it may not be implied in the absence of express statutory provision. Claimant rejoins that the grant of any authority to make the carrier pay the fees of the claimant's attorney represents an abrogation of the principle on which the carrier would rely, and argues persuasively that the intent of section 675 was, in cases in which an insurance carrier refused to pay a valid claim for first-party benefits and forced the claimant to retain an attorney to take his claim to arbitration, to indemnify the claimant against economic loss in exacting payment from the recalcitrant carrier. To achieve that objective the arbitrator must have authority to direct the carrier to pay all attorney's fees; to the extent that any portion thereof [was] excluded, and thus left for payment by the client, the purpose of the statute would be frustrated.

We agree with claimant and hold that in exercising the authority conferred on him under section 675 to direct payment by insurance carriers of reasonable fees of claimant's attorneys, the arbitrator in making his determination may include services rendered by the attorney in substantiating the claim for counsel fees, including efforts expended in addressing any legal issues which may be involved as well as time spent in assembling and presenting factual data to support the claim.

Accordingly, the order of the Appellate Division should be reversed, with costs, and the judgment of Supreme Court confirming the award, reinstated.[4]

[4]In announcing our decision we note, as indicated (supra, n.2), that pursuant to legislative authority the Superintendent of Insurance has now issued regulations limiting the amount of fees which may be awarded by an arbitrator in a section 675 arbitration. To the extent that there may previously have been anxiety in some quarters that arbitrators were being accorded unbridled authority to fix unreasonably high legal fees this anxiety should now be allayed. [Footnote by the court; prior footnotes omitted.]

Defenses of Insurer   Within limits, an insurer may invoke ~ertain defenses to avoid paying a claim that would otherwise be valid. The defenses of concealment, breach of warranty, or misrepresentation might be available.

Concealment   Intentional failure by an insurance applicant to disclose a material fact constitutes concealment and is a good defense if the insurer granted coverage while unaware of the concealment. Examples are a driver's failure to reveal convictions for drunken driving when applying for automobile liability insurance, and a homeowner's failure when applying for fire insurance to reveal illegal storage of large amounts of gasoline in the basement.[5] The essence of concealment is (intentional) nondisclosure of a material fact. The doctrine of concealment is relevant primarily to property and liability insurance but less so to life insurance

[5]If the insurer's application form specifically addressed such questions to the applicant, a false answer would constitute misrepresentation.

(where application forms are so detailed that misrepresentation rather than concealment is likely to occur).

Breach of policy warranties   A "warranty" in an insurance policy is a written statement, description, or undertaking by means of which an applicant for insurance assures the insurer of the literal truth of certain facts. Suppose that Donald Morton seeks to insure the contents of his warehouse against theft. The statement in the policy that "A watchman will be on duty at all times" is a warranty. At common law, breach of a warranty was a complete defense for the insurer regardless of the materiality of the breach. Thus, if on a Monday night there was no watchman on duty, the warranty was breached. If goods were stolen on Tuesday night after the watchman returned to work, the insurer had a good defense despite the probability that the breach on Monday had nothing to do with the theft.

Many insurers took advantage of this common law treatment of warranties by drafting complex and detailed warranty clauses that often deprived insureds of the coverage they expected. Over time, the courts began to construe insurance policies so as to minimize, where possible, the number and scope of warranties made. Today many states have a statute providing that a breach of a warranty is a ground for avoiding the policy only if the breach is material, i.e., if it contributes significantly to the loss. In marine insurance and in states not having a warranty statute, the strict law of warranty (as modified by the courts) is still in effect. However, for the reason noted in the following discussion of misrepresentation, *life* insurance has by statute been largely removed from coverage by the law of warranty. Consequently, life insurers no longer have breach of warranty as a defense to payment of claims.

Misrepresentation   In the law of insurance, a "representation" is an oral or written statement of fact made by an applicant for insurance for the purpose of inducing an insurer to extend cover-

age. A misrepresentation (i.e., a false representation) upon which an insurer relies in issuing a policy is a ground for avoiding the policy, *but only if the misrepresentation is material*. An applicant for life insurance who states that she is in perfect health when in fact she has recently received hospital treatment for a severe heart attack has made a material misrepresentation. If the insurance company relied on the misrepresentation in issuing a policy, the company may rescind (cancel) the contract. If through its own investigation the insurer learned the true state of the applicant's health before issuing the policy, the insurer has not relied on the misrepresentation. But where there was no investigation, or where the insurer investigated but did not learn the truth, the insurer usually will be held to have relied on the applicant's misrepresentation. In the majority of states the defense is good even though the misrepresentation was unintentional.

Only a *material* misrepresentation will give the insurer a defense. In contrast, at common law, even an *immaterial* breach of warranty provided a defense. To mitigate the harshness of the common law warranty doctrine, most states today by statute require that statements made in an application for *life* insurance shall be considered representations and not warranties. Under such statutes, therefore, the inaccuracy of a statement must now be material for a life insurer to have a defense.

Significance of Incontestability   Most life and some health insurance policies contain a clause stating that the policy is "incontestable" after the passage of 1 or 2 years. Incontestability means that the insurer may not avoid the policy for concealment, breach of warranty, or misrepresentation. Statutes requiring the inclusion of incontestability clauses in life insurance policies are in effect in most states and were enacted in part to counter the harshness of the common law doctrine of insurance warranties. Today incontestability clauses are commonly used in life insurance policies even where not required by law, since the protection afforded to purchasers of life insurance enhances its marketability.

Rights at Variance with Policy Provisions

Insureds and other claimants may have rights that are inconsistent with the language of their policies. So may insurers.

Rights of claimants As indicated earlier in this chapter, the older law of insurance enabled insurers to draft insurance policies in such a restrictive way that insureds and other claimants often were deprived of expected benefits. Many denials of benefits were so surprising and harmful to claimants that the courts developed interpretive techniques as a means of controlling abuse and overreaching by the insurers. For instance, instead of interpreting a description of insured property as a warranty (to which the property had to conform exactly to remain covered by the insurance), the courts came to treat a mere description as no more than an identification of the covered property, with no warranty significance. Thus, today a 1979 car might be inaccurately described as a 1980 model and yet be covered. Insurers responded by drafting their warranty provisions more carefully, and the courts reacted by denying warranty status to new wordings. Case law became confusing and some decisions appeared arbitrary as the courts developed techniques for providing claimants with rights at variance with policy provisions.

Today, many doctrines are invoked to recognize rights that are inconsistent with policy language. They include waiver, estoppel, and election. A *waiver* is a voluntary relinquishment of a known right. In insurance cases, true waivers by insurance companies are rare, but the courts have often found a waiver in conduct falling considerably short of a voluntary relinquishment of a right.[6] *Estoppel* requires a showing of detrimental reliance by an insured on

some representation made by the insurer or reasonably inferred from the insurer's conduct. Here, too, the courts have often departed from the traditional requirements of the doctrine and have held the insurer liable. *Election* is a doctrine under which an insurer, by taking one course of action, is held to have disqualified itself from taking another course of action. Suppose that Mary Morton is late in paying her automobile insurance premium. Failure to pay a premium on time normally results in termination (lapse) of insurance coverage. However, some courts hold that an insurance company, by accepting late payment, is precluded from asserting a lapse in coverage. By "electing" to accept the late premium, the company becomes liable for any covered claim arising during what would have been the lapse period.

Most of the seemingly arbitrary insurance decisions can be explained by reference to broader principles of law than those represented by the doctrines that were actually applied. These broader principles are: (1) An insurer will be denied any unconscionable advantage in an insurance transaction. (2) The reasonable expectations of applicants and intended beneficiaries will be honored.[7] These principles explain what appear to be misapplications of the more technical doctrines of waiver, estoppel, and election that have been used to determine the rights of claimants.

Rights of insurers Where defenses such as concealment and misrepresentation are not expressly provided for in an insurance policy, they are nevertheless available to an insurer as rights at variance with policy provisions. Also, like any other contracting party, an insurer may have the insurance contract "reformed" by a court to correct errors. An error may occur, for example, in the preparation of the policy or may arise from a mutual mistake about some matter such as the age of the insured.

---

[6]Robert E. Keeton, *Insurance Law*, West Publishing Co., St. Paul, Minn., 1971, p. 343.

[7]Ibid., p. 341.

Case 29.3 **Pini v. Allstate Insurance Co. and State Farm Fire & Casualty Co.**
499 F. Supp. 1003 (E.D. Pa. 1980)

Fabio and Patricia Pini (plaintiffs) had two fire insurance policies on their property, one with Allstate Insurance Co. and another with State Farm Fire and Casualty Co. (defendants). The property was destroyed by fire. Plaintiff demanded payment from the insurers. After negotiations, the insurers refused to pay. Plaintiffs brought suit to compel payment, but did so more than one year after the loss. Defendants, claiming that plaintiffs failed to institute suit within the one year prescribed by the insurance contracts and Pennsylvania law, moved to dismiss the complaint for failure to state a claim upon which relief can be granted.

TROUTMAN, D.J. . . . The relevant inquiry focuses upon whether an insurer who denies an insured's claim . . . with sufficient time remaining for the insured to comply with [a contract clause imposing a one-year limit] for instituting suit has waived, expressly or impliedly, enforcement of this provision.

Pennsylvania courts acknowledge the validity and "binding nature" of such clauses. The insured's failure to adhere to policy conditions constitutes an "absolute bar" to suit unless the insurer waives its right to rely thereon or its conduct estops it from doing so. Where the insurer affirmatively misleads the insured about the possibility of settlement, dissuades him from filing suit or induces him to believe that it will not enforce the limitations period, courts construe this conduct as violative of the insurer's duty of "utmost good faith and fair dealing." To prevent the insurer from profiting from its own misbehavior, courts do not interpret [the limitations] clause strictly. Importantly, the insured must be given an opportunity to establish a fact question on this issue.

In the case at bar plaintiff adduces no question of fact. The parties agree that plaintiffs promptly notified defendants of the loss, which occurred in April 1979. Five months later Allstate rejected plaintiff's proof of loss for the stated reason that "the amount of the Proof is excessive of the actual loss and is not supported by documentation." In November 1979 counsel for State Farm indicated that defendants were "still conducting an investigation" and that plaintiffs should "await . . . later correspondence before proceeding further." However, on March 24, 1980, State Farm issued formal denial of coverage. Allstate apparently never made a formal statement indicating whether or not it would pay plaintiff's claim.

Clearly, State Farm expressed its intention not to pay within sufficient time for plaintiff to file suit. Even if State Farm denied the claim in bad faith, plaintiffs still had sufficient time within which to comply with the terms of the policy. Admittedly, Allstate's indication to the same effect was not as clear. Allstate did reject plaintiffs' proof of loss within sufficient time for plaintiffs to file suit, and State Farm's formal denial of payment put plaintiffs on notice that representations which State Farm had made previously concerning settlement and payment no longer existed. Plaintiffs should not have sat idly watching the one-year time period elapse. Moreover, negotiations between the parties did not toll [suspend] the limitations period.

Accordingly, defendants' motions to dismiss the complaint will be granted.

Types of Insurers; Key Terminology

Classified by organization, there are two major types of insurers: stock companies and mutual companies. A *stock insurance company* is a corporation established to sell insurance for a profit. Like any other corporation, a stock insurance company has a charter, a board of directors, officers, other employees, and shareholders. The shareholders may receive profits in the form of corporate dividends declared by the board of directors. The shareholders are not necessarily customers of the company.

A *mutual insurance company* has no shareholders. Rather, it is owned by its policyowners who, by purchasing insurance from the company, acquire a right to elect the directors who, in turn, select the officers. Only policyholders may have an ownership interest in a mutual insurance company. A mutual company is "nonprofit" in the sense that there are no shareholders and therefore no dividend distributions of the kind usually associated with corporations.

The insurance business has developed some special terminology. The meaning of "dividend" is an example. As normally understood, a dividend is a share of corporate profits paid to a shareholder. In insurance, the meaning of dividend is quite different. In deciding what premium to charge for insurance coverage, an insurance company must estimate the cost of providing the insurance before knowing what the actual losses and the expenses of administration will be. The premium charged is an estimation of the company's cost of providing the insurance. The actual cost is determined after the company has accumulated data about actual losses. If the actual cost is less than the amount of premiums collected from all insureds, the company may "adjust" the premium downward and pay the policyowner a "dividend." This "dividend" may be viewed as a refund of a part of the price initially charged for the insurance, although it is more accurate to say that an insurance dividend reflects the difference between (a) the premium charged plus earnings from investing the premium and (b) the lower amount justified by the actual loss and expense experience of the insurer. Under the federal income tax law, a policyowner dividend is treated not as income but as a nontaxable refund of an "overcharge."

Insurance policies may be "participating" or "nonparticipating." Under a *participating* policy, the policyowner receives dividends and thus participates in any benefits resulting from a lower than expected loss experience. Under a *nonparticipating* policy, the policyowner receives no dividends; consequently the insurance company receives the benefits of a lower than expected loss experience. Typically, a participating policy has a higher premium than a nonparticipating policy of the same type and amount of coverage does; but where loss experience is favorable, dividends paid under a participating policy could result in a lower final insurance cost to the policyowner. Stock companies issue both participating and nonparticipating insurance, but mutual companies usually issue participating policies. Nonparticipating policies are common for property and liability coverages, whereas participating policies are common for life insurance coverage.

PERSONAL RISKS: LIFE AND HEALTH INSURANCE

Policies of life and health insurance provide protection against a number of general risks: premature death, temporary and permanent disability, unemployment, and outliving one's financial resources. In a family context, insurance can provide reimbursement for medical expenses, a replacement for income lost due to disability, and, at death, funds to cover the cost of the last illness, burial, unpaid debts, taxes, and similar expenses. Insurance can also provide surviving family members with funds for maintaining their standard of living or adjusting to a lower one if necessary, for supporting minor children, and for meeting special needs such as education and paying off a mortgage on the family residence. In a business context, a firm can insure the lives of key personnel whose untimely death would create great financial hardship for the firm. Firms can also use insurance to enhance the availability of credit to the firm, to assure the continuation of business (where, for example, surviving partners need a large fund with which to discharge their obligation to the heirs of a dead partner), and to fund employee benefit plans in an effort to attract and hold talented employees. Determining how (or whether) to meet these family and business needs with insurance requires familiarity with the basic features of life insurance and health insurance, a brief survey of which now follows.

Life Insurance

Types of Life Insurance   There are four basic classes of contracts sold by life insurance companies: term life insurance contracts, whole-life insurance contracts, endowment life insurance contracts, and annuities.[8] The first three classes enable a person to provide or

---

[8]The discussion of life and health insurance is based on S.S. Huebner and Kenneth Black, Jr., *Life Insurance*, Prentice-Hall, Inc., Englewood Cliffs, N.J., 1976.

accumulate a fund for use or investment and are associated in varying degrees with the risk of premature death. When people refer to "life insurance," they usually mean term insurance, whole-life insurance, or endowment insurance —or one of the many combinations or variants of these three basic types. The fourth class of contract, the *annuity,* is a device for systematically *using up* (liquidating) an existing fund. An annuity protects against the risk of outliving one's financial resources and is similar in principle to a life insurance "settlement option" providing a periodic income. The topic of annuities is beyond the scope of this book, but settlement options are discussed later in this chapter.

Term life insurance is a contract that furnishes life insurance protection for a limited number ("term") of years (commonly 1 or 5 years) or for some other fixed period, for an annual premium that remains the same throughout the term. The face value of the policy is payable only if death occurs during the term, and nothing is paid if the insured survives beyond the term. The premium is increased at each renewal because more benefits are paid out by the insurer as the age of insured persons increases and more insured persons die. The purchaser of term insurance receives insurance protection only, and there is usually no buildup of cash values. The premium for term insurance is relatively low when compared to the premiums for other types of life insurance for a given age and face amount, because term insurance does not provide coverage past a given age, usually 65 or 70. However, term insurance is often renewable until that age without proof of insurability. Where a person requires substantial amounts of "pure protection" and is not interested in maintaining coverage beyond retirement, term insurance may be the best choice.

Whole-life insurance (also called "straight," "ordinary," or "lifetime" insurance) is a contract of "permanent" insurance, so called for two reasons. First, the insured is permitted (but not required) to pay premiums throughout life and thereby to keep the policy in effect for life. Second, even if the insured eventually quits paying premiums, there is a buildup of cash values that can be applied to keep the policy in effect for a period of time after the insured quits paying premiums. How long the policy will remain in effect after premium payment ceases, or at what face value, depends on the amount of the cash-value buildup.

Paying for whole-life insurance is almost always accomplished by means of the "level-premium" technique. Suppose Mary Johnson pays a $500 annual premium for her whole-life insurance. The premium is "level" because the amount is fixed at $500 for the duration of the contract. In the early years of the policy, the premium amount paid by Mary and the others in her mortality grouping is far more than is needed to pay claims and expenses that will arise during the early years. The excess amount is retained and invested by the insurer. The resulting fund, called a "legal reserve fund," is* the source of the "cash surrender value" that a whole-life policy accumulates. The legal reserve fund will be sufficient to pay the increasingly frequent claims that will arise in future years. In a sense, the legal reserve fund is intended to be exhausted. If there were a million insureds in a particular mortality grouping and no persons were added to the group, all of the premiums and earnings paid into the legal reserve fund would eventually be paid out as claims, administrative expenses of the insurer, and profits if the insurer is one for profit. Thus, a whole-life policy is basically insurance with a forced-savings feature that finances, in advance, long-term insurance benefits for the policyowner and any beneficiary.

There are many varieties of whole-life policies. One, the *limited-payment life policy*, is especially attractive to people who prefer to have a whole-life policy that is "paid up" by the end of their working lives. A paid-up policy is one on which no future premium payments are due, but under which the insurance company is liable for the full benefits specified by the contract. In a limited-payment life policy, premium payments are made for a limited number of years—20, for example—but are larger than where premiums are payable throughout life. These larger payments may be viewed as payment in advance for whole-life coverage.

Because of the cash-value feature, a whole-life policy can be used as collateral for a loan (as can an endowment policy). Or, where the policyowner wishes to quit paying premiums before the policy is fully paid up, the cash value can be applied in a variety of ways to preserve a lesser degree of insurance coverage. If the policy is a participating one, as most are, dividends can be taken in cash, applied to reduce premiums, applied to the purchase of additional insurance, or treated in some other way.

Endowment insurance is a contract under which the insured pays premiums for a specified number of years called the "endowment period" and at the end of that time *receives the face amount of the policy*. If the insured dies before that time, the face amount is paid to a beneficiary, as in other types of insurance.

An endowment policy has two basic elements: a savings fund resulting from the accumulation and investment of a portion of the premium, and term insurance whose face amount decreases as the endowment policy savings fund increases. At any time during the endowment period, the amount of the savings element plus the face amount of the decreasing term insurance equals the face amount of the endowment policy. An endowment policy develops a cash value.

To provide sufficient funds to pay the face amount due at the end of the endowment period, the insurer must build a large savings element into the premium. Consequently, an endowment policy premium for a given face amount is higher than is the premium for any other type of insurance, especially where the endowment period is relatively short. Where protection from premature death is the main concern, as in a young family with limited finances, endowment insurance would not be suitable. In the event of early death, term or even whole-life insurance would provide much more insurance proceeds per premium dollar than endowment insurance would.

Settlement Options A life insurance policy "matures" when the insured dies or when the insured survives the endowment period of an endowment policy. At the maturity of the policy, the "proceeds" (the face amount of the policy) are available to the person entitled to them under the terms of the policy, usually a beneficiary. Exactly how the beneficiary will receive the proceeds depends on what "settlement option" (way of receiving the proceeds) was chosen. The insured may choose a settlement option when the policy is purchased or may postpone the decision until relevant financial circumstances are known. Often, the choice of settlement options is left, intentionally or unintentionally, for the beneficiary to make when the policy matures. The typical life insurance contract provides the following basic settlement options: (1) a right to receive a lump-sum settlement in cash; (2) a right to leave the proceeds (principal) with the company, to receive the interest in periodic payments, and to withdraw principal from time to time or to specify how the principal is to be disposed of; (3) a right to have principal together with interest paid in equal installments over a fixed number of years; (4) a right to have payments of a specified amount until principal and interest are exhausted; and (5) any of a variety of life income options that serve the same function as an annuity.

Health Insurance

Health insurance protects mainly against the general risk of temporary and permanent disability resulting from injury or illness. Policies and plans of health insurance are so varied in their provisions that we can pursue only a general discussion of health insurance.[9]

Basic Coverages The expression "health insurance" encompasses two major categories of insurance protection: (1) disability income insurance and (2) medical expense insurance. *Disability income insurance* provides periodic payments to the insured as a substitute for income lost as a result of illness, disease, or injury. Some disability income policies cover only those disabilities resulting from *accidental injury*. Others cover disabilities resulting from both *accidental injury and sickness*. Usually, payments under such policies do not begin until the expiration of a stated period after the disability occurs. And, as might be expected, the amount and duration of payments are carefully limited. *Medical expense insurance* provides payments for medical care. "Medical care" includes hospital expenses, surgical expenses, nonsurgical expenses, and nursing expenses. As in disability insurance policies, medical benefits are limited in amount and duration.

Health insurance policies typically contain exclusions from coverage. Some policy provisions exclude risks that the insurer considers too great to cover, such as those encountered in military service. Some clauses exclude coverage of preexisting disabilities or health conditions in an attempt to limit "adverse selection" (the greater-than-normal tendency of poor risks to seek insurance). The desire to limit adverse selection also accounts in part for the exclusion of suicide and self-inflicted injuries. And, to prevent duplication of coverage and benefit payments, virtually all policies exclude coverage where the insured receives workers' compensation or other medical insurance benefits.

Types of Policies and Plans People can acquire health insurance in so many ways that they may unwittingly have overlapping cover-

---

[9]For a more detailed but still general treatment of health insurance, see Huebner and Black, op. cit., Chapters 16–18, 33, and 34.

age and a higher than necessary health insurance cost. Health insurance can be acquired by means of individual health insurance policies, group health insurance policies, social security, and private noncommercial health insurance plans such as Blue Cross and Blue Shield. Other sources of health insurance coverage include life insurance disability "riders" (supplemental agreements that expand coverage) and even automobile insurance policies that provide medical expense coverage (limited, of course, to medical expenses relating to covered automobile accidents).

Group health insurance is widely used and should be distinguished from *individual* health insurance. Normally a person seeking individual insurance must provide evidence of insurability, whereas a company that issues group insurance (life or health, for example) undertakes to insure every person in the group without regard to the insurability of individuals. In group insurance, the insurer issues one detailed *master contract* to the group policyholder (e.g., an employer) but only brief certificates to individual insureds such as employees. Also, many group policies are "experience-rated"; that is, the premium charged depends to some extent on the claims record of the group. Experience rating gives a group an incentive to keep claims at a minimum.

Case 29.4   Morrison Assurance Co. v. Armstrong
264 S.E.2d 320 (Ga. App. 1980)

Armstrong, an employee of Morrison, Inc., was injured and disabled during the course of her employment, and she received workers' compensation benefits. She also had a separate policy of group insurance issued by defendant-appellant Morrison Assurance Company to Morrison, Inc., the master policyholder. The "limitations" clause of the group policy certificate provided: "Benefits shall not be payable for . . . (e) Occupational injury or disease incurred in the course of working for an employer *other than the Group Policyholder*, who is subject to the Workmen's Compensation law." (Emphasis supplied). Because of this language, Armstrong thought the group policy provided benefits in addition to those she had received as workers's compensation. However, when Armstrong submitted expense claims under the group policy, the insurer denied liability, contending that the claimed benefits were excluded by a provision in the master policy. That provision excluded benefits for injuries incurred while working for *any* employer subject to the workers' compensation law, including the group policyholder. Armstrong brought suit seeking expenses, penalties, and attorney fees. The trial court granted summary judgment in favor of Armstrong, and the insurer appealed, contending that the exclusionary clause in the master policy controlled over the terms of the certificate.

CARLEY, J. . . . The law is very clear that "a contract of group insurance is made up of the master group policy and the certificate, which must be construed together. The certificate holder is bound by the provisions of the group policy, the certificate being evidence of coverage thereunder." [Citations.] The reasoning behind this is that the contracting parties in group insurance are primarily the employer and the insurer, and even though the group policy is in the custody of another, the fact is "well known" to the parties since the certificate contains a disclaimer that it is not the whole contract and it is within the power of the insured to compel production of the master policy. . . .

Because of this disclaimer and the long line of decisions upholding provisions of the master policy over conflicting terms of the certificate upon which the group insured has relied, we must reverse [the decision of the trial court], albeit reluctantly. Justice is not well served by this rule of law. To insist, after a person has paid to secure benefits from an insurance company, that the document upon which she has relied, and the only one in her possession, was merely "an instrument which contained a reference to another instrument in which were embodied the limitations" of her actual coverage . . . in our view is unreasonable. We finds its application particularly harsh where, as here, the insurer and the master policyholder are component companies of the same corporate structure. This rule applicable to group policy situations is inconsistent with the established general principle that insurance contracts are always to be construed in favor of the insured against the insurer, particularly where exclusions are in issue. Certainly it violates the spirit of the trend toward consumer protection now recognized in all areas of the law. . . . But . . . we conclude that this court is powerless to provide the remedy. However, "if this is a harsh rule, and if it does not have the approval of the people of the State, there is a definite way, a plain way, and a legal way, whereby it may be changed . . . A very simple and brief enactment of the legislature . . . is all that is required. . . . " [Citation.]

Judgment reversed.

PROPERTY RISKS: PROPERTY AND LIABILITY INSURANCE

Property Insurance

Property insurance indemnifies a person who has an insurable interest in physical property (real or personal) for its loss or for the loss of its income-producing ability. Property insurance protects against loss from certain "perils." A *peril* is a cause of loss such as fire, flood, theft, or vandalism.

Property insurance may be provided by means of either a "specified-perils" or an "all-risk" ("all-perils") contract. In a *specified-perils* contract, the insurer will make indemnity only for losses resulting from the particular peril or perils specified in the contract. A farmer's insurance against hail damage to crops is an example of a specified-perils contract. In an *all-risk* contract, the insurer will indemnify the insured for loss resulting from any peril except those specifically excluded by the contract. A homeowner's "personal property floater" is an all-risk contract because, despite certain exclusionary clauses and other limitations of liability, covered losses will be compensated for even though the particular peril was not spelled out in the contract. All-risk contracts are useful where the exact nature of the peril is difficult to predict.

The risk undertaken by a property insurer is subject to limits imposed by the policy. Many policies impose a "deductible," and all policies contain clauses of exclusion. A deductible is an amount of loss, specified in the policy, that the insured must absorb before he or she is entitled to payment from the insurer. Deductible amounts are common in automobile and homeowners' insurance. They serve to minimize insurance costs (and premiums) by eliminating small claims and claims that are particularly susceptible to moral hazard. Clauses of exclusion serve in property insurance, as in other kinds, to confine the insured risk to manageable proportions. Damage resulting from an act of war is a typical exclusion.

A property loss may be "direct" or "indirect." A *direct loss* is one resulting from damage to the physical property itself. Collision damage to a taxicab is an example. An *indirect loss* is one that occurs as a *consequence* of a direct loss. Loss of income while a taxicab is out of service because of collision damage is one kind of indirect loss. The extra expense of renting a car as a substitute for a taxicab that is temporarily out of service because of collision damage is another.

The following list is representative of the kinds of property insurance available for protection against personal or business losses. Most or all coverages are available on a single-peril, multiple-peril, "package," or all-risk basis. Some coverages are limited to direct losses, most encompass indirect losses, and a few (such as business interruption insurance) protect primarily against indirect losses.

1 *Fire insurance.* Provides indemnity against losses to insured buildings, contents, ships in port, and so on, due to accidental fire. Loss due to a "friendly" fire may not be covered, as where, for example, a valuable object is accidentally tossed into the firebox of a furnace. If a friendly fire escapes and becomes "hostile," the resulting damage is covered.

2 *Automobile collision insurance.* Covers loss to the insured vehicle from its collision with another object. Does *not* cover bodily injury or liability arising from the collision; separate coverages are required for noncollision losses.

3 *Crime insurance.* Pays for losses caused by the criminal acts of others, such as burglary and other forms of theft.

4 *Inland marine insurance.* Originally provided protection for goods transported other than by ocean. Now is often used to cover a variety of transportation and nontransportation losses, whether or not incurred on waterways.

5 *Accounts receivable insurance.* Protects against an inability to collect an account because of damage to records that prove the existence of the account.

6 *Business interruption insurance.* Protects against losses due to an inability of a business to operate because of fire or other hazards such as flood.

Liability Insurance

A person or firm faces two broad types of liability for damages—liability for breach of contract and liability for a wide variety of torts. Liability insurance does *not* cover liability for breach of contract, nor does it cover losses resulting from other speculative activities such as trading in the stockmarket. Liability insurance protects only against tort liability, including, however, tort liability assumed by contract.

The sources and types of tort liability fall into several somewhat overlapping categories. They include:

1 Liability for one's own torts—negligent driving, professional malpractice, false imprisonment of a suspected shoplifter, libel and slander, and so on.

2 Liability of an employer for torts committed by employees in the course of their employment, including many intentional torts.

3 Liability for loss resulting from defective products, whether based on negligence, breach of a warranty, or strict liability in tort.

4 Liability resulting from ownership of property. For example, the strict liability attending the ownership of hazardous property such as a reservoir, and liability to guests, business invitees, and certain classes of trespassers for losses resulting from the negligent maintenance of one's home or business premises.

Most of the tort exposures listed above may be insured against, although insurers commonly exclude from coverage some intentional torts committed by the insured. A policy might exclude assault and battery committed by the insured; but where the insured is a journalist, the policy might cover libel, since a charge of libel is a normal risk of journalism.

The following list is representative of liability coverage:

1 *Employer's liability insurance.* One type provides coverage for workers' compensation claims. Another protects the employer against claims of persons other than employees—business invitees, for example.

2 *Errors and omissions insurance.* Protects the insured from liability to a customer resulting from the insured's error or oversight. An insurance salesperson, for example, might forget to include a requested coverage, or an architect might fail to provide adequate roofing material.

3 *Malpractice insurance.* Protects professionals such as doctors, lawyers, and accountants from liability for negligence in the practice of their professions.

4 *Fidelity (guaranty) insurance.* Protects against loss due to embezzlement and other dishonesty of employees and other persons holding positions of trust.

5 *Automobile liability insurance.* Protects a motor vehicle operator or owner from liability to third persons as a result of the operation of the vehicle. About half of the states have some form of "no-fault" automobile insurance law under which claims for personal injury (and, in Massachusetts, for property damage) must be made against the claimant's own insurance company,

regardless of who was at fault. The aim of such laws is to reduce the cost of automobile insurance by reducing litigation and other expenses, but many no-fault laws are ineffective for this purpose because the right to litigate to establish fault has been preserved even for rather small claims.

6 *Homeowners' liability insurance.* A coverage protecting a homeowner from damage claims of invitees and others.

Subrogation and Coinsurance

Two concepts have special significance in property and liability insurance. The first, an insurance company's right of *subrogation* (right to be substituted as a claimant against a person responsible for loss), applies mainly to liability insurance. Suppose that a teller in a bank embezzles funds from a customer's account and that the bank must make good the loss. At this point the bank has a right to recover the amount of the loss from the teller. Suppose now that the bank has a policy of fidelity insurance and that the insurance company rather than the bank must make good the loss. Upon payment of the bank's claim, the insurer acquires the right of the bank (is "subrogated to" the right of the bank) to collect the amount of the loss from the teller.

The second concept, *coinsurance*, applies to the insuring of commercial property.[10] A coinsurance clause is used by property insurers to prevent customers who underinsure commercial property from taking "unfair" advantage of a common method of setting rates for property insurance. Property rates are fixed at a certain amount per $1,000 of coverage on the preliminary assumption that all customers will carry their full share of the group risk by insuring their property for substantially full value. But if Webster and Smith own identical office buildings worth $100,000 each, and Webster insures

---

[10]"Coinsurance" has other meanings that are beyond the scope of this chapter. One applies to reinsurance and another to health insurance.

hers for $20,000 while Smith insures his for $100,000, Smith pays a total premium that is five times larger than Webster's. This difference in premiums would be "fair" if large and small claims were in the equal balance implied by the flat premium rate per $1,000 of coverage. In fact, however, there are more small claims than large ones because there are more partial than total losses. If all claims were paid in full, the group of insureds that pay less in premiums would receive proportionately more in claims "payout" than would the group that insures for full value. Rather than reduce the premium rate when a person approaches insuring for full value, the insurer uses the coinsurance clause to reduce the claims payout to the group that underinsures. Coinsurance is used in lieu of a reduced-premium ("graded-rate") system because such a system would require an expensive property appraisal each time a policy is issued or renewed. The coinsurance technique is statistically fair because it assures a rough equality of payout per premium dollar to all groups of insureds, but it creates a trap for unwary underinsureds who expect their losses to be fully covered.

A coinsurance clause works as follows: The clause provides that if the owner insured his or her property for at least a given percent of its value (usually 80 percent), then any loss will be paid in full up to the face amount of the policy. In contrast, if the owner insures the property for less than the required percentage, the owner must bear part of the loss and will recover from the insurance company only the amount indicated by the following formula, which is one of several that have been developed for different situations.

$$\text{Recovery} = \text{Actual loss} \times \frac{\text{Face amount of insurance}}{80\% \times \text{"actual cash value" of property}}$$

Webster in the preceding paragraph insured her $100,000 office building for only $20,000.

Suppose she sustains a fire loss of $20,000. She will recover only $5,000 from the insurer, since recovery ($5,000) equals:

$$\text{Actual loss (\$20,000)} \times \frac{\text{Face amount of insurance (\$20,000)}}{80\% \times \$100,000, \text{ the actual cash value of the property (\$80,000)}}$$

Suppose now that Smith insures his $100,000 office building for $80,000. The coinsurance requirement is met. If Smith sustains a $20,000 fire loss, it will be paid in full. However, if the value of the building increases and there is no corresponding increase in the amount of insurance, Smith will not be in compliance with the coinsurance requirement and will have to bear part of the loss. People who insure *residential* property often are subject to a "replacement cost clause" whose purpose is similar to that of a coinsurance clause.

REGULATION OF THE INSURANCE BUSINESS

Insurance is aggressively marketed. The persuasion of sellers, the financial significance of insurance to buyers and sellers, the confusing complexity of insurance contracts, and the ignorance of much of the insuring public make insurance an obvious subject of abuse and, consequently, of governmental regulation. As noted earlier in this chapter, the courts try to strike a fair balance between insureds and insurers by denying any unconscionable advantage to insurers and attempting to honor the reasonable expectations of insurance purchasers and beneficiaries. But the judiciary is only one component in the web of federal and state insurance regulation.

Federal Regulation
In 1944, the Supreme Court held that an insurance company that conducts business across state lines is engaged in interstate commerce

and is therefore subject to the regulatory power of the federal government, specifically to the requirements of the Sherman Antitrust Act.[11] Prior to that decision, insurance regulation had largely been the responsibility of the states. After the decision, Congress enacted the McCarran-Ferguson Act to clarify the regulatory situation, especially as to the applicability of antitrust law to the insurance industry.

Under the McCarran Act, the regulation and taxation of insurance is left mainly to the states. However, the McCarran Act only partially exempts the insurance industry from the federal antitrust laws. Those laws (the Sherman Act, the Clayton Act, and the Federal Trade Commission Act) apply to the "business of insurance" *to the extent that the business of insurance is not regulated by state law.* "Business of insurance" means essentially the relationship between an insurance company and its policyholders. Where a state fails to regulate a harmful business practice falling within the meaning of business of insurance, federal law applies. And, since the McCarran Act exempts only the business of insurance from antitrust coverage, federal antitrust law applies to any aspect of an insurance company's business that lies outside the relationship between the company and its policyholders (if there is a sufficient jurisdictional relationship to interstate commerce). For example, an insurance company that conspired with an automobile glass franchisor to fix the price of replacement glass was subject to Sherman Act liability. Moreover, under the McCarran Act, all boycotts and acts of coercion and intimidation that might be engaged in by insurance companies remain subject to federal antitrust regulation regardless of whether that kind of misconduct is subject to state regulation.

State Regulation

At the state level, insurance regulation is carried out mainly by a state administrative agency usually known as the "insurance commission." One goal of the insurance commission is to ensure the financial soundness of insurance companies so that they can carry out their obligations. Therefore the insurance commission regulates insurance company investments and takes other measures intended to assure preservation of capital and reserves.

Another major regulatory goal is the reasonable and fair treatment of policyholders, insureds, and beneficiaries. This goal accounts for regulatory measures such as the licensing of agents and brokers and the requirement that insurance contracts contain a variety of protective provisions such as nonforfeiture clauses in cash-value life insurance policies. The insurance commissions also prohibit the inclusion of certain particularly burdensome contractual provisions, such as one requiring any suit against an insurer to be commenced within a period shorter than that provided for in the applicable statute of limitations.

ROLES OF INSURANCE AGENTS AND BROKERS

Under the law of agency, an agent is a person who makes contracts on behalf of another person, the "principal," and is subject to the principal's instructions and control. An "insurance agent" represents an insurance company (the principal) by selling insurance to third persons and acting as the insurer's agent in the process of contract formation. An "insurance broker" does not represent a company but, rather, places an order for insurance on behalf of the buyer and is therefore the *buyer's* agent. The rights and duties of principals, agents, and third persons are discussed in the agency chapters of this volume.

The primary job of an insurance agent is to sell a financial product. Whether out of a desire to sell more product or to be of greater service to clients, many insurance agents have in recent years taken on the role of financial adviser, and

---

[11]*United States v. South-Eastern Underwriters Association,* 322 U.S. 533.

many have enrolled in courses of study designed to sharpen their advising skills. But insurance agents face special problems when they serve both as sellers and advisers.

A seller who avoids deception and other illegality is free to advertise the product, and to engage in a variety of promotional practices, including those calculated to induce purchases on the basis of emotional appeals. Despite the prevalence of consumer protection law, the buyer bears considerable responsibility for judging the suitability of the product, or of the amount of the product, for the buyer's need. A financial adviser, on the other hand, may be a fiduciary who is subject to a more stringent standard of professional conduct than a seller. Financial advisers tend to work in areas of technical complexity. They usually undertake to analyze a client's personal problem and to offer a reasonable solution. A client uninformed about technical matters tends to defer to the judgment of the adviser who, because of that deference, is in a position to take advantage of the client or to harm him or her through negligence or incompetence. A client may reasonably expect the financial adviser to possess some minimal level of analytical ability and technical knowledge, to be open and honest in making recommendations, to proceed with care and discretion in the best interests of the client, and to reveal conflicts of interest. Where an insurance agent gives planning advice and also sells a financial product that he or she recommends for putting the plan into effect, a conflict of interests is evident. Such conflicts of interest do not go unnoticed by the courts when overreaching in the sale of insurance is alleged.

SUMMARY

Insurance is a contractual method of transferring risk from an insured to an insurer who distributes it by means of pooling and reinsurance. Since insurance is a system for distributing loss, an insured should not be allowed to profit in the event of casualty but, rather, should be limited to indemnity for loss actually suffered. The principle of indemnity underlies the requirement of an insurable interest, a financial stake that a person seeking insurance has in property or in someone's life or health.

An insurance policy is a contract of adhesion. As such it is subject not only to ordinary rules of contract law, but also to legal controls commonly imposed on contracts of adhesion. Depending on the circumstances, an insurance contract may or may not be assignable. An insurer has a duty to make prompt payment of valid claims, and liability insurers may have a duty to defend the insured in a lawsuit. Insureds have a duty to make prompt presentment of claims and sometimes to give assistance and cooperation in lawsuits. Within limits, the insurer may invoke the defenses of concealment, breach of a policy warranty, and misrepresentation.

Policies of life and health insurance protect against the risks of premature death, disability, unemployment, and outliving one's financial resources. The three basic types of life insurance contracts—term, whole-life, and endowment—provide or help a person accumulate a fund, whereas the annuity contract is used to liquidate an existing fund. Health insurance provides disability income and medical expense reimbursement. Group health or life insurance policies insure all in the group without regard to insurability of individuals, and the policies are experience-rated.

Property insurance protects against the loss of physical property or its income-producing ability. Liability insurance protects against tort liability. Subrogation, the right to be substituted as a claimant against a person responsible for loss, applies mainly to liability insurance. Coinsurance is used to prevent persons who underinsure their property from receiving disproportionate benefits.

Insurance is subject to federal and state regulation. Most insurance regulation is carried out by administrative agencies at the state level. Their goals are to ensure the financial soundness of insurers and to assure fair treatment of policy-holders, insureds, and beneficiaries.

An insurance agent is a salesperson working on behalf of an insurer. An agent who adopts the role of a financial adviser might also acquire the liability of a fiduciary.

STUDY AND DISCUSSION QUESTIONS

1   What are the two basic meanings of "the insured"?

2   Explain how insurers distribute risk of loss by *(a)* pooling and *(b)* reinsurance.

3   *(a)* What is the principle of indemnity? *(b)* Explain whether a coordination-of-benefits clause is consistent with the principle of indemnity.

4   *(a)* What is an insurable interest? *(b)* How is the principle of indemnity related to the requirement of an insurable interest? *(c)* How is "insurable interest" related to "moral hazard"?

5   *(a)* In property insurance, what circumstances give rise to an insurable interest? Why does the interest need to exist only at the time of loss? *(b)* In life insurance, what circumstances give rise to an insurable interest? Why does the interest need to exist only when the policy is taken out?

6   An insurance policy is a contract of adhesion. How does this fact affect the enforceability of an insurance policy?

7   Why are the rules of offer and acceptance of special importance in the formation of a contract of insurance?

8   *(a)* Why is a contract of life insurance more freely assignable than a contract of property or liability insurance is? *(b)* Under what circumstances will the assignability of life insurance be limited?

9   What are the general duties of the insurer? The insured?

10   *(a)* Describe the insurer's defenses of con-cealment, breach of a policy warranty, and misrepresentation. *(b)* In life insurance, what is the significance of treating statements made in an application as representations and not as warranties? *(c)* What is the significance of incontestability?

11   *(a)* What is the meaning of "rights at variance with policy provisions"? *(b)* Define waiver, estoppel, and election, and explain how each confers upon insureds or claimants rights at variance with policy provisions. *(c)* What "rights at variance" do insurers have?

12   *(a)* How does a stock insurance company differ from a mutual insurance company? *(b)* In insurance usage, what is the meaning of "dividend"? *(c)* How does a participating insurance policy differ from a nonparticipating one?

13   In function, how does an annuity differ from contracts of life insurance?

14   Describe the features and main use of *(a)* term life insurance, *(b)* whole-life insurance, and *(c)* endowment insurance.

15   Explain the meaning and use of a "level" premium.

16   Why are settlement options necessary? Name some.

17   *(a)* What basic coverages does health insurance provide? *(b)* What exclusions from coverage do health insurance policies typically contain? Why? *(c)* How does a group health (or life) insurance policy differ from an individual policy?

18   Distinguish between a specified-perils and an all-risk (all-perils) contract of property insurance.

19   Explain the meaning and significance of *(a)* deductible amount, *(b)* direct loss, and *(c)* indirect loss.

20   *(a)* What kind of liability does liability insurance cover? *Not* cover? *(b)* Explain the meaning and purpose of subrogation. Of coinsurance.

21   *(a)* To what extent does the federal government regulate the insurance industry? *(b)* Illustrate how the state insurance regulators attempt to accomplish the two main regulatory goals.

22 *(a)* How does an insurance agent differ from an insurance broker? *(b)* What potential liability confronts an insurance agent who takes on the role of financial adviser? Why is there a problem?

CASE PROBLEMS

1 Chadwick's car was badly damaged in a collision. The fair market value of the car just before the collision was $1,650. Immediately afterward the salvage value was $100. Chadwick sought reimbursement from his insurer. The insurer's adjuster made five offers of settlement ranging downward from $1,250 to $800. Chadwick then submitted a written demand for $1,450. The insurer did not answer the letter or make a counterproposal. Chadwick sued the insurer for $1,450 plus an amount for rental of a replacement car, storage costs for the damaged car, a "bad faith" penalty, and attorney's fees. The jury returned a verdict in favor of Chadwick for $1,550 in damages plus $387 as a bad faith penalty and $800 for attorney's fees. The insurer appealed. Should the verdict in favor of Chadwick be upheld?

2 Perry Brown's 1974 Buick caught fire, and Brown sought recovery for a total loss from his insurer. After negotiations, the insurer's adjuster confirmed a settlement agreement of $3,200. In the meantime, Brown consulted an attorney whose first demand was for $4,500, well above the price of a comparable vehicle located by one of the adjusters. About 2 months before filing suit against the insurer, the attorney demanded $5,400. Brown rejected a pretrial settlement of $3,800. Some 18 months after the loss, an independent appraiser engaged by the insurer estimated the loss at $3,363. The jury returned a verdict in favor of Brown for $3,950, and the trial judge awarded Brown an attorney's fee of $1,316.66. The insurer appealed the award of the attorney's fee. Should the award be upheld?

3 A prisoner alleged that the Sheriff's Department of Nassau County, New York, negligently deprived him of medical care and that the deprivation aggravated injuries from which he suffered during imprisonment. The Sheriff's Department brought an action for declaratory judgment to determine whether its insurer had a duty to defend the persons accused of negligence. The insurer denied that the alleged negligence constituted a covered "occurrence," defined in the policy as "an accident, including continuous or repeated exposure to conditions, which results in bodily injury or personal damage neither expected nor intended from the standpoint of the insured." Did the insurer have a duty to defend?

4 Customers of Diamond Tours and Travel, Inc., brought suit against Diamond, alleging gross misrepresentations by Diamond about a charter tour of Club Islandia, in Jamaica, West Indies. Diamond had a policy of professional liability insurance with American Home Assurance Company. Diamond referred the suit to the insurer, which disclaimed coverage on the ground that the policy did not insure Diamond against its own fraud. The insurer then brought an action for a declaratory judgment to confirm the validity of its disclaimer. Should the court decide in favor of the insurer?

5 Lisa Roberts, a passenger in a car, was injured when it was involved in an accident on October 27, 1978. The insurer, through its adjuster, sent a letter acknowledging the claim and stating that it would be processed when the enclosed forms were properly completed and returned. On December 28, 1978, Roberts' counsel forwarded to the insurer doctors' bills for $766 and copies of all required documents except the attending physicians' report form. At the end of January 1979 Roberts' counsel inquired about the failure to receive payment. The adjuster said there was no payment because he had not received the attending physicians' forms. Roberts' counsel stated that he had no duty to provide the forms and repeated this contention in two subsequent letters. On March 12, 1979, the insurer began to pay Roberts' claim. Thereafter, Roberts sued the insurer, seeking a penalty for the delay plus interest and an attorney's fee. She sued on the basis of a statute giving an insurer 30 days to make payment after receiving reasonable proof of loss. The insurer contended that Roberts had a duty to provide the physicians' forms and that because she had not done so, the delay was her fault. The trial court awarded her the amounts requested. Should it have done so?

6 Phillips applied for life insurance. The application asked the question: "Have you ever been told you had any of the following" listed diseases? Phillips answered "No" for each of the illnesses in the list. Phillips died, his widow sought payment of the face amount of the policy, and the insurer refused to pay. The widow brought suit against the insurer. The insured produced evidence that Phillips had been treated for pulmonary emphysema, hemotysis, chronic brain syndrome associated with the consumption of alcohol, hypertension, and epilepsy, along with other long-standing physical problems for which he had been hospitalized. The trial court awarded the insurer summary judgment on the ground of material misrepresentation. The widow appealed on the ground that Phillips spoke truthfully because he had never been told the names of any of the illnesses. Should the summary judgment for the insurer be upheld?

PART SEVEN

COMMERCIAL PAPER

Chapter 30
**Introduction to the
Law of Commercial Paper**

Chapter 31
Negotiability of Commercial Paper

Chapter 32
**Issue, Transfer, and
Negotiation of Commercial Paper**

Chapter 33
**Holder in Due Course;
Defenses to Liability on the Instrument**

Chapter 34
Liability of the Parties; Discharge

Chapter 35
Checks; Relationship between Bank and Customer

Chapter

30

Introduction to the Law of Commercial Paper

Centuries ago merchants began to devise ways of making payment for property and services without having to carry large amounts of money. The bill of exchange (nowadays called a "draft") was used in Europe for that purpose as early as the fourteenth century. During the Middle Ages, international traders used the bill of exchange in the settlement of their accounts. With the growth of banking, a special kind of draft called a check came into wide use. Today the great majority of all business transactions in the United States are settled by check. Checks and other kinds of drafts constitute one kind of "commercial paper." Checks and drafts serve as a temporary, safe, and efficient substitute for money.

Another kind of commercial paper, the promissory note, is used primarily as a means of credit extension. In its simplest form, a promissory note is the written promise of a person to pay a sum of money to another person at some

future date. Although of ancient origin, promissory notes did not become commercially important until the modern credit era.

This chapter discusses the nature of commercial paper and the nature of the law governing such paper. It also presents the major types and business uses of commercial paper and provides a look ahead at the topics to be covered in subsequent chapters dealing with the law of commercial paper.

NATURE OF COMMERCIAL PAPER AND COMMERCIAL PAPER LAW

There are many kinds of commercial documents in the contemporary business world. The business person daily comes in contact with such documents as stocks, bonds, warehouse receipts, and bills of lading, to name just a few. The functions and uses of commercial documents vary. Some documents are used primarily as evidence of ownership; others are used as substitutes for money in transactions involving cash or credit. Those documents used for money are of special importance and are called "commercial paper." A document classified as commercial paper is distinguished from other documents used in business by the fact that it is payable in *money*. Commercial paper also is *negotiable* (easily transferable with maximum safety to transferees).

Nature of Commercial Paper

Negotiable Character of Commercial Paper When only two parties are involved in a business transaction (e.g., buyer and seller or borrower and lender), there is no need for a special class of documents with a separate body of law. The law of contracts and sales generally is adequate to protect the rights and enforce the duties of each party. However, over many years the practice has developed of one party or the other transferring legal rights and duties to a third person. In such instances, the law of assignments, discussed at some length in Chapter 17, prescribes the rights and duties of the third party (the assignee).

An assignee receives the assignor's rights, but *subject to* any defense of the person responsible for performing the obligation represented by the assigned right. Even an assignee who *purchases* an assigned right ordinarily takes it subject to all defenses. Because of dissatisfaction with the possibility of being denied payment or other performance as a result of a dispute between the original contracting parties, merchants long ago developed specialized documents to meet their needs. A major need was to have a document payable in money that would be easily transferable from merchant to merchant *and that would be honored despite quarrels between the original contracting parties.* Originally the law pertaining to these specialized documents was a part of the "law merchant." Later it was called the law of "negotiable

instruments." The benefit of a negotiable instrument can be seen by examining the legal and economic consequences of negotiability and nonnegotiability.

Legal significance of negotiability Suppose that A hires B, a doctor, to give physical examinations to A's employees at a total cost of $2,000. A lacks the cash to pay for the examinations, and on the day before the date set for the examinations, A signs a "simple" contract (the ordinary, *in*formal contract discussed in Chapter 9) to pay B 6 months from the date of the examinations. Suppose also that B needs cash to purchase an X-ray machine and that before performing the examinations B sells (assigns) the contract to C for $1,500. Under the law of assignments, C is an assignee and takes the contract subject to any defenses to payment that A might have. For instance, if B unjustifiably refuses to make the examinations, A will have a complete defense to payment, and C (who is merely an assignee) can collect nothing from A when A's promised payment comes due.

Now suppose that A signed a negotiable promissory note (one kind of *formal* contract discussed in Chapter 9) for $2,000 payable to B or to bearer. If B properly transfers the note to C, and if C meets certain requirements, C will be called a "holder in due course" and will take the note free from A's "personal" defenses (but not from A's "real" defenses).[1] B's unjustified refusal to make the examinations constitutes failure of consideration, a personal defense that A may not assert against C. Thus, A must pay C the $2,000 promised and file a lawsuit against B to recover damages for breach of contract. The legal effect of negotiability is to protect most purchasers and other deserving transferees of commercial paper from most defenses of the debtor A, who is usually a buyer or a borrower. Figure 30.1 illustrates a typical set of transactions involving the transfer of a negotiable instrument to a holder in due course. A in the

---

[1] Personal and real defenses are discussed in Chapter 33.

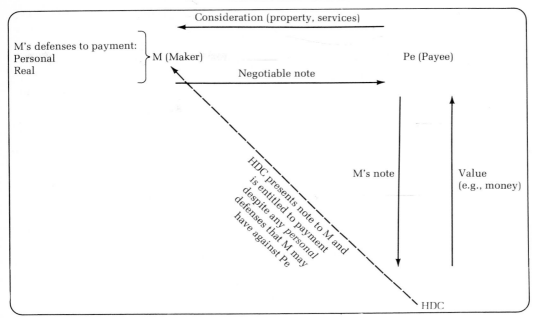

Figure 30.1 Legal Significance of Negotiability

preceding paragraphs is the "maker," B is the payee, and C is the holder in due course (HDC).

Occasionally, a document, such as a promissory note, is lacking one or more of the requirements of a negotiable instrument. Such lack does not make the note worthless or nontransferable. Under the law of assignments, most contract rights are freely assignable, and a creditor who receives such a document may transfer (sell or give) it to another. However, the transferee of a nonnegotiable document takes it subject to all defenses of the maker.

Economic significance of negotiability Given a choice between a negotiable instrument and a nonnegotiable document of the same face value, a potential purchaser (transferee) is likely to favor, and to pay more for, the document that has the least risk of noncollection. The law of commercial paper does not do away with all risks of noncollection, but it reduces the risks. For this reason commercial paper is said to be more "marketable" than nonnegotiable docu-

ments. There are two factors that reduce the risks of loss to a purchaser of commercial paper and that therefore make it more marketable: (1) most defenses are "cut off," that is, not assertable by the debtor-maker and (2) if the debtor does not pay the obligation when it comes due, the transferee usually may recover from ("have recourse to") the transferor.

Dual Nature of Commercial Paper The various kinds of commercial paper are, simultaneously, contracts and a species of property.

In its contractual aspects, commercial paper is subject to most of the general principles of law governing other kinds of contracts. However, negotiable instruments are not ordinary contracts. They are "formal" contracts that by law have been given special attributes so that the *currency* and the *credit* functions will be better served. If the creators of drafts and notes make them negotiable, i.e., put them into negotiable form when creating them, the resulting contracts will, by law, confer certain rights and impose certain liabilities upon various persons without regard to the intentions of the original parties to the instruments. For example, many a maker of a negotiable note has been surprised to learn that he or she must pay the full amount of the note to a transferee despite having failed to receive the thing for which the note was given. As shocking as the situation may be to the person who must make payment, the special protection given the transferee enhances the marketability of commercial paper, and thus tends to increase the amount of credit available to the debtor.

Commercial paper is also a species of property that may be bought and sold. As property, commercial paper is subject to some of the rules of property law. For example, just as delivery of a deed to land is a requirement for conveying title to the grantee, so delivery of a negotiable instrument is a requirement for conveying ownership of the instrument. An ordinary contract would usually be effective whether or not delivered. Warranty law relating to commercial paper has its origin in property law and is discussed in Chapter 34.

Nature of the Law of Commercial Paper

Aims of the Law   The law of commercial paper is designed to enhance the credit and the currency functions of commercial paper. The law accomplishes this aim by providing rules the effect of which is to reduce the risks of noncollection that transferees of commercial paper face, and by making the creditor's transfer of commercial paper convenient. Freeing certain transferees from personal defenses of persons who issue commercial paper is one of the many ways of reducing the risk of noncollection. The simple techniques that the law provides for transferring commercial paper contribute to ease of circulation and to convenience in the use of commercial paper.

At the same time, however, the law of commercial paper protects the vital interests of debtors and other persons who might be asked to make payment. For example, defenses such as insanity and infancy, called "real" defenses, are available against any transferee of commercial paper. In addition, some non-Code law provides protection for consumer-debtors, as we shall see in Chapters 31 and 33.

Sources of the Law   Article 3 of the Uniform Commercial Code (UCC), entitled "Commercial Paper," provides most of the law governing commercial paper. The article is mainly concerned with those rules of law that give commercial paper its special qualities as a type of formal contract. Article 4 of the Code, entitled "Bank Deposits and Collections," also pertains to commercial paper.[2] Article 3 is the chief source of the law discussed in the first five chapters of this part of the book. Article 4 serves as the chief source of the law discussed in the last chapter of the part.

Nonnegotiable documents are not commercial paper as the expression is used in Article 3, and rights and liabilities under them are prescribed by other law, principally by the law of contracts. Whether a document is negotiable depends on the language ("form") of the document. The language that must be used to create the kinds of negotiable instruments that constitute commercial paper is discussed in some detail in Chapter 31.

There are other kinds of negotiable instruments that do not call for the payment of money, such as corporate securities and documents of title. Article 8 of the UCC governs negotiable corporate securities, and Article 7 governs documents of title. Such documents are discussed in other parts of this book.

---

[2]UCC, Official Text, sec. 3-103(2). The UCC is reprinted in Appendix 1. All states except Louisiana have adopted the UCC, and Louisiana has adopted, in substance, several articles of the UCC, including Articles 3 and 4. The immediate predecessor of Article 3 was the Uniform Negotiable Instruments Law (NIL), which had been adopted by many states. Some cases in this book may make reference to the NIL.

TYPES OF COMMERCIAL PAPER

Article 3 lists four types of commercial paper: a draft, a check, a certificate of deposit, and a note. These documents (or "instruments") can be classified as either "three-party paper" or "two-party paper." Drafts and checks involve three parties. Notes and certificates of deposit involve only two parties.

Drafts

Nature of Drafts　A *draft* (or "bill of exchange," as the instrument is called in international business transactions) is an order to pay money. There are three parties to a draft: the drawer, the drawee, and the payee. The party who orders the payment to be made is the *drawer*.[3] The party who is ordered to make the payment is the *drawee*. The drawee can be any individual or firm willing to act as a payor of money. The party, named on the face of the draft, to whom the payment is to be made is the *payee*. A draft may be made payable to bearer

---

[3]Business people, and even lawyers and judges, often refer to the drawer of a draft as "the maker." The terminology is inaccurate but fortunately is not misleading.

(e.g., "Pay bearer," "Pay to the order of bearer"), to a designated third person (e.g., "Pay to the order of Paul Smith," "Pay to the order of the Treasurer of Moro County"), or to the drawer ("Pay to the order of [the drawer]").

Kinds of Drafts　Drafts are either demand drafts or time drafts. A *demand draft* is one payable literally on demand of the payee or other holder. Such drafts usually begin with the words "On demand pay" or "At sight pay." A *time draft* is one payable at a definite time, as shown in Figure 30.2. Another example of a time draft is one reading "sixty days after date pay." A draft reading "Sixty days after sight pay" is a time draft, but requires the "acceptance" of the drawee to fix the maturity date of the instrument. *Acceptance* is the drawee's written engagement (promise) to pay the draft when it falls due. The most usual form of acceptance consists of the word "Accepted" written across the face of the instrument, followed by the date of acceptance and the signature of the drawee.

From the time a draft is drawn, the drawee is customarily referred to as a "party" to the instrument. Actually, the drawee does not become a party unless and until he or she accepts

Figure 30.2 Draft.

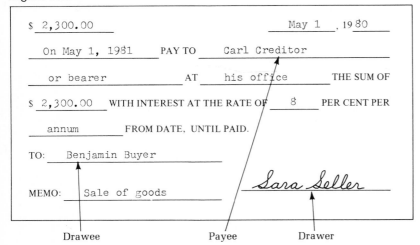

the draft, i.e., by signature agrees to pay it. Until then the drawee has no obligations under the instrument. After a drawee accepts a draft, the individual or firm is usually referred to as "the acceptor." A time draft drawn by the seller on the purchaser of goods and accepted by the purchaser is called a "trade acceptance." The reason for distinguishing trade acceptances from ordinary time drafts is explained in the section of this chapter entitled Use of Drafts in Financing Sales.

Checks

A *check* is a draft drawn on a bank and payable on demand [3-104(2)(b)].[4] The *drawer* is a customer who has an account at the *drawee* bank. The *payee* may be any individual or firm, named on the face of the check, whom the drawer wishes to receive payment. Although a check is a form of draft in that it is an order to pay money, the Code classifies "check" separately from "draft" because there are some rules of law that apply to checks but that do not apply to other kinds of drafts.

Typically, checks are made out on printed forms having blank spaces for the date of the instrument, the payee's name, the amount to be paid, and the drawer's signature, as in Figure 30.3.

However, a check need not necessarily be made out on a printed form. In a notable case, a depositor sent a bank a letter directing it to make a payment of a specified amount to the order of a certain payee. Later the depositor sent a telegram to the bank directing it to make another payment. The court held that "The signed letter and telegram satisfy the requirements for a check in the Uniform Commercial Code."[5]

When a bank draws a check on itself, the instrument is called a "cashier's check." When a bank draws a check on another bank in which the first bank has money on deposit, the check is referred to as a "bank draft."

The drawee of a "traveler's check" may be a bank, but ordinarily is not. When the drawee is not a bank, the so-called traveler's check is not a check at all. It is classified as a draft and is subject to the laws relating to drafts.

Promissory Notes

Nature of Promissory Notes A *promissory note*, usually referred to simply as a "note," is a writing in which one party promises to pay a

---

[4]Numbers within brackets in the text refer to sections of the UCC.

[5]*United Milk Products Co. v. Lawnsdale National Bank*, 392 F.2d 876 (7th Cir. 1968).

Figure 30.3 Check (by permission of Security Pacific National Bank).

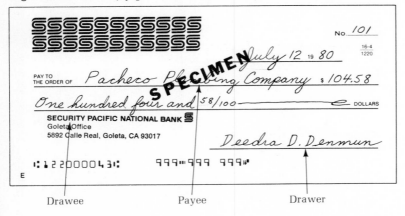

Drawee   Payee   Drawer

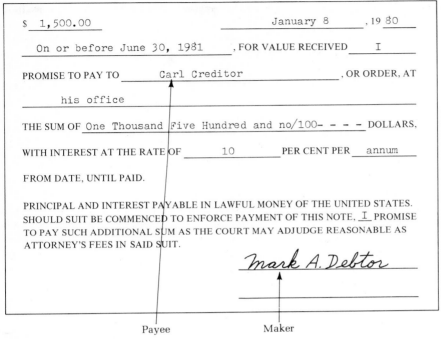

$ __1,500.00__   __January 8__ , 19 __80__

__On or before June 30, 1981__ , FOR VALUE RECEIVED __I__

PROMISE TO PAY TO _____ Carl Creditor _____ , OR ORDER, AT

__his office__

THE SUM OF __One Thousand Five Hundred and no/100- - - -__ DOLLARS,

WITH INTEREST AT THE RATE OF __10__ PER CENT PER __annum__

FROM DATE, UNTIL PAID.

PRINCIPAL AND INTEREST PAYABLE IN LAWFUL MONEY OF THE UNITED STATES. SHOULD SUIT BE COMMENCED TO ENFORCE PAYMENT OF THIS NOTE, __I__ PROMISE TO PAY SUCH ADDITIONAL SUM AS THE COURT MAY ADJUDGE REASONABLE AS ATTORNEY'S FEES IN SAID SUIT.

Mark A. Debtor

Payee   Maker

Figure 30.4 Promissory Note.

sum of money to another party. The party making the promise is the *maker*. The party, named on the face of the note, to whom payment is promised is the *payee*. There is an operational difference between a note and a check or draft. A drawer of a check orders payment from a fund of money held by a depositary. A drawer of a draft orders payment from a fund or against some existing or future obligation of the drawee to the drawer. A maker of a note simply makes a promise to pay money. There is no fund or obligation to be drawn upon.

Kinds of Promissory Notes A note may be a *demand* note (that is, payable on demand) or a *time* note (payable at a definite time). Figure 30.4 shows a simple form of a "single payment" time note.

Among the more complicated time notes are mortgage notes, collateral notes, judgment notes, and installment notes.

A *mortgage note* is a note secured by a mortgage on specified property, real or personal. Usually, the note states that it is secured by a mortgage and gives enough information about the mortgage (date, parties, description of property mortgaged) to make it identifiable. In some states trust deeds have largely replaced mortgages when the security is real property. Where a note is secured by a trust deed, the note is called a "trust deed note."[6]

A *collateral note* is a note accompanied by collateral. Collateral is something of value used to secure the repayment of the loan. Stocks and bonds are the most common kinds of collateral because they are readily convertible to cash. Other usual kinds of collateral are warehouse receipts, bills of lading, life insurance policies, and accounts receivable. Usually, the collateral

---

[6]Real property mortgages and trust deeds are discussed in Chapter 22.

note refers to the collateral and authorizes its sale upon default.

A *judgment note* is "a promissory note, embodying an authorization to any attorney, or to a designated attorney, or to the holder, or the clerk of the court, to enter an appearance [in court] for the maker and confess a judgment against him for a sum therein named, upon default of payment of the note."[7] The advantage of such a note is that on default by the maker, the holder may obtain judgment on the note without service of summons and without a trial. However, there is danger in allowing a plaintiff to secure judgment without a trial: the defendant may have had a defense that would have been good against the plaintiff if the defendant had the opportunity to plead and prove the case. Because of this danger, in many states confession-of-judgment clauses in notes have been made illegal or ineffective, either by statute or by court decisions.

An *installment note* is one in which the principal is payable in stated amounts at specified times. If the note is interest-bearing, as it almost invariably is, the interest is payable periodically on the unpaid balance until the note is paid in full. Usually, the note contains an "acceleration clause." The clause may provide that the entire unpaid principal (plus accrued interest) shall automatically become due and payable upon any default in payment of the principal or interest, or the clause may provide that after any default the holder may, at his or her election, declare the whole amount to be due and payable.

Instead of including installment provisions in a single note, the maker may issue a series of notes with each note representing one installment. The notes are so worded as to become due periodically, generally at the beginning of each successive month. The notes are usually "bound together" by a default clause appearing in each note. The clause describes the series of notes and provides that nonpayment of a note, or of the interest thereon, shall automatically (or perhaps at the election of the holder) make all unpaid notes of the series immediately due and payable.

Certificates of Deposit

A *certificate of deposit* (called a "CD") is defined as "an acknowledgment by a bank of receipt of money with an engagement to repay it" [3-104(2)(c)].[8] The bank (as broadly defined in the Code) is the *maker*. The *payee*, ordinarily an individual or a business firm, deposits money with the maker and receives a CD calling for repayment with interest. There are two classes of CDs: demand certificates and time certificates. A time certificate is often referred to as a "TCD." Although a CD is a form of promissory note, the Code gives CDs a separate classification because there are some rules of law that apply to CDs, but not to other kinds of notes. Figure 30.5 shows a TCD.

When compared with passbook savings accounts, CDs have advantages and disadvantages. There are two principal advantages: (1) normally, a higher rate of interest is paid on a CD than on a savings account and (2) because CDs are negotiable instruments, they are easily transferable and may be sold or used to pay a debt, or they may serve as security for a loan. As to disadvantages, the payee of a TCD must leave the money on deposit for a fixed time, and for CDs in general there is a minimum deposit required, usually $1,000 or some multiple of $1,000.

---

[7]Quoted with permission, from *Black's Law Dictionary*, Copyright © 1979 by West Publishing Co.

[8]"Bank" is defined broadly enough in the Code to include savings and loan associations and other business organizations legally empowered to engage in the business of banking. Cf. James J. White and Robert J. Summers, *Handbook of the Law Under the Uniform Commercial Code*, West Publishing Company, St. Paul, Minn., 1972, p. 552, fn. 2.

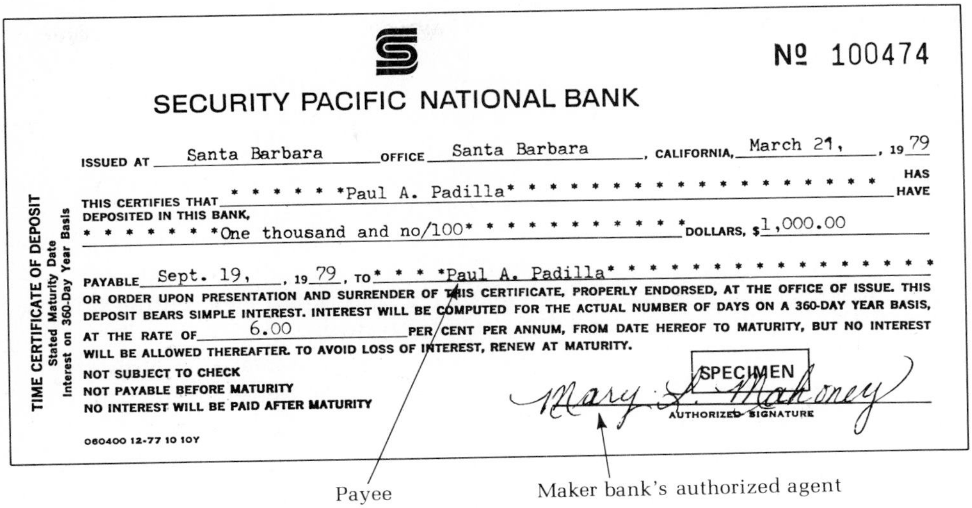

Nº 100474

SECURITY PACIFIC NATIONAL BANK

ISSUED AT Santa Barbara OFFICE Santa Barbara, CALIFORNIA, March 21, 1979

THIS CERTIFIES THAT * * * * * *Paul A. Padilla* HAS/HAVE DEPOSITED IN THIS BANK,

* * * * * * *One thousand and no/100* * * * * * * * * * * *DOLLARS, $1,000.00

PAYABLE Sept. 19, 1979, TO* * * *Paul A. Padilla* * * * * * * * * * * * * * * * * * * OR ORDER UPON PRESENTATION AND SURRENDER OF THIS CERTIFICATE, PROPERLY ENDORSED, AT THE OFFICE OF ISSUE. THIS DEPOSIT BEARS SIMPLE INTEREST. INTEREST WILL BE COMPUTED FOR THE ACTUAL NUMBER OF DAYS ON A 360-DAY YEAR BASIS, AT THE RATE OF 6.00 PER CENT PER ANNUM, FROM DATE HEREOF TO MATURITY, BUT NO INTEREST WILL BE ALLOWED THEREAFTER. TO AVOID LOSS OF INTEREST, RENEW AT MATURITY.

NOT SUBJECT TO CHECK
NOT PAYABLE BEFORE MATURITY
NO INTEREST WILL BE PAID AFTER MATURITY

SPECIMEN

Mary L. Mahoney
AUTHORIZED SIGNATURE

TIME CERTIFICATE OF DEPOSIT
Stated Maturity Date
Interest on 360-Day Year Basis

060400 12-77 10 10Y

Figure 30.5 Time Certificate of Deposit (by permission of Security Pacific National Bank).

USES OF COMMERCIAL PAPER

Uses of Drafts

Drafts are used for a variety of purposes, but mainly for financing the sale of goods and for transferring credits from one community or country to another.

Use of Drafts in Financing Sales The most common use of drafts is in financing the sale of goods. Drafts are especially useful for this purpose when buyer and seller are strangers, are located at a distance from each other, and feel the need for a reliable intermediary to handle the transaction. Suppose that Sally Seller is in Boston, that Robert Buyer is in San Francisco, and that the parties have agreed to the use of a sight draft (demand draft). When Seller ships the goods, she obtains from the carrier a bill of lading (a contract for the carriage and delivery of the goods). She then draws a sight draft on Buyer for the price of the goods and shipping costs. Seller may make the draft payable to her own order, but let us assume (as is much more likely to be the situation) that she makes it payable to the order of her bank. She attaches the bill of lading and an invoice (itemized account of the goods) to the draft and takes it to her bank in Boston for collection. The bank forwards the draft with attached documents to its correspondent bank in San Francisco. When the draft arrives at the San Francisco bank, that bank notifies Robert Buyer of its arrival and requests Buyer to pay the amount specified in the draft. Upon receipt of payment, the bank delivers the bill of lading to Buyer so that he can claim the goods when they arrive. The bank remits the amount collected to the Boston bank, and the Boston bank credits the amount to its customer, Sally Seller.

As previously noted, a time draft drawn by the seller (drawer) on the purchaser of goods (drawee) and accepted by the purchaser is called a "trade acceptance." Trade acceptances are generally less risky and therefore are more readily discounted (sold) to banks than are ordinary drafts or promissory notes. By writing the word "accepted" on such a draft, the drawee acknowledges that it arose out of the sale of goods to him or her.

Use of Drafts in Transferring Credits   As we have noted, in ancient times drafts were called bills of exchange. Their origin was in the usages of international traders. A merchant in London who wanted to buy goods from a merchant in Venice would go to a London money exchanger and pay the individual or firm the price of goods located in Venice. The London money exchanger (drawer) would draw a bill of exchange on a correspondent exchanger in Venice (drawee), ordering the drawee to pay the seller of the goods (payee). When a merchant in Venice purchased goods from a merchant in London, a money exchanger in Venice would draw a bill of exchange on a correspondent exchanger in London, payable to the London seller. In this way the money exchangers in the leading cities of international trade were *drawers* of some bills and *drawees* on others. The money exchangers met from time to time at "merchant fairs" and settled their accounts, often with very little money changing hands. Bills of exchange are used to this day for transferring credits from country to country.

When credits are transferred from one locality to another within a country, the transfer is often accomplished by means of a *bank draft*. Suppose that a Memphis business person is about to leave for Chicago to conclude a business transaction requiring settlement in funds located in Chicago. For some purposes a cashier's check is an acceptable way of transferring credit. But a cashier's check drawn on a Memphis bank is payable in Memphis, and in this illustration the settlement of the transaction requires funds located in Chicago. To meet the requirement, the Memphis business person purchases from a Memphis bank a bank draft drawn on a Chicago bank in which the Memphis bank has funds on deposit.

Uses of Checks

Most people are familiar with the use of checks as a means of payment. Actually, a check operates only as a conditional payment of the obligation for which it is given. It does not become final payment until it clears the bank on which it was drawn [3-802(1)(b) and comment 3].[9] If the check is dishonored (i.e., not paid by the drawee bank), or if the drawer orders the bank to stop payment, the right to sue on the original obligation is "revived."

There are several advantages in using checks as a means of payment. The following are among the more important advantages:

1   It is more convenient, and often is more economical, to mail checks than to "make the rounds" paying bills by cash.

2   It is safer to carry or to mail checks, other than checks payable to bearer, than it is to carry or mail money.

3   The fact that the drawer can stop payment on a check is a protection in certain situations, as where the drawer discovers that the goods for which the check was given are defective. It is a comparatively simple matter to stop payment on a check; it is sometimes difficult, or even impossible, to recover a payment made in currency.

4   After a check has cleared the bank and is returned to the drawer, it operates as a receipt for the payment made.

Checks are not exclusively used to purchase goods and to pay debts. They are often used to make gifts to individuals, churches, educational institutions, and charitable organizations.

Uses of Promissory Notes

Promissory notes can be used for a variety of purposes, but their chief uses are as a means of

---

[9]There is one qualification to the rule that a check operates as conditional payment. If the giver and the recipient of the check agree that it constitutes *the* payment (that is, that the check is unconditional payment), acceptance of the check discharges the obligation for which it was given.

borrowing money, as a means of buying on credit, and as a convenient method for evidencing a preexisting debt.

Use of Notes in Borrowing Money Business firms and individuals alike find it necessary or desirable to borrow money from time to time. A lender ordinarily requires the borrower to evidence the obligation to repay by signing a promissory note. Typically, the borrower signs a note bearing interest. The principal may be due at a fixed time in the future (e.g., 30 or 60 days) or may be payable in installments. Sometimes lenders are willing to lend solely on the basis of the borrower's personal note. Often, however, they will insist that some third person co-sign the note, or that the note be backed by some form of collateral security. Real property mortgage notes, chattel mortgage notes, and collateral notes are forms of notes in which the security is property.

Use of Notes in Credit Sales Notes are frequently used in financing the sale of goods, as in the financing of conditional sales contracts. When used for that purpose, the notes are commonly installment notes, bearing interest. The conditional sales contract has achieved wide popularity because it permits the purchaser to use the article (or service) while he or she is paying for it and permits the seller to retain "legal title" (one variety of an Article 9 "security interest") to the article as security for the payment of the purchase price. Usually, the seller discounts the note at, and assigns the contract to, a finance company or bank. Thus, the seller immediately receives money from the transaction rather than having to collect installment payments over a long period of time.

Use of Notes in Evidencing Preexisting Debts The use of a note is a convenient means of evidencing a preexisting debt, as, for example, where the debt arose out of a loan to a friend, and the debt has existed for some time. Obtaining a note as evidence of a preexisting debt results in several advantages to the creditor. Among them are (1) a note minimizes the chance of future disputes about the amount of indebtedness, (2) a note can be made interest-bearing, (3) a note can provide that the maker will pay the creditor the cost of collection, and (4) the delivery of the note to the creditor starts the statute of limitations running again.

SUMMARY AND A LOOK AHEAD

Early in this chapter it was noted that commercial paper serves as a temporary substitute for money and facilitates the extension of credit. Commercial paper is effective in these functions because it is easy to transfer and because people have confidence that they will be able to collect money with a minimum of difficulty.

When only two parties are involved in a loan or a sale transaction, there is little need for a specialized negotiable instrument. However, in the contemporary world of mass marketing of goods and services, purchasers sign checks and notes in great quantities. These checks and notes ordinarily are not held by the sellers but usually are transferred, for money, to a third person. Under the law of assignments, an assignee acquires no greater rights than the original creditor possessed. Thus, if the instrument involved is nonnegotiable, a few losses sustained by a few assignees could provoke widespread concern, which could erode the market value of assigned paper. The law of commercial paper was developed by merchants to minimize this difficulty by providing techniques for reducing the risks of loss in the purchase of commercial paper.

A principal aim of the law of commercial paper is to reduce those risks that would unduly impair the marketability of commercial paper. Two techniques are central to that purpose: (1) freeing transferees from the personal defenses of parties to the instrument and (2) making transferors liable for payment in the event that makers or drawees fail to pay. Other techniques and rules contribute to the easy transfer of commercial paper.

Understanding these techniques and rules requires attention to three major questions regarding commercial paper: (1) What constitutes *negotiable form* of an instrument? (2) What constitutes a *proper method of transfer*? (3) Who may be a *holder in due course*? Chapter 31 explains what is required for an instrument to be negotiable in form. Chapter 32 discusses the techniques of transfer required for commercial paper to serve its various functions. Chapter 33 discusses the requirements for, significance of, and limits on, holder in due course status. Chapters 34 and 35 deal with related matters: the liabilities of various persons involved in commercial paper transactions and the techniques used by banks in transferring funds and collecting payments.

The law of commercial paper is complex and can be confusing. Understanding the law will be aided by keeping in mind such questions as the following: What specific purpose does this particular rule of commercial paper serve? Does the rule enhance the marketability of commercial paper? Contribute to its convenient use? Or does the rule serve to protect the vital interests of makers and drawers?

STUDY AND DISCUSSION QUESTIONS

1   Negotiable drafts and notes (commercial paper) serve the currency and credit functions better than nonnegotiable drafts and notes do. Explain how this is so by explaining and illustrating *(a)* the legal significance of negotiability and *(b)* the economic significance of negotiability.

2   *(a)* Commercial paper is a type of "formal" contract. Explain or illustrate the significance of the formal character of commercial paper. *(b)* Commercial paper is a species of property. How is that fact significant?

3   What are the principal aims of the law of commercial paper?

4   In general, what constitutes commercial paper as that expression is used in Article 3 of the UCC?

5   *(a)* What are the four specific types of commercial paper? *(b)* Define each.

6   Explain the meaning of each term in the following pairs of terms: *(a)* demand draft and time draft; *(b)* drawee and acceptor; *(c)* cashier's check and bank draft; *(d)* mortgage note and collateral note; *(e)* judgment note and installment note.

7   *(a)* What is the "operational difference" between a note and a check or draft? *(b)* As compared with passbook savings accounts, a certificate of deposit has some advantages and disadvantages. What are they?

8   Explain how drafts are used *(a)* in financing the sale of goods and *(b)* in transferring credits from one locality to another within a country.

9   *(a)* Explain how notes are used in credit sales. *(b)* List some advantages of using notes to evidence preexisting debts.

10   The law of commercial paper, like most other law, attempts to balance the competing interests of various groups of people. *(a)* What interests seem to be in conflict in a commercial paper transaction? *(b)* One aim of the law of commercial paper is to reduce those risks that would unduly impair the marketability of commercial paper. What two basic techniques are used to accomplish that purpose? *(c)* Why is it important to enhance the marketability of commercial paper?

Where an instrument is in the hands of the original parties, there is generally no need to distinguish between commercial paper that is negotiable and paper that is not. Where an instrument has been or is to be transferred by the payee to another individual or business firm, the legal and economic consequences resulting from the use of negotiable or nonnegotiable instruments are substantially different. It often becomes important, therefore, to know whether an instrument is negotiable.

As stated in Chapter 30, when a negotiable instrument is transferred to a person who meets the requirements for a holder in due course, the holder takes the instrument free of most defenses, such as fraud or lack of consideration. Thus, a holder in due course has a special position in the law: such holder has more rights than the original party (payee) who transferred the instrument to the holder. In order for a holder to achieve this special position, the instrument must be negotiable in form.

This chapter is primarily concerned with the requirements for negotiability, that is, the requirements concerning the *form* that an instrument must meet in order to be negotiable. Other topics considered are terms and omissions that do not affect negotiability, instruments deprived of negotiability by statute, and rules for interpreting ambiguities that occur with considerable frequency in negotiable instruments.

REQUIREMENTS FOR NEGOTIABILITY

The requirements for negotiability are set forth in Section 3-104(1) of the Uniform Commercial Code (UCC), as follows:

Any writing to be a negotiable instrument within this Article must

(**a**)   be signed by the maker or drawer; and

(**b**)   contain an unconditional promise or order to pay a sum certain in money . . . ; and

(**c**)   be payable on demand or at a definite time; and

(**d**)   be payable to order or to bearer.

A careful reading of the section discloses that there are eight important requirements for negotiability.

1   a writing;

2   signature by maker or drawer;

3   promise or order to pay;

4   unconditional character of promise or order;

5   payment in money;

6   payment of a sum certain;

7   payment on demand or at a definite time;

8   payment to order or to bearer.

Unless an instrument meets all of these eight requirements for negotiability, the instrument is not negotiable. A nonnegotiable instrument may be valid, enforceable, and transferable under principles of contract law, but the instrument is simply not given the benefits of negotiability stated in Chapter 30.

Instrument in Writing

To be negotiable, an instrument must be in writing. "'Writing' includes printing, typewriting, or any other intentional reduction to tangible form" [1-201(46)].[1] The requirement can be met by a combination of various kinds of writing, as in an instrument that is partly printed, partly typed, and partly handwritten. The hand-

writing may be in pencil, but for obvious reasons the use of ink is much wiser. The Code does not specify any particular kind of material to be used. A negotiable instrument may even be written on wood or cloth. Customarily, individuals and business firms use standard forms printed on paper.

Signature by Maker or Drawer

The instrument must be signed by the maker or drawer. The word "maker" applies to a note or certificate of deposit. The word "drawer" applies to a check or draft. The drawee's signature is not required for the negotiability of checks and drafts.

Normally, a person signs an instrument by writing his or her name on it. However, a signature need not necessarily consist of the maker's or drawer's name. It may consist of one's initials, a trade name, an assumed name, a mark, or even a thumb print [3-401]. Broadly stated, "signed" includes any symbol executed or adopted by a party with present intention to authenticate a writing [1-201(39)].

"Signed" does not necessarily mean handwritten. A signature may be typewritten or applied by rubber stamp, or it may be printed, lithographed, or applied by other mechanical means. Any other rule would be impractical for large corporations issuing thousands of payroll and dividend checks. Neither does "signed" mean subscribed at the end of the document. The signature of the drawer or maker may appear in the body of the instrument or even on the reverse side of the instrument. Although an unusual type or placement of signature may meet the law's requirement, a person should be wary of taking an instrument that is signed in some unusual way. If suit is brought on the instrument, the plaintiff may have difficulty proving that the name or symbol was placed on the instrument by the defendant and was intended as the person's signature.

---

[1]Numbers within brackets in the text refer to sections of the UCC.

Promise or Order to Pay

To be negotiable, the instrument must contain a promise or order to pay. If the instrument is a note, it must contain a promise to pay. A *promise* is an undertaking to pay. The undertaking to pay can best be expressed by using the word "promise" (for example, "I promise to pay"; "The undersigned promises to pay"). However, the law has never required that the maker actually use the word "promise." Any language of similar import is sufficient ("The undersigned undertakes to pay"). On the other hand, mere acknowledgment of a debt ("IOU $50"; "Due Richard Roe $50") is not sufficient to constitute a promise [3-102(1)(c)]. Some courts have held that if an acknowledgment of indebtedness is accompanied by words of negotiability ("Due Richard Roe or order $50") or by a statement that the indebtedness is to be paid (as, "to be paid on demand"), the requirement of a promise has been fulfilled.

If the instrument is a draft or check, it must contain an order to pay. An *order* is a direction to pay and must be more than an authorization or request. The usual language for expressing an order to pay is "Pay to. . . ."

> The prefixing of words of courtesy to the direction—as 'please pay' or 'kindly pay'—should not lead to a holding that the direction has degenerated into a mere request. On the other hand, . . . language—such as 'I wish you would pay'—would not qualify as an order. . . . [3-102, comment 2].

An order to pay must identify with reasonable certainty the person who is directed to make the payment (i.e., the drawee). The order may be directed to two or more such persons jointly ("to A and B") or in the alternative ("to A or B"). Although an order may be addressed to two or more drawees jointly or in the alternative, it may not be addressed to two or more drawees in succession (i.e., may not be addressed "to A, and if he does not pay, to B"). An order so addressed might require the holder to make more than one presentment (demand for payment) of the instrument before taking action against the drawer or others. Unless the holder has recourse the *first* time the instrument is dishonored, the value of the instrument as a substitute for money would be impaired.

Unconditional Character of Promise or Order

The promise or order must be unconditional. Some instruments clearly contain an unconditional promise or order to pay, as in a note reading "On demand I promise to pay the bearer the sum of fifty dollars." The question of whether a promise or order is conditional arises only when the instrument contains some additional language relating to the promise or order to pay. Additional language interferes with free transferability if it raises a question about the effect of the language. A potential purchaser may refuse to take such an instrument because he or she cannot or will not take time to determine if a condition has been satisfied. Section 3-105 deals with the effect of certain additional language relating to the promise or order to pay. The most important provisions of the section are discussed in the following paragraphs.

Effect of Express Conditions If the promise or order is expressly conditioned on the happening or nonhappening of an event, the instrument is nonnegotiable. For example, a promise to pay "if I marry the widow Abigail Smythe" is expressly conditioned on the happening of an event, and an instrument containing such a promise is nonnegotiable. The promise or order must be to pay in all events, not just on the occurrence of one event.

Effect of Words Denoting "Subject To" A promise or order is conditional if the instrument states that it is "subject to" or "governed by" another agreement [3-105(2)(a)]. The intent of the Code provision is to make clear that the conditional or unconditional character of the paper is to be determined solely by what is expressed on the face of the instrument itself. Some courts and legal writers refer to this rule as the "four corner" rule. If the holder must look to another agreement (that is, outside the four corners of the instrument) to see whether the promise or order is subject to some condition, the instrument is nonnegotiable regardless of the provisions of the other agreement.

Effect of Reference to Another Agreement   In family circles, negotiable instruments may be issued as a gift. Thus, a parent who has a son or daughter in college may send him or her a check as a present. In business circles, negotiable instruments are almost invariably issued as part of some agreement (usually referred to as the "underlying agreement" or "underlying transaction"). If a check, draft, or promissory note merely *refers* to the underlying agreement or transaction, without making payment depend on the maker's or drawer's satisfaction with the underlying agreement or transaction, the reference does not make the order or promise conditional. Thus, a promise is not made conditional by the statement that "This note is given for the purchase of goods as per contract of August 22, 19xx."

Case 31.1   Holly Hill Acres, Ltd. v. Charter Bank of Gainesville
314 So. 2d 209 (Fla. App. 1975)

Holly Hill Acres, Ltd. (Holly Hill) purchased some real estate from Rogers and Blythe. In payment, Holly Hill signed and delivered to Rogers and Blythe a promissory note together with a purchase money mortgage on the land to secure the note. Rogers and Blythe then transferred the note and mortgage to Charter Bank of Gainesville (Bank) as security for a loan from the Bank. Alleging a default on each of the notes, Bank (plaintiff-appellee) brought suit to collect the amount of the Holly Hill note. Holly Hill answered, alleging that agents of Rogers and Blythe had committed fraud in inducing Holly Hill to purchase the real estate. The trial court held that the appellee Bank was a holder in due course of the note and entered a summary judgment against Holly Hill. Holly Hill appealed.

SCHEB, J. . . . The note . . . contains the following stipulation:

This note with interest is secured by a mortgage on real estate, of even date herewith, made by the maker thereof in favor of the said payee, and shall be construed and enforced according to the laws of the State of Florida. *The terms of said mortgage are by this reference made a part hereof.* [Emphasis supplied.]

The note having incorporated the terms of the purchase money mortgage was not negotiable. The appellee Bank was not a holder in due course; therefore, the appellant was entitled to raise against the appellee any defenses which could be raised between the appellant and Rogers and Blythe. Since appellant asserted an affirmative defense of fraud, it was incumbent on the appellee to establish the non-existence of any genuine issue of any material fact or the legal insufficiency of appellant's affirmative defense. Having failed to do so, appellee was not entitled to judgment as a matter of law; hence, we reverse.

The note, incorporating by reference the terms of the mortgage, did not contain the unconditional promise to pay required by Section 3-104(1)(b). Rather, the note falls within the scope of Section 3-105(2)(a). Although negotiability is now governed by the Uniform Commercial Code, this was the Florida view even before the UCC was adopted. E.g., the Supreme Court in *Brown v. Marion Mortgage Co.*, 145 So. 413 (Fla. 1932), held that certain bonds which were "to be received and held subject to" a certain mortgage were non-negotiable.

Appellee Bank relies upon *Scott v. Taylor*, 58 So. 30 (Fla. 1912), as authority for the proposition that its note is negotiable. Scott, however, involved a note which stated: "this note secured by mortgage." Mere reference to a note being secured by mortgage is a common commercial practice and such reference in itself does not impede the negotiability of the note. There is . . . a significant difference in a note stating that it is "secured by a mortgage" from one which provides, "the terms of said mortgage are by this reference made a part hereof." In the former instance the note merely refers to a separate agreement which does not impede its negotiability, while in the latter instance the note is rendered non-negotiable. See Section 3-105(2)(a); 3-119. [In a footnote the court quoted a Comment to Section 3-119: " . . . The negotiability of an instrument is always to be determined by what appears on the face of the instrument alone, and if it is negotiable in itself a purchaser without notice of a separate writing is in no way affected by it. *If the instrument itself states that it is subject to or governed by any other agreement, it is not negotiable under this Article*; but if it merely refers to a separate agreement or states that it arises out of such an agreement, it is negotiable." (Emphasis supplied.)]

As a general rule the assignee of a mortgage securing a non-negotiable note, even though a bona fide purchaser for value, takes subject to all defenses available as against the [mortgagee-assignor]. Appellant raised the issue of fraud as between himself and the other parties to the note; therefore it was incumbent on the appellee Bank, as movant for a summary judgment, to prove the non-existence of any genuinely triable issue.

Accordingly, the entry of a summary final judgment is reversed and the cause remanded for further proceedings.

Effect of Reference to Account to Be Debited; "Particular Fund" Doctrine A promise or order otherwise unconditional is not made conditional by the fact that the instrument indicates a particular account to be debited or any other fund or source from which reimbursement is expected. (*Example:* "Pay to the order of Paul Payee and charge the amount to merchandise account.") On the other hand, if the instrument makes clear that it is to be paid *only out of* a particular fund ("I promise to pay out of this year's wheat crop"), the promise or order is conditional. It is conditional because payment is contingent upon the existence and sufficiency of the fund.

The Code provides for two important exceptions to the particular fund doctrine. The first exception provides that short-term instruments issued by a government, or governmental agency or unit, are not rendered nonnegotiable by the fact that payment is limited to a particular fund or to the proceeds of particular taxes or other sources of revenue. The second exception applies primarily to instruments issued by partnerships and other unincorporated associations.

Such instruments often limit payment to the assets of the association by expressly excluding the liability of individual members of the association. If the promise or order is limited to a payment out of "the entire assets" of the partnership or other unincorporated association, the limitation does not render the instrument nonnegotiable. The Code goes even further by extending the policy to instruments that are issued on behalf of a trust or estate and that limit payment to the entire assets of the trust or estate.

Case 31.2   Glendora Bank v. Davis
267 P. 311 (Cal. 1928)

SHENK, J. The plaintiff [Glendora Bank] sued the defendant [E. A. Davis] on a promissory note. . . . The only question here involved is whether the promissory note is nonnegotiable in form. . . . The note . . . appears to be negotiable in form except that immediately preceding the signature of the maker is the following provision: "This note is given in payment of merchandise and is to be liquidated by payments received on account of sale of such merchandise." . . .

The trial court found and concluded: "That said promissory note is nonnegotiable. . . ."

We think the conclusion of the trial court was correct. . . . It is clear that the last clause of the note, above quoted, is susceptible of no other reasonable interpretation than that payment of the note or any part thereof was to be made out of receipts from the sale of the merchandise for which the note was given and that this provision is "a promise to pay out of a particular fund" the existence of which depended on the contingency of the sale of the merchandise which might not take place at all or might take place to some, but to an uncertain extent. These factors were fatal to the negotiability of the note. . . .

The judgment is affirmed.

Payment in Money;
Payment of a Sum Certain

The promise or order must be to pay *money*. As stated in Chapter 30, commercial paper is distinguished from other types of negotiable documents by the fact that each kind of commercial

paper calls for the payment of money. The Code defines money as a "medium of exchange authorized or adopted by a domestic or foreign government as a part of its currency" [1-201(24)]. In the United States at the present time, coins and currency of the United States are legal tender, that is, money. Thus, an instrument payable in wheat or corn is not negotiable. However, if the *payee* is given the option of demanding wheat or money, the instrument would be negotiable. It would not be negotiable if the *maker* or *drawee* could choose to pay in wheat or money.

The payment to be made must be a *sum certain*. The Code does not require absolute certainty. Section 3-106 allows several provisions to be included in an instrument because they are beneficial to the payee or a holder, and would therefore increase the ease with which the instrument may be transferred. For example, a promissory note bearing interest at the rate of 6 percent per annum is held to be a promise to pay a sum certain. Although the sum to be paid must be calculated, the amount due from the maker can easily be determined, and the payment of interest certainly benefits the holder of the note and enhances its marketability. Similarly, the sum payable is a sum certain even though it is to be paid with stated different rates of interest before and after default, or with a stated discount (or conversely, a stated penalty) if paid before the date fixed for payment, or with a stated addition if paid after the date fixed for payment ("late charges.") The sum payable is a sum certain even though the instrument calls for installment payments. For example, Mary promises to pay $1,000 in installments of $100 each on the first day of each month.

Many notes contain a provision regarding collection costs and attorney's fees. Such a provision might read: "If suit is instituted to collect this note, I promise to pay, as attorney's fees, such sum as the court may adjudge to be reasonable." Such a provision is obviously beneficial to the payee. As one would expect, therefore, such a provision does not make the note nonnegotiable. The sum payable is a sum certain even though it is to be paid "with costs of collection or an attorney's fee or both upon default" [3-106(1)(e)].

Payment on Demand or at a Definite Time

An instrument will not pass readily from hand to hand as a substitute for money unless potential holders can tell from the face of the instrument when (i.e., at what time) payment can be expected. Accordingly, the Code provides that in order to be negotiable an instrument must be payable either on demand or at a definite time.

Instrument Payable on Demand An instrument is payable on demand if it contains a promise or order to pay "on demand," "at sight," or "on presentation," or if no time of payment is stated [3-108]. The words "on demand" occur mainly in notes; the words "at sight" or "on presentation" occur mainly in drafts. Checks are payable on demand because "no time of payment is stated." Included in this class of demand instruments is any instrument bearing a blank for the insertion of a date of payment, but which was issued without a date having been inserted.

Case 31.3   **Master Homecraft Co. v. Zimmerman**
222 A.2d 440 (Pa. Super. Ct. 1966)

Master Homecraft Company (plaintiff) contracted to remodel the home of Edward and Alice Zimmerman (defendants). In connection with this work, the defendants on August 4, 1964 executed a note in the principal amount of $9,747. The pertinent part of the note read:

Case 31.3
Continued

"$9,747.00   No.——
(Total amount of note)   Pittsburgh, Pa. 8/4/64

"For value received, I/we or either of us promise to pay to the order of MASTER HOMECRAFT COMPANY, the sum of Nine Thousand Seven Hundred Forty-seven Dollars in _____ monthly installments of $_____each, beginning on the_____day of_____, 19__, and continuing on the same day of each and every month thereafter until the full amount thereof is paid. . . ."

Master Homecraft brought suit on the note. The proceedings which followed were complicated, but the net result was a judgment for defendants, and plaintiff appealed. One of the questions considered by the appellate court was the effect on the instrument of the unfilled installment blanks: "in _____ monthly installments of $_____each."

SPAULDING, J. The law is clear that a motion to strike a judgment . . . will be granted only when there are defects apparent on the face of the record. [Citations.] In the instant case there were no such defects because both the time of default and the amount due were ascertainable from the face of the instrument.

The Uniform Commercial Code provides: "Instruments payable on demand include those payable at sight or on presentation and *those in which no time for payment is stated*." Sec. 3-108 (Emphasis added.) Under this section, the note in question is a demand note, due and payable immediately. This presumption as to payment existed long before the Code . . . and applies whether or not the note is negotiable. As was said in *Liberty Aluminum Products Co. v. Cortis*, 14 Pa. D. & C.2d 624, 625 (1958): "Even if this were not so [under the Code], the logic of the situation compels this conclusion. The parties have the right to use a [printed form containing blanks] and tailor it to their needs. And the failure to include installment payments simply and clearly means that none were intended."

The note is not rendered defective because the blanks for alleged installment payments appear unused. On its face the note designates a principal sum of $9,747. The failure to fill in the monthly installment blanks does not indicate that no principal sum was intended.

On this issue the court below stated: "This court does not know the reason for the failure to complete the note. The parties to this note either inadvertently or unintentionally failed to complete the blanks." This conclusion is without support in the record. The empty blanks could also mean that no installment payments were intended. *Liberty Aluminum v. Cortis, supra*, at 626. . . . Speculation as to the intent of the parties in not filling in the blanks involves matters [beyond] the record and is not relevant. . . .

[Judgment reversed.]

Instrument Payable at a Definite Time

Under Section 3-109(1), an instrument is payable at a definite time if the time of payment is expressed in any of the following ways.

1 On a stated date; for example, "I promise to pay on February 10, 19xx. . . ."

2 On or before a stated date; for example, "I promise to pay on or before February 10, 19xx. . . ."

3 At a fixed period after a stated date; for example, "March 1, 19xx. I promise to pay thirty days after date." (If no date is stated, the instrument is nonnegotiable. However, under Section 3-115 a holder of the instrument may fill in the date and the instrument thereby becomes negotiable.)

4 At a fixed period after sight; for example, "Sixty days after sight, pay," meaning "Sixty days after this draft is presented for acceptance, pay."

5 At a definite time but subject to an acceleration-of-payment provision. The acceleration may be at the option of the maker or drawer, as in the note above reading "I promise to pay on or before February 10, 19xx . . ."; or the acceleration may be at the option of the holder, as in a note or draft that authorizes the holder to demand payment at any time the holder feels insecure;[2] or the acceleration may be automatic upon the occurrence of some event, as where a note provides that it "shall become immediately due and payable upon any default in payment of interest or principal." Thus, if an instrument is otherwise payable at a definite time, the definiteness of the time of payment is not impaired by an acceleration provision.

Subsection 3-109(2) provides that "An instrument which by its terms is . . . payable only upon an act or event uncertain as to time of occurrence is not payable at a definite time, even though the act or event has occurred." For example, suppose Daisy signs a note "payable 30 days after the death of my Uncle Abner." When Uncle Abner dies, the note does not become negotiable. However, Daisy may be held liable under the principles of contract law.

_____

[2] A holder who exercises such an option to accelerate must have a good-faith belief that the prospect of payment or performance is impaired [Sec. 1-208].

Case 31.4   Barton v. Scott Hudgens Realty & Mortgage, Inc.
222 S.E.2d 126 (Ga. App. 1975)

Barton and others (Barton) sought help from Scott Hudgens Realty & Mortgage, Inc. (SHRAM) in locating a person or firm willing to make a commitment for an "acceptable loan" around $300,000. The parties agreed that if SHRAM succeeded in getting such a commitment, it would be entitled to a finder's fee of $3,000. Accordingly, Barton signed a document containing the following pertinent language:

"By execution of this document the undersigned hereby acknowledges and promises to pay to the order of Scott Hudgens Realty & Mortgage, Inc., a Delaware corporation, at Atlanta, Georgia, or at such other place or to such other party or parties as the holder hereof may from time to time designate, the principal sum of three thousand dollars ($3,000). This amount is due and payable upon evidence of an acceptable

Case 31.4
Continued

permanent loan of $290,000 for Barton-Ludwig Cains Hill Place Office Building, Atlanta, Georgia, from one of SHRAM's investors and upon acceptance of the commitment by the undersigned."

SHRAM obtained a commitment for $290,000. Barton, claiming that the commitment was unacceptable, refused to borrow the money. Thereupon, SHRAM (plaintiff) brought suit upon the document. Barton (defendant) admitted execution of the "promissory note" (his wording) and further admitted execution of the loan commitment, but he denied that an "acceptable permanent loan" was obtained and therefore denied that the "promissory note" was due and payable on the date alleged. There was a judgment for the plaintiff, and defendant appealed. One of the issues on appeal was whether the document signed by Barton was a negotiable instrument. The following excerpts deal only with that issue.

DEEN, J. Under Code Section 3-104(1)(c) a negotiable instrument must "be payable on demand or at a definite time." The "note" here was not payable on demand under the language of Section 3-108 [Payable on Demand] and under Section 3-109(2) "an instrument which by its terms is otherwise payable only upon an act or event uncertain as to time of occurrence is not payable at a definite time even though the act or event has occurred." The language of the "promissory note" therefore reveals that it was not payable on demand or at a definite time, and was therefore not negotiable. . . .

The "promissory note" is rather a contract to pay money when certain contingencies are satisfied—"upon evidence of an acceptable permanent loan . . . and upon acceptance of the [loan] commitment."

Payment to Order or to Bearer

To be negotiable, an instrument must contain "words of negotiability." The usual words of negotiability are "to order" or "to bearer." These words, or their equivalent, are necessary to show that the instrument is intended to be freely transferable from hand to hand. For example, the words "Pay to Smith Company" indicate that only Smith Company is to receive payment. Lack of the word "bearer" or "order" makes the instrument nonnegotiable in form. (Recall, however, that lack of negotiability is significant mainly because transferees of a nonnegotiable instrument take it subject to all defenses of the maker or drawer. A nonnegotiable instrument is still freely assignable, and

transferable, if it represents a claim for money.)

The paragraphs that follow distinguish between order and bearer paper. The distinction is often significant, for two main reasons. First, the method of transferring order paper differs from that for transferring bearer paper. Second, the number of people who become liable for payment of an instrument depends in part on the number of signers. Order paper differs from bearer paper as to the number of signatures required for transfer. Methods of transfer and the liability of parties are discussed in later chapters.

Instrument Payable to Order An instrument is payable to order when it is payable to the order of, or assigns of, any person ("Pay to the order of Paul Payee"), or to such person or his order ("Pay to Paul Payee or his order") [3-110(1)]. An instrument may be payable to the order of any individual or business firm named by the maker or drawer, including the maker or drawer or the drawee (if there is one), or it may be payable to the order of two or more persons together ("A, B, and C") or in the alternative ("A, B, or C").[3]

An instrument need not necessarily be payable to the order of a named person or of named persons. It may be payable to the order of (1) an estate, trust, or fund, (2) a partnership or other unincorporated association, or (3) an office or an officer by his or her title as such ("Pay to the order of the Swedish Consulate"; "Pay to the

order of the Treasurer of the Country Club" [3-110(1)(e), (f), (g)].

Instrument Payable to Bearer An instrument is payable to bearer when by its terms it is payable to "bearer," to the "order of bearer," to a specified person "or bearer," or to "cash," to the "order of cash," or any other words that do not purport to designate a specific payee [3-111, and comment 2].

Language such as "Pay to the order of bearer" usually results from the use of a printed form containing the words "Pay to the order of" followed by a blank space that is intended for the name of the payee but in which the word "bearer" is inserted. Under the Code, an instrument so worded is known as a bearer instrument. Note, however, that when such a form is issued with the payee space left blank, the instrument is not bearer paper but incomplete order paper.

---

[3]The question of who may properly indorse an instrument payable to the order of two or more persons or to the order of a payee other than a named person is discussed in the next chapter.

Case 31.5   **Broadway Management Corp. v. Briggs**
332 N.E.2d 131 (Ill. App. 1975)

Conan Briggs (defendant) signed a note that read in part: "*Ninety Days* after date, I, we, or either of us, promise to pay to the order of *Three Thousand Four Hundred Ninety Eight and 45/100----------Dollars*." (The underlined words and symbols had been typed in; the words not underlined were in print.) There were no blanks on the face of the instrument. Any unused spaces had been filled in with dashes. The note was not paid at maturity, and Broadway Management Corporation (plaintiff) brought suit on the note. There was a judgment for plaintiff, and defendant appealed.

CRAVEN, J. The trial court determined this instrument to be nonnegotiable paper, yet applied certain elements of the law of negotiable instruments in arriving at its conclusion. We believe the instrument to be negotiable. . . .

The critical question of whether this is order or bearer paper is to be determined by Article 3 of the Uniform Commercial Code, which governs negotiable instruments. If this is bearer paper, the plaintiff's possession was sufficient to make it a holder. . . . Section 1-201(20). On the other hand, if the instrument is order paper, it becomes apparent that the payee cannot be determined upon the face of the instrument. . . .

Case 31.5
Continued

Under the Code, an instrument is payable to bearer only when by its term it is payable to:

"(**a**) bearer or the order of bearer; or

"(**b**) a specified person or 'bearer' or

"(**c**) 'cash' or the order of 'cash,' or any other indication which does not purport to designate a specific payee." (UCC, Sec. 3-111; Ill. Rev. Stat. 1971, Ch. 26, 3-111.)

The official comments to the section note that an instrument made payable "to the order of_____" is not bearer paper, but an incomplete order instrument unenforceable until completed in accordance with authority. UCC, Sec. 3-115.

The instrument here is not bearer paper. We cannot say that it "does not purport to designate a specific payee." Rather we believe the wording of the instrument is clear in its implication that the payee's name is to be inserted between the promise and the amount, so that the literal absence of blanks is legally insignificant. [In other words, since the payee's name was not inserted in the blank reserved for the payee's name, the instrument was an incomplete order instrument.]

Reversed and remanded. . . .

TERMS AND OMISSIONS NOT AFFECTING NEGOTIABILITY

Terms Not Affecting Negotiability

Under Section 3-112 of the Code, the negotiability of an instrument is not affected by any of the following terms (provisions):

1 A statement that collateral has been given as security and that in case of default the collateral may be sold.

2 A promise to maintain or protect collateral or to give additional collateral. For example, a note may state that it is secured by a deposit of securities having a current market value of $4,800 and that on written demand from the holder, the maker agrees to deposit such additional collateral satisfactory to the holder as may be necessary to maintain the value of the collateral at $4,800. Normally, such a note would contain a provision that if the maker fails to provide the additional collateral, the holder may sell the collateral previously deposited and apply the proceeds of such sale to the debt owed.

3 A term authorizing a confession of judgment on the instrument "if it is not paid when due." This Code provision is important

in the handful of states that permit a clause to be inserted in a negotiable instrument authorizing the confession of judgment. The subsection makes it plain that the confession of judgment clause is not an acceleration clause, and, therefore it can be used in a negotiable instrument only if the instrument is not paid when due. Clauses permitting a judgment to be confessed at any time, therefore, destroy negotiability.[4]

4 A term purporting to waive the benefit of any law for the advantage or protection of the obligor, as, for example, a waiver of a homestead exemption.[5]

---

[4]William D. Hawkland, *A Transactional Guide to the Uniform Commercial Code*, Joint Committee on Continuing Legal Education of the American Law Institute and the American Bar Association, Philadelphia, 1964, vol. 1, pp. 476–477, as quoted with approval in *Marengo State Bank v. Meyers*, 232 N.E.2d 75, 80 (Ill. App. 1967).

[5]In the legal sense, a homestead is the land and buildings occupied by the owner as a home and exempted by law from seizure or sale for debts.

5 A term in a draft that provides that by endorsing or cashing the draft the payee acknowledges full satisfaction of an obligation owed to the payee by the drawer.

Omissions Not Affecting Negotiability

Commercial paper sometimes contains a reference to the consideration for which the instrument was given. Although such a reference may be valuable for record purposes, it is not essential and its omission has no effect on negotiability. Neither is it essential for negotiability that the instrument state the place where it is drawn or where it is payable [3-112(1)(a)].

It is customary and advisable for a maker or drawer to date a negotiable instrument. However, if an instrument meets all the requirements for negotiability, including that of being payable on demand or at a definite time, the negotiability of the instrument is normally not affected by the fact that it is undated [3-114(1)].

Negotiability Not Affected by Antedating or Postdating

Antedating or postdating has no effect on the negotiability of an instrument [3-114(1)]. However, there may be some effect on the time of payment if the instrument is payable on demand or at a fixed period after date. Thus, if a demand instrument is issued January 20 but is dated February 1, payment cannot be demanded until February 1, and if an instrument that is payable "thirty days after date" is issued on January 20 but is dated February 1, it is not payable until 30 days after the stated date. In the few cases that have come before the courts, it has been stated that the legal effect of postdating a check is to convert it into a draft payable at a definite time.

INSTRUMENTS DEPRIVED OF NEGOTIABILITY BY STATUTE

An instrument may meet all Code requirements for negotiability and yet, when used for a certain purpose, be classified as nonnegotiable under the provisions of a special statute. The emergence of the consumer protection movement with its opposition to the "holder in due course doctrine" has resulted in the enactment of a special statute by several of the states.

One of the first states to enact a special statute was Massachusetts. The statute was limited, at the time of its adoption, to consumer *goods*. It made nonnegotiable any promissory note resulting from the sale of consumer goods. The statute was involved in, and a significant paragraph is quoted in, the case below. Subsequently, the statute was amended to cover consumer credit sales of *services*, as well as goods. Some other states have adopted the Uniform Consumer Credit Code, which is similar to the "goods or services" statute of Massachusetts.

Case 31.6   **Alcoa Credit Co. v. Nickerson**
5 U.C.C. Rep. 152 (Mass. Dist. Ct. App. Div. 1968)

YESLEY, J. In this action of contract transferred from the Superior Court, the plaintiff [Alcoa Credit Co.] seeks to recover a balance of $1605.62 allegedly due on a promissory note dated February 3, 1964, made by the defendants [Mr. and Mrs. Nickerson] to the order of Beautiful Homes, Inc. (Homes), and endorsed by it to the plaintiff, the holder. The plaintiff also seeks an attorney's fee for collection as provided therein.

The note was given pursuant to a written contract dated January 6, 1964 between Homes and the defendants for the residing of defendants' home in Kingston, Massachusetts, with aluminum shingles for a price of $1850.00. The trial justice found that at the time the contract was signed, Homes' salesman stated to the defendants that the aluminum shingles "would not chip or fade for twenty years and that they would save 10% on the defendants' heating bill"; that the defendants "relied on these representations" in signing the contract and also the note upon completion of the work; that in the spring of 1966 the defendants complained to Homes and to the plaintiff that the shingles had failed to comply with the representations made by Homes; that they had changed in color and the paint had not adhered to them; and that the heating bills had not been reduced. The trial justice found that these complaints were substantiated and that they would have afforded a defense to an action on the note by Homes, the payee. He ruled that the defense was also available in this action since, as he further ruled, the note was a "consumer note" subject to the provisions of GL c 255, sec. 12C; and he found for the defendants.

The plaintiff contends that it took [the note] as a holder in due course free of any such defense (GL c 106, sec. 3-305). It presented requests for rulings which, if granted, would have required the court to rule that the plaintiff as a holder in due course was entitled to recover, and that the note sued upon was not a "consumer note" within the meaning of said statute. The denial of these requests squarely presents the issue before us.

It is uncontroverted that if the note could not properly have been ruled a "consumer note," the plaintiff would have been entitled to rulings that it was a negotiable instrument under the Uniform Commercial Code (GL c 106, sec. 3-104) and that the plaintiff was a holder in due course (sec. 3-302). The nub of the question then is whether the note was a "consumer note" within the meaning of GL c 255, sec. 12C which provides in pertinent part as follows:

> "If any contract for sale of consumer goods on credit entered into in the Commonwealth between a retail seller and a retail buyer requires or involves the execution of a promissory note, such note shall have printed on the face thereof the words 'consumer note,' and such a note with the words 'consumer note' printed thereon shall not be a negotiable instrument within the meaning of the Uniform Commercial Code—Commercial Paper. For the purposes of this section 'consumer goods' means tangible personal property used or bought for use primarily for personal, family or household purposes."

The plaintiff contends that the contract here was for the furnishing of a service, i.e., the installation of aluminum siding rather than for the sale of goods. A note in the 1964 Annual Survey of Massachusetts Law at page 61 takes the same position and we are inclined to accept it. We note that in Chapter 255D (added to the *General Laws by St. 1966*, c 284), entitled "Retail Installment Sales and Services," the definition of "Goods" (section 1) specifically includes "goods which are . . . to become incorporated into a structure" and the rendering of services which are defined as "any work or labor . . . furnished . . . in the delivery (or) installation . . . of goods."

This would have disposed of the question but for the fact that the face of the note, at the top and to the left of the caption "Promissory Note," contains the words "Consumer Note," in large, bold print, with each letter capitalized. The plaintiff contends that these words should be given no effect. It argues that since the contract pursuant to which the note was given was not "for sale of consumer goods" the presence of those words could not per se convert into a "consumer note," a creature of statute, one which does not fit into the statutory definition thereof. We do not agree that the court should have ruled that the words "consumer note" are a nullity. In our opinion, the court could properly find that the parties to the note intended that the words "consumer note" should have meaning and should be a part of their agreement. No particularized meaning for such words has been suggested other than as given by said statute, nor any reason for the inclusion of such words on the note apart from such statute. We agree with the trial justice that "as far as the parties are concerned the note is a consumer note," and as such nonnegotiable. We know of no policy of the law that would prevent parties from agreeing that a note should be nonnegotiable. See cases cited in *Brannan's Negotiable Instruments Law* (4th ed.) sec. 1 (bottom of page 23).

Since it appears from an examination of the note that it is a printed form prepared by the plaintiff, it can hardly complain that by virtue of inclusion thereon of the words "consumer note" it finds itself holding a nonnegotiable note. If those words were not intended to be applicable to the note in question, it would have been a simple matter to strike them.

. . . In view of our holding, the report should be dismissed.

RULES FOR INTERPRETING COMMON AMBIGUITIES

Commercial paper will not readily pass from hand to hand as a substitute for money or produce maximum value as a credit instrument if it contains ambiguities that only the courts can resolve. The Uniform Commercial Code codifies in Section 3-118 various common law rules for the interpretation of ambiguities that occur with considerable frequency in the various kinds of negotiable instruments. Rules for the interpretation of instruments, documents, and statutes are commonly referred to as "rules of construction." Chief among the Code rules for construing negotiable instruments are the following:

1 Where there is doubt whether the instrument is a draft or a note, the holder may treat it as either. A draft drawn on the drawer is treated as a note.

2 Where there is a discrepancy between handwritten terms and typewritten or printed terms, the handwritten terms control. Where there is a discrepancy between typewritten terms and printed terms, the typewritten terms control.

3 Where the sum payable is expressed in words and also in figures, and there is a discrepancy between the two amounts, the sum payable is that expressed in words. However, if the words are ambiguous, the sum payable is that expressed in figures.

4 Where a provision for interest does not specify the rate of interest, the rate is the judgment rate at the place of payment. If the

instrument is dated, the interest will run from the date of the instrument; if it is undated, the interest will run from the date the instrument was issued.

5 Unless the instrument specifies otherwise, where two or more persons sign as maker, drawer, acceptor, or indorser, and do so as part of the same transaction, they are jointly and severally liable. In other words, the payee or the holder has the discretion to bring an action against all of the signers to enforce their personal obligations or against any one or more of them separately. This rule of interpretation is to be applied even though the instrument contains such words as "I promise to pay."

SUMMARY

In some situations there is a substantial difference in legal effect between instruments that are negotiable and those that are not. To be negotiable (and to perform its currency or its credit function), an instrument must meet eight requirements.

1 The instrument must be in *writing*. "Writing" includes handwriting, typewriting, printing, or any other reduction to tangible form.

2 The instrument must be *signed* by the maker or drawer. "Signed" includes any name or symbol executed with present intention to authenticate the instrument.

3 The instrument must contain a *promise or order*. A "promise" is an undertaking to pay and must be more than an acknowledgment of an obligation. An "order" is a direction to pay and must be more than an authorization or request.

4 The promise or order must be *unconditional*. In general, a promise or order is conditional if the instrument states that *(a)* it is subject to an express condition, or *(b)* it is subject to, or governed by, another instrument, or *(c)* payment is to be made only out of a particular fund ("particular fund doctrine"). However, the particular fund doctrine does not apply where the instrument containing such a promise or order is issued by a government or a governmental agency or unit, or where the promise or order is limited to payment out of the entire assets of a partnership or unincorporated association.

A promise or order otherwise unconditional is not made conditional by the fact that the instrument states that it arises out of a separate agreement, or by the fact that the instrument refers to a fund to be debited or a source from which reimbursement is expected.

5 The promise or order must be to pay *money*. An instrument is payable in money if the payee or holder is given the discretion to demand goods or money.

6 The payment to be made must be a *sum certain*. The sum payable is a sum certain even though it is to be paid with interest, in installments, or with costs of collection or an attorney's fee (or both) upon default.

7 The instrument must be payable *on demand or at a definite time*. An instrument that is payable at a fixed period "after date" is payable at a definite time only if the instrument is dated. Except as just indicated, the absence of a date does not affect the negotiability of an instrument. Neither is the negotiability affected by the fact that the instrument was antedated or postdated.

8 An instrument must be payable *to order* of the payee or *to bearer*. The words "to order" and "to bearer" are called "words of negotiability."

The Code permits the inclusion of certain terms (provisions) that do not affect negotiability. Some examples are a provision giving the holder the power to sell collateral in the event of default, a provision authorizing confession of judgment if the instrument is not paid when due, and a provision waiving the benefit of any law intended for the protection of the obligor.

Negotiability of an instrument is not affected by the omission of a statement of any consideration. Neither is negotiability affected by the omission of any reference to where the instrument is drawn or payable.

Recent opposition to the "holder in due course" doctrine has resulted in statutes declaring certain instruments nonnegotiable even though the instruments meet the eight requirements for negotiability.

The Code contains rules governing the interpretation of ambiguous terms that occur frequently in the various types of commercial paper. This chapter concluded with a brief discussion of those rules.

STUDY AND DISCUSSION QUESTIONS

1 List eight requirements that commercial paper must meet in order to be negotiable.

2 *(a)* "A signature need not necessarily consist of the maker's or drawer's name." Explain. *(b)* "A person should be wary of taking an instrument that is signed in some unusual way." Why?

3 *(a)* Explain the difference between a promise to pay and an order to pay. *(b)* List the instruments in which one would find a promise to pay; an order to pay. *(c)* Why does the UCC permit a draft to be addressed to two or more drawees in the alternative but not to two or more drawees in succession?

4 *(a)* Explain the difference in legal effect between an instrument that states that it is "subject to" a certain contract and an instrument that states that it is made "in accordance with" or "as per" a certain contract. *(b)* What is the reason for the difference in legal effect?

5 "Subject to two important exceptions, a promise or order is conditional if the instrument states that it is to be paid out of a particular fund or source." *(a)* What is the reason for the rule that such a promise or order is conditional? *(b)* What are the two exceptions to the rule?

6 *(a)* State whether you agree, partly agree, or disagree with the following statement, and why: An instrument may be negotiable though it calls for payment in money or in goods. *(b)* List and give examples of provisions allowed by the Code that may make uncertain the sum to be paid. Why are these exceptions permitted?

7 When is an instrument by its terms payable: *(a)* on demand? *(b)* at a definite time?

8 *(a)* Give three examples of instruments payable to order. *(b)* When is an instrument by its terms payable to bearer? *(c)* Is an instrument that says "Payable to the order of cash" classified as order paper or bearer paper? Why? *(d)* What is the significance of classifying an instrument as either order or bearer paper?

9 *(a)* What effect does omission of the date of an instrument have on negotiability? *(b)* What effect does postdating an instrument have?

10 Which term prevails where an instrument contains a discrepancy between: *(a)* a handwritten term and a printed term? *(b)* a typewritten term and a printed term? *(c)* a term expressing the sum payable in figures and a term expressing the sum payable in words?

CASE PROBLEMS

1 Each of the names at the top of the note below was in the handwriting of the person named. Does the instrument meet the requirement that to be negotiable an instrument "must be signed by the maker or drawer"?

$1,600   August 15, 19—

Edward Lukowiak, Jos. M. Lukowiak, Anna Lukowiak, Helen Lukowiak,

On demand after date promise to pay to the order of
E.J. Field, Sixteen Hundred Dollars at 5%.

---

2 Is the following installment note negotiable? Which two of the eight requirements are in doubt?

May 5, 1977

I promise to pay to the order of Dr. Richard Rowe the sum of twenty dollars ($20.00) each month, beginning June 5, 1977, until I have paid four hundred and eighty dollars ($480.00). In case of death of maker, all payments not due at date of death are canceled.

John Doe

---

3 A note made payable to the order of payee stated, "This note with interest is secured by a mortgage on real estate." The payee sold the note to Jones. On the due date of the note, Jones sought payment from the maker. The maker refused payment on the ground that the payee had committed fraud in the sale of the real estate to the maker. Whether the maker could assert the defense of fraud depended on whether the note was negotiable. Was it negotiable?

4 A contractor's note, properly dated and signed, read: "I promise to pay to the order of Paul Payee within the next sixty days the sum of five thousand dollars ($5,000) from the jobs now under construction." Is the note a negotiable instrument? Which of the eight requirements is in doubt?

5 The Nation-Wide Check Corporation sells money orders through 4,000 agents in seventeen states. On the face of each money order is printed "Pay the sum of." When an order is purchased, the agent, with the machine furnished by Nation-Wide, stamps in the amount. On the lower portion of the money order are the words "Payable to" preceding a blank line, and beneath this is the word "From," likewise preceding a blank line. It is the usual practice to deliver to the purchaser the order with the name of the remitter and payee in blank, and the purchaser thereafter fills in the blanks. Ralph Remitter purchased a $50 money order from Nation-Wide, filled in his name on the "From" line and the name of Carl Creditor on the "Payable to" line, and mailed the money order to him. Is the money order negotiable? Which of the eight requirements is in doubt?

6 A note, otherwise negotiable, contained a statement that collateral had been given to secure the obligation on the note. The reference to the collateral security was followed by this provision: "If, in the judgment of the holder of this note, said collateral depreciates in value, the undersigned agrees to deliver when demanded additional security to the satisfaction of said holder." Does that provision make the note nonnegotiable?

7 In an 1871 case, the court held the note below to be negotiable. Would the note be negotiable if it were dated today?

$125.00   Buffalo, March 25, 1868

Six months after date I promise to pay to G. W. Lowe, or order, one hundred and twenty-five dollars for value received, with interest, waiving the right of appeal and of all valuation, appraisement, stay and execution laws.

Moses Anderson

Chapter

32

Issue, Transfer, and Negotiation of Commercial Paper

The major aim of the law of commercial paper is to have instruments that are easily transferable and, because highly marketable, accepted as substitutes for money. The marketability of commercial paper is enhanced by freeing transferees who qualify as holders in due course from most defenses of makers and drawers. A transferee cannot have this special status in the law unless three circumstances exist: (1) the instrument must be negotiable in form; (2) the person or persons transferring the instrument must use a special method of transfer called "negotiation"; and (3) the transferee must have the characteristics of a holder in due course or be an assignee of one. The eight requirements for an instrument to be negotiable were discussed in Chapter 31. The requirements to be a holder are discussed briefly in this chapter and in Chapter 33. The requirements for holder in due course status are discussed extensively in Chapter 33.

This chapter deals with the transfer aspect of commercial paper. Specifically, it deals with the issue, transfer, and negotiation of commercial paper, and with the way the various rules of transfer help fulfill the aims of the law of commercial paper.

ISSUE

We noted in Chapter 30 that commercial paper is both a contract and a species of property; that as a species of property, it is subject to some of the rules of property law; and that just as a deed to land must be delivered by the grantor in order to make it legally effective, so a note, draft, or check must be delivered by the maker or drawer in order to make it legally effective. The delivery of an instrument by the maker or drawer with the intention of granting rights in it is technically referred to as its "issue," although the term "issuance" is sometimes used.

659

Issue and Delivery

Meaning of Issue and Delivery *Issue* means the first delivery of an instrument to another. *Delivery*, with respect to instruments, means voluntary transfer of possession [1-201(14)].[1] Thus, there would be no delivery where the payee of a check, seeing the check on the drawer's desk, picks it up without authority while the drawer is out of the office. And there have been several cases in which the court held that a note found in the maker's effects after his or her death was not enforceable against the maker's estate, for want of delivery.[2] The subject of delivery is discussed in connection with personal property in Chapter 20.

There is no delivery if a drawer or maker hands a negotiable instrument to his or her own agent with instructions to take the instrument to the payee. Delivery does not take place until the agent turns over the instrument to the payee. However, where the drawer or maker turns over an instrument to an agent of the *payee*, there is a delivery of the instrument. The question has arisen several times as to whether mailing an instrument to the payee constitutes delivery. An important consideration is whether the Postal Service is an agent of the sender or an agent of the payee. The courts have held that the act of mailing constitutes delivery if the mailing was with the express or implied authority of the payee, but not if such authority was lacking.[3]

---

[1] Numbers within brackets in the text refer to sections of the Uniform Commercial Code.

[2] William E. Britton, *Bills and Notes*, 2d ed., West Publishing Company, St. Paul, 1961, p. 119, and cases there cited.

---

[3] Ibid., p. 120, and cases there cited. See Chapter 36 for discussion of express and implied authority.

Case 32.1   Bryan v. Bartlett
435 F.2d 28 (8th Cir. 1970)

This case involved a suit by Lem C. Bryan (plaintiff), receiver of the Arkansas Loan and Thrift Corporation (AL&T), against the nine directors of the corporation to recover payment on promissory notes that had been executed by them in favor of AL&T. Each note was for $70,400 and was signed by one of the defendants. Attached to each note as security for payment was a stock certificate of 64 shares in the Savings Guaranty Corporation, a subsidiary of AL&T. For the most part, the same persons were officers and directors of both corporations. At the time the notes were executed they were given into the possession of E. M. Clem, the president of Savings Guaranty Corporation.

The defendant directors asserted lack of consideration, no delivery to AL&T, and various other defenses. The following excerpt is from that part of the court's opinion that dealt with the defense of no delivery.

GIBSON, Cir. J. . . . It is a prerequisite to liability on a negotiable instrument that the instrument be delivered by the maker. The defendants contend that there was no delivery in this case. They argue that Clem held the notes solely as agent for them, that they were never delivered to AL&T, and that the receiver obtained possession only by virtue of a court order which cannot be construed as voluntary delivery. We agree that the transfer from Clem to the receiver cannot be considered to be the sort of delivery requisite to establishing the effectiveness of the notes in question. However, as we construe the facts in this case, the transfer of possession from the defendants to Clem was sufficient to constitute the necessary delivery [to AL&T].

The purpose of requiring a delivery is to make manifest the intention of the maker of a note that it be operative. Thus, even though a person executes a note in proper form, where he retains possession and control over it, it can reasonably be assumed that he did not intend for it to be effective. "Delivery" is defined in the NIL as a transfer of possession from one person to another (Sec. 191), and in the UCC as a voluntary transfer of possession [Sec. 1-201(14)]. Of course, it is an elementary principle of agency that delivery to a principal's agent is the equivalent of delivery to the principal. Where an instrument is no longer in the possession of a party whose signature is on it, there is a presumption of delivery. 11 *Am. Jur.* 2d, *Bills & Notes,* sec. 272 (1963).

Applying these principles to the instant case, we think it is clear that there was delivery of the notes in question to AL&T. . . . The delivery by the defendants to Clem was clearly a voluntary transfer of possession. There is no conflict in the evidence as to that point. It is also clear that this transfer amounted to a relinquishment of control over the instrument. There was never any further attempt by any of the defendants to discover what was being done with the notes or to insure that they not be used for any purpose which might entail liability on their parts. . . . It is evident that in putting the notes in his possession, without any further attempt at control over them, the defendants intended them to be readily accessible to AL&T for any purposes which might be deemed useful. If the defendants truly intended the notes not to be used by AL&T or to be used for strictly limited purposes, the means were readily available to assure the limited use. They could either have not executed them until the appropriate time, or having executed them retained possession of them, or put them in the possession of a completely independent party with clearly limited instructions and authority. Since none of these things was done, and since it is clear that the defendants intended to relinquish possession and control of the notes to a person intimately associated with AL&T, the conclusion is inescapable that they were delivered to AL&T.

To Whom Instrument May Be Issued Issue refers only to the *first* delivery of an instrument, and then only where that delivery is to a holder or a remitter [3-102(1)(a)]. "Holder" is defined more fully in Chapter 33. But in regard to the issue of an instrument, the *holder* is the person who receives possession of the instrument from the maker or drawer. To determine whether an instrument has been legally issued, it is important to know if the instrument is bearer paper or order paper. Where a negotiable instrument is drawn payable to bearer, delivery to any person constitutes delivery to a holder. Where a negotiable instrument is drawn payable to the order of a named payee, only a delivery to the named payee constitutes delivery to a holder.

A *remitter* is a person who purchases ("remits" payment for) a bank draft or cashier's check that is payable to the order of someone other than himself or herself. A common example of a remitter is a debtor who purchases a bank draft made payable to the order of a creditor. When the bank hands over the draft to the purchaser, there is a delivery "to a remitter." Thus, there has been an issue of the instrument, but as yet there is no holder of the instrument. When the remitter delivers the draft to the payee, the payee becomes a holder.

Delivery to a holder or remitter may be actual or "constructive." Constructive delivery occurs when an instrument is made available to a person without any restrictions as to its availability. The following case illustrates this principle.

Case 32.2   Billingsley v. Kelly
274 A.2d 113 (Md. App. 1971)

Note: Although Huffner's name does not appear in the title of this case, he was one of the two defendants in the trial court and, along with Kelly, is an appellee in this Court of Appeals case.

BARNES, J. Henry E. Billingsley joined with Paul J. Kelly and Jack R. Huffner to form Urban Systems, Inc., a Maryland Corporation, in the fall of 1966. . . . Billingsley, Kelly and Huffner each owned a one-third interest in the Corporation and together constituted its board of directors. The Corporation met with less than immediate financial success and became indebted to each of the three principals for unpaid salary. The Corporation had an additional obligation to Billingsley for personal funds he had expended on behalf of the Corporation. On March 11, 1968, the Corporation executed four promissory notes. Two of these notes were made payable to the order of Billingsley; one in the amount of $6,868.81 for unpaid salary; the other in the amount of $16,083.42 for personal expenditures in behalf of the Corporation. Both of these notes were indorsed [signed] by Kelly and Huffner as individual guarantors. A third note made payable to the order of Kelly in the amount of $13,830.98 for unpaid salary was indorsed by Huffner and Billingsley as individual guarantors. A fourth note made payable to the order of Huffner in the amount of $13,280.98 for unpaid salary was indorsed by Kelly and Billingsley as individual guarantors. Payment on each of the four notes, dated March 11, 1968, was due on demand and each was entitled to 6% interest from July 1, 1967. Having made a fruitless demand for payment from the Corporation as maker . . . Billingsley sued Kelly and Huffner for the balance due on March 24, 1969. The Circuit Court, sitting without a jury, found that Kelly and Huffner were liable to Billingsley in the amount claimed but also that Billingsley was liable to Kelly and Huffner on their notes. The trial court determined that the amount due Kelly and Huffner was more than that due Billingsley and thus entered judgment for the Appellees, Kelly and Huffner, . . .

Billingsley raises four points on appeal. . . .

[The remainder of this excerpt from the Court's opinion involves only Billingsley's second contention.]

Billingsley contends that since the Appellee, Huffner, never took possession of the note issued him by the Corporation, such note never became a valid negotiable instrument and thus is not enforceable against him as an indorser.

All four of the notes were executed in Billingsley's office on March 11, 1968. At that time Kelly had the corporate seal in his office. It was agreed that Billingsley would hold the notes until he obtained the seal and impressed it upon each note after which each of the parties could take possession of his note. Shortly after this was accomplished, Kelly obtained delivery of his note. Huffner, however, never bothered to pick up his note. It is also undisputed that Billingsley retained the notes for the sole purpose of placing the seal on them and that there was no reason why Huffner could not have taken physical possession of his note at any time.

. . . In terms of the Uniform Commercial Code, . . . the question comes down to whether or not Huffner can be considered a "holder" of the instrument. Sec. 1-201(20) defines "holder" as "a person who is in possession of . . . an instrument . . . drawn, issued or indorsed to him or to his order or to bearer or in blank." Since it is undisputed that Huffner never took actual possession of the note, he could only qualify as a "holder" if construed to be in constructive possession of the note. . . .

This court recognized and applied the concept of constructive delivery in regard to negotiable instruments in *Miller v. Hospelhorn*, 176 Md. 356, 4 A.2d 728 (1939). Unless changed by the adoption of the Uniform Commercial Code in Maryland, *Miller* still represents the law on the subject in this state. Use of the constructive delivery concept was specifically provided for in the former Negotiable Instruments Law of Maryland which defined "delivery" as the "transfer of possession, actual or constructive, from one person to another." The definition of "delivery" in the Uniform Commercial Code as currently enacted in Maryland is as follows: " 'Delivery' with respect to instruments . . . means voluntary transfer of possession." The "constructive possession" concept is not specifically mentioned as it was in the prior Negotiable Instruments Law but neither is it specifically negated. . . . Stringent requirements of delivery and possession . . . are to avoid fraud by requiring the best possible evidence of intent. If there is any evidence more reliable than delivery and possession on a question such as this, it would have to be the in-court admission of the adverse party. Prudent use of the "constructive delivery" doctrine in the past has apparently worked no great hardship upon the conduct of commercial transactions and there is no reason to believe that it should in the future. . . .

It can be seen from Billingsley's own testimony that reception of the notes by him was in his capacity as an individual and constituted a delivery from the corporate maker to him, as opposed to no delivery and a mere retention by him in his corporate capacity as maker. . . .

We find that Billingsley's reception of the note from the corporate maker constituted constructive delivery to Huffner giving him constructive possession and thus qualifying him as a holder under UCC.

Case 32.2
Continued

[The court also found for the appellees on the appellant's other three contentions.]

Judgment affirmed, the appellant to pay costs.

Issue of Incomplete Instruments

Suppose that Donna draws a check complete in every respect except that the two lines for the amount of the payment are left blank. She gives the check to the payee, Peter, with instructions to "fill in the amount I owe you." The check is issued even though it is an incomplete instrument. The issuance of incomplete instruments may be dangerous, but the practice is convenient and relatively frequent. Not to give effect to instruments completed by others than the issuers would disrupt the flow of commercial paper and would unnecessarily raise doubts about the collectibility of such paper. Of course, an incomplete instrument cannot be enforced until completed [3-115]. The subject of incomplete instruments is discussed in Chapter 34.

TRANSFER AND NEGOTIATION

Meaning and Methods of Transfer

After an instrument has been issued, it may be transferred one or more times during its lifetime. If an instrument is nonnegotiable, its transfer is merely an assignment, and all transferees take the instrument subject to any defenses that might exist. The transferee of a nonnegotiable document is an assignee and has no greater rights than the transferor.

If the instrument is negotiable in form, it may be transferred either by negotiation or by assignment. Where the transfer of a negotiable instrument is accomplished by a "negotiation" and the transferee meets the requirements for a holder in due course, the holder takes the instrument free from most defenses. Thus, the transferee can acquire better rights in the instrument than the transferor had. For example,

suppose a person buys defective goods from a merchant, giving a check in payment. If the merchant negotiates the check to a transferee who qualifies as a holder in due course, the transferee can collect on the check. The drawer's defense of defective goods is cut off. Where the transfer of a negotiable instrument is accomplished by an "assignment," the transferee ordinarily is a mere assignee and acquires only the rights that the transferor had. (As is explained in the next chapter, if an assignee acquires a negotiable instrument from a holder in due course, the assignee ordinarily acquires the *full rights* of a holder in due course, including the right to take the instrument free from personal defenses).

Meaning and Methods of Negotiation

Negotiation is the transfer of a negotiable instrument in such form that the transferee becomes a holder [3-202(1)]. As used here, a *holder* is a person in possession of bearer paper or of order paper that has been properly indorsed (signed by the transferor). Thus, there are two methods of negotiation: (1) if an instrument is payable to order (i.e., is payable to the order of a named payee), it is negotiated by delivery together with any necessary indorsement; and (2) if the instrument is payable to bearer, it is negotiated by delivery alone [3-202(1)]. *Delivery* has here the same meaning it has in connection with the issue of an instrument; that is, delivery is a voluntary transfer of possession. The term "order paper" refers not only to an instrument that is made out to the order of a named payee but also to an instrument that is indorsed to some named person. Order paper and bearer paper are discussed in more detail in the section entitled In-Blank or Special Indorsement.

What happens if the holder-transferor of order paper forgets to add his or her indorsement? In that event the transfer constitutes an *assignment*. Until the indorsement is supplied, a transferee is merely an assignee and is subject to any defenses learned of before the indorsement is supplied. However, a transferee for value is better off than an ordinary assignee. The transferee may become a holder in due course. If the transferee has given value for the instrument, the transferee has "the specifically enforceable right to have the unqualified indorsement of the transferor" [3-201(3)].

Legal Requirements for Indorsement

An *indorsement* is a signature, customarily found on the back of commercial paper and made by a person other than a maker, drawer, or acceptor of the paper. The rights and liabilities of the indorser and of the transferee depend on whether the signature meets the legal requirements for indorsement and upon the type of indorsement used. Code provisions govern where an indorsement must be written, who may indorse, and what constitutes a proper signature for an indorsement.

Where Indorsement Must Be Written An indorsement must be written "on the instrument or on a paper so firmly affixed thereto as to become a part thereof" [3-202(2)]. Although the Code provides that an indorsement must be written on the instrument, it does not specify where on the instrument the indorsement is to be written. Customarily, indorsements are written on the back of the instrument, beginning at the "top," but there is no custom as to which end is the top. Some checks and drafts have a printed instruction at one end to "Write indorsement here." Occasionally, a signature is so placed on the instrument that it is not clear in what capacity the person signed. Under the Code, such a signature is an indorsement.

If a negotiable instrument is negotiated many times, there may be a lack of space on the back of the instrument for all necessary indorsements. A paper attached to an instrument for the purpose of carrying indorsements is called an "allonge." A paper clipped or pinned to an instrument is not so firmly affixed as to become a part of the instrument. It is therefore not an allonge, and anything written on it cannot qualify as an indorsement.

Case 32.3   James Talcott, Inc. v. Fred Ratowsky Associates, Inc.
2 U.C.C. Rep. 1134 (Pa. Ct. Com. Pleas, 1965)

Plaintiff, James Talcott, Inc., was the purchaser of a note on which Fred Ratowsky Associates, Inc. was an accommodation party (a person who lends credit to an instrument by signing it as a favor to the person requesting accommodation). Before the plaintiff purchased the note, it had been indorsed to the Sayve Corporation of America. The Sayve Corporation attached a piece of paper to the note and wrote its indorsement on the attached paper. There was a default in the payment of the note, and plaintiff sued the accommodation party. The defendant, Fred Ratowsky Associates, Inc., contended (1) that the attached paper was not an allonge, and that therefore Sayve Corporation's signature was ineffective to make the plaintiff a holder; and (2) that as an accommodation party the defendant was liable only to the holder of the note. The following

Case 32.3
Continued

excerpt is from that part of the court's opinion that deals with the defendant's first contention.

SHELLEY, J. . . . The parties . . . have entered into a stipulation for the trial of this case without a jury. The parties have also stipulated the facts. We adopt their stipulation as our findings of fact and incorporate the same herein for reference. . . .

Defendant contends that the attached paper was not an "allonge." The answer to the question must be found in an interpretation of the Uniform Commercial Code which provides [in Sec. 3-202(2)] that "an indorsement must be written by or on behalf of the holder and on the instrument or on a paper so firmly affixed thereto as to become a part thereof," as applied to the circumstances of this case.

The Negotiable Instruments Act [Sec. 31] provided that "the indorsement must be written on the instrument itself or upon a paper attached thereto. . . ." A comparison of the provisions of the two acts indicates that the legislature intended by the provision of the Uniform Commercial Code to sanction the use of the "allonge" but added the additional provision that the "allonge" be not merely attached to the instrument but required that it be *firmly affixed* to the note. There is no doubt that the reason for this added requirement was that it was not intended to establish the loose and undesirable practice of making regular indorsements of commercial paper by a writing on the back of any other paper or document to which it might have been temporarily attached, as by pinning, especially when there is ample space for the indorsement on the back of the instrument itself. . . .

For some unexplained reason, neither the original note nor the instrument purporting to be an "allonge" was exhibited to us at any time during the litigation; only photostatic copies were attached to the pleadings. We have no way of determining the method of attachment of the alleged "allonge" except by the use of the word "clipped" in the stipulation of facts. As we understand the word "clip," it means to "clasp" or "fasten with a clip," which usually denotes a temporary method of attachment and is not nearly as secure as the method of stapling or riveting or the use of an adhesive preparation, such as glue, mucilage, or paste.

An examination of the note indicates that there was sufficient space on the back of the note for a second indorsement. . . .

We, accordingly, conclude that the paper attached to the note was not an "allonge." . . .

The UCC defines a holder as "a person who is in possession of . . . an instrument issued or indorsed to him or to his order. . . ." [Sec. 1-201(20)]. Because the paper attached to the note was not an "allonge," it is clear that . . . plaintiff was not in possession of an instrument indorsed to it or to its order and, therefore, was not a holder. [However, defendant Ratowsky was nevertheless held liable as an accommodation party, since an accommodation party is liable not just to holders, but also to "takers" for value.]

Who May Indorse To be effective, an indorsement must be written by or on behalf of the holder [3-202(2)]. A person may indorse an instrument on behalf of the holder only if the person has actual or apparent authority to do so.[4] "Any unauthorized signature is wholly inoperative as that of the person whose name is signed . . ." [3-404(1)]. This provision applies alike to a forgery and to a signature made by an agent exceeding his or her actual or apparent authority. A person who takes an instrument indorsed by an agent runs considerable risk unless there is assurance that the agent has the requisite authority.

We saw in the previous chapter that an instrument may be made payable to two or more persons together ("A, B, and C") or in the alternative ("A, B, or C"). An instrument payable to the order of A, B, and C is payable to all of them and may be negotiated only by indorsement of all of them. An instrument payable to the order of A, B, or C is payable to any one of them and therefore requires the indorsement of only one of them [3-116].

We also saw that an order instrument need not be made payable to the order of a named person or persons. It may be made payable to the order of any of the following.

1 An estate, trust, or fund ("Pay to the order of the Estate of John Doe, Deceased"; "Pay to the order of the Community Fund"). The authorized representative of the estate, trust, or fund may indorse the instrument. Any money collected on the instrument is, of course, collected for the benefit of the estate, trust, or fund.

2 A partnership or other unincorporated association. Such an instrument is payable to the

partnership or other unincorporated association and may be indorsed by any duly authorized person.

3 An office, or an officer by his or her title as such ("Pay to the order of the Swedish Consulate"; "Pay to the order of the Treasurer of the Country Club"). Such an instrument may be indorsed by the incumbent of the office or a successor [3-110(1)(e), (f), (g)].

It is not unusual for checks to be made payable to a named person with the addition of words describing the person as agent or officer of a specified individual or organization (e.g., "Jane Doe, Attorney for Rachel Roe"; "Carl Kasch, Treasurer of the Country Club"). In all such instances

> it is commercial understanding that the description is not added for mere identification but for the purpose of making the instrument payable to the principal, and that the agent or officer is named as payee only for convenience in enabling him to cash the check [3-117, comment 1].

Section 3-117 incorporates this commercial understanding by providing that the instrument is payable to the principal, but the agent or officer may indorse the instrument.

The same section provides that an instrument made payable to a named person with the addition of words describing the person "as fiduciary for a specified person or purpose is payable to the payee and may be negotiated, discharged, or enforced by him." Examples of wording on such instruments are: "Pay to the order of John Doe, Trustee of the Smithers Trust" and "Pay to the order of Jane Doe, Administrator of the Estate of Rachel Roe."

---

[4]Authority of an agent is discussed in Chapter 36, p. 750.

Case 32.4   Bates v. City of New York
10 U.C.C. Rep. 151 (N.Y. Sup. Ct. 1971)

In a previous case brought against the City of New York for personal injuries received by Bruce Baglio, there was a judgment against the City. As a result of the judgment, the City issued a check on Manufacturers Hanover Trust Co. payable "to the order of Joseph Baglio as Administrator of the Est. of Bruce Baglio Dec'd." The check was indorsed "Joseph Baglio" and was presented to the National Bank of North America for deposit in Joseph Baglio's *personal* account. The National Bank credited the amount of the check to Baglio's personal account and collected the amount from the drawee bank. The administrator Baglio converted the proceeds of the check to his personal use. Thereafter he was dismissed as administrator, and one Bates was appointed as administratrix. Administratrix Bates sued the City of New York, the depositary bank (National Bank), and the drawee bank (Manufacturers Hanover Trust Co.) for the face amount of the check. The two banks moved to dismiss the complaint.

BLOOM, J. . . . UCC sec. 3-117 provides that an instrument made payable to a named person with the addition of words describing him "as a fiduciary for a specified person or purpose is payable to the payee and may be negotiated, discharged, or enforced by him." It is plain then that the check was properly indorsed. In the absence of any allegations as to specific knowledge by the drawee bank, with whom the payee had no direct dealings, of the payee's tortious and criminal activities, no liability can attach to the drawee bank for honoring a properly indorsed check.

But the defendant National stands on a different footing. It credited to Baglio's personal account a check payable to him as a fiduciary. Presumably it also paid out to Baglio sums drawn on his personal account into which estate funds had been mingled. Nonetheless, no liability attaches to it either. Its liability is limited to cases where it has *knowingly* participated in the diversion of funds; and in the absence of adequate notice to the contrary, it may assume that, in spite of the commingling of funds, estate funds will be properly applied by the fiduciary.

Accordingly the motion [to dismiss the complaint] is granted with respect to the defendant banks.

What Constitutes Proper Signature for an Indorsement When an instrument is made payable to a person under a misspelled name or a trade name (e.g., a check made payable to the order of "Tim's Tire Retread Shop"), the person may indorse in the trade name or misspelled name, or in his or her own name, or both [3-203]. The preferred procedure is to sign in both names. In fact, Section 3-203 provides that a person paying or giving value for the instrument may require indorsement in both names.

Where an instrument is payable to the order of a corporation, the name of the corporation should appear in the indorsement. If it does not, and the indorsement consists merely of the signature of the corporation's agent, followed by a designation of his position (for example, "John

Doe, Secretary-Treasurer"), has the instrument been indorsed by the corporation? The Code has no provision directly in point, but in the following case the court held that "such an indorsement is legally sufficient" to constitute an indorsement by the corporation. The subject of indorsements by agents is discussed more fully in Chapter 34.

Case 32.5   **American National Bank & Trust Co. v. Scenic Stage Lines, Inc.**
276 N.E.2d 420 (Ill. App. 1971)

The defendant, Scenic Stage Lines of Savanna, Inc. (Scenic), purchased some buses from the Hausman Bus Sales, Inc. (Hausman). As a part of the transaction, Scenic executed and delivered its note made payable to the order of Hausman. Hausman delivered the note for value to the American National Bank & Trust Co. of Chicago. At the time of the transfer there appeared on the back of the note the handwritten words "Eugene Tarkoff, Sec.-Treas." There was a default on the note, and the bank sued the maker (Scenic). Since the note contained a confession of judgment clause, there was no trial, and plaintiff received a judgment. The defendant (Scenic) moved to vacate the judgment. The trial court denied the motion, and defendant appealed.

On appeal, defendant raised several legal issues, only one of which is discussed in the following excerpt from the appellate court's opinion.

VAN DEUSEN, J. . . . The initial question here . . . is whether or not a note made payable to a corporation by its corporate name can be legally indorsed by the signature of an individual followed by a description of his position but without reference in the indorsement itself to the entity for which he purports to act. The Uniform Commercial Code does not deal directly with this issue. Article 3 of the Code dealing with liability of parties does provide in Sec. 3-403—Signature by Authorized Representative—that where the instrument names the person represented and the representative signs in a representative capacity, the representative is not liable. In the Code comment on this section the commentator points out that the unambiguous way to make the representation clear is to sign "Peter Pringle by Arthur Adams, Agent" but that any other definite indication is sufficient, as where the instrument reads "Peter Pringle promises to pay" and it is signed "Arthur Adams, Agent."

There is a strong inference to be drawn from Sec. 3-403 that where the note names the corporation as payee, an indorsement signed by its agent in his own name, followed by a description of his position, is a sufficient indication that the individual signer is acting as agent for the named payee and that such an indorsement is legally sufficient. To hold otherwise would place the plaintiff Bank in the anomalous position of not being able to bring suit against Scenic Stage Lines, the maker of the note, because the indorsement is legally

Case 32.5
Continued

insufficient to convey any rights to the Bank against the maker, and [would] also . . . deny the plaintiff Bank any rights against Tarkoff as an individual indorser because of the terms of Sec. 3-403 of UCC. Such a result would seem to be untenable.

[The Court found for the defendant on each of the other issues.]
Judgment affirmed.

Types and Uses of Indorsements

The types and uses of a variety of indorsements commonly used by holders (i.e., payees and indorsers) to negotiate commercial paper can be described by the application of three sets of terms. An indorsement is either "in blank" or "special"; it is also either "unqualified" or "qualified"; it is also either "nonrestrictive" or "restrictive." Suppose a check has been made payable to the order of John Doe. To negotiate the check, John may elect to sign it on the back as in Figure 32.1. This indorsement is in blank, unqualified, and nonrestrictive.

Or, John might have elected to indorse the check as in Figure 32.2. This indorsement is special, qualified, and restrictive. Many combinations of the three sets of terms are possible. These sets of terms are examined in the following pages.

In-Blank or Special Indorsement   An indorsement *in blank* is so called because it does not specify who the transferee is to be. The payee merely signs his or her name. The check issued to John Doe in the illustration in Figure 32.1 was indorsed in blank. The legal effect of an indorsement in blank is to convert order paper to bearer paper. Thus, the instrument can be further negotiated by delivery alone [3-204(2)].

Keeping possession of or mailing bearer paper (such as a check indorsed in blank) involves serious risk. Suppose that John Doe indorses his check in blank and it is lost or stolen. A finder or thief of bearer paper is a holder because the Code defines "holder" in part as anyone *in possession of* bearer paper. A holder of bearer paper, even though a thief, has the power to negotiate the instrument to another person. If the thief's transferee meets the requirements of a holder in due course, the person who was the owner at the time the paper was stolen (e.g., John Doe in our illustration) is deprived of all rights in the instrument. His or her only recourse is to track down the thief.

John could protect himself from loss by using a "special" indorsement. A *special indorsement* specifies a person to receive payment. In Figure 32.2, the words "Pay Jane Doe, (signed) John Doe" is a special indorsement. The legal effect of a special indorsement is to maintain the "order" character of the check. Thus, in the illustration above, Jane's indorsement is required for further negotiation of the check [3-204(1)]. If the check is lost or stolen before Jane indorses it, neither she nor John has much cause for worry. The drawee bank must follow John's instructions as to whom to pay. By his special indorsement, John instructed the bank to pay Jane. If the drawee disregards that instruction by paying a forger, the drawee must absorb the loss and attempt to track down the person to whom payment was made.

Although words of negotiability must appear on the *face* of an instrument to make it negotiable in form, their presence in or absence from an *indorsement* has no effect on the negotiability of the instrument. The absence of "pay to the

Figure 32.1

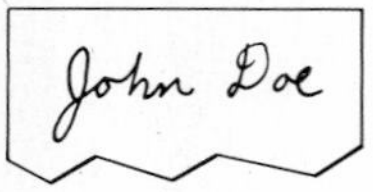

John Doe

Figure 32.2

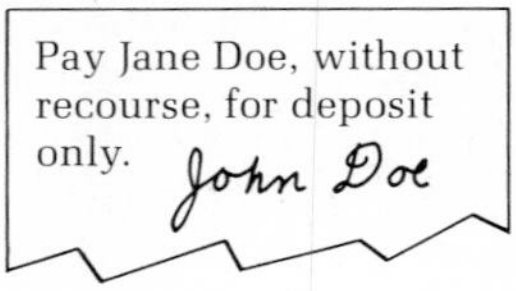

Pay Jane Doe, without recourse, for deposit only.   John Doe

order of" from a special indorsement does not destroy the negotiability of a negotiable instrument. The use of such words in an indorsement does not make a nonnegotiable instrument negotiable. Indorsements simply give evidence of proper transfer, and they create liability on the part of indorsers; they neither create nor destroy negotiability.

Where an instrument is bearer paper on its face and carries no indorsement, the holder can convert it to order paper by a special indorsement [3-204(1)]. Suppose that Jane draws a check payable to bearer and delivers it to Beatrice. Beatrice can protect herself against loss or theft by naming herself the indorsee in a special indorsement: "Pay to the order of myself, (signed) Beatrice Bearer."

A holder may convert a blank indorsement into a special indorsement by writing appropriate words above the signature of the indorser [3-204(3)]. Suppose that Rachel acquires an instrument that is payable to bearer because the last indorsement is in blank (as in Figure 32.3 below). Figure 32.4 shows how Rachel can convert the blank indorsement in Figure 32.3 into a special indorsement.

Unqualified or Qualified Indorsement   One of the consequences of indorsing a negotiable instrument is that the indorser may be liable for the amount due under the instrument if others fail to pay. The indorser may be the payee of an order instrument or a transferee who wishes to negotiate the instrument. To avoid liability on the instrument, the indorser must make a "qualified" indorsement. In Figure 32.2, by the use of the words "without recourse," John Doe makes a *qualified indorsement.* Unless an indorser qualifies his or her indorsement by use of "without recourse" or words of similar meaning, the indorsement is an *unqualified indorsement* [3-414(1)]. The indorsements in Figures 32.3 and 32.4 are all unqualified. Thus, Pauline Payee and John Doe may each be held liable to transferees for the face amount of the instrument if it is not paid by the maker or drawee.

Nonrestrictive or Restrictive Indorsement   Unless a restriction is stated in the indorsement, the indorsement is *nonrestrictive* (as in Figure 32.1). Most *restrictive* indorsements are enforceable, but some are not. The Code lists four categories of restrictive indorsements. Three of them merit discussion here: (1) indorsements that are conditional (these are partially enforceable); (2) indorsements purporting to prohibit further transfer of an instrument (these are not enforceable); and (3) indorsements for deposit or collection (these are enforceable and are widely used).

Conditional indorsement   Since a negotiable instrument is used as a substitute for money, it may be transferred by a holder to a merchant as payment for goods or services. Suppose, however, the merchant is to deliver the goods or perform the services in the future. A conditional indorsement gives the holder some protection against liability in the event the merchant fails to perform. The holder might sign on the back of the instrument as follows: "Pay to Able Typewriter Company provided they deliver a typewriter to me on or before March 1, (signed) Paul Payee." The legal effect of such an indorsement is that Paul is not liable to Able, if Able cannot collect on the instrument from the maker or drawee, unless Able delivers a typewriter on or before March 1. However, as we shall see in Chapter 33, Paul *is liable* to a transferee of the

Figure 32.3   **Figure 32.4**

instrument who meets the requirements for a holder in due course.

Indorsement purporting to prohibit further transfer   Suppose John Doe, a payee, indorses his paycheck as follows: "Pay Jane Doe only, and no one else. Further transfer of this instrument is hereby prohibited, (signed) John Doe." Despite the clear language, the indorsement is unenforceable [3-206(1)]. The reason is simple. Commercial paper cannot serve its function as a substitute for money if indorsers can prevent further negotiation. Therefore, the Code renders ineffective any restrictive indorsement to the extent that it purports to prevent further transfer of a negotiable instrument. Thus, Jane Doe may indorse the paycheck and deliver it to a transferee. The transferee may collect from the drawee bank.

Indorsement for deposit or collection   An indorsement for deposit or collection is useful and does not prevent the further negotiation of commercial paper. This kind of restrictive indorsement includes the words "For deposit," "For collection," "Pay any bank," or other words signifying a purpose of deposit or collection [3-205(c)] (see Figure 32.2). With the exception of certain banks to be discussed later, any transferee under a deposit or collection indorsement must pay or apply any value given for the instrument "consistently with the indorsement." To the extent that the transferee does so, the transferee becomes a holder for value. This means that the transferee may become a holder in due course by meeting the other requirements for such a holder [3-206(3)]. If the transferee does not make the payment in accordance with the instruction given in the restrictive indorsement, the transferee is liable to the indorser for any loss resulting from the transferee's failure to heed the restriction.

An illustration will clarify the operation of indorsements for deposit or collection. Suppose that John Doe, the payee of a check drawn to his order, indorses the check "For deposit only, (signed) John Doe," delivers it to A, his bookkeeper, and tells A to deposit the check in Doe's bank account. Instead, A takes the check to the bank, in which A also has an account, and has the bank apply the proceeds of the check to a debt that A owes the bank. In ignoring Doe's restrictive indorsement, the bank has failed to apply payment consistently with Doe's indorsement. The bank therefore is not a holder for value and cannot become a holder in due course of the check. Moreover, the bank has converted Doe's property and is liable to Doe for the amount of the check.

But not all banks are required to observe Doe's restrictive indorsement. Suppose that the drawer of Doe's check drew it on a Denver bank, that A's account is in a bank located in Philadelphia, and that for the check to "clear" (that is, be paid by the Denver bank), it must be processed by a bank in Indianapolis. The Denver bank (drawee of the check) is the "payor" bank; the Indianapolis bank is an "intermediary" bank; and A's Philadelphia bank is the "depositary" bank. Because intermediary and payor banks must handle checks in bulk, it is impractical for them to determine whether all restrictive indorsements have been heeded. Therefore, the Code permits intermediary and payor banks to ignore all restrictiv indorsements except those of the immediate ransferors of such banks and those of persons presenting restrictively indorsed instruments for payment. In the situation described in this illustration, only the depositary bank (A's bank) is required to heed Doe's restrictive indorsement.

Practical and Economic Significance of Indorsements

The special, the qualified, and the restrictive indorsement each serves a "narrowing" function beneficial to the indorser. The special indorsement protects the indorser if the instrument is lost or stolen. The qualified indorsement limits the indorser's liability in the event that others fail to pay. The conditional indorsement enables the indorser to limit the indorser's liability, and another type of restrictive indorsement enables the indorser to specify a use to which the proceeds of an instrument are to be put. But some of these benefits are not without cost.

The law of commercial paper is calculated to increase the transferability and value of commercial paper by minimizing the amount of risk that a purchaser will incur in accepting it. An indorser who routinely uses qualified indorsements may undermine the marketability of his or her paper by suggesting the existence of more risk than there is. The use of a conditional indorsement can produce the same result. Suppose that John Doe has a note payable to his order and that he indorses it "Pay to Ann Aker if she delivers 5,000 advertising circulars to my store by March 1, 19xx, (signed) John Doe." Suppose also that Aker delivers the circulars on time, and that Aker then attempts to negotiate the note to Cromwell. For safety, Cromwell must determine whether Aker delivered the circulars. Whether on the ground of inconvenience or doubt about the collectibility of the note, Cromwell might refuse to purchase it or might offer a substantially reduced price for it.

Special Rules on Effectiveness of Indorsement

To enhance the convenience and marketability of commercial paper, the Code provides that "An indorsement is effective for negotiation only when it conveys the entire instrument or any unpaid residue" [3-202(3)]. Thus, an indorsement containing the direction to "Pay B one-half" is not effective as a negotiation. It operates only as a partial assignment of the indorser's rights. Under the law of some states, partial assignments are not enforceable. Where partial assignments are enforceable, the transferee cannot personally qualify as a holder in due course, but will acquire the rights of the transferor. Similarly, an indorsement containing the direction to "Pay B two-thirds and C one-third" is ineffective as a negotiation. It operates as two partial assignments of the indorser's

rights. Partial assignments and their enforceability are discussed in Chapter 17.

Section 3-207 provides that negotiation is effective to transfer an instrument even though the negotiation (1) is made by a person without capacity, such as a minor or a corporation exceeding its powers; (2) is obtained by fraud, duress, or mistake; (3) is part of an illegal transaction; or (4) is made in breach of duty. In these situations the transferor ordinarily has the right to rescind the transfer of the instrument. However, title to the instrument passes to the transferee. Consequently, if the instrument is further negotiated to a person who is a holder in due course, the right of rescission may be cut off. Holder-in-due-course status and defenses are discussed in the next chapter.

SUMMARY

A negotiable instrument is issued when it is delivered by the maker or drawer to a holder or a remitter. Delivery means a voluntary transfer of possession, and does not include transfer by a thief or a finder of a lost instrument. To issue a negotiable instrument, the maker or drawer ordinarily delivers order paper or bearer paper to a holder. Anyone to whom bearer paper is delivered is the holder. An order instrument is issued only if delivered to the named payee. Delivery may be actual or constructive. To avoid impeding the flow of commercial paper, the Code allows the issue of incomplete instruments.

After an instrument has been issued, it may be transferred. If an instrument is nonnegotiable, its transfer is merely an assignment, and all transferees take the instrument subject to any defenses. A negotiable instrument may be transferred either by assignment or by negotiation. If the transfer is by negotiation, any transferee who meets the requirements to be a holder in due course takes the instrument free from most defenses.

Negotiation is the transfer of a negotiable instrument in such a way that the transferee becomes a holder. Bearer paper may be negotiated by delivery alone. Order paper may be negotiated only by delivery together with an indorsement. Delivery of order paper without an indorsement amounts to an assignment. However, a transferee for value may require the indorsement of the transferor and become a holder in due course.

Code provisions govern where an indorsement must be written, who may indorse, and what constitutes a proper signature for an indorsement. Many of these provisions enhance the convenience and marketability of commercial paper.

There are various kinds of indorsements. An indorsement is at the same time either in blank or special, qualified or unqualified, and restrictive or nonrestrictive. A special indorsement specifies a person to receive payment. An in-blank indorsement is merely the signature of the indorser. The effect of an in-blank indorsement is to make the instrument bearer paper. Thus, the holder may further negotiate the instrument by delivery alone. The effect of a special indorsement is to make the instrument order paper, thus requiring both delivery and indorsement for further negotiation. The character of an instrument may change back and forth as transferors change back and forth between in-blank and special indorsements.

A qualified indorsement is one where the indorser adds the words "without recourse." Without such words, the indorser may be liable for the face amount of the instrument to a transferee who is unable to collect from either the maker or the drawee. There are several kinds of restrictive indorsements. Neither the qualified nor the restrictive indorsement impairs further negotiation of the instrument. The special, the qualified, and the restrictive indorsement each serves a narrowing function beneficial to the indorser. However, the marketability of the instrument may suffer from the use of qualified or conditional indorsements.

STUDY AND DISCUSSION QUESTIONS

1 Define, or otherwise explain the meaning of, these terms with respect to commercial paper: *(a)* issue, and *(b)* delivery.

2 Has delivery taken place when the maker or drawer: *(a)* hands the instrument to his or her own agent? *(b)* hands it to an agent of the payee? *(c)* hands it to a third person without restriction to be held until the payee picks it up? *(d)* mails it to the payee?

3 "There is no issue of an instrument until it is delivered to a holder or a remitter." Who or what is a remitter?

4 Why does the Code allow the issue of signed but otherwise incomplete instruments?

5 *(a)* What is the legal significance of negotiation? *(b)* How may negotiation of a bearer instrument be accomplished? Negotiation of an order instrument?

6 Suppose that a person purchases a negotiable order instrument but that the transferor forgets to indorse it. What is the legal position of the transferee?

7 To be effective, must an indorsement be written on the back of a negotiable instrument? Explain.

8 Who may indorse an instrument that is payable to the order of: *(a)* two or more named persons? *(b)* a named person with the addition of words describing the person as an agent or officer of a specified person or organization? *(c)* an unincorporated association?

9 Fully describe in the three sets of descriptive terms the following indorsement of a check made out to Jane Doe as payee: "Pay John Doe, without recourse, (signed) Jane Doe."

10 *(a)* What is a special indorsement? *(b)* For

what purpose is a special indorsement normally used? *(c)* Explain why a special indorsement is preferable to an in-blank indorsement for this purpose.

11 *(a)* For what purpose is a qualified indorsement normally used? *(b)* What language is required for making a qualified indorsement?

12 *(a)* For what purposes are restrictive indorsements used? *(b)* Why is an indorsement purporting to prohibit further transfer not enforceable?

13 *(a)* Illustrate how an indorsement for deposit or collection works. *(b)* Are all banks required to heed an indorsement for deposit or collection? Explain.

14 Suppose a person always uses qualified and conditional indorsements when indorsing checks and notes. *(a)* What might be the economic consequence of this practice? *(b)* Would the economic consequence be the same for both kinds of indorsements?

15 *(a)* What is the effect of the following indorsement: "Pay Mary Roe one-half, and Tom Roe one-half, (signed) Jane Doe"? *(b)* Mary Roe indorses her paycheck "Mary Roe," a thief steals it and gives it to his spouse, and the spouse cashes it at the spouse's bank. Mary Roe may rescind her indorsement as to which person or persons? Explain.

CASE PROBLEMS

1 At the beginning of a legal action or during the course of the action, a plaintiff obtained a writ of attachment against the property of the defendant. Such a writ commands the sheriff to seize the property of the defendant and hold it as security for the satisfaction of such judgment as the plaintiff may be awarded. Is a negotiable note that is still in the possession of the maker subject to attachment by a creditor of the payee?

2 Paul fraudulently induced Mary to issue him a note reading: "July 2, 19xx. Sixty days after date I promise to pay Paul the sum of seven hundred dollars ($700.00), together with interest at the rate of 8 percent per annum. Value received. (signed) Mary." The day after Paul received the note, he indorsed and sold it to Albert, who took it without notice of the fraud. Is Albert subject to Mary's defense of fraud?

3 Thomas Jones, the payee of a negotiable instrument, transferred it to Frank White, who transferred it to Robert Grondahl, who transferred it to Arthur Benson, who transferred it to Kermit Smith. At the time of the transfer to Smith, the instrument bore the indorsements shown below. *(a)* Is Smith a holder of the instrument? Explain. *(b)* What difference does status as a holder make to Smith?

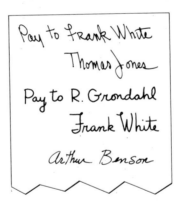

4 On May 16, 1969 the Bank of Hollywood Hills of Hollywood Hills, Florida, issued a cashier's check in the amount of $2,000 payable to "Richard and Grace Grimaldi." Four days later Richard indorsed the check "Grace Grimaldi by Richard Grimaldi" and presented it to a teller of the Beach National Bank located at Fort Myers Beach, Florida, where the Grimaldis had a joint account. The teller cashed the check and paid the full amount to Richard. On May 20 the cashier's check routinely arrived at the Bank of Hollywood Hills for payment. That bank refused to honor the check. Was it justified in refusing to honor the check? Explain.

5 The payee of a check indorsed it "for deposit" and then delivered it for safekeeping to a "friend." The friend had a third person deposit the check in an account with a bank. The depositary bank sent the check to an intermediary bank for collection. That bank forwarded the check to the drawee bank, where it was paid. After the depositary bank received the payment, the third person withdrew the proceeds of the check and turned them over to the "friend," who then absconded. The depositary bank became insolvent, and so the payee sued the intermediary bank. Judgment for whom?

Chapter

33

Holder in Due Course;
Defenses to Liability
on the Instrument

The benefits of negotiability were discussed in Chapter 30. As stated there, a holder in due course of a negotiable instrument is given a special status in the law. The formal requirements for a negotiable instrument and the proper methods to negotiate such an instrument were discussed in Chapters 31 and 32. This chapter is devoted to three other important topics: the requirements to become a holder in due course; the various defenses against liability on the instrument; and some recent changes limiting the rights of purchasers of consumer notes.

HOLDER IN DUE COURSE

Meaning of Holder

To be a holder in due course a person first must be a holder. The Uniform Commercial Code (UCC) defines a *holder* as "a person who is in possession of . . . an instrument . . . drawn, issued, or indorsed to him or to his order or to bearer or in blank" [1-201(20)].[1] As stated in Chapter 32, the holder of a bearer instrument may be any person who is in possession of it. Bearer instruments include any instrument payable on its face to bearer, and any instrument (bearer paper or order paper) indorsed in blank.

The payee of an order instrument may be the holder if the instrument has never been indorsed, although it is not customary to speak of the payee as a holder. If an order instrument has been indorsed by the payee and transferred to the indorsee, the indorsee is the holder. When there are successive indorsements, the instrument is order paper if the last indorsement is a

---

[1]Numbers within brackets in the text refer to sections of the UCC.

special indorsement. The last special indorsee is the holder, provided that the indorsee has possession and the instrument contains all necessary prior indorsements. "All necessary prior indorsements" means the indorsement of all parties who took the paper as order paper. Their signatures are required as evidence that those parties authorized the transfer of the instrument.

Special Status of Holder in Due Course

A holder in due course (HDC) takes a negotiable instrument free from most defenses, although some defenses are good even against a holder in due course. This freedom of a holder in due course from personal defenses is what gives the HDC his or her special place in the law, since, unlike a mere assignee, the HDC may acquire better rights than his or her transferor had. How this is so is explained later in this chapter. Figure 33.1 illustrates a typical set of transactions involving the transfer of a negotiable instrument to a holder in due course.

Requirements for Holder in Due Course

To be a holder in due course a holder must take the instrument (1) for value; (2) in good faith; and (3) without notice that it is overdue, or that it has been dishonored, or that there is any defense against or claim to it on the part of any person [3-302(1)]. It is plain from these requirements that one who steals a *bearer* instrument may be a "holder" (because in possession of a bearer instrument) but will never become a holder in due course.

Ordinarily, when the payee of an order negotiable instrument wishes to transfer it to a holder, the payee properly indorses and delivers the instrument to the holder, who then must meet all three requirements in order to qualify as a holder in due course. As stated in Chapter 32, a person who takes an order instrument that has not been properly indorsed is not at the time of the taking a holder and consequently cannot be a holder in due course at that time. But if later the instrument is properly indorsed, the transferee may become a holder. The trans-

Figure 33.1 Holder in Due Course Status—The Basic Situation.

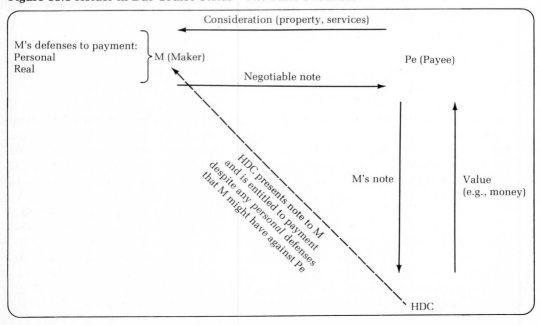

feree could then become a holder in due course if the instrument was taken for value and in good faith and if, prior to receipt of the indorsement, the transferee had received no notice of any of the facts mentioned in requirement (3) above.

Value To qualify as a holder in due course the holder must give value for the instrument. Thus, if the payee of a negotiable instrument indorses and delivers it to a transferee as a gift, the transferee does not qualify as a holder in due course. Furthermore, although an unperformed promise constitutes consideration in the general law of contracts, and constitutes "value" in the law of sales, an *un*performed promise *does not* constitute value in the law of commercial paper. Giving value for an instrument means *performing* the promise made by the holder.

Money, goods, or services Ordinarily, the holder purchases an instrument for money, goods, or services. A purchaser becomes a holder for value as soon as any part of the agreed consideration is performed, but becomes a holder for value only to the extent that the agreed consideration has been performed.

A common situation involving this principle is in the field of banking. When the customer of a bank deposits for collection an "item" (check or other negotiable instrument), the bank credits the customer's account with the amount of the item. Ordinarily, the customer has no *right* to draw against the item until it "clears" (is collected by the bank). The bank's act in crediting its customer's account with the item does not constitute value. In effect, the bank *promises* to give value. However, if the bank permits the depositor to draw against the item before it is collected, the bank becomes a holder for value "to the extent to which credit given for the item has been withdrawn" [4-208(1)(a)].

If, as is typically the case, a customer deposits checks from time to time and from time to time makes withdrawals, when are the proceeds of a particular check withdrawn? The Code requires the application of the "first in, first out" rule. To illustrate, suppose a customer opens a checking account on March 1 by depositing a weekly salary check of $200, deposits similar checks on March 8 and on March 15, and withdraws $200 on March 17 and $200 on March 19. Under the "first in, first out" rule, the bank has given value on the check deposited March 1 at the time of the first withdrawal (March 17) and on the check deposited March 8 at the time of the second withdrawal (March 19).

Case 33.1 Falls Church Bank v. Wesley Heights Realty, Inc.
256 A.2d 915 (D.C. App. 1969)

HOOD, C. J. The sole issue on this appeal is whether, and under what circumstances, may a depositary bank achieve the status of holder in due course of negotiable paper deposited with it by a customer. The facts are undisputed.

The appellees [Wesley Heights Realty, defendants in the lower court] drew a check for $1,400.00, payable to the order of a customer of appellant [plaintiff] bank. The customer deposited this check in his account with the bank and was given a provisional credit of this amount. The customer was permitted to withdraw $140.00 from this account prior to the bank's discovering that appellees had stopped payment on the $1,400.00 check. When the check was returned to the bank dishonored, the bank's customer had "skipped," leaving no credits in his account on which to charge the $140.00. The bank, thereupon, made demand on appellees for that amount and when appellees refused, this action was brought.

At trial appellees moved for, and were granted, judgment on grounds that the bank "was an agent for collection only and did not have a security interest and was not a holder in due course for value."

. . . The Uniform Commercial Code, which controls in this case, expressly provides that a bank acquires a security interest in items deposited with it to the extent that the provisional credit given the customer on the item is withdrawn. UCC, sec. 4-208. It further provides that, for purposes of achieving the status of holder in due course, the depositary bank gives value to the extent that it acquires a security interest in the item in question. UCC, sec. 4-209.

We agree that appellant bank is deemed by the Uniform Commercial Code to be an agent of its customers (sec. 4-201) but under the scheme of the Code, a "bank may be a holder in due course while acting as a collecting agent for its customer." *Citizens Bank of Booneville v. National Bank of Commerce*, 334 F.2d 257, 261 (10th Cir. 1964).

As a holder in due course as to $140.00, appellant's claim cannot be defeated except by those defenses set out in UCC, sec. 3-305(2), none of which are herein alleged. The judgment below is, accordingly,

Reversed with instructions to enter judgment for appellant [in the amount of $140].

Other types of value A holder gives value for an instrument "to the extent that he acquires a security interest in or lien on the instrument otherwise than by legal process" [3-303(a)]. For example, suppose that Peter, the payee of a $5,000 note, desires to borrow $2,000 from Harriet. They agree that if Peter will indorse and deliver the note to Harriet to be held as security for the loan, Harriet will lend him the $2,000. The parties carry out the agreement. Harriet has a security interest in the note and therefore is a holder for value to the extent of $2,000. A person who acquires a lien on an instrument *by legal process* (such as an attaching creditor) is *not* a holder in due course.

A holder gives value for an instrument "when he takes the instrument in payment of . . . an antecedent claim" [3-303(b)]. For example, suppose that Harold has a claim against Peggy for $1,000. Peggy is short of cash but has a note in that amount made by her father that is payable to her order. Harold agrees to discharge the claim if Peggy will indorse the note to him. Peggy indorses and delivers the note to Harold, and Harold discharges the claim. Harold is a holder for value and if the note is not paid, may have recourse against Peggy's father.

A holder gives value for an instrument "when he gives a negotiable instrument for it or makes an irrevocable commitment to a third person" [3-303(c)]. Thus, a holder may purchase a note from the payee by giving a personal check.

Good Faith Article 1 of the UCC has a definition of good faith that applies to the Code as a whole. "*Good faith* means honesty in fact in the conduct or transaction concerned" [1-201(19)]. So far as the law of commercial paper is concerned, the Code definition seems to be an adoption of the pre-Code subjective test or "white heart" test of good faith. The test was stated by one court as follows:

A purchaser lacks the good faith requirement for attaining due course status only if he has actual knowledge of fraud or other defect in the instrument or if he consciously ignores facts which would lead him to discover the defect. The test is said to be subjective, for a purchaser may be a holder in due course if he purchases with a "white heart" but an empty head.[2]

In determining whether a finance company that has purchased commercial paper is a good faith purchaser (and thus a holder in due course), the courts are showing an increasing tendency to examine the extent of the finance company's knowledge of the transaction that gave rise to the instrument, as well as the closeness of relationship between the finance company and the dealer from whom it purchased the paper. For example, a company that is controlled by the payee or that buys great numbers of instruments from the payee at substantial discounts is likely to be aware of questionable trade practices of the payee. Failure to investigate obviously suspicious circumstances can amount to bad faith.

Without Notice The final requirement for holder in due course status is that the holder must take the instrument without notice (1) that it is overdue, or (2) that it has been dishonored, or (3) that there is a defense against it or claim to it on the part of any person [3-302(1)(c)].

There is a close relationship between the "without notice" requirement and the requirement of good faith. However, there is a significant difference between the two. *Good faith* means actual good faith, whereas *without notice* does not necessarily mean without actual notice. Under the Code, a person has notice of a fact "when he has actual knowledge of it," or "when he has received a notice or notification of it," or "when from all the facts and circumstances known to him at the time in question he *has reason to know* that it exists" [1-201(25)]. A holder who acquires an instrument for value in good faith will not qualify as a holder in due course if the holder knows, or has reason to know of the existence of any one of the facts listed in (1), (2), or (3) above.

Notice that instrument is overdue A person can be a holder in due course of an overdue instrument provided the instrument is taken without notice that it is overdue. A holder who takes a *time* instrument that is payable in one lump sum can usually tell from the face of the instrument whether it is overdue. But a holder who takes a time instrument payable in installments may not be able to determine from either the face or back of the instrument whether there has been a default in the payment of an installment. If a time instrument contains an acceleration clause, it is rarely possible to determine from the instrument itself whether acceleration has occurred. However, if the holder learns from some outside source or has "reason to know" that any part of the principal amount is overdue or that acceleration of the instrument has occurred, the holder has notice that the instrument is overdue [3-304(3)(a), (b)].

The purchaser of a *demand* instrument has notice that it is overdue "if he has reason to know . . . that he is taking it after demand has been made or more than a reasonable length of time after its issue" [3-304(3)(c)]. The same subsection provides that a reasonable time for a check drawn and payable within the states and territories of the United States and the District of Columbia is presumed to be 30 days. The Code gives no guidelines for determining what is a reasonable time for demand notes or drafts. Courts have tended to hold that a reasonable length of time after issue is shorter for checks than for drafts; shorter for drafts than for notes; and shorter for noninterest notes than for interest notes. In determining whether an instrument is overdue the courts consider factors such as: the distance between the maker or drawer and the payee; the relationship between the parties (family or business); and the locale (rural or urban).

[2]*Financial Credit Corp. v. Williams*, 229 A.2d 712, 716 (Md. 1967).

Most time instruments and most demand instruments other than checks provide for the payment of interest. Whereas notice that there has been a default in payment of any part of the principal prevents the purchaser from being a holder in due course, "knowledge . . . that there has been default in payment of interest on the instrument" does not do so [3-304(4)(f)]. The reason for the difference in result is that a default in payment on principal may be an indication that the obligor has, or believes he or she has, a good defense, whereas delay in interest payments is of such common occurrence that little significance is attached to it.

Notice that instrument has been dishonored   Negotiable instruments may be dishonored in several ways. If a note or certificate of deposit is presented to the maker for payment and payment is refused, such refusal is a dishonor. A check or draft is dishonored when the instrument is presented to the drawee for acceptance or payment and acceptance or payment is refused. A holder who purchases an instrument with notice that it has been dishonored is taking risks beyond those normally associated with the taking of commercial paper. Such a purchaser is a speculator and does not deserve to be accorded the special status enjoyed by a holder in due course.

Notice that there is a defense or claim   A holder cannot be a holder in due course if the instrument is taken with notice that there is a defense or claim against it. A party being sued on a negotiable instrument may assert a variety of defenses. The usual contract law defenses, such as fraud, duress, and mistake, are discussed in Chapter 13. A holder who purchases a negotiable instrument and knows of, or has reason to know of, such a defense or claim against the instrument, does not qualify as a holder in due course.

To be denied the status of holder in due course, a holder need not be aware of any specific defense or claim. A holder who purchases an instrument will not be accorded the status

of a holder in due course if (1) the instrument is incomplete on its face; or (2) the instrument is irregular on its face; or (3) there are other defects.

(1) Incomplete paper: Incomplete paper means an instrument that has a material omission. Material omissions include lack of a named payee on the face of order paper and lack of an amount in the space for payment. Ordinarily, the lack of a date is immaterial. However, suppose a note or draft is payable "————after date." In such an instance the lack of a date is a material omission, and a purchaser of the instrument would not achieve the status of a holder in due course. A purchaser of incomplete paper is charged with notice of a claim or defense even though the claim or defense is not related to the omission.

The Code does permit a holder to fill in the blanks of incomplete paper [3-115]. Thus, in the above illustration, the payee or holder could fill in the date and negotiate the instrument to a holder for value without notice of the original omission; and the purchaser would qualify as a holder in due course [3-407(3)]. The purchaser may qualify as a holder in due course though he or she has knowledge of the original omission. Knowledge that an incomplete instrument has been completed does not charge the purchaser with notice of a defense or claim, unless the purchaser has notice that the completion was improper [3-304(4)(d)]. For example, a bank may take a check as a holder in due course even though a blank is filled in in the presence of a teller.

(2) Irregular paper: A holder who purchases an instrument that is irregular on its face will not be accorded the status of a holder in due course. A forged or altered instrument is irregular if the instrument "bears visible evidence" of the forgery or alteration. Rarely is a signature so crudely made that it would be recognized as a forgery by someone unfamiliar with the signature of the individual whose name the forger has used. However, a holder who takes an instru-

ment on which an item such as a signature, or the amount payable, or the date, was visibly altered ("doctored"), is charged with notice of a claim or defense even though the claim or defense is not related to the alteration. An alteration that merely corrects an obvious error in the instrument does not give notice of a claim or defense.

An instrument may be irregular for reasons other than forgery or alteration. For example, an instrument stamped "paid" or "nsf" (not sufficient funds), is irregular on its face. A purchaser for value of such an instrument would not qualify as a holder in due course.

(3) Other defects: A holder who purchases a negotiable instrument will not be accorded the status of holder in due course if the holder has notice of other defects. Such defects exist if the obligation of any party is voidable in whole or in part, or if all parties have been discharged, or if a fiduciary has negotiated the instrument in violation of a duty [3-304(1),(2)]. However, knowledge that any person negotiating the instrument is or was a fiduciary "does not of itself give the purchaser notice of a defense or claim" [3-304(4)(e)]. There are other facts, knowledge of which does not of itself give the purchaser notice of a defense or claim. They are: (1) that the instrument is antedated or postdated; (2) that it was issued or negotiated in return for an executory promise or accompanied by a separate agreement, unless the purchaser has notice that a defense or claim has arisen from the terms thereof; and (3) that any party has signed for accommodation [3-304(4)].

Case 33.2   Texico State Bank v. Hullinger
220 N.E.2d 248 (Ill. App. 1966)

Action by the Texico State Bank against Hullinger. At the end of the trial, the plaintiff bank moved for a directed verdict. The motion was denied, and the plaintiff appealed.

SMITH, J. . . . As we view it, the relevant facts are not in dispute. On June 2, 1964, defendant Hullinger executed and delivered to one Walter Sledge his two checks for $3,500 and $3,000. Sledge took the $3,500 check to his bank, plaintiff bank, and obtained a bank draft for it. On the next day, June 3, he took the $3,000 check to plaintiff bank and received a bank draft for $2,400 and deposit credit for $600. On the next day, June 4, defendant stopped payment on both checks and the usual merry-go-round developed. The bank drafts delivered to Sledge by the plaintiff bank entered the ebb and flow of commerce, were in the hands of holders in due course, and the plaintiff bank was required to and did honor its drafts. The demands on the defendant to honor his checks were refused.

We find it difficult to understand why plaintiff is not a holder in due course of the defendant's checks and why there was any issue for a jury to try in this case. Ill. Rev. Stat. 1965, ch. 26, secs. 3-302 to 3-305 [Uniform Commercial Code], define a holder in due course as a holder who takes an instrument (a) for value, (b) in good faith, and (c) without notice that it is overdue or has been dishonored, or of any defense against or claim to it on the part of any person.

Nowhere is there any evidence in this record that this plaintiff accepted and honored these checks with any notice, express or implied, of any infirmities in them. There is evidence in the record—of doubtful relevancy and propriety—that Sledge's credit with his bank and in the community was elastic—so elastic in fact that his own checks bounced with regularity all over the place. It further appears that he ultimately went into bankruptcy—an evidentiary tidbit bearing on nothing in this record. Whatever may have been [Sledge's] financial record, it had nothing to do with the integrity of defendant's [Hullinger's] checks or with any notice express or implied that the defendant could not or would not honor his commercial paper or that any person had a defense against or claim to any part of them. "It is a purchaser who knows at the time of the purchase of an asserted defense, or of facts or circumstances which may create a defense who is precluded from being a holder in due course, and then on the theory of 'bad faith.'" *National Currency Exchange, Inc. #3 v. Perkins,* 52 Ill. App. 2d 215, 221; 201 N.E.2d 668, 672. It is clear that the plaintiff [bank] as purchaser of these two checks had no notice of any of the infirmities set forth in Ill. Rev. Stat. 1965, ch. 26, sec. 3-304.

We have already observed that plaintiff is a holder in due course. There is no legal or factual defense to this suit on record. The trial court should have directed a verdict for the plaintiff in the sum of $6,500. It didn't.

Reversed and remanded.

Payee as Holder in Due Course

A payee may be a holder in due course to the same extent and under the same circumstances as any other holder [3-302(2)]. One of the requirements discussed above is that the holder must take the instrument without notice of any defense. Where there is a defense, the payee will usually have knowledge of it, since normally the payee deals directly with the maker or drawer. Thus, if Paul fraudulently induced Dora to draw a check payable to his order, Paul will have knowledge of the fraud. However, the payee does not necessarily have knowledge of a defense where the payee and the maker or drawer of the instrument deal through an intermediary. For example, suppose a seller of goods requires the buyer to pay by bank draft. The buyer fraudulently induces his or her bank to draw a draft payable to the order of the seller. The bank forwards the draft to the seller. Since the payee (the seller) takes the draft for value

(delivery of goods), in good faith, and without notice of any claim or defense, the payee is a holder in due course. The bank may not assert the defense of fraud against the payee-holder.

Holder through a Holder in Due Course; Shelter Provision

The transfer of an instrument "vests in the transferee such rights as the holder has therein" [3-201(1)]. Therefore, if a transferor is a holder in due course, the transferor's rights as such holder vest in the transferee even if the transferee cannot qualify as a holder in due course. For example, suppose that Hortense, the holder in due course of a note, indorses it to Arnold, who takes the note as a gift. Arnold cannot qualify as a holder in due course in his own right; but he is a holder through a holder in due course and therefore is given the same special status as the law gives to holders in due course.

The transferee, now having the rights of a holder in due course, can transfer those rights to another transferee, and so on down the line. All transferees subsequent to a holder in due course are commonly referred to as holders "through" a holder in due course. The UCC provision that gives holders through a holder in due course the same freedom from claims and defenses that a holder in due course enjoys is often referred to as the "shelter provision." The policy behind the shelter provision is to assure the holder in due course a free market for the paper.

There is an exception to the rule that the transfer of an instrument vests in the transferee such rights as the transferor has therein: a transferee who has been *a party to* any fraud or illegality affecting the instrument, or who as a prior holder had notice of a defense or claim against the instrument, cannot improve his or her position by taking from a later holder in due course [3-201(1)]. Attempts by such transferees

to improve their position by selling paper to a holder in due course and receiving it back will be of no avail. In Figure 33.2, H_2 takes the note *free of* M's personal defenses. In Figure 33.3, H_1 takes the note *subject to* M's defenses.

DEFENSES TO LIABILITY ON THE INSTRUMENT

As stated previously, the major benefit of achieving the status of a holder in due course is that such a holder takes the instrument free of all claims to it and all defenses against it except a very limited number. The few defenses that are available against all holders, including a holder in due course, are commonly called "real defenses." Defenses available only against holders not having the rights of a holder in due course are commonly called "personal defenses."

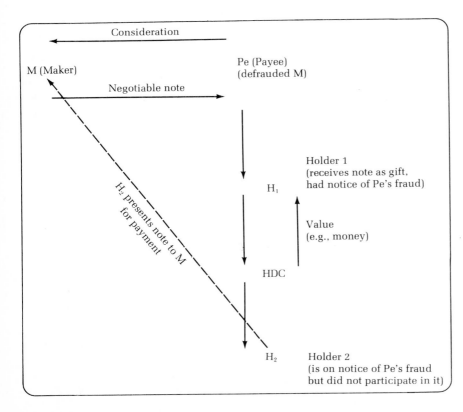

Figure 33.2
Shelter Provision.

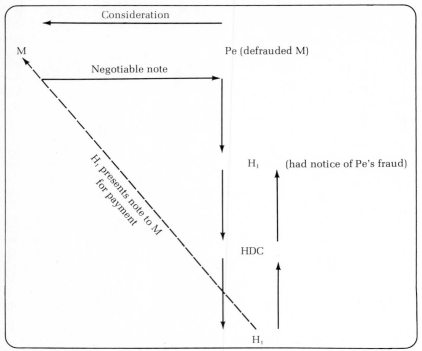

Figure 33.3 Shelter Provision—A Variation.

Real Defenses

There are seven major "real defenses," that a party may assert, even against a holder in due course. They are: (1) infancy to the extent that it is a defense to a simple contract; (2) such other incapacity, duress, or illegality of the transaction as renders the obligation of the party a nullity; (3) such fraud as induces the party to sign the instrument with neither knowledge nor reasonable opportunity to obtain knowledge of its character or its essential terms; (4) discharge in insolvency proceedings; (5) any other discharge of which the holder has notice when the holder takes the instrument; (6) unauthorized signature; and (7) material alteration. These defenses are discussed below, with the exception of the defense of "other discharge." That defense is discussed in Chapter 34.

Infancy (Minority) Infancy is a defense against a holder in due course "to the extent that

it is a defense to a simple contract" under the state law governing the transaction [3-305(2)]. As indicated in Chapter 14, there is considerable variation in state law on such important matters as the age of majority for purposes of contracting, the effect of misrepresentation of age, and the requirements for disaffirming a contract after having received performance from the other contracting party. If state law permits a minor to rescind his or her contract, minority (infancy) is, for that contract, a real defense under the UCC. For example, a minor's contract for a luxury usually may be rescinded, but in a few states a minor's contract for "necessaries" is enforceable to the extent of their fair value. Under the Code, therefore, minority is ordinarily a real defense as to contracts for luxuries but sometimes is not as to contracts for necessaries. In most transactions where a negotiable instrument is given and the maker, drawer, acceptor, or indorser is a minor, the defense of infancy may be available against a holder in due course.

Other Incapacity; Duress; Illegality The defense of "other incapacity" includes such incapacities as insanity, drunkenness, and lack of corporate capacity to do business. The defenses of duress and illegality are discussed in Chapters 13 and 15, respectively. Illegality in connection with commercial paper is most frequently a matter of instruments issued in violation of state or local laws prohibiting gambling or usury. These defenses—other incapacity, duress, and illegality—are available as a defense against a holder in due course only when the obligation of the party is a "nullity," that is, void. Whether the obligation is void or only voidable is left to the law of the state.

Case 33.3   Universal Acceptance Corp. v. Burks
7 U.C.C. Rep. 39 (D.C. Ct. General Sessions, 1969)

HYDE, J. Plaintiff [Universal Acceptance Corporation] is suing the defendant [Burks] on a promissory note, dated February 14, 1967, given in payment of merchandise purchased from the District TV Co., Inc. and negotiated to plaintiff on March 3, 1967. The only defense of merit raised by the defendant is that [in the interval of time between the transaction entered into by] the defendant and District TV Co. and the negotiation of the note to the plaintiff, the certificate of incorporation of the District TV Co. had been revoked by a proclamation under DC Code, sec. 29-938 and, therefore, the contract was null and void and the plaintiff could not recover thereon. The plaintiff contends that as a bona fide purchaser for value it is a holder in due course, and that even if the District TV Co. had lost its charter any defense available to the defendant as a result thereof would not be good against the plaintiff. . . .

Section 28:3-305(2)(a)(b) of the Code provides:

"To the extent that a holder is a holder in due course he takes the instrument free from . . . (2) all defenses of any party to the instrument with whom the holder has not dealt except

"(a) infancy, to the extent that it is a defense to a simple contract; and

(b) such other incapacity, or duress, or illegality of the transaction, as renders the obligations of the party a nullity; . . ."

The comment under this section says:

"5. Paragraph (b) of subsection (2) is new. It covers mental incompetence, guardianship, ultra vires acts or *lack of corporate capacity to do business,* any remaining incapacity of married women, or any other incapacity apart from infancy. Such incapacity is largely statutory. Its existence and effect is left to the law of each state. If under the local law the effect is to render the obligation of the instrument entirely null and void, the defense may be asserted against a holder in due course. If the effect is merely to render the obligation voidable at the election of the obligor, the defense is cut off."

. . . Therefore, the question to be decided is whether our statute, DC Code sections 29-937 and 29-938, renders the contracts of a corporation, which has lost its articles of incorporation thereunder, null and void or merely voidable at the election of the obligor.

The language of our Code which must be interpreted is that which says that upon failure of the corporation to comply ". . . the articles of incorporation shall be void and all powers conferred upon such corporation are declared inoperative, and, in the case of a foreign corporation, the certificate of authority shall be revoked and all powers conferred thereunder shall be inoperative."

It is my judgment that sections 29-937 and 29-938 make the contracts of a corporation which has lost its articles of incorporation thereunder null and void and not merely voidable at the election of the obligor. Therefore, the defense of illegality under section 28:3-305(2)(a)(b) of the Code is not cut off from an obligor of a negotiable note even as to a holder in due course.

Judgment will be entered for the defendant.

Fraud A person may be fraudulently induced to sign a negotiable instrument in either of the following ways.

1 The person may be induced to sign an instrument by a fraudulent representation unrelated to the nature of the instrument or its terms. Often this kind of misrepresentation pertains to the consideration for which the instrument is given, as where a farm implement salesperson knowingly misrepresents the work a tractor can do and thereby induces the farmer to sign an installment note for the purchase price of the tractor. This type of fraud is commonly called "fraud in the inducement." It is a personal defense and is not available against a holder in due course.

2 The maker or drawer may be induced to sign an instrument by a fraudulent representation relating to the character of the instrument itself; or, though the person is aware that the instrument is commercial paper, he or she signs without knowing one or more of its essential terms. This type of fraud is commonly called "fraud in the factum" or "fraud in the essence." It is a real defense if the person signing the instrument had "no reasonable opportunity to obtain knowledge of its character or essential terms" [3-305(2)(c)]. If the person signing has a reasonable opportunity and the ability to obtain knowledge of the true character of the document being signed, the defense is a personal defense.

Case 33.4 Burchett v. Allied Concord Financial Corp.
356 P.2d 186 (N.M. 1964)

Mr. and Mrs. Burchett and Mr. and Mrs. Beevers filed separate complaints against the defendant, Allied Concord Financial Corporation, to have certain notes and mortgages held by the defendant corporation canceled and declared void. Since both cases were against the same defendant and involved substantially similar facts, the cases were consolidated for trial. The trial court's judgment voided the notes and mortgages. The defendant corporation appealed both cases; the cases were consolidated on appeal.

CARMODY, J. . . . The facts, except for one small detail, are the same. It seems that a man named Kelly represented himself as selling Kaiser aluminum siding for a firm named Consolidated Products. . . . In each case, Kelly talked to the husband and wife (appellees) at their homes, offering to install aluminum siding on each of their houses for a certain price in exchange for the appellees' allowing their houses to be used for advertising purposes as a "show house," in order to further other sales of aluminum siding. Kelly told both of the families that they would receive $100 credit on each aluminum siding contract sold in a specified area, and that this credit would be applied toward the contract debt, being the cost of the installation of the siding on the appellees' houses. The appellees were assured, or at least understood, that by this method they would receive the improvements for nothing.

Following the explanation by Kelly, both families agreed to the offer and were given a form of a printed contract to read. While they were reading the contract, Kelly was filling out blanks in other forms. After the appellees had read the form of the contract submitted to them, they signed, *without reading*, the form or forms filled out by Kelly, assuming them to be the same as that which they had read and further assuming that what they signed provided for the credits which Kelly assured them they would receive. Needless to say, what appellees signed were notes and mortgages on the properties to cover the cost of the aluminum siding, and contracts containing no mention of credits for advertising or other sales. . . .

Within a matter of days after the contracts were signed, the aluminum siding was installed, although in neither case was the job completed to the satisfaction of the appellees. Sometime later, the appellees received letters from appellant [Concord Financial Corp.] informing them that appellant had purchased the notes and mortgages which had been issued in favor of Consolidated Products and that appellees were delinquent in their first payment. Upon the receipt of these notices, appellees . . . instituted these proceedings. . . .

In both cases, the trial court found that the notes and mortgages, although signed by the appellees, were fraudulently procured. The court also found that the appellant paid a valuable consideration for the notes and mortgages, although at a discount, and concluded as a matter of law that the appellant was a holder in due course. . . .

. . . The only real question in the case is whether, under these facts, appellees, by substantial evidence, satisfied the provisions of the statute relating to their claimed defense as against a holder in due course.

In 1961 our legislature adopted, with some variations, the Uniform Commercial Code. The provision of the code applicable to this case appears as section 50A-3-305(2)(c), NMSA, which, so far as material, is as follows:

> "To the extent that a holder is a holder in due course he takes the instrument free from . . .
>
> (2) all defenses of any party to the instrument with whom the holder has not dealt except . . .

(c) such misrepresentation as has induced the party to sign the instrument with neither knowledge nor reasonable opportunity to obtain knowledge of its character or its essential terms;."

. . . We believe that the official comments following sec. 3-305(2)(c), Comment No. 7, provide an excellent guideline for the disposition of the case before us. We quote the same in full:

"7. Paragraph (c) of subsection (2) is new. It follows the great majority of the decisions under the original Act in recognizing the defense of 'real' or 'essential' fraud, sometimes called fraud in the essence or fraud in the factum, as effective against a holder in due course. The common illustration is that of the maker who is tricked into signing a note in the belief that it is merely a receipt or some other document. The theory of the defense is that his signature on the instrument is ineffective because he did not intend to sign such an instrument at all. Under this provision the defense extends to an instrument signed with knowledge that it is a negotiable instrument, but without knowledge of its essential terms.

"The test of the defense here stated is that of excusable ignorance of the contents of the writing signed. The party must not only have been in ignorance, but must also have had no reasonable opportunity to obtain knowledge. In determining what is a reasonable opportunity all relevant factors are to be taken into account, including the age and sex of the party, his intelligence, education, and business experience; his ability to read or to understand English, the representations made to him and his reason to rely on them or to have confidence in the person making them; the presence or absence of any third person who might read or explain the instrument to him, or any other possibility of obtaining independent information; and the apparent necessity, or lack of it, for acting without delay.

"Unless the misrepresentation meets this test, the defense is cut off by a holder in due course."

We believe that the test set out in Comment No. 7 above quoted is a proper one and should be adhered to by us. . . . Applying the elements of the test to the case before us, Mrs. Burchett was 47 years old and had a ninth grade education, and Mr. Burchett was approximately the same age, but his education does not appear. Mr. Burchett was foreman of the sanitation department of the city of Clovis and testified that he was familiar with some legal documents. Both the Burchetts understood English and there was no showing that they lacked ability to read. Both were able to understand the original form of contract which was submitted to them. As to the Beevers, Mrs. Beevers was 38 years old and had been through the ninth grade. Mr. Beevers had approximately the same education, but his age does not appear. However, he had been working for the same firm for about nine years and knew a little something about mortgages, at least to the extent of having one upon his property. Mrs. Beevers was employed in a supermarket, and it does not appear that either of the Beevers had any difficulty with the English language and they made no claim that they were unable to understand it. Neither the Beevers nor the Burchetts had ever had any prior association with Kelly and the papers were signed upon the very day that they first met him. There was no showing of any reason why they should rely upon Kelly or have confidence in him. The occurrences took place in the homes of appellees, but other than what appears to be Kelly's "chicanery," no reason was given which would warrant a reasonable person in acting as hurriedly as was done in this case. None of the appellees attempted to obtain any independent information either with respect to Kelly or Consolidated Products, nor did they seek out any other person to read or explain the instruments to them. As a matter of fact they apparently didn't believe this was necessary because, like most people, they wanted to take advantage of "getting something for nothing." . . .

We recognize that the reasonable opportunity to obtain knowledge may be excused if the maker places reasonable reliance on the representations. The difficulty in the instant case is that the reliance upon the representations of a complete stranger (Kelly) was not reasonable, and all of the parties were of sufficient age, intelligence, education, and business experience to know better. In this connection, it is noted that the contracts clearly stated, on the same page which bore the signatures of the various appellees, the following:

"No one is authorized on behalf of this company to represent this job to be 'A SAMPLE HOME OR A FREE JOB'." . . .

Although we have sympathy with the appellees, we cannot allow it to influence our decision. They were certainly victimized, but because of their failure to exercise ordinary care for their own protection, an innocent party cannot be made to suffer. . . .

We determine under these facts as a matter of law that both the Burchetts and the Beevers had a reasonable opportunity to obtain knowledge of the character or the essential terms of the instruments which they signed, and therefore appellant as a holder in due course took the instruments free from the defenses claimed by the appellees. . . .

The judgments will be reversed and the cause is remanded to the district court with directions to dismiss appellees' complaints. IT IS SO ORDERED.

Bankruptcy One purpose of bankruptcy or insolvency proceedings is to permit a hopelessly over-burdened debtor a "fresh start." The debtor may be the maker, drawee, drawer, or an indorser of a negotiable instrument. In the event of a lawsuit, the debtor's discharge in bankruptcy or other insolvency proceedings from primary or secondary liability on the instrument is a good defense, even against a holder in due course.

Unauthorized Signature; Material Alteration *Unauthorized signature* includes both a forgery and a signature made by an agent exceeding his or her actual or apparent authority. A defense of unauthorized signature is good even against a holder in due course, unless the defendant ratified the signature or is precluded from denying it [3-404]. For example, suppose the Drew Candle Company employs Ann as a bookkeeper. Ann is authorized to draw checks on the company bank account provided the checks are co-signed by the controller. Suppose further that Ann draws a check payable to her friend Pierre without securing the signature of the controller of Drew Company. Even if the check is negotiated to a holder in due course, the Drew Company may assert the defense of unauthorized signature. However, Drew Company may be precluded from denying Ann's authority if it is careless in the handling of its checks, for example, if they are not kept in a secure place under proper supervision. The unauthorized signature may be that of the maker, drawer, acceptor, or indorser.

A *material alteration* may be a partial defense against a holder in due course or no defense at all. It is no defense where the alteration was assented to by the defendant or was due to some fault on the part of the defendant. For example, if the amount shown on the face of a negotiable instrument is raised by the payee while the maker or drawer looks on, a holder in due course may collect the increased amount from the maker or drawer. Where the defendant did not assent and was not at fault, the defendant has a defense against a holder in due course *but only to the extent of the alteration*, since "a subsequent holder in due course may in all cases enforce the instrument according to its original tenor" [3-407(3)]. For example, suppose David draws a check for $200 payable to Pamela. If Pamela, without David's knowledge or negligence, raises the amount of the check to $1,200 and negotiates the check to a holder in due course, David may be held liable only for the original amount, $200.

Personal Defenses

Personal defenses are those defenses not allowed against a holder in due course. The major personal defenses include all the ordinary contract law defenses, and lack of delivery of the instrument.

Ordinary Contract Defenses Unless a person has the rights of a holder in due course,

the person takes the instrument subject to all defenses of any party that would be available in an action on a simple contract. The major defenses available—fraud in the inducement, duress, undue influence, and mistake—are discussed in Chapter 13. Breach of warranty (discussed in Chapter 26) and failure of performance, sometimes called "failure of consideration" (discussed in Chapter 18) are also personal defenses. Thus, a purchaser of defective goods who signs a negotiable instrument payable to the seller may refuse to pay the instrument so long as it is in the hands of the payee-seller. However, if the instrument is negotiated by the payee to a holder in due course, the maker or the drawer must pay the holder and bring a separate lawsuit against the seller for breach of contract.

A holder may bring suit against a party other than the maker or drawer, and that other party may have a personal defense. For example, suppose Paul indorses a negotiable instrument to Thomas and writes, "Pay to Thomas only if he delivers a typewriter to me before Oct. 1." If the typewriter is not delivered on time, Paul has a defense against Thomas (breach of a conditional indorsement), but this defense is not permitted against a subsequent holder in due course.

Nondelivery of Instrument Nondelivery is a personal defense not available against a holder in due course. For example, suppose that near the end of the month Dora drew a check that she intended to deliver to the payee after the first of the month. The payee managed to obtain possession of the check without Dora's knowledge and indorsed it to Harry. When Dora discovered that the check was missing, she stopped payment on it. When Harry presented the check to the drawee bank for payment, he was informed of the stop-payment order. He then sued Dora on the check. If Harry is a holder in due course, Dora is not permitted to assert the defense of nondelivery against him. Dora's only recourse is against the payee.

Occasionally, an instrument is delivered by the maker or the drawer with the understanding that the delivery will not become effective unless a specified condition precedent occurs (as, for example, unless a particular service is performed). Occasionally, also, an instrument is delivered with the understanding that it is to be used for a special purpose. The defenses of conditional delivery and delivery for a special purpose are personal defenses. Nondelivery includes lack of delivery by the maker or the drawer to the payee at issuance and lack of delivery by a payee or holder to an indorsee or transferee at negotiation.

Case 33.5   **Watkins v. Sheriff of Clark County, Nevada**
453 P.2d 611 (Nev. 1969)

THOMPSON, J. This appeal tenders an issue of law as to whether the statutory offense of obtaining money under false pretenses embraces one who negotiates bearer paper to a holder in due course. Following a preliminary examination, Freddie Watkins was ordered to stand trial in the district court for having violated NRS 205.380. In that court he sought release from restraint by a petition for habeas corpus, was denied relief and has appealed.

The Silver Slipper Gambling Hall & Saloon issued its payroll check for $185.59 to Mrs. Reggie Bluiett, an employee, who indorsed it in blank and left it on the dresser in her home. The following day she learned that the check was missing along with other items of property. On that day Freddie Watkins purchased two tires from Western Auto with Mrs. Bluiett's payroll check. The tires cost $73.21 and Watkins received the balance in cash. Watkins was subsequently charged with having obtained money under false pretenses from Joseph H. Hudson, the owner of Western Auto.

An essential element of this statutory offense is that the accused intend to cheat or defraud the person from whom the money is obtained.* Case law imposes the additional requirement that the person from whom the money is obtained sustain injury or damage. [Citations.]

Western Auto did not incur injury or damage since it was a holder in due course, having given value, in good faith and without notice of any claim to the instrument on the part of any person. NRS 104.3302 [UCC 3-302]. Theft is not a defense against a holder in due course. NRS 104.3305 [UCC 3-305]. Western Auto was protected against the claim of the rightful owner. It received a valid, enforceable payroll check and was not damaged. Accordingly, the statutory

---

*NRS 205.380 reads: "Every person who shall knowingly and designedly, by any false pretense or pretenses, obtain from any other person or persons any chose in action, money, goods, wares, chattels, effects or other valuable thing, with intent to cheat or defraud any person or persons of the same, is a cheat, and on conviction shall be imprisoned in the state prison not less than 1 year nor more than 10 years, or by a fine of not more than $5,000, or by both fine and imprisonment, and be sentenced to restore the property so fraudulently obtained, if it can be done. Should the value of any chose in action, money, goods, wares, chattels, effects, or any other valuable thing so, as aforesaid, fraudulently obtained, not exceed in value the sum of $100, every person so offending is a cheat, and is guilty of a misdemeanor, and shall be sentenced to restore the property so fraudulently obtained, if it can be done."

Case 33.5
Continued

offense charged to Watkins was not committed by him and his petition for habeas corpus must be granted.

We, therefore, reverse the district court and order that Freddie Watkins be released from custody or restraint upon this particular charge. The state may charge Watkins with whatever offense is warranted by the evidence in its possession.

FEDERAL CHANGES IN THE HOLDER IN DUE COURSE DOCTRINE

In recent years, consumer groups have voiced strong opposition to the holder in due course doctrine. They object to the idea that a maker or drawer of an instrument is not permitted to assert a legitimate defense, such as fraud in the inducement, failure of consideration, or breach of warranty, simply because the payee transfers a negotiable instrument for value to a third person. Case 33.4 at page 688 illustrates rather graphically the plight of the maker. A credit purchaser of goods who executes an installment instrument and who has a legitimate defense must pay a holder in due course in full. The maker or the drawer (debtor) is required to seek recourse in a separate action against the seller of the goods (the original payee of the installment instrument).

In 1976 the Federal Trade Commission (FTC) adopted a regulation that denies holder in due course status to anyone who purchases certain types of commercial paper. Thus, the regulation allows the maker or the drawer with a valid defense to refuse to pay the holder, except, as noted later, where the consumer pays by check.

The regulation preserves all claims and defenses that a consumer may have even against a good faith purchaser for value without notice of any defects. *Consumer* means a person who acquires goods or services for personal, family, or household use. For example, the regulation covers purchases of automobiles, home improvement contracts, and health spa memberships. The regulation does not cover purchases of real estate or securities, or purchases over

$25,000. It does not cover public utility services.

In the typical consumer credit transaction, the consumer's installment note is promptly transferred to a finance company, which purchases the note at a discount. The FTC regulation puts the transferee on notice that the transferee is not a holder in due course, but a mere assignee, by requiring a credit note to contain a prominently printed notice as follows:

NOTICE

ANY HOLDER OF THIS CONSUMER CREDIT CONTRACT IS SUBJECT TO ALL CLAIMS AND DEFENSES WHICH THE DEBTOR COULD ASSERT AGAINST THE SELLER OF GOODS OR SERVICES OBTAINED PURSUANT HERETO OR WITH THE PROCEEDS HEREOF. RECOVERY HEREUNDER BY THE DEBTOR SHALL NOT EXCEED AMOUNTS PAID BY THE DEBTOR HEREUNDER.

The above notice puts upon purchasers of commercial paper the burden of "policing" consumer financing. The notice also makes difficult the practice long engaged in by disreputable sellers of setting up a financing corporation to receive commercial paper, selling shoddy goods or services, and then leaving town. If purchasers of commercial paper are careful to check for fraud and other misconduct of their transferors, consumers will receive protection not formerly available to them. If the policing activities are not effective, however, finance companies may pay less for consumer obligations since the risk of nonpayment would be greater. Ultimately, the seller of the goods or services may raise the price to the consumer to compensate for a higher discount rate. The FTC rule does not cover a consumer who purchases goods or services and pays by check. The check need not contain the notice, and a purchaser of the check may qualify as a holder in due course.

A merchant may not circumvent the FTC regulation by arranging for the consumer to borrow money from a lender and pay cash to the merchant. The regulation provides specifically that when the merchant arranges for the loan, the credit instrument must contain the specified notice, and the lender has no greater rights than the seller of the goods. The lender is denied the status of a holder in due course only when the merchant refers consumers to the lender or is affiliated with the lender by control or by business arrangement.

There is a monetary limitation under the FTC regulation. The maker or the drawer who has a defense may refuse to pay further sums on the instrument and may recover amounts previously paid. However, the consumer may not assert a claim against the holder of the instrument for damages in excess of the amount paid. If the maker or the drawer seeks a larger award for consequential damages, for instance, the party must institute an action in state court against the merchant who sold the person the goods or services.

SUMMARY

A holder in due course of a negotiable instrument occupies a privileged position in the law. A person cannot be a holder in due course unless the person is a holder. A *holder* is any person who is in possession of bearer paper, or who is the payee or indorsee of order paper. To qualify as a *holder in due course*, a holder must take the instrument (1) for value, (2) in good faith, and (3) without notice.

A holder gives *value* to the extent that the holder performs the agreed consideration, as by paying money, delivering goods, or performing services, or to the extent that he or she acquires

a security interest in or lien on the instrument. There is also a taking for value when the holder takes the instrument in payment of an antecedent claim, or when the holder gives a negotiable instrument for it, or when he or she makes an irrevocable commitment to a third person.

To be a holder in due course, the purchaser must take the instrument in *good faith*, that is, "honesty in fact in the conduct or transaction concerned." The holder also must take the instrument *without notice* that it is overdue or that it has been dishonored or that there is any defense against it or claim to it on the part of any person. A person has notice of a fact when the person has actual knowledge of it, or has reason to know that it exists.

A transferee who does not meet all the requirements of a holder in due course may take advantage of the "shelter provision." The transferee receives the same rights as the transferor held. Thus, the transferee from a holder in due course acquires the transferor's special status and is referred to as a holder "through" a holder in due course.

The major advantage of being a holder in due course or a holder through a holder in due course is that such a holder takes the instrument free of all defenses except a very limited number of defenses, commonly called "real defenses." There are seven major real defenses, including infancy (minority); such other incapacity, duress, or illegality of the transaction as renders the obligation of the party a "nullity"; fraud in the essence; bankruptcy; unauthorized signature; and material alteration of the instrument. However, where the defense of alteration is a real defense, it is a defense only to the extent of the alteration.

Defenses that are not real defenses are called "personal defenses." Personal defenses are good only against holders who do not have the rights of a holder in due course. Personal defenses include all the ordinary contract law defenses and nondelivery of the instrument.

A regulation adopted by the Federal Trade

Commission has made major changes in the holder in due course doctrine in order to protect consumers. The regulation covers credit instruments given for the purchase of goods and services for personal, family, or household use.

STUDY AND DISCUSSION QUESTIONS

1 Define or otherwise explain the meaning of "holder" as that term is used in the law of commercial paper.

2 *(a)* Explain the following statement: In the law of commercial paper, value is not the same thing as consideration. *(b)* John Doe deposits a check in his bank. Under what circumstances, and to what extent, does the bank become a holder for value of that item? *(c)* Explain the "first in, first out" rule.

3 Explain why the following statement is not correct: A holder lacks the good faith requirement of a holder in due course only if he or she has actual knowledge of fraud or other defect in the instrument.

4 Criticize the following definition: A holder in due course is a holder who takes the instrument for value, in good faith, before it is overdue, and without notice of any defense against it.

5 *(a)* Explain the two ways a demand instrument may become overdue. *(b)* When is a check overdue? *(c)* What factors do the courts consider in determining whether an instrument is overdue?

6 Explain how the following instruments might be dishonored: *(a)* promissory note; *(b)* check; *(c)* draft.

7 *(a)* Define and give an example of incomplete paper. *(b)* Explain how a purchaser may become a holder in due course of incomplete paper. *(c)* Define and give an example of irregular paper. *(d)* Explain and give an illustration of the following statement: A holder who takes an instrument that is incomplete or irregular is charged with notice of a defense even though the defense is not related to the omission or irregularity.

8 Mary draws up and signs a note payable to the order of Paul Payee. Mary fraudulently induces Martha to sign as comaker. Without authority from Martha, Mary delivers the note to Paul. Is it possible for Paul to be a holder in due course? Explain.

9 *(a)* Explain and give an example of a holder through a holder in due course. *(b)* What is the economic significance of the shelter provision? *(c)* What kind of transferees may not benefit from the shelter provision?

10 Give an example of each of the following real defenses: "other incapacity"; duress; illegality.

11 *(a)* What is the meaning of "fraud in the inducement"? Is that type of fraud a personal or a real defense? *(b)* What is the meaning of "fraud in the factum"? Is it a personal or a real defense?

12 In what way does each of the following statements need to be qualified in order to make it accurate? *(a)* The defense of unauthorized signature is good against a holder in due course. *(b)* The defense of material alteration is good against a holder in due course.

13 State the FTC regulation concerning commercial paper and explain the justification for the rule.

CASE PROBLEMS

1 The payee of a negotiable promissory note placed a special indorsement on it and transferred it to Gunther Gilmore. Gilmore transferred the note to Harold Horton but forgot to indorse it. Horton took the note for value, in good faith, and without notice that it was overdue, or that it had been dishonored, or that there was any defense against it. When Horton discovered that the note had not been indorsed to him, he requested and received his transferor's indorsement. *(a)* Could Horton be a holder in due course at the time he took the instrument? *(b)* Under what circumstances, if any, could Horton become a holder in due course at the time the instrument was indorsed to him?

2 Ferrante was a subcontractor on a job for which O. P. Ganjo, Inc., was a contractor. Ferrante proceeded so slowly with his plastering job that Ganjo became concerned that the subcontract might not be completed in time to allow Ganjo to complete its contract on time. When Ferrante was urged to speed up the work, he stated that he did not have funds enough to pay his workers. However, he said that he had a $3,000 promissory note payable to his order that he had received on his last job. Ganjo agreed to discount the note for $2,800, payable $1,000 at the time of the transfer of the instrument, and the balance of $1,800 if and when the transferor (Ferrante) completed the plastering job. Ferrante indorsed and transferred the note to Ganjo, and Ganjo paid the $1,000 in cash. Before the plastering job was completed, Ferrante became involved in financial difficulties and departed for parts unknown. Ganjo sued the maker of the $3,000 note, who proved he had a personal defense to the note. Was the Ganjo Corporation a holder in due course?

3 Mr. and Mrs. Anderson signed a contract and note for the installation of twelve jalousie windows. After the Atlantic Storm Window Company installed the windows, it negotiated the note to a bank. The Andersons refused to make payments on the note because, as they claimed, the windows had been defectively installed. The bank sued the Andersons. The Andersons contended that the bank had not purchased the note in good faith because it had failed "to communicate with the payee and/or the makers of the note to determine whether the work had been satisfactorily completed." Did the bank purchase the note in good faith?

4 Mr. and Mrs. Ingel signed a contract with Allied Aluminum Associates for the installation of aluminum siding and an installment note for the contract price. Allied sold the note to a credit corporation with which it had done business in the past. The Ingels, claiming fraud on the part of Allied, refused to make payments to the credit corporation, and were sued by that corporation. At the trial the defendants attempted to introduce evidence that plaintiff corporation was aware of complaints against Allied by various previous customers. The trial judge excluded the evidence on the ground that it was not germane to the issue of whether the plaintiff credit corporation was a holder in due course. If the purchase was not for personal, family, or household use, was the evidence properly excluded?

5 American Kosher Provision, Inc., executed a note in the amount of $52,000, payable in "11 consecutive weekly installments of $1,000 each, except the final installment which shall be the balance of $41,000 on March 10, 1966." The note was several times indorsed and finally came into the hands of the National State Bank of Elizabeth, N.J., a purchaser for value. At some time before the note came into the bank's possession, the $41,000 had visibly been changed to $42,000. After making ten payments of $1,000 each, the Kosher Provision company defaulted, and the bank sued the indorsers. The defendants contended that plaintiff bank was not a holder in due course by reason of that portion of UCC section 3-304 that provides that the purchaser has notice of a defense if the instrument bears such visible evidence of alteration as to call into question its validity or terms. Is the defendants' contention correct?

6 Saale purchased a quantity of steel coil from a Japanese supplier. The coil arrived in damaged condition. Saale filed a claim with his insurance company. The insurer said it would pay the claim in full; but that to determine the amount of the loss, the insurance company would take possession of the goods and sell them at auction. The auction was conducted by the insurer's agent without any participation by Saale. Interstate Steel Co., the successful bidder, asked whether credit terms could be arranged. The insurer's agent stated that any arrangement Interstate could make with Saale would be satisfactory to his company. Saale agreed to accept a $50,000 down payment and to take a note payable to his order for the rest of the price.

Soon thereafter Interstate informed Saale that the goods delivered to it by the insurance company were not of the quality represented and that it would make no further payment. Saale sued Interstate on the note. Interstate's defense was fraud and failure of consideration by the insurance company. Interstate asserted that because Saale was the payee of the note he could not be a holder in due course and thus took the note subject to all defenses. Is the contention correct?

7 Jean Devereaux drew a check payable to Lloyd Garrett and delivered the check to him. Garrett intended to cash the check at the drawee bank, but on the way to the bank he lost the check. The bank had him sign a stop-payment order. Someone found the check, forged Garrett's indorsement, and cashed the check at the L. Q. Liquor Store. Thereafter, Garrett learned from the drawee bank that the L. Q. Liquor Store had presented the check for payment and that payment had been refused. Garrett immediately went to the liquor store, identified himself, and demanded surrender of the check. Was he entitled to the check?

Chapter

34

Liability of the Parties; Discharge

Two kinds of liability are associated with commercial paper: contractual liability and warranty liability. The Uniform Commercial Code (UCC) imposes contractual liability "by operation of law" on the *signers* of commercial paper. The existence of contractual liability (liability "on the instrument") means generally that signers are liable or potentially liable for payment of the amount specified in the instrument. The Code also imposes warranty liability, but on nonsigners as well as on signers. Breach of a warranty may occur when a person *transfers* commercial paper or when a person *presents* it for payment.

A person who fulfills the contractual obligations imposed by the Code is discharged (released) from liability. A person may also be discharged from liability by the actions of others. The liability of parties on the instrument, discharge from liability on the instrument, and liability for breach of warranty are discussed in this chapter.

LIABILITY OF PARTIES ON THE INSTRUMENT

A person may sign an instrument as maker, drawer, acceptor, indorser, accommodation party, or guarantor. There are differences in the liability of the various types of signers. Liability of a party may be affected when a signature is made by an agent of the party or by a forger.

699

Liability of Particular Parties

A party to (signer of) commercial paper may have either "primary" or "secondary" liability on the instrument. *Primary liability* on an instrument means that a party ("primary party") is liable for payment immediately and unconditionally when the instrument comes due. Primary liability on a *demand* instrument arises when the instrument is issued. Primary liability on a *time* instrument arises when the due date arrives. *Secondary liability* on an instrument means a party ("secondary party") is liable for payment only upon the happening of certain "conditions precedent" to liability: "presentment," "dishonor," and notice of dishonor. These are discussed later in this chapter.

Liability of Primary Parties The *maker* of a note or certificate of deposit (CD), and the *acceptor* of a draft or check are primary parties. By signing the instrument a maker or an acceptor promises to pay the amount shown on the instrument at the time of the signing, or the amount inserted later by an authorized agent if the instrument is incomplete at the time of signing [3-413(1)].[1] Certification of a check by a drawee bank is a type of acceptance and is discussed in Chapter 35.

Primary liability is unconditional; that is, a primary party is liable immediately when the instrument comes due. As a practical matter, holders normally try to collect payment from the primary party before bringing suit, but there is no requirement that they do so. Consequently, when sued, a primary party cannot delay the lawsuit on the ground of failure to make presentment (demand) for payment.

When a draft or check is *issued*, there is no primary party (that is, no maker or acceptor). The drawer is a signer, but as will be discussed in the next section, is a secondary party. The drawee is not a signer, and unless and until there is acceptance, the drawee is not liable on the instrument to anyone. Of course, if the drawee accepts a draft or certifies a check, the drawee becomes an "acceptor" and is then a primary party.

Liability of Secondary Parties The *drawer* of a check or draft and the *indorser* of any commercial paper are secondary parties. When a draft or check is issued, there is no primary party, but there is always a secondary party, the drawer. The drawer's liability is secondary because it is conditional. By signing a draft or check, a drawer "engages" (promises) that upon *"dishonor" and any necessary "notice* of dishonor or protest," he or she will pay the amount of the draft or check to the holder or to any indorser who "takes up" the instrument (acquires it and pays the holder) [3-413(2)]. The drawee's dishonor of the instrument and the drawer's receipt of notice of the dishonor are conditions that must be met before the drawer will be liable for payment.

As an instrument circulates from hand to hand, the signatures of indorsers may be added to the paper. Thus, a note or CD, which has no secondary party at issuance, may acquire a secondary party through negotiation of the instrument. By signing, an unqualified indorser of commercial paper makes a promise (conditioned on dishonor and notice) to pay the instrument. The promise is made to any *subsequent* indorser who takes up the instrument, and to any holder [3-414]. Thus, liability of indorsers is in relation to the order of signing. For example, suppose A, the payee of an order instrument, indorses and delivers it to B, who in turn indorses and delivers it to C. If C is unable to collect from the maker or drawee, C may collect from indorser B, and B in turn may collect from A. But if C had skipped B and had received payment from A, A could not collect from B because B's engagement as an indorser is made to subsequent indorsers, not to prior ones. As stated in Chapter 33, a qualified indorsement (one "without recourse") eliminates the indorser's contrac-

---

[1] Numbers within brackets in the text refer to sections of the UCC.

tual liability. A qualified indorser may be liable for certain warranties, however. Warranty liability is discussed later in this chapter.

Normally, a secondary party becomes liable on an instrument only after (1) "presentment" of the instrument; (2) "dishonor" of the instrument; and (3) "notice of dishonor." For instruments accepted or payable outside the United States, a fourth condition precedent, called "protest," may be required. A *protest* is a document or certificate of dishonor signed and sealed by a public official such as a United States Consul or a notary public authorized to certify that the instrument was dishonored. Protest will not be discussed further in this chapter. The other conditions precedent are discussed below.

Requirement of presentment   *Presentment* is a demand for acceptance or payment [3-504]. The demand is made by a holder upon a maker or an acceptor ("primary parties"), a drawee, or some other person authorized to accept or to make payment. Presentment may be made in person, by mail, or through a clearing house. If it is made by mail, the time of presentment is determined by the time of receipt of mail. The time for presentment is critical to establish liability of a secondary party. If presentment is delayed, secondary parties may be discharged from liability. The subject of discharge will be discussed in the second part of this chapter.

Some instruments specify a date for presentment. If no date is specified, demand for payment or acceptance must be made within a "reasonable" time. A reasonable time for presentment depends upon the kind of instrument and the circumstances of the case. For uncertified checks

the following are presumed to be reasonable periods within which to present for payment or to initiate bank collection: (a) with respect to the liability of the drawer, thirty days after date or issue, whichever is later; and (b) with respect to the liability of an indorser, seven days after his indorsement [3-503(2)].

These time periods are merely presumed reasonable. A court may find them unreasonably short, for example, where the holder lives in an isolated area or is delayed by circumstances beyond his or her control. A reasonable time to present a demand note or draft ordinarily would be much longer than allowed for a check. A court considers such factors as the community (rural or urban) and the relationship of the parties (business or family).

Requirement of dishonor   *Dishonor* is a refusal or failure to pay or accept an instrument that has been properly presented [3-507(1)]. Dishonor may take several forms. Dishonor of a note or CD occurs if the maker refuses to pay on the due date. Dishonor of a check or draft occurs if the drawee refuses to accept (or certify, if a check) the instrument, or having accepted, refuses to pay on the due date.

However, return of an instrument for lack of a proper indorsement is not a dishonor [3-507(3)]. Nor is the exercise of the right to a proper presentment. The person to whom presentment is made (maker, drawee, acceptor) may require exhibition of the instrument, identification of the presenter, evidence of the presenter's authority to make presentment for another, and presentment of the instrument at the place specified in the instrument for payment or acceptance [3-505(1)]. If the place for presentment has not been specified (as in the ordinary check), the holder ordinarily must present the instrument at the business location or residence of the party who is to accept or pay.

Failure of the presenter to comply with any of these requirements invalidates the presentment; but the presenter has a reasonable time to comply, and the time for acceptance or payment runs *from* the time of compliance [3-505(2)]. Thus, the person who is to accept or pay has the full time allowed by the Code to investigate the situation. Deferring *acceptance* until the close of the next business day does not constitute dishonor. Nor is it a dishonor to defer *payment* of most commercial paper pending a reasonable examination to determine whether it is properly payable. However, if payment is not made by the close of business on the day of presentment, the instrument is dishonored [3-506].

Requirement of notice After an instrument has been dishonored, secondary parties (drawers and indorsers) must be given timely notice if they are to be held liable. Notice of dishonor must be given within time limits prescribed by the Code, usually 3 business days. Collecting banks have a shorter time to give notice of dishonor, up to 2 business days. The notice may be given in any reasonable manner, either orally or in writing. Unlike presentment, notice of dishonor sent by mail is given when sent even though it may never be received by the secondary party [3-508(4)].

Liability of Accommodation Parties An *accommodation party* is a person who signs an instrument for the purpose of lending his or her name to another party to the instrument [3-415(1)]. A common situation involves a person who wishes to buy goods on credit and to give a promissory note. The seller may refuse to extend credit if the buyer is a minor or has a poor credit rating. The seller may agree to sell the goods if another person (with good credit) will sign the note as an accommodation party.

An accommodation party may sign an instrument in any capacity, for example, as maker, drawer, acceptor, or indorser. Usually, accommodation parties sign either as comaker or indorser. The contractual liability of an accommodation party is determined by the capacity in which the party signs. If the party signs as maker or acceptor, the person incurs the liability of a primary party; if the party signs as drawer or indorser, the person's liability is secondary (i.e., presentment, dishonor, and notice are required to establish liability).

An accommodation party may be liable even though the party received no consideration for signing. However, an accommodation party has no liability on the instrument to the party accommodated. An accommodation party who pays the instrument has a right of recourse against the party accommodated [3-415(5)]. For example, the father who co-signs a note so his son may buy a car and who pays the note when the son defaults, may recover from his son.

Case 34.1 **Commerce National Bank v. Baron**
336 F. Supp. 1125 (E.D. Pa. 1971)

Plaintiff-payee, Commerce National Bank in Lake Worth, Florida, instituted this action to collect the amounts due on two overdue notes from defendant-maker, Stanley M. Baron.

LORD, J. . . . Throughout this litigation, the defendant has submitted to this court a myriad of constantly changing defenses. These have included that he is not liable on the notes due to an oral agreement between the parties, that he is liable under the notes but only after plaintiff first proceeds against one R. H. Bailey, who the defendant alleges was the recipient of the proceeds, that he signed the notes as an accommodation to Bailey, that he signed the notes as an accommodation to the plaintiff, that he signed the notes but is relieved of any liability on account of a fraud perpetrated by the plaintiff. . . .

It appears to this court that the defendant has created a smokescreen, which, when penetrated reveals an attempt to evade responsibility from a debt he voluntarily assumed. Nevertheless, we shall now dispose of the legal defenses which defendant has finally decided to pursue. [One of] these defenses [is] that defendant was an accommodation party for R. H. Bailey and the plaintiff must exhaust its remedies against Bailey as a condition to its proceeding against him. . . .

This action is governed by the Uniform Commercial Code. . . . The UCC defines an accommodation party as "one who signs the instrument in any capacity for the purpose of lending his name to *another party* to it." Sec. 3-415(1) [emphasis supplied]. Bailey was not a party to these notes. Therefore, defendant cannot claim the status of being an accommodation party to him.

The defense that plaintiff had to exhaust its remedies against Bailey as a condition precedent to its proceedings against the defendant is but another attempt to clothe the defendant with the status of [a secondary] accommodation party. Nevertheless, even if defendant were an accommodation party, the legal effect would not be altered. The plaintiff would still not be required to proceed against Bailey or any other person before instituting any action against defendant. The defendant would be an accommodation maker and "an accommodation maker or acceptor is [a primary party and is] bound on the instrument without any resort to his principal,. . . ." Sec. 3-415, Official Comment 1.

Defendant further attempts to evade liability by alleging that the parties entered into an agreement whereby the defendant would not be liable until the Bank had first proceeded against Bailey. A similar contention was pursued and rejected in *American National Bank v. Knab Co.*, 158 F.Supp. 695 (E.D. Wis. 1958). It is clear that . . . a maker of a note for which there was consideration will not be permitted to vary or contradict its terms by showing a prior or contemporaneous oral agreement that he was not to be bound. To permit the defendant to pursue this defense would render totally meaningless the effect of the written instrument. The parol evidence rule prohibits this very thing. . . .

For the foregoing reasons, each of the defenses pursued by the defendant is rejected. . . .

[Judgment for plaintiff.]

Liability of Guarantor A *guarantor* is a signer of commercial paper who adds "Payment guaranteed" or equivalent words to the signature. By such language a guarantor promises that if the instrument is not paid when due, he or she will pay it without resort to any other party. A secondary party who guarantees payment *waives* presentment, notice of dishonor, and protest and thus acquires a liability that is indistinguishable from that of a comaker.

A signer who adds "Collection guaranteed" or equivalent words or his to her signature promises that if the instrument is not paid when due, he or she will pay it, but only if (1) the holder has first proceeded against the maker or acceptor by suit and execution, or (2) the holder can show that legal action would be useless, for example because of the insolvency of the maker or acceptor. A secondary party who guarantees collection waives presentment, notice of dishonor, and protest.

Effect on Liability of
Signatures by Agents and Forgers

Signature by Authorized Agent Agents are frequently authorized to sign commercial paper on behalf of their principals. The effect of an authorized agent's signature on an instrument varies according to the way the agent signs. In the following illustrations Arnold Andrews is an agent and Pamela Prince is his principal. Suppose that Andrews is authorized to sign a negotiable instrument on Prince's behalf and wishes to bind her as maker, drawer, acceptor, or indorser without binding himself on the instrument. The safest and commercially most acceptable way for Andrews to accomplish his intention is to sign the instrument

"Pamela Prince
By Arnold Andrews, Agent."

Andrews escapes liability as a signer because he has done two things: He has named the person represented, and he has shown that he signed his own name in a representative capacity.

If Andrews uses forms of signature that do not do *both* of these things, he may be held personally liable [3-403(2)]. The following examples illustrate the dangers of an agent's signing incorrectly.

Suppose Andrews merely signs his own name: "Arnold Andrews." Andrews is liable on the instrument. Parol evidence is not admissible to show that Andrews intended to sign as an agent for Prince. Prince is not liable on the instrument because her name does not appear on it. However, under agency law, she may be liable, as an "undisclosed principal," on the underlying debt for which the instrument was given.[2]

Suppose Andrews signs a negotiable instrument: "Arnold Andrews, Agent." Andrews is liable on the instrument. However, parol evidence is admissible between the immediate parties (but not against a holder in due course) to prove that the agent was not intended to be liable [3-403(2)(b)]. Prince is not liable since her name is not on the instrument. Under agency

law, this signature designates a "partially disclosed principal." If the identity of the partially disclosed principal is discovered, both agent and principal may be liable on the underlying debt for which the instrument was given.

Suppose Andrews signs both names as follows:

"Pamela Prince
Arnold Andrews."

Andrews is liable on the instrument because he signed it. Prince is liable on the instrument because she authorized Andrews to sign her name. Parol evidence is admissible between the immediate parties to show that Andrews was not intended to be liable, but parol evidence is not allowed to defeat liability to a holder in due course.

Unauthorized Signature   *Unauthorized signature* includes both a forgery and a signature by an agent who exceeds his or her actual, implied, or apparent authority in signing the principal's name [1-201(43)]. An unauthorized signature is inoperative as that of the person whose name is signed unless that person ratifies it or is precluded (prevented) from denying it [3-404(1)]. The Code precludes persons who are negligent and persons in certain "imposter" and "fictitious payee" situations from denying their unauthorized or fraudulently procured signatures. An unauthorized signature *is* effective to impose upon the actual signer (forger or agent) liability to persons who in good faith pay the instrument or take it for value [3-404(1)].

Section 3-406 of the Code provides that "Any person who by his negligence substantially contributes to . . . the making of an unauthorized signature is precluded from asserting the . . . lack of authority against a holder in due course. . . ." Many business people sign commercial paper by means of a rubber stamp. If the owner of such a stamp negligently gives unauthorized persons access to it, and the negligence substantially contributes to the making of

---

[2]Obligations of principal and agent are discussed in Chapter 36.

an unauthorized signature (as drawer, maker, acceptor, or indorser), the owner will be precluded from asserting lack of authority. This rule benefits not only holders in due course, but also any "drawee or other payor who pays the instrument in good faith and in accordance with the reasonable commercial standards of the drawee's or payor's business" [3-406].

Liability on Instruments Made Out to Imposters or Fictitious Payees Suppose that a principal is induced by a dishonest agent to sign a payroll check made out to a nonexistent worker, and that the agent gets possession of the check, signs the name of the payee on the back of the check, and cashes it at a supermarket. The supermarket then presents the check to the drawee bank and receives payment. Having learned of the fraud, the principal (the drawer of the check) immediately demands that the drawee bank repay to the principal's account the amount paid to the supermarket. Is the principal entitled to repayment? The answer is no. The drafters of the Code have taken the position that "the loss should fall upon the employer as a risk of his business enterprise rather than upon the subsequent holder or drawee," because "the employer is normally in a better position to prevent such forgeries by reasonable care in the selection or supervision of his employees; or, if he is not, is at least in a better position to cover the loss by fidelity insurance," the cost of which is "properly an expense of his business rather than of the business of the holder or drawee." A

similar principle applies where the payee is an imposter rather than a nonexistent employee. (An imposter is a person who pretends to be someone else, e.g., an existing employee.)

How is this result accomplished by the Code? What has happened to the Code principle stated in Chapter 32 that only a holder can negotiate an instrument? The dishonest agent (who signed the name of the nonexistent worker-payee) is not a holder as that term is usually understood, because the agent was not named as payee. However, to protect purchasers and payors of negotiable instruments, Section 3-405(1) of the Code confers holder status on the dishonest agent in our example, and on other dishonest persons. That section provides in part that

> an indorsement by any person in the name of a named payee is effective if (a) an imposter . . . has induced the maker or drawer to issue the instrument to him or his confederate in the name of the payee, or (b) a person signing as or on behalf of a maker or drawer intends the payee to have no interest in the instrument.

Although Section 3-405 may seem to encourage dishonesty, it should be remembered that the persons who do the defrauding are still subject to criminal penalties for their dishonesty, to civil suits for damages, and, as signers, to liability on the instrument. These rules apply also to situations where the wrongdoer is not an agent of the maker or drawer.

Case 34.2 Philadelphia Title Insurance Co. v. Fidelity-Philadelphia Trust Co.
212 A.2d 222 (Pa. 1965)

Edmund Jezemski and Paula Jezemski were husband and wife, estranged and living apart. Mrs. Jezemski, without her husband's knowledge, arranged for a mortgage to be placed upon some real estate that Mr. Jezemski had inherited from his mother. The arrangements were made through John McAllister, an attorney, and Anthony Di Benedetto, a real estate dealer. They arranged to have the deal closed on a specified date in the office of plaintiff, Philadelphia Title

Insurance Co. Shortly before that date, Mrs. Jezemski represented to McAllister and Di Benedetto that her husband would be unable to attend on the appointed date. She came to McAllister's office in advance of the settlement date, accompanied by a man whom she introduced to McAllister and Di Benedetto as her husband. She and this man, in the presence of McAllister and Di Benedetto, executed the papers necessary for a mortgage. On the settlement date, McAllister, Di Benedetto, and Mrs. Jezemski went to the office of the plaintiff.

Plaintiff's settlement clerk, accepting the word of McAllister and Di Benedetto that the papers had been signed by Mr. Jezemski, gave Mrs. Jezemski a check of the amount stated in the mortgage note and the mortgage. The check was drawn on the defendant bank, Fidelity-Philadelphia Trust Co., and was made payable to Edmund Jezemski and Paula Jezemski. Mrs. Jezemski indorsed the check, and some person other than Mr. Jezemski indorsed Mr. Jezemski's name on the check. Mrs. Jezemski received payment of the check. When the forgery was discovered, the Title Company sued the drawee bank (Fidelity-Philadelphia) to recover the sum, which was charged against the Title Company's account in payment of the check in question. There was judgment for defendant, and plaintiff appealed.

COHEN, J. . . . The parties do not dispute the proposition that as between payor bank (Fidelity-Philadelphia) and its customer (Title Company), ordinarily, the former must bear the loss occasioned by the forgery of a payee's indorsement (Edmund Jezemski) upon a check drawn by its customer and paid by it. . . . Uniform Commercial Code Sec. 3-404 provides, *inter alia,* that "(1) Any unauthorized signature [Edmund Jezemski's] is wholly inoperative as that of the person whose name is signed unless he ratifies it or is precluded from denying it. . . ."

However, the [defendant bank argues] that this case falls within an exception to the above rule, making the forged indorsement of Edmund Jezemski's name effective so that Fidelity-Philadelphia was entitled to charge the account of its customer, the Title Company, who was the drawer of the check. The exception asserted by the bank is found in Sec. 3-405(1)(a) of the Uniform Commercial Code which provides:

> "An indorsement by any person in the name of a named payee is effective if (a) an impostor by the use of the mails or otherwise has induced the maker or drawer to issue the instrument to him or his confederate in the name of the payee; . . ."

. . . In effect, the only argument made by the Title Company to prevent the applicability of Section 3-405(1)(a) is that the imposter, who admittedly played a part in the swindle, *did not "by the mails or otherwise"* induce the Title Company to issue the check within the meaning of Section 3-405(1)(a). The argument must fail. . . .

Both the words of Section 3-405(1)(a) and the Official Comment thereto leave no doubt that the imposter can induce the drawer to issue him or his confederate a check within the meaning of the section even though he does not carry out his impersonation before the very eyes of the drawer. Section 3-405(1)(a) says the inducement might be by "the mails or otherwise." . . .

Moreover, the Legislature's use of the word "otherwise" and the Comment, which suggests that results should not turn upon "the type of fraud which the particular imposter committed," indicates that the Legislature did not intend to limit the applicability of the section to cases where the imposter deals directly with the drawer (face-to-face, mails, telephone, etc.). Naturally, the Legislature could not have predicted and expressly included all the ingenious schemes designed and carried out by imposters for the purpose of defrauding the makers and drawers of negotiable instruments. Something had to be left for the courts by way of statutory construction. For purposes of imposing the loss of one of two "innocent" parties, either the drawer who was defrauded or the drawee bank which paid out on a forged indorsement, we see no reason for distinguishing between the drawer who was duped by an impersonator communicating directly with him through the mails and a drawer who is duped by an impersonator communicating indirectly with him through third persons. Thus, both the language of the Code and common sense dictate that the drawer must suffer the loss in both instances. . . .

Judgment affirmed.

DISCHARGE FROM LIABILITY ON THE INSTRUMENT

As a negotiable instrument is transferred from hand to hand, signers (except qualified indorsers) are or may become liable on the instrument. And, as the instrument is transferred, the liability of various persons may be terminated ("discharged") by a variety of methods. The discharge of one party may result in the discharge of one or more other parties to the instrument.

In a lawsuit brought against a signer to compel payment of an instrument, the signer may assert discharge as a defense. In general, discharge (by whatever method) is a personal defense and will be effective only against a person who is not a holder in due course. But some discharges are good even against a holder in due course. This part of the chapter deals with some common methods of discharge and with the effect of discharge on the rights of a holder in due course.

Methods of Discharge

Payment or Tender of Payment A party (maker, drawer, indorser, acceptor, etc.) who makes full payment to a holder is discharged from liability on the instrument [3-603(1)]. Discharge will not result, however, if the payment was made in bad faith, as where the person making the payment knows that the holder acquired the instrument by theft. Neither will a payment that is inconsistent with a restrictive indorsement ordinarily result in discharge.

The discharge of a party who has no recourse on the instrument usually results in the discharge of all other parties [3-601(3)]. Thus, if a maker or drawer makes payment in full to a holder and is thereby discharged, all other parties such as indorsers and accommodation parties are also discharged.

Usually an instrument is given for the purpose of discharging some underlying obligation. For example, a tenant mails the landlord a check for a month's rent. Where an instrument is taken for an underlying obligation, unless otherwise agreed the underlying obligation (here, to pay rent) is not discharged until the check is actually paid. However, the landlord's taking the instrument suspends the landlord's right to sue for nonpayment until the instrument is overdue or dishonored.

If a party tenders (offers) full payment to the holder at or after the maturity date of the instrument, and the holder improperly refuses the tender, the party making the tender is discharged to the extent of all subsequent liability for interest, costs, and attorney's fees [3-604(1)]. However, the tendering party is not discharged as to the principal (the face amount of the instrument), nor as to the interest accrued to the date of the tender.

Although improper refusal of a valid tender does not wholly discharge the party making the tender, it does wholly discharge any party who has a right of recourse against the party making the tender [3-604(2)]. For example, assume that Martin executes a note payable to the order of Paula, who indorses it to Harriett; that at the maturity of the note Martin properly tenders to Harriett the amount of principal and interest due; and that Harriett, being mistaken as to the amount of interest due, improperly refuses the tender. Harriett's refusal of Martin's tender wholly discharges Paula from her secondary liability on the instrument. The result is that if Harriett later is unable to collect from Martin, she may not collect from Paula, because Paula (having been discharged) is lost to Harriett as an alternative source of payment. (However, Paula remains secondarily liable to *subsequent* holders in due course who take the instrument without notice of the discharge.)

Fraudulent and Material Alteration After an instrument gets into circulation, it may be altered by a holder or by some other person who is rightfully or wrongfully in possession of it. An *alteration* may consist of a deletion, an addition, or a substitution; or it may consist of the completion of an incomplete instrument "otherwise than as authorized" [3-407(1)(b)]. In some cir-

cumstances an alteration discharges any party (maker, drawer, indorser, etc.) whose contract is thereby changed; in other circumstances it does not.

An alteration can result in discharge only when the following requisites for discharge exist.

1 The alteration must be made by a *holder* of the instrument or by the holder's authorized representative. An alteration made by a "stranger" to the instrument has no effect on the liability of the parties. Only misconduct by the holder should result in discharging the party whose contract the holder changed. A holder who has not misbehaved should not be penalized for the misconduct of a stranger.

2 The alteration must be a material one. It is material if it changes the contract of any party *in any respect*. A change is not material which does no more than correct an obvious error in the instrument.

3 The alteration must be made for a fraudulent purpose.

As against the holder who made or authorized the fraudulent, material alteration, the alteration discharges any party whose contract is thereby changed unless the party assents to the alteration or is precluded from asserting it as a defense [3-407(2)(a)]. As against a *subsequent* holder in due course, there is no discharge. The subsequent holder in due course may enforce the instrument according to its original tenor, i.e., according to its original terms.

Suppose that M makes and delivers to P a note for $100 payable to P's order. P indorses and delivers it to X (a holder), who fraudulently raises the amount to $2,100 and then negotiates the note to H. As to X, M and P are discharged because X's alteration was fraudulent and material. If H is *not* a holder in due course, M and P are discharged as to H. If H *is* a holder in due course, M and P are liable to H for $100, the amount originally specified in the note. Moreover, if, in preparing the note, M negligently left spaces in which additional words or figures could easily be inserted, or if M consented to the alteration, H may recover the full $2,100.

Sometimes a person signs an instrument that is incomplete. What happens if a thief or a "faithless employee" makes an unauthorized completion of the instrument and transfers it? The signer is discharged as to a mere holder, but a holder in due course may enforce the instrument *as completed* [3-407(3)]. This is so without regard to whether the signer was negligent. Indeed, a holder in due course will prevail *even though the paper was not delivered by the maker or drawer* [3-115(2)] (e.g., if it was stolen). One reason for favoring the holder in due course in this situation is that loss should fall on the party whose conduct in signing incomplete paper has made fraud possible, rather than on the innocent purchaser. Moreover, favoring the holder in due course increases the marketability of commercial paper.

Suppose that Donna Drawer, an employer, signs 40 payroll checks, otherwise leaves them blank for her agent to fill out, and places them in her office safe. That night a thief breaks open the safe, takes the signed checks, fills them out for $100 in the names of fictitious payees, and negotiates them. As to any holder in due course, Drawer will be liable for the amount stated in the completed instruments.

Unexcused Delay As noted earlier in this chapter, the liability of a secondary party is conditioned on presentment, dishonor, and notice of dishonor, unless one or more of these acts is excused. Presentment or notice of dishonor might be excused where, for example, the secondary party to be charged with liability waives presentment or notice, or where the holder by reasonable diligence cannot make presentment or give notice. Unless excused, however, presentment and notice of dishonor are required, and any unexcused delay in making presentment or giving notice results in a total or a partial discharge of the party who would otherwise be liable.

The holder's unexcused delay in making presentment or in giving notice of dishonor *completely* discharges an *indorser* from liability on the instrument [3-501(1)]. In *Hane v. Exten*,[3] for example, Mr. and Mrs. Exten were indorsers of an installment note which by its terms became due 30 days after a default by the maker. The maker defaulted. Hane then acquired the note, held it for almost 18 months before demanding payment, and sued the Extens in their capacities as indorsers. The appellate court affirmed the trial court's holding that presentment and notice are required to charge an indorser, that the 18 months far exceeded the "reasonable" time allowed by the Code for presentment in the kind of situation here involved, and that Hane had not given the Extens timely notice of dishonor. The indorsers were discharged from liability.

In contrast, unexcused delay does not necessarily discharge a *maker, drawer,* or *acceptor.* Suppose that the acceptor of a "domiciled" draft (one "payable at" a particular bank or other specified location) has on deposit with the bank an amount sufficient to pay the draft on its maturity date; that on the date of maturity the bank is solvent; and that the holder, without excuse, delays presenting the draft until the bank becomes insolvent. In such a situation the acceptor may discharge his or her liability on the domiciled instrument by assigning in writing to the holder whatever rights regarding the deposited amount the acceptor might have against the insolvent bank [3-502(1)(b)]. Thus, where funds were available on the maturity date of domiciled paper and the bank later failed, the holder must absorb any loss caused by the holder's unexcused delay in presenting the instrument. The same rule applies to the maker of a domiciled note *and* to the drawer of *any* check or draft.

But a holder's delay in presenting commercial paper is not enough, in itself, to cause dis-

---

[3]259 A.2d 290 (Md. App. 1969).

charge. If a drawee or a domiciliary bank remains solvent, as most do, the maker, drawer, or acceptor remains liable for the full time prescribed by the applicable statute of limitations, despite the holder's delay in seeking payment. The purpose of this rule is to avoid imposing loss on holders whose delay is harmless and to avoid unjustly enriching the drawer or other party who normally has received goods or other consideration for the issue of the instrument.

Cancellation or Renunciation Perhaps to make a gift or pay a creditor, the holder of an instrument may discharge any party by canceling the instrument (i.e., by "destroying or mutilating it") or by canceling the party's signature (i.e., by "striking out" the signature). A holder may renounce his or her rights in an instrument by signing and delivering a written renunciation, or by surrendering the instrument itself to the party to be discharged [3-605(1)]. If the holder cancels the signature of a party to the instrument, the cancellation discharges that person's liability; but it does not affect the holder's title to the instrument [3-605(2)]. The holder still owns the instrument and may negotiate or collect the instrument. Because a cancellation appears on the instrument itself, subsequent holders are on notice of it. But evidence of a renunciation normally does not appear on the instrument and therefore is ineffective against a holder in due course without notice.

Case 34.3   **Greene v. Cotton**
457 S.W.2d 493 (Ky. App. 1970)

B. C. Cotton and his wife (plaintiffs) executed a promissory note payable to S. R. Jones. Before the note was fully paid, Jones died. Greene and another person were appointed executors of his estate. The Cottons instituted this action, the purpose of which was to have the court hold that Jones had released the Cottons from liability on the note. The defendants (the two executors) denied that Jones had released the Cottons from liability and filed a counterclaim for the unpaid balance of the note and accrued interest. There was a judgment for plaintiffs and defendants appealed.

DAVIS, Commissioner. The critical question is whether a writing by S. R. Jones legally accomplished the cancellation and release of a promissory note which B. C. Cotton and his wife, appellees, had executed to Jones. The circuit court held that it did. There are other questions presented by appellants, but our view of the case makes it unnecessary to consider or discuss them.

On August 17, 1955, the Cottons executed and delivered to S. R. Jones their promissory note in the sum of $72,000 bearing 5% interest and secured by mortgage on real estate in Grant County owned by the Cottons. Various payments on the note had reduced the principal due to $38,400 at the date of the death of Jones on May 2, 1967.

The appellants, executors of the will of Jones, found among Jones' effects a key to a lockbox at Citizens Bank of Dry Ridge. Upon inspecting the contents of that lockbox, they found an envelope bearing the typewritten address:

"To admrs. of my estate
S. R. Jones"

Within the envelope was found a typewritten paper signed by S. R. Jones, which recited:

"I, S. R. Jones hereby request that if B. C. Cotton be living at the time of my death and if there is an unpaid balance on his note and mortgage to me, that same be released and the note and mortgage returned to him marked paid. Dated July 7, 1966.

/s/ S. R. Jones"

. . . The trial judge recited as one finding of fact:

"S. R. Jones intended to renounce the note and his right, title and interest therein, without the necessity of actually relinquishing control of the note itself."

That finding, so far as it is considered, as a *factual* finding, is obviously not clearly erroneous, so it will not be disturbed.

But that finding of fact does not lead to the trial court's conclusion of law [that] the *intended* release legally accomplished its purpose. . . .

Patently, Jones was mindful when the release was typed that Cotton might make further payments on the note—indeed that it might be fully paid. Clearly, he did not purport to remit the debt except on the contingency that Jones should die before the death of B. C. Cotton. Most importantly, Jones never delivered the release to Cotton and never parted with dominion over it. Nobody but Jones, or his qualified personal representatives at his death, had any right to enter the lockbox. If Jones had elected to sue on the note, Cotton could not have interposed the release as a defense. If Jones had changed his mind, he could have destroyed the release or modified it, and Cotton would have had no recourse. In short, we agree with the trial judge that Jones thought he had done all that was legally required; but that fact, without more, did not accomplish the intended result.

Section 3-605(1)(b), in treating the legal requirements for cancellation and renunciation of a note, provides that the result may be achieved:

"(b) by renouncing his right by a writing signed *and delivered* or by surrender of the instrument to the party to be discharged." [Emphasis supplied.] . . .

It follows that the court erred in entering judgment for appellees [plaintiffs] and dismissing the appellants' [defendants'] counterclaim on the note.

The judgment is reversed for proceedings consistent with the opinion.

Impairment of Right of Recourse; Impairment of Collateral Unless they agree to the contrary, the liability of unqualified indorsers is established by the order in which they indorse. That order is presumed to be the order in which their signatures appear on the instrument

[3-414]. Thus, in the event that an instrument is dishonored, an indorser who pays the instrument has a right of recourse not only against the drawer, maker, or acceptor, but also against any prior unqualified indorser who has received timely notice of dishonor. However, if the holder of an instrument impairs the right of recourse of an indorser or some other party, that party is discharged to the extent of the impairment.

Impairment of recourse takes many forms, for example, a cancellation of a signature or an agreement not to sue. A holder's granting an extension of time for payment is also an impairment of recourse, because the extension prevents collection on the date originally contemplated by the various parties to the instrument. Impairment of recourse is illustrated in the following paragraphs.

Suppose that Martha issues a note to the order of Peter; that the note is successively indorsed to Agnes, Betty, Carl, and Harold; and that Harold discharges Carl from liability by canceling Carl's indorsement. Harold's discharge of Carl does not impair the right of recourse of Betty or Agnes because neither person had a right of recourse against Carl, a *subsequent* indorser.

But suppose that, instead of discharging Carl, Harold discharged Agnes by canceling her indorsement. When Betty and Carl indorsed the instrument, they might have done so in the expectation that Agnes would pay if others did not. If Harold canceled Agnes' indorsement without the consent of Betty and Carl, Harold has impaired their right of recourse and has discharged them from liability [3-606(1)]. Had Harold discharged Martha (the maker), he would thereby have discharged all other parties. This follows from the rule that an Article 3 discharge of a party who has no right of recourse on the instrument, such as Martha, discharges all other parties [3-601(3)(b)].

The impairment-of-recourse principle applies also to parties who are not indorsers but who have a right of recourse. For example, an accommodation maker has a right of recourse against the party accommodated. If the holder of a note *knows* that comaker A signed it for the accommodation of comaker B, and the holder releases comaker B without the consent of comaker A, the release discharges comaker A.

An unjustifiable impairment of collateral has the same effect as impairment of recourse. It discharges the party whose rights against others are jeopardized. Suppose that when Martha issued the note to Peter, she also pledged shares of stock to Peter as "collateral" (security) for payment of the note; that Peter indorsed the note and transferred the collateral to Agnes; that Agnes indorsed the note to Betty but, without Peter's consent, returned the collateral to Martha. By returning the shares to Martha, Agnes has prevented Peter from having access to the collateral in the event that Peter must pay the note. Peter's collateral is thereby impaired, and Peter is thus discharged, to the extent of the impairment, from liability to Agnes and Betty [3-606(1)(b)].

Reacquisition of Instrument An instrument is sometimes acquired by a person who was a prior holder. When such a reacquisition occurs, any intervening party is discharged as against the reacquiring party and subsequent holders not in due course [3-208]. For example, suppose that Paul indorses a note to Andrew, who indorses it to Brent, who indorses it back to Paul. The reacquisition of the instrument by Paul discharges Andrew and Brent as to Paul. Were this not true, Paul would have recourse against Andrew and Brent if the note is not paid when due, and then Andrew and Brent each would have a cause of action against Paul on his original indorsement. The purpose of the rule discharging intervening indorsers is to prevent such circular legal actions.

After reacquisition, the reacquirer (Paul, in the example) may keep the instrument until maturity and then seek to collect on it, or may decide to negotiate it again before maturity. If the reacquirer (Paul) decides to negotiate it, he may cancel (strike out) the intervening indorsements. Where the reacquirer negotiates after striking out the intervening indorsements, the intervening indorsers (Andrew and Brent in the example) are discharged *even against* subsequent holders in due course. The reason for this result is that cancellation of (for example, drawing a line through) a prior indorsement is notice to all subsequent takers that the prior indorser has been discharged.

Other Methods of Discharge   The Code provisions considered above relate to the most common methods of discharging liability on commercial paper. However, there are other methods of discharge, recognized by the general law of contracts, that apply to negotiable instruments [3-601(2)]. Thus, a party may be discharged from liability on an instrument by mutual rescission, novation, substituted contract, accord and satisfaction, contract not to sue, and impossibility of performance. These methods of discharge were discussed in Chapter 18. Other discharges, some of which were discussed in Chapter 33, arise apart from the UCC and the general law of contracts. Examples are a discharge in bankruptcy and a discharge imposed by a statute that renders gambling transactions illegal or void. As noted in the next chapter, certification of a check may also result in discharge.

Case 34.4   **Chancellor, Inc. v. Hamilton Appliance Co., Inc.**
418 A.2d 1326 (N.J. Dist. Ct., Small Claims Div., 1980)

Hamilton Appliance Co. (defendant) purchased from Chancellor, Inc., a wholesale distributor, 12 Pioneer home stereo systems for a total of $2,785.64. A dispute arose as to the quality of the merchandise, the wholesale price as of the time of sale, the goods that could be returned to the plaintiff seller, and the total amount actually owed by the defendant buyer. Plaintiff issued the defendant a credit of $1,805.76, leaving a balance due of $979.88. The defendant mailed a check to plaintiff in the amount of $734.88 with a notation on the front, "paid in full." The check was accompanied by a letter that summarized the dispute and explained how the amount was calculated. Plaintiff indorsed the reverse side of the check with the words "without prejudice," deposited it, and advised the defendant that the check was accepted without prejudice to the plaintiff's rights. Plaintiff then brought suit for $245.

SAUNDERS, J.S.C. This contract action raises the novel issue whether Section 1-207 of the UCC has altered the common-law principle of accord and satisfaction affecting "full payment checks." More specifically, the question is whether a disputed claim is extinguished when the debtor tenders to the creditor a check marked "paid in full" and the creditor deposits the check after indorsing it "without prejudice" and notifies the debtor he is reserving his right to contend for the balance of the claim. . . .

The court finds that there was a genuine dispute between the parties as to the amount of money due from defendant to plaintiff. . . . The New Jersey rule has been that when a check is tendered as payment for an unliquidated claim on the condition that it be accepted in full payment, the creditor is deemed to have accepted this condition by depositing the check for collection notwithstanding any obliteration or alteration. . . .

Plaintiff argues that Section 1-207 alters the common-law accord and satisfaction principle and permits the creditor to accept and cash the check offered and to sue the debtor for the balance if the creditor explicitly reserves his rights.

Section 1-207 states:

> A party who with explicit reservation of rights performs or promises performance or assents to performance in a manner demanded or offered by the other party does not thereby prejudice the rights reserved. Such words as "without prejudice," "under protest" or the like are sufficient.

There are no cases in New Jersey interpreting this section of the Code. . . . The reported decisions in other jurisdictions interpreting Section 1-207 and discussing its effect on the common-law rule of accord and satisfaction have not been in agreement.

Only New York has held that Section 1-207 has altered the common-law rule. [Citations.] Four courts have acquiesced to this view in dicta. Conversely, two courts have held specifically that Section 1-207 does not change existing law. . . .

The New York cases which have concluded that Section 1-207 permits a party to reserve his rights while cashing a check offered in full payment are distinguishable [from the case before this court]. [They] were decided on the strength of the New York Annotations to the Code. . . . The New York annotation clearly deals with the effect of Section 1-207 on the "full payment check" and concludes that the rule of accord and satisfaction has been changed [in New York]. However, . . . the New Jersey Study Comment did not adopt the New York Study Commission's report and conducted its own analysis of the Code. It gave no indication that, in adopting Section 1-207, the New Jersey Legislature would change the common-law rule. . . .

The plaintiff argues that the legislature intended Section 1-207 to redefine the law of accord and satisfaction and to restrict the use of the "full payment check." A review of the Comments to Section 1-207 and its legislative history reveals no such intent. The New Jersey Study Comment does not mention the rule on accord and satisfaction. The Comment only states that Section 1-207 is in accord with its predecessor statute, Section 49 of the Uniform Sales Act. Section 49 did not purport to alter the rule of common-law accord and satisfaction. Its language spoke only to the acceptance of goods, not payments. . . . It would appear that the legislature adopted Section 1-207 presupposing that it reflected existing law.

Similarly, the UCC Comments to Section 1-207 do not reflect a legislative intent to change the common-law rule. Comment One states that "This section provides machinery for the *continuation of performance along the lines contemplated by the contract* despite a pending dispute . . ." [Emphasis supplied.] An accord and satisfaction involves a new contract, not the contemplated performance of the original contract. By using the "full payment check" the buyer is seeking to fulfill [discharge], not continue, its duty to pay. . . .

The court does not find any evidence in either the legislative history of the commentaries to Section 1-207 supporting the plaintiff's position that the law of accord and satisfaction has been altered [in New Jersey].

If the court were to conclude that a creditor could reserve his rights on a "full payment check," a convenient and informal device for the resolution of disagreements in the business community would be seriously impeded. The court is hesitant to impair such a valuable, informal settlement tool where there is no indication that the legislature intended that result. I find that the acceptance by the creditor of a check offered by the debtor in full payment of a disputed debt is an accord and satisfaction of the debt and no condition of protest or attempted reservation of rights can affect the legal quality of the action. I hold that Section 1-207 has not altered the common-law rule of accord and satisfaction.

Judgment for the defendant.

Effect of Discharge on Holder in Due Course

As noted throughout the above discussion, and in Chapter 33, most methods of discharge are not effective against a holder in due course who was without notice of the discharge when he or she took the instrument. Generally, discharge of a party is a personal defense that is cut off by a subsequent holder in due course who is without notice of it. For example, where a maker pays a note before its maturity and does not cancel it or compel its surrender, a subsequent holder in due course may require the maker to pay again. However, some discharges, such as a discharge in bankruptcy, are real defenses and are good even against a holder in due course.

WARRANTY LIABILITY

As previously noted, a negotiable instrument is not merely a contract; it is also a species of property subject to sale. Sellers of goods make certain warranties (i.e., guaranties). So do sell-

ers and other transferors of commercial paper. Warranties made by transferors of negotiable instruments who receive consideration are called "transfer warranties." Other warranties are made by transferees who present commercial paper for payment or acceptance and are called "presentment warranties." Presentment warranties are also made by *any prior transferor,* whether or not that person received consideration for the instrument.

The existence of warranty liability becomes especially important where a person from whom payment is sought has no liability on the instrument. Examples of parties with no *contractual* liability include: a qualified indorser, a signer who has been discharged from liability, and a person who has negotiated an instrument without signing it. Yet, signers and nonsigners alike are liable for any actual damages resulting from their breach of a warranty. Moreover, when there is a breach of a transfer warranty by a transferor-indorser, the transferee need not expend time and effort to enforce contractual liability of the parties. The transferee may immediately rescind the transfer by returning the instrument to the transferor, and receive back anything paid for it.

Warranties Made by Sellers of Commercial Paper

Any person, including a thief, who transfers a negotiable instrument and receives consideration for it makes five warranties. The warranties made by sellers concern (1) title, (2) signatures, (3) alterations, (4) insolvency proceedings, and (5) defenses. If the person transfers the instrument without signing it (as, for example, in the transfer of bearer paper), the warranties run only to that person's immediate transferee. If the transfer is by indorsement, the warranties run to *any* subsequent holder who takes the instrument in good faith [3-417(2)]. The remedies of damages or rescission, mentioned in the preceding paragraph, apply to breach of any of the five warranties.

Warranty Concerning Title A seller of a negotiable instrument warrants "that he has good title to the instrument or is authorized to obtain payment or acceptance on behalf of one who has a good title and [that] the transfer is otherwise rightful" [3-417(2)(a)]. This warranty is breached when a bearer instrument that has been found or stolen is sold by the finder or thief; or when there is a sale of an instrument on which a necessary indorsement has been forged; or when the transferor purports to act on behalf of another person but is unauthorized to do so; or when the transferor has authority to act on behalf of another but the person for whom the transferor acts does not have a good title to the instrument.

Warranty Concerning Signatures A seller of commercial paper warrants that all signatures are genuine or authorized [3-417(2)(b)]. Thus, a transferee may sue the seller (or rescind if the seller has indorsed) if the signature of a maker, drawer, acceptor, or indorser is forged or unauthorized.

Warranty Concerning Alterations A seller of commercial paper warrants that the instrument has not been materially altered [3-417(2)(c)]. Thus, suppose that D drew a check for $100 payable to the order of P; that P indorsed the check in blank and delivered it to X; and that X raised the check to $2,100 and then negotiated it by delivery to H for $2,100. As we saw earlier in this chapter, if H is a holder in due course, P and D are liable to H for $100, the original tenor of the instrument. But H also has a cause of action for breach of warranty against X. When X transferred the check to H and received consideration, X warranted that the check had not been materially altered. A breach of warranty entitles H to a recovery of actual damages: here, $2,000 plus cost of litigation.

Warranty Concerning Insolvency Proceedings A seller of a negotiable instrument warrants "that he has no knowledge of any insolvency proceeding instituted with respect to the maker or acceptor or the drawer of an unaccepted instrument" [3-417(2)(e)]. Were it not for this warranty, a holder of bearer paper who *knows* that insolvency proceedings have been instituted against a maker, drawer, or acceptor could avoid almost certain loss by negotiating the instrument, without indorsement, to an unsuspecting transferee.

Warranty Concerning Defenses The warranty concerning defenses varies according to the type of seller. A seller who transfers a negotiable instrument and makes an unqualified indorsement, or transfers without indorsement, warrants flatly that "no defense of any party is good against him" [3-417(2)(d)]. On the other hand, a seller who makes a *qualified* indorsement (one "without recourse") warrants only that he or she has no knowledge of a defense of any party [3-417(3)]. This less burdensome warranty is consistent with the qualified indorser's freedom from *contractual* liability, yet imposes warranty liability if the seller acts in bad faith.

Warranties Made by Presenters and All Prior Transferors

When a holder or other person presents any negotiable instrument to a maker, drawee, or acceptor, and receives payment, or presents a draft or check to a drawee and obtains an acceptance, the presenter impliedly makes three warranties ("presentment warranties") to the payor or acceptor. The warranties concern (1) title, (2) signatures, and (3) alterations. In addition, these three warranties are made by all prior transferors (sellers and nonsellers). Without these warranties the payor or acceptor may suffer a loss. For example, suppose the presenter of an instrument receives payment in full from the maker or drawee. Shortly thereafter, the payor discovers that a necessary indorsement was forged. Can the payor recover from the presenter the money paid? If the presenter is not an indorser (signer), the payor has no contractual recourse to the presenter. However, the payor may recover from the presenter for breach of warranty.

Warranty Concerning Title A person who obtains payment or acceptance warrants (and any prior transferor warrants) to the payor or acceptor that "he has a good title to the instrument or is authorized to obtain payment or acceptance on behalf of one who has a good title" [3-417(1)(a)]. For example, suppose that M makes a note payable to the order of P, that P loses the note without having indorsed it, and that X finds it. Suppose further that X forges P's in-blank indorsement and sells the note to H, and that H presents the note to M for payment and receives payment. No one can get title to an order instrument through a forged indorsement. Thus, P remains the owner of the note and can collect payment from M even though M has already made payment. Because H was not required to and did not indorse the note, H is not a party to it and has no contractual liability to M. However, when H presented the note to M, H impliedly warranted that he had good title. By not having title, H has breached the "presentment" warranty of title and is liable to M for damages. In turn, H has a cause of action against X for breach of X's "transfer" warranty of title. X, a "prior transferor," has also made a presentment warranty of title to M and is liable to M for its breach.

Case 34.5 **Oak Park Currency Exchange, Inc. v. Maropoulos**
363 N.E.2d 54 (Ill. App. 1977)

John Bugay possessed a check drawn to the order of Henry Sherman, Inc., and fraudulently indorsed "Henry Sherman" on the reverse side. Bugay sought the assistance of defendant, James Maropoulos, in cashing it. Defendant took Bugay to the plaintiff, Oak Park Currency Exchange, Inc., where defendant was known. At the currency exchange defendant identified himself, and the exchange agreed to cash the check if defendant would indorse it. He indorsed the check, received the money, and gave it immediately to Bugay.

Plaintiff indorsed and deposited the check in Belmont National Bank. The indorsement "Henry Sherman" was subsequently found to be a forgery. The bank sought and received payment back from plaintiff. Plaintiff, in turn, sought payment from defendant on his indorsement and for breach of warranty and filed this suit. The trial court directed a verdict in favor of defendant, and plaintiff appealed.

GOLDBERG, P. J. . . . In this court, plaintiff urges that defendant breached his warranty of good title when he obtained payment of a check on which the payee's indorsement was forged and that there was sufficient evidence to support a directed verdict in favor of plaintiff. Plaintiff's contentions are based exclusively on Section 3-417(1) of the Code. Defendant contends that an accommodation indorser does not make warranties under Section 3-417(1) and that the trial court properly directed a verdict for the defendant.

A party who signs an instrument "for the purpose of lending his name to another party to . . ." that instrument is an accommodation party. Section 3-415(1). Such a party "is liable in the capacity in which he has signed . . ." Section 3-415(2). Therefore defendant is an accommodation indorser and would be liable to plaintiff under his indorser's contract, provided that he had received timely notice that the check had been presented to the drawee bank and dishonored. Section 3-414. Because these conditions precedent to the contractual liability of an indorser have not been met, defendant is not liable on his contract as an accommodation indorser.

Furthermore, the drawee bank, American National, did not dishonor the check but paid it. This operated to discharge the liability of defendant as an accommodation indorser.

The portion of the Code upon which plaintiff seeks to hold defendant liable is Section 3-417 entitled "Warranties on Presentment and Transfer." . . . Section 3-417(1) sets out warranties which run only to a party who "pays or accepts" an instrument upon presentment. We note that presentment is defined as "a demand for acceptance or payment made upon the maker, acceptor, drawee, or other payor . . ." Section 3-504(1). As applied to the instant case, the warranties contained in Section 3-417(1) . . . run only to the payor bank and not to any other transferee who acquired the check. In the case before us, plaintiff is not a payor or acceptor of the draft. . . . The case before us involves a transferee, not a party who paid or accepted the instrument. Thus it appears that reliance by plaintiff upon subsection 3-417(1) was misplaced. . . .

An additional theory requires affirmance of the judgment appealed from. Subsection 3-417(2) of the Code provides that one "who transfers an instrument and receives consideration warrants to his transferee . . ." that he has good title. . . . The evidence presented in the case at bar establishes that defendant received no consideration for his indorsement. Though Mrs. Panveno [plaintiff's employee] testified that she saw Bugay hand defendant some money as the two left the currency exchange, she also testified that defendant stated that he was doing a favor for his friend; that she was not paying close attention to the two men and that she did not watch them as they walked away from her. Thus her testimony was considerably weakened by her own qualifying statements and it was strongly and directly contradicted by the positive and unshaken testimony of defendant that he received nothing in return for his assistance. The simple fact standing alone that this witness saw Bugay hand some money to defendant, even if proved, would have no legal significance without additional proof of some type showing that the payment was consideration for defendant's indorsement.

Judgment affirmed.

Warranty Concerning Signature of Maker or Drawer A person who obtains payment or acceptance warrants (and any prior transferor warrants) that "he has no knowledge that the signature of the maker or drawer is unauthorized . . ." [3-417(1)(b)]. This warranty is *not* given by a holder in due course acting in good faith to (1) a maker with respect to the maker's own signature; or (2) a drawer with respect to the drawer's own signature; or (3) an acceptor if the holder in due course took the draft after the acceptance or if the holder in due course obtained the acceptance without knowledge that the drawer's signature was unauthorized.

Suppose that an employee of M forges M's signature to a bearer note, that the employee sells the note to X, and that X sells the note to H, a holder in due course who *later* learns of the forgery but presents the note to M for payment anyway. If M detects the forgery and refuses to pay the note, H cannot collect from M because forgery of a maker's signature is a real defense good against even a holder in due course. But if M *pays* the note, later discovers the forgery, and brings suit to recover from H the amount paid, M may lose. Under Section 3-418, payment is final in favor of a holder in due course, unless the holder in due course breached a warranty. Section 3-417(1)(b) expressly exempts H from warranting no knowledge of the forgery of the *maker's own* signature where H obtains payment in good faith, in the honest belief, for example, that M negligently permitted the forgery. The justification is that as between two innocent parties, the one to bear the loss should be the maker, since presumably the maker can take precautions to verify his or her own signature before payment is made. Also, the fact that payment to a holder in due course is final tends to minimize litigation and to enhance the marketability of commercial paper.

Warranty Concerning Alterations A person who obtains payment or acceptance warrants (and any prior transferor warrants) to the payor or acceptor that the instrument has not been materially altered [3-417(1)(c)]. This warranty is subject to exceptions similar to the exceptions relating to signature warranties; that is, holders in due course acting in good faith do not warrant to makers, drawers, or most acceptors that the instrument has not been materially altered. Again, the justification is that upon presentment these parties would likely discover an alteration made after they signed the instrument.

SUMMARY

The Code imposes contractual liability on signers of commercial paper. A signer may have either primary or secondary liability on an instrument. A primary party (a maker or an acceptor) is liable for payment immediately when the instrument comes due. A secondary party (a drawer or an indorser) is liable for payment only upon the happening of certain conditions precedent to liability: presentment, dishonor, and notice of dishonor.

The liability of any accommodation party is determined by the capacity in which he or she signs. For example, an accommodation maker has primary liability; an accommodation indorser has secondary liability. A guarantor is a drawer or indorser who promises to pay an instrument that is not paid when due by the primary party, without resort to any other party.

Liability on a negotiable instrument may be affected by the signatures of agents and forgers. If an authorized agent signs incorrectly, the agent may be personally liable on an instrument, although the agent may intend that only the principal be liable. An unauthorized signature is generally inoperative, but does make the unauthorized *signer* liable. A principal may be liable on an instrument obtained by a dishonest employee and made payable to an imposter or a fictitious payee.

As an instrument goes its rounds, the liability of various persons may be terminated, that is, discharged. The discharge of one party may result in the discharge of other parties to the instrument. Among the methods of discharge are payment, tender of payment, fraudulent and material alteration, unexcused delay in presentment or in notice of dishonor, cancellation or renunciation, impairment of right of recourse, impairment of collateral, and reacquisition. Most methods of discharge are not effective against a subsequent holder in due course who ·was without notice of the discharge when he or she took the instrument.

Because a negotiable instrument is a species of property subject to sale, sellers of commercial paper make "transfer" warranties to transferees. Transfer warranties concern title, signatures, alterations, insolvency proceedings, and defenses. "Presentment" warranties are made by persons who receive payment on an instrument, or acceptance of a draft or check, and by all prior transferors. These warranties are made to payors and acceptors and concern title, signatures, and alterations.

STUDY AND DISCUSSION QUESTIONS

1 *(a)* Distinguish between primary and secondary liability on an instrument. *(b)* Do all instruments have primary parties? Explain.

2 *(a)* To whom does the drawer make a promise to pay? *(b)* To whom does an unqualified indorser make a promise to pay?

3 Briefly explain the meaning and purpose of *(a)* presentment, *(b)* dishonor, and *(c)* notice of dishonor.

4 How long, and why, may acceptance or payment be delayed without the delay being considered a dishonor?

5 *(a)* How is the nature of an accommodation party's liability determined? *(b)* To whom may an accommodation party be liable? *(c)* Against whom may an accommodation party have recourse?

6 What is the significance of indorsing "Payment guaranteed"? "Collection guaranteed"?

7 *(a)* What two things must an agent's form of signature contain in order for the agent to avoid liability on the instrument? *(b)* Under what circumstances may an agent introduce parol evidence to avoid such liability?

8 John Doe receives a check made payable to his order. A thief steals it, indorses it in Doe's name, and transfers it for value to Holder. *(a)* Is Doe liable on the instrument? Why? *(b)* Is the thief? Why?

9 A person might by his or her negligence substantially contribute to the unauthorized signing of a check and thereby be precluded from asserting lack of authority against a holder in due course. *(a)* Describe such a situation. *(b)* Why is the holder in due course favored in such a situation?

10 Who is liable on an instrument made out to an "imposter" or a "fictitious payee"? Why?

11 *(a)* Under what circumstances will payment not discharge a maker, acceptor, or indorser of an instrument? *(b)* What effect does a person's taking a check have on the *underlying* obligation? *(c)* Under what circumstances will tender of payment discharge the tendering party? *(d)* Whom does a tender of payment discharge? Whom does it not discharge?

12 *(a)* Under what circumstances might the alteration of an issued negotiable instrument result in the discharge of a person whose contract has thereby been changed? *(b)* If an alteration discharges a party to the instrument, against whom would the discharge be effective? Explain or illustrate.

13 *(a)* Whom does unexcused delay completely discharge? *(b)* Under what circumstances will unexcused delay discharge a maker, drawer, or acceptor? *(c)* Ordinarily, unexcused delay will not discharge a maker or acceptor. Why?

14 *(a)* For what reasons might a holder discharge a signer by cancellation or renunciation? *(b)* How is cancellation done? *(c)* How is renunciation done?

15 *(a)* What is meant by "impairment of recourse"? *(b)* Explain how the discharge of one party might result in the unintentional discharge of another or of others. *(c)* Illustrate impairment of collateral.

16 *(a)* Why does reacquisition of an instrument result in the discharge of intervening indorsers? *(b)* Suppose that a party reacquires an instrument and cancels the signature of an intervening indorser. What liability has that indorser to a subsequent holder in due course? Why?

17 *(a)* Who makes a transfer warranty? *(b)* To whom is a transfer warranty made by an indorser?

18 *(a)* Explain or illustrate how each of the following "transfer" warranties made by sellers is breached: warranty of title; warranty concerning signatures; and warranty against alterations. *(b)* How does a qualified indorsement affect the warranty concerning defenses? Why?

19 How do presentment warranties differ from transfer warranties with regard to *(a)* who makes them, and *(b)* who receives them?

20 *(a)* Explain or illustrate the presentment warranty of title. *(b)* Why does a holder in due course acting in good faith *not* warrant the signature of the maker, drawer, or most acceptors upon presentment to those parties?

CASE PROBLEMS

1 Danje Fabrics hired Caulder as its accounts payable bookeeper. Specialty Dyers, in the business of dyeing fabrics, had dyed fabrics for Danje for years. Specialty Dyers periodically submitted to Danje correct invoices for work done. Caulder made out checks to Specialty Dyers for the amounts specified in the invoices. Caulder submitted the checks, together with the original invoices and adding machine tapes, to the Danje officials authorized to sign the checks. Those officials signed the checks. Caulder then took twenty-seven of the checks and diverted them into an account that he had opened at Citibank in the name of Specialty Dyers. Citibank collected the amounts of the checks from the drawee, Morgan Guaranty Trust Co. Caulder withdrew the funds from the Citibank account and disappeared. Danje brought action against Morgan for wrongfully debiting Danje's account on the basis of forged instruments. Is Morgan (the drawee) liable to Danje?

2 Defendant executed and delivered to plaintiff a note dated July 14, 1967. In the body of the note appeared the words, "Due and payable ten months and seventeen days after date of execution." In the upper left corner was the typed notation "Due June 1, 1968." About 6 months after the note became due, plaintiff gave it to his bank for collection. An officer of the bank, observing that the due date was incorrectly stated in the notation at the upper left corner, penciled in the date "5/31/68" above the typed date of June 1, 1968. Did this change constitute an alteration that precluded the payee from collecting on the note?

3 Brannan created Sunrise Resources, Inc.,

for the purpose of investing in oil leases, and was seeking capital for that enterprise. Baird executed a note for $100,000 payable to the order of Brannan. The note was executed on a standard printed note form. Beneath his signature Baird wrote that the note was conditioned on Sunrise Resources, Inc., obtaining a minimum of $500,000 in subscriptions. Baird delivered the note to Brannan. Brannan cut off the conditional part of the note, and pledged the note as an apparently complete document to a bank as security for a loan. The bank sued on the note. Baird pleaded as a defense the material alteration of the instrument. Was the defense good?

4 John Doe issued the following draft to Paula Payee:

> February 1, 1979
> Thirty days after date, pay to the order of
> Paula Payee the sum of one thousand eight hundred dollars ($1,800.00). This draft is payable at
> First State Bank, Arrow Head, Arizona.
>   To: First State Bank
>   Arrow Head, Arizona   *John Doe*

On the date the draft was due, Doe had sufficient funds on deposit at First State Bank in Arrow Head, Arizona, to pay the draft. Three months later Doe withdrew the funds. Payee presented the draft at First State Bank on January 15, 1980. The bank dishonored the draft. Payee immediately sought payment from Doe. Doe refused to pay on the ground that Payee's delay in presenting the draft was unexcused and resulted in Doe's discharge. Was Doe discharged?

5 Howard executed and delivered to K & S International, Inc., an installment note in the amount of $2,200 for the unpaid portion of the purchase price of a farm combine. The payee, K & S, indorsed and transferred the note to its

bank. Upon default by Howard in his payments, K & S paid in full the amount that was due the bank on the note. The bank returned the note to K & S, and that company brought an action on the note against Howard. Howard defended on the ground that under the UCC his liability was discharged by the reacquisition of the instrument by a prior party. Was the defense sound?

6 Martin Maker executed and delivered to Paula Payee a 30-day note in the amount of $195 payable to the order of Payee. Payee indorsed the note in blank and "without recourse" and sold it to Alfred Anderson. Anderson indorsed the note in blank and "without recourse" sold it to Betty Brown. Brown, without indorsing the note, sold it to Harold Holder. After the due date of the note, Holder presented it to Maker for payment. Maker refused to pay, correctly stating that he had given the note to Paula Payee for a gambling debt and that a state statute made gambling instruments null and void. *(a)* Assume that Holder sued Brown for breach of warranty. Judgment for whom? *(b)* Assume that Holder sued Anderson for breach of warranty. Judgment for whom? *(c)* Assume that Holder sued Payee for breach of warranty. Judgment for whom?

7 Martin Maker executed a note payable to the order of Paula Payee. Payee lost the note. Fred Forger, the finder, forged Payee's indorsement and sold the note to Georgia Goodenough, who indorsed and sold the note to Harold Holder. Neither Goodenough nor Holder was aware of the forgery. Holder presented the note at maturity, and Maker paid it. Later Maker discovered that the signature on the instrument was a forgery. *(a)* Assume that Maker sued Holder for breach of warranty. Judgment for whom? *(b)* Assume that instead of suing Holder, Maker sued Goodenough for breach of warranty. What judgment?

Chapter

35

Checks; Relationship between Bank and Customer

Nearly all business firms and individuals beyond the age of childhood have a checking account. They issue checks drawn on their bank; and they deposit for collection checks, drafts, matured bonds, interest coupons, and various other instruments calling for payment in money. In banking parlance, any such instrument is referred to as an "item."

Previous chapters in this series dealt with many important aspects of checks. As pointed out in Chapter 30, a check performs a currency function; it is a substitute for money. Although a check is not a credit instrument (it cannot be payable in installments), it is freely transferable and a transferee may purchase a check and become a holder in due course. Thus, the topics covered in Chapters 31 through 34, which apply to all negotiable instruments, govern the relationship of the parties to a check.

There are additional laws, however, that apply to checks and banks. Article 4 of the Uniform Commercial Code (UCC) is devoted to

the subject of Bank Deposits and Collections. Much of the Article is complex and of importance only to firms and individuals in the banking business. This chapter is concerned primarily with Part 4 of the Article, which deals with the relationship between a bank and its customers.

CHECKS

Special Nature of Checks

As noted previously, a check is a particular kind of draft. Two features distinguish a check from other kinds of drafts: a check is always drawn on a bank, and a check is always payable on demand. Figure 35.1 illustrates the relationship among the persons normally involved in issuing and cashing a check.

A check is an order to the bank to pay a specified amount from the drawer's account. A

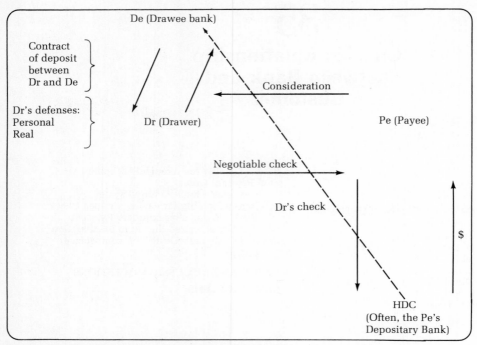

Figure 35.1 Negotiable Check—The Basic Situation.

check does not "of itself" operate as an assignment [3-409(1)].[1] It is not an assignment because it does not show an intention to make a *present transfer* of the right to the specified

[1]Numbers within brackets in the text refer to sections of the UCC. The phrase "of itself" makes clear that a check *may* operate as an assignment where, from all the facts, "and particularly from other agreements, express or implied," there was an intent to assign [Comment 1].

sum. Since a check is not an assignment, the drawee bank is not liable to the payee or holder if it refuses to pay the check, even though there are sufficient funds on deposit to cover the check. However, the bank may be liable to the drawer for refusing to pay. The bank's liability for wrongful refusal to pay is discussed later in this chapter.

Case 35.1   Lambeth v. Lewis
150 S.E.2d 462 (Ga. App. 1966)

Plaintiff Lambeth sued to recover on a check that had been issued to him as payee by a person since deceased. Defendant, the administrator of decedent's estate, filed a demurrer to plaintiff's petition. The trial court overruled the demurrer, and the defendant appealed.

JORDAN, J. . . . The petition affirmatively showed that the plaintiff had not presented the check to the bank for payment, or otherwise negotiated it, during the drawer's lifetime.

(1) A check does not of itself operate as an assignment of any part of the drawer's funds deposited with the bank upon which the check is drawn (UCC, sec. 3-409), but is merely an order upon a bank to pay from the drawer's account. It may be revoked at any time by the drawer before it has been certified, accepted or paid by the bank, and is revoked by operation of law 10 days after the death of the drawer although the drawee bank is not liable where it has in good faith honored such instrument without knowledge of the depositor's death. (Code sec. 4-405.) . . .

The mere execution of the check sued upon in this case did not create an indebtedness on the part of the drawer since the order to pay was revoked by his death without prior presentment by the payee; and since the drawer's estate could only be held liable for debts created by the decedent in his lifetime, it necessarily follows that the plaintiff here must rely upon the underlying claim, if any, and not the check as the basis for recovery.

(2) The petition in this case alleged that the plaintiff had performed certain personal services for the drawer of the check during his lifetime and that the check was given for a valuable consideration, but it expressly declared upon (relied upon) the check itself as the basis of the plaintiff's cause of action and not upon any underlying claim of indebtedness which the check might have represented. The petition did not therefore state a cause of action against the decedent's estate; and the trial court erred in overruling the defendant administrator's general demurrer.

Judgment reversed.

Certified Checks

Certification is the acceptance of a check by a drawee bank which, by stamping the word "certified" on the face of the check, becomes primarily liable on it. Usually the drawer seeks certification at the request of the payee who is unwilling to rely on the credit of the drawer alone. Unless otherwise agreed, a bank is under no obligation to certify a check [3-411(2)]. Usually, however, banks are quite willing to certify a check, provided the drawer has sufficient funds to cover it. Before certifying a check, the bank places a "hold" on the drawer's account for the amount of the check.

Where the bank certifies a check at the request of the *payee* or a *holder*, the drawer and all prior indorsers are discharged [3-411(1)]. Thus, certification procured by the payee or holder

> differs in effect from mere acceptance of bills [i.e., drafts] other than checks in that it is not an added obligation but a substituted obligation. . . . Where the holder of a check sees fit, instead of receiving money, to take the obligation of a bank for payment, the transaction is of the same effect as if he drew the money and then bought the bank's obligation with it.[2]

---

[2]*Wachtel v. Rosen*, 164 N.E. 326 (N.Y. 1928).

Where the bank certifies a check at the request of the *drawer,* the drawer is not discharged from liability. The certification merely adds, to the drawer's secondary liability on the check, the primary liability of the certifying bank. Thus, in the event a lawsuit is initiated it is important to determine who requested certification—the holder or the drawer.

RELATIONSHIP BETWEEN BANK AND CUSTOMER

Contract between Bank and Customer

By opening a checking account, an individual or business firm enters into a contract with the bank. The technical complexities of banking operations are so great that it is not feasible to include in a printed contract all the rights and duties of the parties. Many of these rights and duties are governed by provisions of the UCC. However, the bank and customer are free to vary the effect of a Code provision, except that no agreement can disclaim a bank's responsibility for its own lack of good faith or its failure to exercise ordinary care [4-103(1)].

Although it is not feasible to include in a printed contract all the terms of the contract, most banks require their checking account customers to sign a form, called a "signature card," that includes some of the principal contract provisions. Often the printed form deals with such matters as the bank's handling of items received from the customer for deposit or collection, the depositor's responsibility when the depositor requests the bank to stop payment on a check, and the service charges to which the account shall be subject. If litigation involves a problem that is not governed by special contract or by statute, courts look to the common law and to banking usage for the solution.

Nature of Bank-Customer Relationship

There is a dual relationship between a bank and its checking account customer: that of debtor and creditor and that of principal and agent. When the customer makes a deposit to the customer's account, the bank becomes a debtor. In the event of the bank's bankruptcy, the customer is a general creditor of the bank. If a customer deposits a check or other item for collection, the relationship as to the particular item is that of principal and agent.[3] The Code provides that "unless a contrary intent clearly appears," a collecting bank "is an agent or sub-agent of the owner of the item and any settlement given for the item is provisional" [4-201(1)].[4] However, at some stage in the bank collection process the agency status of a collecting bank changes to that of debtor, a debtor of its customer. Thus, upon *collection* of payment of the item deposited for collection, a debtor-creditor relationship results. A bank also acts as an agent for the customer in honoring checks properly drawn on the account payable to the customer's order.

When Bank May Charge Customer's Account

It is fundamental that when the bank honors a check properly drawn on the customer's account, or certifies a customer's check, it *debits,* or charges, the customer's account for the amount of the check. There are several situations where the bank's right to charge the customer's account may be questioned.

Payment of Overdraft In the absence of some arrangement with the bank for permitting overdrafts, the customer has no right to overdraw an account; and the bank has no obligation to pay an overdraft. If the bank chooses to honor a check creating an overdraft, the bank is authorized by the UCC to do so [4-401(1)]. The authorization carries with it the customer's implied promise to reimburse the drawee bank.

---

[3]The relationship of principal and agent is discussed in Chapter 36.

[4]"Collecting bank" means any bank handling the item for collection. The collection process is illustrated in Chapter 32 at page 672.

Because the obligation to repay the overdraft is without interest, many banks offer a special kind of checking account ("ready reserve checking account") that allows the customer to overdraw an account by a stated number of dollars. The customer is charged interest on the overdraft.

Payment of Altered Check   We saw in Chapter 33 that where a holder in due course takes an instrument that has been altered, the holder may enforce the instrument according to its original tenor [3-407(3)]. The Code gives parallel protection to a drawee bank by providing that if the bank in good faith makes payment of an altered check, it may charge the customer's account according to the original tenor of the check (i.e., the original amount)[4-401(2)(a)]. For example, if a customer issues a check in the amount of $100 and a holder alters the amount to $2,100 and the check is paid in good faith by the drawee bank, the bank may charge the drawer's account with only $100. However, where a bank pays a raised check, it may charge the drawer's account with the full amount paid if (1) the drawer's negligence substantially contributed to the alteration, and (2) payment by the bank was made in good faith and in accordance with reasonable commercial standards in the banking business [3-406].

Payment of Check Incomplete **When Issued** A check containing a material omission, such as lack of amount or lack of a named payee, will not be honored by the bank. However, the payee or holder of an incomplete check may fill in the missing information and present the check for payment. The Code provides that if the bank in good faith makes payment of a completed item, it may charge the customer's account according to the manner in which the item has been completed [4-401(2)(b)]. To illustrate, suppose that a customer signs a blank check and delivers it to the payee, telling that person to "fill it in for the amount I owe you," and the payee fills it in for twice the amount. If the bank in good faith pays the check, it may charge the drawer's account with the amount of the check as com-

pleted. Thus, the risk of loss is on the signer who, by issuing an incomplete instrument, made loss possible. The bank is protected even though it has knowledge of the completion, as for instance if the payee fills in the amount in the presence of a bank employee. The bank is not allowed to charge the customer's account if it is on notice that the completion was improper.

Payment of Stale Check   Banks generally call checks that are outstanding for 6 months or more "stale" checks. The drawee bank is not obligated to pay a check, other than a certified check, that is presented to it more than 6 months after the check is issued. If the bank chooses to honor a stale check, it may charge the customer's account, provided the payment is made in good faith [4-404].

Payment of Postdated Check   Postdating a check has no effect on its negotiability. A postdated check therefore is freely transferable and may be negotiated to a holder in due course. A few courts have indicated that the legal effect of postdating a check is to convert it into a time draft. If a holder presents the check to the drawee bank for payment before the specified date, the bank may properly refuse payment. The reason is that the bank could be held liable to its customer for paying a postdated check early, charging the customer's account, and thereby reducing the balance in the account to a point where currently payable checks are dishonored. A bank will not be held liable for paying a postdated check if the drawer's own negligence is the cause of the drawer's loss or if the drawer postdated the check for a fraudulent purpose.

Bank's Liability
for Wrongful Dishonor

A bank is liable to its customer for damages caused by the wrongful dishonor of the customer's check [4-402]. Since a bank is liable only for a "wrongful dishonor," it is not liable where the check was dishonored for lack of funds, or for lack of necessary indorsement, or for other good reasons. A bank is liable for wrongful dishonor only to the drawer. A payee or other holder of a check who is harmed by the bank's wrongful dishonor has no right of recovery against the bank.

Wrongful dishonor includes intentional refusal to pay a check, brought about by a mistake. Where the dishonor occurs through mistake, the bank's liability is limited to "actual damages proved." The Code *rejects* the view that the wrongful dishonor of a check necessarily de-

fames the drawer by a reflection on the drawer's credit and therefore entitles the drawer to an award without proof that damage has occurred.[5] The Code recognizes, however, that actual damages may include damages for an arrest or prosecution of the customer or other consequential damages, where such consequential damages are proximately caused by the wrongful dishonor of the check.

_____

[5]See discussion of the tort of libel, in Chapter 5.

Case 35.2   Bank of Louisville Royal v. Sims
435 S.W.2d 57 (Ky. App. 1968)

CLAY, Commissioner. Appellee [Sims, plaintiff in lower court] recovered $631.50 for the wrongful dishonor of two small checks. This sum included the following items of damage: $1.50 for a telephone call; $130 for two weeks lost wages; and $500 for "illness, harassment, embarrassment and inconvenience." The trial court, trying the case without a jury, found that the dishonor was due to a mistake and it was not malicious.

KRS 355.4-402 [UCC 4-402] provides:

"A payor bank is liable to its customers for damages *proximately caused* by the wrongful dishonor of an item. *When the dishonor occurs through mistake, liability is limited to actual damages proved.* If so proximately caused and proved, damages may include damages for an arrest or prosecution of the customer or *other consequential damages.* Whether any consequential damages are proximately caused by the wrongful dishonor is a question of fact to be determined in each case." [Emphasis added by the court.]

This statute does not define "consequential" damages but it is clear they must be proximately caused by the wrongful dishonor. . . . As in other cases of breach of contract, "proximately caused" damages, whether direct or consequential, would be those which could be reasonably foreseeable by the parties as the natural and probable result of the breach. [Citations.]

The plaintiff deposited for her account with appellant [Bank of Louisville Royal] a check for $756, drawn on an out-of-town bank. In order to permit such a check to clear, it was apparently customary for the bank to delay crediting the account for a period of three days. By mistake one of appellant's clerks posted a ten-day hold on this check, and during that period two of plaintiff's checks were dishonored and returned with the notation "Drawn Against Uncollected

Funds." Apparently she had some difficulty getting the matter straightened out.

The plaintiff had respiratory trouble and, because of it and a case of "nerves," her doctor advised her to take a two-week leave of absence from her place of employment, which she did. She testified she was embarrassed, humiliated, and mortified; but her principal complaint seems to be of the difficulty and delay in getting the bank to correct its mistake.

In *American National Bank v. Morey*, 113 Ky. 857, 69 S.W.759, it was held that if there was no basis for punitive damages for the dishonor of a check, recovery cannot be had for humiliation or mortification. It was also held that plaintiff's "nervous chill" was not the natural result of the dishonor or such a thing as could be reasonably anticipated. In *Berea Bank and Trust Co. v. Mokwa*, 194 Ky. 556, 239 S.W. 1044, it was recognized that loss of time could be a proper item of damages provided it was the direct and proximate result of the bank's refusal to honor a check.

On the authority of *Morey*, the plaintiff was not entitled to recover for her hurt feelings or for her "nerves." It followed, therefore, that she was likewise not entitled to recover for her two weeks lost time from work even if her mental state actually contributed to this loss. From the proximate cause standpoint, these nebulous items of damage bore no reasonable relationship to the dishonor of her two checks and consequently they could not be classified as "actual damages proved." (Had the action of the bank been willful or malicious, justifying a punitive award, damages of this kind might have been recoverable as naturally flowing from this type of tortious misconduct, but we do not have that question here.)

The charge for the telephone call was a proper item of damages.

The judgment is reversed, with direction to enter judgment for the plaintiff in the sum of $1.50.

Stop-Payment Order

Customer's Right to Stop Payment   Because a check is not an assignment of funds, but is a mere order to pay, it is subject to countermand by the person who ordered the payment. The Code recognizes the right of the customer to instruct the drawee bank not to pay a certain check by issuing a stop-payment order [4-403(1)]. However, the drawer's stop order affects only the relationship between the drawer and the drawee. The stop order *does not* rescind the drawer's engagement to pay the holder, and the holder may bring suit on the check, against the drawer, when the bank dishonors the check by giving effect to the stop order. Whether the holder will prevail depends on the usual factors

—for example, whether the holder is in due course or, if not, whether the drawer has a personal defense. Thus, as further explained later in this chapter in the section entitled *Bank's Rights after Improper Payment*, a stop-payment order will protect the drawer in certain situations but not in others. Ordinarily, there is a small charge to the customer for the bank's inconvenience in stopping payment.

A stop-payment order may be given orally or in writing. An oral order is binding on the bank for only 14 calendar days unless confirmed in writing within that period. A written order is effective for 6 months but may be renewed by the customer, in writing [4-403(2)].

To bind the bank, the stop-payment order

must be received in time to give the bank a reasonable opportunity to act on the order before it has either certified or paid the check. After the bank has certified a check (and has charged the customer's account) the drawer can no longer stop payment. A certification is the bank's own engagement (promise) to pay, and the bank is not required to impair its own credit by refusing payment for the convenience of the drawer [4-403; Comment 5].

Case 35.3 **National Newark & Essex Bank v. Giordano**
268 A.2d 327 (N.J. Super. 1970)

The defendant, Giordano, agreed to purchase from Joseph Fiero two trucks for use in his business. To enable Giordano to do so, the plaintiff bank agreed to lend him $9,500. The bank thereupon drew a check in that amount payable to the order of Fiero. Shortly after the defendant delivered the check to Fiero, he discovered the trucks were defective and requested the bank to stop payment on the check. The bank refused, claiming it could not stop payment on its own check. Thereafter, the bank sued Giordano, demanding judgment for the amount due under the loan agreement, plus interest and costs.

SUGRUE, J. . . . The primary issue raised is whether a bank may stop payment on its own check.

The question does not appear to have been decided in this state previously but there is a clear weight of authority in other jurisdictions which denies a bank the right to countermand its own check. [Citations.]

A check drawn by the bank upon itself is commonly referred to as a cashier's check. . . . [When a bank issues a cashier's check it] undertakes to draw the amount represented from its own resources. It must therefore of necessity be said that issuance of the cashier's check constitutes an acceptance of it by the issuing bank. In drawing the instrument, the bank represents that as drawee, it will honor the draft when presented. The requirements for an acceptance as set forth in NJSA 12A:3-410(1)[UCC 3-410(1)] are fulfilled by the affixing of the signature of the agent of the issuing bank. The rule may thus be stated that a cashier's check is accepted for payment when issued.

Under the provisions of NJSA 12A:4-303, a stop order, whether or not effective under other rules of law to terminate or suspend the bank's right or duty to pay an item, comes too late to terminate or suspend such right or duty if it is received after the bank has accepted or certified the item. Since a cashier's check is accepted when issued, NJSA 12A:4-303 in effect makes it impossible to stop payment on a cashier's check once it has been issued.

In addition to the statutory prohibition against stopping payment on a cashier's check, the nature and usage of these checks require such a rule. A cashier's check circulates in the commercial world as the equivalent of cash. People accept a cashier's check as a substitute for cash because the bank stands behind it rather than an individual. In effect the bank becomes a guarantor of the value of the check and pledges its resources to the payment of the amount represented upon presentation. To allow the bank to stop payment on such an instrument would be inconsistent with the representation it makes in issuing the check. Such a rule would undermine the public confidence in the bank and its checks and thereby deprive the cashier's check of the essential incident which makes it useful. People would no longer be willing to accept it as a substitute for cash if they could not be sure that there would be no difficulty in converting it into cash.

In support of his position defendant relies on NJSA 12A:4-403 which is entitled "Customer's Right to Stop Payment." The section authorizes a customer to order the bank to stop payment on any item payable for his account. A cashier's check is not one payable for the customer's account but rather for the bank's account. . . .

Defendant further relies on *Citizens National Bank of Englewood v. Ft. Lee Savings & Loan Assoc.*, 89 N.J. Super. 43, 213 A.2d 315 (1965). That case however involved a "bank check" drawn by one bank on its account in another bank rather than a cashier's check as in the case at bar. . . . The principal difference insofar as the present case is concerned is that a "bank check" is, in effect, an ordinary check since it is not accepted when issued and may be dishonored by the bank upon which it is drawn when it is presented for payment. This difference undermines the basic defense offered by the defendant at trial. Defendant's offer to post a bond to insure the plaintiff that it would not be damaged by stopping payment on the check is no defense to the plaintiff's action. The bank could not stop payment on its cashier's check as a matter of law. . . .

Judgment will be entered in favor of the plaintiff and against the defendant in the amount of $10,841.60.

Bank's Liability for Paying Stopped Check
The drawee bank may be liable to the customer for the loss resulting from the payment of a check contrary to a binding stop-payment order [4-403(3)]. It is no defense to the bank that it paid the check by mistake. Often a bank, by agreement with its customer, tries to limit or disclaim liability for paying a check contrary to a stop-payment order. However, a bank may not by such an agreement absolve itself from liability for bad faith or for *negligently* paying a check contrary to a stop-payment order [4-103(1)].

Bank's Rights after Improper Payment
Suppose a bank pays a check contrary to the drawer's stop-payment order and the customer demands that the bank credit the drawer's account for the amount of the check. The bank may or may not be required to do so. If the drawer's stop-payment order has a valid basis, the drawee bank must credit the drawer's account and seek payment from the person who in justice should make payment. If there was no legitimate basis for the stop-payment order, the drawee is not required to credit the drawer's account.

These results follow from the fact that the drawee bank has a right of "subrogation" that at least partially protects the bank from loss due to its failure to honor the drawer's stop-payment order. Under Section 4-407 of the UCC, a payor (drawee) bank that makes payment in violation of a stop-payment order is subrogated to (i.e., succeeds to or takes over) (1) the rights of the payee or holder against the drawer, and (2) the rights of the drawer against the payee or holder. Thus, where the bank ignores the stop-payment order and pays the amount of the check to a holder in due course, the bank succeeds to the right of the holder in due course to have payment from the drawer free of the drawer's personal defenses. If the drawer made the stop-payment order on the basis of a personal defense, the bank is not required to credit the drawer's account. The same principle applies where the bank pays the check to a payee or other holder *not* in due course. If, for example, the drawer stopped payment because the payee by fraud induced the drawer to issue the check, the drawer has a good defense as against the payee, and the bank may not charge the drawer's account. However, since the bank also succeeds to the *drawer's* rights, the bank has a legal basis for recovering the amount of the check from the fraudulent payee.

Case 35.4   **Universal C.I.T. Credit Corp. v. Guaranty Bank & Trust Co.**
161 F. Supp. 790 (D. Mass. 1958)

The plaintiff credit corporation (hereafter referred to as "C.I.T.") had a checking account with the defendant bank (Guaranty). On October 1, 1956, plaintiff drew on defendant bank two checks totaling $11,766, payable to the order of McCarthy Motor Sales, Inc. (McCarthy). On the same day (Oct. 1), McCarthy indorsed the checks and deposited them in its bank, the Worcester County Trust Company (Worcester), for collection. Worcester gave McCarthy provisional credit for the deposit and allowed it to withdraw the full $11,766. At 9:10 A.M. on October 2, C.I.T.'s representative presented to Guaranty a written stop-payment order. Later that day when Worcester presented the two checks for payment, Guaranty overlooked the stop-payment order and gave Worcester full credit of $11,766. Later Guaranty asked Worcester to take back the checks, but it refused to do so. Guaranty then debited C.I.T.'s account for $11,766. C.I.T. sued to recover the amount of the charge.

The events occurred after Massachusetts had enacted the UCC but before its effective date. Although the case was decided under the Massachusetts version of the NIL, the court pointed out that the results would have been the same had the UCC been in effect.

WYSANKI, District Judge. . . . The initial question relates to the effect of C.I.T.'s order to Guaranty to stop payment upon the (two) checks. C.I.T., as the drawer of the checks, had an absolute right to order payment stopped; Guaranty, the drawee bank making payment thereon, acted at its peril. . . .

The next issues are whether Worcester was a holder in due course of the checks, and whether . . . Guaranty is subrogated to (succeeds to) Worcester's claim against C.I.T.

Unquestionably under presently effective Massachusetts law, Worcester did not become a holder for value of the checks merely by taking those checks for collection only, even if simultaneously Worcester gave McCarthy a provisional credit based thereon.

But Worcester went further than to enter a provisional credit. Worcester, though it was not required so to do, allowed McCarthy to draw to the full amount of the credit before it had been collected. . . .

The majority of courts have ruled, pursuant either to the N.I.L. or to the common law, that a bank in Worcester's position is a holder in due course to the extent of its advances. [Citations.] . . .

In short, barring some clear agreement by both parties that the bank will not claim any such security rights, when the bank gives the customer the exceptional privilege of drawing against an uncollected item, a privilege to which under his contract the depositor has no right, the bank, while not purchasing the item, is entitled to security to the extent of its advances, and is to that extent a holder in due course—that is, a person who has given value.

This court having concluded that under Massachusetts law (as indeed under the law in most other states, under the N.I.L., and under the Commercial Code) Worcester was a holder in due course for the amount of its advances, . . . it follows that Guaranty . . . is subrogated to Worcester's rights against C.I.T. on the checks. It is usually said that to avoid circuity of action, C.I.T. is not allowed to recover from Guaranty. But perhaps (see comment to Commercial Code, Section 4-407), a sounder way of stating the matter is that C.I.T. is not allowed to recover because it has not borne its burden of showing that it suffered loss from Guaranty's disregard of the stop-payment order; C.I.T. suffered no loss because it would have been liable to Worcester as a holder in due course in any event.

Whichever form of statement is used, judgment must enter for defendant Guaranty. . . .

Effect of Unauthorized Signature or Alteration

Ordinarily, a bank may not charge a customer's account where a check or other item contains an unauthorized signature or has been materially altered. A bank that pays (or certifies) such an item may be required to credit the customer's account for the amount of the improper payment and to absorb any loss or collect the amount from someone else. However, the bank's liability may depend on whether the customer gave timely notice of unauthorized signatures or alterations.

Banks generally furnish their checking account customers with monthly statements of account accompanied by canceled checks and other items in support of debit entries. Where such an account and supporting items are sent to a customer or are made available to the customer in some reasonable manner, the customer is under a duty to examine them promptly and carefully, and to give the bank prompt notice of any unauthorized signature or alteration [4-406(1)]. If the customer makes a negligent inspection or fails to give prompt notice and as a result the bank suffers loss, the customer may not assert against the bank the customer's own unauthorized signature or any alteration. The bank would suffer loss, for example, where the customer's failure to give prompt notice of a forgery enabled the forger to "skip town" and avoid payment.

An unauthorized signature may be that of the drawer, the payee, or a special indorsee. The signature may be unauthorized because it is a forgery or because an agent of the drawer or indorser signed on behalf of the drawer or indorser without authority.

If an altered check (that is, one on which the amount is raised) is discovered, the bank ordinarily is *not* required to credit the customer's account for the full amount of the check. A bank that makes a good-faith payment of an altered check may charge the customer's account according to the original tenor of the altered item [4-401(2)], and the bank may charge the customer's account for the *whole* amount of an altered item if the customer's own negligence substantially contributed to the alteration [3-406]. Leaving open spaces on the face of the check so that alteration is easy is one example of such negligence. Moreover, where the customer has signed and issued an incomplete item, the bank may charge the account according to the tenor of the item *as completed* [4-401(2)(b)]. This is so also where the customer negligently leaves a signature stamp and blank checks unprotected, resulting in an agent's affixing the stamp to a check and cashing it at the drawee bank.

Where a series of checks containing unauthorized signatures or alterations made by the same wrongdoer is paid by the bank and charged to the customer's account over a period of time, the customer may receive only partial or no protection. The customer may not assert an unauthorized signature on, or alteration of, any item paid in good faith by the bank *after* the first item and statement have been available to the customer for 14 days, and *before* the bank receives notification from the customer of any such unauthorized alteration or signature [4-406(2)(b)].

For example, suppose Carl Customer received his January bank statement with canceled checks on February 1. One of the checks paid in January was forged. On February 20 the bank, acting in good faith and without having received notice of the forgery, paid a second check drawn on Customer's account by the same forger. Since the second check was paid more than 14 days after February 1, Customer may not require the bank to credit his account for the amount of the second check. Suppose, however, that the second forgery was paid by the bank on February 10. If Customer promptly notifies the bank of the January forgery, the bank must credit his account for that check. If Customer gave his prompt notice within 14 days after the January statement was available, the bank must also credit his account for the second check paid, because February 10 is within 14 days of his receiving the first statement.

The bank is not protected, whether there is one check or a series of checks, even though the customer does not act promptly or is negligent, if the customer can prove the *bank* was negligent in not discovering the unauthorized signature of the drawer or an alteration, provided the customer reports the impropriety to the bank within 1 year from the time the customer's statement is available [4-406(3) and (4)].

The drawee bank must credit the customer's account for any check paid that contains the unauthorized signature of an indorser. The indorser may be the payee or a special indorsee. The Code provides that the customer must discover and report to the bank the unauthorized indorsement within 3 years from the time the customer's bank statement is made available. Some states, such as California, have shortened the period to 1 year.

Case 35.5 **Jackson v. First National Bank of Memphis**
403 S.W.2d 109 (Tenn. App. 1966)

In 1963 the Greater St. Matthews Church, an unincorporated association, opened an account in the First National Bank of Memphis (defendant). The account specified that withdrawal checks were to be signed by Cleve Jordan,

Financial Secretary, and Milton Jackson, Trustee. The account also specified that statements and canceled checks were to be mailed to Jordan. Some fifty checks were drawn between August 1963 and August 1964, on which Jordan was named as the payee and on which the signature of Jackson was forged. The monthly statements and canceled checks had been mailed to Jordan. When the Church discovered the fraud, Jackson brought an action against the bank for and on behalf of the Church. The trial court gave a decree to the Church in the amount of the forged checks, and the defendant bank appealed.

BEJACH, J. . . . Under the above quoted statute [UCC sections 3-406 and 4-406], a drawee bank which pays the check on a forged signature is deemed to have made the payment out of its own funds and not the depositor's, provided the depositor has not been guilty of negligence or fault that misled the bank. In such situation, the burden is upon the bank to show that the loss was due to the negligence of the depositor, rather than to its failure to exercise its legal duty.

In the instant case, the negligence of the depositor relied on by the bank is its failure to examine the checks and report the forgery, thus preventing a repetition thereof. The fallacy of this argument is that the checks were mailed to Cleve Jordan, Financial Secretary of the Church, who was the forger. He was an unfaithful servant, and obviously his knowledge and information on the subject would not be reported by him to the Church, nor imputed to it. He had been a faithful and trusted member of the Church and one of its officers for about twenty years, and, consequently, the Church cannot be held guilty of negligence in employing an unfaithful agent. The contention is made, however, that the church officials, other than Cleve Jordan, himself, should have called on Jordan for an accounting from time to time, and that the Church was negligent in its failure to perform this duty. The proof shows that the Church did from time to time call on Cleve Jordan for production of the checks and records of the Church, but that he made excuses, said he forgot to bring them, or made other excuses. Under these circumstances, in view of his previous good record and reputation, we cannot say that the Bank carried the burden of showing negligence on the part of the Church.

In *Farmers' and Merchants' Bank v. Bank of Rutherford* (1905), 115 Tenn. 64, 88 S.W. 939, the Supreme Court held that, "It is negligence in a drawee bank to pay a forged check drawn on it in the name of its customer, whose signature is well known to it, where the cashier does not examine the signature closely, but relies on the previous indorsements." It is argued on behalf of the Bank that such examination of the signature card, which admittedly was not made in the instant case, is not practical under modern banking methods. Such may be true as a practical matter, but, if so, the Bank, because of that fact, cannot escape the consequences and must, under that decision, be held guilty of negligence.

We think, however, that the Bank must be held to be guilty of negligence in another and much stronger aspect of the instant case. The Bank account here involved was that of a church, which obviously involved trust funds, and the counter signature of Milton Jackson, Trustee, whose signature has been forged, was required on all checks. In the case of *Fidelity and Deposit Co. of Maryland v. Hamilton National Bank* (1938), 23 Tenn. App. 20, 126 S.W.2d 359, . . . this court held that one who takes paper from a trustee importing upon its face its fiduciary character, is bound to inquire of the transferor the right to dispose of it. A long list of cases is cited as authority for this proposition. Any adequate inquiry made in the instant case by the Bank would have disclosed the situation that Cleve Jordan was forging the name of Milton Jackson, Trustee, and would have prevented a repetition of such forgery.

There is another and a stronger reason why the Bank must be held guilty of negligence and held responsible for the result of the forgery here involved. All of the checks, recovery for which was granted in the instant case, were made payable to Cleve Jordan, personally; and many of them bear the indorsement of the Southland Racing Company, which is the corporation operating the dog racing track in Arkansas across the Mississippi River from Memphis. These circumstances, and especially the one that the checks were made payable to Cleve Jordan, personally, should have put the Bank on inquiry as to whether or not the funds represented by these checks were being withdrawn for unauthorized purposes. Any inquiry would have disclosed the true situation and prevented further depletion of the Church's bank account. The bank account being of a trust fund and the checks withdrawing the same being made to one of the authorized signers of checks, was sufficient to put the Bank on notice that the funds were being improperly withdrawn, or should at least have required the Bank to make inquiry as to whether or not the withdrawals involved were authorized. . . .

The decree of the lower court, together with interest thereon, will be affirmed against the defendant First National Bank of Memphis, Inc. and its surety on the appeal bond. The costs of the cause will also be judged against the Bank and its surety.

As indicated in Chapter 34 in the section on presentment warranties, a drawee bank is not obliged to pay a check containing a forged signature, even to a holder in due course. If the bank *does* make payment, the bank normally may not charge the customer's account. Nor may the bank retrieve the payment from a holder in due course, since payment to a holder in due course is final [3-418]. Instead, the bank must collect the amount of the mistaken payment from someone else or absorb the loss itself. From whom may the bank collect? The answer depends in large part on whose signature was forged.

Suppose that X forges Drawer's signature to a check made out to X; that X indorses the check to Holder (a holder in due course), and that the drawee by mistake makes a payment to Holder that is "final" as the word final is defined in Section 4-213. Despite the forgery of the drawer's signature, the drawee bank cannot recover from Holder the money paid by mistake unless Holder breached a presentment warranty. This she did not do, since a holder in due course does not make the presentment warranty relating to the drawer's own signature. Neither did Holder breach the presentment warranty of title, since that warranty pertains only to forged indorsements. However, the bank may collect the amount from X. X, the forger, has knowledge that the drawer's signature is unauthorized. As a prior transferor, X has therefore breached a presentment warranty.

Suppose now that Drawer issues a check to the order of Payee, that X steals the check from Payee and forges Payee's indorsement, and that X sells the check to Watkins who presents it to and receives payment from the drawee bank. Watkins cannot be a holder (and therefore cannot be a holder in due course) because Payee did not *negotiate* the instrument; negotiation requires Payee's signature and delivery of the instrument. The bank may have payment from either Watkins or X. Since there was no negotiation, Watkins did not acquire title and is in breach of the presentment warranty of title. X, the forger and a thief, lacks title and therefore is also in breach of the presentment warranty of title.

Effect of Customer's Death or Incompetence

As stated earlier, the bank acts as the agent of its customer in two respects: (1) when a customer deposits an item for collection, the initial relationship is that of principal and agent; and (2) when a customer deposits funds that the bank is to pay on the customer's behalf, the bank acts as an agent in paying those funds. It is the general rule in agency law that the death of the principal, or the adjudication of his or her incompetency, terminates the authority of an agent, even before the agent learns of the death or adjudication (see Chapter 38). If this rule were applied to banks, it would be completely unworkable. In view of the tremendous volume of items handled, banks could not possibly verify the continued life and competency of its customers. Accordingly, the Code provides that neither the death nor incompetency of a customer revokes the bank's authority to pay or collect an item or to account for proceeds of its collection "until the bank knows of the fact of death or of an adjudication of incompetence and has reasonable opportunity to act on it" [4-405(1)].

Furthermore, even though the bank knows of its customer's death, it may for 10 days after the date of death pay or certify checks drawn on, or prior to, that date [4-405(2)]. If there is any reason such a check should not have been paid, the executor or administrator of the decedent's estate may recover the payment from the payee or holder of the check. There is one *exception* to the provision that a bank may pay or certify a check within 10 days after the drawer's death: a bank may not do so if it was ordered to stop payment by a person claiming an interest in the account.

SUMMARY

Two features distinguish a check from other types of drafts: a check is always drawn on a bank, and it is always payable on demand. Since usually a check is not an assignment but merely an order on a bank to pay the sum specified, the drawee bank is not liable to the payee or the holder if it refuses to pay the check, even though there are sufficient funds in the drawer's account to cover the check.

Certifying a check constitutes an acceptance of the check and makes the certifying drawee bank primarily liable on the instrument. Where the payee or holder procures certification, the drawer and all indorsers who indorsed the check prior to the certification are discharged. Where the drawer procures certification, the drawer remains secondarily liable on the check.

On payment of a properly drawn check, the bank may charge the account of the drawer, even though the charge creates an overdraft. If the bank in good faith pays an altered check, it may charge the customer's account according to the original tenor of the check. If the bank in good faith pays a check that is incomplete when issued, it may charge the customer's account according to the tenor of the completed item, unless the bank has notice that the completion was improper. The bank may charge the customer's account for a stale check paid in good faith. In certain circumstances, the bank may be liable to its customer for paying a postdated check before the specified date.

A bank is liable to its customer for wrongful dishonor of the customer's check. When a wrongful dishonor occurs by mistake, liability is limited to actual damages proved.

A customer may instruct the drawee bank to stop payment of the customer's check. When a bank pays a check contrary to a stop-payment order, it may be liable for any loss that the drawer suffered by reason of such payment. However, the bank succeeds to the right the payee or holder of the check has against the drawer, and to the rights the drawer has against the payee or holder.

The customer is under a duty to examine monthly bank statements and canceled checks with reasonable care and promptness, and to give prompt notice to the bank if any unauthorized signature or alteration is discovered. The bank must credit the customer's account for improper payments made by the bank. The bank is not protected if the customer establishes the bank's negligence in paying an altered item or a check with an unauthorized signature.

The Code places an absolute time limit beyond which a customer may not assert an alteration or unauthorized signature. For an alteration or the unauthorized signature of the customer, the limit is 1 year from the time the customer's bank statement is available; for an unauthorized indorsement, the limit is 3 years in most states and 1 year in some.

If a drawee bank pays a check containing a forged signature, the bank normally may not charge the account of the customer, nor may the bank retrieve the payment from a holder in due course, since such a payment is final. Depending on whose signature was forged, the bank may collect from others, however.

Neither the death nor incompetence of a customer revokes the bank's authority to pay a check or collect an item until the bank knows of the death or adjudication of incompetency. Upon learning of a death, the bank may for 10 days after the date of death, pay or certify checks drawn on or prior to that date, unless ordered to stop payment by a person claiming an interest in the account.

STUDY AND DISCUSSION QUESTIONS

1 In what ways does a check differ from other drafts?

2 What is the difference in legal effect between certification of a check at the request of the *holder* and certification of a check at the request of the *drawer?*

3 *(a)* When and why is the basic relationship between a checking account customer and the person's bank that of creditor and debtor? *(b)* When and why is the relationship that of principal and agent?

4 *(a)* Under what circumstances may a bank that has paid a raised check charge the customer's account with the altered amount? *(b)* Explain how the rule of law regarding payment of altered checks differs from that regarding payment of checks incomplete when issued.

5 *(a)* Define a stale check. *(b)* Under what circumstances, if any, is the bank protected if it pays or certifies a stale check drawn by its customer? *(c)* Explain why a bank may be liable to its customer for paying a postdated check before the specified date.

6 *(a)* Explain and give an example of a wrongful dishonor. *(b)* How are damages measured when a check is dishonored by mistake?

7 *(a)* In what form may a stop-payment order be made? *(b)* When must the order be received? *(c)* Explain in what way the following statement is inaccurate: A bank by agreement with its depositor may absolve itself from liability for paying a check contrary to a stop-payment order.

8 Suppose that a bank has paid a check over a stop-payment order and that the bank is subrogated to the rights of the drawer. *(a)* Does the bank succeed to the drawer's rights on the check, or to the drawer's rights with respect to the transaction out of which the check arose? *(b)* Explain why the opposite answer would not make sense.

9 *(a)* Define "unauthorized signature." *(b)* List and give examples of situations where the payor bank may properly charge the customer's account for a check containing an unauthorized signature.

10 From whom may a drawer bank collect or retrieve the amount of a forged check that has been mistakenly but "finally" paid?

11 "Even though the bank knows of its customer's death, it may for 10 days after the date of his death pay or certify checks drawn by him on or prior to that date." *(a)* What is the exception to the provision? *(b)* What is the time limit for paying a check when the bank does not know of its customer's death or incompetency?

CASE PROBLEMS

1 Marvin Newman owed Belle Epstein $1,200. In 1955 he gave her an undated check for $1,200 as evidence of this debt. At time of issue the printed dateline read: "Detroit, Michigan," _____ , 195__ . Later someone acting without authority dated the check by inserting "April 16" in the first blank, by writing a "6" over the printed "5," and by inserting a "4" in the second blank. Epstein indorsed the check and it was presented to the drawee bank and paid by it on April 17, 1964. Newman sued the bank for failure to exercise ordinary care in paying the check. At the trial he testified that he had paid all but $300 of the debt to Epstein and that she told him she had destroyed the check. He contended that the check was "on its face stale and altered," and that therefore it should

not have been paid without consulting him. Judgment for whom?

2 An uncle drew a $500 check payable to his nephew and had his bank certify it. He sent the check to his nephew, with a note saying that it was intended as a wedding gift and was not to be cashed until after he and his fiancee were married. An automobile accident caused the wedding to be postponed 7 months. After the wedding the nephew presented the check to the drawee bank, but the bank refused to pay on the ground that it did not pay stale checks without consulting the drawer. The nephew knew that his uncle had started on a round-the-world trip without leaving an address where he could be reached. Does the nephew have to wait until the uncle returns before he can collect on the check?

3 Plaintiff sued to recover damages for the wrongful refusal of drawee bank to honor her check. She claimed that by reason of the wrongful dishonor her credit had been injured, that she had been greatly humiliated and had endured great mental suffering, and that she had suffered a chill so severe that she had to be taken to her mother-in-law's home. She prayed for damages in the amount of $1,000. The judge instructed the jury that if at the time the check was presented to the defendant, the plaintiff had in her bank to her credit sufficient funds to pay the check, and the defendant refused to honor it, they should find for her "a sum in damages as would fairly compensate her for any loss or impairment of credit she sustained, and for any humiliation or mortification of her feelings she had been subjected to." The jury awarded a verdict in the amount of $600 and there was a judgment on the verdict. On appeal the sole question was whether there was error in the instructions to the jury. Do you think there was error in the instructions?

4 On November 20 Owens wrote a check to the Extra Good Candy Co. in payment of Christmas candy bags to be delivered to his store on December 10. On November 21 Owens got a better buy, and telephoned the bank not to pay the candy company check. He meant to cancel the order for the candy, but forgot to do so. On November 27 the candy company indorsed the check to the W Wholesale Co. in payment of a bill. On December 5 the W Wholesale Co. presented the check to the drawee bank and received payment. Owens sued the bank. What decision?

5 The A Corporation had a checking account in the X Bank. B, the president of the A Corporation was authorized to draw checks on the account. C had been employed by the corporation for many years. She forged B's signature to several checks each month between July 1, 1960 and December 14, 1967, when the A Corporation discovered the forgeries and notified the bank. The corporation sued the bank to compel it to credit the corporation's account with each of the forged checks.

The trial court, sitting without a jury, found that (1) the bank had been instructed to mail the monthly bank statements and canceled checks to the corporation's secretary, C, and had done so; (2) the bank established that the corporation had failed to use reasonable care and promptness to examine the statements and checks; and (3) the corporation established lack of ordinary care on the part of the bank in paying the forged checks. What should be the judgment of the court?

6 Guy Hartsook died on July 13, 1961. In November of that year, his half-brother filed a claim against the estate based on a check in the amount of $1,050 that had been given to him by the decedent on December 20, 1960. The administratrix denied liability, claiming the check was stale after 6 months and was a nullity. Did the check become a nullity as a result of the payee's failure to cash it within 6 months after its date?

PART EIGHT

AGENCY

Chapter

36

Creation of Agency; Contract Rights and Obligations of Principal, Agent, and Third Party

When a person agrees to work for and under the direction or control of another, a principal-agent relationship (that is, an agency) is created. Special rules, called the "law of agency," govern this relationship. Since a business enterprise is seldom carried on by one person without the assistance of others, the law of agency pervades all business activities. This area of the law also applies to those who, while not actively engaged in business, make use of the services of such people as insurance and real estate agents and stockbrokers, or who may employ household help.

The law of agency deals with the relationship

between principal and agent; the circumstances under which an agent may bind a principal in contract and in tort; and the relationship and obligations that arise between principal, agent, and third parties. Most agency rules are merely special applications of contract and tort law considered in earlier chapters. However, where a principal-agent relationship is involved, some agency law is unique and appears to be inconsistent with basic rules of contracts and torts. Such departures from normal legal principles are recognized by the courts as desirable allocations of the risks that arise in the normal conduct of business.

Agency law requires business owners, who generally have greater financial resources than do their employees, to compensate persons who suffer injuries caused by their agents. To accomplish this socially desirable end, a tort of an agent only tenuously related to the agent's duties frequently is considered a proper charge against the principal as a cost of doing business. Because of the liberal views of the courts in this regard, in more and more situations principals are bound in contract and in tort by the actions of their agents.

This chapter discusses the creation of the principal-agent relationship; the power of an agent to bind a principal in contract; and the contract rights and obligations which arise out of a contract entered into by an agent on behalf of a principal. The next chapter considers the circumstances under which a principal may be liable for an agent's torts. The last chapter in this series treats of the obligations of principals and agents to each other and the termination of the agency relationship.

ESTABLISHMENT OF PRINCIPAL-AGENT RELATIONSHIP

Principal is the word used to designate the person who empowers another to act on his or her behalf. An *agent* is the person who works on behalf of and subject to the control or direction of a principal. An agent may affect the principal's legal relations with third parties just as though the principal were present and personally acting. In carrying on negotiations, entering into contracts, buying or selling goods or property, or by performing physical labor for the principal, the agent's acts may legally bind (obligate) the principal.

To establish a principal-agent relationship, four elements must be present: (1) parties competent to be principal and agent, (2) who mutually agree, (3) that one (the agent) will act for or on behalf of the other (the principal), and (4) that the agent will be subject to the principal's direction or control.

Who Can Be a Principal; Who Can Be an Agent

Principal Any person who has the legal capacity to perform an act may be a principal and empower an agent to carry out that act.[1] Generally, a minor may appoint an agent, but a contract entered into by an agent on behalf of a minor may be disaffirmed by the minor just as though the minor personally had entered into it.[2] An insane person is without competence to be a principal.

Corporations and other organizations Corporations (to the extent their charters allow), partnerships, and governmental agencies may all be principals and appoint agents. Generally, an unincorporated association, club, or society, not given by law the right to contract in its own name, is not a legal entity and cannot appoint an agent. The courts get around this impediment by holding that the individuals within the organizations who actually engage the services of agents and those members who concur in that

---

[1] Contracts which require personal performance cannot be delegated; see Chapter 17, p. 327.

[2] As to a minor's power to disaffirm and a minor's liability for necessaries, see Chapter 14, pp. 251, 258.

action, are the principals. However, the Supreme Court in 1921 held that a labor union, because of its size, purpose, and organization, was a legal entity separate and apart from its members, despite the absence of an authorizing statute.[3] Several states apply this rule to other types of large unincorporated associations. In many states there are procedural statutes which authorize unincorporated associations to sue and be sued in their organization names. Some courts construe these statutes to authorize such associations to become principals.

Disclosed, partially disclosed, and undisclosed principals Principals may be classified into three categories: disclosed, partially disclosed, and undisclosed.

1 A *disclosed principal* is one whose identity is known to the third party at the time of the transaction. In common practice the word "principal," with no qualifying objective, refers to a disclosed principal. Let us assume that Arthur (an agent) gives Thomas (a third party) a business card which reads, "Bovine Cattle Company, A. Arthur, Sales Representative." Here, Bovine Cattle Company (a principal) is a disclosed principal.

2 But assume that the card says only, "A. Arthur, Sales Representative, 123 Hill Street, Arcadia, Montana." If Arthur does not tell Thomas that Bovine Cattle Company is his principal, Thomas knows that there is a principal lurking in the background but does not know his or her identity. In this instance, Bovine Cattle Company is a *partially disclosed principal.*

3 Lastly, assume that Arthur's business card carries only his name and address; the fact that he is an agent is not revealed, and Arthur, following directions from Bovine and using Bovine's money, purchases some cattle. The invoice shows that Arthur is the purchaser. In this example, Bovine Cattle Company is an *undisclosed principal*.

Agent Any individual capable of comprehending the act to be undertaken is qualified to serve as an agent. Of course, if the individual is so young or is so devoid of mental capacity as not to be able intelligently to understand the duties he or she is directed to perform for the principal, the capacity to act as an agent is lacking. A contract made by an agent on behalf of a principal is considered to be the contract of the principal and not that of the agent. Therefore, a minor, who may not legally obligate himself or herself by contract may still serve as an agent and engage in a contract for a competent principal.

A corporation, to the extent its charter and bylaws permit, or a partnership may be agents.

General and special agents In agency law, a *general agent* is one authorized by a principal to conduct a series of transactions or duties involving a continuity of service. A *special agent* does not have a continuity of service. A general agent might be, for example, a salesman regularly working in a specified territory; a special agent might be designated by a principal to sell one specific piece of property, such as an automobile. The terms "general agent" and "special agent" are also in common usage in some businesses; the meaning they give to these titles depends upon the particular business involved. For instance, in the insurance industry, a general agent sells insurance policies of many different companies; a special agent represents a single company.

Gratuitous agent An agent who works or performs services without compensation may be called a gratuitous agent. A gratuitous agent binds his or her principal under the same rules as one who is paid for the service.

Independent contractors; employees Agents may also be categorized as independent contractors or as employees. Both types of agents

---

[3]*United Mine Workers of America v. Coronado Coal Co.,* 259 U.S. 344 (1921).

perform work or services for and under the direction of a principal. The distinction between an independent contractor-agent and employee-agent rests upon the degree of control or right to control that the principal may exercise over the agent's physical conduct in the performance of the work or duties involved. If the principal has *no right* to control such physical conduct, the agent is called an independent contractor. If the principal *has the right* to control the agent's physical conduct in the performance of the work, he or she is an employee. A more complete analysis of the principal's right to control

appears under the heading Principal's Direction and Control of Agent, at pages 749–750.

Mutual Agreement to Establish Agency Relationship

The principal and agent must mutually agree that the agent will work for and on behalf of the principal. That agreement may be formally or informally expressed, or it may be manifested soley by the actions of the parties.

The case which follows demonstrates that *absent* a manifestation of agreement by each of the parties, there is no agency.

Case 36.1 **Botticello v. Stefanovicz**
411 A.2d 16 (Conn. 1979)

Mary and Walter Stefanovicz, the defendants, were husband and wife. In 1943 they acquired a farm as tenants in common, a form of land-holding in which each is the owner of an undivided one-half interest. In 1965 the plaintiff, Botticello, became interested in the land. He talked to Walter about its purchase and offered $75,000. They ultimately agreed upon a price of $85,000 and Walter gave plaintiff a lease with an option to purchase. Plaintiff did not have a title search made and he did not inquire whether Mary had any interest in the land. He entered into the agreement believing that Walter was the sole owner of the land. While these negotiations were going on, Mary told Walter that she would not sell for less than $85,000. She did not at any time authorize Walter to sell her share of the property.

Soon after entering into the agreement, plaintiff went into occupancy of the land under the lease and made improvements upon it. Six years later, in 1971, he exercised his option to purchase. The defendants refused to honor the option and the plaintiff sued both Mary and Walter to force them to convey the land to him. The trial court, finding for the plaintiff, ordered both Mary and Walter to perform the agreement. On appeal, Mary claims, among other issues, that she, as a principal, did not authorize the sale by her husband, as her agent, of her interest in the land and therefore she is not bound by the Botticello contract and is not subject to an order for specific performance.

PETERS, Assoc. J. . . . Agency is defined as "'the fiduciary relationship which results from manifestation of consent of one person to another that the other shall act on his behalf and subject to his control, and consent by the other so to act. . . .' Restatement (Second), 1 Agency sec. 1." . . . Thus the three elements required to show the existence of an agency relationship include: (1) a manifestation by the principal that the agent will act for him; (2) acceptance by the agent of the undertaking; and (3) an understanding between the parties that the principal will be in control of the undertaking. . . ."

The existence of an agency relationship is a question of fact. . . . The burden of proving agency is on the plaintiff . . . and it must be proved by a fair preponderance of the evidence. . . . Marital status cannot in and of itself prove the agency relationship. . . . Nor does the fact that the defendants owned the land jointly make one the agent for the other. . . .

The finding [of the lower court] . . . discloses that Mary and Walter discussed the sale of the farm, and that Mary remarked that she would not sell it for $75,00, and would not sell it for less than $85,000. A statement that one will not sell for *less than* a certain amount is by no means the equivalent of an agreement to sell for that amount, See Restatement (second), Contracts sec. 25, ... Moreover, the fact that one spouse tends more to business matters than the other does not, absent other evidence of agreement or authorization, constitute the delegation of power as to an agent. What is most damaging to the plaintiff's case is the court's uncontradicted finding that, although Mary may have acquiesced in Walter's handling of many business matters, Walter *never* signed any documents as agent for Mary prior to 1966. Mary had consistently signed any deed, mortgage, or mortgage note in connection with their jointly held property. [Mary did not sign the Botticello contract, nor did Walter sign as her agent; he alone signed it as though he were the sole owner.]

In light of the foregoing, it is clear that the facts found by the court fail to support its conclusion that Walter acted as Mary's authorized agent. . . .

There is error as to the judgment against the defendant Mary Stefanovicz; the judgment as to her is set aside and the case is remanded. . . .

[It is so ordered.]

Agency by Informal Agreement Most agency relationships come into being by informal arrangements. Except in the special situations next to be discussed, no formalities are needed to establish an agency. All that is necessary is some manifestation of consent both by the principal and by the agent that the agent will act on behalf of or for the principal, subject to the latter's direction or control. A consideration is not necessary. For example, when Mrs. Arthur tells her neighbor, Mrs. Baxter, "Do me a favor and buy me a dozen eggs when you're at the market," and Mrs. Baxter replies, "O.K.," an agency is established and Mrs. Baxter becomes a gratuitous agent for that transaction.

Agency by Formal Agreement For certain agencies to be valid, manifestations of consent must be in writing. By application of what is known as the *equal dignities rule*, followed in most states, it is necessary that an agent's authority be expressed with at least the same formality as is prescribed for the act that the agent undertakes to perform for the principal. So, if a contract that an agent is to enter into on behalf of the principal must be in writing or under seal, then the grant of authority for the agent to engage in the contract must be in writing or under seal. This rule finds application particularly when the contract is subject to the Statute of Frauds. That statute requires contracts for several kinds of transactions to be in writing, such as contracts for the conveyance of real property and for the sale of goods of a value of more than $500.[4] Because of the equal dignities rule, if an agent is to execute a contract that is subject to the Statute of Frauds, the agency agreement must be in writing. It is common for states also to require certain types of agency contracts not covered by the Statute of Frauds to be in writing. For instance, in California a real estate agent, when representing a seller of

property, cannot claim a commission for finding a buyer unless the agreement between the agent and his or her principal (the seller) is in writing. Powers of attorney, which are formal grants of authority from a principal to an agent (not necessarily a lawyer), also must be in writing.

Agency by Implied Agreement The agreement of the principal and agent to establish an agency relationship need not be expressed in words. It may be implied from the parties' actions. Under certain circumstances, as brought out in the following case, a principal's consent may even be manifested by nonaction.

---

[4]For discussion of Statute of Frauds see Chapter 16, p. 292.

Case 36.2   **Weingart v. Directoire Restaurant, Inc.**
333 N.Y.S.2d 806 (N.Y. 1972)

In April, 1968, plaintiff, Weingart, drove his Cadillac automobile to the front of the defendant restaurant. Buster Douglas, dressed in a doorman's uniform, was standing in front of the door. Plaintiff gave Douglas the keys to his car with a $1 tip and asked him to park the car. Douglas gave the plaintiff a claim check and the plaintiff went into the restaurant. About 45 minutes later the plaintiff came out and asked Douglas for his car. Douglas could not find it and the car was never returned to Weingart, its owner. Plaintiff claimed that he had bailed (temporarily transferred the possession of the property) to the defendant restaurant and he sued the restaurant for its value.

The court had for consideration the pre-trial issue, raised by appropriate pleadings, of whether Douglas was an employee of the restaurant.

KASSAL, J. The issue here is whether defendant restaurant by permitting an individual to park patrons' cars thereby held him out as its "employee" for such purposes. Admittedly, this individual, one Buster Douglas, is not its employee in the usual sense but with the knowledge of defendant, he did station himself in front of its restaurant, wore a doorman's uniform [which he himself had purchased] and had been parking its customers' autos. The parties stipulated [agreed] that if he were held to be defendant's employee, this created a bailment between the parties. . . .

Defendant did not maintain any sign at its entrance or elsewhere that it would provide parking for its customers (nor, apparently, any sign warning to the contrary).

Buster Douglas parked cars for customers of the defendant's restaurant and at least three or four other restaurants on the block. . . . Defendant clearly knew of and did not object to Douglas' activities. . . .

Defendant's witness testified . . . "I told this Buster . . . that you are a free agent and you do whatever you want to do. I am tending bar in the place and what you do in the street is up to you. I will not stop you, but we are not hiring you or anything like that, because at this time, we didn't know *what* we were going to use the parking lot or get a doorman and put on a uniform or what. . . ."

. . . Although Douglas was not an actual employee of the restaurant, defendant held him out as its authorized agent or "employee" for the purpose of parking its customers' cars, by expressly consenting to his standing, in uniform, in front of its door to receive customers, to park their cars and issue receipts therefor, which services were rendered without charge to the restaurant's customers, except for any gratuity paid to Douglas. . . .

Plaintiff was justified in assuming that Douglas represented the restaurant in providing his services and that the restaurant had placed him there for the convenience of its customers. . . .

There was no suitable disclaimer posted outside the restaurant that it had no parking facilities or that entrusting one's car to any person was at the driver's risk. . . .

The fact that Douglas received no compensation directly from defendant is not material. . . .

Even if such person did perform these services for several restaurants, it does not automatically follow that he is a free lance entrepreneur, since a shared employee working for other small or moderately sized restaurants in the area would seem a reasonable arrangement, in no way negating the authority of the attendant to act as doorman and receive cars for any one of these places individually. . . .

It is thus my finding that a bailment for mutual benefit existed. . . .

Accordingly, I am setting down this matter for trial on these issues. . . .

[It is so ordered.]

Agent to Act for Principal

Inherent in the principal-agent relationship is the understanding that an agent will act for and on behalf of the principal. As both parties must agree to the establishment of the agency, an agent may not, except in an emergency, appoint a substitute agent to serve in his or her place without the consent of the principal. Because an agent agrees to act on behalf of the principal, the agent assumes an obligation of loyalty to the principal and cannot take personal advantage of the business opportunities the agency position uncovers. A principal, in turn, reposes trust and confidence in the agent. These obligations, embodied in the expression that a principal-agent relationship is a fiduciary relationship, are discussed at length in the third chapter of this series (Chapter 38).

Principal's Direction and Control of Agent

The fact that a principal has the right to direct an agent's work distinguishes agency from other relationships. There are different degrees of control that a principal can exercise over an agent, extending from the authority to direct only *what* an agent should do, to *how* the agent should physically perform the work.

If control is limited to the authority to direct only *what* is to be done, the agent is an *independent contractor*. Among agents of this type are: a purchasing agent for a group of stores; a lawyer who carries on negotiations for a client; a real estate or insurance broker; and a factor (a business organization that lends money on accounts receivable). It should be noted that not all independent contractors affect the legal relations of their principals with third parties. An independent contractor who does not bind his or her principal to a third party is engaged merely in selling a commodity or a service and is not an agent. For example, consider a roofing contractor whom Paul hires to repair a roof. The contractor (unless the parties specifically agree otherwise) purchases materials and employs workers on his own account and not for Paul's account. The roofer is an independent contractor but not an agent.

There is also the type of agent over whom a principal has the right to direct or control not only *what* should be done but *how* the work should be physically performed. Among agents of this category are policemen, hospital nurses, airline pilots, and bank tellers. An agent over whom a principal may direct this degree of control is normally called an "employee."

POWER OF AGENT TO BIND PRINCIPAL IN CONTRACT

An agent has the power to bind a principal in contract to the extent the principal authorizes or approves such action. This authority may arise in several ways: (1) the authority may be manifested by the principal *to the agent* (called *actual authority*); (2) it may be manifested by the principal *to a third party* (*apparent authority*); or (3) it may be manifested by the principal's affirming the agent's action after the

action is completed (called *ratification*). In addition, a principal may under certain circumstances be *estopped* to deny the purported agent's authority. This means that under certain circumstances, to be discussed later, a principal may not disavow an agent's claimed authority to act.

Power of Agent Arising from Actual Authority

An agent's power to bind the principal is manifested to the agent by the principal either directly (express authority), or by implication (implied authority). Either manifestation conveys *actual authority* to the agent to act for the principal.

Express Authority of Agent   The written or oral instructions that a principal spells out to an agent constitute the agent's *express* authority to act on the principal's behalf.

Implied Authority of Agent   While it is possible for a principal to express minutely the kind of authority an agent may exercise and to express equally minutely any circumstances which might limit that authority or restrict its use, usually an agent's express authority is defined by the principal in more general terms. The principal's express words are extended by those implications and inferences that the agent may properly draw from the principal's words and actions, from the circumstances surrounding the agency, from the customs of the trade and the community where the agency is to be performed, and from the relations of the parties. The totality of the implications and inferences which an agent may thus reasonably believe he or she possesses is called an agent's *implied authority*. As was said in *Fairfield Lease Corp. v. Radio Shack Corp.*, 256 A.2d 690 (Conn. 1968): "The law presumes that an employer intends his employees to have such powers as are reasonably necessary for him to carry on his work for the employer and such other powers as are reasonably necessary for him to carry into effect the powers thus implied." For example, a principal may give an agent the general direction to "manage my furniture store," and agree to pay the agent a certain salary for that work. The principal's direction thus given is a statement of express authority to the agent. From it the agent may imply authority to do all acts reasonably consistent with that general direction, depending on the place where the store is located, its size, the general character of the store and the community which it serves. These reasonable implications constitute the agent's implied authority. The agent would have authority, among others, to hire and fire employees, to purchase necessary stock, and to place advertisements in the local newspapers.

Power of Agent Arising from Apparent Authority

Apparent Authority Defined Apparent authority is that authority which a *third party* reasonably believes an agent possesses when that belief is based upon some act of the *principal* or some condition which the principal permits to exist.

How Apparent Authority Arises Frequently, a third party's impressions of the extent of an agent's authority is broader than the authority the agent really possesses. Suppose there is a store where the salespeople customarily have authority to warrant the freshness of a product (e.g., that fish has been freshly caught). On a certain day a salesperson, Agnes, is firmly instructed by her employer to make no such warranty, if asked. Agnes therefore has neither an express nor an implied authority to give such a warranty. However, in response to the question and disregarding her instructions, Agnes assures a customer that the fish was freshly caught. The customer, not knowing the limitation upon Agnes' authority, but relying on her *apparent* authority to warrant the freshness of the fish, buys some. If the fish is not as warranted, the purchaser has an action against the employer for breach of warranty. The employer clothed Agnes with the *apparent authority* to make the warranty because it was customary for salespeople to express the condition of the commodity being sold and, so far as the customer was concerned, there was no notice given that Agnes did not possess the authority commonly possessed by salespeople.

Apparent authority may also arise, for example, under a situation such as this: Arthur is discharged from his position as salesman for the Pure Brush Company. The brush company, relying on Arthur's declarations, erroneously believes that he had returned all of his samples and order books. A few days after his discharge, using samples and an order book he has kept, Arthur solicits and receives orders for brushes. Payments are given him as deposits and he keeps the money. Of course the brushes are never delivered to the customers as Pure Brush had no knowledge of the transactions. Is the brush company obligated on the sales Arthur has made without authority? Yes, because he had the *apparent* authority to take the orders. The brush company, by not getting back all the samples and order books, permitted third-party purchasers to have the impression that Arthur had the actual authority to take orders for their merchandise.

In certain circumstances apparent authority may be present even though no actual authority ever existed. This situation was present in the *Weingart v. Directoire Restaurant* case (Case 36.2, above). There, the restaurant allowed Douglas to have the appearance of being its agent (a parking attendant) and the patron reasonably relied on that apparent agency. Therefore, the restaurant was held liable when Douglas failed to return the patron's car.

Whether or not apparent authority is present is essentially a question of the facts in any particular case. A court will consider whether the principal has permitted, or has taken appropriate steps to prevent, a third party from reaching the conclusion that an agent has authority to bind the principal. How a court weighs such evidence is reflected in the next case.

Case 36.3   **Hagel v. Buckingham Wood Products, Inc.**
261 N.W.2d 869 (N.D. 1978)

Gary and Susan Hagel, the plaintiffs, in response to an advertisement, asked Midwestern Homes for information about the prefabricated homes that company was selling. Midwestern Homes is the name under which the defendant, Buckingham Wood Products, does business. The Hagels received a catalog from Midwestern Homes with a letter which stated in part, "Our design and drafting department is at your service [and] door-to-door, roof-to-floor, you get more in a MIDWESTERN HOME." The Hagels were contacted by Koch who said that he was a representative of Midwestern Homes. He discussed the various styles of prefabricated homes his company sold. Koch also said that he was a local builder-contractor involved in constructing prefabricated homes. The Hagels selected one of the prefabricated homes from the catalog and signed a single agreement with Koch for the purchase and construction of the home. Koch then ordered the home from Midwestern at a price agreed upon between him and Midwestern. Koch began construction. A Midwestern crane assisted in raising the prefabricated walls. Koch apparently ran out of money and he abandoned the work. The Hagels then brought suit against Buckingham and Koch for damages for breach of contract, claiming that Koch was Buckingham's agent. The trial court entered judgment against Koch but dismissed the complaint against Buckingham, holding that Koch was its agent only for the sale of its homes but not for their construction. The Hagels appealed, claiming that Koch was at least the apparent (ostensible) agent of Buckingham, doing business as Midwestern Homes, for the construction of the prefabricated home.

SAND, J. . . . [The] letter [attached to the catalog] created the atmosphere under which the Hagels and Koch discussed the selection, purchase, and construction of the . . . home. It also justified Hagels' belief that Koch was an agent of Midwestern Homes. . . . This, [together with the testimony of Pooley, defendant Buckingham's witness] clearly establishes that the letter was designed to carry the message, by implication, that Midwestern Homes not only sold, but also constructed the homes. Pooley's testimony clearly establishes that at the time this letter was composed in the 1950's, it was the practice of Midwestern Homes to not only sell, but also to construct homes. The Hagels should not be blamed for the error or oversight of Midwestern Homes by not revising the letter after a change of business practice occurred. . . .

Nor did the following language, as found on page 4 of the catalog, correct the impression. "Your Midwestern Homes dealer is unique in the industry. . . . he's not just a salesman . . . he's a builder. He's a local businessman who has earned an excellent reputation through years of building experience. He is a Midwestern Homes dealer because of his qualifications."

. . . "An agency is either actual or ostensible [apparent]. It is actual when the agent really is employed by the principal. It is ostensible when the principal intentionally or by want of ordinary care causes a third person to believe another to be his agent, who really is not employed by him. . . .

"An agent's apparent authority results from statements, conduct, lack of ordinary care, or other manifestations of the principal's consent, whereby third persons are justified in believing that the agent is acting within his authority. Therefore, the scope of apparent authority is determined not only by what the principal knows and acquiesces in, but also by what the principal should, in the exercise of ordinary care and prudence, know his agent is doing.

"Thus, if a principal acts or conducts his business, either intentionally or through negligence, or fails to disapprove of the agent's acts or courses of action so as to lead the public to believe that his agent possesses authority to act or contract in the name of the principal, the principal is bound by the acts of the agent within the scope of his apparent authority as to persons who have reasonable grounds to believe that the agent has such authority and in good faith deal with him." . . .

"A third person dealing with a known agent may not act negligently with regard to the extent of the agent's authority or blindly trust the agent's statements in such respect. Rather, he must use reasonable diligence and prudence to ascertain whether the agent is acting and dealing with him within the scope of his powers. . . ."

Midwestern Homes, by want of ordinary care, caused the Hagels to believe Koch was its ostensible agent for both the sale and construction of the home. . . . Midwestern Homes is bound by the mere ostensible authority it created and permitted to continue. . . .

We believe the principal, after allowing or permitting the creation of an ostensible agency relationship, is obligated to correct the erroneous impression. . . .

Failure to correct an ostensible agency relationship will make the principal liable to third parties which acted thereunder in good faith. . . . We believe that he who creates an erroneous impression and stands to gain from the transaction [the sale of the house by Midwestern] should be held liable for the resulting damages . . . to the innocent third party. . . . We have difficulty in trying to separate the sale contract from the construction contract. . . . We therefore conclude the trial court erred in determining that Midwestern is not liable for Koch's failure to complete the construction of the home.

Accordingly, that portion of the judgment dismissing the complaint and action against Midwestern Homes is hereby reversed . . . and the case is remanded for entry of judgment . . . [accordingly].

Estoppel to Deny Agent's Authority

Where a third party deals with an individual on the basis of the latter's apparent authority to enter into a transaction for a principal, the court may say that the principal is *estopped* from denying the authority of the presumed agent. What does "estopped" mean? It means that the principal is not allowed to deny the presumed agent's authority to represent the principal. Estoppel can arise where (1) the third party has changed position in the reasonable belief that the person with whom he or she entered into a transaction was authorized to act on behalf of the principal; or (2) the principal intentionally or carelessly caused the third party to rely on the agent's presumed authority; or (3) the principal knew that a third party believed that an unauthorized person was acting for the principal but even so the principal did not take reasonable steps to dispel reliance on the unauthorized representation. The principle of estoppel is illustrated by the following case.

Case 36.4   Cairo Cooperative Exchange v. First Nat'l Bank
608 P.2d 1370 (Kan. 1980)

Plaintiff, Cairo Cooperative Exchange, in 1969 named Jones its manager in charge of one of its branches. Jones was authorized to act for the plaintiff in all of its transactions with the defendant, First National Bank, where the plaintiff maintained an active checking account. Between 1969 and 1976 Jones wrote 101 checks payable to various Cairo customers even though no money was owed them. He then endorsed the names of the payees, adding "for deposit only" on 91 of them. None of the checks was deposited in the bank. Instead, Jones cashed the checks at the bank, keeping the money for himself. In all, through the improper issuance and fraudulent endorsement of these checks, about $55,000 was charged against Cairo's account at the bank. The plaintiff brought an action against the bank to recover the amounts wrongfully paid out to Jones by the bank. Defendant denied liability, claiming that Jones was plaintiff's agent and the plaintiff was estopped (precluded) to deny his authority to cash the checks. A summary judgment was entered for the defendant and the plaintiff appealed.

SPENCER, J. . . . There can be little doubt that defendant . . . bank . . . had the duty to apply the proceeds of the checks consistently with the restrictive endorsement ["for deposit only"], i.e. to deposit the proceeds in plaintiff's account rather than to pay cash to Jones. . . . However, in this case there are facts and circumstances which preclude the assertion of plaintiff's claim. . . .

It was . . . concluded by the trial court that, because of the implied or apparent authority of Jones, payments to him were the equivalent of payments to the plaintiff and, when money was paid to Jones, the bank was discharged of its obligation on the endorsements although Jones thereafter allegedly misappropriated the funds; . . . Because it was Jones who placed the restrictive endorsements on the checks, it was within his apparent authority to waive the effect of the restrictive endorsements on behalf of the plaintiff. . . .

Equitable estoppel is the effect of voluntary conduct whereby one is precluded, both at law and in equity, from asserting rights against another who has relied on such conduct. One asserting equitable estoppel must show that another party, by its acts, representations, admissions, or silence when there is a duty to speak, induced the one asserting the doctrine to believe certain facts existed. . . .

Plaintiff had the means of ascertaining the facts and Jones' scheme to defraud from the date the first restrictively endorsed check cleared the bank and was returned to plaintiff. [Plaintiff received monthly bank statements from defendant bank.] Its failure to do anything to notify defendant of the wrongful acts of Jones amounts to an inducement to defendant to believe the cashing of the restrively endorsed checks by order of Jones was at least condoned by plaintiff. In our opinion, such conduct precludes the assertion of any claim against defendant by reason of these checks. . . .

Where, as here, one of two innocent parties must suffer because of wrongdoing of a third person, the one who trusted the third person and placed the means in his hands to commit the wrong must bear the loss.

. . . The undisputed facts permit only the conclusion that defendant is entitled to judgment as a matter of law.

Affirmed.

Ratification of Agent's Acts

Meaning and Legal Effect of Ratification   As an agency is a consensual arrangement between a principal and an agent, an individual who professes to act for another but lacks actual or apparent authority, or an agent who exceeds his or her authority, does not bind the principal for whom the act was undertaken. However, the person for whom the act was undertaken can affirm it. After affirmance, called *ratification*, the transaction is treated as though it had been authorized originally. Ratification is based on the fiction that the principal's affirmance relates back to the date the individual purported to act in his or her behalf and establishes an authorization as of that time. No new consideration need move to the principal and the ratification may be without the knowledge or assent of the third party to the transaction.

Ratification may be implied from conduct (including, under appropriate circumstances, nonaction), which indicates that the principal consents to be a party to the transaction from its inception. Ratification of an unauthorized agreement will be inferred if the principal, having full knowledge of it, (1) accepts any performance under the agreement, (2) fails in timely fashion to repudiate the agent's acts of entering into the agreement, or (3) brings a legal action to enforce it.

The principle of ratification is illustrated in the case of *Perry v. Meredith*, 281 S.2d 649 (Ala. 1980). There, Perry, a candidate for political office, mentioned to a printer whom he met at a party, that he would be ordering campaign materials from him. However, Perry was short of funds and instructed his staff not to incur any debts on his behalf. Nevertheless, one of his office staff, without authority, ordered and received printed campaign material from Meredith. Although the materials were used in the campaign, the printer's bills were not paid. When Meredith sued for payment, the court held that Perry's actions in permitting the materials to be used constituted a ratification of the unauthorized order. In accepting the benefits of his agent's contract, the principal (Perry) ratified his agent's act and was therefore liable to Meredith, the innocent third party.

Requirements for Ratification   Ratification can be effected only under the following circumstances.

1   The presumptive agent must have purport-

ed to act on behalf of the individual who subsequently ratifies (though a few courts permit ratification by an undisclosed principal); and

2 The principal must be capable of authorizing the transaction both at the time of the act and when ratifying; and

3 The principal must have knowledge of all material facts involved in the transaction or consciously ratify without such knowledge; and

4 The principal must affirm the act in its entirety or not at all; and

5 The affirmance must occur before the third party withdraws from the transaction or before the circumstances so change that it would be inequitable to hold the third party to the transaction; and

6 The principal must observe the same formalities in approving the act purportedly done in his or her behalf as would have been required initially to authorize it.

Responsibilities of Principal and Agent after Ratification Ratification brings about some interesting changes in the relationship of the parties and in their respective rights and obligations. Until the act is ratified, the purported agent has acted without authority. Therefore, the purported agent is liable in damages to the third party to the transaction. He or she may also be liable in tort to the third party for the misrepresentation. The nature of these two liabilities will be discussed later. As the agent acted without authority, neither the principal nor the third party is bound or required to perform the agreement made by the purported agent. After ratification the situation changes. The "purported agent" is established as the agent of the principal for the purpose of the transaction; the agent's liability to the third party disappears, and the principal and third party are bound to each other under the agreement made by the agent and are required to perform according to its terms. In addition, the agent may now be entitled to compensation for his or her services if compensation is a condition of the agency.

CONTRACTUAL RIGHTS AND OBLIGATIONS OF PRINCIPAL, AGENT, AND THIRD PARTY

Rights and Obligations Where Agent Acted within Scope of Authority—Principal Disclosed or Partially Disclosed

Principal Disclosed When an agent, acting within the scope of authority and purporting to act for the principal, contracts with a third party, the contract is as much a contract of the principal as it would have been had the principal personally entered into it. The agent is a mere middleman and not a party to the contract. Therefore, the principal and the third party have contractual rights and duties directly with respect to each other. Each may require the performance by the other of the agreement that was entered into between the agent and the third party. Since the contract is that of the principal and not that of the agent, the agent can neither require performance nor be forced to make good a failure on the part of the principal to perform unless there is a specific agreement between the third party and the agent to the contrary.

If a principal denies liability under an agreement entered into by an agent who purported to act for the principal, by claiming that the agent had no authority so to act, the third party who asserts the principal's obligation has the burden of proving that the agent had authority so to act or that the principal ratified the contract or that the principal is estopped to deny the agent's authority.

Principal Partially Disclosed Generally, the rules applicable in disclosed principal situations apply also when the principal is partially disclosed. However, there is one very important difference. Unlike an agent for a disclosed principal, an agent for a partially disclosed principal is a party to the contract and both the partially disclosed principal and the agent are liable upon it. The reason for this is that when a principal is partially disclosed, it is highly unlikely the third party relies *entirely* on the unnamed principal for performance. It is inferred that the third party looks to performance also by the agent who engaged in the transaction. Accordingly, in the absence of agreement to the contrary, the partially disclosed principal and the agent are subject to separate liability for the full amount of the damages and, upon breach of contract, each can be sued individually. If the third party secures a judgment against the principal, after learning his or her identity, the agent's liability is not absolved. The liability of both the principal and the agent terminates when the full amount of the damages has been paid by either one.

For example, assume that a central purchasing agency which buys for a number of different companies buys a carload of tires from the Firestone factory without disclosing that Ace Tire Company is the principal in that transaction. The agency takes delivery of the tires and tranships them to Ace Tire. Firestone is not paid for the tires. In making the sale, Firestone relied on the credit of the central purchasing agency as well as that of the partially disclosed principal whose existence but not whose name was known to Firestone. Therefore, both the central purchasing agency and Ace Tire are liable for the indebtedness and a judgment can be secured against either or both.

Rights and Obligations Where Agent Acted outside Scope of Authority—Principal Disclosed or Partially Disclosed

The third party to a transaction has the obligation to ascertain whether an agent with whom the third party deals has the authority he or she purports to have. If an agent has acted outside the scope of his or her authority, and the disclosed or partially disclosed principal (a) has not ratified the unauthorized act, or (b) is not estopped from asserting the purported agent's lack of authority, then the principal is not bound by the agent's act. In that event, the third party has no right of action against the principal.

However, if the entire risk of doing business with the agent of another is cast upon the third party, there would be a monumental impediment to the free and rapid conduct of business. Before transactions are made final, the third party might feel the need to first communicate with the principal to ascertain whether or not the agent had the principal's authorization. Instead, the law gives the third party several remedies against an agent who, without authority, induces a third party to enter into an agreement. It is presumed that when an agent asserts in a business transaction that he or she is acting for a principal, the agent impliedly warrants that he or she has the authority to obligate the principal. An agent or purported agent who acts without authority is liable to the third party for breach of that implied warranty. An agent may also, of course, be liable to the third party for breach of an express warranty of authority if one had been made. In addition, as discussed in the preceding section, an agent for a *partially disclosed* principal may be liable on the contract itself. In certain situations, particularly under Section 3-404(1) of the UCC, an agent for a *disclosed principal* may also be liable on the contract.[5] Instead of these remedies, the third party may choose to sue the purported agent in tort for the loss suffered from relying on the misrepresentation, another remedy available to the third party. It should be noted, however, that there can be no action against an agent by the third party if, at the time of the transaction, the third party knew or had cause to know that the purported agent was acting without or beyond the scope of authority.

Rights and Obligations Where Principal Undisclosed

In General There is an anomaly in the law of agency that permits an agent to bind an undisclosed principal to a contract and gives the third party and the undisclosed principal the right to hold each other to the agreement. This exten-

---

[5] See Chapter 34, p. 704.

sion of rights and obligations arises despite the fact that the third party, when entering into the undertaking, believed it was with the agent alone because the agent, at that time, represented himself to be the principal.

It may be quite proper for a principal to instruct an agent not to inform a third party with whom that agent deals that he or she is actually acting as an agent. Such a device may be helpful, for instance, in acquiring property at the market price rather than at some inflated price the seller might impose if the financial reputation of the true purchaser were known. To illustrate, agents, without revealing the name of the true purchaser, bought a large block of land in New York City at fair market prices, and the undisclosed principal (the Rockefeller family) then donated the land to the United Nations on which to erect its buildings. Doing business as an undisclosed principal, however, raises problems that will now be considered.

Rights of Undisclosed Principal against Third Party   As in a transaction in which the principal is disclosed, an undisclosed principal can be bound by, or secure the benefits of, an agent's acts only if the agent acted within the scope of his or her authority. An agent who acts for an undisclosed principal holds himself or herself out to the third party as though such agent were the contracting party. No apparent authority is involved. Therefore, the concept of apparent authority, which so frequently binds a disclosed principal to a contract, is lacking. Instead, the law of agency substitutes this test: if the agent's act is usual or necessary to a transaction that the agent is authorized to undertake, the act is said to be within the scope of the agent's authority and is binding upon the undisclosed principal. Thus, if the third party breaches the contract he or she may be sued by the undisclosed principal. However, the third party is under no obligation to an undisclosed principal under the following circumstances:

1   Where the personal performance by the agent is required by the contract (as when an agent promises, as a condition of the contract, to oversee the work); or

2   Where the credit of the agent is relied on by the third party (as where an agent personally promises to pay the debt); or

3   Where the agent fraudulently conceals that he or she is acting for another (as where the agent, in response to the question, states that no agency is involved); or

4   Where the agent or principal knows or reasonably should know that the third party would refuse to do business with the principal yet does not disclose that an agency exists.

If none of the four situations listed above are present, the fact that an agent, acting within the scope of authority, fails to disclose to the third party that he or she is acting for an undisclosed principal does not affect the rights of either the principal or the third party, both of whom are bound by and can enforce the contract entered into by the agent.

Rights of Third Party against Undisclosed Principal   A third party, when entering into an agreement with an agent acting for an undisclosed principal, does not know that the person with whom he or she is dealing is, in fact, an agent. The third party believes that the agent is the principal in the transaction. In most circumstances the law gives the third party the right, when the principal is revealed, to seek performance from *either* the agent *or* the previously undisclosed principal, whichever one he or she chooses to hold responsible. Thus, if A contracts with B, and B turns out to be an agent for undisclosed principal X, A is no worse off than if the contract has been with B alone, *or* A may elect to hold X responsible for performance of the contract when X's identity is revealed.

Rights of Agent for Undisclosed Principal against Third Party   An agent for an undisclosed principal occupies a different legal status from an agent for a disclosed principal with respect to rights against the third party. We saw that an agent for a *disclosed* principal is not a party to the contract; therefore, if such an agent acts within the scope of his or her authority, the agent has no rights under the contract and no obligations to the third party. On the other hand, since an agent for an *undisclosed* principal *is a party to the contract*, the agent as well as the principal can bring action against the third party for breach of contract. The mere fact that the third party later discovers the existence and identity of the principal does not prevent the agent, as promisee to the contract, to demand performance.

Rights of Third Party against Agent for Undisclosed Principal An agent for an undisclosed principal is the promisor on a contract entered into with the third party. The agent, therefore, is obligated to the third party on the contract and can be personally held to its performance. This obligation of the agent is distinct from the obligation of the undisclosed principal to the third party which may be enforced when the identity of that individual is discovered. The law thus gives the third party what may be considered a windfall in that both the agent and the undisclosed principal may be held to the agreement. This does not mean that the third party may secure two performances— one from the agent and another from the undisclosed principal. The third party must choose, or, as it is called, *elect* whether to hold the agent or the now-revealed principal to the obligation.

Formerly, courts generally held that the filing of suit against either the principal or the agent, when the identity of the undisclosed principal became known, constituted an election to hold responsible only the one who was sued— thereby letting the other one "off the hook." Most jurisdictions now permit legal action to be instituted against either the principal or the agent, or both, without charging the plaintiff third party with having made an election. If the suit is against both the principal and the agent, either of the defendants may, by motion, require the plaintiff to elect which one should be continued as the defendant. If no such motion is made, the plaintiff is considered to have made an election when a judgment is entered against *one* of the defendants. If a judgment is entered against *both* the principal and the agent at the same time (no election having been required), the plaintiff may seek satisfaction from either or both of them, but there can be no recovery in a total amount exceeding the face of the judgment.

Of course, if the third party sues the agent, not knowing that that individual is merely the representative of a hidden principal, a judgment against the agent does not constitute an election because, under that circumstance, the third party has not exercised a choice between the two. When the principal becomes known, and if the judgment in the action against the agent has not been satisfied, the third party may proceed in a *new action* against the principal. This could be of great financial benefit to the third party who now might have recourse against a more financially secure defendant, well able to pay a judgment.

The case that follows makes clear that if an agent wishes to free himself or herself from liability as a contracting party, the third party must have knowledge or be made aware that the agent is acting for a principal.

Case 36.5   **Brown v. Owen Litho Service, Inc.**
                  384 N.E.2d 1132 (Ind. 1979)

Hicks, a salesman for Owen Litho, the plaintiff in the trial court, called on Brown at his home and entered into an oral agreement with Brown to print four issues of Brown's magazine, "Fishing Fun." There was nothing at Brown's home to indicate that it was a corporate office or that he was acting as a corporate officer. Owen Litho printed the four issues. Payment for the first and part payment for the second issue were made by checks issued by "J.J. Brown Publishing, Inc." Owen was not paid for the remainder of the work and sued Brown for the amount due. Brown denied personal liability, claiming that he had ordered the printing as the agent for J.J. Brown Publishing, Inc. Brown also alleged that he had fully disclosed that he was an agent for that company before the agreement was reached and that, in any event, Owen had notice that he was acting for J.J. Brown Publishing, Inc., because the corporation's checks were used to make the two payments on account. Owen denied that Hicks had been told of Brown's agency and also denied that it had any other knowledge of the agency. The trial court held for Owen and entered judgment against Brown individually for the amount of the unpaid bill. Brown appealed, claiming that he had no personal liability as he was merely an agent for a disclosed principal which was responsible for the debt.

SULLIVAN, J. . . . The defense of agency in avoidance of contractual liability is an affirmative defense and the burden of establishing the disclosure of the agency relationship and the corporate existence and identity of the principal is upon him who asserts an agency relationship. . . .

It is well established that an agent, in order to avoid personal liability, must, at the time of contracting, disclose both the capacity in which he acts and the existence and identity of his principal. . . . It is not sufficient that the third person has knowledge of facts and circumstances which would, if reasonably followed by inquiry, disclose the existence and identity of the principal. . . . It is not the duty of third persons to seek out the identity of the principal. Rather, the weight of authority holds that the duty to disclose the identity of the principal is upon the agent. . . . Thus, unless the third person knows or unless the facts are such that a reasonable person would know of the principal's existence and identity, the agent must be held liable in the same manner as if he were the principal. Actual knowledge brought by the agent or, what is the same thing—that which to a reasonable man is equivalent to actual knowledge—is the criterion of the law. . . .

Whether a principal is disclosed, partially disclosed or undisclosed depends upon the representations of the agent and the knowledge of the third party at the time of the transaction. [Owen wrote one letter, signed by the secretary to Owen's manager, to J.J. Brown Publishing, Inc. All other correspondence from Owen was addressed to Brown personally or to "Fishing Fun Magazine."]

The existence of checks drawn on a corporate account as it relates to the issue of disclosure has not received a great deal of judicial attention. However, . . . courts have not been receptive to the contention that such a check constitutes disclosure of the agency and the existence and identity of the principal. . . . Most jurisdictions hold that disclosure which occurs subsequent to the execution of a contract has no bearing upon the relations created at the time of the transaction and will not relieve the agent from personal liability . . . The Connecticut Supreme Court held that payment made by seven checks drawn on the corporate account was not sufficient notice of agency: "[where] the defendant made no attempt to have the plaintiff charge or bill the corporation instead of himself." . . . It was the defendant's credit, not the corporation's, on which the plaintiff had relied. . . .

. . . Under these facts, a trier of fact could reasonably conclude that Owen Litho did not know or that a reasonable person would not have known of Brown's agency and the existence and identity of his principal. . . .

The judgment is affirmed.

Rights and Obligations between Undisclosed Principal and Agent

Rights of Undisclosed Principal   The undisclosed principal's rights against his or her agent are the same as though the agent had been acting for a disclosed principal. These rights will be considered at length in the chapter that follows.

Rights of Agent   The agent's rights against a principal are the same as though the existence and identity of the principal had been known to the third party. In addition, an agent who, acting within the scope of authority, enters into a contract for an undisclosed principal, may secure "exoneration" from the principal for whatever performance the third party forces the agent to render. *Exoneration* is the repayment to the agent, or the assumption by the principal, of the obligation. The agent has this right of exoneration because, as between principal and agent, the principal is primarily obligated on the contract.

SUMMARY

Agency is a consensual agreement whereby one person (the principal) authorizes another (the agent) to act on the principal's behalf and subject to the principal's control. Depending upon the degree of control a principal exercises, an agent may be an independent contractor or an employee.

Anyone may be appointed an agent, but only an individual capable of entering into a contract may be a principal. The principal-agent relationship may be established in writing or, unless a statute provides otherwise, orally or implied from the conduct of the parties.

An agent has the power to bind a principal to legal obligations when acting within the scope of authority established by the principal. Authority vested in the agent by a principal may be actual or apparent (ostensible). Actual authority arises expressly from the written or spoken words of the principal to the agent or implicitly from the agent's reasonable inferences therefrom. Apparent authority results from a manifestation by a principal *to a third person* that causes the third person reasonably to believe that an individual has authority to act for the principal. Apparent authority may be greater or smaller than an agent's actual authority. When a person without authority purports to act for another, the person for whom the unauthorized agent acts may affirm (ratify) the act. Under certain circumstances the principal may be estopped (legally prevented) from asserting that the act was unauthorized.

If a party to a transaction knows that it is being conducted by an agent for a principal and the identity of such principal is revealed, the principal is a "disclosed principal"; if the principal's identity is not revealed, the principal is a "partially disclosed principal." If a party to a transaction believes that the person with whom the business is being conducted is acting for himself or herself, when, in fact, such person is acting for another, such third party is called an "undisclosed principal."

An agent, acting within the scope of authority, incurs no obligation on a contract entered into on behalf of a disclosed principal. The principal alone is responsible and may require performance by the third party.

When an agent, acting within the scope of authority, engages in a contract for an undisclosed principal, both the principal and the agent are parties to the contract. Either can require performance from the third party unless the agent fraudulently concealed the fact that he or she was acting for a principal or unless the third party had a right to expect performance by the agent personally. In that event, only the agent can require performance. When the third party discovers the identity of the undisclosed principal he or she can, with few exceptions, hold the principal to the contract. However, since the liability of an agent and his or her undisclosed principal is not a joint liability, the third party must choose (elect) from which of the two he or she will require performance.

STUDY AND DISCUSSION QUESTIONS

1 *(a)* Indicate, in general terms or by specific examples, the importance of agency to the economy; to the individual business person. *(b)* Define: "agency."

2 *(a)* What must the parties do to create a principal-agent relationship? *(b)* What qualifications must an individual possess to become an agent? *(c)* What qualifications must an individual possess to become a principal? *(d)* Is an individual who is qualified to be an agent also qualified to be a principal? Explain.

3 Distinguish between an independent contractor and an employee.

4 *(a)* In the law of agency, what does the term "right to control" mean? *(b)* If a principal does not exercise the right to control the physical actions of an agent in the performance of his or her assigned work, is the agency relationship affected? *(c)* Can a person who is hired as an employee bind his or her employer in contract? Explain.

5 *(a)* Distinguish between actual authority and apparent authority. *(b)* In what factual circumstances would one kind of authority exist without the other?

6 *(a)* What is meant by "ratification" in the law of agency? *(b)* What conditions must exist before it can be said that an act was ratified? *(c)* Does a third party have any recourse against either the principal or the agent if the principal does not ratify an agent's unauthorized act? Explain.

7 *(a)* Where an agent, acting within the scope of his or her authority for a disclosed principal, enters into a contract for the principal, who are the parties to the contract? *(b)* If the third party fails to perform according to the contract terms, does the agent have a right of action against him or her? Does the principal? Why or why not in each situation? *(c)* If the principal fails to perform according to the contract terms, does the third party have a right of action against the principal? Against the agent? Why or why not in each situation?

8 *(a)* Distinguish between a disclosed principal, a partially disclosed principal, and an undisclosed principal. *(b)* Does an agent for an undisclosed principal have a greater or lesser degree of apparent authority than an agent for a disclosed principal? Give reasons for your conclusion.

9 *(a)* Why do you suppose the law permits a third party who dealt with an agent for an undisclosed principal to hold the undisclosed principal liable on a contract when the third party, at the time of entering into the contract, had no idea that he or she was dealing with anyone but the agent? *(b)* Under what circumstances would an undisclosed principal have a right of action against the third party who had entered into a contract with an agent for the undisclosed principal?

CASE PROBLEMS

1 Plaintiff's manager went to defendant's store to buy a chain to use in a hoist. Defendant's sales representative was told the purpose for which the chain was to be used. The manager purchased a type of chain that the salesperson assured him would do the job. When this chain was used on the hoist, it broke and a quantity of glass was broken. Plaintiff sued the defendant for the value of that glass. Was the salesperson authorized to make the warranty?

2 W was the general manager of a radio station owned by defendants who lived in another state. W entered into a contract on behalf of the radio station to purchase certain "jingles" and materials to be used to enliven announcements. About a year later W left the employ of the station. The new manager cancelled the contract, stating that W was without authority to enter into a contract for the defendants. Plaintiff sues for breach of contract. Did W have authority to enter into the contract binding the radio station?

3 The plaintiff, the Lohr Funeral Home, ordered from Sample, the defendant's distributor, a custom-built funeral coach. Plaintiff traded to Sample a used funeral coach as part payment on the one ordered. Plaintiff heard nothing about the order and on several occasions telephoned to the defendant that manufactured the vehicles. A representative of the defendant each time said that the plaintiff "would be taken care of." Plaintiff was later told that Sample could not be located and had gone into bankruptcy. Plaintiff did not file a claim in bankruptcy but instituted action against defendant to recover the value of the vehicle it had turned in

to Sample when the order was placed. On the issues of apparent authority and ratification, judgment was rendered for the plaintiff. The defendant appealed. *(a)* Did Sample have the authority to make the manufacturer liable for the coach the funeral home gave up? *(b)* Did the manufacturer ratify Sample's actions?

4 Cochrane was in the business of selling motel supplies. He was also the principal officer and manager of a corporation which owned a motel. Cochrane, in his own name, purchased mattresses which subsequently were used by the motel. Cochrane was not authorized to obligate the motel for the purchase. The mattresses were not paid for and the plaintiff sued the motel company, claiming that it was liable as an undisclosed principal. Should the motel company be required to pay for the mattresses?

5 M, a member of X Church, asked P, a printer, what it would cost to print the minutes of a meeting of the church. P quoted a price of $9 a page. The price was satisfactory to M. P then prepared proofs of the printing and delivered them to M at his home. P heard nothing from M and so P telephoned him several times. In none of the conversations did M object to the prepared proofs. Eventually P learned that the contract had gone to another printer. P sued the X Church for the cost of the proofs and for lost profit. At the trial it was established that the Church had authorized nothing more than the securing of bids. There was a judgment for the Church. P then initiated suit against M. M denied liability, contending that he had acted only as an agent in the transaction; that he had never agreed to pay $9 per page; and that he had no authority to place an order for the printing. The lower court gave a judgment for the plaintiff (P, the printer), Defendant (M) appealed. Should the judgment be affirmed?

6 Fred Dearborn, a plumbing contractor, purchased from the plaintiff various articles of heating equipment that Fred installed in a house owned by his wife, Leah, and in which both lived. The bill for the supplies was unpaid. Plaintiff sought to subject Leah's property to the payment of the indebtedness on the theory that Leah was the undisclosed principal of Fred in the transaction. The master to whom the case was referred concluded that there was no agency because the plaintiff intended to give credit only to Fred, although there was testimony that Leah had requested Fred to purchase the equipment and install it in the house. The court followed the master's recommendation and held that, since the plaintiff believed it was dealing only with Fred and relied solely on Fred's credit, the plaintiff cannot now seek payment from Leah, and ordered a dismissal. Was the court correct in ordering a dismissal?

Chapter

37

Principal's Liability for Torts of Agents

The previous chapter discussed the contractual rights and liabilities of principals, agents, and third parties with whom agents deal. This chapter takes up the liability of principals for the torts of agents.

The nature and elements of specific torts—civil wrongs involving intentional or negligent injury to persons or to the property, reputation, or business of others—have been discussed in Chapters 5, 6, and 7. This chapter is limited to answering the question, "Under what circumstances does the law of agency impose legal responsibility upon a principal for the torts of an agent?"

At the outset, it should be borne in mind that an individual who is injured through the tort of an employee may have a cause of action for that injury against *both* the employer (principal) and the employee (agent). The employee is liable because everyone is accountable for his or her own wrongful actions. However, an employee may not have the financial resources or insur-

ance coverage with which to satisfy a judgment for damages. Therefore, the injured person usually attempts to force the employer to pay for the injuries the employee caused. The employer's liability, depending upon the factual situation, may rest solely on tort law (discussed in Chapters 5 and 6), or may rest solely on agency theories of the law. To illustrate, let us assume, for example, that the owner of a store directs an employee "to throw out" a disagreeable customer. The employee does so and the customer is injured. Or let us assume that the store owner hires a truck driver without making any attempt to ascertain if the individual can competently drive the truck. Someone is injured because of the driver's negligence. In both these instances the employer is *directly* liable under tort law because, in the first illustration, the store owner *ordered* the commission of the tort and in the second he *negligently hired* an incompetent employee. The employer, in both situations, is also *indirectly* (vicariously) liable under agency law because the injuries resulted from the tortious actions of an employee who was acting within the scope of employment. In either illustration, the injured person normally would seek recovery in a law suit against the employer (rather than the employee), basing the claim for damages upon both tort and agency theories. More commonly, an employer's liability arises when an employee, while acting in the scope of employment, *negligently* injures someone although the employer neither ordered the act nor negligently contributed to it. For instance, an employee, while doing an errand for her employer in the course of driving her own car home from work, negligently injures a pedestrian. Under agency law, the employer is liable for the injuries.

This chapter does not deal with an employer's direct liability in tort, but solely with the basis for an employer's indirect liability under agency law. We will see that a principal's (employer's) liability for the tort of an agent (employee) is determined by two factors: (1) the degree of control that the principal may exercise over the agent, and (2) the scope of the agent's employment.

LIABILITY FOR TORTS RESULTING IN PHYSICAL INJURY

In the last chapter it was observed that a principal has different rights of control over different types of agents. As to independent contractor-type agents, we have seen that the principal has the right to direct *what* work or service is to be performed but the principal has no right to control their physical activities in the performance of their work. Because of this absence of control, except under special circumstances to be discussed later, the principal has no responsibility to third parties for the torts of these agents which result in physical injury to third persons.

A principal may exert a great deal of control, however, over other agents; over these, the principal controls or has the right to control their *physical activity* in the performance of the work. The actual *exercise* of the control is not essential; it is the *right* to control that is determinative. Agents over whom a principal has this degree of control were, in the previous chapter, called *employees*. However, at common law and in current decisions of many courts, as well as in treatises on the law of agency, including the *Restatement of the Law of Agency*, these agents are called *servants* and their principals are called *masters*. Because these archaic terms are so universally used, "master" and "servant" will be used in this chapter to mean that category of principal and agent wherein the principal has the right to control the physical activities of the agent. Because this right to control is present, fault-free masters (principals) are obligated to respond in damages to third persons for loss or harm caused by their servants (agents) while acting within the scope of their employment. This rule is called *respondeat superior*.

Doctrine of Respondeat Superior

Statement of the Doctrine   The literal meaning of *respondeat superior* is "Let the master respond." The phrase is a shorthand method of saying that a master must respond in damages for the torts that a servant commits within the scope of employment, even though the master may have been free from fault. The tort may have been (1) an intended physical harm done by the servant in connection with his or her employment, such as a battery; (2) an intentional wrongful act that does not result in physical harm, such as a trespass, defamation, or misrepresentation; or (3) a negligent act that results in physical harm or loss to a third person. The doctrine of respondeat superior is unique to the law of agency, since normally a person who is without fault is not liable for the torts of another. The question naturally arises: What is the justification, if any, for this unique doctrine?

Rationale of the Doctrine   Whether there is legal justification for the doctrine of respondeat superior has been much debated. It has been said that making one person pay for another's fault violates common sense. On the other hand, it has been argued that a person who has the power of controlling the acts of another should be held responsible for the results of those acts; that since a master gets the benefit of his or her servant's acts, the master should bear the burden of them; that although the master may be without fault, the injured person may be equally without fault and that as between two persons who are equally free of fault, one who initiates the enterprise should bear the loss; that the wrongful acts of servants committed in the course of employment are a cost of conducting business and should be handled as are other costs of business; that making masters liable tends to make them exert greater care in the selection and supervision of their servants, and that this heightened degree of care redounds to the public's benefit; that making the master liable for torts of servants committed in the course of employment can be justified as a condition that the law imposes upon masters for the privilege of utilizing the services of others in household and business affairs; and that the master has the "deeper pocket" out of which to respond in damages. Whatever justification is adopted for casting upon the master the respondeat superior responsibility, the costs which the master is required to bear are normally represented by insurance premiums. These premiums become an element calculated in the cost of the articles the master sells. The ultimate result is that in every purchase the consuming public pays some portion of the cost of the master's tort liability.

The question of whether there is justification for the doctrine of respondeat superior is, of course, a philosophical one. But the doctrine has also raised various practical problems with which the courts have wrestled.

1 In doubtful cases, what criteria are available for determining whether an individual was a "servant" at the time the tort was committed?

2 Where a servant works for two masters or was a "borrowed" servant, how can it be determined which person was the master?

3 What principles should guide courts in determining whether the servant was acting within the scope of his or her employment?

4 Can the master ratify a willful tort of a servant committed outside the scope of employment?

Each of these problems deserves consideration.

Problems in the Application of the Doctrine

Was the Tort Feasor a Servant? Since the doctrine of respondeat superior applies only to the torts of servants, it is important to know whether a person who committed a tort was or was not a servant at the time of the wrongful act. Since the employer need not *exercise* his or her right of control, frequently it is not clear whether a master-servant or some other relationship exists. The courts must therefore consider all of the circumstances surrounding the employment in order to reach a decision. The *Restatement of the Law of Agency* has performed a valuable service by compiling a list of factors to aid in making this decision. In the words of the *Restatement:*

The relation of master and servant is indicated by the following factors: (1) an agreement for close supervision or *de facto* close supervision of the . . . work [to be performed]; (2) work which does not require the services of one highly educated or skilled; (3) the supplying of tools by the employer; (4) payment by the hour or month; (5) employment over a considerable period of time with regular hours; (6) full-time employment by one employer; (7) employment in a specified area or over a fixed route; (8) the fact that the work is part of the regular business of the employer; (9) the fact that the community regards those doing such work as servants; (10) the belief by the parties that there is a master and servant relationship; and (11) an agreement that the work cannot be delegated.[1]

A person should not jump to the conclusion that because these factors indicate a master and servant relationship, the absence or opposite of one of the factors necessarily indicates that such a relationship does not exist. For example, a job that does not require the services of a highly skilled or educated person usually indicates that a master and servant relationship exists, but the fact that a job requires the services of an educated or skilled person does not necessarily prove that the relationship is not that of master and servant. Some kinds of servants are necessarily highly educated and skilled persons. For instance, an airline pilot and a lawyer employed on the internal legal staff of a corporation are both considered to be servants in agency law. Furthermore, because of the great variety of contractual arrangements possible between persons who want work performed and persons who agree to do work, contracts between them may contain different factors. Some factors, considered by themselves, might quite clearly indicate the existence of a master and servant relationship, whereas other factors may indicate the existence of a principal and nonservant agent relationship.

When a case involving conflicting factors is before a court, the court has to weigh the factors to determine where the balance lies. It is not surprising, therefore, that courts have sometimes reached opposite conclusions when considering substantially similar facts.[2] To illustrate one such situation, let us suppose that a filling station lessee handles a national brand of gasoline, uses the signs and advertising of the oil company, wears its emblems, and abides by all its selling practices. Suppose further that an employee of the lessee negligently fails to remove oil drippings from the pavement near the gasoline pumps and that a customer who slips on the oil is injured. Under circumstances such as these some courts have held, dependent upon the degree of control maintained by the oil company over the lessee, that the filling station lessee is a servant of the oil company and therefore the company is liable. Other courts have held that the lessee is an independent contractor or business person and therefore he, and not the oil company, is liable for the tort (negligence) of the employee. Questions such as this arise frequently with franchises. A franchise is a business such as Chicken Delight, Taco Bell, or Arthur Murray Dance Studio, which bears the name of a national organization but, after payment of a fee, is locally owned and operated under rules of the organization.

The test applied by a court to determine whether a master-servant relationship exists, is demonstrated in the following case.

---

[1]*Restatement of the Law (Second) Agency*, sec. 220, comment h. Copyright 1958 by the American Law Institute, Philadelphia. Reprinted with permission.

[2]The word *court* is used to mean either the judge or the jury or both.

Case 37.1   Hamilton v. Family Record Plan, Inc.
217 N.E.2d 113 (Ill. 1966)

Logullo entered into a contract with the Family Record Plan pursuant to which he was to conduct door-to-door selling of photograph albums for baby pictures. The agreement specified that Logullo was an independent contractor, could apply his time as he saw fit, could hire assistants, and could engage in other business or selling endeavors. It also provided that he had to sell at least one album each week, that he was required to make a written report of his calls, and that he was not allowed to make more than one approach to each customer. He attended weekly company sales meetings and was given lists of referrals whom he was required to solicit. Logullo used his own automobile to visit potential customers. On his way to make a solicitation he was involved in an accident. The Family Record Plan was sued for damages. The jury returned a verdict for the plaintiff. The court entered judgment for the defendant notwithstanding the verdict, on the ground that there was not sufficient showing that Logullo was the servant of the defendant at the time of the accident. Plaintiff appealed.

BRYANT, J. . . . The first question that we shall decide is whether there was enough evidence for the jury to properly reach the conclusion that Logullo was a servant of the Family Record Plan rather than an independent contractor. . . . It has often been said . . . that whether a relationship is one of master and servant or one of independent contractorship is difficult to determine because many times some elements of each relationship are present.

An independent contractor is often defined as one who renders service in the course of a recognized occupation, and who executes the will of the person for whom the work is done with respect to the result to be accomplished, rather than the means by which the result is accomplished. . . . The right to control the manner of doing the work is probably the most important single consideration in determining whether the relationship is that of an employee or an independent contractor. . . .

The question we must answer, therefore, is how much Logullo was controlled by Family Record Plan in his work of selling the photograph albums. . . . He was directed to call on certain persons whose names appeared on the lists which were passed out each Monday morning. . . . The representatives were also instructed to call "only once" on the prospective customers. This is surely a limitation on the manner in which the work was to be performed rather than on the ends sought to be achieved. All this is evidence of a master-servant relationship. . . .

The contract entered into between the Family Record Plan and Logullo specifically states that the latter was to be an independent contractor. This, however, is not conclusive of the issue. As is stated in a comment on subsection (2) of the *Restatement Second, Agency* §220, "It is not determinative that the parties believe or disbelieve that the relation of master and servant exists, except insofar as such belief indicates an assumption of control by the one and submission to control by the other." . . . Moreover, it has been held that in determining the relationship of the parties, their conduct and the surrounding circumstances may be examined, even though there is an express, unambiguous contract, since to hold otherwise would be to invite masters to avoid their liabilities and responsibilties by paper contracts which do not express the true relationship between the parties. In other words, even though the parties to this contract expressly agreed that their relationship would be one of employer and independent contractor, if their conduct of the business was such as to be inconsistent with this contract, the writing cannot be permitted to protect the employer from liability as against an innocent third party. Whether such an inconsistency existed was, in our opinion, a question for the jury's determination. We believe there was enough evidence to sustain the finding by the jury that Logullo was the servant of the Family Record Plan so as to make that company liable for his torts under the doctrine of *respondeat superior*.

Reversed.

Whose Servant Was the Tort Feasor? For the doctrine of respondeat superior to apply, not only must the tort feasor be a servant but he or she must also, at the time of the wrongful act, be a servant of the master who is to be charged with the dereliction. Legal obligations may depend upon whether the servant was then serving two masters; whether the servant was "lent" by his or her master to another master for the time being; or whether the servant was the subservant of another servant.

The tort feasor serving two masters It has been said that "It is a doctrine as old as the Bible itself, and the common law of the land follows it, that a man cannot serve two masters at the same time; he will obey the one and betray the other."[3] However, it is possible for a person to be the servant of one employer for some acts and the servant of another for other acts, even though the acts are performed at the same time, if the two employments are not mutually inconsistent or incompatible. The classic case where a court found such a situation to exist was *Gordon v. S. M. Byers Motor Car Co.* [164 A. 334 (Pa. 1932)]. There, the owner of a gasoline tank truck, in an effort to effect its sale, had its driver demonstrate the truck by delivering a load of gasoline to a customer of the prospective customer. While delivering the gasoline, with the prospective purchaser present, the driver negligently caused a disastrous fire. The court found that the driver's negligent act occurred while he was serving two masters—the owner of the truck in demonstrating it, and the prospective purchaser in delivering gasoline to the customer. A judgment was therefore rendered against both.

The borrowed servant Because business and trades are becoming increasingly specialized in today's world of commerce, workers of different employers often work on the same premises. When an employee of one employer is assisting another employer, whose "servant" is the employee? Let us say that the Jones Company hires an exterminator to fumigate its mill; that Jones Company assigns one of its employees to help the exterminator; that the employee's negligence in heating a chemical causes a fire; and that the fire damages the Jones Company's building. Who should bear the loss? The answer depends on which employer is the master of the worker at the time of the negligent act. Should it be the Jones Company who, as the general master, "lent" the servant to the exterminator (the special master) who "borrowed" the servant for the time being?

Some courts assess the damage against the concern "in whose business" the negligent servant was then working. Courts that follow this practice would hold the exterminator liable. Other courts apply the so-called control test and charge the negligence to the employer who had the authority to exercise full control over the employee.[4] Courts that apply this test assume that the employee remains the servant of his or

---

[3]*McFarland v. Dixie Machine & Equipment Co.*, 153 S.W.2d 67 (Mo. 1941).

[4]*Restatement*, sec. 227.

her general employer as long as the servant furthers the interests of the general employer while performing the work for which he or she was lent. In our hypothetical case it appears that the Jones Company retained control over its employee who was assisting the exterminator. Under this theory we would expect that the Jones Company would bear the loss.

Now assume that the circumstances had been slightly different. Assume that pursuant to request, the Jones Company had sent one of its employees to the exterminator's plant where he was temporarily to work as an assistant on a crew servicing other companies' plants. Under these circumstances, if the "borrowed servant" was negligent, probably only the borrowing master would be held for the resulting loss.

The borrowed servant problem commonly arises where an owner has rented out heavy machinery or other equipment and provides a driver to operate it. Usually, the equipment is of considerable value and the operator is specially trained. The operator is required to obey the directions of the special employer who rented the machine while, at the same time, he or she must operate and care for the equipment in the manner ordered by the general employer. In cases presenting this situation the operator is usually held to remain the employee of the general employer. Therefore, the general employer would be liable for an injury negligently caused by the employee while operating the machine.

The court in the following case discusses the law of borrowed servants and comments upon the "whose business test."

Case 37.2   Marsh v. Tilley Steel Company
606 P.2d 355 (Cal. 1980)

Maxwell Construction was the general contractor in the construction of a freeway in Pasadena, California. Marsh, the plaintiff, was a workman employed by Maxwell. Wynglarz, a skilled crane operator, was an employee of defendant, Tilley Steel, a subcontractor responsible for installing the reinforced steel in Maxwell's concrete work. As the efficient completion of the freeway required close cooperation between Maxwell and defendant, their superintendents informally agreed that when either party required the use of a particular kind of crane but did not have one available, the necessary crane and its operator could be temporarily borrowed from the other party. No compensation would be made for such use and the operators involved would continue to report to their own respective supervisors and remain on the payrolls of their own companies.

One day, on his supervisor's orders, Wynglarz moved his crane to a Maxwell work-site to assist Maxwell in placing concrete forms. By means of the crane the forms were loaded on a truck. The crane and truck were moved to another location where the truck was to be unloaded. Plaintiff, Marsh, standing on the truck, attached the forms to the crane's boom so that they could be lifted off the truck. Plaintiff then jumped off the truck to signal Wynglarz where the load should be set down. Before he could do so, however, he noticed the boom swinging over his head and the forms sliding toward him. Plaintiff dived under the truck for safety. One of the forms struck him and he was permanently injured.

Plaintiff sued defendant, Tilley Steel, Wynglarz's employer, for the injury he had sustained. At the trial, the court held that at the time of the accident Wynglarz was a special employee of Maxwell, the plaintiff's employer; therefore, that plaintiff's remedy was limited to his workers' compensation claim against Maxwell, and that he had no remedy against defendant Tilley, Wynglarz's general employer. A nonsuit was entered against the plaintiff. The plaintiff appealed, alleging that the court had misapplied the law involving special employment of a borrowed servant.

RICHARDSON, J. . . . When an employer—the "general" employer—lends an employee to another employer and relinquishes to a borrowing employer all right of control over the employee's activities, a "special employment" relationship arises between the borrowing employer and the employee. During this period of transferred control, the special employer becomes solely liable under the doctrine of respondeat superior for the employee's job-related torts. . . .

The special employment relationship and its consequent imposition of liability upon the special employer flows from the borrower's power to supervise the details of the employee's work. Mere instruction by the borrower on the result to be achieved will not suffice. Moreover, California courts have held that evidence of the following circumstances tend to negate the existence of a special employment: The employee is (1) not paid by and cannot be discharged by the borrower, (2) a skilled worker with substantial control over operational details, (3) not engaged in the borrower's usual business, (4) employed for only a brief period of time, and (5) using tools and equipment furnished by the lending employer. . . . Additionally, where the servants of two employers are jointly engaged in a project of mutual interest, each employee ordinarily remains the servant of his own master and does not thereby become the special employee of the other. . . .

Here defendant loaned a crane and its skilled operator for less than a day to complete tasks of mutual interest to defendant and Maxwell. Wynglarz, the crane operator, remained on defendant's payroll; there was evidence that, though Maxwell could request a substitute operator, it could not discharge Wynglarz . . . While Wynglarz might rely on informational signals, he retained unlimited discretion to operate the crane as he deemed necessary to achieve the results Maxwell desired. The evidence permits the inference that Wynglarz was simply acting under defendant's orders to do a specific task for Maxwell. Hence, there was ample basis upon which a jury might reasonably have concluded that Wynglarz was not Maxwell's special employee [borrowed servant] when the accident occurred, but remained solely the employee of defendant. . . . Under such circumstances, defendant would, on a respondeat superior basis, remain liable for Wynglarz' job-related negligence, and the granting of a non-suit was, accordingly, improper.

. . . We reject defendant's suggestion that . . . analysis [should] focus solely on the question of whose business the tortfeasor was about at the time of the accident. . . . Defendant urges that this test, sometimes called the "whose business" analysis, best implements the "risks of the enterprise" principle which we have said is the main justification supporting the respondeat superior doctrine. . . .

We disagree. Among potentially liable employers, those who have the right to control the employee's activities at any given time are in the best position to predict, evaluate, absorb, and reduce the risk that these activities will injure others. . . .We recognized the relevance of a "whose business" analysis in determining which employer or employers had *control* of the tortfeasor at the time of injury. . . . Used in isolation, however, the "whose business" test offers little hope of an improved risk allocation, and, further, has been criticized as "ambiguous and sterile," implying that only one employer may be simultaneously served. . . .

. . . Where general and special employers share control of an employee's work, a "dual employment" arises, and the general employer remains concurrently and simultaneously, jointly and severally liable for the employee's torts. . . .

[The court also discussed the facts with reference to workmen's compensation laws.]

. . . We conclude that a jury could have found Wynglarz to have remained solely in defendant's employ. For that reason alone a nonsuit was improper.

The judgment is reversed.

The subservant   A servant-type agent may, on occasion, secure a substitute or may employ someone, whom we call a subservant, to assist him or her in the work. In either event, the servant becomes a master, with a master's liability concerning the actions of the subservant. However, if the conditions of the servant's employment were such that there was authorization expressly or impliedly, to employ the subservant, both the servant and the principal are liable for the subservant's torts. For example, assume that a truck driver (Archie) is sick so he asks his brother (Bill) to drive for him that day. While Bill is driving, he is Archie's servant. If the substitution was with the permission of Archie's employer, then both Archie and the employer are liable if Bill drives negligently.[5]

Was the Tort Committed within Scope of Employment?   For the doctrine of respondeat superior to apply, the servant's tort must have occurred while he or she was acting within the scope of employment. To be within the scope of employment an act must: (1) be of the same general nature as, or incidental to, authorized work; (2) have a reasonable connection in time and place with such work; and (3) be intended by the servant as a part of his or her duties. Stated negatively, a servant is not acting within the scope of employment where the act is different from that authorized, or is far beyond the authorized time and space limits, or is too little motivated by a purpose to serve the master. If the servant's tort consists of the intentional use of force, the elements required to bring the act within the scope of employment change. Although the tort may not be for the purpose of

---

[5]*Restatement*, sec. 255.

serving the master, if it is related to the work and was not entirely unexpected by the master, the use of force is within the scope of employment.[6] Perhaps the elements can be reduced to this statement: Whether or not a servant was acting within the scope of employment when he or she committed a tort depends upon the degree of departure from the standards that the employer could reasonably have expected of the servant.

General nature of employment A servant is acting within the general nature of his or her employment when engaged in any activity that can reasonably be regarded as incidental to the work that the servant was authorized to perform. Suppose a debt collector uses abusive language and threats in order to intimidate an old lady into paying a bill. As a result, she suffers emotional distress. The collector has committed a tort which might be considered to be reasonably incidental to the work. For a court to determine whether an act was incidental to a servant's employment requires consideration of such questions as whether or not the act was commonly done by the servant or by others in the master's employ; whether or not the act was within the master's business and, if so, whether the master had ever permitted such an act to be performed by a servant; whether or not the harm caused by the servant was done by an instrumentality furnished by the master; and whether or not the master could reasonably have anticipated that the servant would act as he or she did.

We have been considering acts that are or may be incidental to a servant's employment. Under certain circumstances the *failure* of a servant to act may constitute conduct within the scope of employment for which the master is liable. That would be the situation, for example, where the servant is instructed to perform a certain act that the master owes to a third person, and the servant fails to perform it.

Time and place of act To invoke the doctrine of respondeat superior, the servant's act must have a reasonable connection in time and place with authorized work, but the fact that the act occurs before or after the normal working hours does not necessarily preclude the master's liability. If the servant's act is performed reasonably within the time he or she is or should be engaged in authorized work, the act may still be within the scope of employment. The time limits are not marked by "when the whistle blows" but begin when the master has a right physically to control the servant's activities and end when that right ceases.[7] For example, driving to and from work is normally not within scope of employment, but if an employer requests an employee to perform an errand on the way home, the trip may be within the scope of employment. Even though a servant's act may have occurred outside working hours, if the employer is being served, it may still be within the scope of employment. For example, let us assume that a store manager is directed by her employer to close the store at 5 P.M. and not to admit any more customers after that hour. A short time after the store had been closed, the manager responds to a knock on the door and allows a late-arriving customer to enter. The manager may be within the scope of employment while the customer is in the store if, in an ensuing argument, the manager assaults the customer. The store may thereupon be liable for the manager's tortious act. The time and place of the tort must be considered in relation to the duties of the employee. This is reflected in the series of cases which hold that an employee is within the scope of an employment if involved in an accident on the way home from an office party the employee was expected to attend, even though the party was held after working hours and away from the regular place of work.

The fact that the act of a servant occurs outside the authorized area of operations does

---

[6] Ibid., secs. 228 and 229.

[7] Ibid., sec. 233.

not necessarily take it out of the scope of employment. If the place of the servant's tortious act is not unreasonably distant from where the employment authorizes, the act may be chargeable to the employer. How far from an authorized place or route is "unreasonably distant" has been interpreted in many ways. Some courts have held three blocks to be unreasonable; others have held several miles to be reasonable. The question is particularly troublesome when the servant's normal duties require him or her to drive from one place to another. If the deviation from the proper or shortest route is only slight, the servant may be said to be on a "detour" and still within the scope of employment. If the deviation is great, the servant may be said to be on a "frolic" of his or her own and outside the scope of employment.[8] The four situations following illustrate the problem.

1 A servant, being directed to take the company truck and to mail a package at the post office, takes the authorized route and on the way has an accident. The servant was clearly acting within the scope of employment and, if the act was due to the servant's negligence, the master is liable.

2 The servant takes the authorized route to the post office. He mails the package and then drives 2 miles farther to visit his sister. He has an accident while turning into her driveway. The servant, at the time of the accident, appears to be serving a purpose entirely unrelated to his employment and can be said to be on a frolic of his own.

3 The servant, after visiting his sister, begins to drive back to the place of work and before reaching the vicinity of the post office has an accident. Some courts would take the extreme view that the servant reentered his scope of employment when he started the return journey from his sister's house. Other courts would take the other extreme view that the servant

continued to be outside the scope of employment until he returned to the place where the deviation began. Perhaps the majority of the courts would adopt the *Restatement's* view that the servant reenters the scope of employment when he is again reasonably near the authorized route if he was then within the time limits of his employment and again acting with intent to serve a master.[9]

4 The servant, instead of taking the direct route to the post office, takes a longer route because he prefers the view on that route. On the way the servant has an accident. Although in taking the longer route the servant was satisfying a personal whim, a court could well hold that at the time of the accident the servant was acting within the scope of employment because he was merely engaged in a detour while still acting in furtherance of the master's business.

Intent of servant To be within the scope of employment the act must be performed with intent to serve the master. If a servant performs an act solely for some personal purpose, the act is not within the scope of employment even though it is performed at the place of employment and during working hours. However, if the servant performs an act partly to serve some purpose of his or her own and partly to serve the employer, the act can be within the scope of employment, provided the intent to serve the master is a substantial part of the dual objective. Thus, an employee who, during duty hours moves an automobile from one parking space to another and, in the process, has an accident, would be outside the scope of employment. However, if the employee is asked by a supervisor to move the vehicle because it is blocking an entrance to the company driveway, a court would probably hold that the employee acted within the scope of employment.

The following case deals with some of the factual issues to be resolved in determining scope of employment.

---

[8]The concept of "detour" and "frolic" first appeared in *Joel v. Morrison*, 6 Carrington & Payne Reps. 501, decided by the Court of the Exchequer in 1833. These words have become famous terms of the law.

[9]*Restatement*, sec. 237.

Case 37.3   **Burger Chef Systems v. Gorvo**
407 F.2d 921 (8th Cir. 1969)

Norris, nineteen years of age, was employed by the defendant, Burger Chef Systems, as assistant manager of one of its restaurants. When in charge, Norris was permitted to use his discretion as to when and for how long he took a lunch period. When he and the manager were on duty, frequently one of them would go to the Kentucky Fried Chicken establishment a short distance away and bring back food for both of them. It was part of Norris's duties to obtain money change and merchandise when required for the restaurant's operation. On the day in question, because the manager was away, Norris was in charge of the restaurant. He needed change and decided to get lunch on the same trip. Driving his own car, he went to the bank and secured the change. He then proceeded toward the Kentucky Fried Chicken establishment. The distance from Burger Chef directly to the bank is 1.6 miles and from Burger Chef to Kentucky Fried Chicken is 2.5 miles. Two separate trips to these places would have required a longer time than one combined trip. After Norris left the bank and before he reached the place where he was to have lunch, he negligently injured the plaintiff, Gorvo. The District Court rendered a judgment for the plaintiff against Burger Chef, Norris's employer, for the damages he sustained and the defendant company appealed.

VOGEL, C.J. . . . It is defendant's position that the evidence shows, as a matter of law, that Norris was on a personal mission at the time of the accident, had materially deviated from his employer's business, and was not performing any act which was of such special direct benefit to his employer as to warrant a jury finding that he was in the course and scope of his employment. . . .

It is plaintiff's position that there was some direct benefit to Burger Chef from Norris combining going to the bank and picking up his lunch in one trip.

If plaintiff is to recover from Burger Chef it can only be under the doctrine of respondeat superior, whereby a master is liable for his servant's torts committed in the course and scope of his employment. *Restatement, Agency,* sec. 219. In *Stokes v. Four-States Broadcasters,* Mo., 1957, 300 S.W.2d 426, 428 the Supreme Court of Missouri stated:

". . . No definite rule has been formulated by which it may be determined in every instance whether the driver of an automobile, in the general employment of another, was acting . . . under the control of his employer at a given time so as to render his employer liable for his negligence in driving the vehicle. That determination must necessarily depend upon the facts and circumstances of each case.

". . . If at the time of the occurrence of the accident the employee has departed from his work to fulfill a personal purpose not connected with his employment, then the relationship of master and servant is temporarily suspended and the master is not liable for his servant's acts during such a period of suspension. . . . Thus, it is the general rule in Missouri that the employment relationship is suspended while the employee is going to and from work or to and from lunch 'unless there is some special direct benefit to the master from the use of said car.' " . . .

An exception to the general going to and from lunch rule is the doctrine of dual purpose travel, a trip in which the employee and employer's purposes are combined, the landmark case on which is *Marks v. Gray,* 1929, 251 N.Y. 90, 167 N.E. 181. . . . In denying workmen's compensation [in that case] Judge Cardozo announced this formula:

> ". . . The test in brief is this: If the work of the employee creates the necessity for travel, he is in the course of his employment, though he is serving at the same time some purpose of his own. . . . If, however, the work has had no part in creating the necessity for travel, if the journey would have gone forward though the business errand had been dropped, and would have been cancelled upon failure of the private purpose, though the business errand was undone, the travel is then personal, and personal the risk."

It is not required that the business purpose be the primary or dominant motive for the trip, but simply that the service of the employer is a concurrent cause of the journey. . . .

In the situation where the performance of the employee's personal business occasions a detour from the route required for the performance of his employer's business, then the question becomes whether there was such a deviation from the business route as would constitute an abandonment or stepping aside from the employment. . . .

To relieve the master from liability of his servant's acts, on the ground that he has deviated from the scope of his employment, the deviation must be so substantial as to constitute an entire departure from such employment for purposes entirely personal to the servant; and, where the servant, notwithstanding the deviation, is still to some extent engaged in the master's business within the scope of his employment, it is immaterial that he may also have combined with this some private purposes of his own. . . .

. . . We are of the opinion that the District Court did not err in submitting to the jury the question of whether Norris was acting in the course and scope of his employment at the time of the accident. . . .

Affirmed.

Use of willful force against another   It is interesting to note that

courts have no hesitancy in imposing liability for acts which are far from those authorized [or may even be specifically prohibited by the employer] but which are likely to be done by over-zealous servants or in reaction to a situation arising out of employment. In this, as in other areas, the master's liability is expanding, but it is still true that an act done from a purely personal motive . . . is not in the scope of employment. . . . [10]

For example, if a servant who is delivering a package for the master sees an old enemy and assaults him, the assault was not committed within the scope of employment. However, if a truck driver whose truck has been rammed by another vehicle jumps out of his truck in great anger and assaults the other driver, modern

---

[10]Warren A. Seavey, *Handbook of the Law of Agency*, West Publishing Co., St. Paul, Minn, sec. 89, p. 155. Quoted with permission of West Publishing Co.

courts would have no hesitancy in holding that the assault was within the scope of employment.

In some situations the occasional use of force is a natural incident of the servant's job. Thus, a "bouncer" in a tavern would be expected to use such means as are necessary to eject an unruly customer. If the servant uses an unreasonable amount of force, the act is tortious and still within the scope of employment.

The next case illustrates that for a servant to be within the scope of employment, the use of willful force must be related to the servant's work.

Case 37.4   **Fitzgerald v. McCutcheon**
                 410 A.2d 1270 (Pa. Super. 1979)

McCutcheon was a policeman employed by the City of Philadelphia. On June 5, 1968, McCutcheon was off duty. That evening he joined Fitzgerald, a neighbor. They drank beer until about one o'clock in the morning. They then went to a club where they played pool and continued to drink beer. They returned to their homes shortly after 2 a.m.; McCutcheon wanted to go out for breakfast. Plaintiff, Fitzgerald, declined. At this point, McCutcheon's wife came out of the house and an argument ensued between her and her husband. She asked plaintiff to remove the keys from McCutcheon's auto. The plaintiff did so. He gave the keys to Mrs. McCutcheon and then went to his own apartment. A short time later, McCutcheon beat upon and broke down the front door of the apartment building in which plaintiff lived. Plaintiff went downstairs; McCutcheon demanded the return of his car keys, refusing to believe that the plaintiff had given the keys to McCutcheon's wife. McCutcheon told plaintiff that he would "place him under arrest for stealing the keys." McCutcheon then drew a gun and shot plaintiff six times. Fortunately, Fitzgerald was not killed.

Plaintiff sued McCutcheon, the City of Philadelphia and the club in an action in trespass. A judgment was recovered by the plaintiff against McCutcheon and the City of Philadelphia. The trial court denied the City's motion for a judgment in its favor notwithstanding the verdict, holding that the verdict could be sustained on principles of respondeat superior. The City appealed this decision.

WIEAND, J. . . . A master is liable for the acts of his servant which are committed during the course of and within the scope of the servant's employment. . . . This liability of the employer may extend even to intentional or criminal acts committed by the servant. . . . Whether a person acted within the scope of employment is ordinarily a question for the jury. . . . Where, however, the employee commits an act encompassing the use of force which is excessive and so dangerous as to be totally without responsibility or reason, the employer is not responsible as a matter of law. If an assault is committed for personal reasons or in an outrageous manner, it is not actuated by an intent of performing the business of the employer and is not done within the scope of employment. . . .

The Restatement (Second) of Agency, sec. 228, defines conduct within the scope of employment as follows: "(1) Conduct of a servant is within the scope of employment if, but only if: (a) it is of the kind he is employed to perform; (b) it occurs substantially within the authorized time and space limits; (c) it is actuated, at least in part, by a purpose to serve the master, and (d) if force is intentionally used by the servant against another, the use of the force is not unexpectable by the master. (2) Conduct of a servant is not within the scope of employment if it is different in kind from that authorized, far beyond the authorized time or space limits, or too little actuated by a purpose to serve the master."

When this principle is applied to the facts of the instant case, it becomes clear beyond peradventure of a doubt that McCutcheon's act of shooting his neighbor was outside the scope of his employment. His acts were motivated by reasons personal to himself and did not further the purpose of his employment as a policeman. He was off duty and not then subject to the right of his employer's control. His act was so outrageous, so criminal, and so incapable of anticipation by his employer, that it must be held as a matter of law to exceed the scope of McCutcheon's employment. To hold a municipality liable for conduct of an off duty policeman under the circumstances of this case on a theory of respondeat superior would be unreasonable and would exceed the legitimate legal and social purposes which sustain the doctrine. . . .

The evidence, therefore, demonstrates unequivocally and inescapably that McCutcheon shot appellee, not in the line of duty as a city policeman, but solely because of a personal animosity generated by a full day and night of off duty activities. For such conduct, the City of Philadelphia cannot be held responsible.

Reversed and remanded for the entry of judgment n.o.v [notwithstanding the verdict] in favor of appellant.

Can a Willful Tort Committed outside Scope of Employment Be Ratified? Just as a nonmaster principal can make himself or herself liable by ratifying an unauthorized *contract* entered into by an agent, a master can make himself or herself liable by ratifying a willful *tort* committed by a servant-type agent outside the scope of employment. For example, a case arose where an employer had money that his employee fraudulently acquired from another and turned over to the employer as a credit against a shortage in the employee's accounts. The employer who retained the funds was held to have ratified the tort and was liable to the defrauded person for the money.

Liability in Unusual Circumstances

There are certain circumstances where, for policy reasons, the law holds a principal responsible for physical injuries caused not only by servants but also by nonservant agents and even by independent contractors who are not agents at all. These circumstances exist when the work (1) involves a nondelegable duty; (2) is inherently dangerous; or (3) is ultrahazardous.

Nondelegable Duties   When the performance of an activity requires the permission of local, state, or other governmental authority, as by license or franchise, implicit within that permission is the requirement that the activity will be performed with due regard to the protection of the public. The franchise holder is not permitted to free himself or herself from this obligation by contracting out the work. Thus, a trucking company that is a certificated common carrier can hire another freight line to carry its cargo, but it cannot divest itself of tort liability for injury to a third party during the course of such transport. A municipality has a nondelegable duty to keep the city's streets safe, as does a public utility that digs trenches in the street in order to bury the utility's pipes and conduits.

Inherently Dangerous Activities   Work is inherently dangerous where it involves such a high degree of risk that it will, in the natural course of events, produce injury unless an equally high degree of care is used. A principal is liable for a tort committed by its agent in the performance of work requiring such care. For instance, where the owner of property that abuts on a street enters into a contract with a company for the erection of a sign to project over a public thoroughfare, the owner will be liable if a passerby is injured because of an employee's negligence in erecting the sign.

Ultrahazardous Activities   An activity is deemed to be ultrahazardous when, despite the high degree of care exercised in its performance, there is still great risk to third parties. Blasting within the city limits is an illustration. A principal who employs another to perform such an ultrahazardous act is liable for any harm that ensues, regardless of the precautions that are taken to protect against injury to third persons. Since strict liability is imposed, it is immaterial whether the principal does the work himself or herself or employs another to do the work for him or her.

A case involving a nondelegable duty follows.

Case 37.5   Westby v. Itasca County
290 N.W.2d 437 (Minn. 1980)

Plaintiff Westby injured his back when his truck overturned as a result of running into a mud slick on a county highway. The road condition was created approximately 1 hour before the accident when a beaver dam located near the road was intentionally destroyed by dynamite to prevent the erosion of the roadbed from water backed up by the dam. The blasting was handled by Claude, a Department of Natural Resources conservation officer, at the request of Gustafson, a county highway maintenance employee. Claude received no compensation for conducting the blasting.

After the explosion, Claude and his son removed the larger pieces of debris that had fallen upon the road, but most of the slippery mud remained. This hazardous condition was not marked or flagged to warn drivers.

Westby sued the county and Claude, claiming damages for the negligent maintenance of the highway. The trial court ruled that Claude was not an agent of the county; that even if he was an independent contractor of the county his negligent act in not warning drivers of the road's condition was not part of the work he was to perform and therefore the county could not be liable for his acts. Plaintiff appealed on the ground that the trial court's rulings on the agency and independent contractor status of Claude were incorrect.

OTIS, J.. . . Restatement (Second) of Agency, sec. 2 (1958) sets forth the relevant rules:

> An independent contractor is a person who contracts with another to do something for him but who is not controlled by the other or subject to the other's right to control with respect to his physical conduct in the performance of the undertaking. He may or may not be an agent.

The Restatement definition includes someone who acts gratuitously. . . .

Claude was acting at the request of the county and on its behalf for the sole purpose of maintaining a county road which was neither the function of the Department of Natural Resources nor of a conservation officer. To the extent that Gustafson's [the county highway employee] conduct was authorized by the county, Claude was an independent contractor of the county as a matter of law. . . .

A principal is liable for the negligent performance of a nondelegable duty by an independent contractor, and road maintenance is such a duty. . . .

The trial court ruled as a matter of law that the failure to clear the mud off of the road was collateral negligence on the part of the independent contractor which relieved the county of liability. However, negligence of an independent contractor is "collateral" only when the negligence is disassociated "from any inherent or contemplated special risk which may be expected to be created by the work." . . . Claude was negligent in failing either to remove the debris, give warning of the hazard, or notify the county of the dangerous conditions of the road.

The risks which were created by the explosion we hold to be inherent in the work which was contemplated. Under these circumstances Claude's negligence was not collateral and Itasca County [the defendant] is therefore vicariously liable as his principal.

Reversed. Judgment for plaintiff Westby will be entered.

LIABILITY FOR TORTS NOT RESULTING IN PHYSICAL INJURY

Thus far in this chapter, consideration has been given to a principal's liability for the physical torts of a servant or nonservant agent. There is still to be considered a principal's liability for those torts which do not result in physical harm—torts such as fraud, misrepresentation, and defamation. As to these torts, a principal is liable when they are committed either by servant or nonservant agents, acting within the scope of actual or apparent authority. In such cases the courts do not distinguish between the agency theories of authority and the doctrine of respondeat superior. Liability is not restricted to situations where an agent commits the tort for the principal's benefit but may extend to situations where the tort was committed for the agent's own purposes.

It is sometimes said that when a person appoints an agent the principal impliedly *assumes* liability for any nonphysical tort that the agent may commit within his or her actual or apparent authority. Such an explanation is pure legal fiction. The truth is that the law *imposes* liability on the principal for reasons of public policy. Courts have felt that when a person appoints an agent and clothes such person with actual or apparent authority, sound public policy requires that any loss caused by the agent's nonphysical tort in the course of the exercise of such authority should be borne by the one who made the tort possible (the principal) rather than by the victim of the tort. As the United States Court of Appeals said in *Gilmore v. Constitution Life Ins. Co.*, 502 F.2d 1345 (10th Cir., 1974), "a principal may not accept the benefits of its agent's endeavors, and reject out of hand detriments arising therefrom. A principal may not turn loose his agent on the general public, and then merely sit back and exercise little or no supervision [over him]."

But sound public policy also requires that the person injured by the tort should not be protected at the expense of the principal unless the injured party acted reasonably. For example, custom in some lines of business limits the apparent authority of an agent to make representations. Where there is such a limitation on apparent authority, a third party is not justified in relying upon a representation that exceeds that authority.

In Chapter 13 we saw that where a contract is induced by the fraud of one of the parties, the other party has a choice of remedies—he or she can rescind the contract or affirm it and bring action in deceit for damages. If rescission is elected, any performance received from the other party must be returned. The same choice of remedies applies where a contract is induced by the fraud of an agent acting within the scope of actual or apparent authority. The defrauded party can rescind the contract or affirm it and sue the principal for damages. There need be added now only that where an agent acted outside the scope of actual or apparent authority, the principal may ratify the fraudulent act and thus become liable to the injured party. If the principal does not ratify, the defrauded person is not without remedy. Although such person has no cause of action against the principal, he or she does have a cause of action against the agent for the fraud practiced by the agent.

In order to forestall liability arising from the fraudulent representations of their agents, many principals insert protective clauses in their contracts or order blanks. Such provisions, called "disclaimers" or "exculpatory clauses," are designed to put the third party on notice that the agent has no authority to make representations other than those stated on the printed form of contract. Such a clause might read as follows: "It is hereby agreed that there are no understandings, representations, or agreements between the parties other than those expressed in this written contract." While a clause such as this usually is held to protect a principal from liability for the deceit of an agent who acts beyond the scope of authority, it will not protect the principal against losing the benefit of the contract. On application of the injured party, courts may order a rescission of the contract. Courts base rescission in such cases on the equitable principle that one should not be allowed to benefit from the fraud of another, at least when the other is, or purports to be, that person's agent.

The following case considers a principal's liability for an agent's fraud.

Case 37.6   **Parsons v. Bailey**
227 S.E.2d 166 (N.C. 1976)

Liberty Financial Corporation indirectly owned Trade Leasing Corporation. Bailey was the President and Sales Manager of Trade Leasing. That company was engaged in the business of leasing equipment of various kinds. It conducted its business through dealers to whom it sold exclusive franchises.

In response to an advertisement, plaintiff (Parsons) talked to Bailey (defendant) about purchasing a franchise for North Carolina. Bailey told Parsons that he was an agent of Trade Leasing and gave plaintiff information about the company and a sample franchise agreement. In the agreement, the abbreviation "TLC" and "LFC" were used to designate Trade Leasing Corporation and Liberty Financial Corporation, respectively. Bailey corresponded with the plaintiff on Trade Leasing stationery and plaintiff called him several times at the Trade Leasing office in Atlanta. The plaintiff ultimately entered into a license agreement for the State of North Carolina. However, the agreement, prepared by Bailey, was between *TFC Corporation* and the plaintiff, Parsons. Plaintiff gave Bailey a cashier's check for $2,500 made payable to *TFC Leasing Corporation*. Approximately 1 month later, plaintiff learned that TFC and Trade Leasing were different companies and he demanded the return of his $2,500. This was refused.

The plaintiff thereupon sued TLC, Liberty Financial (LFC), TFC, and Bailey, claiming that there had been material misrepresentation and that Bailey was the agent of all the defendant corporations. Liberty Financial and Trade Leasing denied that Bailey had acted as their agent. The court directed verdicts in their favor. The plaintiff appealed the directed verdict.

HEDRICK, J. . . .

"The general rule is that a principal is responsible to third parties for injuries resulting from the fraud of his agent committed during the existence of the agency and within the scope of the agent's actual or apparent authority from the principal, even though the principal did not know or authorize the commission of the fraudulent acts." . . .

It makes no difference that the agent was acting in his own behalf and not in the interest of the principal when the fraudulent act was perpetrated unless the third parties had notice of that fact. . . .

"It would seem to be clear that if the agent is purporting to act as an agent and doing the things which such agents normally do, and the third person has no reason to know that the agent is acting on his own account, the principal should be liable because he has invited third persons to deal with the agent within the limits of what, to such third persons, would seem to be the agent's authority. To go beyond this, however, and to permit the third persons to recover in every case where the agent takes advantage of the standing and position of his principal to perpetrate fraud would seem to be going too far." . . .

In the present case, there seems to be sufficient evidence to support a finding that Bailey was an agent of Trade Leasing at the time he was negotiating with plaintiff. Plaintiff's case against Trade Leasing must fail, however, because there is no evidence in this record to support a finding that he was acting within the scope of authority of such agency when he was negotiating with the plaintiff. . . . The very contract signed by plaintiff and Bailey which defrauded plaintiff . . . and the very check given by plaintiff to Bailey made payable to TFC show conclusively . . . that plaintiff had notice that Bailey was not acting as the agent of Trade Leasing. . . .

The judgment appealed from is affirmed.

SUMMARY

A master is liable for physical harms caused by a servant, acting within the scope of employment, even though the master was not negligent in the selection of the servant and even though the servant was acting contrary to instructions. This rule is called the doctrine of *respondeat superior*. When a servant is "lent" by one employer to another, there are conflicting views as to whether the lending (i.e., the general) employer or the borrowing (the special) employer is, for the time being, the master and liable under respondeat superior.

In general, a servant is acting within the scope of employment if the act (1) is of the same general nature as, or incidental to, the authorized work; (2) is reasonably connected with the work in time and place; and (3) is intended by the servant as a part of the work. A servant who is making a delivery in a company automobile does not necessarily depart from the scope of employment when there is a deviation from a prescribed route. The master is liable if the deviation is a mere *detour*, but is not liable if the departure is a *frolic* of the servant. If the deviation is a frolic, the courts are not agreed on when the servant reenters the scope of employment. The majority view is that reentry occurs when the servant reaches a point reasonably close to the authorized route, intending to reengage in the authorized work.

Courts now recognize that a *master* may be liable for the *willful torts* of a servant. However, courts are less inclined to find a willful tort within the scope of employment than they are to find a negligent tort within the scope of employment.

A principal *(master or nonmaster)* may be liable for a servant's or nonservant's tort that does not involve physical injury if the injury was committed in the scope or course of the servant's or agent's employment. Among such torts could be, for example, defamation of a competitor by an officer of a company or false arrest of a customer, caused by a salesperson.

A *principal* (nonmaster) generally is *not* liable for torts involving physical injury caused by a nonservant agent if the principal was free from negligence in selecting the agent. For reasons of public policy, however, even though there was no negligence in the selection of the agent, a principal will be liable for physical injuries caused by an agent's activities if (1) the duty performed by the agent was personal to the principal and therefore not delegable; or (2) the work was inherently dangerous and precautions and safeguards adequate for the danger involved were not taken; or (3) the work was of such hazardous nature that it involved risk of injury to third persons regardless of any precautions that were taken to prevent tbe injury.

STUDY AND DISCUSSION QUESTIONS

1 *(a)* What is meant by the doctrine of respondeat superior? *(b)* What are some important reasons for such a doctrine in the law of agency? *(c)* What problems are commonly associated with the application of that doctrine?

2 *(a)* How can one tell whether a tort feasor was or was not a "servant"? *(b)* Under what circumstances would a master not be liable for torts of his or her servant? *(c)* If a servant is, at the time of the tort, working for two different employers, which of them might be liable for the servant's tort?

3 *(a)* If a servant engages someone else to help in his or her work and this subservant commits a tort, under what circumstances is the servant, but not the servant's employer, liable for the tort? *(b)* Under what circumstances are both the servant and employer liable?

4 *(a)* Define "scope of employment." *(b)* When is a servant within the scope of employment? *(c)* If, at the time a servant commits a tort the servant is acting both for his or her employer and for himself or herself, can the servant be said to be within the scope of his or her employment? Explain.

5 *(a)* Why are the time when, and the place where, a tort is committed important factors in determining scope of employment? *(b)* What is meant by "detour" in relation to scope of employment? *(c)* How much of a departure from a directed route transforms a detour into a frolic? *(d)* What is a "frolic" in the law of master and servant?

6 *(a)* What effect do explicit directions by a master to a servant concerning the degree of care the servant should exercise in his or her work have on the master's liability for the servant's torts? *(b)* Do you think it is fair for a master to be liable for the willful torts of his or her servant? Why or why not? *(c)* Can an employer be liable for a fraud or misrepresentation of his or her servant? Explain.

7 *(a)* Under what circumstances may an employer be liable for the physical torts of a nonservant agent? *(b)* What types of work would involve an employer's nondelegable duty? *(c)* What is the difference between inherently dangerous and ultrahazardous work?

8 *(a)* Can an employer be liable for the fraud or misrepresentation of a nonservant agent? Explain. *(b)* What is meant by a "disclaimer" or "exculpatory clause" by a principal in sales contracts or order forms? *(c)* In what way do such clauses protect the principal? *(d)* Why do they fail to give him or her full protection?

CASE PROBLEMS

1 Gage, employed by H, was a skilled mechanic who worked on tractor motors. He was sent by H to R's farm to repair a tractor. When Gage finished the work, R asked him to look at the motor on R's water pump. When Gage started it up, a pump part which Gage had failed to fasten, flew out, hitting W who was standing nearby. Is Gage, H, or R liable to W for the injury he sustained?

2 The Double Play Tavern sponsored a semi-professional baseball team. The players enjoyed playing baseball but they did not work for, nor were they otherwise employed by, the tavern. They received no compensation. The tavern furnished the balls, the bats, the equipment, and the team's share of the umpire expenses. These expenses were deducted by the tavern as business expenses in its tax returns. The tavern's name was carried on the uniforms furnished the players. One evening the Double Play team was engaged in the final contest of the season. The winning team would be the champion. In the last half of the ninth inning the score was 0 to 0. Hjort, the Double Play left fielder, dropped a high fly and the winning run scored. Hjort, in disgust and anger, picked up the dropped ball and threw it out of the field. The ball struck a girl walking across the street. She sued Double Play for the injuries she sustained. From a judgment for the plaintiff, the defendant, Double Play Tavern, appealed. Should the judgment be affirmed?

3   W was an advertising manager for Oil Daily, a publication. His duties required him to travel throughout nineteen states soliciting business. Late one evening he was driving his own car to Dallas, Texas, his home office. On his route, he drove 21 miles past Durant, Oklahoma, to Denison, Texas, but being too tired to continue, he decided to return to Durant and spend the remainder of the night with a friend. He did not find his friend at home, so W slept in his (W's) automobile. The next morning he proceeded on his way back to Denison, which was on the road to Dallas. Shortly before arriving at Denison, W fell asleep while driving and his car collided with plaintiff's vehicle. Plaintiff sued Oil Daily for damages. Oil Daily contended that W had deviated from his route and therefore at the time of the accident W was not within the scope of his employment. At the conclusion of the trial the defendant moved for a directed verdict. The motion was denied. Should the ruling be affirmed?

4   B was the manager and operator of the Clovis Club, a "Sho-Bar" owned by DuPree, the defendant. B's duties included supervising the employees and seeing that the customers were entertained. At the conclusion of the last act, when the bar was about to close, B, to amuse the customers, discharged into the air a pistol loaded with blank ammunition. Then he suddenly pointed the pistol at plaintiff's midsection and fired. The resulting explosion singed the plaintiff, and he sued DuPree. DuPree denied that B was acting within the scope of his employment when he discharged the pistol. What test or tests should be applied to determine whether or not the defendant is liable?

5   N was employed by the U.S. Forest Service in Mississippi. He had agreed to accept transfer to Tennessee. N was authorized to travel to Tennessee with his wife to find a new home preparatory to their change of place of duty. In accordance with Forest Service regulations, mileage and per diem were paid to N. While N and his wife were riding through the neighborhood in which they were considering the purchase of a home, N, driving his own vehicle, collided with an automobile driven by the plaintiff. Plaintiff sued the United States to recover damages resulting from the accident. Was N within the scope of his employment at the time of the accident?

6   H was employed by the defendant as the caretaker of an apartment house owned by the defendant. For some unknown reason, H shot one of the tenants who resided in the apartment house. The defendant continued to employ H and secured legal counsel to defend him in a criminal action arising out of the incident. The injured tenant sued the landlord for the damages he sustained, claiming that the defendant had, by retaining H in his employ and furnishing him counsel, ratified H's wrongful act. From a judgment for the defendant, the plaintiff appealed. Should the judgment be sustained?

Chapter
38
Obligations of Principals and Agents to Each Other; Termination of Agency

In the preceding chapters we examined the obligations of agents and principals to third persons. We saw that an agent who acts within the scope of actual or apparent authority has the power to bind a principal contractually. We also saw that where an agency relationship is that of master and servant, the master may be liable for the physical and nonphysical torts of a servant; and that where the relationship is that of principal and nonservant agent, the principal may be liable for the nonphysical torts of an agent, but that only in certain exceptional situations will the principal be liable for the physical torts of an agent.

In this chapter we do not distinguish between servant and nonservant agents because the obligations of a nonservant agent and a principal to each other are generally the same as the ob-

ligations present in the master-servant relationship.[1] We will therefore treat these obligations in the terms of principal and agent. First, we will discuss the obligations of agents and principals to each other and then the remedies available for violations of those obligations. The chapter closes with a discussion of termination of agencies.

OBLIGATIONS OF AGENT TO PRINCIPAL

From the discussion in the two preceding chapters, it is evident that an agent, by unauthorized

---

[1]*Restatement of the Law (Second)* American Law Institute, Philadelphia, 1958, secs. 429 and 461.

actions, may impose unwanted or onerous legal obligations upon a principal in contract as well as in tort. A principal, therefore, places great trust and confidence in an agent and assumes that he or she will follow the principal's instructions and will neither intentionally nor negligently act improperly in the performance of the agency. It is said that a *fiduciary* relationship exists between them, meaning a relationship of trust and confidence. In response to the reliance of the principal on an agent, an agent who acts either for a consideration or gratuitously, assumes in law a number of obligations to the principal. Those obligations can generally be characterized as follows: the duty to obey the reasonable instructions of the principal; to perform personally the duties of the agency; to use at least normal care and skill in the performance of those duties; and to be loyal to the principal's best interests. The scope of an agent's fiduciary responsibilities is demonstrated by the following case.

Case 38.1   **Campagna v. United States**
474 F. Supp. 573 (D.C. N.J. 1979)

Over many years Mr. Campagna performed renovation services for the Mautner-Glick Corporation upon various buildings that company owned or managed. When Mr. Campagna died, Mrs. Campagna, his widow (the plaintiff), continued to operate the business. A memorandum of understanding was entered into between Mautner-Glick and Mrs. Campagna whereby that company agreed to pay for all renovation work, labor, services, and materials furnished by her. This included the payment of the wages of her employees and the payment to the government of the amounts withheld from her employees for the purpose of paying taxes.

Mrs. Campagna, believing that there had been an overpayment by Mautner-Glick of withholding taxes, sued the United States for a refund. The Government filed a complaint against Mautner-Glick as an additional defendant. Pursuant to the Federal Rules of Civil Procedure, the District Court filed a memorandum opinion which states in part:

BIUNNO, Dist. J. [There is no proof that Mautner-Glick either paid Mrs. Campagna the gross wages of her employees so that she could pay their withholding taxes or that Mautner-Glick deducted and paid the government the necessary withholding taxes and remitted the balance to her.] The court finds that the monthly summary sheets . . . and the weekly payroll sheets . . . are false and unreliable records.

. . . The arrangement here, . . . was one in which Mautner-Glick undertook to serve as Mrs. Campagna's agent in the handling of the funds on the three buildings [on which Mrs. Campagna did renovation work] and doing the necessary bookkeeping and accounting. The relation was one of trust and confidence placed in Mautner-Glick. . . .   That trust and confidence were betrayed.

The relationship of an agent to his principal is not that of mere debtor and creditor, but is one of a fiduciary nature. The agent is held to a high standard of honesty, must admit to no selfish interest and cannot delegate the performance of discretionary duties. . . .

An agent stands in fiduciary relationship to his principal, and is under a duty to be careful, skillful, diligent and loyal in the performance of his principal's business and for failure so to act he subjects himself to liability to his principal.

Even one who undertakes *gratuitously* to act for another in a matter of trust and confidence shall not, in the same transaction, act for himself against the one relying on his integrity. . . .

An agent is not permitted to assume two distinct and opposite characters in the same transaction, in one of which he acts for himself and in the other pretends to act for his principal.

Officers of corporations are held to the same standard when acting for the corporation in connection with corporate dealings with others.

When an agent places himself in a position where his own interests may conflict with those of his principal, courts do not stop to inquire whether the agent has obtained an advantage or not. It is enough to show that he has attempted to assume two distinct, opposite and conflicting characters in the same transaction. . . .

In all transactions between persons occupying relations, whether legal, natural or conventional in their origin, in which confidence is naturally inspired, is presumed, or, in fact, reasonably exists, the *burden of proof* is thrown upon the person in whom confidence is reposed, and who has acquired an advantage, *to show affirmatively*, not only that no deception was practiced therein, no undue influence used, and that all was fair, open and voluntary, *but also that is was well understood.*

. . . The court finds that . . . there was a relationship of trust and confidence between [Mrs. Campagna] and Mautner-Glick. . . . Mautner-Glick did not "pay" the "labor", i.e., the total gross wages. . . .

Under these circumstances, Mrs. Campagna, while unable to establish her claim for refund from the United States (largely, the court believes, for lack of support from Mautner-Glick in another breach of duty) is entitled to have judgment against Mautner-Glick on her counter claim for indemnity, in the full amount of all federal withholding taxes and FICA taxes paid by or collected from her . . . together with interest. . . .

Judgment accordingly.

Duty to Obey Reasonable Instructions

An agent is under a duty to obey reasonable instructions given by his or her principal. An agent is also required to refrain from doing acts that the principal has not expressly or impliedly authorized. For example, if a sales agent is instructed to accept only cash payments, acceptance of a check violates the duty of obedience, even though the agent is convinced that the check is good and, in good faith, believes that the best interests of the principal are being served.

The statement that an agent has a duty to obey *reasonable* instructions is more accurate than the statement, sometimes found in the cases, that an agent has a duty to obey *lawful* instructions. An instruction may be lawful without being reasonable, but an instruction cannot be reasonable unless it is also lawful.

There is an exception to the rule that an agent has a duty to obey reasonable instructions. In emergency situations an agent may deviate from the instructions received to the extent that the agent in good faith deems necessary to protect the interests of the principal. An emergency situation is one that the agent reasonably believes was unforeseen by the principal and that requires action by the agent before he or she has an opportunity to inform the principal of the unforeseen event and to ask for revised instructions. For instance, a vehicle bearing perishable provisions breaks down at night. The driver (D), who is not authorized to obligate the principal by contract, is unable to reach the employer (E) by telephone. D asks a farmer to tow the truck to the nearest garage and assures the farmer that E will pay the charges for that service. E would be liable for the charges.

Duty to Perform Service Personally

Absent the express or implied consent of a principal, an agent is without authority to dele-
gate the duty of performance. An old adage of the law is: *Delegatus non potest delegare* (A delegate cannot delegate). The reason for the rule is obvious—since the risks of agency are substantial, a person should be subject to these risks only when represented or served by someone of his or her own choosing.

As indicated above, an agent can delegate the duty of performance if the agent has implied authority to do so. It is usually held that implied authority is present: (1) if the act that the agent seeks to delegate is purely ministerial as, for example, the clerical act of filling in the blanks of a printed purchase order with data furnished to the delegate by the agent; (2) if a well-established trade custom sanctions the delegation, as where it is customary for purchasing agents to purchase through brokers; (3) if the principal knows, or has reason to know, that it is impractical for the agent to perform the duty personally, as where the holder of a check that is drawn on, let us say, a Chicago bank, deposits the check for collection in a San Francisco bank, and (4) if an unforeseen contingency arises where it is impracticable for the agent to communicate with the principal to secure instructions, as illustrated in the preceding section. An agent's duty to perform personally is discussed in the following case.

Case 38.2   Greenberg v. Skurski
602 P.2d 178 (Nev. 1979)

Nine individuals, the defendants in this case, were an investment group. They owned, as tenants in common, certain commercial property called Starlite Industrial Park. By a written document they appointed one of their number, Mayer Greenberg, as their agent and attorney in fact with regard to the property. A real estate consultant, working on behalf of the owners, sent to Skurski, the plaintiff in the original action and the respondent here, and to other real estate brokers a brochure describing the property. Skurski and certain of his clients who were interested in its purchase, and some of the owners, carried on negotiations for its sale. Skurski later telephoned to Greenberg's office and talked to Eric Staniek, one of the nine owners. In the conversation

Skurski offered to purchase the property and Staniek said they "had a deal." The other owners claimed that they had not authorized Staniek to act for them and the sale was not consummated.

Skurski then sued all nine owners of the property to recover the real estate commission he allegedly had earned. The district court entered a judgment in his favor against all of the members of the investment group, having found that Staniek, as a subagent of Greenberg, was empowered to negotiate for and bind all members of the group in the sale of the property. The defendants in the original action denied that Staniek had authority to bind them in the transaction with Skurski and they appealed the judgment.

THOMPSON, J. . . . The document appointing Mayer Greenberg agent and attorney in fact for each tenant in common does not authorize the appointment of a subagent. There is no evidence to suggest that [the other owners] authorized Eric Staniek to act for them.

A subagent is a person appointed by an agent empowered to do so, to perform functions undertaken by the agent for the principal, but for whose conduct the agent agrees with the principal to be primarily responsible. . . . We read nothing in the record suggesting that the principals empowered Mayer Greenberg to appoint a subagent, nor may the record be read to indicate that . . . Greenberg agreed with his principals to be responsible for the conduct of . . . Staniek.

The agency relationship normally is grounded on the trust and confidence the principal places in his agent. Consequently, the law has come to look upon that relationship as personal in nature. It is for this reason that agency duties ordinarily cannot be delegated without the express authority of the principal where the duties involve any personal discretion, skill or judgment.

There is no question but that the duties placed upon Mayer Greenberg to act for the principals with regard to Starlite Industrial Park involved the personal discretion, skill or judgment of Greenberg. His personal performance was called for and his duty to so perform was not assignable to Eric Staniek or anyone else without the consent of his principals. . . .

[The requirement that a precondition of entitlement to a broker's commission is that he produce a buyer who is ready, willing and able to purchase the property upon the terms prescribed by the sellers was then discussed.]

The judgment below is reversed. . . .

Duty to Use Care and Skill

Unless otherwise agreed, an agent owes a duty to his or her principal to use reasonable care and skill in performing required duties. The employee does not guarantee that he or she will make no mistakes or that he or she possesses and will exercise the *highest* degree of skill and diligence. The law contemplates merely that a principal is entitled to expect that the agent has the degree of ability commonly possessed in the locality by one employed in the sort of work the agent undertakes. For example, a person who applies for a job in a machine shop impliedly represents that he or she can operate the machines with the proficiency of other operators in that job market; or a lawyer who agrees, either gratuitously or for a fee, to prepare a will, impliedly represents that the will shall comply with the applicable law. If an agent does not exercise the standard of care and skill that others in like trade or profession would use, the agent is liable for any losses the principal suffers.

Duty to Be Loyal to Principal

The most pervasive obligation that an agent assumes is the obligation to be loyal to his or her principal. Loyalty cannot be defined with precision. It depends much upon the generally accepted standards in the community. Of cardinal importance to this obligation is an employee's duty to refrain from placing himself or herself in a position that would ordinarily encourage a conflict between the agent's own interests and those of the principal. In requiring an employee to refrain from placing himself or herself in such a position, the law acts on the basis that it should preclude the possibility, however slight, that an agent will allow the dictates of self-interest to supersede the obligation to his or her principal.[2] Faced with a case requiring resolution of the question of whether there has been a breach of the obligation of loyalty, a court must choose between applying the public policy of encouraging initiative and the public policy of protecting the economic security of established enterprises. Therefore, with but slight change in the facts of any situation, a different conclu-

---

[2]*Robertson v. Chapman*, 152 U.S. 673 (1893).

sion could be justified as to whether an agent has violated the duty of loyalty to a principal.

For convenience, the agent's duty of loyalty will be treated under six general headings: (1) duty to communicate notice or knowledge; (2) duty to account to principal; (3) duty not to act for third person; (4) duty not to receive secret compensation; (5) duty not to use confidential information; and (6) duty not to appropriate principal's economic opportunities.

Duty to Communicate Notice or Knowledge

An agent has a general duty to keep the principal fully and promptly informed of all facts that materially affect the subject matter of the agency. The requirement of full disclosure applies even where the agent acquires the information outside the scope of employment. The duty extends to any information coming to the agent's knowledge that would put the employer in a more favorable bargaining or bidding position for future business. However, if information that would normally be of interest to a principal is received by an agent in confidence from a third party, the agent need not reveal it to the principal, for to do so would be a breach of confidence. Suppose, for example, that an attorney has two separate clients, X and Y. While representing X, the attorney acquires confidential information from Y that would be useful to X. The attorney cannot violate his or her confidence to Y by disclosing the information to X. The result of an agent's failure to communicate information is revealed in the following case.

Case 38.3   Miles v. Perpetual Savings & Loan Co.
388 N.E.2d 1364 (Ohio 1979)

Mr. and Mrs. Miles, the plaintiffs (appellee in this appeal), entered into an agreement to purchase a dwelling. In conjunction with the purchase, Miles met with Russell, president of the Perpetual Savings & Loan Co., the appellant, for the purpose of securing a mortgage loan upon the property. During discussions concerning the loan, Miles inquired about a termite inspection of the property and he was told that it was the savings and loan company's policy to require the inspection and that such matters were customarily handled by them. On September 5, 1975, Miles met with Russell and executed the documents to secure the loan and to make the down payment on the property. One of the documents indicated that a termite inspection had been made at a cost of $15. Later the same day the Savings & Loan was informed that the inspection showed that the house was termite infested and that treatment would cost $450. Russell discussed this with the *seller* of the property and her real estate agent. At no time did anyone tell Mr. or Mrs. Miles that termites were found in the house. Three days later the Savings & Loan recorded the deed and mortgage and the settlement proceeds were distributed to the parties to the transaction. A month later Miles went into possession of the property. A few days later they discovered termite damage.

The Mileses filed suit against the Savings & Loan for its failure to tell them the contents of the termite inspection report and claimed damages in an amount sufficient to pay the costs required to have the termite condition rectified. The trial court entered a judgment in Miles' favor. The savings and loan company appealed.

PER CURIAM [By the Court] . . . One who acts as an agent for another becomes a fiduciary with respect to matters within the scope of the agency relation. . . . An agent owes his principal a duty to disclose all material information which the agent learns concerning the subject matter of the agency relation and about which the principal is not apprised. . . . Furthermore, where a principal suffers loss through his agent's failure to function in accordance with his duty, the agent becomes liable to the principal for the resulting damage. . . .

Because of the facts at bar, we conclude that appellant, through its president, Russell, assumed the role of appellee's agent for the purpose of securing the termite inspection. From that relationship arose a duty to inform them of the results of the inspection, and the breach of that duty resulted in the damages found by the jury to have been sustained by appellees. . . .

During the course of the trial, Russell stated that he was acting as agent for [Mr. and Mrs. Miles only] in the settlement of the [sale of the house]. The record shows also that when appellees questioned Russell with regard to obtaining a termite inspection of the property, they were told that it was customary for appellant to handle such matters and that appellant [the savings and loan company] would do so in this instance. In reliance that the inspection would be conducted and the results made available to them, no separate inspection was initiated by appellees. . . .

. . . Therefore, appellant was duty bound to disclose the material facts relating to the termite infestation before recording the deed and distributing the purchase money proceeds.

[Exemplary damages were also discussed.]

The judgment of the Court of Appeals with respect to the award of compensatory damages is affirmed. . . .

Duty to Account to Principal If an agent receives money or property from the principal or from a third person to which the principal is entitled, the agent must keep a record of the transaction and must account for the money or property received. Furthermore, a careful agent will not mix the principal's funds with his or her own. A lawyer, for example, usually establishes a "Trustee Account" in which there is deposited all collections or other moneys that the lawyer holds for the clients' benefit. Some lawyers, out of an abundance of caution, maintain their Trustee accounts in banks other than those in which they maintain their personal accounts.

Duty Not to Act for Third Person An agent cannot represent both parties to a transaction unless both parties know of the dual relationship and consent to it. If the agent represents both parties, but with the consent of only one of them, the transaction is voidable at the election of the nonconsenting principal. If neither principal knew of the dual representation, the transaction is voidable at the election of either principal. If both parties consent to be represented by a common agent, there is a danger that the agent might, in the transaction, prefer one principal over the other. From a practical standpoint, therefore, such a dual agency relationship should be undertaken only under the most unique circumstances. However, if the sole function of an agent is merely to bring a buyer and seller together, not speaking for either in fixing the price or terms, he or she may serve both parties without violating any confidences or representing conflicting interests. An agent who acts in this capacity is called a "middleman." A real estate broker who lists property for sale is frequently a middleman.

An agent may not, without his or her principal's knowledge, be the third party in a transaction in which the agent is acting for a principal, even though the agent innocently believes that he or she is acting in the best interests of the principal. This situation can arise when the agent is engaged either in selling or in buying for a principal. An agent who is employed to sell property must not purchase the property for himself or herself unless the principal's consent to do so has been received. If the agent conceals the fact that he or she is the purchaser, the agent violates the duty of loyalty even though paying the going market price for the property. However, when the terms of the agency agreement allow the agent to retain anything above the selling price set by the principal, the agent may pay the set price and be freed from the restraint against purchasing. An agent cannot circumvent the prohibition against buying property he or she is employed to sell by having a spouse or someone else buy the property for the agent's benefit, for an agent cannot do indirectly what may not be done directly. If an agent locates property of the kind he or she is employed to purchase, the agent may not, without the principal's consent, buy it for himself or herself. The following case deals with the strict interpretation the courts give to the rule that an agent may not, without notice to the principal, buy property the agent has agreed to sell for the principal.

Case 38.4   **Sierra Pacific Industries, Inc. v. Carter**
              163 Cal. Rptr. 764 (Cal. 1980)

Sierra Pacific, the plaintiff, owned certain real property which it desired to sell. Carter, the defendant, was a real estate agent who was acquainted with the property. Relying on Carter's representation as to the value of the property, the plaintiff orally commissioned him to sell the property for an asking price of

$85,000 of which the plaintiff would receive $80,000 and Carter would receive $5,000. Carter showed the property to various people but was unable to sell it. After several months, Carter sold the property for $85,000 to his daughter and son-in-law. Carter retained $5,000 and turned over the balance ($80,000) to Sierra Pacific. Carter did not inform Sierra Pacific of his relationship to the buyers.

When Sierra Pacific learned that the buyers were Carter's daughter and son-in-law, that company instituted action against Carter alleging that he had breached his fiduciary duty as an agent and sought recovery of the $5,000 commission retained by him. The jury entered a general verdict in Carter's favor and a judgment was entered accordingly. The plaintiff, Sierra Pacific, moved for a new trial on the ground, among others, that the verdict was contrary to the law as the facts established a breach of Carter's fiduciary obligation to them. The court granted the motion for a new trial, which could result in Carter's loss of the commission, and Carter appealed claiming that no violation of fiduciary duties had occurred.

RHODES, Assoc. J. . . . An agent bears a fiduciary relationship to his or her principal which requires, among other things, disclosure of all information in the agent's possession relevant to the subject matter of the agency. . . . An agent may not compete with the principal, nor may he or she act as agent for another whose interests conflict with those of the principal. . . .

In the context of an agreement to sell land on another's behalf, the general duties inherent in every agency become more specific. A real estate agent must refrain from dual representation in a sale transaction unless he or she obtains the consent of both principals after full disclosure. . . . This means under most circumstances that if the agent is related to the buyer in a way which suggests a reasonable possibility that the agent him or herself (sic) could indirectly be acquiring an interest in the subject property, the relationship is a "material fact" which must be disclosed. . . .

There is no question that Carter concealed information material to this transaction from his principal, Sierra Pacific. He claims that he was exempted from the disclosure requirement, however, on the basis of a so-called "net listing." Under a net listing agreement the seller agrees to take a fixed sum of money for his property and the broker is entitled to all additional sums as his commission. It is true that under this type of arrangement, a broker may not be obligated to disclose any relationship he has to the buyer. . . .

In order to exempt a broker from the strict requirement of disclosure a real estate sales agreement must include a net sale price determined by the seller *without influence by the agent.* . . .

Here, uncontradicted evidence shows that Sierra Pacific officials agreed to the $85,000 figure based on an estimate Carter made at their request. It is irrelevant whether $85,000 represented a fair price, or whether the officials also relied in part on their own recent experience in acquiring property. "It cannot be overemphasized that the key factor in permitting the real estate broker this relief [provided under the net listing exception] is the independent and completely uninfluenced determination of the net sales price by the seller." . . .

It is thus evident that Carter owed a duty of disclosure to his principal, Sierra Pacific. It is equally evident that the duty was breached. . . . Apart from any actual and proximately caused loss on the price it received for its property, Sierra Pacific was entitled to recover the commission it paid to Carter. . . . "A real estate broker must act in good faith in the discharge of his duties as agent. . . . By misconduct, breach of conduct [sic] or wilful disregard, in a material respect, of an obligation imposed upon him by the law of agency he may forfeit his right to compensation."

We thus are led to the inescapable conclusion that Carter is liable to Sierra Pacific as a matter of law for a minimum of $5,000 and that the jury's verdict to the contrary was in error. . . .

The order granting a new trial is therefore affirmed with instructions to the court below to direct a verdict against the defendant. . . . The only triable issue remaining concerns the extent of plaintiff's damages. . . .

Duty Not to Receive Secret Compensation

To minimize the dangers that may arise from divided loyalties, the law directs that an agent may neither (1) make a secret profit on a transaction conducted for the principal; nor (2) accept a benefit of any kind from anyone who might influence the agent's actions on behalf of the principal. Assume that an agent, A, is authorized to sell the automobile of principal, P, for $500. A sells the car for $750 and pockets the difference. P is entitled to the $250 profit that A secretly made and, in addition, P may refuse to pay A the commission that would have been earned had the agent sold the automobile for the authorized price of $500. If P has already paid the commission, P may recover it. To illustrate the second situation, let us again assume that P wants to sell a car for $500. A finds a buyer, T, who is willing to pay $750. A tells T that he will try to get P to reduce the price to $500 if T will split the difference between $500 and $750 with him, A. Of course, P does not know of these arrangements. The sale is consummated and A pockets the $125 "bribe." In this situation P has a choice of remedies when the facts are discovered: P may at her option rescind the sale (because P's agent acted for T as well as for P), or go through with the sale. In either event, P can recover from A the $125 A received.[3]

Duty Not to Use Confidential Information

The law is well settled that an employee is subject to the obligation not to use for his or her own benefit, or for the benefit of a competitor, confidential information that the employee gains in the course of employment. This obligation continues after the employee leaves the employment in which the confidential information was learned. It is not necessary that the restriction be spelled out in the employment contract, for it is implicit in any hiring. A business concern's confidential information usually takes the form of, but is not limited to, trade secrets and customer lists. A principal's remedies for an employee's violation of confidentiality is a suit to recover the profits made by the employee through the use of that information, and suits to enjoin the employee and third parties from its further use.

A trade secret consists of any information, procedure, process, and so forth, used in a business that may give the firm an economic advantage over its competitors (see "Violating Trade Secrets," Chapter 7, p. 136). A unique

---

[3] *Restatement*, secs. 403 and 407.

process for giving synthetic fibers a suedelike texture is an example of a trade secret. To be a "secret" the firm must reasonably protect the information from the knowledge of its competitors and from the public. Merely to say that one of its industrial processes is a trade secret, without keeping the process confidential, is not sufficient to entitle the process to protection as a trade secret.

It is inevitable that when an employee changes his or her place of employment the employee will bring to the new job some knowledge gained from the former one. Though an employee has no right to use in the new employment the trade secrets learned in the previous work, the employee does have the right to use the skills and knowledge thus acquired. The line of demarcation between a learned skill and a former employer's trade secret is often difficult to draw. In such situations the difficulty must be resolved on a case-by-case basis.

Another aspect of the obligation of an agent to keep inviolate a principal's secrets is the obligation of professional people, such as attorneys, not to reveal, or to place themselves in a position where they might be tempted to reveal, information gained in confidence from clients.

Customer lists are compilations of the names of customers and potential customers of a business. For example, department stores compile lists of their charge accounts and stock brokers compile the names of people who evidence interest in financial matters. The lists are developed through the expenditure of time, money, and usually advertising effort. They are generally trade secrets representing a source of patronage and constitute an interest in property. Faced with a case involving the reputed misuse of a customer list by a former employee, a court must consider both the right of a business establishment to protect its property from invasion and the right of an individual to seek employment elsewhere or to become the owner of a business and to use the general business information acquired in prior employments. To resolve this conflict the courts will usually permit an individual to solicit the customers of a former employer if such customers are openly engaged in business or can be discovered in directories, the Yellow Pages of the telephone book, and similar sources.

The "shop-right" privilege also deserves mention as a variant of the obligation of an employee to protect information arising in the course of employment. It may be that an employee, during employment or while using the employer's materials and equipment, conceives and perfects an invention. If the duties of the employee are to conduct research and to invent, then the product of the employee's labors belongs to his or her employer and any patent the inventor secures should be assigned to the employer. But if the duties to conduct research and make inventions are outside the scope of the employment, the employer is not entitled to the invention but only to a shop-right interest in it. Such an interest entitles the employer to a nonexclusive right to make use of the invention without paying the employee any royalties therefor. The employee-inventor retains the ownership and, subject to the shop-right interest, full rights over the invention.

The next case deals with the confidentiality of information concerning the financial condition of a company gained by an individual who occupies a fiduciary relationship to that company.

Case 38.5   Diamond v. Oreamuno
248 N.E.2d 910 (N.Y. 1969)

Oreamuno was the chairman of the board of directors and Gonzalez was the president of Management Assistance, Inc. (MAI). MAI was in the business of financing computer installations. Under its lease provisions MAI was required to maintain and repair their computers, but because of lack of capacity it engaged IBM to service the machines. As a result of a sharply increased charge for such services, MAI suffered a decrease of about 75% in its net earnings. Before this information was made public, Oreamuno and Gonzalez sold a large block of their MAI stock at the then current price of $28 per share. After the information concerning the drop in earnings was made public, the value of MAI stock dropped to $11 per share. By selling before the drop in earnings was made public, the defendants were able to realize $800,000 more for their securities than they would have realized had they sold their shares after the drop in earnings was made public. The plaintiff, an MAI stockholder, brought a derivative action seeking to have the defendants account to the corporation for this sum as they were "forbidden to use [such] information . . . for their own personal profit or gain." A motion to dismiss the complaint for failure to state a cause of action was granted by the Supreme Court, special term; the Supreme Court, Appellate Division, reinstated the complaint and the defendants appealed.

FULD, C.J. . . . As a general proposition, a person who acquires special knowledge or information by virtue of a confidential or fiduciary relationship with another is not free to exploit that knowledge or information for his own personal benefit but must account to his principal for any profits derived therefrom. . . . This, in turn, is merely a corollary of the broader principle, inherent in the nature of the fiduciary relationship, that prohibits a trustee or agent from extracting secret profits from his position of trust.

. . . The defendants take the position that, although it is admittedly wrong for an officer or director to use his position to obtain trading profits for himself in the stock of his corporation, the action ascribed to them did not injure or damage MAI in any way. Accordingly, the defendants continue, the corporation should not be permitted to recover the proceeds. . . . It is true that the complaint before us does not contain any allegation of damages to the corporation but this has never been considered to be an essential requirement for a cause of action founded on a breach of fiduciary duty. . . . This is because the function of such an action, unlike an ordinary tort or contract case, is not merely to compensate the plaintiff for wrongs committed by the defendant, but, as the court declared many years ago . . . "to *prevent* them, by removing from agents and trustees all inducement to attempt dealing for their own benefit in matters which they have undertaken for others, or to which their agency or trust relates."

. . . The primary concern, in a case such as this, is not to determine whether the corporation has been damaged but to decide, as between the corporation and the defendants, who has a higher claim to the proceeds derived from the exploitation of the information. In our opinion, there can be no justification for permitting officers and directors, such as the defendants, to retain for themselves profits which, it is alleged, they derived solely from exploiting information gained by virtue of their inside position as corporate officials. . . . And a similar view has been expressed in the *Restatement, 2d, Agency* (§ 388, comment c):

"c. *Use of confidential information.* An agent who acquires confidential information in the course of his employment or in violation of his duties has a duty . . . to account for any profits made by the use of such information, although this does not harm the principal. . . . So, if [a corporate officer] has 'inside' information that the corporation is about to purchase or sell securities, or to declare or to pass a dividend, profits made by him in stock transactions undertaken because of his knowledge are held in constructive trust for the principal."

. . . The concept underlying the present cause of action is hardly a new one. . . . Under Federal law (Securities Exchange Act of 1934, § 16(b)), for example, it is conclusively presumed that, when a director or officer or 10% shareholder buys and sells securities of his corporation within a six-month period, he is trading on inside information. The remedy which the Federal statute provides in that situation is precisely the same as that sought in the present case under State law, namely, an action brought by the corporation or on its behalf to recover all profits derived from the transactions.

In view of the practical difficulties inherent in an action under the Federal law, the desirability of creating an effective common-law remedy is manifest. . . . For all that appears, the present derivative action is the only effective remedy now available against the abuse by these defendants of their privileged position. . . .

The order appealed from should be affirmed. . . .

Duty Not to Appropriate Principal's Economic Opportunities An agent must reveal to the principal all economic opportunities that the agent has reason to believe the principal would be interested in and could financially handle. An *economic opportunity* is the opportunity to engage in a transaction upon which a potential profit can be made. The following illustrates such a situation. A is a geologist working for P Oil Company. A's duty is to discover probable oil-bearing formations and to report them to P for its determination whether or not to purchase the property in which they lie. A discovers a property with great oil-bearing potential. Instead of reporting this to P Oil Company, the principal, A purchases the property for himself. When A personally took advantage of the economic opportunity the property represented, a fiduciary duty owed by A to P was violated. In effect, A was competing with his principal—hardly a demonstration of loyalty. If the principal does not take advantage of the opportunity, then the agent is free to appropriate it to his or her own benefit. An interesting aspect of the economic opportunity rule is revealed by the case which follows.

Case 38.6   **Group Association Plans, Inc. v. Colquhoun**
292 F. Supp. 564 (D.C. 1968)

Defendant Colquhoun was a soliciting agent of the plaintiff company, an insurance broker specializing in the sale of group insurance plans. Each series of negotiations leading to the establishment of a group insurance plan takes a considerable period of time and numerous conferences. Colquhoun had a written employment contract with the plaintiff that was due to terminate on May 31, 1966. The plaintiff wanted to renew the contract and discussed it with Colquhoun. Colquhoun asked for an increase in salary which was refused. On May 31, 1966, Colquhoun tendered his written resignation to the plaintiff and the next day went to work for a competitor company. Instead of discontinuing his solicitation of business from concerns that he had solicited while he was employed by the plaintiff, and letting other employees of that firm take up and continue the negotiations, Colquhoun continued his negotiations with those prospective customers in behalf of his new employer. Colquhoun succeeded in consummating the sale of group insurance plans to at least three of such prospects. The plaintiff brought suit to restrain these activities and to recover damages.

HOLTZOFF, Dist. J. . . . There is a common law duty involved. An employee who is in the process of securing business for his employer and works on the matter as part of his employment on his employer's time for which his employer pays him, may not, upon terminating his employment, continue negotiations in behalf of himself or in behalf of a new employer. In a sense he is delivering the proceeds or the fruits of his work for one employer to his new employer if he continues solicitations for the latter. This is such an activity that is clearly a breach of an agent's duty at common law irrespective of contract.

Judge Cardozo, in his usual inimitable style, in the case of *Meinhard v. Salmon*, 249 N.Y. 458, 464, 164 N.E. 545, . . . discussed a situation involving two joint adventurers, where one of them dealt with the property of the joint adventure for his own benefit and without disclosing the facts to his partner. Judge Cardozo said:

> "Many forms of conduct permissible in a workaday world for those acting at arm's length, are forbidden to those bound by fiduciary ties. A trustee is held to something stricter than the morals of the market place. Not honesty alone, but the punctilio of an honor of the most sensitive, is then the standard of behavior. As to this there has developed a tradition that is unbending and inveterate. Uncompromising rigidity has been the attitude of courts of equity when petitioned to undermine the rule of undivided loyalty by the 'disintegrating erosion' of particular exceptions."

Although the relation between a principal and agent is not technically that of a trustee and a *cestui que trust*, nevertheless there is a fiduciary relation between them. For this reason, Judge Cardozo's words are applicable to the instant case just as he applied them to the situation of two joint adventurers. . . .

This Court concludes, therefore, that in continuing negotiations with customers or prospective customers with whom he had been negotiating in his employer's behalf after terminating his employment, the defendant Colquhoun was guilty of a breach of duty to his former employer.

Accordingly, the Court will render judgment granting a permanent injunction against both defendants from continuing and accepting the fruits of the illegal course of action to which the Court has referred, and awarding damages as to the three prospective customers to whom the individual defendant succeeded in selling insurance plans in behalf of his new employer. . . . The measure of damages is the income derived by the corporate defendant, the new employer, from the business done with these three concerns, less the expenses incurred in conducting it. . . . The judgment for damages will run only against the corporate defendant and not against the individual defendant. The injunction will run against both.

OBLIGATIONS OF PRINCIPAL TO AGENT

The obligations owed by a principal to an agent stem from the principal-agent relationship. Some of the obligations are expressed; others are implicit within such a relationship. Among the obligations of the principal are the undertakings (1) to pay any compensation due the agent; (2) to retain the agent for the agreed tenure; (3) to provide the agent with means to accomplish the work; and (4) to compensate agent for injuries.

Duty to Compensate Agent for Services

The principal's duties to an agent primarily center around the obligation to compensate the agent for services rendered unless the agent has agreed to serve gratuitously. If the rate of compensation is not specified, a reasonable rate is implied. If there is a customary rate within the community for such services, the customary rate is usually held to be the reasonable rate.

When compensation is dependent upon the result attained, the agent earns a commission, fee, or bonus. For example, payment of a commission is the customary practice in the real estate business. Unless there is some other specific agreement, a real estate broker undertakes to find a buyer who is ready, able, and willing to purchase the principal's property at the price and terms directed. If he or she finds such a buyer, he or she earns a commission even though the principal decides not to make the sale. If the principal lists property for sale with several real estate brokers, the first broker to find a ready, able, and willing buyer is entitled to the commission; the time, effort, and money the other brokers may have expended to find a buyer are lost. If the owner sells the property through his or her own efforts, none of the realtors is entitled to a commission. Real estate brokers frequently require persons who list property with them to enter into exclusive agency contracts or, preferably, exclusive sales contracts. Under either form of contract the broker agrees, for the period of time stipulated, to exert his or her best efforts to find a purchaser. When an exclusive *agency contract* is used, the owner may, during the agreed agency period, sell the property through his or her own efforts without being obligated to pay a commission. When an exclusive *sales contract* is used, the owner is obligated to pay the agreed commission even if he or she finds a buyer through his or her own efforts. Which type of contract serves a principal better depends upon the particular circumstances then present.

A principal is obligated to keep whatever accounts are necessary to establish the amounts of money due the agent for services rendered. If the agent is an employee, the principal also must make deductions from the agent's salary for Social Security, disability insurance, income tax, and so forth, and augment those deductions as required by state or federal law.

Duty to Continue Employment for Term of Contract

A principal has the duty to continue an agent's employment according to the terms of the express or tacit agreement between them. An agency may be at will, or for a reasonable period, or for some fixed time, or for the accomplishment of a stated purpose. An agreement to pay salary by fixed time units, as by the week, month, or year, is evidence, in connection with other factors, to establish the term of employment. Usually, a promise by the principal to give an employee "permanent employment" is held to be employment for a reasonable period only according to such conditions as may exist, rather than for the life of the employee. If the agent promises to work for a fixed period or until a stated objective is accomplished, there is a duty on the part of the principal to permit the agency to continue for that length of time, provided the agent satisfactorily performs the assigned duties. Thus, although a principal has the *power* to terminate an employment, the *right* to do so may be limited by the circumstances. The right to discharge an employee is further constrained by union agreements and civil rights legislation.

Duty to Provide Means to Accomplish the Work

A principal is obligated to furnish an agent with the means necessary to accomplish the task for which he or she was hired. For example, a salesperson should usually be furnished samples or descriptive literature; and a brickmason, paid by the number of bricks laid in a day, should be supplied with the bricks, mortar, and scaffolding required to do the job. The employer is also obligated not to interfere unreasonably with the agent's performance of duties. An employer should not place the agent in such a position that the agent's possibility of future employment is jeopardized. For instance, an employer should not require an agent to perform an illegal or unethical act.

Duty to Compensate Agent for Injuries; Workers' Compensation Laws

At the beginning of this chapter it was stated that the obligation of a nonservant agent and the principal to each other are *generally* the same as the obligations present in the master-servant relationship. In discussing the right of an agent to be compensated for injuries suffered in the course of employment, we must revert to the distinction between nonservant agents and servants. Unless a specific understanding to the contrary exists, a *nonservant* agent is not entitled to compensation for injuries sustained while performing services for a principal. A *servant*, however, *is* entitled to be compensated for injuries sustained in the scope of employment. This distinction arises from the fact that a principal does not have the right to control the physical activities of a nonservant agent; a master *has* the right to control the physical activities of a servant (discussed at length in Chapter 36).

Under the common law, a worker (servant) injured in the course of employment had great difficulty in securing compensation for work-related injuries. If the claim went to trial, the worker had two almost insurmountable obstacles to overcome: the fellow-servant rule and the assumption-of-risk rule. Under the former, a worker could not recover if the injuries were caused by another worker (fellow servant). Under the latter rule a worker was held to have assumed all of the risks of the place of employment and of the tools and machinery upon which he or she worked. Therefore, if an injury was, for example, sustained because a press did not have a guardrail, if a workroom was poorly lit and had a slippery floor, or if protective clothing was not furnished, the worker was presumed to have assumed the risks that might flow from an employment voluntarily entered into. Even if a servant in a particular case was able to overcome the impediments to recovery presented by these two rules, compensation might still be barred because the worker had been contributorily negligent.

All states now have workers' compensation acts.[4] These statutes are substitutes for the common law in this field. The fellow-servant and assumption-of-risk rules have been eliminated. Compensation for injuries is independent of any negligence on the part of either the worker or the employer. A speedy administrative proceeding takes the place of court trial. Recovery is allowed according to a fixed scale applicable to all workers according to the nature of the injury sustained. Payment is assured because each employer is required to carry workers' compensation insurance or to satisfy financial responsibility laws. Workers' compensation laws are also of benefit to employers because the employers' liability is limited to the amount of their insurance premiums.

REMEDIES FOR VIOLATION OF DUTIES

Remedies Available to Principal

When an agent fails to observe a duty owed to a principal, some remedy is always available. Under proper circumstances the principal may have several different remedies, as for instance, the principal may:

1 terminate the agent's contract of employment,

---

[4]In the federal system there are the Federal Employer's Liability Act, 45 USC 51; the Longshoremen's & Harbor Worker's Compensation Act, as amended, 33 USC 901; and the Merchant Marine Act (the Jones Act), as amended, 46 USC 1160.

2 withhold compensation otherwise due the agent,

3 recover any secret profit the agent may have made in violation of his or her agency obligations,

4 recover, or impose a trust upon, any money or property gained or held by the agent to which the principal is entitled,

5 restrain the agent, by court injunction, from continuing to breach the agency obligations,

6 recover damages from the agent for breach of the contract of employment,

7 recover damages from the agent that may have been assessed against the principal for the agent's wrongdoing, or

8 rescind a contract entered into by the agent based on a bribe or other improper inducement of a third party or based on an improper relationship between the agent and a third party.

It will be observed that the remedies are of various kinds—some are "self-help" remedies, while others require court action. Some of the remedies apply only where the agent has had contractual dealings with a third party; others apply only where the agent committed a tort; and still others may apply in both situations. The choice of one of the remedies in the above list may bar resort to some other remedy. For example, if the principal seeks rescission of the agency contract, it would be inconsistent to ask for an injunction restraining the agent from future violations of agency duties. Often, however, several of the remedies are at the same time available to a principal. Thus, a principal may have the right to terminate the agency agreement, to withhold compensation from the agent, and also to recover a secret profit made by the agent. The question whether an agent who has been disloyal may be forced to repay all salaries received during the period of his or her disloyal actions is not susceptible to a simple answer. That subject is dealt with at length in the next case.

Case 38.7   **Hartford Elevator, Inc. v. Lauer**
289 N.W.2d 280 (Wis. 1980)

From 1972 until 1975 Lauer, the defendant, misappropriated funds belonging to his employer, the plaintiff. After Lauer was convicted of the crime, the employer filed a civil action to recover the money misappropriated and also to secure repayment of all salary and bonuses paid to Lauer during the 3-year period during which the misappropriations took place. The trial court concluded that Lauer's contract of employment imposed a duty of loyalty upon him and therefore the employer was entitled to recover the amount misappropriated plus all salary and bonuses paid to Lauer during the entire period of the breach of duty. Lauer appealed so much of the decision as holds that he must return the salary and bonuses he had received.

ABRAHAMSON, J. . . . The only question before us on appeal is whether the trial court erred in concluding as a matter of law that an employee who breaches his duty of loyalty must return to the employer compensation he received for services rendered during the period of the breach.

. . . There is no question that the employee in the case at bar, a general manager, owed a fiduciary duty to the employer, breached that duty and is liable for the breach. . . .

The general rule appears to be that an agent who is dishonest in the performance of his duties forfeits the right to compensation. This rule is derived from the broader principle of contract law that a party who violates an agreement should not be permitted to recover under the contract. However, these rules are not rigid, inflexible or without exceptions. . . .

Sec. 456 of the Restatement (Second) of Agency (1957) sets forth the liability of the employer to the defaulting employee for compensation as follows:

"If a principal properly discharges an agent for breach of contract, or the agent wrongfully renounces the employment, the principal is subject to liability to pay to the agent, with a deduction for the loss caused the principal by the breach of contract:

"(a) the agreed compensation for services properly rendered for which the compensation is apportioned in the contract, whether or not the agent's breach is wilful and deliberate; and (b) the value, not exceeding the agreed ratable compensation, of services properly rendered for which the compensation is not apportioned if, but only if, the agent's breach is not wilful and deliberate." . . .

The Comments to this section of the Restatement explain apportioned and unapportioned services as follows:

"b. *Apportioned services.* If an agent is paid a salary apportioned to periods of time . . . he is entitled to receive the stipulated compensation for periods or items properly completed before his renunciation or discharge. This is true even if, because of unfaithfulness or insubordination, the agent forfeits his compensation for subsequent periods or items.

"c. *Unappropriated services.* If the agent has rendered services, compensation for which is not apportioned in the contract of service, and his renunciation or other breach of contract is not wilful, he is entitled to an amount equal to the fair value of his services. . . . A breach of contract is wilful and deliberate . . . only when the agent, in complete disregard of his contractual obligations, fails to perform or misperforms the promised services and has no substantial moral excuse for so doing. . . ."

If the agent sues the principal for compensation, sec. 469 of the Restatement . . . provides that the employer may defend the suit by proving disloyalty and insubordination. . . .

Comment e to sec. 469 states that if the principal in ignorance of the agent's faulty conduct pays the agent, the principal can maintain an action to recover the amount.

In addition, because agents and trustees are classed together for many purposes as fiduciaries, it is instructive to look at the Restatement (Second) of Trusts (1957) which speaks to the effect of a breach of trust on the trustee's compensation. Sec. 243 provides:

"If the trustee commits a breach of trust, the court may in its discretion deny him all compensation or allow him a reduced compensation or allow him full compensation."

The Comment to this section explains . . . that the reduction or denial of compensation is not in the nature of an additional penalty for the breach but is based in the fact that the trustee has not rendered . . . the services for which compensation is given. . . .

It is clear that the agent is liable for damages in the event of a breach of duty and that any losses he caused may be offset against any claim he may have for compensation. However, we do not adopt the rigid, mechanical rule urged by the employer that compensation is automatically denied to the agent during the period in which he has committed a wilful and significant breach of duty or loyalty. . . .

We conclude that whether the agent should be denied all or any part of his compensation during the period in which he breached his duty or loyalty depends on consideration and evaluation of the relevant circumstances with a view to avoiding unjust enrichment of or unjust deprivation to either the employer or employee. The circumstances to be considered include, but are not limited to, the nature and extent of employee's services and breach of duty; the loss, expenses and inconvenience caused to the employer by the employee's breach; and the value to the employer of the services properly rendered by the employee. . . .

The burden of proof to establish a right of the employer to recover compensation paid to the employee as a result of the employee's breach of duty owed to the employer is upon the employer. . . .

Because the trial court . . . incorrectly concluded that it had no alternative but to deny the employee the entire compensation for the entire period during which he misappropriated funds, we reverse the judgment and remand the matter to the trial court to determine whether the employee should be denied all or any part of his compensation.

Judgment reversed and remanded. . . .

Remedies Available to Agent

The remedies of an agent against a principal are generally founded upon breach of express or implied contract. Just as some of the remedies available to a principal may be cumulative, so some of the remedies available to an agent may be cumulative. Where appropriate, the agent may do one or more of the following:

1   terminate his or her employment,

2   recover damages for the principal's breach of contract,

3   rescind the employment agreement and recover the value of services rendered,

4   secure reimbursement for payments made by the agent for the principal,

5   secure indemnity for personal liability sustained while performing an authorized act for the principal,

6   secure exoneration from liability for a tort committed under the direction of the principal,

7   enforce a lien, if so authorized by statute.

TERMINATION OF AGENCY

Methods of Termination

An agency relationship may terminate by reason of some limitation in the agency agreement; by subsequent mutual assent; by decision of one of the parties; or by operation of law.

Termination by Provision in Agency Agreement   Where an agency is created for an object or purpose specified in the agency agreement, the agency terminates automatically when the object or purpose has been accomplished. Similarly, if the agreement states that the agency is

to exist for a specified period of time, the agency terminates automatically at the end of the specified time.

Termination by Subsequent Mutual Assent   Since an agency is created by mutual assent, it can be terminated by mutual assent.

Termination by Decision of One Party   Because an agency is a consensual arrangement, either the principal or the agent terminates it if there is manifested to the other either orally, in writing, or through actions that the agency relationship no longer continues.[5]

However, an agreement establishing an agency may provide that for the agreed period neither party may terminate the agency unless justified by the conduct of the other or by supervening circumstances. If either the principal or the agent improperly terminates the agency, such person is liable to a suit for damages by the other party.

Termination by Operation of Law   This phrase is somewhat misleading. It seems to imply that some methods of termination result from operation of law and that others do not. In reality, termination occurs only where the law says it can or does occur. However, the phrase

---

[5]*Restatement*, sec. 119. It has been said that an "agency coupled with an interest" may not be revoked in violation of its terms. An example of an agency coupled with an interest is a pledge delivered by A to B, where B is authorized to sell the pledged property in the event A defaults in paying the debt and to remit to A any surplus that B receives from the sale. However, such a relationship, although in the form of an agency, is not an agency as that word is used in the *Restatement of Agency, Second* (sec. 118d) but is a power given as a security interest. The holder of a security interest has rights other than those possessed by an agent (*Restatement*, secs. 138 and 139; also Warren A. Seavey, *Handbook of the Law of Agency*, West Publishing Company, St. Paul, 1964, sec. 11c).

is a useful one and has long been used to denote methods of termination that do not result from some limitation in the agency agreement, or from mutual assent, or from a decision of one of the parties. Termination *by operation of law* occurs in the following ways.

Death of principal or agent   The general rule is that the death of the principal or agent terminates an agency. Upon the death of the principal, any agreement for personal services made between an agent and a third party is ineffective, even if they are unaware of the death. This may impose hardship upon the agent, whose contract with the third party was made under the implied warranty of authority to act for the principal. With the death of the principal the agency relationship expired, and the agent's acts thereafter were made without authority. The agent may, therefore, be liable for a suit for damages for breach of the implied warranty.[6] The third party may also suffer because the contract was not binding and a third party cannot recover from the estate of the principal for breach of contract. The hardships resulting from the application of the rule that the death of the principal terminates the agent's authority has caused some states and some courts to take a more liberal attitude, and they have modified the rule.

Insanity of principal or agent   Although the general rule is that the insanity of either a principal or an agent terminates the authority of the agent, in a few states the courts hold that an agent has power to bind a principal who has become insane if the principal has not been judicially declared insane, if the third person had no knowledge of the insanity, and if injustice can be prevented in no other way.

Loss of qualification of principal or agent The failure of a principal to obtain or retain in effect a required license may result in the termination of the agent's authority. Similarly, the failure of an agent to obtain or retain in

effect a required license may result in the termination of authority to represent the principal. For instance, if P employs A as her lawyer to represent her in a legal matter, and thereafter A is disbarred, the disbarment terminates A's authority to represent P.

Impossibility of performance   The authority of the agent is terminated when the accomplishment of the agency purpose becomes impossible. Thus, if A is employed to effect the sale of P's automobile to T, the destruction of the automobile terminates A's authority.

Subsequent illegality   A change of law that makes performance of the agent's duties illegal terminates the agency relation. Suppose that the P Company, engaged primarily in the manufacture and sale of slot machines, employs A to manage its interstate sales department. Subsequent enactment of a federal statute making the interstate shipment of slot machines illegal would terminate the agency relationship of P and A.

Important change of circumstances   The authority of an agent terminates when there is such a change in the affairs of the principal, or in the subject matter of the agency, or in external events, that the agent should reasonably infer that the principal would not desire the agent to act under the changed circumstances. Suppose that a farmer employs an agent to sell his farm because he cannot borrow enough money to buy the equipment necessary to farm the land properly. If the agent later learns that the farmer inherited a large sum of money or that oil had been struck on the adjacent farm, the changed circumstances might result in a revocation of the agent's authority.

Notice to Third Persons of Termination

Notice Where Termination Is by Act of Party or Parties   When an agency is terminated by act of the parties or of one of them, the principal should give prompt notice of the termination to all persons who may have learned of the agency.

---

[6]Seavey, *Handbook*, secs. 48 B and 124.

Failure to give notice may leave the agent with apparent authority and, as we have seen, one who has apparent authority to represent another has the power to bind him or her contractually to third persons who act in reliance on the apparent authority.

Persons who are entitled to notice of the termination fall into two groups. One, those who are known to have dealt with the agent or who are known to have been negotiating with him or her at the time of the termination. To cut off the agent's apparent authority that has been manifested to this class of individuals, the principal must notify each of them either orally or by written communication that the agency was terminated. If the letter is properly addressed, stamped, and mailed, the principal has done all that he or she could do and the notification is legally effective even though the addressee does not receive it. Two, the second class comprises those who have done business with the agent but whose identity the principal may have no way of ascertaining (usually those who have dealt with the agent on a cash basis) and those who have not dealt with the agent but may have in some way learned that he or she was representing the principal. To terminate the authority that was apparent to those third parties, the principal should publish notice of termination in a newspaper of general circulation in the area where the agent was representing, or was purported to be representing, the principal.

Notice Where Termination Is by Operation of Law The general rule is that the law does not require notification in order to cut off an agent's apparent authority where the termination of the agency relationship is by operation of law. However, in some instances the courts have protected a person who was not notified of the termination or of the fact causing the termination. Evidently, the general rule is not an inflexible one, and a court may choose not to apply it if its application would cause great hardship to a third person.

SUMMARY

In return for the trust and confidence that a principal reposes in an agent, the agent owes fiduciary duties to the principal. Besides the duty to perform the work assigned, an agent's primary obligation to the principal is that of loyalty. Loyalty involves dealing openly with the principal and making full disclosures of all matters concerning the agency. It is obvious that an agent must account for the money and property that comes into his or her possession to which the principal is entitled. An essential aspect of loyalty in this context is that an agent cannot represent both the principal and a third party to a transaction without the consent of both those parties. Furthermore, an agent cannot himself or herself become the third party to a transaction without the consent of the principal, as otherwise the agent would be representing possible opposing interests at the same time. The same considerations dictate that an agent should not directly or indirectly use to personal advantage confidential information that is gained through the agency relationship or make a secret profit on an agency transaction.

When an agent violates fiduciary obligations, the principal has the right to terminate the agency and to withhold any compensation that would be due the agent had there been no violation of duty. In addition, the principal has a cause of action for damages against the agent that the principal may have sustained because of the agent's violation of duty. The principal may also rescind a contract that the agent made with a third person where the third party used improper means (e.g., bribery) to induce the agent to enter into the contract.

A principal's obligations to an agent involve paying the compensation expressly or tacitly agreed between them and permitting the agent to accomplish the work for which the agent was hired. Upon breach of such obligations, the agent has contract actions against the principal.

An agency agreement, being personal between the parties, terminates at the will of either of them or when its purposes are accomplished. It is terminated by operation of law if either of the parties dies, becomes insane, or ceases to be qualified to act. An agency is also terminated by operation of law when the purposes of the agency become impossible or illegal of performance.

An agent's *apparent* authority to act for a principal may continue after the agent's *actual* authority to do so has ceased, as the agent may still appear to a third party to be authorized to act for the principal. To terminate this continuing apparent authority, actual notice must be given to third parties who have done business with the agent and a notice by publication must be given to those who may have known of the existence of the agency but had not done business with the agent.

STUDY AND DISCUSSION QUESTIONS

1 *(a)* Why is the distinction between servants and nonservant agents, which was so important in the previous agency chapter, unimportant in this agency chapter? *(b)* Why does the law hold agents to a high standard of conduct? *(c)* State four main duties an agent owes to a principal.

2 *(a)* What is meant by "reasonable instructions" in the law of agency? *(b)* What discretion does an agent have who has received from a principal instructions as to how the work or service is to be performed?

3 *(a)* Why is an agent generally precluded from delegating to another his or her duty of performance? *(b)* Under what circumstances may an agent delegate to another his or her duty of performance? *(c)* Assume that A and his brother, B, are both experienced bus drivers; that A is employed by a bus company but B is unemployed; that one day A is sick so he asks B to drive his bus that day; and that B does so. Has

A violated any duty he owes to his employer? Explain.

4 *(a)* What is meant by an agent's duty of loyalty to a principal? *(b)* State six areas in which it can be said that an agent owes a duty of loyalty to a principal.

5 *(a)* A traveling salesperson, while on business in a city removed from her home office, learns that certain supplies used by her employer can be acquired there at a very low price. Should she inform her employer of this opportunity? What agency principle is involved? *(b)* The article the sales representative sells is in short supply with deliveries promised to customers in the sequence of their orders. A customer gives the salesperson $100 to backdate his order. What agency principle is involved?

6 *(a)* X, a former employee of the Y Company, now works for himself. May X solicit Y's customers whose names X learned through his employment by Y? Why or why not? *(b)* Would your answer be any different if X had personally secured these customers for Y? Why or why not? *(c)* What is meant by "trade secret"? By "shop-right" privilege?

7 *(a)* State three main duties a principal owes to an agent. *(b)* Contrast an exclusive agency contract and an exclusive sales contract.

8 *(a)* State four ways in which an agency relationship may be terminated. *(b)* If an agency relationship was created by a writing, may it be terminated by oral notice of revocation or renunciation? What is the theory behind the legal rule? *(c)* Under what circumstances is an agency terminated by "operation of law"? *(d)* Assume that an agent, who has no knowledge of the death of his or her principal, enters into an agreement with a third party in the name of the deceased principal. Is there a contract? Why or why not?

9 *(a)* What third parties should be notified when an agency is terminated? *(b)* By what means should those third parties be notified?

CASE PROBLEMS

1 Plaintiff was a motion picture actress under written contract of employment with the defendant motion picture company. The contract required her to abide by the rules and regulations of the producing company and to report for rehearsals promptly. She was repeatedly late for rehearsals and on some occasions could not be reached to be told when she was needed for work. On January 22, the defendant caused a letter to be delivered to the actress directing her to be present at the studio every morning not later than 8:30 A.M., "irrespective of whether you are cast or not." Plaintiff did not report for work on January 24, 25, or 26. She was discharged on January 27. Plaintiff brought suit for the wages due her for the unexpired period of her contract, claiming that she had no work to do on any part of the 3 days that she was absent; that the order to report every day was not reasonable; and her violation of the order did not justify a rescission of her contract. The court charged the jury that if the motion picture company did not have any general rule requiring actresses to be present not later than 8:30 A.M. "irrespective of whether they were cast or not," and if Lola May had not been instructed to act on the days in question, then she did not breach her contract. Would you agree that this was a proper charge? Explain.

2 Brink was an insurance broker who held himself out as an insurance expert. Hardt ran a business which was located in a rented building. The lease required Hardt to pay the rent for the full lease period even if the building were to be damaged by fire. Hardt asked Brink to secure a fire insurance policy for his business. Brink did not investigate the terms of Hardt's lease and secured a policy of insurance covering only Hardt's machinery and merchandise; it did not cover damage to the building, reimbursement for rent that would have to be paid, or for such losses as Hardt would suffer if the building was not usable because of a fire. There was a fire which rendered the building unusable, but because of the lease provisions Hardt was required to pay rent on the building for the remainder of the lease period. Hardt thinks Brink should compensate him for the loss. Is Hardt correct?

3 Helen, the plaintiff, bought a "package tour" to Las Vegas from a travel agency. The agency, in turn, booked Helen on a tour that was put together, or "wholesaled" by another agency. At the airport, the wholesaler agency misdirected Helen's baggage; in addition, she was not given accommodations in the hotel she had been told she would be registered in but was forced to accept accommodations a distance from the city's activities. Helen asserts that she should be compensated for the inconvenience she suffered. (*a*) Is she entitled to such compensation? (*b*) If so, which agency is liable, the one from which she purchased the tour or the wholesaler agency in charge of the tour?

4 The San Antonio Development Company, Inc., purchased certain property from the plaintiff. As specified in the offer of purchase, the plaintiff paid a real estate commission to Strehlow, the President of San Antonio. The plaintiff later learned that the entire purchase price was put up by Strehlow and two associates and that soon after the sale was completed San Antonio conveyed the property without consideration to a partnership consisting of Strehlow and the same two associates. The plaintiff then brought action to recover the real estate commission that was paid to Strehlow on the ground that he was a principal and not an agent in the transaction. As the plaintiff sold the property at a price agreeable to him and voluntarily paid a normal real estate commission, can he now successfully require a refund of that commission?

5 The Board of Directors of Queen Fisheries, Inc., in December 1965, employed Williams for a period of 3 years as its president and general manager. Williams, in addition to his managerial duties, operated a lighterage service using Queen's equipment as though the lighterage service were his own business. On November 10, 1966, Williams was relieved of his managerial duties and was notified that he was no longer an officer and director of the Queen Fisheries. He continued to write checks on the lighterage account. On December 14, 1966, Williams was notified that his employment with Queen was terminated effective December 31, 1966. Williams brought suit against Queen Fisheries, Inc., alleging breach of his employment contract. Queen Fisheries denied liability and demanded, among other relief, the return of the salary that had been paid to Williams during 1966. The lower court held that Queen was not liable to Williams for breach of his employment contract and that Williams could retain the money he had received as salary. Both the plaintiff and the defendant appealed. Should the verdict of the lower court be sustained?

6 The Edison Company is a large organization with many stores. Joe worked for Edison as a buyer of products that were sold in Edison's stores. Jaclyn was a manufacturer of goods of the kind sold in Edison's stores. In order to assure themselves that Edison would buy their merchandise, Jaclyn repeatedly and covertly gave Joe sums of money. Joe's superiors in the Edison organization found out that Joe was accepting these gifts but a year passed before Joe was fired. Edison refused to pay Jaclyn for merchandise received, asserting that since Jaclyn had given Edison's salesman a commercial bribe, Edison was not obligated to pay for the goods. Should Edison be required to pay Jaclyn?

7 Plaintiff had a written contract with the defendant hospital whereby he was appointed its medical director for a period of 10 years, with the sole authority to select its professional personnel. The agreement stated that "it may not be revoked or altered by The Hospital during that period." One year later the president of the hospital association wanted the plaintiff to appoint certain doctors as assistant medical directors. Plaintiff asserted his sole authority under the contract and the hospital notified him that his association with the hospital was terminated. The plaintiff sued to enjoin the hospital from terminating his services as medical director. The defendant answered that "even if just cause [for cancelling the contract] were lacking, they have the power to terminate the agency or employment relationship, subject only to an action for damages if, in so doing, there is a wrongful breach of the contract." Was the defendant's position correct?

PART NINE

PARTNERSHIPS; MINOR BUSINESS ORGANIZATIONS

Chapter 39

Formation of Partnerships;
Rights and Liabilities of Partners

Chapter 40

Partnership Property

Chapter 41

Termination of Partnerships
Addendum: Limited Partnerships and
Minor Business Organizations

Chapter

39

Formation of Partnerships; Rights and Liabilities of Partners

The partnership is a common form of business organization that is of ancient lineage. References to partnerships can be traced as far back as the Hammurabian Code of Babylon and the Roman law. Eventually, the law of partnerships became a part of the English common law; however, in the United States it is now codified with modifications as the Uniform Partnership Act within the statutory law of almost all of the states.[1] In the states that have not yet adopted the Uniform Partnership Act, the act nevertheless influences the decisions of the courts.

This discussion of partnerships is based main-

ly upon the Uniform Partnership Act, hereafter referred to as the UPA. The first chapter deals with the nature and formation of partnerships, and the rights and liabilities of partners. The two succeeding chapters deal with partnership property and the termination of partnerships, including the division of assets.

The three chapters do not cover the subject of limited partnerships. The limited partnership is a less common form of business organization, entirely distinct from that of the general commercial partnership being considered here. The law relating to limited partnerships is codified in the United States as the Uniform Limited Partnership Act, often referred to as the ULPA. The three chapters are followed by an addendum

---

[1]The Uniform Partnership Act (reprinted in Appendix 2) was drafted by the National Conference of Commissioners on Uniform State Laws, after years of consideration.

that tabulates the principal differences between general partnerships and limited partnerships, and describes briefly various minor forms of business organizations.

MEANING OF PARTNERSHIP

Partnership under the Common Law

A partnership is a business organization composed of two or more persons, without limit as to number. Although such an association gives the appearance of being a distinct legal entity, the common law considers a partnership to be merely an aggregate or collection of the persons who compose it. Not being a legal entity or having a personality of its own, a partnership under the common law has no rights or duties separate from those of its members. The rights of the organization to hold or own property, to sue and be sued, and to engage in contracts, for instance, are viewed as belonging to the members of the partnership and not to the organization as such. All of the partnership property is jointly owned by the several partners. The title is held in their names and the property may be inherited by the widow or other heirs of the partner on his or her death. It has been said that

there is "no other relationship known to the law which, in its nature, is so complicated as is a partnership."[2]

Partnership under the Uniform Partnership Act

Modern case law and the UPA depart somewhat from the common law aggregate theory of partnerships; and partnerships are, in certain circumstances, being recognized as possessing characteristics of separate legal entities. For example, it will be noted in the two succeeding chapters that a partnership, under the UPA, can hold and convey property in its partnership name similar to the manner in which a corporation holds property; partnership creditors are given priority in partnership assets in the event of dissolution; partnership property, as such, is not part of the estate of a deceased partner; and the continuance of a partnership business after the death of one of its members is possible. As revealed in the following case, a partnership may be considered an entity, rather than an aggregate of individuals, and thus become guilty of a regulatory offense.

---

[2]Reed Rowley, *Rowley on Partnership*, 2d ed., Bobbs-Merrill, Indianapolis, 1960, p. 15.

Case 39.1   People v. Smithtown General Hospital
399 N.Y.S.2d 993 (N.Y. 1977)

The defendant hospital is a partnership of forty-two individuals. The hospital was alleged to have permitted an unauthorized person to participate in a surgical procedure upon an uninformed, nonconsenting patient and falsifying its records. The defendant hospital moved to dismiss the indictment, contending that because it was a general partnership it was not subject to the criminal law since a partnership is not an entity separate and apart from the aggregate of individuals who are its members. The opinion of the court entered with regard to that motion follows.

JASPAN, J. . . . While the criminal liability of corporations and individuals acting in the name of a corporation is expressly set forth in the Penal Law . . . no similar provision is found with respect to partnerships and no reported case has been found in this State which deals directly with this issue.

The legislative pattern is probably grounded upon the common law concepts of a partnership as opposed to that of the entity known as a corporation. But the definition of "person" in the Penal Law [a "human being, and where appropriate, a public or private corporation . . . a partnership . . . "] and the mandate of that law . . . that it be liberally construed provide an opportunity for rationalization in the interests of promoting justice and effecting the objects of the law.

A partnership has been defined as a relationship with no legal being as distinct from the members who comprise it. . . . But that is a generalization which invites exceptions. . . .

The partnership can be either an entity or an aggregate of its members depending upon the nature of its activities and in the case of criminal law depending also upon the nature of the infraction. . . .

The concept of a partnership as an entity liable for certain of its criminal activities independent of culpability by its respective members was expressly considered in *United States v. A & P Trucking Co.*, 358 U.S. 121. . . . Two partnerships were charged, as entities, with violations of [a statute] which makes it a crime to knowingly violate some Interstate Commerce Commission regulations. . . .

The Supreme Court [of the United States], relying upon a definition of persons . . . similar to that [above quoted] held that impersonal entities can be guilty of knowing or wilful violations of regulatory statutes through the doctrine of respondeat superior and that a partnership may be considered an entity separate and apart from the aggregate of its members.

The operation of a hospital is so intertwined with the public interest as to legally justify the imposition of extensive controls by all levels of government. . . . The health care is provided by the facility and not necessarily by any of its proprietors. Accreditation, when given, is provided to the institution, and not to the component members of the named proprietor. The hospital is in every sense an entity and not just an aggregate of the 42 individual partners. . . .

In civil law, two or more persons conducting a partnership may sue or be sued in the partnership name. I now hold that this defendant may be charged in an indictment as an entity with the commission of crimes related to the discharge of its primary obligations as a general hospital even though there is no showing of culpability on the part of the individual's partners.

The motion to dismiss the indictment . . . is denied. . . .

FORMATION OF PARTNERSHIPS

The UPA defines a partnership as "an association of two or more persons to carry on as co-owners a business for profit" [6(1)].[3] To understand more fully the nature of a partnership,

---

[3]Numbers in brackets in the text of this series of chapters refer to sections of the UPA.

the formation of a partnership, and the relationships that arise out of membership in such a business organization, this definition must be analyzed.

Requisites for Partnership

Analysis of the UPA definition reveals three requirements for a partnership: (1) an agreement between or among the members of the association; (2) a business for profit; and (3) partners to be co-owners of the business.

An Agreement   There can be no partnership in the absence of an agreement. If by their agreement the parties intend a relation that includes the essential elements of a partnership, a partnership results. It results even though the individuals did not realize they were creating a partnership relation or even though they were trying to avoid creating such a relation in order to escape some of its legal consequences. Conversely, if by their agreement the parties intend a relation that lacks some requisite for a partnership, there is no partnership even though the persons thought they were forming a partnership. Where the agreement does not make clear whether the associates intended a partnership relation, their intention may be determined by examining the way they have been conducting the business of the enterprise.

An agreement is a requirement for a partnership, but the law does not specify the form the agreement must take. Although a partnership agreement need not necessarily be in writing, the rights and liabilities of the partnership members are so affected by the terms of their agreement that the preferred practice is to reduce the partnership agreement to writing.

A Business for Profit   A partnership association must be designed to carry on a trade, occupation, or profession for profit [2]. It may, of course, conduct more than a single business. Courts are not in agreement as to whether an association organized to conduct an isolated transaction for profit is a partnership. Some courts hold that such an organization is merely a joint venture; nevertheless, they will apply partnership law to such an organization as though it were a partnership.[4]

Partners to Be Co-owners   Lastly, to establish a partnership there must be agreement that the several members will be the co-owners of the business. This ownership of the business is to be distinguished from the ownership of the property used in the business. The partnership as a business entity, not the members, owns the property. Co-ownership involves the sharing of the profits and the losses of the enterprise and the right to engage in its management, unless the partners agree to the contrary.

The receipt by a person of a share of the profits of an enterprise is prima facie evidence that he or she is a partner in the business, but this presumption does not conclusively prove that the individual who is entitled to a share of the firm's profits is a partner. A court may inquire into the basis for such entitlement to determine whether the other requisites to establish a partnership are present. For example, A lends $5,000 to B to assist him in his business. They agree that in lieu of interest A will be paid a designated percentage of the profits earned in the business. A is merely B's creditor and is not a partner in the enterprise. Or it may be that B hires C as his store manager, agreeing to pay her 25 percent of the store's profits as her salary. In this situation there is merely an employer-employee relationship and not a partnership. In each of these situations there is no community of ownership in the business itself, a primary requisite for partnership.

Frequently, it is difficult to determine whether a business arrangement is a partnership. In deciding whether a partnership exists, a court takes into consideration all of the circumstances surrounding the understanding between the parties [7]. When one associate claims that a

---

[4]Alan R. Bromberg, *Crane and Bromberg on Partnership*, West Publishing Company, St. Paul, 1968, sec. 35, p. 192.

partnership was formed and the other denies it, strict proof is required to establish the existence of a partnership. A lesser degree of proof is required to establish the existence of a partnership when an action is brought by a third person who, having relied on the manner in which the entity was doing business, asserts that it was a partnership. The tests applied by one court to determine whether or not a partnership existed appears in the following case.

Case 39.2   Stone-Fox, Inc. v. Vandehey Development Co.
611 P.2d 1195 (Or. 1980)

A property known as Family Acres was owned by Vern Vandehey and Jack P. Leonard as tenants in common. They had no oral or written partnership agreement. They developed and subdivided the tract and sold lots within it, sharing profits, losses, and management. Vandehey conveyed his undivided interest in the property to the Vandehey Development Company (VDC). Four days earlier he had signed on behalf of VDC an agreement to sell the entire property to the plaintiff, Stone-Fox, Inc. Leonard did not sign the agreement of sale and the documents were not executed in the name of a partnership or joint venture, nor was there a written authorization by Leonard for Vandehey or VDC to sell the property. The deposit the plaintiff made when executing the agreement of sale was later returned to him by Leonard for the reason that at the time the agreement was signed VDC had no interest in the property. The following week VDC and Leonard, the defendants, executed an agreement for the sale of Family Acres to another party.

The plaintiff immediately filed suit against VDC and Leonard for specific performance of the agreement executed by VDC asserting that a partnership existed between VDC and Leonard and that the agreement with the plaintiff was an enforceable partnership obligation. The lower court held that there was no partnership and entered a decree for the defendants. The plaintiff appealed.

JOSEPH, Presiding Judge. . . . A partnership is an association of two or more persons to carry on a business for profit as co-owners. . . . "Person" includes corporations as well as individuals. . . . Tenancy in common "does not of itself establish a partnership, whether such co-owners do or do not share any profits made by the use of the property," . . . nor does "the sharing of gross returns" have that effect. . . . A partnership may exist for a single transaction, in which case it is called a joint venture. . . . Partnership law controls joint ventures. . . . It is well established that a partnership dealing in real property can be demonstrated by parol evidence . . . and partnership may be shown from the objective conduct of the alleged partners.

In *Hayes v. Killinger* . . . 235 Or. at 471, 385 P.2d at 750, the Supreme Court set out the criteria for determining when a partnership exists in the eyes of the law:

"The essential test in determining the existence of a partnership is whether the parties intended to establish such a relation. Given the multiplicity of legal consequences that flow from a partnership, we should not surprise the parties into such a relationship against their will. However, a disinclination to assume the burdens of a partnership does not necessarily preclude the creation of that relationship, since the substance of legal intent rather than the actual intent may be controlling. In the absence of an express agreement codifying the relationship, the status may be inferred from the conduct of the parties in relation to themselves and to third parties. In other words, if they function as a partnership, they must assume the attendant duties and liabilities. . . .

"In placing the conduct of these parties in the framework of a partnership, no one factor is absolutely determinative; the entire factual setup must be examined as a whole. But when faced with the intricate transactions that arise, this court looks mainly to the right of a party to share in the profits, his liability to share losses, and the right to exert some control over the business. Those are deemed the earmarks of a partnership. . . . "

In this case, VDC and Leonard acknowledged that they shared in profits and losses and that each had the right of control in the Family Acres project. They contend nonetheless that these factors alone are not sufficient to establish a partnership, since they also describe incidents of co-tenancy. Like partners, co-tenants share equally in profits and liabilities. . . . But whereas co-tenants also hold an undivided interest in real property . . . one co-tenant cannot bind another to a real property transaction without written authorization. . . .

The relationship of VDC and Leonard in the Family Acres project involved more than joint land ownership. They were engaged in a business endeavor, which consisted of acquiring, subdividing and selling a parcel of real property. The project entailed construction of curbs, grading of roads and installation of gas, electricity, sewer and water lines, as well as platting and financing. Each had supervisory power over the operation. The profits and losses were to be shared. In short, despite defendants' "disinclination to assume the burdens of a partnership" . . . there was "such an amalgam of funds, of property, of skills, of risks, of control or of interest as would create a joint adventure." . . .

Once a partnership or joint venture is established, agency need not be proven to show that one partner or venturer was authorized to act for another [when the act is within the normal scope of the partnership business]. . . . VDC bound the venture by signing the . . . agreement as seller of the whole undivided interest in Family Acres. . . .

Defendants here maintain that their intent was that Leonard had to approve the sale; but his formal assent was not necessary, as we have seen, to bind the partnership. . . .

We conclude that plaintiff is entitled to a decree of specific performance of the . . . agreement. . . .

Partnership Name

When a partnership is formed, the partners normally adopt a name under which the business of the firm will be conducted. As a partnership grows and prospers, considerable value may attach to the name. The name adopted may consist of the names of the partners or one or some of them, as for example, "Mary Henry and Peter Jones, Realtors," or "Mary Henry and Sons." Often the name adopted is an assumed or fictitious name, such as "Tasty Food Cafe" or "Modern Barber Shop."

In most states the choice and use of a fictitious name is governed by statute. A partnership that does business under such a name may be required to give public notice in a newspaper of its formation and to file a certificate in the public records of the county where it does business or maintains its principal office. The certificate must list the names and addresses of the partners. By referring to the certificate, creditors are able to discover the identity of the individuals responsible for the debts of a partnership. In some states a partnership that does not file the required certificate is subject to a penalty; in other states the partnership is merely precluded from bringing suit until it complies with the filing statute.

The listing in a fictitious-name certificate of persons as members of a partnership is evidence that they are partners; but such evidence is not conclusive, since their names may have been used without actual or implied permission.

THE MEMBERS OF A PARTNERSHIP

Who May Be a Partner

The General Rule   Each partner is a principal in the conduct of the business affairs of the organization. As a principal, a partner must be legally competent to enter into partnership contracts. Therefore, as a general rule, any person who can legally enter into contracts may become a member of a partnership.

Even though a person is legally qualified to be a partner, "no person can become a member of a partnership without the consent of all the partners." This doctrine, recognized in Section 18(g) of the UPA, is technically known as "delectus personae" (literally, choice of the person). The rationale for the doctrine is that a partnership is necessarily based on mutual trust and confidence, and therefore a person should and does have the right to choose his or her partners. The doctrine of delectus personae applies in the formation of partnerships, but its chief application is in the addition of new members to partnerships already in existence.

Application of the General Rule to Special Classes of Persons   Under ordinary contract law, a *minor* may enter into contracts; thus, it follows that minority furnishes no legal impediment for an individual to become a member of a partnership. As a member of a partnership a minor is entitled to all of the rights and priviliges of an adult partner, including the right to share in the partnership profits. But since under contract law a minor may disaffirm contracts, a minor may at any time during minority disaffirm the agreement to be a member of the partnership.

If a minor disaffirms the agreement, his or her status as a partner is repudiated from the date of membership and the minor is freed of personal liability to former copartners and to the partnership creditors. However, any contributions made to the partnership assets by the minor remain subject to the claims of those creditors who extended credit to the firm prior to the minor's disassociation from the partnership. In some jurisdictions, a minor's contributions to the partnership are also liable to the claims of the copartners for losses sustained by the partnership prior to disassociation, unless the minor had been fraudulently induced to enter into the partnership. If so induced, the minor could, of course, compel the former partners to return whatever contributions he or she may have made to the partnership assets.

The UPA defines *persons*, for the purpose of interpreting the act, as: "Individuals, partnerships, corporations, and other associations" [1]. Therefore, if a corporation's charter so authorizes, the *corporation* may become a member of a partnership with all of the rights and liabilities of an individual member of the partnership. A *partnership*, too, as a business entity, may become a partner with other individuals, with corporations, or with other partnerships.

Types of Partners

The UPA provides for only one type of partner. Each member is a general partner within the organization.[5] Each is personally liable to third persons for all obligations of the partnership. In addition, each partner has an equal right to manage the partnership business unless the partnership agreement provides otherwise.

A descriptive title is sometimes given to an individual associated with a partnership. The title describes the status of that individual within the enterprise with respect to persons outside the partnership, who are usually referred to as third persons. Among other titles are: dormant partners; secret partners; incoming, retiring, continuing, and surviving partners; and partners by estoppel.

A *dormant or silent partner* is a true member of a partnership with all the rights and liabilities

---

[5]There is no "limited partner" in a partnership organized under the UPA. A limited partner exists only in a limited partnership organized under the ULPA, or other statutory authority. See Addendum to Partnerships, pp. 883–886.

as such, but whose association with the firm is not generally known to persons with whom it does business. The dormant partner's name is not used in the firm's business, and usually such partner takes no part in the management of its affairs. If a dormant partner does take an active part in the management of its affairs, he or she is sometimes referred to as a "secret partner," rather than as a dormant partner.

An individual who becomes a member of an existing partnership is called an "incoming partner." A "retiring partner" is one who ceases to be a member of an association that is continued by the remaining or "continuing partners." Those partners who continue a partnership business after the death of a member are called "surviving partners."

Sometimes a person appears to be a partner when he or she is not. An individual who is not, in fact, a member of a partnership might represent himself or herself to a third person as a member, or permit another so to represent him or her. In these circumstances, if the third person in good faith relies upon the representation and extends credit to the firm, the individual who was falsely represented to be a partner becomes what is called a "partner by estoppel" or an "ostensible partner" [16]. Although a partner by estoppel is not, in fact, a partner in the enterprise, the partnership is liable to a third person who gives the firm credit based upon the misrepresentation as if that individual were a partner. The partnership, having received benefit from the misrepresentation, becomes responsible to the third party. The following case shows how a partner by estoppel situation may arise.

Case 39.3   Anderson Hay and Grain Co. v. Dunn and Welch
467 P.2d 5 (N.M. 1970)

Lincoln Management controlled all the concessions at the Ruidoso Race Track. It subleased the feed concession there to Virgil Welch. In that agreement

Welch was described as an independent contractor. In order to obtain the sublease, Welch was required to have Sam Dunn guarantee the note securing the sublease. Dunn had an interest in Lincoln Management. Dunn and Welch entered into a written agreement whereby Dunn was given sole right to maintain the accounting records, inventory controls, and accounts receivable of the concession for the purpose of protecting him from liability to creditors of the feed concession which might arise from his guarantee of the note but not for the purpose of establishing a partnership. A bank account was opened in the name of Ruidoso Downs Feed Concession and both Dunn and Welch were authorized to sign checks and to make withdrawals. Welch filed a partnership income tax return for the concession for the year 1968.

Anderson Hay and Grain Co. (plaintiff) extended credit to the concession on the strength of Dunn's financial responsibility, and the grain company contacted Dunn for payments on account. After the signing of the sublease contract, Kenneth Newton, president of Lincoln Management, supposedly sent a letter to Anderson Hay and Grain (the receipt whereof was denied) advising that Welch would be responsible for all debts incurred by the Ruidoso Downs Feed Concession. Action was commenced by Anderson Hay and Grain Co. to recover more than $13,000 allegedly owed to it by defendants Welch and Dunn. The trial court awarded judgment against Welch and dismissed the complaint against Dunn. The plaintiff appealed.

TACKETT, J. . . . The only issue before this court is whether Dunn was a partner in the operation of the Ruidoso Downs Feed Concession. . . . The public conduct of both Dunn and Welch lead to the conclusion that they were partners, and Dunn and Welch allowed themselves to be so held out. . . .

Section 66-1-16, N.M.S.A., 1953 Comp., [UPA, sec. 16] is as follows:

1 When a person, by words spoken or written or by conduct, represents himself, or consents to another representing him or any one, as a partner in an existing partnership or with one (1) or more persons not actual partners, he is liable to any such person to whom such representation has been made, who has, on the faith of such representation, given credit to the actual or apparent partnership, and if he has made such representation or consented to its being made in a public manner he is liable to such person, whether the representation has or has not been made or communicated to such person so giving credit by or with the knowledge of the apparent partner making representation or consenting to its being made.
(a) When a partnership liability results, he is liable as though he were an actual member of the partnership.
(b) When no partnership liability results, he is liable jointly with the other persons, if any, so consenting to the contract or representation as to incur liability, otherwise separately.

2 When a person has been thus represented to be a partner in an existing partnership, or with one (1) or more persons not actual partners, he is an agent of the persons consenting to such representation to bind them to the

Case 39.3
Continued

same extent and in the same manner as though he were a partner in fact, with respect to persons who rely upon the representation. Where all the members of the existing partnership consent to the representation, a partnership act or obligation results; but in all other cases it is the joint act or obligation of the person acting and the persons consenting to the representation.

Dunn, by his conduct, actions and words, furnishes substantial evidence that he and Welch were partners. . . . It is immaterial that the parties do not designate the relationship as a partnership, or realize that they are partners, for the intent may be implied from their acts. . . .

If Dunn did not want to be considered or held out as a partner in the feed business, he should not have allowed himself to be so associated. He consented to being held out as a partner by his actions. . . . Consent can be implied by conduct. Holding out as a partner may be construed from acts and conduct. . . . When appellant demanded money from Dunn on account, Dunn never said he was not a partner. When payments were past due, appellant called Dunn on the telephone and Dunn would send a check. A reasonable conclusion to draw from such occurrences is that Dunn was the responsible partner. It is sufficient if the course of conduct is such as to induce a reasonable and prudent man to believe that which the conduct would imply. . . .

Dunn conducted himself so as to induce appellant to deal with him in the belief that he was a partner and, by so doing, created a partnership by estoppel. . . .

The statutory tests for partnership by estoppel require (1) credit must have been extended on the basis of partnership representations; or (2) that the alleged partner must have made or consented to representations being made in a public manner, whether or not such representations were actually communicated to the person extending credit. . . . By these statutory tests, Dunn is a partner by estoppel.

The trial court erred in not so finding. . . .

The case is reversed and remanded to the trial court with instructions to reinstate it on the docket and enter a new judgment against Dunn and Welch. . . .

RIGHTS AND DUTIES OF PARTNERS

Since each partner owns an undivided share of the partnership business, each partner is a principal in the partnership enterprise and has all of the rights and liabilities accruing to any owner. In addition, since more than one individual owns the partnership business, each may, by his or her actions in behalf of the partnership, affect the rights and liabilities of his copartners and of the partnership as a business organization. Therefore, in a partnership

each partner acts as a principal in his own behalf and as an agent for his co-partners; the functions, duties, rights and liabilities of the partners in a great measure comprehending those of agents, and the general rules of law applicable to agents apply with equal force in determining the rights and liabilities of partners.[6]

This dual relationship affects (1) the rights and duties of partners between or among themselves; and (2) the powers and liabilities of partners with respect to third persons.

Rights of Partners

Right to Participate in Management It is basic to the partnership concept that each partner has an equal right with the other copartners to manage the firm's business [18(e)]. The right to participate in the conduct of the partnership business is not limited by the value or the kind of contribution that the several partners may have made to the enterprise. For example, one member of a partnership may contribute as his share of the enterprise the sum of $10,000, another member contributes certain patents that she owns, and the third contributes $2,000 and his experience. Each of these partners is entitled to an equal voice in the conduct of the business.

Where a partnership consists of more than two members, decisions concerning its ordinary business transactions may be made by a majority of the members [18(h)]. However, certain acts are so far outside the usual course of business that they must be authorized by all of the partners. Among such acts are: assigning the partnership property for the benefit of creditors, or selling the goodwill of the business, or doing any other act that would make impossible the continuance of the ordinary business of the partnership; confessing a judgment; and submitting a partnership claim or liability to arbitration [9(3)].

Partners, among themselves, may limit their spheres of activities and powers. For example, three partners may agree that one of them will be the "inside man" who will run the machine shop but will enter into no contracts for the firm except the hiring of shop employees; the second

partner will be the purchasing agent for the partnership; and the third will devote full time to the sale of the firm's products. Such an arrangement will, of course, limit the managerial authority of each of the partners. It does not, however, affect the firm's liability to a third party who does business with a partner without knowledge of the limitation upon the scope of that partner's authority. If a partner exceeds his or her agreed upon authority, such partner is liable to the copartners for any losses which may result.

Right to Have Access to Partnership Books Each partner has the right to have access at all times to the partnership books and to make copies of them if he or she so desires [19]. The right may be important to a partner in that partner's management capacity. It may be equally important for private purposes, as, perhaps, for the purpose of determining or checking on his or her share of the firm's profits. Usually, the firm's books are more readily accessible if they are kept at the firm's principal place of business. The UPA requires the books to be kept at such place, unless the partners agree otherwise [19].

Right to Share in Profits In the absence of an agreement to the contrary, each partner is presumed to have an equal share in the business, and therefore each is entitled to an equal portion of the profits. Such a presumption exists even though the several partners may have contributed to the partnership money, property, or services of unequal value. Partners who do not wish this presumption to apply should enter into an agreement that stipulates the share of the profits each is to receive.

Right to Be Compensated for Services Unless the members of a partnership have agreed otherwise, a partner is entitled to no compensation for any services performed for the enterprise [18(f)]. That partner's remuneration is his or her share of the partnership profits, which are divided among the several partners. Where some partners devote their entire time to the partnership business while other partners are

---

[6]*Lindly v. Seward*, 5 N.E.2d 998 (Ind. App. 1937).

partially or totally inactive, there may be an express or implied agreement that the working partners will receive compensation in addition to their portion of the profits.

It is possible that a partner who has not rendered the services called for in the partnership agreement may be charged with the cost of hiring someone to do the work that that partner failed to perform; or the other partners may be allowed compensation for the value of their services to the partnership in addition to their share of the firm's profits.

Where controversy arises regarding the right to compensation, or indeed regarding any of the rights and duties of partners among themselves, the partners should seek to settle their controversy amicably. Appeal to the courts may prove useless. Courts are loath to settle claims of partners against each other except in connection with the dissolution of the partnership. A leading authority on partnership law reflected this view of the courts when he wrote: ". . . partners should not seek to have the courts operate their affairs; if they cannot get along amicably, they should dissolve [the partnership] and wind up [its affairs]."[7]

---

[7]Bromberg, *Crane and Bromberg*, sec. 72.

Right to Indemnity and to Repayment Because each partner is an owner of the partnership, each is personally responsible for the firm's obligations, whether they arise out of contract or tort [15]. Moreover, a partner is entitled to be *indemnified* by the partnership for any partnership obligation that he or she was required to discharge in the ordinary and proper course of the firm's affairs or for the preservation of its property [18(b)]. A partner who makes a payment in aid of the partnership business, or an advance to the partnership beyond the amount of capital he or she agreed to contribute, is also entitled to *repayment* and to interest from the date of the payment or advance [18(c)]. If the partnership or copartners be required to pay damages to a third person because of the tort of a partner, the partnership or the aggrieved members may secure *reimbursement* from the wrongdoing partner. Upon dissolution of the partnership, a partner is entitled to be *repaid* his or her capital contribution and any advances that that partner may have made that were not repaid prior to dissolution[18(a)]. A frequently discussed case which examines the application of Section 18 of the UPA to an unusual situation is the case of *Levy v. Leavitt* which follows.

Case 39.4   Levy v. Leavitt
178 N.E. 758 (N.Y. 1931)

Levy, the plaintiff, joined with Leavitt, the defendant, in a venture wherein the defendant would purchase a large quantity of bacon from the government with the expectation of an early profitable resale. Plaintiff paid defendant $50,000, and it was agreed between them that plaintiff would receive 20 percent of the net profits or stand 20 percent of the net loss, should a loss occur. Their agreement was silent as to how the venture would be financed or conducted, but it was understood that the defendant would manage the venture and the plaintiff would perform no services and make no further capital contributions.

Claiming that Leavitt had violated the Lever Act (a World War I act restricting certain exports), the government, after delivery of the bacon, caused it to be impounded, and the defendant was unable to deliver it to overseas purchasers. By the time Leavitt obtained the release of the bacon, it had so deteriorated that although he made extraordinary efforts to sell the bacon both in the United States and in Europe, it could not be sold. The bacon was ultimately destroyed by public authorities. As a result, the venture lost the entire purchase price of the bacon, amounting to $700,000. The defendant then managed to have a special act of Congress passed whereby the government consented to the Court of Claims' hearing defendant Leavitt's claim for indemnification. Defendant was ultimately successful in having the claim allowed and paid.

Levy, the plaintiff, brought an action for an accounting. Defendant Leavitt sought repayment of the reasonable value of his services in attempting to sell the bacon and interest on moneys that he advanced to the venture in the conduct of its business. The referee denied this allowance, and defendant Leavitt appealed.

LEHMAN, J. . . . Upon the accounting, the defendant has been denied the right to charge as an expense of the joint venture or partnership the reasonable value of any services rendered by the defendant, and interest on any moneys which he loaned or furnished to the venture in the conduct of its business. The rights and obligations of the partners as between themselves arise from and are fixed by their agreement. . . . Here the [partnership] agreement was oral and informal. There is nothing to show that the parties considered or discussed whether the defendant should be entitled to compensation for his services or to any interest for moneys he might furnish. The question then is whether from the relations of the parties and the circumstances of the transaction, an implication of a promise of compensation for services rendered or of interest upon moneys paid arises.

. . . "In the case of joint partners, the general rule is, that one is not entitled to charge against another, a compensation for his more valuable or unequal services bestowed on the common concern, without a special agreement; for it is deemed a case of voluntary management." [*Bradford v. Kimberly*, 3 Johns, Ch. 431, 435] . . . In the business of a partnership the services of a partner are rendered for the common benefit in the performance of an obligation created by the partnership agreement, and the resultant benefit is divided pro rata as provided in the partnership contract. Those profits constitute, in the absence of other agreement, the stipulated reward for services to be rendered, and there is no right to other compensation based on the reasonable value of the services actually rendered. Inequality in the value of services rendered, even the fact that the services were extraordinary and that, at the time the contract was made, the parties did not contemplate that such services would be required in the course of the partnership business, would not alone justify the award of compensation outside the share of profits accruing to the partner rendering the services. . . .

Though the evidence shows that unexpected obstacles called forth extraordinary exertions by the defendant in attempting to sell the bacon, nevertheless his services at that time were performed in compliance with the obligation he had assumed, when the partnership was formed, to devote his efforts to the resale of the bacon. There are no circumstances which would support an inference that the services were performed at the special request of his copartners or under a special agency or employment, or that the partners agreed to pay any compensation for such services. Certainly none which would require such an inference as a matter of law.

. . . The defendant's right to charge against the plaintiff's share in the partnership funds, interest on moneys furnished by the defendant, like his right to charge compensation for his services, depends upon the contract made between the parties. . . . The Partnership Law . . . provides: . . . "A partner, who in aid of the partnership makes any payment or advance beyond the amount of capital which he agreed to contribute, shall be paid interest from the date of the payment or advance." And . . . "no partner is entitled to remuneration for acting in the partnership business, except that a surviving partner is entitled to reasonable compensation for his services in winding up the partnership affairs."

. . . Where the express contract of partnership fails to provide for payment of special compensation for services rendered, the burden of proving that the parties intended such payment rests upon the person claiming such compensation. Where the express contract fails to provide for payment of interest on moneys furnished by a partner beyond the amount which he agreed to contribute, the burden of proving that the parties intended that no such interest should be paid rests upon the other partners. . . . The distinction . . . rests upon an inherent difference between the obligation of a partner to render services in the partnership business and the obligation to provide capital. . . . Therefore, where a partner pays money to the partnership beyond his partnership obligation, it is a reasonable inference that the parties intended that such payment should be a loan and should bear interest.

The judgment should be modified in accordance with this opinion and as modified affirmed.

Duties of Partners

Duty to Share in Losses If there are not enough assets to make payments on partnership debts or to pay creditors in full, the deficiency is a loss that is chargeable against all of the partners. Each partner shares the loss in the same proportion that he or she is entitled to share in the partnership profits [18(a)]. Therefore, if there is no agreement between or among them as to responsibility for losses, the partners will share losses equally unless they had agreed to share the profits in unequal proportions. The obligation to share losses is discussed in detail and illustrated in connection with the winding up of partnerships.

Duty to Render Service to Partnership Each partner normally is expected to work on behalf of the partnership to the extent of his or her ability and to exercise reasonable care, skill, and diligence. The obligations of the several partners to work for the organization may, of course, be limited in any way by agreement among themselves. As in the case of a dormant partner, such an agreement may excuse a partner entirely from performing active service.

Where a partner breaches the duty to perform services for the partnership there may be varying consequences, extending from the excuse of the breach to a dissolution of the partnership. If a partner's failure to perform services is caused by physical disability, the action taken by the other partners would depend upon the expected duration of the disability and the terms of the partnership agreement. If the disability is temporary, the partner would probably continue as a member of the partnership; if the disability renders the partner permanently unable to furnish services as contemplated in the formation of the partnership, ground for dissolution of the partnership by court decree would exist [32(1)(b)].

Fiduciary Duties   When an individual enters into a partnership that person necessarily places great confidence in his or her copartners. Each partner accepts the possibility of personal loss should there be any mismanagement or wrongdoing by any of the other partners. Each of the members, therefore, has the right to expect the highest degree of good faith from the other partners; that is to say, each partner occupies a fiduciary position with regard to all the copartners and owes them a high degree of loyalty. None of them should maintain any activity that conflicts with the interests of the partnership. In addition, each partner must refrain from taking any advantage of his or her copartners by the slightest misrepresentation or concealment of material facts. Growing out of this fiduciary relationship are certain duties. Among the most important are: (1) the duty to furnish full information; (2) the duty not to profit secretly; and (3) the duty not to compete with the partnership business.

Duty to furnish information   On demand of the copartners, a partner is required to render full information affecting the affairs of the business [20]. If one of the partners obtains information about partnership matters or about other matters that he or she knows would be of interest to the partnership, that partner is under an obligation to make full disclosure to them because, as comanagers, the other partners are equally entitled to the knowledge.

Duty not to profit secretly   A partner is not privileged secretly to use partnership property or funds for private benefit or for payment of personal debts. If he or she uses partnership money, not only must the money "borrowed" be accounted for but also whatever profits were made through its use. Although a partner has a fiduciary duty to the firm, he or she may deal as an individual with the partnership, provided that partner acts in good faith and the firm receives a fair consideration in return. A partner violates his or her fiduciary duty if that partner buys property in his or her own name for the purpose of selling it to the company for a profit, or if that partner sells partnership property and gains a secret profit from the transaction, or if that partner makes a secret commission out of any partnership business; and he or she must account to the partnership for any profit improperly made.

Duty not to compete   Because of his or her fiduciary responsibility a partner may not, without the consent of the copartners, compete with the partnership business or take personal advantage of an economic opportunity that he or she knows or should know is within the ambit of the partnership business. For instance, in a frequently cited case the court held that a partner could not take or renew in his or her own name a lease to property occupied by or useful to the firm even though the lease was not to begin until after the partnership agreement terminated.[8]

As a general rule, a partner need not account for profits made in an independent transaction that is outside the scope of the partnership business. Moreover, if the partnership agree-

---

[8]*Meinhard v. Salmon*, 164 N.E. 545 (N.Y. 1928).

ment does not obligate a partner to devote full time to the firm's business, that partner may be a partner in another firm at the same time and derive income from that firm also. But if the partnership agreement obligates a partner to devote full time to the business, he or she may be required to pay over to the partnership any money earned in another enterprise carried on during normal working hours.

As shown in the following case, the fiduciary relationship and duties continue to exist even though there is a conflict between the partners.

Case 39.5   **W.A. McMichael Construction Co., v. D & W Properties, Inc.**
356 So. 2d 1115 (La. 1978)

W. A. McMichael Construction Company, the plaintiff, was a member of a partnership in which D & W Properties, Inc., the defendant, was the managing partner. The principal asset of the partnership was an option to lease 34+ acres of land from Alice McCrary at the annual rental of $24,000. The defendant, as the managing partner, endeavored to sublease the property to others. In July, 1974, it reported to the other partners that it was having no success in renting the property. After that time the plaintiff failed to pay its part of the partnership expenses. On October 9, 1974, D & W entered into an agreement with a bank to lease it slightly more than 1 acre of the 34+ acres of the McCrary tract for $20,500 a year, leaving the remainder of the land available for further development.

On October 16th, D & W, through its president, Delaney, offered the plaintiff $23,000 for its interest in the partnership. The next day the plaintiff accepted the offer and transferred all of its interest in the partnership to the defendant. The plaintiff was not told about the agreement with the bank when it sold its partnership interest to the defendant. After the plaintiff withdrew as a partner, all of the partnership's right to lease the McCrary tract was transferred to another partnership of which D & W was the general partner. The new partnership exercised the option to lease the McCrary property and then it entered into the sublease with the bank.

When the plaintiff, McMichael Construction, learned about the bank lease, it filed suit to set aside the agreement by which it withdrew from the partnership, alleging that the managing partner (D & W, the defendant) had breached its fiduciary duty when it failed to disclose to the plaintiff the true status of the partnership affairs during the negotiations for the plaintiff's withdrawal. The lower court agreed and entered a judgment for the plaintiff. The defendant appealed.

HALL, J. . . . The law applicable to the case at bar may be summarized as follows: The relationship of partners is fiduciary and imposes upon them the obligation of the utmost good faith and fairness in their dealings with one another with respect to partnership affairs. Each partner must refrain from taking any advantage of another partner by the slightest misrepresentation or concealment of material facts. The obligation is especially stringent on a partner who is managing the business, his duty being analogous to that of a trustee. The fiduciary duty of partners is particularly applicable when one partner seeks to purchase the interest of another partner. Such a sale will be sustained only when it is made in good faith, for a consideration, and on a full and complete disclosure of all important information as to value. The duty of disclosure holds true despite the fact that the relations between the partners have become strained or are in conflict. The fiduciary duty continues through the sale or purchase of a partner's interest or through termination and liquidation of the partnership. . . .

Even if Delaney's failure to disclose the existence of the agreement to lease was unintentional, or a mere oversight or negligence on his part, as urged by the defendants, the failure to disclose is not any less a breach of the managing partner's fidicuary duty. . . .

The judgment of the district court [as amended] is affirmed. . . .

POWERS AND LIABILITIES OF PARTNERS

Powers of Partners to Obligate Partnership

Power to Obligate by Contract A partner may obligate the partnership of which he or she is a member when the partner acts in the ordinary course of the partnership business or otherwise when the partner has the consent of all copartners. The ordinary rules of agency, discussed in Chapter 36, determine (1) whether a partnership is bound to perform an agreement entered into by a partner in its behalf; and (2) whether the partnership can enforce a contract against a third person with whom one of its partners has contracted.[9]

A partnership is bound by a contract entered into by one of its partners in its behalf if that partner had actual or apparent authority to engage in the undertaking. Apparent authority is present when the third person, taking into consideration business usages in the locality, reasonably believes that the partner is carrying on the business of the partnership in the usual

way [9(1)]. If the partnership is engaged in ordinary commercial transactions that involve buying and selling for profit, it may be considered to be a "trading partnership." A partner in such a firm has a much broader scope of authority than does a partner in a firm that has a limited field of endeavor, such as the operation of a fishing boat.

In the eyes of a third person who has no notice to the contrary, each partner has apparent authority to undertake the general management of the firm within the scope of its usual business. Therefore, a partner who follows normal business practices may bind the firm when he or she borrows money on the firm's credit, executes a negotiable instrument in the name of the firm, or pledges the firm's assets as security for the firm's indebtedness. A partner also has apparent authority to sell such property as the partnership business usually sells; to purchase such merchandise as the partnership normally uses; to hire employees necessary to carry on the business; to insure property; to enforce claims against third persons; and to compromise and pay its debts.

Notwithstanding an agreement among partners that limits the authority of the various partners, third persons without notice of such

---

[9]UPA, sec. 4(3) provides that "The law of agency shall apply under this act."

limitations are not bound by them. So, if a partner who is instructed by his or her copartners to make no purchases nevertheless contracts a purchase for the partnership, the contract is binding on the firm provided the third person had no notice of the limitation on the partner's authority and the partner reasonably appeared to be carrying on the partnership business in the usual manner.

Where a partner purports to engage his or her partnership in a contract outside the usual business of the partnership, the third person cannot enforce the contract against the partnership unless the partner had been specifically authorized to make the contract.

An unauthorized contract entered into by a partner may be ratified by the partnership under the principles of agency law (see Chapter 36, pp. 755–756). Thus, if after notice, the partnership fails to repudiate an unauthorized contract or retains the benefits of the unauthorized contract, the partnership has ratified the contract and may be estopped from asserting the partner's lack of authority to enter into it.

Power to Obligate by Admissions or Representations The legal rights and obligations of a partnership may be affected by a partner's admissions or representations to a third person concerning partnership affairs. Such an admission or representation made while the partner acts for the partnership may be used in evidence against the firm [11]. For example, partner A, after business hours, drives a partnership vehicle to a wholesaler to procure some material urgently required by the partnership the next day. On the way A negligently drives into B. A tells B that he was engaged in partnership business at the time of the accident. This admission against the interest of the partnership is admissible evidence against the partnership if it seeks to deny liability on the theory that A was acting outside the scope of the partnership business in driving the vehicle after business hours.

Power to Obligate by Knowledge or Notice A partnership is also charged with knowledge of all matters relating to its affairs that comes to the attention of any of its members; and a partnership will be bound by a notice received by one of its members regarding a transaction within the scope of its business [12]. Knowledge of a matter that affects the partnership is also imputed to each member of the partnership. However, if the knowledge of a partner concerns a fraud committed by him or her against the partnership, such knowledge is not imputed to the copartners. For example, Jane Jones, a partner in Sunset Realty Company, uses company money to buy a car for her mother. In an action by the partnership to void the purchase, the firm is not estopped from asserting that Jones acted without authority.

Power to Obligate by Tort Where a partner, while acting in the ordinary course of partnership business, negligently injures a third person, the partnership is liable for the injury to the same extent as the partner who caused the injury [13]. Such a situation could arise, for instance, when a partner, while driving the firm's vehicle to make a delivery to a customer, negligently injures a third party. A partnership is also liable for a tortious act committed by a partner with the authority of his or her copartners. Since willful and malicious acts generally are not within a partner's authority, a partnership will usually not be held liable for such an act by one of its members. However, if a willful tort is committed in the interest of the partnership and in furtherance of its usual business, the partnership may be liable to the injured person. Under such circumstances, partnerships have been held liable for a partner's willful trespass, fraudulent representations, defamation, and conversion.

If a partnership or a partner within the scope of the partner's apparent authority receives money or property from a third person, which is then misapplied, "the partnership is bound to make good the loss" [14].

Power to Obligate by Criminal Act   Since a criminal act is generally personal to the actor, requiring a mens rea (loosely, criminal intent), under ordinary circumstances the partner who commits a criminal act, and not his or her copartners, may be found guilty thereof. Of course, if some or all of the copartners participate in the criminal act, each of the participants may also be found guilty.

Some criminal offenses are statutory and regulatory in nature, requiring no criminal intent. Such offenses are commonly called "strict liability" offenses. When a partner commits such an offense in the course of partnership business, the partnership may be liable for the wrongful act even though the act had not been authorized by the other partners. For example, assume that there is an ordinance that makes the burning of refuse within the city limits punishable by fine, and that partner A, without partner B's knowledge or consent, burns partnership refuse within the city limits. The ordinance is one imposing strict liability, and the partnership is liable to a fine for the offense. (Compare with Case 39.1.)

Liabilities of Partners

Because each partner is a principal in the partnership, each is legally liable for its debts and obligations. Accordingly, a creditor has a remedy against the partnership, as a business organization, and against each partner personally.

The nature of the action to enforce the personal liability of a partner for a partnership debt or obligation depends, however, upon the character of the obligation. Where it arises out of a partnership contract, the partners are said to be "jointly" liable [15(b)]. This means that if a creditor, through legal action, seeks payment from a partner as distinct from the partnership entity, the creditor must bring action against all of the partners jointly.

A different rule pertains when the obligation arises out of a tort committed by a partner in the ordinary course of the partnership business. In that circumstance, the partners are said to be "jointly and severally" liable [15(a)]. This means that the injured party may, at his or her discretion, bring an action against the partnership and against all of the partners to enforce their personal obligations or against any one or more of them separately. This distinction between cases arising out of contract and those arising out of tort follows the common law. Many states have eliminated this distinction, and both contract and tort actions are joint and several. The partner who committed the tort may, in any case, be ordered by a court to reimburse the copartners for any loss they sustained because of his or her wrongful act. The last case in this chapter illustrates the principle, based on agency law, that each partner is liable for the tort of a copartner committed within the course and scope of the partnership business.

Case 39.6   Martin v. Barbour
558 S.W.2d 200 (Mo. 1977)

Martin, the plaintiff, suffering from stomach pains, consulted Dr. Barbour, one of the defendants in this suit. Dr. Barbour operated upon the plaintiff in February, 1970. After that time the plaintiff was examined weekly either by Dr. Barbour or by Dr. Egle, with whom Dr. Barbour practiced in partnership and who is also a defendant in this suit. Dr. Barbour operated upon Martin again in April, 1970. Following that operation the plaintiff could no longer control his bowels; he was incontinent. Martin was examined by a specialist who found that Martin's inner sphincter muscle had been severed. The specialist attempted to correct the condition with another operation but it was not successful.

Because of his condition, the plaintiff sustained a permanent total disability and was unable to continue to work. He filed suit against both Dr. Barbour and Dr. Egle for malpractice based upon Dr. Barbour's negligence in performing the original operation. The jurors returned a verdict for the plaintiff. The Circuit Court sustained the defendant's motion to set aside the verdict and the plaintiff appealed to the Supreme Court.

HOUSER, Special Judge. . . . [The Judge noted that "We find proof of causation (of negligent injury to the plaintiff from the operation) sufficient to submit the case to the jury."]

Plaintiff's case against Dr. Egle, who did not assist or participate in either of the operations performed by Dr. Barbour and did not consult or treat plaintiff until after the operations, is based upon the contention that the two doctors were partners acting concurrently in treating plaintiff. . . .

Having proved that a partnership between the two doctors existed in January, 1970 an inference arises that the partnership continued to exist. . . . For defendants to take the position that the law of partnerships does not apply, the burden was theirs to demonstrate when the partnership terminated. This they failed to do. "Pursuant to general rules, partners in the practice of medicine are all liable for an injury to a patient resulting from the lack of skill or the negligence, either in omission or commission, of any one of the partners within the scope of their partnership business. . . . " 70 C.J.S. Physicians and Surgeons, sec. 54b, p. 977. "And where several physicians are in partnership, they may be held liable in damages for the professional negligence of one of the firm." 60 Am. Jur. 2d, Partnership, sec. 166, p. 86. "It is plain, too, that when physicians and surgeons are in partnership, all are liable in damages for the professional negligence of one of the firm, for the act of one, within the scope of the partnership business, is the act of each and all, as fully as if each is present, participating in all that is done." 61 Am. Jur. 2d, Physicians, Surgeons, etc., sec. 166, p. 295. . . . On this record Dr. Egle is liable for Dr. Barbour's professional negligence on the basis of their partnership. There is no merit in the contention that fraudulent concealment by one partner may not be imputed to another partner. "The individual partners . . . are liable in a civil action for the fraudulent misconduct of a partner within the course or scope of the transactions and business of the partnership, whether such misconduct be by fraudulent representation or otherwise, even though the copartners had no knowledge of the fraud and did not participate therein; . . . "

Accordingly, the order of November 25, 1975 is reversed and the cause is remanded with directions to enter judgment in accordance with the verdict in favor of the plaintiff and against both defendants. . . .

SUMMARY

A *partnership* is an association of persons who either formally or informally agree to carry on as co-owners a business for profit. As this definition reveals, there are three requisites for a partnership: (1) an agreement between or among associates; (2) the carrying on of a business for profit; and (3) co-ownership of the business by the various associates. The common law considered a partnership to be merely an aggregate or collection of the persons who compose the firm. Under modern case law and the Uniform Partnership Act (UPA), a partnership is considered to be a legal entity for the purpose of owning and conveying real property, entering into contracts, suing and being sued in the partnership name, and for certain other purposes.

Any person who is legally competent to enter into a contract may, subject to the law of the state concerned, become a partner. Under the UPA, "person" includes "individuals, corporations, partnerships, and other associations." However, no person can become a member of a partnership without the consent of all the partners. The receipt by a person of a share of the profits is some evidence that that person is a partner in the business; but the evidence is not conclusive, since the person may be receiving such profits in the capacity of creditor or landlord or employee, or in some other capacity.

The UPA specifies the rights and obligations of partners. The members of a partnership may, however, by agreement, establish rights and obligations between or among themselves different from those set out in the UPA. Unless the partnership agreement provides otherwise, partners share equally in the profits of their business enterprise. They each contribute to defray any losses the partnership sustains, in the same proportion as they share in the profits. Partners generally receive no compensation for their services to the partnership; their remuneration is their share of the profits.

In the absence of an agreement to the contrary, all partners have equal rights in the management and conduct of the partnership business. If the partnership has more than two members, a majority of them may make the necessary business decisions. However, certain extraordinary actions that would diminish the capability of the partnership to continue in business require the unanimous agreement of the partners.

Each partner owes a fiduciary responsibility to his or her copartners. Among these fiduciary duties are: that he or she inform the copartners of all matters coming to his or her attention that affect the business; that he or she not use the partnership property or its business for private gain; that he or she not compete with the partnership business; and that he or she not personally take advantage of an economic opportunity that the partnership should enjoy.

A partner is a principal in the partnership in that each partner is an owner of the enterprise; and, being also an agent for the copartners, the partner can affect their legal rights and liabilities. A partner may bind the partnership in contract if such partner has actual or apparent authority to do so. The partner has apparent authority if he or she reasonably appears to the third person to be carrying on the partnership business in the usual way. A partner may also bind the partnership by admissions or representations concerning its affairs. Notice or knowledge acquired by a partner in the ordinary course of business may affect the legal rights and liabilities of the partnership. Such knowledge is imputed to the other partners.

A partner may subject the partnership and the copartners to tort liability for loss or injury that he or she causes a third person in the ordinary course of business. Except for strict liability offenses, generally a partner's crimes do not generate partnership criminal liability.

Although a partnership obligation may be created by the act of only one partner, all partners are liable on all partnership obligations. The partners are jointly liable for partnership debts and other nontortious obligations; and they are jointly and severally liable for tortious obligations. The partner committing the tort may, however, be ordered by a court to reimburse the other partners for any loss they sustained because of his or her wrongful act.

STUDY AND DISCUSSION QUESTIONS

1 (a) What is a partnership? (b) State at least three ways the Uniform Partnership Act has modified the common law concept of a partnership.

2 Are these statements true, partly true, or false? Give reasons for answers. (a) If two people call themselves partners, under the UPA they are partners. (b) It is not necessary that individuals enter into a written agreement in order to form a partnership. (c) Frequently a court must examine the way parties carry on a business enterprise in order to determine whether the enterprise is a partnership.

3 Define or otherwise explain the meaning of: (a) general partner; (b) dormant partner; (c) surviving partner; (d) partner by estoppel.

4 (a) What is the relationship of the law of agency to the law of partnership? (b) Explain the duties that a partner owes to the partnership of which he or she is a member. (c) Why should a partner be subject to such duties?

5 What is the rationale for each of these rules? (a) No person can become a member of a partnership without the consent of all the partners. (b) In the absence of an agreement to the contrary, a partner is not entitled to compensation for the efforts he or she expends in behalf of the partnership.

6 Are these statements true, partly true, or false? Give reasons for answers. (a) A partner, without the consent of the copartners, has authority to borrow money to carry on the business of the partnership. (b) If a partner, contrary to the instructions of the copartners, purchases on credit articles normally used in the partnership business, he or she alone is obligated on the contract of purchase. (c) A partner has apparent authority to sell merchandise manufactured by the partnership for sale.

7 (a) Under what circumstances would a partnership be liable for the willful tort of one of the partners in the firm? (b) If the partnership is liable, would the wrong-doing partner be individually liable?

8 Under what circumstances would a partnership become liable for the criminal act of one of the partners?

CASE PROBLEMS

1 Roberts owned a building in which he ran a restaurant. He closed the restaurant but left on it a sign reading, "Roberts' Town and Country Restaurant." About a year later Roberts rented the building together with all of its equipment to Hanna, to operate a restaurant there. The rent was to be a percentage of the gross receipts. A representative of Havelock Meats called on Hanna and allowed him to purchase meat on credit. Hanna at first paid the meat bills but 3 months later absconded, leaving a large unpaid bill. The meat company demands payment from Roberts. Is he obligated to pay the bill?

2 Croysdill desired to be designated distributor to sell tools manufactured by Quinco Tool Products. Crawford agreed to furnish Croysdill with such financial resources as would become necessary. In June, Croysdill and Crawford went together to the Quinco company. They told Quinco's officers that Crawford and Croysdill would be associated in a business to be

called Associated Tool Supply. Croysdill would be the manager and Crawford would be "the financial backer." Relying on Crawford's financial worth and credit standing, Quinco made Associated Tool Supply a distributor and sold tools to it on credit. In July, Crawford filed a certificate of fictitious firm name in accordance with applicable state law. That certificate showed Croysdill to be the sole proprietor of Associated Tool Supply. Approximately 6 months later, the Quinco company was told that Crawford was not a partner in Associated Tool Supply.

Was Crawford liable to the Quinco company for the tools purchased by Associated Tool Supply from Quinco: *(a)* between the date of the visit of Crawford and Croysdill to Quinco and the date of the publication of the fictitious firm name certificate? *(b)* between the date of the publication of the certificate and the date of notice to Quinco that Crawford was not a partner in Associated Tool Supply?

3 A, then 17 years of age, entered into a partnership with B, aged 25. A and B each agreed to contribute $2,500 to the partnership. B contributed his entire share, but A contributed only $1,000. The partnership began to do business, but A refused to make any further contributions to the partnership capital, although requested by B to do so. Instead, A said that he was disassociating himself from the partnership and demanded the return of his $1,000 contribution. B contended that A had to pay into the partnership the balance of his agreed contribution amounting to $1,500 and that A was liable to B for the damages arising out of A's wrongful dissolution of the partnership. Were B's contentions legally sound?

4 Hauke arranged with Frey to establish bowling alleys in a building which Hauke owned. It was agreed between them that Frey would act as the manager of the business and receive a salary from the revenues of the enterprise, and that Hauke would receive a monthly sum for the use of the building. The bank account of their enterprise was in their joint names, and signatures of both Hauke and Frey were required to make a withdrawal. The contract for the purchase of the bowling equipment was signed by both Hauke and Frey. It was the intention of the parties to establish a corporation in which they would each own shares of stock. Before the corporation was organized Hauke discharged Frey and brought an action in equity to prevent Frey from interfering in any manner with the operation of the bowling alleys. Frey contested the action. In a case involving this state of facts the court held against the plaintiff, Hauke, and for the defendant, Frey. What do you think was the basis for the court's decision?

5 Salmon and Meinhard engaged in a joint venture to lease a certain building. Each contributed equal amounts to the venture. It was understood that Salmon would manage the building. When the lease was near its end, the owner of the property asked Salmon if he desired to engage in a new lease of the building and of some adjoining property. Salmon, without telling Meinhard about the transaction, entered into the new lease in his own name. When Meinhard learned of the new lease, he demanded that it be held in trust as an asset of the joint venture between himself and Salmon. Was Meinhard justified in making this demand?

6 While an employee of the Adams-Baker-Clarke partnership was driving a partnership automobile in the course of his employment, he negligently ran over Paulson. Paulson brought suit against Baker for the damages Paulson alleged he sustained. Adams and Clarke were not made parties defendant. There was judgment for Paulson, and Baker contended on appeal that all the members of the partnership should have been made defendants in the action brought by Paulson. Is Baker correct?

7 A, B, and C were partners in the Blank Welding Company. The partnership had contracts to perform welding work on certain government ships. All three of the partners were indicted for defrauding the government. The indictment was based upon inflated partnership payrolls submitted by partner A to government paying agents. Assume that partner A was in charge of the partnership bookkeeping; that he, without the knowledge of partners B and C "padded the payrolls," which caused the partnership to be overpaid for the work performed; and that the overpayments were made a part of the regular partnership receipts that were divided equally between all three partners. If these facts were proved, would you expect that partners A, B, and C would each be found guilty of the offense of defrauding the government?

Chapter
40
Partnership Property

The Uniform Partnership Act (UPA) is concerned in part with the interests of individual partners and of the partnership firm as a whole in partnership property. This chapter discusses the characteristics of partnership property, the unique title by which it is held, the transfer of such property, and the rights of partners and of creditors in it. Before undertaking that discussion it is necessary to define what is meant by partnership property.

Partnership property consists of: (1) the real and personal property contributed by partnership members to the firm's capital at the time of the formation of the business; (2) the property acquired with the funds of the partnership; (3)

the tangible and intangible property created or manufactured by the partnership business; (4) the profits it earns, and (5) the good will it develops [8, 18(a), and 40(a)]. A partnership does not require any particular form of capitalization, and it need have no minimum amount of money or property in order to begin business.

A partnership can acquire, hold, and convey real and personal property. The acquisition and transfer of property by a partnership, and the ability of creditors to reach such property to satisfy personal debts of partnership members, present unique problems not arising in other business organizations.

839

ACQUISITION OF PARTNERSHIP PROPERTY

Acquisition under the Common law

Under the common law, legal title to real property could be held only by an individual or other legal entity. A partnership was not considered to be a legal entity but only an aggregate of the individuals who comprised its membership. It followed that a partnership could not, as such, acquire or convey the title to real property. A purported conveyance of real property to a partnership was not effective, even though partnership funds were used to make the purchase and the partnership took possession of the property. When the members of a partnership desired their firm to purchase real property, the title was taken in the name of one or more of the partners or, for convenience, in the name of a third person, as trustee.

The acquisition and transfer of personal property could be accomplished at common law by a mere change of possession. Therefore, the holding and transfer of personal property did not present partnerships with the problems involved in real-property transactions.

Acquisition under the Uniform Partnership Act

The UPA has modified the common law and treats a partnership as a legal entity for the purpose of acquiring real property. Section 8(3) states: "Any estate in real property may be acquired in the partnership name." The key word in the quoted sentence is *may*. Since this authority of a partnership to acquire property directly in its own name is only permissive and does not preclude the indirect method necessary under the common law, real property may be acquired by a partnership in either of two ways: (1) in its own name; or (2) in the name of one or more of its partners (or in that of a third person).

The following case demonstrates the practical application of the UPA rule that property acquired with partnership funds is partnership property unless the partners agree otherwise.

Case 40.1   **Gauldin v. Corn**
                  595 S.W.2d 329 (Mo. 1980)

Corn, the defendant in the original action and the respondent in this appeal, entered into a partnership with appellant-plaintiff, Gauldin, for the purpose of raising cattle and hogs. They agreed to own the business equally but no formal agreement was executed. The defendant and the plaintiff contributed equally to establish the business. The bulk of the partnership profits were put back into the business. Some of the profits were used to improve the land, to fence part of it, to top-dress and seed the soil, and to build a barn and another building for processing cattle and hogs. The buildings were fixed to, and could not be removed from, the land but the partners never talked about ownership of the buildings. The land on which the enterprise was conducted was owned first by defendant's (Corn's) parents and later was acquired by Corn and his wife. The partnership paid no rent for the use of the land.

In 1975 Corn told Gauldin that, because of ill-health, he was getting out of the business. Gauldin, the plaintiff, continued to operate the business alone and offered Corn $7,500 for the latter's share of the *removable* partnership assets. About 1 year later Corn accepted $7,500 from Gauldin for his interest in all the removable assets and agreed to allow Gauldin to continue the business on his land for the following 2 months.

Gauldin filed suit for a dissolution of the partnership and an accounting of his interest in the buildings placed by the partnership upon Corn's land. The trial court held that the assets of the partnership had already been divided and that Gauldin was not entitled to any part of the value of the nonremovable buildings that had been placed on Corn's land. Gauldin appealed, maintaining that since the improvements were acquired with partnership funds and were used in the partnership business and since there was no agreement between the partners as to the disposition of the property, he was entitled to one-half of their value.

GREENE, J. . . . There appear to be no Missouri cases which directly address the question of how to treat improvements made, with partnership funds for partnership purposes, on land owned by one of the partners. [The court then discusses the answers to this question reached by other jurisdictions.]

We agree . . . that the rule is "well established" that improvements made upon lands owned by one partner, if made with partnership funds for purposes of partnership business, are the personal property of the partnership, and the non-landowning partner is entitled to his proportionate share of their value. . . . The cases . . . [are] . . . consistent with the language contained in Missouri's Uniform Partnership Law . . . [U.P.A. sec. 8] which states, in part:

> "1. *All property* originally brought into the partnership stock or *subsequently acquired by purchase or otherwise, on account of the partnership is partnership property.*
> 2. *Unless the contrary intention appears, property acquired with partnership funds is partnership property.*"
>]Emphasis added.]

It is clear . . . that the general rule, governing the disposition of improvements upon dissolution of a partnership is activated only where, as here, there is no agreement between the partners which controls such disposition. It matters not that the landowning partner contributed the use of his land to the partnership, that the non-landowning partner knew that the improvements, when made, could not be removed from the land, or that a joint owner with the landowning partner was not joined in the suit for dissolution and accounting of the partnership. Thus the trial court, after finding that the partners had no agreement regarding the dispostion of fixed assets upon dissolution of the partnership, should have applied the rule, that we have approved here, and should have awarded plaintiff his proportionate share of the value of the improvements at the time of dissolution of the partnership.

We therefore reverse the judgment of the trial court awarding plaintiff nothing. . . .

CONVEYANCE OF PARTNERSHIP PROPERTY

Because a partnership may become the owner of real property in either of two ways, different procedures are required for a partnership to effect the conveyance of its property, depending on the method by which the property was acquired.

Conveyance of Property Held in Name of Partnership

Conveyance in Partnership Name   When legal title to real property is acquired in the partnership name, the legal title can be conveyed only by an instrument in the partnership name [8(3)]. To illustrate, let us suppose that Jones Brothers, a partnership consisting of Dan Jones, Jack Jones, and Tom Jones, desires to sell to Rachel Buyers some real property held in the partnership name, and that Jack and Tom authorize Dan to execute the deed. To transfer the legal title, the deed must be signed "Jones Brothers." If Dan follows normal procedure, he will add "By Dan Jones," or "By Dan Jones, Partner."

Now let us suppose that Dan Jones purports to convey the property in the partnership name, although he was given no authority to do so. The question then arises: Did Dan have apparent authority to sell the property and execute the deed? As we saw in the previous chapter, a partner has apparent authority to act only when that partner is carrying on the business of the partnership in the usual manner. If Jones Brothers is in the business of buying and selling real estate, Dan may well have had apparent authority to sell the property in question. If he had apparent authority, the sale would be as final as though he had had actual authority. On the other hand, if the partnership is operating a shoe store, Dan would not have had apparent authority to convey the building in which the shoe store is located.

Our series of assumed situations leads to this question: Where a partner, A, who has no actual or apparent authority to convey partnership property purports to convey it in the name of the partnership, does A's act bind the partnership? The question cannot be answered by a simple "yes" or "no." The UPA provides that the partnership may recover the property unless it was conveyed by the grantee (the party to whom A conveyed the property) to a holder who took the property for value and without knowledge that A, in making the conveyance, had exceeded his or her authority [10(1)]. If the partnership recovers the property from the grantee, the grantee has a cause of action for damages against A, from whom the purported conveyance was received. The basis of such liability would be A's implied warranty to the purchaser that authority existed for A to make the conveyance.

Conveyance in Partner's Name   As we saw in the previous section, legal title to real property *acquired in the partnership name* can be conveyed only by an instrument in the partnership name. It follows that if a conveyance of such property is executed by a partner in his or her own name, legal title to the property does not pass. However, the conveyance may not be entirely without effect. If the partner who executed the conveyance had actual or apparent authority to convey the property, the conveyance passes all of the interest that the partnership had in the property even though the purchaser has not received a deed in the name of the partnership as it should have. The purchaser's interest is called an "equitable interest" in the property.[1] The defect in the title may be corrected by another deed or by subsequent legal action.

If the partner did not have actual or apparent authority, the deed is of no legal effect and conveys nothing to the purported grantee. Consequently, if the purported grantee is in possession of the property, the partnership is entitled to the return of the property.

---

[1]See Chapter 2, Law in the United States, for a discussion of "equity principles."

The following case involves a partnership whose regular business was not the buying and selling of real property. Nonetheless, one partner, without the written consent of his copartner as required by the Statute of Frauds, entered into an agreement in his own name to sell certain partnership real property. The case holds that the agreement was not binding upon the copartner. Had the partnership business been the buying and selling of real property, the agreement to sell would have been binding.

Case 40.2   **Ellis v. Mihelis**
384 P.2d 7 (Cal. 1963)

Elias Mihelis and his brother, Pericles Mihelis, the defendants, owned and operated a ranch in partnership. They decided to sell the property and agreed that Pericles would handle the negotiations and submit any prospective sale arrangements to Elias. Pericles listed the property with a broker, telling him that he was the owner of the property. Pericles, in his own name, entered into a contract of sale of the property to the plaintiff, Ellis. Pericles orally told his brother about the terms of the sale and Elias voiced no objection. About a month after the deposit money had been placed in escrow and before the title was transferred to the purchaser, Elias stated that he had changed his mind and did not want to sell the property. As a result, Pericles did not convey the ranch to the purchaser. The plaintiff, Ellis, brought suit against both Pericles and Elias Mihelis for specific performance of the contract of sale and for damages. The trial court found, among other things, that Pericles and Elias operated the ranch as partners, that the ranch was an asset of the partnership, and that each partner orally authorized the other to sell the ranch for the partnership. A judgment was entered decreeing specific performance and damages against both Pericles and Elias Mihelis. They appealed.

GIBSON, C.J. . . . Although plaintiff may rely on the agreement [to sell the land], it does not follow that he may hold Elias, who did not sign it or authorize Pericles in writing to act as his agent. In seeking to overcome the requirement of the statute of frauds that an agreement for the sale of real property must be signed by the party to be charged or by an agent who has authority in writing, plaintiff contends that there is an overriding provision in the Uniform Partnership Act . . . which is applicable to the facts of this case and which empowered Pericles to bind Elias in the absence of written authority. It may be helpful in this connection to keep in mind that there is no evidence that defendants were in the business of buying and selling real estate or that the sale of the ranch was in the usual course of the partnership business.

The Uniform Partnership Act makes it clear that, unless it is otherwise provided therein, the usual rules of law and equity, including the law of agency, apply. . . . As a provision overriding the statute of frauds plaintiff relies on Section 15009 [of the Calif. Corp. Code (UPA, sec.9)] which reads in part:

"(1) Every partner is an agent of the partnership for the purpose of its business, and the act of every partner, including the execution in the partnership name of any instrument, for apparently carrying on in the usual way the business of the partnership of which he is a member binds the partnership, unless the partner so acting has in fact no authority to act for the partnership in the particular matter, and the person with whom he is dealing has knowledge of the fact that he has no such authority. (2) An act of a partner which is not apparently for carrying on the business of the partnership in the usual way does not bind the partnership unless authorized by the other partners. (3) Unless authorized by the other partners . . . one or more but less than all the partners have no authority to: (a) Assign the partnership property in trust for creditors or on the assignee's promise to pay the debts of the partnership. (b) Dispose of the good will of the business. (c) Do any other act which would make it impossible to carry on the ordinary business of a partnership. . . ."

A contract executed by one partner alone to sell partnership real estate is binding on the other partners provided the partnership is in the business of buying and selling real estate and the property covered by the contract is part of the stock held for sale. . . .

Since it does not appear that the sale of the ranch was in the usual course of the partnership business, a contract to sell it would come within subdivision (2) of section 15009, not subdivision (1), even if the ranch were a partnership asset as found by the trial court. Accordingly, the statute of frauds would be applicable and Pericles could not bind Elias without authority in writing.

. . . The statute of frauds precludes enforcement of the agreement against Elias, and the judgment must be reversed as to him. On the record now before us Pericles could be compelled as a joint tenant to convey his half interest in the ranch . . . but the case was obviously not tried on that theory, and a reversal is also necessary as to Pericles. . . .

The judgment is reversed.

Conveyance of Property Held in Name of One or More Partners

As we have seen, partnership property may be held in the name of one (or more) of the partners instead of in the partnership name. Where a partner holds the record title, such partner has the power to convey the property by an instrument in his or her own name. Such a conveyance effectively transfers the partnership interest in the property.

However, if the partner had neither actual nor apparent authority to make the transfer, the partnership may recover the property "unless the purchaser, or his assignee, is a holder for value, without knowledge" of the partner's lack of authority [10(3)]. If the partnership's attempt to secure the return of the property is unsuccessful (as it would be if the property had been conveyed to a holder for value, without knowledge), the partnership's recourse would be to seek compensation for the value of the property from the partner who acted wrongfully. Where all of the partners, as individuals, join in the conveyance, they cannot later, acting as a partnership, defeat the conveyance [10(5)].

PARTNERSHIP PROPERTY DISTINGUISHED FROM PROPERTY SEPARATELY OWNED BY A PARTNER

Importance of the Distinction

The fact that a partnership uses certain property in the furtherance of its business does not necessarily mean that the property belongs to the partnership. Most partnerships rent the store or office space they use and some partnerships rent equipment for the firm's use. More important for our present purpose is the fact that many partnerships use property that belongs to a partner—or at least that belonged to the partner at the time such partner turned the property over to the partnership for its use. Months or even years later a dispute may arise as to whether the partner had retained ownership of the property or had transferred it to the partnership.

Whether the ownership of the property was retained by the partner or was passed on to the partnership may be important not only to the members of the firm but also to creditors of the firm. If the property continued to be individually owned, it is not subject to seizure by creditors of the firm without first securing a judgment against the partner who owns the property. On the other hand, if the property became partnership property, it is subject to seizure by a creditor of the firm in an action against it.

Methods of Determining Whether Property is Partnership Property

Whether property remained individually owned or became partnership property depends upon the *intent of the parties* at the time the property was turned over to the partnership for use in its business. However, such intent is frequently difficult to determine. Methods of determining intent vary according to the situation involved.

Determination by Agreement The difficulty of determining the intent of the parties regarding ownership of property is greatly reduced whenever the partners take time to reach a definite understanding about their intent. The difficulty is further reduced whenever that understanding is put into writing. Even though the agreement is in writing, the written agreement is by no means conclusive so far as third persons are concerned. However, in any litigation involving the rights or claims of third persons, the written agreement between the partners is usually admissible evidence.

Determination in Absence of Agreement If intent regarding ownership of property turned over to a partnership was not made clear in an oral or written agreement and litigation results, the court will have to make its decision on the basis of all available facts. Among the types of facts that courts consider are: (1) circumstances surrounding the use of the property by the partnership; (2) the source of funds used to procure the property; (3) the record title to the property; and (4) other indicia of ownership, such as who pays the taxes on the property and how its ownership was reported to credit agencies.

Circumstances surrounding use of the property Inasmuch as the use of property by a partnership does not conclusively establish that the property is owned by the partnership, courts take into consideration the circumstances surrounding the use of the property. One of the circumstances to which courts attach special importance is the relationship among the partners. Where the partners are all close relatives, and one of the partners turns over property to the partnership for its use, a court is more likely to conclude that the property was intended to be partnership property than where the partners are merely business associates.

Another circumstance to which courts may attach considerable importance is the status of the firm's business at the time a partner permits the partnership to have possession of the property. If the business is starting or if its success is becoming doubtful, the intent of the partner who owned the property was probably to retain its ownership and thereby to prevent its seizure by firm creditors in the event of failure of the enterprise.

Perhaps more important than either of the circumstances mentioned is the nature of the property turned over to the partnership. If the property is of a type that may be consumed in the course of the partnership business, there is a strong presumption that the property was intended to be partnership property. Thus, if X, a potato grower, permits a grocery store partnership of which he is a member to have possession of potatoes X has grown, X probably intended to give up separate property interest in the potatoes. However, if the partnership owns a warehouse (rather than a store), and X stores potatoes in it, X probably intends to retain separate ownership of them.

Funds used to procure the property   Where partnership funds are used to effect a purchase and title is taken in the partnership name, the purchased property belongs to the partnership [8(1)]. Where property is purchased with partnership funds, and the title is taken in the name of one of the partners, there is a *presumption* that the partnership owns the property. [8(2)]. This presumption exists even where the property is not used by the partnership, but the presumption is particularly persuasive where the property is used in the course of the partnership business.

Record title to the property   Where nonpartnership funds are used to effect a purchase, and the title is taken in the name of the partnership, there is a strong indication that the firm is the owner notwithstanding the source of the funds used to make the purchase.

Other indicia of ownership   Other facts may also aid a court in determining whether particular property was intended to be partnership property or to remain the property of a partner. The court may seek answers to such questions as: Who pays the taxes, insurance premiums, mortgage payments, and upkeep charges on the property? Who pays the rent for the use of the property? Who collects and retains rents if there are tenants other than the partnership in occupancy? Who claims depreciation on the property for income tax purposes? Who claims the property as an asset for credit rating purposes? Still another indication of ownership may be whether the partnership or the partner made claims against an insurance carrier for loss of, or damage to, the property. However, it should be noted that a partner, as an owner of the business, has an insurable interest in partnership property and that that partner can insure his or her interest in it against loss.

The following case deals with the presumption that property purchased with partnership funds is partnership property.

Case 40.3   Reiners v. Sherard
233 N.W.2d 579 (S.D. 1975)

Sherard, a successful farmer, befriended Reiners, then about 13 years old and "without a good home." Sherard took Reiners into his home and treated him as a son. Later they entered into a livestock feeding partnership in which they were to share equally in the profits and losses. To finance the partnership operation they obtained the assurance of credit from the Production Credit Association (PCA). The account with PCA was created as a common fund. Whenever cattle or sheep were sold, the proceeds were deposited with PCA to pay off current loans. Whenever either partner needed cash for personal expenses he simply wrote a draft on the PCA account and deposited the funds to his own account. Each purchased real property in his individual name with funds from the PCA account. No annual accounting of profits and losses was ever made and no attempt was made to assure that each partner withdrew an equal amount for living expenses.

A guardian was appointed for Reiners after the partnership had been in existence for a number of years, and two actions arose: one an action by the guardian against Sherard for an accounting of the profits of the partnership and another which involved a mortgage foreclosure. [The court's opinion concerning the latter action is omitted.] The trial court found in the accounting action that Reiners owed Sherard approximately $19,000.00. Reiners' guardian appealed both actions which were consolidated for this appeal.

DOYLE, J. . . . The facts of this case demonstrate the unfortunate results which accrue when good friends or relatives become partners and fail to keep adequate records. At the dissolution of the partnership, it often happens that a clear view of the initial agreement is clouded by the years and there is suspicion on both sides that one partner has taken advantage of the other. So it appears to be here. . . .

The first issue is whether the trial court erred in finding that [any] real property purchased with partnership funds became property of the individual partners and not of the partnership. . . .

The applicable statutory law is stated in [UPA, sec. 8(2)]: "Unless the contrary intention appears, property acquired with partnership funds is partnership property." This statute creates a . . . presumption that property purchased with partnership money becomes partnership property. . . . However, the "presumption . . . is rebuttable and the same is true with respect to the presumption that the partnership owns the property that it uses in the conduct of the firm business." . . . [The evidence introduced at the trial rebutted the presumption].

The trial court, then, was left to balance the facts presented to it [as to the use of partnership funds for the benefit of the individual partners]. Several factors were urged on the court as favorable to the finding that the land was property of the partnership. First, of course, the land had been purchased with partnership funds and taxes on it had been paid with partnership funds. However, we believe that the probative value of these facts is severely limited in this case because of the manner in which the two men conducted their affairs. Each drew funds for every personal or business purpose conceivable from the same PCA account. To say that these funds could be used only to purchase property for the partnership would be to say that the partners had intended to have little or no property in their individual names. Thus, we agree with the trial court in its finding that the mere payment of taxes and of the purchase price of property is not persuasive when such payments come from a common fund used by both partners for all expenses. Furthermore, the cases are explicit in their view that the property purchased with partnership funds does not automatically become the property of the partnership. . . .

The plaintiff [the guardian] further argues that the fact that the crops from the land in question were used in the partnership feeding business should lead to a finding that the land was intended to be partnership property. Again, however, the mere fact that the partnership uses property is not dispositive. . . . "Use of the property alone is not sufficient because an owner may intend to contribute only the use, as distinguished from the ownership, to the partnership."

Finally, the plaintiff would argue that even if these particular factors alone do not persuade the court that the property is partnership property, the facts [taken] together should. . . .

. . . "Property acquired with partnership funds or by the partners individually for the use of the partnership does not necessarily constitute a partnership asset. In the absence of supervening rights of creditors, such property may, as between the partners at least, be owned by them individually as tenants in common or otherwise, as distinguished from the partnership, *if such was their intention* in the acquisition and holding thereof. . . ."

Thus, although Reiners is undoubtedly correct in stating that the ownership of the land by a partnership may sometimes be shown by the payment of purchase price, taxes and by the use of the land, . . . no single factor or combination of factors is necessarily dispositive of the issue. Each case presents a search for the intent of the parties. . . .

The trial court . . . found that the partners did not intend the land in question to be the property of the partnership. Several factors support this conclusion. First, none of the land was ever listed in applications to PCA as a partnership asset. Instead, the land was listed in the names of the individuals, i.e., "Sherard owns 560 acres and Reiners owns 320." Second, the partners once traded certain tracts of the land in question to each other. Such conduct would, of course, be illogical and unnecessary if the partnership owned the land. . . . Third, there was no evidence that either man made a representation to anyone before the commencement of this litigation that the land farmed by the partnership was the property of the partnership. We find the factors cited above in support of the trial court's determination [that the real property purchased with partnership funds became property of the individual partners and not of the partnership] to be persuasive. . . . We find the trial court's determination was not "clearly erroneous." . . .

Affirmed. . . .

PROPERTY RIGHTS OF A PARTNER

Since at common law a partnership was considered an aggregate of its members, all the members of a partnership were the owners of the partnership property. The view that each partner was a part owner of the property could, and frequently did, produce undesirable results. For example, a creditor of a partner, or the widow or other heir of a deceased partner, was frequently able to force a sale of partnership property even though such sale was against the best interests of the firm and might result in the firm's liquidation.

The UPA may not have eliminated all the confusion that existed at common law regarding a partner's property rights. However, the act makes a distinct contribution by devoting an entire part (Part V) to "Property Rights of a Partner." The first section of Part V establishes in each partner *dual property rights*, namely: (1) each partner's "rights in specific partnership property"; and (2) each partner's "interest in the partnership" [24]. In other words, there is a distinction between *specific partnership property* and an *interest in the partnership*. These concepts will now be examined.

Partner's Rights in
Specific Partnership Property

Nature of Partner's Rights in Specific Partnership Property Specific partnership property is any item of real or personal property owned by a partnership. The UPA states that "A partner is a co-owner with his partners of specific partnership property holding as a *tenant in partnership*" [Italics added][25(1)]. Tenancy in partnership is a form of ownership created by the UPA that applies only to specific partnership property. This new legal concept gives a partner practically none of the rights to use, control, or dispose of property that are commonly associated with ownership.

One of the purposes of creating this new kind of ownership was to prevent the undesirable results that occurred under the common law view of ownership of partnership property mentioned above. The UPA prevents those results by providing that tenancy in partnership has certain "incidents." The incidents are really rules governing tenancy in partnership, and we shall sometimes refer to them as "rules."

Rules Relating to Partner's Rights in Specific Partnership Property Two peculiar incidents of tenancy in partnership concern the right of a partner to possess and to transfer specific partnership property.[2]

1 "A partner . . . has an equal right with his partners to possess specific partnership property for partnership purposes; but he has no right to possess such property for any other purposes without the consent of his partners" [25(2)(a)]. For example, a partner has the right to use a partnership vehicle in order to conduct or further the partnership business, but has no right, without the consent of the copartners, to use the vehicle for personal pleasure. Similarly, while a partner has the right to use partnership funds for partnership business, such partner has no right to use them to pay personal obligations.

2 "A partner's right in specific partnership property is not assignable except in connection with the assignment of rights of all the partners in the same property" [25(2)(b)]. As here used, "assignment" includes any form of transfer, whether by sale, mortgage, pledge, or otherwise. The quoted rule is a necessary consequence of the partnership relation [25(2)(b), official comment]. Its meaning is perhaps best understood through an example. Suppose that A and B are partners and that A attempts to sell his interest in a partnership truck to C. If the law were to recognize the sale, then C would have some right to possess the truck. Obviously, this would be impossible because it would take away from the partnership firm its right to use the truck whenever it so desired. If C were to have a joint use of the vehicle with the partnership, then C would become, in effect, a partner in the firm so far as the truck is concerned. But a partnership is a voluntary association of all of its members. One partner cannot make a stranger a member of the firm without the consent of all the members.

Since a partnership, as an entity, is the owner of the specific property of the firm, would a partner be guilty of larceny if he or she steals partnership property? The answer to that question appears in the case that follows.

---

[2]The other incidents of tenancy in partnership are discussed under Creditors' and Heirs' Rights, this chapter, at page 851; 854.

Case 40.4   **Patterson v. Bogan and Kerr**
             198 S.E.2d 589 (S.C. 1973)

Defendants Bogan and Kerr owned an automobile junk yard. They sold the business to the plaintiff, Patterson, who took possession of the junk yard. The defendants claimed that they had sold Patterson only a one-half interest in the business and that they were partners. Patterson claimed that he had purchased the entire business and owed the defendants nothing. Bogan and Kerr demanded the return of the business but Patterson refused. Then, to compel the plaintiff to return the property, the defendants secured a warrant for the plaintiff's arrest for the crime of larceny. Patterson was arrested and released on bail.

At a preliminary hearing the magistrate dismissed the charge against the plaintiff, who forthwith instituted this action for damages against the defendants for the tort of malicious prosecution. Bogan and Kerr claimed that they had not acted maliciously but solely to secure the return of the property. The trial judge, over the objection of the defendants, instructed the jury that "a copartner in the business cannot be convicted of larceny of the partnership property or for defrauding the partnership." A judgment was rendered against the defendants. Patterson was awarded $5000 in actual damages and $15,000 in punitive damages. Bogan and Kerr appealed.

LEWIS, Justice. . . . As a general rule, a partner cannot be convicted of larceny of partnership property. . . . Wharton [*Criminal Law.* sec. 500] states the rule as follows: "As each partner is the ultimate owner of an undivided interest in all the partnership property, none of such property can be said, with reference to any partner, to be the property of another. It is therefore generally held that a partner cannot be convicted of larceny of partnership property which he has appropriated to his own use." . . .

It is argued that the Uniform Partnership Act, adopted in 1950, "firmly settled the point that a partnership is a *separate entity* from the partners themselves, and its property is treated as such, pointing out that Code Section [U.P.A. 25(2)] expressly provides that individual partners have no right to use partnership property except on partnership business. This statement is the premise for the further contention that since the partnership is a separte entity, larceny of partnership property by a partner is not larceny of his own property but that of the separate partnership entity.

The decision in *Chitwood v. McMillan*, 189 S.C. 262, 1 S.E.2d 162, decided prior to the adoption of the Uniform Partnership Act, recognized the principle that for certain purposes "a partnership under the law is an entity, separate and distinct from the persons who compose it." The Uniform Partnership Act apparently recognizes this principle. This, however, does not change the nature of the ownership or right to possession of personal property of the partnership.

Partners own such partnership property [through their joint ownership of the partnership business] and each has an equal right to its possession and control.

The instruction to the jury that a partner could not be convicted of larceny of partnership property was in accord with the rule adopted in this State.

Plaintiff testified that he purchased the entire junk yard business from defendants; while defendants said that they only sold him a one-half interest therein and that plaintiff held the property as a partner in the business. In either event, as the sole owner or a partner, plaintiff could not have been guilty of larceny. . . . By their own admissions, the motive of defendants in procuring the arrest of plaintiff was to compel the return of the property in question. A warrant signed for this purpose would constitute an abuse of the process of the courts and would constitute evidence of malice. . . .

Judgment affirmed.

Partner's Interest in the Partnership

Nature of Partner's Interest in the Partnership A partner's interest in the partnership (that is, interest in the firm's *business* as distinguished from rights in the firm's *property*) "is his share of the profits and surplus, and the same is personal property" [26]. *Surplus* means any funds of a dissolved partnership that remain after the payment of all partnership debts and other prior obligations.[3]

Rules Relating to Assignment of Partner's Interest in the Partnership The rules concerning the assignment by a partner of an interest in the partnership are as follows.

1 A partner may sell, mortgage, or otherwise assign his or her *interest* in the partnership to anyone. The assignee does not become a member of the partnership unless the assignee and the other members so agree.[4]

2 The assignment of a partner's interest in the partnership entitles the assignee to receive, in accordance with his or her agreement (with the assigning partner), the profits to which the assigning partner would otherwise be entitled.

3 Unless the assignee of a partner's interest in the partnership is made a member of the partnership by agreement with the other partners, such assignee (*a*) has no right to participate in the management or administration of the partnership business; (*b*) cannot require any information or account of partnership transactions; and (*c*) has no right to inspect partnership books.

4 A conveyance by a partner of his or her interest in the partnership does not of itself dissolve the partnership, but it may justify the partners who have not assigned their interest to bring about the dissolution of the partnership [27(1) and 31(1)(c)]. In the event of dissolution, the assignee is entitled to participate in any surplus remaining after the payment of all debts and other prior obligations [27(2)].

CREDITORS' AND HEIRS' RIGHTS AGAINST PARTNER'S PROPERTY RIGHTS

As previously discussed, under the UPA the property rights of a partner include *rights in specific partnership property* and an *interest in the partnership*. This last section of the chapter will answer two important questions concerning a partner's property rights. One, can the creditors of a partner have recourse against either of

---

[3]Termination of partnerships is discussed in the next chapter.

[4]This rule and the following two rules are based on UPA, sec. 27(1).

these rights? Two, do heirs have any legal claim against either of these rights of a deceased partner?

Creditors' Rights against Partner's Property Rights

We noted that one of the incidents of a tenancy in partnership is that a partner's *right in specific partnership property* is not assignable, except in connection with the assignment of the rights of all partners in the same property. Inasmuch as a partner cannot assign his or her right in specific partnership property for personal purposes, there is no way in which a personal creditor of a partner can attach a partner's right in such property. Accordingly, the UPA provides as one of the incidents of a tenancy in partnership that "A partner's right in specific partnership property is not subject to attachment or execution, except in a claim against the partnership" [25(2)(c)]. The remedy of a creditor of an individual partner is not to proceed against the partner's right in specific partnership property but to proceed against the partner's interest in the partnership. This the creditor can reach.

A partner's *interest in the partnership* is an *intangible* property right. Therefore, a creditor who holds a judgment against a partner may not levy execution directly against the partner's interest in the partnership. To reach that inter-

est the creditor must secure a *charging order* from a competent court. Such an order is in the nature of an attachment. The order charges the debtor-partner's interest with the unsatisfied amount of the judgment debt [28(1)]. Based upon the charging order, the creditor can then have a receiver appointed to collect whatever profits would otherwise be made by the partnership to the debtor-partner. The creditor may, upon a showing of necessity to assure the payment of the amount owing by the debtor-partner, foreclose the charging order and cause the partner's interest to be sold at a judicial sale. This interest may be redeemed at any time before sale by one or more of the partners using their own personal money; or it may be redeemed through the use of partnership funds, if all of the partners consent to such expenditure [28(2)].

If the interest that has been charged is not redeemed by the partnership or by one of the partners, it may be purchased by a third party at the foreclosure sale. The purchaser does not then become a partner in the business. He or she becomes only an assignee of the debtor-partner's interest in the partnership with the rights discussed at page 851. That a sale under a charging order has no effect on specific partnership property is illustrated by the next case.

Case 40.5   Bohonus v. Amerco
602 P.2d 469 (Ariz. 1979)

A summary judgment was entered by the Superior Court against Bohonus, the appellant, in favor of Amerco, the appellee, for an unpaid private debt owing by Bohonus to Amerco. The court granted Amerco's request for a charging order and directed the sale of appellant's interest in the assets and property of a business in which Bohonus was a partner, including the liquor license owned by the partnership. The appellant, Bohonus, then filed a motion to quash [set aside] the sale as being contrary to Arizona partnership law because partnership property had been sold by the sheriff.

HAYS, Justice. . . . The first issue before us is: "May the trial court order the sale of partnership property to satisfy the individual debt of a partner." . . .

We . . . now look at the partnership statute. Arizona Revised Statutes sec. 29-225(B) (3) [sec. 25(c), U.P.A.] says:

"A partner's right in specific partnership property is not subject to attachment or execution, except on a claim against the partnership. . . ."

Arizona Revised Statutes sec. 29-224 [sec. 24, U.P.A.] sets forth the extent of the property rights of the partner:

"The property rights of a partner are:
1. His rights in specific partnership property.
2. His interest in the partnership.
3. His right to participate in the management."

A.R.S. sec. 29-226 [sec. 26, U.P.A.] defines a partner's interest:

"A partner's interest in the partnership is his share of the profits and surplus, and the same is personal property."

A.R.S. sec. 29-228 [sec. 28, U.P.A.] reads, in pertinent part, as follows;

"A. On due application to a competent court by any judgment creditor of a partner, the court which entered the judgment, order, or decree, or any other court, may charge the interest of the debtor-partner with payment of the unsatisfied amount of such judgment debt with interest thereon; and may then or later appoint a receiver of his share of the profits, and of any other money due or to fall due to him in respect of the partnership, and make all other orders, directions, accounts and inquiries which the debtor partner might have made, or which the circumstances of the case may require."

With the foregoing statutes in mind, we note that it is only a partner's interest in the partnership which may be charged and, in some jurisdictions, sold. It cannot be overemphasized that "interest in the partnership" has a special limited meaning in the context of the Uniform Partnership Act and hence in the Arizona statutes.

. . . The fact of the receivership provision enforces the conclusion that only the "interest in the partnership" may be charged and we find no provision therein for sale of assets or property of the partnership. . . .

We concur with appellee's position that the charged interest of a debtor-partner can be sold, but further enforcement of the creditor's rights must be pursuant to statute. . . . This in no wise makes the sale of the partnership assets valid.

. . . The Uniform Partnership Act, which, as we have stated, prohibits the sale of partnership property in order to satisfy the nonpartnership debts of individual partners, has been contravened by the lower court's order. This order must be rectified. . . .

For the foregoing reasons, we reverse and remand to the trial court for proceedings consistent with this opinion.

Heirs' Rights against Deceased Partner's Property Rights

At common law, the heirs of a deceased partner could inherit the partner's right in partnership property. Under the UPA tenancy-in-partnership concept, a partner's *right in specific partnership property* does not pass to his or her heirs in the event of death but vests in the surviving partner or partners for partnership purposes [25(2)(d)].

Since a deceased partner's right in specific partnership property vests in the surviving partner or partners, it cannot be a source of support for the decedent's spouse or next of kin. Accordingly, the UPA provides as one of the incidents of a tenancy in partnership that "A partner's right in specific partnership property is not subject to dower, curtesy, or allowance to widows, heirs, or next of kin" [25(2)(e)].

The *interest in the partnership* that was owned by a deceased partner at the time of his or her death *is* part of the estate. It is personal property and, like any other personal property in an estate, may pass to heirs or legatees according to the provisions of the will; or, if there is no will, by the laws of intestacy of the state concerned [26]. The legal right to inherit real or personal property when an individual dies leaving or without leaving a valid will, and the meaning of "dower," "curtesy," and other terms related to inheritances, are explained in Chapter 23, *Wills, Estates, and Trusts.*

SUMMARY

Partnership property includes all of the real and personal property that belongs to a partnership. This property may be acquired in the name of one or more of the partners (a procedure under the common law), or in the name of the partnership (a procedure authorized by the UPA).

The legal title to property acquired in the name of a partner can be conveyed only by an instrument in the partner's name. The legal title to property acquired in the name of a partnership can be conveyed only by an instrument in the partnership name. If a partner transfers partnership property without authority, the property may be recovered by the partnership, unless it was conveyed to a bona fide purchaser who had no knowledge of the partner's lack of authority.

Partners may permit their firm to use their separate property without conveying its ownership to the partnership. Frequently, it is difficult to tell whether particular property used by a partnership is property of the firm or is the separate property of a partner. The determining factor is the intent of the parties, usually revealed by oral or written agreement or, in the absence of such agreement, by the circumstances surrounding the transfer and use of the property. Property that is owned by the partnership is called "specific partnership property."

A partner does not own, in the usual sense, specific partnership property. A partner can possess such property only for partnership purposes but cannot assign or otherwise dispose of it unless all of the partners join in the assignment. Partnership property may be levied upon by a judgment-creditor of the partnership but not by a judgment-creditor of a partner.

Each partner owns an undivided portion of the partnership business. This is called a partner's "interest" in the partnership. Generally, this interest is represented by a percentage of the profits and surplus of the partnership. It is personal property and in the event of a partner's death it becomes a part of the deceased partner's estate, subject to will or to the laws of intestacy. A judgment-creditor of a partner can levy upon a partner's interest in the firm by securing and then foreclosing a charging order directed against such interest.

STUDY AND DISCUSSION QUESTIONS

1   What different kinds of property are included in the term "partnership property"?

2 Distinguish between the acquisition of property by a partnership under the common law and under the UPA.

3 Under what circumstances may partnership property be conveyed by: *(a)* an instrument in the name of the partnership? *(b)* an instrument in the name of one of the partners?

4 Assume that partnership property is held in the name of partner A and that she conveys the property to a third party without the consent of her partner B. What rights, if any, does B have to the property?

5 Partners A and B agree that certain property owned by A will be used by the partnership, but that the title to the property will remain in A's name. Under what circumstances could that property be subjected to a partnership debt?

6 Partner A invested $12,000 in the A-B partnership. B's sole contribution to the partnership assets was a patent. In the event of a dispute between A and B as to the ownership of a building occupied by the partnership, what factors will a court consider in determining to whom the property belongs?

7 Distinguish between a partner's "rights in specific partnership property" and a partner's "interest in the partnership."

8 What is meant by "tenancy in partnership"?

9 Compare a partner's right to convey his or her "interest in the partnership" of which that partner is a member with the right to convey his or her "rights in specific partnership property."

10 Under what circumstances, if any, can the creditor of a partner proceed against the property rights of a partner?

CASE PROBLEMS

1 A and B operated a garage in partnership under the name "Veterans' Garage." Using the firm's money, A and B purchased certain land that adjoined their garage. The UPA was in effect in the state, and title to the land was taken in the name "Veterans' Garage." A and B contracted to sell the land. When the deed of conveyance of the land is prepared, should it provide for a conveyance by the Veterans' Garage or by A and B?

2 A and B were partners trading as "A and B, a copartnership." The partnership owned 40 acres of farm land. Title to the land was in A's name. A, in his own name and without mentioning the partnership, conveyed the 40 acres of land to X. The sale of the property was made without B's knowledge and for other than partnership purposes. When B discovered that the land had been conveyed to X, he brought suit against X for the return of the property. X contended that since A alone held the record title to the property, A had conveyed good title. Who should win?

3 Gerlach and Pratt were partners in a firm called the Allentown Supply Company. Gerlach secured in his own name the title to the building, which was occupied by the partnership, and to two adjoining lots. The consideration for the purchase was paid in part out of the firm's funds and in part out of Gerlach's personal funds. Gerlach, however, was credited in the capital account of the partnership with the amount of money he had personally paid to effect the purchase. The property was carried on the partnership books as an asset. The partnership also paid the applicable taxes and insurance premiums. The partnership paid no rent to Gerlach for the use of the property. Gerlach subsequently died. His widow claimed that the property that her husband had purchased and the title to which was in his name at the date of his death, was an asset of his estate. Was her contention correct?

4 A and B were partners in a commercial business. Each partner insured his life for $15,000, making the policy payable to his spouse. The firm accountant, without instructions from the partners, paid from partnership funds the premiums as they became due. After this procedure had been followed for 5 years, an Internal Revenue agent informed the accountant that such payments were not tax deductible by the partnership. For the next 3 years the firm accountant charged the premiums against the individual accounts of the two partners. At the end of that period, partner A died. Was the sum payable under A's insurance policy an asset of the partnership or was it the personal property of A's widow?

5   Lester Rider and his son, Ross, operated a farm in partnership. They had an oral understanding that they would equally divide all profits and losses. Periodically Lester withdrew money from the partnership account and purchased real property in his own name. When Lester died, his widow claimed all of such property as his will provided that she was his sole heir. Ross claims that the property is partnership property. He submits to the court income tax returns showing the property to have been listed as partnership property and insurance policies on the buildings showing that the property was insured as partnership property. Should those exhibits be considered by the court in settling the question as to who is entitled to the property? If so, what would be the rationale by which property standing in the name of one partner is considered to be property of a partnership?

6   W. B. Napier, R. C. Napier, and Duff were partners. The partnership maintained a balance of $5,000 in the partnership account in the State Street Bank. W. B. Napier, individually, gave to the State Street Bank his note for $500. When the note fell due, he told the bank to charge $500 against the partnership account. The bank did so. The bank marked the note paid and returned it to him. Was the action of the bank proper?

7   A partnership existed between Martin, Sidney, and Herman Ellis and their father, Abraham Ellis. Abraham died, and Martin and Sidney Ellis filed a bill in equity in the common pleas court (the court having jurisdiction over the dissolution of partnerships and the sale of a dissolved partnership's property) to dissolve the partnership and to sell the partnership property. Herman Ellis challenged the jurisdiction of the court. He asserted that since Abraham Ellis had a one-fourth interest in the partnership, and that since his estate was then being administered in the orphans' court (the court having jurisdiction over estate matters), prior approval of that court must be obtained before the property could be sold. Was Herman correct?

Chapter

41

Termination of Partnerships
Addendum: Limited Partnerships and Minor Business Organizations

A partnership does not have a perpetual existence. It comes to an end through a two-step process. The first step is the *dissolution* of the partnership. The second step is the *winding up* of its affairs. When the winding up is completed, the partnership is said to be terminated, and it ceases to exist.

Normally, the winding-up step follows immediately after the dissolution step. However, the winding-up step is sometimes bypassed, as

where the business is continued without interruption by a sole surviving partner or by a new partnership consisting of members of the old partnership either alone or in conjunction with others. Such a continuance raises special legal problems.

The first two parts of this chapter deal with the dissolution of a partnership and the winding up of partnership affairs. The last part of the chapter deals with continuance of the business of a dissolved partnership without a winding up of its affairs.

Following the Problems at the end of this chapter is an addendum that briefly describes limited partnerships and other business organizations, but not including corporations. Corporations are the subject of Chapters 42–46.

DISSOLUTION OF PARTNERSHIPS

The Uniform Partnership Act (UPA) defines dissolution as "the change in the relation of the partners caused by any partner ceasing to be associated in the carrying on, as distinguished from the winding up, of the business" [29]. A simpler definition is that dissolution "designates the point in time when the partners cease to carry on the business together."[1] Dissolution should not be confused with termination. The UPA expressly provides that "on dissolution the partnership is not terminated, but continues until the winding up of partnership affairs is completed" [30].

Dissolution may be brought about in a number of ways: (1) by an act of the partners or the occurrence of an event not in violation of the partnership agreement; (2) by an act of a partner in violation of the agreement; (3) by automatic operation of law; and (4) by court decree.

Dissolution Not in Violation of Partnership Agreement

Dissolution of a partnership may be brought about without violation of the partnership agreement: by the conclusion of the agreed term of the partnership or the consummation of its purpose; by the act of any partner in a partnership at will; by the agreement of all of the partners at any time; by the expulsion of a partner from the firm in accordance with power conferred by the agreement [31(1)]; or, in certain circumstances, by the addition of a partner.

Dissolution by Conclusion of Term or Consummation of Purpose   It is common for partners, when they organize their partnership, to limit its life to a definite term. For example, let us assume that when the partners organize their partnership they agree that it will continue for a period of 5 years. When the fifth year ends, the partnership is automatically dissolved. Partners may also condition the life of their partnership, either with or without a time limitation, upon the consummation of its purpose, or upon the occurrence of a particular event. When the purpose is consummated or the event occurs, the partnership is automatically dissolved. For example, a partnership or joint venture formed to print and sell programs during a certain state fair is dissolved when the fair closes; a partnership formed to train and race a particular horse is dissolved if and when the horse is sold or dies.

Dissolution by Act of a Partner in a Partnership at Will   Where a partnership agreement does not specify the date or circumstances that would bring about dissolution, the organization is called a partnership at will. Where members of a dissolved partnership continue to carry on the partnership business without making a new agreement, the organization continuing the business is also called a partnership at will. Since there is no fixed time for the dissolution of a partnership at will, any partner may dissolve such a partnership at any time. A partner may cause dissolution by simply leaving the partnership; or a partner may cause dissolution in any manner by which a partnership not at will may be dissolved [23(1); 31(1)(b)]. If a partner elects to dissolve a partnership at will, the action is not a breach of the partnership agreement even though the partnership was operating profitably and its dissolution results in a monetary loss to the copartners. Therefore, under ordinary circumstances, the partner who brings about the dissolution of a partnership at will is not liable in

---

[1]Commissioners' Notes to UPA, sec. 29, 7 *Uniform Laws Ann.*, pp. 165–166, 1949.

damages to copartners who may desire to continue its business.

Dissolution by Agreement of All the Partners   Since a partnership is a consensual association, the partners may by unanimous assent dissolve their association at any time, without regard to the term or purpose for which they established the partnership. If a partner assigns his or her interest in the partnership, or if the partner's interest is the subject of a charging order, the remaining partners have the right by their unanimous action to dissolve the partnership [31(1)(c)].

Dissolution by Expulsion of a Partner   The UPA provides that dissolution of a partnership may occur without violation of the partnership agreement where the expulsion is in accordance with a power of expulsion conferred by the agreement [31(1)(d)]. The agreement may specify a number of specific causes for expulsion, as for example, failure of a partner to pay an assessment or failure of a partner to perform the duties set out in the partnership agreement. In addition, the agreement may authorize the expulsion of a partner when such expulsion is in the best interest of the firm as determined by the other partners under conditions set forth in the partnership agreement. One of the conditions might be, for example, that the expulsion of a partner shall not be effective until the partner is notified in writing why the expulsion "is in the best interest of the firm."

An expelled partner is entitled to be paid in cash the net amount due him or her from the firm. This is determined by computing the net worth of the partnership and then the expelled partner's share of that net worth. It may be one-half, one-third, or some other share that the partners established in their partnership agreement. The value of this share is then diminished by any debts or obligations owing by the expelled partner to the firm. The remainder is the sum that should be paid to such individual.

A partnership agreement that authorizes the expulsion of a member would normally provide for giving notice of expulsion to the expelled member and the manner in which the expelled partner's share of the value of the business is paid.

Dissolution by Addition of a Partner   Older cases considered a partnership dissolved when a new partner is added. More recent cases hold that there is a dissolution in such event except where the partnership agreement permits the admission of a new partner without dissolution. As the admission of a new partner requires the unanimous assent of the original partners and does not involve a partner ceasing to be associated, the later cases reflect the better view. It should be noted that the UPA does not state that the admission of a new partner into a preexisting partnership dissolves the firm. The act merely provides, in effect, that the money or property contributed by a newly admitted member is liable for partnership obligations arising before admission as though he or she had been a partner when such obligations were incurred. However, the new partner is not *personally* liable (as are the old partners) to those who were partnership creditors prior to the admission of the new partner [17].

Dissolution in Violation of Partnership Agreement

Because a partnership is a voluntary association of its members, any partner has the *power* to dissolve the association at any time despite the terms of the partnership agreement. The agreement merely circumscribes a partner's *authority* to exercise his or her power to dissolve the partnership. If a partner withdraws from a partnership in contravention of the agreement, such person breaches the partnership contract and causes dissolution of the partnership. In that event UPA Section 38 prescribes certain consequences: (1) the withdrawing partner is entitled to receive payment for the value of his or her interest in the partnership; (2) in the computation of the monetary worth of such interest, the value of the partnership goodwill is excluded; (3) the outgoing partner is liable in damages to the remaining partners for any injury they may have suffered because of the breach of the partnership agreement.

Under the common law, a partner who assigned his interest in the partnership to someone other than a copartner automatically caused a dissolution of the partnership. Under the UPA, such assignment does not *of itself* dissolve the partnership. For instance, a dissolution would not usually result where a partner assigns all or part of an interest in a partnership to a bank as security for a loan while continuing to perform all of his or her duties as a partner. Nor would an automatic dissolution result where the assignment is by a dormant partner,[2] since such a partner performs no duties. However, if a partner assigns an interest in a partnership and also refuses to perform agreed duties for the enterprise, courts would hold that such partner has brought about dissolution in contravention of the partnership agreement.

Dissolution by Automatic Operation of Law

Dissolution of a partnership is brought about automatically by the death of a partner; by the bankruptcy of a partner or of the partnership; or by subsequent illegality of the partnership business.

Dissolution by Death of a Partner The UPA provides that the death of a partner dissolves a partnership [31(4)]. This provision accords with the historic view that the mutual obligations and personal inducements upon which a partnership was founded come to an end when a partner dies. Based upon that view, the older cases hold that a partnership, being contractual, must terminate when one of its members can no longer perform. These cases also hold that should a partnership *business* be continued by the surviving partners without entering into a new partnership agreement, the business is, in fact, being conducted by a new partnership composed of the surviving partners. This conclusion is adhered to even though the original partners may have agreed among themselves that the partnership would continue after the death of any of its members and no new formal partnership agreement had been entered into by the surviving partners. There is little practical justification for such a narrow view. Therefore, some of the more recent cases and several state statutes have departed from the older view and the clear words of the UPA. These cases give effect to the continuation agreement and hold that after the death of a partner the partnership may continue according to the terms of the agreement.[3]

Dissolution by Bankruptcy Dissolution is also caused by bankruptcy of a partner or of the partnership [31(5)]. Under the federal Bankruptcy Reform Act, a trustee takes charge of the bankrupt's assets and disposes of them for the benefit of creditors.[4] If an individual partner is declared a bankrupt, the partner's interest in the partnership would be disposed of in the bankruptcy action, and a dissolution of the partnership occurs automatically. If either a partner or a partnership is declared insolvent under a state insolvency law, automatic dissolution likewise results.

Dissolution by Subsequent Illegality Any event that makes it unlawful for a partnership business to be carried on, or unlawful for any of its members to engage in the business, causes the automatic dissolution of the partnership

---

[2]The subject of dormant partners is discussed in Chapter 39, p. 822.

[3]Alan R. Bromberg, *Crane and Bromberg on Partnership*, West Publishing Company, St. Paul, 1968, sec. 77, p. 432.

[4]Explained at length in Chapter 49.

[31(3)]. Automatic dissolution under such circumstances may be illustrated by the following examples. *Example 1:* A partnership carries on the business of selling intoxicating liquor at retail. A newly enacted state law makes the retail sale of liquor illegal. Upon the effective date of such law the partnership is dissolved. *Example 2:* Several individuals are partners in a law firm. One of its members is named to a judicial position that precludes the incumbent from practicing law. When the member assumes the judicial position, the partnership is dissolved.

Dissolution by Court Decree

There are a number of circumstances that do not automatically cause dissolution of a partnership but that may justify a court in decreeing dissolution on the application of a partner. There are even some unusual circumstances where dissolution may occur as a result of a court decree on the application of a third person.

Dissolution for Cause on Application of a Partner A court might decree dissolution of a partnership on the application of a partner because of the incapacity or the misconduct of a partner; or because the business of the partnership can be continued only at a loss; or because of other circumstances that make dissolution equitable.

Incapacity of a partner A partner may be declared insane or may be shown to be of such unsound mind as to be incapable of performing the partnership contract. The occurrence of physical disability may also make impossible the substantial performance of a partner's duties. It would be unfair to the other partners to require them to retain in the partnership a member who, over an extended period of time, is unable to carry on the work agreed to be performed when the partnership was organized. It would be equally unfair to force a partner to leave a profitable business organization because he or she suffers a temporary disability. Therefore,

the dissolution of a partnership because of the incapacity of a partner to perform partnership duties is not automatic but is a matter for decision by a competent court [32(1)(a),(b)]. Problems such as these are commonly anticipated when a partnership is organized. The partners usually include in their agreement a provision for the conduct of the business and for the equitable settlement of a partner's interest in the firm in the event of permanent disability, as that term is defined in the agreement.

Misconduct of a partner On proper application, a court will decree the dissolution of a partnership when a partner has been guilty of such conduct as tends to prejudice the carrying on of the partnership business [32(1)(c)], or when the partner willfully and persistently commits a breach of the partnership agreement, or otherwise so acts in partnership affairs that the copartners find it is not reasonably practical to carry on the business in partnership with that person [32(1)(d)]. Any conduct by a partner that is productive of serious and permanent injury to the partnership business is a valid basis for the firm's dissolution by court decree on the application of the injured members of the firm. Such conduct might involve acts with regard to customers, sources of supply, or the public that cause the firm to be brought into disrepute or its credit and goodwill impaired. For example, there may be cause for dissolution when a partner in a retail establishment repeatedly treats its customers so disdainfully that customers never return to the store.

Unprofitable business Since a partnership is an association designed to carry on a business for profit, dissolution of the partnership would normally follow if the business can be carried on only at a loss [32(1)(e)]. When faced with such a situation, the partners will usually agree to dissolve the partnership and thus obviate the expense and burden of legal action to achieve the same end. However, there may be circumstances that lead some of the partners to believe that the business would be profitable in the future if continued, and so they oppose immediate dissolution of the partnership. In the presence of a conflict of this type, a judicial dissolution may be sought in order to settle the conflict.

Other circumstances Section 32(1)(f) of the UPA provides that on application by or for a partner, the court shall decree a dissolution whenever "other circumstances render a dissolution equitable." The following are examples of situations in which partners may find it necessary to seek, under this authority, a court decree ordering the dissolution of a partnership. *Example 1:* Partners A and B have irreconcilable differences with regard to the management of

the firm or with regard to B's right to have access to the partnership books. Their ultimate recourse is to bring an action for the dissolution of the partnership. *Example 2:* Partner X refuses to participate in the conduct of the partnership business to the extent that X does not properly perform partnership duties. The circumstances are such that copartners Y and Z are in doubt whether X has caused a dissolution of the partnership. Under these circumstances, Y and Z may seek a dissolution by court order. The basis for a court-ordered dissolution for irreconcilable differences between partners is discussed in the following case.

Case 41.1   **Cooper v. Isaacs**
448 F.2d 1202 (D.C. Cir. 1971)

Burton Cooper and Leslie Isaacs were partners in the firm of Lesco Associates, engaged in the sale and distribution of janitorial supplies. Their partnership agreement provided that it might be terminated by (1) the sale of its interests, (2) mutual consent, (3) retirement of a partner, (4) death of a partner, or (5) incompetency of a partner. Cooper filed a complaint in the District Court asking for a dissolution of the partnership because irreconcilable d ifferences had arisen between the partners regarding matters of policy. In h.s answer Isaacs alleged that the filing of the complaint constituted a wrongful dissolution in contravention of the partnership agreement. He asserted that he, therefore, was entitled to continue the business in the name of the partnership, pursuant to sec. 41-337 of the District of Columbia Partnership Act (UPA, sec. 38). After the pleadings had been filed, Cooper moved for the appointment of a receiver, and Isaacs moved for an injunction prohibiting Cooper from interfering with the business. The District Court appointed a receiver *pendente lite* [during the suit] for the partnership business, and denied Isaacs' motion. Isaacs appealed.

TAMM, J. . . . In determining whether the District Judge's appointment of a receiver *pendente lite* was a permissible exercise of his authority, we must first decide whether appellee [plaintiff in the lower court] Cooper's filing of his complaint requesting dissolution of the partnership on the ground of irreconcilable differences regarding business policy was itself a wrongful dissolution of the partnership in contravention of the partnership agreement. If it was, then appellant Isaacs was entitled to relief under section 41-337, and the appointment of the receiver was improper as a matter of law. . . .

Since a dissolution based upon irreconcilable differences is not one of [the] events [enumerated in the partnership agreement], the filing of a complaint seeking this relief is, according to Isaacs, a dissolution in contravention of the partnership agreement. . . .

Section 41-330 of the Act [UPA, sec. 31] provides:

"Dissolution is caused . . . (6) By *decree of court* under section 44-331" [UPA, sec. 32] [emphasis added].

Turning to section 41-331, we find the following provisions:

1 On application by or for a partner the court shall decree a dissolution whenever . . .

(**c**) a partner has been guilty of such conduct as tends to affect prejudically the carrying on of the business;

(**d**) a partner wilfully or persistently commits a breach of the partnership agreement, or otherwise so conducts himself in matters relating to the partnership business that it is not reasonably practicable to carry on the business in partnership with him; . . .

(**f**) other circumstances render a dissolution equitable.

Courts interpreting these provisions have consistently held that serious and irreconcilable differences between the parties are proper grounds for dissolution by decree of court. . . . Since the Act provides for dissolution for cause by decree of court and Cooper has alleged facts which would entitle him to a dissolution on this ground if proven, his filing of his complaint cannot be said to effect a dissolution, wrongful or otherwise, under the Act; dissolution would occur only when decreed by the court or brought about by other actions. This reasoning is subject to the proviso that the court below does not eventually conclude that Cooper's complaint is "groundless." If this occurs, the date the complaint was filed will be deemed the time of dissolution. . . . However, in deciding this appeal we cannot assume that the complaint will prove to be "groundless."

A partnership agreement can presumably change this result, but the terms of the agreement must be quite specific to effect such a change. This is so because the provisions of the Act regarding dissolution by decree of court were clearly designed to allow partners to extricate themselves from business relationships which they felt had become intolerable without exposing themselves to liability in the process, and this sound policy should apply unless expressly negated, and perhaps even then.

We do not believe it can be said at this time, with the case in its present posture, that the partnership agreement involved here was clearly meant to exclude the possibility of dissolution of the partnership by decree of court under section 41-331. . . .

We thus conclude that without further inquiry into the claims made by the parties, it is impossible to say that the mere filing of the complaint by Cooper constituted a wrongful dissolution.

Case 41.1
Continued   . . . In circumstances similar to these, several courts have held the appointment of a receiver to be proper, and we find the reasoning of these decisions persuasive. Accordingly we affirm the District Judge's appointment of the receiver *pendente lite.*

Affirmed.

Dissolution on Application of a Third Person   A conveyance by a partner of his or her interest in a partnership does not of itself dissolve the partnership. An assignee of a partner, whether by purchase or by the foreclosure of a charging order, does not thereby become a member of the partnership (see Chapter 40). An *assignee of a partner* therefore is not ordinarily entitled to force the dissolution of a partnership. Neither is a *creditor of a partnership* entitled to force its dissolution. A judgment-creditor may, however, force the sale of partnership property to satisfy the judgment held against the *firm.* The forced sale may bring about the bankruptcy of the partnership or at least may so deplete the assets of the firm as to cause the partners to dissolve the partnership. In either event, the creditor brings about *indirectly* a result that the creditor had no power to bring about directly.

WINDING UP OF PARTNERSHIP AFFAIRS

The dissolution of a partnership brings to an end the *normal* working relationships among the several partners. However, as already noted, the partnership does not cease to exist when it is dissolved. Instead, it usually enters a phase where the winding up of its affairs is accomplished.[5] This part of the chapter is devoted to a discussion of who conducts the winding up and

how the winding up is carried out.

Who Conducts the Winding Up

Unless otherwise agreed, the partners who have not wrongfully dissolved the partnership (or the legal representative of the last surviving partner not bankrupt) have the right to wind up the partnership affairs [37]. By agreement, the partners who are entitled to take charge of the winding up usually designate one of their number or someone else to act for them. Under appropriate circumstances a court may designate the partner or a third-party receiver who will conduct the winding up. In some states, if dissolution is brought about by the death of a partner, the law requires that the winding up must be conducted by the personal representative of the deceased partner.

In Chapter 39 it was shown that a partner is not entitled to compensation for services to the partnership unless there is an agreement to the contrary and the partner must look to the profits of a partnership for compensation. Likewise, if a dissolution of a partnership is brought about by causes other than the death of a partner, courts generally hold that no compensation is due to the partner who conducts the winding up, unless there was an agreement to the contrary. However, if the dissolution was brought about by the death of one of the partners, the surviving partner who winds up the partnership affairs is entitled to reasonable compensation for such services [18(f)]. The right of partners to participate in the winding up of a dissolved partnership is discussed in the next case.

---

[5]Continuation of the business of a dissolved partnership without a winding up is discussed at p. 873.

Case 41.2   **Stark v. Utica Screw Products, Inc.**
425 N.Y.S.2d 750 (N.Y. 1980)

Stark, the plaintiff, orally entered into a partnership with Henning to act as sales representatives for various firms. They adopted the partnership name of Stark, Henning & Co. In 1975 the partnership contracted with Utica Screw Products, the defendants, to act as its sales representative in New York State. In October, 1976, Stark sent a letter to Henning terminating the partnership, stating that thereafter each of them would act as individual salesmen. A copy of that letter was sent to Utica Screw Products. In reply, Utica stated that all commissions already earned by Stark, Henning & Co. would be paid to the partnership and that any further commissions earned in the territory would be sent to the representative who was so employed.

The defendant than retained Henning as its sales representative for the next 11 months. Stark filed suit against Utica. The plaintiff contended that some commissions were still due for orders the partnership had negotiated before the partnership was dissolved. Utica contended that Stark had no standing (right) to bring the law suit as Henning did not concur in that action. The trial court decision, in pertinent part, follows.

HYMES, J. . . . Upon dissolution of a partnership, any partner has the right to participate in the winding up of a partnership. He needs no authority from his co-partners. A unilateral letter of dissolution does not cut off the partnership relationship. On dissolution the partnership continues until the winding up of the partnership affairs is completed. . . . The only way in which a partnership is wound up is through an accounting. . . .

The duty imposed upon the partner who is engaged in winding up the partnership business is one of agency. . . . The general agency of one partner for his co-partner ceases, but each partner has the equal duty and power to do whatever is necessary to collect the debts of the partnership. . . .

After the dissolution of a partnership, a partner may bind the partnership by any appropriate action necessary to wind up the partnership affairs or to complete transactions unfinished at the time of dissolution. . . . While a partner would not be entitled to remuneration for winding up the partnership affairs, he would be allowed reasonable expenses incurred in performing these services. . . . Such expenses could include the commencement of an action to collect on accounts due and payable to the partnership and the hiring of counsel for that purpose. . . .

A partner cannot bar his co-partner from suing to collect debts due the partnership. Any judgment recovered by Stark would be for the benefit of the partnership and not for himself individually. It would then be up to the parties to wind up the partnership through an accounting. . . .

The defendant was incorrect in assuming that the dissolution of the partnership voided the contract with the plaintiff. The dissolution of a partnership operates only with respect to future transactions. All past transactions and obligations of the partnership continue until all pre-existing matters are terminated. The partnership continues to be responsible for its obligations and debts, and third parties are responsible to the partnership for obligations which they owe said partnership. "The contractual rights of the latter (partnership) continues to be enforceable though only by action . . . in the name of all. . . . " (*Horst v. Roehm*, 84 Fed. Rep. 565, aff'd 178 U.S. 1).

Where the major consideration in the earning of commissions is procurement of orders for the defendant, the employee is entitled to commissions on the sales he obtained during the period of his employment. . . . [The court determined that the partnership should be paid on all sales effected until October, 1976.]

Judgment is awarded to the plaintiff. . . .

The Winding-Up Process

The winding up of a partnership involves the *liquidation* of the partnership business and the settling of its affairs. The partnership's unfinished business is completed; other steps are taken as necessary to preserve the partnership assets; its debts are collected and liabilities discharged; its property is converted to cash; and an accounting is made.

If the partnership business is very involved, especially if the partnership has interests in different cities and owns much property that must be converted to cash, the winding up may be a lengthy process. If the partnership business is simple in nature, with few outstanding obligations, the winding up can be accomplished within a very short period of time.

Completing Unfinished Business The partnership must continue to carry out the terms of its executory contracts as if there had been no dissolution. Executory contracts to which the partnership is a party, that is, those in which some performance is owing by or to the partnership, are not affected by the dissolution even though the dissolution comes about because of the death of a partner. Of course, if the other party to a partnership contract agrees to the rescission of its contract, performance is no longer required. If the contract is one of purchase by the partnership, the person in charge of the winding up may use partnership funds to pay for the property contracted to be purchased. If the contract is one of sale by the partnership, the property is delivered to the purchaser and payment is received in accordance with the contract terms.

Preserving Assets In order to complete pending business advantageously and to preserve the value of partnership assets, the person in charge of the winding up may, if necessary, make new purchases and even augment the partnership inventory. Such action may require borrowing money in the name of the partnership. The partnership and its members are liable for any debts contracted or for any torts committed by the winding-up partner as a part of the winding-up process to the same extent as they would have been liable had the partnership not been dissolved [35(1)(a)].

Collecting Debts and Discharging Liabilities The person who conducts the winding up must use his or her best efforts to collect any debts due to the partnership. If necessary, a lesser sum than is due may be accepted as full payment of a debt. Suit may be brought in the name of the partnership (if permitted by local practice) against a firm debtor and partnership funds may be used to pay for necessary legal services.

Incident to the winding-up process, partnership debts must be paid and other liabilities discharged, even if so doing necessitates selling real and personal property of the partnership in order to raise necessary funds. The dissolution of a partnership does not relieve the firm or its members from debts or other liabilities incurred prior to the dissolution. If the law were otherwise, members of a partnership could free themselves from their partnership obligations to third persons by the mere expedient of dissolving the firm.

Converting Assets to Cash After all of the partnership debts have been paid, the partners are entitled to have the remaining partnership property converted into cash and applied to the payment of whatever amounts may be owing to them [38(1)]. However, the most ready buyers of partnership property are often the partners themselves. Therefore, the remaining partnership property may, with the consent of the other partners, be sold to one (or more) of their number; or the property may be transferred to one (or more) of the partners to satisfy a partnership debt owing to such member. The remaining partnership property may be equitably distributed in kind among the partners.

Making an Accounting An accounting (or an account) is a statement of all of the transactions of the person who conducts the winding-up process. The accounting should show the total assets and debts of the partnership at the date of dissolution and at the conclusion of the winding up. It should also itemize the winding-up receipts and disbursements. In addition, the accounting should show the value of each partner's interest in the remaining assets of the business as of the date the winding up is concluded. If there are no remaining assets, the accounting should show the sums each partner is required to contribute to satisfy the firm's creditors. Settlement of accounts is covered more fully later in the chapter. What an accounting entails is discussed in the following case.

Case 41.3   Polikoff v. Levy
270 N.E.2d 540 (Ill. 1971)

A joint venture of some forty-nine persons, including Ben Polikoff, acquired land and constructed on it a motor hotel known as the State House Inn. Subsequently the persons who had taken the initiative in forming the joint venture organized the State House Inn Corporation and transferred all the assets of the venture to the new corporation. Polikoff filed suit for dissolution, naming as defendants Maurice S. Levy and all the other members of the joint venture, and the State House Inn Corporation. Plaintiff alleged that the transfer of the assets was without his consent and over his objection, and that such transfer constituted a wrongful dissolution of the joint venture. The complaint prayed that the court wind up the affairs of the joint venture.

The defendants, in answer, offered to return to the plaintiff the sum he had invested in the joint venture and alleged that the rights of other members of the venture would be unduly and harshly prejudiced by its dissolution. The trial court ordered that the joint venture be wound up by a public judicial sale of all its assets and that the net proceeds of such sale be distributed to the members of the joint venture. The court also approved the accountings filed by the defendants.

Both sides appealed from the decree of the court.

CRAVEN, J. . . . It is clear that defendants have no right to buy plaintiff's, Ben Polikoff's, interest in the joint venture. A co-venture is governed substantially by the same rules which govern a partnership. The settled law is that where, as here, a partner or joint venturer retires without himself causing a wrongful dissolution, the copartners or co-venturers have no right to buy the retired partner's or co-venturer's interest. . . . Plaintiff here did not wrongfully withdraw from the joint venture nor cause a wrongful dissolution. Section 42 of the Illinois Uniform Partnership Act is not applicable here since plaintiff did not cause a wrongful dissolution.

Actually, by transfer of certain joint venture or partnership assets to a corporation, defendants caused a wrongful dissolution of the partnership since the partnership agreement specified no duration or term of the partnership. . . .

The established procedure in winding up a dissolved joint venture where the dissolution was not caused in contravention of the agreement, unless the agreement creating the joint venture provides otherwise or all joint venturers agree otherwise, is to convert its assets into cash by sale, discharge its liabilities, and distribute the surplus, if any, to its members. Section 38(1) of the Illinois Uniform Partnership Act so provides. . . .

Where the co-venturers cannot agree on the method of sale at dissolution, a public judicial sale is the only available method of conversion of the assets. Equitable principles and possible unfavorable results of a forced judicial sale cannot compel disregard for the application of the ordinary and traditional methods of final settlement of a business relationship. The parties have failed to provide by their agreement a possibly more favorable method of liquidation. The trial court properly decreed a public judicial sale in the instant case.

[Plaintiff's appeal attacks] that portion of the trial court decree which approved defendant's accounting. . . .

Each partner of a partnership or co-venturer of a co-venture is entitled to a "formal account" as to partnership or co-venture operations and affairs. . . .

An accounting is a statement of receipts and disbursements. A final account of a partnership or co-venture should show all of the detailed financial transactions of the business and the true status of the firm's assets. . . .

In an accounting on dissolution of a partnership or co-venture, the same type of account is required as that of a trustee. The account should list all receipts and disbursements made and the original vouchers, bills and cancelled checks should be tendered or available for inspection to support the items listed. It should include a listing of original contributions and current assets and liabilities.

While it is apparent that the account in the instant case must cover many years, will consist of many items, and will require production of many documents, yet in order for the account to be of any value or to fulfill the duty of accounting it cannot be merely a summary or lump listing of types of items. Simply because a matter has become complicated or voluminous does not excuse the duty of giving "true and full information". . . . While the burden may be considerable, this does not eliminate the requirement of a proper account where a duty to account exists. . . . This cause is remanded . . . with directions to order the filing of proper and sufficient accountings and for further proceedings in accordance with the views herein expressed.

Affirmed in part, reversed in part, and remanded with directions.

Transactions Not Incident to Winding Up

It is not unusual for a partnership to incur liabilities in the course of the winding up of its affairs through an act of the person in charge of the winding up. A partnership may also incur liability through an act of a partner who is not in charge of the winding-up activities. Although such a partner has no *express authority* to act for the partnership,[6] he or she may have the *power* (through apparent authority) to bind the partnership where (1) the nature of the transaction is such that the partnership would be bound if the dissolution had not taken place, and (2) the third person had no knowledge or notice of the dissolution.

In order to protect themselves against the possibility of being liable on unauthorized transactions, the partners should give prompt notice of dissolution. As to persons who had extended credit to the partnership prior to dissolution, "notice" means actual notice. As to persons who knew of the partnership but had not extended credit to it prior to dissolution, constructive notice may be given by advertisement in a newspaper of general circulation in the place (or in each place, if more than one) at which the partnership business was regularly carried on [35].

---

[6]UPA, sec. 33: "Except so far as may be necessary to wind up partnership affairs or to complete transactions begun but not then finished, dissolution terminates all authority of any partner to act for the partnership."

Settlement of Partnership Accounts

Order of Payment The ultimate objective of the winding-up process is to pay all of the partnership debts and then to repay to the partners the capital contributions they made to the firm, together with their respective shares of any surplus funds that remain. In the settlement of accounts among partners, the assets of the partnership are its property and such additional contributions of the partners as may be necessary for the payment of its liabilities [40(a)]. The liabilities of the partnership rank in order of payment as follows [40(b)]:

1 those owing to partnership creditors other than the partners of the firm

2 those owing to any of the partners for loans or advancements made to the partnership

3 those owing to partners as repayment for their capital contributions

4 those owing to the partners for their share of profits, if any

Provided no creditor's priority of claim is affected, the partners may, by agreement, change the order of payment among themselves.

Settlement of Accounts among Partners Unless a partnership agreement provides otherwise, partners share equally in partnership profits regardless of the varying amounts of their contributions to the firm's capital (see Chapter 39, p. 825). The UPA also provides that, absent contrary provisions in their agreement, each partner "must contribute towards the losses, whether of capital or otherwise, sustained by the partnership according to his share of the profits" [18(a)]. Therefore, a problem arises on dissolution of a partnership that does not have enough assets to pay all of its creditors. How much must each partner contribute to defray partnership losses when partners, entitled to share equally in profits, have contributed different amounts to the capital of the firm? How the courts handle this problem can best be explained by illustration.

Let us assume that partner A made a capital contribution of $10,000; partner B made a contribution of $5,000 and services; and partner C made no money contribution but agreed to devote expert knowledge to the firm. Let us also assume that the partners had agreed to divide the partnership profits *equally*. Suppose that after completion of the winding up, the partners find that the partnership has paid all of its bills except $2,500 to creditor X and $1,100 to partner A, who had loaned that amount to the business. The firm has no money or property to meet these obligations. How are the partnership accounts to be settled?

Most courts would settle the partnership accounts in this type of situation as follows.[7]

1   Obligations of firm (assumed):
    To X . $2,500 (for amount due)
    To A . . 1,100 (for loan to partnership)
    To A . 10,000 (for capital contribution)
    To B . . 5,000 (for capital contribution)
    To C. . . . — (no money contribution)
    Total obliga-
    tions $18,600

2   Contributions required: Since the partners had agreed to share equally in the profits, they must contribute equally to cover the losses. Therefore, A, B, and C must share equally the loss of $18,600, or $6,200 each.

3   Contributions now required:
    By A . . none (original contribution $10,000; loss $6,200; balance due A, $3,800)
    By B . $1,200 (original contribution $5,000; loss $6,200; balance required from B, $1,200)
    By C . $6,200 (original money contribution: none; $6,200 required from C)
    Total contributions required: $7,400

4   Distribution of total contributions ($7,400):
    To X . $2,500 (to pay creditor's bill)
    To A . . 1,100 (to repay loan)
    To A . . 3,800 (partial return of original contribution)
Proof that under this method of settling accounts, all partners share equally the loss of $18,600:
    A loses $6,200 ($10,000 original contribution, less $3,800)
    B loses $6,200 ($5,000 original contribution plus new contribution of $1,200)
    C loses $6,200 ($6,200 new contribution)

Some courts would distribute the loss only among partners A and B and assess no monetary contribution against partner C because C contributed services but not money to the partnership.[8]

If any of the partners (but not all of them) in the above example is insolvent, or if one or more of the partners is not subject to the jurisdiction of the court in a suit brought by a partnership creditor, or if one of the partners otherwise refuses to contribute his or her share, the distribution changes. The solvent partner or partners then must contribute the additional amount necessary to pay the firm's liabilities [40(d)] and the partners who pay the debts have claims against the noncontributing partners which can be enforced by suit.

[7]Bromberg, *Crane and Bromberg*, sec. 65, p. 367, note 14.

[8]*Kovacik v. Reed*, 315 P.2d 314 (Cal. 1957).

Case 41.4   **Petersen v. Petersen**
169 N.W.2d 228 (Minn. 1969)

William Petersen owned and operated a hatchery business. In 1946 his son, Donald Petersen, joined him in the business and they formed a partnership. William contributed his hatchery business, which included cash, machinery, equipment, inventory, and accounts receivable, having a total value of $41,000. Donald contributed nothing, but he took over the active management of the hatchery. During the following years William only helped out in the business as needed. The taxes and costs of upkeep of the property were paid out of the partnership funds. Depreciation on the building and equipment was deducted on the partnership tax returns, and the net income was divided equally between William and Donald. The partnership property continued, however, to be held in William's name. Donald, in 1964, prepared a list of his assets on which he included one-half the assets of the hatchery business.

In October 1964, Donald died. The total value of the partnership property at the date of Donald's death was $18,572.89. William claimed that he was entitled to the return of his capital investment in the partnership before Donald's estate could recover anything. Since he had contributed $41,000 to its capital, William asserted there were no assets left for Donald's estate. Donald's widow, the plaintiff in this action, brought suit against William Petersen to compel a division of the partnership assets. The plaintiff contended, and the trial court found, that the conduct of the parties established an agreement for the equal division of the total assets of the partnership without a prior return of capital to William. From this judgment William appealed.

GALLAGHER, J. . . . The law in Minnesota on the distribution of partnership property upon dissolution of the partnership is governed by Minn. St. 323.39, part of the Uniform Partnership Act [UPA, sec. 40], which establishes the following priority: (1) Payment of debts to creditors other than partners; (2) payment of debts to partners for other than capital contributions; (3) payment to partners for capital contributions; and (4) payment to partners of their share of the profits. It is established beyond question in this state, as elsewhere, that the capital contributed by a partner is a debt of the partnership which must be paid after the outside creditors but before there is any division of the profits. . . . However, the . . . authorities, including sec. 323.39, make it equally clear that the right of a partner to receive back the capital he contributed is subject to a contrary agreement among the partners. Before setting out the rules for distribution of assets, sec. 323.39 provides:

> "In settling accounts between partners after dissolution, the following rules shall be observed, *subject to any agreement to the contrary.* . . ."
> [Italics supplied.]

It is also clear from past cases that a contrary agreement of the type referred to above need not be in writing. Where it is not written it is in effect an implied-in-fact contract and may be established in the same manner as any other contract. . . .

In this case the trial judge . . . based his decision on the following facts, all of which are supported in the record:

1 The capital contributed by William was listed on the partnership tax returns and all depreciation was taken on those returns;

2 All taxes on the property as well as repairs and improvements were paid out of partnership funds;

3 The list prepared by Donald 3 months before his death included one-half the partnership assets as part of what he believed to be his property;

4 The conduct of defendant before and immediately after Donald's death tends to support plaintiff's claim;

5 The fondness William showed for his son as evidenced by his demonstrated intent to leave all the assets to Donald. (William testified that his will so provided.)

. . . While the deceased did not contribute any capital to the business, for all but the very early years of the partnership, he operated it with very little help from his father. Although contributing nothing more than occasional assistance during this period, William continued to receive half of the income. The conduct of the parties makes it entirely reasonable to infer that William put up the capital and Donald provided the labor under an agreement by which each was to own half of the business, including both capital and profits.

Affirmed.

Priorities between Types of Creditors

There are no priorities among the general creditors of a partnership whose claims are allowable. However, since a partner is personally liable for the obligations of a partnership of which the partner is a member, there may be a question as to priorities between the creditors of the firm and the creditors of individual partners. This question particularly arises when the partnership is in liquidation or the assets of a partner are in the possession of a court for distribution, as, for example, in the event of a partner's death. To establish an order of priorities in such situations, the UPA provides that a partner's personal assets are then primarily subject to the claims of his or her personal creditors and the partnership's assets are primarily subject to the claims of partnership creditors [40(h)]. This has been called the *jingle rule*. An example of the application of this rule would be present where a partner has died and his or her estate is being administered in a probate court. In that event, the individual creditors of the deceased partner are paid out of the deceased partner's estate *before* any payment is made from that source to discharge the debts of the partnership of which the deceased had been a member.

Because of a provision of the Bankruptcy Reform Act of 1978, the same rule as to priority between creditors is not followed when a partnership is a bankrupt debtor (11 USC 723). In this situation, if there are insufficient assets to pay in full all claims against it, the trustee of the debtor partnership may collect the deficiency from its individual partners. In seeking payment to cover that deficiency, the trustee stands on an *equal footing* with the individual partners' creditors and *not after* the personal creditors have first been paid. Thus, let us say that partnership AB is bankrupt and does not have sufficient assets to pay $6,000 owing its creditors. Assume that partner A has no assets but partner B has assets of $4,000. Further assume that B owes a personal debt to X of $2,000. B may not claim that the debt to X should be paid before any portion of his assets are used to pay the partnership debt. Instead, B's assets of $4,000 are divided between the trustee and X in proportion to the amounts owing to each. B is obligated to pay the $6,000 partnership debt (since A has no assets) and the $2,000 personal debt, totalling $8,000. Therefore, the trustee will receive $3,000 (six-eighths of $4,000) and X will receive $1,000 (two-eighths of $4,000.).

CONTINUANCE OF BUSINESS OF A DISSOLVED PARTNERSHIP

When a partnership is dissolved and liquidated, some measure of forced sale is involved. Therefore, a monetary sacrifice usually occurs. Liquidation may also cause loss in the value of the firm's goodwill. To prevent the possibility of economic loss being forced upon innocent partners, the UPA provides that a member who has been expelled from a partnership or has caused its dissolution in contravention of the partnership agreement cannot force a winding up of the partnership business if the remaining partners desire to continue it.

The UPA also furnishes a basis, should the partners so agree, for the continuance of a dissolved partnership's business under other circumstances without a winding up [38, 41, 42, and 43]. As an eminent authority on partnership law has said:

Partnerships have evolved with the economy. Concepts which were appropriate in a simpler day for 2- or 3-man firms without written agreements need modification today for large firms with elaborate structures and continuity agreements. In the latter cases, dissolution is an empty and useless notion. It is time we recognize in this respect, as we do in many others, that the partnership is what the partners make it.[9]

When the *business* of a dissolved partnership continues without a winding up of its affairs, the law assumes that the continuing business is carried on by a new entity, either a new partnership composed of the remaining partners and such other persons as they may add, or by an entity composed of the sole surviving partner. However, the circumstance that a new entity carries on the business is of no practical importance because the creditors of the dissolved partnership are also creditors of the new entity continuing the business [41].

Continuance of the business after dissolution but without a winding up most often occurs where the dissolution was caused by the completion of the partnership term; by the expulsion or wrongful withdrawal of a partner; or by the retirement, authorized withdrawal, or death of a partner.

Continuance after Completion of Partnership Term

The continued partnership may be either a partnership at will or a partnership for a new term agreed upon by its members. In the absence of an agreement between the partners to the contrary, the rights and duties of the partners remain the same as they were before the partnership reached the conclusion of its term. Creditors' rights against the partners as individuals remain unaffected by the technical

[9]Bromberg, op. cit., sec. 78a, p. 444. Quoted with the permission of West Publishing Co.

dissolution through which the partnership has passed.

Continuance after Expulsion or Wrongful Withdrawal of a Partner

As discussed on page 859, when a partnership has been dissolved by the expulsion of a partner or by the withdrawal of a partner in contravention of the partnership agreement, and the dissolution may be said to have been brought about by a partner's wrongdoing, the business of the partnership may be continued by the remaining partners without going through the winding-up process. If the law were to provide otherwise, innocent members of a partnership would be penalized by the act of a wrong-doing partner. The primary problems arising in such a

dissolution concern the obligations of the dissolving and continuing partners to the firm's creditors, and a determination of the value of the wrong-doing partner's interest in the firm as of the date of dissolution. Since the dissolution of a partnership does not discharge any existing liabilities of a partner to the partnership creditors, the partner who causes the dissolution remains liable to anyone who is a partnership creditor on the date of the dissolution [36(1)], but is not liable to those who become creditors subsequent thereto.

The next case deals with the payments to be made to a partner who wrongfully caused the dissolution of a partnership, the business of which is continued by the non-wrongdoing partner.

Case 41.5   **Laddon v. Whittlesey**
                 408 A.2d 93 (Md. 1979)

In 1973, Laddon, the appellant, and Whittlesey, the appellee, entered into a partnership to operate an automobile wrecking business. There was no formal partnership agreement. It was agreed between them that Laddon would spend most of his time running the business and would receive a weekly salary. Whittlesey would work only about one-half day per week and receive no salary. Laddon suffered a heart attack and while he was sick Whittlesey attended to the business. By April, 1974, Laddon was able to work for a few hours each day and he and Whittlesey became increasingly antagonistic over how the business should be conducted. In June, 1974, Laddon said that he would not put any more money into the business.

In September, 1974, Whittlesey filed a complaint seeking a judicial dissolution of the partnership and asking that he, Whittlesey, be permitted to continue the business after its dissolution. Laddon, in his answer, concurred that the partnership should be dissolved but he objected to its continuance by Whittlesey. Instead, he asked that the business be wound up and the assets disposed of at public sale.

Numerous court hearings followed in the ensuing 4 years, during which time Whittlesey ran the business. The court ultimately determined that the partnership had been dissolved as of June, 1974, caused by the wrongful acts of defendant Laddon. It also determined that as of June, 1975 Whittlesey had contributed to the firm's capital $19,123.75 more than had been contributed by his partner, Laddon. The court ordered Laddon to pay to Whittlesey one-half of the excess capital contribution ($9,561.87) and also to pay Whittlesey's attorney's fee, the appraisal fees, and the accountant's fees. Laddon appealed the order directing the payment of these sums.

LOWE, J. . . . The Uniform Partnership Act . . . like most uniform acts, was intended to anticipate problems and simplify solutions. . . . Subtitle 6 [UPA secs. 26–43] anticipated the problems of Dissolution and Winding Up of partnerships . . . when a surviving partner desires to continue the business with the same name or when the business is dissolved or terminated.

If dissolution is mutually agreed upon, each partner may have the partnership property applied to discharge its liabilities and the surplus applied to pay in cash the net amount owing each partner. [UPA sec. 38]. . . . If the dissolution is not mutual and amicably agreed upon, but caused by the wrongful conduct of a partner, the innocent partner is entitled not only to his net share of the surplus after liabilities, but also to damages caused by the wrongdoer. . . .

The innocent partners are given a conditional option either to continue the business or to wind it up and terminate it. If they desire to continue the business in the same name, they must, among other things, pay the partner who wrongfully causes the dissolution the value of his interest in the partnership . . . as of the date of the dissolution . . . less damages recoverable as above-mentioned. . . . If the business is not continued, the innocent partner has the right to wind up the partnership affairs . . . ; nonetheless, the partner who caused the dissolution wrongfully is entitled to be paid in cash the net amount of the surplus after repayment of liabilities . . . although his share is subject to diminution for whatever damages were caused by his wrongful breach of the partnership agreement. . . .

While all partnership rights to an accounting of any partner's interest . . . accrue at the date of dissolution . . . , dissolution does not terminate the partnership. Only in the best of all possible partnership worlds will dissolution and termination coincide, but more often than is desirable a partnership will begin to disintegrate commensurate with a developing animosity between partners. At some point during that period, dissolution may be caused intentionally or unconsciously by wrongful conduct of a recalcitrant partner, but the "partnership" business limps on.

. . . Perhaps, recognizing that there will be times when this arms length period between partners will require business to be conducted for the preservation of the business partnership assets, the Act has provided among its delineation of rights and duties of partners . . . [UPA sec. 18] that:

> "(2) The partnership must indemnify every partner in respect of payments made and personal liabilities reasonably incurred by him in the ordinary and proper conduct of its business, or for the preservation of its business or property."

In addition thereto,

> "(3) A partner who, in aid of the partnership makes any payment or advance beyond the amount of capital which he agreed to contribute, shall be paid interest from the date of the payment or advance."

Unless there is some agreement for salary for specified services among or between the partners.

> "(6) No partner is entitled to remuneration for acting in the partnership business, except that a surviving partner is entitled to reasonable compensation for his services in winding up the partnership affairs.

Thus, the [trial] court must first determine whether it will . . . permit [the appellee, Whittlesey] to continue the business, or, . . . that the "partnership business be wound up and disposed of at public or private sale." . . .

Even assuming the court will again on remand determine that Laddon was the wrongful cause of dissolution . . . if it is to be continued by Whittlesey, Laddon is nonetheless entitled to be paid the value of his interest effective the date of dissolution, less damages for breach of the agreement. . . .

Assuming, as we must, that the partnership is still in a state of being "wound up," the court must distinguish between debts incurred of a continuing nature prior to dissolution . . . which continue to be obligations of the partners . . . and any new capital contributions (as for purchases of inventory, etc.) which may have been volunteered in anticipation of continuing the business as prayed by the appellee. Any new capital contributions would hardly be chargeable to the appellant. . . . But if either partner was compelled to pay the liabilities incurred prior to the dissolution to preserve the partnership assetts, he is entitled to recover from the partnership whether designated as winding up partner or not. . . . Only if the partnership assets are insufficient to recompense him for these payments, is he entitled to recover from the other partner pursuant to that partner's obligation under [the UPA].

On the other hand, if Whittlesey is to be permitted to continue the business as his own, such prior incurred capital contributions and liability payments as he may have made after the date of dissolution should not be made Laddon's obligation. To do otherwise would be to benefit the continuing business and the surviving partner at the expense of the withdrawing partner. . . .

The court erred [with regard to attorney's fees and other charges] absent some adequate explanation. . . . The court should have ascertained and charged the partnership only with liabilities incurred by the partnership. . . . Laddon would be responsible, if at all, only if it were a justifiable partnership liability which the partnership assets cannot pay upon distribution. . . . This is not an award to the winding up partner . . . nor is it justified in the records as a partnership indemnification of a partner for the preservation of its business or property. . . .

Judgment reversed. . . .

Continuance after Retirement or Authorized Withdrawal of a Partner

When a partner retires or voluntarily withdraws from a partnership, but *not* in contravention of the agreement, the change in the relationship of the parties dissolves the original partnership by the express will of the partners [31(1)(b) and (c)]. The business of the newly constituted partnership may be continued without a winding up.

Unless the partnership agreement contains a controlling provision, a retiring (or withdrawing) partner and the continuing partners must agree upon the method by which the value of the outgoing partner's interest in the firm is determined. The valuation is computed as of the date the partnership is dissolved. If the value of the outgoing partner's interest is to be paid in installments or if such partner does not withdraw his or her full share but leaves all or some of it in the partnership, he or she is entitled to (1) interest on the value of the share left in the partnership, or (2) if such person so elects, instead of interest, as much of the profits of the continuing business as are attributable to the use of that share [42].

The outgoing partner is an ordinary creditor of the continuing partnership to the extent that the value of his or her interest in the business remains unpaid. However, the creditors of the partnership on the date of the partner's retirement or withdrawal from the firm have a claim against the continuing partnership and its members that is prior to a claim of the outgoing partner. The outgoing partner remains personally liable for partnership debts incurred *before* the dissolution [36(1), 41(8), and 42]. Such person generally is not liable for partnership obligations incurred subsequent to the dissolution. However, if appropriate notice is not given to firms that have done business with the former partnership, the outgoing partner may, on estoppel principles, be liable for subsequently incurred obligations.[10]

---

[10]Estoppel is discussed in connection with Power Arising from Apparent Authority, Chapter 36, pp. 751–753.

Continuance after Death of a Partner

Unless the partnership agreement provides otherwise, the representative of a deceased partner may elect to require the winding up of the partnership and the distribution of its net assets, or to permit the continuation of the partnership business.

If the representative elects to permit the continuation of the business, or if the partnership agreement authorizes continuance, and the surviving partners decide to continue it, the value of the deceased partner's interest is ascertained as of the date of death. This value is determined by application of a formula set out in the partnership agreement or one agreed upon by the surviving partners and the representative of the deceased partner. An important element in computing the value of the deceased partner's interest may be the value placed upon the partnership goodwill. If the surviving partner(s) want to continue the partnership business and the representative of the deceased partner does not object, then some arrangement must be reached as to the payment of the deceased partner's share. If the estate is not to be immediately paid in a lump sum, the representative has the right to elect whether the estate will receive (1) interest on the deceased partner's share left in the business, or (2) so much of the profits of the continuing business as are attributable to the use of that share. The representative is entitled to make only a single election between interest and profits. Profits may not be chosen and later the choice changed to interest because the business proved not to be as profitable as had been anticipated.

The estate of the deceased partner is an ordinary creditor of the continuing business. However, creditors of the partnership on the date of the partner's death have a claim prior to that of the estate of the deceased partner (or to the separate creditors of the deceased partner) against the continuing business and those who comprise it. The deceased partner's estate remains liable to any partnership creditor whose claim arose prior to the partner's death [36(1), 41(8), and 42].

The final case in this chapter concerns the value to be attached to a deceased partner's share when the winding up of the partnership of which he was a member continues over an extended period.

Case 41.6

Matter of Trust Estate of Schaefer
283 N.W.2d 410 (Wis. 1979)

Ben Schaefer owned thirteen parcels of real estate in partnership with Arthur Schaefer. Ben died in 1969. The co-executor of Ben's estate and the trustee under Ben's will, brought this action for a declaration whether the interest of Ben's estate in the property is (1) 50 percent of the valuation at the date of his death plus 50 percent of the profits from the date of death until final settlement of the partnership, or (2) 50 percent of the valuation of the partnership assets at the final settlement of the partnership accounts, which has not as yet occurred. Since Ben's death, the property has appreciated in value. Therefore, the second method of valuation would be more beneficial to the estate. The probate court determined that Section 42 of the Uniform Partnership Act [see Appendix 2, page 1246] controlled and therefore the trustee's interest is limited to 50 percent of the partnership assets valued at the date of death plus interest or profits accruing since then until the date of final settlement. The trustee appealed from that decree, claiming, among other things, that it is entitled to the appreciated value of the property.

BROWN, Presiding Judge. . . . When a partner dies, the partnership is dissolved. . . . On dissolution, however, the partnership is not terminated; it continues until the wind-up of the partnership affairs is completed. . . . Winding up is the process of settling partnership affairs after dissolution. Partners, or those claiming through a deceased partner, may agree to settle the partnership affairs without a liquidation of the assets (by agreeing to a cash settlement or in-kind distribution). However, absent an agreement, winding-up involves reducing the assets to cash (liquidation), paying creditors, and distributing to partners the value of their respective interests. . . .

Ordinarily, upon distribution due to death of a partner, it is the duty and responsibility of the surviving partner to wind up the partnership with due diligence and pay the estate of the deceased partner the value of his interest in the partnership. . . . The surviving partner, however, need not wind up the partnership if he has a right to continue the business. . . .

Arthur Schaefer's right, as surviving partner, to continue the business is controlled by [sec. 41, UPA]. Under [that section] the business may be continued if the legal representative of the deceased partner assigns the deceased partner's rights to the . . . surviving partner . . . [or] the business may be continued by the surviving partner if the legal representative of the deceased partner consents to the continuation without liquidation of the partnership affairs. . . . Specific consent is not required. Acquiescence by the legal representatives in the continuation of the business is sufficient. . . . The record is clear that the legal representatives did not consent to or acquiesce in the continuation of the business. . . .

Therefore, . . . the business was not continued pursuant to sec. [41], but was instead a slow wind-up due to the pending litigation [Ben's widow sought to have the court decree that there was no partnership. The case went to the Supreme Court of the State of Wisconsin which held that the real estate in question was partnership property].

Under the circumstances, the rights of the partners are controlled by sec. [38, UPA]. . . . The business was being wound up albeit slowly, because of the litigation. . . .

Where the business is not continued but is being wound up, the value of the deceased partner's interest is not determined by the date of death value plus interest or profits, as is the case if the business is continued. . . .

. . . The deceased partner's interest is not determined until the wind-up is complete. After the creditors have been paid, all profits are shared by the surviving partners and the deceased partner, as well as losses based on their predissolution ratios (in this case 50%). Therefore, where the business is wound up rather than continued under the conditions set forth in [UPA sec. 42], the deceased partner's interest is the value of his interest at the date of liquidation (when wind-up is complete). This value includes assets appreciation during the winding-up period and is subject to any losses incurred during that time. . . .

In the present case, . . . there was no agreement to continue the business. . . . Therefore, sec. [UPA 42] does not apply. Section [UPA 38] applies and the estate is entitled to 50% of the proceeds, including asset appreciation, at the time of liquidation or final settlement. . . .

Decree reversed and case remanded for liquidation of all assets and distribution of the surplus, after payment to creditors, to the deceased partner's estate and the surviving partner, 50% to each, unless otherwise agreed.

SUMMARY

A partnership comes to an end through a two-step process. First there is a dissolution; then a winding up. Completion of the winding up terminates a partnership as a business organization.

A dissolution may be consistent with the partnership agreement or in violation of it. Dissolution is consistent if the reason therefor was within the contemplation of the parties when they entered into the partnership.

Since a partnership is a voluntary association, any of its members has the power to bring the association to an end at any time even though such action may be contrary to the partnership agreement. If a partner causes a dissolution in contravention of the agreement, that partner is liable to the copartners in damages because of breach of contract.

A partnership is automatically dissolved by operation of law when the continuance of the partnership becomes illegal or when a partner dies. In some states, death does not automatically dissolve a partnership if the agreement specifically permits its continuance in such event.

Dissolution of a partnership may also be ordered by a court. Among the reasons for judicial dissolution are: when there is existence of a fundamental disagreement among the partners as to how the business should be conducted; when a party is guilty of misconduct; and when the business cannot be carried on at a profit.

A winding up (the second stage of the termination process) involves completing pending partnership business; collecting debts; discharging liabilities; converting partnership property into cash; making an accounting; paying partnership obligations; and distributing among its members any balance remaining. If the partnership assets are not sufficient to pay all of the firm's debts and to repay contributions to the capital of the partnership, the partners must make up the deficit from their personal resources.

Under certain circumstances a partnership business may be continued without a winding up of the firm. However, the continuing firm is, in legal effect, a new partnership comprised of its continuing members.

Upon the death or retirement of a partner, the business may, with the consent of the outgoing partner or of the representative of the deceased partner, be continued by the surviving partners. The representative of the deceased partner may elect to receive the value of the deceased partner's interest in cash or to let that interest remain in the firm. In the latter event the representative receives for the deceased partner's estate, at the representative's further election, either interest on the share left in the business or the profits earned by the share.

Creditors of a dissolved firm are also creditors of any partnership that continues the partnership business. All of the members of the firm on the date of the dissolution are liable for the partnership debts on the date of the dissolution. Normally, only continuing partners are personally liable for debts contracted by the partnership after the date of dissolution.

STUDY AND DISCUSSION QUESTIONS

1 Distinguish between the "dissolution" and the "winding up" of a partnership.

2 Enumerate five circumstances that would cause the dissolution of a partnership without violating the partnership agreement.

3 When a partner withdraws from the firm before the conclusion of the partnership term, and does so without the consent of his or her partners, is such partner entitled to the return of his or her contribution to the partnership? Explain.

4 If a partnership consists of four members and one of the partners dies, is the partnership automatically dissolved? Explain.

5 If a partner, by ill-tempered actions, causes the firm to lose customers, what recourse do the other partners have against that partner?

6 (a) Who conducts the winding up of a partnership? (b) Is the individual paid for such services? Why or why not?

7 (a) What effect, if any, does the dissolution of a partnership have on the rental obligations under an unexpired lease? Why? (b) Under what circumstances may a partnership in winding up engage in new contracts of purchase?

8 At the conclusion of the winding up of a partnership, in what order are the partnership liabilities paid?

9 Explain the relationship between a dissolved partnership and the entity that continues the business of the original partnership after its dissolution.

CASE PROBLEMS

1 Edward and Martha entered into a partnership for a term of years ending in December 1951. Edward was to be the manager of the business and to receive a salary for his services. Martha was to receive rent for a building owned by her and occupied by the partnership. Each was to share equally in the partnership profits and losses. After 1951, without any further agreement of the parties, the business continued. From that date Martha received rent but Edward made no division of the profits. In April 1960 Edward informed Martha that her interest in the business had ceased in 1951 and he excluded her from any participation in it. Martha immediately filed suit for an accounting, the appointment of a receiver, and the winding up of the partnership. The court determined that Martha was entitled to an equal division of the profits of the partnership until such time as the business was sold by the receiver. Was the court correct in making that determination?

2 Napoli and Domnitch were partners engaged in the building and operation of apartment houses. The partnership agreement did not specify any definite term for its duration or any event that was to terminate it. However, the agreement did provide that in the event of the dissolution of the partnership, the value of the dissolving partner's interest would be determined by appraisers appointed by the partners. The continuing partner could, at his option, then purchase the dissolved partner's interest at the value so found and pay the purchase price in sixty monthly installments. Napoli brought an action for the dissolution of the partnership, contending that he had an unqualified right to dissolve the partnership because it was a "partnership at will." Domnitch, the defendant, al-

leged that Napoli's action was a breach of the partnership agreement and sought damages for the dissolution of the partnership. *(a)* Was Napoli correct in contending that he had an unqualified right to dissolve the partnership? *(b)* Was Domnitch correct in contending that Napoli was liable in damages?

3 Andrew Leapes, Leonard Mimoni, and Emanuel Patrikes operated the Times Square Service Station as partners. J. C. H. Service Stations, Inc., had rented the property to the partnership by a written lease having a termination date of August 31, 1943. Sometime prior to October 31, 1942, Leapes was inducted into the military service and Mimoni received an order by his draft board to appear for formal induction. In October 1942, all three defendants gave J. C. H. Service Stations, Inc., plaintiff, written notice that the leased premises would be vacated on November 30, 1942, pursuant to the authority of the Soldiers' and Sailors' Civil Relief Act of 1940. Section 304 of that act provides that persons in the military service and those ordered to report for induction, may, by notice in writing, terminate any lease entered into before entering military service.

The premises were vacated as of November 30, and the landlord made a reasonable, but unsuccessful, effort to rerent the premises for the period December 1942 through August 1943. The partnership did not pay rental on the filling station for December 1942, nor for January to August 1943 inclusive. J. C. H. Service Stations, Inc., filed suit against Leapes, Mimoni, Patrikes, and against their partnership for the rent due under the lease. Leapes and Mimoni filed no answer. Patrikes filed an answer denying liability. Which of the four defendants, if any, were liable on the filling station lease?

4 A and B formed a partnership to which A contributed $20,000 and B $50,000. The partnership owned a hardware store. A managed the business; B, as a "silent partner," took no active part in it. They agreed to share the profits of the business equally. During the first 5 years of the partnership's existence the store made a profit. Each of the partners received about $15,000 per year. Then a large discount store was built nearby, and the partnership's hardware business diminished. For the next 3 years the business suffered a loss of about $3,000 per year. B asked A to liquidate the partnership, but A refused. B, therefore, brought an action against A to force a dissolution of the partnership. A, in his answer, asserted that B had received a generous return on his investment during the prior years; that the partnership was losing very little money; that he had plans for increasing its business; and that therefore the partnership should not be dissolved. Do these facts establish a cause of action for dissolution of the partnership?

5   C and M were equal partners in the business of fire insurance adjusting. M had possession and control of all the partnership assets. The partnership was dissolved at C's request. Thereafter C brought an action for an accounting. M claimed compensation for his expenses and services in winding up the partnership. Should the court allow the partnership assets to be charged with amounts to cover (*a*) M's expenses? (*b*) M's services?

ADDENDUM: LIMITED PARTNERSHIPS AND MINOR BUSINESS ORGANIZATIONS

The two principal types of business organizations, other than sole proprietorships, are partnerships and corporations. Business enterprises may, however, be organized in other forms. Some of those forms of organization assume aspects of both a partnership and a corporation in order to obtain extended business life, opportunity for financial gain with the least possible personal liability, and minimization of tax burdens and governmental controls.

The first part of this addendum deals with limited partnerships. The concluding part identifies various minor organizational forms.

LIMITED PARTNERSHIPS

There is a need in business for some type of organization which would extend to investors in a partnership the same freedom from the risks of personal liability as is enjoyed by corporation stockholders. In response to this need, the National Conference of Commissioners on Uniform State Laws in 1916 drafted the Uniform Limited Partnership Act (ULPA). That act was approved by the American Bar Association and adopted, with slight modifications, by all states except one (Louisiana). The act authorizes the formation of *limited partnerships* composed of one or more general partners and one or more *limited partners*. The general partner(s) manages the enterprise and is subject to all the liabilities that may be imposed on a partner in a regular (general) business partnership. Under that act, a limited partner has no right to manage the affairs of the enterprise and usually is not subject to personal liability for the contracts or the torts of the firm. Limited partnerships have encouraged the investment of risk capital in new and sometimes daring enterprises. They have been found particularly useful in attracting capital into ventures having a relatively limited scope or duration, such as the construction of real estate projects, the drilling of oil wells in unproven areas, and the financing of theatrical productions.

With the experience gained over the years through the use of limited partnerships, it has been found in practice that a limited partner can exercise certain restricted controls over the business enterprise and still properly retain his or her immunity from personal liability. These, and other changes in the original act, are incorporated in the Uniform Limited Partnership Act (1976), commonly referred to as the Revised Uniform Limited Partnership Act. The revised act is designed to supersede the 1916 formulation; it is slowly being enacted by the states. Because of the similarity in name and organization, limited partnerships are often confused with "ordinary" or "general" partnerships. The salient distinguishing features of these two forms of business organizations are summarized in the following tabulation. The numbers in brackets in the left column indicate the UPA section. The bracketed numbers in the right column refer to the sections of the *revised* ULPA.

TABLE 41.1 Comparison of General and Limited Partnerships

General Partnership	Limited Partnership under Revised ULPA
Basic Law	
The Uniform Partnership Act (UPA).	The revised Uniform Limited Partnership Act (ULPA) and, to the extent applicable, the Uniform Partnership Act (UPA) [1105].
Purpose	
It may carry on for profit any business, trade, or profession authorized by its certificate [2; 6].	Except as otherwise limited by its certificate, a limited partnership may engage in any business that a partnership without limited partners may carry on [106].
Formation	
No formal agreement is required [7].	A certificate in the form required by statute must be signed and publicly filed in the office of the Secretary of State. Among other things, the certificate must state the firm's and partners' names; the general character of the business; its duration and location; the contribution made by each partner; termination of membership; and right to receive distributions from the partnership [201; 204; 206].
Membership	
All partners are of one class: *general partners*. A contribution to the firm's capital is not a prerequisite to membership [9; 18].	A limited partnership consists of at least one general partner and one limited partner. A general partner may also invest in the firm as a limited partner [404]. Contributions to the firm by either class of partners may be in money, property, or services [201].
Management	
Each partner has, except as may be agreed between the partners, an equal voice in the firm's management [18].	A general partner has all of the rights and powers of a partner in a partnership without limited partners [403]. A limited partner generally exercises no control over the business; however, voting upon such matters as a change in the nature of the business or in the removal of a partner is not considered to be participation in the control of the business [303].
Admission of Additional Partners	
The unanimous consent of all partners is required before a new member may be added to an existing partnership [18].	Additional general partners may be admitted only with the specific written consent of all partners, both general and limited [401]. Additional limited partners may be admitted as specified in the partnership agreement or upon the written consent of all of the partners, or as assignee of a limited partner [301; 704].

TABLE 41.1 Continued

General Partnership	Limited Partnership under Revised ULPA
Assignment of a Partner's Interest	
An assignment of a partner's interest may be a cause for the dissolution of the partnership [27; 32].	Except as provided in the partnership agreement, a partnership interest is assignable in whole or in part [402; 702].
Liability of Partners	
All partners are jointly liable for the firm's contract debts and jointly and severally liable for its tort obligations arising in the ordinary course of its business [15].	A general partner of a limited partnership is subject to the restrictions and liabilities of a partner in a partnership without limited partners [403]. A limited partner is not personally liable for the obligations of a limited partnership unless he or she takes part in the control of its business. If the participation in control is not substantially the same as the powers exercised by a general partner, the limited partner is personally liable only to those persons who do business with the firm and who have actual knowledge of the limited partner's participation in control [303].
Profits or Income	
All partners share equally in the profits unless their agreement provides otherwise [18].	Profits and losses are allocated as specified in the partnership agreement. If not stated therein, profits and losses are allocated on the basis of the value of each partner's contribution [503].
Withdrawal of Contribution	
All partners must agree, and the firm's creditors must be protected, before a partner may withdraw his or her contribution from the firm's capital [25].	Withdrawal of contribution may be accomplished as specified in the partnership agreement except that a withdrawal may not result in partnership liabilities exceeding the fair value of partnership assets [601; 607].
Death of a Partner	
Death of a partner dissolves the partnership unless the members had agreed to its continuance in such an event. Absent such an agreement, if the enterprise continues it is a new partnership [31].	Death of a general partner dissolves a limited partnership *unless* (1) there was more than one general partner and the certificate permits the firm to be carried on by the remaining general partners, or (2) within 90 days, the limited partners agree in writing to continue the business and to the appointment of additional general partners, if necessary. A deceased limited partner's personal representative may exercise all of the limited partner's rights in the partnership [705; 801].

TABLE 41.1 Continued

General Partnership	Limited Partnership under Revised ULPA
Dissolution	
Dissolution may be pursuant to the terms of the agreement; by action of one or more of the partners; or by operation of law [31; 32].	A limited partnership is dissolved upon the happening of the conditions therefor stated in its certificate; by the written consent of all of the partners; by the withdrawal of a general partner unless continued with other general partners; or by entry of a decree of judicial dissolution [801].
Distribution of Assets Upon Dissolution	
Assets are distributed in the following order: 1 To creditors (other than partners). 2 To partners (other than for capital and profits). 3 To partners to repay capital contributions. 4 To partners for profits, in the proportions described in the partnership agreement; if the agreement is silent, then equally among the partners [18(a); 40].	The assets of a limited partnership are distributed in the following order: 1 To creditors. 2 Except as provided in the agreement, to partners (both general and limited) in satisfaction of previously declared distributions. 3 Except as provided in the agreement, to partners (a) for return of their contributions and then (b) the remainder is divided among all the partners in the same proportions in which they share in the distribution of profits [804].

MINOR BUSINESS ORGANIZATIONS

Subchapter S Corporation   A Subchapter S Corporation, while a true corporation, may elect to be taxed in many respects as though it were a partnership. This form of business organization is analyzed in Chapter 43, "Financial Structure of Corporations."

Professional Service Corporation   A professional service corporation is a special form that many states allow to designated professional classes such as doctors, lawyers, architects, and accountants. Under this type of organization, the professional members become entitled to the retirement and tax savings advantages of corporate employees while at the same time they retain personal responsibility to their clients.[11]

---

[11]For example, Cal. Corp. Code, sec. 13400.

Business Trust   A business trust, often called a Massachusetts trust because of its wide use in that state, has a trust form rather than a corporate form. Trustees hold the title to its property and manage its business. The interest of the beneficial owners is represented by trust certificates. The trust and the trustees are liable for the contract and tort obligations of the enterprise and the beneficiaries of the trust assume no personal liability. If the holders of the trust certificates exercise ultimate control over the trustees, and the existence of the trust is challenged, the court may hold that the organization is not a business trust but is a relationship in the nature of a partnership or joint stock company. In the event the court so holds, any liability found to exist would be cast on the beneficiaries of the trust.

Joint Stock Company   A joint stock company combines characteristics of both a corporation and a partnership. Such a company acquires existence by articles of association, which resemble a corporation charter. Ownership interest in the company usually is represented by transferrable shares of stock. Thus, the members do not have the inherent right to control the composition of the organization as do the partners in a partnership. A joint stock company is generally not dissolved by the death of a member. Its contracts are made and its business is managed by trustees or a board of directors. However, unlike shareholders in a corporation, the members of a joint stock company have the liability of partners in an ordinary business partnership. In the absence of statutory provisions to the contrary, a joint stock company is subject to the same rules about suing and being sued as is a partnership.

Cooperative[12]   A cooperative is an association for the benefit of its members that may take the form of a corporation, a partnership, or any other type of organization, including a club or social group. The possible personal liability of its members is dependent upon the form of organization used and the degree of individual control or right to control its activities that is present. Cooperatives have been found useful for many purposes. For instance, they are frequently organized for the mutual marketing of farm produce, for the operation of retailer-owned wholesale grocery establishments, for

providing goods and services to consumers, and for furnishing rural telephone and electric services.

The cooperative ownership of real property is growing in favor and may be cast in a number of forms. In some, the members share ownership of an entire building and each member pays a monthly carrying charge for the portion of the building used or occupied by such member. Cooperative ownership is different from a condominium. In most condominiums, but not in all, each member has the legal ownership of the apartment or office he or she occupies and an undivided ownership with the other occupants of the building in the halls, lobbies, elevators, and other facilities used in common. Because each member is an owner of the common areas, each is vicariously liable for the torts of the common employees and for negligence in the maintenance of the common areas.

Mining Partnership   A mining partnership, recognized in some states, is similar to a general partnership but is restricted to mining activities.[13]

Joint Venture or Syndicate   A joint venture or syndicate has all of the characteristics of a general partnership except that it is organized to accomplish a single or limited purpose. Since such an organization is, in effect, a temporary partnership, partnership law is applicable to it and to its members.

---

[12]See Chapter 21, p. 404.

[13]For example, Cal. Pub. Resources Code, sec. 2351.

PART TEN

CORPORATIONS

Chapter 42
Nature and Formation of Corporations

Chapter 43
The Financial Structure of Corporations

Chapter 44
The Management Structure of Corporations

Chapter 45
Securities Regulation

Chapter 46
Foreign Corporations

Chapter

42

Nature and
Formation of Corporations

The corporation-for-profit is the most important form of business organization in the United States. Since World War II, the number of partnerships has increased only 84 percent as compared to an increase of over 430 percent in the number of corporations. This remarkable growth is due primarily to an increase in the number of small incorporated businesses with assets of less than $100,000. By 1971, there were over a million such companies in the United States. However, these small corporations collectively owned only 1 percent of total corporate assets, whereas the 200 largest corporations owned 60 percent of all corporate assets.

In 1979, the 1000 largest industrial corporations and the 50 largest retail corporations employed approximately 21 million persons—nearly a fifth of the nonagricultural labor force of the nation.[1] An understanding of the legal framework within which corporations operate is useful to every executive, employee, shareholder, consumer, and taxpayer in our modern free enterprise system.

This chapter briefly traces the development of corporation law and discusses important legal

---

[1] All figures in the paragraph are based upon *Statistical Abstract of the U.S.*, 1980, U.S. Dept. of Commerce.

principles relating to the nature and formation of modern business corporations. Subsequent chapters in this series deal with the financing, management, and regulation of business corporations.

DEVELOPMENT OF MODERN CORPORATION LAW

The idea that a state can breathe life into a fictitious legal person known as a "corporation" originated in ancient Rome and spread to England, and thence to the American Colonies. However, the Constitutional Convention defeated a federal incorporation provision, and therefore there is no basis in our Constitution for federal incorporation of private businesses. Initially, our corporations were formed by special acts of the various state legislatures. These acts became unnecessary as the pressure of the industrial revolution forced the states to enact incorporation laws, sometimes called "enabling statutes." The first of these was passed by North Carolina in 1795. Although these early statutes were highly restrictive, they provided an established procedure under which any business could be incorporated.

During the 1800s, the restrictions on incorporation were relaxed as the states began to compete for the taxable income and employment generated by the larger corporations. In 1899, the *Delaware General Corporation Law* was revised so as to offer maximum freedom from restriction. By 1975, nearly half of the companies listed on the New York Stock Exchange had been incorporated in Delaware. Although the laws governing the formation of corporations have been liberalized, state and federal regulation of corporations *after* their formation has increased.

State Corporation Law
Except for overriding safeguards provided by the federal Constitution, each state has been relatively free to enact and amend statutes providing for the formation and regulation of corporations. Most corporation law is statutory, but the law that governs corporations is also found in applicable provisions of each state's constitution and in interpretive court decisions.

Each state has a *general corporation law* that establishes: incorporation requirements, guidelines for financing a corporation, the rights and duties of directors and shareholders, and the procedure for dissolving a corporation. These statutes vary in detail from state to state. The *Model Business Corporation Act*, which was first published by the American Bar Association in 1950,[2] was designed as a guide by which general corporation statutes could be revised to meet the needs of modern small as well as large corporations. Thirty-six states have partially or substantially adopted the Model Act.[3] California and Delaware are among the states that have not done so.

Each state has a variety of *regulatory statutes* that govern, and often restrict, the business activities of existing corporations. The principal types of state statutes that regulate corporations are:

1 Securities laws called "blue-sky" laws that establish criteria for permits to issue stock[4] and regulate the sale of corporate securities (Blue-sky laws are discussed in Chapter 45, Securities Regulation.)

2 Relevant provisions of Articles 8 and 9 of the

---

[2] American Bar Association, Committee on Corporation Laws (Section of Corporation, Banking and Business Law), *Model Business Corporation Act* (revised January 1, 1979). The Model Act is reproduced in Appendix 3, p. 1247.

[3] Alabama, Alaska, Arkansas, Connecticut, Colorado, District of Columbia, Georgia, Illinois, Iowa, Kansas, Kentucky, Louisiana, Maine, Maryland, Massachusetts, Michigan, Mississippi, Montana, Nebraska, New Jersey, New Mexico, New York, North Carolina, North Dakota, Oregon, Rhode Island, South Carolina, South Dakota, Tennessee, Texas, Utah, Vermont, Virginia, Washington, Wisconsin, and Wyoming.

[4] In all states except Delaware and Nevada.

Uniform Commercial Code that deal with the transfer of corporate securities and the pledge of stock as security for loans

3 Laws that regulate certain kinds of corporations, such as banks and public utilities

4 Corporate tax laws

5 Antimonopoly laws

6 Laws that regulate the in-state activities of foreign corporations organized in another state (or a foreign country)

State statutes are subject to interpretation by the courts. The accumulated body of court decisions is collectively referred to as *case law*. Many important areas of corporation law have developed in the courts. The special legal rules that apply to close corporations and the law that defines the fiduciary duty of directors are examples of such case law. (Close corporations are discussed at p. 896. The fiduciary duty of directors is discussed in Chapter 44.)

Federal Corporation Law
The monopolistic practices of large corporations in the post-Civil War period led to the enactment of corrective federal statutes, such as the Interstate Commerce Act (1888), the Sherman Antitrust Act (1890), and the Federal Trade Commission Act (1914). The stock market crash of 1929 and the ensuing Great Depression spurred Congress to enact further regulatory legislation, such as the Securities Act (1933) and the Securities Exchange Act (1934). The federal agencies created by such statutes have broad power to prosecute violations of these laws. At first, individuals who were wronged by corporations had to refer such grievances to the appropriate regulatory agency. Since 1947, individuals have been allowed to seek direct redress in the federal courts. The case law that resulted from court interpretations of federal regulatory statutes has burgeoned into what is loosely referred to as "federal corporation law."

NATURE OF MODERN CORPORATIONS

The nature of a modern business corporation can best be clarified by examining its chief characteristics and by comparing it with partnerships and other types of corporations.

Chief Characteristics of Corporations
A Legal Entity The word "corporation" means *body*. A corporation may therefore be thought of as a legal body or person whose rights and obligations are separate and distinct from those of its shareholders. The idea of a corporation as a legal "person," or entity, has far-reaching significance. The Supreme Court has held that the Constitution of the United States entitles the corporate person to equal protection of the laws. The corporate body is protected from unreasonable searches and seizures and from deprivation of its property without due process of law. In court, the corporation is a "client," and can claim the privilege of not testifying to matters discussed with its attorney.

A corporation can buy and sell property; it can sue and be sued; it is subject to criminal prosecution; and it is a taxpayer. By contrast, partnerships do not pay taxes and are not subject to criminal prosecution. Whether a corporation has one shareholder or millions, it is treated as a separate legal entity.

A Creature of the State Chief Justice Marshall, in *Dartmouth College v. Woodward*, said: "A corporation is an artificial being, invisible, intangible, and existing only in contemplation of law. Being a mere creature of law, it possesses only those properties which the charter of its creation confers upon it, either expressly or as incidental to its very existence."[5] The term "charter" is sometimes used as a synonym for the articles of incorporation which must be filed with the state as the first step in the incorporation of a business. *Dartmouth* held that a charter is a contract between the corporation and

---

[5] 17 U.S. 518, 636 (1819).

the state and that the enactment of any state law which impairs the obligations of a contract is prohibited by the Constitution of the United States. State legislatures circumvented the *Dartmouth* decision by reserving in the general corporation statutes the power to amend or repeal part or all of such statutes. The practical result is that most corporations are subject to future amendments of the statutes under which they were formed.

Free Transferability of Shares A *share* of stock is a proportionate ownership interest in the corporation. As a general rule, that ownership interest is evidenced by a *stock certificate*. (Ownership shares that are "uncertificated," that is, not represented by a stock certificate, are now permitted under the Model Act, sec. 23, as revised January 1, 1979, and under recent revisions to the Uniform Commercial Code, Article 8, sections 407 and 408.) A transfer in share ownership does not affect the separate legal existence of a corporation. To transfer shares, the owner simply endorses and delivers his or her stock certificate to the transferee. The free transferability of shares has been a major factor in the development of the national stock exchanges and in the prodigious industrialization of the United States.

Limited Liability Investors prefer corporations over other forms of business organizations because a stockholder's potential loss is limited to his or her investment in the corporation's shares. Creditors' claims may exhaust corporate assets, but, normally, creditors cannot reach the personal assets of individual stockholders.

Perpetuity of Existence The death or illness of a corporate director, officer, or shareholder does not affect the life of a corporation. The Model Act (4a)[6] provides that a corporation shall have perpetual existence unless limited to a shorter period by the articles of incorporation. A few statutes limit the duration of a corporation's life, but permit renewal of the term. However,

a corporation may be terminated at any time. (Voluntary dissolutions by the shareholders, as well as involuntary corporate dissolutions, are discussed in Chapter 44.)

Centralization of Management The board of directors controls and manages the business affairs of a corporation "except as may be otherwise provided in the articles" (35). Centralization of management makes it possible for corporations to function with maximum efficiency. At the same time, stockholders who are not active in the business may share in the profits.

Corporations Distinguished from Partnerships

Basic differences between business corporations and partnerships are summarized in Table 42.1.

Types of Corporations

Profit and Nonprofit Corporations A *corporation-for-profit* is organized to conduct a business that is expected to make profits. Profits are distributed to the stockholders as dividends at the discretion of the board of directors. The rights and liabilities of stockholders are determined by the articles, the terms printed on stock certificates, and the law relating to share ownership. Upon liquidation, the corporation's creditors are the first to be paid; any remaining assets are distributed to the stockholders.

A *nonprofit corporation* is formed for charitable, religious, educational, or fraternal purposes. Schools, hospitals, churches, service organizations, and social clubs are examples of organizations that may organize as nonprofit corporations. Some of them issue stock, but most of them grant memberships instead. The rights and liabilities of members are normally determined in the bylaws. The corporate entity protects members from personal liability, but nonprofit corporations are increasingly subject to governmental regulation.

Many nonprofit corporations obtain needed capital by issuing bonds or other debt securities. The issuance of such securities generally requires the approval of the same state agency

---

[6]The section numbers of the Model Act are given in parentheses throughout this series of chapters.

TABLE 42.1

Comparison of Corporations and Partnerships

	Corporation	Partnership
Entity	A legal entity or "person," and taxable as such.	Not a legal entity but has certain characteristics of one (see pp. 816, 840).
Creation	Created by the state upon application of organizers in required legal form.	Created by formal or informal agreement of its members (see p. 818).
Transferability of interest	Shares evidencing ownership are ordinarily transferred without consent of corporation or other stockholders.	All partners (co-owners of business) must consent to admission of new member to partnership (see p. 821.)
Liability	Personal liability for corporate obligations limited to each stockholder's investment in shares.	Personal liability for partnership obligations goes beyond a partner's original investment in the business (see pp. 828, 833, 869, 870).
Duration	Perpetual corporate life unless limited by statute or articles, but shareholders may terminate.	Partnership life not perpetual (see pp. 858 and 860, especially p. 860).
Management	Stockholders' management authority generally limited to voting in elections of directors and on amendments to articles.	Partners manage business and act as agents of partnership unless otherwise provided in the partnership agreement (see pp. 824–25, 831–32).
Purposes and powers	Limited to purposes and powers enumerated in articles and state corporation statute.	Purposes and powers determined by agreement of members, without state approval (see pp. 818, 825, 845, 877).

that regulates the issuance of securities by profit corporations. The assets of nonprofit corporations can be distributed to members only when the corporation is dissolved.

Private, Public, and Quasi-Public Corporations *Private corporations* are organized by private individuals for private purposes and include nonprofit entities as well as business corporations for profit. *Public corporations*[7] are created for governmental purposes by the state or federal government or, in some instances, by

a local unit of government. The Federal Deposit Insurance Corporation, the Federal Land Bank, incorporated cities, and sanitation districts are examples of public corporations. A public corporation, such as the Tennessee Valley Authority and the California State Compensation Insurance Fund, may also be created to operate a public business.

Distinctions between private and public corporations are not always clear. *Quasi-public corporations* are privately organized for profit, but they affect the public interest to such an extent that they are subject to special regulation by state or federal agencies. Examples of such corporations are banks, insurance companies, savings and loan associations, railroads, and

[7]A public corporation should be distinguished from a "publicly held" private corporation-for-profit whose shares are sold to the public. When a substantial amount of "closely held" stock is sold to a large number of persons, the process is referred to as "going public."

other public utilities. Governmental regulation of these corporations is proportionate to the special power or monopolistic privilege granted to them. Most states permit quasi-public corporations to be formed under general business corporation statutes. However, the appropriate regulatory agency must approve the articles of incorporation before they can be accepted for filing by the designated officer of the state.

Domestic and Foreign Corporations A corporation is described as "domestic" in the state of its incorporation. From the standpoint of every other state or nation, it is a "foreign" corporation. Thus, X Corporation, chartered in New York, is a domestic corporation in New York, regardless of the residence of its shareholders. X is viewed as a foreign corporation by every state other than New York. A corporation chartered in one nation is sometimes referred to as an "alien" corporation by other nations.

Aggregate and Sole Corporations In 1769, Blackstone distinguished an *aggregate* corporation from a corporation *sole*. An aggregate corporation which corresponds to today's corporation with many shareholders, he defined as "many persons united together in one society, and maintained by a perpetual succession of members, so as to continue forever."[8]

A corporation *sole*, which in some respects resembles today's "one-man business corporation," consists of a single individual who incorporates to obtain the special advantages of perpetual existence as a separate legal entity. The corporation sole was initiated in medieval England as a means of providing perpetual succession of church lands. Thus, the office of the "Bishop of Exeter" was incorporated as a corporation sole with church lands held in that corporate name. If Jones, who held the office of Bishop of Exeter died, Smith might be appointed to the office as head of the one-man corporation, but the lands would not have to be trans-

ferred from Jones to Smith because they would always be held by the corporation sole. Today many state statutes provide for a corporation sole. A typical statutory provision states that such a corporation may be formed by the "presiding officer of any religious denomination, society, or church, for the purpose of administering and managing the affairs, property, and temporalities thereof."[9]

Close Corporations A majority of the business corporations chartered each year are close corporations. A *close corporation* has two basic characteristics:

1 Its shares are not traded in the securities market.
2 It has relatively few stockholders, all of whom usually participate in management and, for practical purposes, act as partners.

The shareholders of certain close corporations may elect to be a *Subchapter S* corporation which is taxed in many respects as though it were a partnership. ("Subchapter S" and other tax options available to close corporations that qualify under revised federal tax laws are discussed in Chapter 43.) If substantially all the stock in a close corporation is held by members of the same family, the company is often described as a *family* corporation. If the stock is held by one individual, the company may be referred to as a *one-man* or *one-person* corporation. If the stock is held by one professional person or by a group of professionals who incorporate, the close corporation is called a *professional* corporation. (Statutory restrictions imposed on professional corporations are discussed in Chapter 44 under "Limitations on Corporate Powers.")

Close corporations are frequently referred to as "closely held" or "closed" corporations. These three terms are used interchangeably. Nevertheless, the term "closed corporation" is

---

[8] William Blackstone, *Commentaries on the Laws of England*, vol. 1, p. 469, Bancroft-Whitney Company, San Francisco, 1916.

[9] Calif. Corp. Code, sec. 10002.

sometimes used to emphasize the shareholders' determination to prevent outsiders from acquiring stock. Restrictions on transfers of stock to outsiders are sometimes included in the articles or bylaws or in separate agreements among the stockholders. (Such restrictions are discussed in Chapter 43.)

It is difficult to organize a close corporation under a statute designed to apply to large publicly held corporations. Many states are adding flexibility to their general corporation statutes by enacting provisions that deal with the unique requirements of close corporations.[10] The Model Act includes options that permit only one incorporator (53) or one director (36) and that allow business to be transacted without a meeting by unanimous written consent of the directors (44) or shareholders (145).

FORMATION OF CORPORATIONS

A business corporation originates as an *idea* for a profitable business. A person or legal entity that is active in transforming that idea into a corporation is called a *promoter*. This part of the chapter deals with legal problems relating to the role of promoters and stock subscribers, the selection of a state in which to incorporate, and the procedure for forming a corporation.

Role of Promoters

Nature and Function of Promoters   The promoter occupies the role of corporate "midwife." He or she discovers a business opportunity, verifies its economic feasibility, and brings incorporators, subscribers, lenders, and management together to form and operate the corporate enterprise. A promoter often makes necessary arrangements for the real property, equipment, materials, and human resources

that the corporation will need to begin business operations.

A promoter is usually self-appointed. He or she is neither an agent of the persons brought into the venture nor an agent of the future corporation (since the corporation cannot be a principal or appoint agents until it legally exists). The term "promoter" is not restricted to an individual. A promoter can be a corporation that organizes another corporation or an existing partnership that incorporates.

Fiduciary Duty of Promoters   Promoters owe a fiduciary duty to the subscribers, the shareholders, and the corporation. A promoter's fiduciary duty requires fair dealing, the exercise of good faith, and disclosure of all material facts concerning transactions on behalf of the corporation. For example, a promoter who buys property in anticipation of selling it to a prospective corporation is liable to the corporation for any *secret* profit realized from the transaction. To avoid liability, the promoter must make a full disclosure to an *independent* board of directors. In situations involving "dummy" directors controlled by the promoter, his or her fiduciary duty can ordinarily be discharged by a full disclosure to all existing shareholders.

Fraud against Future Shareholders   Does a promoter's fiduciary duty to the corporation require that its future shareholders be informed of prior transactions that materially affect the value of their shares? There is conflicting case law on this question, but the majority rule is that a promoter's duty of full disclosure stretches the length of any promotional plan that provides for part of the originally authorized shares to be sold to future subscribers.

In the classic *Old Dominion Copper* cases, two promoters formed the corporation and then transferred overvalued property to the corporation in exchange for its stock. The transaction was approved by a dummy board of directors and by all the existing stockholders. Additional stock was then issued and sold to the general public at a price that greatly exceeded its true

---

[10]Arkansas, California, Delaware, Florida, Iowa, Kansas, Kentucky, Maine, Maryland, Nevada, New Jersey, New York, North Carolina, Rhode Island, South Carolina, Wisconsin.

value. When the promoters' transaction was discovered several years later, the corporation sued to recover the promoters' hidden profit. One promoter was sued in the Massachusetts courts, and the other was sued in the federal court in New York.

The Massachusetts court took the position, followed by a majority of courts, that nondisclosure of the facts to future stockholders constitutes an actionable wrong to the corporation. Accordingly, a $2 million judgment was entered against the promoter.[11] In contrast, the federal court expressed the view, followed by a minority of state courts, that a corporation has no cause of action if its original shareholders consent to a promoter's stock transaction with full knowledge of the facts. This ruling does not adversely affect the rights of shareholders who purchase the later stock issue because their injuries constitute an independent cause of action against the promoter.[12]

State and federal security regulation has reduced the incidence of fraudulent stock promotion schemes. Many statutes now provide that a corporation cannot offer to sell its securities without a permit. State agencies that grant such permits may require the promoters and the corporation to make a full disclosure in a verified written statement of prior transactions that affect the value of the shares proposed to be issued. A similar disclosure is required for securities subject to the jurisdiction of the United States Securities and Exchange Commission. (See Chapter 45, Securities Regulation.)

Liability of Corporation on Promoter's Contracts As a general rule, a newly formed corporation does not automatically become a party to preincorporation contracts made by the promoter on behalf of the proposed corporation. The justification for the rule is that the corporate person has rights and duties that are separate from those of the promoter. Consequently, the new corporation has the right to choose those preexisting contracts which it will assume and those which it will reject.

There are various legal theories by which a newly incorporated business can become liable on a promoter's preincorporation contract. Many courts favor the *adoption* theory. According to this theory, a contract between a promoter and a third person contains an implied continuing offer to the corporation, which it can accept after it is formed. Adoption is *express* if the directors or shareholders vote a resolution of adoption; it is *implied* if the corporation accepts benefits or performs obligations under the terms of the contract. Other theories by which a corporation may become a party to a promoter's preincorporation contract—*ratification, assignment*, and *novation* —have previously been discussed. (Ratification is discussed in the Agency part of this volume, beginning on p. 755. Assignment and novation are discussed in the Contracts part, beginning on pp. 316 and 338 respectively.)

Promoter's Liability on Contracts Promoters must usually assume personal liability on preincorporation contracts made for the benefit of the proposed corporation. If the corporation is never formed or if the newly formed corporation fails to act on the contract, the promoter remains personally liable. A promoter's liability may even continue after the corporation acts affirmatively on such contracts, depending on the action taken by the corporation or the legal theory applied, or both.

Under the adoption theory, the promoter continues to be liable on the contract adopted by the corporation. Under the assignment theory, the liability of the promoter (assignor) continues even if the corporation (assignee) agrees to perform the promoter's duties under the contract. In either situation, a promoter who is forced to pay damages for the corporation's breach of contract can seek indemnification from the corporation. When there is a

[11] *Old Dominion Copper Min. & Smelt. Co. v. Bigelow*, 89 N.E. 193 (Mass. 1909); affirmed, 225 U.S. 111 (1912).

[12] *Old Dominion Copper Min. & Smelt. Co. v. Lewisohn*, 210 U.S. 206 (1908).

novation, the promoter is immediately discharged from liability.

A promoter and a third party may enter into an informal agreement called a "contingency contract." In reality, it is not a contract at all; it is merely a "gentlemen's agreement." The promoter makes no promises except in the name of the proposed corporation and on its credit. The third party makes promises with the understanding that the promises are not to be effective until the corporation comes into existence and accepts the promises made in its behalf. The promoter is not liable under such agreements because he or she has not given any consideration to support the promises of the third party.

Case 42.1   RKO-Stanley Warner Theatres, Inc. v. Graziano [& Jenofsky]
355 A.2d 830 (Pa. 1976)

Defendant Jenofsky was a promoter of a corporation to be known as Kent Enterprises, Inc. Before the corporation was formed, he negotiated a contract with RKO-Stanley Warner Theatres, Inc. (RKO) to purchase the Kent Theatre for $70,000. Paragraph 19 of the agreement stated:

"It is understood by the parties hereto that it is the intention of the Purchaser to incorporate. Upon condition that such incorporation be completed by closing, all agreements, covenants, and warranties contained herein shall be construed to have been made between Seller and the resultant corporation and all documents shall reflect same."

Jenofsky filed the articles for the proposed corporation 12 days prior to the scheduled settlement date, at which time he failed to deposit the purchase money and notes into escrow. RKO filed an action in equity for specific performance of the contract. Jenofsky contended that his completion of the incorporation process released him under Paragraph 19 from any personal liability resulting from the nonperformance of the agreement. The trial court's judgment was for RKO, and Jenofsky appealed.

EAGEN, J. The legal relationship of Jenofsky to Kent Enterprises, Inc., at the date of the execution of the agreement of sale was that of promoter. . . . As such, he is subject to the general rule that a promoter, although he may assume to act on behalf of a projected corporation and not for himself, will be held personally liable on contracts made by him for the benefit of a corporation he intends to organize. . . . This personal liability will continue even after the contemplated corporation is formed and has received the benefits of the contract, unless there is a novation or other agreement to release liability.

The imposition of personal liability upon a promoter where that promoter has contracted on behalf of a corporation is based upon the principle that one who assumes to act for a nonexistent principal is himself liable on the contract in the absence of an agreement to the contrary. . . . As stated in Comment (a) under Section 326 of the Restatement of Agency, Second:

"there is an inference that a person intends to make a present contract with an existing person. If, therefore, the other party knows that there is no principal capable of entering into such a contract, there is a rebuttable inference that, although the contract is nominally in the name of the nonexistent person, the parties intend that the person signing as agent should be a party, unless there is some indication to the contrary."

However, even though a contract is executed by a promoter on behalf of a proposed corporation, where the person with whom the contract is made agrees to look to the corporation alone for responsibility, the promoter incurs no personal liability with respect to the contract. . . .

Jenofsky contends the parties, by their inclusion of Paragraph 19 in the agreement, manifested an intention to release him from personal responsibility upon the mere formation of the proposed corporation, provided the incorporation was consummated prior to the scheduled closing date. However, while Paragraph 19 does make provision for recognition of the resultant corporation as to the closing documents, it makes no mention of any release of personal liability. Indeed, the entire agreement is silent as to the effect the formation of the projected corporation would have upon the personal liability of Jenofsky. Because the agreement fails to provide expressly for the release of personal liability, it is, therefore, subject to more than one possible construction. . . .

As found by the court below, this agreement was entered into on the financial strength of Jenofsky . . . [as an individual]. Therefore, it would have been illogical for RKO to have consented to the release of his personal liability upon the mere formation of a resultant corporation prior to closing. For it is a well-settled rule that a contract made by a promoter, even though made for and in the name of a proposed corporation, in the absence of a subsequent adoption (either expressly or impliedly) by the corporation, will not be binding upon the corporation. . . . If, as Jenofsky contends, the intent was to release personal responsibility upon the mere incorporation prior to closing, the effect of the agreement would have been to create the possibility that RKO, in the event of nonperformance, would be able to hold no party accountable; there being no guarantee that the resultant corporation would ratify the agreement. Without express language in the agreement indicating that such was the intention of the parties, we may not attribute this intention to them. Therefore, we hold that the intent of the parties in entering into this agreement was to have Jenofsky . . . personally liable until such time as the intended corporation was formed and ratified the agreement.

Judgment affirmed.

Role of Subscribers;
Share Subscriptions

Anyone who offers to purchase stock from an issuing corporation is a *subscriber* (2e). The offer itself is called a "subscription" or "share subscription." If the corporation is in existence, the usual contract principles apply. If the corporation is yet to be formed, special problems arise in determining the subscriber's liability to the corporation. Two important questions are:

- May a share subscription be revoked prior to acceptance?
- What constitutes an acceptance of a subscription?

There are conflicting opinions as to whether a subscriber's preincorporation share subscription may be revoked prior to acceptance by the corporation. A majority of courts treat a subscription as a continuing offer to purchase stock —an offer which may be revoked at any time before its acceptance. Some courts regard a subscription as a contract among the subscribers. Under this minority view, a subscription is irrevocable unless the consent of all subscribers is obtained. The Model Act (17) provides a compromise: A subscription for shares of a proposed corporation is irrevocable for 6 months, unless the subscription agreement pro-

vides otherwise or unless all the subscribers consent to a revocation.

There is conflict also as to what constitutes acceptance of a preincorporation share subscription. The majority view is that completion of the incorporation process amounts to acceptance of the subscriber's offer. A few courts require some act to evidence acceptance, e.g., listing the subscriber as a shareholder in the stock records or issuing a stock certificate in his or her name. As a general rule, actual communication of acceptance to the shareholder is not required.

A subscription agreement usually obligates the subscriber to pay cash for the shares agreed to be purchased. (Consideration for shares is discussed in Chapter 43.) Subscriptions are payable at the time stated in the agreement or, if the time is not stated, at such time as is fixed by the board of directors (17). If the subscriber defaults when a "call" for payment is made, the corporation may proceed to collect the amount due in the same manner as it collects other debts.

Case 42.2   **Molina v. Largosa**
                  465 P.2d 293 (Haw. 1970)

This was an action by Molina (plaintiff) against Largosa (defendant) to rescind a stock subscription contract and to recover the purchase price of the stock. Judgment for defendant, and plaintiff appealed.

WONG, Circuit Judge.* On April 15, 1963, plaintiff Henry Molina attended a meeting to discuss the formation of a corporation [which] was to engage in selling stereo equipment under the trade name Specialties Unlimited. . . . At the meeting, Molina signed a "subscription form" for the purchase of $2,000 worth of stock. . . . On May 3, 1963, Molina paid $2,000, which Largosa [the promoter] deposited in a bank account under the name Specialties Unlimited.

On June 25, 1963, the officers filed the corporation's Articles of Association, and an affidavit as required by R.L.H. Sec. 172-13 (HRS Sec. 416-15). The

---

*Because of the unusual length of some of the court cases selected for this series of chapters, more than the usual number of deletions were necessary. However, in each case the material essential to illustrate the point of law discussed in the textual material has been retained. To improve readability and to save space, some deletions have not been noted.

affidavit lists Henry Molina as having subscribed 40 shares and paid $2,000, and a total subscription price for all subscriptions of $11,750. Thereafter the corporation failed.

Plaintiff contends that because the subscription form did not set out the total capital of the proposed corporation and his proportionate interest in it, there was no valid subscription contract. As a general proposition, in the absence of any statutory requirement, no particular form is required if the intent of the parties can be collected from the writing. . . .

Although the subscription form did not state the total capital and Molina's interest, these were ascertainable by merely adding up the investments of all subscribers. This information is also obtainable from the affidavit filed with the corporation's Articles, which listed all subscribers, and the respective amounts invested. . . .

Upon filing of the said Articles and affidavit, the corporation came into existence. [The majority view is that completion of the incorporation process amounts to acceptance by the corporation of a subscriber's offer, thereby finalizing the subscription contract.] In this jurisdiction, however, the mere fact of incorporation does not amount to an acceptance by the corporation of a subscriber's offer. There must be an expressed or implied acceptance of that offer. After payment of the subscription price by Molina, not only was his name listed as a stockholder in the affidavit filed with the corporation's Articles, but Molina himself made inquiries concerning his stock certificate, and from time to time requested Largosa to sell his shares. The acceptance by the corporation of Molina's offer and Molina's acknowledgment of such acceptance are, therefore, clearly supported by the record.

Molina may not now rescind his contract. . . . It should be noted that even if he were entitled to rescission, his action should be against the corporation and not the promoter. . . .

In the case of a subscription contract, however, the objective is a valid incorporation pursuant to the terms of the contract. Once that is accomplished, the contract has been performed. There is no need for a discharge by novation of the promoter from liability as the promoter is liable only if there is a failure of such incorporation. . . .

Largosa promised to form a corporation, and he performed his promise. Plaintiff Molina got just what he paid for: stock in a corporation. There was no failure of consideration in the contract; only a failure of a corporation in which Molina had purchased stock. Clearly, if the corporation had succeeded, Molina would have been entitled to his share of the stock appreciation and any dividends declared. . . .

[The judgment for defendant is] affirmed.

Selection of State of Incorporation

Many factors should be taken into account in selecting the state of incorporation. If the corporation will operate chiefly within one state, the business should normally be incorporated in that state. Some corporations operate extensively within a number of states. The selection of a jurisdiction in which to incorporate would then depend on the relative flexibility and freedom from restriction offered by the corporation statutes in those states. It is also desirable to select a state in which the courts have thoroughly interpreted the corporation statutes. A well-developed body of appellate case law eliminates uncertainty as to the meaning of those statutes.

If the corporation will operate within a number of states, the organizers should also consider the relative impact of fees and taxes levied by those states. The states vary greatly in the amount of organization fees, franchise taxes, income taxes, and stock issuance and transfer taxes charged. There is also a difference in the legal cost and in the degree of difficulty encountered in complying with varying statutory requirements for incorporating a business and for qualifying the corporation to do business in foreign jurisdictions.

Requirements for Incorporating and Commencing Business

Incorporation requirements differ from state to state, but all state statutes require the drafting and filing of a corporate charter, commonly referred to as "articles of incorporation." In order to commence business, most states also require the corporation to adopt bylaws, hold an organization meeting, and qualify and issue the first stock offering.

Drafting and Filing Articles of Incorporation; Role of Incorporators Articles of incorporation may be likened to a self-imposed constitution. The articles, together with applicable statutes of the state of incorporation, provide the legal framework within which a corporation must operate. State statutes confer broad powers on corporations, but the specific objectives of incorporators and the rights of prospective stockholders are spelled out in the articles. All general corporation laws (54) require the articles to include basic information, such as the corporation's name, purposes, and term of existence. The articles must also specify the classes of shares and the number of shares of each class

which the corporation is authorized to issue. In addition, the articles may include optional provisions, such as stock transfer restrictions, or an enumeration of corporate transactions which require approval by the stockholders.

The articles of incorporation must be *signed by the incorporator(s)*, and most states require acknowledgment of the signatures or verification of the articles.[13] Modern statutes have reduced the function of an incorporator to signing the articles; and, as a general rule, an incorporator who takes no part in company management is *not* exposed to legal liability. Some states require three incorporators but a majority of states require only one (53). The statutory qualifications for incorporators also vary. Some states impose citizenship or residence requirements, or require incorporators to subscribe for shares. The Model Act (53) permits a domestic or foreign corporation to be an incorporator, and Delaware even extends the privilege to a partnership or association.

The signed articles of incorporation and required filing fees are forwarded to the secretary of state (or other official designated in the corporation statute). If the articles conform to law, they are *filed by the secretary of state*. In Model Act jurisdictions, the secretary then issues a "certificate of incorporation" (55). A few states, including Delaware and Illinois, require that a certified copy of the articles be filed in the county where the corporation's office is located. Several states require that the articles be published in a local newspaper.

In suits by or against a corporation, it is sometimes important to know the date on which its existence commenced. The Model Act (56)

---

[13]A signature is "acknowledged" when a notary public certifies on the document that he or she knows the identity of the person signing the document and that such person appeared in person and acknowledged the signature to be his or her own. A document is "verified" when a person signs a written recital at the end of the document which states under penalty of perjury that the signer has personal knowledge that the facts stated in the document are true.

provides that corporate existence begins "upon the issuance of the certificate of incorporation. States which do not require the issuance of a certificate usually provide that corporate exis- tence commences upon the filing of the articles of incorporation. This date-of-filing rule is even followed in some of the states that issue certifi- cates of incorporation.

Case 42.3   State ex rel. Carlton v. Triplett
517 P.2d 135 (Kan. 1973)

Lawyers Tom Triplett and William Crank, and their secretary Barbara Samuelson, assisted in the incorporation of Air Capital International, Inc. These three persons acted as incorporators and signed the articles of incorpora- tion. None of them ever served as an officer or director of the corporation.

The then-existing state statute provided that a corporation came into existence upon the filing of its articles with the secretary of state *and* with the register of deeds in the county where the corporation's office was to be located. Air Capital never became a corporation because its articles were never filed with the register of deeds.

The statute also provided that a corporate entity must exist before it can commence doing business as a corporation. Air Capital complied with all other prerequisites before commencing business in August of 1967. Therefore, there was no corporate entity to shield the officers from personal liability for debts and other obligations incurred on behalf of the "corporation." Directors could only escape such liability by dissenting to such "corporate" transactions in writing.

Air Capital International, Inc. declared bankruptcy in 1971. The State of Kansas (plaintiff) then brought an action against the incorporators (defendants) to recover employment taxes due. Judgment for defendants, and plaintiff appealed.

FOTH, Commissioner. The appellant [State of Kansas, plaintiff] advances two basic theories for the claimed liability of appellees [the defendant incorporators], *viz.*, that it is imposed by statute, or that it is imposed by the law of partnership. The first contention requires an examination of the corporation code in effect at the time the corporation was sought to be formed and when the taxes accrued. . . .

It is apparent that [the] statute imposed no liability on the appellees. It is stipulated that they were neither "officers" nor "directors" of the purported corporation. Since there *was* no corporation, they could not be actual officers or directors, and they never held themselves out to be such. . . .

There remains the question of whether appellees are liable under a common law partnership theory. . . .

We think the proper rule is well put in 18 Am. Jur. 2d, Corporations, Sec. 134:

"A signer of articles of incorporation *who takes no active part in the management of the company and does not contract debts or incur liabilities* or authorize or ratify contracts cannot be held liable by creditors of the company, either individually or as a partner. . . ." [Emphasis added.]

We find nothing in our law to the contrary. The appellees here took no part in the management of the company, and incurred no debts or liabilities in the company's name. They thus incurred no personal liability under the rule quoted above. . . .

Judgment [for defendants is] affirmed.

Drafting and Adopting Bylaws Bylaws may be described as private corporate laws which bind the directors, officers, and shareholders of a corporation and which govern its internal affairs. Most general corporation statutes (27) provide that the bylaws may contain any provision regulating the internal management of the corporation which is not inconsistent with law or the articles of incorporation. The bylaws usually include provisions which establish:

• The time and place of shareholders' and directors' meetings
• The manner in which notice of such meetings shall be given
• Quorum requirements for such meetings
• The qualifications and duties of directors and officers
• The procedure for filling vacancies on the board

Unlike the articles of incorporation, the bylaws are not normally required to be filed with a designated officer of the state.

Most state statutes provide that the power to adopt the original bylaws and the power to alter, amend, or repeal existing bylaws "shall be vested in the board of directors unless reserved to the shareholders by the articles" (27). However, amendments adopted by the directors are usually "subject to repeal or change by action of the shareholders." The requirements for amending the bylaws tend to differ somewhat in the various jurisdictions.

Holding an Organization Meeting Most general corporation statutes provide that the board of directors shall hold an organization meeting "for the purpose of adopting bylaws, electing officers, and transacting such other business as may come before the meeting" (57). With respect to "other business" considered by the board, the directors usually adopt resolutions that name the corporation's bank, direct the officers to qualify the initial stock issue with appropriate state and federal agencies, and authorize a corporate seal.

As a general rule, the law does not provide that a corporation must have a corporate seal, but it may be indirectly required by statutes which provide that a corporate seal must be affixed to certain documents. For example, most states require that the signatures of corporate officers on documents affecting title to real property must be authenticated by the corporate seal. In addition, banks, creditors, and governmental agencies traditionally require that the corporate seal be affixed to certified copies of board resolutions. The seal is customarily kept in the possession of the corporate secretary as a precaution against unauthorized signatures.

Qualifying and Issuing Stock The shares which are initially proposed to be sold, and all subsequent stock offerings, must be qualified and issued in accordance with state blue-sky laws. As discussed in Chapter 45, some stock offerings must also be registered with the United States Securities and Exchange Commission prior to issuance.

Qualifying and issuing stock is not ordinarily considered a part of the incorporation process. However, there are two major reasons why a corporation should not commence business until its shares are qualified, fully paid, and issued:

1 Some statutes provide that a corporation may not transact business or incur debt until the minimum amount of capital prescribed in the statute or in the articles of incorporation has been paid to the corporation in exchange for shares. The statutory minimum usually ranges from $500 to $1000. Directors and officers who fail to observe requirements for minimum paid-in capital are personally liable for debts incurred by the corporation during the period of noncompliance.

2 Most courts consider inadequate capitalization to be a factor in determining whether creditors have the right to disregard the corporate entity and hold its directors, officers, and stockholders personally liable for corporate debts. (Additional dangers of inadequate capitalization are discussed in Chapter 43.)

RECOGNITION OR DISREGARD OF CORPORATENESS

Recognition of Corporateness

A defectively formed corporation is open to attack. Creditors may contend that the shareholders of a defectively formed corporation are partners with unlimited personal liability for the debts of the enterprise. Debtors who are sued by a defective corporation may challenge its capacity to contract or to sue. Subscribers may seek to escape liability on subscription contracts by asserting that the proposed corporation never came into existence. The corporation itself may deny its own "corporateness" to avoid liability to creditors. The state may also cite failure to comply with statutory requirements for incorporation as the basis for a court order requiring the corporation to forfeit its charter or to cease operations.

The courts may decide the question of "corporateness" by holding that an organization is a de jure corporation, a de facto corporation, a corporation by estoppel, or no corporation. The legal distinctions between these classifications are discussed below.

De Jure Corporation   A de jure corporation has all the legal characteristics of a corporation. Its corporateness is "impregnable to assault in the courts from any source" including the state.[14] Thus, a de jure corporate entity is a legal fortress which shields its shareholders from personal liability for corporate obligations.

To form a perfectly legal or de jure corporation, there must be a valid statute which permits the enterprise to incorporate, and the incorporation procedure in the statute must be strictly followed. A de jure corporation also results if there is substantial compliance with the *mandatory* provisions of the statute. Failure to follow the *directory* provisions of the statute does not affect the legal existence of the corporation. Case law determines whether a given provision is mandatory or directory.

De Facto Corporation   What happens if the organizers of a business association do not comply with the law to the extent required to create a corporation de jure? The courts may recognize the association as a corporation de facto—that is, a corporation for most purposes—but only if the association could have been validly incorporated under an existing statute and only if the organizers attempted in good faith to comply with the mandatory provisions of the statute. For an association to qualify as a de facto corporation, there must also be a "corporate user"; that is, the association must operate as a corporation.

The legal existence of a corporation de facto

---

[14]*Henderson v. School District No. 44*, 242 P. 979, 980 (Mont. 1926).

can only be challenged by the state. It may initiate a quo warranto proceeding which, literally, asks the corporation: "By what *authority* are you doing business?" and has as its purpose forfeiture of the corporate charter. However, it is improbable that the state would attempt to take the life of a de facto corporation unless its operations adversely affected the public interest.

The de facto doctrine is based on the idea that injustice should not result from honest mistakes or omissions. The doctrine is often applied to prevent creditors from holding innocent shareholders liable because an incorporation attempt, made in good faith, falls short of the mandatory requirements in the statute. To discourage unfair attacks on corporations, the Model Act (56) provides that issuance of a certificate of incorporation is conclusive evidence that all conditions have been met. The net effect is that even a corporation with some defects in its formation is redefined as a de jure corporation once the certificate has been issued.

Corporation by Estoppel If the de facto doctrine is inapplicable, an attack on corporateness may be blocked by the theory of estoppel. An *estoppel to deny corporateness* has three requirements:

1 Representation by an enterprise that it is a corporation
2 Reasonable reliance on such representation by the other party
3 Fair and equitable conduct by the party asserting estoppel

A person who contracts with a defectively formed corporation cannot avoid contractual liability by claiming that the corporation does not legally exist. Similarly, an association that represents itself to be a corporation cannot escape liability by denying its own corporateness. With reference to that contract, the parties are estopped from asserting a position inconsistent with corporate existence. The estoppel theory applies only to the parties in that transaction, as opposed to the de facto doctrine which recognizes corporate existence for most purposes.

Case 42.4   **Bukacek v. Pell City Farms, Inc.**
   237 So. 2d 851 (Ala. 1970)

James Bukacek was having serious financial problems. Bukacek and others agreed to form "Pell City Farms, Inc." Once formed, the corporation was to pay Bukacek's debts. In exchange, Bukacek was to deed his 300-acre farm to the corporation. Bukacek deeded the land to Pell City Farms, Inc.; but its articles of incorporation had not as yet been filed with the designated officer of the state. After the corporation was formed, Bukacek participated in corporate business involving the farm and took an active role as an officer, director, and stockholder. However, he later asserted that at the time he signed the deed, the corporation did not legally exist. He therefore argued that the corporation had been incapable of taking title to real property and that he still owned the farm. Bukacek (plaintiff) sued in equity to quiet title to the land. Judgment for Pell City Farms, Inc. Bukacek appealed.

MADDOX, J. . . . . Assuming, without deciding, that we would subscribe to

Case 42.4
Continued

the broad view that no corporation was here formed prior to the filing of the Articles of Incorporation, we think the fact situation here presented shows that while Pell City Farms, Inc. may not have been a corporation de jure—or perhaps even de facto—insofar as the transaction here is concerned, it should be regarded practically as a corporation, being recognized as such by the parties themselves. In other words, the incidents of corporate existence may exist as between the parties by virtue of an estoppel. . . .

Bukacek was one of the incorporators; he dealt with the corporation as a corporation both before and after the Articles of Incorporation were filed. Under such facts, Bukacek is estopped to deny the existence of the corporation at the time he voluntarily executed a deed transferring property to the corporation even though the Articles of Incorporation had not been filed at that time.

Our ruling here is limited. It is based on equitable grounds which preclude the [plaintiff] here from denying corporate existence. As against the state, of course, a corporation cannot be created by agreement of the parties . . . but . . . they may, by their agreements or their conduct estop themselves from denying the fact of the existence of the corporation. We hold, therefore, that Bukacek is estopped to deny the existence of Pell City Farms, Inc., even though it may have been neither de facto nor de jure at the time he executed the deed making the corporation, *by its corporate name*, the grantee. . . .

Decree [for Pell City Farms, Inc.] is affirmed.

No Corporation; Liability of Purported Agent   No corporation results when:

1   An incorporation effort is so defective that it falls short of the requirements of a de facto corporation, or

2   Business associates operate as a corporation without any intention of complying with the incorporation statute.

Many statutes (146) impose joint and several liability on persons who act as a corporation without authority. Some courts impose partnership liability on those who are *actively* involved in the promotion or management of the enterprise but limit the liability of *inactive* "shareholders" to their capital investment. Most courts impose personal liability on the innocent "shareholders" as well as the associates who operate the purported "corporation." Under agency law, a person who purports to act on behalf of a named principal impliedly warrants that the principal exists and that he or she is authorized to act in the principal's behalf. Consequently, an "agent" who purports to act for a corporate principal that fails to meet the criteria of a de facto corporation is personally liable for the contractual obligations of the nonexistent principal.

Disregard of Corporateness

The preceding discussion shows that the law will bend to recognize a defectively formed corporation if the interests of justice would be served. Similarly, the courts will refuse to recognize a perfectly formed corporation in order to impose personal liability on anyone who uses the corporate entity to sanction fraud, perpetrate a crime, circumvent a statute, accomplish a wrongful purpose, or promote injustice. Such wrongdoers are usually controlling shareholders who are active in management. If warranted by the facts, the courts will go behind the legal fiction of a separate corporate entity to reach the wrongdoers.

To disregard corporateness, the courts must "pierce the corporate veil." Case law in this area has developed the *alter ego doctrine,* which enables the courts to recognize an individual as the corporation's other self—its alter ego. It follows logically that, if justice demands it, the individual who is the moving force behind the corporate entity can be held to account for its obligations and wrongful acts. Conversely, the obligations and wrongful acts of the individual can be recognized as those of the corporation.

Disregard in Close-Corporation Situations
Courts most frequently apply the alter ego doctrine to pierce the corporate veil of one-person corporations. The doctrine applies to close corporations:

1 If the interests of a corporation and its controlling shareholder(s) are so united that separateness does not exist; *and*

2 If recognition of a corporate entity apart from the shareholder(s) behind it, would sanction fraud or promote injustice.[15]

---

[15]*Minifie v. Rowley,* 202 P. 673 (Cal. 1921).

Facts which tend to show unity of interest and ownership are: inadequate capitalization to meet the anticipated requirements of the corporation's business; commingling of a principal shareholder's personal and corporate business; and failure to hold board meetings, keep corporate minutes, or observe other corporate formalities.[16] Facts which evidence "injustice" include incorporation to evade a statute or to avoid a contractual obligation.

The alter ego doctrine is typically used to impose personal liability on shareholders for the benefit of creditors or other injured third parties, but the doctrine can be used to benefit the shareholders. For example, if the owner of a business incorporates the enterprise and forms a one-person corporation which operates with the same employees, the merit rating given to the proprietorship by the state unemployment agency is transferable to the corporation.[17]

---

[16]The California Corporation Law (revised January 1, 1977) is cited as an exception. Shareholders of a close California corporation may agree to manage it like a partnership, and failure to observe corporate formalities relating to directors' and shareholders' meetings "shall not be considered a factor tending to establish that the shareholders have personal liability for corporate obligations."

[17]*Packard Clothes, Inc. v. Director of Div. of Employment Sec.,* 61 N.E.2d 528 (Mass. 1945).

Case 42.5   **Kugler v. Koscot Interplanetary, Inc.**
293 A.2d 682 (N.J. Super. 1972)

Glenn Turner was chairman of the board of Koscot Interplanetary, Inc., which he incorporated in Florida in 1967. Within its "retail" organization Koscot sold positions, known as "supervisor" and "distributor," for $2,000 and $5,000 respectively. A like amount of cosmetics (at retail prices) was credited to the buyers, who had to resell the cosmetics to recoup their "investment." There was also a "wholesale" plan whereby Koscot paid a finder's fee to any person in the organization who enrolled a new distributor or supervisor. These fees were unrelated to retail sales and were paid solely for bringing new investors into Koscot's marketing program.

Investors were recruited at "Golden Opportunity Meetings" and on "Golden Opportunity Tours" (charter flights to Koscot's home office in Florida).

Prospective investors were told to bring certified checks. Great efforts were exerted to "get the check." When the plane landed in Florida, potential investors toured company facilities and attended "GO" meetings. Unsubstantiated claims of huge earnings were made at these meetings. At times, piles of cash and contracts were dropped into the laps of the potential investors. They were told that building a sales organization was not difficult, when, in fact, it was extremely difficult. Some of the fraudulent statements were attributed to Turner, who was credited with Koscot's "success." The distributor's training manual contained a biographical sketch of Turner captioned: "The Founder and Chairman of the Board, Sharecropper on His Way to Harvest the World."

Starting in 1969, Koscot sold a total of 624 "supervisor" positions and 387 "distributor" positions to New Jersey residents. Their total investment in the scheme exceeded $3 million. Turner, who owned 95 percent of Koscot's stock was the direct beneficiary of the earnings that arose from Koscot's unlawful practices.

Kugler (plaintiff) was state attorney general for New Jersey. He brought an action for violation of the Consumer Fraud and Corporation Acts of New Jersey against Koscot Interplanetary, Inc. and its principal stockholder, Glenn Turner (defendants). The attorney general contended that defendants employed fraudulent practices in connection with the sale of Koscot distributorships. Defendant Turner denied this contention and claimed that, as a stockholder, he was not liable for corporate acts.

MEHLER, J. While it is fundamental that a corporation is an entity wholly separate and distinct from the individuals who compose and control it . . . and that the entity may not as a general rule be disregarded, the principle is not without its exceptions. . . .

"Where the corporate form is used by individuals for the purpose of evading the law, or for the perpetuation of fraud, the courts will not permit the legal entity to be interposed so as to defeat justice. *Trachman v. Trugman*, 117 N.J. Eq. 167, 170, 175 A. 147, 149 (Ch. 1934)." . . .

[Plaintiff] has demonstrated that Koscot is the *alter ego* of Turner and that Turner, for his financial gain, utilized Koscot to engage in unlawful practices proscribed by the Consumer Fraud Act. Hence, the fact that Koscot is a corporate entity does not immunize Turner from being held to account for Consumer Fraud Act violations committed on his behalf. . . .

[Judgment for plaintiff.]

Disregard in Parent-Subsidiary Situations   Courts can use the alter ego doctrine to pierce the corporate veil of undercapitalized, wholly owned subsidiaries and impose liability on affluent parent corporations. As in close-corporation situations, a plaintiff who seeks to hold a parent corporation liable for the debts or wrongs of its subsidiary must prove:

1   Unity of interest and ownership between the parent and its subsidiary; and

2   Use of the subsidiary to promote fraud,

sharp practice, unfair advantage, or illegality; or to evade a statute or contractual obligation.

In general, the courts will not disregard the corporateness of a subsidiary or hold the parent corporation liable for the torts of the subsidiary so long as their separate corporate status is maintained.

The evidence required to disprove the separateness of a parent and its subsidiary is similar to the evidence required in close-corporation situations: intermingling of funds and accounting records; interlocking directorates; failure to observe separate corporate formalities; inadequate capitalization of the subsidiary to meet normal business needs; domination by the parent to an extent that makes the subsidiary a mere agent or instrumentality of the parent; or failure by the two companies to represent themselves publicly as separate corporations. Even if a parent-subsidiary relationship does not exist, corporateness may be disregarded if one corporation uses another as an agency for accomplishing a wrongful purpose.

Case 42.6   Shirley v. Drackett Products Co.
182 N.W.2d 726 (Mich. App. 1970)

Julia Shirley (plaintiff) purchased a can of Vanish toilet bowl cleaner from a local store. As directed on the can, Shirley sprinkled the cleaner into the interior of the bowl and scrubbed vigorously with a short-handled brush. The resulting fumes made her cough and choke, and she had to be taken to the hospital and placed under oxygen. Shirley's doctor indicated that she would be permanently disabled as a result of the incident. Plaintiff brought an action against the distributor, The Drackett Products Company, for negligence and for breach of warranty. A jury returned a verdict of $100,000 in favor of plaintiff. Defendant appealed.

BROWN, J. As a general rule, a vendor who distributes a product acquired in the open market is not liable for its negligent manufacture. [Citations.] However, that rule is not applicable in view of the facts in this case.

Vanish is manufactured by The Drackett Company. The defendant bore the corporate name "The Drackett Products Company" and was a wholly-owned subsidiary and the exclusive distributor of all of the manufacturer's products. The parent and subsidiary had their principal offices at the same address. . . . There were interlocking officers and directors and there was some interchange of employees. The subsidiary (the defendant) existed solely as the distributing arm of the manufacturer and the manufacturer's only source of revenue was from the sales of its subsidiary. Where a corporation is so organized and so controlled as to make it a mere instrumentality or an agent of another corporation, its separate existence as a distinct corporate entity will be ignored and the two corporations will be regarded in legal contemplation as one unit. These facts may be held to deny this defendant the insulation from liability that ordinarily protects a retailer or distributor. The trial court's ruling that the facts warranted piercing the corporate veil was sustained by the evidence. . . .

Judgment affirmed.

SUMMARY

The corporation-for-profit is by far the most influential form of business organization in the United States. The Constitution did not provide for federal incorporation of private businesses and early American corporations could only be formed by a special act of a state legislature. As a result of rapid industrialization, the states enacted general corporation laws which permit any legal business to incorporate by complying with the statutory requirements.

State corporation statutes have been influenced in varying degrees by the Model Business Corporation Act developed by the American Bar Association. Other sources of corporation law are state constitutions and regulatory statutes, and court decisions. Since the turn of the century, court decisions interpreting federal regulatory legislation, such as the Securities Act (1933), have developed into a body of "federal corporation law."

The chief characteristics of business corporations are:

1 Status as a legal "entity"
2 Existence by authority of the state
3 Free transferability of stock
4 Limitation of each stockholder's liability to the amount of his or her capital investment
5 Perpetual existence
6 Centralization of management in a board of directors

A *promoter* transforms an idea for a business into a corporation. The promoter owes a fiduciary duty to the subscribers, the shareholders, and the corporation. Under the majority view, this fiduciary duty is also owed to future shareholders if future stock issues are contemplated in the original promotional plan.

A corporation is not automatically liable on a promoter's preincorporation contract. Under the prevailing "adoption" theory, the third party impliedly extends a continuing offer which may be "accepted" by the corporation after it is formed. However, the promoter usually remains liable on preincorporation contracts even if contractual liability is accepted by the corporation or imposed on it under any theory except novation.

A subscriber's offer to purchase shares from the issuing corporation is called a "subscription." The Model Act provides that a subscription for shares of a proposed corporation is irrevocable for 6 months unless the agreement provides otherwise or unless all subscribers consent to the revocation. Completion of the incorporation process usually constitutes acceptance of preincorporation subscriptions. A few courts require the corporation's acceptance to be evidenced by some additional act. Important steps required by most state statutes to incorporate and to commence business as a corporation are: drafting and filing articles of incorporation, drafting and adopting bylaws, holding an organization meeting, and qualifying and issuing stock.

The existence of a de jure corporation, which results from substantial compliance with the mandatory provisions of a valid enabling statute, cannot be attacked, even by the state. A good faith attempt to comply with such provisions, which fails to do so, may result in a corporation de facto, if the business operates as a corporation. If the requirements of a de facto or a de jure corporation are not met, but a business represents itself to be a corporation and contracts as such, it is recognized as a corporation by estoppel for that transaction only. The parties are estopped from denying corporate existence as a means of escaping contractual liability.

The courts will disregard the corporate entity and hold the involved individuals personally liable: (1) if a corporation is used for a wrongful purpose, and (2) if the interests of the wrongdoers and the corporation are united so that separateness does not exist. Courts most frequently "pierce the corporate veil" in cases involving unlawful use of a close corporation that is the alter ego of its principal shareholder(s). The doctrine of corporate disregard can also be applied to hold a parent corporation liable for its subsidiary's acts and obligations if the facts show unity of interest and use by the parent of the subsidiary for a wrongful purpose. Unity of interest and ownership may also be evidenced by inadequate capitalization, failure to observe corporate formalities, and commingling of personal-corporation business or of parent-subsidiary business.

STUDY AND DISCUSSION QUESTIONS

1   What are the three sources of state corporation law?

2   *(a)* Identify the Model Business Corporation Act. *(b)* What are some of its objectives? *(c)* What influence has the act had on contemporary state corporation law?

3   List five or six principal types of state statutes which regulate corporations after they have been formed.

4   Explain the origin and meaning of the term "federal corporation law."

5   *(a)* List the chief characteristics of a business corporation. *(b)* Explain the advantages that arise from each such characteristic.

6   What are the chief differences between a corporation and a partnership?

7   Distinguish between the following kinds of corporations: *(a)* profit and nonprofit; *(b)* private, public, and quasi-public; *(c)* domestic and foreign; *(d)* aggregate and sole.

8   *(a)* Explain the meaning of the term "close corporation." *(b)* Are the terms "close corporation," "closely held corporation," and "closed corporation" interchangeable? Explain.

9   *(a)* In the formation of corporations, who or what is a promoter? *(b)* Discuss the chief functions of a promoter. *(c)* What are the principal

elements of his or her fiduciary duty? *(d)* Does this fiduciary duty extend to future shareholders? Explain.

10   Under what circumstances does a corporation become liable on preincorporation contracts entered into by the promoter on behalf of the corporation?

11   *(a)* Define "share subscription." *(b)* Under what circumstances, if any, may a share subscription be revoked?

12   Discuss factors to be considered in selecting the state of incorporation.

13   *(a)* What basic information is required to be included in articles of incorporation? *(b)* What provisions are commonly included in bylaws?

14   State whether you agree, partly agree, or disagree with the following statement, and why: "Once the incorporation process is completed, the corporation has the characteristic of limited liability, irrespective of whether stock has been issued."

15   *(a)* In what respects do the following differ: a *de jure* corporation and a *de facto* corporation? *(b)* Why are the differences important?

16   What factor, or combination of factors, must be present to justify a court in disregarding corporateness?

CASE PROBLEMS

1   The Rippee brothers, who purported to act for Northwest Tech-Manuals, Inc., signed two 2-year leases of commercial space with Heintze Corporation as lessor. Heintze was unaware that Northwest was not incorporated when the first lease was signed on May 1. Northwest completed its incorporation on June 17, and the second lease was signed July 15. Northwest paid rent on both leases for a year and then abandoned them. Heintze sued Northwest and the Rippee brothers individually to recover unpaid rent. *(a)* Is Heintze entitled to recover from Northwest

on either or both leases? *(b)* Are the Rippee brothers personally liable on either or both leases?

2   In 1922, the Baum family incorporated the Baum Realty Company in Nebraska, and transferred an office building to the corporation in exchange for its stock. Shortly thereafter, four members of the family incorporated Baum Holding Company, and transferred about half of the realty company's shares to the holding company in exchange for holding company shares. Nebraska's incorporation statute was not amended to permit one corporation to hold and own stock in another corporation until 1941. Thereafter, Baum Holding Company operated in full compliance with the amended statute. However, there was evidence, such as participation in the election of directors, that the stockholders had recognized the holding company as a corporation from its inception. In 1951, a dispute arose between the majority and minority factions of the holding company's stockholders. The minority stockholders instituted a suit which involved two issues: *(a)* Is the holding company a corporation *de facto* ? *(b)* Are plaintiffs estopped from denying that the holding company is a corporation? How would you hold on each issue?

3   Mr. and Mrs. Conway contracted to have their house remodelled by Trend Set Construction Corporation. The contract was signed by the Conways and by Marilyn Samet as president of Trend Set. The Conways sued Trend Set for breach of contract and obtained a default judgment for $10,647.33. Then, upon discovering that no certificate of incorporation had been prepared, acknowledged, or filed, as required by the state enabling statute, the Conways sued Samet individually. They alleged that no corporation existed and that Samet had impliedly warranted Trend Set to be a corporation on whose behalf she had authority to act. Defendant Samet claimed that Trend Set was a de facto corporation, that she was not personally liable, and that it was not her fault that the attorney, employed by her to incorporate Trend Set, had failed to comply with the statute. *(a)* Is Trend Set a corporation de facto? *(b)* Is Samet individually liable on the contract?

4   James Day contracted with Filmlab, Inc., for a franchise to use its name and trademark to operate a film developing business. The corporate secretary signed the contract on behalf of Filmlab. Later, Day learned that Filmlab had not given him all the property rights that he had bargained for. Day sued Filmlab and its principal stockholder, Kenneth Dietel, for breach of contract. Day contended that Dietel was liable because Filmlab was Dietel's alter ego. Evidence at the trial showed that Dietel was a director and vice president of Filmlab at the time the contract was signed. There was no evidence that Dietel had commingled corporate assets with his personal assets or that he had engaged in fraudulent representations. The court found that Filmlab had breached its contract with Day, and entered a judgment for $10,000 against Filmlab and Dietel. Dietel appealed, contending that he should not be held personally liable for corporate debts. Is his contention correct?

5   Maloney was the controlling stockholder, and served as a director and as president of the Marlin Electric Company. Under an employment contract with the company, Maloney also performed the duties of managing officer. As such, he fixed his own salary and made all final decisions concerning Marlin's affairs, but the board of directors reviewed and routinely approved Maloney's decisions. Maloney was killed while flying the company plane on company business and his widow applied for death benefits under the Worker's Compensation Act. The insurance carrier, Aetna Casualty, denied liability on the ground that Maloney was not Marlin's employee. Aetna argued that Marlin could not have an arm's-length employment contract with Maloney because he owned most of Marlin's shares and had authority over his own employment. Was Maloney an employee of the corporation at the time of the fatal crash, or was the corporation Maloney's alter ego?

6 All the stock of the Long Island Railroad (LIRR) was owned by the Metropolitan Transportation Authority (MTA), a public corporation. One of LIRR's trains struck and killed a man. The administrator of the decedent's estate sued MTA for the wrongful death which was caused by LIRR's negligence. There was no evidence that MTA and LIRR had commingled their corporate business. Is MTA liable to plaintiff?

7 McDaniel, owner of an 800-acre farm, was approached by ABC, Inc. about leasing her farm to a new corporation which ABC, Inc. proposed to form. McDaniel expressed interest in becoming an investor of the proposed corporation, and actively participated with others in the organizational meetings. At one of the later meetings, a contract regarding the financial structure of the proposed corporation and a proposed lease of the McDaniel farm were read, but neither was signed. Thereafter, the investors' group decided, with McDaniel's knowledge and consent, to commence the spring planting of 200 acres of McDaniel's farm. After the planting, the group decided to abandon the idea of forming the new corporation. A creditor who supplied seed for the planting sued McDaniel for the unpaid bill, claiming that she was a member of the promoters' group, and as such, was liable on the seed contract. Is McDaniel liable on the seed contract?

How does a business corporation get the money it needs to organize, survive, and grow? All corporations-for-profit must issue and sell shares of stock (equity securities). This method of raising capital is called *equity financing*. Initially, promoters and other investors transfer cash or other property to the corporation in exchange for its shares. Additional working capital is obtained from retained earnings, sales and leasebacks, installment purchases, and other sources common to most businesses. Borrowing money from individuals (or from institutions such as banks) is called *debt financing*. The sale of bonds (debt securities) is a form of borrowing used most often by larger corporations.

This chapter explores two methods of raising capital that are unique to business corporations:

- The sale of bonds
- The sale of shares

A discussion of the more usual types of bonds and shares is included for the benefit of students who are or may become investors in securities, owners of small incorporated businesses, or directors responsible for issuing securities that meet the special needs of a given corporation. The last two parts of the chapter deal with transfers of securities and corporate distributions, including dividend payments.

DEBT FINANCING

Few statutes restrict a corporation's borrowing power. Delaware and Model Act states permit corporations to mortgage a major portion of their assets without shareholder approval (78).[1] However, corporate borrowing may be limited by the corporation's articles or bylaws, by economic factors such as high interest rates, or by the practical requirements of creditors. For example: A newly formed close corporation may not have well-established credit. Banks may, therefore, require the principal stockholders to personally guarantee the repayment of loans made to the corporation. Thus, the corporation's credit is limited to the personal borrowing capacity of its key stockholders.

Nature of Bonds (Debt Securities)

Definition of Bonds A *bond* is a long-term promissory note which obligates the corporation to pay the bondholder: (1) the amount of the loan (principal) on a stated maturity date and (2) a fixed rate of interest on principal, payable at regular intervals until maturity. The term "bond" can be used, in a more restricted sense, to refer to an obligation secured by a lien on corporate property. Unsecured bonds are called *debentures*. Thus, in the common phrase, bonds and debentures, the word "bonds" clearly refers only to secured obligations.

Characteristics of Bonds The most important legal characteristics of bonds are:

1 They create a debtor-creditor relationship between the corporation and its bondholders, and
2 They are negotiable securities, which are readily transferable [UCC, 8-105(1)].[2]

If a corporation defaults on its bond payments, the holders of secured bonds may satisfy the bond indebtedness by selling the property which the corporation pledged as collateral. Debenture holders have no such recourse. They are merely creditors, but as such, their claims against unencumbered corporate assets are superior to the claims of shareholders in the event that the corporation is dissolved.

Issuance of Bonds

In most instances, state law permits a corporation's board of directors to incur debt and issue bonds without the approval of the shareholders. Nevertheless, the articles of incorporation may require shareholder approval or otherwise limit the board's power to borrow. The specific terms and provisions of a given bond issue are generally determined by two practical considerations:

• The financial objectives of the corporation
• The necessity of attracting potential investors

The contractual rights and obligations of the corporation and its bondholders and any description of property securing payment by the corporation are usually set forth in an agreement called an *indenture*.

Types of Bonds

The many possible combinations of bond provisions often result in varieties of bonds that defy

---

[1]The section numbers of the Model Business Corporations Act are given in parentheses throughout this series of chapters.

[2]The numbers within brackets in the text of this series of chapters refer to sections of the Uniform Commercial Code.

easy classification. However, bonds are ordinarily identified by their distinguishing features. For example: Bonds secured by the issuing corporation's real property or equipment are called *mortgage* bonds. Bonds issued to owners whose names and addresses are registered on the books of the corporation are described as *registered* bonds; principal and interest payments on these bonds are made only to the bondholders of record. (The term "registered" is also used to describe securities registered with the Securities and Exchange Commission, as detailed in Chapter 45.) Interest coupons payable to the bearer are attached to *coupon* bonds, which may or may not be registered as to the principal amount. *Bearer* bonds are unregistered as to both principal and interest. Bonds that are callable before maturity at the option of the corporation are said to be *redeemable*. Some bonds are convertible to shares at the option of the holder; if the market price of the issuing corporation's stock rises, these *convertible* bonds may be exchanged for shares which can then be sold at a profit.

EQUITY FINANCING

A corporation's initial stock issue usually provides most of the capital needed to commence business. Thereafter, earnings retained from net income are the most important source of funds available for operating and expanding the business. Nevertheless, subsequent stock issues may provide additional capital for business expansion, such as the acquisition or improvement of land, buildings, machinery, and other equipment.

Nature of Shares (Equity Securities)

Shares, like bonds, are negotiable securities and are readily transferable [UCC 8-105(1)], but shareholders and bondholders have a significantly different relation to the issuing corporation. Shareholders actually *own* the corporation, whereas its bondholders are merely creditors.

Stock ownership typically includes a threefold right to participate in corporate earnings, in net assets upon liquidation, and in the election of directors. Most statutes permit these rights to be restricted (15, 16, 58), but a shareholder's right to vote on charter amendments which affect his or her shares is usually inviolate (60).

A share does not confer upon the holder a vested title to specific property owned by the corporation. Rather, a *share of stock* is a proportionate ownership interest, or equity, in the corporation as a whole. Each shareholder's interest is generally evidenced by a *stock certificate* for a stated number of shares of a designated type. Recent additions to the Uniform Commercial Code permit the issuance of "uncertificated" securities which are not represented by a stock certificate [UCC, 8-407 and 8-408]. This option is reflected in the 1979 edition of the Model Act. It provides that "the shares of a corporation shall be represented by certificates or shall be uncertificated shares" but declares that the rights and obligations of the holders of such securities "shall be identical" (23). Minnesota, West Virginia, and a few other states have enacted statutory provisions which permit corporations to issue uncertificated securities, but the extent to which they will be used remains to be seen. The text discussion will, for the most part, exclude any consideration of uncertificated securities.

Issuance of Shares

Authority to Issue Shares   A business corporation can only offer and sell the classes of shares, up to the maximum number of shares of each class, that are authorized in the articles. Each proposed issue must also qualify under state and federal statutes (discussed in Chapter 45) which specifically regulate the issuance and sale of securities. These laws and regulations are designed to protect the public from fraudulent stock schemes. If shares of a proposed issue are not authorized in the articles or if shares are sold in violation of state or federal statutes, the sale is illegal. If a sale is illegal, shareholders can rescind their subscription agreements and recover any consideration given to the corporation in exchange for its shares.

Consideration for Shares Stock subscriptions may be paid in installments, but a stock certificate cannot be issued and delivered to the subscriber until the shares represented by the certificate are fully paid. (In the case of uncertificated shares, the corporation furnishes an "Initial Transaction Statement" which includes a description of the class and number of shares owned, the date they are issued to the stockholder, and a notation of any restrictions on transfer; UCC, 8-408.) Shares are deemed to be fully paid and nonassessable when the corporation has received the full issuance price of the shares. Shares may be issued in exchange for cash, or for any tangible or intangible property other than promissory notes; shares may also be exchanged for services performed prior to the issuance of the shares, but not for future services (19).

The directors fix the value of property and services given to the corporation in exchange for its shares. If the property or services are overvalued so that the consideration given for the shares is inadequate, the shares are described as "bonus," "discount," or "watered" shares. Courts generally hold shareholders liable to the corporation for the true value of watered shares. Alternatively, the corporation may be permitted to treat watered shares as voidable and rescind the stock purchase transaction. In that case, the corporation would return the overvalued property to the shareholder and demand surrender of the shares for cancellation.

Case law is based on the same policies that underlie statutory provisions requiring shares to be issued for full value. If $10,000 of authorized stock is issued to Alice in exchange for machinery worth only $5,000 and another $10,000 of stock is issued to Bill in exchange for realty worth only $3,000, the ownership interests of stockholders who give full value for their shares would be diluted. The issuance of watered shares would also be misleading to creditors who are entitled to rely on the underlying capital investment of the stockholders. The liability of shareholders who purchase stock for less than full value, and the potential liability of directors who issue shares for overvalued or unlawful consideration are discussed in Chapter 44.

Case 43.1   Smith v. Panorama Country Club
538 S.W.2d 268 (Tex. App. 1976)

The Panorama Country Club was organized as a golf and country club under the Texas Non-Profit Corporation Act. The club's shareholder-members, all of whom owned homes adjacent to the club's golf course, financed its development by purchasing bonds secured by a mortgage on the club's facilities. The club had difficulty making the interest payments on the bonds, and the shareholders voted to issue $421,000 of additional stock and apply the proceeds to the redemption of the bonds. The articles did not specifically authorize the issuance of stock for that purpose.

Smith and three others (plaintiffs) refused to submit their bonds for redemption. The club (defendant) deposited sufficient funds in a bank escrow to redeem plaintiffs' bonds when due. Plaintiffs sued for a decree declaring that defendant could not lawfully issue stock or use the proceeds to redeem its mortgage bonds. Judgment for the club, and Smith appealed.

KEITH, J. . . . [The] Texas Non-Profit Corporation Act does not prohibit the issuance of stock, and stock corporations can be organized under it if they otherwise qualify. Stock is traditional in some non-profit organizations, particularly country clubs. . . .

We are not impressed with plaintiffs' argument that the stock issued by Club is "simply evidence of a debt of the . . . corporation to the investor." The stock, according to our record and the findings of the court, was validly issued as authorized. Plaintiff admitted that the Club was unable to sell new memberships and could not pay its bond indebtedness and other debts as they accrued. Yet, the principal and interest on the bonds had to be paid when due or the Club's property was subject to foreclosure by the bondholders.

The membership of the Club determined that there was an alternative method of preserving the Club's assets: the issuance of the stock and the retirement of the mortgage bonds. We are not persuaded that in so doing any of the rights of plaintiffs or other members of the Club were infringed. . . .

The judgment of the trial court is affirmed.

Classes of Shares

The Model Act (15) provides that the shares authorized in the articles may be issued as one class, or may be divided into two or more classes. Common and preferred shares are the two principal classes of stock issued by business corporations, but there are many kinds of common and preferred shares. The corporate articles must set forth the "designations, preferences, limitations and relative rights" of each class of authorized stock (15). The Model Act (58d,e, f,g) permits the articles to be amended to create new classes of shares and to change the number of authorized shares as well as the rights and preferences of both issued and unissued shares.

Common Stock If a corporation has only one class of stock, it is usually held to be "common stock," even if the articles do not use the term. If there is more than one class of stock, common stock is "common" in the sense that its rights to dividends and to corporate assets upon dissolution are inferior to the rights of other classes of shares. Dividends are not paid on common shares until dividends on preferred shares are

paid. If a corporation fails, the investment of the common shareholders (who stand last in line) may be wiped out by the distribution of assets to creditors and preferred shareholders. The advantage of owning common stock is that it is not restricted to the fixed rate of return paid on most preferred shares and debt securities. After fixed obligations are paid, any net profit that is retained in the business, or paid out as dividends, will enhance the per-share value of common stock.

Preferred Stock Many corporations do not issue preferred stock, but if they do, the contractual rights of preferred stock are superior to those of common stock. The superior rights of preferred shares usually involve preferences as to dividends and assets upon liquidation. Preferred shares may be issued in series, and the articles may vary the dividend and liquidation preferences and the redemption, conversion, and voting rights of each series (16). In the alternative, the articles may authorize the directors to create such series and to determine their relative rights and preferences. This flexibility permits the promoters or directors to devise an endless variety of preferred shares so that a given issue of preferred stock may offer any number of optional features. For example: "Convertible" preferred shares may be exchanged, in a specified ratio, for shares of another series or class, such as common stock. The conversion privilege is generally at the option of the *holder*. In contrast, the *corporation* has an option to reacquire "redeemable" preferred shares at the redemption price fixed in the articles (15,16). Preferred shareholders normally do not have a voice in management, but some preferred shares entitle the holders to elect a specified number of directors if dividends are not paid for a stated number of quarters.

The dividend preferences of preferred shares may also vary. For example: If a dividend preference is "cumulative," dividends in arrears (earned but unpaid for 1 or more years) must be fully paid before dividends are paid on subordinate shares. If a dividend preference is "cumulative-to-the-extent-earned," dividends must be paid only for those prior fiscal periods in which funds were available to pay dividends. Upon liquidation of the corporation, cumulative preferences usually entitle the shareholders to dividends in arrears and to the return of the par value of their preferred shares. A "noncumulative" preference only entitles the shareholders to dividends earned and unpaid in the current fiscal period. Preferred shares may also be characterized as participating or nonparticipating: "Participating" shares receive a basic preferential dividend and participate in further dividends on a prescribed basis with other classes of shares. "Nonparticipating" shares are only entitled to a basic preferential dividend.

Voting and Nonvoting Stock   Most statutes (15) permit the articles to limit the right to elect directors to one or more classes of voting stock. If the articles are silent as to voting rights, each outstanding share of authorized stock is entitled to one vote. However, the right to vote in board elections is usually conferred on common stock and denied to any preferred shares that may be authorized. This traditional pattern may be altered by limiting voting rights to any small class of shares. For example: Common stock may be divided into two classes—Class A with voting rights and a larger Class B without such rights. If the small class of voting shares is purchased by the promoters, they can control the corporation as well as the public's investment in a large class of nonvoting shares. New York Stock Exchange rules prohibit the listing of companies with publicly held, nonvoting common shares.

Par and No-Par Stock   The promoters or directors determine the number and value of shares to be initially issued and sold. If the articles fix a "par" value for any authorized class of shares, it is *par stock*. The par value of *one* share of par stock, of any authorized class or series, must be printed on the certificates evidencing such shares. The Model Act (18) authorizes the directors to fix the price at which an issue of par stock will be sold. With the exception of treasury stock, the price cannot be fixed at less than the par value stated in the articles. The par value of authorized shares—both issued and unissued—can only be changed by amending the articles with the approval of the shareholders.

The unsophisticated investor often fails to distinguish par value from the book value or from the market value of a share. If a corporation has only one class of stock, the *book value* of one share is determined as follows: "shareholders equity" (the total issuance price of outstanding shares + retained earnings) divided by the total number of outstanding shares. The *market value* of a share is usually something other than book value because existing economic conditions cause the selling price of stock to fluctuate.

The concept of no-par stock was developed to avoid the confusion created by conflicting par, book, and market valuations. The directors fix the "stated" value of *no-par stock* at the time that no-par shares are issued, but the per-share value assigned by the directors is not printed on the stock certificates. Directors who act in good faith may issue additional no-par shares at a higher or lower stated value, in contrast to par shares which may not be sold for less than par (18).

Nebraska prohibits the issuance of no-par stock. In California, corporations formed after 1976 are not permitted to issue par stock. All other states permit shares to be issued with or without par (15), but common shares with a par value of $10 to $25 are still favored. The par value of preferred shares is usually fixed at $100 or a multiple of that sum. This facilitates the computation of preferred dividends, which are usually expressed as a percentage of par.

Illustrative example The following example shows how the classes of shares discussed above can be used to design a plan of equity financing that allows management to adapt to changing economic conditions:

ABC, Inc., a fast-growing Illinois corporation, issued 100,000 shares of common stock with a $10 par (a capitalization of $1 million). Substantial retained earnings increased the book value of ABC common to $20 per share. The directors, who owned 70,000 shares, anticipated that their book value would increase rapidly for at least 5 years. The issuance of additional common stock would have the effect of diluting this increase by spreading it over a greater number of shares.

The corporation, which had already borrowed to the limit at the bank, needed an additional $400,000 to purchase machinery. Acting on the board's recommendation, the common shareholders amended the articles so as to authorize $100-par preferred shares, to be issued in series. The amendment provided that, at any time within 5 years of issuance, the corporation had the right to call and redeem the stock at par or to convert it into common stock (at the book value of common

as of the time of conversion). The board was empowered to establish the rights and preferences of each series. The directors voted to issue 4000 shares of series A preferred stock with an annual dividend of 10 percent. When the preferred shares were issued, most of them were purchased by the minority common stockholders.

The new issue permits the board to adjust to almost any eventuality: (1) If a major recession occurs, the directors can eliminate the burden of paying a 10-percent dividend on preferred shares ($40,000 annually) by exercising the conversion privilege. At a book value of $20, five shares of common would be exchanged for each preferred share. The 20,000 new shares of common required for the conversion would still leave the directors with a margin of control (70,000 out of 120,000 outstanding common shares). (2) If times are good, the corporation can pay the preferred dividend while the book value of common shares is rising sharply. The corporation will then be in a position to exercise the conversion privilege and exchange the preferred shares for a relatively fewer number of new common shares. (3) If earnings are very high, the directors can opt to redeem and cancel the preferred shares.

Options, Rights, and Warrants Delaware and Model Act states permit a corporation to issue options to purchase its shares (20). *Options* are classified as securities. Option holders have a right to purchase a stated number of shares of an authorized class at a specified price if the option is exercised within a given time period. Stock options are also given to key employees as incentive compensation, but such programs require shareholder approval. Certificates evidencing options, called "warrants," are often issued as an incentive to investors in connection with the sale of other securities. Short-term options, called "rights," are frequently issued to shareholders (in nonnegotiable form) so that they may protect their existing stock interests by buying pro rata shares of a new issue. (See discussion of preemptive rights in Chapter 44.)

Allocations to Capital Accounts (Stated Capital, Capital Surplus, and Retained Earnings)

The total amount of stock authorized in the articles is referred to as "authorized capital stock." As the authorized shares are sold, they become "issued and outstanding." A portion of the issuance price must be set aside in the "capital stock" account, which appears on the equity side of the corporate balance sheet. This account is referred to in the Model Act as "stated capital" (2j), a term now generally preferred. *Stated capital* is equal to: the aggregate par value of outstanding shares + the allocation to stated capital from the issuance price of outstanding no-par shares. Stated capital may be increased by issuing additional shares or by transferring all or part of the corporation's total "surplus" (the excess of net assets over stated capital) to stated capital (21).

A corporation's capital strength is measured in terms of its stated capital. All states have statutory safeguards which protect shareholders and creditors against any decrease in stated capital that would impair a corporation's financial capability. In general, stated capital must always exceed the total of: the liquidation preferences payable on outstanding preferred shares + the aggregate par value of outstanding shares without liquidation preferences (69).

If par shares are issued for more than their par value (18), the excess (sometimes called "paid-in surplus") is allocated to the capital surplus account. As a general rule, the issuance price of no-par shares must be set aside as stated capital unless the directors allocate a portion of the consideration to capital surplus within 60 days of issuance (18, 21). The creation of a capital surplus account provides some financial flexibility, but distributions from this account are subject to statutory restrictions, discussed later in the chapter. *Capital surplus* (also called

"unearned surplus") consists of a corporation's entire surplus other than earned surplus (2m).

Retained earnings consist of all profits earned, retained, and accumulated by the corporation from its inception. This accumulated net income is also called "earned surplus." Both terms are used to describe the account from which dividends are normally paid.

> *Illustrative example* Allocations to capital accounts, as required in equity financing, become more meaningful if applied to a situation which a growing close corporation might experience. Suppose that the articles of X Corporation authorize 100,000 shares of $1 par stock and 100,000 shares of no-par stock. If X initially issues and sells all its authorized $1 par shares at $1.50 per share, their aggregate par value (100,000 shares × $1 par) must be set aside as stated capital. The paid-in surplus (100,000 shares × $.50) is allocated to capital surplus.
>
> Let us assume that 5 years later, X has retained earnings in cash of $100,000 but that increased production requires an outlay of $300,000 for additional plant and equipment. If the directors issue half of the authorized no-par shares at $2 per share and put the entire amount (50,000 shares × $2) into stated capital, the $100,000 increase in capitalization added to X's retained earnings of $100,000 and a bank loan of $100,000 will provide the funds needed for business growth. The remaining authorized stock (50,000 no-par shares) can be issued to meet future capital needs without amending the articles.

LEGAL FACTORS AFFECTING DEBT-EQUITY RATIO

A corporation's financial structure always includes equity financing and usually includes some form of debt financing. The question is: How much capital should a corporation raise by selling bonds and how much by selling shares? To determine the most beneficial debt-equity mix, the organizers must assess the corporation's future growth potential, earning capability, and need for borrowed capital. In close corporations, the personal financial circumstances of the proposed stockholders are also a factor. This section deals with some of the legal aspects of debt-equity financing which corporate management should bear in mind.

Trading on Equity (Leverage)

Corporations may offer the underlying capital strength of the common shares as security for the repayment of a proposed bond issue. In effect, these corporations are "trading on the equity" of their common shares (playing the "leverage" game) to induce outsiders to buy bonds. A corporation generally expects that the added investment in the business from the sale of bonds will generate profits which exceed the fixed rate of interest payable to the bondholders. The extra profit (reflected in higher dividends or retained earnings) enhances the per-share value of common stock.

If a corporation with a high debt-to-equity ratio is very profitable, earnings derived from the total investment will yield a disproportionately high return on equity capital. The greater the proportion of debt, in relation to the amount of equity capital invested in the business, the faster the common stock will appreciate. However, a high debt-equity ratio is a high-risk choice. If the corporate business is not a financial success and revenues are insufficient to cover the interest on the bonds, losses on common shares are magnified and the common stockholders may lose their investment.

Illustrative example Risk-Takers, Inc., issued $100,000 of common stock and $1 million of 10-percent mortgage bonds secured by a major portion of the corporation's assets. First-year gross receipts (on the combined debt-equity investment) were $300,000. Business expenses and interest paid on the bonds totaled $200,000. The net profit—$100,000—represented a 100-percent return on the capital invested in common stock. However, a net loss of $100,000 would cause the corporation to become insolvent: The equity of the common stockholders would be wiped out, and the bondholders would have to sell the corporation's assets to satisfy the bond indebtedness.

Thin Incorporation

A *thin corporation* is financed with a relatively high ratio of debt to equity. In such situations, most of the borrowed capital is invested by outsiders. Historically, "thin incorporation" enables a corporation to maximize deductions of interest from taxable income. Nevertheless, if the debt-equity ratio is "too thin," tax authorities can treat loans from shareholders as contributions to share equity. As a consequence, interest payments may be disallowed and treated as dividends,[3] and shareholders may not be able to write loans off as "bad debts" if the corporation fails.

---

[3]Int. Rev. Code of 1954, 26 U.S.C.A., sec. 7482(*a*).

Case 43.2   Tanzi v. Fiberglass Swimming Pools, Inc.
414 A.2d 484 (R.I. 1980)

Richard Tanzi and his parents formed a family corporation, Fiberglass Swimming Pools, Inc., in 1968, with a capital stock investment of $3,000. In the spring of each year, when swimming pool construction commenced, Richard met the operating capital needs of the business by advancing his personal funds to Fiberglass. In 1972 Richard and his widowed mother, Lucy, advanced $43,000 of personal funds to Fiberglass to purchase excavating equipment. Not until a year later did the corporation issue promissory notes to the Tanzis in the amount of their advances.

Fiberglass became insolvent in 1976, and Richard petitioned the court for appointment of a receiver. The receiver liquidated the corporation's assets, and proposed to distribute them pro rata to the Fiberglass' creditors exclusive of the Tanzis. The Tanzis claimed that their advances to the corporation were bona fide loans, and that they should rank equally with the other creditors in the distribution of the assets. The trial court held that the Tanzis' advances were a "contribution to capital used for the operation of the corporation" and rejected the theory that Richard and his mother were creditors of the corporation, thereby holding that the Tanzis were not entitled to receive reimbursement for any part of their "loans." The Tanzis appealed.

KELLEHER, J. The dispute essentially concerned the nature of cash advances made to Fiberglass by Richard Tanzi, its president, operator-owner, and controlling shareholder, and his mother, Lucy Tanzi.

. . . As a matter of law there is nothing to prevent bona fide transactions between a corporation and its principal shareholder, including those which result in the shareholder's becoming a creditor of the corporation. . . . The question of what treatment is to be accorded such claims most often arises in receivership or bankruptcy proceedings. Even though a shareholder loan is not *per se* invalid, obviously the transaction is subject to strict judicial scrutiny. The general rule would also permit corporate directors and officers as well as shareholders to attain creditor status for loans advanced to the corporation. It goes without saying that courts are particularly watchful in all these situations because of the fiduciary status that officers and dominant shareholders must observe *vis-a-vis* the corporation when the individual acts both for himself and for the corporation. . . . We have not previously articulated standards regarding the distinction between a bona fide debt and a contribution to capital.

In *Weyerhaeuser Co. v. Clark's Material Supply Co.*, 413 P.2d 180 (1966), the Supreme Court of Idaho found that the transaction under review did not meet the requirements of a valid loan and hence the shareholder and his wife could not share in the distribution of the corporate assets. In reaching its decision, the court considered the following factors: the husband and wife were not listed on the corporate records as creditors; no note was executed; and they did not regard the security advanced earlier as a loan until after a decision was reached in litigation concerning the appointment of the corporate receiver.

In *In re Mader's Store for Men*, 254 N. W. 2d 171 (1977), the court collected and analyzed cases in which advances to a corporation were subordinated on the capital contribution theory and extracted the following relevant factors: (1) was the claimant in a position to control corporate affairs "at least to the extent of determining the form of the transaction"; (2) were the advances intended to be repaid in the ordinary course of the corporation's business; and (3) was the paid-in stated capital "unreasonably small in view of the nature and size of the business in which the corporation was engaged." In our view, the *Mader* court correctly indicated that a breach of fiduciary duties was not a prerequisite to treating shareholder advances as capital contributions. . . . "Inequity enough to justify subordination exists when it is shown that a claim which is in reality a proprietary interest is seeking to compete on an equal basis with true creditors' claims."

Interestingly, the *Mader* court cited numerous bankruptcy decisions also relied upon by the receiver in the present case. These bankruptcy cases and their legal principles have . . . [considered the following criteria] in determining the treatment of the disputed advancements: the adequacy of capital contribution, the ratio of shareholder loans to capital, the amount of shareholder control, the availability of similar loans from outside lenders, and certain relevant questions, such as, whether the ultimate financial failure was caused by undercapitalization, whether the note included repayment provisions and a fixed maturity date, whether a note or debt document was executed, whether proceeds were used to acquire capital assets, and how the debt was treated in the corporate records.

Applying the criteria enunciated earlier to the facts in this case, we conclude that the trial court was justified in finding that the cash advancements to Fiberglass were contributions to risk capital rather than bona fide loans to the corporation. We feel that the initial risk capital of $3,000 was inadequate to sustain corporate sales in excess of $200,000. Furthermore, Richard Tanzi completely controlled the corporation, a factor to which the trial court specifically alluded as follows: "As long as it [Fiberglass] was making profits, he was taking the profits out. When he needed money to buy additional assets or run the business, he put money in." On balance, the transaction itself bore very few earmarks of an arm's length bargain. The note lacked either interest, repayment, or default provisions and had no fixed maturity date. . . . Finally, the belated execution of the promissory note strongly suggests that it was an attempt in form rather than in substance to protect the family investment. Surely, under these circumstances, in which repayment safeguards were virtually nonexistent, an outside lender would have been foolhardy to risk its funds. The Tanzis' "loan," therefore, qualified as a contribution to capital that was correctly subordinated to the claims of the general creditors.

Accordingly, the Tanzis' appeal is denied and dismissed, and the judgment appealed from is affirmed.

The Deep-Rock Doctrine

In some situations, the promoters or controlling shareholders may themselves purchase a high ratio of bonds as compared to shares. Such stockholders are not "trading on equity" because they own the total investment in the corporation's debt and equity securities. Promoters of high-risk business ventures may form this type of "thin" corporation in the mistaken belief that loans from controlling shareholders will rank with debts owed to outside creditors in event of insolvency or liquidation. However, a landmark case[4] established the "deep-rock" doctrine, which holds that the claims of outside creditors against the unsecured assets of a bankrupt corporation rank ahead of debts owing to controlling shareholders.

Subchapter S and Section 1244 Provisions

Income which a corporation pays out as dividends is often subject to double taxation. The corporation pays taxes on its income and then, the shareholders pay taxes on the dividends. Subchapter S of the Internal Revenue Code[5] permits close corporations to avoid taxes on net income by passing it to the shareholders, pro rata, as ordinary income. A similar pass-through of certain corporate losses is also permitted. A Subchapter S election requires the consent of all the shareholders who, in effect, elect to be taxed as partners. However, they retain the benefits of limited liability. A Subchapter S option is available to "small business" corporations that:

1 Derive income from an active source (such as the sale of goods and services) as opposed to a passive source (such as rental property), and

2 Have only one class of stock which is initially issued to no more than 15 stockholders who must be United States citizens or resident aliens.

Some "small business" corporations, as defined in the Internal Revenue Code, may also qualify their shares as Section 1244 stock.[6] Shareholders may deduct losses on "1244" shares as "ordinary" losses, up to a maximum of

$25,000 per shareholder per year. Any additional loss is deductible as a capital loss. The tax benefits available under Section 1244 and Subchapter S tend to offset most of the advantages of debt financing and encourage the organizers of close corporations to invest in stock.

TRANSFER OF SECURITIES AND RECORD OWNERSHIP

Transfer of Securities

The rules that govern the transfer of stocks, bonds, and debentures are set out in Article 8 of the Uniform Commercial Code. The rules in Article 8 are similar to rules in Article 3 governing the transfer of ordinary negotiable instruments. Every investor has a right to transfer his or her securities by sale, pledge, or gift, or by the terms of a will. A bearer bond is transferred by mere delivery of the instrument. The transfer of registered securities (stocks and bonds) requires indorsement as well as delivery of the certificate to the new owner [UCC, 8-309]. In this context, the term "registered securities" refers to their registration on the corporate books, as distinguished from registration with the Securities and Exchange Commission, discussed in Chapter 45. The new owner of a security in registered form may register the transfer on the books of the issuer, but failure to do so will ordinarily not affect the new owner's title to the transferred shares.

Under the UCC [8-407], a security is either certificated or uncertificated. Both involve corporate stock or bonds "of a type commonly dealt in on securities exchanges or markets." The principal difference is that a *certificated security* is represented by a written instrument issued in bearer or registered form, whereas an *uncertificated security* is not evidenced by any written instrument, and its transfer must be registered upon books maintained for that purpose by the issuer [UCC 8-102(a)(b)]. Likewise, the granting of a security interest in an uncertificated securi-

---

[4]*Taylor v. Standard Gas and Elec. Co.*, 306 U.S. 307 (1939).

[5]Int. Rev. Code of 1954, 26 U.S.C.A., sec. 1371–1377, as amended.

[6]Int. Rev. Code of 1954, 26 U.S.C.A., sec. 1244(*a*), (*b*), as amended.

ty can only be accomplished by appropriate entries upon the issuer's books.

The concept of an uncertificated security creates special problems where corporate shares or bonds are used as collateral for debts. For example, in the ordinary use of certificated stock shares as collateral, the debtor delivers the endorsed collateral certificates to the creditor. Since this is not possible with uncertificated securities, a "registered pledge" is used; that is, recitals are registered on the issuer's books which state that the securities have become collateral for a debt. Inasmuch as words recited on the corporate books have been substituted for the physical delivery used in a pledge of certificated securities, the resulting secured transaction involving uncertificated securities more closely resembles an assignment of rights than a true pledge.

The holder of a certificated security may exchange it for an uncertificated security if the issuing corporation authorizes and regularly maintains a system for issuing both types of securities. The certificate that represents a given security is simply indorsed by the owner and surrendered to the corporation for an equivalent uncertificated security [UCC 8-407 and 8-408].

Indorsements and Stock Powers An indorsement may be "special" (to a named transferee) or "in blank" with only the signature of the registered owner [UCC, 8-308(2)] . In either event, corporations customarily require the transferor's signature to be guaranteed by a bank or trust company [UCC, 8-312 and 8-402(1)(a)]. This procedure discourages forged or unauthorized indorsements.

Indorsements can be made on an assignment form printed on the reverse side of the certificate or on a separate document called a "stock power" which must then be delivered with the certificate [UCC, 8-308(1)]. Banks usually require borrowers to execute stock powers covering securities pledged as collateral for a loan. Once the loan is repaid, the stock power is

voided, and the securities are returned to the borrower. At such time as a pledge of an uncertificated security is registered in the corporate records and upon release of such registered pledge, the issuer shall immediately provide the security holder and the former pledgee with a "transaction statement" summarizing the status of the security involved [UCC 8-408].

Bona Fide Purchasers A *bona fide purchaser* is a "purchaser for value in good faith and without notice of any adverse claim who takes delivery of a security in bearer form or of one in registered form issued to him or indorsed to him in blank" [UCC, 8-302]. A bona fide purchaser acquires title to the security free from any adverse claim [UCC, 8-301(2)]. For example: If Alice indorses her stock certificate "in blank," and Bill steals it and sells it to Carol (who has no knowledge of the theft), Carol is a bona fide purchaser. Carol acquires a good title as against Alice, who cannot recover the stock.

Lost or Stolen Certificates If a certificate is lost, destroyed, or stolen, a new certificate may be obtained by following the procedure set out in the Uniform Commercial Code. However, the true owner must notify the corporation of the loss "within a reasonable time after he has notice of it" [UCC, 8-405(1)]. An indorsement by an unauthorized party—such as a forger, thief, or finder—cannot ordinarily pass a good title unless the corporation issues a new certificate registered to a bona fide purchaser [UCC, 8-311(a)]. Suppose that Bill steals Alice's unindorsed certificate, forges her signature, and sells it to Carol, a bona fide purchaser. If Carol has the certificate transferred into her name on the books of the corporation, she acquires a good title and can keep the shares. Nevertheless, if Alice, the true owner, promptly notifies the corporation of her loss, she can require the corporation to issue her a new certificate for the same number of shares [UCC, 8-404(2)]. If an overissue would result, the corporation must purchase equivalent shares on the market and deliver them to Alice [UCC, 8-104].

Case 43.3   **Weller v. American Telephone and Telegraph Co.**
290 A.2d 842 (Del. Ch. 1972)

In 1968, Mrs. Gertrude Weller, a 94-year-old widow, was invited to live with Kenneth Jumper and his wife. Advanced age and poor health caused Weller gradually to surrender responsibility for her business affairs to Jumper. When Weller went to live with her nephew in 1970, she discovered that Jumper had used a form containing her signature to open a joint trading account with Merrill Lynch, Pierce, Fenner & Smith, Inc., a stock brokerage firm. Weller had believed Jumper when he told her that he was depositing her dividend checks in her bank. Actually, Jumper had forged Weller's signature on her stock certificates and had sold them on the market to a bona fide purchaser. Merrill Lynch had guaranteed that the signatures that Jumper forged on the stock certificates were Weller's.

Several weeks after discovering the fraud, Weller notified General Electric (GE) and American Telephone and Telegraph (AT&T) and requested them to issue replacement certificates. The corporations refused. Weller (plaintiff) filed an action against AT&T and GE (defendants) to recover damages arising from the unauthorized registration of stock upon forged indorsements. AT&T and GE, in turn, sued Merrill Lynch as a third-party defendant.

The case raised two issues: (1) Was Weller entitled to judgment against AT&T and GE? (2) Were AT&T and GE entitled to recover their loss, if any, from Merrill Lynch? The trial court held that Merrill Lynch could not have reasonably interpreted the trading agreement as authorizing the guarantee of forged signatures. Summary judgment was granted against Merrill Lynch to the extent of any liability on the part of GE and AT&T. The trial court then granted judgment for defendants GE and AT&T, and Weller appealed. Merrill Lynch defended.

MARVEL, Vice Chancellor. Section 8-404(2) of the Uniform Commercial Code provides that where an issuer has registered a transfer of a security in the name of a person not entitled to it, such issuer on demand must deliver a like security to the true owner, provided *inter alia*, the owner has [notified] the issuer of the wrongful taking complained of within a reasonable time after he has notice of a lost or wrongfully taken certificate. Section 8-405(1). . . [UCC] Article 1 provides that a person has "notice" of a fact when he has actual knowledge of it. . . . "What is a reasonable time for taking any action depends on the nature, purpose, and circumstances of such action." Section 1-204(2).

In the case at bar, I am satisfied that Mrs. Weller, a lonely and trusting person of advanced years and of infirm mind and body, had every reasonable right to trust a family which took her in and which she had known intimately before she moved into its home. In light of her reliance on the perpetrator of the acts which deprived her of title to her securities and her own age and decrepitude, I do not think Mrs. Weller can be charged with unreasonable action in not checking her accounts from time to time. I therefore conclude in view of all of the surrounding circumstances that Mrs. Weller notified the issuers of her stolen securities within a reasonable time.

[The appellate court held that Weller was not entitled to damages but ordered GE and AT&T to issue replacement shares to her, together with accrued and unpaid dividends.]

Corporation's Duty to Transfer   A corporation has a duty to transfer registered securities upon request of the new owner [UCC, 8-401]. The corporation must record the transfer on the corporate books, cancel the surrendered certificate, and issue and deliver a new certificate registered in the transferee's name. If the corporation fails to do so, the new owner may recover damages for conversion or, in some instances, may obtain a decree compelling transfer. The new owner may also hold the corporation liable for unreasonable delay. Nevertheless, the corporation has a duty to inquire into any adverse claim if timely written notice is received before the transfer is recorded. This duty of inquiry may be discharged by any reasonable means [UCC, 8-403(1)(a) and (2)].

Restrictions on Transfer   The general rule is that securities are freely transferable. Most exceptions relate to stock transfers. For example, a corporation may refuse to transfer shares securing a shareholder's debt to the corporation until the debt is paid. Also, the issuance and transfer of a given class of shares may be restricted to a specific group of stockholders, such as corporate employees.

Some statutes prohibit stock transfers made in anticipation of a corporation's insolvency. However, most restraints on transfer are contained in the articles or bylaws, or in "buy-sell" or "right-of-first-refusal" agreements among the stockholders. Restrictions on future dispositions of stock are necessary to preserve continuity of control—a significant factor in close corporations: The original stock issue is usually purchased by the organizers, who often serve as officers and directors, and may wish to prevent incompatible outsiders from buying shares. Sales of stock to outsiders are usually restricted by providing that each shareholder must first offer his or her stock to the corporation or to the remaining shareholders, or both. At the same time, the shareholders of a close corporation can create a market for their stock by mutually agreeing to buy the shares of persons who die or who may simply desire to cash out their investment. Internal conflicts are avoided if the tendered shares are apportioned in a way that permits the remaining stockholders to maintain their relative ownership interest in the corporation.

Restrictive agreements usually permit transfers by gift or upon death to members of the shareholder's family. The shares so transferred generally remain subject to the terms of the agreement. An absolute prohibition on stock transfers constitutes an unreasonable interference with a person's right to transfer property, and agreements that contain such prohibitions are void. Similarly, the courts will not enforce stock transfer restrictions which do not have a reasonable purpose or which do not provide a clear, fair formula for pricing and apportioning shares to the remaining shareholders.

A corporation that is not a party to a restrictive agreement cannot refuse to record a transfer made in violation of the agreement. However, the transfer does not alter the rights and liabilities of the parties to the agreement. Stock transfer restrictions are generally binding on transferees if their stock certificates contain a summary of the restrictions and specify where the full text may be found. Unless conspicuously noted on the certificate, any restriction imposed by the issuing corporation is ineffective "except against a person with actual knowledge of it" [UCC, 8-204].

Record Ownership

The Model Act (52) requires corporations to keep a record of the name and address of each shareholder and the number and class of shares that he or she holds. Corporations must be currently informed as to the identities of shareholders in order to pay dividends, send notices of meetings, solicit proxies, and determine voting eligibility of shareholders. A list of the record owners of registered bonds must be kept for similar reasons. Such records are updated as transfers of securities and their transferees are registered in the corporate books.

If uncertificated securities are authorized and issued, the issuing corporation is required—at least annually, and upon the reasonable written request of the registered owner—to furnish him or her with a dated written statement summarizing the security holder's interest in the corporation. The statement must describe the issue of which the uncertificated security is a part, the number of shares or units registered to the security holder, and the date the security was issued or transferred to him or to her. The statement must also include a statement as to liens, stock transfer restrictions, or adverse claims of which the issuer has knowledge [UCC, 8-408].

The corporation treats persons registered on the corporate books as the true owners of outstanding securities. Until the securities are transferred in the corporate records, the former owner is entitled to exercise all the rights and powers of ownership [UCC, 8-207]. It is therefore important for the new owner to request the corporation to record the transfer. An adult who takes title to securities as "custodian" for a named minor (or an executor or administrator of a deceased security-holder's estate) has the right to transfer the security.

DIVIDENDS AND OTHER CORPORATE DISTRIBUTIONS

Dividend Distributions

Shareholders expect to profit from the resale of their shares or from dividends. Corporations usually reinvest most of their earnings in the business, but publicly held corporations generally distribute some of the profits to the shareholders as regular quarterly dividends. An "extra" dividend may be declared if it is warranted by year-end profits.

Cash and Property Dividends   Distributions to the shareholders from earned surplus are called dividends (45a). Unless one or more classes of shares are entitled to preferential dividends, all shareholders participate in dividends on a pro rata basis. Dividends on preferred shares and most dividends on common shares are paid in cash. Distributions of the corporation's unencumbered property (e.g., products or even shares of a subsidiary) are called "property dividends" or "dividends-in-kind," but this type of dividend is less common.

Authority to Declare Dividends; the Business Judgment Rule   A few statutes permit the articles to require "mandatory" dividends or construe "guaranteed" dividends as mandatory dividends, but such provisions are rare. Most statutes (45) give the directors the exclusive power to declare dividends in their sound business judgment and discretion. A court will not substitute its business judgment for that of the directors unless they clearly act unreasonably, fraudulently, or in bad faith. This "business judgment" rule even applies to dividends on preferred shares.

Profits realized from selling shares receive favorable capital-gains tax treatment, whereas dividends are taxable as ordinary income. As a result, the directors-shareholders of close corporations, who often receive comfortable salaries as officers or employees, may opt to reinvest profits in the business. If the directors act reasonably and in good faith, their business judgment will be upheld against a minority shareholder who sues to compel dividends.

In exercising their business judgment, directors should consider the risks involved in accumulating earnings which could otherwise be distributed to the shareholders without detriment to the business. Severe federal tax penalties are imposed on retained earnings which exceed anticipated business needs. An unwarranted retention of profits can also be used to support other facts showing bad faith or oppression by the directors. If they own controlling shares, they may be held liable for breach of their fiduciary duty to minority shareholders. To avoid these hazards, the directors should allocate excess earnings to reserves for specified capital improvements. Such actions should be reflected in formal resolutions contained in the corporate minute book.

The *Ford* case below demonstrates that at some point in the accumulation of earnings beyond expected business needs, the stockholders may be able to compel a dividend return on their investment.

Case 43.4   Dodge v. Ford Motor Co.
170 N.W. 668 (Mich. 1919)

The Ford Motor Co. initially issued 1000 of its authorized $100-par shares in 1903. In 1908, the articles were amended to increase the corporation's authorized capital stock to 20,000 shares. The 19,000 unsubscribed shares were then distributed to the shareholders as a stock dividend. This required a transfer of $1.9 million (19,000 shares × $100 par) from earned surplus to stated capital, which increased from $100,000 to $2 million. From 1911 to 1916, Ford paid dividends equal to 5 percent of stated capital per month and also paid twelve special dividends in total amount of $43 million (a return of $500 to $1 on the original shares). The directors continued to declare regular monthly dividends of 5 percent, but special dividends were discontinued in 1916. In that year, the corporation had a $112 million surplus, $54 million cash on hand, and anticipated an annual profit of $60 million. Total liabilities were $18 million and the estimated cost of planned expansion was $24 million.

John F. and Horace E. Dodge (plaintiffs) filed an action to compel the Ford Motor Company and its directors (defendants) to declare a special dividend. Plaintiffs also sought to enjoin the reinvestment of earned surplus beyond the maximum capital stock (stated capital) which was then permitted by the Michigan statute.

OSTRANDER, C.J. It has been the policy of this state, unlike that of most states, to limit the aggregate of capital which, in the first instance, may be employed in corporate enterprises; but the history of legislation is not evidence of a continuing state policy which limits the capital assets of corporations. . . . The purpose of any [business] organization is earnings—profit. Undistributed profits belong to the corporation and may be lawfully employed as capital. . . .

The case for [Dodge] must rest upon the claim that the withholding of a special dividend is [an] arbitrary action of the directors requiring judicial interference. . . . This court, in *Hunter v. Roberts, Throp & Co.,* 83 Mich 63, 71, 47 N.W. 131, 134 [1890], recognized the

> "principle of law that the directors of a corporation, and they alone, have the power to declare a dividend. Courts of equity will not interfere unless [the directors] refuse to declare a dividend when the corporation has a surplus of net profits which it can, without detriment to its business, divide among its shareholders, and when a refusal to do so would amount to such an abuse of discretion as would constitute a fraud, or breach of that good faith which they are bound to exercise towards the stockholders."

In Cook on Corporations (7th Ed.) section 545, it is expressed [that] "a reasonable use of the profits to provide additional facilities for the business cannot be objected to or enjoined by the stockholders." . . .

Mr. Henry Ford is the dominant force in the business of the Ford Motor Company. . . . The record convinces that he has the attitude towards shareholders of one who has distributed to them large gains and that they should be content to take what he chooses to give. His testimony creates the impression also that he thinks the Ford Motor Company has made too much money, and that, although large profits might be still earned, a sharing of them with the public, by reducing the price of the output of the company, ought to be undertaken. . . .

There should be no confusion of the duties which Mr. Ford conceives that he and the stockholders owe to the general public and the duties which in law he and his codirectors owe to protesting, minority stockholders. A business corporation is organized primarily for the profit of the stockholders. . . . [No] one will contend that, if the avowed purpose of the defendant directors was to sacrifice the interests of the shareholders, it would not be the duty of the courts to interfere. . . .

Assuming the [directors'] general plan and policy of expansion [to be] for the best ultimate interest of the company and therefore of its shareholders, what does it amount to in justification of a refusal to declare and pay a special dividend or dividends? . . . If the total cost of proposed expenditures had been immediately withdrawn from the cash surplus on hand, there would have remained nearly $30,000,000. . . . So that, without going further, it would appear that, accepting and approving the plan of the directors, it was their duty to distribute on or near the 1st of August, 1916, a very large sum of money to the stockholders.

[The appellate court affirmed the lower court's decree ordering a $19 million special dividend of excess liquid assets not required to carry out the corporate business, but it reversed the lower court's order restraining reinvestment of earned surplus.]

Legal Restrictions on Dividends The most important legal restraints on dividends are contractual. These restraints may be found in: the articles of incorporation, preferred share agreements, bond indentures, loan contracts that prohibit dividends until the corporation repays the lender, and securities exchange rules that bind the corporation. All such restraints are binding on the directors. The directors must also comply with statutory restrictions on dividends imposed by the state of incorporation and by other states in which the corporation does business.

Each state has a variety of statutes which limit a corporation's power to pay dividends. These statutes protect the interests of creditors and shareholders by preserving the capital strength required to carry on the corporation's business. The common law view is that dividends should not impair a corporation's capital. An invasion of stated capital or of capital surplus to pay dividends would convey a false impression of the corporation's profitability. As a general rule, statutory definitions restrict the term "dividends" to distributions from earned surplus (retained earnings) or current earnings. As discussed in Chapter 42, directors who vote to declare an illegal dividend are liable to the corporation (48a).

Statutory Tests for Dividends There are four major statutory tests of the validity of a dividend:

1 The *earned-surplus test* followed by a majority of states (45) provides that dividends may only be paid from earned surplus (retained earnings). This accumulated net income may be used to pay dividends even in profitless years. "Wasting asset" corporations that extract coal, oil, and other minerals, are often permitted to declare dividends from net income before deducting depletion allowances (45b).

2 The *current* or *recent earnings test* followed by a few states is sometimes called the "nimble dividend" rule (alternative 45a). This rule permits dividends to be paid from net profits for the

current or preceding accounting period, even if the corporation's net assets are less than stated capital (creating a negative surplus). However, directors must be "nimble" to declare such dividends before the profits are charged against the accumulated deficit. In effect, "nimble dividends" are distributions out of capital.

3 The *balance sheet surplus test* holds that total assets must exceed the combined total of liabilities and stated capital after the proposed dividend is paid.

4 The *insolvency test* is recognized by all states (45). Any dividend that would render a corporation insolvent—that is, unable to "pay its debts as they become due in the usual course of business"—is prohibited (2n). Apart from statutory restrictions, dividends that would cause corporate insolvency are enjoined at common law as an illegal invasion of creditors rights. Such dividends are also prohibited by the Uniform Fraudulent Transfer Act.

Persons Entitled to Dividends The directors ordinarily close the stock transfer books for a stated period, and fix a future "record date" to determine which shareholders are entitled to receive a dividend (30). The corporation may pay dividends to shareholders "of record" on that date without liability to transferees whose interests are unknown to the corporation [UCC, 8-207(1)]. Nevertheless, the recipient may be required to pay the dividend to others who have an interest in the shares. A seller and a buyer can contractually agree to the disposition of a particular dividend. If there is no agreement, the seller (transferor) is entitled to dividends declared before the transfer. The buyer (transferee) is entitled to dividends declared after the transfer. However, listed stock purchased during the 5 business days prior to the record date is "ex dividend" (without dividend) to the buyer.

Status of Declared but Undistributed Dividends If the directors declare a cash dividend, it becomes a debt owing to the shareholders. As creditors, they are entitled to recover the dividend from the unencumbered assets of the corporation if it is dissolved or becomes insolvent. The directors cannot rescind or revoke a validly declared cash dividend without the shareholders' consent. Stock dividends are not true dividends and may be revoked prior to distribution.

Other Corporate Distributions

Stock Dividends   A corporation may issue new shares to its existing stockholders as a "share" or "stock" dividend. The dividend shares are usually of the same class as the shares entitled to the dividend and are distributed in a fixed ratio. For example, if a 5-percent stock dividend is declared on common stock, one share of common will be issued and distributed for each block of 20 shares owned by the common stockholders. Dividend shares may be of another class or series if authorized by the articles or by the holders of a majority of outstanding shares of the same class as the proposed dividend.

Stock dividends are merely "psychological" dividends. The shareholders receive certificates evidencing the dividend shares, but the corporation does not, in fact, distribute any of its assets. The new shares do not increase the total value of the recipients' holdings. In the corporate books, stated capital is increased by the total amount of the stock dividend and earned surplus is reduced by the same amount. However, this capitalization of surplus does not alter the combined total of: stated capital + paid-in surplus + earned surplus (retained earnings). Thus, the shareholders' equity is simply represented by an increased number of shares. The book value of each share is diluted, but the total value of each shareholder's proportionate ownership interest in the corporation is unchanged. Stock dividends are not taxable as income because no profit is realized by the recipients unless the shares are later sold at an appreciated market value.

Stock Splits   A stock split resembles a stock dividend in that the new shares do not increase the total value of the recipients' shares. However, a stock split does not increase stated capital. Instead, the articles are amended to reduce the par value of the shares being split. If 100 shares of $100-par stock are split into 200 shares of $50-par stock, total stated capital ($10,000) remains the same. The chief purpose of a stock split is to reduce the market price of shares traded on an exchange to the customary price range of $20 to $75 per share. If the market price of a stock falls below that range, a *reverse stock split*, in which two or more shares become one, may be employed to increase the market price of the shares.

Case 43.5   Keller Industries, Inc. v. Fineberg
203 So. 2d 644 (Fla. App. 1967)

All the common stock of Silby-Dolcourt Chemical Industries was owned by Fineberg and others. Keller Industries agreed to buy their stock for $600,000 payable in Keller stock. Sellers received 15,000 shares of Keller's stock as a down payment on the Silby shares when the agreement was signed on February 14, 1964. The agreement fixed the value of Keller's shares at the price quoted on the New York Stock Exchange 2 years later—the close of business February 13, 1966. Additional shares in amount of any unpaid balance were to be delivered to sellers on February 14, 1966, but the total consideration was not to exceed 30,000 shares. The agreement further provided that this number would be "proportionately adjusted for any *stock split*" (Emphasis added). It was also agreed that the sellers would not be held to account for any of the original 15,000 shares should their value exceed $600,000 on the settlement date. In the meantime, sellers received a stock dividend of 3,000 shares on the original Keller shares.

At the time of settlement, Keller claimed that the stock dividend received by sellers should be credited against the purchase price. Sellers (plaintiffs) claimed that the stock dividend was an incident of absolute ownership, akin to a cash dividend, and filed suit against Keller (defendant). Judgment for plaintiffs, and defendant appealed.

SWANN, J. . . . The question before us is whether the term *stock split* as used in the agreement, encompasses *stock dividends*. We hold that it does not. . . .

"A substantial and conclusive difference exists between a 'stock split' and a 'stock dividend': in [a stock split], a division of the shares of stock . . . takes place without any change in . . . the then existing status on the corporate books of the earned surplus and capital accounts; in [a stock dividend], an addition of shares of stock and a division of, at least, some of the earnings or profits of the corporation take place, such division being reflected on the corporate books by an irreversible allocation of corporate funds from the earned surplus to the capital account." In re *Trust Estate of Pew*, 398 Pa. 523, 158 A.2d 552, 555 (1960). . . .

Keller has argued that [construing the language of the agreement to exclude stock dividends] leads to the result that "Seller" would be entitled to a total payment in excess of $600,000. It concedes, however, that had the dividend been paid in cash it would have been considered an incident of ownership for which Keller would not have been entitled to credit in the computation of the final purchase payment in 1966.

. . . The agreement provided specifically that the shares due to "seller" on the settlement date should not draw any dividends [on behalf of Seller]. No such restrictions were imposed on the initial 15,000 shares.

Accordingly, the judgment is affirmed.

Distributions from Capital Surplus (46) Distributions from capital surplus (unearned surplus) amount to a partial liquidation of corporate assets and are regulated by statute. State statutes differ, but all states prohibit distributions from capital surplus that would cause insolvency. Distributions from capital surplus are also restricted to protect the dividend and liquidation preferences of preferred shareholders.

Restrictions vary, depending upon the source of capital surplus (i.e., whether capital surplus is created from paid-in surplus, from an upward revaluation of corporate assets, from a reduction of par value not related to a stock split, or from donated surplus). For example, distributions from capital surplus may be limited to stock dividends if the source is an unrealized capital increment created by an accounting write-up— that is, an upward revaluation of corporate assets. The amount and the source of any distribution from capital surplus must be disclosed to the shareholders at the time of the distribution (46e). In general, such distributions must be authorized by the articles or approved by a majority of the holders of all outstanding shares (46b). Some statutes (6a, c) forego this requirement if a corporation redeems or repurchases shares from capital surplus for special purposes, such as eliminating fractional shares or buying out dissenting shareholders.

Redemption or Repurchase of Outstanding Shares   The articles may authorize the corporation to redeem designated classes of shares at a fixed price (15). The corporation's right of redemption is exercisable by the directors and initiates an *involuntary* sale by the shareholders. A *voluntary* sale to the corporation by holders of any class of shares is an ordinary purchase transaction. Preferred stock is often subject to redemption. Common stock may be purchased but, with rare exceptions, may not be redeemed.

In order to reacquire stock by redemption or purchase, the corporation must distribute cash to the shareholders. It follows that a corporation's power to reacquire shares is limited by statutes similar to those which limit dividend distributions. For example, the Model Act (66) prohibits any redemption or acquisition that would render the corporation insolvent. A corporation may pay cash or give promissory notes for reacquired shares, but only to the extent of "unrestricted and unreserved" earned surplus or unearned capital surplus. However, distributions from unearned capital surplus must be authorized by the articles or by the holders of a majority of shares.

A corporation may resell or cancel purchased shares or may hold them as treasury stock (6, 68). (Treasury shares cannot be voted and are not entitled to dividends.) In contrast to purchased shares, redeemed shares cannot be reissued and must be canceled (67). Authorized capital stock is reduced by the number of redeemed or purchased shares that are canceled.

The stated capital account is reduced in the amount represented by all the canceled shares. Redemption and purchase effectively reduce a corporation's ability to pay dividends.

SUMMARY

Corporations raise capital by selling shares (*equity financing*) and by borrowing funds from bondholders and from traditional business sources (*debt financing*).

A *bond* is similar to a long-term corporate promissory note (usually secured by corporate assets) which creates a debtor-creditor relationship between the corporation and the bondholder. There are many types of bonds. Mortgage bonds, secured by the issuing corporation's property, are the most common. Unsecured bonds are called debentures. Bondholders' rights, including the right to exhaust security in event of nonpayment, are usually set forth in an agreement called an *indenture*.

A *share of stock* is a proportionate ownership interest in a corporation. Before the corporation can issue a stock certificate to the shareholder, the shares must be fully paid (in cash, property other than promissory notes, or services). Typically, shareholders have a right to participate in: corporate earnings (dividends), net assets upon liquidation, and control of corporate management (the election of directors). The articles of incorporation can vary, deny, or limit the rights of any class of authorized stock and can make any class redeemable at the corporation's option or convertible at the shareholders' option. There are two principal classes of stock: common and preferred. *Common* stock, which is subordinate to the liquidation and dividend preferences of *preferred* stock, is typically superior with respect to voting rights. The value of a par share (fixed in the articles) or the stated value of a no-par share (fixed by the directors) does not necessarily bear any relation to the book or market valuation of the share.

A portion of the issuance price of all outstanding shares must be allocated to stated capital (traditionally called *capital* stock). Any remainder is allocated to capital (unearned) surplus, which includes a corporation's entire surplus other than accumulated profits (earned surplus). Earned surplus, the primary source of dividends and of operating capital after business operations commence, is now commonly referred to as "retained earnings."

Trading on the equity of common shares to induce outsiders to buy bonds (or incorporating with a "thin ratio" of equity-to-debt) magnifies the impact of profits or losses on common shares. Tax authorities will disallow interest deductions on debts owed to shareholders if the corporation's debt-equity ratio is "too thin." Moreover, the *deep-rock doctrine* ranks the claims of outside creditors ahead of debts owing to controlling shareholders. Equity financing of close corporations is encouraged by Subchapter S and Section 1244 provisions of the Internal Revenue Code.

Transfers of stocks and bonds (negotiable securities) are governed by Article 8 of the Uniform Commercial Code. The transfer of securities issued in "bearer" form is completed by delivery to the transferee, but the transfer of "registered" securities also requires indorsement by the registered owner. A forged indorsement cannot ordinarily pass a good title unless the corporation subsequently issues a new certificate to a bona fide purchaser, who must be without notice of any adverse claim. If the true owner promptly notifies the corporation when the loss becomes apparent, the corporation is liable to the true owner for an equivalent number of shares. The transfer of registered securities must be recorded in the corporation's books upon the request of the new owner, subject to the corporation's duty to inquire into known adverse claims.

The courts will enforce reasonable agreements restricting share transfers if the restrictions are noted conspicuously on the certificates. Absolute prohibitions on transfer will not be upheld.

Up-to-date corporate records of registered securities promote correct payments of interest and principal to holders of registered bonds and proper distribution of dividends and notices to shareholders. These records are also necessary to verify proxies and the voting eligibility of shareholders.

Typically, the directors have the exclusive power to declare dividends—pro rata distributions of cash or property to the shareholders. State statutes differ, but, in most instances, dividends are limited to distributions from earned surplus (retained earnings) or "current" earnings. Once declared, a cash dividend is a debt owing to shareholders of record or to shareholders who have sold listed shares during the 5 days prior to the designated record date.

A *stock dividend* creates the illusion of a property distribution but is not a true dividend. Earned surplus is reduced, and stated capital is increased without altering the shareholders' proportionate interests, which are merely represented by more shares. A *stock split* reduces the par value of outstanding shares and increases their number proportionately so that total stated capital is unchanged.

State regulation of corporate distributions is designed to preserve the capital strength of the corporation for the benefit of its shareholders and creditors. Distributions from stated capital or from capital surplus are subject to stringent statutory restrictions. Distributions from sources other than retained earnings must be authorized in the articles or approved by the shareholders, who must be advised of the source when distribution is made. Any distribution which would render the corporation insolvent is prohibited.

Shares which are redeemed or repurchased by the corporation must generally be paid for from earned surplus. The use of other corporate funds is restricted by statutes similar to those governing dividend distributions. Redeemed shares must be canceled, but repurchased shares may be resold, canceled, or held as treasury stock. Treasury stock held by the corporation has no dividend or voting rights.

STUDY AND DISCUSSION QUESTIONS

1 Discuss factors which can limit a corporation's borrowing power.

2 *(a)* What is a bond? *(b)* What are the two chief characteristics of bonds?

3 What is an indenture agreement?

4 Distinguish between: *(a)* mortgage bonds and debentures and *(b)* registered bonds and bearer bonds.

5 How does a corporation obtain funds *(a)* to commence business? *(b)* to operate and expand the business?

6 *(a)* What is a share of stock? *(b)* What basic rights do shareholders normally have? *(c)* How does a shareholder's relation to the corporation differ from that of a bondholder?

7 What authority does a corporation need to legally offer, sell, and issue its shares?

8 Distinguish between: *(a)* common and preferred shares *(b)* voting and nonvoting shares, *(c)* par and no-par shares, and *(d)* options, rights and warrants. Give examples showing how each is used.

9 *(a)* How does capital stock (stated capital) differ from authorized capital stock? *(b)* How do funds accumulate in earned surplus (retained earnings) as compared to unearned capital surplus?

10 Explain what is meant by *(a)* "trading on equity," *(b)* "thin" incorporation, *(c)* the "deep-rock" doctrine, *(d)* a Subchapter S election, and *(e)* qualification under Section 1244. Discuss the possible advantages or disadvantages of each of the above.

11 *(a)* What is required to complete the transfer of bearer bonds? *(b)* What is required to complete the transfer of registered bonds and shares?

12 *(a)* What is a bona fide purchaser? *(b)* What special right attaches to securities transferred to a bona fide purchaser?

13 *(a)* Under what circumstances is a corporation required to transfer securities? *(b)* What steps must a corporation take to transfer registered securities?

14 Why is it important for a new owner to record the transfer of registered shares on the books of the corporation?

15 *(a)* Discuss some of the important contractual restrictions on dividends. *(b)* Explain the primary purpose of statutory restrictions on dividends. *(c)* Discuss the statutory tests of a valid dividend. In your answer, stress the majority view.

16 *(a)* Why is a "record date" important in connection with the declaration of a dividend? In your answer, discuss the rights of transferees who are not of record when the dividend is paid. *(b)* What is the status of an undistributed dividend that has been validly declared?

17 Explain the similarities and the differences between a stock dividend and a stock split.

18 Explain the basis for statutory restrictions on distributions from unearned capital surplus.

19 Discuss the similarities and the differences between a redemption and a purchase of shares by the corporation.

CASE PROBLEMS

1 Haselbush agreed to buy 10,000 shares of X Corporation's stock for $20,000 and gave a promissory note in that amount. The corporation issued 10,000 shares in Haselbush's name but held the stock certificate pending payment of the note. When Haselbush failed to pay the note, the corporation sued to collect. Haselbush countersued and asked the court to cancel the note. He argued that the corporation's acceptance of inadequate consideration (the note) had resulted in the issuance of watered stock and that the transaction was illegal and therefore voidable. X claimed that the stock had not been "issued" because the certificate had not been delivered to Haselbush. Should the court order cancellation of the note?

2 Norton owned a business that manufactured vending machines. He agreed to sell his business to Digital, Inc., in exchange for 600,000 shares of Digital stock. As a down payment, Digital issued and delivered 300,000 shares to Norton. Acting under the purchase contract, Digital deposited the remaining 300,000 shares in a bank escrow. The escrowed shares were to be distributed to Norton on the basis of one share for each $2.66 of future profits that Digital earned from Norton's vending machine business. Any shares remaining in escrow at the end of 18 months were to be returned to Digital. Digital held its next shareholders meeting before it had realized any profits from Norton's business. However, the escrowed shares were registered in Norton's name, and Norton therefore claimed that he was entitled to vote all 600,000 shares. Is Norton's contention correct?

3 Parsons agreed to sell 700 shares of Concrete, Inc., to ABC, Inc., for $264,000. The purchase price was payable in installments, and the certificate which was issued to ABC was deposited in escrow. On the same day, Smith (president of ABC) executed a stock assignment. It read: "For value received, ABC, Inc., hereby sells, assigns, and transfers 700 shares of Concrete, Inc., represented by certificate #41 to Nancy White" (Smith's daughter). Smith put the assignment in a sealed envelope and gave it to White's husband. He was instructed to give it to White after Smith's death. In the meantime, ABC paid Parsons in full, and the certificate for the Concrete shares was delivered to ABC. Smith kept the certificate in his safety deposit box. For several years, ABC voted Concrete's shares at shareholders' meetings, and ABC and Concrete filed consolidated income tax returns on the premise that ABC, Inc., owned the Concrete shares. When Smith died, White learned of the assignment. She then sued to compel ABC to indorse and deliver the certificate for the Concrete shares to her. Did the assignment which Smith signed on behalf of ABC transfer the Concrete shares to White?

4 George Riggs, the president of Midwest Steel, purchased 400 shares of Midwest stock and signed a right-of-first-refusal agreement at the time of the purchase. The agreement required Riggs to offer his shares, at book, to certain corporate officers and then to the company before selling the shares to outsiders. A summary of the agreement, which made no provision for transfers by inheritance, was printed on the stock certificate. Riggs died and bequeathed his shares to his wife, Mary, who was not a party to the agreement. The corporate officers and Midwest claimed an absolute right to acquire the shares, and Midwest refused to transfer the stock to Mary. Mary sued to compel the corporation to do so. (*a*) Is Mary entitled to judgment? (*b*) Do the officers and Midwest have any rights under the agreement?

5 Fuel, Inc., and its sole stockholders (Able and Ball) signed a restrictive stock transfer agreement which was also signed by three "key" employees (Fry and Ball's two sons). The agreement provided: (*a*) that Able and Ball must each offer their shares to the corporation and then to each other before transferring any shares to outsiders; (*b*) that upon the death of either stockholder, his estate must sell and the corporation must buy the decedent's shares; and (*c*) that upon the death of the survivor, his estate must sell his shares equally to the three key employees. In 1972, Able died, and the corporation bought his shares. Ball then sold all his stock to his sons. As a result, when Ball died, his sons already owned all the stock. Fry demanded that Ball's sons sell him one-third of their shares. They refused, and Fry sued to compel the sale. Is Fry entitled to purchase one-third of the stock?

6 Helen Cole owned all the outstanding stock

of Realty, Inc., except 2 percent which was held by Trust Bank. Helen operated Realty, Inc., as a "one-woman" corporation and was president, treasurer, and a director from 1961 to 1970. During that period, Realty accumulated a cash balance of $19,000 and earned surplus of $40,000. The corporation could have distributed a dividend from excess profits, which accumulated steadily, without detriment to the business, but the directors held no meetings and declared no dividends. Helen did increase her own salary; she also converted $7,000 of excess corporate assets to her own use. Trust Bank sued to compel declaration of a dividend. Helen Cole and Realty, Inc., claimed that there were insufficient funds in "current taxable income" from which to declare a dividend and that use of earned surplus would amount to an invasion of capital. *(a)* Is this contention correct? *(b)* Should the court order a dividend?

7 Four accountants formed a professional corporation and signed a buy-sell agreement whereby CPA, Inc., agreed to repurchase the shares of each accountant at book value upon death, incapacity, or retirement. To the extent allowed by law, CPA, Inc., was to repurchase the shares with a corporate promissory note. The remaining shareholder-accountants contracted to buy any shares in excess of the corporation's financial capability. When Hall retired, his shares had a book value of $200,000. CPA, Inc., had retained earnings of $7,000 and a capital surplus of $135,000—a total of $142,000. The remaining accountants attempted to sidestep any personal obligation to buy shares in excess of that amount by authorizing CPA, Inc., to give Hall a note for $200,000 in exchange for his stock. Hall contended that CPA, Inc., could not lawfully issue a note in excess of $142,000 and sued for specific performance. Should the court order the remaining stockholders to purchase any shares in excess of $142,000?

8 Realty Co. was incorporated by eight doctors to construct a medical building. They purchased $36,000 of common stock, $57,000 of bonds, and obtained additional capital by borrowing $134,000 from banks in exchange for amortized notes secured by a mortgage of the building. The bonds had a fixed maturity date but made no provision for the amortization of principal. If the corporation defaulted on its bond payments, individual bondholders could not enforce payment without the consent of a majority of all bondholders, that is, a majority of the eight doctors. The rights of bondholders did not rank equally with outside creditors, but were subordinate to them. For 7 years Realty Co. deducted the interest which accrued, but was not paid, on the bonds. The Internal Revenue Service construed the bonds as shares, disallowed the interest deductions to the corporation, and compelled it to pay additional income taxes. Was IRS correct in treating the bonds as shares?

Chapter

44

The Management Structure of Corporations

The management power structure of corporations may be described as a pyramid of delegated authority. At the top, the state creates the corporation and empowers it with all the author-ity contained in the articles of incorporation and the general corporation law. Next in the pyramid of authority are the shareholders who have the right to elect the directors and the ultimate

942

power over the bylaws. The bylaws delegate authority to the directors and confer upon them the power to appoint or remove corporate officers. To facilitate the day-to-day operation of the business, directors adopt resolutions delegating specific duties and responsibilities to the officers. They, in turn, delegate particular duties to subordinate personnel.

Each director, officer, and manager of a corporation should keep this pyramid of delegated authority in mind. Before acting on behalf of the corporation, he or she should ask: "Do I have authority to enter into this transaction under state law, the articles, and the bylaws (or a resolution of the board of directors)? The rules of agency law which explain delegations of authority and define "scope of authority" (discussed in Chapter 36) form the foundation upon which the corporate management structure is erected. The powers and duties of shareholders, directors, and officers may appear to overlap, especially in close corporations where the same person frequently serves in all three capacities. Nevertheless, there is a traditional separation of corporate powers which mandates the distinct roles played by the shareholders, directors, and officers.

A corporation's powers and its potential liabilities for unauthorized or illegal acts are discussed in the first part of this chapter. The second part examines the managerial role of shareholders, their legal rights and remedies, and their potential liabilities. The last part outlines the respective duties and liabilities of directors and officers.

THE CORPORATE ENTITY: POWERS AND LIABILITIES

The constitution and statutes of the state of incorporation establish the limits within which a corporation must operate. Its articles of incorporation cannot confer greater powers than those conferred on corporations by the state. The corporate entity is generally liable for acts beyond its corporate powers and for illegal acts committed by directors or by officers and other agents in the process of discharging their corporate duties.

Sources of Corporate Powers

The term *corporate powers* refers to a corporation's legal capacity to carry out its business purposes. A corporation's powers may be express or implied. They are derived from the state constitution, applicable statutes of the state of incorporation, the corporation's articles, and interpretive court decisions.

Express Powers The powers granted in state statutes or specified in the articles are referred to as "express powers." Corporation statutes set out the general powers which are traditionally granted to all business corporations, including the power to exist in perpetuity, to sue and be sued, to acquire or transfer real or personal property, to have a seal, and to make bylaws. The Model Act[1] and the Delaware statute specifically include a corporation's power to make gifts for charitable or educational purposes (4m); to adopt profit sharing, pension, or stock option plans as incentive compensation for directors, officers, or employees (4o); to be a partner or joint venturer (4p); to guarantee obligations of others (4h); and to indemnify against personal liability those directors, officers, and other agents who act for the corporation in good faith and without negligence (5).

The incorporators have wide discretion in drafting the articles of incorporation. All states require the articles to set forth the corporation's business purposes, but they may usually be stated in broad terms, such as "for any lawful purpose." Neither the Model Act (54) nor the Delaware statute require the articles to restate the powers listed in the incorporation statute.

---

[1] The section numbers of the *Model Business Corporations Act* are given in parentheses throughout this series of chapters.

Implied Powers Narrow interpretations of express powers can hamper a corporation's business operations. To prevent this, the courts developed the doctrine of implied powers, which gives corporations authority to do things that are reasonably necessary to carry out express powers and purposes (4q). For example, a railroad has implied power to operate a hotel for the convenience and safety of passengers.

Limitations on Corporate Powers

Limitations in Statutes All states have special statutes which protect the public by limiting the powers of particular kinds of corporations, such as banks, savings and loan associations, public utilities, and insurance companies. Most states have now enacted statutes which permit incorporation by professionals, such as doctors and lawyers, who have a similar responsibility to the public. Professionals often pursue their practices in corporate form in order to qualify for tax-deductible benefits, such as health insurance and retirement plans. As a general rule, incorporation does *not* give professionals the advantage of limited liability. However, the privilege is made available in the Professional Corporation Supplement which was added to the Model Act in 1979. The Supplement includes an optional clause which, if enacted into law, would provide that a shareholder of a professional corporation shall in no respect have greater personal liability than a shareholder of a nonprofessional corporation.

Limitations in Articles The articles may limit the broad powers granted to corporations in a general corporation statute. For example, the articles may restrict a corporation to a particular business, or require the shareholders to approve certain transactions, such as the purchase of real property. These limitations on a corporation's power and authority serve to guide the directors and officers who must use the shareholders' investment for the purposes stated in the articles.

Effect of Ultra Vires Acts

"Ultra vires" means *beyond the powers* of a corporation. Thus, if the articles limit a corporation's purpose to manufacturing machine tools, a contract to purchase wood for the purpose of making yo-yos would be ultra vires. What is the legal effect of ultra vires acts?

The Ultra Vires Defense The idea that a corporation's acts or contracts could be ultra vires was first used in the courts by parties defending suits for breach of contract. The defending party (the corporation itself or the other parties to the contract) would attempt to escape liability for contractual obligations by claiming that the contract was ultra vires—outside the scope of the corporation's powers. It was argued that the corporation lacked legal capacity to contract ultra vires and that the contract was therefore void. This defense was often unrelated to the contractual intent of the parties or to the merits of the case.

As the states liberalized their enabling statutes, they granted broader powers to corporations. Over the years, this process diminished the applicability of the ultra vires defense. Modern statutes (7) do not recognize lack of corporate capacity to contract (ultra vires) as a defense in suits seeking to impose liability for breach of contract. The practical result is that a corporation may, in fact, contract in excess of its powers, but corporations that do so must suffer the consequences of contractual liability to the other party.

Although a few courts still recognize the ultra vires defense, its applicability is generally limited to executory (wholly unperformed) contracts. Parties who have benefited from a partially performed contract are estopped from raising the ultra vires defense. Courts will not disturb a fully performed ultra vires contract.

Ultra Vires as Grounds in Direct Suits Most jurisdictions permit ultra vires acts to be used as grounds for "direct" suits (7abc, 94c). For example: The state attorney general may sue to enjoin or dissolve a corporation engaged in unauthorized business, or a shareholder may seek to enjoin the corporation's ultra vires acts. The corporation itself may bring an action to restrain the ultra vires acts of directors and officers or to recover damages from them for acts already committed.

Corporate Liability for Torts and Crimes

Directors and corporate agents sometimes engage in acts which are legally within the corporation's powers (*intra vires*) but which, nevertheless, infringe on the legal rights of others. Such infringement may constitute a tort against an individual or a crime against the state. Vicarious liability for the torts and crimes of directors and corporate agents may be imposed on the corporate principal.

Corporate Liability for Torts Under the agency law doctrine of respondeat superior, an injured party may hold the corporation liable for the wrongful acts (torts) of employees *acting within the general scope of their authority*, even if the corporate employer has instructed the employee not to commit the tort. The rule of respondeat superior imposes liability on the corporation for the unintentional tort of negligence as well as intentional torts, such as trespass, fraud, or conversion. The wrongful intent of the employee is imputed to the corporation as a matter of law. Many statutes authorize exemplary or punitive damages against an individual who willfully or maliciously commits a tort, but such damages may not be levied against the corporate employer unless it authorizes or ratifies the wrongful act of its employee.

Corporate Liability for Crimes The early common law view was that a corporation lacked both a mind capable of criminal intent and a body capable of imprisonment and, therefore, could not be criminally liable. The present trend is to impute the criminal intent of administrators, officers, and directors to the corpora-

tion[2] and to hold it liable for crimes which "high managerial agents" commit during the performance of authorized tasks. This concept of corporate criminality is reflected in a growing number of state statutes, including the Model Penal Code and the New York Penal Law. Recognition of corporate criminality is also evident in federal statutes such as the Sherman Act, the Social Security Act, the Internal Revenue Code, and the Securities Act of 1933. An individual who commits a crime is subject to punishment by fine or imprisonment, or both; whereas a corporation that is found to be criminally liable is only subject to fine. For example, the Foreign Corrupt Practices Act of 1977 provides for fines up to $1 million against any corporation convicted of bribing foreign officials or certain other persons to obtain business.

SHAREHOLDERS: POWERS, RIGHTS, AND LIABILITIES

Powers of Shareholders; Extraordinary Transactions

Shareholders have an important role in the corporate management structure. As the owners of a majority of voting shares, the "majority" shareholders exercise *indirect* control over corporate activities and policies by electing and removing directors (36, 39). Majority shareholders usually have the *direct* power to amend the articles (59). Majority shareholders also have the ultimate power to adopt, amend, and repeal the bylaws. Although most statutes initially give the directors this power, their actions are generally subject to repeal or change by the shareholders (27).

In addition, the shareholders exercise direct managerial power over extraordinary corporate transactions such as:

[2]*United States v. Park*, 421 U.S. 658 (1975). See also, T. McAdams and C. B. Tower, "Personal Accountability in the Corporate Sector," 16 *Am. Bus. Law J.* 67 (1978).

• Mergers or consolidations (73)

• Sales or leases that dispose of substantially all corporate assets other than in the regular course of business (79)

• Reductions in stated capital (69)

• Voluntary dissolutions (83, 84)

• Loans to directors (47)

• Stock option plans benefiting officers and directors

The directors cannot complete such transactions without shareholder approval.

Election and Removal of Directors[3] Shareholders meet annually and elect directors by a majority of the shares voted. The directors hold office until the next such meeting or until their successors are elected and qualified (36). If the directors serve staggered terms (37), the shareholders vote on the directorships that are vacated as of each annual meeting.

The shareholders have the power, at common law, to remove a director "for cause"—such as dishonesty or gross abuse of discretion. Some statutes require the holders of a specified percentage of outstanding shares to vote for the director's removal. The holders of only 10 percent of the shares of a New York or California corporation may petition the court to remove a director for cause if the required majority of directors or shareholders are unwilling to act. The Model Act (39) permits majority shareholders to remove directors with or without cause at a meeting called for that purpose; special rules apply to corporations with cumulative voting. (Cumulative voting is discussed on p. 950.) The articles or bylaws may also impose special rules for the removal of directors.

Amendment of Articles The shareholders may amend the articles (or "charter") for a variety of reasons (58). For example, the articles may be amended to change the corporation's name, purpose, or duration; the number or par

[3]See *Petition of Directors of Willoughby Walk Co-op,* Case 44.1, p. 948.

value of authorized shares; or the relative rights and preferences of issued or unissued shares. The corporate charter can also be amended to create new classes of shares or to deny or grant the right to acquire additional shares to shareholders of any class.

Typically, an amendment to the charter is first proposed and approved by the board. All shareholders entitled to vote must receive proper written notice of the proposed amendment and of the meeting at which it is to be considered (59). If approved by a majority of shares voted at the meeting (59, 60), verified articles of amendment (describing the amendment proceedings) are filed with the secretary of state (61, 62). If the proceedings conform to law and all fees and franchise taxes are paid, the secretary issues a certificate of amendment (62, 63).

Acquisitions by Merger, Consolidation, Share Exchange, Sale, or Lease Corporations can often expand quickly and economically by acquiring other corporations. The method of acquisition should be evaluated in light of applicable state and federal tax statutes, security regulations, and antitrust laws.

• A *merger* occurs when an existing corporation acquires all the assets and assumes all the liabilities of one or more corporations which then cease to exist (76). The *surviving* corporation usually exchanges its securities for the outstanding shares of the *disappearing* corporations (71). The merger of a substantially or wholly owned subsidiary into the parent corporation is called a *short* merger.

• A *consolidation* occurs when a new corporation is created for the express purpose of consolidating the assets and liabilities of two or more constituent corporations which then cease to exist (76). Their outstanding shares are usually exchanged for securities issued by the consolidated corporation (72).

• A *share exchange* occurs when *all* of a corporation's outstanding shares are exchanged for shares issued by another corporation, and both corporations continue to exist in a parent-subsidiary relation. Such exchanges are subject to special procedures (72A). Acquisition of a portion of another corporation's outstanding shares is not similarly restricted.

• A *sale, lease, or exchange of all—or substantially all—of a corporation's assets for a purpose not in the regular course of business* is an extraordinary transaction. However, such sale, lease, or exchange for the purpose of expanding existing operations is not considered to be extraordinary.

The extent to which shareholder approval is required can be an additional consideration in selecting the method for acquiring another corporation. Each of the corporations involved in a merger (71, 73) or consolidation (72, 73) must give notice to all their shareholders, even if the corporate charter limits voting to specified shares (73). The corporations must each complete a statutory procedure similar to the procedure required to amend the charter and must jointly sign the articles of merger or consolidation (74). Short mergers are effected by unilateral action of the surviving parent corporation; the subsidiary's shareholders are entitled to notice, but shareholder approval is not required of either corporation (75).

A share exchange requires that both corporations pass board resolutions (72A) and sign articles of exchange (74), but only the shareholders of the corporation to be acquired need approve the transaction (73). Corporations which propose to make an extraordinary disposition of assets outside the regular course of business must secure majority approval of directors as well as shareholderrs.

Appraisal Rights of Dissenting Shareholders (80, 81) Shareholders who object to a proposed merger, consolidation, or extraordinary disposition of corporate assets have a right to demand that their shares be appraised and purchased by the corporation which originally issued them. Such rights do not extend to the shareholders of a surviving parent corporation

in a short merger or to the owners of shares registered on a national securities exchange. However, a few statutes extend appraisal and purchase rights to shareholders who oppose certain amendments to the articles of incorporation, such as a change in the corporation's purposes or in the rights and preferences of its shares.

In any event, the dissenting shareholders must have objected *in writing*, whereupon the corporation must make a written offer to purchase their shares. If the offer is unacceptable, the corporation or its dissenting shareholders may file suit in the corporation's name to determine the fair value of the shares. The court's valuation is binding on the corporation and its dissenting shareholders.

Corporate Dissolutions Thousands of corporations quit doing business each year. However, a formal corporate dissolution can only occur by: (1) legislative act of the state of incorporation; (2) expiration of the period for which the corporation was formed; (3) involuntary judicial dissolution by decree of an equity court—pursuant to suit by the attorney general (94–96) to forfeit the corporate charter for causes such as nonpayment of taxes or abuse of corporate powers, or pursuant to suit by shareholders seeking to dissolve the corporation because of mismanagement or a deadlock of control (97); (4) action by a majority of incorporators prior to the issuance of shares or prior to the commencement of business (82); (5) written consent of all shareholders (83); or (6) corporate action consisting of a resolution adopted by the directors, written notice to the shareholders, and approval by a majority of voting shares (84).

To effect a voluntary dissolution, a statement of intent must first be filed with the secretary of state (85). After the corporation liquidates its assets, pays its creditors, and distributes the remaining proceeds to the shareholders (86, 87), articles of dissolution must also be filed (93). Suit upon any claim existing prior to dissolution may be brought against the corporation, its directors, officers, or shareholders, within 2 years after the date of dissolution (105).

Shareholders' Meetings

Annual and Special Meetings Most states require the bylaws to fix a time for the *annual shareholders' meeting*, the primary purpose of which is to elect the board of directors. If a place is not designated in the bylaws, meetings are held at the corporation's registered office. Any shareholder may seek a court order compelling an annual meeting if none is held for 13 months. As a general rule, a *special shareholders' meeting* may be called by the directors, by holders of 10 percent or more of the shares entitled to vote, or by any other persons authorized in the articles or bylaws (28).

The shareholders of publicly held corporations rarely have a voice in developing the proposals presented by management, but every shareholder has a basic right to participate in shareholders' meetings by offering resolutions and by arguing and voting for or against the resolutions that are presented. Shareholders have recently used such meetings as a forum in which to debate social policy issues, such as environmental control and nondiscrimination in employment.

Notice of Meetings and Waiver of Notice Some states permit the bylaws to dispense with notice of annual shareholders' meetings if the date and hour are stated in the articles or bylaws. Most states require that the shareholders who are eligible to vote at an annual or special meeting must receive timely written notice of the place, day, and hour of the meeting, *and* of the proposals which the shareholders are to consider (29, 73, 79). Actions taken at a meeting for which notice has not been properly given are not legally effective unless shareholders waive notice requirements by attending the meeting or by signing a written waiver of notice (144).

Case 44.1   Petition of Directors of Willoughby Walk Co-op
428 N.Y.S.2d 574 (N.Y. App. 1980)

A shareholder and member of the board of directors of the Willoughby Walk Cooperative Apartments, Inc. brought an action seeking to set aside the election of directors. The petitioner claims that the election of one of the directors violated statutes and a section of the cooperative's bylaws which prohibits a transfer of membership within 10 days preceding the annual stockholders' meeting. The specified director, Mr. Garland Core-Shuler, 5 days before the election, had his name added to that of his roommate, Virginia Shuler, on the stock certificate allotted to their apartment. Mr. Core-Shuler stated that it was through his own oversight that it was registered solely in the name of his roommate and that he helped to pay for the cooperative stock allotted and does in fact pay for the maintenance charges. It was also shown that Core-Shuler had long been actively concerned in the cooperative's affairs.

At a shareholders' meeting, on November 19, 1979, the petitioner voiced objections, but the majority of the shareholders elected Core-Shuler to serve on the board of directors. Six months later the petitioner initiated action to set aside the election. The petition was denied and the petitioner appealed.

HIRSCH, J. . . . The petitioner's full participation at the election meeting on November 19, 1979, after having heatedly contested Core-Shuler's eligibility for directorship, is understandable and would not prejudice his position. However, his participation at numerous subsequent meetings takes on a different connotation, rendering untenable his contention that the Board is illegally constituted. This is particularly true where on at least one occasion he accepted Core-Shuler's seconding to motions made by petitioner. This, in effect, is an acknowledgment of Core-Shuler's membership on the Board of Directors and acts as a waiver of petitioner's rights to contest the election. . . .

A discharge of the Board, as this petition demands, would necessitate vacating all actions on which the Board has given its approval since November. This would not only disrupt the affairs of the cooperative, but would be highly prejudicial to the interests of the cooperators. On this ground alone, the petition could properly be denied . . .

The provision in the by-laws relied upon by petitioner must be read together with other portions of the by-laws and with relevant statutes. Section 604 of the Business Corporation Law provides for the fixing of a "record date" to establish shareholder ownership, but only for the purpose of determining which shareholders are entitled to notice or to vote or receive payment of dividends. No reference is made as to eligibility for membership on a cooperative's Board. The statute obviously does not deal with eligibility for Board membership nor was it contemplated to do so.

Focusing on the statutory language of another material statute, Section 60 of the Cooperative Corporations Law, one finds that members of a cooperative corporation are elected from among themselves. It appears that a person who is a member of the corporation as of the date of Board elections is an eligible candidate.

Article III, Section 8 of the Willoughby Walk cooperative by-laws restricts the transfer of membership to a period in excess of ten days of the annual meeting. This article must be read within its context. It is patent that Section 8 is concerned with transfers occasioned by (a) the death of a shareholder and (b) and (c) the sale of an apartment viewed from a consideration of options available to the cooperative upon such contingency. Nowhere in Section 8 is there reference to Board membership. The utilization of this provision to claim ineligibility of a Board member and thereby to nullify the votes of the majority of cooperators who elected Mr. Core-Shuler is misguided. . . .

The court finds the Core-Shuler transfer to be without substance or significance and the ten day restriction a mere technicality, having no effect on the eligibility of Mr. Core-Shuler as a candidate. . . .

Accordingly, petition is denied.

Quorum and Voting Requirements Most states require a quorum to consist of at least one-third of a corporation's outstanding shares (32). Some states require a simple majority. If a quorum is not present at a shareholders' meeting, the shareholders have only the power to adjourn. To accommodate close corporations (which normally have 1 to 10 shareholders) the articles or bylaws may provide for greater-than-normal quorum and voting requirements at shareholders' meetings (32, 143).

Most statutes require shareholders' actions to be approved by a simple majority of the voting shares represented at any meeting where a quorum is present. Nevertheless, the articles or bylaws may specify that certain actions require the approval of more than a simple majority of voting shares.

Acting without a Meeting; Written Consent Nearly all statutes (145) provide that shareholders may act without a meeting by unanimous written consent. The Delaware statute only requires the written consent of a quorum.

Voting Rights of Shareholders

The voting rights of a given share are determined by state statutes, relevant provisions of the articles and bylaws, pertinent board resolutions, and the terms printed on the share certificate. Although corporations may issue nonvoting stock, most shares carry voting rights—usually one vote for each outstanding share (33). Unissued shares and treasury stock may not be voted.

Voting Eligibility The corporate stock transfer books are closed as of a "record date" (for a period of 10 to 50 days before a meeting) to determine the shareholders entitled to vote (30). Only holders of voting shares as of the record date have the right to vote at shareholders' meetings. The directors often appoint inspectors to judge the voting eligibility of shareholders.

Cumulative Voting Each share of stock entitles the holder to one vote for each vacancy on the board. Without cumulative voting, 51 percent of the shares voted at a meeting at which a quorum is present can elect all the directors. Cumulative voting permits a shareholder to cast all of his or her votes (shares owned × directors to be elected) for one candidate. The formula for

determining the minimum number of shares (X) required to elect one director is:

$$X = \frac{\text{total shares voting}}{\text{number of directors to be elected} + 1} + 1$$

Thus, dissenting minority shareholders who own a sufficient block of shares can vote cumulatively and elect one or more directors. Large, publicly held corporations often view dissent on the board as disruptive and avoid incorporating in states that require cumulative voting.

A majority of states permit the articles to provide for cumulative voting, but no major industrial state, except California, gives shareholders an absolute right to cumulate votes in board elections. The Model Act provides alternatives for either mandatory or permissive cumulative voting (33). The act also provides the means for diminishing the effects of cumulative voting (37) by permitting directors to be elected for longer, staggered terms. In a hypothetical nine-person board, minority shareholders would obviously need more votes to elect 1 of 3 directors for a 3-year term than 1 of 9 directors for a 1-year term.

Proxy Voting A shareholder can vote his or her shares in person or appoint another to do so. The appointee and the authorization which the shareholder signs, are both referred to as a *proxy*. A few states permit oral proxies, but most statutes require a proxy to be in writing; unless the proxy declares otherwise, its duration is limited to 11 months (33). Proxies can be limited to a particular transaction, but most proxies authorize the appointee to vote on all matters submitted to the shareholders. Anyone who complies with Securities and Exchange Commission rules may solicit proxies from shareholders of publicly held corporations. Shares represented by proxies are counted in determining whether a quorum is present at a meeting.

Revocation of Proxies Proxies are governed by agency law rules. Unless a proxy is "coupled with an interest," it is revocable at any time or upon the death of the shareholder. The concept of an irrevocable proxy originated with contracts to purchase shares in installments, wherein the seller contractually agrees to give the buyer a proxy to vote the shares being purchased for such period as the buyer is not in default. Such proxies are irrevocable because they are coupled with the buyer's property interest in the shares. Liberal court decisions have interpreted a "property interest" to include almost any interest in shares. For example, one court has held that a *proxy coupled with an interest* resulted from a buy-sell agreement between two shareholders which gave each a "first option" to buy the other's controlling shares in event of sale, and which provided for cross-proxies authorizing the survivor to vote the shares of the decedent.[4] The trend is to uphold irrevocable proxies regardless of the "property interest" requirement.

Voting Trusts and Agreements   Any number of shareholders may sign an agreement transferring their shares to a trustee who is instructed to vote the shares in a specified manner. Title to the shares is held by the voting trustee, who issues in exchange "certificates of beneficial interest" to the shareholders. The shareholders retain the right to inspect the corporation's books and records (52).

Under most statutes (34), a voting trust is irrevocable for any term up to 10 years and can only be terminated in the manner provided in the trust agreement. A voting trust avoids the risk that a court may set an "irrevocable" proxy aside, but the purpose of both devices is the same—to consolidate control of board elections in one or in a few persons. Voting trusts created to consolidate control or for any other proper purpose will be upheld. However, the courts will void a voting trust and declare it to be against public policy if it promotes monopoly,

oppresses minority shareholders, or perpetrates a fraud.

Preemptive Rights

The common law rule is that shareholders have a right to preserve their proportionate stock interests by purchasing shares of a new issue ahead of others. This concept of preemptive rights is designed to prevent the dilution of the existing shareholders' equity in a corporation when additional shares are issued. All states, except New Hampshire, recognize preemptive rights, but most states permit the articles to limit or deny such rights. In some states, including California, Delaware, New Jersey, Michigan, Massachusetts, and Pennsylvania, preemptive rights are recognized only if they are established in the articles. These alternatives are reflected in optional provisions of the Model Act (26, 26-A).

Even if the articles do not provide for preemptive rights, a corporation's directors cannot use a new stock issue to obtain an unfair advantage over minority shareholders. For example, if a new stock issue or a resale of treasury shares is designed to dilute the voting strength of minority shareholders, an equity court can order a preemptive right where none previously existed. However, some statutes and most courts do not permit preemptive rights to be applied to shares issued for noncash consideration, to shares issued as a result of merger or consolidation, or to shares issued pursuant to an incentive stock option plan for employees. The general consensus is that shareholders who have benefited from this type of stock acquisition are not justified in claiming preemptive rights.

The size of the corporation often determines whether its charter should authorize preemptive rights. On the one hand, shareholders of close corporations may find that preemptive rights are crucial to voting control. On the other hand, most shareholders of publicly held corporations own only a small proportion of outstand-

---

[4]*State ex rel. Everett Trust & Sav. Bank v. Pacific Waxed Paper Co.*, 157 P.2d 707 (Wash. 1945).

ing shares and are, therefore, unconcerned about preemptive rights. Large corporations may also find that investment bankers are reluctant to underwrite a public issue affected by the preemptive rights of existing stockholders.

Even if large corporations are not bound by preemptive rights, the theory is often implemented by issuing stock rights which entitle existing shareholders to buy proportionate shares of a new issue.

Case 44.2   Schwartz v. Marien
373 N.Y.S.2d 122 (N.Y. App. 1975)

Smith, Marien, and Dietrich each owned one-third (50 shares) of the outstanding stock of Superior Engraving Co. When Smith died in 1959, the corporation purchased his shares as treasury stock. When Marien died in 1961, his shares passed to his wife and three sons. Thereafter, Dietrich, his daughter Margaret Schwartz, and two of Marien's sons constituted the four-member board. When Dietrich died in 1968, the Mariens called a special board meeting and the third Marien son was elected to fill the Dietrich vacancy. The three Marien directors then voted to have the corporation sell one share of treasury stock to each of them. The three treasury shares gave voting control of the corporation to the Marien family. Margaret Schwartz was denied the right to buy treasury shares to equalize Dietrich holdings.

Schwartz (plaintiff) sued the Marien brothers (defendants) for breach of their fiduciary duty as directors and controlling shareholders. Plaintiff's motion for summary judgment was denied, and she appealed.

JONES, J. . . . While preemptive rights as such do not attach to treasury stock in the absence of specific provision in the certificate [articles] of incorporation, members of a corporate board of directors nevertheless owe a fiduciary responsibility to the shareholders in general and to individual shareholders in particular to *treat all shareholders fairly and evenly.* [Emphasis added.]

Departure from precisely uniform treatment of stockholders may be justified where a bona fide business purpose indicates that the best interests of the corporation would be served by such departure. The burden of coming forth with proof of such justification shifts to the directors, where, as here, a prima facie case of unequal stockholder treatment is made out. Particularly is this so, when it appears that the directors favored themselves individually over the complaining shareholder. Additionally, disturbance of equality of stock ownership in a corporation closely held for several years by the members of two families calls for special justification in the corporate interest; not only must it be shown that it was sought to achieve a bona fide independent business objective, but as well that such objective could not have been accomplished substantially or effectively by other means which would not have disturbed proportionate stock ownership.

[The case was remanded to the trial court with instructions to proceed in accordance with the above opinion.]

Shareholders' Right to Examine Corporate Books

Common Law Right of Inspection Shareholders or their agents, if they act in good faith, have a common law right to inspect corporate books and records for any proper purpose. As owners, the shareholders have a right to inspect the records in order to: determine the corporation's financial condition or the propriety of dividends, discover mismanagement, and obtain shareholders lists required in any organized opposition to management. Some courts limit inspection rights by holding that a proper purpose must be related to the shareholder's economic interest in the corporation.

If a shareholder is denied inspection rights, his or her remedy is to obtain a writ of mandamus. However, a denial of inspection rights will be upheld if the corporation proves that the shareholder has an improper purpose,[5] such as aiding a competitor, discovering business secrets, or developing "sucker lists" for personal business purposes. If a shareholder already has the information, this fact tends to show a lack of good faith, which is also a proper ground for denying inspection.

---

[5]*State ex rel. Pillsbury v. Honeywell, Inc.*, 191 N.W.2d 406 (Minn. 1971).

Statutory Right of Inspection All states have statutes which supplement a shareholder's common law right of inspection. Each corporation must mail an annual financial statement to its shareholders. In the interim, if any of them makes a written request, the corporation must provide the most recent financial statement available (52). Books of account, minutes of shareholders' and directors' meetings, and shareholders' lists must be made available at the corporation's registered office (52). At meetings, shareholders also have an absolute right to inspect lists of shareholders and their holdings (31). In addition to rights granted by state law, shares that are subject to the proxy rules of the Securities Exchange Commission entitle the holder to demand a shareholders' mailing list.

Any corporate official who denies a proper demand for inspection is liable for a penalty equal to 10 percent of the value of a stockholder's shares. Most statutes attempt to reduce capricious demands by limiting the right of inspection to shareholders who have owned their shares for 6 months or to holders of 5 percent of outstanding shares (52). Delaware gives shareholders the right of inspection regardless of the size or duration of their holdings.

Case 44.3   Weigel v. O'Connor
373 N.E.2d 421 (Ill. App. 1978)

O'Connor, Shapiro, and Weisberg were board chairman, president, and secretary, respectively, of Weigel Broadcasting Company. No dividend had ever been paid on the company's outstanding common shares, two-thirds of which were held by O'Connor and Shapiro. Corporate employees told John Weigel, a minority shareholder, that the corporation's officers were diverting profits to their personal use by trading company advertising for goods and services. (O'Connor privately admitted that he had taken such trade-outs in the form of trips.) Inside sources also told Weigel of $1,000 kickbacks paid to an advertising agent named Foristal. One such report involved delivery of a key to an airport locker containing a television set.

When Weigel (plaintiff) was denied the right to inspection, he sought a writ of mandamus compelling the corporation and certain officers (defendants) to produce specified corporate records. Plaintiff also sought assessment against the defendant officers of the statutory penalty for refusal to allow inspection. The trial court held that plaintiff had established a proper purpose for inspection with reference to some of the requested documents and ordered defendants to produce them. Plaintiff's demand was dismissed as to the remaining books and records on the ground that a proper purpose for their examination had not been established. The court did not assess the statutory penalty. Plaintiff appealed, contending that once a proper purpose for examining requested documents had been established, "the court could not properly limit the documents which were subject to inspection."

LINN, Justice. . . . We agree with plaintiff's contention that it is improper to allow only piecemeal inspection when the record indicates that the shareholder has presented sufficient evidence of a proper purpose and the trial court has so held.

It is elementary that if corporate mismanagement or the misuse of corporate property exists, it will best be shown by a total examination of all reasonably required books and records of the corporation. . . .

Accordingly, we conclude that the cause must be remanded to the trial court with directions to broaden the writ of mandamus to include all books and records requested in the plaintiff's demand, and for the court to conduct a hearing on the issue of the statutory penalty.

Shareholders' Rights of Action

Individual Suits and Class Actions   An *individual* shareholder can sue the corporation to enforce inspection rights, payment of dividends on preferred stock ahead of common, or other rights under a share contract. Individual suits are also filed to recover dividends declared, but unpaid, or to enjoin ultra vires acts. A group of shareholders can collectively pursue individual causes of action arising out of the same transaction by bringing a *class* action against the corporation. The individuals joining in the suit commence the action in their own names and on behalf of "all others similarly situated." Other members of the class must usually be given notice of any resulting judgment and may elect to benefit from the judgment by paying a pro rata share of litigation costs.

Shareholders' Derivative Suits   If a third party wrongs a corporation so that the value of its shares is depreciated, each shareholder suffers a pro rata share of the damage. However, the shareholder(s) cannot recover the damage by filing suit in their own names. Such suits must be filed in the corporate name. This rule avoids a multiplicity of suits by individual stockholders and protects corporate creditors by retaining judgment funds in the corporation. All stockholders benefit equally because recovery by the corporation appreciates the value of all its shares.[6]

The directors normally initiate suits in the corporate name, but directors who serve at the pleasure of a controlling shareholder-officer, may hesitate to sue that person for misappropriation of corporate funds. If directors fail to act in such situations or in situations involving misconduct by outsiders, one or more shareholders may act on behalf of the corporation by filing a *derivative* suit in its name. This concept has been extended to permit shareholders to defend suits against the corporation, in its name, when the directors unjustifiably fail to do so.[7]

In past years shareholders have used derivative suits to harass directors and officers with unwarranted accusations of mismanagement. These tactics have been used to intimidate management into making a lucrative out-of-court settlement or purchasing the complaining shareholder's stock at a favorable price. Abuse

arising from such "strike" suits has led to restrictive statutes and court rules.

In order to file a derivative suit, a stockholder must now own his or her shares at the time of the wrongdoing and must show that the directors (and in some states, the shareholders) refused a demand to commence suit on behalf of the corporation. Federal courts (and many state courts) require that settlements be submitted to them for approval and that all the corporation's shareholders be notified. This procedure is designed to preclude an unfair advantage to the shareholder(s) who file the action. The court may also require a shareholder who owns less than a prescribed percentage or dollar value of shares to give security sufficient to cover the litigation expenses of the parties (49). In event of a favorable judgment, the shareholder can generally recover reasonable litigation expenses from the corporation.

Derivative suits and class actions are both initiated by stockholders, but there is an important difference: A *derivative suit* is commenced *for* the corporation against third parties, and the judgment recovered is the property of the corporation. A *class action* is a direct suit *against* the corporation for invasion of its shareholders' property rights, and if a judgment is recovered, it is the property of the shareholders.

---

[6]*Smith v. Bramwell*, 31 P.2d 647 (Or. 1934).

[7]*Eggers v. National Radio Co.*, 208 Cal. 308, 311 (1929).

Case 44.4   Harff v. Kerkorian
324 A.2d 215 (Del. Ch. 1974)

The directors of Metro-Goldwyn-Mayer, Inc. declared a cash dividend on common shares in 1973. At that time, Philip and Stephanie Harff owned debentures which were convertible to MGM shares at the option of the holder. The Harffs (plaintiffs) brought a derivative action on behalf of the corporation and against its directors (defendants) to recover the amount of the dividend paid. The complaint alleged that the dividend had damaged MGM's capital position and future prospects. The trial court dismissed the action on the ground that the Harffs were not MGM stockholders and, therefore, could not maintain the derivative suit,

The Harffs (plaintiffs) also brought a class action on behalf of all debenture holders against MGM and its directors (defendants). The complaint alleged that the dividend (1) evidenced self-dealing by defendant Kirk Kerkorian and other controlling shareholder-directors and (2) impaired the value of the conversion feature offered by the debentures, thereby causing a decline in their market value. Defendants moved to dismiss on the ground that a cause of action was not stated because plaintiffs did not allege that defendants breached any of the terms of the indenture agreement which governed the rights of debenture holders. The court granted summary judgment in favor of defendants.

Plaintiffs appealed from both judgments.

QUILLEN, Chancellor. . . . The derivative action was developed by equity to enable stockholders to sue in the corporation's name where those in control of the corporation refused to assert a claim belonging to the corporation. The nature of the derivative suit is two-fold: first, it is the equivalent of a suit by the stockholder to compel the corporation to sue; and second, it is a suit by the corporation, asserted by the stockholders in its behalf, against those liable to it. Suits by stockholders alleging mismanagement on the part of directors are of course included within the umbrella of a derivative action.

Under Delaware law only one who was a stockholder at the time of the transaction or one whose shares devolved upon him by operation of law may maintain a derivative action. For purposes of a derivative action, an equitable owner is considered a stockholder. But Delaware law seems clear that stockholder status at the time of the transaction being attacked and throughout the litigation is essential.

The holder of an option to purchase stock is not an equitable stockholder of the corporation. Debenture holders are not stockholders and their rights are determined by their contracts. A holder of a convertible bond "does not become a stockholder, by his contract, in equity any more than at law." *Parkinson v. West End St. Ry. Co.*, 53 N.E. 891, an opinion by Justice Holmes. . . . The conclusion is inescapable that plaintiffs are creditors of MGM and simply do not have standing to maintain a stockholder's derivative action under Delaware law. The derivative cause of action is therefore dismissed.

The basis upon which plaintiffs assert the class claim is an alleged breach by defendants of their fiduciary duty to refrain from acting in their own self interest. . . . The authorities cited by plaintiffs for the proposition that creditors can maintain an action against management for rights which exist independently of the Indenture Agreement all involved either fraud or insolvency. It is apparent that unless there are special circumstances, e.g. fraud, insolvency, or violation of a statute, the rights of debenture holders are confined to the terms of the Indenture Agreement. . . . The fact that the market value of the common stock is not sufficiently attractive to make conversion profitable at a particular time does not give rise to a cause of action against management. . . . As plaintiffs have failed to allege any default under the Indenture, the class claim must be dismissed.

[The Supreme Court of Delaware later held, on appeal, that plaintiff's class action had sufficiently alleged fraud by the directors so as to constitute a default under the Indenture Agreement, and ordered a trial on the issue of fraud. *Harff v. Kerkorian*, 347 A.2d 133 (Del. 1975). The lower court's ruling in the derivative suit was affirmed.]

Minority Shareholders' Actions Majority shareholders (and the directors and officers acting for them) owe minority shareholders a fiduciary duty of due diligence and fair dealing. If policies adopted by majority shareholders (or by others acting for them) fraudulently or negligently impair the investment of minority shareholders, they may obtain relief in a court of equity. For example, minority shareholders can recover damages from a majority that sells controlling shares to purchasers who foreseeably would loot the corporate treasury.[8] (See *De-Baun v. First West. Bank & Trust Co.*, Case 44.5, p. 958.) Similarly, many courts will award minority shareholders a pro rata interest in any premium (in excess of fair market value) paid to majority stockholders for their shares because they represent voting control of the corporation. Liability of controlling shareholders is discussed further at page 958.

Any shareholder may also petition the court for appointment of a receiver, if: (1) a deadlock among directors threatens irreparable injury to the corporation; (2) the acts of those in control are illegal, oppressive, or fraudulent; (3) a deadlock among shareholders prevents the election of directors; or (4) corporate assets are being misapplied or wasted (97, 98, 102).

Shareholders' Liabilities

The fact that a shareholder's liability is limited to his or her capital investment is perhaps the most important characteristic of a modern corporation, but there are exceptions to the rule. As discussed in Chapter 42, creditors that prove unity of interest may "pierce the corporate veil"

and hold a controlling shareholder liable for corporate debts. Personal liability may also be imposed on shareholders who use the corporation for fraudulent purposes. Other liabilities which frequently arise are discussed in the following paragraphs.[9]

Liability for True Value of Shares The holder of fully paid shares is not obligated to the corporation or its creditors (25). Conversely, a shareholder who pays less than the full subscription price is liable for the deficiency (17). If the shareholder dies, the estate is liable. However, neither the executor of an estate nor an innocent purchaser of unpaid shares can be held personally liable for the deficiency (25).

Shares are sometimes issued for overvalued property. A majority of state statutes and the Model Act (19) do not impose liability on the shareholder if there is no fraud and the directors value such property "in good faith." Of course, if the facts show fraud on the part of the shareholder or bad faith on the part of the directors, the shareholder is liable for the amount of any underpayment that results. In the absence of statute, courts use a variety of theories to impose liability on the stockholder. The end result, in most cases, is equivalent to the liability imposed on shareholders under the *true value* rule. This rule holds the shareholder liable to the corporation (or to its creditors) for the difference between the inflated value and the true value of the property. Stated another

---

[8]*Gerdes v. Reynolds*, 28 N.Y.S.2d 622 (1941).

[9]One kind of statutory liability which is imposed very infrequently is liability for wages due corporate employees. For example, under New York law, the ten largest shareholders are jointly and severally liable for wages due employees of corporations whose shares are not publicly traded. Such statutes are contrary to the idea of limited liability and tend to discourage incorporation.

way, the shareholder must pay the difference between the true value of the property and the issuance price of his or her shares.

Liability for Unlawful Dividends and Distributions Some statutes permit a corporation to recover from shareholders who know that a dividend or other corporate distribution is unlawful. The Model Act (48) permits corporations to hold directors jointly and severally liable for such distributions, but the directors can recover from recipients who are aware of the illegality. The trustee or receiver of an insolvent corporation can even recover from innocent shareholders.

Liability of Controlling Shareholders The courts have not clearly defined the duties that controlling shareholders-directors of close corporations owe to minority stockholders. One problem area that arises frequently, especially in close corporations, involves injuries suffered by minority shareholders as the result of the sale of controlling shares. In a number of cases, the selling price of controlling shares has been found to include a premium which is paid for voting control of the corporation in excess of the fair market value of the stock. A growing number of courts will compel majority shareholders to disgorge the premium paid to them for control and will redistribute the amount of the premium ratably among *all* shareholders.[10] Equal rights attach to each share of stock of any given class. Under the law, the shareholders

also tend to be treated equally, regardless of the size of their holdings. Thus, in most situations, the courts will prevent controlling shareholders from deriving a greater benefit from their *per-share investment* in stock and will equalize inequities suffered by minority shareholders.[11]

A second problem area relates to the potential liability of controlling shareholder-directors who refuse to declare dividends. As discussed in Chapter 43, the courts will ordinarily uphold the directors' business judgment, but a growing number of decisions grant relief if dividends are suppressed "in bad faith" for a wrongful purpose. Examples are: to force a minority shareholder to sell his or her stock,[12] to further the personal interests of directors,[13] or to depress the price of the corporation's stock.[14] Relief may be in the form of a decree ordering the declaration of a dividend or a decree ordering the majority shareholders to pay damages to minority shareholders. As discussed in Chapter 42, courts will impose personal liability on controlling shareholders who use the corporate entity to sanction fraud, perpetrate a crime, circumvent a statute, accomplish a wrongful purpose, or promote injustice.

---

[11]*Donahue v. Rodd Electrotype Co.* Case 44.6, p. 963.
[12]*Patton v. Nicholas*, 279 S.W.2d 848 (Tex. 1955).
[13]*Gottfried v. Gottfried*, 73 N.Y.S.2d 692 (Sup. Ct. 1947).
[14]*Cochran v. Channing Corp.*, 211 F. Supp. 239 (S.D.N.Y. 1962).

---

[10]*Brown v. Halbert*, 76 Cal. Rptr. 781 (Cal. App. 1969).

Case 44.5   **DeBaun v. First Western Bank & Trust Co.**
120 Cal. Rptr. 354 (Cal. App. 1975)

   In 1955, Johnson formed Alfred S. Johnson, Inc. Johnson initially purchased all the corporation's outstanding stock (100 shares), but he later sold a few shares to key employees (10 shares to Stephens and 20 shares to DeBaun). When Johnson died in 1965, he left his 70 controlling shares to First Western Bank & Trust Co. (Bank) as trustee of a trust created by his will. DeBaun and

Stephens continued to run the business, and profits rose steadily. By 1968, Alfred S. Johnson, Inc. (Corporation) had $198,000 of liquid assets and a net worth of $220,000.

Raymond Mattison owned S.O.F. Fund, Inc. and offered to have it purchase Johnson's shares, which Bank held as trustee. The down payment was to be $50,000. The balance of $200,000 was to be paid over 5 years, and payment was to be secured by Corporation's assets. Bank's decision to accept the offer was based on Mattison's "friendly reception by fellow Jonathan Club members." A Dun & Bradstreet report suggested that S.O.F. Fund no longer existed and indicated that Mattison and his other entities had a history of financial failures and legal troubles. Bank knew that its own assets included an unsatisfied judgment against Mattison and asked his attorney about pending litigation. His attorney referred Bank to courthouse records. The courthouse records, which Bank failed to check, showed that Mattison and his entities had potential liability exceeding $1 million under 38 unsatisfied judgments, 22 recorded abstracts of judgment, 54 pending suits, and 18 tax liens.

Bank's staff doubted that it was legal to permit Mattison, as a shareholder, to secure the personal obligation which arose from the purchase of Johnson's stock with Corporation's assets. However, Bank concealed these facts to induce DeBaun and Stephens (as stockholders and directors) to approve the sale to Mattison. Bank then gave Mattison a proxy to vote the 70 shares but retained them as additional security. Bank soon learned that Mattison was looting the corporation but took no action until it was hopelessly insolvent. Pursuant to the security agreement, Bank sold Corporation's remaining assets for $60,000. After tax liens were satisfied, only $35,000 remained in the Johnson trust.

DeBaun and Stephens brought a derivative action on behalf of the Corporation (plaintiff) and against Bank (defendant) to recover damages resulting from its sale of controlling shares to Mattison. The trial court held the Bank liable to Corporation for $473,836 in damages (the corporation's net worth as of transfer date plus 10 years of projected, after-tax earnings). Defendant appealed.

THOMPSON, J. . . . "In any transaction where the control of the corporation is material," the controlling majority shareholder must exercise good faith and fairness "from the viewpoint of the corporation and those interested therein." *Remillard Brick Co. v. Remillard-Dandini Corp.*, 109 Cal. App. 2d 405, 420; 241 P.2d 1966. That duty of good faith and fairness encompasses an obligation of the controlling shareholder in possession of facts "such as to awaken suspicion that a potential buyer of his shares may loot the corporation, . . . to conduct a reasonable and adequate investigation of the buyer." *(Insuranshares Corp. v. Northern Fiscal Corp.*, 35 F. Supp. 22, 25 (E.D. Pa. 1940).)

[As trustee of Johnson's shares] Bank was the controlling majority shareholder. It became directly aware of facts that would have alerted a prudent person that Mattison was likely to loot the corporation. . . . Armed with knowledge of those facts, Bank owed a duty to Corporation and its minority shareholders to act reasonably with respect to its dealings in the controlling shares with Mattison. It breached that duty. Knowing that the information could be obtained from the public records, Bank closed its eyes to that obvious source. . . . Had Bank investigated, it would have precluded its dealings with [Mattison] except under circumstances where his obligation was secured beyond question and his ability to loot Corporation precluded.

Bank, however, elected to deal with Mattison in a fashion that invited his looting of Corporation's assets. . . . By fraudulently concealing its nature from DeBaun and Stephens, Bank obtained corporate approval of a security agreement which hypothecated corporate assets to secure Mattison's obligation to it. Thus, to permit it to sell its majority shares to Mattison, Bank placed the assets and business of Corporation in peril. . . . The judgment is affirmed.

DIRECTORS, OFFICERS, AND EMPLOYEES: POWERS, DUTIES, AND LIABILITIES

Powers of the Board of Directors

The Model Act (35) provides that "all corporate powers shall be exercised by or under authority of . . . a board of directors." Nevertheless, the board's power is always subject to the shareholder's statutory power to elect and remove directors and to vote on extraordinary transactions. Although the board delegates the daily management of corporate affairs to designated corporate officers, this delegation does not diminish the directors' responsibility for corporate policy decisions. Each director has a right to inspect corporate records in order to carry out his or her duties, but an individual director can only act for the corporation when he or she is authorized as an officer or agent.

Number of Directors Ten states require a minimum of three directors[15] and twelve states follow the Model Act (36) which requires only one director.[16] The remaining states offer a

---

[15]Alabama, Colorado, Hawaii, Maryland, Mississippi, Montana, New Hampshire, North Dakota, Oklahoma, and Utah.

[16]Arizona, Delaware, Florida, Michigan, Missouri, New Jersey, New Mexico, Oregon, South Dakota, Texas, West Virginia, and Wisconsin.

compromise: Although there is a general requirement of three directors, the number of directors need not exceed the number of shareholders. In effect, if there is only one shareholder, there need be only one director. This trend reflects the growing importance of a close corporation owned by a single shareholder-director. The articles or bylaws must fix the number of directors (36) but need not set out their qualifications (35).

Election and Removal of Directors by Board The Model Act (38) provides that a majority of directors, even if less than a quorum, can elect a director to fill a predecessor's unexpired term. The articles may also give the board of directors the power to increase the size of the board. If the directors do so, they can fill "vacancies" created by the new directorships "until the next election of directors by the shareholders" (38).

Most statutes also permit the board to remove a director who has been declared insane or convicted of a felony. The articles or governing statute determine whether the board has the power to remove a director "for cause." Of course, such provisions do not affect the shareholders' inherent power to remove directors.

Powers of Board and Executive Committee The board of directors has the power to take any action related to managing the corporate enterprise which the articles or state statutes permit.

The board is generally empowered to fix the compensation of the individual directors (35). The directors may also adopt, amend, or repeal bylaws, unless the articles reserve this power to the shareholders (27). As part of managing the ordinary business affairs of the corporation, the directors normally approve or ratify reports and authorize officers to take important actions (e.g., opening bank accounts, borrowing money, and signing contracts).

The articles or bylaws may also authorize the directors (by majority vote of the full board) to establish an executive committee, which must be composed entirely of board members. Such committees can exercise all board powers, within the limits of the authorizing resolution, excepting the power to initiate extraordinary transactions. New York Stock Exchange rules now require all listed corporations to establish an audit committee consisting of outside directors charged with the duty of working cooperatively with the corporation's independent public accountants.

Formal Actions of the Board

The directors usually meet as a board at regular intervals. The directors' actions are reflected in formal board resolutions.

Adoption of Board Resolutions Resolutions can generally be adopted by a majority of the directors voting at any meeting at which a quorum is present (40). (A quorum normally consists of a majority of the number of directors specified in the articles or bylaws.) Most statutes (44) also acknowledge the need for swift, informal action, especially in close corporations, by permitting the directors to adopt resolutions without a meeting by giving their unanimous written consent to one or any number of specified transactions or policy statements.

All resolutions are recorded in the corporate minute book. Third parties, such as banks, frequently require the secretary to furnish certified copies of resolutions evidencing corporate actions. Management and corporate counsel are keenly aware that resolutions may be scrutinized by potential suitors. Minority shareholders, governmental agencies, or creditors may use the minute books to obtain evidence against the corporation.

Directors' Meetings; Notices and Waivers Traditionally, the directors can only act when the board is properly convened. Notice of regular board meetings is not required if the time and place is fixed in the bylaws or by standing resolution. Notice of special meetings must be given as prescribed in the bylaws (43). The directors may waive notice of any meeting by attending the meeting or by signing a written waiver of notice before or after the meeting.

Authority of Officers and Employees

Officers and employees are *agents* of the corporation. They have implied authority, under agency law rules, to take actions required to carry out the express authority found in state statutes, articles, bylaws, and board resolutions.

Election of Officers The directors elect (and remove) the corporate officers and fix their salaries (35, 50, 51). As a general rule, the bylaws provide for a president, one or more vice presidents, a secretary, and a treasurer (50) and describe the general duties and authority of each officer. In addition, specific duties and responsibilities are assigned to the officers by the board. One person may hold more than one office but, in most states, the same person cannot be president and secretary. However, a growing minority of states have eliminated this prohibition to accommodate the needs of close corporations.

Limitations on Authority of Officers and Employees A certified copy of the board resolution authorizing a given transaction can apprise involved third parties of any limits on a corporate officer's authority. However, the duties which officers or employees customarily perform tend to define their authority. Thus, prior conduct may estop the corporation from denying the agency authority of an officer or employee in a subsequent transaction. The unauthorized acts of officers and employees can bind the corporation if it later ratifies such acts.

Duties of Directors, Officers, and Employees

Duty of Obedience, Due Diligence, and Loyalty Directors are *not* corporate agents, but their basic duties are similar to those duties arising from the agency relation which officers and employees bear to the corporate principal. Directors, officers, and employees have a duty of *obedience* (to act *intra vires*) and a duty to exercise *due diligence*. Stated another way, they must not be negligent, either in acting or failing to act. Their express and implied authority must be exercised with the care which an ordinarily prudent person in a like position would exercise. Directors, officers, and subordinates also have a *fiduciary duty of loyalty* that is "influenced in action by no consideration other than the welfare of the corporation."[17]

Fiduciary Duty of Directors, Officers, and Employees Directors, officers, employees and, in some situations, controlling shareholders, owe a fiduciary duty to the corporation (and to its minority shareholders). State and federal statutes define fiduciary duty in broad terms, such as "loyalty, good faith, and fair dealing." Courts have used similar phrases, such as "honest conduct" and "independent judgment" to define the fiduciary duty. These elements are emphasized in a classic opinion by Justice Cardozo,[18] whose warning should be heeded by officers and other corporate agents as well as directors:

Any adverse interest of a director will be

subjected to a scrutiny rigid and uncompromising. He may not profit at the expense of his corporation and in conflict with its rights; he may not for personal gain divert unto himself the opportunities which in equity and fairness belong to his corporation.

Conflicts of Interest Conflicts of interest between a director, officer, or employee—and the corporation—arise in many ways. For example, a director may: have an interest in a competing business; contract with an outside company owned by the director to furnish goods or services to the corporation; use corporate funds or employees in an outside venture; accept secret profits or commissions on corporate transactions; use influence to prevent the corporation from competing with an outside business; or disclose trade secrets to an outside business. Early courts held these "self-dealing" activities to be voidable at the corporation's option. The view followed by Delaware, California, and Model Act states (41) is that a contract between a corporation and one or more directors is neither void nor voidable if:

1 The contract is "fair and reasonable to the corporation," or

2 The conflict is fully disclosed or known to the *disinterested* directors, or to the shareholders, and either body approves or ratifies the transaction without counting the vote or consent of the *interested* parties.

A like standard of fairness and full disclosure applies to any contractual conflict of interest involving a corporate officer or employee.

Self-dealing is unavoidable when directors fix their own compensation (35) or adopt incentive stock option plans which benefit them as directors or as officer-employees (20). Incentive rights or options that are not to be issued to "shareholders generally" must be approved by a majority of shares entitled to vote. In the ab-

---

[17]*Meinhard v. Salmon*, 164 N.E. 545, 546 (1928).
[18]Ibid.

sence of fraud, the directors' judgment as to the adequacy of the consideration given for such options is conclusive. However, minority shareholders may bring suit to limit or deny incentive compensation which does not bear a reasonable relation to the services rendered. Court rulings in these suits are often based on the premise that the holders of majority shares do not have unlimited freedom to give away corporate property against the protest of the minority.[19]

[19]*Roger v. Hill*, 289 U.S. 582 (1933).

Case 44.6   Donahue v. Rodd Electrotype Co.
328 N.E.2d 505 (Mass. 1975)

Harry Rodd and Joseph Donahue purchased 80 percent and 20 percent respectively of the outstanding shares of Rodd Electric, a close corporation. Rodd gradually gave most of his stock as gifts to his children, including his sons, Charles and Frederick. Charles succeeded Rodd as president, and Frederick replaced Donahue as plant superintendant. Rodd continued to serve on the board until he retired in 1970. At that time, Rodd gifted more stock to his children, and he also sold two shares to each of them at the book value of $800 per share. Rodd then offered to sell 45 shares to the corporation at $800 per share. The two remaining directors (Rodd's attorney and his son, Charles) voted to acquire the Rodd shares as treasury stock, even though the corporation's best offer to Donahue, shortly before the Rodd purchase, had only been $200 per share. The directors also elected Frederick to succeed his father on the board.

When Donahue and his wife learned of the stock purchase, they offered their shares to the corporation at the price paid to Rodd—$800 per share. The corporation declined, claiming that it was not financially able to do so.

Donahue died, but his widow and son (plaintiffs) sued the corporation, its directors, and Harry Rodd (defendants). Plaintiffs characterized the corporation's purchase of Rodd's shares as an unlawful distribution of corporate assets to controlling shareholders and a breach of their fiduciary duty to minority shareholders. Their complaint asked the court to rescind the corporate purchase of Rodd's shares and to compel Rodd to repay the purchase monies, with interest, to the corporation. Defendants argued (1) that the stock purchase was within the corporation's powers and met the test of good faith and inherent fairness required of fiduciaries; and (2) that a shareholder has no right to equal opportunity when a corporation purchases treasury stock. The appellate court upheld the trial court's judgment for defendants. Plaintiffs appealed to the state Supreme Court.

TAURO, Chief Justice. . . . In previous opinions, we have alluded to the distinctive nature of the close corporation, but have never defined precisely what is meant. We deem a close corporation to be typified by: (1) a small number of stockholders; (2) no ready market for the corporate stock; and (3) substantial majority stockholder participation in the management, direction and operations of the corporation.

As thus defined, the close corporation bears striking resemblance to a partnership. The stockholders "clothe" their partnership "with the benefits peculiar to a corporation, limited liability, perpetuity and the like." In essence, though, the enterprise remains one in which ownership and management are in the same hands. Just as in a partnership, the relationship among the stockholders must be one of trust, confidence and absolute loyalty if the enterprise is to succeed. . . .

Although the corporate form provides advantages for the stockholders, the minority is vulnerable to a variety of oppressive devices, termed "freeze-outs," which the majority may employ. In particular, the power of the board of directors, controlled by the majority, to declare or withhold dividends and to deny the minority employment is easily converted to a device to disadvantage minority stockholders.

The minority can, of course, initiate suit against the majority and their directors. However, in practice, the plaintiff will find difficulty in challenging policies considered to be within the judgment of the directors "unless a plain abuse of discretion is made to appear." Thus, minority stockholders, cut off from all corporation-related revenues, must either suffer their losses or seek a buyer for their shares.

At this point, the true plight of the minority stockholder in a close corporation becomes manifest. In a large public corporation, the oppressed or dissident minority stockholder could sell his stock to extricate some of his invested capital [but] in a close corporation, the minority stockholders may be trapped in a disadvantageous situation. No outsider would knowingly assume the position of the disadvantaged minority. To cut losses, the minority stockholder may be compelled to deal with the majority. This is the capstone of "freeze-out" schemes designed to compel the minority to relinquish stock at inadequate prices.

Because of the inherent danger to minority interests, we hold that stockholders in the close corporation owe one another substantially the same fiduciary duty in the operation of the enterprise that partners owe to one another—the "utmost good faith and loyalty." Stockholders in close corporations may not act out of avarice, expediency or self-interest in derogation of their duty of loyalty to the other stockholders and to the corporation. . . .

In cases involving close corporations, *we have held stockholders participating in management to a standard of fiduciary duty more exacting than the traditional good faith and inherent fairness standard because of the trust and confidence reposed in them by the other stockholders.* . . . In these cases, we have imposed a duty of loyalty more exacting than that duty owed by a director to his corporation. [Emphasis added.]

Under settled Massachusetts law, a domestic corporation, unless forbidden by statute, has the power to purchase its own shares [but] "the purchase must be made in good faith and without prejudice to creditors and stockholders."

When the corporation is a close corporation, the purchase is subject to the additional requirement, in the light of our holding in this opinion, that if the stockholder whose shares were purchased was a member of the controlling group, the controlling stockholders must cause the corporation to offer each stockholder an equal opportunity to sell a ratable number of his shares to the corporation at an identical price.

Purchase by the corporation confers substantial benefits on the members of the controlling group whose shares were purchased: (1) provision of a market for shares; (2) access to corporate assets for personal use. The rule of equal opportunity in stock purchases by close corporations provides equal access to these benefits for all stockholders. We hold that, in any case in which the controlling stockholders have exercised their power over the corporation to deny the minority such equal opportunity, the minority shall be entitled to appropriate relief.

[The case was remanded to the trial court with instructions to enter judgment requiring: (1) Harry Rodd to repurchase his shares to the corporation for the original purchase price, plus interest, or (2) the corporation to purchase 45 shares from plaintiffs at the price paid to Rodd.]

The Corporate Opportunity Doctrine The corporate opportunity doctrine prohibits directors and officers from seizing business opportunities which belong to the corporation. Although case law does not clearly define the elements of a corporate opportunity, an opportunity is generally held to belong to the corporation if:

1 A director or officer becomes aware of the opportunity in his or her corporate capacity, or

2 The corporation customarily deals in such an opportunity, or

3 It is developed with corporate capital, facilities, or personnel.

A clear example of the courts' application of the corporate opportunity doctrine is found in the leading case of *Guth v. Loft, Inc.*[20] Guth was president of Loft, a corporation that manufactured soft drinks and syrups, and distributed Coca-Cola. While Guth was president, he learned that the formula for Pepsi-Cola was for sale and secretly formed a rival corporation to produce and market Pepsi-Cola. Guth overextended his personal credit to acquire controlling shares. To ease the financial strain, he used Loft's credit, as well as its plant, equipment, and employees, to produce Pepsi for the new corporation which was soon worth millions. Loft claimed that Guth had improperly seized a corporate opportunity for himself and brought a successful suit to impress a "constructive trust" on Guth's Pepsi-Cola stock in favor of Loft. In effect, the court interpreted Guth's operation as a "trust" and ordered him as trustee to turn the Pepsi stock over to Loft:

"The rule, referred to as the rule of corporate opportunity, is merely one of the manifestations of the general rule that demands of an officer or director the utmost good faith in his relation to the corporation which he represents. . . . If an officer or director of a corporation, in violation of his duty as such, acquires gain or advantage for himself, the law charges the interest so acquired with a [constructive] trust for the

---

[20]*Guth v. Loft, Inc.*, 5 A.2d 503 (Del. 1939).

benefit of the corporation, at its election, while it denies to the betrayer all benefit and profit. The rule does not rest upon the narrow ground of injury or damage to the corporation resulting from a betrayal of confidence, but upon a broader foundation of a wise public policy that, for the purpose of removing all temptation, extinguishes all possibility of profit flowing from the breach of the confidence imposed by the fiduciary relation. . . . Guth took without limit or stint from a helpless corporation. Cunning and craft supplanted sincerity. Frankness gave way to concealment. He did not offer the Pepsi-Cola opportunity to Loft, but captured it for himself. He thrust upon Loft the hazard, while he reaped the benefit. His time was paid for by Loft. A genius in his line he may be, but the law makes no distinction between the wrongdoing genius and the one less endowed."

A corporate opportunity is not usually held to exist if:

1 The directors' best efforts cannot obtain financing for the project, or

2 Involvement by the corporation would be ultra vires, or

3 The director or officer involved discloses his or her interest and a *disinterested* majority of directors votes against the proposal.

Such opportunities are then open to exploitation by any director, officer, or employee.

Insider Trading in Corporation's Shares
Directors, officers, employees, and controlling shareholders ("insiders") have access to information which may not be known to other shareholders or the general public ("outsiders"). The waning majority view is that, *in the absence of fraud*, insiders may profit from share transactions with outsiders and owe them no duty to disclose inside information affecting the value of the shares. Nevertheless, if the outsiders prove to the court that facts which were *material* to the stock transaction were *intentionally conceal-*

ed by the insiders, they will be held liable for the *common law tort of fraud and deceit*. The minority view holds that insiders have a fiduciary duty to disclose such information. The party injured by nondisclosure can usually recover the "extra" profit realized by the insider—the difference between the price paid for shares and their value if the undisclosed facts had been known.

Liabilities of Directors and Officers

Directors and officers who abuse the corporate powers entrusted to them are generally liable to the corporation for breach of the duty of obedience, due diligence, or loyalty. In addition, state or federal statutes impose civil or criminal liability on officers or directors for willful nonpayment of taxes, denial of shareholders' inspection rights, and violation of antitrust laws and other such offenses. Many states impose personal liability on directors or officers who contract on behalf of the corporation before its initial shares are issued, and impose criminal liability on those responsible for an illegal stock issue. Directors and officers have also been increasingly exposed to civil and criminal liability under federal securities regulations discussed in the next chapter.

Liability for Ultra Vires Acts The corporation may hold directors, officers, and other agents liable for damages resulting from their ultra vires acts. Liability may be avoided in some cases if the directors or managerial agents act in good faith or upon the advice of counsel, or if the shareholders ratify the ultra vires transaction.

Special Liabilities of Directors Directors are liable to the corporation for negligence. "Dummy" directors who fail to attend meetings, to keep informed on corporate affairs, or to review financial statements or legal opinions prepared by the corporation's accountants or attorneys, are liable for any injury which such omissions cause the corporation. A growing number of state and federal statutes impose civil sanctions on directors who cause the corporation to issue shares for overvalued or unlawful consideration, or unlawfully to declare dividends (48*a*), reacquire shares (48*b*), distribute assets in disregard of creditors' rights (48*c*), or unlawfully lend corporate funds to a director, officer, or employee (47).

Special Liabilities of Officers   A corporate officer who contracts in excess of his or her authority is personally liable to third parties for breach of implied warranty of authority. An officer who fails to disclose the corporate principal as a party to the contract may also be held personally liable by the third party. This liability can easily be avoided if the officer signs the contract so as fully to disclose his or her agency authority (for example: "ABC, INC., by Gloria Bruce, Vice President"). An officer may also incur personal liability by signing a corporate contract as a guarantor.

The Model Act (136) imposes criminal liability on officers (as well as directors) for failure to file required reports, or for filing false reports with the secretary of state or other regulatory authority. As discussed in Chapter 46, a corporation engaged in business beyond the borders of the state of incorporation must comply with the laws in the other state (e.g., obtain required licenses or qualify to do business as a foreign corporation.) If the officers fail to do so, they are personally liable for state license fees, taxes, and penalties imposed by the "host" states.

Indemnification of Directors, Officers, and Agents   The prevailing business judgment rule holds that directors are not liable for errors in judgment if they act in good faith, without negligence, and in the best interests of the corporation. The Model Act (35) specifically protects directors who act in reliance on data, opinions, reports, or financial statements which a knowledgeable officer, employee, lawyer, public accountant, or board committee represents to be correct.

A corporation can indemnify directors, officers, employees, or other agents against personal liability in any proceeding resulting from any act or decision made, in good faith and without negligence, on behalf, or at the request of the corporation (5). In the alternative, the corporation may purchase insurance that provides such indemnification. Protection is usually unavailable or is subject to the court's discretion in cases involving directors who knowingly violate a state or federal statute.

SUMMARY

A corporation's legal capacity is circumscribed by:

1   *Express powers* contained in state statutes or specified in the articles of incorporation, and

2   Those *implied powers* which courts interpret as reasonably required to carry out express powers.

Statutes or articles may also restrict a corporation's powers. For example, a statute may deny limited liability to professional corporations, or the articles may prohibit the corporation from owning real estate.

The corporation, its officers, or its directors may be held liable for acts beyond the corporate powers (ultra vires). The corporation may also be held liable for acts within its legal powers (intra vires) if the conduct infringes on the legal rights of private persons (torts) or the general public (crimes). Under the doctrine of respondeat superior, the corporation is liable for torts which an agent commits while engaged in corporate business. Similarly, vicarious liability may be imposed on the corporation for crimes committed by "high managerial agents" in the course of authorized corporate business. Corporate liability does not diminish the personal liability of the tort-feasor or criminal.

The shareholders exercise indirect control over corporate policies by electing or removing directors. Directors are elected for designated terms but may be removed with or without cause by a majority of the shares voted at a meeting called for that purpose. The shareholders may also amend articles to modify corporate purposes, or to alter the number, par value, rights, or classes of authorized shares; and changes in the bylaws are generally subject to the shareholders' approval. Other extraordinary transactions which require shareholder approval include merger, consolidation, sale, or lease of substantially all corporate assets *not* in the ordinary course of business, and voluntary dissolutions.

Shareholders exercise their powers by voting in annual or special meetings. Shareholders may offer resolutions and may argue and vote for or against resolutions offered by management. Proper notice of shareholders' meetings may be waived in writing or by actual attendance. Actions are usually effected by majority vote of the shares represented at any meeting in which a quorum (one-third of outstanding voting shares) is present. Shareholders may act without a meeting by unanimous written consent.

A shareholder is entitled to one vote for each voting share held as of a fixed "record date" preceding a shareholders' meeting. Most statutes give minority shareholders greater influence by permitting their votes (shares owned × directors to be elected) to be cumulated for a single candidate. Agency law permits shares to be voted by proxy. The trend is to uphold shareholders' agreements which create irrevocable proxies or voting trusts, whether or not such proxies are "coupled with a property interest." Statutory recognition of preemptive rights (a shareholder's right to preserve proportionate stock interests and voting rights by buying shares of a new issue) may be limited or denied in the articles.

In addition to voting rights, shareholders have a right to:

• Inspect corporate books and records,
• Institute individual suits and class actions

for the purpose of enforcing rights under a share contract, and

• Initiate derivative suits in the corporation's name to enforce its rights against third parties (if directors fail or refuse to do so).

Under certain circumstances, a shareholder may be held liable for unlawful dividends or distributions and for the "true value" of shares acquired in exchange for overvalued property. Minority shareholders may sue majority shareholders for breach of their fiduciary duty of due diligence and fair dealing. Controlling shareholder(s) of close corporations may also be liable for dividends suppressed "in bad faith" or for the sale of controlling shares in situations involving fraud or wrongful purpose.

Corporate affairs and policies are controlled by a board of directors, which derives its power from the articles and state statutes. The number of directors fixed in the articles cannot be less than the statutory minimum. The board of directors may act by formal resolution adopted by a majority of the directors voting at a regular or special meeting at which a quorum is present or by unanimous written consent without a meeting. The board may also establish an executive committee, but its authority may not extend to initiating extraordinary transactions.

The directors elect officers, who carry out broad policies and assume the duties and authority prescribed in the bylaws and board resolutions. Directors and corporate agents (officers, employees, and others) owe the corporation a duty of obedience, due diligence, and loyalty. The *fiduciary duty* of loyalty includes an obligation to exercise honesty and independent judgment. A director may contract with his corporation if the contract is fair and reasonable, or if the conflict of interest is known to the *disinterested* directors or to the shareholders and either body approves the transaction without counting the vote or consent of the *interested* director(s). Under the *corporate opportunity doctrine*, fiduciaries cannot seize business opportunities which belong to (and have not been rejected by) the corporation. An insider's fiduciary duty does not extend to stock purchases or sales involving outsiders, if there is no fraud.

STUDY AND DISCUSSION QUESTIONS

1 Distinguish between: *(a)* a corporation's express and implied powers and *(b)* the limitations placed on corporate powers by state statutes and by the articles of incorporation.

2 *(a)* What is the meaning of the term ultra vires? *(b)* Why have most states abolished the ultra vires defense? *(c)* In what three ways can the ultra vires concept be used in direct suits?

3 *(a)* How are corporations affected by the doctrine of respondeat superior? *(b)* How can a corporation which is sued on a tort claim avoid exemplary or punitive damages? *(c)* How does the early common law view of corporate criminality differ from the modern view?

4 How do the shareholders exercise their managerial power?

5 Why must the shareholders approve amendments to the articles of incorporation?

6 What is the end result of a merger, short merger, consolidation, share exchange, and sale or lease of substantially all of a corporation's assets?

7 How does the statutory procedure for amending articles and effecting acquisitions protect the shareholders' power to exercise control over such transactions?

8 *(a)* Under what circumstances do dissenting shareholders have appraisal rights? *(b)* Why are such rights important?

9 Distinguish between voluntary and involuntary dissolutions and give one example of each.

10 Statutory provisions covering annual shareholders' meetings generally: *(a)* require a time for such meetings to be fixed—in what instru-

ment? *(b)* permit shareholders to compel such meetings—how and under what circumstances? *(c)* permit special meetings to be called—by whom?

11 Under what circumstances is a shareholder deemed to have waived notice of a meeting?

12 At shareholders' meetings, what is the minimum statutory requirement: *(a)* for a quorum? *(b)* for an affirmative vote of shareholders?

13 Describe an alternative procedure by which most statutes permit shareholders to act without a meeting.

14 *(a)* How are the voting rights of shareholders determined? *(b)* What is the effect of a "record date?"

15 *(a)* How does cumulative voting benefit minority stockholders? *(b)* What special provisions can the incorporators include in the articles to diminish the effects of cumulative voting?

16 *(a)* What is a proxy? *(b)* What is the difference between an irrevocable proxy and a voting trust?

17 Describe one or more situations in which a shareholder can be held personally liable to the corporation or its creditors.

18 *(a)* What limitations are there on the authority of an individual director? *(b)* How do statutory requirements affecting the size of the board of directors reflect the growing importance of close corporations? *(c)* How can the board of directors alter the composition of an existing board? *(d)* What limits are there on the powers of an executive committee appointed by the board? *(e)* Give examples of powers that vest exclusively in the board of directors.

19 *(a)* What is the usual statutory requirement for a quorum of the board? *(b)* How does the minimum statutory requirement for approving a resolution at a board meeting differ from the usual requirement for adopting a resolution by written consent of the directors?

20 Is it necessary to give directors notice of *(a)*

regular meetings? *(b)* special meetings? Give exceptions.

21 *(a)* Describe the source(s) of express and implied authority of officers. *(b)* Under what circumstances is the corporation estopped from denying an officer's authority?

22 What are the three special "duties" which directors and officers owe to the corporation?

23 *(a)* May insiders profit from share transactions with outsiders without disclosing inside corporate information affecting the value of the shares? *(b)* In your answer, explain how the common law tort of fraud and deceit applies in such transactions.

24 Under what circumstances may directors and officers avoid personal liability for ultra vires acts?

25 Discuss some of the situations which can expose directors and officers to personal liability.

26 How does the business judgment rule serve to protect those who act on behalf of the corporation?

CASE PROBLEMS

1 Pillsbury had no interest in the affairs of Honeywell, Inc., until he learned that Honeywell was manufacturing bombs for the Vietnam war. Pillsbury was opposed to the war and bought one share of Honeywell stock in order to make his views known to management and the stockholders. Pillsbury immediately demanded shareholders' lists and all corporate records dealing with weapons and munitions production. When Honeywell refused, Pillsbury sued for a writ of mandamus. Should the court compel Honeywell to make the records available to Pillsbury for inspection?

2 The bylaws of American Insurance, Inc., provided for a board of eight directors and a quorum of at least five directors. A contract with

Management Corp. was reviewed and approved by unanimous vote of six directors present at a meeting of American's board. Three of the directors who voted were also on the board of Management; two of the three were the president and secretary, respectively, of both corporations. Upon further review, American found the contract to be against its best interests and served notice of termination on Management. Management sued American for breach of contract and $180,000 in damages. American claimed that the contract was voidable because it had not been authorized by a quorum of disinterested directors. Is Management entitled to recover from American?

3 Ed Ash and his wife, Fay, owned 74 percent of Lumber Corporation's stock. The corporation borrowed $240,000 in exchange for demand notes payable to Ed, who was board chairman and president of the corporation. Ed was very wealthy and never required substantial payments on the notes, but when Fay filed for divorce, Ed stated: "I'll run the corporation into the ground as long as Fay has an interest in it." That year, Ed enforced payment of $140,000 on the notes. He then used his influence to cause the corporation (which was left with a deficit of $120,000) to file a notice of election to dissolve. Fay filed a shareholder's derivative suit against Ed for breach of his fiduciary duty to the corporation and its shareholders. Is Fay entitled to judgment on behalf of the corporation?

4 Glen's employment as president of Law Books, Inc., was "at will" and not for a stated term. In April, he agreed to become president of a competitor on June 1st. In May, Glen obtained confidential salary data on selected editors and other key personnel of Law Books, Inc., and in some cases personally assisted in their recruitment by the competitor. Glen quieted the fears of Law Books' directors by telling them that there was "no danger of a raid." Glen and 12 recruits resigned on May 30th and started working for Law Books' competitor the next day. Law Books sued Glen for breach of his fiduciary duty. Glen contended that his employment was "at will" and that, therefore, he did nothing wrong. Is Glen's contention correct?

5 Calvin and his sister, Thelma, were directors and controlling shareholders of Baseball Club, Inc., a close corporation. In 1961, the board voted to double Calvin and Thelma's salaries as president and vice president, which were increased to $75,000 and $50,000, respectively. The salaries of three employees who were related to them were also increased substantially. Gripe, a minority stockholder, challenged the increases as void for self-dealing and filed a derivative suit which sought an injunction to restrain the corporation from paying the increased amount. Gripe did not present evidence showing the salary increases to be unreasonable. Should the court grant the injunction?

6 Abel and Brooks were directors, and president and vice president, respectively, of Quarry, Inc., a limestone mining business. The two men owned 100 percent of Quarry's outstanding shares, which they agreed to sell and transfer to Construction, Inc., as of October 20th. On October 10th, Brooks, on his own behalf, leased land which reports from Quarry's files showed to be suitable for a limestone quarry. Brooks did not tell Abel or Construction, Inc., about the lease. Construction acquired Quarry as a wholly owned subsidiary and elected new directors to serve on Quarry's board. The new board learned of Brooks's actions and authorized Quarry to file suit to compel Brooks to transfer the lease to the corporation. Should the court compel Brooks to transfer the lease to Quarry?

7 Kritzer located a possible site for Radiant Coils, Inc. (RC), of which he was president and

a director, and used company funds to purchase the land in his own name. He later resold the land and repaid RC, but kept the $140,000 profit which he made on the transaction. When a competitor offered to sell its plant and equipment to RC, Kritzer declined in RC's behalf even though RC could have financed the transaction. Kritzer then formed a one-man corporation (BK) which bought the plant and equipment and leased them to RC. The monthly rental permitted BK to recover the purchase price from RC in the first 6 years of the lease term. RC shareholders brought a derivative suit against Kritzer for breach of his fiduciary duty to RC. The court was asked to order Kritzer to transfer the land profits and BK stock to RC. Should the court make the order?

8 Arn and Ball organized Supply, Inc., and served as its directors and officers. Arn was the sole stockholder and personally guaranteed a $20,000 loan made to the corporation. No capital was invested by Ball, who did locate a suitable building, worth $70,000, which could be purchased for $30,000 at a mortgage foreclosure sale. The corporation did not have the required cash or credit so Arn bought the building for its benefit. He obtained financing and "temporarily" took title in his own name. Ball knew that the corporation was making the monthly loan payment of $500 and entering it in the books as "rent." The payments were shown as income on Arn's tax return. He also took the depreciation and listed the building as a personal asset on his financial statements. After 2 years, the corporation went into receivership. The receiver sued Arn, alleging his building purchase to be a breach of his fiduciary duty to the corporation. Should the court order Arn to deed the property to the corporation subject to the existing mortgage?

Chapter

45

Securities Regulation

Business growth and development depend primarily on a free flow of funds from the investing public. Regulatory measures, such as state and federal disclosure requirements, discourage fraudulent practices and engender public confi-

dence in the securities that are issued and sold. The first part of this chapter presents an overview of state and federal securities regulation. The rest of the chapter deals with federal requirements for registering new issues and trading in existing securities. Liabilities that federal securities laws impose on violators are also discussed.

OVERVIEW OF STATE AND FEDERAL SECURITIES REGULATION

Nature and Scope of State Securities Regulation

The constitutional power to regulate interstate commerce rests with the federal government. It could, therefore, assume exclusive control of securities transactions that occur in or affect interstate commerce. Nevertheless, the federally enacted Securities Act of 1933 expressly preserves state jurisdiction to regulate security issues, including those affecting interstate commerce. The result is that a corporation's issue of securities may be subject to registration with *both* state and federal agencies.

Blue-Sky Laws and Anti-takeover Statutes Each state has enacted statues designed to protect the public from speculative stock promotion schemes that have no more basis than "so many feet of 'blue sky.'" These statutes are collectively referred to as "blue-sky laws."[1] Although they differ in detail, most blue-sky laws contain provisions that (1) require the corporate issuer to register proposed securities with a designated state agency; (2) require brokers (and others who deal in securities) to register or obtain a license; (3) prohibit fraud in the sale of securities; and (4) impose severe penalties for submitting false or misleading registration data.

In addition, about half of the states have enacted statutes designed to discourage corporate raids, that is, attempts by "outsiders" to wrest control of a lucrative incorporated business from the existing stockholders. These "anti-takeover" statutes throw numerous stumbling blocks in the path of outsiders who at-

tempt to take over domestic corporations (or foreign corporations with substantial in-state assets). For example, the takeover group may be required to make a full disclosure of its plan at a hearing or in a formal filing with the state, or a waiting period may be imposed.

Disparities in State Securities Regulation The securities laws enacted by the various state legislatures lack uniformity. Some states, such as Delaware and Connecticut, have opted for minimal blue-sky regulation. Others, such as New York and California, tend to maximize the regulatory authority of the state. The differences in state securities laws place an undue burden on corporations attempting to qualify a securities issue for multistate sale. Disparities in state enforcement also create problems. For example, it is often difficult (if not impossible) to extradite violators who flee across state lines.

Disparities between State and Federal Securities Regulation A securities issue may be subject to differing state and federal statutes, a factor that further complicates the task of qualifying securities for simultaneous sale in different states. Nevertheless, concurrent state-federal regulation has the advantage of distributing the regulatory burden. State law can, and frequently does, regulate securities and transactions that are exempted from federal regulation.

Nature and Scope of Federal Securities Regulation

Federal securities laws, Securities and Exchange Commission rules, and interpretive court decisions have evolved into a highly specialized field known as "federal corporation law." The purpose of this chapter is to acquaint the reader with some of the more important concepts involved in this complex area of law. The material presented here can only provide a limited understanding of the obligations and liabilities that federal securities regulation imposes on the corporation, its directors and officers, and others who participate in the registration, issuance, or sale of securities. In order to

---

[1] *Hall v. Geiger-Jones Co.*, 242 U.S. 539 (1917).

avoid liability for negligence or for violation of federal securities laws, directors who make decisions involving regulated securities should be guided by ethical accountants and lawyers who are knowledgeable in the field.

General Purposes of the 1933 and 1934 Acts
The basic framework of the federal securities law is contained in the Securities Act of 1933 and the Securities Exchange Act of 1934. The purpose of the 1933 act is to regulate the *issuance* of new securities by corporations. The purpose of the 1934 act is to regulate *trading*, that is, the sale or purchase of existing securities among investors. The 1934 act controls credit in securities markets by means of "margin rules" established by the Federal Reserve System's board of governors. Both acts contain registration and antifraud provisions that require disclosure of securities information to investors. Registration provides investors with material information pertaining to securities offered to the general public. Antifraud provisions are designed to discourage fraudulent practices in the sale of securities, whether or not they are registered.

Administration of Federal Securities Statutes: The SEC   The 1934 act created the Securities and Exchange Commission (SEC) to administer the 1933 and 1934 acts. The SEC's broad rule-making power now includes administration of a number of other federal securities statutes.[2] In 1977 Congress also put the SEC in charge of investigating violations of the Foreign Corrupt Practices Act. The act, discussed later in this chapter, prohibits corporations from paying bribes to obtain business from foreign governments, and mandates internal accounting controls designed to prevent violations by directors and officers. In 1979 the SEC established rules

requiring outside auditors to verify that proper internal safeguards against corrupt practices had been established. New statutes and amendments and a growing body of federal court decisions have quickened the pace of changes in SEC rules.

Scope of Registration Requirements under the 1933 Act   The Securities Act of 1933 requires issuers of nonexempt securities to publish data that enable the investing public to judge the financial soundness of the issuing corporation and the quality of the proposed securities. The data, in narrative and tabular form, are provided to investors in a *prospectus*, the first part of a comprehensive *registration statement* that the issuer must file with the SEC. The content of the prospectus and of the registration statement as a whole may differ, but both must accurately present all material facts needed to make an informed decision.

Scope of Registration-Reporting Requirements under the 1934 Act   The Securities Exchange Act of 1934 requires securities traded on any national securities exchange to be registered with the exchange and with the SEC. Most unlisted shares (as opposed to bonds) traded in interstate commerce must also be registered with the SEC. These securities are usually traded over-the-counter. Less information is required to register traded securities under the 1934 act than to register initial issues under the 1933 act. However, Section 15(d) of the 1934 act requires issuers of registered securities to file periodic reports with the SEC. Section 12 also requires periodic reports to be filed by corporations with 500 shareholders and assets exceeding $1 million, even if the corporation's securities are not registered under the 1933 act.

Annual report form 10-K calls for facts about the corporation's current management, outstanding securities, and business operations, including a certified financial statement for the preceding fiscal year. Quarterly report form

---

[2]The following federal statutes applying to securities of particular industries are not discussed: Public Utility Holding Company Act of 1935, Trust Indenture Act of 1939, Investment Company Act of 1940, Investment Advisors Act of 1940, and Securities Investor Protection Act of 1970.

10-Q requires audited operating statements and a statement of condition, which may be in summarized form. Form 8-K is an early-warning report that, under revised 1977 rules, must be filed within 15 days of "any materially important events," such as changes in corporate control or auditors, and accounting write-ups or write-downs (upward or downward revaluation of an asset due to a change in its market value).

The 1934 act also requires securities exchanges, national securities associations, and brokers and dealers to register with the SEC. Brokers and dealers may be exempted if, for example, their business is exclusively intrastate and they do not use any facility of a national exchange.

Civil and Criminal Liabilities under Federal Securities Laws The 1933 and 1934 acts impose civil and criminal liability on directors, officers, and others, including lawyers and accountants, who promote fraud or participate in deceptive or manipulative practices in connection with a purchase or sale of securities. There are no exemptions from the numerous antifraud provisions in the acts.

A person who violates federal securities laws, as well as an *aider-abettor* (one who knowingly participates in or benefits from a securities violation), is subject to *civil liability*. The SEC may commence a civil suit against violators to recover money damages on behalf of injured parties, may ask the court to enjoin violations, or may seek both money damages and injunctive relief.[3]

If an injunction is ignored, the violator may also be punished for contempt of court. Injured parties can also file suits to recover damages from persons who willfully misrepresent or fail to disclose any fact that is material to the sale of a security. The most common example of such nondisclosure is the omission from a registration statement or periodic report of some material fact. Where the acts do not provide a statutory cause of action that is appropriate to a given situation, the federal courts have created implied rights to facilitate the filing of damage suits by injured parties.

A person who willfully violates any federal statute administered by the SEC is also subject to *criminal liability*. Uniform criminal penalties were imposed by the Securities Acts Amendments of 1975. A maximum penalty of $10,000 and 5 years in prison may be imposed on any person who (1) willfully violates a federal securities statute or SEC rules and regulations or (2) willfully falsifies or omits any material fact that is necessary to accurately present data required in a registration statement, application, report, or other required document filed with the SEC. However, a securities exchange that commits any of these violations may be fined up to $500,000.

---

[3]*SEC v. Texas Gulf Sulphur*, Case 45.5, p. 995.

Case 45.1   United States v. Weiner [Equity Funding Case]
578 F.2d 757 (9th Cir. 1978)

Equity Funding Corporation of America (Equity) sold "equity funding" programs to participants who purchased mutual funds and pledged them as security for loans, using the proceeds to buy life insurance from Equity. The operation was legitimate until 1964. At that time, one of the most colossal frauds in modern times began. The Equity scandal involved more than 20 of the corporation's officers, directors, and accountants, who conspired closely over a period of years to create more than $62,000,000 of nonexistent corporate assets. Their machinations included midnight typing parties where fictitious insurance policies were prepared from names selected at random from telephone directories and reflected as assets of Equity's life-insurance subsidiary. A variety of other phony documents was also fabricated to back up falsified financial statements which were used to inflate the market value of Equity's stock. Nineteen persons—mostly employees—pleaded guilty to criminal fraud charges under the 1933 Act.

This case involved three independent public auditors: J. S. Weiner, who performed audits for Equity, starting in the early 1960s; M. A. Lichtig, who supervised the field work and reported directly to Weiner; and S. Block, who replaced Lichtig when he became chief accounting officer for Equity in 1968. The indictment charged that the defendants (1) falsely certified that Equity's financial statements fairly presented the company's condition in conformity with generally accepted accounting principles (GAAP) and (2) willfully made false and misleading statements of material facts about specific accounts in financial statements filed with the SEC as part of a securities registration. The trial judge instructed the jury that three elements were required to warrant a conviction: First, "that the defendant in the specific document named in the count made a false statement of material fact, or omitted a material fact required to make the statements therein not misleading." Second, "that the document named in each count had been filed with the [government agencies] named in the count." Third, "that the defendant under consideration acted willfully and knowingly." The jury convicted the auditors on various counts of criminal fraud related to the manipulation of stock prices. Defendants appealed.

The appellate court found that the first two elements required for conviction were self-evident, but further explored whether ". . . there is sufficient evidence from which the jury could find that defendants willfully and knowingly produced the documents containing erroneous information." Various Equity Funding officials testified to the falsity of unsupported entries which appeared in financial statements and to the personal involvement of the defendants. For example, the evidence showed that an account called "Funded Loans and Accounts Receivable" (FLAR) was used as an umbrella for various falsified entries. There was evidence that Lichtig was present at a meeting where a company employee was directed to prepare a reconciliation for a $10,000,000 "plug" in the FLAR account. When Block was conducting an audit, he questioned some accounting procedures. Equity's controller then offered Block a trip to Rome in exchange for his cooperation. Thereafter, Block was told to handle the $10,000,000 gap in the funded loans asset himself. No further questions were raised by Block, although a check of the schedules supplied would have revealed the falsity of the claimed assets. Block also asked company officials for a job with Equity Funding, thus bringing his independence sharply into question.

The appellate court's opinion noted that, in 1969, Equity acquired Investors Planning Corporation (Investors) for $10,000,000. The financial statement reflected the value of the acquisition at about $27,800,000. This overvaluation was accomplished by an improper write-up of Investor's future ("trail") commissions, which were uncertain because customers could withdraw from making payments on Investors' plans at any time. Nevertheless, a total of $17,874,290 was booked in Clients Contractual Receivables and added to the FLAR balance. The write-up was fraudulently substantiated by (1) a letter to the auditors from Stanley Goldblum, Equity's president, advising that a sale of the trail commissions was in progress and that he would personally guarantee the sale and (2) the routing of Equity's own funds through two of its subsidiary "shell" corporations to show a $2,000,000 down payment on the fictitious sale from a nonexistent outside purchaser.

When the fraud was uncovered in 1973, Touche Ross & Co. was appointed to audit Equity's financial statements in accordance with GAAP as well as generally accepted auditing standards (GAAS). The total final adjustment of the FLAR account alone was a deduction of $62,305,353 to eliminate the items related to false or improper entries. A partner in Touche Ross & Co. testified that the accounting treatment of Investors' trail commissions (accruing the commissions in the year of purchase as well as recording the excess value) was contrary to GAAP. The Court's decision is of major importance to accountants.

. . . CHOY, GOODWIN, AND THOMPSON, JJ. . . . Since backup [for entries in financial statements] often was not even fabricated, the jury could infer that the auditors either completely failed to audit the areas in disregard of GAAS or consciously failed to audit in "cooperation" with Equity Funding officials, thus purposely avoiding the false entries. If the questionable areas had been audited and no backup found, the failure of the auditors to reflect that fact in their report would have clearly contravened GAAS and the purpose of an independent audit. . . .

. . . Even if [the independent public accountants] did not initially know or indeed learn the step-by-step fictitious entries and improper manipulations, their consistent failure to apply GAAS and GAAP after they knew some kind of major fraud was afoot provided a basis from which the jury could reasonably infer defendants' knowing and willful participation in the fraud.

We have not previously ruled on the propriety of instructions which state that compliance or noncompliance with GAAS or GAAP is relevant to the determination of a defendant's intent. In *United States v. Simon*, 425 F.2d 796 (1969), proof of compliance with GAAS was deemed "evidence which may be very persuasive but not necessarily conclusive that [defendant] acted in good faith." [Citations]

The prosecution introduced into evidence the Statement on Auditing Standards (1973) issued by the Committee on Auditing Procedure, American Institute of Certified Public Accountants. The Statement explains [that]:

"The responsibility of the independent auditor for failure to detect fraud arises only when such failure clearly results from failure to comply with generally accepted auditing standards.''

In our case, failure to apply generally accepted auditing standards is relevant to the issue of knowledge and willfullness. . . . The judge's instruction, which stated that evidence regarding compliance with GAAS and GAAP was not conclusive, but was relevant, was a proper statement. The weight to be given the evidence was for the jury's determination.

Defendants also assert that the court erred in instructing the jury on the issue of knowledge. The jury was instructed that proof of negligence was insufficient to support a conviction, and that proof of good faith constituted a complete defense to the charges. The court went on to instruct the jury that, in determining intent, the jury could consider whether defendants acted in "reckless, deliberate . . . disregard for truth or falsity," and could infer from proof of such acts that defendants acted willfully and knowingly.

The instruction was given before our decision in *United States v. Jewell*, 552 F.2d 697 (1976), where we held:

> ". . . To act 'knowingly' is not necessarily to act only with positive knowledge, but also to act with an awareness of the high probability of the existence of the fact in question. When such awareness is present, 'positive' knowledge is not required."

. . . The jury instruction was proper. Affirmed.

[In 1975, the *Report of the Special Committee on Equity Funding*, prepared at the request of the American Institute of CPAs, concluded that customary auditing procedures, properly applied, would have led to the detection of the fraud and that major changes in GAAS and GAAP were unnecessary.]

THE 1933 ACT: REGISTRATION OF NEW SECURITIES ISSUES; EXEMPTIONS; LIABILITIES

The Securities Act of 1933 was enacted to ensure that truthful securities information is provided to investors before they buy. Specifically, the act seeks to prevent the exploitation of unsophisticated investors. Financially sophisticated investors (persons who can evaluate the economic risks of investment and can afford to take such risks) do not need the same degree of protection. The extent to which investors may, or may not, need protection affects the manner in which the SEC and the courts interpret the registration provisions of the act as well as exemptions from those provisions.

Registration of Securities under the 1933 Act

Section 5 of the 1933 act broadly provides that if a security does not qualify for one of the exemptions discussed below, the security must be *registered* before it is offered or sold through the use of the mails or any facility of interstate commerce, including securities exchanges. Generally, the issuing corporation must file a registration statement with the SEC and provide investors with a prospectus. The registration statement and the prospectus must supply sufficient information to enable unsophisticated investors to evaluate the financial risk involved in buying a given security. However, it is important to note that registration does not ensure that an issue of securities is meritorious or that the purchaser will not suffer a loss on his or her investment.

Content of the Registration Statement   The registration statement must set forth all facts that are material to a proposed sale of securities, including (1) the plan for distributing the securities, the proposed use of the proceeds by the issuer, and a description of the rights and limitations placed on the securities being offered; (2) the names and remuneration of directors and principal officers, names of persons who control the company and who own 10 percent or more of the company's securities, and details about material transactions between any such persons and the company; (3) information about pending legal proceedings; and (4) detailed financial statements certified by an independent public accountant, accompanied by his or her signed consent authorizing their use in the registration statement. Similar information in summary form is reflected in the prospectus, which also includes a balance sheet and statement of income and expense.[4] Over the years, the SEC has so expanded the list of information required in a registration prospectus that the prospectus has been criticized as too complex for the ordinary investor to use as an analytic tool.

Activities Permitted Before, During, and After Registration   *Before* filing the registration statement and prospectus with the SEC, a corporation can contract with an underwriter to handle the distribution of a proposed issue. The underwriter's commission ("spread") and the offering price of the securities are usually fixed in an amendment to the registration statement just prior to the expiration of the 20-day waiting period required for the registration to become effective.

During the waiting period, the issuing corporation and interested investors may exchange *oral* offers to buy and sell the proposed securities. However, written advertising ("free writing") is generally limited to a sketchy, preliminary "red herring" prospectus, so-called because it bears a red legend stating that a registration statement has been filed but has not become effective.

After the effective date, the securities covered in the registration statement can legally be offered and sold to investors. In the typical situation, delivery of the securities must be accompanied (or preceded) by delivery of a prospectus. During the period of distribution, free writings are usually limited to the publication of "tombstone ads" that are presented in a format resembling a tombstone. The advertisement is a limited notice of the securities offering that tells prospective investors where and how to obtain a prospectus. Under the 1933 act, other advertising, whether by newspaper, radio, television, speech, letter, or brochure, is generally prohibited. The statutory policy behind the restriction is to prevent the investing public from being influenced by slanted publicity initiated by the issuer and to encourage investment decisions based on the data in the formal prospectus.

Definitions That Determine Whether Registration Is Required

The broad statutory language used to define terms related to the issuance and sale of securities, coupled with liberal SEC and court interpretations, has extended the protective umbrella of registration to cover a great variety of situations involving unwary investors. Interpretations of terms, such as "security," "distribution," "issuer," or "underwriter," discussed below, can include or exclude thousands of investors from the coverage of the acts.

Meaning of a Security   The 1933 act [2(1)][5] defines a security as:

. . . any note, stock, treasury stock, bond,

---

[4]With few exceptions, valuations of assets must be based upon historical cost (SEC Regulation S-X). Financial accounting Standards Board, Statement no. 33 (1979), in addition requires valuation of assets using general price level methods as well as current value methods.

[5]The section numbers of the 1933 and 1934 acts are given in brackets in this chapter.

debenture, evidence of indebtedness, certificate of interest or participation in any profit-sharing agreement, . . . preorganization certificate or subscription, transferable share, investment contract, . . . fractional undivided interest in oil, gas, or other mineral rights, or, in general, any interest or instrument commonly known as a "security," or any certificate of interest or participation in, . . . receipt for, . . . or right to subscribe to or purchase, any of the foregoing.

A substantial body of case law has broadly interpreted many of the terms that the 1933 act uses to define a security. The net effect has been to expand the statutory definition. For example, in the *Howey* case[6] the U.S. Supreme Court interpreted "investment contract" to include *any transaction whereby* (1) *a person invests in an ownership share of* (2) *a common enterprise* (3) *in which management is separate from the investor who expects to profit solely from the efforts of others.* Investments that meet the *Howey* test—even sales of citrus groves, bottled whiskey, cattle, condominiums, limited partnerships, and variable annuities coupled with contracts to manage such assets, as well as ordinary promissory notes—have been construed as "investment contracts" or "securities."

As such, they are subject to the registration and antifraud provisions of the Securities Acts.

Conversely, the courts have held that an investment that falls within the plain terms of the statutory definition but does not meet the threefold criteria of the *Howey* decision is not a security and is not covered by the act. For example, the courts have excluded notes that "simply formalize an open-account debt incurred in the ordinary course of business."[7] Such notes are commonly executed for consumer financing (secured by home mortgages, assignments of accounts receivable, and the like) or represent "character" loans to bank customers. Notes that bear a "strong family resemblance" to these cited examples do not meet the *Howey* test and therefore do not come under the protective umbrella of the acts.

Offer and Sale of Securities The 1933 act [2(3)] defines an *offer* of securities to include any attempt or offer to dispose of a security for value. Solicitations of an offer to buy securities are also included within the meaning of the term. A *sale* of securities includes every contract for the sale or disposition of a security for value. Any principal or agent who actively solicits an order, participates in negotiations, or arranges a sale of securities is subject to all applicable provisions of the acts, including prohibitions against fraudulent practices.

[6]*SEC v. W. J. Howey Co.*, 328 U.S. 293 (1946).

[7]*Exchange National Bank v. Touche Ross & Co.*, 544 F.2d 1126 (2d Cir. 1976).

Case 45.2   Rubin v. United States
101 S. Ct. 698 (1981)

Defendant William Rubin was convicted of conspiring to violate the fraud provision in the 1933 Securities Act (§17-a). The Court of Appeals affirmed, and the Supreme Court granted certiorari.

Rubin, a former accountant, was president of Tri-State Energy, a mining company that sought a loan from Bankers Trust Company. Rubin prepared a false financial statement for submission to the bank. The balance sheet listed a $7.5 million account receivable and included a copy of a contract that purportedly formed the basis of this account. No such item existed, and the signature on the contract had been forged. To secure the loan, Tri-State pledged worthless stock in six companies which Rubin represented was worth $1.7 million. He arranged for fictitious quotations to appear in a service reporting over-the-counter transactions used by the bank in evaluating pledged securities. Tri-State also planted a fictitious advertisement in an overseas newspaper and showed it to the bank, representing it to be a price quotation on some of the pledged securities. Bankers Trust loaned $475,000, taking the securities as pledged collateral. Rubin later paid $5,000 to two bank officials as inducements to make further loans.

Rubin appealed from conviction of violating the 1933 Act. Rubin claimed that the pledge of stock to the bank was not an "offer or sale" as defined in the statute.

BURGER, Chief Justice. Petitioner [Rubin] does not deny that he engaged in a conspiracy to commit fraud through false representations to Bankers Trust concerning the stock pledged; he does not deny that the shares were "securities" under the Act. Rather, he contends narrowly that these pledges did not constitute "offers" or "sales" under 17(a) of the Act. To sustain this contention, petitioner argues that Tri-State deposited the stocks with the bank only as collateral security for a loan, not as a transfer or sale. From this he argues that the implied power to dispose of the stocks could ripen into title and thereby constitute a "sale" only by effecting foreclosure of the various pledges, an event that could not occur without a default on the loans.

The terms "offer" and "sale" in §17(a) are defined in §2(3) of the Act:

The term "sale" or "sell" shall include every contract of sale or *disposition* of a security or *interest* in a security, for value. The term . . . "offer" shall include every attempt or *offer to dispose of,* or solicitation of an offer to buy, a security or *interest* in a security, for value." [Emphasis added.]

Obtaining a loan secured by a pledge of shares of stock unmistakably involves a "disposition of . . . and interest in a security, for value." Although pledges transfer less than absolute title, the interest thus transferred nonetheless is an "interest in a security." . . . Bankers Trust parted with substantial consideration—specifically, a total of $475,000—and obtained the inchoate but valuable interest under the pledges and concomitant powers. It is not essential under the terms of the Act that full title pass to a transferee for the transaction to be an "offer" or a "sale." . . . The Uniform Sale of Securities Act, a model "blue sky" statute, adopted in many states, defined "sale" in language almost identical to that now appearing in §2(3). In *Cecil B. De Mille Productions, Inc. v. Woolery,* 61 F.2d 45 (CA9 1932), the Court of Appeals construed this provision of the model statute as adopted by California and held that the definition of "sale" embraced a pledge. Congress subsequently enacted the definition from the uniform Act almost verbatim.

Treating pledges as included among "offers" and "sales" comports with the purpose of the Act and specifically, with that of §17(a). We frequently have observed that these provisions were enacted to protect against fraud and promote the free flow of information in the public dissemination of securities. The economic considerations and realities present when a lender parts with value and accepts securities as collateral security for a loan are similar in important respects to the risk an investor undertakes when purchasing shares. Both are relying on the value of the securities themselves, and both must be able to depend on the representations made by the transferor of the securities, regardless of whether the transferor passes full title or only a conditional and defeasible interest to secure repayment of a loan. . . . We therefore hold that pledges here were "offers" or "sales" under §17(a); accordingly, the judgment of the Court of Appeals is Affirmed.

Case 45.3   **Goodman v. Epstein**
582 F.2d 388 (7th Cir. 1978)

In June, 1972, a partnership was formed to develop residential units on 100 acres in Westmont, Illinois. Goodman and other investors were limited partners. Epstein and other developers were general partners. The limited partnership agreement provided that limited partners had no right to participate in the management of the enterprise and no power to subject the partnership to any liability or obligation. The limited partners were obligated to make periodic contributions of capital as the project progressed, at the general partners' request. The general partners failed to agree on site plans or to obtain environmental agency permits. Although the general partners abandoned the project in March, 1973, they asked the limited partners to make a capital contribution of $500,000 in April. No mention was made of the abandonment of the project or of the use to which the capital would be put. A final capital call was made in June.

The limited partners (plaintiffs) sued to recover $1,061,500 from the general partners (defendants). The action was based on common law fraud under state law, and on antifraud provisions of the 1934 Act and SEC Rule 10b-5, which require a full disclosure of facts material to the sale of a security. The trial judge instructed the jury that *if* they found a limited partnership interest to be a security, it was purchased *when* plaintiffs signed the agreement that committed them to acquire the interest. Plaintiffs claimed that the jury was improperly instructed on applicable law and appealed from a verdict for defendants.

JUNAIG, J. . . . The basic test enunciated by the Supreme Court for determining the existence of a security involves three elements: (1) an investment in a common venture (2) premised on a reasonable expectation of profits (3) to be derived from the entrepreneurial or managerial efforts of others.

United Housing Foundation, Inc. v. Forman, 421 U.S. 837 (1975). . . . A limited partner's interest in a limited partnership is an "investment contract" or "security," even though it does not have the normal trappings of what a lay person may think of as a security. . . . The evidence adduced at trial reveals no debatable question of the plaintiffs' interests meeting all three of the *Howey/Forman* tests.

In light of the weighty authority for considering a limited partnership interest to be a "security" within the protective scope of the federal securities laws, the trial judge should have given plaintiffs' requested instruction that plaintiffs' interests were securities. The item which constitutes grounds for reversal is the trial Court's instruction . . . which was read to the jury as follows:

> "If you find that a limited partnership interest obtained by a plaintiff constituted a security, the purchase occurred when such a plaintiff was committed . . . by agreement to acquire such interest; even if such plaintiff was to perform his obligations under the agreement after a lapse of time, *each subsequent capital contribution . . . does not constitute a purchase of a security.*" [Emphasis added]

We agree with plaintiffs that this instruction amounted to an incorrect peremptory direction to the jury that only the Agreement itself could be considered the purchase of a security and that such direction clearly eliminated any chance of the plaintiffs' obtaining a favorable verdict. . . . What we have here is *not* a one-shot deal. The seller-defendants were required to perform certain management functions which were the primary determinants of the value of the securities sold. Any "meeting-of-the-minds" which occurred when the Agreement was signed clearly involved a series of payments, and, potentially, a whole series of "investment decisions" which could be made based on the progress, or lack of progress, in development.

We find that, when an investment decision remained to be made at the time of a call for a capital contribution, the contributions by each Limited Partner in response to the call constituted a separate "purchase" of a security and, therefore, *any material representations or omissions at that time were "in connection with the purchase or sale" of a security.* [Emphasis added]

[The case was reversed and remanded for a new trial.]

Public Offerings (Distributions); Issuers, Underwriters, and Dealers A *public offering* is a "distribution" of securities to the general public. Any such distribution or public offering is presumed to be made to a substantial number of unsophisticated investors. For that reason *the 1933 act requires distributions to be registered.*

Distributions of securities are generally made in two ways: the corporation that issues the securities ("issuer") may sell them directly to others, or the corporation may enlist the services of an investment banking firm ("underwriter"). The underwriter usually sells securities *for* the issuing corporation on a "best efforts" basis, without incurring liability for unsold shares. An underwriter may also make a "firm commitment" to purchase securities *from* an issuer in order to resell them to the investing public. In either event, an underwriter always receives the securities from the issuer *with a view to distribution and participates in the risks and profits of distribution*. In fact, there can be no "underwriting" unless there is a distribution. Since a distribution of securities must be registered, it follows that *securities sold by an underwriter must be registered under the 1933 act*. A *dealer*, who buys securities for resale and distribution, is not an underwriter *unless* the buy-sell price spread exceeds the customary commission payable to brokers who sell for the account of others.

The *issuer* is usually a corporation, but the 1933 act [2] defines the term so as to include "every person who issues or proposes to issue any security." This broad definition encompasses unincorporated businesses as well as corporations. As explained later in this chapter, an issuer can make *exempt private offerings of unregistered securities* as well as *public offerings of registered securities*. To prevent the *resale* of unregistered securities to the public, the term "issuer" has also been interpreted to include controlling persons, that is, owners of more than 10 percent of the issuer's stock who have the power directly or indirectly to control the management policies of the issuer. As a result, securities that are purchased as part of an exempt private offering are subject to registration if the controlling person resells ("reissues") the securities to the public (a substantial number of unsophisticated investors). Furthermore, anyone who buys the controlling person's unregistered shares with a view to distribution is included in the definition of an underwriter and, therefore, the securities cannot be resold unless they are registered. Suppose that Bill purchases controlling shares ($1 million) of unregistered stock issued by ABC, Inc. under the private-offering exemption, with the intent of reselling $500,000 to his cousin Cathy, knowing

full well that she plans to resell the stock in $10,000 lots to fifty of her friends at the country club. Bill is an "issuer," because he is a controlling person who is reselling ("reissuing") to the public through Cathy. She, perhaps unwittingly, becomes an "underwriter," because she is purchasing a controlling person's unregistered shares "with a view to distribution." Her shares are subject to the act's prohibition against *distributions* of unregistered shares.

Exempted Securities

The 1933 act provides a number of exemptions from registration, but the exemptions extend *only* to registration and prospectus requirements. *There are no exemptions from the antifraud provisions of the Securities Acts*. Exemptions from registration fall into two classes: exempted *securities* and exempted *transactions*. An issuer who plans to claim an exemption should seek the advice of attorneys and accountants who specialize in security regulation. Liability for an improperly claimed exemption can usually be avoided by obtaining an SEC ruling ("no action" letter) prior to the issuance of the securities. Representative examples of securities exemptions available under Section 3 of the 1933 act are discussed below. These exemptions are granted for a variety of reasons: the instrument being sold (such as commercial paper) is not functionally a security and should not be burdened with a registration requirement, the security involves such a small segment of the public that exposure to risk is minimal, or another agency already regulates the security issue so that the public is protected.

Short-term Commercial Paper Under Section 3(a)(3), notes, drafts, bills of exchange, bankers' acceptances, and other types of commercial paper are exempted, provided they (1) arise out of current business transactions or the proceeds are used for current transactions (such as the purchase of a plant or machinery) and (2) have a maturity of not more than 9 months. The exemption does not apply if the commercial paper is advertised for sale to the public. Courts have held that a note must bear a "strong family resemblance" to the type discounted by banks to qualify as exempt short-term commercial paper.

Small Public Offerings: SEC Regulation A   Regulation A exempts securities that are part of a small public offering not exceeding $1.5 million ($300,000 if the offering is on behalf of a holder other than the issuing company). However, the issuer must make a "notification" filing with the SEC (which is somewhat simpler than regular registration) and must furnish investors with an "offering circular" disclosing relevant information. Although the availability of the Regulation A exemption is limited, small public offerings have definite advantages: the required financial statements are simpler; the SEC can process the forms more quickly; and, consequently, legal and accounting costs are somewhat lower.

Securities Offered and Sold by Closely Held Corporations   Under SEC Rule 240 certain limited offers and sales by closely held corporate issuers are exempt from registration. Broadly stated, this exemption is available if (1) the aggregate sales proceeds of the securities issue do not exceed $100,000 in the 12-month period preceding sale; (2) no advertising or commissions are involved; (3) all the stock of the issuer is owned by no more than 100 persons; (4) the securities contain a "restricted securities" legend; and (5) the SEC is notifed within 10 days after each issue.

Intrastate Issues   The intrastate exemption applies to securities that are part of an issue that is offered and sold exclusively to residents of the issuer's state of incorporation. There is no fixed limit on the number of offerees or the size of the offering. However, SEC Rule 147 requires that at least 80 percent of the issuer's gross revenues must come from operations within the state. To preserve the exemption, the securities must also "rest" in the hands of resident purchasers for at least 9 months before an out-of-state offer or resale is made. The issuer is solely responsible for determining the residence of each purchaser and will be held liable for an illegal issue if any shares are sold outside the state during distribution. If a purchaser is a nonresident, the issuer's good faith or reliance on the purchaser's statements as to his or her residence is not a defense to the illegality of the issue. Rule 147 is so restrictive that the exemption is seldom used.

Government Issues and Issues Regulated by Agencies Other Than the SEC   Securities issued by the United States government, by any state, or by any other political subdivision are exempted from the registration requirements of the 1933 act. Securities of issuers that are subject to regulatory supervision by any specialized state or federal agency other than the SEC are also exempted. Common examples are securities of state or federally chartered banks and savings institutions, issues of farmers' cooperatives, and insurance and endowment policies. Similarly exempted are securities of common carriers, which are subject to regulation by the Interstate Commerce Commission.

Issues of Nonprofit Organizations   The constitutional separation of church and state is a factor in the exemption of securities issued by religious organizations. However, the nonprofit status of such groups is the chief policy reason for the exemption. Securities covered by the nonprofit exemption also include issues of associations or corporations organized for educational, social, recreational, or charitable purposes.

The nonprofit exemption has been abused with increasing frequency in recent years. For example, fraudulent promoters have attempted to finance hospital construction by selling mortgage bonds that are represented to be a deductible "charitable" investment with a high rate of return. To curtail such practices, the SEC and the courts have taken the position that a charitable exemption will be lost if there is a single "substantial noncharitable purpose." The SEC and the courts are not restricted to the purposes declared in the issuer's articles and examine each case in light of all the surrounding facts.[8]

Exchanges between the Issuer and Its Existing Security Holders Securities exchanged exclusively by the issuer and its existing security holders are exempted if no commission is paid for soliciting the exchange.

Exempted Transactions

In general, exempt *securities* retain their exempt status when they are resold. Securities exchanged between an issuer and its security holders are a notable exception in that resales come under the rules applicable to exempted transactions. The exemption of a *transaction* under Section 4 of the 1933 act does not necessarily exempt a subsequent transaction involving the same securities. In *Thompson Ross Securities Co.*,[9] controlling shareholders acquired exempt securities in an exchange and then sought to make a *distribution* of the unregistered securities. The shareholders claimed that the securities had acquired a permanent exemption. The SEC rejected this view because the sale was fraught with all the dangers attendant upon a new offering of securities to the public.

Private Offerings (Transactions by Issuer Not Involving Any Public Offering) If an issuer does not contemplate that any part of a securities issue will be distributed to the public, the transaction may qualify as a *private offering*. The issuer's offering is "private" because it is limited to a *small number of sophisticated investors*. Private offerings are exempt from registration because the possibility of injury to the public is remote. However, the SEC and the courts have made it clear that even sophisticated investors cannot "fend for themselves" unless they have *access* to the same kind of

information that registration would provide. If the information is not furnished to the investor, his or her relation to the issuing company must afford effective access to such information. For example, an offering to company executives who have both sophistication and access would be exempt but an offering to all employees who, as a class, are members of the investing public would not be exempt, even if the issuer provides them with all of the required information.[10]

Requirements for an exempt private offering of restricted securities: SEC Rule 146 The indefinite nature of terms such as "access" and "fend for themselves" led to SEC Rule 146, which was designed to provide more objective criteria for the private-offering exemption. Broadly stated, the rule outlines the manner in which the securities are offered, the nature of the offerees, the number of purchases, and the kind of information to which they are entitled. As amended in 1978, this rule limits the number of purchasers to thirty-five, permits little or no advertising or promotional activity, and requires offerees (or their representatives) to have access to the same data that registration would provide, as well as the ability to evaluate such data.

Purchasers must *take for investment and not for immediate resale*. Unregistered securities sold under the private-offering exemption are called "restricted securities" because their *resale* is restricted. In fact, an offering is neither private nor exempt unless the issuing company notifies the purchaser in writing that he or she must bear the economic risk of investment for an indefinite period of time. The purchaser must sign an "investment letter" stating that the purchase is for investment and agreeing that the securities will not be resold without registration or further exemption under the act. The certificate representing such shares must bear a legend warning that resale of the securities is

---

[8]*SEC v. Children's Hospital*, 214 F. Supp. 883 (1963).
[9]6 SEC 111 (1940).

[10]*SEC v. Ralston Purina Co.*, 346 U.S. 119 (1953).

restricted. The SEC requires the issuer to file a report of private-offering transactions.

Requirements for resales of restricted securities: SEC Rule 144   The private-offering exemption is lost if any purchaser takes "with a view to distribution," that is, with a view to reselling the securities to a number of unsophisticated investors. An issuer who attempts to use a purchaser as a conduit (underwriter) to distribute unregistered securities is subject to civil and criminal liability. Conversely, a legitimate purchase of restricted securities for *investment* does not expose the issuer to liability for an illegal sale of unregistered securities.

Now, let us consider the plight of the individual who attempts to sell securities acquired in a private offering. As discussed earlier, the SEC and the courts will treat a purchaser who is a control person as an issuer and will treat a person who buys from a control person for distribution as an underwriter. The end result is that their securities must be registered before a lawful resale can occur. However, *only the issuing corporation* can take advantage of the private-offering exemption or can register securities. What if the issuing corporation cannot subsequently be persuaded to register its restricted securities? Are the purchasers of an exempt private offering condemned to hold the securities forever?

Until recently, a purchaser of restricted securities was barred from selling them in the public marketplace. However, SEC Rule 144, adopted in 1972, permits *limited* resales of restricted securities. A resale of securities in strict compliance with the requirements of this regulation is *not* deemed to be a distribution. Thus, the seller is not faced with the problem of causing the securities to be registered. Rule 144 does make certain distinctions among control persons, noncontrol persons, and affiliates of the issuer (usually a parent or subsidiary), but all of them are permitted to sell limited amounts of restricted securities in ordinary trading transactions. The investing public is protected by a

requirement that adequate information about the issuer be available, such as a recent form 10-K report filed with the SEC. The sellers cannot solicit buyers, and the securities must be sold through a broker.

As previously discussed, purchasers of an exempt private offering must assume the economic risk of the investment. Rule 144 interprets this requirement to mean that purchasers of restricted securities must hold them for at least 2 years prior to resale. To avoid a disruption of trading markets due to resales of restricted securities, Rule 144 strictly limits the number of shares that can be sold in each quarter. The SEC must be notified when an order to sell restricted securities is placed with a broker. Because of these requirements, SEC Rule 144 is popularly called the "2 year and dribble" rule.

There are a number of regulations that cover resales in specific situations. For example, SEC Rule 237 covers resales by noncontrol persons who hold restricted securities of a domestic corporation for 5 years or more.

Other Exempted Transactions   The complex private-offering exemption just discussed was drafted to meet the needs of larger corporations. In 1980, the SEC's newly established Office of Small Business Policy announced Rule 242 that permits certain issuers to offer and sell up to $2 million in securities in a single offering. Offerings made to "accredited investors" (institutional investors, the issuer's officers and directors, employee benefit plan investors, and persons purchasing at least $100,000 of securities, as well as up to thirty-five "non-accredited" purchasers) need not be accompanied by any mandated written disclosures. The Rule is available only to corporations and excludes partnerships, investment companies, and companies in oil or mining activities. Rule 242 has been widely acclaimed for removing barriers to small firms seeking to raise additional new capital.

There are three other types of exempted transactions that deserve mention here.

Transactions involving sales of promissory notes secured by first liens on real property This exemption is limited to sales (totaling $250,000 or more) of first trust-deed notes originated by state or federally regulated lending institutions. Banks and savings institutions often raise cash for new investments by selling exempted interests in existing loan portfolios.

Transactions by individual investor (person other than issuer-underwriter-dealer) This exemption applies only to the trading transactions of individual investors with respect to securities already issued. The exemption is designed to facilitate routine trading activities on securities exchanges.

Transactions by brokers and dealers The exempt status of a transaction by an individual investor (discussed above) is not altered if the transaction is effected through a broker or through a dealer acting as a broker. It follows that the broker or dealer should be entitled to a similar exemption. With few exceptions, ordinary brokerage transactions and transactions in which a dealer is not acting as an underwriter are exempt. As a result, a dealer can usually buy and sell securities that have been registered or have been available on the market for a minimum period (normally 40 days) without first providing the purchaser with a prospectus.

Liabilities under the 1933 Act

There are two main sources of civil liability under the 1933 act: the registration provisions and the antifraud provisions.

The *registration provisions* of Section 11 cre-ate a statutory cause of action in favor of purchasers who rely on materially false or misleading data in a registration statement. A purchaser can recover losses, up to the full price paid for securities, from (1) the issuer; (2) every person who signs the registration statement; (3) every person who is a director when the statement is filed or who consents to be named therein as a person about to become a director; (4) every accountant, engineer, appraiser, or other expert who prepares or bears responsibility for a report or valuation and consents to its use in the registration statement; and (5) every underwriter. However, all participants, except the issuer, may benefit from the defense that they acted with "due diligence." As illustrated in the *BarChris* case, which appears below, the due diligence defense is available only to those who have *reasonable grounds* to believe that the filed registration statement did not omit or misrepresent any material facts.

The *antifraud provisions* of Section 17(a) impose civil liability on those who perpetrate or who aid and abet any fraud in connection with any offer and sale of securities. This catch-all provision prohibits sellers from using any device or scheme to defraud. Section 12 specifically prohibits false or misleading statements in a prospectus or other document, as well as oral misrepresentations, used to induce a sale of securities. Securities and transactions that are exempt from registration under the 1933 act remain subject to its antifraud provisions. Criminal liability may also be imposed for *willful* violations of any provision contained in the act.

Case 45.4   Escott v. BarChris Construction Corp.
283 F. Supp. 643 (S.D.N.Y. 1968)

BarChris was in the business of contracting to build and equip bowling alleys. The introduction of automatic pin-setting machines made bowling very popular, and BarChris's sales leaped from $800,000 in 1956 to $9,000,000 in 1960. BarChris had two financing plans. Customers could make a small cash down payment and agree to execute notes for the balance to BarChris upon completion of the job; BarChris would then discount the notes to a factor. In the alternative, BarChris would construct and equip the interior of a bowling alley (excluding the outer shell of the building) and sell it to the factor. The factor would then lease it to a customer or to BarChris's subsidiary, which could operate the facility or sublease it to a customer. In both situations, BarChris acted as a guarantor; in the event a customer defaulted, BarChris was liable to the factor for 100 percent of any unpaid balance on the customer's notes and leases.

BarChris had to expend substantial sums before receiving reimbursement. As operations expanded, the company experienced a growing need for cash. In 1959, BarChris sold additional common stock. By 1961, the company needed more working capital and decided to issue convertible debentures. The registration statement was filed with the SEC in March, 1961, and became effective May 16th. By the close of financing on May 24th, overexpansion in the industry was causing a number of bowling alley operators to fail. Some of BarChris's customers were in arrears on payments which BarChris had guaranteed to the factor. The company was unable to pay the interest due on its debentures and filed a bankruptcy petition.

Escott and 60 other debenture holders (plaintiffs) sued under Section 11 of the 1933 Act to recover damages from BarChris Construction Corporation and its directors, officers, attorneys, public auditors, and underwriters (defendants). Plaintiffs alleged that BarChris's registration statement had been misleading in that it contained false statements and omitted facts which were material to the sale of the debentures. Defendants had each signed the registration statement or a consent that his "expert" opinion be reflected in the statement.

The court found that the registration statement had overstated BarChris's current assets by $609,689. Contingent liabilities were understated by $375,795 as of December 31, 1960, and by $618,853 as of April 30, 1961. The prospectus also failed to disclose contingent guarantor liability to factors of $1,350,000. (BarChris's contingent liability as guarantor on sale-leaseback financing was incorrectly shown as 25 percent instead of 100 percent of total customer obligations to the factor.) First quarter 1961 gross profits were overstated by $350,755, and the backlog of unfilled orders was overstated by $4,490,000. The prospectus incorrectly reflected that loans from officers to the company of $386,615 had been repaid. In addition, the proceeds of the debenture sales were not used for the purposes stated in the prospectus. Instead, $1,067,736 was used to pay off debts, and $120,000 was lent to a friend of one of the officers.

The court concluded that the errors in the registration statement-prospectus were material from the standpoint of an average, prudent investor. The auditing firm Peat, Marwick, Mitchell & Co. was found to be the only "expert" (within the meaning of Section 11) that had contributed to the registration statement.

In order to successfully defend against liability, each defendant had to sustain the burden of proving "due diligence." The court's findings on this point, as presented in the excerpts quoted below are limited to the defendants named in each subhead.

MCLEAN, District J. . . . Section 11(b) of the Act provides that:

[No person, other than the issuer, shall be liable if that person can prove that he or she relied on the authority of an expert, or made a reasonable investigation and believed on reasonable grounds that the statements made in the registration statement were true and that there was no omission of a material fact required to make the statements therein not misleading.]

I turn now to the question of whether defendants have proved their due diligence defenses. The position of each defendant will be separately considered.

Russo Russo was the chief executive officer of BarChris. He was familiar with all aspects of the business. He was personally in charge of dealings with the factors. He talked with customers about their delinquencies.

Russo prepared the list of jobs which went into the backlog figure. It was Russo who arranged for the temporary increase in BarChris's cash in banks on December 31, 1960, a transaction which borders on the fraudulent. In short, Russo knew all the relevant facts. He could not have believed that there were no untrue statements or material omissions in the prospectus. Russo has no due diligence defenses.

Vitolo and Pugliese They were the founders of the business who stuck with it to the end. Vitolo was president and Pugliese was vice president. Vitolo and Pugliese are each men of limited education. It is not hard to believe that for them the prospectus was difficult reading, if indeed they read it at all.

But whether it was or not is irrelevant. The liability of a director who signs a registration statement does not depend upon whether or not he read it or, if he did, whether or not he understood what he was reading.

And in any case, Vitolo and Pugliese were not as naive as they claim to be. They were members of BarChris's executive committee. At meetings of that committee BarChris's affairs were discussed at length. They must have known what was going on. Certainly they knew of the inadequacy of cash in 1961. They knew of their own large advances to the company which remained unpaid. They knew that they had agreed not to deposit their checks until the financing proceeds were received. They knew and intended that part of the proceeds were to be used to pay their own loans.

The position of Vitolo and Pugliese is not significantly different from Russo's. They could not have believed that the registration statement was wholly true and that no material facts had been omitted. And in any case, there is nothing to show that they made any investigation of anything which they may not have known about or understood. They have not proved their due diligence defenses.

Kircher Kircher was treasurer of BarChris. He is a certified public accountant and an intelligent man. He was thoroughly familiar with BarChris's financial affairs. He knew the terms of BarChris's agreements with [the factor]. He knew of the customers' delinquency problem. He knew how the financing proceeds were to be applied and he saw to it that they were so applied. He arranged the officers' loans and he knew all the facts concerning them.

Kircher worked on the preparation of the registration statement. He conferred with Grant [BarChris's attorney] and on occasion with Ballard [the underwriter's attorney]. He read the prospectus and understood it. He knew what it said and what it did not say. Kircher's contention is that he had never before dealt with a registration statement, that he did not know what it should contain, and that he relied wholly on Grant, Ballard, and Peat, Marwick to guide him. . . . In effect, he says that if they did not know enough to ask the right questions and to give him the proper instructions, that is not his responsibility.

There is an issue of credibility here. In fact, Kircher was not frank in dealing with Grant and Ballard. He withheld information from them. But even if he had told them all the facts, this would not have constituted the due diligence contemplated by the statute. Knowing the facts, Kircher had reason to believe that the expertised portion of the prospectus, i.e., the 1960 figures, was in part incorrect. He could not shut his eyes to the facts and rely on Peat, Marwick for that portion.

As to the rest of the prospectus, knowing the facts, he did not have a reasonable ground to believe it to be true. On the contrary, he must have known that in part it was untrue. Kircher has not proved his due diligence defenses.

Auslander Auslander was an "outside" director, i.e., one who was not an officer of BarChris. He was chairman of the board of Valley Stream National Bank. In February 1961 Vitolo asked him to become a director of BarChris. As an inducement, Vitolo said that when BarChris received the proceeds of a forthcoming issue of securities, it would deposit $1,000,000 in Auslander's bank.

In considering Auslander's due diligence defenses, a distinction is to be drawn between the expertised and non-expertised portions of the prospectus. As to the former, Auslander knew that Peat, Marwick had audited the 1960 figures. He believed them to be correct because he had confidence in Peat, Marwick. He had no reasonable ground to believe otherwise.

As to the non-expertised portions, however, Auslander is in a different position. He seems to have been under the impression that Peat, Marwick was responsible for all the figures. This impression was not correct, as he would have realized if he had read the prospectus carefully. Auslander made no investigation of the accuracy of the prospectus. He relied on the assurance of Vitolo and Russo, and upon the information he had received in answer to his inquiries back in February and early March. These inquiries were general ones, in the nature of a credit check. The information which he received in answer to them was also general, without specific reference to the statements in the prospectus, which was not prepared until some time thereafter.

It is true that Auslander became a director on the eve of the financing. He had little opportunity to familiarize himself with the company's affairs. The question is whether, under such circumstances, Auslander did enough to establish his due diligence defense with respect to the non-expertised portions of the prospectus.

Section 11 imposes liability in the first instance upon a director, no matter how new he is. He is presumed to know his responsibility when he becomes a director. He can escape liability only by using that reasonable care to investigate the facts which a prudent man would employ in the management of his own property. In my opinion, a prudent man would not act in an important matter without any knowledge of the relevant facts, in sole reliance upon representations of persons who are comparative strangers and upon general information which does not purport to cover the particular case. To say that such minimal conduct measures up to the statutory standard would, to all intents and purposes, absolve new directors from responsibility merely because they are new. This is not a sensible construction of Section 11, when one bears in mind its fundamental purpose of requiring full and truthful disclosure for the protection of investors.

I find and conclude that Auslander has not established his due diligence defenses with respect to the misstatements and omissions in those portions of the prospectus other than the audited 1960 figures:

Peat, Marwick . . . Section 11(b) provides that:
[No person shall be liable with regard to any part of a registration statement made upon his or her authority as an expert, if that person can prove that he or she made a reasonable investigation and believed on reasonable grounds that the statements therein were true and that there was no omission of a material fact required to make the statements not misleading.]

This defines the due diligence defense for an expert. Peat, Marwick has plead it. Peat, Marwick's work was [mostly] performed by a senior accountant, Berardi. He was not yet a C.P.A. He had no previous experience with the bowling industry. This was his first job as a senior accountant. He could hardly have been given a more difficult assignment.

The purpose of reviewing events subsequent to the date of a certified balance sheet (referred to as an S-1 review) is to ascertain whether any material change has occurred in the company's financial position which should be disclosed in order to prevent the balance sheet figures from being misleading. The scope of such a review is limited. It does not amount to a complete audit.

Berardi made the S-1 review in May 1961. He devoted a little over two days to it. He did not discover any of the errors or omissions pertaining to the state of affairs in 1961, all of which were material. The question is whether, despite his failure to find out anything, his investigation was reasonable within the meaning of the statute.

What Berardi did was to look at a consolidated trial balance as of March 31, 1961 which had been prepared by BarChris, compare it with the audited

December 31, 1960 figures, and read certain minutes. He did not examine any "important financial records" other than the trial balance. He asked questions, he got answers which he considered satisfactory, and he did nothing to verify them.

Berardi did not discover that BarChris was holding up checks in substantial amounts because there was no money in the bank to cover them. He did not know of the . . . officers' loans. Since he never read the prospectus, he was not even aware that there had ever been any problem about loans from officers.

During the 1960 audit Berardi had obtained some information from factors as to delinquent notes. He made no inquiry of factors about this in his S-1 review. He was content with [the controller's] assurance that no liability theretofore contingent had become direct.

There had been a material change for the worse in BarChris's financial position. The change was sufficiently serious so that failure to disclose it made the 1960 figures misleading. Berardi did not discover it. As far as results were concerned, his S-1 review was useless.

Accountants should not be held to a standard higher than that recognized in their profession. I do not do so here. Berardi's review did not come up to that standard. He did not take some of the steps which Peat, Marwick's written program prescribed. He did not spend an adequate amount of time on a task of this magnitude. Most important of all, he was too easily satisfied with glib answers to his inquiries.

This is not to say that he should have made a complete audit. But there were enough danger signals in the materials which he did examine to require some further investigation. Generally accepted accounting standards required such further investigation under these circumstances. It is not always sufficient merely to ask questions.

Here again, the burden of proof is on Peat, Marwick. I find that that burden has not been satisfied. I conclude that Peat, Marwick has not established its due diligence defenses.

[Note: The court also found that BarChris's controller, in-house counsel, its lawyer-director, another "outside" director, a director-underwriter, and the underwriters consisting of eight investment banking firms led by Drexel & Co. had all failed to establish the due diligence defenses.]

THE 1934 ACT: FAIR DEALING AND TRADING IN EXISTING SECURITIES; LIABILITIES

The 1934 act establishes standards for fair dealing and trading in securities. The courts construe these provisions so as to maximize remedies available to investors. This part of the chapter focuses on two aspects of fair dealing: the trading activities of corporate insiders and proxy and tender-offer solicitations. Liabilities under the 1934 act are also discussed.

Insider Trading under the 1934 Act

Purchases or Sales by Insiders Who Have Material Inside Information The term "insiders" as used in SEC Rule 10b-5 has been interpreted to extend beyond directors, officers, and controlling shareholders and to include employees, attorneys, accountants, investment bankers, and others who have access to inside information. Under Section 10(b) of the 1934 act and SEC Rule 10b-5, it is unlawful for an insider who has *material inside information* to purchase or sell the company's securities, irrespective of whether the insider deals directly or through an exchange. In effect, the insider is required to refrain from dealing in the company's securities until the information is released and the investing public has had a reasonable time to react to it.

Information is *material* if it is reasonably likely to affect the market price of the corporation's shares. The question is "At what point does indefinite information about an energy-saving invention, contemplated merger, tender offer, or possible oil discovery become sufficiently material to require the insider to disclose the information or to abstain from trading in the corporation's shares?" Although the *Texas Gulf Sulphur* case below attempts to deal with this question, the courts are still working out the answer on a case-by-case basis.

A second question of equal importance is "Does the insider with material information owe a duty of disclosure to everyone in the market place?" In *Chiarella v. United States*,[11] the Supreme Court held that there can be no conviction for fraud under Section 10(b) unless there is a duty to speak, and that such a duty does not arise from the mere possession of nonpublic market information. Chiarella was an employee for an outside printing company that prepared confidential tender-offer material for lawyers retained by the offeror corporations. He decoded the information and used it to buy stock in five target corporations, which he later sold at a profit. The Court of Appeals upheld a jury's criminal conviction of Chiarella for violating Section 10(b) of the 1934 Act. In so doing,

the court extended liability to Chiarella as a remote purchaser, buying through an exchange, from unidentified shareholders of target corporations, from which no inside information had leaked. In reversing the decision of the Court of Appeals, the Supreme Court rejected the notion that the mere use of material information not generally available is fraudulent. The Court said that Chiarella's use of the information was not a fraud unless there was a duty to speak. Such a duty must arise from a *prior relation with the sellers*, which was not present inasmuch as Chiarella had no prior dealings with them. "He was not their agent, he was not a fiduciary, he was not a person in whom the sellers had placed their trust and confidence. He was, in fact, a complete stranger who dealt with the sellers only through impersonal market transactions." The *Chiarella* Court's added requirement of a duty to speak as an element of a Section 10(b) concealment violation makes it difficult to distinguish the statutory offense from the common law tort of fraud and deceit in connection with insider trading in corporate shares discussed at page 966.

Insiders often disclose "tips" to relatives, friends, and others ("tippees") who are also prohibited from trading in the corporation's shares.[12] In *Texas Gulf Sulphur*, an insider ("tipper") was held liable for profits realized by the tippees who purchased shares as a result of the tip. Tippees as well as insider-tippers who purchase shares without disclosing material inside information can be compelled to disgorge profits to the corporation and to persons from whom the securities were purchased.

Suppose Alfred, an insider-tipper tips Barbara (tippee) that the corporation's year-end statement will show unexpectedly high profits, and Barbara buys stock from Cox without disclosing the tip. If the tip proves to be erroneous and the stock drops in price, can Barbara sue to

---

[11]100 S. Ct. 1108 (1980).

[12]*Tarasi v. Pittsburg National Bank*, 555 F.2d 1152 (3d Cir. 1977).

recover damages from Alfred under Rule 10b-5? Some decisions have denied recovery, holding that the plaintiff is in pari delicto (equal fault) because she bought the shares from the seller without disclosing the tip. However, there is federal case law that supports the view that a tippee cannot be in equal fault because the tipper, as the source of the inside information, creates the possibility of tippee violations by making the initial disclosure. If a court follows this line of reasoning, Barbara would be permitted to recover.

Case 45.5   **S.E.C. v. Texas Gulf Sulphur Co.** [On remand]
446 F.2d 1301 (2d Cir. 1971)

The now famous Texas Gulf Sulphur (TGS) case was an action by the SEC against TGS and thirteen directors, officers, and employees for alleged violations of Section 10(b) of the 1934 Act and Rule 10b-5. In 1963 TGS drilled an exploratory hole near Timmins, Ontario, which produced a remarkably high copper content. TGS sealed the hole and, after acquiring the surrounding land, resumed drilling on March 31, 1964. On April 11th, New York papers reported rumors of a rich TGS strike. On April 13th, TGS management issued a press release designed to quell the rumors. The release stated that the rumors were without factual basis, that most of the areas drilled in eastern Canada were barren, and that:

> "The work done to date has not been sufficient to reach definite conclusions and any statement as to size and grade of ore would be premature and possibly misleading. When we have progressed to the point where reasonable and logical conclusions can be made, TGS will issue a definite statement to its stockholders and the public."

At the time of the core drill of November 12, 1963, TGS directors, officers, employees, and their "tippees," owned only 1,135 shares of TGS stock and no calls (the right to purchase additional shares at a fixed price). By March 31, 1964, when drilling resumed, insiders and tippees had acquired 12,300 calls and an additional 7,100 shares. On February 20, 1964, TGS issued stock options to three members of top management and to two other employees as part of their compensation. Between November 12, 1963 and May 15, 1964, the market price of TGS stock rose from $18 to $58 per share.

The SEC's complaint asked the court to (1) enjoin TGS and individual defendants from publishing deceptive and misleading information such as the April 12th press release and (2) compel rescission of the defendants' purchases and stock options. At the first trial, the court found that the April 12th press release was not "false, misleading or deceptive" and was not issued "in connection with the purchase or sale of any security." In the absence of a showing that the release was intended to manipulate the price of TGS stock to the advantage of TGS or its insiders, the court held that the issuance of the press release did not constitute a violation of Section 10(b) or Rule 10b-5. The complaint was dismissed as to all defendants except Clayton and Crawford.

On appeal, the circuit court interpreted the legislative purpose of Section 10(b) as follows:

> ". . . The intent of the Securities Exchange Act of 1934 is the protection of investors against fraud. Therefore, it would seem elementary that the Commission has a duty to police management so as to prevent corporate practices which are reasonably likely fraudulently to injure investors. . . . When materially misleading corporate statements or deceptive insider activities have been uncovered, the courts have broadly construed the statutory phrase 'in connection with the purchase or sale of any security.' "

The circuit court interpreted the essence of Rule 10b-5 as follows:

> "Anyone who, trading for his own account in the securities of a corporation has 'access, directly or indirectly, to information intended to be available only for a corporate purpose and not for personal benefit of anyone,' may not take 'advantage of such information knowing it is unavailable to those with whom he is dealing,' i.e., the investing public. Insiders, as directors or management officers, are, of course, by this Rule, precluded from so unfairly dealing, but the rule is also applicable to one possessing the information who may not be strictly termed an 'insider' within the meaning of Section 16(b) of the Act. . . . It is here no justification for insider activity that disclosure was forbidden by the legitimate objective of acquiring . . . land surrounding the exploration site; if the information was . . . material, its possessors should have kept out of the market until disclosure was accomplished."

The court held that all transactions in TGS stock or calls by individuals who knew of the drilling results were made in violation of 10b-5. Referring to Darke, a TGS geologist, the court noted that, although his tippees were not defendants, their conduct was equally reprehensible. The three members of top management who accepted their stock options without disclosing the ore discovery to the option committee were held to have violated the Rule. The appeals court also concluded that the April 12 press release was issued "in a manner reasonably calculated to affect the market price of TGS stock and to influence the investing public." The trial court's judgment against Clayton and Crawford was affirmed, and the trial court's dismissal of all other defendants (except one) was reversed. The case was remanded to the trial court to decide (1) whether the release was misleading to the reasonable investor and, if found to be misleading, whether the court should enjoin further deceptive statements and (2) what remedies should be invoked against individual defendants who profited from inside information in violation of Rule 10b-5.

Following the hearing on remand, the trial court (1) enjoined defendants Clayton and Crawford from future violations of 10b-5; (2) denied injunctions against TGS and other defendants, although each was found to have violated

10b-5; (3) required the stock option of Kline, the one member of top management who had not voluntarily returned his option to the corporation, to be cancelled; and (4) required defendants to disgorge profits on their stock to TGS and also required Darke to pay to TGS the profits realized by his tippees. Defendants appealed.

WATERMAN, Circuit J. . . . The district court required Holyk, Huntington, Clayton, and Darke to pay to TGS the profits they had derived (and, in Darke's case, also the profits which his tippees had derived) from their TGS stock between their respective purchase dates and April 17, 1964, when the ore strike was fully known to the public. The payments are to be held in escrow in an interest-bearing account for a period of five years, subject to disposition in such manner as the court might direct upon application by the SEC or other interested persons, or on the court's own motion. [The total escrow settlement fund amounted to $2,700,000. Former stockholders who sold shares between the time of the discovery and the public announcement, and who contended they would not have sold had they known of the discovery, were permitted to recover from this fund.] At the end of five years any money remaining undisposed of would become the property of TGS. . . .

Appellants, of course, contend that the required restitution is indeed a penalty assessment. This contention overlooks the realities of the situation. In our prior opinion we found that these appellants had violated the Act by their purchases of TGS stock before there had been a public disclosure of the ore discovery. Restitution of the profits on these transactions merely deprives the appellants of the gains of their wrongful conduct. Nor does restitution impose a hardship in this case. The court's order requires only restitution of the profits made by the violators prior to general knowledge of the ore strike on April 17, 1964, and, in effect, leaves the appellants all the profits accrued after that date. It would severely defeat the purposes of the Act if a violator of Rule 10b-5 were allowed to retain the profits from his violation. The district court's order corrects this by effectively moving the purchase dates of the violators' purchases up to April 17, 1964.

[The judgment was affirmed as to each appellant except as to the order cancelling Kline's stock option, which was reversed and remanded for a hearing on the appropriateness of that remedy.]

Short-Swing Transactions Section 16(b) of the 1934 act defines *short-swing transactions* as those in which a director, officer, or beneficial owner of more than 10 percent of any class of nonexempt securities buys and sells (or sells and buys) the company's securities within a 6-month period. Such transactions are prohibited. As described above, Section 16(b) covers only directors, officers, and stockholders, but their short-term trading activities are sometimes referred to as insider short-swing trading. It should be noted that Section 16(b) uses the term "insider" in a narrow sense, whereas Section 10(b) and Rule 10b-5 use the term in a broad sense to include all persons who possess material inside information.

Short-swing transactions present problems involving conflicts of interest. A Section 16 insider might have the power to take measures that might enhance the short-term value of his or her shares but which would be detrimental to the company in the long-term For example, a controlling stockholder-director could cause the corporation to pay dividends from profits that are needed for anticipated operating costs. Section 16 discourages unfair use of inside information by requiring insiders to report holdings and transactions in their company's securities to the SEC. The company, or any security holder acting on behalf of the company, can sue to require the insider to pay short-swing profits to the corporation. As a general rule, an insider cannot avoid liability simply because he or she acts in good faith, does not possess or use inside information, or does not intentionally violate the statute. However, these factors have been viewed as mitigating circumstance in some cases.[13]

---

[13]*Foremost-McKesson, Inc. v. Provident Securites Co.*, 423 U.S. 232 (1976).

Case 45.6   Tyco Laboratories, Inc. v. Cutler-Hammer, Inc.
490 F. Supp. 1 (S.D.N.Y. 1980)

Action by Tyco Laboratories, Inc. seeking a declaratory judgment that it was not liable for short-swing profits realized on the sale of Cutler-Hammer, Inc. (C-H) stock. Defendant C-H counterclaimed asserting that Tyco was liable for such profits under §16(b) of the 1934 Act. Tyco had been purchasing C-H common stock commencing in November, 1977. On April 7, 1978 Tyco purchased additional shares, bringing its total holdings to 12 percent of the total number of outstanding C-H shares, thus qualifying it as a beneficial owner of more than 10 percent of a registered security under §16(a) of the 1934 Act. A few days later, a rival purchaser, Koppers Company, Inc. acquired approximately 21 percent of the voting stock of C-H. Between April 10 and June 9, 1978, Tyco quickly purchased an additional 1,374,100 shares of C-H stock at a cost of $92,560,997. On June 12, 1978, Tyco sold its entire holdings of C-H common stock to Eaton Corporation for $55 per share.

Thereafter, C-H demanded that Tyco pay over its short-swing profits on the sale of the 1,374,100 shares of C-H stock purchased after April 7, 1978 in the sum of $7,900,410. Tyco admitted that this sum was correct, but claimed (1) that because its buying and selling transactions arose out of a contest for control of C-H, they fell within the "unorthodox transaction" exception to §16(b), and (2) that Congress did not intend to impose automatic liability upon 10 percent shareholders who make short-swing cash-for-stock profits unless they had "access to inside information," and that Tyco did not have or use any inside information in its transactions.

WARD, J. Section 16(b) of the Act was originally intended to apply in an automatic, almost mechanistic fashion, which came to be known as the "objective approach." As the Supreme Court stated:

"In order to achieve its goals, Congress chose a relatively arbitrary rule capable of easy administration. The objective standard of Section 16(b) imposes strict liability upon substantially all transactions occurring within the statutory time period, regardless of the intent of the insider or the existence of actual speculation. This approach maximized the ability of the rule to eradicate speculative abuses by reducing difficulties in proof. Such arbitrary and sweeping coverage was deemed necessary to insure the optimum prophylactic effect."

However, in response to a series of cases requiring the application of the statute to transactions which were not classic purchases and sales for cash, such as stock conversions, mergers, and stock options, the Supreme Court approved a narrow exception to the generally broad and arbitrary reach of section 16(b). The court held that when a transaction is "unorthodox" and not clearly within the reach of the statute, the opportunity for speculative abuse should be assessed before section 16(b) liability is imposed.

"In deciding whether borderline transactions are within the reach of the statute, the courts have come to inquire whether the transaction may serve as a vehicle for the evil which Congress sought to prevent—the realization of short-swing profits based upon access to inside information—thereby endeavoring to implement congressional objectives without extending the reach of the statute beyond its intended limits." *Kern County Land Co. v. Occidental Petroleum Corp.*, 411 U.S. 582 (1973).

This "subjective" or "pragmatic approach" was designed to mitigate the harshness of the application of section 16(b)'s strict liability standard to situations which, although arguably involving some equivalent of a section 16(b) purchase and sale, could not possibly allow for insider speculation and profiteering on non-public information.

Tyco contends that inasmuch as its purchases of C-H stock and the sale of that stock to Eaton occurred in the context of a "control contest type of situation," the sale was an "unorthodox" transaction within the *Kern County* exception to section 16(b) liability.

The Court finds Tyco's arguments without merit. Its assertion that section 16(b) when read in light of its legislative purpose and economic reality, establishes that Congress did not intend to impose automatic liability upon ten percent shareholders who make short-swing cash-for-stock trades and profits unless they had "access to inside information" is supported by neither the legislative history of section 16(b) nor the case law applying it. . . . Congress specifically envisioned a statutory scheme which imposes automatic liability on any and all ten percent shareholders who buy and sell an issuer's securities within a six-month period, irrespective of whether they had access to or misused inside information.

. . . Tyco's claim that the existence of a "control contest type of situation" renders the transaction at issue here "unorthodox" within the meaning of *Kern County* and warrants an inquiry into whether Tyco had access to inside information when it traded in C-H stock is without merit. [In *Kern County*] after considering the purpose of section 16(b) the Supreme Court stated:

> "Although traditional cash-for-stock transactions that result in a purchase and sale or a sale and purchase within the six-month, statutory period are clearly within the purview of §16(b), the courts have wrestled with the question of inclusion or exclusion of certain 'unorthodox' transactions."

. . . The Court defined "unorthodox" as including those "transactions not ordinarily deemed a sale or purchase" and listed the categories of transactions to which the term had been applied:

> stock conversions, exchanges pursuant to mergers and other corporate reorganizations, stock reclassifications, and dealings in options, rights, and warrants.

Nowhere in *Kern County*, however, did the Supreme Court state or suggest that a "control contest type of situation" makes a securities transaction "unorthodox." On the contrary, what the Supreme Court actually stated is that a "cash-for-stock" transaction is orthodox and results in automatic section 16(b) liability. . . .

In any event, . . . two factors must exist in order to remove even an "unorthodox" transaction from the ambit of section 16(b) liability: . . . (1) The unlikelihood of actual access to inside information in an atmosphere of hostility by a party adverse in interest; and (2) the utter inability of the unsuccessful party to control the course of events.

Tyco's complaint asserting that it lacked access to inside information, . . . satisfies part of the test. There are no facts alleged in Tyco's complaint however, which would indicate that its sale of C-H stock was "involuntary" or that it was "utterly unable to control the course of events." . . .

In conclusion, the Court finds that Tyco's extensive cash purchases of C-H stock after becoming a 10% stockholder and subsequent sale of their entire block of C-H stock within approximately two months subjects them to liability under section 16(b).

Accordingly, C-H's motion for judgment on the pleadings upon its counterclaim is granted.

Proxy and Tender-Offer Solicitations

Proxy Solicitations   A *proxy* is a written authorization by which a stockholder gives to another person the authority to vote the stockholder's shares. The term "proxy" is also used to refer to the person appointed in the written proxy.

Prior to the annual meeting of shareholders, companies customarily solicit proxies from their shareholders. These proxies authorize one or more directors to vote the stockholders' shares for reelection of the board and for approval of the corporation's auditors as well as a variety of other management proposals. SEC rules require that any solicitation by management, or by minority shareholders, must disclose all material facts pertaining to the matters on which the shareholders are being asked to vote. In addition, the shareholders must be given an opportunity to vote "yes" or "no" on each proposal. The SEC has effectively used its proxy rules to require submission of specified financial statements in the annual report to stockholders at the time their votes are solicited for the election of directors. All proxy material must be filed with the SEC in advance of circulation.

In recent years, reform-minded stockholders have attempted to stimulate corporate social responsibility by soliciting proxy support for a broad spectrum of controversial issues. In *Medical Committee for Human Rights v. SEC*, 432 F.2d 659 (D.C. Cir. 1970), the issue was whether the committee, as a shareholder, could require the Dow Chemical Company to include in the proxy material for the annual meeting a proposal that prohibited Dow from manufacturing napalm used in warfare. Under the 1934 act, Section 14(a), and SEC Rule 14a-8(c), management could omit from its proxy statement any proposal that clearly appeared to be "primarily for the purpose of promoting general economic, political, racial, religious, social, or similar causes." In upholding the committee's right to include the anti-napalm proposal in the proxy material, the court reasoned that the overriding purpose of Section 14(a) was to assure corporate shareholders of their right to control important decisions that affect them in their capacity as stockholders and owners of the corporation. As now revised, SEC Rule 14a-8 permits management to omit from proxy statements proposals that are contrary to state law in the issuer's domicile or that request action on general economic, political, racial, religious, or social causes *not related to the issuer's business* or not within the control of the issuer.

Tender Offers   Outside corporations or persons may solicit proxies from shareholders of a "target" corporation to gain approval of a merger. As an alternative, the "corporate raiders" may make a *tender offer*, that is, an offer to the shareholders of the target company to buy their stock at a set price. A tender offer is most commonly used to acquire voting control of the target corporation through stock ownership.

Abuse resulting from the "urge to merge"

boom in the 1960s led to enactment in 1968 of the Williams Act amendments to the Exchange Act and to further amendments in 1970. These amendments provide that any person or corporation seeking to acquire more than 5 percent of a company's securities, whether by direct purchase or tender offer, must furnish the shareholders of the target corporation with specified information that must also be filed with the SEC. This information includes disclosure of the offerors' names and stock interests, the purpose of the take-over bid, and the details of any planned merger or other disposition of the target corporation's assets. Any special agreements to obtain shareholder support for the tender offer must also be fully disclosed. The offer of payment to large stockholders of a higher price for their shares than is paid to other shareholders is prohibited. Any recommendation for or against the tender offer that is made by the directors of the target company to its shareholders must be preceded by an SEC filing.

The company itself may make a tender offer to its own shareholders for some specific corporate purpose, such as reacquiring a sufficient number of shares to establish an employee stock-option plan, or "going private." Going private involves a reduction in the number of shareholders below SEC jurisdictional limits. To accomplish this, a control group, or the corporation itself, may purchase shares on the market or may make a tender offer to the shareholders, or both. In any event, this type of transaction generally involves the acquisition of more than 5 percent of the corporation's shares, and is therefore subject to the SEC's tender-offer regulations.

The antifraud provisions of the Williams Act specifically prohibit the omission or misrepresentation of any fact likely to influence a reasonable shareholder's decision in connection with a proxy or tender-offer solicitation.[14]

---

[14]*T. S. C. Industries, Inc. v. Northway, Inc.*, 426 U.S. 438 (1976).

Case 45.7   **Mills v. Electric Auto-Lite Co.**
396 U.S. 375 (1970)

Plaintiffs Mills and other minority shareholders of the Electric Auto-Lite Company brought a class action and derivative suit to obtain an order setting aside a merger of Auto-Lite into Mergenthaler Linotype Company. For 2 years prior to the merger, Mergenthaler owned more than 50 percent of Auto-Lite's stock and nominated and dominated all eleven of Auto-Lite's directors. During this period, American Manufacturing Company (AMC) had effective control of Mergenthaler and, through it, controlled Auto-Lite's board of directors. Auto-Lite, Mergenthaler, and AMC were all named as defendants.

Plaintiffs alleged that the proxy statement which Auto-Lite's management had sent to the shareholders to solicit votes in favor of the merger was misleading, in violation of Section 14(a) of the 1934 Act and SEC Rule 14a-9. The proxy statement told Auto-Lite shareholders that their board of directors recommended approval of the merger. However, the shareholders were not informed that the directors were all nominees of Mergenthaler and under its control and domination. The trial court found that the proxy statement had failed to state a material fact, in violation of Section 14(a) and Rule 14a-9, and granted plaintiffs' motion for summary judgment.

The court then held a hearing to determine if there was a causal connection between the violation and the injury claimed by plaintiffs. The court found that Mergenthaler and AMC owned 54 percent of Auto-Lite's shares and that the votes obtained by proxy from the plaintiffs as minority stockholders were necessary to obtain the required two-thirds approval of the proposed merger. The trial court concluded that a causal connection between the proxy solicitation and the plaintiffs' damaged had been established, and referred the matter to a special master to determine appropriate relief. Defendants appealed.

The Court of Appeals affirmed the trial court's conclusion that the proxy statement was materially deficient but reversed on the question of causation. The court reasoned that it could hardly attempt to determine if thousands of shareholders had relied on the material omissions from the proxy solicitation material in deciding to give their proxies. It was therefore held that the issue of damage to minority shareholders should be resolved by determining whether the terms of the merger were fair to the minority shareholders. Proof of fairness could then be used to sustain a finding that a sufficient number of shareholders would have approved the merger if there had been no deficiency in the proxy statement. This ruling was appealed to the United States Supreme Court.

HARLAND, Justice. As we stressed in *J.I. Case Co. v. Borak*, 377 U.S. 426 (1964), Section 14(a) stemmed from a congressional belief that "fair corporate suffrage is an important right that should attach to every equity security bought on a public exchange." The provision was intended to promote "the free exercise of the voting rights of stockholders" by ensuring that proxies would be solicited with "explanation to the stockholder of the real nature of the questions for which authority to cast his vote is sought." The decision [of the Court of Appeals] by permitting all liability to be foreclosed on the basis of a finding that the merger was fair, would allow the stockholders to be bypassed, at least where the only legal challenge to the merger is a suit for retrospective relief after the meeting has been held. A judicial appraisal of the merger's merits could be substituted for the actual and informed vote of the stockholders. . . . Such a result would subvert the congressional purpose of ensuring full and fair disclosure to shareholders.

Further, recognition of the fairness of the merger as a complete defense would confront small shareholders with an additional obstacle to making a successful challenge to a proposal recommended through a defective proxy statement. The risk that they would be unable to rebut the corporation's evidence of the fairness of the proposal, and thus to establish their cause of action, would be bound to discourage such shareholders from the private enforcement of the proxy rules that "provide a necessary supplement to Commission action."

Section 14(a) declares it "unlawful" to solicit proxies in contravention of Commission rules, and SEC Rule 14a-9 prohibits solicitations "containing any statement which . . . is false or misleading with respect to any material fact, or which omits to state any material fact necessary in order to make the statements therein not false or misleading. . . ."

Where the misstatement or omission in a proxy statement has been shown to be "material," as it was found to be here, that determination itself indubitably embodies a conclusion that the defect was of such a character that it might have been considered important by a reasonable shareholder who was in the process of deciding how to vote. This requirement that the defect have a significant *propensity* to affect the voting process is found in the express terms of Rule 14a-9, and it adequately serves the purpose of ensuring that a cause of action cannot be established by proof of a defect so trivial, or so unrelated to the transaction for which approval is sought, that correction of the defect or imposition of liability would not further the interests protected by Section 14(a).

There is no need to supplement this requirement, as did the Court of Appeals, with a requirement of proof of whether the defect actually had a decisive effect on the voting. Where there has been a finding of materiality, a shareholder has made a sufficient showing of causal relationship between the violation and the injury for which he seeks redress if, as here, he proves that the proxy solicitation itself, rather than the particular defect in the solicitation materials, was an essential link in the accomplishment of the transaction. This objective test will avoid the impracticalities of determining how many votes were affected, and by resolving doubts in favor of those the statute is designed to protect, will effectuate the congressional policy of ensuring that the shareholders are able to make an informed choice when they are consulted on corporate transactions.

Case 45.7
Continued
For the foregoing reasons we conclude that the judgment of the Court of Appeals should be vacated and the case remanded to that court for further proceedings consistent with this opinion.

It is so ordered.

Liabilities under the 1934 Act

Liability for Trading Activities *Buyers* and *sellers* may both have a cause of action or be subjected to civil and criminal liability for a variety of misconduct related to trading activities governed by the 1934 act. Section 18 imposes liability for false or misleading statements made in registration statements or other documents filed under the act, subject to defenses similar to the due diligence defenses available under the 1933 act. Section 9 bans manipulation of security prices by creating a false or misleading appearance of active trading. Section 15(c) establishes liability for "churning," that is, excessive buying and selling of over-the-counter shares by a broker in order to increase commissions from customers. A 1964 amendment [15(c)(5)] extends the SEC's power to suspend trading in situations involving suspected violations, irrespective of whether the securities are listed or unlisted.

Liability under Section 10b and SEC Rule 10b-5 Section 10(b) of the 1934 act sets out a sweeping prohibition against fraud, leaving it to the SEC to define the term. SEC Rule 10b-5 incorporates the prohibitions against sellers in Section 17(a) of the 1933 act, and applies them to both sellers and buyers:

It shall be unlawful for any person, directly or indirectly, by use of any means or instrumentality of interstate commerce, or of the mails, or of any facility of any national securities exchange . . . to make any untrue statement of a material fact or to omit to state a material fact necessary in order to make the statements made, in the light of the circumstances under which they were made, not misleading, or to engage in any act, practice, or course of business which operates . . . as a fraud or deceit upon any person, *in connection with the purchase or sale of any security.*[15] [Emphasis added]

This wording covers listed and unlisted and registered and unregistered securities, in all buy-sell transactions, whether completed in direct dealings between individuals[16] or through an exchange.

The courts have used the rule's broad prohibition against "*any* device, scheme, or artifice to defraud" to attack a wide variety of fraudulent practices.[17] These include brokers' making wild predictions to customers without knowing or investigating the facts,[18] dealers' charging customers prices not reasonably related to market prices,[19] high-pressure ("boiler room") selling of securities to strangers by long-distance telephone,[20] and a parent corporation's exercising control over a subsidiary to manipulate the relative market prices of the two stocks so that the exchange ratio in a subsequent merger is unfair to the subsidiary's shareholders.[21]

---

[15] See *Goodman v. Epstein*, Case 45.3, p. 982, and *SEC v. Texas Gulf Sulphur Co.*, Case 45.5, p. 995, for illustrations of the application of SEC Rule 10b-5.

[16] *Myzel v. Fields*, 386 F.2d 718 (8th Cir. 1967).

[17] See *Rubin v. United States*, Case 45.2, p. 980.

[18] *Gottreich v. San Francisco Investment Corporation*, 552 F.2d 866 (9th Cir. 1977).

[19] *Charles Hughes & Co. v. SEC*, 139 F.2d 434 (2d Cir. 1943).

[20] *Barnett v. United States*, 319 F.2d 340 (8th Cir. 1963).

[21] *Schlick v. Penn-Dixie Cement Corp.*, 507 F.2d 374 (2d Cir. 1974).

Court interpretations, although not always consistent, have expanded the meaning of Rule 10b-5 beyond its literal wording, which has been applied to attempted frauds as well as consummated frauds. The right to damages in private suits is limited to actual buyers or sellers.[22] Nevertheless, the rule has been held to apply where a security holder is fraudulently persuaded *not* to sell his or her shares.[23]

Corporations that buy or sell their own shares are also vulnerable under Rule 10b-5. For example, a corporation that buys shares back without disclosing material facts to the seller is liable for damages under Rule 10b-5.[24] In another case, a corporation that sold stock for inadequate consideration was permitted, under Rule 10b-5, to recover from a fraudulent buyer.[25]

Congress clearly gave the SEC the right to prosecute violations of Section 10b. However, it was not until 1947 that federal courts first established the principle that injured parties have an implied right to bring a direct suit to recover damages from the wrongdoer.[26] A large number of private suits under Section 10b followed, and by 1961 the resulting body of case decisions was described as a "federal substantive corporation law."[27] The first *Texas Gulf Sulphur* decision[28] was perhaps the high point of Section 10b litigation. Despite the fact that there was no proof of a wrongful purpose or intent to deceive, the corporation's publication of a misleading press release was held to be a violation of Section 10b. The court said that "the

investing public may be injured as much by one's misleading statement containing inaccuracies caused by negligence as by a misleading statement published intentionally to further a wrongful purpose."

Since *Texas Gulf*, the Supreme Court has discouraged Section 10b suits in several areas. *Hochfelder* below clearly holds that a private cause of action to recover damages for negligence alone will not prevail under Rule 10b-5 in the absence of "scienter," that is, an intent to deceive, manipulate, or defraud. In 1977, the Court decided *Sante Fe Industries v. Green*, 430 U.S. 462. In that case, minority shareholders sued to set aside a "short form" merger between Sante Fe and Kirby Lumber Corporation. That merger had been carried out in compliance with Delaware's merger statute. The shareholders did not ask the Delaware court to appraise the fair value of dissenting shares and to require Sante Fe to purchase them. Instead, the plaintiffs sued in the federal court, claiming that the merger was "manipulative and deceptive" under Section 10(b). The Supreme Court rejected this contention. It found that Sante Fe had made no omission or misstatement in the Information Statement accompanying the notice of merger and construed Congress' use of the term "manipulative" as referable to such practices as wash sales, matched orders, or rigged prices intended to mislead investors by artificially affecting market activity. The court held that Congress did not intend to apply the word manipulative to corporate mismanagement in which shareholders were treated unfairly by a fiduciary, particularly where there was an adequate remedy under state law. The Court concluded: "There may well be a need for uniform federal fiduciary standards to govern mergers such as that challenged in this complaint. But those standards should not be supplied by judicial extension of Section 10(b) and Rule 10b-5 to cover the corporate universe."

---

[22]*Santa Fe Industries, Inc. v. Green*, 430 U.S. 462 (1977).

[23]*Silverman v. Bear Stearns & Co.*, 331 F. Supp. 1334 (E.D.Pa. 1971).

[24]*Kohler v. Kohler Co.*, 319 F.2d 634 (7th Cir. 1963).

[25]*Hooper v. Mountain States Securities Corp.*, 282 F.2d 195 (5th Cir. 1960).

[26]*Kardon v. National Gypsum Co.*, 83 F. Supp. 613 (E.D.Pa. 1947).

[27]*McClure v. Borne Chemical Co.*, 292 F.2d 824 (3d Cir. 1967).

[28]*SEC v. Texas Gulf Sulphur Co.*, 401 F.2d 833 (2d Cir. 1968).

Case 45.8   **Ernst & Ernst v. Hochfelder**
425 U.S. 185 (1976)

Leston Nay was president and principal shareholder of First Securities, a brokerage firm. Ernst & Ernst, certified public accountants, performed audits for the firm for 20 years. During that period, Nay induced Hochfelder and others to invest funds in fictional high-yield "escrow" accounts. Nay converted these funds to his own use. This led to Nay's suicide. His suicide note described First Securities as bankrupt and the escrow accounts as "spurious." The fraud had not been discovered because Nay had a rule that only he could open mail addressed to him, even if it arrived in his absence.

Hochfelder brought suit against Ernst in the federal courts under Rule 10b-5. Hochfelder disclaimed fraud or intentional misconduct by Ernst, but argued that Ernst had "aided and abetted" Nay's fraud. The complaint alleged that (1) the accountants' failure to discover the "mail rule" amounted to negligent nonfeasance, (2) discovery would have required Ernst to report the "mail rule" to the SEC in the periodic reports which Ernst prepared for Nay's firm, and (3) this would have led to an investigation that would have uncovered Nay's fraudulent scheme. The District Court granted Ernst's motion for summary judgment and dismissed the action. The Court of Appeals reversed. Ernst appealed to the Supreme Court.

POWELL, Justice. We granted certiorari to resolve the question whether a private cause of action for damages will lie under § 10(b) and Rule 10b-5 in the absence of "scienter." We conclude that it will not and therefore we reverse. . . .

Section 10(b) makes unlawful the use or employment of "any manipulative or deceptive device or contrivance" in contravention of Commission rules. The words "manipulative or deceptive" used in conjunction with "device or contrivance" strongly suggest that § 10(b) was intended to proscribe knowing or intentional misconduct. [Citations]

In its *amicus curiae* brief, however, the Commission contends that nothing in the language "manipulative or deceptive device or contrivance" limits its operation to knowing or intentional practices. In support of its view, the Commission cites the overall congressional purpose in the 1933 and 1934 Acts to protect investors against false and deceptive practices that might injure them. . . . The argument simply ignores the use of the words "manipulative," "device," and "contrivance," terms that make unmistakable a congressional intent to proscribe a type of conduct quite different from negligence. Use of the word "manipulative" is especially significant. . . . It connotes intentional or willful conduct designed to deceive or defraud investors by controlling or artificially affecting the price of securities. . . .

Thus, despite the broad view of Rule 10b-5 advanced by the Commission in this case, its scope cannot exceed the power granted the Commission by Congress under § 10(b). . . . When a statute speaks so specifically in terms of manipulation and deception, and of implementing devices and contrivances—the commonly understood terminology of intentional wrongdoing—and when its history reflects no more expansive intent, we are quite unwilling to extend the scope of the statute to negligent conduct.

The judgment of the Court of Appeals is reversed.

THE FOREIGN CORRUPT PRACTICES ACT OF 1977

Purpose and Prohibitions

Following a series of international scandals involving payment of bribes by American corporations to foreign officials for the purpose of obtaining business, Congress enacted the Foreign Corrupt Practices Act of 1977 to discourage such practices. The act prohibits issuers subject to the registration and reporting provisions of the Securities Exchange Act of 1934 as well as domestic concerns not subject to the 1934 act from using any instrumentality of interstate commerce to corruptly offer or give anything of value to foreign officials and certain other persons for the purpose of obtaining or retaining business.

Penalties

A director, stockholder, officer, or agent who acts for a corporation in willful violation of the Foreign Corrupt Practices Act is subject to maximum penalties of $10,000 and 5 years in prison. Although criminal penalties imposed on those who violate federal statutes administered by the SEC were standardized under the Securities Acts Amendments of 1975, the Foreign Corrupt Practices Act of 1977 provides an exception: corporations that violate the act are subject to a fine of up to $1 million.

Accounting Standards

The act also amended Section 13(b) of the Securities Exchange Act to require reporting companies to make and keep books, records, and accounts that, in reasonable detail, accurately and fairly reflect the transactions and dispositions of assets of the issuer. The act prohibits keeping inaccurate books, maintaining off-the-book accounts, and related practices. Reporting companies are also required to devise and maintain a system of internal accounting controls sufficient to ensure (1) that corporate payments are made only with the specific authorization of management, (2) that all transactions—including payments made abroad—are accurately recorded so as to permit preparation of financial statements in accordance with generally accepted accounting principles, (3) that accountability is maintained for the corporation's assets, including cash payments, (4) that access to assets is permitted only in accordance with management authorization, and (5) that recorded accountability for assets is compared with existing assets at reasonable intervals and appropriate action is taken with respect to any differences. The SEC's enforcement responsibilities under the act extend to conducting investigations, bringing civil injunction actions, commencing administrative proceedings, and referring cases to the Justice Department for criminal prosecution. The act reinforces the obligation of corporations to disclose illegal or materially questionable corporate practices.[29]

SUMMARY

The underlying theory of state and federal securities laws is twofold: (1) to protect the

---

[29]SEC Accounting Release No. 242, February 16, 1978.

investors, and (2) to increase public confidence in securities markets. Concurrent state-federal jurisdiction over securities issues, as well as broad differences in state blue-sky laws, cause major problems for corporations that plan multistate securities issues.

The SEC administers the Securities Act of 1933, which regulates initial issuance of securities, and the Securities Exchange Act of 1934, which regulates trading in securities after issuance. The 1933 act requires issuers to file a registration statement, including a prospectus, with the SEC. The 1934 act (1) requires securities traded on a national exchange, and unlisted shares traded over-the-counter, to be registered with the SEC; (2) requires national securities exchanges, associations, and most brokers and dealers to register; and (3) requires issuers of registered securities, or any corporation with 500 shareholders and assets over $1 million to file periodic reports with the SEC.

A person who willfully violates the 1933 or 1934 act, or any SEC rules, is subject to criminal penalties (5 years in prison and a fine of not more than $10,000, except that a fine not to exceed $500,000 may be imposed on a securities exchange). Civil liability may be imposed on violators through (1) suits by the SEC for money damages, as well as an injunction restraining future violations; (2) causes of action created by statute in favor of injured parties; and (3) suits by private parties under the doctrine of implied rights recognized by the courts. There are no exemptions from the numerous antifraud provisions of the acts.

Under the 1933 act, registration must occur before any nonexempt security is offered or sold through the use of the mails or any facility of interstate commerce. Securities can be sold only after the effective date of the registration statement. Delivery of the securities must be accompanied or preceded by a prospectus.

Court interpretations of the meaning of various statutory terms help to define the scope of the acts. The 1933 act defines a security to include an "investment contract," a term which the *Howey* rule defines to encompass any agreement to invest funds in an ownership share of a common enterprise in which the investor expects to profit solely from the managerial efforts of others. If promissory notes meet these criteria, they are treated as securities. Other important terms are distribution (public offering), issuer (includes unincorporated businesses and control persons), and underwriter (one who participates in the risks and profits of a distribution).

Under the 1933 act, there are two classes of exemptions from the requirements of registration: securities and transactions. Exempted securities include small offerings, short-term commercial paper, intrastate issues, offerings by closely held corporations, government issues, issues regulated by agencies other than the SEC, issues of nonprofit organizations, and exchanges between an issuer and its existing security holders. Exempted transactions include most trading activities of individual investors with respect to outstanding securities, transactions by brokers and dealers, and private offerings. Resales of restricted securities (issued as part of a private offering) can be made on the open market, but only through a broker, on a 2-year-and-dribble basis. Detailed restrictions and conditions are imposed on the exemption of securities and transactions. The principle underlying these restrictions is to protect the unsophisticated investor.

Persons who participate in the filing of a registration statement or other document required by the SEC must prove that they acted with due diligence in order to avoid liability for any false or misleading data or omission in any such document. A willful violation of the registration or antifraud provisions of the 1933 act subjects the violator to civil or criminal liability, or both.

Two types of insider trading are prohibited by the 1934 act and Rule 10b-5: (1) purchases or sales by insiders or tippees who have access to corporate information not available to the public and (2) short-swing transactions (in which insiders buy and sell, or sell and buy, their company's securities within any 6-months period). The 1934 act [14] also requires compliance with SEC rules before any person solicits proxies or makes a tender offer to shareholders of a company whose securities are registered under the 1934 act.

Buyers and sellers may both have a cause of action or be subjected to civil and criminal liability for a variety of misconduct related to trading activities governed by the 1934 act. The antifraud provisions of the 1934 act and Rule 10b-5 permit injured parties to recover damages from violators for a broad range of deceptive, manipulative, or fraudulent practices. There is a general statutory prohibition against any misrepresentation or omission of a fact that is material to an investor's decision to buy and sell (or sell and buy) any security, when filing any document with the SEC or otherwise making it public.

The Foreign Corrupt Practices Act of 1977 applies to corporations subject to the registration and reporting provisions of the 1934 act as well as to other domestic firms involved in international commerce. The 1977 act requires the maintenance of an exacting system of internal accounting controls. These controls are designed to reinforce statutory prohibitions against bribing foreign officials (and certain others) in order to keep or obtain business. An extraordinary penalty not to exceed $1 million may be imposed on corporations that violate the act.

STUDY AND DISCUSSION QUESTIONS

1 Explain the purpose of *(a)* blue-sky laws and *(b)* anti-takeover statutes.

2 Compare the advantages and disadvantages of concurrent state-federal jurisdiction over the issuance of securities.

3 Explain the meaning of the term "federal corporation law."

4 What is the basic coverage of *(a)* the Securities Act of 1933? and *(b)* the Securities Exchange Act of 1934?

5 Explain the role of the SEC and the extent and importance of its rule-making authority.

6 What is the statutory purpose of the registration provisions of the 1933 act?

7 *(a)* Under what circumstances do securities have to be registered under the 1934 act? *(b)* Under what circumstances are periodic reports required to be filed under the 1934 act? *(c)* How does the SEC regulate national securities exchanges and brokers and dealers?

8 *(a)* Under what circumstances must securities be registered under the 1933 act? *(b)* How are securities registered?

9 *(a)* What kinds of information are required in a registration statement? *(b)* How does the required information relate to the purpose of the 1933 act?

10 *(a)* Explain what activities are permitted with reference to a proposed sale of securities prior to filing the registration statement, during the waiting period, and after the effective date. *(b)* How do these restrictions help to protect unsophisticated investors?

11 *(a)* What is a distribution? *(b)* To whom does the term "issuer" apply? *(c)* How does the role of an underwriter differ from that of a dealer or broker?

12 What precautions would you recommend to an issuer that plans to claim an exemption in connection with a proposed issue of securities?

13 List at least five examples of securities exemptions, and explain what you believe to be the chief policy reason for each exemption.

14 What is the basic difference between a securities exemption and a transaction exemption?

15 What factors determine whether a securities issue qualifies as a private offering?

16 What are the social policy reasons underlying the requirements for the private-offering exemptions?

17 *(a)* How is the SEC's jurisdiction over resales of restricted securities preserved by including "controlling persons" within the meaning of the term issuer? *(b)* Explain the significance of the 2-year-and-dribble rule.

18 *(a)* Why is the exemption of transactions by individual investors important? *(b)* How is this exemption related to the exemption of transactions by brokers and dealers? *(c)* Under what circumstances are transactions by dealers *not* exempt?

19 *(a)* What are some of the reasons for proxy and tender-offer solicitations? *(b)* Why does the SEC regulate such solicitations?

20 Give two examples of unlawful trading activities for which the 1934 act imposes liability.

21 *(a)* How do controls established by the Foreign Corrupt Practices Act help to implement its purpose? *(b)* What are the maximum penalties imposed on individual and corporate violators? *(c)* How do these penalties differ from criminal penalties standardized by the Securities Acts Amendments of 1975?

CASE PROBLEMS

1 Heller (a commercial lender) agreed to a continuing loan to Benson Finance Co. (a family corporation). The loan was to equal 80 percent of the outstanding balance on Benson's notes receivable that showed some payment on account from customers within the prior 90-day period. Heller lent Benson $3 million before an audit disclosed that Benson had falsified its accounts to show a 6-month profit instead of a $186,965 loss. Benson also gave Heller several bad checks. When Heller terminated the credit

agreement, Benson offered to sell its stock to Bankshares Corporation and gave Heller as a credit reference. In response to Bankshares' telephone inquiry, Heller stated that Benson met its obligations promptly and that its operation was above-average. Heller also told Bankshares that if it did not acquire Benson, Heller would lend Benson additional funds. Heller's next audit showed that Benson was still "doctoring the books," but Heller never advised Bankshares.

Bankshares acquired Benson and paid off Heller's $3 million loan before discovering that Benson was insolvent by $650,000 at the time of the purchase. Bankshares sued for $1 million damages in connection with the purchase of Benson's stock. The complaint charged responsible officers and directors within the Benson family, and Heller, with the common law tort of fraud and with violations under Section 10(b) of the 1934 act and SEC Rule 10b-5. Is Bankshares entitled to judgment against Benson family members, and against Heller as an aider-abettor, on both counts?

2 In 1955, Beef Inc. initiated a voluntary program whereby employees lent funds deducted from payroll to the company on 6 percent promissory notes with maturities of 1 to 5 years. The employees were never given financial data about the company. Bank made a substantial loan to Beef Inc. based on financial statements that included the details of the notes owed to employees. Bank's loan agreement required Beef Inc. to pledge its assets to secure the loan and to subordinate the notes owed to employees. These facts were concealed from Beef's employees with Bank's knowledge. Bank encouraged continuation of the employee note program because it provided cash to satisfy Beef's debt to Bank. Bank also prevented Beef from paying interest or honoring the notes as they matured. In 1972, Beef Inc. became insolvent, and its assets were sold to satisfy Bank's loan.

The employee noteholders, who received

nothing, commenced a class action against Beef Inc. and against Bank as an aider-abettor. At the trial it was stipulated that the notes were securities transmitted by mail or in interstate commerce and that Beef's failure to register the notes was a violation of the 1933 act. The court found Beef liable to the employees under the antifraud provisions of the 1933 act [12] and the 1934 act [10(b)] because of misleading statements and omissions with reference to the note program. Was Bank liable as an aider-abettor?

3 Fifty investors lent Jones (doing business as Wine Imports) $21 million, which was evidenced by Imports' promissory notes. The money was purportedly used to import industrial wines that were to be resold at a substantial profit. Actually, the money from new investors was used to pay a return of 30–100 percent on existing notes. The hoax, known only to Jones, depended on a continuous increase in the number of investors. Jones had little direct contact with any of the investors, excepting Smith and Brown who, in turn, approached Rich, a businessman of "mature experience." Smith and Brown promised a 45 percent return on notes purchased through them and offered Rich a 10 percent commission on any funds that he solicited from others. Rich invested $270,000 of his own money and obtained additional funds from new investors by guarantying them a profitable return. These investors later caused Rich to be adjudicated a bankrupt. Lawler (Rich's trustee in bankruptcy) sued Smith and Brown for damages arising from the sale of unregistered securities in violation of the 1933 act. Is Lawler entitled to judgment? Your answer should discuss *(a)* whether the notes were securities and *(b)* whether Smith and Brown offered and sold securities in violation of the registration provisions of the 1933 act, or *(c)* whether Smith and Brown properly contended that Rich's purchase was the result of an exempt private offering.

4 Oil Co. did not register its offering of limited interests in a California partnership organized to drill oil wells in Wyoming. There was no public advertising. A California broker who knew Davis, a petroleum engineer who had invested most of his $1 million in oil ventures, telephoned Davis in Texas. Oil Co. mailed Davis drilling logs and maps. Davis was one of four offerees. Each of them put up $25,000. Davis "invested" an additional $100,000 by guarantying a note that Oil Co. owed a supplier. The wells did not produce enough to pay the note, and the supplier got a $50,000 judgment against Davis. He sued to rescind his purchase, alleging that the oil interests were unregistered securities sold in violation of the 1933–1934 acts. Did Oil Co. correctly contend that its sale of limited partnership interests was an exempt private offering? Discuss fully.

5 Bank's manager gave a bank customer and her attorney a hush-hush tip that Bank was backing a merger between Meridian Inc. and Paragon Plastics. The tippees were told that bank "big shots" were buying Meridian stock in anticipation of the merger. The customer bought 1,200 shares of Meridian at $8 per share; the attorney bought call options; neither of them told the sellers about the merger. The merger fell through, and Meridian stock dropped to $1 per share. The customer and her attorney sued Bank and its manager for damages arising from false statements made in connection with the purchase of a security. The defendant-tippers claimed that the plaintiffs were in pari delicto (in equal fault) because they had not advised their sellers of the tip at the time they had purchased the Meridian shares. *(a)* Are the plaintiff-customer and attorney as much at fault as Bank and its manager? *(b)* If so, should the claim of in pari delicto prevent them from recovering from Bank under Section 10(b) of the 1934 act and SEC Rule 10b-5?

6 Buckley, a securities broker, told Allen that the price of certain shares would rise. Buckley knew that his prediction was not based on special knowledge about the issuing companies or on proper investigation and analysis. Allen relied on Buckley's representations and purchased the recommended stocks. The market price of the stock declined. Buckley contended that Allen's loss was due to a general decline in market prices. Allen sued to recover damages from Buckley. Is Buckley liable to Allen under Section 10(b) of the 1934 act and SEC Rule 10b-5?

7 In 1964 Mapco, Inc. issued warrants which provided that on April 1, 1972, each warrant was to be automatically converted into one-half share of common stock. The warrant holder could then purchase the other one-half share at its market value. Prior to April 1, 1972, a holder who surrendered one warrant and paid $9 could buy one share of common stock. Donald Ross, Mapco's financial vice president, acquired 3,616 warrants and held them for more than 6 months. In February and March, 1972, Mapco common was selling on the New York Exchange for $41–$43 per share. During that period, Ross exchanged 1,100 warrants plus $9 per share for 1,100 shares, which he immediately sold.

Morales brought a shareholder's derivative suit, under Section 16(b) of the 1934 Act, to recover for Mapco-Ross' short-swing profits. Ross contended that his sale of 1,100 shares related back to the acquisition of the warrants more than 6 months prior to the sale. Was the immediate sale of the 1,100 shares a violation of Section 16(b) of the 1934 Act?

Chapter

46

Foreign Corporations

A corporation is "domestic" in the state of its incorporation and "foreign" in all other states and countries. Under the Constitution, each sovereign state is permitted to grant powers and privileges to its domestic corporations. Clearly, such franchises cannot extend into the jurisdiction of another sovereign state without its consent. It follows that a domestic corporation may not transact local business in any other state without its permission. All states have granted such permission, and, in doing so, they have enacted laws regulating the activities of foreign corporations. In general, the amount of statutory regulation varies with the extent to which the interests of residents may be affected by the in-state activities of a foreign corporation.

A corporation whose presence is limited to transporting goods by common carrier across a "host" state (any state other than the state of incorporation) is clearly engaged in *interstate* commerce. However, a corporation is engaged in *intrastate* commerce in such "host" state if its business activities extend into that state to the point that it is doing business there. For example, a foreign corporation that carries on manufacturing operations or maintains a warehouse to stock goods in a host state is usually considered to be doing business in that state. Although the line of demarcation between interstate commerce and "doing business" intrastate has not been neatly defined by state statutes or the courts, the distinction is important. On the one hand, a foreign corporation that engages in interstate commerce does not have to qualify to do business in the host state. On the other hand, a corporation that transacts local business in the host state is subject to all its regulatory statutes and must qualify to do business.

The first part of this chapter examines the nature and extent of the power of a host state to regulate foreign corporations engaging in interstate or intrastate activities. The last two parts of the chapter deal with state taxation and court jurisdiction of foreign corporation and with state regulation of foreign corporations "doing business" in the host state. The chief sources of the law upon which this discussion is based are the United States Constitution, state statutes pertaining to the activities of foreign corporations, and applicable court decisions—particularly those of the federal courts.

POWER OF HOST STATE
OVER FOREIGN CORPORATIONS

Power of Host State over
Foreign Corporations Engaged in
Interstate Commerce

Under the commerce clause of the Constitution (Article 1, Section 8), the power to control interstate commerce is reserved to the federal government. As a result, state law cannot restrict a foreign corporation's activities in interstate commerce. In addition, state statutes cannot require corporations chartered by Congress, such as national banks, to register to do business. These corporations, as well as foreign corporations engaged exclusively in interstate commerce, are relatively free from regulation by the host state. However, the Tenth Amendment of the Constitution gives each state the power to enact laws that protect the health, safety, morals, and welfare of its residents. To this end, the state can impose reasonable nondiscriminatory regulation, such as inspection of incoming food or limitation of truck size, on foreign entities as well as residents. The Supreme Court has held that such state statutes do not unreasonably burden or interfere with interstate commerce.

Case 46.1   Aldens, Inc. v. Packel
379 F. Supp. 521 (M.D. Pa. 1974)

Aldens, Inc. operated a retail mail-order business solely from a location in Illinois, the state of incorporation. Although the corporation had no office, sales personnel, telephone listing, or property in Pennsylvania, sales to customers residing in that state amounted to approximately $15 million per year (7 percent of Aldens's total sales). Mail orders were accepted in Illinois and shipped by mail, parcel post, or common carrier from outside Pennsylvania. Aldens's standard credit agreement, used throughout the United States, provided for a monthly finance charge of 1.75 percent (an annual percentage rate of 21 percent). A Pennsylvania statute prohibited finance charges for revolving charge accounts in excess of 15 percent. Aldens (plaintiff) contended that the statute burdened interstate commerce and should, therefore, be declared unconstitutional. The state attorney general (defendant) contended that a statute regulating credit practices was a proper exercise of the state's power to protect the welfare of residents.

MUIR, District J. The statute involved in the case at bar is distinguishable from taxing and licensing statutes in that it involves an exercise of the state's police power to protect local customers from overreaching and deception. The state has considerable power in this area even though interstate commerce is affected. . . . We are not here dealing with an exaction for the privilege of doing business with Pennsylvania residents, but with a statute reasonably calculated to protect consumers residing in Pennsylvania from unfair credit practices. . . .

The plaintiff points out that every case upholding a statute seeking to protect the public's health, safety, morals, or welfare involves some local activity or physical presence of the regulated entity within the regulating state. However, the physical presence is often transitory. Thus, a state can regulate the highway speed of trucks engaged solely in interstate commerce, *South Carolina State Highway Department v. Barnwell Bros.*, 303 U.S. 177 (1938), or control the emission of smoke from ships involved in interstate commerce while the ships are docked at the port of the regulating jurisdiction. *Huron Portland Cement Co. v. City of Detroit*, 362 U.S. 440 (1960). The interest of the state in protecting its citizens is so strong that the state may even prohibit certain dangerous products from entering the state at all. *Rasmussen v. Idaho*, 181 U.S. 198 (1901).

In my view, application of the Pennsylvania Goods and Services Installment Sales Act to Aldens does not depend upon Aldens' physical presence in Pennsylvania. Aldens' annual solicitation of over two million Pennsylvania residents and its sales of almost $15,000,000 per year indicates an exploitation of the Pennsylvania market and requires Aldens to conform with the Act which protects Pennsylvania consumers in those types of transactions in which Aldens engages. To hold otherwise would expose Pennsylvania consumers to the type of credit sales practices which the Pennsylvania legislature deemed unfair and prohibited in Pennsylvania. In *Robertson v. People of the State of California*, 328 U.S. 440 (1946), the Supreme Court, in upholding provisions of the California Insurance Code which prohibited the sale of insurance in California by unadmitted foreign insurance companies stated the following:

> "It is quite obvious . . . that if appellant's contentions were accepted and foreign insurers were to be held free to disregard California's reserve requirements and then to clothe their agents or others acting for them with their immunity, not only would the state be made helpless to protect her people against the grossest forms of unregulated or loosely regulated foreign insurance, but the result would be inevitably to break down also the system for control of purely local insurance business. In short, the result would be ultimately to force all of the states to accept the lowest standard for conducting the business permitted by one of them or, perhaps, by foreign countries."

Similarly, if Pennsylvania cannot regulate the finance charges of mail order businesses, then the ultimate result could be that all retailers would do business through the mails from a state whose service charge ceiling was the highest. . . . I have concluded that the national interest in the free flow of interstate commerce does not outweigh the interest of Pennsylvania in protecting its consumers from unreasonable service charge rates on installment credit accounts.

[Note: The above decision was affirmed by the Circuit Court of Appeals in 524 F.2d 38 (3rd Cir. 1975). The court noted that the Pennsylvania statute regulating finance charges was not an unreasonable burden on interstate commerce and that Congress, in the Federal Truth in Lending Act (15 U.S.C. Sections 1601–1665), had expressly deferred such matters to state authority. Certiorari denied 425 U.S. 943.]

Power of Host State over Foreign Corporations Engaged in Intrastate Commerce

Extent of Host State's Power   Every corporation is subject to the statutes of its state of incorporation. In addition, a corporation that engages in extensive intrastate business activities in another state is subject to a high degree of regulation by the host state. Such corporations must qualify (register) to do business in that state and conform to all other statutes applicable to foreign corporations. However, the Model Act (106)[1] provides that a host state cannot regulate the organization or internal affairs of a foreign corporation, such matters being reserved to the state of incorporation.

"Doing Business" as an Issue in Suits   Whether a particular foreign corporation is doing business intrastate or is merely engaged in interstate commerce is a question which must ultimately be decided by the courts. This question is often a key issue in suits involving foreign corporations. For example:

• If a suit to enjoin a foreign corporation from transacting intrastate business without a license is brought by a resident competitor (or by the host state), the unlicensed corporation usually

---

[1]The section numbers of the *Model Business Corporations Act* are given in parentheses throughout this chapter.

claims that it is not doing local business but is engaged solely in interstate commerce.

• If an unlicensed foreign corporation sues a resident in the host state, the defendant typically seeks to escape liability by arguing that the corporation is doing local business without a license and is, therefore, barred from using state courts.

Because court decisions depend upon the facts and circumstances in each case—no two of which are exactly alike—resulting case law is endless and conflicting. A few states have attempted to resolve the uncertainty of court decisions by enacting statutes which define "doing business." However, foreign corporations have consistently litigated statutory definitions, arguing that they conflict with the right to engage in interstate commerce.

The Model Act does not attempt to define "doing business." Instead, the act enumerates specific activities in which a foreign corporation can engage without qualifying to do business (106). Such activities include suing or defending suits, holding corporate meetings, maintaining a bank account or stock transfer office, effecting sales through independent contractors, soliciting orders through agents or by mail for acceptance outside the state, creating and collecting debts, and conducting an isolated transaction completed within 30 days.

Case 46.2   Allenberg Cotton Co. v. Pittman
419 U.S. 20 (1974)

An independent Mississippi broker negotiated a contract with Ben Pittman, a Mississippi cotton farmer, on behalf of Allenberg Cotton Company, Inc., a Tennessee cotton merchant. The broker had no authority to bind Pittman, who agreed to plant, cultivate, and harvest a crop of cotton on his land, deliver it to a named company for ginning, and then turn over the ginned cotton to Allenberg at a local warehouse. The "forward" contract for Pittman's crop was prepared and signed by Allenberg, who then asked the Mississippi broker to obtain Pittman's signature. Allenberg resold the future cotton to customers in interstate and foreign commerce. The resale contracts were reflected in the price of cotton futures on a national commodities exchange.

Allenberg had no office or warehouse in Mississippi and no employees who solicited business or otherwise operated in the state. All cotton which Allenberg purchased from various Mississippi farmers was customarily delivered to the same local warehouse for sorting and grading. From there, the cotton was shipped to Allenberg's customers.

Pittman (defendant) failed to deliver his cotton crop, and Allenberg (plaintiff) sued for breach of contract. The trial court found for Allenberg. The Mississippi Supreme Court then reversed the judgment, holding (1) that Allenberg's transactions with Mississippi farmers were complete upon delivery of the cotton at the local warehouse and, therefore, were wholly intrastate in nature; (2) that it was irrelevant that Allenberg subsequently sold the cotton in interstate commerce; and (3) that Mississippi law did not permit Allenberg, as an unlicensed corporation doing business intrastate, to maintain a suit in state courts. Allenberg contended that its purchase transaction with Pittman was solely in interstate commerce and appealed to the U.S. Supreme Court.

DOUGLAS, Justice. [Allenberg's*] arrangements with Pittman and the broker are representative of a course of dealing with many farmers whose cotton, once sold to [Allenberg], enters a long interstate pipeline. That pipeline ultimately terminates at mills across the country or indeed around the world, after a complex sorting and matching process designed to provide each mill with the particular grade of cotton which the mill is equipped to process.

Each bale of cotton, even though produced on the same farm, may have a different quality. Traders or merchants like Allenberg, with the assistance of the Department of Agriculture, must sample each bale and classify it according to grade, staple length, and color. Similar bales, whether from different farms or even from different collection points, are then grouped in multiples of 100 into "even-running lots." This grouping process typically takes place in card files in the merchant's office; when enough bales have been pooled to make an even-running lot, the entire lot can be targeted for a mill equipped to handle cotton of that particular quality, and the individual bales in the lot will then be shipped to the mill from their respective collection points. It is true that title often formally passes to the merchant upon delivery of the cotton at the warehouse, and that the cotton may rest at the warehouse pending completion of the classification and grouping processes; but these fleeting events are an

---

[*To improve readability, "Allenberg" has been substituted for "appellant" in this case.]

integral first step in a vast system of distribution of cotton in interstate commerce.

The Court held in *Shafer v. Farmers Grain Co.* 268 U.S. 189 (1925), that a pervasive state regulatory scheme governing the purchase of wheat for interstate shipment was not permissible since the

> "buying for shipment [was] as much a part of interstate commerce as the shipping. . . . The right to buy it for shipment, and to ship it, in interstate commerce is not a privilege derived from state laws and which they may fetter with conditions, but is a common right, the regulation of which is committed to Congress and denied to the States by the commerce clause of the Constitution."

Much reliance is placed on *Eli Lilly & Co. v. Sav-on-Drugs, Inc.* 366 U.S. 276 (1961)[*] for sustaining Mississippi's action. The case is not in point. . . . [Allenberg] has no office in Mississippi, nor does it own or operate a warehouse there. It has no employees soliciting business in Mississippi or otherwise operating there on a regular basis; its contracts are arranged through an independent broker, whose commission is paid either by [Allenberg] or by the farmer himself. These facts are in sharp contrast to the situation in *Eli Lilly*, where Lilly operated a New Jersey office with 18 salaried employees whose job was to promote the use of Lilly's products. There is no indication that the cotton which makes up [Allenberg's] "perpetual inventory" in Mississippi is anything other than what [Allenberg] has claimed it to be, namely, cotton which is awaiting necessary sorting and classification as a prerequisite to its shipment in interstate commerce.

In short, [Allenberg's] contacts with Mississippi do not exhibit the sort of localization or intrastate character which we have required in situations where a State seeks to require a foreign corporation to qualify to do business. Whether there were local tax incidents of those contracts which could be reached is a different question on which we express no opinion. Whether the course of dealing would subject [Allenberg] to suits in Mississippi is likewise a different question on which we express no view. We hold only that Mississippi's refusal to honor and enforce contracts made for interstate or foreign commerce is repugnant to the Commerce Clause.

The judgment is reversed and the cause remanded for proceedings not inconsistent with this opinion.

[*See Case 46.4, p. 1023.]

STATE TAXATION AND COURT JURISDICTION OF FOREIGN CORPORATIONS

Between the two extremes of interstate commerce and doing business intrastate, there are degrees of activity which may subject a foreign corporation to taxation and to court jurisdiction in the host state. A corporation may engage in a wide range of activities that go beyond transporting goods in interstate commerce without qualifying to do business. Nevertheless, the foreign corporation may be active enough to be taxed by the host state and sued in its courts. Generally, a corporation is active enough to be taxed and sued if it maintains certain minimum contacts within the host state, and the state confers benefits and protection upon the agents or property of the corporation.

Minimum-Contacts and Benefits-and-Protection Theories

Business convenience may require a corporation to maintain certain minimum contacts in a foreign state. For example, a Texas corporation may send sales agents into Utah to solicit orders for acceptance in Texas. This activity does not require qualification to do business in Utah. Nevertheless, the corporation profits from its transactions in the host state, and agents driving corporate automobiles in Utah also benefit from police and fire protection. The U.S. Supreme Court has held that a corporation which maintains minimum contacts and receives business benefits under the protection of a host state's laws should, in return, bear any reasonable burden. Under these related theories of "minimum contacts" and "benefits and protection," a state can tax a foreign corporation or make it answer in the courts for the consequences of its in-state activities, even if they fall short of "doing business."

State Taxation of Foreign Corporations

Property Taxes   Each state can tax any property that is permanently situated within its borders, even if the property is used by a foreign corporation to carry on interstate business. A problem arises in situations involving personal property that is in the host state for only part of the tax year. In *Braniff Airways, Inc. v. Nebraska State Board of Equalization and Assessment,*[2] the question was whether Nebraska could levy an apportioned personal property tax on the flight equipment of a foreign corporation engaged solely in interstate commerce. The U.S. Supreme Court found that regular stops by the carrier constituted minimum contacts in the host state which were sufficient to confer jurisdiction to tax. The Court held that requiring Braniff to pay a nondiscriminatory share of the local tax burden was not an unwarranted interference with interstate commerce. In general, any state that furnishes benefits and protection may levy an apportioned tax on the value of personal property which a foreign corporation uses in interstate commerce, even if other states tax the same property.

State Income Taxes   The U.S. Supreme Court has also upheld an apportioned nondiscriminatory tax on the net in-state income of foreign corporations if their interstate activities involve minimum contacts and benefits and protection.[3] The impact of this position is limited by the Federal Interstate Income Law of 1959.[4] This statute grants immunity from state income taxes to any foreign corporation that limits its source of in-state income and activity to soliciting orders which are accepted and shipped from outside the state.

---

[2]347 U.S. 590 (1954).

[3]*Northwestern States Portland Cement Co. v. Minnesota; Williams v. Stockham Valves & Fittings, Inc.*, 358 U.S. 450 (1959).

[4]15 U.S.C.A. Sections 381–384.

Case 46.3   Complete Auto Transit, Inc. v. Brady
430 U.S. 274 (1977)

General Motors shipped motor vehicles from its out-of-state assembly plants, by rail, to Jackson, Mississippi. Complete Auto Transit, Inc., a Michigan corporation, had a contract to pick up the vehicles and deliver them to GM dealers throughout Mississippi. The state levied a 5 percent tax on Auto Transit's gross in-state income "for the privilege of . . . doing business within this state." The state required the taxpayer "insofar as practicable" to add the tax to and collect it with the gross sales price paid by retail customers.

Auto Transit (plaintiff) sued for a refund of $165,000 in taxes which were paid, under protest, to the state of Mississippi (defendant). The plaintiff argued that its transportation activities within the state were part of an interstate movement and that the tax assessment was, therefore, unconstitutional. The trial court and the Mississippi Supreme Court sustained the assessment. Plaintiff appealed to the U.S. Supreme Court.

BLACKMUN, Justice. The Mississippi Supreme Court . . . concluded:

"It will be noted that Taxpayer has a large operation in this State. It is dependent upon the State for police protection and other State services the same as other citizens. It should pay its fair share of taxes so long, but only so long, as the tax does not discriminate against interstate commerce, and there is no danger of interstate commerce being smothered by cumulative taxes of several states. There is no possibility of any other state duplicating the tax involved in this case."

Auto Transit's attack is based solely on decisions of this Court holding that a tax on the "privilege" of engaging in an activity in the State may not be applied to an activity that is part of interstate commerce. *Spector Motor Service v. O'Connor*, 340 U.S. 602 (1951). This rule . . . deems irrelevant any consideration of the practical effect of the tax. The rule reflects an underlying philosophy that interstate commerce should enjoy a sort of "free trade" immunity from state taxation.

Mississippi, in its turn, relies on decisions of this Court stating that "it was not the purpose of the commerce clause to relieve those engaged in interstate commerce from their just share of state tax burden, even though it increases the cost of doing the business." [Citations.] These decisions have considered not the formal language of the tax statute but rather its practical effect, and have sustained a tax against Commerce Clause challenge when the tax is applied to an activity with a substantial nexus with the taxing State, is fairly apportioned, does not discriminate against interstate commerce, and is fairly related to the services provided by the State.

The prohibition against state taxation of the "privilege" of engaging in commerce that is interstate was reaffirmed in *Spector,* a case similar on its facts to the instant case. . . . The Court recognized that "where a taxpayer is engaged both in intrastate and interstate commerce, a state may tax the privilege of carrying on intrastate business and, within reasonable limits, may compute the amount of the charge by applying the tax rate to a fair proportion of the taxpayer's business done within the state, including both interstate and intrastate."

It held, nevertheless, that a tax on the "privilege of doing business" is unconstitutional if applied against what is exclusively interstate commerce. . . . The possibility of defending [this rule] in the abstract does not alter the fact that the Court has rejected the proposition that interstate commerce is immune from state taxation. . . .

If Mississippi had called its tax one on "net income" or on the "going concern value" of Auto Transit's business, the Spector rule could not invalidate it. There is no economic consequence that follows necessarily from the use of the particular words, "privilege of doing business," and a focus on that formalism merely obscures the question whether the tax produces a forbidden effect. Simply put, the Spector rule does not address the problems with which the Commerce Clause is concerned. Accordingly, we now reject the rule of *Spector Motor Service Inc. v. O'Connor*, that a state tax on the "privilege of doing business" is per se unconstitutional when it is applied to interstate commerce.

There being no objection to Mississippi's tax on Auto Transit except that it was imposed on nothing other than the "privilege of doing business" that is interstate, the judgment of the Supreme Court of Mississippi is affirmed.

Expansion of State Court Jurisdiction

The International Shoe Decision The U.S. Supreme Court's landmark opinion in *International Shoe Co. v. State*[5] discarded the traditional doing-business test and applied the minimum-contacts and benefits-and-protection theories to the question of local court jurisdiction. The State of Washington filed suit in its courts to recover unemployment compensation taxes from International Shoe Co., a Delaware corporation engaged in interstate commerce. The company maintained some sales personnel in Washington who solicited orders that were approved and filled at the principal office in Missouri. Although these minimum contacts did not constitute doing business in Washington, the U.S. Supreme Court held that they were sufficient to establish the company's presence in the state, thereby satisfying the due process requirements of the Fourteenth Amendment. The *International Shoe* decision established that an unlicensed foreign corporation can be sued in the host state if traditional notions of fair

play and substantial justice are not offended. The Supreme Court declared that such notions would not be offended if:

1 The suit is reasonable;

2 There are "certain minimum contacts" that establish the foreign corporation's presence in the state;

3 The corporation has enjoyed the benefits and protection of the state's laws; *and*

4 Court jurisdiction (including service of process) in the host state better serves the convenience of resident parties and witnesses.

Long-Arm Statutes On the one hand, the ruling in *International Shoe* limited the jurisdiction of state courts to suits arising from a foreign corporation's contacts within the state. On the other hand, the decision to drop the doing-business test encouraged the enactment of "long-arm" statutes which have expanded the list of activities that subject foreign corporations to suit within a host state. Examples of such activities are:

---

[5]326 U.S. 310 (1945).

- Causing tortious injury to residents
- Selling defective goods resulting in product liability
- Owning real property within the state
- Contracting to insure a person or property within the state
- Producing substantial revenue by selling interstate to users within the state

STATE REGULATION OF FOREIGN CORPORATIONS "DOING BUSINESS"

The Constitution permits the host state to impose any reasonable restriction on foreign corporations as a condition of doing business within the state. The Fourteenth Amendment prohibits any state from abridging privileges and immunities of citizens of the United States, but a corporation is not a citizen within the meaning of this clause. Therefore, it is possible for a host state to impose on foreign corporations requirements for qualifying to do business which are more burdensome than conditions imposed on domestic corporations.

Qualifying to Do Business

The Constitution provides that state laws must not interfere with interstate commerce. Subject to this proviso, all corporations must comply with state statutes designed to protect the welfare of residents (e.g., health and safety regulations and usury laws). As previously discussed, minimum contacts may subject a foreign corporation to the jurisdiction of local courts and state taxing authorities. However, a foreign corporation whose in-state business operations are extensive enough to constitute transacting business locally is subject to the full regulatory authority of the host state. Such corporations must qualify to do business and comply with statutes regulating foreign corporations as well as all other state and local laws, regulations, and ordinances which may be applicable.

When to Qualify State statutes and court decisions have not clearly fixed the point at which a foreign corporation's activities constitute doing business in a host state. In general, collateral acts which are incidental to a transaction in interstate commerce, such as occasional sales of samples or repossessed items and receipt of notes and mortgages for goods sold, do not require qualification. A number of courts have also held that preliminary acts, such as signing contracts preparatory to doing business, do not require a foreign corporation to qualify. However, sending personnel and materials into the state in performance of a contract is doing business. Similarly, shipping goods into the host state, storing them there, and later selling them to various resident customers is usually held to require qualification. Treatment of foreign corporations in similar circumstances is not necessarily uniform: For example, a few state statutes provide that mere ownership of real estate is not doing business; in other states, the courts have held that such ownership requires qualification to do business.

State court decisions requiring a foreign corporation to qualify are often appealed on constitutional grounds that the state is unduly burdening interstate commerce or un easonably denying a property right in violation of the due process clause of the Fourteenth Amendment. The U.S. Supreme Court must ultimately decide these issues. To avoid litigation costs, the management of many smaller corporations follow the maxim: "When in doubt, qualify to do business."

How to Qualify Each state has statutes (106–124) which set forth general requirements for "qualifying" to do business. To comply with these statutes, a foreign corporation must usually:

1 Furnish a copy of its articles and any other required data to the secretary of state;

2 Maintain a registered office within the state; and

3 Designate an agent authorized to accept service of process in the host state.

Most statutes provide that a foreign corporation cannot register to do intrastate business under a name deceptively similar to that of a domestic corporation (108) or be licensed to transact business which a domestic corporation is not permitted to transact (106). All states require a qualifying foreign corporation to pay annual license fees and franchise taxes proportionate to the property which it owns and the business which it transacts within the state. Once licensed, the foreign corporation is also required to file annual reports (125, 126).

Penalties Imposed on Unlicensed Corporations "Doing Business"

A foreign corporation which is doing business without having first qualified may be subject to severe penalties. Most statutes (121) provide that even if the corporation has qualified to do business, its license may be revoked for failure to pay taxes, file reports, or maintain a registered agent within the state on whom process may be served.

Denial of Access to Courts State statutes (124) deny the right to bring an action in state courts to a foreign corporation doing local business until it is licensed and has paid all fees, taxes, and penalties in arrears. The majority rule is that contracts entered into by a non-qualified foreign corporation are valid, but unenforceable by the corporation until it has qualified. Qualification is usually retroactive so that the corporation may sue and recover on a previously unenforceable contract. However, in Arkansas, Mississippi, and Vermont, such contracts are void and unenforceable, even if the foreign corporation subsequently qualifies to do business.

The statutory purpose for denying court access to unlicensed foreign corporations engaged in intrastate commerce is to protect the innocent public and to punish the wrongdoing corporation. In furtherance of this purpose, all jurisdictions permit qualified parties to sue an unlicensed corporation on contracts entered into prior to qualification. All states (124), except Nevada, permit a foreign corporation to defend against such suits.

Statutory Liability, Fines, and Penalties The various states impose statutory penalties (ranging from $100 to $10,000) on foreign corporations that transact local business without qualifying to do business. A few states also impose fines upon the offending corporation's officers or hold them personally liable for all debts and contracts for so long as the failure to qualify continues. Liability is imposed on the theory that if a foreign corporation is operating without authority, its agents and officers must have acted as a partnership.

Case 46.4   Eli Lilly and Company v. Sav-on-Drugs, Inc.
366 U.S. 276 (1961)

Eli Lilly and Company was an Indiana corporation dealing in pharmaceuticals. Eighteen salaried "detailmen" or representatives worked under a district manager in Lilly's Newark, New Jersey, office. The representatives visited retail pharmacists, physicians, and hospitals to encourage orders of Lilly's products from independent wholesalers in New Jersey. The wholesalers were supplied by interstate shipments from Lilly.

Lilly (plaintiff) sued Sav-on-Drugs (defendant), a New Jersey corporation, to enjoin its retail sales of Lilly's products at prices lower than those fixed under the New Jersey Fair Trade Act. The trial court dismissed Lilly's complaint under a statute that denied the right to bring an action in state courts to any foreign corporation transacting local business in New Jersey without first qualifying to do business with the secretary of state. The New Jersey Supreme Court upheld the decision and rejected Lilly's argument that enforcement of this statute against Lilly was forbidden by the commerce clause of the federal Constitution. Lilly appealed to the U.S. Supreme Court.

BLACK, Justice. The record shows that the New Jersey trade in Lilly's pharmaceutical products is carried on through both interstate and intrastate channels. . . . It is well established that New Jersey cannot require Lilly to get a certificate of authority to do business in the State if its participation in this trade is limited to its wholly interstate sales to New Jersey wholesalers. Under the authority of the so-called "drummer" cases . . . Lilly is free to send salesmen into New Jersey to promote this interstate trade without interference from regulations imposed by the State. On the other hand, it is equally well settled that if Lilly is engaged in intrastate as well as interstate aspects of the New Jersey drug business, the State can require it to get a certificate of authority to do business. In such a situation, Lilly could not escape state regulation merely because it is also engaged in interstate commerce. We must then look to the record to determine whether Lilly is engaged in intrastate commerce in New Jersey.

The findings of the trial court, based as they are upon uncontroverted evidence presented to it, show clearly that Lilly is conducting an intrastate as well as an interstate business in New Jersey. . . . Eighteen "detailmen," working out of a big office in Newark, New Jersey, with Lilly's name on the door and in the lobby of the building, and with Lilly's district manager and secretary in charge, have been regularly engaged in work for Lilly which relates directly to the intrastate aspects of the sale of Lilly's products. These eighteen "detailmen" have been traveling throughout the State of New Jersey promoting the sales of Lilly's products, not to the wholesalers, Lilly's interstate customers, but to the physicians, hospitals and retailers who buy those products in intrastate commerce from the wholesalers. To this end, they have provided these hospitals, physicians and retailers with up-to-date knowledge of Lilly's products and with free advertising and promotional material designed to encourage the general public to make more intrastate purchases of Lilly's products. And they sometimes even directly participate in the intrastate sales themselves by transmitting orders from the hospitals, physicians and drugstores they service to the New Jersey wholesalers.

The record clearly supports the judgment of the New Jersey Supreme Court and that judgment must therefore be and is affirmed.

SUMMARY

A graphic approximation of a host state's power to regulate, tax, and subject a foreign corporation to suit in state courts, as affected by the degree of the corporation's in-state activities, appears in Table 46.1.

A host state has little power over a foreign corporation if it is engaged purely in interstate commerce and does not maintain minimum contacts in the state. The state's power to tax and to assert court jurisdiction over foreign corporations (1) arises when activities go beyond shipping goods through a host state by common carrier and (2) is usually related to the degree of the corporation's minimum contacts within the host state and the benefits and protection it provides. If a foreign corporation is held to be doing business locally, it is subject to the full regulatory authority of the host state and must qualify to do business as required by state statute.

STUDY AND DISCUSSION QUESTIONS

1 In your own words, compare (*a*) "domestic" and "foreign" corporations, (*b*) state of incorporation and host state, and (*c*) interstate and intrastate activities of foreign corporations.

2 Describe two areas of a foreign corporation's activities which are virtually immune from regulation by a host state.

TABLE 46.1

Host State's Power over Foreign Corporation's In-State Activities

Degree of Corporation's Activities →	High Activity "Doing Business"	Moderate Activity "Minimum Contacts" (Not doing business)	Negligible Activity Interstate Commerce (no minimum contacts)
Regulation by Host State	Must (1) qualify to do business and (2) comply with all applicable state and local laws	(1) Need not qualify to do business but (2) is subject to minimal regulation (in addition to taxation and court jurisdiction)	(1) Need not qualify to do business but (2) is subject to reasonable nondiscriminatory regulation (e.g., inspection of incoming food) that does not unduly burden interstate commerce
Taxation by Host State	Subject to all applicable state taxes	Subject to taxes reasonably related to benefits and protection provided by state	Generally not subject to taxation by host state
State Court Jurisdiction (as expanded under long-arm statutes)	Complete state court jurisdiction (foreign corporation may defend suit, but cannot sue prior to qualification)	Subject to jurisdiction of state courts for consequences of in-state activities if traditional notions of fair play and convenience of witnesses are served	Generally not subject to jurisdiction of state courts

3 Can a host state subject a foreign corporation in interstate commerce to taxation and local court jurisdiction? Discuss related factors and theories on which you base your answer.

4 Discuss factors, if any, which limit the amount of state taxes that can be levied on a foreign corporation's *(a)* real property, *(b)* personal property, and *(c)* income.

5 Under what circumstances would you recommend that a foreign corporation register to do business in a host state? Give examples which illustrate your answer.

6 Give at least three of the major statutory requirements for qualifying to do business.

7 What circumstances would cause a host state to revoke a foreign corporation's license to do business?

8 Under what circumstances can a foreign corporation's officers and agents be held personally liable, as partners, for corporate debts and contracts?

CASE PROBLEMS

1 Fairfield, Inc., and Midland, Inc., foreign corporations, entered Delaware to hold public auction sales of jewelry and oriental rugs. Fairfield held auctions on four separate days, and Midland conducted eleven separate auctions. The auctions, which were advertised extensively, were held in premises leased in Delaware. Numerous bids were solicited from the public (Delaware residents) at each auction. Wier, a competitor residing in Delaware, brought an action in the state court to permanently enjoin Fairfield and Midland from doing in-state business without qualifying with the secretary of state. The two corporations contended that the isolated auction transactions did not constitute doing business. Should Fairfield and Midland be enjoined from transacting further business in Delaware until they comply with statutory qual-ification requirements? In your answer discuss *(a)* whether Fairfield and Midland's presence in Delaware was sufficient to satisfy "due process" requirements so that local courts had jurisdiction for service of process and *(b)* whether Fairfield and Midland's activities in Delaware were sufficient to constitute "doing business" so as to warrant granting the injunction requested by Wier.

2 Uniroyal Belgique (Uniroyal-B) was a Belgian corporation. It manufactured tires used on Opel automobiles which were imported and sold by General Motors. A Buick dealer in Illinois sold Connelly's father one of about 800 Opels which were sold in the state each year. Connelly, who went to Colorado with his father, was injured in an accident caused by a defective tire. Connelly alleged negligence in a product liability suit filed against Uniroyal-B in Illinois. Uniroyal-B was served with process in Belgium. The corporation moved to quash service, contending *(a)* that Uniroyal-B did not have sufficient minimum contacts to subject it to court jurisdiction in Illinois and *(b)* that the Illinois long-arm statute applied to "the commission of a tortious act within this State" and therefore excluded a cause of action arising in Colorado. It was undisputed that convenience of witnesses would be best served by an Illinois suit. Did the Illinois court have jurisdiction over Uniroyal-B for purposes of Connelly's suit? In your answer, discuss items *(a)* and *(b)* above.

3 Face Inc. was a New Jersey corporation. It operated a cocktail bar, the Lounge, located in New Jersey just across the state line from Pennsylvania. In 1973 and 1974, the corporation ran a daily newspaper advertisement in Philadelphia which induced underage drinkers in Pennsylvania to drive to New Jersey to drink at the Lounge. McCollum, a young Pennsylvania resident, drove to the Lounge; its personnel carelessly and negligently continued to serve the youth after he became visibly intoxicated. On the way home, McCollum caused an accident that resulted in the death of Hugh Hart and Maureen Laphen. Their parents, as their executors, sued Face for wrongful death (negligence) in Pennsylvania. Face contended that it had never done business in Pennsylvania and had no place of business and no contacts within the state to justify jurisdiction under the state long-arm statute. The Pennsylvania statute provided that "the doing by any person in this Commonwealth of a series of similar acts for the purpose of thereby realizing pecuniary benefit" was sufficient to confer court jurisdiction. The trial court ruled that Pennsylvania had no jurisdiction over Face, Inc. The decedents' parents appealed. Should the appellate court reverse the trial court's judgment?

4 Nobel, Inc. was a New York corporation. Wood was a Michigan resident. Nobel retained Wood to solicit mail orders from clothing shops in Michigan. Wood drew $250 per week against a 4-percent commission on goods sold. On occasion, Nobel sales personnel also put up display booths at fashion shows in Michigan. Although the sales volume was not large, these business activities continued over a period of years. All orders were accepted and shipped by Nobel from New York, but complaints from Michigan customers were handled by Wood. While traveling on business for Nobel, Wood crossed the centerline on a Michigan road and struck an oncoming car. Wood and two girls riding in the other car were killed in the head-on collision. The girls' father filed a wrongful death action for negligence against Nobel. The trial court held that it lacked jurisdiction over Nobel and dismissed the complaint. On appeal, should the trial court's ruling be sustained?

5 Whitin, Inc., a Massachusetts corporation, manufactured printing presses which were advertised in trade journals in South Dakota.

Perfection, Inc., a Minnesota corporation, acted as an independent dealer under a contract to distribute Whitin products in South Dakota. Libby, Perfection's president, visited Drier at his printing shop in South Dakota and sold him a new printing press. At the time, Libby made certain warranties as to the performance of the Whitin press. The press, which Whitin shipped to Drier from Massachusetts, was defective. Whitin paid half the cost of sending Perfection's experts to South Dakota to make repairs. Drier corresponded with Whitin about the problem, and Whitin also sent its "troubleshooter" to South Dakota to work on the press, but it continued to malfunction. Drier sued Perfection and Whitin for breach of warranty, and the jury awarded damages to Drier. Whitin appealed, contending that it was not "present" in South Dakota and that local courts had no jurisdiction. South Dakota's long-arm statute provided that any corporation transacting "any business within the state" was subject to state court jurisdiction. Was Whitin subject to the jurisdiction of the South Dakota court?

6 Oil Producer Co., a Louisiana corporation that owned oil, gas, and mineral leases in Mississippi, found a sand bridge in its oil well and hired Parks to remove the sand. Parks's sand bailing operations came to an abrupt halt when a wire snapped, leaving the bailing mechanism in the well. Oil Producer filed a negligence suit against Parks in Mississippi. Assume that Parks correctly contended that Oil Producer was doing intrastate business without qualifying and, therefore, lacked standing to sue. If Oil Producer subsequently qualifies to do business, should it be permitted to pursue a cause of action which arose prior to qualification? In your answer, distinguish between the majority and minority views.

PART ELEVEN

TRADE REGULATION

Chapter 47

**Introduction to Antitrust Law;
The Sherman Act**

Chapter 48

**The Clayton, Robinson-Patman, and
Federal Trade Commission Acts**

Chapter

47

Introduction to Antitrust Law; The Sherman Act

The term "antitrust law" refers to a broad system of federal and state law that seeks to promote business competition and to prohibit monopoly power. "Monopoly" literally means "a single seller," and monopoly power may therefore be defined as the power of a single large seller to use predatory means to exclude competitors from a market or to fix prices at arbitrarily high levels. Underlying antitrust law is a fundamental precept of capitalism: Scarce resources can most efficiently be allocated to satisfy consumer wants at the lowest price through a competitive free enterprise system. Such a system is incompatible with monopoly power and the high prices that result from the abuse of such power.

Perhaps unknowingly, each one of us is affect-ed by antitrust law. It applies to manufacturing and service industries that produce over 70 percent of the national income and distribute their products to national markets. The prices we pay for the things we buy each day are often lower because of antitrust law. There is virtually no nationwide industry that has not been involved with antitrust suits.

The first part of this chapter traces briefly the origin of antimonopoly sentiment in the English common law and the early development of antitrust law in the United States. The rest of the chapter examines the Sherman antitrust statute and the interpretative court decisions that have developed an organized body of law aimed at anticompetitive behavior. Chapter 48 will then look at the three other major antitrust statutes—the Clayton Act, Robinson-Patman Act, and Federal Trade Commission Act—and their impact on business today.

DEVELOPMENT OF ANTITRUST LAW

Restraints of Trade under Early Common Law

Antecedents of modern antitrust legislation first appeared in the English common law. In 1415, one of the earliest decisions arose in Dyer's case[1] where the court refused to enforce John Dyer's agreement with the buyer of his shop, that he would not practice his dyer's trade within the town. The court concluded that such agreements were void as a restraint on trade and competition. In 1623, Parliament enacted the Statute of Monopolies[2] which declared that "all monopolies" are "contrary to the laws of this realm, and so are and shall be utterly void." The Statute also prescribed that injured parties could recover treble damages, thus establishing an early precedent for the American Sherman Act provision for damages, discussed later in this chapter.

The Statute's rigid condemnation of *all* monopolies was steadily eroded by court decisions in the century that followed, culminating in the famous case of *Mitchel v. Reynolds.*[3] Reynolds; a baker, sold his business to Mitchel, and as part of the deal agreed not to compete as a baker in the vicinity for 5 years. When Reynolds breached this covenant, Mitchel sued for damages, and won. Even though the covenant was against competition, the court held that it was only a *partial* restraint, since it was limited as to time and place. In essence, the court said that if a *partial* or *ancillary* restraint is reasonable it is lawful. In contrast, a *general* restraint primarily for the purpose of restricting competition is invalid.

The historical significance of *Mitchel* is that it reflected the idea that there are "good" trade restraints as well as those that are "bad." If the restraint is "reasonable" as determined by examining its purpose and probable effect on competition, it is lawful. The decision was a direct precedent for the "rule of reason" eventually adopted by the United States Supreme Court[4] as the standard for determining whether a particular restraint on competition is lawful or unlawful under the antitrust laws.

Restraints of Trade in the Era of Laissez-Faire

In the century that followed *Mitchel*, the doctrine of laissez-faire as expounded by Adam Smith in the *Wealth of the Nations* was the dominant philosophy of the emerging capitalism. Its basic premise was that each entrepreneur by competitively seeking his own self-interest would be led as if by an "unseen hand" to further the welfare of all. In such an automatic economy, government should not interfere with business except to umpire the rules of the competitive game. In general, during the eighteenth and nineteenth centuries, decisions of English and American courts reflected laissez-faire views, and tended to favor restraints on competition that arose from contracts between entrepreneurs. For example, in 1892, the English court upheld a combination of steamship companies that was formed to restrict competition by reducing rates below cost in certain areas, giving discounts to shippers dealing exclusively with them, and refusing to deal with shippers who patronized their competitors.[5] The court held that these practices were merely weapons in a competitive war, and that the competitive goal justified any harm to the injured competitors.

About the same time, the American Supreme Court was also reflecting the laissez-faire view

---

[1]Y. B. 2 Hen. V. vol. 5, pl. 26.
[2]21 Jac. 1, c. 3 (1623).
[3]1 P. Williams 181, 24 Eng. Rep. 347 (K.B. 1711).

[4]*Standard Oil Co. of New Jersey v. United States,* 221 U.S. 1 (1911).
[5]*Mogul Steamship Co. v. McGregor Gow & Co.* (1889) 23 Q.B.D. 598, Aff'd. (1892) A.C. 25.

that business contracts which obviously injured competition would not be disturbed unless they involved a total restraint on competition. For example, an Oregon company bought a steamship from a California seller who required the buyer to agree not to use the ship for a period of 10 years in California waters where the seller operated. The court held that, even though the vessel was removed from shipping competition in a state with a 2000-mile coastline by the terms of the agreement, it did not amount to an unlawful *general* restraint on competition. Since the covenant was held to be only a *partial* restraint, it was lawful and enforceable.[6]

The Rise of Trusts in the United States

Rapid industrial expansion and growth of national markets after the Civil War encouraged large corporations to form industrial combines, or trusts, to fix prices, control production, divide markets, and freeze out competitors. The type of trust most commonly used was easily formed: Each corporation would cause a majority of its stockholders to transfer their shares to a board of trustees which included a representative from each company that was a party to the combine. The board of trustees would then issue trust certificates to the stockholders in exchange for their shares. These certificates gave the owners the right to any dividends declared by the trustees out of the pooled earnings of the combine.

With a majority of the outstanding shares of each member corporation firmly in hand, the board of trustees of the trust could control the election of the directors of each member company in the trust. The anticompetitive policies and practices of the trust could then be uniformly imposed upon all of the member corporations in the combine. At the same time each of these companies had retained its separate identity, and remained autonomous on all management

decisions other than those involving the monopolistic policies of the combine.

Enactment of Laws to Promote Competition

During the last quarter of the nineteenth century, trusts began controlling railroads as well as production and distribution of fuel oil, sugar, whiskey, and other commodities. The "captains of industry" who operated these trusts became ruthless. They cut prices below the cost of production in areas where small competitors operated, and after they were forced out of business, boosted prices to monopoly levels. A monopolistic industry with no competitors would also dictate low wages to workers immigrating by the millions from Europe, or drifting to the cities because free western land was no longer available. Railroads charged high rates to helpless farmers by using various devices, including secret rebates to powerful shippers. In one way or another, the monopolists exploited the three groups constituting a majority of the American population—workers, farmers, and consumers.

Responding to a public outcry for regulation and reform, a few state legislatures enacted "antitrust" laws aimed at restricting the monopolies. Hence, the term "antitrust" referred to trusts created by competitors who pooled their economic resources and transferred decision making to a trustee. Today, however, antitrust legislation is not limited to trusts but regulates a wide variety of practices which have the same anticompetitive effect. These include industrial combinations arising from devices such as holding companies, corporate mergers, interlocking directorates, formal or informal agreements between companies, or cooperative understandings between members of a trade association.

Since the activities of the trusts were nationwide in scope, it is not surprising that state antitrust legislation was largely ineffective. Similarly, the common law, based upon case precedents, was ineffective for three reasons: (1) Although the common law was quick enough to

---

[6]*Oregon Steam Navigation Co. v. Winsor*, 87 U.S. 64 (1873).

condemn outright monopolies, the courts (functioning in a laissez-faire environment) were hesitant to strike them down. (2) Although certain unfair competitive practices and agreements were illegal at common law, they could be attacked in the courts only when one of the parties brought suit, which seldom occurred. There was no legal basis for either the general public or government to attack unfair competition, and no statute absolutely prohibiting it. (3) Since the common law could only be applied within a particular state jurisdiction, state courts were ineffective in dealing with interstate abuses of the trusts.

Responding to the rising clamor for national corrective regulation, Congress enacted the Interstate Commerce Act (1887), directed against abuses of the railroads. Soon this was followed by the Sherman Antitrust Act (1890) aimed at the anticompetitive practices of the industrial trusts and monopolies. These two major legislative milestones reflect two distinct approaches to government's problem of dealing with monopoly: (1) Recognize it as socially necessary—as in the case of a railroad or public utility—and *regulate* the prices it charges at a level that is fair to the consumer and yields a reasonable rate of return to the company. (2) Recognize the monopoly as socially undesirable—for example, a petroleum cartel—and either break it into a number of small competing firms or stop it from becoming a monopoly. This is the approach Congress took in adopting the Sherman Act and later, the Clayton Act, Federal Trade Commission Act, and Robinson-Patman Act. Today, federal antitrust law is founded upon these four basic statutes that regulate competition in interstate commerce. Most states have laws patterned after the federal laws to deal with the intrastate dimension.

THE SHERMAN ACT

The significance of the Sherman Act was recently stated by the U.S. Supreme Court:

Antitrust laws in general, and the Sherman Act in particular, are the Magna Carta of free enterprise. They are as important to the preservation of economic freedom and our free-enterprise system as the Bill of Rights is to the protection of our fundamental personal freedoms. And the freedom guaranteed each and every business, no matter how small, "is the freedom to compete—to assert with vigor, imagination, devotion, and ingenuity whatever economic muscle it can muster."[7]

Purpose and Scope of the Act

Purpose An immediate aim of the Sherman Act was to satisfy public demand for a curb on anticompetitive practices of John D. Rockefeller's oil empire. The broad congressional purpose was to promote competition by slowing down the trend toward concentration in industry. Another major congressional objective was to create a broad federal court jurisdiction for the development of a new body of federal antitrust law that could reflect common law principles without being bound by them.

Scope The two basic sections of the Sherman Act[8] are:

1 Every contract, combination in the form of trust or otherwise, or conspiracy, in restraint of trade or commerce among the several states, or with foreign nations, is hereby declared to be illegal. . . .

2 Every person who shall monopolize, or attempt to monopolize, or combine or conspire with any other person or persons, to monopolize any part of the trade or commerce among the several States, or with foreign nations, shall be deemed guilty of a felony. . . .

The conspicuous absence of any wording defining key terms such as "restraint of trade," "combination," and "monopolize" left to the

[7]*United States v. Topco Associates, Inc.*, 405 U.S. 596 (1972).
[8]15 U.S.C.A. §§ 1–7.

judiciary the task of developing the legal meaning of these words on a case-by-case basis. Since the Sherman Act was passed as an exercise of congressional power to regulate interstate commerce, there remained for court clarification this important question: At what point does a local contract restraining trade substantially affect interstate commerce so as to violate the Sherman Act?

Although Sections 1 and 2 were purposely vague in some respects, they were clear in others. Both sections provide that violations are punishable as crimes. Both sections are *proscriptive* rather than *prescriptive*, that is, they tell businesses (in vague language) what they *cannot* do, rather than what they can do. Initially, the Act created no administrative agency to implement its provisions with regulations, consult with business persons, or respond to their inquiries. The need for such an agency was eventually met in 1914 with the creation of the Federal Trade Commission.

Enforcement of the Act

The provisions of the Sherman Act as well as other federal antitrust laws are enforced by private or governmental civil suits. In addition, the government may initiate criminal proceedings against violators.

Private Actions; Standing to Sue   Most antitrust cases in the federal courts are commenced by private parties, not the government. Special statutes authorize private enforcement by empowering any person "injured in his business or property by reason of anything forbidden in the antitrust laws"[9] to bring a *private action* to recover treble damages plus reasonable attorney's fees. Private litigants may also ask the court to grant injunctive relief against violations.[10] Damage awards in recent cases have been very substantial. For example, in *Trans World Airlines, Inc. v. Hughes*[11] the

damage award was $137 million after trebling, and attorney's fees totaled $7.5 million.

In order to prevail in a private treble damage suit, the plaintiff must have standing to sue, that is, be able to prove that: (1) the defendant violated the antitrust laws, (2) the violation was a substantial or direct cause of an injury to the plaintiff which can be measured with some certainty in money terms, and (3) the defendant's illegal act affected activities of the plaintiff that are under the protective umbrella of the antitrust laws.

In determining whether a plaintiff has standing to sue, the central focus of the courts is upon the *directness* of the injury suffered by the plaintiff as a result of the defendant's wrongful antitrust violation. To illustrate, the courts have determined damage was so indirect that the following plaintiffs were held not to have standing under the antitrust laws: shareholders suing derivatively on behalf of their injured corporation, creditors of a corporation allegedly injured by antitrust violations, a partner (as opposed to the partnership) suing for injuries to the partnership, suppliers suing for sales losses because of injury to a customer, franchisors suing to recover lost profits caused by injuries to franchisees, and an indirect purchaser-owner of a building whose contractor purchased blocks from suppliers allegedly charging monopolistic prices.[12]

Government Enforcement   The Sherman Act makes available to the federal government a wide variety of powerful enforcement tools:

1   Under Sections 1 and 2, as amended, restraints and monopolies are declared to be felonies, subject to criminal prosecution. Violators are punishable by a fine up to $1 million against a corporation, or $100,000 against an

---

[9]Section 4 of the Clayton Act, 15 U.S.C. § 15.
[10]15 U.S.C. § 26.
[11]409 U.S. 363 (1973).

[12]*Kaufman v. Dreyfus Fund*, 434 F.2d 727 (3d Cir. 1970); *Loeb v. Eastman Kodak Co.*, 183 F.704 (1910); *Hauer v. Bankers Trust N.Y. Corp.* 65 F.R.D. 1 (1974); *Milk Producers v. Bergjans Farm Dairy, Inc.* 368 F.2d 679 (1966); *Nationwide Auto Appraiser Serv. Inc. v. Ass'n of Cas. & Sur. Cos.*, 382 F.2d 925 (1967); *Illinois Brick Co. v. State of Illinois*, 421 U.S. 720 (1977).

individual or 3 years imprisonment, or both. The Justice Department's current policy is to proceed criminally if a company engages in "hard core" violations such as "price fixing, bid rigging, market and territorial allocation schemes, and various predatory practices."[13] The Department's recent emphasis on criminal enforcement is illustrated by the fact that in 1978, businessmen spent more time in jail for price fixing than in the previous 89 years since the Sherman Act was passed. The Department often permits companies engaged in lesser offenses to enter nolo contendere (no contest) pleas. Such pleas result in a judgment against the defendant that is not admissible to prove the defendant's liability in any subsequent civil suit, for example, a suit filed by a private party.

2 Section 4 of the Sherman Act also empowers the Department of Justice to bring a *civil action for injunction* against a violation of any provision of the Act.[14] Courts have used their power to restrain violations in a variety of ways, including ordering a defendant to divest itself of ownership of another company ("divestiture"), dissolution of a corporation, or divorcement and cessation by a company from conducting operations that would restrain trade.

3 Property being transported in interstate or foreign commerce pursuant to a contract or conspiracy that violates Section 1 is subject to *seizure and forfeiture* to the United States.

4 Recent legislation authorizes each state's *attorney general to commence civil actions* in the name of the state for treble damages for injury sustained by natural persons residing in the state arising from violations of the Sherman Act.[15] This legislation was intended to permit recovery by a state attorney general on behalf of large numbers of consumers. However, the Supreme Court's ruling in *Illinois Brick* that only direct purchasers from a violator have standing to sue, raises doubts as to how extensively the new legislation will be used.

Proving "Commerce" Jurisdiction under Sections 1 and 2 Under the Constitution, Congress can regulate only interstate commerce, not intrastate commerce. Therefore, Congress provided in the Sherman Act that federal courts are without jurisdiction to decide an antitrust case unless the restraint has a significant impact on interstate or foreign commerce.

Interstate commerce Either of two tests is used to meet the interstate commerce jurisdiction required by the Sherman Act:

1 Did the activities occur within the *flow of commerce?* The "flow of commerce" test applies only if a restraint is imposed directly upon goods or services while moving in interstate commerce. Consequently, under this test the volume or size of the restraint may be relatively small.[16]

2 Even though the activities occured wholly intrastate, did they have a substantial and adverse *effect* on commerce? Thus, a wholly intrastate activity will meet the jurisdictional requirement if it substantially affects interstate commerce, and is not merely inconsequential or remote.[17] "The test of jurisdiction is not that the acts complained of affect a business engaged in interstate commerce, but that the conduct complained of affects the interstate commerce of such business."[18]

In practice, a relatively small amount of direct or indirect interstate activity will be held by the courts to "substantially affect" interstate commerce. Thus, Sherman Act jurisdiction under the "effect on commerce" theory has been held to apply to a manufacturer's agreement with wholesalers to boycott a single local retailer,

---

[13]Department of Justice *Release*, October 21, 1978, p. 4.
[14]15 U.S.C.§4.
[15]15 U.S.C. § 15c (1976), amending Section 4 of the Clayton Act. See *Illinois Brick Co. v. Illinois*, 431 U.S. 720 (1977).

[16]*United States v. Yellow Cab Co.*, 332 U.S. 218 (1947).
[17]*Northern Cal. Pharmaceutical Ass'n v. United States*, 306 F.2d 379 (9th Cir. 1962).
[18]*C.A. Page Publishing Co. v. Work*, 178 F. Supp. 184 (S.D. Cal. 1959).

thereby reducing the manufacturer's shipments in interstate commerce,[19] and to a beet producers' agreement to fix beet prices to local processing refineries which in turn ship sugar in interstate commerce.[20]

---

[19]*Klor's Inc. v. Broadway-Hale Stores, Inc.*, Case 47.7.

[20]*Mandeville Island Farms, Inc. v. American Crystal Sugar Co.*, 334 U.S. 219 (1948).

Case 47.1   **McLain v. Real Estate Board of New Orleans**
444 U.S. 232 (1980)

Treble damage private antitrust class action by McLain and other real estate vendors (petitioners) against an association of real estate brokers in New Orleans (respondents) alleging that they had conspired to fix prices (brokers' commissions) in violation of Section 1 of the Sherman Act. The trial court's dismissal of the complaint for lack of "commerce" jurisdiction was affirmed by the Court of Appeals, and petitioners appealed to the Supreme Court.

BURGER, Chief Justice. The allegations of the complaint pertinent to establishing federal jurisdiction are: (1) that the activities of the respondents are "within the flow of interstate commerce and have an effect upon that commerce"; (2) that the services of respondents were employed in connection with the purchase and sale of real estate by "persons moving into and out of the Greater New Orleans area"; (3) that respondents "assist their clients in securing financing and insurance involved with the purchase of real estate in the Greater New Orleans area," which "financing and insurance are obtained from sources outside of Louisiana and move in interstate commerce into the State of Louisiana through the activities" of the respondents; and (4) that respondents have engaged in an unlawful restraint of "interstate trade and commerce in the offering for sale and sale of real estate brokering services." . . . Petitioners advance two independent theories to support federal jurisdiction: (1) that respondents' activities occurred within the stream of interstate commerce; and (2) that even if respondents' activities were wholly local in character they depended upon and affected the interstate flow of both services and people. . . . It can no longer be doubted . . . that the jurisdictional requirement of the Sherman Act may be satisfied under either the "in commerce" or the "effect on commerce" theory.

Although the cases demonstrate the breadth of Sherman Act prohibitions, jurisdiction may not be invoked under that statute unless the relevant aspect of interstate commerce is identified; it is not sufficient merely to rely on identification of a relevant local activity and to presume an interrelationship with some unspecified aspect of interstate commerce. To establish jurisdiction a plaintiff must allege the critical relationship in the pleadings. . . . Petitioners need not make the more particularized showing of the effect on interstate commerce caused by the alleged conspiracy to fix commission rates and if these allegations are controverted must proceed to demonstrate by submission of evidence beyond the pleadings either that the defendants' activity is itself in interstate commerce or, if it is local in nature, that it has an effect on some other appreciable activity demonstrably in interstate commerce. In a civil action under the Sherman Act, liability may be established by proof of either an unlawful purpose or an anticompetitive effect. Nor is jurisdiction defeated in a case relying on anticompetitive effects by plaintiff's failure to quantify the adverse impact of defendant's conduct.

Since the financing depended on a valid and insured title, in *Goldfarb v. Virginia State Bar* [421 U.S. 773] we concluded that title examination [by lawyers] was ''an integral part'' of the interstate transaction of obtaining financing for the purchase of residential property and, because of the ''inseparability'' of the attorneys' services from the title examination process, we held that the legal services were in turn an ''integral part of an interstate transaction.'' By placing the *Goldfarb* holding on the available ground that the activities of the attorneys were within the stream of interstate commerce, Sherman Act jurisdiction was established.

It is clear that an appreciable amount of commerce is involved in the financing of residential property in the Greater New Orleans area and in the insuring of titles to such property. The presidents of two of the many lending institutions in the area stated in their deposition testimony that those institutions committed hundreds of millions of dollars to residential financing during the period covered by the complaint. The testimony further demonstrated that this appreciable commercial activity has occurred in interstate commerce. Funds were raised from out-of-state investors and from interbank loans obtained from interstate financial institutions. Multistate lending institutions took mortgages insured under federal programs which entailed interstate transfers of premiums and settlements. Mortgage obligations physically and constructively were traded as financial instruments in the interstate secondary mortgage market. Before making a mortgage loan in the Greater New Orleans area, lending institutions usually, if not always, required title insurance, which was furnished by interstate corporations.

To establish federal jurisdiction in this case, there remains only the requirement that respondents' activities which allegedly have been infected by a price-fixing conspiracy be shown ''as a matter of practical economics'' to have a not insubstantial effect on the interstate commerce involved. It is clear, as the record shows, that the function of respondent real estate brokers is to bring the buyer and seller together on agreeable terms. . . . Ultimately, whatever stimulates or retards the volume of residential sales, or has an impact on the purchase price, affects the demand for financing and title insurance, those two commercial activities that on this record are shown to have occurred in interstate commerce. Where, as here, the services of respondent real estate brokers are often employed in transactions in the relevant market, petitioners at trial may be able to show that respondents' activities have a not insubstantial effect on interstate commerce.

We therefore conclude that it was error to dismiss the complaint at this stage of the proceedings. The judgment of the Court of Appeals is vacated and the case is remanded for further proceedings consistent with this opinion.

Foreign commerce Restraints which affect the flow of services or goods imported into or exported from the United States meet the jurisdictional requirement of "commerce . . . with foreign nations." Once such foreign jurisdiction is established, the Sherman Act will apply to activities of United States citizens or foreign nationals, within the United States or within a foreign country, and before or after the goods actually flow in commerce. Generally, the Sherman Act will not be enforced against an act of a foreign nation or its authorized agent. However, the Foreign Sovereign Immunities Act of 1976[21] applies the Sherman Act to "commercial activities" of a foreign state which have a "direct effect" in the United States.

Proving Conspiracy under Section 1 The words "contract, combination . . . or conspiracy" clearly require proof that at least *two* persons agreed to act in concert so as to restrain trade. Courts have used "combination" and "conspiracy" interchangeably[22] and because it is often impossible to obtain direct evidence of a contract, combination, or conspiracy to restrain trade, circumstantial evidence is sufficient.[23] For example, where a dealer's association distributed to its members a list of wholesalers who sold directly to consumers and the members ceased to deal with the listed wholesalers, a conspiracy to boycott was inferred.[24]

Consciously parallel behavior, that is, uniform business conduct by competitors who are aware of each other's actions, would seem to be circumstantial evidence from which an agree-ment could be inferred. However, standing alone, it is generally insufficient to prove a conspiracy.[25] The doctrine of conscious parallelism was probably extended to its furthest limit in *Interstate Circuit, Inc. v. U.S.*[26] where motion picture distributors and exhibitors were accused of conspiring to impose minimum admission prices on competing exhibitors. Although there was no direct testimony that the defendant distributors and exhibitors had conspired, communicated with each other, or ever met, the Supreme Court affirmed the conviction and said: "Acceptance by competitors without previous agreement of an invitation to participate in a plan, the necessary consequence of which, if carried out, is restraint of interstate commerce is sufficient to establish an unlawful conspiracy under the Sherman Act."

In the later *Theatre Enterprises case*[26], the plaintiff film exhibitor claimed a conspiracy among the defendant distributors to refrain from leasing films to him. Defendants produced evidence showing why each acting separately and not in concert, had refused to deal with the plaintiff. The Supreme Court, in affirming a jury verdict for the defendants, said:

To be sure, business behavior is admissible circumstantial evidence from which the fact finder may infer agreement. But this court has never held that proof of parallel business behavior conclusively establishes agreement, or, phrased differently, that such behavior itself constitutes a Sherman Act offense. Circumstantial evidence of consciously parallel behavior may have made heavy

---

[21]38 U.S.C. §§ 1602–1611.

[22]*Perma Life Mufflers, Inc. v. International Parts Corp.*, 392 U.S. 134 (1968).

[23]*United States v. General Motors Corp.*, 384 U.S. 127 (1966).

[24]*Eastern States Retail Lumber Dealers' Ass'n v. United States*, 234 U.S. 600 (1914).

[25]*FTC v. Lukens Steel Co.*, 454 F. Supp. 1183 (D. D.C., 1978).

[26]306 U.S. 208 (1939). See also, *Theatre Enterprises, Inc. v. Paramount Film Distrib. Corp.* 346 U.S. 537 (1954).

inroads into the traditional judicial attitude toward conspiracy; but "conscious parallelism" has not read conspiracy out of the Sherman Act entirely.

Conscious parallelism, together with evidence of exchange of pricing data at meetings or through correspondence, can be enough to infer a conspiracy.[27] A corporation is a separate legal person and because it can act only through its agents, it is incapable of conspiring with its officers or employees.[28] Hence, any such "con-

spiracy" does not meet the two-actor requirement of Section 1. However, wholly owned subsidiaries can conspire among themselves, or with the parent corporation.[29] Under well-established doctrines of criminal conspiracy, a defendant convicted is liable for all of the acts of his co-conspirators. As long as a defendant remains active in the conspiracy, he is liable for the actions of others which occur before or after his participation.

---

[27]*Gainsville Utilities Dept. v. Florida Power & Light Co.*, 573 F.2d 292 (5th Cir. 1978).

[28]*Solomon v. Houston Corrugated Box Co.*, 526 F.2d 389 (5th Cir. 1976).

[29]*Balian Ice Cream Co. v. Arden Farms Co.*, 104 F. Supp. 796 (S.D. Cal. 1952).

Case 47.2   **Esco Corp. v. United States**
340 F. 2d 1000 (9th Cir. 1965)

Esco and three other distributors of stainless steel pipe were criminally charged with violating Section 1 of the Sherman Act by conspiring to fix prices. The other defendants pleaded nolo contendere, but Esco elected to proceed with trial by jury, and was found guilty. Esco appealed, claiming that although there was some proof of a conspiracy among the other defendants, there was no proof of an Esco connection.

BARNES, Circuit Judge. While particularly true of price-fixing conspiracies, it is well recognized law that any conspiracy can ordinarily only be proved by inferences drawn from relevant and competent circumstantial evidence, including the conduct of the defendants charged. A knowing wink can mean more than words. Let us suppose five competitors meet on several occasions, discuss their problems, and one finally states—"I won't fix prices with any of you, but here is what I am going to do—put the price of my gidget at X dollars; now you all do what you want." He then leaves the meeting. Competitor number two says—"I don't care whether number one does what he says he's going to do or not; nor do I care what the rest of you do, but I am going to price my gidget at X dollars." Number three makes a similar statement—"My price is X dollars." Number four says not one word. All leave and fix "their" prices at "X" dollars.

We do not say the foregoing illustration *compels* an inference in this case that the competitors' conduct constituted a price-fixing conspiracy, *including an agreement to so conspire*, but neither can we say, as a matter of law, that an inference of no agreement is compelled. As in so many other instances, it remains a question for the trier of fact to consider and determine what inference appeals to it (the jury) as most logical and persuasive, after it has heard all the evidence as to what these competitors had done before such meeting, and what actions they took thereafter, or what actions they did not take.

An accidental or incidental price uniformity, or even "pure" conscious parallelism of price is, standing alone, not unlawful. Nor is an individual competitor's sole decision to follow a price leadership, standing alone, a violation of law. But we do not find that factual situation here. . . . It is not necessary to find an express agreement, either oral or written, in order to find a conspiracy, but it is sufficient that a concert of action be contemplated and that the defendants conform to the arrangement. Mutual consent need not be bottomed on express agreement, for any conformance to an agreed or contemplated pattern of conduct will warrant an inference of conspiracy. Thus not only action, but even a lack of action, may be enough from which to infer a combination or conspiracy.

Applying these rules to the facts at hand, the jury came to an opposite conclusion from that which appellant urges, and the fact that Esco's involvement was in but two of ten allegedly conspirational situations does not absolve Esco from participation in the entire conspiracy if its involvement in the two was unlawful and knowingly and purposely performed. We hold that sufficient evidence existed for the jury to find participation in a price-fixing conspiracy. . . . Finding no error, we affirm.

Court Interpretations of Section 1

The Supreme Court's initial response to the Sherman Act was to strip it of its vitality by narrow interpretation. Only 5 years after passage of the Act, the Court held that its provisions did not apply to a trust of sugar manufacturers in Pennsylvania because they were not engaged in "interstate commerce" within the meaning of the act.[30] The Court reasoned that even though the sugar would eventually be shipped in interstate commerce, the manufacture of it was purely a local activity.

Commencing in 1897, the Court flip-flopped in the other direction, holding to a strict literal interpretation that Section 1 prohibited *every* restraint of trade.[31] Such a rigid interpretation

could be used to invalidate every normal business deal by arguing that it restrains trade because the contractually obligated parties are no longer free to deal with others. Retreat from this arbitrary position was inevitable. It came with the Court's decision in the landmark case, *Standard Oil Company of New Jersey v. United States.*[32]

The Rule of Reason In *Standard Oil*, the Court rejected its earlier position that *all* contracts in restraint of trade were prohibited by the Sherman Act and applied what has come to be called the *Rule of Reason*. The Court ruled that the congressional intent was to prohibit only those contracts that *unreasonably* restrained trade. This rule of reason, that is, the process of determining if a defendant's conduct is sufficiently anticompetitive to constitute an

---

[30]*United States v. E. C. Knight Co.*, 156 U.S. 1 (1895).
[31]*United States v. Trans-Missouri Freight Ass'n.*, 166 U.S. 290 (1897).

[32]221 U.S. 1 (1911).

"unreasonable restraint," is very much a part of antitrust law today in Section 1 cases.

The Developing Doctrine of Per Se Unreasonableness The question yet remained: If firms combine to fix prices at *reasonable* levels, does such action nevertheless constitute an *unreasonable* restraint of trade under Section 1? The Supreme Court has answered this question in the affirmative, holding that certain actions are per se illegal. In *United States v. Trenton Potteries Co.*,[33] Justice Stone speaking for the Court said:

> The aim and result of every price-fixing agreement, if effective, is the elimination of one form of competition. *The power to fix prices, whether reasonably exercised or not, involves power to control the market and to fix arbitrary and unreasonable prices.* The reasonable price fixed today may through economic and business changes become the unreasonable price of tomorrow. Once established, it may be maintained unchanged because of the absence of competition secured by the agreement for a price reasonable when fixed. *Agreements which create such potential power may well be held to be in themselves ["per se"] unreasonable or unlawful restraints, without the necessity of minute inquiry whether a particular price is reasonable as fixed and without placing on the government in enforcing the Sherman Law the burden of ascertaining from day to day whether it has become unreasonable through the mere variation of economic conditions.* [Emphasis added.]

Certain types of restrictive agreements are so inherently anticompetitive it can be said as a *matter of law* that they unreasonably restrain trade, and are therefore illegal under Section 1 of the Act. If an activity is illegal per se, proof of that activity is sufficient to establish its anticompetitive nature, and it is not necessary to present evidence that the activity unreasonably restrained trade. Obviously, it takes less effort to establish a per se violation than is required in other Section 1 cases where proof must be presented that the restraint is unreasonable. Thirty years after *Trenton*, the Supreme Court summarized the nature of per se violations as follows:

> There are certain agreements or practices which because of their pernicious effect on competition and lack of any redeeming virtue are conclusively presumed to be unreasonable and therefore illegal without elaborate inquiry as to the precise harm they have caused or the business excuse for their use. This principle of *per se* unreasonableness not only makes the type of restraints which are proscribed by the Sherman Act more certain to the benefit of everyone concerned, but it also avoids the necessity for an incredibly complicated and prolonged economic investigation into the entire history of the industry involved, as well as related industries, in an effort to determine at large whether a particular restraint has been unreasonable—an inquiry so often wholly fruitless when undertaken. . . . [34]

It is only after considerable experience with certain business relationships that courts classify them as per se violations of the Sherman Act.[35] Joint activities in interstate commerce that are regularly recognized as per se violations include horizontal price fixing, vertical price fixing,

---

[33]273 U.S. 392 (1927).

[34]*Northern Pac. Railway Co. v. United States*, 356 U.S. 1 (1958). In the period between *Trenton* and *Northern Pacific Railway*, the only notable departure from per se rules was in *Appalachian Coals, Inc. v. United States*, 268 U.S. 344 (1933), during the emergency conditions of the Great Depression, when many sick industries, including bituminous coal, were trying to avoid failure by entering into price-fixing and market allocation agreements. The Court held that the coal producers' agreement was not an undue restraint of trade under the Sherman Act.

[35]*United States v. Topco Associates, Inc.*, 405 U.S. 596 (1972).

restricting production, horizontal division of customers or geographical markets, concerted refusals to deal (group boycotts), promoting reciprocal dealing arrangements, tying contracts, as well as other restraints. Generally, all kinds of anticompetitive restraints that are not per se violations are judged under the "rule of reason" to determine if the particular restraint is unreasonable and therefore unlawful.

Horizontal price fixing When two or more competitors at the same level—such as two manufacturers, two wholesalers, or two retailers—agree to establish a minimum or maximum price, or to charge a set price for a product, the result is a *horizontal price-fixing* agreement. Such an agreement by its very nature eliminates price competition and is the most common per se violation of the antitrust law. Once the prosecution has proved the existence of horizontal price fixing, it is no defense to argue that it was necessary to prevent "ruinous competition," "financial disaster," or the "evils of price cutting." Additionally, the fact that the prices fixed are equal to the fair market price or are otherwise reasonable is considered irrelevant.

Case 47.3 Catalano, Inc. v. Target Sales
446 U.S. 635 (1980)

Class action by beer retailers (plaintiffs) in the Fresno, California area, seeking treble damages and injunctive relief against a group of wholesalers (defendants) alleging that they had horizontally conspired and agreed to eliminate the industry practice of granting short-term trade credit to the retailers on beer purchases. A violation of Section 1 of the Sherman Act was alleged. The trial court denied plaintiffs' motion requesting that the court declare that defendants' conduct amounted to a per se violation; and the plaintiff appealed. The Court of Appeals (9th Circuit) held that a horizontal agreement among competitors to fix credit terms does not necessarily contravene the antitrust laws, and certiorari was granted by the United States Supreme Court.

PER CURIAM. According to the Petition, prior to the agreement wholesalers had competed with each other with respect to trade credit, and the credit terms for individual retailers had varied substantially. After entering into the agreement, respondents uniformly refused to extend any credit at all. . . . In *Broadcast Music, Inc. v. Columbia Broadcasting System, Inc.*, 441 U.S. 1 (1979) we said:

> In construing and applying the Sherman Act's ban against contracts, conspiracies, and combinations in restraint of trade, the Court has held that certain agreements or practices are so "plainly anticompetitive" and so often "lack any redeeming virtue" that they are conclusively presumed illegal without further examination under the rule of reason generally applied in Sherman Act cases.

A horizontal agreement to fix prices is the archetypal example of such a practice. It has long been settled that an agreement to fix prices is unlawful *per se*. It is no excuse that the prices fixed are themselves reasonable. In *United States v. Socony-Vacuum Oil Co.*, 310 U.S. 150 (1940) we held that an agreement among competitors to engage in a program of buying surplus gasoline on the spot market in order to prevent prices from falling sharply to be unlawful without any inquiry into the reasonableness of the program, even though there was no direct agreement on the actual prices to be maintained. In the course of that opinion, the Court made clear that

> the machinery employed by a combination for price-fixing is immaterial. Under the Sherman Act a combination formed for the purpose and with the effect of raising, depressing, fixing, pegging, or stabilizing the price of a commodity in interstate or foreign commerce is illegal *per se*.

> . . . It is virtually self-evident that extending interest-free credit for a period of time is equivalent to giving a discount equal to the value of the use of the purchase price for that period of time. . . . An agreement to terminate the practice of giving credit is thus tantamount to an agreement to eliminate discounts, and thus falls squarely within the traditional *per se* rule against price fixing. . . . Under the reasoning of our cases, an agreement among competing wholesalers to refuse to sell unless the retailer makes payment in cash either in advance or upon delivery is "plainly anticompetitive." Since it is merely one form of price-fixing, and since price-fixing agreements have been adjudged to lack any "redeeming virtue," it is conclusively presumed illegal without further examination under the rule of reason.

> Accordingly, the judgment of the Court of Appeals is reversed, and the case is remanded for further proceedings consistent with this opinion. It is so ordered.

Vertical price fixing   If a manufacturer sells to a wholesaler (or a wholesaler sells to a retailer) on condition that the buyer will not resell the product below a set minimum price, or on condition that the buyer will only resell at a stated fixed price, the contract is called a *vertical price-fixing agreement*. This process, whereby a seller at one level of the chain of distribution fixes the resale price terms of a buyer at a different level, is also called *resale price maintenance*. Until 1937, the Supreme Court held that resale price maintenance contracts in interstate commerce were per se violations of Section 1 even though the buyer's state legislature had enacted a *fair trade* law permitting such contracts. However, in that year Con-gress enacted the Miller-Tydings Act exempting resale price maintenance contracts from the Sherman law *if* there was a fair trade law in effect in the buyer's state. Since most states had enacted fair trade laws, the effect of the Miller-Tydings Act was to make most resale price maintenance agreements legal.[36] In 1976, Congress repealed the Miller-Tydings Act with the result that resale price maintenance in interstate commerce once again constituted a per se violation of Section 1. Today, such vertical price-fixing agreements are unlawful to the same extent as prior to 1937. Thus, it is a

---

[36]However, South Carolina remains as the only state with a "fair trade" resale price maintenance law in effect.

violation of the Sherman Act for a manufacturer to establish suggested retail prices and then refuse to sell to wholesalers that are selling to retailers who do not observe such prices. However, it is still lawful for a seller to establish suggested resale prices, and to unilaterally announce that it will refuse to sell to its immediate customers who do not maintain such prices.[37]

There is an important distinction between

[37]*United States v. Parke, Davis & Co.*, 362 U.S. 29 (1960); *United States v. Colgate & Co.*, 250 U.S. 300 (1919); *FTC v. Beech-Nut Packing Co.*, 257 U.S. 441 (1922).

vertical price fixing and other vertical nonprice restraints. Generally, vertical restraints not involving price fixing—for example, a manufacturer's allocation of market territory among franchised retailers—are subject to the rule of reason, and are not per se violations. Some manufacturers own their own retail outlets and occasionally enter into price-fixing agreements with other independent retailers. Such arrangements may be classified by the courts as both "horizontal" and "vertical" thus violating Section 1 with both types of unlawful restraints.

Case 47.4   **Canadian American Oil Co. v. Union Oil Co. of Calif.**
577 F.2d 468 (9th Cir. 1978)

Treble damage action by Canadian Oil (plaintiff and appellant), owner of two high-volume service stations in the San Francisco Bay area, against Union Oil, contending that it had violated Section 1 of the Sherman Act by engaging in resale price maintenance. In 1972, Union Oil contracted with Canadian to supply it with 13 million gallons of gasoline per year, at Union's standard "posted dealer purchase price." However, all parties understood that Canadian would shortly be entitled to a 2 cents per gallon discount from that price, which Union would give in the form of a sign rental agreement. Canadian was also led to believe that within a few months it would be given a jobbership, that is, a wholesale distributorship. Canadian began selling Union gas at their two stations 2 to 5 cents below the prevailing market prices for other major brand gasoline in the area. Competing Union dealers complained about the price cutting to Union, which then urged Canadian to keep its retail price within 2 cents of the prevailing market price. When Canadian persisted in its price-cutting practices, Union refused the promised jobbership and sign rental benefits and exercised its 90-day termination clause on the gasoline supply contract. Canadian commenced suit, the trial court dismissed the complaint, and Canadian appealed.

PER CURIAM. The district court recognized that the appellants lost both the two-cent per gallon discount on the price and the opportunity for a jobbership in retaliation for appellants' "renegade pricing policies." The court nevertheless held that Union's conduct was outside the ambit of *Simpson v. Union Oil Company*, 377 U.S. 13, and *Lehrman v. Gulf Oil Corporation*, 464 F. 2d 26, because "the element of coercive leverage inherent in the pricing policy is missing. . . . "At most, the undisputed facts establish that when plaintiffs exercised their independent pricing discretion, Union attempted to keep them in line by coercive techniques independent of its widespread pricing program. . . . The coercion applied to plaintiffs had no more effect on the gasoline industry than the regulation of the prices charged by plaintiffs in their local operations." [Note: In *Simpson*, Union had required Simpson and other lessees of its retail outlets to sign product consignment agreements as well as station leases, both agreements being of one year's duration. Under the consignment agreement Union retained title to the delivered gas and retained control of the retail price charged. When Simpson undercut Union's fixed price, Union refused to renew the lease-consignment agreements. The Supreme Court held that the "consignment" device was an indirect attempt to unlawfully engage in resale price maintenance.]

These conclusions rest upon a mischaracterization of the conduct attributed to Union and upon a misreading of both *Simpson* and *Lehrman*. The district court apparently assumed that *Simpson* did not apply because Union's price support system was not on its face a forbidden price-fixing agreement, and that *Lehrman* did not apply because the coercive techniques used to force appellants to raise their prices did not involve withdrawal of the company's price support program. The district court's restrictive reading of *Simpson* and *Lehrman* is unjustified.

Resale price maintenance in violation of the Sherman Act is an actionable wrong whenever the restraint of trade or monopolistic practice has an impact on the market, and "it matters not that the complainant may be only one merchant." (*Simpson, supra.*) *Lehrman* extended this principle to find jurisdiction under the Sherman Act for an independent service station operator in Texas: "Because of the broad scope of the price support mechanism, however inherently compatible with competition, the treatment of Lehrman when he disobeyed Gulf's price 'suggestions' transformed a practice benign on its face into a coercive practice with untold geographical potential for deterring Gulf retailers from freely determining their own retail prices. . . ."

Judge Wisdom rejected Gulf's preferred distinction that its price support program was a facially benign business practice subject to intermittent anticompetitive abuse "as applied" only on a case-by-case basis, while in Simpson, the single, intrastate operator was permitted Sherman Act jurisdiction because Union's "consignment agreement" was anticompetitive "on its face." Judge Wisdom noted that . . . "It would be exceedingly unfortunate if large enterprises could, without federal antitrust liability, use small, intrastate operators as a way of making known certain unspoken and unwritten features of broadly utilized business practices which are not anticompetitive on their face."

For Sherman Act purposes, it matters not at all whether Union chose to drive appellants out of its market by exercising a 90-day option to cancel their dealer contract or by withdrawing its price supports. The impact is identical. Independent dealers similarly situated to appellants in either event received the message that obdurate price cutters faced dealer contract cancellation.

We cannot say that the omnipresent threat of dealer contract cancellation for failure to conform one's retail prices to those announced by Union's price support program is not coercive. The effect of Union's conduct is to eliminate effective intrabrand price competition among Union dealers within its Western Region. Viewed in the aggregate, an absence of effective intrabrand price competition produces a substantial economic impact upon interstate commerce.

The district court assumed that no coercive effect upon other dealers could have been exerted when Union withheld the jobbership and withheld the sign rental discount because other dealers in the area had not been promised similar benefits. That assumption overlooks the practical effect of Union's action. The point is that other dealers were made aware that Union would retaliate against any dealer who failed to follow Union's pricing dictates. Especially is that true on this record where Union undertook retaliatory action in response to complaints from Union dealers who were following Union's pricing policies. Union's alleged conduct in violation of the antitrust laws adversely affected the appellants and potentially created anticompetitive effects upon other dealers in the ten states comprising Union's Western Region.

The judgment is reversed and the cause is remanded for further proceedings consistent with the views herein expressed.

Restricting production   Competitive theory holds that many producers competing with each other will maximize production at minimum prices. However, if producers combine and agree to fix prices, the effort cannot be effective unless the producers also agree to restrict production and sales. Since price fixing and manipulation of production are closely interrelated, an agreement to manipulate production to achieve an anticompetitive objective is a per se violation.[38]

Dividing markets or customers   It is illegal per se for *horizontal* competitors (that is, at the same level) to geographically apportion market territory among themselves, to allocate customers while agreeing not to solicit each other's customers, or to divide product markets.[39] However, *vertical* division of markets or customers is *not* a per se violation, and courts evaluate such arrangements under the rule of reason, as illustrated by the *Sylvania* decision which follows. Here the test of reasonableness is whether the procompetitive effect of the restraint on interbrand competition outweighs the anticompetitive effect of eliminating intrabrand competition.

[38]*United States v. Addyston Pipe & Steel Co.*, 85 F. 271 (6th Cir. 1898); *Hartford-Empire Co. v. United States*, 323 U.S. 386 (1945).

[39]*United States v. Topco Associates, Inc.*, *supra.*

Case 47.5   **Continental TV, Inc. v. GTE Sylvania, Inc.**
433 U.S. 36 (1977)

Continental TV (plaintiff) held a franchise from GTE Sylvania (defendant), a manufacturer of television sets, to sell its TV products. GTE marketed its products through a limited number of franchised retailers, who were restricted to selling only from the locations at which they were franchised. The franchise agreements did not establish exclusive territory, and Sylvania retained sole discretion to increase the number of retailers in an area in light of the success or failure of existing retailers in developing their market. Sylvania's franchise program increased its market share of national television sales from 1 percent in 1962 to 5 percent in 1965. Continental was one of Sylvania's more successful franchise retailers in the San Francisco area. When Sylvania refused Continental's request for a franchise to open another retail outlet in Sacramento, Continental announced it intended to proceed without a franchise. Sylvania then terminated Continental's San Francisco franchise.

Thereupon Continental sued Sylvania for treble damages, alleging that the franchise location restrictions were a per se violation of Section 1 of the Sherman Act. The trial court (relying on *Schwinn & Co. v. U.S.*, 388 U.S. 365) instructed the jury that once Sylvania had parted with title to its products any attempt to control their resale including the location restriction on dealers, was a violation of Section 1 of the Sherman Act, regardless of the reasonableness of the restriction. Based on those instructions, the jury awarded plaintiff $1,774, 515 damages, and Sylvania appealed. The Court of Appeals reversed, stating that the sales location limitation clause should be judged under the rule of reason, and that the provision did not constitute a per se violation. Continental appealed to the Supreme Court.

POWELL, Associate Justice. In the present case, it is undisputed that title to the televisions passed from Sylvania to Continental. Thus, the *Schwinn per se* rule applies unless Sylvania's restriction on location falls outside *Schwinn's* prohibition against a manufacturer attempting to restrict a "retailer's freedom as to where and to whom it will resell the products." As the Court of Appeals conceded, the language of *Schwinn* is clearly broad enough to apply to the present case. Unlike the Court of Appeals, however, we are unable to find a principled basis for distinguishing *Schwinn* from the case now before us.

Both Schwinn and Sylvania sought to reduce but not to eliminate competition among their respective retailers through the adoption of a franchise system. The Schwinn franchise plan included a location restriction similar to the one challenged here. These restrictions allowed Schwinn and Sylvania to regulate the amount of competition among their retailers by preventing a franchisee from selling franchised products from outlets other than the one covered by the franchise agreement.

Sylvania argues that if *Schwinn* cannot be distinguished, it should be reconsidered. Although *Schwinn* is supported by the principle of *stare decisus*, we are convinced that the need for clarification of the law in this area justifies reconsideration. *Schwinn* itself was an abrupt and largely unexplained departure from *White Motor Co. v. United States*, 372 U.S. 253, where only four years earlier the Court had refused to endorse a *per se* rule for vertical restrictions. The great weight of scholarly opinion has been critical of the decision, and a number of the federal courts confronted with analogous vertical restrictions have sought to limit its reach.

The market impact of vertical restrictions is complex because of their potential for a simultaneous reduction of intrabrand competition and stimulation of interbrand competition. Significantly, the Court in *Schwinn* did not distinguish among the challenged restrictions on the basis of their individual potential for intrabrand harm or interbrand benefit. Restrictions that completely eliminated intrabrand competition among Schwinn distributors were analyzed no differently than those that merely moderated intrabrand competition among retailers. The pivotal factor was the passage of title: All restrictions were held to be *per se* illegal where title had passed, and all were evaluated and sustained under the rule of reason where it had not. The location restriction at issue here would be subject to the same pattern of analysis under *Schwinn*.

Vertical restrictions reduce intrabrand competition by limiting the number of sellers of a particular product competing for the business of a given group of buyers. Location restrictions have this effect because of practical constraints on the effective marketing area of retail outlets. Although intrabrand competition may be reduced, the ability of retailers to exploit the resulting market may be limited both by the ability of consumers to travel to other franchised locations and, perhaps more importantly, to purchase the competing products of other manufacturers. None of these key variables, however, is affected by the form of the transaction by which a manufacturer conveys his products to the retailers.

Vertical restrictions promote interbrand competition by allowing the manufacturer to achieve certain efficiencies in the distribution of his products. These "redeeming virtues" are implicit in every decision sustaining vertical restrictions under the rule of reason. Economists have identified a number of ways in which manufacturers can use such restrictions to compete more effectively against other manufacturers. For example, new manufacturers and manufacturers entering new markets can use the restrictions in order to induce competent and aggressive retailers to make the kind of investment of capital and labor that is often required in the distribution of products unknown to the customer. Established manufacturers can use them to induce retailers to engage in promotional activities or to provide service and repair facilities necessary to the efficient marketing of their products. Service and repair are vital for many products, such as automobiles and major household appliances.

Economists have also argued that manufacturers have an economic interest in maintaining as much intrabrand competition as is consistent with the efficient distribution of their products. Although the view that the manufacturer's interest necessarily corresponds with that of the public is not universally shared, even the leading critic of vertical restrictions concedes that *Schwinn's* distinction between sale and nonsale transactions is essentially unrelated to any relevant economic impact.

We conclude that the distinction drawn in *Schwinn* between sale and nonsale transactions is not sufficient to justify the application of a *per se* rule in one situation and a rule of reason in the other. . . . Vertical restrictions, in varying forms, are widely used in our free market economy. As indicated above, there is substantial scholarly and judicial authority supporting their economic utility. There is relatively little authority to the contrary. Certainly, there has been no showing in this case, either generally or with respect to Sylvania's agreements, that vertical restrictions have or are likely to have a "pernicious effect on competition" or that they "lack . . . any redeeming virtue." Accordingly, we conclude that the *per se* rule stated in *Schwinn* must be overruled. In so holding we do not foreclose the possibility that particular applications of vertical restrictions might justify *per se* prohibition under *Northern Pac. R. Co.* But we do make clear that departure from the rule of reason standard must be based upon demonstrable economic effect rather than—as in *Schwinn*—upon formalistic line drawing.

In sum, we conclude that the appropriate decision is to return to the rule of reason that governed vertical restrictions prior to *Schwinn*. When anticompetitive effects are shown to result from particular vertical restrictions they can be adequately policed under the rule of reason, the standard traditionally applied for the majority of anticompetitive practices challenged under Section 1 of the Act. Accordingly, the decision of the Court of Appeals is affirmed.

Although the *Sylvania* court held that vertical nonprice restrictions are to be judged under the rule of reason, it also noted that horizontal restrictions and vertical resale price maintenance would remain per se illegal. The District Court on remand granted Sylvania's motion for summary judgment, holding that the sales location clause did not constitute an unreasonable restraint of trade since it stimulated competition, and enabled Sylvania to increase its market share by a method that was least restrictive of competition (461 F. Supp. 1046, 1978).

An unusual sequel to *Sylvania* was the *Cernuto* case which follows. There a manufacturer—at the request of a competing distributor—withdrew its product in retaliation against a distributor who was undercutting the price of other distributors. The manufacturer's conduct thus had the appearance of vertical nonprice activity which, according to *Sylvania*, should be judged under the rule of reason. However, the court noted that the transaction took on the character of *horizontal* price-fixing activity because the manufacturer's withdrawal of the product from the dealer was at the request of the dealer's competitor at the same level. The court then explored whether the manufacturer's conduct should possibly be considered a per se horizontal price-fixing violation of Section 1.

Case 47.6   Cernuto, Inc. v. United Cabinet Corporation
595 F.2d 164 (3rd Cir. 1979)

This was a treble damage Sherman Act challenge by Cernuto, Inc. a distributor of kitchen cabinets (plaintiff and appellant) against United Cabinet Corporation, a manufacturer of cabinets, the Lappin Company, the manufacturer's representative, and Famous Furnace, a retail competitor of Cernuto. In 1974 United through Lappin, its sales representative, agreed to supply Cernuto with United cabinets for at least a 2-year period. In return, Cernuto agreed to promote, display, and sell United's cabinets, and thereafter Cernuto advertised

United's products. Following the complaint of defendant Famous Furnace, a retail competitor, that Cernuto was cutting prices, United terminated Cernuto's supply of cabinets 3 months after the distributorship contract had been executed. Cernuto sued, and appealed from an adverse summary judgment.

ADAMS, Circuit Judge. The *per se* violations of the Sherman Act—those requiring no proof of an actually harmful impact—are specific exceptions to the general rule of reason. Among those business practices that have been treated as *per se* violations are price-fixing, resale price maintenance, group boycotts, tying arrangements, and certain types of reciprocal dealing. The question we must consider is whether the conduct at issue here—a manufacturer deliberately withdrawing its product from a distributor that resold it for prices less than its competitors at the request of a competitor—should be classified as a *per se* violation of the Act. . . . The activity under consideration in this case must be seen to have a pernicious effect on competition without having any redeeming virtue. The pernicious effect is apparent: one competitor has succeeded in excluding another from dealing in United cabinets through a combination with United and its agent, and in so doing, has eliminated the possibility of price competition by the foreclosed dealer. Although this harm may have its impact solely in the market for United kitchen cabinets, rather than in the general market for kitchen cabinets, it is not for that reason, beyond the reach of the antitrust laws.

The difficult problem here, as we read the case law, is whether the business decision that has been brought into question has the same redeeming pro-competitive virtues that have been relied upon in rejecting a *per se* rule in other arguably similar cases. The conduct at issue, it might be said, is merely a decision by a manufacturer to terminate a customer. It is therefore, the argument goes, comparable to the conduct at issue in *Continental T.V. Inc. v. GTE Sylvania, Inc.*, a case notable for the importance the Supreme Court placed on the pro-competitive aspects of the manufacturer's marketing plan. There, the Court upheld the right of a company to terminate a distributor of its television sets when that distributor began to sell them at an outlet outside of its alloted territory. The Supreme Court reasoned that the manufacturer's exclusive-franchise marketing plan was in fact beneficial to competition among the various television manufacturers and should therefore be governed by a "rule of reason."

The ultimate reach of the *Sylvania* decision is still uncertain, and continues to be a subject of considerable controversy, but we are not persuaded that the law's tolerance of reasonable restraints designed to improve the manufacturer's competitive position may be converted into a blanket allowance of *any* marketing decision made by a manufacturer.

Two of the most crucial differences between the conduct under consideration here and other accepted manufacturer actions are, upon analysis, readily apparent. When a manufacturer acts on its own, in pursuing its own market strategy, it is seeking to compete with other manufacturers by imposing what may be defended as reasonable vertical restraints. This would appear to be the rationale of the *Sylvania* decision. However, if the action of a manufacturer or other supplier is taken at the direction of its customer, the restraint becomes primarily horizontal in nature in that one customer is seeking to suppress its competition by utilizing the power of a common supplier. Therefore, although the termination in such a situation is, itself, a vertical restraint, the desired impact is horizontal and on the dealer, not the manufacturer, level.

The importance of the horizontal nature of this arrangement is illustrated by *United States v. General Motors Corp.*, 384 U.S. 127 (1966). Although General Motors, the manufacturer, was seemingly imposing vertical restraints when it pressured recalcitrant automobile dealers not to deal with discounters, the Supreme Court noted that in fact these restraints were induced by the dealers seeking to choke off aggressive competitors at their level, and found a *per se* violation, rejecting the suggestion that only unilateral restraints were at issue. So here, if United and Lappin acted at Famous' direction, both the purpose and effect of the termination was to eliminate competition at the retail level, and not, as in *Sylvania*, to promote competition at the manufacturer level. Accordingly, the pro-competitive redeeming virtues so critical in *Sylvania* may not be present here.

Equally important, the motivating factor in Famous' efforts and therefore the resulting conspiracy was—at least according to Cernuto's theory of the case—price. "Price is the central nervous system of the economy, and an agreement that interferes with the setting of price by free market forces is illegal on its face." *U.S. v. Nat'l Society of Prof. Engineers*, 435 U.S. 679. It is true that the alleged combination in the case at hand did not set prices at an exact level. But . . . if the purpose and effect of the challenged conduct is to restrain price movement and the free play of market forces, it is then illegal *per se*. . . . The thrust of Famous' communication to United was that Cernuto "was selling United products in Famous' territory and that Cernuto was a low price volume dealer." Cernuto is a discount house and it must be presumed, was prepared to sell United cabinets at prices lower than those offered by Famous. Famous' concern, understandably, was that Cernuto's low prices would force Famous' own prices down if it were to compete effectively in selling United cabinets. By prevailing upon United and Lappin to terminate their contract with Cernuto, Famous effectively eliminated the threatened competition and was able to maintain prices at its own preferred levels. It is just this type of conduct that the antitrust laws were designed to reach.

Thus, . . . the situation present in this case may be fairly considered to raise the possibility of a *per se* violation of the Sherman Act. . . . The judgment of the district court will be reversed, and the case will be remanded for action consistent with this opinion.

Jointly refusing to deal—group boycotts   In the absence of any purpose to create or maintain a monopoly, one may freely exercise his or her own independent discretion to deal or not deal with another party. Nevertheless, joint action for the purpose of restricting a competitor's access to markets or sources of supply are per se violations of Section 1. Examples of illegal per se group boycotts include refusals to sell, refusals to buy,[40] picketing by a trade association to force retailers to remove a competitor's product, joint cancellation of advertising in a local newspaper in order to eliminate competition against the sole remaining newspaper,[41] and an agreement between member teams of a sports association that they will not negotiate with prospective players until 4 years after graduation from high school.[42] However, not all group boycotts are per se violations of Section 1. If coercion or an anticompetitive purpose are not present, the joint activity will be evaluated by the courts under the rule of reason.[43]

---

[40]*United States v. Hilton Hotels Corp.*, 467 F.2d 1000 (9th Cir. 1972).

[41]*Greenspun v. McCarran*, 105 F. Supp. 662 (D. Nev. 1952).

[42]*Denver Rockets v. All-Pro Management, Inc.*, 325 F. Supp. 1049 (C.D. Cal. 1971).

[43]*Hatley V. American Quarter Horse Ass'n.*, 552 F.2d 646 (5th Cir. 1977).

Case 47.7   **Klor's Inc. v. Broadway-Hale Stores, Inc.**
359 U.S. 207 (1959)

Private treble damage action brought by Klor's, Inc., a retail appliance store (plaintiff) against its next-door competitor, Broadway-Hale Stores, Inc., a department store chain, and ten national manufacturers and their distributors (defendants). Klor's claimed that the defendants conspired among themselves either not to sell to Klor's or to do so only at discriminatory prices and highly unfavorable terms in violation of Sections 1 and 2 of the Sherman Act. Defendants contended that the controversy was "purely a private quarrel" between Klor's and the department store chain, which did not amount to a "public wrong" prohibited by the Sherman Act. The District Court's dismissal of the complaint and summary judgment for defendants was affirmed by the Court of Appeals, and Klor's appealed.

BLACK, Associate Justice. We think Klor's allegations clearly show one type of trade restraint and public harm the Sherman Act forbids. . . . Section 1 of the Sherman Act makes illegal any contract, combination or conspiracy in restraint of trade, and Section 2 forbids any person or combination from monopolizing or attempting to monopolize any part of interstate commerce. In the landmark case of *Standard Oil Co. v. United States*, this Court read Section 1 to prohibit those classes of contracts or acts which the common law had deemed to be undue restraints of trade and those which new times and economic conditions would make unreasonable. . . . It emphasized, however, that there were classes of restraints which from their "nature or character" were unduly restrictive, and hence forbidden by both the common law and the statute. . . . Group boycotts, or concerted refusals by traders to deal with other traders, have long been held to be in the forbidden category. They have not been saved by allegations that they were reasonable in the specific circumstances, nor by a failure to show that they "fixed or regulated prices, parcelled out or limited production, or brought about a deterioration in quality." *Fashion*

Originators' Guild v. Federal Trade Comm'n, 312 U.S. 457. Even where they operated to lower prices or temporarily to stimulate competition they were banned.

Plainly the allegations of this complaint disclose such a boycott. This is not a case of a single trader refusing to deal with another, nor even of a manufacturer and a dealer agreeing to an exclusive distributorship. Alleged in this complaint is a wide combination consisting of manufacturers, distributors and a retailer. This combination takes from Klor's its freedom to buy appliances in an open competitive market and drives it out of business as a dealer in the defendant's products. It deprives the manufacturers and distributors of their freedom to sell to Klor's at the same prices and conditions made available to Broadway-Hale, and in some instances forbids them from selling to it on any terms whatsoever. It interferes with the natural flow of interstate commerce. It clearly has, by its "nature" and "character," a "monopolistic tendency." As such it is not to be tolerated merely because the victim is just one merchant whose business is so small that his destruction makes little difference to the economy. Monopoly can as surely thrive by the elimination of such small businessmen, one at a time, as it can by driving them out in large groups. In recognition of this fact the Sherman Act has consistently been read to forbid all contracts and combinations "which tend to create a monopoly," whether "the tendency is a creeping one or one that proceeds at full gallop." The judgment of the Court of Appeals is reversed and the cause is remanded to the District Court for trial.

Reciprocal dealing Sometimes a company buys large quantities of goods from a supplier who also needs the products of the company it supplies. For example, an automobile manufacturer may buy large quantities of steel from a supplier whose nationwide selling organization regularly needs automobiles. If the automobile manufacturer uses its purchasing power leverage to coerce the steel supplier to buy its automobiles, the arrangement is called "reciprocal dealing" or "reciprocity." Reciprocity arising from coercion, or even a "voluntary" reciprocal buying arrangement in which one of the parties departs from the usual criteria of product selection (quality, price, service, time of delivery), can be a per se violation of Section 1 of the Sherman Act. Key factors considered by the courts in determining whether reciprocity is illegal per se include: the relative size and purchasing volume of the parties; the existence

of power to exert "leverage" pressure on a supplier, regardless of whether the leverage was actually used in a purchasing agreement; and the maintenance of facilities such as a "trade relations department" to exert purchasing power coercion.

Other per se violations There are other joint per se restraints that occur less frequently than those discussed. For example, collusive bidding ("bid-rigging") includes agreements to select one from the group to make the lowest bid while the others refrain from bidding, comparing bids prior to submission, creating a bid depository where competitors compare bids and fix the bid price, or split profits made by the successful bidder. In addition, arrangements to refrain from advertising prices, and most tying contracts are per se unreasonable restraints.

In order to establish an unlawful tying arrangement, three elements must be proved: (1)

the scheme in question involves two distinct items and provides that one (the tying product) may not be obtained unless the other (the tied product) is also purchased; (2) the tying product possesses sufficient economic power appreciably to restrain competition in the tied product market; and (3) a "not insubstantial" amount of commerce is affected by the arrangement. It has been held that a trademark can be a tying product. Tying contracts may also violate the Clayton Act, discussed in the next chapter.

Proving Monopolization under Section 2

Three distinct offenses are listed in Section 2: to "monopolize, or attempt to monopolize, or combine or conspire . . . to monopolize" any part of interstate or foreign commerce. Unlike the prohibitions of Section 1 which always require at least two actors, a violation of Section 2 can result from a *single firm's* outright acquisition of a monopoly position, or attempting to monopolize. However, a Section 2 violation can also result from a plurality of actors as, for example, when two companies combine or conspire to monopolize. It should be further noted that two companies can conspire to restrain trade so as to violate Section 1, but not Section 2 because the amount of trade they are restraining is not sufficient to constitute a monopoly or an attempt to monopolize their industry. On the other hand, any conspiracy or combination to monopolize necessarily is a conspiracy in restraint of trade which also violates Section 1. Two elements are necessary to establish criminal or civil liability for monopolization under Section 2: (1) The *acquisition of monopoly power*, that is, the power to control prices or exclude competitors in a relevant market, and (2) deliberateness or a *general intent to monopolize*. A thorough comprehension of these complex concepts requires an understanding of the basic principles of economics as well as antitrust law.[44]

Monopoly Power in a Relevant Market
Courts consider many factors in determining whether a firm has the monopoly power to control prices or exclude competitors in a relevant market. They are: (1) the size of the market share, (2) whether the size of the firm was achieved through "natural growth" or by acquiring competitors, (3) the number of competitors and their financial strength, (4) whether the defendant engaged in unlawful exclusionary practices to prevent entry into the market by potential competitors, and (5) the extent to which the defendant used unduly coercive tactics to suppress competition.[45] The most important of these factors is the size of the market share. Although there are no judicially approved precise formulas, 80 percent or more of the market is generally considered to constitute market power and 50 percent or less is insufficient evidence that such power exists. If a defendant has 50 to 80 percent of the market share, courts will then examine the other factors more closely in order to decide whether the defendant has market power.[46]

A key question in Section 2 cases is: "What is a relevant market?" Generally, it consists of (1) the geographic area of effective competition in which a particular product is traded and (2) the market area for other substitute products with which the particular product is interchangeable. In the language of economists (who are often used as expert witnesses in antitrust cases) product interchangeability is referred to as *cross*-elasticity of demand, that is, the degree in which users of product A will shift to buying product B in response to a drop in the price of B. If the number of users of product A that shifts to purchasing B is relatively high, it is said that A and B have a high degree of cross-elasticity of demand, or (in the terminology of the courts) a high degree of interchangeability.

---

[44]See Ernest Gellhorn, *Antitrust Law and Economics*, West Publishing Co., St. Paul, 1976.

[45]*United States v. Aluminum Co. of America*, 148 F.2d 416 (2nd Cir. 1945).

[46]*Yoder Bros. Inc. v. California-Florida Plant Corp.*, 537 F.2d 1347 (5th Cir. 1976).

The terms "monopoly power," "relevant market," and "cross-elasticity of demand" were applied by the Supreme Court in the leading case of *United States v. duPont de Nemours and Company*[47] in which the United States brought a Section 2 civil action charging duPont with monopolizing the cellophane industry. During the period involved, duPont produced almost 75 percent of the cellophane in the United States, but cellophane constituted less than 20 percent of all "flexible packaging material" sales. The central question was: Does the "relevant market" include only the product cellophane, or is cellophane competing in a larger market of "flexible packaging materials" (such as saran, foil, and wax paper) that are interchangeable?

The trial court found that duPont cellophane was competing in the larger market, and that the interchangeable products in that market had a high degree of cross-elasticity of demand. Pointing out that duPont furnished less than 7 percent of wrappings for bakery products, 25 percent for candy, 32 percent for snacks, and 35 percent for meat and poultry, the trial court concluded that duPont did not have monopoly power in the flexible packaging material market. In upholding this decision, the Supreme Court said:

> The "market" which one must study to determine when a producer has monopoly power will vary with the part of commerce under consideration. The tests are constant. That market is composed of products that have reasonable interchangeability for the purposes for which they are produced—price, use, and qualities considered. While the application of the tests remains uncertain, it seems to us that duPont should not be found to monopolize cellophane when that product has the competition and interchangeability with other wrappings that this record shows.

---

[47]351 U.S. 377 (1956).

General Intent to Monopolize Deliberate conduct, the probable result of which is to obtain monopoly, meets the "general intent" requirement necessary to establish Section 2 liability. Obviously, if a firm acquires monopoly power while restraining trade in violation of Section 1, it has also clearly violated Section 2. Intent to monopolize is proved if it can be shown that the single firm engaged in predatory activities such as injuring actual competitors, excluding potential competitors, erecting barriers to entry into the market ("limit pricing"), and refraining from maximizing profits until competitors are driven out of the market ("predatory pricing").

An across-the-board price set at or above marginal cost should not ordinarily form the basis for an antitrust violation, but setting prices below marginal cost may well form the basis for such a violation. It has been held that average variable cost can be used as evidence of marginal cost, in determining whether a setting of price forms the basis of an antitrust violation.[48] Proof of an *attempt to monopolize* is sufficient when it is shown that the defendant employed "methods, means and practices which would, if successful, accomplish monopolization, and which, though falling short, nevertheless approach so close as to create a dangerous probability of it.[49]

Conduct That Is Not Monopolization; Oligopoly Monopoly power may be lawfully obtained through superior business acumen or product, or as the result of historic accident and by natural, as distinguished from predatory, means. A defendant firm that has acquired monopoly power in this manner will argue (usually without success) that its monopoly position was "thrust upon" it and that its market dominance did not come about as the result of any wrongful conduct under Section 2. In the

---

[48]*Janich Bros. Inc. v. American Distilling Co.*, 570 F.2d 848 (9th Cir. 1977).

[49]*American Tobacco Co. v. United States*, 221 U.S. 106 (1911).

duPont case, discussed earlier, the Supreme Court in illustrating a lawful monopoly said: "A retail seller may have in one sense a monopoly on certain trade because of location, as an isolated country store or filling station, or because no one else makes a product of just the quality or attractiveness of his product. . . ." However, in the leading cases [50] involving the "thrust upon" defense to monopolization, the defendant was found to be liable, because of predatory practices that accompanied the firm's growth to monopoly power.

In the absence of concerted action to fix prices or engage in other anticompetitive conduct, the "thrust upon" or "historic accident" defense to a Section 2 monopolization charge is probably available to most firms in *oligopolistic industries.* Economists use the term "oligopoly" (literally, "a few sellers") to refer to an industry in which a smaller number of firms account for

substantially all of that industry's output. For example, one study conducted by Congress showed that three or less companies in the United States held a market share of 75 percent or more for aluminum, automobiles, telephone equipment, typewriters, cigarettes, soap, cereal, and many other kinds of products.

Concentration in American industry often arose because of historic accident, ownership of a valuable patent, or natural growth up to the point where a few firms found themselves participating in what is sometimes called a "shared monopoly." The mere size of a firm that grew in this manner is not, of itself, a violation of Section 2. However, if one or more firms in an oligopoly jointly participate in predatory activity that presents a probability of creating monopoly power, Section 2 has been violated. In the *Eastman Kodak* case below, which the court described as "one of the largest and most significant private antitrust suits in history," the Court focused on present legal elements that must be proved to establish liability for monopolization under Section 2.

---

[50]*United States v. Aluminum Co. of America,* 148 F.2d 416 (2nd Cir. 1945); *United States v. Grinnell Corp.,* 384 U.S. 563 (1966).

Case 47.8   **Berkey Photo, Inc. v. Eastman Kodak Co.**
                   603 F.2d 263 (2nd Cir. 1979)

Treble damage action under both Sections 1 and 2 of the Sherman Act by Berkey Photo, Inc. (plaintiff), a supplier of photofinishing services, against Eastman Kodak Co. (defendant). Berkey charged, among other things, that Eastman had willfully acquired and exercised monopoly power in the film, color print paper, and camera markets in violation of Section 2 of the Sherman Act, causing it to lose sales in the markets for these products. The jury returned a treble damage verdict which, with attorney fees, exceeded $87 million, from which Eastman Kodak appealed.

The appellate court confirmed four relevant product markets, each nationwide in scope: (1) The film market in which Kodak had monopoly power, annual sales since 1952 always exceeding 82 percent of the nationwide volume on a unit basis, and 88 percent of revenues. (2) The still camera market, in which Kodak was dominant with no less than 61 percent of industry annual unit sales from 1954 to 1973. This success was largely due to introduction in 1972 of the small 110 "Pocket Instamatic" which could be loaded only with a special cartridge containing a newly developed film, Kodacolor II. (3) Photofinishing services and photofinishing equipment, furnished by Kodak's Color Print and Processing Laboratories (CP&P) accounting for but 10 percent of the market in 1976, the remainder going to the 600 independent photofinishers in the United States. (4) Color photographic paper, with Kodak's market share dropping from 94 percent in 1968 to 67 percent in 1975.

Berkey contended that, in violation of Sherman Section 2, Kodak exercised monopoly power by (a) designing the Kodacolor II film in the special cartridge so that buyers of the camera could only buy Kodak film, thus foreclosing competitors in the film market; (b) introducing a new film requiring special new developing equipment thereby foreclosing independent photofinishers from the developing business, and (c) that Kodak's failure to "predisclose" the 110 Pocket Instamatic to competitors foreclosed them from making competing film that was compatible with the 110 design or "format."

KAUFMAN, Circuit Judge. To millions of Americans, the name Kodak is virtually synonymous with photography. . . . Snapshots may be taken with a Kodak camera, on Kodak film, developed by Kodak's CP&P, and printed on Kodak photographic paper. The firm has rivals at each stage of this process, but in many of them it stands, and has long stood, dominant. . . . Berkey competes with Kodak in providing photofinishing services. . . . It does not manufacture film, but it does purchase Kodak film for resale to its customers, and it also buys photofinishing equipment and supplies, including color print paper, from Kodak. . . . Kodak has been Berkey's competitor in some markets and its supplier in others. In this action, Berkey claims that every aspect of the association has been infected by Kodak's monopoly power in the film, color print paper, and camera markets, willfully acquired, maintained, and exercised in violation of Section 2 of the Sherman Act. Berkey alleges that these violations caused it to lose sales in the camera and photo-finishing markets and to pay excessive prices to Kodak for film, color print paper, and photofinishing equipment.

MONOPOLY POWER

Kodak, then, is indeed a titan in its field, and accordingly has almost inevitably invited attack under § 2 of the Sherman Act. Section 2 . . . is aimed primarily not at improper conduct but at a pernicious market structure in which the concentration of power saps the salubrious influence of competition. Indeed, there is little argument over the principle that existence of monopoly power—"the power to control prices or exclude competition"—is the primary requisite to a finding of monpolization. The Supreme Court has informed us that "monopoly power, whether lawfully or unlawfully acquired, may itself constitute an evil and stand condemned under §2 even though it remains unexercised." *U.S. v. Griffith*, 334 U.S. 100. . . . If a finding of monopoly power were all that were necessary to complete a violation of Section 2, our task in this case would be considerably lightened. Kodak's control of the film and color paper markets clearly reached the level of a monopoly. And, while the issue is a much closer one, it appears that the evidence was sufficient for the jury to find that Kodak possessed such power in the camera market as well. But our inquiry into Kodak's liability cannot end there.

REQUIREMENT OF ANTICOMPETITIVE CONDUCT

Thus, while proclaiming vigorously that monopoly power is the evil at which Section 2 is aimed, courts have declined to take what would have appeared to be the next logical step—declaring monopolies unlawful *per se* unless specifically authorized by law. . . . [Thus, Judge Hand, in *U.S. v. Aluminum Co. of America*, 148 F. 2d 416] . . . having stated that "Congress did not condone 'good trusts' and condemn 'bad' ones; it forbad all," declared with equal force, "The successful competitor, having been urged to compete, must not be turned upon when he wins." Hand, therefore, told us that it would be inherently unfair to condemn success when the Sherman Act itself mandates competition. Such a wooden rule, it was feared, might also deprive the leading firm in an industry of the incentive to exert its best efforts. Further success would yield not rewards but legal castigation. . . . The key to analysis, it must be stressed, is the concept of market power. . . . The mere possession of monopoly power does not *ipso facto* condemn a market participant. But to avoid the proscription of § 2, the firm must refrain at all times from conduct directed at smothering competition.

MONOPOLY POWER AS A LEVER IN OTHER MARKETS

It is clear that a firm may not employ its market position as a lever to create—or attempt to create—a monopoly in another market. Kodak, in the period relevant to this suit, was never close to gaining control of the markets for photofinishing equipment or services and could not be held to have attempted to monopolize them. Berkey nevertheless contends that Kodak illicitly gained an advantage in these areas by leveraging its power over film and cameras. Accordingly, we must determine whether a firm violates Section 2 by using its monopoly power in one market to gain a competitive advantage in another, albeit without an attempt to monopolize the second market. We hold, as did the lower court, that it does. This rule is linked to the prohibition against tying arrangements in the sale of goods and services.

ATTEMPT TO MONOPOLIZE CAMERA MARKET

There is little doubt that the evidence supports the jury's implicit finding that Kodak had monopoly power in cameras. . . . [According to Berkey] Kodak persistently refused to make film available for most formats other than those in which it made cameras. Since cameras are worthless without film, this policy effectively prevented other manufacturers from introducing cameras in new formats. . . . For eighteen months after its introduction, Kodacolor II was available only in the 110 format. Thus it followed that any consumer wishing to use Kodak's "remarkable new film" had to buy a 110 camera. Since Kodak was the leading—and at first the only—manufacturer of such devices, its camera sales were boosted at the expense of its competitors. For the reasons explained below, we do not believe any of these contentions is sufficient on the facts of this case to justify an award of damages to Berkey. We therefore reverse this portion of the judgment.

PREDISCLOSURE

We hold that . . . as a matter of law, Kodak did not have a duty to predisclose information about the 110 system to competing camera manufacturers. . . . A firm may normally keep its innovations secret from its rivals as long as it wishes, forcing them to catch up on the strength of their own efforts after the new product is introduced. It is the possibility of success in the marketplace, attributable to superior performance, that provides the incentives on which the proper functioning of our competitive economy rests. If a firm that has engaged in the risks and expenses of research and development were required in all circumstances to share with its rivals the benefits of those endeavors, this incentive would very likely be vitiated. . . .

Clearly, then the policy considerations militating against predisclosure requirements for monolithic monopolists are equally applicable here. The first firm, even a monopolist, to design a new camera format has a right to the lead time that follows from its success. The mere fact that Kodak manufactured film in the new format as well, so that its customers would not be offered worthless cameras, could not deprive it of that reward. Nor is this conclusion altered because Kodak not only participated in but dominated the film market. Kodak's ability to pioneer formats does not depend on its possessing a film monopoly. Had the firm possessed a much smaller share of the film market, it would nevertheless have been able to manufacture sufficient quantities of 110-size film to bring the new camera to market. It is apparent, therefore, that the ability to introduce the new format without predisclosure was solely a benefit of integration and not, without more, a use of Kodak's power in the film market to gain a competitive advantage in cameras.

RESTRICTION OF KODACOLOR II TO THE 110 FORMAT

For eighteen months after the 110 system introduction, Kodacolor II was available only in the 110 format. Berkey asserts . . . that since consumers were led to believe that Kodacolor II was superior to Kodacolor X, they were more likely to buy a Kodak 110, rather than a Berkey camera, so that the new film could be used. . . . We shall assume *arguendo* that Kodak violated Section 2 of the Sherman Act if its decision to restrict Kodacolor II to the 110 format was not justified by the nature of the film but was motivated by a desire to impede competition in the manufacture of cameras capable of using the new film. This might well supply the element of coercion we found lacking in the previous section. . . .

But to prevail, Berkey must prove more, for injury is an element of a private treble damages action. Berkey must, therefore, demonstrate that some consumers who would have bought a Berkey camera were dissuaded from doing so because Kodacolor II was available only in the 110 format. This it has failed to establish. The record is totally devoid of evidence that Kodak or its retailers actually attempted to persuade customers to purchase the Pocket Instamatic because it was the only camera that could use Kodacolor II, or that, in fact, any consumers did choose the 110 in order to utilize the finer-grained film. . . .

FILM AND COLOR PAPER CLAIMS

. . . Excessive prices, maintained through exercise of a monopolist's control of the market, constituted one of the primary evils that the Sherman Act was intended to correct. Where a monopolist has acquired or maintained its power by anticompetitive conduct, therefore, a direct purchaser may recover the overcharge caused by the violation of Section 2.

But unless the monopoly has bolstered its power by wrongful actions, it will not be required to pay damages merely because its prices may later be found excessive. Setting a high price may be a use of monopoly power, but it is not in itself anticompetitive. . . . If a firm has taken no action to destroy competition it may be unfair to deprive it of the ordinary opportunity to set prices at a profit-maximizing level. [The Court remanded the issue of monopolization of film and color paper with instructions for the trial court to receive further evidence as to whether Kodak had exercised coercion or engaged in anticompetitive conduct that would render its monopoly pricing wrongful and unlawful. The trial court's judgment was reversed as to the $45,750,000 treble damage award to Berkey for lost profits arising from Kodak's introduction of the 110 camera. All other portions of the judgment were reversed and the case was remanded for new trial.]

SUMMARY

Antecedents of modern antitrust law appeared in the early English Statute of Monopolies in 1623, and in court decisions which held that if a *partial* restraint on trade was *reasonable* it was lawful. In the era of laissez-faire, courts interpreted most restraints on trade as lawful. The rise of monopolistic trusts after the Civil War led to enactment of the Sherman Act in 1890, and later the Clayton Act, Federal Trade Commission Act, and Robinson-Patman Act. Federal antitrust law is based upon these four statutes.

The Sherman Act was passed to promote competition, retard concentration in industry, and to create a broad federal court jurisdiction to develop a new body of antitrust law. The

Act's two basic provisions are: Section 1, which prohibits contracts or conspiracies in restraint of trade; and Section 2 which prohibits monopolization. The Sherman Act is enforced: (1) By civil treble damage suits brought by those private parties who have "standing" to sue, that is, whose injury is causally and directly linked to the defendant's wrongful antitrust conduct. (2) By the government in a civil suit for injunction and damages, or in a criminal proceeding punishable by fine up to $1 million against a corporation or $100,000 against an individual, or 3 years imprisonment, or both. If a defendant is permitted to enter a nolo contendere plea, the result is a judgment against the defendant that is not admissible to prove liability in any subsequent civil suit by a private party such as a competitor of the defendant. (3) By seizure and forfeiture to the United States of property being transported in interstate commerce pursuant to a conspiracy that violates Section 1.

To establish a violation of Section 1 or 2 of the Sherman Act, interstate or foreign "commerce" jurisdiction must be proved by showing that the defendant's activities either (1) occurred within the *flow of commerce*, or (2) had a substantial and adverse *effect on commerce*, even though such effect is produced indirectly by intrastate activity. An additional element that must be proved in all cases is *intent* to contract, combine, or conspire (Section 1) or to monopolize (Section 2). However, intent may be inferred by circumstantial evidence. With few exceptions, consciously parallel behavior, standing alone, is insufficient to prove a conspiracy.

In the *Standard Oil* case, the Supreme Court held that Congress intended by Section 1 to prohibit only those contracts that *unreasonably* restrain trade. Under this "Rule of Reason," if a restraint was reasonable, it was lawful. Most Section 1 cases are judged under this rule of reason. However, certain agreements or practices have such a deadly effect on competition that they are conclusively presumed to be unreasonable and therefore illegal without the necessity of proof or unreasonableness. Such agreements, called per se violations, include horizontal and vertical price fixing (resale price maintenance), restricting production, dividing markets or customers, refusing to deal (group boycotting), reciprocal dealing arrangements, and most tying contracts. However, vertical nonprice restraints, such as allocation of market territory to franchised retailers, are judged under the rule of reason.

To prove a violation of Section 2, the plaintiff must show: (1) The defendant acquired monopoly power, that is, the power to control prices or exclude competitors in a relevant market. In determining a relevant market, courts first define the *product* (e.g., paint or automotive paint) and then define the geographic area of effective competition in which the product, as well as any interchangeable substitute product, is traded. (2) The defendant had a general intent to monopolize, that is, engaged in deliberate conduct the probable result of which is to obtain monopoly. This is shown by predatory activities such as injury or excluding competitors, erecting barriers to entry, or adopting "predatory pricing" policies.

Monopoly power may be lawfully obtained if superior business acumen or historic accident thrust upon the defendant a monopoly position. This "thrust upon" defense is usually not successful because predatory practices are found to have accompanied the firm's growth. However, if there is no predatory activity, most firms in oligopolistic industries can successfully avail themselves of this defense.

STUDY AND DISCUSSION QUESTIONS

1 Explain the meaning of "antitrust law."

2 How did court decisions under the early common law interpret *(a)* the covenant of the seller of a business not to compete with the buyer, *(b)* the Statute of Monopolies?, *(c)* partial restraints of trade?

3 How did laissez-faire doctrine influence decisions of English and American courts in their treatment of monopolistic shipping industry practices in the nineteenth century?

4 Explain how the trust device can be used to achieve control of a number of corporations.

5 In the late nineteenth century, how did abuses by the rising trust adversely affect *(a)* consumers, *(b)* farmers, and *(c)* workers?

6 What was the most significant major objective of Congress in passing the Sherman Act?

7 The Sherman Act prohibits what activities in Section 1? In Section 2?

8   Name three methods of enforcing the Sherman Act. Which is the most commonly used?

9   *(a)* What is meant by "standing to sue"? *(b)* What test do the courts use to determine if a plaintiff has "standing"?

10   What is the punishment for a criminal violation of the Sherman Act by an individual? By a corporation?

11   Sherman Act jurisdiction over "commerce with foreign nations" applies to what classes of persons with respect to their activities in what geographic locations?

12   With respect to the "rule of reason," *(a)* explain its meaning in the field of antitrust law, *(b)* trace its origins in the common law, and *(c)* identify the landmark decision of the Supreme Court that introduced the concept.

13   How does the doctrine of per se unreasonableness relate to the rule of reason? Of what advantage is it to a plaintiff to prove a per se violation of the Sherman Act?

14   Explain *(a)* vertical price fixing, *(b)* resale price maintenance, *(c)* the Miller-Tydings Act, and *(d)* state fair trade laws.

15   Which type of violation of the Sherman Act is easiest for a plaintiff to prove, vertical price fixing or a nonprice vertical restraint? Why?

16   Is it a violation of the Sherman Act to divide markets or customers *(a)* horizontally? *(b)* vertically? If so, is the violation judged under the rule of reason or as a per se violation?

17   How can reciprocal dealing adversely effect competition?

18   What factors do courts consider in determining whether a firm has the monopoly power to control prices or exclude competition in a relevant market?

19   What evidence is considered relevant by courts in proving intent to monopolize?

20   *(a)* What is meant by "oligopoly"? *(b)* How is it possible to achieve monopoly power lawfully?

CASE PROBLEMS

1   Checker Corp. manufactured taxicabs. It entered into a contract with Yellow Cab Co. and other cab operating companies in New York, Chicago, Pittsburgh, and Minneapolis whereby they agreed to buy their cabs exclusively from Checker. The agreement only involved purchase of 5000 cabs in the four cities. Collectively these purchases constituted a very small percentage of all cabs bought in the United States. The government, in a civil action against the Checker Corp. and the Yellow Cab Co. charged them with violating Section 1 of the Sherman Act. The trial court dismissed the complaint for failure to state factors showing that the transaction affected interstate commerce and the United States appealed. Decision?

2   In Richmond, Virginia, thirty-five of thirty-eight savings associations used the "escrow accounting method" for tax and insurance prepayments advanced by mortgage borrowers. Eight of these firms had changed to the escrow method from the "capitalization method" within the past 3 years. Brown, a borrower, brought an action against the savings associations alleging violations of Section 1 of the Sherman Act. Brown noted that lending institutions must pay more interest on borrowers' advances under the capitalization method and its elimination was therefore an economic motive for conspiring to use the escrow method. Brown also claimed that parallel behavior of the associations established intent to restrain trade. Although most of the defendant firms belonged to the same trade association, there was no evidence that they had exchanged information on accounting methods. Did the defendant savings association engage in a conspiracy in violation of Section 1?

3 Paper Companies was a group of ten manufacturing firms that accounted for 90 percent of the shipments of corrugated containers from plants in the Southeastern United States. From 1955 to 1963, these firms regularly exchanged price information among themselves, but no agreements to adhere to a price schedule were made. When a seller requested and received price information from a competitor, it affirmed its willingness to furnish such information in return. Frequently, after two competitors exchanged price information, they would usually quote the same price to a buyer. The exchange of price information had the effect of stabilizing prices within a fairly narrow range, but with supply exceeding demand in the container market, prices drifted downward over an 8-year period. Did the Paper Companies violate the price-fixing agreement of Section 1 of the Sherman Act?

4 Harvey operated a retail gas station that purchased its gas from Fearless Farris Wholesale, Inc., which was wholly owned by Farris. Farris also owned all of the stock of five other corporations, each of which operated a retail gas station. When the 1973 gas shortage set in, Farris as president of the wholesale corporation decided to cut off deliveries to Harvey and sold its gas to the five retail gas corporations whose stock Farris owned. Harvey brought a treble damage action against Fearless Farris Wholesale and the five incorporated gas stations claiming that their actions constituted a "combination or conspiracy in restraint of trade" violating Section 1 of the Sherman Act. Farris claimed that since he owned all the stock in the wholesale company as well as the five corporate gas stations, and was the sole decision maker, he could not conspire with himself, and that the two-actor requirement of the Sherman Act had not been met, and the case should be dismissed. Harvey claimed that all six corporations are separate legal entities—therefore there are six parties capable of conspiring. Does the alleged conspiracy meet the "two-actor" requirement of Section 1 of the Sherman Act?

5 Chicken Delight, a fast food franchising company in interstate commerce, required its franchisees to purchase certain essential cooking equipment, dry-mix food items, and trademark-bearing packaging exclusively from Chicken Delight, as a condition of getting a franchise and trademark license. A class action suit was filed against Chicken Delight alleging violation of Section 1 of the Sherman Act for an unlawful tying arrangement. Chicken Delight claimed that the trademark and franchise license were not separate and distinct from the equipment, food items, and packaging, but that all of these constituted an integrated franchise system to be treated as a combined sale. Was the franchise system an unlawful tying arrangement?

6 Jerrold Electronics manufactured a new community television three-channel antenna system, but often only one channel was available at the time the system was installed. Jerrold's sales contract required the system buyer to: (1) purchase the equipment, (2) enter into a service maintenance contract with Jerrold to insure proper operation of the equipment, and (3) agree that if additional TV channels became available, the buyer would purchase the additional necessary equipment from Jerrold. The FTC claimed this agreement was an unlawful tying arrangement in violation of Section 1 of the Sherman Act. Jerrold argued that during the development period following introduction of the systems to the market, the success of the system and payment depended on overcoming reluctance of utility companies to have men of unknown ability working on their poles thus making it desirable to install the system under the supervision of Jerrold's employees whose ability was known to the utility company; that the service contracts were also essential to the successful marketing of the systems in order to prevent a wave of system failures at the start which could undermine buyer confidence.

However, the service contract arrangement was continued for many months after the TV systems were successfully in operation. Was Jerrold's contract an unlawful tie-in under Section 1 of the Sherman Act?

7 Mercy Hospital, in a treble damage action against Rex Hospital, claimed it had violated Section 1 of the Sherman Act by conspiring to block expansion of Mercy's hospital so as to enable Rex to monopolize the hospital business in the area. Rex claimed that there was no "commerce" jurisdiction to justify suit under the Sherman Act. A substantial number of the patients at Mercy Hospital came from out of state. A large proportion of Mercy's revenue came from insurance companies outside the state or from federal government Medicaid or Medicare programs. Mercy Hospital also paid a management fee to a Delaware corporation based in Georgia. Mercy planned to finance its $4 million hospital expansion by borrowing from out-of-state lending institutions. Up to 80 percent of Mercy's medicines and supplies came from out-of-state sellers. Is there "commerce" jurisdiction sufficient for Mercy to proceed with its suit under the Sherman Act under either the "flow of commerce" or the "effect on commerce" theory?

8 Before going out of business Inglis Baking Company manufactured and distributed wholesale bread. It brought a treble damage action against Continental Bakeries alleging it attempted to monopolize in violation of Section 2 of the Sherman Act, by engaging in predatory below-cost sales, in order to drive the weaker wholesalers out of the market. Specifically, Inglis claimed Continental set its prices below marginal cost (increment to total cost that results from producing an additional increment of output), and as evidence of marginal cost, Inglis introduced data showing average variable cost (total variable costs divided by output). For the

month of July 1972, average variable costs were 20.60 cents per loaf, during which month Continental sold bread for 17.2 cents per loaf. At this time there was considerable excess capacity at Continental and other bakeries. Oven time was available during periods when wages were already being paid, and excess space was available on delivery trucks. The only additional short-run expenses for incremental increases in production were ingredients, wrappers, fuel, and commission. Continental argues that, because it had excess capacity in July 1972, marginal cost data should have been used, and that Inglis has failed to prove below-cost pricing. Has Inglis proved that Continental engaged in predatory below-cost selling?

9 Aeromotor, Inc. manufactured 70 percent of the windmills marketed in the United States and distributed them through selected independent distributors who were assigned particular geographic sales territory. Under Aeromotor's announced policy, distributors could sell outside their territories if: (1) the goods first came to their territories; (2) the items were placed in stock; and (3) the distributors were not "actively soliciting business outside their assigned territory." There was no evidence that interbrand competition was harmed by Aeromotor's policy of requiring shipment first into a distributor's territory before he could sell elsewhere. Cowley held the distributorship for the state of Arizona, and in violation of the agreement, began selling windmills to Carder in Colorado without first shipping the windmills through Arizona. Carder then resold the windmills at lower prices than the authorized Aeromotor dealer for Colorado, who complained to Aeromotor. Aeromotor terminated Cowley's contract, and Cowley and Carder sued Aeromotor, alleging illegal territorial restraints in violation of Section 1 of the Sherman Act. Did Aeromotor's policy restricting distributors' sales outside of assigned territory violate Section 1 of the Sherman Act?

Chapter

48

The Clayton,
Robinson-Patman, and
Federal Trade Commission
Acts

In the 25 years following the Sherman Act of 1890, there was growing criticism of its shortcomings. Small business objected that the act focused on breaking up monopolies after they were formed, but did little or nothing to stop anticompetitive practices in their beginning stages. Labor unions claimed that, contrary to the intent of Congress, injunctions authorized by the act for use against monopolistic business practices had been twisted by court interpretation into a powerful tool to suppress organized

labor's only weapons—strikes, pickets, and boycotts. Other critics argued that the general and vague language of the act and conflicting court interpretations of the rule of reason made it difficult or impossible for firms to know precisely what conduct was prohibited.

Responding to these objections, Congress enacted the Clayton Act in 1914. At the same time, the Federal Trade Commission Act was passed, creating the Federal Trade Commission (FTC) to administer certain portions of the antitrust laws. The first three parts of this chapter survey the scope and effect of these acts as well as the Robinson-Patman Act of 1936 which amended the Clayton Act. The last part of the chapter reviews various exemptions to the antitrust laws.

THE CLAYTON ACT

Scope

The Clayton Act[1] was enacted to prohibit four types of anticompetitive business practices involving interstate commerce: price discrimination (Section 2), exclusive dealing and tying contracts (Section 3), anticompetitive corporate mergers (Section 7), and interlocking directorates (Section 8). The Clayton Act dealt with probabilities, not certainties. Thus, in each section, the particular conduct under attack was declared unlawful if it *tended* "to substantially lessen competition." The underlying philosphy of the Clayton Act was to strike at monopolistic practices in their incipiency.

Section 2—Price Discrimination Section 2, as amended, prohibits discrimination in prices charged different purchasers of commodities—if such discrimination tends to substantially lessen competition or to create a monopoly—unless the price differential is justified by a difference in the "grade, quality, or quantity of the commodity sold," or is justified by the cost of selling or transporting the goods or by the need to meet competition. Two important exceptions were: (1) Any seller could refuse to sell to a buyer if such refusal was not designed to restrain trade, and (2) a seller could change his prices in response to market conditions such as deterioration of perishable goods, obsolescense of seasonal goods, distress sales under court process, or sales in discontinuance of business.

Section 2 was meant to put a stop to the practice of using territorial or local price dis-

crimination as a means of eliminating competitors. For example, the Standard Oil Company of New Jersey in the early 1900s would force a local competing firm out of business by selling oil below the price Standard charged in other territories as well as below the cost of the competing firm. Section 2 was strengthened by the Robinson-Patman Act amendments, discussed later in this chapter.

Section 3—Exclusive Dealing and Tying Contracts Section 3 applied to exclusive dealing contracts, that is, to sales of goods on condition that the buyer would not "use or deal in" the goods of a competitor of the seller. Such sales are prohibited if they would "substantially lessen competition or tend to create a monopoly in any line of commerce." The most typical form of exclusive dealing is an agreement between a supplier and distributor which prohibits the distributor from dealing in goods of the supplier's competitors. Such agreements should be distinguished from an *exclusive distributorship* in which a supplier agrees to deal with a single distributor in a given territory. Another common exclusive dealing arrangement is a *requirement contract* which provides that the buyer will obtain all of its requirements of a product from a single supplier. Exclusive distributorships and requirement contracts are illegal only if they have an anticompetitive effect.[2]

In addition to the Department of Justice, other groups of potential private plaintiffs who might claim a Section 3 violation are: (1) Buyers or lessees under exclusive dealing arrangements that preclude them from buying or leasing on more favorable terms elsewhere, and (2) competitors of the seller (or lessor) who are foreclosed from the buyer's (or lessee's) market because of the exclusive dealing arrangement. Section 3 also prohibits "tying contracts." A tying contract is one in which a seller (or lessor) will sell (or lease) a product (the "tying" product) only on condition that the buyer (or lessee)

---

[1]15 U.S.C. §§ 12-27.

[2]See discussion at p. 1068.

also purchase (or lease) a second distinct product which is not desired (the "tied" product). Tying contracts are discussed in detail later in this chapter.

Clayton Section 3 and Sherman Section 1 compared It was noted in Chapter 47 that Section 1 of the Sherman Act also prohibits exclusive dealing and tying contracts. Both statutes apply to an agreement between seller and buyer that forecloses competitors from a substantial share of the market. However, the two acts differ in the following ways: (1) The Clayton Act applies only to the lease or sale of "goods, wares, merchandise, machinery, supplies, or other commodities," but the Sherman Act applies to a broader range of activity including real estate transactions and services such as advertising. (2) The Clayton Act applies to a person who is "engaged in commerce" and who does certain acts "in the course of such commerce"; the Sherman Act is much broader, covering acts which are in the "flow of interstate commerce" as well as those that "affect interstate commerce." (3) The Clayton Act requires only a showing that the exclusive dealing arrangement might *tend* to create a monopoly or lessen competition whereas the Sherman Act is much narrower in this respect as the arrangement must actively and unreasonably restrain trade to be unlawful. Because of these differences, a plaintiff might prevail in a Section 3 case under the Clayton Act but not have sufficient evidence to prevail under the stricter language of Section 1 of the Sherman Act.

Tests of competitive effect of exclusive dealing To determine if an exclusive dealing contract will substantially lessen competition or tend to create a monopoly in an action under the Clayton Act the court first defines the relevant market and then attempts to measure the effect of the exclusive dealing arrangement on competition in that market. This approach is the same as that used in cases under Section 1 of the Sherman Act. Two tests have been used by

the courts to measure competitive effect: (1) the "quantitative substantiality" test, and (2) the "qualitative substantiality" test.

Under the *quantitative* test, if the exclusive dealing contract covers a *substantial quantity of the relevant market*, it is held to substantially lessen competition and there is no need for further inquiry into other economic competitive factors. The quantitative test was first applied in *Standard Oil Company of California v. U.S.*,[3] in which Standard was charged with violating Section 3 of the Clayton Act because its contracts with 537 distributors required them to purchase all of their requirements from Standard. The Supreme Court held that Standard had violated Section 3 because its contracts covered a sufficient share of the market so as to substantially lessen competition. The Court rejected Standard's argument that consideration should be given to such qualitative economic factors as evidence that competition had flourished despite use of requirement contracts, their duration and reasonableness in relation to the legitimate needs of the industry. It was reasoned that evaluation of such data placed too great a burden on the judiciary. The decision has been criticized because Standard's 6.7 percent relevant market share would hardly seem enough to permit a sole defendant to substantially lessen competition as required by the court's "quantitative" test. The test now appears to be used primarily to evaluate exclusive dealing contracts when the defendant dominates the relevant market.

In *Tampa Electric Co. v. Nashville Coal Co.*[4] the Supreme Court departed from the quantitative test used in *Standard Oil* and required a *qualitative economic evaluation* of the anticompetitive effect of a contract to supply a power utility's coal requirements. The Court held that such evaluation should consider the relative

---

[3]337 U.S. 293 (1949).
[4]365 U.S. 320 (1961).

market strength of the parties, the volume of trade involved in the contract compared with the total volume in the relevant market, the probable immediate and future effect of the contract on competition, and whether it continued to flourish despite the restrictive agreement. It is uncertain whether the quantitative or qualitative test will be used in a particular case. However, the qualitative test seems to be favored in those cases where the seller does not dominate the market and where there is a relatively small percentage of competitors' business being cut out of the market (referred to as "market foreclosure") because of the exclusive dealing contract. In such cases, courts have permitted the defendant to try to prove the reasonableness of exclusive dealing by showing that it mutually benefited the parties in such ways as ensuring the buyer a source of supply at a fixed price or providing the seller with a sure outlet as well as fixed selling costs.[5]

Tying contracts Generally, the tests of legality of tying arrangements are the same, regardless of whether the plaintiff brings its action under Section 1 of the Sherman Act, or Section 3 of the Clayton Act. Unlike other forms of exclusive dealing which are judged under the rule of reason, tying contracts are almost always held to be per se violations when the plaintiff has shown: (1) that the seller has sufficient economic power with respect to the tying product to appreciably restrain free competition in the market for the tied product[6] and (2) that the tying arrangement affects a "not insubstantial amount of commerce."[7] However, after the plaintiff has made out such a prima facie case, the tying arrangement may be justified by the defendant showing that it is a small company trying to break into the market, or that the

arrangement was necessary to protect a firm's goodwill.[8]

Requisites of tying contracts A tying arrangement is not unlawful unless the tying and tied products are distinct. In deciding this issue under either Clayton or Sherman, courts consider such factors as whether the products are priced separately, are physically separate, have separate markets, and whether consumers view them as separate items. For example, in *Times-Picayune Publishing Co. v. U.S.*,[9] the Supreme Court held that a newspaper's refusal to sell advertising in its morning edition unless the advertiser also purchased space in the afternoon edition was not an unlawful tying contract because the products were identical and the markets were the same. On the other hand, in *Siegel v. Chicken Delight, Inc.*,[10] the court held that two distinct products were involved where the franchise agreement required the franchisee to purchase exclusively from Chicken Delight (the franchisor) dry-mix food items and packaging bearing the Chicken Delight trademark (the "tied" products). The court considered the franchisee's right to use the franchisor's trademark (the "tying" product) as separate and distinct, and concluded that the tying agreement was unlawful.

An illegal tying arrangement does not require that the *same party* offer both the tying product and the tied product. A violation occurs if the offeror of the tying product has some economic interest in the tied product, such as a contractual benefit arising from the tied product or stock ownership in the company manufacturing it. Since the Clayton Act applies only to "goods, wares, and merchandise," courts have held that *both* the tying and tied products must fall into these personal property categories in order for it to be a Clayton Section 3 violation. Inasmuch as

[5]*American Motor Inns, Inc. v. Holiday Inns*, Inc., 521 F.2d 1230 (3d Cir. 1975).

[6]*Northern Pac. Ry. v. United States*, 336 U.S. 1 (1958).

[7]*United States Steel Corp. v. Fortner Enterprises, Inc.* 429 U.S. 610 (1977).

[8]*United States v. Jerrold Electronic Corp.*, 187 F. Supp. 545 (E.D. Pa. 1960), aff'd 365 U.S. 567 (1961).

[9]345 U.S. 594 (1953).

[10]448 F.2d 43 (9th Cir. 1971).

the Sherman Act jurisdiction is not restricted to such categories, a sale of electricity tied to light bulbs might be a violation of Section 1 of the Sherman Act, but could not possibly violate Section 3 of the Clayton Act.

Section 7—Corporate Mergers This "antimerger section" as amended by the Celler-Kefauver Act of 1950, prohibits (1) the acquisition by one corporation of the stock of another corporation "where in any line of commerce in any section of the country, the effect . . . may be substantially to lessen competition, or to tend to create a monopoly," and (2) the acquisition by a corporation subject to the jurisdiction of the Federal Trade Commission (FTC) of the *assets* (as distinguished from the stock) of another corporation if such acquisition would substantially lessen competition or tend to create a monopoly. However, a corporation may purchase stock of another corporation for investment, provided there is no attempt or motive to lessen competition. Likewise, a corporation is permitted to form a subsidiary to carry on a part of its business when the effect of such formation is not to substantially lessen competition. Today, proposed corporate mergers are often challenged by both the FTC and the Department of Justice.

Celler-Kefauver amendment The Celler-Kefauver Act of 1950 corrected a glaring defect of the Clayton Act which originally prohibited mergers where the effect would be to lessen competition between the acquiring corporation and the "target" corporation. The new and obviously sounder standard is the test used in Clayton Section 3: "to substantially lessen competition" generally, and not just competition between the two firms. The amendment also plugged another loophole in the original statute by making Section 7 apply to a corporate acquisition effected through purchase of the *assets* of the target corporation. Before the amendment, Section 7 had only prohibited anticompetitive mergers accomplished through purchase by one

corporation of another's *stock*. Since the Celler-Kefauver amendment, a very substantial body of case law has developed from the growing number of private suits attacking proposed mergers. Frequently the plaintiff in such suits is the target company of an unfriendly takeover.

Relevant market under Section 7 Chapter 47, beginning at page 1055, discussed the importance of defining a firm's "relevant product and geographic market" in a Sherman Section 2 monopolization case. These concepts are equally basic to any analysis of a merger under Clayton Section 7. In a proposed merger, a narrowly defined product or geographic market will result in a greater anticompetitive effect. Conversely, a broadly defined product line or geographic market will result in a smaller adverse effect on competition. Therefore, the entire issue of the probable anticompetitive effect of a merger often depends upon the relevant "product" and "geographic" market definition that the trial court accepts. The Supreme Court in the landmark *Brown Shoe*[11] case developed an elaborate test for defining relevant product markets for purposes of Section 7 mergers. First, the product line ("line of commerce") must be defined, and then the relevant geographic market for that product ("section of the country"). Up to this point the approach is similar to that used in Section 2 cases under the Sherman Act discussed in Chapter 47. However, in defining the relevant geographic market the Court outlined two further steps that must be taken: (1) Define the "outer boundary market" using criteria similar to those used in monopolizing cases, and then (2) further define *geographic submarkets* within those outer boundaries using the following "practical indicia": the industry or public recognition of the submarket as a separate economic entity, the product's peculiar characteristics and uses, unique production facilities, distinct customers,

---

[11]*Brown Shoe Co. v. United States,* 370 U.S. 294 (1962).

distinct prices, sensitivity to price changes, and specialized vendors. Once these submarkets are defined, the Court said "it is necessary to examine the effects of a merger in each such economically significant submarket to determine if there is a reasonable probability that the merger will substantially lessen competition. If such a probability is found to exist, the merger is proscribed." Similarly, the Court said there can be *product submarkets* as well as geographic submarkets. In this case the product (shoes) was further broken down into submarket categories—men's, women's, and children's shoes.

The Court then applied these principles to the facts of the merger between the Brown and Kinney shoe companies. Both were manufacturers who also operated retail outlets. Thus, the merger was vertical as well as horizontal. The "outer boundary market" was found to be the entire nation, and a geographical submarket was determined to be "every city of 10,000 or more population and its immediate surrounding area" in which both a Kinney and a Brown store were located. Basing its analysis primarily upon a review of market shares of the two companies before the merger, the Court held that both the vertical and horizontal aspects of the merger violated Section 7 of the Clayton Act. In the wake of *Brown Shoe,* courts have not consistently applied its "practical indicia" but most frequently the uses of the product and its interchangeability from the viewpoint of buyers have been the criteria.

The definition of the product line is also crucial to the outcome of a Section 7 merger. For example, in the leading case of *United States v. E. I. du Pont de Nemours & Co.,*[12] the government charged du Pont with a violation of Section 7 by reason of its acquisition of 23 percent of the stock of General Motors (GM). Du Pont sold paint to GM as well as to many

industrial users other than auto manufacturers. The case turned on whether du Pont's product line was paint in general or automotive paint. If paint in general, GM's purchases were foreclosing competitors of du Pont from only 3.5 percent of the total industrial paint market, an inconsequential amount. On the other hand, if du Pont's product line was *automotive* paint, GM's purchases were 24 percent of total automotive uses. The Supreme Court held that the "line of commerce" was automotive paint, thus greatly exaggerating the impact of the merger upon du Pont's competitors. Having adopted the narrower product line definition, it was then easy for the Court to conclude that the merger foreclosed a substantial share (24 percent) of the market, and that the stock acquisition was unlawful.

Substantial lessening of competition After determining the relevant product line and geographic market and submarkets the plaintiff in a Section 7 case must prove, and the court must find, that the effect of the merger "may be substantially to lessen competition, or to tend to create a monopoly." Generally, the approach of the FTC and Department of Justice, as well as the courts, is to examine market concentration as measured by market share percentages of the merging firms before and after the merger. Since the percentage-of-market-share allowed depends on whether the merger is horizontal, vertical, or conglomerate, each type of merger must be evaluated separately.

1 *Horizontal mergers* arise from the combination of two firms at the same level, such as two manufacturers, two wholesalers, or two retailers. Such mergers are considered unlawful and are challenged by the Department of Justice which has primary enforcement responsibility with respect to mergers and acquisitions. Although corporate combinations may violate Sections 1 and 2 of the Sherman Act, most challenges are made under Section 7 of the Clayton Act, since it is easier to prove a case under that

---

[12]353 U.S. 586 (1957).

section. The Department has published *Merger Guidelines*[13] for the information of firms contemplating merger. These guidelines focus on market structure and market shares. For example, a proposed horizontal merger in a highly concentrated market, where the shares of the four largest firms amount to 75 percent or more, will be challenged when the following market share percentages are present:

If Acquiring Firm Has:	and Acquired Firm Has:
4%	4% or more
10%	2% or more
15%	1% or more

Regardless of these percentages, if there is a *trend* toward concentration in an industry, a merger will be challenged. In addition, any horizontal merger may be questioned if it appears that it may be "disruptive" to competition.

If one of the merging firms faces the clear probability of being a *failing company* and it has made a good faith effort toward being acquired by a firm that would not produce anticompeti-

[13]*Department of Justice Merger Guidelines*, May 30, 1968.

tive effects (for example, a conglomerate, discussed below), then the merger will ordinarily not be challenged. Generally, the Department will not accept as justification for a horizontal merger the claim that it will produce economies or improve efficiency. Section 7 of the Clayton Act was applied to a horizontal merger in the *Von's Grocery* case which follows.

2 *Vertical mergers* arise when a firm at one level, such as a manufacturer, acquires a firm at a different level, such as a wholesaler or a supplier. Regardless of whether such mergers arise from an acquisition that is "backward" into a supplying market, for example, a wholesaler acquiring a manufacturer, or "forward" into a purchasing market, they will be challenged if they tend to raise barriers to entry by restricting a potential competitor's equal access to potential customers or to potential suppliers. The Department will ordinarily challenge a merger if the market share of the supplying firm is 10 percent or more and if the purchasing firm accounts for 6 percent or more of the total purchases in that market, unless it clearly appears that there are no significant barriers to entry into the business of the purchasing firm. Regardless of these percentages, a vertical merger may also be challenged if there is a significant trend toward vertical integration in the entire industry.

Case 48.1   United States v. Von's Grocery Co.
384 U.S. 270 (1966)

Civil action by the United States charging that the acquisition by Von's Grocery Company of its direct competitor Shopping Bag Food Stores, both large retail grocery companies in Los Angeles, California, violated Section 7 of the Clayton Act. The sole question was whether the District Court properly concluded that the government had failed to prove a violation of Section 7. The facts are stated in the opinion.

BLACK, Associate Justice. From 1948 to 1958 the number of Von's stores in the Los Angeles area practically doubled from 14 to 27, while at the same time the number of Shopping Bag's stores jumped from 15 to 34. During that same decade, Von's sales increased fourfold and its share of the market almost doubled while Shopping Bag's sales multiplied seven times and its share of the market tripled. The merger of these two highly successful, expanding and aggressive competitors created the second largest grocery chain in Los Angeles with sales of almost $172,488,000 annually. In addition the findings of the District Court show that the number of owners operating single stores in the Los Angeles retail grocery market decreased from 5,365 in 1950 to 3,818 in 1961. . . . During roughly the same period, from 1953 to 1962, the number of chains with two or more grocery stores increased from 96 to 150. While the grocery business was being concentrated into the hands of fewer and fewer owners, the small companies were continually being absorbed by the larger firms through mergers. . . . These facts alone are enough to cause us to conclude contrary to the District Court that the Von's Shopping Bag merger did violate § 7. Accordingly, we reverse.

. . . To arrest [the] "rising tide" toward concentration into too few hands and to halt the gradual demise of the small businessman, Congress decided to clamp down with vigor on mergers. [By the Celler-Kefauver amendment] it both revitalized § 7 of the Clayton Act by "plugging its loophole" and broadened its scope . . . [By using terms] in § 7 which look not merely to the actual present effect of a merger but instead to its effect upon future competition, Congress sought to preserve competition among many small businesses by arresting a trend toward concentration in its incipiency before that trend developed to the point that a market was left in the grip of a few big companies. . . .

The facts of this case present exactly the threatening trend toward concentration which Congress wanted to halt. The number of small grocery companies in the Los Angeles retail grocery market had been declining rapidly before the merger and continued to decline rapidly afterwards. This rapid decline in the number of grocery store owners moved hand in hand with a large number of significant absorptions of the small companies by the larger ones. In the midst of this steadfast trend toward concentration, Von's and Shopping Bag, two of the most successful and largest companies in the area, jointly owning 66 grocery stores merged to become the second largest chain in Los Angeles. This merger cannot be defended on the ground that one of the companies was about to fail or that the two had to merge to save themselves from destruction by some larger and more powerful competitor. What we have on the contrary is simply the case of two already powerful companies merging in a way which makes them even more powerful than they were before.

Von's primary argument is that the merger between Von's and Shopping Bag is not prohibited by § 7 because the Los Angeles grocery market was competitive before the merger, has been since, and may continue to be in the future. Even so, § 7 requires not merely an appraisal of the immediate impact of the merger upon competition, but a prediction of its impact upon competitive conditions in the future; this is what is meant when it is said that the amended § 7 was intended to arrest anticompetitive tendencies in their incipiency. . . .

Congress passed the Celler-Kefauver Act to prevent such a destruction of competition. Our cases . . . have faithfully endeavored to enforce this congressional command. We adhere to them now.

Reversed and remanded.

3 *Conglomerate mergers* arise where there is no visible relation between the business of two uniting firms. Conglomerate mergers experienced an explosive growth in the 1960s. The Department of Justice defines such mergers as any merger that is neither horizontal nor vertical. The Department also classifies as "conglomerate" a *market extension merger* or a *product extension merger*. A market extension merger takes place if the two firms sell the same product in different geographic markets. The *Falstaff* case below is illustrative. A *product extension merger* arises when the product of the target firm is in the same general category as the products of the acquiring firm, but they do not directly compete with such products. Two types of conglomerate mergers likely to be challenged because of their anticompetitive effect are: mergers creating a danger of reciprocal buying, and mergers involving a potential entrant into the market.

The *potential entrant doctrine* holds that the forbidden anticompetitive effect may exist if one of the two merging firms is a potential entrant into the market. Prohibiting such a merger not only increases the chances that the potential entrant will stimulate competition by actually entering the market, but the mere fact that it is "on the edge of the market" has a stimulating effect on competition between firms that are already there. The potential entrant doctrine may be applied to a horizontal merger, as in *Falstaff* which follows, or to a large conglomerate firm that could potentially enter a new product market, thus introducing the danger of market dominance. Antitrust policy is concerned that market dominance may result from merger with a powerful conglomerate because: (1) its strength may enable it to sell below cost in a product or geographic market and drive out weaker competitors; (2) economies of scale may enable it to eliminate smaller competitors by underpricing them even without selling below cost; (3) the danger of reciprocal buying is increased, foreclosing suppliers from competing to meet the needs of either merging firm; (4) barriers to entry are potentially increased; and (5) it has the potential for accelerating the trend toward concentration in industry with all of the social ills associated with such concentration.

Conflicting court decisions, the cost and complexity of gathering economic data relevant to a merger, wide differences among experts in interpreting such data, the absence of rigid criteria—all these factors make the outcome of a planned merger very uncertain. Proposed legislation would significantly curtail conglomerate mergers by prohibiting firms with $2.5 billion in annual sales or $2 billion in assets from further acquisitions. Sponsors of this "Big is Bad Bill" contend that further concentration of economic and political power in such large corporations is a social evil. Opponents of the legislation argue that increased efficiency resulting from bigness may reduce prices, and thus stimulate competition.

Case 48.2   United States v. Falstaff Brewing Corporation
410 U.S. 526 (1973)

Civil action under Section 7 of the Clayton Act by the United States to enjoin Falstaff Brewing Corp., the nation's fourth largest brewer, from acquiring a firm which was the largest seller of beer in New England. In 1963, Falstaff extended its geographic market into New England by acquiring the Narragansett Brewing Company. Prior to 1965, Falstaff had no beer sales in the New England area, although of the three largest brewers in the nation that did *not* sell beer in New England, Falstaff's brewery was the closest to that market. While beer sales in New England increased approximately 9.5 percent in the 4 years preceding the acquisition, the eight largest sellers increased their share of these sales from approximately 74 to 81.2 percent. The parties agreed that the relevant product market was beer, and the six New England states composed the geographic market. The number of brewers operating plants in this market decreased from thirty-two in 1935 to eleven in 1957, to six in 1964.

After trial, the district court upheld the merger and rejected the government's contention that Falstaff at the time of the acquisition was a potential entrant into the New England market and that the merger deprived that market of additional competition Falstaff would have provided. The court also found that Falstaff's management had consistently decided not to attempt to enter the New England market unless it could acquire an existing company with a strong distribution system such as that possessed by Narragansett. The government appealed directly to the Supreme Court.

WHITE, Associate Justice. Section 7 of the Clayton Act forbids mergers in any line of commerce where the effect may be substantially to lessen competition or tend to create a monopoly. The section proscribes many mergers between competitors in a market. . . . Suspect also is the acquisition by a company not competing in the market but so situated as to be a potential competitor and likely to exercise substantial influence on market behavior. Entry through merger by such a company, although its competitive conduct in the market may be the mirror image of that of the acquired company, may nevertheless violate § 7 because the entry eliminates a potential competitor exercising present influence on the market.

In the case before us, Falstaff was not a competitor in the New England market, nor is it contended that its merger with Narragansett represented an entry by a dominant market force. It was urged, however, that Falstaff was a potential competitor so situated that its entry by merger rather than *de novo* violated § 7. The District Court, however, relying heavily on testimony of Falstaff officers, concluded that the company had no intent to enter the New England market except through acquisition and that it therefore could not be considered a potential competitor in that market. Having put aside Falstaff as a potential *de novo* competitor, it followed for the District Court that entry by a merger would not adversely affect competition in New England.

The District Court erred as a matter of law. The error lay in the assumption that because Falstaff, as a matter of fact, would never have entered the market *de novo*, it could in no sense be considered a potential competitor. More specifically, the District Court failed to give separate consideration to whether Falstaff was a potential competitor in the sense that it was so positioned on the edge of the market that it exerted beneficial influence on competitive conditions in that market.

The specific question with respect to this phase of the case is not what Falstaff's internal company decisions were but whether, given its financial capabilities and conditions in the New England market, it would be reasonable to consider it a potential entrant into that market. Surely, it could not be said on this record that Falstaff's general interest in the New England market was unknown; and if it would appear to rational beer merchants in New England that Falstaff might well build a new brewery to supply the northeastern market then its entry by merger becomes suspect under § 7. The District Court should therefore have appraised the economic facts about Falstaff and the New England market in order to determine whether in any realistic sense Falstaff could be said to be a potential competitor on the fringe of the market with likely influence on existing competition. . . . We remand this case to the District Court to make the proper assessment of Falstaff as a potential competitor.

Section 8—Interlocking Directorates Section 8 attacked the potential anticompetitive effects of interlocking directorates by providing that "no person at the same time shall be a director in any two or more corporations, if any one of them has capital, surplus, and undivided profits aggregating more than $1 million" and if it would constitute a violation of the antitrust laws should competition between the corporations be eliminated. Inasmuch as one legal test is whether a hypothetical merger of the two companies would tend to reduce competition with other firms, there often is sufficient cross-elasticity (interchangeability) of demand for the products of two apparently noncompeting companies to prohibit the same director from serving on both boards. In recent years, the hazard of a Section 8 violation coupled with the growing popularity of derivative[14] suits by stockholders against directors for negligence or breach of duty has discouraged the earlier practice of recruiting as an outside director an officer-director of another corporation.

---

[14]Derivative suits are defined and explained in Chapter 44, p. 954.

Case 48.3   United States v. Sears, Roebuck & Co.
111 F. Supp. 14 (S.D.N.Y. 1953)

Suit by the United States under Section 8 of the Clayton Act, against Sears, Roebuck & Co. and B. F. Goodrich Company, seeking an order directing the resignation of S. Weinberg as a director of both companies. Both corporations were of the size required by the statute, and were engaged in commerce as the term is used in the Clayton Act. Both firms competed in the retail sale of many items such as refrigerators, washers, automotive supplies, radio and television sets. The principal question was whether Sears and Goodrich were "competitors, so that the elimination of competition between them would constitute a violation of any of the provisions of any of the antitrust laws."

WEINFELD, District Judge. Section 8 was but one of a series of measures which finally emerged as the Clayton Act, all intended to strengthen the

Sherman Act, which through the years, had not proved entirely effective. Congress had been aroused by the concentration of control by a few individuals or groups over many gigantic corporations which in the normal course of events should have been in active and unrestrained competition. Instead, and because of such control, the healthy competition of the free enterprise system had been stifled or eliminated. Interlocking directorships on rival corporations had been the instrumentality of defeating the purpose of the antitrust laws. They had tended to suppress competition or to foster joint action against third party competitors. The continued potential threat to the competitive system resulting from these conflicting directorships was the evil aimed at. Viewed against this background, a fair reading of the legislative debates leaves little room for doubt that, in its efforts to strengthen the antitrust laws, what Congress intended by Section 8 was to nip in the bud incipient violations of the antitrust laws by removing the opportunity or temptation to such violations through interlocking directorates.

Assume that Sears and Goodrich are selling refrigerators competitively in a town of 30,000 population, the effective and easy means is at hand, through a price-fixing agreement or the withdrawal of either Sears or Goodrich from the territory or an agreement not to sell the refrigerators in the same area, to eliminate or lessen competition. . . . [A director] might, if he felt the interests of an interlocking corporation so required, either initiate or support a course of action resulting in price-fixing or division of territories or a combination of his competing corporations as against a third competitive corporation. The fact that this has not happened up to the present does not mean that it may not happen hereafter.

. . . Price fixing and territorial division between competitors are *per se* violations of § 1 of the Sherman Act, without regard to the amount of commerce affected. No showing of industry domination is required. It is the character of the restraint and not the amount of commerce affected that taints the transaction.

Since Sears and Goodrich are competitors, since a price-fixing or division of territory agreement would eliminate competition between them, and since such an agreement would *per se* violate at least one "of the provisions of . . . the antitrust laws," namely § 1 of the Sherman Act, it follows that § 8 forbids defendant Weinberg to be a director of both corporations.

The government's motion for summary judgment is granted.

Enforcement

Section 4 of the Clayton Act authorizes individuals who suffer business injury arising from a violation of the antitrust laws to bring a civil suit for treble damages and attorney fees. In addition, Section 11 empowered the Federal Trade Commission to hold hearings and to issue cease and desist orders against violations. Failure to comply with such an order could result in a civil penalty of $5,000 for each day the noncompliance continues. The Justice Department shares with the Federal Trade Commission civil enforcement authority over the Clayton Act.

THE ROBINSON-PATMAN ACT

Historical Background

In the 20 years that followed the Clayton Act, certain defects appeared which required remedial legislation. Large grocery, drug, and other chain stores were able to use their buying power and to employ various devices to purchase goods at lower prices than their smaller competitors. These devices included: receiving payments in lieu of brokerage fees, purchasing through a wholly owned subsidiary that masqueraded as a "wholesaler," and receiving larger advertising and promotional allowances than were given to smaller competitors. In some cases, suppliers sold to chain stores at lower prices than they charged the wholesalers who distributed to the small retail outlets. These practices, which were not forbidden by the Clayton Act, involved suppliers discriminating in price between different *customers* at the same level. However, as the courts had interpreted the Clayton Act, the focus was on the anticompetitive effect of price discrimination at the *supplier's level,* but not on the possible anticompetitive effect of supplier price discrimination at the *customer level.* In the midst of the Great Depression, the outcry of small retailers and wholesalers against the chain stores eventually reached Congress. It passed the Robinson-Patman Act in 1936.[15]

Purpose and Scope

Purpose   The primary aim of the Robinson-Patman Act was to limit the buying power of large chain stores and other buyers so as to prevent them from coercing suppliers to furnish discriminatory concessions on prices or services and thereby to prevent such buyers from gaining an unfair advantage over their smaller competitors. Since the act is enforceable against sellers as well as buyers that participated in discriminatory discounts, a secondary objective was to discourage sellers from offering such discounts.

Critics contend that these goals have not been effectively realized. They argue that enforcement has been mostly against small sellers or against buyers engaged in genuine competition, and that fear of prosecution has led sellers to substitute price uniformity for price competition. The complexity of the statue has also made it difficult and costly to establish a violation, with the result that FTC enforcement has reduced to a trickle in recent years and the Supreme Court rarely accepts appeals from lower courts requesting interpretation of the act. Nevertheless, the act is still on the books, numerous private treble damage suits are founded upon it, and it continues to have nationwide impact on pricing decisions of manufacturers, wholesalers, and retailers.

Scope   The Robinson-Patman Act amended Section 2(a) of the Clayton Act to provide:

That it shall be unlawful for any person engaged in commerce, in the course of such commerce, either directly or indirectly, to discriminate in price between different purchasers of commodities of like grade and quality, where either or any of the purchases involved in such discrimination are in commerce, where such commodities are sold for use, consumption, or resale within the United States or any Territory thereof or the District of Columbia, or any insular possession or other place under the jurisdiction of the United States, and where the effect of such discrimination may be substantially to lessen competition or tend to create a monopoly in any line of commerce, or to injure, destroy, or prevent competition with any person who either grants or knowingly receives the benefit of

---

[15]15 U.S.C. § 13.

such discrimination, or with customers of either of them: *Provided*, That nothing herein contained shall prevent differentials which make only due allowance for differences in the cost of manufacture, sale or delivery resulting from the differing methods or quantities in which such commodities are to such purchasers sold or delivered: . . . *And provided further*, That nothing herein contained shall prevent persons engaged in selling goods, wares, or merchandise in commerce from selecting their own customers in bona fide transactions and not in restraint of trade: *And, provided further*, That nothing herein contained shall prevent price changes from time to time where in response to changing conditions affecting the market for or the marketability of the goods concerned, such as but not limited to actual or imminent deterioration of perishable goods, obsolescence of seasonal goods, distress sales under court process or sales in good faith in discontinuance of business in the goods concerned.

Court Interpretation of Robinson-Patman Act

Proving "Commerce" Jurisdiction A person charged with a violation of Section 2(a) of the Robinson-Patman Act must be "engaged in interstate, as distinguished from intrastate commerce." In other words, the transaction must involve two or more states. For example, the act applies to a seller in one state who sells to a buyer in the same state at a favorable price, but who sells to a competing buyer in another state at a discriminatory higher price. Thus, Section 2(a) of the Robinson-Patman Act, by requiring that one of the two transactions must be "in the course" of interstate commerce, imposes a narrower "commerce" test than the Sherman Act test which includes intrastate transactions that substantially *affect* interstate commerce as well as those that are actually in interstate commerce.

Proving Discrimination To establish price discrimination under Section 2(a) of the Robinson-Patman Act it must be shown that (1) in the "course of commerce" there were (2) two or more sales of (3) commodities (as distinguished from services) which were (4) of like grade or quality to (5) two or more purchasers (6) about the same time, involving (7) discriminatorily different prices which (8) may injure competition. The act does not apply to retail sales because normally such sales do not injure competition between businesses. There is no violation if a discriminatory price is quoted but the buyer refuses to accept it, inasmuch as a sale is not completed. Likewise, there is no violation if the two sales occur at substantially different times. The allowable time span between sales varies with the durability or perishability of the goods and the volatility of their market. Thus the sale of 100 boxes of bolts to two different buyers 2 weeks apart at different prices might be considered as having occurred at substantially the same time, but if the boxes had contained perishable tomatoes, the sale would probably be treated as having occurred at different times.

Since the act applies to a seller dealing with *different* purchasers there is no violation if the seller sells at uniform prices to bona fide independent distributors who resell to their customers. However, in certain circumstances, the FTC's "indirect purchasers" doctrine may apply. This doctrine attributes sales to a seller that are made by others under the domination and control of the original seller. For example, the doctrine has been applied where a supplier exercises an abnormal degree of control over redistribution by his wholesale customers, so that their discriminatory sales are treated as those of the supplier. Since Section 2(a) of the Robinson-Patman Act refers to "commodities" and not services, discriminatory pricing of electricity, lease rentals, broadcasting network time, or terms of bank loan are not prohibited. Such practices, however, might violate provisions of the Sherman Act or the Federal Trade Commission Act, discussed later in this chapter.

Proving Commodities Are of Like Grade and Quality   Obviously a price differential based upon differences in grade is not discriminatory —large eggs appropriately sell for more than small. Unfortunately, in a specific case, determining whether the goods are of like grade and quality is not always as easy as classifying eggs. For example, the Supreme Court has held that if a seller produces a certain kind of canned milk, the fact that a private label is placed on its cans that are sold to a chain store does not make it different from its cans which bear a major advertising brand label.[16] However, even where the products have the same brand, if there is an actual difference in grade or quality, the seller may charge whatever different prices he chooses, regardless of whether those differentials are proportionate to the differences in the seller's costs. Clearly, the seller who establishes various prices based upon differences in grade and quality is not engaging in price discrimination under the act if all buyers are given the same opportunities to purchase.

Proving Injury to Competition   Section 2(a) of the Robinson-Patman Act does not render price discrimination automatically illegal but applies only if the plaintiff can prove that the price differentials may "tend to create a monopoly in any line of commerce, or to injure, destroy, or prevent competition. . . ." The act is aimed at preventing probable injury to competitors of the seller (*primary line injury*), to buyers (*secondary line injury*), to customers of buyers (*tertiary line injury*), and even to competitors of the buyer's customer (*fourth line injury*). For example, in *Perkins v. Standard Oil Company of California*,[17] Standard sold gasoline at a favored price to another oil company, Signal. Signal resold to its subsidiary Western

Hyway, which in turn sold to its subsidiary, Regal, whose sales at cut-rate prices caused injury to Regal's competitor, Perkins. The Court of Appeals termed Regal's harm to Perkins "fourth level injury" and held that since Section 2(a) quoted above only suggests three levels of injury, Perkins was not entitled to recover under the act. The Supreme Court reversed, and in ruling for Perkins pointed out that "the competitive harm done him by Standard is certainly no less because of the presence of an additional link in this particular distribution chain."

Two customers situated in different geographic markets are clearly not competing. Hence, they cannot suffer competitive injury if one of them receives a favored price from a discriminating supplier. For example, if a manufacturer sells a can opener to a retailer in Boston for $1.00 and to a retailer in Seattle for $1.25, although the latter price is discriminatory, it has not injured the retailer in Seattle who is not competing with the retailer in Boston. However, if such discrimination impairs competition with the *seller*, Section 2 would be violated.

Competitive injury generally does not result when a supplier sells at different prices to buyers who are differentiated *by function*. For example, a supplier of tires may sell at a given price to wholesalers of replacement tires, but sell at a lower price to an automobile manufacturer who markets the tires as part of an automobile in a different functional distribution system. Courts assume that since the buyers perform different functions, they are not competing with each other; therefore, the price differentials cannot injure competition. The decisive test in cases involving functional discounts is: Does the price differential have a significant anticompetitive effect? Functional discounts commonly exist because of cost savings. A seller's charge per unit will be less to the wholesaler who processes a carload than to the

---

[16]*FTC v. The Borden Co.*, 383 U.S. 637 (1966).
[17]89 S.Ct. 1871 (1969).

retailer who buys only a few items. Even if the amount of the functional discount is significantly higher than the cost savings, the FTC has been reluctant to challenge such discounts unless there is a clear anticompetitive effect.

Case 48.4   **Utah Pie Co. v. Continental Baking Co.**
386 U.S. 685 (1967)

Suit for treble damages and injunctive relief by Utah Pie Company against Continental Baking Company, Carnation Company, and Pet Milk Company (defendants) charging price discrimination under the Robinson-Patman Act. Utah Pie was a small bakery, with 18 employees, that operated in the Salt Lake City area for 30 years. It was the last to enter the frozen pie market in 1957, having been preceded by Pet, Continental, and Carnation. However, Utah Pie was immediately successful and built a new plant in 1958 which gave it a competitive advantage over the three larger defendants. During the period covered by the suit (1957–1961), Utah Pie's share of the market varied from 66 to 45 percent, but its sales volume steadily increased over the 4 years. For the same period, the market shares of the other defendants were: Carnation, 10 to 8 percent; Continental 1 to 8 percent; Pet, 16 to 29 percent. The jury found for Utah Pie on the price discrimination charge, the Court of Appeals reversed on the ground that Utah Pie had failed to prove a prima facie case, and appeal was taken to the Supreme Court.

WHITE, Associate Justice. We disagree with the Court of Appeals in several respects. First, there was evidence from which the jury could have found considerably more price discrimination by Pet with respect to "Pet-Ritz" and "Swiss Miss" pies than was considered by the Court of Appeals. In addition to the seven months during which Pet's prices in Salt Lake were lower than prices in the California markets, there was evidence from which the jury could reasonably have found that in ten additional months the Salt Lake City prices for "Pet-Ritz" pies were discriminatory as compared with sales in western markets other than California. Likewise, with respect to "Swiss Miss" pies, there was evidence in the record from which the jury could have found that in 5 of the 13 months during which the "Swiss Miss" pies were sold prior to the filing of this suit, prices in Salt Lake City were lower than those charged by Pet in either California or some other western markets. . . . With respect to whether Utah would have enjoyed Safeway's business absent the Pet contract with Safeway, . . . there were other companies seeking the Safeway business, including Continental and Carnation, whose pies may have been excluded from the Safeway shelves by what the jury could have found to be discriminatory sales to Safeway. . . . The Court of Appeals almost entirely ignored other evidence which provides material support for the jury's conclusion that Pet's behavior satisfied the statutory test regarding competitive injury. This evidence bore on the issue of Pet's predatory intent to injure Utah Pie. As an initial matter, the jury could have concluded that Pet's discriminatory pricing was aimed at Utah Pie; Pet's own management, as early as 1959, identified Utah Pie as an "unfavorable factor," one which "dug holes in our operation" and posed a constant "check" on Pet's performance in the Salt Lake City market. Moreover, Pet candidly admitted that during the period when it was establishing its relationship with Safeway, it sent into Utah Pie's plant an industrial spy to seek information that would be of use to Pet in convincing Safeway that Utah Pie was not worthy of its custom. Pet denied that it ever in fact used what it had learned against Utah Pie in competing for Safeway's business. . . . But even giving Pet's view of the incident a measure of weight does not mean the jury was foreclosed from considering the predatory intent underlying Pet's mode of competition. Finally, Pet does not deny that the evidence showed it suffered substantial losses on its frozen pie sales during the greater part of the time involved in this suit. . . .

It seems clear to us that the jury heard adequate evidence from which it could have concluded that Pet had engaged in predatory tactics in waging competitive warfare in the Salt Lake City market. Coupled with the incidence of price discrimination attributable to Pet, the evidence as a whole established, rather than negated, the reasonable possibility that Pet's behavior produced a lessening of competition proscribed by the Act.

Utah Pie's case against Continental is not complicated. Continental was a substantial factor in the market in 1957. But its sales of frozen 22-ounce dessert pies, sold under the "Morton" brand amounted to only 1.3% of the market in 1958, 2.9% in 1959, and 1.8% in 1960. . . . Then in June 1961, it took the steps which are the heart of Utah Pie's complaint against it. Effective for the last two weeks of June, it offered its 22-ounce frozen apple pies in the Utah area at $2.85 per dozen. It was then selling the same pies at substantially higher prices in other markets. The Salt Lake City price was less than its direct cost plus an allocation for overhead.

We again differ with the Court of Appeals. Its opinion that Utah was not damaged as a competitive force apparently rested on the fact that Utah's sales volume continued to climb in 1961 and on the court's own factual conclusion that Utah was not deprived of any pie business which it otherwise might have had. But this retrospective assessment fails to note that Continental's discriminatory below-cost price caused Utah Pie to reduce its price to $2.75 [per dozen]. The jury could have . . . reasonably concluded that a competitor who is forced to reduce his price to a new all-time low in a market of declining prices will in time feel the financial pinch and will be a less effective competitive force. . . . We think there was sufficient evidence from which the jury could find a violation of § 2(a) by Continental. . . .

We need not dwell long upon the case against Carnation. . . . After Carnation's temporary setback in 1959 it instituted a new pricing policy to regain business in the Salt Lake City market. The new policy involved a slash in price of 60¢ per dozen pies, which brought Carnation's price to a level admittedly well below its costs, and well below the other prices prevailing in the market. The impact of the move was felt immediately, and the two other major sellers in the market reduced their prices. Carnation's banner year, 1960, in the end involved eight months during which the prices in Salt Lake City were lower than prices charged in other markets. . . . The trend continued during the eight months in 1961 that preceded the filing of the complaint in this case, . . . and in all but August 1961 the Salt Lake City delivered price was 20¢ to 50¢ lower than the prices charged in distant San Francisco. . . . We cannot say that the evidence precluded the jury from finding it reasonably possible that Carnation's conduct would injure competition.

. . . Sellers may not sell like goods to different purchasers at different prices if the result may be to injure competition in either the sellers' or the buyers' market unless such discriminations are justified as permitted by the Act. This case concerns the sellers' market. In this context, the Court of Appeals placed heavy emphasis on the fact that Utah Pie constantly increased its sales volume and continued to make a profit. But we disagree with its apparent view that there is no reasonably possible injury to competition as long as the volume of sales in a particular market is expanding and at least some of the competitors in the market continue to operate at a profit. Nor do we think that the Act only comes into play to regulate the conduct of price discriminators when their discriminatory prices consistently undercut other competitors. It is true that many of the primary line cases that have reached the courts have involved blatant predatory price discriminations employed with the hope of immediate destruction of a particular competitor. On the question of injury to competition such cases present courts with no difficulty, for such pricing is clearly within the heart of the proscription of the Act. Courts and commentators alike have noted that the existence of predatory intent might bear on the likelihood of injury to competition. In this case there was some evidence of predatory intent with respect to each of these respondents. There was also other evidence upon which the jury could rationally find the requisite injury to competition. . . . We believe that the Act reaches price discrimination that erodes competition as much as it does price discrimination that is intended to have immediate destructive impact. In this case, the evidence shows a drastically declining price structure which the jury could rationally attribute to continued or sporadic price discrimination. The jury was entitled to conclude that "the effect of such discrimination," by each of these respondents, "may be substantially to lessen competition . . . or to injure, destroy, or prevent competition with any person who either grants or knowingly receives the benefit of such discrimination. . . ." The statutory test is one that necessarily looks forward on the basis of proven conduct in the past. Proper application of that standard here requires reversal of the judgment of the Court of Appeals.

Defenses to Liability under the Act

Sellers use two principal defenses to avoid liability under the Robinson-Patman Act: (1) that their price differentials are justified under Section 2(a) by "differences in the cost of manufacture, sale, or delivery resulting from the differing methods or quantities" involved, and (2) that lowering the "price or furnishing of services or facilities . . . was made in good faith to meet an equally low price of a competitor. . . ." The burden of proving a defense rests upon the person claiming it.

Cost Justification   A seller accused of a Section 2 discrimination because of the lower price charged large chain stores as opposed to small retailers may try to show that economies realized in large-quantity sales justify the lower per-unit selling price. The seller who deals with a very large number of customers obviously cannot establish different cost-reflecting prices for each customer. Instead, customers may be grouped for pricing purposes according to their dollar-volume of purchases and the seller's costs are then averaged for each group. The FTC as well as the courts accept such cost averaging provided that the different classes are not established in such an arbitrary manner that they result in discrimination.

An arbitrary cost-averaging system was used in *United States v. Borden Co.*[18] Borden distributed milk at 8.5 percent discount to two large grocery chains, but sold to independent grocers at discounts ranging from 5.5 percent down to nothing. In a price discrimination suit under Section 2(a) Borden defended on the ground that lower costs from quantity purchases by the chains justified the lower prices charged. In support of its claim, Borden submitted data which had classified the independents into four groups with the two chains in a fifth group. However, some independents had larger volumes than the chain stores. Average cost computed for each group tended to support the

differences in discounts. The Supreme Court held that the grouping of purchasers according to whether they were chain stores or independents (rather than classifying them on the basis of cost-saving factors such as volume of purchases,) was an arbitrary and illegal price discrimination. The Court said:

> A balance is struck by the use of classes for cost justification which are composed of members of such selfsameness as to make the averaging of the cost of dealing with the group a valid and reasonable indicium of the cost of dealing with any specific group member. High on the list of "musts" in the use of the average cost of customer groupings under the proviso of § 2(a) is a close resemblance of the individual members of each group on the essential point or points which determine the costs considered. . . . Turning first to Borden's justification, we note that it not only failed to show that the economies relied upon were isolated within the favored class but affirmatively revealed that members of the classes utilized were substantially unlike in the cost saving aspects considered. For instance the favorable cost comparisons between the chains and the larger independents were for the greater part controlled by the higher average volume of the chain stores in comparison to the average volume of the 80-member class to which these independents were relegated.

Generally, discounts based upon the customer's annual volume of purchases cannot be defended on the ground that they are justified by cost savings to the seller. A 10 percent discount on the purchase price of a single carload delivery of 100,000 units obviously involves a cost saving. The same discount to a buyer who annually purchases the same quantity, but in 20 shipments, is obviously not based upon cost savings. The more probable explanation is that the seller designed the annual discount to attract a larger market share.

---

[18]370 U.S. 460 (1962).

The cost defense has been widely criticized for the enormous complexity involved in determining and defining "cost" as well as the uncertainty arising from disagreement among experts as to the accounting standards to be used in interpreting cost data. The Supreme Court has noted the "elusiveness of cost data" and the Attorney General has described the cost justification defense as "illusory." Because the defense has rarely been successful, it is generally considered to be a poor investment of accounting time and legal expense.

Meeting Competition   Section 2(b) provides:

> Upon proof being made, at any hearing on a complaint under this section, that there has been discrimination in price or services or facilities furnished, the burden of rebutting the prima facie case thus made by showing justification shall be upon the person charged with a violation of this section, and unless justification shall be affirmatively shown, the Commission is authorized to issue an order terminating the discrimination: *Provided, however,* That nothing herein contained shall prevent a seller rebutting the prima facie case thus made by showing that his lower price or the furnishing of services or facilities to any other purchaser or purchasers was made in good faith to meet an equally low price of a competitor, or the services or facilities furnished by a competitor.

The defense of "meeting competition" is not available to a seller who knowingly goes below the standard of meeting the competitor's price by undercutting it. Nor can the defense be claimed by a seller who knowingly meets an unlawful discriminatory price quoted by a competitor. However, a seller is permitted to make a good faith competitive price reduction to retain an old customer, and may also quote the same price in order to take a new customer away from a competitor.[19] The seller must be pre- pared to show reasonable reliance on the buyer's representations as to the low prices quoted by competitors. However, the *buyer* who lies about competitors' low prices may be violating Section 2(f) by inducing and receiving an illegal discriminatory price from the seller.

Both the courts and the FTC have consistently denied the defense of meeting competition to sellers whose products, because of intrinsic superior quality or intense public demand, normally command a price higher than that usually received by sellers of competitive goods. For example, the defense was denied when the price of Lucky Strikes was dropped to the level of a "poorer grade of cigarettes."[20] Similarly, the seller cannot use the defense by meeting the price quoted by the competitor for goods in a larger quantity than that furnished the seller.

The Supreme Court has held that the "meeting competition" defense is not available to a supplier who charges a discriminatorily low price to assist a selected retail dealer in matching the price of another *retail competitor* engaged in a price war.[21] This conclusion was reached by interpreting "equally low price of a competitor" as used in Section 2(b) to mean "equally low price of a competitor of the seller." The Court reasoned that "to allow a supplier to intervene and grant discriminatory price concessions designed to enable its customer to meet the lower price of a retail competitor who is unaided by his supplier would discourage rather than promote competition. . . . To permit a competitor's supplier to bring his often superior economic power to bear narrowly and discriminatorily to deprive the otherwise resourceful retailer of the very fruits of his efficiency and convert the normal competitive struggle between retailers into an unequal contest between one retailer and the combination of another retailer and his supplier is hardly an element of reasonable and fair competition."

---

[19]*Sunshine Biscuits, Inc. v. FTC*, 306 F.2d 48 (7th Cir. 1962).

[20]*Porto Rican American Tobacco Co. v. American Tobacco* Co., 30 F.2d 234 (2d Cir. 1929).

[21]*FTC v. Sun Oil Co.*, 371 U.S. 505 (1963).

Case 48.5   **United States v. U.S. Gypsum Co.**
                438 U.S. 422 (1978)

U.S. Gypsum and five other major gypsum board producing firms and many of their executives (defendants) were charged by the government with criminal violation of Section 1 of the Sherman Act by engaging in the practice "verifying" (exchanging information) with each other with respect to the offering prices quoted to a specific customer. The government charged that the purpose of this verification system was to fix prices.

The defendants claimed that in each instance the interseller verification between any two of the competing firms was for the purpose of ensuring compliance with Section 2(b) of the Robinson-Patman Act which permits a supplier to lower its price to a buyer in order to meet the price of a competitor. They also contended that if a seller lowered its price without verifying the competitor's price there would be a risk of Robinson-Patman liability for price discrimination, and that interseller verification was absolutely necessary because buyers often lied about offering prices they had received, and other means of price confirmation were not available. On appeal from a conviction, the Court of Appeals reversed. The Supreme Court then granted certiorari.

BURGER, Chief Justice. Section 2(a) of the Robinson-Patman Act embodies a general prohibition of price discrimination between buyers when an injury to competition is the consequence. The primary exception to the § 2(a) bar is the meeting competition defense which is . . . in § 2(b) of the Act. . . .

In *FTC v. A. E. Staley Manufacturing Co.*, 324 U.S. 746, the Court provided the first and still the most complete explanation of the kind of showing which a seller must make in order to satisfy the good-faith requirement of the Section 2(b) defense:

> "Section 2(b) does not require the seller to justify price discriminations by showing that in fact they met a competitor's price. But it does place on the seller the burden of showing that the price was made in good faith to meet a competitor's. . . . We agreed with the Commission that the statute at least requires the seller, who has knowingly discriminated in price to show the existence of facts which would lead a reasonable and prudent person to believe that the granting of a lower price would in fact meet the equally low price of a competitor."

Application of these standards to the facts in *Staley* led to the conclusion that the Section 2(b) defense had not been made out. The record revealed that the lower price had been based simply on reports of salesmen, brokers, or purchasers with no efforts having been made by the seller "to investigate or verify" the reports or the character and reliability of the informants. Similarly in *Corn Products v. FTC*, 324 U.S. 726, the Section 2(b) defense was not allowed because "the only evidence said to rebut the prima facie case . . . of price discriminations was given by witnesses who had no personal knowledge of the transactions, and was limited to statements of each witness' assumption or conclusion that the price discriminations were justified by competition."

Staley's "investigate or verify" language coupled with the *Corn Products*' focus on "personal knowledge of the transactions" have apparently suggested to a number of courts that, at least in certain circumstances, direct verification of discounts between competitors may be necessary to meet the burden of proof requirements of the § 2(b) defense. . . . The Court of Appeals . . . concluded that only a very narrow exception to Sherman Act liability should be recognized; that exception would cover the relatively few situations where the veracity of the buyer seeking the matching discount was legitimately in doubt, other reasonable means of corroboration were unavailable to the seller, and the interseller communication was for the sole purpose of complying with the Robinson-Patman Act. Despite the court's efforts to circumscribe the scope of the exception it was constrained to recognize, we find its analysis unacceptable.

A good-faith belief, rather than absolute certainty, that a price concession is being offered to meet an equally low price offered by a competitor is sufficient to satisfy the Robinson-Patman's Section 2(b) defense. While casual reliance on uncorroborated reports of buyers or sales representatives without further investigation may not, as we noted earlier, be sufficient to make the requisite showing of good faith, nothing in the language of Section 2(b) or the gloss on that language in *Staley* and *Corn Products* indicates that direct discussions of price between competitors are required. Nor has any court, so far as we are aware even imposed such a requirement.

The so-called problem of the untruthful buyer, which concerned the Court of Appeals does not in our view call for a different approach to the Section 2(b) defense. The good-faith standard remains the benchmark against which the seller's conduct is to be evaluated, and we agree with the government and the FTC that this standard can be satisfied by efforts falling short of interseller verification in most circumstances where the seller has only vague, generalized doubts about the reliability of its commercial adversary—the buyer. . . . It is difficult to predict all the factors the FTC or a court would consider in appraising a seller's good faith in matching a competing offer in these circumstances. Certainly, evidence that a seller had received reports of similar discounts from other customers or was threatened with a termination of purchases if the discount were not met, would be relevant in this regard. Efforts to corroborate the reported discount by seeking documentary evidence or by appraising its reasonableness in terms of available market data would also be probative as would the seller's past experience with the particular buyer in question.

There remains the possibility that in a limited number of situations a seller may have substantial reasons to doubt the accuracy of reports of a competing offer and may be unable to corroborate such reports in any of the generally accepted ways. . . . Both economic theory and common human experience suggest that interseller verification—if undertaken on an isolated and infrequent basis with no provision for reciprocity or cooperation—will not serve its putative function of corroborating the representations of unreliable buyers regarding the existence of competing offers. Price concessions by oligopolists generally yield competitive advantages only if secrecy can be maintained; when the terms of the concessions are made publicly known, other competitors are likely to follow and any advantage to the initiator is lost in the process. Thus, if one seller offers a price concession for the purpose of winning over one of his competitor's customers, it is unlikely that the same seller will freely inform its competitor of the details of the concession so that it can be promptly matched and diffused.

The other variety of interseller verification is, like the conduct charged in the instant case, undertaken pursuant to an agreement, either tacit or express, providing for reciprocity among competitors in the exchange of price information. Such an agreement would make little economic sense, in our view, if its sole purpose were to guarantee all participants the opportunity to match the secret price concessions of other participants under Section 2(b) of the Robinson-Patman Act, for in such circumstances, each seller would know that his price concession could not be kept from his competitors and no seller participating in the information exchange arrangement would therefore, have any incentive for deviating from the prevailing price level in the industry. . . . Instead of facilitating use of the Section 2(b) defense, such an agreement would have the effect of eliminating the very price concessions which provide the main element of competition in oligopolistic industries and the primary occasion for resort to the meeting competition defense.

Especially in oligopolistic industries such as the gypsum board industry, the exchange of price information among competitors carries with it the added potential for the development of concerted price-fixing arrangements which lie at the core of the Sherman Act's prohibitions.

We are left, therefore on the one hand with doubts about both the need for and the efficacy of interseller verification as a means of facilitating compliance with Section 2(b) of the Robinson-Patman Act, and on the other, with recognition of the tendency for price discussions between competitors to contribute to the stability of oligopolistic prices and open the way for the growth of prohibited anticompetitive acitivity. To recognize even a limited "controlling circumstance" exception for interseller verification in such circumstances would be to remove from scrutiny under the Sherman Act conduct falling near its core with no assurance, and indeed with serious doubts, that competing antitrust policies would be served thereby. In *Automatic Canteen v. FTC*, 346 U.S. 61, the Court suggested that as a general rule the Robinson-Patman Act should be construed so as to insure its coherence with "the broader antitrust policies that have been laid down by Congress;" that observation buttresses our conclusion that exchange of price information—even when putatively for purposes of Robinson-Patman Act compliance—must remain subject to close scrutiny under the Sherman Act.

[The decision of the Court of Appeals remanding the case for new trial was affirmed. In 1979, the Court followed the principles of *Gypsum* in *A&P Co. v. FTC*, 99 S.Ct. 925.]

Prohibited Indirect Price Discrimination

Obviously a supplier who wishes to engage in illegal price discrimination could evade Section 2(a) by charging uniform prices to all customers while secretly paying a phony "brokerage" commission to a favored buyer's agent or by paying such buyer a fictitious "promotional allowance." The following three subsections were included in the Robinson-Patman Act for the purpose of preventing such indirect price discrimination.

Unlawful Brokerage Section 2(c) of the Robinson-Patman Act establishes an independent per se prohibition of certain kinds of "kickbacks" to favored customers:

It shall be unlawful for any person . . . to pay or grant, or to receive or accept, anything of value as a commission, brokerage, or other compensation, or any allowance or discount in lieu thereof, except for services rendered in connection with the sale or purchase of goods, wares, or merchandise, either to the other party to such transaction or to an agent, representative, or other intermediary therein where such intermediary is acting in fact for or in behalf, or is subject to the direct or indirect control, of any party to such transaction, other than the person by whom such compensation is so granted or paid.

The section expressly prohibits a seller from paying brokerage to an intermediary who acts for or in behalf of the buyer, or under the buyer's control. Since Section 2(c) creates a per se violation, it is unnecessary to show that the unlawful brokerage payment was injurious to competition. Courts have interpreted the section to prohibit buyers and their brokers from receiving compensation for "brokerage" ser-

vices rendered to *sellers* in connection with a sale. The effect of these decisions, which also reflect the policy of the FTC, is to eliminate the phrase "except for services rendered" from the subsection, with the result that brokerage payments by the seller to the buyer or buyer's broker for any reason are absolutely prohibited.

An unusual interpretation of Section 2(c) arose in *Rangen, Inc. v. Sterling Nelson & Sons*,[22] where a seller paid a bribe to a state purchasing agent to influence the sale. The court held that an injured competitor was entitled to bring a treble damage suit under Section 2(c). Decisions of the courts include commercial bribes to agents of buyers as violations of Section 2(c) where the effect of such bribes is to injure competition.

Following passage of the Robinson-Patman Act, large buyers argued that their purchasing organization had saved the seller its ordinary brokerage expense and that, therefore, a price reduction to them was lawful because it was justified by cost savings to the seller. A number of courts have rejected this argument, but other decisions have recognized a distinction between bona fide cost savings to the seller and brokerage. For example, in *Central Retailer-Owned Grocers, Inc. v. FTC*,[23] Central operated as a purchasing agent that consolidated orders from member retail grocers, and purchased at quantity discounts from suppliers. Central paid suppliers, and billed the members at slightly higher prices, the difference representing its operating cost. Any profits were distributed as dividends to the members in proportion to their purchases. Government counsel showed that the amount of price reductions Central obtained

---

[22]351 F.2d 851 (9th Cir. 1965).
[23]319 F.2d 410 (7th Cir. 1963).

from the suppliers was nearly the same as the brokerage commissions paid by the suppliers to other buyers, and claimed that Central was in effect functioning as a broker in violation of Section 2(c). The FTC agreed, but the court in setting aside the Commission's order, held that Central was functioning not as a broker, but as a buyer, and that the discounts obtained were justified by cost savings arising from quantity purchases.

Discriminatory Payments and Services Sellers often promote the sale of their products by furnishing their customers with services such as advertising, give-away samples, merchandise displays, and demonstrations. Alternatively, sellers may pay their customers to engage in promotional activities. It follows that a seller desiring to evade the prohibition of a direct price discrimination under Section 2(a) might attempt to discriminate indirectly by making payments or furnishing services to different buyers on unequal terms. Subsection 2(d) and (e) of the Robinson-Patman Act as interpreted by the courts, make it a per se violation for a seller to engage in either discriminatory payments or services. Therefore it is no defense that the discrimination did not injure competition or that it was justified by cost savings to the seller.

Section 2(d) which relates to *payments by the seller* to a customer for promotional services, provides:

That it shall be unlawful for any person engaged in commerce to pay or contract for the payment of anything of value to or for the benefit of a customer of such person in the course of such commerce as compensation or in consideration for any services or facilities furnished by or through such customers in connection with the processing, handling, sale or offering for sale of any products or commodities manufactured, sold, or offered for sale by such person, unless such payment or consideration is available on proportionally

equal terms to all other customers competing in the distribution of such products or commodities.[24]

Section 2(e) applies to *services furnished by the seller* to a customer:

That it shall be unlawful for any person to discriminate in favor of one purchaser against another purchaser or purchasers of a commodity bought for resale, without or with processing, by contracting to furnish or furnishing, or by contributing to the furnishing of, any services or facilities connected with the processing, handling, sale, or offering for sale of such commodity so purchased upon terms not accorded to all purchasers on proportionately equal terms.

Courts have interpreted the "meeting competition" defense of Section 2(b) as also applying to Sections 2(d) and (e). Thus a supplier accused of making advertising payments to a favored buyer on unequal terms with other customers can defeat liability by showing that the payment was necessary to meet a similar advertising payment offered by the supplier's competitor. Likewise, apparent inconsistencies in Section 2(d) and (e) have been harmonized by the courts, and for all practical purposes the sections are construed similarly. For example, Section 2(d) requires the seller who pays a favored customer for promotional services to offer proportionately equal payments to other *competing customers*. Although the corresponding phrase used in Section 2(e) is "all purchasers," the courts have interpreted it to mean "competing customers—the same as in Section 2(d).[25] However, "competing customers" has been held to also include those purchasing for resale from the seller's customer. Thus, in *FTC v. Fred Meyer, Inc.*,[26] where a seller offered promotional allowances to

---

[24]15 U.S.C. § 13(d).
[25]FTC v. Simplicity Pattern Co., 360 U.S. 55 (1959).
[26]390 U.S. 341 (1968).

direct-buying retailers, it was required to extend proportionally equal allowances to nondirect buying competing retailers who purchased through intermediaries.

Courts have interpreted the requirement of two contemporaneous sales transactions for purposes of Sections 2(d) and (e) in the same manner as that requirement has been interpreted with respect to Section 2(a). Similarly, the courts have required customers to handle products of the seller "of like grade and quality" in order to claim equality. The standard used is the same as that under Section 2(a). Thus, a supplier of Canadian bacon who made promotional payments to a buyer was held not to have violated Section 2(d) by refusing to make proportional payments to other buyers that distributed different pork products of the seller.[27]

The requirement of both sections that the seller who provides payments or services to a customer must make them "available on proportionally equal terms" to all other competing customers has been frequently interpreted by the courts. The seller must go beyond merely complying with the request of competing customers for like treatment by actually notifying them of the availability of payments or services on a proportional basis.

A seller is not excused from the obligation of making payments or services available to the favored buyer's competitors simply because the size or type of their operations are not adaptable to the seller's promotional plan. For example, if a seller offers payments to those buyers who promote the seller's goods by radio advertising, a buyer in a rural area where advertising is not practical would not have the benefit of the discount. Therefore, to avoid the possibility of a Section 2(d) violation, the seller is required to broaden the promotion plan to include alternate forms of advertising such as newspapers or handbills.

Diversity and flexibility in the seller's promotional plan are also necessary to meet the statutory requirement that the payments or services be on "proportionately equal terms." For example, in *State Wholesale Grocers v. Great Atlantic & Pacific Tea Co.*,[28] suppliers of A & P purchased from A & P advertising space in *Woman's Day*, a magazine that A & P owned, published, and distributed in its nationwide chain of stores. In a treble damage action the court held that, although the suppliers were not violating Section 2(e) because they were not furnishing any services or facilities, they were violating Section 2(d) by paying A & P for services without making similar payments available on proportionately equal terms to competitors of A & P. It was immaterial that these competitors had no magazine in which the defendant suppliers could also have purchased advertising space. The suppliers could nevertheless have made proportionately equal cash payments to A & P's competitors for use in other promotional advertising media such as newspapers. Suppliers' uncertainty as to the legality of particular promotional allowance programs was significantly reduced when the FTC published its useful and authoritative *Guides for Advertising Allowances and Other Merchandising Payments and Services*.[29]

Buyer Inducement of Discrimination   Section 2(f) provides:

> That it shall be unlawful for any person engaged in commerce, in the course of such commerce, knowingly to induce or receive a discrimination in price which is prohibited by this section.

Since the subsection refers only to a buyer who has induced or received a discriminatory *price*, it does not apply to a buyer who induces promotional allowances or services that are for-

---

[27]*Atlanta Trading Corp. v. FTC*, 258 F.2d 365 (2d Cir. 1958).

[28]258 F.2d 831 (7th Cir. 1938).
[29]16 CFR, § 240 (1969, amended in 1972).

bidden by Sections 2(d) and (e). However, Section 5 of the FTC Act has been interpreted to prohibit as an unfair method of competition such buyer inducement and receipt of discriminatory promotional benefits. Courts have held that *scienter* is a necessary element of a violation of Section 2(f), that is, the buyer must know that he is receiving a lower price than that which the seller is charging other customers.

THE FEDERAL TRADE COMMISSION ACT

Simultaneously with the passage of the Clayton Act in 1914, Congress enacted the Federal Trade Commission Act.[30] This act created the Federal Trade Commission (FTC), a bipartisan agency to provide day-to-day enforcement of the antitrust laws. The Commission was specifically charged with enforcement of Sections 2, 3, 7, and 8 of the Clayton Act. Section 5 of the FTC Act conferred upon the FTC broad authority to proceed against "unfair methods of competition" and "unfair or deceptive acts or practices."[31] In enacting Section 5, Congress

---

[30]15 U.S.C. §§ 41-58.
[31]This phrase was added by the Wheeler-Lea amendments in 1938.

recognized the limitless ingenuity of business persons to circumvent existing laws by developing anticompetitive practices that were not specifically forbidden by the antitrust statutes. Therefore, the FTC was given comprehensive authority to prosecute any practice that it considered anticompetitive, subject to final review by the courts. In exercising this broad authority, the FTC considers whether the particular practice (1) offends public policy; (2) is immoral, unethical, oppressive, or unscrupulous; or (3) causes substantial injury to consumers particularly with respect to their purchases of the necessities of life. Courts have also interpreted Section 5 as conferring upon the FTC the nonpenal power to enforce against *any* violation of antitrust laws. However, private treble damage suits cannot be brought under Section 5.

Since 1914, many statutes have extended the FTC's jurisdiction into the area of consumer protection. These statutes, as well as the manner in which the FTC conducts enforcement hearings, issues cease-and-desist orders, and promulgates trade regulation rules that have the force of law, have already been discussed in Chapter 4. The case below illustrates the broad discretion which the FTC is authorized to exercise in prosecuting "unfair methods of competition" that are not specifically prohibited by the Sherman Act or the Clayton Act.

Case 48.6   FTC v. Sperry and Hutchinson Co.
405 U.S. 233 (1972)

The FTC (plaintiff) issued a cease-and-desist order against defendant Sperry and Hutchinson Co. (S&H), a leading seller of trading stamps, restraining continuation of its policy of commencing suit against trading stamp exchanges that would trade "gold stamps" for Sperry's green stamps, or pay cash for S&H green stamps. This arrangement enabled the housewife to consolidate various types of stamps into one kind which could then be exchanged for merchandise, but S&H objected to such exchanges on the ground that they lessened consumer patronage of its franchised retailers and decreased its stamp business. During the period from 1957 to 1965, Sperry threatened or filed more than 250 suits against unauthorized stamp exchanges, or against unauthorized purchase of stamps by firms that did not have an S&H franchise. Many of these suits successfully urged that trading exchanges were wrongfully interfering with contracts between S&H and its franchisees or infringing on trademark rights. S&H contended that its activities were not subject to FTC Section 5 of the FTC Act. The FTC appealed from an adverse judgment of the Court of Appeals.

WHITE, Associate Justice. In reality, the question is a double one: First, does Section 5 empower the Commission to define and proscribe an unfair competitive practice, even though the practice does not infringe either the letter or the spirit of the antitrust laws? Second, does Section 5 empower the Commission to proscribe practices as unfair or deceptive in their effect upon consumers regardless of their nature or quality as competitive practices or their effect on competition? We think the statute, its legislative history, and prior cases compel an affirmative answer to both questions. . . .

Legislative and judicial authorities alike convince us that the Federal Trade Commission does not arrogate excessive power to itself if, in measuring a practice against the elusive, but congressionally mandated standard of fairness, it, like a court of equity, considers public values beyond simply those enshrined in the letter or encompassed in the spirit of the antitrust laws.

[Note: The effect of the decision was to sustain the FTC's theory that its authority under Section 5 was to be interpreted broadly. The Supreme Court specifically held that unfair competitive practices are not limited to those that have anticompetitive effect, nor are unfair practices in commerce confined to purely competitive behavior.]

ANTITRUST EXEMPTIONS AND EXTRATERRITORIALITY

It has been estimated that approximately one-fourth of America's national income originates in the sectors of economy that are exempt from antitrust law.

Exemptions from antitrust law may be of two types: "express" or "implied." Express exemptions are found in the antitrust statutes or in regulatory statutes for certain industries, particularly public utilities. Since antitrust law reflects a national policy of major importance to the competitive economic system, courts interpret it liberally so as to give it the broadest possible coverage. Conversely, antitrust exemptions are construed very strictly so as to limit their applicability as much as possible. Implied exemptions arise from court interpretations that

are necessary to reconcile conflicts between antitrust law and other statutes or the Constitution. An example is the Noerr-Pennington doctrine discussed below.

Express Exemptions

Labor Organizations   Section 6 of the Clayton Act attempted to exempt labor unions from the antitrust laws, and Section 20[32] granted unions relief from some injunctions. Nevertheless, the use of federal court injunctions against unions under the Sherman Act was not effectively limited until the Norris-La Guardia Act of 1932.[33] A labor union's immunity from antitrust law is confined to a "labor dispute" as defined in that Act. A union will also lose its exempt status

---

[32]29 U.S.C. §52.
[33]29 U.S.C. §§101–115; *United States v. Hutcheson*, 312 U.S. 219 (1941).

if its primary intent is to restrain trade, or if it conspires with nonlabor groups to monopolize. In a landmark case,[34] a union, electrical contractors, and the suppliers in New York City all agreed that (1) contractors would hire union labor and buy only from the suppliers and (2) suppliers would sell only in New York to contractors who hired union labor. The Supreme Court held that the arrangement was an unlawful conspiracy under Section 1 of the Sherman Act. In denying the union's claim of exemption, the court said: "When the unions participated with a combination of business men who had complete power to eliminate all competition among themselves and to prevent all competition from others, a situation was created not included within the exemptions of the Clayton and Norris-LaGuardia Acts."

The "labor" exemption of the Clayton Act has been held not to apply to organizations representing learned professions, primarily because the members are usually independent contractors, not employees. Thus a county bar association's publication of a "minimum fee schedule"[35] and a ban on competitive bidding by a professional engineer's association[36] have been held to be nonexempt violations of the antitrust laws. Even professional sports are subject to the Sherman Act, with the notable exception of baseball.[37]

Agricultural Cooperatives   Section 6 of the Clayton Act and Section 1 of the Capper-Volstead Act[38] establish an exemption for farmers' cooperative associations that are formed to market agricultural products. Like the labor exemption, the agricultural exemption is lost if the organization combines with outside firms to restrain trade.[39]

Patents and Copyrights   Federal legislation enacted under constitutional authority[40] expressly confers limited monopoly privileges on those who invent or publish. Although such rights inherently conflict with the antitrust objective of promoting competition, they are recognized in order to encourage innovative inventions and creative publications. Patents and copyrights are limited monopolies in the sense that the products or writings that have benefited from the special privileges granted, must nevertheless compete in the market with similar or related products.

Generally, courts have resolved the conflict between the competition objective of the Sherman Act and the monopoly objectives of patent laws by interpreting patent and copyright privileges narrowly and by overruling any attempt of the owners to extend and expand such privileges into familiar areas of anticompetitive behavior. For example, in *Morton Salt Co. v. G. S. Suppiger Co.*,[41] Suppiger owned a patent on a machine used in the canning industry for depositing predetermined amounts of salt in tablet form to the contents of cans. It licensed the use of the machine to canneries on condition that they use the patented machines only with tablets that were sold by Suppiger. Morton claimed these were unlawful tying contracts that tended to lessen competition in violation of Section 3 of the Clayton Act. The Supreme Court struck down the tying contract. Sidestepping the issue of whether Section 3 was violated, the Court reached its decision on the ground that it is against public policy for a court of equity to lend

[34]*Allen Bradley Co. v. Local Union No. 3, International Brotherhood of Electrical Workers*, 325 U.S. 797 (1945).

[35]*Goldfarb v. Virginia State Bar*, 421 U.S. 733 (1975); See also, *Boddicker v. Arizona State Dental Ass'n.*, 549 F.2d 626 (9th Cir. (1977). In that case a local dental association's requirement that membership was conditional upon the dentist's maintaining membership also in the national association was held to be subject to Sherman Act jurisdiction, and not protected by the "learned profession" exemption. The case was remanded for trial on the issue of whether the arrangement was an unlawful tie-in.

[36]*United States v. Nat'l Soc'y of Professional Engineers*, 404 F. Supp. 457; aff'd 55 L.Ed.2d 637 (1978).

[37]*Toolson v. New York Yankees, Inc.*, 346 U.S. 356 (1953).

[38]7 U.S.C. §§291–292.

[39]*Case-Swayne Co. v. Sunkist Growers, Inc.*, 389 U.S. 384 (1967).

[40]U.S. Constitution, Art. 1, sec. 8, clause 8.

[41]314 U.S. 488 (1942).

its aid to protect a patent monopoly when the owner is misusing it as an "effective means of restraining competition with its sale of an unpatented article." This *patent misuse doctrine* prohibits the owner from obtaining an injunction against infringement so long as the patent is being used in an anticompetitive manner that is outside the scope of the granted patent.

Implied Exemptions

Regulated Enterprises; The Parker Doctrine

In addition to the express statutory exemptions from antitrust law already discussed, federal statutes expressly provide limited exemption for many industries affected with the public interest. For example, insurance carriers may exchange information in establishing their rates without violating the Sherman Act. Broader exemptions are extended to industries regulated under federal law such as telephone, airlines, railroads, television and radio broadcasting, interstate pipeline, stock and grain exchanges, and ocean shipping. Nevertheless, there has been a continuing trend toward deregulation and encouragement of competition.

The majority of industries which affect the public interest are regulated by commissions established by state law. A broad implied exemption for such "state action" was established by the Supreme Court in *Parker v. Brown*,[42] where a raisin packer sued under the Sherman Act to enjoin the California Director of Agriculture from carrying out a statutory price-fixing program to market raisins. The program involved pro rata restrictions on sales, first proposed by the producers, but modified and established by the state. In holding that this "state action" was exempt from the antitrust laws, the Court said:

> The prorate program here was never intended to operate by force of individual agreement or combination. It derived its authority and its efficacy from the legislative command of the state and was not intended to operate or become effective without that command. . . . True, a state does not give immunity to those who violate the Sherman Act by authorizing them to violate it or by declaring that their action is lawful. Here, although the organization of a prorate zone is proposed by the producers, and a prorate program, approved by the Commission, must also be approved by referendum of the producers, it is the state, acting through the Commission, which adopts the program and which enforces it with penal sanctions, in the execution of a governmental policy.

In recent cases, the Court has further clarified *Parker*. Thus, in *Goldfarb* discussed earlier, the Court held that a minimum lawyer fee schedule approved by the state bar was nevertheless subject to the Sherman Act. The Court stated: "The fact that the State Bar is a state agency for some limited purposes does not create an antitrust shield that allows it to foster anticompetitive practices for the benefit of its members." The Court's current view is that a company affecting the public interest such as a utility can appropriately have its natural monopoly powers regulated by the state and simultaneously be required to comply with antitrust standards to the extent that it engages in business activity in the competitive sector of the economy.

---

[42]317 U.S. 341 (1943).

Case 48.7   **California Retail Liquor Dealers Association v. Midcal Aluminum, Inc.**
445 U.S. 97 (1980)

Petition for writ of mandate by Midcal Aluminum, Inc., a wine distributor, in the California Court of Appeal, seeking to enjoin the California Department of Alcoholic Beverage Control (ABC) from enforcing a statute requiring all wine producers and wholesalers to file with ABC fair trade contracts fixing prices or price schedules. Under the statute, all wine producers and wholesalers were also required to post their price schedules and were prohibited from selling wine to retailers at other than the posted price. A wholesaler selling below the established prices was subject to fine or license revocation. Midcal was charged by ABC with failure to post prices, and selling wines for less than the posted prices.

The court of appeal ruled that the scheme restrained trade in violation of the Sherman Act and enjoined ABC from enforcing the price-control system, rejecting claims that the scheme was immune from Sherman liability under the "state action" doctrine of *Parker v. Brown*. The decision was appealed to the United States Supreme Court by California Retail Liquor Dealers Association, an intervenor.

POWELL, Associate Justice. The issue in this case is whether those state laws are shielded from the Sherman Act by . . . the "state action" doctrine of *Parker v. Brown*. . . . The State is divided into three trading areas for administration of the wine pricing program. A single fair trade contract or schedule for each brand sets the terms for all wholesale transactions in that brand within a given trading area. Similarly, state regulations provide that the wine prices posted by a single wholesaler within a trading area bind all wholesalers in that area. . . . The State has no direct control over wine prices, and it does not review the reasonableness of the prices set by wine dealers.

The threshold question is whether California's plan for wine pricing violated the Sherman Act. This Court has ruled consistently that resale price maintenance illegally restrains trade. . . . For many years, however, the Miller-Tydings Act of 1937 permitted tbe States to authorize resale price maintenance. The goal of that statute was to allow the States to protect small retail establishments that Congress thought might otherwise be driven from the marketplace by large-volume discounters. But in 1975 that congressional permission was rescinded. The Consumer Goods Pricing Act of 1975 repealed the Miller-Tydings Act and related legislation. Consequently, the Sherman Act's ban on resale price maintenance now applies to fair trade contracts unless an industry or program enjoys a special antitrust immunity.

California's system for wine pricing plainly constitutes resale price maintenance in violation of the Sherman Act. The wine producer holds the power to prevent price competition by dictating the prices charged by wholesalers. As Mr. Justice Hughes pointed out in *Dr. Miles Medical Co. v. Park & Sons Co.*, 220 U.S. 373, such vertical control destroys horizontal competition as effectively as if wholesalers "formed a combination and endeavored to establish the same restrictions . . . by agreement with each other.

Thus, we must consider whether the State's involvement in the price-setting program is sufficient to establish antitrust immunity under *Parker v. Brown*, 317 U.S. 341. That immunity for state regulatory programs is grounded in our federal structure. "In a dual system of government in which, under the

Constitution, the states are sovereign, save only as Congress may constitutionally subtract from their authority, an unexpressed purpose to nullify a state's control over its officers and agents is not lightly to be attributed to Congress." In *Parker* . . . the Court expressly noted, "a state does not give immunity to those who violate the Sherman Act by authorizing them to violate it, or by declaring that their action is lawful. . . ."

Several recent decisions have applied *Parker's* analysis. In *Goldfarb v. Virginia State Bar*, the Court concluded that fee schedules enforced by a state bar association were not mandated by ethical standards established by the State Supreme Court. The fee schedules therefore were not immune from antitrust attack. "It is not enough . . . that anticompetitive conduct is prompted by state action; rather, anticompetitive conduct must be compelled by direction of the State acting as a sovereign." Similarly, in *Cantor v. Detroit Edison Co.*, a majority of the Court found that no antitrust immunity was conferred when a state agency passively accepted a public utility's tariff. In contrast, Arizona rules against lawyer advertising were held immune from Sherman Act challenge because they "reflected a clear articulation of the State's policy with regard to professional behavior" and were "subject to pointed reexamination by the policymaker—the Arizona Supreme Court—in enforcement proceedings." *Bates v. State Bar of Arizona*, 433 U.S. 350.

Only last Term, this Court found antitrust immunity for a California program requiring state approval of the location of new automobile dealerships. *New Motor Vehicle Bd. of Calif. v. Orrin W. Fox Co.*, 439 U.S. 96 (1978). That program provided that the State would hold a hearing if an automobile franchisee protested the establishment or relocation of a competing dealership. In view of the State's active role, the Court held, the program was not subject to the Sherman Act. The "clearly articulated and affirmatively expressed" goal of the state policy was to "displace unfettered business freedom in the matter of the establishment and relocation of automobile dealerships.

These decisions establish two standards for antitrust immunity under *Parker*. First, the challenged restraint must be "one clearly articulated and affirmatively expressed as state policy"; second, the policy must be "actively supervised" by the State itself. The California system for wine pricing satisfies the first standard. The legislative policy is forthrightly stated and clear in its purposes to permit resale price maintenance. The program, however, does not meet the second requirement for *Parker* immunity. The State simply authorizes price-setting and enforces the prices established by private parties. The State neither establishes price nor reviews the reasonableness of the price schedules; nor does it regulate the terms of fair trade contracts. The State does not monitor market conditions or engage in any "pointed reexamination" of the program. The national policy in favor of competition cannot be thwarted by casting such a gauzy cloak of state involvement over what is essentially a private price fixing arrangement. As *Parker* teaches, "a state does not give immunity to those who violate the Sherman Act by authorizing it, or by declaring that their action is lawful. . . ."

The judgment of the California Court of Appeal . . . is affirmed.

Lobbying: the Noerr-Pennington Exemption
The First Amendment right of citizens to petition the government has been interpreted by
courts to impliedly exempt from the antitrust
laws lawful lobbying to obtain legislative or
executive action, even if it is intended to restrain trade or eliminate competition. However,
this "Noerr-Pennington Exemption"[43] is lost if
lobbying is used as a sham to cover other
activities that directly restrain trade.

Extraterritoriality of Antitrust Laws

Generally, agreements by American firms to
divide world markets, assign export quotas, or
fix prices overseas are subject to the antitrust
laws. Beginning in the 1940s, the Department
of Justice sought to break up large international
cartels of American and foreign companies dom-
inating markets for such commodities as magne-
sium alloys, matches, titanium compounds, and
roller bearings. Enforcement has primarily focused on foreign activity by American or foreign
firms that has a serious anticompetitive effect
within the United States, but increasing attention is now being given by the Department as
well as by private plaintiffs to the extraterritorial
(outside of the United States) anticompetitive
activities of multinational corporations.

*Effect of Antitrust Law on American Compe-
tition Abroad* American antitrust policy conflicts sharply with the view of many other
free-world nations which hold that antitrust
notions should be discarded in the highly competitive areas of world trade. The United States
is virtually alone among major trading nations in
the extent to which it imposes a variety of
antitrust restrictions on exporters who wish to
combine to penetrate foreign markets. For example, two American widget manufacturers
form a joint marketing venture to distribute
their products in France. Since they are combining to fix prices, a potential per se violation

of Section 1 of the Sherman Act is involved.
Suppose the same two firms learn that a German firm plans to discontinue manufacturing
widgets, and they persuade it to join an
American-based venture which will then export
widgets to Germany and distribute them there.
Since the German firm is an actual or potential
competitor who might market its products in
the United States, the plan might be construed
under the "potential entrant" doctrine as an
unlawful merger that would tend to lessen
competition in violation of Section 7 of the
Clayton Act.

In contrast with American efforts to give
antitrust laws extraterritorial effect, many foreign governments openly encourage export cartels by offering antitrust exemption, outright
subsidies, or tax incentives. Such foreign export
monopolies disadvantage American medium
and small firms that are prevented by the
antitrust laws from combining to meet world
competition. The problem is aggravated by recent expansion of trade with state-controlled,
centrally planned nonmarket economies, such
as those of the Iron Curtain countries. These
nations usually deal through a state trading
agency which can use its superior bargaining
power to play American firms off against each
other.

The negotiating ability of state trading monopolies is actually strengthened by the United
States' antitrust laws which prohibit American
sellers from exchanging price information. For
example, suppose an Iron Curtain state trading
agency, receives a fleet auto quotation of $6,000
per car from Ford, and says: "Chrysler offered
to deliver a comparable car for $5,000, can you
meet that price?" Ford is prohibited by existing
antitrust law from verifying the claimed lower
bid with Chrysler, from conferring with them
on price, or from comparing proposals which
have been offered to the two companies
separately.[44] Foreign competitors unrestricted

---

[43]*Eastern Railroad Presidents Conference v. Noerr-
Motor Freight, Inc.*, 365 U.S. 127 (1961); *United Mine
Workers v. Pennington*, 381 U.S. 657 (1965).

[44]See Case 48.5 at p. 1086.

by antitrust considerations can obviously bargain much more effectively with such state-controlled agencies.

Webb-Pomerene Export Trade Act In token recognition of the competitive disadvantage of American firms in world markets, Congress in 1918 passed the Webb-Pomerene Export Trade Act[45] exempting from the Sherman Act an export trade association provided it does *not* (1) restrain trade within the United States, (2) restrain exports by domestic competitors of the association, and (3) engage in domestic activity that will lessen competition or fix prices in the United States. The very few trade associations that have been organized under the Act account for only 3 percent of total American exports.

Failure of the act to stimulate exports is due to several factors: (1) uncertainty as to the permissible limits of the antitrust exemption under conflicting government policy and court decisions; (2) delay in obtaining favorable clearances from the Department of Justice, thus making it impossible to act with the speed required for most international transactions; and (3) the failure of the act to provide antitrust exemption for export services, thus restricting access to such foreign markets as computer servicing and engineering construction. Recently there has been mounting pressure for amendment of the act to correct these deficiencies, as well as to broaden antitrust exemptions to permit the formation of natural resource sellers' cartels that equalize America's bargaining position against the growing number of foreign cartels imposing higher prices on American consumers.

Comity Foreign governments have expressed growing concern over the lack of comity (respect for sovereignty) that is evidenced by the effort of the United States to give extraterritorial effect to its antitrust laws. In coming years, with growing pressure to increase exports as a means of improving America's balance of

payments, it appears predictable that some revisions in the antitrust laws will be made to reconcile the conflict between antitrust policy in the United States and the realities of a world in which trade is characterized by cartels, monopolistic state-controlled trading agencies, agreements dividing markets, and joint venture export marketing arrangements.

SUMMARY

The Clayton Act of 1914 was passed to strike at anticompetitive and monopolistic practices in their incipiency. The act prohibits price discrimination (Section 2 as amended by the Robinson-Patman Act), exclusive dealing and tying contracts (Section 3), mergers (Section 7), and interlocking directorates (Section 8). The act also requires that the prohibited activities must occur "in the course of commerce" and the actor must be "engaged in commerce"—a much narrower "commerce" definition than that used in the Sherman Act.

In all cases, the prohibited conduct must "tend to substantially lessen competition, or to create a monopoly." In applying this standard of exclusive dealing and tying contracts, courts use one of two tests: (1) The "quantitative substantiality" test which is met if the contract covers a substantial quantity of the relevant market, and (2) the "qualitative substantiality" test which judges the contract's anticompetitive effect by examining qualitative factors such as relative market strength of the parties, the probable immediate and future effect of the contract on competition, and whether it continued to flourish despite the restrictive agreement.

Most tying contracts are held to be per se violations when it is shown that (1) the seller has market power with respect to the tying product, and (2) the arrangement affects a "not insubstantial amount of commerce." For a tying arrangement to be unlawful, the tying and tied products must both be distinct *commodities*, inasmuch as

---

[45]15 U.S.C. §§61–66.

the Clayton Act does not apply to services or real estate transactions. In contrast, the Sherman Act applies to a tie-in between a service (e.g., electric power) and a commodity (e.g., light bulbs).

Section 7, as amended by the Celler-Kefauver Act of 1950, prohibits acquisition by one corporation of the stock or assets of another if it would tend to substantially lessen competition or tend to create a monopoly. In evaluating anticompetitive effect of a merger, the definition of "relevant market" is important. To determine this, courts first define the product, and then the relevant geographic market for that product. The relevant geographic market is further subdivided into (1) the "outer boundary market" and (2) one or more submarkets, using economic criteria established by case law. Finally, the court examines whether there is a reasonable probability that the merger will substantially lessen competition in each of the submarkets.

To determine if a merger will substantially lessen competition, the government and the courts examine market concentration as measured by market share percentages, using different percentage-of-market-share guidelines, depending on whether the merger is horizontal, vertical, or conglomerate. Under the "potential entrant" doctrine, the forbidden anticompetitive effect will be found to exist if one of the two merging firms is a potential entrant into the market. The doctrine has the effect of encouraging a firm to expand by branching de novo into a market, rather than by merging with a firm already in that market.

The Clayton Act is enforced by private civil treble damage suits, and by administrative proceedings instituted by the FTC, usually seeking a cease-and-desist order against conduct prohibited by the act. There is a civil penalty for each day of noncompliance with a cease-and-desist order. Corporations and their directors and agents who violate any penal provision of the antitrust laws are also subject to criminal prosecution.

The purpose of the Robinson-Patman Act, which amended the Clayton Act, was to prevent large chain stores from using their buying power to coerce suppliers into furnishing discriminatory services or prices, and thus to prevent such buyers from gaining an unfair advantage over smaller competitors. Section 2(a) of the Robinson-Patman Act prohibits price discrimination between different purchasers of commodities of like grade and quality in the "course of commerce" if the effect may be to substantially lessen competition or tend to create a monopoly. To constitute a violation, the transaction must involve two or more states, two or more sales of commodities (not services), to two or more purchasers at about the same time, at discriminatorily different prices, which injures competition. The act is aimed at preventing injury to competitors of the seller (primary line injury), to buyers (secondary line injury), to customers of buyers (tertiary line injury), and competitors of the buyer's customer (fourth line injury).

Sellers charged with Robinson-Patman violations may assert two defenses: (1) that price differentials were justified by differences in costs, and (2) that prices were lowered in good faith to meet an equally low price of a competitor.

To prevent circumvention of the Robinson-Patman Act, Sections 2(c) through 2(e) prohibit sellers from paying favored buyers unlawful "brokerage" or "kickbacks," or from discriminating by providing favored buyers with services or promotion allowances not available to other customers on "proportionately equal terms." Section 2(f) prohibits *buyers* from knowingly inducing or receiving a discrimination in price.

The Federal Trade Commission Act of 1914 created the FTC and conferred upon it broad jurisdiction to enforce Sections 2, 3, 7, and 8 of the Clayton Act as well as "unfair methods of competition" and "unfair or deceptive acts or practices." The Supreme Court has held that such practices are not limited to those that have an anticompetitive effect, nor are such practices confined to purely competitive behavior.

Exemptions to antitrust law are express, such as those for labor organizations, agricultural cooperatives, and owners of patents or copyrights. Generally, the Supreme Court has interpreted these exemptions narrowly. Implied exemptions arise from court interpretations, such as the *Parker* doctrine. As modified by later decisions, it holds that state regulatory action is immune from the antitrust laws. However, a firm may be regulated by the state in some areas and simultaneously be required to comply with antitrust standards in other areas involving business activity in the competitive sector of the economy. Another implied exemption from antitrust law, the *Noeer-Pennington* rule, exempts lawful lobbying from the antitrust laws, even if it is intended to restrain trade or eliminate competition.

Agreements by American firms to divide world markets, as well as foreign activity by American or foreign firms that has a serious anticompetitive effect within the United States, are subject to the antitrust laws. The Webb-Pomerene Export Trade Act exempted export trade associations from the antitrust laws, but uncertainty as to the extent of that exemption has discouraged formation of such associations. American firms, restricted by federal antitrust laws, compete at a disadvantage in world markets that are characterized by cartels, monopolistic state-controlled trading agencies, agreements dividing markets, and joint venture export marketing arrangements.

STUDY AND DISCUSSION QUESTIONS

1   (*a*) What shortcomings of the Sherman Act did the Clayton Act attempt to correct? (*b*) In your opinion, how effective have Sections 2, 3, 7, and 8 of the Clayton Act been in correcting the defects of the Sherman Act?

2   (*a*) Define exclusive dealing and tying contracts. (*b*) How does an exclusive dealing contract differ from an exclusive distributorship? (*c*) Compare and contrast Section 1 of the Sherman Act and Section 3 of the Clayton Act with respect to (*i*) the "commerce" jurisdictional requirements and (*ii*) the products or services covered.

3   Explain how the competitive effect of exclusive dealing and tying arrangements is measured under (*a*) the "quantitative substantiality" test and (*b*) the "qualitative substantiality" test.

4   (*a*) Are violations of the Clayton Act civil or criminal offences, or both? (*b*) What different classes of plaintiffs commence proceedings for violations of the Clayton Act, and what remedies does the act provide for each kind of plaintiff?

5   (*a*) What business practices led to the Robinson-Patman amendment to Section 2 of the Clayton Act? (*b*) What was the primary aim of the Robinson-Patman Act? (*c*) In broad terms, explain the scope of the Robinson-Patman Act. (*d*) What are the eight elements of a violation of Section 2(a) of the Robinson-Patman Act?

6   Under the Robinson-Patman Act, when are the following commodities "of like grade and quality": (*a*) Identical goods bearing different brand labels? (*b*) Goods of different quality bearing identical brand labels?

7   Explain how the "cost justification" defense to a Robinson-Patman price discrimination charge is affected by (*a*) classifying customers into groups and averaging costs for each group; (*b*) averaging costs of annual purchases of customers who purchase the same quantity, but for whom the number of shipments differ.

8   (*a*) Why and in what manner does the Robinson-Patman Act prevent indirect price discrimination? (*b*) Is it necessary to show that an unlawful brokerage payment injured competition in order to establish a violation of Section 2(c) of the Robinson-Patman Act? (*c*) Can the

seller's payment of a bribe to the purchasing agent of a customer violate the Robinson-Patman Act? *(d)* Is it a per se violation for a seller to engage in discriminatory payments or services to the buyer? *(e)* Can a seller accused of making advertising payments to a buyer on unequal terms with other customers in violation of Section 2(d) of the Robinson-Patman Act, assert as a defense that such payments were necessary to "meet competition"? *(f)* What is meant by the Robinson-Patman provision that the seller who provides payments or services to a customer must make them "available on proportionally equal terms"? *(g)* What practical problems face a seller in trying to comply with the provision quoted in question *(f)* above, and how can those problems be resolved? *(h)* If a buyer knowingly induces the seller to pay him a discriminatory promotional allowance, has the buyer violated the Robinson-Patman Act?

9 *(a)* What groups are expressly exempted from the antitrust laws? *(b)* What limits have court decisions placed upon these exemptions?

10 Under the *Parker* doctrine, as modified by later decisions of the courts, how extensive must "state action" be in order to be exempt from the antitrust law?

11 *(a)* To what extent is extraterritorial effect given to the antitrust laws? *(b)* What factors arising from the antitrust laws place American firms at a competitive disadvantage in world markets? *(c)* What factors account for the relatively few export trade associations formed under the Webb-Pomerene Act? *(d)* What is meant by "comity"?

CASE PROBLEMS

1 Park, Inc. developed 500 mobile home sites for sale. Park, Inc. then contracted to permit four dealers (Dealers) to display model mobile homes in the park, and to simultaneously offer prospective buyers a mobile home and a lot on which to place it. The Dealers paid Park Inc. $200 for every mobile home that was displayed and sold in the park. Park, Inc. agreed to reserve 288 spaces for sale to Dealers' customers. Dealers' customers were told they must purchase their mobile home from Dealers in order to buy a lot in the park. Lots in the area were very scarce, and Dealers' sales of mobile homes depended upon helping the buyer also find a lot. Mobile, Inc., a competing dealer, sold mobile homes from 1971 to 1975 that filled 90 percent of the mobile park vacancies in the area. But thereafter, because of Park, Inc.'s contract with Dealers, Mobile, Inc. was able to sell only six mobile homes to buyers who also bought lots from Park, Inc. During the same period, Dealers sold 247 homes to buyers who also bought lots from Park, Inc. Mobile, Inc. turned away six prospects a week because Park, Inc. refused to sell lots to them.

Mobile, Inc. brought an antitrust suit against Park, Inc. and Dealers, claiming that they had entered into a per se unlawful contract tying the sale of lots to the sale of mobile homes. Park, Inc. and Dealers claimed that the antitrust laws relating to tying contracts only apply to a *single* seller of two distinct products who uses the market power of one product to force purchase of the other; and that since there were *different* sellers of lots and homes, there could be no violation. Was the contract between Park, Inc. and Dealers an unlawful tying arrangement in violation of either Section 3 of the Clayton Act, or Section 1 of the Sherman Act, or both?

2 Five cemeteries (Cemetery Group) followed a pattern of selling burial lots only on condition that the buyer also purchase a grave marker from or through the cemetery as well as the services necessary to install the marker. Moore, a gravestone manufacturer, brought a private antitrust action alleging that these arrangements were unlawful tie-ins under Section 3 of the Clayton Act and Section 1 of the Sherman Act. Cemetery Group claimed that cemetery lots and gravemarkers must necessarily be sold as a single product and that they are not two distinct products. As justification for the joint sale of lots and markers, they also claimed that such sales were necessary to retain neatness and aesthetic quality control of the cemetery grounds. The trial court entered judgment for the defendants, and Moore appealed.

Assume that there is sufficient interstate commerce involved to meet the "commerce" jurisdictional requirement, and that a noncompetitive higher price is charged by Cemetery Group for gravemarkers because of their market power over cemetery lots. (a) Are cemetery lots sold with gravemarkers and installation services distinct products? (b) Is there a possible violation of either Section 3 of the Clayton Act or Section 1 of the Sherman Act arising from a tying arrangement? (c) Assuming for argument, that the sale of lots and gravemarkers is a tie-in, is it justified in order to promote goodwill of customers who may be favorably impressed with neatness and aesthetic appearance of the cemetery?

3 Brunswick Corp., one of the two largest manufacturers of bowling equipment, sold its products to local bowling centers on credit. In 1960, more than a fourth of these centers were in default and in satisfaction of its claims as a creditor, Brunswick took over 222 such centers. In 1965, after these acquisitions, Brunswick's gross revenue was more than seven times greater than the total for the eleven next largest bowling chains. Four of the defaulting centers that Brunswick took over were in markets competing with centers owned by Pueblo Bowl-O-Mat, Inc.

Pueblo brought a treble damage suit against Brunswick under Section 7 of the Clayton Act. Pueblo claimed that because of its size, Brunswick had the capacity to drive smaller competitors out of business, and that its merger with the four defaulting bowling centers would therefore substantially lessen competition. Pueblo claimed as damages the amount of additional profit it would have realized had Brunswick let

the local bowling centers close, instead of taking them over and operating them. The jury awarded $6.5 million and Brunswick appealed, claiming that antitrust damages should not be available where the sole injury claimed was that Brunswick kept the competing bowling centers from closing, thereby denying Pueblo an anticipated increase in market shares. Did Pueblo sustain antitrust injury?

4 Bank X proposed to merge with Bank Y. Government opposed the merger, and claimed that the relevant geographic market was the four-county area around Philadelphia in which most of both banks' customers resided. If the merger was permitted, the merged firms would control 30 percent of the commercial banking business in the four-county area. The two banks contended that the "greater part of the Northeastern United States" was the geographic market; and that since the merged firms would only have less than 5 percent of the total business of this larger market, the effect of the merger would not be to "substantially lessen competition." (a) What is the "relevant geographic market"? (b) Should the merger be permitted?

5 Bank A (acquiring bank) proposed to acquire Bank T (target bank). The Bank Merger Act required the regulatory banking agency (FDIC) to evaluate the merger according to antitrust standard under Section 7 of the Clayton Act. The "line of commerce" (product market) was demand deposits. However, a dispute arose as to the "section of the country" (geographic market). The uncontradicted survey of Banks A and T showed that Bank A had 91 percent of its demand deposits in the southern half of Pike County and 6 percent in the northern half. Bank T had 95 percent of its demand deposits in the northern half and 3 percent in the southern half. There was strong competition from other banks in the northern half of Pike County. There was good freeway access to all parts of the county, but the evidence showed that small demand depositors tend to bank near their residences.

Banks A and T claimed that the northern and southern halves of the county were separate geographic markets. The FDIC ruled that all of Pike County was the geographic market, and denied the merger as anticompetitive. FDIC also held that the merger should not be approved because if Bank A remained a separate entity in the southern half of Pike County, it would be an "actual potential entrant" into the northern half, and would therefore have a pro-competitive effect on the entire county. However, the evidence showed that it was not viable for Bank A to enter the northern half by establishing branches because of the strong competition already there. Banks A and T filed suit seeking to set aside the FDIC ruling. (*a*) What is the appropriate "geographic market"? (*b*) Should the FDIC ruling be set aside and the merger approved?

6 In 1969 Beatrice Foods, a multinational company doing business primarily in food-related services, acquired the Tip Top Brush Company and 1 year later acquired the Essex Graham Company merging them together. At the time of the merger, Tip Top was a leading manufacturer of paint brushes and rollers, ranking third with 7.6 percent of the shipments in the brush-and-roller market and ranking eighth in the roller submarket with 3.7 percent. Essex manufactured paint rollers, ranking thirteenth with 2.3 percent in the brush-and-roller market and ranking fifth in the roller submarket with 7 percent. The merger of Tip Top and Essex resulted in the 1969 top four-firm concentration figure in the brush-and-roller market increasing from 41.3 percent and the top eight-firm figure from 62.5 to 64.8 percent. The merger of Tip Top and Essex resulted in Tip Top becoming the third ranking firm in the roller submarket and the four-firm concentration figure increasing from 58 to 61 percent and the eight-firm figure rising from 78 to 80 percent. The FTC found increased concentration in the relevant markets as a result of the merger, although prior to the merger there was a trend of rising

competition in both markets. Is this merger in violation of Section 7 of the Clayton Act?

7 JLG, Inc. manufactured self-lifting work platforms. Burr, under a distributorship agreement in effect 1976–1978, purchased and resold JLG platforms. While this agreement was in effect, JLG in 1977 offered Burr a new distributorship agreement, the effect of which would be to sell platforms to Burr at less favorable prices than JLG was selling to other platform distributors who were competing with Burr. Burr refused to enter into the proposed new distributorship agreement, continued to purchase platforms under the existing agreement, and brought suit against JLG under Section 2(a) of the Robinson-Patman amendment to the Clayton Act, claiming price discrimination. JLG argued that since Burr never signed the proposed new contract or bought platforms under its terms, Burr cannot be one of at least two "purchasers" required by Robinson-Patman to constitute a price discrimination. Was JLG liable for unlawful price discrimination?

8 A&P, a grocery chain, asked its long-time supplier, Borden Co., to supply it with "private label" (as opposed to "brand label") milk. A&P refused Borden's initial offering price and solicited other offers from competitors, resulting in a lower offer from one of Borden's competitors. A&P told Borden that its offer "was not even in the ball park" and that a $50,000 reduction in its offer wouldn't be "a drop in the bucket." Borden then, in good faith, submitted a new offer lower than the competitor's offer, and A&P accepted. Borden did not know that its new offer was, in fact, lower than the competitor's offer.

The FTC charged A&P for misleading Borden by failing to inform it that its second offer was better than its competitor's offer, and thus with violating Section 2(f) of the Robinson-Patman Act by knowingly inducing or receiving price discrimination from Borden. A&P argued that it could not be liable for inducing discrimination because Borden's price, although below that charged to other customers, was cut in order to "meet competition," and since Borden could not be liable under Sections 2(a) and (b) for discrimination, A&P could not be liable under Section 2(f). The FTC contended that A&P is liable even though Borden had the "meeting competition" defense. Is A&P liable for knowingly inducing price discrimination?

9   Some years before the Michigan Public Service Commission was created, Detroit Edison initiated a "lamp program" under which it furnished light bulbs to consumers at no charge. The cost of the bulbs was reflected in the regular electricity rates charged to the customer. In 1916, the Commission approved the program. Michigan statutes regulated electric utilities, but not the distribution of light bulbs. Edison's "lamp program" furnished the southeastern Michigan area with 50 percent of the light bulbs used.

Cantor, a retail druggist selling light bulbs, brought a private treble damage Sherman action against Edison. Edison claimed (1) that its "lamp program" was approved by the State, that it could not discontinue it without further State approval, and that it would be unjust to hold a private company liable under federal law when it was simply obeying the command of the sovereign state; (2) Congress did not intend to superimpose antitrust law in an area already regulated by the state, and therefore, under the *Parker* doctrine, Edison was impliedly exempt from the Sherman Act. Was Edison's "lamp program" exempt from federal antitrust law?

10   Trucking Unlimited, a group of highway carriers, commenced suit under Section 1 of the Sherman Act against Cal Motor Associates, a group of competing motor carriers. The complaint alleged that Cal Motor Associates instituted proceedings before California and federal courts as well as agencies regulating the trucking industry to resist and defeat applications by Trucking Unlimited to acquire operating rights or to transfer those rights. It was further claimed that Cal Motor Associates instituted actions without probable cause, and regardless of the merits of the cases, in order to discourage and prevent Trucking Unlimited from having meaningful access to the administrative agencies and the courts, all for the purpose of putting Trucking Unlimited out of business and to monopolize the highway common carrier business. Cal Motor Associates claimed that under the *Noerr* doctrine, they had a First Amendment right to petition government through the courts, and that, regardless of their purpose, they were immune from Sherman Act liability. Assuming Trucking Unlimited's claims are true, is Cal Motor Associates exempt from Sherman Act liability under the *Noerr* doctrine?

PART TWELVE

BANKRUPTCY

Chapter 49
Bankruptcy

Chapter

49
Bankruptcy

Anyone, even the largest of corporations, can experience financial difficulty or financial failure. If a bankrupt business must close down, employees lose their jobs and may lose back wages and pension benefits. General (unsecured) creditors may be unable to collect unpaid debts. Tax authorities lose a source of revenue and may be unable to collect unpaid taxes. Customers must look elsewhere for goods and services, suppliers lose a customer, and proprietors and shareholders may lose all or most of their investment.

Financial difficulty occurs for a variety of reasons—because of mismanagement, unfavorable business conditions, or other circumstances —and creditors react differently to it. Some creditors continue to extend credit in the hope that the financial setback is temporary. Some

cut off credit immediately and take aggressive collection measures under state "grab" law (law that permits unpaid creditors to seize and sell property of the debtor). Creditors whose claims are too small to warrant expensive collection measures hope for a voluntary settlement by the debtor.

As for debtors, some will attempt a voluntary settlement of debts in an effort to keep their businesses going. Where financial difficulty is serious, a debtor might elect to go out of business and, under state law, to make an assignment of remaining business assets for the benefit of creditors. Occasionally, a debtor makes as few payments as possible and hides the remaining assets in fraud of creditors. Or a debtor might pay some creditors in full and ignore the others.

Some state insolvency statutes favor local creditors over out-of-state creditors; and under state statutes, debtors usually are not discharged from their debts unless all creditors consent to a discharge. The difficulty that overburdened debtors experience in continuing or in reentering business, the relative weakness of such creditors as unpaid employees and small suppliers, the ability of some creditors to shut down a business by "grabbing" all of a debtor's productive assets under state law, the tendency of some creditors to seek (or debtors to give) unfair advantage over other creditors, the expense of litigation, and inadequate or discriminatory state insolvency statutes—these and other factors led in 1898 to the enactment of the federal Bankruptcy Act. That act was superseded in 1978 by the so-called Bankruptcy Reform Act, which is referred to in this chapter as the Bankruptcy Code.

This chapter deals with the federal law of bankruptcy. In the first part of the chapter the purposes and scope of the Bankruptcy Code, its relationship to state insolvency law, and the nature of the bankruptcy court and bankruptcy administration are discussed. The remainder of the chapter is devoted to the three principal kinds of bankruptcy proceedings: liquidation ("straight" bankruptcy), business reorganizations, and repayment plans for debtors with regular income.

FEDERAL BANKRUPTCY LAW AND ADMINISTRATION

Purposes of Federal Bankruptcy Law

Federal bankruptcy law has two main purposes or goals: (1) to provide for a more evenhanded treatment of creditors than state insolvency law typically does, and (2) to allow debtors to escape from impossible burdens of debt so that they may more quickly return to productive business activities.

Although some bankrupt persons are incompetent as business managers, many more are

not. It is presumed that the "fresh-start" policy of bankruptcy law has more beneficial consequences than detrimental ones. One aspect of the fresh-start policy is the practice of permitting some firms to stay in business while they attempt to recover their financial health. Permitting financially distressed firms to stay in business, especially large ones such as the Penn Central Transportation Company (Conrail), tends to minimize the disruption of employment and to maintain the flow of goods and services to the public.

Relationship of Federal Bankruptcy Law to State Insolvency Law

Article I, Section 8 of the United States Constitution states that "The Congress shall have power . . . to establish . . . uniform laws on the subject of bankruptcies throughout the United States." The Bankruptcy Code, together with interpretive court decisions (and procedural rules and standards published by the U.S. Supreme Court), constitutes our national bankruptcy law.

Under the supremacy clause of the Constitution, the federal bankruptcy law prevails over conflicting state law. However, although Congress probably could preempt (displace) all state insolvency law, it has chosen not to do so. The Bankruptcy Code looks to state law for the resolution of a number of bankruptcy issues. Usually, the state law of property and of contracts will be followed for the purpose of determining, for example, what property the debtor owns. By express provision of the Code, a debtor may elect to have state law govern what property of the debtor (residence, tools, clothing, and so on) is exempt from the claims of creditors. State insolvency law that does not defeat the purposes of the Bankruptcy Code will usually be allowed to stand.

Coverage and Organization of the Federal Bankruptcy Code

Most individuals, partnerships, and corporations are covered by the Bankruptcy Code and thus may voluntarily seek relief from debts or may be subjected to involuntary bankruptcy proceedings. *Not* covered by the Bankruptcy Code are insurance companies, banks, savings and loan associations, building and loan associations, credit unions, and similar organizations. Such organizations are regulated by administrative agencies under special state or federal statutes. Financial failure of regulated businesses is left to the regulatory agencies, which are considered to be better equipped than the courts to resolve such problems.

Railroads and municipal corporations receive special treatment under the Bankruptcy Code. Traditionally, railroads have been regulated as a part of interstate commerce, and financially distressed railroads have been reorganized under "equity receivership" rather than being subjected to straight bankruptcy or to reorganization proceedings available to other corporations. Today, railroads may be reorganized or liquidated under Chapter 11 of the Bankruptcy Code, but they are not otherwise eligible for bankruptcy. Municipal corporations are not liquidated, but they may seek "adjustment" of their debts under Chapter 9 of the Code, if state law authorizes them to do so.

The Bankruptcy Code is divided into eight odd-numbered chapters. Chapter 1 contains various general provisions, such as definitions and rules of construction, and states who may be a debtor (i.e., who is eligible for relief from debts) in different kinds of cases under the Code. Chapter 3, entitled Case Administration, indicates how a case is begun and deals with the administrative powers of bankruptcy officials. Chapter 5 contains much of the substantive law of bankruptcy. Chapter 5 deals with *(a)* what property constitutes the debtor's estate, *(b)* the powers of the trustee in bankruptcy to avoid (set aside) transactions that would diminish the debtor's estate, *(c)* the order in which distributions from the estate will be made to creditors, and *(d)* the duties and benefits of the debtor. Chapters 1, 3, and 5 apply to any kind of case under the Code.

Chapters 7, 9, 11, and 13 of the Code deal with particular kinds of bankruptcy proceedings. Chapter 7 deals with liquidation, also known as straight bankruptcy; Chapter 9 with the adjustment of municipal debt; Chapter 11 with corporate reorganizations; and Chapter 13 with plans for the adjustment of debts of individuals with regular income. Liquidation, corporate reorganizations, and Chapter 13 plans will be discussed later in this chapter. Railroad reorganizations, the adjustment of municipal debt, and the liquidation of stockbrokers and commodity brokers under Subchapters III and IV of Chapter 7 are beyond the scope of this book. Chapter 15 concerns a pilot program in which the office of United States Trustee is established on a 5-year trial basis.

Bankruptcy Court and Bankruptcy Administration

The Bankruptcy Court   On April 1, 1984, a new bankruptcy court system becomes effective.[1] Under the new system there is a United States bankruptcy court for each federal judicial district. Bankruptcy judges will be appointed by the President for terms of 14 years. Appointments will be subject to Senate confirmation.

Although the new bankruptcy court is technically an "adjunct" to the federal district court, present and future bankruptcy judges have full power to render binding decisions on all aspects of a bankruptcy case. This is so because the bankruptcy court has been directed by Congress to exercise all of the district court's bankruptcy jurisdiction, a jurisdiction that has been expanded by the Bankruptcy Code to encompass all controversies affecting the debtor and the debtor's estate [28 U.S.C. 1471(e)].[2] The bankruptcy court may abstain from exercising

---

[1] Under the present system, "bankruptcy court" means essentially the federal district court of the district in which the alleged bankrupt resides. Bankruptcy judges (formerly called referees) currently are appointed by the judges of the federal district courts for terms of 7 years.

[2] Numbers within brackets in the text refer to titles and their sections in the United States Code; thus, here, Title 28, U.S.C., section 1471, subsection e.

its jurisdiction if the court believes that a particular matter can be better handled by some other court; the bankruptcy court's decision to abstain or not to abstain is not reviewable [28 U.S.C. 1471(b),(d)].

Final judgments, orders, and decrees of the bankruptcy court are subject to appeal. If all the parties to an appeal agree, an appeal from a final order of the bankruptcy court goes directly to the U.S. Court of Appeals [28 U.S.C. 1293(b)]. Otherwise, an appeal of a final order is to the district court (or to a panel of three bankruptcy judges where the panel system has been set up to displace the district court in the review of bankruptcy appeals) [28 U.S.C. 1334(a); 160(a)].

Bankruptcy Administration Bankruptcy is not merely a judicial proceeding. It also involves the administration of the debtor's estate for the benefit of creditors. Two officials have major responsibility for administering the estate: the trustee in bankruptcy and the bankruptcy judge.

The trustee in bankruptcy is responsible for collecting, liquidating, and distributing the debtor's estate. These tasks require the trustee to inspect the property and business of the debtor, to decide whether to adopt or reject executory contracts and leases, to operate the business of the debtor under certain circumstances, and to perform a variety of routine tasks relating to the administrative process. One of the trustee's major duties is to act on behalf of the general (unsecured) creditors. To discharge that duty, the trustee must guard the estate against unfounded claims of creditors, resist doubtful exemption claims of the debtor, and avoid (set aside) various transactions by means of which the debtor or others may have dissipated the estate. The trustee possesses extensive legal powers for carrying out these tasks. Many of the trustee's powers, especially the trustee's powers of avoidance, are discussed later in this chapter.

The bankruptcy judge has a number of administrative duties. Appointing trustees is one of them. In a *liquidation* case, the judge appoints an interim trustee who may be displaced by a trustee elected by the creditors [11 U.S.C. 701; 702(c)]. In a *business reorganization* case, the judge has a limited power to appoint a trustee. If requested to do so by a party in interest (e.g., a creditor or a shareholder), the judge may appoint a trustee "for cause"; that is, because of dishonesty or incompetence of the debtor or, where the debtor is a corporation, because of dishonesty or incompetence of its management [11 U.S.C. 1104]. Unless the court orders otherwise, the debtor may continue to operate the business. Such a debtor, called a "debtor in possession," has the powers, rights, and duties of a reorganization trustee [11 U.S.C. 1107(a)]. The word "trustee" includes "debtor in possession." In addition to appointing trustees, the bankruptcy judge supervises their activities in the administration of debtors' estates.

Before the enactment of the Bankruptcy Code, the bankruptcy judge had extensive administrative contact with the trustee (whose responsibility runs primarily to unsecured creditors) and with creditors' lawyers. Because of the judge's involvement in day-to-day administrative activities, the judge was vulnerable to a charge of bias in favor of unsecured creditors and their representatives when rendering judicial decisions. To separate the judicial and the administrative functions in a bankruptcy case, and thus to prevent judicial bias or an appearance of bias, several provisions of the Bankruptcy Code reduce the judge's administrative involvement. To separate further the judicial from the administrative function, the Code has established on an experimental basis a system of United States Trustees. In ten pilot districts the United States Trustee handles most administrative matters, including the appointment of trustees; and the judge's function is primarily that of deciding disputes. In most districts, however, the bankruptcy judge retains substantial administrative duties under the Bankruptcy Code.

The role of the United States Trustee will not be discussed further in this chapter because so few exist.

KINDS OF FEDERAL BANKRUPTCY PROCEEDINGS

Liquidation (Straight Bankruptcy)

The purpose of a Chapter 7 liquidation proceeding is to convert the debtor's nonexempt assets into cash, to distribute it in accordance with the scheme of distribution provided by the Bankruptcy Code, and to grant the honest debtor a discharge from most of the remaining debts.

Commencement of a Straight Bankruptcy Proceeding Any "person" except a railroad or a regulated business of the type discussed earlier in this chapter may file a *voluntary* petition to liquidate under Chapter 7 [11 U.S.C. 109(b)]. *Person* includes individuals, partnerships, and corporations, but not governmental units [11 U.S.C. 101(30)]. Therefore, municipal corporations may not file under Chapter 7. The filing fee is $60 and may be paid in installments. No one is exempted from payment of the filing fee.

Most persons who qualify for a voluntary liquidation may be subjected to an *involuntary* liquidation proceeding. Farmers and charitable corporations may not be subjected to any kind of involuntary bankruptcy proceeding [11 U.S.C. 303(a)]. A *farmer* is a person (individual, partnership, or corporation) whose gross income in the taxable year prior to bankruptcy was more than 80 percent from a farming operation owned or operated by that person [11 U.S.C. 101(17)].

A person cannot be declared an involuntary bankrupt unless three requirements or conditions have been met. First, the petitioning creditor or creditors must have claims of at least $5,000 in unsecured debts. Second, where the number of creditors is twelve or more, three of them must join in the involuntary petition; otherwise, only one petitioning creditor is required. Third, the alleged debtor must have given the creditor or creditors a *ground for relief.* Under the Code there are two grounds for relief, which replace the numerous, outmoded "acts of bankruptcy" found in earlier bankruptcy law. One ground is that "the debtor is generally not paying such debtor's debts as such debts become due." The other is that the debtor has, within 120 days of the filing of the involuntary petition, made a general assignment for the benefit of creditors [11 U.S.C. 303(h)].

These requirements serve several interrelated purposes. They provide specific, numerical guidance to the court and thus facilitate the administration of bankruptcy law. They also identify the level of financial ill health at which creditors may seek protection against the wishes of the debtor. And they serve, in part, to protect the debtor from unfounded, trivial, or harassing claims. The debtor has another important protection. If the allegations for an involuntary petition are not proved, the court may grant court costs to the debtor; and, if a trustee was appointed and took possession of the debtor's property, the court may award damages to the debtor. A bad faith petitioner may be liable for both compensatory and punitive damages even though no trustee was appointed [11 U.S.C. 303(i)].

Collection and Liquidation of Debtor's Estate The collection and liquidation of the debtor's estate can involve considerable litigation. Issues may include what property belongs to the debtor's estate, what powers the trustee has to set aside transactions in order to acquire property for the estate, and what exemption claims by the debtor the trustee should honor.

Property of the debtor's estate The debtor's estate consists of a broad range of property interests either owned by the debtor as of the commencement of the bankruptcy case or recoverable for the estate by the trustee from someone other than the debtor. Section 541 of the Bankruptcy Code spells out what constitutes the debtor's estate. Included in the estate are the following:

1   All legal and equitable interests of the debtor in property as of the commencement of the bankruptcy case, *except (a)* certain powers over property exercisable by the debtor solely for the benefit of others, and *(b)* the debtor's beneficial interest under a spendthrift trust which is valid under state law. A spendthrift trust is one set up to protect the beneficiary from his or her improvident spending habits. Where state law recognizes such a trust, creditors may not reach trust funds, and the beneficiary may dispose of funds only as they are received The Bankruptcy Code makes spendthrift trust provisions that are enforceable under state law effective also against the trustee in bankruptcy.

It should be noted that a secured creditor's security interest does *not* become a part of the debtor's estate. A security interest in collateral is by its nature the property of the creditor. Unless the secured transaction can be set aside under the trustee's avoiding powers, only the debtor's "equity" in the collateral is included in the debtor's estate. The trustee does, however, receive the collateral itself for purposes of administration.

2   All interests of the debtor and the debtor's spouse in community property *if* the community property is under the sole, equal, or joint management or control of the debtor.

3   Any interest in property held by others than the debtor and recoverable by the trustee for the debtor's estate under various provisions of the Bankruptcy Code. The powers of the trustee to recover property for the estate are discussed later in this chapter.

4   Certain property acquired by the debtor within 180 days after the date of the filing of the petition. This property includes inheritances, property acquired as a result of a divorce decree or a property settlement with the debtor's spouse, and property acquired by the debtor as a beneficiary of a life insurance policy or of a death benefit plan.

5   Income and other proceeds from property of the estate, and any interest or property that the estate acquires after the commencement of the case. (Earnings from services performed by an *individual* debtor after the commencement of the case are *not* included in the debtor's estate.)

Trustee's powers to collect and liquidate the estate   To administer the debtor's estate properly, the trustee in bankruptcy must gain possession, custody, or control of the property, regardless of who actually has the property. In carrying out his or her duties, the trustee has the benefit of *(a)* certain "legal mechanisms" of the Bankruptcy Code, *(b)* powers to use, sell, or lease property and to borrow money, *(c)* powers to assume or reject executory contracts and unexpired leases, and *(d)* powers to avoid a variety of transactions.

Two legal mechanisms are central in the collection and liquidation of the estate. They are the "automatic stay" and the "turnover" provisions of the Code. A *stay* is a halting or a suspension of legal action. The filing of a petition in bankruptcy automatically stays the commencement or continuation of other legal proceedings affecting the debtor's estate until the bankruptcy case is over or until the stay is vacated by the bankruptcy court. The stay enables the bankruptcy court to exercise its jurisdiction efficiently, and it enables the trustee to preserve and administer the estate. Some actions, such as criminal actions against the debtor, are excluded from the operation of the automatic stay [11 U.S.C. 363].

The *turnover* provisions require holders of property to which the debtor's estate is entitled to deliver it to the trustee [11 U.S.C.542; 543]. The estate is entitled, for example, to any property that the trustee may use, sell, or lease in the administration of the estate, including property subject to a security interest. The estate is also entitled to any property that the debtor is permitted later to exempt from the estate.

Case 49.1   **Collomb v. Wyatt**
6 B.R. 947 (E.D.N.Y. 1980)

Pauline Collomb (plaintiff) transferred the proceeds of a life insurance policy to the Wyatts (defendant debtors) as consideration for their promise to support her. The Wyatts used the money to purchase a residence, to which they took legal title. Plaintiff resided there for a time, during which the Wyatts supported her. Then, alleging that the debtors ceased to support her, plaintiff brought an action in state court to impress a constructive trust on the real estate. Plaintiff was awarded judgment and attempted to foreclose on the constructive trust. However, the judicial sale that had been scheduled was stayed when the debtors filed a Chapter 13 petition. Plaintiff then brought this suit seeking the termination of the automatic stay thereby permitting the judicial sale of the real estate.

PARENTE, B.J. . . . . A constructive trust is an equitable duty to convey [property] to another on the ground that he would be unjustly enriched if he were permitted to retain it. Equity converts the holder of legal title in property subject to a constructive trust into a trustee *ex maleficio* [trustee "out of misconduct"] who is charged with the equitable duty to convey the property to another. . . .

Plaintiff is stayed from foreclosing on her constructive trust . . . if the Court finds that the subject matter of the constructive trust constitutes property of the [debtors'] estate. . . .

Before resolving the issue of whether the subject matter of the constructive trust constitutes property of the debtors' estate, it is imperative to identify the plaintiff's interest and the debtors' interest in the property in question. Under state law, a constructive trust creates a dual ownership of the property; legal title remains with the trustee *ex maleficio* and the equitable right to said property is awarded to the benficiary. Thus, the debtors as trustees *ex maleficio* retain their legal title to the property and the plaintiff is considered in equity as the beneficial owner of the property. . . .

Under the Bankruptcy Code, the commencement of a bankruptcy case creates an estate which, pursuant to Section 541(a)(1), consists of "all legal or equitable interests of the debtor in the property as of the commencement of the case."

The legislative history, however, indicates that where the debtor holds bare legal title to property without any equitable interest, or holds property in trust for another, only those rights which the debtor . . . had . . . pass to the estate under Section 541. Thus, in the case at bar . . . the debtors' estate includes only the bare legal title without any equitable interest in the property. . . .

Premised on the foregoing analysis, the Court concludes that the debtors' legal title to the real property constitutes property of the estate under Section 541(a). Therefore, since plaintiff is attempting to enforce her state court judgment against property of the estate . . . the filing of the debtors' Chapter 13 petition . . . stays the commencement of the judicial sale of debtors' real property. . . .

Plaintiff's request for a vacatur of the automatic stay brings into question the grounds for authorizing such relief. . . . [One ground is] for cause, as expressed in Section 362(d)(1). . . . Cause includes lack of adequate protection of a creditor's interest in the debtor's property. . . . Although the term "adequate protection" is not defined in . . . the Bankruptcy Code, Section 361 offers three non-exclusive methods of providing adequate protection. . . . [One is some form of relief provided by the debtor as will] result in the realization by [the creditor] of the indubitable equivalent of such entity's interest in such property.

The debtors have proposed to pay plaintiff 40 percent of her claim over three years under the Chapter 13 plan. . . .

The filing of the petition in bankruptcy does not modify the equitable rights of the parties, and all obligations of a legal or equitable nature remain undisturbed thereby. Thus, the estate, like the debtor prior to the filing of a petition under Chapter 13, is under an equitable duty to convey the property to the beneficiary.

Premised on the foregoing, the indubitable equivalent of plaintiff's interest in debtors' real property would be the payment of $7,274.80 by the debtors. Since the debtors only proposed to pay 40 percent of the plaintiff's interest in said property, the debtors have failed to propose a method of adequately protecting plaintiff's interest . . . and thus plaintiff is entitled to relief from the automatic stay. . . .

Settle judgment.

Especially in reorganization cases, but sometimes in liquidation cases and in Chapter 13 plans, the trustee needs to use, sell, or lease property that is subject to the claims of persons such as secured creditors, or to borrow money in a manner that might threaten existing security or other interests. The Bankruptcy Code provides essentially that the trustee may use, sell, or lease encumbered property (e.g., in order to liquidate the debtor's estate or to keep the debtor's business in operation) so long as the security interest or lien is adequately protected [11 U.S.C. 363(e)]. The property may not be sold free and clear of an encumbrance unless, for example, the holder of the interest consents or the price received for the property is greater than the value of the interest [11 U.S.C. 363(f)].

As compared to the situation under prior bankruptcy law, the trustee has broader powers to obtain secured credit. These broader powers were made necessary by the frequent refusal of holders of "floating liens" under Article 9 of the Uniform Commercial Code (UCC) to extend further credit or to subordinate their liens. Such liens may encumber all of the business property of the debtor, and under prior bankruptcy law, their holders could force liquidation of the debtor's business even though liquidation might be ill-advised. Under the Bankruptcy Code, the trustee may obtain unsecured credit or, if necessary, secured credit. Where property of the estate is already encumbered, the trustee may grant a junior lien on that property. Where lenders refuse to extend credit on an unsecured or a junior lien basis, the court may authorize the trustee to grant a lien equal in priority or senior to existing interests, *if* there is adequate protection of the holders of existing interests [11 U.S.C. 364].

Subject to court approval, the trustee may assume, reject, or assign executory contracts and unexpired leases of the debtor [11 U.S.C. 365(a)]. These powers enable the trustee to reject improvident or burdensome transactions, to retain for the estate any beneficial transaction that is assumable under state law, and to assign any contract or lease that is assignable under state law. Some contract clauses or provisions in state law are intended to prevent the trustee from assuming contracts upon the debtor's bankruptcy or insolvency, even though the contracts would otherwise be assumable. The Bankruptcy Code invalidates such clauses and provisions of state law [11 U.S.C. 365(e)]. Consequently, the parties to a contract can no longer use the mere fact of bankruptcy or insolvency to deny to the trustee the debtor's rights and benefits under a contract or lease. The trustee's rejection of a contract or lease constitutes a breach of it and gives the aggrieved party a claim against the debtor's estate.

The trustee's powers to avoid transactions are of two major kinds: (1) powers to avoid prebankruptcy transactions which usually involve no wrongdoing by the debtor or others, and (2) powers to avoid wrongful transactions.

Powers to avoid transactions involving no wrongdoing can be explained by an illustration. Suppose that Sam Supplier (S) sells some business equipment to Brenda Buyer (B), retains a purchase-money security interest in the equipment, and allows B to have possession of the property while paying for it. At the time of the sale, Cora Creditor (C) has a perfected security interest in B's business property and in "any business property which B may hereafter acquire." To perfect his purchase-money security interest, and thus to acquire priority over C's security interest, S must file a financing statement within 10 days after B receives possession of the equipment. S fails to do so. B fails to pay the debt she owes C, C brings foreclosure action, and the court renders a judgment against B in favor of C. As a result of the judgment in her favor, C has a *judicial lien* on so much of B's property as was covered by C's perfected security interest. Because S failed to perfect his security interest in the business equipment, C's security interest prevails and C is entitled to the equipment as part of her collateral.

What has this to do with bankruptcy? Suppose a situation somewhat different from the one described in the preceding paragraph. Suppose that S sells the equipment to B, that S fails to perfect his security interest, that there is no such person as C, and that a month after receiving possession of the equipment, B files a petition in bankruptcy. The Bankruptcy Code gives the trustee the *status* of a judicial lien creditor such as C whether or not such a person exists [11 U.S.C. 544(a)(1)]. Thus, the Bankruptcy Code confers upon the trustee the power to defeat S's unperfected security interest and to acquire the business equipment for the debtor's estate. (S would, of course, have a claim as an unsecured creditor for the price of the equipment.) The Code confers upon the trustee other statuses: the status of a hypothetical creditor who has received a judgment, has attempted to collect on it, and has had execution returned unsatisfied; and the status of a hypothetical bona fide purchaser of real property from the debtor. These statuses enable the trustee to overturn a variety of prebankruptcy transactions [11 U.S.C. 544(a)(2),(3)]. In addition, the trustee succeeds to the rights of certain *actual* creditors, that is, those who hold *unsecured*, allowable claims [11 U.S.C. 544(b)]. The trustee may avoid any transfer by the debtor that such existing, unsecured creditors could have avoided but did not.

The trustee's powers to avoid wrongful transactions are well known. Transactions that are wrongful in a bankruptcy sense fall into two major categories: *fraudulent transfers* and *preferential transfers* (preferences). Such transfers are wrongful because they deprive the debtor's estate of assets to which it may be entitled, or because they undermine a fundamental bankruptcy policy, that is, equality of distribution among creditors.

The trustee may avoid any fraudulent transfer of the debtor's property made within 1 year before the filing of the petition in bankruptcy, regardless of who made the transfer. The trustee may also avoid any fraudulent obligation incurred by the debtor within the 1-year period preceding bankruptcy [11 U.S.C. 548]. The fraud may be either actual or constructive. The fraud is *actual* if the transfer or obligation involved an intent to hinder, delay, or defraud creditors. The fraud is *constructive* (involving no specific intention to defraud) if the debtor received less than a reasonable equivalent value for the transfer or obligation *and* (1) the debtor was insolvent or became insolvent as a result of the transaction, or (2) the debtor was engaged in business, or was about to engage in a business or transaction, for which any property remaining with the debtor was an unreasonably small capital, or (3) the debtor intended to incur, or believed that the debtor would incur, debts that would be beyond the debtor's ability to pay as the debts matured.

The trustee may avoid preferential payments or transfers (preferences). A *preference* is a transfer of property that enables an unsecured creditor to receive a greater percentage of his or her claim against a debtor than the creditor would have received in a distribution of the debtor's assets pursuant to a Chapter 7 liquidation. Preferences occur in a variety of ways. Sometimes, for example, a debtor faced with impending bankruptcy voluntarily pays a favor-

ite creditor-supplier in full and leaves other creditors to share whatever remains. Sometimes a creditor coerces a debtor into making a preferential transfer. Frequently, the preference takes the form of a security interest given just before bankruptcy and long after an extension of credit that was originally intended to be unsecured.

The determination of what constitutes a preference and what does not requires the application of some specific Code rules. A payment or other transfer is a preference (and is therefore avoidable by the trustee) if the transfer (1) was to or for the benefit of a creditor on account of an *antecedent* (prior unsecured) debt, (2) was made "on or within" 90 days before the filing of the bankruptcy petition, (3) was made when the debtor was insolvent, and (4) conferred upon the creditor more than the creditor would have been entitled to receive in a bankruptcy liquidation case [11 U.S.C. 547(b)]. The debtor is presumed insolvent during the 90-day period [11 U.S.C. 547(f)]. Preferences made within the 90-day period are vulnerable to the trustee's attack regardless of whether the creditor had reasonable cause to believe that the debtor was insolvent.

With regard to preferences made to "insiders," (i.e., the debtor's relatives, partners, directors, controlling persons, and so on) the trustee has additional powers of avoidance. Preferences made to insiders within the 90-day period before bankruptcy are avoidable under the rule stated in the preceding paragraph. The trustee may also avoid preferences made to insiders between the beginning of the 90-day period and 1 year before bankruptcy *if* the insider had reasonable cause to believe that the debtor was insolvent at the time of the transfer [11 U.S.C. 547(b)].

Some transactions that appear technically to be preferences are not, and therefore they are not avoidable by the trustee. Consider, for example, a supplier of inventory who delivers goods to an insolvent retailer 30 days before the retailer's bankruptcy and, a few days later, receives full payment out of the proceeds from the resale of the goods. The supplier has extended unsecured credit and could be said to have received a preferential payment on account of an antecedent debt. However, the payment is not so treated under the Bankruptcy Code. The trustee cannot avoid an otherwise preferential payment of a debt incurred in the ordinary course of the debtor and creditor's business or financial affairs where the payment was made (1) in the ordinary course of business according to ordinary business terms, and (2) not later than 45 days after the debt was incurred [11 U.S.C. 547(c)(2)]. The rule applies to consumer transactions as well as to commercial transactions.

Similar rules apply to other apparently preferential transactions. Suppose, for example, that a bank intends to make a secured loan to an insolvent debtor, but the execution of the security documents occurs a few days after credit is extended. What kind of transaction has occurred, a secured loan or a preference? If the transfer was "intended . . . to be a contemporaneous exchange for new value" and was "in fact a substantially contemporaneous exchange," the transfer is a secured transaction and the trustee may not avoid it [11 U.S.C. 547(c)(1)]. Such rules encourage suppliers and lenders to continue to do business with insolvent persons while there is a chance that they might recover their financial health. And the rules do no harm to general creditors because the protected suppliers and lenders have not depleted the debtor's estate.

Case 49.2   Matter of Duffy
3 B.R. 263 (S.D.N.Y. 1980)

Peter L. Duffy leased a car from Avis Rent-A-Car System on a long-term basis. Duffy made no rental payments until July 30, 1979, when, after a conversation with an Avis representative, Duffy forwarded to Avis a check for $400 postdated to August 3, 1979. The check cleared and was honored by the drawee bank on August 6, 1979, which was 88 days before the debtor filed his Chapter 7 petition for relief in bankruptcy. Thus, the check was delivered to Avis more than 90 days before the filing, but was cashed within the 90-day period. The trustee challenged the $400 payment to Avis as a voidable preference.

SCHWARTZBERG, B.J. . . . . The undisputed facts established at the trial are as follows: . . .

7. The $400 payment by the debtor to Avis was on account of an antecedent debt owed by the debtor before such payment was made.

8. Avis presented no evidence to rebut the presumption of the debtor's insolvency for the 90 days preceding the filing of the petition. . . .

9. The $400 payment to Avis enabled Avis to receive more than it would receive if the payment had not been made and Avis [had] received payment of its debt by way of distribution in this case, as specified in 11 U.S.C. Section 547(b)(5). . . .

. . . This court must first determine whether or not the $400 payment by the debtor to Avis accrued within the proscribed [prohibited] 90-day period so as to trigger the voidable preference provisions. . . . If the 90-day requirement has been met, reference must then be made to the exception to the trustee's avoiding power referred to by Avis in its answer, namely, a substantially contemporaneous exchange for a new value given to the debtor. . . .

That a payment of a debt by check is a transfer of property is manifestly expressed in the broad definition of "transfer" under the Bankruptcy Code. . . . It is clear that payment of the debt did not occur when the debtor delivered the postdated check to Avis. A check itself does not vest in the payee any title to or interest in the funds held by the drawee bank. See U.C.C. Section 3-409. The check is simply an order to the drawee bank to pay the sum stated and does not constitute a transfer and delivery of the fund until it is paid. The date of payment, and not the date of delivery [of the check] is crucial in determining when the preferential transfer occurred. . . .

Avis argues that once the check is paid, payment should revert to the date the check was delivered, citing [federal income tax cases]. These tax cases are inapposite since they address the issue of when a cash basis taxpayer is entitled to deduct a business expense. For income tax purposes, the delivery of a check is treated in the same manner as a cash payment. The concept of the timing of a transfer of property within the framework of the preference provisions [of bankruptcy law] requires a different focus. . . .

Having found that the $400 payment . . . amounted to a preferential payment of an antecedent indebtedness, there next remains for consideration the affirmative defense that the transfer was a contemporaneous exchange for new value within the meaning of Code Section 547(c)(1), which provides as follows:

> (c) The trustee may not avoid under this section a transfer—(1) to the extent that such transfer was—(A) intended by the debtor and the creditor to or for whose benefit such transfer was made to be a contemporaneous exchange for new value given to the debtor; and (B) in fact a substantially contemporaneous exchange. . . .

Avis argues that it gave new value to the debtor when it accepted the $400 payment because of its forbearance from repossesing the leased vehicle. The term "new value" is defined in Code Section 547(a)(2) as follows:

> (2)"new value" means money or money's worth in goods, services, or new credit, or release by a transferee of property previously transferred to such transferee in a transaction that is neither void nor voidable by the debtor or the trustee under any applicable law, *but does not include an obligation substituted for an existing obligation* [emphasis added].

The basic concept underlying bankruptcy legislation, and of particular significance in dealing with preferences, is the fundamental goal of equality of distribution. A creditor who gives new value in exchange for the receipt of a payment from the debtor has not depleted the debtor's estate to the detriment of other creditors. In the instant case, a forbearance by Avis from repossessing the rented vehicle does not enhance the value of the debtor's estate [and does not] offset the diminution of his estate. . . . While Avis's forbearance from reclaiming possession of the rented vehicle might constitute consideration to support a contract, it is nevertheless not "new value" within the meaning of [the Bankruptcy Code]. Such forbearance was of no economic solace to the creditors of this estate. . . .

The trustee in bankruptcy is entitled to an order directing Avis to return the $400 payment made to it by the debtor as a voidable preference.

Settle order on notice.

The debtor's exemptions As a part of the fresh-start policy, the Bankruptcy Code permits an *individual* debtor to exempt certain property from the debtor's estate. Under pre-Code bankruptcy law, the debtor was entitled to whatever exemptions were permitted by the law of the debtor's state. Because of variations in state exemption laws, exemptions were nonuniform; and in many states the exemptions were or became inadequate to provide individuals with the desired fresh start.

Under the Bankruptcy Code, individual debtors are given a choice between the exemptions provided by state law and the rather generous federal exemptions provided by the Code itself.[3] Under the Code, an individual may exempt a variety of property interests. These federal exemptions include $7,500 equity in a residence, $1,200 equity in one motor vehicle, ordinary household furnishings and personal apparel, $500 in jewelry, $750 in books and tools of the debtor's trade, any unmatured life insurance contract owned by the debtor (other than a credit life insurance contract), up to $4,000 cash surrender or loan value of an unmatured life insurance contract on the life of and owned by the debtor, alimony and child support, certain rights in pension or profit sharing plans, and awards from personal injury causes of action [11 U.S.C. 522]. To the extent that the federal residence exemption is not used, the debtor may exempt up to $7,500 of any kind of property, including cash. Regardless of whether the debtor chooses the state or the federal exemptions, waivers of exemptions in favor of unsecured creditors are unenforceable.

A consumer-debtor may redeem exempt property that is subject to a security interest by paying to the secured creditor the amount of the allowed secured claim [11 U.S.C. 722]. The right to redeem applies to tangible personal property intended primarily for personal, family, or household use. The debtor could, for example, redeem an automobile that would otherwise be repossessed.

Distribution of the Estate Three kinds of creditors may be involved in the distribution of the debtor's estate: secured creditors, unsecured creditors called "priority" creditors, and unsecured creditors other than priority creditors. For convenience, nonpriority unsecured creditors are referred to in the remainder of this chapter as "general" creditors. The rights of various creditors depend on rules governing proof of claim, allowability of claims, and priority of payments.

Proof of claim The distribution process begins with the filing of a document called a "proof of claim." A proof of claim is prima facie evidence of the validity and the amount of the claim [Bankruptcy Rule 301]. Only unsecured

---

[3]States are permitted to reject ("opt out" of) the federal exemptions alternative. In states that do so, debtors are limited to state exemptions and to certain non-Code federal exemptions. As of June 1, 1981, 17 states have "opted out." They are: Alabama, Arizona, Arkansas, Florida, Georgia, Illinois, Indiana, Iowa, Kansas, Kentucky, Louisiana, Nebraska, Ohio, South Dakota, Tennessee, Virginia, and Wyoming. Opt-out legislation is pending in Missouri.

creditors are required to file proofs of claim (or to have such documents filed on their behalf). A secured creditor need not file a proof of claim. However, a secured creditor whose secured claim exceeds the value of the collateral is an unsecured creditor as to the amount of the deficiency, and a proof of claim is required for the recovery of the deficiency. Where a proof of claim is required, it must be filed within 6 months after the first date set for the first meeting of creditors, unless the time for filing has been extended [Bankruptcy Rule 302(e)]. Unless a proof of claim is timely filed, a claim cannot be "allowed" even though the claim is otherwise valid.

Allowability of claims Only allowed claims are eligible for payment out of the debtor's estate, and then, of course, allowed claims will be paid only to the extent that funds are available. What claims are allowed?

Upon the filing of a proof of claim, the claim is "deemed allowed" unless a party in interest, such as a creditor or the trustee, objects to the allowance of the claim. If there is an objection, the bankruptcy court must decide whether the claim is to be allowed. Claims filed after the 6-month limit will not be allowed. Where the debtor has a defense to an alleged debt (e.g., fraud or failure of consideration), a claim for payment of the debt will not be allowed. The Bankruptcy Code lists other claims that will and will not be allowed [11 U.S.C. 502; 503]. Where a claim is valid but contingent or unliquidated, the court must estimate the amount of the claim for purposes of allowance so that the closing of the case will not be unduly delayed [11 U.S.C. 502(c)(1)].

Some otherwise allowable claims are disallowed, at least temporarily, to foster efficient administration of the bankruptcy case. Suppose that Cora Creditor made a large, unsecured loan to Daniel Debtor 18 months before his bankruptcy; that 30 days before his bankruptcy she received a preferential payment for a small part of the loan; that the trustee in bankruptcy had the preference set aside; and that Cora has not yet paid the preferential amount to the debtor's estate. Cora files a proof of claim for the difference between the preferential payment she received and the amount of the loan. Will Cora's claim be allowed? No. Before her claim will be allowed, she must pay to the estate the amount of the preferential transfer [11 U.S.C. 502(d)]. This rule gives the trustee leverage in this and in similar situations to collect preferential and other improper payments.

Suppose, in contrast to the situation just described, that Creditor made a $10,000 loan to Debtor 18 months before his bankruptcy, and that in the same week he sold to her, on credit, $1,000 worth of goods. This situation involves mutual debts, and Creditor has a right of "setoff," which entitles her to reduce her $10,000 claim against Debtor by the $1,000 that she owes Debtor [11 U.S.C. 553]. Thus, instead of having to pay the estate the $1,000 (which might be distributed to creditors of higher priority than herself) and then filing a claim for $10,000 (which might not be paid because of lack of funds), Creditor has only $9,000 at risk.

Priority of payments Secured creditors have property rights (security interests) that the trustee did not acquire. Consequently, secured claims are paid in full if the collateral is sufficiently valuable. Where the amount of the secured claim exceeds the value of the collateral, the claimant is a general creditor as to the deficiency and must share available funds with other general creditors of the claimant's class.

Subject to the rights of secured creditors, other claimants whose claims have been allowed may receive a share (called a "dividend") of the debtor's estate. There are six classes of claims specified in the general distribution scheme of Section 726. The first of these six classes is the category designated "priority claims," so called because the Bankruptcy Code gives them priority of payment over the other five classes in the general distribution scheme. The remaining five classes include the general creditors.

Priority claims are subdivided into six classes of priorities. If funds are sufficient, the claims in the first class of priorities are paid in full, and any excess is applied to the claims of the next class of priorities. Where funds are insufficient to pay a class of priority claims in full, each claimant of that class receives the same percentage of his or her claim that the other claimants of that class receive. That percentage is called a "pro rata share." The principle of pro rata distribution is applied throughout the general scheme of distribution. Where all priority claims are paid, there may be sufficient funds for general creditors and other claimants to receive at least a pro rata share.

What are the priority claims, and why are priority claimants favored by the Bankruptcy Code? Priority claims fall into the following six categories.

1 *First priority claims:* These consist chiefly of administrative expenses, such as reimbursement for the costs of preserving the debtor's estate; compensation of trustees, examiners, accountants, attorneys, the debtor's attorney, appraisers, and others for expenses incurred and for services rendered; and expenses incurred by creditors who, for example, file involuntary petitions against debtors, recover concealed or transferred property for the estate, and prosecute criminal offenses relating to the bankruptcy case or to the business or property of the debtor. In general, first priority status tends to encourage the preservation and early collection of the debtor's estate.

2 *Second priority claims:* These consist of unsecured claims arising in the ordinary course of the debtor's business in the interval following the filing of an involuntary petition against the debtor but before an order for relief or the appointment of a trustee. Priority status for such claims tends to forestall the cutting off of goods, services, and operating credit at the slightest hint of financial difficulty, and therefore to give the debtor an early opportunity to escape bankruptcy.

3 *Third priority claims:* These consist of claims for up to $2,000 for wages, salaries, or commissions (including vacation, severance, and sick leave pay) earned within 90 days preceding bankruptcy or preceding the cessation of the debtor's business, whichever occurs first. Third priority status protects employees from undue hardship. It can be argued that the status forestalls an early desertion of a financially troubled debtor-employer by employees.

4 *Fourth priority claims:* These consist of limited unsecured claims for contributions to employee benefit plans.

5 *Fifth priority claims:* These consist of unsecured claims by individual consumer creditors, to the extent of $900 for each such creditor, arising from a prebankruptcy deposit of money in connection with the purchase of services or property (or the leasing of property) for personal, family, or household use. This priority status enhances consumers' chances of recovering prepayments for goods not delivered or services not rendered.

6 *Sixth priority claims:* These consist of claims for federal, state, and local taxes. This priority is said to be justified by the need of government to protect the revenue-raising power. The sixth priority is discussed further under the heading of Nondischargeable Debts.

The Bankruptcy Code has made a significant change in priorities as between the creditors of a bankrupt partnership and the creditors of a bankrupt partner. Suppose that the XY partnership, partner X, and partner Y each files a petition in bankruptcy; that the claims of all secured creditors have been satisfied; that the funds of the partnership are now exhausted; and that there are some funds left in the estates of X and Y, but not enough to satisfy the claims of all unsecured creditors. Under a long-standing rule of partnership law (called the "jingle rule" because of its supposedly spurious logic), creditors of the partnership have first claim to assets of the partnership, and creditors of individual partners have first claim to assets of individual partners. Under the jingle rule, in the situation described here, the unsecured creditors of each partner would receive shares of the funds remaining in that partner's estate, and the unsecured creditors of the partnership (the funds of which have now been exhausted) would receive nothing from that partner's estate until the claims of the partner's creditors are satisfied. The Bankruptcy Code changes part of the jingle rule, insofar as it applies to cases covered by the Code. The partnership creditors still have first claim to the partnership assets, but now the creditors of the partnership estate receive a share (via the partnership trustee) in the remaining assets of each partner. The partnership creditors share pro rata with the unsecured creditors of the individual partner [11 U.S.C. 723]. This rule is consistent with the rule that general partners are liable for the debts of the partnership.

Discharge; Nondischargeable Debts Debtors who seek liquidation under Chapter 7 or 11, or who propose a Chapter 13 repayment plan, may receive a discharge from most debts that remain unpaid after the distribution of the debtor's estate or the performance of the plan. Most debtors are eligible for a discharge only once every 6 years. However, a wage earner or other debtor who is carrying out a Chapter 13 repayment plan may be eligible for discharge more frequently. The 6-year bar does not apply to a Chapter 13 debtor who pays 70 percent of the unsecured claims under a repayment plan that was proposed by the debtor in good faith and that represents the debtor's best efforts [11 U.S.C. 727(a)(9)].

Grounds for denying discharge A debtor who is eligible for a discharge will be denied a discharge for engaging in any of a variety of activities prohibited by the Bankruptcy Code. The grounds for denying discharge include the debtor's fraudulent transfer or concealment of property (within 1 year before filing a bankruptcy petition) with intent to hinder, delay, or defraud a creditor or an officer of the estate;

unjustifiably concealing or destroying business records or failing to keep adequate business records; making a false oath, a fraudulent account, or a false claim in connection with the bankruptcy case; failing to explain satisfactorily any loss of assets or deficiency of assets to meet the debtor's liabilities; and refusal of the debtor to obey lawful orders of the court [11 U.S.C. 727].

The Bankruptcy Code makes a significant departure from prior bankruptcy law regarding denial of discharge. Under prior law, a debtor could be denied a discharge for obtaining money or credit on the basis of a materially false financial statement, whether it was prepared by the debtor or not. Financial statements are difficult to construct with total accuracy; yet, any omission, even of a long-forgotten contingent liability (such as that of a debtor who co-signed a parent's promissory note), can render a financial statement materially false. Moreover, some lenders make a practice of hurrying borrowers through the process of listing creditors, intending later to use omissions to oppose the debtor's discharge. To combat such practices, the Bankruptcy Code does not list as a ground for denial of discharge the issuing of a false financial statement.

Nondischargeable debts Although an individual debtor may receive a discharge, certain kinds of debts are not covered by it and therefore remain binding on the debtor [11 U.S.C. 523]. These include the following:

1 Debts for taxes for which a governmental unit receives sixth priority status, for which a required return was not timely filed, or with respect to which the debtor made a fraudulent return or a willful attempt at evasion. In general, taxes more than 1 to 3 years old (depending on the kind of tax) *are* discharged, in the absence of fraud, late filing, and the like. It is debts for taxes that are less than 1 to 3 years old that receive sixth priority status and that are not discharged.

2 Debts contracted on the basis of the debtor's

false pretenses, false representations, or actual fraud. It should be noted that a materially false written financial statement *can* be the basis for denying discharge of a particular debt (but not for denying a general discharge) where the debtor issued the statement with *intent to deceive* and the creditor *reasonably relied* on it.

3 Debts not scheduled by the debtor or others in time to permit a creditor without notice of the case to make a timely filing of a proof of claim.

4 Debts resulting from the debtor's embezzlement or larceny, or from the debtor's fraud or defalcation while acting in a fiduciary capacity.

5 Debts arising from alimony, maintenance, or child support awards.

6 Debts arising from the debtor's willful and malicious injury of another entity or willful and malicious injury to or conversion of an entity's property.

7 Debts arising from certain educational loans.

8 Governmental fines and penalties, except those relating to dischargeable taxes, for example.

Case 49.3   **In re Mazzola**
             4 B.R. 179 (D. Mass. 1980)

LAVIEN, B.J. The plaintiffs in this proceeding, Wayne and Gayle LaVangie, seek to bar the discharge of the debtors . . . pursuant to . . . provisions of . . . the Bankruptcy Code. The plaintiffs allege the debtors made false oaths on their petition and transferred and concealed property within one year preceding the filing of the petition. . . .

The debtors filed a joint petition under Chapter 7 of the Bankruptcy Code on October 15, 1979. At the time of filing, the debtor Dennis Mazzola was the sole stockholder of the Dennis M. Construction Co., Inc., and was engaged in the home construction industry. Just prior to the filing of the bankruptcy, the plaintiffs had been involved in bitter litigation with the debtors . . . over a claim of faulty home construction. In fact, in August of 1979, the plaintiffs obtained an attachment on two parcels of property owned by the debtors jointly. In early September of 1979 the debtors accomplished the dissolution of the attachment, sold the properties speedily, deposited the $14,000 received from the sale in the checking account of Dennis M. Construction Co., Inc., and used the proceeds to pay the corporation's creditors. The debtors then abandoned their defense [of the litigation with the LaVangies] and filed a petition in bankruptcy on October 15, 1979. The testimony adduced at trial revealed several false answers in the debtors' schedules and statement of affairs. . . .

The purpose of section 727(a)(4)(A) [barring a discharge if the debtor knowingly and fraudulently, in or in connection with the case, made a false oath or account] is to ensure that dependable information is supplied for those interested in the administration of the bankruptcy estate on which they can rely without the need for the trustee or other interested parties to dig out the true facts in examinations or investigations. The trustee and creditors are entitled to honest and accurate signposts on the trail showing what property has passed through the bankrupt's hands during a period prior to his bankruptcy. A false statement in the schedules or statement of affairs due to mere mistake or inadvertence is insufficient for the denial of a discharge; fraudulent intent is necessary to bar a discharge. A reckless disregard of both the serious nature of the information sought and the necessary attention to detail and accuracy in answering may rise to the level of fraudulent intent necessary to bar a discharge. . . .

There is no question in the present case that the schedule and statement of affairs filed by the debtors contained numerous false statements. The debtors concede the false statements exist. The determinative issue with regard to the ultimate granting or denial of discharge is whether those false statements were knowingly and fraudulently made so as to fall within the prohibition of section 727(a)(4)(A).

After hearing and observing Mr. Mazzola at trial, the court finds the explanations offered by Mr. Mazzola for the false statements in the documents not credible. The present facts do not reflect mere mistake or inadvertence but rather are indicative at the very least of such a cavalier and reckless disregard for truthfulness as to cause the court to find fraudulent intent. The court finds Mr. Mazzola's explanation for the false answer to question 12b on the statement of affairs to be particularly disturbing. Question 12b clearly asks the debtors whether they have transferred any real or tangible personal property during the year immediately preceding the filing of the petition. . . . The debtors answered "No" to the question. Mr. Mazzola stated at trial, under oath, that he interpreted the question to ask if he currently owned any property. The court cannot accept this explanation as credible. Mr. Mazzola is not an unintelligent individual inexperienced in real estate transactions as is evidenced by the fact that for many years he made his living building homes and buying and selling real estate. Mr. Mazzola's alleged interpretation of question 12b cannot be deemed a reasonable and honest misinterpretation of the question. The question is entitled, in bold face, "Transfers of property." There is nothing that could justify any genuine belief that "transfer" meant "present ownership." In fact, the entire page of the statement of affairs asks questions *only* about transfers. The pleadings further belie the credibility of this explanation, as the debtors' answer to the plaintiffs' complaint states that the debtor simply overlooked these properties. Indeed, even this contradictory explanation leaves much to be desired in the area of credibility inasmuch as these properties were subject to a controversial attachment obtained by the plaintiffs during the state court litigation between the parties and had been sold only one month prior to the filing of the bankruptcy petition.

None of this even attempts to explain why the transfer of the $14,000 from the sale of these properties to the corporation was not mentioned in the answer. Likewise, the explanations of the other false statements fall short of being credible. Mr. Mazzola claimed he failed to disclose the sole ownership of the corporation's stock because he believed it to have no value and that he failed to list the attachment because he considered it to be illegal and because it was dissolved approximately two weeks after it was granted. Individually any one of these explanations might appear plausible in the abstract, but when combined with the fact of the existence of the bitterly contested state court proceedings, the speed of the conveyances when the attachment was dissolved, the immediate transfer of the sale proceeds to the corporation which was not a party to the lawsuit, the subsequent abandonment of the state court proceeding, and the almost simultaneous filing [in bankruptcy] coupled with the blatantly false answers, there is simply too much self-serving "misunderstanding" and "mistake." . . .

I find that the statements were made with a calculated disregard for the importance of documents which were signed under penalty of perjury and on which a determination on the request for a discharge would be made. This reckless disregard for the truth is the equivalent of the fraudulent intent necessary to bar a discharge. . . .

It is hereby ordered that the debtors Dennis Joseph Mazzola and Anne Tresa Mazzola be denied discharges in bankruptcy due to their false oaths in violation of 11 U.S.C. Section 727(a)(4)(A). . . .

Discharge hearing; reaffirmation; protection of discharge A discharge in bankruptcy is not an automatic protection against the payment of discharged debts. As many debtors have been shocked to learn, the discharge must be pleaded by the debtor as a defense to any action subsequently brought to enforce a discharged debt. Primarily to protect the debtor, the Bankruptcy Code requires that an individual debtor appear in person before the court to receive his or her discharge or to hear the reason why a discharge has not been granted [11 U.S.C. 524(d)]. More specifically, the mandatory hearing serves three purposes: (1) to impress upon the debtor the judicial nature and the seriousness of the bankruptcy remedy; (2) to provide the debtor with an explanation by the court of the discharge and with a warning about the reaffirmation of discharged debts (a debtor who reaffirms discharged debts may be required to pay them despite the discharge); and (3) to determine whether any reaffirmation agreement the debtor wishes to make complies with the requirements of the Bankruptcy Code.

Under prior bankruptcy law, uninformed debtors were often persuaded to give up the protection afforded them by the discharge. Now, for a reaffirmation agreement to be enforceable, it must satisfy four conditions: (1) the agreement must have been made before the granting of the discharge; (2) the debtor must be given 30 days after the agreement becomes enforceable to rescind it; (3) the court must have held the discharge hearing, the debtor must have attended, and the debtor must have been warned about the legal effect and consequences of reaffirmation; and (4) if there is a reaffirmation of a consumer debt not secured by the debtor's real property, the court must approve the agreement. The agreement is to be approved only *(a)* where it will not impose an undue hardship on the debtor or the debtor's dependents and will be in the best interests of the debtor, or *(b)* where the agreement was entered into in good faith to redeem consumer property or to settle litigation relating to exceptions to the discharge [11 U.S.C. 524(c)].

The laws of some states have penalized discharged debtors for exercising certain of their discharge rights. In the case of *Perez v.*

Campbell, 402 U.S. 637 (1971), for example, an Arizona financial responsibility law permitted suspension of a driver's license for the uninsured debtor-driver's failure to pay an automobile personal injury judgment that had been discharged in bankruptcy. The Supreme Court held, by a 5 to 4 vote, that the suspension provision of the Arizona law was in conflict with bankruptcy law and therefore was void under the supremacy clause of the United States Constitution. The Bankruptcy Code follows and expands on that case by providing, in essence, that a governmental unit may not penalize or discriminate against a debtor or the debtor's associates solely because of the debtor's failure to pay a discharged debt or because of the debtor's status as a debtor under bankruptcy law. Thus, the fresh-start policy of the Bankruptcy Code prevails over the state policy of protecting favored creditors.

Business Reorganizations

The main purpose of a Chapter 11 reorganization proceeding is to allow a financially troubled firm to stay in business while it undergoes a process of financial rehabilitation. Reorganization is essentially a process of negotiation in which the debtor firm and its creditors develop a plan for the adjustment and discharge of debts. The plan may provide for a change of management and even for the liquidation of the firm. However, a continuation of the business is the usual goal.

Most of the substantive rules and principles of bankruptcy law that apply to Chapter 7 liquidations apply also to Chapter 11 reorganizations. Most individuals, partnerships, and corporations that are eligible for Chapter 7 liquidation are eligible for Chapter 11 reorganization. Like Chapter 7 cases, reorganization cases may be voluntary or involuntary; and the conditions for forcing a debtor into involuntary liquidation apply to involuntary reorganizations as well. The trustee's powers, the law of fraudulent and preferential transfers, the grounds for denial of discharge, and many other aspects of bankruptcy law are the same or nearly the same for Chapter 11 cases as for Chapter 7 cases. Consequently, the discussion here is limited to topics of special significance to reorganization cases.

Role of Creditors' Committee As soon as practicable after the court enters an order for relief under the reorganization chapter, the court must appoint a committee of unsecured creditors (but may *not* preside at the initial meeting). Ordinarily, the committee will consist of the seven largest unsecured creditors willing to serve; however, a committee formed prior to the order for relief will become the official committee if it was fairly chosen and is representative of the various claims against the debtor. At the request of a party in interest, the court (1) may change the composition of the committee to make it representative and (2) may appoint additional committees, such as a committee of equity security holders [11 U.S.C. 1102].

The committee has a number of powers and duties. The principal tasks of the committee are to investigate the financial affairs of the debtor; to determine whether the business should continue to be operated; to determine whether to request the appointment of a trustee to displace the debtor in possession; and to consult with the debtor or trustee in the administration of the case [11 U.S.C. 1103]. In carrying out these tasks, the committee may question the debtor, who must appear and submit to examination under oath at the initial meeting of creditors [11 U.S.C. 343]. Subject to court approval, the committee may select lawyers, accountants, and other agents to represent or to perform services for the committee.

Plan for Satisfaction of Creditors' Claims Either the debtor or any other party in interest may file a plan for reorganization. For the first 120 days after the date of the order for relief, only the debtor may file a plan (unless a trustee has been appointed). If the debtor files a plan within that time, the debtor has an additional 60 days to obtain creditors' acceptances of (agreements to) the plan. The time allowed the debtor for filing and obtaining acceptances may be reduced (or extended) "for cause," such as the debtor's unreasonable delay in proposing a plan [11 U.S.C. 1121]. After the necessary acceptances have been obtained, the plan is presented to the court for confirmation. Acceptance and confirmation are discussed in more detail later in this chapter.

Mandatory and permissive provisions of the plan A plan of reorganization must do the following things: (1) designate classes of claims and ownership interests; specify any class of claims or interests that is not impaired under the plan; and specify the treatment of any class that is impaired under the plan; (2) provide the same treatment for each claim or interest of a particular class unless the holder of a particular claim or interest agrees to a less favorable treatment; (3) provide adequate means for carrying out the plan; (4) if the debtor is a corporation, prohibit (in the corporate charter) the issuance of nonvoting equity securities and protect the voting rights, if any, of security holders; (5) in the selection of officers, directors, and trustees, contain only provisions that are consistent with the interests of creditors, security holders, and public policy.

As to permissive provisions, the plan may, for example, impair any class of claims (secured or unsecured) or any class of interests; settle or adjust any claim or interest belonging to the debtor or to the estate; or liquidate the business [11 U.S.C. 1123]. A claim or interest is "impaired" where the plan alters the legal, equitable, or contractual rights of its holder; where the plan fails to cure a pre-reorganization default by the debtor; or where the plan provides for payment of less than the full amount or value of a claim or interest [11 U.S.C. 1124]. Impairment may be necessary if funds are insufficient to pay claims in full. However, impairment gives the affected class a ground upon which to oppose confirmation of the plan.

Confirmation of the plan Confirmation is the act of the bankruptcy court in approving a plan of reorganization and thereby giving effect to its provisions. The court may confirm a plan only if the requirements of the Bankruptcy Code are met [11 U.S.C. 1129(a)]. Confirmation makes the plan binding not only on the debtor but also on creditors, equity security holders, and others, whether or not their claims are impaired, and whether or not they have accepted the plan. Confirmation also discharges all debts except those of *individual* debtors for which a discharge is denied under Section 523.

Ordinarily, a plan may not be confirmed unless the holders of impaired claims or interests accept (consent to) the plan by the requisite majority vote. A class of *creditors* (secured or unsecured) has accepted the plan when holders of a simple majority in number and two-thirds in dollar amount of allowed claims approve the plan. A class of *ownership interests* has accepted the plan when holders of two-thirds in dollar amount of allowed interests approve the plan [11 U.S.C. 1126(c),(d)].

Consent of an impaired class is *not* necessary for confirmation if the plan treats the impaired class in a manner that is "fair and equitable" [11 U.S.C. 1129(b)]. A plan may be fair and equitable if, for example, the members of the impaired class receive under the plan (1) the present value of the amount of their allowed claims, or (2) a pro rata share of their claims in a situation where junior classes of claims or interests receive nothing. The consent of an unimpaired class is not necessary for confirmation.

What are the rights of dissenting minorities of impaired classes that accept the plan? Those minorities are protected by the requirement that all members of a class, dissenters and nondissenters alike, receive at least the value that they would obtain as a result of a Chapter 7 liquidation [11 U.S.C. 1129(a)]. That value will, of course, be zero if funds are exhausted by claims of higher priority.

A plan of reorganization might provide for the

issuance of securities in exchange for a claim against or an ownership interest in the debtor. Unless a creditor or other entity purchases a claim with a view to distributing securities to be received under the plan, an issue of such securities is not subject to the registration requirement of Section 5 of the Securities Act of 1933, nor to state or local registration requirements [11 U.S.C. 1145]. The exemption of such securities from the registration requirements is due largely to the existence in the Bankruptcy Code of substantial disclosure requirements that apply to the solicitation of acceptances needed for the confirmation of a plan of reorganization [see 11 U.S.C. 1125; 1126].

Repayment Plans for Debtors with Regular Income

Chapter 13 of the Bankruptcy Code permits an *individual* debtor to develop a repayment plan and, upon completion of payments under the plan, to receive a discharge from most remaining debts [11 U.S.C. 1328]. The predecessor of Chapter 13 was limited to wage earners. The present Chapter 13 is available (on a voluntary basis only) to any individual (except a stockbroker or a commodity broker) who has regular income, unsecured debts of less than $100,000, and secured debts of less than $350,000. The debts must be noncontingent and liquidated; that is, they must be owing and unpaid at the time of the debtor's application for relief.

Much of the bankruptcy law previously discussed applies to Chapter 13 cases. Especially notable are those provisions of the Code that prohibit governmental discrimination against debtors, restrict the enforceability of reaffirmation agreements, and provide federal exemptions for an individual debtor.

Typically, the plan proposed by the debtor will be either a composition or an extension plan. In a composition plan the debtor pays creditors less than 100 percent of their claims, on a pro rata basis for each class of claims. In an extension plan the debtor pays the full amount, but over a longer period than originally agreed. Payments under a plan (whether composition or extension) must be completed within 3 years after confirmation, or within 5 years if the court approves. Regardless of the kind of plan, the debtor must give the trustee control of the debtor's future income, the trustee makes payments of claims, and the debtor has the benefit of injunctive relief against creditors while the plan is being carried out.

Unsecured creditors do not vote on Chapter 13 plans; but for a Chapter 13 plan to be confirmed, unsecured creditors must receive at least what they would receive in a Chapter 7 liquidation. Priority claims must be paid in full (so long as funds are available), unless particular priority claimants agree otherwise [11 U.S.C. 1322(a)(2)]. As explained in the following paragraph, the plan may unilaterally modify the rights of most other claimants (secured and unsecured), so long as all claims in a class receive the same treatment.

Chapter 13 permits a plan to modify not only the rights of unsecured nonpriority creditors (as prior law did) but also the rights of holders of most secured claims, including claims secured by an interest in real estate [11 U.S.C. 1322(b)(2)]. However, the plan cannot modify the rights of a claimant whose claim is secured by an interest in the debtor's principal residence. A plan may be confirmed without the consent of a secured creditor in either of two situations: (1) where the creditor retains his or her lien and the property to which the lien applies has a value not less than the allowed amount of the secured claim; or (2) where the debtor surrenders to the claimant the property securing the claim [11 U.S.C. 1325(a)(5)].

If the plan was a composition, the Chapter 13 discharge upon completion of the plan bars another discharge for 6 years, unless the debtor has made 70 percent of the payments under the plan, the plan was proposed in good faith, and the plan was the best effort of the debtor [11 U.S.C. 727(a)(9)].

SUMMARY

Federal bankruptcy law has two main purposes: (1) to provide for an evenhanded treatment of creditors, and (2) to provide overburdened debtors with a "fresh start" in business. Bankruptcy law is essentially federal law, but the Bankruptcy Code looks to state law for the resolution of some bankruptcy issues.

Two officials have major responsibility for administering the debtor's estate. The trustee in bankruptcy is responsible for collecting, liquidating, and distributing the estate. The bankruptcy judge (or the United States Trustee) appoints trustees. The judge supervises the activities of appointed trustees and renders judicial decisions as the need arises.

The purpose of a Chapter 7 liquidation proceeding is to convert the debtor's nonexempt assets into cash, to distribute this cash in accordance with the scheme of distribution provided by the Bankruptcy Code, and to grant the honest debtor (individual, partnership, or corporation) a discharge from most of the remaining debts. The trustee in bankruptcy has broad powers to collect the property for the estate and to avoid transactions that improperly dissipate the estate. An individual debtor is entitled to exempt certain property from the estate. To the extent that funds permit, the remaining property is distributed to priority unsecured creditors and then to others, such as nonpriority unsecured creditors. The security interests of secured parties do not become a part of the debtor's estate. The claim of a secured creditor is paid in full if the collateral is sufficiently valuable.

There are several grounds for a general denial of a discharge; and certain kinds of debts, such as alimony, are excepted from the discharge. An individual debtor must appear in person before the bankruptcy court to receive his or her discharge. The court must warn the debtor about the legal effect and consequences of any reaffirmation agreement, and the court must determine whether any reaffirmation agreement the debtor wishes to make complies with the requirements of the Bankruptcy Code. Governmental units may not discriminate against a debtor solely because of the debtor's failure to pay a discharged debt.

The main purpose of a Chapter 11 business reorganization is to allow a financially troubled firm (individual, partnership, or corporation) to stay in business while it undergoes a process of financial rehabilitation. Most of the substantive rules and principles of bankruptcy law that apply to Chapter 7 liquidations apply also to Chapter 11 reorganizations. Topics of special significance to reorganization cases include the role of creditors' committees, the content of the plan for the satisfaction of creditors' claims, and the requirements for confirmation of the plan.

Chapter 13 of the Bankruptcy Code permits individual debtors (wage earners and others except stock and commodity brokers) to develop a repayment plan and, upon the completion of payments under the plan, to receive a discharge from most remaining debts. Much of the bankruptcy law previously discussed applies to Chapter 13 cases. Typically, the plan proposed by the debtor will be either a composition or an extension plan. Regardless of the kind of plan, the debtor must give the trustee control of the debtor's future income, the trustee makes payments of claims, and the debtor has the benefit of injunctive relief against creditors while the plan is being carried out.

STUDY AND DISCUSSION QUESTIONS

1 For what reasons was the Bankruptcy Act of 1898 enacted?

2 (a) What are the purposes of the federal bankruptcy law? (b) How is federal bankruptcy law related to state insolvency law? (c) Briefly describe the coverage and organization of the Bankruptcy Code.

3 *(a)* Given that a bankruptcy court is an "adjunct" to its federal district court, how is it that bankruptcy judges have power to render binding decisions on all aspects of a bankruptcy case? *(b)* What are the main duties of a trustee in bankruptcy? *(c)* What are the main duties of a bankruptcy judge?

4 *(a)* Why was the bankruptcy judge vulnerable to a charge of bias in favor of unsecured creditors when rendering judicial decisions? *(b)* What steps have been taken in the Bankruptcy Code to decrease that vulnerability?

5 *(a)* What is the purpose of a Chapter 7 liquidation proceeding? *(b)* Who is eligible for a voluntary Chapter 7 proceeding? *(c)* Who may be subjected to an involuntary Chapter 7 proceeding? Under what circumstances?

6 *(a)* What purposes are served by the two bankruptcy grounds for relief? *(b)* How is a debtor protected from an unfounded, trivial, or harassing charge of bankruptcy?

7 *(a)* What two broad classes of property become part of the debtor's estate? *(b)* How does the Bankruptcy Code treat spendthrift trust provisions? *(c)* Does a secured party's security interest become part of the debtor's estate? Explain.

8 *(a)* What is the function of the automatic stay? Of the turnover provisions of the Code? *(b)* Under what general circumstances may the trustee use, sell, or lease property that is subject to a creditor's security interest? *(c)* Under what circumstances may the trustee obtain secured credit for the estate?

9 *(a)* Why is the trustee empowered to assume, reject, or assign executory contracts and unexpired leases? *(b)* Where the trustee rejects such a contract or lease, what right has the aggrieved party? *(c)* How does the Code treat contract clauses that are intended to prevent the trustee from assuming a contract upon the debtor's bankruptcy? Why?

10 Why is the trustee given the status of a hypothetical lien creditor and similar statuses?

11 *(a)* A fraudulent transfer may involve either actual or constructive fraud. Under bankruptcy law, how does constructive fraud differ from actual fraud? *(b)* What fraudulent transfers may a trustee avoid?

12 *(a)* What is a preferential transfer (preference)? Give an example of a preference. *(b)* Why is a preference considered to be a wrongful transaction? *(c)* Give an example of a transaction that appears technically to be a preference but is not a preference. Why is the transaction not classified as a preference? *(d)* Under what circumstances may the trustee avoid a preference made to an insider?

13 *(a)* What debtors are entitled to exemptions? Why are exemptions permitted? *(b)* Why does the Bankruptcy Code provide for federal exemptions as an alternative to those provided by state law?

14 *(a)* In the distribution of the debtor's estate, what function is served by a proof of claim? *(b)* Who must file a proof of claim? Must secured creditors file? Explain. *(c)* Where filing is required, what is the effect of failing to file within the prescribed 6 months?

15 *(a)* How is a claim allowed? *(b)* What is the meaning or effect of allowance of a claim? *(c)* Give an example of a claim that will not be allowed. *(d)* Why are some otherwise allowable claims disallowed, at least temporarily? Give an example of such a claim. *(e)* Illustrate setoff.

16 *(a)* Under Chapter 7, who is entitled to a share of the debtor's estate? Are secured creditors so entitled? Explain. *(b)* Explain the principle of pro rata distribution. *(c)* There are six classes of priority claims. Select two and explain why claims of those classes are given priority. *(d)* How has the Bankruptcy Code changed the jingle rule?

17 *(a)* How often may a debtor be granted a

discharge in bankruptcy? *(b)* List two grounds for the denial of a discharge. Is obtaining money on the basis of a materially false financial statement such a ground? Why? *(c)* Even though a debtor receives a discharge, some debts are not covered by it. List three kinds of debts that are not dischargeable in a liquidation proceeding.

18 *(a)* What purposes are served by the mandatory discharge hearing? *(b)* What is a reaffirmation agreement? How is it treated under the Bankruptcy Code? *(c)* May a state suspend a driver's license because the driver failed to pay an automobile personal injury judgment that had been discharged in bankruptcy? Explain.

19 *(a)* What is the main purpose of a Chapter 11 business reorganization proceeding? *(b)* In a business reorganization, how is the membership of the creditors' committee established? *(c)* What are the principal tasks of the committee?

20 *(a)* How is a plan of reorganization developed? *(b)* A plan may impair any class of claims or ownership interests. What is meant by impairment? *(c)* Define acceptance and confirmation as those terms are used in bankruptcy.

21 *(a)* Explain the relationship between impairment of a claim, acceptance of a plan, and confirmation of a plan. *(b)* What are the rights of dissenting minorities of classes that accept the plan or whose claims or interests are unimpaired by the plan? *(c)* A plan of reorganization may provide for the issuance of securities in exchange for a claim against (or an ownership interest of) the debtor. Are such securities subject to securities registration requirements? Explain.

22 With regard to Chapter 13 repayment plans for debtors with regular incomes, explain *(a)* who may file for Chapter 13 relief, *(b)* how a composition plan differs from an extension plan, and *(c)* in general, what the debtor must do, what protection the debtor receives, and how the plan is carried out.

23 *(a)* Unsecured creditors do not vote on Chapter 13 plans. How, then, are their interests protected? *(b)* Unlike its predecessor, Chapter 13 permits a repayment plan to modify the rights of most secured creditors without their consent. Under what circumstances will a plan be confirmed without the consent of a secured creditor? *(c)* Is an extension plan subject to the rule that completion of a plan bars another discharge for 6 years? Explain.

CASE PROBLEMS

[*Note:* The Bankruptcy Reform Act of 1978 (the Bankruptcy Code) took effect on October 1, 1979. Assume that it applies to all of the problems that follow. The problems are hypothetical cases that illustrate a number of new bankruptcy rules and principles.]

1 Johnson owned and operated a small farm from which he derived about half of his gross income. The other half he earned from a job as a clerk in a local farm supply store that was Johnson's major supplier of fuels, seed, fertilizer, equipment, and tools. Johnson had unpaid open accounts with his employer and with two other farm supply stores. He owed his employer $7,000 and he owed the other two suppliers $2,000 each. A local bank held a chattel mortgage on his farm equipment (worth $12,000) to secure a farm loan of $7,500 for operating expenses. The bank also held a $50,000 mortgage on Johnson's farm, which was worth $70,000 in the prevailing real estate market. Due to a partial crop failure and to a truckers' strike that prevented him from marketing his crops, Johnson was unable to pay any of his debts except the monthly payments on the real estate mortgage. Against Johnson's wishes, all the creditors except his employer joined in a Chapter 7 liquidation petition to have Johnson declared a bankrupt. Will the liquidation petition succeed?

2 Franklin filed a voluntary petition in bankruptcy. At that time she had debts of $100,000 and, among other holdings, the following interests in property: *(a)* business equipment worth $5,000, which was subject to a $3,000 chattel mortgage in favor of her bank, *(b)* an automobile worth $1,000, which she intended to claim as exempt property, and *(c)* as trustee for her ill brother, legal title to a $10,000 fund left to her by her mother solely for the brother's support, the remainder, if any, to go to the Memorial Hospital at the brother's death. Five months after filing the petition, Franklin inherited $25,000 from her uncle. Three months later, at the death of another uncle, she received $50,000 as the beneficiary of an insurance policy on that uncle's life. In the meantime, after the filing of the petition, Franklin's business realized a net profit of $10,000, and Franklin earned $8,000 as a consultant to another firm. The trustee in bankruptcy claimed for the debtor's estate all the property described above. To what property was the trustee entitled?

3 Pursuant to a plan for reorganizing Widget Corporation, the trustee was authorized to operate the debtor's business. One creditor, First Bank, held a security interest in "all of Widget Corporation's business equipment and inventory, and in all other such assets or proceeds of such assets that Widget Corporation may hereafter acquire." Widget Corporation owed First Bank a secured debt of $23,000. The value of the equipment covered by the security interest was $10,000, and the production cost of the inventory was $13,000. To acquire funds to operate the business, the trustee proposed a sale of the inventory and a refinancing plan for the business equipment. First Bank refused to extend further credit. Of all the banks in the area, only Second State Bank was willing to extend operating credit, and then only if it received a security interest that would prevail over all others. First Bank refused to subordinate its lien. The wholesale value of the invento-

ry was $26,000. Upon request of the trustee, the bankruptcy court authorized the trustee to grant Second State Bank a senior security interest in half the inventory (and in half its proceeds), to sell all of it, and to use the proceeds in continuing the production of widgets. The bankruptcy court's order was agreeable to Second State Bank, but First Bank appealed it. Should the appellate court uphold the order?

4 Jones owned an apartment building worth $100,000. Having recently suffered serious business reverses and needing immediate cash to pay creditors, Jones sold the building to his brother-in-law, Frampton, for $50,000. That amount was not enough to pay Jones's debts. Ten months later Jones's creditors forced Jones into involuntary bankruptcy. The trustee brought action against Frampton to recover the apartment building for the debtor's estate. Frampton defended on the ground that the sale of the apartment building to him was not a fraudulent conveyance as the trustee contended, but was, rather, a legitimate business transaction that produced for Jones much needed immediate cash at a time when Jones had no knowledge that creditors would eventually force him into bankruptcy. Was the sale of the apartment building a fraudulent conveyance?

5 Bago Corporation, a manufacturer of industrial packaging, experienced financial difficulty as the result of a strike by its employees and eventually could not meet its debt service charges and other expenses. In an attempt to keep the company afloat, Thomas, its chief financial officer, made an unsecured loan of $10,000 to the company. Four months later the strike ended, but by then the market for industrial packaging had softened. Fearing that the company might fail, Thomas sought repayment of the loan. In settlement of the loan, the president of Bago Corporation paid Thomas $10,000 out of the proceeds of recent bag sales. Six months after repayment of the loan, creditors of Bago filed a Chapter 7 petition and forced the company into bankruptcy. Liquidation of company assets produced sufficient funds to pay priority claims, but only enough to pay 10 percent of the claims of nonpriority unsecured creditors. Consequently, the trustee brought suit to avoid as a preferential transfer Bago's repayment of the $10,000 to Thomas. Thomas defended on the ground that the repayment of the loan did not occur on or within 90 days before the filing of the bankruptcy petition and therefore could not be considered a preferential payment. Was the repayment of the loan a preferential transfer?

6 In the bankruptcy situation described in the preceding problem, Bagging Suppliers, Inc. delivered on credit to Bago a load of packaging materials 60 days before the filing of the petition in bankruptcy. Ten days later, Bago paid Bagging Suppliers in full for the materials, less the 2 percent discount allowed to regular customers of Bagging Suppliers for prompt payment of open accounts. The trustee sought to avoid the payment as a preference. Was the payment of Bagging Suppliers a preference?

7 In the liquidation of Blotto, Inc., the following creditors filed timely proofs of claim: *(a)* three employees who had not been paid their wages of $1,000 each for 1 month preceding Blotto's bankruptcy; *(b)* 100 customers of Blotto, each of whom, prior to Blotto's bankruptcy, had paid Blotto a $50 unsecured deposit on pen and pencil sets that Blotto never delivered; *(c)* Second Bank, to which Blotto owed $8,000 secured by a valid, perfected security interest in collateral worth $4,000; *(d)* various administrative officials, lawyers, and accountants whose claims totaled $5,000. The trustee realized $14,500 upon liquidation of the debtor's estate. How much of its claim does each creditor or class of creditors receive?

8 Recognizing that his driveway paving company was in serious financial difficulty, Morton sought and received an unsecured loan of $2,000 from City Small Loan Co. In applying for the loan, Morton intentionally overstated his assets and understated his liabilities, thereby rendering his written financial statement materially false. Five months later Morton was forced into bankruptcy. Funds from the liquidation of Morton's estate were insufficient for unsecured nonpriority creditors to receive a dividend. One of those creditors was First Bank, which held an allowed unsecured claim for $10,000. Realizing that Morton would receive a substantial inheritance approximately a year after bankruptcy, First Bank requested the bankruptcy court to deny Morton a discharge. Should the discharge be denied?

9 In a Chapter 7 proceeding, Swanson received a discharge from her debts. Unsecured nonpriority creditors received only 12 percent of their allowed claims. A week before the discharge was granted, Swanson signed a reaffirmation agreement with her brother-in-law, Hayes, a plumbing contractor who had sold Swanson an air conditioning unit on open account for Swanson's business. The agreement required Swanson to pay, in monthly installments, $3,000 in business debts covered by the discharge. A week after signing the agreement, Swanson had second thoughts and sought to rescind the agreement. Hayes pointed out that the agreement was enforceable under state law. May Swanson rescind the reaffirmation agreement?

10 Sadiron Corporation was undergoing a Chapter 11 reorganization. The debtor proposed a plan that called for all classes of creditors to receive 50 percent of their claims. There was one class of bonds (secured by the total assets of the corporation) and one class of debentures (unsecured debt). Most of the bondholders objected to the plan, and the requisite majority could not be persuaded to vote for it. May the plan be confirmed without the consent of the bondholders?

11   Jones, the sole proprietor of a small business, encountered financial difficulty and sought relief under Chapter 13 of the Bankruptcy Code. In developing her repayment plan, she proposed to pay all creditors in full, but to extend the time for payment and to deprive secured creditors of their contractual rights to repossess collateral or to foreclose mortgages. Two secured creditors objected to the plan: Jones's major supplier of inventory, and the bank that held the mortgage on Jones's residence. May the repayment plan be confirmed over their objections?

APPENDIXES

APPENDIX

1

Uniform
Commercial Code*

Authors' Note: Within recent years, Articles 8 and 9 of the Uniform Commercial Code have been substantially amended. Not all states have adopted the amended versions of those Articles. Consequently, this Appendix includes the 1962 and the 1977 versions of Article 8, and the 1962 and the 1972 versions of Article 9. As of May 1979, two states—Minnesota and West Virginia—have adopted the 1977 version of Article 8, together with a few related 1977 amendments of Articles 1, 5, and 9. As of September 1979, twenty-eight states have adopted the 1972 version of Article 9, together with a few related 1972 amendments of Articles 1, 2, and 5. A list of the thirty-one states is found in Chapter 28 of this volume.

You will notice in Articles 8 and 9 and in a few sections in other Articles some underlined passages and some bracketed passages. The underlined material is new language, added for the 1977 version of Article 8 and for the 1972 version of Article 9. The bracketed material is 1962 language that has been deleted from the amended versions of Articles 8 and 9.

For the 1977 version of Article 8, read everything except the bracketed material. For the 1962 version of Article 8, read everything except the underlined material. Similarly, for the 1972 version of Article 9, read everything except the bracketed material; for the 1962 version of Article 9, read everything except the underlined material.

ARTICLE 1: GENERAL PROVISIONS

Part 1 Short Title, Construction, Application and Subject Matter of the Act

§1–101. Short title. This act shall be known and may be cited as Uniform Commercial Code.

§1–102. Purposes; Rules of Construction; Variation by Agreement.

(1) This Act shall be liberally construed and applied to promote its underlying purposes and policies.

(2) Underlying purposes and policies of this Act are

(a) to simplify, clarify and modernize the law governing commercial transactions;

(b) to permit the continued expansion of commercial practices through custom, usage and agreement of the parties;

(c) to make uniform the law among the various jurisdictions.

(3) The effect of provisions of this Act may be varied by agreement, except as otherwise provided in this Act and except that the obligations of good faith, diligence, reasonableness and care prescribed by this Act may not be disclaimed by agreement but the parties may by agreement determine the standards by which the performance of such obligations is to be measured if such standards are not manifestly unreasonable.

(4) The presence in certain provisions of this Act of the words "unless otherwise agreed" or words of similar import does not imply that the effect of other provisions may not be varied by agreement under subsection (3).

(5) In this Act unless the context otherwise requires

(a) words in the singular number include the plural, and in the plural include the singular;

(b) words of the masculine gender include the feminine and the neuter, and when the sense so indicates words of the neuter gender may refer to any gender.

§1–103. Supplementary General Principles of Law Applicable. Unless displaced by the particular provisions of this Act, the principles of law and equity, including the law merchant and the law relative to capacity to contract, principal and agent, estoppel, fraud, misrepresentation, duress, coercion, mistake, bankruptcy, or other validating or invalidating cause shall supplement its provisions.

§1–104. Construction Against Implicit Repeal. This Act being a general act intended as a unified coverage of its subject matter, no part of it shall be deemed to be impliedly repealed by subsequent legislation if such construction can reasonably be avoided.

§1–105. Territorial Application of the Act; Parties' Power to Choose Applicable Law.
(1) Except as provided hereafter in this section, when a transaction bears a reasonable relation to this state and also to another state or nation the parties may agree that the law either of this state or of such other state or nation shall govern their rights and duties. Failing such agreement this Act applies to transactions bearing an appropriate relation to this state.

(2) Where one of the following provisions of this Act specifies the applicable law, that provision governs and a contrary agreement is effective only to the extent permitted by the law (including the conflict of laws rules) so specified:

Rights of creditors against sold goods. Section 2–402.

Applicability of the Article on Bank Deposits and Collections. Section 4–102.

Bulk transfers subject to the Article on Bulk Transfers. Section 6–102.

Applicability of the Article on Investment Securities. Section 8–106.

[Policy and scope of the Article on Secured Transactions. Sections 9–102 and 9–103.]

Perfection provisions of the Article on Secured Transactions. Section 9–103.

§1–106. Remedies to Be Liberally Administered.
(1) The remedies provided by this Act shall be liberally administered to the end that the aggrieved party may be put in as good a position as if the other party had fully performed but neither consequential or special nor penal damages may be had except as specifically provided in this Act or by other rule of law.

(2) Any right or obligation declared by this Act is enforceable by action unless the provision declaring it specifies a different and limited effect.

§1–107. Waiver or Renunciation of Claim or Right After Breach. Any claim or right arising out of an alleged breach can be discharged in whole or in part without consideration by a written waiver or renunciation signed and delivered by the aggrieved party.

§1–108. Severability. If any provision or clause of this Act or application thereof to any person or circumstances is held invalid, such invalidity shall not affect other provisions or applications of the Act which can be given effect without the invalid provision or application, and to this end the provisions of this Act are declared to be severable.

§1–109. Section Captions. Section captions are parts of this Act.

Part 2   General Definitions and Principles of Interpretation

§1–201. General Definitions *(1977 Amendments)*. Subject to additional definitions contained in the subsequent Articles of this Act which are applicable to specific Articles or Parts thereof, and unless the context otherwise requires, in this Act.

(1) "Action" in the sense of a judicial proceeding includes recoupment, counterclaim, set-off, suit in equity and any other proceedings in which rights are determined.

(2) "Aggrieved party" means a party entitled to resort to a remedy.

(3) "Agreement" means the bargain of the parties in fact as found in their language or by implication from other circumstances including course of dealing or usage of trade or course of performance as provided in this Act (Section 1–205 and 2–208). Whether an agreement has legal consequences is determined by the provisions of this Act, if applicable; otherwise by the law of contracts (Section 1–103). (Compare "Contract".)

(4) "Bank" means any person engaged in the business of banking.

(5) "Bearer" means the person in possession of an instrument, document of title, or certificated security payable to bearer or indorsed in blank.

(6) "Bill of lading" means a document evidencing the receipt of goods for shipment issued by a person engaged in the business of transporting or forwarding goods, and includes an airbill. "Airbill" means a document serving for

air transportation as a bill of lading does for marine or rail transportation, and includes an air consignment note or air waybill.

(**7**) "Branch" includes a separately incorporated foreign branch of a bank.

(**8**) "Burden of establishing" a fact means the burden of persuading the triers of fact that the existence of the fact is more probable than its non-existence.

(**9**) "Buyer in ordinary course of business" means a person who in good faith and without knowledge that the sale to him is in violation of the ownership rights or security interest of a third party in the goods buys in ordinary course from a person in the business of selling goods of that kind but does not include a pawnbroker. All persons who sell minerals or the like (including oil and gas) at wellhead or minehead shall be deemed to be persons in the business of selling goods of that kind. "Buying" may be for cash or by exchange of other property or on secured or unsecured credit and includes receiving goods or documents of title under a pre-existing contract for sale but does not include a transfer in bulk or as security for or in total or partial satisfaction of a money debt.

(**10**) "Conspicuous": A term or clause is conspicuous when it is so written that a reasonable person against whom it is to operate ought to have noticed it. A printed heading in capitals (as: Non-Negotiable Bill of Lading) is conspicuous. Language in the body of a form is "conspicuous" if it is in larger or other contrasting type or color. But in a telegram any stated term is "conspicuous". Whether a term or clause is "conspicuous" or not is for decision by the court.

(**11**) "Contract" means the total legal obligation which results from the parties' agreement as affected by this Act and any other applicable rules of law. (Compare "Agreement".)

(**12**) "Creditor" includes a general creditor, a secured creditor, a lien creditor and any representative of creditors, including an assignee for the benefit of creditors, a trustee in bankruptcy, a receiver in equity and an executor or administrator of an insolvent debtor's or assignor's estate.

(**13**) "Defendant" includes a person in the position of defendant in a cross-action or counterclaim.

(**14**) "Delivery" with respect to instruments, documents of title, chattel paper, or certificated securities means voluntary transfer of possession.

(**15**) "Document of title" includes bill of lading, dock warrant, dock receipt, warehouse receipt or order for the delivery of goods, and also any other document which in the regular course of business or financing is treated as adequately evidencing that the person in possession of it is entitled to receive, hold and dispose of the document and the goods it covers. To be a document of title a document must purport to be issued by or addressed to a bailee and purport to cover goods in the bailee's possession which are either identified or are fungible portions of an identified mass.

(**16**) "Fault" means wrongful act, omission or breach.

(**17**) "Fungible" with respect to goods or securities means goods or securities of which any unit is, by nature or usage of trade, the equivalent of any other like unit. Goods which are not fungible shall be deemed fungible for the purposes of this Act to the extent that under a particular agreement or document unlike units are treated as equivalents.

(**18**) "Genuine" means free of forgery or counterfeiting.

(**19**) "Good faith" means honesty in fact in the conduct or transaction concerned.

(**20**) "Holder" means a person who is in possession of a document of title or a certificated [a] instrument or an investment security drawn, issued or indorsed to him or to his order or to bearer or in blank.

(**21**) To "honor" is to pay or to accept and pay, or where a credit so engages to purchase or discount a draft complying with the terms of the credit.

(**22**) "Insolvency proceedings" includes any assignment for the benefit of creditors or other proceedings intended to liquidate or rehabilitate the estate of the person involved.

(**23**) A person is "insolvent" who either has ceased to pay his debts in the ordinary course of business or cannot pay his debts as they become due or is insolvent within the meaning of the federal bankruptcy law.

(**24**) "Money" means a medium of exchange authorized or adopted by a domestic or foreign government as part of its currency.

(**25**) A person has "notice" of a fact when

(**a**) he has actual knowledge of it; or

(**b**) he has received a notice or notification of it; or

(**c**) from all the facts and circumstances known to him at the time in question he has reason to know that it exists.

A person "knows" or has "knowledge" of a fact when he has actual knowledge of it. "Discover" or "learn" or a word or phrase of similar import refers to knowledge rather than to reason to know. The time and circumstances under which a notice or notification may cease to be effective are not determined by this Act.

(**26**) A person "notifies" or "gives" a notice or notification to another by taking such steps as may be reasonably required to inform the other in ordinary course whether or not such other actually comes to know of it. A person "receives" a notice or notification when

(**a**) it comes to his attention; or

(**b**) it is duly delivered at the place of business through which the contract was made or at any other place held out by him as the place for receipt of such communications.

(**27**) Notice, knowledge or a notice or notification received by an organization is effective for a particular transaction from the time when it is brought to the attention of the individual conducting that transaction, and in any event from the time when it would have been brought to his attention if the organization had exercised due diligence. An organization exercises due diligence if it maintains reasonable routines for communicating significant information to the person conducting the transaction and there is reasonable compliance with the routines. Due diligence does not require an individual acting for the organization to communicate information unless such communication is part of his regular duties or unless he has reason to know of the transaction and that the transaction would be materially affected by the information.

(**28**) "Organization" includes a corporation, government or governmental subdivision or agency, business trust, estate, trust, partnership or association, two or more persons having a joint or common interest, or any other legal or commercial entity.

(**29**) "Party", as distinct from "third party", means a person who has engaged in a transaction or made an agreement within this Act.

(**30**) "Person" includes an individual or an organization (See Section 1–102).

(**31**) "Presumption" or "presumed" means that the trier of fact must find the existence of the fact presumed unless and until evidence is introduced which would support a finding of its non-existence.

(**32**) "Purchase" includes taking by sale, discount, negotiation, mortgage, pledge, lien, issue or re-issue, gift or any other voluntary transaction creating an interest in property.

(**33**) "Purchaser" means a person who takes by purchase.

(**34**) "Remedy" means any remedial right to which an aggrieved party is entitled with or without resort to a tribunal.

(**35**) "Representative" includes an agent, an officer of a corporation or association, and a trustee, executor or administrator of an estate, or any other person empowered to act for another.

(**36**) "Rights" includes remedies.

(**37**) "Security interest" means an interest in personal property or fixtures which secures payment or performance of an obligation. The retention or reservation of title by a seller of goods notwithstanding shipment or delivery to the buyer (Section 2–401) is limited in effect to a reservation of a "security interest". The term also includes any interest of a buyer of accounts[,] or chattel paper[, or contract rights] which is subject to Article 9. The special property interest of a buyer of goods on identification of such goods to a contract for sale under Section 2–401 is not a "security interest", but a buyer may also acquire a "security interest" by complying with Article 9. Unless a lease or consignment is intended as security, reservation of title thereunder is not a "security interest" but a consignment is in any event subject to the provisions on consignment sales (Section 2–326). Whether a lease is intended as security is to be determined by the facts of each case; however, (a) the inclusion of an option to purchase does not of itself make the lease one intended for security, and (b) an agreement that upon compliance with the terms of the lease the lessee shall become or has the option to become the owner of the property for no additional consideration or for a nominal consideration does make the lease one intended for security.

(**38**) "Send" in connection with any writing or notice means to deposit in the mail or deliver for transmission by any other usual means of communication with postage or cost of transmission provided for and properly addressed and in the case of an instrument to an address specified thereon or otherwise agreed, or if there be none to any address reasonable under the circumstances. The receipt of any writing or notice within the time at which it would have arrived if properly sent has the effect of a proper sending.

(**39**) "Signed" includes any symbol executed or adopted by a party with present intention to authenticate a writing.

(**40**) "Surety" includes guarantor.

(**41**) "Telegram" includes a message transmitted by radio, teletype, cable, any mechanical method of transmission, or the like.

(**42**) "Term" means that portion of an agreement which relates to a particular matter.

(**43**) "Unauthorized" signature or indorsement means one made without actual, implied or apparent authority and includes a forgery.

(**44**) "Value". Except as otherwise provided with respect to negotiable instruments and bank collections (Sections 3–303, 4–208 and 4–209) a person gives "value" for rights if he acquires them

(a) in return for a binding commitment to extend credit or for the extension of immediately available credit whether or not drawn upon and whether or not a chargeback is provided for in the event of difficulties in collection; or

(b) as security for or in total or partial satisfaction of a pre-existing claim; or

(c) by accepting delivery pursuant to a pre-existing contract for purchase; or

(d) generally, in return for any consideration sufficient to support a simple contract.

(**45**) "Warehouse receipt" means a receipt issued by a person engaged in the business of storing goods for hire.

(**46**) "Written" or "writing" includes printing, typewriting or any other intentional reduction to tangible form. As amended 1962 and 1972.

§1–201. General Definitions (1977 Amendments).

Subject to additional definitions contained in the subsequent Articles of this Act which are applicable to specific Articles or Parts thereof, and unless the context otherwise requires, in this Act:

* * *

(5) "Bearer" means the person in possession of an instrument, document of title, or certificated security payable to bearer or indorsed in blank.

* * *

(14) "Delivery" with respect to instruments, documents of title, chattel paper, or certificated securities means voluntary transfer of possession.

* * *

(20) "Holder" means a person who is in possession of a document of title or an instrument or [an] a certificated investment security drawn, issued, or indorsed to him or his order or to bearer or in blank.

* * *

§1–202. Prima Facie Evidence by Third Party Documents. A document in due form purporting to be a bill of lading, policy or certificate of insurance, official weigher's or inspector's certificate, consular invoice, or any other document authorized or required by the contract to be issued by a third party shall be prima facie evidence of its own authenticity and genuineness and of the facts stated in the document by the third party.

§1–203. Obligation of Good Faith. Every contract or duty within this Act imposes an obligation of good faith in its performance or enforcement.

§1–204. Time; Reasonable Time; "Seasonably".

(1) Whenever this Act requires any action to be taken within a reasonable time, any time which is not manifestly unreasonable may be fixed by agreement.

(2) What is a reasonable time for taking any action depends on the nature, purpose and circumstances of such action.

(3) An action is taken "seasonably" when it is taken at or within the time agreed or if no time is agreed at or within a reasonable time.

§1–205. Course of Dealing and Usage of Trade.

(1) A course of dealing is a sequence of previous conduct between the parties to a particular transaction which is fairly to be regarded as establishing a common basis of understanding for interpreting their expressions and other conduct.

(2) A usage of trade is any practice or method of dealing having such regularity of observance in a place, vocation or trade as to justify an expectation that it will be observed with respect to the transaction in question. The existence and scope of such a usage are to be proved as facts. If it is established that such a usage is embodied in a written trade code or similar writing the interpretation of the writing is for the court.

(3) A course of dealing between parties and any usage of trade in the vocation or trade in which they are engaged or of which they are or should be aware give particular meaning to and supplement or qualify terms of an agreement.

(4) The express terms of an agreement and an applicable course of dealing or usage of trade shall be construed wherever reasonable as consistent with each other; but when such construction is unreasonable express terms control both course of dealing and usage of trade and course of dealing controls usage of trade.

(5) An applicable usage of trade in the place where any part of performance is to occur shall be used in interpreting the agreement as to that part of the performance.

(6) Evidence of a relevant usage of trade offered by one party is not admissible unless and until he has given the other party such notice as the court finds sufficient to prevent unfair surprise to the latter.

§1–206. Statute of Frauds for Kinds of Personal Property Not Otherwise Covered.

(1) Except in the cases described in subsection (2) of this section a contract for the sale of personal property is not enforceable by way of action or defense beyond five thousand dollars in amount or value of remedy unless there is some writing which indicates that a contract for sale has been made between the parties at a defined or stated price, reasonably identifies the subject matter, and is signed by the party against whom enforcement is sought or by his authorized agent.

(2) Subsection (1) of this section does not apply to contracts for the sale of goods (Section 2–201) nor of securities (Section 8–319) nor to security agreements (Section 9–203).

§1–207. Performance or Acceptance Under Reservation of Rights. A party who with explicit reservation of rights performs or promises performance or assents to performance in a manner demanded or offered by the other party does not thereby prejudice the rights reserved. Such words as "without prejudice", "under protest" or the like are sufficient.

§1–208. Option to Accelerate at Will. A term providing that one party or his successor in interest may accelerate payment or performance or require collateral or additional collateral "at will" or "when he deems himself insecure" or in words of similar import shall be construed to mean that he shall have power to do so only if he in good faith believes that the prospect of payment or performance is impaired. The burden of establishing lack of good faith is on the party against whom the power has been exercised.

§1–209. Subordinated Obligations. An obligation may be issued as subordinated to payment of another obligation of the person obligated, or a creditor may subordinate his right to payment of an obligation by agreement with either the person obligated or another creditor of the person obligated. Such a subordination does not create a security interest as against either the common debtor or a subordinated creditor. This section shall be construed as declaring the law as it existed prior to the enactment of this section and not as modifying it. Added 1966.

Note: *This new section is proposed as an optional provision to make it clear that a subordination agreement does not create a security interest unless so intended.*

ARTICLE 2: SALES

Part 1 Short Title, General Construction and Subject Matter

§2–101. Short Title. This Article shall be known and may be cited as Uniform Commercial Code—Sales.

§2–102. Scope; Certain Security and Other Transactions Excluded From This Article. Unless the context otherwise requires, this Article applies to transactions in goods; it does not apply to any transaction which although in the form of an unconditional contract to sell or present sale is intended to operate only as a security transaction nor does this Article impair or repeal any statute regulating sales to consumers, farmers or other specified classes of buyers.

§2–103. Definitions and Index of Definitions.

(1) In this Article unless the context otherwise requires

(a) "Buyer" means a person who buys or contracts to buy goods.

(b) "Good faith" in the case of a merchant means honesty in fact and the observance of reasonable commercial standards of fair dealing in the trade.

(c) "Receipt" of goods means taking physical possession of them.

(d) "Seller" means a person who sells or contracts to sell goods.

(2) Other definitions applying to this Article or to specified Parts thereof, and the sections in which they appear are:

"Acceptance". Section 2–606.
"Banker's credit". Section 2–325.
"Between merchants". Section 2–104.

"Cancellation". Section 2–106(4).
"Commercial unit". Section 2–105.
"Confirmed credit". Section 2–325.
"Conforming to contract". Section 2–106.
"Contract for sale". Section 2–106.
"Cover". Section 2–712.
"Entrusting". Section 2–403.
"Financing agency". Section 2–104.
"Future goods". Section 2–105.
"Goods". Section 2–105.
"Identification". Section 2–501.
"Installment contract". Section 2–612.
"Letter of Credit". Section 2–325.
"Lot". Section 2–105.
"Merchant". Section 2–104.
"Overseas". Section 2–323.
"Person in position of seller". Section 2–707.
"Present sale". Section 2–106.
"Sale". Section 2–106.
"Sale on approval". Section 2–326.
"Sale on return". Section 2–326.
"Termination". Section 2–106.

(3) The following definitions in other Articles apply to this Article:

"Check". Section 3–104.
"Consignee". Section 7–102.
"Consignor". Section 7–102.
"Consumer goods". Section 9–109.
"Dishonor". Section 3–507.
"Draft". Section 3–104.

(4) In addition Article 1 contains general definitions and principles of construction and interpretation applicable throughout this article.

§2–104. Definitions: "Merchant"; "Between Merchants"; "Financing Agency".

(1) "Merchant" means a person who deals in goods of the kind or otherwise by his occupation holds himself out as having knowledge or skill peculiar to the practices or goods involved in the transaction or to whom such knowledge or skill may be attributed by his employment of an agent or broker or other intermediary who by his occupation holds himself out as having such knowledge or skill.

(2) "Financing agency" means a bank, finance company or other person who in the ordinary course of business makes advances against goods or documents of title or who by arrangement with either the seller or the buyer intervenes in ordinary course to make or collect payment due or claimed under the contract for sale, as by purchasing or paying the seller's draft or making advances against it or by merely taking it for collection whether or not documents of title accompany the draft. "Financing agency" includes also a bank or other person who similarly intervenes between

persons who are in the position of seller and buyer in respect of the goods (Section 2–707).

(3) "Between merchants" means in any transaction with respect to which both parties are chargeable with the knowledge or skill of merchants.

§2–105. Definitions: Transferability; "Goods"; "Future" Goods; "Lot"; "Commercial Unit".

(1) "Goods" means all things (including specially manufactured goods) which are movable at the time of identification to the contract for sale other than the money in which the price is to be paid, investment securities (Article 8) and things in action. "Goods" also includes the unborn young of animals and growing crops and other identified things attached to realty as described in the section on goods to be severed from realty (Section 2–107).

(2) Goods must be both existing and identified before any interest in them can pass. Goods which are not both existing and identified are "future" goods. A purported present sale of future goods or of any interest therein operates as a contract to sell.

(3) There may be a sale of a part interest in existing identified goods.

(4) An undivided share in an identified bulk of fungible goods is sufficiently identified to be sold although the quantity of the bulk is not determined. Any agreed proportion of such a bulk or any quantity thereof agreed upon by number, weight or other measure may to the extent of the seller's interest in the bulk be sold to the buyer who then becomes an owner in common.

(5) "Lot" means a parcel or a single article which is the subject matter of a separate sale or delivery, whether or not it is sufficient to perform the contract.

(6) "Commercial unit" means such a unit of goods as by commercial usage is a single whole for purposes of sale and division of which materially impairs its character or value on the market or in use. A commercial unit may be a single article (as a machine) or a set of articles (as a suite of furniture or an assortment of sizes) or a quantity (as a bale, gross, or carload) or any other unit treated in use or in the relevant market as a single whole.

§2–106. Definitions: "Contract"; "Agreement"; "Contract for Sale"; "Sale"; "Present Sale"; "Conforming" to Contract; "Termination"; "Cancellation".

(1) In this Article unless the context otherwise requires "contract" and "agreement" are limited to those relating to the present or future sale of goods. "Contract for sale" includes both a present sale of goods and a contract to sell goods at a future time. A "sale" consists in the passing of title from the seller to the buyer for a price (Section 2–401). A "present sale" means a sale which is accomplished by the making of the contract.

(2) Goods or conduct including any part of a performance are "conforming" or conform to the contract when they are in accordance with the obligations under the contract.

(3) "Termination" occurs when either party pursuant to a power created by agreement or law puts an end to the contract otherwise than for its breach. On "termination" all obligations which are still executory on both sides are discharged but any right based on prior breach or performance survives.

(4) "Cancellation" occurs when either party puts an end to the contract for breach by the other and its effect is the same as that of "termination" except that the cancelling party also retains any remedy for breach of the whole contract or any unperformed balance.

§2–107. Goods to Be Severed From Realty: Recording.

(1) A contract for the sale of [timber,] minerals or the like (including oil and gas) or a structure or its materials to be removed from realty is a contract for the sale of goods within this Article if they are to be severed by the seller but until severance a purported present sale thereof which is not effective as a transfer of an interest in land is effective only as a contract to sell.

(2) A contract for the sale apart from the land of growing crops or other things attached to realty and capable of severance without material harm thereto but not described in subsection (1) or of timber to be cut is a contract for the sale of goods within this Article whether the subject matter is to be severed by the buyer or by the seller even though it forms part of the realty at the time of contracting, and the parties can by identification effect a present sale before severance.

(3) The provisions of this section are subject to any third party rights provided by the law relating to realty records, and the contract for sale may be executed and recorded as a document transferring an interest in land and shall then constitute notice to third parties of the buyer's rights under the contract for sale.

Part 2 Form, Formation and Readjustment of Contract

§2–201. Formal Requirements; Statute of Frauds.

(1) Except as otherwise provided in this section a contract for the sale of goods for the price of $500 or more is not enforceable by way of action or defense unless there is some writing sufficient to indicate that a contract for sale has been made between the parties and signed by the party against whom enforcement is sought or by his authorized agent or broker. A writing is not insufficient because it omits or incorrectly states a term agreed upon but the contract is not enforceable under this paragraph beyond the quantity of goods shown in such writing.

(2) Between merchants if within a reasonable time a

writing in confirmation of the contract and sufficient against the sender is received and the party receiving it has reason to know its contents, it satisfies the requirements of subsection (1) against such party unless written notice of objection to its contents is given within 10 days after it is received.

(3) A contract which does not satisfy the requirements of subsection (1) but which is valid in other respects is enforceable

(a) if the goods are to be specially manufactured for the buyer and are not suitable for sale to others in the ordinary course of the seller's business and the seller, before notice of repudiation is received and under circumstances which reasonably indicate that the goods are for the buyer, has made either a substantial beginning of their manufacture or commitments for their procurement; or

(b) if the party against whom enforcement is sought admits in his pleading, testimony or otherwise in court that a contract for sale was made, but the contract is not enforceable under this provision beyond the quantity of goods admitted; or

(c) with respect to goods for which payment has been made and accepted or which have been received and accepted (Sec. 2–606.)

§2–202. Final Written Expression: Parol or Extrinsic Evidence. Terms with respect to which the confirmatory memoranda of the parties agree or which are otherwise set forth in a writing intended by the parties as a final expression of their agreement with respect to such terms as are included therein may not be contradicted by evidence of any prior agreement or of a contemporaneous oral agreement but may be explained or supplemented

(a) by course of dealing or usage of trade (Section 1–205) or by course of performance (Section 2–208); and

(b) by evidence of consistent additional terms unless the court finds the writing to have been intended also as a complete and exclusive statement of the terms of the agreement.

§2–203. Seals Inoperative. The affixing of a seal to a writing evidencing a contract for sale or an offer to buy or sell goods does not constitute the writing a sealed instrument and the law with respect to sealed instruments does not apply to such a contract or offer.

§2–204. Formation in General.

(1) A contract for sale of goods may be made in any manner sufficient to show agreement, including conduct by both parties which recognizes the existence of such a contract.

(2) An agreement sufficient to constitute a contract for sale may be found even though the moment of its making is undetermined.

(3) Even though one or more terms are left open a contract for sale does not fail for indefiniteness if the parties have intended to make a contract and there is a reasonably certain basis for giving an appropriate remedy.

§2–205. Firm Offers. An offer by a merchant to buy or sell goods in a signed writing which by its terms gives assurance that it will be held open is not revocable, for lack of consideration, during the time stated or if no time is stated for a reasonable time, but in no event may such period of irrevocability exceed three months; but any such term of assurance on a form supplied by the offeree must be separately signed by the offeror.

§2–206. Offer and Acceptance in Formation of Contract.

(1) Unless otherwise unambiguously indicated by the language or circumstances

(a) an offer to make a contract shall be construed as inviting acceptance in any manner and by any medium reasonable in the circumstances;

(b) an order or other offer to buy goods for prompt or current shipment shall be construed as inviting acceptance either by a prompt promise to ship or by the prompt or current shipment of conforming or non-conforming goods, but such a shipment of non-conforming goods does not constitute an acceptance if the seller seasonably notifies the buyer that the shipment is offered only as an accommodation to the buyer.

(2) Where the beginning of a requested performance is a reasonable mode of acceptance an offeror who is not notified of acceptance within a reasonable time may treat the offer as having lapsed before acceptance.

§2–207. Additional Terms in Acceptance or Confirmation.

(1) A definite and seasonable expression of acceptance or a written confirmation which is sent within a reasonable time operates as an acceptance even though it states terms additional to or different from those offered or agreed upon, unless acceptance is expressly made conditional on assent to the additional or different terms.

(2) The additional terms are to be construed as proposals for addition to the contract. Between merchants such terms become part of the contract unless:

(a) the offer expressly limits acceptance to the terms of the offer;

(b) they materially alter it; or

(c) notification of objection to them has already been given or is given within a reasonable time after notice of them is received.

(3) Conduct by both parties which recognizes the existence of a contract is sufficient to establish a contract for sale although the writings of the parties do not otherwise establish a contract. In such case the terms of the particular contract consist of those terms on which the writings of the

parties agree, together with any supplementary terms incorporated under any other provisions of this Act.

§2–208. Course of Performance or Practical Construction.

(1) Where the contract for sale involves repeated occasions for performance by either party with knowledge of the nature of the performance and opportunity for objection to it by the other, any course of performance accepted or acquiesced in without objection shall be relevant to determine the meaning of the agreement.

(2) The express terms of the agreement and any such course of performance, as well as any course of dealing and usage of trade, shall be construed whenever reasonable as consistent with each other; but when such construction is unreasonable, express terms shall control course of performance and course of performance shall control both course of dealing and usage of trade (Section 1–205).

(3) Subject to the provisions of the next section on modification and waiver, such course of performance shall be relevant to show a waiver or modification of any term inconsistent with such course of performance.

§2–209. Modification, Rescission and Waiver.

(1) An agreement modifying a contract within this Article needs no consideration to be binding.

(2) A signed agreement which excludes modifcation or rescission except by a signed writing cannot be otherwise modified or rescinded, but except as between merchants such a requirement on a form supplied by the merchant must be separately signed by the other party.

(3) The requirements of the statute of frauds section of this Article (Section 2–201) must be satisfied if the contract as modified is within its provisions.

(4) Although an attempt at modification or rescission does not satisfy the requirements of subsection (2) or (3) it can operate as a waiver.

(5) A party who has made a waiver affecting an executory portion of the contract may retract the waiver by reasonable notification received by the other party that strict performance will be required of any term waived, unless the retraction would be unjust in view of a material change of position in reliance on the waiver.

§2–210. Delegation of Performance; Assignment of Rights.

(1) A party may perform his duty through a delegate unless otherwise agreed or unless the other party has a substantial interest in having his original promisor perform or control the acts required by the contract. No delegation of performance relieves the party delegating of any duty to perform or any liability for breach.

(2) Unless otherwise agreed all rights of either seller or buyer can be assigned except where the assignment would materially change the duty of the other party, or increase materially the burden or risk imposed on him by his contract, or impair materially his chance of obtaining return performance. A right to damages for breach of the whole contract or a right arising out of the assignor's due performance of his entire obligation can be assigned despite agreement otherwise.

(3) Unless the circumstances indicate the contrary a prohibition of assignment of "the contract" is to be construed as barring only the delegation to the assignee of the assignor's performance.

(4) An assignment of "the contract" or of "all my rights under the contract" or an assignment in similar general terms is an assignment of rights and unless the language or the circumstances (as in an assignment for security) indicate the contrary, it is a delegation of performance of the duties of the assignor and its acceptance by the assignee constitutes a promise by him to perform those duties. This promise is enforceable by either the assignor or the other party to the original contract.

(5) The other party may treat any assignment which delegates performance as creating reasonable grounds for insecurity and may without prejudice to his rights against the assignor demand assurances from the assignee (Section 2–609).

Part 3   General Obligation and Construction of Contract

§2–301. General Obligations of Parties.
The obligation of the seller is to transfer and deliver and that of the buyer is to accept and pay in accordance with the contract.

§2–302. Unconscionable Contract or Clause.

(1) If the court as a matter of law finds the contract or any clause of the contract to have been unconscionable at the time it was made the court may refuse to enforce the contract, or it may enforce the remainder of the contract without the unconscionable clause, or it may so limit the application of any unconscionable clause as to avoid any unconscionable result.

(2) When it is claimed or appears to the court that the contract or any clause thereof may be unconscionable the parties shall be afforded a reasonable opportunity to present evidence as to its commercial setting, purpose and effect to aid the court in making the determination.

§2–303. Allocation or Division of Risks.
Where this Article allocates a risk or a burden as between the parties "unless otherwise agreed", the agreement may not only shift the allocation but may also divide the risk or burden.

§2–304. Price Payable in Money, Goods, Realty, or Otherwise.

(1) The price can be made payable in money or otherwise. If it is payable in whole or in part in goods each party is a seller of the goods which he is to transfer.

(2) Even though all or part of the price is payable in an

interest in realty the transfer of the goods and the seller's obligations with reference to them are subject to this Article, but not the transfer of the interest in realty or the transferor's obligations in connection therewith.

§2–305. Open Price Term.

(1) The parties if they so intend can conclude a contract for sale even though the price is not settled. In such a case the price is a reasonable price at the time for delivery if

    (a) nothing is said as to price; or

    (b) the price is left to be agreed by the parties and they fail to agree; or

    (c) the price is to be fixed in terms of some agreed market or other standard as set or recorded by a third person or agency and it is not so set or recorded.

(2) A price to be fixed by the seller or by the buyer means a price for him to fix in good faith.

(3) When a price left to be fixed otherwise than by agreement of the parties fails to be fixed through fault of one party the other may at his option treat the contract as cancelled or himself fix a reasonable price.

(4) Where, however, the parties intend not to be bound unless the price be fixed or agreed and it is not fixed or agreed there is no contract. In such a case the buyer must return any goods already received or if unable so to do must pay their reasonable value at the time of delivery and the seller must return any portion of the price paid on account.

§2–306. Output, Requirements and Exclusive Dealings.

(1) A term which measures the quantity by the output of the seller or the requirements of the buyer means such actual output or requirements as may occur in good faith, except that no quantity unreasonably disproportionate to any stated estimate or in the absence of a stated estimate to any normal or otherwise comparable prior output or requirements may be tendered or demanded.

(2) A lawful agreement by either the seller or the buyer for exclusive dealing in the kind of goods concerned imposes unless otherwise agreed an obligation by the seller to use best efforts to supply the goods and by the buyer to use best efforts to promote their sale.

§2–307. Delivery in Single Lot or Several Lots.
Unless otherwise agreed all goods called for by a contract for sale must be tendered in a single delivery and payment is due only on such tender but where the circumstances give either party the right to make or demand delivery in lots the price if it can be apportioned may be demanded for each lot.

§2–308. Absence of Specified Place for Delivery.
Unless otherwise agreed

    (a) the place for delivery of goods is the seller's place of business or if he has none his residence; but

    (b) in a contract for sale of identified goods which to the knowledge of the parties at the time of contracting are in some other place, that place is the place for their delivery; and

    (c) documents of title may be delivered through customary banking channels.

§2–309. Absence of Specific Time Provisions; Notice of Termination.

(1) The time for shipment or delivery or any other action under a contract if not provided in this Article or agreed upon shall be a reasonable time.

(2) Where the contract provides for successive performances but is indefinite in duration it is valid for a reasonable time but unless otherwise agreed may be terminated at any time by either party.

(3) Termination of a contract by one party except on the happening of an agreed event requires that reasonable notification be received by the other party and an agreement dispensing with notification is invalid if its operation would be unconscionable.

§2–310. Open Time for Payment or Running of Credit; Authority To Ship Under Reservation.
Unless otherwise agreed

    (a) payment is due at the time and place at which the buyer is to receive the goods even though the place of shipment is the place of delivery; and

    (b) if the seller is authorized to send the goods he may ship them under reservation, and may tender the documents of title, but the buyer may inspect the goods after their arrival before payment is due unless such inspection is inconsistent with the terms of the contract (Section 2–513); and

    (c) if delivery is authorized and made by way of documents of title otherwise than by subsection (b) then payment is due at the time and place at which the buyer is to receive the documents regardless of where the goods are to be received; and

    (d) where the seller is required or authorized to ship the goods on credit the credit period runs from the time of shipment but post-dating the invoice or delaying its dispatch will correspondingly delay the starting of the credit period.

§2–311. Options and Cooperation Respecting Performance.

(1) An agreement for sale which is otherwise sufficiently definite (subsection (3) of Section 2–204) to be a contract is not made invalid by the fact that it leaves particulars of performance to be specified by one of the parties. Any such specification must be made in good faith and within limits set by commercial reasonableness.

(2) Unless otherwise agreed specifications relating to assortment of the goods are at the buyer's option and except as otherwise provided in subsections (1) (c) and (3) of Section

2–319 specifications or arrangements relating to shipment are at the seller's option.

(3) Where such specification would materially affect the other party's performance but is not seasonably made or where one party's cooperation is necessary to the agreed performance of the other but is not seasonably forthcoming, the other party in addition to all other remedies

(a) is excused for any resulting delay in his own performance; and

(b) may also either proceed to perform in any reasonable manner or after the time for a material part of his own performance treat the failure to specify or to cooperate as a breach by failure to deliver or accept the goods.

§2–312. Warranty of Title and Against Infringement; Buyer's Obligation Against Infringement.

(1) Subject to subsection (2) there is in a contract for sale a warranty by the seller that

(a) the title conveyed shall be good, and its transfer rightful; and

(b) the goods shall be delivered free from any security interest or other lien or encumbrance of which the buyer at the time of contracting has no knowledge.

(2) A warranty under subsection (1) will be excluded or modified only by specific language or by circumstances which give the buyer reason to know that the person selling does not claim title in himself or that he is purporting to sell only such right or title as he or a third person may have.

(3) Unless otherwise agreed a seller who is a merchant regularly dealing in goods of the kind warrants that the goods shall be delivered free of the rightful claim of any third person by way of infringement or the like but a buyer who furnishes specifications to the seller must hold the seller harmless against any such claim which arises out of compliance with the specifications.

§2–313. Express Warranties by Affirmation, Promise, Description, Sample.

(1) Express warranties by the seller are created as follows:

(a) Any affirmation of fact or promise made by the seller to the buyer which relates to the goods and becomes part of the basis of the bargain creates an express warranty that the goods shall conform to the affirmation or promise.

(b) Any description of the goods which is made part of the basis of the bargain creates an express warranty that the goods shall conform to the description.

(c) Any sample or model which is made part of the basis of the bargain creates an express warranty that the whole of the goods shall conform to the sample or model.

(2) It is not necessary to the creation of an express warranty that the seller use formal words such as "warrant" or "guarantee" or that he have a specific intention to make a warranty, but an affirmation merely of the value of the goods or a statement purporting to be merely the seller's opinion or commendation of the goods does not create a warranty.

§2–314. Implied Warranty: Merchantability; Usage of Trade.

(1) Unless excluded or modified (Section 2–316), a warranty that the goods shall be merchantable is implied in a contract for their sale if the seller is a merchant with respect to goods of that kind. Under this section the serving for value of food or drink to be consumed either on the premises or elsewhere is a sale.

(2) Goods to be merchantable must be at least such as

(a) pass without objection in the trade under the contract description; and

(b) in the case of fungible goods, are of fair average quality within the description; and

(c) are fit for the ordinary purposes for which such goods are used; and

(d) run, within the variations permitted by the agreement, of even kind, quality and quantity within each unit and among all units involved; and

(e) are adequately contained, packaged, and labeled as the agreement may require; and

(f) conform to the promises or affirmations of fact made on the container or label if any.

(3) Unless excluded or modified (Section 2–316) other implied warranties may arise from course of dealing or usage of trade.

§2–315. Implied Warranty: Fitness for Particular Purpose.
Where the seller at the time of contracting has reason to know any particular purpose for which the goods are required and that the buyer is relying on the seller's skill or judgment to select or furnish suitable goods, there is unless excluded or modified under the next section an implied warranty that the goods shall be fit for such purpose.

§2–316. Exclusion or Modification of Warranties.

(1) Words or conduct relevant to the creation of an express warranty and words or conduct tending to negate or limit warranty shall be construed wherever reasonable as consistent with each other; but subject to the provisions of this Article on parol or extrinsic evidence (Section 2–202) negation or limitation is inoperative to the extent that such construction is unreasonable.

(2) Subject to subsection (3), to exclude or modify the implied warranty of merchantability or any part of it the language must mention merchantability and in case of a writing must be conspicuous, and to exclude or modify any implied warranty of fitness the exclusion must be by a writing and conspicuous. Language to exclude all implied warranties of fitness is sufficient if it states, for example, that "There are no warranties which extend beyond the description on the face hereof."

(3) Notwithstanding subsection (2)

(a) unless the circumstances indicate otherwise, all implied warranties are excluded by expressions like "as is", "with all faults" or other language which in common understanding calls the buyer's attention to the exclusion of warranties and makes plain that there is no implied warranty; and

(b) when the buyer before entering into the contract has examined the goods or the sample or model as fully as he desired or has refused to examine the goods there is no implied warranty with regard to defects which an examination ought in the circumstances to have revealed to him; and

(c) an implied warranty can also be excluded or modified by course of dealing or course of performance or usage of trade.

(4) Remedies for breach of warranty can be limited in accordance with the provisions of this Article on liquidation or limitation of damages and on contractual modification of remedy (Sections 2–718 and 2–719).

§2–317. Cumulation and Conflict of Warranties Express or Implied. Warranties whether express or implied shall be construed as consistent with each other and as cumulative, but if such construction is unreasonable the intention of the parties shall determine which warranty is dominant. In ascertaining that intention the following rules apply:

(a) Exact or technical specifications displace an inconsistent sample or model or general language of description.

(b) A sample from an existing bulk displaces inconsistent general language of description.

(c) Express warranties displace inconsistent implied warranties other than an implied warranty of fitness for a particular purpose.

§2–318. Third Party Beneficiaries of Warranties Express or Implied.

Note: *If this Act is introduced in the Congress of the United States this section should be omitted. (States to select one alternative.)*

Alternative A—A seller's warranty whether express or implied extends to any natural person who is in the family or household of his buyer or who is a guest in his home if it is reasonable to expect that such person may use, consume or be affected by the goods and who is injured in person by breach of the warranty. A seller may not exclude or limit the operation of this section.

Alternative B—A seller's warranty whether express or implied extends to any natural person who may reasonably be expected to use, consume or be affected by the goods and who is injured in person by breach of the warranty. A seller may not exclude or limit the operation of this section.

Alternative C—A seller's warranty whether express or implied extends to any person who may reasonably be expected to use, consume or be affected by the goods and who is injured by breach of the warranty. A seller may not exclude or limit the operation of this section with respect to injury to the person of an individual to whom the warranty extends. As amended 1966.

§2–319. F.O.B. and F.A.S. Terms.

(1) Unless otherwise agreed the term F.O.B. (which means "free on board") at a named place, even though used only in connection with the stated price, is a delivery term under which

(a) when the term is F.O.B. the place of shipment, the seller must at that place ship the goods in the manner provided in this Article (Section 2–504) and bear the expense and risk of putting them into the possession of the carrier; or

(b) when the term is F.O.B. the place of destination, the seller must at his own expense and risk transport the goods to that place and there tender delivery of them in the manner provided in this Article (Section 2–503);

(c) when under either (a) or (b) the term is also F.O.B. vessel, car or other vehicle, the seller must in addition at his own expense and risk load the goods on board. If the term is F.O.B. vessel the buyer must name the vessel and in an appropriate case the seller must comply with the provisions of this Article on the form of bill of lading (Section 2–323).

(2) Unless otherwise agreed the term F.A.S. vessel (which means "free alongside") at a named port, even though used only in connection with the stated price, is a delivery term under which the seller must

(a) at his own expense and risk delive the goods alongside the vessel in the manner usual in that port or on a dock designated and provided by the buyer; and

(b) obtain and tender a receipt for the goods in exchange for which the carrier is under a duty to issue a bill of lading.

(3) Unless otherwise agreed in any case falling within subsection (1) (a) or (c) or subsection (2) the buyer must seasonably give any needed instructions for making delivery, including when the term is F.A.S. or F.O.B. the loading berth of the vessel and in an appropriate case its name and sailing date. The seller may treat the failure of needed instructions as a failure of cooperation under this Article (Section 2–311). He may also at his option move the goods in any reasonable manner preparatory to delivery or shipment.

(4) Under the term F.O.B. vessel or F.A.S. unless otherwise agreed the buyer must make payment against tender of the required documents and the seller may not tender nor the buyer demand delivery of the goods in substitution for the documents.

§2–320. C.I.F. and C.&F. Terms.

(1) The term C.I.F. means that the price includes in a lump sum the cost of the goods and the insurance and freight to the named destination. The term C.&F. or C.F. means that the price so includes cost and freight to the named destination.

(2) Unless otherwise agreed and even though used only in connection with the stated price and destination, the term C.I.F. destination or its equivalent requires the seller at his own expense and risk to

(a) put the goods into the possession of a carrier at the port for shipment and obtain a negotiable bill or bills of lading covering the entire transportation to the named destination; and

(b) load the goods and obtain a receipt from the carrier (which may be contained in the bill of lading) showing that the freight has been paid or provided for; and

(c) obtain a policy or certificate of insurance, including any war risk insurance, of a kind and on terms then current at the port of shipment in the usual amount, in the currency of the contract, shown to cover the same goods covered by the bill of lading and providing for payment of loss to the order of the buyer or for the account of whom it may concern; but the seller may add to the price the amount of the premium for any such war risk insurance; and

(d) prepare an invoice of the goods and procure any other documents required to effect shipment or to comply with the contract; and

(e) forward and tender with commercial promptness all the documents in due form and with any indorsement necessary to perfect the buyer's rights.

(3) Unless otherwise agreed the term C. & F. or its equivalent has the same effect and imposes upon the seller the same obligations and risks as a C.I.F. term except the obligation as to insurance.

(4) Under the term C.I.F. or C. & F. unless otherwise agreed the buyer must make payment against tender of the required documents and the seller may not tender nor the buyer demand delivery of the goods in substitution for the documents.

§2–321. C.I.F. or C. & F.: "Net Landed Weights"; "Payment on Arrival"; Warranty of Condition on Arrival. Under a contract containing a term C.I.F. or C. & F.

(1) Where the price is based on or is to be adjusted according to "net landed weights", "delivered weights", "out turn" quantity or quality or the like, unless otherwise agreed the seller must reasonably estimate the price. The payment due on tender of the documents called for by the contract is the amount so estimated, but after final adjustment of the price a settlement must be made with commercial promptness.

(2) An agreement described in subsection (1) or any warranty of quality or condition of the goods on arrival

places upon the seller the risk of ordinary deterioration, shrinkage and the like in transportation but has no effect on the place or time of identification to the contract for sale or delivery or on the passing of the risk of loss.

(3) Unless otherwise agreed where the contract provides for payment on or after arrival of the goods the seller must before payment allow such preliminary inspection as is feasible; but if the goods are lost delivery of the documents and payment are due when the goods should have arrived.

§2–322. Delivery "Ex-Ship".

(1) Unless otherwise agreed a term for delivery of goods "ex-ship" (which means from the carrying vessel) or in equivalent language is not restricted to a particular ship and requires delivery from a ship which has reached a place at the named port of destination where goods of the kind are usually discharged.

(2) Under such a term unless otherwise agreed

(a) the seller must discharge all liens arising out of the carriage and furnish the buyer with a direction which puts the carrier under a duty to deliver the goods; and

(b) the risk of loss does not pass to the buyer until the goods leave the ship's tackle or are otherwise properly unloaded.

§2–323. Form of Bill of Lading Required in Overseas Shipment; "Overseas".

(1) Where the contract contemplates overseas shipment and contains a term C.I.F. or C. & F. or F.O.B. vessel, the seller unless otherwise agreed must obtain a negotiable bill of lading stating that the goods have been loaded on board or, in the case of a term C.I.F. or C. & F., received for shipment.

(2) Where in a case within subsection (1) a bill of lading has been issued in a set of parts, unless otherwise agreed if the documents are not to be sent from abroad the buyer may demand tender of the full set; otherwise only one part of the bill of lading need be tendered. Even if the agreement expressly requires a full set

(a) due tender of a single part is acceptable within the provisions of this Article on cure of improper delivery (subsection (1) of Section 2–508); and

(b) even though the full set is demanded, if the documents are sent from abroad the person tendering an incomplete set may nevertheless require payment upon furnishing an indemnity which the buyer in good faith deems adequate.

(3) A shipment by water or by air or a contract contemplating such shipment is "overseas" insofar as by usage of trade or agreement it is subject to the commercial, financing or shipping practices characteristic of international deep water commerce.

§2–324. "No Arrival, No Sale" Term. Under a term "no arrival, no sale" or terms of like meaning, unless otherwise agreed,

(a) the seller must properly ship conforming goods and if they arrive by any means he must tender them on arrival but he assumes no obligation that the goods will arrive unless he has caused the nonarrival; and

(b) where without fault of the seller the goods are in part lost or have so deteriorated as no longer to conform to the contract or arrive after the contract time, the buyer may proceed as if there had been casualty to identified goods (Section 2–613).

§2–325. "Letter of Credit" Term; "Confirmed Credit".

(1) Failure of the buyer seasonably to furnish an agreed letter of credit is a breach of the contract for sale.

(2) The delivery to seller of a proper letter of credit suspends the buyer's obligation to pay. If the letter of credit is dishonored, the seller may on seasonable notification to the buyer require payment directly from him.

(3) Unless otherwise agreed the term "letter of credit" or "banker's credit" in a contract for sale means an irrevocable credit issued by a financing agency of good repute and, where the shipment is overseas, of good international repute. The term "confirmed credit" means that the credit must also carry the direct obligation of such an agency which does business in the seller's financial market.

§2–326. Sale on Approval and Sale or Return; Consignment Sales and Rights of Creditors.

(1) Unless otherwise agreed, if delivered goods may be returned by the buyer even though they conform to the contract, the transaction is

(a) a "sale on approval" if the goods are delivered primarily for use, and

(b) a "sale or return" if the goods are delivered primarily for resale.

(2) Except as provided in subsection (3), goods held on approval are not subject to the claims of the buyer's creditors until acceptance; goods held on sale or return are subject to such claims while in the buyer's possession.

(3) Where goods are delivered to a person for sale and such person maintains a place of business at which he deals in goods of the kind involved, under a name other than the name of the person making delivery, then with respect to claims of creditors of the person conducting the business the goods are deemed to be on sale or return. The provisions of this subsection are applicable even though an agreement purports to reserve title to the person making delivery until payment or resale or uses such words as "on consignment" or "on memorandum". However, this subsection is not applicable if the person making delivery

(a) complies with an applicable law providing for a consignor's interest or the like to be evidenced by a sign, or

(b) establishes that the person conducting the business is generally known by his creditors to be substantially engaged in selling the goods of others, or

(c) complies with the filing provisions of the Article on Secured Transactions (Article 9).

(4) Any "or return" term of a contract for sale is to be treated as a separate contract for sale within the statute of frauds section of this Article (Section 2–201) and as contradicting the sale aspect of the contract within the provisions of this Article on parol or extrinsic evidence (Section 2–202).

§2–327. Special Incidents of Sale on Approval and Sale or Return.

(1) Under a sale on approval unless otherwise agreed

(a) although the goods are identified to the contract the risk of loss and the title do not pass to the buyer until acceptance; and

(b) use of the goods consistent with the purpose of trial is not acceptance but failure seasonably to notify the seller of election to return the goods is acceptance, and if the goods conform to the contract acceptance of any part is acceptance of the whole; and

(c) after due notification of election to return, the return is at the seller's risk and expense but a merchant buyer must follow any reasonable instructions.

(2) Under a sale or return unless otherwise agreed

(a) the option to return extends to the whole or any commercial unit of the goods while in substantially their original condition, but must be exercised seasonably; and

(b) the return is at the buyer's risk and expense.

§2–328. Sale by Auction.

(1) In a sale by auction if goods are put up in lots each lot is the subject of a separate sale.

(2) A sale by auction is complete when the auctioneer so announces by the fall of the hammer or in other customary manner. Where a bid is made while the hammer is falling in acceptance of a prior bid the auctioneer may in his discretion reopen the bidding or declare the goods sold under the bid on which the hammer was falling.

(3) Such a sale is with reserve unless the goods are in explicit terms put up without reserve. In an auction with reserve the auctioneer may withdraw the goods at any time until he announces completion of the sale. In an auction without reserve, after the auctioneer calls for bids on an article or lot, that article or lot cannot be withdrawn unless no bid is made within a reasonable time. In either case a bidder may retract his bid until the auctioneer's announcement of completion of the sale, but a bidder's retraction does not revive any previous bid.

(4) If the auctioneer knowingly receives a bid on the seller's behalf or the seller makes or procures such a bid, and notice has not been given, the liberty for such bidding is reserved, the buyer may at his option avoid the sale or take the goods at the price of the last good faith bid prior to the completion of the sale. This subsection shall not apply to any bid at a forced sale.

Part 4 Title, Creditors and Good Faith Purchasers

§2–401. Passing of Title; Reservation for Security; Limited Application of This Section. Each provision of this Article with regard to the rights, obligations and remedies of the seller, the buyer, purchasers or other third parties applies irrespective of title to the goods except where the provision refers to such title. Insofar as situations are not covered by the other provisions of this Article and matters concerning title become material the following rules apply:

(1) Title to goods cannot pass under a contract for sale prior to their identification to the contract (Section 2–501), and unless otherwise explicitly agreed the buyer acquires by their identification a special property as limited by this Act. Any retention or reservation by the seller of the title (property) in goods shipped or delivered to the buyer is limited in effect to a reservation of a security interest. Subject to these provisions and to the provisions of the Article on Secured Transactions (Article 9), title to goods passes from the seller to the buyer in any manner and on any conditions explicitly agreed on by the parties.

(2) Unless otherwise explicitly agreed title passes to the buyer at the time and place at which the seller completes his performance with reference to the physical delivery of the goods, despite any reservation of a security interest and even though a document of title is to be delivered at a different time or place; and in particular and despite any reservation of a security interest by the bill of lading

(a) if the contract requires or authorizes the seller to send the goods to the buyer but does not require him to deliver them at destination, title passes to the buyer at the time and place of shipment; but

(b) if the contract requires delivery at destination, title passes on tender there.

(3) Unless otherwise explicitly agreed where delivery is to be made without moving the goods,

(a) if the seller is to deliver a document of title, title passes at the time when and the place where he delivers such documents; or

(b) if the goods are at the time of contracting already identified and no documents are to be delivered, title passes at the time and place of contracting.

(4) A rejection or other refusal by the buyer to receive or retain the goods, whether or not justified, or a justified revocation of acceptance revests title to the goods in the seller. Such revesting occurs by operation of law and is not a "sale".

§2–402. Rights of Seller's Creditors Against Sold Goods.

(1) Except as provided in subsections (2) and (3), rights of unsecured creditors of the seller with respect to goods which have been identified to a contract for sale are subject to the buyer's rights to recover the goods under this Article (Section 2–502 and 2–716).

(2) A creditor of the seller may treat a sale or an identification of goods to a contract for sale as void if as against him a retention of possession by the seller is fraudulent under any rule of law of the state where the goods are situated, except that retention of possession in good faith and current course of trade by a merchant-seller for a commercially reasonable time after a sale or identification is not fraudulent.

(3) Nothing in this Article shall be deemed to impair the rights of creditors of the seller

(a) under the provisions of the Article on Secured Transactions (Article 9); or

(b) where identification to the contract or delivery is made not in current course of trade but in satisfaction of or as security for a pre-existing claim for money, security or the like and is made under circumstances which under any rule of law of the state where the goods are situated would apart from this Article constitute the transaction a fraudulent transfer or voidable preference.

§2–403. Power to Transfer; Good Faith Purchase of Goods; "Entrusting".

(1) A purchaser of goods acquires all title which his transferor had or had power to transfer except that a purchaser of a limited interest acquires rights only to the extent of the interest purchased. A person with voidable title has power to transfer a good title to a good faith purchaser for value. When goods have been delivered under a transaction of purchase the purchaser had such power even though

(a) the transferor was deceived as to the identity of the purchaser, or

(b) the delivery was in exchange for a check which is later dishonored, or

(c) it was agreed that the transaction was to be a "cash sale", or

(d) the delivery was procured through fraud punishable as larcenous under the criminal law.

(2) Any entrusting of possession of goods to a merchant who deals in goods of that kind gives him power to transfer all rights of the entruster to a buyer in ordinary course of business.

(3) "Entrusting" includes any delivery and any acquiescence in retention of possession regardless of any condition expressed between the parties to the delivery or acquiescence and regardless of whether the procurement of the entrusting or the possessor's disposition of the goods have been such as to be larcenous under the criminal law.

(4) The rights of other purchasers of goods and of lien creditors are governed by the Articles on Secured Transactions (Article 9), Bulk Transfers (Article 6) and Documents of Title (Article 7).

Part 5   Performance

§2–501. Insurable Interest in Goods; Manner of Identification of Goods.

(1) The buyer obtains a special property and an insurable interest in goods by identification of existing goods as goods to which the contract refers even though the goods so identified are non-conforming and he has an option to return or reject them. Such identification can be made at any time and in any manner explicitly agreed to by the parties. In the absence of explicit agreement identification occurs

(a) when the contract is made if it is for the sale of goods already existing and identified;

(b) if the contract is for the sale of future goods other than those described in paragraph (c), when goods are shipped, marked or otherwise designated by the seller as goods to which the contract refers;

(c) when the crops are planted or otherwise become growing crops or the young are conceived if the contract is for the sale of unborn young to be born within twelve months after contracting or for the sale of crops to be harvested within twelve months or the next normal harvest season after contracting whichever is longer.

(2) The seller retains an insurable interest in goods so long as title to or any security interest in the goods remains in him and where the identification is by the seller alone he may until default or insolvency or notification to the buyer that the identification is final substitute other goods for those identified.

(3) Nothing in this section impairs any insurable interest recognized under any other statute or rule of law.

§2–502. Buyer's Right to Goods on Seller's Insolvency.

(1) Subject to subsection (2) and even though the goods have not been shipped a buyer who has paid a part or all of the price of goods in which he has a special property under the provisions of the immediately preceding section may on making and keeping good a tender of any unpaid portion of their price recover them from the seller if the seller becomes insolvent within ten days after receipt of the first installment on their price.

(2) If the identification creating his special property has been made by the buyer he acquires the right to recover the goods only if they conform to the contract for sale.

§2–503. Manner of Seller's Tender of Delivery.

(1) Tender of delivery requires that the seller put and hold conforming goods at the buyer's disposition and give the buyer any notification reasonably necessary to enable him to take delivery. The manner, time and place for tender are determined by the agreement and this Article, and in particular

(a) tender must be at a reasonable hour, and if it is of goods they must be kept available for the period reasonably necessary to enable the buyer to take possession; but

(b) unless otherwise agreed the buyer must furnish facilities reasonably suited to the receipt of the goods.

(2) Where the case is within the next section respecting shipment tender requires that the seller comply with its provisions.

(3) Where the seller is required to deliver at a particular destination tender requires that he comply with subsection (1) and also in any appropriate case tender documents as described in subsections (4) and (5) of this section.

(4) Where goods are in the possession of a bailee and are to be delivered without being moved

(a) tender requires that the seller either tender a negotiable document of title covering such goods or procure acknowledgement by the bailee of the buyer's right to possession of the goods; but

(b) tender to the buyer of a non-negotiable document of title or of a written direction to the bailee to deliver is sufficient tender unless the buyer seasonably objects, and receipt by the bailee of notification of the buyer's rights fixes those rights as against the bailee and all third persons; but risk of loss of the goods and of any failure by the bailee to honor the non-negotiable document of title or to obey the direction remains on the seller until the buyer has had a reasonable time to present the document or direction, and a refusal by the bailee to honor the document or to obey the direction defeats the tender.

(5) Where the contract requires the seller to deliver documents

(a) he must tender all such documents in correct form, except as provided in this Article with respect to bills of lading in a set (subsection (2) of Section 2–323); and

(b) tender through customary banking channels is sufficient and dishonor of a draft accompanying the documents constitutes non-acceptance or rejection.

§2–504. Shipment by Seller.

Where the seller is required or authorized to send the goods to the buyer and the contract does not require him to deliver them at a particular destination, then unless otherwise agreed he must

(a) put the goods in the possession of such a carrier and make such a contract for their transportation as may be reasonable having regard to the nature of the goods and other circumstances of the case; and

(b) obtain and promptly deliver or tender in due form any document necessary to enable the buyer to obtain possession of the goods or otherwise required by the agreement or by usage of trade; and

(c) promptly notify the buyer of the shipment.

Failure to notify the buyer under paragraph (c) or to make a proper contract under paragraph (a) is a ground for rejection only if material delay or loss ensues.

§2–505. Seller's Shipment Under Reservation.

(1) Where the seller has identified goods to the contract by or before shipment:

(a) his procurement of a negotiable bill of lading to his own order or otherwise reserves in him a security interest in the goods. His procurement of the bill to the order of a financing agency or of the buyer indicates in addition only the seller's expectation of transferring that interest to the person named.

(b) a non-negotiable bill of lading to himself or his nominee reserves possession of the goods as security but except in a case of conditional delivery (subsection (2) of Section 2–507) a non-negotiable bill of lading naming the buyer as consignee reserves no security interest even though the seller retains possession of the bill of lading.

(2) When shipment by the seller with reservation of a security interest is in violation of the contract for sale it constitutes an improper contract for transportation within the preceding section but impairs neither the rights given to the buyer by shipment and identification of the goods to the contract nor the seller's powers as a holder of a negotiable document.

§2–506. Rights of Financing Agency.

(1) A financing agency by paying or purchasing for value a draft which relates to a shipment of goods acquires to the extent of the payment or purchase and in addition to its own rights under the draft and any document of title securing it any rights of the shipper in the goods including the right to stop delivery and the shipper's right to have the draft honored by the buyer.

(2) The right to reimbursement of a financing agency which has in good faith honored or purchased the draft under commitment to or authority from the buyer is not impaired by subsequent discovery of defects with reference to any relevant document which was apparently regular on its face.

§2–507. Effect of Seller's Tender; Delivery on Condition.

(1) Tender of delivery is a condition to the buyer's duty to accept the goods and, unless otherwise agreed, to his duty to pay for them. Tender entitles the seller to acceptance of the goods and to payment according to the contract.

(2) Where payment is due and demanded on the delivery to the buyer of goods or documents of title, his right as against the seller to retain or dispose of them is conditional upon his making the payment due.

§2–508. Cure by Seller of Improper Tender or Delivery; Replacement.

(1) Where any tender or delivery by the seller is rejected because non-conforming and the time for performance has not yet expired, the seller may seasonally notify the buyer of his intention to cure and may then within the contract time make a conforming delivery.

(2) Where the buyer rejects a non-conforming tender which the seller had reasonable grounds to believe would be acceptable with or without money allowance the seller may if he seasonably notifies the buyer have a further reasonable time to substitute a conforming tender.

§2–509. Risk of Loss in the Absence of Breach.

(1) Where the contract requires or authorizes the seller to ship the goods by carrier

(a) if it does not require him to deliver them at a particular destination, the risk of loss passes to the buyer when the goods are duly delivered to the carrier even though the shipment is under reservation (Section 2–505); but

(b) if it does require him to deliver them at a particular destination and the goods are there duly tendered while in the possession of the carrier, the risk of loss passes to the buyer when the goods are there duly so tendered as to enable the buyer to take delivery.

(2) Where the goods are held by a bailee to be delivered without being moved, the risk of loss passes to the buyer

(a) on his receipt of a negotiable document of title covering the goods; or

(b) on acknowledgement by the bailee of the buyer's right to possession of the goods; or

(c) after his receipt of a non-negotiable document of title or other written direction to deliver, as provided in subsection (4) (b) of Section 2–503.

(3) In any case not within subsection (1) or (2), the risk of loss passes to the buyer on his receipt of the goods if the seller is a merchant; otherwise the risk passes to the buyer on tender of delivery.

(4) The provisions of this section are subject to contrary agreement of the parties and to the provisions of this Article on sale on approval (Section 2–327) and on effect of breach on risk of loss (Section 2–510).

§2–510. Effect of Breach on Risk of Loss.

(1) Where a tender or delivery of goods so fails to conform to the contract as to give a right of rejection the risk of their loss remains on the seller until cure or acceptance.

(2) Where the buyer rightfully revokes acceptance he may to the extent of any deficiency in his effective insurance coverage treat the risk of loss as having rested on the seller from the beginning.

(3) Where the buyer as to conforming goods already identified to the contract for sale repudiates or is otherwise in breach before risk of their loss has passed to him, the seller may to the extent of any deficiency in his effective insurance coverage treat the risk of loss as resting on the buyer for a commercially reasonable time.

§2–511. Tender of Payment by Buyer; Payment by Check.

(1) Unless otherwise agreed tender of payment is a condition to the seller's duty to tender and complete any delivery.

(2) Tender of payment is sufficient when made by any means or in any manner current in the ordinary course of business unless the seller demands payment in legal tender and gives any extension of time reasonably necessary to procure it.

(3) Subject to the provisions of this Act on the effect of an instrument on an obligation (Section 3–802), payment by check is conditional and is defeated as between the parties by dishonor of the check on due presentment.

§2–512. Payment by Buyer Before Inspection.

(1) Where the contract requires payment before inspection non-conformity of the goods does not excuse the buyer from so making payment unless

(a) the non-conformity appears without inspection; or

(b) despite tender of the required documents the circumstances would justify injunction against honor under the provisions of this Act (Section 5–114).

(2) Payment pursuant to subsection (1) does not constitute an acceptance of goods or impair the buyer's right to inspect or any of his remedies.

§2–513. Buyer's Right to Inspection of Goods.

(1) Unless otherwise agreed and subject to subsection (3), where goods are tendered or delivered or identified to the contract for sale, the buyer has a right before payment or acceptance to inspect them at any reasonable place and time and in any reasonable manner. When the seller is required or authorized to send the goods to the buyer, the inspection may be after their arrival.

(2) Expenses of inspection must be borne by the buyer but may be recovered from the seller if the goods do not conform and are rejected.

(3) Unless otherwise agreed and subject to the provisions of this Article on C.I.F. contracts (subsection (3) of Section 2–321), the buyer is not entitled to inspect the goods before payment of the price when the contract provides

(a) for delivery "C.O.D." or on other like terms; or

(b) for payment against documents of title, except where such payment is due only after the goods are to become available for inspection.

(4) A place or method of inspection fixed by the parties is presumed to be exclusive but unless otherwise expressly agreed it does not postpone identification or shift the place for delivery or for passing the risk of loss. If compliance becomes impossible, inspection shall be as provided in this section unless the place or method fixed was clearly intended as an indispensable condition failure of which avoids the contract.

§2–514. When Documents Deliverable on Acceptance; When on Payment. Unless otherwise agreed documents against which a draft is drawn are to be delivered to the drawee on acceptance of the draft if it is payable more than three days after presentment; otherwise, only on payment.

§2–515. Preserving Evidence of Goods in Dispute. In furtherance of the adjustment of any claim or dispute

(a) either party on reasonable notification to the other and for the purpose of ascertaining the facts and preserving evidence has the right to inspect, test and sample the goods including such of them as may be in the possession or control of the other; and

(b) the parties may agree to a third party inspection or survey to determine the conformity or condition of the goods and may agree that the findings shall be binding upon them in any subsequent litigation or adjustment.

Part 6   Breach, Repudiation and Excuse

§2–601. Buyer's Rights on Improper Delivery. Subject to the provisions of this Article on breach in installment contracts (Section 2–612) and unless otherwise agreed under the sections on contractual limitations of remedy (Sections 2–718 and 2–719), if the goods or the tender of delivery fail in any respect to conform to the contract, the buyer may

(a) reject the whole; or

(b) accept the whole; or

(c) accept any commercial unit or units and reject the rest.

§2–602. Manner and Effect of Rightful Rejection.

(1) Rejection of goods must be within a reasonable time after their delivery or tender. It is ineffective unless the buyer seasonably notifies the seller.

(2) Subject to the provisions of the two following sections on rejected goods (Section 2–603 and 2–604),

(a) after rejection any exercise of ownership by the buyer with respect to any commercial unit is wrongful as against the seller; and

(b) if the buyer has before rejection taken physical possession of goods in which he does not have a security interest under the provisions of this Article (subsection (3) of Section 2–711), he is under a duty after rejection to hold them with reasonable care at the seller's disposition for a time sufficient to permit the seller to remove them; but

(c) the buyer has no further obligations with regard to goods rightfully rejected.

(3) The seller's rights with respect to goods wrongfully rejected are governed by the provisions of this Article on Seller's remedies in general (Section 2–703).

§2–603. Merchant Buyer's Duties as to Rightfully Rejected Goods.

(1) Subject to any security interest in the buyer (subsection (3) of Section 2–711), when the seller has no agent or place of business at the market of rejection a merchant

buyer is under a duty after rejection of goods in his possession or control to follow any reasonable instructions received from the seller with respect to the goods and in the absence of such instructions to make reasonable efforts to sell them for the seller's account if they are perishable or threaten to decline in value speedily. Instructions are not reasonable if on demand indemnity for expenses is not forthcoming.

(2) When the buyer sells goods under subsection (1), he is entitled to reimbursement from the seller or out of the proceeds for reasonable expenses of caring for and selling them, and if the expenses include no selling commission then to such commission as is usual in the trade or if there is none to a reasonable sum not exceeding ten per cent on the gross proceeds.

(3) In complying with this section the buyer is held only to good faith and good faith conduct hereunder is neither acceptance nor conversion nor the basis of an action for damages.

§2–604. Buyer's Options as to Salvage of Rightfully Rejected Goods.

Subject to the provisions of the immediately preceding section on perishables if the seller gives no instructions within a reasonable time after notification of rejection the buyer may store the rejected goods for the seller's account or reship them to him or resell them for the seller's account with reimbursement as provided in the preceding section. Such action is not acceptance or conversion.

§2–605. Waiver of Buyer's Objections by Failure to Particularize.

(1) The buyer's failure to state in connection with rejection a particular defect which is ascertainable by reasonable inspection precludes him from relying on the unstated defect to justify rejection or to establish breach

(a) where the seller could have cured it if stated seasonably; or

(b) between merchants when the seller has after rejection made a request in writing for a full and final written statement of all defects on which the buyer proposes to rely.

(2) Payment against documents made without reservation of rights precludes recovery of the payment for defects apparent on the face of the documents.

§2–606. What Constitutes Acceptance of Goods.

(1) Acceptance of goods occurs when the buyer

(a) after a reasonable opportunity to inspect the goods signifies to the seller that the goods are conforming or that he will take or retain them in spite of their non-conformity; or

(b) fails to make an effective rejection (subsection (1) of Section 2–602), but such acceptance does not occur until the buyer has had a reasonable opportunity to inspect them; or

(c) does any act inconsistent with the seller's ownership; but if such act is wrongful as against the seller it is an acceptance only if ratified by him.

(2) Acceptance of a part of any commercial unit is acceptance of that entire unit.

§2–607. Effect of Acceptance; Notice of Breach; Burden of Establishing Breach After Acceptance; Notice of Claim or Litigation to Person Answerable Over.

(1) The buyer must pay at the contract rate for any goods accepted.

(2) Acceptance of goods by the buyer precludes rejection of the goods accepted and if made with knowledge of a non-conformity cannot be revoked because of it unless the acceptance was on the reasonable assumption that the non-conformity would be seasonably cured but acceptance does not of itself impair any other remedy provided by this Article for non-conformity.

(3) Where a tender has been accepted

(a) the buyer must within a reasonable time after he discovers or should have discovered any breach notify the seller of breach or be barred from any remedy; and

(b) if the claim is one for infringement or the like (subsection (3) of Section 2–312) and the buyer is sued as a result of such a breach he must so notify the seller within a reasonable time after he receives notice of the litigation or be barred from any remedy over for liability established by the litigation.

(4) The burden is on the buyer to establish any breach with respect to the goods accepted.

(5) Where the buyer is sued for breach of a warranty or other obligation for which his seller is answerable over

(a) he may give his seller written notice of the litigation. If the notice states that the seller may come in and defend and that if the seller does not do so he will be bound in any action against him by his buyer by any determination of fact common to the two litigations, then unless the seller after seasonable receipt of the notice does come in and defend he is so bound.

(b) if the claim is one for infringement or the like (subsection (3) of Section 2–312) the original seller may demand in writing that his buyer turn over to him control of the litigation including settlement or else be barred from any remedy over and if he also agrees to bear all expense and to satisfy any adverse judgment, then unless the buyer after seasonable receipt of the demand does turn over control the buyer is so barred.

(6) The provisions of subsections (3), (4) and (5) apply to any obligation of a buyer to hold the seller harmless against infringement or the like (subsection (3) of Section 2–312).

§2–608. Revocation of Acceptance in Whole or in Part.

(1) The buyer may revoke his acceptance of a lot or commercial unit whose non-conformity substantially impairs its value to him if he has accepted it

(a) on the reasonable assumption that its non-conformity would be cured and it has not been seasonably cured; or

(b) without discovery of such non-conformity if his acceptance was reasonably induced either by the difficulty of discovery before acceptance or by the seller's assurances.

(2) Revocation of acceptance must occur within a reasonable time after the buyer discovers or should have discovered the ground for it and before any substantial change in condition of the goods which is not caused by their own defects. It is not effective until the buyer notifies the seller of it.

(3) A buyer who so revokes has the same rights and duties with regard to the goods involved as if he had rejected them.

§2–609. Right to Adequate Assurance of Performance.

(1) A contract for sale imposes an obligation on each party that the other's expectation of receiving due performance will not be impaired. When reasonable grounds for insecurity arise with respect to the performance of either party the other may in writing demand adequate assurance of due performance and until he receives such assurance may if commercially reasonable suspend any performance for which he has not already received the agreed return.

(2) Between merchants the reasonableness of grounds for insecurity and the adequacy of any assurance offered shall be determined according to commercial standards.

(3) Acceptance of any improper delivery or payment does not prejudice the aggrieved party's right to demand adequate assurance of future performance.

(4) After receipt of a justified demand failure to provide within a reasonable time not exceeding thirty days such assurance of due performance as is adequate under the circumstances of the particular case is a repudiation of the contract.

§2–610. Anticipatory Repudiation.

When either party repudiates the contract with respect to a performance not yet due the loss of which will substantially impair the value of the contract to the other, the aggrieved party may

(a) for a commercially reasonable time await performance by the repudiating party; or

(b) resort to any remedy for breach (Section 2–703 or Section 2–711), even though he has notified the repudiating party that he would await the latter's performance and has urged retraction; and

(c) in either case suspend his own performance or proceed in accordance with the provisions of this Article on the seller's right to identify goods to the contract notwithstanding breach or to salvage unfinished goods (Section 2–704).

§2–611. Retraction of Anticipatory Repudiation.

(1) Until the repudiating party's next performance is due he can retract his repudiation unless the aggrieved party has since the repudiation cancelled or materially changed his

position or otherwise indicated that he considers the repudiation final.

(2) Retraction may be by any method which clearly indicates to the aggrieved party that the repudiating party intends to perform, but must include any assurance justifiably demanded under the provisions of this Article (Section 2–609).

(3) Retraction reinstates the repudiating party's rights under the contract with due excuse and allowance to the aggrieved party for any delay occasioned by the repudiation.

§2–612. "Installment Contract"; Breach.

(1) An "installment contract" is one which requires or authorizes the delivery of goods in separate lots to be separately accepted, even though the contract contains a clause "each delivery is a separate contract" or its equivalent.

(2) The buyer may reject any installment which is non-conforming if the non-conformity substantially impairs the value of that installment and cannot be cured or if the non-conformity is a defect in the required documents; but if the non-conformity does not fall within subsection (3) and the seller gives adequate assurance of its cure the buyer must accept that installment.

(3) Whenever non-conformity or default with respect to one or more installments substantially impairs the value of the whole contract there is a breach of the whole. But the aggrieved party reinstates the contract if he accepts a non-conforming installment without seasonably notifying of cancellation or if he brings an action with respect only to past installments or demands performance as to future installments.

§2–613. Casualty to Identified Goods.

Where the contract requires for its performance goods identified when the contract is made, and the goods suffer casualty without fault of either party before the risk of loss passes to the buyer, or in a proper case under a "no arrival, no sale" term (Section 2–324) then

(a) if the loss is total the contract is avoided; and

(b) if the loss is partial or the goods have so deteriorated as no longer to conform to the contract the buyer may nevertheless demand inspection and at his option either treat the contract as avoided or accept the goods with due allowance from the contract price for the deterioration or the deficiency in quantity but without further right against the seller.

§2–614. Substituted Performance.

(1) Where without fault of either party the agreed berthing, loading, or unloading facilities fail or an agreed type of carrier becomes unavailable or the agreed manner of delivery otherwise becomes commercially impracticable but a commercially reasonable substitute is available, such substitute performance must be tendered and accepted.

(2) If the agreed means or manner of payment fails

because of domestic or foreign governmental regulation, the seller may withhold or stop delivery unless the buyer provides a means or manner of payment which is commercially a substantial equivalent. If delivery has already been taken, payment by the means or in the manner provided by the regulation discharges the buyer's obligation unless the regulation is discriminatory, oppressive or predatory.

§2–615. Excuse by Failure of Presupposed Conditions.
Except so far as a seller may have assumed a greater obligation and subject to the preceding section on substituted performance:

(a) Delay in delivery or non-delivery in whole or in part by a seller who complies with paragraphs (b) and (c) is not a breach of his duty under a contract for sale if performance as agreed has been made impracticable by the occurrence of a contingency the non-occurrence of which was a basic assumption on which the contract was made or by compliance in good faith with any applicable foreign or domestic governmental regulation or order whether or not it later proves to be invalid.

(b) Where the causes mentioned in paragraph (a) affect only a part of the seller's capacity to perform, he must allocate production and deliveries among his customers but may at his option include regular customers not then under contract as well as his own requirements for further manufacture. He may so allocate in any manner which is fair and reasonable.

(c) The seller must notify the buyer seasonably that there will be delay or non-delivery and, when allocation is required under paragraph (b), of the estimated quota thus made available for the buyer.

§2–616. Procedure on Notice Claiming Excuse.
(1) When the buyer receives notification of a material or indefinite delay or an allocation justified under the preceding section he may by written notification to the seller as to any delivery concerned, and where the prospective deficiency substantially impairs the value of the whole contract under the provisions of this Article relating to breach of installment contracts (Section 2–612), then also as to the whole,

(a) terminate and thereby discharge any unexecuted portion of the contract; or

(b) modify the contract by agreeing to take his available quota in substitution.

(2) If after receipt of such notification from the seller the buyer fails so to modify the contract within a reasonable time not exceeding thirty days the contract lapses with respect to any deliveries affected.

(3) The provisions of this section may not be negated by agreement except in so far as the seller has assumed a greater obligation under the preceding section.

Part 7   Remedies

§2–701. Remedies for Breach of Collateral Contracts Not Impaired.
Remedies for breach of any obligation or promise collateral or ancillary to a contract for sale are not impaired by the provisions of this Article.

§2–702. Seller's Remedies on Discovery of Buyer's Insolvency.
(1) Where the seller discovers the buyer to be insolvent he may refuse delivery except for cash including payment for all goods theretofore delivered under the contract, and stop delivery under this Article (Section 2–705).

(2) Where the seller discovers that the buyer has received goods on credit while insolvent he may reclaim the goods upon demand made within ten days after the receipt, but if misrepresentation of solvency has been made to the particular seller in writing within three months before delivery the ten day limitation does not apply. Except as provided in this subsection the seller may not base a right to reclaim goods on the buyer's fraudulent or innocent misrepresentation of solvency or of intent to pay.

(3) The seller's right to reclaim under subsection (2) in subject to the rights of a buyer in ordinary course or other good faith purchaser under this Article (Section 2–403). Successful reclamation of goods excludes all other remedies with respect to them. As amended 1966.

§2–703. Seller's Remedies in General.
Where the buyer wrongfully rejects or revokes acceptance of goods or fails to make a payment due on or before delivery or repudiates with respect to a part or the whole, then with respect to any goods directly affected and, if the breach is of the whole contract (Section 2–612), then also with respect to the whole undelivered balance, the aggrieved seller may

(a) withhold delivery of such goods;

(b) stop delivery by any bailee as hereafter provided (Section 2–705);

(c) proceed under the next section respecting goods still unidentified to the contract;

(d) resell and recover damages as hereafter provided (Section 2–706);

(e) recover damages for non-acceptance (Section 2–708) or in a proper case the price (Section 2–709);

(f) cancel.

§2–704. Seller's Right to Identify Goods to the Contract Notwithstanding Breach or to Salvage Unfinished Goods.
(1) An aggrieved seller under the preceding section may

(a) identify to the contract conforming goods not already identified if at the time he learned of the breach they are in his possession or control;

(b) treat as the subject of resale goods which have demonstrably been intended for the particular contract even though those goods are unfinished.

(2) Where the goods are unfinished an aggrieved seller may in the exercise of reasonable commercial judgment for the purposes of avoiding loss and of effective realization either complete the manufacture and wholly identify the goods to the contract or cease manufacture and resell for scrap or salvage value or proceed in any other reasonable manner.

§2–705. Seller's Stoppage of Delivery in Transit or Otherwise.

(1) The seller may stop delivery of goods in the possession of a carrier or other bailee when he discovers the buyer to be insolvent (Section 2–702) and may stop delivery of carload, truckload, planeload or larger shipments of express or freight when the buyer repudiates or fails to make a payment due before delivery or if for any other reason the seller has a right to withhold or reclaim the goods.

(2) As against such buyer the seller may stop delivery until
(a) receipt of the goods by the buyer; or
(b) acknowledgement to the buyer by any bailee of the goods except a carrier that the bailee holds the goods for the buyer; or
(c) such acknowledgement to the buyer by a carrier by reshipment or as warehouseman; or
(d) negotiation to the buyer of any negotiable document of title covering the goods.

(3)
(a) To stop delivery the seller must so notify as to enable the bailee by reasonable diligence to prevent delivery of the goods.
(b) After such notification the bailee must hold and deliver the goods according to the directions of the seller but the seller is liable to the bailee for any ensuing charges or damages.
(c) If a negotiable document of title has been issued for goods the bailee is not obliged to obey a notification to stop until surrender of the document.
(d) A carrier who has issued a non-negotiable bill of lading is not obliged to obey a notification to stop received from a person other than the consignor.

§2–706. Seller's Resale Including Contract for Resale.

(1) Under the conditions stated in Section 2–703 on seller's remedies, the seller may resell the goods concerned or the undelivered balance thereof. Where the resale is made in good faith and in a commercially reasonable manner the seller may recover the difference between the resale price and the contract price together with any incidental damages allowed under the provisions of this article (Section 2–710), but less expenses saved in consequence of the buyer's breach.

(2) Except as otherwise provided in subsection (3) or unless otherwise agreed resale may be at public or private sale including sale by way of one or more contracts to sell or of identification to an existing contract of the seller. Sale may be as a unit or in parcels and at any time and place and on any terms but every aspect of the sale including the method, manner, time, place and terms must be commercially reasonable. The resale must be reasonably identified as referring to the broken contract, but it is not necessary that the goods be in existence or that any or all of them have been identified to the contract before the breach.

(3) Where the resale is at private sale the seller must give the buyer reasonable notification of his intention to resell.

(4) Where the resale is at public sale
(a) only identified goods can be sold except where there is a recognized market for a public sale of futures in goods of the kind; and
(b) it must be made at a usual place or market for public sale if one is reasonably available and except in the case of goods which are perishable or threaten to decline in value speedily the seller must give the buyer reasonable notice of the time and place of the resale; and
(c) if the goods are not to be within the view of those attending the sale the notification of sale must state the place where the goods are located and provide for their reasonable inspection by prospective bidders; and
(d) the seller may buy.

(5) A purchaser who buys in good faith at a resale takes the goods free of any rights of the original buyer even though the seller fails to comply with one or more of the requirements of this section.

(6) The seller is not accountable to the buyer for any profit made on any resale. A person in the position of a seller (Section 2–707) or a buyer who has rightfully rejected or justifiably revoked acceptance must account for any excess over the amount of his security interest, as hereinafter defined (subsection (3) of Section 2–711).

§2–707. "Person in the Position of a Seller".

(1) A "person in the position of a seller" includes as against a principal an agent who has paid or become responsible for the price of goods on behalf of his principal or anyone who otherwise holds a security interest or other right in goods similar to that of a seller.

(2) A person in the position of a seller may as provided in this Article withhold or stop delivery (Section 2–705) and resell (Section 2–706) and recover incidental damages (Section 2–710).

§2–708. Seller's Damages for Non-acceptance or Repudiation.

(1) Subject to subsection (2) and to the provisions of this Article with respect to proof of market price (Section 2–723), the measure of damages for non-acceptance or repudiation by the buyer is the difference between the market price at the time and place for tender and the unpaid contract price together with any incidental damages provided in this Article (Section 2–710), but less expenses saved in consequence of the buyer's breach.

(2) If the measure of damages provided in subsection (1) is inadequate to put the seller in as good a position as performance would have done then the measure of damages is the profit (including reasonable overhead) which the seller

would have made from full performance by the buyer, together with any incidental damages provided in this Article (Section 2–710), due allowance for costs reasonably incurred and due credit for payments or proceeds of resale.

§2–709. Action for the Price.

(1) When the buyer fails to pay the price as it becomes due the seller may recover, together with any incidental damages under the next section, the price

(a) of goods accepted or of conforming goods lost or damaged within a commercially reasonable time after risk of their loss has passed to the buyer; and

(b) of goods identified to the contract if the seller is unable after reasonable effort to resell them at a reasonable price or the circumstances reasonably indicate that such effort will be unavailing.

(2) Where the seller sues for the price he must hold for the buyer any goods which have been identified to the contract and are still in his control except that if resale becomes possible he may resell them at any time prior to the collection of the judgment. The net proceeds of any such resale must be credited to the buyer and payment of the judgment entitles him to any goods not resold.

(3) After the buyer has wrongfully rejected or revoked acceptance of the goods or has failed to make a payment due or has repudiated (Section 2–610), a seller who is held not entitled to the price under this section shall nevertheless be awarded damages for non-acceptance under the preceding section.

§2–710. Seller's Incidental Damages.

Incidental damages to an aggrieved seller include any commercially reasonable charges, expenses or commissions incurred in stopping delivery, in the transportation, care and custody of goods after the buyer's breach, in connection with return or resale of the goods or otherwise resulting from the breach.

§2–711. Buyer's Remedies in General; Buyer's Security Interest in Rejected Goods.

(1) When the seller fails to make delivery or repudiates or the buyer rightfully rejects or justifiably revokes acceptance then with respect to any goods involved, and with respect to the whole if the breach goes to the whole contract (Section 2–612), the buyer may cancel and whether or not he has done so may in addition to recovering so much of the price as has been paid

(a) "cover" and have damages under the next section as to all the goods affected whether or not they have been identified to the contract; or

(b) recover damages for non-delivery as provided in this Article (Section 2–713).

(2) Where the seller fails to deliver or repudiates the buyer may also

(a) if the goods have been identified recover them as provided in this Article (Section 2–502); or

(b) in a proper case obtain specific performance or replevy the goods as provided in this Article (Section 2–716).

(3) On rightful rejection or justifiable revocation of acceptance a buyer has a security interest in goods in his possession or control for any payments made on their price and any expenses reasonably incurred in their inspection, receipt, transportation, care and custody and may hold such goods and resell them in like manner as an aggrieved seller (Section 2–706).

§2–712. "Cover"; Buyer's Procurement of Substitute Goods.

(1) After a breach within the preceding section the buyer may "cover" by making in good faith and without unreasonable delay any reasonable purchase of or contract to purchase goods in substitution for those due from the seller.

(2) The buyer may recover from the seller as damages the difference between the cost of cover and the contract price together with any incidental or consequential damages as hereinafter defined (Section 2–715), but less expenses saved in consequence of the seller's breach.

(3) Failure of the buyer to effect cover within this section does not bar him from any other remedy.

§2–713. Buyer's Damages for Non-Delivery or Repudiation.

(1) Subject to the provisions of this Article with respect to proof of market price (Section 2–723), the measure of damages for non-delivery or repudiation by the seller is the difference between the market price at the time when the buyer learned of the breach and the contract price together with any incidental and consequential damages provided in this Article (Section 2–715), but less expenses saved in consequence of the seller's breach.

(2) Market price is to be determined as of the place for tender or, in cases of rejection after arrival or revocation of acceptance, as of the place of arrival.

§2–714. Buyer's Damages for Breach in Regard to Accepted Goods.

(1) Where the buyer has accepted goods and given notification (subsection (3) Section 2–607) he may recover as damages for any non-conformity of tender the loss resulting in the ordinary course of events from the seller's breach as determined in any manner which is reasonable.

(2) The measure of damages for breach of warranty is the difference at the time and place of acceptance between the value of the goods accepted and the value they would have had if they had been as warranted, unless special circumstances show proximate damages of a different amount.

(3) In a proper case any incidental and consequential damages under the next section may also be recovered.

§2–715. Buyer's Incidental and Consequential Damages.

(1) Incidental damages resulting from the seller's breach include expenses reasonably incurred in inspection, receipt, transportation and care and custody of goods rightfully rejected, any commercially reasonable charges, expenses or commissions in connection with effecting cover and any

other reasonable expense incident to the delay or other breach.

(2) Consequential damages resulting from the seller's breach include

(a) any loss resulting from general or particular requirements and needs of which the seller at the time of contracting had reason to know and which could not reasonably be prevented by cover or otherwise; and

(b) injury to person or property proximately resulting from any breach of warranty.

§2–716. Buyer's Right to Specific Performance or Replevin.

(1) Specific performance may be decreed where the goods are unique or in other proper circumstances.

(2) The decree for specific performance may include such terms and conditions as to payment of the price, damages, or other relief as the court may deem just.

(3) The buyer has a right of replevin for goods identified to the contract if after reasonable effort he is unable to effect cover for such goods or the circumstances reasonably indicate that such effort will be unavailing or if the goods have been shipped under reservation and satisfaction of the security interest in them has been made or tendered.

§2–717. Deduction of Damages From the Price. The
buyer on notifying the seller of his intention to do so may deduct all or any part of the damages resulting from any breach of the contract from any part of the price still due under the same contract.

§2–718. Liquidation or Limitation of Damages; Deposits.

(1) Damages for breach by either party may be liquidated in the agreement but only at an amount which is reasonable in the light of the anticipated or actual harm caused by the breach, the difficulties of proof of loss, and the inconvenience or nonfeasibility of otherwise obtaining an adequate remedy. A term fixing unreasonably large liquidated damages is void as a penalty.

(2) Where the seller justifiably withholds delivery of goods because of the buyer's breach, the buyer is entitled to restitution of any amount by which the sum of his payments exceeds

(a) the amount to which the seller is entitled by virtue of terms liquidating the seller's damages in accordance with subsection (1), or

(b) in the absence of such terms, twenty per cent of the value of the total performance for which the buyer is obligated under the contract or $500, whichever is smaller.

(3) The buyer's right to restitution under subsection (2) is subject to offset to the extent that the seller establishes

(a) a right to recover damages under the provisions of this Article other than subsection (1), and

(b) the amount or value of any benefits received by the buyer directly or indirectly by reason of the contract.

(4) Where a seller has received payment in goods their reasonable value or the proceeds of their resale shall be treated as payments for the purposes of subsection (2); but if the seller has notice of the buyer's breach before reselling goods received in part performance, his resale is subject to the conditions laid down in this Article on resale by an aggrieved seller (Section 2–706).

§2–719. Contractual Modification or Limitation of Remedy.

(1) Subject to the provisions of subsections (2) and (3) of this section and of the preceding section on liquidation and limitation of damages,

(a) the agreement may provide for remedies in addition to or in substitution for those provided in this Article and may limit or alter the measure of damages recoverable under this Article, as by limiting the buyer's remedies to return of the goods and repayment of the price or to repair and replacement of non-conforming goods or parts; and

(b) resort to a remedy as provided is optional unless the remedy is expressly agreed to be exclusive, in which case it is the sole remedy.

(2) Where circumstances cause an exclusive or limited remedy to fail of its essential purpose, remedy may be had as provided in this Act.

(3) Consequential damages may be limited or excluded unless the limitation or exclusion is unconscionable. Limitation of consequential damages for injury to the person in the case of consumer goods is prima facie unconscionable but limitation of damages where the loss is commercial is not.

§2–720. Effect of "Cancellation" or "Rescission" on Claims for Antecedent Breach. Unless the contrary
intention clearly appears, expressions of "cancellation" or "rescission" of the contract or the like shall not be construed as a renunciation or discharge of any claim in damages for an antecedent breach.

§2–721. Remedies for Fraud. Remedies for material
misrepresentation or fraud include all remedies available under this Article for non-fraudulent breach. Neither rescission or a claim for rescission of the contract for sale nor rejection or return of the goods shall bar or be deemed inconsistent with a claim for damages or other remedy.

§2–722. Who Can Sue Third Parties for Injury to Goods.
Where a third party so deals with goods which have been identified to a contract for sale as to cause actionable injury to a party to that contract

(a) a right of action against the third party is in either party to the contract for sale who has title to or a security interest or a special property or an insurable interest in the goods; and if the goods have been destroyed or converted a right of action is also in the party who either bore the risk of loss under the contract for sale or has since the injury assumed that risk as against the other;

(b) if at the time of the injury the party plaintiff did not bear the risk of loss as against the other party to the contract for sale and there is no arrangement between them for disposition of the recovery, his suit or settlement is, subject to his own interest, as a fiduciary for the other party to the contract;

(c) either party may with the consent of the other sue for the benefit of whom it may concern.

§2–723. Proof of Market Price: Time and Place.

(1) If an action based on anticipatory repudiation comes to trial before the time for performance with respect to some or all of the goods, any damages based on market price (Section 2–708 or Section 2–713) shall be determined according to the price of such goods prevailing at the time when the aggrieved party learned of the repudiation.

(2) If evidence of a price prevailing at the times or places described in this Article is not readily available the price prevailing within any reasonable time before or after the time described or at any other place which in commercial judgment or under usage of trade would serve as a reasonable substitute for the one described may be used, making any proper allowance for the cost of transporting the goods to or from such other place.

(3) Evidence of a relevant price prevailing at a time or place other than the one described in this Article offered by one party is not admissible unless and until he has given the other party such notice as the court finds sufficient to prevent unfair surprise.

§2–724. Admissibility of Market Quotations.
Whenever the prevailing price or value of any goods regularly bought and sold in any established commodity market is in issue, reports in official publication or trade journals or in newspapers or periodicals of general circulation published as the reports of such market shall be admissible in evidence. The circumstances of the preparation of such a report may be shown to affect its weight but not its admissibility.

§2–725. Statute of Limitations in Contracts for Sale.

(1) An action for breach of any contract for sale must be commenced within four years after the cause of action has accrued. By the original agreement the parties may reduce the period of limitation to not less than one year but may not extend it.

(2) A cause of action accrues when the breach occurs, regardless of the aggrieved party's lack of knowledge of the breach. A breach of warranty occurs when tender of delivery is made, except that where a warranty explicitly extends to future performance of the goods and discovery of the breach must await the time of such performance the cause of action accrues when the breach is or should have been discovered.

(3) Where an action commenced within the time limited by subsection (1) is so terminated as to leave available a remedy by another action for the same breach such other action may be commenced after the expiration of the time limited and within six months after the termination of the first action unless the termination resulted from voluntary discontinuance or from dismissal for failure or neglect to prosecute.

(4) This section does not alter the law on tolling of the statute of limitations nor does it apply to causes of action which have accrued before this Act becomes effective.

ARTICLE 3: COMMERCIAL PAPER

Part 1   Short Title, Form and Interpretation

§3–101. Short Title. This Article shall be known and may be cited as Uniform Commercial Code—Commercial Paper.

§3–102. Definitions and Index of Definitions.

(1) In this Article unless the context otherwise requires
   (a) "Issue" means the first delivery of an instrument to a holder or a remitter.
   (b) An "order" is a direction to pay and must be more than an authorization or request. It must identify the person to pay with reasonable certainty. It may be addressed to one or more such persons jointly or in the alternative but not in succession.
   (c) A "promise" is an undertaking to pay and must be more than an acknowledgement of an obligation.
   (d) "Secondary party" means a drawer or endorser.
   (e) "Instrument" means a negotiable instrument.

(2) Other definitions applying to this Article and the sections in which they appear are:

"Acceptance". Section 3–410.
"Accommodation party". Section 3–415.
"Alteration". Section 3–407.
"Certificate of deposit". Section 3–104.
"Certification". Section 3–411.
"Check". Section 3–104.
"Definite time". Section 3–109.
"Dishonor". Section 3–507.
"Draft". Section 3–104.
"Holder in due course". Section 3–302.
"Negotiation". Section 3–202.
"Note". Section 3–104.
"Notice of dishonor". Section 3–508.
"On demand". Section 3–108.
"Presentment". Section 3–504.
"Protest". Section 3–509.
"Restrictive Indorsement". Section 3–205.
"Signature". Section 3–401.

(3) The following definitions in other Articles apply to this Article:

"Account". Section 4–104.
"Banking Day". Section 4–104.
"Clearing house". Section 4–104.

"Collecting bank". Section 4–105.
"Customer". Section 4–104.
"Depositary Bank". Section 4–105.
"Documentary Draft". Section 4–104.
"Intermediary Bank". Section 4–105.
"Item". Section 4–104.
"Midnight deadline". Section 4–104.
"Payor bank". Section 4–105.

(4) In addition Article 1 contains general definitions and principles of construction and interpretation applicable throughout this Article.

§3–103. Limitations on Scope of Article.

(1) This Article does not apply to money, documents of title or investment securities.

(2) The provisions of this Article are subject to the provisions of the Article on Bank Deposits and Collections (Article 4) and Secured Transactions (Article 9).

§3–104. Form of Negotiable Instruments; "Draft"; "Check"; "Certificate of Deposit"; "Note".

(1) Any writing to be a negotiable instrument within this Article must

(a) be signed by the maker or drawer; and

(b) contain an unconditional promise or order to pay a sum certain in money and no other promise, order, obligation or power given by the maker or drawer except as authorized by this Article; and

(c) be payable on demand or at a definite time; and

(d) be payable to order or to bearer.

(2) A writing which complies with the requirements of this section is

(a) a "draft" ("bill of exchange") if it is an order;

(b) a "check" if it is a draft drawn on a bank and payable on demand;

(c) a "certificate of deposit" if it is an acknowledgement by a bank of receipt of money with an engagement to repay it;

(d) a "note" if it is a promise other than a certificate of deposit.

(3) As used in other Articles in this Act, and as the context may require, the terms "draft", "check", "certificate of deposit" and "note" may refer to instruments which are not negotiable within this Article as well as to instruments which are so negotiable.

§3–105. When Promise or Order Unconditional.

(1) A promise or order otherwise unconditional is not made conditional by the fact that the instrument

(a) is subject to implied or constructive conditions; or

(b) states its consideration, whether performed or promised, or the transaction which gave rise to the instrument, or that the promise or order is made or the instrument matures in accordance with or "as per" such transaction; or

(c) refers to or states that it arises out of a separate agreement or refers to a separate agreement for rights as to prepayment or acceleration; or

(d) states that is drawn under a letter of credit; or

(e) states that it is secured, whether by mortgage, reservation of title or otherwise; or

(f) indicates a particular account to be debited or any other fund or source from which reimbursement is expected; or

(g) is limited to payment out of a particular fund or the proceeds of a particular source, if the instrument is issued by a government or governmental agency or unit; or

(h) is limited to payment out of the entire assets of a partnership, unincorporated association, trust or estate by or on behalf of which the instrument is issued.

(2) A promise or order is not unconditional if the instrument

(a) states that it is subject to or governed by any other agreement; or

(b) states that it is to be paid only out of a particular fund or source except as provided in this section. As amended 1962.

§3–106. Sum Certain.

(1) The sum payable is a sum certain even though it is to be paid

(a) with stated interest or by stated installments; or

(b) with stated different rates of interest before and after default or a specified date; or

(c) with a stated discount or addition if paid before or after the date fixed for payment; or

(d) with exchange or less exchange, whether at a fixed rate or at the current rate; or

(e) with costs of collection or an attorney's fee or both upon default.

(2) Nothing in this section shall validate any term which is otherwise illegal.

§3–107. Money.

(i) An instrument is payable in money if the medium of exchange in which it is payable is money at the time the instrument is made. An instrument payable in "currency" or "current funds" is payable in money.

(2) A promise or order to pay a sum stated in a foreign currency is for a sum certain in money and, unless a different medium of payment is specified in the instrument, may be satisfied by payment of that number of dollars which the stated foreign currency will purchase at the buying sight rate for that currency on the day on which the instrument is payable or, if payable on demand, on the day of demand. If such an instrument specifies a foreign currency as the medium of payment the instrument is payable in that currency.

§3–108. Payable on Demand.
Instruments payable on demand include those payable at sight or on presentation and those in which no time for payment is stated.

§3–109. Definite Time.

(1) An instrument is payable at a definite time if by its terms it is payable

(a) on or before a stated date or at a fixed period after a stated date; or

(b) at a fixed period after sight; or

(c) at a definite time subject to any acceleration; or

(d) at a definite time subject to extension at the option of the holder, or to extension to a further definite time at the option of the maker or acceptor or automatically upon or after a specified act or event.

(2) An instrument which by its terms is otherwise payable only upon an act or event uncertain as to time of occurrence is not payable at a definite time even though the act or event has occurred.

§3–110. Payable to Order.

(1) An instrument is payable to order when by its terms it is payable to the order or assigns of any person therein specified with reasonable certainty, or to him or his order, or when it is conspicuously designated on its face as "exchange" or the like and names a payee. It may be payable to the order of

(a) the maker or drawer; or

(b) the drawee; or

(c) a payee who is not maker, drawer or drawee; or

(d) two or more payees together or in the alternative; or

(e) an estate, trust or fund, in which case it is payable to the order of the representative of such estate, trust or fund or his successors; or

(f) an office, or an officer by his title as such in which case it is payable to the principal but the incumbent of the office or his successors may act as if he or they were the holder; or

(g) a partnership or unincorporated association, in which case it is payable to the partnership or association and may be indorsed or transferred by any person thereto authorized.

(2) An instrument not payable to order is not made so payable by such words as "payable upon return of this instrument properly indorsed."

(3) An instrument made payable both to order and to bearer is payable to order unless the bearer words are handwritten or typewritten.

§3–111. Payable to Bearer.
An instrument is payable to bearer when by its terms it is payable to

(a) bearer or the order of bearer; or

(b) a specified person or bearer; or

(c) "cash" or the order of "cash", or any other indication which does not purport to designate a specific payee.

§3–112. Terms and Omissions Not Affecting Negotiability.

(1) The negotiability of an instrument is not affected by

(a) the omission of a statement of any consideration or of the place where the instrument is drawn or payable; or

(b) a statement that collateral has been given to secure obligations either on the instrument or otherwise of an obligor on the instrument or that in case of default on those obligations the holder may realize on or dispose of the collateral; or

(c) a promise or power to maintain or protect collateral or to give additional collateral; or

(d) a term authorizing a confession of judgment on the instrument if it is not paid when due; or

(e) a term purporting to waive the benefit of any law intended for the advantage or protection of any obligor; or

(f) a term in a draft providing that the payee by indorsing or cashing it acknowledges full satisfaction of an obligation of the drawer; or

(g) A statement in a draft drawn in a set of parts (Section 3–801) to the effect that the order is effective only if no other part has been honored.

(2) Nothing in this section shall validate any term which is otherwise illegal. As amended 1962.

§3–113. Seal.
An instrument otherwise negotiable is within this Article even though it is under a seal.

§3–114. Date, Antedating, Postdating.

(1) The negotiability of an instrument is not affected by the fact that it is undated, antedated or postdated.

(2) Where an instrument is antedated or postdated the time when it is payable is determined by the stated date if the instrument is payable on demand or at a fixed period after date.

(3) Where the instrument or any signature thereon is dated, the date is presumed to be correct.

§3–115. Incomplete Instruments.

(1) When a paper whose contents at the time of signing show that it is intended to become an instrument is signed while still incomplete in any necessary respect it cannot be enforced until completed, but when it is completed in accordance with authority given it is effective as completed.

(2) If the completion is unauthorized the rules as to material alteration apply (Section 3–407), even though the paper was not delivered by the maker or drawer; but the burden of establishing that any completion is unauthorized is on the party so asserting.

§3–116. Instruments Payable to Two or More Persons.
An instrument payable to the order of two or more persons

(a) if in the alternative is payable to any one of them and may be negotiated, discharged or enforced by any of them who has possession of it;

(b) if not in the alternative is payable to all of them and may be negotiated, discharged or enforced only by all of them.

§3–117. Instruments Payable With Words of Description.
An instrument made payable to a named person with the addition of words describing him

(a) as agent or officer of a specified person is payable to his principal but the agent or officer may act as if he were the holder;

(b) as any other fiduciary for a specified person or

purpose is payable to the payee and may be negotiated, discharged or enforced by him;

(c) in any other manner is payable to the payee unconditionally and the additional words are without effect on subsequent parties.

§3–118. Ambiguous Terms and Rules of Construction.

The following rules apply to every instrument:

(a) Where there is doubt whether the instrument is a draft or a note the holder may treat it as either. A draft drawn on the drawer is effective as a note.

(b) Handwritten terms control typewritten and printed terms, and typewritten control printed.

(c) Words control figures except that if the words are ambiguous figures control.

(d) Unless otherwise specified a provision for interest means interest at the judgment rate at the place of payment from the date of the instrument, or if it is undated from the date of issue.

(e) Unless the instrument otherwise specifies two or more persons who sign as maker, acceptor or drawer or indorser and as a part of the same transaction are jointly and severally liable even though the instrument contains such words as "I promise to pay."

(f) Unless otherwise specified consent to extension authorizes a single extension for not longer than the original period. A consent to extension, expressed in the instrument, is binding on secondary parties and accommodation makers. A holder may not exercise his option to extend an instrument over the objection of a maker or acceptor or other party who in accordance with Section 3–604 tenders full payment when the instrument is due.

§3–119. Other Writings Affecting Instrument.

(1) As between the obligor and his immediate obligee or any transferee the terms of an instrument may be modified or affected by any other written agreement executed as a part of the same transaction, except that a holder in due course is not affected by any limitation of his rights arising out of the separate written agreement if he had no notice of the limitation when he took the instrument.

(2) A separate agreement does not affect the negotiability of an instrument.

§3–120. Instruments "Payable Through" Bank.

An instrument which states that it is "payable through" a bank or the like designates that bank as a collecting bank to make presentment but does not of itself authorize the bank to pay the instrument.

§3–121. Instruments Payable at Bank.

Note: *If this Act is introduced in the Congress of the United States this section should be omitted. (States to select either alternative.)*

Alternative A—A note or acceptance which states that it is payable at a bank is the equivalent of a draft drawn on the bank payable when it falls due out of any funds of the maker or acceptor in current account or otherwise available for such payment.

Alternative B—A note or acceptance which states that it is payable at a bank is not of itself an order or authorization to the bank to pay it.

§3–122. Accrual of Cause of Action.

(1) A cause of action against a maker or an acceptor accrues

(a) in the case of a time instrument on the day after maturity;

(b) in the case of a demand instrument upon its date or, if no date is stated, on the date of issue.

(2) A cause of action against the obligor of a demand or time certificate of deposit accrues upon demand, but demand on a time certificate may not be made until on or after the date of maturity.

(3) A cause of action against a drawer of a draft or an indorser of any instrument accrues upon demand following dishonor of the instrument. Notice of dishonor is a demand.

(4) Unless an instrument provides otherwise, interest runs at the rate provided by law for a judgment

(a) in the case of a maker, acceptor or other primary obligor of a demand instrument, from the date of demand;

(b) in all other cases from the date of accrual of the cause of action. As amended 1962.

Part 2 Transfer and Negotiation

§3–201. Transfer: Right to Indorsement.

(1) Transfer of an instrument vests in the transferee such rights as the transferor has therein, except that a transferee who has himself been a party to any fraud or illegality affecting the instrument or who as a prior holder had notice of a defense or claim against it cannot improve his position by taking from a later holder in due course.

(2) A transfer of a security interest in an instrument vests the foregoing rights in the transferee to the extent of the interest transferred.

(3) Unless otherwise agreed any transfer for value of an instrument not then payable to bearer gives the transferee the specifically enforceable right to have the unqualified indorsement of the transferor. Negotiation takes effect only when the indorsement is made and until that time there is no presumption that the transferee is the owner.

§3–202. Negotiation.

(1) Negotiation is the transfer of an instrument in such form that the transferee becomes a holder. If the instrument is payable to order it is negotiated by delivery with any necessary indorsement; if payable to bearer it is negotiated by delivery.

(2) An indorsement must be written by or on behalf of the holder and on the instrument or on a paper so firmly affixed thereto as to become a part thereof.

(3) An indorsement is effective for negotiation only when

it conveys the entire instrument or any unpaid residue. If it purports to be of less it operates only as a partial assignment.

(4) Words of assignment, condition, waiver, guaranty, limitation or disclaimer of liability and the like accompanying an indorsement do not affect its character as an indorsement.

§3–203. Wrong or Misspelled Name.
Where an instrument is made payable to a person under a misspelled name or one other than his own he may indorse in that name or his own or both; but signature in both names may be required by a person paying or giving value for the instrument.

§3–204. Special Indorsement; Blank Indorsement.

(1) A special indorsement specifies the person to whom or to whose order it makes the instrument payable. Any instrument specially indorsed becomes payable to the order of the special indorsee and may be further negotiated only by his indorsement.

(2) An indorsement in blank specifies no particular indorsee and may consist of a mere signature. An instrument payable to order and indorsed in blank becomes payable to bearer and may be negotiated by delivery alone until specially indorsed.

(3) The holder may convert a blank indorsement into a special indorsement by writing over the signature of the indorser in blank any contract consistent with the character of the indorsement.

§3–205. Restrictive Indorsements.
An indorsement is restrictive which either

   (a) is conditional; or

   (b) purports to prohibit further transfer of the instrument; or

   (c) includes the words "for collection", "for deposit", "pay any bank", or like terms signifying a purpose of deposit or collection; or

   (d) otherwise states that it is for the benefit or use of the indorser or of another person.

§3–206. Effect of Restrictive Indorsement.

(1) No restrictive indorsement prevents further transfer or negotiation of the instrument.

(2) An intermediary bank, or a payor bank which is not the depositary bank, is neither given notice nor otherwise affected by a restrictive indorsement of any person except the bank's immediate transferor or the person presenting for payment.

(3) Except for an intermediary bank, any transferee under an indorsement which is conditional or includes the words "for collection", "for deposit", "pay any bank", or like terms (subparagraphs (a) and (c) of Section 3–205) must pay or apply any value given by him for or on the security of the instrument consistently with the indorsement and to the extent that he does so he becomes a holder for value. In addition such transferee is a holder in due course if he otherwise complies with the requirements of Section 3–302 on what constitutes a holder in due course.

(4) The first taker under an indorsement for the benefit of the indorser or another person (subparagraph (d) of Section 3–205) must pay or apply any value given by him for or on the security of the instrument consistently with the indorsement and to the extent that he does so he becomes a holder for value. In addition such taker is a holder in due course if he otherwise complies with the requirements of Section 3–302 on what constitutes a holder in due course. A later holder for value is neither given notice nor otherwise affected by such restrictive indorsement unless he has knowledge that a fiduciary or other person has negotiated the instrument in any transaction for his own benefit or otherwise in breach of duty (subsection (2) of Section 3–304).

§3–207. Negotiation Effective Although It May Be Rescinded.

(1) Negotiation is effective to transfer the instrument although the negotiation is

   (a) made by an infant, a corporation exceeding its powers, or any other person without capacity; or

   (b) obtained by fraud, duress or mistake of any kind; or

   (c) part of an illegal transaction; or

   (d) made in breach of duty.

(2) Except as against a subsequent holder in due course such negotiation is in an appropriate case subject to rescission, the declaration of a constructive trust or any other remedy permitted by law.

§3–208. Reacquisition.
Where an instrument is returned to or reacquired by a prior party he may cancel any indorsement which is not necessary to his title and reissue or further negotiate the instrument, but any intervening party is discharged as against the reacquiring party and subsequent holders not in due course and if his indorsement has been cancelled is discharged as against subsequent holders in due course as well.

Part 3   Rights of a Holder

§3–301. Rights of a Holder.
The holder of an instrument whether or not he is the owner may transfer or negotiate it and, except as otherwise provided in Section 3–603 on payment or satisfaction, discharge it or enforce payment in his own name.

§3–302. Holder in Due Course.

(1) A holder in due course is a holder who takes the instrument

   (a) for value; and

   (b) in good faith; and

   (c) without notice that it is overdue or has been dishonored or of any defense against or claim to it on the part of any person.

(2) A payee may be a holder in due course.

(3) A holder does not become a holder in due course of an instrument:

   (a) by purchase of it at judicial sale or by taking it under legal process; or

   (b) by acquiring it in taking over an estate; or

(c) by purchasing it as part of a bulk transaction not in regular course of business of the transferor.

(4) A purchaser of a limited interest can be a holder in due course only to the extent of the interest purchased.

§3–303. Taking for Value.
A holder takes the instrument for value

(a) to the extent that the agreed consideration has been performed or that he acquires a security interest in or a lien on the instrument otherwise than by legal process; or

(b) when he takes the instrument in payment of or as security for an antecedent claim against any person whether or not the claim is due; or

(c) when he gives a negotiable instrument for it or makes an irrevocable commitment to a third person.

§3–304. Notice to Purchaser.

(1) The purchaser has notice of a claim or defense if

(a) the instrument is so incomplete, bears such visible evidence of forgery or alteration, or is otherwise so irregular as to call into question its validity, terms or ownership or to create an ambiguity as to the party to pay; or

(b) the purchaser has notice that the obligation of any party is voidable in whole or in part, or that all parties have been discharged.

(2) The purchaser has notice of a claim against the instrument when he has knowledge that a fiduciary has negotiated the instrument in payment of or as security for his own debt or in any transaction for his own benefit or otherwise in breach of duty.

(3) The purchaser has notice that an instrument is overdue if he has reason to know

(a) that any part of the principal amount is overdue or that there is an uncured default in payment of another instrument of the same series; or

(b) that acceleration of the instrument has been made; or

(c) that he is taking a demand instrument after demand has been made or more than a reasonable length of time after its issue. A reasonable time for a check drawn and payable within the states and territories of the United States and the District of Columbia is presumed to be thirty days.

(4) Knowledge of the following facts does not of itself give the purchaser notice of a defense or claim

(a) that the instrument is antedated or postdated;

(b) that it was issued or negotiated in return for an executory promise or accompanied by a separate agreement, unless the purchaser has notice that a defense or claim has arisen from the terms thereof;

(c) that any party has signed for accommodation;

(d) that an incomplete instrument has been completed, unless the purchaser has notice of any improper completion;

(e) that any person negotiating the instrument is or was a fiduciary;

(f) that there has been default in payment of interest on the instrument or in payment of any other instrument, except one of the same series.

(5) The filing or recording of a document does not of itself constitute notice within the provisions of this Article to a person who would otherwise be a holder in due course.

(6) To be effective notice must be received at such time and in such manner as to give a reasonable opportunity to act on it.

§3–305. Rights of a Holder in Due Course.
To the extent that a holder is a holder in due course he takes the instrument free from

(1) all claims to it on the part of any person; and

(2) all defenses of any party to the instrument with whom the holder has not dealt except

(a) infancy, to the extent that it is a defense to a simple contract; and

(b) such other incapacity, or duress, or illegality of the transaction, as renders the obligation of the party a nullity; and

(c) such misrepresentation as has induced the party to sign the instrument with neither knowledge nor reasonable opportunity to obtain knowledge of its character or its essential terms; and

(d) discharge in insolvency proceedings; and

(e) any other discharge of which the holder has notice when he takes the instrument.

§3–306. Rights of One Not Holder in Due Course.
Unless he has the rights of a holder in due course any person takes the instrument subject to

(a) all valid claims to it on the part of any person; and

(b) all defenses of any party which would be available in an action on a simple contract; and

(c) the defenses of want or failure of consideration, non-performance of any condition precedent, non-delivery, or delivery for a special purpose (Section 3–408); and

(d) the defense that he or a person through whom he holds the instrument acquired it by theft, or that payment or satisfaction to such holder would be inconsistent with the terms of a restrictive indorsement. The claim of any third person to the instrument is not otherwise available as a defense to any party liable thereon unless the third person himself defends the action for such party.

§3–307. Burden of Establishing Signatures, Defenses and Due Course.

(1) Unless specifically denied in the pleading each signature on an instrument is admitted. When the effectiveness of a signature is put in issue

(a) the burden of establishing it is on the party claiming under the signature; but

(b) the signature is presumed to be genuine or authorized except where the action is to enforce the obligation of a purported signer who has died or become incompetent before proof is required.

(2) When signatures are admitted or established, production of the instrument entitles a holder to recover on it unless the defendant establishes a defense.

(3) After it is shown that a defense exists a person claiming the rights of a holder in due course has the burden of establishing that he or some person under whom he claims is in all respects a holder in due course.

Part 4   Liability of Parties

§3–401. Signature.

(1) No person is liable on an instrument unless his signature appears thereon.

(2) A signature is made by use of any name, including any trade or assumed name, upon an instrument, or by any word or mark used in lieu of a written signature.

§3–402. Signature in Ambiguous Capacity.
Unless the instrument clearly indicates that a signature is made in some other capacity it is an indorsement.

§3–403. Signature by Authorized Representative.

(1) A signature may be made by an agent or other representative, and his authority to make it may be established as in other cases of representation. No particular form of appointment is necessary to establish such authority.

(2) An authorized representative who signs his own name to an instrument

(a) is personally obligated if the instrument neither names the person represented nor shows that the representative signed in a representative capacity;

(b) except as otherwise established between the immediate parties, is personally obligated if the instrument names the person represented but does not show that the representative signed in a representative capacity, or if the instrument does not name the person represented but does show that the representative signed in a representative capacity.

(3) Except as otherwise established the name of an organization preceded or followed by the name and office of an authorized individual is a signature made in a representative capacity.

§3–404. Unauthorized Signatures.

(1) Any unauthorized signature is wholly inoperative as that of the person whose name is signed unless he ratifies it or is precluded from denying it; but it operates as the signature of the unauthorized signer in favor of any person who in good faith pays the instrument or takes it for value.

(2) Any unauthorized signature may be ratified for all purposes of this Article. Such ratification does not of itself affect any rights of the person ratifying against the actual signer.

§3–405. Impostors; Signature in Name of Payee.

(1) An indorsement by any person in the name of a named payee is effective if

(a) an impostor by use of the mails or otherwise has induced the maker or drawer to issue the instrument to him or his confederate in the name of the payee; or

(b) a person signing as or on behalf of a maker or drawer intends the payee to have no interest in the instrument; or

(c) an agent or employee of the maker or drawer has supplied him with the name of the payee intending the latter to have no such interest.

(2) Nothing in this section shall affect the criminal or civil liability of the person so indorsing.

§3–406. Negligence Contributing to Alteration or Unauthorized Signature.
Any person who by his negligence substantially contributes to a material alteration of the instrument or to the making of an unauthorized signature is precluded from asserting the alteration or lack of authority against a holder in due course or against a drawee or other payor who pays the instrument in good faith and in accordance with the reasonable commercial standards of the drawee's or payor's business.

§3–407. Alteration.

(1) Any alteration of an instrument is material which changes the contract of any party thereto in any respect, including any such change in

(a) the number or relations of the parties; or

(b) an incomplete instrument, by completing it otherwise than as authorized; or

(c) the writing as signed, by adding to it or by removing any part of it.

(2) As against any person other than a subsequent holder in due course

(a) alteration by the holder which is both fraudulent and material discharges any party whose contract is thereby changed unless that party assents or is precluded from asserting the defense;

(b) no other alteration discharges any party and the instrument may be enforced according to its original tenor, or as to incomplete instruments according to the authority given.

(3) A subsequent holder in due course may in all cases enforce the instrument according to its original tenor, and when an incomplete instrument has been completed, he may enforce it as completed.

§3–408. Consideration.
Want or failure of consideration is a defense as against any person not having the rights of a holder in due course. (Section 3–305), except that no consideration is necessary for an instrument or obligation thereon given in payment of or as security for an antecedent obligation of any kind. Nothing in this section shall be taken to displace any statute outside this Act under which a promise is enforceable notwithstanding lack or failure of

consideration. Partial failure of consideration is a defense pro tanto whether or not the failure is in an ascertained or liquidated amount.

§3–409. Draft Not as Assignment.

(1) A check or other draft does not of itself operate as an assignment of any funds in the hands of the drawee available for its payment, and the drawee is not liable on the instrument until he accepts it.

(2) Nothing in this section shall affect any liability in contract, tort or otherwise arising from any letter of credit or other obligation or representation which is not an acceptance.

§3–410. Definition and Operation of Acceptance.

(1) Acceptance is the drawee's signed engagement to honor the draft as presented. It must be written on the draft, and may consist of his signature alone. It becomes operative when completed by delivery or notification.

(2) A draft may be accepted although it has not been signed by the drawer or is otherwise incomplete or is overdue or has been dishonored.

(3) Where the draft is payable at a fixed period after sight and the acceptor fails to date his acceptance the holder may complete it by supplying a date in good faith.

§3–411. Certification of a Check.

(1) Certification of a check is acceptance. Where a holder procures certification the drawer and all prior indorsers are discharged.

(2) Unless otherwise agreed a bank has no obligation to certify a check.

(3) A bank may certify a check before returning it for lack of proper indorsement. If it does so the drawer is discharged.

§3–412. Acceptance Varying Draft.

(1) Where the drawee's proffered acceptance in any manner varies the draft as presented the holder may refuse the acceptance and treat the draft as dishonored in which case the drawee is entitled to have his acceptance cancelled.

(2) The terms of the draft are not varied by an acceptance to pay at any particular bank or place in the United States, unless the acceptance states that the draft is to be paid only at such bank or place.

(3) Where the holder assents to an acceptance varying the terms of the draft each drawer and indorser who does not affirmatively assent is discharged. As amended 1962.

§3–413. Contract of Maker, Drawer and Acceptor.

(1) The maker or acceptor engages that he will pay the instrument according to its tenor at the time of his engagement or as completed pursuant to Section 3–115 on incomplete instruments.

(2) The drawer engages that upon dishonor of the draft and any necessary notice of dishonor or protest he will pay the amount of the draft to the holder or to any indorser who takes it up. The drawer may disclaim this liability by drawing without recourse.

(3) By making, drawing or accepting the party admits as against all subsequent parties including the drawee the existence of the payee and his then capacity to indorse.

§3–414. Contract of Indorser; Order of Liability.

(1) Unless the indorsement otherwise specifies (as by such words as "without recourse") every indorser engages that upon dishonor and any necessary notice of dishonor and protest he will pay the instrument according to its tenor at the time of his indorsement to the holder or to any subsequent indorser who takes it up, even though the indorser who takes it up was not obligated to do so.

(2) Unless they otherwise agree indorsers are liable to one another in the order in which they indorse, which is presumed to be the order in which their signatures appear on the instrument.

§3–415. Contract of Accommodation Party.

(1) An accommodation party is one who signs the instrument in any capacity for the purpose of lending his name to another party to it.

(2) When the instrument has been taken for value before it is due the accommodation party is liable in the capacity in which he has signed even though the taker knows of the accommodation.

(3) As against a holder in due course and without notice of the accommodation oral proof of the accommodation is not admissible to give the accommodation party the benefit of discharges dependent on his character as such. In other cases the accommodation character may be shown by oral proof.

(4) An indorsement which shows that it is not in the chain of title is notice of its accommodation character.

(5) An accommodation party is not liable to the party accommodated, and if he pays the instrument has a right of recourse on the instrument against such party.

§3–416. Contract of Guarantor.

(1) "Payment guaranteed" or equivalent words added to a signature mean that the signer engages that if the instrument is not paid when due he will pay it according to its tenor without resort by the holder to any other party.

(2) "Collection guaranteed" or equivalent words added to a signature mean that the signer engages that if the instrument is not paid when due he will pay it according to its tenor, but only after the holder has reduced his claim against the maker or acceptor to judgment and execution has been returned unsatisfied, or after the maker or acceptor has become insolvent or it is otherwise apparent that it is useless to proceed against him.

(3) Words of guaranty which do not otherwise specify guarantee payment.

(4) No words of guaranty added to the signature of a sole maker or acceptor affect his liability on the instrument. Such words added to the signature of one of two or more makers

or acceptors create a presumption that the signature is for the accommodation of the others.

(**5**) When words of guaranty are used presentment, notice of dishonor and protest are not necessary to charge the user.

(**6**) Any guaranty written on the instrument is enforcible notwithstanding any statute of frauds.

§3–417. Warranties on Presentment and Transfer.

(**1**) Any person who obtains payment or acceptance and any prior transferor warrants to a person who in good faith pays or accepts that

(**a**) he has a good title to the instrument or is authorized to obtain payment or acceptance on behalf of one who has a good title; and

(**b**) he has no knowledge that the signature of the maker or drawer is unauthorized, except that this warranty is not given by a holder in due course acting in good faith

(**i**) to a maker with respect to the maker's own signature; or

(**ii**) to a drawer with respect to the drawer's own signature, whether or not the drawer is also the drawee; or

(**iii**) to an acceptor of a draft if the holder in due course took the draft after the acceptance or obtained the acceptance without knowledge that the drawer's signature was unauthorized; and

(**c**) the instrument has not been materially altered, except that this warranty is not given by a holder in due course acting in good faith

(**i**) to the maker of a note; or

(**ii**) to the drawer of a draft whether or not the drawer is also the drawee; or

(**iii**) to the acceptor of a draft with respect to an alteration made prior to the acceptance if the holder in due course took the draft after the acceptance, even though the acceptance provided "payable as originally drawn" or equivalent terms; or

(**iv**) to the acceptor of a draft with respect to an alteration made after the acceptance.

(**2**) Any person who transfers an instrument and receives consideration warrants to his transferee and if the transfer is by indorsement to any subsequent holder who takes the instrument in good faith that

(**a**) he has a good title to the instrument or is authorized to obtain payment or acceptance on behalf of one who has a good title and the transfer is otherwise rightful; and

(**b**) all signatures are genuine or authorized; and

(**c**) the instrument has not been materially altered; and

(**d**) no defense of any party is good against him; and

(**e**) he has no knowledge of any insolvency proceeding instituted with respect to the maker or acceptor or the drawer of an unaccepted instrument.

(**3**) By transferring "without recourse" the transferor limits the obligation stated in subsection (2) (d) to a warranty that he has no knowledge of such a defense.

(**4**) A selling agent or broker who does not disclose the fact that he is acting only as such gives the warranties provided in this section, but if he makes such disclosure warrants only his good faith and authority.

§3–418. Finality of Payment or Acceptance.
Except for recovery of bank payments as provided in the Article on Bank Deposits and Collections (Article 4) and except for liability for breach of warranty on presentment under the preceding section, payment or acceptance of any instrument is final in favor of a holder in due course, or a person who has in good faith changed his position in reliance on the payment.

§3–419. Conversion of Instrument; Innocent Representative.

(**1**) An instrument is converted when

(**a**) a drawee to whom it is delivered for acceptance refuses to return it on demand; or

(**b**) any person to whom it is delivered for payment refuses on demand either to pay or to return it; or

(**c**) it is paid on a forged indorsement.

(**2**) In an action against a drawee under subsection (1) the measure of the drawee's liability is the face amount of the instrument. In any other action under subsection (1) the measure of liability is presumed to be the face amount of the instrument.

(**3**) Subject to the provisions of this Act concerning restrictive indorsements a representative, including a depositary or collecting bank, who has in good faith and in accordance with the reasonable commercial standards applicable to the business of such representative dealt with an instrument or its proceeds on behalf of one who was not the true owner is not liable in conversion or otherwise to the true owner beyond the amount of any proceeds remaining in his hands.

(**4**) An intermediary bank or payor bank which is not a depositary bank is not liable in conversion solely by reason of the fact that proceeds of an item indorsed restrictively (Sections 3–205 and 3–206) are not paid or applied consistently with the restrictive indorsement of an indorser other than its immediate transferor.

Part 5 Presentment, Notice of Dishonor and Protest

§3–501. When Presentment, Notice of Dishonor, and Protest Necessary or Permissible.

(**1**) Unless excused (Section 3–511) presentment is necessary to charge secondary parties as follows:

(**a**) presentment for acceptance is necessary to charge the drawer and indorsers of a draft where the draft so provides, or is payable elsewhere than at the residence or place of business of the drawee, or its date of payment depends upon such presentment. The holder may at his option present for acceptance any other draft payable at a stated date;

(b) presentment for payment is necessary to charge any indorser;

(c) in the case of any drawer, the acceptor of a draft payable at a bank or the maker of a note payable at a bank, presentment for payment is necessary, but failure to make presentment discharges such drawer, acceptor or maker only as stated in Section 3–502(1)(b).

(2) Unless excused (Section 3–511)

(a) notice of any dishonor is necessary to charge any indorser;

(b) in the case of any drawer, the acceptor of a draft payable at a bank or the maker of a note payable at a bank, notice of any dishonor is necessary, but failure to give such notice discharges such drawer, acceptor or maker only as stated in Section 3–502(1)(b).

(3) Unless excused (Section 3–511) protest of any dishonor is necessary to charge the drawer and indorsers of any draft which on its face appears to be drawn or payable outside of the states, territories, dependencies and possessions of the United States, the District of Columbia and the Commonwealth of Puerto Rico. The holder may at his option make protest of any dishonor of any other instrument and in the case of a foreign draft may on insolvency of the acceptor before maturity make protest for better security.

(4) Notwithstanding any provision of this section, neither presentment nor notice of dishonor nor protest is necessary to charge an indorser who has indorsed an instrument after maturity. As amended 1966.

§3–502. Unexcused Delay; Discharge.

(1) Where without excuse any necessary presentment or **notice** of dishonor is delayed beyond the time when it is due

(a) any indorser is discharged; and

(b) any drawer or the acceptor of a draft payable at a bank or the maker of a note payable at a bank who because the drawee or payor bank becomes insolvent during the delay is deprived of funds maintained with the drawee or payor bank to cover the instrument may discharge his liability by written assignment to the holder of his rights against the drawee or payor bank in respect of such funds, but such drawer, acceptor or maker is not otherwise discharged.

(2) Where without excuse a necessary protest is delayed beyond the time when it is due any drawer or indorser is discharged.

§3–503. Time of Presentment.

(1) Unless a different time is expressed in the instrument the time for any presentment is determined as follows:

(a) where an instrument is payable at or a fixed period after a stated date any presentment for acceptance must be made on or before the date it is payable;

(b) where an instrument is payable after sight it must either be presented for acceptance or negotiated within a reasonable time after date or issue whichever is later;

(c) where an instrument shows the date on which it is payable presentment for payment is due on that date;

(d) where an instrument is accelerated presentment for payment is due within a reasonable time after the acceleration;

(e) with respect to the liability of any secondary party presentment for acceptance or payment of any other instrument is due within a reasonable time after such party becomes liable thereon.

(2) A reasonable time for presentment is determined by the nature of the instrument, any usage of banking or trade and the facts of the particular case. In the case of an uncertified check which is drawn and payable within the United States and which is not a draft drawn by a bank the following are presumed to be reasonable periods within which to present for payment or to initiate bank collection:

(a) with respect to the liability of the drawer, thirty days after date or issue whichever is later; and

(b) with respect to the liability of an indorser, seven days after his indorsement.

(3) Where any presentment is due on a day which is not a full business day for either the person making presentment or the party to pay or accept, presentment is due on the next following day which is a full business day for both parties.

(4) Presentment to be sufficient must be made at a reasonable hour, and if at a bank during its banking day.

§3–504. How Presentment Made.

(1) Presentment is a demand for acceptance or payment made upon the maker, acceptor, drawee or other payor by or on behalf of the holder.

(2) Presentment may be made

(a) by mail, in which event the time of presentment is determined by the time of receipt of the mail; or

(b) through a clearing house; or

(c) at the place of acceptance or payment specified in the instrument or if there be none at the place of business or residence of the party to accept or pay. If neither the party to accept or pay nor anyone authorized to act for him is present or accessible at such place presentment is excused.

(3) It may be made

(a) to any one of two or more makers, acceptors, drawees or other payors; or

(b) to any person who has authority to make or refuse the acceptance or payment.

(4) A draft accepted or a note made payable at a bank in the United States must be presented at such bank.

(5) In the cases described in Section 4–210 presentment may be made in the manner and with the result stated in that section. As amended 1962.

§3–505. Rights of Party to Whom Presentment Is Made.

(1) The party to whom presentment is made may without dishonor require

(a) exhibition of the instrument; and

(b) reasonable identification• of the person making

presentment and evidence of his authority to make it if made for another; and

(c) that the instrument be produced for acceptance or payment at a place specified in it, or if there be none at any place reasonable in the circumstances; and

(d) a signed receipt on the instrument for any partial or full payment and its surrender upon full payment.

(2) Failure to comply with any such requirement invalidates the presentment but the person presenting has a reasonable time in which to comply and the time for acceptance or payment runs from the time of compliance.

§3–506. Time Allowed for Acceptance or Payment.

(1) Acceptance may be deferred without dishonor until the close of the next business day following presentment. The holder may also in a good faith effort to obtain acceptance and without either dishonor of the instrument or discharge of secondary parties allow postponement of acceptance for an additional business day.

(2) Except as a longer time is allowed in the case of documentary drafts drawn under a letter of credit, and unless an earlier time is agreed to by the party to pay, payment of an instrument may be deferred without dishonor pending reasonable examination to determine whether it is properly payable, but payment must be made in any event before the close of business on the day of presentment.

§3–507. Dishonor; Holder's Right of Recourse; Term Allowing Re-Presentment.

(1) An instrument is dishonored when

(a) a necessary or optional presentment is duly made and due acceptance or payment is refused or cannot be obtained within the prescribed time or in case of bank collections the instrument is seasonably returned by the midnight deadline (Section 4–301); or

(b) presentment is excused and the instrument is not duly accepted or paid.

(2) Subject to any necessary notice of dishonor and protest, the holder has upon dishonor an immediate right of recourse against the drawers and indorsers.

(3) Return of an instrument for lack of proper indorsement is not dishonor.

(4) A term in a draft or an indorsement thereof allowing a stated time for re-presentment in the event of any dishonor of the draft by nonacceptance if a time draft or by nonpayment if a sight draft gives the holder as against any secondary party bound by the term an option to waive the dishonor without affecting the liability of the secondary party and he may present again up to the end of the stated time.

§3–508. Notice of Dishonor.

(1) Notice of dishonor may be given to any person who may be liable on the instrument by or on behalf of the holder or any party who has himself received notice, or any other party who can be compelled to pay the instrument. In addition an agent or bank in whose hands the instrument is dishonored may give notice to his principal or customer or to another agent or bank from which the instrument was received.

(2) Any necessary notice must be given by a bank before its midnight deadline and by any other person before midnight of the third business day after dishonor or receipt of notice of dishonor.

(3) Notice may be given in any reasonable manner. It may be oral or written and in any terms which identify the instrument and state that it has been dishonored. A misdescription which does not mislead the party notified does not vitiate the notice. Sending the instrument bearing a stamp, ticket or writing stating that acceptance or payment has been refused or sending a notice of debit with respect to the instrument is sufficient.

(4) Written notice is given when sent although it is not received.

(5) Notice to one partner is notice to each although the firm has been dissolved.

(6) When any party is in insolvency proceedings instituted after the issue of the instrument notice may be given either to the party or to the representative of his estate.

(7) When any party is dead or incompetent notice may be sent to his last known address or given to his personal representative.

(8) Notice operates for the benefit of all parties who have rights on the instrument against the party notified.

§3–509. Protest; Noting for Protest.

(1) A protest is a certificate of dishonor made under the hand and seal of a United States consul or vice consul or a notary public or other person authorized to certify dishonor by the law of the place where dishonor occurs. It may be made upon information satisfactory to such person.

(2) The protest must identify the instrument and certify either that due presentment has been made or the reason why it is excused and that the instrument has been dishonored by nonacceptance or nonpayment.

(3) The protest may also certify that notice of dishonor has been given to all parties or to specified parties.

(4) Subject to subsection (5) any necessary protest is due by the time that notice of dishonor is due.

(5) If, before protest is due, an instrument has been noted for protest by the officer to make protest, the protest may be made at any time thereafter as of the date of the noting.

§3–510. Evidence of Dishonor and Notice of Dishonor.

The following are admissible as evidence and create a presumption of dishonor and of any notice of dishonor therein shown:

(a) a document regular in form as provided in the preceding section which purports to be a protest;

(b) the purported stamp or writing of the drawee, payor bank or presenting bank on the instrument or accompanying it stating that acceptance or payment has been refused for reasons consistent with dishonor;

(c) any book or record of the drawee, payor bank, or any collecting bank kept in the usual course of business which shows dishonor, even though there is no evidence of who made the entry.

§3–511. Waived or Excused Presentment, Protest or Notice of Dishonor or Delay Therein.

(1) Delay in presentment, protest or notice of dishonor is excused when the party is without notice that it is due or when the delay is caused by circumstances beyond his control and he exercises reasonable diligence after the cause of the delay ceases to operate.

(2) Presentment or notice or protest as the case may be is entirely excused when

(a) the party to be charged has waived it expressly or by implication either before or after it is due; or

(b) such party has himself dishonored the instrument or has countermanded payment or otherwise has no reason to expect or right to require that the instrument be accepted or paid; or

(c) by reasonable diligence the presentment or protest cannot be made or the notice given.

(3) Presentment is also entirely excused when

(a) the maker, acceptor or drawee of any instrument except a documentary draft is dead or in insolvency proceedings instituted after the issue of the instrument; or

(b) acceptance or payment is refused but not for want of proper presentment.

(4) Where a draft has been dishonored by nonacceptance a later presentment for payment and any notice of dishonor and protest for nonpayment are excused unless in the meantime the instrument has been accepted.

(5) A waiver of protest is also a waiver of presentment and of notice of dishonor even though protest is not required.

(6) Where a waiver of presentment or notice of protest is embodied in the instrument itself it is binding upon all parties; but where it is written above the signature of an indorser it binds him only.

Part 6   Discharge

§3–601. Discharge of Parties.

(1) The extent of the discharge of any party from liability on an instrument is governed by the sections on

(a) payment or satisfaction (Section 3–603); or

(b) tender of payment (Section 3–604); or

(c) cancellation or renunciation (Section 3–605); or

(d) impairment of right of recourse or of collateral (Section 3–606); or

(e) reacquisition of the instrument by a prior party (Section 3–208); or

(f) fraudulent and material alteration (Section 3–407); or

(g) certification of a check (Section 3–411); or

(h) acceptance varying a draft (Section 3–412); or

(i) unexcused delay in presentment or notice of dishonor or protest (Section 3–502).

(2) Any party is also discharged from his liability on an instrument to another party by any other act or agreement with such party which would discharge his simple contract for the payment of money.

(3) The liability of all parties is discharged when any party who has himself no right of action or recourse on the instrument

(a) reacquires the instrument in his own right; or

(b) is discharged under any provision of this Article, except as otherwise provided with respect to discharge for impairment of recourse or of collateral (Section 3–606).

§3–602. Effect of Discharge Against Holder in Due Course.
No discharge of any party provided by this Article is effective against a subsequent holder in due course unless he has notice thereof when he takes the instrument.

§3–603. Payment or Satisfaction.

(1) The liability of any party is discharged to the extent of his payment or satisfaction to the holder even though it is made with knowledge of a claim of another person to the instrument unless prior to such payment or satisfaction the person making the claim either supplies indemnity deemed adequate by the party seeking the discharge or enjoins payment or satisfaction by order of a court of competent jurisdiction in an action in which the adverse claimant and the holder are parties. This subsection does not, however, result in the discharge of the liability

(a) of a party who in bad faith pays or satisfies a holder who acquired the instrument by theft or who (unless having the rights of a holder in due course) holds through one who so acquired it; or

(b) of a party (other than an intermediary bank or a payor bank which is not a depositary bank) who pays or satisfies the holder of an instrument which has been restrictively indorsed in a manner not consistent with the terms of such restrictive indorsement.

(2) Payment or satisfaction may be made with the consent of the holder by any person including a stranger to the instrument. Surrender of the instrument to such a person gives him the rights of a transferee (Section 3–201).

§3–604. Tender of Payment.

(1) Any party making tender of full payment to a holder when or after it is due is discharged to the extent of all subsequent liability for interest, costs and attorney's fees.

(2) The holder's refusal of such tender wholly discharges any party who has a right of recourse against the party making the tender.

(3) Where the maker or acceptor of an instrument payable otherwise than on demand is able and ready to pay at every place of payment specified in the instrument when it is due, it is equivalent to tender.

§3–605. Cancellation and Renunciation.

(1) The holder of an instrument may even without consideration discharge any party

(a) in any manner apparent on the face of the instrument or the indorsement, as by intentionally cancelling the instrument or the party's signature by destruction or mutilation, or by striking out the party's signature; or

(b) by renouncing his rights by a writing signed and delivered or by surrender of the instrument to the party to be discharged.

(2) Neither cancellation or renunciation without surrender of the instrument affects the title thereto.

§3–606. Impairment of Recourse or of Collateral.

(1) The holder discharges any party to the instrument to the extent that without such party's consent the holder

(a) without express reservation of rights releases or agrees not to sue any person against whom the party has to the knowledge of the holder a right of recourse or agrees to suspend the right to enforce against such person the instrument or collateral or otherwise discharges such person, except that failure or delay in effecting any required presentment, protest or notice of dishonor with respect to any such person does not discharge any party as to whom presentment, protest or notice of dishonor is effective or unnecessary; or

(b) unjustifiably impairs any collateral for the instrument given by or on behalf of the party or any person against whom he has a right of recourse.

(2) By express reservation of rights against a party with a right of recourse the holder preserves

(a) all his rights against such party as of the time when the instrument was originally due; and

(b) the right of the party to pay the instrument as of that time; and

(c) all rights of such party to recourse against others.

Part 7   Advice of International Sight Draft

§3–701. Letter of Advice of International Sight Draft.

(1) A "letter of advice" is a drawer's communication to the drawee that a described draft has been drawn.

(2) Unless otherwise agreed when a bank receives from another bank a letter of advice of an international sight draft the drawee bank may immediately debit the drawer's account and stop the running of interest pro tanto. Such a debit and any resulting credit to any account covering outstanding drafts leaves in the drawer full power to stop payment or otherwise dispose of the amount and creates no trust or interest in favor of the holder.

(3) Unless otherwise agreed and except where a draft is drawn under a credit issued by the drawee, the drawee of an international sight draft owes the drawer no duty to pay an unadvised draft but if it does so and the draft is genuine, may appropriately debit the drawer's account.

Part 8   Miscellaneous

§3–801. Drafts in a Set.

(1) Where a draft is drawn in a set of parts, each of which is numbered and expressed to be an order only if no other part has been honored, the whole of the parts constitutes one draft but a taker of any part may become a holder in due course of the draft.

(2) Any person who negotiates, indorses or accepts a single part of a draft drawn in a set thereby becomes liable to any holder in due course of that part as if it were the whole set, but as between different holders in due course to whom different parts have been negotiated the holder whose title first accrues has all rights to the draft and its proceeds.

(3) As against the drawee the first presented part of a draft drawn in a set is the part entitled to payment, or if a time draft to acceptance and payment. Acceptance of any subsequently presented part renders the drawee liable thereon under subsection (2). With respect both to a holder and to the drawer payment of a subsequently presented part of a draft payable at sight has the same effect as payment of a check notwithstanding an effective stop order (Section 4–407).

(4) Except as otherwise provided in this section, where any part of a draft in a set is discharged by payment or otherwise the whole draft is discharged.

§3–802. Effect of Instrument on Obligation for Which It is Given.

(1) Unless otherwise agreed where an instrument is taken for an underlying obligation

(a) the obligation is pro tanto discharged if a bank is drawer, maker or acceptor of the instrument and there is no recourse on the instrument against the underlying obligor; and

(b) in any other case the obligation is suspended pro tanto until the instrument is due or if it is payable on demand until its presentment. If the instrument is dishonored action may be maintained on either the instrument or the obligation; discharge of the underlying obligor on the instrument also discharges him on the obligation.

(2) The taking in good faith of a check which is not postdated does not of itself so extend the time on the original obligation as to discharge a surety.

§3–803. Notice to Third Party. Where a defendant is sued for breach of an obligation for which a third person is answerable over under this Article he may give the third person written notice of the litigation, and the person notified may then give similar notice to any other person who is answerable over to him under this Article. If the notice states that the person notified may come in and defend and that if the person notified does not do so he will in any action against him by the person giving the notice be bound by any determination of fact common to the two

litigations, then unless after seasonable receipt of the notice the person notified does come in and defend he is so bound.

§3–804. Lost, Destroyed or Stolen Instruments. The owner of an instrument which is lost, whether by destruction, theft or otherwise, may maintain an action in his own name and recover from any party liable thereon upon due proof of his ownership, the facts which prevent his production of the instrument and its terms. The court may require security indemnifying the defendant against loss by reason of further claims on the instrument.

§3–805. Instruments Not Payable to Order or to Bearer. This Article applies to any instrument whose terms do not preclude transfer and which is otherwise negotiable within this Article but which is not payable to order or to bearer, except that there can be no holder in due course of such an instrument.

ARTICLE 4: BANK DEPOSITS AND COLLECTIONS

Part 1   General Provisions and Definitions

§4–101. Short Title. This Article shall be known and may be cited as Uniform Commercial Code—Bank Deposits and Collections.

§4–102. Applicability.

(1) To the extent that items within this Article are also within the scope of Articles 3 and 8, they are subject to the provisions of those Articles. In the event of conflict the provisions of this Article govern those of Article 3 but the provisions of Article 8 govern those of this Article.

(2) The liability of a bank for action or non-action with respect to any item handled by it for purposes of presentment, payment or collection is governed by the law of the place where the bank is located. In the case of action or non-action by or at a branch or separate office of a bank, its liability is governed by the law of the place where the branch or separate office is located.

§4–103. Variation by Agreement; Measure of Damages; Certain Action Constituting Ordinary Care.

(1) The effect of the provisions of this Article may be varied by agreement except that no agreement can disclaim a bank's responsibility for its own lack of good faith or failure to exercise ordinary care or can limit the measure of damages for such lack or failure; but the parties may by agreement determine the standards by which such responsibility is to be measured if such standards are not manifestly unreasonable.

(2) Federal Reserve regulations and operating letters, clearing house rules, and the like, have the effect of agreements under subsection (1), whether or not specifically assented to by all parties interested in items handled.

(3) Action or non-action approved by this Article or pursuant to Federal Reserve regulations or operating letters constitutes the exercise of ordinary care and, in the absence of special instructions, action or non-action consistent with clearing house rules and the like or with a general banking usage not disapproved by this Article, prima facie constitutes the exercise of ordinary care.

(4) The specification or approval of certain procedures by this Article does not constitute disapproval of other procedures which may be reasonable under the circumstances.

(5) The measure of damages for failure to exercise ordinary care in handling an item is the amount of the item reduced by an amount which could not have been realized by the use of ordinary care, and where there is bad faith it includes other damages, if any, suffered by the party as a proximate consequence.

§4–104. Definitions and Index of Definitions.

(1) In this Article unless the context otherwise requires

(a) "Account" means any account with a bank and includes a checking, time, interest or savings account;

(b) "Afternoon" means the period of a day between noon and midnight;

(c) "Banking day" means that part of any day on which a bank is open to the public for carrying on substantially all of its banking functions;

(d) "Clearing house" means any association of banks or other payors regularly clearing items;

(e) "Customer" means any person having an account with a bank or for whom a bank has agreed to collect items and includes a bank carrying an account with another bank;

(f) "Documentary draft" means any negotiable or non-negotiable draft with accompanying documents, securities or other papers to be delivered against honor of the draft;

(g) "Item" means any instrument for the payment of money even though it is not negotiable but does not include money;

(h) "Midnight deadline" with respect to a bank is midnight on its next banking day following the banking day on which it receives the relevant item or notice or from which the time for taking action commences to run, whichever is later;

(i) "Properly payable" includes the availability of funds for payment at the time of decision to pay or dishonor;

(j) "Settle" means to pay in cash, by clearing house settlement, in a charge or credit or by remittance, or otherwise as instructed. A settlement may be either provisional or final;

(k) "Suspends payments" with respect to a bank means that it has been closed by order of the supervisory authorities, that a public officer has been appointed to take it over or that it ceases or refuses to make payments in the ordinary course of business.

(2) Other definitions applying to this Article and the sections in which they appear are:

"Collecting bank". Section 4–105.
"Depositary bank". Section 4–105.
"Intermediary bank". Section 4–105.
"Payor bank". Section 4–105.
"Presenting bank". Section 4–105.
"Remitting bank". Section 4–105.

(3) The following definitions in other Articles apply to this Article:

"Acceptance". Section 3–410.
"Certificate of deposit". Section 3–104.
"Certification". Section 3–411.
"Check". Section 3–104.
"Draft". Section 3–104.
"Holder in due course". Section 3–302.
"Notice of dishonor". Section 3–508.
"Presentment". Section 3–504.
"Protest". Section 3–509.
"Secondary party". Section 3–102.

(4) In addition Article 1 contains general definitions and principles of construction and interpretation applicable throughout this Article.

§4–105. "Depositary Bank"; "Intermediary Bank"; "Collecting Bank"; "Payor Bank"; "Presenting Bank"; "Remitting Bank".

In this Article unless the context otherwise requires:

(a) "Depositary bank" means the first bank to which an item is transferred for collection even though it is also the payor bank;

(b) "Payor bank" means a bank by which an item is payable as drawn or accepted;

(c) "Intermediary bank" means any bank to which an item is transferred in course of collection except the depositary or payor bank;

(d) "Collecting bank" means any bank handling the item for collection except the payor bank;

(e) "Presenting bank" means any bank presenting an item except a payor bank;

(f) "Remitting bank" means any payor or intermediary bank remitting for an item.

§4–106. Separate Office of a Bank.

A branch or separate office of a bank [maintaining its own deposit ledgers] is a separate bank for the purpose of computing the time within which and determining the place at or to which action may be taken or notices or orders shall be given under this Article and under Article 3. As amended 1962.

Note: *The brackets are to make it optional with the several states whether to require a branch to maintain its own deposit ledgers in order to be considered to be a separate bank for certain purposes under Article 4. In some*

states "maintaining its own deposit ledgers" is a satisfactory test. In others branch banking practices are such that this test would not be suitable.

§4–107. Time of Receipt of Items.

(1) For the purpose of allowing time to process items, prove balances and make the necessary entries on its books to determine its position for the day, a bank may fix an afternoon hour of 2 P.M. or later as a cut-off hour for the handling of money and items and the making of entries on its books.

(2) Any item or deposit of money received on any day after a cut-off hour so fixed or after the close of the banking day may be treated as being received at the opening of the next banking day.

§4–108. Delays.

(1) Unless otherwise instructed, a collecting bank in a good faith effort to secure payment may, in the case of specific items and with or without the approval of any person involved, waive, modify or extend time limits imposed or permitted by this Act for a period not in excess of an additional banking day without discharge of secondary parties and without liability to its transferor or any prior party.

(2) Delay by a collecting bank or payor bank beyond time limits prescribed or permitted by this Act or by instructions is excused if caused by interruption of communication facilities, suspension of payments by another bank, war, emergency conditions or other circumstances beyond the control of the bank provided it exercises such diligence as the circumstances require.

§4–109. Process of Posting.

The "process of posting" means that usual procedure followed by a payor bank in determining to pay an item and in recording the payment including one or more of the following or other steps as determined by the bank:

(a) verification of any signature;

(b) ascertaining that sufficient funds are available;

(c) affixing a "paid" or other stamp;

(d) entering a charge or entry to a customer's account;

(e) correcting or reversing an entry or erroneous action with respect to the item. Added 1962.

Part 2 Collection of Items: Depositary and Collecting Banks

§4–201. Presumption and Duration of Agency Status of Collecting Banks and Provisional Status of Credits; *Applicability of Article; Item Indorsed "Pay Any Bank".*

(1) Unless a contrary intent clearly appears and prior to the time that a settlement given by a collecting bank for an item is or becomes final (subsection (3) of Section 4–211 and Sections 4–212 and 4–213) the bank is an agent or sub-agent

of the owner of the item and any settlement given for the item is provisional. This provision applies regardless of the form of indorsement or lack of indorsement and even though credit given for the item is subject to immediate withdrawal as of right or is in fact withdrawn; but the continuance of ownership of an item by its owner and any rights of the owner to proceeds of the item are subject to rights of a collecting bank such as those resulting from outstanding advances on the item and valid rights of setoff. When an item is handled by banks for purposes of presentment, payment and collection, the relevant provisions of this Article apply even though action of parties clearly establishes that a particular bank has purchased the item and is the owner of it.

(2) After an item has been indorsed with the words "pay any bank" or the like, only a bank may acquire the rights of a holder

(a) until the item has been returned to the customer initiating collection; or

(b) until the item has been specially indorsed by a bank to a person who is not a bank.

§4–202. Responsibility for Collection; When Action Seasonable.

(1) A collecting bank must use ordinary care in

(a) presenting an item or sending it for presentment; and

(b) sending notice of dishonor or non-payment or returning an item other than a documentary draft to the bank's transferor [or directly to the depositary bank under subsection (2) of Section 4–212] (*see note to Section 4–212*) after learning that the item has not been paid or accepted, as the case may be; and

(c) settling for an item when the bank receives final settlement; and

(d) making or providing for any necessary protest; and

(e) notifying its transferor of any loss or delay in transit within a reasonable time after discovery thereof.

(2) A collecting bank taking proper action before its midnight deadline following receipt of an item, notice or payment acts seasonably; taking proper action within a reasonably longer time may be seasonable but the bank has the burden of so establishing.

(3) Subject to subsection (1) (a), a bank is not liable for the insolvency, neglect, misconduct, mistake or default of another bank or person or for loss or destruction of an item in transit or in the possession of others.

§4–203. Effect of Instructions. Subject to the provision of Article 3 concerning conversion of instruments (Section 3–419) and the provisions of both Article 3 and this Article concerning restrictive indorsements only a collecting bank's transferor can give instructions which affect the bank or constitute notice to it and a collecting bank is not liable to prior parties for any action taken pursuant to such instructions or in accordance with any agreement with its transferor.

§4–204. Methods of Sending and Presenting; Sending Direct to Payor Bank.

(1) A collecting bank must send items by reasonably prompt method taking into consideration any relevant instructions, the nature of the item, the number of such items on hand, and the cost of collection involved and the method generally used by it or others to present such items.

(2) A collecting bank may send

(a) any item direct to the payor bank;

(b) any item to any non-bank payor if authorized by its transferor; and

(c) any item other than documentary drafts to any non-bank payor, if authorized by Federal Reserve regulation or operating letter, clearing house rule or the like.

(3) Presentment may be made by a presenting bank at a place where the payor bank has requested that presentment be made. As amended 1962.

§4–205. Supplying Missing Indorsement; No Notice from Prior Indorsement.

(1) A depositary bank which has taken an item for collection may supply any indorsement of the customer which is necessary to title unless the item contains the words "payee's indorsement required" or the like. In the absence of such a requirement a statement placed on the item by the depositary bank to the effect that the item was deposited by a customer or credited to his account is effective as the customer's indorsement.

(2) An intermediary bank, or payor bank which is not a depositary bank, is neither given notice nor otherwise affected by a restrictive indorsement of any person except the bank's immediate transferor.

§4–206. Transfer Between Banks. Any agreed method which identifies the transferor bank is sufficient for the item's further transfer to another bank.

§4–207. Warranties of Customer and Collecting Bank on Transfer or Presentment of Items; Time for Claims.

(1) Each customer or collecting bank who obtains payment or acceptance of an item and each prior customer and collecting bank warrants to the payor bank or other payor who in good faith pays or accepts the item that

(a) he has a good title to the item or is authorized to obtain payment or acceptance on behalf of one who has a good title; and

(b) he has no knowledge that the signature of the maker or drawer is unauthorized, except that this warranty is not given by any customer or collecting bank that is a holder in due course and acts in good faith

(i) to a maker with respect to the maker's own signature; or

(ii) to a drawer with respect to the drawer's own signature, whether or not the drawer is also the drawee; or

(iii) to an acceptor of an item if the holder in due course took the item after the acceptance or obtained the acceptance without knowledge that the drawer's signature was unauthorized; and

(c) the item has not been materially altered, except that this warranty is not given by any customer or collecting bank that is a holder in due course and acts in good faith

(i) to the maker of a note; or

(ii) to the drawer of a draft whether or not the drawer is also the drawee; or

(iii) to the acceptor of an item with respect to an alteration made prior to the acceptance if the holder in due course took the item after the acceptance, even though the acceptance provided "payable as originally drawn" or equivalent terms; or

(iv) to the acceptor of an item with respect to an alteration made after the acceptance.

(2) Each customer and collecting bank who transfers an item and receives a settlement or other consideration for its warrants to his transferee and to any subsequent collecting bank who takes the item in good faith that

(a) he has a good title to the item or is authorized to obtain payment or acceptance on behalf of one who has a good title and the transfer is otherwise rightful; and

(b) all signatures are genuine or authorized; and

(c) the item has not been materially altered; and

(d) no defense of any party is good against him; and

(e) he has no knowledge of any insolvency proceeding instituted with respect to the maker or acceptor or the drawer of an unaccepted item.

In addition each customer and collecting bank so transferring an item and receiving a settlement or other consideration engages that upon dishonor and any necessary notice of dishonor and protest he will take up the item.

(3) The warranties and the engagement to honor set forth in the two preceding subsections arise notwithstanding the absence of indorsement or words of guaranty or warranty in the transfer or presentment and a collecting bank remains liable for their breach despite remittance to its transferor. Damages for breach of such warranties or engagement to honor shall not exceed the consideration received by the customer or collecting bank responsible plus finance charges and expenses related to the item, if any.

(4) Unless a claim for breach of warranty under this section is made within a reasonable time after the person claiming learns of the breach, the person liable is discharged to the extent of any loss caused by the delay in making claim.

§4–208. Security Interest of Collecting Bank in Items, Accompanying Documents and Proceeds.

(1) A bank has a security interest in an item and any accompanying documents or the proceeds of either

(a) in case of an item deposited in an account to the extent to which credit given for the item has been withdrawn or applied;

(b) in case of an item for which it has given credit available for withdrawal as of right, to the extent of the credit given whether or not the credit is drawn upon and whether or not there is a right of charge-back; or

(c) if it makes an advance on or against the item.

(2) When credit which has been given for several items received at one time or pursuant to a single agreement is withdrawn or applied in part the security interest remains upon all the items, any accompanying documents or the proceeds of either. For the purpose of this section, credits first given are first withdrawn.

(3) Receipt by a collecting bank of a final settlement for an item is a realization on its security interest in the item, accompanying documents and proceeds. To the extent and so long as the bank does not receive final settlement for the item or give up possession of the item or accompanying documents for purposes other than collection, the security interest continues and is subject to the provisions of Article 9 except that

(a) no security agreement is necessary to make the security interest enforceable (subsection (1) (b) of Section 9–203); and

(b) no filing is required to perfect the security interest; and

(c) the security interest has priority over conflicting perfected security interests in the item, accompanying documents or proceeds.

§4–209. When Bank Gives Value for Purposes of Holder in Due Course.
For purposes of determining its status as a holder in due course, the bank has given value to the extent that it has a security interest in an item provided that the bank otherwise complies with the requirements of Section 3–302 on what constitutes a holder in due course.

§4–210. Presentment by Notice of Item Not Payable by, Through or at a Bank; Liability of Secondary Parties.

(1) Unless otherwise instructed, a collecting bank may present an item not payable by, through or at a bank by sending to the party to accept or pay a written notice that the bank holds the item for acceptance or payment. The notice must be sent in time to be received on or before the day when presentment is due and the bank must meet any requirement of the party to accept or pay under Section 3–505 by the close of the bank's next banking day after it knows of the requirement.

(2) Where presentment is made by notice and neither honor nor request for compliance with a requirement under Section 3–505 is received by the close of business on the day after maturity or in the case of demand items by the close of business on the third banking day after notice was sent, the presenting bank may treat the item as dishonored and charge any secondary party by sending him notice of the facts.

§4–211. Media of Remittance; Provisional and Final Settlement in Remittance Cases.

(1) A collecting bank may take in settlement of an item

(a) a check of the remitting bank or of another bank on any bank except the remitting bank; or

(b) a cashier's check or similar primary obligation of a remitting bank which is a member of or clears through a member of the same clearing house or group as the collecting bank; or

(c) appropriate authority to charge an account of the remitting bank or of another bank with the collecting bank; or

(d) if the item is drawn upon or payable by a person other than a bank, a cashier's check, certified check or other bank check or obligation.

(2) If before its midnight deadline the collecting bank properly dishonors a remittance check or authorization to charge on itself or presents or forwards for collection a remittance instrument of or on another bank which is of a kind approved by subsection (1) or has not been authorized by it, the collecting bank is not liable to prior parties in the event of the dishonor of such check, instrument or authorization.

(3) A settlement for an item by means of a remittance instrument or authorization to charge is or becomes a final settlement as to both the person making and the person receiving the settlement

(a) if the remittance instrument or authorization to charge is of a kind approved by subsection (1) or has not been authorized by the person receiving the settlement and in either case the person receiving the settlement acts seasonably before its midnight deadline in presenting, forwarding for collection or paying the instrument or authorization,—at the time the remittance instrument or authorization is finally paid by the payor by which it is payable;

(b) if the person receiving the settlement has authorized remittance by a non-bank check or obligation or by a cashier's check or similar primary obligation of or a check upon the payor or other remitting bank which is not of a kind approved by subsection (1)(b),—at the time of the receipt of such remittance check or obligation; or

(c) if in a case not covered by sub-paragraphs (a) or (b) the person receiving the settlement fails to seasonably present, forward for collection, pay or return a remittance instrument or authorization to it to charge before its midnight deadline,—at such midnight deadline.

§4–212. Right of Charge-Back or Refund.

(1) If a collecting bank has made provisional settlement with its customer for an item and itself fails by reason of dishonor, suspension of payments by a bank or otherwise to receive a settlement for the item which is or becomes final, the bank may revoke the settlement given by it, charge back the amount of any credit given for the item to its customer's account or obtain refund from its customer whether or not it is able to return the items if by its midnight deadline or within a longer reasonable time after it learns the facts it

returns the item or sends notification of the facts. These rights to revoke, charge-back and obtain refund terminate if and when a settlement for the item received by the bank is or becomes final (subsection (3) of Section 4–211 and subsections (2) and (3) of Section 4–213).

[(2) Within the time and manner prescribed by this section and Section 4–301, an intermediary or payor bank, as the case may be, may return an unpaid item directly to the depositary bank and may send for collection a draft on the depositary bank and obtain reimbursement. In such case, if the depositary bank has received provisional settlement for the item, it must reimburse the bank drawing the draft and any provisional credits for the item between banks shall become and remain final.]

Note: *Direct returns is recognized as an innovation that is not yet established bank practice, and therefore, Paragraph 2 has been bracketed. Some lawyers have doubts whether it should be included in legislation or left to development by agreement.*

(3) A depositary bank which is also the payor may charge-back the amount of an item to its customer's account or obtain refund in accordance with the section governing return of an item received by a payor bank for credit on its books. (Section 4–301).

(4) The right to charge-back is not affected by

(a) prior use of the credit given for the item; or

(b) failure by any bank to exercise ordinary care with respect to the item but any bank so failing remains liable.

(5) A failure to charge-back or claim refund does not affect other rights of the bank against the customer or any other party.

(6) If credit is given in dollars as the equivalent of the value of an item payable in a foreign currency the dollar amount of any charge-back or refund shall be calculated on the basis of the buying sight rate for the foreign currency prevailing on the day when the person entitled to the charge-back or refund learns that it will not receive payment in ordinary course.

§4–213. Final Payment of Item by Payor Bank: When Provisional Debits and Credits Become Final; When Certain Credits Become Available for Withdrawal.

(1) An item is finally paid by a payor bank when the bank has done any of the following, whichever happens first:

(a) paid the item in cash; or

(b) settled for the item without reserving a right to revoke the settlement and without having such right under statute, clearing house rule or agreement; or

(c) completed the process of posting the item to the indicated account of the drawer, maker or other person to be charged therewith; or

(d) made a provisional settlement for the item and failed to revoke the settlement in the time and manner permitted by statute, clearing house rule or agreement.

Upon a final payment under subparagraphs (b), (c) or (d) the payor bank shall be accountable for the amount of the item.

(2) If provisional settlement for an item between the presenting and payor banks is made through a clearing house or by debits or credits in an account between them, then to the extent that provisional debits or credits for the item are entered in accounts between the presenting and payor banks or between the presenting and successive prior collecting banks seriatim, they become final upon final payment of the item by the payor bank.

(3) If a collecting bank receives a settlement for an item which is or becomes final (subsection (3) of Section 4–211, subsection (2) of Section 4–213) the bank is accountable to its customer for the amount of the item and any provisional credit given for the item in an account with its customer becomes final.

(4) Subject to any right of the bank to apply the credit to an obligation of the customer, credit given by a bank for an item in an account with its customer becomes available for withdrawal as of right

(a) in any case where the bank has received a provisional settlement for the item—when such settlement becomes final and the bank has had a reasonable time to learn that the settlement is final;

(b) in any case where the bank is both a depositary bank and a payor bank and the item is finally paid,—at the opening of the bank's second banking day following receipt of the item.

(5) A deposit of money in a bank is final when made but, subject to any right of the bank to apply the deposit to an obligation of the customer, the deposit becomes available for withdrawal as of right at the opening of the bank's next banking day following receipt of the deposit.

§4–214. Insolvency and Preference.

(1) Any item in or coming into the possession of a payor or collecting bank which suspends payment and which item is not finally paid shall be returned by the receiver, trustee or agent in charge of the closed bank to the presenting bank or the closed bank's customer.

(2) If a payor bank finally pays an item and suspends payments without making a settlement for the item with its customer or the presenting bank which settlement is or becomes final, the owner of the item has a preferred claim against the payor bank.

(3) If a payor bank gives or a collecting bank gives or receives a provisional settlement for an item and thereafter suspends payments, the suspension does not prevent or interfere with the settlement becoming final if such finality occurs automatically upon the lapse of certain time or the happening of certain events (subsection (3) of Section 4–211, subsections (1) (d), (2) and (3) of Section 4–213).

(4) If a collecting bank receives from subsequent parties settlement for an item which settlement is or becomes final and suspends payments without making a settlement for the item with its customer which is or becomes final, the owner of the item has a preferred claim against such collecting bank.

Part 3 Collection of Items: Payor Banks

§4–301. Deferred Posting; Recovery of Payment by Return of Items; Time of Dishonor.

(1) Where an authorized settlement for a demand item (other than a documentary draft) received by a payor bank otherwise than for immediate payment over the counter has been made before midnight of the banking day of receipt the payor bank may revoke the settlement and recover any payment if before it has made final payment (subsection (1) of Section 4–213) and before its midnight deadline it

(a) returns the item; or

(b) sends written notice of dishonor or nonpayment if the item is held for protest or is otherwise unavailable for return.

(2) If a demand item is received by a payor bank for credit on its books it may return such item or send notice of dishonor and may revoke any credit given or recover the amount thereof withdrawn by its customer, if it acts within the time limit and in the manner specified in the preceding subsection.

(3) Unless previous notice of dishonor has been sent an item is dishonored at the time when for purposes of dishonor it is returned or notice sent in accordance with this section.

(4) An item is returned:

(a) as to an item received through a clearing house, when it is delivered to the presenting or last collecting bank or to the clearing house or is sent or delivered in accordance with its rules; or

(b) in all other cases, when it is sent or delivered to the bank's customer or transferor or pursuant to his instructions.

§4–302. Payor Bank's Responsibility for Late Return of Item.
In the absence of a valid defense such as breach of a presentment warranty (subsection (1) of Section 4–207), settlement effected or the like, if an item is presented on and received by a payor bank the bank is accountable for the amount of

(a) a demand item other than a documentary draft whether properly payable or not if the bank, in any case where it is not also the depositary bank, retains the item beyond midnight of the banking day of receipt without settling for it or, regardless of whether it is also the depositary bank, does not pay or return the item or send notice of dishonor until after its midnight deadline; or

(b) any other properly payable item unless within the time allowed for acceptance or payment of that item the bank either accepts or pays the item or returns it and accompanying documents.

§4–303. When Items Subject to Notice, Stop-Order, Legal Process or Setoff; Order in Which Items May be Charged or Certified.

(1) Any knowledge, notice or stop-order received by, legal process served upon or setoff exercised by a payor bank, whether or not effective under other rules of law to terminate, suspend or modify the bank's right or duty to pay an item or to charge its customer's account for the item, comes too late to so terminate, suspend or modify such right or duty if the knowledge, notice, stop-order or legal process is received or served and a reasonable time for the bank to act thereon expires or the setoff is exercised after the bank has done any of the following:

(a) accepted or certified the item;

(b) paid the item in cash;

(c) settled for the item without reserving a right to revoke the settlement and without having such right under statute, clearing house rule or agreement;

(d) completed the process of posting the item to the indicated account of the drawer, maker or other person to be charged therewith or otherwise has evidenced by examination of such indicated account and by action its decision to pay the item; or

(e) become accountable for the amount of the item under subsection (1) (d) of Section 4–213 and Section 4–302 dealing with the payor bank's responsibility for late return of items.

(2) Subject to the provisions of subsection (1) items may be accepted, paid, certified or charged to the indicated account of its customer in any order convenient to the bank.

Part 4   Relationship between Payor Bank and Its Customer

§4–401. When Bank May Charge Customer's Account.

(1) As against its customer, a bank may charge against his account any item which is otherwise properly payable from that account even though the charge creates an overdraft.

(2) A bank which in good faith makes payment to a holder may charge the indicated account of its customer according to

(a) the original tenor of his altered item; or

(b) the tenor of his completed item, even though the bank knows the item has been completed unless the bank has notice that the completion was improper.

§4–402. Bank's Liability to Customer for Wrongful Dishonor. A payor bank is liable to its customer for damages proximately caused by the wrongful dishonor of an item. When the dishonor occurs through mistake liability is limited to actual damages proved. If so proximately caused and proved damages may include damages for an arrest or prosecution of the customer or other consequential damages. Whether any consequential damages are proximately caused by the wrongful dishonor is a question of fact to be determined in each case.

§4–403. Customer's Right to Stop Payment; Burden of Proof of Loss.

(1) A customer may by order to his bank stop payment of any item payable for his account but the order must be received at such time and in such manner as to afford the bank a reasonable opportunity to act on it prior to any action by the bank with respect to the item described in Section 4–303.

(2) An oral order is binding upon the bank only for fourteen calendar days unless confirmed in writing within that period. A written order is effective for only six months unless renewed in writing.

(3) The burden of establishing the fact and amount of loss resulting from the payment of an item contrary to a binding stop payment order is on the customer.

§4–404. Bank Not Obligated to Pay Check More Than Six Months Old. A bank is under no obligation to a customer having a checking account to pay a check, other than a certified check, which is presented more than six months after its date, but it may charge its customer's account for a payment made thereafter in good faith.

§4–405. Death or Incompetence of Customer.

(1) A payor or collecting bank's authority to accept, pay or collect an item or to account for proceeds of its collection if otherwise effective is not rendered ineffective by incompetence of a customer of either bank existing at the time the item is issued or its collection is undertaken if the bank does not know of an adjudication of incompetence. Neither death nor incompetence of a customer revokes such authority to accept, pay, collect or account until the bank knows of the fact of death or of an adjudication of incompetence and has reasonable opportunity to act on it.

(2) Even with knowledge a bank may for 10 days after the date of death pay or certify checks drawn on or prior to that date unless ordered to stop payment by a person claiming an interest in the account.

§4–406. Customer's Duty to Discover and Report Unauthorized Signature or Alteration.

(1) When a bank sends to its customer a statement of account accompanied by items paid in good faith in support of the debit entries or holds the statement and items pursuant to a request or instructions of its customer or otherwise in a reasonable manner makes the statement and items available to the customer, the customer must exercise reasonable care and promptness to examine the statement and items to discover his unauthorized signature or any alteration on an item and must notify the bank promptly after discovery thereof.

(2) If the bank establishes that the customer failed with respect to an item to comply with the duties imposed on the customer by subsection (1) the customer is precluded from asserting against the bank

(a) his unauthorized signature or any alteration on the item if the bank also establishes that it suffered a loss by reason of such failure; and (**b**) an unauthorized signature or alteration by the same wrongdoer on any other item paid in good faith by the bank after the first item and statement was available to the customer for a reasonable period not exceeding fourteen calendar days and before the bank receives notification from the customer of any such unauthorized signature or alteration.

(**3**) The preclusion under subsection (2) does not apply if the customer establishes lack of ordinary care on the part of the bank in paying the item(s).

(**4**) Without regard to care or lack of care of either the customer or the bank a customer who does not within one year from the time the statement and items are made available to the customer (subsection (1)) discover and report his unauthorized signature or any alteration on the face or back of the item or does not within 3 years from that time discover and report any unauthorized indorsement is precluded from asserting against the bank such unauthorized signature or indorsement or such alteration.

(**5**) If under this section a payor bank has a valid defense against a claim of a customer upon or resulting from payment of an item and waives or fails upon request to assert the defense the bank may not assert against any collecting bank or other prior party presenting or transferring the item a claim based upon the unauthorized signature or alteration giving rise to the customer's claim.

§4–407. Payor Bank's Right to Subrogation on Improper Payment. If a payor bank has paid an item over the stop payment order of the drawer or maker or otherwise under circumstances giving a basis for objection by the drawer or maker, to prevent unjust enrichment and only to the extent necessary to prevent loss to the bank by reason of its payment of the item, the payor bank shall be subrogated to the rights

(**a**) of any holder in due course on the item against the drawer or maker; and

(**b**) of the payee or any other holder of the item against the drawer or maker either on the item or under the transaction out of which the item arose; and

(**c**) of the drawer or maker against the payee or any other holder of the item with respect to the transaction out of which the item arose.

Part 5   Collection of Documentary Drafts

§4–501. Handling of Documentary Drafts; Duty to Send for Presentment and to Notify Customer of Dishonor. A bank which takes a documentary draft for collection must present or send the draft and accompanying documents for presentment and upon learning that the draft has not been paid or accepted in due course must seasonably notify its customer of such fact even though it may have discounted or bought the draft or extended credit available for withdrawal as of right.

§4–502. Presentment of "On Arrival" Drafts. When a draft or the relevant instructions require presentment "on arrival", "when goods arrive" or the like, the collecting bank need not present until in its judgment a reasonable time for arrival of the goods has expired. Refusal to pay or accept because the goods have not arrived is not dishonor; the bank must notify its transferor of such refusal but need not present the draft again until it is instructed to do so or learns of the arrival of the goods.

§4–503. Responsibility of Presenting Bank for Documents and Goods; Report of Reasons for Dishonor; Referee in Case of Need. Unless otherwise instructed and except as provided in Article 5 a bank presenting a documentary draft

(**a**) must deliver the documents to the drawee on acceptance of the draft if it is payable more than three days after presentment; otherwise, only on payment; and

(**b**) upon dishonor, either in the case of presentment for acceptance or presentment for payment, may seek and follow instructions from any referee in case of need designated in the draft or if the presenting bank does not choose to utilize his services it must use diligence and good faith to ascertain the reason for dishonor, must notify its transferor of the dishonor and of the results of its effort to ascertain the reasons therefor and must request instructions.

But the presenting bank is under no obligation with respect to goods represented by the documents except to follow any reasonable instructions seasonably received; it has a right to reimbursement for any expense incurred in following instructions and to prepayment of or indemnity for such expenses.

§4–504. Privilege of Presenting Bank to Deal With Goods; Security Interest for Expenses.

(**1**) A presenting bank which, following the dishonor of a documentary draft, has seasonably requested instructions but does not receive them within a reasonable time may store, sell, or otherwise deal with the goods in any reasonable manner.

(**2**) For its reasonable expenses incurred by action under subsection (1) the presenting bank has a lien upon the goods or their proceeds, which may be foreclosed in the same manner as an unpaid seller's lien.

ARTICLE 5: LETTERS OF CREDIT

§5–101. Short Title. This Article shall be known and may be cited as Uniform Commercial Code—Letters of Credit.

§5–102. Scope.

(**1**) This Article applies

(**a**) to a credit issued by a bank if the credit requires a documentary draft or a documentary demand for payment; and

(**b**) to a credit issued by a person other than a bank if the credit requires that the draft or demand for payment be accompanied by a document of title; and

(**c**) to a credit issued by a bank or other person if the credit is not within subparagraphs (a) or (b) but conspicuously states that it is a letter of credit or is conspicuously so entitled.

(**2**) Unless the engagement meets the requirements of subsection (1), this Article does not apply to engagements to make advances or to honor drafts or demands for payment, to authorities to pay or purchase, to guarantees or to general agreements.

(**3**) This Article deals with some but not all of the rules and concepts of letters of credit as such rules or concepts have developed prior to this act or may hereafter develop. The fact that this Article states a rule does not by itself require, imply or negate application of the same or a converse rule to a situation not provided for or to a person not specified by this Article.

§5–103. Definitions.

(**1**) In this Article unless the context otherwise requires

(**a**) "Credit" or "letter of credit" means an engagement by a bank or other person made at the request of a customer and of a kind within the scope of this Article (Section 5–102) that the issuer will honor drafts or other demands for payment upon compliance with the conditions specified in the credit. A credit may be either revocable or irrevocable. The engagement may be either an agreement to honor or a statement that the bank or other person is authorized to honor.

(**b**) A "documentary draft" or a "documentary demand for payment" is one, honor of which is conditioned upon the presentation of a document or documents. "Document" means any paper including document of title, security, invoice, certificate, notice of default and the like.

(**c**) An "issuer" is a bank or other person issuing a credit.

(**d**) A "beneficiary" of a credit is a person who is entitled under its terms to draw or demand payment.

(**e**) An "advising bank" is a bank which gives notification of the issuance of a credit by another bank.

(**f**) A "confirming bank" is a bank which engages either that it will itself honor a credit already issued by another bank or that such a credit will be honored by the issuer or a third bank.

(**g**) A "customer" is a buyer or other person who causes an issuer to issue a credit. The term also includes a bank which procures issuance or confirmation on behalf of that bank's customer.

(**2**) Other definitions applying to this Article and the sections in which they appear are:

"Notation of Credit". Section 5–108.

"Presenter". Section 5–112(3).

(**3**) Definitions in other Articles applying to this Article and the sections in which they appear are:

"Accept" or "Acceptance". Section 3–410.

"Contract for sale". Section 2–106.

"Draft". Section 3–104.

"Holder in due course". Section 3–302.

"Midnight deadline". Section 4–104.

"Security". Section 8–102.

(**4**) In addition, Article 1 contains general definitions and principles of construction and interpretation applicable throughout this Article.

§5–104. Formal Requirements; Signing.

(**1**) Except as otherwise required in subsection (1)(c) Section 5–102 on scope, no particular form of phrasing is required for a credit. A credit must be in writing and signed by the issuer and a confirmation must be in writing and signed by the confirming bank. A modification of the terms of a credit or confirmation must be signed by the issuer or confirming bank.

(**2**) A telegram may be a sufficient signed writing if it identifies its sender by an authorized authentication. The authentication may be in code and the authorized naming of the issuer in an advice of credit is a sufficient signing.

§5–105. Consideration.
No consideration is necessary to establish a credit or to enlarge or otherwise modify its terms.

§5–106. Time and Effect of Establishment of Credit.

(**1**) Unless otherwise agreed a credit is established

(**a**) as regards the customer as soon as a letter of credit is sent to him or the letter of credit or an authorized written advice of its issuance is sent to the beneficiary; and

(**b**) as regards the beneficiary when he receives a letter of credit or an authorized written advice of its issuance.

(**2**) Unless otherwise agreed once an irrevocable credit is established as regards the customer it can be modified or revoked only with the consent of the customer and once it is established as regards the beneficiary it can be modified or revoked only with his consent.

(**3**) Unless otherwise agreed after a revocable credit is established it may be modified or revoked by the issuer without notice to or consent from the customer or beneficiary.

(**4**) Notwithstanding any modification or revocation of a revocable credit any person authorized to honor or negotiate under the terms of the original credit is entitled to reimbursement for or honor of any draft or demand for payment duly honored or negotiated before receipt of notice of the modification or revocation and the issuer in turn is entitled to reimbursement from its customer.

§5–107. Advice of Credit; Confirmation; Error in Statement of Terms.

(**1**) Unless otherwise specified an advising bank by advising a credit issued by another bank does not assume any obligation to honor drafts drawn or demands for payment made under the credit but it does assume obligation for the accuracy of its own statement.

(2) A confirming bank by confirming a credit becomes directly obligated on the credit to the extent of its confirmation as though it were its issuer and acquires the rights of an issuer.

(3) Even though an advising bank incorrectly advises the terms of a credit it has been authorized to advise, the credit is established as against the issuer to the extent of its original terms.

(4) Unless otherwise specified the customer bears as against the issuer all risks of transmission and reasonable translation or interpretation of any message relating to a credit.

§5–108. "Notation Credit"; Exhaustion of Credit.

(1) A credit which specifies that any person purchasing or paying drafts drawn or demands for payment made under it must note the amount of the draft or demand on the letter or advice of credit is a "notation credit".

(2) Under a notation credit

(a) a person paying the beneficiary or purchasing a draft or demand for payment from him acquires a right to honor only if the appropriate notation is made and by transferring or forwarding for honor the documents under the credit such a person warrants to the issuer that the notation has been made; and

(b) unless the credit or a signed statement that an appropriate notation has been made accompanies the draft or demand for payment the issuer may delay honor until evidence of notation has been procured which is satisfactory to it but its obligation and that of its customer continue for a reasonable time not exceeding thirty days to obtain such evidence.

(3) If the credit is not a notation credit

(a) the issuer may honor complying drafts or demands for payment presented to it in the order in which they are presented and is discharged pro tanto by honor of any such draft or demand;

(b) as between competing good faith purchasers of complying drafts or demands the person first purchasing has priority over a subsequent purchaser even though the later purchased draft or demand has been first honored.

§5–109. Issuer's Obligation to Its Customer.

(1) An issuer's obligation to its customer includes good faith and observance of any general banking usage but unless otherwise agreed does not include liability or responsibility

(a) for performance of the underlying contract for sale or other transaction between the customer and the beneficiary; or

(b) for any act or omission of any person other than itself or its own branch or for loss or destruction of a draft, demand or document in transit or in the possession of others; or

(c) based on knowledge or lack of knowledge of any usage of any particular trade.

(2) An issuer must examine documents with care so as to ascertain that on their face they appear to comply with the terms of the credit but unless otherwise agreed assumes no liability or responsibility for the genuineness, falsification or effect of any document which appears on such examination to be regular on its face.

(3) A non-bank issuer is not bound by any banking usage of which it has no knowledge.

§5–110. Availability of Credit in Portions; Presenter's Reservatior of Lien or Claim.

(1) Unless otherwise specified a credit may be used in portions in the discretion of the beneficiary.

(2) Unless otherwise specified a person by presenting a documentary draft or demand for payment under a credit relinquishes upon its honor all claims to the documents and a person by transferring such draft or demand or causing such presentment authorizes such relinquishment. An explicit reservation of claim makes the draft or demand non-complying.

§5–111. Warranties on Transfer and Presentment.

(1) Unless otherwise agreed the beneficiary by transferring or presenting a documentary draft or demand for payment warrants to all interested parties that the necessary conditions of the credit have been complied with. This is in addition to any warranties arising under Articles 3, 4, 7 and 8.

(2) Unless otherwise agreed a negotiating, advising, confirming, collecting or issuing bank presenting or transferring a draft or demand for payment under a credit warrants only the matters warranted by a collecting bank under Article 4 and any such bank transferring a document warrants only the matters warranted by an intermediary under Articles 7 and 8.

§5–112. Time Allowed for Honor or Rejection; Withholding Honor or Rejection by Consent; "Presenter".

(1) A bank to which a documentary draft or demand for payment is presented under a credit may without dishonor of the draft, demand or credit

(a) defer honor until the close of the third banking day following receipt of the documents; and

(b) further defer honor if the presenter has expressly or impliedly consented thereto. Failure to honor within the time here specified constitutes dishonor of the draft or demand and of the credit [except as otherwise provided in subsection (4) of Section 5–114 on conditional payment].

Note: *The bracketed language in the last sentence of subsection (1) should be included only if the optional provisions of Section 5–114(4) and (5) are included.*

(2) Upon dishonor the bank may unless otherwise instructed fulfill its duty to return the draft or demand and the documents by holding them at the disposal of the presenter and sending him an advice to that effect.

(3) "Presenter" means any person presenting a draft or demand for payment for honor under a credit even though that person is a confirming bank or other correspondent which is acting under an issuer's authorization.

§5–113. Indemnities.

(1) A bank seeking to obtain (whether for itself or another) honor, negotiation or reimbursement under a credit may give an indemnity to induce such honor, negotiation or reimbursement.

(2) An indemnity agreement inducing honor, negotiation or reimbursement

(a) unless otherwise explicitly agreed applies to defects in the documents but not in the goods; and

(b) unless a longer time is explicitly agreed expires at the end of ten business days following receipt of the documents by the ultimate customer unless notice of objection is sent before such expiration date. The ultimate customer may send notice of objection to the person from whom he received the documents and any bank receiving such notice is under a duty to send notice to its transferor before its midnight deadline.

§5–114. Issuer's Duty and Privilege to Honor; Right to Reimbursement (*1977 Amendments*).

(1) An issuer must honor a draft or demand for payment which complies with the terms of the relevant credit regardless of whether the goods or documents conform to the underlying contract for sale or other contract between the customer and the beneficiary. The issuer is not excused from honor of such a draft or demand by reason of an additional general term that all documents must be satisfactory to the issuer, but an issuer may require that specified documents must be satisfactory to it.

(2) Unless otherwise agreed when documents appear on their face to comply with the terms of a credit but a required document does not in fact conform to the warranties made on negotiation or transfer of a document of title (Section 7–507) or of a certificated security (Section 8–306) or is forged or fraudulent or there is fraud in the transaction

(a) the issuer must honor the draft or demand for payment if honor is demanded by a negotiating bank or other holder of the draft or demand which has taken the draft or demand under the credit and under circumstances which would make it a holder in due course (Section 3–302) and in an appropriate case would make it a person to whom a document of title has been duly negotiated (Section 7–502) or a bona fide purchaser of a <u>certificated</u> security (Section 8–302); and

(b) in all other cases as against its customer, an issuer

acting in good faith may honor the draft or demand for payment despite notification from the customer of fraud, forgery or other defect not apparent on the face of the documents but a court of appropriate jurisdiction may enjoin such honor.

(3) Unless otherwise agreed an issuer which has duly honored a draft or demand for payment is entitled to immediate reimbursement of any payment made under the credit and to be put in effectively available funds not later than the day before maturity of any acceptance made under the credit.

[(4) When a credit provides for payment by the issuer on receipt of notice that the required documents are in the possession of a correspondent or other agent of the issuer

(a) any payment made on receipt of such notice is conditional; and

(b) the issuer may reject documents which do not comply with the credit if it does so within three banking days following its receipt of the documents; and

(c) in the event of such rejection, the issuer is entitled by charge back or otherwise to return to the payment made.]

[(5) In the case covered by subsection (4) failure to reject documents within the time specified in sub-paragraph (b) constitutes acceptance of the documents and makes the payment final in favor of the beneficiary.]

Note: *Subsections (4) and (5) are bracketed as optional. If they are included the bracketed language in the last sentence of Section 5–112(1) should also be included.*

§5–115. Remedy for Improper Dishonor or Anticipatory Repudiation.

(1) When an issuer wrongfully dishonors a draft or demand for payment presented under a credit the person entitled to honor has with respect to any documents the rights of a person in the position of a seller (Section 2–707) and may recover from the issuer the face amount of the draft or demand together with incidental damages under Section 2–710 on seller's incidental damages and interest but less any amount realized by resale or other use or disposition of the subject matter of the transaction. In the event no resale or other utilization is made the documents, goods or other subject matter involved in the transaction must be turned over to the issuer on payment of judgment.

(2) When an issuer wrongfully cancels or otherwise repudiates a credit before presentment of a draft or demand for payment drawn under it the beneficiary has the rights of a seller after anticipatory repudiation by the buyer under Section 2–610 if he learns of the repudiation in time reasonably to avoid procurement of the required docu-

ments. Otherwise the beneficiary has an immediate right of action for wrongful dishonor.

§5–116. Transfer and Assignment.

(1) The right to draw under a credit can be transferred or assigned only when the credit is expressly designated as transferable or assignable.

(2) Even though the credit specifically states that it is nontransferable or nonassignable the beneficiary may before performance of the conditions of the credit assign his right to proceeds. Such an assignment is an assignment of [a contract right] an account under Article 9 on Secured Transactions and is governed by that Article except that

(a) the assignment is ineffective until the letter of credit or advice of credit is delivered to the assignee which delivery constitutes perfection of the security interest under Article 9; and

(b) the issuer may honor drafts or demands for payment drawn under the credit until it receives a notification of the assignment signed by the beneficiary which reasonably identifies the credit involved in the assignment and contains a request to pay the assignee; and

(c) after what reasonably appears to be such a notification has been received the issuer may without dishonor refuse to accept or pay even to a person otherwise entitled to honor until the letter of credit or advice of credit is exhibited to the issuer.

(3) Except where the beneficiary has effectively assigned his right to draw or his right to proceeds, nothing in this section limits his right to transfer or negotiate drafts or demands drawn under the credit.

§5–117. Insolvency of Bank Holding Funds for Documentary Credit.

(1) Where an issuer or an advising or confirming bank or a bank which has for a customer procured issuance of a credit by another bank becomes insolvent before final payment under the credit and the credit is one to which this Article is made applicable by paragraphs (a) or (b) of Section 5–102(1) on scope, the receipt or allocation of funds or collateral to secure or meet obligations under the credit shall have the following results:

(a) to the extent of any funds or collateral turned over after or before the insolvency as indemnity against or specifically for the purpose of payment of drafts or demands for payments drawn under the designated credit, the drafts or demands are entitled to payment in preference over depositors or other general creditors of the issuer or bank; and

(b) on expiration of the credit or surrender of the beneficiary's rights under it unused any person who has given such funds or collateral is similarly entitled to return thereof; and

(c) a charge to a general or current account with a bank if specifically consented to for the purpose of indemnity against or payment of drafts or demands for payment drawn under the designated credit falls under the same rules as if the funds had been drawn out in cash and then turned over with specific instructions.

(2) After honor or reimbursement under this section the customer or other person for whose account the insolvent bank has acted is entitled to receive the documents involved.

ARTICLE 6: BULK TRANSFERS

§6–101. Short Title.
This Article shall be known and may be cited as Uniform Commercial Code—Bulk Transfers.

§6–102. "Bulk Transfers"; Transfers of Equipment; Enterprises Subject to This Article; Bulk Transfers Subject to This Article.

(1) A "bulk transfer" is any transfer in bulk and not in the ordinary course of the transferor's business of a major part of the materials, supplies, merchandise or other inventory (Section 9–109) of an enterprise subject to this Article.

(2) A transfer of a substantial part of the equipment (Section 9–109) of such an enterprise is a bulk transfer if it is made in connection with a bulk transfer of inventory, but not otherwise.

(3) The enterprises subject to this Article are all those whose principal business is the sale of merchandise from stock, including those who manufacture what they sell.

(4) Except as limited by the following section all bulk transfers of goods located within this state are subject to this Article.

§6–103. Transfers Excepted From This Article.
The following transfers are not subject to this Article:

(1) Those made to give security for the performance of an obligation;

(2) General assignments for the benefit of all the creditors of the transferor, and subsequent transfers by the assignee thereunder;

(3) Transfers in settlement or realization of a lien or other security interests;

(4) Sales by executors, administrators, receivers, trustees in bankruptcy, or any public officer under judicial process;

(5) Sales made in the course of judicial or administrative proceedings for the dissolution or reorganization of a corporation and of which notice is sent to the creditors of the corporation pursuant to order of the court or administrative agency;

(6) Transfers to a person maintaining a known place of

business in this State who becomes bound to pay the debts of the transferor in full and gives public notice of that fact, and who is solvent after becoming so bound;

(7) A transfer to a new business enterprise organized to take over and continue the business, if public notice of the transaction is given and the new enterprise assumes the debts of the transferor and he receives nothing from the transaction except an interest in the new enterprise junior to the claims of creditors;

(8) Transfers of property which is exempt from execution. Public notice under subsection (6) or subsection (7) may be given by publishing once a week for two consecutive weeks in a newspaper of general circulation where the transferor had its principal place of business in this State an advertisement including the names and addresses of the transferor and transferee and the effective date of the transfer.

§6–104. Schedule of Property, List of Creditors.

(1) Except as provided with respect to auction sales (Section 6–108), a bulk transfer subject to this Article is ineffective against any creditor of the transferor unless:

(a) The transferee requires the transferor to furnish a list of his existing creditors prepared as stated in this section; and

(b) The parties prepare a schedule of the property transferred sufficient to identify it; and

(c) The transferee preserves the list and schedule for six months next following the transfer and permits inspection of either or both and copying therefrom at all reasonable hours by any creditor of the transferor, or files the list and schedule in (a public office to be here identified).

(2) The list of creditors must be signed and sworn to or affirmed by the transferor or his agent. It must contain the names and business addresses of all creditors of the transferor, with the amounts when known, and also the names of all persons who are known to the transferor to assert claims against him even though such claims are disputed. If the transferor is the obligor of an outstanding issue of bonds, debentures or the like as to which there is an indenture trustee, the list of creditors need include only the name and address of the indenture trustee and the aggregate outstanding principal amount of the issue.

(3) Responsibility for the completeness and accuracy of the list of creditors rests on the transferor, and the transfer is not rendered ineffective by errors or omissions therein unless the transferee is shown to have had knowledge.

§6–105. Notice to Creditors.

In addition to the requirements of the preceding section, any bulk transfer subject to this Article except one made by auction sale (Section 6–108) is ineffective against any creditor of the transferor unless at least ten days before he takes possession of the goods or pays

for them, whichever happens first, the transferee gives notice of the transfer in the manner and to the persons hereafter provided (Section 6–107).

§6–106. Application of the Proceeds.

In addition to the requirements of the two preceding sections:

(1) Upon every bulk transfer subject to this Article for which new consideration becomes payable except those made by sale at auction it is the duty of the transferee to assure that such consideration is applied so far as necessary to pay those debts of the transferor which are either shown on the list furnished by the transferor (Section 6–104) or filed in writing in the place stated in the notice (Section 6–107) within thirty days after the mailing of such notice. This duty of the transferee runs to all the holders of such debts, and may be enforced by any of them for the benefit of all.

(2) If any of said debts are in dispute the necessary sum may be withheld from distribution until the dispute is settled or adjudicated.

[(3) If the consideration payable is not enough to pay all of the said debts in full distribution shall be made pro rata.]

Note: *This section is bracketed to indicate division of opinion as to whether or not it is a wise provision, and to suggest that this is a point on which State enactments may differ without serious damage to the principle of uniformity.*

In any State where this section is omitted, the following parts of sections, also bracketed in the text, should also be omitted, namely:

Section 6–107(2) (e).

6–108(3) (c).

6–109(2).

In any State where this section is enacted, these other provisions should be also.

Optional Subsection (4)

[(4) The transferee may within ten days after he takes possession of the goods pay the consideration into the (specify court) in the county where the transferor had its principal place of business in this state and thereafter may discharge his duty under this section by giving notice by registered or certified mail to all the persons to whom the duty runs that the consideration has been paid into that court and that they should file their claims there. On motion of any interested party, the court may order the distribution of the consideration to the persons entitled to it.]

Note: *Optional subsection (4) is recommended for those states which do not have a general statute providing for payment of money into court.*

§6–107. The Notice.

(1) The notice to creditors (Section 6–105) shall state:

(a) that a bulk transfer is about to be made; and

(b) the names and business addresses of the transferor and transferee, and all other business names and addresses used by the transferor within three years last past so far as known to the transferee; and

(c) whether or not all the debts of the transferor are to be paid in full as they fall due as a result of the transaction, and if so, the address to which creditors should send their bills.

(2) If the debts of the transferor are not to be paid in full as they fall due or if the transferee is in doubt on that point then the notice shall state further:

(a) the location and general description of the property to be transferred and the estimated total of the transferor's debts;

(b) the address where the schedule of property and list of creditors (Section 6–104) may be inspected;

(c) whether the transfer is to pay existing debts and if so the amount of such debts and to whom owing;

(d) whether the transfer is for new consideration and if so the amount of such consideration and the time and place of payment; [and]

[(e) if for new consideration the time and place where creditors of the transferor are to file their claims.]

(3) The notice in any case shall be delivered personally or sent by registered or certified mail to all the persons shown on the list of creditors furnished by the transferor (Section 6–104) and to all other persons who are known to the transferee to hold or assert claims against the transferor.

Note: *The words in brackets are optional. See Note under § 6–106.*

§6–108. Auction Sales; "Auctioneer".

(1) A bulk transfer is subject to this Article even though it is by sale at auction, but only in the manner and with the results stated in this section.

(2) The transferor shall furnish a list of his creditors and assist in the preparation of a schedule of the property to be sold, both prepared as before stated (Section 6–104).

(3) The person or persons other than the transferor who direct, control or are responsible for the auction are collectively called the "auctioneer". The auctioneer shall:

(a) receive and retain the list of creditors and prepare and retain the schedule of property for the period stated in this Article (Section 6–104);

(b) give notice of the auction personally or by registered or certified mail at least ten days before it occurs to all persons shown on the list of creditors and to all other persons who are known to him to hold or assert claims against the transferor; [and]

[(c) assure that the net proceeds of the auction are applied as provided in this Article (Section 6–106).]

(4) Failure of the auctioneer to perform any of these duties does not affect the validity of the sale or the title of the purchasers, but if the auctioneer knows that the auction constitutes a bulk transfer such failure renders the auctioneer liable to the creditors of the transferor as a class for the sums owing to them from the transferor up to but not exceeding the net proceeds of the auction. If the auctioneer consists of several persons their liability is joint and several.

Note: *The words in brackets are optional. See Note under § 6–106.*

§6–109. What Creditors Protected; [Credit for Payment to Particular Creditors].

(1) The creditors of the transferor mentioned in this Article are those holding claims based on transactions or events occurring before the bulk transfer, but creditors who become such after notice to creditors is given (Sections 6–105 and 6–107) are not entitled to notice.

[(2) Against the aggregate obligation imposed by the provisions of this Article concerning the application of the proceeds (Section 6–106 and subsection (3) (c) of 6–108) the transferee or auctioneer is entitled to credit for sums paid to particular creditors of the transferor, not exceeding the sums believed in good faith at the time of the payment to be properly payable to such creditors.]

Note: *The words in brackets are optional. See Note under § 6–106.*

§6–110. Subsequent Transfers. When the title of a transferee to property is subject to a defect by reason of his non-compliance with the requirements of this Article, then:

(1) a purchaser of any of such property from such transferee who pays no value or who takes with notice of such non-compliance takes subject to such defect, but

(2) a purchaser for value in good faith and without such notice takes free of such defect.

§6–111. Limitation of Actions and Levies. No action under this Article shall be brought nor levy made more than six months after the date on which the transferee took possession of the goods unless the transfer has been concealed. If the transfer has been concealed, actions may be brought or levies made within six months after its discovery.

ARTICLE 7: WAREHOUSE RECEIPTS, BILLS OF LADING AND OTHER DOCUMENTS OF TITLE

Part 1   General

§7–101. Short Title. This Article shall be known and may be cited as Uniform Commercial Code—Documents of Title.

§7–102. Definitions and Index of Definitions.

(1) In this Article, unless the context otherwise requires:

(a) "Bailee" means the person who by a warehouse receipt, bill of lading or other document of title acknowledges possession of goods and contracts to deliver them.

(b) "Consignee" means the person named in a bill to whom or to whose order the bill promises delivery.

(c) "Consignor" means the person named in a bill as the person from whom the goods have been received for shipment.

(d) "Delivery order" means a written order to deliver goods directed to a warehouseman, carrier or other person who in the ordinary course of business issues warehouse receipts or bills of lading.

(e) "Document" means document of title as defined in the general definitions in Article 1 (Section 1–201).

(f) "Goods" means all things which are treated as movable for the purposes of a contract of storage or transportation.

(g) "Issuer" means a bailee who issues a document except that in relation to an unaccepted delivery order it means the person who orders the possessor of goods to deliver. Issuer includes any person for whom an agent or employee purports to act in issuing a document if the agent or employee has real or apparent authority to issue documents, notwithstanding that the issuer received no goods or that the goods were misdescribed or that in any other respect the agent or employee violated his instructions.

(h) "Warehouseman" is a person engaged in the business of storing goods for hire.

(2) Other definitions applying to this Article or to specified Parts thereof, and the sections in which they appear are:

"Duly negotiate". Section 7–501.

"Person entitled under the document". Section 7–403(4).

(3) Definitions in other Articles applying to this Article and the sections in which they appear are:

"Contract for sale". Section 2–106.

"Overseas". Section 2–323.

"Receipt" of goods. Section 2–103.

(4) In addition Article 1 contains general definitions and principles of construction and interpretation applicable throughout this Article.

§7–103. Relation of Article to Treaty, Statute, Tariff, Classification or Regulation. To the extent that any treaty or statute of the United States, regulatory statute of this State or tariff, classification or regulation filed or issued pursuant thereto is applicable, the provisions of this Article are subject thereto.

§7–104. Negotiable and Non-Negotiable Warehouse Receipt, Bill of Lading or Other Document of Title.

(1) A warehouse receipt, bill of lading or other document of title is negotiable

(a) if by its terms the goods are to be delivered to bearer or to the order of a named person; or

(b) where recognized in overseas trade, if it runs to a named person or assigns.

(2) Any other document is non-negotiable. A bill of lading in which it is stated that the goods are consigned to a named person is not made negotiable by a provision that the goods are to be delivered only against a written order signed by the same or another named person.

§7–105. Construction Against Negative Implication. The omission from either Part 2 or Part 3 of this Article of a provision corresponding to a provision made in the other Part does not imply that a corresponding rule of law is not applicable.

Part 2   Warehouse Receipts: Special Provisions

§7–201. Who May Issue a Warehouse Receipt; Storage Under Government Bond.

(1) A warehouse receipt may be issued by any warehouseman.

(2) Where goods including distilled spirits and agricultural commodities are stored under a statute requiring a bond against withdrawal or a license for the issuance of receipts in the nature of warehouse receipts, a receipt issued for the goods has like effect as a warehouse receipt even though issued by a person who is the owner of the goods and is not a warehouseman.

§7–202. Form of Warehouse Receipt; Essential Terms; Optional Terms.

(1) A warehouse receipt need not be in any particular form.

(2) Unless a warehouse receipt embodies within its written or printed terms each of the following, the warehouseman is liable for damages caused by the omission to a person injured thereby:

(a) the location of the warehouse where the goods are stored;

(b) the date of issue of the receipt;

(c) the consecutive number of the receipt;

(d) a statement whether the goods received will be delivered to the bearer, to a specified person, or to a specified person or his order;

(e) the rate of storage and handling charges, except that where goods are stored under a field warehousing arrangement a statement of that fact is sufficient on a non-negotiable receipt;

(**f**) a description of the goods or of the packages containing them;

(**g**) the signature of the warehouseman, which may be made by his authorized agent;

(**h**) if the receipt is issued for goods of which the warehouseman is owner, either solely or jointly or in common with others, the fact of such ownership; and

(**i**) a statement of the amount of advances made and of liabilities incurred for which the warehouseman claims a lien or security interest (Section 7–209). If the precise amount of such advances made or of such liabilities incurred is, at the time of the issue of the receipt, unknown to the warehouseman or to his agent who issues it, a statement of the fact that advances have been made or liabilities incurred and the purpose thereof is sufficient.

(3) A warehouseman may insert in his receipt any other terms which are not contrary to the provisions of this Act and do not impair his obligation of delivery (Section 7–403) or his duty of care (Section 7–204). Any contrary provisions shall be ineffective.

§7–203. Liability for Non-Receipt or Misdescription.
A party to or purchaser for value in good faith of a document of title other than a bill of lading relying in either case upon the description therein of the goods may recover from the issuer damages caused by the non-receipt or misdescription of the goods, except to the extent that the document conspicuously indicates that the issuer does not know whether any part or all of the goods in fact were received or conform to the description, as where the description is in terms of marks or labels or kind, quantity or condition, or the receipt or description is qualified by "contents, condition and quality unknown," "said to contain" or the like, if such indication be true, or the party or purchaser otherwise has notice.

§7–204. Duty of Care; Contractual Limitation of Warehouseman's Liability.
(1) A warehouseman is liable for damages for loss of or injury to the goods caused by his failure to exercise such care in regard to them as a reasonably careful man would exercise under like circumstances but unless otherwise agreed he is not liable for damages which could not have been avoided by the exercise of such care.

(2) Damages may be limited by a term in the warehouse receipt or storage agreement limiting the amount of liability in case of loss or damage, and setting forth a specific liability per article or item, or value per unit of weight, beyond which the warehouseman shall not be liable; provided, however, that such liability may on written request of the bailor at the time of signing such storage agreement or within a reasonable time after receipt of the warehouse receipt be increased on part or all of the goods thereunder,

in which event increased rates may be charged based on such increased valuation, but that no such increase shall be permitted contrary to a lawful limitation of liability contained in the warehouseman's tariff, if any. No such limitation is effective with respect to the warehouseman's liability for conversion to his own use.

(3) Reasonable provisions as to the time and manner of presenting claims and instituting actions based on the bailment may be included in the warehouse receipt or tariff.

(4) This section does not impair or repeal . . .

Note: *Insert in subsection (4) a reference to any statute which imposes a higher responsibility upon the warehouseman or invalidates contractual limitations which would be permissible under this Article.*

§7–205. Title Under Warehouse Receipt Defeated in Certain Cases.
A buyer in the ordinary course of business of fungible goods sold and delivered by a warehouseman who is also in the business of buying and selling such goods takes free of any claim under a warehouse receipt even though it has been duly negotiated.

§7–206. Termination of Storage at Warehouseman's Option.
(1) A warehouseman may on notifying the person on whose account the goods are held and any other person known to claim an interest in the goods require payment of any charges and removal of the goods from the warehouse at the termination of the period of storage fixed by the document, or, if no period is fixed, within a stated period not less than thirty days after the notification. If the goods are not removed before the date specified in the notification, the warehouseman may sell them in accordance with the provisions of the section on enforcement of a warehouseman's lien (Section 7–210).

(2) If a warehouseman in good faith believes that the goods are about to deteriorate or decline in value to less than the amount of his lien within the time prescribed in subsection (1) for notification, advertisement and sale, the warehouseman may specify in the notification any reasonable shorter time for removal of the goods and in case the goods are not removed, may sell them at public sale held not less than one week after a single advertisement or posting.

(3) If as a result of a quality or condition of the goods of which the warehouseman had no notice at the time of deposit the goods are a hazard to other property or to the warehouse or to persons, the warehouseman may sell the goods at public or private sale without advertisement on reasonable notification to all persons known to claim an interest in the goods. If the warehouseman after a reasonable effort is unable to sell the goods he may dispose of them in any lawful manner and shall incur no liability by reason of such disposition.

(4) The warehouseman must deliver the goods to any person entitled to them under this Article upon due demand made at any time prior to sale or other disposition under this section.

(5) The warehouseman may satisfy his lien from the proceeds of any sale or disposition under this section but must hold the balance for delivery on the demand of any person to whom he would have been bound to deliver the goods.

§7–207. Goods Must Be Kept Separate; Fungible Goods.

(1) Unless the warehouse receipt otherwise provides, a warehouseman must keep separate the goods covered by each receipt so as to permit at all times identification and delivery of those goods except that different lots of fungible goods may be commingled.

(2) Fungible goods so commingled are owned in common by the persons entitled thereto and the warehouseman is severally liable to each owner for that owner's share. Where because of overissue a mass of fungible goods is insufficient to meet all the receipts which the warehouseman has issued against it, the persons entitled include all holders to whom overissued receipts have been duly negotiated.

§7–208. Altered Warehouse Receipts.

Where a blank in a negotiable warehouse receipt has been filled in without authority, a purchaser for value and without notice of the want of authority may treat the insertion as authorized. Any other unauthorized alteration leaves any receipt enforceable against the issuer according to its original tenor.

§7–209. Lien of Warehouseman.

(1) A warehouseman has a lien against the bailor on the goods covered by a warehouse receipt or on the proceeds thereof in his possession for charges for storage or transportation (including demurrage and terminal charges), insurance, labor, or charges present or future in relation to the goods, and for expenses necessary for preservation of the goods or reasonably incurred in their sale pursuant to law. If the person on whose account the goods are held is liable for like charges or expenses in relation to other goods whenever deposited and it is stated in the receipt that a lien is claimed for charges and expenses in relation to other goods, the warehouseman also has a lien against him for such charges and expenses whether or not the other goods have been delivered by the warehouseman. But against a person to whom a negotiable warehouse receipt is duly negotiated a warehouseman's lien is limited to charges in an amount or at a rate specified on the receipt or if no charges are so specified then to a reasonable charge for storage of the goods covered by the receipt subsequent to the date of the receipt.

(2) The warehouseman may also reserve a security interest against the bailor for a maximum amount specified on the receipt for charges other than those specified in subsection (1), such as for money advanced and interest. Such a security interest is governed by the Article on Secured Transactions (Article 9).

(3)

(a) A warehouseman's lien for charges and expenses under subsection (1) or a security interest under subsection (2) is also effective against any person who so entrusted the bailor with possession of the goods that a pledge of them by him to a good faith purchaser for value would have been valid but is not effective against a person as to whom the document confers no right in the goods covered by it under Section 7–503.

(b) A warehouseman's lien on household goods for charges and expenses in relation to the goods under subsection (1) is also effective against all persons if the depositor was the legal possessor of the goods at the time of deposit. "Household goods" means furniture, furnishings and personal effects used by the depositor in a dwelling.

(4) A warehouseman loses his lien on any goods which he voluntarily delivers or which he unjustifiably refuses to deliver. (As amended in 1966.)

§7–210. Enforcement of Warehouseman's Lien.

(1) Except as provided in subsection (2), a warehouseman's lien may be enforced by public or private sale of the goods in block or in parcels, at any time or place and on any terms which are commercially reasonable, after notifying all persons known to claim an interest in the goods. Such notification must include a statement of the amount due, the nature of the proposed sale and the time and place of any public sale. The fact that a better price could have been obtained by a sale at a different time or in a different method from that selected by the warehouseman is not of itself sufficient to establish that the sale was not made in a commercially reasonable manner. If the warehouseman either sells the goods in the usual manner in any recognized market therefor, or if he sells at the price current in such market at the time of his sale, or if he has otherwise sold in conformity with commercially reasonable practices among dealers in the type of goods sold, he has sold in a commercially reasonable manner. A sale of more goods than apparently necessary to be offered to insure satisfaction of the obligation is not commercially reasonable except in cases covered by the preceding sentence.

(2) A warehouseman's lien on goods other than goods stored by a merchant in the course of his business may be enforced only as follows:

(a) All persons known to claim an interest in the goods must be notified.

(b) The notification must be delivered in person or sent

by registered or certified letter to the last known address of any person to be notified.

(c) The notification must include an itemized statement of the claim, a description of the goods subject to the lien, a demand for payment within a specified time not less than ten days after receipt of the notification, and a conspicuous statement that unless the claim is paid within that time the goods will be advertised for sale and sold by auction at a specified time and place.

(d) The sale must conform to the terms of the notification.

(e) The sale must be held at the nearest suitable place to that where the goods are held or stored.

(f) After the expiration of the time given in the notification, an advertisement of the sale must be published once a week for two weeks consecutively in a newspaper of general circulation where the sale is to be held. The advertisement must include a description of the goods, the name of the person on whose account they are being held, and the time and place of the sale. The sale must take place at least fifteen days after the first publication. If there is no newspaper of general circulation where the sale is to be held, the advertisement must be posted at least ten days before the sale in not less than six conspicuous places in the neighborhood of the proposed sale.

(3) Before any sale pursuant to this section any person claiming a right in the goods may pay the amount necessary to satisfy the lien and the reasonable expenses incurred under this section. In that event the goods must not be sold, but must be retained by the warehouseman subject to the terms of the receipt and this Article.

(4) The warehouseman may buy at any public sale pursuant to this section.

(5) A purchaser in good faith of goods sold to enforce a warehouseman's lien takes the goods free of any rights of persons against whom the lien was valid, despite noncompliance by the warehouseman with the requirements of this section.

(6) The warehouseman may satisfy his lien from the proceeds of any sale pursuant to this section but must hold the balance, if any, for delivery on demand to any person to whom he would have been bound to deliver the goods.

(7) The rights provided by this section shall be in addition to all other rights allowed by law to a creditor against his debtor.

(8) Where a lien is on goods stored by a merchant in the course of his business the lien may be enforced in accordance with either subsection (1) or (2).

(9) The warehouseman is liable for damages caused by failure to comply with the requirements for sale under this section and in case of willful violation is liable for conversion. As amended in 1962.

Part 3 Bills of Lading: Special Provisions

§7–301. Liability for Non-Receipt or Misdescription; "Said to Contain"; "Shipper's Load and Count"; Improper Handling.

(1) A consignee of a non-negotiable bill who has given value in good faith or a holder to whom a negotiable bill has been duly negotiated relying in either case upon the description therein of the goods, or upon the date therein shown, may recover from the issuer damages caused by the misdating of the bill or the non-receipt or misdescription of the goods, except to the extent that the document indicates that the issuer does not know whether any part or all of the goods in fact were received or conform to the description, as where the description is in terms of marks or labels or kind, quantity, or condition or the receipt or description is qualified by "contents or condition of contents of packages unknown", "said to contain", "Shipper's weight, load and count" or the like, if such indication be true.

(2) When goods are loaded by an issuer who is a common carrier, the issuer must count the packages of goods if package freight and ascertain the kind and quantity if bulk freight. In such cases "shipper's weight, load and count" or other words indicating that the description was made by the shipper are ineffective except as to freight concealed by packages.

(3) When bulk freight is loaded by a shipper who makes available to the issuer adequate facilities for weighing such freight, an issuer who is a common carrier must ascertain the kind and quantity within a reasonable time after receiving the written request of the shipper to do so. In such cases "shipper's weight" or other words of like purport are ineffective.

(4) The issuer may be inserting in the bill the words "shipper's weight, load and count" or other words of like purport indicate that the goods were loaded by the shipper; and if such statement be true the issuer shall not be liable for damages caused by the improper loading. But their omission does not imply liability for such damages.

(5) The shipper shall be deemed to have guaranteed to the issuer the accuracy at the time of shipment of the description, marks, labels, number, kind, quantity, condition and weight, as furnished by him; and the shipper shall indemnify the issuer against damage caused by inaccuracies in such particulars. The right of the issuer to such indemnity shall in no way limit his responsibility and liability under the contract of carriage to any person other than the shipper.

§7–302. Through Bills of Lading and Similar Documents.

(1) The issuer of a through bill of lading or other document embodying an undertaking to be performed in part by

persons acting as its agents or by connecting carriers is liable to anyone entitled to recover on the document for any breach by such other persons or by a connecting carrier of its obligation under the document but to the extent that the bill covers an undertaking to be performed overseas or in territory not contiguous to the continental United States or an undertaking including matters other than transportation this liability may be varied by agreement of the parties.

(2) Where goods covered by a through bill of lading or other document embodying an undertaking to be performed in part by persons other than the issuer are received by any such person, he is subject with respect to his own performance while the goods are in his possession to the obligation of the issuer. His obligation is discharged by delivery of the goods to another such person pursuant to the document, and does not include liability for breach by any other such persons or by the issuer.

(3) The issuer of such through bill of lading or other document shall be entitled to recover from the connecting carrier or such other person in possession of the goods when the breach of the obligation under the document occurred, the amount it may be required to pay to anyone entitled to recover on the document therefor, as may be evidenced by any receipt, judgment, or transcript thereof, and the amount of any expense reasonably incurred by it in defending any action brought by anyone entitled to recover on the document therefor.

§7–303. Diversion; Reconsignment; Change of Instructions.

(1) Unless the bill of lading otherwise provides, the carrier may deliver the goods to a person or destination other than that stated in the bill or may otherwise dispose of the goods on instructions from

(a) the holder of a negotiable bill; or

(b) the consignor on a non-negotiable bill notwithstanding contrary instructions from the consignee; or

(c) the consignee on a non-negotiable bill in the absence of contrary instructions from the consignor, if the goods have arrived at the billed destination or if the consignee is in possession of the bill; or

(d) the consignee on a non-negotiable bill if he is entitled as against the consignor to dispose of them.

(2) Unless such instructions are noted on a negotiable bill of lading, a person to whom the bill is duly negotiated can hold the bailee according to the original terms.

§7–304. Bills of Lading in a Set.

(1) Except where customary in overseas transportation, a bill of lading must not be issued in a set of parts. The issuer is liable for damages caused by violation of this subsection.

(2) Where a bill of lading is lawfully drawn in a set of parts,

each of which is numbered and expressed to be valid only if the goods have not been delivered against any other part, the whole of the parts constitute one bill.

(3) Where a bill of lading is lawfully issued in a set of parts and different parts are negotiated to different persons, the title of the holder to whom the first due negotiation is made prevails as to both the document and the goods even though any later holder may have received the goods from the carrier in good faith and discharged the carrier's obligation by surrender of his part.

(4) Any person who negotiates or transfers a single part of a bill of lading drawn in a set is liable to holders of that part as if it were the whole set.

(5) The bailee is obliged to deliver in accordance with Part 4 of this Article against the first presented part of a bill of lading lawfully drawn in a set. Such delivery discharges the bailee's obligation on the whole bill.

§7–305. Destination Bills.

(1) Instead of issuing a bill of lading to the consignor at the place of shipment a carrier may at the request of the consignor procure the bill to be issued at destination or at any other place designated in the request.

(2) Upon request of anyone entitled as against the carrier to control the goods while in transit and on surrender of any outstanding bill of lading or other receipt covering such goods, the issuer may procure a substitute bill to be issued at any place designated in the request.

§7–306. Altered Bills of Lading. An unauthorized alteration or filling in of a blank in a bill of lading leaves the bill enforceable according to its original tenor.

§7–307. Lien of Carrier.

(1) A carrier has a lien on the goods covered by a bill of lading for charges subsequent to the date of its receipt of the goods for storage or transportation (including demurrage and terminal charges) and for expenses necessary for preservation of the goods incident to their transportation or reasonably incurred in their sale pursuant to law. But against a purchaser for value of a negotiable bill of lading a carrier's lien is limited to charges stated in the bill or the applicable tariffs, or if no charges are stated then to a reasonable charge.

(2) A lien for charges and expenses under subsection (1) on goods which the carrier was required by law to receive for transportation is effective against the consignor or any person entitled to the goods unless the carrier had notice that the consignor lacked authority to subject the goods to such charges and expenses. Any other lien under subsection (1) is effective against the consignor and any person who permitted the bailor to have control or possession of the goods unless the carrier had notice that the bailor lacked such authority.

(3) A carrier loses his lien on any goods which he

voluntarily delivers or which he unjustifiably refuses to deliver.

§7–308. Enforcement of Carrier's Lien.

(1) A carrier's lien may be enforced by public or private sale of the goods, in block or in parcels, at any time or place and on any terms which are commercially reasonable, after notifying all persons known to claim an interest in the goods. Such notification must include a statement of the amount due, the nature of the proposed sale and the time and place of any public sale. The fact that a better price could have been obtained by a sale at a different time or in a different method from that selected by the carrier is not of itself sufficient to establish that the sale was not made in a commercially reasonable manner. If the carrier either sells the goods in the usual manner in any recognized market therefor or if he sells at the price current in such market at the time of his sale or if he has otherwise sold in conformity with commercially reasonable practices among dealers in the type of goods sold he has sold in a commercially reasonable manner. A sale of more goods than apparently necessary to be offered to ensure satisfaction of the obligation is not commercially reasonable except in cases covered by the preceding sentence.

(2) Before any sale pursuant to this section any person claiming a right in the goods may pay the amount necessary to satisfy the lien and the reasonable expenses incurred under this section. In that event the goods must not be sold, but must be retained by the carrier subject to the terms of the bill and this Article.

(3) The carrier may buy at any public sale pursuant to this section.

(4) A purchaser in good faith of goods sold to enforce a carrier's lien takes the goods free of any rights of persons against whom the lien was valid, despite noncompliance by the carrier with the requirements of this section.

(5) The carrier may satisfy his lien from the proceeds of any sale pursuant to this section but must hold the balance, if any, for delivery on demand to any person to whom he would have been bound to deliver the goods.

(6) The rights provided by this section shall be in addition to all other rights allowed by law to a creditor against his debtor.

(7) A carrier's lien may be enforced in accordance with either subsection (1) or the procedure set forth in subsection (2) of Section 7–210.

(8) The carrier is liable for damages caused by failure to comply with the requirements for sale under this section and in case of willful violation is liable for conversion.

§7–309. Duty of Care; Contractual Limitation of Carrier's Liability.

(1) A carrier who issues a bill of lading whether negotiable or non-negotiable must exercise the degree of care in relation to the goods which a reasonably careful man would exercise under like circumstances. This subsection does not repeal or change any law or rule of law which imposes liability upon a common carrier for damages not caused by its negligence.

(2) Damages may be limited by a provision that the carrier's liability shall not exceed a value stated in the document if the carrier's rates are dependent upon value and the consignor by the carrier's tariff is afforded an opportunity to declare a higher value or a value as lawfully provided in the tariff, or where no tariff is filed he is otherwise advised of such opportunity; but no such limitation is effective with respect to the carrier's liability for conversion to its own use.

(3) Reasonable provisions as to the time and manner of presenting claims and instituting actions based on the shipment may be included in a bill of lading or tariff.

Part 4 Warehouse Receipts and Bills of Lading: General Obligations

§7–401. Irregularities in Issue of Receipt or Bill or Conduct of Issuer. The obligations imposed by this Article on an issuer apply to a document of title regardless of the fact that

(a) the document may not comply with the requirements of this Article or of any other law or regulation regarding its issue, form or content; or

(b) the issuer may have violated laws regulating the conduct of his business; or

(c) the goods covered by the document were owned by the bailee at the time the document was issued; or

(d) the person issuing the document does not come within the definition of warehouseman if it purports to be a warehouse receipt.

§7–402. Duplicate Receipt or Bill; Overissue. Neither a duplicate nor any other document of title purporting to cover goods already represented by an outstanding document of the same issuer confers any right in the goods, except as provided in the case of bills in a set, overissue of documents for fungible goods and substitutes for lost, stolen or destroyed documents. But the issuer is liable for damages caused by his overissue or failure to identify a duplicate document as such by conspicuous notation on its face.

§7–403. Obligation of Warehouseman or Carrier to Deliver; Excuse.

(1) The bailee must deliver the goods to a person entitled under the document who complies with subsections (2) and (3), unless and to the extent that the bailee establishes any of the following:

(a) delivery of the goods to a person whose receipt was rightful as against the claimant;

(b) damage to or delay, loss or destruction of the goods for which the bailee is not liable [, but the burden of establishing negligence in such cases is on the person entitled under the document];

Note: *The brackets in (1) (b) indicate that State enactments may differ on this point without serious damage to the principle of uniformity.*

(c) previous sale or other disposition of the goods in lawful enforcement of a lien or on warehouseman's lawful termination of storage;

(d) the exercise by a seller of his right to stop delivery pursuant to the provisions of the Article on Sales (Section 2–705);

(e) a diversion, reconsignment or other disposition pursuant to the provisions of this Article (Section 7–303.) or tariff regulating such right;

(f) release, satisfaction or any other fact affording a personal defense against the claimant;

(g) any other lawful excuse.

(2) A person claiming goods covered by a document of title must satisfy the bailee's lien where the bailee so requests or where the bailee is prohibited by law from delivering the goods until the charges are paid.

(3) Unless the person claiming is one against whom the document confers no right under Sec. 7–503(1), he must surrender for cancellation or notation of partial deliveries any outstanding negotiable document covering the goods, and the bailee must cancel the document or conspicuously note the partial delivery thereon or be liable to any person to whom the document is duly negotiated.

(4) "Person entitled under the document" means holder in the case of a negotiable document, or the person to whom delivery is to be made by the terms of or pursuant to written instructions under a non-negotiable document.

§7–404. No Liability for Good Faith Delivery Pursuant to Receipt or Bill. A bailee who in good faith including observance of reasonable commercial standards has received goods and delivered or otherwise disposed of them according to the terms of the document of title or pursuant to this Article is not liable therefor. This rule applies even though the person from whom he received the goods had no authority to procure the document or to dispose of the goods and even though the person to whom he delivered the goods had no authority to receive them.

Part 5   Warehouse Receipts and Bills of Lading: Negotiation and Transfer

§7–501. Form of Negotiation and Requirements of "Due Negotiation".

(1) A negotiable document of title running to the order of a named person is negotiated by his indorsement and delivery. After his indorsement in blank or to bearer any person can negotiate it by delivery alone.

(2)

(a) A negotiable document of title is also negotiated by delivery alone when by its original terms it runs to bearer.

(b) When a document running to the order of a named person is delivered to him the effect is the same as if the document had been negotiated.

(3) Negotiation of a negotiable document of title after it has been indorsed to a specified person requires indorsement by the special indorsee as well as delivery.

(4) A negotiable document of title is "duly negotiated" when it is negotiated in the manner stated in this section to a holder who purchases it in good faith without notice of any defense against or claim to it on the part of any person and for value, unless it is established that the negotiation is not in the regular course of business or financing or involves receiving the document in settlement or payment of a money obligation.

(5) Indorsement of a non-negotiable document neither makes it negotiable nor adds to the transferee's rights.

(6) The naming in a negotiable bill of a person to be notified of the arrival of the goods does not limit the negotiability of the bill nor constitute notice to a purchaser thereof of any interest of such person in the goods.

§7–502. Rights Acquired by Due Negotiation.

(1) Subject to the following section and to the provisions of Section 7–205 on fungible goods, a holder to whom a negotiable document of title has been duly negotiated acquires thereby:

(a) title to the document;

(b) title to the goods;

(c) all rights accruing under the law of agency or estoppel, including rights to goods delivered to the bailee after the document was issued; and

(d) the direct obligation of the issuer to hold or deliver the goods according to the terms of the document free of any defense or claim by him except those arising under the terms of the document or under this Article. In the case of a delivery order the bailee's obligation accrues only upon acceptance and the obligation acquired by the holder is that the issuer and any indorser will procure the acceptance of the bailee.

(2) Subject to the following section, title and rights so acquired are not defeated by any stoppage of the goods represented by the document or by surrender of such goods by the bailee, and are not impaired even though the negotiation or any prior negotiation constituted a breach of duty or even though any person has been deprived of possession of the document by misrepresentation, fraud, accident, mistake, duress, loss, theft or conversion, or even

though a previous sale or other transfer of the goods or document has been made to a third person.

§7–503. Document of Title to Goods Defeated in Certain Cases.

(1) A document of title confers no right in goods against a person who before issuance of the document had a legal interest or a perfected security interest in them and who neither

(a) delivered or entrusted them or any document of title covering them to the bailor or his nominee with actual or apparent authority to ship, store or sell or with power to obtain delivery under this Article (Section 7–403) or with power of disposition under this Act (Sections 2–403 and 9–307) or other statute or rule of law; nor

(b) acquiesced in the procurement by the bailor or his nominee of any document of title.

(2) Title to goods based upon an unaccepted delivery order is subject to the rights of anyone to whom a negotiable warehouse receipt or bill of lading covering the goods has been duly negotiated. Such a title may be defeated under the next section to the same extent as the rights of the issuer or a transferee from the issuer.

(3) Title to goods based upon a bill of lading issued to a freight forwarder is subject to the rights of anyone to whom a bill issued by the freight forwarder is duly negotiated; but delivery by the carrier in accordance with Part 4 of this Article pursuant to its own bill of lading discharges the carrier's obligation to deliver.

§7–504. Rights Acquired in the Absence of Due Negotiation; Effect of Diversion; Seller's Stoppage of Delivery.

(1) A transferee of a document, whether negotiable or non-negotiable, to whom the document has been delivered but not duly negotiated, acquires the title and rights which his transferor had or had actual authority to convey.

(2) In the case of a non-negotiable document, until but not after the bailee receives notification of the transfer, the rights of the transferee may be defeated

(a) by those creditors of the transferor who could treat the sale as void under Section 2–402; or

(b) by a buyer from the transferor in ordinary course of business if the bailee has delivered the goods to the buyer or received notification of his rights; or

(c) as against the bailee by good faith dealings of the bailee with the transferor.

(3) A diversion or other change of shipping instructions by the consignor in a non-negotiable bill of lading which causes the bailee not to deliver to the consignee defeats the consignee's title to the goods if they have been delivered to a buyer in ordinary course of business and in any event defeats the consignee's rights against the bailee.

(4) Delivery pursuant to a non-negotiable document may be stopped by a seller under Section 2–705, and subject to the requirement of due notification there provided. A bailee honoring the seller's instructions is entitled to be indemnified by the seller against any resulting loss or expense.

§7–505. Indorser Not a Guarantor for Other Parties.
The indorsement of a document of title issued by a bailee does not make the indorser liable for any default by the bailee or by previous indorsers.

§7–506. Delivery Without Indorsement: Right to Compel Indorsement.
The transferee of a negotiable document of title has a specifically enforceable right to have his transferor supply any necessary indorsement but the transfer becomes a negotiation only as of the time the indorsement is supplied.

§7–507. Warranties on Negotiation or Transfer of Receipt or Bill.
Where a person negotiates or transfers a document of title for value otherwise than as a mere intermediary under the next following section, then unless otherwise agreed he warrants to his immediate purchaser only in addition to any warranty made in selling the goods

(a) that the document is genuine; and

(b) that he has no knowledge of any fact which would impair its validity or worth; and

(c) that his negotiation or transfer is rightful and fully effective with respect to the title to the document and the goods it represents.

§7–508. Warranties of Collecting Bank as to Documents.
A collecting bank or other intermediary known to be entrusted with documents on behalf of another or with collection of a draft or other claim against delivery of documents warrants by such delivery of the documents only its own good faith and authority. This rule applies even though the intermediary has purchased or made advances against the claim or draft to be collected.

§7–509. Receipt or Bill: When Adequate Compliance With Commercial Contract.
The question whether a document is adequate to fulfill the obligations of a contract for sale or the conditions of a credit is governed by the Articles on Sales (Article 2) and on Letters of Credit (Article 5).

Part 6 Warehouse Receipts and Bills of Lading: Miscellaneous Provisions–

§7–601. Lost and Missing Documents.

(1) If a document has been lost, stolen or destroyed, a court may order delivery of the goods or issuance of a substitute document and the bailee may without liability to any person comply with such order. If the document was negotiable the claimant must post security approved by the

court to indemnify any person who may suffer loss as a result of non-surrender of the document. If the document was not negotiable, such security may be required at the discretion of the court. The court may also in its discretion order payment of the bailee's reasonable costs and counsel fees.

(2) A bailee who without court order delivers goods to a person claiming under a missing negotiable document is liable to any person injured thereby, and if the delivery is not in good faith becomes liable for conversion. Delivery in good faith is not conversion if made in accordance with a filed classification or tariff or, where no classification or tariff is filed, if the claimant posts security with the bailee in an amount at least double the value of the goods at the time of posting to indemnify any person injured by the delivery who files a notice of claim within one year after the delivery.

§7–602. Attachment of Goods Covered by a Negotiable Document. Except where the document was originally issued upon delivery of the goods by a person who has no power to dispose of them, no lien attaches by virtue of any judicial process to goods in the possession of a bailee for which a negotiable document of title is outstanding unless the document be first surrendered to the bailee or its negotiation enjoined, and the bailee shall not be compelled to deliver the goods pursuant to process until the document is surrendered to him or impounded by the court. One who purchases the document for value without notice of the process or injunction takes free of the lien imposed by judicial process.

§7–603. Conflicting Claims; Interpleader. If more than one person claims title or possession of the goods, the bailee is excused from delivery until he has had a reasonable time to ascertain the validity of the adverse claims or to bring an action to compel all claimants to interplead and may compel such interpleader, either in defending an action for non-delivery of the goods, or by original action, whichever is appropriate.

ARTICLE 8: INVESTMENT SECURITIES (INCORPORATING 1977 AMENDMENTS)

Part 1   Short Title and General Matters

§8–101. Short Title. This Article shall be known and may be cited as Uniform Commercial Code—Investment Securities.

§8–102. Definitions and Index of Definitions

(1) In this Article, unless the context otherwise requires:

[(a) A "security" is an instrument which

(i) is issued in bearer or registered form; and

(ii) is of a type commonly dealt in upon securities exchanges or markets or commonly recognized in any area in which it is issued or dealt in as a medium for investment; and

(iii) is either one of a class or series or by its terms is divisible into a class or series of instruments; and

(iv) evidences a share, participation or other interest in property or in an enterprise or evidences an obligation of the issuer.]

(a) A "certificated security" is a share, participation, or other interest in property of or an enterprise of the issuer or an obligation of the issuer which is

(i) represented by an instrument issued in bearer or registered form;

(ii) of a type commonly dealt in on securities exchanges or markets or commonly recognized in any area in which it is issued or dealt in as a medium for investment; and

(iii) either one of a class or series or by its terms divisible into a class or series of shares, participations, interests, or obligations.

(b) An "uncertificated security" is a share, participation, or other interest in property or an enterprise of the issuer or an obligation of the issuer which is

(i) not represented by an instrument and the transfer of which is registered upon books maintained for that purpose by or on behalf of the issuer;

(ii) of a type commonly dealt in on securities exchanges or markets; and

(iii) either one of a class or series or by its terms divisible into a class or series of shares, participations, interests, or obligations.

(c) [(b)] A "security" is either a certificated or an uncertificated security. If a security is certificated, the terms "security" and "certificated security" may mean either the intangible interest, the instrument representing that interest, or both, as the context requires. A writing [which] that is a certificated security is governed by this Article and not by [Uniform Commercial Code—Commercial Paper] Article 3, even though it also meets the requirements of that Article. This Article does not apply to money. If a certificated security has been retained by or surrendered to the issuer or its transfer agent for reasons other than registration of transfer, other temporary purpose, payment, exchange, or acquisition by the issuer, that security shall be treated as an uncertificated security for purposes of this Article.

(d) [(c)] A certificated security is in "registered form" [when] if

(i) it specifies a person entitled to the security or the rights it [evidences] represents, and [when]

(ii) its transfer may be registered upon books maintained for that purpose by or on behalf of [an] the issuer, or the security so states.

(e) [(d)] A certificated security is in "bearer form" [when] if it runs to bearer according to its terms and not by reason of any indorsement.

(2) A "subsequent purchaser" is a person who takes other than by original issue.

(3) A "clearing corporation" is a corporation registered as a "clearing agency" under the federal securities laws or a corporation:

    (**a**) at least [ninety] 90 percent of [the] whose capital stock [of which] is held by or for one or more [persons (other than individuals)]organizations, none of which other than a national securities exchange or association, holds in excess of 20 percent of the capital stock of the corporation, and each of [whom] which is

        (**i**) [is] subject to supervision or regulation pursuant to the provisions of federal or state banking laws or state insurance laws, [or]

        (**ii**) [is] a broker or dealer or investment company registered under the [Securities Exchange Act of 1934 or the Investment Company Act of 1940] federal securities laws, or

        (**iii**) [is] a national securities exchange or association registered under [a statute of the United States such as the Securities Exchange Act of 1934,] the federal securities laws; and [none of whom, other than a national securities exchange or association, holds in excess of twenty per cent of the capital stock of such corporation; and]

    (**b**) any remaining capital stock of which is held by individuals who have purchased [such capital stock] it at or prior to the time of their taking office as directors of [such] the corporation and who have purchased only so much of the capital stock as [may be] is necessary to permit them to qualify as [such] directors.

(4) A "custodian bank" is [any] a bank or trust company [which] that is supervised and examined by state or federal authority having supervision over banks and [which] is acting as custodian for a clearing corporation.

(5) Other definitions applying to this Article or to specified Parts thereof and the sections in which they appear are:

"Adverse claim".	Section [8–301] 8–302.
"Bona fide purchaser".	Section 8–302.
"Broker".	Section 8–303.
"Debtor".	Section 9–105.
"Financial intermediary".	Section 8–313.
"Guarantee of the signature".	Section 8–402.
"Initial transaction statement".	Section 8–408.
"Instruction".	Section 8–308.
"Intermediary Bank".	Section 4–105.
"Issuer".	Section 8–201.
"Overissue".	Section 8–104.
"Secured Party".	Section 9–105.
"Security Agreement".	Section 9–105.

(6) In addition Article 1 contains general definitions and principles of construction and interpretation applicable throughout this Article.

§8–103. Issuer's Lien. A lien upon a security in favor of an issuer thereof is valid against a purchaser only if:

    (**a**) the security is certificated and the right of the issuer to [such] the lien is noted conspicuously [on the security] thereon; or

    (**b**) the security is uncertificated and a notation of the right of the issuer to the lien is contained in the initial transaction statement sent to the purchaser or, if his interest is transferred to him other than by registration of transfer, pledge, or release, the initial transaction statement sent to the registered owner or the registered pledgee.

§8–104. Effect of Overissue; "Overissue".

(1) The provisions of this Article which validate a security or compel its issue or reissue do not apply to the extent that validation, issue, or reissue would result in overissue; but if:

    (**a**) [if] an identical security which does not constitute an overissue is reasonably available for purchase, the person entitled to issue or validation may compel the issuer to purchase [and deliver such a] the security [to] for him and either to deliver a certificated security or to register the transfer of an uncertificated security to him, against surrender of [the] any certificated security [, if any, which] he holds; or

    (**b**) [if] a security is not so available for purchase, the person entitled to issue or validation may recover from the issuer the price he or the last purchaser for value paid for it with interest from the date of his demand.

(2) "Overissue" means the issue of securities in excess of the amount [which] the issuer has corporate power to issue.

§8–105. Certificated Securities Negotiable; Statements and Instructions Not Negotiable; Presumptions.

(1) Certificated securities governed by this Article are negotiable instruments.

(2) Statements (Section 8–408), notices, or the like, sent by the issuer of uncertificated securities and instructions (Section 8–308) are neither negotiable instruments nor certificated securities.

(3) [(2)] In any action on a security:

    (**a**) unless specifically denied in the pleadings, each signature on [the] a certificated security [or], in a necessary indorsement, on an initial transaction statement, or on an instruction, is admitted;

    (**b**) [when] if the effectiveness of a signature is put in issue, the burden of establishing it is on the party claiming under the signature, but the signature is presumed to be genuine or authorized;

    (**c**) [when] if signatures on a certificated security are admitted or established, production of the [instrument] security entitles a holder to recover on it unless the defendant establishes a defense or a defect going to the validity of the security; [and]

    (**d**) if signatures on an initial transaction statement are admitted or established, the facts stated in the statement are presumed to be true as of the time of its issuance; and

    (**e**) [(d)] after it is shown that a defense or defect exists, the plaintiff has the burden of establishing that he or some person under whom he claims is a person against whom the defense or defect is ineffective (Section 8–202).

§8–106. Applicability. The law (including the conflict of law rules) of the jurisdiction of organization of the issuer governs the validity of a security, the effectiveness of registration by the issuer, and the rights and duties of the issuer with respect to:

(a) registration of transfer of a certificated security;

(b) registration of transfer, pledge, or release of an uncertificated security; and

(c) sending of statements of uncertificated securities. [are governed by the law (including the conflict of laws rules) of the jurisdiction of organization of the issuer.]

§8–107. Securities [Deliverable] Transferable; Action for Price.

(1) Unless otherwise agreed and subject to any applicable law or regulation respecting short sales, a person obligated to [deliver] transfer securities may [deliver] transfer any certificated security of the specified issue in bearer form or registered in the name of the transferee, or indorsed to him or in blank, or he may transfer an equivalent uncertificated security to the transferee or a person designated by the transferee.

(2) [When] If the buyer fails to pay the price as it comes due under a contract of sale, the seller may recover the price of:

(a) [of] certificated securities accepted by the buyer; [and]

(b) uncertificated securities that have been transferred to the buyer or a person designated by the buyer; and

(c) [(b) of] other securities if efforts at their resale would be unduly burdensome or if there is no readily available market for their resale.

§8–108. Registration of Pledge and Release of Uncertificated Securities. A security interest in an uncertificated security may be evidenced by the registration of pledge to the secured party or a person designated by him. There can be no more than one registered pledge of an uncertificated security at any time. The registered owner of an uncertificated security is the person in whose name the security is registered, even if the security is subject to a registered pledge. The rights of a registered pledgee of an uncertificated security under this Article are terminated by the registration of release.

Part 2   Issue—Issuer

§8–201. "Issuer".

(1) With respect to obligations on or defenses to a security, "issuer" includes a person who:

(a) places or authorizes the placing of his name on a certificated security (otherwise than as authenticating trustee, registrar, transfer agent, or the like) to evidence that it represents a share, participation, or other interest in his property or in an enterprise, or to evidence his duty to perform an obligation [evidenced] represented by the certificated security; [or]

(b) creates shares, participations or other interests in his property or in an enterprise or undertakes obligations, which shares, participations, interests, or obligations are uncertificated securities;

(c) [(b)] directly or indirectly creates fractional interests in his rights or property, which fractional interests are [evidenced] represented by certificated securities; or

(d) [(c)] becomes responsible for or in place of any other person described as an issuer in this section.

(2) With respect to obligations on or defenses to a security, a guarantor is an issuer to the extent of his guaranty, whether or not his obligation is noted on [the] a certificated security or on statements of uncertificated securities sent pursuant to Section 8–408.

(3) With respect to registration of transfer, pledge, or release (Part 4 of this Article), "issuer" means a person on whose behalf transfer books are maintained.

§8–202. Issuer's Responsibility and Defenses; Notice of Defect or Defense.

(1) Even against a purchaser for value and without notice, the terms of a security include:

(a) if the security is certificated, those stated on the security;

(b) if the security is uncertificated, those contained in the initial transaction statement sent to such purchaser, or if his interest is transferred to him other than by registration of transfer, pledge, or release, the initial transaction statement sent to the registered owner or registered pledgee; and

(c) those made part of the security by reference, on the certificated security or in the initial transaction statement, to another instrument, indenture, or document or to a constitution, statute, ordinance, rule, regulation, order or the like, to the extent that the terms [so] referred to do not conflict with the [stated] terms stated on the certificated security or contained in the statement. [Such] A reference under this paragraph does not of itself charge a purchaser for value with notice of a defect going to the validity of the security, even though the certificated security or statement expressly states that a person accepting it admits [such] notice.

(2) [(a)] A certificated security in the hands of a purchaser for value or an uncertificated security as to which an initial transaction statement has been sent to a purchaser for value, other than [one] a security issued by a government or governmental agency or unit, even though issued with a defect going to its validity, is valid [in the hands of a] with respect to the purchaser [for value and] if he is without notice of the particular defect unless the defect involves a violation of constitutional provisions, in which case the

security is valid [in the hands of] with respect to a subsequent purchaser for value and without notice of the defect. [(b) The rule of subparagraph (a)] This subsection applies to an issuer [which] that is a government or governmental agency or unit only if either there has been substantial compliance with the legal requirements governing the issue or the issuer has received a substantial consideration for the issue as a whole or for the particular security and a stated purpose of the issue is one for which the issuer has power to borrow money or issue the security.

(3) Except as [otherwise] provided in the case of certain unauthorized signatures [on issue] (Section 8–205), lack of genuineness of a certificated security or an initial transaction statement is a complete defense, even against a purchaser for value and without notice.

(4) All other defenses of the issuer of a certificated or uncertificated security, including nondelivery and conditional delivery of [the] a certificated security, are ineffective against a purchaser for value who has taken without notice of the particular defense.

(5) Nothing in this section shall be construed to affect the right of a party to a "when, as and if issued" or a "when distributed" contract to cancel the contract in the event of a material change in the character of the security [which] that is the subject of the contract or in the plan or arrangement pursuant to which [such] the security is to be issued or distributed.

§8–203. Staleness as Notice of Defects or Defenses.

(1) After an act or event [which creates] creating a right to immediate performance of the principal obligation [evidenced] represented by [the] a certificated security or [which] that sets a date on or after which the security is to be presented or surrendered for redemption or exchange, a purchaser is charged with notice of any defect in its issue or defense of the issuer if:

(a) [if] the act or event is one requiring the payment of money [or], the delivery of certificated securities, the registration of transfer of uncertificated securities, or [both] any of these on presentation or surrender of the certificated security [and such], the funds or securities are available on the date set for payment or exchange, and he takes the security more than one year after that date; and

(b) [if] the act or event is not covered by paragraph (a) and he takes the security more than [two] 2 years after the date set for surrender or presentation or the date on which [such] performance became due.

(2) A call [which] that has been revoked is not within subsection (1).

§8–204. Effect of Issuer's Restrictions on Transfer.

[Unless noted conspicuously on the security a] A restriction on transfer of a security imposed by the issuer, even though otherwise lawful, is ineffective [except] against [a] any person [with] without actual knowledge of it [.] unless:

(a) the security is certificated and the restriction is noted conspicuously thereon; or

(b) the security is uncertificated and a notation of the restriction is contained in the initial transaction statement sent to the person or, if his interest is transferred to him other than by registration of transfer, pledge, or release, the initial transaction statement sent to the registered owner or the registered pledgee.

§8–205. Effect of Unauthorized Signature on [Issue] Certificated Security or Initial Transaction Statement.

An unauthorized signature placed on a certificated security prior to or in the course of issue or placed on an initial transaction statement is ineffective, [except that] but the signature is effective in favor of a purchaser for value of the certificated security or a purchaser for value of an uncertificated security to whom such initial transaction statement has been sent, if the purchaser is [and] without notice of the lack of authority and [if] the signing has been done by:

(a) an authenticating trustee, registrar, transfer agent, or other person entrusted by the issuer with the signing of the security [or], of similar securities, or of initial transaction statements or [their] the immediate preparation for signing of any of them; or

(b) an employee of the issuer, or of any of the foregoing, entrusted with responsible handling of the security or initial transaction statement.

§8–206. Completion or Alteration of [Instrument] Certificated Security or Initial Transaction Statement.

(1) [Where] If a certificated security contains the signatures necessary to its issue or transfer but is incomplete in any other respect:

(a) any person may complete it by filling in the blanks as authorized; and

(b) even though the blanks are incorrectly filled in, the security as completed is enforceable by a purchaser who took it for value and without notice of [such] the incorrectness.

(2) A complete certificated security [which] that has been improperly altered, even though fraudulently, remains enforceable, but only according to its original terms.

(3) If an initial transaction statement contains the signatures necessary to its validity, but is incomplete in any other respect:

(a) any person may complete it by filling in the blanks as authorized; and

(b) even though the blanks are incorrectly filled in, the statement as completed is effective in favor of the person to whom it is sent if he purchased the security referred to therein for value and without notice of the incorrectness.

(4) A complete initial transaction statement that has been improperly altered, even though fraudulently, is effective in favor of a purchaser to whom it has been sent, but only according to its original terms.

§8–207. Rights and Duties of Issuer With Respect to Registered Owners and Registered Pledgees.

(1) Prior to due presentment for registration of transfer of a certificated security in registered form, the issuer or indenture trustee may treat the registered owner as the person exclusively entitled to vote, to receive notifications, and otherwise to exercise all the rights and powers of an owner.

(2) Subject to the provisions of subsections (3), (4), and (6), the issuer or indenture trustee may treat the registered owner of an uncertificated security as the person exclusively entitled to vote, to receive notifications, and otherwise to exercise all the rights and powers of an owner.

(3) The registered owner of an uncertificated security that is subject to a registered pledge is not entitled to registration of transfer prior to the due presentment to the issuer of a release instruction. The exercise of conversion rights with respect to a convertible uncertificated security is a transfer within the meaning of this section.

(4) Upon due presentment of a transfer instruction from the registered pledgee of an uncertificated security, the issuer shall:

(a) register the transfer of the security to the new owner free of pledge, if the instruction specifies a new owner (who may be the registered pledgee) and does not specify a pledgee;

(b) register the transfer of the security to the new owner subject to the interest of the existing pledgee, if the instruction specifies a new owner and the existing pledgee; or

(c) register the release of the security from the existing pledge and register the pledge of the security to the other pledgee, if the instruction specifies the existing owner and another pledgee.

(5) Continuity of perfection of a security interest is not broken by registration of transfer under subsection (4) (b) or by registration of release and pledge under subsection (4) (c), if the security interest is assigned.

(6) If an uncertificated security is subject to a registered pledge:

(a) any uncertificated securities issued in exchange for or distributed with respect to the pledged security shall be registered subject to the pledge;

(b) any certificated securities issued in exchange for or distributed with respect to the pledged security shall be delivered to the registered pledgee; and

(c) any money paid in exchange for or in redemption of part or all of the security shall be paid to the registered pledgee.

(7) [(2)] Nothing in this Article shall be construed to affect the liability of the registered owner of a security for calls, assessments, or the like.

§8–208. Effect of Signature of Authenticating Trustee, Registrar, or Transfer Agent.

(1) A person placing his signature upon a certificated security or an initial transaction statement as authenticating trustee, registrar, transfer agent, or the like, warrants to a purchaser for value of the certificated security or a purchaser for value of an uncertificated security to whom the initial transaction statement has been sent, if the purchaser is without notice of the particular defect, that:

(a) the certificated security or initial transaction statement is genuine; [and]

(b) his own participation in the issue or registration of the transfer, pledge, or release of the security is within his capacity and within the scope of the [authorization] authority received by him from the issuer; and

(c) he has reasonable grounds to believe that the security is in the form and within the amount the issuer is authorized to issue.

(2) Unless otherwise agreed, a person by so placing his signature does not assume responsibility for the validity of the security in other respects.

Part 3 [Purchase] Transfer

§8–301. Rights Acquired by Purchaser [; "Adverse Claim"; Title Acquired by Bona Fide Purchaser].

(1) Upon [delivery] transfer of a security to a purchaser (Section 8–313), the purchaser acquires the rights in the security which his transferor had or had actual authority to convey unless the purchaser's rights are limited by Section 8–302 (4). [except that a purchaser who has himself been a party to any fraud or illegality affecting the security or who as a prior holder had notice of an adverse claim cannot improve his position by taking from a later bona fide purchaser. "Adverse claim" includes a claim that a transfer was or would be wrongful or that a particular adverse person is the owner of or has an interest in the security.]

[(2) A bona fide purchaser in addition to acquiring the rights of a purchaser also acquires the security free of any adverse claim.]

(2) [(3)] A [purchaser] transferee of a limited interest acquires rights only to the extent of the interest [purchased] transferred. The creation or release of a security interest in a security is the transfer of a limited interest in that security.

§8–302. "Bona Fide Purchaser"; Adverse Claim"; Title Acquired by Bona Fide Purchaser.

(1) A "bona fide purchaser" is a purchaser for value in good faith and without notice of any adverse claim:

(a) who takes delivery of a certificated security in bearer form or [of one] in registered form, issued [to him] or indorsed to him or in blank;

(b) to whom the transfer, pledge or release of an uncertificated security is registered on the books of the issuer; or

(c) to whom a security is transferred under the provisions of paragraph (c), (d) (i), or (g) of Section 8–313(1).

(2) "Adverse claim" includes a claim that a transfer was or would be wrongful or that a particular adverse person is the owner of or has an interest in the security.

(3) A bona fide purchaser in addition to acquiring the

rights of a purchaser (Section 8–301) also acquires his interest in the security free of any adverse claim.

(**4**) Notwithstanding Section 8–301(1), the transferee of a particular certificated security who has been a party to any fraud or illegality affecting the security, or who as a prior holder of that certificated security had notice of an adverse claim, cannot improve his position by taking from a bona fide purchaser.

§8–303. "Broker". "Broker" means a person engaged for all or part of his time in the business of buying and selling securities, who in the transaction concerned acts for, [or] buys a security from, or sells a security to, a customer. Nothing in this Article determines the capacity in which a person acts for purposes of any other statute or rule to which [such] the person is subject.

§8–304. Notice to Purchaser of Adverse Claims.

(**1**) A purchaser (including a broker for the seller or buyer, but excluding an intermediary bank) of a certificated security is charged with notice of adverse claims if:

(**a**) the security, whether in bearer or registered form, has been indorsed "for collection" or "for surrender" or for some other purpose not involving transfer; or

(**b**) the security is in bearer form and has on it an unambiguous statement that it is the property of a person other than the transferor. The mere writing of a name on a security is not such a statement.

(**2**) A purchaser (including a broker for the seller or buyer, but excluding an intermediary bank) to whom the transfer, pledge, or release of an uncertificated security is registered is charged with notice of adverse claims as to which the issuer has a duty under Section 8–403(4) at the time of registration and which are noted in the initial transaction statement sent to the purchaser or, if his interest is transferred to him other than by registration of transfer, pledge, or release, the initial transaction statement sent to the registered owner or the registered pledgee.

(**3**) [(2)] The fact that the purchaser (including a broker for the seller or buyer) of a certificated or uncertificated security has notice that the security is held for a third person or is registered in the name of or indorsed by a fiduciary does not create a duty of inquiry into the rightfulness of the transfer or constitute constructive notice of adverse claims. [If,] However, if the purchaser (excluding an intermediary bank) has knowledge that the proceeds are being used or [that] the transaction is for the individual benefit of the fiduciary or otherwise in breach of duty, the purchaser is charged with notice of adverse claims.

§8–305. Staleness as Notice of Adverse Claims. An act or event [which] that creates a right to immediate performance of the principal obligation [evidenced] represented by [the] a certificated security or [which] sets a date on or after which [the] a certificated security is to be presented or surrendered for redemption or exchange does not [of] itself constitute any notice of adverse claims except in the case of a [purchase] transfer:

(**a**) after one year from any date set for [such] presentment or surrender for redemption or exchange; or

(**b**) after [six] 6 months from any date set for payment of money against presentation or surrender of the security if funds are available for payment on that date.

§8–306. Warranties on Presentment and Transfer of Certificated Securities; Warranties of Originators of Instructions.

(**1**) A person who presents a certificated security for registration of transfer or for payment or exchange warrants to the issuer that he is entitled to the registration, payment, or exchange. But, a purchaser for value and without notice of adverse claims who receives a new, reissued, or re-registered certificated security on registration of transfer or receives an initial transaction statement confirming the registration of transfer of an equivalent uncertificated security to him warrants only that he has no knowledge of any unauthorized signature (Section 8–311) in a necessary indorsement.

(**2**) A person by transferring a certificated security to a purchaser for value warrants only that:

(**a**) his transfer is effective and rightful; [and]

(**b**) the security is genuine and has not been materially altered; and

(**c**) he knows of no fact which might impair the validity of the security.

(**3**) [Where] If a certificated security is delivered by an intermediary known to be entrusted with delivery of the security on behalf of another or with collection of a draft or other claim against [such] delivery, the intermediary by [such] delivery warrants only his own good faith and authority, even though he has purchased or made advances against the claim to be collected against the delivery.

(**4**) A pledgee or other holder for security who redelivers [the] a certificated security received, or after payment and on order of the debtor delivers that security to a third person, makes only the warranties of an intermediary under subsection (3).

(**5**) A person who originates an instruction warrants to the issuer that:

(**a**) he is an appropriate person to originate the instruction; and

(**b**) at the time the instruction is presented to the issuer he will be entitled to the registration of transfer, pledge, or release.

(**6**) A person who originates an instruction warrants to any person specially guaranteeing his signature (subsection 8–312 (3)) that:

(**a**) he is an appropriate person to originate the instruction; and

(**b**) at the time the instruction is presented to the issuer

(**i**) he will be entitled to the registration of transfer, pledge, or release; and

(**ii**) the transfer, pledge, or release requested in the

instruction will be registered by the issuer free from all liens, security interests, restrictions, and claims other than those specified in the instruction.

(7) A person who originates an instruction warrants to a purchaser for value and to any person guaranteeing the instruction (Section 8–312(6)) that:

(a) he is an appropriate person to originate the instruction;

(b) the uncertificated security referred to therein is valid; and

(c) at the time the instruction is presented to the issuer

(i) the transferor will be entitled to the registration of transfer, pledge, or release;

(ii) the transfer, pledge, or release requested in the instruction will be registered by the issuer free from all liens, security interests, restrictions, and claims other than those specified in the instruction; and

(iii) the requested transfer, pledge, or release will be rightful.

(8) If a secured party is the registered pledgee or the registered owner of an uncertificated security, a person who originates an instruction of release or transfer to the debtor or, after payment and on order of the debtor, a transfer instruction to a third person, warrants to the debtor or the third person only that he is an appropriate person to originate the instruction and at the time the instruction is presented to the issuer, the transferor will be entitled to the registration of release or transfer. If a transfer instruction to a third person who is a purchaser for value is originated on order of the debtor, the debtor makes to the purchaser the warranties of paragraphs (b), (c)(ii) and (c)(iii) of subsection (7).

(9) A person who transfers an uncertificated security to a purchaser for value and does not originate an instruction in connection with the transfer warrants only that:

(a) his transfer is effective and rightful; and

(b) the uncertificated security is valid.

(10) [(5)] A broker gives to his customer and to the issuer and a purchaser the applicable warranties provided in this section and has the rights and privileges of a purchaser under this section. The warranties of and in favor of the broker acting as an agent are in addition to applicable warranties given by and in favor of his customer.

§8–307. Effect of Delivery Without Indorsement; Right to Compel Indorsement. [Where] If a certificated security in registered form has been delivered to a purchaser without a necessary indorsement he may become a bona fide purchaser only as of the time the indorsement is supplied[,]; but against the transferor, the transfer is complete upon delivery and the purchaser has a specifically enforceable right to have any necessary indorsement supplied.

§8–308. [Indorsement, How Made; Special Indorsement; Indorser Not a Guarantor; Partial Assignment] Indorsements; Instructions.

(1) An indorsement of a certificated security in registered form is made when an appropriate person signs on it or on a separate document an assignment or transfer of the security or a power to assign or transfer it or [when the] his signature [of such person] is written without more upon the back of the security.

(2) An indorsement may be in blank or special. An indorsement in blank includes an indorsement to bearer. A special indorsement specifies [the person] to whom the security is to be transferred, or who has power to transfer it. A holder may convert a blank indorsement into a special indorsement.

(3) [(5)] An indorsement purporting to be only of part of a certificated security representing units intended by the issuer to be separately transferable is effective to the extent of the indorsement.

(4) An "instruction" is an order to the issuer of an uncertificated security requesting that the transfer, pledge, or release from pledge of the uncertificated security specified therein be registered.

(5) An instruction originated by an appropriate person is:

(a) a writing signed by an appropriate person; or

(b) a communication to the issuer in any form agreed upon in a writing signed by the issuer and an appropriate person.

If an instruction has been originated by an appropriate person but is incomplete in any other respect, any person may complete it as authorized and the issuer may rely on it as completed even though it has been completed incorrectly.

(6) [(3)] "An appropriate person" in subsection (1) means [(a)] the person specified by the certificated security or by special indorsement to be entitled to the security [; or].

(7) "An appropriate person" in subsection (5) means:

(a) for an instruction to transfer or pledge an uncertificated security which is then not subject to a registered pledge, the registered owner; or

(b) for an instruction to transfer or release an uncertificated security which is then subject to a registered pledge, the registered pledgee.

(8) In addition to the persons designated in subsections (6) and (7), "an appropriate person" in subsections (1) and (5) includes:

(a) [(b) where] if the person [so specified] designated is described as a fiduciary but is no longer serving in the described capacity,[—] either that person or his successor; [or]

(b) [(c) where] if the [security or indorsement so specifies] persons designated are described as more than one person as fiduciaries and one or more are no longer serving in the described capacity,[—]the remaining fiduciary or fiduciaries, whether or not a successor has been appointed or qualified; [or]

(c) [(d) where] if the person [so specified] designated is an individual and is without capacity to act by virtue of death, incompetence, infancy, or otherwise,[—]his executor, administrator, guardian, or like fiduciary; [or]

(d) [(e) where] if the [security or indorsement so

specifies] persons designated are described as more than one person as tenants by the entirety or with right of survivorship and by reason of death all cannot sign,[—] the survivor or survivors; [or]

(**e**) [(f)] a person having power to sign under applicable law or controlling instrument; [or] and

(**f**) [(g)] to the extent that the person designated or any of the foregoing persons may act through an agent,[—] his authorized agent.

(**9**) [(4)] Unless otherwise agreed, the indorser of a certificated security by his indorsement or the originator of an instruction by his origination assumes no obligation that the security will be honored by the issuer but only the obligations provided in Section 8–306.

(**10**) [(6)] Whether the person signing is appropriate is determined as of the date of signing and an indorsement made by or an instruction originated by [such a person] him does not become unauthorized for the purposes of this Article by virtue of any subsequent change of circumstances.

(**11**) [(7)] Failure of a fiduciary to comply with a controlling instrument or with the law of the state having jurisdiction of the fiduciary relationship, including any law requiring the fiduciary to obtain court approval of the transfer, pledge, or release, does not render his indorsement or an instruction originated by him unauthorized for the purposes of this Article.

§8–309. Effect of Indorsement Without Delivery. An indorsement of a certificated security, whether special or in blank, does not constitute a transfer until delivery of the certificated security on which it appears or, if the indorsement is on a separate document, until delivery of both the document and the certificated security.

§8–310. Indorsement of Certificated Security in Bearer Form. An indorsement of a certificated security in bearer form may give notice of adverse claims (Section 8–304) but does not otherwise affect any right to registration the holder [may possess] possesses.

§8–311. Effect of Unauthorized Indorsement or Instruction. Unless the owner or pledgee has ratified an unauthorized indorsement or instruction or is otherwise precluded from asserting its ineffectiveness:

(**a**) he may assert its ineffectiveness against the issuer or any purchaser, other than a purchaser for value and without notice of adverse claims, who has in good faith received a new, reissued, or re-registered certificated security on registration of transfer or received an initial transaction statement confirming the registration of transfer, pledge, or release of an equivalent uncertificated security to him; and

(**b**) an issuer who registers the transfer of a certificated security upon the unauthorized indorsement or who registers the transfer, pledge, or release of an uncertificated security upon the unauthorized instruction is subject to liability for improper registration (Section 8–404).

§8–312. Effect of Guaranteeing Signature, [or] Indorsement or Instruction.

(**1**) Any person guaranteeing a signature of an indorser of a certificated security warrants that at the time of signing:

(**a**) the signature was genuine; [and]

(**b**) the signer was an appropriate person to indorse (Section 8–308); and

(**c**) the signer had legal capacity to sign.

[But the guarantor does not otherwise warrant the rightfulness of the particular transfer.]

(**2**) Any person guaranteeing a signature of the originator of an instruction warrants that at the time of signing:

(**a**) the signature was genuine;

(**b**) the signer was an appropriate person to originate the instruction (Section 8–308) if the person specified in the instruction as the registered owner or registered pledgee of the uncertificated security was, in fact, the registered owner or registered pledgee of such security, as to which fact the signature guarantor makes no warranty;

(**c**) the signer had legal capacity to sign; and

(**d**) the taxpayer identification number, if any, appearing on the instruction as that of the registered owner or registered pledgee was the taxpayer identification number of the signer or of the owner or pledgee for whom the signer was acting.

(**3**) Any person specially guaranteeing the signature of the originator of an instruction makes not only the warranties of a signature guarantor (subsection (2)) but also warrants that at the time the instruction is presented to the issuer:

(**a**) the person specified in the instruction as the registered owner or registered pledgee of the uncertificated security will be the registered owner or registered pledgee; and

(**b**) the transfer, pledge, or release of the uncertificated security requested in the instruction will be registered by the issuer free from all liens, security interests, restrictions, and claims other than those specified in the instruction.

(**4**) [But] The guarantor under subsections (1) and (2) or the special guarantor under subsection (3) does not otherwise warrant the rightfulness of the particular transfer, pledge, or release.

(**5**) [(2)] Any person [may guarantee] guaranteeing an indorsement of a certificated security [and by so doing warrants not only the signature (subsection 1)] makes not only the warranties of a signature guarantor under subsection (1) but also warrants the rightfulness of the particular transfer in all respects. [But no issuer may require a guarantee of indorsement as a condition to registration of transfer.]

(**6**) Any person guaranteeing an instruction requesting the transfer, pledge, or release of an uncertificated security makes not only the warranties of a special signature guarantor under subsection (3) but also warrants the rightfulness of the particular transfer, pledge, or release in all respects.

(7) [But] No issuer may require a special guarantee of signature (subsection (3)), a guarantee of indorsement (subsection (5)), or a guarantee of instruction (subsection (6)) as a condition to registration of transfer, pledge, or release.

(8) [(3)] The foregoing warranties are made to any person taking or dealing with the security in reliance on the guarantee, and the guarantor is liable to [such] the person for any loss resulting from breach of the warranties.

§8–313. When [Delivery] Transfer to [the] Purchaser Occurs: [; Purchaser's Broker] Financial Intermediary as [Holder] Bona Fide Purchaser; "Financial Intermediary".

(1) [Delivery] Transfer of a security or a limited interest (including a security interest) therein to a purchaser occurs only [when]:

(a) at the time he or a person designated by him acquires possession of a certificated security; [or]

(b) at the time the transfer, pledge, or release of an uncertificated security is registered to him or a person designated by him;

(c) [(b)] at the time his [broker] financial intermediary acquires possession of a certificated security specially indorsed to or issued in the name of the purchaser; [or]

(d) [(c)] at the time [his broker] a financial intermediary, not a clearing corporation, sends him confirmation of the purchase and also by book entry or otherwise identifies [a specific security in the broker's possession] as belonging to the purchaser [; or]

(i) a specific certificated security in the financial intermediary's possession;

(ii) a quantity of securities that constitute or are part of a fungible bulk of certificated securities in the financial intermediary's possession or of uncertificated securities registered in the name of the financial intermediary; or

(iii) a quantity of securities that constitute or are part of a fungible bulk of securities shown on the account of the financial intermediary on the books of another financial intermediary;

(e) [(d)] with respect to an identified certificated security to be delivered while still in the possession of a third person, not a financial intermediary, [when] at the time that person acknowledges that he holds for the purchaser; [or]

(f) with respect to a specific uncertificated security the pledge or transfer of which has been registered to a third person, not a financial intermediary, at the time that person acknowledges that he holds for the purchaser;

(g) [(e)] at the time appropriate entries to the account of the purchaser or a person designated by him on the books of a clearing corporation are made under Section 8–320[.];

(h) with respect to the transfer of a security interest where the debtor has signed a security agreement containing a description of the security, at the time a written notification, which, in the case of the creation of the security interest, is signed by the debtor (which may be a copy of the security agreement) or which, in the case of the release or assignment of the security interest created pursuant to this paragraph, is signed by the secured party, is received by

(i) a financial intermediary on whose books the interest of the transferor in the security appears;

(ii) a third person, not a financial intermediary, in possession of the security, if it is certificated;

(iii) a third person, not a financial intermediary, who is the registered owner of the security, if it is uncertificated and not subject to a registered pledge; or

(iv) a third person, not a financial intermediary, who is the registered pledgee of the security, if it is uncertificated and subject to a registered pledge;

(i) with respect to the transfer of a security interest where the transferor has signed a security agreement containing a description of the security, at the time new value is given by the secured party; or

(j) with respect to the transfer of a security interest where the secured party is a financial intermediary and the security has already been transferred to the financial intermediary under paragraphs (a), (b), (c), (d), or (g), at the time the transferor has signed a security agreement containing a description of the security and value is given by the secured party.

(2) The purchaser is the owner of a security held for him by [his broker] a financial intermediary, but [is not the holder] cannot be a bona fide purchaser of a security so held except [as] in the circumstances specified in [subparagraphs] paragraphs [(b)] (c), (d)(i), and [(e)] (g) of subsection (1). [Where] If a security so held is part of a fungible bulk, as in the circumstances specified in paragraphs (d)(ii) and (d)(iii) of subsection (1), the purchaser is the owner of a proportionate property interest in the fungible bulk.

(3) Notice of an adverse claim received by the [broker] financial intermediary or by the purchaser after the [broker] financial intermediary takes delivery of a certificated security as a holder for value or after the transfer, pledge, or release of an uncertificated security has been registered free of the claim to a financial intermediary who has given value is not effective either as to the [broker] financial intermediary or as to the purchaser. However, as between the [broker] financial intermediary and the purchaser the purchaser may demand [delivery] transfer of an equivalent security as to which no notice of [an] adverse claim has been received.

(4) A "financial intermediary" is a bank, broker, clearing corporation or other person (or the nominee of any of them) which in the ordinary course of its business maintains security accounts for its customers and is acting in that capacity. A financial intermediary may have a security interest in securities held in account for its customer.

§8–314. Duty to [Deliver] Transfer, When Completed.

(1) Unless otherwise agreed, [where] if a sale of a security is made on an exchange or otherwise through brokers:

(a) the selling customer fulfills his duty to [deliver when] transfer at the time he:

(i) [he] places [such] a certificated security in the possession of the selling broker or of a person designated by the broker; [or if requested causes an acknowledgment to be made to the selling broker that it is held for him; and]

(ii) causes an uncertificated security to be registered in the name of the selling broker or a person designated by the broker;

(iii) if requested, causes an acknowledgment to be made to the selling broker that [it] a certificated or uncertificated security is held for [him; and] the broker; or

(iv) places in the possession of the selling broker or of a person designated by the broker a transfer instruction for an uncertificated security, providing the issuer does not refuse to register the requested transfer if the instruction is presented to the issuer for registration within 30 days thereafter; and

(b) the selling broker, including a correspondent broker acting for a selling customer, fulfills his duty to [deliver] transfer at the time he:

(i) [by placing the] places a certificated security [or a like security] in the possession of the buying broker or a person designated by [him or] the buying broker;

(ii) causes an uncertificated security to be registered in the name of the buying broker or a person designated by the buying broker;

(iii) places in the possession of the buying broker or of a person designated by the buying broker a transfer instruction for an uncertificated security, providing the issuer does not refuse to register the requested transfer if the instruction is presented to the issuer for registration within 30 days thereafter; or

(iv) [by effecting] effects clearance of the sale in accordance with the rules of the exchange on which the transaction took place.

(2) Except as [otherwise] provided in this section and unless otherwise agreed, a transferor's duty to [deliver] transfer a security under a contract of purchase is not fulfilled until he:

(a) [he] places [the] a certificated security in form to be negotiated by the purchaser in the possession of the purchaser or of a person designated by the purchaser; [him or at the purchaser's request causes an acknowledgment to be made to the purchaser that it is held for him.]

(b) causes an uncertificated security to be registered in the name of the purchaser or a person designated by the purchaser; or

(c) [at the purchaser's request] if the purchaser requests, causes an acknowledgment to be made to the purchaser that [it] a certificated or uncertificated security is held for [him] the purchaser.

(3) Unless made on an exchange, a sale to a broker purchasing for his own account is within [this] subsection (2) and not within subsection (1).

§8–315. Action Against [Purchaser] Transferee Based Upon Wrongful Transfer.

(1) Any person against whom the transfer of a security is wrongful for any reason, including his incapacity, [may] as against anyone except a bona fide purchaser, may:

(a) reclaim possession of the certificated security wrongfully transferred; [or]

(b) obtain possession of any new certificated security [evidencing] representing all or part of the same rights; [or]

(c) compel the origination of an instruction to transfer to him or a person designated by him an uncertificated security constituting all or part of the same rights; or

(d) have damages.

(2) If the transfer is wrongful because of an unauthorized indorsement of a certificated security, the owner may also reclaim or obtain possession of the security or a new certificated security, even from a bona fide purchaser, if the ineffectiveness of the purported indorsement can be asserted against him under the provisions of this Article on unauthorized indorsements (Section 8–311).

(3) The right to obtain or reclaim possession of a certificated security or to compel the origination of a transfer instruction may be specifically enforced and [its] the transfer of a certificated or uncertificated security enjoined and [the] a certificated security impounded pending the litigation.

§8–316. Purchaser's Right to Requisites for Registration of Transfer, Pledge, or Release on Books. Unless otherwise agreed, the transferor of a certificated security or the transferor, pledgor, or pledgee of an uncertificated security [must] on due demand must supply his purchaser with any proof of his authority to transfer, pledge, or release or with any other requisite [which may be] necessary to obtain registration of the transfer, pledge, or release of the security; but if the transfer, pledge, or release is not for value, a transferor, pledgor, or pledgee need not do so unless the purchaser furnishes the necessary expenses. Failure within a reasonable time to comply with a demand made [within a reasonable time] gives the purchaser the right to reject or rescind the transfer, pledge, or release.

§8–317. [Attachment or Levy Upon Security] Creditors' Rights.

(1) Subject to the exceptions in subsections (3) and (4), no attachment or levy upon a certificated security or any share or other interest [evidenced] represented thereby which is outstanding [shall be] is valid until the security is actually seized by the officer making the attachment or levy, but a

certificated security which has been surrendered to the issuer may be [attached or levied upon at the source] reached by a creditor by legal process at the issuer's chief executive office in the United States.

(2) An uncertificated security registered in the name of the debtor may not be reached by a creditor except by legal process at the issuer's chief executive office in the United States.

(3) The interest of a debtor in a certificated security that is in the possession of a secured party not a financial intermediary or in an uncertificated security registered in the name of a secured party not a financial intermediary (or in the name of a nominee of the secured party) may be reached by a creditor by legal process upon the secured party.

(4) The interest of a debtor in a certificated security that is in the possession of or registered in the name of a financial intermediary or in an uncertificated security registered in the name of a financial intermediary may be reached by a creditor by legal process upon the financial intermediary on whose books the interest of the debtor appears.

(5) Unless otherwise provided by law, a creditor's lien upon the interest of a debtor in a security obtained pursuant to subsection (3) or (4) is not a restraint on the transfer of the security, free of the lien, to a third party for new value; but in the event of a transfer, the lien applies to the proceeds of the transfer in the hands of the secured party or financial intermediary, subject to any claims having priority.

(6) [(2)] A creditor whose debtor is the owner of a security [shall be] is entitled to [such] aid from courts of appropriate jurisdiction, by injunction or otherwise, in reaching [such] the security or in satisfying the claim by means [thereof as is] allowed at law or in equity in regard to property [which] that cannot readily be [attached or levied upon] reached by ordinary legal process.

§8–318. No Conversion by Good Faith [Delivery] Conduct. An agent or bailee who in good faith (including the observance of reasonable commercial standards if he is in the business of buying, selling, or otherwise dealing with securities) has received certificated securities and sold, pledged, or delivered them or has sold or caused the transfer or pledge of uncertificated securities over which he had control according to the instructions of his principal, is not liable for conversion or for participation in breach of fiduciary duty although the principal [has] had no right [to dispose of them] so to deal with the securities.

§8–319. Statute of Frauds. A contract for the sale of securities is not enforceable by way of action or defense unless:

(a) there is some writing signed by the party against whom enforcement is sought or by his authorized agent or broker, sufficient to indicate that a contract has been made for sale of a stated quantity of described securities at a defined or stated price; [or]

(b) delivery of [the] a certificated security or transfer

instruction has been accepted, or transfer of an uncertificated security has been registered and the transferee has failed to send written objection to the issuer within 10 days after receipt of the initial transaction statement confirming the registration, or payment has been made, but the contract is enforceable under this provision only to the extent of [such] the delivery, registration, or payment; [or]

(c) within a reasonable time a writing in confirmation of the sale or purchase and sufficient against the sender under paragraph (a) has been received by the party against whom enforcement is sought and he has failed to send written objection to its contents within [ten] 10 days after its receipt; or

(d) the party against whom enforcement is sought admits in his pleading, testimony, or otherwise in court that a contract was made for the sale of a stated quantity of described securities at a defined or stated price.

§8–320. Transfer or Pledge Within [a] Central Depository System.

(1) In addition to other methods, a transfer, pledge, or release of a security or any interest therein may be effected by the making of appropriate entries on the books of a clearing corporation reducing the account of the transferor, pledgor, or pledgee and increasing the account of the transferee, pledgee, or pledgor by the amount of the obligation, or the number of shares or rights transferred, pledged, or released, if the security is shown on the account of a transferor, pledgor, or pledgee on the books of the clearing corporation; is subject to the control of the clearing corporation; and

(a) [(1)] if [a security] certificated,

(i) [(a)] is in the custody of [a] the clearing corporation, another clearing corporation, [or of] a custodian bank or a nominee of [either subject to the instructions of the clearing corporation] any of them; and

(ii) [(b)] is in bearer form or indorsed in blank by an appropriate person or registered in the name of the clearing corporation, [or] a custodian bank, or a nominee of [either] any of them; or [and]

(b) if uncertificated, is registered in the name of the clearing corporation, another clearing corporation, a custodian bank, or a nominee of any of them;

[(c) is shown on the account of a transferor or pledgor on the books of the clearing corporation;

then, in addition to other methods, a transfer or pledge of the security or any interest therein may be effected by the making of appropriate entries on the books of the clearing corporation reducing the account of the transferor or pledgor and increasing the account of the transferee or pledgee by the amount of the obligation or the number of shares or rights transferred or pledged.]

(2) Under this section entries may be made with respect to like securities or interests therein as a part of a fungible bulk and may refer merely to a quantity of a particular

security without reference to the name of the registered owner, certificate or bond number, or the like, and, in appropriate cases, may be on a net basis taking into account other transfers, [or] pledges, or releases of the same security.

(**3**) A transfer [or pledge] under this section [has the effect of a delivery of a security in bearer form or duly indorsed in blank (Section 8–301) representing the amount of the obligation or the number of shares or rights transferred or pledged] is effective (Section 8–313) and the purchaser acquires the rights of the transferor (Section 8–301). A pledge or release under this section is the transfer of a limited interest. If a pledge or the creation of a security interest is intended, [the making of entries has the effect of a taking of delivery by the pledgee or a secured party (Sections 9–304 and 9–305)] the security interest is perfected at the time when both value is given by the pledgee and the appropriate entries are made (Section 8–321). A transferee or pledgee under this section [is a holder] may be a bona fide purchaser (Section 8–302).

(**4**) A transfer or pledge under this section [does] is not [constitute] a registration of transfer under Part 4 [of this Article].

(**5**) That entries made on the books of the clearing corporation as provided in subsection (1) are not appropriate does not affect the validity or effect of the entries [nor] or the liabilities or obligations of the clearing corporation to any person adversely affected thereby.

§8–321. Enforceability, Attachment, Perfection, and Termination of Security Interests.

(**1**) A security interest in a security is enforceable and can attach only if it is transferred to the secured party or a person designated by him pursuant to a provision of Section 8–313(1).

(**2**) A security interest so transferred pursuant to agreement by a transferor who has rights in the security to a transferee who has given value is a perfected security interest, but a security interest that has been transferred solely under paragraph (i) of Section 8–313(1) becomes unperfected after 21 days unless, within that time, the requirements for transfer under any other provision of Section 8–313(1) are satisfied.

(**3**) A security interest in a security is subject to the provisions of Article 9, but:

(**a**) no filing is required to perfect the security interest; and

(**b**) no written security agreement signed by the debtor is necessary to make the security interest enforceable, except as otherwise provided in paragraph (h), (i), or (j) of Section 8–313(1).

The secured party has the rights and duties provided under Section 9–207, to the extent they are applicable, whether or not the security is certificated, and, if certificated, whether or not it is in his possession.

(**4**) Unless otherwise agreed, a security interest in a

security is terminated by transfer to the debtor or a person designated by him pursuant to a provision of Section 8–313(1). If a security is thus transferred, the security interest, if not terminated, becomes unperfected unless the security is certificated and is delivered to the debtor for the purpose of ultimate sale or exchange or presentation, collection, renewal, or registration of transfer. In that case, the security interest becomes unperfected after 21 days unless, within that time, the security (or securities for which it has been exchanged) is transferred to the secured party or a person designated by him pursuant to a provision of Section 8–313(1).

Part 4   Registration

§8–401. Duty of Issuer to Register Transfer, Pledge, or Release.

(**1**) [Where] If a certificated security in registered form is presented to the issuer with a request to register transfer[,] or an instruction is presented to the issuer with a request to register transfer, pledge, or release, the issuer [is under a duty to] shall register the transfer, pledge, or release as requested if:

(**a**) the security is indorsed or the instruction was originated by the appropriate person or persons (Section 8–308); [and]

(**b**) reasonable assurance is given that those indorsements or instructions are genuine and effective (Section 8–402); [and]

(**c**) the issuer has no duty [to inquire into] as to adverse claims or has discharged [any such] the duty (Section 8–403); [and]

(**d**) any applicable law relating to the collection of taxes has been complied with; and

(**e**) the transfer, pledge, or release is in fact rightful or is to a bona fide purchaser.

(**2**) [Where] If an issuer is under a duty to register a transfer, pledge, or release of a security, the issuer is also liable to the person presenting a certificated security or an instruction [it] for registration or his principal for loss resulting from any unreasonable delay in registration or from failure or refusal to register the transfer, pledge, or release.

§8–402. Assurance that Indorsements and Instructions Are Effective.

(**1**) The issuer may require the following assurance that each necessary indorsement of a certificated security or each instruction (Section 8–308) is genuine and effective:

(**a**) in all cases, a guarantee of the signature ([subsection (1) of] Section 8–312(1) or (2)) of the person indorsing a certificated security or originating an instruction including, in the case of an instruction, a warranty of the taxpayer identification number or, in the absence thereof, other reasonable assurance of identity: [and]

(**b**) [where] if the indorsement is made or the instruction is originated by an agent, appropriate assurance of authority to sign;

(**c**) [where] if the indorsement is made or the instruction is originated by a fiduciary, appropriate evidence of appointment or incumbency;

(**d**) [where] if there is more than one fiduciary, reasonable assurance that all who are required to sign have done so; and

(**e**) [where] if the indorsement is made or the instruction is originated by a person not covered by any of the foregoing, assurance appropriate to the case corresponding as nearly as may be to the foregoing.

(**2**) A "guarantee of the signature" in subsection (1) means a guarantee signed by or on behalf of a person reasonably believed by the issuer to be responsible. The issuer may adopt standards with respect to responsibility [provided such standards] if they are not manifestly unreasonable.

(**3**) "Appropriate evidence of appointment or incumbency" in subsection (1) means:

(**a**) in the case of a fiduciary appointed or qualified by a court, a certificate issued by or under the direction or supervision of that court or an officer thereof and dated within [sixty] 60 days before the date of presentation for transfer, pledge, or release; or

(**b**) in any other case, a copy of a document showing the appointment or a certificate issued by or on behalf of a person reasonably believed by the issuer to be responsible or, in the absence of [such a] that document or certificate, other evidence reasonably deemed by the issuer to be appropriate. The issuer may adopt standards with respect to [such] the evidence [provided such standards] if they are not manifestly unreasonable. The issuer is not charged with notice of the contents of any document obtained pursuant to this paragraph (b) except to the extent that the contents relate directly to the appointment or incumbency.

(**4**) The issuer may elect to require reasonable assurance beyond that specified in this section, but if it does so and, for a purpose other than that specified in subsection (3)(b), both requires and obtains a copy of a will, trust, indenture, articles of co-partnership, by-laws, or other controlling instrument, it is charged with notice of all matters contained therein affecting the transfer, pledge, or release.

§8–403. [Limited Duty of Inquiry] Issuer's Duty as to Adverse Claims.

(**1**) An issuer to whom a certificated security is presented for registration [is under a duty to] shall inquire into adverse claims if:

(**a**) a written notification of an adverse claim is received at a time and in a manner [which affords] affording the issuer a reasonable opportunity to act on it prior to the issuance of a new, reissued, or re-registered certificated security, and the notification identifies the claimant, the registered owner, and the issue of which the security is a part, and provides an address for communications directed to the claimant; or

(**b**) the issuer is charged with notice of an adverse claim from a controlling instrument [which] it has elected to require under [subsection (4) of] Section 8–402(4).

(**2**) The issuer may discharge any duty of inquiry by any reasonable means, including notifying an adverse claimant by registered or certified mail at the address furnished by him or, if there be no such address, at his residence or regular place of business that the certificated security has been presented for registration of transfer by a named person, and that the transfer will be registered unless within [thirty] 30 days from the date of mailing the notification, either:

(**a**) an appropriate restraining order, injunction, or other process issues from a court of competent jurisdiction; or

(**b**) there is filed with the issuer an indemnity bond, sufficient in the issuer's judgment to protect the issuer and any transfer agent, registrar, or other agent of the issuer involved[,] from any loss [which] it or they may suffer by complying with the adverse claim [is filed with the issuer].

(**3**) Unless an issuer is charged with notice of an adverse claim from a controlling instrument which it has elected to require under [subsection (4) of] Section 8–402(4) or receives notification of an adverse claim under subsection (1) [of this section, where], if a certificated security presented for registration is indorsed by the appropriate person or persons the issuer is under no duty to inquire into adverse claims. In particular:

(**a**) an issuer registering a certificated security in the name of a person who is a fiduciary or who is described as a fiduciary is not bound to inquire into the existence, extent, or correct description of the fiduciary relationship; and thereafter the issuer may assume without inquiry that the newly registered owner continues to be the fiduciary until the issuer receives written notice that the fiduciary is no longer acting as such with respect to the particular security;

(**b**) an issuer registering transfer on an indorsement by a fiduciary is not bound to inquire whether the transfer is made in compliance with a controlling instrument or with the law of the state having jurisdiction of the fiduciary relationship, including any law requiring the fiduciary to obtain court approval of the transfer; and

(**c**) the issuer is not charged with notice of the contents of any court record or file or other recorded or unrecorded document even though the document is in its possession and even though the transfer is made on the indorsement of a fiduciary to the fiduciary himself or to his nominee.

(**4**) An issuer is under no duty as to adverse claims with respect to an uncertificated security except:

(a) claims embodied in a restraining order, injunction, or other legal process served upon the issuer if the process was served at a time and in a manner affording the issuer a reasonable opportunity to act on it in accordance with the requirements of subsection (5);

(b) claims of which the issuer has received a written notification from the registered owner or the registered pledgee if the notification was received at a time and in a manner affording the issuer a reasonable opportunity to act on it in accordance with the requirements of subsection (5);

(c) claims (including restrictions on transfer not imposed by the issuer) to which the registration of transfer to the present registered owner was subject and were so noted in the initial transaction statement sent to him; and

(d) claims as to which an issuer is charged with notice from a controlling instrument it has elected to require under Section 8–402(4).

(5) If the issuer of an uncertificated security is under a duty as to an adverse claim, he discharges that duty by:

(a) including a notation of the claim in any statements sent with respect to the security under Sections 8–408(3), (6), and (7); and

(b) refusing to register the transfer or pledge of the security unless the nature of the claim does not preclude transfer or pledge subject thereto.

(6) If the transfer or pledge of the security is registered subject to an adverse claim, a notation of the claim must be included in the initial transaction statement and all subsequent statements sent to the transferee and pledgee under Section 8–408.

(7) Notwithstanding subsections (4) and (5), if an uncertificated security was subject to a registered pledge at the time the issuer first came under a duty as to a particular adverse claim, the issuer has no duty as to that claim if transfer of the security is requested by the registered pledgee or an appropriate person acting for the registered pledgee unless:

(a) the claim was embodied in legal process which expressly provides otherwise;

(b) the claim was asserted in a written notification from the registered pledgee;

(c) the claim was one as to which the issuer was charged with notice from a controlling instrument it required under Section 8–402(4) in connection with the pledgee's request for transfer; or

(d) the transfer requested is to the registered owner.

§8–404. Liability and Non-Liability for Registration.

(1) Except as [otherwise] provided in any law relating to the collection of taxes, the issuer is not liable to the owner, pledgee, or any other person suffering loss as a result of the registration of a transfer, pledge, or release of a security if:

(a) there were on or with [the] a certificated security the necessary indorsements or the issuer had received

an instruction originated by an appropriate person (Section 8–308); and

(b) the issuer had no duty [to inquire into] as to adverse claims or has discharged [any such] the duty (Section 8–403).

(2) [Where] If an issuer has registered a transfer of a certificated security to a person not entitled to it, the issuer on demand [must] shall deliver a like security to the true owner unless:

(a) the registration was pursuant to subsection (1); [or]

(b) the owner is precluded from asserting any claim for registering the transfer under [subsection (1) of the following section] Section 8–405(1); or

(c) [such] the delivery would result in overissue, in which case the issuer's liability is governed by Section 8–104.

(3) If an issuer has improperly registered a transfer, pledge, or release of an uncertificated security, the issuer on demand from the injured party shall restore the records as to the injured party to the condition that would have obtained if the improper registration had not been made unless:

(a) the registration was pursuant to subsection (1); or

(b) the registration would result in overissue, in which case the issuer's liability is governed by Section 8–104.

§8–405. Lost, Destroyed, and Stolen Certificated Securities.

(1) [Where] If a certificated security has been lost, apparently destroyed, or wrongfully taken, and the owner fails to notify the issuer of that fact within a reasonable time after he has notice of it and the issuer registers a transfer of the security before receiving [such a] notification, the owner is precluded from asserting against the issuer any claim for registering the transfer under [the preceding section] Section 8–404 or any claim to a new security under this section.

(2) [Where] If the owner of [the] a certificated security claims that the security has been lost, destroyed, or wrongfully taken, the issuer [must] shall issue a new certificated security or, at the option of the issuer, an equivalent uncertificated security in place of the original security if the owner:

(a) so requests before the issuer has notice that the security has been acquired by a bona fide purchaser; [and]

(b) files with the issuer a sufficient indemnity bond; and

(c) satisfies any other reasonable requirements imposed by the issuer.

(3) If, after the issue of [the] a new certificated or uncertificated security, a bona fide purchaser of the original certificated security presents it for registration of transfer, the issuer [must] shall register the transfer unless registration would result in overissue, in which event the issuer's liability is governed by Section 8–104. In addition to any

rights on the indemnity bond, the issuer may recover the new certificated security from the person to whom it was issued or any person taking under him except a bona fide purchaser or may cancel the uncertificated security unless a bona fide purchaser or any person taking under a bona fide purchaser is then the registered owner or registered pledgee thereof.

§8–406. Duty of Authenticating Trustee, Transfer Agent, or Registrar.

(1) [Where] If a person acts as authenticating trustee, transfer agent, registrar, or other agent for an issuer in the registration of transfers of its certificated securities or in the registration of transfers, pledges, and releases of its uncertificated securities, [or] in the issue of new securities, or in the cancellation of surrendered securities:

(a) he is under a duty to the issuer to exercise good faith and due diligence in performing his functions; and

(b) [he has] with regard to the particular functions he performs, he has the same obligation to the holder or owner of [the] a certificated security or to the owner or pledgee of an uncertificated security and has the same rights and privileges as the issuer has in regard to those functions.

(2) Notice to an authenticating trustee, transfer agent, registrar or other [such] agent is notice to the issuer with respect to the functions performed by the agent.

§8–407. Exchangeability of Securities.

(1) No issuer is subject to the requirements of this section unless it regularly maintains a system for issuing the class of securities involved under which both certificated and uncertificated securities are regularly issued to the category of owners, which includes the person in whose name the new security is to be registered.

(2) Upon surrender of a certificated security with all necessary indorsements and presentation of a written request by the person surrendering the security, the issuer, if he has no duty as to adverse claims or has discharged the duty (Section 8–403), shall issue to the person or a person designated by him an equivalent uncertificated security subject to all liens, restrictions, and claims that were noted on the certificated security.

(3) Upon receipt of a transfer instruction originated by an appropriate person who so requests, the issuer of an uncertificated security shall cancel the uncertificated security and issue an equivalent certificated security on which must be noted conspicuously any liens and restrictions of the issuer and any adverse claims (as to which the issuer has a duty under Section 8–403(4)) to which the uncertificated security was subject. The certificated security shall be registered in the name of and delivered to:

(a) the registered owner, if the uncertificated security was not subject to a registered pledge; or

(b) the registered pledgee, if the uncertificated security was subject to a registered pledge.

§8–408. Statements of Uncertificated Securities.

(1) Within 2 business days after the transfer of an uncertificated security has been registered, the issuer shall send to the new registered owner and, if the security has been transferred subject to a registered pledge, to the registered pledgee a written statement containing:

(a) a description of the issue of which the uncertificated security is a part;

(b) the number of shares or units transferred;

(c) the name and address and any taxpayer identification number of the new registered owner and, if the security has been transferred subject to a registered pledge, the name and address and any taxpayer identification number of the registered pledgee;

(d) a notation of any liens and restrictions of the issuer and any adverse claims (as to which the issuer has a duty under Section 8–403(4)) to which the uncertificated security is or may be subject at the time of registration or a statement that there are none of those liens, restrictions, or adverse claims; and

(e) the date the transfer was registered.

(2) Within 2 business days after the pledge of an uncertificated security has been registered, the issuer shall send to the registered owner and the registered pledgee a written statement containing:

(a) a description of the issue of which the uncertificated security is a part;

(b) the number of shares or units pledged;

(c) the name and address and any taxpayer identification number of the registered owner and the registered pledgee;

(d) a notation of any liens and restrictions of the issuer and any adverse claims (as to which the issuer has a duty under Section 8–403(4)) to which the uncertificated security is or may be subject at the time of registration or a statement that there are none of those liens, restrictions or adverse claims; and

(e) the date the pledge was registered.

(3) Within 2 business days after the release from pledge of an uncertificated security has been registered, the issuer shall send to the registered owner and the pledgee whose interest was released a written statement containing:

(a) a description of the issue of which the uncertificated security is a part;

(b) the number of shares or units released from pledge;

(c) the name and address and any taxpayer identification number of the registered owner and the pledgee whose interest was released;

(d) a notation of any liens and restrictions of the issuer and any adverse claims (as to which the issuer has a duty under Section 8—403(4)) to which the uncertificated security is or may be subject at the time of registration or a statement that there are none of those liens, restrictions or adverse claims; and

(e) the date the release was registered.

(4) An "initial transaction statement" is the statement sent to:

(a) the new registered owner and, if applicable, to the registered pledgee pursuant to subsection (1);

(b) the registered pledgee pursuant to subsection (2); or

(c) the registered owner pursuant to subsection (3).

Each initial transaction statement shall be signed by or on behalf of the issuer and must be identified as "Initial Transaction Statement."

(5) Within 2 business days after the transfer of an uncertificated security has been registered, the issuer shall send to the former registered owner and the former registered pledgee, if any, a written statement containing:

(a) a description of the issue of which the uncertificated security is a part;

(b) the number of shares or units transferred;

(c) the name and address and any taxpayer identification number of the former registered owner and of any former registered pledgee; and

(d) the date the transfer was registered.

(6) At periodic intervals no less frequent than annually and at any time upon the reasonable written request of the registered owner, the issuer shall send to the registered owner of each uncertificated security a dated written statement containing:

(a) a description of the issue of which the uncertificated security is a part;

(b) the name and address and any taxpayer identification number of the registered owner;

(c) the number of shares or units of the uncertificated security registered in the name of the registered owner on the date of the statement;

(d) the name and address and any taxpayer identification number of any registered pledgee and the number of shares or units subject to the pledge; and

(e) a notation of any liens and restrictions of the issuer and any adverse claims (as to which the issuer has a duty under Section 8–403(4)) to which the uncertificated security is or may be subject or a statement that there are none of those liens, restrictions, or adverse claims.

(7) At periodic intervals no less frequent than annually and at any time upon the reasonable written request of the registered pledgee, the issuer shall send to the registered pledgee of each uncertificated security a dated written statement containing:

(a) a description of the issue of which the uncertificated security is a part;

(b) the name and address and any taxpayer identification number of the registered owner;

(c) the name and address and any taxpayer identification number of the registered pledgee;

(d) the number of shares or units subject to the pledge; and

(e) a notation of any liens and restrictions of the issuer and any adverse claims (as to which the issuer has a duty under Section 8–403(4)) to which the uncertificated security is or may be subject or a statement that there are none of those liens, restrictions, or adverse claims.

(8) If the issuer sends the statements described in subsections (6) and (7) at periodic intervals no less frequent than quarterly, the issuer is not obliged to send additional statements upon request unless the owner or pledgee requesting them pays to the issuer the reasonable cost of furnishing them.

(9) Each statement sent pursuant to this section must bear a conspicuous legend reading substantially as follows: "This statement is merely a record of the rights of the addressee as of the time of its issuance. Delivery of this statement, of itself, confers no rights on the recipient. This statement is neither a negotiable instrument nor a security."

ARTICLE 9: SECURED TRANSACTIONS; SALES OF ACCOUNTS [, CONTRACT RIGHTS] AND CHATTEL PAPER

Part 1   Short Title, Applicability and Definitions

§9–101. Short Title. This Article shall be known and may be cited as Uniform Commercial Code—Secured Transactions.

§9–102. Policy and [Scope] Subject Matter of Article.

(1) Except as otherwise provided [in Section 9–103 on multiple state transactions and] in Section 9–104 on excluded transactions, this Article applies [so far as concerns any personal property and fixtures within the jurisdiction of this state]

(a) to any transaction (regardless of its form) which is intended to create a security interest in personal property or fixtures including goods, documents, instruments, general intangibles, chattel paper or accounts [or contract rights]; and also

(b) to any sale of accounts [contract rights] or chattel paper.

(2) This Article applies to security interests created by contract including pledge, assignment, chattel mortgage, chattel trust, trust deed, factor's lien, equipment trust, conditional sale, trust receipt, other lien or title retention contract and lease or consignment intended as security. This Article does not apply to statutory liens except as provided in Section 9–310.

(3) The application of this Article to a security interest in a secured obligation is not affected by the fact that the obligation is itself secured by a transaction or interest to which this Article does not apply.

Note: *The adoption of this Article should be accompanied by the repeal of existing statutes dealing with conditional sales, trust receipts, factor's liens where the factor is given a non-possessory lien, chattel mortgages, crop mortgages, mortgages on railroad equipment, assignment of accounts and generally statutes regulating security interests in personal property.*

Where the state has a retail installment selling act or small loan act, that legislation should be carefully examined to determine what changes in those acts are needed to conform them to this Article. This Article primarily sets out rules defining rights of a secured party against persons dealing with the debtor; it does not prescribe regulations and controls which may be necessary to curb abuses arising in the small loan business or in the financing of consumer purchases on credit. Accordingly there is no intention to repeal existing regulatory acts in those fields [.] by enactment or re-enactment of Article 9. See Section 9–203(4) and the Note thereto.

[§9–103. Accounts, Contract Rights, General Intangibles and Equipment Relating to Another Jurisdiction; and Income Goods Already Subject to a Security Interest].

[(**1**) If the office where the assignor of accounts or contract rights keeps his record concerning them is in this state, the validity and perfection of a security interest therein and the possibility and effect of proper filing is governed by this Article; otherwise by the law (including the conflict of laws rules) of the jurisdiction where such office is located.]

[(**2**) If the chief place of business of a debtor is in this state, this Article governs the validity and perfection of a security interest ad the possibility and effect of proper filing with regard to general intangibles or with regard to goods of a type which are normally used in more than one jurisdiction (such as automotive equipment, rolling stock, airplanes, road building equipment, commercial harvesting equipment, construction machinery and the like) if such goods are classified as equipment or classified as inventory by reason of their being leased by the debtor to others. Otherwise, the law (including the conflict of laws rules) of the jurisdiction where such chief place of business is located shall govern. If the chief place of business is located in a jurisdiction which does not provide for perfection of the security interest by filing or recording in that jurisdiction, then the security interest may be perfected by filing in this state. [For the purpose of determining the validity and perfection of a security interest in an airplane, the chief place of business of a debtor who is a foreign air carrier under the Federal Aviation Act of 1958, as amended, is the designated office of the agent upon whom service of process may be made on behalf of the debtor.]]

[(**3**) If personal property other than that governed by subsections (1) and (2) is already subject to a security interest when it is brought into this state, the validity of the

security interest in this state is to be determined by the law (including the conflict of laws rules) of the jurisdiction where the property was when the security interest attached. However, if the parties to the transaction understood at the time that the security interest attached that the property would be kept in this state and it was brought into this state within 30 days after the security interest attached for purposes other than transportation through this state, then the validity of the security interest in this state is to be determined by the law of this state. If the security interest was already perfected under the law of the jurisdiction where the property was when the security interest attached and before being brought into this state, the security interest continues perfected in this state for four months and also thereafter if within the four month period it is perfected in this state. The security interest may also be perfected in this state after the expiration of the four month period; in such case perfection dates from the time of perfection in this state. If the security interest was not perfected under the law of the jurisdiction where the property was when the security interest attached and before being brought into this state, it may be perfected in this state; and in such case perfection dates from the time of perfection in this state.]

[(**4**) Notwithstanding subsections (2) and (3), if personal property is covered by a certificate of title issued under a statute of this state or any other jurisdiction which requires indication on a certificate of title of any security interest in the property as a condition of perfection, then the perfection is governed by the law of the jurisdiction which issued the certificate.]

[[(**5**) Notwithstanding subsection (1) and Section 9–302, if the office where the assignor of accounts or contract rights keeps his records concerning them is not located in a jurisdiction which is a part of the United States, its territories or possessions, and the accounts or contract rights are within the jurisdiction of this state or the transaction which creates the security interest otherwise bears an appropriate relation to this state, this Article governs the validity and perfection of the security interest and the security interest may only be perfected by notification to the account debtor.]]

§9–103. Perfection of Security Interests in Multiple State Transactions.

(**1**) Documents, instruments and ordinary goods.

(**a**) This subsection applies to documents and instruments and to goods other than those covered by a certificate of title described in subsection (2), mobile goods described in subsection (3), and minerals described in subsection (5).

(**b**) Except as otherwise provided in this subsection, perfection and the effect of perfection or non-perfection of a security interest in collateral are governed by the law of the jurisdiction where the collateral is when the last event occurs on which is based the assertion that the security interest is perfected or unperfected.

(c) If the parties to a transaction creating a purchase money security interest in goods in one jurisdiction understand at the time that the security interest attaches that the goods will be kept in another jurisdiction, then the law of the other jurisdiction governs the perfection and the effect of perfection or non-perfection of the security interest from the time it attaches until thirty days after the debtor receives possession of the goods and thereafter if the goods are taken to the other jurisdiction before the end of the thirty-day period.

(d) When collateral is brought into and kept in this state while subject to a security interest perfected under the law of the jurisdiction from which the collateral was removed, the security interest remains perfected, but if action is required by Part 3 of this Article to perfect the security interest,

(i) if the action is not taken before the expiration of the period of perfection in the other jurisdiction or the end of four months after the collateral is brought into this state, whichever period first expires, the security interest becomes unperfected at the end of that period and is thereafter deemed to have been unperfected as against a person who became a purchaser after removal;

(ii) if the action is taken before the expiration of the period specified in subparagraph (i), the security interest continues perfected thereafter;

(iii) for the purpose of priority over a buyer of consumer goods (subsection (2) of Section 9–307), the period of the effectiveness of a filing in the jurisdiction from which the collateral is removed is governed by the rules with respect to perfection in subparagraphs (i) and (ii).

(2) Certificate of title.

(a) This subsection applies to goods covered by a certificate of title issued under a statute of this state or of another jurisdiction under the law of which indication of a security interest on the certificate is required as a condition of perfection.

(b) Except as otherwise provided in this subsection, perfection and the effect of perfection or non-perfection of the security interest are governed by the law (including the conflict of laws rules) of the jurisdiction issuing the certificate until four months after the goods are removed from that jurisdiction and thereafter until the goods are registered in another jurisdiction, but in any event not beyond surrender of the certificate. After the expiration of that period, the goods are not covered by the certificate of title within the meaning of this section.

(c) Except with respect to the rights of a buyer described in the next paragraph, a security interest, perfected in another jurisdiction otherwise than by notation on a certificate of title, in goods brought into this state and thereafter covered by a certificate of title issued by this state is subject to the rules stated in paragraph (d) of subsection (1).

(d) If goods are brought into this state while a security interest therein is perfected in any manner under the law of the jurisdiction from which the goods are removed and a certificate of title is issued by this state and the certificate does not show that the goods are subject to the security interest or that they may be subject to security interests not shown on the certificate, the security interest is subordinate to the rights of a buyer of the goods who is not in the business of selling goods of that kind to the extent that he gives value and receives delivery of the goods after issuance of the certificate and without knowledge of the security interest.

(3) Accounts, general intangibles and mobile goods.

(a) This subsection applies to accounts (other than an account described in subsection (5) on minerals) and general intangibles and to goods which are mobile and which are of a type normally used in more than one jurisdiction, such as motor vehicles, trailers, rolling stock, airplanes, shipping containers, road building and construction machinery and commercial harvesting machinery and the like, if the goods are equipment or inventory leased or held for lease by the debtor to others, and are not covered by a certificate of title described in subsection (2).

(b) The law (including the conflict of laws rules) of the jurisdiction in which the debtor is located governs the perfection and the effect of perfection or non-perfection of the security interest.

(c) If, however, the debtor is located in a jurisdiction which is not a part of the United States, and which does not provide for perfection of the security interest by filing or recording in that jurisdiction, the law of the jurisdiction in the United States in which the debtor has its major executive office in the United States governs the perfection and the effect of perfection or non-perfection of the security interest through filing. In the alternative, if the debtor is located in a jurisdiction which is not a part of the United States or Canada and the collateral is accounts or general intangibles for money due or to become due, the security interest may be perfected by notification to the account debtor. As used in this paragraph, "United States" includes its territories and possessions and the Commonwealth of Puerto Rico.

(d) A debtor shall be deemed located at his place of business if he has one, at his chief executive office if he has more than one place of business, otherwise at his residence. If, however, the debtor is a foreign air carrier under the Federal Aviation Act of 1958, as amended, it shall be deemed located at the designated office of the agent upon whom service of process may be made on behalf of the foreign air carrier.

(e) A security interest perfected under the law of the jurisdiction of the location of the debtor is perfected until the expiration of four months after a change of the debtor's location to another jurisdiction, or until perfection would have ceased by the law of the first jurisdiction, whichever period first expires. Unless perfected in the new jurisdiction before the end of that period, it becomes unperfected thereafter and is deemed to have been unperfected as against a person who became a purchaser after the change.

(4) Chattel paper.

The rules stated for goods in subsection (1) apply to a possessory security interest in chattel paper. The rules stated for accounts in subsection (3) apply to a non-possessory security interest in chattel paper, but the security interest may not be perfected by notification to the account debtor.

(5) Minerals.

Perfection and the effect of perfection or non-perfection of a security interest which is created by a debtor who has an interest in minerals or the like (including oil and gas) before extraction and which attaches thereto as extracted, or which attaches to an account resulting from the sale thereof at the wellhead or minehead are governed by the law (including the conflict of laws rules) of the jurisdiction wherein the wellhead or minehead is located.

§9–103. Perfection of Security Interests in Multiple State Transactions *(1977 Amendments)*.

* * *

(3) Accounts, general intangibles and mobile goods.
  (a) This subsection applies to accounts (other than an account described in subsection (5) on minerals) and general intangibles (other than uncertificated securities) and to goods.

* * *

(6) Uncertificated securities.

The law (including the conflict of laws rules) of the jurisdiction of organization of the issuer governs the perfection and the effect of perfection or non-perfection of a security interest in uncertificated securities.

§9–104. Transactions Excluded From Article. This Article does not apply

(a) to a security interest subject to any statute of the United States to the extent that such statute governs the rights of parties to and third parties affected by transactions in particular types of property; or
(b) to a landlord's lien; or
(c) to a lien given by statute or other rule of law for services or materials except as provided in Section 9–310 on priority of such liens; or
(d) to a transfer of a claim for wages, salary or other compensation of an employee; or
[(e) to an equipment trust covering railway rolling stock; or]
(e) to a transfer by a government or governmental subdivision or agency; or
(f) to a sale of accounts[, contract rights] or chattel paper as part of a sale of the business out of which they arose, or an assignment of accounts [, contract rights] or chattel paper which is for the purpose of collection only, or a transfer of a [contract] right to payment under a contract to an assignee who is also to do the performance under the contract or a transfer of a single account to an assignee in whole or partial satisfaction of a preexisting indebtedness; or
(g) to a transfer of an interest in or claim in or under any policy of insurance, except as provided with respect to proceeds (Section 9–306) and priorities in proceeds (Section 9–312); or
(h) to a right represented by a judgment (other than a judgment taken on a right to payment which was collateral); or
(i) to any right of set-off; or
(j) except to the extent that provision is made for fixtures in Section 9–313, to the creation or transfer of an interest in or lien on real estate, including a lease or rents thereunder; or
(k) to a transfer in whole or in part of [any of the following:] any claim arising out of tort; [any deposit, savings, passbook or like account maintained with a bank, savings and loan association, credit union or like organization.]; or
(l) to a transfer of an interest in any deposit account (subsection (1) of Section 9–105), except as provided with respect to proceeds (Section 9–306) and priorities in proceeds (Section 9–312).

§9–105. Definitions and Index of Definitions.

(1) In this Article unless the context otherwise requires:
  (a) "Account debtor" means the person who is obligated on an account, chattel paper [, contract right] or general intangible;
  (b) "Chattel paper" means a writing or writings which evidence both a monetary obligation and a security interest in or a lease of specific goods, but a charter or other contract involving the use or hire of a vessel is not chattel paper. When a transaction is evidenced both by such a security agreement or a lease and by an instrument or a series of instruments, the group of writings taken together constitutes chattel paper;
  (c) "Collateral" means the property subject to a security interest, and includes accounts [, contract rights] and chattel paper which have been sold;
  (d) "Debtor" means the person who owes payment or other performance of the obligation secured, whether or not he owns or has rights in the collateral, and includes the seller of accounts [, contract rights] or

chattel paper. Where the debtor and the owner of the collateral are not the same person, the term "debtor" means the owner of the collateral in any provision of the Article dealing with the collateral, the obligor in any provision dealing with the obligation, and may include both where the context so requires;

(e) "Deposit account" means a demand, time savings, passbook or like account maintained with a bank, savings and loan association, credit union or like organization, other than an account evidenced by a certificate of deposit;

(f) [(e)] "Document" means document of title as defined in the general definitions of Article 1 (Section 1—201) [;], and a receipt of the kind described in subsection (2) of Section 7–201;

(g) "Encumbrance" includes real estate mortgages and other liens on real estate and all other rights in real estate that are not ownership interests.

(h) [(f)] "Goods" includes all things which are movable at the time the security interest attaches or which are fixtures (Section 9–313), but does not include money, documents, instruments, accounts, chattel paper, general intangibles, [contract rights and other things in action,] or minerals or the like (including oil and gas) before extraction. "Goods" also includes standing timber which is to be due and removed under a conveyance or contract for sale, the unborn young of animals, and growing crops.

(i) [(g)] "Instrument" means a negotiable instrument (defined in Section 3–104), or a security (defined in Section 8–102) or any other writing which evidences a right to the payment of money and is not itself a security agreement or lease and is of a type which is in ordinary course of business transferred by delivery with any necessary indorsement or assignment;

(j) "Mortgage" means a consensual interest created by a real estate mortgage, a trust deed on real estate, or the like;

(k) An advance is made "pursuant to commitment" if the secured party has bound himself to make it, whether or not a subsequent event of default or other event not within his control has relieved or may relieve him from his obligation.

(l) [(h)] "Security agreement" means an agreement which creates or provides for a security interest;

(m) [(i)] "Secured party" means a lender, seller or other person in whose favor there is a security interest, including a person to whom accounts [, contract rights] or chattel paper have been sold. When the holders of obligations issued under an indenture of trust, equipment trust agreement or the like are represented by a trustee or other person, the representative is the secured party;

(n) "Transmitting utility" means any person primarily engaged in the railroad, street railway or trolley bus business, the electric or electronics communications transmission business, the transmission of goods by pipeline, or the transmission or the production and transmission of electricity, steam, gas or water, or the provision of sewer service.

(2) Other definitions applying to this Article and the sections in which they appear are:

"Account". Section 9–106.
"Attach". Section 9–203.
"Construction mortgage". Section 9–313 (1).
"Consumer goods". Section 9–109 (1).
["Contract right". Section 9–106.]
"Equipment". Section 9–109 (2).
"Farm products". Section 9–109 (3).
"Fixture". Section 9–313.
"Fixture filing". Section 9–313.
"General intangibles". Section 9–106.
"Inventory". Section 9–109 (4).
"Lien creditor". Section 9–301 (3).
"Proceeds". Section 9–306 (1).
"Purchase money security interest". Section 9–107.
"United States". Section 9–103.

(3) The following definitions in other articles apply to this Article:

"Check". Section 3–104.
"Contract for sale". Section 2–106.
"Holder in due course". Section 3–302.
"Note". Section 3–104.
"Sale". Section 2–106.

(4) In addition Article 1 contains general definitions and principles of construction and interpretation throughout this Article.

§9–105. Definitions and Index of Definitions *(1977 Amendments)*.

(1) In this Article unless the context otherwise requires:

* * *

(i) "Instrument" means a negotiable instrument (defined in Section 3–104), or a certificated security (defined in Section 8–102) or . . .

* * *

§9–106. Definitions: "Account"; ["Contract Right";] "General Intangibles".

"Account" means any right to payment for goods sold or leased or for services rendered which is not evidenced by an instrument or chattel paper[.], whether or not it has been earned by performance. ["Contract right" means any right to payment under a contract not yet earned by performance and not evidenced by an instrument or chattel paper.] "General intangibles" means any personal property (including things in action) other than goods, accounts, [contract rights,] chattel paper, documents, [and] instruments, and money. All rights to payment earned or unearned under a charter or other contract involving the use or hire of a vessel and all rights incident to the charter or contract are [contract rights and neither] accounts [nor general intangibles].

§9–107. Definitions: "Purchase Money Security Interest". A security interest is a "purchase money security interest" to the extent that it is

(a) taken or retained by the seller of the collateral to secure all or part of its price;

(b) taken by a person who by making advances or incurring an obligation gives value to enable the debtor to acquire rights in or the use of collateral if such value is in fact so used.

§9–108. When After-Acquired Collateral Not Security for Antecedent Debt. Where a secured party makes an advance, incurs an obligation, releases a perfected security interest, or otherwise gives new value which is to be secured in whole or in part by after-acquired property his security interest in the after-acquired collateral shall be deemed to be taken for new value and not as security for an antecedent debt if the debtor acquires his rights in such collateral either in the ordinary course of his business or under a contract of purchase made pursuant to the security agreement within a reasonable time after new value is given.

§9–109. Classification of Goods; "Consumer Goods"; "Equipment"; "Farm Products"; "Inventory". Goods are

(1) "consumer goods" if they are used or bought for use primarily for personal, family or household purposes;

(2) "equipment" if they are used or bought for use primarily in business (including farming or a profession) or by a debtor who is a non-profit organization or a governmental subdivision or agency or if the goods are not included in the definitions of inventory, farm products or consumer goods;

(3) "farm products" if they are crops or livestock or supplies used or produced in farming operations or if they are products of crops or livestock in their unmanufactured states (such as ginned cotton, wool-clip, maple syrup, milk and eggs), and if they are in the possession of a debtor engaged in raising, fattening, grazing or other farming operations. If goods are farm products they are neither equipment nor inventory;

(4) "inventory" if they are held by a person who holds them for sale or lease or to be furnished under contracts of service or if he has so furnished them, or if they are raw materials, work in process or materials used or consumed in a business. Inventory of a person is not to be classified as his equipment.

§9–110. Sufficiency of Description. For the purposes of this Article any description of personal property or real estate is sufficient whether or not it is specific if it reasonably identifies what is described.

§9–111. Applicability of Bulk Transfer Laws. The creation of a security interest is not a bulk transfer under Article 6 (see Section 6–103).

§9–112. Where Collateral Is Not Owned by Debtor. Unless otherwise agreed, when a secured party knows that collateral is owned by a person who is not the debtor, the owner of the collateral is entitled to receive from the secured party any surplus under Section 9–502 (2) or under Section 9–504 (1), and is not liable for the debt or for any deficiency after resale, and he has the same right as the debtor

(a) to receive statements under Section 9–208;

(b) to receive notice of and to object to a secured party's proposal to retain the collateral in satisfaction of the indebtedness under Section 9–505;

(c) to redeem the collateral under Section 9–506;

(d) to obtain injunctive or other relief under Section 9–507 (1); and

(e) to recover losses caused to him under Section 9–208 (2).

§9–113. Security Interests Arising Under Article on Sales. A security interest arising solely under the Article on Sales (Article 2) is subject to the provisions of this Article except that to the extent that and so long as the debtor does not have or does not lawfully obtain possession of the goods

(a) no security agreement is necessary to make the security interest enforceable; and

(b) no filing is required to perfect the security interest; and

(c) the rights of the secured party on default by the debtor are governed by the Article on Sales (Article 2).

§9–114. Consignment.

(1) A person who delivers goods under a consignment which is not a security interest and who would be required to file under this Article by paragraph (3) (c) of Section 2–326 has priority over a secured party who is or becomes a creditor of the consignee and who would have a perfected security interest in the goods if they were the property of the consignee, and also has priority with respect to identifiable cash proceeds received on or before delivery of the goods to a buyer, if

(a) the consignor complies with the filing provision of the Article on Sales with respect to consignments (paragraph (3) (c) of Section 2–326) before the consignee receives possession of the goods; and

(b) the consignor gives notification in writing to the holder of the security interest if the holder has filed a financing statement covering the same types of goods before the date of the filing made by the consignor; and

(c) the holder of the security interest receives the notification within five years before the consignee receives possession of the goods; and

(d) the notification states that the consignor expects to

deliver goods on consignment to the consignee, describing the goods by item or type.

(2) In the case of a consignment which is not a security interest and in which the requirements of the preceding subsection have not been met, a person who delivers goods to another is subordinate to a person who would have a perfected security interest in the goods if they were the property of the debtor.

Part 2 Validity of Security Agreement and Rights of Parties Thereto

§9–201. General Validity of Security Agreement. Except as otherwise provided by this Act a security agreement is effective according to its terms between the parties, against purchasers of the collateral and against creditors. Nothing in this Article validates any charge or practice illegal under any statute or regulation thereunder governing usury, small loans, retail installment sales, or the like, or extends the application of any such statute or regulation to any transaction not otherwise subject thereto.

§9–202. Title to Collateral Immaterial. Each provision of this Article with regard to rights, obligations and remedies applies whether title to collateral is in the secured party or in the debtor.

§9–203. Attachment and Enforceability of Security Interest; Proceeds; Formal Requisites.

[(1) Subject to the provisions of Section 4–208 on the security interest of a collecting bank and Section 9–113 on a security interest arising under the Article on Sales, a security interest is not enforceable against the debtor or third parties unless

(a) the collateral is in the possession of the secured party; or

(b) the debtor has signed a security agreement which contains a description of the collateral and in addition, when the security interest covers crops or oil, gas or minerals to be extracted or timber to be cut, a description of the land concerned. In describing collateral, the word "proceeds" is sufficient without further description to cover proceeds of any character.]

(1) Subject to the provisions of Section 4–208 on the security interest of a collecting bank and Section 9–113 on a security interest arising under the Article on Sales, a security interest is not enforceable against the debtor or third parties with respect to the collateral and does not attach unless

(a) the collateral is in the possession of the secured party pursuant to agreement, or the debtor has signed a security agreement which contains a description of the collateral and in addition, when the security

interest covers crops growing or to be grown or timber to be cut, a description of the land concerned; and

(b) value has been given; and

(c) the debtor has rights in the collateral.

(2) A security interest attaches when it becomes enforceable against the debtor with respect to the collateral. Attachment occurs as soon as all of the events specified in subsection (1) have taken place unless explicit agreement postpones the time of attaching.

(3) Unless otherwise agreed a security agreement gives the secured party the rights to proceeds provided by Section 9–306.

(4) [(2)] A transaction, although subject to this Article, is also subject to . . . . *, and in the case of conflict between the provisions of this Article and any such statute, the provisions of such statute control. Failure to comply with any applicable statute has only the effect which is specified therein.

Note: *At* * *in subsection (4) insert reference to any local statute regulating small loans, retail installment sales and the like.*

The foregoing subsection (4) is designed to make it clear that certain transactions, although subject to this Article, must also comply with other applicable legislation.

This Article is designed to regulate all the "security" aspects of transactions within its scope. There is, however, much regulatory legislation, particularly in the consumer field, which supplements this Article and should not be repealed by its enactment. Examples are small loan acts, retail installment selling acts and the like. Such acts may provide for licensing and rate regulation and may prescribe particular forms of contract. Such provisions should remain in force despite the enactment of this Article. On the other hand if a retail installment selling act contains provisions on filing, rights on default, etc., such provisions should be repealed as inconsistent with this Article except that inconsistent provisions as to deficiencies, penalties, etc., in the Uniform Consumer Credit Code and other recent related legislation should remain because those statutes were drafted after the substantial enactment of the Article and with the intention of modifying certain provisions of this Article as to consumer credit.

§9–203. Attachment and Enforceability of Security Interest; Proceeds; Formal Requisites (1977 Amendments).

(1) Subject to the provisions of Section 4–208 on the security interest of a collecting bank, Section 8–321 on security interests in securities and Section 9–113 on a security interest arising under the Article on Sales, a security interest is not enforceable against the debtor or third parties with respect to the collateral and does not attach unless:

(a) the collateral is in the possession of the secured party pursuant to agreement, or the debtor has signed a security agreement which contains a description of the collateral and in addition, when the security interest covers crops growing or to be grown or timber to be cut, a description of the land concerned; [and]

(b) value has been given; and

(c) the debtor has rights in the collateral.

* * *

§9–204. [When Security Interest Attaches;] After-Acquired Property; Future Advances.

[(1) A security interest cannot attach until there is agreement (subsection (3) of Section 1–201) that it attach and value is given and the debtor has rights in the collateral. It attaches as soon as all of the events in the preceeding sentence have taken place unless explicit agreement postpones the time of attaching.]

[(2) For the purposes of this section the debtor has no rights

(a) in crops until they are planted or otherwise become growing crops, in the young of livestock until they are conceived;

(b) in fish until caught, in oil, gas or minerals until they are extracted, in timber until it is cut;

(c) in a contract right until the contract has been made;

(d) in an account until it comes into existence.]

[(3) Except as provided in subsection (4) a security agreement may provide that collateral, whenever acquired, shall secure all obligations covered by the security agreement.]

[(4) No security interest attaches under an after-acquired property clause

(a) to crops which become such more than one year after the security agreement is executed except that a security interest in crops which is given in conjunction with a lease or a land purchase or improvement transaction evidenced by a contract, mortgage or deed of trust may if so agreed attach to crops to be grown on the land concerned during the period of such real estate transaction;

(b) to consumer goods other than accessions (Section 9–314) when given as additional security unless the debtor acquires rights in them within ten days after the secured party gives value.]

(1) Except as provided in subsection (2), a security agreement may provide that any or all obligations covered by the security agreement are to be secured by after-acquired collateral.

(2) No security interest attaches under an after-acquired property clause to consumer goods other than accessions (Section 9–314) when given as additional security unless the debtor acquires rights in them within ten days after the secured party gives value.

(3) (5) Obligations covered by a security agreement may include future advances or other value whether or not the advances or value are given pursuant to commitment (subsection (1) of Section 9–105).

§9–205. Use of Disposition of Collateral Without Accounting Permissible.
A security interest is not invalid or fraudulent against creditors by reason of liberty in the debtor to use, commingle or dispose of all or part of the collateral (including returned or repossessed goods) or to collect or compromise accounts [contract rights] or chattel paper, or to accept the return of goods or make repossessions, or to use, commingle or dispose of proceeds, or by reason of the failure of the secured party to require the debtor to account for proceeds or replace collateral. This section does not relax the requirements of possession where perfection of a security interest depends upon possession of the collateral by the secured party or by a bailee.

§9–206. Agreement Not to Assert Defenses Against Assignee; Modification of Sales Warranties Where Security Agreement Exists.

(1) Subject to any statute or decision which establishes a different rule for buyers or lessees of consumer goods, an agreement by a buyer or lessee that he will not assert against an assignee any claim or defense which he may have against the seller or lessor is enforceable by an assignee who takes his assignment for value, in good faith and without notice of a claim or defense, except as to defenses of a type which may be asserted against a holder in due course of a negotiable instrument under the Article on Commercial Paper (Article 3). A buyer who as part of one transaction signs both a negotiable instrument and a security agreement makes such an agreement.

(2) When a seller retains a purchase money security interest in goods the Article on Sales (Article 2) governs the sale and any disclaimer, limitation or modification of the seller's warranties. Amended in 1962.

§9–207. Rights and Duties When Collateral is in Secured Party's Possession.

(1) A secured party must use reasonable care in the custody and preservation of collateral in his possession. In the case of an instrument or chattel paper reasonable care includes taking necessary steps to preserve rights against prior parties unless otherwise agreed.

(2) Unless otherwise agreed, when collateral is in the secured party's possession

(a) reasonable expenses (including the cost of any insurance and payment of taxes or other charges) incurred in the custody, preservation, use or operation of the collateral are chargeable to the debtor and are secured by the collateral;

(b) the risk of accidental loss or damage is on the debtor

to the extent of any deficiency in any effective insurance coverage;

(c) the secured party may hold as additional security any increase or profits (except money) received from the collateral, but money so received, unless remitted to the debtor, shall be applied in reduction of the secured obligation;

(d) the secured party must keep the collateral indentifiable but fungible collateral may be commingled;

(e) the secured party may repledge the collateral upon terms which do not impair the debtor's right to redeem it.

(3) A secured party is liable for any loss caused by his failure to meet any obligation imposed by the preceding subsections but does not lose his security interest.

(4) A secured party may use or operate the collateral for the purpose of preserving the collateral or its value or pursuant to the order of a court of appropriate jurisdiction or, except in the case of consumer goods, in the manner and to the extent provided in the security agreement.

§9–208. Request for Statement of Account or List of Collateral.

(1) A debtor may sign a statement indicating what he believes to be the aggregate amount of unpaid indebtedness as of a specified date and may send it to the secured party with a request that the statement be approved or corrected and returned to the debtor. When the security agreement or any other record kept by the secured party identifies the collateral a debtor may similarly request the secured party to approve or correct a list of the collateral.

(2) The secured party must comply with such a request within two weeks after receipt by sending a written correction or approval. If the secured party claims a security interest in all of a particular type of collateral owned by the debtor he may indicate that fact in his reply and need not approve or correct an itemized list of such collateral. If the secured party without reasonable excuse fails to comply he is liable for any loss caused to the debtor thereby; and if the debtor has properly included in his request a good faith statement of the obligation or a list of the collateral of both the secured party may claim a security interest only as shown in the statement against persons misled by his failure to comply. If he no longer has an interest in the obligation or collateral at the time the request is received he must disclose the name and address of any successor in interest known to him and he is liable for any loss caused to the debtor as a result of failure to disclose. A successor in interest is not subject to this section until a request is received by him.

(3) A debtor is entitled to such a statement once every six months without charge. The secured party may require payment of a charge not exceeding $10 for each additional statement furnished.

Part 3   Rights of Third Parties; Perfected and Unperfected Security Interests; Rules of Priority

§9–301. Persons Who Take Priority Over Unperfected Security Interests; Right of "Lien Creditor".

(1) Except as otherwise provided in subsection (2), an unperfected security interest is subordinate to the rights of

(a) persons entitled to priority under Section 9–312;

(b) a person who becomes a lien creditor [without knowledge of the security interest and] before [it] the security interest is perfected;

(c) in the case of goods, instruments, documents, and chattel paper, a person who is not a secured party and who is a transferee in bulk or other buyer not in ordinary course of business, or is a buyer of farm products in ordinary course of business, to the extent that he gives value and receives delivery of the collateral without knowledge of the security interest and before it is perfected;

(d) in the case of accounts [, contract rights,] and general intangibles, a person who is not a secured party and who is a transferee to the extent that he gives value without knowledge of the security interest and before it is perfected.

(2) If the secured party files with respect to a purchase money security interest before or within ten days after the debtor receives possession of the collateral [comes into possession of the debtor], he takes priority over the rights of a transferee in bulk or of a lien creditor which arise between the time the security interest attaches and the time of filing.

(3) A "lien creditor" means a creditor who has acquired a lien on the property involved by attachment, levy or the like and includes an assignee for benefit of creditors from the time of assignment, and a trustee in bankruptcy from the date of the filing of the petition or a receiver in equity from the time of appointment. [Unless all the creditors represented had knowledge of the security interest such a representative of creditors is a lien creditor without knowledge even though he personally has knowledge of the security interest.]

(4) A person who becomes a lien creditor while a security interest is perfected takes subject to the security interest only to the extent that it secures advances made before he becomes a lien creditor or within 45 days thereafter or made without knowledge of the lien or pursuant to a commitment entered into without knowledge of the lien.

§9–302. When Filing Is Required to Perfect Security Interest; Security Interests to Which Filing Provisions of This Article Do Not Apply.

(1) A financing statement must be filed to perfect all security interests except the following:

(a) a security interest in collateral in possession of the secured party under Section 9–305;

(b) a security interest temporarily perfected in instruments or documents without delivery under Section 9–304 or in proceeds for a 10 day period under Section 9–306;

[(c) a purchase money security interest in farm equipment having a purchase price not in excess of $2500; but filing is required for a fixture under Section 9–313 or for a motor vehicle required to be licensed;]

(c) a security interest created by an assignment of a beneficial interest in a trust or a decedent's estate;

(d) a purchase money security interest in consumer goods; but filing is required [for a fixture under Section 9—313 or for a motor vehicle required to be licensed;] for a motor vehicle required to be registered; and fixture filing is required for priority over conflicting interests in fixtures to the extent provided in Section 9–313;

(e) an assignment of accounts [or contract rights] which does not alone or in conjunction with other assignments to the same assignee transfer a significant part of the outstanding accounts [or contract rights] of the assignor;

(f) a security interest of a collecting bank (Section 4–208) or arising under the Article on Sales (see Section 9–113) or covered in subsection (3) of this section;

(g) an assignment for the benefit of all the creditors of the transferor, and subsequent transfers by the assignee thereunder.

(2) If a secured party assigns a perfected security interest, no filing under this Article is required in order to continue the perfected status of the security interest against creditors of and transferees from the original debtor.

[(3) The filing provisions of this Article do not apply to a security interest in property subject to a statute

(a) of the United States which provides for a national registration or filing of all security interests in such property; or

Note: *States to select either Alternative A or Alternative B.*

Alternative A—

(b) of this state which provides for central filing of, or which requires indication on a certificate of title of, such security interests in such property.

Alternative B—

(b) of this state which provides for central filing of security interests in such property, or in a motor vehicle which is not inventory held for sale for which a certificate of title is required under the statutes of this state if a notation of such a security interest can be indicated by a public official on a certificate or a duplicate thereof.]

[(4) A security interest in property covered by a statute described in subsection (3) can be perfected only by registration or filing under that statute or by indication of the security interest on a certificate of title or duplicate thereof by a public official.]

(3) The filing of a financing statement otherwise required by this Article is not necessary or effective to perfect a security interest in property subject to

(a) a statute or treaty of the United States which provides for a national or international registration or a national or international certificate of title or which specifies a place of filing different from that specified in this Article for filing of the security interest; or

(b) the following statutes of this state; [[list any certificate of title statute covering automobiles, trailers, mobile homes, boats, farm tractors, or the like, and any central filing statute*.]]; but during any period in which collateral is inventory held for sale by a person who is in the business of selling goods of that kind, the filing provisions of this Article (Part 4) apply to a security interest in that collateral created by him as debtor; or

(c) a certificate of title statute of another jurisdiction under the law of which indication of a security interest on the certificate is required as a condition of perfection (subsection (2) of Section 9–103).

(4) Compliance with a statute or treaty described in subsection (3) is equivalent to the filing of a financing statement under this Article, and a security interest in property subject to the statute or treaty can be perfected only by compliance therewith except as provided in Section 9–103 on multiple state transactions. Duration and renewal of perfection of a security interest perfected by compliance with the statute or treaty are governed by the provisions of the statute or treaty; in other respects the security interest is subject to this Article.

§9–302. When Filing is Required to Perfect Security Interest; Security Interests to Which Filing Provisions of This Article Do Not Apply *(1977 Amendments).*

(1) A financing statement must be filed to perfect all security interest[s] except the following:

* * *

(f) a security interest of a collecting bank (Section 4–208) or in securities (Section 8–321) or arising under the Article on Sales (see Section 9–113) or covered in subsection (3) of this section;

* * *

§9–303. When Security Interest Is Perfected; Continuity of Perfection.

(1) A security interest is perfected when it has attached and when all of the applicable steps required for perfection have been taken. Such steps are specified in Sections 9–302, 9–304, 9–305 and 9–306. If such steps are taken before the

*****Note:** It is recommended that the provisions of certificate of title acts for perfection of security interests by notation on the certificates should be amended to exclude coverage of inventory held for sale.

security interest attaches, it is perfected at the time when it attaches.

(2) If a security interest is originally perfected in any way permitted under this Article and is subsequently perfected in some other way under this Article, without an intermediate period when it was unperfected, the security interest shall be deemed to be perfected continuously for the purposes of this Article.

§9–304. Perfection of Security Interest in Instruments, Documents, and Goods Covered by Documents; Perfection by Permissive Filing; Temporary Perfection Without Filing or Transfer of Possession.

(1) A security interest in chattel paper or negotiable documents may be perfected by filing. A security interest in money or instruments (other than instruments which constitute part of chattel paper) can be perfected only by the secured party's taking possession, except as provided in subsections (4) and (5) of this section and subsections (2) and (3) of Section 9–306 on proceeds.

(2) During the period that goods are in the possession of the issuer of a negotiable document therefor, a security interest in the goods is perfected by perfecting a security interest in the document, and any security interest in the goods otherwise perfected during such period is subject thereto.

(3) A security interest in goods in the possession of a bailee other than one who has issued a negotiable document therefor is perfected by issuance of a document in the name of the secured party or by the bailee's receipt of notification of the secured party's interest or by filing as to the goods.

(4) A security interest in instruments or negotiable documents is perfected without filing or the taking of possession for a period of 21 days from the time it attaches to the extent that it arises for new value given under a written security agreement.

(5) A security interest remains perfected for a period of 21 days without filing where a secured party having a perfected security interest in an instrument, a negotiable document or goods in possession of a bailee other than one who has issued a negotiable document therefor

    (a) makes available to the debtor the goods or documents representing the goods for the purpose of ultimate sale or exchange or for the purpose of loading, unloading, storing, shipping, transshipping, manufacturing, processing or otherwise dealing with them in a manner preliminary to their sale or exchange, [;or] but priority between conflicting security interests in the goods is subject to subsection (3) of Section 9–312; or

    (b) delivers the instrument to the debtor for the purpose of ultimate sale or exchange or of presentation, collection, renewal or registration of transfer.

(6) After the 21 day period in subsections (4) and (5) perfection depends upon compliance with applicable provisions of this Article.

§9–304. Perfection of Security Interest in Instruments, Documents, and Goods Covered by Documents; Perfection by Permissive Filing; Temporary Perfection Without Filing or Transfer of Possession *(1977 Amentments)*.

(1) A security interest in chattel paper or negotiable documents may be perfected by filing. A security interest in money or instruments (other than certificated securities or instruments which constitute part of chattel paper) can be perfected only by the secured party's taking possession, except as provided in subsections (4) and (5) of this section and subsections (2) and (3) of Section 9–306 on proceeds.

* * *

(4) A security interest instruments (other than certificated securities) or negotiable documents is perfected without filing or the taking of possession for a period of 21 days from the time it attaches to the extent that it arises for new value given under a written security agreement.

(5) A security interest remains perfected for a period of 21 days without filing where a secured party having a perfected security interest in an instrument (other than a certificated security), a negotiable document or goods in possession of a bailee other than one who has issued a negotiable document therefor:

* * *

    (b) delivers the instrument to the debtor for the purpose of ultimate sale or exchange or of presentation collection, renewal, or registration of transfer.

(6) After the 21 day period in subsections (4) and (5) perfection depends upon compliance with applicable provisions of this Article.

§9–305. When Possession by Secured Party Perfects Security Interest Without Filing. A security interest in letters of credit and advices of credit (subsection (2) (a) of Section 5–116), goods, instruments, money, negotiable documents or chattel paper may be perfected by the secured party's taking possession of the collateral. If such collateral other than goods covered by a negotiable document is held by a bailee, the secured party is deemed to have possession from the time the bailee receives notification of the secured party's interest. A security interest is perfected by possession from the time possession is taken without relation back and continues only so long as possession is retained, unless otherwise specified in this Article. The security interest may be otherwise perfected as provided in this Article before or after the period of possession by the secured party.

§9–305. When Possession by Secured Party Perfects Security Interest Without Filing *(1977 Amendments)*. A security interest in letters of credit and advices of credit (subsection (2)(a) of Section 5–116), goods, instruments (other than certificated securities), money, negotiable documents, or chattel paper may be perfected by the secured party's taking possession of the collateral. If such collateral other than goods covered by a negotiable document is held by a bailee, the secured party is deemed to have possession from the time the bailee receives notification of the secured party's interest. A security interest is perfected by possession from the time possession is taken without relation back and continues only so long as possession is retained, unless otherwise specified in this Article. The security interest may be otherwise perfected as provided in this Article before or after the period of possession by the secured party.

§9–306. "Proceeds"; Secured Party's Rights on Disposition of Collateral.

(1) ["Proceeds" includes whatever is received when collateral or proceeds is sold, exchanged, collected or otherwise disposed of. The term also includes the account arising when the right to payment is earned under a contract right.]
"Proceeds" includes whatever is received upon the sale, exchange, collection or other disposition of collateral or proceeds. Insurance payable by reason of loss or damage to the collateral is proceeds, except to the extent that it is payable to a person other than a party to the security agreement. Money, checks, deposit accounts, and the like are "cash proceeds". All other proceeds are "non-cash proceeds".

(2) Except where this Article otherwise provides, a security interest continues in collateral notwithstanding sale, exchange or other disposition thereof [by the debtor] unless [his action was] the disposition was authorized by the secured party in the security agreement or otherwise, and also continues in any identifiable proceeds including collections received by the debtor.

(3) The security interest in proceeds is a continuously perfected security interest if the interest in the original collateral was perfected but it ceases to be a perfected security interest and becomes unperfected ten days after receipt of the proceeds by the debtor unless

[(a) a filed financing statement covering the original collateral also covers proceeds; or]
(a) a filed financing statement covers the original collateral and the proceeds are collateral in which a security interest may be perfected by filing in the office or offices where the financing statement has been filed and, if the proceeds are acquired with cash proceeds, the description of collateral in the financing statement indicates the types of property constituting the proceeds; or
(b) a filed financing statement covers the original collateral and the proceeds are identifiable cash proceeds; or
(c) [(b)] the security interest in the proceeds is perfected before the expiration of the ten day period.
Except as provided in this section, a security interest in proceeds can be perfected only by the methods or under the circumstances permitted in this Article for original collateral of the same type.

(4) In the event of insolvency proceedings instituted by or against a debtor, a secured party with a perfected security interest in proceeds has a perfected security interest only in the following proceeds:
(a) in identifiable non-cash proceeds[;] and in separate deposit accounts containing only proceeds;
(b) in identifiable cash proceeds in the form of money which is [not] neither commingled with other money [or] nor deposited in a [bank] deposit account prior to the insolvency proceedings;
(c) in identifiable cash proceeds in the form of checks and the like which are not deposited in a [bank] deposit account prior to the insolvency proceedings; and
(d) in all cash and [bank] deposit accounts of the debtor [if other cash] in which proceeds have been commingled with other funds, [or deposited in a bank account,] but the perfected security interest under this paragraph (d) is
(i) subject to any right of set-off; and
(ii) limited to an amount not greater than the amount of any cash proceeds received by the debtor within ten days before the institution of the insolvency proceedings [and commingled or deposited in a bank account prior to the insolvency proceedings less the amount of cash proceeds received by the debtor and paid over to the secured party during the ten day period,] less the sum of (I) the payments to the secured party on account of cash proceeds received by the debtor during such period and (II) the cash proceeds received by the debtor during such period to which the secured party is entitled under paragraphs (a) through (c) of this subsection (4).

(5) If a sale of goods results in an account or chattel paper which is transferred by the seller to a secured party, and if the goods are returned to or are repossessed by the seller or the secured party, the following rules determine priorities:
(a) If the goods were collateral at the time of sale, for an indebtedness of the seller which is still unpaid, the original security interest attaches again to the goods and continues as a perfected security interest if it was perfected at the time when the goods were sold. If the security interest was originally perfected by a filing which is still effective, nothing further is required to continue the perfected status; in any other case, the secured party must take possession of the returned or repossessed goods or must file.
(b) An unpaid transferee of the chattel paper has a security interest in the goods against the transferor. Such security interest is prior to a security interest asserted under paragraph (a) to the extent that the transferee of the chattel paper was entitled to priority under Section 9–308.
(c) An unpaid transferee of the account has a security interest in the goods against the transferor. Such security interest is subordinate to a security interest asserted under paragraph (a).

(d) A security interest of an unpaid transferee asserted under paragraph (b) or (c) must be perfected for protection against creditors of the transferor and purchasers of the returned or repossessed goods.

§9–307. Protection of Buyers of Goods.

(1) A buyer in ordinary course of business (subsection (9) of Section 1–201) other than a person buying farm products from a person engaged in farming operations takes free of a security interest created by his seller even though the security interest is perfected and even though the buyer knows of its existence.

(2) In the case of consumer goods [and in the case of farm equipment having an original purchase price not in excess of $2500 (other than fixtures, see Section 9–313)], a buyer takes free of a security interest even though perfected if he buys without knowledge of the security interest, for value and for his own personal, family or household purposes [or his own farming operations] unless prior to the purchase the secured party has filed a financing statement covering such goods.

(3) A buyer other than a buyer in ordinary course of business (subsection (1) of this section) takes free of a security interest to the extent that it secures future advances made after the secured party acquires knowledge of the purchase, or more than 45 days after the purchase, whichever first occurs, unless made pursuant to a commitment entered into without knowledge of the purchase and before the expiration of the 45 day period.

§9–308. Purchase of Chattel Paper and [Non-Negotiable] Instruments.

[A purchaser of chattel paper or a non-negotiable instrument who gives new value and takes possession of it in the ordinary course of his business and without knowledge that the specific paper or instrument is subject to a security interest has priority over a security interest which is perfected under Section 9–304 (permissive filing and temporary perfection). A purchaser of chattel paper who gives new value and takes possession of it in the ordinary course of his business has priority over a security interest in chattel paper which is claimed merely as proceeds of inventory subject to a security interest (Section 9–306), even though he knows that the specific paper is subject to the security interest.]

A purchaser of chattel paper or an instrument who gives new value and takes possession of it in the ordinary course of his business has priority over a security interest in the chattel paper or instrument

    (a) which is perfected under Section 9–304 (permissive filing and temporary perfection) or under Section 9–306 (perfection as to proceeds) if he acts without knowledge that the specific paper or instrument is subject to a security interest; or

    (b) which is claimed merely as proceeds of inventory subject to a security interest (Section 9–306) even though he knows that the specific paper or instrument is subject to the security interest.

§9–309. Protection of Purchasers of Instruments and Documents.

Nothing in this Article limits the rights of a holder in due course of a negotiable instrument (Section 3–302) or a holder to whom a negotiable document of title has been duly negotiated (Section 7–501) or a bona fide purchaser of a security (Section 8–301) and such holders or purchasers take priority over an earlier security interest even though perfected. Filing under this Article does not constitute notice of the security interest to such holders or purchasers.

§9–309. Protection of Purchasers of Instruments [and], Documents and Securities *(1977 Amendments).*

Nothing in this Article limits the rights of a holder in due course of a negotiable instrument (Section 3–302) or a holder to whom negotiable document of title has been duly negotiated (Section 7–501) or a bona fide purchaser of a security (Section [8–301] 8–302) and such holders or purchasers take priority over an earlier security interest even though perfected. Filing under this Article does not constitute notice of the security interest to such holders or purchasers.

§9–310. Priority of Certain Liens Arising by Operation of Law.

When a person in the ordinary course of his business furnishes services or materials with respect to goods subject to a security interest, a lien upon goods in the possession of such person given by statute or rule of law for such materials or services takes priority over a perfected security interest unless the lien is statutory and the statute expressly provides otherwise.

§9–311. Alienability of Debtor's Rights: Judicial Process.

The debtor's rights in collateral may be voluntarily or involuntarily transferred (by way of sale, creation of a security interest, attachment, levy, garnishment or other judicial process) notwithstanding a provision in the security agreement prohibiting any transfer or making the transfer constitute a default.

§9–312. Priorities Among Conflicting Security Interests in the Same Collateral.

[(1) The rules of priority stated in the following sections shall govern where applicable: Section 4–208 with respect to the security interest of collecting banks in items being collected, accompanying documents and proceeds; Section 9–301 on certain priorities; Section 9–304 on goods covered by documents; Section 9–306 on proceeds and repossessions; Section 9–307 on buyers of goods; Section 9–308 on possessory against nonpossessory interests in chattel paper or non-negotiable instruments; Section 9–309 on security interests in negotiable instruments, documents or securities; Section 9–310 on priorities between perfected security interests and liens by operation of law; Section 9–313 on security interests in fixtures as against interests in real estate; Section 9–314 on security interests in accessions as against interest in goods; Section 9–315 on conflicting security interests where goods lose their identity or become part of a product; and Section 9–316 on contractual subordination.]

(1) The rules of priority stated in other sections of this Part and in the following sections shall govern when applicable: Section 4–208 with respect to the security interests of collecting banks in items being collected, accompanying documents and proceeds; Section 9–103 on security interests related to other jurisdictions; Section 9–114 on consignments.

(2) A perfected security interest in crops for new value given to enable the debtor to produce the crops during the production season and given not more than three months before the crops become growing crops by planting or otherwise takes priority over an earlier perfected security interest to the extent that such earlier interest secures obligations due more than six months before the crops become growing crops by planting or otherwise, even though the person giving new value had knowledge of the earlier security interest.

[(3) A purchase money security interest in inventory collateral has priority over a conflicting security interest in the same collateral if

(a) the purchase money security interest is perfected at the time the debtor receives possession of the collateral; and

(b) any secured party whose security interest is known to the holder of the purchase money security interest or who, prior to the date of the filing made by the holder of the purchase money security interest, had filed a financing statement covering the same items or type of inventory, has received notification of the purchase money security interest before the debtor receives possession of the collateral covered by the purchase money security interest; and

(c) such notification states that the person giving the notice has or expects to acquire a purchase money security interest in inventory of the debtor, describing such inventory by item or type.]

(3) A perfected purchase money security interest in inventory has priority over a conflicting security interest in the same inventory and also has priority in identifiable cash proceeds received on or before the delivery of the inventory to a buyer if

(a) the purchase money security interest is perfected at the time the debtor receives possession of the inventory; and

(b) the purchase money secured party gives notification in writing to the holder of the conflicting security interest if the holder had filed a financing statement covering the same types of inventory (i) before the date of the filing made by the purchase money secured party, or (ii) before the beginning of the 21 day period where the purchase money security interest is temporarily perfected without filing or possession (subsection (5) of Section 9–304); and

(c) the holder of the conflicting security interest receives the notification within five years before the debtor receives possession of the inventory; and

(d) the notification states that the person giving the notice has or expects to acquire a purchase money security interest in inventory of the debtor, describing such inventory by item or type.

(4) A purchase money security interest in collateral other than inventory has priority over a conflicting security interest in the same collateral or its proceeds if the purchase money security interest is perfected at the time the debtor receives possession of the collateral or within ten days thereafter.

(5) In all cases not governed by other rules stated in this section (including cases of purchase money security interests which do not qualify for the special priorities set forth in subsections (3) and (4) of this section), priority between conflicting security interests in the same collateral shall be determined [as follows:

(a) in the order of filing if both are perfected by filing, regardless of which security interest attached first under Section 9–204(1) and whether it attached before or after filing;

(b) in order of perfection unless both are perfected by filing, regardless of which security interest attached first under Section 9–204(1) and, in the case of a filed security interest, whether it attached before or after filing; and

(c) in the order of attachment under Section 9–204(1) so long as neither is perfected.]

according to the following rules:

(a) Conflicting security interests rank according to priority in time of filing or perfection. Priority dates from the time a filing is first made covering the collateral or the time the security interest is first perfected, whichever is earlier, provided that there is no period thereafter when there is neither filing nor perfection.

(b) So long as conflicting security interests are unperfected, the first to attach has priority.

[(6) For the purpose of the priority rules of the immediately preceding subsection, a continuously perfected security interest shall be treated at all times as if perfected by filing if it was originally so perfected and it shall be treated at all times as if perfected otherwise than by filing if it was originally perfected otherwise than by filing.]

(6) For the purposes of subsection (5) a date of filing or perfection as to collateral is also a date of filing or perfection as to proceeds.

(7) If future advances are made while a security interest is perfected by filing or the taking of possession, the security interest has the same priority for the purposes of subsection (5) with respect to the future advances as it does with respect to the first advance. If a commitment is made before or while the security interest is so perfected, the security

interest has the same priority with respect to advances made pursuant thereto. In other cases a perfected security interest has priority from the date the advance is made.

§9–312. Priorities Among Conflicting Security Interests in the Same Collateral *(1977 Amendments).*

(**7**) If future advances are made while a security interest is perfected by filing [or], the taking of possession, or under Section 8–321 on securities, the security interest has the same priority for the purposes of subsection (5) with respect to the future advances as it does with respect to the first advance. If a commitment is made before or while the security interest is so perfected, the security interest has the same priority with respect to advances made pursuant thereto. In other cases a perfected security interest has priority from the date the advance is made.

* * *

§9–313. Priority of Security Interests in Fixtures.

[(**1**) The rules of this section do not apply to goods incorporated into a structure in the manner of lumber, bricks, tile, cement, glass, metal work and the like and no security interest in them exists under this Article unless the structure remains personal property under applicable law. The law of this state other than this Act determines whether and when other goods become fixtures. This Act does not prevent creation of an encumbrance upon fixtures or real estate pursuant to the law applicable to real estate.]

[(**2**) A security interest which attaches to goods before they become fixtures takes priority as to the goods over the claims of all persons who have an interest in the real estate except as stated in subsection (4).]

[(**3**) A security interest which attaches to goods after they become fixtures is valid against all persons subsequently acquiring interests in the real estate except as stated in subsection (4) but is invalid against any person with an interest in the real estate at the time the security interest attaches to the goods who has not in writing consented to the security interest or disclaimed an interest in the goods as fixtures.]

[(**4**) The security interests described in subsections (2) and (3) do not take priority over

    (**a**) a subsequent purchaser for value of any interest in the real estate; or

    (**b**) a creditor with a lien on the real estate subsequently obtained by judicial proceedings; or

    (**c**) a creditor with a prior encumbrance of record on the real estate to the extent that he makes subsequent advances

if the subsequent purchase is made, the lien by judicial proceedings is obtained, or the subsequent advance under the prior encumbrance is made or contracted for without knowledge of the security interest and before it is perfected. A purchaser of the real estate at a foreclosure sale other than an encumbrancer purchasing at his own foreclosure sale is a subsequent purchaser within this section.]

(**1**) In this section and in the provisions of Part 4 of this Article referring to fixture filing, unless the context otherwise requires

    (**a**) goods are "fixtures" when they become so related to particular real estate that an interest in them arises under real estate law

    (**b**) a "fixture filing" is the filing in the office where a mortgage on the real estate would be filed or recorded of a financing statement covering goods which are or are to become fixtures and conforming to the requirements of subsection (5) of Section 9–402

    (**c**) a mortgage is a "construction mortgage" to the extent that it secures an obligation incurred for the construction of an improvement on land including the acquisition cost of the land, if the recorded writing so indicates.

(**2**) A security interest under this Article may be created in goods which are fixtures or may continue in goods which become fixtures, but no security interest exists under this Article in ordinary building materials incorporated into an improvement on land.

(**3**) This Article does not prevent creation of an encumbrance upon fixtures pursuant to real estate law.

(**4**) A perfected security interest in fixtures has priority over the conflicting interest of an encumbrancer or owner of the real estate where

    (**a**) the security interest is a purchase money security interest, the interest of the encumbrancer or owner arises before the goods become fixtures, the security interest is perfected by a fixture filing before the goods become fixtures or within ten days thereafter, and the debtor has an interest of record in the real estate or is in possession of the real estate; or

    (**b**) the security interest is perfected by a fixture filing before the interest of the encumbrancer or owner is of record, the security interest has priority over any conflicting interest of a predecessor in title of the encumbrancer or owner, and the debtor has an interest of record in the real estate or is in possession of the real estate; or

    (**c**) the fixtures are readily removable factory or office machines or readily removable replacements of domestic appliances which are consumer goods, and before the goods become fixtures the security interest is perfected by any method permitted by this Article; or

    (**d**) the conflicting interest is a lien on the real estate obtained by legal or equitable proceedings after the security interest was perfected by any method permitted by this Article.

(**5**) A security interest in fixtures, whether or not perfected, has priority over the conflicting interest of an encumbrancer or owner of the real estate where

    (**a**) the encumbrancer or owner has consented in writing to the security interest or has disclaimed an interest in the goods as fixtures; or

(b) the debtor has a right to remove the goods as against the encumbrancer or owner. If the debtor's right terminates, the priority of the security interest continues for a reasonable time.

(6) Notwithstanding paragraph (a) of subsection (4) but otherwise subject to subsections (4) and (5), a security interest in fixtures is subordinate to a construction mortgage recorded before the goods become fixtures if the goods become fixtures before the completion of the construction. To the extent that it is given to refinance a construction mortgage, a mortgage has this priority to the same extent as the construction mortgage.

(7) In cases not within the preceding subsections, a security interest in fixtures is subordinate to the conflicting interest of an encumbrancer or owner of the related real estate who is not the debtor.

(8) [(5)] When [under subsections (2) or (3) or (4) a] the secured party has priority over [the claims of all persons who have interests in] all owners and encumbrancers of the real estate, he may, on default, subject to the provisions of Part 5, remove his collateral from the real estate but he must reimburse any encumbrancer or owner of the real estate who is not the debtor and who has not otherwise agreed for the cost of repair of any physical injury, but not for any diminution in value of the real estate caused by the absence of the goods removed or by any necessity of replacing them. A person entitled to reimbursement may refuse permission to remove until the secured party gives adequate security for the performance of this obligation.

§9–314. Accessions.

(1) A security interest in goods which attaches before they are installed in or affixed to other goods takes priority as to the goods installed or affixed (called in this section "accessions") over the claims of all persons to the whole except as stated in subsection (3) and subject to Section 9–315(1).

(2) A security interest which attaches to goods after they become part of a whole is valid against all persons subsequently acquiring interests in the whole except as stated in subsection (3) but is invalid against any person with an interest in the whole at the time the security interest attaches to the goods who has not in writing consented to the security interest or disclaimed an interest in the goods as part of the whole.

(3) The security interests described in subsections (1) and (2) do not take priority over

(a) a subsequent purchaser for value of any interest in the whole; or

(b) a creditor with a lien on the whole subsequently obtained by judicial proceedings; or

(c) a creditor with a prior perfected security interest in the whole to the extent that he makes subsequent advances.

If the subsequent purchase is made, the lien by judicial proceedings obtained or the subsequent advance under the prior perfected security interest is made or con-

tracted for without knowledge of the security interest and before it is perfected. A purchaser of the whole at a foreclosure sale other than the holder of a perfected security interest purchasing at his own foreclosure sale is a subsequent purchaser within this section.

(4) When under subsections (1) or (2) and (3) a secured party has an interest in accessions which has priority over the claims of all persons who have interests in the whole, he may on default subject to the provisions of Part 5 remove his collateral from the whole but he must reimburse any encumbrancer or owner of the whole who is not the debtor and who has not otherwise agreed for the cost of repair of any physical injury but not for any diminution in value of the whole caused by the absence of the goods removed or by any necessity for replacing them. A person entitled to reimbursement may refuse permission to remove until the secured party gives adequate security for the performance of this obligation.

§9–315. Priority When Goods are Commingled or Processed.

(1) If a security interest in goods was perfected and subsequently the goods or a part thereof have become part of a product or mass, the security interest continues in the product or mass if

(a) the goods are so manufactured, processed, assembled or commingled that their identity is lost in the product or mass; or

(b) a financing statement covering the original goods also covers the product into which the goods have been manufactured, processed or assembled. In a case to which paragraph (b) applies, no separate security interest in that part of the original goods which has been manufactured, processed or assembled into the product may be claimed under Section 9–314.

(2) When under subsection (1) more than one security interest attaches to the product or mass, they rank equally according to the ratio that the cost of the goods to which each interest originally attached bears to the cost of the total product or mass.

§9–316. Priority Subject to Subordination. Nothing in this Article prevents subordination by agreement by any person entitled to priority.

§9–317. Secured Party Not Obligated On Contract of Debtor. The mere existence of a security interest or authority given to the debtor to dispose of or use collateral does not impose contract or tort liability upon the secured party for the debtor's acts or omissions.

§9–318. Defenses Against Assignee; Modification of Contract After Notification of Assignment; Term Prohibiting Assignment Ineffective; Identification and Proof of Assignment.

(1) Unless an account debtor has made an enforceable agreement not to assert defenses or claims arising out of a

sale as provided in Section 9–206 the rights of an assignee are subject to

(**a**) all the terms of the contract between the account debtor and assignor and any defense or claim arising therefrom; and

(**b**) any other defense or claim of the account debtor against the assignor which accrues before the account debtor receives notification of the assignment.

(**2**) So far as the right to payment or a part thereof under an assigned contract has not been fully earned by performance, [right has not already become an account,] and notwithstanding notification of the assignment, any modification of or substitution for the contract made in good faith and in accordance with reasonable commercial standards is effective against an assignee unless the account debtor has otherwise agreed but the assignee acquires corresponding rights under the modified or substituted contract. The assignment may provide that such modification or substitution is a breach by the assignor.

(**3**) The account debtor is authorized to pay the assignor until the account debtor receives notification that the [account] amount due or to become due has been assigned and that payment is to be made to the assignee. A notification which does not reasonably identify the rights assigned is ineffective. If requested by the account debtor, the assignee must seasonably furnish reasonable proof that the assignment has been made and unless he does so the account debtor may pay the assignor.

(**4**) A term in any contract between an account debtor and an assignor [which] is ineffective if it prohibits assignment of an account [or contract right to which they are parties is ineffective] or prohibits creation of a security interest in a general intangible for money due or to become due or requires the account debtor's consent to such assignment or security interest.

Part 4   Filing

§9–401. Place of Filing; Erroneous Filing; Removal of Collateral.

First Alternative Subsection (1)

(**1**) The proper place to file in order to perfect a security interest is as follows:

(**a**) when the collateral is timber to be cut or is minerals or the like (including oil and gas) or accounts subject to subsection (5) of Section 9–103, or when the financing statement is filed as a fixture filing (Section 9–313) and the collateral is goods which [at the time the security interest attaches] are or are to become fixtures, then in the office where a mortgage on the real estate [concerned] would be filed or recorded;

(**b**) in all other cases, in the office of the [[Secretary of State]].

Second Alternative Subsection (1)

(**1**) The proper place to file in order to perfect a security interest is as follows:

(**a**) when the collateral is equipment used in farming operations, or farm products, or accounts [, contract rights] or general intangibles arising from or relating to the sale of farm products by a farmer, or consumer goods, then in the office of the . . . . in the county of the debtor's residence or if the debtor is not a resident of this state then in the office of the . . . . in the county where the goods are kept, and in addition when the collateral is crops growing or to be grown in the office of the . . . . in the county where the land [on which the crops are growing or to be grown] is located;

(**b**) when the collateral is [goods which at the time the security interest attaches are or are to become fixtures] timber to be cut or is minerals or the like (including oil and gas) or accounts subject to subsection (5) of Section 9–103, or when the financing statement is filed as a fixture filing (Section 9–313) and the collateral is goods which are or are to become fixtures, then in the office where a mortgage on the real estate [concerned] would be filed or recorded;

(**c**) in all other cases, in the office of the [[Secretary of State]].

Third Alternative Subsection (1)

(**1**) The proper place to file in order to perfect a security interest is as follows:

(**a**) when the collateral is equipment used in farming operations, or farm products, or accounts [, contract rights] or general intangibles arising from or relating to the sale of farm products by a farmer, or consumer goods, then in the office of the . . . . . . in the county of the debtor's residence or if the debtor is not a resident of this state then in the office of the . . . . . . in the county where the goods are kept, and in addition when the collateral is crops growing or to be grown in the office of the . . . . . . in the county where the land [on which the crops are growing or to be grown] is located;

(**b**) when the collateral is [goods which at the time the security interest attaches are or are to become fixtures] timber to be cut or is minerals or the like (including oil and gas) or accounts subject to subsection (5) of Section 9–103, or when the financing statement is filed as a fixture filing (Section 9–313) and the collateral is goods which are or are to become fixtures, then in the office where a mortgage on the real estate [concerned] would be filed or recorded;

(**c**) in all other cases, in the office of the [[Secretary of State]] and in addition, if the debtor has a place of business in only one county of this state, also in the office of . . . . . . of such county, or, if the debtor has no place of business in this state, but resides in the state, also in the office of . . . . . . of the county in which he resides.

Note: *One of the three alternatives should be selected as subsection (1).*

(**2**) A filing which is made in good faith in an improper place or not in all of the places required by this section is nevertheless effective with regard to any collateral as to which the filing complied with the requirements of this Article and is also effective with regard to collateral covered by the financing statement against any person who has knowledge of the contents of such financing statement.

(**3**) A filing which is made in the proper place in this state continues effective even though the debtor's residence or place of business or the location of the collateral or its use, whichever controlled the original filing, is thereafter changed.

Language in double brackets is Alternative Subsection (3).

[[(3) A filing which is made in the proper county continues effective for four months after a change to another county of the debtor's residence or place of business or the location of the collateral, whichever controlled the original filing. It becomes ineffective thereafter unless a copy of the financing statement signed by the secured party is filed in the new county within said period. The security interest may also be perfected in the new county after the expiration of the four-month period; in such case perfected dates from the time of perfection in the new county. A change in the use of the collateral does not impair the effectiveness of the original filing.]]

(**4**) [If collateral is brought into this state from another jurisdiction, the] The rules stated in Section 9–103 determine whether filing is necessary in this state.

(**5**) Notwithstanding the preceding subsections, and subject to subsection (3) of Section 9–302, the proper place to file in order to perfect a security interest in collateral, including the fixtures, of a transmitting utility is the office of the [[Secretary of State]]. This filing constitutes a fixture filing (Section 9–313) as to the collateral described therein which is or is to become fixtures.

(**6**) For the purposes of this section, the residence of an organization is its place of business if it has one or its chief executive office if it has more than one place of business.

Note: *Subsection (6) should be used only if the state chooses the Second or Third Alternative Subsection (1).*

§9–402. Formal Requisites of Financing Statement; Amendments; Mortgage as Financing Statement.

(**1**) A financing statement is sufficient if it gives the names of the debtor and the secured party, is signed by the debtor [and the secured party], gives an address of the secured party from which information concerning the security interest may be obtained, gives a mailing address of the debtor and contains a statement indicating the types, or describing the items, of collateral. A financing statement may be filed before a security agreement is made or a security interest otherwise attaches. When the financing statement covers crops growing or to be grown [or goods which are or are to become fixtures], the statement must also contain a description of the real estate concerned. When the financing statement covers timber to be cut or covers minerals or the like (including oil and gas) or accounts subject to subsection (5) of Section 9–103, or when the financing statement is filed as a fixture filing (Section 9–313) and the collateral is goods which are or are to become fixtures, the statement must also comply with subsection (5). A copy of the security agreement is sufficient as a financing statemen if it contains the above information and is signed by [both parties.] the debtor. A carbon, photographic or other reproduction of a security agreement or a financing statement is sufficient as a financing statement if the security agreement so provides or if the original has been filed in this state.

(**2**) A financing statement which otherwise complies with subsection (1) is sufficient [although] when it is signed [only] by the secured party instead of the debtor if it is filed to perfect a security interest in

    (**a**) collateral already subject to security interest in another jurisdiction when it is brought into this state, or when the debtor's location is changed to this state. Such a financing statement must state that the collateral was brought into this state or that the debtor's location was changed to this state under such circumstances; or

    (**b**) proceeds under Section 9–306 if the security interest in the original collateral was perfected. Such a financing statement must describe the original collateral; or

    (**c**) collateral as to which the filing has lapsed; or

    (**d**) collateral acquired after a change of name, identity or corporate structure of the debtor (subsection (7)).

(**3**) A form substantially as follows is sufficient to comply with subsection (1):

Name of debtor (or assignor) . . . .
Address. . . . .
Name of secured party (or assignee) . . . .
Address. . . . .

    1. This financing statement covers the following types (or items) of property:
    (Describe) . . . .
    2. (If collateral is crops) The above described crops are growing or are to be grown on:
    (Describe Real Estate) . . . .
    [**3.** (If collateral is goods which are or are to become fixtures) The above described goods are affixed or to be affixed to:
    (Describe Real Estate).]

3. (If applicable) The above goods are to become fixtures on*
(Describe Real Estate) . . . .
and this financing statement is to be filed [[for record]] in the real estate records. (If the debtor does not have an interest of record) The name of a record owner is . . . .
4. (If [proceeds or] products of collateral are claimed) [Proceeds—] Products of the collateral are also covered.

(use	. . . .
whichever	Signature of Debtor (or Assignor)
is	. . . .
applicable)	Signature of Secured Party (or Assignee)

(4) A financing statement may be amended by filing a writing signed by both the debtor and the secured party. An amendment does not extend the period of effectiveness of a financing statement. [The term "financing statement" as used in this Article means the original financing statement and any amendments but if] If any amendment adds collateral, it is effective as to the added collateral only from the filing date of the amendment. In this Article, unless the context otherwise requires, the term "financing statement" means the original financing statement and any amendments.

(5) A financing statement covering timber to be cut or covering minerals or the like (including oil and gas) or accounts subject to subsection (5) of Section 9–103, or a financing statement filed as a fixture filing (Section 9–313) where the debtor is not a transmitting utility, must show that it covers this type of collateral, must recite that it is to be filed [[for record]] in the real estate records, and the financing statement must contain a description of the real estate [[sufficient if it were contained in a mortgage of the real estate to give constructive notice of the mortgage under the law of this state]]. If the debtor does not have an interest of record in the real estate, the financing statement must show the name of a record owner.

(6) A mortgage is effective as a financing statement filed as a fixture filing from the date of its recording if (a) the goods are described in the mortgage by item or type, (b) the goods are or are to become fixtures related to the real estate described in the mortgage, (c) the mortgage complies with the requirements for a financing statement in this section other than a recital that it is to be filed in the real estate records, and (d) the mortgage is duly recorded. No fee with reference to the financing statement is required other than

the regular recording and satisfaction fees with respect to the mortgage.

(7) A financing statement sufficiently shows the name of the debtor if it gives the individual, partnership or corporate name of the debtor, whether or not it adds other trade names or the names of partners. Where the debtor so changes his name or in the case of an organization name, identity or corporate structure that a filed financing statement becomes seriously misleading, the filing is not effective to perfect a security interest in collateral acquired by the debtor more than four months after the change, unless a new appropriate financing statement is filed before the expiration of that time. A filed financing statement remains effective with respect to collateral transferred by the debtor even though the secured party knows of or consents to the transfer.

(8) [(5)] A financing statement substantially complying with the requirements of this section is effective even though it contains minor errors which are not seriously misleading.

Note: *Language in double brackets is optional.*

Note: *Where the state has any special recording system for real estate other than the usual grantor-grantee index (as, for instance, a tract system or a title registration or Torrens system) local adaptations of subsection (5) and Section 9–403(7) may be necessary. See Mass. Gen. Laws Chapter 106, Section 9–409.*

§9–403. What Constitutes Filing; Duration of Filing; Effect of Lapsed Filing; Duties of Filing Officer.

(1) Presentation for filing of a financing statement and tender of the filing fee or acceptance of the statement by the filing officer constitutes filing under this Article.

(2) Except as provided in subsection (6) a [(2) A] filed financing statement [which states a maturity date of the obligation secured of five years or less is effective until such maturity date and thereafter for a period of sixty days. Any other filed financing statement] is effective for a period of five years from the date of filing. The effectiveness of a filed financing statement [on the expiration of such sixty day period after a stated maturity date or] on the expiration of [such five] the five year period [, as the case may be] unless a continuation statement is filed prior to the lapse. If a security interest perfected by filing exists at the time insolvency proceedings are commenced by or against the debtor, the security interest remains perfected until termination of the insolvency proceedings and thereafter for a period of sixty days or until expiration of the five year period, whichever occurs later. Upon [such] lapse the security interest becomes unperfected, unless it is perfected without filing. If the security interest becomes unperfected upon lapse, it is deemed to have been unperfected as against a person who became a purchaser or lien creditor before lapse. [A filed financing statement which states that the

*Where appropriate substitute either "The above timber is standing on. . . ." or "The above minerals or the like (including oil and gas) or accounts will be financed at the wellhead or minehead of the well or mine located on. . . ."

obligation secured is payable on demand is effective for five years from the date of filing.]

(3) A continuation statement may be filed by the secured party [(i) within six months before and sixty days after a stated maturity date of five years or less, and (ii) otherwise] within six months prior to the expiration of the five year period specified in subsection (2). Any such continuation statement must be signed by the secured party, identify the original statement by file number and state that the original statement is still effective. A continuation statement signed by a person other than the secured party of record must be accompanied by a separate written statement of assignment signed by the secured party of record and complying with subsection (2) of Section 9–405, including payment of the required fee. Upon timely filing of the continuation statement, the effectiveness of the original statement is continued for five years after the last date to which the filing was effective whereupon it lapses in the same manner as provided in subsection (2) unless another continuation statement is filed prior to such lapse. Succeeding continuation statements may be filed in the same manner to continue the effectiveness of the original statement. Unless a statute on disposition of public records provides otherwise, the filing officer may remove a lapsed statement from the files and destroy it.[.] immediately if he has retained a microfilm or other photographic record, or in other cases after one year after the lapse. The filing officer shall so arrange matters by physical annexation of financing statements to continuation statements or other related filings, or by other means, that if he physically destroys the financing statements of a period more than five years past, those which have been continued by a continuation statement or which are still effective under subsection (6) shall be retained.

(4) Except as provided in subsection (7) a) [(4) A] filing officer shall mark each statement with a [consecutive] file number and with the date and hour of filing and shall hold the statement or a microfilm or other photographic copy thereof for public inspection. In addition the filing officer shall index the statements according to the name of the debtor and shall note in the index the file number and the address of the debtor given in the statement.

[(5) The uniform fee for filing, indexing and furnishing filing data for an original or a continuation statement shall be $. . . . . . .]

(5) The uniform fee for filing and indexing and for stamping a copy furnished by the secured party to show the date and place of filing for an original financing statement or for a continuation statement shall be $. . . . . . . if the statement is in the standard form prescribed by the [[Secretary of State]] and otherwise shall be $. . . . . . . , plus in each case, if the financing statement is subject to subsection (5) of Section 9–402, $. . . . . . . The uniform fee for each name more than one required to be indexed shall be $. . . . . . . The secured party may at his option

show a trade name for any person and an extra uniform indexing fee of $. . . . . . . shall be paid with respect thereto.

(6) If the debtor is a transmitting utility (subsection (5) of Section 9–401) and a filed financing statement so states, it is effective until a termination statement is filed. A real estate mortgage which is effective as a fixture filing under subsection (6) of Section 9–402 remains effective as a fixture filing until the mortgage is released or satisfied of record or its effectiveness otherwise terminates as to the real estate.

(7) When a financing statement covers timber to be cut or covers minerals or the like (including oil and gas) or accounts subject to subsection (5) of Section 9–103, or is filed as a fixture filing, [[it shall be filed for record and]] the filing officer shall index it under the names of the debtor and any owner of record shown on the financing statement in the same fashion as if they were the mortgagors in a mortgage of the real estate described, and, to the extent that the law of this state provides for indexing of mortgages under the name of the mortgagee, under the name of the secured party as if he were the mortgagee thereunder, or where indexing is by description in the same fashion as if the financing statement were a mortgage of the real estate described.

Note: *In states in which writings will not appear in the real estate records and indices unless actually recorded the bracketed language in subsection (7) should be used.*

§9–404. Termination Statement.

(1) If a financing statement covering consumer goods is filed on or after . . . . , then within one month or within ten days following written demand by the debtor after there is no outstanding secured obligation and no commitment to make advances, incur obligations or otherwise give value, the secured party must file with each filing officer with whom the financing statement was filed, a termination statement to the effect that he no longer claims a security interest under the financing statement, which shall be identified by file number. In other cases whenever [Whenever] there is no outstanding secured obligation and no commitment to make advances, incur obligations or otherwise give value, the secured party must on written demand by the debtor send the debtor, for each filing officer with whom the financing statement was filed, a termination statement to the effect that he no longer claims a security interest under the financing statement, which shall be identified by file number. A termination statement signed by a person other than the secured party of record must [include or] be accompanied by [the assignment or] a separate written statement of assignment signed by the secured party of record [that he has assigned the security interest to the signer of the termination statement. and] complying with subsection (2) of Section 9–405, including payment of the required fee. [The uniform fee for filing and indexing such

an assignment or statement thereof shall be $ . . . .] If the affected secured party fails to file such a termination statement as required by this subsection, or to send such a termination statement within ten days after proper demand therefor he shall be liable to the debtor for one hundred dollars, and in addition for any loss caused to the debtor by such failure.

(2) On presentation to the filing officer of such a termination statement he must note it in the index. [The filing officer shall remove from the files, mark "terminated" and send or deliver to the secured party the financing statement and any continuation statement, statement of assignment or statement of release pertaining thereto.] If he has received the termination statement in duplicate, he shall return one copy of the termination statement to the secured party stamped to show the time of receipt thereof. If the filing officer has a microfilm or other photographic record of the financing statement, and of any related continuation statement, statement of assignment and statement of release, he may remove the originals from the files at any time after receipt of the termination statement, or if he has no such record, he may remove them from the files at any time after one year after receipt of the termination statement.

(3) If the termination statement is in the standard form prescribed by the [[Secretary of State]], the uniform fee for filing and indexing [a] the termination statement [including sending or delivering the financing statement] shall be $. . . . ., and otherwise shall be $. . . . ., plus in each case an additional fee of $. . . . . . . for each name more than one against which the termination statement is required to be indexed.

Note: *The date to be inserted should be the effective date of the revised Article 9.*

§9–405. Assignment of Security Interest; Duties of Filing Officer; Fees.

(1)A financing statement may disclose an assignment of a security interest in the collateral described in the financing statement by indication in the financing statement of the name and address of the assignee or by an assignment itself or a copy thereof on the face or back of the statement. [Either the original secured party or the assignee may sign this statement as the secured party.] On presentation to the filing officer of such a financing statement the filing officer shall mark the same as provided in Section 9–403(4). The uniform fee for filing, indexing and furnishing filing data for a financing statement so indicating an assignment shall be $. . . . . if the statement is in the standard form prescribed by the [[Secretary of State]] and otherwise shall be $. . . . ., plus in each case an additional fee of $. . . . . . for each name more than one against which the financing statement is required to be indexed.

(2) A secured party may assign of record all or part of his rights under a financing statement by the filing in the place where the original financing statement was filed of a separate written statement of assignment signed by the secured party of record and setting forth the name of the secured party of record and the debtor, the file number and the date of filing of the financing statement and the name and address of the assignee and containing a description of the collateral assigned. A copy of the assignment is sufficient as a separate statement if it complies with the preceding sentence. On presentation to the filing officer of such a separate statement, the filing officer shall mark such separate statement with the date and hour of the filing. He shall note the assignment on the index of the financing statement, or in the case of a fixture filing, or a filing covering timber to be cut, or covering minerals or the like (including oil and gas or accounts subject to subsection (5) of Section 9–103, he shall index the assignment under the name of the assignor as grantor and, to the extent that the law of this state provides for indexing the assignment of a mortgage under the name of the assignee, he shall index the assignment of the financing statement under the name of the assignee. The uniform fee for filing, indexing and furnishing filing data about such a separate statement of assignment shall be $. . . . . if the statement is in the standard form prescribed by the [[Secretary of State]] and otherwise shall be $. . . . . . ., plus in each case an additional fee of $. . . . . . . for each name more than one against which the statement of assignment is required to be indexed. Notwithstanding the provisions of this subsection, an assignment of record of a security interest in a fixture contained in a mortgage effective as a fixture filing (subsection (6) of Section 9–402) may be made only by an assignment of the mortgage in the manner provided by the law of this state other than this Act.

(3) After the disclosure or filing of an assignment under this section, the assignee is the secured party of record.

§9–406. Release of Collateral; Duties of Filing Officer; Fees.

A secured party of record may by his signed statement release all or a part of any collateral described in a filed financing statement. The statement of release is sufficient if it contains a description of the collateral being released, the name and address of the debtor, the name and address of the secured party, and the file number of the financing statement. A statement of release signed by a person other than the secured party of record must be accompanied by a separate written statement of assignment signed by the secured party of record and complying with subsection (2) of Section 9–405, including payment of the required fee. Upon presentation of such a statement of release to the filing officer he shall mark the statement with the hour and date of filing and shall note the same upon the margin of the index of the filing of the financing statement. The uniform fee for filing and noting such a statement of release shall be $. . . . . . if the statement is in the standard form prescribed by the [[Secretary of State]] and otherwise shall be $. . . . . . ., plus in each case an additional fee of $. . . . . . for each name more than one against which the statement of release is required to be indexed.

[[§9–407. Information From Filing Officer]].

[[(1) If the person filing any financing statement, termination statement, statement of assignment, or statement of release, furnishes the filing officer a copy thereof, the filing officer shall upon request note upon the copy the file number and date and hour of the filing of the original and deliver or send the copy to such person.]]

[[(2) Upon request of any person, the filing officer shall issue his certificate showing whether there is on file on the date and hour stated therein, any presently effective financing statement naming a particular debtor and any statement of assignment thereof and if there is, giving the date and hour of filing of each such statement and the names and addresses of each secured party therein. The uniform fee for such a certificate shall be $. . . . . . . [plus $. . . . . . . for each financing statement and for each statement of assignment reported therein.] if the request for the certificate is in the standard form prescribed by the [[Secretary of State]] and otherwise shall be $. . . . . . . [plus $. . . . . . . for each financing statement and for each statement of assignment reported therein.] Upon request the filing officer shall furnish a copy of any filed financing statement or statement of assignment for a uniform fee of $. . . . . . . per page.]]

Note: *This section is proposed as an optional provision to require filing officers to furnish certificates. Local law and practices should be consulted with regard to the advisability of adoption.*

§9–408. Financing Statements Covering Consigned or Leased Goods.

A consignor or lessor of goods may file a financing statement using the terms "consignor," "consignee," "lessor," "lessee" or the like instead of the terms specified in Section 9–402. The provisions of this Part shall apply as appropriate to such a financing statement but its filing shall not of itself be a factor in determining whether or not the consignment or lease is intended as security (Section 1–201(37)). However, if it is determined for other reasons that the consignment or lease is so intended, a security interest of the consignor or lessor which attaches to the consigned or leased goods is perfected by such filing.

Part 5   Default

§9–501. Default; Procedure When Security Agreement Covers Both Real and Personal Property.

(1) When a debtor is in default under a security agreement, a secured party has the rights and remedies provided in this Part and except as limited by subsection (3) those provided in the security agreement. He may reduce his claim to judgment, foreclose or otherwise enforce the security interest by any available judicial procedure. If the collateral is documents the secured party may proceed either as to the documents or as to the goods covered thereby. A secured party in possession has the rights, remedies and duties provided in Section 9–207. The rights and remedies referred to in this subsection are cumulative.

(2) After default, the debtor has the rights and remedies provided in this Part, those provided in the security agreement and those provided in Section 9–207.

(3) To the extent that they give rights to the debtor and impose duties on the secured party, the rules stated in the subsections referred to below may not be waived or varied except as provided with respect to compulsory disposition of collateral (subsection (3) of Section 9–504 and [(subsection (1) of] Section 9–505) and with respect to redemption of collateral (Section 9–506) but the parties may by agreement determine the standards by which the fulfillment of these rights and duties is to be measured if such standards are not manifestly unreasonable:

(a) subsection (2) of Section 9–502 and subsection (2) of Section 9–504 insofar as they require accounting for surplus proceeds of collateral;

(b) subsection (3) of Section 9–504 and subsection (1) of Section 9–505 which deal with disposition of collateral;

(c) subsection (2) of Section 9–505 which deals with acceptance of collateral as discharge of obligation;

(d) Section 9–506 which deals with redemption of collateral; and

(e) subsection (1) of Section 9–507 which deals with the secured party's liability for failure to comply with this Part.

(4) If the security agreement covers both real and personal property, the secured party may proceed under this Part as to the personal property or he may proceed as to both the real and the personal property in accordance with his rights and remedies in respect of the real property in which case the provisions of this Part do not apply.

(5) When a secured party has reduced his claim to judgment the lien of any levy which may be made upon his collateral by virtue of any execution based upon the judgment shall relate back to the date of the perfection of the security interest in such collateral. A judicial sale, pursuant to such execution, is a foreclosure of the security interest by judicial procedure within the meaning of this section, and the secured party may purchase at the sale and thereafter hold the collateral free of any other requirements of this Article.

§9–502. Collection Rights of Secured Party.

(1) When so agreed and in any event on default the secured party is entitled to notify an account debtor or the obligor on an instrument to make payment to him whether or not the assignor was theretofore making collections on the collateral, and also to take control of any proceeds to which he is entitled under Section 9–306.

(2) A secured party who by agreement is entitled to charge back uncollected collateral or otherwise to full or limited recourse against the debtor and who undertakes to collect from the account debtors or obligors must proceed in a commercially reasonable manner and may deduct his reasonable expenses of realization from the collections. If the security agreement secures an indebtedness, the secured party must account to the debtor for any surplus, and unless otherwise agreed, the debtor is liable for any deficiency. But, if the underlying transaction was a sale of accounts [, contract rights,] or chattel paper, the debtor is entitled to any surplus or is liable for any deficiency only if the security agreement so provides.

§9–503. Secured Party's Right to Take Possession After Default.

Unless otherwise agreed a secured party has on default the right to take possession of the collateral. In taking possession a secured party may proceed without judicial process if this can be done without breach of the peace or may proceed by action. If the security agreement so provides the secured party may require the debtor to assemble the collateral and make it available to the secured party at a place to be designated by the secured party which is reasonably convenient to both parties. Without removal a secured party may render equipment unusable, and may dispose of collateral on the debtor's premises under Section 9–504.

§9–504. Secured Party's Right to Dispose of Collateral After Default; Effect of Disposition.

(1) A secured party after default may sell, lease or otherwise dispose of any or all of the collateral in its then condition or following any commercially reasonable preparation or processing. Any sale of goods is subject to the Article on Sales (Article 2). The proceeds of disposition shall be applied in the order following to

(a) the reasonable expenses of retaking, holding, preparing for sale or lease, selling, leasing and the like and, to the extent provided for in the agreement and not prohibited by law, the reasonable attorneys' fees and legal expenses incurred by the secured party;

(b) the satisfaction of indebtedness secured by the security interest under which the disposition is made;

(c) the satisfaction of indebtedness secured by any subordinate security interest in the collateral if written notification of demand therefor is received before distribution of the proceeds is completed. If requested by the secured party, the holder of a subordinate security interest must seasonably furnish reasonable proof of his interest, and unless he does so, the secured party need not comply with his demand.

(2) If the security interest secures an indebtedness, the secured party must account to the debtor for any surplus, and, unless otherwise agreed, the debtor is liable for any deficiency. But if the underlying transaction was a sale of accounts [, contract rights,] or chattel paper, the debtor is entitled to any surplus or is liable for any deficiency only if the security agreement so provides.

(3) Disposition of the collateral may be by public or private proceedings and may be made by way of one or more contracts. Sale or other disposition may be as a unit or in parcels and at any time and place and on any terms but every aspect of the disposition including the method, manner, time, place and terms must be commercially reasonable. Unless collateral is perishable or threatens to decline speedily in value or is of a type customarily sold on a recognized market, reasonable notification of the time and place of any public sale or reasonable notification of the time after which any private sale or other intended disposition is to be made shall be sent by the secured party to the debtor, if he has not signed after default a statement renouncing or modifying his right to notification of sale. In the case of consumer goods no other notification need be sent. In other cases notification shall be sent to any other secured party from whom the secured party has received (before sending his notification to the debtor or before the debtor's renunciation of his rights) written notice of a claim of an interest in the collateral [and except in the case of consumer goods to any other person who has a security interest in the collateral and who has duly filed a financing statement indexed in the name of the debtor in this state or who is known by the secured party to have a security interest in the collateral]. The secured party may buy at any public sale and if the collateral is of a type customarily sold in a recognized market or is of a type which is the subject of widely distributed standard price quotations he may buy at private sale.

(4) When collateral is disposed of by a secured party after default, the disposition transfers to a purchaser for value all of the debtor's rights therein, discharges the security interest under which it is made and any security interest or lien subordinate thereto. The purchaser takes free of all such rights and interests even though the secured party fails to comply with the requirements of this Part or of any judicial proceedings

(a) in the case of a public sale, if the purchaser has no knowledge of any defects in the sale and if he does not buy in collusion with the secured party, other bidders or the person conducting the sale; or

(b) in any other case, if the purchaser acts in good faith.

(5) A person who is liable to a secured party under a guaranty, indorsement, repurchase agreement or the like and who receives a transfer of collateral from the secured party or is subrogated to his rights has thereafter the rights and duties of the secured party. Such a transfer of collateral is not a sale or disposition of the collateral under this Article.

§9–505. Compulsory Disposition of Collateral; Acceptance of the Collateral as Discharge of Obligation.

(1) If the debtor has paid sixty per cent of the cash price in the case of a purchase money security interest in consumer

goods or sixty per cent of the loan in the case of another security interest in consumer goods, and has not signed after default a statement renouncing or modifying his rights under this Part a secured party who has taken possession of collateral must dispose of it under Section 9–504 and if he fails to do so within ninety days after he takes possession the debtor at his option may recover in conversion or under Section 9–507(1) on secured party's liability.

(2) In any other case involving consumer goods or any other collateral a secured party in possession may, after default, propose to retain the collateral in satisfaction of the obligation. Written notice of such proposal shall be sent to the debtor [and except in the case of consumer goods to any other secured party who has a security interest in the collateral and who has duly filed a financing statement indexed in the name of the debtor in this state or is known by the secured party in possession to have a security interest in it. If the debtor or other person entitled to receive notification objects in writing within thirty days from the receipt of the notification or if any other secured party objects in writing thirty days after the secured party obtains possession the secured party must dispose of the collateral under Section 9–504.] if he has not signed after default a statement renouncing or modifying his rights under this subsection. In the case of consumer goods no other notice need be given. In other cases notice shall be sent to any other secured party from whom the secured party has received (before sending his notice to the debtor or before the debtor's renunciation of his rights) written notice of a claim of an interest in the collateral. If the secured party receives objection in writing from a person entitled to receive notification within twenty-one days after the notice was sent, the secured party must dispose of the collateral under Section 9–504. In the absence of such written objection the secured party may retain the collateral in satisfaction of the debtor's obligation.

§9–506. Debtor's Right to Redeem Collateral. At any time before the secured party has disposed of collateral or entered into a contract for its disposition under Section 9–504 or before the obligation has been discharged under Section 9–505(2) the debtor or any other secured party may unless otherwise agreed in writing after default redeem the collateral by tendering fulfillment of all obligations secured by the collateral as well as the expenses reasonably incurred by the secured party in retaking, holding and preparing the collateral for disposition, in arranging for the sale, and to the extent provided in the agreement and not prohibited by law, his reasonable attorneys' fees and legal expenses.

§9–507. Secured Party's Liability for Failure to Comply With This Part.

(1) If it is established that the secured party is not proceeding in accordance with the provisions of this Part disposition may be ordered or restrained on appropriate terms and conditions. If the disposition has occurred the debtor or any person entitled to notification or whose security interest has been made known to the secured party prior to the disposition has a right to recover from the secured party any loss caused by a failure to comply with the provisions of this Part. If the collateral is consumer goods, the debtor has a right to recover in any event an amount not less than the credit service charge plus ten per cent of the principal amount of the debt or the time price differential plus 10 per cent of the cash price.

(2) The fact that a better price could have been obtained by a sale at a different time or in a different method from that selected by the secured party is not of itself sufficient to establish that the sale was not made in a commercially reasonable manner. If the secured party either sells the collateral in the usual manner in any recognized market therefor or if he sells at the price current in such market at the time of his sale or if he has otherwise sold in conformity with reasonable commercial practices among dealers in the type of property sold he has sold in a commercially reasonable manner. The principles stated in the two preceding sentences with respect to sales also apply as may be appropriate to other types of disposition. A disposition which has been approved in any judicial proceeding or by any bona fide creditors' committee or representative of creditors shall conclusively be deemed to be commercially reasonable, but this sentence does not indicate that any such approval must be obtained in any case nor does it indicate that any disposition not so approved is not commercially reasonable.

ARTICLE 10: EFFECTIVE DATE AND REPEALER

See Article 11 for Transition Provisions for those jurisdictions adopting the 1972 amendments.

SECTION

10–101. Effective Date.
10–102. Specific Repealer; Provision for Transition.
10–103. General Repealer.
10–104. Laws Not Repealed.

§10–101. Effective Date. This Act shall become effective at midnight on December 31st following its enactment. It applies to transactions entered into and events occurring after that date.

§10–102. Specific Repealer; Provision for Transition.

(1) The following acts and all other acts and parts of acts inconsistent herewith are hereby repealed:

(Here should follow the acts to be specifically repealed including the following:

Uniform Negotiable Instruments Act
Uniform Warehouse Receipts Act
Uniform Sales Act
Uniform Bills of Lading Act
Uniform Stock Transfer Act
Uniform Conditional Sales Act

Uniform Trust Receipts Act
Also any acts regulating:
Bank collections
Bulk sales
Chattel mortgages
Conditional sales
Factor's lien acts
Farm storage of grain and similar acts
Assignment of accounts receivable)

(**2**) Transactions validly entered into before the effective date specified in Section 10–101 and the rights, duties and interests flowing from them remain valid thereafter and may be terminated, completed, consummated or enforced as required or permitted by any statute or other law amended or repealed by this Act as though such repeal or amendment had not occurred.

Note: *Subsection (1) should be separately prepared for each state. The foregoing is a list of statutes to be checked.*

§10–103. General Repealer. Except as provided in the following section, all acts and parts of acts inconsistent with this Act are hereby repealed.

§10–104. Laws Not Repealed.

[(**1**)] The Article on Documents of Title (Article 7) does not repeal or modify any laws prescribing the form or contents of documents of title or the services or facilities to be afforded by bailees, or otherwise regulating bailees' businesses in respects not specifically dealt with herein; but the fact that such laws are violated does not affect the status of a document of title which otherwise complies with the definition of a document of title (Section 1–201).

[(**2**) This Act does not repeal. . . . *, cited as the Uniform Act for the Simplification of Fiduciary Security Transfers, and if in any respect there is any inconsistency between that Act and the Article of this Act on investment securities (Article 8) the provisions of the former Act shall control.] As amended 1962.

Note: *At* in subsection (2) insert the statutory reference to the Uniform Act for the Simplification of Fiduciary Security Transfers if such Act has previously been enacted. If it has not been enacted, omit subsection (2).*

ARTICLE 11: EFFECTIVE DATE AND TRANSITION PROVISIONS

Notes *This material has been numbered Article 11 to distinguish it from Article 10, the transition provision of the 1962 Code, which may still remain in effect in some states to cover transition problems from pre-Code law to the original Uniform Commercial Code. Adaptation may be necessary in particular states. The terms "[old Code]" and "[new Code]" and "[old U.C.C.]" and "[new U.C.C.]" are used herein, and should be suitably changed in each state.*

This draft was prepared by the Reporters and has not been passed upon by the Review Committee, the Permanent Editorial Board, the American Law Institute, or the National Conference of Commissioners on Uniform State Laws. It is submitted as a working draft which may be adapted as appropriate in each state. The "Discussions" were written by the Reporters to assist in understanding the purpose of the drafts.

§11–101. Effective date. This Act shall become effective at 12:01 A.M. on _____, 19__.

§11–102. Preservation of Old Transition Provision. The provisions of [here insert reference to the original transition provision in the particular state] shall continue to apply to [the new U.C.C.] and for this purpose the [old U.C.C. and new U.C.C.] shall be considered one continuous statute.

§11–103. Transition to [New Code]—General Rule. Transactions validly entered into after [effective date of old U.C.C.] and before [effective date of new U.C.C.], and which were subject to the provisions of [old U.C.C.] and which would be subject to this Act as amended if they had been entered into after the effective date of [new U.C.C.] and the rights, duties and interests flowing from such transactions remain valid after the later date and may be terminated, completed, consummated or enforced as required or permitted by the [new U.C.C.]. Security interests arising out of such transactions which are perfected when [new U.C.C.] becomes effective shall remain perfected until they lapse as provided in [new U.C.C.], and may be continued as permitted by [new U.C.C.], except as stated in Section 11–105.

§11–104. Transition Provision on Change of Requirement of Filing. A security interest for the perfection of which filing or the taking of possession was required under [old U.C.C.] and which attached prior to the effective date of [new U.C.C.] but was not perfected shall be deemed perfected on the effective date of [new U.C.C.] if [new U.C.C.] permits perfection without filing or authorizes filing in the office or offices where a prior ineffective filing was made.

§11–105. Transition Provision on Change of Place of Filing.

(**1**) A financing statement or continuation statement filed prior to [effective date of new U.C.C.] which shall not have lapsed prior to [the effective date of new U.C.C.] shall remain effective for the period provided in the [old Code], but not less than five years after the filing.

(**2**) With respect to any collateral acquired by the debtor subsequent to the effective date of [new U.C.C.], any effective financing statement or continuation statement described in this section shall apply only if the filing or filings are in the office or offices that would be appropriate to perfect the security interests in the new collateral under [new U.C.C.].

(**3**) The effectiveness of any financing statement or continuation statement filed prior to [effective date of new

U.C.C.] may be continued by a continuation statement as permitted by [new U.C.C.], except that if [new U.C.C.] requires a filing in an office where there was no previous financing statement, a new financing statement conforming to Section 11–106 shall be filed in that office.

(4) If the record of a mortgage of real estate would have been effective as a fixture filing of goods described therein if [new U.C.C.] had been in effect on the date of recording the mortgage, the mortgage shall be deemed effective as a fixture filing as to such goods under subsection (6) of Section 9–402 of the [new U.C.C.] on the effective date of [new U.C.C.].

§11–106. Required Refilings.

(1) If a security interest is perfected or has priority when this Act takes effect as to all persons or as to certain persons without any filing or recording, and if the filing of a financing statement would be required for the perfection or priority of the security interest against those persons under [new U.C.C.], the perfection and priority rights of the security interest continue until 3 years after the effective date of [new U.C.C.]. The perfection will then lapse unless a financing statement is filed as provided in subsection (4) or unless the security interest is perfected otherwise than by filing.

(2) If a security interest is perfected when [new U.C.C.] takes effect under a law other than [U.C.C.] which requires no further filing, refiling or recording to continue its perfection, perfection continues until and will lapse 3 years after [new U.C.C.] takes effect, unless a financing statement is filed as provided in subsection (4) or unless the security interest is perfected otherwise than by filing, or unless under subsection (3) of Section 9–302 the other law continues to govern filing.

(3) If a security interest is perfected by a filing, refiling or recording under a law repealed by this Act which required further filing, refiling or recording to continue its perfection, perfection continues and will lapse on the date provided by the law so repealed for such further filing, refiling or recording unless a financing statement is filed as provided in subsection (4) or unless the security interest is perfected otherwise than by filing.

(4) A financing statement may be filed within six months before the perfection of a security interest would otherwise lapse. Any such financing statement may be signed by either the debtor or the secured party. It must identify the security agreement, statement or notice (however denominated in any statute or other law repealed or modified by this Act), state the office where and the date when the last filing, refiling or recording, if any, was made with respect thereto, and the filing number, if any, or book and page, if any, of recording and further state that the security agreement, statement or notice, however denominated, in another filing office under the [U.C.C.] or under any statute or other law repealed or modified by this Act is still effective. Section 9–401 and Section 9–103 determine the proper place to file such a financing statement. Except as specified in this subsection, the provisions of Section 9–403(3) for continuation statements apply to such a financing statement.

§11–107. Transition Provisions as to Priorities. Except as otherwise provided in [Article 11], [old U.C.C.] shall apply to any questions of priority if the positions of the parties were fixed prior to the effective date of [new U.C.C.]. In other cases questions of priority shall be determined by [new U.C.C.].

§11–108. Presumption that Rule of Law Continues Unchanged. Unless a change in law has clearly been made, the provisions of [new U.C.C.] shall be deemed declaratory of the meaning of the [old U.C.C.].

APPENDIX

2

Uniform Partnership Act

Part I   Preliminary Provisions

§1. Name of Act. This act may be cited as Uniform Partnership Act.

§2. Definition of Terms. In this act, "Court" includes every court and judge having jurisdiction in the case.

"Business" includes every trade, occupation, or profession.

"Person" includes individuals, partnerships, corporations, and other associations.

"Bankrupt" includes bankrupt under the Federal Bankruptcy Act or insolvent under any state insolvent act.

"Conveyance" includes every assignment, lease, mortgage, or encumbrance.

"Real property" includes land and any interest or estate in land.

§3. Interpretation of Knowledge and Notice.

(1) A person has "knowledge" of a fact within the meaning of this act not only when he has actual knowledge thereof, but also when he has knowledge of such other facts as in the circumstances shows bad faith.

(2) A person has "notice" of a fact within the meaning of this act when the person who claims the benefit of the notice:

(a) States the fact to such person, or

(b) Delivers through the mail, or by other means of communication, a written statement of the fact to such person or to a proper person at his place of business or residence.

§4. Rules of Construction.

(1) The rule that statutes in derogation of the common law are to be strictly construed shall have no application to this act.

(2) The law of estoppel shall apply under this act.

(3) The law of agency shall apply under this act.

(4) This act shall be so interpreted and construed as to effect its general purpose to make uniform the law of those states which enact it.

(5) This act shall not be construed so as to impair the obligations of any contract existing when the act goes into effect, nor to affect any action or proceedings begun or right accrued before this act takes effect.

§5. Rules for Cases Not Provided for in This Act. In any case not provided for in this act the rules of law and equity, including the law merchant, shall govern.

Part II   Nature of Partnership

§6. Partnership Defined.

(1) A partnership is an association of two or more persons to carry on as co-owners a business for profit.

(2) But any association formed under any other statute of this state, or any statute adopted by authority, other than the authority of this state, is not a partnerhsip under this act, unless such association would have been a partnership in this state prior to the adoption of this act; but this act shall apply to limited partnerships except in so far as the statutes relating to such partnerships are inconsistent herewith.

§7. Rules for Determining the Existence of a Partnership. In determining whether a partnership exists, these rules shall apply:

(1) Except as provided by section 16 persons who are not partners as to each other are not partners as to third persons.

(2) Joint tenancy, tenancy in common, tenancy by the entireties, joint property, common property, or part ownership does not of itself establish a partnership, whether such co-owners do or do not share any profits made by the use of the property.

(3) The sharing of gross returns does not of itself establish a partnership, whether or not the persons sharing them

1239

have a joint or common right or interest in any property from which the returns are derived.

(4) The receipt by a person of a share of the profits of a business is prima facie evidence that he is a partner in the business, but no such inference shall be drawn if such profits were received in payment:

(a) As a debt by installments or otherwise,

(b) As wages of an employee or rent to a landlord,

(c) As an annuity to a widow or representative of a deceased partner,

(d) As interest on a loan, though the amount of payment vary with the profits of the business,

(e) As the consideration for the sale of a good-will of a business or other property by installments or otherwise.

§8. Partnership Property.

(1) All property originally brought into the partnership stock or subsequently acquired by purchase or otherwise, on account of the partnership, is partnership property.

(2) Unless the contrary intention appears, property acquired with partnership funds is partnership property.

(3) Any estate in real property may be acquired in the partnership name. Title so acquired can be conveyed only in the partnership name.

(4) A conveyance to a partnership in the partnership name, though without words of inheritance, passes the entire estate of the grantor unless a contrary intent appears.

Part III   Relations of Partners to Persons Dealing with the Partnership

§9. Partner Agent of Partnership as to Partnership Business.

(1) Every partner is an agent of the partnership for the purpose of its business, and the act of every partner, including the execution in the partnership name of any instrument, for apparently carrying on in the usual way the business of the partnership of which he is a member binds the partnership, unless the partner so acting has in fact no authority to act for the partnership in the particular matter, and the person with whom he is dealing has knowledge of the fact that he has no such authority.

(2) An act of a partner which is not apparently for the carrying on of the business of the partnership in the usual way does not bind the partnership unless authorized by the other partners.

(3) Unless authorized by the other partners or unless they have abandoned the business, one or more but less than all the partners have no authority to:

(a) Assign the partnership property in trust for creditors or on the assignee's promise to pay the debts of the partnership,

(b) Dispose of the good-will of the business,

(c) Do any other act which would make it impossible to carry on the ordinary business of a partnership,

(d) Confess a judgment,

(e) Submit a partnership claim or liability to arbitration or reference.

(4) No act of a partner in contravention of a restriction on authority shall bind the partnership to persons having knowledge of the restriction.

§10. Conveyance of Real Property of the Partnership.

(1) Where title to real property is in the partnership name, any partner may convey title to such property by a conveyance executed in the partnership name; but the partnership may recover such property unless the partner's act binds the partnership under the provisions of paragraph (1) of section 9, or unless such property has been conveyed by the grantee or a person claiming through such grantee to a holder for value without knowledge that the partner, in making the conveyance, has exceeded his authority.

(2) Where title to real property is in the name of the partnership, a conveyance executed by a partner, in his own name, passes the equitable interest of the partnership, provided the act is one within the authority of the partner under the provisions of paragraph (1) of section 9.

(3) Where title to real property is in the name of one or more but not all the partners, and the record does not disclose the right of the partnership, the partners in whose name the title stands may convey title to such property, but the partnership may recover such property if the partner's act does not bind the partnership under the provisions of paragraph (1) of section 9, unless the purchaser or his assignee, is a holder for value, without knowledge.

(4) Where the title to real property is in the name of one or more or all the partners, or in a third person in trust for the partnership, a conveyance executed by a partner in the partnership name, or in his own name, passes the equitable interest of the partnership, provided the act is one within the authority of the partner under the provisions of paragraph (1) of section 9.

(5) Where the title to real property is in the names of all the partners a conveyance executed by all the partners passes all their rights in such property.

§11. Partnership Bound by Admission of Partner.
An admission or representation made by any partner concerning partnership affairs within the scope of his authority as conferred by this act is evidence against the partnership.

§12. Partnership Charged with Knowledge of or Notice to Partner.
Notice to any partner of any matter relating to partnership affairs, and the knowledge of the partner acting in the particular matter, acquired while a partner or then present to his mind, and the knowledge of any other partner who reasonably could and should have communicated it to

the acting partner, operate as notice to or knowledge of the partnership, except in the case of a fraud on the partnership committed by or with the consent of that partner.

§13. Partnership Bound by Partner's Wrongful Act.
Where, by any wrongful act or omission of any partner acting in the ordinary course of the business of the partnership or with the authority of his co-partners, loss or injury is caused to any person, not being a partner in the partnership, or any penalty is incurred, the partnership is liable therefor to the same extent as the partner so acting or omitting to act.

§14. Partnership Bound by Partner's Breach of Trust.
The partnership is bound to make good the loss:

(a) Where one partner acting within the scope of his apparent authority receives money or property of a third person and misapplies it; and

(b) Where the partnership in the course of its business receives money or property of a third person and the money or property so received is misapplied by any partner while it is in the custody of the partnership.

§15. Nature of Partner's Liability. All partners are liable
(a) Jointly and severally for everything chargeable to the partnership under sections 13 and 14.

(b) Jointly for all other debts and obligations of the partnership; but any partner may enter into a separate obligation to perform a partnership contract.

§16. Partner by Estoppel.
(1) When a person, by words spoken or written or by conduct, represents himself, or consents to another representing him to any one, as a partner in an existing partnership or with one or more persons not actual partners, he is liable to any such person to whom such representation has been made, who has, on the faith of such representation, given credit to the actual or apparent partnership, and if he has made such representation or consented to its being made in a public manner he is liable to such person, whether the representation has or has not been made or communicated to such person so giving credit by or with the knowledge of the apparent partner making the representation or consenting to its being made.

(a) When a partnership liability results, he is liable as though he were an actual member of the partnership.

(b) When no partnership liability results, he is liable jointly with the other persons, if any, so consenting to the contract or representation as to incur liability, otherwise separately.

(2) When a person has been thus represented to be a partner in an existing partnership, or with one or more persons not actual partners, he is an agent of the persons consenting to such representation to bind them to the same extent and in the same manner as though he were a partner in fact, with respect to persons who rely upon the represen-tation. Where all the members of the existing partnership consent to the representation, a partnership act or obligation results; but in all other cases it is the joint act or obligation of the person acting and the persons consenting to the representation.

§17. Liability of Incoming Partner. A person admitted as
a partner into an existing partnership is liable for all the obligations of the partnership arising before his admission as though he had been a partner when such obligations were incurred, except that this liability shall be satisfied only out of partnership property.

Part IV   Relations of Partners to One Another

§18. Rules Determining Rights and Duties of Partners.
The rights and duties of the partners in relation to the partnership shall be determined, subject to any agreement between them, by the following rules:

(a) Each partner shall be repaid his contributions, whether by way of capital or advances to the partner-ship property and share equally in the profits and surplus remaining after all liabilities, including those to partners, are satisfied; and must contribute towards the losses, whether of capital or otherwise, sustained by the partnership according to his share in the profits.

(b) The partnership must indemnify every partner in respect of payments made and personal liabilities reasonably incurred by him in the ordinary and proper conduct of its business, or for the preservation of its business or property.

(c) A partner, who in aid of the partnership makes any payment or advance beyond the amount of capital which he agreed to contribute, shall be paid interest from the date of the payment.

(d) A partner shall receive interest on the capital contributed by him only from the date when repay-ment should be made.

(e) All partners have equal rights in the management and conduct of the partnership business.

(f) No partner is entitled to remuneration for acting in the partnership business, except that a surviving partner is entitled to reasonable compensation for his services in winding up the partnership affairs.

(g) No person can become a member of a partnership without the consent of all the partners.

(h) Any difference arising as to ordinary matters connected with the partnership business may be decided by a majority of the partners; but no act in contravention of any agreement between the partners may be done rightfully without the consent of all the partners.

§19. Partnership Books. The partnership books shall be kept, subject to any agreement between the partners, at the principal place of business of the partnership, and every partner shall at all times have access to and may inspect and copy any of them.

§20. Duty of Partners to Render Information. Partners shall render on demand true and full information of all things affecting the partnership to any partner or the legal representative of any deceased partner or partner under legal disability.

§21. Partner Accountable as a Fiduciary.

(1) Every partner must account to the partnership for any benefit, and hold as trustee for it any profits derived by him without the consent of the other partners from any transaction connected with the formation, conduct, or liquidation of the partnership or from any use by him of its property.

(2) This section applies also to the representatives of a deceased partner engaged in the liquidation of the affairs of the partnership as the personal representatives of the last surviving partner.

§22. Right to an Account. Any partner shall have the right to a formal account as to partnership affairs:

(a) If he is wrongfully excluded from the partnership business or possession of its property by his co-partners,

(b) If the right exists under the terms of any agreement,

(c) As provided by section 21.

(d) Whenever other circumstances render it just and reasonable.

§23. Continuation of Partnership beyond Fixed Term.

(1) When a partnership for a fixed term or particular undertaking is continued after the termination of such term or particular undertaking without any express agreement, the rights and duties of the partners remain the same as they were at such termination, so far as is consistent with a partnership at will.

(2) A continuation of the business by the partners or such of them as habitually acted therein during the term, without any settlement or liquidation of the partnership affairs, is prima facie evidence of a continuation of the partnership.

Part V Property Rights of a Partner

§24. Extent of Property Rights of a Partner. The property rights of a partner are (1) his rights in specific partnership property, (2) his interest in the partnership, and (3) his right to participate in the management.

§25. Nature of a Partner's Right in Specific Partnership Property.

(1) A partner is co-owner with his partners of specific partnership property holding as a tenant in partnership.

(2) The incidents of this tenancy are such that:

(a) A partner, subject to the provisions of this act and to any agreement between the partners, has an equal right with his partners to possess specific partnership property for partnership purposes; but he has no right to possess such property for any other purpose without the consent of his partners.

(b) A partner's right in specific partnership property is not assignable except in connection with the assignment of rights of all the partners in the same property.

(c) A partner's right in specific partnership property is not subject to attachment or execution, except on a claim against the partnership. When partnership property is attached for a partnership debt the partners, or any of them, or the representatives of a deceased partner, cannot claim any right under the homestead or exemption laws.

(d) On the death of a partner his right in specific partnership property vests in the surviving partner or partners, except where the deceased was the last surviving partner, when his right in such property vests in his legal representative. Such surviving partner or partners, or the legal representative of the last surviving partner, has no right to possess the partnership property for any but a partnership purpose.

(e) A partner's right in specific partnership property is not subject to dower, curtesy, or allowances to widows, heirs, or next of kin.

§26. Nature of Partner's Interest in the Partnership. A partner's interest in the partnership is his share of the profits and surplus, and the same is personal property.

§27. Assignment of Partner's Interest.

(1) A conveyance by a partner of his interest in the partnership does not of itself dissolve the partnership, nor, as against the other partners in the absence of agreement, entitle the assignee, during the continuance of the partnership, to interfere in the management or administration of the partnership business or affairs, or to require any information or account of partnership transactions, or to inspect the partnership books; but it merely entitles the assignee to receive in accordance with his contract the profits to which the assigning partner would otherwise be entitled.

(2) In case of a dissolution of the partnership, the assignee is entitled to receive his assignor's interest and may require an account from the date only of the last account agreed to by all the partners.

§28. Partner's Interest Subject to Charging Order.

(1) On due application to a competent court by any judgment creditor of a partner, the court which entered the judgment, order, or decree, or any other court, may charge the interest of the debtor partner with payment of the

unsatisfied amount of such judgment debt with interest thereon; and may then or later appoint a receiver of his share of the profits, and of any other money due or to fall due to him in respect of the partnership, and make all other orders, directions, accounts and inquiries which the debtor partner might have made, or which the circumstances of the case may require.

(2) The interest charged may be redeemed at any time before foreclosure, or in case of a sale being directed by the court may be purchased without thereby causing a dissolution:

(a) With separate property, by any one or more of the partners, or

(b) With partnership property, by any one or more of the partners with the consent of all the partners whose interests are not so charged or sold.

(3) Nothing in this act shall be held to deprive a partner of his right, if any, under the exemption laws, as regards his interest in the partnership.

Part VI   Dissolution and Winding Up

§29. Dissolution Defined. The dissolution of a partnership is the change in the relation of the partners caused by any partner ceasing to be associated in the carrying on as distinguished from the winding up of the business.

§30. Partnership not Terminated by Dissolution. On dissolution the partnership is not terminated, but continues until the winding up of the partnership affairs is completed.

§31. Causes of Dissolution. Dissolution is caused:

(1) Without violation of the agreement between the partners,

(a) By the termination of the definite term or particular undertaking specified in the agreement,

(b) By the express will of any partner when no definite term or particular undertaking is specified,

(c) By the express will of all the partners who have not assigned their interests or suffered them to be charged for their separate debts, either before or after the termination of any specified term or particular undertaking,

(d) By the expulsion of any partner from the business bona fide in accordance with such a power conferred by the agreement between the partners;

(2) In contravention of the agreement between the partners, where the circumstances do not permit a dissolution under any other provision of this section, by the express will of any partner at any time;

(3) By any event which makes it unlawful for the business of the partnership to be carried on or for the members to carry it on in partnership;

(4) By the death of any partner;

(5) By the bankruptcy of any partner or the partnership;

(6) By decree of court under section 32.

§32. Dissolution by Decree of Court.

(1) On application by or for a partner the court shall decree a dissolution whenever:

(a) A partner has been declared a lunatic in any judicial proceeding or is shown to be of unsound mind,

(b) A partner becomes in any other way incapable of performing his part of the partnership contract,

(c) A partner has been guilty of such conduct as tends to affect prejudicially the carrying on of the business,

(d) A partner willfully or persistently commits a breach of the partnership agreement, or otherwise so conducts himself in matters relating to the partnership business that it is not reasonably practicable to carry on the business in partnership with him,

(e) The business of the partnership can only be carried on at a loss,

(f) Other circumstances render a dissolution equitable.

(2) On the application of the purchaser of a partner's interest under sections 27 or 28:

(a) After the termination of the specified term or particular undertaking,

(b) At any time if the partnership was a partnership at will when the interest was assigned or when the charging order was issued.

§33. General Effect of Dissolution on Authority of Partner. Except so far as may be necessary to wind up partnership affairs or to complete transactions begun but not then finished, dissolution terminates all authority of any partner to act for the partnership,

(1) With respect to the partners,

(a) When the dissolution is not by the act, bankruptcy or death of a partner; or

(b) When the dissolution is by such act, bankruptcy or death of a partner, in cases where section 34 so requires.

(2) With respect to persons not partners, as declared in section 35.

§34. Right of Partner to Contribution from Co-Partners after Dissolution. Where the dissolution is caused by the act, death or bankruptcy of a partner, each partner is liable to his co-partners for his share of any liability created by any partner acting for the partnership as if the partnership had not been dissolved unless

(a) The dissolution being by act of any partner, the partner acting for the partnership had knowledge of the dissolution, or

(b) The dissolution being by the death or bankruptcy of a partner, the partner acting for the partnership had knowledge or notice of the death or bankruptcy.

§35. Power of Partner to Bind Partnership to Third Persons after Dissolution.

(1) After dissolution a partner can bind the partnership except as provided in paragraph (3).

(a) By any act appropriate for winding up partnership affairs or completing transactions unfinished at dissolution;

(b) By any transaction which would bind the partnership if dissolution had not taken place, provided the other party to the transaction

(I) Had extended credit to the partnership prior to dissolution and had no knowledge or notice of the dissolution; or

(II) Though he had not so extended credit, had nevertheless known of the partnership prior to dissolution, and, having no knowledge or notice of dissolution, the fact of dissolution had not been advertised in a newspaper of general circulation in the place (or in each place if more than one) at which the partnership business was regularly carried on.

(2) The liability of a partner under paragraph (1b) shall be satisfied out of partnership assets alone when such partner had been prior to dissolution

(a) Unknown as a partner to the person with whom the contract is made; and

(b) So far unknown and inactive in partnership affairs that the business reputation of the partnership could not be said to have been in any degree due to his connection with it.

(3) The partnership is in no case bound by any act of a partner after dissolution

(a) Where the partnership is dissolved because it is unlawful to carry on the business, unless the act is appropriate for winding up partnership affairs; or

(b) Where the partner has become bankrupt; or

(c) Where the partner has no authority to wind up partnership affairs; except by a transaction with one who

(I) Had extended credit to the partnership prior to dissolution and had no knowledge or notice of his want of authority; or

(II) Had not extended credit to the partnership prior to dissolution, and, having no knowledge or notice of his want of authority, the fact of his want of authority has not been advertised in the manner provided for advertising the fact of dissolution in paragraph (1bII).

(4) Nothing in this section shall affect the liability under section 16 of any person who after dissolution represents himself or consents to another representing him as a partner in a partnership engaged in carrying on business.

§36. Effect of Dissolution on Partner's Existing Liability.

(1) The dissolution of the partnership does not of itself discharge the existing liability of any partner.

(2) A partner is discharged from any existing liability upon dissolution of the partnership by an agreement to that effect between himself, the partnership creditor and the person or partnership continuing the business; and such agreement may be inferred from the course of dealing between the creditor having knowledge of the dissolution and the person or partnership continuing the business.

(3) Where a person agrees to assume the existing obligations of a dissolved partnership, the partners whose obligations have been assumed shall be discharged from any liability to any creditor of the partnership who, knowing of the agreement, consents to a material alteration in the nature or time of payment of such obligations.

(4) The individual property of a deceased partner shall be liable for all obligations of the partnership incurred while he was a partner but subject to the prior payment of his separate debts.

§37. Right to Wind Up. Unless otherwise agreed the partners who have not wrongfully dissolved the partnership or the legal representative of the last surviving partner, not bankrupt, has the right to wind up the partnership affairs; provided, however, that any partner, his legal representative or his assignee, upon cause shown, may obtain winding up by the court.

§38. Rights of Partners to Application of Partnership Property.

(1) When dissolution is caused in any way, except in contravention of the partnership agreement, each partner, as against his co-partners and all persons claiming through them in respect of their interests in the partnership, unless otherwise agreed, may have the partnership property applied to discharge its liabilities, and the surplus applied to pay in cash the net amount owing to the respective partners. But if dissolution is caused by expulsion of a partner, bona fide under the partnership agreement and if the expelled partner is discharged from all partnership liabilities, either by payment or agreement under section 36(2), he shall receive in cash only the net amount due him from the partnership.

(2) When dissolution is caused in contravention of the partnership agreement the rights of the partners shall be as follows:

(a) Each partner who has not caused dissolution wrongfully shall have,

(I) All the rights specified in paragraph (1) of this section, and

(II) The right, as against each partner who has caused the dissolution wrongfully, to damages for breach of the agreement.

(b) The partners who have not caused the dissolution wrongfully, if they all desire to continue the business in the same name, either by themselves or jointly with others, may do so, during the agreed term for the partnership and for that purpose may possess the partnership property, provided they secure the payment by bond approved by the court, or pay to any partner who has caused the dissolution wrongfully, the value of his interest in the partnership at the dissolution, less any damages recoverable under clause (2aII) of this section, and in like manner indemnify him against all present or future partnership liabilities.

(**c**) A partner who has caused the dissolution wrongfully shall have:

(**I**) If the business is not continued under the provisions of paragraph (2b) all the rights of a partner under paragraph (1), subject to clause (2aII), of this section,

(**II**) If the business is continued under paragraph (2b) of this section the right as against his co-partners and all claiming through them in respect of their interests in the partnership, to have the value of his interest in the partnership, less any damages caused to his co-partners by the dissolution, ascertained and paid to him in cash, or the payment secured by bond approved by the court, and to be released from all existing liabilities of the partnership; but in ascertaining the value of the partner's interest the value of the good-will of the business shall not be considered.

§39. Rights Where Partnership Is Dissolved for Fraud or Misrepresentation.
Where a partnership contract is rescinded on the ground of the fraud or misrepresentation of one of the parties thereto, the party entitled to rescind is, without prejudice to any other right, entitled,

(**a**) To a lien on, or a right of retention of, the surplus of the partnership property after satisfying the partnership liabilities to third persons for any sum of money paid by him for the purchase of an interest in the partnership and for any capital or advances contributed by him; and

(**b**) To stand, after all liabilities to third persons have been satisfied, in the place of the creditors of the partnership for any payments made by him in respect of the partnership liabilities; and

(**c**) To be indemnified by the person guilty of the fraud or making the representation against all debts and liabilities of the partnership.

§40. Rules for Distribution.
In settling accounts between the partners after dissolution, the following rules shall be observed, subject to any agreement to the contrary:

(**a**) The assets of the partnership are:

(**I**) The partnership property,

(**II**) The contributions of the partners necessary for the payment of all the liabilities specified in clause (b) of this paragraph.

(**b**) The liabilities of the partnership shall rank in order of payment, as follows:

(**I**) Those owing to creditors other than partners,

(**II**) Those owing to partners other than for capital and profits,

(**III**) Those owing to partners in respect of capital,

(**IV**) Those owing to partners in respect of profits.

(**c**) The assets shall be applied in order of their declaration in clause (a) of this paragraph to the satisfaction of the liabilities.

(**d**) The partners shall contribute, as provided by section 18 (a) the amount necessary to satisfy the liabilities; but if any, but not all, of the partners are insolvent, or, not being subject to process, refuse to contribute, the other partners shall contribute their share of the liabilities, and, in the relative proportions in which they share the profits, the additional amount necessary to pay the liabilities.

(**e**) An assignee for the benefit of creditors or any person appointed by the court shall have the right to enforce the contributions specified in clause (d) of this paragraph.

(**f**) Any partner or his legal representative shall have the right to enforce the contributions specified in clause (d) of this paragraph, to the extent of the amount which he has paid in excess of his share of the liability.

(**g**) The individual property of a deceased partner shall be liable for the contributions specified in clause (d) of this paragraph.

(**h**) When partnership property and the individual properties of the partners are in possession of a court for distribution, partnership creditors shall have priority on partnership property and separate creditors on individual property, saving the rights of lien or secured creditors as heretofore.

(**i**) Where a partner has become bankrupt or his estate is insolvent the claims against his separate property shall rank in the following order:

(**I**) Those owing to separate creditors,

(**II**) Those owing to partnership creditors,

(**III**) Those owing to partners by way of contribution.

§41. Liability of Persons Continuing the Business in Certain Cases.

(**1**) When any new partner is admitted into an existing partnership, or when any partner retires and assigns (or the representative of the deceased partner assigns) his rights in partnership property to two or more of the partners, or to one or more of the partners and one or more third persons, if the business is continued without liquidation of the partnership affairs, creditors of the first or dissolved partnership are also creditors of the partnership so continuing the business.

(**2**) When all but one partner retire and assign (or the representative of a deceased partner assigns) their rights in partnership property to the remaining partner, who continues the business without liquidation of partnership affairs, either alone or with others, creditors of the dissolved partnership are also creditors of the person or partnership so continuing the business.

(**3**) When any partner retires or dies and the business of the ·dissolved partnership is continued as set forth in paragraphs (1) and (2) of this section, with the consent of the retired partners or the representative of the deceased partner, but without any assignment of his right in partnership property, rights of creditors of the dissolved partnership and of the creditors of the person or partnership continuing the business shall be as if such assignment had been made.

(**4**) When all the partners or their representatives assign their rights in partnership property to one or more third persons who promise to pay the debts and who continue the business of the dissolved partnership, creditors of the dissolved partnership are also creditors of the person or partnership continuing the business.

(**5**) When any partner wrongfully causes a dissolution and the remaining partners continue the business under the provisions of section 38(2b), either alone or with others, and without liquidation of the partnership affairs, creditors of the dissolved partnership are also creditors of the person or partnership continuing the business.

(**6**) When a partner is expelled and the remaining partners continue the business either alone or with others, without liquidation of the partnership affairs, creditors of the dissolved partnership are also creditors of the person or partnership continuing the business.

(**7**) The liability of a third person becoming a partner in the partnership continuing the business, under this section, to the creditors of the dissolved partnership shall be satisfied out of partnership property only.

(**8**) When the business of a partnership after dissolution is continued under any conditions set forth in this section the creditors of the dissolved partnership, as against the separate creditors of the retiring or deceased partner or the representative of the deceased partner, have a prior right to any claim of the retired partner or the representative of the deceased partner against the person or partnership continuing the business, on account of the retired or deceased partner's interest in the dissolved partnership or on account of any consideration promised for such interest or for his right in partnership property.

(**9**) Nothing in this section shall be held to modify any right of creditors to set aside any assignment on the ground of fraud.

(**10**) The use by the person or partnership continuing the business of the partnership name, or the name of a deceased partner as part thereof, shall not of itself make the individual property of the deceased partner liable for any debts contracted by such person or partnership.

§42. Rights of Retiring or Estate of Deceased Partner When the Business Is Continued. When any partner retires or dies, and the business is continued under any of the conditions set forth in section 41 (1, 2, 3, 5, 6), or section 38(2b) without any settlement of accounts as between him or his estate and the person or partnership continuing the business, unless otherwise agreed, he or his legal representative as against such persons or partnership may have the value of his interest at the date of dissolution ascertained, and shall receive as an ordinary creditor an amount equal to the value of his interest in the dissolved partnership with interest, or, at his option or at the option of his legal representative, in lieu of interest, the profits attributable to the use of his right in the property of the dissolved partnership; provided that the creditors of the dissolved partnership as against the separate creditors, or the representative of the retired or deceased partner, shall have priority on any claim arising under this section, as provided by section 41(8) of this act.

§43. Accrual of Actions. The right to an account of his interest shall accrue to any partner, or his legal representative, as against the winding up partners or the surviving partners or the person or partnership continuing the business, at the date of dissolution, in the absence of any agreement to the contrary.

Part VII   Miscellaneous Provisions

§44. When Act Takes Effect. This act shall take effect on the. . . . . day of. . . . . one thousand nine hundred and. . . . .

§45. Legislation Repealed. All acts or parts of acts inconsistent with this act are hereby repealed.

APPENDIX

3

Model Business Corporation Act* *(with Revisions through January 1, 1979)*

Section 1. Short Title. This Act shall be known and may be cited as the "[supply name of state] . . . Business Corporation Act."

Section 2. Definitions. As used in this Act, unless the context otherwise requires, the term:

(a) "Corporation" or "domestic corporation" means a corporation for profit subject to the provisions of this Act, except a foreign corporation.

(b) "Foreign corporation" means a corporation for profit organized under laws other than the laws of this State for a purpose or purposes for which a corporation may be organized under this Act.

(c) "Articles of incorporation" means the original or restated articles of incorporation or articles of consolidation and all amendments thereto including articles of merger.

(d) "Shares" means the units into which the proprietary interests in a corporation are divided.

(e) "Subscriber" means one who subscribes for shares in a corporation, whether before or after incorporation.

(f) "Shareholder" means one who is a holder of record of shares in a corporation. If the articles of incorporation or the by-laws so provide, the board of directors may adopt by resolution a procedure whereby a shareholder of the corporation may certify in writing to the corporation that all or a portion of the shares registered in the name of such shareholder are held for the account of a specified person or persons. The resolution shall set forth (1) the classification of shareholder who may certify, (2) the purpose or purposes for which the certification may be made, (3) the form of certification and information to be contained therein, (4) if the certification is with respect to a record date or closing of the stock transfer books within which the certification must

be received by the corporation and (5) such other provisions with respect to the procedure as are deemed necessary or desirable. Upon receipt by the corporation of a certification complying with the procedure, the persons specified in the certification shall be deemed, for the purpose or purposes set forth in the certification, to be the holders of record of the number of shares specified in place of the shareholder making the certification.

(g) "Authorized shares" means the shares of all classes which the corporation is authorized to issue.

(h) "Treasury shares" means shares of a corporation which have been issued, have been subsequently acquired by and belong to the corporation, and have not, either by reason of the acquisition or thereafter, been cancelled or restored to the status of authorized but unissued shares. Treasury shares shall be deemed to be "issued" shares, but not "oustanding" shares.

(i) "Net assets" means the amount by which the total assets of a corporation exceed the total debts of the corporation.

(j) "Stated capital" means, at any particular time, the sum of (1) the par value of all shares of the corporation having a par value that have been issued, (2) the amount of consideration received by the corporation for all shares of the corporation without par value that have ben issued, except such part of the consideration therefor as may have been allocated to capital surplus in a manner permitted by law, and (3) such amounts not included in clauses (1) and (2) of this paragraph as have been transferred to stated capital of the corporation, whether upon the issue of shares as a share dividend or otherwise, minus all reductions from such sum as have been effected in a manner permitted by law. Irrespective of the manner of designation thereof by the laws under which a foreign corporation is organized, the stated capital of a foreign corporation shall be determined on the same basis and in the same manner as the stated capital

*Reprinted with the permission of the American Law Institute–American Bar Association Committee on Continuing Professional Education.

of a domestic corporation, for the purpose of computing fees, franchise taxes and other charges imposed by this Act.

(k) "Surplus" means the excess of the net assets of a corporation over its stated capital.

(l) "Earned surplus" means the portion of the surplus of a corporation equal to the balance of its net profits, income, gains and losses from the date of incorporation, or from the latest date when a deficit was eliminated by an application of its capital surplus or stated capital or otherwise, after deducting subsequent distributions to shareholders and transfers to stated capital and capital surplus to the extent such distributions and transfers are made out of earned surplus. Earned surplus shall include also any portion of surplus allocated to earned surplus in mergers, consolidations or acquisitions of all or substantially all of the outstanding shares or of the property and assets of another corporation, domestic or foreign.

(m) "Capital surplus" means the entire surplus of a corporation other than its earned surplus.

(n) "Insolvent" means inability of a corporation to pay its debts as they become due in the usual course of its business.

(o) "Employee" includes officers but not directors. A director may accept duties which make him also an employee.

Section 3. Purposes. Corporations may be organized under this Act for any lawful purpose or purposes, except for the purpose of banking or insurance.

Section 4. General Powers. Each corporation shall have power:

(a) To have perpetual succession by its corporate name unless a limited period of duration is stated in its articles of incorporation.

(b) To sue and be sued, complain and defend, in its corporate name.

(c) To have a corporate seal which may be altered at pleasure, and to use the same by causing it, or a facsimile thereof, to be impressed or affixed or in any other manner reproduced.

(d) To purchase, take, receive, lease, or otherwise acquire, own, hold, improve, use and otherwise deal in and with, real or personal property, or any interest therein, wherever situated.

(e) To sell, convey, mortgage, pledge, lease, exchange, transfer and otherwise dispose of all or any part of its property and assets.

(f) To lend money and use its credit to assist its employees.

(g) To purchase, take, receive, subscribe for, or otherwise acquire, own, hold, vote, use, employ, sell, mortgage, lend, pledge, or otherwise dispose of, and otherwise use and deal in and with, shares or other interests in, or obligations of, other domestic or foreign corporations, associations, partnerships or individuals, or direct or indirect obligations of the United States or of any other government, state,

territory, governmental district or municipality or of any instrumentality thereof.

(h) To make contracts and guarantees and incur liabilities, borrow money at such rates of interest as the corporation may determine, issue its notes, bonds, and other obligations, and secure any of its obligations by mortgage or pledge of all or any of its property, franchises and income.

(i) To lend money for its corporate purposes, invest and reinvest its funds, and take and hold real and personal property as security for the payment of funds so loaned or invested.

(j) To conduct its business, carry on its operations and have offices and exercise the powers granted by this Act, within or without this State.

(k) To elect or appoint officers and agents of the corporation, and define their duties and fix their compensation.

(l) To make and alter by-laws, not inconsistent with its articles of incorporation or with the laws of this State, for the administration and regulation of the affairs of the corporation.

(m) To make donations for the public welfare or for charitable, scientific or educational purposes.

(n) To transact any lawful business which the board of directors shall find will be in aid of governmental policy.

(o) To pay pensions and establish pension plans, pension trusts, profit sharing plans, stock bonus plans, stock option plans and other incentive plans for any or all of its directors, officers and employees.

(p) To be a promoter, partner, member, associate, or manager of any partnership, joint venture, trust or other enterprise.

(q) To have and exercise all powers necessary or convenient to effect its purposes.

Section 5. Indemnification of Officers, Directors, Employees and Agents.

(a) A corporation shall have power to indemnify any person who was or is a party or is threatened to be made a party to any threatened, pending or completed action, suit or proceeding, whether civil, criminal, administrative or investigative (other than an action by or in the right of the corporation) by reason of the fact that he is or was a director, officer, employee or agent of the corporation, or is or was serving at the request of the corporation as a director, officer, employee or agent of another corporation, partnership, joint venture, trust or other enterprise, against expenses (including attorneys' fees), judgments, fines and amounts paid in settlement actually and reasonably incurred by him in connection with such action, suit or proceeding if he acted in good faith and in a manner he reasonably believed to be in or not opposed to the best interests of the corporation, and, with respect to any criminal action or proceeding, had no reasonable cause to believe his conduct was unlawful. The termination of any action, suit or proceeding by judgment, order, settlement, conviction, or upon a plea of nolo contendere or its equivalent, shall not, of itself, create a presumption that the person did not act in good faith and in a manner which he reasonably believed to be in or not opposed to the best interests of the corporation, and, with respect to any criminal action or proceeding, had reasonable cause to believe that his conduct was unlawful.

(**b**) A corporation shall have power to indemnify any person who was or is a party or is threatened to be made a party to any threatened, pending or completed action or suit by or in the right of the corporation to procure a judgment in its favor by reason of the fact that he is or was a director, officer, employee or agent of the corporation, or is or was serving at the request of the corporation as a director, officer, employee or agent of another corporation, partnership, joint venture, trust or other enterprise against expenses (including attorneys' fees) actually and reasonably incurred by him in connection with the defense or settlement of such action or suit if he acted in good faith and in a manner he reasonably believed to be in or not opposed to the best interests of the corporation and except that no indemnification shall be made in respect of any claim, issue or matter as to which such person shall have been adjudged to be liable for negligence or misconduct in the performance of his duty to the corporation unless and only to the extent that the court in which such action or suit was brought shall determine upon application that, despite the adjudication of liability but in view of all circumstances of the case, such person is fairly and reasonably entitled to indemnity for such expenses which such court shall deem proper.

(**c**) To the extent that a director, officer, employee or agent of a corporation has been successful on the merits or otherwise in defense of any action, suit or proceeding referred to in subsections (a) or (b), or in defense of any claim, issue or matter therein, he shall be indemnified against expenses (including attorneys' fees) actually and reasonably incurred by him in connection therewith.

(**d**) Any indemnification under subsections (a) or (b) (unless ordered by a court) shall be made by the corporation only as authorized in the specific case upon a determination that indemnification of the director, officer, employee or agent is proper in the circumstances because he has met the applicable standard of conduct set forth in subsections (a) or (b). Such determination shall be made (1) by the board of directors by a majority vote of a quorum consisting of directors who were not parties to such action, suit or proceeding, or (2) if such a quorum is not obtainable or, even if obtainable a quorum of disinterested directors so directs, by independent legal counsel in a written opinion, or (3) by the shareholders.

(**e**) Expenses (including attorneys' fees) incurred in defending a civil or criminal action, suit or proceeding may be paid by the corporation in advance of the final disposition of such action, suit or proceeding as authorized in the manner provided in subsection (d) upon receipt of an undertaking by or on behalf of the director, officer, employee or agent to repay such amount unless it shall ultimately be determined that he is entitled to be indemnified by the corporation as authorized in this section.

(**f**) The indemnification provided by this section shall not be deemed exclusive of any other rights to which those indemnified may be entitled under any by-law, agreement, vote of shareholders or disinterested directors or otherwise, both as to action in his official capacity and as to action in another capacity while holding such office, and shall continue as to a person who has ceased to be a director, officer, employee or agent and shall inure to the benefit of the heirs, executors and administrators of such a person.

(**g**) A corporation shall have power to purchase and maintain insurance on behalf of any person who is or was a director, officer, employee or agent of the corporation, or is or was serving at the request of the corporation as a director, officer, employee or agent of another corporation, partnership, joint venture, trust or other enterprise against any liability asserted against him and incurred by him in any such capacity or arising out of his status as such, whether or not the corporation would have the power to indemnify him against such liability under the provisions of this section.

Section 6. Right of Corporation to Acquire and Dispose of its Own Shares. A corporation shall have the right to purchase, take, receive or otherwise acquire, hold, own, pledge, transfer or otherwise dispose of its own shares, but purchases of its own shares, whether direct or indirect, shall be made only to the extent of unreserved and unrestricted earned surplus available therefor, and, if the articles of incorporation so permit or with the affirmative vote of the holders of a majority of all shares entitled to vote thereon, to the extent of unreserved and unrestricted capital surplus available therefor.

To the extent that earned surplus or capital surplus is used as the measure of the corporation's right to purchase its own shares, such surplus shall be restricted so long as such shares are held as treasury shares, and upon the disposition or cancellation of any such shares the restriction shall be removed pro tanto.

Notwithstanding the foregoing limitation, a corporation may purchase or otherwise acquire its own shares for the purpose of:

(**a**) Eliminating fractional shares.

(**b**) Collecting or compromising indebtedness to the corporation.

(**c**) Paying dissenting shareholders entitled to payment for their shares under the provisions of this Act.

(**d**) Effecting, subject to the other provisions of this Act, the retirement of its redeemable shares by redemption or by purchase at not to exceed the redemption price.

No purchase of or payment for its own shares shall be made at a time when the corporation is insolvent or when such purchase or payment would make it insolvent.

Section 7. Defense of Ultra Vires. No act of a corporation and no conveyance or transfer of real or personal property to or by a corporation shall be invalid by reason of the fact that the corporation was without capacity or power to do such act or to make or receive such conveyance or transfer, but such lack of capacity or power may be asserted:

(a) In a proceeding by a shareholder against the corporation to enjoin the doing of any act or the transfer of real or personal property by or to the corporation. If the unauthorized act or transfer sought to be enjoined is being, or is to be, performed or made pursuant to a contract to which the corporation is a party, the court may, if all of the parties to the contract are parties to the proceeding and if it deems the same to be equitable, set aside and enjoin the performance of such contract, and in so doing may allow to the corporation or to the other parties to the contract, as the case may be, compensation for the loss or damage sustained by either of them which may result from the action of the court in setting aside and enjoining the performance of such contract, but anticipated profits to be derived from the performance of the contract shall not be awarded by the court as a loss or damage sustained.

(b) In a proceeding by the corporation, whether acting directly or through a receiver, trustee, or other legal representative, or through shareholders in a representative unit, against the incumbent or former officers or directors of the corporation.

(c) In a proceeding by the Attorney General, as provided in this Act, to dissolve the corporation, or in a proceeding by the Attorney General to enjoin the corporation from the transaction of unauthorized business.

Section 8. Corporate Name. The corporate name:

(a) Shall contain the word "corporation," "company," "incorporated" or "limited," or shall contain an abbreviation of one of such words.

(b) Shall not contain any word or phrase which indicates or implies that it is organized for any purpose other than one or more of the purposes contained in its articles of incorporation.

(c) Shall not be the same as, or deceptively similar to, the name of any domestic corporation existing under the laws of this State or any foreign corporation authorized to transact business in this State, or a name the exclusive right to which is, at the time, reserved in the manner provided in this Act, or the name of a corporation which has in effect a registration of its corporate name as provided in this Act, except that this provision shall not apply if the applicant files with the Secretary of State either of the following: (1) the written consent of such other corporation or holder of a reserved or registered name to use the same or deceptively similar name and one or more words are added to make such name distinguishable from such other name, or (2) a certified copy of a final decree of a court of competent jurisdiction establishing the prior right of the applicant to the use of such name in this State.

A corporation with which another corporation, domestic or foreign, is merged, or which is formed by the reorganization or consolidation of one or more domestic or foreign corporations or upon a sale, lease or other disposition to or exchange with, a domestic corporation of all or substantially all the assets of another corporation, domestic or foreign, including its name, may have the same name as that used in this State by any of such corporations if such other corporation was organized under the laws of, or is authorized to transact business in, this State.

Section 9. Reserved Name. The exclusive right to the use of a corporate name may be reserved by:

(a) Any person intending to organize a corporation under this Act.

(b) Any domestic corporation intending to change its name.

(c) Any foreign corporation intending to make application for a certificate of authority to transact business in this State.

(d) Any foreign corporation authorized to transact business in this State and intending to change its name.

(e) Any person intending to organize a foreign corporation and intending to have such corporation make application for a certificate of authority to transact business in this State.

The reservation shall be made by filing with the Secretary of State an application to reserve a specified corporate name, executed by the applicant. If the Secretary of State finds that the name is available for corporate use, he shall reserve the same for the exclusive use of the applicant for a period of one hundred and twenty days.

The right to the exclusive use of a specified corporate name so reserved may be transferred to any other person or corporation by filing in the office of the Secretary of State a notice of such transfer, executed by the applicant for whom the name was reserved, and specifying the name and address of the transferee.

Section 10. Registered Name. Any corporation organized and existing under the laws of any state or territory of the United States may register its corporate name under this Act, provided its corporate name is not the same as, or deceptively similar to, the name of any domestic corporation existing under the laws of this State, or the name of any foreign corporation authorized to transact business in this State, or any corporate name reserved or registered under this Act.

Such registration shall be made by:

(a) Filing with the Secretary of State (1) an application for registration executed by the corporation by an officer thereof, setting forth the name of the corporation, the state or territory under the laws of which it is incorporated, the date of its incorporation, a statement that it is carrying on or doing business, and a brief statement of the business in which it is engaged, and (2) a certificate setting forth that such corporation is in good standing under the laws of the state or territory wherein it is organized, executed by the Secretary of State of such state or territory or by such other official as may have custody of the records pertaining to corporations, and

(b) Paying to the Secretary of State a registration fee in the amount of . . . for each month, or fraction thereof, between the date of filing such application and December 31st of the calendar year in which such application is filed.

Such registration shall be effective until the close of the calendar year in which the application for registration is filed.

Section 11. Renewal of Registered Name [Text omitted].

Section 12. Registered Office and Registered Agent.
Each corporation shall have and continuously maintain in this State:

(a) A registered office which may be, but need not be, the same as its place of business.

(b) A registered agent, which agent may be either an individual resident in this State whose business office is identical with such registered office, or a domestic corporation, or a foreign corporation authorized to transact business in this State, having a business office identical with such registered office.

Section 13. Change of Registered Office or Registered Agent.
A corporation may change its registered office or change its registered agent, or both, upon filing in the office of the Secretary of State a statement setting forth:

(a) The name of the corporation.

(b) The address of its then registered office.

(c) If the address of its registered office is to be changed, the address to which the registered office is to be changed.

(d) The name of its then registered agent.

(e) If its registered agent is to be changed, the name of its successor registered agent.

(f) That the address of its registered office and the address of the business office of its registered agent, as changed, will be identical.

(g) That such change was authorized by resolution duly adopted by its board of directors.

Such statement shall be executed by the corporation by its president, or a vice president, and verified by him and delivered to the Secretary of State. If the Secretary of State finds that such statement conforms to the provisions of this Act, he shall file such statement in his office and upon such filing the change of address of the registered office, or the appointment of a new registered agent, or both, as the case may be, shall become effective.

Any registered agent of a corporation may resign as such agent upon filing a written notice thereof, executed in duplicate, with the Secretary of State, who shall forthwith mail a copy thereof to the corporation at its registered office. The appointment of such agent shall terminate upon the expiration of thirty days after receipt of such notice by the Secretary of State.

If a registered agent changes his or its business address to another place within the same . . . . *, he or it may change such address and the address of the registered office of any corporation of which he or it is registered agent by filing a statement as required above except that it need be signed only by the registered agent and need not be responsive to (e) or (g) and must recite that a copy of the statement has been mailed to the corporation.

Section 14. Service of Process on Corporation.
The registered agent so appointed by a corporation shall be an agent of such corporation upon whom any process, notice or demand required or permitted by law to be served upon the corporation may be served.

Whenever a corporation shall fail to appoint or maintain a registered agent in this State, or whenever its registered agent cannot with reasonable diligence be found at the registered office, then the Secretary of State shall be an agent of such corporation upon whom any such process, notice or demand may be served. Service on the Secretary of State of any such process, notice, or demand shall be made by delivering to and leaving with him, or with any clerk having charge of the corporation department of his office, duplicate copies of such process, notice or demand. In the event any such process, notice or demand is served on the Secretary of State, he shall immediately cause one of the copies thereof to be forwarded by registered mail, addressed to the corporation at its registered office. Any service so had on the Secretary of State shall be returnable in not less than thirty days.

The Secretary of State shall keep a record of all processes, notices and demands served upon him under this section, and shall record therein the time of such service and his action with reference thereto.

Nothing herein contained shall limit or affect the right to serve any process, notice or demand required or permitted by law to be served upon a corporation in any other manner now or hereafter permitted by law.

Section 15. Authorized Shares.
Each corporation shall have power to create and issue the number of shares stated in its articles of incorporation. Such shares may be divided into one or more classes, any or all of which classes may consist of shares with par value or shares without par value, with such designations, preferences, limitations, and relative rights as shall be stated in the articles of incorporation. The articles of incorporation may limit or deny the voting rights of or provide special voting rights for the shares of any class to the extent not inconsistent with the provisions of this Act.

Without limiting the authority herein contained, a corporation, when so provided in its articles of incorporation, may issue shares of preferred or special classes:

(a) Subject to the right of the corporation to redeem any of such shares at the price fixed by the articles of incorporation for the redemption thereof.

(b) Entitling the holders thereof to cumulative, noncumulative or partially cumulative dividends.

(c) Having preference over any other class or classes of shares as to the payment of dividends.

---

*Supply designation of jurisdiction, such as county, etc., in accordance with local practice.

(d) Having preference in the assets of the corporation over any other class or classes of shares upon the voluntary or involuntary liquidation of the corporation.

(e) Convertible into shares of any other class or into shares of any series of the same or any other class, except a class having prior or superior rights and preferences as to dividends or distribution of assets upon liquidation, but shares without par value shall not be converted into shares with par value unless that part of the stated capital of the corporation represented by such shares without par value is, at the time of conversion, at least equal to the aggregate par value of the shares into which the shares without par value are to be converted or the amount of any such deficiency is transferred from surplus to stated capital.

Section 16. Issuance of Shares of Preferred or Special Classes in Series. If the articles of incorporation so provide, the shares of any preferred or special class may be divided into and issued in series. If the shares of any such class are to be issued in series, then each series shall be so designated as to distinguish the shares thereof from the shares of all other series and classes. Any or all of the series of any such class and the variations in the relative rights and preferences as between different series may be fixed and determined by the articles of incorporation, but all shares of the same class shall be identical except as to the following relative rights and preferences, as to which there may be variations between different series:

(a) The rate of dividend.

(b) Whether shares may be redeemed and, if so, the redemption price and the terms and conditions of redemption.

(c) The amount payable upon shares in event of voluntary and involuntary liquidation.

(d) Sinking fund provisions, if any, for the redemption or purchase of shares.

(e) The terms and conditions, if any, on which shares may be converted.

(f) Voting rights, if any.

If the articles of incorporation shall expressly vest authority in the board of directors, then, to the extent that the articles of incorporation shall not have established series and fixed and determined the variations in the relative rights and preferences as between series, the board of directors shall have authority to divide any or all of such classes into series and, within the limitations set forth in this section and in the articles of incorporation, fix and determine the relative rights and preferences of the shares of any series so established.

In order for the board of directors to establish a series, where authority so to do is contained in the articles of incorporation, the board of directors shall adopt a resolution setting forth the designation of the series and fixing and determining the relative rights and preferences thereof, or so much thereof as shall not be fixed and determined by the articles of incorporation.

Prior to the issue of any shares of a series established by

resolution adopted by the board of directors, the corporation shall file in the office of the Secretary of State a statement setting forth:

(a) The name of the corporation.

(b) A copy of the resolution establishing and designating the series, and fixing and determining the relative rights and preferences thereof.

(c) The date of adoption of such resolution.

(d) That such resolution was duly adopted by the board of directors.

Such statement shall be executed in duplicate by the corporation by its president or a vice president and by its secretary or an assistant secretary, and verified by one of the officers signing such statement, and shall be delivered to the Secretary of State. If the Secretary of State finds that such statement conforms to law, he shall, when all franchise taxes and fees have been paid as in this Act prescribed:

(1) Endorse on each of such duplicate originals the word "Filed," and the month, day, and year of the filing thereof.

(2) File one of such duplicate originals in his office.

(3) Return the other duplicate original to the corporation or its representative.

Upon the filing of such statement by the Secretary of State, the resolution establishing and designating the series and fixing and determining the relative rights and preferences thereof shall become effective and shall constitute an amendment of the articles of incorporation.

Section 17. Subscriptions for Shares. A subscription for shares of a corporation to be organized shall be irrevocable for a period of six months, unless otherwise provided by the terms of the subscription agreement or unless all of the subscribers consent to the revocation of such subscription.

Unless otherwise provided in the subscription agreement, subscriptions for shares, whether made before or after the organization of a corporation, shall be paid in full at such time, or in such installments and at such times, as shall be determined by the board of directors. Any call made by the board of directors for payment on subscriptions shall be uniform as to all shares of the same class or as to all shares of the same series, as the case may be. In case of default in the payment of any installment or call when such payment is due, the corporation may proceed to collect the amount due in the same manner as any debt due the corporation. The by-laws may prescribe other penalties for failure to pay installments or calls that may become due, but no penalty working a forfeiture of a subscription, or of the amounts paid thereon, shall be declared as against any subscriber unless the amount due thereon shall remain unpaid for a period of twenty days after written demand has been made therefor. If mailed, such written demand shall be deemed to be made when deposited in the United States mail in a sealed envelope addressed to the subscriber at his last post-office address known to the corporation, with postage thereon prepaid. In the event of the sale of any shares by reason of any forfeiture, the excess of proceeds realized over the amount due and unpaid on such shares shall be paid to the delinquent subscriber or to his legal representative.

Section 18. Consideration for Shares. Shares having a par value may be issued for such consideration expressed in dollars, not less than the par value thereof, as shall be fixed from time to time by the board of directors.

Shares without par value may be issued for such consideration expressed in dollars as may be fixed from time to time by the board of directors unless the articles of incorporation reserve to the shareholders the right to fix the consideration. In the event that such right be reserved as to any shares, the shareholders shall, prior to the issuance of such shares, fix the consideration to be received for such shares, by a vote of the holders of a majority of all shares entitled to vote thereon.

Treasury shares may be disposed of by the corporation for such consideration expressed in dollars as may be fixed from time to time by the board of directors.

That part of the surplus of a corporation which is transferred to stated capital upon the issuance of shares as a share dividend shall be deemed to be the consideration for the issuance of such shares.

In the event of the issuance of shares upon the conversion or exchange of indebtedness or shares, the consideration for the shares so issued shall be (1) the principal sum of, and accrued interest on, the indebtedness so exchanged or converted, or the stated capital then represented by the shares so exchanged or converted, and (2) that part of surplus, if any, transferred to stated capital upon the issuance of shares for the shares so exchanged or converted, and (3) any additional consideration paid to the corporation upon the issuance of shares for the indebtedness or shares so exchanged or converted.

Section 19. Payment for Shares. The consideration for the issuance of shares may be paid, in whole or in part, in cash, in other property, tangible or intangible, or in labor or services actually performed for the corporation. When payment of the consideration for which shares are to be issued shall have been received by the corporation, such shares shall be deemed to be fully paid and nonassessable.

Neither promissory notes nor future services shall constitute payment or part payment for the issuance of shares of a corporation.

In the absence of fraud in the transaction, the judgment of the board of directors or the shareholders, as the case may be, as to the value of the consideration received for shares shall be conclusive.

Section 20. Stock Rights and Options. Subject to any provisions in respect thereof set forth in its articles of incorporation, a corporation may create and issue, whether or not in connection with the issuance and sale of any of its shares or other securities, rights or options entitling the holders thereof to purchase from the corporation shares of any class or classes. Such rights or options shall be evidenced in such manner as the board of directors shall

approve and, subject to the provisions of the articles of incorporation, shall set forth the terms upon which, the time or times within which and the price or prices at which such shares may be purchased from the corporation upon the exercise of any such right or option. If such rights or options are to be issued to directors, officers or employees as such of the corporation or of any subsidiary thereof, and not to the shareholders generally, their issuance shall be approved by the affirmative vote of the holders of a majority of the shares entitled to vote thereon or shall be authorized by and consistent with a plan approved or ratified by such a vote of shareholders. In the absence of fraud in the transaction, the judgment of the board of directors as to the adequacy of the consideration received for such rights or options shall be conclusive. The price or prices to be received for any shares having a par value, other than treasury shares to be issued upon the exercise of such rights or options, shall not be less than the par value thereof.

Section 21. Determination of Amount of Stated Capital. In case of the issuance by a corporation of shares having a par value, the consideration received therefor shall constitute stated capital to the extent of the par value of such shares, and the excess, if any, of such consideration shall constitute capital surplus.

In case of the issuance by a corporation of shares without par value, the entire consideration received therefor shall constitute stated capital unless the corporation shall determine as provided in this section that only a part thereof shall be stated capital. Within a period of sixty days after the issuance of any shares without par value, the board of directors may allocate to capital surplus any portion of the consideration received for the issuance of such shares. No such allocation shall be made of any portion of the consideration received for shares without par value having a preference in the assets of the corporation in the event of involuntary liquidation except the amount, if any, of such consideration in excess of such preference.

If shares have been or shall be issued by a corporation in merger or consolidation or in acquisition of all or substantially all of the outstanding shares or of the property and assets of another corporation, whether domestic or foreign, any amount that would otherwise constitute capital surplus under the foregoing provisions of this section may instead be allocated to earned surplus by the board of directors of the issuing corporation except that its aggregate earned surplus shall not exceed the sum of the earned surpluses as defined in this Act of the issuing corporation and of all other corporations, domestic or foreign, that were merged or consolidated or of which the shares or assets were acquired.

The stated capital of a corporation may be increased from time to time by resolution of the board of directors directing that all or a part of the surplus of the corporation be transferred to stated capital. The board of directors may direct that the amount of the surplus so transferred shall be deemed to be stated capital in respect of any designated class of shares.

Section 22. Expenses of Organization. Reorganization and Financing. The reasonable charges and expenses of organization or reorganization of a corporation, and the reasonable expenses of and compensation for the sale or underwriting of its shares, may be paid or allowed by such corporation out of the consideration received by it in payment for its shares without thereby rendering such shares not fully paid or assessable.

Section 23. Shares Represented by Certificates and Uncertificated Shares. The shares of a corporation shall be represented by certificates or shall be uncertificated shares. Certificates shall be signed by the chairman or vice-chairman of the board of directors or the president or a vice president and by the treasurer or an assistant treasurer or the secretary or an assistant secretary of the corporation, and may be sealed with the seal of the corporation or a facsimile thereof. Any of or all the signatures upon a certificate may be a facsimile. In case any officer, transfer agent or registrar who has signed or whose facsimile signature has been placed upon such certificate shall have ceased to be such officer, transfer agent or registrar before such certificate is issued, it may be issued by the corporation with the same effect as if he were such officer, transfer agent or registrar at the date of its issue.

Every certificate representing shares issued by a corporation which is authorized to issue shares of more than one class shall set forth upon the face or back of the certificate, or shall state that the corporation will furnish to any shareholder upon request and without charge, a full statement of the designations, preferences, limitations, and relative rights of the shares of each class authorized to be issued, and if the corporation is authorized to issue any preferred or special class in series, the variations in the relative rights and preferences between the shares of each such series so far as the same have been fixed and determined and the authority of the board of directors to fix and determine the relative rights and preferences of subsequent series.

Each certificate representing shares shall state upon the face thereof:

(a) That the corporation is organized under the laws of this State.

(b) The name of the person to whom issued.

(c) The number and class of shares, and the designation of the series, if any, which such certificate represents.

(d) The par value of each share represented by such certificate, or a statement that the shares are without par value.

No certificate shall be issued for any share until such share is fully paid.

Unless otherwise provided by the articles of incorporation or by-laws, the board of directors of a corporation may provide by resolution that some or all of any or all classes and series of its shares shall be uncertificated shares, provided that such resolution shall not apply to shares represented by a certificate until such certificate is surrendered to the corporation. Within a reasonable time after the issuance or transfer of uncertificated shares, the corporation shall send to the registered owner thereof a written notice containing the information required to be set forth or stated on certificates pursuant to the second and third paragraphs of this section. Except as otherwise expressly provided by law, the rights and obligations of the holders of uncertificated shares and the rights and obligations of the holders of certificates representing shares of the same class and series shall be identical.

Section 24. Fractional Shares. A corporation may (1) issue fractions of a share, either represented by a certificate or uncertificated, (2) arrange for the disposition of fractional interests by those entitled thereto, (3) pay in cash the fair value of fractions of a share as of a time when those entitled to receive such fractions are determined, or (4) issue scrip in registered or bearer form which shall entitle the holder to receive a certificate for a full share or an uncertificated full share upon the surrender of such scrip aggregating a full share. A certificate for a fractional share or an uncertificated fractional share shall, but scrip shall not unless otherwise provided therein, entitle the holder to exercise voting rights, to receive dividends thereon, and to participate in any of the assets of the corporation in the event of liquidation. The board of directors may cause scrip to be issued subject to the condition that it shall become void if not exchanged for certificates representing full shares or uncertificated full shares before a specified date, or subject to the condition that the shares for which scrip is exchangeable may be sold by the corporation and the proceeds thereof distributed to the holders of scrip, or subject to any other conditions which the board of directors may deem advisable.

Section 25. Liability of Subscribers and Shareholders. A holder of or subscriber to shares of a corporation shall be under no obligation to the corporation or its creditors with respect to such shares other than the obligation to pay to the corporation the full consideration for which such shares were issued or to be issued.

Any person becoming an assignee or transferee of shares or of a subscription for shares in good faith and without knowledge or notice that the full consideration therefor has not been paid shall not be personally liable to the corporation or its creditors for any unpaid portion of such consideration.

An executor, administrator, conservator, guardian, trustee, assignee for the benefit of creditors, or receiver shall not be personally liable to the corporation as a holder of or subscriber to shares of a corporation but the estate and funds in his hands shall be so liable.

No pledgee or other holder of shares as collateral security shall be personally liable as a shareholder.

Section 26. Shareholders' Preemptive Rights. The shareholders of a corporation shall have no preemptive right to acquire unissued or treasury shares of the corporation, or securities of the corporation convertible into or carrying a right to subscribe to or acquire shares, except to the extent, if any, that such right is provided in the articles of incorporation.

Section 26A. Shareholders' Preemptive Rights [Alternative]. Except to the extent limited or denied by this section or by the articles of incorporation, shareholders shall have a preemptive right to acquire unissued or treasury shares or securities convertible into such shares or carrying a right to subscribe to or acquire shares.

Unless otherwise provided in the articles of incorporation,

(a) No preemptive right shall exist

(1) to acquire any shares issued to directors, officers or employees pursuant to approval by the affirmative vote of the holders of a majority of the shares entitled to vote thereon or when authorized by and consistent with a plan theretofore approved by such a vote of shareholders; or

(2) to acquire any shares sold otherwise than for cash.

(b) Holders of shares of any class that is preferred or limited as to dividends or assets shall not be entitled to any preemptive right.

(c) Holders of shares of common stock shall not be entitled to any preemptive right to shares of any class that is preferred or limited as to dividends or assets or to any obligations, unless convertible into shares of common stock or carrying a right to subscribe to or acquire shares of common stock.

(d) Holders of common stock without voting power shall have no preemptive right to shares of common stock with voting power.

(e) The preemptive right shall be only an opportunity to acquire shares or other securities under such terms and conditions as the board of directors may fix for the purpose of providing a fair and reasonable opportunity for the exercise of such right.

Section 27. By-laws. The initial by-laws of a corporation shall be adopted by its board of directors. The power to alter, amend or repeal the by-laws or adopt new by-laws, subject to repeal or change by action of the shareholders, shall be vested in the board of directors unless reserved to the shareholders by the articles of incorporation. The by-laws may contain any provisions for the regulation and management of the affairs of the corporation not inconsistent with law or the articles of incorporation.

Section 27A. By-laws and Other Powers in Emergency [Optional]. The board of directors of any corporation may adopt emergency by-laws, subject to repeal or change by action of the shareholders, which shall, notwithstanding any different provision elsewhere in this Act or in the articles of incorporation or by-laws, be operative during any emergency in the conduct of the business of the corporation resulting from an attack on the United States or any nuclear or atomic disaster. The emergency by-laws may make any provision that may be practical and necessary for the circumstances of the emergency, including provisions that:

(a) A meeting of the board of directors may be called by any officer or director in such manner and under such conditions as shall be prescribed in the emergency by-laws;

(b) The director or directors in attendance at the meeting, or any greater number fixed by the emergency by-laws, shall constitute a quorum; and

(c) The officers or other persons designated on a list approved by the board of directors before the emergency, all in such order of priority and subject to such conditions, and for such period of time (not longer than reasonably necessary after the termination of the emergency) as may be provided in the emergency by-laws or in the resolution approving the list shall, to the extent required to provide a quorum at any meeting of the board of directors, be deemed directors for such meeting.

The board of directors, either before or during any such emergency, may provide, and from time to time modify, lines of succession in the event that during such an emergency any or all officers or agents of the corporation shall for any reason be rendered incapable of discharging their duties.

The board of directors, either before or during any such emergency, may, effective in the emergency, change the head office or designate several alternative head offices or regional offices, or authorize the officers so to do.

To the extent not inconsistent with any emergency by-laws so adopted, the by-laws of the corporation shall remain in effect during any such emergency and upon its termination the emergency by-laws shall cease to be operative.

Unless otherwise provided in emergency by-laws, notice of any meeting of the board of directors during any such emergency may be given only to such of the directors as it may be feasible to reach at the time and by such means as may be feasible at the time, including publication or radio.

To the extent required to constitute a quorum at any meeting of the board of directors during any such emergency, the officers of the corporation who are present shall, unless otherwise provided in emergency by-laws, be deemed, in order of rank and within the same rank in order of seniority, directors for such meeting.

No officer, director or employee acting in accordance with any emergency by-laws shall be liable except for willful misconduct. No officer, director or employee shall be liable for any action taken by him in good faith in such an emergency in furtherance of the ordinary business affairs of the corporation even though not authorized by the by-laws then in effect.

Section 28. Meetings of Shareholders. Meetings of shareholders may be held at such place within or without this State as may be stated in or fixed in accordance with the by-laws. If no other place is stated or so fixed, meetings shall be held at the registered office of the corporation.

An annual meeting of the shareholders shall be held at such time as may be stated in or fixed in accordance with the by-laws. If the annual meeting is not held within any thirteen-month period the Court of. . . . . may, on the application of any shareholder, summarily order a meeting to be held.

Special meetings of the shareholders may be called by the board of directors, the holders of not less than one-tenth of all the shares entitled to vote at the meeting, or such other persons as may be authorized in the articles of incorporation or the by-laws.

Section 29. Notice of Shareholders' Meetings. Written notice stating the place, day and hour of the meeting and, in case of a special meeting, the purpose or purposes for which the meeting is called, shall be delivered not less than ten nor more than fifty days before the date of the meeting, either personally or by mail, by or at the direction of the president, the secretary, or the officer or persons calling the meeting, to each shareholder of record entitled to vote at such meeting. If mailed, such notice shall be deemed to be delivered when deposited in the United States mail addressed to the shareholder at his address as it appears on the stock transfer books of the corporation, with postage thereon prepaid.

Section 30. Closing of Transfer Books and Fixing Record Date. For the purpose of determining shareholders entitled to notice of or to vote at any meeting of shareholders or any adjournment thereof, or entitled to receive payment of any dividend, or in order to make a determination of shareholders for any other proper purpose, the board of directors of a corporation may provide that the stock transfer books shall be closed for a stated period but not to exceed, in any case, fifty days. If the stock transfer books shall be closed for the purpose of determining shareholders entitled to notice of or to vote at a meeting of shareholders, such books shall be closed for at least ten days immediately preceding such meeting. In lieu of closing the stock transfer books, the by-laws, or in the absence of an applicable by-law the board of directors, may fix in advance a date as the record date for any such determination of shareholders, such date in any case to be not more than fifty days and, in case of a meeting of shareholders, not less than ten days prior to the date on which the particular action, requiring such determination of shareholders, is to be taken. If the stock transfer books are not closed and no record date is fixed for the determination of shareholders entitled to notice of or to vote at a meeting of shareholders, or shareholders

entitled to receive payment of a dividend, the date on which notice of the meeting is mailed or the date on which the resolution of the board of directors declaring such dividend is adopted, as the case may be, shall be the record date for such determination of shareholders. When a determination of shareholders entitled to vote at any meeting of shareholders has been made as provided in this section, such determination shall apply to any adjournment thereof.

Section 31. Voting Record. The officer or agent having charge of the stock transfer books for shares of a corporation shall make a complete record of the shareholders entitled to vote at such meeting or any adjournment thereof, arranged in alphabetical order, with the address of and the number of shares held by each. Such record shall be produced and kept open at the time and place of the meeting and shall be subject to the inspection of any shareholder during the whole time of the meeting for the purposes thereof.

Failure to comply with the requirements of this section shall not affect the validity of any action taken at such meeting.

An officer or agent having charge of the stock transfer books who shall fail to prepare the record of shareholders, or produce and keep it open for inspection at the meeting, as provided in this section, shall be liable to any shareholder suffering damage on account of such failure, to the extent of such damage.

Section 32. Quorum of Shareholders. Unless otherwise provided in the articles of incorporation, a majority of the shares entitled to vote, represented in person or by proxy, shall constitute a quorum at a meeting of shareholders, but in no event shall a quorum consist of less than one-third of the shares entitled to vote at the meeting. If a quorum is present, the affirmative vote of the majority of the shares represented at the meeting and entitled to vote on the subject matter shall be the act of the shareholders, unless the vote of a greater number or voting by classes is required by this Act or the articles of incorporation or by-laws.

Section 33. Voting of Shares. Each outstanding share, regardless of class, shall be entitled to one vote on each matter submitted to a vote at a meeting of shareholders, except as may be otherwise provided in the articles of incorporation. If the articles of incorporation provide for more or less than one vote for any share, on any matter, every reference in this Act to a majority or other proportion of shares shall refer to such a majority or other proportion of votes entitled to be cast.

Neither treasury shares, nor shares held by another corporation if a majority of the shares entitled to vote for the election of directors of such other corporation is held by the corporation, shall be voted at any meeting or counted in determining the total number of outstanding shares at any given time.

A shareholder may vote either in person or by proxy executed in writing by the shareholder or by his duly authorized attorney-in-fact. No proxy shall be valid after eleven months from the date of its execution, unless otherwise provided in the proxy.

[Either of the following prefatory phrases may be inserted here: "The articles of incorporation may provide that" or "Unless the articles of incorporation otherwise provide"] . . . at each election for directors every shareholder entitled to vote at such election shall have the right to vote, in person or by proxy, the number of shares owned by him for as many persons as there are directors to be elected and for whose election he has a right to vote, or to cumulate his votes by giving one candidate as many votes as the number of such directors multiplied by the number of his shares shall equal, or by distributing such votes on the same principle among any number of such candidates.

Shares standing in the name of another corporation, domestic or foreign, may be voted by such officer, agent or proxy as the by-laws of such other corporation may prescribe, or, in the absence of such provision, as the board of directors of such other corporation may determine.

Shares held by an administrator, executor, guardian or conservator may be voted by him, either in person or by proxy, without a transfer of such shares into his name. Shares standing in the name of a trustee may be voted by him, either in person or by proxy, but no trustee shall be entitled to vote shares held by him without a transfer of such shares into his name.

Shares standing in the name of a receiver may be voted by such receiver, and shares held by or under the control of a receiver may be voted by such receiver without the transfer thereof into his name if authority so to do be contained in an appropriate order of the court by which such receiver was appointed.

A shareholder whose shares are pledged shall be entitled to vote such shares until the shares have been transferred into the name of the pledgee, and thereafter the pledgee shall be entitled to vote the shares so transferred.

On and after the date on which written notice of redemption of redeemable shares has been mailed to the holders thereof and a sum sufficient to redeem such shares has been deposited with a bank or trust company with irrevocable instruction and authority to pay the redemption price to the holders thereof upon surrender of certificates therefor, such shares shall not be entitled to vote on any matter and shall not be deemed to be outstanding shares.

Section 34. Voting Trusts and Agreements among Shareholders. Any number of shareholders of a corporation may create a voting trust for the purpose of conferring upon a trustee or trustees the right to vote or otherwise represent their shares, for a period of not to exceed ten years, by entering into a written voting trust agreement specifying the terms and conditions of the voting trust, by depositing a counterpart of the agreement with the corporation at its registered office, and by transferring their shares to such trustee or trustees for the purposes of the agreement. Such trustee or trustees shall keep a record of the holders of voting trust certificates evidencing a beneficial interest in the voting trust, giving the names and addresses of all such holders and the number and class of the shares in respect of which the voting trust certificates held by each are issued, and shall deposit a copy of such record with the corporation at its registered office. The counterpart of the voting trust agreement and the copy of such record so deposited with the corporation shall be subject to the same right of examination by a shareholder of the corporation, in person or by agent or attorney, as are the books and records of the corporation, and such counterpart and such copy of such record shall be subject to examination by any holder of record of voting trust certificates, either in person or by agent or attorney, at any reasonable time for any proper purpose.

Agreements among shareholders regarding the voting of their shares shall be valid and enforceable in accordance with their terms. Such agreements shall not be subject to the provisions of this section regarding voting trusts.

Section 35. Board of Directors. All corporate powers shall be exercised by or under authority of, and the business and affairs of a corporation shall be managed under the direction of, a board of directors except as may be otherwise provided in this Act or the articles of incorporation. If any such provision is made in the articles of incorporation, the powers and duties conferred or imposed upon the board of directors by this Act shall be exercised or performed to such extent and by such person or persons as shall be provided in the articles of incorporation. Directors need not be residents of this State or shareholders of the corporation unless the articles of incorporation or by-laws so require. The articles of incorporation or by-laws may prescribe other qualifications for directors. The board of directors shall have authority to fix the compensation of directors unless otherwise provided in the articles of incorporation.

A director shall perform his duties as a director, including his duties as a member of any committee of the board upon which he may serve, in good faith, in a manner he reasonably believes to be in the best interests of the corporation, and with such care as an ordinarily prudent person in a like position would use under similar circumstances. In performing his duties, a director shall be entitled to rely on information, opinions, reports or statements, including financial statements and other financial data, in each case prepared or presented by:

(a) one or more officers or employees of the corporation whom the director reasonably believes to be reliable and competent in the matters presented,

(b) counsel, public accountants or other persons as to matters which the director reasonably believes to be within such person's professional or expert competence, or

(c) a committee of the board upon which he does not serve, duly designated in accordance with a provision of the articles of incorporation or the by-laws, as to matters within its designated authority, which committee the director reasonably believes to merit confidence, but he shall not be considered to be acting in good faith if he has knowledge concerning the matter in question that would cause such reliance to be unwarranted. A person who so performs his duties shall have no liability by reason of being or having been a director of the corporation.

A director of a corporation who is present at a meeting of its board of directors at which action on any corporate matter is taken shall be presumed to have assented to the action taken unless his dissent shall be entered in the minutes of the meeting or unless he shall file his written dissent to such action with the secretary of the meeting before the adjournment thereof or shall forward such dissent by registered mail to the secretary of the corporation immediately after the adjournment of the meeting. Such right to dissent shall not apply to a director who voted in favor of such action.

Section 36. Number and Election of Directors. The board of directors of a corporation shall consist of one or more members. The number of directors shall be fixed by, or in the manner provided in, the articles of incorporation or the by-laws, except as to the number constituting the initial board of directors, which number shall be fixed by the articles of incorporation. The number of directors may be increased or decreased from time to time by amendment to, or in the manner provided in, the articles of incorporation or the bylaws, but no decrease shall have the effect of shortening the term of any incumbent director. In the absence of a by-law providing for the number of directors, the number shall be the same as that provided for in the articles of incorporation. The names and addresses of the members of the first board of directors shall be stated in the articles of incorporation. Such persons shall hold office until the first annual meeting of shareholders, and until their successors shall have been elected and qualified. At the first annual meeting of shareholders and at each annual meeting thereafter the shareholders shall elect directors to hold office until the next succeeding annual meeting, except in case of the classification of directors as permitted by this Act. Each director shall hold office for the term for which he is elected and until his successor shall have been elected and qualified.

Section 37. Classification of Directors. When the board of directors shall consist of nine or more members, in lieu of electing the whole number of directors annually, the articles of incorporation may provide that the directors be divided into either two or three classes, each class to be as nearly equal in number as possible, the term of office of directors of the first class to expire at the first annual meeting of shareholders after their election, that of the second class to expire at the second annual meeting after their election, and that of the third class, if any, to expire at the third annual meeting after their election. At each annual meeting after such classification the number of directors equal to the number of the class whose term expires at the time of such meeting shall be elected to hold office until the second succeeding annual meeting, if there be two classes, or until the third succeeding annual meeting, if there be three classes. No classification of directors shall be effective prior to the first annual meeting of shareholders.

Section 38. Vacancies. Any vacancy occurring in the board of directors may be filled by the affirmative vote of a majority of the remaining directors though less than a quorum of the board of directors. A director elected to fill a vacancy shall be elected for the unexpired term of his predecessor in office. Any directorship to be filled by reason of an increase in the number of directors may be filled by the board of directors for a term of office continuing only until the next election of directors by the shareholders.

Section 39. Removal of Directors. At a meeting of shareholders called expressly for that purpose, directors may be removed in the manner provided in this section. Any director or the entire board of directors may be removed, with or without cause, by a vote of the holders of a majority of the shares then entitled to vote at an election of directors.

In the case of a corporation having cumulative voting, if less than the entire board is to be removed, no one of the directors may be removed if the votes cast against his removal would be sufficient to elect him if then cumulatively voted at an election of the entire board of directors, or, if there be classes of directors, at an election of the class of directors of which he is a part.

Whenever the holders of the shares of any class are entitled to elect one or more directors by the provisions of the articles of incorporation, the provisions of this section shall apply, in respect to the removal of a director or directors so elected, to the vote of the holders of the outstanding shares of that class and not to the vote of the outstanding shares as a whole.

Section 40. Quorum of Directors. A majority of the number of directors fixed by or in the manner provided in the by-laws or in the absence of a by-law fixing or providing for the number of directors, then of the number stated in the articles of incorporation, shall constitute a quorum for the transaction of business unless a greater number is required by the articles of incorporation or the by-laws. The act of the majority of the directors present at a meeting at which a quorum is present shall be the act of the board of directors, unless the act of a greater number is required by the articles of incorporation or the by-laws.

Section 41. Director Conflicts of Interest.

No contract or other transaction between a corporation and one or more of its directors or any other corporation, firm, association or entity in which one or more of its directors are directors or officers or are financially interested, shall be either void or voidable because of such relationship or interest or because such director or directors are present at the meeting of the board of directors or a committee thereof which authorizes, approves or ratifies such contract or transaction or because his or their votes are counted for such purpose, if:

(**a**) the fact of such relationship or interest is disclosed or known to the board of directors or committee which authorizes, approves or ratifies the contract or transaction by a vote or consent sufficient for the purpose without counting the votes or consents of such interested directors; or

(**b**) the fact of such relationship or interest is disclosed or known to the shareholders entitled to vote and they authorize, approve or ratify such contract or transaction by vote or written consent; or

(**c**) the contract or transaction is fair and reasonable to the corporation.

Common or interested directors may be counted in determining the presence of a quorum at a meeting of the board of directors or a committee thereof which authorizes, approves or ratifies such a contract or transaction.

Section 42. Executive and Other Committees.

If the articles of incorporation or the by-laws so provide, the board of directors, by resolution adopted by a majority of the full board of directors, may designate from among its members an executive committee and one or more other committees each of which, to the extent provided in such resolution or in the articles of incorporation or the by-laws of the corporation, shall have and may exercise all the authority of the board of directors, except that no such committee shall have authority to (i) declare dividends or distributions, (ii) approve or recommend to shareholders actions or proposals required by this Act to be approved by shareholders, (iii) designate candidates for the office of director, for purposes of proxy solicitation or otherwise, or fill vacancies on the board of directors or any committee thereof, (iv) amend the by-laws, (v) approve a plan of merger not requiring shareholder approval, (vi) reduce earned or capital surplus, (vii) authorize or approve the reacquisition of shares unless pursuant to a general formula or method specified by the board of directors, or (viii) authorize or approve the issuance or sale of, or any contract to issue or sell, shares or designate the terms of a series of a class of shares, provided that the board of directors, having acted regarding general authorization for the issuance or sale of shares, or any contract therefor, and, in the case of a series, the designation

thereof, may, pursuant to a general formula or method specified by the board by resolution or by adoption of a stock option or other plan, authorize a committee to fix the terms upon which such shares may be issued or sold, including, without limitation, the price, the dividend rate, provisions for redemption, sinking fund, conversion, voting or preferential rights, and provisions for other features of a class of shares, or a series of a class of shares, with full power in such committee to adopt any final resolution setting forth all terms thereof and to authorize the statement of the terms of a series for filing with the Secretary of State under this Act.

Neither the designation of any such committee, the delegation thereto of authority, nor action by such committee pursuant to such authority shall alone constitute compliance by any member of the board of directors, not a member of the committee in question, with his responsibility to act in good faith, in a manner he reasonably believes to be in the best interests of the corporation, and with such care as an ordinarily prudent person in a like position would use under similar circumstances.

Section 43. Place and Notice of Directors' Meetings; Committee Meetings.

Meetings of the board of directors, regular or special, may be held either within or without this State.

Regular meetings of the board of directors or any committee designated thereby may be held with or without notice as prescribed in the by-laws. Special meetings of the board of directors or any committee designated thereby shall be held upon such notice as is prescribed in the by-laws. Attendance of a director at a meeting shall constitute a waiver of notice of such meeting, except where a director attends a meeting for the express purpose of objecting to the transaction of any business because the meeting is not lawfully called or convened. Neither the business to be transacted at, nor the purpose of, any regular or special meeting of the board of directors or any committee designated thereby need be specified in the notice or waiver of notice of such meeting unless required by the by-laws.

Except as may be otherwise restricted by the articles of incorporation or by-laws, members of the board of directors or any committee designated thereby may participate in a meeting of such board or committee by means of a conference telephone or similar communications equipment by means of which all persons participating in the meeting can hear each other at the same time and participation by such means shall constitute presence in person at a meeting.

Section 44. Action by Directors without a Meeting.

Unless otherwise provided by the articles of incorporation or by-laws, any action required by this Act to be taken at a meeting of the directors of a corporation, or any action which may be taken at a meeting of the directors or of a committee, may be taken without a meeting if a consent in writing, setting forth the action so taken, shall be signed by all of the directors, or all of the members of the committee, as the case may be. Such consent shall have the same effect as a unanimous vote.

Section 45. Dividends. The board of directors of a corporation may, from time to time, declare and the corporation may pay dividends in cash, property, or its own shares, except when the corporation is insolvent or when the payment thereof would render the corporation insolvent or when the declaration or payment thereof would be contrary to any restriction contained in the articles of incorporation, subject to the following provisions:

(a) Dividends may be declared and paid in cash or property only out of the unreserved and unrestricted earned surplus of the corporation, except as otherwise provided in this section.

[Alternative] (a) Dividends may be declared and paid in cash or property only out of the unreserved and unrestricted earned surplus of the corporation, or out of the unreserved and unrestricted net earnings of the current fiscal year and the next preceding fiscal year taken as a single period, except as otherwise provided in this section.

(b) If the articles of incorporation of a corporation engaged in the business of exploiting natural resources so provide, dividends may be declared and paid in cash out of the depletion reserves, but each such dividend shall be identified as a distribution of such reserves and the amount per share paid from such reserves shall be disclosed to the shareholders receiving the same concurrently with the distribution thereof.

(c) Dividends may be declared and paid in its own treasury shares.

(d) Dividends may be declared and paid in its own authorized but unissued shares out of any unreserved and unrestricted surplus of the corporation upon the following conditions:

(1) If a dividend is payable in its own shares having a par value, such shares shall be issued at not less than the par value thereof and there shall be transferred to stated capital at the time such dividend is paid an amount of surplus equal to the aggregate par value of the shares to be issued as a dividend.

(2) If a dividend is payable in its own shares without par value, such shares shall be issued at such stated value as shall be fixed by the board of directors by resolution adopted at the time such dividend is declared, and there shall be transferred to stated capital at the time such dividend is paid an amount of surplus equal to the aggregate stated value so fixed in respect of such shares; and the amount per share so transferred to stated capital shall be disclosed to the shareholders receiving such dividend concurrently with the payment thereof.

(e) No dividend payable in shares of any class shall be paid to the holders of shares of any other class unless the articles of incorporation so provide or such payment is authorized by the affirmative vote or the written consent of the holders of at least a majority of the outstanding shares of the class in which the payment is to be made.

A split-up or division of the issued shares of any class into a greater number of shares of the same class without increasing the stated capital of the corporation shall not be construed to be a share dividend within the meaning of this section.

Section 46. Distributions from Capital Surplus. The board of directors of a corporation may, from time to time, distribute to its shareholders out of capital surplus of the corporation a portion of its assets, in cash or property, subject to the following provisions:

(a) No such distribution shall be made at a time when the corporation is insolvent or when such distribution would render the corporation insolvent.

(b) No such distribution shall be made unless the articles of incorporation so provide or such distribution is authorized by the affirmative vote of the holders of a majority of the outstanding shares of each class whether or not entitled to vote thereon by the provisions of the articles of incorporation of the corporation.

(c) No such distribution shall be made to the holders of any class of shares unless all cumulative dividends accrued on all preferred or special classes of shares entitled to preferential dividends shall have been fully paid.

(d) No such distribution shall be made to the holders of any class of shares which would reduce the remaining net assets of the corporation below the aggregate preferential amount payable in event of involuntary liquidation to the holders of shares having preferential rights to the assets of the corporation in the event of liquidation.

(e) Each such distribution, when made, shall be identified as a distribution from capital surplus and the amount per share disclosed to the shareholders receiving the same concurrently with the distribution thereof.

The board of directors of a corporation may also, from time to time, distribute to the holders of its outstanding shares having a cumulative preferential right to receive dividends, in discharge of their cumulative dividend rights, dividends payable in cash out of the capital surplus of the corporation, if at the time the corporation has no earned surplus and is not insolvent and would not thereby be rendered insolvent. Each such distribution when made, shall be identified as a payment of cumulative dividends out of capital surplus.

Section 47. Loans to Employees and Directors. A corporation shall not lend money to or use its credit to assist its directors without authorization in the particular case by its shareholders, but may lend money to and use its credit to assist any employee of the corporation or of a subsidiary, including any such employee who is a director of the corporation, if the board of directors decides that such loan or assistance may benefit the corporation.

Section 48. Liabilities of Directors in Certain Cases.
In addition to any other liabilities, a director shall be liable in the following circumstances unless he complies with the standard provided in this Act for the performance of the duties of directors:

(a) A director who votes for or assents to the declaration of any dividend or other distribution of the assets of a corporation to its shareholders contrary to the provisions of this Act or contrary to any restrictions contained in the articles of incorporation, shall be liable to the corporation, jointly and severally with all other directors so voting or assenting, for the amount of such dividend which is paid or the value of such assets which are distributed in excess of the amount of such dividend or distribution which could have been paid or distributed without a violation of the provisions of this Act or the restrictions in the articles of incorporation.

(b) A director who votes for or assents to the purchase of the corporation's own shares contrary to the provisions of this Act shall be liable to the corporation, jointly and severally with all other directors so voting or assenting, for the amount of consideration paid for such shares which is in excess of the maximum amount which could have been paid therefor without a violation of the provisions of this Act.

(c) A director who votes for or assents to any distribution of assets of a corporation to its shareholders during the liquidation of the corporation without the payment and discharge of, or making adequate provision for, all known debts, obligations, and liabilities of the corporation shall be liable to the corporation, jointly and severally with all other directors so voting or assenting, for the value of such assets which are distributed, to the extent that such debts, obligations and liabilities of the corporation are not thereafter paid and discharged.

Any director against whom a claim shall be asserted under or pursuant to this section for the payment of a dividend or other distribution of assets of a corporation and who shall be held liable thereon, shall be entitled to contribution from the shareholders who accepted or received any such dividend or assets knowing such dividend or distribution to have been made in violation of this Act, in proportion to the amounts received by them.

Any director against whom a claim shall be asserted under or pursuant to this section shall be entitled to contribution from the other directors who voted for or assented to the action upon which the claim is asserted.

Section 49. Provisions Relating to Actions by Shareholders.
No action shall be brought in this State by a shareholder in the right of a domestic or foreign corporation unless the plaintiff was a holder of record of shares or of voting trust certificates therefor at the time of the transaction of which he complains, or his shares or voting trust certificates thereafter devolved upon him by operation of law from a person who was a holder of record at such time.

In any action hereafter instituted in the right of any domestic or foreign corporation by the holder or holders of record of shares of such corporation or of voting trust certificates therefor, the court having jurisdiction, upon final judgment and a finding that the action was brought without reasonable cause, may require the plaintiff or plaintiffs to pay to the parties named as defendant the reasonable expenses, including fees of attorneys, incurred by them in the defense of such action.

In any action now pending or hereafter instituted or maintained in the right of any domestic or foreign corporation by the holder or holders of record of less than five per cent of the outstanding shares of any class of such corporation or of voting trust certificates therefor, unless the shares or voting trust certificates so held have a market value in excess of twenty-five thousand dollars, the corporation in whose right such action is brought shall be entitled at any time before final judgment to require the plaintiff or plaintiffs to give security for the reasonable expenses, including fees of attorneys, that may be incurred by it in connection with such action or may be incurred by other parties named as defendant for which it may become legally liable. Market value shall be determined as of the date that the plaintiff institutes the action or, in the case of an intervenor, as of the date that he becomes a party to the action. The amount of such security may from time to time be increased or decreased, in the discretion of the court, upon showing that the security provided has or may become inadequate or is excessive. The corporation shall have recourse to such security in such amount as the court having jurisdiction shall determine upon the termination of such action, whether or not the court finds the action was brought without reasonable cause.

Section 50. Officers.
The officers of a corporation shall consist of a president, one or more vice presidents as may be prescribed by the by-laws, a secretary, and a treasurer, each of whom shall be elected by the board of directors at such time and in such manner as may be prescribed by the by-laws. Such other officers and assistant officers and agents as may be deemed necessary may be elected or appointed by the board of directors or chosen in such other manner as may be prescribed by the by-laws. Any two or more offices may be held by the same person, except the offices of president and secretary.

All officers and agents of the corporation, as between themselves and the corporation, shall have such authority and perform such duties in the management of the corporation as may be provided in the by-laws, or as may be determined by resolution of the board of directors not inconsistent with the by-laws.

Section 51. Removal of Officers. Any officer or agent may be removed by the board of directors whenever in its judgment the best interests of the corporation will be served thereby, but such removal shall be without prejudice to the contract rights, if any, of the person so removed. Election or appointment of an officer or agent shall not of itself create contract rights.

Section 52. Books and Records: Financial Reports to Shareholders; Examination of Records. Each corporation shall keep correct and complete books and records of account and shall keep minutes of the proceedings of its shareholders and board of directors and shall keep at its registered office or principal place of business, or at the office of its transfer agent or registrar, a record of its shareholders, giving the names and addresses of all shareholders and the number and class of the shares held by each. Any books, records and minutes may be in written form or in any other form capable of being converted into written form with a reasonable time.

Any person who shall have been a holder of record of shares or of voting trust certificates therefor at least six months immediately preceding his demand or shall be the holder of record of, or the holder of record of voting trust certificates for, at least five per cent of all the outstanding shares of the corporation, upon written demand stating the purpose thereof, shall have the right to examine, in person, or by agent or attorney, at any reasonable time or times, for any proper purpose its relevant books and records of accounts, minutes, and record of shareholders and to make extracts therefrom.

Any officer or agent who, or a corporation which, shall refuse to allow any such shareholder or holder of voting trust certificates, or his agent or attorney, so to examine and make extracts from its books and records of account, minutes, and record of shareholders, for any proper purpose, shall be liable to such shareholder or holder of voting trust certificates in a penalty of ten per cent of the value of the shares owned by such shareholder, or in respect of which such voting trust certificates are issued, in addition to any other damages or remedy afforded him by law. It shall be a defense to any action for penalties under this section that the person suing therefor has within two years sold or offered for sale any list of shareholders or of holders of voting trust certificates for shares of such corporation or any other corporation or has aided or abetted any person in procuring any list of shareholders or of holders of voting trust certificates for any such purpose, or has improperly used any information secured through any prior examination of the books and records of account, or minutes, or record of shareholders or of holders of voting trust certificates for shares of such corporation or any other corporation, or was

not acting in good faith or for a proper purpose in making his demand.

Nothing herein contained shall impair the power of any court of competent jurisdiction, upon proof by a shareholder or holder of voting trust certificates of proper purpose, irrespective of the period of time during which such shareholder or holder of voting trust certificates shall have been a shareholder of record or a holder of record of voting trust certificates, and irrespective of the number of shares held by him or represented by voting trust certificates held by him, to compel the production for examination by such shareholder or holder of voting trust certificates of the books and records of account, minutes and record of shareholders of a corporation.

Each corporation shall furnish to its shareholders annual financial statements, including at least a balance sheet as of the end of each fiscal year and a statement of income for such fiscal year, which shall be prepared on the basis of generally accepted accounting principles, if the corporation prepares financial statements for such fiscal year on that basis for any purpose, and may be consolidated statements of the corporation and one or more of its subsidiaries. The financial statements shall be mailed by the corporation to each of its shareholders within 120 days after the close of each fiscal year and, after such mailing and upon written request, shall be mailed by the corporation to any shareholder (or holder of a voting trust certificate for its shares) to whom a copy of the most recent annual financial statements has not previously been mailed. In the case of statements audited by a public accountant, each copy shall be accompanied by a report setting forth his opinion thereon; in other cases, each copy shall be accompanied by a statement of the president or the person in charge of the corporation's financial accounting records (1) stating his reasonable belief as to whether or not the financial statements were prepared in accordance with generally accepted accounting principles and, if not, describing the basis of presentation, and (2) describing any respects in which the financial statements were not prepared on a basis consistent with those prepared for the previous year.

Section 53. Incorporators. One or more persons, or a domestic or foreign corporation, may act as incorporator or incorporators of a corporation by signing and delivering in duplicate to the Secretary of State articles of incorporation for such corporation.

Section 54. Articles of Incorporation. The articles of incorporation shall set forth:

(a) The name of the corporation.

(b) The period of duration, which may be perpetual.

(c) The purpose or purposes for which the corporation is organized which may be stated to be, or to include, the transaction of any or all lawful business for which corporations may be incorporated under this Act.

(d) The aggregate number of shares which the corporation shall have authority to issue; if such shares are to consist of one class only, the par value of each of such shares, or a statement that all of such shares are without par value; or, if such shares are to be divided into classes, the number of shares of each class, and a statement of the par value of the shares of each such class or that such shares are to be without par value.

(e) If the shares are to be divided into classes, the designation of each class and a statement of the preferences, limitations and relative rights in respect of the shares of each class.

(f) If the corporation is to issue the shares of any preferred or special class in series, then the designation of each series and a statement of the variations in the relative rights and preferences as between series insofar as the same are to be fixed in the articles of incorporation, and a statement of any authority to be vested in the board of directors to establish series and fix and determine the variations in the relative rights and preferences as between series.

(g) If any preemptive right is to be granted to shareholders, the provisions therefor.

(h) Any provision, not inconsistent with law, which the incorporators elect to set forth in the articles of incorporation for the regulation of the internal affairs of the corporation, including any provision restricting the transfer of shares and any provision which under this Act is required or permitted to be set forth in the by-laws.

(i) The address of its initial registered office, and the name of its initial registered agent at such address.

(j) The number of directors constituting the initial board of directors and the names and addresses of the persons who are to serve as directors until the first annual meeting of shareholders or until their successors be elected and qualify.

(k) The name and address of each incorporator.

It shall not be necessary to set forth in the articles of incorporation any of the corporate powers enumerated in this Act.

Section 55. Filing of Articles of Incorporation.

Duplicate originals of the articles of incorporation shall be delivered to the Secretary of State. If the Secretary of State finds that the articles of incorporation conform to law, he shall, when all fees have been paid as in this Act prescribed:

(a) Endorse on each of such duplicate originals the word "Filed," and the month, day and year of the filing thereof.

(b) File one of such duplicate originals in his office.

(c) Issue a certificate of incorporation to which he shall affix the other duplicate original.

The certificate of incorporation, together with the duplicate original of the articles of incorporation affixed thereto by the Secretary of State, shall be returned to the incorporators or their representative.

Section 56. Effect of Issuance of Certificate of Incorporation.

Upon the issuance of the certificate of incorporation, the corporate existence shall begin, and such certificate of incorporation shall be conclusive evidence that all conditions precedent required to be performed by the incorporators have been complied with and that the corporation has been incorporated under this Act, except as against this State in a proceeding to cancel or revoke the certificate of incorporation or for involuntary dissolution of the corporation.

Section 57. Organization Meeting of Directors.

After the issuance of the certificate of incorporation an organization meeting of the board of directors named in the articles of incorporation shall be held, either within or without this State, at the call of a majority of the directors named in the articles of incorporation, for the purpose of adopting by-laws, electing officers and transacting such other business as may come before the meeting. The directors calling the meeting shall give at least three days' notice thereof by mail to each director so named, stating the time and place of the meeting.

Section 58. Right to Amend Articles of Incorporation.

A corporation may amend its articles of incorporation, from time to time, in any and as many respects as may be desired, so long as its articles of incorporation as amended contain only such provisions as might be lawfully contained in original articles of incorporation at the time of making such amendment, and, if a change in shares or the rights of shareholders, or an exchange, reclassification or cancellation of shares or rights of shareholders is to be made, such provisions as may be necessary to effect such change, exchange, reclassification or cancellation.

In particular, and without limitation upon such general power of amendment, a corporation may amend its articles of incorporation, from time to time, so as:

(a) To change its corporate name.

(b) To change its period of duration.

(c) To change, enlarge or diminish its corporate purposes.

(d) To increase or decrease the aggregate number of shares, or shares of any class, which the corporation has authority to issue.

(e) To increase or decrease the par value of the authorized shares of any class having a par value, whether issued or unissued.

(f) To exchange, classify, reclassify or cancel all or any part of its shares, whether issued or unissued.

(g) To change the designation of all or any part of its shares, whether issued or unissued, and to change the preferences, limitations, and the relative rights in respect of all or any part of its shares, whether issued or unissued.

(h) To change shares having a par value, whether issued or unissued, into the same or a different number of shares without par value, and to change shares without par value, whether issued or unissued, into the same or a different number of shares having a par value.

(i) To change the shares of any class, whether issued or unissued, and whether with or without par value, into a different number of shares of the same class or into the same or a different number of shares, either with or without par value, of other classes.

(j) To create new classes of shares having rights and preferences either prior and superior or subordinate and inferior to the shares of any class then authorized, whether issued or unissued.

(k) To cancel or otherwise affect the right of the holders of the shares of any class to receive dividends which have accrued but have not been declared.

(l) To divide any preferred or special class of shares, whether issued or unissued, into series and fix and determine the designations of such series and the variations in the relative rights and preferences as between the shares of such series.

(m) To authorize the board of directors to establish, out of authorized but unissued shares, series of any preferred or special class of shares and fix and determine the relative rights and preferences of the shares of any series so established.

(n) To authorize the board of directors to fix and determine the relative rights and preferences of the authorized but unissued shares of series theretofore established in respect of which either the relative rights and preferences have not been fixed and determined or the relative rights and preferences theretofore fixed and determined are to be changed.

(o) To revoke, diminish, or enlarge the authority of the board of directors to establish series out of authorized but unissued shares of any preferred or special class and fix and determine the relative rights and preferences of the shares of any series so established.

(p) To limit, deny or grant to shareholders of any class the preemptive right to acquire additional or treasury shares of the corporation, whether then or thereafter authorized.

Section 59. Procedure to Amend Articles of Incorporation. Amendments to the articles of incorporation shall be made in the following manner:

(a) The board of directors shall adopt a resolution setting forth the proposed amendment and, if shares have been issued, directing that it be submitted to a vote at a meeting of shareholders, which may be either the annual or a special meeting. If no shares have been issued, the amendment shall be adopted by resolution of the board of directors and the provisions for adoption by shareholders shall not apply. The resolution may incorporate the proposed amendment in restated articles of incorporation which contain a statement that except for the designated amendment the restated articles of incorporation correctly set forth without change

the corresponding provisions of the articles of incorporation as theretofore amended, and that the restated articles of incorporation together with the designated amendment supersede the original articles of incorporation and all amendments thereto.

(b) Written notice setting forth the proposed amendment or a summary of the changes to be affected thereby shall be given to each shareholder of record entitled to vote thereon within the time and in the manner provided in this Act for the giving of notice of meetings of shareholders. If the meeting be an annual meeting, the proposed amendment of such summary may be included in the notice of such annual meeting.

(c) At such meeting a vote of the shareholders entitled to vote thereon shall be taken on the proposed amendment. The proposed amendment shall be adopted upon receiving the affirmative vote of the holders of a majority of the shares entitled to vote thereon, unless any class of shares is entitled to vote thereon as a class, in which event the proposed amendment shall be adopted upon receiving the affirmative vote of the holders of a majority of the shares of each class of shares entitled to vote thereon as a class and of the total shares entitled to vote thereon.

Any number of amendments may be submitted to the shareholders, and voted upon by them, at one meeting.

Section 60. Class Voting on Amendments. The holders of the outstanding shares of a class shall be entitled to vote as a class upon a proposed amendment, whether or not entitled to vote thereon by the provisions of the articles of incorporation, if the amendment would:

(a) Increase or decrease the aggregate number of authorized shares of such class.

(b) Increase or decrease the par value of the shares of such class.

(c) Effect an exchange, reclassification or cancellation of all or part of the shares of such class.

(d) Effect an exchange, or create a right of exchange, of all or any part of the shares of another class into the shares of such class.

(e) Change the designations, preferences, limitations or relative rights of the shares of such class.

(f) Change the shares of such class, whether with or without par value, into the same or a different number of shares, either with or without par value, of the same class or another class or classes.

(g) Create a new class of shares having rights and preferences prior and superior to the shares of such class, or increase the rights and preferences or the number of authorized shares, of any class having rights and preferences prior or superior to the shares of such class.

(h) In the case of a preferred or special class of shares, divide the shares of such class into series and fix and determine the designation of such series and the variations in the relative rights and preferences between the shares of such series, or authorize the board of directors to do so.

(i) Limit or deny any existing preemptive rights of the shares of such class.

(j) Cancel or otherwise affect dividends on the shares of such class which have accrued but have not been declared.

Section 61. Articles of Amendment. The articles of amendment shall be executed in duplicate by the corporation by its president or a vice president and by its secretary or an assistant secretary, and verified by one of the officers signing such articles, and shall set forth:

(a) The name of the corporation.

(b) The amendments so adopted.

(c) The date of the adoption of the amendment by the shareholders, or by the board of directors where no shares have been issued.

(d) The number of shares outstanding, and the number of shares entitled to vote thereon, and if the shares of any class are entitled to vote thereon as a class, the designation and number of outstanding shares entitled to vote thereon of each such class.

(e) The number of shares voted for and against such amendment, respectively, and, if the shares of any class are entitled to vote thereon as a class, the number of shares of each such class voted for and against such amendment, respectively, or if no shares have been issued, a statement to that effect.

(f) If such amendment provides for an exchange, reclassification or cancellation of issued shares, and if the manner in which the same shall be effected is not set forth in the amendment, then a statement of the manner in which the same shall be effected.

(g) If such amendment effects a change in the amount of stated capital, then a statement of the manner in which the same is effected and a statement, expressed in dollars, of the amount of stated capital as changed by such amendment.

Section 62. Filing of Articles of Amendment. Duplicate originals of the articles of amendment shall be delivered to the Secretary of State. If the Secretary of State finds that the articles of amendment conform to law, he shall, when all fees and franchise taxes have been paid as in this Act prescribed:

(a) Endorse on each of such duplicate originals the word "Filed," and the month, day and year of the filing thereof.

(b) File one of such duplicate originals in his office.

(c) Issue a certificate of amendment to which he shall affix the other duplicate original.

The certificate of amendment, together with the duplicate original of the articles of amendment affixed thereto by the Secretary of State, shall be returned to the corporation or its representative.

Section 63. Effect of Certificate of Amendment. The amendment shall become effective upon the issuance of the certificate of amendment by the Secretary of State, or on such later date, not more than thirty days subsequent to the filing thereof with the Secretary of State, as shall be provided for in the articles of amendment.

No amendment shall affect any existing cause of action in favor of or against such corporation, or any pending suit to which such corporation shall be a party, or the existing rights of persons other than shareholders; and, in the event the corporate name shall be changed by amendment, no suit brought by or against such corporation under its former name shall abate for that reason.

Section 64. Restated Articles of Incorporation. A domestic corporation may at any time restate its articles of incorporation as theretofore amended, by a resolution adopted by the board of directors.

Upon the adoption of such resolution, restated articles of incorporation shall be executed in duplicate by the corporation by its president or a vice president and by its secretary or assistant secretary and verified by one of the officers signing such articles and shall set forth all of the operative provisions of the articles of incorporation as theretofore amended together with a statement that the restated articles of incorporation correctly set forth without change the corresponding provisions of the articles of incorporation as theretofore amended and that the restated articles of incorporation supersede the original articles of incorporation and all amendments thereto.

Duplicate originals of the restated articles of incorporation shall be delivered to the Secretary of State. If the Secretary of State finds that such restated articles of incorporation conform to law, he shall, when all fees and franchise taxes have been paid as in this Act prescribed:

(1) Endorse on each of such duplicate originals the word "Filed," and the month, day and year of the filing thereof.

(2) File one of such duplicate originals in his office.

(3) Issue a restated certificate of incorporation, to which he shall affix the other duplicate original.

The restated certificate of incorporation, together with the duplicate original of the restated articles of incorporation affixed thereto by the Secretary of State, shall be returned to the corporation or its representative.

Upon the issuance of the restated certificate of incorporation by the Secretary of State, the restated articles of incorporation shall become effective and shall supersede the original articles of incorporation and all amendments thereto.

Section 65. Amendment of Articles of Incorporation in Reorganization Proceedings. Whenever a plan of reorganization of a corporation has been confirmed by decree or order of a court of competent jurisdiction in proceedings for the reorganization of such corporation, pursuant to the provisions of any applicable statute of the United States relating to reorganizations of corporations, the articles of incorporation of the corporation may be amended, in the manner provided in this section, in as many respects as may be necessary to carry out the plan and put it into effect, so long as the articles of incorporation as amended contain only such provisions as might be lawfully contained in original articles of incorporation at the time of making such amendment.

In particular and without limitation upon such general power of amendment, the articles of incorporation may be amended for such purpose so as to:

(**A**) Change the corporate name, period of duration or corporate purposes of the corporation;

(**B**) Repeal, alter or amend the by-laws of the corporation;

(**C**) Change the aggregate number of shares or shares of any class, which the corporation has authority to issue;

(**D**) Change the preferences, limitations and relative rights in respect of all or any part of the shares of the corporation, and classify, reclassify or cancel all or any part thereof, whether issued or unissued;

(**E**) Authorize the issuance of bonds, debentures or other obligations of the corporation, whether or not convertible into shares of any class or bearing warrants or other evidences of optional rights to purchase or subscribe for shares of any class, and fix the terms and conditions thereof; and

(**F**) Constitute or reconstitute and classify or reclassify the board of directors of the corporation, and appoint directors and officers in place of or in addition to all or any of the directors or officers then in office.

Amendments to the articles of incorporation pursuant to this section shall be made in the following manner:

(**a**) Articles of amendment approved by decree or order of such court shall be executed and verified in duplicate by such person or persons as the court shall designate or appoint for the purpose, and shall set forth the name of the corporation, the amendments of the articles of incorporation approved by the court, the date of the decree or order approving the articles of amendment, the title of the proceedings in which the decree or order was entered, and a statement that such decree or order was entered by a court having jurisdiction of the proceedings for the reorganization of the corporation pursuant to the provisions of an applicable statute of the United States.

(**b**) Duplicate originals of the articles of amendment shall be delivered to the Secretary of State. If the Secretary of State finds that the articles of amendment conform to law, he shall, when all fees and franchise taxes have been paid as in his Act prescribed:

(**1**) Endorse on each of such duplicate originals the word "Filed," and the month, day and year of the filing thereof.

(**2**) File one of such duplicate originals in his office.

(**3**) Issue a certificate of amendment to which he shall affix the other duplicate original.

The certificate of amendment, together with the duplicate original of the articles of amendment affixed thereto by the Secretary of State, shall be returned to the corporation or its representative.

The amendment shall become effective upon the issuance of the certificate of amendment by the Secretary of State, or on such later date, not more than thirty days subsequent to the filing thereof with the Secretary of State, as shall be provided for in the articles of amendment without any action thereon by the directors or shareholders of the corporation and with the same effect as if the amendments had been adopted by unanimous action of the directors and shareholders of the corporation.

Section 66. Restriction on Redemption or Purchase of Redeemable Shares.
No redemption or purchase of redeemable shares shall be made by a corporation when it is insolvent or when such redemption or purchase would render it insolvent, or which would reduce the net assets below the aggregate amount payable to the holders of shares having prior or equal rights to the assets of the corporation upon involuntary dissolution.

Section 67. Cancellation of Redeemable Shares by Redemption or Purchase.
When redeemable shares of a corporation are redeemed or purchased by the corporation, the redemption or purchase shall effect a cancellation of such shares, and a statement of cancellation shall be filed as provided in this section. Thereupon such shares shall be restored to the status of authorized but unissued shares, unless the articles of incorporation provide that such shares when redeemed or purchased shall not be reissued, in which case the filing of the statement of cancellation shall constitute an amendment to the articles of incorporation and shall reduce the number of shares of the class so cancelled which the corporation is authorized to issue by the number of shares so cancelled.

The statement of cancellation shall be executed in duplicate by the corporation by its president or a vice president and by its secretary or an assistant secretary, and verified by one of the officers signing such statement, and shall set forth:

(**a**) The name of the corporation.

(**b**) The number of redeemable shares cancelled through redemption or purchase, itemized by classes and series.

(**c**) The aggregate number of issued shares, itemized by classes and series, after giving effect to such cancellation.

(**d**) The amount, expressed in dollars, of the stated capital of the corporation after giving effect to such cancellation.

(**e**) If the articles of incorporation provide that the cancelled shares shall not be reissued, the number of shares which the corporation will have authority to issue itemized by classes and series, after giving effect to such cancellation.

Duplicate originals of such statement shall be delivered to the Secretary of State. If the Secretary of State finds that such statement conforms to law, he shall, when all fees and franchise taxes have been paid as in this Act prescribed:

(1) Endorse on each of such duplicate originals the word "Filed," and the month, day and year of the filing thereof.

(2) File one of such duplicate originals in his office.

(3) Return the other duplicate original to the corporation or its representative.

Upon the filing of such statement of cancellation, the stated capital of the corporation shall be deemed to be reduced by that part of the stated capital which was, at the time of such cancellation, represented by the shares so cancelled.

Nothing contained in this section shall be construed to forbid a cancellation of shares or a reduction of stated capital in any other manner permitted by this Act.

Section 68. Cancellation of Other Reacquired Shares. A corporation may at any time, by resolution of its board of directors, cancel all or any part of the shares of the corporation of any class reacquired by it, other than redeemable shares redeemed or purchased, and in such event a statement of cancellation shall be filed as provided in this section.

The statement of cancellation shall be executed in duplicate by the corporation by its president or a vice president and by its secretary or an assistant secretary, and verified by one of the officers signing such statement, and shall set forth:

(a) The name of the corporation.

(b) The number of reacquired shares cancelled by resolution duly adopted by the board of directors, itemized by classes and series, and the date of its adoption.

(c) The aggregate number of issued shares, itemized by classes and series, after giving effect to such cancellation.

(d) The amount, expressed in dollars, of the stated capital of the corporation after giving effect to such cancellation.

Duplicate originals of such statement shall be delivered to the Secretary of State. If the Secretary of State finds that such statement conforms to law, he shall, when all fees and franchise taxes have been paid as in this Act prescribed:

(1) Endorse on each of such duplicate originals the word "Filed," and the month, day and year of the filing thereof.

(2) File one of such duplicate originals in his office.

(3) Return the other duplicate original to the corporation or its representative.

Upon the filing of such statement of cancellation, the stated capital of the corporation shall be deemed to be reduced by that part of the stated capital which was, at the time of such cancellation, represented by the shares so

cancelled, and the shares so cancelled shall be restored to the status of authorized but unissued shares.

Nothing contained in this section shall be construed to forbid a cancellation of shares or a reduction of stated capital in any other manner permitted by this Act.

Section 69. Reduction of Stated Capital in Certain Cases. A reduction of the stated capital of a corporation, where such reduction is not accompanied by any action requiring an amendment of the articles of incorporation and not accompanied by a cancellation of shares, may be made in the following manner:

(A) The board of directors shall adopt a resolution setting forth the amount of the proposed reduction and the manner in which the reduction shall be effected, and directing that the question of such reduction be submitted to a vote at a meeting of shareholders, which may be either an annual or a special meeting.

(B) Written notice, stating that the purpose or one of the purposes of such meeting is to consider the question of reducing the stated capital of the corporation in the amount and manner proposed by the board of directors, shall be given to each shareholder of record entitled to vote thereon within the time and in the manner provided in this Act for the giving of notice of meetings of shareholders.

(C) At such meeting a vote of the shareholders entitled to vote thereon shall be taken on the question of approving the proposed reduction of stated capital, which shall require for its adoption the affirmative vote of the holders of a majority of the shares entitled to vote thereon.

When a reduction of the stated capital of a corporation has been approved as provided in this section, a statement shall be executed in duplicate by the corporation by its president or a vice president and by its secretary or an assistant secretary, and verified by one of the officers signing such statement, and shall set forth:

(a) The name of the corporation.

(b) A copy of the resolution of the shareholders approving such reduction, and the date of its adoption.

(c) The number of shares outstanding, and the number of shares entitled to vote thereon.

(d) The number of shares voted for and against such reduction, respectively.

(e) A statement of the manner in which such reduction is effected, and a statement, expressed in dollars, of the amount of stated capital of the corporation after giving effect to such reduction.

Duplicate originals of such statement shall be delivered to the Secretary of State. If the Secretary of State finds that such statement conforms to law, he shall, when all fees and franchise taxes have been paid as in this Act prescribed:

(1) Endorse on each of such duplicate originals the word "Filed," and the month, day and year of the filing thereof.

(2) File one of such duplicate originals in his office.

(3) Return the other duplicate original to the corporation or its representative.

Upon the filing of such statement, the stated capital of the corporation shall be reduced as therein set forth.

No reduction of stated capital shall be made under the provisions of this section which would reduce the amount of the aggregate stated capital of the corporation to an amount equal to or less than the aggregate preferential amounts payable upon all issued shares having a preferential right in the assets of the corporation in the event of involuntary liquidation, plus the aggregate par value of all issued shares having a par value but no preferential right in the assets of the corporation in the event of involuntary liquidation.

Section 70. Special Provisions Relating to Surplus and Reserves. The surplus, if any, created by or arising out of a reduction of the stated capital of a corporation shall be capital surplus.

The capital surplus of a corporation may be increased from time to time by resolution of the board of directors directing that all or a part of the earned surplus of the corporation be transferred to capital surplus.

A corporation may, by resolution of its board of directors, apply any part or all of its capital surplus to the reduction or elimination of any deficit arising from losses, however incurred, but only after first eliminating the earned surplus, if any, of the corporation by applying such losses against earned surplus and only to the extent that such losses exceed the earned surplus, if any. Each such application of capital surplus shall, to the extent thereof, effect a reduction of capital surplus.

A corporation may, by resolution of its board of directors, create a reserve or reserves out of its earned surplus for any proper purpose or purposes, and may abolish any such reserve in the same manner. Earned surplus of the corporation to the extent so reserved shall not be available for the payment of dividends or other distributions by the corporation except as expressly permitted by this Act.

Section 71. Procedure for Merger. Any two or more domestic corporations may merge into one of such corporations pursuant to a plan of merger approved in the manner provided in this Act.

The board of directors of each corporation shall, by resolution adopted by each such board, approve a plan of merger setting forth:

(a) The names of the corporations proposing to merge, and the name of the corporation into which they propose to merge, which is hereinafter designated as the surviving corporation.

(b) The terms and conditions of the proposed merger.

(c) The manner and basis of converting the shares of each corporation into shares, obligations or other securities of the surviving corporation or of any other corporation or, in whole or in part, into cash or other property.

(d) A statement of any changes in the articles of incorporation of the surviving corporation to be effected by such merger.

(e) Such other provisions with respect to the proposed merger as are deemed necessary or desirable.

Section 72. Procedure for Consolidation. Any two or more domestic corporations may consolidate into a new corporation pursuant to a plan of consolidation approved in the manner provided in this Act.

The board of directors of each corporation shall, by a resolution adopted by each such board, approve a plan of consolidation setting forth:

(a) The names of the corporations proposing to consolidate, and the name of the new corporation into which they propose to consolidate, which is hereinafter designated as the new corporation.

(b) The terms and conditions of the proposed consolidation.

(c) The manner and basis of converting the shares of each corporation into shares, obligations or other securities of the new corporation or of any other corporation or, in whole or in part, into cash or other property.

(d) With respect to the new corporation, all of the statements required to be set forth in articles of incorporation for corporations organized under this Act.

(e) Such other provisions with respect to the proposed consolidation as are deemed necessary or desirable.

Section 72–A. Procedure for Share Exchange. All the issued or all the outstanding shares of one or more classes of any domestic corporation may be acquired through the exchange of all such shares of such class or classes by another domestic or foreign corporation pursuant to a plan of exchange approved in the manner provided in this Act.

The board of directors of each corporation shall, by resolution adopted by each such board, approve a plan of exchange setting forth:

(a) The name of the corporation the shares of which are proposed to be acquired by exchange and the name of the corporation to acquire the shares of such corporation in the exchange, which is hereinafter designated as the acquiring corporation.

(b) The terms and conditions of the proposed exchange.

(c) The manner and basis of exchanging the shares to be acquired for shares, obligations or other securities of the acquiring corporation or any other corporation, or, in whole or in part, for cash or other property.

(d) Such other provisions with respect to the proposed exchange as are deemed necessary or desirable.

The procedure authorized by this section shall not be deemed to limit the power of a corporation to acquire all or part of the shares of any class or classes of a corporation through a voluntary exchange or otherwise by agreement with the shareholders.

Section 73. Approval by Shareholders.

(a) The board of directors of each corporation in the case of a merger or consolidation, and the board of directors of the corporation the shares of which are to be acquired in the case of an exchange, upon approving such plan of merger, consolidation or exchange, shall, by resolution, direct that the plan be submitted to a vote at a meeting of its shareholders, which may be either an annual or a special meeting. Written notice shall be given to each shareholder of record, whether or not entitled to vote at such meeting, not less than twenty days before such meeting, in the manner provided in this Act for the giving of notice of meetings of shareholders, and, whether the meeting be an annual or a special meeting, shall state that the purpose or one of the purposes is to consider the proposed plan of merger, consolidation or exchange. A copy or a summary of the plan of merger, consolidation or exchange, as the case may be, shall be included in or enclosed with such notice.

(b) At each such meeting, a vote of the shareholders shall be taken on the proposed plan. The plan shall be approved upon receiving the affirmative vote of the holders of a majority of the shares entitled to vote thereon of each such corporation, unless any class of shares of any such corporation is entitled to vote thereon as a class, in which event, as to such corporation, the plan shall be approved upon receiving the affirmative vote of the holders of a majority of the shares of each class of shares entitled to vote thereon as a class and of the total shares entitled to vote thereon. Any class of shares of any such corporation shall be entitled to vote as a class if any such plan contains any provision which, if contained in a proposed amendment to articles of incorporation, would entitle such class of shares to vote as a class and, in the case of an exchange, if the class is included in the exchange.

(c) After such approval by a vote of the shareholders of each such corporation, and at any time prior to the filing of the articles of merger, consolidation or exchange, the merger, consolidation or exchange may be abandoned pursuant to provisions therefor, if any, set forth in the plan.

(d) (1) Notwithstanding the provisions of subsections (a) and (b), submission of a plan of merger to a vote at a meeting of shareholders of a surviving corporation shall not be required if:

(i) the articles of incorporation of the surviving corporation do not differ except in name from those of the corporation before the merger.

(ii) each holder of shares of the surviving corporation which were outstanding immediately before the effective date of the merger is to hold the same number of shares with identical rights immediately after,

(iii) the number of voting shares outstanding immediately after the merger, plus the number of voting shares issuable on conversion of other securities issued by virtue of the terms of the merger and on exercise of rights and warrants so issued, will not exceed by more than 20 per cent the number of voting shares outstanding immediately before the merger, and

(iv) the number of participating shares outstanding immediately after the merger, plus the number of participating shares issuable on conversion of other securities issued by virtue of the terms of the merger and on exercise of rights and warrants so issued, will not exceed by more than 20 per cent the number of participating shares outstanding immediately before the merger.

(2) As used in this subsection:

(i) "voting shares" means shares which entitle their holders to vote unconditionally in elections of directors;

(ii) "participating shares" means shares which entitle their holders to participate without limitation in distribution of earnings or surplus.

Section 74. Articles of Merger, Consolidation or Exchange.

(a) Upon receiving the approvals required by Sections 71, 72 and 73, articles of merger or articles of consolidation shall be executed in duplicate by each corporation by its president or a vice president and by its secretary or an assistant secretary, and verified by one of the officers of each corporation signing such articles, and shall set forth:

(1) The plan of merger or the plan of consolidation;

(2) As to each corporation, either (i) the number of shares outstanding, and, if the shares of any class are entitled to vote as a class, the designation and number of outstanding shares of each such class, or (ii) a statement that the vote of shareholders is not required by virtue of subsection 73(d);

(3) As to each corporation the approval of whose shareholders is required, the number of shares voted for and against such plan, respectively, and, if the shares of any class are entitled to vote as a class, the number of shares of each such class voted for and against such plan, respectively.

(b) Duplicate originals of the articles of merger, consolidation or exchange shall be delivered to the Secretary of State. If the Secretary of State finds that such articles conform to law, he shall, when all fees and franchise taxes have been paid as in this Act prescribed:

(1) Endorse on each of such duplicate originals the word "Filed," and the month, day and year of the filing thereof.

(2) File one of such duplicate originals in his office.

(3) Issue a certificate of merger, consolidation or exchange to which he shall affix the other duplicate original.

(c) The certificate of merger, consolidation or exchange together with the duplicate original of the articles affixed thereto by the Secreatry of State, shall be returned to the surviving, new or acquiring corporation, as the case may be, or its representative.

Section 75. Merger of Subsidiary Corporation. Any corporation owning at least ninety per cent of the outstanding shares of each class of another corporation may merge such other corporation into itself without approval by a vote of the shareholders of either corporation. Its board of directors shall, by resolution, approve a plan of merger setting forth:

(A) The name of the subsidiary corporation and the name of the corporation owning at least ninety per cent of its shares, which is hereinafter designated as the surviving corporation.

(B) The manner and basis of converting the shares of the subsidiary corporation into shares, obligations or other securities of the surviving corporation or of any other corporation or, in whole or in part, into cash or other property.

A copy of such plan of merger shall be mailed to each shareholder of record of the subsidiary corporation.

Articles of merger shall be executed in duplicate by the surviving corporation by its president or a vice president and by its secretary or an assistant secretary, and verified by one of its officers signing such articles, and shall set forth:

(a) The plan of merger;

(b) The number of outstanding shares of each class of the subsidiary corporation and the number of such shares of each class owned by the surviving corporation; and

(c) The date of the mailing to shareholders of the subsidiary corporation of a copy of the plan of merger.

On and after the thirtieth day after the mailing of a copy of the plan of merger to shareholders of the subsidiary corporation or upon the waiver thereof by the holders of all outstanding shares duplicate originals of the articles of merger shall be delivered to the Secretary of State. If the Secretary of State finds that such articles conform to law, he shall, when all fees and franchise taxes have been paid as in this Act prescribed:

(1) Endorse on each of such duplicate originals the word "Filed," and the month, day and year of the filing thereof,

(2) File one of such duplicate originals in his office, and

(3) Issue a certificate of merger to which he shall affix the other duplicate original.

The certificate of merger, together with the duplicate original of the articles of merger affixed thereto by the Secretary of State, shall be returned to the surviving corporation or its representative.

Section 76. Effect of Merger, Consolidation or Exchange. A merger, consolidation or exchange shall become effective upon the issuance of a certificate of merger, consolidation or exchange by the Secretary of State, or on such later date, not more than thirty days subsequent to the filing thereof with the Secretary of State, as shall be provided for in the plan.

When a merger of consolidation has become effective:

(a) The several corporations parties to the plan of merger or consolidation shall be a single corporation, which, in the case of a merger, shall be that corporation designated in the plan of merger as the surviving corporation, and, in the case of a consolidation, shall be the new corporation provided for in the plan of consolidation.

(b) The separate existence of all corporations parties to the plan of merger or consolidation, except the surviving or new corporation, shall cease.

(c) Such surviving or new corporation shall have all the rights, privileges, immunities and powers and shall be subject to all the duties and liabilities of a corporation organized under this Act.

(d) Such surviving or new corporation shall thereupon and thereafter possess all the rights, privileges, immunities, and franchises, of a public as well as of a private nature, of each of the merging or consolidating corporations; and all property, real, personal, and mixed, and all debts due on whatever account, including subscriptions to shares, and all other choses in action, and all and every other interest of or belonging to or due to each of the corporations so merged or consolidated, shall be taken and deemed to be transferred to and vested in such single corporation without further act or deed; and the title to any real estate, or any interest therein, vested in any of such corporations shall not revert or be in any way impaired by reason of such merger or consolidation.

(e) Such surviving or new corporation shall thenceforth be responsible and liable for all the liabilities and obligations of each of the corporations so merged or consolidated; and any claim existing or action or proceeding pending by or against any of such corporations may be prosecuted as if such merger or consolidation had not taken place, or such surviving or new corporation may be substituted in its place. Neither the rights of creditors nor any liens upon the property of any such corporation shall be impaired by such merger or consolidation.

(f) In the case of a merger, the articles of incorporation of the surviving corporation shall be deemed to be amended to the extent, if any, that changes in its articles of incorporation are stated in the plan of merger; and, in the case of a consolidation, the statements set forth in the articles of consolidation and which are required or permitted to be set forth in the articles of incorporation of corporations organized under this Act shall be deemed to be the original articles of incorporation of the new corporation.

When a merger, consolidation or exchange has become effective, the shares of the corporation or corporations party to the plan that are, under the terms of the plan, to be converted or exchanged, shall cease to exist, in the case of a merger or consolidation, or be deemed to be exchanged in the case of an exchange, and the holders of such shares shall thereafter be entitled only to the shares, obligations, other securities, cash or other property into which they shall have been converted or for which they shall have been exchanged, in accordance with the plan, subject to any rights under Section 80 of this Act.

Section 77. Merger, Consolidation or Exchange of Shares between Domestic and Foreign Corporations.
One or more foreign corporations and one or more domestic corporations may be merged or consolidated, or participate in an exchange, in the following manner, if such merger, consolidation or exchange is permitted by the laws of the state under which each such foreign corporation is organized:

(a) Each domestic corporation shall comply with the provisions of this Act with respect to the merger, consolidation or exchange, as the case may be, of domestic corporations and each foreign corporation shall comply with the applicable provisions of the laws of the state under which it is organized.

(b) If the surviving or new corporation in a merger or consolidation is to be governed by the laws of any state other than this State, it shall comply with the provisions of this Act with respect to foreign corporations if it is to transact business in this State, and in every case it shall file with the Secretary of State of this State:

(1) An agreement that it may be served with process in this State in any proceeding for the enforcement of any obligation of any domestic corporation which is a party to such merger or consolidation and in any proceeding for the enforcement of the rights of a dissenting shareholder of any such domestic corporation against the surviving or new corporation;

(2) An irrevocable appointment of the Secretary of State of this State as its agent to accept service of process in any such proceeding; and

(3) An agreement that it will promptly pay to the dissenting shareholders of any such domestic corporation, the amount, if any, to which they shall be entitled under provisions of this Act with respect to the rights of dissenting shareholders.

Section 78. Sale of Assets in Regular Course of Business and Mortgage or Pledge of Assets.
The sale, lease, exchange, or other disposition of all, or substantially all, the property and assets of a corporation in the usual and regular course of its business and the mortgage or pledge of any or all property and assets of a corporation whether or not in the usual and regular course of business may be made upon such terms and conditions and for such consideration, which may consist in whole or in part of cash or other property, including shares, obligations or other securities of any other corporation, domestic or foreign, as shall be authorized by its board of directors; and in any such case no authorization or consent of the shareholders shall be required.

Section 79. Sale of Assets Other Than in Regular Course of Business.
A sale, lease, exchange, or other disposition of all, or substantially all, the property and assets, with or without the good will, of a corporation, if not in the usual and regular course of its business, may be made upon such terms and conditions and for such consideration, which may consist in whole or in part of cash or other property, including shares, obligations or other securities of any other corporation, domestic or foreign, as may be authorized in the following manner:

(a) The board of directors shall adopt a resolution recommending such sale, lease, exchange, or other disposition and directing the submission thereof to a vote at a meeting of shareholders, which may be either an annual or a special meeting.

(b) Written notice shall be given to each shareholder of record, whether or not entitled to vote at such meeting, not less than twenty days before such meeting, in the manner provided in this Act for the giving of notice of meetings of shareholders, and, whether the meeting be an annual or a special meeting, shall state that the purpose, or one of the purposes, is to consider the proposed sale, lease, exchange, or other disposition.

(c) At such meeting the shareholders may authorize such sale, lease, exchange, or other disposition and may fix, or may authorize the board of directors to fix, any or all of the terms and conditions thereof and the consideration to be received by the corporation therefor. Such authorization shall require the affirmative vote of the holders of a majority of the shares of the corporation entitled to vote thereon, unless any class of shares is entitled to vote thereon as a class, in which event such authorization shall require the affirmative vote of the holders of a majority of the shares of each class of shares entitled to vote as a class thereon and of the total shares entitled to vote thereon.

(d) After such authorization by a vote of shareholders, the board of directors nevertheless, in its discretion, may abandon such sale, lease, exchange, or other disposition of assets, subject to the rights of third parties under any contracts relating thereto, without further action or approval by shareholders.

Section 80. Right of Shareholders to Dissent and Obtain Payment for Shares.
(a) Any shareholder of a corporation shall have the right to dissent from, and to obtain payment for his shares in the event of, any of the following corporate actions.

(1) Any plan of merger or consolidation to which the corporation is a party, except as provided in subsection (c);

(2) Any sale or exchange of all or substantially all of the property and assets of the corporation not made in the usual or regular course of its business, including a sale in dissolution, but not including a sale pursuant to an

order of a court having jurisdiction in the premises or a sale for cash on terms requiring that all or substantially all of the net proceeds of sale be distributed to the shareholders in accordance with their respective interests within one year after the date of sale;

(3) Any plan of exchange to which the corporation is a party as the corporation the shares of which are to be acquired;

(4) Any amendment of the articles of incorporation which materially and adversely affects the rights appurtenant to the share of the dissenting shareholders in that it:

(i) alters or abolishes a preferential right of such shares;

(ii) creates, alters or abolishes a right in respect of the redemption of such shares, including a provision respecting a sinking fund for the redemption or repurchase of such shares;

(iii) alters or abolishes a preemptive right of the holder of such shares to acquire shares or other securities;

(iv) excludes or limits the right of the holder of such shares to vote on any matter, or to cumulate his votes, except as such right may be limited by dilution through the issuance of shares or other securities with similar voting rights; or

(5) Any other corporate action taken pursuant to a shareholder vote with respect to which the articles of incorporation, the bylaws, or a resolution of the board of directors directs that dissenting shareholders shall have a right to obtain payment for their shares.

(b) (1) A record holder of shares may assert dissenters' rights as to less than all of the shares registered in his name only if he dissents with respect to all the shares beneficially owned by any one person, and discloses the name and address of the person or persons on whose behalf he dissents. In that event, his rights shall be determined as if the shares as to which he has dissented and his other shares were registered in the names of different shareholders.

(2) A beneficial owner of shares who is not the record holder may assert dissenters' rights with respect to shares held on his behalf, and shall be treated as a dissenting shareholder under the terms of this section and Section 31 if he submits to the corporation at the time of or before the assertion of these rights a written consent of the record holder.

(c) The right to obtain payment under this section shall not apply to the shareholders of the surviving corporation in a merger if a vote of the shareholders of such corporation is not necessary to authorize such merger.

(d) A shareholder of a corporation who has a right under this section to obtain payment for his shares shall have no right at law or in equity to attack the validity of the corporate action that gives rise to his right to obtain payment, nor to

have the action set aside or rescinded, except when the corporate action is unlawful or fraudulent with regard to the complaining shareholder or to the corporation.

Section 81. Procedures for Protection of Dissenters' Rights.

(a) As used in this section:

(1) "Dissenter" means a shareholder or beneficial owner who is entitled to and does assert dissenters' rights under Section 80, and who has performed every act required up to the time involved for the assertion of such rights.

(2) "Corporation" means the issuer of the shares held by the dissenter before the corporate action, or the successor by merger or consolidation of that issuer.

(3) "Fair value" of shares means their value immediately before the effectuation of the corporate action to which the dissenter objects, excluding any appreciation or depreciation in anticipation of such corporate action unless such exclusion would be inequitable.

(4) "Interest" means interest from the effective date of the corporate action until the date of payment, at the average rate currently paid by the corporation on its principal bank loans, or, if none, at such rate as is fair and equitable under all the circumstances.

(b) If a proposed corporate action which would give rise to dissenters' rights under Section 80(a) is submitted to a vote at a meeting of shareholders, the notice of meeting shall notify all shareholders that they have or may have a right to dissent and obtain payment for their shares by complying with the terms of this section, and shall be accompanied by a copy of Sections 80 and 81 of this Act.

(c) If the proposed corporate action is submitted to a vote at a meeting of shareholders, any shareholder who wishes to dissent and obtain payment for his shares must file with the corporation, prior to the vote, a written notice of intention to demand that he be paid fair compensation for his shares if the proposed action is effectuated, and shall refrain from voting his shares in approval of such action. A shareholder who fails in either respect shall acquire no right to payment for his shares under this section or Section 80.

(d) If the proposed corporate action is approved by the required vote at a meeting of shareholders, the corporation shall mail a further notice to all shareholders who gave due notice of intention to demand payment and who refrained from voting in favor of the proposed action. If the proposed corporate action is to be taken without a vote of shareholders, the corporation shall send to all shareholders who are entitled to dissent and demand payment for their shares a notice of the adoption of the plan of corporate action. The notice shall (1) state where and when a demand for payment must be sent and certificates of certificated shares must be deposited in order to obtain payment, (2) inform holders of uncertificated shares to what extent transfer of shares will be restricted from the time that demand for payment is received, (3) supply a form for demanding payment which includes a request for certification of the date on which the shareholder, or the person on whose behalf the shareholder dissents, acquired beneficial ownership of the shares, and (4) be accompanied by a copy of Sections 80 and 81 of this Act. The time set for the demand and deposit shall be not less than 30 days from the mailing of the notice.

(e) A shareholder who fails to demand payment, or fails (in the case of certificated shares) to deposit certificates, as required by a notice pursuant to subsection (d) shall have no right under this section or Section 80 to receive payment for his shares. If the shares are not represented by certificates, the corporation may restrict their transfer from the time of receipt of demand for payment until effectuation of the proposed corporate action, or the release of restrictions under the terms of subsection (f). The dissenter shall retain all other rights of a shareholder until these rights are modified by effectuation of the proposed corporate action.

(f) (1) Within 60 days after the date set for demanding payment and depositing certificates, if the corporation has not effectuated the proposed corporate action and remitted payment for shares pursuant to paragraph (3), it shall return any certificates that have been deposited, and release uncertificated shares from any transfer restrictions imposed by reason of the demand for payment.

(2) When uncertificated shares have been released from transfer restrictions, and deposited certificates have been returned, the corporation may at any later time send a new notice conforming to the requirements of subsection (d), with like effect.

(3) Immediately upon effectuation of the proposed corporate action, or upon receipt of demand for payment if the corporate action has already been effectuated, the corporation shall remit to dissenters who have made demand and (if their shares are certificated) have deposited their certificates the amount which the corporation estimates to be the fair value of the shares, with interest if any has accrued. The remittance shall be accompanied by:

(i) the corporation's closing balance sheet and statement of income for a fiscal year ending not more than 16 months before the date of remittance, together with the latest available interim financial statements;

(ii) a statement of the corporation's estimate of fair value of the shares; and

(iii) a notice of the dissenter's right to demand supplemental payment, accompanied by a copy of Sections 80 and 81 of this Act.

(g) (1) If the corporation fails to remit as required by subsection (f), or if the dissenter believes that the amount remitted is less than the fair value of his shares, or that the interest is not correctly determined, he may send the corporation his own estimate of the value of the shares or of the interest, and demand payment of the deficiency.

(2) If the dissenter does not file such an estimate within 30 days after the corporation's mailing of its remittance, he shall be entitled to no more than the amount remitted.

(h) (1) Within 60 days after receiving a demand for payment pursuant to subsection (g), if any such demands for payment remain unsettled, the corporation shall file in an appropriate court a petition requesting that the fair value of the shares and interest thereon be determined by the court.

(2) An appropriate court shall be a court of competent jurisdiction in the county of this state where the registered office of the corporation is located. If, in the case of a merger or consolidation or exchange of shares, the corporation is a foreign corporation without a registered office in this state, the petition shall be filed in the county where the registered office of the domestic corporation was last located.

(3) All dissenters, wherever residing, whose demands have not been settled shall be made parties to the proceeding as in an action against their shares. A copy of the petition shall be served on each such dissenter; if a dissenter is a nonresident, the copy may be served on him by registered or certified mail or by publication as provided by law.

(4) The jurisdiction of the court shall be plenary and exclusive. The court may appoint one or more persons as appraisers to receive evidence and recommend a decision on the question of fair value. The appraisers shall have such power and authority as shall be specified in the order of their appointment or in any amendment thereof. The dissenters shall be entitled to discovery in the same manner as parties in other civil suits.

(5) All dissenters who are made parties shall be entitled to judgment for the amount by which the fair value of their shares is found to exceed the amount previously remitted, with interest.

(6) If the corporation fails to file a petition as provided in paragraph (1) of this subsection, each dissenter who made a demand and who has not already settled his claim against the corporation shall be paid by the corporation the amount demanded by him, with interest, and may sue therefor in an appropriate court.

(i) (1) The costs and expenses of any proceeding under subsection (h), including the reasonable compensation and expenses of appraisers appointed by the court, shall be determined by the court and assessed against the corporation, except that any part of the costs and expenses may be apportioned and assessed as the court may deem equitable against all or some of the dissenters who are parties and whose action in demanding supplemental payment the court finds to be arbitrary, vexatious, or not in good faith.

(2) Fees and expenses of counsel and of experts for the respective parties may be assessed as the court may deem equitable against the corporation and in favor of any or all dissenters if the corporation failed to comply substantially with the requirements of this section, and may be assessed against either the corporation or a dissenter, in favor of any other party, if the court finds that the party against whom the fees and expenses are assessed acted arbitrarily, vexatiously, or not in good faith in respect to the rights provided by this section and Section 80.

(3) If the court finds that the services of counsel for any dissenter were of substantial benefit to other dissenters similarly situated, and should not be assessed against the corporation, it may award to these counsel reasonable fees to be paid out of the amounts awarded to the dissenters who were benefitted.

(j) **(1)** Notwithstanding the foregoing provisions of this section, the corporation may elect to withhold the remittance required by subsection (f) from any dissenter with respect to shares of which the dissenter (or the person on whose behalf the dissenter acts) was not the beneficial owner on the date of the first announcement to news media or to shareholders of the terms of the proposed corporate action. With respect to such shares, the corporation shall, upon effectuating the corporate action, state to each dissenter its estimate of the fair value of the shares, state the rate of interest to be used (explaining the basis thereof), and offer to pay the resulting amounts on receiving the dissenter's agreement to accept them in full satisfaction.

(2) If the dissenter believes that the amount offered is less than the fair value of the shares and interest determined according to this section, he may within 30 days after the date of mailing of the corporation's offer, mail the corporation his own estimate of fair value and interest, and demand their payment. If the dissenter fails to do so, he shall be entitled to no more than the corporation's offer.

(3) If the dissenter makes a demand as provided in paragraph (2), the provisions of subsections (h) and (i) shall apply to further proceedings on the dissenter's demand.

Section 82. Voluntary Dissolution by Incorporators.

A corporation which has not commenced business and which has not issued any shares, may be voluntarily dissolved by its incorporators at any time in the following manner:

(a) Articles of dissolution shall be executed in duplicate by a majority of the incorporators, and verified by them, and shall set forth:

(1) The name of the corporation.

(2) The date of issuance of its certificate of incorporation.

(3) That none of its shares has been issued.

(4) That the corporation has not commenced business.

(5) That the amount, if any, actually paid in on subscriptions for its shares, less any part thereof disbursed for necessary expenses, has been returned to those entitled thereto.

(6) That no debts of the corporation remain unpaid.

(7) That a majority of the incorporators elect that the corporation be dissolved.

(b) Duplicate originals of the articles of dissolution shall be delivered to the Secretary of State. If the Secretary of State finds that the articles of dissolution conform to law, he shall, when all fees and franchise taxes have been paid as in this Act prescribed:

(1) Endorse on each of such duplicate originals the word "Filed," and the month, day and year of the filing thereof.

(2) File one of such duplicate originals in his office.

(3) Issue a certificate of dissolution to which he shall affix the other duplicate original.

The certificate of dissolution, together with the duplicate original of the articles of dissolution affixed thereto by the Secretary of State, shall be returned to the incorporators or their representative. Upon the issuance of such certificate of dissolution by the Secretary of State, the existence of the corporation shall cease.

Section 83. Voluntary Dissolution by Consent of Shareholders.

A corporation may be voluntarily dissolved by the written consent of all of its shareholders.

Upon the execution of such written consent, a statement of intent to dissolve shall be executed in duplicate by the corporation by its president or a vice president and by its secretary or an assistant secretary, and verified by one of the officers signing such statement, which statement shall set forth:

(a) The name of the corporation.

(b) The names and respective addresses of its officers.

(c) The names and respective addresses of its directors.

(d) A copy of the written consent signed by all shareholders of the corporation.

(e) A statement that such written consent has been signed by all shareholders of the corporation or signed in their names by their attorneys thereunto duly authorized.

Section 84. Voluntary Dissolution by Act of Corporation.

A corporation may be dissolved by the act of the corporation, when authorized in the following manner:

(a) The board of directors shall adopt a resolution recommending that the corporation be dissolved, and directing that the question of such dissolution be submitted to a vote at a meeting of shareholders, which may be either an annual or a special meeting.

(b) Written notice shall be given to each shareholder of record entitled to vote at such meeting within the time and in the manner provided in this Act for the giving of notice of meetings of shareholders, and, whether the meeting be an annual or special meeting, shall state that the purpose, or one of the purposes, of such meeting is to consider the advisability of dissolving the corporation.

(c) At such meeting a vote of shareholders entitled to vote thereat shall be taken on a resolution to dissolve the corporation. Such resolution shall be adopted upon receiving the affirmative vote of the holders of a majority of the shares of the corporation entitled to vote thereon, unless any class of shares is entitled to vote thereon as a class, in which event the resolution shall be adopted upon receiving the affirmative vote of the holders of a majority of the shares of each class of shares entitled to vote thereon as a class and of the total shares entitled to vote thereon.

(d) Upon the adoption of such resolution, a statement of intent to dissolve shall be executed in duplicate by the corporation by its president or a vice president and by its secretary or an assistant secretary, and verified by one of the officers signing such statement, which statement shall set forth:

(1) The name of the corporation.

(2) The names and respective addresses of its officers.

(3) The names and respective addresses of its directors.

(4) A copy of the resolution adopted by the shareholders authorizing the dissolution of the corporation.

(5) The number of shares outstanding, and, if the shares of any class are entitled to vote as a class, the designation and number of outstanding shares of each such class.

(6) The number of shares voted for and against the resolution, respectively, and, if the shares of any class are entitled to vote as a class, the number of shares of each such class voted for and against the resolution, respectively.

Section 85. Filing of Statement of Intent to Dissolve.

Duplicate originals of the statement of intent to dissolve, whether by consent of shareholders or by act of the corporation, shall be delivered to the Secretary of State. If the Secretary of State finds that such statement conforms to law, he shall, when all fees and franchise taxes have been paid as in this Act prescribed:

(a) Endorse on each of such duplicate originals the word "Filed," and the month, day and year of the filing thereof.

(b) File one of such duplicate originals in his office.

(c) Return the other duplicate original to the corporation or its representative.

Section 86. Effect of Statement of Intent to Dissolve.

Upon the filing by the Secretary of State of a statement of intent to dissolve, whether by consent of shareholders or by act of the corporation, the corporation shall cease to carry on its business, except insofar as may be necessary for the winding up thereof, but its corporate existence shall contin-

ue until a certificate of dissolution has been issued by the Secretary of State or until a decree dissolving the corporation has been entered by a court of competent jurisdiction as in this Act provided.

Section 87. Procedure after Filing of Statement of Intent to Dissolve.

After the filing by the Secretary of State of a statement of intent to dissolve:

(a) The corporation shall immediately cause notice thereof to be mailed to each known creditor of the corporation.

(b) The corporation shall proceed to collect its assets, convey and dispose of such of its properties as are not to be distributed in kind to its shareholders, pay, satisfy and discharge its liabilities and obligations and do all other acts required to liquidate its business and affairs, and, after paying or adequately providing for the payment of all its obligations, distribute the remainder of its assets, either in cash or in kind, among its shareholders according to their respective rights and interests.

(c) The corporation, at any time during the liquidation of its business and affairs, may make application to a court of competent jurisdiction within the state and judicial subdivision in which the registered office or principal place of business of the corporation is situated, to have the liquidation continued under the supervision of the courts as provided in this Act.

Section 88. Revocation of Voluntary Dissolution Proceedings by Consent of Shareholders. *(Text omitted).*

Section 89. Revocation of Voluntary Dissolution Proceedings by Act of Corporation. *(Text omitted).*

Section 90. Filing of Statement of Revocation of Voluntary Dissolution Proceedings. *(Text omitted).*

Section 91. Effect of Statement of Revocation of Voluntary Dissolution Proceedings.

Upon the filing by the Secretary of State of a statement of revocation of voluntary dissolution proceedings, whether by consent of shareholders or by act of the corporation, the revocation of the voluntary dissolution proceedings shall become effective and the corporation may again carry on its business.

Section 92. Articles of Dissolution.

If voluntary dissolution proceedings have not been revoked, then when all debts, liabilities and obligations of the corporation have been paid and discharged, or adequate provision has been made therefor, and all of the remaining property and assets of the corporation have been distributed to its shareholders, articles of dissolution shall be executed in duplicate by the corporation by its president or a vice president and by its secretary or an assistant secretary, and verified by one of the officers signing such statement, which statement shall set forth:

(a) The name of the corporation.

(b) That the Secretary of State has theretofore filed a

statement of intent to dissolve the corporation, and the date on which such statement was filed.

(c) That all debts, obligations and liabilities of the corporation have been paid and discharged or that adequate provision has been made therefor.

(d) That all the remaining property and assets of the corporation have been distributed among its shareholders in accordance with their respective rights and interests.

(e) That there are no suits pending against the corporation in any court, or that adequate provision has been made for the satisfaction of any judgment, order or decree which may be entered against it in any pending suit.

Section 93. Filing of Articles of Dissolution. Duplicate originals of such articles of dissolution shall be delivered to the Secretary of State. If the Secretary of State finds that such articles of dissolution conform to law, he shall, when all fees and franchise taxes have been paid as in this Act prescribed:

(a) Endorse on each of such duplicate originals the word "Filed," and the month, day and year of the filing thereof.

(b) File one of such duplicate originals in his office.

(c) Issue a certificate of dissolution to which he shall affix the other duplicate original.

The certificate of dissolution, together with the duplicate original of the articles of dissolution affixed thereto by the Secretary of State, shall be returned to the representative of the dissolved corporation. Upon the issuance of such certificate of dissolution the existence of the corporation shall cease, except for the purpose of suits, other proceedings and appropriate corporate action by shareholders, directors and officers as provided in this Act.

Section 94. Involuntary Dissolution. A corporation may be dissolved involuntarily by a decree of the . . . . court in an action filed by the Attorney General when it is established that:

(a) The corporation has failed to file its annual report within the time required by this Act, or has failed to pay its franchise tax on or before the first day of August of the year in which such franchise tax becomes due and payable; or

(b) The corporation procured its articles of incorporation through fraud; or

(c) The corporation has continued to exceed or abuse the authority conferred upon it by law; or

(d) The corporation has failed for thirty days to appoint and maintain a registered agent in this State; or

(e) The corporation has failed for thirty days after change of its registered office or registered agent to file in the office of the Secretary of State a statement of such change.

Section 95. Notification to Attorney General. The Secretary of State, on or before the last day of December of each year, shall certify to the Attorney General the names of all corporations which have failed to file their annual reports or

to pay franchise taxes in accordance with the provisions of this Act, together with the facts pertinent thereto. He shall also certify, from time to time, the names of all corporations which have given other cause for dissolution as provided in this Act, together with the facts pertinent thereto. Whenever the Secretary of State shall certify the name of a corporation to the Attorney General as having given any cause for dissolution, the Secretary of State shall concurrently mail to the corporation at its registered office a notice that such certification has been made. Upon the receipt of such certification, the Attorney General shall file an action in the name of the State against such corporation for its dissolution. Every such certificate from the Secretary of State to the Attorney General pertaining to the failure of a corporation to file an annual report or pay a franchise tax shall be taken and received in all courts as prima facie evidence of the facts therein stated. If, before action is filed, the corporation shall file its annual report or pay its franchise tax, together with all penalties thereon, or shall appoint or maintain a registered agent as provided in this Act, or shall file with the Secretary of State the required statement of change of registered office or registered agent, such fact shall be forthwith certified by the Secretary of State to the Attorney General and he shall not file an action against such corporation for such cause. If, after action is filed, the corporation shall file its annual report or pay its franchise tax, together with all penalties thereon, or shall appoint or maintain a registered agent as provided in this Act, or shall file with the Secretary of State the required statement of change of registered office or registered agent, and shall pay the costs of such action, the action for such cause shall abate.

Section 96. Venue and Process. Every action for the involuntary dissolution of a corporation shall be commenced by the Attorney General either in the . . . . court of the county in which the registered office of the corporation is situated, or in the . . . . . . court of . . . . . . county. Summons shall issue and be served as in other civil actions. If process is returned not found, the Attorney General shall cause publication to be made as in other civil cases in some newspaper published in the county where the registered office of the corporation is situated, containing a notice of the pendency of such action, the title of the court, the title of the action, and the date on or after which default may be entered. The Attorney General may include in one notice the names of any number of corporations against which actions are then pending in the same court. The Attorney General shall cause a copy of such notice to be mailed to the corporation at its registered office within ten days after the first publication thereof. The certificate of the Attorney General of the mailing of such notice shall be prima facie evidence thereof. Such notice shall be published at least once each week for two successive weeks, and the first publication thereof may begin at any time after the summons has been returned. Unless a corporation shall have been served with summons, no default shall be taken against it earlier than thirty days after the first publication of such notice.

Section 97. Jurisdiction of Court to Liquidate Assets and Business of Corporation. The . . . . courts shall have full power to liquidate the assets and business of a corporation:

(a) In an action by a shareholder when it is established:

(1) That the directors are deadlocked in the management of the corporate affairs and the shareholders are unable to break the deadlock, and that irreparable injury to the corporation is being suffered or is threatened by reason thereof; or

(2) That the acts of the directors or those in control of the corporation are illegal, oppressive or fraudulent; or

(3) That the shareholders are deadlocked in voting power, and have failed, for a period which includes at least two consecutive annual meeting dates, to elect successors to directors whose terms have expired or would have expired upon the election of their successors; or

(4) That the corporate assets are being misapplied or wasted.

(b) In an action by a creditor:

(1) When the claim of the creditor has been reduced to judgment and an execution thereon returned unsatisfied and it is established that the corporation is insolvent; or

(2) When the corporation has admitted in writing that the claim of the creditor is due and owing and it is established that the corporation is insolvent.

(c) Upon application by a corporation which has filed a statement of intent to dissolve, as provided in this Act, to have its liquidation continued under the supervision of the court.

(d) When an action has been filed by the Attorney General to dissolve a corporation and it is established that liquidation of its business and affairs should precede the entry of a decree of dissolution.

Proceedings under clause (a), (b) or (c) of this section shall be brought in the county in which the registered office or the principal office of the corporation is situated.

It shall not be necessary to make shareholders parties to any such action or proceeding unless relief is sought against them personally.

Section 98. Procedure in Liquidation of Corporation by Court. In proceedings to liquidate the assets and business of a corporation the court shall have power to issue injunctions, to appoint a receiver or receivers pendente lite, with such powers and duties as the court, from time to time, may direct, and to take such other proceedings as may be requisite to preserve the corporate assets wherever situated, and carry on the business of the corporation until a full hearing can be had.

After a hearing had upon such notice as the court may direct to be given to all parties to the proceedings and to any other parties in interest designated by the court, the court may appoint a liquidating receiver or receivers with authority to collect the assets of the corporation, including all amounts owing to the corporation by subscribers on account of any unpaid portion of the consideration for the issuance of shares. Such liquidating receiver or receivers shall have authority, subject to the order of the court, to sell, convey and dispose of all or any part of the assets of the corporation wherever situated, either at public or private sale. The assets of the corporation or the proceeds resulting from a sale, conveyance or other dispostion thereof shall be applied to the expenses of such liquidation and to the payment of the liabilities and obligations of the corporation, and any remaining assets or proceeds shall be distributed among its shareholders according to their respective rights and interests. The order appointing such liquidating receiver or receivers shall state their powers and duties. Such powers and duties may be increased or diminished at any time during the proceedings.

The court shall have power to allow from time to time as expenses of the liquidation compensation to the receiver or receivers and to attorneys in the proceeding, and to direct the payment thereof out of the assets of the corporation or the proceeds of any sale or disposition of such assets.

A receiver of a corporation appointed under the provisions of this section shall have authority to sue and defend in all courts in his own name as receiver of such corporation. The court appointing such receiver shall have exclusive jurisdiction of the corporation and its property, wherever situated.

Section 99. Qualifications of Receivers. A receiver shall in all cases be a natural person or a corporation authorized to act as receiver, which corporation may be a domestic corporation or a foreign corporation authorized to transact business in this State, and shall in all cases give such bond as the court may direct with such sureties as the court may require.

Section 100. Filing of Claims in Liquidation Proceedings. In proceedings to liquidate the assets and business of a corporation the court may require all creditors of the corporation to file with the clerk of the court or with the receiver, in such form as the court may prescribe, proofs under oath of their respective claims. If the court requires the filing of claims it shall fix a date, which shall be not less than four months from the date of the order, as the last day for the filing of claims, and shall prescribe the notice that shall be given to creditors and claimants of the date so fixed. Prior to the date so fixed the court may extend the time for

the filing of claims. Creditors and claimants failing to file proofs of claim on or before the date so fixed may be barred, by order of court, from participating in the distribution of the assets of the corporation.

Section 101. Discontinuance of Liquidation Proceedings. The liquidation of the assets and business of a corporation may be discontinued at any time during the liquidation proceedings when it is established that cause for liquidation no longer exists. In such event the court shall dismiss the proceedings and direct the receiver to redeliver to the corporation all its remaining property and assets.

Section 102. Decree of Involuntary Dissolution. In proceedings to liquidate the assets and business of a corporation, when the costs and expenses of such proceedings and all debts, obligations and liabilities of the corporation shall have been paid and discharged and all of its remaining property and assets distributed to its shareholders, or in case its property and assets are not sufficient to satisfy and discharge such costs, expenses, debts and obligations, all the property and assets have been applied so far as they will go to their payment, the court shall enter a decree dissolving the corporation, whereupon the existence of the corporation shall cease.

Section 103. Filing of Decree of Dissolution. In case the court shall enter a decree dissolving a corporation, it shall be the duty of the clerk of such court to cause a certified copy of the decree to be filed with the Secretary of State. No fee shall be charged by the Secretary of State for the filing thereof.

Section 104. Deposit with State Treasurer of Amount Due Certain Shareholders. Upon the voluntary or involuntary dissolution of a corporation, the portion of the assets distributable to a creditor or shareholder who is unknwon or cannot be found, or who is under disability and there is no person legally competent to receive such distributive portion, shall be reduced to cash and deposited with the State Treasurer and shall be paid over to such creditor or shareholder or to his legal representative upon proof satisfactory to the State Treasurer of his right thereto.

Section 105. Survival of Remedy After Dissolution. The dissolution of a corporation either (1) by the issuance of a certificate of dissolution by the Secretary of State, or (2) by a decree of court when the court has not liquidated the assets and business of the corporation as provided in this Act, or (3) by expiration of its period of duration, shall not take away or impair any remedy available to or against such corporation, its directors, officers, or shareholders, for any right or claim existing, or any liability incurred, prior to such dissolution if action or other proceeding thereon is commenced within two years after the date of such dissolution. Any such action or proceeding by or against the corporation may be prosecuted or defended by the corporation in its corporate name. The shareholders, directors and officers shall have power to take such corporate or other action as shall be appropriate to protect such remedy, right or claim. If such corporation was dissolved by the expiration of its period of duration, such corporation may amend its articles of incorporation at any time during such period of two years so as to extend its period of duration.

Section 106. Admission of Foreign Corporation. No foreign corporation shall have the right to transact business in this State until it shall have procured a certificate of authority so to do from the Secretary of State. No foreign corporation shall be entitled to procure a certificate of authority under this Act to transact in this State any business which a corporation organized under this Act is not permitted to transact. A foreign corporation shall not be denied a certificate of authority by reason of the fact that the laws of the state or country under which such corporation is organized governing its organization and internal affairs differ from the laws of this State, and nothing in this Act contained shall be construed to authorize this State to regulate the organization or the internal affairs of such corporation.

Without excluding other activities which may not constitute transacting business in this State, a foreign corporation shall not be considered to be transacting business in this State, for the purposes of this Act, by reason of carrying on in this State any one or more of the following activities:

(a) Maintaining or defending any action or suit or any administrative or arbitration proceeding, or effecting the settlement thereof or the settlement of claims or disputes.

(b) Holding meetings of its directors or shareholders or carrying on other activities concerning its internal affairs.

(c) Maintaining bank accounts.

(d) Maintaining offices or agencies for the transfer, exchange and registration of its securities, or appointing and maintaining trustees or depositaries with relation to its securities.

(e) Effecting sales through independent contractors.

(f) Soliciting or procuring orders, whether by mail or through employees or agents or otherwise, where such orders require acceptance without this State before becoming binding contracts.

(g) Creating as borrower or lender, or acquiring, indebtedness or mortgages or other security interests in real or personal property.

(h) Securing or collecting debts or enforcing any rights in property securing the same.

(i) Transacting any business in interstate commerce.

(j) Conducting an isolated transaction completed within a period of thirty days and not in the course of a number of repeated transactions of like nature.

Section 107. Powers of Foreign Corporation. A foreign corporation which shall have received a certificate of authority under this Act shall, until a certificate of revocation or of withdrawal shall have been issued as provided in this Act, enjoy the same, but no greater, rights and privileges as a domestic corporation organized for the purposes set forth in the application pursuant to which such certificate of authority is issued; and, except as in this Act otherwise provided, shall be subject to the same duties, restrictions, penalties and liabilities now or hereafter imposed upon a domestic corporation of like character.

Section 108. Corporate Name of Foreign Corporation.

No certificate of authority shall be issued to a foreign corporation unless the corporate name of such corporation:

(a) Shall contain the word "corporation," "company," "incorporated," or "limited," or shall contain an abbreviation of one of such words, or such corporation shall, for use in this State, add at the end of its name one of such words or an abbreviation thereof.

(b) Shall not contain any word or phrase which indicates or implies that it is organized for any purpose other than one or more of the purposes contained in its articles of incorporation or that it is authorized or empowered to conduct the business of banking or insurance.

(c) Shall not be the same as, or deceptively similar to, the name of any domestic corporation existing under the laws of this State or any foreign corporation authorized to transact business in this State, or a name the exclusive right to which is, at the time, reserved in the manner provided in this Act, or the name of a corporation which has in effect a registration of its name as provided in this Act except that this provision shall not apply if the foreign corporation applying for a certificate of authority files with the Secretary of State any one of the following:

(1) a resolution of its board of directors adopting a fictitious name for use in transacting business in this State which fictitious name is not deceptively similar to the name of any domestic corporation or of any foreign corporation authorized to transact business in this State or to any name reserved or registered as provided in this Act, or

(2) the written consent of such other corporation or holder of a reserved or registered name to use the same or deceptively similar name and one or more words are added to make such name distinguishable from such other name, or

(3) a certified copy of a final decree of a court of competent jurisdiction establishing the prior right of such foreign corporation to the use of such name in this State.

Section 109. Change of Name by Foreign Corporation.

Whenever a foreign corporation which is authorized to transact business in this State shall change its name to one under which a certificate of authority would not be granted to it on application therefor, the certificate of authority of such corporation shall be suspended and it shall not thereafter transact any business in this State until it has changed its name to a name which is available to it under the laws of this State or has otherwise complied with the provisions of this Act.

Section 110. Application for Certificate of Authority.

A foreign corporation, in order to procure a certificate of authority to transact business in this State, shall make application therefor to the Secretary of State, which application shall set forth:

(a) The name of the corporation and the state or country under the laws of which it is incorporated.

(b) If the name of the corporation does not contain the word "corporation," "company," "incorporated," or "limited," or does not contain an abbreviation of one of such words, then the name of the corporation with the word or abbreviation which it elects to add thereto for use in this State.

(c) The date of incorporation and the period of duration of the corporation.

(d) The address of the principal office of the corporation in the state or country under the laws of which it is incorporated.

(e) The address of the proposed registered office of the corporation in this State, and the name of its proposed registered agent in this State at such address.

(f) The purpose or purposes of the corporation which it proposes to pursue in the transaction of business in this State.

(g) The names and respective addresses of the directors and officers of the corporation.

(h) A statement of the aggregate number of shares which the corporation has authority to issue, itemized by classes, par value of shares, shares without par value, and series, if any, within a class.

(i) A statement of the aggregate number of issued shares itemized by classes, par value of shares, shares without par value, and series, if any, within a class.

(j) A statement, expressed in dollar, of the amount of stated capital of the corporation, as defined in this Act.

(k) An estimate, expressed in dollars, of the value of all property to be owned by the corporation for the following year, wherever located, and an estimate of the value of the property of the corporation to be located within this State during such year, and an estimate, expressed in dollars, of the gross amount of business which will be transacted by the corporation during such year, and an estimate of the gross amount thereof which will be transacted by the corporation at or from places of business in this State during such year.

(l) Such additional information as may be necessary or appropriate in order to enable the Secretary of State to determine whether such corporation is entitled to a certificate of authority to transact business in this State and to determine and assess the fees and franchise taxes payable as in this Act prescribed.

Such application shall be made on forms prescribed and

furnished by the Secretary of State and shall be executed in duplicate by the corporation by its president or a vice president and by its secretary or an assistant secretary, and verified by one of the officers signing such application.

Section 111. Filing of Application for Certificate of Authority. Duplicate originals of the application of the corporation for a certificate of authority shall be delivered to the Secretary of State, together with a copy of its articles of incorporation and all amendments thereto, duly authenticated by the proper officer of the state or country under the laws of which it is incorporated.

If the Secretary of State finds that such application conforms to law, he shall, when all fees and franchise taxes have been paid as in this Act prescribed:

(a) Endorse on each of such documents the word "Filed," and the month, day and year of the filing thereof.

(b) File in his office one of such duplicate originals of the application and the copy of the articles of incorporation and amendments thereto.

(c) Issue a certificate of authority to transact business in this State to which he shall affix the other duplicate original application.

The certificate of authority, together with the duplicate original of the application affixed thereto by the Secretary of State, shall be returned to the corporation or its representative.

Section 112. Effect of Certificate of Authority. Upon the issuance of a certificate of authority by the Secretary of State, the corporation shall be authorized to transact business in this State for those purposes set forth in its application, subject, however, to the right of this State to suspend or to revoke such authority as provided in this Act.

Section 113. Registered Office and Registered Agent of Foreign Corporation. Each foreign corporation authorized to transact business in this State shall have and continuously maintain in this State:

(a) A registered office which may be, but need not be, the same as its place of business in this State.

(b) A registered agent, which agent may be either an individual resident in this State whose business office is identical with such registered office, or a domestic corporation, or a foreign corporation authorized to transact business in this State, having a business office identical with such registered office.

Section 114. Change of Registered Office or Registered Agent of Foreign Corporation. A foreign corporation authorized to transact business in this State may change its registered office or change its registered agent, or both, upon filing in the office of the Secretary of State a statement setting forth:

(a) The name of the corporation.

(b) The address of its then registered office.

(c) If the address of its registered office be changed, the address to which the registered office is to be changed.

(d) The name of its then registered agent.

(e) If its registered agent be changed, the name of its successor registered agent.

(f) That the address of its registered office and the address of the business office of its registered agent, as changed, will be identical.

(g) That such change was authorized by resolution duly adopted by its board of directors.

Such statement shall be executed by the corporation by its president or a vice president, and verified by him, and delivered to the Secretary of State. If the Secretary of State finds that such statement conforms to the provisions of this Act, he shall file such statement in his office, and upon such filing the change of address of the registered office, or the appointment of a new registered agent, or both, as the case may be, shall become effective.

Any registered agent of a foreign corporation may resign as such agent upon filing a written notice thereof, executed in duplicate, with the Secretary of State, who shall forthwith mail a copy thereof to the corporation at its principal office in the state or country under the laws of which it is incorporated. The appointment of such agent shall terminate upon the expiration of thirty days after receipt of such notice by the Secretary of State.

If a registered agent changes his or its business address to another place within the same . . . . *, he or it may change such address and the address of the registered office of any corporation of which he or it is registered agent by filing a statement as required above except that it need be signed only by the registered agent and need not be responsive to (e) or (g) and must recite that a copy of the statement has been mailed to the corporation.

Section 115. Service of Process on Foreign Corporation. The registered agent so appointed by a foreign corporation authorized to transact business in this State shall be an agent of such corporation upon whom any process, notice or demand required or permitted by law to be served upon the corporation may be served.

Whenever a foreign corporation authorized to transact business in this State shall fail to appoint or maintain a registered agent in this State, or whenever any such registered agent cannot with reasonable diligence be found at the registered office, or whenever the certificate of authority of a foreign corporation shall be suspended or revoked, then the Secretary of State shall be an agent of such corporation upon whom any such process, notice, or demand may be served. Service on the Secretary of State of any such process, notice or demand shall be made by delivering to and leaving with him, or with any clerk having

*Supply designation of jurisdiction, such as county, etc., in accordance with local practice.

charge of the corporation department of his office, duplicate copies of such process, notice or demand. In the event any such process, notice or demand is served on the Secretary of State, he shall immediately cause one of such copies thereof to be forwarded by registered mail, addressed to the corporation at its principal office in the state or country under the laws of which it is incorporated. Any service so had on the Secretary of State shall be returnable in not less than thirty days.

The Secretary of State shall keep a record of all processes, notices and demands served upon him under this section, and shall record therein the time of such service and his action with reference thereto.

Nothing herein contained shall limit or affect the right to serve any process, notice or demand, required or permitted by law to be served upon a foreign corporation in any other manner now or hereafter permitted by law.

Section 116. Amendment to Articles of Incorporation of Foreign Corporation *(Text omitted).*

Section 117. Merger of Foreign Corporation Authorized to Transact Business in This State *(Text omitted).*

Section 118. Amended Certificate of Authority *(Text omitted).*

Section 119. Withdrawal of Foreign Corporation *(Text omitted).*

Section 120. Filing of Application for Withdrawal *(Text omitted).*

Section 121. Revocation of Certificate of Authority *(Text omitted).*

Section 122. Issuance of Certificate of Revocation *(Text omitted).*

Section 123. Application to Corporations Heretofore Authorized to Transact Business in This State *(Text omitted).*

Section 124. Transacting Business without Certificate of Authority. No foreign corporation transacting business in this State without a certificate of authority shall be permitted to maintain any action, suit or proceeding in any court of this State, until such corporation shall have obtained a certificate of authority. Nor shall any action, suit or proceeding be maintained in any court of this State by any successor or assignee of such corporation on any right, claim or demand arising out of the transaction of business by such corporation in this State, until a certificate of authority shall have been obtained by such corporation or by a corporation which has acquired all or substantially all of its assets.

The failure of a foreign corporation to obtain a certificate of authority to transact business in this State shall not impair the validity of any contract or act of such corporation, and shall not prevent such corporation from defending any action, suit or proceeding in any court of this State.

A foreign corporation which transacts business in this State without a certificate of authority shall be liable to this State, for the years or parts thereof during which it transacted business in this State without a certificate of authority, in an amount equal to all fees and franchise taxes which would have been imposed by this Act upon such corporation had it duly applied for and received a certificate of authority to transact business in this State as required by this Act and thereafter failed all reports required by this Act, plus all penalties imposed by this Act for failure to pay such fees and franchise taxes. The Attorney General shall bring proceedings to recover all amounts due this State under the provisions of this Section.

Section 125. Annual Report of Domestic and Foreign Corporations. Each domestic corporation, and each foreign corporation authorized to transact business in this State, shall file, within the time prescribed by this Act, an annual report setting forth:

(a) The name of the corporation and the state or country under the laws of which it is incorporated.

(b) The address of the registered office of the corporation in this State, and the name of its registered agent in this State at such address, and, in case of a foreign corporation, the address of its principal office in the state or country under the laws of which it is incorporated.

(c) A brief statement of the character of the business in which the corporation is actually engaged in this State.

(d) The names and respective addresses of the directors and officers of the corporation.

(e) A statement of the aggregate number of shares which the corporation has authority to issue, itemized by classes, par value of shares, shares without par value, and series, if any, within a class.

(f) A statement of the aggregate number of issued shares, itemized by classes, par value of shares, shares without par value, and series, if any, within a class.

(g) A statement, expressed in dollars, of the amount of stated capital of the corporation, as defined in this Act.

(h) A statement, expressed in dollars, of the value of all the property owned by the corporation, wherever located, and the value of the property of the corporation located within this State, and a statement, expressed in dollars, of the gross amount of business transacted by the corporation for the twelve months ended on the thirty-first day of December preceding the date herein provided for the filing of such report and the gross amount thereof transacted by the corporation at or from places of business in this State. If, on the thirty-first day of December preceding the time herein provided for the filing of such report, the corporation had not been in existence for a period of twelve months, or in the case of a foreign corporation had not been authorized to transact business in this State for a period of twelve months, the statement with respect to business transacted shall be furnished for the period between the date of incorporation or the date of its authorization to transact business in this State, as the case may be, and such thirty-first day of December. If all the property of the corporation is located in this State and all of its business is transacted at or from places of business in this State, or if the corporation elects to pay the annual franchise tax on the basis of its entire stated capital, then the information required by this subparagraph need not be set forth in such report.

(i) Such additional information as may be necessary or appropriate in order to enable the Secretary of State to determine and assess the proper amount of franchise taxes payable by such corporation.

Such annual report shall be made on forms prescribed and furnished by the Secretary of State, and the information therein contained shall be given as of the date of the execution of the report, except as to the information required by subparagraphs (g), (h) and (i) which shall be given as of the close of business on the thirty-first day of December next preceding the date herein provided for the filing of such report. It shall be executed by the corporation by its president, a vice president, secretary, an assistant secretary, or treasurer, and verified by the officer executing the report, or, if the corporation is in the hands of a receiver or trustee, it shall be executed on behalf of the corporation and verified by such receiver or trustee.

Section 126. Filing of Annual Report of Domestic and Foreign Corporations *(Text omitted).*

Section 127. Fees, Franchise Taxes and Charges to be Collected by Secretary of State *(Text omitted).*

Section 128. Fees for Filing Documents and Issuing Certificates *(Text omitted).*

Section 129. Miscellaneous Charges *(Text omitted).*

Section 130. License Fees Payable by Domestic Corporations *(Text omitted).*

Section 131. License Fees Payable by Foreign Corporations *(Text omitted).*

Section 132. Franchise Taxes Payable by Domestic Corporations *(Text omitted).*

Section 133. Franchise Taxes Payable by Foreign Corporations *(Text omitted).*

Section 134. Assessment and Collection of Annual Franchise Taxes *(Text omitted).*

Section 135. Penalties Imposed upon Corporations *(Text omitted).*

Section 136. Penalties Imposed upon Officers and Directors.
Each officer and director of a corporation, domestic or foreign, who fails or refuses within the time prescribed by this Act to answer truthfully and fully interrogatories propounded to him by the Secretary of State in accordance with the provisions of this Act, or who signs any articles, statement, report, application or other document filed with the Secretary of State which is known to such officer or director to be false in any material respect, shall be deemed to be guilty of a misdemeanor, and upon conviction thereof may be fined in any amount not exceeding . . . . dollars.

Section 137. Interrogatories by Secretary of State.
The Secretary of State may propound to any corporation, domestic or foreign, subject to the provisions of this Act, and to any officer or director thereof, such interrogatories as may be reasonably necessary and proper to enable him to ascertain whether such corporation has complied with all the provisions of this Act applicable to such corporation. Such interrogatories shall be answered within thirty days after the mailing thereof, or within such additional time as shall be fixed by the Secretary of State, and the answers thereto shall be full and complete and shall be made in writing and under oath. If such interrogatories be directed to an individual they shall be answered by him, and if directed to a corporation they shall be answered by the president, vice president, secretary or assistant secretary thereof. The Secretary of State need not file any document to which such interrogatories relate until such interrogatories be answered as herein provided, and not then if the answers thereto disclose that such document is not in conformity with the provisions of this Act. The Secretary of State shall certify to the Attorney General, for such action as the Attorney General may deem appropriate, all interrogatories and answers thereto which disclose a violation of any of the provisions of this Act.

Section 138. Information Disclosed by Interrogatories.
Interrogatories propounded by the Secretary of State and the answers thereto shall not be open to public inspection nor shall the Secretary of State disclose any facts or information obtained therefrom except insofar as his official duty may require the same to be made public or in the event such interrogatories or the answers thereto are required for evidence in any criminal proceedings or in any other action by this State.

Section 139. Power of Secretary of State.
The Secretary of State shall have the power and authority reasonably necessary to enable him to administer this Act efficiently and to perform the duties therein imposed upon him.

Section 140. Appeal from Secretary of State *(Text omitted).*

Section 141. Certificates and Certified Copies to Be Received in Evidence *(Text omitted).*

Section 142. Forms to Be Furnished by Secretary of State *(Text omitted).*

Section 143. Greater Voting Requirements. Whenever, with respect to any action to be taken by the shareholders of a corporation, the articles of incorporation require the vote or concurrence of the holders of a greater proportion of the shares, or of any class or series thereof, than required by this Act with respect to such action, the provisions of the articles of incorporation shall control.

Section 144. Waiver of Notice. Whenever any notice is required to be given to any shareholder or director of a corporation under the provisions of this Act or under the provisions of the articles of incorporation or by-laws of the corporation, a waiver thereof in writing signed by the person or persons entitled to such notice, whether before or after the time stated therein, shall be equivalent to the giving of such notice.

Section 145. Action by Shareholders without a Meeting. Any action required by this Act to be taken at a meeting of the shareholders of a corporation, or any action which may be taken at a meeting of the shareholders, may be taken without a meeting if a consent in writing, setting forth the action so taken, shall be signed by all of the shareholders entitled to vote with respect to the subject matter thereof.

Such consent shall have the same effect as a unanimous vote of shareholders, and may be stated as such in any articles or document filed with the Secretary of State under this Act.

Section 146. Unauthorized Assumption of Corporate Powers. All persons who assume to act as a corporation without authority so to do shall be jointly and severally liable for all debts and liabilities incurred or arising as a result thereof.

Section 147. Application to Existing Corporations *(Text omitted).*

Section 148. Application to Foreign and Interstate Commerce *(Text omitted).*

Section 149. Reservation of Power. The . . . . . . * shall at all times have power to prescribe such regulations, provisions and limitations as it may deem advisable, which regulations, provisions and limitations shall be binding upon any and all corporations subject to the provisions of this Act, and the . . . . . . * shall have power to amend, repeal or modify this Act at pleasure.

Section 150. Effect of Repeal of Prior Acts *(Text omitted).*

Section 151. Effect of Invalidity of Part of This Act *(Text omitted).*

Section 152. Repeal of Prior Acts *(Text omitted).*

[Professional Corporation Supplement, added to the Model Business Corporation Act in 1979, is omitted.]

*Insert name of legislative body.

GLOSSARY

Some of the definitions in this glossary are quoted in whole or in part, with permission, from Black's Law Dictionary, Copyright © 1979, by West Publishing Company. Quoted definitions are indicated by quotation marks and the symbol (c).

Abatement Generally, plea in abatement. A form of pleading which asserts that an action is without legal effect; if the plea is sustained, the entire action is ended. Also, in inheritance law, a required reduction or nonpayment of a gift stated in a will.

Acceptance An offeree's manifestation of assent to the terms of an offer, usually needed for a contract to arise. Also, *in the law of sales:* a buyer's act of taking as the buyer's own property the particular goods covered by a contract, whether by words or by action or silence when it is time to speak. Also, *in the law of commercial paper*, a drawee's act of writing the word "accepted" across the face of a draft (or the word "certified" across the face of a check), or signing on the face of the instrument, and thereby becoming a primary party to the instrument. Also, *in the law of bankruptcy*, an agreement by a class of creditors (or holders of ownership interests) to a plan for satisfaction of claims against the debtor's estate. A class accepts by means of a vote.

Accommodation party A person who signs an instrument for the purpose of lending his or her name (credit) to another party to the instrument.

Accord and satisfaction The reaching of a new agreement and the performance of it or the acceptance of it by both parties as a substitute for the original contract. Usually associated with settlement of a disputed claim.

Account receivable (account) A right to payment for goods sold or leased or for services rendered.

Acknowledgment Certification by a notary public as to the identity of a person who signs a document.

Adhesion contracts See *Contract of adhesion.*

Adjective law See *Procedural law.*

Administrative agency A public officer, board, bureau, or commission—other than legislatures and courts—having power to determine private rights and obligations by making rules and rendering decisions.

Administrative law The law concerning the powers and procedures of administrative agencies, including the law governing judicial review of administrative action.

Administrator In estate or inheritance law: a person or entity, not designated by a decedent's will, appointed by a court to administer a decedent's estate.

Admiralty jurisdiction The power of the district courts of the United States to entertain and decide cases involving maritime contracts, torts, injuries, and so on. See *Maritime law.*

Affirmation (to affirm) The ratification of an act, statement, or promise. In the law, it is used primarily to express agreement to be held to a voidable transaction, as the affirmance or ratification of a minor's voidable contract or the ratification by a principal of an agent's voidable action on the principal's behalf.

After-acquired property clause A clause in a security agreement that gives a creditor a security interest in both present and future assets of the debtor instead of a security interest only in specific assets on hand at the creation of the secured transaction.

Agency A relationship in which one person acts for or represents another by the latter's authority; where one person acts for another either in the relationship of principal and agent, master and servant, or employer and employee.

1285

Agent A person authorized by another to act for him or her; one entrusted with another's business.

Agreement See *Contract*.

Allowed claim In bankruptcy law, a valid claim against the debtor's estate. An allowed claim will be paid to the extent that funds are available.

Amicus curiae "Means, literally, friend of the court. A person with strong interest in or views on the subject matter of an action may petition the court for permission to file a brief, ostensibly on behalf of a party but actually to suggest a rationale consistent with its own views. Such amicus curiae briefs are commonly filed in appeals concerning matters of broad public interest." (c)

Analogy As used in the development of law, a technique of applying a principle or a rule of law to a situation essentially similar to, but not exactly the same as, the case originally decided.

Annuity A contractual device for systematically using up (liquidating) an existing fund; a type of contract sold by some life insurance companies.

Apparent authority The authority which, though not actually granted, the principal knowingly permits an agent to exercise or which the principal holds the agent out as possessing.

Appellant One who files an appeal. The various grounds for an appeal are discussed in Chapter 3.

Appellee The party opposite the appellant. Usually, the party who won at the trial level.

Arbitration A nonjudicial method of resolving civil disputes, informal and voluntary in most cases. Discussed in Chapter 3.

Armed Services Procurement Regulations (ASPR) A system of regulations prescribed by the Secretary of Defense under authority of Chapter 137, Title 10, of the United States Code, having the force and effect of law, which establish uniform policies and procedures applicable to the procurement of supplies, services, and construction by Department of Defense agencies.

Authority The power of an agent to affect the legal relations of a principal by acts done in accordance with the principal's manifestations of consent.

Authority by estoppel Authority that is not actual, but is apparent only, being imposed on the principal because the conduct of the principal has been such as to mislead a third party, so that it would be unjust to let the principal deny it.

Automatic stay A suspension of legal action. In bankruptcy law, a suspension of legal action (other than the bankruptcy proceeding itself) until the bankruptcy case is over or until the stay is vacated by the bankruptcy court.

Articles of incorporation A legal document, filed with a designated state official, that meets the requirements of the state's incorporation statute before a person or persons can commence doing business as a corporation. The articles, sometimes called "corporate charter," provide the framework within which the corporation must operate.

Artisan "One skilled in some kind of trade, craft, or art requiring manual dexterity; e.g., a carpenter, plumber, tailor, mechanic." (c)

Assignee A person to whom an assignment is made.

Assignment A transfer of rights, usually of contract rights.

Assignor The maker of an assignment.

Assumpsit A common law form of action to recover damages for breach of contract.

Attachment A seizure of property, through legal process, for the purpose of protecting the claim of a creditor. An attachment normally occurs at the outset of a lawsuit.

Attachment of a security interest In the law of secured transactions, the name given to the process of creating (agreeing to) a security interest in personal property and of making it enforceable against the debtor.

Bailment A transaction in which the owner of personal property (bailor) retains title to it but puts someone else (bailee) in possession for a limited purpose such as repair or storage.

Bearer paper See *Commercial paper*.

Bequest A gift by will of personal property.

Bilateral contract "A contract formed by the exchange of promises in which the promise of one party is consideration supporting the promise of the other." (c)

Bill of lading A document of title issued by a railroad or other carrier that lists the goods accepted for transport and that sometimes states the terms of the shipping agreement. See *Document of title*. A *through bill* of lading is one issued by a carrier for transport of goods over its own lines for a certain distance, and then over connecting lines to the destination. A *destination bill* of lading is one to be issued at the destination point instead of the sending point so that the documents will be available when the goods arrive.

Bill of Rights The First Ten Amendments to the

Constitution of the United States. The Bill of Rights confers a number of rights intended to protect individuals from governmental oppression.

Blue-sky laws   State statutes that protect investors against fraudulent schemes by regulating the issuance, sale, and/or transfer of securities.

Board of Contract Appeals   An organization set up within each of the major contracting departments and agencies of the federal government to hear and settle disputes arising under their contracts.

Board of directors   One or more persons elected and authorized by the shareholders of a corporation to manage the corporation and its affairs.

Bona fide   "In or with good faith; honestly, openly, and sincerely; without deceit or fraud." (c)

Bonds   With reference to corporate financing, a bond is a certificate or other evidence of debt that obligates the corporation to pay the bondholder a fixed rate of interest on the principal at regular intervals and to pay the principal on a stated maturity date.

Bulk sale   The sale of a whole stock in trade of a business.

Bylaws   Self-made regulations or rules adopted by a corporation to regulate and govern its internal actions and affairs.

C&F (CF)   An abbreviation meaning that the price includes in a lump sum the cost of goods and the cost of freight to the named destination.

CIF   An abbreviation meaning that the price includes in a lump sum the cost of goods and the cost of insurance and freight to the named destination.

COD   An abbreviation of "collect on delivery."

Call   A demand of payment, either in installments or portions, made upon subscribers of shares by directors of a corporation. Also, a negotiable option contract under which the bearer has the right to buy a certain number of shares of stock at an agreed price before a fixed date.

Case law   The accumulated body of court decisions that form an important part of the law of a particular subject.

Case surrender value   A dollar value of an insurance policy, generated from premium payments that exceed the amount needed to pay claims against and expenses of the insurer. The excess payments are retained and invested by the insurer, and the accumulation is held in a *legal reserve fund*.

Cause of action   Legal basis for a lawsuit.

Caveat emptor   A Latin phrase meaning "Let the buyer beware."

Cease-and-desist order   A command from an administrative agency to stop a challenged practice. A cease-and-desist order is similar to an injunction.

Certificate of competency   A certificate issued by the Small Business Administration attesting to the competency, as to capacity and credit, of a prospective small business contractor to perform a government contract.

Certificate of incorporation   A document, issued by some states, that grants an organization permission to do business as a corporation.

Certificated securities   Stocks or bonds evidenced by a written instrument in bearer or registered form. In contrast, uncertificated securities are not evidenced by a written instrument.

Certified check   A check that has been accepted by the drawee bank. See *Acceptance*.

Certiorari   "Latin: To be informed of. Writ issued by a superior court requiring an inferior court to produce a certified record of a particular case. Most commonly used [by] the Supreme Court of the United States as a device to choose the cases it wishes to hear." (c)

Chancery   Equity. A *court of chancery* is a *court of equity*. See *Equity*.

Charter   An instrument by which the state creates a corporation and confers on it the right, power, and authority to do business under the corporate form. The term "charter" is sometimes used to refer to the articles of incorporation.

Chattel   A term often used to refer to movable, tangible things which are not firmly attached to real property.

Chattel mortgage   A writing evidencing a secured transaction in personal property, that is, a mortgage evidencing both a monetary obligation and a security interest in personal property. The debtor has possession of the property, but the creditor has, as his or her security interest, title to the property or, in some states, a lien (claim) against it.

Chattel paper   A writing which evidences both a monetary obligation and a security interest in specific goods.

Civil law   In the United States, that law under which a person (the plaintiff) may sue another (the defendant), for example, in a lawsuit involving a contract or tort, to obtain redress for a wrong committed by the defendant. The expression "civil law" is also used to describe those legal systems (e.g., the French) whose law is centered around a comprehensive legislative code.

Class-action shareholder suit An action brought against a corporation by some of its shareholders on behalf of themselves and other shareholders similarly situated.

Close corporation A corporation whose stock is held by one stockholder or by a relatively small group of stockholders who actively participate in management. The stock is generally subject to restrictions on transfer.

Coinsurance A method used by property insurers to prevent customers who underinsure commercial property from receiving a disproportionately high payout per premium dollar for losses.

Collateral Something of value that can be converted into cash by a creditor if the debtor defaults.

Collusive bidding Bid-rigging. An agreement to select one from a group to make a low bid while the others refrain from bidding or bid higher amounts, to compare bids prior to submission, to create a bid depository where competitors compare bids and fix the bid price, or to split profits made by successful bidder.

Commercial impracticability A basis upon which the parties to a sales contract may be excused from their performance obligations. The essence of commercial impracticability is an unexpected occurrence which seriously impairs a party's ability to perform.

Commercial paper Negotiable instruments payable in money: negotiable drafts, checks, notes, and certificates of deposit. Commercial paper is *bearer paper* if it can be negotiated by delivery alone. Commercial paper is *order paper* if, in addition to delivery, an indorsement is required by law for negotiation.

Common law In England, a body of law *common* to the whole population, produced primarily by the efforts of judges in various parts of England to harmonize their decisions with those of judges in other parts of the country. The English common law became a basis for the development of a common law in the United States. In the United States, common law is decisional or case law as supplemented by decisions in equity. See *Equity*.

Common stock A class of corporate stock that usually represents the voting control of a corporation. Such stock carries rights to dividends and, upon dissolution of the corporation, to corporate assets; but such rights are subordinate to the rights of preferred stock, if any.

Compensatory damages Damages awarded to a plaintiff to compensate him or her for harm suffered, such as medical bills or lost profits. In tort cases, it includes general damages for embarrassment, pain, or suffering.

Composition agreement An arrangement between a debtor and two or more creditors whereby the debtor agrees to turn his or her assets over to the creditors, and the creditors agree to accept their pro rata portions in full satisfaction of their claims.

Composition plan In bankruptcy law, a plan for the adjustment or settlement of debt in which the debtor pays creditors less than 100 percent of their claims on a pro rata basis for each class of claims. In contrast, under an *extension plan*, the debtor pays the full amount, but over a longer period than originally agreed.

Condition A qualification or limitation of a grant or of an agreement.

Conditional sale contract A contract evidencing a secured transaction in which a buyer of goods receives possession of them and the seller-creditor retains title to them until the buyer makes payment.

Confirmation In bankruptcy law, the act of the bankruptcy court in approving a plan of reorganization or some other plan for the adjustment or settlement of debt.

Conscious parallelism In antitrust law, uniform pricing or other business conduct by competitors not acting in concert, but who are aware of each other's actions.

Consent order An order of an administrative agency under which a person agrees to discontinue a challenged practice. Under a consent order the respondent does not admit any violation of law.

Consideration In contract law, a bargained-for legal detriment incurred in exchange for a promise.

Consignment A transfer of possession of property for the purpose of transportation or sale. The consignor retains title to (ownership of) the property.

Conspiracy An unlawful combination between two or more persons or corporations to do an illegal act or to accomplish a lawful end through illegal means; it may be a civil wrong *and* a criminal offense.

Construction As applied to a statute, the process of discovering and explaining the legal effect which the statute is to have. Construing a statute may involve interpreting unclear language, but it mainly involves such tasks as determining the purpose or policy of the statute, deciding how the provisions of a complex statute are related, and deciding to what specific people or things the statute applies.

Constructive trust A device imposed by a court of equity to compel one who unfairly holds a property interest to convey that interest to another to whom it justly belongs.

Consumer goods See *Consumer product.*

Consumer product As used in the Magnuson-Moss Warranty Act, any tangible personal property that is distributed in commerce and that is normally used for personal, family, or household purposes, including any such property intended to be attached to or installed in any real property.

Contract A promise or set of promises for the breach of which the law gives a remedy or for the performance of which the law in some way recognizes as a duty. In the law of sales, a contract consists of the total legal obligation that results from the parties' agreement, as that agreement is affected by the UCC and by any other applicable rules of law. *Contract* should be distinguished from *agreement.* An agreement is the bargain of the parties in fact, as found in their language or by implication from other circumstances, such as course of performance.

Contract of adhesion A contract in which a party, usually the buyer, has no meaningful choice with regard to some or all the terms of the contract, for example, an insurance contract.

Contract for sale See *Sale.*

Contract to sell See *Sale.*

Contracting officer An official designated to enter into or administer contracts for the United States and authorized to make related determinations and findings.

Conversion Unauthorized and wrongful exercise of dominion and control over personal property of another, in a manner inconsistent with the rights of the owner.

Corporate opportunity doctrine A doctrine that prohibits a person who has a fiduciary relation to a corporation from seizing business opportunities which rightfully belong to the corporation.

Corporation A legal entity created by authority of a statute as an artificial person whose rights, obligations, and liabilities are separate and distinct from those of its shareholders.

Corporation sole A unique corporate form granted to the titular head of a church or state and, upon his

or her death, to the named successor, thus perpetuating ownership of church or state properties.

Cost-type contract A form of government contract that provides for the payment to the contractor of allowable costs incurred in its performance and, if so provided in the contract, a fixed fee, or an additional fee dependent upon the relationship the allowable costs bear to target costs or dependent upon accomplishment of established performance objectives.

Course of dealing In the law of sales, a pattern of prior business transactions (not just the performance of one transaction) which can establish a background for the interpretation of the immediate transaction.

Course of performance In the law of sales, the carrying out of a particular transaction. There can be no course of performance unless there are repeated occasions for performance, such as several deliveries of coal to be made pursuant to a single contract of sale.

Court of Claims A special court created by Congress for the purpose, among others, of hearing and determining contract claims against the United States.

Cover A buyer's arrangement for the purchase of goods in substitution for goods which the seller failed to deliver.

Criminal law In the United States, that body of state or federal law that defines offenses against the public and provides punishments for their commission.

Cumulative voting A system, permitted by most state statutes, whereby a shareholder can cast all of his or her votes (shares owned multiplied by the number of directors to be elected) for one candidate.

Cure The act of correcting a defective tender or delivery of goods.

Debtor in possession In bankruptcy law, a debtor who is allowed to continue to operate the business after the commencement of bankruptcy proceedings. The debtor in possession has the rights and duties of a trustee in bankruptcy.

Debtor's estate In the law of bankruptcy, the various property interests either owned by the debtor at the commencement of a bankruptcy case or recoverable for the estate by the trustee in bankruptcy from someone other than the debtor.

Deceit (action for deceit) An action at law based upon a misrepresentation or contrivance by which one deceives another who has no means of detecting the fraud, to the injury and damage of such person.

De facto corporation An organization that operates as a corporation, whose organizers have made an unsuccessful attempt in "good faith" to comply with the state enabling statute. Only the state can challenge the existence of a de facto corporation.

De jure corporation A corporation that has all the legal characteristics of a corporation and whose incorporators have substantially complied with the enabling statute of the state of incorporation.

Delegatee See *Delegation.*

Delegation The authorizing, by a person under a duty of performance, of another person to render the required performance. The person who does the authorizing is the *delegator.* The person authorized to carry out the performance is the *delegatee.*

Delegator See *Delegation.*

Demise As used in law, a transfer of real property or of an interest in real property.

Demurrer A document, filed by the defendent in a lawsuit, by which the defendant challenges the court's jurisdiction or the legal sufficiency of the plaintiff's complaint. Usually a form of pleading which admits the facts alleged but asserts that they do not constitute a cause of action. Discussed in Chapter 3.

De novo See *Trial de novo.*

Derivative suit An action filed in the corporate name by one or more shareholders to enforce a corporate cause of action.

Destination bill of lading See *Bill of lading.*

Destination contract A contract in which the seller is required to make delivery at the point of destination.

Devise A gift by will of real property.

Directed verdict A verdict entered for either the plaintiff or the defendant, not as a result of jury deliberation, but as a result of the judge ordering the entry. A directed verdict is ordered only if the facts are so clear that the jury could not reasonably reach a verdict for the other party. Discussed in Chapter 3.

Disaffirmance The setting aside or avoiding of a contract or obligation which can be avoided legally.

Discharge To extinguish an obligation, whether by performance or otherwise. The termination of a contractual obligation.

Disclaimer A denial, especially a denial that a warranty was made or is effective.

Discount In a general sense, to sell for less than face value. In banking, the taking of interest in advance.

Dishonor Refusal or failure to pay or accept a negotiable instrument that has been properly presented for payment or acceptance.

Dissolution The termination of a corporation by legislative act, by judicial decree, by voluntary action of the shareholders, or by expiration of the period of time for which the corporation was formed. With reference to a partnership, dissolution is a preparatory step to its termination (see Chapter 41).

Dividends Distribution from corporate assets (usually earned surplus), made on a pro rata basis to shareholders of a designated class of stock, as authorized by the corporation's board of directors. Also, *in the law of insurance,* the difference between (a) the premium charged for a policy plus earnings from investing the premium and (b) the lower amount justified by the actual loss and expense experience of the insurer. An insurance dividend may be viewed as a refund of a part of the premium initially charged for the insurance.

Dock receipt See *Document of title.*

Dock warrant See *Document of title.*

Document of title A writing that is treated as adequately evidencing that the person in possession of it is entitled to receive, hold, and dispose of the document and the goods it covers. Documents of title include *bills of lading, dock warrants, dock receipts, and warehouse receipts.*

Domestic corporation A corporation which is doing business in the state of incorporation.

Double jeopardy A second prosecution after a prior prosecution for the same offense, transaction, or omission.

Drawee The person, bank, or firm that is ordered by the drawer of a draft or check to make payment to a payee.

Drawer The person, bank, or firm that issues a draft or check and thereby orders the drawee to make payment to the payee.

Due process The administration of law in accordance with rules and forms which have been established for the protection of private rights. *Procedural due process* requires a fair hearing or the right to one. *Substantive due process* requires that laws not be arbitrary, unreasonably discriminatory, or demonstrably irrelevant to the matter which the law purports to govern.

Duress Any wrongful or illegal coercion, by threat or other means, that overcomes the free will or judgment of a person and induces the person to do something he or she otherwise would not do.

Ecclesiastic law   Law developed and enforced by church authorities. In the United States, ecclesiastical law is not enforceable by governmental authority.

Emancipation   "The act by which one who was under the control of another is set at liberty and made his own master." (c)

Enforceable contract   One for the breach of which the law gives a remedy.

Enjoin   Prohibit. Ordinarily, a party files a lawsuit and requests the court to issue an injunction against the defendant; the injunction "enjoins" the defendant from certain conduct.

Equity   A body of law developed by the English Courts of Chancery to supplement the rigid common law of the time. The Courts of Chancery developed new remedies and flexible procedures for cases where the remedy at law (damages) was inadequate. The word equity implies fairness and a wise discretion in the formulation and application of equitable remedies. Also, an ownership interest in property.

Equity securities   Shares of capital stock representing a shareholder's proportionate ownership interest in the corporation as a whole.

Estoppel   "Estoppel is a bar or impediment which precludes allegation or denial of a certain fact or state of facts, in consequence of previous allegation or denial or conduct or admission, or in consequence of a final adjudication of the matter in a court of law." (c)

Exclusive dealing contract   A contract in which a buyer (e.g., a retailer) agrees to deal exclusively with the goods of one seller.

Executed contract   One that has been fully performed by both parties.

Execution (of judgment at law)   The process of procuring a writ of execution from the clerk of court and having the sheriff seize the defendant's property and sell it to satisfy the judgment.

Executive committee   In a corporation, a committee composed entirely of board members who are authorized by majority vote of the board of directors to make corporate management decisions (not involving extraordinary transactions) during intervals between board meetings.

Executor   A person or entity designated by a testator in a will to carry out the testator's wishes concerning the disposition of the testator's property after his or her death.

Executory contract   One in which neither party has rendered the promised performance.

Exoneration   An act freeing another from blame; the discharge of an obligation.

Experience rating   In insurance, the process of adjusting the premium to reflect, for renewal years, the actual loss experience of the insured.

Ex post facto law   A law imposing a criminal sanction upon a person for an act that, when committed, was not criminal. Ex post facto laws are unconstitutional.

Express authority   The authority explicitly given by a principal to an agent, either in writing or orally.

Express contract   One in which the terms of the contract are stated in words, either written or spoken.

Express powers   In constitutional law, the powers specifically named by a constitution. The Constitution of the United States specifically grants certain powers (called "express" or "enumerated" powers) to the federal government.

Express warranty   See *Warranty*.

Ex rel.   Abbreviation for "ex relatione," meaning "upon relation" or information. "Legal proceedings which are instituted by the attorney general (or other proper person) in the name and behalf of the state, but on the information and at the instigation of an individual who has a private interest in the matter." (c) See, for example, Case 42.3, *State ex rel. Carlton v. Triplett*.

Extension plan   See *Composition plan*.

FAS   Free alongside a vessel.

FOB (*fob*)   Free on board.

Face value   The nominal value of a security as expressed on its face, for example, the par value of a share of stock, or the amount due and payable on a bond, according to its terms.

Federal Procurement Regulations (FPR)   A system of regulations prescribed by the Administrator of General Services under the Federal Property and Administrative Services Act of 1949 (5 U.S.C. 630) which establish uniform policies and procedures applicable to the procurement of personal property and nonpersonal services (including construction) by the executive agencies of the government except the Department of Defense.

Fiction   An assumption of law that something that is or may be false is true. It is a legal fiction to say that a corporation is a person. Also, an assumption of law of a state of facts that does not exist or that has never existed.

Fictitious name A counterfeit, feigned, or pretended name taken by a person, differing in some essential particular from his or her true name; a name adopted to identify a business concern.

Fiduciary relationship A relation between persons regarding a business, contract, or property, or regarding the general business or estate of one of them, of such a character that each must repose trust and confidence in the other and must exercise the utmost degree of fairness and good faith.

Field warehousing A secured transaction for the financing of business inventory. The inventory used as collateral is segregated in a fenced-off area of the borrower's premises and is placed under the control of an independent warehouse.

Financing statement A writing that is filed in the public records to give notice of the creditor's security interest in collateral.

Firm offer In the law of sales, an offer in which the offeror promises to hold the offer open, usually for a certain period of time.

Fixture An article that was personal property but which has been attached to real property with the intent that it become a permanent part of the real property.

Floating lien A security interest in both present and future assets of the debtor instead of a security interest only in specific assets on hand at the creation of the secured transaction. Floating liens are created by the use of *after-acquired property clauses*.

Foreign corporation A corporation that is doing business in a state other than the state of incorporation.

Formal advertising Under statutes and regulations applicable to the federal government, the public invitation for a reasonable time to prospective bidders to submit bids upon a proposed procurement; a process involving the letting of a contract after open, competitive bidding subsequent to advertising for bidders for a sufficient time with specifications sufficiently descriptive to permit full and free competition consistent with the procurement of the property and services needed, and thereupon the award of the contract to the lowest and best responsive responsible bidder.

Formal contract A contract to which the law gives special effect because of the form used in creating it;

for example, a negotiable instrument such as a check is a formal contract because to create a negotiable instrument, a person must use a particular form or style of language.

Four-corner rule In the law of commercial paper, the rule that whether an instrument is unconditional is to be determined solely by what is expressed on the face of the instrument.

Franchise A contract in which the owner (franchisor) of intangible property such as a trademark or trade name, authorizes another (franchisee) to use such property in the operation of a business within described territory.

Fraud "An intentional perversion of truth for the purpose of inducing another in reliance upon it to part with something of value or to surrender a legal right; a false representation of a matter of fact, whether by words or by conduct, by misleading or false allegations, or by concealment of that which should have been disclosed, which deceives and is intended to deceive another so that the person deceived shall act upon it to his or her legal injury." (c)

Fraudulent transfer In bankruptcy law, a transfer of property by the debtor within 1 year preceding bankruptcy, where the debtor was insolvent when the transfer was made and where the debtor received less than a reasonable equivalent value for the transfer. A fraudulent transfer can occur under circumstances other than those just described. Also called a *fraudulent conveyance*.

Full warranty A written consumer product warranty that meets the four minimum standards or requirements of the Magnuson-Moss Warranty act.

Fungible Equivalent. Goods are fungible if by their nature or by usage of trade one unit is the equivalent of any other unit.

Future-advances clause A clause in a security agreement that permits the collateral of the debtor to be used to secure future loans.

Future goods Goods which are not both existing and identified to the contract for their sale.

Garnishment A legal procedure by means of which a creditor acquires money or other property of a debtor where the property is in the hands of some other person, such as a bank or an employer.

General Accounting Office A government agency established by the act of June 10, 1921 (31 U.S.C. 41–61), headed by the Comptroller General, to make investigations of matters relating to the receipt, disbursement, and application of public funds and to report the results to the Congress with appropriate recommendations.

Good faith   In the law of sales, honesty in fact in the conduct or transaction concerned. With regard to a merchant, good faith is honesty in fact and the observance of reasonable commercial standards of fair dealing in the trade.

Goodwill   The "advantage or benefit that has been acquired by a proprietor in carrying on a business, whether connected with the premises in which the business is conducted, with the name under which it is managed, or with any other matter carrying with it a benefit to the business." (c)

Government contract   Any type of commitment that obligates the federal government to an expenditure of funds; the instrument by which the federal government agrees to purchase supplies, services, construction, research and development, or other things.

Grab law   Law, usually state law, that permits unpaid creditors to seize and sell the property of the debtor.

Graded rate   In property insurance, a reduced premium rate that is applied when a person approaches insuring his or her property for full value. Graded rates reflect the fact that there are more partial than full losses and are a means, seldom used, for assuring that people who underinsure their property receive no more indemnity per dollar of premiums than do people who insure for full value.

Grantee   One to whom a grant is made. In property law, the person to whom real property is granted and conveyed.

Grantor   "The person by whom a grant is made. A transferor of property." (c)

Group boycott   Joint refusal to deal. Joint action for the purpose of restricting a competitor's access to markets or sources of supplies

Group insurance   Insurance in which the insurer undertakes to insure every person in the group without regard to the insurability of individuals. The insurer issues one detailed *master contract* to the group policyholder, but only brief certificates to individual members of the group. Many group policies are experience rated.

Guarantor   In the law of commercial paper, a signer who adds "Payment guaranteed" or equivalent words to the signature and thereby promises that if the instrument is not paid when due, he or she will pay it without insisting on resort to any other party.

Hearsay evidence   Statements, made in court by a witness, involving not personal knowledge or observation but mere repetition of what he or she has heard others say.

Heir   Under modern law, a person who inherits from another real or personal property or an interest in such property. Formerly, one who inherits by virtue of the laws of descent and distribution.

Holder   A person who is in possession of an instrument drawn, issued, or indorsed to him or to his order or to bearer or in blank.

Holder in due course   A *holder* who takes an instrument for value, in good faith, and without notice that it is overdue or that it has been dishonored or that there is any defense against or claim to it on the part of any person.

Horizontal merger   A combination of two firms at the same level, e.g., two manufacturers, two wholesalers, or two retailers.

Identification   In the law of sales, the act of designating goods as the subject of a particular contract of sale.

Illusory   Deceptive. For example, an "illusory promise is an expression that is cloaked in promissory terms [but that] actually promises nothing because it leaves to the speaker [or writer] the choice of performance or nonperformance." (c)

Impairment   In bankruptcy law, the adverse impact of a plan of reorganization that gives a claimant less than the full value of his or her claim or interest.

Implied contract   One in which the terms of the contract are wholly or partly inferred from conduct or from surrounding circumstances.

Implied powers   In constitutional law, powers that are not specifically named in a constitution but which are necessary and proper for carrying out the express powers. See *Express powers*.

Implied warranty   See *Warranty*.

Incentive contract   A form of government contract that provides for a graduated compensation to the contractor dependent upon the degree of accomplishment of defined target objectives.

Incontestability   An inability, imposed by law or by contract, of an insurer to avoid a policy for concealment, breach of warranty, or misrepresentation. Also, a non-contest clause in a will.

Incorporation   The process (as established in state statutes) by which a corporation is formed.

Incorporator Person who organizes a corporation by signing and filing the articles of incorporation with the designated officer of the state.

Indemnification (to indemnify) The compensation or payment of a damage another sustains. In legal terms, it may also mean to give security against the possibility of future damage or loss; for instance, an insurance company undertakes to *indemnify* its policy holders against loss.

Indemnity Reimbursement for loss.

Indemnity principle The theory that in the event of casualty an insured should be limited to reimbursement (indemnity) for loss actually suffered, because insurance is a system for distributing losses and not for generating a profit for insureds. The principle is especially applicable in liability, property, and health insurance.

Independent contractor One who, exercising an independent employment, contracts to do certain work according to his or her own methods and without being subject to the control of an employer except as to the results to be accomplished.

Indictment An accusation in writing found and presented by a grand jury that a person named in the indictment has done some act or has been guilty of some omission which by law is a public offense.

Indorsement A signature customarily found on the back of commercial paper; made by a person other than a maker, drawer, or acceptor; and ordinarily resulting in secondary liability on the instrument. An indorsement is in-blank or special, nonrestrictive or restrictive, *and* unqualified or qualified. A *special indorsement* maintains the order character of an order instrument or gives order character to a bearer instrument. A *restrictive indorsement* specifies a use to which the proceeds of the instrument must be put. A *qualified indorsement* protects the indorser from liability on the instrument but not for liability for breach of warranty.

Informal contract One for which the law does not prescribe a particular form in order for the contract to be enforceable.

Information In criminal law, a formal accusation of crime similar to an indictment but preferred (made) by a competent prosecuting official, such as a district attorney instead of by a grand jury.

Inherently dangerous activity "Danger inhering in an instrumentality or condition itself at all times, so as to require special precautions to prevent injury, [the danger involved arising] not from the mere casual or

collateral negligence of others with respect thereto under the particular circumstances." (c)

Inheritance Something obtained by operation of law from a person who dies without leaving a valid will and, under modern usage, by virtue of the provisions of a will.

Injunction An equitable remedy in which a court orders a person to do or to refrain from doing something.

In re the matter of; regarding. "The usual method of entitling a judicial proceeding in which there are not adversary parties but merely some [matter]concerning which judicial action is to be taken, such as a bankrupt's estate." (c) See, for example, Case 28.2, *In re Bishop.*

Insanity A mental derangement due to a disease of the mind. An insane person is without legal competence to enter into a contract or to make a will; proof of insanity may free an accused person from responsibility for a criminal act. Tests for insanity differ in contract law, probate law, and criminal law.

Insurable interest A financial stake in property or in someone's life that will justify the person who has that stake in insuring the property or life.

Insurance A contractual means of transferring and distributing the risk of financial loss.

Inter alia Latin: Among other things.

Interlocking directorates A practice in which members on the board of directors of one corporation also serve as directors of other corporations.

Interpretation The process of discovering and explaining the meaning of any unclear language, for example, of a statute or a contract. See *Construction.*

Interstate commerce Commercial intercourse, communication, transportation of persons or property between or among two or more states of the Union.

Inter vivos "Between the living; from one living person to another. Where property passes by conveyance, the transaction is said to be inter vivos, to distinguish it from [a transfer upon death]." (c)

Intestate "Without making a will. A person is said to die intestate when he dies without making a will." (c)

Intrastate Activity or territory that is wholly within a state of the Union.

Intra vires doctrine "An act is said to be intra vires (within the power) of a person or corporation when it is within the scope of his or its powers or authority." (c)

Ipso facto "By the fact itself; by the mere fact." (c)

Issue Under the laws of descent and distribution, all persons who have descended from a common ancestor; also, the child or children of an individual and of their children.

Jingle rule The rule of partnership law that the creditors of partners have first claim to assets of the partners and that creditors of the partnership have first claim to the partnership assets. This rule has been modified by the Bankruptcy Code for situations to which the Code applies.

Joint and several liability The liability of the various defendants is said to be joint and several when a plaintiff, at his option may sue and establish liability of persons separately, or sue all of them together. For example, if a plaintiff is a victim of a tort committed by several tortfeasors, they have joint and several liability, that is, the plaintiff may sue only one, or elect to sue all of them.

Joint tortfeasors Includes: (1) persons who have acted together by agreement for the purpose of injuring another; and (2) persons who have acted independently but have caused a single indivisible injury.

Judgment nonwithstanding the verdict ("judgment n.o.v.") A judgment entered by the judge for the losing party in a jury trial, thus reversing the verdict of the jury. The trial judge will overrule the jury only if there is no substantial evidence to support their decision.

Jurisdiction The power of a court to hear and decide cases.

Jurisprudence "The philosophy of law, or the science which treats of the principles of . . . law and legal relations." (c) Also, a body of law.

Laches See *Statute of limitations*.

Law merchant A forerunner of modern commercial law, based on the customs of merchants.

Legacy A bequest (gift by will) of money.

Legal entity An entity, other than a natural person, existing in contemplation of law and having the legal rights and duties of a separate person, for example, a corporation.

Legal fiction See *Fiction*.

Legal reserve fund See *Cash surrender value*.

Level premium A life insurance premium fixed at a certain amount for the duration of the contract. The premium is larger than needed to pay claims and expenses during the early years of the contract. The excess is invested to provide funds to pay increasingly frequent future claims.

Libel "A method of defamation expressed by print, writing, pictures, or signs. In its most general sense, any publication that is injurious to the reputation of another." (c)

Lien A claim or charge against property. A lien may be imposed by contract but is usually allowed by law to secure, for example, the claims of mechanics or other artisans for work done on property, or to secure the claim of a government for unpaid taxes.

Limited partnership A partnership consisting of one or more general partners, jointly and severally responsible as ordinary partners, by whom the business is conducted, and one or more special partners, who are not liable for the debts of the partnership beyond the funds contributed, and who do not participate in the firm's management.

Limited warranty A written consumer product warranty that does not conform with the standards imposed by the Magnuson-Moss Warranty Act for a full warranty.

Liquidated damages An amount of money provided for as a remedy for breach of contract by the contract itself.

Liquidation proceeding A bankruptcy proceeding the object of which is to convert the debtor's nonexempt assets into cash, to distribute it in accordance with the scheme of distribution provided by the Bankruptcy Code, and to grant the honest debtor a discharge from most of the remaining debts.

"Long-arm" statute A statute conferring jurisdiction over out-of-state defendants.

Majority shareholders Shareholders who collectively own a majority of the voting shares of a corporation and who exercise control over the corporation by electing directors, amending articles, and making decisions on extraordinary transactions.

Mandamus "We command." A command issued by a court of competent jurisdiction to an inferior court, corporation, or person.

Maritime law The law relating to harbors, ships, and seafarers. See *Admiralty jurisdiction*.

Master contract In group insurance, the detailed insurance policy held by the group policyholder, to be contrasted with the brief certificate held by each member of the group.

Merchant   In the law of sales, a person who deals in goods of the kind involved in the transaction. Also, a person who by occupation holds himself or herself out as having knowledge or skill peculiar to the practices or goods involved in the transaction, and a person to whom such knowledge or skill may be attributed by his or her employment of an intermediary who by occupation holds himself or herself out as having such knowledge or skill.

Merger   In corporation law, the absorption of one corporation by another: the latter acquires all the assets and assumes all the liabilities of the "target" corporation which then ceases to exist.

Minor   A person under the age at which the law recognizes a capacity to contract. The age of "majority," 21 at common law, is now 18 in many states.

Minority shareholders   Shareholders whose collective voting rights are insufficient to elect a corporation's board of directors or otherwise control management decisions.

Model Business Corporation Act   A model corporation statute designed by The American Law Institute and the American Bar Association to meet the changing needs of modern business corporations and to encourage a greater degree of uniformity in state laws governing the incorporation and operation of corporations. (See Appendix 3.)

Monopoly power   In antitrust law, the power to fix prices, exclude competitors, or control the market in a given geographical area.

Moral hazard   Any characteristic of a potential recipient of insurance proceeds that will increase the frequency or severity of loss—poor health habits or a tendency toward fraud, for example.

Moral turpitude   An act which is regarded as immoral; conduct which is contrary to justice and honesty.

Necessaries   "Food, clothing, lodging, medical service, and a suitable place of residence; [they are considered absolutely necessary; also whatever else] is ordinarily necessary and suitable, in view of the rank, position, fortune, earning capacity, and mode of living of the [spouse or parent]." (c)

Negotiation   With reference to contracts, the exploring or discussing through oral or written communication of the terms and conditions of a contract preliminary to the making of a final contract. With reference to commercial paper, the *transferring* of a negotiable instrument to another.

Nolo contendere   A plea to a criminal charge which neither admits nor denys guilt. Such a plea cannot be used as an admission of guilt for purposes of a related civil suit.

Nominal damages   Usually $1.00. Awarded to a plaintiff who wins a case and receives a judgment but is unable to prove any harm or loss.

Nonprofit corporation   A corporation that is formed for charitable, religious, educational, or fraternal purposes which are not profit-oriented. No part of income may be distributed to members, and assets can only be distributed to members when the corporation is dissolved.

No-par stock   Authorized stock to which "no par" value is assigned by the articles of incorporation. Upon issuance, the directors fix the per-share subscription price, but the amount is not stated on the certificate.

n.o.v. (non obstante veredicto)   Notwithstanding the verdict. A judgment entered by order of a court for the plaintiff although there has been a jury verdict for the defendant.

Novation   The substitution of a new obligation for an old one with the result that the old obligation is thereby extinguished.

Nullity   "Nothing; no proceeding; an act or proceeding in a cause which the opposite party may treat as though it had not taken place, or which has absolutely no legel force or effect." (c)

Obligee   A person to whom an obligation or duty is owed.

Obligor   A person who owes a duty to someone else, that is, a person who has an obligation to perform.

Offer   A statement or other conduct by which the offeror confers upon the offeree a legal power to accept the offer and thereby to create a contract.

Open term   Some aspect or detail of a contract which the parties have not agreed upon but have, instead, left undecided.

Option   An offer for which the offeree pays (or gives other valuable consideration) to keep the offer open for a stated period of time. Sometimes called *option contract.*

Order paper   See *Commercial paper.*

Output contract   A contract in which one party agrees to purchase the total production of the other party. Also, a contract in which the seller agrees to sell his or her total production to the other party.

Pari delicto   Parties equally at fault.

Par stock   Shares of stock that have been assigned a

fixed "par" value in the articles of incorporation. The par value of one share is printed on each certificate evidencing par stock.

Penal damages A harsh monetary penalty provided for by a contract, to coerce the performance of the contract. Penal damages clauses are not enforceable because the amount of damages provided for is not related to actual damages caused by breach of the contract.

Per capita Literally, "by the head." In inheritance laws, a method of distribution of the estate of a decedent where the persons designated are to receive equal shares, taking in their own right.

Per curiam By the court. Opinion of the whole court, as contrasted with an opinion written by one justice.

Perfection In the law of secured transactions, the name of the process by which a security interest is made enforceable against subsequent lien creditors and certain other persons having a right in the collateral.

Perfect tender rule A rule of law, often relaxed by the UCC, that a buyer may elect to reject goods if the goods or the tender of delivery fails in any respect to conform to the contract.

Peril A cause of loss such as fire, flood, theft, or vandalism.

Per se In and of itself; inherently.

Personal property floater A type of property insurance that applies to movable property, whatever its location.

Per stirpes A method of distribution of the estate of a decedent whereby heirs take the shares their respective deceased ancestor (e.g., parent, grandparent, etc.) would have taken if he or she had been living.

Piercing the corporate veil The process whereby a court disregards the separateness of the corporation from its shareholders and holds them liable for fraudulent or other wrongful conduct that injures third parties.

Plea bargain A plea of guilty to a lesser charge in exchange for an agreed punishment or for the recommendation by the prosecutor to the judge of a lesser punishment than may have been imposed for the offense originally charged.

Pledge A transaction in which a debtor gives possession of the debtor's personal property to the creditor as security for repayment of a loan.

Police power The power vested in a state legislature to make laws for the welfare of the state and its residents.

Pooling A process of treating as a single group a large number of individual risks of a certain kind so that the total loss likely to be sustained by the group of insureds can be accurately estimated.

Power The ability to do any act; in agency law, the *authority* to do an act which the grantor might himself or herself lawfully perform; an authority by which one person enables another to do some act for him or her.

Predatory pricing In antitrust law, the prohibited practice of refraining from maximizing profits until competitors are driven out of the market.

Preempt To take exclusive control, as where the federal government, in accordance with the Constitution, expressly denies the states the right to regulate an activity, or enacts a comprehensive scheme of regulation which by implication precludes state regulation.

Preemptive right The right of a stockholder to preserve his or her proportionate stock interest by purchasing shares of a new issue ahead of others.

Preference In bankruptcy law, a transfer of property by the debtor that enables an unsecured creditor to receive a greater percentage of his or her claim against the debtor than the creditor would have received in a distribution of the debtor's assets pursuant to a Chapter 7 liquidation.

Preferential transfer See *Preference.*

Preferred stock A class of stock that has superior rights to dividends and, upon dissolution of the corporation, to corporate assets.

Present sale See *Sale.*

Pretermitted In inheritance law, a child or other descendant not mentioned or provided for in an ancestor's will and who had not been otherwise provided for by the testator. Also, sometimes used to designate a spouse who is not provided for in a will.

Price discrimination In antitrust law, a practice whereby a seller charges two or more buyers different prices for an identical product or service.

Prima facie "On the face of it; . . . a fact presumed to be true unless disproved by some evidence to the contrary." (c)

Primary party A signer of a negotiable instrument who is liable for payment immediately and unconditionally when the instrument comes due. To be contrasted with a *secondary* party, whose liability is conditional because it normally does not arise until after presentment, dishonor, and notice of dishonor.

Prime contract   A contract between the government and a contractor. Such a contractor is a *prime contractor*.

Primogeniture   An English system whereby the eldest son had the exclusive right to inherit the estate of his ancestor. Not used in the United States.

Principal   A person primarily liable for an obligation; a person who, being competent to do an act for his or her own benefit on his or her own account, authorizes another to serve as his or her agent for such purpose.

Priority claim   In bankruptcy law, an allowed, unsecured claim that is, by statute, to be paid before claims of lower rank may be paid. The Bankruptcy Code lists six classes of priority claims.

Private corporation   A profit or nonprofit corporation organized by individuals, as opposed to one formed by the government.

Private law   Law dealing with the relationships among private persons and organizations.

Privity of contract   A relationship that exists between contracting parties because of the contract. A person usually must be in privity of contract in order to bring suit on it. However, the absence of privity of contract between a manufacturer and a remote purchaser of goods is not ordinarily a good defense to a suit brought against the manufacturer by a plaintiff on the ground of negligence or breach of warranty.

Probate   The act or process of proving the validity of a will; also, the name generally given to all proceedings within the jurisdiction of a probate court.

Procedural due process   See *Due process*.

Procedural law   That law which specifies the formal steps to be followed in enforcing or asserting rights, duties, privileges, or immunities. Also called "adjective" law.

Promise   A manifestation of intention to act or to refrain from acting in a specified way, so made as to justify a promisee in understanding that a commitment has been made.

Promissory estoppel   A doctrine or rule of law that forbids or "estops" a promisor to avoid liability for the consequences of a promise on which the promisee has justifiably relied (sometimes called the "doctrine of justifiable reliance").

Promotor   The person(s) who plans the organization of a corporation.

Promulgate   To announce officially; to make known publicly as important or obligatory.

Proof of claim   In bankruptcy law, a document by means of which a creditor seeks payment from the debtor's estate.

Pro rata   Proportionate.

Pro rata share   Where funds are insufficient to pay a class of bankruptcy claims in full, the percentage of the claim that each creditor of that class will receive.

Proxy   A person who is authorized by another person to represent or act for him or her at a meeting. With reference to corporations, a person authorized to vote a shareholder's shares at a shareholders' meeting. The term is used also to mean the writing that authorizes a person to vote the shares of another at a shareholders' meeting.

Public corporation   A corporation created for governmental purposes by any agency or subdivision of state or federal government.

Public law   Law dealing with the organization of government and with the relation of the government to the people.

Puffing   See *Sales puffing*.

Punitive damages   "Damages other than compensatory damages that may be awarded against a person to punish him for outrageous conduct [or to set] an example for similar wrongdoers." (c)

Purchase-money security interest   A security interest taken or retained by a seller or other financer in financing the purchase or leasing of the collateral.

Qualified indorsement   See *Indorsement*.

Quasi   Resembling, possessing some of the attributes of something else. An administrative agency may have a quasi-judicial and a quasi-legislative function. In its *quasi-judicial* function it hears and disposes of disputes in the manner of a court. In its *quasi-legislative* function it makes rules and regulations of relatively general application, in the manner of a legislature.

Quasi contract   A restitutionary remedy for an obligation imposed by law, intended to prevent the unjust enrichment of a person upon whom a benefit has been conferred. Under the law of quasi contract, the plaintiff may recover the reasonable value of the property or services conferred, despite the absence of a contract.

Quasi-judicial   See *Quasi*.

Quasi-legislative   See *Quasi*.

Quasi-public corporation A profit corporation privately organized for purposes which affect the public interest to an extent requiring special state or federal regulation, for example, a bank or insurance company.

Quiet title A proceeding filed for the purpose of establishing one's ownership of property.

Quorum The number of qualified persons (usually a majority of the entire body) required to be present at a meeting in order to conduct business. With reference to corporations, the number of qualified persons (shares represented in person or by proxy) required to conduct business lawfully at a shareholders' meeting. Also, the number of directors required to be present to conduct business lawfully at a directors' meeting.

Ratable Proportional.

Ratification Confirmation of a previous act or promise. With reference to a minor, a manifestation by a minor, upon reaching majority, of an intention to be bound by a contract entered into during the period of minority. With reference to agency law, "the adoption and confirmation by one party with knowledge of all material facts, of an act or contract performed or entered into in his behalf by another who, at the time, assumed without authority to act as his agent." (c)

Reaffirmation agreement An agreement by a debtor to pay a debt that has been discharged in bankruptcy.

Redemption The exercise by a corporation of a right to buy back outstanding shares at a fixed price.

Reformation A contractual remedy in which a court rewrites or corrects a contract so that it reveals the bargain of the parties.

Regular dealer A person (or firm) who owns, operates, or maintains a store, warehouse, or other establishment in which materials, articles, or equipment are bought, kept in stock, and sold to the public in the usual course of business.

Reinsurance A contractual arrangement in which an insurance company transfers a part of the group risk it has assumed to another insurer called a reinsurer.

Release A discharge from liability.

Relevant market The geographic area of effective competition in which a particular product as well as other interchangeable products are traded.

Remand To send back; usually the sending back of a court record or case by a higher court to the court from which a decision, order, or judgment originated, for the purpose of having the originating court take the action dictated by the higher court.

Reorganization proceeding In bankruptcy law, a proceeding in which a debtor firm and its creditors negotiate a plan for the adjustment and discharge of debts. A reorganization permits a financially troubled firm to stay in business while it undergoes a process of financial rehabilitation.

Replevin An action taken to acquire possession of goods.

Requirements contract A contract in which one party agrees to purchase from the other party all the goods or services which the purchasing party needs in his or her business.

Resale price maintenance In antitrust law, the practice of a seller fixing the resale price terms of the buyer at a lower level in the chain of distribution. This practice is also known as "*vertical price-fixing.*"

Rescission (to rescind) The setting aside or avoiding of a contract, transaction, or other obligation that can be set aside legally. Used primarily with reference to the avoidance of an agreement, such as the repudiation of a sales contract by one of the parties to it or a principal's repudiation of an unauthorized act by an agent undertaken beyond his or her authority.

Res ipsa loquitur A Latin expression meaning "the thing (or incident) speaks for itself." Under the doctrine of *res ipsa loquitur*, the defendant may be required to prove that he or she was *not* negligent where the injury-causing instrumentality was completely within the control of the defendant.

Respondeat superior A maxim meaning "Let the master answer." The doctrine under which a master (employer) can be held liable for the wrongful acts of his or her servant (employee) performed within the scope of employment.

Restitution In the law of contracts, compensation for or the return of partial performances. In general, the return of a thing.

Resulting trust A trust relationship imposed by a court of equity to carry into effect the presumed intentions of the parties.

Restrictive endorsement See *Indorsement.*

Reverse, to An order reversing, overthrowing or setting aside a judgment, order, or decree previously entered by a court.

Revocation of offer The withdrawal of the offer by the offeror.

Rider An attachment to an insurance policy that modifies the contract in some way.

Rule of reason In antitrust law, the rule that conduct which unreasonably restrains trade is illegal.

Sale (of goods) The passing of title to goods from the seller to the buyer, in return for a consideration called the price. In a *present sale*, title passes at the time the sales transaction is entered into. In a *contract to sell*, title passes to the buyer at some future time. UCC Article 2 covers both present sales and contracts to sell. The term *contract for sale* includes present sales and contracts to sell.

Sale on approval A sale of goods in which the buyer is not obligated until the buyer accepts, that is, approves, the goods.

Sale or return A transaction in which the buyer of goods purchases them for resale but has a right to return to the seller any unsold goods.

Sales puffing Exaggeration and other nonfactual seller's talk intended to induce a sale.

Sanction A punishment. However, sanction may also mean "approval."

Scienter A necessary element of the tort of fraud and deceit which requires the plaintiff to prove that at the time false representations were made, the defendant knew they were false. Scienter is a necessary element required to be proved in most violations of federal antitrust and securities laws.

Seasonably In a timely manner.

Secondary party See *Primary party*.

Secret lien A claim against the property of another person, the acquisition of which is unknown to the general public because the claim has not been filed in the public records or otherwise has not been made known to the public.

Secured transaction Any arrangement made by agreement of the parties for the purpose of providing a creditor with a backup source of payment if the debtor defaults. In a *surety* arrangement, a person or a firm makes a backup promise to pay the debt in the event that the debtor defaults. In a *secured transaction in personal property*, personal property is the collateral and may be sold in the event of the debtor's default.

Secured transaction in personal property See *Secured transaction*.

Security An investment in a common enterprise in which the investor usually profits solely from the efforts of others. If the investment is in a corporation, it is usually evidenced by a stock or bond certificate issued in bearer or registered form.

Security agreement An agreement between the debtor and the creditor that the creditor is to have a security interest in the collateral. Unless the creditor is to possess the collateral, the security agreement must be in writing.

Security interest Some interest in property, such as possession or title, which a creditor retains or acquires to secure the payment of a debt.

Separation of powers In constitutional law, the doctrine that each branch of government (judicial, legislative, executive) should be allowed to exercise its constitutional prerogatives without undue interference by the other branches.

Servant A person employed to perform work or services for another, whose physical conduct in the performance of the work or service and the means by which it will be accomplished are subject to the control of the person, (generally called a "master" or "employer") for whom it is being performed.

Settlement option Any of several ways of receiving the proceeds of a life insurance policy upon its maturity.

Shareholder A person who owns a proportionate ownership interest in a corporation; usually such ownership is evidenced by a stock certificate.

Share of stock An equity security that represents a proportionate ownership interest in a corpration and evidences the rights which the shareholde has in the management, profits, and assets of the corporation.

Shelter provision The provision of the Uniform Commercial Code that gives holders through a holder in due course the same freedom from claims and defenses that a holder in due course enjoys. The shelter provision reflects the principle that a person may assign whatever rights he or she has.

Shipment contract A contract in which the seller is required or authorized to send goods to the buyer and is not required to deliver them at a particular destination.

Shop-right privilege The right of an employer to use without payment of royalties an invention conceived by an employee in the course of employment, or through use of the employer's facilities, the employee not having been hired to perform such work.

Shortswing transactions Those transactions under Section 16 of the Securities Exchange Act of 1934, in which a director, officer, or beneficial owner of more than 10 percent of any class of nonexempt securities buys and sells (or sells and buys) the company's securities within a 6-month period. The profits from such transactions belong to the corporation.

Slander "The speaking of base and defamatory words tending to prejudice another in his reputation, office, trade, business, or means of livelihood; oral defamation." (c)

Small business concern Generally, an independently owned and operated concern, not dominant in the field of operations in which it is bidding, that, with its affiliates, employs fewer than 500 employees, or that is certified as a small business concern by the Small Business Administration.

Special indorsement See *Indorsement*.

Specific performance An equitable remedy under which a person is entitled to a contractual performance rather than to money damages for breach of the contract. Specific performance is granted where the remedy at law (damages) is inadequate.

Specification A clear and accurate description of the technical requirements for a material, product, or service to be purchased, including the procedure for determining that the requirements have been met.

Standing In antitrust law, a doctrine requiring the plaintiff to prove that the defendant's violation was a substantial or direct cause of the plaintiff's injury which can be measured with some certainty in money terms, and that the defendant's illegal act affected legally protected activities of the plaintiff.

Stare decisis Latin. To abide by, or adhere to. A doctrine that precedents set by decisions in previous cases are to be followed in later cases involving the same point unless there is a compelling reason to depart from precedent.

Stated capital That portion of the issuance price of the outstanding shares of stock that is set aside in the capital stock account.

Statute of frauds A statute intended "to close the door on numerous frauds and perjuries. Its chief characteristic is the provision that no suit or action shall be maintained on certain classes of contracts or engagements unless there shall be a note or memorandum thereof in writing signed by the party to be charged or by his authorized agent." (c)

Statute of limitations "A statute prescribing limitations to the right of action on certain described causes of action or criminal prosecutions; that is, declaring that no suit shall be maintained on such causes of action, nor any criminal charge be made, unless brought within a specified period of time after the right accrued."(c) A statute of limitations applies to the remedy at law. In equity there is also a limit (called "laches") on the time that a person has to bring suit. Under the equitable principle of *laches*, suit is barred if not brought with a *reasonable* time.

Stock certificate A certificate issued by a corporation to a named person as owner of a given number of shares of stock in the corporation. The certificate is written evidence of the owner's proportionate equity interest in the corporation.

Stock subscription A contract whereby a person agrees to purchase a specified number and class of shares of a new stock issue.

Stop-payment order The instruction by a drawer of a check to the drawee not to pay a certain check.

Straight bankruptcy See *Liquidation proceeding*.

Strict liability in tort A liability imposed by the law regardless of the care or skill of the defendant, as, for example, when injury results from a defective product or from an ultrahazardous activity. The liability is called "strict" because the plaintiff need not prove fault (negligence or fraud).

Subcontract; subcontractor "Where a person has contracted to perform certain work and [such person] in turn engages another to perform the whole or a part of that [work] which is included in the original contract, the agreement with such third person is called a *subcontract*, and such person is called a *subcontractor*."(c)

Subrogation "The substitution of one person in the place of another with reference to a lawful claim, demand, or right, so that he who is substituted succeeds to the right of the other in relation to the debt or claim, and its rights, remedies, or securities." (c)

Substantial evidence rule A rule requiring the courts to accept an administrative agency's findings of fact when they are based on substantial evidence.

Substantive due process See *Due process*.

Substantive law That law which is concerned with the recognition of rights, duties, privileges, and immunities (as contrasted with that law which is concerned with procedure).

Sum certain In the law of negotiable instruments, an amount payable that is sufficiently calculable for an instrument to be classified as a negotiable instrument.

Summary Short, abbreviated, as a summary hearing before an administrative agency.

Surety See *Secured transaction.*

Tender An offer of performance by one party to a contract which, if unjustifiably refused, places the other party in default and permits the party making the tender to exercise remedies for breach of contract.

Tender offer The offer by a corporation or person to purchase the shares of stock from shareholders of a "target corporation" in exchange for money or other securities. A tender offer is most commonly used to acquire voting control of the "target corporation."

Tenor In the law of negotiable instruments, the amount originally intended. Where the face amount of a stolen negotiable instrument has been raised without the consent of the maker, a holder in due course ordinarily may enforce the instrument only in accordance with its original tenor.

Testate With a will. A person who dies leaving a will is said to die testate.

Testator A person who dies leaving a will.

Third-person beneficiary In the law of contracts, a person who is not a party to a contract but who is intended to receive benefits from it.

Through bill of lading See *Bill of lading.*

Tort "A legal wrong committed upon the person or property of another; it may be either (1) a direct invasion of some legal rights of the individual; (2) the infraction of some public duty by which special damage accrues to the individual; or (3) the violation of some private obligation by which some damage accrues to the individual." (c)

Totten trust A trust, not recognized in all states, created by the deposit by one person of his or her own money in his or her own name as trustee for another. Generally considered a tentative or revocable trust.

Trademark "A distinctive mark, motto, device, or emblem which a manufacturer stamps, prints, or otherwise affixes to the goods he produces, so that [the goods] may be identified in the market and their origin be vouched for." (c)

Trade name "A name used in trade to designate a particular business . . . or the place at which the business is located, or a class of goods, but which is not a technical trade-mark either because not applied or affixed to goods sent into the market or because not capable of exclusive appropriation by anyone as a trade-mark." (c)

Treasury stock Stock issued by a corporation but subsequently reacquired by the corporation.

Trial de novo A new trial held in an appellate court.

Trust An estate in real or personal property the legal title to which is vested in a trustee, while the equitable title is held by a beneficiary or beneficiaries who bear no contractual relations among themselves. Also, an obligation arising out of a confidence reposed in a person, for the benefit of another, to apply property or services faithfully according to such confidence. A trust arises when property is given to one person with direction that it be used and applied for the benefit of another.

Trustee in bankruptcy A bankruptcy official responsible for collecting, liquidating, and distributing the debtor's estate.

Tucker Act The Act of March 3, 1887, 24 Stat. 505, as amended (28 U.S.C. 1491) which established the Court of Claims and gave congressional consent to suits against the United States on all claims founded upon contract, express or implied, but not sounding in tort.

Turnover In bankruptcy law, the act of delivering to the trustee in bankruptcy property that belongs to the debtor's estate.

Tying contract A contract in which a seller sells a product only on condition that the buyer also purchases a distinct second product which is not desired.

Ultrahazardous activity An activity that necessarily involves a risk of serious harm, which risk cannot be eliminated by the exercise of utmost care.

Ultra vires act A corporate act or action that is beyond the scope of authority and powers conferred upon the corporation by law or by the articles of incorporation.

Unconscionable Conduct (not necessarily amounting to fraud, misrepresentation, or duress) that results in the oppression or unfair surprise of one contracting party by the other.

Undue influence The overcoming of the free will of a person by unfair persuasion; usually involves misuse of a position of confidence or relationship.

Unenforceable contract One that the law will not enforce by direct legal proceedings but may recognize in some indirect way as creating some duty of performance.

Unilateral contract "A contract formed by the exchange of a promise for an act." (c)

Uniform Limited Partnership Act An act approved

by the National Conference of Commissioners on Uniform State Laws in 1916 and revised in 1976, defining the formation of a limited partnership and the rights and obligations of its general partners and limited partners to each other and to third persons dealing with the limited partnership.

Usage of trade   In the law of sales, any practice or method of dealing having such regularity of observance in a place, vocation, or trade as to justify an expectation that it will be observed with respect to the transaction in question.

Usury   The charging of any rate of interest in excess of that permitted by law.

Value   In the law of *sales*, any promise or other consideration sufficient to support a simple contract. In the law of *commercial paper*, *performed* consideration.

Verification   A person's statement, signed under penalty of perjury, that facts recited in a document are true and correct.

Vertical merger   A combination in which a firm at one level acquires a firm at a different level, e.g., a manufacturer acquiring a wholesaler.

Vertical price fixing   See *Resale price maintenance*.

Vicarious act   An act performed or exercised by one party for another. In agency law, an agent's or servant's act which may bind the principal or master.

Voidable contract   One that a party may enforce or set aside (avoid) as that person wishes.

Void contract   An attempt at contracting which never produced a contract because some essential contractual element was missing.

Vest   To become established; to take effect; "to give an immediate, fixed right of present or future enjoyment." (c)

Walsh-Healey Public Contracts Act   The Act of June 30, 1936, as amended (41 U.S.C. 35–45), prescribing rules governing contracting by agencies of the United States and remedies for violation of the Act.

Wanton act   A malicious and unjustifiable act; a heedless and reckless disregard for another's rights; careless of the consequences.

Warehouse receipt   See *Document of title*.

Warranty   A statement, promise, or other representation that a thing has certain qualities or that the seller has title to the thing. Also, an obligation imposed by law that a thing will have certain qualities. Warranties made by means of a statement or other affirmation of fact are called *express warranties*. Warranties imposed by law are called *implied warranties*. In the law of sales, a *warranty of merchantability*, whether express or implied, assures the recipient that the goods are of fair, average quality. A sales *warranty of fitness for a particular purpose* assures the buyer that the goods are fit for the buyer's particular purpose.

Warranty of fitness   See *Warranty*.

Warrant of merchantability   See *Warranty*.

Warranty of title   See *Warranty*.

Will   In estate or inheritance law, a declaration of a person's wishes as to how his or her property will be disposed of, to take effect after death. Until death, a will is said to be ambulatory and may be revoked.

With reserve   With regard to auctions, an expression indicating that the auctioneer, on behalf of the owner, reserves the right to withdraw the goods from bidding.

Without reserve   With regard to auctions, an expression indicating that the owner of the goods will sell them to any bidder no matter how low the bid is, if a bid is made within a reasonable time.

Writ   A writing, issued by a court or other competent tribunal and directed to the sheriff or to some other officer, for the purpose of carrying out an order or sentence of the court.

Wunderlich Act   The Act of May 11, 1954 (41 U.S.C. 321), providing that a decision of a board of contract appeals is final and conclusive upon the contractor unless a court of competent jurisdiction finds it was fraudulent, capricious, or arbitrary, or was so grossly erroneous as necessarily to imply bad faith, or was not supported by the evidence.

Index